A NEW ENGLISH-CHINESE DICTIONARY OF AUTOMOTIVE ENGINEERING
(Revised Third Edition)

张蔚林 编

新英汉（第三版）汽车技术词典

内容提要

本书收录了汽车设计、制造、研究、检测、结构、使用、修理、运输、管理、材料等方面,以及与汽车专业关系紧密的词汇十万余条,供汽车专业科研人员、工程技术人员和大中专院校师生学习参考。

图书在版编目(CIP)数据

新英汉汽车技术词典 / 张蔚林编. —3 版. —北京:人民交通出版社股份有限公司,2017.4
ISBN 978-7-114-13455-5

Ⅰ.①新… Ⅱ.①张… Ⅲ.①汽车工程—词典—英、汉 Ⅳ.①U46-61

中国版本图书馆 CIP 数据核字(2016)第 271557 号

书　　名:	新英汉汽车技术词典(第三版)
著　作　者:	张蔚林
责任编辑:	林宇峰
出版发行:	人民交通出版社股份有限公司
地　　址:	(100011)北京市朝阳区安定门外外馆斜街 3 号
网　　址:	http://www.ccpress.com.cn
销售电话:	(010)59757973
总　经　销:	人民交通出版社股份有限公司发行部
经　　销:	各地新华书店
印　　刷:	北京市密东印刷有限公司
开　　本:	787×1092　1/32
印　　张:	57.625
字　　数:	3063 千
版　　次:	2000 年 6 月　第 1 版　2006 年 1 月　第 2 版 2017 年 4 月　第 3 版
印　　次:	2017 年 4 月　第 3 版　第 1 次印刷　总第 4 次印刷
书　　号:	ISBN 978-7-114-13455-5
印　　数:	0001—1000 册
定　　价:	160.00 元

(有印刷、装订质量问题的图书由本公司负责调换)

前　言

《新英汉汽车技术词典》(第二版)出版至今已有十一年。这十一年对人类历史来说,只不过是"白驹过隙"的瞬间,但对汽车技术的发展却是堪称具有划时代意义的飞跃阶段。十一年间汽车技术发生了令人炫目的巨变。为了给读者提供一部可跟上汽车技术发展速度的英汉汽车技术词典,我社再次邀请《新英汉汽车技术词典》(第二版)主编张蔚林教授对《新英汉汽车技术词典》(第二版)进行了大幅度的改编,删除过时的旧词,增添这十一年间随着汽车技术的发展出现的新词。为了区别于《新英汉汽车技术词典》(第二版),我社将改编后的词典定名为《新编英汉汽车技术词典》(第三版)。

《新编英汉汽车技术词典》(第三版)保留了《新英汉汽车技术词典》(第二版)的特色:对那些仅简单地给出"英汉名词对照"并不能让读者明确其含义的众多词条都作了简洁而明确的诠释,让读者在查阅英文术语的同时,还可以进一步了解汽车新理论,新功能、新结构,新材料等方面的相关知识,使这部《新编英汉汽车技术词典》(第三版)真正起到"词典"的作用。

《新编英汉汽车技术词典》(第三版)由张蔚林教授担任主编。此外,参与词汇收集、整理、校订的还有张平、秦嵩生、李维维、杨琦、孙守增、冯小华、廖发良、张昊、张月玲。

由于水平和条件有限,谬误和遗漏在所难免,欢迎广大读者批评指正,以便再版时修正。

人民交通出版社股份有限公司
2017 年 3 月 3 日

目 录

使用说明 ………………………………………… (1)
词典正文 ………………………………………… (1-1838)

使用说明

一、本词典的全部词条,不论是单词或由几个单词组成的词组,均连贯起来视作整体,然后按字母顺序排列。例如:

  cleanability
  cleaner
  cleaning agent
  clean master

二、单词的词类一般可从词尾或汉语词义中辨认出来,如"-tion""-ment"为名词,"××的"为形容词。但是有些动词和名词比较难辨,因此遇有难辨的词汇,则在动词后加注[动],其他词类均不加注。

三、凡词义中注有[英]或[美]的,表示该词为英国或美国用语。

四、单词上所附的圆括号( )表示相同含义的不同拼写形式。如friction(al) loss 表示 friction loss 或 frictional loss,意义都是"摩擦损失"。

五、汉语词义中的圆括号,是注释或为词义的一部分。

A ①埃（10^{-10} m，见 angstrom）②安培（ampere）

AA ［英］汽车协会（Automobile Association）

AAA 美国轿车协会（American Automobile Association）

A-ABS 主动控制式防抱死制动系统［Active-Control Anti-lock Brake 的简称，本田公司"车辆横向运动主动控制系统"的商品名。该系统是在原防抱死制动系统上增加了一个横摆率（yaw rate）传感器和一个横向加速度（lateral acceleration）传感器（简称横 G 传感器），并共用原 ABS 系统的车轮速度传感器、制动液压系统，以及原左右轮驱动力控制系统（见 ATTS）的控制元件和传感器等。当横摆率传感器和横 G 传感器测得车辆在高速行驶下改变车道或转向中紧急制动而造成侧滑，或出现过度转向时，电子控制模块便发出指令，对汽车制动力及驱动力进行控制，以抑制车辆的侧滑和过度转向现象，确保车辆稳定性］

AABS ①主动控制式防抱死制动系统（active control antilock brake system 的简称）②高级安全气囊系统（advanced air bag system 的简称）

AAC ［美］汽车广告协会（Automotive Advertising Council）

AAC 主动式空气（进气量）控制（阀）［active air control（valve）的简称］

AALA 美国出租汽车协会（American Automotive Leasing Association）

AAMA ［美］汽车附件制造商协会（Automotive Accessories Manufacturers' Association）

AAMVA 美国汽车管理协会（American Association of Motor-Vehicle Administrators）

AAMVM 美国汽车制造商协会（American Association of Motor Vehicle Manufactures）

A-arm （独立悬架的）A 形横臂（由两根杆件构成的 A 形横向布置的控制臂，亦称 A-fram），（因其形似鸟胸骨，故亦称 wishbone，鸟胸）叉骨形横（控制）臂

AAS ①主动适应性换挡系统（商品名，active adaptive shift 的简称）②自动调节悬架系统（商品名，Auto Adjusting Suspension 的简称，该系统通过可变阻尼减振器来改变悬架的刚度，有软、硬两种模式可供选换）③（奥迪 A8 的）适应性空气悬架（adaptive air suspension 的简称，其双管减振器阻尼连续可变，并可提供 4 种不同离地间距）

AASHTO 美国公路与运输公务员协会（American Association of State

Highways and Transportation Officials 的简称)

AAV 防(熄火后)继燃阀(anti after burn valve 的简称)

ABA 美国客车协会(American Bus Association 的简称)

abampere (CGS 电磁制)绝对安培(1CGS 绝对安培 =10 安培)

abandoned ①报废的,废弃的②报废车,废车,报废物品(一般加冠词 the)

abbreviated injury scale 简化伤害基准,受伤简略分度(汽车交通事故中,乘员受伤严重程度的简易划分标准,伤害程度分为 6 等,伤害部位分为 7 处,现被国际广泛采用,简称 AIS)

abbreviated name 简称(车辆、系统、设备、方法、组织、公司等的全名的)

ABC ①下止点后(after bottom center 的简称,= after bottom dead centre)②(奔驰公司的)主动式车身控制系统(电子控制液压悬架的商品名,active body control 的简称)

ABCD 见 air-bag collapsible dash

ABCM (汽车)防抱死制动控制模块(antilock brake control module 的简称,即控制防抱系统的车用微型电子计算机,亦写作 ABC module)

abcoulomb 绝对库仑,绝库,CGS 电磁制库仑(电磁制电量单位,=10 库仑)

ABC suspension system 主动车身控制悬架系统(active body control suspension system 的简称,Benz 公司轿车悬架系统商品名)

ABC + T (宝马公司的)自动稳定性控制加牵引力控制(系统)(automatic stability control plus traction control 的简称)

ABD 自动锁紧式差速器(automatic braking differential 的简称)

ABDC 在下止点后(after bottom dead centre 的简称)

abdomen injury 下腹伤

Abel tester (燃油和液体润滑油的)阿倍尔闪点测定仪

aberration ①色差,像差②偏差③反常④畸变,变体

ABF (福特公司 2005 年推出的汽车配件商对汽车生产厂的配件)直销体制

ABG 酒精混合汽油(掺酒精的汽油,alcohol blended gasoline 的简称)

ability factor 工作性能比指标(如:评价汽车动力性能,即汽车总质量与发动机最大输出功率之比的比功率 kW/t 等)

ability of survive (车辆)在恶劣使用条件下运行仍能保持完好性能的能力

ABN 空气传播的噪声(air borne noise 的简称)

abnormal combustion 异常燃烧(发动机的爆震、早燃等不正常燃烧的总称)

abnormal engine noise diagnosis equipment 发动机异响诊断设备

abnormal injection 异常喷油(间断喷油,波动喷油,不齐喷油,二次喷油等不正常喷油的总称)

abnormal knocking 异响(超过技术文件规定的不正常响声)

aboard 在车上(参见 on board)

abort ①故障,失灵,失效②出故障的,失灵的,失效的(= aborted)

abortive failure 早期失效(低于统计寿命情况下的失效)

abort sensing-control system 故障感知与控制系统(简称 ASC system,指自动发现故障并进行必要处理,以维持基本功能的计算机控制系统)

above-head visibility (车内乘员的)头上方视野(如采用全景式玻璃车顶,以改善头上方视野)

above throttle valve EGR system 节气门前 EGR 系统（再循环废气的入口设在节气门前方的 EGR 系统，见 EGR）

ABP(valve) 气制动比例分配(阀) [air brake proportioning (valve) 的简称]

ABR 丙烯腈丁二烯橡胶（acrylonitrile butadiene rubber 的简称）

abrasion 磨损，磨耗

abrasive ①研磨用具，磨料 ②研磨用的，磨料的（= abradant）③磨损，磨损的（= abrasion）

abrasive paper 砂纸

abrasive test 耐磨试验，磨损试验

abrasive wear 磨料磨损（由于硬质颗粒或硬质突出物沿固体表面强制相对运动而造成的磨损）

abrasive wheel 砂轮

ABRS （汽车）安全气囊式乘员拘束性保护系统（air bag restraint system 的简称）

ABRSV RES 耐磨的，抗磨料磨损的（abrasive resistant 的简称）

abruption ①中断，断裂，破裂 ②隔断 ③断路，断开

abrupt slope 陡坡

abrupt stop （汽车的）突然停车，猛然停车（一般指碰撞停车，其减速度约为 1～4g）

ABS ①丙烯腈-丁二烯-苯乙烯共聚物（acrylonitrile-butadiene-styrene 的简称）②美国标准局（American Bureau of Standards 的简称）③防抱死制动系统（anti-lock braking system, anti-block brake system, anti-brake-skid system 等的简称）

ABS actuator （防抱死制动系的制动）压力调节器（见 pressure modulator）

ABS/ASR 见 ASR②

ABS/ASR system for regulating differential slip on rear-wheel drive vehicle 后轮驱动车辆左、右轮滑差控制式 ABS/ASR 系统（当在左、右轮地面摩擦系数不同处起步时，若左、右驱动轮出现速度差，则将差速锁锁住，直到速度差降到某规定值时开锁的 ABS/ASR）

abscissa 横坐标

ABS electronic control module 防抱死制动系统电子控制模块（简称 ABSECM 亦称 ABS controller, ABS electronic control unit, 后者简称 ABSECU）

absolute 绝对的，纯粹的

absolute alcohol 纯酒精（无水乙醇）

absolute coordinate 绝对坐标（指相对于某一特定坐标系的原点来标示某一可编程点的位置坐标，见 relative coordinate）

absolute error 绝对误差 [测量结果减去被测量的（约定）真值，见 conventional true valve]

absolute filtration 绝对滤度（指在规定条件下可通过滤件的颗粒的最大直径）

absolute humidity 绝对湿度 [指直接测定的单位体积（m^3）的空气中水蒸气的质量（g），单位：g/m^3，见 relative humidity]

absolute position sensor 绝对位置传感器 [只要接通电源，便会对所测部件的位置或角度产生明显且唯一的电压、频率或其他模拟量输出，故又称绝对输出传感器（absolute output sensor），如节气门和加速踏板位置传感器等。比较 incremental position sensor]

absolute pressure 绝对压力（以绝对真空为零点的压力，等于大气压与表压力的代数和）

absolute system ①绝对（值）系统（恒用全值表示的数据处理所有变量的系统）②绝对方式（数字控制系统中用绝对坐标值表示运动的方

式，见 absolute coordinate）

absolute temperature 绝对温度（即开尔文温度，见 Kelvin temperature）

absolute traffic capacity 绝对通行能力（道路可通过的最大交通量）

absolute value ①绝对值②（模量的）模

absolute viscosity 绝对黏度［亦称动力黏度（dynamic viscosity），见 kinetic viscosity］

absolute zero 绝对零度（= -273.16℃）

absorb ①吸收②（吸收振动时指）减振③（吸收冲击时指）缓冲

absorbed natural gas 吸附天然气（吸附存储在某种材料上，要用时，再从材料上逸出的天然气。天然气汽车储存天然气的一种方式）

absorbed power ①（人体）吸收的功率（乘坐舒适性的评价基准）②（减振体等）吸收的能量，吸收的功率

absorbent charcoal 活性炭（= activated charcoal）

absorbent-type filter 吸附式滤清器，吸收式滤清器（内有吸收性材料，如毡、纸等，= absorptive-type filter）

(absorption and reaction) combination type muffler （吸收与反射）复合式消声器

Absorption by resonance （噪声的）共振吸收法

absorption canister （污染物）吸附罐

absorption characteristic 吸收特性（液力减速器吸收功率与转速之间的关系特性）

absorption dynamometer 吸收式测功机（能量）

absorption meter ①（测定溶质浓度的）吸光光度计，吸收光度计，吸收式比色计②（液体）溶气计（测定液体内溶解的气体量）

absorption refrigeration 吸热式制冷，吸热式冷冻

absorptive muffler 吸收型消声器（利用吸声材料吸收废气能量的消声器）

absorptive type filter 吸附式滤清器

ABS override button 防抱死制动系统超越按钮（可断开防抱死系统，而由驾驶员做常规控制）

ABS relay valve 气制动防抱死系统（中用来控制制动气压的电控）继动阀

ABS return pump ABS 回流泵（将制动液抽回总泵的电动机泵或活塞泵）

ABS/TCS 防抱死制动/牵引力控制系统（antilock brake system/traction control system 的简称，将防止制动力或牵引力大于路面附着力，导致车轮抱死或滑转的防抱死和牵引力控制两个系统合二而一的联合控制系统，亦称 ABS/TRC system，其中 TRC 为 traction control 的简称）

abstract （论文等的）摘要

ABSV 空气旁通电磁阀（air bypass solenoid valve 的简称）

3/3 ABS valve 三位三通型 ABS（车轮制动液压调控）阀

abs visc 绝对黏度（见 absolute viscosity）

ABS warning lamp 防抱死制动系统（发生故障时连续闪光的）警报灯（多为琥珀色）

ABS with (anti-spin) traction control 带（防滑转）牵引力控制的防抱死制动系统［当驱动车轮由于牵引力大于路面附着力而产生滑转时即通过下列方式减少牵引力，阻止滑转：①对滑转的车轮施加制动②控制节气门或副节气门开度调节器（throttle regulator）的直流电动机，减小节气门（或副节气门）开度③向动力系控制模块"PCM"发出信号，减小点火提前角④让一个或数个汽缸熄火］

ABS with dynamic rear proportioning

带后轮制动力动态比例分配的防抱死制动系统

ABS without vaccum booster 无真空助力器的防抱死制动系统（亦称 hydraulic boost type ABS，指其制动总泵无真空助力器，而是利用储能器或动力转向系的液压助力的防抱死制动系统）

A-BUS 汽车位串行通用接口系统（Automotive Bit-Series Universal Interface System，汽车单线式多路复用电路系统，用一根导线连接各种电气和电子系统，采用数字数据的串行传输法，在单一的传输线上按时间顺序传输一连串的比特）

abuse 乱用，误用，不合理地使用，滥用

abuse test 非正常使用条件下的试验（在人为的超常规使用条件下进行的试验）

abuse tolerance （汽车变速器等的）耐滥用性，不合理使用允许度

abut 使接触（特指齿轮啮合）

abutment ①止动件（较正规用语为 stop）②（使）接触，啮合③支座，凸台

abutment joint 对接接头（= abutting joint）

abutment oil (piston) ring 无开口间隙的（活塞）组合油环

abutment pump 外啮合凸轮转子泵

abutting collar 凸环，凸圈，凸出圆肩，耳盘

abutting end ①端面②对接端，衔接端

ABV ①防回火阀（见 anti backfire valve）②旁通空气阀（见 air bypass valve）

AC ①交流电（alternating current 的简称）②整流/充电器（adapter/charger 的简称）

A/C (a/c) ①空调装置（air conditioner 的简称）②（六角形、方形等的）对角线长度，对角

ACAC 风冷式空调（air-cooling air conditioning 的简称）

Academy of Sciences 科学院（简称 AS）

ACAP ［美］（汽车工程师学会的）汽车腐蚀和防护委员会（Automotive Corrosion and Prevention Committee 的简称）

ACAV 电路自动分析检验仪（automatic circuit analyzer and verifier 的简称）

a-c beta （晶体管）集电极对基极的交流电流短路放大系数，共发射极交流电流短路放大系数（$= \Delta I_C / \Delta I_B$）

AC cars （英国）AC 汽车公司（福特控股）

ACCEL ①加速（accelerate 的简称）②加速器，加速踏板（accelerator 的简称）③加速度表（accelerometer 的简称）

accelerate 加速，加快，促进

accelerated test (ing) 快速试验，加速试验，强化试验（利用增加负载等方法，缩短试验时间）

accelerated weathering test 天气自然作用的加速试验，加速风蚀暴露试验（参见 exposure test）

accelerating ability 加速能力，加速性能

accelerating coil 见 accelerating winding

accelerating jet 加速油泵（出油）喷管（亦称 acceleration jet, accelerating pump jet，或简称 pump jet）

accelerating pump (outlet ball check) valve 加速泵（球式止回）出油阀

accelerating pump piston （化油器的）加速泵柱塞（= accelerating pump plunger）

accelerating system 加速油系（= accelerator-pump system）

accelerating winding 加速线圈（电压

调节器或电流限制器中用以提高触点振动频率的线圈,亦称 accelerating coil)

acceleration ①加速度(简称 acc,符号 a,$a=\dfrac{\mathrm{d}v}{\mathrm{d}t}$)②加速作用

acceleration(adhesion)force coefficient 加速(所要求的附着)力系数(为加速滑转率的函数)

acceleration/coast cycle (汽车)加速-滑行(行驶)循环(一种节油驾驶法)

acceleration, cruise, idle, deceleration system (排气有害物含量测定的)加速、稳速(常用车速)、怠速、减速试验循环

acceleration-decceleration sensor 加速度-减速度传感器

acceleration due to gravity 重力加速度(亦称 acceleration of gravity)

acceleration enrichment 加速(混合气)加浓

acceleration from dead stop [美]起步加速(度)(自静止不动状态加速,=acceleration from rest, starting acceleration,以汽车从静止起步加速到某一车速的时间来表明其加速能力和动力性好坏)

acceleration hesitation 加速迟滞(加速初始的降速现象)

acceleration index 加速度指数(车辆加速度与重力加速度之比)

acceleration-insensitive 对加速度不敏感的

acceleration jet 加速量孔

acceleration limit (汽车的)加速度极限(汽车所能达到的最大加速度)

acceleration mass (加速度仪内的)加速质量(重锤等)

acceleration mode ①(汽车多工况试验中的)加速工况②(电子控制喷油系统等的控制模式中的)加速模式(指电子控制模块收到节气门开度以及进气管压力或空气流量剧增的信号时,加浓空气/燃油混合气的工作模式)

acceleration of gravity 重力加速度(代号 g,$g=9.8\,\mathrm{m/s^2}$)

acceleration performance 加速性能(指汽车迅速提高车速,发动机迅速提高转速的能力)

acceleration pumpwell (化油器)加速油泵泵筒;加速补偿油井,加速泵油井(简称 accelerating well、acceleration well)

acceleration resistance 加速阻力

acceleration sensor 加速度传感器(亦称 G sensor,将加速度值转换为电信号输出)

acceleration slip rate (汽车的)加速滑转率[亦写作 acceleration spin rate,或称驱动滑移率(drive slip 或 spin rate)。驱动中,如起步加速时,若牵引力大于车轮与路面的附着力,将导致车轮滑转,驱动轮的滑转程度用滑转率 λ_d 或 λ_a 表示,$\lambda_a=(V_w-V_v)\,V_w\times100\%$,式中:$V_w$—车轮瞬时线速度,m/s;$V_v$—汽车瞬时平移速度,m/s。当在地面上车轮无滑转地纯滚动时,滑转率 $\lambda_a=0$;汽车不动,车轮原地纯滑转时,滑转率 $\lambda_a=100\%$,而当 $0<\lambda_a<100\%$ 时,表示车轮边滚动边滑转,见 brake slip rate]

acceleration slip regulation 加速滑移调节(简称 ASR,指防止加速过猛,致使车轮驱动力超过地面附着力打滑时对驱动力进行的调节或控制,一般该系统与 ABS 组成一体。亦称 ASC,acceleration slip control,详见 ASR)

acceleration smoke characteristic (柴油机等的)加速排烟特性

acceleration squat (汽车的)加速仰头(加速时质量转移,车身后部下沉,头部扬起的现象)

acceleration test 加速试验（①测定发动机从低速迅速加速到预定高速所需的时间②车辆原地起步换挡加速或从某一稳定车速开始换挡加速的方法测定加速过程的时间、和行驶距离，以确定汽车的加速能力）

acceleration transducer ①加速度传感器②加速度计（＝accelerometer）

acceleration vector of center of mass 质心加速度矢量（汽车质心或簧上质心的三维加速度矢量）

acceleration wearoff test 快速磨损试验（在台架上向发动机供应磨料，以加速主要零件磨料磨损，缩短试验时间）

accelerator ①（汽车的）加速踏板（指控制节气门开度的脚踏板，亦称 accelerator pedal、throttle pedal、foot throttle、accel pedal，美称 gas pedal）②加速拉钮③加速剂（加速反应过程的化学添加剂）

accelerator foot rest 加速踏板的踏脚板

accelerator interlock 加速踏板（与自动变速器等之间的）互锁机构

accelerator lever 加速踏板杆件

accelerator pedal bracket 加速踏板支架

accelerator pedal joint 加速踏板铰轴

accelerator pedal lever 加速踏板推杆

accelerator pedal sensor 加速踏板传感器（向电子控制模块提供加速踏板是否踩踏及其位置信息）

accelerator pump delivery ball valve 加速油泵出油口单向球阀

accelerator pump discharge nozzle 加速油泵喷管

accelerator pump lever 加速油泵推臂

accelerator pump piston （化油器）加速油泵柱塞

accelerator pump rod 加速油泵推杆

accelerator pump spring guide 加速油泵回位弹簧导片

accelerator-pump system （化油器）加速油系（＝accelerating system）

accelerograph 加速度记录仪，加速度时间曲线仪

accelerometer ①（测定加速度用）加速度表，加速表，加速计②（研究机械振动用的）机械振动仪；加速传感器

accelerometer type impact sensor (with piezoelectric element) （具有压电元件的）加速度计式碰撞传感器

accel heel point 加速踏板后支点（简称 AHP，指驾驶员踩踏加速踏板过程中，其脚后跟与地板的假拟接触点）

acceptability （对车内异味、噪声、振动等的）①可接受程度②容忍性，容忍度

acceptable reliability level 可接受的可靠性水平（简称 ARL）

acceptance ①接收②接受

acceptance test 验收试验（＝acceptance trial，检查是否符合所要求的技术条件）

access ①（客车座位间）通道 ②（存储器的）存取

access door 观察窗孔，检修孔，检修门（＝access hole、access opening、inspection door）

accessibility 易接近性，可达性

accessible 易接近的

access mode （汽车计算机控制系统）存取模式，访问方式

access motion time （汽车计算机控制系统的）存取时间（指从传感器信息输入电子控制模块到该模块输出控制信号的时间，亦称 access time）

access of repair 修理用孔口，修理

用窗孔

accessory ①附件，附加装置，辅助设备，附属物②附加的，附属的，辅助的

accessory belts ①附属装置驱动带②辅助装置传动带

accessory drive ①辅助传动②辅助机构的驱动装置，附件驱动机构（= auxiliary drive）

accessory equipment 辅助设备，辅助装备，附加装置（= auxillary equipment）

accessory horsepower ①驱动辅助机构所消耗的功率（= accessory power consumption）②（发动机）附件消耗功率；附件功率

accessory shaft 副轴

access ramp （互通式立体交叉的）入口；进出口，引道，进出坡道，连接匝道，匝道；接坡，进口坡，进入匝道（简称 ramp）

acceterated test ratio ①快速试验强化比（快速试验与常规试验所加负载的比）②强化试验时间比（快速试验与常规试验所用时间的比）

accident 车祸；事故

accidental ①偶然的，意外的②附属的③非本质的

accident (al) error 偶然误差，随机误差

accident blackspot （交通）事故多发地点（见 traffic black spot）

accident brake 紧急制动器（= emergency brake）

accident damage （车辆等因）事故（造成的）损坏（亦称 accident defect，accident fault）

accident data recorder 事故数据记录器（简称 ADR，亦称 black box 黑匣子）

accident-free 无事故的，无故障的

accident occurrence probability 事故发生概率

accident proneness （驾驶员的）事故倾向性（由于驾驶员的心理、生理素质形成的，但是经过训练培养可以改变）

accident shifting （变速器）挂错挡；乱挡

acclivity 上坡道（= upward slope，向上的斜坡）

accommodation ①适应，调节②供应，供给③便利，设备④安置，容纳⑤（特指）（眼睛）视线（的焦点从某一距离上的一物体）转移（至另一距离上的一物体的过程，即改变聚焦的过程）

accordion door 摺门，折叠门

accountability 负有责任

accountable 负有责任的

ACC signal 空调离合器（接合）信号（air-conditioning clutch signal 的简称，该信号由空调开关发送至电子控制模块，电子控制模块收到该信号后，立即使发动机急速相应提高）

ACC system 自适应性巡航控制系统（adaptive cruise control system 的简称，当定速巡航系统工作时，该系统可测得前方车辆的车速，自动调整巡行车速，以保持与前车间的安全距离）

accumlation wear average 平均累计磨损

accumulated engine rpm indicator 发动机曲轴累计转数计数器

accumulated errors 累积误差，积累误差（= cumulative error）

accumulated fuel delivery rate 累计喷油率（在发动机每一做功循环中，从喷油始点开始累计的喷油量与循环喷油量之比，以% 表示，亦称喷油百分率）

accumulating three-point drive 累进式三点（传动带）传动（指第一传动带盘带动第二传动带盘，而第二

传动带盘用另一根传动带带动第三传动带盘的三点式传动)

accumulator ①(专指各种能量的)存储器(如:可充电的蓄电池,液压系统存储压力的液压箱,气压系统的储气筒,供热系统的热存储器等) ②(泛指一般的)储蓄装置(如集尘器等) ③(在电子控制系统中指)累加器(在其中存放中间或最终算术运算结果、供以后使用的一种寄存器) ④储能电路 ⑤(特指自动变速器行星齿轮机构液压系内的)储能减振器(用于离合器的称为 high accumulator,用于制动带的称为 low accumulator)

accumulator acid 电解液(见 electrolyte)

accumulator bag 储气囊

accumulator battery 蓄电池(= storage battery)

accumulator box ①蓄电池箱 ②蓄电池外壳(= accumulator case, battery box, battery jar)

accumulator capacity ①蓄电池容量(= battery capacity) ②蓄能器容量

accumulator car 蓄电池车,电瓶车(参见 electric motor car)

accumulator cell 单格电池

accumulator circuit ①蓄压器的油路 ②蓄压器气路 ③蓄电池电路

accumulator-drier (汽车空调系统位于蒸发器出口处的制冷剂)干燥-存集器(用于制冷剂除湿并存集过量的制冷剂)

accumulator drive ①蓄电池驱动(装置) ②储能器驱动

accumulator jar ①蓄电池外壳(= battery jar) ②储气筒 ③蓄能瓶

accumulator metal 蓄电池极板合金

accumulator-orifice tube air conditioning system 集液器-节流孔式膨胀管空调系统(其蒸发器出口和压缩机入口间装有一集液器,用以捕集气态制冷剂中的液滴,使进入压缩机的气态制冷剂得到滤清和干燥。此外,该系统使一带缩径式节流孔的膨胀管代替膨胀阀,故名)

accumulator piston (液压系统)蓄压器活塞

accumulator plate 蓄电池极板

accumulator separators 蓄电池电极隔板

accumulator terminal 蓄电池接线柱

accumulator tester 蓄电池充电检查仪

accumulator traction 蓄电池驱动(= battery traction)

accumulator-type fuel injection system 高压储油歧管式燃油喷射系统(见 common rail injection system)

accumulator valve ①(液压)储能器(的)控制阀 ②(气压系统)储压器(的)控制阀 ③(自动变速器液压控制系统的)蓄压阀(用于缓冲液压波动,保证离合器和制动器平顺接合,以减小换挡冲击)

accuracy ①精确度,准确度,精密度 ②正确,准确 ③精密准确(性)

accuracy life 丧失精确性前的使用期限,可保证精度的使用期限

accuracy of measurement ①测量准确度(指一个参数的测量结果与该参数真值相符合的程度,测量中系统误差越大,测量准确度越低) ②测量精确度(测量中,系统误差会使测量值偏离真值,降低测量的准确度,而随机误差会使测定值产生离散,降低测量的精密度"precision",两者是相互独立的,但都影响测量结果,在测量结果中综合考虑这两者后,测定值与实值的吻合程度称为测量精确度)

accuracy rate ①精确度,精密度,精度; ②准确率

accurate position indicator 精确位置指示器(简称 API)

accurate press-fit technique 精密压配合技术（可确保密封，而无须O形密封环）

accurate to dimension 精确符合加工尺寸的

accurate within 0.0001mm 精度达0.0001mm

ACCUS 美国汽车竞赛委员会（Automobile Competition Committee for the United States 的简称）

A/C cut-out relay （由电子控制模块控制的）空调系统断开继电器（关闭空调时，该继电器断开空调离合器电路）

AC-DC inverter 交流-直流转换器（如：将混合动力车的发电机发出的三相交流电转变为给蓄电池充电的直流电的转换器）

AC drive(s) （电动汽车的）交流驱动装置（指作为电动汽车动力源的三相交流电动机）

AC dynamo 交流发电机（=alternator）

ACE ①先进的清洁能源（advanced clean energy 的简称，一般指生物柴油氢，二甲醚，天然气等）②空气调节设备（air conditioning equipment）③自动检测设备（automatic checkout equipment）④（悬架的）主动转弯加强装置（active curve energizer 的简称）

ACEA 欧洲汽车制造商协会（European Vehicle Manufacturers' Association 的简称）

ace-class 顶级的

a-c electric drive 交流电驱动

Acetaldehyde 乙醛

acetal plastics 缩醛塑料（RCH(OR)$_2$）

acetone 丙酮（CH_3COCH_3）

acetonitrile 乙腈（氰甲烷）

acetylene 乙炔（CH≡CH）；亚次乙基（=CHCH=）

acetylene (gas) generator 乙炔发生器

acetylene gas tank 乙炔气罐

acetylene welder ①乙炔气焊接设备（如：气焊枪）②气焊工

acetylene welding 乙炔焊（的），气焊（的）

ACEV 先进的清洁能源车（advanced clean energy vehicle 的简称）

AC-firing 交流点火（指安全气囊点火器等由交流脉冲点火）

ACG 美国通用汽车零部件集团（American General Motors Automotive Components Group Worldwide 的简称，1995年改名 Delphi Automotive Systems）

AC generator 交流发电机（=alternator）

acid ①酸②酸的（=acidic）

acid brittleness 酸蚀脆性（=pickle brittleness）

acid content 含酸量，酸含量（亦称acidic content）

acid-cured 酸性硫化的，冷硫化的，冷补的（=cold-vulcanized, cold-cured）

acid electrolyte fuel cell 酸电解液燃料电池

acid fume 酸雾，酸烟

acidified oil 含酸油料，酸化油料

acidimeter 酸度计，酸液比重计（=acidometer）

acid-impregnated ①含酸的②酸浸渍的

acidity ①酸度，见 gasoline acidity ②酸性（=acidness）

acid lead 耐酸铜铅合金

acidless 非酸性的，不含酸的，无酸的（=acid-free, non-acid, free from acid）

acid number 酸值（亦称 acid value, 为总酸值"total acid number 或 total acid value, TAN 或 TAV"的简称。

定义为:中和1g试样所含的酸性成分需要的氢氧化钾mg数)

acid-proof coating 耐酸保护层,防酸面层,防酸涂料

acid rain 酸雨(CO_x、NO_x、SO_x等排放物,进入大气,与雨云相遇形成硝酸、硫酸、碳酸等化合物,溶于雨滴落下,称为酸雨,对林业、农业危害很大)

acid refining oil 酸精制机油

acid siphon (蓄电池)加酸虹吸管

acid storage battery 酸蓄电池

acid tanker 酸罐车(装有耐酸内衬的容罐、吸排装置和安全设施,用于运输酸性液体)

ACID test cycle (汽车的)加速、稳速、怠速、减速试验循环(=acceleration, cruise, idle, deceleration test cycle 的简称)

acid tester 酸度计(=acidometer)

acid trailer 运酸液的挂车

acid valve 酸值(简称 AV,见 gasoline acidity)

acid vapo(u)r (蓄电池)酸蒸气

ACIR 汽车撞车伤害度调查(automotive crash injury research 的简称)

ACIS 声控进气系统(acoustic control induction system 的简称,指利用进气气流惯性产生增压效应,以提高进气效率。目前已实际使用的进气惯性增压系统有多种结构,但基本上都是通过改变进气气流通道有效长度,即:低速工况下,使进气气流通道较长,高速工况下,使气气流通道较短,以保证在发动机低、高速工况下均能充分利用进气气流惯性作用产生的反射压力波,实现进气增压)

ACIS valve ACIS 的进气通道(长度)控制阀(见 ACIS)

Ackermann angle 阿克曼角(指阿克曼转向机构的车辆处于直行位置时车轮的前束或前张角)

Ackermann axle 阿克曼式前桥(指阿克曼转向机构车辆的前转向桥,两端具有转向节和主销)

Ackermann centre 阿克曼(瞬间转向)中心(指装用阿克曼转向机构的汽车的瞬时转向中心。理想的阿克曼转向机构,可保证汽车转向时,其转向桥左、右车轮中心延长线交点降落在后轴中心线延长线上,汽车的全部车轮均绕该交点做无滑移纯滚动,该交点便是阿克曼瞬时转向中心)

Ackermann geometry 梯形转向传动机构(见 Ackermann steering 及 steering geometry)

Ackermann steer angle 阿克曼转角(指汽车回驶中心在汽车后轴延长线上时,轴距与后轴回转半径之比的反正切,= arc tan(L/R),亦写作 Ackermann steering angle)

Ackermann steering 阿克曼转向机构(转向桥本身不动,而由转向杆系拉动转向节臂,使转向桥左、右两端的转向轮绕转向桥左、右两端的转向节主销转动而实现车辆转向的机构,1817年由英国人 Lankensperger 发明,但其英国专利注册人为其代理人 Rudolph Ackermann,故名,亦称 Ackermann steering gear, Ackermann steering mechanism, axle-pivot steering, king-pin steering, steering knuckle type steering, 后经法国人 Jeantaud 改进,将左、右转向节臂向内斜,在直行位置时,左、右转向节臂中心线的延长线相交于后桥中心,转向时前、后桥四个车轮均绕同一瞬时中心回转。改进后的转向机构称 Ackermann Jeantaud steering,简称 Jeantaud steering, 但在英语国家仍称 Ackermann steering。由于这种转向杆系用于非独立悬架前桥时,多呈梯形,故我国亦称梯形转向机构)

Ackermann steering linkage 阿克曼转向机构杆系（指由转向垂臂，各种横、直拉杆和转向节臂组成的杆系）

ACLD 空冷式，空冷的（air cooled）

ACM ①空调系统控制模块（air condition system control module 的简称，即控制汽车空调的车用微型计算机）②安全气囊控制模块［详见 air bag (system) control module］

Acme 爱克米螺纹（指顶角为29°的英制梯形螺纹 Acme screw thread）

acme 顶点，极点，最高点

acoustic 听觉的；有声的，声响的；声学的

acoustic absorption 消声，吸声（亦称 acoustical attenuation）

acoustical absorptivity 消声能力，消声效率，消声率

acoustical foam 吸声泡沫（塑料）

acoustical frequency 声频

acoustical liner 吸声衬里，消声衬垫

acoustic (al) power 声功率

acoustical reduction factor 隔声系数，消声系数

acoustical transmission factor 传声系数

acoustic barrier 隔声屏

acoustic board 吸声板，消声板

Acoustic Control Induction System 声控制型进气系统（见 ACIS）

acoustic (depth) sounding 声波探测法，回声探测法

acoustic emission 噪声污染，噪声排放

acoustic holography 声像全息摄影

acoustic hood 隔声罩

acoustic inspection 声响检查

acoustic-laminated glass （可消减风声高频道路噪声的车用）消声夹层玻璃

acoustic material 隔声材料，消声材料

acoustic output 声响输出（单位时间内声源输出的能量，单位：W）

acoustic signal 声频信号

acoustic tread pattern 消声胎面花纹，减噪胎面花纹

acoustic treatment 消声处理

acoustic vehicle detector 车辆（位置和速度等的）声学检测装置

ACP 副控制仪表板（auxiliary control panel 的简称）

acquisition ①（无线电）探测②取得，获得③获得物

ACRE ①（使用前的）自动检查和（待机）准备装置（automatic checkout and readiness equipment 的简称）②自动检测和读出装置（automatic checkout and reading equipment 的简称）

acre 英亩（约4050m²）

acrolein 丙烯醛（CH_2CHCHO）

acronym （由组成一条术语的各个名词的第一个字母组成的）缩写词，简称

across corners 对角（见 A/C③）

across flats 对边，对面（见 A/F②）

Acro system cylinder head 空气室式燃烧室气缸盖（= aircell cylinder head）

acrotorque 最大转矩

ACRS （汽车乘员的）气垫保护系统，气垫拘束性安全装置（air cushion restraint system 的简称）

acrylate 丙烯酸盐（类）聚合物

acrylic 丙烯酸的，丙烯酸类的，丙烯酸系的（如：acrylic plastics 丙烯酸塑料，acrylic polymers 丙烯酸聚合物，acrylic resins 丙烯酸树脂，crylic glass 丙烯酸玻璃等）

acrylonitrile butadiene rubber 丙烯腈丁二烯橡胶（合成橡胶的一种，简称 ABR）

acrylonitrile-butadiene-styrene 丙烯腈-丁二烯-苯乙烯（汽车上广泛使

用的一种塑料,简称 ABS)

ACS ①空气调节系统,空调系统(air conditioning system 的简称)②自适应性系统(adaptive control system 的简称,指能够自动适应自身状态或外界条件变化的控制系统)③自适应性巡行系统(见 adaptive cruise system)

ACS-O 检修孔(access opening 的简称)

ACSP ①美国通用汽车公司 AC 火花塞分部生产的火花塞②美国通用汽车公司 AC 火花塞分部(ACSP 为 AC Spark Plug 的简称,其中 AC 为该分部创始人名的头两个字母)

ac strain ga(u)ge 交流式应变仪(用于测定发动机转矩)

AC supply 交流电源

a/c system (汽车)空调系统(air conditioner system)

ACT ①自动控制运输系统(automatic control transportation 的简称)②进气温度(指被吸入化油器或燃油喷射系统进气歧管的空气的温度,air charge temperature 的简称,= manifold air temperature)③进气温度传感器(air charge temperature sensor 的简称,见 IAT)

ACTE 自动检查试验装置,自动测试装置(automatic checkout test equipment 的简称)

acting force 作用力

actinium 锕(Ac)

action radius 见 active radius

activated carbon 活性炭(= absorbent carbon, activated charcoal, absorbent charcoal,简称 charcoal 或 active carbon)

activated carbon canister ①(泛指各种)活性炭容器②(特指)活性炭罐(亦称 activated charcoal trap)

activated radical combustion engine 活性分子团燃烧式发动机,活性分子团点燃式发动机(该机利用排气终了后缸内残存废气中的活性分子团引燃新鲜混合气,与常规发动机比较,油耗减少 27%~29%,HC 排放减少 50%,简称 ARC engine)

activating ①(使…)活化,激活②(蓄电池的)充电(特指对较长期存放的蓄电池添加电解液和补充电作业)

activating pressure (离合器)接合压力

activation 活化,激活

activator ①加速器②激励器③活化剂④提高灵敏度装置

active ①活动的,活性的②有效的③有源的④主动的

active area 工作面积,有效面积

active battery thermal management system 主动式蓄电池室温度控制系统(用于保持电动汽车蓄电池室相对恒温的系统,冬季加热,夏季送凉)

Active Brake Limited Slip system (日产公司的)主动式制动防滑系统

active braking time 有效制动时间(从制动力开始作用到制动力全部消失时,所经历的时间,不包括驾驶员反应时间和制动系统滞后时间。若车辆在制动力消失前停止,则车辆停止时间为该时间终点)

active carbon 活性炭(通常制成丸状、粒状或粉状的多孔性炭,其特点是由于微孔结构,每单位体积具有极大的面积,因而能吸收大量的气体或液体等,= active charcoal)

active carbon canister (蒸发排放物控制系统中的)活性炭罐(利用罐中的活性炭吸收、储存燃油蒸气等蒸发排放物,= charcoal canister 详见 charcoal canister storage system)

active carbon treatment 活性炭处理(吸收有机杂质)

active circuit 有源电路(指电路本

身有电动势或其他电源）

active coil （弹簧）有效圈

Active-Control Anti-lock Brake 主动控制式防抱死制动系统（见 A-ABS）

active control engine mount 主动控制式发动机支座（用于按需开缸或闭缸式发动机，可根据发动机的工作缸数改变支座的减振特性，以减少振动和噪声）

active control suspension 见 active suspension

active cruise control system 主动式巡航系统（简称 ACC system，见 radar cruise control system）

active current 有效电流（交流电中与电压相位相同的那一部分电流，它与电压的乘积便是有效功率）

active display （电子仪表的）主动显示（指可自动发光的显示方式）

Active ECS 见 active electronic suspebtion

active electronic suspension 电子控制主动式悬架（亦简称 active suspension，由电子控制模块，各种传感器和执行器及其动力源组成，不仅可以根据涉及汽车的运行状况对悬架的弹簧刚度和阻尼特性作最佳控制，而且对车身的侧倾、纵倾、制动点头、加速后座，车身高度等进行调控。为了实现上述控制，一般悬架的减振器由液压或气压执行器所替代，由电子控制模块对其阻尼特性作实时调节，以实现上述功能，保证最佳行驶平顺性和操纵稳定性）

active element 有源元件（主要对电路起提供整流、开关和放大功能的元件。有源元件在电路中也可以起电阻和电容的作用或能量形式转化作用，如晶体管、集成电路、光敏半导体器件或光发射半导体器件）

active engine brake 主动型发动机制动（电子控制模块随时把握车辆的行驶姿势和状态。当根据转向角传感器、加速踏板和车速传感器等的信息推断出汽车转弯或在弯道上行驶减速时，即在控制变速器挂低挡的同时，自动启用发动机制动，以协助减速。直线高速行驶中突见前方红灯慌忙踩踏制动时，该系统亦可协助减速停车。此外，平时由该系统缓慢减速亦可减少制动系统的磨耗）

active engine mount 主动型发动机支座（①指装有同步减振系统等的发动机反振动波支座"synchronous cancellation system for engine vibration" ②指装有可使支座连续变形、发动机特定频率的振动波不致通过支座传至车架或车身的执行机构的支座系统）

active filter （汽车电子控制系统中只允许某一规定的频率范围内的电信号通过的）有源滤波器

active flank （齿轮的）有效齿面（指与相互啮合的齿轮齿面接触的区域，其面积的最大值就是可用齿面的面积）

Active four （三菱公司 Diamond 牌轿车上采用的）主动式四轮驱动系统（商品名，包括四轮防抱死制动，四轮驱动，四轮转向，四轮独立悬架等众多新机构）

active headlight system 主动前照灯系统（可在汽车临转向前照亮驾驶员目光所投向的要转向的弯道，简称 AHL system）

active headrest 主动式头枕（发生碰撞时，头枕可在火药型气体发生器的作用下紧靠头部，减少头部二次碰撞的伤害程度）

active hood 见 AH

active hybrid film integrated circuit 有源混合膜集成电路（指至少有一个有源元件的混合膜集成电路）

active steering system 主动转向系统（简称 ASS，电子控制模块根据车速、横向加速度和转向盘转角等传感器的信息判断汽车出现危害其行驶稳定性的状态时，便会通过转向盘柱中部的电动机-行星齿轮机构对转向轮施加减小转向角或反向转向的干涉性修正。这种修正是独立于驾驶者的转向操作进行的，而且会让驾驶者感觉不到。该系统一般与汽车的电子控制稳定性系统耦合使用）

active suspension (system) 主动式悬架（系统），（电子控制式悬架系统，能根据悬架上质量的加速度，主动地调节悬架的高度或刚度，以控制车身侧倾、振动等，亦称 active suspention control system）

active torque control 4WD 主动式转矩控制型 4 轮驱动

Active Torque Transfer System 主动式转矩分配系统（亦称 Active terque transmission system，见 ATTS）

active transduser ①有源换能器②（汽车电子控制系统中的）有源传感器（其输出信号要依靠电源或外电源提供能量）

active transmission 有效转换（如输入信号从一个电平到另一个电平并能产生激励的转换）

Active TRC system （丰田公司的）主动型牵引力控制系统（商品名，通过对四轮独立的制动控制，抑制因驱动大于轮胎与路面附着力而产生的某一车轮的滑转，该系统与 ABS, EBD, brake assist, VSC, DAC 及 HSAC 组成一个总体，相互配合，协同工作）

active valve transmission 见 AVT

active voltage 有效电压（在交流电路中与电流相位相同的一部分电压）

active volt-amperes 有功功率，有效功率（交流电路中有效电压与电流的乘积或有效电流与电压的乘积，单位为 watt，有效功率为 1 瓦指有效电流 1 安流过 1 伏电压所做的功，亦称 active power）

active yaw control system 主动式横摆控制系统

activity ①活性，活力，活动能力，作用效能②占空系数

ACT sensor 进气空气温度传感器（air charge temperature sensor 的简称，= manifold air temperature sensor）

actual 实际的，在使用（运行，作用）中进行或发生的，有效的

actual capacity of an accumulator ①蓄电池有效容量②蓄能器有效容量

actual cycle 实际循环

actual displacement ①（转子发动机的）实际排量（指旋转活塞每自转一转的排量，为单室排量的三倍）②实际位移③实际工作容积

actual efficiency 实际效率（= practical efficiency）

actual gum 溶于燃油的胶质（参见 dissolved gum）

actual horsepower 有效功率（参见 effective horsepower）

actual load 实际载荷，有效载荷

actual mixing ratio （可燃混合气的）实际空燃比

actual operating conditions 实际运行（工作）状况，实际使用状况

actual output ①有效功率②实际输出

actual-service test 实际使用条件下的试验（简称 actual test）

actual special energy requirement 实际所需比能（指压缩机等压缩单位质量或单位容积的气体，其驱动轴所需的能，分别称为实际质量比能或实际容积比能。实际容积比能就是比功率，但国际标准 ISO 提出，应尽量避免使用比功率 special power

Active Hybrid　主动式混合动力车（BMW 混合动力车商品名，有 5 series，7 series 等多个型号，全电力行驶时最高车速可达 60km/h，加速时发动机参与驱动）

Active Hydraulic Suspension System　主动式液压悬架系统（日产公司研制的一种电子控制式液压悬架的商品名。该悬架系统的液压源为发动机驱动的液压泵，由电子控制模块根据行车状况控制输入四个车轮悬架液压缸的液压，使汽车始终保持稳定状态）

active length　有效长度

active level　有效电平（如在时序电路中能产生激励的数字输入信号的电平）

active life　使用寿命，使用期限

active mass　①有效质量，作用质量 ②放射性材料，活性材料（= active material）

Active matic　（日本 MAZDA 公司）手动-自动一体式变速器（商品名）

active metal　活性金属

active muffler system　主动型消声器系统（见 active noise control system）

active noise cancellation　主动式消声（如：利用反相噪声消声等，见 antinoise）

active noise control system　（车内噪声）主动消声系统（电子控制系统测得车内的噪声超过规定值时，即通过微型声响装置发出可精确抵消该噪声的频率的反相声波，利用该反相声波消声的系统，亦称 anti-noise system）

active particulate filter　（柴油机的）主动式微粒物滤清器（使用多孔陶瓷滤件，见 diesel engine emission standards）

active power　（电机等的）有效功率（有效电流与电压的乘积，见 active current）

active radius　①行动半径，作用半径 ②（车辆的）运行半径（亦写作 action radius）

active reaction power steering system　主动式反作用力型动力转向系（以转向时产生的各种反作用力作为输入信号，向驾驶者提供车辆转向实时状况和改善动力转向系转向手感，以及对车辆因各种干扰而产生的转向误差进行自动补偿和修正的反馈信息）

Active Rear Steer System　主动式后轮转向系统（见 ARS）

active repair time　有效修理时间（扣除停歇的修理延续时间）

active restraint　（指安全带等需要乘员动手使用的）主动式乘员保护装置（或系统）

active ride control (system)　行驶平顺性自动控制（系统）

active roll-mitigation system　主动式防翻车系统（只要传感器测得某一车轮离地抬升趋势达到规定阈值，便制动减速，避免翻车）

active safety system　主动安全系统（指汽车在驾驶人员主动操作下确保安全的系统，如：性能优越的制动系统、安全稳定的转向系统等。相对无须驾驶人员操作即可在发生事故时，减少伤害的被动安全系统"passive safety system"，如：安全气囊等而言）

active (seat) belt　（汽车乘员的）主动式安全带（指由乘员自己带挂的安全带）

active sensor　主动式传感器（如：既可测定车轮转速，又可测定其旋转方向，测速范围可从 0km/h 开始的半导体式脉冲车轮转速传感器）

Active Stability Control System　稳定性主动控制系统（见 ASC system）

active steering effort　操舵力（驾驶员作用于转向盘的力）

Active Hybrid　主动式混合动力车（BMW混合动力车商品名，有5 series，7 series等多个型号，全电力行驶时最高车速可达60km/h，加速时发动机参与驱动）

Active Hydraulic Suspension System　主动式液压悬架系统（日产公司研制的一种电子控制式液压悬架的商品名。该悬架系统的液压源为发动机驱动的液压泵，由电子控制模块根据行车状况控制输入四个车轮悬架液压缸的液压，使汽车始终保持稳定状态）

active length　有效长度

active level　有效电平（如在时序电路中能产生激励的数字输入信号的电平）

active life　使用寿命，使用期限

active mass　①有效质量，作用质量　②放射性材料，活性材料（= active material）

Active matic　（日本MAZDA公司）手动-自动一体式变速器（商品名）

active metal　活性金属

active muffler system　主动型消声器系统（见 active noise control system）

active noise cancellation　主动式消声（如：利用反相噪声消声等，见 antinoise）

active noise control system　（车内噪声）主动消声系统（电子控制系统测得车内的噪声超过规定值时，即通过微型声响装置发出可精确抵消该噪声的频率的反相声波，利用该反相声波消声的系统，亦称 antinoise system）

active particulate filter　（柴油机的）主动式微粒物滤清器（使用多孔陶瓷滤件，见 diesel engine emission standards）

active power　（电机等的）有效功率（有效电流与电压的乘积，见 active current）

active radius　①行动半径，作用半径　②（车辆的）运行半径（亦写作 action radius）

active reaction power steering system　主动式反作用力型动力转向系（以转向时产生的各种反作用力作为输入信号，向驾驶者提供车辆转向实时状况和改善动力转向系转向手感，以及对车辆因各种干扰而产生的转向误差进行自动补偿和修正的反馈信息）

Active Rear Steer System　主动式后轮转向系统（见 ARS）

active repair time　有效修理时间（扣除停歇的修理延续时间）

active restraint　（指安全带等需要乘员动手使用的）主动式乘员保护装置（或系统）

active ride control (system)　行驶平顺性自动控制（系统）

active roll-mitigation system　主动式防翻车系统（只要传感器测得某一车轮离地抬升趋势达到规定阈值，便制动减速，避免翻车）

active safety system　主动安全系统（指汽车在驾驶人员主动操作下确保安全的系统，如：性能优越的制动系统、安全稳定的转向系统等。相对无须驾驶人员操作即可在发生事故时，减少伤害的被动安全系统 "passive safety system"，如：安全气囊等而言）

active (seat) belt　（汽车乘员的）主动式安全带（指由乘员自己带挂的安全带）

active sensor　主动式传感器（如：既可测定车轮转速，又可测定其旋转方向，测速范围可从0km/h开始的半导体式脉冲车轮转速传感器）

Active Stability Control System　稳定性主动控制系统（见 ASC system）

active steering effort　操舵力（驾驶员作用于转向盘的力）

active steering system 主动转向系统（简称 ASS，电子控制模块根据车速、横向加速度和转向盘转角等传感器的信息判断汽车出现危害其行驶稳定性的状态时，便会通过转向盘柱中部的电动机-行星齿轮机构对转向轮施加减小转向角或反向转向的干涉性修正。这种修正是独立于驾驶者的转向操作进行的，而且会让驾驶者感觉不到。该系统一般与汽车的电子控制稳定性系统耦合使用）

active suspension（system） 主动式悬架（系统），（电子控制式悬架系统，能根据悬架上质量的加速度，主动地调节悬架的高度或刚度，以控制车身侧倾、振动等，亦称 active suspention control system）

active torque control 4WD 主动式转矩控制型4轮驱动

Active Torque Transfer System 主动式转矩分配系统（亦称 Active torque transmission system，见 ATTS）

active transduser ①有源换能器 ②（汽车电子控制系统中的）有源传感器（其输出信号要依靠电源或外电源提供能量）

active transmission 有效转换（如输入信号从一个电平到另一个电平并能产生激励的转换）

Active TRC system （丰田公司的）主动型牵引力控制系统（商品名，通过对四轮独立的制动控制，抑制因驱动大于轮胎与路面附着力而产生的某一车轮的滑转，该系统与 ABS, EBD, brake assist, VSC, DAC 及 HSAC 组成一个总体，相互配合，协同工作）

active valve transmission 见 AVT

active voltage 有效电压（在交流电路中与电流相位相同的一部分电压）

active volt-amperes 有功功率，有效功率（交流电路中有效电压与电流的乘积或有效电流与电压的乘积，单位为 watt，有效功率为1瓦指有效电流1安流过1伏电压所做的功，亦称 active power）

active yaw control system 主动式横摆控制系统

activity ①活性，活力，活动能力，作用效能 ②占空系数

ACT sensor 进气空气温度传感器（air charge temperature sensor 的简称，= manifold air temperature sensor）

actual 实际的，在使用（运行，作用）中进行或发生的，有效的

actual capacity of an accumulator ①蓄电池有效容量 ②蓄能器有效容量

actual cycle 实际循环

actual displacement ①（转子发动机的）实际排量（指旋转活塞每自转一转的排量，为单室排量的三倍）②实际位移 ③实际工作容积

actual efficiency 实际效率（= practical efficiency）

actual gum 溶于燃油的胶质（参见 dissolved gum）

actual horsepower 有效功率（参见 effective horsepower）

actual load 实际载荷，有效载荷

actual mixing ratio （可燃混合气的）实际空燃比

actual operating conditions 实际运行（工作）状况，实际使用状况

actual output ①有效功率 ②实际输出

actual-service test 实际使用条件下的试验（简称 actual test）

actual special energy requirement 实际所需比能（指压缩机等压缩单位质量或单位容积的气体，其驱动轴所需的能，分别称为实际质量比能或实际容积比能。实际容积比能就是比功率，但国际标准 ISO 提出，应尽量避免使用比功率 special power

一词）

actual state 实际状态

actual stopping distance （汽车的）实际制动停车距离（等于汽车制动距离和反应距离的总和。参见 braking distance 和 reaction distance）

actual stress 实际应力，有效应力（= true stress）

actual tire force on road 轮胎对路面的实际作用力

actual-use test conditions （符合）实际使用（状况的）试验条件

actual volume rate of flow （流体的）实际体积流量

actual zero point 绝对零点，基点

actuate ①（使）…起作用，开动 ②激励，激活

actuating line 促动管（线）路，执行管路（气制动系中将压缩空气能转化为机械能的制动气室的管路系统）

actuating medium 工作介质，工质

actuating signal （控制系统的）执行信号

actuating switch 促动开关，执行开关

actuating system of braking system 制动系的执行系统，促动系统（指包括制动踏板—制动主缸—管道—轮缸或踏板—气制动阀—制动气室等在内的控制装置和传能装置的总称）

actuator 执行元件，执行器，执行机构（如：电子控制系统中执行电子控制模块的指令的各种电磁阀、继电器、步进电动机、电磁开关，以及制动系中的轮缸等）

actuator arm 执行臂，促动臂（如：真空点火提前机构中膜片推动断电器底板的推杆）

actuator pressure sensor （电控液压制动系）执行机构输入压力传感器（监控输入执行机构的液压传感器，见 brake actuator）

acuity 分辨能力

acute ①尖的，尖锐的 ②剧烈的，强烈的，急剧的 ③高音的

acute angle 锐角

acute-angle bevel drive 锐角锥齿轮传动

ACV ①空气控制阀（air control valve）②气垫车（air cushion vehicle）③报警单向阀（alarm check valve）④自动控制阀（automatic control valve）

A/D 模数转换，模拟数字转换（analog to digital conversion 的简称）

AD ①最新发展（advanced development 的简称）②气动力减速器（aerodynamic decelerator 的简称）③空气干电池（air dry cell）④公元（Anno Domini 的简称）

ADAC 全德汽车俱乐部（德文 Allgemeiner Deutscher Automobilclub 的简称，是德国一家向会员提供多种服务的非营利性组织，ADAC 的汽车碰撞测试要求严格，且更具权威）

adaptability to driving （驾驶人员的）驾驶适应性

adaptability to road and weather condition （对）道路及气候的适应性

adaptable 可适应的，善于适应的，适合的，可装配的

adaptation ①适应，适合 ②采用（某种新技术等）

adaptation to driver's behavior and traffic situation 驾驶人员操作习惯和交通状况的自适应能力（指电子控制系统随驾驶员操作习惯和道路交通条件改变其控制程序或控制量，以维持最佳控制的能力，亦称学习能力"learning ability"）

adapter ①适配器，转接器 ②异径接头（特指将两个尺寸不同部件连接在一起的装置或部件，如：将套筒

扳手的扭杆接装与之尺寸不同的套筒扳头的附件）③插座、灯座、接头

adapter shaft 连接轴，接装轴，套接轴

adapter sleeve （滚动轴承的）紧定套

adapter-type bearing 装在紧定套上的滚动轴承（靠轴承锥形内孔紧定在轴上）

adaptive 自适应的（在汽车电子控制系统中，指具有可根据受控装置实时状况自动改变控制量的系统或装置）

adaptive coefficient 发动机适应性系数（指发动机的转矩适应性系数 m 和转速适应性系数 n 的乘积，该系数愈大，则发动机适应负荷变化的性能愈好）

adaptive control 自适应控制（指可自动根据受控过程或对象以及外部作用条件的变化，改变控制参数及控制量，以维持事先选定的某一优化值的控制方式。如果能随上述变化，使控制目标作随机改变，则称最佳自适应控制"adaptive optimal control"）

adaptive cruise control with steer assist 带（弯道行驶时）自动跟随转向的适应性定速巡航系统

adaptive cruise system 自适应性定速巡航系统（简称 ACS，亦称 adaptive cruise control system，简称 ACC system 或智能定速巡航系统 intelligent cruise system，简称 ICS。当无前车时按所设定的车速以稳定的车速行驶；当有前车时，车速随前车而变，与前车保持稳定的间距，因此该系统又称为 inter-vehicular distance keeping system 车间距离保持系统，简称 IDK system，在市区走走停停交通条件下可大幅度减轻驾驶疲劳，确保行车安全）

adaptive data 适应性数据（电子系统适应性控制所需的各种数据）

adaptive driving beam system 见 adaptive front-lighting system

adaptive front-lighting system 适应性（汽车）前照灯照明系统（简称 AFS，亦称"intelligent lighting system"智能灯光照明系统或"beam controllable head-lighting system"照射光束可控前照灯照明系统。该系统可①根据车速改变照射距离，根据环境黑暗程度调节照射光亮度及照射光斑照度分布②根据转向盘或前轮转向角，改变照射方向，实现动态弯道照明）

adaptive fuel control 喷油量适应性控制（当喷油器内有油垢沉积，或燃油压力调节器磨损引起油压降低时，实际喷出的燃油量将少于电子控制模块指令脉冲宽度的喷油量，使空燃比失准。电子控制模块在闭路控制中根据 O_2 传感器的信息测得这一情况时，即启动喷油量适应性控制，加大喷油指令脉冲宽度，使空燃比保持要求值。如果这一状态继续时间超过某一规定值，电子控制模块将改变原指令脉冲宽度，使之固定为当前值）

adaptive fuzzy controller 自适应性模糊控制器

adaptive idle speed strategy （发动机电子控制系统的）怠速适应性控制模式（当测得向怠速空气装置发出的怠速空气控制量指令不足以产生该控制量所对应的怠速转速时，电子控制模块将发出一新的控制量指令取代原指令，以达到所要求的怠速转速。如果在闭路运转中，新的控制量可保证所要求的稳速怠速，则经过规定的时间后，该新控制量将被存储，供以后遇到同样情况时使用，即所谓的学习过程"learning process"）

adaptive lighting　自适应性照明（技术）（见 intelligent lighting）

adaptive memory　自适应性存储器

adaptive monitoring software　（汽车电子控制系统的）自适应性监测软件

adaptive optimal control　最佳自适应控制（见 adaptive control）

adaptive programming　自适应性编程（汽车自适应控制性系统的自动程序编制，如：汽车的自适应预选车速定速巡行控制系统可自动分析驾驶员在汽车非定速巡行控制工况下的加速/减速习惯，并归类存储，编入其控制程序内，进而参照该习惯模式控制车速）

adaptive shift（point）control（function）　（电子控制无级连续变速器的）适应性换挡（点）控制（功能）（简称 ASC, 电子控制模块可根据车速、加速踏板位置、行驶阻力、坡道阻力、转向阻力等传感器的信息从存储的数百种换挡模式中选出最符合驾驶者的驾驶操作习惯、道路和行车条件以及最能节油、环保和充分发挥车辆性能的换挡点的控制功能）

adaptive software strategy　适应性的软件策略（指不增加或不改变硬件设备，仅通过软件处理实现适应性控制的策略）

adaptive strategy　（电子控制系统的）适应式控制策略（指其电子控制模块可连续地调整其按理想状态拟定的控制参数量值，以补偿因传感器或其他影响主要功能的部件的制造误差，磨损或退化造成的不足，使受控系统始终保持理想状态。如果电子控制模块除上述适应性功能外，还具有存储与借鉴以往实施过的适应性控制模式，使当前进行的适应性控制更加完善的功能，则称该电子控制模块具有学习能力"learning capability"）

adaptive suspension system　自适应性悬架系统（电子控制模块根据车速、转向角、离地间隙、制动压力、加速度、节气门开度、横摆加速度，侧倾加速度传感器等信息，通过执行机构不断改变悬架弹簧和减振器的阻尼，即软硬程度，以保持悬架的最佳工况状态和车身高度）

adaptive variable suspension　阻尼可变适应性悬架

adaptor　①接头，灯座　②转接装置（= adapter）

adaptor plate　转接板，（指可接装形状或尺寸与原件不同的代用件的接装板或板形接头, = adapter plate）

ADAS　①先进的驾驶者支援系统（advanced driver assistance system 的简称）②自动数据获取系统（automatic data acquisition system 的简称）

Adblue　尿素［欧洲市场出售的尿素喷射式催化转化器用尿素（urea）的商品名］

A/D converter　模/数转换器，A/D 转换器（analog-to-digital converter 的简称）

ADD　（分时四轮驱动系统的）自动分离差速器（automatic disconnecting differential 的简称）

added resistance　附加电阻

addendum　齿顶高（圆柱齿轮指齿顶圆与分度圆的径向距离；锥齿轮指上述两圆沿锥母线度量的距离；环面蜗杆指分度圆与喉圆之间、圆柱蜗杆指分度圆柱面与齿根圆柱面之间的距离）

addendum angle　（锥齿轮的）齿顶角（顶锥角与分锥角之差）

addendum flank　（齿轮轮齿的）上齿面（指齿顶曲面与分度曲面之间的齿面）

adder　加法器［①其输出表示诸输

入之和的部件②产生两个或多个数之和的装置,亦称加法电路"add(ed) circuit"]

adder-subtractor 加减器

addition ①加,加法,补充,添加②附加物,添加剂

addition agent 添加剂

additional charge (蓄电池的)补充充电

additional load 附加载荷,补充荷载

additional resistance coil 附加电阻线圈

additional retarding braking system 辅助减速系统,辅助缓速制动系统(在下长坡时,辅助驾驶员控制或降低车速, = auxiliary brake)

additional safety factor 额外安全系数,附加安全系数

additional seat (客车座椅边,可折叠、收合的)加座(亦称 folding seat)

additional sphere (可控型油-气悬架系统的)附加球囊型减振器(亦称 addition damper, 该球囊经一电子控制模块控制的调节阀与主球囊相通,当该调节阀关闭时,悬架阻尼特性为硬模式,开启时转为软模式)

additional temperature error 温度附加误差(指仪表和附件环境温度偏离规定值时所引起的仪表值变化)

additional voltage error 电压附加误差(指仪表测试电压偏离规定电压时引起的仪表值变化量)

addition decreasing freezing point 冰点降低(添加)剂,防冻剂

addition increasing viscosity number 黏度指数提高(添加)剂

additive ①附加的,增加的,添加的②附加物,添加剂③加法,加法的

additive engine oil 加有添加剂的发动机润滑油,掺有添加剂的机油,含有添加剂的机油(亦称 additive blended oil, additive treated oil)

additized 加有添加剂的

add load control (底盘测功机滚筒等的)加载控制装置;加载控制

add-oil level 润滑油面准线(应按此线高度加注润滑油)

add-on ①加载,加上,加添上②加装的,由工厂、出售商或用户加装在标准设计上的(如空调设备等)③加装的设备或装置

add on ABS 见 non-integrated ABS

add-on power-booster steering arrangement 附加助力转向装置,附加动力转向装置

add-ons 附加装置,添增组件

address ①地址(计算机中用于标识存放数据的存储器存储单元的一组代码)②寻址(指通过地址来访问或查取该数据项等)

addressable program storage 可寻址程序存储器(具有固定位置与地址码的程序存储单元)

address bus (计算机的)地址总线(由地址寄存器向存储器或输入级传输地址的单向总线)

address format 地址格式(电子控制系统中①指令中地址部分的安排形式②各个地址的安排形式)

addressing mode 寻址方式

address register 地址寄存器(电子控制系统中指①存放一个地址的寄存器,②在某项指令执行过程中临时保存该指令地址的存储单元)

ADECS 汽车柴油机电子控制系统(automotive diesel electronic control system 的简称)

ADF 空气动力阻力系数(aerodynamic drag factor 的简称)

ADFR 遥控自动定向仪,自动遥控测向仪(remote-controlled automatic direction finder 的简称)

adhere 附着,黏着于;黏住

adhesion ①黏附,黏着,胶着

②（路面与轮胎间的）附着力（亦称 adhesion force，实际上指二者摩擦力）③（橡皮对金属的）胶着力 ④（电线的）接头

adhesion coefficient 附着系数（亦称 adhesive coefficient, adhesion factor）

adhesion of lubricant 润滑剂的附着性能

adhesion strength ①黏着力，黏附力 ②黏着强度

adhesion test ①黏着力试验，黏着强度试验 ②附着力试验

adhesion (-type) tyre 高抓着力轮胎，高附着性轮胎（亦称 adhesive-tire）

adhesion utilization （制动时）附着力利用率（制动减速度与地面最大附着系数之比）

adhesion weight ①附着重量（亦称 adhesive weight，为附着质量的旧称）②（有时亦指贴在轮辋上的车轮）平衡重块

adhesion wheel 驱动轮，主动车轮（参见 traction wheel）

adhesive ①附着的，黏着的，易黏的 ②黏合胶，胶合剂，黏性物质 ③附着力；黏着现象

adhesive bonding aluminum body 铝板黏结车身

adhesive force tyre on road 轮胎在路面上的附着力［有纵向附着力和侧向附着力之分，adhesive force 或称 adhesion force 一般指纵向附着力（longitudinal adhesive force）］

adhesive tape 胶带，绝缘胶带

adhesive tread of tire 高抓着力的（越野胎）胎面

adhesive wear 黏附磨损，黏着磨损（指相互接触的表面之间局部黏着而造成的磨损）

adhesive weight （贴在轮辋上平衡车轮的小铅块）平衡重块

ADHP 气动液压泵（air-drawn hydraulic pump 的简称）

adiabatic 绝热的（= adiathermal, adiathermic，既不传热的，也不损失热量，也不获得热量，因而热效率高的）

adiabatic change 绝热变化（一定量的气体在既不输出热量，也不输入热量的情况下产生的绝热膨胀和绝热压缩等的总称）

adiabatic engine 绝热发动机（指减少或断绝冷却损失从而大幅度提高燃烧热效率的各类发动机，亦称 low heat rejection engine）

adiabatic exponent 绝热指数

adiabatic/turbo compounding (version) 绝热-涡轮增压复合型（发动机）

adiabator 保温材料；绝热材料

adiathermancy ①绝热性 ②不透红外线性

ADIS 先进的驾驶员信息系统（参见 advanced driver information system）

adjacent frequency system （与车载无线通信系统）频率相邻的系统

adj sp 可调速率，可调速度（adjustable speed 的简称）

adjustability 可调性，可调程度，可调能力

adjustable condenser 可变电容器

adjustable cup-holder （车厢内的大小）可调式（饮水）杯架

adjustable-guide-blade control cam 几何结构（可变型涡轮机的）角度可调导向叶片的控制凸轮

adjustable-height draw bar （全挂车）高度可调的牵引杆

adjustable jack table 带可调节千斤顶的工作台

adjustable jet ①可调量孔（= adjustable orifice）②可调喷嘴（= adjustable nozzle）③可调喷射流

adjustable lever 可调（长度的）杠杆，可调（长度）的臂杆

adjustable pedal 可调踏板（高度，角度，踏程，软、硬可调）

adjustable range 可调范围（指各种调整装置，参数的可调上、下限之间的区域）

adjustable roof van 车顶高度可调的厢式货车

adjustable shock absorber 可调式减振器（软、硬程度，即其阻尼—位移特性可调的减振器）

adjustable spanner 活扳手（指常见的可调到适用于各种不同尺寸的螺母和螺栓的开口扳手，美称 adjustable wrench，= shifting spanner, screw wrench, female wrench，用于车身作业的称 coach wrench，俗称 crescent wrench，或 monkey wrench 因其形似而得名）

adjustable speed governor 全程式速度调节器（参见 variable speed governor）

adjustable steering column （长度、倾斜度可调的）可调式转向柱，可调节式转向盘柱

adjustable stop 可调挡块，可调限位挡块，可调限位装置（= adjustable dog）

adjustable style hydraulic tube fitting 可调式液压管接头

adjustable tread 可调轮距

adjustable wrench ［美］活动扳手（见 adjustable spanner）

adjusted data 经修正的数据，经校核的资料

adjusted part throttle （新车出厂）调好的节气门限定开度，（制造厂在新车出厂前调好的限制走合期负荷的节气门最大开度）

adjusted power 修正功率（指将某种大气状态下测得的功率换算成所规定的标准大气状态下的功率）

adjuster 调节器，调节装置，调节件（如：seat adjuster 汽车座椅的前、后位置，靠背斜度等的调节装置，adjuster 后常跟一名词说明该调节装置具体是什么，如 adjuster cam，表示该调节装置为一凸轮，可译为调节凸轮，如制动蹄与制动鼓面的间隙调节凸轮）

adjusting ①（起）调节（作用）的 ②调整（= adjustment①）

adjusting cam （间隙等的）调整凸轮

adjusting eccentric screw 偏心调节螺钉

adjusting gauge 调整（作业用的）量规（如厚薄规等）

adjusting nut 调整螺母

adjusting pull-rod end 拉杆的（长度）调节端

adjusting resistance winding 调节电流、电压用的电阻线圈

adjusting ring 调整环

adjusting screw 调节螺钉（如怠速油量调节螺钉等）

adjusting shim 调整垫片

adjusting sleeve 调节套管（如：转向横拉杆端调节转向轮前束用的内螺纹套管）

adjustment ①调整作业，调整动作，调整过程 ②调整工具，调整手段，（装置上进行某项）调整（的）部件 ③（可进行）调整（的）余地，（剩下的可）调整（冲程、长度、域值、大小等）余量

adjustment for altitude （喷油量的）高度校正，海拔校准

adjustment for wear 磨损（补偿）调整

adjustment in direction 方向修正，方位调整

adjustment of ignition timing 点火正时调整，点火正时（= adjustment of ignition, distributor timing control, spark control）

adjustment table 调整数据表，调整

参数表

adjustment test 调整试验（对车辆或发动机的各可调因素进行综合调整，使其处于最佳技术状态的试验）

adjustomatic shock absorber 自动调节（阻尼特性）的减振器

ADMB ［美］自动路-轨两用型客车（可在普通路面及轨道上行驶，automated dual mode bus 的简称）

ADM-EV 先进的动态阻尼器—电动机型电动汽车（指利用电动机质量作为非悬架质量的动态阻尼质量的轮内驱动型电动汽车，可显著降低其轮胎接地力的波动，其中 ADM 为 advanced-dynamic-damper-motor 的简称）

administration ①经营，管理，治理（多指政府行政或法规管理）②（管理）局，处，署

administrative preventive maintenance time 维护准备时间

administrative time ①修理准备时间②（因组织管理不善的）停歇时间

administrative transportation 后勤运输

admissible stress 许用应力，容许应力

admissible test 资格鉴定，认证试验

admission ①许可进入，进入，接收，容纳②（常用于表示）进气（= induction, inlet）

admission line ①（示功图上的）进气曲线②进气管道

admission stroke 进气冲程（= inlet stroke, induction stroke）

admittance wave （发动机的）进道气流波

admixture ①掺和，混合②掺和剂，掺合剂，混合物，杂质，掺料

adopt 采取，采用，选用，接受，（正式）通过；仿效

adorn （车身或车内）装饰，配饰（各种增加美观的饰件等）

adornment （车内的）装饰物

ADR 见 accident data recorder

A-drier A 型烤房（指其空间可分为上、下两层区的车身油漆烘干室。上层为烘干区，下层为加热区。车身由加热区入口进入烤房后即被提升至上层烘干区，烘干后再下降至加热区，由加热区出口送出烤房。车身通过烤房的路线似 A 字形，故名。由加热区加热的热空气聚集于上层烘干区，不会逸散、节能高效）

ADS ①自动数据处理系统（automatic data processing system 的简称）②节气门自动控制执行件（automative throttle actuator 的简称）

adsorbed oil film 吸附的油膜

adsorbent storage （利用活性炭或其他介质的吸附能力存储气体燃料的低压）吸附存储法

adsorbing matter 吸附体，吸附物质，吸附材料

adsorption ①吸附，吸附作用②表面吸收，表面吸着（特指固体表面与气体或液体接触时，气体或液体中的成分附着于固体表面的现象）

adsorption affinity 吸附力，吸附亲和力

adsorption canister 活性炭罐（= activated carbon canister）

adsorptive power 吸附能力

adulterated oil ①脏油（含有杂质的机油）②品质低劣的机油

adult occupant （汽车的）成年乘员

advance ①将…提前，使…前移，增加，提高，促进；前进，上升，上涨②提前量（通常指点火、喷油、进气门开启等的时刻提到活塞到达上止点前，以及排气门开启时刻提前到活塞到达下止点前的曲轴转角度数）③提前的，超前的，位于前沿的（= advancing）④已提前的，

先进的，程度高的（= advanced）⑤与提前有关的

advance angle （点火，喷油等的）提前角（一般用上止点前曲轴转角度数表示）

advance capsule 真空点火提前装置（= vaccum advance unit）

advance curve （点火、喷油等）提前特性曲线（提前角随发动机转速、进气管真空度而变化的曲线）

advanced ①先进的，高级的②被提前的，（已）提前的

advanced-class 高级的，高档的，先进的，最新的

advanced development 远景（产品的）开发（研制）（特指新机型的性能完善性研制）

advanced driver information system 先进的驾驶员信息系统（简称 ADIS，为驾驶员服务的电子控制信息系统的总称）

advance device （机械式点火、喷油等的）提前装置，提前器

advance device fly weight spring （离心式）提前装置的飞锤弹簧

advanced high-mounted stop lamp 先进型高位制动灯（可通过点亮面积的大小向后方行驶的车辆传达制动减速度大小的信息）

advanced high strength steel 见 AHSS

advance diaphragm （双膜片真空点火提前分电器的）点火提前膜片（亦称 primary diaphragm）

advanced ignition （点火正时失调造成的火花点火式发动机电火花在非最佳时刻之前出现）过早点火

advanced inflatable tubular structure 见 AITS

advance direction sign 前置指路标志，预告方向标志

advanced opening of admission valve 进气门提前开启度（= early opening of inlet valve, admission valve lead）

advanced public transportation systems 先进的公共运输系统（简称 APTS，ITS 的子系统）

advanced rural transportation systems 先进的乡村运输系统（简称 ARTS，ITS 的子系统）

Advanced Safety Vehicle 先进的安全汽车（见 ASV）

Advanced Total Traction Engineering System for All Electronic Torque Split 先进的电子控制转矩分配牵引力系统（见 E-TS）

advanced traffic management system 先进的交通管理系统（简称 ATMS，ITS 的子系统）

advanced traveler information systems 先进的旅行者信息系统，先进的车辆驾驶者信息系统（简称 ATIS，= advanced driver information system，ITS 的子系统）

advanced vehicle control system 先进的车辆控制系统（简称 AVCS，= automatic vehicle control system）

advance fire 早燃，过早点火（参见 early ignition）

advance plate （断电器的）活动盘，点火提前盘

advancer （各种）提前装置（器，机构，件的通称）

advance stop （分电器真空膜片等的）点火提前冲程限制件

AdvanceTrac （Ford 集合 ABS、EBD、TCS、ESC、RSC 等功能的）先进牵引系统（商品名）

advance weight （离心式点火提前机构的）重锤，飞锤（centrifugal-advance-mechanism weight 的简称）

advancing edge 前沿，前边缘，上升边（= front edge, leading edge, rising edge）

advancing side 受拉部分（如：传动带的紧张侧）

advection heat 对流热

advective cooling 对流冷却

adverse-condition test 恶劣（困难）条件下的试验，苛刻条件试验

adverse effect 反作用，有害影响，不利影响

adverse grade ①向下坡度；②过陡的坡度（亦称 adverse slope）

adverse terrain 难通行的地面，不易通过的地面

adverse-weather lamp 恶劣天候行车灯（如：雾灯，= fog light）

adverse wind 迎面风，逆风，顶风（= contrary wind, head wind, head-on wind, opposing wind）

advertised horsepower 公告马力，宣传马力，制造厂标定马力（亦称 Detroit horsepower）

advertised load 制造厂公告的载荷

ADVISOR （美国能源部再生能量实验室开发的）高级汽车仿真器（Advanced Vehicle Simulator 的简称，是一种针对民用轿车，基于 MAT-LAB/SMULINK 软件环境的免费仿真软件，其代码完全公开，提供图形用户操作界面，用户可通过点击各部件及其源文件修改参数，也可通过参数对话框进行参数修改。用户可以利用其内部提供的通用子模块来组装所需的汽车模块进行仿真。其主要功能：估计汽车燃油经济性，比较各种循环工况下的油耗与排放，考核汽车驱动链间的工作，评价混合动力车的控制逻辑，进行控制参数的优化匹配，以燃油经济性或最大动力性为优化目标进行汽车参数设计）

advisory 咨询的，推荐的，建议的

advisory speed sign 推荐车速标志，建议车速标志（如在急弯处或危险地点推荐的最高安全车速）

AEA 汽车电器协会（Automotive Electric Association 的简称）

AEB 自动紧急制动器（Automatic Emergency Brake 的简称，当雷达探测器或摄像机等测得与前方障碍物的相对速度及距离必须立即停车或减速才能避免碰撞时即在电子控制模块的控制下酌情制动停车或减速）

AECD 辅助排放控制装置，辅助排放物净化装置（auxiliary emission control device 的简称）

AEI ①在喷油结束后（after end of injection）②（美国 SAE 的）汽车工程国际版（月刊，automotive engineering international 的简称）

AEL ［美］（环保局的）汽车排放试验室（Automotive Emission Laboratory 的简称）

A/ELR 自动-紧急锁死式安全带伸缩器［Automatic/Emergency Locking Retractor 的简称，是一种自动锁死与紧急锁死功能可切换的安全带伸缩装置。所谓自动锁死安全带伸缩装置（automatic locking retractor，简称 ALR）是指拉出多长，便自动锁死在该长度上，而不能再拉长。紧急锁死安全带伸缩装置（emergency locking retractor，简称 ELR）则是在一般情况下可任意拉长、缩短，但遇紧急情况，如汽车突然减速，安全带受到急剧拉力时，便会立即锁死拉紧］

A end （液力传动机构的）A 端，主动部分

Aeolus （古代西方神话中的）风神伊俄勒斯（我国东风汽车公司的英文名）

Aeolus-Citroën Automobile Company Ltd 神龙汽车有限公司（其中 Aeolus 为风神，代表东风集团，Citroën 音译雪铁龙，故名神龙）

AER （位于车身后部的）后发动机室（rear engine room 的简称）

aer 空气动力学，气体动力学（aerodynamics 的简称)

AERA ［美］汽车发动机大修工作者协会 (Automotive Engine Rebuilders Association 的简称)

aerate 充气；暴露于空气中使与空气混合；使与氧化合

aerated bath nitriding 空气搅拌液体渗氮法

aerated plastic 泡沫塑料 (= foam plastic, expanded plastic, sponge plastic)

aeration ①充气，通风，鼓风②(空气以微小气泡状态混入液力系统工作液中的)混气现象，乳化状态③(工作液中)混入的空气 (= entrained air)

aeration-cooling (车厢内的)通风降温

aerator 充气器，打气机，鼓风机，通风装置，通风机

aerial ①天线的②空气的③高架的，空中的④气体的⑤天线，天线系统 (= 美 antenna)

aerial lead-in 天线的引入线

aerial system ①高架道路系统②天线系统

aerial transport system 高架(轨)道运输系统

aerial tuning capacitor 天线调谐电容器 (简称 ATC)

Aero acoustic noise (汽车高速行驶时产生的)气流噪声

Aero-Acoustic Wind Tunnel Test 高速气流风洞声响试验 (测试汽车行驶空气动力噪声)

Aero Car (美国工程师莫尔顿·泰勒 20 世纪 50~90 年代研制的)飞行汽车 (的名称)

aerocar 气垫车

aerodromometer 气流速度计，气速表

aerodynamic add-on device (车身的)空气动力附加装置，空气动力附件，风力附件 (装在车身外部可提高汽车空气动力稳定性及减少空气阻力的多种附加板件及装置的通称，= aerodynamic attachment，简称 AOA device，亦称 aerodynamic control device)

aerodynamic(al) ①空气动力(学)的②符合空气动力学原理的(指流线型的、空气阻力小的等)

aerodynamic angle of attack 气动迎角 (指车辆行驶时合成气流速度在车辆对称平面内的投影与车辆纵向轴线间的夹角)

aerodynamic appearance (车辆的)空气动力学外形

aerodynamic atomization (燃油的)气流雾化，空气动力粉碎

aerodynamic brake 见 air brake②

aerodynamic centre 风压中心 (指汽车运动时所受气流侧向力合力的作用点)

aerodynamic characteristics 空气动力特性 (曲线)

aerodynamic (clean) body 流线型车身，(符合)空气动力学(原理的)的车身

aerodynamic coefficient 空气动力(学)系数 (汽车运动时各种空气力和力矩作用的程度的空气阻力系数，升力系数和侧向力系数等的通称)

aerodynamic drag factor 空气阻力系数 (指汽车空气阻力与气流密度、车辆正面投影面积和速度平方的乘积的 1/2 的比值，亦称 air resistance coefficient)

aerodynamic efficiency 空气动力效率，空气动力系数 (空气阻力系数的倒数)

aerodynamic force 空气动力 (行驶时，气流对车辆的各种作用力)

aerodynamic force coefficients 空气动力系数 (见 longitudinal、side、 vertical aerodynamic force coefficients)

aerodynamic form 流线型（=streamline form）

aerodynamic lift 空气动力学升力，空气浮力

aerodynamic loading 空气动力负荷

aerodynamic moment coefficients （汽车）空气动力矩系数

aerodynamic moments 空气动力学作用力矩，空气动力力矩

aerodynamic motion variables （汽车）空气动力学运动变量（如：环境风速，风向角，相对风速，合成气流速度，气动侧偏角，气动迎角等）

aerodynamic noise 空气动力噪声，空气动力学噪声（行驶时，气流引起的噪声）

Aero Dynamic Port 空气动力学进气道（简称 AD port，其入口处较大，越靠近燃烧室进气道口径越小，借以增加进气流速，在燃烧室内形成较强的进气涡流）

aerodynamic properties 空气动力学特性（见 aerodynamics②）

aerodynamic reaction 空气动力反作用（力）

aerodynamic resistance 空气阻力（=aerodynamic drag，指空气流在汽车行驶方向的分力）

aerodynamic resistance coefficient 空气阻力系数（若令 F—空气阻力，A—车辆正面面积，ρ—空气密度，v—相对速度，则：$F=\dfrac{1}{2}C_{D}\rho Av$，式中：$C_{D}$—空气阻力系数）

aerodynamic retarder 空气动力缓速器

aerodynamics ①空气动力学②空气动力学特性（=aerodynamic properties）

aerodynamic screen 空气动力筛屏板（一种装在驾驶室顶上的空气阻力减少装置，板的中部具有很多筛眼，两翼形状按空气动力学原理制成）

aerodynamic sideforce 空气动力（学）侧向力

aerodynamic sideslip angle 空气动力侧偏角（①合成气流速度与 X_0 轴在 $X-Y$ 平面内的投影之间的夹角②因空气动力作用而形成或增加的侧偏角）

aerodynamic simulation system （车辆的）空气动力模拟系统

aerodynamic stability （汽车的）空气动力学稳定性（汽车受高速行驶时的空气升力，及侧向力等作用时的方向和行驶稳定性等）

aero (dynamic) stabilizer 空气动力稳定装置（利用空气动力改善车辆操纵稳定性和减少或对抗空气动力的影响而保持汽车稳定性的各种装置的总称）

aerodynamic suction 空气动力吸力

aerodynamic tool 气动工具；空气动力器械

aerodynamic torque converter 空气动力（学）变矩器，可压缩性流体变矩器（使用可压缩性流体，作为变矩器的工作介质）

aerodynamic tunnel （进行空气动力试验用的）风洞

aero-fairing encasement （装在车身上减小空气阻力的）空气（动力）导流罩板

aerofoil （=美 airfoil）①翼形，翼型②翼板，翼形板③导风罩，导风板（特指各种翼形的导风装置，如用于赛车，以产生负升力或向下的压力，使车轮紧压路面的压风板等）

aerogel 气凝胶（接触空气即可凝固）

aeromobile 气垫车（可离开地面浮行的汽车）

aeronautical 航空的，飞行的

aero part 空气动力学板件（安装在车身上控制气流方向，减少空气动力阻力，及将空气流引向需要冷却的部位的各种板件的总称，亦称 aero kit）

aero parts （车身上安装的改善）空气动力学（的）部件

aeroseal ①气封，气垫密封②防止漏气的密封件

aerosol ①烟雾，尘雾（浮游状态分散在大气中的固体微粒和液体微粒或雾的总称）②喷雾器

aerosoloscope 空气中微粒测算器，空气微粒测定仪

aerospace ①航空航天，航天②航空航天技术，航天技术③航天航空工业，航天工业

aero-stabilizer 空气动力稳定装置（运用空气动力学改善汽车稳定性的附加装置的通称）

aerostatic bearing 空气静力轴承，气垫轴承

Aerotwin 双飞片（Bosch公司最新发明"无支架雨刮片"的商品名）

aeroview 俯瞰图，鸟瞰图

aero wheel cover 空气流整流型车轮罩（对行驶时车轮四周的空气流进行"整流"，以降低空气阻力）

AESI ［美］汽车环境系统公司（Automotive Environmental System, lnc. 的简称）

aesthetic impact （车身外形等的）美学效果

aether 乙醚；乙太（= ether）

AETS 发动机自动测试系统（automatic engine test system）

A/F ①空燃比（air-fuel ratio）②六角形，方形等物件各对边间的宽度（= width across the flats）

AFC ①自动频率控制（automatic frequency control 的简称）②酒精轿车（alcohol-fueled car 的简称）③空气燃油混合比调节装置（air fuel controller 的简称）④碱性燃料电池（alkaline fuel cell 的简称）

AFC 碱性燃料电池（alkaline fuel cell 的简称）

AFCO 自动断油装置（automatic fuel cutoff 的简称）

AFD 主动型前桥差速器（active front differential 的简称）

A/F distribution 可燃混合气分配（air-fuel distribution 的简称）

AFE 汽车燃油经济性（automotive fuel economy 的简称）

AFER 空气燃油当量比（air fuel equivalence ratio 的简称）

AFES 平均燃油经济性标准（average fuel economy standards 的简称）

affix ①附加物，添加剂；附标，附录，附件②附加，黏上，贴上；使固定

AFL 见 AFS④

AFR ①空气燃油比（air-fuel ratio 的简称）②容许故障率（acceptable failure rate 的简称）

A-frame ①A形框架，A形机架②（货车拖带挂车的）A形拖架③（悬架）A形臂（= A-arm）

A-frame control arm （独立悬挂的）A型架控制臂（简称 A-frame 或 A-arm）

AFS ①辅助燃料供给系统（auxiliaryfuel supply System 的简称）②美国货运系统（American Freight System 的简称）③美国铸造工作者协会（American Foundrymen's Society 的简称）④（汽车）适应性前照灯系统（adaptive front-lighting system 的简称，可根据车速和转向角度在水平方向自动调整灯光照射方向的系统，亦简称 AFL）⑤空燃比传感器（air/fuel sensor 的简称）⑥空气流量传感器（air flow sensor 的简称）

AFSHTC 空燃比传感器加热温度控制（air/fuel sensor heating temperature control 的简称)

aft ①在后部,在尾部,在车尾;到后部,到尾部②后部的,尾部的

aft end 尾部,后端面(= after end)

after body 车身后部(简称 aftbody)

after bottom dead centre (在)下止点后,(在)下死点后(= after bottom center)

afterburner 后燃器(再次燃烧废气中的碳氢化合物和一氧化碳净化排气的装置,其中备有点火或可使排气着火的机构)

after burning ①(发动机熄火后)继燃,再燃(指发动机停机后,熄不了火,仍继续燃烧的现象)②(废气净化)后燃处理(指使废气中残存的 HC 和 CO 在排气系内排出前完全燃烧)③排气管放炮(点火不良,缺火,混合气过浓等原因,以致未完全燃烧的混合气体在排气管或消声器内燃烧的现象)④(发动机正常燃烧过程中的)后燃,后燃(见 aftercombustion period)

after-combustion period 后燃期,补燃期(从汽缸出现最高燃烧温度起,到燃烧基本结束为止的一段时间,以曲轴转角表示,= after burning④)

after cooler 后置冷却器,后冷却器,后冷器(如压缩空气输出口后面的冷却器,柴油机增压空气进入汽缸前的冷却器等)

after-crash door automatic opening system 碰撞后车门自动开启系统

after-dripping 残滴,残漏(喷油器喷油终止时,由喷口漏出的残油,= dribbling)

after fire ①排气管放炮,排气管喷火(= banging, back fire in exhaust)②见 after ignition

after glow (发动机起动后冷却水温仍未达到某规定值,如:40℃时电热塞对进气进行的)后加热

after-ignition (点火开关断开后,发动机由于缸内炽热点等原因仍然不熄火的)断电继燃,继燃现象(亦称 after run, after running, running on, after fire, post ignition, dieseling)

after impact skidding 碰撞后滑移

after injection (多段喷射式柴油机主喷射后的)后喷射(= follow-up injection)

aftermarker installation (汽车等)出售后(由用户等)加装(各种设备和装置)

aftermarket part ①黑市购入的零件(泛指非正规市场购入的零件)②售后由车主加装的零件

aftermarket service and maintenance (车辆等)出售后的保用期维护;出售后的维护服务,售后服务及维护(亦称 after sale service, after care)

after-start enrichment 起动加浓(指发动机起动时的混合气加浓)

after-treatment device 后处理装置(如催化转化器等排气后处理装置)

AF05 type dummy AF05 型假人(NHTSA 开发的小身材女性碰撞试验用假人)

AFV 代用燃料车辆(alternative fuel vehicle 的简称)

Ag 银(silver 的化学符号)

a.g. 气隙,火花塞间隙(air gap 的简称)

AGC ①自动增益控制,自动增益调整(automatic gain control 的简称)②(钢板锻压,线材控制过程中的厚度、直径、尺寸的)自动测量—调整装置(automatic gauge controller 的简称)

age ①时代②寿命③时效;老化

age coating of a lamp 灯泡(内表面)老化发黑层(长期使用产生的

钨蒸发覆层）

aged ①老化的②经过时效（处理）的

aged car 超龄轿车，老龄轿车（使用期超过额定使用寿命的轿车，亦写作 aging car）

aged catalyst （已）老化的催化剂（相对新鲜催化剂 fresh catalyst 而言）

age-hardening 时效硬化（合金的时效处理硬化，见 aging）

ageing （亦写作 aging）①老化（指汽车零件材料的性能随使用时间的增加而逐渐衰退的现象）②时效（消除铸件内应力，使其形状和性质稳定化的一种热处理。在常温下 6~8 个月放置称为自然时效；在高温下进行的时效处理称为高温时效；将工件置于一定温度的炉中升温至 500~600℃，再经较长时间保温后缓慢冷却，称人工时效）

ageing-resistant 耐老化的，防老化的（亦写作 aging-resistant）

ageing stability 老化稳定性，耐老化性

age limit 寿命极限，使用年限

agent ①代理人，代销商②（化学）剂；介质

agglomeration ①结块，成团②烧结③集团（如：由 Hyundai 和 Kia 联合组成的 Hyundai Automotive Group）

agglomerator （从燃油或机油中清除水分的）聚集式水分离器

aggregate ①总计，合计②总数的，总计的，总的③（沥青混合料等的）集料，骨料（aggregate body 运送沙石等集料、通常具有自卸功能的散装货物运输车身）

aggressive agent 腐蚀性材料，腐蚀性介质（亦称 aggressive medium）

aggressive strategy （企业为争夺市场份额而采取的）开拓性的战略，挑战性的战略

agile 灵便的，轻便的，灵活的

agility 车辆机动能力，车辆机动性（包括加速度、爬坡能力、转弯半径、操纵稳定性、倾翻角等）

Ag-impregnated zeolite 含银沸石（具有高脱湿温度的 HC 吸附剂）

agitation 搅拌，拌和

agitator 搅拌器，搅拌装置，搅动装置，拌和器

agitator truck 水泥混凝土搅拌车（= mix truck，transit mix truck）

AGLS 自动润滑脂润滑系统（automatic grease lubrication system 的简称）

agricultural automobile 农用汽车

agrol fluid 酒精汽油混合燃油（一种代汽油燃料，含乙醇 78%，汽油 22%）

AGT 汽车用燃气轮机（automotive gas turbine 的简称）

AGVS 自动导航车辆系统（Automated Guide Vehicle System 简称，20 世纪 50 年代美国 Barrett Electronic 公司为提高仓库自动化水平而开发的）自动导航车辆系统（的商品名，成为智能车辆的雏形）

ah 安培小时（ampere-hour 的简称）

AH 主动发动机罩（active hood 的简称，当发生人-车碰撞时，发动机罩可主动升起，防止行人撞向风窗玻璃，而使行人头部接触其可变形柔性表面）

AHC 悬架高度调节系统（可对车身高度进行高"HI"，正常"N"和低"LO"三级手动开关电动调节）

AHC suspension 主动式车身高度控制悬架（active height control suspension 的简称）

ahm 安培小时计（ampere-hour meter 的简称）

AHP 加速踏板后支点（accel heel point 的简称）

AHR 主动式头枕约束性保护系统

(active head restraint system 的简称，发生追尾等碰撞时可根据碰撞力的大小自动控制头枕的前移幅度，防止乘员头骨损伤)

AH rim AH 轮辋，双峰轮辋 (double hump rim 的简称，指圈上设计有双平峰或凹峰的轮辋。当轮胎泄气时，借助于双峰仍可夹持变瘪的轮胎行驶一定的距离，见 flat hump, round hump)

AHS ①先进的巡行支援公路系统 (Advanced cruise-assist Highwaysystem 的简称，指由公路设施向驾驶员提供信息、警告和操作干预等保证安全的巡行支援系统) ②自动化公路系统 (参见 automated highway system)

AHSS 先进高强度钢 (advanced high strength steel 的简称，包括双相钢、复相钢、马氏体钢等，通过相变组织强化来达到高强度的汽车用钢，其强度范围为 500~1500MPa，具有高的、碰撞吸能性、疲劳强度、成型性和低的平面各向异性以及轻等优点)

AI ①空气喷射（见 air injection）②防冻（见 anti-icing）③人工智能（见 artificial intelligence）

AIA 美国汽车进口商会 (Automobile Importers of America 的简称)

AIADA 美国国际汽车经销商协会 (American International Automobile Dealers Association 的简称)

AICC system （汽车）智能化定速巡行自动控制系统，智能化巡航车速自动控制系统 (autonomous intelligent cruise control system 的简称)

AII 安全气囊造成的伤害 (airbag-induced injuries 的简称)

aimer 校准器（前照灯光轴方向调整时，能吸着于前灯玻璃的一种光轴标准工具）

aiming of head lamp 前照灯对光（调整光轴方向）

aiming screw （前照灯的）对光螺钉

air ①空气②空气的③气动的（air-actuated 的简称）④通风，充气，气动

AIR 见 air injection reaction system

air absorber 气室式缓冲器，气囊式减振器（利用压缩密封在气囊或通过止回阀充入气室内的空气而获得减振、缓冲效果的装置的通称，亦称 air shock absorber 或 air shocks）

air adjust screw 空气调节螺钉（用来调节空气旁通流量，以控制怠速混合气浓度，简称 AAS）

air-air 空气对空气，风冷-气（如增压式柴油机用新鲜冷空气来冷却增压空气的中间冷却系统等）

air/air ratio 见 air ratio

air-and-oil spring 油气弹簧（以液体传递载荷，以空气气囊等作为弹性元件的弹簧形式）

air-and-water extractor （装在空气压缩机和风动工具，如喷枪等之间的）压缩空气脱水器，亦称空气耦合器，用于滤除压缩空气中的水分，此外还可调节压缩空气的压力，亦称 air transformer）

air application time 气制动作用时间，气制动滞后时间（气制动系统制动阀开启至制动管道内气压达到规定值所需的时间）

air-assisted hydraulic brake 空气助力液压制动，气动液压制动（一种利用压缩空气作为伺服气室动力源，伺服气室输出力直接作用于液压制动主缸活塞，以助踏板力不足的液压制动系统，俗称"气顶油"，亦称 air servo brake, air-operated hydraulic brake, air-over-hydraulic brake, combined compressed air hydraulic brake)

AIRB 二次空气旁通阀（air bypass 的简称）

air bag （汽车乘员）安全气囊（一般由高强度轻质尼龙布制成。驾驶员的安全气囊多装于转向盘中央，助手座安全气囊则装于仪表板区其座位前方。安全气囊系统由发出碰撞信号的传感器，收到碰撞信号后立即产生使气囊瞬间充气膨胀所需气体的气体发生源和膨胀后保护乘员免受伤害的气囊组成）

air-bag collapsible dash 装有折叠式安全气囊的（驾驶室）仪表板（简称 ABCD）

air bag deployment 安全气囊膨胀，安全气囊膨开

air bag disable switch 安全气囊放气开关

airbag-induced injuries 安全气囊造成的伤害（简称 AII）

air bag inflating pressure sensor 安全气囊充气压力传感器

air bag module ①安全气囊总成（包括气囊，充气装置及气囊外壳等，= air bag unit）②安全气囊系统控制模块（air bag control module 的简称）

air bag restraint system 安全气囊拘束性乘员保护系统（即安全气囊系统，由气囊、碰撞传感器、气体发生器和安全控制模块等组成的被动安全系统）

air-bag sensing system 安全气囊的（碰撞）传感系统（可分为多点机电式传感系统 "multipoint electromechanical sensing system" 和单点电子式传感系统 "single-point electronic sensing system" 两大类，前者又称为分布式传感系统 "distributed sensing system"，后者又称为中央式传感系统 "central sensing system"。多点式传感系统由两个或四个装在汽车碰撞挤压破损区内的碰撞判别传感器 "crash discrimination sensor" 和装在乘座舱电子控制模块内的一个机电式待爆传感器 "arming sensor" 组成。当发生碰撞时，待爆传感器触点首先接通，给充气装置点火器电路加上 12V 电压，使充气装置处于待爆状态。如果碰撞严重到足以使挤压破损区内的任一个碰撞判别传感器的触点闭合，则充气装置点火器的电路便经判别传感器触点接地，而在瞬间引爆充气装置。早期的单点式电子传感系统使用一个应变仪式加速度传感器 "strain gage acceleration sensor" 取代多点式传感系统中的各外置式碰撞传感器和一个作为保险传感器 "safing sensor" 的水银开关 "mercury switch"。碰撞中，当车辆的减速度值 ΔV 超过所规定的阈值时，水银开关闭合，引爆充气系统。20 世纪 80 年代后期，使用单通道压电晶体加速度计 "single-channel piezoelectric accelerometer" 代替应变仪式加速度传感器，使用簧片开关 "read switch" 代替水银开关。20 世纪 90 年代，开始使用全电子双通道型电子加速度计 "dual-channel electronic accelerometer"，而不再需要机械式安全开关）

air bag (system) control module 安全气囊系统控制模块（简称 ACM，其功能为①监控安全气囊警告灯②监控安全气囊系统全部部件③控制安全气囊系统的诊断功能，因此亦称安全气囊系统诊断模块 air bag system diagnostic module，简称 ASDM。④记录碰撞。ACM 记录一定数量的碰撞后便需更换⑤某些 ACM 还起减速度传感器的作用，与安全气囊的其他传感器一起监控车速的突然急剧减速并在确认出现上述情况时引爆安全气囊的充气系统。这类 ACM 多位于汽车客舱中部，故亦称 center air bag sensor assembly ⑥大部分 ACM 都备有后备电源，

当蓄电池因碰撞而中断供电时,该备用电源可使气囊膨胀,因而这样的 ACM 也称诊断/储能模块"diagnostic/energy reserve module",简称 DERM)

air bag system diagnostic module 安全气囊系统诊断模块[亦称安全气囊系统控制模块,= ACM,因它具有连续监测安全气囊系统全部部件的诊断功能,故名,见 air bag (system) control module]

air bearing 空气轴承,气垫轴承,气浮轴承

air bellows (波纹状)空气气囊(空气悬架中起弹簧作用的弹性元件)

air-belt system (汽车乘员的)充气式安全带系统(亦称 inflatable seat-belt system)

air bleed ①排气,放气(如排除制动液内的空气)②渗气,引入空气(如化油器中通过空气量孔,吸入空气,使汽油泡沫化)③起上述作用的孔或通道

air bleed adjuster screw 空气补偿量孔调节螺钉

air bleeder 起 air bleed 作用的装置,孔、管、口、道和部件的通称

air bleed passage [美]空气补偿量孔(=[英]compensating jet,亦称 air bleed jet,指将空气引入主油系,适当降低其吸油真空度,减少主喷管出油量,防止混合气过浓,保证中等负荷时得到理想的经济混合气体的空气管和空气量孔系统)

airborne ①悬空的(脱离地面的)②空气中悬浮的

air borne noise 空气传播的噪声(简称 ABN)

airborne particles 空气中悬浮的微粒

air bottle (压缩空)气瓶,储气筒,气罐

air bound 气隔,气阻,气锁

air brake ①气制动器,气制动(= air operated brake, air-pressure brake, compressed-air brake, pneumatic brake,指以压缩空气作为动力的行车制动器或制动系统)②(指利用空气动力阻力,使高速行驶的车辆减速的阻挡式风力减速装置)风阻制动器,空气动力制动器(亦称 air-resistance brake, aerodynamic 或 atmospheric brake)

air brake chamber 见 brake chamber

air brake control valve 见 brake valve

air brake dynamometer 气制动机械式测功器

air brake foot control 气制动踏板

air brake force limiter 气制动力限制器

air brake oil separator 气制动系油液分离器

air brake proportioning (valve) 气制动比例分配(阀)(参见 apportion valve)

air brake releasing valve 气制动放气阀

air brake system 气制动系统(见 air brake)

air breather filter (曲轴箱)通气口滤清器,通风口滤清器

air-breathing ability (发动机的)吸气能力,充气能力

air bridge (Ferrari F12 位于前保险架的)进风道(该进风道围绕车身两侧,行驶时空气由该风道经后轮上方的电子控制开闭的通风口冷却后轮制动器)

airbrush ①气动雨刷,气动刷②(喷漆用)喷枪③用喷枪喷

AIRB solenoid 二次空气喷射系统中的空气旁通阀电磁阀(air injection reactor bypass valve solenoid 的简称,在无须二次空气喷射的工况下,如起动时,该电磁阀不通电,空气泵输入的空气经旁通阀排至大气,而

当要求二次空气喷射时,如正常运转后,该电磁阀通电,空气泵输入的空气经该阀送至空气换向阀,见AIRD)

air buffer 空气缓冲器,气压减振器(＝pneumatic buffer)

air burner 喷灯

air by-pass (solenoid) valve 空气旁通(电磁)阀[简称AB(S)V]

air car 气垫(汽)车

air casing (气波增压器的)空气室

air-cell ①(空气室式柴油机燃烧室的)空气室(＝air chamber, energy chamber) ②空气电池

air-cell chamber 空气室式燃烧室

air-cell cylinder head 空气室式汽缸盖(＝aero system cylinder head)

air-cell diesel 空气室式柴油机(＝air-chamber diesel)

air-chamber ①空气室②空气室式燃烧室(＝air-cell chamber) ③制动气室(见brake chamber)

air charge (新鲜)空气充量(被吸入燃油喷射系统的新鲜空气)

air charge temperature 进气温度(指被吸入燃油喷射系统的空气的温度,简称ACT)

air check valve (脉冲式二次空气喷射系统中的)空气单向阀(防止废气流回进气系)

air choke (阻)风门

air cleaner [美]空气滤清器(＝[英]air filter)

air cleaner efficiency and capacity test apparatus 空气滤清器效率及流量试验装置

air cleaner gauze 空气滤清器滤网

air cleaner hair 空滤器(发状)金属滤丝(滤网)

air cleaner oil cup 空气滤清器油环

air cleaner test dust 空气滤清器试验用(的特制标准)粉尘

air cleaner type crankcase ventilating system 空气滤清器型曲轴箱通风系(进气管真空抽吸型曲轴箱通风系的一种,见air filter storage system)

air clearance 气隙

air clutch 气动离合器

air cock 空气开关,放气开关,排气开关

air compensating jet 空气补偿量孔

air compressor 空气压缩机,空压机

air compressor relay 空气压缩机继电器(控制空气压缩机电源的通-断)

air compressor truck ①车载式空气压缩机②空压机汽车,(＝compressor truck)

air con 空调装置(air conditioner的简称)

air-conditioned 带空气调节装置的(＝climatized)

air conditioner system (汽车等的)空气调节系统(亦写作air conditioning system, 简称a/c system)

air-conditioning clutch 空调(系统的压缩机)离合器(简称ACC,该离合器由空调开关直接控制接合,或空调开关闭合后由电子控制模块控制接合)

air conditioning clutch switch 空调离合器开关(向电子控制模块发送空调离合器是否接通的信息)

air conditioning control 空气调节装置操纵件(控制空调装置工况的手操纵件)

air conditioning switch 空调开关

air conditioning test 空调试验(试验内容包括:风速分布,风量、温度和温度分布、空气和尘埃分析等)

air conditions 天气状况,气候条件,大气条件

air conduit 空气导管,空气管道

air con ECU 空调系统电子控制模块

（air conditioner ECU 的简称）

air consumption 空气消耗量（如：内燃机每小时所消耗的空气量，按质量计）

air control ①气动操纵，气动控制②空气量调节，供气量控制

air control shutter 空气节流阀，阻风门

air control (vacuum) motor （恒温式进气系的）冷热空气流量阀门（真空）控制器

air control valve （二次）空气（喷射）量控制阀（根据发动机负荷，转速控制供给排气管的二次空气量，简称ACV）

air coolant 冷却（用）空气

air cooled flat twin engine 卧式双缸风冷发动机

air-cooled intercooler （废气涡轮增压废气的）空（气）冷（却）式中间冷却器

air-cored （线圈）无芯的，无铁芯的

air correction jet 空气补偿量孔

air course ①空气流②空气流通路线

aircraft caterer's delivery truck 航空食品装运车

aircraft refueller 飞机加油车

aircraft service vehicle 机场服务车辆；（机场）地勤车辆

aircraft shunt bus 机场联运客车

aircraft towing vehicle （机场的）飞机牵引车

air cure 热空气硫化，热补

air current 空气流，气流

air cushion ①气垫，空气垫，气幕②安全气囊（=air bag）

air-cushioned seat 气垫座椅，空气悬架座椅

air cushion restraint system （汽车乘员的）气垫拘束型保护系统

air cushion shock absorber 气垫减振器（参见 pneumatic buffer）

aircushion vehicle 气垫车（简称ACV，=air cushion car, free air suspension vehicle, hovercraft, levitated vehicle, terrain-hugging vehicle）

air cylinder ①（气压系中的）气动缸，气压缸②（真空系中的）大气缸，空气缸

AIRD 空气换向阀（air director valve 的简称）

air dam （装在大型货车驾驶室顶上及货车与轿车保险杠下面的）导风板，阻风板（减少空气阻力或空气升力。装在驾驶室顶的亦称导流罩：wind deflector, air shield, 装在保险杠下面的亦称保险杠下挡风裙，阻力裙：under bumper apron, air dam skirt）

air damper ①阻风门，风挡，调节风门②空气阻尼器，气压减振器，气动缓冲器（=pneumatic shock absorber）

air deflector ①空气偏导器，气流导向器，气流换向器，空气导流板（改变气流方向的装置）②（装在驾驶室顶，用以减少空气阻力损失的）导风板，导流罩（=英 air shield）

air-disc brake 气压式盘式制动器

air divert valve （二次空气喷射系统的）空气换向阀（改变空气流向的控制阀）

air draft [美] 通风，气流（=[英] air draught）

air drag reduction device 减小空气阻力的装置（=drag reducing device）

air drain 排风道，排风管道

air-driven 气动的，风动的，压缩空气驱动的（有时称 air drawn）

air dryer 空气干燥器（清除空气中的水分和杂质）

AIRD solenoid 二次空气喷射系统中的空气换向阀（air injection reactor

air diverter solenoid 的简称,其功用为按照电子控制模块的指令,当空气泵泵入的空气经空气旁通阀输入换向阀后:①在暖机运转中,换向阀将空气引入排气歧管,使其中的 HC 燃烧,此外还可使催化转化器迅速升温②发动机达到正常工作温度后,换向阀将空气引入催化转化器,使 HC、CO 充分氧化,见 AIRB)

air duct 空气管道(如汽车的暖风与通风管道)

air dynamical part (减小空气阻力的)空气动力学部件

air dynamometer 空气动力测功器,气涡流测动机,气力测功器(用叶轮等搅动空气而吸收动力的简易测功器)

air-efficient 具有空气动力效应的,空气阻力系数小的

air electrode (金属-空气电池的)空气电极

air engine ①往复式气动机,往复式气动马达(压缩空气驱动的微型往复式气动机,为 air motor 的一种)②热空气发动机(用空气做工质的外燃机,亦称 hot air engine。Stirling engine 是其中的一种,但目前 Stirling engine 大多用氢代替空气做工质)③空气压缩机

air escape valve (气制动中的)放气阀,泄气阀

air-excess factor (混合气的)过量空气系数($=\dfrac{实际空气燃料比}{理论空燃比}$,参见 theoretical air-fuel ratio)

air exhaust 抽气,排气

air exhaust filter (空压机的)排气滤清器

air-fast 不透气的;气密的,密封的;不通气的

air-filler tyre 充气轮胎

air filter ①空气滤清器(= [美] air cleaner) ②(滤网等)空气滤清件

air filter bowl 空气滤芯的杯形外壳

air filter checker 空气滤清器滤芯通气性能检测器

air filter element 空气滤清器滤芯

air filter in oil bath 油浴式空气滤清器 (= oil bath air filter, oil bath cleaner, oil-type air cleaner)

air filter intake silencer 空气滤清器进气消声器

air filter storage system 空气滤清器储存系统(将燃油箱等的燃油蒸气引入空气滤清器内的吸附材料,如活性炭存储,进而随新鲜空气进入进气歧管,以减少燃油蒸气排放污染并达到节油目的)

air filter tell-tale 空气滤清器警报灯(监控空气滤清器堵塞程度的信号灯)

air fix (汽车)胎压测定和充气箱(是一种便携式带压力表及充气管的压缩空气箱,可同时进行轮胎的充气和胎压测定作业)

air flap 通风口(单向)活门

air flow ①空气流,气流②空气流量

air flow bubble 气流剥离生成的紊流泡泡(亦称 separation bubble,参见 air flow separation)

air flow divider (空)气流分流器

air flow meter 空气流量计

air flow sensor 空气流量传感器(汽油喷射系统中的重要传感元件,它提供的空气流量信号为发动机控制模块控制燃比,即喷油量的基础信息,可分为测定体积流量的翼片式、卡尔曼涡式空气流量传感器和测定质量流量的热线式、热膜式、声速式空气流量传感器两大类。体积流量式还必须进行密度修正)

air flow separation 气流剥离(指汽车高速行驶时,紧贴车身表面的空气附着层气流与车身表面产生分离

的现象,见 separation③)

air-flow tuner plus (装在轿车上的)气流调节附件(降低风阻的尾翼的商品名)

airfoil 空气动力学导流板(亦称 aerofoil,如装在车尾产生负升力的压流板等)

airfoil-section blade 翼形叶片

airfoil shield 顶装导风罩(参见 Drag foiler)

air force 空气动力,空气反作用力,空气负荷

air fork 气动拨叉

air fountain 空气喷流

air-free 抽了空气的,无空气的,真空的

air friction ①空气摩擦阻力②空气摩擦

air-friction dynamometer 空气摩擦制动式测功机(利用风扇叶轮旋转形成的空气扰流和产生的摩擦阻力来吸收能量,= fan dynamometer)

air-fuel equivalence ratio 空气燃油当量比

air-fuel ratio 空燃比(每循环充入汽缸的空气量与燃料量的质量比)

air-fuel ratio feedback control system 空燃比反馈控制系统(根据氧传感器的反馈信号,将混合比控制在理论混合比附近的系统)

air gap (芯与衔铁之间的)气隙;(火花塞)跳火间隙,间隙

air gap of ignition signal generator (无断电器式电子点火系统的)点火信号发生器空气间隙(指信号转子的凸起端与感应线圈的中心端相对时二者之间的间隙。当空气间隙不符合规定的标准值时,通过传感线圈的磁通将偏离规定值,以致信号发生器产生的脉冲电压偏离要求。这是造成点火时错混和缺火的常见原因。一般空气间隙为0.2~0.4mm,可用传感线圈上安装的两个螺钉进行调整)

air gauge 气压表,压缩空气压力表

air governor (燃油喷射系的)气压式调整器(为气动式调速器的一种,由发动机带动的调速泵装置供给气压进行控制的调速器)

air guide spray control spray control direct injection (进气)气流导向型(汽缸内)直接喷射

air gulp system (为防止减速时送入进气歧管的混合气体过浓,以致未燃烧的 HC 进入排气系统,造成排气管等放炮而将二次空气喷入或吸入进气歧管的)减速空气增补系统

air gulp valve (air gulp system 中由发动机真空控制的)减速空气增补阀(用于将二次空气引入进气歧管,以防止减速时混合气体过浓,亦称 diverter valve)

air gun 压缩空气喷枪

air heater ①热风加热器②空气预热器

air hold fitting 气压式气门压具(顶置式气门发动机的气门拆装专用工具,拧入火花塞孔中,将压缩空气输入汽缸,使气门保持关闭状态,可在不拆卸缸盖的条件下,完成更换气门弹簧、气门座等作业)

air horn ①气喇叭(亦称 pneumatic horn)②进气(喇叭)口(在其空气通道的上部,= air inlet)③(美)空气由空气滤清器进入化油器或进气歧管的通道

air-hydraulic intensifier 气动 - 液压增压器

air-hydraulic power unit 气动-液压式动力装置(运用压缩空气的压力推动液压系统工作的装置,亦称 air-over-hydraulic unit)

air inclusions ①(液压系统)气阻②(金属内的)气体夹杂物

air induction system ①(柴油机和直接喷射式汽油机的)进气系统

②（无空气泵，利用气流脉冲原理通过吸气阀将新鲜空气吸至排气门区，以促使未燃烧的 HC 进一步燃烧的）二次空气吸入系统（简称 AIS）

air inflation indicator 轮胎气压计，充气指示器，胎压表（= tyre gauge, tyre pressure gauge）

airing 乘车兜风

air-injected catalyst system 空气喷射触媒净化系统，空气喷射催化系统（喷入新鲜空气，促进 HC、CO 的氧化）

air injection engine 空气喷射柴油发动机（高压空气喷射燃料的一种早期柴油机，亦称 air injection diesel）

air injection reaction system 空气喷射反应净化系统（向汽油机排气系统中喷入新鲜空气，使废气中 HC 和 CO 产生氧化反应而减少其排放量的装置，亦写作 air injection reactor system，或简称 air injection reactor，air injection system，有时称 air injector system，简称 AIS 或 AIR。这一系统一般由电子控制模块控制，故亦称 electronic air injection reaction system，简称 EAIR）

air injection switch 见 air switching valve

air inlet ①进气口，进风口，进气道②（特指）（化油器体的）进气段（英，= 美 air horn，指阻风门及加速泵喷嘴区）③进气

air inlet blower and evaporator assembly （空调系统）鼓风机与蒸发器总成

air inlet heating device （柴油机）空气进气预热装置，进气预热装置（= air intake heater）

air inlet housing （通风机）进风罩

air inlet strainer 进空气滤清器，进气过滤器（美，非正式用语）

air input 进气；进气量

air-in screen 进气滤网

air insulation 空气绝缘

air intake ①（喷油系统，空调，热风系统，冷却水散热器等的）进气孔，进气口②进气量③进气（美，= 英 air admission, air admittance, air induction, air inlet）

air-intake control lever （汽车通风-暖风系统的）进气口控制柄

air intake grill(e) （散热器等的）吸气栅格，通风护栅

air intake silencer （空气）进气消声器（一般装在空气滤清器上）

air intake stator ①（气波增压器）空气进口壳体②（涡轮增压机）进气导流叶栅

air intake tip （空气）进气管端管

air leak 空气泄漏，漏气

airless 无空气的

airless injection （柴油机）无气喷射（利用燃料本身的高压喷射使燃料雾化的方法，即目前柴油机通用的燃油喷射方法，亦称 solid injection）

airless spraying 无气喷雾，无气喷漆（指涂料等不是依靠压缩空气而是依靠本身高压喷雾）

airless tire 不充气轮胎，实心轮胎

air-lifter damper 气动举升式减振器（重载时，驾驶员可利用车内的轮胎充气系统等气压源，将减振器升到标准高度）

air lift force 空气浮力，空气（动力）升力（汽车高速行驶时，由于空气动力学的作用，产生的使汽车浮升的力）

airline 空气管路，气压管路（包括硬管、软管和通道）

airline coach 机场用大客车（= airport bus）

air line lubrication 气压供油中央润滑

airload 空气动力负荷，风载

air lock 气锁、气阻、气塞

air-lock switch 气阻开关,气阻式开关（利用受控气阻切断通路,气阻解除时,通路自动接通）

air louver 空气调节孔,空调口;放气窗孔

air management kit 改善车辆空气动力特性的各种装置的通称（如各种导风板等）

air management system 空气管理系统（将新鲜空气喷入排气系统,以促使 HC、CO 等氧化的电子控制二次空气喷射系统的商品名）

air management valve （二次空气喷射系统中的）空气控制阀（指换向阀 air divert valve 和开关阀 air switching valve 等控制空气流向的电磁或真空阀）

air mass flow 空气质量流量（按质量计的空气流量）

air mass sensor 进气空气质量流量传感器（见 intake air mass flow sensor）

Air Master 一种空气助力制动器的商品名（参见 air servo-brake）

Airmatic （奔驰车的）空气弹簧减振系统（商品名）

AIRMATIC Dual Control 双控自动空气悬架系统（奔驰公司生产的电子控制悬架系统,可根据路面状况改变悬架阻尼及刚度）

air meter 空气流量计,气流计,风速表,量气计

air micrometer ①（测千分之一毫米的）气动测微仪②（用于空气喷枪等喷射系统精确控制喷气量的）（空）气量精调器

air mix heater （热-冷）空气混合式暖风装置（将通过电热芯的热空气与冷空气混合制暖的暖风系统）

air momentum drag （气垫车）气垫装置的起动加速阻力

air monitor 大气（质量）监测器,空气（质量）监测装置

air motor 气动马达,气马达,气动机

air-oil actuator 气控液压执行器,气顶油执行器

air oil cooler 机油空气冷却器（风冷却机油冷却器）

air-oil heat exchanger 空气-机油热交换器（风冷式机油散热器）

air-oil suspension 液压-空气悬架,油-气悬架

airometer 空气流量计,空气流速计,风速计

air operated grease oil drum pump 桶装润滑油脂（气动）抽油泵

air-operated linkage brake 气动杆系制动器,气动机械式制动器

air operated oil changer 气动换机油器

air outlet 空气出口,出气口

air (-over) hydraulic booster ①气动-液压助力器 [= air-(over) hydraulic braking-force assistor, 由制动踏板控制的制动气压来推动制动主缸的助力装置] ②气动-液压增压器 [air-(over) hydraulic intensifier, 主缸输出的液压经压缩空气增压器增压后推动轮缸的增压装置]

air-over-hydraulic brake system 气动液压制动系统 [在这种制动系中,制动踏板控制气系的气压推动制动液压主缸输出控制车轮制动器的制动液压,这一套气压转变为液压的装置亦称 air-over-hydraulic booster（气动-液压）加力器]

air over hydraulic intensifier 见 air hydraulic booster②

air over hydraulic jack 气动液压式千斤顶

air pack （汽车轮胎用）高压空气充气罐（该罐可随车携带,直接对轮胎充气）

air-packed labyrinth seal 迷宫式气封

air painter 喷漆器,压缩空气油漆

air

喷枪（= air painting sprayer）
air permeability 透气性
air-permeable material （可）透气性材料
air pin 气压顶销，气压推力销
air-polluting 污染空气的，（造成）空气污染的
air pollution control 空气污染控制，空气污染净化，空气净化
air pollution index 大气污染指数（简称 API，指大气污染的程度：API < 50 最高质量；API = 51～99 二级质量；API = 100～199 三级质量，轻度污染；API = 200～299 四级质量，严重污染，并对人体心肺部有害）
Air Pollution Research Advisory Committee [美]大气污染研究咨询委员会
air pollution with lead particles 铅微粒空气污染，铅空气污染
air-powered master cylinder 气顶油制动主缸，气动（助力）液压主缸
air-power steering unit 气动助力转向装置，气动力转向装置（= air steering unit，一般利用汽车气制动或油气悬架的压缩空气作为加力装置的动力源，由控制阀、动力缸组成，通常为联杆型，参见 linkage-type power steering）
air pressure ①压缩气压力，气动压力 ② 大气压力（= atmospheric pressure）③轮胎气压（= tyre pressure）
air-pressure bead lock system （轮胎的）气压式胎圈锁定系统（用空气压力固定胎圈）
air pressure ga（u）ge 气压表
air pressure governor （气动）空气压力调节器
air pressure modulation valve （气制动系统）制动气压调节阀
air pressure oil drain （汽车发动机、变速器等更换滑油时使用的）气压式废油排放器
air pressure reducer 减（气）压阀
air pressure test ①在压缩空气条件下进行的试验（例如在压缩空气下进行火花塞的跳火试验）②（测定气压的）气压试验
airproof 密封的，气密的，不漏气的
air proportional EGR system 空气比例式 EGR 系统（根据发动机吸入的空气量将一定百分比的废气做再循环的废气再循环系统）
air-pumping noise 泵气噪声（如：轮胎花纹与路面间的空气在行驶中不断被压缩、泵出而产生的噪声）
air purifier （车内）空气净化器（有两种类型：一种是用过滤器滤净空气中的尘埃，而用活性炭吸净空气中的臭味；另一种是用高压放电吸尘。此外，有的还组装有杀菌灯和负离子发生器）
air quality control system 空气质量控制系统（简称 AQCS 或 AQS）
air quench hardening glass （汽车用）风冷钢化玻璃（用快速气流做骤冷介质的钢化玻璃）
air ratio 空气/空气比，过量空气系数（指实际吸入汽缸的空气量与进入汽缸的燃料完全燃烧理论上所需的空气量的质量比，= coefficient of excess air，亦称 air/air ratio。理论空燃比混合气的过量空气系数 $\alpha = 1$）
air reaction 空气反作用力
air reel 高压空气软管卷盘
air regulator 空气流量调节器（简称 AR）
air relay ①气压继电器，气动继电器②气动替续器③气动（自动）转换，气压继动④电触式气动量仪
air reservoir 储气筒，储气罐（= air tank）

air-resistance horsepower 克服空气阻力所消耗的功率，风阻功率，风阻马力（=air-resistance power）

air-resistance of autotrain 汽车列车的空气阻力

air-retaining liner （无内胎轮胎的）气密层，密封层

air sack 气阻（=air lock）

air scarf 头颈暖风系统

air scoop 空气口，进气道，进气孔，进气喇叭口（特指装在发动机罩或车身其他构件上，朝向汽车前进方向的高压通风或冷却用风的进气口）

air screw （气垫车等用）螺旋桨

air scrubber （一般指）湿式空气滤清器

air seat （驾驶员或乘员的）气垫座

air select valve （带二次空气喷射的双级式催化净化器中使用的）空气选择阀（该阀由电磁阀按照电子控制模块的指令来控制，根据发动机运转工况将空气引至排气孔口或双级式催化转化器的三元催化剂床和氧化催化剂床之间的区域）

air sensor 空气（质量）传感器（用于监测车内空气质量，当其中污染物含量过高时，即关闭风门，以阻止车外空气进入车内空调系统）

air separation 气泡析出（指工作液体压力低于某一界限值时，液体中空气、蒸气等初期以气泡的形式析出，气泡析出时的压力称气泡析出压力，"gas separation pressure"，压力再进一步降低，发展成空穴，见cavitation，空穴受压爆炸是造成局部高压、噪声、液系统性能下降、表面穴蚀的原因）

air separation property （工作液体的）气泡析出性（见 air separation）

air servicer 气动系统维修车

air set 空气中凝固，常温凝固；自然硬化

air shield （装在车顶，特别是货车或厢式车挂车顶，以减小空气阻力的）导风板，导流罩（=美 air deflector, wind deflector，见 air dam）

air shift 气动换挡

air shock absorber 空气弹簧式减振器

air silencer with wet air filter 带湿式空气过滤器的进气消声器

air siren 汽笛，报警汽笛

air snap 气动卡扣

air snatch 抢气（多缸发动机，因进气系布置不当，点火次序和配气相位选择不当，使进气管中气流相互干扰，降低充气量的现象）

air space 气隙，气隔

air speed 空气流速，气速（简称 AS）

air spoiler ①扰流板，导流器②（特指车顶尾部向上翘起的）压流板（用于改变车身后部的气流，使后轮紧压地面，亦称 rear spoiler）

air spring 空气弹簧（指起减振弹簧作用的空气气囊）

air-spring air escape valve 空气弹簧排气阀（当必须降低空气弹簧高度时，该阀与相应的空气弹簧高度控制阀一同开启，同时关闭空气压缩机，直至达到所要求的平衡高度）

air spring and strut assembly 空气弹簧带滑柱总成

air-spring height control valve 空气弹簧高度控制阀（见 air spring valve）

air-spring suspension control module 空气弹簧悬架（电子）控制模块（一般装在行李舱内，根据各悬架的高度传感器、车速传感器及转向盘转角传感器和高度控制开关等的信息，通过空气压缩机、空气弹簧高度控制阀、放气阀等执行器控制车身高度和悬架的阻尼特性）

air spring（type）suspension 空气

弹簧式悬架（以气体弹簧为弹性元件的悬架）

air spring valve 空气弹簧阀（为一常闭式电磁阀，装在每个空气弹簧的顶部，该阀开启时压缩空气进入或排出空气弹簧，以控制空气弹簧的高度，亦称 air spring height control valve）

air steering unit 气压式动力转向装置（= air-power steering unit）

air-storage tank 储气筒，储气罐

air strain and silencer 带消声装置的空气滤清器，进气消声滤清器

air strainer 空气滤清器，空气滤网（美非正规用语，= air filter）

air strangler ①阻风门（= air choke）②挡风板

airstream deflector 导风板，导风器，气流偏导装置（用于减少空气阻力装置）

air-stream eddy current 空气涡流

air suction ①吸入空气，吸气②（特指废气再燃烧净化系中的）二次空气吸入（简称 AS，利用排气脉冲负压，将新鲜空气吸入排气管，使废气中的 CO、HC 再燃烧而净化）

air suspended type 大气浮动式（制动增压器），大气式（制动增压器）（不踩踏制动踏板时，增压缸活塞或膜片两侧保持大气压力。踩踏制动踏板后，活塞或膜片的一侧接负压而产生增压作用，参见 vacuum suspended type）

air suspension ①气垫，空气弹簧②空气悬架，空气弹簧式悬架（亦称 pneumatic suspension，见 air spring suspension）

air-suspension seat 空气弹簧座

air suspension switch 空气悬架开关（此开关断开时，控制模块断电，空气悬架系统不起调节作用）

air swirl 空气旋流，空气涡流

air swirler 旋流式空气喷嘴，离心式空气喷嘴，空气旋流装置

air switch ①气路开关②气动开关③电触式气动量测仪

air switching solenoid 见 air switching valve

air switching valve （废气净化系中的二次空气喷射系统的）气路开关阀（简称 ASV，由真空膜片控制，当冷机运转时真空作用于膜片，该阀通向排气歧管的空气喷射通道开放。当发动机热起后，真空被切断，该阀通向排气歧管的通道关闭，而通向催化转化器空气喷射通道开放。亦称 air injection switch。该阀的真空由电子控制模块控制的气路开关电磁阀 air switching solenoid 或冷却水温真空控制阀控制）

AIR system （美通用公司货车发动机的）空气喷射（氧化）反应系统（air injection reactor system 的简称，将新鲜空气喷至排气门区域，利用废气的高热，使废气中的 HC、CO 等燃烧的后处理净化系，亦称 Thermactor system，air pump system）

air system plumbing （车身的）通风系统管道

air tank 压缩空气罐，储气筒

air-temperature EGR control 废气再循环的（空）气温（度）控制（法）（由发动机的起动温度或大气温度来自动控制废气再循环阀的开度）

air temperature indicator 空气温度指示器，空气温度表

air-temperature sending resistor 空气温度传感电阻

air temperature sensing fan drive 空气温度传感式风扇驱动（装置）（可根据通过散热器芯后的空气温度，确定实现最佳风冷效果的风扇转速）

air temperature sensor 空气温度传

感器

air tight ①气密的，不漏气的，密封的，密闭的②气密性，气密

air tightness 气密度，气密性

air-tight seal 气密封件，气封

air-to-air charge cooling （增压）充气的空气冷却（增压器充入汽缸内的压缩空气的鼓风冷却）

air-to-air heat exchanger 空气对空气热交换器，（一般指压缩空气或增压空气的）风冷装置，中间风冷器

air-to-air intercooler 空冷型（增压）空气中间冷却器（装于增压器和进气歧管之间，用空气来冷却增压空气）

air tool 气动工具（= pneumatic tool）

airtow 飞机牵引车，机场用牵引车

air tower 压缩空气塔，压缩空气储存器，供气柜，供气柱

air toxic emission 毒化空气污染物，毒害空气排放（主要指氧化合、分解的碳氢化合物）

air transformer 空气耦合器（空气压缩机和风动装置，如喷枪等之间的连接装置，用于滤清和调压，亦称 air and water extractor）

air-tread amphibian 充气履带式水陆两用车

air tube ①内胎②空气管道；通风管道；空气软管

air tunnel 风洞（参见 aerodynamic tunnel）

air tyre 充气轮胎（= pneumatic tyre，美称 air tire）

air utilization ratio 空气利用率（一循环中用于燃烧的空气量占汽缸内已有空气量的质量百分比）

air valve ①节气门，节流阀②气制动阀（气制动系中，按照制动踏板踏下和松开的位置使制动管路充气或放气的部件）③（电子喷油系统的低温起动旁通）空气阀（绕过节气门将辅助空气送入进气歧管，以提高起动怠速，为快怠速装置的一种）

air valve lapper 气门-气门座气动研磨机，气动气门研磨机

air vent 空气出口，通风孔（简称 AV）

air vent window 通风窗（= ventilation window）

air volume ①空气容积，空气容量②空气体积

air volume flow 空气容积流量（按容积计的空气流量）

air washer 湿式空气滤清器

air-water valve （轮胎的）气-液型气门嘴（用于充气或同时充气、充液的气门嘴）

air wheel ①低压轮胎车轮②气胎车轮

air wrench 气动扳手，风动扳手

airy ①通风的②（车身或车身、车内构件线条）流畅的

air zero gas 零点气（见 zero grade gas）

AIS ①（汽车乘员事故的）简化伤害分级（abbreviated injury scale 的简称。目前广泛用于撞伤急救，AIS-1—轻伤，AIS-2—中伤，AIS-3—无生命危险的重伤，AIS-4—有生命危险的重伤，AIS-5—重伤且存活难定）②二次空气喷射系统（air injection system 的简称）

AI shift 人工智能型自动变速器（Artificial Intelligence Shift 的简称，日本丰田公司一种电子计算机控制自动变速器的商品名。其电子控制模块装有类似人脑判断能力的逻辑电路，可同时对多项输入信息作综合性地相互关联分析并在瞬间做出决断，在各种行驶工况下均能根据节气门开度、发动机转速、车速、加速度、制动减速度，以及对驾驶

者以往驾驶意图的记录等信息和对驾驶者现时驾驶意图的推断、对道路坡度等的推算,自动选择符合每位驾驶者意愿和道路状况的换挡模式,操作在经济模式、运动模式、常规模式间切换)

Aisin-Wamer (Volvo 的) 五挡自动变速器 (商品名)

aisle width at seat cushions (公共汽车) 座椅间的通道宽度

AIT 美国工业运输公司 (American Industrial Transport, Inc)

AITS 高级筒状气囊结构 (advanced inflatable tubular structure 的简称,用作头部安全气囊或侧面安全气囊等)

ajar ①(车门) 半开 (未关严,微开) ②不协调 (不调和)

AKI 抗爆震(燃)指数 (anti-knock index 的简称)

AK materials AK 合成橡胶材料 (指耐热老化温度为 70℃,最大耐油浸泡胀率为 10% 的橡胶材料,参见 type and class of elastomeric materials)

Al ①铝 (aluminium 的简称及元素符号) ②自动调制稀混合气 (= autolean mixture)

AL 加速度级,加速水平 (acceleration level 的简称)

ALA 美国汽车驾驶者联盟 (American League of Automobilists 的简称)

ALABC (美国) 先进的铅—酸电池联合开发组织 (由汽车工业与政府共同投资研制供电动汽车使用的新型铅酸电池)

alarm 警报,警报信号,警报器

alarm annunciator 警报信号器,事故指示装置

alarm buzzer 蜂鸣报警器

alarm check valve 报警(装置)检验阀(简称 ACV)

alarmed 装有警报器的

alarm pressure ①报警压力(当压力达到此限时,即报警)②最大允许压力

alarm signal system 警报信号系统

alarm valve 警报阀,安全阀

ALB (本田公司的) 防抱死制动系统 (的商品名,Anti Lock Brake System 的简称)

albronze 铝铜合金,铝青铜

ALC (汽车的) 高度自动调平控制 (见 automatic level control)

ALCL 见 ALDL

alcohol ①酒精,乙醇 (C_2H_5OH) ②醇 (ROH)

alcohol auto 见 alcohol fueled car

alcohol base fuel 酒精燃料

alcohol blended gasoline 掺酒精的汽油 (简称 alcogas)

alcohol blending effect 酒精掺和效应 (燃用酒精汽油时,由于酒精的热值低,汽车有乏力反应)

alcohol-drinking driver 酒后开车者,酗酒驾驶员

alcohol fuel cell 乙醇燃料电池,酒精燃料电池

alcohol-fueled car 乙醇燃料轿车,酒精轿车 (简称 AFC,亦称 alcohol car, alcohol engine car, alcohol auto)

alcoholometer 酒精比重计,乙醇比重计 (= alcoholometer)

alcohol safety interlock system 酒后驾驶锁死系统 (防止酒后驾驶的装置)

alcohol sensor (驾驶者饮酒的) 酒精(浓度)传感器

Alcokey 酒精(检测)钥匙(当按压钥匙上的开门按钮时,装在钥匙内的传感器自动接通,驾驶者对着钥匙吹气,若酒精含量超过规定,钥匙上的红灯亮,同时发动机锁死,以防醉酒驾车)

A4LD 轻型车用带超速挡的四挡自

动变速器（用于后轮驱动式车辆，其液力变矩器、离合器由电子控制模块控制，Automatic Four-speed Light-Duty 的简称）

aldehyde ①醛（结构式中带 CHO 甲醇基的化合物的总称，RCHO 为光化学烟雾及排气臭味的成分之一）②乙醛（=ethanal）

ALDL （汽车自诊断系统的）诊断（数据通信）总线（assembly line diagnostic link 的简称，亦称 assembly link data link，或 assembly line communication link，简称 ALCL。一般装在仪表板下方或转向盘柱与收音机之间的故障诊断总线盒。该盒表面具有若干插口，数目随车型而异，通常有一个诊断接地插口和各系统的故障诊断测试插口，外接诊断设备插口，或系统运转插口。如：将一跨接线插入通用公司的 12 插口诊断总线盒的 A、B 两插口，则计算机控制系统将读出其故障存储器内的故障代码，并通过仪表板上的故障闪光灯的闪光次数，输出故障代码，若故障灯先闪一次，稍停后再连闪两次，表示汽车存在代码为 12 的故障，查表即可知故障的具体内容）

aldural 高强度铝合金

alert ①警报，报警信号②发出警报

alerting ability （紧急情况下驾驶员的）机敏控制能力，机警性；瞬时反应能力

Alfa-Romeo 阿尔法-罗密欧（意大利的一家汽车制造公司，以生产赛车著名）

Alfin 铝铁铸合的（指采用铝铁铸合法制成，见 Alfin process）

Alfin brake drum 铸合式制动鼓（指采用铝铁铸合法制成、带有铝合金制动鼓的铸铁轮辋）

Alfin cylinder barrel （风冷式发动机的）铸合式缸筒（用铝铁铸合法加有铝合金散热片的铸铁缸筒）

Alfin piston 铸合式活塞（指采用铝铁铸合法嵌铸有铸铁环槽的铝合金活塞）

Alfin process 铝铁铸合法（由 Fairchild Engine and Airplane co. 首创的一种特殊铸造法，通过铝铁合金中介层将铸铁件与铝合金件相互结合的一种异金属铸合法）

alfresco driving 敞篷驾驶（指将车篷放下，开敞篷车，alfresco 为露天的意思）

algae based fuel 海藻基燃油（见 photo bioreactor system）

algae ethanol （车用）海藻乙醇（亦称 algae oil，见 photo bioreactor system）

algorithm ①算法（对求解某一问题的明确规定的程序、步骤、规则和完整的说明）②（计算机控制系统具体执行的）控制程序

align 排列，（直线）对准，对正，校正，校直，对光，使…成一直线，列成一行

aligner 定位器，校直器，调整器，校准试验台；前轮定位仪

aligning capacitor 微调电容器

aligning punch 中心冲

aligning stiffness 回正刚度，回正力矩刚度（轮胎侧偏角的单位增量所对应的回正力矩的增量，= aligning torque stiffness）

aligning stiffness coefficient 回正刚度系数，回正力矩刚度系数（自由滚动车轮的回正刚度或称回正力矩刚度与垂直负荷的比值，= aligning torque stiffness coefficient）

aligning torque 回正力矩［复原力矩，稳定力矩；由路面作用在轮胎上的力矩矢量，使轮胎绕轮胎坐标系 Z'轴（见 tire axis system）旋转的分量，= self aligning torque］

aligning torque camber stiffness （车

轮的）外倾回正力矩刚度（单位外倾角所产生的外倾推力引起的回正力矩）

aligning torque coefficient 回正力矩系数（回正力矩与垂直负荷的比值）

aligning torque compliance effect （汽车轮胎的）回正力矩致生效应（由弹性轮胎的回正力矩对车轮转向角等的影响）

aligning torque compliance steer ①（汽车的轮胎）回正力矩致生偏转现象（由车轮的侧偏角和外倾角所引起的转弯力和外倾推力，使轮胎产生的自回正力矩对汽车行驶方向的影响）②（汽车的轮胎）回正力矩致生偏转角（由于上述影响，使汽车行驶方向偏转的角度）

aligning torque compliance steer coefficient （汽车的轮胎）回正力矩致生偏转系数（即弹性轮胎的单位回正力矩对汽车行驶方向引起的偏转角）

aligning torque slip angle stiffness （车轮的）侧偏回正力矩刚度（即单位侧偏角产生的转弯力所引起的回正力矩，参见 cornering force）

alignment ①定中心，对中，对正，定位，调准，使…在一条直线上 ②直线度，对中度，对正的程度，定位的正确度

alignment change correcting ability （悬架）抑制和修正车轮定位变化的能力

alignment chart 诺莫图，列线图（由三条标度线组成，两条标度线上的已知值的连线，与第三条标度线的交点，即为所求的值）

alignment check （汽车）车轮定位检查

alignment clip 钢板弹簧定位夹，弹簧夹，回弹夹（当钢板弹簧反向变形，即车桥离开车架时，将载荷从主片传至以下各片，以免主片单独承载，此外还可防止各片横向相对移动，= alignment spring clip，亦称 rebound clip）

alignment gauge ①定位仪（如前轮定位仪等）②直线调准仪，直线对准仪表

alignment mark 对准标记，定位标记

alignment reserve 调整余量，对中余量

alignment scope 调准用示波器

alignment test 车轮定位测试

aliquation 成层，层化，起层

ALIS 汽车导航信息系统（参见 Automobile Leading Information System）

alitizing （钢铁表面的）渗铝法

alive 带电的，通电流的

alkali 碱，强碱，碱性，碱质

alkali fastness 耐碱度，抗碱性，抗碱强度（= fastness to alkali）

alkali-metal anode （金属-空气电池的）碱金属阳极

alkaline degreasing 碱溶液去脂，碱液清除油污

alkaline electrolyte 碱性电解液

alkaline fuel cell 碱性燃料电池（简称 AFC）

alkaline storage battery 碱性蓄电池（使用碱溶液作为电解液的二次电池的统称，按其极板活性材料的种类，可分为铁镍蓄电池、镉镍蓄电池、银镉蓄电池、锌蓄电池等。与铅蓄电池比较，具有质量小、机械强度高等优点）

alkalinity 碱度，碱性，含碱量

alkane 烷（属）烃，（链）烷（C_nH_{2n+2}）

alki （掺水）酒精

alky gas 酒精汽油混合燃料

alkyl 烷基，烃基（= alkyl radical）

all-alloy engine 全合金发动机（缸盖、缸体、曲轴箱、油底壳均由轻合金制造的发动机）

all aluminium body 全铝车身

All ant 阿兰特（美国 Cadillac 生产的一种两座跑车名）

Allanté traction control system 阿兰特型牵引力控制系统（通用公司20世纪90年代初推出的 ABS/TCS 系统的商品名。该系统的特点是：将 ABS 系统与发动机电子控制模块组合在一起，当测出某侧驱动轮因牵引力大于路面附着力而滑转时，ABS 系统首先向该车轮施加制动，使该车轮保持10%的滑移率，以获得最佳牵引力。若施加制动后，车轮仍继续滑转，则发动机电子控制模块将切断一个汽缸供油，直至切断全部汽缸供油，并点亮仪表板上的滑转指示灯）

all-around efficiency 总效率

All Data Electronic Retrieval system [美] 全数据电子检索系统（向维修人员提供车辆维修信息与资料的电子计算机信息系统）

all dog clutch transmission 全齿套变速器（全部前进挡都靠齿套换挡的常啮式变速器）

all-electric traction 全电力驱动

Allen key 内六方螺钉起子

Allen（screw）driver 内六方螺钉旋具

Allen（screw）wrench 内六方（螺钉）扳手，内六方（螺钉）弯头扳手（= hexagonal key wrench）

all-enveloping body 流线型（轿车）车身（指当今最流行的车身造型，即：翼子板、前照灯、散热器护栅等均包合成一条平滑的车身轮廓线）

all-gear drive 全齿轮传动

alliance （技术开发或商务上的）联盟，合作单位，合伙人（等）

alligator ①水陆两用车②传动带卡子，传动带搭扣③鳄口工具，鳄鱼口形扳手，管子钳，管子扳手④龟裂

alligator bonnet 鳄鱼（口）形发动机罩（指铰链装于后部而从前面开启的发动机罩，= alligator-type bonnet）

alligator clip 弹簧夹，鳄鱼夹

all-independent suspension 全独立悬架

all-indirect gearbox 无直接挡的变速器

all-in-one-piece cylinders 整体式汽缸体

all linkage type steering system 全拉杆式转向装置（一种多轴挂车上应用的转向装置形式）

all-mains 可由任何电源供电的，可调节以适应于各种电压的

All-mode 4×4 system （日产公司的）全模式四轮驱动系统（该系统具有 2WD "两轮驱动"，Auto "自动"和 4WD Lock "四轮驱动锁定"等按钮操控的多种驱动模式，故称全模式。选择 2WD 模式时，仅前轮驱动，选择 Auto 时，若前驱动轮打滑，则将相应的动力传至后轮参与驱动。选择 4WD Lock 键时，动力分别按 57/43% 的比例传给前、后轮，实现全四轮驱动）

all-out braking （指产生最大制动力的）全力制动

allowable 容许的，许可的，允许的，许用的，可以承认的

allowable forward displacement （在安全带等保护装置达到其最大保护能力之前）允许（乘员向）前移（动力）距离

allowance 容许限度，许可限度，容限；余量；公差；修正

allowance error 容许误差，许用误差

allowance test 容差试验，公差配合试验

alloy 合金

alloy wheel 合金车轮（由铝、镁等合金制成的车轮，多用于赛车或其他高速车）

Alloy wheel 合金车轮（通常为铝合金）

all-plastic car 全塑料车身轿车

all-purpose 多用的，万能的，通用的（= general purpose），多效的

all-red period 全红灯交通期间，禁止车辆通行期间，交通封闭期间

all-round safety compartment 全面安全座舱（可满足各种安全因素的轿车座舱 = all-around safety compartment）

all-round visibility 周围视野，四周可见度

all-season 4×4 radial tire 全天候四轮驱动子午轮胎

all-service vehicle 多用途车辆（= all-purpose vehicle）

all-silent body 全隔音车身

all-silent gearbox 无声变速器

all solid-state engine analyzer 全固体电路发动机分析仪

all-speed governor 全程式调速器（= variable-speed governor）

all-speed traction control 全速度域牵引力控制（系统）

all-steel body 全钢车身（一般指整体钢壳车身，相对于木构架加铝或钢板件的车身而言）

all-steel radial tyre 全钢丝子午胎

all-surface capability 各类地面通过能力，全路面通过能力

all-surface transit 全路面通行（可在各种路面上通行）

all-synchromesh transmission ［美］全同步器式变速器（指全部前进挡位都装有同步器的变速器，= 英 all-synchromesh gear box）

all terrain undercarriage 高通过性底盘

all-terrain vehicle 全地域车辆，越野车辆，高通过性车辆（= offroad vehicle）

all-time AWD 全时全轮驱动系统（All-Time All-Wheel driving system 的简称）

all-transistorized 全部晶体管化的，完全用晶体管的

all-up weight 总重（总质量的旧称）

all wave rectifier circuit 全波整流电路

all-weather head 全天候（车厢）顶盖（指可启开的车顶）

all-weather test facility 全天候试验设备，全天候试验室（①指可在任何气候条件下进行测试②指可模拟任何气候条件）

all-welded aluminium body 全焊接铝车身

all-wheel drive 全轮驱动（的）（= four-wheel drive，all-wheel powered）

all(-wheel) position tire 通用轮胎

all-wheel steering 全轮转向的（= four wheel steering，all-wheel control）

allyl plastic(s) 丙烯塑料

Almen tester 阿尔门润滑剂性能测定仪

Al-Mg alloy 铝镁合金（= aluminium magnesium alloy）

alnico 铝镍钴磁铁（汽车电气-电子系统中使用的一种高保磁力合金磁石）

alpax 铝硅合金（铝87%，硅13%）

alphabetic code 字母代码（指不含数字的，由字母字符构成的信息集代码）

alpha key α键，V 形圆顶键（截面形状与轴的 60°V 形键槽和套的半圆形键槽相配合）

alphanumeric code （汽车电子控制系统中使用的）字母数字代码（指由字母、数字、二进制字符或其组合组成的信息集的代码）

alphanumeric display （汽车电子系

统中指计算机内所存储的信息，如故障代码等，由计算机控制在必要时输出的各种）数字字母显示装置

Alpha Rockwell hardness α 级洛氏硬度（洛氏硬度计上的 α 级硬度）

alpha silicon carbide α 碳化硅（一种耐高温材料，作为汽车用燃气轮机的内部零件，可在 2500°F 下正常运行）

Alphatron α 粒子电离压力计

Alphatron (vacuum) gauge α-电离真空计

alpine edition 登山型，登山版（高通过性越野车）

alpine road 高山道路，山（岭）道（路）

ALR （乘员安全带的）自动长度调节和紧急锁紧式收紧装置（automatic length adjusting and locking retractor 的简称，见 automatic locking retractor）

Al-Si alloy 铝硅合金（= aluminium-silicon alloy）

alternate ①交替，交流，交变 ②交替的，交流的，交变的，可供选择的，替代的，新一代的（= alternative）

alternate distributor 交替式分电器（具有双组触点）

alternate engine 正在研制的第二代发动机，未来的替代发动机

alternate test 标准件比较故障测定试验，新旧件比较试验（取下旧件，换装新件，若使用新、旧件时的机械性能相同，说明旧件完好）

alternating bending test 交变弯曲疲劳试验

alternating current 交流电流，交流电（一般简称 AC）

alternating impact test 交变冲击疲劳试验

alternating injection suppression （电子喷油系统的）交替停喷（曲轴每两转，改变一次喷油缸的数目，以调节发动机转矩）

alternating load 交变载荷

alternating motion 往复运动，交变运动

alternating-tension-and-compression fatigue strength 交变拉-压疲劳强度

alternation ①轮流，交替，反复变换 ②半个周期

alternative ①二者择一的；交替的，交变的；替代的；比较的；可供选择的 ②替代物，代用品，替代方案；两者之一，可采用的方法，可能性，（供选择的）比较方案

alternative assemblies 可供选择的总成，可替代的组件

alternative fuel 代用燃料，燃油代用品

alternative gear ratios 可变传动比；可供用户选择的（变速器或主传动）不同传动比

alternative/mixed fuel engine 代用燃料/混合燃料发动机（一般指可单独使用甲醇、乙醇、天然气等代燃料，而又可使用甲醇汽油，乙醇汽油等混合燃料的内燃机，参见 flexible fuel engine，dual fuel engine）

alternative solution 可替代的解决方法，可供选择的另一解决方法

alternative strain 交变应变

alternative stroking test apparatus 交变冲程的试验装置

alternative wheelbases 供订购者选择的不同尺寸轴距

alternator 交流发电机（= alternating current generator，用二极管整流的输出为直流电，不用二极管整流的输出为交流电的发电机）

alternator charging light 发电机充电信号灯（当交流发电机不充电时发出灯光信号，一般装在仪表板上）

alternator regulator 交流发电机调节器（调控其输出电压）

alternator scope （汽车等用）交流发电机性能测试示波器

alternator with neutral-point diodes 带中性点二极管的交流发电机（指在中性点上接入两个二极管。当交流发电机转速超过 2000~3000r/min 时，取出定子星形联结的中性点上的电压用于充电。与未装中性点二极管的交流发电机比较，当转速为 5000r/min 左右时，发电机的输出约可提高 10%）

altimeter （海拔）高度计，测高仪，高程计，高度表

altimetric pressure transducer （海拔）高度-气压传感器（为一种气压计式高度传感器，通过测定大气压力确定海拔高度的传感器件）

altitude 高度；海拔高度；标高；水位；高线，顶垂线

altitude chamber 气压试验室，压力室，（海拔）高度试验室，高空模拟室

altitude compensating 海拔补偿（在控制供油量的系统中，为了保持正确的混合比，对海拔高度所做的补偿，或称 altitude adjustment, altitude mixture control 海拔高度调节，海拔高度控制）

altitude grade gasoline 高原地区用汽油，高海拔级汽油

altitude of fifth wheel coupling leading edge （半挂牵引车上的）半挂车转盘式牵引座的后端离地高度

altitude-pressure compensator （发动机燃油系的）海拔高度补偿器（供油量随海拔高度的变化而变化）

altitude sensor 海拔高度传感器（一般装在空气滤清器处，为绝对大气压力传感器或表压力传感器"barometric pressure sensor"的另一种称谓）

altitude test ①高原试验，高海拔试验②高空试验

altometer 经纬仪

AL-TPWS 自定位轮胎压力警报系统（autonomous locating tyre pressure warning system 的简称，可自动确定胎压低于规定值的轮胎）

ALU 算术和逻辑部分（见 arithmetic and logical unit）

aluman 铝锰合金

alumel （一种耐高温的）镍铝锰合金（镍 94%，铝 2%，锰 2.5%，硅 1%，铁 0.5%，多用作高温热电偶材料）

alumetized 镀铝的，渗铝的，铝粉涂料涂覆的（见 alumetizing）

alumetizing ①镀铝②表面涂覆铝粉涂料的③渗铝（使钢或铸铁工件的工作表面饱和一层铝原子，亦写作 aluminizing, aluminising, 有时称 a-luminium impregnation）

alumina 矾土；氧化铝（Al_2O_3），铝氧粉

alumina beads 氧化铝微珠（用作某些催化转化器的催化剂陶瓷载体）

alumina ceramic capacitor (type) MAP sensor 氧化铝陶瓷电容器型进气空气压力传感器（MAP 为 manifold absolute pressure 的简称）

aluminised glass reflector 镀铝玻璃反射镜

aluminithermic weld(ing) 热铝焊接

aluminium 铝（Al=美 aluminum）

aluminium-based catalyst 铝基催化剂

aluminium (based) grease 铝基滑脂（采用铝肥皂制成的滑脂，在金属表面上的附着性好，耐压、耐水，多用于转向拉杆接头、万向节等处，亦称 chassis grease, mobile grease, = aluminium soap grease）

aluminium bearing 铝基合金轴瓦

aluminium brazing 铝合金焊料硬钎焊

aluminium-chromium cylinder 铬铝

合金汽缸
aluminium foil 铝箔
aluminium "honeycomb" material 蜂窝状铝材（一种新的、按质量比具有高机械强度和耐冲击强度的车身构件材料）
aluminium-oxide ceramics coatings 氧化铝陶瓷镀复层
aluminium oxide isolator （火花塞芯的）氧化铝绝缘体
aluminium paint 银色漆，铝粉漆
aluminium solder 铝合金焊料软钎焊
aluminium-tin bearing 铝锡合金轴瓦
aluminized 渗铝的；镀铝的；涂复铝粉涂料的
aluminum ［美］铝（= aluminium）
aluminum/air battery 铝-空气电池（用铝材料作阳极，大气中的氧作阴极，在其发电反应中铝逐步变为氢氧化铝，这种电池不能再充电，亦称 alumium/air cell）
aluminum bonnet 铝（合金）发动机罩
aluminum high-voltage wire 高（电）压铝线
aluminum wheel 氧化铝砂轮
ALVINN 神经网络自主控制型陆地车辆（Autonomous Land Vehicle in Neural Net 的简称，美国 Carnegie Mellon 研制的智能车辆车名）
alw 容差，余量，公差，间隙（allowance 的简称）
A/m 安培/米（ampere/metre，为国际单位制的磁场强度单位，参见 oersted）
AM 调幅（amplitude modulation 的简称）
AMA ①［美］轿车制造商协会（Automobile Manufacturers Association 的简称）②美国摩托车协会（American Motorcycle Association 的简称）

Amalgamated Society of Engineers 工程师联合会（简称 ASE）
amber flasher 黄色闪光标牌，黄色闪光灯
amber lens （车灯）黄色散光玻璃
amber period （交通灯的）黄灯期间
amber signal ①黄色交通信号灯（= amber light）②黄色交通信号
ambience （汽车内、外的）①环境②气氛③格调
ambient ①大气的，周围的，环境的②周围空间，环绕空间
ambient ①周围的（温度、光线、环境等）②产生轻松气氛的、柔和的（车内照明、音乐等）
ambient density 周围介质密度
ambient functional test ①周围介质条件下的功能试验②大气环境下的功能试验
ambient LED lighting （车内使用彩色等）发光极管（产生的）轻松、柔和气氛的照明
ambient meter 故障预警表（向驾驶者警报行车中即将发生的故障等的灯光预警装置，正常状态下为蓝色，预测到即将发生的故障时变为红色）
ambient pressure 环境压力（指周围的大气压力）
ambient sensor （汽车自动温度控制系统使用的）车外温度传感器
ambient switch 见 ambient temperature switch
ambient temperature battery 常温蓄电池（如铅酸电池，镍锡电池等在常温下工作的蓄电池）
ambient temperature switch ①车外温度（控制）开关（特指汽车空调系统中由车外环境温度控制的开关。当车外温度较低时，该开关使空调系统的压缩机延迟运转，简称 ambient switch）②（泛指所有的由环境）温度控制（的）开关

ambient wind angle 环境风向角，外界风向角（指环境风速与地面坐标系 X 轴之间的夹角）

ambient wind velocity 环境风速，外界风速（指车辆周围的大气风速在地面坐标系 $X-Y$ 平面内的投影）

ambinocular field 左、右单眼总视区，左、右单眼总能见区（指左、右两单眼可见区的总和。除双眼视区以外还包括左眼能见到，右眼见不到；和右眼见到，左眼见不到的区域）

ambulance（car） 救护车，急救车

AMC ①美国（汽车货运协会的）搬运工作者会议（American Movers Conference 的简称）②美国汽车公司（American Motor Corporation 的简称）

American Association of Motor Vehicle Administrators 美国汽车管理者协会（简称 AAMVA）

American Association of Motor Vehicle Manufacturers 美国汽车制造商协会（简称 AAMVM）

American Association of State Highways and Transportation Officials 美国各州公路及运输公务员协会（简称 AASHTO）

American Automobile Association 美国轿车协会（简称 AAA）

American Automotive Leasing Association 美国汽车租赁协会（简称 AALA）

American Bureau of Standard 美国标准局（简称 ABS）

American Bus Association 美国客车协会（简称 ABA）

American Engineering Standards Committee 美国工程标准委员会（简称 AESC）

American ESV Crash Performance Specification 美国试验安全车碰撞性能标准（见 ESV）

American Industrial Transport, Inc 美国工业运输公司

American League of Automobilists 美国汽车驾驶者联盟（简称 ALA）

American National coarse thread 美国粗螺纹（参见 Seller's thread）

American National Standard code for information interchange 见 ASCII

American National Standard Thread Form 美国标准螺纹

American Public Transit Association 美国公共交通协会（简称 APTS）

American Society of Traffic and Transportation 美国交通运输学会（简称 ASTT）

American Standard 美国标准（简称 AS）

American Standard Wire Gange 美国标准线规（不测钢线、铜线，简称 ASW）

American Steel and Wire Gauge 美国线径规（测钢丝、铜丝及其他金属丝，简称 ASWG）

American Tank-Automotive Center 美国陆军坦克和机动车辆试验中心（简称 ATAC）

American taper pipe thread 美国标准锥管螺纹

American Truck Dealers 美国载货汽车经销商（协会）（简称 ATD）

American Trucking Association 美国汽车货运协会（简称 ATA）

American wire gauge 美国线规（简称 AWG，参见 Brown and sharpe wire gauge）

ameripol 人造橡胶

Amer Std 美国标准（American Standard 的简称）

amesdial 测微仪

amethyst grey 紫晶灰（车身颜色）

AM/FM/CD audio system （车用）调幅/调频/CD 光盘音响系统

aminoplastics 氨基塑料，氨基树脂，聚酰胺塑料（= aminoplast）

ammeter 安培计，电流表（amperemeter 或 amperometer 的简称）

ammonia 氨（NH_3）

ammonia gas reductant （选择催化还原废气净化系统中使用的）氨气还原剂

ammonia-plus-hydrogen fuel 氨加氢混合燃油

ammunition vehicle 军火运载车辆

amortisseur 阻尼器，缓冲器，减振器；阻尼线圈；消声器

amortization ①折旧②缓冲，减振

amount ①量②总计，总和③等于，相当于④结果，效果⑤要旨，要点

amount of crown 拱高，拱度

amount of deflection ①弯度，挠度②偏移量，变位量

amount of man-hours per 100km run （汽车）每100公里行程的（维修）工时数（额）

amount of man-hours per one repair service 每次修理服务的工时数（额）

amount of valve lift 气门升高度，气门升起高度值

amp 放大器（amplifier 的简称，放大信号波形、电压或电流的器件）

AMPA ［日］汽车材料和零部件协会（Automobile Material and Parts Association 的简称）

amperage 安培数，电流量，电流强度

ampere 安，安培（国际单位制中电流强度单位，代号 A，简称 amp）

ampere density 电流密度（参见 current density）

ampere-hour 安培小时（简称 a·h, ah 或 AH, 指每小时通过导体1安培的电流量）

ampere-hour capacity （蓄电池）安培小时容量（亦称 ampere-hour efficiency, amperage capacity, 简称 A·H capacity）

ampere-hour drain 安培小时耗电量

ampere-second 安培·秒（每秒钟内通过导体1安培的电流量）

ampere turn 安（培）匝（数）（磁势的单位，代号 At 或 at, 1安匝等于1安培电流通过1圈导线时产生的磁动势，有时亦称 ampere winding, 参见 magneto motive force）

ampere volt 伏安（培）

amperite 镇流电阻器，镇流管，限流器

amphibian ①水陆两用车（简称 amph, 参见 alligator）②水陆两用的，两栖的

amphibian truck 水陆两用载货汽车（= amphibious truck, swimming truck, amphibious cargo vehicle, 简称 amph. trk. 或 amphtrk）

amphibious hover craft 水陆两用气垫船（车）

amphibious tracklayer 履带式水陆两用车，水陆两用履带式牵引车（简称 amphtrac）

ample dimensions 宽裕的尺寸，大小足够的尺寸

ample power 大功率，强功率

amplification ①放大；放大系数，放大率②加强，强化

amplification factor 放大因素，放大系数

amplified inverted signal 放大的反向信号

amplifier 放大器（在汽车电子系统中，指不改变波形而对输入信号的电压、电流或功率加以放大的装置、部件、系统或电路，简称 amp）

amplifier tuning condenser 放大器调谐电容器

amplifying relay valve （气制动系的）加速阀（简称 relay valve）

amplitude 辐（角），振幅；幅度，大小

amplitude modulation 幅度调制，调

幅（指按照要求使一固定频率载波信号的强度或振幅随调制信号变化的一种调制方法或电路，简称 AM）
amplitude of exciting force 激（振）力幅（指激振力的最大幅值）
amplitude of harmonic strain 简谐应变幅值（指简谐应变的最大值）
amplitude of oscillation 摆幅
amplitude of vibration 振幅
amplitude processing method （对机件实测载荷时间历程统计进行处理的）幅度计数法（直接给出载荷的变化值，即幅度，然后按幅度级整理出相应的载荷谱）
ampule （电器元件的）筒形玻璃壳体
AMRC [美] 陆军机动性研究中心（Army Mobility Research Center 的简称）
Amsler's universal tester 阿姆斯勒万能材料试验机（或称 Amsler type universal testing machine）
AMT ①（电子）自动控制式机械变速器（automatic-mechanical transmission 的简称，指由电子控制模块根据加速踏板、制动踏板等传递的驾驶者的意图和发动机转速、车速及原挡位所表征的车辆运行状态，按存储的最佳换挡规律，通过相应的执行机构实现自动换挡操作的传统齿轮式机械变速器）②手动电子控制式机械变速器（automatic-manual transmission 的简称，automatic-mechanical transmission 的另一种称谓。由电子控制系统根据驾驶者手动操纵的按开关式挡位选择板和加速踏板、制动踏板等的信息，由电子控制模块选择最适合当时行驶条件的挡位，通过执行机构实现自动换挡的机械式齿轮变速器）
Amtics 先进的（汽车）交通信息与通信系统（Advanced Mobile Traffic Information and Communication System 的简称）
amtrack （二次大战中使用的小型）水陆两用履带式登陆车（亦写作 amtrac）
amyl 戊（烷）基（$C_5 M_{11}$）
amyl nitrite 亚硝酸（正）戊酯（$C_5 H_{11} ONO$）（有异香的黄绿色液体，沸点 96℃，可提高柴油的十六烷值）
Amyl Zimate 戊基抗氧剂（美国 Dupont 公司出品的一种抗氧化剂的商品名）
An 标准大气压（normal atmosphere 的简称）
anacom 模拟计算机（analogue computer 的简称）
anaerobic 厌氧的，厌气的（如汽缸垫用的厌氧密封膏剂 anaerobic sealants 等）
anallobar 增压区，气压上升区
analmatic 自动检查和分析装置
analog data 模拟数据（用连续变化量表示的数据）
analog (data) recorder 模拟数据记录器
analog display （汽车仪表等的）模拟显示（一般利用长度按比例表示温度、压力、转速等，以别于数字显示）
analog IC 模拟集成电路（亦称线性集成电路"linear IC"）
analog input 模拟量输入（指与被传感量成正比的传感器的电压等连续物理量信号）
analog pressure control solenoid 模拟型压力控制电磁阀（相对于数字型脉冲宽度调制压力控制电磁阀而言）
analog processing 模拟处理（使用模拟式信号分析设备对试验数据的模拟连续信号进行处理）
analog quantity 模拟量（相对数字量而言，一般指流速、压力、流

量、温度、电压、电流等通常连续变化的物理量）
analog signal 模拟信号（指表示连续物理量的电压或电流信号）
analog signal interface 模拟信号接口
analog (-to) digital converter 模（拟）—数（字）转换器（将输入的连续量模拟信号变换成各种脉冲式数字信号，简称 AD converter，ADC）
analog transmission （在汽车电子控制系统中指）以连续波形传输信息数据的能力
analog type sensor 模拟型传感器〔指其输出是与所传感物理量的变化相对应的连续变化的电量，二者间的关系可以是线性的，或非线性的，但后者要修正成线性信号。其输出要先输入模/数（A/D）转换器转换为数字信号后，才能由计算机处理〕
analog ue ①模拟的，类比的，相似的，比拟的（亦写作 analog 或 analogous）②模拟，模拟量；模拟装置，模拟设备，模拟系统（在汽车电子控制系统中指其输出为其输入的连续函数，且无分立的数值，仅为连续变化量的装置或电路）
analogue cluster 模拟式组合仪表，组合式模拟仪表板
analog ue computer 模拟计算机（简称 anacom）
analog ue integrated circuit 模拟集成电路（指对表示连续物理量的电流或电压进行放大、转换、调制、传输、运算等的集成电路，可分为线性与非线性的两种，当不发生误解时，"集成"二字可从术语中省略）
analogue resolution（of a linear or non-linear ADC or DAC） （线性或非线性 ADC 或 DAC 的）模拟分辨率（台阶宽度标称值）
analogue signal processing circuit 模拟信号处理电路
analogue simulation 相似模拟（连续过程的模拟）
analog ue-to-digital processor 模—数字处理器（模拟—数字转换器的模拟部分的集成电路，它加上外部定时器，计数和算术运算部分才构成一个完整的模拟—数字转换器）
analogue to time to digital 模拟-时间-数字转换（简称 ATD）
analyser 分析仪，分析器（各种分析仪器，装置的通称）
analysis ①分析（法），解析（法）②分析（学），解析（学）
analysis by weight method （组合、杂质等的）重量分析法（重量分析法的旧称）
analysis of market needs 市场需要量分析
analysis of variance 方差分（解）析
analysis sample 分析用试样，分析样本
analytical investigation 分析研究
analytical model 解析模型（一种应用分析技术的计算机模拟模型）
anatomy ①分析，解析②解剖③组织，构造
ancestor 始祖车型（原始车型）
anchor ①支座,固定件,系紧件②电枢,衔铁③拴住,固定,系紧,支撑
anchorage ①固定，系紧，拴定②支撑装置，固定装置，紧固件③（垫车轮的）停车三角木④固定点，紧固点
anchor bolt ①（泛指一般的）紧固螺栓（任一种穿过被紧固件，一端由螺母固定的螺栓，如：地脚螺栓、系紧螺栓、支撑螺栓）②（特指将起动机或交流发电机总成紧固

在一起的两根长的）贯穿式紧固螺栓（＝through bolt）

anchor bracket 支架，托架，底架，安装底板

anchored wrist pin 固定式活塞销

anchoring point 固定点，支撑点

anchor pin ①连杆销②（制动器）蹄片销③支撑销，销轴

anchor (pin) boss 转向节主销孔凸台（＝swivel pin boss）

anchor wire （灯丝的）支撑线，桩线

ancillaries ①（特指交流发电机、动力转向泵、进气增压器、燃油泵、冷却水泵等装在发动机上或发动机旁，由发动机驱动的）发动机附件②（泛指）附件

ancillary equipment 辅助设备，外围设备，附属设备

ANC-NO 汽车噪声标准值（automobile noise criteria number 的简称）

AND "与"（计算机中逻辑运算的一种；或称逻辑乘法，logical product, collation operation 的简称）

ANDC 汽车新闻数据中心（Automotive News Data Center 的简称）

AND gate(circuit) "与"门，"与"门电路（有两个输入和一个输出，只有当两个输入全为 1 时，输出为 1，否则，输出均为 0。与门电路可实现逻辑乘法，亦称 logical multiply）

AND NOT-gate "与非"门（在与门输出端连接一非门，即为与非门。只要输入有一个为 0，则输出为 1，只有全部输入为 1 时，输出才为 0，亦称 exclusion）

"AND-OR" circuit "与/或"电路（在与门输出端接一个或门，即为与/或门，当与门的两个输入均为 1 时，其输出为 1）

android 人形机器人

anechoic chamber 隔声室，无回声室，吸声室，消声室（＝anechoic room, echoless chamber, echoless room）

anelasticity 滞弹性（指在弹性范围内，应变时间滞后于应力的现象）

anemobarometer 风速风压计

anemometer 风速表，风速计

anemorumbometer 风速风向仪（亦称 anemoscope）

aneroid ①无液的，不用液体的②膜盒（的），波纹盒（的）（中空，或充有挥发性液体）

aneroid air speed metering element 膜盒式空气流速计测器

aneroid altimeter 膜盒式高度表

aneroid battery 干电池

aneroid chamber ①真空膜盒②气压计盒

aneroid-type thermostat 金属波纹盒式恒温器（其中充填部分丙酮，乙醚或类似的挥发性液体）

ANG ①吸附型天然气（见 absorbed natural gas）②噪声发生器（acoustic noise generator 的简称）③美国天然气公司（American Natural Gas Company 的简称）④角，角度（angle 的简称）

angle ①角，角度②成一定角度的，斜的③角型件

angle between spray orifices （喷嘴的）喷孔夹角（孔式喷油嘴针阀体头部各喷孔轴线间的夹角）

angle bevel gear 斜交伞齿轮（简称 angle gear）

angle block gauge 量角规，角度块规（＝angle gauge block）

angle brace 角撑，斜撑，拱角拉条

angle bracket 斜撑架，斜角形托架

angle control （紧固件拧紧力矩的）回转角控制，转角控制，角度控制法（指将螺纹紧固件拧到刚好与紧固面接触后再拧转某一规定的角度）

angled big-end cap joint 连杆大头盖

斜角接合

angled nozzle 斜喷嘴（按一定角度倾斜安装的喷嘴）

angle gauge 量角器，角规，测角仪（亦称 angle meter）

angle head open spanner 弯头开口扳手

angle in circular segment 圆周角

angle-nose pliers 弯头钳（钳腿弯成90°的手钳）

angle of action 作用角（亦称 angle of application）

angle of approach 见 approach angle

angle of arrival 见 angle of incidence

angle of attach 见 approach angle

angle of chord 弦角（弦所对应的圆心角）

angle of contact 接触角，包角

angle of cord （轮胎的帘）线角

angle of departure 见 departure angle

angle of eccentricity ①（转子发动机的）主轴转角 ②偏心轴转角 ③偏心角（亦称 eccentric angle）

angle of elevation 仰角

angle of external friction 外摩擦角（土壤对车轮外部摩擦系数的反正切）

angle of incidence 入射角（入射光线与入射点的垂线的夹角，亦称 angle of arrival）

angle of internal friction 内摩擦角（土壤对车轮内部摩擦系数反正切）

angle of lock ①锁止角（指允许的最大转角，由锁止件限定的转角等，= lock angle）②（特指）最大转向角（= steering lock angle）

angle of pitch 见 vehicle pitch angle

angle of polarization 偏振角

angle of reflection 反射角

angle of refraction 折射角（= refraction angle，指入射光线与出射点垂线间的夹角）

angle of repose （散装货物的）安息角，天然倾角，静止角，休止角

angle of retarded closing （气门等的）迟关角，延迟关闭角，迟后关闭角

angle of roll 见 vehicle roll angle

angle of rotation 旋转角

angle of slip 见 side slip angle

angle of torsion 扭转角（= angle of twist）

angle of tractor fifth wheel coupling longitudal swinging 牵引车转盘式牵引座纵向摇摆角

angle of train 方位角，方向角（简称 AT）

angle of turn 回转角，转角

angle parking 斜列停车，斜向停车（车辆停放排列方向对车道方向保持一定的斜角，亦称 echelon parking）

angle pipe 弯管，角管

angle plate （液压马达）斜盘

angle screwdriver 双弯头螺钉起子（指每一端均有与起子杆身成直角的起子头，亦称 double-offset screwdriver）

angle-spring clutch 斜置弹簧离合器（弹簧压力斜向作用在传力套上，并通过压杆作用在压盘上）

angle steering column 倾斜式转向柱

angle strut 角铁支撑件（= angle support）

angle/time sensor 转角/时间传感器（向电子控制模块提供旋转件转速信号的传感件）

angle transmission 角传动，角传动装置（如圆锥齿轮传动，亦称 angular drive, angle drive）

angle (turning) indicator 转角指示仪（调整转向轮用）

angle-type axial piston pump 弯体式轴向活塞泵

angle type check valve 弯管止回阀，弯管单向阀（出入口成一定夹角的

止回阀）

angle valve 斜气门嘴（= angular valve）

angle wrench 斜口扳手（= skew wrench）

angstrom 埃（长度单位，代号 Å，$1Å = 10^{-10}$ m $= 10^{-4}$ μm。目前被广泛接受并较为合理的是 nanometer 毫微米，纳米，$= 10^{-9}$ m，即十亿分之一米。纳米技术可实现电子器件的超微型化）

angular 角形的，角状的，有角度的，成角度的，斜的，倾斜角，多角的，用角度量的

angular acceleration 角加速度（$\alpha = d\omega/dt$，式中：ω—角速度）

angular addendum （锥齿轮）齿顶高

angular advance 角度提前量

angular contact bearing 向心推力滚动轴承，角接触滚动轴承［指能同时承受径向载荷与轴向载荷的滚动轴承，其中向心推力球轴承称为 angular（contact）ball bearing，向心推力滚子轴承称为 angular（contact）roller bearing］

angular displacement 角位移

angular distance 角距

angular force 旋转力，角向力

angular gear ratio 角传动比

angular impact 斜碰撞（与汽车纵向平面成一锐角的正面碰撞，= angular collision）

angularity ①斜度，倾度②曲率，弯曲率，曲线度③成（一定）角度，棱角

angular member 角形构件，弯曲构件

angular misalignment ①（传动轴的）角偏差，角位移，偏斜（在传动系中两相互连接的传动轴，既不在一条直线上，又不平行，而形成夹角）②角度误差，角度失准

angular momentum 角动量，动量矩（= moment of momentum）

angular motion 角运动（转动，= rotation）

angular-motion transducer 角位移传感器，角运动传感器，转角传感器

angular output shaft （执行机构的）转角输出轴（将输入的控制指令变成一定的转角输出）

angular pipe union 弯管接头

angular pitch 齿距角（整个圆周即 360°与圆周上的齿数的比值）

angular rate sensor 角速度传感器，角度变化率传感器（单位 deg/sec）

angular rate signal （摆动角传感器等输出的）角速度信号，角度变化率信号（单位 deg/sec）

angular section 斜截面

angular-shaped groove 三角形（或梯形）槽

angular strain 角应变（指用切应变表示的应变，见 shear strain）

angular valve 直角形气门（= angle valve）

angular velocity 角速度（$\omega = d\varphi/dt$，式中：φ—平面角）

angular wheel 锥齿轮，锥形轮

ANGV （使用吸附型天然气为燃料的）吸附型天然气汽车（absorbed natural gas vehicle 的简称）

anhydrous 无水的，脱水的（简称 anh）

aniline point 苯胺点，苯胺溶液临界温度（石油燃料与同体积的苯胺刚好能够混合的最低温度，高苯胺点表示燃料的着火品质好。简称 an. pt）

anilol(e) 酒精苯胺混合液（一种高辛烷值汽油的添加液）

animation （电子计算机辅助设计的）总装整机（指通过计算机系统将各个部件的计算机辅助设计图样组装成可运转的仿真整机或整个系统）

anion 阴离子
anionic 阴离子的
anionic surface active agent 阴离子表面活性剂（在水溶液中其界面活性部分为阴离子）
anionite 阴离子交换剂（= anion-exchanger）
anion radical 阴离子团
aniseikon 光电探伤器，光电检疵装置（用来检察零件等的裂缝、变形等）
anisobaric ①不等压②不等压的
anisotropy 各向异性（当从不同方向测定时，机械性质不同）
ANL ①噪声自动限制器（automatic noise limiter 的简称）②退火（anneal 的简称）
anneal（ing） 退火（钢材的普通热处理工艺，加热到钢的临界点以上或以下，保温然后缓慢冷却，以降低硬度，增加塑性，消除内应力，细化晶粒，提高机械性能）
annealing furnace 退火柜（对金属、合金、玻璃等制品退火的可控气氛烘箱或加热炉）
Anno Domini 公元（简称 A.D.）
annoy （车辆产生的频率在100Hz以上的噪声）引起（乘员听觉上的）不舒适感，烦躁感
annoyance index 噪声指数
annual energy-saving rate 年节能率
annual inspection 年度检修，年检
annual overhaul 年度大修，年度解体检修
annual repair 全年需修量，年修理量
annual SAE congress 美国汽车工程师学会年会
annual trade show 年度展销会
annual traffic 年交通量，年运输量；年周转量
annual use 年度使用（时间），年度工作（时间）

annual vehicle registration 车辆年度登记
annular 环状的，环形的
annular ball bearing 径向球轴承
annular combustion chamber 环形燃烧室
annular float 环形浮子
annular gap 环形间隙（= circular gap）
annular gasket 密封垫圈，密封环
annular gear 环状齿轮，齿圈，齿环（包括环状的内、外齿轮，亦称 annulus gear 或简称 annulus）
annular seal space 密封腔（一般指旋转轴与静壳体间需要安装密封件处的环状空间）
annular slot nozzle 环口喷（油）嘴（亦称 annular jet nozzle；或简称 annular jet，= ring nozzle）
annular space 环形间隔，环形空间
annulus （复数 annuli 或 annuluses）①环状物，环形体（如环形套筒、外齿圈、内齿轮、气门座圈等）②环状空间（如环隙、环形通道等）③环形的，环的
annunciator （汽车电子控制系统可指明故障电路故障性质等的）声响警报器
anode 正极，阳极，板极，屏极
anode coating 见 anodic oxidation
anode current 阳极电流
anode efficiency 阳极效率（在电路中指输入的电能与输出电能之比，在电镀中指从阳极实际溶下的质量与理论上溶下的质量之比）
anode rays 阳极射线
anodic electro painting 见 electrophoretic painting
anodic metal ①阳极金属（金属原电池腐蚀时，在内电路中电位较低的活性金属）②作为阳极用的金属
anodic oxidation 阳极氧化处理（用电化学方法，在作为阳极的金属表

面上形成一种防腐蚀和美观的薄膜，= anodic oxydation treatment, anodization 或 anodic coating，其动词为 anodize 或 anodise。anodizing 或 anodising 指进行阳极处理的，如：anodizing bath 或 anodizing tank 阳极处理溶槽。anodized 指经过阳极处理的，如：anodized piston，经阳极处理的活塞。阳极处理生成的薄膜称为 anode oxide layer 或 anodic coating film。由于它是零件表面最后一道处理工序，因而有人又称为 anodized finish。与它过程相反，为了对金属表面层做清洁性处理，如：除锈等，称为 anodic scouring 阳极蚀洗）

anodize 对…作阳极化处理，阳极电镀［如：silver anodized（阳极镀银的）］

anolyte 阳极电解液（环绕阳极部分的电解液）

anomalous 反常的，异常的；不规则的

anomalous fracture 不规则破损（裂碎等），异常破损

anomaly 反常（的事物、情况、现象）

anotron （冷阴极充气）整流管

an. pt 苯胺点（见 aniline point）

ANS 消声系统，防噪声系统（antinoise system 的简称，见 antinoise）

ANSI 美国国家标准协会（American National Standards Institute 的简称）

anstatic agent 抗静电剂

answer ①答案，解答②响应，反应③回答信号（简称 A 或 ans）

ansymmetrical leaf spring 非对称式钢板弹簧（指其夹紧部分的长度不相等的钢板弹簧）

ANSYS 分析系统（analysis system 的简称）

antechamber 预燃室（antecombustion chamber 的简称）

antechamber system of injection （燃油）预燃室喷射系统

antechamber (type) engine 预燃室式发动机（一般多指预燃室式柴油机）

antenna （美）天线（= aerial）

antenna motor （驱动）天线（升降机构的）电动机

antenna trimmer 伸缩式天线杆，拉杆天线杆

anthropometer 人体条件测定装置（用于研究汽车乘坐区安全舒适性等）

anthropometric data 人体尺寸数据

anthropometric (test) dummy 人体试验用模型，假人（= anthropomorphic dummy）

anthropometric value 人体测定值

anthropomorphic test device （汽车各种）人体模拟试验用装置（如假人等，简称 ATD）

anthropotomy 人体解剖学

anti-acid coat 抗酸镀层，防酸涂层，耐酸面层

anti afterburn valve 防（熄火后）继燃阀（简称 AAV）

antiager 防（抗）老化剂

anti-air-pollution 防止空气污染

anti-alarm "Plus" with interior monitor 防盗警报带车内监视器

anti aquaplaning air jet （汽车的）防水层浮滑空气喷射装置（一般装在汽车前轮的前方，将路面的水层吹开）

anti-aquaplaning system （汽车的）防浮滑装置（见 aquaplaning）

anti-attrition 减磨的，防止磨损的

antibackfire valve ①防回火阀（简称 ABV，指在减速工况时将空气由空气泵引入进气歧管以防止回火的阀门）②（空气喷射净化系的）防排气管放炮阀

antibacklash check valve （液压转向

机构）防止产生背隙的止回阀（单向阀）

anti-backlash spring 消隙弹簧（防止因齿隙而反撞的弹簧）

anti-block(ing) system 见 anti-locking brake system

antibouncer 防回跳减振装置

anti-brake-skid system 见 anti-locking brake system

anti-brake-skid system 制动防滑系统（简称 ABS system，为 antilock brake system 的别称）

antiburst 抗破裂，抗挣断，抗撞破

antiburst door lock 可防振开的门锁（在冲碰时不会自动打开）

anti-carbon 防积炭的，抗积炭的

antichamber 预燃室（= antechamber）

anti-chip coating 防碎石涂层（在底涂层和表面涂层之间的弹性涂层，以保护车身板件免受碎石等击伤破损）

anticipate ①预先防止，预防，预先处理②预测，预见③超前，超过

anticipated load 预载荷

anticipated value 期望值，预期值

anticlockwise direction 反时针方向，逆时针方向，左向

anticollision device 防撞（车）装置

anti-compounding valve 防并用阀（货车气制动系统防止驾驶员同时使用气制动器和弹簧制动器的安全阀，亦称 differential protection valve）

Anticorodal-600 Jaguar Land Rover 全铝承载式车身使用的铝合金板材的商品名

anti-corrosion oil 防锈油（= anticorrosive oil）

anti-corrosion treatment 防腐蚀处理

anticorrosive 防腐蚀的

anticorrosive coating 防蚀涂料，耐蚀涂层，防腐蚀覆盖层

anticrash guard (head) lamp 带防护罩的前照灯

anticrash side steel beam （车身的）侧面防撞钢梁

anticreep ①防蠕变②防蠕动

anti-dazzle 防眩（= anti-glare）的

anti-dazzle driving mirror 防眩后视镜（亦称 anti-dazzle rear view mirror, antiglare rear-view mirror, anti-dazzle mirror, non-glare mirror, dipping mirror, anti glare driving mirror）

anti-dazzle filament 防眩灯丝（前照灯近光灯丝 = dimming filament, anti-glare filament）

anti-dazzle pedal （前照灯）变光踏板，近光踏板（= dimmer pedal）

anti-dazzle screen 防眩遮护罩，防眩屏蔽

anti-dazzle switch （前照灯）变光开关（= dimmer button）

anti-dazzle visor 遮阳防眩板（=［美］sun visor）

anti-dazzling windshield glass 防眩风窗玻璃

antidetonation cylinder head 防爆震汽缸盖

antidetonation fuel 抗爆燃料（如：高辛烷值汽油、高十六烷值柴油等燃料，= antiknock fuel）

antidetonation injection 抗爆震喷射

antidetonator （汽油）抗爆剂（= anti-detonation agent, antidetonating fluid）

antidiesel 防（汽油机）炽热点火（指防止汽油机在断开点火电路后仍不能熄火、继续运转的现象）

anti-dieseling solenoid （汽油机）防继燃电磁开关（点火开关断开后，发动机继续燃烧时切断油路）

anti-dieseling throttle-stop （汽油机）防继燃阻气门（继燃时切断气路）

anti-dieseling valve 见 overrun fuel cut-off

anti-disturbance 防干扰的，反扰动

的，抗拢动的

antidive control （汽车制动时）点头控制（装置）

anti-diving moment 反点头力矩（参见 diving moment）

antidraft ventilation 非直吹式通风（指避免式防止汽车高速行驶时外来风直吹乘员的通风模式, = draftless ventilation, draft-proof ventilation, no-draft ventilation）

anti-draft ventilation glass （轿车车身）前角窗玻璃（指前门窗前部可旋转防直吹式通风的角窗玻璃，亦称 door ventilation glass）

anti-drag 反阻力的，减阻力的

anti-drive end hsg （转子发动机的）非驱动端缸盖, 前端盖（参见 crank end hsg）

antidrum 防振消声板；消声筒

anti-drum(ing) compound 防振消声复合料（以沥青或橡胶为基料的复合黏性料, 用于涂敷板件内面, 以消减振动等引起的噪声）

anti-drunken-driving 反酗酒驾驶的, 防酒后开车的

anti-emission device 排放净化装置

anti-extrusion ring O 形密封环挡圈

antifading 抗衰退（的），抗衰减（的）

anti-flutter adhesive 抗颤振黏合剂

antiflywheel end 曲轴前端, 曲轴非飞轮端

antifoam additive 防泡沫添加剂

antifouling composition 防腐剂, 防污剂, 防腐蚀剂, 防脏剂（亦称 antifouling compound）

antifouling paint 防污漆

antifreeze ①防冻②防冻的（= anti-icing）③防冻（添加）剂（指加入冷却水中, 以降低其冰点的乙二醇等化学材料, 亦称 antifreeze additive, antifreezer; antifreeze agent, antifreeze compound, antifreeze dope）

antifreeze coolant 防冻液（指加有防冻添加剂的冷却水, 亦称 antifreeze fluid, antifreeze solution）

antifreeze (driver's) seat 防寒座椅（驾驶员的电热座椅）

antifretting coating 防侵蚀覆盖层, 防腐蚀涂层

antifriction ①减磨②减磨剂, 润滑剂（= lubricant）

anti-friction ball bearing 球轴承

antifriction bearing 滚动轴承（= rolling bearing, 使用滚子或球作轴承减摩元件的滚动轴承的总称）

anti-friction bearing pillow 滚动轴承座

anti-friction material ①耐磨材料；减摩材料②润滑剂（= lubricant）

anti-friction metal （滑动轴承的）减摩合金（如：巴氏合金等）

anti-friction roller ①（滚动轴承的）滚子②（起减摩作用的）支撑滚子, 支撑滚棒

anti-friction thrust bearing 推力滚动（滚子或球）轴承

anti-frost screen ①防霜风窗玻璃②防霜冻屏

antifrother 防泡沫剂, 防起泡添加剂

antigalling coating 防表面擦伤涂层

anti-glare 防眩（= anti-dazzle）

anti-glare glass 防眩玻璃（= antidazzle glass, non-glare glass, tinted glass）

anti-glare lens 防眩前照灯配光镜

anti-glare light 防眩灯, 近光灯（= anti-dazzle light, dim light）

anti-glare paint 防眩涂料, 无光漆

anti-heat glazing 抗热车窗玻璃（可防阳光热辐射, 降低车内温度）

antihunt 防摆动的, 防转速不稳定的

anti-icer(s) ①防止汽油结冰的化学添加剂②防止（在风窗上）结冰

的装置③防冻设备
anti-icing 防冻的（= anti-freeze）
anti-impact bumper 防撞保险杠
anti-interference condenser 抗干扰电容器
anti-interference ignition cable 高压阻尼线（可抑制电火花对无线电干扰的高阻抗高压线）
anti-jackknife device （铰接式汽车列车的）防折褶装置（该装置多安装在挂车列车的牵引或拖挂装置中，防止挂车相对牵引车折褶，亦称 anti-jack-knifing device，参见 jack-knife）
anti-jamming performance （多普勒雷达系统的）防欺骗干扰性能
anti-joy ride device （防不顾安全只图娱乐高速开车的）防飙车装置
anti-judder link 防止杆系振动的连接杆件
anti-kickback attachment 防反冲装置，防逆转装置
anti-knock 防爆震（的）
anti-knock additive 抗爆（添加）剂（减轻爆燃倾向的汽油添加剂，亦称 anti-knock agent, anti-knock compound, anti-knock component, ant-knock dope, ant-knock fluid, ant-knock substance）
antiknock fuel 抗爆震燃料（高辛烷值汽油，= antipinking fuel, knock-free fuel, non-detonating fuel, non-knocking fuel）
antiknock index （车用汽油的）抗爆指数（等于马达法辛烷值和研究法辛烷值的平均值，即 1/2（RON + MON），美国材料试验标准 ASTM 与美国联邦汽车规格均采用该指数值作为划分汽油等级的抗爆性指标）
antiknock performance （车用汽油的）抗爆性（指汽油在汽油机内燃烧时不易产生爆燃的性能，以往常用辛烷值表示，最近美国 SAE、ASTM、API 建议用抗爆指数表示，亦称 antiknock property, anti-knock quality）
antiknock petrol 抗爆汽油（高辛烷值燃油）
antiknock rating ①抗爆震指数②抗爆值的标定
antiknock requirements （对汽油）抗爆性（的）要求
antiknock sensitivity 抗爆敏感度（指研究法辛烷值与马达法辛烷值的差值，= RON-MON）
antiknock value 抗爆值，防爆震值（表示燃油的抗爆性能，如辛烷值）
anti-lacerative glass 防碎玻璃
anti-lock braking system 防抱死制动系统（简称 ABS，指在制动过程中，调节与控制制动管路压力，以防止因车轮制动力大于车轮与路面附着力，导致车轮抱死，而将车轮的滑移率控制在最佳范围的系统，亦称 antiblocking system。由反映车轮转速等的传感器，根据传感器的输入信号，确定车轮的滑移状态，而向制动力控制装置发出制动力控制指令的控制器 controller，或制动控制模块，如 EBCM, ABSCM 等及根据控制器的信号调节与控制各车轮制动器制动管路压力的调节器 modulator 三大部分组成）
antilock controller 防抱死（制动系统）的控制器（见 anti-lock braking system）
antilock mode （制动系的）防抱死工况
antilock modulator 防抱死（制动系统的）调节器（见 anti-lock braking system）
antilock outboard sensor 外装式（制动系）防抱死传感器（一般指装于车轴头上的车轮转速传感器）
antimagnetic 抗磁性的，反磁性的，

防磁的

antimagnetic disc 反磁盘,防磁(性)盘

antimony 锑(Sb)(轴承减磨层用合金材料)

antimony fume (熔化蓄电池极板等散放的)含锑烟雾,锑烟

antinoise ①防噪声的,消声的 ②反相噪声(指与噪声频率、振幅相同但相位相反的人为噪声,二者"相遇"产生相消干涉而消减原噪声,用于主动式消声系统,见 active muffler system)

anti-noise paint 消声漆

antinoise speaker (积极式消声系统的)反噪声波放大器

anti-noise system 消声系统(简称 ANS)

antioxidant 抗氧化剂

anti-oxidant 抗氧化的

anti-percolation device 防气湿装置;防热湿装置(防止汽车长期高速行驶等原因,化油器浮子室内的燃油受热烘烤、强烈蒸发而导致混合气过浓的装置。从主喷油管导出这类燃油蒸气的管或孔,称为 anti percolator,有时该词亦表示上述装置)

antipercolator 见 anti-percolation device

anti-pinch system 防(车门、窗)夹(手等的)系统

anti-pinking 抗爆震(的)(= anti-knock)

antipinking fuel 见 anti-knock fuel

anti-pitch rod (汽车悬架系统的)抗纵倾杆(防止簧上质量产生纵倾,绕纵倾轴俯仰振动,参见 pitch)

anti-pitch stiffness (汽车悬架系统的)(抗)纵倾刚度(指簧上质量纵倾角的单位增量所对应的纵倾力矩的增量,参见 pitch)

anti-polluting altitude-compensating high efficiency carburetor 高效防污染海拔高度补偿式化油器

anti-pollution device 防污染装置(亦称 anti-pollution package)

antipollution law 防污染法

antique car ①老式轿车,旧型轿车 ②古典汽车(美国指第一次世界大战前生产的名牌汽车)

antiradar device 抗雷达干扰装置

anti-rattler ①防振器,防振装置 ②消声涂层,减振涂层

anti-rattle spring 减振弹簧(= spreader spring)

antiresonance mass 抗共振质量,消共振质量

antiriot police car 抗暴警车

anti-roll bar (汽车悬架系统中的)抗侧倾杆(亦称 stabilizer "横向稳定器",为一根横向布置的扭力杆,可耦合左、右车轮的垂直位移,从而减少车身在侧倾中的摇晃,简称 roll-bar,但勿与翻车保护杆混淆,美称 anti-sway bar)

anti-roll-over 抗翻倾、翻车的

anti-rotating pin 防转销(防止相邻两零件相对转动)

anti-run-on valve 防(发动机断开点火后)继燃阀

antirust coat 防锈镀层,防锈涂层,防锈面层

anti-rust treatment 防锈蚀处理(亦称 rust proofing treatment)

anti-scaling compound 防垢剂(简称 antiscale,亦称 antiscale composition)

antiscuff coatings 防擦伤涂层,防擦镀层(= scuff-resistant coating)

antiseize compound 防熔黏剂,防咬合剂(防止滑动面,由于过热、过压产生熔黏、咬合等现象的润滑剂 antiseize lubricant 等)

antishimmy device 防摆振装置(指各种防止或减轻汽车转向轮绕主销

持续振动的装置,见 shimmy)
antisiphon airbleed 防止虹吸作用的排气孔
anti-skid braking system (汽车的)防抱死制动系(简称 ABS 或 ASBS,亦称 anti-slip 或 anti-lock braking system,指每当制动力,趋于超过车轮与路面附着力,而使车轮趋向抱死时,即减小制动力,防止车轮抱死的系统,因而该系统也称 anti-wheel lock system)
antiskid capability 防滑性能
antiskid depth 胎面防滑花纹高度(= skid depth)
anti-skid final drive 防滑差速器
anti-skid system brake balanced exhaust valve 防抱死系统的气制动压力平衡放气阀
anti-skid tester 防滑制动系测试台,制动系防滑试验台
antiskid tread 轮胎防滑胎面
anti-slipping chain (车轮)防滑链
anti-smog 防烟雾(的)
anti-snake stabilizer (汽车列车)防摆稳定装置,防蛇行装置
anti-spin (out) system 防(驱动车轮的)滑转系统(指防止驱动力大于车轮与路面附着力时车轮原地滑转,而及时减小驱动力的系统,见 ASR)
anti-spin regulation 见 ASR
antisplash guard 挡泥板(= dirt guard, mudguard, slush guard, splash guard)
anti-spray flap 见 mud flap
antispray guard 防油喷溅护板(= antispray plate)
antisquat function (电子控制悬架系统及车身高度调平系统在汽车突然起步加速时的)抗(车身)后坐功能
antisquat system 防车头上扬系统,防抬头系统(装在后悬架上,可将加速时产生的使车尾下沉的力转变为使车身后部上扬的垂直力,以减轻加速时车头抬升现象)
antisqueak spring 带消声衬片的钢板弹簧
anti-squeal shim (装在制动分泵活塞或盘式制动器制动蹄摩擦块后面的)制动啸声消除垫片,消声垫
anti-squish swirl 反挤压涡流(燃烧涡流的一种,膨胀冲程,活塞离开上止点下行时,由于燃烧气体的膨胀和深坑型燃烧室的收口形状,使坑内高压燃气向挤压涡流"squish swirl"相反的方向流入不断扩大的活塞顶隙空间,这种涡流称反挤压涡流)
antistatic agent 抗静电物,抗(静)电剂
anti-static solid tyre (可导电的)防静电实心轮胎
antisway bar [美]防横摇稳定杆,防侧倾稳定杆(= anti-roll bar)
antisymmetric 不对称的,非对称的
anti-theft steering lock 防盗转向盘锁
anti-tire blow-out & overload system 防爆胎与超载系统(当根据有关传感器的信息确认轮胎的载荷和爆破危险有一项超过规定的阈值时即制动停车,同时发动机熄火,直到危险完全消除方能再次行驶)
antivibration device 防振装置,避振器,减振器(亦称 antivibration damp, antivibrator, shock absober, damber)
anti-vibration mounting 防振支座,减振座架
anti-wear 抗磨损的
antiwear properties 抗磨损特性,耐磨特性
antiwelding film 防止摩擦面咬合的油膜
anti-windup spring 抗扭转变形弹

簧，抗卷曲弹簧（参见 sping wind-up）

anvil ①砧，铁砧②电键的下触点

AO 压缩空气操纵的，压缩空气控制的，气动的（air operated 的简称）

AOA device 附加型空气动力装置（aerodynamic add-on device 的简称）

AOC ①自动超载控制（automatic overload control 的简称）②空冷却机油冷却器（air oil cooler 的简称）

AOD-E transmission （福特公司的）AOD-E 型自动变速器（在原 AXOD-E "automatic transaxle overdrive" 型和 E4OD 型自动变速器的基础上重新设计的电子控制式自动变速器的商品名）

AOT 带超速挡的自动变速器（见 automatic overdrive transmission）

A/P 压气机（air pump 的简称）

A-P ①前-后，前至后（anterior-posterior, anterior to posterior 的简称）②汽车产品（automotive products 的简称）

APA 汽车零部件和附件（automotive parts and accessories 的简称）

A-panel （轿车车身的）前侧板，A 板（连接前车门的前边与前翼子板后边的板件）

APC ①自动相位调整（automatic phase control 的简称）②自动功率调整（automatic power control 的简称）③自动程序控制（automatic program control 的简称）

aperiodic 非周期的，非调谐的，直指的

aperiodic damping 非周期阻尼（阶跃响应不出现过冲的阻尼，亦称过阻尼"overdamping"，见 periodic damping）

aperture 小孔，口，孔径，口径，开度

Aperture Construction Method （本身的）大件结构法（使用数量尽可能少的大尺寸板件制造车身，以便减少易于腐蚀的焊、铆接缝）

aperture correction factor 孔口（流阻）修正系数

aperture panel （轿车车身的）侧主板（含门、侧窗洞及后翼子板的大型板件，亦称 side aperture panel）

aperture stop 气流管道内的流量限制或封闭件（如：节气门等）

apex ①顶，顶点，顶峰，尖，最高点②（三角转子）角顶③三角胶带（断面呈三角形）

apex seal assembly （转子发动机旋转活塞的）径向密封片总成（包括主密封片、密封角片、密封销及弹簧等）

apex to crown （锥齿轮的）分锥顶点至齿顶圆所在平面的距离

API ①美国石油学会（American Petroleum Institute 的简称）②精确位置指示器（accurate position indicator 的简称）③大气污染指数，大气质量指数（air pollution index 的简称，主要指大气中悬浮粉尘总量 TSP，二氧化硫 SO_2 及氮氧化物 NO_x 的含量）

API certification mark 美国石油协会认证标志（如：机油容器上的 API 机油质量认证标志）

A-pillar （轿车车身、货车驾驶室的）前立柱，前柱，A-立柱（= front pillar, A-post, front post, front standing pillar, 支撑顶盖，安装风窗玻璃与前门的立柱）

a pilot run 小批量试生产

API service symbol ［美］石油协会（润滑油）等级与黏度标志（一般印在润滑油容器外表面）

APL 认可的零部件及材料清单（Approved Parts and Material List）

A-post （轿车车身或货车驾驶室的）前柱（见 A-pillar）

aposteriori [拉丁语]（根据）经验的；归纳的，由结果追溯到原因的
aposteriori probability 后验概率（经验概率，= posterior probability 的简称）
app ①仪表，器件，设备（apparatus 的简称）②附录（appendix 的简称）
apparant crank initiation COD 表面启裂 COD 值（指 COD 阻力曲线外推到稳定裂纹扩展量为零时的 COD 阻力值，见 COD 及 COD resistance curve）
apparatus 器械，仪器，装置，设备
apparent ①表观的，视在的，表面上的②视在功率（交流电路中的有效电压和有效电流的乘积，= volt·amperes，单位：伏安 V·A）③透明的
apparent power 表观功率，视在功率
apparent road speed 近似道路速度，近似行驶速度；计算行驶速度
apparent weight 毛重，视重
Appealing （车辆等新产品）令人感兴趣的，有吸引力的
appearance 外表，外观，外形，外貌
appearance fracture test 断裂外观试验
appearance inspection 外观检查，外表检视
appearance of a vehicle 车容（车内外的整洁、卫生、美观等状况）
appendage ①附件，附具，附属品②备件，配件，备用仪表
appendix 附录，附表，附件
appliance ①用具，设备②救火车，消防车（fireappliance 的简称，= fire engine）
appliance circuit 仪表用电路
appliance outlet 设备（电源）插口
applicable 可应用的，适用的

application ①应用②加，施加③申请
application counter （车辆）驾驶动作（如：制动、换挡）统计器
application factor 工件的使用条件系数（在设计计算时考虑工作条件、加载方式等对耐久性、寿命影响的系数）
application oil groove 润滑油槽，润滑油道
application pressure 作用压力，使动压力，驱动压力
application valve 控制阀门，操纵阀门
applied force 施加的力，作用力
applied stress 工作应用，作用应力（指工件在使用中，单位面积上所受到的力）
apply ①施加②使用③镀，涂，敷④安装（如：apply oil 加机油，apply brake 踩制动器，apply tire 安装轮胎）
apply valve 作用阀（液压系统中使某装置或器件进入工作状态或位置，或开始起作用的控制阀）
appointments 车身内部装饰
apportion 按比例分配
apportioning valve （制动力）比例分配阀（随制动强度或载荷变化而使前后轮制动力按近似理想比例来分配的装置，目前多称 proportioning valve）
apportionment of tractor-trailer-braking 牵引车-挂车制动力比例分配
AP position sensor 加速踏板位置传感器（accelerator pedal position sensor 的简称）
appraisal 评价，估价，鉴定，鉴别
approach angle 接近角，前通过角（切于静载前轮轮胎外缘且垂直于 Y 平面的外缘与 Z 平面之间所夹的最大锐角，前轴前方任何固定在车辆上的刚性件均在该平面内，表示

汽车接近土丘等障碍物时，不致发生碰撞的范围，= angle of approach, angle of attack, 亦称 front overhang angle "前悬角")

approach speed 接近速度

approval 批准，认可，通过（计划，方案，设计，规划，设备、装置、车辆等）

approval test 验收试验；鉴定试验

approved design 已经审定的设计；已经核准的结构

approximate ①近似的，大约的，约略的②近似于，接近于，使接近，使近似③近似，接近，近似法，近似值

approximate value 近似值

approximation ①近似，接近，近似法，近似值②模拟，模拟法③概算，略计

APP sensor 加速踏板位置传感器（accelerator petal position sensor 的简称）

appts 仪器，装置，设备（apparatus 的简称）

appurtenances [复]附属物，附属装置，辅助机组，辅助工具，配件，附件，附属建筑，从属设备

appx. 附录（参见 appendix）

APR [法]标致-雷诺（联营）公司（Association Peugeot-Renault 的简称）

APRA [美]汽车零部件修复工作者协会（Automotive Parts Rebuilders Association 的简称）

APRAC [美]大气污染研究咨询委员会（Air Pollution Research Advisory Committee 的简称）

apron ①挡板，护板②（垂挂在车轮后面等处的）挡泥板③（整个车身侧面向下延伸的或位于车身正前面保险杠下方的）裙板（均起减少空气动力阻力的作用等）④停车等用的车库前面的广场，道路加宽的部分

apron bus 机场客车（机场内接送旅客用车）

apron ring 在活塞裙下部的活塞环

AP&T 轮胎气压与温度自动监测系统（auto tire air pressure and temperature monitering system 的简称）

APT （出厂前制造厂）调好的部分开启节气门（factory adjusted part throttle 的简称，确保走合期内发动机在规定的部分负荷下运转）

APTA 美国公共交通协会（American Public Transit Association 的简称）

APTS 先进的公共运输系统（Advanced Public Transportation System 的简称）

APU 辅助动力装置（auxiliary power unit 的简称）

APV 多用途车辆，通用车辆（all-purpose vehicle 的简称）

AQCS 见 AQS②

AQL ①验收（合格）质量标准（acceptable quality level 的简称）②平均质量水平（average quality level 的简称）

AQS ①（车内）空气质量监控系[air quality (supervision) system 的简称]②（车内）控制系统（air quality control system 的简称，= AQCS）

aqua 水溶液

aqua ammonia(e) 氨水（$NH_4OH + nH_2O$）

aqua communis 普通水

aqua distillata 蒸馏水

aqua fortis （浓）硝酸

aquaplaning （路面的积水层使车轮与路面间脱离接触而产生的）浮滑现象、飘滑现象、水滑现象（严重时会使制动和转向操作均失去作用，=[美] hydroplaning）

aquastat 水温自动调节器

aquazole 水氮杂茂（一种乳化柴油）
aqueous alcohol 含水酒精
aqueous caustic 苛性碱液
aqueous electrolyte battery 含水电解液蓄电池（一般用高导离子性的酸或碱溶液作为电解液的蓄电池，如：铅酸蓄电池等）
aqueous fluid resistance （橡胶等）耐水类流体浸泡变质特性，耐含水流体特性
aqueous ingredients 含水量
aqueous solution 水溶液
aqueous vapo（u）r 水蒸气，水汽
AR ①空气流量调节器（air regulator 的简称）②驱动轴减速比（axle ratio 的简称）
Aramid fiber 芳香族聚酰胺纤维（亦称 polyamide fiber，具有极强的拉伸和耐热特性，多用来制作纤维强化材料）
24-A-rated 24-安额定电流的（指用电器件，如：30 安额定电流者，称 30-A-rated）
arbitary-shaped radiator 异形散热器（任意形状的散热器）
arbitrary 任意的（任选的，随机的，任一个的）
arbitrary sequence computer 任意顺序计算机（所执行的每一条指令都明确规定即将执行的下一条指令的地址，即：将要执行的任一条指令都是由刚刚执行过的上一条指令所规定）
arbitration 判优（①汽车计算机控制系统中，指当两个网点或两个以上的网点同时开始传输帧或帧内响应数据时，分辨哪一帧或帧内响应数据应继续传输②对多路复用系统或多路处理的优先权的管理）
arbour 柄轴，心轴，刀杆（= arbor）
arc ①弧，电弧，弧光，圆弧，弧线，弓形线；拱，扇形物，弧形板②拱形的，弧的，弧形的，圆弧的，电弧的③产生电弧；击穿，飞弧，电弧放电
ARC 行驶平顺性主动控制（系统）（activeride control system 的简称）
arc-contact worm 圆弧圆柱蜗杆（= Hollow flank worm，ZC-worm，齿面为圆环面的包络曲线的圆柱蜗杆，通常它做成凹齿，其齿面的变形曲面为圆环面的外表面）
ARC engine 活性分子团燃烧式发动机（参见 Activated Radical Combustion engine）
arc-free 无火花的，无电弧的，不产生电弧的，不产生火花的，不放电的
arch ①半圆形，弓形；弓形物，弧形物，弓架结构，拱，拱门②见 wheel arch
arched-head piston 拱顶活塞，凸顶活塞（= arched top piston, dome head piston）
arched tire 拱形轮胎（外径与普通充气轮胎大致相等而横断面成拱形）
Archimedes screw 阿基米德螺旋（= Archimedes spiral，动点沿一直线作等速运动，同时该直线又绕与其直交的轴线做等角速旋转时，该动点在该直线旋转平面上的轨迹）
Archimedes worm 阿基米德蜗杆（见 straight sided axial worm）
architecture 组织结构（主要指应用结构和通信协议）
arch top 拱（形车）顶
arcing voltage 起弧电压，跳火电压
arc length 弧长
arc line 弧线
arcminute 1/60 弧度，分弧度
arc of action （齿轮）作用弧，啮合弧（亦称 arc of contact）
arc over 产生电弧，跳火（= jump over）

arc thickness （齿轮的）弧线厚度
arctic operation （汽车在）北极地区运行，严寒地区运行
arctic shield （汽车发动机等冬季用的）防寒护罩
arctic test 在寒冷气候条件下的试验
arc welder 电弧焊机
arc welding 电弧焊，弧焊（为熔焊的一种，指利用电弧放电时产生的热量将焊接件加热至熔化状态完成的焊接方法）
ardnous service 恶劣条件下的使用
ARE（空调系统鼓风机）与蒸发器总成（air inlet blower and evaporator assembly）
area ①面积②表面③区域；范围，场地
area closed sign 封锁区标志（对该区域实行交通封锁的标志）
area deformation 表面变形，表面面积变化
area factor （汽车空气阻力的）迎面面积系数
area licensing scheme 区域牌照制（简称ALS，防止某一地区汽车太多而造成交通阻塞，挂有该地区的区域牌照的车辆才允许驶入的制度）
area of ball imprint 小球压痕面积，铜球压印面积，球迹面积
area of stress concentration 应力集中区
area of tire impression 轮胎印痕面积（指轮胎充气后在静负荷下的接地投影面积。和轮胎接地面积的概念不同，后者是指轮胎充气后在静负荷下的花纹接地面积）
area ratio 面积比，面积利用系数
area ratio of combustion chamber passage 燃烧室通道面积比（指主、副燃烧室之间连接通道的截面积与活塞面积之比）
areometer 液体比重计

ARG ①［英］（利兰汽车公司）奥斯汀-罗孚部（Austin Rover Group 的简称）②汽车备用玻璃（automotive replacement glass 的简称）
argon 氩（Ar 或 A）
argon arc (spot) welding 氩弧（点）焊
argon rectifier 氩整流器
AR-HUD （向驾驶者视野，如：风窗玻璃上清晰投射汽车的运行数据、安全情报等影像的）逼真型抬头显示（augmented-reality HUD 的简称，见 HUD）
arithmetical difference 算术差
arithmetic and logical unit 算术和逻辑部分［在计算机中央处理器（CPU）内，进行加减演算（+·-），逻辑演算（与·或），比较演算（=·>）等演算的部分，简称 ALU］
arithmetic mean 算术平均，算术均数
arithmetic sum 算术和
Arizona road dust （供试验空气滤清器用的）（美国）亚利桑那州道路埃尘
ARL 可接受的可靠性水平（acceptable reliability level 的简称）
arm 臂，杠杆，手柄，手把，摇把；支撑臂，支臂，悬臂，辐条
armature ①电枢（直流发电机的电枢由铁心、电枢绕组和换向器成，装在电枢轴上，在固定于发电机外壳内壁上的磁极间转动，切割磁力线而感生电流；直流电动机电枢的结构与发电机相似，当电流通过其绕组导线时，电枢将在此时产生的电磁转矩作用下转动，而输出转矩）②衔铁（由电磁吸力作用而驱动触点等的导磁件）③（电缆）铠装
armature arm 衔铁（触点）臂
armature brake （电动机）电枢制动

器（一般装在电枢轴端，防止电动机达到危险转速或在切断电源后制动电枢）

armature coil 电枢绕组，电枢线圈（= armature loop, armature winding）

armature contact points 衔铁触点

armature core 电枢芯子，电枢芯，电枢矽钢片芯，电枢铁芯

armature gap ①衔铁间隙 ②电枢间隙

armature groove 电枢（铁芯上的）绕组槽

armature growler 电枢测试器，电枢线圈短路测试仪

armature pinion 电枢轴驱动小齿轮

armature reaction 电枢反应，电枢反作用（指流过电枢线圈的电流所产生的磁力线使主磁场的磁力线畸变的现象）

armature shaft 电枢轴

armature shift type 电枢移动式（起动机电枢做轴向移动而使起动机驱动小齿轮与飞轮齿圈啮合的方式）

armature slot 电枢嵌线槽

armature spindle 电枢芯轴

armature terminal A 接线柱（直流发电机输出端接线柱或调节器的相应接线柱，旧称输出接线柱，= output terminal）

armature tester 电枢测试器（俗称 growler，用于测试电枢线圈的短路或断线等故障）

armature type relays 电枢式继电器

armature winding 电枢绕组

arm for direction indicator 方向指示器（指臂），方向指针，方向箭头（= direction arrow, direction indicator arm, trafficator arm, signal-arm, indicator arm）

arm indicator ①臂式转向指示器 ②杠杆式测量仪表

arming and disarming method (of antitheft system) （防盗系统的）启用和解除方法

arming sensor （安全气囊的）待爆传感器（见 air bag sensing system）

arm of ratchet 棘轮爪臂

arm of steering wheel 转向盘辐（= steering wheel spoke）

arm of wheel 轮辐（= wheel spoke）

armored cable 铠装电缆（用金属编织层包覆的电缆）

armored frame 加强的车架（机架）

armored glass 嵌有铁丝网的安全玻璃（= wired glass）

armored hose 铠装软管

armored vehicle 装甲车辆

arm rest ①（座椅上的）靠手，肘靠 ②（拾音器的）臂架

ARMS 汽车零售管理系统（automotive retail management system 的简称）

arm shaft 臂轴（指固定各种臂件的轴）

arm span （人）两臂伸展宽度

4-arm wheel nut wrench 十字形四头螺母扳手（美称 4-way lug wrench）

army all-purpose engine oil 军用多用途发动机润滑油，军用全能机油

army grade 军用级

Army Mobility Research Center 美国陆军机动性研究中心（简称 AMRC）

army repair workshop 军用汽车修理车间，军（用汽）车修理厂

army specification 军用规范，军用规格

aromatic compound 芳香族化合物（苯 C_6H_6 及含有苯核结构的化合物的总称）

aromatic electrolytic membrane （氢燃料电池等的）芳香族电解质（质子交换）膜（具有良好的低温氢离子传导性和耐热性能，可在零下 20℃ 起动，在 95℃ 高温下亦可发电）

Aromatic-free diesel fuel 无芳香烃柴

油机用燃油
aromatic fuel 芳香烃燃料
aromatic hydrocarbon 芳香烃
aromatics 芳香族添加剂
Around View Monitor （周围）全景监视器（可观测到车辆周围情况的可视监测系统）
ARQ 自动误差查寻装置（automatic error quest equipment 的简称）
arrangement in parallel 平行排列
arrangement of cylinders 汽缸排列（参见 cylinder set-up）
arrangement of ribs 肋的布置，加强（劲）肋（拱）排列，冷却片布置
arrangement plan 布置方案，布置计划
arranger 传动装置
array computer 阵列计算机（见 vector computer）
array logic （汽车电子控制系统中的）阵列逻辑（电路），数组逻辑（电路），（指其多条输入/输出引线交点成矩形网络状的逻辑电路，用于作编码器或译码器）
arrester ①制动器，限止器，止动器，停机装置，镇定装置，行程限制器，挡板②过压熔断丝（亦写作 arrestor）
arrester catch 挡块，卡子，制止器，销挡，掣子（亦称 arresting stop）
arresting device 行程限制器，止动装置，挡块（亦称 arresting gear）
arrest point 转化点，驻点，临界点
arrow 指针，箭头
arrowheaded 箭头形的，镞状的
arrow line 箭头线
ARS 主动式后轮转向系统（Active Rear Steer System 的简称，丰田公司的电子控制式四轮转向系统的商品名。该系统可根据汽车行驶条件、轮胎状况、乘员、装载状况、路面状况的变化，通过对后轮转向角的控制，实现车身侧偏角≈0 的高转向稳定性控制）
arsenate 砷酸盐（砷酸酯）
art ①制品，产品，物体②项目③条款；章程④技术，技巧；艺术⑤人造的，人工的，模拟的，假的（= artificial）
art department （汽车外形）美术设计室
arterial highway 主干公路，公路干线（交通流量相当高，但不是立体交叉的高速公路，指 primary state highways, major urban arterial highways 等，简称 arterial，亦称 arterial road, trunk road, main highway）
arterial street 城市干道
artic 牵引车-半挂车汽车列车（articulated vehicle 的简称）
articized vehicle 供严寒地带使用的车辆
artics 鞍式牵引车带半挂车列车
artics tanker （汽车）半挂油罐列车
articulate ①铰链接合，铰接②铰接的
articulated axle （独立悬架）铰接桥，铰接轴（见 swing axle）
articulated bus 铰接客车（由铰接装置相连通、互相连接、乘客可在其中走动的两个刚性车厢体所组成的客车）
articulated con-rod 铰接式连杆（一个曲轴销上装有两个相互铰接的连杆，多用于 V 形发动机，= hinged con-rod）
articulated cross shaft 万向节轴，万向节十字轴（亦称 articulating link, shaft cardon joint shaft）
articulated frame 腰折式车架，铰接式车架（由前、后两部分铰接组成，可减少转向半径，提高机动性）
articulated haulage vehicle 铰接式运输车辆
articulated lorry 铰接式货车（一般

指拖带挂车或半挂车的货运车辆)

articulated mirror 铰接式(后视)镜,万向转动(视)镜

articulated passenger carrier 鞍式牵引客车

articulated six-wheeler 三轴铰接式车辆(指双轴牵引车带单轴挂车组成的链接式列车)

articulated steer (铰接式车架车辆的)铰接转向,扭腰式转向(前、后轮场绕铰接垂直轴线转向,亦写作articulation steering)

articulated suspension 铰接式悬架

articulated tanker 铰接式液罐车

articulated traffic 拖挂运输

articulated trailer 铰接式挂车

articulated wheeled off-the-road vehicle 轮式铰接型越野车辆(车身由前后铰接的两部分组成,前后两部分可作相对转动)

articulation 铰接,关节,活络连接,活节头

articulation joint 铰接

artification intelligent 人工智能(亦称artificial intelligence,简称AI,指电子计算机对所馈送的信息能按照人类的方式进行推理、决策和处理的系统反应能力,以及学习能力)

artificial atmosphere 人工气氛,人工大气环境

artificial barrier 人造障碍,人造壁障

artificial climate laboratory 人工气候试验室

artificial cooling 强制冷却

artificial environment 人造环境,人工环境

artificial gasoline 合成汽油

Artificial Intelligence Shift 人工智能型自动变速器(见 AI shift)

artificial leather 人造革(亦称 artificial substitute, imitation leather)

artificial neural net 人工神经网络(简称 neural nets, NNs, 亦称 connection model 连接模型,一种模拟人类神经系统行为、用于生物型电子计算机系统、由海量神经元组成的分布式并行信息存储-处理系统。其信息是通过神经元的兴奋模式存储在网络上的,信息处理是通过大量神经元之间同时相互作用的动态过程完成的)

artillery wheel (炮车用的)宽辐轮

artmobile 流动艺术展览车

art of driving 驾驶技术

ARTS ①先进的道路运输系统(Advanced Road Transportation System 的简称,日本 ITS 的开发项目之一)②先进的乡村交通系统(Advanced Rural Transportation System 的简称)

ARV 装甲抢救车(armored recovery vehicle 的简称)

AS ①吸入空气(参见 air suction)②科学院(Academy of Science 的简称)③空气流速(air speed 的简称)④美国标准(参见 American Standard 的简称)⑤自动洒水车(Automatic sprinkler 的简称)⑥自动同步器(automatic synchronizer 的简称)

ASA 美国标准协会[American Standard(s) Association 的简称]

asbestonite 石棉制绝热材料

asbestos (bakelite brake) lining (制动蹄的)石棉(酚醛塑料)摩擦衬片

asbestos-free 无石棉的,非石棉的(特指制动蹄摩擦片、离合器摩擦片等,由不含石棉的材料制成,以防石棉公害)

asbestos packing 石棉垫料,石棉垫

asbestos plug 石棉塞

ASBS 见 anti-skid braking system

ASC ①(发动机)轴向层状充气(axially-stratified-charge 的简称)②防车轮滑转控制(系统)(anti-spin control 的简称，见 ASR）③自动稳定性控制系统（automatic stability system 的简称的简称）

ASCC 自动程序控制计算器（automa-tic sequence-controlled calculator 的简称）

ASCD 自动速度控制装置（Auto Speed Control Device 的简称，日产公司预先车速控制系统的商品名，即使松开加速踏板上坡，该系统也可以维持汽车以所选定的车速行驶，见 cruise control system）

ascending grade 爬坡度，上坡度，升坡

ascending handles （公共汽车）登车扶手（= ascension handle, assist handle）

ascending speed 上坡速度

ascending stroke （活塞）向上冲程，上升冲程（= up stroke，如：直列式内燃机的压缩、排气冲程）

ascent 上升，上坡，上升坡，斜坡路

ASCII 美国国家信息交换标准码（American National Standard Code for Information 的简称，使用七位编码字符组成的编码字符集，若为 8 位，则包括奇偶校验，用于数据的处理和通信系统有关设备间的信息交换，其字符集由 128 个代码组成，其中 96 个是大、小写英文字母、数字和符号，32 个为控制符）

ASC system 稳定性主动控制系统（Active Stability Control System 的简称，日本三菱公司一种电子计算机四轮制动力独立控制系统的商品名，电子控制模块根据转向盘转角、节气门开度、制动压力信息判断驾驶员的意图，根据四个车轮的转速、横向加速度、前后方向的加速度、横摆角加速度信号判断车辆的运动状态，并与计算机内存储的理想运动状态进行比较，通过对发动机驱动力及各个车轮制动力的分别控制，实现汽车稳定性的最佳控制）

ASD ①自动防滑差速器（automatic slip-control differential 的简称）②自动切断（油、气、电）（auto shut down 的简称）

ASDM 安全气囊系统诊断模块（见 air bag system diagnostic module）

ASD relay type fuel pump 自动断路继电器型燃油泵（automatic shut-down relay type fuel pump 的简称，若点火开关接通后 0.5s 发动机仍不起动，发动机电子控制模块便切断 ASD 电路，电压不再经 ASD 继电器供给油泵，油泵停止泵油）

ASE ①自动稳定装置（参见 automaticstabilization equipment 的简称）②工程师联合会（Amalgamated Society of Engineers 的简称）③汽车用斯特林发动机（automotive Stirling engine 的简称）

4A service 四 A 服务（anytime、anywhere、anybody、anything service 的简称，指能实现在任何时间、地点、对任何对象、项目提供服务的系统）

ASF （轿车的）全铝空间车架（aluminium space fram 的简称）

AS&G 见 auto-stop & go

ash 灰，灰分

ash box （车内的）烟灰盒（亦称 ash pan, ash tray, ash pit）

ash content 灰分，含灰量

ash-forming material （燃油中）形成灰分的物质，成灰物质

ashless 无灰的

ASHRAE 美国采暖、制冷、空气调节工程师协会（American Society of Heating, Refrigerating and Air-Conditioning Engineers 的简称）

ASHRAE comfort chart （评价车辆空气调节系统性能的）空气温、湿

度舒适范围图（参见 ASHRAE）

ash tree brown （仪表板等）梣木褐色的（仪表板等）

ASIA ［美］汽车维修行业协会（Automotive Service Industry Association 的简称）

ASIC （按用户要求设计的）专用集成电路（application-specific integrated circuit 的简称，一般指门阵列或可编程逻辑装置）

ASIS ①（紧急）故障传感及处理系统（abort sensing and implementation system 的简称）②防止酒后驾驶的安全联锁装置（alcohol safety interlock system 的简称）③美国工业安全协会（American Society for Industrial Security 的简称）

asist grip 扶手（客车上供乘员手扶的构件，= handrail, banisters）

Askania servo mechanism 喷管式液压伺服机构，喷管式液压随动机构（由喷管、操作缸或液动机组成。改变喷管的位置即可改变液压的分配和流量）

ASL （自动变速器的）自动挂挡安全锁（automatic shift lock 的简称，起动后必须将制动踏板踩到底才能挂挡的安全锁止机构）

ASLE 美国润滑工程师学会（American Society of Lubrication Engineers 的简称）

aslope 带斜度的，有坡度的

ASM ①美国金属协会（American Society for Metals 的简称）②加速模拟工况（acceleration simulating mode 的简称）

ASME 美国机械工程师学会（American Society of Mechanical Engineers 的简称）

ASME CODE 美国机械工程师学会标准

aspect angle 视界角，视线角

aspect ratio ①纵横（尺寸）比，高宽（尺寸）比，（平均）长度（与）直径（之）比②形态比，形数比③展弦比

asperity 粗糙度

aspest ratio of tyre （轮胎的）①高/宽比（其断面高度与宽度之比）②扁平率（= 轮胎断面高度/轮胎断面宽度 ×100%）

asphalt 沥青

asphalt distribution truck 沥青洒布车

asphaltic concrete road 沥青混凝土路

asphalt surface course 沥青路面，面层

aspheric mirror 非球面（后视）镜

aspirated 吸气的，吸入的

aspirated volume 吸气容积，吸入容积，吸气量，吸入的空气量

aspirating stroke 吸气冲程，进气冲程（参见 induction stroke）

aspiration 吸入，吸气

aspiration noise ①吸气噪声，进气噪声②（汽车行驶时由门、窗等缝隙进入车内的气流引起的）漏风噪声（亦称 leakage noise）

aspirator ①吸气器，吸出器（泛指利用吸力将气流或液流吸出的装置）②气压输出孔③喉管

aspirator controlled EGR system 吸气喉管真空控制式 EGR 系统（见 EGR venturi）

aspirator-type air injection system 吸气式空气喷射系统，吸气式喷气净化系统［利用排气负压脉冲，将新鲜空气吸入排气管内，使废气中的 CO, HC 氧化。亦称 aspirator air (injection) system, pulse air injection system, pulse air inducton reactor, air suction system, 简称 ASS］

aspirator valve ①吸气器阀，呼吸阀，吸气阀，进气门②指二次空气吸入系统"air induction system"中的单向排气脉冲吸气阀（通过吸气

管道将进气系的空气滤清器区与排气系的排气门口区连接，当排气压力低于空气滤清器内的压力时，该阀在进排气压力差的作用下开放，而将新鲜空气吸入排气气流，使废气中未烧尽的 HC、CO 进一步氧化燃烧，以净化排气，而当排气压力高于空气滤清器区的进气压力时，该阀关闭，防止废气流入新鲜空气中，参见 air induction system②）

ASPS （汽车座椅的）防（乘员在车辆碰撞时向前下方）溜滑保护系统（anti-submarining protection system 的简称，车辆正面碰撞时，与安全带相配合将人限制在座椅上，并产生下沉力，防止人体向前下方溜滑所造成的创伤）

ASQC 美国质量控制协会（American Society of Quality Control 的简称）

ASR ①（报废车拆散后将有用件、油、液及切碎的有用金属分类回收后，剩下的）汽车废渣（automobile shredder residue 的简称，由于这类废渣多带有污染物，故各国法令规定，必须深埋）②防（汽车加速时，车轮）滑转系统［anti-spin regulation, acceleration slip regulation 的简称，亦称 anti-spin device, anti-slip (out) system, 都是通过调节与控制作用于驱动车轮上的牵引力来防止猛加速时，牵引力大于路面附着力，以致车轮滑转，车辆失去操纵稳定性，故亦称 acceleration spin regulation, 仍简称 ASR。一般 ASR 与防抱死制动系共用一个电子控制模块和各种传感器，并借助于对趋于滑转的车轮施加制动或同时降低发动机输出动力控制作用于车轮上的牵引力，即：是通过控制牵引力来控制车轮滑移的，故又称牵引力控制系统"traction control system"，简称 TCS, 有时称 ASR traction control system, 与制动器合在一起时称 ABS/ASR］

ASR brake pressure modulator 防滑转控制制动压力调节器

ASR braking intervention 防滑转系统的制动干涉（指利用对车轮施加制动力的方法消耗车轮驱动力防滑转）

ASR deactivation switch 防滑转控制解除开关（在沙地和松砾石路面上行车时，断开 ASR 系统，以便在上述路面上获得最大牵引力）

ASR deactivation valve 防滑转系统的断开阀（在砂地或松软地面上行驶时断开 ASR 系统，亦称 shuttle valve）

ASR engine torque-control intervention 防滑转系统的发动机转矩控制干涉（用减少节气门开度控制供油量或调整点火正时，或二者同时采用的方法减小发动机的输出转矩，以降低车轮驱动力防其滑转）

ASR for controlling differential slip on wheels 车轮（间）滑转差控制型 ASR 系统（其中 controlling 有时亦写作 regulating, 指具有通过制动的方法消除各车轮间的滑转差，以保持车辆稳定性功能的 ASR 系统）

ASR hydraulic unit 防车轮滑转系统的液压装置（除共用常规液压制动系和 ABS 系已有的液压系统零部件外，还包括 ASR 阀、储能器或储能室等 ASR 专用件）

ASR selecting switch 防滑转控制选择开关（由驾驶者选择是否启用 ASR 系统的手动开关）

ASR slip-threshold switch 防车轮滑转系统的滑转控制阈设定开关（用于设置和调定 ASR 系统对车轮滑转的控制范围）

ASR TCS with ignition and fuel-injection intervention 通过减少点火提前角和喷油缸数干预的防滑转牵引力控制系统

ASR traction control system 防滑转牵引力控制系统

ASR with brake torque control 制动力控制式防车轮滑转系统（通过对车轮施加制动力的防车轮滑转系统）

ASR with braking intervention using stored energy 使用储备能量的制动干涉式防滑转系统（为了加速防滑转响应，在 ASR 系中装有储能器，由专门的液压泵或利用常规制动泵或 ABS 的回油泵向该储能器充压，以备 ASR 作用时使用）

ASS 见 active steering system

ass 总成；装配（assembly 的简称）

assay ①试验，化验，试料，试样 ②[动]试验，化验

ASSE 美国安全工程师学会（American Society of Safety Engineers 的简称）

assemblage department 装配车间（= assembling department）

assemble 装配，总装，组装

assembled camshaft 组合式凸轮轴（分段组合而成）

assembled car （用不同厂牌总成装配的）拼装式汽车

assembler ①汇编程序（见 assembly program）②收集器③装配器④装配工人

assembler program 汇编程序（简称 assembler，计算机只能理解由1和0组成的计算机语言，将人容易理解的汇编语言写成的程序翻译成计算机语言的程序称为汇编，即 assembly，执行汇编作业的程序称为汇编程序）

assembling department 装配车间（= assemblage department, assembling shop）

assembling drawing 装配图（亦写作 assembly drawing）

assembling play 装配间隙（= assembling clearance）

assembly 总成

assembly cleanliness 装配清洁度（未经磨合的总成或整车，按规定方法解体后，用在规定部位采集到的杂质微粒的尺寸、质量轻重、数量多少来表示）

assembly exchange repairing method 总成互换修理法

assembly integrity testing device 装配完整性检验装置

assembly language 汇编语言（汽车电子计算机控制系统使用的一种程序设计语言，一般是指将信息转换为二进制字符表示）

assembly line 装配线，总装线

assembly line method 流水作业总线法

assembly-line testing 装配线试验，总装配线试验

assembly plant 装配工厂，总装厂（亦写作 assembling plant）

assembly program 汇编程序（= assembly routine, assembler，见 assembly language）

ASSESS （汽车）预防性安全系统效果模拟器（A Survey Simulator to Evaluate Safety System 的简称，通过计算系统模拟汽车的各种预防性安全系统的实际效果的软件及硬件）

assistance ①援助，帮助，支援②辅助设备

assistant driver ①驾驶员助手②副驾驶员

assist handle 登车扶手（= ascending handle）

assist strap （车身内）皮带拉攀

assn 学会，协会（association 的简称）

Associated Commercial Vehicle 联营车（简称 ACV）

Associated Truck Lines [美]联合汽车运输公司

Association of Diesel Specialists [美] 柴油机专家协会

Association of International Automobile Dealers （美国）国际汽车经销商协会

Association Peugeot-Renault [法] 标致-雷诺（联营）公司

assortment 分级，分类；品种，种类

assumed design speed （公路）假定设计车速（快车群的最高平均行驶车速）

assumed load 假定载荷，计算载荷

assumption 假设（设定条件）

assurance coefficient 安全系数，保险系数（= assurance factor，亦称 safety factor）

assy ①机组，组件，总成 ②装配，总装，组装（assembly 的简称）

AST （复合动力电动车控制系统中使用的）主动式换挡变速器（active shift transmission 的简称，可根据汽车行驶工况自动变换驱动电动机与传动系统之间的速比，使电动机保持最佳转速）

astatine 砹 Ar（卤族元素）（= astatium）

ASTE 美国工具工程师学会（American Society of Tool Engineers 的简称）

astern 倒车的，向后的，在后的，后退的

astern power 倒车功率（内燃机反转功率）

astern (pressure) stage （燃气轮机的）倒车级

astern running test （发动机）倒车试验（反转的内燃机在规定的倒车工况下，能否运转一段时间并发出规定功率的试验）

ASTM ①美国试验材料学会（American Society for Testing Materials 的简称）②美国试验材料标准（American standard of testing materials 的简称）

ASTMD 975 classification of Diesel Fuel Oils （美国 ASTM 的）柴油分类（包括 1—D、2—D 和 4—D 三级，其中 1—D 级为黏度低，挥发性较好的柴油，适用于速度和负荷经常变化的发动机；2—D 级为挥发性较差的柴油，适用于工业及重型车辆的发动机；4—D 级为黏度高，挥发性差的柴油，适用于低速、中速柴油机）

ASTME 美国工具与制造工程师学会（American Society of Tool and Manufacturing Engineers 的简称）

ASTM slope 美国材料试验学会黏度-温度特性曲线图

Aston Martin 阿斯顿马丁（英国汽车公司名，美国福特公司拥有 75% 股份）

Aston Martin linkage 阿斯顿马丁杆系（一种杆式悬架杆系，以其制造商命名）

astroroof 电动天窗（= power sunroof 或 power window in the roof of vehicle）

AST&T 美国交通运输学会（American Society of Traffic and Transportation 的简称）

ASV 先进的安全汽车（Advanced Safety Vehicle 的简称，日本 ITS 的开发项目之一）

ASW 美国线（径）规，参见 American standard wire (gauge)

ASWAN Automotive Federation 东南亚国家联盟汽车联合会

asymmetrical beam （前照灯的）非对称式光束（其光斑两侧光强不同）

asymmetrical beam double filament bulb 非对称式光束双灯丝灯泡

asymmetrical power distribution 非对称式驱动力分配（指全轮驱动车辆前、后轮驱动力分配不同，亦称

asymmetrical power split)
asymmetrical rim 非对称式轮辋（其凹槽偏离车轮的中心线，参见 symmetric rim）
asymmetrical wear 不对称磨损
asymmetric damping characteristics 非对称衰减特性，非对称阻尼特性
asymmetric tire 胎面花纹不对称的轮胎
asymmetry 不对称（性），不平衡（度）偏位（性）
asymptotic line 渐近线
asymptotic stability 渐近稳定性（对指定的工作点而言，扰动或控制输入有任何小而短暂的改变时，汽车将逼近由工作点所规定的运动状态）
asynchronous 异步的，非同步的，不同步的
asynchronous device transmission （汽车计算机控制系统的）异步装置传输（异步装置指其操作速度与其相互连接的机器之间无关，即无须考虑其操作速度的装置，如键盘输入设备与操作员的操作速度无关，这类装置传输数据方式为一次一个字符，每一字符前有一个起始位，后有一个停止位，其输入装置识别起始位后，才开始读入数据）
asynchronous serial communication 异步串行通信（汽车计算机控制系统大都采用此种通信模式，指运行速度或频率与所连接的系统的速度或效率无关的串行通信，见 serial communication）
5AT 五挡自动变速器（5-speed automatic transmission 的简称）
AT ①存取时间（参见 access time 的简称）②安匝数（参见 ampere turn）③方位角（angle of train）④自动变速器（automatic transmission 的简称）
ATA ①美国汽车货运协会（American Trucking Association 的简称）②汽车运输技术协会（Automobile Transportation Technical Association 的简称）
atbas metal 镍铬钢（镍22％，铬8％，硅 1.8％，铜 1％，锰 0.25％，碳0.25％，其余为铁）
ATC ①上止点后（after top center 的简称）②自动温度控制（automatic temperature control 的简称）
ATC module 自动温度控制模块（automatic temperature control module 的简称，该模块通过 C^2D 总线：①接收 BCM 来自日照强度、环境温度、车内温度、空调蒸发器温度等传感器和 PCM 输入的冷却水温等信息并在其显示板上显示②将驾驶者通过显示板上的旋钮、按钮等产生的各种温度调控信息经 C^2D 总线传给 BCM，由 BCM 发出指令，经各种执行器执行）
at critical 在临界状态下
ATC system 牵引力自动控制系统（automatic traction control system 的简称，见 TCS）
ATD ①模拟—时间—数字转换（参见 analogue to time to digital）②人体模拟试验装置（anthropomorphic test device 的简称）③人体模拟试验假人（anthropomorphic test dummy 的简称）④美国载货汽车经销商（协会）（American Truck Dealers 的简称）
ATDC 上死点后（after top dead centre 的简称）
ATE 自动检验设备，自动测试设备（Automatic Test Equipment 的简称）
A terminal 输出终端（= output terminal）
ATF （汽车）自动变速器用油液（automatic transmission fluid 的简称）
at focus test （汽车大灯等的）焦点试验，焦点光度试验（指大灯光源等安装在厂方规定位置，并按照规

定对好光后，从规定的各测量点测定其光束的光度）

ATF oil 自动变速器用油液（指具有SAE10W级黏度、较高的氧化稳定性及黏度指数的自动变速器专用油，automatic transmission fluid oil 的简称）

at full throttle 节气门全开，油门全开

ATIS 先进的旅行者信息系统（Advanced Traveler Information System 的简称，最早称 ADIS—Advanced Driver Information System，当时仅限于车内导行，交通信息，现在已扩大到向家居、办公室、公用电话、手携式信息机及车内信息系统等，提供全面的导行，交通及出行信息）

Atkinson cycle 埃特金森循环（以发明者英国人 James Atkinson 命名的高膨胀比热力学循环，经美国人 Miller 改良后实际应用于内燃机，因此，亦称 Miller cycle "米勒循环"。Atkinson 循环热效率高，泵气损失小，但采用这种循环的发动机要使用电动等进气增压装置才能输出较高的功率，见 Miller cycle）

Atkinson cycle ICE 埃特金森循环内燃机（其中 ICE 为 internal combustion engine 的简称，丰田公司2004年型 Prius 内燃机-电机复合动力车上使用的电动增压式内燃机，见 Atkinson cycle）

ATL ［美］联合汽车运输公司（Associated Truck Lines 的简称）

Atlas alloy 阿特拉斯合金（一种铜、铝、铁合金。铜90%，铁1%，铝9%）

Atlas bronze 阿特拉斯青铜（一种铝、铅青铜合金，铝9%，铅9%，余为铜）

atm ①大气（atmosphere 的简称）②大气压（atmospheric pressure 的简称）

atm drg 空气阻力（atmospheric drag 的简称）

atmosphere ①大气②环境③大气压（压力单位，代号 atm，一个标准大气压等于在0℃时水银柱高760mm时的压力）

atmosphere-pressure sensor 大气压力传感器

atmospheric ①大气的，大气压的，大气中的，常压的（简称 a）②（车内灯光、显示屏等）令人兴奋、愉悦、动情、有感染力的（照明效果等）

atmospheric contamination 大气污染（多用 atmospheric pollution）

atmospheric corrosion 大气腐蚀（金属或合金制件与大气中的氧、二氧化碳、水蒸气，硫及硫化物，氯化物等接触而产生的腐蚀）

atmospheric crack 老化裂纹，风化裂纹

atmospheric deceleration 风阻减速，空气阻力减速（车辆在大气中自由滑行时，由于空气阻力的作用而形成的减速）

atmospheric duct ①大气含尘量②大气中的飞尘

atmospheric environment 大气环境

atmospheric funnel 在正常大气压气流下试验的风洞

atmospheric line （示功图）大气压力线

atmospheric pollutants 大气污染物

atmospheric pollution law 防止大气污染法

Atmospheric Pollution Simulation Program 大气污染模拟程序

atmospheric pressure （标准）大气压（简称 atm；1atm = 1.0133bar = 1.0332kg/cm^2 =760mm 水银柱）

atmospheric pressure compensating 气压补偿，大气压力补偿

atmospheric pressure tyre 常压轮胎，

大气压轮胎（胎压与大气压相等）
atmospheric pressure valve （膜片室等的通）大气压力（的）阀
atmospheric static condition 标准大气条件
atmospheric valve 大气阀（真空系统中通大气的阀）
ATMS 先进的交通管理系统（advanced traffic management system 的简称，指美国提出并已逐步实施的高速公路计算机实时全面管理系统）
ATO 汽车列车自动驾驶装置（automatic train operation 的简称）
atom 原子
atomic 原子的，原子能的
atomic energy 原子能
atomic fuel 核燃料
Atomic gold （车身外壳的）原子金（色）
atomic hydrogen welding 氢原子焊（亦写作 atomic H welding，或简称 atomic welding）
atomiser 喷雾器，雾化器，喷油嘴，喷嘴（亦写作 atomizer）
atomization 喷雾，雾化
atomized fuel 雾化燃料
atomizer cone ①雾化锥体，雾化锥 ②喉管 ③喷嘴，喷嘴喇叭口（亦写作 atomizing cone）
atomizing pressure 雾化压力，喷雾压力（使液体雾化，喷成雾状所需的压力）
ATOP 车载式无线通信平台（终端）（Automotive Telematics On-board unit Platform 的简称）
ATPG system 自动测试程序/模式产生系统（automation test program/pattern generator system 的简称，一种自动测试软件系统，用于产生进行数字电路测试时所执行的测试程序）
AT-PZEV （按美加利福尼亚排放标准的）先进技术部分零排放车（Advanced Technology Partial Zero Emission Vehicle 的简称，指除了达到美加州排放标准规定的超级超低排放车"SULEV"要求以外，尚符合零燃油蒸发物排放标准和 240000km 使用期内排放控制系统质量保证，以及为加州大气资源局"California Air Resources Board"认可为先进的未来型燃料电池车的车辆）
a-tr 自耦变压器（auto-transformer 的简称）
atramentizing （钢件在90°的磷酸锌溶液中）磷化处理，渗磷，镀磷（防腐蚀）
ATRSC 防翻车稳定性控制系统（anti-rollover stability control 的简称）
ATS ①汽车列车自动停车装置（automatic train stop 的简称）②高架轨道运输系统（aerial transport system 的简称）③见 IAT
AT selector 自动变速器选挡杆，自动变速器换挡杆（automatic transmission selector 的简称）
Att （消声器的）消声量，减音量（attenuation 的简称，= noise reduction）
attachment ①附着，固定 ②附加装置，附件
attachment axle 附加的非驱动桥
attachment clip 紧固夹头，固定夹，固定箍
attachment driving shaft 辅助传动轴
attachment face 安装面，接合面
attachment flange 连接突缘；固定突缘
attachment of rubber to metal 橡胶与金属的黏结
attachment plug （连接）插头，（电）插销（亦写作 attaching plug）
attachment point 固定点，安装点
attachment screw 装合螺钉，连接螺钉，止动螺钉
attack 破坏，腐蚀，锈蚀

attack angle ①（可有效防止高速行驶时车身浮升的）后压风板角 ②见 approach angle

attemperator ①温度调节器 ②恒温箱

Attention Assist 注意力警示系统（可自动监测驾驶者的驾驶风格和操作动作，通过与其正常的操作动作对比，发现驾驶者疲劳、动作迟缓或注意力不集中时即发出相应警示）

attenuate ①减少，减弱，衰减 ②稀释，阻尼

attenuater ①衰减器，阻尼器 ②增益调整器，增益控制器（= attenuator）

attenuation ①减少，减弱，降低（多指噪声或排放）②衰减（信号在传输系统中的减小）③阻尼（= damping，运动过程中系统能量的耗散作用）④稀释（= dilution，冲淡溶液的浓度）⑤阻光度，不透明度（= opacity）

attenuator ①减压器 ②衰减器，增益控制器 ③阻尼器 ④消声器（参见 attenuater）

attitude angle （汽车）姿势角，方位角（= vehicle attitude angle）

attitude change （汽车的）姿势变化（参见 vehicle attitude change）

attitude control signal （车身高度自动调平系统电子控制模块向执行机构发出的）车身姿势控制信号

attitude sensor （车身）姿势传感器，位置传感器

atto- 微微微，渺，毫尘（10^{-18}，简称 a，亦称 attoa）

attoa 微微微（= atto）

attraction force 引力

attrition 磨耗，磨损

ATTS 主动式转矩分配系统（Active Torque Transfer System 的简称，日本本田公司前桥驱动式轿车用的电子控制式左、右轮驱动转矩传输—分配系统的商品名。前桥驱动式轿车，如果在转向中急踩加速踏板，由于车辆载荷后移，将产生一个绕质心的与车辆转向方向相反的横摆力矩，造成车辆不能完全按照驾驶员所希望的方向转向，即：不足转向。此时 ATTS 的电子控制模块根据发动机转速传感器、进气压力传感器、四个车轮的转速传感器、转向盘转角传感器、横向加速度传感器及横摆角速度传感器等的信号，确定车辆的挡位、加速度、回转状态，并与内存的车辆正常转向或回转姿势作比较，从而判定车辆的不足转向程度，向左、右轮驱动转矩分配机构发出最佳左右驱动力分配指令，使外侧前轮驱动力加大，以产生与驾驶员所希望的转向方向一致的横摆力矩，而抵消不足转向）

ATU ①高通过性底盘（all terrain undercarriage 的简称）；②辅助测试装置（auxiliary test unit 的简称）

ATV ①在节气门上方（above the throttle valve 的简称）②高通过性全地形越野车辆（all-terrain vehicle 的简称）

ATWO （三菱公司的）主动式综合车轮最佳（控制）系统（商品名，Active Total Wheels Optimum System 的简称，该系统包括牵引力控制、弯道稳定性控制、防抱死控制、四轮转向控制和四轮独立悬架控制等综合电子控制系统）

ATX 自动变速驱动桥（带自动变速器的前轮驱动一体式车桥"automatic transaxle"的简称）

Au 金（gold, aurum）

Audi 奥迪（德国大众公司"Volkswagen"的分公司）

audibility 可闻度

audible alarm 声响警报

audible inspection 听诊检查，声响检查

audible knock 听觉可分辨的爆震声，听觉可分辨的敲击声

audible limit 能闻度极限

audio frequency 声频（声波可听见时的频率。一般指频率范围在 30～20000Hz 的任一波动）

audiolloy 铁镍透磁合金（铁 52%，镍 48%）

audiolocator 声波定位器

audiometry 听觉测定法

audio noise meter 噪声计

audio system 音响系统（指收音及声响录、放系统）

Audio-Video Network （实现汽车视频-音响系统数字化的）音频视频网络（简称 AV network）

Audio-Video Support System 音频视频支持系统（用于播放图像和音响的软件，简称 AVSS）

audio/visual comunication 声响/图像通信，声响/图像传输

audio-visual warning 声响-图像警报，声/光警报

audio warning control 声响警告操纵件（向行人及其他车辆发出声响警告的操纵件，不包括有特殊优先权的车辆，如消防车的声响警告）

auditory area （声的）可闻范围，可闻阈

Audi TT 奥迪 TT（奥迪跑车名，TT 为 Tourist Trophy "旅行者大奖赛"的简称，为 20 世纪初颇具盛名的一项汽车赛事，Audi TT 荣获德国 1999 年最佳跑车称号，排量 1781mL）

audit test 鉴定性试验，检验性试验，审查性试验

aud snl 声频信号（audio signal 的简称）

augment 扩张，扩大，增大，增加

augmented-reality 增加真实感的，更加逼真的，增强实体感的（车用投影式显示图像等）

Aunt Minnie test 利用汽车在寒冷气候下多次短距离低速行驶的方法进行的机油腐蚀性试验

aural ①听觉的②听到的③声响的④辉光的⑤气氛的⑥预兆的

aural and visual 视听的

auralization 听觉

austempering 等温淬火，奥氏体回火

austenic 奥氏体的

austerity car 简易小排量汽车

Austin Rover Group [英]（利兰车公司）奥斯汀-罗孚部

autag [英]燃气轮机用煤油

authentic ①可信的，可靠的，切实的，有根据的②真正的，真的③认证了的，正式的

authentic car ①鉴定过的（古旧）轿车②仿真轿车

authorised street parking 在街道指定场地上停放车辆

authorization test （汽车安全、公害防止装置等的）核准试验，评价试验，审定试验，认可试验，认定试验

authorized axle laden mass 允许轴载质量（由主管部门根据使用条件而规定的汽车最大轴载质量）

authorized dealer 特约销售商，指定经销商（一般带售后服务）

authorized emergency maintenance and service vehicle 道路紧急维修作业专车，道路抢险专车

authorized load capacity 额定载荷能力，额定承载量，允许承载量

authorized pressure 许可压力，指定的最高压力

authorized service shop （制造厂）特约检修服务站，指定维护站

authorized total mass 法定总质量，容许总质量（由主管部门根据使用

条件而规定的汽车总质量,等于整车整备质量和允许装载质量之和,参见 complete vehicle kerb mass)

authorzied maximum towed mass 允许最大拖挂质量(车辆管理部门根据牵引车的特性和交通条件而规定的拖挂质量)

autilock warning lamp (仪表板上的)防抱死系统警报灯(用于监视防抱死制动系统的状况)

auto ①[美]轿车(automobile 的简称)②自动(的)(automatic 的简称)

auto air con 自动空调(系统,可根据车外气候条件及发动机工况自动起动或停机)

auto air conditioner ①自动空调系统(电子控制模块根据车内各部分的温度、大气温度、日光照射程度、水温等预设定最佳温度分布自动调节制冷量,送风量及送风方向等)②(轿)车用空调

auto anti-glare room mirror 车内自动防炫后视镜

Auto Auction Association 轿车拍卖商协会

auto /auto head on collision 车对车正面碰撞,汽车间迎面相撞

auto avalanche rectifiers diode 车用雪崩整流二极管

autobahn (欧洲、澳洲等地)高速公路(的一种称呼)

Autobahn (德国的)汽车高速国道

autobi 摩托车(autocycle, autobike 的简称)

autobody 汽车车身

auto bonnet 汽车发动机室罩

autobulb 车用灯泡

autobus 公共汽车,客车

autoCAD-drawing 全自动计算机辅助设计绘图

autocade 汽车队列,一长列汽车(= motorcade)

AUTOCAP 汽车用户诉讼程序(automotive consumer action program 的简称)

autocar ①轿车(目前已不大通用)②客车(当前在一些欧洲国家使用,如法国)

autocentre 汽车中心,汽车展销中心,汽车制造中心

autochangeover (备用系统)自动接通机构

auto-changer (多盘式 CD 机的)自动换盘器

autochoke 自动阻风门(见 automatic choke)

autoclave ①密封蒸锅,密蒸器,高压箱,高压锅,(生产轮胎中使用的)高压硫化箱②(用高压蒸锅)蒸煮

auto company 汽车公司,汽车制造公司

auto conglomerate 汽车工业集团,汽车集团

auto consumption credit 汽车消费信贷

auto consumption finance service 汽车消费融资服务(包括汽车融资租赁和消费信贷等)

autoconvective lapse rate 自动对流速率,自动对流梯度

autocorrection 自动校正

auto court [美]汽车旅馆(= motel, motorist hotel)

autocrane 汽车起重机,汽车吊(= autohoist, autolift)

autocycle 机器脚踏车,机动自行车(装有发动机的助力式自行车,= autobi, auto-bike, autobicycle)

autodelivery car 分发货物用汽车,送货车

auto dimming mirror 自动减光后视镜(防止后车前照灯强光反射)

autodio frequency 声频(简称 AF)

auto-domain 汽车业,汽车界

auto-driving school 汽车驾驶学校（见 auto-school）

auto electric equipment 汽车电器设备

auto electronics ①汽车电子装置,汽车电子设备（汽车各个部分电子装置的统称, = vehicle electronics）②汽车电子学

auto emission standard 汽车（污染物）排放标准

autoexcitation 自激励,自激,自激振荡

auto exhaust reactors 汽车排气净化反应器

auto financing company 汽车金融公司（指由汽车企业、非银行金融机构出资,为汽车厂商维护销售体系,提供市场信息,整合销售策略,为经销商提供信贷、营运资金及设备等融资,为汽车用户提供消费信贷、租赁、维修融资及保险业务的金融公司）

auto financing lease 汽车融资租贷（出租人根据承租人对出卖人、租赁汽车的选择,向出卖人购买汽车提供给承租人使用,承租人支付租金）

auto fleet （汽）车队

autoformer 自耦变压器

auto fuel economy standard 汽油油耗标准

auto-gantry vehicle washing equipment 自动龙门型整车清洗装备

autogas （汽车用）液化石油气（= LPG,在英国广泛使用的商品名）

autogenous soldering 气钎焊

autographic load strain recorder 载荷-应变自动记录器

autohitch 自动挂钩

auto hoist 汽车起吊装置

auto hold function （电动驻车制动器的）自动驻车功能（商品名）

auto-ignition ①自燃,自着火（= autogenous ignition, spontaneous ignition）②继燃（发动机在点火开关断开后仍继续点火运转, = running-on, dieseling）

autoignition temperature 自燃温度,自燃点

auto industry 汽车工业,汽车产业

autoinhibition 自动抑制作用

autoist 汽车驾驶员,汽车驾驶者

autojumble （主要销售旧式汽车、古典汽车二手配件的）露天汽车配件集市

autolean mixture 自动变稀混合气（简称 ALM）

auto-leveling system 车身高度自动调节系统

auto lift 汽车举升装置

auto light kit （汽车的）成套自动灯具（汽车行驶时,外界光线暗于某规定值时自动点亮,而高于该规定值时自动熄灭）

auto loader 自动装载机,自动装卸车,汽车装载机

autolube （干底壳式发动机,如四冲程摩托车用发动机的）加压式机油计量系统

auto luber ①（汽车等的）自动集中润滑器（通过管道与各润滑点相连,利用真空、压缩空气或手动等将润滑脂一次同时自动地压入各润滑点,亦称 multiluber）②汽车润滑工

auto maker 汽车制造者,汽车制造厂家

automaker 汽车市场

automated dual mode bus [美]自动换行的双运行模式客车（可在普通路面及轨道上行驶）

automated guideway transit 自动双模汽车（简称 AGT）

automated handling ①自动化搬运,自动化装卸②自动化管理,自动化操纵

automated highway system 自动化公路系统（简称 AHS，参见 ITS）

automated mechanical transmission controls 机械变速器的自动控制装置

automated parking system 自动化驻车系统，自动化车辆停放系统

automated transit system 自动化快速运输系统，自动化公共交通系统

automatic ①自动的，自动化的②自动装置，自动机械③（俚）自动变速器或装有自动变速器的汽车

automatic advance（mechanism） 自动点火提前装置（①指机械飞重式或真空膜片式自动点火提前机构②电子点火提前装置）

automatic air-conditioning（system） （可自动保持所设定温度的）自动空调系统

automatic air-recirculation（control）system 车内空气自动循环控制系统（如：当交通高峰期，车外排放污染严重时，空调系统自动关闭由车外吸入新鲜空气的进气门，而进入车内空气循环模式，经过规定的时间后，进气门自动开启，重新回到引入车外新鲜空气的空调循环模式）

automatic air suspension system 自动空气悬架系统（可在各种载荷条件下使车身保持正确的高度，并可根据传感器提供的车速，车轮上、下跳振的幅度和速度及汽车的加、减速度信号使悬架在软"soft"，中"medium"，硬"hard"或"firm"等不同的阻尼模式间转换，而无须驾驶者操纵，在各种驾驶与路面条件下提供良好的车辆操纵性，行驶平顺性和稳定性）

automatic alignment 自动对正，自动定位

automatically variable illumination 自动变光照明

automatic blade adjustment system ①（风扇）叶片自动调节系统②（进风口导向）叶栅自动调节系统

automatic block system 自动锁闭装置，自动封闭装置

automatic boost control 增压自动控制，自动增压调节（器）

automatic brake 自动制动器，特指①挂车在与牵引车脱开后自动制动的装置；②当牵引车和挂车的制动管路渗漏或破裂时，使挂车自动制动的装置③由电子控制模块根据测距雷达的信号控制的、于紧急情况下防止撞车或非紧急情况下保持车距的自动制动、减速系统

automatic chassis leveling ①底盘高度自动调平②底盘高度自动调平装置

automatic checkout test equipment 自动检查试验装置，自动测试装置

automatic choke 自动阻风门，自动风门（简称 autochoke，发动机或进气温度低时自动关闭，发动机升温或进气温度高时自动开启）

automatic circuit analyzer and verifier 自动电路分析检验仪（简称 ACAV）

automatic clock switch 时控开关，自动时钟开关

automatic closing（system） （汽车车门，窗玻璃，顶盖等的）自动关闭系统

automatic control box （自动变速器的）控制阀体（=美·control valve body）

automatic cruise（control）system 自动定速巡行控制系统（指可在各种行驶条件变化的情况下，始终保持稳定的设定车速的计算机自动控制系统，电子控制模块不断地比较车速传感器传来的实际车速与驾驶人员所设定的车速，并及时向供油量执行机构或换挡执行机构发出增减

供油量或挡位变换指令，以消除实际车速与设定车速的差值）

automatic cycling equipment 自动循环运作的设备

automatic data processing system 自动数据处理系统（简称ADPS）

automatic dimmer 前照灯自动变光器（亦称automatic beam changer, automatic head light dimmer, automatic head lamp dimmer）

automatic dimming （汽车远光灯的）自动防炫减光

automatic door tell-tale 车门自动警报灯（警告某个车门未关闭好的信号灯）

automatic driving car 无人驾驶车（一般指由埋设的信号缆线或无线电信号导向，由各种伺服机构控制转向、变速、制动等的自动驾驶汽车）

automatic-driving support （驾驶员辅助系统的）自动驾驶支持（功能）（可根据摄像机和雷达传感器取得的信息，自动控制车速并保持与前车及并行车辆的安全距离）

Automatic/Emergency Locking Restractor 自动—紧急锁死式安全带伸缩器（见A/ELR）

automatic engine shutdown system 发动机自动停机系统（如：当水温高于或低于某规定值时，即通过断油继电器自动断油停机）

automatic engine stop tell-tale 发动机自动停机警报灯（表示发动机由于故障已自动停机的警报灯）

automatic falling occupant protecting net 自动降落式（汽车）乘员保护网（撞车时，保护网即自动落在乘员前方防止撞伤）

automatic fault isolation testing system 自动故障分离检验系统

automatic fog alert system 雾情自动报警系统

Automatic Four speed Light-Duty 见A4LD

automatic freight handling car 自动装卸货车

automatic front wheel drive engagement （分时四轮驱动车辆的）前轮驱动自动接合（装置）

automatic fuel saving device 自动节油装置

automatic gearbox ①［英］自动变速器（=［美］automatic transmission）②（指）自动变速器系统内的（行星齿轮换挡机构等）齿轮机构

automatic gearbox indicator 自动变速器（挡位）指示器

automatic gear changing 自动换挡，自动变速（=automatic gear shifting）

automatic guided vehicle system 车辆自动导行系统

automatic high beam system （前照灯）远-近光自动切换系统（夜间行驶时电子控制模块根据摄像系统测出的前方明暗程度及对向车光照情况等信息自动控制远、近光灯的切换）

automatic hill holder 自动坡地驻车制动器

automatic hitch 自动挂钩

automatic hydraulic transmission ［美］液力自动变速器

automatic idle speed motor （装在多点式汽油喷射系统节气门体上的）自动急速控制电动机（由电子控制模块根据节气门开度、冷却水温、发动机转速、变速器挡位和制动等信息控制的可逆转电动机，用于控制节气门旁通空气道的阀门开启度。当节气门完全关闭时，该阀开启，让足够的空气绕过节气门进入发动机，维持其无负荷最低速空转。在减速期间该阀开启，防止发动机熄火或补偿此时已开始从进气孔壁上蒸发的燃油所形成的过浓混合气。在发动机怠速运转过程中，控制最佳怠速空气流量，保证使用空调或动力转向时所要求的怠速转速）

automatic inclination compensation （汽车）倾斜自动补偿（装置）

automatic injector 自动喷油器（高压油泵输入的燃油压力超过某规定值时自动开闭喷嘴的喷油器，如一般汽车柴油机使用的喷油器）

automatic inspection data accumulator 检测数据自动存储器

automatic inspection machine 自动检验机

automatic interlock 自动连锁

automatic length adjusting and locking retractor （乘员安全带的）自动长度调节和锁死式收紧装置（见 automatic locking retractor）

automatic level (ling) device （汽车悬架系统的）①车身高度自动调平装置（亦称 height corrector, height regulator, level control, levelling control system 等，指可在汽车行驶过程中自动调整各悬架点的高度，从而使整车无论在空车、重载或遇颠簸及不平衡载时均能保持既定的水平高度，以防止前照灯光线偏斜，保持重心稳定，提高汽车安全性、舒适性的装置或系统）②自动液面高度控制装置

automatic load compensator （汽车气液悬架）自动载荷补偿器

automatic-locking retractor （汽车乘员安全带的）自动锁紧式收紧装置（简称 ALR，指自动锁死在拉出的长度上，而不能再拉长，亦称 automatic length adjusting and locking retractor）

automatic longitudinal control 自动纵向控制（指对车辆加速、减速、稳速、停车等纵向工况的控制，简称 ALC）

automatic lubricator 自动润滑器

automatic-manual transmission 见 AMT②

automatic mechanical timing advance unit 机械式自动提前器（如：感应元件为飞锤的离心式机械点火提前或喷油提前装置）

automatic-mechanical transmission 见 AMT①

automatic mixture control 混合气成分的自动调整，混合气成分自动控制

automatic noise level (l) er 噪声自动限制器（亦称 automatic noise limiter）

automatic oiling 自动润滑（= automatic lubrication）

automatic overdrive transmission 带超速挡的自动变速器（简称 AOT）

automatic overload control 自动超载控制

automatic parking system 自动驻车系统（车辆自动驾驶系统的一个子系统，参见 AVCS）

automatic parking system 全自动驻车系统（亦称智能驻车系统 intelligent parking system，由左、右及后方等多组测距或避障雷达等组成，驾驶人员只需将车辆倒至驻车位前方，按下自动驻车按钮，车辆便可在该系统的操控下自动安全倒入车位）

automatic particle counter 微粒自动计量仪（测量排气的污染微粒）

automatic passenger counter （汽车）乘客自动记数装置

automatic position system （汽车）自动定位系统（简称 APS，利用卫星信号，在车载电子地图上显示出汽车的行车位置，行驶路线）

automatic power control 自动功率调

整

automatic preset 自动预置，自动预调

automatic radiator shutter 散热器的自控百叶窗

automatic-range-only radar 自动测距雷达，自动无线电测距

automatic recording instrument 自动记录仪

automatic reset 自动复位

automatic retractor （汽车乘员安全带的）自动收紧器

automatic reverse-park assist 自动倒车—驻车辅助系统

automatic reversing 自动换向

automatic ride control suspension 行驶平顺性自动控制悬架

automatics ①自动机，自动装置②自动学

automatic seat belt system （汽车乘员的）自动安全带系统

automatic selective overdrive 自动选挂式超速挡

automatic shift 自动换挡（在自动变速器中，特指由于自动控制装置的作用按照事先制定的换挡规律 "automatic shift schedule" 实现的换挡）

automatic slip-control differential 自动防滑差速器（自动防滑锁止式差速器，简称 ASD。当某一侧车轮由于附着力低于驱动力而打滑时，电子控制模块即通过执行机构将差速器锁死，使左右两侧车轮以相同转速运行）

automatic speed control 见 cruise control

automatic stability control system 稳定性自动控制系统

automatic starting device 自动起动装置

automatic steering control system 自动转向控制系统（自动驾驶系统的一个子系统，参见 AVCS）

automatic supervision 自动监视（装置），自动监测（装置）

automatic switch off 自动断路（机构）

automatic synchronizer 自动同步器（简称 AS）

automatic test equipment 自动测试设备

automatic throttle 自动节流阀，自动节气门

automatic throttle-valve actuator 节气门自动控制执行器（如：在 ASR 系统中，当出现驱动轮滑转率超过规定阈值时，自动减小节气门开度的执行器件）

automatic timer 自动定时仪，自动记时器，自动延时调节器

automatic time switch 自动定时开关

automatic timing corrector 自动正时校正器

automatic top 自动开启式车顶板，自动折叠式车顶篷

automatic topping-up 自动加满，自动充满（气、液等），自动添足

automatic traffic control system 交通自动控制系统（简称 ATC system）

automatic transaxle 自动变速驱动桥（简称 ATX，自动变速器直接装在驱动桥壳内，多见于发动机横置式的带自动变速器的前轮驱动一体式车桥。装在这种车桥壳内的自动变速器带有超速挡机构者称 automatic transaxle overdrive，简称 AXOD）

automatic transmission 自动变速器，自动变速箱（自动实现换挡的液力变速器）

automatic transmission fluid 自动变速器用油液（简称 ATF）

automatic transmission fluid anti-shudder durability （自动变速器工作油液的）抗黏滑寿命（不致产生规定程度以上的黏滑现象的使用期限，见 shudder ②）

automatic trouble locating arrangement 自动故障诊断装置,故障(点)自动定位装置

automatic tuning control 自动调谐控制(简称 ATC)

automatic vehicle control system 自动汽车控制系统,汽车自动驾驶系统(简称 AVCS,一般包括自动转向控制系统"automatic steering control system",定速巡行自动控制系统"autonomous cruise speed system",综合防碰撞系统"integrated collision avoidance system")

automatic vehicle diagnostic system 汽车自动诊断系统

automatic vehicle guiding system 自动化车辆导航系统(简称 AVGS,其中 guiding,有时写作 guided)

automatic vehicle identification system 自动车辆识别系统(简称 AVIS 系先进的交通管理系统的子系统,参见 ATMS)

automatic vehicle location 车辆自动定位(简称 AVL,为 ITS 系统中先进的交通管理系统的子系统,参见 ATMS)

automatic vehicle monitoring system 自动汽车监测系统(简称 AVMS,ITS 的子系统)

automatic vehicle traffic counting 车辆通过台数自动计数,车辆交通量自动计数

automatic volume control ①自动响度控制②自动容量控制(简称 AVC)

automatic wear adjuster ①(制动器、离合器等的摩擦材料的)磨损自动补偿装置②磨损(造成的间隙的)自动调节装置

automatic weighting machine (车辆)自动台秤,自动称重机,自动秤

automatic window (汽车的)自动升降窗,自动窗(= power window)

automatic wiper (风窗)自动刮水器,自动雨刮

automatic zero set 自动调零(简称 AZS)

automation ①自动②自动器,自动机,自动装置③自动学④自动化(其复数为 automata)

automatization 自动化

automatograph ①自动记录仪②(点火系统故障)检测示波器(= autoscope)

automaton 自动机械,自动装置(= automat)

auto mechanika (德国每两年举行一次的)汽车保修机具展览会名

auto meter 汽车仪表;车用仪表

automicrometer 自动千分尺,自动测微仪

automobile ①[美]轿车(通常指用于城市道路及公路上的内燃机四轮轿车,亦称 car, passenger car, =[英]motorcar)②(在欧洲指各种四轮及四轮以上的)汽车,机动车的通称

automobile-assisted recreation 驱车游乐,开车游乐

Automobile Association [英]汽车协会(简称 AA)

auto (mobile) clock (装在)汽车(上的)时钟

automobile club 汽车俱乐部(= motor club)

automobile composition 汽车总布置,汽车组成布置图

automobile design ①汽车设计②汽车结构

automobile diffusion rate 轿车普及率(= diffusion rate of car,单位为车数/1000 人)

automobile-dominated transport system ①轿车为主的交通体系②汽车为主的运输体系

automobile engineering circle 汽车工程界

automobile exhibition 汽车展览会,轿车展览,轿车展览品,汽车展示(＝motor car exhibition, automobile show, motor car show)

auto (mobile) jack 车用千斤顶(＝car jack, lifting jack, lifting screw)

automobile laundry 汽车清洗间

Automobile Leading Information System 汽车导航信息系统,(由地面中心电子计算机通过车内的导行系统引导驾驶员选择最佳的行车路线,简称 ALIS)

automobile maintenance industry 汽车维修业,汽车维修行业

automobile noise criteria number 汽车噪声评价值

automobile park ①汽车停车场,轿车停车场②轿车群;汽车群③车队(＝fleet of cars)

automobile performance diagram 汽车(行驶)特性曲线图(包括驱动力、行驶阻力,及各挡下的发动机转速等相对车速的曲线图)

automobile racer 竞赛汽车,赛车

automobile scale 汽车地秤

automobile shredder residue 见 ASR

automobile tax 汽车税,[美]轿车税

automobile terms 汽车术语,汽车名词

automobile track (供汽车试验或竞赛用)汽车跑道

automobile trading firm 汽车贸易公司

automobile train 汽车列车

Automobile Transportation Technical Association [日]汽车运输技术协会

automobile transport trailer 装运轿车的平板挂车

automobile wagon 厢式轿车,旅行车(＝station wagon)

Automobile Warranty and Repair Act (美国联邦政府有关部门制定的)轿车保用和修理法

automobile works 轿车厂(＝motor-car works)

automobilism 汽车使用方法,汽车驾驶方法

automobilist 驾驶汽车者,使用汽车者

automobilization 汽车化,汽车普及化(亦称 automobility)

automonitor 自动监控器

automotive ①自行的,自身带有驱动动力的(＝self-propelling)②自动车的,机动车的,汽车的,与汽车有关的(简称 auto)③汽车业的,汽车界的

automotive adhesive 汽车用黏合剂

automotive area 汽车界(亦称 automotive community, autosense, automotive field)

automotive avigraph 车用导航仪

Automotive Bit-Serial Universal Interface System 见 A-BUS

automotive communication protocol 汽车通信协议[简称 ACP,如：SAE 1939 汽车通信协议(SAE 1939 automotive communication protocol),由 CAN 2.0b 协议扩展产生,传输速率 1 b/s]

automotive crane 汽车吊,汽车起重机(指在汽车底盘上装置起重设备、完成吊装任务的汽车)

automotive crash injury 汽车撞车伤害度

automotive diagnosis 汽车诊断(复数为 diagnoses,在不解体或仅卸下个别小件的条件下,使用诊断设备确定汽车技术状况,查明故障部位及原因的检查分析)

automotive emission 汽车排放(指从汽车排入大气环境的一切排放物,包括尾气排放、噪声排放、无线电干扰排放等)

automotive encyclopedia 汽车百科全书

automotive engine additives 汽车发动机用添加剂（发动机用燃油、润滑油等添加剂的总称）

automotive environment 汽车境域，汽车环境（指在汽车车身范围内）

automotive excellence 汽车精品，特优汽车

automotive fatigue design 汽车疲劳设计

automotive folklore ①汽车界的习惯说法、做法和习俗 ②与汽车有关的传说

automotive-grade 车用等级的（指器械、设备、工具或材料的性能、质量或规格符合汽车使用要求的）

automotive inspection station 汽车检测站（亦称 detecting test station of vehicle）

automotive interior design 汽车车身内部设计（包括乘员座位、仪表、安全装置等）

automotive leading information system 汽车导行信息系统（指引导汽车行驶的信息系统，如：引导汽车选择最佳路线、避开交通阻塞、道路损坏的路段等）

automotive microcircuitry 汽车用微电子电路；汽车用微电子装置

automotive operating materials 汽车运行材料（主要指燃料、润滑材料、轮胎，以及液力变矩器油、电解液等汽车在运行中消耗的非金属材料）

automotive operation engineering (automotive operations engineering) 汽车运用工程（包括汽车自出厂到报废期间的使用、维修、检测等所有技术、经济内容）

automotive parts identification scheme 汽车零件明细表

Automotive Products ［英］汽车产品公司（简称 AP）

automotive rear vision 汽车后视界，汽车后方视野

automotive repair industry 汽车维修行业，汽车维修产业，汽车修理业

automotive safety product 车用安全产品

Automotive Safety Standards Advisory Committees （美国）汽车安全标准咨询委员会（简称 ASSAC）

Automotive Service Council （美国）汽车维修协会（民间组织）

automotive service fluid 汽车使用液（燃油、润滑油，冷却液、制动液及液力传动系工作液等的总称）

Automotive Service Industry Association ［美］汽车维修行业协会（简称 ASIA）

automotive software 汽车（电子控制系统用）软件

automotive technography 汽车技术发展史

automotive transportation enterprise 汽车运输企业

automotive truck 载货汽车，货车（= autotruck, ［英］motor lorry, motor truck, 简称 truck）

automotive vehicle 机动车辆；汽车（= motor vehicle, mechanical vehicle, self-propelled vehicle）

automotive vehicle-related 与汽车有关的

automotive visibility 汽车视界，汽车视野

auto-navigation system 汽车导航系统，汽车导行系统（见 routes guidance system）

autonomic 自调的，自行调节的（= self-regulating，注意这里指的自调是系统本身的自调能力，与 auto-regulating"对其他机构或系统进行自动调节"不同）

autonomous 自动的（对国家、地

区、组织指自治的，有自治权的，对个人指自主的，有自主权的。用在汽车技术中指无人驾驶的、自动的，=driverless、automatic)

autonomous control system (of troubled vehicle) （故障的）自主控制系统（包括自动故障检测，自动故障排除或补救，以及自动控制恢复行驶等）

autonomous driving vehicle 自动驾驶汽车，无人驾驶汽车（指不用人操纵的汽车）

autonomous(intelligent) cruise control (system) （汽车）（智能化）自动定速巡行控制（系统）(简称 AICC 系统。自动驾驶系统 AVCS 的子系统，根据雷达测距装置等传感系统的信息由车载电子计算机自动完成稳速、加速、减速、制动以及保持与前车的安全距离等控制实现汽车自动定速巡行的系统)

autonomous locating tyre pressure warning system 自定位轮胎压力警报系统（见 AL-TPWS）

autonomous parking system （汽车）自主驻车系统（车载电脑实时分析摄像、雷达等获取的信息，自主寻找驻车位并向转向、变速、制动系统发出相应指令完成驻车全过程）的

autonomy ①自主权②（论及汽车时指）无人驾驶自由汽车

auto-off headlight 自动熄灭式前照灯

auto-oiled 自动加油的，自动润滑的

autooscillation 自振

auto park 停车场

autopilot 自动驾驶仪

auto-polo 一种乘汽车进行的击球运动

auto proving ground 汽车认证基地（按规定标准在该基地对汽车进行试验、检测，取得认证技术资料）

auto refitting plant 汽车改装厂

auto-reversive 自动倒车的，自动换向的

autorich （混合气）①自动加浓的 ②自动加浓

AUTOSAR （由多家汽车生产厂家和供应商联合组建的）汽车开放型系统结构联盟［Automotive Open System Architecture 的简称，任务是制定汽车电气电子设备的开放性系统的工业标准（open industry standards），见 open system］

autoscope ①（汽车的一种）前视镜（驾驶员可以看到前方受遮蔽的交通情况，而不必伸出头来看路边的情况）②（检查发动机点火系统的故障）汽车点火系诊断示波器（= engine scope）

autosense ①自动感知的，自动传感的②汽车自动诊断装置

auto shelter 汽车软篷罩（盖住整个汽车，防风蚀雨淋，= weather guard auto shelter）

auto show 汽车展示会，汽车展销会，汽车展览会（= automotive show, automobile show）

autosizing 自动尺寸监控

auto-spark-retard device 点火自动迟后装置

auto speed control device 自动速度控制装置（简称 ASCD）

auto stability ①自稳定性②汽车稳定性

auto starting guarder 汽车起动保护器（通过电子延时电路"electronic delay circuit"控制起动机的起动时间和起动时机，达到保护起动机，延长电池寿命，防止误起动的目的）

Auto-stop & go 自动停机-起动系统（stop and go, 简称 AS&G, 踩踏制动踏板时发动机自动停机，松开制动踏板时发动机自动起动，节油和

减排。停机期间导航系统和车载音响设备等不受影响。起动后车速低于 5 km/h 时自动停机功能不起作用)

autostrada (以后演变为)①高速公路干线②(只准汽车行驶)汽车专用路(复数 autostrade)

auto therm air cleaner system 自动温控空气滤清系,恒温进气滤清系(见 heated air intake system)

autothermic piston 防热膨胀活塞,抗热变形活塞(在活塞销座孔处铸入钢片,抑制热膨胀变形, = thermic piston,使用殷钢片者,称为 Invar strut piston)

auto throttle 自动节气门

auto timer 自动计时器,自动定时钟

auto track ①自动跟踪②汽车跑道③汽车轮辙

auto/trailer combination 汽车挂车列车(亦称 autotrain)

auto transformer 自耦变压器

auto transporter 运输汽车(特指轿车)的汽车引车

autovulcanization 自动硫化

auto wash shop 汽车洗车站(一般指露天洗车站)

autoweak ①(混合气)自动变稀的②自动弱化的

auto wind tunnel 汽车风洞(用于测试汽车的空气动力学参数)

auto-wrap safety belt (汽车乘员的)自动载挂式安全带

aut sign ①自动信号(automatic signal 的简称)②自动发送信号(automatic signalling 的简称)

autur [美]燃气轮机燃料

aux. 辅助的;辅助装置(= auxiliary)

auxiliaries 附件

auxiliary accelerating pump 辅助加速泵(冷机起动后加速时将一部分辅助燃油喷入进气管,使混合气变浓,该泵是由水温感知阀控制的真空膜片泵,简称 AAP)

auxiliary air control valve 辅助空气控制阀(简称 AACV)

auxiliary air gap (火花塞的)辅助间隙,副间隙(亦称 auxiliary spark gap,用以减轻火花塞积污)

auxiliary air-valve 辅助空气阀(冷机运转期间该阀开启,将一部分额外空气绕过节气门引入进气系统,以提高冷机运转期间的怠速转速, = compensating air valve)

auxiliary brake 辅助制动器(一般指汽车的排气缓速器"exhaust retarder"和装在传动轴上的电磁缓速器"electromagnetic retarder",以及利用液力变矩器的油液作为工作介质的液力缓速器"hydrodynamic retarder"等,但有时亦包括驻车制动器"parking brake")

auxiliary chamber method (内燃机燃烧的)副室法(柴油机指预燃室、涡流室、空气室等。层状燃烧发动机指装有火花塞的副燃室,在其中形成的浓混合气点燃后,窜入主燃烧室点燃稀混合气,参见 stratified engine)

auxiliary connecting rod 副连杆

auxiliary drive shaft 辅助传动轴(指汽车上除驱动车轮行驶以外的任一传动轴)

auxiliary driving lamp (汽车的)辅助前照灯(补充前照灯远光的不足,如:雾灯等)

auxiliary facia 副仪表板(亦称 console)

auxiliary frame 副车架

auxiliary fuel 辅助燃油(如柴油机冷机起动用燃油等,亦称 auxiliary fluid, starting fuel, starting fluid。用辅助燃油实现的点火称为 auxiliary fuel ignition,供给辅助燃油的系统称为 auxiliary fuel supply system)

auxiliary gear box 辅助变速器(①指

在齿轮变速器前或后面加装的、一般为两档的副变速器，可使主变速器的挡位数增加一倍②指装在一般齿轮变速器后的外加行星齿轮式超速传动器，提供传动比＝0.7～0.8的超速挡③指扩大液力变矩器传动比范围并获得倒挡和空挡的液力变矩器辅助行星齿轮变速器)

auxiliary pole （直流电机等的）辅助电极（如换向极，整流辅助极"commutating pole"，罩极，屏蔽极"consequent pole"，间极"intermediate pole"等）

auxiliary seal ring 辅助密封圈（指起辅助密封作用的弹性件，按其截面可分为O形圈、V形圈、楔形环等）

auxiliary servomotor ①辅助伺服电动机②辅助伺服液动机（液压马达）

auxiliary spring 副钢板弹簧（＝supplementary spring, helper spring, overload spring, 在小负荷时只有主钢板弹簧工作，当负荷增加到一定程度后副钢板弹簧与主钢板弹簧一起承受载荷)

auxiliary spring bracket 副钢板弹簧托架

auxiliary spring leaf 副钢板弹簧片（亦称 tension leaf）

auxiliary tank ①副（油）箱，辅助（油）箱②副储气筒③（空气弹簧式悬架中的）辅助气室（增加气室容积或悬架阻尼的附加气室)

auxiliary venturi 副喉管，二级喉管（＝secondary venturi）

auxiliary view 辅助视图

auxiliary windshield wiper （汽车风窗）副刮水器

AUX-IN 音频接口

A.V. ①酸值（acid value 的简称）②实际速度（actual velocity）③通风孔（air vent 的简称）④视听的，声光的（audiovisual 的简称）⑤平均值（average value 的简称）

availability ①可获得性，可（利）用性，可达性，利用率②（设备及仪器仪表等的）有效性（指在某时刻或时间段内具有或维持其规定功能的能力）

availability factor （设备的）时间利用系数，时间利用率（在所考查的一段时间内，机器、设备的实际工作时间与总时间之比）

available 可获得的，可购得的，可找到的

available factor 利用率（设备有用运转时间与包括准备工作等所占用的辅助时间在内的总时间之比）

available space （可供容纳乘客、行李等的）有效空间

available spline slip 花键有效滑动量

available time 有效时间，可用时间

avalanche breakdown （汽车电子控制系统集成电路半导体元件，由于强电场感应碰撞电离使载流子急剧积累增加而引起的非破坏性的）雪崩击穿

avalanche diode （电子控制系统中使用的）雪崩二极管（亦称 silicon breakdown diode，指反/正向电阻比很高，当反向电压达到其工作点后，便会产生雪崩击穿，于是其电压降可基本上维持稳定的二极管，在反向偏置的情况下能传导很大的电流，多用于要求稳压或限压的系统中，旧称齐纳二极管"zener diode"）

AVC 自动车辆分类（automatic vehicle classification 的简称）

AVCS ①（富士重工的）主动式气门控制系统（由电子控制模块根据发动机工况和汽车运行状态自动控制气门的可变升程和正时，active valve control system 的简称）②先进的车辆控制系统（advanced vehicle control system 的简称)

AVCSS 先进的车辆控制与安全系统 (advanced vehicle control and safety system 的简称)

average ①平均的②平均值(简称 avg 或 av.)③平均,计算出平均值

average bias current 平均偏置电流(器件处于静态时,进入差动输入端电流的算术平均值,= meanbias current)

average charge-transfer efficiency 平均电荷转移效率(简称 ACTE,总电荷转移效率的 n 次根,n 为电荷转移次数)

average cost of vehicle maintenance and repair 汽车维修平均费用(指汽车某类维修作业所耗费用的平均值)

average current input 平均输入电流(用直流电流表测得的点火系输入电流)

average days during major repair of vehicle 汽车大修平均车日(汽车大修从开工到竣工检验合格平均所占用的天数)

average days in plant during major repair of vehicles 汽车大修平均在场车日(汽车进厂大修到竣工出厂的平均天数)

average fuel consumption 平均燃油消耗量(平均油耗,行驶距离或工作时间除以该距离或时间内所消耗的全部燃油)

average ground speed (车辆的)平均行驶速度,平均车速(行程与行驶时间的比值)

average haul distance 平均运距(在相应的时期和范围内运送旅客或货物的平均距离)

average headway 平均车头间距,平均车头时距(参见 headway)

average highway 一般公路,普通公路

average leakage current density 平均漏电流密度(器件有源区内单位面积上的平均漏电流,亦称平均暗电流密度,平均热生电流密度)

average man-hours of vehicle maintenance and repair 汽车维修平均工时(指汽车某类维修作业所耗工时的平均值)

average of plastic strain ratio value 平均塑性应变比(指金属薄板平面上,与主作用力方向成 0°,45° 和 90° 三个方向测得的塑性应变比值的加权平均值)

average plug 均热式火花塞(参见 spark plug's heat range)

average rate of change 平均变化率

average rate of pressure rise 平均压力增长率(指燃烧压力增长过程中,以曲轴转角表示的单位时间内的压力平均增长量)

average selection (汽车防抱死制动系统控制方式的)平均选择(指以某组全部车轮的平均瞬时速度值作为信号,来控制该组车轮制动力的防抱死制动系统)

average service conditions 平均运行(工作)状况,一般使用状况

average sound-energy density 平均声(音)能(量)密度(一个声波振动周期内声能密度的平均值,见 sound-energy density)

average sound-energy flux density (平均)声能通量密度[单位时间内通过垂直于声波传播方向称 sound intensity(声强),单位 W/m^2,与声源振幅成正比,与声源的距离平方成反比]

average speed 平均速度(= mean speed, average velocity, mean velocity)

average speed indicator (汽车上的)车速表

average spot speed (通过道路上某一定点的)定点平均车速

average travel distance per vehicle-day 平均车日行程（车辆在工作车日内的平均行驶里程）

average trip length 路程（旅程）平均长度

average unit pressure 平均单位压力，平均压强

average value 平均值（简称 AV）

avex rivet 心杆端头塞封式空心单面压装铆钉，塞封式空心单面压装铆钉（单面空心压装铆钉之一种，参见 blind rivet）

avg 平均的;平均(值)(＝average)

AVI 自动车辆识别（Automatic Vehicle Identification 的简称）

aviation ①航空②航空学③（集合词）飞机，军用飞机④飞机制造业

AVM 自动车辆监督检查装置（automatic vehicle monitoring 的简称）

AV network 见 Audio-Video network

avoidance ①（车辆）避让，躲避（行人）②防止，避免

AVO meter （安伏欧）万用（电）表，三用电表，安伏欧计（亦写作 avometer）

AVP 自动驻车入库系统（auto vehicle parking 的简称）

AVS 适应性阻尼可变悬架（adaptive variable suspension 的简称）

AVSS 见 Audio-Video Support System

AVT （英国 Lotus 公司的）主动气门传动系统（商品名，active valve transmission 的简称，无凸轮轴气门驱动系统，由电子控制模块根据发动机工况的要求，直接通过液压挺杆系统精确控制气门开、闭和升程）

A/W 实际重力（actual weight 的简称）

awaiting parts 维修用备件

awaiting repair time 等候修复的时间

AWARE 早期报警设备（advance warning equipment 的简称）

AWC 全轮（驱动力）控制系统（all wheel control 的简称）

AWCD 全天候底盘测功机（all weather chassis dynamometer 的简称）

AWD 全轮驱动（all-wheel-drive 的简称）

AWG 美国线规（参见 American wire gauge 的简称）

AWL 平均工作负载（average workload 的简称）

awl 锥子，钻子

awning 凉篷，雨篷

AWP ①维修用备件（awaiting parts 的简和）②平均工作压力（average work pressure 的简称）③实际工作压力（actual working pressure，亦写作 awp）④年工作计划（annual work program 的简称）

A-4WS 主动式四轮转向系统（active four-wheel steering system 的简称）

axial 轴的，轴线的②轴向

axial air compressor 轴流式空（气）压（缩）机，轴流式压气机（亦称 axial-flow compressor）

axial angle （光）轴角

axial cam 轴向凸轮，圆柱凸轮

axial chamber width 见 axial width of the center housing

axial compressor engine ①带轴流式增压器的发动机②带轴流式空压机的发动机

axial deflection 轴向变形量（指在轴向方向产生的变形量）

axial diametral pitch 轴向节径（圆周率 π 除以轴向齿距，mm，为轴向模数 "axial module" 的倒数）

axial double mechanical seal 轴向双端面机械密封

axial engine ①具有一只轴流式空压机的燃气涡轮机②汽缸与驱动轴平行的活塞发动机

axial entry impeller 轴向进口叶轮

axial flow ①轴流式的②轴向气流,轴向流动,轴对称气流

axial flow turbine (废气涡轮增压器中的)轴流式涡轮(指废气轴加流过涡轮工作轮的涡轮机)

axial flow type converter 轴流式转化器(排气催化转化系统中,排出的废气沿轴向流动与催化剂接触,参见 radial flow type converter)

axial flux linear induction motor 轴向磁通直线感应电动机

axial internal clearance (滚动轴承的)轴向内间隙(内外圈间的轴向移动量, = end play,参见 internal clearance)

axiality 同心度,同轴度,同轴线度

axial length ①轴长②轴向长度

axially-stratified-charge (engine) 轴向层状充气(发动机)[指其燃烧室的混合气沿轴向分层,亦称 axially stratification charge (engine)]

axial module (齿轮的)轴向模数(轴向齿距除以圆周率 π)

axial pitch 轴向齿距(指斜齿圆柱齿轮或圆柱蜗杆的一个轴平面内,两个相邻同侧齿廓之间的轴向距离)

axial plane 轴平面(指任一个包含轴线的平面)

axial play of piston rings 活塞环轴向间隙

axial plunger motor 轴向柱塞马达(柱塞或活塞沿平行泵体或缸体中心线方向往复运动的柱塞式气动机、液动机的总称,亦称 axial piston motor)

axial profile 轴向轮廓(指轴平面所截的截面轮廓,如:轴向齿廓等)

axial pump 轴向泵(活塞或柱塞沿泵筒中心线方向往复运动的各种泵的总称)

axial seal ①轴向密封件(利用与轴垂直的平面和轴向的接触压力,密封旋转部分的密封件)②(转子发动机的)端面密封,端面密封装置,端面密封条

axial strain 轴向应变(指平行于物体纵轴线的平面上的线性应变,亦称)纵向应变

axial stratification (分层充气式发动机燃烧室内混合气沿纵轴方向的)轴向分层

axial thrust bearing 轴向推力轴承,轴向止推轴承

axial turbo-supercharger 轴流式涡轮增压器(= axial turbocharger, axial turboblower)

axial velocity 轴向速度

axial wheel (液力变矩器)轴流式叶轮

axial width (密封环等的)轴向宽度,轴向厚度

axis ①轴,轴线,中心线②坐标轴线

axis of abscissa 横坐标轴,横轴

axis of coordinates 坐标轴

axis of ordinate 纵坐标轴,纵轴

axis of revolution 回转轴(亦称 axis of rotation)

axis parallelism (平行轴的)中心线平行度

axis pin 销轴

axis system 坐标系(= coordinates)

axle ①轴②车桥(如汽车的前、后桥)

axle-and-wheel aligner 桥-轮定位仪(即:前轮定位仪或四轮定位仪)

axle arm ①驱动桥定位臂②车桥臂件

axle base 轴距(指汽车相邻两轴的轴线间的距离,三轴和三轴以上汽车的各轴距之和,亦称 wheel space)

axle beam (汽车)非驱动桥的桥梁,如:前桥梁;(前桥)工字梁

axle bearing (驱动桥)半轴轴承

axle block 轴座

axle bush 轴套

axle-by-axle split brake system 前后桥分开的双管路制动系统

axle camber （前桥工字梁拱曲而造成的车轮外倾）桥致外倾

axle cap 车轮帽，车轮罩，轴头盖

axle casing 桥壳，驱动桥壳（= 美 axle housing，亦称 axle tube, axle case, axle carrier, axle box 或 differential case, differential casing 及 differential housing）

axle chuckle 驱动桥噪声

axle collar 轴环，轴肩

axle control （防抱死制动系的）车桥控制，轴控制（指同一车轴上的各个车轮的制动力，由同一个指令控制）

axle drive 主减速器（= final drive）

axle drive bevel gear 主减速器主动锥齿轮，主传动主动锥齿轮（= crown wheel）

axle drive pinion 主减速器驱动小锥齿轮

axle end 半轴轴端；半轴轴颈

axle (-ground) clearance 车桥离地间距

axle half tube （独立悬架断开式）驱动桥半轴管

axle half tube gaiter 断开式驱动桥的半轴管套

axle housing 见 axle casing

axle housing ball end 桥壳球形端

axle housing cap 桥壳罩

axle input 驱动桥（半轴）的输入转矩

axle key 轴键

axle leading arm 驱动桥（悬架）的后置纵臂

axle lift （货车可提升的车桥的）升降机构

axle load 车桥载荷，轴荷（亦称 axle weight, weight on the axle, weight per axle）

axle loaden mass 轴载质量，轴荷

axle load restriction 轴载荷限制，车桥载荷限制

axle neck 轴头，轴颈（亦称 axle journal）

axle pad （前、后桥）钢板弹簧垫块

axle pin 转向节主销（= king pin）

axle pin rake 主销后倾（= caster）

axle pivot steering 主销式转向（机构）（= Akermann steering）

axle ratio ①驱动桥减速比②发动机转速与驱动车轮转速比

axle (rebuild) stand （修理汽车用）车桥支架

axle rubber bumper 车桥的橡胶缓冲垫

axle semitrailing arm 驱动桥（悬架的）前置斜（控制）臂

axle shaft ①（非独立悬架整体式驱动桥的）半轴（见 differential axle，指将转矩传给车轮的左、右半轴）②（独立悬架式驱动桥中，连接差速器与左、右半轴的）短轴

axle shaft （汽车驱动桥的）半轴

axle shaft bearing 驱动桥半轴轴承（亦称 half-axle bearing）

axle shaft gear （汽车的）半轴齿轮

axle shaft housing （驱动桥）半轴壳

axle-shaft mounted 装在半轴上的驱动

axle shaft oil seal 半轴油封

axle shaft puller 驱动桥半轴拉器

axle shaft sleeve 半轴套管（简称 axle sleeve, = axle tube①）

axle side shake 车桥横向摆振

axle spacing 轴距

axle-split hybrid drive （前、后）桥分动式混合动力车（亦写作 axle-split drive HV，其动力系统由分别驱动前、后桥的两台电动机和一台内燃机组成）

axle spread （货车等的）并装双桥两悬架中心线的间距，（亦称）有

效轴距（effective wheel base）

axle straightening tool　车桥校直工具（亦称 axle straightener, axle straightening iron）

axle stub　轴头

axle tools　前后桥维修工具

axle trailing arm　驱动桥前置纵臂

axle tramp　①左、右车轮在轴上异相颠振②车桥-悬架系统在汽车急加速时由于悬架扭振而引起的共振

axle tubes　①半轴套管②驱动桥壳（= axle housing）

axle (wheel) load tester　轴（轮）重仪

axle wind-down　（汽车制动时）后桥壳（产生的绕其过重心横轴线的）向下方向的角振动

axle wind-up　①（汽车加速时）后桥壳（产生的绕其过重心横轴线的）向上方向的角振动②有时用于表示向上方向和向下方向的两种角振动

AXOD　（一种）带超速挡的自动变速驱动桥（用于某些前轮驱动轿车，其液力变矩器离合器由电子控制模块控制，automatic transaxle overdrive 的简称）

AXOD-E　（福特公司）电子控制带超速挡的自动变速驱动桥（商品名，electronic automatic overdrive transaxle 的简称）

AYC system　主动式横摆控制系统（Active Yaw Control System 的简称，三菱公司后轮驱动式轿车左右驱动车轮的驱动力分配机构的商品名。后轮驱动车辆在转向或改变车道的过程中加速时，常常会产生不足转向趋势。遇到这类情况电子控制模块通过执行机构使外侧后轮的驱动力大于内侧后轮的驱动力，产生减少不足转向方向的横摆力矩，使不足转向得到抑制，而提高车辆的转向操纵稳定性。当车辆在左、右轮路面附着系数不同的道路上起步或行驶时，电子控制模块便使高附着系数一侧车轮的驱动力增大，低附着系数一侧车轮的附着力减少，以提高车辆的起步加速性能和恶劣道路的通过性能及行驶稳定性）

Aytron-Mother ring test method A. M.　电路故障点测试法（借助惠斯登电桥原理，诊断电路内的故障点的一种定位测试法）

az　见 azimuth

azimuth　方位，方位角，地平经度（简称 az）

azimuthal　①方位的，方位角的②水平的

azote　氮 N （= nitrogen）

azotize　①氮化，渗氮②使与氮化合

azran　方位-距离（azimth-range 的简称）

AZS　自动调零（automatic zeroset 的简称）

AZUSA tracking system　方位-速度-高度电子跟踪系统（= azimuth speed altitude tracking system 的简称）

B 100 纯生物柴油（100% bio-diesel 的简称）

BA 英国协会（British Association 的简称，该协会以设计各种电器和精密仪器用小、微直径螺纹著称）

babbit ①巴氏合金，巴比特合金，(1862 年由 Isaac Babbit 发明，因而得名。一般分为：锡基巴氏合金，含铜 2%～8%，含锑 5%～15%；铅基巴氏合金，含锡 1%～10%，含锑 10%～15%，= babbit metal, babbit's metal 简称，babbit) ②滑动轴承的巴氏合金耐磨层③巴氏合金的④浇挂巴氏合金

babbit-lined metal （浇挂有）巴氏合金（的）轴瓦，巴氏合金轴承

baby car ①微型轿车（美俚语，= mini car, cycle car, midget car) ②婴儿车

baby compressor 小功率压缩机，小型压缩机

baby enclave （汽车成人座椅上安装固定）婴幼儿（座椅的）飞地

baby seat （供体重在 20 磅以内的）婴儿（坐的）座椅（通常是面朝后地装在驾驶座旁的前座上）

BAC 血液中酒精浓度（blood alcohol concentration 的简称）

back ①反面，背面，后部；（座位）靠背，靠垫，基座②后部的，后面的，背后的；后回的，反向的，逆转的，倒的③后退，倒车，返回，反向，逆转④加背层，加衬里，装上椅背

back astern 倒车，倒驶，向后开车

back axle 后桥，后轴（指车辆最后面的车轴，= rear axle）

back axle ratio 后桥主减速器传动速比

back bench-type seat （车厢的）长凳式后座椅（= rear bench-type seat, back single-cross seat, rear single-cross seat）

back bias voltage 反馈偏压

backblast 废气冲击；反冲，反喷

back bone chassis 中央独梁式底盘（由一管状中央独梁式结构承载汽车的全部动力与传动系统，而板件构成的车身结构则装在该管梁前端的两短纵梁及数根横梁上，亦写作 backbone，英多称 tubular frame）

backbone tray frame 中央独梁半承载式车架，中央独梁盘形车架（中央梁式车架与部分车身底板制成一体，为 semiframe-less construction 或 tray-type frame 的一种）

back clearance （活塞环等的）背隙

back cone angle 背锥角（锥齿轮轴线与背锥母线之间的夹角）

back cone distance 背锥距（背锥顶点沿背锥母线与分度圆锥面的距离）

back cone tooth profile （锥齿轮的）背锥齿廓（指其齿面被背锥所截的截线）

back corner panel （货车驾驶室的）后角板，后角围板，（后部拐角处的壁板）

back current ①反向电流②逆流，回流

back cushion （座椅等的）靠背垫

back door 背门（车身背部的车门，亦称 tail gate）

back draft 逆流通风

back driver ①坐在后座上的驾驶指导者②后座式驾驶者

back dumping 后方倾卸

backed 有支座的，带支架的；带靠背的

back eddy （车辆高速行驶时）车身后方的空气涡流

backedge 后缘，后沿（= following edge）

back elevation 后视图（= rear elevation）

back e. m. f. 反电动势（back electromotive force 的简称，亦称 counter e. m. f.）

back entrance 后方入口（= rear entrance）

back exit 后方出口（= rear exit）

backface 反面，背面

backfall 山坡，斜坡，倾斜

back feed phase 反馈相位

back fire（= back firing, back flash, back kick, pop back）①进气管回火（指进、排气门叠开期间，汽缸内的高温燃气倒流入进气管，遇新鲜混合气而在进气管内急剧燃烧的现象）②排气管放炮（废气中未燃烧的 HC 在排气系统的排气管造成消声器内爆燃），消声器放炮（此时亦称 explosion in silencer 或 back shot）③（发动机起动时）逆转④引起回火；导致排气系统放炮

backfire test 回火试验，耐回火能力试验

back firing ①见 fire②重复回火或排气系统放炮

back fit 重新磨合，再磨合，修合

back flow ①回流，逆流②（特指）内燃机进气回流（指四缸或四缸以下的发动机进气门同时关闭时出现的进气空倒流的现象）

back flow scavenging （二冲程发动机的）回流扫气，环流扫气（亦称 loop scavenging，有时用德语 Schnürle scavenging，进气口与排气口位于汽缸下部同一侧或两侧，使充量从进气口进入汽缸，冲向对面的缸壁，然后向汽缸上部迂回流动，驱使废气从排气口排出的扫气方式）

back flush 逆流冲洗，反向冲洗（如：利用新鲜空气从相反的方向洗净排气分析器的采样系管道）

back gauge 车轮内侧间距（= wheel gauge）

back gear ①倒挡齿轮②倒挡

back-geared 带倒挡的

back glass wiper and washer 后窗玻璃刮水器和冲洗器

back ground noise 背景噪声，本底噪声

back guide monitor technology 倒车引导监测技术

backhoe （铲斗向后方挖掘的）反铲挖土机

back impact （发动机）反冲，（进气管）回火

backing block ①止动块②车轮下的垫楔木

backing light ①倒车灯②（向车）后照（射的）灯，（= back up light, reversing light, back up lamp）

backing plate （支撑）底板（亦称 back plate，如：安装制动蹄等的制动器底板）

backing presser 背压,反压力
backing ring (油封)护圈
back lamp 后(车)灯,尾灯
backlash (由于松动等原因造成齿轮或杆系之类的机械系统中的过大的间隙)齿隙(= back play)
backlash adjuster 背隙调节机构,背隙调节器
backlash circuit 间断电路
backlash eliminator 齿隙消除装置
backlash in the steering (转向机构中松旷造成的)自由行程
backlash spring 背隙消除弹簧
backlash valve 背隙补偿阀
backless (车厢内)无靠背座椅;无靠背的
back light ①[美](汽车车身的)后窗,后玻璃(= back window, rear window,亦称 rear light, back light)②从后方照射
back light blinds 后窗玻璃遮光帘
backlight defogging system [美]后窗玻璃除雾系统(一般用热风或埋设在玻璃上的电热丝,= 英 rear screen heater,因而亦称后窗玻璃加热器)
backlight frame 后窗框架
backlining 衬板,背衬
back metal (滑动轴承的)轴瓦基片
back mirror 后视镜(= rear-view mirror, reference mirror, retrospection mirror, observation mirror, back-view mirror)
back monitor camera 车后监控摄像机(简称 BMC)
back-mounted 背面安装的
back nut 锁紧螺母,后螺母
back of (piston) ring 活塞环内表面(接触活塞的一面)
back panel (车身或驾驶室)后壁板,后围板
back plate ①(泛指各种)后板,后挡板,护板;底板②(特指)鼓式制动器制动蹄的固定底板和盘式制动器制动钳摩擦块的金属底板③[美]离合器盖(= 英 clutch cover)④(有时指)信号板
back pressure 反压,背压(①指作用方向相反的压力,如:压力的反作用力,弹簧膜片式气压储能器的弹簧压力,机械密封件密封应对端面间流体膜平均压力等②指任何限制、阻碍气流或液流沿其流动方向流动的压力,或各种阻碍流体流动的限制压力。如:在内燃机排气系中阻碍废气流沿排气方向流动的压力③指反馈压力,回授压力)
back pressure control 背压控制,反馈压力控制(简称 BPC)
back pressure test 背压试验(如:测定内燃机主要性能参数随排气背压变化的试验,见 exhaust back pressure)
back pressure transducer 背压传感器(如:排气压力传感器,简称 BPT)
backrest ①(座椅)靠背②后支架
back-scattered laser light (由激光照射点)反射回的散射激光
back seat box bracket (轿车)后座椅的箱形支架
backseat driving ①坐在后座上指挥驾驶②后座式驾驶
back shaft 后轴
back shield 后遮板,后挡板
back side panel (货车驾驶室)后侧壁板,后侧板(后部两侧的壁板)
back single-cross seat (车厢内)长条横排后座(= back bench type seat)
back spring 回动弹簧,复位弹簧
back-to-back ①背靠背(指座位布置)②背至背间的距离
back-to-back test 总成的成对试验(如:成对变速器的功率闭路循环

试验等）

back-to-chest vibration（applied to the human body） （作用于人体的）前、后方向的振动，胸-背方向的振动

back up 后援，备份（在汽车电子系统中）①指当主要设备发生故障时，通过备用设备能接替其工作的一种预防性措施②指在误操作或数据丢失的情况下，可使迅速恢复工作的设施③指主要设备发生故障时，能接替其工作的设备或部件④指电源断开后，由蓄电池供电防止存储元件存储的程序、参数和数据等因停电而丢失的系统⑤指将信息复制到软盘、硬盘或磁带上，一旦原始软盘上的信息被无意改动或破坏时，可使用该软盘进行恢复）

back-up battery 后备电池，备用电池

backup camera system 倒车摄像系统（供驾驶员观察车后障碍物）

back-up collision intervention 防止倒车碰撞（功能或系统。目前有两类：①当车辆两侧和后方的3D传感器测得与包括其他车辆在内的障碍物的距离接近规定的极值时立即发出相应的声响、图像警报②在发出警报的同时还可自动制动减速或停车）

back-up guide monitor 倒车引导监视器

back-up lamp ①后照灯（泛指各种向车后方向照射的灯）②（特指，挂倒挡时，自动发亮的）倒车灯（=［英］reversing lamp，亦称back up light，backing light）③（补充标准前照灯的各种）灯具（如探照灯，雾灯等）

back-up radar 倒车雷达

back up ring ①保护圈，垫圈②（密封圈的）护圈，支撑环，挡圈（防止O形圈等辅助密封圈在轴向压力作用下被挤到缝隙中去的零件）

back-up service （汽车出售后的）保用期服务，售后服务

backup system 后备系统，备份系统，后备保险系统（指机构或装置发生重大故障时，能保证其继续正常运转的支持系统）

back valve 单向阀，止回阀（=check valve，non-return valve，one-way valve）

back view 后视图（=rear view）

back voltage 逆电压（指阻碍电流变化的电压。如：当线圈中的电流变化时，产生的自感电动势，其方向，即电势差正副值的方向，总是阻碍线圈中原电流的变化）

back wall （客车车厢）后壁，后围（亦称rear wall，由后围骨架、后围蒙板、后围护板、后窗玻璃及所属车身附件组成）

back wall pillar （客车车厢的）后壁立柱，后围立柱（指后围骨架两侧支撑顶盖及安装后玻璃的立柱）

backward and forward bending test 交变弯曲疲劳试验，前后（方向）弯曲（疲劳）试验

backward turnover 向后翻倾

back（ward）visibility （车辆）后方视野（=rear visibility）

backwash ①汽车行驶时车身后面的空气涡流②冲击；冲洗

back wheel 后轮（=rear wheel）

back wind lower panel （轿车车身）后围上盖板（指后窗下部与行李盖或后置发动机罩前缘连接的外层盖板，=rear waist panel，upper back panel，rear deck panel）

back-window frame 后窗框架

back-window glass 后窗玻璃

back window ledge （汽车）后窗下部的平台，后窗台，后窗挡架

bad condition of vehicle 汽车不良技术状况（指汽车不符合技术文件规

定的任一要求的状况,参见 good condition of vehicle)

bad conductor 不良导体

bad contact ①接触不良②不良触点,烧损触点

bad earth 搭铁不良,接地不良(=美 bad ground)

badge (在镀铬牌上用彩色瓷釉制成的)厂徽(有时也用文字或图形表示车型、车种,如:V-12, 16V, 3.0L等)

badge engineering 冒牌销售(指将某种型号的车辆只在外形上稍加改动,便以不同的型号和牌名推出销售)

bad visibility 不良的能见度,不良视野

baffle ①隔板,挡板,防护板,隔音板,遮光板,遮热板,导流板,反射板②挡住,堵住,阻断;用隔音板隔音;反射,导流

baffle chamber 消声室

baffled piston (二冲程发动机)带导流顶的活塞

baffle plate 隔板(①油箱,油底壳,消声器内的隔板②液力偶合器的环形挡板)

baffler ①消声器;减声器;阻尼器②挡板,隔板③折流板,导流板④节流阀,阻风门

baffle separator 隔板(= plate separator)

baffling 用节流阀调节;节流,阻尼

baffling wind 顶风,逆风(= head wind)

bag 包、袋、囊

bag analysis 袋式分析(用定容取样器将样气收集进取样袋再进行分析的方法。为质量"mass"分析法,用于监视性或合格性试验)

bag filter 滤袋式滤清器(带有灰尘收集器的空气滤清器)

baggage [美]行李,辎重(简称 bag, = [英] luggage)

baggage allowance (随带)行李质量限额,容许行李随带量

baggage car 行李车

baggage carrier (汽车车身内的)行李架(= luggage carrier, luggage holder)

baggage compartment (汽车车身后部的)行李舱(= trunk, luggage compartment, luggage boot, luggage locket, trunk compartment)

baggage grid (在车顶上的)栅格式行李架(= luggage grid)

Ba-grease 钡基润滑脂

bag sampling (废气分析等用的)气袋取样法(见 bag analysis)

bag (type) tank 软(油)箱,囊(袋)式油箱,储气囊,燃料气袋

bail clamp 夹紧箍卡,卡夹

bail wire (汽油滤清器油杯的)压环,钢丝固定卡

bainite (金相)巴菌体,贝氏体

bake 烘,烤;烧干;烧硬

bakelite 酚醛塑料,胶木,电木(用甲醛、石炭酸缩合成的树脂,因发明人 Bakelite 而得名)

bakelite terminal (点火高压线套接火花塞的)胶木接头

bake out ①退火②烘烤

baker's van 厢式面包运送车

balance ①平衡,对称,均衡②天平,秤③配重,平衡器,平衡块;平衡力;平衡表④使平衡,使均衡,与…保持平衡;(用天平)秤;衡量,权衡

balance bar ①平衡杆②秤杆

balance beam 平衡梁(亦称 equalizing beam)

balanced attenuator (无源集成电路的)补偿衰减器(具有补偿四端网络的衰减器)

balanced bridge 平衡电桥

balanced full trailer 平衡式全挂车

（单轴全挂车，车轴位于货厢重心附近，因而车厢可保持平衡；有时亦采用双轴或多轴结构，此时各车轴亦装于货厢重心附近）

balance disk （装在离心泵轴上的）盘形平衡装置，平衡盘

balanced-life design （总成各部件的）等寿命设计

balanced mechanical seal 平衡式机械密封（指载荷系数K<1的机械密封）

balanced pressure indicator 平衡压力计（测量内燃机工作时各汽缸内的瞬时压力）

balanced relief valve 平衡式卸荷阀

balanced spool (type) valve 平衡式滑柱阀（为液压控制系中广泛使用的液流方向控制滑柱阀，滑柱左右两方向所受的油压保持平衡，因而只要很小的外力便能使滑柱移向所要求的方向）

balanced suspension （双轴并装后桥的）平衡臂式悬架

balanced two-terminal-pair network （无源集成电路中的）补偿四端网络（亦称平衡双端对偶网络，指输入端可互换，输出端也同时互换的网络）

balance patch （轮胎的）平衡补片

balance piston 平衡活率

balancer ①平衡机，平衡装置②平衡重（＝balance weight）

balance shaft （装有平衡块的）平衡轴（用于平衡曲轴连杆机构的离心惯性力和往复惯性力）

balance tube 平衡管，均压管（＝air vent, air vent tube, balance pire）

balance weight 平衡重，平衡配量，配重（＝balancer②，亦称balancing weight, counter weight, pullback weight）

balance-weight crankshaft （带）平衡重的曲轴，配重曲轴（＝counter balanced crankshaft）

balancing-centering machine 平衡钻中心孔机床（用于曲轴钻中心孔，以减少机械加工后的动不平衡和去重工作量）

balcony lift 平台式举升器，平台式升降机

bald （被）磨光了的，磨成光面的（如轮胎胎面花纹等，＝worn-out）

baldness （轮胎胎面花纹）（被）磨光，（成）光面（指其花纹凸起部分已磨到花纹沟底）

bale trailer 袋装货物挂车，捆包货物挂车

bale wagon 运捆包货物的厢式货车

balk ①大梁，梁木②横向系杆③障碍物④阻止，中止

balk ring 同步环，阻尼环（在同步式变速器中，防止齿轮过早啮合的旋转件，亦称baulk ring或block ring）

ball ①球②球状物③滚珠④球头，球端⑤（球销式万向节中的）球环⑥使成球形

ball-and-nnt steering 循环球-螺母式转向机（＝recirculating ball steering）

ball-and-socket geer shifter 球窝式变速杆

ball-and-socket joint 球节，球形连接（见spherical connection）

ball and socket steering knuckle 球销式转向节，（一种不用主销而用球销和前悬架控制杆件铰接的无主销式转向节）

ball and trunion (universal) joint 球销式万向节（由一根两端轴颈上装有球环的销轴将双торца槽壳与球头轴连接起来组成的一种允许轴向滑动的径向自承式非等速万向节，亦称pin and ball trunnion universal joint, pot joint muff coupling joint）

ball-and-worm steering system 循环

球-蜗杆式转向系

ballast ①压载物,压重,镇重②镇流器,镇流电阻③装镇重物

ballastable all-purpose tractor 可加镇重(以提高驱动轮载荷,从而增加车轮与路面的附着力,多用于沙砾路等)的多用途牵引车

ballastable engineering sectionalized tractor 可加镇重的积木式工程机械用牵引车

ballasted ignition system 镇流电阻点火系统(指点火线圈初级绕组串联附加电阻或电阻丝的点火系统,该附加电阻电路称为镇流点火电路"ballasted ignition circuit",所使用的附加电阻为镇流电阻"ballast resistor",该点火线圈称为镇流点火线圈"ballasted ignition coil"。起动时该电阻短路,改善起动性能。高速时,初级电流小,电阻温度低,阻值小,从而改善高速点火特性,低速时初级电流大,电阻温度高,阻值增大,可限制初级电流而避免点火线圈过热)

ballasted weight (牵引车的)配重,镇重(物)

ballast resistor 平衡电阻,镇流电阻,附加电阻(简称 Bal Res,见 ballasted ignition system)

ballast truck 运碎石的底卸式货车

ball-bank indicator 钢球式横向加速度测定仪

ball bearing 球轴承

ball bearing felt packing 球轴承填密毡

ball bearing housing 球轴承座,球轴承外圈座

ball bearing nut steering gear 循环球螺杆螺母式转向机构

ball-bearing puller 球轴承拉器(用来拆卸装在轴或轴承座内的球轴承,亦称 ball-bearing extractor)

ball-bearing with clamping sleeve 装在紧定套上的球轴承

ball bearing with double side shield 两面带防尘侧盖的球轴承 (= double shield ball bearing)

ball bearing with filling slot 带装球缺口的球轴承 (= filling slot-type bearing, ball bearing with loading groove, notched type bearing)

ball bearing with flanged outer race 外圈有止推凸缘的球轴承

ball bearing with shoulder ring in outer race 外圈带止推肩的球轴承 (= snap ring bearing)

ball bearing with side plate 带防尘侧盖的球轴承

ball bonding 球形接头,球铰节

ball cage (球轴承的)球保持架 (= ball holder, ball retainer, ball distance ring)

ball cam ①滚球式凸轮②球形凸轮

ball check housing 单向球阀阀体 (= ball valve housing)

ball check type hydraulic self-sealing coupling 单向球阀式液压自密封接头

ball circuit screw 循环球螺杆

ball circuit type 循环球式 (= circulating ball type)

ball collar thrust bearing 带推力环的推力球轴承

ball cup ①球窝,球头座,球座②(径向推力球轴承)外圈

ball distance ring 球保持架 (= ball cage)

ball electrolyte tester 小球式电解液试验器(可代替比重计,测试电解液浓度)

ball end ①球头销②球面枢轴

ball-end tappet 球头挺杆(与凸轮接触的部分成球状)

ball gear-change lever 球头变速杆 (= ball gearshift lever)

ball governor 球形重锤式离心调速

器（=fly-ball governor）

ball-grease bearing 微钢珠-滑脂轴承（由极小的钢珠加油脂组成，其摩擦系数仅0.001）

ball guide channel （循环球式转向机的）滚球导槽

ball hardness 钢球压入硬度（布氏硬度）

ball head ①球头②（球销式万向节中的）球头轴（具有横向定位销孔和传动连接结构的拳形元件）

ball headed aiming screw （前照灯的）球头对光螺钉

ball indentation test 布氏硬度试验（用压入小钢球确定硬度的试验，=ball test, ball pressure test）

ball-in-tube sensor （安全气囊系统的）球-筒式减速度传感器（在一筒壳内装有一个由永久磁定位于管端的镀金钢球，当车身减速度大到作用于钢球的惯性力超过永久磁铁的吸力时，钢球即冲向管的触点端）

ball joint 球节，球形连接（见spherical connection）

ball joint and kingpin wear indicator （转向轮）球节和主销磨损指示仪（并可测车轮偏摆量，传动轴脉动量等）

ball joint axis inclination （独立悬架前轮的）转向轴线内倾（独立悬架的转向轴线指上下悬架臂球节中心的连线，相当于一般非独立悬架的主销，因此亦可称为主销内倾，=steering axis inclination, king pin axis inclination）

ball joint inclination 球形万向节夹角，球节倾斜角

ball joint rockerarm （气门）球节式摇臂（指不装在摇臂轴上而装在球形座上的摇臂）

ball joint separator 球节分解器（压出球节用的工具）

ball joint steering knuckle 球节式转向节（独立悬架用球节代替主销的转向节）

ball journal 球轴颈

ball latch sleeve （齿轮变速器自锁机械的）销球套（筒），球销套筒

ball nut steering gear 循环球螺杆螺母式转向器（=ball screw type, recirculating-ball type, circulating-ball type, ball-and-worm type, ball bearing nut steering gear）

balloon ①低压轮胎②气囊③装低压轮胎

balloon tyre 球形断面低压胎（20世纪20年代推出的一种球形断面、高-宽基本相同的低压胎的名称，流行于20世纪20~30年代。目前亦指客车和货车使用的充气压力为0.294~0.49MPa的宽断面低压胎。轿车用的宽断面低压胎，则多称low pressure balloon tire, 其充气压力更低，一般在0.15~0.2MPa, 亦称doughnut tire）

ball piston pump 钢球活塞式油泵（由带钢球孔道，钢球和泵壳等组成，钢球孔道起缸筒的作用，钢球起活塞的作用）

ball pivot 支枢球头

ball plug 球形柱塞

ball pressure test 布氏硬度试验（见ball indentation test）

ball proof 防弹的

ball race 球轴承座圈

ball race cage （球轴承）座圈保持架

ball reciprocating bearing 允许轴做旋转运动和直线往复运动的滚珠轴承（=reciprocating bearing）

ball recirculating steering gear 循环球式转向器

ball retainer （球轴承）球保持架（见ball cage）

ball ring （球销式万向节的）球环

（可在销轴轴颈上旋转并通过滤针和轴颈将载荷从双柱槽壳"housing"传给球头的球形元件）
ball roller screw 球头圆柱螺钉
ball screw type 循环球式（转向器）（= ball nut type, circulating ball type）
ball seat ①球阀阀座②球节的球窝
ball seating 球窝座
ball socket 球窝，球座（球头节中与球头配合的球面凹窝件）
ball spline Rzeppa universal joint 滚球花键球笼式万向节（借助于球式或柱式滚动花键可轴向相对运动的盘形球笼式万向节）
ball stud 球头销，球销（亦称 ball pin）
ball test ①布氏硬度试验（见 ball indentation test）②（汽车用安全玻璃的）钢球试验（分 227g 钢球试验和 2260g 钢球试验两项，前者测试在小而硬的物体冲击下的耐冲击强度，后者测试耐穿透能力）
ball thrust bearing 推力球轴承
ball thrust bearing with outside band 带外罩的推力球轴承
ball thrust bearing with outside retainer 带外保持架的推力球轴承
ball track 球轴承滚道
ball tube （循环球式转向机的）滚球循环导管
ball valve housing 单向（止回）球阀阀体（= ball check valve housing）
ball yoke （球叉式万向节的）球叉（在其内侧径向平面内具有曲面球槽并与轴制成一体的叉形件）
BAMA 英国汽车制造商协会（British Automobile Manufacturer's Association 的简称）
BAMP 大气压与进气歧管绝对压力传感器（barometric and manifold absolute pressure sensor 的简称）
banana spring 弧形卷簧（中心线呈弧形的螺旋弹簧）

band ①带，条，箍，圈；扁钢，带钢，频带，谱带，光带，波段；区域，范围，地带，条纹②带形的，带状的，带式的③用带绑扎，打捆，结合，联合
bandage ①带，带状物，箍带，铁箍②上箍带，用带捆起
B1 and B2 NO$_X$ and PM emission level （欧共同体1999/96指令中规定的重型车辆柴油机）2005年和2008年的 NO$_X$ 和微粒物排放限值[B1为2005年限估，B2为2008年限值，即俗称的欧4（Euro 4）和欧5（Euro 5）标准]
band brake 带式制动器（见 transmission band）
band clip 箍，卡箍，箍带（=[美]clamp）
band cover （用来封闭筒状零件上的孔、宽缝等的）宽带卡箍，宽箍（形）盖（箍的两端由螺栓上紧）
band eliminator filter 带阻滤波器
band filter ①带通滤波器②带阻滤波器
band gap （频）带隙
band level （噪声的）频带级，带强级
band noise 频带噪声
band of frequencies 频带，波段（= frequency band）
band pass filter 带通滤波器
band seal 密封条
band selector 波段开关（= band switch）
band speedometer 带式刻度车速里程表
band tire 实心轮胎；载重轮胎
band wagon （游行队伍的）乐队花车
band wheel ①带式制动器的鼓轮②皮带传动轮
band width 频带宽度，带宽（指带的上、下界频率差，单位赫兹，

见 frequency range)

banger (指仍能使用的)破旧廉价车

banger racing 旧车赛(指门窗玻璃及修饰件等均已拆除的破旧汽车在狭小的车道上进行的汽车赛事)

banging 爆破声,敲击声,冲击声(如消声器内放炮声,轮胎爆破声)

banjo ①(泛指)各种形状像班卓琴(一种五弦琴,中间粗大,呈鼓形,两头或一头细长)的构件 ②(特指一种形似班卓琴的)软管或硬管的直角管接头 "banjo coupling" ③(特指)整体式桥壳(见 banjo axle housing)

banjo oiler (弯曲)长颈润滑油加注器

banjo (type) axle housing 整体式(驱动)桥壳与之相对的是可分式桥壳(split axle housing)

banked battery 并联电池组

banking angle ①(车辆转弯时)侧倾角 ②(弯道)外缘超高角(亦写作 bank angle)

banking loss 急速运转时燃料消耗

bank line 道路边缘,路肩线

bank of cylinders 气缸体

bank of gear 在同一轴上的一排齿轮

bantam ①吉普车的俗称(原意矮脚鸡,见 jeep)②小型设备

bantam type spark plug 矮型火花塞(= compact type spark plug)

Banzai (日本)万岁公司(生产汽车检测设备车的厂家及其商标名)

BAP 大气绝对压力(barometric absolute pressure 的简称)

bar ①巴(压力单位,1 bar = 10^5 Pa) ②棒,杆,棒料,棒材,条钢;横木 ③(电流)汇流,母线

barb bolt 基础螺栓,地脚螺栓,倒钩螺栓

Barber-Greene (后倾式自卸汽车的)开度可控式后栏板(商品名,用于控制卸料速度)

BARC 英国汽车竞赛俱乐部(British Automobile Racing Club 的简称)

bar chart 见 bar graph

barcode 条形码(亦写作 bar code)

bare 裸的,暴露的;无外壳的,无遮蔽的,无屏蔽的,无绝缘的

bare back 不带半挂车的鞍式牵引车(口语)

bare chassis dry weight 底盘干重量(底盘干质量的旧称,不包括燃料、冷却液、备胎、随车工具、驾驶室和车厢时的汽车质量)

bare chassis kerb weight 底盘整备重量(底盘整备质量的旧称,见 curb mass)

bare engine gross power 不带附件的发动机功率

bare pipe 无螺纹管,裸管,无绝缘管

bare shell 裸板件(附件如铰链、锁扣等均完全拆除的车身板件)

bare structure 无外壳结构,裸结构

bare universal joint 无套万向节

bare weight 空(车)重,净重,裸重,干重,不带附件的本体质量

bare wire 裸线(= naked wire)

bar gauge 棒状量规,棒形计测器(如:棒形量缸表、棒形标准间隙规)

bargraph 柱状图(用柱状直线表示各项指标或参数所占%比的条线图, = bar chart)

barium 钡(Ba)

barium detergent 钡洗涤剂

barium titanate 钛酸钡

barndoor tailgate (厢式)车身双扇后门(简称 barndoor gate)

BARO 表压力(见 barometric pressure)

baroceptor 气压敏感元件,气压传感器

barograph 气压记录仪,自计气压

计，自计高度计
barometer ①（大）气压（力）表，气压计，晴雨表②标记
barometric and manifold absolute pressure sensor 大气压力及进气管绝对压力传感器（一种双作用式传感器，可用于测定大气压力及进气管绝对压力，简称 BMAP）
barometric pressure 大气压（亦称大气绝对压力"barometric absolute pressure"，指用压力表测得的大气压力，故亦称表压力。美国政府规定从 1995 年 1 月起，一律用 BARO 作为它的简称，取代各公司自定的名称，如：Ford 的 PS 等）
barometric pressure sensor （汽车发动机电子控制系统用的）大气压力传感器（它提供的信息供动力控制模块随海拔高度调节混合气浓度等，美国政府规定该传感器从 1995 年 1 月起，一律使用 SAE 推荐的简称"BARO"表示）
barometrograph 气压计，气压自动记录仪
barometry 气压测定法
barothermohydrograph 气压温度湿度记录仪
bar pressure 大气压力，大气压（barometric pressure 的简称）
barrel ①桶（石油工业常作为计量单位，简称 bar）。②圆桶，桶状物，（如：滚子轴承的球面滚子，衬套，汽缸套筒，滚筒）③（有时指）安装阻风门的筒形体壳部分④（特指空气与燃油蒸气混合的腔室及其壳体）混合腔，混合室，混合腔筒（亦称 mixing chamber）⑤（柴油机喷油泵柱塞偶件中的）柱塞套（柱塞在该套中做往复运动）⑥装桶；装成桶⑦滚磨，磨研⑧高速行驶
barrel assemble （球面滚子轴承的）球面滚子-保持架总成
barrel bearing 向心球面滚子轴承
barrel-contoured 筒状的
barrel crank case （不能分开的）整体式曲轴箱，筒式曲轴箱
barrel cranking motor 桶式起动机（供小飞轮式发动机用的起动机，其驱动小齿轮接有一桶形重物，以增加其转动惯量）
barrel sleeve 汽缸套（见 cylinder liner）
barrel spring （两端直径小中间直径大的）鼓形螺旋弹簧
barrel tappet 空心筒形（气门）挺杆，筒形空心（气门）跟随件（=［美］·barrel valve lifter）
barricade ①路障，栅栏②隔板，屏蔽板③设路障于…，阻塞，遮住
barrier ①路障，隔板，障碍，屏障，栅栏②（特指汽车碰撞试验用的）障壁③阻挡层
barrier collision test （汽车）障壁碰撞试验（亦称 barrier impact test, barrier crash test）
barrier effect ①（指防腐涂层等对金属件的）保护作用，防腐蚀作用②屏障效应
barrier potential 势垒（位垒，阻挡层）
barrier potential difference 势垒差（阻挡层电位差）
barrier ring 阻挡环，隔环
barrier voltage 阻挡层电压
bar the engine 用手起动摇把转动发动机
BAS ①（突发状态时的）紧急制动系统（见 brake assist system）②英国标准协会（British Association of Standard 的简称）
basal crach 底面裂缝
base ①基础，基座，底板；基点，基线，基面，基数②轮距，跨距③三极管基极④基本的
base bearing 主轴承
base bearing bushing （曲轴）主轴

承瓦（= crankshaft bearing shell, mainbearing shell）

base bearing cap 曲轴主轴承盖

base bias 基极偏压

base blend （加有添加剂的混合燃油的）基础油

base chamber （发动机）曲轴箱（= crankcase, engine base, bottom chamber）

base circle （渐开线或摆线圆柱齿轮的）基圆（指形成渐开线或摆线齿廓的发生线或发生圆在其圆周上作纯滚动的假想圆）

base coat 底涂层（见 ground coat）

base current 基极电流

base cylinder （渐开线圆柱齿轮的）基圆柱面（形成其齿轮渐开螺旋面齿面的发生平面在它上面作纯滚动运动的假想圆柱面）

base data 基本数据，基本参数

base diameter 基圆直径（指渐开线和摆线圆柱齿轮的基圆柱面和基圆的直径）

base engine strategy （发动机控制模块，即发动机控制用电子计算机的）发动机基本控制模式（通常该模式又分为以下四个分模式：①起动②节气门关闭运转③节气门部分开启运转④节气门全开运转。控制模块根据输入信号，确认发动机所处的运转状态后，根据程序中设计的该状态下的基本控制模式，对点火、供油等进行控制，以获得最佳油耗，排放和操纵性）

base explosion 曲轴箱内爆燃，油底壳放炮（= crankcase explosion）

base face 基准面

base frequency 基础频率（见 fundamental frequency）

base gasoline 基体汽油，基础汽油（相对于抗爆剂等添加剂而言）

base helix 基圆螺旋线（渐开线斜齿轮的基圆柱面与形成该齿轮齿面的渐开螺旋面的交线）

base helix angle （渐开线斜齿轮的）基圆螺旋角（指其基圆螺旋线的螺旋角，见 helix angle）

base ignition setting 基本点火正时，基础点火正时（指发动机处于静止状态时调定的点火正时，亦称 base ignition timing, basic timing，在该基础上发动机运转过程中的点火时刻由点火提前机构自动调节）

base lead 基极导线，基极引线

base lead angle （渐开线斜齿轮和渐开线蜗杆的）基圆导程角（指其基圆螺旋线的导程角，见 lead angle）

baseline test 基础试验

base metal ①（电镀、喷镀等的）被镀覆金属，②（镀层）基体金属 ③（焊接时的）被焊接件金属 ④（熔焊的）基体金属⑤（合金中的）主要成分，母体金属（= basic metal）⑥母材，基料（= parent metal）⑦任意两种金属中电位较低的一种，贱金属（noble metal 的反义）⑧碱金属

base metal attack （漆层下的）基本金属腐蚀

base metal catalyst 普通金属催化剂（用一种或一种以上的普通金属，如：铜、铬、镍、钴作为原料的催化剂）

base mounted fuel injection pump 平底安装式喷油泵（安装底部为平面并以托架和柴油机连接的喷油泵）

base oil 原料油，基础油

base package 组合草图，总装草图（见 package drawing）

base pitch 基圆齿距（指摆线轮的一个端平面上，两个相邻而同侧的齿廓之间相对应的基圆弧长）

base plane 基准平面，基面，底平面（= basal plane, basic plane）

base plate 底板，垫板，座板，基座，基板，基底，支撑板（简称

BP)
base point 基点
base pressure 基准压力
base pulse width （喷油器）基本喷油量，脉冲宽度（电子控制模块根据所要求的燃油质量流量和喷油器常数确定的喷油量初始控制脉冲宽度，见 effective injector pulse width）
base radius 基圆半径
base ring ①轮辋上用于固定轮胎胎圈的挡圈、弹性挡圈、锁圈等的总称②基环座圈
base stock ①基本原料，基本组分②加有添加剂的润滑油的基础油
base 10 system （常规使用的）10进制
base 16 system 16进制
base 2 system （计算机中使用的）二进制（用0与1两个符号表示数的逢2进1制）
base 8 system 8进制
base tread 基层胎面，底层胎面（花纹沟下的胎面层，= under tread）
base unit 基本单位［简称bu．，指在规定的量制中基本量的单位，国际单位制中的基本单位有七个：米m，千克kg，秒s，安（培）A，开（尔文）K，坎（德拉）cd，摩（尔）mol
base voltage 基极电压
basic ①基本的，基础的，基准的，根本的②碱性的
basic dynamic capacity （轴承的）基本额定动载荷量
basic engine ①基础发动机（按美国汽车工程师学会的规定，是指只包括下列机内附件的发动机：燃油泵、机油泵、冷却液泵及装在机内的废气净化装置。当用电动燃油泵等附件时，才包括发电机，亦称 bare engine）②发动机（系列）的基本型③（各种变型发动机的）基础发动机

basic form of thread （螺纹的）基本牙形（亦称 basic profile of thread）
basic ignition setting 基本点火正时（= basic ignition timing，指发动机静态调定的点火正时，作为自动点火提前装置或发动机电子控制模块根据转速、负荷等进行动态调整点火正时的基础）
basic ion 阳离子，正离子
basic operating motor vehicle 基本（可）运转机动车辆（只包括发动机、车架及其他车辆行驶所必需的机构和机械部分，不包括车身及一切非驾驶操纵用的附属装置）
basic point 基础点，基点
basic sediment and water （燃油箱）底部沉积物及水（简称 BS&W）
basic size 基本尺寸，主要尺寸
basic specification 基本参数，主要特性，简要说明，基本技术条件
basic system voltage （汽车电器系统的）标称电压，名义电压（如6v，12v或24v，亦称 nominal voltage）
basic warranty （新车等的）基本质保期［如：4yrs/50000 miles（4年/5万英里）］
basin shaped combustion chamber （发动机的）盆形燃烧室（指燃烧室在活塞顶内的部分呈盆形，分深盆形和浅盆形两种）
basis ①基础，基准，基线，基数②基本原理③主要成分
basis hole system （公差配合中的）基孔制，孔基准制（= hole basis system，hole basis，hole base system，basic hole system）
basis shaft system （公差配合中的）基轴制，轴基准制（= shaft basis system，shaft base system，basic shaft system）
basket rack 行李架
bastard (-cut) file 次粗牙锉，次粗

（齿）锉

batch ①一批，一组，一捆②配料

batch board （载货汽车的）货槽隔板，货厢隔板（将货厢隔成几个空间）

batch test 分批抽查，批量试验

batch truck 斗式车厢载货汽车

batch (type) sample 分批取样，非连续采样，抽采取样（=noncontinuous sampling）

bath ①浴，浸，泡②（浸泡，浴用的）池，槽，器具

bath lubrication 油浴润滑（亦称 bath oiling）

bath resistance 电镀液电阻，电解质电阻

bath-splash lubrication 油浴飞溅润滑

bath tub combustion chamber （汽油机）浴盆形燃烧室（顶置气门式燃烧室的一种，进、排气门纵向布置，其横剖面呈倒浴盆形，故亦名倒浴盆形燃烧室"reverse bath tub combustion chamber"）

bath tub test （车辆）水浴密封试验（驶过水沟以检查其密封性）

bath unit trailer 浴室挂车，拖挂的活动浴室

batten ①板条，撑条，压条②车厢壁板支撑③万能曲线尺

battery 蓄电池（特指由一组单格电池串联成的汽车用电池，其总电压为各单格电池电压之和）

battery acid 蓄电池酸液，电解液（亦称 battery fluid, battery liquid, battery solution, battery electrolyte, 用相对密度为1.840的纯硫酸与一定比例的纯水配制而成）

battery analyzer 蓄电池充电检验器；蓄电池故障诊断仪

battery-battery hybrid car 双蓄电池复合动力汽车（动力装置一套驱动电动机和一套内燃机-发电机充电系统及两套蓄电池组成，中、小负荷下，一套大蓄电池供电，并向小蓄电池充电，大负荷下，两套蓄电池同时供电）

battery bearer ①蓄电池托架（亦称 battery carrier, battery cradle, battery support, battery bracket, battery rack, battery holder）②蓄电池搬运工具

battery block （多由聚丙烯制成的）蓄电池壳（体）（亦称 battery case, battery cupboard, battery jar）

battery box 蓄电池箱（亦称 battery crate, accumulator box, battery container, battery tray）

battery cable terminals （蓄电池接线柱的）接线夹头，接线夹（带拧紧螺丝，=battery clamp, battery clip, 注意：不是指 battery terminal post "蓄电池接线桩"）

battery cable to earth 蓄电池搭铁线

battery capacity 蓄电池容量（单位为安培小时，即放电电流与时间的乘积 $A \cdot h$）

battery car 蓄电池车，电瓶车

battery carrying strap 蓄电池吊带（=battery suspension strap）

battery cell 蓄电池单元，单格电池，单体电池

battery change-over switch 蓄电池转换开关

battery charge ①蓄电池充电状态，蓄电池充电程度（=state of battery charge 或 battery charging condition, 指蓄电池尚存留的电量，一般用尚存电量为额定容量的%表示）②蓄电池充电（指对蓄电池充电）

battery charge indicator 蓄电池充电状态指示器，蓄电池充电程度指示器（亦称 battery state indicator, battery charging condition indicator）

battery charger 蓄电池充电器，蓄电池充电机（分限流式和限压式两

大类)

battery charging condition tell-tall
蓄电池充电状况（不良）警报灯

battery cold cranking amperes 蓄电池低温启动安培（指在规定的低温起动容量测试条件下蓄电池所能提供的电量的安培数，简称 CCA 或 CCA'S。一般美国生产的蓄电池均标明在蓄电池壳上，有时还连用×××minutes RC 字样说明其额定容量）

battery cold cranking rating 蓄电池低温启动容量（指蓄电池在发动机低温启动时的供电能力。美国规定完全充电的蓄电池在 -18℃，连续放电 30 秒，单格电池端电压不低于 1.2v 的条件下所输出的电量。我国规定在 -18℃下，以 5min 放电率连续放电至单格电池为 1v 所输出的电量，单位：安培）

battery compartment 蓄电池室（指汽车上装放蓄电池的独立空间，通常轿车在发动机室或后座下面，客车和货车则有独立的蓄电池箱"battery box"）

battery connector ①蓄电池接线夹②（特指以蓄电池为动力源的电动汽车的）蓄电池充电插头

battery cover 蓄电池壳盖（板）

battery cut-out relay 蓄电池断电器

battery cycle life 蓄电池（充电放电）循环寿命（常用次数来表示）

battery diffusion 蓄电池渗漏电解液

battery discharge controller （当电动汽车蓄电池的电压下降到规定值时，触发蓄电池放电警报装置和/或断开电源的）蓄电池放电控制器

battery discharge indicator 蓄电池放电指示器（以额定容量的%数表示的蓄电池的尚存电量来指示其放电程度的指针式或数字式指示仪表）

battery drain 从蓄电池中放出电解液

battery-driven 蓄电池（供电）驱动的

battery earth 蓄电池搭铁，蓄电池接地

battery ECU （混合动力车驱动用）蓄电池（的）电子监测模块（通过各个传感器，监测电池的残存电量、内阻、充电和放电状况、高压件绝缘及电池的温度和强冷却效率等，并将监测结果输入混合动力车的动力管理电子控制模块进行分析和处理，将故障代码输入车载故障诊断系统显示、存储。见 power management ECU）

battery-electricmotor drive 蓄电池-电动机驱动

battery electric vehicle 电瓶车（亦称 battery electrics）

battery exchange system （电瓶汽车的）电瓶更换系统（将用完的电瓶换成新充满电的电瓶）

battery filler ①蓄电池加液工具②蓄电池加液口（= battery filling hole）

battery filler cover 蓄电池加液孔盖

battery filling plug 蓄电池注液孔塞（= battery filler plug）

battery fluid 见 battery acid

battery/flywheel hybrid 蓄电池/储能飞轮复合动力汽车（动力装置为一套内燃机—发电机—蓄电池—电动机系统，一套储能飞轮，在怠速及中、小负荷下，多余能量，由储能飞轮储存。短时间大负荷时，蓄电池与储能飞轮同时输出功率，驱动汽车）

battery ground strap 蓄电池搭铁条

battery heater 蓄电池加热器（防止电解液冻结和低温下蓄电池输出容量下降）

battery hookup 蓄电池的联结方式（指由两个或两个以上的蓄电池组成一个 12v 或 24v 电源系统时，各蓄电池的连接方式，分并联与串联

两种)

battery hybrid 蓄电池复合动力汽车（以蓄电池为储能装置的内燃机-电动机复合动力汽车）

battery ignition (system) 蓄电池点火（系）(亦称 coil ignition, Kettering ignition, 以蓄电池为电源, 通过点火线圈将蓄电池电压升到点火高压的点火系统称)

battery isolating switch control 蓄电池断路器操纵件（使蓄电池和电器线路间断路的手操纵件）

battery jar sill 蓄电池壳底内槛条

battery lead ①蓄电池接线柱②蓄电池接线

batteryless injection system (小型两冲程发动机的电子控制) 无蓄电池喷射系统

battery master switch (汽车的) 电源总开关（断开蓄电池, 即: 切断汽车全部用电器件的电源总开关）

battery negative terminal 蓄电池负极接线柱

battery-operated (蓄) 电池供电的, 用电池作电源的

battery paste (蓄电池极板) 糊状活性物质

battery plate 蓄电池极板

battery (plate) separator 蓄电池隔板

battery plug 电源插头

battery positive terminal 蓄电池正极接线柱

battery post 蓄电池接线柱

battery-powered vehicle (完全由蓄电池供电驱动的) 蓄电池车, 电瓶车 (= battery traction vehicle, battery electric vehicle)

battery quick charger 蓄电池快速充电机（指可以在短时间内将放电状态的蓄电池恢复到可以起动发动机的程度的充电机, 俗称 battery charge counter, 除快速充电功能外, 快速充电机大多具有普通充电功能和用作为发动机起动外接电源）

battery rating 蓄电池（容量）的额定值（指在规定条件下, 蓄电池的标准容量值）

battery rectifier 蓄电池充电用整流器

battery reserve capacity 蓄电池的实际容量（指发电系统不工作的情况下, 蓄电池实际上所能提供给汽车电气系统的电量）

battery reserve capacity rating 蓄电池的额定实际容量,（我国一般称）蓄电池额定容量（在美国指完全充电的蓄电池电解液平均温度为 26.6℃时, 连续以 25A 电流放电到单格电池电压降到 1.75 所经过的时间。在我国则指以 20h 放电率的放电流, 在电解液平均温度为 30℃时, 连续放电, 单格电池电压降到 1.75v 蓄电池所输出的电量。容量单位为安培小时, 即为放电电流与放电时间的乘积)

battery rundown protection system 蓄电池完全放电保护系统

battery saver (以蓄电池为电源的汽车用电设备的) 节电器

battery scanning method 蓄电池逐个增减串接法（电瓶车车速的控制方法之一, 利用机械继电器依次增加或减少串于供电电路中的电瓶数, 来控制电流）

battery sensor 蓄电池传感器（向电子控制模块提供其电压信号）

battery shedding (由于老化或反复过充电, 或充电电流过大, 温度过高造成的) 蓄电池极板活性物质脱落

battery skin (起蓄电池作用的车身) 蓄电板件〔指具有蓄电功能的碳素纤维复合材料制成的车身外壳板件, 可起到常规蓄电池相同的作用向汽车供电, 这种蓄电池亦称车身结构板件蓄电池（structural battery）〕

battery slow charger 慢速充电机

battery starter tester 起动机接合时蓄电池技术状况检验仪

battery state sensor 蓄电池状态传感器

battery syringe 蓄电池电液注射管

battery temperature sensor 蓄电池温度传感器（靠近蓄电池，向电子控制模块提供蓄电池周围温度信息）

battery terminal ①蓄电池的接线柱，接线桩（= battery lead 或 post）②"B"接线柱（指与蓄电池连接的交流发电机输出接线柱或交流发电机调节器的相应接线柱）③有时指连接电缆接蓄电池一端的接线夹

battery tester 蓄电池试验器（= battery gauge, battery meter)①一般指检查蓄电池充电状态的电压表或电解液比重计，或叉状检验器，蓄电池检验叉"battery prod"②有时特指检查单格电池状态的仪具，称 battery cell tester）

battery tray （一般轿车装在发动机室侧面的）蓄电池托架

battery vent plung 蓄电池通气孔塞

battery voltage correction mode （汽车动力控制模块的）蓄电池电压修正模式（当蓄电池电压降到某规定值时，为防止电火花减弱，控制模块 PCM 将①加浓混合气②若发动机处于急速，增大节气门开度③延长点火线圈一次绕组通电时间）

battery voltage-supplied RAM 蓄电池供电（压）型随机存取存储器（其中 RAM 为 random access memory 的简称）

battery warmer 蓄电池保温箱

battle wagon ①［英］高级汽车，高级轿车，高级旅行车②战车

baud 波特（信息传送速率单位，1波特＝1bit/每秒。每秒所传送的 bit 数量称为 baud rate"波特率"）

baulk ring （同步器式变速器中的）同步环，阻尼环，摩擦环（防止变速器齿轮过快啮合，亦称 block ring，blocking ring）

Baumé areometer 玻美比重计（亦称 Baume' hydrometer）

Baumé scale (of specific gravity) 玻美比重度

BAV 放气阀，空气排出阀（bleed air valve 的简称）

bay ①跨距，跨度②舱，室，隔间③底板，机架，台，座，支柱

Bayerische Motoren Werke 宝马公司（BMW 的德文全称）

bay front 半圆前挡板（鞍式挂车车厢上的前挡板）

bayonet ①接装卡销（例如卡口灯泡的卡销）②卡口

bayonet cap 卡口式灯头

bayonet-coupled bulb 卡口灯泡

bayonet joint 卡口连接，卡口接头

bayonet joint seat （由卡口连接的壳体和壳盖的壳体上的）卡口凹边，卡口座边

bayonet lamp holder 卡口灯头

bayonet lock 卡扣，卡锁

bayonet oil level gauge 带卡口的机油尺

bayonet radiator cap 卡扣式散热器加水口盖，卡口式散热器盖

bayonet socket 卡口灯座，卡口插座（亦称 bayonet base, bayonet fitting）

B battery 乙电池，B 电池（指屏极电池）

BBC 在下止点前（before bottom center 的简称）

BBS 积木式，积木式结构（building block system 的简称）

B-CAN （汽车）车身控制器局域网（Body-Controller area network 的简称，用传输速率较低"33.33 kb/s"的总线连接灯光、刮水器、门锁、空调）

BCD 800 circuit 见 bidirectional data

BCM 车身控制模块（控制空调及车身的电器系统的车载计算机，body control module 的简称，旧称 body computer module，也简称 BCM）

BCS 博世（公司）汽车维修服务（的连锁经营模式维修店，Bosch Car Service 的简称）

BC valve 强制怠速工况下，进气管真空度控制阀（简称 BCV，见 boost control valve）

BDC 下止点，下死点（bottom dead centre 的简称，指活塞顶面离曲轴中心线最近的止点）

BDF 生物柴油（bio-diesel fuel 的简称）

BDV 击穿电压（breakdown voltage 的简称）

BE ①工学士（bachelor of engineering 的简称）②玻美（度，比重计）③助推发动机（booster engine 的简称）

beach wagon 厢式轿车，旅行车（见 station wagon 的简称）

beacon flasher 闪光信号装置

beacon light 标志灯（如急救车上的红色闪光灯），警号灯，信号灯

bead ①珠，滴，泡②边，缘③焊缝④轮胎胎圈（轮胎安装在轮辋上的部分，由胎圈芯 "bead core" 和胎圈包布 "chafer" 等组成）

bead base （轮胎）胎圈底部（轮胎与轮辋胎圈座 "beat seat of rim" 接触的部位）

bead blasting （旧漆皮等的）喷（玻璃）珠除漆法

bead breaker 胎圈翻边机

bead bundle 轮胎胎圈的胎圈钢丝圈（= bead ring，亦称 bead coil，bead cord）

bead chafer （轮胎）胎圈包布（贴在胎圈外部的胶布层，直接与轮辋的胎圈座接触，有时亦称 bead wrapping）

bead core 胎圈芯（由钢丝圈 "bead ring"，三角胶条 "apex" 和胎圈芯包布 "bead core flipper" 所制成的胎圈部件）

bead (core) flipper （轮胎）胎圈芯包布（包在钢丝圈和三角胶条外面的胶布亦称 bead wire guard）

bead diameter at rim seat 在轮辋座上的胎圈直径

beaded edge rim 卷边轮辋，软边胎轮辋

beaded (-edge) tire 软边轮胎，楔式轮胎（轮胎胎圈为软边结构，有一楔形边用来嵌入轮辋卷边内，如：自行车的轮胎）

bead edge 胎圈出边（指其包皮、胎趾胶、帘布被挤出的现象）

beader 卷边装置，翻边机

bead face 轮胎胎圈底部（= bead base）

bead filler （轮胎）胎圈的填胶层（在胎圈包布 "chafer" 和外帘布层 "outer plies" 之间，将后者箍紧在胎圈钢丝圈 "bead ring" 上的硬橡胶片）

bead fit pressure 胎圈密合压力

bead flange （轮辋夹持轮胎胎圈，给轮胎提供轴向支撑的凸缘）轮缘（= rim flange。其中一件式轮辋两侧均为固定轮缘 "fixed flange,"二件~四件式轮辋的一侧和五件式轮辋的两侧轮缘为可卸式轮缘 "detachable flange"）

bead-forming ring 轮胎胎圈钢丝圈（= bead wire ring）

bead hammer （大型轮胎拆卸用的）滑锤式胎圈拆卸器，胎圈拆卸锤

bead heel （轮胎胎圈的）胎踵（胎圈外侧与轮辋胎圈座圆角接触的部位，简称 heel）

beadless tire 直边式轮胎［相对于楔边式而言，见 beaded (-edge) tire］

bead lock band　胎圈锁箍

bead lock ring　轮辋锁圈（装在轮辋锁圈槽内，锁止挡圈或座圈的弹性圈）

bead lock-style rim　胎圈锁形轮辋

bead of air spring　（空气悬架中）空气弹簧的密封沿口

bead radius　（轮辋）胎圈座圆角半径

bead reinforcement　（轮胎）胎圈加强层

bead reinforcing strip　（轮胎）胎圈加强带

bead ring　（组成轮胎胎圈芯的）钢丝圈（由包胶钢丝按一定断面形状排列制成的刚性环，见 bead bundle）

bead ring wrapper　钢丝圈缠绕布（缠在钢丝圈外或接头处的胶布条）

bead seater band ring　轮辋的胎圈座环

bead seater　（无内胎轮胎装在轮辋上充气时用的）胎圈压装器（在充气前，压装器将胎圈压在轮辋的突缘上，在充气过程中，逐步将压装器沿突缘的斜边紧压下去，胎圈与轮辋之间形成气密结合"air tight seal"，直到轮胎内的气压将其压紧在轮辋上为止）

bead seat mat　（汽车座椅的）木珠网坐垫

bead seat (of rim)　（轮辋向胎圈提供径向支撑的）胎圈座

bead separator　（将胎圈剥离轮辋的）轮胎拆卸器，胎圈剥离器

bead set　（车轮轮辋上的）胎圈挡锁装置（平式轮辋等的挡圈、锁圈及座圈等轮胎锁挡件的总称）

bead stiffener　轮胎胎圈加强层

bead toe　（轮胎胎圈）的胎趾（胎圈内侧的端边）

bead tyre　卷边轮胎

bead unseating test　轮胎胎圈脱座试验（用实验方法确定从车轮辋圈上压出胎圈所需施加的载荷）

bead weld (ing)　堆焊

bead width　（轮胎）胎圈宽度（指胎圈外表面至内表面胎趾"bead toe"的最短距离）

bead wire isolation　胎圈钢丝圈隔离胶（加贴在钢丝圈外帘布层间的薄胶片）

bead wire ring　轮胎胎圈钢丝圈（= bead-forming ring, bead wire bundles, bead bundles, bead wire tape）

bead wire wrap　钢丝圈缠绕布（缠绕在钢丝圈外或接头处的胶布条）

bead wrapping　见 bead chafer

beam　①梁，横梁，横杆②束，射束（指仅仅朝向某一方向具有鲜明的单一指向性的发射的电波、音波和光波，以及离子、电子等粒子流，并以朝着特定的方向集中各种波和粒子流能量为目的）③（汽车前照灯的）灯光（如：远光"high beam"，近光"low beam"）

beam adjusting disk plate　（前照灯主光轴等的）调光盘座（板）

beam axle　梁式轴，梁式车桥（原意为工字形截面梁非驱动车桥，现指任一种整体式非独立悬架车桥）

beam axle/leal spring combination　梁式车桥-钢板弹簧组合结构

beam camber　梁拱度（梁向上的拱起度）

beam center　（灯光的）光束中心（指光束最亮区域）

beam channel　槽钢，槽铁，U形铁，U型钢

beam control　灯光亮度控制，亮度调节，远近光调节

beam controllablehead-lighting system　照射光束可控前照灯照明系统（见 adaptive front-lighting system）

beam crane　梁式起重机

beam deflector switch　（前照灯）变光开关（= dimmer switch, DIM-switch, dip-switch)

beam distribution graph （车身的）弯曲变形分布图（两条曲线分别表示车身底板和外壳沿纵轴各点的弯曲变形，即挠度值）

beam element （汽车前照灯），发光元件

beamforming system （多声源混合噪声分离评价的）波束混成系统

beam frequency 弯曲振动频率

beam indicator lamp （前照灯）远近光指示灯（= beam indicator, high-low-beam head light indicator, 有的只指示远光灯亮）

beaming ①弯曲（见 beaming test）②聚束，辐射

beaming curve （车辆构架等的）弯曲曲线（在静载或动载弯曲试验条件下取得的曲线，一般是横坐标表示位置，纵坐标表示弯曲变形位移量）

beaming limit 抗弯极限，弯曲极限（= beaming resistance limit）

beaming stiffness 抗弯刚度

beaming test （车身底盘构架等的）抗弯试验，弯曲试验 亦称 beam test

beam lead integrated circuit 梁式引线集成电路

beam of light 光束

beam of radiation （光线等的）射束

beam over windscreen （汽车的）风窗篷条

beam pattern （汽车前照灯）光照模式（指灯光的照射点的形状，即：光斑形状和照射强度）

beam selector （前照灯）变光开关

beam spreading （前照灯）光束锥照射角

beam switch button 前照灯变光按钮开关，前照灯变光踏钮开关（见 dimmer button）

beam trammel 游标卡尺，梁式卡尺，梁式圆规

beam wind 横风，侧风（= cross wind）

bearable 可支撑的，能承受的

bear box 轴承箱，轴承壳体

bearer ①支座，支架，支撑件，承载体②车厢下横梁③运载工具（参见 crossbearer）

bearing ①轴承，轴瓦②支撑座，支撑点③支承的，承载的，支持的

bearing accuracy 定位精度

bearing block （组合式）轴承座（包括底座和用螺栓固定在底座上的盖或上座）

bearing bond 轴瓦减磨层浇铸（轴瓦的减磨合金和钢瓦片之间的结合）

bearing burning-out 轴承烧熔（烧坏）

bearing bush （起轴承作用的）衬套，轴套（= bearing bushing）

bearing cage （滚动轴承）轴承隔圈，轴承保持架（保持滚柱或球间相对位置的隔环）

bearing cap ①轴承盖（如：主轴承盖，连杆轴承盖）②轴承壳（防尘）盖（= bearing cover）

bearing clearance 轴承间隙（指滑动轴承内表面和轴颈间的间隙）

bearing cone ①（可调向心球）轴承的内圈②圆锥滚子轴承的简称（= taper roller bearing）

bearing crush （滑动轴承轴瓦）压紧量（参见 crush height）

bearing cup ①轴承外圈②（滑动轴承）轴瓦（见 bearing shell）

bearing cup inserter 锥轴承外圈（或轴瓦的）压装工具

bearing driver 安装轴承用的心棒（压入轴承用）

bearing extractor 轴承拆卸器，轴承拉器

bearing face ①承载表面②轴承的工

作面③支承面④（特指螺母或螺栓头紧压其所紧固的零件表面的）压紧面

bearing flaking 轴承表面剥落（压碎）

bearing gauge 轴承量规，同心度量规

bearing insert ①轴瓦②轴套

bearing journal 轴承支撑的轴颈

bearing kelmet 油膜轴承合金（含铅20%~45%的铅青铜）

bearing lip （滑动轴承）轴瓦定位凸耳（为防止错动，设置在轴承瓦片背面端部等处的凸起部分，供轴瓦定位用，= bearing lug）

bearing loss 旋转损失（见 spin loss）

bearing material （浇挂在）滑动轴承（或轴瓦工作面上的）减磨材料（层）（特指 white metal）

bearing metal ①轴承合金②轴瓦

bearing packer 轴承加滑脂工具

bearing packing 轴承密封填料

bearing parting line 轴瓦剖分线

bearing plate 承重板，支撑板，垫板，底垫

bearing point 支撑点

bearing puller 轴承拉器（通过拉拔的方法拆卸各种轴承的工具）

bearing race 滚动轴承，（座）圈，包括内、外（座）圈

bearing race snap 轴承外圈上的止推环肩

bearing release lever （离合器）分离叉

bearing remover 轴承拆卸工具（= bearing replacer）

bearing retainer ①轴承护圈②滚动轴承保持架（亦称 bearing retaining ring）

bearing rib 轴承凸肩

bearing ring 滚动轴承（座）圈（亦称 bearing race，内、外圈及推力轴承中圈的通称）

bearing ring with aligning seat 带调心座的（滚动）轴承圈

bearing scope 拉瓦（指由于轴承间隙不当引起过热，或机油中杂质使轴瓦表面起痕、拉毛的现象）

bearing scraper 滑动轴承刮刀

bearing scuff 轴承拉伤，拉瓦（发动机曲轴轴颈在运转时将轴承表面拉毛或刮伤的现象）

bearing separator 轴承拆卸器（特指一般爪式轴承拉器无法使用的场合用的弯爪式拉器）

bearing shell 轴瓦（浇挂有巴氏合金减磨层的两块半圆形钢片）

bearing shield （滚动）轴承防尘圈

bearing sleeve 轴承衬套，轴承套，轴套（支撑轴颈，起滑动轴承作用的衬套）

bearing spacer 轴承隔圈

bearing spread 轴承（的）过盈量，盈量（指轴承制造直径稍大于其座孔直径，以保证轴承与其座孔的压配合）

bearing spring 支撑弹簧，托簧

bearing strip 轴瓦补偿垫片

bearing surface 支承表面，轴承工作表面

bearing tension indicator 轴承紧度指示器

bearing thrust plate 轴承止推片（承受轴承所受推力）

bearing thrust washer 轴承推力垫圈，轴承止推环

bearing track 轴承（滚柱或球的）滚道

bearing-up pulley 传动带张紧轮

bearing wheel 支撑轮

beating file （车身板件的）敲平手锉，锉刀式敲平手锤

beat noise （轮胎的噪声和发动机、驱动系噪声相互干扰而产生的60~120Hz，变动周期2~4次/秒的）敲击噪声

beat of pointer (仪表)指针的摆动
beaver back 海狸背型(车身后部的一种造型,后背的下部向外倾斜成斜坡形)
beck cone (锥齿轮的)背锥,背锥面(通常指锥齿轮轮齿的大端端面的圆锥面,它与分度锥面同心且垂直相交)
Becker's soap-bubble method 拜克肥皂泡法(用于在等压条件下测量正常燃烧速度)
bed ①(平)机座,底座,基础②试验台架③固定在基础之中,安装,嵌入
bedding-in oil (新轴承)磨合期用的机油
bed in ①磨合②嵌入
bed of face 支撑面(或配合面)的刮配,磨合
bed of fuel 燃料层
bed plate ①底板,底座,座板(= bed piece)②(特指内燃机的)下曲轴箱(在曲轴箱和油底壳之间的箱体,设有主轴承座及安装平面,有时包括油底壳)
beefier 功率、性能强大的车辆
Beema (德国)宝马(BMW 的俚称,= Beemer)
beep ①大型吉普车(见 jeep)②(汽车喇叭的)嘟嘟声,高频笛音③按喇叭,发嘟嘟声
Beer-Lambert law 拜耳-朗伯特定律(亦称 Beer Lambert relationship 拜耳-郎伯特关系式,表示光通过某介质时被吸收的量随该介质的厚度及其克分子浓度变化而变化的关系,用于测定柴油机等的排烟浓度)
beer tank (运输)啤酒(的)槽车
Beetle 甲壳虫牌(轿车,德国大众汽车公司,在二次大战后投产的省油普及型空冷后置发动机轿车)
BEF 见 brake efficiency factor
before bottom (dead) center 在下止点前,在下止点前(简称 BBC)
before control (事)前控制,事先控制(为 after control 的反义)
before exhaust valve opening 在排气门开启前(简称 BEVO)
beforehand 事先,预先
beginning circle of involute profile 渐开线的起始圆(指开始有渐开线轮廓的圆)
beginning of delivery 泵油始点(高压油泵柱塞移至喷油开始时的位置,以针阀被顶起为标志的,= beginning of injection)
behavio(u)r ①(指机器设备的)(运转)状态,(工作)情况(使用)性能,(作用)方式②(指性能,状态的)(变化)特性,(变化)曲线③(泛指)特点、特性,性能功效,作用,状态
BEL 公共汽车专用车道(见 bus exclusive lane)
Belgian block test surface (汽车加振试验用)比利时条石试验路面([美],=[英] Belgian pavé,亦称 Belgian pavement,指汽车强化试验用凹凸石砌路面,在比利时常见,故名)
belisha ①(指示行人可优先横过马路的)黄色闪光信号灯(亦称 belisha beacon, 或 beacon, 美国称 beacon beam)②危险信号(标志)装置,危险信号灯,航标灯(Belisha 是英国一位运输大臣的名字)
Beijing Jeep Corporation Ltd. 北京吉普车有限公司
bell ①钟,铃,钟声②钟形罩,钟形物③喇叭口,漏斗,扩散管
Belleville oil seal 俾利维利油封(一种垫圈式膜片弹簧密封圈)
Belleville (-type) spring ①(离合器等使用的)膜片弹簧(一般为中心开孔,沿孔圆周有切口的锥形圆弹簧片)②(进、排气门的转阀器

的）碟形弹簧（指在气门弹簧力作用下变形，迫使滚珠在转阀器罩盖斜面滑槽内转动的盘形弹簧）

bell housing 钟形壳，钟形罩（如：发动机的飞轮—离合器壳等）

bell-mouthed cylinder 喇叭口缸孔（如：缸孔上部因热变形而直径略大）

bellows ①防尘波状套管；波纹管，波纹套②（空气弹簧等的波状）气囊

bellows framed door 拉门，折叠式门

bellows-pressure gauge 波纹箱式压力计

bellows-type actuator 波纹管式执行器

bellows type air spring 波囊式空气弹簧（亦称 bellows-type pneumatic spring，由夹有帘线的橡胶囊和充入其内腔的压缩空气构成的一种空气弹簧）

bell-shape (d) flex spline （谐波齿轮传动中的）钟形柔轮（指柔轮的基本形状成钟形者）

bell type Rzeppa universal joint 钟形壳球笼式等速万向节，薛帕式万向节（见 Rzeppa universal joint）

belly dumper 底卸式自卸汽车（= bottom dumper）

below-standard size car 小于标准尺寸的轿车

below the throttle valve 在节气门下方，节气门后方（简称 BTV）

below throttle valve EGR system 节气门后的废气再循环系统（再循环废气的入口设在节气门后方）

belt ①带，皮带，钢带；传动带②（特指）轮胎的带束层（子午胎和带束斜交胎胎面基部下、沿胎面中心线圆周方向箍紧胎体的材料层）③车身腰线④（汽车乘员的）安全带⑤用带系住，系上带子

belt airbag 安全带气囊（安全带贴身的一面装有带爆发装置的带状气囊，临碰撞前的瞬间气囊爆发而形成充气软垫，分散、消减乘员所受的冲击力）

belt anchorage （汽车乘员）安全皮带（在车身上的）固定点（= belt mounting）

belt bias tyre 带束斜交轮胎（指具有与子午胎相同的带束层箍紧的斜交轮胎胎体的充气轮胎）

belt brake 带式制动器（= band brake）

belt chassis dynamometer 履带式底盘测功机（用履带模拟路面）

belt composition 传动带润滑剂

belt cone 锥形传动带轮，皮带级轮，皮带塔轮

belt connector 传动带接头，传动带搭扣

belt creep 传动带蠕变而拉长打滑（= creep of belt）

belt drive 传动带传动（= belt gear, pulley drive）

belted ①用安全带扣住的，用带系住的②带束的（指轮胎）

belted-bias tire 带束斜交轮胎，斜交束带轮胎（以带束层箍紧斜交轮胎胎体的充气轮胎）

belt edge filler （子午胎）钢丝束带的压边带（由高强度橡胶制成，压贴钢丝束带两侧边，防止束带错动）

belted radial ply tire 带束子午线轮胎（简称 belted radial tire，由于子午线轮胎均有带束层，故多简称 radial ply tire 或 radial tire，即子午胎）

belt horsepower 传动带（传动）功率

belt idle pulley 传动带惰轮，中介轮，导轮（亦称 belt ider, mule ider，当该惰轮同时起调节传动带松紧作用时亦称）张紧轮，紧度调节轮（为 tension adjuster 的一种，

= belt tensioning pulley)
belting ①传动带②传动带传动
belt intersection ①传动带交点②（车身）腰线交点
belt lacing 皮带搭扣（参见 lace①）
belt-line ①［美］（汽车车身的）腰线（指绘制车身侧视图时概括整个车身下部两侧的上边线条，=［英］waist rail line，亦称 door belt fascia, belt rail）②装饰带线③流水线④环行路
belt-line production 流水线生产
belt moulding 车身装饰条带，车身模制嵌条（= body belt moulding）
belt mounting 见 belt anchorage
belt puller （汽车乘员）安全带的拉紧装置
belt pulley crown diameter 皮带轮轮脊直径（最大直径）
belt/pulley-type continuously variable transmission 传动带-传动带盘式无级变速器
belt retractor 安全带收紧器（将安全带自动收回其卷筒，调节带的长短，以适应人体，并且在发生事故时，将带锁死的装置）
belt sag 传动带垂度
belt seat 有安全带的座椅
belt slack 传动带松动
belt slip 传动带打滑
belt tension adjuster 传动带张紧度调节装置（亦称 belt tightener, belt tensioner, belt tension）
belt tensioning pulley 传动带张紧轮（亦称 belt tension, idle pulley, belt tightening puller）
belt tension release lever 传动带放松杆，传动带张紧杆
belt transmission 传动带传动（= belt drive）
belt type automatic transmission 传动带型无级变速器，传动带型自动变速器，传动带式自动变速机构

belt up 戴上安全带
belt width 皮带宽度
BEM 边界元法（见 boundary element method）
bench ①台，工作台，架，座②（试验）台架，试验装置
bench board 操纵台，控制盘
bench charge 台架充电（蓄电池从车上拆下，在台架上充电）
bench life （由）台架试验（确认的）的耐久性，台架试验寿命
benchmark ①标准，规范②水准点③标准检查程序（亦写作 bench mark）④以…为标准
bench-scale experiment 实验室试验，台架试验，台试（亦称 bench test）
bench seat （车身内）长凳座位，长条座椅
bench test failure 台架试验中发生的（零件）损坏或故障
bench work 钳工工作，钳工作业
bend ①弯管，弯头，弯道，弯曲处②弯曲③使弯曲
bend alloy 弯管时填充管子用的易熔合金
bend elastic constant 弯曲（的）弹性常数（见 elastic constant）
bending ①弯曲，挠曲；弯曲度②（使其他物体）弯曲的，挠曲的
bending deflection 挠度，挠偏转，弯曲变形
bending fatigue life 弯曲疲劳寿命
bending fatigue resistance 弯曲疲劳强度
bending light （汽车前照灯的）转向随动照明
bending moment 弯曲力矩，弯矩（参见 moment of deflection）
bending radius 弯曲半径
bending strength 抗弯强度（工件在弯曲断裂前所承受的最大正压力）
Bendix drive type starter 邦迪克斯起动机，邦迪克斯起动电动机（惯

性啮合式起动机，亦称 Bendix stater，inertia-type starter）

Bendix screw 邦迪克斯（驱动机构）螺旋齿螺杆

bendix-tracta joint 见 tracta joint

Bendix type brake tester 邦迪克斯型制动试验台（滚筒式制动试验台，亦称 Bendix brake tester, roller-type tester）

Bendix-Weiss constant velocity joint 邦迪克斯-韦斯式等速万向节（球叉式万向节，= weiss universal joint）

bend loss （管路）弯头阻力损失

bend safer 弯道安全设施

bend test 弯曲试验（对试件施加静弯矩或弯曲力，测量其相应的挠度，直至断裂）

bend the throttle ①踩下加速踏板 ②按下节气门按钮

Benett type side slip tester （汽车车轮的）回转型侧偏试验台（试验台的车轮支撑件可转动，根据其转动量，可直接测出车轮的侧偏角，亦称 pivot type side slip tester）

benlin（e） ①驾驶员座位与客座分隔开的华贵轿车 ②老式四轮轿车

bent ①弯曲，弯头 ②弯曲的，弓形的

bent axis axial piston pump 弯体式轴向活塞泵

bent-axis motor 缸筒斜置式液力马达（缸筒轴线相对于驱动轴线斜置，亦称 tilted-body motor）

bent frame 弯曲形状的车架，曲线形状的车架（= curved frame）

bentone（-thickened）grease 膨润土润滑脂，皂土（稠化）润滑油（稠化）（加有膨润土、皂土等增稠剂，= bentonite grease）

Benz ①本茨（德国人 Carl Benz，首次将燃用煤气的 otto 四冲程内燃机改成的小汽油机，装在一辆三轮车上，1886 年 1 月 26 日为其专利正式立案之日。后人多将这一天作为第一辆内燃机汽车的诞生日）②（德国）奔驰牌轿车名

benzene 苯（C_6H_6）

benzin（e） 轻质汽油，挥发油，石油精，石油醚［亦称 ligroin（e）］

benzolene（亦写作 benzoline） 苯汽油

Benz's classes 奔驰轿车的级别（奔驰轿车分 A, C, E, S 四级，C 级为其初级车，E 级为其中级车，S 级为其高级车。休闲车用 M 表示，厢式车用 V 表示，越野车用 G 表示，型号中的数字 280、300、500 等分别表示排量为 2.8 升，3 升和 5 升，型号最后的字母：L 表示加长型，Diesel 表示柴油车，如 S600L 表示为 6 升排量的加长型高级轿车。此外，还有在法国生产的 Smart，两个跑车系列 CLK 和 SLK，以及 SUV 系列 M 级）

Bernoulli's theory 伯努利理论

berth bus 卧铺客车（= sleeper bus）

beryllium copper spring 铍铜弹簧，铜铍合金弹簧（铍 Be2.25%，有时含有少量的镍铬等，余为铜）

bespoke ①定制的，预定的，已预定出去的 ②预约

best balance vortex incline degree （发动机汽缸进气口的）最佳平衡涡流斜角［指进气口斜角度可保证形成的进气涡流（vortex）中的横涡（swirl）-纵涡（tumble）比呈最佳平衡值］

best fuel economy spark timing 最佳燃油经济性点火正时（简称 BFEST）

best injection timing 最佳喷油正时（简称 BIT）

best seller 畅销车

best-straight-linearity error 最佳直线性误差（指实际值与标称值的正、负差值达到的最小极值）

beta method β法（一种分析和控制汽车动态特性的理论和方法）

between-axles cab （位于前后桥中间、颠簸最小处的）桥间驾驶室

bevel ①锥，锥体②斜面，斜角③斜角的，锥面的

bevel cone friction clutch 锥形摩擦离合器

bevel drive shaft （一端或两端均装有）锥齿轮（的）传动轴（多用于驱动顶置式凸轮轴）

bevel friction gear 斜摩擦轮

bevel gear 锥齿轮（分度曲面为圆锥面的齿轮，见 reference surface）

bevel (gear) differential 锥齿轮差速器（由行星锥齿轮机构所构成的差速器）

bevel gear drive 锥齿轮传动（主动轴与从动轴轴线成直角或不在一条直线上的锥齿轮传动机构）

bevel gear pair 锥齿轮副（指一对轴线相交的锥齿轮）

bevel gear pair with small teeth difference 少齿差锥齿轮副（由齿数差很少的锥齿轮组成的齿轮副）

bevel gear transmission 见 bevel gear drive

bevel hub 锥形孔轮毂

bevel/hypoid gear pair 准双曲面圆锥形齿轮副（指一对轴线交错的圆锥形齿轮传动）

bevel joint ①斜接，斜面对接②斜接切口（= bevelled joint, diagonal joint, skew joint）

bevelled claw-clutch 斜齿牙嵌爪形离合器

bevel (l) ing ①斜切，斜削②偏斜，倾斜③做斜边，倒斜角

bevel piston ring 外斜面活塞环，外倒角活塞环

bevel seated valve 锥形工作面阀门，锥形座面气门（= taper-seat valve, conical valve）

bevel type final drive （汽车的）锥形齿轮型主传动，伞齿轮式主减速器

beverage holder （轿车驾驶座边等处的圆形）饮料瓶座，茶杯架

beverage tanker 饮料罐车（装备有相应的吸、排系统，运输液状食品的罐车）

BEVO 在排气门开启前（见 before exhaust valve opening）

bezel of head lamp （汽车前照灯玻璃）边框（= head lamp case rim, head-lamp glass-rim, lamp moulding, rim of head lamp）

BFC 制动力系数（见 brake force coefficient）

BGR 已燃气比率(见 burned gas ratio)

B_H （用钢球或硬质合金球试验的）布氏硬度（Brinell hardness）的简称（亦写作 B_h）

b. hp 制动功率，制动马力（brake horse-power 的简称，亦写作 bhp 或 BHP）

Bi 铋（bismuth）

bias ①偏差，偏移，偏置，偏压，偏流，偏斜，不按直线前进的倾向，位移，斜线，斜痕②（在液力传动的叶轮中特指叶片的）边斜角（设计流线处的叶片进、出口边相对于轴平面的斜角）③斜的，偏置的，偏动的④使偏，偏重，加偏压；使…有偏差，使倾向一方

bias balancing interaxle differential 前后驱动轮速差平衡用桥间差速器

bias charge （电子控制系统中电荷转移器的）偏置电荷（在模拟应用中确定无信号电平、并注入所有势阱中的电荷）

biasing 见 variable torque dividing

bias magnet 偏阻磁块（安全气囊系统传感器中防止汽车正常加、减速等所引起的振动使传感器误触发的磁铁）

bias plate （轴向柱塞泵的）斜盘
bias (ply) tyre ［美］斜交（帘布层）轮胎（帘布层和缓冲层各相邻层帘线交叉，且与胎面中心成小于90°角排列的充气轮胎，亦称diagonal 或 crossply ［英］tyre）
bias voltage （输入）偏置电压（input bias voltage 的简称）
biaxial 双轴的
bib cock 排放开关，排放旋塞，弯嘴旋塞（= bibcock, draining cock, drain cock, discharge cock, purge cock, dain tap）
bichromate dipped finish 重铬酸盐浸渍处理（将金属浸入重铬酸钠与硫酸的水溶液中，以清除积垢及氧化皮）
bicurvature 双曲率
bicycle carrier （位于轿车后端或车顶的）自行车架
bidirectional bus 双向总线
bidirectional data link 双向数据链路（可在两终端或两电子控制模块间相互发送或接收信息的一条通信线路，亦称 universal asynchronous receiver/transmitter。通用公司将可在发动机电子控制模块"ECM"和车身电子控制模块"BCM"之间以及二者与其他控制模块间相互传递和接受信息的链路，称为"BCD 800 circuit"）
bidirectional diagnostics interface 双向诊断接口
bidirectional diode thyristor （电子控制系统中使用的）双向两极可控硅，双向二极闸流管（一种具有两个在电压/电流特性的第一和第三象限内，有基本上相同的开关特性的引出端的半导体开关元件）
bidirectional vehicle 双向行驶车辆（两头都可向前行驶的车辆）
bifilar bulb （汽车）双丝灯泡（①一根灯丝为远光，一根灯丝为近光的双丝前照灯灯泡 ②一根灯丝为制动灯，另一根为尾灯的双丝尾灯灯泡，= double-filament bulb, two filament bulb）
bifilar winding ①双线绕法 ②双线绕阻；双股绕组，双线无感线圈
bi-focal headlamp 双焦点大灯（装有带两个焦点的分段式单反射镜或双反射镜，通常使用单灯丝灯泡，作为四灯制前照灯的近光灯，亦称 homofocal 或 homo-focus headlamp）
bi-fuel vehicle 两用燃料汽车（具有两套相互独立的燃油系统，分别但不可同时供油，如汽油/压缩天然气两用燃料汽车等）
bifunctional Litronic Headlight 电子控制远-近光双功能前照灯（简称 bi-Litronic，该灯内装有一个高亮度气体放电灯泡，可由电子系统控制移动到远光或近光位置，而由同一反射镜反射出远光或近光，见 Litronic）
bifurcated 分叉的
big-block engine 大功率、大转矩的发动机（特指 20 世纪 60~70 年代美国生产的铸铁缸体和缸盖，使用常规化油器的 V 型 8 缸发动机）
big-end 连杆大头（连杆曲轴端）
big-end bearing 连杆大头轴承（亦称 bottom-end bearing, crankpin bearing, = ［美］connecting rod bearing 及 rod bearing）
big-end bearing cap 连杆大头轴承盖，曲轴连杆轴承盖
big-end bearing shell 连杆大头轴瓦，曲轴连杆轴瓦
big-end bolt 连杆（大头）螺栓
big-end half bearing 连杆大头对轴承（连杆大头对开式滑动轴承）
big foot car 大脚汽车（一种车轮大，车身小的汽车）
bigge ①水陆两用汽车车体的水下部分 ②舱底 ③弯度，凸度，拱度，挠

度，上弯度
big repair 大修（理）（= major repair, heavy repair, capital repair）
big-rig motor home 大型旅居车（旅游车之一种，车厢内有4~6人的卧床，有炊事等生活设备）
bihexagon 12角形的（螺母、螺栓头、套筒等）
bilateral ①双向的，双向作用的②两面的，两侧的
bilateral servo 双输入伺服系统，双输入随动系统，（指由两个输入信号控制或输出的一部分作为输入反馈的伺服系统）
bilateral tolerance 双向公差
bi-Litronic 见 bifunctional Litronic Headlight
billion [美、法] 十亿（10^9）；[英、德] 万亿（10^{12}）
bimanualness 双手操作，双手控制
bi-metal cut-out switch 双金属断路开关，双金属切断开关
bimetallic 双金属的（指用两种膨胀系数不同的金属制成的）
bimetallic actuator 双金属促动器，双金属片型执行元件（亦称 bimetallic motor）
bimetallic circuit flat fuse 电路的双金属片熔片
bimetallic corrosion 双金属腐蚀（= couple corrosion, galvanic corrosion，指暴露在电解液中的两种不同金属件接触时产生的电化学腐蚀）
bimetallic oil pressure sensor 双金属式油压（表）传感器
bimetal (lic) spring 双金属弹簧
bimetal (lic) switch 双金属温控开关（由两种热膨胀系数不同的金属制成的温度控制的开关）
bimetal vacuum switching valve 双金属式温控真空阀（根据水温或进气温度等控制各种真空通道的阀门，简称 BVSV）
Bimmer BMW 宝马公司的俚称
bimotor (ed) 双发动机（的）
binary ①二，双②二部分组成的③双成分的④二元的⑤二自由度的⑥二进制的⑦双燃料的
binary circuit 二进制电路（用二进制信号工作的电路）
binary code 二进制代码（只使用1，0两个符号的计算机代码）
binary coding number system 二进制代码记数制（指使用二进制代码、逢二进一的记数制，在计算机内一切信息的存放、处理、传送均采用二进制的形式）
binary digit 二进制数（常简称 bit，比特，①指二进制数字1和0中的任一个②二进制中的位，二进制字串中有一个数字0或1，表示有1位，如32位，表示由32个0或1组成的串③一组脉冲中的一个单脉冲）
binary form 二进制形式（指用1和0两个数的各种组合来表现各种数码的形式，亦称 binary notation）
binary inverter 二进制反相器（仅有一个输入端和一个输出端，当输入端的信号为0时，输出端产生信号1，而输入端为1时，输出端为0）
binary mass balancing 两个自由度系统的质量平衡
binary notation 见 Binary form
binary signal 二进制信号（指由0和1表示的二进制的量化信号）
bind 结合，黏合，连接
binder ①黏结剂②使二者结合或连接的器件（如 binder bolt 连接螺栓）
bind in 卡住，阻塞
binding ①（起）黏合、胶合、黏结，束缚，约束（作用）的②（汽车地毯、软垫等用条形材料做的）滚边，包边③（装筛件，板件的）

压条，压缝条④阻滞、卡死、咬合（如制动蹄对制动鼓或制动钳摩擦块对制动盘的卡滞）

binding end cap ①压条端封（压条等的端头保护件）②端部封盖，端封盖

binding force 结合力，内聚力（= binding power）

bind metal 浇铸轴承合金（参见 castin metal）

binnacle （汽车驾驶室内的）仪表盘（通常指组合在圆形外壳内的一组仪表，带或不带开关件，多位于转向盘柱附近）

binocular field 双眼可见区，双眼能见区

binocular parallax 两点视差（从与物体不在一条直线上的两点观察该物体时产生的物体位置上的视差）

Binz 宾治（总厂设在德国南部 Stuttgart 的著名汽车改装厂，以改装 Benz 车为主，从 1936 年起一直为不同的车型提供改装服务）

bio-alcohol 生物乙醇

bio-degradable 可生物降解的（指可被细菌腐烂的）

bio-diesel ①生物柴油［以植物果实和动物脂肪为原料与醇类交酯化反应（transesterification reaction）获得的压燃机用含氧、不含硫、低排放清洁燃料］②植物油柴油［指作为柴油机代用燃料的植物油，如：菜籽油（rape oil），亦称（rape seed oil）或（colza oil）］

bio-diesohol 生物乙醇-柴油混合燃料（见 diesohol）

bio-gas 生物基天然气

biological ①生物学（上）的②生物制品，生物制剂

biomass-derived methanol 植物源甲醇（汽车的绿色燃料）

biomass fuel 生物燃料（参见 biodiesel）

biometrics data （驾驶人员的脉搏和心电图等的）生理状态测定数据

bionics 仿生（电子）学

bioplastics 生物塑料（亦写作 Bio-Plastics，指由植物原料而不是传统的石油类原料制成的塑料）

biopolar transistor 双极型晶体管（晶体管分为场效应和双极晶体管两大类。凡由两个 P-N 节构成的，均被称为双极型晶体管）

biosensor （乘员和驾驶人员的）生理信息传感器（如：用来获取驾驶者心跳次数，以便判断是否处于临睡状态的脉搏传感器等）

bi-pass 双行道，双行车路，双通

biphase ①双相②双相的，两相的

bipolar ①双极②双极的；双极型的；双极性的③双向的，两种性质相反的

bipolar heater 双极（性）预热器，双极（性）预热塞

bipolar integrated circuit 双极型集成电路（以双极型晶体管为基本有源元件构成的集成电路）

birds-eye view 鸟瞰图，俯视图

birefraction 双折射（亦称 refrangence，光射入各向异性物质后，折射光线分裂为振动方向相互垂直的两束光的现象）

Birfield tyre constant velocity joint 伯尔菲德型（球笼式）等速方向节（早期的 Rzeppa 型球笼式万向节有分度杆，改进后的 Rzeppa 型又称 Birfield 型，用钟形壳和星形套的圆弧滚道对称地偏离万向节中心，而靠内，外子午滚道的交叉使钢球定位）

birotary engine 双缸转子发动机

birr 机械、车轮等转动时的噪声

bismuth 铋（Bi）（熔点 271℃，为熔断丝的易熔合金原料之一）

BIST （系统或器件的）内置自检测（功能，built-in self-test 的简称）

bistable amplifier 双稳态放大器
bistable circuit 双稳态电路（只有两个输出组态或输出图形的时序电路，通常指单激励双稳态电路）
bistatic antenna （车用微波雷达的）发射-接收分置式天线
bistatic sonar 收发分置式声呐
bit 见 binary digit
BIT ①最佳喷油正时（best injection timing 的简称）②车载信息终端（board information terminal 的简称）
BITE 装在机内的自检测设备（built-in test equipment 的简称）
bit holes （气门头上的研磨工具）卡装凹孔
32-bit microcontroller 32 位微处理器（亦写作 thirty-two bit microcontroller，指字长为 32 个二进制位的微处理器）
bitone horn （汽车）双音喇叭（指两只具有不同音调的喇叭组成的喇叭组）
bit-oriented organization （存储器的）按位编排（存储器的一种排列，其中每个存储区由一个存储单元构成）
bit stock 钻柄，手摇钻柄
bitumen mat （车身壁板等的）沥青底层，沥青涂层，沥青垫层（隔声、防振等）
bituminous concrete 沥青混凝土
bituminous macadam road 沥青碎石路
bituminous paint 沥青涂料（用于金属件的保护涂层）
bivalve 双阀的，双气门的
BIW 白车身（未涂漆的车身，body in white 的简称）
biweekly inspection 每半个月的定期检查；两周一次的定期检查
Bi-Xenonheadlight incl. bending light 带弯道转向照明的双氙气前大灯
BL 英国利兰公司（British Layland 的简称，为 Rover Group 的旧称）
black bolt 粗制螺栓
black box ①黑匣子（记录事故的录音装置，亦称 crash recorder）②控制单元，控制器（= control unit）
black chromium plating （装饰性）黑镀铬（层）光亮黑色镀铬
blackening ①发黑处理②（指灯泡用久后由于灯丝金属沉积而使）灯泡玻璃发黑（的现象，bulb blackening 的简称）
black in （轴承）按涂色刮配
black lead ①黑铅；石墨②在润滑剂中加石墨
black light 不可见光（肉眼看不见的光线，如：红外线、紫外线等）
black nut ①防松螺母，锁止螺母，保险螺母（= check nut）②（未磨光的）黑皮螺母
black-out device 遮光装置
black-out dial 发光表盘，荧光表盘（指无灯光照明的表盘，= luminous dial）
black out head lamp 带遮光罩的（防空式）前照灯
black over-fender 黑色翼子板
blacksmith ①锻工②锻的，锻造的
black smoke 黑烟（通常指柴油机排出的小于 1μm 的碳粒烟尘）
black washer 粗制垫圈，黑皮垫圈（bright washer 的反义词）
bladder type pneumatic spring 囊状空气弹簧
blade ①零件的扁平部分②扁平的直零件（如：起子口，刮水片，转子的叶片，刀片等）
blade angle ①（动液传动装置叶轮元件等的）叶片角（指叶片骨线沿液流方向的切线与泵轮旋转方向的夹角，流线上各点的叶片角是不同的，一般只注明叶片进、出口的叶片角）②刀片安装角③风扇叶片偏斜角

blade angle shift （自动变速器的）叶片转位换挡，叶片角度换挡（指改变动液元件叶片的角度以改变其转矩传递能力的换挡）

blade angle system （动液传动装置叶轮元件等的）叶片角制（分为A制与B制，指确定叶片角的方式）

blade connector 片形（电）接头，（带片状连接端的连线片）

bladed impeller （离心泵等）叶片式泵轮

bladed tread design 刀槽形胎面花纹结构

blade height ratio 叶片高度比（叶片长度 L 与叶片圆平均直径 D 之比 L/D）

blade opening coefficient 叶片开度系数（叶片间最狭窄部分的距离与叶片间距的比值）

blade pitch 叶片节距（= blade spacing）

blade plan form 叶片平面展开形状

blade rim 叶轮轮辋

blade rubber 刮水的橡胶刮片

blade socket 片式插座

blade terminal （电）片式插头，接线片（带片状的连接端）

blade-tip clearance （涡轮）叶片端（与壳体内表面的）间隙

blade wheel 叶轮（= vane wheel）

blanch ①镀锡②使变白，粉饰

blank ①空白的②空间③（计）空位，间隔④熄灭脉冲⑤熄灭，作废，使无效

blank cover 塞，盖，堵片，堵盖

blank flange 管子突缘盖，突缘盖，无孔突缘，管口盖板

blank gasoline 无添加剂的汽油

blanking piece ①（封闭孔口的平形金属）盖板（= banking plate）②（堵孔的）堵头（= blanking plug）

blank run （发动机）空转

blank terminal （电子器件的）空引出端（无内部连接，可用做外部连接线的支撑、对器件功能无影响的引出端）

blast ①鼓风，吹风②喷砂；喷丸，喷射③爆炸

blast engine 鼓风机（= blowing engine）

blaster 喷砂装置，喷丸装置

blast lamp 喷灯（= blow lamp）

blast type 强风式（如风冷式发动机的冷却方式，火花塞的高压气流清洗方式等）

blast wave 冲击波

bleed ①排放，排出（指：将液压系统内的工作油液排空、放净或排出、放泄渗入液压系统内的空气）②（排放工作油液或空气的阀门、螺钉、螺塞等的总称，= bleeder）③分压，分泄④分流

bleed air valve ①（液压系统的）空气排出阀②空气补给阀（化油器式发动机中，在节气门与喉管之间补给二次空气的单向阀，简称BAV）

bleeder ①排放装置（排放油液、空气、水等的阀，开关，螺塞，螺钉的通称）②分压器，分泄电阻（见 bleeder resistor）

bleeder plug 排放（油、液、空气的）螺塞（= bleeding plug）

bleeder resistor 泄漏电阻，分泄电阻（必要时可引泄或吸放一定量电流的电阻器）

bleeder screw 排放（油、流、空气的）螺钉（= bleeding screw）

bleeder type filter 分流式滤清器（见 bypass filter）

bleeder valve 排放（油液，空气的）阀门（= bleeding valve）

bleed-off flow control 分流控制，旁通控制（= bypass control）

bleed-off metering system ①（液力传动）泄流阀调节系统②（柴油

机）高压泵溢油计量系统

blend ①混合，配料，②混合物，掺和汽油，合金③（曲线，曲面等不同线段的）过渡部分，接合部分

blend composition （燃油的）混合组分

blended synthetic metallic motor oil 掺添合成金属添加剂的发动机润滑油

blending octane value 掺和辛烷值（简称 BOA，即乙醇或甲醇等与汽油掺和后的辛烷值，一般掺入 5% 的酒精可提高 2 个 MON，亦称 blend octane number）

blenometer 弹簧弹力测定仪

blik 镀锡铁皮，镀锡钢皮，白铁皮

blind ①帘，幕，幔，百叶窗，屏风，遮阳板，遮光板，挡板，防护板，罩；塞子，螺旋塞②封闭的，堵死的，无出口的，不通的；隐蔽的，不显露的

blind area （驾驶员）视野盲区，视野死角区（= blind zone）

blind axle ①死轴，非旋转车轴；支撑轴，②非驱动桥（= dead axle, trailing axle）

blind corner 盲区弯道（山区公路上看不见的弯道或看不到尽头的弯道）

blind corner monitoring system （驾驶人员视线）盲区监视系统（简称 BCMS，显示驾驶者视线盲区死角的实时影像系统，亦称 blind-spot monitoring system、blind-spot information system）

blinder 遮光器件（如：遮光罩，遮阳板等）

blind fastener 单面紧固件，单面系固件（指只从构件单面紧固的连接件，如：木螺钉、铁钉、单面装压铆钉等）

blind hole 盲孔（= closed hole）

blinding ①填塞，堵死②炫目的，致盲的

blinding glare 眩光

blind joint 无间隙接头

blind operation 盲目操作（不靠视觉，仅凭仪表等进行驾驶等）

blind rivet 空心（单面装压）铆钉（详见 pop rivet）

blind roller 散热器帘卷轴

blind-side 盲侧（左座驾驶车辆的右侧、右座驾驶车辆的左侧盲区）

blind-side swipes （向）盲侧（变换车道时发生的）碰撞

blind spot 死角；盲点（驾驶员在正常驾驶位置上无论用眼或通过后视镜均看不见的区域）

blind-spot looking sensor 盲点（障碍物）观测传感器（亦称 blind-spot warning sensor, blind-sport detecting sensor）

blind spot monitor system （简称 BSM，亦称 blind area monitor system, 简称 BAM system）

Blindspotter 盲区警戒员（美 Eaton Vorad 公司研制的大型汽车列车用车侧障碍物雷达控测-警报系统的商品名）

blind spot viewer （汽车用）盲点观察器（装在驾驶员前方的荧光屏，以观察盲区的情况）

blind van 无窗式厢式车身

blink code （故障指示灯用闪光次数和每次闪光的停歇时间显示故障部位及内容的）闪光代码

blinker 闪光灯，闪光信号灯（= flasher lamp, blinking light）

blinking trafficator 转向闪光信号灯，转向闪光指示灯（= flashing trafficator, blinking turn signal）

blink rate ①眨眼率（指眼睑在规定条件下的眨眼频率）②闪视率，闪光率

BLIS （Ford 车的后方）盲区监测系统（blind location inspecting system

的简称，当车后部的雷达测得有车辆靠近或进入车后盲区时立即在后视镜上亮出警告光点）

blister ①气泡，水泡；局部隆起，起泡②（铸件）缩孔，砂眼，气孔③（轮胎）鼓包④（车身）流线型外罩，泡形罩（简称 BLSR）

blister fender （轿车等车身的）翼子板

blistering of paint 漆层表面起泡

BLM 无刷式电动机（brushless motor 的简称）

BLMC 英国利兰（德）汽车公司（British Leyland Motor Corporation 的简称）

block ①各种块状物（如：滑块，垫块，金属块）②滑车（组），滑轮③（汽缸）体④（疲劳载荷中的）载荷单元（指连续施加的恒幅载荷循环的特定次数，或同样重复的有限长度的谱载荷序列）⑤（计算机控制系统的）字块（指作为一个整体来处理的一串字或一个字符串），信息块（作为一个单位来处理的一组信息），地址块（存储器地址的一个连续范围或区域）⑥阻塞，障碍物⑦堵塞，断路

blockage area ratio 阻塞面积比（风洞中汽车模型的正面面积与风洞测定部位截面积之比，其值愈大，阻塞效应愈显著）

blockage effect 阻塞效应（汽车安放在风洞内以后，风的通过截面积减小，而汽车周围的风速相应增加的效应）

block brake 蹄式制动器（= shoe brake）

block-cast cylinder （多缸发动机）整体铸造缸体

block clutch 蹄式离合器

block construction 单元结构，积木式结构

block control 联锁式控制机构

block diagram 方框图，框图

block gauge 块规

block head cylinder 整体汽缸（汽缸盖与汽缸体铸成一整体）

blocking ①堵塞，阻塞；闭锁，联锁，镇定②单元化，模块化③（电子计算机控制系统信息传输、存储、处理中的）组块（指两个或更多的记录组成一个连续的记录组合，亦称"块"，以节省存储空间和提高计算机处理能力）④堵塞的，闭锁的

blocking capacitor 隔流电容器，阻直流电容器，级间耦合电容器（= block condenser）

blocking ring 见 baulk ring

block-mounted sensor 装在缸体上的传感器（如爆振传感器等）

block nut 锁紧螺母（= jam nut）

block-oriented organization （存储器的）按字块排列（储存器的排列方式，一个存储区构成一个字块）

block representation 方框图、方块图表示法

Block Shift technology （ROLLS-ROYCE Azure 的 8 挡自动变速器的）直接换挡技术（如：从 8 挡降到 4 挡，可不经过 7、6、5 挡）

block test 台架试验

block tire 实心轮胎（= band tire）

blood alcohol concentration 血液中酒精浓度（简称 BAC，亦称 blood alcohol content 或 blood alcohol level）

blooming （特指车身漆层表面上形成的）乳白色薄蒙膜层（由于上漆时寒冷潮湿所改）

blow ①鼓风，送风②烧损，漏气，爆炸，冲击③（熔断丝）熔断

blow-back （由于进气门关闭过迟或气门黏着而造成的）①进气歧管回火（= explosion in the carburettor）②部分混合气被压回进气歧管

blow-by ①从…中漏出，窜出，漏气

②（特指）窜气（发动机燃烧室内的燃气或可燃混合气经汽缸与活塞间隙窜入曲轴箱）

blow-by meter 曲轴箱窜气量测量计，窜气计量仪

blow-down ①放，排（如放水、排气）②扰动，增压③（特指四冲程发动机从排气门开启到活塞到达下止点，两冲程发动机从排气孔开启到进气孔开启的一段时间内，由于汽缸内气体的高压而产生的）膨胀排气

blower ①废气涡轮增压器（俚）②鼓风机③风扇（如汽车暖气或通风装置用的风扇等）

blower-cooled engine 鼓风式风冷发动机

blower guide ring 鼓风机导向环（引导风向）

blower impeller 鼓风机叶轮

blower scavenging system （二冲程发动机的）增压扫气系；增压换气式（利用增压器压送的新鲜空气扫除汽缸内的废气）

blower switch （汽车暖风和通风系）风扇开关

blow gun 喷枪（如：用压缩空气喷净车身管缝内的尘埃用的扁口喷枪）

blowing piston （活塞环磨损了的）漏气活塞

blow moulded plastic fuel tank 气压模铸塑料油箱

blown ①破损而漏气的（汽缸垫等）②被烧断的（熔丝等）③废气涡轮增压的（＝super charged）

blown down period （内燃机的）膨胀排气期（见 blowdown）

blown oil engine 增压式柴油机

blown-out tire （因被刺穿等原因而）爆破的轮胎（通常脱离轮辋，＝flat tire，deflated tire，collapsed tire）

blown-up tire 充足气的轮胎

blow off ①放气，排出②（轮胎）放炮③喷出④（混合气流速大于燃烧速度时产生的）吹灭（现象）

blow-off valve （增压器中防止增压压力过高的弹簧）安全阀，放气阀（亦称 boost control valve）

blow (-) out ①鼓风②（轮胎）爆裂③吹灭，熄弧④（熔断丝）熔断，烧断⑤（用压缩空气）吹通（堵塞的管路等）

blowout coil 灭火线圈，减弧线圈，清除火花线圈

blowout patch 补胎胶布，补胎垫

blow pipe ①吹管，火焰喷灯，焊枪，焊炬（＝blow lamp，［美］blow torch）②压缩空气输送管（＝blast pipe）

blow (-pipe) lamp 喷灯，焊灯（＝［美］blow torch）

blow-through turbocharger （火花点火式发动机用）直充式增压器（其压缩机直接将增压空气充入进气歧管）

blow torch 见 blow lamp

blow-up tire 充气轮胎，气胎（＝airfilled tire，air inflated tire，pneumatic tire）

Blue6 蓝6［德 Mercedes-Bens 公司对其满足 Euro 6（欧6）排放标准的柴油机货车的称谓。原符合 Euro 7 者称 Blue 7］

Bluebird 蓝鸟（日本 Nisson 轿车牌名）

blue control lamp 前照灯远光指示灯（＝beam indicator lamp）

Bluecore-2 （美 Cambridge Silicon Radio 公司"CSR"支持车载免提移动电话的）蓝牙外部芯片（可在40～85℃温度范围内工作）

BlueDIRECT （Mercedes-Bens S 级轿车和 CLS 的运动型轿车配备的新型 V6、V8）汽油直接喷射式高效发动机（商品名，据称其油耗可降低

24%，输出功率却进一步提高）

BlueEFFICIENCY （Mercedes-Benz 提出的）创新、优化、环保、高效理念［包含一整套具体的技术方案（BlueEFFICIENCY techniques）］

Blue e-motion VW公司电动车名（外形酷似该公司的"高尔夫"，由装在前部的85 kW电动机驱动，续行里程150 km）

blue flame 蓝焰（混合气燃烧过程中的焰前反应的第二阶段，即紧跟在冷焰后形成。冷焰中形成的大量甲醛在一定的温度下爆炸性的分解成醛基，发出蓝色辉光，故名）

blue gasoline 蓝色汽油（加抗爆剂后染成蓝色，表明为有毒的高辛烷值汽油）

blueing 发蓝处理（使钢铁件表面形成一层均匀致密带有磁性的Fe_3O_4，呈蓝黑色、黑色或棕褐色，厚度一般为$0.6 \sim 0.8 \mu m$的薄膜）

BlueLink （Hyundai的）车载通信系统（商品名，可连接智能手机和服务中心，为行车提供紧急救援、远程车辆控制及语言导航等服务）

Blue Metallic （汽车车身外壳的）金属光泽蓝色，蓝金属漆色

Blueprint ①（设计）蓝图②行动方案③型板

Blue-Ray player （高清晰度）蓝光播放装置

blue smoke 蓝烟（柴油机排烟的一种形态，通常由未完全燃烧的燃油和润滑油的微滴形成，尺寸一般小于$0.4 \mu m$）

Blue Tec system 蓝色技术系统（大型货车上安装的柴油机排放微粒物过滤再生装置，和尿素选择性NOx还原催化净化装置组成的排放净化系统的商品名，见DPF、SCR）

bluetooth 蓝牙（实现快速方便的数据与语音通信的无线网络技术，基于蓝牙技术，可实现使用任一种蜂窝式移动电话或车内音响系统在开车途中与外界的免提语音通信）

bluff body 宽型车身（指就其长度而言，显得较宽的车身，特指头部宽广、竖立的非流线型车身，风阻大，亦称钝体车身）

blunt angle 钝角

blunt nose 方头型（车身），钝头型车身（车头成方形，空气阻力大）

BM ①故障最少化②（交通）堵塞最小化（breakdown minimum 的简称）

BMC ①英国汽车公司（British Motor Corporation的简称，英国Rover Group 在称为 British Leyland 之前的旧称）②车后监控摄像机（back monitor camera 的简称）

BMCS 机动车辆安全运输局（Bureau of Motor Carrier Safety的简称）

BMD （废气分析的）取样袋少量稀释法（Bag Mini-Diluter的简称，在美国已成为传统定容取样法"CVS"的可接受的替代方法）

BMEP 平均有效制动压力（亦写作bmep，brake mean effective pressure 的简称）

BMEP balancer 平均有效制动压力平衡检测仪（检测各缸的压缩压力是否均等）

bmep required curve （汽车的）平均制动有效压力需用曲线（表示汽车在各种不同速度下克服总行驶阻力所需的bmep）

BMS 盲区监视系统（见blind corner monitoring system）

BMSC module （汽车全自动空调系统的）鼓风机电动机转速控制模块（blower motor speed control module的简称）

BMW ［德］宝马公司（Bayarische Motoren work 巴伐利亚发动机制造厂的简称，1916年创建，1928年生产第一辆轿车）

BMW i3 宝马 i3（宝马公司四人乘全电动锂离子电池轿车名，由 125 kW 电动机后轮驱动）

BMW i8 宝马 i8（宝马公司前、后分离动力装置型混合动力车的车名，该车前轮由锂离子电池和 125 kW 的电动机驱动，后轮由 164 kW 的三缸涡轮增压式发动机驱动，续行距离 130～160 km，0→100 km/h 7.9s，此外可加选购件：小型汽油机-发电机组在汽车行驶中发电，以延长续行里程）

BMW modic 11 宝马专用维修电脑 11 型（商品名）

BMW serials 宝马车系列（主要有 3、5、7 和 8 四个系列，其中 3 系列为中档轿车，5 系列为高档轿车，7 系列为豪华轿车，8 系列为超级豪华轿车。宝马车型号的第一个数字为系列号，第二、三个数字为排量，最后一个字母：i 表示燃油喷射，A 表示自动变速器，C 表示双座跑车，S 表示超级豪华。如：318iA，表示该车为 3 系列，排量 1800cc，燃油喷射，自动变速器。850Si 表示该车为 8 系列，5000cc 排量，超豪华型，燃油喷射）

board ①板，挡板，栏板，护板，壁板；仪表板；镶板、铺板，（电路）印刷板，插件板；配电板②操纵台，控制屏

board edge iron 包边（主板边缘的加强护板）

board information terminal 车载信息终端（简称 BIT）

boarding 车身内壁板，镶板，铺板

board tail （汽车的）船尾形后端（指逐渐变细的后端，形似船尾）

board test ①（指对）印刷电路板（的）测试②（电器）模拟板试验（研制阶段，将整个电器或系统做成模拟板进行的测试）

boat (launching) trailer 游艇运载挂车

bobbin 线轴，绕线筒，绕线管

bobbin frame 线圈架，点火线圈架

bobweight 配重，平衡重（=balance weight）

bodge （因未使用合适的工具和材料，技术差，作业马虎而造成的）劣质修理（结果，或修理过程）

bodily harm （事故等造成的对）人体的伤害（=bodily injury）

body ①体，主体，物体，机体，机身躯干，壳体②（特指）车身（汽车的上部可见结构，相对底盘、驱动系统而言）③螺栓的杆部

body accessories 车身附件（指有独立功能并成为一个分总成的机构，如：门锁、刮水器、后视镜、座椅等）

body assembly ①（指使用各种构件和板件）装配车身，车身装配②（指由车身骨架、车身附件、地板座椅、门窗及全部外复件构成的）车身总成（简称 body）

body belt mo(u)lding 车身装饰条带，车身模制嵌条（=body line moulding）

body builder ①车身制造者，车身制造师②车身制造商，车身制造厂（=body maker, carriage builder, carriage manufacturer, coach maker）

body bulkhead 见 bulkhead

body bumping tool 车身修整工具，车身板件敲击校正工具

body CAN 见 comfort CAN

body capacity 车身容量，车身容积

body ceilling 车身内顶板，车身内篷板

body center pillar （车身）中间立柱

body-chassis constructure （指车身本体挠性悬置于车架上的）非承载式车身结构（亦称 body-chassis frame construction, separate frame construction）

body checking tram 测定车身变形量的梁式卡尺

body-coloured （指）与车身颜色相同的，车身色的（保险杠等）

body computer module 见 BCM

body contact terminal （车身上的）搭铁接线柱（= earth terminal）

body control module 见 BCM

body coordinate axis 车身坐标轴线（高度零线一般取汽车满载时车架纵梁上缘面或地板上平面或通过前轮中心的水平线；宽度零线取汽车的纵向对称中心线；长度零线通常取汽车的前轮中心的垂线）

body design 车身设计，车身结构

body diameter of axle shaft 半轴非花键部分的直径

body diameter of screw 螺钉杆身直径（指螺钉头部以下无螺纹部分的杆径）

body division 车身分块（从工艺性的角度出发，将车身外覆盖件分成若干块便于冲压和焊装）

body drag 车身的迎风阻力，车身空气阻力

body fabric 车身内部蒙布，车身装饰用织物

body fashion ①车身造型，车身风格；流行的车身式样（= body style）②（指）将车身制成所设计的风格的外形，制造出所设计造型的车身式样

body file 车身板件用手锉，车身作业用成型锉刀

body filler 车身填隙料，车身填充料，车身板件接缝填料

body flange 指车身两块板件搭接处所形成的突缘

body frame （客车）车身骨架（指为保证车身强度和刚度而构成的空间框架结构，亦称 body skeleton）

body-frame car 车架式车身轿车（参见 frame car，相对于承载式车身而言）

body framing ①车身构件总成②车身构件和装配

body front assembly （长头或短头货车和轿车的）车头板件总成

body front panel 车身前部板件

body glass 车身用玻璃（如：车门窗玻璃等）

body guide （自动倾卸车身升降时用）车身导架

body hardware 车身附件（如：车门铰链，门锁，玻璃升降机构，发动机罩铰链等）

body hold down bracket （非承载式车身的）车身托架，车身底架

body insulation ①车身隔热、隔音②车身隔热、隔音材料

body integral with frame 承载式车身，无车架式车身，整体式车身（= body integral with chassis, chassisless body, frameless body, unitized body, integral body and frame）

body-integrated bump （与车身制成整体的）车身一体式保险杠

body integrity （碰撞后）车身完整度

body interior equipment 车身内部设备

body interior light ①车内照明②车内灯（具）（=［美］room lamp）

body in white 白车身（指已经焊装好但尚未喷漆的白皮车身，简称 BIW）

body iron 车身用薄钢板（亦称 body sheet）

body jack 车身（修复用）千斤顶（直接顶在车身板件碰撞后的变形处，或通过校正工具顶压、拉拔变形扳板，使之恢复原形）

body jig ①车身尺寸检测工具，车身尺寸测量设备②车身规尺，车身样板③车身装配架；车身焊接台

body knock 车体前后摇动

body lead 车身用铅料（用于填补车身板件凹痕和缝隙的铅锡合金，用喷灯加热后，在其尚处于塑性状态时涂于需修补处，以获得光滑表面）

body level regulater 车身高度调平装置

body line ①车身外形线，车身轮廓线，车身造型线（= contour flow, skin line）②车身装配线

body line moulding 车身装饰条带（= body belt moulding）

body lip 车身凸出部分

body mechanism 车身机构（指能满足车身上一定功能要求的机械组件，= mechanical hardware of body）

body-mounted bracket （货车）车身枕梁撑架（参见 outrigger bracket）

body mounting 车身悬架，车身软支撑，车身挠性支撑（在非承载式车身结构中，为了隔绝振动和噪声，车身通过多个橡胶垫安装在车架上）

body number 车身号码，车身编号（制造厂打在车身上的识别号，每车一号，=［美］·VIN）

body-on-frame construction 车身-车架式结构（指车身装在车架上的结构形式，相对无车架的承载式单壳车身"unibody"而言）

body plan ①正面图，横剖型线圈②车身设计图，车身布置图

body rail 车身的纵梁

body rattle （由于板件松旷，或装配不良造成的行驶时产生的）车身振动噪声

body repair jack unit 车身整形修理用的顶拉装置（如：body jack）

body rigidity 车身刚度

body roll 车身侧倾（见 roll）

body roll gradient 车身侧倾度（车身侧倾角与侧向加速度关系曲线上，侧向加速度值为 $2m/s^2$ 处的平均斜率，= roll rate of body）

body roll sensitivity 车身侧倾敏感性，车身侧倾增益（指输入增加规定量时，车身侧倾的稳态响应增益的增加量，亦称 body roll compliance, body roll gain, body roll susceptibility）

body rumble 车身振动噪声（车辆以 30～60km/h 的速度在不规则凹凸的路面上行驶时汽车内产生的振动噪声，参见 road noise）

body sealer ①车身密封件②车身用密封膏（密封车身接缝处用的膏剂，其主要成分多为硅胶）

body sealing test 车身密封试验（如：人工淋雨试验或汽车在干燥的尘土路上尾随前车的粉尘试验）

body shell 车身本体（亦称 main body, white body, body in white complete①对轿车指车身结构件及覆盖件焊接总成，并包括前翼板，车门、发动机罩，行李舱盖，但不包括附件及装饰件的未上漆车身②对客车指车身骨架，车身外覆盖件及车门等构成的组合体③对货车指驾驶室本身，不包括附件、装饰及非金属件的驾驶室焊接总成，亦称 cab body）

body side moulding （沿）车侧面（塑料、硬橡胶，有时带金属装饰条的）加固和保护条（防侧面碰撞）

body side sill 车身底边梁

body silencing ①车身隔音②车身消声（指行驶时其构件振动声的消减）

body size hole 通孔，穿通孔，贯穿孔，贯通孔

body skeleton 车身骨架（指去掉发动机、传动系统、行驶部以及所有的装置、附件和可拆卸的板件后的裸空间构架，通常指承载式轿车车身骨架，及客车车身骨架 = body frame)

body skirt 车身裙部（客车指基准腰线以下的车身部分的总称，轿车指腰线以下车身表面部分的总称）

body space ①车身容积 ②安装车身的空间位置

body spoon （车身板件修理用）钣金勺

body squeak 车身吱吱声

body station （车身振动试验等时的）车身测量点

body strength calculation 车身强度计算

body stripe （沿车身侧面下部的）装饰带（通常在跑车上用大的字母标示制造者和/或车型名称）

body structural member 车身结构件（支撑覆盖件的全部车身结构零件）

body structure 车身构架，车身结构（指能形成结构及支撑覆盖件的全部车身结构零件，亦称 body structural member）

body style 车身造型，车身风格，车身样式（= fashion①）

body styling 车身造型设计，车身外形式样设计

body styling kit 车身流线型附件套装（指一整套改善车身流线型、提高其空气动力特性的附加板件，如：装在驾驶室上的导风板，车尾的压风板，车裙板等）

body subframe 车身底板副车架，车身下辅助车架

body support runner （货车）车身枕梁，车身纵枕梁，车身纵梁（直接垫在车架大梁上，= chassis runner，亦称 bottom side）

body surface pressure test 车身表面压力分布试验

body sweeps 车身用曲线规，车身用曲线板

body's wind pressure meter 车身风压计（测定气流对车身的压力及其与汽车行进方向的夹角）

body terminal 车身上的搭铁接线柱（= earth terminal）

body tipped endways 后倾卸式车箱（= end dump body）

body tipped sideways 侧倾卸式车箱（= side dump body）

body-to-frame insulator 车身与车架之间的弹性隔振件

body tub （非承载式车身除去所有可卸下的板件，如门、窗等以后的梁）车身骨架

body varnish ①车身（光亮）漆 ②车身装饰品

body warning device 车内警报信号装置

body wax 车身蜡，车身抛光蜡

body wear plate 车身防磨耗覆盖板

body weathering ①车身的天气作用试验 ②车身抗天气作用的防护（措施）（参见 weathering）

body with portion over cab 一部分在驾驶室顶上的车厢

bodywork ①车身（= vehicle body，指②非承载式车身的装在底盘上的整个车身结构 ③承载式车身的整个车身板件总成） ④车身制造工艺，车身修理工艺，车身制造作业，车身维修作业（= coach work）

boggy ground 沼泽地（= marshy ground）

bogie （汽车的）双轴并装车桥带车轮总成（亦写作 bogey 或 bogey axle）

bogie arm 双轴并装车桥平衡臂

bogie spread 并装车桥跨距（指两最外端的车轴中心线之间的距离）

bogie suspension （汽车）双轴并装后桥悬架

boil 沸腾，起泡，冒泡（发动机冷却系水箱）开锅

boiler 锅炉（各种蒸气发生装置的通称）

boiling of the radiator 散热器沸腾，水箱冷却水过热，水箱开锅（亦称 boil over）

boiling point 沸点（亦称 boiling temperature）

boiling point-gravity constant 沸点比重值（美国石油学会评定柴油燃料的一项指标，= boiling point-gravity number）

boil-off loss 汽化损失，蒸发损失

bollard ①（装设在行人安全岛或人行道上的）标柱，护柱 ②（在道路安全地带接近端设置的）缓冲设施（在美国一般称 buffer）③ 系缆柱，系缆桩

bolometer （热敏电阻式）辐射热量测仪，电阻式测辐射计

bolster ①支持物 ②（车辆的）横梁（货车货箱底板的横梁，亦称 crosssill）③ 承梁，枕木，枕垫 ④车坐垫和靠背垫 ⑤（牵引车）鞍座 ⑥（用支持物）支持，支撑，垫起

bolster and cover （货车车身底板纵、横梁的）梁端盖板（亦称 sill end cover）

bolster body tractor 鞍式牵引车（= bolster-type tractor）

bolster body trailer 长货挂车，鞍式长货半挂车（= bolster-type trailer）

bolster bolt 货车（车身底板的）纵拱梁连接螺栓（亦称 sill bolt）

bolster kingpin 鞍式牵引架主销

bolster-type trailer 鞍式长货半挂车（= bolster body trailer）

bolt ①螺栓 ②用螺栓紧固

bolt cap 螺栓头（= bolt head）

bolt coupling 螺栓连接

bolt die 板牙，螺丝板（= screwing die）

bolted-on 用螺栓装上的

bolted splice 螺栓搭接，螺栓拼接

bolt-loosening test 螺栓的松动性试验

bolt-on goodies （装在车身外面的）额外附件（如附加的车灯等非必要件）

bolt-on kit （指车主可以自己装上去的）整套加装件（如装在车身上的导流板，装在发动机点火系内的晶体管点火组件等）

bolt-on wing （直接用）螺栓紧固（而不是焊接的）翼子板

bolt shackle 螺栓钩环，（钢板弹簧）吊耳销，U 型钩横销

bolt stay 拉杆螺栓

bolt type clip 带螺栓的夹箍，用螺栓收紧的夹箍

bomb ①高压容器，氧气瓶 ②弹，弹形试验用器

bomb calorimeter 热值测定弹，弹形量热器（一种测量燃料热值的弹形仪器。参阅 oxygen bomb）

bond ①合同，契约 ②（用黏结、浇铸、附着、胶合、焊接、铆接、紧固等方法将两个单件）结合，连接，复合，搭接

bondability 可结合性

bonded-in liner ①浇铸的衬面 ②黏结或铆接在制动蹄上的摩擦片

bonded-in PTFE seal （轴承的）黏合式聚四氟乙烯衬面油封

bonded windscreen 黏结式风窗玻璃（直接黏在车身板件内，而不用橡胶玻璃框条的风窗玻璃）

bonderite （钢的）磷酸盐薄膜防锈处理（层），磷化处理

bonding agent 黏结剂，黏合剂，黏合胶

bonding of rubber to metal 橡胶金属黏接

bonding wire ①（发动机和车架间的）搭铁线，接地线（= earth cable）②接合线；焊线

bond line 接合缝，搭接缝，黏结缝

bond master （环氧树脂类的）强力黏合剂

bond metal ①烧结金属 ②烧结金属

制件

bond strap （单独使用的带接头的）搭铁线

bonnet ①罩，帽；机罩，保护罩 ②（特指）发动机罩（=[美] hood）③加罩

bonnet badge （装在发动机）罩前（端中央的）车徽（表明厂家或车型的标志件）

bonnet bumper 发动机罩座面上的减振橡胶条（= bonnet bump rubber）

bonnet damper （行人保护系统装在）发动机罩（上的）减振软垫（当根据遥感型加速度传感器、卫星定位系统及压力传感器等的信息确认车头已撞上行人时，火药式执行机构即通过爆炸使发动机罩后端升起，通过该减振软垫减轻对行人头部的冲击）

bonnet door （发动机）罩上的小门

bonneted （说明汽车时，指）长头的（发动机装在驾驶室前方的发动机罩下的常规式货车等，[美]亦称 cab-behind-engine, conventional, [英] normal-control）

bonnet latch 发动机罩扣钩，发动机罩锁扣（亦称 engine hood latch, hood safety catch, bonnet fastener, bonnet lock, bonnet fastener-clip）

bonnet liner 发动机罩的（消声）内衬（贴在发动机罩内面，用来消减发动机噪声）

bonnet release 发动机罩锁栓松脱机构（如，在车内便可松开发动机罩锁扣的拉柄等）

bonnet stay 发动机罩撑杆（亦称 bonnet support stay）

bonus loader 装载车（指装有起重机、举升叉或其他举升装置，用于装载的车辆）

BOO 制动 on/off 开关（brake on/off 的简称，踩下制动踏板时，点亮制动信号灯，并向 PCM 发出使变矩器或离合器分离的信号的开关件）

bookmobile 汽车图书馆，流动图书馆

boom 起重臂，悬臂

Boomerang-shaped LED lights 回力棒形 LED（发光二极管）灯光组

boom hoist 悬臂式起重机，臂式吊车

booming ①行驶时干扰气流所产生的噪声（如，行车时开启车窗所产生的噪声等）②低频共振噪声（特指排气系统发出的此类噪声）

boost ①助推；加强，强化 ②（特指）进气增压

boost charge （蓄电池的）快速充电（指以大电流短时间充电, = fast charge）

boost coil （磁电机）起动线圈（= booster coil）

boost(composition)fuel feed stroke （柴油机喷油泵调节齿杆的进气）增压（补偿）供油行程

boost control ①（增压式发动机）增压压力控制装置 ②增压控制，增压调节 ③（利用发动机进气管负压的）真空控制装置（= vacuum control, 如真空点火提前装置）④涡轮增压式柴油机低速运转时的喷油量自动控制装置

boost cylinder 助力缸（亦称 booster cylinder）

booster ①助力器，加力器（一般指增加踏板力的制动助力装置）②（电压）升压器，放大级

booster battery （起动用串联的）辅助蓄电池（组）

booster brake 加力制动器，助力制动器（不用于脚制动器的助力装置，指脚制动器以外的制动器，供紧急情况下增加车辆的制动效果）

booster cable 外接电源线（一般为两端均带接线夹的备用外接线，如

将救援车的蓄电池接到故障车上用的接线)

booster coil ①(磁电机)起动线圈(=boost coil) ②增加火花强度的辅助线圈

booster compressor 进气增压(用)空气压缩机

booster crack point (制动踏板行程中的)助力器作用始点

booster magneto 起动磁电机

booster runout 输入力过大,以致助力器的输出力小于输入力的现象

booster starter 辅助起动电源;外接起动电源机组(通常由一小型汽油机和发动机组成,起动时,供给汽车辅助电流)

booster venturi (化油器)小喉管

boost gauge 增压压力计,增压压力表(=[美]boost gage)

boosting battery 升压蓄电池(用以提升输出电压)

boosting charge 快速充电,急充电(=booster charge)

boosting voltage 附加电压,升压电压

boost pressure 增压压力(指进气增压系统充量增压后达到的压力,通常为增压式内燃机进气管内的压力)

boost pressure connection (柴油机调速器进气增压补偿器膜片室连接进气歧管以获取进气增压的)增压连通管

boost pressure ratio 增压比(指增压器出口压力与环境大气压力或增压器进口压力的比值,简称pressure ratio)

boost sensor 增压进气压力传感器

boost start (由)外接电源(提供电力的)起动

boost valve (液压系统内的)增压阀

BOO switch 制动器合/断开关(见brake on/off switch)

boot ①轿车后部行李舱(亦称boot或luggage compartment,=[美]trunk) ②橡胶防尘罩;罩、套 ③轮胎爆裂救急用垫料(件) ④(锁住违章停放车辆的)夹锁(见wheel clamp)

booted version 追加后行李舱型(指在原舱门式后背的车形上追加行李舱的变形车型)

boot handle 后行李舱盖把手

boot lid lock-striking plate (轿车车身等的)行李舱盖锁扣碰板

boot spoiler 见rear spoiler

borax 硼砂($Na_2B_4O_7 \cdot 10H_2O$,熔焊和钎焊时作为熔剂)

BoÁrdan tube-micro switch type pressure switch 布尔登管微型开关型压力开关(布尔登管为一端封闭的薄壁空心弯铜管,其封闭端称为自由端,压力油进入该管后,管的伸直与回弯度与油压成比例,当油压达到或低于某规定值时,其自由端正好到达推动微型开关闭合或断开的位置,使所控制的电路断开或接通,或向电子控制模块发出接通或断开信号)

border ①边界,边缘,界限;缘,框,壁 ②接壤,毗邻,接近;镶边

border line oil film 边界润滑油膜

bore ①(镗成的)孔 ②孔径,内径;缸径 ③镗孔;镗缸,扩孔

bore area 内孔表面积

bore-out-of-round 孔失圆度,内圆失圆度

bore scope 窥孔镜,内孔探测镜

bore spacing 孔间中心距(如:多缸发动机的汽缸中心距)

bore-to-stroke ratio (发动机汽缸的)径-程比,缸径-冲程比(简称B/S ratio,或B/S)

boric steel 硼钢(=boron steel)

boring ①镗孔 ②镗孔的

boron 硼B

boronization 渗硼（在金属表面使硼原子渗入扩散而形成硼化物FeB、Fe$_2$B表层的化学热处理工艺，可使钢件表面有极好的耐磨性及一定的抗腐蚀性和抗氧化性，亦称boronizing）

borosiliconizing 渗硼渗硅处理

borrow 借位（计算机中央处理器按位求差时的算术负进位，向上位数借）

BOS 制动优先系统（brake override system 的简称，驾驶者万一误操作、同时踩踏制动踏板和加速踏板时，仅制动起作用）

Bosch ①[德]波许（股份有限）公司（创建于1886年，世界上首先开发生产柴油机喷油泵）②波许公司产品的商品名

Bosch's Motronic 波许（公司推出的第一套）发动机多功能电子控制系统（的商品名）

boss ①轴套②凸台，凸座，凸起部（如：活塞销孔座）

boss eddy 叶轮根部的涡流

boss（joint）bolt 轮毂（接合）螺栓

boss ratio 内外径比

bottle 瓶，罐

bottle car 瓶罐运输车（如，清凉饮料运送车）

bottle（d）gas 高压瓶装气（如：瓶装煤气，瓶装液化石油气，瓶装液态丁烷）

bottle jack 瓶式千斤顶（螺旋举升器，呈瓶形，故名）

bottle neck （交通）瓶颈（指由于道路狭窄或车辆拥挤而造成的交通堵塞不畅处）

bottler's body [美]瓶罐运输车身（通常为厢式车身，供运送箱装瓶罐之用，=[英]brewer's dray）

bottom ①底部，根部，底；基础，根基，根源②残渣，沉淀物③最低的，最下面的，底层的，底部的④（特指悬架）被压至其冲程的最低点，以致引起（车身）颠簸⑤（特指汽车底部）碰到路面或地面

bottom board （车厢）地板（一般指可拆卸式地板）

bottom boom 底桁，下部构架

bottom bushing 一端不通的衬套，盲端套筒

bottom centre （往复活塞式内燃机活塞冲程等的）下止点，下死点（=bottom dead centre，简称BDC，指活塞冲程中离燃烧室最远的一点）

bottom clearance ①径向间隙，底隙②（齿轮传动中的）顶隙（谐波齿轮指在波发生器作用下，柔性齿轮与刚性齿根在半径方向上的间隙；在圆柱齿轮副中，指一齿轮齿根圆柱面与配对齿轮齿顶圆柱面之间在连心线上的距离；在锥齿轮副中，指一齿轮齿顶圆锥面与配对齿轮齿根圆锥面间，沿两背锥公母线的距离）

bottom dead-center indicator 下止点标记（=lower deadcenter indicator）

bottom diameter （螺纹）内径；底径

bottom dump ①（自卸汽车的）底卸（货物由车身底部卸出，=bottom discharge）②底卸式自卸车辆（=bott-dump truck，centerdump truck，floor-hopper truck，belly dumper，bottom-dump tipper，bottom dumper）

bottom end ①下端，底端②指发动机曲轴箱内所有的运动件及其轴承③（特指）连杆大头（=big end）④发动机曲轴转速的低速区

bottom-end bearing （连杆）大头轴承（=big-end bearing）

bottom end of stroke （活塞等的）冲程的下止点

bottom end torque (发动机)低速(运转时的)转矩

bottom-feed injector (汽油喷射的)底部进油喷射器(在喷孔附近进油,可减少常规喷射器的汽油蒸发)

bottom feed type 底部供油式

bottom gear 头挡,(最低速前进挡,= first gear)

bottom half (曲轴箱、轴瓦等的下半部分)下瓦片,下曲轴箱

bottoming ①车辆在凹凸不平的路面上行驶时,悬架达到其冲程的止点 ②在行驶中,因各种原因轮胎的胎体被短暂压平在轮辋上 ③汽车底部(某处)与路面凸起处接触

bottom land 见 bottom of tooth space

bottom of tooth space 齿槽底面(指齿槽底部,被齿根曲面所包含的那一部分齿槽表面,= bottom land)

bottom-opening thermostat 底部开启式恒温器

bottom plate 垫板,底板

bottom (radiator) tank (冷却系散热器的)下水箱

bottom rib of piston 活塞底肋

bottom ring ①裙部活塞环(安装在活塞裙部下端的,裙部底环) ②活塞环衬环;活塞环胀圈

bottom settling and water 底部沉淀及积水(简称BS&W)

bottom side ①底、底部、下部、底边 ②车身底架纵梁(参见 body support runner)

bottom sill ①(车身的)门槛(板) ②(车身的)底梁

bottom view 仰视图,底视图,下视图

bounce ①跳动弹起 ②(汽车的)跳振(指汽车簧上质量绕汽车坐标系y轴的回转振动和沿z轴方向的平行振动的复合振动且以后者为主) ③(气门、触点等高速运动时)颤振或跳振(以致闭合不良) ④(减振器性能试验等中的)汽车加振(加振系统对车辆的一角按一定的频率和速度施加向下的压力,促使其上、下振动,以测试悬架系统的有关性能)

bounce control (主动式悬架对车身)跳振控制(对装在车身上的垂直加速度传感器测出的车身瞬时垂直加速度进行积分,算出车身的绝对跳振速度,通过压力控制阀对悬架减振器施加与该绝对速度成比例的反向控制液压,这一控制方法亦称 skyhook damper control)

bounce cylinder (自由活塞燃气发生器的)缓冲汽缸

bounce test (悬架、减振器等的)加振试验(由加振系统施加使之上、下振动的加振力,测试其有关性能)

bouncing control system (主动式悬架的)防车辆(上、下)跳振系统(通过加速度传感器测得车辆的垂直加速度值,给悬架一与垂直振动成比例的阻尼压力)

bouncing of car body 汽车车身的垂直振动

bouncing pin indicator (测定最大爆发压力或燃料的爆震特性的)跳针式指示仪,爆震测量仪

bound ①界、界限、边界 ②弹跳、跳回 ③限制、约束 ④接合、黏合

boundary condition 边界状态,边界条件,极限条件

boundary dimensions 轮廓尺寸,边界尺寸

boundary element method 边界元法(简称BEM,用于分析声辐射问题)

boundary (film) lubrication 边界润滑(见 boundary friction)

boundary friction 边界摩擦(摩擦面间仅有若干个分子层厚且不连续的极薄的润滑油膜,局部发生固体

boundary layer 边界层，临界层，界面层，（亦写作 bounding layer）
boundary science 边缘科学
bound energy 结合能
bounding medium 黏合介质
Boundon cable 波登拉索（指操纵阻风门、节气门等的套管拉索，详见 Boudon wire）
bounds on error 误差界限
bound vortex 附体涡流，附着涡流，束缚涡流
Bourdon tube pressure (or temperature) switch 波登管式压力（或温度）开关
Bourdon tube (pressure 或 temperature) gauge 波登管式（压力或温度）计（波登管为一端封闭的圆弧形金属管，该管弧度随管内压力或温度的变化而变，借以带动指针指示温度压力，亦称弹簧管式压力或温度计）
BOV 混合汽油辛烷值（blending octane value 的简称）
bow ①弓，弓形物②使弯曲，弯曲成弓形③（kow for…车辆的性能等）适应…的要求
Bowden brake 波顿制动器（拉索操纵的鼓式机械制动器）
Bowden cable ①波顿安全电缆（电缆有金属编织层覆盖的铠装，当发生漏电，电流流经铠装层时，即可触动继电器，切断供电电路）②见 Bowden wire
Bowden wire 波顿软索（钢丝套筒软索，钢丝套筒内装有可拉动的钢索，用以传递纵向运动，如阻风门的拉索，用这种拉索实现的控制称 Bowden control，英国人 Bowden 发明，因而得名，= bowden cable, pushpull cable）
bowl ①碗、杯（状物）②浮子室，凹腔③球，球形物④转筒，辊筒⑤（板簧）夹箍
bowl cover 碗状盖，盖碗
bowl-in-crown combustion chamber 活塞顶凹腔燃烧室（= bowl-in-piston, bowl-in-piston chamber, bowl-in piston type combustion chamber）
bowl mill 球磨机（= ball mill）
bowser 加油车，油罐车，油槽车，水柜车
bow spring 半椭圆形钢板弹簧
bow supporter 弓形车顶支柱，车篷的弧形支撑杆
bow type spring 半椭圆形钢板弹簧
box ①箱，盒；外壳，套，罩；盒形小室；单元组件；接线盒；车厢②（排气系统的）消声器（= silencer）③装箱，做成箱形；给…装上外壳
box beam 箱形断面梁（亦称 box girder）
box body 厢式货车车身（= box van body，[美] panel body）
box car 厢式汽车
boxed frame 箱形梁架（指由两槽钢焊成箱形梁制成的框架等）
boxed rod 箱形断面连杆（指工字形连杆两侧加焊加强板，而呈箱形断面）
boxed weight 装箱重量（包括皮重，装箱质量的旧称，= crated weight）
boxer engine 汽缸水平对置式发动机
box member 箱形断面构件
box section frame 箱形断面车架（指车架构件断面呈箱形，而不是常规的"["形，= box-type frame）
box spanner 套筒板手（=[美] box wrench）
box/stake truck 仓栅式汽车（具有仓笼式、棚栏式结构的车箱，用于运输散装颗粒食物、畜禽等货物的专用汽车）
box thread 阴螺纹，内螺纹

box van ①箱式货车车厢（= box van body）②箱式货车（= box truck, boxed truck）③（泛指各种）箱式汽车

Boyle's law 玻意耳定律（在温度保持不变时，理论气体的容积与其压力成反比，即PV = 常数，亦称Mariotte's law）

boy motor vehicle 少儿汽车（= juvenile motor vehicle）

boy racer ①儿童赛车②（指仅注重外表赛车，但并不要求有很高的车速和功率的）低档车

bp ①沸点（boiling point的简称）②（发动机）制动功率（brake power的简称）

BPA 旁通空气（bypass air的简称）

BPC ①背压控制（back pressure control的简称）②英国石油公司（British Petroleum Corporation的简称）

BP-FS 见brake pre-fill system

B-pillar （轿车车身）中柱（指位于前车门后的中间立柱，支撑车顶和安装前门的门锁碰板，而在四门式车型上还要安装后门的铰链，亦称center pillar, center post, B-post, middle standing pillar）

BPMV （ABS的）制动压力调节阀（brake pressure regulating valve的简称）

B Point （踏板的）踵点（如：加速踏板踏下时脚后跟与地板表面接触的交点）

B post （四门轿车车身的）中支柱[见 centre (standing) pillar]

B-power 阳极电源, 乙电源（简称BP）

bps 每秒钟传递的位数（bit per second的简称）

BPT ①背压传感器（back pressure transducer的简称）②基点, 原点, 小数点（basic point的简称）

B. P. V 商务车（business purpose vehicle的简称）

Br ①溴（bromine）②黄铜（brass）

BR 丁二烯橡胶（见 butadiene rubber 及 polybutadiene rubber）

brace ①支撑件（指为提高结构刚性，在两个或多个构件间起支撑作用而设置的支撑杆、臂、架、筋、条、板等）②（曲柄式手摇钻或螺丝起子的）曲柄③支撑, 拉紧

braced 被支撑、拉紧的

braced-tread tyre 子午线轮胎（= radial-ply tyre）

brace ring （制动鼓的外）加强边环

bracing ①（起）支撑（拉紧作用）的支撑件（= brace①）

bracket ①托架, 支架, 悬臂架②装托架

bracket crane 悬臂式起重机

bracket lamp （装在车厢壁上的）壁灯

bracket plate 支撑板, 托板

bracket value 曲线图上的独立点值

braid ①条带, 编织的带子, 编织物②编织；用编织物装饰

braided grounding strap （蓄电池）编织搭铁线

braided hose 包有编织外皮的橡胶软管（多用于燃油管或制动管道）

braided packing （由石棉、棉线等编织成断面为长方形、圆形等的）编织密封带, 编织密封件, 编织填料

brain waves 脑电波

brake ①制动器, 制动装置②测功器（目前多用dynamometer一词）③见 station wagon④制动

brake actuating lever 制动拉杆, 制动操纵杆（= brake operating lever, brake bar）

brake actuator ①（电子控制制动系统"ECB"的）制动执行机构（由②制动主缸输出液压、储压器液

压、车轮制动缸输入液压等的传感器②正常制动及 ABS、TRC、VSC、BAS 等制动工况的液压回路切换电磁阀③上述各制动工况下的车轮制动缸输入液压增、减控制阀等组成,根据电子控制模块的指令,控制前、后、左、右车轮的制动液压)④见 brake apply device ⑤见 brake chamber

brake adjuster 制动器(蹄片间隙)调节器;制动器调节机构(亦称 brake-adjusting mechanism)

brake adjusting spanner 制动(蹄与鼓间隙)调节扳手(=[美] brake wrench)

brake adjustment screw 制动器间隙调整螺钉

brakeage 制动作用,制动器动作,制动力,制动装置

brake (air) bleeder (液压制动系)空气排除器(如,用来排除渗入制动液压系统内的空气的排气螺钉等,亦称 brake flusher)

brake air chamber 制动气室(见 brake chamber)

brake anchorage 制动蹄支承轴,制动蹄支承销(亦写作 brake anchor)

brake ant-roll (back down) device (汽车在坡道上停车时,在制动踏板松开后,仍保证有足够制动压力的)防坡道下滑安全制动装置

brake application time 制动(持续)时间,制动器作动(持续)时间

brake apply device 制动踏板踩压装置(可照规定将所要求大小的踩踏力加在制动踏板上,供制动试验等时使用,以避免人力造成的误差,亦称 brake actuator 或 brake depressor)

brake-applying handle 制动手柄(一般指驻车制动手柄,= brake handle)

brake arm (某些带制动助力机构的制动系统中,将助力传至制动蹄驱动件的)制动助力臂

brake assistor 制动加力器,制动助力器(= brake booster, power brake, servo brake)

brake assist system 紧急制动助力系统(简称 BAS 或 BA。驾驶人遇到紧急情况,而陷于慌乱状态时,一般会快速踩踏制动踏板,但踩踏力却较小,而导致制动力不足,这时电子控制模块根据制动踏板传感器的上述踩踏速度和踩踏力信号可推定驾驶员欲紧急制动的意图而发出指令,使制动力增加,实现紧急制动的电子控制制动系统)

brake back plate 制动器底板(安装制动蹄总成及其他非旋转件的基体件,亦写作 brake backing plate, = brake anchor plate, brake bottom plate, blake spider)

brake balancer 制动器平衡仪(调整各车轮的制动器,保证均衡制动)

brake band 制动带

brake band clamp (带式制动器)制动带夹,制动带固定夹(亦称 brake band catch, brake band clevis)

brake-band lining 制动带摩擦衬带

brake beams 制动杠杆系

brake bias (汽车的)制动偏斜,偏制动(左右两侧的车轮制动效应不同的现象)

brake bleeder tank 排除液压制动系统内的空气时用来盛装制动液的容器

brake bleeder tube 制动系(液压系统)排气管

brake block 制动蹄

brake bonder 制动蹄摩擦片黏结机,制动蹄摩擦片烘箱(指在制动蹄和蹄片表面涂敷黏结剂,将涂好黏结剂的蹄片和蹄夹紧并送入烘箱内烘干的全套机具及烘箱)

brake booster 制动助力器，制动加力器（= brake servo，指增加制动踏板踩力的真空、气压或液压装置）

brake-by-wire system 线控制动系统（①指制动踏板不是通过机械、液压或气压方式而是通过传感元件发出的电信号向制动系电子控制模块发送驾驶员的制动踏板踩力大小，快慢，强弱等信息的制动系统②指全电控电力制动系统，亦称 fully electrical brake system，指从制动踏板开始，直到各车轮制动器的整个制动系统的工作过程均由导线输送的电子计算机指令来控制，制动力亦来自电动装置，不再使用气动和液压系统的制动系）

brake cable （某些机械式制动系或驻车制动器的）制动拉索（= brake wire）

brake caliper （盘式制动器）制动钳（制动时将制动块总成紧压于制动盘上的部件）

brake caliper guider 制动钳导板

brake caliper mounting bracket 制动钳安装架（安装其推力机构和制动衬块总成的零件，亦称 brake body carrier）

brake caliper plate yoke 制动钳板臂（浮钳式盘式制动器将油缸推力传到对应一侧制动块的传力件）

brake caliper spring 制动钳（回位）弹簧

brake cam shaft 制动器凸轮轴

brake camshaft lever 制动器凸轮轴臂

brake cap 制动器盖

brake chamber （气制动）制动气室（= air brake chamber，有时亦称 brake actuator, brake motor, = ［美］air chamber，将制动气压转变为驱动制动器凸轮等的机械力的部件）

brake chamber cover 制动气室盖

brake chamber push rod sealing cup 制动气室推杆（密封）皮碗

brake chatter 制动震颤（在制动时，制动装置本身产生振动的现象，有时发出尖叫声）

brake clearance 制动器间隙（指制动鼓与制动蹄摩擦衬片或制动盘与制动衬块之间的间隙）

brake clevis 制动拉杆叉形头（连接叉）

brake compensating device 制动（力）补偿装置

brake compressor 气制动压气机

brake conduit 制动主管道

brake cone 锥形制动器的制动锥

brake control force （施加于）制动器控制（制动器动作的）力

brake control (initial) movement 制动初始操作动作（按 SAE 的规定，指制动踏板垫中心或制动杆端最初的 3.175mm 行程范围内的制动操作动作）

brake cross lever 制动器横向传动杆

brake cylinder （液压制动系的）轮缸（指将制动主缸产生的液压，转换成推动制动蹄或制动块的作用力，直接顶推制动蹄或制动块的部件）

brake cylinder boot 制动轮缸护罩

brake cylinder casing （液压）制动轮缸缸体，制动轮缸体壳

brake cylinder clamps 制动轮缸夹钳（拆卸制动蹄时压紧车轮制动缸活塞用）

brake cylinder hone 制动缸研磨头

brake cylinder piston cup 制动轮缸活塞皮碗

brake disc （盘式制动器的）制动盘（指装在轮毂上、随车轮一起旋转，受制动块总成压紧后起制动作用的盘形旋转件，亦写作 brake disk，=［美］brake rotor）

brake dive （汽车的）制动点头（制动时，由于载荷由后向前转移，使车头下栽的现象）

brake doctor 制动蹄片磨修机

brake dragging 制动器卡滞，制动器拖滞（由于制动蹄与鼓之间的间隙调整不当，蹄片复位弹簧减弱等原因，使制动蹄片与鼓不能脱离接触的现象，亦写作 brake drag）

brake drum （鼓式制动器的）制动鼓（指装在轮毂上，随车轮一起旋转的鼓形壳件，其内鼓面受到制动蹄压紧后，起制动作用）

brake drum dust cover 制动鼓防尘罩，制动鼓防尘盖板，

brake drum gauge 制动鼓量规

brake drum lathe 制动鼓车床

brake drum thermal (storage) capacity 制动鼓热容量，制动鼓储热能力（$Q_b = CW_b \Delta t$，其中：C 为比热。W_b 为制动鼓质量，Δt 为制动鼓温升）

brake drum-to-shoe gauge 制动鼓-制动蹄两用卡钳（可测量制动鼓内径，制动蹄总成外径）

braked wheel 被制动车轮

brake dynamometer 制动式测功器

brake eccentric 制动器偏心轮

brake efficiency 制动器效能（亦写作 efficiency of brake，或称 brake effectiveness，常用 brake efficiency factor 表示）

brake efficiency factor 制动器效能因素（简称 BEF，指制动器的输入量，包括力矩、力、压力等，与输出力矩之间的比例关系，常用来表示制动器的效能，注意与 braking efficiency factor 不同）

brake electrohydraulic booster system 电控液压制动助力系统（简称 brake elec hyd boost system，由制动踏板触动的电路开关开启液压助力油路，推动液压制动主缸工作）

brake enegy regeneration efficiency （车辆的）制动能量再生率（制动能量回收率，亦称 brake energy collection rate）

brake equalizer 制动器平衡杆

brake facing 见 brake lining

brake fade 制动器（效能）衰退（指由于受热或水浸等原因，制动器摩擦力显著降低的现象，亦写作 brake fading）

brake failure 制动器（完全）失效

brake feel （驾驶员的）制动感（①对制动踏板踩踏力与车辆实际产生的制动力之间的关系感②对制动踏板软、硬等的踩踏感）

brake final temperature 制动终止时（摩擦片）温度

brake flange ①制动蹄固定盘②制动器突缘

brake fluid 制动液（= braking fluid, brake oil）

brake fluid dispenser 制动液加注器

brake fluid inlet port （液压制动系统制动缸液压室的）进液孔

brake fluid reservoir 制动液室，制动液箱（一般指直接位于制动主缸顶面或其他较高且易于接近处的透明塑料容器，内有液面高度传感器；双管路制动系统具有两个储液腔）

brake fluid safety meter 制动液沸点测定仪（通过测定其沸点，确定制动液内吸收的水分。制动液容易吸收水分，吸收水分后不仅制动系统内部容易生锈，而且会影响制动性能，是十分危险的，制动液内水分越多，沸点越高）

brake fluid tank 制动液容器

brake flusher ①（液压制动系统）制动液自动更换装置②液压制动系统排气装置（= brake air bleeder, brake bleeder）

brake flushing 压力冲洗制动系统管

路，高压液流冲洗制动器

brake force （制动器的）制动力

brake force coefficient 制动力系数（简称BFC）

brake force limiter 制动力限制器

brake force parallel distribution type dual-circuit brake system 见front/rear split type dual-circuit brake system

brake frictional torque 制动器摩擦力矩

brake friction pad spring （盘式制动器）制动块（回位）弹簧

brake gear 制动装置，制动机构，制动传动机构

brake grabbing 制动咬死（grabbing of brakes，亦称brake gripping，= gripping of brake）

brake grease baffle 制动器挡油环

brake hand lever 制动器手把，制动器手操纵杆（= brake handle）

brake head 制动蹄块

brake hop 制动时车轮的垂直跳动

brake horsepower （用马力为单位表示的发动机）制动功率（通常指发动机在不带附件的情况下在试验台上测得的输出功率，相当于指示功率减去机械损失。由于发动机输出功率试验台、即测功机"dynamometer"，早先叫作"brake"，故将该试验台上测出的发动机输出功率称为brake horse power，亦简称brake power，现多称有效功率，并用千瓦"kW"为单位，见effective power）

brake horsepower-hour （发动机）制动功率小时

brake hose 制动软管

brake housing ①制动器壳②制动器底板

brake hub 制动器毂

brake hydraulic pressure sensor 制动液压传感器（简称BHPS）

brake hysteresis 制动器滞后（施加形放松制动过程中，对于某相同的制动力矩"braking torque"，两制动作用力"braking application force"的差值，亦称brake lag）

brake initial temperature 制动初始时（摩擦片）温度

brake interlocks for door （客车的）车门和制动器联锁装置（当车门处于半开、全开或未关牢状态时，制动器将车制动）

brake jamming 制动器咬死

brake lag ①制动器滞后（见brake hysteresis）②制动迟后时间，制动迟后距离（指驾驶员踩踏或放松制动踏板瞬间起至制动蹄与制动鼓实际接触或分离为止所经过的时间或距离，= brake time lag，brake distance lag）

brake lamp 制动（信号）灯（具）（= stop lamp）

brake latch （手）制动器锁销

brake legislation 制动法规

brake lever 制动杆，制动手柄

brake-lever guide 制动杆导槽

brake-lever latch 驻车制动杆锁销

brake lever pawl 制动手柄锁棘销

brake lever sector 驻车制动杆扇形齿板

brake light 制动信号灯（光）（位于车身尾部踩踏制动踏板时便自动发亮的红色信号灯光，亦称stop light）

brake line 制动管路（制动系统各种管路的总称。对整车，actuating line"促动管路"，指控制装置和执行装置间的管路，feed line"供能管路"，指连接制动能源与控制装置的管路，pilot line"操纵管路"，指各控制装置之间的管路，仅起控制另一个控制装置的作用。对汽车列车，control line"控制管路"，指控制制动能或信号由牵引车传给挂车的管路，emergency line"应急管路"，指由牵引车向挂车传送应急

制动能量的专用管路，supply line "供给管路"，指将制动能或信号从牵引车传给挂车的管路。在单管路牵引车制动系统中，既可作供给管路，又可作控制管路的，称 common line "共用管路"）

brake lining ①（制动蹄）摩擦衬片 ②（制动钳）摩擦衬块（亦称 brake friction lining, brake bush, brake facing, 表示盘式制动器的制动衬块时，多称 brake pad）

brake lining area 制动摩擦衬片面积（= braking surface, braking area, brake surface, brake friction area）

brake lining grinder 制动蹄片光磨机

brake lining refacer 制动蹄片重装机

brake lining spreader base 制动蹄擦片黏结作业用座板

brake lining test 制动摩擦片试验（包括物理试验和摩擦性能试验。物理试验测定其硬度、密度、压缩强度及变形、弯曲强度等。摩擦性能是测定摩擦系数和磨耗率及其与温度的关系）

brake-lining wear-indicator 制动摩擦衬片磨损指示器（亦称 brake wear detector）

brake linkage 机械式制动杆系

brake lug （带式制动器的）制动带支架（=［美］brake lining support）

brake master cylinder （液压制动系统）制动主缸（将踏板等的控制力和助力器的助力等转变为制动液压的部件）

brake master cylinder reservoir cover 液压制动主缸储油室盖

brake master cylinder T-pipe 制动主缸三通接头

brake mean effective pressure 平均有效压力（指有效功与汽缸工作容积之比，表示单位汽缸工作容积所做的有效功，平均有效压力 P_e = 平均指示压力 P_1 - 平均机械损失压力 P_m。平均有效压力 P_e 与发动机的总转矩成正比，可以认为 P_e 反映的是单位汽缸容积所发出的转矩）

brake moisture sensing unit 制动液"湿度"传感器（指装在制动主缸储液室内的温度传感器。制动液吸入空气中的水分后，其沸点和气阻温度均会降低。通过测定其沸点温度判断其含水量，故亦称 brake moisture sensor 简称 BMS）

brake monitor 制动（器）监测器

brake noise 制动（时发出的）噪声

brake OK monitor 制动系统完好状态监测器（亦称 brake warning, 行驶前自动指示制动系统各处是否完好的灯光信号装置）

brake on differential shaft （作用于）差速器轴的制动器

brake on/off switch 制动器接合/断开开关（向发动机电子控制模块发送制动器工况，即：施加制动与放松制动的信息的开关型传感器件，简称 BOO switch）

brake on transmission shaft （作用于）变速器轴的中央制动器

brake operating lever 制动器操纵杆

brake out of adjustment 调整不当的制动器；制动器失调

brake over-ride system 见 BOS

brake pad assembly 制动摩擦衬块总成（指盘式制动器中压紧在制动盘上产生摩擦力的块形摩擦件及其背板总成）

brake pad back plate 制动摩擦衬块背板（指固定盘式制动器制动摩擦衬块的零件）

brake pad wear indicator （盘式）制动摩擦衬块磨损指示器（有机械式和电子式两种，当衬块磨损到规定值时，前者产生警告噪声，后者接通一警报灯）

brake pedal 制动踏板
brake-pedal-travel sensor 制动踏板行程传感器（＝brake pedal travel switch）
brake pedal travel switch 制动踏板行程开关（装在制动主缸内，根据主缸活塞行程，向控制模块提供制动踏板位置信息）
brake pipe 制动管（＝brake tube）
brake piping 制动管路（＝brake line）
brake piston 液压制动缸活塞
brake plate flange 制动盘安装凸缘，制动盘安装盘
brake power （发动机的）有效功率（旧称制动功率，为指示功率减去机械损失功率所剩的功率，即：在飞轮或其他作有用功的输出元件上由测功机测出的输出功率，以往用米制马力 PS 或英制马力 hp 为单位，后者英美仍沿用至今。国际单位制用千瓦 kW 为单位，1hp ＝ 0.7457kW ＝ 1.0139Ps，用马力表示时，亦称 brake horse power, shaft horse power "制动马力，轴马力，输出马力"）
brake pre-fill system （制动液）预充满型制动系统（简称 BP-FS，每次松开制动踏板的瞬间即将制动系液压器件和管道内充满制动液，以缩短下次制动时的空驶距离）
brake (pressure) limiting valve 制动压力限制阀
brake (pressure) modulator valve (assembly) （中型、重型货用防抱死气压制动系统的）制动（压力）调节阀（总成），亦称 brake pressure modulation valve
brake pull cable 制动器拉索
brake pulling 制动跑偏（亦称 brake deviation，由于左右制动力不平衡而汽车在制动时向左或右偏移的现象，＝brake steer①）

brake push-out pressure 制动蹄接触压力
brake ratchet 制动器的棘轮机构
brake reaction time （驾驶员的）制动反应时间（从产生制动意念起，到将放在加速踏板上的脚移至制动踏板并开始踏踩踏板止所需的最短时间）
brake release 制动放松，松开制动
brake release spring 制动器复位弹簧
brake reservoir 制动液储液室
brake resistance 制动阻力
brake retarder 见 retarder
brake rods 制动杆系
brake rod yoke 制动拉杆端叉
brake rotor （［美］盘式制动器的）制动盘（＝brake disk）
brake scotch （垫在车轮下的）制动三角木
brake service department 制动检修工间，制动系维护工间
brake service tool 制动系维护工具
brake servo 制动助力器，制动器加力装置，制动助力机构（见 brake booster）
brake servo motor ①（对于气压制动系指）制动气室（＝brake chamber 或 air chamber）②（对于液压制动系指）轮缸（＝wheel cylinder）
brake shield （盘式制动器的）护板（一般由前、后两半组成，装在制动盘的内侧）
brake shoe 制动蹄（通常指制动蹄加制动摩擦衬片总成，亦称 brake block）
brake shoe adjusting cam 制动蹄-鼓间隙调整凸轮
brake shoe adjusting gauge 制动蹄调整量具；制动蹄调整器
brake shoe anchor bolt 制动蹄支承销（＝brake shoe anchor pin）
brake shoe anchor pin cam 制动蹄支

承销凸轮

brake shoe and drum gauge 制动蹄鼓测量器（量蹄外径、鼓内径）

brake shoe（automatic）adjuster 制动蹄（自动）调整装置（自动调整制动蹄与制动鼓间隙的装置）

brake shoe carrier 制动蹄座

brake shoe efficiency factor 制动蹄效能因素［摩擦片表面的圆周力 F 与加施在两制动蹄上的作用力 f_1、f_2 之比，即制动蹄效能因素 $C = F/(f_1 + f_2)/2$］

brake（shoe）expander 制动蹄片张开装置

brake shoe grinder 制动蹄片磨削装置

brake shoe heel （接近支撑销的）制动蹄端，制动蹄根部

brake shoe hold down spring 制动蹄限位弹簧（使蹄总成靠压在制动器底板上的弹簧）

brake-shoe return spring 制动蹄复位弹簧，制动蹄回位弹簧（= brake-shoe back-moving spring, brake-shoe check spring, brake-shoe pull-off spring）

brake shoe tappet （液压制动系统轮缸活塞的）制动蹄推杆

brake slave cylinder 见 brake wheel cylinder

brake snubbing （使汽车减速但不停车的）轻踩踏制动，轻刹制动，点刹

brake specific biological activity （发动机）单位制动马力生物活性排放量（简称 BS-BA，亦称比生物活性排放量）

brake specific emission （发动机）单位制动马力排放量［每 $kW·h$ 所排放出的污染物的质量，以 $g/(kW·h)$ 表示，亦称比排放量］

brake specific fuel consumption （发动机）制动马力燃油消耗率（每制动马力小时的油耗，单位：1b/制动马力小时，g/制动马力小时，简称 BSFC，bsfc，亦称比油耗）

brake specific HC emission （发动机）制动马力碳氢化合物排放率，（每制动马力小时的碳氢化合物排放量，简称 BSHC，亦称 HC 比排放量）

brake specific NO_x emission （发动机）制动马力氮氧化物排放率（简称 $BSNO_x$、发动机每制动马力小时的 NO_x 排放量，亦称比 NO_x 排放量）

brake specific solids emission （发动机）制动马力固态微粒排放率（简称 BSSE，发动机每制动与力小时的颗料排放量，亦称比固态微粒排放量）

brake squeak 制动刺耳尖声，制动啸声

brake steer ①（汽车的）制动偏转（现象），制动跑偏（指制动时汽车向左侧或右侧偏转的现象，= brake pulling）②制动转向（利用制动车轮的方法，使车辆转向）

brake stop 制动停车

brake stop intervention（for driver asleep at the wheel）（对驾驶者开车期间瞌睡的）制动停车干涉（功能）

brake strap 制动带

Brake SW 见 brake switch

brake swept area 制动鼓（或盘）的工作面积

brake switch 制动（踏板控制）开关（简称 brake SW. 指由制动踏板控制的在制动时断开或接通有关电路的开关，见 BOO）

brake system air pressure 气制动系统的气压

brake system performance monitor 制动系性能监测器

brake tandem master cylinder 串列

双腔式制动主缸（由两个工作室组成，且活塞依次串列，用于双回路液力制动系统，亦称 series dual-chamber brake master cylinder）

brake temperature limit 制动器温度极限，制动器最高允许温度

brake test ①（汽车）制动试验，（包括路试和台试）②（发动机）制动测功试验

brake tester 制动（器）试验台（＝brake testing stand, brake bench）

brake thermal efficiency （发动机）制动热效率，有效热效率（发动机曲轴所输出的有用功 W_e 和燃料燃烧所产生的热量 Q_1 之比，即 $\eta_e = AW_e/Q_1$）

brake toggle 制动器凸轮

brake torque 制动力矩（见 braking torque）

brake torque control system with out stored energy （ABS 和 ASR）不使用存储能量的制动力矩控制系统（无高压储能器，而使用一回油泵"return pump"或自吸式循环泵"self-priming recirculation pump"作为 ABS 和 ASR 系统升压工况"build"的液压源）

brake torque control system with stored energy （ABS 和 ASR）带存储能量的制动力矩控制系统（当需要增加制动力时，电子控制模块经电磁阀接通高压储能器与车轮分泵间的液压通路，高压制动电液迅速输入车轮分泵，缩短制动响应时间）

brake valve ①（气压制动驱动系中的）气制动阀（指汽车及挂车制动时，可随着制动踏板行程的变化，改变制动管路中气压的部件，有单腔、双腔、三腔式多种，分别控制单回路、双独立回路和三独立回路式制动系的管路压力，＝air brake valve, air brake control valve,

control valve）②（有时指气制动系的）制动踏板

brake valve air intake valve spring 气制动阀进气阀弹簧

brake warning buzzer 制动故障警报蜂鸣器

brake warning lamp 制动故障警报灯（具）

brake warning light 制动系故障警报灯（光）（见 brake OK monitor）

brake wheel cylinder 制动轮缸（亦称 brake slave cylinder）

brake with two leading shoes 双领蹄式的制动器（参见 leading shoe）

brake worm control 制动器蜗杆式间隙调节装置（lash adjusting device 的一种）

brake wrench 见 brake adjusting spanner

braking adhesion coefficient 制动附着系数（在给定工作点下，车轮没有抱死时制动力系数所能达到的最大值，见 braking force coefficient）

braking axle 制动桥（装制动车轮的车桥）

braking bag （Benz ESF 2009 安全概念车上安装的）（起）制动（作用的）气囊（该气囊实际上是一个装在车头下方的爆炸推进装置，可在雷达测得临碰撞前 80μs 起爆而膨胀，将一特制的与车身连接的钢板压至路面，而与路面产生可使汽车形成 2G 的减速度的摩擦力，与此同时膨胀的气囊将车身前端顶高 8 cm，以避免追尾钻撞）

braking by grades 分级制动

braking curve ①（前后车轮）制动力分配曲线②制动力（随时间变化的）曲线

braking cylinder ①制动液压缸②止动油缸，液压止动油缸

braking deceleration 制动减速度

braking deceleration coefficient 制动

减速度系数（指制动减速度与重力加速度的比值）

braking deviation　制动跑偏

braking distance　①（汽车的）制动距离（从踩下制动踏板施加制动力开始，到松开制动踏板取消制动力为止，汽车在制动条件下行驶的距离）②（汽车的）制动停车距离（= full-stop braking distance，从踩下制动踏板开始到汽车完全停止汽车所移动的距离，包括车轮滚动距离和滑动距离）

braking drag　制动拖滞（制动蹄或制动块松开不彻底）

braking (driving) stiffness　制动（驱动）刚度（纵向滑移率的单位增量所对应的纵向力的增量）

braking (driving) stiffness coefficient　制动（驱动）刚度系数[车轮的制动（驱动）刚度与垂直负荷的比值]

braking effect　制动效果；制动作用

braking effectiveness test　制动效能试验（测定制动踏板力和汽车制动减速度关系的试验）

braking efficiency　制动效率（指以一定的减速度制动时，其制动减速度系数与防止车轮抱死所需的轮胎-路面附着系数之比，当制动效率为1，即=100%时，轮胎-路面附着性能得到最充分利用。注意：其意义不同于 brake efficiency）

braking efficiency control valve　制动力调控阀，制动力调节阀

braking efficiency factor　制动因数（总制动力 F 与作用在汽车一个或若干个轴上的静载荷 G 之比：制动因数 $Z=F/G$，有时亦简称 braking factor）

braking effort　①制动力，制动作用力（= braking force）②制动效果

braking energy source　制动能源

braking failure　制动失效

braking figures　制动性能数据

braking force　制动力（由制动力矩作用而产生的与汽车行驶方向相反的纵向力）

braking force/braking slip　制动力对制动滑移率比

braking force coefficient　制动力系数（制动力与垂直负荷的比值）

braking force diagonal distribution type dual circuit brake system　见 diagonal (ly) split type dual-circuit brake system

braking force distribution rate　制动力分配率（各车轴上的制动力与总制动力之比或前、后桥制动力之比，亦称 braking force distribution ratio）

braking force limit　（汽车的）制动力极限（由制动桥的动载荷和有效道路附着系数所决定的最大制动力）

braking force of brake　制动器的制动力[指制动时轮胎周缘克服制动器摩擦力矩所需的力，亦称 brake application force（制动器作用力）。注意：不同于 tyre-ground braking force]

braking frequency　制动频率

braking heat dissipation　制动热消散（制动产生的热量经过传导、辐射、对流的方式消散）

braking heat effect　制动热效应（制动时，制动鼓、制动蹄和轮胎等的温度上升对制动性能的影响）

braking hop　（车轮）制动跳动，制动跳振

braking in a turntest　转弯制动试验（用以评价汽车在弯道行驶施加制动时的行驶方向稳定性能）

braking intervention　制动干涉（指当驱动轮因驱动力大于路面附着力而滑转时，对驱动轮施加的制动）

braking in turn test　弯道制动试验，

转向制动试验

braking jack-knifing 制动折叠（制动时牵引车与挂车成人字形折叠的现象）

braking maneuver 制动操作，制动动作（＝braking action）

braking mechanics 制动力学

braking mechanism ①制动机构②制动机理

braking nose dive （汽车）制动点头

braking performance chart （汽车的）制动性能图（车速、制动减速度及驾驶员反应时间、停车距离的关系曲线图）

braking power 制动功率

braking pressure switch 制动压力开关（见 switch type braking sensor）

braking ratio ①前、后轮制动力分配比，前、后车轮制动力比②用重力加速度 g 表示的制动减速度值

braking regulations （汽车）制动规程

braking rotorassembly 制动转子总成（①指电磁缓速器中的转子总成②指液力缓速器中的转轮总成）

braking sensor 制动传感器（向电子控制模块提供施加制动与否的信息）

braking severity 制动的猛烈程度，制动的剧烈程度

braking signal switch 制动信号灯开关

braking skid 制动滑移

braking stability 制动稳定性

braking statorassembly 制动定子总成（①指电磁缓速器中的定子线圈总成②指液力缓速器中的定轮总成）

braking swerve 制动甩尾

braking system hysteresis 制动系统滞后（施在制动与放松制动的过程中，对应某一相同的制动力矩，两制动控制力的差值，见制动控制力

"brake control force"）

braking time 制动时间（指驾驶员踩上制动踏板到车辆停止时所经历的时间，包括制动机构反应时间、制动力增长时间、主制动时间、放松制动时间，较 stopping time 少一段驾驶员反应时间）

braking time lag 见 brake lag②

braking tire traction 制动时轮胎和道路间的附着力（简称 braking traction）

braking torque 制动力矩（由制动作用力引起的制动鼓或制动盘与制动蹄或制动块的摩擦力，与其作用点到旋转轴线间距离的乘积）

braking trace 制动轨迹，制动轮印迹，（车轮的）制动拖印

braking weight transfer 制动时质量转移

braking with the motor 发动机制动（＝engine braking）

braking work 制动功（W_f）（瞬时总制动力 F_f 和有效制动距离微元 ds 乘积在有效制动距离 s 范围内的积分 $\int_0^s F_f ds$）

branch 支路，支管，支线；分流，分支

branch box 分动箱；分流器

branched duct 歧管，（分）支管

branching ①分支，分流，分部，支线②（在汽车电子控制系统中指在某一程序的执行过程中，执行的指令离开规定的次序，即：改变指令的执行顺序的）转移，跳转（一般多使用 jump 一词）

brand awareness （汽车）品牌的知名度

brand name 品牌（产品牌名）

brass ①黄铜（铜60%～90%，锌40%～10%），黄铜制品②黄铜制的，含黄铜的，黄铜色的③镀铜，覆盖黄铜层

brassing ①用黄铜镀覆的②黄铜覆盖层，黄铜镀层

brass punch 黄铜冲（轴承内、外圈，衬套等的拆装工具）

Brayton cycle 布雷敦循环（燃气轮机用的等压循环）

Brayton-cycle hot-air engine 布雷敦循环热空气发动机（简称 Brayton-cycle engine）

braze ①铜焊，铜钎焊（指用铝合金、铜锌合金等焊料进行的被焊接件不熔化的焊接。由于其钎料的熔点较高，又称为硬钎焊, = brazing）②用锌铜合金钎焊，用黄铜钎焊③用黄铜制造，用黄铜镶饰

brazing filler metal 黄铜钎料，硬钎料（指熔点高于450℃的铜锌合金的钎焊焊料, = hard solder, brazing solder）

bread-board ①试验电路板，模拟电路板②实验性的，试验的（= brassboard）

bread board experiment 试验板实验（设计集成电路等时，事先用试验电路板进行的模拟试验）

breadth 宽度，幅度，跨度，间距

break ①断裂，破损②裂缝，裂口③断开，断路④中断，停顿⑤将整件（如整车）拆成散件⑥（触点等）分开，断开

breakage ①断裂，破裂，损坏，毁坏②失事③（电）击穿

break away （指汽车轮胎接地面上的合力大于附着力时车辆的）侧向滑移，侧滑（前轮侧滑称为飘出，转向半径增加，横摆角速度减小；后轮侧滑称为甩尾，横摆角速度及后轮侧偏角均急增。这两种侧滑的结果都将造成车辆偏离所希望的方向）

breakaway connector 拔脱式管接头，拉脱式管接头

breakaway coupling 超载断开式联轴节

breakaway release 断开式安全装置

breakaway torque ①起动转矩（指克服惯性等阻力，使发动机等由静止到开始转动所需的力矩）②打滑转矩（指制动时，大于制动蹄与制动鼓间的摩擦力矩而使制动器打滑的力矩）③（机件不致受到破坏的）破损极限力矩（= breakdown torque）

breakaway valve （当挂车与牵引车事故性脱离时，使挂车自动制动的）安全阀

break down （动）①（汽车因故障而）停车②绝缘（材料）失效③破损

breakdown point ①击穿点②屈服点③（油膜）破坏点

breakdown potential 击穿电压（= break-down voltage, disruptive 或 flash over voltage, 见 Paschen's law）

breakdown recovery 将故障车拖（或运）至修理处或指定地点

breakdown service ①指在条件许可的情况下，对故障车的就地援助和修复②指无条件就地修理时将故障车拖（或运）至修理厂修复

breakdown speed 损坏（临界）速度

breakdown test 断裂试验，耐久力试验，击穿试验，耐电压试验，折断试验，稳定性试验，破坏性试验（= breaking test）

breakdown time ①（混合料燃烧过程中的）诱导期②故障时间（指营运车辆因机件损坏等故障影响其正常运行的停车时间）

breakdown truck （英）故障或事故车拖车（美称 tow truck）

breakdown vehicle ①（公路事故或故障车辆的）应急抢修车②（特指将事故或故障车辆拖运至修理厂等的）急救车、救济车，亦称 break-down service vehicle（包括：breakdown tractor, breakdown crane, breakdown ruck, breakdown van)

breaker ①（轮胎）缓冲层（斜交胎胎面与胎体之间或子午胎胎面与带束层之间的胶布层或胶层，亦称 breaker ply, cord breaker）②断路器，开关③（分电器的）断电器 ④（将已无使用价值，但某些零部件尚可利用的车辆拆成散件出售）拆车人

breaker and distributor column 分电器-断电器轴

breaker arm 断电器臂

breaker bolt 安全螺栓（见 beak-out torque）

breaker cam 断电器凸轮（= breaker point cam）

breaker camshaft 断电器凸轮轴

breaker cover 分电盘盖，断电器盖

breakerless distributor 无触点式分电器

breakerless transistorized ignition system 无断电器式晶体管点火系（亦简称 breakerless ignition system，指没有常规点火系的断电器，由电感式、霍尔效应式或光电脉冲式等点火信号发生器的信号通过晶体管电路接通或断开点火线圈一次绕组的电路，使点火线圈产生点火高压的点火系统）

breaker lever 断电器臂，断电器触点臂

breaker plate 断电器底板

breaker point 断电器触点（= break contact，包括断电器臂上的活动触点及底板上的固定触点）

breaker point cam 断电器触点凸轮（= breaker cam）

breaker points clearance 断电器触点间隙（= breaker point gap）

breaker points feeler gauge 断电器触点间隙规

breaker strip 缓冲胶片（加贴在轮胎缓冲层或带束层上、下的胶片）

breaker's yard 拆车场（见 breaker④）

breaker timing 断电器正时（使断电器凸轮按规定时刻顶开断电器触点）

breaker-triggered transistorized ignition system 触点式晶体管点火系

breaker-type distributor 断电器或分电器

break-in ①磨合期，走合期（= break-in period）②磨合，走合，磨合运转（亦称 break-in run，［美］= run in）

break-in coating （新件的）磨合涂层（改善磨合条件，防止新件在磨合中过热、咬死和擦伤）

breaking force 致断力，（造成）断裂（的）力

breaking point ①强度极限，破损强度，断裂强度（breaking strength）②断裂点，转折点

break in grade 坡度转折点，坡度变更点

break-in period 磨合期

break-in scuffing 磨合（期）拉缸（故障）

break off ①拆断，断开，脱开②停顿，暂停工作

breakout box 测试接线盒（电子测试设备与汽车相应的电气和电子电路连接的接线盒）

break-out torque 安全装置（如：转矩超过某故定值时而断开的安全螺栓"breaker bolt"）的断开转矩

breakover （车身板件的）凹瘪区

break-over angle （汽车的）纵向通过角（= ramp angle）

break pin hitch 带剪切销的牵引装置

break point ①停止点，中断点，间歇点，变换点，转折点②破乱点（层流火焰变为紊乱火焰的过渡点）③（汽车电子控制系统的）断点

(指程序由于外部干扰或收到暂停指令而暂停执行或转移的点,有时亦指该暂停指令)

break shock 断路冲击(电路断电时的电压冲击)

break through 突破,击穿

break time 断电器触点开启时间(参见 dwell period)

breakup ①分解,破裂,分裂;拆散,脱开,脱钩,摘下挂车②(特指)将整车拆成散件并出售其可用的零件(=[美] part out)

breast hook (汽车的)前挂钩

breathalyse (对汽车驾驶者作)呼气法血液酒精含量测试(亦写作 breathalyze)

breathalyser (用呼气法对驾驶者)血液酒精浓度(进行检测的)测试仪(亦写作 breathalyzer)

breathalyser test 用呼气法对驾驶员血液酒精浓度的检测(简称 breath test)

breather ①换气装置(阀、孔、管件等)②进、排气装置③换气的

breather cheek valve (二冲程发动机曲轴箱等的)单向进气阀

breather valve 换气阀(如储液罐内用来保持罐内规定气压的自动进气和放气的恒压阀)

breathing characteristics (气孔的)通气特性,(气门的)进、排气特性,(发动机的)充气特性

breath test 见 breathalyser test

breeches pipe Y 字形排气管(其两个分支接发动机的双排气歧管,此后该两个分支管合为一根管,并经一个消声器由一根排气尾管将废气排至大气)

breed 品种,种类

brewer's body (啤酒瓶等的)瓶桶运输车

BRG 见 British Racing Green

bridge ①桥,电桥②跨接,越过,跨过

bridge circuit for power steering control valve (液压)动力转向控制阀的桥式液压回路

bridge crane 桥式吊车,桥式起重机

bridge ignitor (安全气囊的)点火器,点火引爆装置

bridge member 桥件,搭接件,跨接件(= bridge piece)

bridge pipe 跨接管,桥式管(如在有两个轮缸的制动器中,连接这两个轮缸的管件)

Bridge Stone Tire Co. Ltd (日本)桥石轮胎有限公司

bridge truck 汽车式架桥车

bridge washer (轮辋上的轮胎气门嘴等用)桥形垫圈(可将其载荷分散到其外缘,状如桥形,故名)

bridging ①跨接,桥接;分流;接通,短路②桥接的,跨接的

Brigg's standard pipe thread 布氏标准管螺纹

brightener 抛光剂,光亮剂,上光蜡

brightness 亮度(= luminance,表面的亮度,常用单位为 cd/m², 简称 B, 参见 candela)

bright stock (未加添加剂的裂化)精制润滑油

bright viewing distance (汽车灯具的)认视距离(指照度为 21x 的点与灯具配光镜之间的距离)

bright washer 精制垫圈,光磨垫圈,抛光垫圈(black washer 的反义词)

brilliance ①光彩,光泽,辉度②亮度,主观亮度(亦写作 brilliancy, = subjective brightness,参见 brightness)

brilliant black (车身外壳的)旋光黑

brilliant silver (车身外壳的)亮银色

Brinell hardness number 布氏硬度值(指用钢球以一定的压力压入工件

表面，保持规定的时间后，测量其压痕表面直径，此后按所给定计算式算出压痕单位面积表面承受的平均压力，即为布氏硬度值）

brisk acceleration 急加速，急剧加速度

Bristol alloy 白铜（锌37%，铜58%，锡5%）

Brithsh Standard Whitworth 英国标准惠式螺纹（简称BSW，至今仍广泛使用的轻小载荷粗牙螺纹）

British Association 见 BA

British Automobile Racing Club 英国汽车竞赛俱乐部（简称BARC）

British Automotive Manufacturer's Association 英国汽车制造商协会（简称BAMA）

British Leyland Public Limited Company 英国利兰公司（英国Rover集团公司的前身，简称BL）

British Motor Corporation 英国汽车公司（英国Rover集团公司在称为British Leyland公司以前的名称，简称BMC）

British Racing Green 英国赛车绿（简称BRG，以前英国官方规定深绿色为正式赛车的颜色）

British Sandard Coarse Thread 英国标准粗牙螺纹（简称BSC）

British Standard Fine Thread 英国标准细牙螺纹（简称BSF）

British Transport Commission 英国运输委员会（简称BTC）

Brit pat 英国专利（British patent）

brittle fracture 脆性断裂（几乎无塑性变形而形成脆性断口的断裂）

brittle lacquer coationg （应力分布试验用的）脆性漆涂层

brittleness 脆性

broach 拉削，扩孔，绞孔（及其工具）

broached-tooth design （两接合面间的）锯齿结构

broadband 宽（频）带

broadband noise 宽频带噪声

broadband sensor 宽带传感器

broadband video detector 宽带视频检波器

broad-beam head lamp 宽光前照灯（亦称 broad-beam light）

broad cut fuel 宽馏分燃料（= wide-boiling-point-range fuel）

broad lace （车身内部）装饰带

broadside impact （车辆）侧向碰撞

broken circuit 断开的电路，断路，开路

broken down vehicle 发生事故、故障或毁坏了的车辆

bromine number 溴值（燃油抗爆剂化学分析用参数，= bromine value）

bronze ①青铜（铜、锡合金，高强度，良导热性，抗腐蚀）②青铜色涂料，青铜色颜料

bronze-backed metal 青铜基片减磨合金轴瓦

bronze bearing 青铜轴承，青铜轴套

bronze bushing 青铜衬套（= bronze bush）

bronze plain bearing 青铜滑动轴承

bronze welding 青铜焊材堆焊；青铜堆焊，青铜焊

brother type universal test bench 并装式万能试验台

brougham ①布鲁姆式轿车（前排座上方无顶盖的敞篷驾驶室厢式古典货柜轿车，4门，4~6窗，4~7座，驾驶室车门为半截式，类似limousine）②电动两门轿车 ③四轮车

Brown and Sharpe wire gauge 美国线径规，美国线规（美国线径基准，亦称 B&S wire-gauge，简称 BS wiregauge，直径0.46in为4/0号，0.00124in为48号，4/0号与48号间按等比级数分为52个号码，= American wire gauge）

Brown Boveri Co. 布朗波渥瑞公司（瑞士，简称 BBC）

Brown taper 布朗锥度

bruise break 冲击内裂（轮胎经冲击后胎里帘线局部断裂的现象）

bruising ①（乘员）撞伤 ②（车辆）碰撞破损，碰撞损坏

brush ①刷 ②电刷

brush collector 电刷集电器，集电刷

brush end （发电机的）换向器端，电刷端

brush film 发电机换向器上的电刷材料形成的污膜

brush lead （发电机换向器）电刷超前量（沿着旋转方向）

brush less DC motor 无电刷式直流电动机（定子装线圈，转子装永久磁铁）

brush shifting device 电刷移位装置（直流电动机消除换向火花用）

brush sponge plating 刷镀（用刷或多孔材料吸收电镀液作为阳极，镀件作为阴极）

brush type distributor 接触式配电器，电刷式配电器

brush-type generator 电刷式发电机（指由电刷-滑环式换向器整流的发动机）

B/S 缸径冲程比（= bore-to-stroke ratio）

BSC 英国标准粗螺纹（British standard coarse thread 的简称）

BSCO 单位制动马力一氧化碳排放量（brake specific CO emission 的简称）

BSF 英国标准细螺纹（British standard fine 的简称）

BSF thread 英国标准细螺纹（British standard fine thread 的简称）

BSHC 制动马力碳氢化合物排放率（brake specific HC emission 的简称）

BSI 英国标准学会（British Standards Institution 的简称）

BSM system 盲区监视系统（blind spot monitor system 的简称，亦称 blind area monitor system，简称 BAM system）

BSNO$_x$ 制动马力氮氧化合物排放率（brake specific NO$_x$ emission 的简称）

BSP thread 英国标准管螺纹（British standard pipe thread 的简称）

BSS 英国标准规格（British standard specification 的简称）

BS solids 制动马力固态微粒排放率（brake-specific solids emission 的简称）

BSW 英国惠氏标准螺纹（目前仍广泛使用，British standard whitworth 的简称）

BSWG 英国标准线规（British standard wire gauge 的简称）

BS wire-gauge ①美国线径规（Brown and Sharpe wire gauge 的简称）②伯明翰线径规（Birmingham wire gauge）

BTC 英国运输委员会（British Transport Commission 的简称）

BTDC 上止点前，（before top dead center 的简称）

BThE 制动热效率，有效热效率（brake thermal efficiency 的简称）

B thread 内螺纹（= internal thread）

btry 蓄电池（battery 的简称）

BTU 英国热量单位（= 252 卡，在标准状态下，1 磅水升高 1°F 所需的热量，British thermal unit 的简称，亦写作 Btu）

BTV ①基本运输车（basic transportation vehicle 的简称）②在节气门下方（below the throttle valve 的简称）

BUA system 倒车辅助系统（backup assist system 的简称，使用倒车雷达等向驾驶者提供车后的固定及移动障碍物的警报声响或图像信息）

bubble ①泡，气泡 ②水准器气泡，

水准仪③起泡，发泡④（初期汽油机采用的）气泡式化油器的简称

bubble car 泡泡车（20世纪50年代流行的一种微型汽车，整车为玻璃所围绕，成肥皂泡形，因而得名，在很小的外形内获得了尽可能大的空间，车门常常在驾驶座的前方，如：BMW Isetta, Heinkel Trojan等）

bubble in the interlayer （汽车用夹层玻璃）胶合层中的气泡

bubble point 饱和压力点

bubble-top （汽车车身后部的）透明防弹罩

bubbling （蓄电池）冒气泡

buck 全尺寸汽车模型

bucket-brigade device 斗链器件（简称BBD，指将电荷存储在半导体中相互分离区域内，通过连接这些区域的多个开关器件，以电荷包的形式转移这些电荷的电荷转移器件）

bucket tappet 斗形挺杆，桶形挺杆（见tappet）

bucket tipping device （装载机）翻斗装置

bucket (-type) seat 斗式座椅（两侧略升高，供乘坐人侧向依靠的硬座椅，多用于跑车）

bucking ①（发动机）抖撞（小负荷，低速或急速时，节气门关闭后出现的一种发动机突然加速一下的现象）②（汽车的）突撞（行驶中，突然加速一下的现象）

bucking coil 补偿线圈，去磁线圈，反磁线圈，反感线圈

buckle ①扣环，搭扣②扣住③弄弯

buckle tongue （安全带）扣舌

buckle up ［美］系上安全带（=belt up）

buckling ①压弯；压弯的（指杆形件等受到轴向压力时的弯曲、翘曲、拱曲）②（钢板弹簧等的）拱度

buffed ①用麂皮打亮的（如，用麂皮擦亮的金属件表面）②经过打磨的

buffer ①缓冲器，缓冲垫，减振装置，阻尼器，保险杆，消声器②用软皮、棉布、毛毡、软刷等进行最后光面抛光及其机具③（在汽车电子计算机系统中指）ⓐ缓冲存储器（平衡两设备间信息流速率差或事件发生时间差的一种临时存储区）ⓑ，（起上述作用的）缓冲程序ⓒ电子计算机内部存储器的一部分，用于临时存放输入或输出的数据的一个区，以加速逻辑运算过程④隔离电路，缓冲电路，防止驱动电路干扰被驱电路

buffer arm 保险杠，防撞杠（=buffer bar, buffer beam, bumper rod, bumper bar）

buffer beam 缓冲梁，减振（扭）杆（=buffer arm, bumper beam）

buffer clearance 缓冲间隙（汽车最大载荷时，悬架止动件的余裕间隙）

buffer fluid 隔离流体（指在双端面密封、串联式机械密封、立式带油杯的单端面机械密封或外加压流体静压式机械密封中，从外部引入的与被密封介质相容的密封流体）

buffering 缓冲，减振，阻尼

buffer stop 缓冲块（防止在冲击负荷下产生刚性撞击及弹性元件产生过大变形的橡胶块等，亦称bump stop，美称snubber）

buffer switch （将传感器输出的模拟信号变换为一定频率的数字信号输入电子控制模块的）缓冲器开关（亦简称buffer）

buffeting （汽车高速行驶时，开启车窗或敞篷时感觉到的）强劲的冲击气流，强气流冲击

buff (ing) wheel 抛光轮（=burnishing wheel, polishing wheel）

bug ①（一切可有可无的装备都不

要的）简易轻型汽车②双座小汽车③（在汽车电子计算机控制系统中指程序中的）错误，缺陷，（系统中的）故障

bug deflector （风窗玻璃的）昆虫挡板（= insect deflector）

buggy 吧吉车（一种钢管制网架状车身的专用单人低座宽轮距车轮越野赛车）

buggy race 吧吉车赛

Buick car 别克轿车（美国 GM 公司生产）

Buick Division （美国通用汽车公司）别克部

building block 积木块（汽车设计与制造的一个新的发展趋势是将各个系统或总成集成化成为汽车的大的结构件，只要像摆积木那样，便可组合成各种形式的新车，这些大的集成结构件称为"building block"）

build-in motor 内装式电动机（多用作电子控制系统的执行器件）

build-in (the bumper) type fog lamp （装在保险杠上的）内置式雾灯

build quality （车辆等的）制造质量（包括工艺水平和材料质量等）

build state （防抱死制动系统的）升压工况（见 pressure increase②）

build-up ①建立，建造②组装（将零件装配成总成或整车）③（车身外形矫正修复过程中）将板件凹陷处敲起，恢复到其原形④（在旧件修理中，指）用堆焊、金属喷镀或镀复等方法修复磨损面，以恢复其原有的尺寸⑤组合式的，组装的

build-up crankshaft 组合式曲轴

build-up time of braking force 制动力增长时间（指制动力开始发生作用至达到一定值时所经历的时间）

build-up tolerance 装配公差，累积公差

build-up welding 堆焊

built-in 机内的，内装的，装入的，嵌入的，插入的；内在的，固有的，固接的

built-in accessories 内装附件

built-in air spoiler 内装式导流板（与保险杠制成一体的导流板，参见 spoiler，某些汽车将雾灯布置在这类导流板上，称为内装式雾灯"built-in fog lamp"）

built-in blinker 嵌入式闪光灯，内装式闪光灯

built-in cab 内置式驾驶室（与车箱做成一体的驾驶室）

built-in check （系统的）自检，内部检查，自动校验

built-in comfort 指车身内部安装的空气调节等保证乘员舒适性的设备

built-in frame ①与车体焊接一体的车架②内装式框架

built-in head lamp 嵌入式前照灯（置在车身壳体内）

built-in headrest 嵌入式头枕（嵌合在座椅靠背内的头枕）

built-in (hydraulic) jack 装在车上的（液压）千斤顶

built-in smoke meter ①车载式烟度计②布置在汽车检测线排放检测工位上的烟度计（= in-line smoke meter）

built-in stress 预加应力，预应力

built-in system 与主体成整件的系统

built-in test 机内试验

built-in test equipment 车载式检验设备，车载诊断设备（为汽车的一部分固定装置）

built-in type 内装式，机内式，固定式

built-up gear 组合机构

built-up piston 组合活塞

built-up rim 组合式轮辋，装配式轮辋

built-up time 增长时间

built-up welding 堆焊（= deposit weld-ing, overlaying welding）

bulb ①灯泡②球形零件，球状物
bulb base 灯泡头，灯头（指灯泡装入灯座的部分）
bulb baynnet socket 卡口式灯座
bulb blackening 灯泡玻璃（由于钨丝金属蒸发沉积在其内表面而）发黑
bulb contacts 灯泡触点
bulb holder 灯座，灯泡插座，灯泡座（=［美］lamp socket）
bulb retaining spring 灯头压紧弹簧
bulb ring 灯泡座盘
bulb screen 灯泡罩（一般指小照明灯泡的遮光罩）
bulb shield 遮光罩（指装在前照灯反射镜上遮去发光体直射光的罩件）
bulb sleeve 灯座套
bulge （车身外表）不平处，隆起处
bulging of tyre 轮胎凸胀（局部鼓出）
bulk ①大量（in bulk = in large amounts 大量地）②（指容量，体积）大体积，大容量（= large volume）③（指货物）散装的，未装箱的（= loose, not packed in box）④（相对"面"而言的）体，体积，整体［如：surface temperature 指表面温度，而 bulk temperature 指（整）体温（度），按体积计算的平均温度］⑤大块的，整体的，大容量的，体的，总体的
bulk breakdown voltage 体击穿电压
bulk carrier ①笨重物搬运车②散装物运输车
bulk-cement delivery tanker 散装水泥罐车
bulk conductivity 体导电率
bulk diode 体效应二极管
bulk factor 体积因素（与体积、体积变化有关的因素，如粉末成型前后的体积比）
bulkhead ①隔壁、隔板，横隔板②（轿车）前围板（= bulk board, 特指轿车发动机室与客厢之间的整个车身宽度的横隔板，=［美］dash panel, dash board, toe board firewall 亦称 front bulkhead）③（轿车）后围板（后座后面客厢与后行李舱之间的隔板，亦称 rear bulkhead）
bulk head connector （轿车）前围板接线板（指驾驶室仪表板上的各种仪表和指示灯的电源接线总板，装在前围板上，故名）
bulkhead of cylinder block 缸体横隔板（作为曲轴轴承的支撑）
bulkhead strut （轿车）前围板撑柱
bulk memory 大容量存储器（= bulk storage）
bulk micromachined structure 体微加工结构（指整块硅片腐蚀而成的结构或电子器件，相对于面微加工结构 surface micromachined structure 而言，后者指多晶硅材料沉积底板表面而成的结构或器件）
bulk modulus 体积弹性模量
bulk oil ①曲轴箱内的机油②桶装机油，听装机油，罐装机油
bulk property 整体特性，整体性能
bulk resistance 体电阻
bulk semitrailer 散装货运半挂车
bulk storage 大容量存储量（= bulk memory, 现多用 mass memory 一词）
bulk transport vehicle 散装货物运输车辆（= bulker, bulk-delivery vehicle, bulk powder vehicle）
bull bar ①护杠（两端向上扩展的保险杠，以保护灯具）②（指前面的）散热器护栅
bulldozer 推土机
bullet connector 插杆式电插头（为一圆柱形杆，插入筒形插杆式插座内，见 snap connector）
bullet-proof tank 防弹油箱
bullet-proof tire 防弹轮胎（= shot-

proof tire)

bullet-resisting glass 防弹玻璃（亦写作 bullet-resistant glass）

bullet-shaped side mirror 子弹头型车侧后视镜（以减少空气阻力）

bullet-shaped van 子弹头型小客车（整车外形像子弹头）

bullet valve 球阀（= ball valve）

bullet vehicle （两车相撞中的撞击被撞车的）施撞车

bump ①冲击，碰撞 ②连续冲击（如：试验所用多次重复的冲击）③颠簸 ④（物体碰撞产生的）冲击声 ⑤（空气压力的）突然改变 ⑥碰撞造成的伤痕 ⑦（路面因车辆行驶造成的）凹凸不平

bump and rebound （悬架的）受压和反弹（悬架运动的两种形式或阶段，为了减少汽车颠簸，二者均需阻尼）

bump clearance of suspension 悬架的极限行程（指从车身平衡位置起，悬架允许的最大压缩行程，即悬架可能的最大动挠度，钢板弹簧的极限压缩量，冲击余隙）

bump damper foam filling 保险杠缓冲结构的泡沫材料

bumper ①缓冲器，减振器，缓冲垫 ②（汽车的）保险杠

bumper arm 保险杠支架，保险杠托架（将保险杠联结于车身式车架的托架，亦称 bumper stay, bumper bracket, bumper iron）

bumper bar （汽车）保险杠（= face bar，指管形或曲面形断面的独立式保险杠，如货车保险杠）

bumper blade 保险杠（一般指平板式略呈弯曲的板形断面的独立保险杠）

bumper damper （汽车）保险杠（后面的）缓冲器，缓冲件，缓冲结构

bumper energy absorber 保险杠（的碰撞）能量吸收装置

bumper face angle 汽车保险杠正面倾角（指保险杠正面与垂直面间的夹角）

bumper face-bar （汽车的）保险杠面杠

bumper filler 保险杠衬板（保险杠和车身板件之间的小衬板，通常用塑料模制）

bumper guard 保险杠护板，保险杠抗撞装置（如防撞块等）

bumper head lamp （装在大型车辆）保险杠上的前照灯（可降低灯光照射高度，防止小轿车等小型车辆驾驶者炫目）

bumper horn 保险杠护角（保险杠上的直立形附件，用于防止与其他车辆的保险杠互相卡结）

bumper insert 保险杠嵌条（镶在保险杠整个宽度上的橡皮嵌条）

bumper jack 汽车保险杠专用举升器

bumper lift 汽车保险杠回升（在摆锤碰撞试验中，碰撞第二阶段，保险杠与摆锤撞面分离后，由于汽车的减振回弹作用，使保险杠向上跳动的高度，见 bumper ramping）

bumper pad 缓冲用防振垫，橡皮垫块，缓冲垫，保险杠镶条（装于保险杠前面的非金属条）

bumper position visual indicator （汽车）保险杠位置视标（一般是在保险杠端部装一垂直杆，杆顶装有小灯或标志球，供驾驶员标测保险杠的位置）

bumper ramping 汽车保险杠的碰撞移距（在摆锤碰撞试验中，碰撞第一阶段，保险杠与摆锤碰撞面分离前，由于汽车的减振回弹作用，使保险杠沿锤面的上移距离，见 bumper lift）

bumper step （载货车）后保险杠登车踏脚板

bumper tester ①减振器试验台，缓

冲器试验台②保险杠试验台
bumper-to-back-of-cab dimension 从保险杠至驾驶室后壁的距离
bumper-to-bumper （车身）汽车，前保险杠至后保险杠长度
bumping ①撞击，冲击②颠簸③形成凹凸不平④（特指）车身板件矫正修理敲击作业
bumping bag 防撞气囊，安全气囊，缓冲气囊
bumping blade 矫正车身板件轻微或较缓的凹陷用的）扁平锤（有的锤面上有锉纹状小齿，以免刮伤板件金属，故亦称 bumping file）
bumping hammer 车身凹陷校正用手锤
bumping out ①敲出②（特指，车身板件变形矫正作业的第一步工序，用平头锤将变形处先）敲回原形
bumping spoon （用手锤敲平矫正车身板件用的）敲击垫匙（锤一边敲击，一边移动该垫，亦称 spring beating spoon）
bumping test 车辆颠簸试验（车辆行驶在坎坷不平的道路或人造搓板跑道上以承受冲击）
bumping tool （车身外壳）矫直锤击工具
bump rubber （限制悬架最大行程的）橡胶挡块
bump score test （在冲击负荷作用下的）撞击伤痕试验
bump start 推车起动（指齿轮变速器式汽车蓄电池电压不足时，推动汽车或让汽车顺坡下溜，然后接合离合器并挂二挡，使汽车起动的方法或过程）
bump steer 颠簸转向（车辆驶过路上凹凸处时，悬架振动引起的车轮偏转和车辆偏行车方向）
bump stop 悬架压缩行程限位挡块（一般为橡胶缓冲块）

bump stress 冲击应力
bump stroke （车辆颠簸行驶时）悬架弹簧压缩行程
bump test ①（连续）冲击试验②（车辆）颠簸试验
bunch light 聚束灯光，聚光，聚光灯
Bunsen flame method （测定燃烧速率的）本生火焰法
burbling ①（进气）气流旋涡，扰流②泡流分离③层流变湍流
Bureau of Motor Carrier Safety ［美］（运输部的）机动车辆安全运输局（简称 BMCS）
Bureau of Standards 美国标准局（简称 BS，Bur st 或 Bur of Stds）
burglar alarm system 防盗窃警报装置
buried layer 埋层（集成电路中，在集电极正下方基片层内埋置的一层电阻率低的杂质原子）
burn 烧，燃烧（burned 已燃烧的，被烧坏或烧损的，burner 燃烧器，如：喷灯，焊枪等）
burncd gas ratio 已燃气比率，（简称 BGR，指燃烧室中已燃混合气与点燃前全部混合气的比率）
burned air 燃耗空气量（发动机每一循环燃烧时消耗之氧气所对应的空气量）
burner-heated catalyst 燃烧器预热式催化转化净化器（用燃油燃烧预热催化剂，以缩短其起燃时间，简称 BHC，参见 electrically heated catalyst）
burner line 燃气轮机燃烧室的火焰管（= burner pipe）
burner section （燃气轮机的）燃烧器
burn-in ①预烧，老化（指电子部件在装用之前，在不同温度下进行数小时的预模拟运行）②烙上，烧牢，焊上

burning ①燃烧（=combustion）②（断电器触点，火花塞电极，排气门等）烧蚀，（在氧化介质中的滑动接触表面，因局部受热而氧化产生的）烧伤③燃烧的

burning behavior 燃烧特性（= burning characteristics）

burning charge （充入汽缸中的）可燃混合气（或燃料）

burning in （曲轴连杆等轴承）紧配跑合（刮研装配后的跑合）

burning oil ①燃油（煤油、轻油、重油等的统称）②（特指）煤油

burning point 着火点，燃烧温度（亦称 burning temperature）

burnish ①光泽，光亮②抛光，磨光，压光③（钢）烧蓝

burn-off 焊穿，烧穿，熔化

burn-out proof 防烧蚀，耐烧毁

burnt ①被烧损的②被烧过的，烧完的

burr 毛刺、飞边

burr walnut 胡桃木薄板料（用于豪华轿车仪表板、车门等复面）

burst 爆炸，爆破（如轮胎爆裂）

bursting pressure （引起轮胎、油箱等）爆破（的）压力

burst(ing) test （软管、轮胎、油箱等的静压）破裂试验

burst-proof door lock 可防振开的门锁

burst speed （飞轮等高速旋转件的）破裂速度

burst tire 爆胎

bus board 汇流条板

bus controller 总线控制器（①指计算机中央处理器与内程序存储器、外存储器之间的接口②指产生总线命令和控制信号的部件）

bush ①套筒，套管，衬套，衬管（[美]=bushing）②用金属衬里，加衬套，加轴套

bush bearing 轴套，整体式滑动轴承（=solid bearing, bushing bearing, 简称 bush 或 bushing）

bushed 装有轴套的，装有衬套的

bushel 蒲式耳，斛（英制容积单位，代号 bush, bsh, bus, bu。1 bush = 8 gallons, 英国原意为 500 磅水的容积，英国 bushel 等于 2219.36 英寸^3，参见 Imperial gallon; 美国 bushel 等于 2150.42 英寸^3, 用以衡量干物容积，不用于衡量液体, 1 美 busher = 4pecks = 32 干 quart = 64 干 pint = 0.3524m^3 ≈ 1.25 英尺^3）

Bush engine 布什发动机（一种改良型司特林发动机，参见 stirling engine）

bush extractor 衬套拉器

bushing lock 轴瓦定位榫，衬套定位榫

bushing renewing tool 轴套更换用工具（简称 bushing tool, 亦称 bushing replacer, 包括 bushing driver "衬套压出冲子", bushing press "衬套压装机", bushing puller "衬套拉器"等，总称为衬套拆装成套工具 "bushing tool set"）

bushing ring 衬环

bush metal ①衬套（轴承）合金，（铜72%，锡14%，黄铜14%）②铜（衬）套

business car 商务用汽车，公务用汽车,营业用汽车（相对娱乐、业余时间游乐用汽车而言，亦称 business purpose vehicle, 简称 B.P.V）

bus lane 公共汽车专用车道（= special bus lane）

bus stop 公共汽车停车站

bus terminal 公共汽车起、终点站，客运站

bus-to-bus communication system 客车间通信系统

bus top 双层公共汽车的上层车厢，双层客车顶层

bus tractor 客车牵引车，带挂车的

客车

butadiene 丁二烯（通常指 $CH_2=CH-CH=CH_2$）

butadiene rubber 聚丁二烯橡胶（简称 BR，亦称 butaprene）

butane 丁烷（$CH_3-CH_2-CH_2-CH_3$）（加压液化后，作为货车燃料）

butanol 丁醇（C_4H_9OH，= butal alcohol）

BUTC 上止点前（before upper dead center 的简称，= BTDC）

butene polymers 丁烯聚合物（= butylene polymers）

butt and collar joint 套筒接合

butt cracks 接头裂缝，端面裂纹

butt end 端面，对接端

butterfly bolt 蝶形头螺栓（参见 fly-headed screw）

butterfly carburetor 蝶形阀式活动喉管化油器（其空燃比籍随转速变化而变化的蝶形阀的开度来控制）

butterfly nut 蝶形螺母（= wing nut）

butterfly opening hood （两侧板可向上翻转的）蝶式发动机罩

butterfly valve 蝶形阀（由两块半圆阀片和中间枢轴组成）

butt joint ①对接，对头接，平接 ②碰焊，对接焊，= butt weld (ing)

butt joint ring （切口端面是平的）对接（密封）环

buttock-cushion 坐垫

buttock to head vibration 人体上下振动（沿人体脊柱方向从臀至头的直线振动，参见 foot to head vibration）

button ①按钮，旋钮；球形捏手，纽扣状物 ②（特指，球销式万向节的）球头钉（为球头轴定位并能承受推力的元件）

button control 按钮操纵，按钮控制（= knob control）

Button-control （电动）按钮控制的

button head 圆头（的）（= round head）

button shift mode 加减按钮换挡模式

button start （汽车发动机的）按钮式起动

button-type clutch facing 离合器片上的圆钮形摩擦衬面

buttress ①（轮胎）胎侧加强部 ②支持物

buttressed thread 锯齿形螺纹，偏梯形螺纹（螺纹的一侧面呈斜形，另一侧面为垂直形者）

butyl 丁(烷)基（$CH_3(CH_2)_2CH_2-$）

butyl alcohol 丁醇（涂料的溶剂）

butylenes 丁烯

butyl rubber 异丁(烯)橡胶，丁基橡胶（见 IIR）

buzzer 蜂鸣器（用电磁线圈激励膜片振动产生低声级的音响器，亦称 buzzer phone）

BV ①击穿电压（break down voltage 的简称）②平衡电压（balanced voltage 的简称）

BVSV 双金属温控真空阀（见 bimetal vacuum switching valve）

B/W display （汽车液晶显示器的）黑白两色显示

by pass 旁通，绕行，旁路

bypass air screw 旁通空气螺钉（如：汽油喷射系统空气流量传感器上的、用于调节混合气中的空气量的螺钉）

bypass clutch control valve 液力变矩器锁止离合器（接合、分离）控制阀（见 CCC valve）

bypass highway 绕行公路

bypass hot-wire air flow sensor 旁通式热线空气（质量）流量传感器（其热线传感头置于主空气通道侧的旁通空气通道内，以免受气流中未滤净的微粒的污损和减少回流空气的影响）

bypass idle-hole 怠速过渡油孔，第二怠速油孔（= secondary idle-hole）

bypass line 旁通管路，支线管道，溢流管（= bypass pipe）

bypass poppet valve （变量轴向柱塞泵的）菌形旁通阀

bypass port ①旁通孔 ②（有时特指制动主缸中的）补偿孔

bypass type oil filter 旁通式机油滤清器（一般指并联主机油管中的精滤器，只过滤全部循环机油的10%~30%，可滤除5~10μm的机械杂质，简称 bypass filter，= bleeder type filter，partial-flow filter）

bypass-type thermostat 旁通式恒温器

bypass valve 旁通阀，溢流阀（一般为减压阀，该阀开启，可溢出部分流体，从而降低工作压力或作用压力，起调节或保护作用）

byte （电子计算机）字节（计算机内存容量的基本度量单位，一般由8位二进制数，即8个bit组成。内存的一个单元存放一个字节，例如：一个字长32位的数，可分成四个字节，分别存在内存的四个单元内，代表一个字符并且作为一个单元来处理，见 bit, word）

Byteflight 宝马安全总线系统（商品名）

Byteflight "字节飞驰"（商品名，频率时间分割多路复用存取"FTD-MA"汽车局域网）

By-wire fuel-cell vehicle 线控燃料电池车

Bèzier curve 贝齐尔曲线（用于汽车外形设计）

C4 微机控制催化转化器（computer controlled catalytic converter 的简称，为通用公司早期计算机空燃比控制触媒净化系统的商品名，该系统以后为 CCC，computer command control 系统所取代）

C3 计算机指令控制（系统）见 computer command control

C ①烛光（candle）②电容（capacitance）③碳（carbon）④阴极（cathode）⑤电池（cell）⑥摄氏温标（Celsius scale）⑦中心（centre）⑧充电（charge）⑨系数（coefficient）⑩库仑（coulomb）⑪舒适（comfort）

Ca ①钙（calcium）②气冷的，空冷的（air-cooling）

CAA ［美］清洁大气净化法（Clean Air Act）

CAAA ［美］清洁大气法修正案（Clean Air Act Amendments）

cab ①货车驾驶室②出租汽车（= taxi cab）

CAB 复合型防抱死制动（系统）Combination Antilock Brake 的简称，指具有防驱动车轮滑转牵引力控制功能的防抱死制动系统（见 ABS with traction control）

cab-ahead-of-engine truck 前置式驾驶室载货汽车，平头式货车［= cab-over(-engine) truck, camel-back truck, forward control truck, cab-forward type truck］

cab air suspension 商用货车驾驶室的空气弹簧悬架系统

cab-along-side-engine motor truck 驾驶室靠发动机侧的货车（驾驶室及操纵机构在发动机舱的一侧，简称 CAE motor truck，= cba-beside-engine truck, half-cab truck）

cab bed 货车驾驶室内的卧铺

cab-behind-engine (motor) truck ［美］长头运货汽车（驾驶室及操纵机构装置在发动机罩之后，如常规运货汽车，简称 CBE motor truck，=［英］normal control truck）

cab-forward type vehicle 驾驶室前置式车辆，平头车（= forward control vehicle）

cab guard 驾驶室护架，（特指自卸车翻斗前壁延伸至驾驶室上方的）驾驶室顶护罩板（= cab shield, cab protector）

cab heater （商用货车）驾驶室暖气装置

cabin ①（指驾驶区与乘客区有隔断的客车的）乘客区客厢②（无隔断的轿车指驾驶区与乘客区的总称）车厢

cabin communication system 车内通话系统（避免驾驶员与后座乘员谈话时回头和分散精力）

cabinet 舱，室，箱，柜，盒

cabin-forward-design （指轿车的）短头式结构（其驾驶员的放脚坑前移至前桥上方，以增大车厢容量）

cabin space 车厢内部空间

cable ①缆索，缆绳，钢索②电缆（指由若干条相互绝缘的导线和保护外套等构成的信号传输或电流传送线或由多股导线编织或缠绕成的粗线或扁线）

cable brake 由拉杆和拉索操纵的制动器（多指驻车制动器）

cable car 缆车，索车（=cable carriage）

cable clamp ①钢索夹子，缆索夹子 ②电缆夹

cable-conduit assembly （柔性传动）钢索-套管总成

cable-controlled 用绳索操纵的，用钢索控制的（=cable-operated，cable-actuated，如，拉索式制动器、离合器等）

cable-dump truck 钢索自卸式货车，用钢索操纵倾倒的货车

cable guide （固定在货车等车身上的裸）缆索导管

cable-laying vehicle 电缆敷设车辆（=wire laying vehicle）

cable lift 绳索升降装置（常用于挂车倾卸）

cable of bead 胎圈钢丝（圈）

cable-operated 用拉索操纵的（=cable-controlled）

cabling ①导线的连接，接线②导线的布置③导线的结构（如：多股线、绞合线等）④线路⑤缆索（多种 coble 的总称）

cab lock tell-tale 驾驶室锁止警报灯（翻转式驾驶室的锁止机构没有锁住的警报灯）

cab meter 出租汽车计价器（=cab mileage meter 出租汽车里程表）

CAB Module 防抱死与牵引力控制复合系统的控制模块（combination Antiblock module 的简称）

cab mounting 驾驶室悬架（驾驶室装在车架上的支撑、减振机构）

caboose-to-engine communication （汽车列车等）驾驶室与尾车间的通信

cab over (the) engine motor truck 平头货车（指整个发动机或其主要部分位于驾驶室下方的货车，简称 COE motor truck）

cabriolet 带可折叠式软篷的活顶轿车（=drophead car 或 soft head car，其中两门的称 cabriolet-coupe，cabriolet-roadster 或简称 roadster，四门的美称 cabriolet-sedan，英称 cabriolet-saloon。当前、后无任何限定词时，cabriolet 一般指两门软篷活顶车）

cabriolet top （活顶汽车的）可折叠式软篷顶

cab signal 车内信号装置，车内警报装置（如将道路通行、停车、注意等信号传至车内，由车内信号装置通知驾驶员的系统等）

cab slant （汽车的）驾驶室流线型，驾驶室斜面型（俗称子弹头型）

cab structural member 驾驶室结构件（保证驾驶室强度、刚度要求的零件总称）

cab-tilt 见 tilt-cab

cab-to-trailer corner clearance 驾驶室对挂车货厢前角间隙［车辆最大转弯时，驾驶室后背与挂车货厢前（左）右角的最小间隙］

cab tyre 汽车轮胎

cabtyre cable 橡皮绝缘软电缆（简称 cabtyre）

CAC （汽车）客户支援中心（Customer Assistance Center 的简称）

CACIS 见 continuous AC ignition system

CACS 汽车综合控制系统（comprehensive automobile control system)

CAD 计算机辅助设计（computer-aided design）

CAD/CAM 计算机辅助设计制造一体化（computer aided design/computer aided manufacture 的简称）

CADD ①计算机辅助设计和绘图（computer aided design and drafting）②计算机辅助模具设计（见 computer aided die design）

cadence braking （路遇滑时）节奏式连踩连松（制动踏板的防滑）制动法（亦称 stab braking）

Cadillac ［美］凯迪莱克（通用公司的轿车生产厂家之一）

CA dimension(s) （货车）CA 尺寸（指驾驶室后背最后点到后轴中心线、若为三轴货车，则为到双后轴的中间线间的距离，其中，CA 为 cab-to-axle 的简称）

cadmium 镉（Cd）

cadmium alloy bearing 镉基合金轴瓦

cadmium-nickel battery 镉镍蓄电池

cadmium-plated 镀镉的（镀镉多用于铝及铝合金制件和螺栓、螺母等钢制件）

cadmium test （蓄电池的）镉棒测试（用镉棒作为辅助电极来测试阴、阳极板的状态，借以检验蓄电池故障）

CAE ①特许汽车工程师，注册汽车工程师（chartered automobile engineer）②计算机辅助工程技术（computer aided engineering）③计算机辅助试验（computer aided experimental）

CAEF ［美］公司平均排放量（corporation average emissions figure 的简称，指政府对各汽车公司生产的各种车型的平均要求排放指标）

caesium 铯（Cs，亦写作 cecum）

caesium vapor rectifier 铯蒸气整流器

CAFC 公司平均燃油消耗量（corporation average fuel-consumption 的简称，美国政府对各汽车公司生产的各种车型的平均燃油消耗量的要求限值）

CaFCP （美国）加利福尼亚燃料电池合作计划（California Fuel-Cell Plan 的简称，由加利福尼亚大气局于 1999 年 4 月启动，政府部门，美、日、德等国主要汽车生产厂家和石油公司参加，原计划目标是 1999～2003 年实现燃料电池车商品化，后该计划延长至 2007 年完成）

CAFE 公司平均燃油经济性（corporation average fuel economy，美国政府要求汽车厂家生产的各种车型的平均燃油经济性）

CAGD 计算机辅助几何设计（computer aided geometric design）

cage ①滚动轴承保持架，滚动轴承的隔圈②笼，笼状物；盒，罩，厢，壳体③差速器壳（differential cage 的简称）④（球笼式万向节的钢球）保持架（为一具有内、外球形支撑表面的环形元件，沿其圆周面上开有一组钢球定位窗孔，将钢球保持在等速平面内）

CAID ①计算机辅助工业（造型）设计（computer aided industrial design）②计算机辅助智能化设计（computer aided intelligent design）

CAI petrol engine （计算机）控制自动点火式汽油机（的简称，不用火花塞而是利用电子系统控制的回流废气的热量点燃混合气）

Cairo grey 开罗金（车身颜色）

caking ①烧结，结炭，结焦②烘烤

CAL ①标定（calibrate）②平均计算寿命（calculated average life）③防撞灯（collision avoidance light）④计算机辅助照明（设计）（computer aided lighting）

cal 卡（热量单位，见 calorie）

cal box ①（全自动传呼公共汽车系统的）呼叫箱，传呼箱 ②公共电话亭

CalcdCI 计算十六烷值（见 calculated cetane index）

calcic 钙的，含钙的，石灰质的

calcium 钙（Ca）

calcium-air cell 钙-空气电池

calcium base grease 钙基润滑脂

calcium carbide 碳化钙（CaC_2，白色固体与水作用生成乙炔，简称 carbide）

calcium-lead battery 钙-铅蓄电池（一种免维护蓄电池，用钙代替常规电池的锑）

Calcium-Plus 一种新型的铅-钙蓄电池的商品名

calculate 计算

calculated carbon aromaticity index 计算碳芳香度指数（简称 CCAI，用以评价柴油的着火性）

calculated cetane index 计算十六烷指数，计算十六烷值（表示柴油着火性能，简称 CCI。CCI，不用于合成燃油以及加有着火性添加剂的燃油等）

calculator 计算器（一般指电子计算机"computer"以外的计算装置或计算人员）

calf design （胎面）细花纹

caliber （管，筒等的）内径（亦写作 calibre）

calibrate ①（对仪表、量具等的刻度示值及其精度等进行）标定、校验、校准 ②标定的，标准的

calibrated ①经校准的，已标定的（多用于指已经标定，在试验、校准或检查中作为标准件使用的，即：)标准的 ②（要加以）标定的

calibrater 标定、标准、测检用器具的通称（亦写作 calibrator）

calibrating gas 校正气（已知浓度的标准气体，用来制定仪器的校正曲线。在美国，校正气精度一般分为：国家标准局标准参比气"NBS standard reference gases"，贵重标准气"golden standards"，初级标准气"primary standards"和工作气"working gases"几种）

calibration ①标定、校准（指在规定条件下，确定测量仪器仪表或实物量具的示值与被测量对应的已知值之间关系的操作）②（确）定刻度，定分度

calibration command （电子控制模块根据各种传感器的输入信息对各执行元器件发出的发动机）运行参数控制量指令（见 engine calibration）

calibration curve 校准曲线（在规定条件下，表示被测量值与仪器仪表实际测得值之间的关系曲线，如：废气分析仪的校正曲线为以校正气浓度为横坐标，以分析仪的读数为纵坐标制成的曲线，亦称 calibration trace）

calibration cycle 校准循环（仪器仪表校准范围极限间上行校准曲线与下行校准曲线的组合）

calibration map ①（汽车电子计算机控制系统的）控制参数曲面（图）（指某一控制量随两种变量的变化而改变的曲面）②校准曲面（指对某一随两种变量而变化的装置或系统的输出进行校准或标定用的校准曲面图）

calibration package 见 calpak

calibration screw 校准用螺钉（指仪器仪表上对其示值进行校准用的螺钉）

calibration table 校准表格（校准曲线的数据表格形式）

calibration test 标定试验

calibre ratio of combustion chamber 燃烧室口径比（半开式和开式燃烧

室中，活塞顶内燃烧室的口径与汽缸直径的比值）

California Air Resources Board ［美］加利福尼亚州大气资源局（简称CARB）

California cycle 加利福尼亚多工况循环（美国加州规定的汽车排气污染试验工况循环）

California's low-emission vehicle standard ［美］加利福尼亚低公害车标准，加州低排放车标准（简称California LEV standard）

California top 带侧壁的折叠式车顶

caliper disc brake 钳盘式制动器（由固定于车轮并随车轮转动的制动盘和固定于车辆固定部位上的制动钳组成，制动钳上的摩擦衬块仅覆盖制动盘工作表面一小部分，分定盘式和浮盘式两种，caliper亦写作calliper）

caliper drag （盘式制动器）制动钳拖滞

caliper frame 制动钳安装架

calking 敛缝，凿密，填密（亦写作caulking）

call 呼叫

cal(l)iper ①（复数）卡钳，卡尺，圆规，两脚规（=calliper gauge）②（钳盘式）制动（器的）卡钳（见brake caliper）

cal(l)iper anchor bracket （盘式制动器的）制动钳安装架（亦称caliper adapter, caliper mounting bracket，由于该支架多为一承受转矩的板状构件，故亦称torque plate）

cal-look ［美］加州风格（指源于美国加利福尼亚州的一种小型轿车外形改装风格，去掉原车的所有镀络件，顶多留一条车侧装饰镀铬条，将车身涂成黄、浅蓝、红等鲜艳的颜色，或加装镀铬双管式或平板型保险杠）

caloric ①热的，热量的，热力的（=calorific）②热量，热质

calorie 小卡，卡［CCS单位制的热量单位，代号cal，即1g的水，每升高1℃所需的热量，在国际单位制中，已为焦耳"joule"代替，1cal（mean）=4.1897J，≈4.2J。由于焦耳"J"也是功的单位，故4.2J/cal焦/卡叫作热功当量］

calorific 热的，热量的，热能的，发热的

calorimetric flow sensor 热测量型空气流量传感器（热线式空气质量流量传感器的一种，与一般热线式传感器不同处在于它将加热功能与传感器功能分开）

calorite 耐热合金（镍65％，铬12％，铁15％，锰8％）

calorize （表面）渗铝，（对…进行）铝化（处理），热镀铝

Calpak 插装式标定程序包，标定软件插块（calibration package的简称，一般为一集成块，直接插在电子控制模块的专门插座上，存储有喷油量的计量数据、控制程序等。当电子控制模块出现影响其执行喷油控制程序的故障时，calpak即充当喷油控制备份电路"fuel back up circuit"向喷油器电磁阀发出喷油脉冲指令，见TBB）

Caltrans （美）加利福尼亚运输局（California Department of Transportation的简称）

CAM ①（汽车）维护（care and maintenance）②计算机辅助制造（computer aided manufacture）③计算机辅助管理（computer aided management）

cam ①凸轮②有时指凸轮轴（如：twin cam engine"双凸轮轴发动机"）

cam-actuated 凸轮作动力的，凸轮驱动的

cam-actuated brake 凸轮促动型鼓式

制动器（制动时，凸轮将制动蹄顶开，紧压制动鼓，简称 cam brake，见 fixed cam brake, floating cam brake）

cam and lever steering gear 见 cam and peg steering gear

cam and peg steering gear 蜗杆指销式转向器（有时，用 worm 代替 cam，用 lever、stud 代替 peg，称 worm and peg, cam and leve, worm and lever, cam and stud 等 steering gear。一根变螺距蜗杆位于转向盘轴的下端，其螺旋槽与装在摇臂轴上的指销啮合，其中，带固定指销的，称 with fixed stud，带滚轮的，称 with roller stud，带双指销的，称 twin-lever type 等）

cam-and-rack steering gear 齿轮-齿条式转向器（具有齿轮-齿条传动副的转向器，= rack and pinion steering gear）

cam-and-roller steering gear 蜗杆滚轮式转向器（指由蜗杆-滚轮传动副组成的转向器，蜗杆 cam 常写作 worm。有双滚轮式 double-roller, twin roller 和单滚轮式 single roller 等多种）

cam-and-roller type free wheel 滚柱式自由轮，滚柱式单向离合器，滚柱式超越离合器

cam angle ①凸轮包角，凸轮工作角 ②（以凸轮转角表示的某一时间的长度或某一过程的延续时间）断电器触点闭合角（指该触点闭合期分电器凸轮所转过的角度，参见 dwell angle）

cam angle tester （断电器触点开、闭期的）凸轮转角测试仪

cam belt （camshaft belt 的简称，凸轮轴的）正时齿轮传动带

camber ①车轮外倾［指车轮中心平面向外倾斜，若向内倾斜，则称 negative camber 负外倾，或内倾，车辆的外倾和负外倾（内倾）统称车辆侧（向）倾（斜）］②车轮外倾角（= camber angle，指车轮外倾后，其中心平面与中心平面接地线垂直平面间的夹角，俗称 Rake angle）③（路面或其他表面）向上拱曲，拱度④（钢板弹簧叶片的）挠曲⑤弯度，曲度，向上弯曲，翘曲，中凸形，上挠度，成弓形，弧线

camber aligning torque 车轮外倾（产生的）回正转矩

camber-and-caster aligner ①转向轮外倾角-主销后倾角调准仪②前轮定位仪

cambered 成拱形的，向上凸起的，拱曲的

cambered axle ①拱形车桥②弯轴

cambered spring 半椭圆形钢板弹簧（= bow spring, half-elliptic spring, semielliptic spring，指由中间向两端平缓翘曲，整体呈半个椭圆形的钢板弹簧，是钢板弹簧中用得最多的一种）

camber effect 外倾效应（见 camber steer effect）

camber of spring （钢板）弹簧挠度（= spring camber，亦称 opening of spring）

camber steer coefficient （汽车的）车轮外倾转向系数（即车轮每外倾 1°引起的转向角偏转度）

camber steer effect （汽车车轮的）外倾转向效应（指车轮具有外倾角时对转向角的影响。其影响程度用 camber steer coefficient 表示，常简称 camber effect）

camber stiffness 外倾刚度（外倾角的单位增量所对应的横向力的增量。通常指在外倾角为 0°时的测定值）

camber stiffness coefficient 外倾刚度系数（自由滚动车轮的外倾刚度与

垂直负荷的比值)

camber thrust 外倾推力(侧偏角为0°时,为保持车轮外倾而作用在车轮上的横向力,即:外倾角在轮胎负荷作用下产生的与车前束侧向阻力相抗衡的推力,亦称 camber thrust force,简称 camber force)

camber torque ①外倾转矩(车轮外倾造成的使车轮前端外张的转矩)②外倾回正力矩,外倾稳定力矩(=camber aligning torque)

camber wear (外倾造成的)轮胎胎面单边均匀磨损

cam brake 凸轮张开式制动器(指利用凸轮的转动使制动蹄张开并压靠到旋转件上面产生制动作用的鼓式制动器,亦称 cam operated brake, cam actuated brake)

cam chain 正时(齿轮)链条(camshaft chain 的简称)

cam contour 见 cam profile

cam design 见 cam profile

cam drive 凸轮驱动(机构),凸轮传动(机构)

camel-top truck 驼箱式载货汽车(车箱高于驾驶室顶)

camera-based headlight 摄像(信息)控制(变光的)前照灯(系统)(电子控制系统根据实时摄像系统的信息判断对向行驶的车辆临近规定的距离时使前照灯减光)

cam face 凸轮表面(=surface of cam)

cam follower ①凸轮随动件(亦称 camshaft follower,指一切随凸轮轮廓而起降或运动,即:将凸轮的转动变为升降或特定运动的部件的总称,如:在发动机气门机构中,靠在凸轮轴凸轮上随凸轮的转动而上、下运动的 valve tappet "气门挺杆",push rod "推杆",及直接由凸轮驱动的 rocker arm "摇臂"等)②(美·特指)带滚轮的气门挺柱(亦称 roller lifter)

cam for relieving compression (发动机起动时使用的)减压缩力凸轮,减压凸轮

cam ground piston 椭圆形活塞(=oval piston, oval section piston, cam shaped piston)

cam heel ①凸轮背面(凸轮非工作面,凸轮曲线的非凸起部分)②凸轮凸尖对面的最低点(有时亦指凸轮基圆"base circle")

camion ①重型载货汽车(参见 heavy-duty lorry)②军用货车

cam lead 凸轮升程(=lead of cam, cam lift, cam rise,指凸轮轮廓线的最高点与基圆半径之差)

camless engine 无凸轮(轴)式发动机(其气门的开启与关闭由电子控制的电动-液压式气门开闭执行器操纵)

cam lobe 凸轮的凸起部,凸轮的工作部分

cam lubricator (一般指润滑断电器)触点凸轮的(油绳)润滑器

camming surface (轴之类的非凸轮零件上的)凸轮面

cam opening angle (断电器)触点断开期间的凸轮转角(参见 dwell angle)

camouflage color (军用车辆的)伪装色

camper ①[英]野营车(=[美] recreational vehicle,供旅行野营的箱式机动车,多备有起居和炊饮设备)②[美]野营挂车(=[英] caravan,指无动力装置由其他车辆拖挂牵引的单轴箱式挂车,亦称 camping trailer)

cam plate 平板形凸轮,凸轮盘

cam profile 凸轮轮廓线(=cam contour,有时亦称 cam design)

cam pump ①由曲轴上的凸轮驱动的机油泵等②由凸轮而不是由曲柄

连杆机构驱动的往复式活塞泵

cam rim 凸轮环（一般指内表面带有凸起工作面的内凸轮环）

cam rise 见 cam lead

cam roller （滚轮式气门挺杆、汽油泵等的）驱动凸轮随动滚轮

CAMS 计算机控制汽车维护系统（Computerized Automotive Maintenance System 的简称）

cam sensor 凸轮轴位置传感器（camshaft position sensor 的简称）

camshaft 凸轮轴，偏心轴

camshaft advance indicator （可变气门正时机构的）凸轮轴提前角指示器

camshaft bearing 凸轮轴轴承，凸轮轴衬套（= camshaft bushing）

camshaft drive 凸轮轴驱动机构（指驱动凸轮轴的机构）

camshaft drive belt 凸轮轴驱动带，正时带

camshaft drive sprocket （曲轴的）凸轮轴驱动链轮

camshaft end play 凸轮轴端隙（凸轮轴的轴向活动量）

camshaft follower 凸轮轴从动件（特指压靠在凸轮上传递往复运动的部件，如：camshaft rocker arm 等）

camshaft follower bracket 凸轮从动件支架（摇臂心轴支架）

camshaft follower shaft 凸轮从动件销轴（如：摇臂的心轴，摇臂绕该轴自由摆动）

camshaft housing （装在顶置双凸轮轴发动机汽缸盖上的）凸轮轴罩（一般除罩住凸轮轴外，还包括气门挺杆）

camshaft in the vee V 形发动机用凸轮轴

camshaft journal 凸轮轴轴颈

camshaft oil pump driving gear 凸轮轴（上的）机油泵驱动齿轮

camshaft phasing control 凸轮轴相位控制（通过对进、排气凸轮轴相位控制，改变进、排气门在发动机不同转速下的开、关时刻，借以调节进、排气门叠开时间的长短）

camshaft position sensor 凸轮轴位置传感器（简称 CMP，美国政府规定从 1995 年 1 月 1 日起使用的标准术语，取代通用和克莱斯勒公司的 SYN 和福特公司的 CID 等，亦称 camshaft reference sensor）

camshaft puller 凸轮轴（端的驱动）传动带盘

camshaft sprocket 凸轮轴链轮（指装在凸轮轴上的驱动链轮）

camshaft thrust spacer 凸轮轴止推隔片（= camshaft thrust plate）

camshaft timing gear 凸轮轴正时齿轮（见 distribution gear）

cam-shaped piston 椭圆形裙部活塞

cam slot 凸轮槽（起凸轮作用的槽形件）

cam-type axial piston pump 斜盘式轴向柱塞泵

cam-type wave generator （谐波齿轮的）凸轮式波发生器（以某种轮廓线的凸轮作为基本构件的积极控制式波发生器，参见 wave generator）

can ①罐，壶，桶②（密封式电动机中定子线圈的）绝缘管（见 canned motor pump）

CAN 控制器局域网（controller area network 的简称，多路传输系统的一种。为有效支持分布式控制或实时控制串行通信网络，20 世纪 80 年代初，德国 Bosch 公司为实现现代汽车众多电子控制系统间联网实时数据交换而开发了 CAN 协议，1991 年 9 月形成技术规范 2.0 版本，1993 年 CAN 规范为国标标准组织 ISO 定为国际标准。自 2000 年起美国制造商也开始用 CAN 代替 J1850。早在 2005 年，CAN 就已占据汽车

网络协议市场的63%）

canal 管路，管道，槽、沟

can bus CAN 总线［按 CAN 标准建立的分布式控制、多主竞争总线，它不使用传统的地址编码方式，而是对数据信息进行编码，其通信速率最高可达1Mb/s（距离40m），能充分满足汽车发动机、自动变速器、防抱死制动、牵引力、动力转向、悬架以及安全气囊和组合仪器等众多控制系统间的连续实时信息交换和动作相互关联与协作的要求，其成本低，可在恶劣的强磁干扰环境下可靠地工作。在不增加新硬件和不降低可靠性的前提下，只要通过软件，便可增加新的系统功能。此外，CAN 总线亦可用来作为某一控制系统内部（如主动式变阻尼悬架系统的各车轮悬架之间）交换信息的通道。CAN 总线在汽车领域几乎成为一种必须采用的技术手段，已成为汽车总线的化名词，目前，奔驰，宝马，大众，沃尔沃，丰田，本田等多家公司都在采用 CAN 总线技术］

cancel 删去，省略，取消，把…作废，约去，消去，抵消，吸收

cancellation ①消除，抵消，补偿②（特指使用可调谐振器或可吸收一定频率范围内的声能的材料来）消声（亦称 absorption）

candela 坎德拉，（新）烛光（国际单位制的发光强度单位，代号为 cd 或 CD。1cd 等于 $1/600000m^2$ 的黑体在101325Pa 的压力和铂凝固温度2042K 下，在垂直方向的发光强度，用来取代原先使用的 candle, international candle 等单位）

candelabra bayonet base （直径15mm 的）小型卡门灯座

candelabra prefocused base （直径15mm 的）小型定焦距凸缘灯座

candidate 候选方案，选择对象，候选对象，选用结构

candidate automotive powerplant 候选的汽车动力装置

candidate oil 润滑油试样

candle （旧）烛光（= international candle, 美国用的发光强度单位，较国际新烛光约大1.6%，已由 candela 替代）

candle-power 烛光（简称 CP, 用烛光表示的灯光的亮度）

candle type suspension 烛式悬架（车轮可沿主销轴线方向移动的独立悬架形式，亦称 sliding pillar type suspension）

candy white 糖果白（车身颜色）

canister ①金属罐，金属筒②（特指汽车蒸发排放物控制系统中收集和存储来自油箱等的燃油蒸气的）活性炭罐

canister purge 活性炭罐扫气（简称 CANP, 亦称活性炭罐清罐，指发动机工作时，利用进气歧管内的真空将新鲜空气通过一滤清层吸入活性炭罐内，新鲜空气通过罐内的活性炭层时便将存储于其中的汽油蒸气和新进入罐内的汽油蒸气带走，经罐端的管道一起送入进气歧管的整个过程，亦称 canister purging, charcoal canister purge, 简称 CCP, 美国政府规定，从1995年1月1日起，不再使用 CANP 这一术语，而一律改用统一名称 EEC, 见 evaporative emission control）

canned gasoline 桶装汽油

canned motor ①（装在）密封（外壳内的）发动机②密封式电动机

canned motor pump 潜水泵，密封式电动机泵（指由密封式电动机直接驱动的无密封件液体泵。由于其电动机的定子绕组由专门的绝缘管密封而与所泵吸的液体隔离，因此，泵轴无须再装密封件来防止所泵吸的液体进入电动机）

canned software 通用软件（预先编好向用户提供的通用化程序）

cannibalize 拼修（拆用其他车的零件来修车，利用旧件修车，= cannibalise）

canning （将…）装入罐内，装入容器内（如：将催化剂装入催化转化器的催化箱内）

cannular 管状的，中空的（亦写作 cannulate）

cannular chamber 环形截面管式燃烧室

canon 标准，准则，规则，典范，规范，定律

canopy 罩，盖，顶篷，遮阳板

canopy rail ①（汽车车身的）风窗篷条（板）（= windscreen rail, beam over windscreen）②帆布顶篷支架

canopy top 篷顶；固定篷布车顶

canopy truck 带篷顶的载货汽车

CANP 见 canister purge

CANP solenoid 活性炭罐（内的燃油蒸气）清扫电磁阀（canister purge solenoid 的简称，见 EVAP solenoid）

cant ①使倾斜；推，撞；切掉棱角；改变方向，翻转②斜面，角，有棱角的木材，倾斜，斜撑③汽车转向轮主销后倾（= caster）④超高（公路弯道上内外侧的倾斜坡度）

cantilever ①悬臂，悬臂梁②支架，支撑木，角撑架③使…伸出悬臂（= cantalever, cantaliver）

cantilever crane 悬臂起重机

cantilever roof 悬臂式车顶（无前侧柱，发生碰撞事故时，驾驶人员等不致被侧柱撞伤）

cantilever spring ①悬臂式钢板弹簧（指倒置的半椭圆形钢板弹簧 = inverted semielliptic spring，弹簧的中央部分由 U 形螺栓等固定在车架上，其一端通过吊耳装在车架上，另一端亦通过吊耳等支撑在车桥上）②1/4 椭圆形弹簧［= (one) quarter elliptic spring，只有倒置的半椭圆形钢板弹簧的一半，即：保留有固定在车架上的中央部分与支撑在车桥上的半段，另外支撑在车架上的半段被截去，因其形似一个椭圆形的 1/4，故名。又由于它实际上是悬臂式弹簧的一半，故亦称 semielliptic cantilever spring］

cantilever traction attachment （牵引车的）悬架式加载装置（增加驱动轮的载重，以提高它与路面的摩擦力，从而加大它可能利用的最大牵引力）

cantrail ①（厢式货车车身的）上边梁（侧围骨架顶边的纵梁，亦称 roof side rail，或写作 cant rail。有时亦指中间的顶盖纵梁，= roof rail）②（客车车身的顶盖两侧部框架的）上边梁（为顶盖两侧的纵向加强件）

canvas ①帆布②帆布制的

canvas top 帆布（车）顶篷（美，指活顶敞篷车的天然织物软顶篷）

cap ①电容（量）（capacitance）②电容器（capacitor）③容量，能力（capacity）

cap ①盖，帽，罩，嘴②灯头

CAP ①（［美］货车的）净化空气装置（Clearer Air Package system 的简称）②曲轴转角相位（指用上止点前、后的转角来表示的曲轴位置，crank angular position 的简称）

capability 能力

capable ①可…的，能…的，易…的②有技能的，有资格的

capacitance ①电容量，电容（电容器所带电量，与其两极间电势差成正比，其比值为一恒量，称作电容，简称 C，其单位为法拉，简称法 F，见 farad）②（各种）容量

capacitance-coupled 电容耦合的

capacitance potentiometer 电容分压器，电容电位计

capacitance-resistance 阻容（简称CR）

capacitive 电容（性）的，容性的

capacitive acceleration sensor 电容式加速度传感器

capacitive accelerometer 电容式加速度计

capacitive discharge 电容放电（①指电容器存储的能量的放电过程②指点火系次级电路分布电容与火花塞静电电容蓄积的静电能量等的放电过程）

capacitive discharge ignition system 电容放电点火系（简称CDI system。先由振荡电路将蓄电池直流变为交流，并经变压器升至 300~500V 高压再整流为直流向电容器充电。点火时，电子控制模块发出的点火信号触发开关元件，使电容器向点火线圈初级绕组充电，而在次级绕组产生 20~30kV 的高压，次级电压上升比普通点火系快 10 倍，但电容器放电时间极短，仅 5~50μs，不适用于稀燃发动机，亦称 capacitor discharge ignition system, condenser discharge capacity discharge ignition system, 简称 CD system）

capacitive humidity sensor 电容式相对湿度传感器（由聚合物薄膜式电容器制成，聚合物薄膜的介电常数与大气相对湿度的变化呈线性关系）

capacitively coupled 电容耦合的

capacitive pressure sensor 电容式压力传感器（由感压膜片改变电容器片间的距离，根据由此而引起的电容的变化，测定感压膜片所受到的压力）

capacitive twist sensor 电容式扭转应变传感器（如：一电容器固定，另一片随曲轴旋转，即可产生与曲轴扭转成比例的电容信号）

capacitor ①电容器（任何两个彼此绝缘而又互相靠近的导体，都可以看作是一个电容器，最简单的电容器是两块互相平行、靠近且绝缘的金属板组成的平行板电容器，旧称 condenser）②化油器的加速油泵油筒③能量暂存器，一次储能器，燃料暂存器

capacitor accumulated energy 电容器存储能量（$Q=1/2CV^2$，式中：C-静电量，F；V-无负载端电压，V）

capacitor charging controller 容电器充电控制器（简称 capacitor controller）

capacitor hybrid vehicle 电容器型混合动力车（不使用常规蓄电池而使用高性能电容器型蓄电系统的内燃机-电动机混合动力车）

capacitor type energy reservoir 电容器型储能器

capacitor type flasher 电容式闪光器（以电容器充电放电来控制继电器动作的闪光器）

capacity ①（内燃机的）排量（= swept volume, displacement，指全部汽缸工作容积的总和，美国仍沿用 in^3 为单位，欧洲则用 cm^3 或 L 为单位）②（容器的）容积，容量（= volume 或 usable volume）③（电容器的）电容量（旧称，现多用 capacitance）④（电动机等的）输出（功率）⑤（泵等的）排量（如：每分钟的可泵液体的升数或加仑数）

capacity cell 电容器型蓄电器

capacity-controlled oil pump 排量可（由电子控制模块根据润滑需要量）控（制的）机油泵

capacity factor ①（设备）功率利用率②负载因素③能容系数（如：液力变矩器等叶轮的能容系数，为

其转速 N 与转矩 T 平方根之比，简称 K factor）

capacity load 满载，满负荷，全容量载荷，额定载荷（＝full load）

capacity of road 道路通过能力（＝road capacity）

capacity of tyre 轮胎的载质量，轮胎的承载能力（＝tyre capacity）

capacity of vehicle 车辆的容量，车辆装载量（＝vehicle capacity）

capacity qualifying circuit 能力鉴定电路（简称CQC，指用来部分或全面评价申报的新研制电路的能力的试验样品）

capacity rating 额定排量，额定容量，额定功率（＝rated capacity，指排量、功率、容量等的额定值）

capacity reactance 电容电抗，容抗（＝capacitive reactance，condensive reactance）

capacity reserve 容量储备，能力储备，功率储备

CAPE 计算机辅助生产工程（computer aided production engineering 的简称）

cap end pressure 盖端压力，（油缸）无活塞杆端压力

capillarity 毛细管作用，毛细管现象

capillary ①毛细管（＝capillary tube）②毛细管的

capillary viscometer 毛细管黏度计（定量的流体流过的时间秒数，表示该流体的黏度）

capital repair 大修，全面拆修（＝big repair，general overhaul）

cap nut 螺盖，封口螺母

cap of connecting rod big end 连杆（大端）轴承盖（＝connecting rod bearing cap）

CAPP 计算机辅助工艺规划设计（computer aided process program 的简称）

capping 见 door capping

cap plies 胎冠缓冲层（＝shock plies）

cap screw 自攻螺钉（见 tap bolt）

capsize mode （剧烈振动引起的汽车行驶方向的）颠覆性振荡模式（如果失控，将导致汽车翻倾）

capsize safety （车辆的抗）倾翻安全性

capstan ①卷扬机，绞盘，立式绞车 ②（磁盘录音机磁带传动的）主动轮驱动盘

capstan screw 绞盘状（带孔的）圆头螺钉，圆杆螺柱（其圆形头部有一个或数个穿通的圆孔，供插入板杆拧紧或拧松螺钉用，似微型绞盘，故名）

capstat 蜡囊式温度调节器（蜡囊体积随温度而变化，借以实现对各种随温度而改变的控制参数的调节功能）

capsule ①囊，膜盒②膜盒式传感器

captain's chair （豪华型轿车等的）老板型座椅

captive （位置）固定不变的，被拴住的

captive nut 固定螺母（指固定在各种构件上，用于加装其他附件等的螺母）

captive plain washer 固定式平垫圈（如，某些螺栓头部下方本身带有的平垫圈）

car ①轿车，小客车（＝passenger car，motor car，［美］automobile，但在欧洲 automobile 指 motor vehicle，见 automobile）②（铁路列车）车厢（［英］carriage coach ②）③［美］有轨电车（＝tramcar）

car accident 汽车事故，车祸（当表示撞车时，＝car crash）

caravan （主要用于英国，指带有旅居设备的单轴无动力）旅居挂车（＝［美］camper，camping trailer）

caravanning 乘旅居挂车度假旅行

caravansary 旅居汽车旅馆（可容纳旅居车队住宿的旅馆，亦定作 caravanserai）

CARB [美]加利福尼亚州大气资源局（California Air Resources Board 的简称）

carb 化油器，汽化器（carburetor 的简称）

car beautification 轿车美容（一般包括清洗，打蜡，仪表及车厢内清洗，吸尘等）

car belt （轿车乘员）安全带

carbide ①碳化物②碳化钙，电石（calcium carbide 的简称）

carbide alloy 硬质合金

carbinol 甲醇 CH_3OH（一般用于复合词中）

car blind 汽车遮光帘（一般指后窗防跟随车辆前照灯光炫目的遮帘）

carbolite 磺烃酚醛塑料

carbon ①碳（代号C）②碳棒，碳（电）刷，石墨③积炭，积炭层（亦称 coke）④使碳化

carbonaceous 含碳的，碳质的

carbonate ①碳酸盐（或酯）②碳酸盐（或酯）的③充碳酸气④质碳化

carbonate deposit 碳酸盐水垢

carbon balance method （燃油消耗量测定的）炭平衡法（发动机排放的总炭量等于发动机所消耗的燃油中的总炭量）

carbon-based seal 石墨基密封片（以石墨为基体，渗金属等的密封片）

carbon bearing ①含碳的；②碳素轴承，石墨轴承

carbon black 炭黑（塑料，特别是轮胎橡胶的填料，可改善其机械性能并使其成黑色）

carbon-black/oil slurries 炭黑浆油（将炭黑微粒与柴油混合，喷入往复式柴油机中使用，以节油）

carbon blaster （金属表面）积炭喷砂清除器

carbon bridge 火花塞电极间形成的（导电）积炭桥

carbon brush 碳（电）刷

carbon built-up （指燃烧室内，活塞顶等处的）积炭（= carbon deposits）

carbon ceramic （制动摩擦片用的）石墨金属陶瓷合金（亦称 carbon ceramal）

carbon composition resistors 碳粉混合物电阻器（用碳粉与合成树脂等混合，压制成各种形状的电阻元件）

carbon content 碳含量

carbon-core leads 碳芯导线（石墨芯点火高压线等）

carbon deposit 积炭（燃油不完全燃烧，一部分炭粒和杂质沉积于内燃机燃烧室壁面和活塞等零件上的现象，亦称 carbon built-up）

carbon dioxide 二氧化碳（CO_2）

carbon electrode 碳电极

carbon-element seal 石墨密封件

carbon equivalent 碳数当量［碳氢化合物浓度（ppm）乘以构成其分子的碳原子数之积，用百分率碳（ppmc）表示的碳氢化合物浓度单位］

carbonfiber reinforced resin 碳素纤维强化树脂

carbon fibre 碳素纤维（质量轻、强度高的纯碳素纤维，用作复合材料、塑料、金属等的增强材料）

carbon fibre reinforced plastics 碳素纤维强化塑料（简称 CFRP，= graphite fiber reinforced plastics，以环氧树脂、酚醛树脂或聚四氟乙烯、聚酯树脂等基体材料，加上碳素纤维或其织物作增强骨架而制成的一种高强度，高弹性，轻的复合材料）

carbon (-filled) canister （燃油蒸发污染控制系的）燃油蒸气活性炭储蓄箱，活性炭罐

carbon film 积炭层

carbon footprint 含碳排放物，碳排放

carbon fouling 炭污（指火花塞电极被积炭堵塞，以致跳火不良或完全缺火）

carbon-free 不含碳的

carbonic oxide 一氧化碳（CO，= carbon monoxide）

carbon-impregnated aluminum 渗铝石墨 = carbon-impregnated with Al

carbonitriding 氰化，碳氮共渗，渗碳渗氮处理（铁合金在碳氮气氛中加热，吸收碳和氮，然后冷却，使表面硬化）

carbonitriding steel 碳-氮共渗钢

carbonization 结焦，形成积炭，碳化

carbonizing ①碳化②积炭

carbon knock 积炭爆震（汽油发动机由于燃烧室积炭，引起的爆震）

carbon mass balance technique 碳量平衡法（根据废气中的碳含量，测定汽车油耗的方法）

carbon miles 积炭清除里程（指汽车发动机清除积炭作业的间隔里程）

carbon monoxide 一氧化碳（CO）

carbon pile regulator 碳堆稳压器，碳堆调压器（通过改变碳堆的电阻，控制发电机的输出）

carbon pin （分电器盖中央的销形）炭柱（上端接插入分电器盖中心高压插孔的点火线圈高压线，下端接分火头）

carbon pole 石墨电极

carbon tracking 积炭形成的漏电通路

carboxylates 羧化物，羧酸盐

carburation ①渗碳作用，渗碳②（特指在化油器内）燃油气化并按正确的比例与空气混合形成内燃机燃烧所要求的混合气的过程（=［美］carburetion）

carburetor （美）化油器（=［英］carburetter, carburettor，使燃油气化并与空气按一定的比例混合形成可燃混合气的装置）

carburetor altitude adjustment 化油器海拔高度（混合比自动）调整（装置）

carburetor anti-icing additive （汽油的）防化油器结冰添加剂

carburetor balancer （装在一台发动机上的两个或两个以上的化油器或双腔、多腔化油器各腔间）吸入空气量平衡器

carburetor barrel 化油器腔（指化油器安装阻风门、喉管、各种量孔、喷嘴、节气门等，实现空气与燃油按准确比例混合形成混合气的筒形主体部分）

carburetor bowl ［美］化油器浮子室（见 float chamber）

carburetor circuits 化油器油系，化油器油路（如：加速油系、怠速油系等）

carburetor float circuit 化油器浮子系（包括浮子室、浮子及由浮子控制的进油阀）

carburetor flow stand 化油器流量试验台（= carburetor flow tester）

carburetor flow test fluid 化油器流量试验液（化油器流量测试专用油，其馏分的沸点范围窄，密度与黏度均作严格控制）

carburetor intake case 化油器进气腔壳体

carburetor-manifold combination 联体式化油器进气歧管（化油器与进气歧管制成一体）

carburetor port signal 化油器真空孔信号（由化油器真空孔引出的真空

carburetor throat 化油器喉管（= carburetor ventury，指化油器腔中直径收缩部分，喉管在收缩处产生压差，并将燃油吸出，见 ventury）

carburettor choke 化油器阻风门，化油器风门

carburettor controls 节气门操纵杆系，节气门操纵拉杆

carburettor engine 化油器式内燃机（指燃料与空气在化油器和进气管内形成混合气的点燃式内燃机，参见 Otto-engine）

carburettor float 化油器浮子

carburettor icing 化油器结冰

carburize 渗碳（carburized 经渗碳的，carburizing 渗碳用的，用于渗碳的，进行渗碳的，carburization 渗碳）

car cap （汽车露天停放时的）防护罩

car-care center 汽车维修中心

car-care council ［美］汽车维修协会

car care product 汽车养护用品（主要指汽车，特别是车身外表和车厢内部的清洁、抛光、养护用剂和工具）

car/car intersection collision 交叉路口两车相撞

car carrier 轿车运载车，（运载轿车的专用车）

carcass（亦写作 carcase） （轮胎的）胎体（通常为由一层或数层帘布组成整体的充气轮胎的受力结构，亦称 cord carcass 或 cord body，［美］casing）

carcass ply （轮胎胎体的）帘布层（指胎体中由覆胶平行帘线组成的布层，= casing ply, cap ply, stabilizer ply）

carcinogen 致癌物质

carcinogenic hydrocarbons 致癌性烃（如：汽车废气中的 $C_{20}H_{12}$ 等多环芳香族化合物，可能引起肺癌）

car consumption tax 轿车消费税

car control for disabled drivers 残疾驾驶者用汽车的驾驶设备

car cover 汽车外罩（汽车露天停放、防尘、防雨、防晒等的软外罩，一般按车身外形制作）

card ①卡片，穿孔卡，程序卡；图表②印刷电路板

cardan click （双）十字轴万向节（产生的）短而尖的噪声（多发生于低速时前转向驱动桥，若有转向操作，会加剧这种噪声）

cardan drive 十字轴万向节驱动，十字轴万向节传动

cardan joint 十字轴式万向节（由一个十字轴连接两个万向节叉组成的非等速万向节，因其发明人意大利的 Cardan 而得名，亦称 Hooke's coupling Hooke 是第一个在汽车上实际应用这种万向节的英国人，亦称 Cardan universal joint）

cardan shaft 十字轴万向节传动轴（指每端均装有一个十字轴式万向节的传动轴）

cardan tube ①十字轴万向节传动轴管身②管状（十字轴）万向节传动轴（= tubular cardan shaft）

card entry system 进出卡系统（通过车门镜或后保险杠上的天线接收出入卡的密码，该系统便自动开启或关闭车门、行李舱门锁）

car finish 轿车车身（最后）涂（喷）漆；车身装饰工序；车身抛光

car follower （车速自动控制系统中的）车辆跟踪装置

cargo ①货物；载货②货物的，载货的

cargo-and-personnel car 客货两用汽车（亦称 cargo-and-personnel carrier）

cargo area ([美]车内)装载面积,载物面积,载货区

cargo bed ①货车的载货平台②平板式货车的平板货台

cargo bus 双排座驾驶室的客货两用车

cargo capacity 载货量

cargo-carrying 载货的,运货的

cargo floor (货车车身的)装货底板,地板(= load floor)

cargo-mile 载货行驶里程

cargo movement 货物流通

cargo organizer (轿车的)行李舱盖

cargo space (厢式货车等的)车厢容积

cargo vehicle 载货汽车,货车(= freight vehicle, motor truck cargo truck 简称 truck)

car icer 冷藏车,冷冻车(= refrigerated van)

car insurance 汽车保险(= motor insurance)

car knocker 轿车修理工;汽车检修工(= car inspector, car repairman)

car leasing industry 轿车租赁业

car-like ride (指各种大型车辆或越野车辆具有)与轿车相似的行驶平顺性

car mat (轿车等的)地板垫

car navi 汽车导航系统(car navigation 的简称)

car navigation computer 车用导航计算机,车用导行计算机

car navigator 汽车导行装置,汽车导航系统(简称 car navi,亦称 car navigation system)

car networking 行车网络(系统)(指由车间通信、Wi-Fi,和公路沿线各项设施的通信系统统一组成的可全面覆盖整个车辆行驶区域的巨大实时信息网络)

car park 汽车停车场

carpeted floor 铺有地毯的车身地板

carpet mats 车身地板脚垫

car phone (装在)汽车(上的)移动电话

car plane 飞行轿车(装有折叠式机翼,可展开成为一架小飞机的轿车,美国研制成的第一辆命名为 star car)

car polish 汽车抛光(油漆或电镀面的打亮上光)

car-pooling program 轿车合用方案(有计划地组织目的地相同的数人轮流共用各自私有的一辆轿车出行或公干,以减少街道行驶车辆数)

car responsiveness 汽车响应性能(如:加速踏板踩下时,汽车加速响应的快慢程度)

carriage ①(原指载客的四轮厢式马车,现专指长途单层客车= motor coach,或铁路列车的一个客车厢, = [美] car) ②可改变其他部件位置的机器的运动件③货运,货物运费

carriage bolt 菌形头方颈螺栓(其颈部插入方孔中)

carriage forward 运费未付,运费由收货人支付

carriage free 运费已付,(收货人)免收运费(= carriage paid)

carriage-way 车道,车行道

carrier ①运载装置,运输车辆②货运公司③支架,托架,行李架载装件(如活塞是活塞环的载装件)④壳体⑤载体⑥载波(指能由信号调制的固定频率的波)⑦载流子(指半导体中的电流载体:电子和空穴)

carrier basket (加装在车顶上的)物架

carrier bearing (支撑)差速器壳(的)轴承

carrier frequency 载频

carrier truck 载货汽车,货车

carrozeria house 车身及造型工作

室，车身造型设计室
carry ①承载，运载，携带，传送，进行②（计算机处理中的）进位；进位数
carry clear signal 进位清除信号
carry digit 进位数字
carry flip-flop 进位触发器，进位寄存器
carrying axle （汽车）承载桥
carrying capacity ①承载量，容许载荷，承载能力②（电）最大允许负载
carrying distance 运载距离，运货里程
carry look-ahead （车用计算机中央处理器的）先行进位电路（清除加法器进位传送延时，以提高加法速度的电路，根据加法器提供的部分进位信号，便可预测最终的进位）
carry-over ①交通绿灯信号延长时间②（计算机的）进位③携带，带出转移
carry-over factor 传递因子
carry-over moment 传递力矩
carry to failure 进行（试验）到损坏
car sharing system ①轿车合乘系统（根据轿车行驶路线由合乘管理中心调度搭载同方向或同路线的乘客，以节约资源，减少排放）②轿车分享系统（公寓区内的住户可通过互联网或手机预约使用该区内其他用户当时空闲的汽车）
car sponge 擦车用（大块）海绵
car stereo 汽车（用）立体声响设备
car taken at random from the assembly line 自装配线上任意选中的汽车，从装配线上随机选取的汽车
car tax 汽车税
cartesian coordinates 笛卡儿坐标，直角坐标（= rectangular coordinates）
car-to-car communication 汽车相互间通信
car to car impact 两车相撞，车撞车
car-to-car proximity information 车对车临近信息
cartography 绘图法，制图法，制图学，绘制图表
car-top camper 车顶野营帐篷（= car-top-tent 带在车上，在使用时撑在车顶上）
car transceiver 车载无线电收发机
car transporter 车辆运输车
car/tree-head on 车对树正面碰撞
cartridge ①筒状物，筒状件（如滤清器的滤筒芯，套筒，一筒胶卷等）②筒状的
cartridge fuse 熔丝管（装在管状外壳内的熔丝）
cart spring 钢板弹簧（= leaf spring）
car tyre 轿车用轮胎
carvac 轿车专用小型便携式吸尘器（car vacuum cleaner 的简称）
car washer ①洗车设备，洗车机②街道清洗车③汽车用清洗剂（= car washings）
car wax 汽车（漆面的含石蜡非研磨用）抛光蜡
car wings 车翼（日产公司开发的第二代完全由乘员语音声控代替行车中手动操作车载IT机器的人—机接口系统的商品名）
CARWINGS 车翼（Nissan 的车载信息系统商品名，可提供交通路况信息、救援、安全等多项行车在线服务）
CAS ①[美]净化空气系（cleaner air system 的简称）②汽车安全中心（center for auto safety 的简称）
CAS/CAD/CAE/CAM integration 计算机辅助造型、设计、工程、制造集成化
cascade ①（电子电路的）级联，串级（如串接的两个放大级，前一级的输出为后一级的输入）②串接、

串联、串行③格,栅,格状物

cascade control (车用电子计算机控制系统的)级联控制,串级控制(各个控制单元按顺序连接的自动控制系统,每个单元控制下一个单元的操作,即:上一个单元的输出为下一单元的输入)

cascade pumps 串联泵

case ①壳,套,箱,盒②表面,表面层③表面的④案例,情况⑤壳装的,有壳件的

cased seal 有内(或外)圈的油封

case for steering gear 转向器外壳

case-harden ①表面硬化(指经淬火或渗碳等提高表层硬度)②表面硬化的(= case-hardened 经表面硬化的,或 case-hardening 进行表面硬化的)

casing ①壳,罩套,箱,盒,外皮,面板②(轮胎的)胎体(见 carcass)

cassette ①箱,盒②盒式的,用盒装的③盒式磁带

cassette memory 盒式存储器(如:插入故障诊断解码、扫描仪内存储有各种车型和电子系统的数据的盒式存储器)

cast ①铸造②铸成的③铸件

cast alloy wheel 整体铸造式合金车轮

cast aluminium 铸制铝合金(指将各种合金元素及铝熔化后铸入砂型或金属型内而制成的铝合金)

cast-aluminum wheel 铸铝车轮

casted rigid axle housing 整体铸造式桥壳(通常中间是可锻铸铁或铸钢铸件,两边压入无缝钢管半轴套管)

castellated coupling 牙嵌式联结(指以矩形牙等相嵌的联结形式)

castellated nut (美)开槽螺母,槽顶螺母,蝶形螺母(= [英] castle nut)

castellated shaft 花键轴

cast en bloc 整体铸造;整体铸件(= cast in block)

caster ([美] = castor)①(转向轮)转向主销纵倾(指从侧向看,转向主销向前、后倾斜。当无特别说明时,指主销向后倾斜,称主销后倾或正后倾"positive caster"。主销向前倾斜,称主销前倾,或负后倾"negative caster 或 minus caster")②主销纵倾距(指主销后倾或负后倾造成的、过车轮中心的铅垂线和主销轴线在车辆纵向对称平面上的投影线与地面的两个交点间的距离,亦称 caster lead, caster offset 及 caster trail 或 mechanical trail, 无特别说明时,一般指主销后倾距或主销正后倾距。主销前倾造成者,称主销前倾距或主销负后倾距"negative caster trail")③主销纵倾角(指主销轴线和过车轮中心的铅垂线在车辆纵向对称平面上的投影线间的夹角, = caster angle, 无特别说明时,指主销后倾角,为正值,负后倾形成的上述夹角,为负值)④(装在小推车底面可向任意方向转动的)脚轮

caster action 主销后倾效应(亦称 caster effect, 由于主销后倾的作用,当转向车轮在行驶中偶受外力而偏转时,车轮便会产生绕主销旋转的回正力矩,从而保证汽车直线行驶稳定性)

caster angle 主销纵倾角 [见 caster ③无特别说明时指主销(正)后倾角, = castor angle]

caster lead 主销纵倾距 [①见 caster ②, 无特别说明时,指主销(正)后倾距②有的文献,为了区别正、负后倾所形成的纵倾距,仅将主销后倾时,主销轴线与地面交点落在车轮中心铅垂线与地面交点的前方而形成的主销(正)后倾距称 caster lead, 可译为主销(正)后倾导

距，而将主销负后倾，即前倾时，主销轴线与地面交点落在车轮中心铅垂线后方形成的主销负后倾距称 caster trail "主销负后倾拖距"]

caster offset　主销纵倾距 [见 caster ②无特别说明时，指主销（正）后倾距。注意，勿将 caster offset 与 kingpin offset 混淆，后者指转向轮外倾和主销内倾所造成的主销轴线与地面的交点和车轮中心平面或车轮接地面中心间的距离]

caster trail　主销纵倾距 [①见 caster ②，无特别说明时，指主销后倾距。②有的文献，为了区别正、负后倾所形成的纵倾距，仅将主销负后倾时，主销轴线与地面交点落在车轮中心铅垂线与地面交点之后的主销负后倾距（称为 caster trail，可译为主销负后倾拖距]

caster wedge　主销后倾角调整用楔铁（一般是插在车桥悬架弹簧座内）

cast hi-alloy　高铬、高镍、高钨、高钴等铸造合金

cast hi-alloy-materials　高合金铸造材料（指高含量铬、镍、钴、钨等合金）

cast-in　铸入的，镶铸的

cast in-block　单（体）铸（造），整体铸造（将整个结构做成一个铸件，= cast enbloc，= monoblock）

casting central tubular chassis　铸制中央管式车架，铸管中梁式底盘

cast-in liner　（铝缸体内）铸入（而不是镶入）的汽缸套

cast-in metal　浇铸轴承合金，浇铸式轴承（将耐磨合金直接浇铸在机体的轴承座上，= bind metal）

cast iron　铸铁

castle circular nut　六角圆顶螺母

castle nut　槽顶螺母（一般带开口销孔，用开口销锁定）

castor　①见 caster ②（可朝任意方向转动的）小脚轮 ③蓖麻

castor oil　蓖麻油（用作赛车发动机的润滑及制动液原料）

castor-wheeled jack　装有小脚轮的举升器，带小脚轮的千斤顶小车（用来拆卸底盘上的总成）

cast plastics　铸造用塑料

cast soldering　铸焊

cast to shape　成形铸造（不再机械加工）

CAT　计算机辅助试验（computer-aidedtest）

catadioptric　反射的，折射的

catalog（ues）　①（产品）目录，（产品）样本（图书）一览表 ②条目，总目，种类

catalyst　催化剂，触媒（指加速化学反应，但本身并不参与化学反应的物质，= catalytic agent，catalyzator，catalyzer）

catalyst attrition　催化剂劣化（由于摩擦、过热等原因造成被催化剂剥落、破损而降低质量的现象，亦称 catalyst degradation 或 catalyst deterioration）

catalyst bed　催化床（指装在称为催化箱的容器中的表面载有同一种催化剂的颗粒状载体层或蜂窝状整体式陶瓷载体块）

catalyst charge　催化料（指填入催化箱内的载有催化剂的颗粒或陶瓷块等）

catalyst coating　（催化剂载体上的）催化剂涂层（= catalyst layer）

catalyst container　催化箱（内部装有催化床，使废气与催化剂接触而产生催化反应的容器，= catalyst housing）

catalyst contamination　见 catalyst poisoning

catalyst degradation　见 catalyst attrition

catalyst deterioration　见 catalyst attrition

catalystic oxidizing converter 氧化型催化转化器(加速 HC 和 CO 氧化为水蒸气和 CO_2 的催化转化器)

catalystic reduction converter 还原型催化转化器(加速 NO_x、CO、H_2 或 HC 起化学还原反应生成 N_2、CO_2 和 H_2O 的催化转化器)

catalyst indicator (装在汽车仪表板上的)催化剂更换指示灯(该灯亮,表明催化剂应予更换)

catalyst poisoning 催化剂中毒,催化剂污染(使用含铅汽油或劣质燃料等原因使铅、磷或硫沉积在催化剂表面,削弱或消除催化剂能力的现象,亦称 catalyst contamination)

catalyst shrinkage 催化剂收缩(由于高温,载体收缩,催化剂作用面积减少的现象)

catalyst substrate 催化剂载体(亦称 catalyst support)

catalytic activity 催化剂活性(指催化转化器的废气净化率)

catalytically cracked gasoline 催化裂化汽油,触媒裂炼汽油

catalytic combustion analyzer 催化燃烧分析仪(根据 CO 等催化氧化时的反应热量,求出其浓度的分析仪)

catalytic control (废气的)催化净化,催化处理

catalytic converter (排气净化的)催化转化器,(借助催化反应减少废气中的碳氢化合物、一氧化碳和氮氧化物的装置。主要由催化箱、载体和催化剂等组成。按催化剂类型可分为氧化、还原或三效等三种,偶见称 catalytic exhaust purifier)

catalytic cracking 催化分解,触媒分解,催化裂化,触媒裂化

catalytic cycle oil 催化循环油

catalytic efficiency 催化剂效率

catalytic gas sensor 催化反应型气体传感器(指表面层为催化剂活性层的气体传感器,该表面层上产生的催化反应会使传感器温度上升,其温度升高与催化反应的气体成分有关,且与其浓度成正比)

catalytic ignition 触媒点火,催化(剂)点火(利用某些金属遇煤气或汽油空气混合气后即产生炽热的特性点火)

catalytic layer 催化剂层(指陶瓷或金属载体上的催化剂薄层,通常为铂膜等)

catalytic muffler 触媒净化式消声器

catalytic precious metal 贵金属催化剂

catalytic rejuvenation 催化剂再生(使催化剂恢复活性的过程)

catalyze (使受)催化(作用)

catalyzed diesel particulate filter 催化转化式柴油机(排放)微粒物滤清器(简称 catalyzed DPF,在常规的柴油机排放微粒滤清器上附加氧化催化剂,促进滤集于滤芯上的碳微粒"soot"高温氧化,经二次空气喷射燃烧,使滤芯再生"regeneration"。这种滤清器亦称第二代"second-generation" DPF)

catalyzed hydrocarbon (HC) trap 催化型碳氢化合物捕集器(用于吸附冷机起动时的 HC 排放物)

catalyzed oxidation test (滑油的)催化氧化试验(在一定的温度和空气流量下,用 Fe、Cu、Pb、Al 等催化剂试验滑油的氧化性)

cat and mouse engine 猫捉鼠型发动机(一种中轴式单纯旋转型发动机,工作室的容积变化是由行星齿轮及曲柄连杆装置来完成的)

cataphoretic painting 阳极电泳涂装(见 electrophoresis)

catastrophic failure 突然失效,突然发生的重大故障(亦称 catastrophe)

catastrophic wear 灾变磨损(由于磨损迅速造成表面损伤,严重缩短

catch 卡、夹、挡、销、键、锁、扣、挂等动作或器件

cat converter 催化转化器（catalyst converter 的简称）

category 等级，类别

category 1 vehicle （RE5 定义的）I 类汽车（指设计和构造目的主要用于运输乘客的四轮或四轮以上的机动车辆。其中，除驾驶员外，不超过 8 个座位的 1 类车辆称 category 1-1 vehicle "1-1 类车辆"。除驾驶座外，多于 8 个座位的 1 类车辆称 category 1-2 vehicle "1-2" 类车辆，见 RE5）

category 2 vehicle （RE5 定义的）2 类车辆（设计和构造目的主要用于运输货物的四轮或四轮以上的车辆）

category 3 vehicle （RE5 定义的）3 类车辆（运输乘客或货物的两轮或三轮机动车辆，其中中如果使用热机，排量不超过 50cm³ 或使用任一种动力最大设计车速不超过 50km/h 的两轮机动车，称 category 3-1 vehicle "3-1 类车辆"，亦称 two-wheeled moped "两轮轻便摩托车"；排量不超过 50cm³，或车速不超过 50km/h 的三轮机动车辆称 category 3-2 vehicle "3-2 类车辆" 或 three-wheeled moped "三轮轻便摩托车"；排量不超过 50cm³ 或最大设计车速在 50km/h 以上的两轮摩托车 "two-wheeled motorcycle" 称 catelogy 3-3 vehicle "3-3 类车辆"；排量在 50cm³ 以下或最大设计车速在 50km/h 以上的三轮车辆 "tricycle" 称 category 3-4vehicle "3-4 类车辆"）

Cat engine 卡特发动机［美］卡特皮勒拖拉机公司发动机的商品名

caterer's body 运输饮食的车厢

caterpillar ①履带车辆（因 Caterpillar 公司而得名）②履带式的 ③Caterpillar［美］卡特皮勒（拖拉机）公司

caterpillar band 履带（＝caterpillar track, caterpillar chain）

caterpillar block 履（带）板（＝track block）

caterpillar Brakesaver 卡特皮勒制动救星（用于重型货车和汽车列车牵引车上的一种电控液压式柴油机排气缓速器的商品名。当节气门位于急速开度，离合器踏板松开后，闭合驾驶室仪表板上的手动开关，该系统便经过电磁阀开启液压源使排气门关闭，同时停止喷油，实现缓速运转，其液压源来自发动机双齿轮副机油泵，若将手动开关置于自动挡，该系统将自动运转，简称 Cat Brakesaver）

caterpillar engine test （润滑油）卡特皮勒发动机试验（使用一种单缸压燃式发动机进行的润滑油质量试验）

cathode ①负极，阴极②负极的，阴极的

cathode-anode area ratio 负极-正极表面积比

cathode efficiency 负极效应（①负极实际发射的电流能量与输入电流能量之比，亦称 emission efficiency ②负极上实际沉积物质量与理论上计算的沉积物质量之比）

cathode luminescence 阴极（射线致）发光，电子致发光，阴极电子激发光

cathode ray oscilloscope 阴极射线示波器，阴极示波器

cathode ray tube 阴极射线管，示波管（简称 C-R-tube, 或 CRT, 将电信号转换成可见图像的器件）

cathodic electropainting 阴极电泳涂装（＝cathode electro-coating 见 electrophoresis）

cathodogram 阴极射线示波图
cation 阳离子,正离子
cation exchange 阳离子交换
CAT system 计算机辅助测试系统(computer aided testing system 的简称)
caulk 凿密,填隙,填缝,敛缝
causal relationship 因果关系
caustic ①苛性的,腐蚀性的②腐蚀性,苛性药物③焦散的
caustic curve 焦散曲线
caustic etching ①(铝件上漆前的)腐蚀性溶液浸洗(如:浸入苛性钠或硝酸溶液中除去表面污垢,锈膜并使表面粗糙)②(对铝件表面)蚀刻(利用腐蚀性溶液在其表面刻出所要求的花纹等)
causticity 腐蚀性,碱度,苛性
caustic potash 苛性钾,氢氧化钾(KOH)
caustic soda 苛性钠,氢氧化钠(NaOH)(= sodalye, sodium hydroxide)
caustic surface 焦散面
caution plate (说明汽车有关性能参数和使用事项的)标牌
CAV ①强制怠速空燃比控制阀(coasting air valve 的简称)②气蚀,穴蚀,空化,空穴(cavitation 的简称)③空腔,型腔(cavity 的简称)
cave ①洞,穴,凹痕,凹槽,内腔,(屏蔽)室②凹进去,下陷,塌下
cavitation ①成穴,空化(指物体在流体中运动时,在其背面产生的流体剥离,形成局部真空的空穴或凹涡现象,这一现象造成的对运动的阻力所产生的能量损失称空穴损失"cavitation loss")②空穴现象(指流体中的空气,蒸汽以气泡形式析出,继而发展成空穴的现象,当空穴爆炸破裂时形成局部高温、高压冲击。这种冲击及其引起的共振、电化学腐蚀会造成与上述液体接触的金属件生成麻坑、穴坑或穿孔现象,称穴蚀 cavitation erosion,或简称 cavitation)③气穴现象,空化作用[指在流体密封件的密封端面局部产生气(或汽)泡的现象,通常发生在压力迅速减小区]
cavitation erosion 见 cavitation
cavity (空)腔,室,洞,孔,凹处
cavity oscillation (空)腔振荡
cavity resonance 空腔谐振(当封闭空腔的固有频率与外界振源的频率相同或成倍比例关系时,产生的共振及其引起的共鸣现象)
cavity sealant 腔室防锈剂(防止腔、室内表面锈腐的防锈油蜡、溶剂及其他各种防锈剂)
CAX 计算机辅助技术集成系统(将各种计算机辅助系统,如 CAD, CAE, CAM, CAS 等作为子系统集成在一起成为一个大的系统。
CB ①(美国 API 滑油分类中的)重级 B 类(滑油)(适用于使用劣质燃油的中、轻负荷柴油机)②触点断电器(contact breaker)③民用波段(citizens' band,如:美国汽车驾驶者间通信或接收—发射无线电信号的波段)
CBC system 弯道制动力控制系统(curve braking control system 的简称)
CBR process 控制燃烧速率法(controlled burn rate process 的简称,通过对燃烧速度的控制和加速来提高燃油经济性的方法)
CBS data (存储在遥控钥匙和便捷乘入系统内的)按车况维护数据(包括车架号,车型整车配置号,代理商号,首次登录日期,目前车况,检查控制数据,故障代码等,可用 KeyReader 读出)
CC ①(美国 API 滑油分类中的)重级 C 类(滑油)(适用于重型、中型低增压柴油机及某些重型汽油

机）②变矩器离合器（converter clutch）③立方厘米（cubic centimeter）

CCC ①气候控制中心（climate control center 的简称，指集中安装有车内空调、通风、暖气、湿度调节等的控制件的组合开关板）②紧接式催化转化器（见 close-coupled catalyst converter）③发动机电子计算机指令控制系统（computer command control system 的简称，电子控制模块根据发动机水温、进气管压力或真空、废气中氧含量、节气门开度、爆燃、车速、变速器挡位等传感器的信息对混合气浓度，点火正时，三元催化转化器的氧化反应区二次空气输入，怠速转速，废气再循环及液力变矩器等进行综合控制）

CCC valve 变矩器锁止离合器控制阀（亦称 cccv，为 converter clutch control valve 的简称。当电子控制模块根据发动机和汽车运行工况，发出变矩器锁止离合器接合的指令时，电磁调节阀将该阀端的液压通路开放，将该阀推至开启位置，于是主液压通过该阀所开启的油道进入锁止离合器，实现变矩器锁止，亦称 bypass clutch control valve，见 TCC shift valve）

CCD 紧密靠近的装置（close-couple device 的简称）

CCD camera CCD 摄像机（CCD 为 charge-coupled device "电荷耦合器件"的简称，指高密度低功耗的半导体存储器件，填补了磁存储器与半导体随机存储器之间的空白，在汽车上用于防碰撞和驻车，倒车障碍物可见系统，以及前照灯检测仪）

C-class (car) 普及型级轿车，紧凑型小型轿车（compact class car 的简称）

CCM （OBDII 系统的）综合部件监测器（complex component monitor 的简称，运用直接监测各传感器的输出或间接根据其他有关传感器的输出来推断某一传感器的输出是否正常等方法，向动力控制模块提供传感器有无故障的信息）

C. C. N 控制论控制参数（Cybernetics Control Number 的简称，反映人的行为倾向的特征参数，用于评价驾驶员是否适合驾驶车辆）

CCO （废气）氧化催化器转化（catalytic converter oxidation 的简称）

C-coupe (Mercedes-Benz 的) C—级三门跑车（全玻璃车顶、C-class sports coupe 的简称）

CCP ①（车内）气候控制板（climate control panel 的简称，指装在仪表板或副仪表板上的空调与暖风、通风系统的小控制板②见 charcoal canister purge）

CCR 电子计算机控制平顺性（系统）（computer command ride 的简称，电子控制模块根据车速、加速度、制动强度和横向加速度等信息，以 1/10 秒的速率改变悬架减振系统的阻尼率，确保汽车无论高速或低速行驶均能获最佳行驶平顺性和操纵性）

CC rating 发动机额定排量（说明书、广告等用语）

CCRM （双电压式燃油泵的）恒定控制继电器模块（constant-controlled relay module 的简称）

CCRO ①（废气）铑（NOx 还原）催化转化器（catalytic converter rhodium 的简称）②氢仪-还原双效催化转仪器（catalytic converter reduction-oxidation 的简称）

CCRV 液压变矩器锁止离合器（控制液压）调节阀（converter clutch regulator valve 的简称）

CCS ①控制燃烧系（con-trolled combustion system 的简称，通过对燃烧的控制来减少废气中的有害排放物的发动机系统）②冷机起动模拟器（cold cranking simulator）③轿车通信系统（car communication system 的简称，该系统包括卫星定位、音响控制、空调控制和车载电话等多项功能）④定速巡行系统（cruise control system 的简称，按下该系统开关，汽车便可自动按驾驶者所选定的车速稳定行驶）

CCV 合成概念车（composite concept vehicle）

CCW 逆时针（方向）（counter clockwise）

C^2D 见 Chrysler collision Detection

CD ①（美国 API 滑油分类中的）重级 D 类（机油，适用于重型高速增压柴油机）②小光盘（compact disk 的简称）

CD auto changer （车用）CD 机的自动换碟器

CDC （减振器的）连续阻尼控制（continuous damping control 的简称）

CDI system 电容放电点火系（见 capacitive discharge ignition system）

CDL 磁心二极管逻辑（core diode logic 的简称）

CDMA on-board terminal device （代）码分（割）多（地）址车载终端装置（CDMA 为 code division multiple address 的简称）

C^2D multiplex transmission system 克莱斯勒（信息）冲突检测多路复用传输系统［其中 C^2D 为 Chrysler Collision Detection 的简称，亦写作 CCD。为克莱斯勒公司研制，而由 Harris 公司商品供应的串行通信网络和总线接口专用集成电路，用于汽车的分布式多路复用系统各部分间数据通信网络，其特点是简单、可靠，亦简称 C^2D bus "C^2D 总线"，该总线实现下列计算机系统（各控制模块）间的互联：车身控制模块"BCM"，动力控制模块"PCM"，传动控制模块"TCM"，乘员安全气囊诊断模块"PASDM"，屏显式行车信息系统模块"OTIS"，电气机械仪表组模块"MIC"防抱死制动系统模块"ABS"，温度自动控制模块"TAC"等］

CD ROM 小光盘式只读存储器（compact disk read only memory system 的简称，指使用小光盘的只读存储装置）

C^2D system ［美］克莱斯勒数据冲突检出信号系统（Chrysler Collision Detection system 的简称，该系统为解决信息传输中两个或两个以上的信息争用同一信道的问题，在每一信息前加有一表示传输先后次序的标识符"ID"，由 8 位二进制字符组成，如：0010 1000, 0100 0100, 其第一个"1"前的"0"越多，越具有优先传输权。上述两列中，0010 1000 优先于 0100 0100）

CDV 小型厢式送货车（Car Derived Van 的简称）

Cd value 汽车车身的空气阻力系数（见 coefficient of drag, 亦写作 CD valve）

Ce 铈（cerium）

CEAPS 常规发动机排放净化系统，往复活塞式发动机排放净化系统（conventional engine anti-pollution system 的简称）

cease 使停止

CEE 欧洲经济共同体

cee spring C 字形弹簧

Ceiba 木棉（见 kapok）

ceiling ①顶篷，天花板 ②升限

ceiling-hung heater 顶篷吊挂式取暖器，悬挂式加热器

ceiling light 车内顶篷灯，（= ceiling lamp, dome light）

ceiling mounted DVDunit 装在车厢顶篷上的DVD装置

ceiling voltage 峰值电压，最高电压

CEL （车装自诊断系统发现发动机有故障，提示驾驶者检修的）检查发动机警报灯（check engine light的简称）

CELECT system （冠明思公司的柴油机）电子控制系统（Cummins Electronic System的简称）

cell ①箱，舱，室；元件，单元②电池③组成蓄电池的单格电池④转子发动机的燃烧室

cellastic tire 带海绵橡胶芯的防弹轮胎

cell balancing （蓄电池各）单格（之间电解液密度的）平衡

cell connecting bar （蓄电池）单格电池（间的）连接条，亦称cell connecting bridge, cell connecting strip, cell connector, cell-to-cell connector)

cell densities （蜂窝状材料的）窝孔密度（单位cells/inch^2)

cell density 单格电池（电流）密度（瓦/小时）

cellophane 赛璐玢，胶膜，玻璃纸

cell stack 一组相连接的单电池（不一定是一个整体）

cell structure 蜂窝结构

cell swept volume （转子发动机的）燃烧室扫气容积（其燃烧室最大与最小容积差）

cell-to-cell connector 单格电池连接条（蓄电池中各单格电池相互之间的串联铅条）

cell-to-cell leakage 蓄电池单格间渗漏（电解液）

cell-type 蜂巢式的，蜂窝式的

400 -cell-type catalytic converter 400蜂巢型催化转化净化器（本田公司由400条壁厚9.91mm、1.25mm×1.2mm方形细管组成的蜂窝状、废气自下而上垂直输入的催化转化净化器的商品名）

cellular 蜂窝状的，格状的；多孔状的，泡沫状的；单元的，单体的

cellular ceramic substrate （催化剂的）多孔陶瓷载体，蜂窝状陶瓷载体

cellular-connected vehicle 采用蜂窝式无线通信系统的connected vehicle，见connected

cellular liner （一种轮胎的）蜂窝状人造橡胶内衬层（该层贴于轮胎内面，当胎面被外物穿透后，多孔状人造橡胶即迅速膨胀而将破孔堵死，防止轮胎泄气）

cellular plastics 泡沫塑料

cellular radiator 蜂窝式散热器

cellular radio system 蜂窝式无线电通信系统（汽车移动式无线电通信制式之一，将电话服务区分成许多互不干扰的小区，即所谓的蜂窝"cells"，每一小区均装备有不同频率的发射台，当呼叫用户由一个小区移到另一个小区时，利用先进的计算机技术，将呼叫用户使用频率切换到另一小区的频率，从而最大限度地扩大移动电话的服务范围。现行的日本NTT制，英国的TACS制，德国的CNET制，美国的AMPS制及北欧的Nordic制全部采用这一制式）

cellular tire 泡沫橡胶芯轮胎（= foam-filled tire）

celluloid ①赛璐珞（含75%硝酸纤维，25%樟脑的固溶体，无色透明，比重1.4，90℃以上变软，易燃）②细胞状的

cellulose ①纤维素②硝化纤维漆，硝化纤维涂料（nitrocellulose lacquer的俗称）

cellulosic ①纤维质的②纤维素质

cellulosic ethanol 纤维素乙醇，纤维酒精（由农业和林业废弃物提炼的

乙醇，用作汽车燃料，可消除炭粒排放）

cellulosic plastics 纤维素系树脂，纤维素系塑料（由纤维素的氢氧基烃酯化作用而成，有醋酸纤维素"cellulose acetate"、硝酸纤维素"cellulose nitrate"、丙酸纤维素"cellulose propionate"等多种）

cell voltage （蓄电池）单格电压

celotex (board) 纤维板（绝缘、隔声材料）

Celsius scale 摄氏（温度）表，摄氏温标（亦写作 Celcius scale，见 centigrade scale）

Celsius thermometer 摄氏温度计（亦称 centigrade thermometer）

cement ①水泥②黏结剂，接合剂

cementation ①表面（硬化）渗碳②渗（铝、铬、锌等）金属（在高温下使 Al、Cr、Zn 等金属扩散渗透入钢件表面，形成耐腐蚀性的保护薄层）③黏结，胶结④硬化

cement carbon 渗碳

cemented ①渗了碳的②胶结了的③烧结的

cemented carbide 烧结碳化物（= sintered carbide）

cemented metal ①渗碳金属②烧结金属

cemented steel （经过）渗碳（的）钢

cement for radiator leaks 散热器渗漏修补胶（= radiator cement）

cementite （金相）渗碳体、碳化铁体（Fe_3C）

cement mixer 混凝土搅拌车（= concrete mixer）

centage 百分率

centare 平方米（= centiare）

center （=［美］centre）①中心②定中心，使置于中心

center air bag sensor (assembly) 见 air bag control module

centeralizing switch （中央）集中开关

center arm-rest bench seats （轿车后座的）中央臂枕式长椅型乘员座椅

center axle （多轴汽车的）中间桥，中间轴

center-axle trailer 中央车轴式挂车（车轴位于挂车重心附近）

center backrest （某些车辆的夹在驾驶座和助手座之间的）中间（加座）靠背

center ball = centering ball

center brake 中央制动器（指设置在变速器箱输出轴后端的鼓式或盘式制动器，因得名，用于驻车）

center console 中央控制板（位于轿车仪表板中部向下延伸的装有多个开关、按键、按钮与拉杆，如：空调控制键，音响按键等的控制板）

center console box （位于轿车驾驶座与助手座之间，与中间控制板连成一体的）中央控制箱（装有换挡杆，驻车制动器拉杆等操纵杆件）

center differential （四轮驱动车辆前、后驱动桥的）桥间差速器（将动力分配给前、后驱动桥，= inter-axle differential）

center differential lock （四轮驱动车辆的）桥间差速器锁（当某车轮打滑空转时，将桥间差速器锁死）

center differential regulator （四轮驱动汽车的）中央差速器调节器（调控前、后轮转矩比，一般分四挡，最高为一挡，其前、后转矩比为50/50）

center drag link 中央连杆（见 center link）

center-dump trailer 底卸式挂车（= bottom-dump trailer）

center floor cover （车身底板上的）中央地板车底导流罩板

center gear （行星齿轮机构的）中心轮，太阳轮（亦写作 centre gear，

指在行星齿轮传动中，与行星轮啮合，处于中心位置且轴线固定的齿轮，= sun gear

centering ①定中心②定中心的

centering ball （球叉式万向节的）定心钢球（亦称分度球，万向节定心并承受轴向推力的销孔钢球，其销孔内的销使万向节各元件保持为一总成）

center injection 中央喷射（指喷油器装在汽缸中央位置，汽油垂直喷于进气涡流中，避免喷入缸内的燃油附着于缸壁）

center line 中心线，轴线（亦写作 central line）

center-line-average（method） 算术平均法，平均高度法（英国及美国一般公认的表面光洁度用参数，简称 CLA）

center-line power take-off 见 center power take-off

center link （独立悬架分段式转向传动杆系中将转向摇臂的力和运动传给左、右分段式横拉杆的）中央连杆（亦称 center drag link，intermediate rod 或 relay rod）

center of air pressure 风压中心（气动力合力的作用线与汽车纵向对称平面的交点，为汽车行驶时受到的风力合力的作用点）

center of gravity 重心（简称 G）

center of parallel wheel motion 平行车轮（瞬时）运动中心（指碰撞或回弹过程中，同一车轿上的两个车轮位移相同时，这一对车轮中心在垂直平面内相对于悬架质量运动线路的曲率中心）

center of sideforce reaction 侧向反作用力中心

center of tire contact 轮胎接地中心（车轮中心平面与地面的交线和车轮旋转中心线在地面上投影的交点）

center of vibration 振动中心

center-opening doors （指车身每侧两扇车门都从车身中间向两边开启的）中央开启式车门

center parking 路中停放车辆，街心驻车（在道路中心线或其附近停放车辆）

center piece 十字头，十字轴，十字架

center pillar = center post，见 middle standing pillar

center pillarless body （小轿车）无中柱式车身（可改善上、下车的方便性）

center pillarless body 无中柱式（小轿车）车身

center pin 销轴

center plate （离合器的）从动盘

center-point linkage 中心点式（转向）拉杆机构

center-point steering 中心点转向（指主销中心线延长线正好落在车轮中心平面与地面的交线上，即主销偏移距为零的转向布置，故亦称 zero offset steering）

center port injection 见 CPI

center power take-off 位于纵向对称轴线上的功率输出轴，中心取力器（= center-line power take-off）

center separation 中间隔板，中间壁，中隔板（= center wall，center side wall，intermediate housing）

center stack （汽车驾驶室内的）中央控制仪表组

center steering linkage 中央式转向杆系机构（转向摇臂经直拉杆带动中央摇臂，中央摇臂通过左、右横拉杆分别带动左、右转向节臂实现转向）

center steering shaft （机械式全四轮转向系中将前轮转向角传至后轮转向器的）中央转向轴

center-to-center tire spacing 并装双

轮胎中心距

center torque-control arm 中央转矩控制臂（见 three-link rear-axle suspension）

center tube ①中央管道②（中央管脊式车架的）中央脊管

center wear （轮胎的异常磨损，由边缘向中心磨损逐渐严重的）凹磨

center-zero electrical meter 中央指零式电气仪表

centigrade ①百分度的，百分温标的，摄氏温度的②百分度，百分温标刻度，摄氏温度（简称℃）

centile 百分位，百分位点（= percentile）

centimeter 厘米（cm，亦写作 centimetre）

centimeter-gram-second system 厘米-克-秒制（基本单位为厘米、克、秒，参见 metric system）

centipoise 厘泊（黏度单位，常用于液体，代号 cP，$= 10^{-2}$ poise，水在 20℃时的动力黏度为 1.0020cP，参见 poise）

centra ［拉丁语］百，一百，centrum 的复数（= centrums）

central 中心的，中央的，重要的，主要的

central air bag sensing system 安全气囊中央传感系统（见 single point electronic sensing system）

central angle 圆心角

central area network （汽车的）中央局域网（简称 CAN，通过网络而不是通过单独的导线通信，因而可靠且可减少导线的数量，易于获得诊断信息，无须改变硬件，仅通过软件即可改变或加减系统功能）

central arm rest （车厢）双座位的中间扶手

central chassis lubrication ①底盘集中润滑②底盘集中润滑装置（指只从一个中心点加注油、脂即可润滑底盘所有部件，= one-shot chassis lubrication, one-shot lubricating system, servo-lubrication）

central collision 迎面碰撞（参见 knock-on collision）

central (controlled) door locking system 中央（控制）门锁系统（可控制车门、行李舱、发动机舱盖等的开锁和上锁）

central cruciform bracing 车架 X 形横梁（亦称 central cross form bracing）

central engine 中置发动机（发动机在驾驶座位之后，底盘中部，亦称 centrally mounted engine）

central frame 中间框架（如：铰接式客车的中间框架）

central frequency 中心频率（滤波器上限频率 f_2 与下限频率 f_1 的几何平均值即 $f_0 = \sqrt{f_2 f_1}$）

central fuel injection 中央单点式燃油喷射（简称 CFI，在原来的进气歧管安装化油器的位置上装有一节气门体，一个或两个由电子控制模块控制的喷嘴装在该节气门体中的节气门上方，将汽油喷至进气空气流中并随空气进入进气歧管，亦称单点式喷射系统、节气门体喷射系统，见 TBI, SPI）

central gear change 变速杆位于地板中间的常规换挡布置形式

central hydraulic system （液力制动、离合器助力和液力转向等共用的）中央液力系

Central Injection System 中央喷射系统（见 CI）

centralization 集中化，统一化

centralized control 集中管理，集中控制，集中操纵（简称 CTC）

centralized data processing 数据集中处理

centralized lubrication pressure indicator 集中润滑系统油压表（显示集

中润滑系统中润滑油工作压力的指示器)

centralized traffic control 交通集中控制,交通集中管理(简称CTC)

central king pin type steering system 中央主销式转向装置(一种全挂车转向装置形式,由转盘架、上下转盘、中央转向主销、滚轮等组成)

central locking 中央门锁(指通过一个电子开关或只要锁上驾驶员车门锁便可锁住所有车门)

central locking hub (带外花键的)中央锁紧式车轮的轮毂(见 central locking wheel)

central locking wheel 中央锁紧式车轮(一般为辐条式车轮,其轮辋辐条的中央是一个内花键套,与轮毂的外花键啮合,而由一个中央锁紧螺母紧固,故名)

central microprocessor 中央微型处理器(在车上安装一台微型处理器控制所有的电子装置)

central pillar (轿车车身的)中央立柱,中柱(亦称 B-post,B-pillar,位于前门后)

central plane of wheel 车轮中心平面(单轮指与车轮轮辋两侧内边缘等距的平面;双轮指与外轮轮辋内缘和内轮轮辋外缘等距的平面)

central port injection 中央多点式(汽油)喷射(系统)[简称 CPI,在其节气门体内装有一中央多孔式喷油器,该喷油器的储油腔具有数量与汽缸数相同的出油孔,这些出油孔由电子控制模块控制的电磁阀板密封并通过相同数量的软管分别与各汽缸进气口处的喷嘴连接,汽油由油泵以规定的压力(由压力调节器调控)泵入该储油腔内。喷油时刻,电子控制模块将电磁阀板升起,储油腔内的燃油便由各出油孔经软管和喷嘴喷至各缸进气门前方,直至电磁阀板下落将出油孔封闭]

central reserve (多车道道路的)中央分隔带(= [美] medial strip, medial divider, dividing strip, 美亦简称 divider, median)

central sensing system (安全气囊的)中央式传感系统(见 air-bag sensing system)

central single-node control system 中央单网点控制系统(相对于分布式多网点控制系统 "distributed multi-node control system" 而言)

central spindle 芯轴,中心轴(如滤清器安装滤芯的轴)

central tubular backbone frame 中央管式脊梁车架

central tunnel (轿车车身结构中的)中央胴体(指构成客厢的车身结构中段)

centre [美]①对正中心,定中心 ②中心(= [英] senter)

centre-arm steering linkage 带中央转向摇臂的转向杆系

centre boss 轮毂

centre differential 中央差速器[指多桥驱动车辆的桥间(或称轴间)差速器, = inter axial differential]

centre distance 中心距(两中心点或平行轴线间的距离)

centre drive 中央驱动(指动力不从曲轴端而从发动机中部输出的结构形式)

centre electrode ①(火花塞)中心电极 ②中央接线柱(= centre terminal, 特指分电器盖炭柱型中心触点)

centre gear ①(行星齿轮机构的)太阳轮(= sun gear) ②中央齿轮

centre gearchange (变速杆位于驾驶座侧地板中线上的常规)中央换挡

centre-girder frame 中央脊梁式车架

centre locking disc (车轮的)轮毂罩(= hub cap)

centre locking nut (辐条式车轮等的)中央锁紧螺母(=spinner)

centre-lock wire wheel 在轮毂上具有中央锁母的钢丝辐条车轮

centre member shell of wire wheel (钢丝)辐条式车轮轮毂

centre of gravity 重心(物体各部分重力作用的集中点,重心的位置不一定都在物体上)

centre position (控制阀)中立位置,中间位置

centre (standing) pillar (四门轿车车身等的)中支柱(简称 B post,亦称 side wall centre post)

centre terminal 见 centre electrode②

centre terminal tower 见 distributor tower

centre tunnel (轿车或客车车身底板中轴线上的)变速器半圆或椭圆盖板

centrifugal 离心的

centrifugal acceleration 离心加速度

centrifugal advance 离心式点火提前(装置)(=centrifugal ignition advance,利用旋转质量的离心力调整点火提前角的机械式装置)

centrifugal air clean [美]离心式空气滤清器(=centrifugal filter, centrifugal purifier,利用离心力将杂质甩除)

centrifugal blower ①离心式鼓风机 ②离心式增压器(=centrifugal supercharger)

centrifugal caster ①离心浇铸机 ②车轮旋转运动所产生的自定心效应 ③(车轮)绕主销轴线的不平衡运动

centrifugal clutch 离心式离合器(达到一定转速后在离心力作用下自动结合)

centrifugal filter fan (离心式空气)滤清器扇轮

centrifugal flow compressor 离心(流)式压缩机

centrifugal force 离心力(简称 cf)

centrifugal governor (指依靠随转速变化的飞重的离心力来调节供油量,从而控制转速的)离心式调节器(亦称 centrifugal regulator)

centrifugal ignition advance 见 centrifugal advance

centrifugal impeller (涡轮增压器压气机的)离心式叶轮(空气轴向流入,压缩后径向流出的叶轮)

centrifugal inertia force (旋转机构由于质量不均匀而产生的)离心惯性力

centrifugal inertia moment 离心惯性力矩

centrifugal oil filter 离心式机油滤清器(利用离心力甩除机油内的机械杂质和水分,=centrifugal oil clarifier, centrifugal oil cleaner, centrifugal oil purifier)

centrifugal pump 离心泵(将流体吸至泵体中心,然后依靠离心力甩出的液泵)

centrifugal spark-advance device 离心式点火提前装置

centrifugal spring (飞重等的)离心力平衡弹簧

centrifugal stress 离心力(产生的)应力

centrifugal turbocharger 离心式涡轮增压器(指其涡轮机和压气机均为离心式,即径流式而非轴流式,一般涡轮增压器多为此型)

centrifugal-vaccum-operated clutch 离心-真空式离合器(起步、行驶时靠离心力接合,换挡时利用发动机真空助力强制分离)

centrifugal weights (离心式调节机构中的)离心重块,离心重锤

centripetal 向心的;应用向心力的

centripetal acceleration 向心加速度(汽车上某一点的加速度矢量的该

点运动轨迹的法线方向上的分量)

centripetal force 向心力

centum 百,一百

CEO 首席执行官(chief executive officer 的简称)

CEPS 转向盘柱助力式电子控制转向系统(见 column assist type electronic power steering system)

cepstrum 倒频谱对数倒频谱,(见 power cepstrum)

ceramal ①金属陶瓷,陶瓷合金(= ceramet, cermet, 为 ceramic metal 的简称。其形容词 cerametallic "金属陶瓷的", "烧结金属的," 为 ceramic-metallic 的简称) ②粉末冶金学,烧结金属学

ceramal resistance 金属陶瓷电阻

ceramic ①陶瓷的,陶瓷材料的,陶质的②陶瓷,陶瓷制品

ceramic capacitive strain ga(u)ge 陶瓷电容式应变仪

ceramic coat 陶瓷涂层,陶瓷覆层(= ceramic coating)

ceramic combustion chamber (绝热发动机的)陶瓷材料燃烧室

ceramic core 陶瓷磁心,粉末烧结磁心(铁氧体等的粉末压缩或烧结成形的磁心,损失小,高频用)

ceramic diesel engine 陶瓷绝热柴油机

ceramic exhaust gas sensor 陶瓷型废气(氧浓度)传感器(指以陶瓷元件作为固态电解质电极的氧浓度传感器, 亦称 Nernst type exhaust gas sensor)

ceramic filter 陶瓷(材料)滤清器

ceramic honeycomb 陶瓷蜂窝体(催化转向器催化剂陶瓷载体的内部结构)

ceramic metal 金属粉末烧结陶瓷(= cermet, ceramal①)

ceramic particle strainer 陶瓷微粒过滤器(用多孔陶瓷材料制成,装于柴油机排气管,过滤废气中的碳粒)

ceramic pickup 陶瓷传感器 = ceramic sensor

ceramic pressure sensor 陶瓷薄膜式压力传感器

ceramic refractory 陶瓷耐火材料

ceramics 陶瓷制品,陶瓷材料

cerium 铈(Ce)

cermet button (离合器)金属陶瓷纽扣式摩擦块(= button-tyne ceramal pad)

certainty facto 置信度,可信度(简称 CF)

certificate ①证书, 执照;证件②认证;发证书;鉴定;检定

certification system 认证体系(合格认证工作的一整套程序和管理体系)

certification test (ing) (由主管部门颁发合格证书、执照等进行的)验证试验,鉴定试验,发照考试

certified automotive engineer ([美]经考核合格,发给执照的)注册汽车工程师(简称 CAE, = [英] chartered automotive engineer)

Certs 证明文件, 证书(certificates 的简称, 说明书、广告等用语)

cervical spine model 颈椎(骨)模型

CES system 综合排放净化系统(combined emission control system 的简称)

CET 发动机出厂检验(calibrated engine testing 的简称)

cetane 十六烷($C_{16}H_{34}$, 柴油中着火性能最好的碳氢化合物)

cetane improver (提高)十六烷值(的)添加剂(亦称 cetane number booster)

cetane index 十六烷指数(为十六烷的计标值, = 柴油中沸点的对数与其20℃时的密度的比值乘以一个系

数，与十六烷的实际值接近，更为常用)

cetane method (柴油)十六烷值(的评价方)法(取十六烷的十六烷值为100, α-甲萘的十六烷值为零，二者按不同容积比组成混合油，在标准的十六烷值试验机上，与要测试的柴油进行对比，当某种容积比的混合油与所测试的柴油的着火性能相同时，该混合油中十六烷值的百分比，即为所测试柴油的十六烷值)

cetane number (柴油的)十六烷值(十六烷值越低，柴油的自燃点越高，工作越粗暴。柴油的十六烷值等于与之燃烧粗暴度相同的标准燃油中十六烷的体积百分比，亦称 cetane rating, 见 cetane method)

cetene 十六烯($C_{16}H_{32}$，其着火性能仅次于十六烷)

cetene number 十六烯值(柴油机燃料着火性指数之一，用十六烯替代十六烷与α-甲萘组成标准油，试验油的十六烯值等于与之着火性相同的标准油中的十六烯体积百分含量，十六烯值100＝十六烷值80)

CEVTM 见 continuous exhaust variable timing mechanism

chain-type CVT 传动链型连续无级变速器 [传动链与钢传动带(steel belt)型 CVT 使用的钢传动带不同。传动链传递的不是压缩力，而是拉力，因而可传递的转矩更大，而且摩擦损失小]

chairman car 设有特别单人座椅的轿车，主席车

chamber 室，腔，舱(等封闭空间)

chamber displacement (转子发动机的)单室排量(转子发动机转子的一个工作面与其旋转线缸壁所形成的容积称单室容积"chamber volume"，其单室容积随转子的旋转而变化，最大容积与最小容积之差，即为转子发动机的单室排量，相当于往复式活塞发动机的单缸排量，亦称 single chamber displacement, swept volume of a single chamber, 参见 equivalent total displacement)

chamber mixture (内燃机的)空间混合(①特指燃油被喷入燃烧室空间，形成油雾，油雾吸收燃烧室内压缩空气的热量而蒸发成为燃油蒸气，与空气混合形成燃油空气混合气，亦称雾化混合，燃烧室喷雾混合，如：柴油机、汽油机燃烧室内直接喷射式内燃机的混合形成方式②以空间混合为主的混合方式的统称)

chamfer ①(圆)槽，斜面，斜口，切角面；倒角，圆角②在…上开槽，挖圆槽，倒棱，倒角，削角，去角边，磨斜，斜切，修切边缘

chamfered (边或角被切成对称的)斜棱的，被倒角的，成坡口的

chamfering ①倒角，倒棱②斜切，坡口加工③倒角的，斜切的

chamois-covered 麂皮包覆的

chamois leather 软羊皮，麂皮(亦称 shammy leather 用于擦拭玻璃、装饰件及漆面的软皮)

chance 机会，偶然事件，意外事件

chance failure 偶然性故障，随机性故障(参见 random failure)

chance variable 随机变量

chance variations ①随机变化②偶然误差

change 变化，变换，改变，变量，更换

changeability 互换性，可变性

changeable 可更换的

change down 低挡，换到低一挡的挡位(＝[美] downshift)

change drive 变速传动

change (gear) lever 变速杆(＝change speed lever)

change gear ratio 挡位速比，传动齿

轮速比（参见 transmission gear ratio）

change gear (s) 变速，换挡（=［美］shift gear）

change-gear transmission ［美］齿轮（换挡）变速器［= change (gear) box, change speed gear box］

change into higher gear 换高挡，换到高一挡（= change up）

change into lower gear 换入低挡，挂低一挡（= change down）

change over ①（发动机等小修或更换零件后）重新调整的时间，更换故障件所费的时间②变换；转换，改变

change over solenoid valve （工况）切换电磁阀

changer 变换器，转换开关，转换装置

change speed gearbox 齿轮变速器（=［美］transmission）

change speed lever 变速杆

change speed motor 变速电动机，多速电机

change valve （自动变速器的）换挡阀（由随车速提高而上升的液压控制，=［美］shift valve）

changing load 交变载荷，变化着的载荷

channel ①通道，信道，磁道，波道，频道，孔道，管道，②槽，凹缝，沟；

channel beam 槽形梁，槽钢梁

channel crossbar （汽车车架的）槽形横梁，U 形（断面）横梁

channel for oiling 润滑油路，润滑油槽

channel frame ①（车架）槽形断面纵梁②由槽形梁组成的车架

channel guide 导槽

channeling leakage （气门等的）沟槽漏气（积炭，使气门某一点或数点形成缝隙或气门工作面烧损产生径向裂缝等引起的漏气现象）

channel of ABS 防抱死制动系统的分路［在 ABS 中，根据某一个车轮的转速传感器的信息，可由一个压力调节阀来控制该车轮或包括该车轮在内的多个车轮制动力的回路称为一个分路（channel）。如：四分路 ABS（four channel ABS），对小轿车或 4×2 货车，指每个车轮都由一个独立的分路控制的 ABS；而对 6×2 和 6×4 货车则指左、右前轮各由一个独立的分路控制，另外两个独立的分路分别控制两个左后轮和两个右后轮的 ABS］

channel of oil piston ring 活塞油环上下（刮油）边之间的槽

channel-section axle 槽形断面车桥

channel steel 槽钢

chap 龟裂，皲裂

Chapman strut 查甫曼式悬架（由一上端装在车架上，下端由两根拉杆限制纵向和横向运动的滑竿式悬架，以发明人 Colin Chapman 命名，为麦弗逊式的发展，多用于后桥悬架）

charabanc （原自法语 char-à-banc，指）长条座椅式大型客车

character ①性质，特性，特征，特点②字母③（车用计算机）字符（指一个字母，一个数字，一个标点符号或其他符号，用于单独或组合表示存储于计算机内的一条信息等）④表现…的特征，描绘

character code 字符编码（指字符集合中，每一个字符的唯一数字表示）

character display （仪表等的）字符显示（用字母、符号和数字的显示）

characteristic ①特性，特征，特点②特性曲线（= characteristics）③特性的，典型的，特有的，表示特性的

characteristic constant 特征常数

characteristic curve 特性曲线（表示输出量稳态值与某一个或数个输入量之间函数关系的曲线，简称characteristics）

characteristic data 特征数据

characteristic equation 特征方程

characteristic family 特性曲线族（= family of characteristics）

characteristic function 特征函数

characteristic map （汽车的）特性曲面（三维特性曲面，一般以转速和负荷为 x、y 轴，z 轴表示 x、y 轴示值的函数所形成的三维特性曲面图）

characteristic material designation 材料规格标称（用简单字母或数字代表材料的技术规格，并作为材料的名称）

characteristics of heat release 放热特性（亦称：放热规律，指混合气在汽缸内燃烧过程中放热量或放热速率随曲轴转角改变而变化的规律）

characteristics of limit maneuver 机动性界限特性（如：汽车的临界车速，最大向心加速度等）

characteristic speed 特征车速（不足转向汽车产生最大横摆角速度增益的前进速度）

characterization ①表征，表示特性 ②鉴定

character of operation 运转特性

charactron 数码管，显像管

charcoal 炭，炭黑

charcoal-burning engine 木炭煤气机（使用车载式木炭煤气发生炉，烧木炭生成煤气作燃料的发动机）

charcoal canister purge 见 canister purge

charcoal canister storage system 活性炭罐存储系统（利用装满活性炭粒的罐存储来自燃油系，特别曲轴箱、油箱的燃油蒸发排放物，并在某种运转工况下再送入进气系）

charcoal filter 活性炭过滤器

charge ①充气，充电，加注，装料 ②充量（特指在进气过程中充入汽缸的新鲜空气或可燃混合气） ③（蓄电池的）充电量 ④（泛指各种）加注物，充填物，装填物（如：装入催化转化器内的催化剂等） ⑤货价，（因服务而索取的）费用 ⑥电荷

charge air ①（柴油机或汽油直喷式汽油机）充入汽缸的空气 ②（汽油机）充入汽缸的可燃混合气中的空气

charge air cooling 进气空气（由增压器输出后进入汽缸前的强制）冷却（= intercooling）

charge air recycling system 增压空气再循环系统（当工况无须增压时，仍不停止增压系统的运转、开启旁通阀使增压空气回流，在增压充气系统内循环，一旦要求增压时，便可立即实现增压的系统）

charge changing process （二冲程发动机）换气过程[指从排气开始，经进气、扫气过程到进、排气门（口）全部关闭为止的整个工质更换过程，亦称 gas exchange process, charge exchange process]

charge characteristic 见 charging characteristic

charge control lamp （发动机充电系统的）充电指示灯，充电警报灯（亦称 charge control light, charge lamp, charge light, charge warning light, charge pilot lamp, charge indicator lamp）

charge (-) cooled （利用新鲜充量来冷却发动机的）充量冷却的，充气冷却的（如 charge-cooled RC engene 用新鲜充量来冷却的转子发动机）

charge-cooling （对）新鲜充量进行

冷却的（指冷却新鲜充量，以增加其密度和质量的，如增压系统的intercooler）

charge current 充电电流（指充电时流入蓄电池的电流，=［英］charging current）

charged ①带电的②充有电的③充满的

charged density ①（充入汽缸的）可燃混合气或空气密度，②充量密度③（蓄电池充电时）电流密度

charge dilution 充量稀释

charge/discharge efficiency （蓄电池等的）充/放电效率（％）

charge heating 混合气（充量）预热，进气预热

charge indicator (lamp) relay 充电指示灯继电器（接通、断开蓄电池充电指示灯的继电器）

charge loss （发动机的）充气损失

charge (-mass) ratio （二冲程发动机的）扫气比（指每个工作循环中，通过进气口的新鲜充量与留在汽缸内的充量的质量比，亦称扫气系数，为扫气利用系数的倒数）

charge motion 充量运动（指汽缸内混合气体的运动）

charge motion control valve 见CMCV

charge of rupture 破坏负载

charge of surety 容许负载，安全负载

charger ①充电器，充电机②加载装置，装料设备③注液器

charge station （美）①（蓄电池的）充电站②（飞轮储能系统的）加能站③（液力储能系统的）升压站（=charging station, charging point）

charge stratification effect （发动机进气的）充气分层效应（①由于雾化不良等因素的影响，混合气本身产生稀浓不匀的分层现象②层状充气对混合气燃烧的影响）

charge stratification method （层状燃烧发动机的）分层充气法，层状充气法

charge temperature sensor 进气温度传感器（简称CTS，用于测定进气温度，以供电子控制模块修正喷油量和点火时刻，见IAT）

charge transfer device （汽车电子控制系统中的）电荷转移器件

charge-transfer loss 电荷转移损失［指集成电路存储器中，前面的电荷包（charge packet）通过器件后，残余电荷衰减到零，存储区处于空置状态，当后面的电荷包转移至此时，信号电荷为补充这些残余电荷所损失的部分］

charging 充电（的），充气（的）；加料（的），加载（的），充加制冷剂（的）

charging characteristic 充电特性（充电机的电流与电压的关系特性）

charging current ①充电电流②电容电流

charging duration （蓄电池）充电持续时间，充电时间（=charging time）

charging efficiency ①（四冲程发动机的）充量系数（指实际充量与理论充量之比，亦称充气系数）②（二冲程发动机的）扫气利用系数（指扫气口关闭后留在缸内的新鲜充量与实际扫气容积之比，亦称扫气效率）

charging piston （某些旧式二冲程发动机中用于压缩新鲜空气供充气之用的）附加活塞

charging pressure （进气）增压压力

charging rate （充电系统的）充电量

charging rectifier 充电整流器

charging resistance 充电电阻

charging set ①增压装置②充电装置

charging station 充电站（=charge station, charging point）

charging stroke 进气冲程（= induction stroke, inlet stroke）

charging system ①充电系统②充气系统③充液系统

charles' low 查理定律（一定质量的气体在体积不变时，其压强与热力学温度成正比）

Charpy (impact) test 摆锤式冲击（强度）试验，夏比（U型或V型）缺口冲击试验（用规定高度上的摆锤对简支梁状态的U型缺口试样，或V型缺口试样进行一次性打击，测量试样折断时的冲击吸收功）

charring 烧焦，烧成炭，炭化（法），焦化（法）

charry 炭化的，炭状的

chart ①图表②制定图表，用图表说明

charter ①（汽车等）租用，包租②执照，特许证③发给执照，租用

chartered automotive engineer ［英］注册汽车工程师（指授予合格证或任职资格证或认证的汽车工程师，=［美］certified automotive engineer, 简称CAE）

chart of automotive model 汽车型谱

chart with contour line 有等（温、压、浓度、力等）量线的图

chase leaks 检漏，查漏（用跟踪法查出漏源）

chassis 底盘（①对于货车等非承载式车身的汽车，［英］指由车架、悬架和车桥组成的车辆单独的下部结构。［美］指供安装车身及驱动，转向及悬架、车桥、车轮系统的车架。我国则定义为实际上是除车身和驾驶室以外可用于行驶的整个车辆。这一定义所包括的内容等于美的chassis cab减去驾驶室。②对于轿车等无独立车架结构的承载式车身的车辆，见running gear）

chassis and body half-integral construction 半承载式车身结构（车身与车架刚性相连，车身分担部分载荷）

chassis and body integral construction 承载式车身，整体式承载车身结构（没有车架，由车身承载）

chassis and cab dry mass 底盘与驾驶室干质量（底盘干质量与完整驾驶室质量之和）

chassis and cab kerb mass 底盘与驾驶室整备质量（底盘整备质量与完整驾驶室质量之和）

chassis black 底盘防锈黑，底盘黑色涂料

chassis-cab 底盘—驾驶室总成（指装有驾驶室、发动机、传动、转向、悬架、车桥、车轮、制动等汽车行驶所需的全套系统的底盘总成，但不包括车身式货箱）

chassis' center tunnel （汽车）底盘（封装变速器-传动轴的）中央管道

chassis channel 车架构件用槽钢

chassis checking gauge 车架尺寸检查量规，车架量杆

chassis cowl 底盘—前围板总成（指装有发动机及传动、转向、悬架等行驶所需的全套系统，但只配备驾驶室前围板的平头货车底盘总成，供厂家制造如牲畜运输车，其中不带风窗玻璃者，称chassis scuttle）

chassis dry mass 底盘干质量（不包括燃料和冷却液的底盘质量）

chassis dynamometer 汽车底盘测功器，底盘测功机（一般为滚筒式试验台，用于测定车轮的输出功率和转矩，进行整车的动力、经济性及排放试验）

chassis earth-return electrical system 车架搭铁电器系，车架接地电器系统

chassis frame （货车）车架（指纵梁与横梁构成的框架结构）

chassis friction horsepower 底盘摩擦功率，车辆摩擦马力（以马力为单

位的底盘各运动件的摩擦消耗功率)

chassis grease 车用底盘滑脂(亦称 mobile grease,参见 aluminium grease)

chassis kerb mass 底盘整备质量(底盘干质量,随车件质量,冷却液质量和不少于油箱容量90%燃油质量之和)

chassis-less body 承载式车身,无车架车身,整体式车身,(= body integral with frame)

chassis-mount 装在车架上的

chassis number 底盘号码,底盘编号

chassis (power) output (汽车)底盘输出功率(指汽车驱动轮上实际输出的驱动汽车行驶的功率,即汽车驱动功率, = road horsepower)

chassis runner 车架纵梁(= body support runner)

chassis scuttle 见 chassis cowl

chassis stop (由)车架(伸出)的(副悬架弹簧件)支撑板或支撑架(当主弹簧件变形过大时,支撑副弹簧件)

chassis straightener 车架矫正装置

chassis-to-ground distance sensor 底盘离地高度传感器(用于悬架自动高度调平、行驶平顺性控制)

chassis with centre tube 中央管梁式车架,脊梁式车架

chatter ①振动,震颤②(零件表面因振动产生的)震纹

ChB 阻风门开度限制器(参见 choke braker)

cheap ①廉价的,便宜的②贬了值的③粗劣的,低劣的,劣质的

check 校核,检验,检查,核对

check ball 球阀式单向阀(由球和弹簧构成,只允许液体向压缩弹簧的方向通过)

check bar (材料试验)试棒;校验棒(作为比较标准)

check bit (车用计算机)校验位(用于检测传输数据中的错误)

check bolt ①防松螺栓,锁紧螺栓②抑制螺栓(如:发生泄漏后用手可切断液压油路的螺栓)

check connector (电子控制系统的)诊断插座

check crack 细裂纹,收缩裂纹,网裂(= contraction crack, shrinkage crack)

checked 检验过的,验算过的,校对过的

check engine (warning) light 发动机故障警报灯(该灯亮,表示发动机系统发生故障,应停机检查,简称 check eng,见 MIL)

checker flag 方格旗(汽车竞赛时判决定胜负用格子旗)

checking ①[美]表面的细裂纹,一般指橡胶表面由于光照和风雨而形成的细裂纹[英]crazing),龟裂②检验,校核

checking by blueing 涂蓝检验,着色检验(用涂色法检查两表面的配合状况或贴合程度等)

checking calculation 验算,检验性计算,验证性核算

checking cylinder 止动油缸,液压止动油缸

checking engine balance 发动机各缸功率平衡检测(一般用 engine analyzer 检测多缸发动机各缸输出功率的差值)

check nut 锁紧螺母,防松螺母

check point ①(故障的)检查点②(路上的车辆)检查站

check ring 限位环,止动环,锁紧环,锁圈

check road 汽车性能试验道路;车辆检验用道路,路试道路

check routine ①(查找故障源的)检查程序②(新车出厂的)检验程序

check sample 质量检验用试样,检查用的试样(=check specimen)

check screw 定位螺钉,止动螺钉

check spring 止动弹簧

check strap 车门开度限制皮带

check sum 检验和(在计算机控制系统数字处理和通信用于校验目的一组数据项的和)

check valve ①单向阀,止回阀(参见 back valve,=one-way valve)②(特制制动主缸内,使液压系保持一定残留压力的)残留阀[亦称 residual (pressure) valve]

check (valve) ball 止回阀球,单向球阀的阀球

check valve pump 止回(液压)泵

check washer 锁止垫圈

cheek 面颊,颊板

cheek brake 蹄式制动器(=shoe brake)

cheek of crankshaft 曲轴曲柄臂

chemical ①化学的,化学用的②化学制品,化学物质,化学成分,化合物③电流强度单位(=0.176A)

chemical brightening 化学抛光(=chemical polishing,浸入化学抛光剂溶液内,改善金属件的光滑度)

chemical change 化学变化

chemical composition 化学成分

chemical conversion coating 化学稳定涂层

chemical emissions 化学有害排出物,排出物的有害化学成分

chemical hazards 化学危险品

chemical luminescence detector 化学发光测定仪,化学发光分析仪(简称 CLD)

chemically correct (air-fuel) ratio 理论空燃比(根据燃料化学成分计算,混合气完全燃烧应有的空气与燃料质量比,=theoretical mixture ratio)

chemically pure 化学纯的,三级纯的(=chemical-pure,简称 chempure 或 CP)

chemical polishing 化学抛光(金属件溶液,浸渍表面光泽法,简称 CP,=chemical brightening)

chemical reaction 化学反应

chemicals 化学(制)品

chemical stability 化学稳定性(指难以反应或反应速度很慢而几乎不反应的性质)

chemical symbol 化学符号

chemical toilet 宿营车上使用的便携式厕具

chemical vaporous deposition 化学气相沉积法(在 900~1200℃ 或 400~600℃ 下,在金属表面形成高硬度的碳化物、氮化物、硼化物薄膜层的方法,简称 CVD 法)

chemico-heat treatment 化学热处理(合金元素的活性原子在一定温度下渗入钢件表层并随后进行适当热处理的复合工艺方法)

chemigum (用化学方法制成的)人造橡胶,丁腈橡胶

chemiluminescence 化学(低温)发光

chemiluminescent 化学发光的

chemiluminescent analyzer 化学发光分析器(通过测量 NO_x 和 O_3 反应产生的化学光强度,求出氮氧化物 NO_x 的浓度的分析仪,简称 CLA,=chemiluminescent detector)

chemiluminescent detector (简称 CLD,见 chemiluminescent analyzer)

chemistry ①化学②(物质的)化学组成,化学成分③(物质的)化学性质

chemosorbent 化学吸附剂

chemosphere 臭氧层(有光化学作用的大气层,地面上空约 30~80km,=ozonosphere,ozone layer)

chequered plate 花钢板,网纹板(=checkered plate)

cherry picker 车载升降台（用于维修高空电线）

chest ①箱，柜，盒，匣②（人体的）胸部

chest depth 乘员胸部处的厚度

chestnut ①栗木，栗树②栗色

chest severity index （人体）胸部（受冲击的）严重程度指数（简称 CSI）

cheveron 人字花纹，人字形断口，V 型符号；锯齿形花饰，波浪纹饰（亦写作 chevron）

cheveron pattern （胎面）人字形花纹

Chevolet cockpit-noise-reducing technology 雪佛兰驾驶室消声技术（由电子控制的声响系统根据装在驾驶室内的麦克风测得的发动机噪声，控制小型喇叭产生与该噪声相应的低频声波消除该噪声）

Chevrolet 雪佛兰（美国通用公司的轿车厂及该厂生产的轿车商标名）

chevron gear 人字（形齿）齿轮（= double helical gear）

chevron seal 人字形迷宫式密封（件）

CHHNAP （美国）加利福尼亚公路氢（燃料）实施计划（California Hydrogen Highway Action Plan 的简称）

chief ①主要部分，最有价值的部分（简称 ch）②主要的，重要的，总…，主…

chief axle 主轴

chief engineer 总工程师（= engineer in chief）

chief executive officer （公司、企业的）首席执行官

child lock （轿车上的）儿童安全锁（一般指接通电源等后，从车内打不开的后车门锁，亦称 child proof lock）

child proof (device) （轿车的）儿童保护机构（如：将该机构的拨杆拨至锁紧位置，车门便不能从车内开启，而只能从车外打开，以防儿童在行车中开门）

child restraint system 儿童约束性安全系统（指儿童专用座椅及其安全带等约束性装置。由于儿童专用座椅都带有各种安全附件，故该术语一般被用作儿童座椅系统的同义词，见 child seat）

child safety door latches 儿童安全车门锁闩

child seat 儿童座椅［特指适合于欧洲经济委员会 ECE-R44 标准中规定的第 1、2 组年龄段（第 1 组为 9 ~ 18kg，或 8 个月 ~ 4 岁，第 2 组为 15 ~ 25kg，或 4 ~ 6 岁）的儿童乘坐的安全座椅，由椅身、安全带系统和（或）防冲击软垫等组成］

child-seat detecting system 儿童座椅检知系统（当测得在助手座或成人座位上装有儿童座椅或坐有儿童时即限制安全气囊展开）

chill ①冷激，冷淬，冷硬，冻结②激冷的，冷冻的，冻结的

chill car 冷藏车（= refrigerator car）

chill crack 冷激裂纹；热裂，火裂（= fire crack）

chill (ed) cast (ing) ①冷激铸件②冷激铸造

chilled distribution （货物的）冷藏配送（一般指温度控制在 0 ~ 5℃ 的冷藏车送货）

chill effect 激冷效应（指燃烧室某部分冷却强度过大，导致该处混合气温度下降，影响燃烧火焰传播的现象）

chiller 冷冻机，冷冻装置

chill point 冻结温度，凝固温度，凝固点，冰冻点

chimney ①烟囱②烟筒状物

China Commission for Conformity of Automotive Products 中国汽车产品

认证委员会

China National Automotive Industry Corporation 中国汽车工业总公司(简称 CNAIC)

chinese six (指两个前转向桥,一个后驱动桥的)六轮栏板式货车

chip (集成电路)晶片,芯片①生产电子部件的一小片半导体材料②一片半导体材料上的一个集成电路,亦称 die,参见 wafer③片状的(电容器,电阻器,载体等)④碎片,削片,屑⑤(车用玻璃)爆边(指边缘出现的贝壳状缺损)

chip resistance of surface coatings 表面涂层抗剥落强度

chip-select input 芯片选通输入,片选输入(指一种当其无效时,阻止向集成电路输入数据或从集成电路输出数据的允许输入,参见 enable z)

chirp ①线性调频脉冲②(ABS 工作时,车轮会有 10%～30% 的滑移率,此时因轮胎滑移而产生的)吱吱声

chisel ①凿,凿刀,錾子②用上述工具完成的作业

chisel truck 叉式装载机(= fork truck)

chloride 氯化物

chloride plate (氯化铅蓄电池阳极板)

chloride (storage) battery 氯化铅蓄电池

chlorinated solvent 氯化物溶剂(三氯乙烯等用以清洗金属零件)

chlorine 氯(Cl)

chlorine-lithium cell 锂氯电池(亦写作 lithium chlorine cell)

chlorofluoromethane refrigerant (汽车空调用的)氟氯烷制冷剂(亦称氟利昂制冷剂"Freon")

chloroprene rubber 氯丁二烯橡胶,氯丁橡胶(简称 CR)

chock ①角垫木(防止汽车溜坡),木楔,楔形垫块②用垫木楔阻,阻塞

choice ①选择,抉择②值得选用的,精选的,上等的

chokage 堵塞,阻滞,障碍

choke ①阻(堵,充,填)塞②阻止,抑制,截流③扼流器,扼流线圈④(发动机)阻风门,风门(简称 ch, = choke valve,[美] strangler)

choke braker 阻风门开度限制器(起动或冷机运转时开度减小,以便增加进气管真空度,增加供油量,使混合气加浓,而在常温或发动机起动后立即使阻风门开度增大,防止混合气过浓,减少 CO、HC 排出量,简称 chB 或 CB)

choke button 阻风门按钮(= choke knob)

choke cleaner 阻风门清洗器(内装清洗合剂,可喷射到阻风门轴、阻风门联杆轴节上)

choke control cable bracket 阻风门拉索支架

choked 在阻风门关闭下运转的(指发动机)

choke knob 阻风门拉钮(仪表板上操纵阻风门的拉钮)

choke opener 阻风门开启器,阻风门强制开启阀(为了减少使用阻风门时浓混合气生成的 CO、HC,发动机热起后,迫使阻风门开到一定开度的装置,亦称 chock braker)

choker ①阻风门②扼流线圈③(管的)闭塞部分④喉管

choke relief valve (阻风门上的)空气补充(单向)阀(= choker check valve)

choke stove 自动风门加热室(在排气歧管,为一热交换室,经废气加热的空气流入自动风门装置,加速其作用)

choke thermostat 扼流式节温器(水

冷发动机中无旁通管时使用的节温器）

choke tube ①（[美]化油器）喉管（= venturi）②阻流管，限流管

choke tube of variable size 可变截面喉管，可变尺寸喉管，活动喉管

choke unloader setting （化油器）阻风门最小闭合间隙调整

choke valve （限制，扼制，阻止气流或液流的）阻流阀门（如，化油器内的阻风门，用于限制进入汽缸的空气量，使混合气加浓，易于冷机起动或冷机运转）

choking ①阻塞，节气，扼流②阻塞的，节气的，扼流的

choking winding 扼流线圈，扼流绕组

cholesteric liquid crystal 胆甾相液晶（因层分子平行排列，相邻平行层指向矢稍有旋转，呈螺旋排列的液晶）

choose 选择，挑选，选定

chop 砍，斩，劈（及所造成的后果）

chopper ①断路器，断续器②斩波器，遮光器③变磁阻转子，磁路截断器

chopper blade 斩光片，斩光板，断续遮光片（如：无触点式电子点火系中光电火花信号发生装置中的斩光片）

chopper method 断续控制法（参见interrupted control method）

chopper switch 闸刀开关

chop shop [美]用可折叠式活顶更换轿车标准钢顶的专业工厂

chord ①弦（简称CD）②弦长

chordal height 弦齿高（①对圆柱齿轮，指法向弦齿厚到齿顶面的最短距离②对直齿锥齿轮，指当量圆柱齿轮上的弦齿高）

chordal tooth thickness （锥齿轮的）弦齿厚（指当量圆柱齿轮上的弦齿厚）

chord force 弦向分力（指平行于基准线的分力）

chord modulus 弦线模量（指在弹性范围内，轴向应力—轴向应变曲线上，任一规定应力或应变处的斜率）

chovr ①转换开关②换向，转接（changeover 的简称）

CHPM 正负检验（check plus minus）

C-H ratio （碳氢化合物的）碳氢比

chroma 孟塞尔色品（度）（Munsell chroma 的简称）

chromate ①铬酸盐②渗铬处理（用铬化合物溶液处理，生成渗铬保护膜）

chromate-phosphate (conversion) coating ①表面渗铬-磷酸②用铬酸盐-磷酸盐溶液处理在金件表面、生成渗铬-磷层

chromate treatment （金属件的）铬酸盐（溶液表面渗铬）处理

chromatic 有色的，色彩的，颜色的，着色的

chromaticity （光的）色品，色度（由颜色的纯度和支配颜色的主波长表示）

chromatograph ①色层（分离）谱，色谱②色层分离法③色（层）谱仪

chrome ①铬（Cr, = chromium）②镀铬③铬合金

chromed 镀铬的（= chrome-plated, 亦称 chromium-plated, chrome-faced）

chrome exhaust tip （汽车的）排气尾管镀铬管头

chrome-flashed 光亮镀铬的

chrome-hardened （钢件）镀硬铬层的

chrome-iron-alloy insert 铬铁合金的镶嵌件（如气门座的铬铁合金镶口等）

chromel 铬镍合金（一种耐高温的

镍基铬合金）

chromel-alumel thermocouple 镍铬铝合金热电偶，铬镍—铝镍温差电偶

chrome manganese steel 铬锰钢（= chromium manganese steel）

chrome work 车身镀铬件的通称

chroming ①镀铬的②镀铬（作业）

chromium 铬（Cr）（chrome①的正规名称）

chromizing 铬化（处理），渗铬（处理）（亦写作 chromising）

chromophotometer 比色计（= chromometer）

chronograph 计时器，时间记录器，记录式计时器

chronometric tachometer 计时式转速计

chronoscope 千分秒表，瞬时计，精密计时器

Chrysler Collision Detection 克莱斯勒防（电子）碰撞（多路传输）系统（简称 C^2D，或 C^2D bus system，指由一条母线连接汽车上的多个计算机控制系统，并可避免总线系统中电子碰撞）

Chrysler Corporation ［美］克莱斯勒（汽车）公司 1998 年与德国 Daimler Benz 公司合并，成为 Daimler-Chrysler 公司

CHU ①卡热单位（caloric heat unit）②摄氏热单位（centigrade heat unit）

chuck 夹具，卡盘

chug ①（发动机不正常燃烧时）粗暴声②（车辆等维护不良，各部机械发出的）嚓嘎声，机械噪声

churning losses 搅动损失（= churn loss，如：齿轮在机油中搅拌的功率损失）

CI ①压燃（compression ignition）②线圈点火（coil ignition）③圆堆（贯入）指数④立方英寸（cubic inch）⑤中央喷射系统（Central Injection 的简称，节气门体单点式汽油喷射系统，见 single point injection system）

CID（cid） （发动机）立方英寸排量［cubic inch (es) displacement 的简称］

CID class （发动机的立方英寸）排量级（英美将发动机的排量按立方英寸分级。如：400CID 表示排量为 400in^3 级的发动机）

CID sensor 汽缸识别传感器（cylinder identification sensor 的简称，电子控制模块根据该传感器的信号确定哪一个汽缸应喷油和点火，见 CMP）

CIE（A）S （车身或车架）碰撞冲击能量吸收结构（crash impact energy absorbing structure 的简称）

cigarette lighter （驾驶室仪表盘附近的电热）点烟器（亦写作 cigaret-lighter）

CIGS thin-film sun battery CIGS 薄膜太阳能电池［CIGS 为以铜（Cu）、铟（In）、镓（Ga）和硒（Se）为原料制成的半导体］

CIH 装在缸盖内的凸轮轴（camshaft in head 的简称，注意：CIH engine 指凸轮轴封装在缸盖内的顶置气门式发动机，不要与 OHC 顶置凸轮轴式发动机相混淆）

CIMS 计算机联控制造系统（computer integrated manufacturing system）

circa （与日期连用）大约［如：circa 2015（大约2015）年］

circle ①圆，圆周②范围③圆周运动

circle-arc tooth 圆弧（轮）齿，格里森齿（= circular tooth, Gleason tooth）

circle-of-sight visibility 周围视野，周围可见度（= all-round visibility）

circlet （小）圈，环；锁环

circling motion 环流，环形，圆周运动（= circular motion, circumferen-

circlip 弹簧卡环,弹簧锁圈,卡簧,弹簧挡圈([美] snap ring,由弹簧钢丝制成的开口环,开口两端带有钳孔,以便于用卡簧专用手钳拆装,一般卡在被锁件的环槽内)

circlip pliers 卡簧专用手钳(其钳爪端头尖细,使用时,插入卡簧开口两端的孔中,将它撑开,以便装卸)

circuit ①环路(如环形赛车跑道)②电路(电流的完整回路)③起相对独立作用的电气—电子元件的组合(如:驱动电路"drive circuit",逻辑电路"logic circuit",微分电路"differential circuit"等)

circuit alarm 电路故障警报

circuit breaker ①断路器,电路保护器(当电流超过某规定值时,即切断电路的装置,其断电电流值一般是可调的)②电路开关器

circuit diagram ①线路图,电路图 ②流程图

circuit pack 线路组件,电路组件,电路单元,电路部分

circuitry ①整机电路,电路(一套设备中全部电路的总称)②电路图,接线图,布线图③电路原理,电路学

circuit tester ①万用表,多用表②电路试验器,线路检测器(最简单的电路检测器为螺钉旋具形的电笔)

circular 圆形的,圆周的(简称 cir)

circular-arc gear 圆弧圆柱齿轮(基本齿条的法向或端面可用齿廓为圆弧或近似圆弧的某种曲线的斜齿圆柱齿轮,亦简称圆弧齿轮)

circular-arc gear drive with small teeth difference 圆弧少齿差齿轮传动(由圆弧少齿差齿轮副、偏心元件及输出机构组成)

circular-arc spurgear 圆弧直齿轮(齿廓曲线为圆弧线或近似圆弧线的圆柱直齿轮)

circular ball type 循环球式(转向机)(= circulating ball type)

circular cam 盘型凸轮,偏心轮(= disc cam)

circular constant 圆周率(π = 3.14158…)

circular dichroism 圆偏振二色性(指线偏振光射入光学活性物质后变为圆偏振光的性质)

circular file 圆锉刀

circular frequency 角速度,角频率

circular grinder 外圆磨床(= cylindrical grinder)

circular head lamp 圆形前照灯

circular helix 圆柱螺旋线(普通螺旋线)

circular key 半圆键

circularly polarized light 圆偏振光[两束线偏振光的电矢量相互垂直,若其振幅相等,固相差为 $\pi/2$ 或 $3\pi/2$,则合成光束的电矢量的光点在它们传播方向的垂直面上将描绘出圆形轨迹,迎着光传播方向,向左(右)旋转者称左(右)圆偏振光]

circular mil 圆密耳(金属丝断面面积单位,等于 5.0674×10^{-4} mm^2,简称 c. m.)

circular motion 圆运动;圆周运动 (= circular movement)

circular oil groove 环形油槽

circular path (车辆转弯)圆形轨迹

circular pitch (齿轮)分度圆周节,周节

circular spline (谐波齿轮传动中的)刚性齿轮,刚轮(相对柔性齿轮而言的普通齿轮)

circular thickness (齿轮的)弧齿厚,分度圆齿厚(= circular tooth thickness)

circular tooth 圆弧齿(= circle-arc tooth)

circular tooth contact 圆弧齿面接触区（一对圆弧齿轮在正常啮合运转条件下，齿面上实际接触的部分）

circular velocity （圆）周速（度）

circular washer 圆垫圈

circulate 循环，环流，环行

circulating 循环的，环流的

circulating ball-and-nut steering gear 循环球-螺母式转向机构（= recirculating ball-and-nut steering gear）

circulating ball type 循环球式（转向机）（= circular ball type, recirculating ball type, ball screw type, ball circuit type）

circulating decimal 循环小数（亦称 recurring decimal, repeating decimal）

circulating lubrication 循环润滑（= circulation lubrication）

circulating pump 循环泵（使液体在一个封闭系统内循环）

circulation 环行，循环，环流，（矢量的）旋转

circulatory turbine （液力变矩器中位于泵轮和涡轮之间的）导轮（泵轮旋转时，工作液以高速流入涡轮，使涡轮旋转而输出动力，由涡轮出来的工作液经过导轮改变方向后又流入泵轮并给涡轮一个反作用力矩，如此循环不已，故偶见文献将导轮称为"循环涡轮"见 reactor）

circumcenter 外接圆圆心

circum circle 外接圆

circumference 圆周；四周，周长

circumference of wheel 轮周（长度）

circumferential backlash 圆周侧隙（将一对相啮合的一个齿轮固定，另一个齿轮所能转过的节圆弧长的最大值）

circumferential fold line pattern （轮胎胎面的）纵向折线花纹

circumferential force 圆周力，切向力（= peripheral force）

circumferential groove 圆周槽，圆环槽（= circular groove）

circumferential highway 环行公路

circumferential lug space （轮胎）圆周花纹间距

circumferential pattern 纵向花纹（按轮胎周向排列的胎面花纹）

circumferential pitch 周节，圆周齿节（见 circular pitch）

circumferential restricting mechanism 周向限制机构（将空间摆动变成平面回转运动，并传至输出元件上的输出机构）

circumferential stress 周向应力

circumferential velocity 圆周速度，切向速度（= peripheral velocity, circumferential speed）

circumfluent 环流的，绕流的

circumgyrate （作）陀螺运动，使旋转

circumscribed circle 外接圆，外切圆（亦称 circumcircle）

circumstance [复] 环境，情况，详情，细节，事件，事实，有关事项

cir mil (s) 圆密耳（circular mil 的简称）

CIS ①惯性系统中心（center of inertia system 的简称）②连续喷油系统（continuous injection system）③见 cylinder identification sensor

CISC 组合仪表(用)计算机（complex instruction set computer 的简称）

CIS-E 见 continuous injection system-electronic

CIS-L 见 continuous injection system-Lambda

cissoidal curve 蔓叶类曲线

cistern truck 液罐车

C³I system ①三线圈（型无分电器式）点火系统（three-coil ignition system 的简称，每两缸火花塞由一个点火线圈提供点火高压，每冲程每缸点火两次的六缸发动机）

②（通用公司的）计算机控制线圈点火系统（商品名，Computer-Controlled Coil Ignition 的简称，见 EIS）

CITA 国际汽车检查委员会（[法]Comitè International de L'Inspèction Technique Automobile 的简称）

Citaro 西踏罗（Daimler-Chrysler 公司推出的高压"35 MPa"氢燃料电池汽车车名，据称其输出功率＞200kW，最高车速200km/h，续航距离200km）

cite 引례，引证（＝citation）

city beam 市内行车灯光，近光（＝low beam）

city car 市区用轿车（通常指长 10～12 英尺的紧凑型轿车）

city cycle 见 urban cycle

city diesel 城市（用低污染）柴油

city driving 城市驾驶，市区行车

city dweller car 城市居民用轿车

city noise 城市噪声

city-suburban route 市区-郊区线路（简称C-S）

city (-type motor) bus 市区公共汽车，城市型客车（＝town bus, town service bus）

CIVIC HYBRID （本田公司）思域（公民）牌混合动力车（该车使用电子控制模块控制的稀燃发动机和助力电动机混合动力系统。正常行驶时由汽油机驱动，急加速时助力电动机与汽油机共同驱动，减速时电动机起发电机作用，将减速能转变为电能由蓄电池回收，备加速时使用）

civil defense sign 民防标志（紧急情况时指标和引导交通的标志）

civil vehicle 民用车辆

CKD 完全拆散的，全套拆卸开的；全套散件组装（一般指将整个车辆的全套散零部件运至外地或国外组装成车，completely knocked down 的简称）

CKD truck set 整套货车散件（往往由装配厂组装成整车）

CKP sensor 曲轴位置传感器（见 crankshaft position sensor，为美国政府规定使用的 SAE 推荐术语，从1995 年元月起取代以往通用和克莱斯勒公司使用的 REF，和福特公司使用的 CPS 等）

CKS 车道保持系统（见 course keeping system）

CL 舒适豪华型（轿车）（comfort luxe 的简称，较 L 型高一级，但不如 GL 型）

Cl 企业商标（Corporate Identity 的简称）

clack ①瓣，瓣阀，活门，阀门 ②发出噼啪声

clack seat 瓣阀座

clack valve 瓣阀（＝clapper valve, flap valve, hinged valve）

clad 金属热压包覆（指在高温高压下，使一金属包覆另一金属表面）

clad （车身等的）外壳、外皮

cladding ①热压包覆的；热压包覆（法）②（独立装配在客车木制或钢制车身框架上的）车身外板（件）

claimed accuracy 规定的精度，要求的精度

claim for damages 索赔

clam bucket （装运、挖掘机械的）抓斗

clamp ①夹子，夹紧装置；卡箍，夹钳；压板 ②箝位电路 ③夹紧；紧固

clamp band 夹箍

clamp coupling 对开套筒夹紧联轴节

clamper ①接线板 ②箝位电路 ③夹子

clamping ①夹紧的 ②箝位（过程）（指保持电路输出为常量）

clamping apparatus 夹具，卡具

clamp (ing) bolt 夹紧螺栓

clamping collar 夹环，夹圈，夹紧

套，钢板弹簧夹

clamping diode 钳压二极管，钳位二极管（跨接于线圈或绕组，拦截电路接通、断开时产生的尖峰电压）

clamping load （作用于离合器片或联轴节盘等上的）夹紧压力

clamping ring 锁圈，锁紧圈，锁环，夹紧环，夹环（＝clamp ring）

clamp load torque （螺钉等的）旋紧力矩（达到规定紧固载荷所需的旋紧力矩，参见 clamp load）

clamp-type end fitting （软管）夹紧式管端接头

clamshell hood 蛤壳形罩

clarification of water 水的滤清，水澄清，水净化

clarifier ①（无线电）干扰清除装置②净化剂，澄清剂③滤清器，澄清器，沉淀槽

clarify ①说明，阐明②（液体）净化，澄清

clash-free shifting 无冲击换挡（＝clashless shifting）

clash gear transmission 滑动齿轮变速器（＝sliding gear transmission）

clasp ①扣子，扣环，扣钩，扣紧物，铰链搭扣，钩环，相互钩挂②扣上，钩住，夹紧，铆固，握紧，抱拢

clasp joint 对扣连接，咬口连接

class ①种类，等级，级②分级

class A ignition miss （发动机）甲类缺火（指发动机在转速低于200r/min 时某汽缸缺火）

class A multiplex system A级多路复用系统（用来取代常规汽车电线系统，减少导线条数的单线多路复用系统，在多节点间通过同一条信号线传输和接受多路信号）

class A thread 外螺纹（＝external thread）

class B ignition miss 乙类缺火（指发动机转速为1000r/min 时某汽缸缺火）

class B multiplex system B级多路复用传输系统（在各节点间传递数据，资源共享，可减去不必要的传感器和系统的其他部件）

class B thread 内螺纹（＝internal thread）

class C multiplex system C级多路复用系统（由信号线传输发动机控制、防抱死控制等实时控制系统的高速率数据信号）

classes of car 轿车的级（轿车一般按发动机排量、最大功率、转矩、轴距、车重等分为若干等级，如德国分为 A、B、C、D 四级，A 级又分为 Aoo、Ao 和 A 三个等级，排量小于1000mL，轴距2000～2200mm 的小型车为 Aoo 级"Aoo class"；排量1000～1300mL，轴距2200～2300mm 的小型车为 Ao 级"Ao-class"；排量1300～1600mL，轴距2300～2450mm 者为 A 级"A-class"；排量1600～2400mL，轴距2450～2600mm 的中档轿车为 B 级"B class"；排量2300～3000mL，轴距2600～2800mm 的高档车为 C 级；排量3000mL 以上，轴距在2800mm 以上的豪华车为 D 级。但随着汽车的发展，新车型不断涌现，分级的标准也在变化，如：有的文献将排量1390mL、轴距2462mm 的 skoda 划分 Ao 级，将排量1769mL、轴距2535mm 的 Nissan 阳光轿车划为 A 级，将排量2794mL、轴距2725mm 的 BMW33oi 划为 B 级等）

classic ①第一流的，经典的②古典的，有古典艺术风格的（如车身造型等）③因历史悠久而著名的

classic car 古典轿车（"古"是相对而言的，如战后年代将1919～1939年生产的名牌车，称为古典车，但到了今天，战后美国20世纪70、80年代生产的名车也已经是古典车

了，甚至 classic car 一词亦用作老旧汽车的通称)

classic piston engine 常规活塞发动机，传统的活塞式发动机

classification 分类，归类，分等，分级，类别

classify ①把…分类，把…分等级，把…归入一类②分成类的

Class-leading 高级的，顶级的，优秀的

class of accuracy 精度等级 = class of precision

class of fit 配合公差等级

clatter ①发咔嗒声②咔嗒声

claw 爪，钩，钳，爪钩，爪形器具，卡爪，卡子；把手，凸起部；齿，销

claw clutch 爪形离合器；牙嵌离合器 (= claw coupling)

claw pole (电机的)爪极 (爪形磁极)

clay buck 见 clay model

clay design interpretation (车身造型设计方案的)黏土模型示样(指车身的1/4或3/8等黏土缩尺模型)

clay model 黏土模型(一般指投产前的全尺寸模型，亦称 clay buck)

CLD (废气有害成分)化学发光分析器 (chemiluminescent detector 的简称)

CLD type fast response NO$_X$ analyzer 光化学分析仪型快速响应 NO$_X$ 分析仪

cleading 护罩，保热套，衬板，套板

clean ①干净的，无杂质的；低污染或无污染的(燃烧燃料、发动机、汽车等)②清洗，清除，清理

Clean Air Amendments Act 清洁大气法修订条例 [1970 年美国联邦政府对 1963 年制定的清洁大气法 CAA (Clean Air Act) 的修订法令，简称 CAAA]

clean air system 空气净化系统(简称 CAS，指80年代美国 Chrysler 公司货车等用的排气净化装置，较早期用的 CAP 更完善，见 clean air package)

clean-air tuning (发动机的)排气净化调整(通过调整来减少排放)

clean alternative fuel (汽车的)清洁代用燃料(如：甲醇，乙醇等)

clean burning engine vehicle 清洁燃烧发动机车辆 (= clean engine vehicle, clean burning vehicle, clean air vehicle, clean vehicle)

cleaner ①各种清洁器具、装置的通称(如滤清器)②清洗液，清洗剂

clean (er) air package 空气净化组件(简称 CAP，美国 Chrysler 公司货车用的排气净化组件的商品名，用以减少废气中的 CO 等)

clean-fuel 清洁燃料(无污染燃油，20世纪90年代美国认定的 clean fuel 有甲醇、M85 甲醇汽油、压缩天然气、液化石油气、重整汽油及氢)

cleaning agent 清洁剂 (= cleaning compound, detergent, cleaning solvent cleansing agent, cleansing fluid)

cleaning gun 压缩空气清洗枪，高压水清洗枪

cleanliness ①清洁度，干净程度②良流线型

cleanliness characteristic (机油)清洁能力特性

cleanliness life (润滑油)清洁寿命(指脏污前之使用期限)

cleanliness of disengagement (离合器等)分离的彻底性

cleanliness of exhaust (汽车发动机)排气的清洁度，废气的清洁程度(指废气中不含有害污染物的程度)

clean master (汽车)零件洗涤台(商品名)

clean oil ①轻质油，透明油，未加裂化油的油料②无添加剂润滑油

③新鲜机油
clean oil lubrication ①清洁机油润滑②全消耗性机油润滑（见 total-loss lubrication）
cleanse 清洗，洗净，清除
cleanser 清洁器，清洗机，吸尘器
cleansing ①净化，纯化，提纯②清洁用的，清洗用的
cleansing filter element 滤清器滤芯
clean substitute fuel 清洁的代用燃料（= non-polluting fuel）
Clean Tax System （车辆的）清洁税制（如：日本规定凡经其国土交通省认定的超低排放汽车最高可减免年度规定税额的70%）
clearage fracture （金属件的）解理断裂（指沿原子结合力最弱的解理面发生开裂的断裂）
clearance ①间隙（= gap）②净空（= headroom）③（可供车辆通行的）间距（= space between obstructions）④余地（= free space）⑤清除（= making clear）
clearance adjustment 间隙调整
clearance and marker lamp （货车的）示高示宽灯（装在牵引车驾驶室前方左右两上角或挂车车身前、后方左、右四上角，表示车宽和车高）
clearance angle 留隙角，后角
clearance circle （汽车回转的）通道圆〔汽车以最大转向角缓慢回转行驶时，①其最外侧车轮接地中心点的轨迹所形成圆的半径称为最小回转半径（minimum turning radius），该半径所做的圆称为"最小半径通过圆"（minimum-turning-radius clearance circle）②其最外侧车轮最外点的轨迹所形成的圆，称为"路缘石通道圆"，该圆的直径称为"curb-to-curb turning diameter"③汽车保险杠最外端等的轨迹所形成的圆称为"整车通过圆"（vehicle clearance circle）〕
clearance envelope （零部件周围的）自由空间
clearance fit 动配合，间隙配合
clearance for expansion 膨胀间隙（温度补偿间隙）
clearance gauge 量隙规，厚薄规，塞尺
clearance height ①（汽车的）净空高度（车辆在桥梁或类似障碍物下通过时，车顶面与桥底面间的距离）②（汽车的）离地间隙（= ground clearance）
clearance hole 孔隙
clearance interval 车辆穿街清尾时间（绿灯信号停止后，已进入交叉口的车辆扫清通过的黄灯时间，= clearance period）
clearance lamp 车宽灯（装在汽车车顶前、后端的两外侧表示车的最大高度和宽度，= clearance light 或 marker lamp）
clearance leakage 间隙（造成的）泄漏
clearance length ①外形长度②间隙长度
clearance line ①（指示车辆绕行的）导向线，引导线②净空线，界限线
clearance loss 由间隙引起的（泄漏）损失
clearanceometer 间隙测量仪，间隙测量器，量隙规，量隙片
clearance slippage ①因间隙造成打滑错动②（因上述现象引起的动力传递）损失
clearance sonar 间距声呐（丰田公司的汽车与障碍物间距离的超声波探测系统的商品名。前/后保险杠上装有超声波测距传感器，每当汽车与障碍物间距离达到规定值时，车内警报装置即发出声响或灯光警告）

clearance space （汽缸）余隙容积（见 cylinder clearance volume）

clearance time (at crossing) （车辆）通过（交叉路口的）时间

clearance volume (of cylinder) （汽缸）余隙容积，最小容积（指活塞位于上止点时活塞上面余留的容积，为燃烧室总容积；对容积式压缩机指压缩循环终了时残留气体所占的压缩腔容积）

clearance width 外廓宽度，外形宽度

clear area ①有效面积②零区③（符号识别）空白区，无字区

clear cut 清晰的轮廓

clear distance 净距离，净空

clear flood mode （电子计算机内燃机控制系统的）清淹工况（发动机起动时）如果发动机因混合气过浓而被淹，则只要将加速踏板踩到节气门保持80%的开度位置，电子控制模块便会使混合气稀到20∶1，直到发动机起动，浸淹工况终止（有的电子控制系统无此工况，仅完全停止喷油，吸入空气）

clear focusing glass 聚焦光玻璃（相对 frosted glass 而言）

clear gasoline （一般指）无铅汽油，无乙基铅添加剂的汽油

clear headroom 净空高度（亦称 clear headway，clear height）

clearing point 清亮点（液晶材料由液晶态变为液态的过程中，呈透明时的温度）

clear lens （前照灯）无色的散光玻璃

clear octane number 净辛烷值（未加四乙基铅等抗爆剂的汽油辛烷值，= clear octane rating）

clear opening ①（管道等的）有效通过面积，净孔②（气门等的）净开度，有效开（启）度（= clear valve opening）

clear sight distance 清晰视距（= clear vision distance）

clear view 良好的视野，清晰的可见度（= clear visibility）

clearway 禁止停车的道路

clear width 净宽，内宽

cleat （绝缘夹板，钉）线夹

cleated tyre chain 带抓地齿的防滑链

cleft welding 裂缝焊补，裂口铺焊

clench nut 压装螺孔塞，（指带螺孔的塞形件，用于薄板构件，将该塞压装于板件事先钻好的孔中，而形成螺孔，= clinch nut）

clerestory ①（客车）靠近车顶的（高位）侧窗②（客车）左、右侧座位之间的通道

clerestory head （一种进、排气门轴向对置、横断面小于缸径的）上延式燃烧室缸盖

Clerk cycle 克拉克循环（二冲程循环，由英人克拉克于1881年实际使用，故名。= two-stroke cycle, two-cycle, two-stroke）

clevice （亦写作 clevis）①（各种）U形夹、箍、卡、栓、钩、环件②各种带U形头的件（如连接叉等）

clevis bolt U形夹的锁紧螺栓

clevis pin U型夹的锁销

click ①棘爪，棘轮机构②咔嗒声；间隙过大时产生的咯哒、咯哒声

click adjustable 棘轮调节的，（利用棘轮机构调节，因而调好后可相对稳定，不致回松）

clicker wheel adjuster ①棘轮式调节装置②带刻度的小齿轮调节装置

click pulley 棘轮

click-type (adjustable) torque wrench 棘轮式（可调）扭力扳手

clickwork 棘轮机构

client ①用户（顾客，买主）②当事人

climate 气候

climate cell 人工气候试验室（亦称 climate test chamber, climatic chamber）

climate control （车内）气候控制系统

climate control system （车用取暖、降温、调湿联合式）空调系统

climatic 气候的

climatic seat 空调座椅

climatic wall 全天候壁（适应风、雨、气温等变化的壁，如旅行车的夹层篷壁等）

climatic wind chamber 人工风模拟试验室

climatic wind tunnel 带人工气候模拟系统（模拟温度、湿度等气候条件的影响）的试验风洞（简称 climatic tunnel）

climatized cabin 带空调装置的驾驶室（见 air-conditioned cabin）

Climatronic 电控气候（大众车电子控制分区域独立可调空调系统的商品名）

climatronic (four) zone air condition system （车内）电子控制（四）分区人工气候空调系统

climax 顶点，极点

climb ①爬坡，攀爬，上坡②爬高速度，爬升距离，爬高段长度

climbing ability 爬坡能力（= grade-climbing ability, 简称 climbability）

climbing slop 上坡道

clinch 铆装式钢板弹簧夹（通常铆在一片弹簧钢板上，可防止钢板间相对移动）

clincher tyre 楔边式轮胎，软边轮胎［如自行车轮胎，= beaded (-edge) tire］

clinching 咬接，咬口，咬边压接，叠边压接

clinch strip 见 chafer

clinometer 测斜仪，倾斜计，坡度仪，侧角器（= inclinometer）

clip ①夹子，夹钳，夹具②剪，夹住，夹紧

clip bolt (nut) ①轮毂螺栓（螺母）②夹紧螺栓（螺母）

clip-on weight （夹在车轮上的）平衡重块

clipped noise 削波噪声

clipper ①尖口钳；剪钳②削波器，限幅器③特快班车

clipping ①修（整毛）边②削剪③限制，限幅，削波④载荷限定（当载荷低于或高于某一限定水平时，将载荷加大或降低至该限定水平的方法）⑤极好的，快速的

clipping circuit 削波电路，限幅电路

clip ring 弹簧卡环，卡环

clip wrench 轮毂螺母扳手（= hub wrench）

c/lock 中控门锁（见 central locking）

clock ①时钟，计时器，时钟机构②时钟脉冲（见 clock pulse）

clocking ①时钟的，计时的，时钟控制的②（将汽车里程表）读数拨（到比实际里程）少（非法行为）

clock pulse 时钟脉冲（数字信息处理系统中，具有确定周期的脉冲顺序，简称 clock）

clock rate （电子计算机，控制模块的）时钟频率（亦称 clock frequency, 指时间脉冲发生器发生脉冲的时间频率，它决定同步计算机完成逻辑或算术运算的选通速率。目前汽车控制模块的时间频率已超过 80MHz, 每秒钟内可执行数百万条指令）

clock signal 时钟信号（电子计算机工作的时间基准脉冲信号，通常使用水晶振荡器作为时钟信号发生器"clock signal generator"）

clock signal 时钟信号

clock-spring type connector （安全气囊系统中实现电气系统与充气器之

间的电气连接的）钟表发条式导电条（既可实现气囊电气系统与充电器间的电气连接，又可保证转向盘的自由转动）

clock synchronization 时钟同步（在汽车的电子控制系统中，由时钟脉冲发生器通过分频器输出多种标准的时钟脉冲，用来测量或指示时间、提供定时的控制信号和操作的同步信号，使整个系统的各个部分保持一定的时间相位关系，使全部操作和过程均按给定的时间和顺序发生，从而确保整个系统实现约定的同步运转）

clock-time ①时钟（机构）定时的②定时（机构）控制的

clockwise 顺时针方向的

clock (-work) -triggered 时钟（机构）触发的

clog 阻塞，堵塞 [clog-free 无堵塞的，畅通的；clogged 被堵塞的，（交通）阻塞的；clogging 阻塞（…）的，（造成）堵塞的，堵塞，粘住，（车轮）陷入泥坑；clogproof 防堵塞的，抗堵塞的，免堵塞的]

close ①关闭，堵塞②接通（电路），使（电路）闭合③接近、靠紧④闭合的，严密的，接近的，狭窄的⑤终止，结束

close analysis 精密分析

close coil （螺旋弹簧两端紧靠在一起的）并圈

close collision （车辆）近距离碰撞

close-control ①精密控制②近距离控制

close-coupled catalyst converter 紧接式催化转化器（安装位置紧接排气出口、排气管温度最高处，发动机起动后便可迅速达到工作温度，简称 CCC）

close-coupled city bus （主车与挂车间有通道相连的）单层城市铰接式公共汽车

close-coupled trailer 两车轴靠得很近（在 1m 以内）的双轴全挂车（轴上无转向装置）

closed 闭合的，闭路的；关闭的，封闭的，紧密的

closed-cell 闭孔的，闭底的，闭窝的

closed-center （滑阀等的）中间关闭式，中心关闭型（滑阀在中间位置或中心位置时全部通路关闭）

closed circuit (= closed loop, closed loop circuit) ①闭路，闭合电路 ②环行线路，闭合环流

closed cooling system 闭路冷却系（亦称 sealed cooling system，带有膨胀箱，整个冷却系统对外界封闭，形成封闭回路，见 radiator expansiontank）

closed-cycle system 闭式循环系统

closed-cycle turbine 闭路循环式燃气轮机（工作气体在机内循环而不向大气排出）

closed end spanner 闭口扳手（ = closed end wrench）

closed-flux ignition coil 闭磁路点火线圈（见 closed magnetic circuit ignition coil）

closed frame 由封闭断面梁组成的车架

closed hole 不通孔，盲孔（ = blind hole, dead hole）

closed liquid cooling system 闭式水冷（却）系统

closed magnetic circuit ignition coil 闭磁路点火线圈（亦称 closed-flux ignition coil, moulded type ignition coil，其铁芯和线圈由树脂材料塑封成一体，形成闭合磁路，磁阻小，漏磁少，耐蚀、耐振、小而轻，能量转换率可达75%，广泛应用于汽车电子点火系统）

closed nozzle （柴油机的）闭式喷油嘴（具有一个受弹簧控制的菌形阀或针阀的喷嘴，见 closed type nozzle)

closed truck 厢式载货汽车 [= box van, 参见 panel (-body) truck]

closed type nozzle (柴油机等的)闭式喷嘴(不喷油时,喷孔为针阀等关闭,简称 closed nozzle)

closed wrench 梅花扳手

close fit 紧配合,静配合,密配合

close-grained 细粒的,细晶粒结构的

close-in 接近中心的,近距离的,近处的

close-limits ①窄的公差带②窄的变化范围,窄上下限范围的

close-loop dwell-angle control (断电器)触点闭合角闭环控制

closely spaced (具有)小间隔的,小间距的

closeness ①接近程度,接近②密闭,狭窄③严密,精密,紧密

closer 关闭器,闭合器

close range 近距离(简称 CR)

close-ratio gearbox 小速比变速器(挡间速比差小,挡数多,换挡快)

close working fit 紧滑配合

closing cam/rocker (在无气门弹簧式气门控制系统中,代替气门弹簧使气门关闭的)气门闭合凸轮/摇臂

closing capacity 闭路电流容量

closing panel 间隙盖板,密封板(亦称 closing plate)

closing pressure 闭合压力,切断压力

closing pressure surge (液压油路)关闭时的压力冲击(波)(= closing shock)

closing rate (对向运动体等的)接近速度(= closing speed, closing velocity)

closing sleeve 夹紧套筒

closing time 停止工作时间,下班时间,截止时间,停业时间

closing voltage 触点闭合电压(参见 cut-in voltage)

closure ①闭合,锁合,关闭,封闭,闭路;截止,停止,终结,结束,停业,末尾;截流②罩子,隔板,挡板,填塞砖,围墙③使…结束

closure test 螺旋弹簧压合试验(将弹簧压缩到各圈相碰)

cloth 布,织物,织品,毛料,丝绸

cloth cleaner 布滤清器,布芯滤清器(亦称 clotch filter)

cloud-based Bluetooth connection system 基于云的蓝牙连接系统

cloud-based car safety management service 基于云的车辆安全管理服务

clouded glass 毛玻璃,磨砂玻璃(亦称 frosted glass)

cloud (y) point 浊点,浑浊点(柴油析出针状石蜡晶体、开始浑浊失去透明度时的温度,= cloud temperature)

cloverleaf head (火花塞装在中央、气门的布置成)苜蓿叶形(四叶形)的汽缸盖

cloverleaf interchange 四叶式立体交叉,苜蓿叶式立体交叉(= cloverleaf intersection, cloverleaf grade separation)

CLT 计算机语言翻译程序(computer language translator)

CLTE 线性热膨胀系数(coefficient of lineate thermal expansion)

clucth (disk) lining 离合器(从动盘)摩擦衬片(见 clutch facing)

clunker [美](噪声很大的)破旧汽车

cluster ①(线)束,簇,组②化学基,化学族③蓄电池组④组件,元件组⑤成群,聚集组合,集成一束,形成凝块

cluster engine 发动机组

cluster gauge 组合仪表（如装在表板上的一套仪表）

cluster gear ①（变速器）中间轴带齿轮组（总成）②塔齿轮（= compound gear）

cluster spring 组合弹簧

clutch ①接合器，联轴器，联动器②（特指汽车的）离合器（使发动机与变速器接合、分离的装置）③接合，咬合

clutch aligning set 离合器对正中心用整套工具

clutch alignment 离合器（盘与飞轮）对正中心

clutch and brake steering （履带式车辆）使用离合器和制动器转向

clutch brake 离合器制动器（由制动踏板控制，用于降低离合器分离后，从动盘及变速器第一轴齿轮转速，以实现快速、无声换挡，= clitch stop②；单片式离合器的从动盘质量小，一般无此装置）

clutch cable 离合器操纵索（从离合器踏板到离合器分离推杆的拉索）

clutch cam ①某些离合器结构中的离合器分离凸轮（起分离杆的作用）②（有时指膜片弹簧式离合器中起分离杆作用的）膜片弹簧（= clutch diaphragm spring）

clutch case 飞轮壳（飞轮带离合器总成的外壳，旧称离合器壳，= clutch casing, clutch housing, bell housing, flywheel casing）

clutch collar 见 clutch sleeve

clutch cover 离合器盖（直接安装在飞轮上。离合器的压盘、分离杆和压紧弹簧等均装在离合器盖内，因而亦称 clutch cover with pressure plate assembly 离合器盖带压盘总成，简称 clutch cover assembly 或 pressure plate assembly）

clutch damper 见 torsional damping arrangement

clutch disk 离合器盘（亦写作 clutch disc，=［美］clutch plate，包括将从动盘紧压于飞轮的压盘 "pressure disk" 和将飞轮的动力通过花键传给变速器第一轴的从动盘 "driven disk"。当无特别说明时，clutch disk 指从动盘）

clutch disk hub 离合器从动盘毂（带内花键孔，与变速器第一轴，即：离合器轴的花键端相啮合。从动盘毂与从动片、摩擦衬片等三部分组成从动盘，美称 clutch plate hub）

clutch drag ①离合器拖滞（指离合器不能彻底分离，踩下踏板后，从动盘及变速器第一轴齿轮仍继续被带动旋转，以致换挡困难）②离合器阻力（例如湿式离合器片在油中旋转时的阻力）

clutch driving drum （履带式车辆的转向）离合器主动鼓

clutch-engagement oscillations 离合器接合时（在传动系中）产生的振动

clutch explosion 离合器爆破（突遇特高转速而爆破，碎片飞溅的现象）

clutch facing ［美］离合器从动盘摩擦衬片［以往用石棉有机材料，有时石棉中编有钢丝，近年来多用无石棉摩擦材料，烧结金属或金属陶瓷材料，= clutch (driven) plate lining 或 clutch lining］

clutch-facing spring 离合器从动盘（扭转减振）弹簧（= clutch-slip spring, torsional damping spring, torque vibration damper spring）

clutch fluid 液压式离合器操纵机构用的驱动液

clutch friction moment test 离合器摩擦力矩试验（测定离合器静摩擦力矩和动摩擦力矩，以检验其后备系数和摩擦系数的试验）

clutch gear ①齿式离合套，齿式啮合套②啮合套换挡机构

clutch grab(ing) 离合器卡滞

clutch (head) (screw) driver 离合头螺钉,旋具(当拧紧力矩达到规定值时,自动松脱)

clutch heat load test 离合器热负荷试验

clutch housing 离合器壳(指飞轮和离合器总成的金属罩盖。液力传动指变矩器总成的外壳, = bell housing, clutch case)

clutch housing (inspection) retiming hole cover 飞轮壳点火正时检查、调整孔盖

clutch housing ventilation vent gauze 离合器壳通风孔滤网

clutching surface of flywheel 与离合器摩擦片接触的飞轮平面

clutch judder 离合器(接合时)抖振(亦称 clutch shudder)

clutch knob 离合器(控制)按钮

clutchless gear-shift 不踩离合器

clutch lever ①离合器分离杆②离合器(脚)踏板(= clutch foot pedal, clutch pedal)

clutch linkage 离合器操纵杆系

clutch lockup solenoid (变矩器)离合器锁止电磁阀

clutch operating lever 离合器操纵系传力杆件;离合器踏板臂,离合器踏板拉杆

clutch operating shaft ①离合器踏板轴②离合器分离轴(指在离合器操纵杆系的分离推杆通过转动来改变并传递推力的轴件,亦称 clutch release shaft, clutch throwout shaft)

clutch out 分离,松离;踩下离合器踏板,松开离合器,分开离合器(= declutch, throwout the clutch, step on the clutch pedal, depress the clutch pedal, press down the clutch pedal, disengage the clutch)

clutch pedal (free) clearance 离合器踏板自由行程(= clutch pedal free travel)

clutch pedal pad 离合器踏板垫

clutch pedal position sensing switch 离合器踏板位置传感开关

clutch pedal rod adjusting yoke 离合器踏板调节叉杆

clutch pilot bearing (位于曲轴端或飞轮中心的)变速器输入轴(第一轴)(伸出端的)轴承

clutch piston return spring (液压操纵的)离合器活塞回位弹簧

clutch plate 见 clutch disk

clutch point (液力变矩器的)耦合器工作点(泵轮和涡轮转速相同的一点)

clutch pop 离合器突然性接合(往往发生于加速后)

clutch pressure assembly 离合器压板总成

clutch pressure controlling automatic transmission (行星齿轮机构)离合器压力控制型自动变速器(可根据车速和负荷的大小调节和控制离合器的接合压力)

clutch pressure lever 离合器压杆

clutch (pressure) operating pin 离合器分离杠杆销轴

clutch pressure plate 离合器压盘(= clutch thrust plate, drive plate, driving plate, throwout plate, 压盘将从动盘紧压在飞轮上,传动飞轮动力)

clutch pressure plate release lever adjusting screw 离合器压板分离杠杆调整螺钉

clutch pressure plate spring insulation washer 离合器压盘弹簧隔热垫圈

clutch pressure ring 离合器压环

clutch pulley 离合轮(在两平行轴组成的传动系统中,两轴之间由链条、传动带或齿轮连接,其中,装有离合器装置的驱动链轮、传动带轮或齿轮称离合轮)

clutch range 耦合区（参见 coupling range）

clutch regulator valve 离合器接合压力控制阀（根据车速和负荷的大小调节和控制离合器的接合压力）

clutch release 离合器分离（参见 declutching）

clutch release bearing 离合器分离轴承，（装在离合器轴上的推力轴承，离合器踏板的踩踏力通过杆系和分离叉传动给该轴承推动压盘，使离合器分离，＝clutch bearing, clutch thrust bearing, clutch withdrawal bearing, [美] clutch throwout bearing）

clutch (release) bearing and sleeve assembly 离合器分离套筒总成（由分离套筒与分离轴承组成，离合器分离叉通过分离套筒推动分轴承轴向移动推动分离杆将压盘推开，实现离合器分离，它同时承受离心力和径向力。一般使用推力球轴承或滑动止推轴承及自动定心式推力轴承，＝[美] clutch yoke）

clutch release cable （某些拉索式离合器操纵机构中的）离合器分离叉拉索

clutch (release) fork 离合器分离叉（离合器中拨动分离轴承的叉形头杠杆，＝withdrawal fork, operating fork, 见 release bearing）

clutch release hitch 带脱钩装置的挂钩（在超载时可自动脱钩，＝stop hitch）

clutch release lever ①离合器分离叉，指一端呈叉形推动分离轴承，使离合器分离而另一端由离合器踏板通过机械、气动或液力驱动的杠杆。注意：不是装在压盘上的使压盘分、合的分离杆，＝clutch (release) fork, withdrawal fork, operation fork, throwout fork, thrust bearing actuating lever, release yoke lever, clutch withdrawal lever, ＝[美] clutch throwout lever, declutching lever②（指装在压盘上，能绕中间支点转动，使压盘分、合的杠杆）压盘分离杠杆，分离杠杆 [亦称 clutch (release) finger]

clutch release lever plate 离合器分离盘（将分离轴承的轴向移动传给分离叉的部件）

clutch release master cylinder （离合液压式操纵机构的）离合器分离主缸

clutch release shaft 离合器分离轴（通过转动在离合器操纵机构两分离推杆叉间传动推拉力的轴件）

clutch (release) slave cylinder （离合器液压式操纵机构的）工作缸（将主缸产生的推力传递给离合器分离机构的液压缸）

clutch (release) sleeve 离合器分离套筒（亦称 clutch collar, clutch thrust ring, 装在离合器分离轴承上与分离轴承组成一个总成，该总成称 clutch yoke）

clutch semi-centrifugal release fingers 离合压盘的半离心式分离杠杆（分离杠杆上装有重块，高速时可产生附加推力）

clutch servo （重型汽车推动离合器液压工作缸的）离合器气动伺服机构，气动助力机构

clutch shaft 离合器轴（由从动盘毂通过花键驱动，将发动机的动力传递至变速器的输入轴，亦称变速器第一轴，＝constant pinion shaft）

clutch shaft and gear 带齿轮的变速器第一轴，带齿轮的离合器轴

clutch shifter 见 clutch release lever

clutch shudder 见 clutch judder

clutch slip 离合器打滑（指离合器从动盘与飞轮和压盘之间打滑）

clutch slippage 离合器滑转量，离合器打滑程度，离合器动力传递损耗

clutch spider hub 离合器带辐条状膜片弹簧的从动盘毂

clutch spring 离合器弹簧（指对压盘施加压紧力的弹性件、螺旋弹簧、膜片弹簧等，= clutch pressure spring）

clutch spring heat insulating washer 离合器弹簧隔热垫圈

clutch start （汽车的）离合器起动（指汽车溜坡或拖、推起动时，由车轮通过变速器，离合器带动发动机起动）

clutch stop ①离合器踏板行程挡块 ② = clutch brake

clutch switch 离合器开关（指由离合器踏板控制的某些电路的开关，如：踩下离合器踏板，发动机制动系统控制电路便自动断开等）

clutch throwout fork 见 clutch release fork

clutch type disc brake 离合盘式制动器（由与车轮一起旋转的转盘和通过花键等固定在车桥上并可做轴向移动的非转盘组成，二者的工作表面均覆盖有摩擦衬片。非转盘紧压转盘即可产生制动作用，亦称全盘式制动器，见 spot type disc brake）

clutch vaccum control 离合器真空控制；离合器真空控制系统

clutch with multiple laminated disc 多片式离合器

clutch yoke 见 clutch (release) bearing and sleeve assembly

clutter ①（雷达显示装置）扰乱回波，混杂信号 ②地物干扰，地面反射干扰 ③混乱，杂乱

clutter filter （雷达）反干扰滤波器

cm 厘米(centimeter 的简称，= 10^{-2} m)

C-matic transmission 法国雪铁龙公司研制的一种半自动变速器的商品名

C-MAX Hybrid 福特公司使用的第二代锂-铁电池的混合动力车车名

C-MAX Energi plug-in hybrid 福特公司的家电插座充电式混合动力车车名（该车上装有充电插座，只要将充电站的充电插头插入该插座，车上的充电系统便可将来自电网的交流电，转换为直流电对车上的液冷却或液加热的动力电池组充电，简称 plug-in hybrid）

CMCV （装在发动机进气歧管内的）进气充量运动控制阀（charge motion control valve 的简称，使进气气流产生强烈的涡流）

C meter 电容测试计，电容表（capacity meter 的简称）

cmm 忽米（= 10^{-5} 米 centimillimetre，亦写作 centimillimeter）

CMOS 互补型金属氧化物硅半导体器件（complementary metal-oxide-silicon semiconductor 的简称，由一个 N-沟 MOS 器件，即一个 N 型金属氧化物场效应晶体管"MOSFEF"和一个 P-沟 MOS 器件，即一个 P 型 MOSFEF 两者串联而成的半导体器件，N 沟和 P 沟半导体在电特性上呈互补态"complementary"，故名，是车用微处理器中使用最为广泛的器件之一。当其第一个 MOS 器件输入为 0 时，与之串联的第二个 MOS 器件输出为 1，第一个输入为 1 时，第二个输出为零，故多用作反相器，亦称 CMOS invertor）

CMOS type on-body camera CMOS 型车载摄像机

CMO 常规矿物质润滑油（conventional mineral oil）

CMP 凸轮轮位置传感器（见 camshaft position sensor。美国政府规定的 SAE 推荐标准用语，从 1995 年 1 月起取代原各厂家使用的 sync，或 CID，该传感器用于识别汽缸，确定哪一缸应点火和喷油）

CMPV 紧凑型多功能车（compact

multi purpose vehicle 的简称）

CMS ①催化剂监测传感器（catalyst monitor sensor 的简称，用于监测催化剂转化效率）②计算机监测系统（computer monitor system 的简称）

CM tire 可监测路面状况的轮胎（course monitoring tire）

CMVSS 加拿大机动车安全标准（Canada Motor Vehicle Safety Standards 的简称）

CNAIC 中国汽车工业总公司（China National Automotive Industry Corp. 1982 年成立，简称中汽公司）

C-NCAP 中国新型小轿车（碰撞安全性）鉴定大纲（China New Car Assessment Program 的简称）

CNG 压缩天然气（compressed natural gas）

CNG-Hydrogen enrichment ratio 压缩天然气-氢强化（混合气的）混合比

CNG 3 stage regulator （压缩天然气汽车发动机的）压缩天然气三级压器（CNG 由高压储气瓶流入调压器，经过三级调压，再流入 CNG 混合器，成为空气天然气混合气进入汽缸）

CNGV 压缩天然气车辆（compressed natural gas vehicle 的简称，指使用压缩天然气为动力源的汽车）

CN improver （柴油的）十六烷值改进剂

Co 钴（cobalt）

coach ①平头式厢式客车（指发动机装在车厢内，全车成厢形的客车）②两门厢式轿车车身（如：Sedan 等的车身）

coach bolt 圆头方颈螺栓（木构件车身用，装入方孔中）

coach-builder （特指专门制造特种车身的）车身制造厂，车身制造商（主要以底盘配制车身）

coach-built body 非承载式厢式车身（指不与底盘构成一个整体式承载结构，而是装在底盘上的独立车厢）

coach-built construction 非承载式车厢—底盘结构（指由安装全部传动—悬架—行驶件的独立底盘和非承载式的独立车身构成的汽车结构）

coach screw 车身木螺钉；方头木螺钉（= log screw）

coach timber 制造车厢用木料

coach work ①（客车）车身设计，制造，装配②车身，车身总成（= body work，指安装在底盘上的整个车身结构，包括构架及全部板件）

co-acting (force) 同时作用的（力等）

coagel 凝聚胶

coagulant 凝结剂

coagulate 凝结

CO_2 air-conditioning system CO_2 空调系统（使用 CO_2 为制冷剂的无公害、高效车用空调系统）

coal-air fuel cell 煤-空气燃料电池

coal-burning engine 烧煤内燃机（有的烧干煤粉，有的烧与柴油混合的煤浆，= coal fueled engine，solid coal fueled engine）

coal cell 煤燃料电池

coal-derived fuel 以煤为原料提炼的车用燃料（合成汽油、甲醇等）

coal-dust diesel engine 煤粉燃料柴油机

coal gas producer 煤气发生炉

coalition ①联合，联盟②结合，合并

coal slurry 煤浆（将精制煤粉与液态载体混合；与柴油混合称柴油煤浆"coal/oil slurry"，与水混合称水煤浆"coal/water slurry"，或 coal water mixture"，简称 CWM，用作柴油机燃料）

Coanda effect ①柯安达效应（流体沿喷口圆边的倒流现象）②附壁作用，附壁效应

CO_2 arc welding CO_2 电弧焊，CO_2 掩弧焊，CO_2 保护焊

coarse 未加工的，粗糙的

coarse acceleration 猛踩、重踩加速踏板

coarse adjustment 粗调（= rough 或 coarse turing）

coarse brake （不必要的）猛踩制动踏板

coarse cleaner 粗滤器（= coarse filter, rough filter）

coarse-clearance fit 松转配合

coarse control 粗控（指大幅度控制量的控制工况，相对于小幅度控制量的精控"fine control"而言，如：在防抱死制动控制中，保持"hold"或升压/降压"build/decay"及慢升压"slow build"属于精控，快速升压"fast build"便属于粗控）

coarse file 中粗锉，粗纹锉

coarse fit 粗配合

coarse-grained 粗晶粒的，粗晶粒结构的

coarse mesh filter 大孔滤网滤清器，粗滤器

coarseness 粗糙度，粒度

coarseness of file 锉刀的粗细度（= fineness of file，美国分为六级：最粗 rough，中粗 coarse，次粗 bastard，细 2nd cut，精 smooth，光 dead smooth）

coarse pitch 粗（螺）距，大螺距

coarse steering （不必要的）猛打转向盘

coarse thread screw 粗纹螺钉，粗牙螺钉

coarse wheel 粗砂轮

coast 滑行，惯性滑行（指汽车不再由发动机驱动，而仅靠其惯性或下坡时重力沿路面的分力行驶）

coasted engine 被车辆惯性滑行带动旋转的发动机，强制急速（工况）发动机

coasting ①滑行②滑行的③滑行距离（汽车断开发动机动力后到完全停车的距离）④（发动机的）强制急速［工况：指车辆行驶中在未挂空挡和未踩离合器踏板的情况下，突然松开加速踏板，如下长坡时，发动机被倒拖，其转速远高于正常急速的运行工况］

coasting air valve 强制急速空气阀（简称 CAV，在发动机强制急速工况中，当发动机进气管真空度高于某一规定值时该阀开启，使适量空气吸入进气管，以防止混合气过浓，减少 HC 排放）

coasting fuel-cut system 强制急速断油系统（简称 CFS，指车辆行驶中，突然松开加速踏板，发动机被倒拖，转速高于正常急速，处于强制急速工况时，切断供油系统的装置）

coasting performance （汽车的）惯性滑行性能（变速器挂空挡或离合器分离后汽车以惯性行驶的性能）

coasting richer system （发动机）强制急速（工况）混合气加浓系统（防止强制急速后期混合气变稀熄火，而排出大量 HC，简称 CRS 或 CstRS）

coast performance ①（液力变矩器）反拖特性（由泵轮驱动发动机运转时的特性）②（汽车的）惯性滑行特性

coast side （齿轮的）不工作齿侧，齿背面

coast-test ①汽车滑行试验（用于测定汽车的滚动阻力系数和空气阻力系数，综合地评价汽车底盘的技术状况，亦称 coastdown test）②（发动机废气排放及噪声级检测中的）减速试验

coat ①涂层，镀层，覆盖层②涂覆，包覆，镀覆

coatability 可涂覆性

coater 涂镀设备，涂漆机，涂覆器，镀膜机

coating-compound type vibration proof material 涂料型防振材料

coaxial 同轴线的，同中心线的，同轴的

coaxial cable 同轴电缆

coaxial drive starter 同轴式起动机（由与起动同轴的电磁开关直接吸动驱动齿轮与飞轮齿环啮合）

coaxial seals 同轴密封件（塑料圈和橡胶圈套在一起，全部或大部由塑料圈作摩擦密封面的组合密封件）

coaxswitch 同轴开关

cobalt 钴（CO）

cobalt additive （铅酸电池）钴添加剂（提高蓄电能力，延长使用寿命）

cock （控制液流开关的）旋塞，开关，阀门

cockpit （汽车，特指赛车的）驾驶室（包括驾驶座、全部仪表的控纵件的区域）

cocktail effect 鸡尾酒效应，混合效应（指混合的有害排放物对环境的危害大于单一的有害排放物）

cocktail shaker piston 鸡尾酒摇酒器型活塞，带冷却油槽的活塞（在活塞顶下方，活塞内腔有一鸡尾酒摇酒器形机油槽，机油从该槽溅出冷却活塞）

cocoa 摩擦痕斑（磨损产生的金属氧化物，外观似可可粉，故名）

CO/CO$_2$/HC heated NDIR analyzer 加热型不分光红外线型CO、CO$_2$、HC分析仪（见NDIR）

cocoon （原意为茧，在汽车技术文献中转意为）裹住，封存（如：①在零件上喷涂一层塑料以防腐蚀 ②将车身完全覆盖住以防生锈库存等）

Cocoon protective interior 茧式（乘员保护）内壳（20世纪90年代后期出现的一种乘员安全保护概念，将各种乘员保护装置组合成一个完整的高强度、高防碰撞性塑料护身内壳，如同虫茧）

cocurrent flow 平行流，并流，伴流

code ①代号（表示事物或概念的字母、数字、文字、标志、符号、颜色或它们的组合）②（计算机控制系统中的）代码（指用处理器可以接受的符号形式表示数据或一个计算机程序，亦称编码）③（有时指）编写代码或编写一个计算机程序 ④密码

code converter 代码转换器（将一种代码翻译成另一种代码的组合电路）

coded （已）编码的，编码的

code data 代码数据（用数字构成的代码，如用01-07表示星期几等）

coded decimal notation （二进制编码的）十进制表示法（= binary-coded decimal notation）

coded intervention type immobilizer （汽车防盗系统的）编码干预式停车装置

coder ①编码器（对数据进行编码的装置）②编码员（执行编码作业，但一般不设计程序的人员）

codriver's seat （驾驶座旁的）助手席，副驾驶座

coeffcient of torque reserve 转矩储备系数（全负荷特性曲线上的最大转矩与标定工况下速度特性曲线上的转矩的比值）

coefficient of adhesion 附着系数

coefficient of admission 充气系数（= coefficient of charge）

coefficient of aerodynamic drag 空气阻力系数（见coefficient of drag）

coefficient of air viscosity 空气黏性系数（表征空气对车身运动所产生的摩擦阻力的一个系数，标准状态下大气的黏性系数取为 $1.7894 \times 10^{-5} Pa \cdot S$）

coefficient of centripetal acceleration effect 向心加速度影响系数（汽车在定转弯半径回转时，转向盘转角增量对向心加速度增量的比值）

coefficient of centripetal acceleration on steering force 操舵力的向心加速度影响系数（汽车在定转弯半径回转时，操舵力增量对向心加速度增量的比值）

coefficient of charge 充气系数（= coefficient of admission）

coefficient of contact （轮胎的）接地系数（接地印痕的长轴与短轴的比值）

coefficient of correction 修正系数，校正系数

coefficient of decay amplitude 减幅系数（指衰减振动曲线两相邻振幅比）

coefficient of drag （汽车的）空气阻力系数（汽车行驶时，空气力在行驶方向的分力称为空气阻力 Fa，$Fa=1/2C_D \rho V^2 A$，式中：ρ—空气密度，V—汽车与空气间的相对速度，A—汽车的正投影面积，而 C_D 便是空气阻力系数，它取决于车身的形状和表面粗糙度）

coefficient of excess air 过量空气系数（发动机实际空气消耗量与燃料完全燃烧所需理论空气量的比值）

coefficient of expansion 膨胀系数（= coefficient of dilatation）

coefficient of friction 摩擦系数

coefficient of intensification 强化系数（衡量内燃机强化程度的一项指标，指平均有效压力 p_e 与活塞平均速度的乘积）

coefficient of molecular change 分子变更系数（汽缸内工质燃烧后与燃烧前的摩尔数的比值。不考虑残余废气，称理论分子变更系数，考虑残余废气，称实际分子变更系数，实用上简称分子变更系数）

coefficient of overacting 负荷强度系数（平均有效压力和活塞平均速度的乘积，表示内燃机热负荷和机械负荷的强烈程度）

coefficient of road adhesion 路面附着系数

coefficient of road resistance 道路阻力系数（道路阻力 F_R = 滚动阻力 fr + 坡度阻力 fg，若以 ψ 表示道路阻力系数，则 $\psi = \dfrac{F_R}{mg}$，式中：m—车辆质量）

coefficient of rolling resistance 滚动阻力系数

coefficient of scavenging 扫气系数（在一个循环中，由进气口进入汽缸内的充量与扫气完毕后留在汽缸里的充量的质量比值）

coefficient of scavenging loss 扫气漏气系数（在一个工作循环内，从排气口排出的新鲜充量与从进气口进入汽缸内的全部新鲜充量的质量比值）

coefficient of sliding resistance （轮胎与地面的）滑动摩擦系数，滑动阻力系数（= coefficient of sliding friction）

coefficient of speed fluctuation 转速波动率（在负荷不变的条件下，一定时间内测得的最大转速 n_{max} 或最低转速 n_{min} 与该时间内的平均转速 n_m 之差除以平均转速 n_m，取其绝对值的百分比，即：$\dfrac{n_{max}(\text{或}\,n_{min}) - n_{min}}{n_m} \times 100\%$）

coefficient of torsional rigidity 扭转刚度系数（扭转力矩与相对扭转角之比值）

coefficient of utilization of ton-kilometers 实载率（指车辆实际完成货物周转量与总行程中载货量充分利用时所完成的货物周转量的比值）

coefficient of wave height （谐波齿轮

的)波高系数(波高与模数之比)

coeficient of residual gas 残余废气系数(在一个工作循环中,残余废气量与充量的比值)

coeifcient of speed reserve 转速储备系数(标定转速与最大转矩转速的比值)

COEI 一氧化碳排放指数(carbon monoxide emission index 的简称)

coelinvar 恒弹性系数的镍、铁、铬磁性材料

COE motor truck 平头载货汽车(cab-over-engine motor truck 的简称)

coercive field 矫顽磁场(将导电材料的极化作用减至零的磁场)

coercive force 抗磁力,矫顽力,矫顽(磁)力(= coercivity force)

coexist ①共存 ②同时产生

co-extrusion (两种金属互相挤压在一起制成零件的)互挤法(如钢棒包铜皮)

COF 见 container-on-frame car

COF ①摩擦系数(coefficient of friction 的简称)②软膜覆晶结合技术(chip on film 或 chip on flex 的简称,指将 IC 直接装在 PCB 柔性线路板上的芯片)

cog ①齿轮 ②齿 ③榫

CO₂ gas shield arc welding 二氧化碳气体保护电弧焊

cog belt (凸轮轴正时齿轮驱动)内齿传动带,带齿传动带(cogged belt 的简称)

cogged belt (正时齿轮用)带齿的橡胶传动带(亦称 toothed belt)

cogging joint 榫齿接合

cog rack 齿条

cog-swapping 换挡(的)(= gear-changing)

cog wheel ①齿轮 ②嵌齿轮

coherence effect (光)相干效应,(物)凝聚效应

cohesion ①内聚性,内聚力 ②附着力,附着性;黏附

cohesive 有黏聚性的,有黏结力的,有附着性的,有结合力的

cohesive failure (接触表面的)黏著破坏

cohesive force ①内聚力 ②黏着力(= force of cohesion)

coil ①线圈,绕组②一匝,一圈③蛇管,盘管④带材卷,薄板卷⑤螺旋状物,卷状物⑥绕制线圈,盘,缠,卷

coil-and-wishbone front suspension 螺旋弹簧-A 型横臂式前轮独立悬架

coil chimney 见 coil tower

coil clutch 弹簧离合器

coil constant 线圈常数(在已知频率的条件下,感应线圈电抗与其实际电阻的比率)

coiled radiator 蛇形管式散热器,盘管式散热器

coiled spring 螺旋弹簧,卷簧

coil file (断电器)触点小锉刀(通常称 point file)

coil ignition (传统的感应)线圈点火(系统)(由点火线圈的初级绕组存储蓄电池能量而在其次级绕组内感生点火高压的点火系统)

coil lead 点火线圈至分电器的高压导线(= [美] coil wire)

coil loading 感应线圈加载,加感(在预定间隔中插入感应线圈,以改善输电线路的性能)

coil (magnetizing) method (磁粉探伤的)绕组磁化法

coil-ohm tester (点火)线圈电阻测试仪,线圈欧姆表

coil-on-plug ignition system (点火)线圈(直接装在)火花塞(上的)点火系(每一个火花塞上都装在一个由电子控制模块控制的点火线圈直接向该火花塞提供跳火高压)

coilover coil-over shock absorber 的简称

coil-over-shock absorber assembly 螺旋弹簧套同中心线减振器总成

coil-over spring wrapped around monotube shock absorber 外螺旋弹簧套装式单筒减振器

coil pickup 电感式传感器，线圈式传感器

coil pipe 蛇形管，螺旋盘管

coil pitch 线圈节距，盘管节距

coil primary induced voltage 线圈初级感应电压（线圈初级绕组由于磁通量变化所感应的电压）

coil pulser 线圈式脉冲发生器

coil-Q 线圈质量因素

coil spring 螺旋弹簧（亦称 helical spring）

coil spring clutch 螺旋弹簧离合器

coil spring damp(en)er 螺旋弹簧减振器（= coil-spring shock absorber）

coil testing ammeter 线圈（测试用）电流表

coil tower （典型的车用）点火线圈盖（其分电器高压线插座伸出壳外似塔形，故名，= coil chimney）

coil type fuel gauge 线圈式燃油油量表

coil type receiver unit ①线圈式表头（燃油表或水温表用的表头的一种，亦称电磁式指示器"electromagnetic indicator"，由两个线圈和与指针成一体的可动转子组成）②线圈式接收器

coin box car washer 投币式洗车机

coincidental starting （汽车发动机）同时拉阻风门起动

coke ①炭②，结焦，覆盖薄积炭层

coke-oven gas engine 焦炉煤气发动机

coking test （机油）结焦试验，积炭试验

CO_2 laser CO_2 激光器（气体激光器的一种，可产生波长 10.6μm 的连续红外激光，输出很高的功率）

cold-and-hot test 低温和高温循环试验，循环冷却和加热试验

cold brake sickness 冷制动故障（在低于给定温度下制动时，制动作用低于规定值的弊病）

cold brittleness 冷脆性（材料在低温下变脆的性质）

cold cap 冷补胎面胶片

cold car ①冷藏车（= refrigerated van）②灵柩车（= cold wagon）

cold chisel 平口凿子（= flat chisel）

cold-condensate corrosion 冷凝腐蚀（特指排气系统后端由于低温废气中腐蚀性成分凝聚而产生的化学腐蚀）

cold corrosion type wear （在低温下运转时的）冷腐蚀型磨损

cold cracking （塑性材料的）低温脆裂，冷裂

cold cranking ability 蓄电池的低温起动能力（指蓄电池的低温起动容量，见 cold cranking rating）

cold cranking rating （蓄电池的）低温起动额定容量（指蓄电池在 -17.8℃下，连续放电 30s 单格电池仍能保持 1.2V 电压所输出的电量）

cold cure 冷硫化，酸性硫化，冷补（= acid-cure）

cold end （热电偶的）冷端，冷接点（= cold junction）

cold filter plugging point （油料等的）滤清器堵塞点（指导致油料低温下凝聚堵塞滤清器的温度）

cold flame 冷焰（冷焰是焰前反应的第一阶段，过氧化物达到临界浓度时出现，只释放出燃料热量的 5%～15%，生成甲醛，发出辐射光，以辐射强度表征冷焰强度）

cold flow point （燃油可自油箱流出的）最低流动温度，冷流温度，冷流点

cold fouling rating (火花塞)耐冷污值(火花塞耐燃烧产物污染的能力或自净能力的额定值)

cold galvanizing 室温电镀(无特别说明时,一般指室温镀锌,包括在富锌涂料中进行的热浸镀和电沉积度锌,亦写作 cold galvanising)

cold gas type(**air bag**) **inflator** (充惰性气体的)冷气体型安全气囊充气装置

cold idle control 冷机怠速控制(发动机低温运转怠速调节)

cold-metal work 白铁工,钣金工

cold mixture ①制冷混合气(指浓混合气,参见 hot mixture)②冷混合气

cold override switch 冷断开关(低于某一温度时断开电路)

cold press molding 冷压模制(仅依靠机械压力的冷模压制成形工艺,见 hot press molding)

cold-proof 抗寒的,防寒的

cold resistance 耐寒性

cold-resistant 耐寒的

cold room test 人工冷室试验,人工低温试验

cold rubber ①冷聚合橡胶(在4℃下进行聚合的苯乙烯-丁二烯橡胶)②低温硫化橡胶

cold running-in 冷磨合(由电动机等外部动力拖动发动机运转磨合)

cold set 冷凝,常温凝固

cold setting (气门间隙)冷机调整

cold slap (发动机)冷运转时活塞敲击缸壁声

cold sparking plug 冷型火花塞(见 cold plug)

cold start ballast resistor 冷机起动镇流电阻(点火线圈的镇流电阻,高速时调节点火线圈输出电压,冷机起动时,提高火花电压, = ballast resistor)

cold-start capability ①(汽车发动机)冷机起动性能,低温起动性能 ②(蓄电池)低温起动容量(见 cold capacity)

cold start coefficient (催化转化器催化剂载体的)冷起动系数(= C_P/GO,式中:C_P—载体热容量,GO—催化剂表面积。为了充分利用排气热量,使催化转化器在冷机起动时迅速达到起燃温度,要求采用 C_P 尽可能小,而 GO 尽可能大的载体,即要求冷起动系数尽可能小,它决于载体材料的孔密度和壁厚)

cold-start enrichment 冷机起动混合气加浓(增加供油量,以补偿燃油冷凝损失)

cold starter (发动机)冷起动装置(= cold-start device)

cold start injector (汽油喷射系统的)冷机起动喷油器(附加喷油器,仅发动机冷机起动时喷油,使冷机混合气加浓)

cold start valve 冷机起动(混合气加浓)阀,冷起动阀

cold (-state) test (ing) 冷态试验(指发动机在其他动力装置带动下进行的多项试验)

cold stator (气波增压器)空气进出口壳体

cold sticking (活塞环)冷机卡滞(在环槽内)

cold storage truck 冷藏车(= cold vans)

cold test ①冷机试验②低温(条件下进行的)试验

cold type spark plug 冷型火花塞(亦称高热值型火花塞"high heat rating type spark plug"。其裙部短,吸热面积小,散热路径短,散热快,易于冷却。此外,其壳体下腔孔径小,容纳的高温气体少,因而温度较低。适用于高转速、高压缩比、火花塞温度易于升高、易于引起早燃的发动机)

cold weather blues (转向助力器等的)低温失灵(现象)

collapse ①(磁场)衰减,(磁力线)收缩②(顶篷等)折叠③(轮胎)爆瘪④(壳件)压叠、挤扁⑤(组件)分拆、拆散⑥(表面)塌陷

collapsible metal roof (敞篷车的)可折叠式金属活顶

collapsible spare tire 见 space-saving spare tire

collapsible steering column (碰撞时)可压叠的转向柱,可压塌式转向柱(冲击能量吸收式转向柱的一种)

collapsible top 折叠式车顶,活动式顶篷(= convertible top, falling top, folding top)

collapsible tube 波纹软管

collapsing 可造成 collapse 的,

collar ①圈,垫圈,环,套,套筒,套管,箍②轴肩;突缘,③系梁,底梁,地脚

collar beam 系杆,系梁

collar bearing 带凸缘边的轴承(= flange bearing)

collateral 间接的,附属的,并联的,侧面的,旁边的,附加的

collation operation "与"逻辑运算(= AND)

collect 收集,采集,聚集,聚积,集中,集合

collection brush (与集电环接触的)集电刷(= collector brush)

collector ①集电极(晶体三极管三个极中的一个,用符号 C 表示,一般该极接负载)②集电器③收集器

collector amplifier 集电极接地放大器(= grounded-collector amplifier, 亦称发射极输出放大器或发射极跟随器"emitter follower,"指一种集电极接地的放大电路,其电压增益小于1,但却有较高的输入电阻和较低的输出电阻)

collector-base junction (晶体管的)集电极-基极结

collector-emitter current 集电极-发射极电流

collector ring ①集电环,集流环②(离心压气机)蜗壳

collector's car 有收藏价值的旧车

collector segment 整流器片,集电器片

collet ①(弹簧)筒夹,(弹性)夹头,有缝夹套,开口夹套,套筒,锁片,锁圈,卡环②(复数)继电器簧片的绝缘块

collide 碰撞,冲突

colliding speed 碰撞速度(亦称 collision speed)

collision ①碰撞,撞击②(汽车多路复用信息传输系统中出现的)冲突(指网络的同一信道上同时出现两个或两个以上的并行传输)

collision accident 撞车事故

collision angle 碰撞角度(指与其他车辆或障壁碰撞时,两车辆纵轴线对称平面之间,或纵轴线对称平面与障壁的垂面之间的角度。该角度在 0~180°的范围内变化。该碰撞角为 0°时,为前面碰撞,90°时为侧面碰撞,180°时为后面碰撞)

collision avoidance light 防撞灯(避免撞车的安全灯,简称 CAL)

collision-avoidance radar braking system 防碰撞雷达(测距)制动系统

collision axis alignment (汽车)碰撞轴线排列(若两车或一车与障碍物的平面在同一平面内,称对中碰撞,否则称偏置碰撞,见 main plane)

collision bumper 保险杠

collision deflector (汽车发生碰撞时,将)碰撞力引导(开,以防止人体脆弱或重要部位受伤的)装置

collision detection （多路复用传输系统中的）冲突检出（信号）（显示系统中出现冲突现象，即：在同一信道上同时出现两个或两个以上的并行传输现象的信号，供逐节判优来解上述争用）

collision mitigation system 碰撞（伤害）减轻系统（简称CMS，该系统根据微波雷达测定的与前方车辆间的相对车速和距离认定：①有相互碰撞或追尾碰撞的危险时即发出声的警报，提醒驾驶者注意②与前方车辆碰撞危险性较大时即自动减速制动，同时收紧安全带向驾驶者发出体感警告③碰撞已难避免时立即强制紧急制动，并强力拉紧安全带，尽力减轻碰撞冲击对乘员的伤害）

collision offset 碰撞偏置〔碰撞中两车主平面的间距，见主平面（main plane in collision）〕

collision-possibility judging and warning radar 碰撞可能性判断与警报雷达

collision prevention device （汽车的）防碰撞装置（= collision avoidance system，指利用超声波，红外线，激光，微波雷达等及时探测车前、后及各盲区的障碍物或来车，发出警报或采取制动等措施，以避免碰撞的系统）

collision-sensing radar （汽车）碰撞感知雷达，碰撞传感雷达

collision speed 碰撞速度（指两车碰撞瞬间的相对速度）

collision warning system 碰撞警报系统

colloidal sol 溶胶，胶状溶液，胶体溶液（colloidal solution的简称）

colloidal suspension ①胶态悬浮②胶态悬浮体

color blindness 色盲

color check 染色探伤（法），（一般多用红色，故亦称red check）

color display （仪表指示灯等的）彩色显示

color polarizer mode 彩色偏振片型（利用彩色偏振片与液晶盒组成的彩色液晶显示类型）

color spot 色斑（如夹层风窗玻璃中，胶合层附着的带色斑点）

color test （汽车前照灯等的）光色试验（测灯光的颜色，显色试验）

color touch screen 触摸（控制式）彩屏

color tube 配线色标管（导线端头用彩色标示该导线用途的绝缘管）

colour back monitor with voice guidance 带声向导向的彩色后方监视器（倒车安全装置）

colo（u）r chart 色样样本

colour code 颜色标识，（供识别的）色标

colour coded ①带色标的（用颜色标示用途、安装部位，连接处等的）②与车身主要部分颜色相同的（如：保险杠等）

colour-keyed ①色彩调和的，颜色协调的②（对汽车保险杠、视镜壳、车门把手等车身配件而言指）与车身同色的（= body-colored）

colour papering technique （车身模型等的）彩箔包覆技术

colour picture 彩色效果图

colour scheme （汽车车身内、外）色彩的调配，色彩的组合，色彩设计图

colour sequence 色灯顺序（在周期内显示各种色灯信号的顺序）

columbium 钶Cb（元素铌"niobium"的旧称）

column ①柱，柱状物②（汽车的）转向盘柱

column assist type electronic power steering system 转向盘柱助力式电子控制动力转向系统（简称CEPS，指助力电动机装于转向盘柱，经减速齿轮将动力传给转向盘柱的动力

转向系,见 electronic power steering system)

column gear shift (换挡杆装在)转向盘柱(上的)变速机构([美],=[英] column gear change)

column-mounted hand brake 操纵杆装在转向盘柱上的驻车制动器

colunm tube 立轴外(套)管,立柱外(套)管(如套在转向盘轴外的柱管)

colza oil 菜(籽)油(见 rape oil)

combat referee gasoline ①(美国)军用仲裁汽油(参见 referee test)②军用副标准汽油(相对于 standard gasoline 而言)

comb gauge 螺纹规;螺距规

combinated road conditions detecting vehicle 综合路况检测车

combination ①组合,联合,复合②带斗的摩托车③汽车列车(一般指牵引车-挂车列车)

combinational logic (汽车电子控制系统中的)组合逻辑电路(不使用存储元件,其输出完全取决于同一时刻的逻辑输入信号)

combinational technologies 混合信号技术(指集成数字-模拟混合信号的技术)

combination antilock module 防抱死与牵引力复合控制系统的控制模块(简称 CAB)

combination brake chamber 组合式气制动室(如:组装有储能弹簧安全装置的气制动室,当制动气压低于某规定值时弹簧伸展,推动制动气制动,防止在制动系漏气或制动气压不足的情况下行车,以保证安全)

combination braking system 组合制动系(产生制动力的能由两种或两种以上方式传递到制动器的制动系)

combination charging and testing unit (电器设备等的)综合充电-试验台

combination head lamp (汽车的)组合式前照灯(前照灯与转向信号灯等组合在一起)

combination integral-remote power steering system 组合整体式遥控动力转向系统

combination meter 组合仪表(指将车速表、发动机转速表、燃油表、冷却水温表等指示仪表和前照灯远光指示灯、转向指示灯、驻车指示灯、挡位指示灯及故障警报灯等指示-警报装置组合在一起的仪表)

combination of vehicles 汽车列车,牵引车带半挂车列车(= combination vehicle)

combination oil bath air cleaner and silencer 组合式油浴空气滤清消声器

combination side-impact head and roll over air bag (汽车)侧面碰撞头部保护和翻车保护气囊

combination TAB/TAD valve 组合式 TAB/TAD 阀(将 TAB 和 TAD 阀合成一体,详见 TAB,TAD valve)

combination tail lamp 组合后灯(简称 combination lamp,指汽车后部的尾灯、制动灯、转向灯及倒车灯、尾部反射器等组合在一起,但仍独立发挥各自机能,以满足车身设计简洁或符合空气动力学、美学等要求的灯具)

combination valve 组合阀(如:液压制动系统的组合式压力调节阀,该阀由一个故障警报灯开关,压差阀"pressure-difference valve"压力控制阀"metering valve"和比例阀等组成)

combinatory (digital) circuit 组合(数字)电路(指对于输入端上数字信号的每一种可能组合,输出端上仅存在一种相对应的数字信号组合的数字电路)

combinatory integral transmission 组

合式整体变速器（主变速器、副变速器组装在一个变速器壳内的多挡位变速器，= combinatory multi-speed transmission，有副变速器前置和后置两种）

combined 联合的，综合的，复合的，合成的

combined BS tester 制动-车速联合试验台（combined brake-speed tester 的简称）

combined city/highway track test 城市与公路跑道综合试验（一般用来试验车辆的燃料经济性）

combined compressed-air and hydraulic brake 组合式气动液压制动器（参见 air-operated hydraulic brake）

combined-cycle engine 混合循环发动机（按混合循环工作的发动机，= mixed cycle engine，dual-cycle engine，Sabathe-cycle engine，composite engine，见 Sabathe cycle）

combined cylinder-block-crankcase unit 汽缸体和曲轴箱铸成一体的整体式发动机体

combined design ①组合式设计 ②组合式结构，（= building block principle design）

combined EGR system 组合式废气再循环系统（指由水冷式 EGR 和排气门控制式 EGR 共同组成的 EGR 系统，见 water cooled EGR 和 valve EGR）

combined error 总和误差，综合误差

combined fuel consumption （各种工况下的）综合平均油耗

combined fuel economy 综合燃油经济性（指按城市与公路工况循环测定并按规定的比例核算的标准燃油经济性）

combined light switch 组合式车灯开关

combined limiting-and-quick release valve （气动制动系的）限压-快释组合阀

combined multi-axle (brake) control 组合式多轴控制（制动系）（用同一指令，对多轴车轮的制动力进行控制）

combined pressure and vacuum relief valve （冷却系加水口盖的）组合式压力-真空安全阀

combined radial and thrust loads 径向与轴向合成载荷

combined retarder 联合式缓速器（见 integrated retarder）

combined seal （金属和软材料）复合油封，（橡胶金属）复合油封

combined type linkage power steering 组合式联杆型（液压）动力转向装置（联杆型动力转向装置的一种，参见 linkage-type power steering。其液压泵、控制阀和动力缸组合成一个总成，参见 separate type linkage power steering）

combustibility 可燃性，易燃性

combustible ①燃料，可燃物质 ②可燃的

combustible charge 可燃混合气充量，充入的可燃混合气

combustible mixture 可燃混合气（= explosive mixture）

combustible products 易燃品，易燃物

combustible zone 易燃层

combustion analyzer （发动机）燃烧分析仪（如：通过对发动机排气的测定来分析燃油喷射系统的调整及燃料的燃烧状况）

combustion arc （转子发动机缸体的）燃烧区，燃烧段（指旋转线缸体壁对应燃烧过程的弧段）

combustion bomb 燃烧弹（一种钢壁弹形试验容器，测量各种燃料参数，如：热值等）

combustion chamber 燃烧室（特指

内燃机燃烧室,内燃机汽缸内的可燃混合气燃烧放热的空间)

combustion chamber cavity (转子发动机转子工作面上的)燃烧室凹坑(亦称 combustion chamber recess)

combustion chamber of wedge form 楔形燃烧室

combustion chamber surface-to-volume ratio 燃烧室面容比(汽缸燃烧室容积最小时,燃烧室表面积与容积之比)

combustion control computer 燃烧控制计算机(美克莱斯勒公司的发动机电子控制系统"Oxygen feedback system"中使用的电子控制模块的商品名)

combustion deposit modifier 燃烧积炭消减剂,燃烧沉积物消除剂(一种消减燃烧沉积物的汽油添加剂,以减轻发动机的表面点火、早燃、火花塞污脏等现象)

combustion duration 燃烧持续期(内燃机每一工作循环内,从燃料燃烧始点到燃烧终点的持续时间,以曲轴转角表示)

combustion (efficiency) tester 燃烧(效率)分析器(主要测试废气中CO的含量,借以判断燃烧状况及空燃比,亦称 CO meter)

combustion engine 内燃机(= internal combustion engine)

combustion environment 燃烧环境(指燃烧时环境的压力、温度等)

combustion-flame propagation (混合气)燃烧火焰的扩散、传播

combustion front 燃烧前沿,燃烧面(已燃气与未燃气的分界面)

combustion gases ①燃气 ②废气(= burned gas,指燃烧产生的气体)

combustion gas turbine 燃气轮机(= gas turbine)

combustion head (带燃烧室的)汽缸盖

combustion mixture gas 可燃混合气(指处于能着火燃烧的浓度界线范围内的空气与燃料的混合气)

combustion modifier 燃烧改善剂,燃烧调节剂

combustion precess 燃烧过程(内燃机广义的燃烧过程包括喷油、混合气形成、着火、放热、火焰扩散和传播、有害成分的生成等过程在内的着火和燃烧全过程,狭义的燃烧过程只包括热焰开始的放热和火焰传播过程)

combustion pressure (可燃混合气在汽缸内)燃烧(所产生的)压力(单位 kg/cm^2 或 bf/in^2)

combustion pressure sensor 燃烧压力传感器(直接测定发动机汽缸内的燃烧压力,以确认是否出现缺火等情况,参见 fiber optical combustion pressure sensor)

combustion products ①易燃品,易燃物 ②燃烧产物

combustion quality (燃料的)燃烧品质(燃料在燃烧过程中的表现及热值,如:汽油的抗爆性、抗早燃性、热值等)

combustion rate 燃烧率(指内燃机燃烧过程中,燃烧室每单位容积、单位曲轴转角或单位时间内烧掉的燃料量或释放的热量,亦称 combustion intensity "燃烧强度")

combustion recorder 燃烧过程自动记录仪

combustion residue(s) 燃烧产生的炭、结胶等沉积物

combustion roughness (柴油机的)燃烧粗暴性,燃烧平顺性

combustion swirl 燃烧涡流(由于燃烧,气体膨胀、活塞下行以及燃烧室形状的导流等因素形成或加强的涡流)

combustion timing sensor 燃烧始点

传感器（在电子控制式柴油发动机中，将燃烧室火焰作为光信号测出，变换为电信号输入计算机的传感器，由装在耐高温的外壳内的石英棒和光电晶体三极管 photo transistor 组成。利用这一传感器可以直接测出开始燃烧的时刻，通过反馈控制而实现柴油喷射时刻的最佳控制）

combustion triangle 燃烧三角（一种计算废气成分的方法）

combustion valve 热值（= caloric value）

combustor ①燃烧器 ②（特指）（燃气轮机的）燃烧室（位于压缩机和涡轮机之间，燃油喷入其中燃烧，= combustion chamber）

CO meter 一氧化碳检测仪（检测废气中 CO 含量的仪器，CO 含量过高表示混合气过浓）

comet head 彗星式燃烧室缸盖（Ricardo 公司研制的涡流室式间接喷射柴油机缸盖系统）

comfort ①舒适，舒适性 ②舒适型〔轿车，一般简称 C 型，为最基本型，或称标准型，比它高一级的是 L 型（luxe）豪华型，再高一级的是 CL 型（comfort luxe）舒适豪华型，最高级的是 GL 型（Grand Luxe）最豪华型〕

comfort auto suspension （日产公司开发的电子控制式）舒适自动悬架系统（商品名，简称 CAS，该系统有两种运行模式可供切换选用：①舒适模式，着重乘坐舒适性，悬架刚度较低 ②硬模式，接近运动车的特性，悬架刚度较高）

comfort CAN （大众公司用于连接车身各控制系统的）舒适 CAN（其通信速率为 62.5kb/s，主要连线连接对象为与车身有关电子控制系统，如：中央门锁、电动窗、照明、后视镜加热、自诊断等对传输速度和实时性要求较低的控制系统，亦称 body CAN）

comfort chart （人体对振动、温度、湿度等的）适应区域图

"comfort-first" design idea （汽车的）"舒适性第一" 的设计理念

comfort system （保证车辆乘坐、驾驶）舒适（的）系统（如车身自动调平系统，各种助力装置等）

coming home function （汽车前照灯系统的）回家功能，送进家门功能（汽车停车关闭电源后前照灯仍可亮一段时间，以便乘车人走进家门）

command 命令（计算机的一种控制信号、指令、数学或逻辑运算符等）

commanded position （电子控制模块）指令（所规定的）位置〔相对于 actual position（实际位置）而言〕

command mode （汽车电子计算机控制系统的）命令模式（指系统处于随时可接受命令库中任何命令的状态，即：主机做提示控制，随时待命，以实施命令所要求的输入/输出功能，亦称 control mode "控制状态"）

CommandView （Jeep 大切诺基的）全景式天窗的商品名

commence 开始，着手，从…开始

commences test 启用试验，试用试验（新系统正式使用前的试用）

commercial 商业的，民用的（简称 coml）

commercial car 商用汽车，营运汽车（以营运服务为目的，包括出租车、公共汽车、长途客车、营运货车等）

commercial class （美国 API 滑油分类中的）重级滑油（用于柴油机和大负荷汽油机，通常简写为 C 类，下分四类，分别用 CA、CB、CC、

CD 表示）

commercialization （研究成果等的）商品化

commercialization （新产品等的）商品化，商业化

commercial oil 营运货车用油（见 commercial class）

commercial type fuel 民用燃料（= commercial grade fuel）

commercial vehicle 商用车辆，营运车辆（在英国包括营运的货车和客车，在美国特指商用载货汽车，简称 CV，= commercial truck）

commercial vehicle operation (system) 营运车辆调度（系统）（简称 CVO，亦称 commercial vehicle operation/fleet management system，简称 CVOMS，包括车辆监控系统、自动定位系统、自动识别系统、计算机调度系统等，为 ITS 的子系统）

commission ①委托，代理，代办 ②职权，权限 ③手续费，佣金 ④委员会 ⑤交付使用，试运行，交工试运转，投产 ⑥命令

commissioning tset 运行试验（为证明安装与运行的正确性，而对设备进行的现场试验）

commnication ①交通 ②联络，通信

common ①公用的，公共的，普通的，通常的，常见的，一般的，常用的，通用的，通约的，公约的，共同的 ②普通，共同，共用，一般

common aisle 公共通道（客车公共汽车内的）通道

commonality 共性，通用性

common apex （锥齿轮的）公共锥顶（一对相配的锥齿轮的锥节的公共顶点）

common base 共基极（晶体管电路）

common battery system 共（用）电池组制，中央电池组制

common collector 共集电极（晶体管电路）

common curvature （钢板弹簧总成）自由状态时的曲率

common emitter 共发射极（晶体管电路）

common line 共用管（线）路（如单管路汽车列车制动系中，既作供给管路，又是控制管路的制动管路，见 brake line）

common mode rejection ratio 共模抑制比（在相同规定的条件下，两个基极输入端加差模电压信号时的增益 G_d 和加共模电压信号时的增益 Gc 之比：G_d/Gc）

common-mode signal 共模电压信号（指等幅同相位的电压信号）

common rail （电子控制燃油喷射系统中，向各汽缸的喷油器供给高压燃油的）共用储油歧管（燃油泵将燃油不断地泵入该歧管内，在该歧管的端部装有一压力调节器，以确保歧管内的油压稳定，不受发动机工况和转速的影响，各汽缸的喷油器直接安装或通过油管接装在该歧管上。喷油时刻，当喷油器的电磁阀开放时，共用储油歧管内的稳压、高压燃油便经喷油器喷出。这种供油结构原来仅用于电子控制式汽油喷射系统，目前亦用于直喷式柴油机）

common-rail direct-injection system 共用储油歧管式直接喷射系统（目前已实用化的有两种：①供油式。高压油泵将燃油泵入带压力调节装置的储油歧管内，再由后者将稳定压力的高压燃油供给喷油器直接喷入发动机各个汽缸内，这种形式多用于直喷式汽油机 ②供压式。多用于直喷式柴油机，由一高压机油泵将机油泵入各缸共用的储油歧管内，在该歧管内保持 200 大气压的稳定机油压力。喷油时，该歧管内的高压机油经管道输入各汽缸的特殊结构的喷油器上部的压力室

内，推动比喷油柱塞面积大7倍的压力活塞，产生200×7＝1400大气压的压力作用于柱塞，而将该喷油器下部燃油室内由燃油泵输入的燃油喷入汽缸。输入喷油器上部压力室的机油压力的大小，及喷油始点和喷油时间的长短，均由电子控制模块根据发动机转速、负荷、冷却水温度等通过储油歧管的压力控制阀和喷油器的电磁阀控制，见HEUT。共用储油歧管式的最大优点是喷油压力不受发动机转速的影响，解决了发动机低速运转时，喷油压力不足的难题。特别是供压式，可产生极高的喷油压力，油雾更加微粒化，燃烧完全，节油，排放干净）

common rail injector （共用储油歧管燃油直接喷射系统使用的）喷油器（供油式共用储油歧管直接喷射系统使用的喷油器与常规喷油器相同，但供压式的却与常规的不同，详见 common rail direct-injection system②）

common rail pressure sensor 共用燃油歧管压力传感器

common return （电器）公共回路（如：车架等公共接地回路）

common terminal 共用接线柱

common timing system 共用正时系统，共用计时装置

common transport 公用运输（参见 public transport）

communal automobile 公用汽车

communicating pipe 连通管

communication drive function （车用网络信息系统的）信息共享驾驶功能（可在多功能显示屏的交通地图上看到附近友人驾驶的车辆，并与之共享路线、交通状况信息）

communications protocol 通信协议（指在计算机网络或控制系统中，为使计算机与终端之间或计算机与被控制对象之间正确地传送信息，对信息传输顺序、信息格式和信息内容等的约定）

Communiport Radio （Delphi公司开发的一种）车装多媒体和通信系统（商品名，该系统应用蓝牙无线技术，由驾驶者通过移动电话实现与拥有大型计算机系统的远程服务中心的直接通信，获取导航信息）

communitator 换向器（指直流发电机和起动机的换向器。直流发电机换向器的作用是将电枢绕组中产生的交流电转换为直流电，起动机换向器的作用是改变进入电枢绕组中的电流方向，从而保证电磁转矩的方向和电枢的旋转方向不变）

commutability 可变换（性），可交换（性）

commutating current 整流电流

commutating pole 整流极，极间极，辅助极（＝interpole，简称 compole，参见 auxiliary pole）

commutation ①整流，换向 ②交换，变换，换算

commutator ①（泛指各种）转接器，转换器，转换开关；交换机，交换台 ②（特指汽车直流电机的）换向器（在直流发电机电枢的电流输出端和起动机电枢的电流输入端，由彼此间用绝缘片隔开的两组钢片组成，起整流的作用，旧称整流子）

commutator end head （电机）换向器端盖

commutator motor 换向器电动机，整流式电动机

commutator pitch 换向器片距

commutator segment 换向器片（＝commutator bar）

commutator (slip ring) end bearing bracket （电机的）后端盖（指非驱动端，即：换向器滑环端的电机转子支承座）

commuter ①上班族个人使用的市区短途往返行驶的车辆（亦称 city commuter）②上班族

commuter car （上班族的）通勤车

compact ①小型的，紧凑的，密集的，坚实的 ②见 compact car①

compact car ①（美国指长 14 英尺 5 英寸~17 英尺，载客 5 人的）紧凑型轿车（简称 compact 或 c-class）②（我国定义为发动机排量大于 1.6L，小于或等于 2.5L 的）中级轿车

compact disc 小激光盘（见 CD）

compact flying taxi 小型飞行出租车（美国宇航局"个人空中交通工具探索"项目研制的飞行汽车，可乘坐 5~10 人）

compact linear-type solenoid 小型线性型电磁阀

compactness ①紧凑度，紧密度，压实度 ②体积小，小型

compact spare tire 窄轮辋备用胎（美国小型轿车为节省备胎存放空间而使用的一种 4 英寸宽轮辋，但直径比标准车轮大一英寸，充气压力 60psi 左右的备用胎，这种备胎仅在紧急情况下临时使用，故亦称 temporary use only spare tire "仅供临时使用备胎"）

compact wagon 小型旅行车（= compact station wagon, compact estate）

companion 成对物之一

companion cylinders （多缸发动机的）同位汽缸（工作过程中活塞位置始终相同的一对汽缸）

company ①公司，商号，商社 ②社团，联队，伙伴

company car 公司轿车（由公司提供给雇员的业务用车或私人用车）

company of limited liability 有限责任公司（简称 company limited 或 Co. Ltd）

comparability 可比性

comparative test 对比试验（= comparison test）

comparator 比较电路，比较器（在车用模拟计算技术中，比较两个输入信号的相位、频率或功率电平，只按规约提供一个输出）

comparator circuit 比较电路［简称 comparator，指将传感器输入的电压信号与基准电压值进行比较的集成电路。一般具有两个输入端和一个输出端。一个输入端输入比较电压，另一个输入传感器电压。当传感器电压低于比较电压时输出为 0，当等于比较电压时输出为 1。如果将比较电压一点点地改变，比较电路就相当于一个模拟/数字（A/D）变换器］

compare 比较，对照，参照

compariso bridge 比较电桥

compartment 室，舱，腔

compartmented tank 内部分隔的（油）箱等容器

compass ①范围，区域 ②音域 ③指南针，罗盘（由于美国公路有正东、正西、正南、正北走向的特征，因而几乎为美国轿车的标准仪表）④（复数）两脚规，圆规 ⑤围绕，绕行 ⑥周围

compatibility 一致性，适应性，兼容性

compatibilitybody 碰撞适应性车身（指能吸收碰撞能量和发生碰撞时可减轻乘员和行人伤害的车身结构）

compatibility crash safety technology （车身结构的）兼容性碰撞安全技术（对车身碰撞能量吸收区的材料作最佳适配，以保证与大、小型车辆碰撞时冲击能量均能得到有效吸收）

compatible 兼容的，协调的

compatible monolithic 兼容型单片

（集成电路）

compct type spark plug　矮型火花塞（指径向与轴向尺寸缩小的小型火花塞）

compensate control　补偿控制

compensated dynamo　带补偿绕组的（直流）发电机

compensated flow control valve　补偿式流量控制阀

compensated magnetic vehicle detector　修正式电磁感应型车辆探测器（当车辆以外的物体通过时，探测器无输出）

compensated relief valve　带压力补偿的安全阀

compensated ring　（密封件中的）补偿环（指具有轴向补偿能力的密封环）

compensated voltage control system　（发电机）负荷补偿式电压控制系统

compensating　补偿（的），补充（的），抵偿（的），均衡（的），平衡（的），校正（的）

compensating air valve　补偿空气阀，辅助空气阀（＝auxiliary air valve）

compensating axle suspension　双轴并装车桥的平衡式悬架（可保证各轴间负荷平衡）

compensating bar　见compensator

compensating (brake) master cylinder　补偿孔式制动主缸（主皮碗移过该量孔后，才产生液压，为最常见的普通型制动主缸）

compensating jet　①（化油器）补偿量孔，亦称compensator jet，＝[美] air bleed passage "空气补偿量孔油道"（在高供油流量工况下，如高速大负荷运转时，吸入空气，使混合比浓度随负荷增大而变稀）②（泛指）各种提供补偿燃油或空气的量孔或喷嘴

compensation　①赔偿 ②补偿 ③调节，调剂 ④平衡

compensation network　补偿网络

compensator　各种起补偿、平衡作用的装置、杆系、部件、电路的通称（如：制动系统中制动蹄不均匀磨损的补偿装置，保证同一车桥左、右车轮同步作用的平衡装置，或制动力分配装置；平衡左、右后轮驻车制动力的平衡臂；平衡式悬架的平衡梁等。当表示起平衡作用的件或装置时，亦称equalizer）

compensator pressure　（液力变速器控制系统的）①变速补偿液压（缓冲压力，改善换挡元件接合压力增长特性的调制液压，亦称trimmer pressure）②加速补偿液压（参见compensator valve）

compensator valve　（自动变速器液压控制系统的）加速补偿液压阀（踩踏加速踏板时，该阀开启，将一股加速补偿液压输入行星齿轮系制动带等的伺服缸内，以加大制动带等的制动压力，阻止制动带等打滑，补偿液压的大小，与加速踏板行程成正比）

compensting port　（特指液压制动主缸连通储液室与活塞皮碗前的压力室的）补偿孔

competence　①能力 ②技能，本领（＝competency）③权限，权限范围

competition car　①（商业上作为竞争对手的）竞争汽车 ②（竞赛用）赛车（＝racer）

competitive　竞争的，有竞争力的

compilation　汇编，编码，编译（将原程序转换为可执行程序，即目标程序的过程）

compile(r)　①（计算机）编译（指将高级语言程序翻译为中间语言、汇编语言或计算机语言）②编译程序（指执行该项翻译的程序）

complement　①补充 ②补码 ③配套

（部分）④余角，余数，余弧

complementary circuit 互补电路，补码电路

complementary metal-oxide-silicon-semi-conductor 互补型金属氧化物硅半导体（简称 CMOS）

complete ①完成，完工 ②完全的，完整的，圆满的

complete alternation 整周期，全循环，整个交变过程

complete annealing 完全退火（使组织发生完全重结晶）

complete disk brake 全盘式制动器（摩擦材料覆盖制动盘全部工作表面的制动器）

complete failure 完全故障（汽车部分或完全丧失工作能力的故障，= total failure）

completely charged （= fully charged）①全充电的 ②充足气的

completely discharged battery 全放电的蓄电池

completely knocked down 全散件的（简称 CKD）

completely seated 完全落座的，座面完全贴合的

completeness 完整性，完全（度），完备性，完善性

complete recharge （蓄电池）再次满充电

complete revolution ①（公转）周转；②一整转

complete vehicle （RE5 定义的）完整车辆（指除喷漆之类小型精加工外，不需要其他进一步加工就能够达到其设计和构造目的的所有车辆，见 RE5）

complete vehicle dry mass 整车干质量（装备有车身、全部电气设备和车辆正常行驶所需要的辅助设备的完整车辆的质量与备用轮胎等选装装置质量之和，不包括燃料和冷却液质量）

complete vehicle kerb mass 整车整备质量（整车干质量、冷却液质量、不少于整个油箱容量 90% 的燃料质量与随车件质量之和）

completion 完成，结束，完工

complex ①复杂的，复式的，多元的，合成的 ②组合体，合成物

complex coordination test 全套设备协调试验（简称 CCT）

complexity 错综性，复杂性

complex shear modulus of elasticity （弹性）复切变模量（以复数形式表示的切变模量，见 shear modulus of elasticity）

complex-split torgue paths type hydro-mechanic drive 复合分流式液力机械传动（由内分流与外分流组合成的液力机械传动），如 VKD 公司的 Variable Kinetic drives（简称 V. K. D），其变矩器在双涡轮内分流的基础上，使第一涡轮的一部分功率经行星齿轮以循环功率的方式返回泵轮，而在泵轮、第一涡轮和行星排之间构成一个外分流液力机械变矩器，其特点是变矩系数提高，效率高

complex steel sheet with zinc chromate 铬酸锌复合钢板（镀铬酸锌防腐复合层的钢板）

complex stiffness 复刚度（用复数形式表示的刚度，见 stiffness）

compliance ①柔（顺）性，柔量 ②顺从，依从 ③随变性，可塑性，配合性，贴合性

compliance characteristics ①随变特性（指外力作用下，汽车的机构或部件变形，导致汽车的某些特性产生变化的规律，参见 roll compliance）②（对外力而言称为）致生特性（参见 lateral force compliance effect）

compliance in suspension 悬架柔性（悬架刚度的倒数）

compliance oversteer 柔性过度转向（使汽车过度转向增大，或使汽车不足转向减小的柔性转向）

compliance steer 柔性转向（亦称随变转向，由悬架系、转向系的柔性变形产生的前、后轮转向角的变化）

compliance steer coefficient 柔性转向系数（由路面作用在轮胎上的力或力矩的单位变化量所对应的柔性转向的变化量）

compliance test ①性能审核试验（审查汽车是否符合某项规定标准的试验）②适应性试验

compliance understeer 柔性不足转向（使汽车不足转向增大，或使汽车过度转向减少的柔性转向）

compliant ①（与规则、标准等）符合的，一致的 ②遵从，服从 ③不受…影响的（如：to be standard compliant 不受标准规定影响的）

complicated 复杂的

compole 整流极，辅助极（= commutating pole 的简称）

component ①部件，组成部分（可能指一个零件，或一个总成）②分量，分力

component built-in type frame 结构件内置式车架

component car 见 kit car

component efficiency 部件效率，组件效率（系统中的某部件、组件、总成的效率）

component force 分力（= component of force）

component interaction （机器名）总成、部件间的相互作用

component location table （电子或电气装置的）元器件位置表（一般都带有电路图，指示元器件的实际位置）

component noise （工作中）部件（产生的）噪声

component (of) velocity 分速度

component reactance 电抗分量

component sharing 部件共用，部件共享（指在不同的型号上用同样部件）

6-component test （轮胎特性的）六维试验（测定垂直方向、前进方向及侧向的作用力和绕该三个方向的力矩等6个项目）

compose 组成，构成

composite ①合成的，复合的，组合的 ②合成物，复合物，组合物

composite antivibrator 复合式减振器（见 elastic pendulum-type torsional vibration balancer）

composite bearing 多层合金轴瓦（= compound bearing）

composite body （由底架和车壳两部分组成的）组合结构车身；非承载式车身

composite chamber 复合燃烧室

composite concentration of exhaust emission 综合排放浓度（指在几种不同工况下测定 CO、HC 等污染物的浓度，再经加权平均所得出的浓度值）

composite concept vehicle 合成概念车（简称 CCV）

composite cycle 混合循环（指沙巴特循环，参见 Sabathe cycle）

composite engine ①复合式动力机组（指由不同的两种发动机，如活塞式发动机和发电机—电动机组成的动力系）②混合循环发动机（参见 combined-cycle engine）

composite force 合力（= resultant force）

composite fuel economy 综合燃油经济性，综合燃料经济性（简称 CFE）

composite gear 复合材料齿轮

composite intake manifold 组合式进气歧管

composite mass of exhaust emission 综合排放质量（由不同工况组成的试验循环测得的排放物的质量，单位：g/km）

composite materials 复合材料

composite metal 双金属，复合金属

composite plating 多金属分层电镀，多层电镀，复合电镀（亦称 composite coating）

composite propeller shaft 合成（材料）传动轴（由纤维加强的环氧树脂制成的新型单件式传动轴）

composite trailer 组合式全挂车（指由常规的半挂车和装有鞍式牵引座的单轴挂车组合成的全挂车）

composite wire 双金属丝

composition ①合成，结合，综合 ②组成，成分，组织，结构 ③混合物；合成物，混合剂，合剂

composition metal 合金（= alloy）

composure ①镇静，沉稳 ②稳定

compound ①复合物，化合物，剂，料 ②复合的，合成的，结合的 ③复合，掺和，调和，结合 ④复激，复卷

compound ball bearing 组合式球轴承

compound bearing 多层合金轴套或轴瓦（= composite bearing）

compound cam 复式凸轮

compound carburetor 多腔分动式化油器（双腔，中、小负荷时由主腔供给经济混合气，当负荷和转速大到规定值时，副腔节气门迅速开启，双腔同时工作，满足大负荷时对混合气数量与质量的要求，亦称 two-stage carburetor, progressive carburettor）

compound casting 双金属铸件

compound (centre) electrode 复合式中心电极（火花塞的包有铜芯的镍基合金电极）

compound diesel engine 复合式柴油机（指在常规的废气涡轮增压式柴油机废气涡轮的废气排出口处再加一个低压涡轮—齿轮减速—液力耦合装置，将废气剩余的能量传至发动机飞轮，以充分利用废气能量的柴油机系统）

compound (ed) oil 混合油，复合油

compound engine ①涡轮反馈式活塞发动机（废气涡轮驱动增压器后的剩余动力又通过传动机构回授给发动机曲轴）②多级膨胀式发动机（见 multipe-expansion engine）③组合式发动机，复式发动机（指由两种不同原动机，如内燃机-电动机组成的动力系统）

compound glass 见 laminated glass

compound horn 高低音喇叭

compounding ①配料，配方，配合；混合，复合 ②复激，复绕

compound intersection 复式交叉口，多路交叉口，复合交叉口（5条以上的多条道路汇合的交叉口，= multiple inter-section, multiway inter-section）

compound mixture （内燃机可燃混合气形成的）复合混合（方式）（指空间混合与油膜混合各占一定比例的混合方式）

compound motor 复绕电动机，复激电动机，串并联电动机（= series-parallel motor，有两个独立的磁场线圈，一个与电枢电路并联，另一个与该电路串联，多用作起动机）

compound oscillating tooth 组合活齿（由滚子和推杆组成的传动构件，参见 oscillating tooth）

compound pendulum 复摆

compound piston ring 组合式活塞环

compound planetary arrangement （自动变速器的）内啮双联行星齿轮机构（这类行星齿轮机构的种类很多，但其基本特点是前、后两排行星齿系共用塔式齿轮作为行星

轮，= compound planetary gearing, compound gearing, compound gear train, 参见 compound planet gear)

compound planetary train 组合行星齿轮系（指由一级或多级行星齿轮传动机构与其他类型齿轮传动机构组成的齿轮系）

compound planet gear 双联行星齿轮，行星齿轮组，塔轮式行星齿轮（两个或两个以上的行星齿轮组成的同心整体塔轮，亦称 planetary cluster pinion, compound pinion gear 或简称 compound planet)

compound rotary CI engine 复式柴油转子发动机，复式转子柴油机（压缩与动力冲程分别在两个转子缸中完成）

compound transmission 组合式变速器（由主、副变速器组成）

compound-valve hemispherical (engine) 双进、排气门半球形燃烧室（发动机），四气门半球形燃烧室（发动机）（简称 CVH）

compound vortex controlled combustion(system) 复合涡流控制燃烧系统（一种副室式层状充气系统，浓混合气送入副室点燃后喷入充有稀混合气的主室，简称 CVCC）

compound wall （不同材料制成的）多层板壁

compound wound machine 复绕式电机；复励式电机

compreg 胶合木材，渗胶压缩木材（= compregnated wood）

comprehend ①理解，了解 ②包含，包括 ③综合

comprehensive 综合的，广泛的，包含的，全面的

comprehensive automobile control system 轿车综合控制系统（简称 CACS，指对汽车各总成作综合控制，如：发动机点火、混合比、防抱死制动、车身调平、自动变速、车内空调等统一集中控制）

comprehensive automobile traffic control techniques 汽车交通综合控制技术，简称 CATCT，参见 ITS

comprehensive data 综合性资料，全面的数据

comprehensive information system of driver 驾驶人综合信息系统（智能运输系统的一个子系统，为驾驶人提供道路交通实时信息）

comprehensive planning 总体规划

comprehensive test stand （汽车）综合试验台（亦称 multi-function test stand）

compress ①压缩，压紧，压榨，压挤，压扁，压制 ②浓缩，缩短，扼要，叙述，摘要 ③收缩器，打包机

compressed air 压缩空气

compressed air atomizer 压缩空气喷雾器

compressed air bearing 压缩空气轴承

compressed air brake 见 air brake

compressed air cooler 强制风冷式冷却器

compressed air engine 压缩空气发动机（见 pneumatic engine）

compressed air gauge 压缩空气压力表

compressed air gear shifting 气动换挡

compressed air starting 压缩空气起动（将压缩空气按一定次序充入汽缸，强制内燃机曲轴旋转的起动方式）

compressed gap ①（密封环等的）端隙，切口间隙（= end clearance）②（活塞环）在压缩状态下的切口间隙

compressed natural gas 压缩天然气（主要成分为甲烷，简称 CNG）

compressed natural gas vehicle 压缩天然汽车（用压缩天然气作燃料的

汽车的通称，其燃料系主要由压缩天然气的压力容器，减压-稳压装置，加温系统及天然气与空气的混合气配制和混合比调节系统等组成，简称 NGV)

compressibility ①可压缩性，压缩性（一般指流体在压力、温度变化时，其体积及密度的变化，用压缩率表示）②压缩系数，压缩率（表示流体压缩性大小的系数，见 compressibility factor)

compressibility-and-recovery test 可压缩（性）和弹性恢复试验

compressibility factor 压缩（性）系数（表示实际气体状态与理想气体状态差异的无量纲因子，$Z = \dfrac{PVm}{RT}$，式中：P—压力，Vm—摩尔容积，R—摩尔气体常数，T—热力学温度)

compressibility influence 压缩效应

compressible ①可压缩的，可压紧的，压缩性的 ②可浓缩的

compressible fluid 可压缩性流体（指体积的弹性系数不为零的流体。一般认为气体是可压缩性流体，液体为非压缩性流体。但在高速运动的液体，亦应考虑为可压缩性流体)

compression ①压缩，压紧，压实 ②加压 ③压缩压力 ④凝缩，浓缩

compressional vibration 压缩振动（纵向振动)

compressional wave 压缩波（纵波)

compression blow-by 压缩冲程中混合气串入曲轴箱

compression bumper 压缩式缓冲器

compression casing （涡轮增压器）压气机壳

compression check （发动机汽缸的）压缩压力检测

compression-deflection resistance （橡皮等弹性材料的）压缩-变形特性

compression end pressure without combustion 燃烧前压缩终点压力（指未着火时，压缩过程终点，汽缸内工质的压力)

compression end temperature without combustion 燃烧前压缩终点温度（指未着火时，压缩过程终点，汽缸内工质的温度)

compression failure ①（材料的）压缩破坏 ②（发动机）由于压缩压力引起的故障或与压缩压力有关的故障（如：造成压缩压力过低的故障等)

compression fatigue 压缩疲劳

compression fittings 压力接头（压缩空气管道的接头)

compression gasoline 压缩汽油（由天然气等压缩成的液态燃油)

compression gauge 汽缸压缩压力表（= compression tester)

compression grease cup 加压式滑脂杯

compression ignition engine 压燃式内燃机（= diesel engine, self-ignition engine, 指压缩汽缸内的空气或可燃混合气，产生高温引起燃料着火的内燃机如：柴油机)

compression inner ring 活塞环衬环（活塞环胀圈)

compression leak (age) 压缩漏气

compression leveling （发动机电子控制的一种模式）等压缩控制（每一个汽缸内的每一个活塞均将其充量压缩至相同的压缩压力)

compression link （受）压缩杆（悬架装置中承受压缩压力的杆件)

compression (loaded) ball joint （承受）压缩载荷式球节

compression loss 压缩损失（在压缩过程中的能量损失)

compression member 抗压件，受压构件，承压件

compression packing 压缩性密封件，

软质衬垫

compression (piston) ring （活塞）压缩环，气环

compression pressure 压缩压力（①指压缩冲程终了时汽缸内的压力 ②指压缩过程中汽缸内的压力）

compression process （内燃机）压缩过程（活塞在汽缸内压缩工质的过程）

compression ratio （内燃机）压缩比（一般指其几何压缩比，即：汽缸最大容积与余隙容积的比值，简称R）

compression refuse collector 旋转板式自装卸垃圾车

compression release valve （柴油机起动）减压阀（= decompression valve）

compression relief cock （压缩压力等的）泄压开关，减压开关

compression retarder ［美］（发动机制动）排气缓速器，压缩缓速器

compression rod （承受）压（力的）杆（件）

compression rubber spring 压缩橡胶弹簧（利用橡胶压缩变形起缓冲和减振作用）

compression seal 压缩密封件，软质密封件（亦写作 compressive seal）

compression set ①加压变形率，压缩系数（受压试件在去掉规定的外加压力后，经过一定的时间，如30min，试件厚度的压缩度变小率）②压缩永久变形，压缩残余变形（= compressive permanent set）

compression shackle （钢板弹簧）承压吊耳

compression spring 压缩弹簧（= coil spring）

compression strength 抗压强度（指构件等加压至破坏前所承受的最大标称压应力）

compression stroke 压缩行程，压缩冲程（= compression travel）

compression swirl 压缩涡流（指压缩过程中引起或加强的工质涡流）

compression temperature 压缩温度

compression test 压缩试验（指拆去火花塞，将压缩压力表拧入火花塞孔内，测汽缸内最高的压缩压力）

compression tester （汽缸）压缩压力表，压缩测试仪

compression turbulence （压缩冲程中形成的）压流紊流

compression type belt （通过压缩方式来传递动力的）压缩型传动带

compression type CVT 压缩型 CVT（指使用压缩型传动带的 CVT）

compression volume （发动机汽缸的）压缩容积（指活塞处于上止点时的汽缸容积，= clearance volume, compression space, minimun cylinder vol-ume，我国一般称为燃烧室容积）

compression washer （螺栓防漏的）压缩垫圈

compression wave 压缩波（正压波）

compressire stress 压应力（指朝向力作用平面的正应力，参见 normal stress）

compressive 压缩的，加压的，挤压的

compressive force 压缩力（= force of compression）

compressive resistance 抗压强度

compressive test 压缩试验［用静压缩力对试件作轴向压缩，在试件不发生屈曲下测量其相应变形（缩短）和压缩力的试验］

compressometer （测量压缩形变的）压缩计，缩度计，压缩变形计

compressor ①压气机、空气压缩机 ②压缩工具（如气门弹簧压缩器）

compressor discharge pressure sensor （汽车空调）压缩机输出压力传感器（亦称 refrigerant pressure sensor

制冷剂压力传感器)

compressor pressure ratio 压气机增压比$\left(=\dfrac{\text{排出空气的绝对压力}}{\text{进入空气的绝对压力}}\right)$

compressor protection switch (汽车空调) 压缩机保护开关 (一种温度、压力传感开关,防止压缩机因漏油或过热而损坏,亦称 superheat switch)

compressor turbine (燃气轮机的) 压气机涡轮,压气机叶轮 (驱动压气机的叶轮, = compressor wheel)

compressur beginning temperature 压缩始点温度 (压缩过程实际开始时,汽缸内工质的温度)

compressure beginning pressure (内燃机) 压缩始点压力 (压缩过程实际开始时,汽缸内工质的压力)

Comprex exhaust pressure wave supercharger 寇姆普列克斯排气压力波增压器,排气压力波增压器,压力波增压器,气波增压器 [利用废气膨胀产生的压力波直接压缩新鲜空气的增压装置,因研制厂 Comprex 而得名,亦称 Comprex pressure wave (super) charger 或简称 Comprex。由①沿径向用隔板隔成许多气道的格栅式压气机转子 "cell-type compressor wheel" ②与转子一端对接的低压空气入口—高气空气出口壳体 "air casing" ③与转子另一端对接的高压废气入口—低压废气出口壳体 "gas casing" 及④由曲轴带动转子以 8000r/min 旋转的传动带传动装置组成。这种增压器既有容积式增压器对节气门响应快的优点,又有涡轮增压器热效率高的特点,且低速时进气压力高,发动机低速转矩大]

comprise 包含,包括,构成,合成,由…组成

comprison colorimeter 比色计

compromise ①折中,兼顾,妥协 ②折中办法,折中方案

compton effect 康普顿效应 (光子与电子冲撞时的效应)

compulsory vehicle inspection 车辆的定期强制检查

compulsory (vehicle) maintenance (车辆的) 强制维护,计划预防维护

computation 计算

computational fluid dynamics 见 CFD

computational study (相对试验研究而言的) 计算研究 (= numerical investigation)

computed value 计算值 (= calculated value)

computer ①(任一种) 计算机,计算器 ②(目前一般指) 电子计算机 [不同厂家用各种不同的术语表示车用电子计算机,如:ECA (electronic control assembly), ECM (electronic control module), ECU (electronic control unit), SMEC (single module engine control), EEC (electronic engine control) 等等,但美国政府规定从 1995 年 1 月 1 日起,一切厂家生产的汽车用电子计算机均必须按 SAE 推荐的术语称 control module,如:发动机控制用电子计算机,必须称 powertrain control module "动力系控制模块",简称 PCM;车身系统控制用计算机,一律称 body control module "车身控制模块",简称 BCM 等]

computer-aided 借助计算机的,电子计算机辅助的 (= computer assisted)

computer aided design and drafting 计算机辅助设计和绘图 (简称 CADD)

computer aided die design 计算机辅助模具设计 (简称 CADD)

computer-aided engineering 计算机

辅助工程技术（简称 CAE）

computer aided experiment　计算机辅助试验（简称 CAE）

computer aided geometric design　计算机辅助几何设计（简称 CAGD）

computer aided industrial design　计算机辅助工业设计（简称 CAID，在汽车工业中，特指应用计算机进行汽车造型的智能化设计过程，故又称 computer aided intelligent design，欧洲则常用 computer aided styling）

computer-aided instruction　计算机辅助教学，机助教学，计算机辅助说明

computer aided manufacture　计算机辅助制造（简称 CAM）

computer-aided post-processing　计算机（控制的）后处理

computer-aided pre-processing　计算机（控制的）前处理

computer-aided technology　计算机辅助技术（包括：计算机辅助设计"CAD"，计算机辅助造型"CAS"，计算机辅助工程分析"CAE"，计算机辅助制造"CAM"，计算机辅助工艺规划设计"CAPP"等）

computer-aided test　计算机辅助试验（简称 CAT）

computer-based　借助计算机的，利用计算机的

computer coil ignition system　计算机控制线圈式点火系

computer command control system　电子计算机指令控制系统（通用公司早期推出的发动机电子控制系统的商品名，简称 CCC 及 C^3 或 C-3）

computer command ride　见 CCR

computer/computer communication　计算机-计算机间通信，计算机间信息传递

computer-controlled brakes　计算机控制式制动系（指在每一个车轮上都装有速度传感器，以电脉冲形式将车轮转速信号输入车载计算机，制动时，由车载计算机控制，使每一个车轮都以相同的或各自最佳的速率制动或减速，以减小急刹时的侧滑倾向）

computer controlled catalytic converter　微机控制催化转化器（简称 C4）

computer controlled dwell　计算机控制点火线圈一次绕组通电时间（简称 CCD）

computer-dependent　与计算机相关的，与计算机有关的，计算机的

computer graphics　①计算机制图 ②计算机制图系统

computerization　计算机化（亦写作 computerization）

computerized　计算机化的，计算机处理的，应用计算机的，计算机控制的，计算机管理的（= computer driven，或简称 computered）

computerized dispatch and fleet management system　计算机化调度和车队管理系统

computerized tomography　计算机控制 X 光断层照相术（简称 CT，一种用 X 光分层透视物体内部，并可屏幕显示或照相的技术）

computer manufacturing integrated system　计算机辅助制造集成系统（集 CAD、CAM、MIS、DSS 等系统于一体，形成从产品设计到产品销售全过程的全面计算机辅导系统，简称 CMIS）

computer on slice　单片（式计算）机

computer-orchestrated brake by wire　计算机（精确）控制的线控制动器

computer-oriented　（与）计算机有关的

computer remote terminal　计算机远程终端（简称 CRT）

computer virus 计算机病毒

computing heating value （燃料的）计算热值（指根据经验公式计算出的燃料热值）

comsat 通信卫星（communication satelite 的简称）

comution system 通信系统（comunication system 的简称）

concave combustion chamber 凹面燃烧室

concave-concave 两面凹的，双凹（形）的

concave-convex 一面凹一面凸的

concave-down （向）下凹的

concave-head piston 凹顶活塞

concave lens 凹透镜

concave mirror 凹面（反射）镜，凹镜

concave-up （向）上凹的

concavity ①凹处，凹面②凹面形，凹度，凹性

concealed fitting 暗接头

concealed headlight 隐蔽式前照灯（使用时才伸出或升起，亦称 pop-up headlight）

concentrate ①集中，聚集，浓缩②浓缩物

concentration cell 浓差电池

concentration of emission 排放浓度（指废气中的有害成分浓度，即：用 $10^{-6} m^3/m^3$、mg/m^3 等单位度量的 NO_X、CO、HC 等有害气体在每 m^3 废气中的排放量）

concentrator 集中器［①数据传输中，兼有控制器和多路复用器功能的器件，并具有存储信息和在低速设备发送某信息前，以高速将该信息发送至另一设备的功能②可以将多个输入信息组合成单个信息（集中）或从一个传输系列所发送的数据中抽出各单个信息（分散）的装置］

concentric circles 同心圆

concentric coil spring（around strut/shock absorber）（套在麦弗逊式悬架的滑柱/减振器外的）同心螺旋弹簧

concentric float 同心式浮子（化油器腔筒与浮子室同心，车辆倾斜时空燃比变动较小）

concentricity ①同心度②同心性；集中，同心

concept car 概念车（用于表示一种尚未有的新的设计思想、式样、风格或结构的样车，亦称 concept vehicle）

concern ①营业，业务，事务关系，关联②与…有关系，对…有重要性，影响到，涉及，参与

concrete ①具体的②混凝土③混凝土制的

concrete mixer ①混凝土搅拌机②混凝土搅拌车（装备有恒定转速的搅拌筒、均匀排料的螺旋叶片、油压动力系统等专用设备，用于搅拌混凝土的罐式汽车）

concurring 同时发生的，并发的

concussion ①撞击，冲击②振动，震荡

concussion spring 减振弹簧，缓冲弹簧

condemned 报废的，失去使用价值的

condensance （电）容量；容抗

condensate ①冷凝物，冷凝液②浓缩物

condensate outlet 冷凝水排出口

condensation ①浓缩②凝结，冷凝③凝露（指表面温度低于环境空气的露点温度时，水蒸气在其表面冷凝成液态水的现象）④凝缩的⑤变浓了的

condensation coefficient （蒸气的）冷凝系数（每秒钟内在任意表面上凝聚的分子数对碰撞该表面上总分子数的比值）

condensation point 凝点（蒸气的凝结温度）

condensation polymerization 凝缩，聚合，缩聚（作用）

condense ①（液体）浓缩 ②（气体）凝结 ③（光线）集中

condensed spark 电容火花

condensed specifications 简要说明，简明技术规范

condenser ①聚光镜，聚光器（= condenser lens）②冷凝器 ③电容器（目前，电容器一词大多用 capacitor）

condenser discharge ignition system 电容放电点火系统（指火花放电能量存储在电容器中，而不储存于点火线圈，点火线圈仅起变换电压作用的点火系。由振荡器、点火变压器和整流电路组成的电容器充电电路，将蓄电池的电压变换成400V左右的直流供电容器充电，点火信号触发晶闸管通导，电容器向点火线圈初级绕组放电，而在其次级绕组中感应出电压升高速度比一般点火线圈式点火系快10倍左右的4000V高压点火脉冲。这里，电容器存储的能量是通过晶闸管传至点火线圈的，因而亦称晶闸管点火系统，但目前其中"condenser"词多用 capacitor）

condenser megaohm tester 电容器兆欧测试仪，电容器高阻表

condenser pump 冷凝泵

condenser type spot welder （电容器储蓄电能，通过变压器，瞬间放出能量的）电容器式点焊机

condensing coil 冷凝蛇行管，冷凝盘管

condensive reactance 电容电抗，容抗（= capacity reactance）

condition ①条件，状况 ②调节（温度、湿度）

conditional branch 条件转移（指在执行程序中离开规定的次序执行某一指令，亦称 conditional jump）

conditional branch instruction 条件转移指令（指完成上述转移的指令）

conditioner （空气温度、湿度等的）调节器

conduct ①传导（热、电等），引导，进行，实施 ②导管

conductance ①电导，电导系数 ②传导性，传导率

conductibility 导电性，导磁性，传导性

conducting film 导电薄膜

conducting probe 试电笔，导电探针

conducting sector 扇形导电板，扇形导体（= sector conductor）

conducting wire 导线

conduction 传导

conduction cooling 传导冷却，导热冷却

conductive coating ①导电涂层 ②导热涂层

conductive discharge （经）导体（的）放电

conductive elastomer 导电弹性材料，导电合成橡胶（一种金属-硅酮化合物，受压时其电阻大幅度下降，呈导电性，可用作汽车上的各种按压开关）

conductive rubber 导电橡胶（电阻系数约为 5×10^4 ohm/cm）

conductive solid tyre 导电实心轮胎

conductivity ①传导性，传导率，传导系数 ②电导率，导电性（= electrical conductivity）③热导率，导热性（= thermal conductivity）

conductivity modulation 电导率调制（使载流子浓度变化而引起半导体电导率的变化）

conductometric analysis 电导率分析（测定）法（根据溶液电导率来确定其溶液中含有物质浓度的方法）

conductor 导体,导线

conduit 导管,管道,通道

cone 锥体,锥形;锥形物(如临时路标等)

cone and cup bearing 锥形滚子轴承(= taper roller bearing)

cone angle 锥角

cone bearing 锥形轴承

cone belt 三角(传动)带(= V-belt)

cone brake 锥形制动器

cone claw clutch 锥形牙嵌式离合器(= cone dog clutch)

cone clutch 锥形离合器(指主动件和从动件的接合表面成锥者,用于齿轮变速器的同步器等)

cone coupling 锥形连接器,锥形连轴节

cone-cup chamber 锥杯形燃烧室

cone distance (圆锥齿轮)分度锥母线长度,锥距(亦称 conical distance)

cone effect (外倾车轮滚动时形成以理论回转中心为锥顶的)滚锥效应

cone (front) back-face rib (圆锥滚子轴承)内圈锥面前-后凸肩

cone gauge 锥度量规,锥度规

cone gear drive 锥齿轮传动

cone-headed 带锥形头的,头部成锥形的,锥形头的

cone of gears 多级塔齿轮

cone pawl clutch 锥形棘爪式离合器(= cone ratchet clutch)

cone penetrometer ①圆锥贯入仪,针入度仪(土壤、滑脂等圆锥贯入度"cone penetration"试验用)②透度仪(测量 X 线穿透力用)

cone (penetrometer) index 圆锥(贯入)指数(美国陆军试验站提出的一种确定土壤坚实度的方法,用以衡量车辆行驶时土壤的阻力和推力特性;用一锥角为 30°底面积为 $0.5in^2$ 的圆锥压头压入土中至车辆作用可能达到的深度时,土壤作用在圆锥压头上的平均阻力,简称 CI。按规定条件冲击土壤 100 次后测得的圆锥指数称为额定圆锥指数 rated cone index,简称 RCI,车辆在同一车辙中通过 50 次后,陷车所需的最小额定圆锥指数,称为车辆圆锥指数"vehicle cone index"简称 VCI)。

cone pulley 锥轮,宝塔(传动带)轮

cone rotor ①锥形转子 ②(锥形制动器的)斜锥制动鼓,锥条制动鼓

cone seat (辐条式车轮辐条锁定螺母的)锥形座

cone-shape(d) 锥形的

cone spring 锥形螺旋弹簧

cone type injector 锥形喷嘴

cone-type steering wheel 喇叭口形转向盘(撞车时,转向盘柱不会碰伤驾驶员胸部,亦称 cone-type handle)

cone washer 锥形垫圈

cone worm ①锥蜗杆(见 spiroid)②锥面包络圆柱蜗杆(见 milled helicoid worm)③锥面包络环面蜗杆(见 TK-worm)

conference 会议,讨论会

conference mobile 会议客车(供召开流动会议用)

confidence (数理统计的)置信,置信度,可靠程度

confidence interval 置信区间

configuration ①形状,外形,轮廓,构形 ②排列(组合),布置(简称 CONFIG)

confine ①限制(在…范围内)②区域,范围,限度

confined heating stability (润滑油等的)极限热稳定性

confirm 使有效,批准,证实,确定

confirmation testing 验证性试验(亦称 confirm test)

conflagrant 快速燃烧的,燃烧着的

conflict （相互）抵触（冲突、矛盾）

conflicting requests 相互矛盾的（互相抵触的）要求

conflicting traffic 交会的交通流，交会的车流

confluence ①汇合，合流 ②群集，集合

conform 一致，符合，遵照，适合

conformability ①适应性，贴合性，一致性，相似性 ②顺从

conformability (of piston ring) **to bore contour** （活塞环）对汽缸壁面的贴合性

conformable 一致的，相似的，适合的，贴合的

conformable oil piston ring （能与缸壁弧面贴合的）挠性活塞油环

conformal coating 保形涂层，敷形涂覆（一般采用渗有柔韧剂的塑料漆面，以使被涂零件与接合件耦合面或接触面形状吻合并可使其免受损伤）

conformity 一致性（对测量仪表而言，指其校准曲线与规定特性曲线，如直线抛物线等的一致性，无特别说明时，指其独立一致性，见 independent conformity）

conformity certification 合格认证（指权威机构确认并通过证书证明某一产品符合相应规范或标准）

confuse 使混乱，混淆，把…混同

congestion management system 交通堵塞管理系统

congestion traffic 交通阻塞（= congested traffic condition）

conglomerate ①（汽车）企业集团，联营公司 ②密聚体，集成物 ③（使）成球形，（使）积聚成团 ④密集的,成团的,聚成球形的 ⑤由不同种类的部分组成的

Congo red 刚果红，直接刚果红（一种酸性溶液的化学试剂）

congress 大会，会议，专业会议

congruent 相同，一致，全等（的），叠合，同余

conic ①锥形的，圆锥形的 ②圆锥曲线，二次曲线

conical 圆锥形的，圆锥体的

conical base solid tyre （底部呈圆锥形的）斜底实心轮胎

conical fit 锥面配合

conical involute gear 锥形渐开线齿轮

conical plug ①锥形塞，锥形螺塞 ②见 conical seat type spark plug

conical roller thrust bearing 推力圆锥滚子轴承（= taper thrust bearing, thrust taper roller bearing）

conical seated valve 锥形座面阀［气门］（= bevel seated valve）

conical seat type spark plug 锥座形火花塞（亦称 tape seat type spark plug，壳体支承面以63°±1°的锥角与汽缸盖火花塞孔相配合、无须用外密封垫圈的火花塞）

conical spiral 圆锥螺旋线（动点在沿圆锥面上一条母直线作等速运动，而该母直线又绕圆柱面的轴线作等角速旋转时，该动点在该圆锥面上的轨迹）

conicity ①锥形，锥度，圆锥度 ②轮胎的锥形效应（由于车轮中心平面两侧的不对称性，即：胎面的外形不是理想的筒形，而呈锥形，因而导致轮胎的滚动轨迹不是直线，而是圆形的效应）

conicity force 克服轮胎锥形效应所需的力（该力的方向与轮胎即车辆运动的方向一致）

conic seat type spark plug 锥座型火花塞（以锥面与缸盖火花塞孔配合的火花塞，= tape seat type）

conic splined joint 锥形花键接合（= tapered splined joint）

conjugate ①共轭的，成对的，配合

的，结合着，连接的 ②结合，配合，配对，共轭，相配

conjugate profile 共轭齿面（指一对在整个啮合过程中，能在保持相切的条件下，按预定的规律而运动的啮合齿廓）

conjugate value 共轭值

conjunction ①连接，结合，契合，联合；关联 ②同时发生 ③逻辑乘法，逻辑乘积 ④结合件

conjunction box 接线盒

conk 工作中断，工作失常，（机械）失灵，出毛病，发生故障

conlight system 光控灯光自动开关系统（light control system 的简称，由外界光控制的自动亮灯、熄灯和变光的系统）

connect 连接，联结，结合，接装

connected （被）连接的②有联系的，有联络的 ③连续的，连贯的 ④ [在通信系统中，指物理单元（physical unit）或逻辑单元（logical unit）已通过物理通路与其主控制机] 连接（好）的（状态）⑤随着通信技术与车载电信系统的发展，装有各种电信设施，具有完善的信息收发、处理、显示、交流和导航、娱乐、防撞、呼救，以及与车辆动力、传动、控制系统联动等功能的智能车辆，即具有"连接-联动"功能的车辆称"connected vehicle"、"connected car"，见 Cnnnectivity Connected Drive 联（合驱）动（BMW 与车辆动力管理系统联动的新一代智能导航系统的商品名。电子控制模块根据该导航系统的路线和路形的预告功能，自动控制变速器的挡位和车速。除常规导航功能外还具有等同于智能手机的功能，如：录音和收发电子邮件、语言信息、广播、电视、各类图像等并可连接两部智能手机）

Connectedconsult service （通过车载通信系统实现的）互助咨询服务，互功咨询服务

Connected Key （具有"近域无车通信 NFC"功能，可存储和传输信息的）联用钥匙（只要将这种钥匙在也具有近域无线通信功能的个人电脑、智能手机或车载导航系统等上方晃一晃，就能获得电脑存储的信息，或将目的地的信息等传给车载导航系统，将车载故障系统的诊断数据传给电脑，将最后停车位置的 GPS 坐标、油箱内油量等信息传手机显示等）

Connected vehicle 见 Connected③

connecting panel （车身板件中起连接和加强作用的）连接板

connecting rod 连杆（起连接作用的杆件的通称，如：①活塞式内燃机中曲轴与活塞之间的连杆，简称 con rod②转向杆系中连接左、右转向梯形臂的转向横拉杆，亦称 tie rod）

connecting rod aligner 连杆校正仪，连杆校正器

connecting rod aligning jig 连杆大小头平行度检验夹具

connecting rod bearing 连杆轴承（为连杆大端轴瓦和连杆小端轴套的通称）

connecting-rod bearing rebore 连杆轴承镗刮机

connecting rod bearing saddle 连杆轴瓦座

connecting rod big end （发动机）连杆大头，连杆曲端端（= crankpin end, connecting rod tip）

connecting-rod blade 连杆（润滑）油勺（在连杆大头下部，= connecting rod oil scoop or dipper）

connecting rod body 连杆杆身（= body of connecting rod, connecting rod shank）

connecting rod bolt 连杆螺栓

connecting rod bushing lock 连杆衬套定位榫舌

connecting rod fork （取下连杆盖后的）连杆大头叉形

connecting rod length 连杆长度（指连杆大端孔中心至小端孔中心的距离）

connecting rod oil duct 连杆（杆身内）油道

connecting rod pressure 沿连杆方向的压力

connecting rod shank 连杆杆身（= connecting rod body，指连杆大、小头间的工字形断面部分）

connecting rod shim 连杆大头分割面调整垫片

connecting rod small end 连杆小头，连杆活塞端（= little end，piston rod end，small end，wrist pin end）

connecting rod small end bushing 连杆小头衬套

connecting rod thrust （沿连杆纵向轴线作用的）连杆推力

connecting sensor 连接传感器，接头传感器（可接到需要诊断的汽车上）

connecting up ①装配，装置，安装 ②布线

connection box 接线盒，接线箱

connection resistance （电器）接线点电阻

connective operation 连接运转，联合操作

Connectivity ①（特指车辆的功能单元间互联或与移动通信-信息系统间连接的难易和实用程度，或相互间数据传输速度的快慢，可实现的功能多少）连接性，连接功能②（特指车辆通信-信息系统与车辆动力系统、控制系统等之间的）联动性，联动功能（如：导航系统与动力系统联动，指根据导航系统预先提供的路线和路形"上、下坡度，转弯半径等"信息自动选择变速器挡位和控制发动机工况等）

connector ①接头，连接器，连接件，接线盒，接线柱，线夹 ②插接器（由插头和插座配合在一起的组件）

Conradson carbon test 康氏积炭试验，康拉得森残炭测定法

con' rod 见 connecting rod

con-rod metal 曲轴连杆轴承轴瓦

consecutive ①串行的，连续的 ②相邻的，依次相连的，顺序的

consecutive sequence computer 连续顺序计算机（按照既定的顺序执行指令的计算机，只有转移指令才可改变执行顺序）

consequent pole （直流电机）间极（亦称罩极、屏蔽极、附加极、交替极，参见 auxiliary pole）

conservation ①守恒；保护，保存（以免损坏，损失）②维护，维修，保养，养护

conserve ①保存，保藏 ②养护

conserving agent 防腐剂

consistence ①一致性，符合，相容（性）②稳定性③稠度，浓度，（= consistency）

consistency check （计算结果，试验数据的）相符性检查，一致性检验

consistency meter 稠度计（= consistency gauge）

consistency of grease 润滑脂稠度

consistent grease 高稠度润滑脂

consistent lubricant 润滑脂，固体润滑剂

console ①托架，角撑架，落地式支架，悬臂（梁）②仪表板，（特指轿车前座之间的）控制台

console indicator unit 台式显示装置，指示仪表台；落地式指示仪表台

console switch 台式开关，台架式开关

consonance 和谐,一致,共鸣
constant ①常数,常量,恒量,不变值,定值②恒定的,稳定的,固定的,不变的
constant acceleration 匀加速度,等加速度
constant acting load 固定载荷,恒定作用载荷(一直作用的载荷)
constant-amplitude loading 恒幅载荷(指所有峰值和谷值均相等的载荷)
constant-amplitude signal 等幅信号,定幅信号
constant-amplitude test 等幅应力疲劳试验
constantan 康铜(电阻值很高且随温度变化系数很小、接近十五定不变的一种铜镍合金,多用作电阻丝)
constant-area orifice 等截面(校准)量孔
constant cell 恒压电池
constant choke carburetor 固定喉管
constant chord height (圆柱齿轮的)固定弦齿高(指固定弦的中点到齿顶面的最短距离)
constant chord thickness 固定弦齿厚(断开线齿轮的一个齿与基本齿条的两个齿对称接触时,分布于该齿两侧齿面上的两条接触线间的最短距离)
constant circulating oiling 等速环流润滑
constant clearance piston 恒定间隙活塞(参见 autothermic piston)
constant coefficient 常数
constant current (type) charge 恒(电)流(式)充电(不管蓄电池的充电状态如何,一直以一定的电流值充电)
constant-deceleration orifice (液压减振器的)等阻尼节流孔
constant depression carburetor 见 constant vacuum carburetor
constant displacement pump 定排量泵(= constant delivery pump)
constant drive overdrive 常驱动型超速挡(一经接合便与驱动车轮常啮合,而阻止滑行)
constant duty 固定工况,不变工况
constant duty engine 固定负荷发动机
constant error 常见误差,固定误差
constant failure (rate) period 正常工作期,稳态失效(率)期,故障稳定期
constant flow ①恒流量(流量不变的)②常流(的)(一直在流着的)
constant flow hydraulic power steering gear 常流式液压动力转向器(工作液压一直处于常流状态的转向器)
constant-frequency pulse 固定频率脉冲
constant gear ratio steering 固定速比式转向(机构)
constant input coast performance 定输入转矩反拖特性(反拖工况下,输入转矩定值时的液力传动装置的特性)
constant input torque performance 定输入转矩特性(输入转矩定值时液力变速器的特性)
constant-level carburettor (浮子室内)油面固定式化油器,定油面式化油器
constant life design 等寿命设计,等寿命结构(主要构件均设计成基本相等的使用寿命)
constant life fatigue diagram 等寿命疲劳图(表达给定疲劳寿命下的应力幅与平均应力,或最大应力与最小应力间的关系)
constant loading fatigue test 等幅加载疲劳试验

constant load type ①等载荷型,定载荷式②(变速器)等推力式(同步啮合器)(推动同步啮合器的力为一定值,变速迅速,但有噪声,多用于赛车)

constantly variable transmission 见 continuously variable transmission

constant maintenance 日常性维护,例行维护

constant-mesh countershaft transmission 带中间轴的常啮合齿轮变速器

constant-mesh gear-box 常啮合式变速器(=[美]constant-mesh transmission,亦称 non-clashing gear set "无冲击式变速器"前进挡的齿轮副均处于常啮合状态,通过各挡接合齿圈式同步器实现挂挡,传递动力)

constant of chemical equilibrium 化学当量常数(简称K)

constant potential recharge 恒(电)压充电(=constant voltage change)

constant power curve 见 driving force curve

constant power distribution (四轮驱动汽车前、后轮)等动力分配(亦称 constant power split)

constant pressure ①等压(压力一直相等)②常压(一直处于压力下)

constant-pressure cycle 等压循环(指由绝热压缩、等压加热、绝热膨胀和等容放热四个过程依次组成的理想循环)

constant-pressure-cycle engine 等压循环发动机(按等压循环工作的发动机,=diesel-cycle engine)

constant pressure exhaust manifold 等压排气管(管内压力基本均匀稳定、容积较大的排气支管)

constant pressure flow controller 等压流量控制器(如:保持管道液压不变的流量控制装置)

constant pressure hydraulic power steering gear 常压式液压动力转向器(工作液压一直处于高压状态的动力转向器,其转向控制阀在中间位置常闭)

constant pressure parking brake 等压力驻车制动器(如弹簧驻车制动器等制动压力不受气压管道压力变动的影响而保持稳定的驻车制动器)

constant pressure turbo-charging 定压增压(废气涡轮增压的一种,进入废气涡轮器的废气压力基本上稳定不变)

constant rate suspension 等刚度悬架

constant running power take-off 常运转式功率输出轴

constant speed characteristics ①负荷特性(指内燃机转速保持不变时,内燃机主要性能参数:油耗、排气温度等随负荷、功率、转矩、平均有效压力的改变而变化的关系)②负荷特性曲线

constant speed control 等速控制(使速度保持不变)

constant-speed fuel economy 等速燃油经济性

constant spray system (汽车发动机的汽油)连续喷射系

constant stroke (fuel) injection pump 固定冲程式喷油泵,不变冲程式高压油泵

constant temperature 等温,恒温

constant vacuum carburetor 等真空度化油器,活动喉管化油器(喉管的通过断面随发动机负荷、转速变化,在整个发动机工作过程中喉管喷油嘴处的真空度始终接近某一最佳值,亦称 constant depression carburetor, variable chock carburetor)

cons tant value control 定值控制(目标值固定不变的控制)

constant velocity 等速，匀速，恒速（简称CV）

constant velocity plane （等速万向节的）等速平面（指等速万向节各传动接触点所在的平面，它垂直于输入轴和输出轴旋转轴线所在的平面，二者的交线平分上述两轴线所构成的钝角）

constant velocity (universal) joint 等速万向节（简称CV joint，指输出轴和输入轴以等于1的瞬时角速度比传递运动的万向节）

constant voltage 直流电压，恒定电压

constant voltage control 恒电压控制（使电压保持恒定）

constant volume cycle 等容循环（指由绝热压缩、等容加热、绝热膨胀和等容放热四个过程依次组成的理想循环，＝Otto cycle）

constant volume cycle engine 等容循环发动机（按等容循环工作的发动机，Otto-cycle engine）

constant volume sampling （废气分析）定容积采样法（简称CVS，用清洁空气按一定的稀释率稀释全部排气，并使其在一定的温度和流量下流动，从中采集定量试样的采样方法）

constituent ①成分 ②分力，分量 ③组成的，成分的，组织的

constitute 构成，组成；设立；制定

constitution ①结构，构造 ②组成，组织③章程，法规④制定，设立

constitution(al) diagram 状态图，平衡图，(金)相图

constrain ①强迫，强制 ②约束（指对物体变形、移动等的任一种限制）

constrained-layer damping technology 约束层阻尼技术（主要采用金属-金属夹层材料"metal-composite-metal sandwich"降低噪声等）

constrained oscillations 强迫摆振；强迫振荡

constrained vibration 强迫振动（＝forced vibration）

constraint ①限制，制约，强制，约束 ②条件，制约条件

constrict ①使收缩；压缩②磨出环形凹槽，使轴颈等磨损，磨细；使变小

constriction 收缩，收窄，压缩

construction ①构造，结构，建筑②解释

constructional drawing 结构图，构造图

construction assistance vehicle 建筑工地运载车辆，建筑辅助运输工具（简称CAV）

construction machinery transporter 工程机械运输车

consumable load （车辆的）消耗性荷载（如由燃油等可消耗材料形成的载荷）

consume 消耗，消费

consumer ①用户，消费者 ②消耗(性)装置

Consumer Information Regulation 用户信息手册（美国NHTSA规定汽车生产厂家必须以小册子的形式向用户说明车辆的：①加速性能②制动性能③轮胎安全系数④汽车旅游帐篷的装载法等，简称CIR）

consumer-oriented 指导用户的，使用户能正确选用（汽油等）的，面向用户的

Consumer Reports 《消费者报告》（美国一份月发行量1200万份的畅销杂志，定期公布美国测试中心对上百辆新车进行的性能测试结果，左右着整个北美地区的购车行为）

consumer selection model 用户选择数学模型（用于市场预测用户对车型等的要求）

consumption lubrication 消耗式润滑（法）（如：将滑油送入缸内润滑，而与燃油一起燃烧完全消耗的润滑方式）

consumption of fuel 燃料消耗（量），油耗

contact ①接触 ②触点，触头，接点 ③保持接触的，由接触引起的，有联系的

contact alloy 触点合金（亦称 contact metal）

contact angle ①接触角，闭合角（参见 dwell angle）②包覆角，包角（如传动带对传动带轮的包角）

contact arcing 触点跳火花，触点跳火

contact area 接触面积，接触区（如：轮胎与地面的接触印痕面积，见 contact patch）

contact area pressure （车轮对地面的）接触面压力，接触压强，压印压力（= footprint pressure）

contact area (pressure) distribution （轮胎的）触地压力分布，印迹压力分布（= footprint pressure distribution）

contact arm （分电器的）活动触点臂

contact assisted transistor ignition system 带触点的晶体管点火系统

contact bounce 触点振动（= contact chatter）

contact breaker 断电器（点火系分电器内的一个弹簧闭合式触点开关，当凸轮将其活动触点臂顶开后，便将点火线圈一次电路切断，而在二次绕组中感生点火高压，简称 CB）

contact breaker cage 断电器壳体

contact breaker current 断电触点电流（指触点断开瞬间流经断电发装置的触点电流）

contact breaker gap 断电器触点间隙

contact breaker plate 断电器底板

contact breaker point 断电器触点（指断电器的固定触点，参见 make and break contact）

contact brush 接触电刷

contact center 接触中心（特指车轮平面与车轮旋转轴线在地面上的投影线的交点）

contact chatter 见 contact bounce

contact-controlled 触点控制的，触点式（的）

contact controlled ignition 触点控制或点火

contact corrosion ①接触腐蚀，接触性侵蚀 ②触点腐蚀

contact coupling （带锥形插头和插座的）接触密封式管接头

contact drop ①接触电压降 ②触点电压降

contact fatigue 接触疲劳（指材料在循环接触应力作用下，产生局部永久性累积损伤，经一定循环次数后表面发生麻点，浅层或深层剥落的过程）

contact gap ①触点间隙 ②接触表面间隙，接触间隙

contacting width 接触宽度

contacting width of edge （密封件的）密封刃口与轴接触的轴向长度

contact length 接触长度（特指沿轮胎平面测定的轮胎印痕的前、后边缘间的距离）

contactless 无触点的

contactless transistor ignition system 无触点晶体管点火系（= breakerless transistorized ignition system）

contact line 接触线

contactor 接触器，触点式开关

contact patch （轮胎与道路）接触印痕（= footprint，有时亦称 contact area）

contact pattern 接触印痕图形

contact pin 触头，触针

contact point 触点
contact point dresser 触点修磨工具
contact potential difference 接触电位差（简称CPD）
contact printed lithography （电路的）平板印刷术
contact sensor 接触型传感器（指直接与被传感参数接触的传感器，如接触式位移传感器等）
contact set （供换新用的）触点组件
contact spring 触点弹簧（使触点保持闭合状态的弹簧）
contact switch ①触模式开关 ②接触式开关
contact triggered 触点触发的，触点控制的
contact-type 接触式
contact welding 接触焊
contact width 接触宽度（特指垂直于轮胎平面方向所测得的轮胎印痕宽度）
contain ①包含，容纳 ②相当于 ③控制，抑制 ④被⋯除尽
container ①容器，箱，罐，外壳 ②（特指）集装箱
container berth 集装箱泊位（放置处）
container carrier 集装箱专用车，集装箱搬运车
container lorry 集装箱货车，集装箱运输车
container-on-frame car 无货箱式集装运输车（简称COF车，集装箱直接装在汽车底架上的运输车）
container platform vehicle 平板式集装箱运输车（具有敞开式平货台，货台上设置有夹紧装置，用于运输各种型号集装箱）
contaminant ①污染，玷污，弄肮 ②（复数）污物，污染物，杂质 ③掺和物
contaminant holding capacity （滤清器）蓄尘能力
contaminant particle 污染物微粒
contaminate 污染，玷污，使变脏，损害，毒害
contaminated oil settling tank 污油沉淀槽（简称COST）
contaminates particle size 污染物粒度
contaminating metal 杂质金属
contamination ①污染 ②污秽，污染物 ③损害，有害 ④混淆
content ①容积，容量，含量 ②含义
content addressable memory 按内容访问存储器（简称CAM，一种不是根据地址，而是根据内容访问的存储口，亦称associative memory, content addressed storage）
continental-type fuse 大陆型熔丝（一种带锥形端盖的陶瓷合金熔丝，标有颜色示值）
contingency ①偶然性，可能发生的事，偶然事故，临时性 ②应急费用，临时费用 ③相切 ④列联
continous bits 连续位元（指一串连续的数据位元，各位元间无停滞时间）
continually varying 连续变化的
continued development ①连续研制，继续开发 ②持续发展（简称CD）
continuity 连续性，持续性，不间断性，连续，连贯
continuity test （电路的）断路检查
continuous 连续的，不断的，长期的，经常的
continuous AC ignition system 连续交流点火系统（一种新型的点火系统，在整个做功冲程中，一直激发高能交流电流，简称CACIS）
continuous adjustable shock absorber 连续可调式减振器
continuous belt ①传动带 ②环形传送带
continuous brake power （发动机的）持续有效功率（指在制造厂规定的

连续工作条件下，发动机能令人满意的运转的厂方推荐功率）

continuous braking system （汽车列车的）连续式制动系（牵引车与挂车的制动力来自同一动力源，驾驶员操纵牵引车制动控制装置即可连续实现对牵引车和挂车的制动）

continuous combustion engine 连续燃烧发动机（如：燃气轮机）

continuous cruising power （发动机的）持续定速运转最大功率（指在标准环境条件下，以标定的转速允许长期连续运行的最大有效功率，简称 continuous power，持续功率）

continuous-delivery measurement type injector test bench 喷油量连续测试型喷油器试验台

continuous drive transmission 连续驱动式变速器（换挡时动力不中断的变速器，参见 power-shift transmission）

continuous dryer 连续（作用）干燥器（= continuous drier）

continuous duty ①连续运转工况，②连续工作制度

continuous exhaust gas analysis 废气连续分析，排气连续分析

continuous exhaust variable timing mechanism 连续可变排气正时机构（简称 CEVTM）

continuous exposure 连续暴露（如：露天大气环境下），持续暴露（试验）

continuous film 连续膜，连续油膜（不断开的油膜）

continuous flow combustion systems （外燃机等的）连续燃烧系统

continuous fuel injection 汽油连续喷射

continuous grade 连续坡度，长坡

continuous hydrocarbon analyzer 连续式 HC 分析仪，连续式 HC 测定仪

continuous injection system 连续燃油喷射系（简称 CIS，分机械式与电子控制式两类，无特别说明时，一般指机械式，见 K-Jetronic）

continuous injection system-electronic 电子控制式连续汽油喷射系（简称 CIS-E，波许公司生产，油泵将汽油泵入燃油分配器供给各汽缸的喷油嘴，将汽油喷至进气门附近，它的特点是在发动机运转过程中连续不停地喷油，故名）

continuous injection system-Lambda 带氧传感器的电子控制连续汽油喷射系统（该系统在 CIS-E 的基础上增加氧传感器-催化转化闭路控制功能，简称 CIS-Lambda）

continuously operating actuator 连续作用式执行器（如：用于调制液压的执行机构）

continuously regenerative-trap system （柴油机微粒排放物的）连续再生捕集系统（简称 CRT system，在这一类微粒排放物捕集系统中装有氧化催化剂，利用废气自身的热量连续烧净捕集器滤件捕集到的炭微粒排放物，但对废气的排放温度有一定要求，而且是必须使用含硫量低的燃油。有的这一类系统不使用催化剂而是在燃油中掺加添加剂，降低滤件积炭的着火温度，也可达到同样的目的。不论用什么方法这一类系统都是在捕集器内清除掉炭微粒排放物，故亦称 internal regenerating trap 或 self-regenerating system）

continuously tracked vehicle 履带车辆

continuously variable 无级变化的（参见 infinitely variable）

continuously variable (intake) valve timing 连续可变（进）气门正时（机构），简称 CVVT，亦写作 continuous variable valve timing

continuously variable (ratio) transmission 无级变速器,连续变速装置(泛指速比可作连续无级变化的变速机构,但目前多指由一个可变工作半径的主动传动带轮、与之相配的从动传动带轮和V形传动带组成的无级变速器,简称CVT,亦称variable belt transmission 或 constant variable transmission, continuously variable unit, infinitely variable transmission, stepless transmission)

continuous maximum power (发动机的)持续运转最大功率(允许发动机在标准环境条件下,以标定转速长期连续运转的最大有效功率, = maximum cruising power)

continuous operation limit 连续运转极限(允许长期连续运转时间,如:起动机的连续运转极限为30s)

continuous output (rating) 持续输出功率(参见 continuous maximum power)

continuous production operation sheet 连续生产作业图表,流水作业图表(简称CPOS)

continuous sampling 连续取样,连续采样(简称CS,如:在发动机废气分析中连续不断地采取废气试样并连续测试, = dynamic sampling)

continuous service brake 见 continuous braking system

continuous side ring 轮辋整体式挡圈

continuous spray pump (汽油连续喷射系统中的)连续喷油泵

continuous torque 持续工作转矩,持续运转转矩(= sustained operating torque)

continuous wave(s) 连续波

conti tyre system 康泰轮胎系统(简称CTS,商品名,一种新型轮胎抗爆破设计,轮胎爆破后仍能以80km/h行驶400km)

contour ①外形,轮廓 ②等高线 ③划轮廓线

contour flow 见 body line

contour line ①轮廓线 ②等高线,恒值线

contracting band brake 收紧式带式制动器

contracting brake 收紧式制动器,抱闸式制动器

contracting chuck 收缩夹头

contracting spring 拉簧

contraction 收缩,收缩作用,收缩量

contraction cavity 缩孔

contraction crack 见 check crack

contractor ①压缩装置,压装工具,(如:将活塞环装入汽缸筒内用的压箍)②承包商,承包人

contradiction 对立,不一致,矛盾

contra-flow ①逆流,反向流动 ②反向电流

contraflow (双车道的一侧车道因维修而关闭时原单向行驶的另一侧的车道)双向行驶

contra-injection 反向喷射,逆向喷油

contrarotation 反(向旋)转,反向转动

contrary ①相反的 ②相反,反面

contrary sign 异号

contrary wind 逆风(参见 adverse wind)

contrast ①对比,对照,对照中的差别,对照物显著的不同,对照法,对比法 ②对比的

contrasting (车身式样、颜色等)极不相同的,迥异的

contrast ratio ①(亮度)对比度(指亮态与暗态亮度之比"highlight-to-low-light ratio")②对比度系数,反差比

contrast rendering factor 对比显现因素(简称CRF,指在给定的照明

系统下的可见度与在参照照明条件下的可见度比，评价照明系统的一个因素）

contrast sensitivity 对比感受性（指可知觉的最小光亮差度，即阈限对比的倒数，亦称对比敏感度，参见 threshold contrast）

contrate gear 端面齿盘（顶锥角与根锥角均为90°的锥齿轮或准双曲面齿轮，= contrate wheel）

contrate gear pair 圆柱齿轮-端面齿盘副（由端面齿盘及与之配对的圆柱齿轮组成，轴交角成90°相交或交错的齿副）

contravariant bridge circuit of three-phase and double-electrode 三相双极性逆变桥式电路

contravariant device 逆变器（可将直流电逆变为三相交流电的装置）

contravariant pipe 逆变管

contre pente （车轮）轮辋胎圈座（上的）内凸缘（用于将气压不足的轮胎胎圈卡在胎圈座上，防止胎圈滑入轮辋槽内，多见于法国产轿车，简称CP，仅在轮辋向外的一侧有这凸缘的称 outboard contre pente，两边都有的称CP2）

contrivance ①工具，用具，设置，装置 ②发明，创造；设计方案

control ①控制，操纵 ②控制装置，控制系统

control algorithm 控制算法（指控制动作的数学表示或过程设计）

control apparatus 调节装置，控制装置，调整设备

control area network 控制区（内的）局域网

control arm 控制臂（①泛指各种起控制作用的臂件 ②在汽车悬架中，特指连接车轮与车身或车架的确定车轮位置及控制或限制车轮的摆动、跳动等运动幅度的各种臂件。一般是一端连接车身或车架，一端连接轮毂，有多种形状、布置方式和连接形式，亦称摆臂"swing arm"简称arm。由于它无论制成何种形状，本质上是车轮与车身或车架的连接杆件，故不少文献直接将其称为连杆"link"）

control arm console （悬架）控制臂的支撑架（亦称 rocker arm console）

control bench ①控制台，操纵台（亦称 control desk）②（质量）控制（工序的）检验台

control board 控制板

control button 控制按钮

control cable 控制索，操纵索（= ［美］ control wire）

control circuit trigger 控制电路触发器

control cycle 控制循环（某一控制过程的完整周期）

control diaphragm return spring 控制膜片回位弹簧

control failure 操纵（系统）失效

control field （汽车计算机控制系统存储器中的）控制字段（用于存储何时执行特定操作的命令的区域）

control fork ①控制叉（泛指各种叉形控制杆件、拨叉等）②（特指柴油机柱塞式喷油泵的拨叉式油量调节机构的装在调节拉杆上、拨动柱塞尾部的调节臂使柱塞转动的叉形零件）调节叉

control frequency 控制频率（每秒的控制周期数）

control gauge 校准量规，标准块规

control gear 操纵机构，控制机构

control handle 操纵杆，控制旋柄，控制手柄

Control-iDrive 控制—智能驾驶（宝马新7系列中可控制700多项功能的控制装置的商品名）

controllability 可控制性

controllablehead-lighting system 照射光束可控前照灯照明系统

controllable hydropneumatic suspension system 可控型液压气动悬架系统（其阻尼特性可由电子控制模块控制，在硬模式"firm mode"和软模式"soft mode"间变化的油气悬架系统）

controlled auto ignition petrol engine 见 CAI petrol engine

controlled burn rate process 见 CBR process

controlled-collapse solution （车辆发生碰撞时，防止转向盘轴柱等伤害驾驶人员而采取的）受控可压折式解决方案

controlled combustion system 控制燃烧系统（简称 CCS，美国通用公司商品名，包括①改良型燃烧室②高温冷却条③恒温控制空气滤清器④超稀混合气⑤高怠速⑥大点火延迟角⑦TCS 和 TVS 等项排放控制措施）

controlled environmental test chamber 可控环境条件试验室，受控人工环境试验室

controlled high traction differential 可控式高牵引力差速器（防滑差速器的一种，见 controlled slip differential）

controlled nonlinear semiconductor resistor 可控非线性半导体电阻器（指可控硅整流元件，可控硅开关元件，可控硅）

controlled separation layer 受控剥离层（由于车身外形的轮廓线的突变等造成的与车身表面剥离的气流边界层）

controlled slip differential 防滑差速器 [= limited-slip differential，种类很多，但都是通过控制锁止作用借以增大锁止系数"differential locking factor"的方法，防止驱动车轮滑转，充分利用路面附着力，以提高其驱动能力，因而又称为 controlled (high) traction differential。按其锁止方式，分为强制锁止式差速器 locking differential 和自锁式差速器 self-locking differential 两大类]

controlled suspension （指刚度可控的）受控变刚度悬架

controlled test 受控试验（试验参数及试验条件可由试验者按需要主动控制）

controlled-turbulence combustion 控制扰动燃烧

controlled variable 受控变量，可控变量

controlled vehicle 指装有减少废气有害物排放系统的车辆，亦称 detoxicated vehicle 或 detoxed vehicle

controlled weight transfer 受控重力转移

controller ①控制器（监控信息传输和系统运转的装置；能处理传感器信息并发出控制指令的装置）②控制件（如：控制杆等）③管理员，主管人

controller area network 见 CAN

controller chip 控制器芯片

control lever ①控制手柄，控制杆，操纵手柄②（美）（自动变速器的）换挡手柄

control lever shaft 操纵轴（由手柄转动的控制轴）

control limit 检验时允许的偏差极限，检验公差范围；控制极限

control line ①（泛指）各种传递控制信号、控制动力的管路和线路②见 brake line

controlling means ①（控制系统的）控制方法，控制手段②（净化系统的）净化措施，净化方法

control module （电子）控制模块（在汽车电子控制系统中，指执行某项控制任务的车用电子计算机"on-board computer"。如：SAEJ1930 术语标准中规定车用发动机计算机称为 power control module，简称

PCM)

control monitor unit 监控装置（简称CMU）

control orifice 控制孔（真空或气压控制信号的引出孔）

control pinion （柴油机柱塞式喷油泵齿杆式油量调节装置的）调节齿圈（指装在控制套筒上，与调节齿杆啮合的齿圈）

control piston cup 控制活塞皮碗

control plunger （燃油喷射系统的喷油量）控制柱塞

control pressure （来自液压、气压管道压力）控制压力（包括正、负压力）

control rack （柴油机柱塞式喷油泵齿杆式油量调节机构的）调节齿杆（与调节齿套或调节齿圈啮合的调节杆，其轴向位置由调速器控制）

control rack travel sensor （柴油机柱塞喷油泵的）喷油量调节齿条行程传感器

control regulation 管理规程，操纵规范，管理规章

control response 控制灵敏度（对控制指令响应的快慢程度）

control ring （活塞刮）油环（= oil-scraper ring）

control rod ①（柴油机柱塞式喷油泵拨叉式油量调节机构的）调节拉杆（调节叉装在该杆上，其轴向位置由调整器控制）②（各种）控制杆件

control room 调度室，操纵间，控制室

controls ①控制杆系②控制件③控制装置

control sleeve gear （柴油机柱塞式喷油泵齿杆式油量调节机构的）调节齿套（上部有齿与调节齿杆啮合，下部有槽带动柱塞转动，亦称control sleeve）

control speed accessory drive （汽车发动机曲轴皮带盘与风扇皮带盘间的）变速附件驱动装置（简称CS-AD）

control stalk （转向盘下方，由转向管柱伸出的，装有灯光、刮水器、转向灯、喇叭等的开关或按钮的）控制柄

control strategy 控制策略（控制软件提供的控制程序和控制模式）

control structure （计算机控制系统的）控制模式［= pattern of control, 车用系统一般有looping（闭环）、sequence（顺序）和selecton（选择）控制等］

control surface （液体动力学的）操纵面，控制面

control techniques ①控制技术②（大气污染的）净化措施，净化技术③（噪声的）静化技术

control-trac four-wheel-drive system 牵引力控制式四轮驱动系统（可自动感知车轮打滑，并根据需要减小打滑轮上的驱动力，增加非打滑轮的驱动力，简称control Trac 4WD system有自动"auto"，高"high"，低"low"三种模式）

control unit ①控制器②见control module

control valve air conditioning system 控制阀式空调系统（指一经运转其压缩机和离合器便不再分离，而由各种控制阀来控制运转工况的车用空调系统）

control valve assembly 控制阀总成（如：装有自动变速器液压系大部分控制阀的铸件或冲压件，亦称hydraulic control block "控制阀组合体"）

control valve body （制动真空增压器的）控制阀体

controversial 有争议的，有争论的

convection ①对流②对流传热

convection current 对流，对流热流，

对流气流,对流电流
convection oven 对流恒温器,对流加热炉(简称 convector)
convector 热空气循环对流加热器,对流加热机(使空气经过热表面而变热的取暖设备)
convenience ①方便②(方便的或可带来方便的)用具,机械,装置,设备
convention ①(社团的)会议(一般指为某一目的而召开的大会)②协定③惯例
conventional ①常规的,传统的,普通的,按惯例,约定俗成的②协议的
conventional cab 常规驾驶室(一般指货车的长头驾驶室,= cab over engine)
conventional engine anti-pollution system 往复式发动机排气净化系统(的总称,简称 CEAPS,以别于转子发动机排气净化系)
conventional linear motor 常规直线电动机(一种特殊形成的感应电动机,其定子和转子不是圆柱而是直线状,不是同心的而是平行的)
conventionally leaded gasoline 常规含铅汽油(美国联邦汽油技术规范,指添加含铅抗爆剂后之含铅量,为每升 0.13~1.12g 的汽油)
conventional oil 普通机油,无添加剂的机油
conventional Otto engine 常规奥托循环发动机(指均质充气汽油机,以区别于 stratified charge Otto engine)
conventional section tyre 普通断面轮胎(指断面的高-宽比为 0.89 以上的充气轮胎)
conventional strain 公称应变
conventional test 常规试验,标准试验
conventional theory 传统理论

conventional tractor 常规型(指长头型)牵引车
converge ①集中(于一点),聚集,会聚,汇合②收敛
convergence ①收敛(如:汽车在有操纵输入或外部扰动输入时,横摆运动响应的收敛性,指汽车以一定车速行驶,突然转动转向盘并立即撒手,汽车的横摆角速度曲线呈振荡式单调型收敛性,最终回复为零的特性)②会聚,集中,会合,聚集③聚焦
convergency of (the) front wheels 前轮前束
convergent beam 聚光光束
convergent lens 放大镜,聚光透镜(亦称 converging lens)
convergent mode of motion 收敛性衰减运动模式
convergent modulation (液力变矩器的)收敛性调节(换挡滞后随节气门的开度增加而减少的换挡规律)
convergent nozzle 收敛形喷嘴
converse piezoelectric activity 反压电作用(压电晶体在电场作用下变形)
converse piezoelectric effect 反压电效应
conversion ①转变,改变,变化,变换②改装,改装用部件③变形
conversion chart 换算表
conversion coating (金属制件的)表面渗层(如渗碳层等)
conversion constant 转换常数(如热功当量)
conversion curve 变换曲线,换算曲线
conversion diagram 换算图表,变换特性曲线
conversion efficiency 转化效率(如:催化转化器的有害成分转化为无害成分的比率)
conversion factor 换算因数,变换系

数,转换系数,换算系数(= conversion coefficient, conversion ratio)

conversion hardware (车辆等的)改装硬件

conversion kit 改装用的成套部件

conversion rate 转化率(指催化转化器净化废气流的速率)

conversion table 换算表,换位表(= conversion chart)

convert 转变,变换,改变

converted traffic 换乘交通量(改换交通手段所增加的交通量,如:由其他交通工具改乘公共汽车时,所增加的交通量)

converter 起转变、变换、转化作用的装置(如:自动变速系的变矩器,废气催化转化器,改变频率的变频器,以及相位变换器,脉冲转换器,电器的转接头,汽车的能量存储转换系统,计算机的模-数转换器等)

converter case (自动变速器)变矩器泵轮带腔壳总成(由泵轮和焊在它上面的腔壳体组成,由曲轴驱动。变矩器的全部叶轮及变速器工作油液均装在该腔壳所形成的密闭空腔内)

converter clutch assembly 变矩器-离合器总成(由四个主要部件:液力变矩器、锁止离合器、单向离合器、换挡离合器组成)

converter clutch control valve 见 CCC valve

converter clutch regulator valve 见 CCRV

converter coupling range 两相式液力变矩器的耦合相(指其变矩比为 1 的工作范围。变矩比大于 1 的工作范围称变矩相"torque conversion range",二者的转换点称耦合点"coupling point")

converter cover (与变矩器泵轮焊在一起的)变矩器腔壳

converter dolly (一般货车拖挂半挂车时使用的)转接挂车(为一只装有鞍式牵引座的单轴全挂车,半挂车的车头支在该牵引座上,便可由一般货车拖走)

converter housing ①自动变速器变矩器不动的外壳 ②催化转化器外壳(亦称 converter shell)

converter lockout 见 converter lockup

converter lockup 液力变矩器锁止(锁止离合器接合,实现由动液传动向机械传动的转换,= converter lockout)

converter phase 变矩相,变矩器相(见 converter range)

converter pressure limit valve 变矩器限压阀

converter pressure regulator valve 液力变矩器调压阀(调节液力变矩器控制系统压力的阀)

converter range (两相式液力变矩器的)变矩范围(指变矩导向元件固定不动,输出转矩与输入转矩之比 >1 时的工作区域,= torque convertion range,亦称 converter phase "变矩相")

converter speed ratio (液力变矩器的)变速比(即涡轮转速与泵轮转速之比)

converter stall speed 变矩器零速度,变速器失速点(指在一定输入转矩下,涡轮不动时的输入转速)

converter torque ratio (液力变矩器的)变矩比(即输出转矩与输入转矩之比)

converter-transmission drive 液力机械传动

converter vehicle 储能式车辆(如:利用飞轮系统存能的车辆等,简称 CVT vehicle)

convertible ①(指装有可折叠的软篷车顶或可卸下的硬顶、软顶折叠或硬顶卸下后即可变成敞篷车

"open car"的）活顶轿车（亦称 convertible car, 简称 CV 或 CVT, conv。其中两门者，称 convertible coupe 或 convertible cabriolet，四门者，称 convertible sedan 或 four door cabriolet) ②（[美]上述软篷活顶车的）软篷（一般由帆布或人造织物制成 = convertible top）③（指行驶机构可变换的）两用车（如：轮胎可换成履带的货车等）④可改换的，可调换的，可变换的，活动的

convertible gas-diesel engine ①可转换式煤气-柴油发动机（经过适当改装即可用柴油而不用煤气）②柴油-煤气双燃料机（以煤气作为主要燃料，柴油作为点火燃料，亦可单纯用柴油作燃料，参见 dual fuel engine, gas-diesel engine)

convertible hard top （车身的）活动硬顶

convertible modular machine 多功能组合式机床

convertible sedan 四门活顶轿车（=[美] cabriolet sedan 或 [英] four door cabriolet, cabriolet saloon [英]）

convertible shovel 两用铲（正反铲）挖土机

convertible top （[美]通常轿车带后窗的）尼龙或帆布等可折叠敞篷车顶（= collapsible top)

convertible top system （敞篷车的）活动顶篷系统

convertible trailer ①易改装的通用挂车（容易改装成运输各种货物）②折合顶篷式敞篷挂车

Conv-EV 传统型电动汽车（conventional electric vehicle 的简称，相对于轮内驱动型电动汽车"IWD-EV"而言）

convex ①中凸的，凸形的，凸面的，凸的；球面形凸起的②凸面，凸状面，球形凸面，凸圆体③钢卷尺

convex cam 凸面凸轮，圆弧凸轮（= convex flank cam）

convex-concave 一面凸一面凹的，凸凹的

convex exterior mirror 外置凸面（后视）镜

convex head piston 凸顶活塞（= dome head piston)

convex head valve 凸头气门

convexity 凸（出高）度，凸起，向上弯曲度，中凸凸状，凸形，凸性

convex lens 凸透镜

convex offset wheel 凸面偏位圆盘车轮（轮辋胎圈座与中心面不在同一平面内）

convey 输送，运输，传送

conveyance ①运输工具，运输车辆 ②运送，运输，搬运，传播

conveying belt 传送带（参见 conveyer belt）

conveyor 输送机，输送器，传送设备，传送装置，传送带（= conveyer)

conveyor chain 传送链

convoy condition 车辆列队行驶状况（成群车辆维持一定顺序和车间距离列队行驶的状况）

COO 首席经营官（chief operating officer 的简称）

cook 烧焦，滑油等烧成积炭

cool ①冷的，凉的，冷藏的，有冷藏设备的②（数额等）整的

coolant 冷却剂，冷却液（目前，一般指加有各种添加剂的水和防冻液的混合液）

coolant analysis service 冷却水分析故障诊断法（对冷却水成分进行定期分析，以诊断发动机的状态）

coolant indicator 冷却液水位与温度指示器，冷却液温度表

coolant level warning light 冷却水液面警报灯，冷却水量警报灯（当冷却水量减少到低于某规定的液面高

度时，该警报灯亮）

coolant over-temperature light 冷却水温过热警报灯

coolant temperature override switch 冷却水温控制式超越开关

coolant temperature sensor 冷却水温度传感器（简称 CTS，见 ECT）

CoolCoat technology （德国 SGSI 公司的防日晒车窗玻璃，可反射 60% 的日照热量而使车内保持较低温度的）凉盾技术（这种玻璃称为 CoolCoat glass 或 heat management glass）

cooled EGR （柴油机 NO_x 排放对策的）冷废气再循环

cooler ①散热器，冷却器，冷凝器②冷却剂；冷却液③（汽车车身的）空调装置（= air conditioner）④（食物等储存用的）冰箱

coolers tat （冷却水温）节温器，调温器，恒温器

cool flame 冷焰

cooling agent 冷却剂（= cooling agency）

cooling gill 冷却叶片，散热片（= cooling fin, cooling rib, radiation gill）

cooling heat loss 冷却热损失（指燃料发出的热量中，被冷却介质带走的份额，以百分比表示，简称 cooling loss）

cooling hole in the radial direction （通风盘式制动器的）径向冷却孔

cooling interval 冷却间隔时间；冷却所需时间

cooling-jacket 冷却水套（= water jacket）

cooling liquid 冷却液

cooling system 冷却系

cooling tan 冷却风扇

cooling test （冷却剂）冷却（能力）试验

cooling water additive 冷却水添加剂（防冻、防蚀或防漏剂等）

cooling water capacity 冷却水容量（一台内燃机冷却系所能容纳的水量）

cooperative ①合作的，协作的，协调的②配合的，协助的③使各方作为一个整体相互协调配合、协调行动的（控制系统等）④共同拥有、共同经营、利益共享的（公司、合作社等）

cooperative chassis control 底盘（各系统的）协同控制

cooperative-vehicle driving safety support system （包括车间、车路间通信及行人、障碍物等探测信息等的）协调型车辆安全行驶支援系统

coordinate ①坐标②坐标系（= coordinate system）③协调

coordinate angle 坐标角

coordinate axis 坐标轴

coordinated accident rescue system 事故协作救援系统，事故救济协作体系

coordinated control 联动控制

coordinates fixed on road 路面固定坐标系（亦称 road-fixed axis system，指固定在路面上的直角坐标系）

coordinates fixed on vehicle 车辆固定坐标系（亦称 vehicle-fixed axis system）

COP 计算机控制脉冲（计算机操作脉冲，computer operated pulses 的简称）

copilot ①自动驾驶装置，自动驾驶仪②副驾驶员

copolyester elastomer 共聚脂弹性材料

copolymer 共聚物，异分子聚合物，协聚合物

copolymerization 共聚反应，共聚作用，异分子聚合（作用）

copper ①铜（Gu，紫铜，红铜）②铜器，铜制品③铜的，铜制的，

铜色的 ④ 用铜皮包，用铜板盖，镀铜

copper-asbestos 铜石棉的，铜皮包石棉的（亦写作 = copper-asbestus）

copper base alloy 铜基合金

copper-coated 镀铜的，包铜的（copper facing, copper plated, copper clad, coppered）

copper core ①（火花塞的）铜中心电极②（高压线芯）铜芯

copper-cored lead 铜芯线

copper facing 见 copper plating

copper/glass gas-tight seal （火花塞的）铜/玻璃气密封件

copper-graphite 铜-石墨的

copper internal washer （火花塞绝缘体与软钢壳间的）内密封钢垫圈

copper lead 耐酸铜铅合金（= acid lead）

copper-loaded 装在铜制容器内的

copper loss 铜损，铜绕组损耗

copper-nickel alloy 铜镍合金

copper-oxide glue 氧化铜黏结剂（由氧化铜和无水磷酸调和而成，可耐 600℃ 的高温）

copperoxide rectifier 氧化铜整流器

copper plate （厚度 < 0.5mm 的）薄铜板，铜皮，紫铜皮

copper plated brush 表面镀铜的电刷

copper strip test 铜片（腐蚀）试验（根据铜片被腐蚀的程度，检验燃油内腐蚀性硫化物的含量）

copper sulphate 硫酸铜（$CuSO_4$）

corbel ①梁托,梁翅,撑架②托、撑

cord ①绳、索、线、缆、带②cords（轮胎的）帘线

cord angle 帘线角（一般指胎体帘布层帘线与胎面中心线的夹角，亦称 cord crown angle）

cord breaker 见 breaker①

cord drive 圆皮带传动，绳索传动（= rope drive）

cord fabric （轮胎）帘布

cordless tyre 无帘线轮胎（胎体不用帘布层的充气轮胎）

cord line （传动带等的）帘线，帘线层

cord ply 轮胎帘布层（= cord layer, 常简称 ply）

cordwood system 积木式（器件的组合方式）

core ①芯子，中心部分②（液力变矩器或耦合器任一叶轮单元的）内环（特指任一叶轮上循环圆的内壁，参见 torus section）③铁心，磁芯④散热器芯子⑤型芯，坭芯⑥（电缆）芯线⑦装填料，装填物

core cooled piston 铸有冷却油道的油冷活塞

cored channel 铸出的通道

cored for lightness 为减少质量而制成空心的

core diameter （螺纹）内径；（螺杆等）杆芯直径

cored out 利用砂芯铸成空心的，砂芯铸造出的空心的，砂芯铸空的

core means of transport 核心运输工具，主要的运输工具

core pin ①中心销，型孔栓②（继电器）线圈铁心

core plug ①（缸体水套上的）防裂塞片（冷却水结冻膨胀时所产生的压力可将该塞片推出，而防止水套冻裂 = [美] freeze plug）②泥芯孔堵头

core-type radiator 蜂窝式散热器，芯型散热器

coriolis force 科里奥利力（既自转又公转的旋转体表面上形成切向力和离心效应力，亦称 geostrophic force）

cork ①软木，软木塞，管塞，栓②软木制的③塞住,用塞子塞住

corner 角，棱角，角落，（道路）转角，拐角；转弯

4-corner air suspension 四轮空气悬架，全轮空气悬架

corner brace 角支柱，角筋（臂），斜撑，角拉条

corner curvature information sensor （车辆主动性导航系统的）弯道曲率信息传感器

cornered piston ring 带沉肩的扭曲活塞环

corner fillet 角镶，填角块

corner fitting 角部附件，包角件；（集装箱等的）角件（装在箱的四角，具有供安装或起吊用的孔洞）

corner impact 角碰撞（对汽车四角的碰撞）

cornering 转向，拐弯，转弯

cornering ability ①（轮胎的）抗侧偏能力（亦称 cornering capacity，常用侧偏刚度表示，见 cornering stiffness）②（车辆的）转弯能力（指车辆以合理的速度安全转弯，车身不致发生侧翻和侧滑的能力，= turning ability，亦称转弯稳定性 cornering stability）

cornering aid construction （汽车的）助转结构（用于改善汽车转弯特性）

cornering breakaway 转向时车轮脱离地面

cornering characteristics （轮胎的）转弯力特性，侧偏特性（亦称 cornering behavior，cornering performance，cornering properties，见 cornering force）

cornering coefficient （轮胎的）转弯力系数（指轮胎每单位垂直负荷下的比转弯力，即：转弯力/侧偏角/垂直负荷，参见 cornering power，我国亦称轮胎的侧偏阻力系数、侧向反作用力系数）

cornering drag 侧偏（滚动）阻力（见 cornering force）

cornering effect （轮胎的）抗侧偏作用，转弯力效应（一般用轮胎的比转弯力来表示，参见 cornering stiffness）

cornering force （汽车的）转弯力[当车轮受外来横向力时，由于车轮弹性及其与地面的摩擦，致使车轮横向变形、形成一定的侧偏角而产生的对外来横向力的反作用力，即：车轮外倾角0°时，为保持该侧偏力，由路面作用在车轮上的横向力。该力分成两个分力，一个为与滚动方向相反的水平分力，称侧偏（滚动）阻力，即 cornering drag，另一个为与滚动方向垂直的水平分力，后者起向心力的作用，使汽车能够转弯，故称转弯力，国外有人称为：frictional-reaction, slip angle force, steering force, tire cornering force, cornering resistance, lateral control force 等，我国亦称偏扭力、拐弯力、侧偏力、侧向反作用力、横偏阻力等]

cornering lamp 转向照明灯（补充前照灯在转向方向上的照明）

cornering power 见 cornering stiffness

cornering ratio 侧向力系数，拐弯比（拐弯时离心力与车辆质量的比值）

cornering resistance ①侧偏阻力（= cornering drag，见 cornering force）②发动机用于克服汽车转向行驶所产生的阻力增加的输出

cornering speed （汽车的）转弯车速

cornering stability 见 cornering ability

cornering stiffness 侧偏刚度（轮胎侧偏角的单位增量所对应的横向力的增量，通常指在轮胎侧偏角为0°时的测定值，= cornering power）

cornering stiffness coefficient 侧偏刚度系数（车轮侧偏刚度与垂直负荷的比值）

cornering tire squeal 转弯时轮胎噪声，轮胎转弯噪声

cornering tire traction 转向时轮胎的

牵引力（即与 cornering drag 方向相反的力，简称 cornering traction）

cornering wear （轮胎）转弯磨损，拐弯磨耗

corner lamp 角灯，侧灯，前小灯

corner panel （车身的）角板；包角板

corner pillar 角柱（= corner post）

corner seals （转子发动机的）角密封装置（将径向密封装置和端面密封装置连接在一起的角端密封系统）

corner steady （旅居车驻车后车身四角的悬臂千斤顶支撑）角撑

cornice （车身）檐板，檐条，雨水槽，雨檐，檐边（亦称 gutter channel, roof drip moulding, rain channel, drip guard rail）

corona discharge 电晕放电

corona ignition 电晕放电点火

corona-resistant 防电晕放电的，电晕放电电阻的

Corporate Average Emissions Figure [美]公司平均废气有害物排出量（简称 CAEF，取公司生产的全部车型的有害物排出量的平均值作为检测标准，计算方法类似于 CAFE）

corporate average fuel economy [美]公司平均油耗，公司平均燃油经济性（指政府对各汽车制造公司生产的各种车型的平均燃料经济性标准，如 1991 年为 27.5miles/gal，即 8.5L/100km，简称 CAFE）

corral 用多辆汽车围成的圈

correct ①校正，修正，校准②正确的，合格的，符合标准的，恰当的，对的

corrected brake horsepower 换算有效功率，修正有效功率（将实测的发动机有效功率换算成标准大气状态下的功率，见 observed brake power）

corrected for CO_2 extraction CO_2 干扰校正（在计算 CO 浓度时排除 CO_2 对 CO 分析仪干扰的校正）

corrected for water vapor extraction 水蒸气干扰校正（在计算 CO 浓度时排除水蒸气对 CO 分析仪干扰的校正）

corrected result 已修正结果（指对系统误差作必要的修正而获得的测量结果）

corrected specific fuel consumption 换算（为标准条件下）的比油耗

correction ①校正，修正，改正，校准②校正值，修正值（为补偿系统误差，以代数加法加于未修正的测量结果的一个值）

correction factor 修正因子（为补偿系统误差而对未修正测量结果所乘的数值因子）

corrective maintenance 校正性维修（指通过校正性保养实现的功能恢复性维修）

corrector 校正器，校正电路

correlation 相互关系，相关（性），相应，对比关系，交互作用，对比

correlation coefficient 相关系数

correlation graph 相关（曲线）图

correlation test 相关性试验

correlation tracking and range 无线电跟踪定位系统，相关跟踪测距系统（简称 COTAR）

correring squeal （车轮）转向时产生的啸声

correspond ①相当，对等，相符，符合②通信

corresponding angles 同位角，对应角

corresponding flanks （齿轮的）同侧齿面（指各个左侧齿面或各右侧齿面）

corridor ①通道（如客车座位的中间通道）②走廊（如两城市间的交通运输走廊）

corrode 腐蚀，侵蚀，锈蚀

corrodibility 腐蚀性

corronium 轴承铜合金（铜80%，锌15%，锡5%）
corrosion 腐蚀，侵蚀，锈蚀
corrosion control ①防腐蚀，防腐蚀措施（= corrosion prevention 或 protection）②防腐蚀件
corrosion cracking 腐蚀断裂，锈蚀缝裂
corrosion current （金属的）腐蚀电流
corrosion fatigue 腐蚀疲劳，锈蚀疲劳（材料在腐蚀环境和循环应力的复合作用下而导致疲劳破坏的现象）
corrosion inhibitor 防腐蚀剂，防锈剂
corrosion product 腐蚀生成物，锈蚀产物
corrosion-proof 防腐的，耐蚀的，不蚀的
corrosion remover 除锈剂，防蚀剂，防腐剂
corrosion resistance 见 corrosion strength
corrosion-resistant 防腐的，耐蚀的，不锈的
corrosion-resistant steel 耐蚀钢，不锈钢（亦称 stainless steel）
corrosion strength 耐腐蚀强度，抗腐蚀强度（= corrosion resistance）
corrosive ①腐蚀性的，侵蚀性的，生锈的②腐蚀剂，腐蚀性物质
corrosive lading 对车箱有腐蚀作用的货物
corrosive wear 腐蚀性磨损（在化学或电化学反应明显的介质中产生的磨损）
corrugated brass boot 皱纹铜皮（防尘）罩
corrugated deck （货车车身的）波纹状底板
corrugated elastic sleeve 波形挠性套
corrugated fin 皱纹状（散热）片，波纹状金属薄片
corrugated road 搓板路（①专门修筑路面成波浪状的试验跑道②在使用过程中由于车轮碾压造成的高低不平呈波浪状路面的道路）
corrugated track 搓板路面的试验道路
corrugated tube 波纹管（= caterpillar tube）
corsa mode （跑车、赛车等的行驶模式之一的）赛道-手动换挡行驶模式
Corson alloy 柯松合金（Cu-Ni-Si 系合金）
Corten-Dolan Theory （根据累计损坏来估算疲劳寿命的）葛坦-多兰理论
corubin 人造刚玉，合成刚玉，人造金刚砂（= synthetic corundum）
corundum 金刚砂（Al_2O_3），刚玉，刚石（研磨剂）
Corvett 克尔维特（[美]通用公司雪佛兰部跑车名）
cosine-cam wave generator 余弦凸轮波发生器（指以余弦变化规律作为凸轮基本轮廓的积极控制式波发生器）
cost ①成本②价格，费用
COST 污油沉淀槽（contaminated oil settling tank 的简称）
cost account 成本核算
cost-benefit analysis 成本-效益分析
cost-cutting 降低成本（的）
cost-effective 成本低的，费用少的
cost-effectiveness analysis (method) 成本-效果分析（法）[工程经济分析（法）之一]
cost-estimate 成本估算，费用估计
cost-free 免费（= free of cost）
coston light 三角信号灯
cost option （新车的）收费选购件
cost per passenger trip 人次（乘车）成本（每人乘车一次的运行成本等）

Cotal gearbox （一种）预选式半自动电控变速器

COTAR 相关跟踪测距系统（correlation tracking and range 的简称）

COTS 检验测试设备（check out test set）

cottar 见 cotter

cotter ①栓销，制销，开口销，开尾销，楔形销②用销固定，用栓固定（=cottar)

cotter bolt 带锁销的螺栓

cottered 用销，栓关紧的

cotter(ed) pin ①具有切口的定位导销，楔槽定位导销②开口销，开尾销（=split pin)

cotton ①棉花，棉织品，棉纱，棉布②棉织品的，棉纱的

cotton covered 纱布包起的，纱包绝缘的

cotton string filter element 棉线滤芯；棉绳滤芯

cotton wood filter 棉绒滤芯滤清器

couch ①底层，层，床②长沙发椅③休息处④底漆，油漆底层⑤压出，含有⑥层的，多层的

coulomb 库（仑）（国际单位制的电荷，电量单位，代号 C 或 Q)

coulomb damping 库仑阻尼，干摩擦阻尼

coulometer 库仑表，库仑计，电量计，电量表（=coulomb-meter）

count 计数，计算

countdown ①递减计数，倒计时，倒数读秒（从大到小倒计数，如 5，4，3…）②（雷达）回答脉冲比，反射脉冲比（发射脉冲数与回答脉冲总数之比，简称 CD）③读，示度④读数漏失

counter ①计数器（在计算机控制系统中累计事件发生次数的寄存器或存储单元；当计算输入脉冲数达到规定的数量后产生一个输出脉冲）②计算器，计量器，测量器③相反物，反面④一对中之一⑤副轴，中间轴⑥相反的，对立的，逆的，副的⑦对抗，反抗，抵消

counter acting force 反作用力

counteraction ①反作用（力）②抵消

counterbalance ①平衡重，平衡块（=balance weight）②使与…平衡

counterbalance valve 背压阀，平衡阀

counterbore（=countersink）①（用平底扩孔钻）扩孔，（平底）锪孔，镗阶梯孔；钻埋头孔 ②平底扩孔钻，平头钻，平底锪钻③埋头孔，锥口孔，沉孔

counterbored piston ring 内沉肩扭曲活塞环

counterbuffer 缓冲器，阻尼器

counterclockwise 逆时针方向（简称 CCKW，=left-handed）

counter current 反向电流，逆流

counter-down 脉冲分频器

counter emf 见 back emf

counter engine wise 与发动机旋转方向相反

counterfeit(ing) part 伪造零件，冒牌零件（对应词为 real part）

counter fire 逆火

counter flange 对接凸缘

counter-flow 逆流（式）的，对向流（的）

counter gear 见 countershaft gear

counter mark （装配用的）对合标记

countermeasure(s) 对策，防范措施

counter part 一对中的一个（两个相互匹配件中的一个）

counterpoise ①见 counter weight ②（接）地（电）线③使平衡，保持均衡，补偿，抵消

counterpressure 反压力，支力，平衡压力

counter pulley 中间传动带轮

countershaft ［美］（变速器）中间

轴，副轴（= lay shaft, intermediate shaft）

countershaft cone （传动带传动）中间轴传动带塔轮，中间轴阶梯传动带轮

countershaftgear 中间轴齿轮（亦称 counter gear）

countershaft transmission ①中间轴式变速器（只有一根中间轴的固定轴式变速器）②定轴式液力变速器（采用固定轴线齿轮机构的液力变速器）

countersink 见 counterbore

countersink bolt 埋头螺栓

counter steering 反向转向（当发现因各种原因汽车后轮滑向某侧时，立即向与其相反的方向打转向盘，可校正汽车的姿势）

counter-stream 逆流

countersunk ①埋头的，沉肩的②埋头孔，锥口孔③埋头钻，锥孔钻

countersunk head bolt 埋头螺栓（= dormant bolt）

counter-timer 时间间隔计数测量器，时间测录仪

counter tube 计算管，计数器

counter weight 平衡重，平衡块（= balance weight, counterpoise, counter balance）

counting accelerometer 计数式加速度计

counting loss 漏计数

counting type sensor 计数型传感器（亦称 pulse type sensor "脉冲型传感器"，为数字型传感器的一种，为一脉冲发生器，其所输出的脉冲数与所传感的物理量成一定的正比关系，对其输出脉冲数进行计数，便可确定其所传感的物理量）

country beam （汽车前照灯的）远光，远光灯（= high beam）

country sedan 旅行车，接站车（= station wagon）

counts per second 每秒钟读数（简称 cps）

coupe 斜背双门小轿车（若为四门应写明 4-door coupe）

couple ①对，双，力偶，热偶，电偶，热电偶，温差电偶②耦合，成对，连接，挂钩

couple corrosion 双金属腐蚀（= bi-metallic corrosion）

coupled 耦合的，成对的，联结的

coupled bus 拖挂式公共汽车

couple distance （轿车的）前后座间距离

coupled suspensions 成对悬架

coupled truck 拖挂式货车，拖挂式载货汽车

coupled wheels （汽车的）并装双轮（= doubled wheels）

couple of forces 力偶

coupler 连接器，耦合器，耦合件，耦合设备，可变电感耦合器；联轴节，管接头，车钩

coupling ①连接器，耦合器，联轴节②挂钩③联结，耦合的

coupling connector 联轴节头

coupling fan （汽车发动机）离合式风扇

coupling head （万向节轴的）接头；（管）接头

coupling pin 连接销，牵引装置插销

coupling plate 联结板

coupling point （液力变矩器的）耦合器点，耦合点（变矩区与耦合区的转折点，变矩区的终点，耦合区的始点，亦称 clutch point，参见 coupling range）

coupling range （液力变矩器的）耦合相，耦合区（指输出转矩与输入转矩之比为1的工作区域，= coupling phase，亦称 clutch range）

coupling rate （原电池腐蚀的金属）电偶腐蚀量，电偶腐蚀率

coupling sleeve ①连接套②（离合器

coupling socket (牵引车上插接挂车电路的) 插座

coupling valve (自动变速器的) 速比变换阀, 变速阀 (见 shift valve)

coupon 试件, 试样

course ①进行, 经过, 过程②路线③教程

course angle (汽车) 行进方向角 (质心处车速在路面上的投影与地面固定坐标系 X 轴的夹角, 等于方位角与侧偏角的代数和, 见 earth-fixed axis system)

course keeping system 车道保持系统 (当测得行驶车辆驶出规定车道时即自动调整方向, 使车辆回到规定车道, 简称 CKS)

course monitoring tire 路况监测轮胎 (①指可根据路面状况, 自动调整气压轮胎②指向电子控制模块传递路况信息的轮胎, 简称 CMtire)

course tracking test 行驶路线跟踪试验 (简称 CTT)

court death [美俚] 参赛汽车

courtesy lamp 门控灯 (开门灯亮, 关闭灯灭, = courtesy light, 有的具有熄灯延时功能)

courtesy of… 由…提供 (文献中的插图或数据, 资料)

coved floor 凹面地板

cove lamp 壁灯 (在车箱壁凹处)

cover ①盖, (机) 罩, 外罩, 外壳②外胎 (相对内胎而言)

coverage ①作用距离, 可达范围, 有效区域②覆盖层, 涂覆层

cover bar 盖板

covered 封闭的, 盖复的, 有盖罩的

covered bus (风窗玻璃等不能开启、有空调设备的) 封闭式客车 (= closed bus, enclosed bus)

covered wire 绝缘导线 (= insulated wire)

cover panel (车身) 覆盖件 (车身骨架的包覆板件, = skin)

cover tyre 外胎

cowl ①帽、罩、壳、盖②保护突出部分并使之成流线型的车身板件③ ([美]轿车和长头货车的) 前围上盖板 (亦称 cowl top panel, cowl top = [英] scuttle panel, windscreen panel, 指风窗下边与发动机罩之间的连接处的外层盖板, 亦称 shroud upper panel, 有时简称 scuttle)

cowl and dash panel assembly ([美]汽车车身) 前围上板及仪表板总成 = [英] scuttle section

cowl drain tube 发动机罩上的排水管

cowling ① = cowl②发动机整流罩 (使绕车身的气流得到改善, 尾迹分离区最小, 保护发动机不受风吹影响并减小空气阻力的导流件)

cowling support 发动机罩撑杆

cowl lamp (装在前风窗玻璃与发动机罩之间的) 前围上盖板灯

cowl side complete panel assembly [美] 前围侧板总成 (位于前围板两侧的挡板总成, = [英] scuttle side panel assembly)

cowl side lower brace (车身的) 前围侧板下撑板

cowl side panel (轿车和长头货车车身的) 前围侧板 (指前围板两侧的挡板)

cowl side upper brace (车身的) 前围侧板上撑板

cowl side upper panel (车身的) 前围上侧板

cowl support bracket 发动机罩支架

cowl top 见 cowl③

cowl upper panel 见 cowl③

cowl vent(ilator) 前围上盖板通风口 = scuttle ventilation)

CP ①烛光 (candle power) ②厘泊 (centipoise) ③时钟脉冲 (clock

pulse）④轮辋的中凹（见 centre pente）⑤控制点（control point）⑥曲轴位置（crankshaft position）⑦偏偏刚度（cornering power 的简称，亦称 cornering stiffness，指轮胎侧偏角的单位增量所对应的转弯力增量，见 cornering force）

CPCS 产品强制认证制度（Compulsory Product Certification System 的）

CPI 中央多点式喷射（系统）（见 central port injection）

C-pillar （轿车车身）后柱，C-立柱（亦称 rear pillar C-post, rear post, dogleg pillar）

CPOD system 儿童座椅安放和定位（朝向）探测系统（child seat present and orientation detection device 的简称，该系统能识别儿童座椅并向安全气囊的电子控制单元提供其安放的相关信息，如朝前、朝后或安放是否正确等，以提高气囊系统的安全性，减少气囊展开时可能对儿童造成的伤害）

cps ①每秒钟读数（counts per second）②周/秒，赫（cycles per second）

CPS 曲轴位置传感器（crankshaft position sensor 的简称）

CP steel 复相钢（complex phase steel 的简称，先进高强度钢的一种，其组织特点是细小的铁素体和高比例的硬相，如：马氏体、贝氏体，含有 Nb、Ti 等元素，具有高的吸收能和扩孔性能，适合于制作车门防撞杠、保险杠、B 立柱等车身板件，见 AHSS）

CQD 遇难呼救信号（come quick, danger 的简称）

Cr 铬（chromium）

CR 压缩比（见 compression ratio, 亦写作 cr）

crabbing （由于汽车失调，纵轴线歪斜而造成的）斜驶，斜行

crab-tracked 前轮轮距大于后轮轮距的（底盘）

crab winch 起重绞车

crack 裂纹，裂缝，龟裂（一般指不致引起断裂的表面裂纹）

crackability （零件等的）易裂纹性

crack detector 裂缝探测仪（= crack follower, crack meter）

cracked 有裂纹的

cracked carbon resistors 裂化碳膜电阻器，热解碳膜电阻器（气化烃通过热瓷棒，裂化而在其表面形成的碳粒电阻薄膜）

cracker 破碎机，粉碎机，破碎工具，割除工具（如切割锈死螺母用工具）

crack extension 裂纹扩展量（裂纹尺寸的增量）

cracking ①形成裂纹，裂缝，龟裂②裂炼（法）（石油提炼中，将大分子裂化为小分子结构）

cracking gasoline 裂化汽油，裂炼汽油

cracking load 破坏负载，开裂载荷

cracking pressure ①开裂压力②（安全阀等的）开阀压力，开启压力（参见 pressure override）

cracking resistance 抗裂强度，抗裂纹强度

crackling 噼啪声，爆裂声

crack opening displacement 裂纹开张位移（指裂纹尖端或裂纹嘴的张开型扩展，简称 COD）

cramp angle （车辆）转向角（= steering angle）

crane ①起重机，吊车②用起重机搬运

crane-lift truck 起重举升汽车［装有起重设备或可升降作业台（斗）的专用汽车］

crane truck ①汽车吊，汽车式起重机，起重汽车②带起重装置的小车

crank ①曲臂摇把②（特指）曲轴

的曲柄，（有时指）曲轴③用摇把或起动机转动发动机

crank angle indicator diagram 以曲轴转角为横坐标的示功图

crank angle selecting unit 曲轴转角选择器

crank angle sensor 曲轴转角传感器（亦称 crankshaft position sensor 曲轴位置传感器，向电子控制模块发送曲轴转速和活塞上止点位置的曲轴转角信号，一般还利用曲轴转角传感器产生汽缸识别信号）

crank angular position 曲轴相位角，曲轴转角位置（简称 CAP）

crank arm angle （多缸发动机的）曲柄工作相位间隔角，曲柄工作相位角（四冲程的 = 720°/缸数；二冲程的 = 360°/缸数）

crank bearing liner ①曲轴轴承衬套 ②曲轴轴承轴瓦

crank bore 连杆大端孔；曲轴主轴承孔

crank brass 曲轴主轴承黄铜轴瓦

crank cap 曲轴主轴承盖

crankcase 曲轴箱（部分围住曲轴回转空间，有主轴承和安装用平面的箱形部件，其上有汽缸、水套、汽缸体）

crankcase bearing saddle 曲轴箱（主）轴承座

crankcase blow-by 曲轴箱串气（燃气由汽缸串漏入曲轴箱）

crankcase bottom half 下曲轴箱（曲轴箱下半部，= crankcase lower half）

crankcase breather 曲轴箱通风阀（见 crankcase bleeder）

crankcase closed system 曲轴箱双通风系统（曲轴箱完全密封，用两个通风装置强制曲轴箱通风的系统）

crankcase compartment 曲轴箱隔室，曲轴箱（内壁隔开的）分间

crankcase compression system （二冲程汽油发动机的）曲轴箱压缩扫气系统，曲轴箱压缩换气系统（利用活塞下行在曲轴箱内对新鲜充量进行预压缩，以便更多的新鲜混合气进入汽缸，亦称 crankcase pre-compression system）

crankcase cover plate 曲轴箱盖板

crankcase door 曲轴箱检查孔盖

crankcase drain cock 曲轴箱放油阀

crankcase drain mileage period （汽车发动机以英里计的）机油更换里程，机油更换期

crankcase drain plug 曲轴箱放油螺塞

crankcase emission （发动机）曲轴箱排放物，曲轴箱有害排出物（指从曲轴箱排至大气的有害物质，主要是窜缸气和机油蒸气）

crankcase emission control system 曲轴箱排放物控制系统

crankcase end cover 曲轴箱端盖（密封曲轴箱端面的部件）

crankcase explosion 曲轴箱内爆燃（放炮）（= base explosion）

crankcase explosion proof door 曲轴箱防爆门（当曲轴箱内的压力超过一定值时，能自动开启的阀门）

crankcase facing 曲轴箱凸缘面（亦称 crankcase flange）

crankcase front (end) cover 曲轴箱前端盖

crankcase gas 见 crankcase vapour

crankcase guard （装在发动机下方的）曲轴箱防护罩

crankcase (oil) dilution 曲轴箱机油被未燃烧的汽油稀释（混合气过浓或燃烧不完全，汽油由活塞缸壁间串入油底壳）

crankcase oil pan （发动机）曲轴箱油底壳；曲轴箱机油盘（亦称 crankcase sump, crankcase lower cover）

crankcase oil seal 曲轴箱油封

crankcase oil tray 曲轴箱油底壳（＝crankcase oil pan）

crankcase partition 上曲轴箱隔板

crankcase pressure 曲轴箱（内因串缸气等造成的）压力

crankcase scavenged diesel engine 曲轴箱扫气型柴油机

crankcase scavenging 曲轴箱扫气（以曲轴箱作为扫气泵的压缩室，利用活塞下行压缩曲轴箱内的新鲜空气经压缩后的新鲜空气通过曲轴箱的扫气通道、经扫气口进入汽缸，实现扫气。扫气口由活塞的位置开、闭）

crankcase sealed system 曲轴箱密封系统，曲轴箱单通风装置（曲轴箱全密封，只用一个通风装置强制曲轴箱通风）

crankcase storage system 曲轴箱储存系统（利用曲轴箱储存蒸发排放物的系统）

crankcase top half 上曲轴箱（曲轴箱上半部，＝crankcase upper half）

crankcase vapo（u）r 曲轴箱蒸气（由漏入曲轴箱内的燃油蒸气、废气以及机油蒸气组成，但一般指燃油蒸气，＝crankcase gas）

crankcase ventilation system 曲轴箱通风系（亦称crankcase ventilator 或 breathering system）

crank center 曲柄中心

crank diameter 曲柄直径（＝crank travel，piston stroke，piston travel）

cranked 成曲柄状的，成中凹状的

cranked frame trailer 低（车）架挂车（亦称cranked trailer, deep-loading trailer, drop frame trailer, low-bed trailer, low-down trailer, low-loading trailer）

cranked wrench 曲柄扳手

crank effort 曲轴回转力矩，曲柄回转力，曲柄的切向力

crank element 曲拐元件（将旋转运动变成摆动或往复直线运动，或将摆动与往复直线运动变为旋转运动的元件）

crank end 曲柄端

crank end hsg （转子发动机的）起动端缸盖，非驱动端缸盖，前端盖，前缸盖，前端缸盖（亦称 anti-drive end hsg，其中 hsg 为 housing 的简称）

crank engine 曲柄连杆式发动机

crank gauge 曲轴轴颈量测器

crank handle （发动机曲轴）起动摇把（＝crank starting handle，简称 cranker）

cranking 摇动，起动，开动

cranking enrichment （混合气）起动加浓

cranking mtor [美]起动机（＝starter motor）

cranking signal （由起动机电磁开关电路向电子控制模块输送的）起动信号

cranking speed 起动时的曲轴转速

cranking torque （转动发动机的）起动转矩

cranking trouble 发动机起动系统故障

crank journal 曲轴主轴颈

crankless engine 无曲轴式发动机（如：利用旋转斜盘机械等将活塞的往复运动转变成动力输出轴的旋转运动的发动机）

crankmobile 汽车吊，起重汽车

crank-operated window 摇柄升降式风窗玻璃

crankpin angle 曲轴连杆轴颈夹角，曲轴销夹角（在多缸发动机中，相邻曲柄的夹角）

crank pin bearing 曲轴连杆轴颈轴承，连杆大端轴承（参见 big-end bearing）

crankpin end of the connecting rod 连杆大端（连杆连接曲轴连杆轴颈

的一端，= connecting rod big end）
crank radius 曲柄半径（从曲轴主轴颈中心线到曲轴连杆轴颈中心线的垂直距离）
crank radius-connecting rod length ratio 曲柄半径与连杆长度（的）比（值）
crank sensor 曲轴位置传感器（crankshaft position sensor 的简称）
crankshaft 曲轴，曲柄轴（将活塞往复运动变为旋转运动、输出发动机动力的主轴）
crankshaft aligner ①曲轴直线性检测仪，曲轴扭曲检测仪②曲轴校正器
crankshaft axis 曲轴中心线
crankshaft bearing bushing ①曲轴主轴承瓦②曲轴连杆轴承衬套
crankshaft bearing cap 曲轴轴承盖
crankshaft bearing cap bolt 曲轴轴承盖螺栓
crankshaft bearing liner 曲轴轴承耐磨衬层
crankshaft bush 曲轴轴承衬套
crank shaft collar 曲轴轴环，曲轴轴肩
crankshaft compensator ①曲轴（伸缩）补偿件②曲轴平衡块
crankshaft counterbalance ①曲轴平衡（= crankshaft balancing）②曲轴平衡块，曲轴配重（= crankshaft-counterweight 或 balance weight, compensator）
crankshaft deflection 曲轴弯曲变形量，曲柄臂间距变化量（曲轴弯曲变形，而在曲柄臂原配重端测得的两臂间距的变化量）
crankshaft degree 曲轴转角度数
crankshaft dynamic balancing machine 曲轴动平衡机
crankshaft end bearing ［美］连杆大头轴承（= big end bearing）
crankshaft flange 曲轴凸缘，曲轴凸缘盘
crankshaft front-bearing seal 曲轴前轴承油封
crankshaft gauge 曲轴轴颈测量仪（测量主轴颈及连杆轴颈的磨损量、失圆度及锥度等）
crankshaft half bearing 对开式曲轴（滑动）轴承，曲轴轴瓦
crankshaft impulse neutralizer 曲轴冲击力平衡装置
crankshaft intermediate main bearing cap 曲轴中间主轴承盖
crankshaft jaw 曲轴起动摇把棘爪，起动爪（亦称 crankshaft ratchet、starting claw 或 starting jaw）
crankshaft journal 曲轴轴颈（一般指曲轴主轴颈）
crankshaft journal bearing 曲轴主轴颈轴承，曲轴主轴承
crankshaft (main) bearing 曲轴主轴承
crankshaft oil seal 曲轴油封，曲轴挡油盘；曲轴抛油圈，曲轴甩油环（亦称 crankshaft oil thrower, crankshaft oil slinger）
crankshaft oil-way 曲轴润滑油路
crankshaft pilot 曲轴后端中央的变速器第一轴导向轴承座孔
crank (shaft) pin 曲柄销，曲轴连杆轴颈
crankshaft position sensor 曲轴位置传感器（简称CKP，向电子控制模块发送发动机转速与曲轴位置信号，该传感器向电子控制模块每发送一个信号，表示有一个汽缸的活塞到达压缩冲程上止点前某一确定位置。发动机电子控制模块根据发动机转速、曲轴位置信号以及大气压力、进气压力和冷却水温信号，确定点火提前角，并向点火控制模块发出最佳点火正时指令及喷油指令。CKP 为美国政府规定从 1995 年 1 月 1 日起使用的标准术语，以取

代通用和克莱斯勒公司的 REF 和福特公司的 CPS 等)

crankshaft pulley 曲轴传动带轮(驱动凸轮轴的带传动轮)

crankshaft reluctor (装在)曲轴(上的)磁阻转子

crankshaft sprocket 曲轴链轮(驱动凸轮轴的链轮)

crankshaft thrust plate 曲轴止推垫片

crankshaft timing gear 曲轴正时齿轮(简称 crankshaft gear)

crankshaft timing sensor 曲轴正时传感器(= crankshaft position sensor)

crankshaft web (曲轴的)曲柄臂(简称 crank web, crank cheek, crank arm, crank throw)

crank (side) plate (转子发动机)前端盖(参见 crank end plate)

crank signal (发动机)起动信号(输入动力系电子控制模块,实现混合气起动加浓)

crank throw ①曲柄半径,曲柄有效长度②曲轴主轴颈中心线与曲轴连杆轴颈中心线的间距,为活塞冲程的 1/2 ②见 crank web

crank thrust bearing 曲轴推力轴承

crank to connecting rod length ratio 曲柄—连杆(长度)比 $C = r/L$,式中:r—曲柄半径,即曲轴主轴颈线与连杆轴颈轴线间距,L—连杆长度,即大、小头孔轴线间距,该比值越大,连杆越短,发动机总高度越小

crank travel 见 crank diameter

crank type compressor 曲轴型压缩机(通过曲轴机构将旋转运动变为活塞往复运动的往复式压缩机的一种)

crank web 曲柄臂(曲轴上支承连杆颈的部分)

crank 18X 曲轴位置传感器(通用公司 type Ⅲ C^3I 型点火系统中除了凸轮轴位置传感器外,装有两个曲轴位置传感器,第一个称"crank 3x",曲轴每转产生 3 个分别相隔 110°、100°和 90°的脉冲信号,第二个称"crank 18x",曲轴每转产生 18 个等间隔的脉冲信号。二者相互对照,供电子控制模块确定各汽缸的点火顺序与时刻)

crash ①碰撞,撞车②破裂声③应急的,紧急的

crash-absorbing 吸收碰撞(能量)的

crash avoidance system 车辆的防碰撞系统

crash barrier (汽车冲撞试验用的)障壁(分为固定壁"fixed barrier"和移动壁"movable barrier"两大类)

crash change of speeds 冲击换挡,无同步器换挡

crash data 碰撞数据

crash detection sensor 碰撞检测传感器

crash discriminating sensor (安全气囊等的)碰撞判别传感器(亦写作 crash discrimination sensor, 见 air bag sensing system)

crash discrimination algorithm (汽车)碰撞判断算法(指如何确认汽车发生了碰撞或怎样才算汽车发生碰撞而不是汽车急制动减速或其他)

crash discrimination circuit (安全气囊控制系统的)碰撞判断电路(接受电子控制模块内的碰撞传感器的信号,并经逻辑分析,确认汽车发生碰撞时触发点火器引爆安全气囊)

crash discrimination sensor 碰撞判断传感器(指安全气囊系统中作为前置传感器、装在汽车碰撞部位前端,如保险杠中心,左、右翼子板

等首先感受碰撞的部位，多使用惯性式磁力或弹簧力定位型惯性质量减速度传感器）

CRASH FEM simulation （车身）碰撞有限元法模拟（crash finite-element-method simulation 的简称）

crash/fire/rescue truck 事故-消防-救援汽车

crash gearbox 无换挡同步器的变速器（因而换挡时，要两次踩离合器）

crash opponent （车对车碰撞事故中的）对方车

crash pad 防撞垫，防振垫

crash predicting technology 碰撞预知系统

crash-proof 防撞的，耐撞击的（= crash-protective）

crash recorder 碰撞记录器（测定、记录行车速度、方向以及制动和指示信号装置使用情况的电子装置，俗称黑匣子 black box；一般可将碰撞前 60 s 内的上述信息回放，以供事故分析用）

crash resistance 碰撞强度，耐碰撞性能

crash sensor （车辆）碰撞传感器（用于测定减速度的临界值，以触发安全气囊）

crash severity （汽车）碰撞严重程度

crash signature 碰撞特征信号（如：汽车发生碰撞时，通过底盘发出的冲击波形）

crash simulation （汽车）碰撞模拟

crash standards （汽车）碰撞标准（对车辆碰撞时，汽车损坏程度及乘员安全要求的标准）

crash stop 紧急停止，紧急制动

crash survivability （车辆等的）碰撞安全性，碰撞免伤亡性能（指发生碰撞事故时，可保护乘员免于伤亡的性能）

crash survival distance 防碰撞伤亡距离（简称 CSD）

crash test （受控）撞车试验，碰撞试验

crash test computational model 碰撞试验计算机模型

crash truck 碰撞肇事救护车，碰撞救援车（= wrecker truck）

crashworthiness 抗撞击能力，耐撞性能

crash zone 碰撞区［指：发生碰撞时汽车车身前端的可挤压变形区（crushable zone），以吸收撞击能量，保护驾驶人员免受撞伤。欧洲货车驾驶室前方均设有 600 mm 的挤压变形区］

crated weight 装箱质量（装箱质量的旧称，= boxed weight）

crater-contoured piston 顶部有火山喷凹坑燃烧室的活塞

crawler （= creeper） ①履带式车辆；履带②缓慢行驶的车辆（如沿街招揽生意的出租车或特大型货车）③（上陡坡时使用的超大速比）爬行挡，超低速挡（= crawler gear, crawling gear 或 creeper gear）

crawler gear 见 crawler③

crawler lane （山区公路供重型货车或其他慢行车辆的）慢行专用车道

crawler-mounted 装有履带的，履带式的，装在履带式车辆上的

crawler-mounted motor lorry 履带式货车（= caterpillar track motor lorry）

crawler track 见 crawler tread

crawler tractor 履带式牵引车（= caterpillar tractor, chaintrack tractor, creeper-type tractor, track-laying tractor）

crawler (-) tread 履带；履带传动，履带式行进装置（= crawler track, cater pillar tread, chain tread, creeper tread）

crawler wheel （履带行走装置）支

重轮，张紧轮，导向轮（= carter pillar wheel, truck wheel）

crawl-under lubrication points 需爬匐着加油的润滑点

craze ①龟裂（网络状细裂纹，= crazing）②出现龟裂，产生网状细裂纹

CRC ①美国汽车与石油工业科学研究协作委员会（Coordinating Research Committee 或 Coordinating Research Council 的简称）②中国汽车拉力锦标赛

CRC F-1、F-2、F-3、F-4 method 汽车燃料 CRC 辛烷值测定法（其中：F-1 称为研究法，F-2 称为马达法，二者都是用铸铁活塞在可变压缩比的单缸发动机内测定车用燃油的辛烷值，参见 laboratory knock-testing method。F-3、F-4 则是用铝活塞测定航空发动机燃油的辛烷值）

CRC-L-38 test CRC-L-38 试验（评价发动机机油在高温下对铜、铅基轴承的腐蚀性试验）

CRD 苛刻道路条件（crushing road conditions 的简称）

CRD ①电容-电阻-二极管网络（capacitor-resistor-diode network）②可控后差速器（controlled rear differential）

CRDI 共用储油歧管直喷式柴油机（common rail direct injection 的简称，common rail 我国不少处译为"共轨"，其实这里的 rail 和轨道毫无关系，见 common rail 和 common rail direct injection system）

CR-DPF 柴油机微粒排放物连续再生过滤器（continuously recycling-diesel particles filter 的简称）

creak detector 噪声检测器

crease ①褶皱，折痕②变皱

creasing machine 折皱机，折缝机，皱纹机

create 创立，建立，引起，产生

credenza （试验安全车）后座前的安全气囊箱

credibility ①可靠性②可信程序，可信性③可接受性

creep ①（传动带）打滑②车辆爬行，缓慢移动③（频率）漂移④轮胎（沿轮辋的）位移⑤（特指自动变速式车辆，怠速挂挡、未踩制动时慢慢前移的趋势）蠕动⑥蠕变（在规定温度及恒定力作用下，材料塑性变形随时间而增加的现象）

creepage ①徐变，蠕变，塑流②渗水，漏电③（腐蚀，特别是锈蚀的）扩展

creep controlled bonding （粗糙表面间在长时间高温低压作用下发生的）蠕变黏结

creep curve 蠕变曲线（指蠕变变形量随时间而变化的曲线）

creeper ①（车下作业）躺板（带脚轮的小平板，车下作业时，可仰卧在上面操作）②见 crawler

creeper tread 见 tread, crawler tread

creeper-type 履带式的

creep length （火花塞）中央绝缘嘴的长度（长者，火花塞温度高，称热型；短者，温度低，称冷型）

creep limit 蠕变极限（在规定温度下，引起材料在一定时间内蠕变总伸长率或恒定蠕变速率不超过规定值的最大应力）

creep rate 蠕变速率（单位时间内的蠕变变形量）

creep recovery 蠕变回复（在规定温度下卸除产生蠕变的作用力后，变形回缩量与时间的关系）

creep resistance 见 creep strength

creep speed （汽车的）蠕动速动，爬坡速度

creep strength 蠕变强度，抗蠕变力（= creep resistance，指材料抵抗蠕变的能力）

CRES 耐蚀钢，不锈钢（corrosion

resistant steel)
cresceleration 幂次加（减）速度［按幂级数递增（递减）的加（减）速度］
crescent ①新月形的，镰形的②新月状物，月牙形部件（特指内齿轮泵内、外齿之间的）月牙形密封分隔板件
crescent (type) gear pump 新月形齿轮泵，月牙形齿轮泵［一种内啮合齿轮泵，在主动齿轮与从动齿轮间具有一月牙型元件，亦称crescent design (geared 或 shaped) pump］
crescent wrench 可调扳手（= adjustable spanner）
crest ①峰，峰值②齿顶面（= top land，指被齿顶曲面所包含的那一部分齿轮表面）；（螺纹）牙顶③达到顶点，升到峰值
crest discharge 峰值流量；峰值放电
crest speed ①（车速分布中的）最多用车速（缓行、制动以外的最多使用车速，亦称 modal speed）②最高速度，峰值速度
crest value 峰值
crest width （齿轮的）端面齿顶厚，齿顶厚（在端平面内，一个齿的两侧端面齿廓之间的齿顶圆弧长）
crevice 缝隙，裂缝
crevice corrosion 隙间腐蚀
crevice effect （燃烧的）缝隙效应（在两个很靠近的相对运动表面之间的可燃气体，常常会失去燃烧能力，不能燃烧完全）
crevice tool （车身等的）缝隙、凹槽的清扫工具；缝隙修整工具
crew cab （货车、公用事务车等）双排座驾驶室（= double cab）
crew comfort （汽车）驾驶人员的舒适性，工作人员的舒适性，工作人员的方便性
crimp 折叠，折皱，翻边，卷边

crimping 卷边，折皱，卷边封口，折皮结口
crimp seal ①锯齿形焊缝②卷边密封件
crinkle finish 波形面饰，皱纹（罩面）漆
criss (-) cross （交叉成）十字形的
criteria criterion 的复数
criteria for evaluation of vehicle tractive performance 汽车动力性（评价）指标（包括汽车的最高车速、加速时间和所能克服的最大坡度）
criterion （判断）标准，规范，准则
critical 临界的，极限的，转折（点）的
critical angle 临界角
critical approach speed 临界接近车速，安全接近速度（如：车辆接近交叉口时可及时停车而不致与横向驶过的车辆相撞的安全车速，= safe approach speed）
critical compression ratio 临界压缩比（简称CCR）
critical conditions 临界条件，临界状态
critical damping 临界阻尼（指单自由度系统自由振动时，使其逐渐返回平衡位置的非周期运动的阻尼作用）
critical damping coefficient 临界阻尼系数（使偏离平衡位置的单自由度系统回到无振动平衡位置的最小线性黏性阻尼系数）
critical failure 致命故障（指使汽车总成造成重大损坏的故障）
critical flow venturi 临界流量文丘里管（CVS取样时，取样器中控制排气流量的装置）
critical fusion frequency （驾驶者视觉的）①临界融合频率（简称CFF，指不同的光在较短的周期内，在视场上交替呈现时，恰能察觉出

恒定刺激的最小频率，高于该频率时不能再察觉出视亮度或颜色的差别）②临界（视觉）停闪频率（视觉感觉不出闪光的频率）

critical inflation pressure of tires 轮胎临界充气压力（其土壤压实性能与刚性轮相等）

critical pressure 临界压力（指在规定条件或定义下某极限压力，如：流体的临界压力指不论温度高低，在观测不到流体气相和液相间不连续性时的最低压力）

critical pressure ratio 临界压力比（指流体的绝对压力与其临界压力之比，亦称 reduced pressure）

critical protrusion 极限伸出长度

critical slant angle （车身的）临界后坡度角（试验车的气动力阻力系数发生突变时的车身后窗倾斜坡度角）

critical speed 临界速度（①临界转速，如：导致振动前的最高转速②临界车速，如：过度转向汽车产生无限大横摆角速度增益时的前进车速）

critical speed of crankshaft 曲轴的临界转速（指作用于曲轴上的干涉力矩的频率与曲轴固有频率相等而产生共振，以改转矩振幅剧增时的曲轴转速）

critical temperature 临界温度（指规定条件或定义下的某极限温度，如：流体的临界温度指不论压力高低，在不能观测到流体的气相与液相间的不连续性的极限温度）

critical temperature resistor 临界温度电阻器（温度达到某特定值时，其电阻值急剧变化，故多用来作为汽车自动控制系统的温度控制开关或温度临界值传感元件，简称 CTR）

critical tracking task （一种）防酒后驾驶装置（简称 CTT）

critical value 临界值，阀值（= thresh-old value）

critical yield stress 临界屈服应力（简称 CYS）

critical zone ①临界区域②驾驶室内最小安全区（指驾驶员实占的空间轮廓）

CRM 客户关系管理（Customer Relationship Management 的简称，指对汽车客户的数据及售前、售中、售后服务支援系统）

CRO 阴极射线示波器（cathode-ray oscillograph, cathode-ray oscilloscope）

crocodile clip 鳄口夹（=［美］aligator clip，用于临时接线的鳄口弹簧夹，如跨接线用的线夹）

cross ①十字形物，十字轴②相交的，交叉的，横的

cross analysis （随机信号分析的）穿越分析（法）（亦称交叉分析，指对信号在时间 T 内，以正或负斜率穿越某值的次数及概率进行的分析）

cross and roller 滚子轴承式十字轴万向节

cross assembly 十字轴总成（十字轴带轴承总成）

cross axle 横轴

cross bar ①横杆，横木，横梁，横臂②十字架，十字头，四通管③（美）十字柄扳手的横扳杆（= tommy bar）

cross-bar tread tire 十字花纹轮胎；横条花纹轮胎

cross beam ①横梁，横臂②十字梁

cross bearer （货车车身）底板支撑横桁梁，底板横枕梁（在车身纵梁和车身底板间，简称 bearer，= cross bolster）

cross bending test 横向弯曲试验（在横向载荷作用下的弯曲）

cross-biased tire （帘线层）交叉斜

交轮胎
cross bow （车顶篷的）横向弓形梁
cross-braced frame X 形加强梁的车架（= diagonally-braced frame）
cross brace(ing) 横拉条，横撑；十字形横撑
cross bracket 十字轴托架
cross breaking 横向断裂的
cross brushes 直角安装的电刷
cross component 侧向分力，横向分力，横向分量
cross-compound cycle （高低压涡轮分别与高低压压气机）交错同轴的燃气轮机循环
cross connection ①交叉连接②横向连接，横接
cross correlation function 互相关函数
cross-country lorry 高通过性货车，越野货车（= cross country cargo carrier, cross country truck, off road truck）
cross-country six-wheeler 三轴越野车（6×6 越野车）
cross country tread pattern （轮胎的）越野花纹（适用于无路条件下行驶的胎面花纹）
CROSS COUPE （大众公司推出的）越野型四门混合动力小轿车（商品名，SUV 与 coupe 结合的一种新车型，四座，前后各装有一台电动机与一台汽油直喷、增压式内燃机组成的四轮驱动混合动力系统）
cross-coupled 交叉连接的，交叉耦合（的）（如：前一元器件的输出端接后一元器件的输入端，而后一元器件的输出端接前一元器件的输入端）
cross-coupling 相互作用，交叉耦合
cross-cut 横切的，正交的
cross-cut file 交纹锉，双纹锉
cross cut point 十字槽触点
cross direction 横向，侧向（简称 CD）
cross draft (gas) producer 平吸式（煤气）发生炉
cross-draught carburettor = side draught carburettor
cross-drive 横向传动
crossed helical gear pair 交错轴斜齿轮副（由两个配对的斜齿轮组成的交错轴齿轮副。注意：斜齿轮的旧称"螺旋齿轮"一词，已停止使用）
crossed polarizer 正交偏振片（偏振方向正交的两偏振片，参见 polarizer）
cross (feed) hair(s) （目镜中的）十字线，瞄准线（亦称 cross wire, hair cross）
cross-feed line ①连于总装配线两旁的部件装配线②与总管道相连的横向分支管道
crossfire ①串扰（不同线路的信号相互干扰）②见 cross firing
crossfire injection （具有两个喷嘴的节气门体汽油喷射系统）交替喷射，交叉喷射
cross firing 多缸同时点火（指多缸发动机，由于高压线之间短路或相互感应而造成两缸以上的火花塞同时点火的故障）
cross flow 横向气流，交叉气流，正交流动，横向流动
cross flow cylinder head 横流式汽缸盖（指进、排气歧管分别布置在缸盖的两侧，因而，其进、排气门各在汽缸相对的一侧，一般见于顶置凸轮轴式发动机，亦称 X-flow cylinder head）
cross-flow radiator 横流式散热器（其进、出水箱位于散热芯的两侧，冷却水由发动机缸体流出的热水流入其进水箱"inlet tank"后横向流过散热芯汇集于出水箱"outlet tank"再流回发动机缸盖）

cross flow scavenging 横流扫气（简称 cross scavenging，= transverse flow scavenging，指进、排气位于汽缸中心线两侧，利用进气口方向与汽缸中心线呈一倾角，使充量从进气口一侧进入汽缸，将废气驱扫出排气口的排气方式）

cross force 横向力（= transverse force）

cross girder ①横梁②小字形桁架

cross handle 十字手柄

crosshead 十字头，滑块

crosshead engine 十字头式发动机（一般指用沿导板滑动的十字头连接活塞杆与连杆的柴油机）

crosshead piston 丁字形头组合式活塞

crosshead screw 十字形槽螺钉

cross helical gear 交错轴斜齿轮

crossing ability （汽车的）通过能力，通过性，越障能力

crossing analysis 穿越分析，交叉分析，跨过分析（分析信号在时间T内以正或负斜率穿越某值的次数及概率，进而获知峰值分布的概率特性）

cross (ing) point 交点，交叉点，相交点，穿过点

crossing point of axes 轴线交点（指两轴线的相交点。对于交错齿轮副指两轴线在垂直于连心线的平面上的投影的交点）

cross joiner 纵、横梁的连接与加固支架

cross joint 四通，十字接头，交叉连接

cross limb wrench 十字棒套筒扳手（在十字棒的四个端头均装有套筒的扳手）

cross mark 十字标记

cross mean value processing method （对机件实测载荷时间历程进行统计处理的）越过均值计数法（仅对主要的极大值和极小数计数）

cross-median crash 横越（车道的）中（央分界）线（和对向来的车辆）碰撞

cross member 横梁，横板，横臂，横件，十字梁（= cross rail）

cross-model evaluation of ride comfort 乘坐舒适性的综合模型评价

cross modulation 交扰调制，变扰调制，交叉调制

cross movement 横向运动

crossover ①跨接②见 CUV

crossover point ①（气门）重叠点（指进、排气门开启曲线的交点，即进、排气门开启高度相等点，用曲轴转角位置来表示）②转折点③（道路）立体交叉点

crossover relief valve circuit 交叉溢流油路（如：回转叶片式液压执行器一侧与另一侧相互连通的溢流阀油路）

crossover utility vehicle 混合型多功能车（简称 crossover vehicle，crossover，见 CUV）

cross peen and finishing hammer （车身扳件修复用的）凿形端式凹陷敲平小手锤

cross-piece ①横杆，横梁②十字构件，十字轴（= cross pins）

cross-pin tester 十字轴（油膜）试验器（一旋转轴在一与之十字交叉的固定轴上转动摩擦，测试在各种工作压力和摩擦力下的油膜状况）

crosspin type joint 十字轴形万向节

cross pipe 十字形管，四通管

cross-ply tire 见 bias tyre

cross point screwdriver 十字头槽螺钉旋具

cross rail 见 cross member

cross scavenging 见 cross-flow scavenging

cross screw 左右交叉螺纹

cross section 横断面，横剖面

cross sectional characteristics （发动机的）万有特性（曲线图，常以功率为纵坐标，转速为横坐标，绘制的功率、转矩、油耗等特性曲线图）

cross shaft ①横轴② ［美］ = rocker shaft③（转向器中转向蜗杆通过滚轮或齿轮驱动的）转向摇臂轴（该轴多通过花键端与转向摇臂连接，亦称 pitman arm shaft。由齿扇驱动者，亦称 sector shaft）

cross-shaped 十字形的

cross sill （车身）横梁（= bolster）

cross-spectral density （多点输入）相交频谱密度近似法，互功率谱密度，互谱

cross speed 侧向速度，侧向分速度

cross-spoke wheel 钢丝交错辐条式车轮

cross steering linkage 转向横拉杆系

cross step processing method （对机件实测载荷时间历程进行统计处理的）穿级计数法

cross strap 安全带（= safety belt）

cross talk 窜线，串话干扰，串声，信号干扰；相互干扰；互相影响（简称 CT）

cross talk voltage 交叉串扰电压（发生交叉效应的串扰电压）

cross threading （拧装螺纹紧固件时的）错扣，咬扣，乱扣，夹扣（现象）

cross-traffic alert （盲区监测系统的）横向行驶车辆警报（功能）

cross travel 横向位移(= side travel)

cross under 穿接（在集成电路内，使一连接从半导体晶片内低阻区通过）

cross valve 三通阀

cross wall 横隔板，横隔壁（= transverse wall）

crosswind pressure sensor 横风压力传感器（装在车身两侧的若干压差传感器，用以测定横向风对汽车的压力，以修正因横风引起的汽车行驶方向的变动，保持汽车的方向稳定性）

crosswind sensitivity 侧风敏感性，横风稳定性（横向风扰动输入时，汽车的响应程度，= side wind sensitivity）

crosswise 横向的，交叉的，成十字状的；相反的

crosswise angle 横向角（如：铰接式客车的副车绕过球铰机构球心的纵向中心线回转的横向扭转角）

crosswise engine 横向布置的发动机（垂直于车辆纵向轴线，= transvesal mounted engine）

crowbar circuit 消弧电路

crowd ①节气门（小于全开的）稳态大开（状态）②人群，群集③拥挤，挤满

crow-flight distance 直线距离（= straight-line distance）

crown ①（道路）拱顶，拱高，拱度②顶部，圆顶部；拱曲部分；冠状物③活塞顶部④（轮胎的）胎冠（外胎两胎肩间的整个部位，包括胎面、缓冲层或带束层和帘布层等）

crown angle 胎冠帘线角（见 cord crown angle）

crown cord angle 胎冠帘线角（轮胎周向中心线与胎冠部位的胎体帘线排列方向所构成的角度，简称 crown angle）

crowned 凸面的，拱形的，鼓形的

crowned roller path （凹面滚子轴承的）凸面滚道

crowned section 拱形断面

crowned spline 鼓形花键

crowned teeth （齿轮的）鼓形齿（经过鼓形修整的轮齿，见 crowning）

crown gear 冠轮（分锥角为90°的

锥齿轮, 如主减速器的从动冠轮或大锥齿轮)

crown-head piston (中部凸起的) 圆顶活塞 (= arched head piston, dome-head piston)

crowning ①拱起, 凸起 ②凸形的 ③鼓形修整(采用齿面或齿廓修形, 使轮齿在齿面中部区域与相啮齿面接触)

crown nut 槽顶螺母, 开槽螺母

crown of piston 活塞顶部

crown of tooth (齿轮)齿顶, 齿冠

crown of tyre 胎冠(外胎两胎肩的整个部位, 包括胎面、缓冲层或带束层和帘布层)

crown wheel 冠齿轮, 冠轮, 主传动从动齿轮, 从动锥齿轮(指锥角为90°的锥齿轮, 如: 主减速器的冠轮或差速器内冠轮 "crown gear", "gear differential crown wheel", "differential master gear", "axle drive bevel gear")

CRPO 容许连续超载的额定(功率) (continuous rating permitting overload power)

CRS ①见 coasting richer system ②儿童级束性安全系统(child restraint system 的简称, 指安全带等防止儿童二次碰撞的安全保护系统)

CRT ①阴极射线管 (cathode ray tube) ②特性响应时间 (characteristic response time) ③计算机远程终端 (computer remote terminal) ④(柴油机的)连续再生型(排放)微粒物捕集器 (continuous regenerating trap 的简称)

CRT touch panel control 阴极射线管触摸板控制

cru 克鲁(蠕变单位: 1 克鲁 = 1000h 发生 10%的蠕变)

cruciform 十字形的, 交叉形的 (= cruci shaped)

cruciform frame ①X 形横梁型车架 ②承载式车身底板的 X 形加强架

cruciform member (X 形车架中部的) X 形加强梁

crude 天然的, 未经加工的, 原状的, 粗制的

crude oil 原油, 石油 (= crude petroleum, base oil, mother oil)

crude oil engine 重油发动机, 原油发动机

crudity 粗糙度

cruise 巡行(以稳定的经济车速行驶)

cruise control brake switch 定速巡行制动控制开关(当踩踏制动踏板时, 该开关断开, 由该开关送至电子控制模块的电压信号消失, 于是, 电子控制模块获知, 车辆正在制动, 而退出定速巡行)

cruise control enable switch 定速巡行控制接合开关(亦称 cruise on/off switch, 该开关控制定速巡行系统的接合与退出)

cruise control (system) (预选车速)定速巡行控制(系统) (可根据道路和行驶条件, 自动控制发动机输出和换挡以保持汽车按驾驶人员所选定的车速稳速行驶, 而无须踩踏加速踏板或操纵换挡杆, 简称 CCS)

cruise control vacuum solenoid 定速巡行真空控制电磁阀(由电子控制模块控制的电磁阀, 用来作为节气门真空执行机构的真空通路控制开关)

cruise error calculation algorithm (巡航控制系统的)车速偏差算法

cruise odor 车辆行驶时的排气臭味

cruiser 巡逻车

cruise resume/accelerate switch 定速巡行系统的复位/加速开关(将该开关推至复位端, 电子控制模块使汽车恢复因制动而取消的原设定速巡行车速。将该开关推至加速端

时，电子控制模块使汽车在原设定的巡行车速基础上加速，直至松开该开关。松开该开关后，车速保持所加至的车速巡行）

cruise set/coast switch 定速巡行设定/滑行开关（定速巡行系统接通后，若汽车处于滑行工况，则按压该开关，电子控制模块便将巡行车速定于按压该开关时的车速；若车处于某定速工况，则按压该开关，汽车将进入滑行工况，车速下降）

cruise switch （定速巡行控制系统的）定速巡行开关（亦称 cruise on/off switch, cruise main switch, 该开关置于"on"位置时，定速巡行系统接通，置于"off"位置时，巡行系统关闭）

cruise velocity （汽车的）巡行车速（相对于加速、减速、怠速等变速而言的等速、稳速）

cruising 巡航的，稳速行驶的

cruising distance ①巡航距离②（电动汽车一次充电的可）行驶距离

cruising power （发动机的）持续输出功率（= continuous output, continuous maximum power）

cruising radius 常速行车半径（根据汽车油箱容量，以常速行驶时，可以往返的最大距离，亦称 cruising range）

cruising speed （汽车的）巡行车速（见 cruise velocity）

cruising switch （汽车定速巡行系统的）巡行控制开关（指定速巡行系统中的主电源开关"cruise main switch"，设定/减速开关"set/coast switch"，复位/加速开关"REC/ACC switch"，取消开关"Cancel switch"的总称）

crumple zone 防撞压损区（指轿车的前、后端被撞时，先受压挤、破损，吸收能量，保护车内乘员安全的构造区，= crush zone, deformation zone）

crush ①压碎，压皱，压坏 ②碰撞

crushability 抗压性；抗碰撞性

crushable construction 易压损结构（一般指强度较低，受挤压、碰撞时易于损坏的结构，在汽车上利用这类结构在撞车时，吸收碰撞能量，保护乘员）

crushable zone 见 crumple zone, zone body concept

crusher （旧车）破碎机

crush height （滑动轴瓦）压紧量；压紧高度（对口平面高出值，装配时轴瓦切口边超出轴承座对口平面的高度，以便装合后轴瓦背紧贴轴承座，简称 crush, = bearing crush, crush pad）

crushing 压碎，轧碎，捣碎

crush pad 见 crush height

crush zone 见 crumple zone

cryogenic 深冷的，低温的（一般指 -100℃以下）

cryogenic liquid fuel 低温液化燃料

cryogenics 低温学（研究物质在很低温度下的性能、效应等）

cryometer 低温计（= cryoscope）

cryophysics 低温物理学，超导物理学

cryotron 冷子管（利用导电材料的低温效应制成的一种磁场微小的变化即可使电流产生大的变化的器件，亦称冷持元件，冷温管）

crypto gear 行星齿轮，行星齿轮机构（= planetary gear, epicyclic gear, sun and planet gear）

crystal ①晶体，晶粒，结晶，水晶制品 ②水晶制的，透明的，结晶的

crystal chromatic light 晶体变色灯（用于检测是否醉酒，未醉时为白色，醉后为特定彩色）

crystal-controlled （石英）晶体控制的

crystalline material 晶体材料
crystallization point 结晶温度，结晶点
crystal pickup 压电晶体传感器
crystal rectifier 晶体二极管整流器
crystal wafer 晶片
c/s 周／秒（c/s），赫（兹）（cycle/second）
CSF 催化炭烟过滤器［catalyzed soot filter，亦称 SCR on Filter system（选择性催化还原-过滤系统）。指在炭烟滤清器上方加装选择性催化剂的排放净化系统］
C-shape column C 形柱
CSI ①胸部（冲击）严重程度指数（chest severity index）②国际汽车运动委员会（Commission Sportive International）
CSI engine 压燃-火花点火（双模式）发动机（compression and spark ignition engine 的简称，部分负荷时压燃，满负荷时电火花点火）
CSL ①（current steering logic）电流控制逻辑（电路）②（current switch logic）电流开关逻辑（电路）
CSMA/CD 带冲突检测的载波侦听多路存取［carrier sense multiple access with collision detection 的简称，有时书写 CSMA，在车-车间、车-路间、车-媒体间使用的多路存取通信系统中防止数据传输碰撞或冲突的一种控制方式。在发送数据前先要侦听（sense）传输媒体（carrier）是否空闲，若空闲，便开始传输，否则等到空闲后再传输，以避免冲突］
cst 厘泡（亦写作 cs，见 centistokes）
C-4 system C-4 系统（计算机控制催化转化器系统 computer controlled catalytic converter system 的简称）
3C system =（**CCC system**）（美通用公司的）计算机控制系统（商品名，computer command control system 的简称）
CTC impact 车对车碰撞（car to car impact 的简称，= car to car crash）
CTL ①互补晶体管逻辑（complementary transistor logic 的简称）②磁心晶体管逻辑（core transistor logic 的简称）
CTM 中央定时器模块（center timer module 的简称，控制安全带、车门半开、前照灯误开等的警告的定时）
CTR 见 critical temperature resistor
CTS 冷却水温传感器（coolant temperature sensor 的简称）
CTT 汽油（中）四乙基铅（含量）测定试验（gasoline tetraethyl lead test）
Cu 铜（copper）
cubby （驾驶室内仪表板上的）文件箱，手套箱，手工具箱，杂物箱（无盖者称 cubby hole）
cube 立方体，立方，三次幂
cubes ［美］立方英寸（= cubic inches）
cub exp 体膨胀系数（coefficient of cubical expansion 的简称）
cubic 立方体的，立方的，三次方的
cubical expansion 体积膨胀（= volume expansion）
cubic capacity （发动机汽缸的）排量，工作容积，立方英寸容积（以 in^3 为排量单位，北美一直沿用至今）
cubic centimeter 立方厘米（体积、容积单位，代号 cc 或 cm^3，= ml，参见 millilitre）
cubic deformation 体积变形
cubic measure 容量，体积
cubic meter 立方米
cu. cm. 立方厘米（cubic centimeter）
cuff valve engine 一种套筒滑阀式气门发动机
Cugnot 居纽（法国人 Nicolas Joseph

Cugnot, 1769 年研制成蒸汽机三轮拖炮车，可乘坐 4 人，时速达 3.6km/h，是世界上第一辆蒸汽机汽车）

culprit ①出事故的原因，故障原因 ②可能出故障的地方，故障所在处 ③肇事者

cult car 畅销车，受车迷喜爱的车

cum 立方米（cubic meter）

cu. mm. 立方毫米（cubic millimeter）

Cummis ECI system 冠明思电子控制（柴油）喷射系统（Cummis electronically controlled injection system 的简称）

cumulative 渐增的，累积的，累计的

cumulative compound（wound）motor 积复激（励）电动机（具有两个磁场线圈的复激电机，如：两挡切换式风窗刮水器用电动机）

cumulative error 累计误差（= accumulated errors）

cumulative failure probability 累积失效概率（汽车在规定的条件下和规定的时间内失效或故障的概率）

cumulative unbalance （组合件的）累积不平衡度

cunife（alloy） 铜镍铁永磁合金

cuno（oil）filter 叠片式滤油器（滤芯由多片薄片叠合而成，机油通过片间微隙过滤）

cup ①杯，碗，杯形物 ②盖，罩，帽 ③（轴承）外圈皮碗

cup-and-ball joint 球窝关节

cup-and-cone bearing 锥形滚子轴承（见 conical roller bearing）

cup angle （圆锥滚珠轴承）外（圈工作面形成的）圆锥角

cup grease 钙基润滑脂，滑脂杯滑脂（由矿物油与钙肥皂制成的滑脂，耐水性强，多用于水泵等的滑脂加注杯中，因而得名，参见 lime soap grease）

cup gum （液压制动系的）杯形胶质密封件，皮碗

cup holder （轿车车厢内的饮水）杯托

cup packing 皮碗，碗形密封件（= cup seal）

cupped 成杯形的，成深凹形的，深拉的

cupped washer （凹）碟形垫圈（- saucer washer）

cupping test（of metals） （金属的）突杯试验（用球形冲头将板状或带状金属板压入规定尺寸的冲模中直至出现穿透裂缝，测定突杯深度值的试验，参见 cupping test value）

cupping test value 突杯深度值（突杯试验中，裂缝开始穿透试样厚度，透光时冲头的压入深度）

cup protector （液压制动器）皮碗防护垫（防止擦伤制动皮碗的垫片等）

cupro-nickel（metal） 铜镍合金，白铜（镍40%，少量铁、锰）

cup seap （液压缸活塞等的）密封皮碗

cup-shape flexspline 杯形柔轮（谐波齿轮传动中，基本形状呈圆柱杯形的柔轮，参见 flexspline）

cup spring 盘形弹簧

cup valve 杯形阀，钟形阀

cup wear （周期性出现于胎面周围的，胎面呈）凹沟形异常磨损

cup wheel 杯形砂轮；碟形轮

curb clearance circle 见 clearance circle②

curb idle 最低限制怠速

curb（ing）rib ［美］（轮胎的）防擦线（摸压在胎侧上部，用以保护胎侧不被擦伤的环形凸起胶棱，亦称 protect rib, scuff rib, sidewall rib, =［英］kerb rib, kerbing rib）

curb level 路缘（石）高度

curb light ①装在路缘石上的照明灯 ②（客车车门槛外边的）路边灯（开门时自动接通）

curb mass ［美］整备质量（=［英］kerb mass，底盘干质量与随车件、冷却液及不少于油箱容量90％的燃油质量之和，称为底盘整备质量；底盘整备质量与完整驾驶室质量之和称为底盘与驾驶室整备质量；整车干质量与随车件，冷却液和不少于油箱容量90％的燃油质量之和称为整车整备质量，但都不包括驾驶员和货载，参见 dry mass）

curb return （交叉口转弯处的）弧形路缘石

curbside parking 路边靠缘石驻车

curb stone 路缘石（=［英］kerb stone）

curb-to-curb turning diameter 见 clearance circles

curb-to-curb width 行车道宽度，路缘（石）之间的宽度

curb-top speed （道路设计等的）最高限制车速

curb weight ［美］整备重量（整备质量的旧称，指车辆或底盘满注燃料、冷却水、润滑油、工作油等液体，并带备胎、随车工具等全部附属装备，但不带驾驶员、乘客与货载时的自重，=［英］kerb side weight，见 curb mass）

cure ①固化，硬化，传变硬②（特指橡胶）硫化（见 vulcanization）

cured 硫化了的，固化了的

cured-in valve 硫化固定的内胎气门嘴

cured-on solid tyre （直接硫化在轮辋上的）黏结式实心轮胎

curie 居里（放射性物质的单位，符号：C）

Curie point 居里点，居里温度［当温度高于此点时，压电晶体（或元件）再不能可靠地保有其原有的压电特性，亦称 Curie Temperature（Tc）］

curium 锔 Cm

current ①流（如：水流、气流、离子流、电流等，无特别说明时，多指电流）②通用的，流行的，现时的，日常的，例行的

current amplifier 电流放大器

current breaker 电流开关，断电器

current capacity 载流容量（亦称 current-carrying capacity）

current-carrying 带电的，载流的

current check 例行检查

current circuit 电路

current collector 集电器

current comparator bridge 电流比较电桥

current consumption 电流消耗（量），耗电量

current density ①电流密度（A/m², = density of current, ampere density）②扩散流密度，弥漫流密度

current distributor 配电线，配电器（如：点火系的分电器，= ignition distributor, spark spacer, ignition timer, 亦称 timer）

current gain 电流增益

current intensity 电流强度

current leakage 电流泄漏，漏电

currentless 无电流的；去激励的

current limiter 电流限制器，限流器

currently accepted 目前通用的

current meter 流速仪；电流计

current mirror 电流镜（指可产生与另一电流量成正比的信号的装置）

current mode car 流行型轿车

current mode logic 电流型逻辑（电路）

current "on" time 通电时间；通电率（如：闪光灯通电时间占整个周期的百分比等）

current output 输出电流

current rating 额定电流度

current-regulated output stage （电子控制系统的）电流调节型输出级

current regulator 电流调节器，稳流器

current repair （汽车）小修，日常修理（= minor repair）

current reverser 电流换向开关

current-sensing power FET 电流感应式功率场效应晶体管（当电流超过某规定值时，该晶体管截止）

current sensor 电流传感器（用于检测电流变化及与电流变化有函数关系的各种变量）

current steering logic 电流导引逻辑（电路）

current supply 供电，电源

current surge diode （电路中的）防电涌冲击二极管

current tap 电插头，分插头

current tap socket 分插座

current transformer 变流器，电流互感器（简称CT）

current-voltage characteristic 伏安特性，电流-电压特性（曲线）

current wave form 电流波形

current winding 电流绕组

cursor 滑标，游标，光标

curtail ①比计划提前结束②比预计的减少

curtain 幕，帘，屏，挡板，隔壁

curtain airbag 帘式安全气囊

curtain area 充复面积（指混合气充入燃烧室的均匀度）

curtain shield inflatable bag system （汽车乘员的）护帘式安全气囊系统

curtain sider 软帘式侧壁货车车厢（软帘可拉开，供车侧装卸）

curtate cycloid 短幅（直线型）摆线（在平面上，某圆沿一直线无滑动地滚动时，该圆内任一点的轨迹，有时亦统称为 trochoid）

curtate epicycloid 短幅外摆线〔在平面上，一动圆（发生圆）沿一固定圆（基圆）的外侧，作外切或内切纯滚动时，位于外切动圆之内或外切动圆之外并与动圆固连的一点的轨迹〕

curtate hypocycloid 短幅内摆线（在一平面上，一动圆沿一固定圆的内侧纯滚动时，位于动圆内并与动圆固连的一点的轨迹）

curtate involute 幅短渐开线（在平面上，一条动直线，沿一个固定圆作纯滚动时，与圆心分别位于动直线的各一侧、与该动直线固连的一点的轨迹）

curvature ①弯曲②曲率（亦称 curvity，$=1/\rho$，式中：ρ—曲率半径）

curvature panel 曲面壁板

curve ①曲线②弯曲处，弯道③弯曲的

curve behavior （汽车的）曲线行驶性能，弯道行驶特性（亦写作 curve behaviour）

curve break 曲线转折点

curve control （汽车稳定性控制系统的）弯道（行驶）控制（功能）

curved frame 弯曲形状的车架（= bent frame）

curved grooved type universal joint 见 Bendix-Weiss constant velocity joint

curved tempered glass 曲面钢化玻璃

curved-tooth bevel gear 弧形齿锥齿轮

curved-top 曲面形顶的，曲顶的

curved windscreen glass 曲面风窗玻璃，弧面风窗玻璃（= curved windshield）

curve fitting 曲线拟合

curve speed （汽车的）弯道行驶速度

curve stability （汽车）曲线行驶稳定性

curvic coupling 弧齿联轴器

curvilinear ①曲线（性的）②曲

线的
cushion ①软垫②各种起软垫作用的器件的通称③缓冲的，减振的，挠性的，弹性的④缓冲，减振
cushion car 安全软垫车（［美］David Forster 设计的一种安全车）
cushion cross member 缓冲横梁，缓冲横挡
cushion cylinder 缓冲缸，减振缸
cushion disk coupling 挠性盘式联轴节，弹性盘式联轴节
cushion drive 挠性传动，柔性传动
cushion gum 垫衬胶（缓冲材料用橡胶的总称，= cushion rubber）
cushion hitch spring （牵引、悬架）联结装置缓冲弹簧
cushioning capacity of tyre 轮胎的缓冲能力
cushion spring ①缓冲弹簧，减振弹簧（有时指装在离合器从动盘上的扭转减振器）②坐垫弹簧
cushion-spring drawbar 弹簧减振式牵引装置
cushion tilt 座椅靠垫倾斜机构
cushion tire 软心轮胎（如：海绵轮胎）
custom ①定制的，按顾客要求专门制作的②常规，常例，习惯，传统
custom-built 见 custom made
custom car 定制汽车（根据订货要求加以改造或加装特别设备的汽车）
custom doped （半导体等）常规掺杂的
customer ①用户②泛指各种消耗水、电、燃料的装置
customer demo unit （向）用户展示（的）样机
customer fuel consumption 用户（实际）油耗（相对于制造厂额定油耗而言，= driver's fuel consumption, "inuse" consumption）
customer-specified 订货人提出规格的
customer support facility 用户支持机构
customer testing 用户（使用）试验
custom-fitting 按订货要求加装的
customizable 可按用户要求订制的
customizing plan （按用户要求的定做方案，用于汽车改装业，指）改装方案
custom-made 订制的
custom-rated engine 额定功率应用户要求做出调整的发动机
cut ①切削，切割，削减，切断②（直线等）相交③切口，被切下之物
cut-and-short 将底盘（或）和车身一部分去除而变短的（车辆）
cut-and-try 试探（法），试凑（法），逐步逼近（法）（= cut-and-trial, try and error）
cutaway ①剖开的，剖面的②剖开，切开，切去
cut-away diagram 剖视图（亦称 cut-away illustration, cut-away view）
CUTE 欧洲清洁城市运输（系统，Clean City Transportation for Europe 的简称）
cut-in ①接入，插入，接通，开动②插入的
cut-in point 工作始点，插入点，切入点
cut-in relay 接通继电器
cut-in voltage 路电压，接通电压，（断电器等的）触点闭合电压（= closing voltage）
cutline 图例、插图的说明文字
cut-off 关断，阻断，断开，截止，关机，停车
cut-off cab 去掉后壁的驾驶室（供加装旅宿车身等用）
cut-off frequency 截止频率（如：吸声材料可有效吸收所有入射声的最低频率）

cut-off point 断开点，截止点，熄火点

cut-off ratio 预胀比，等压膨胀比，等压容积比（等压循环或混合循环中，等压膨胀阶段最大容积与最小容积之比）

cut-off signal 停车信号，断电信号，关闭信号

cut-off size 可通过滤芯的最大微料尺寸

cut-off valve 断流阀，截流阀，关闭阀，切断阀，隔离阀

cut-off wheel ①缺口齿轮（齿轮圆周被切去一部分的齿轮）②切割轮（如：金刚石切割轮）

cut (-) out ①切断，断路，关闭，中止；切开，切口②所有停止、中断机械或电路工作的装置③（特指汽车发动机充电电路中防止蓄电池电流逆流的）截流继电器，断流器（= cut-out relay，亦称 cut off relay）

cut-out catalytic converter （可）断开式催化转化器（可随着发动机工况及排气净化要求断开或接通的催化转化器）

cutting blowpipe （气体火焰）切割吹管，切割焊枪，切割器（= cutting torch）

Cutting edge ①（技术等发展的）尖端，最前沿，领先阶段②优势

cut (ting) in speed ①接通速度（指发电机的输出高于蓄电池端电压而开始充电时的转速等）②（发电机的）空载转速（负载为零，端电压达额定电压值时的转速）③换挡（时的）车速

CUV ①混合型多功能车（crossover utility vehicle 的简称，指集运动型多用途车，微型厢式货车与轿车等的特点于一身的新型车辆，有时亦简称 crossover）②基于小轿车平台的多功能车（car-based utility vehicle 的简称，即：基于小轿车的crossover utility vehicle）

Cv 定容比热（const volume specific heat 的简称）

CV 传统汽车（conventional vehicle 的简称，指电动汽车和混合动力汽车等以外的常规汽油车和柴油车）

C/V 受控通风（controlled-ventilation）

CVCC 见 compound vertex combustion chamber

CVH 见 compound-valve hemispherical engine

CV joint 见 constant velocity joint

CVO 商用车辆管理（系统）（Commercial Vehicle Operation 的简称，智能车辆公路系统 IVHS 的子系统）

CV (R) T 见 continuously variable (ratio) transmission

CVS 定容取样法（用清洁空气稀释全部排气并使之在规定温度下流动，定量采集其中一部分作为试样的取样方法）

CVT input shaft 无级变速器的输入轴（指由液力变矩器经行星齿轮式前进/倒车变换机构将发动机转矩输入无级变速器的传动轴，亦称 CVT primary shaft, CVT drive shaft。从无级变速器将转矩输出至主减速器的输出轴称 output shaft, secondary shaft 或 driven puller shaft）

CVT steel belt puller 无级变速器的传动钢带轮（由有效半径可变的主动传动带轮"drive puller, primary puller"和从动传动带轮"driven puller, secondary puller"组成。其主、从动传动带盘均由一个锥面固定盘"fixed taper disc"和一个锥面活动盘"moving taper disc, movable disc"组成。无级变速器电子控制模块"CVT ECM"根据车辆运行情况对转矩的要求通过电动或液压机构推动活动盘，轴向移动，改变其与锥面固定盘的间距，从而改变

主、从传动带轮间 V 形钢带槽的宽度,即其有效传动直径,而实现主、从动传动轮间的速比的无级连续变换)

CVTC 连续可变气门正时控制 (Continuously Variable Timing Control 的简称)

CVTS 见 CVVT

CVT vehicle ①见 converter vehicle ②装有在连续无级变速器的车辆

CVU 无级变速器 (continuously variable unit 的简称)

CVVT 连续可变气门正时 (continuously variable valve timing 的简称,亦称 CVTC, continuously valve timing control 的简称, CVTS, continuously valve timing system 的简称)

cw ①顺时针 (clock-wise) ②连续波,等幅波 (continuous wave)

C-washer C 形垫圈,开口垫圈

c'weight 平衡重 (counter weight)

CWM 水煤浆 (coal water mixture)

cwt [英]担 (= hundred weight, 符号为 cwt, [英] lcwt = 1121b, [美] lcwt = 1001b, lwt = 45.36kg)

CW transmission 等幅波传送, 连续波传送 (= continuous wave transmission 的简称)

cyanidation 氰化, 氰化处理, 碳氮共渗 (兼施渗碳及渗氮, 以提高表面硬度、耐磨性和抗疲劳强度, = cyanide carburizing, cyanide case hardening, cyanide hardening, cyaniding)

cyanide 氰化物

cyaniding under low temperature 软氰化, 低温氰化 (以渗氮为主的低温碳氮共渗)

cyanoacrylates 氰(基)丙烯酸酯, 丙烯腈 (丙烯酸类树脂为基料的高性能黏合剂, 可黏合橡胶、塑料和金属)

cyanogen 氰 (NCCN = dicyanogen)

cyber ①(电子计算机系统等对车辆的)自动控制②控制论 (cybernetics 的简称, 研究信息的传递与控制的理论)

cybernate 使受计算机化自动仪控制

cybernetics (用作单数) 控制论 (神经机械学, 研究人脑思维活动与微机之比较, 以求用微机代替人脑)

cybernetics control number 行为特征参数 (说明一个人的行为特征类型, 简称 C.C.N)

Cybrid 电动-液压动力转向系统 (商品名, 见 electro-hydraulic power steering)

cycle car (指载重 7.5 英担, 皮带或链传动, 由单缸式双缸空冷发动机驱动的) 小型轿车

cycle charging (蓄电池) 循环充电

cycle counter 频率计, 周期计数器

cycle life 以循环次数表示的寿命 (亦称 cyclic life)

cycle ratio 循环比 (指实际累积循环数与根据具有相同特征循环的 S/N 曲线所估计的疲劳寿命之比, 见 S-N curve)

cycles per second 每秒钟循环数 (简称 cps)

cycles-to-failure 断裂或破坏前应力循环次数

cycle temperature 周期性变化的温度

cycle time 周期 (完成一个循环所需的时间, 即: 一个循环起始和终止的时间间隔, 在汽车内燃机上是用曲轴转角度数来表示循环周期的)

cycle timer 周期时间记录器, 循环时间记录器

cycle-to-cycle distribution 各循环与循环间的混合气分配

cycle-to-mileage ratio 循环里程比 (试验台负荷循环数与相应的以英里为单位的行驶里程的比值)

cycle welding (金属等的)合成树脂结合剂焊接法

cyclic 循环的,周期的,交变的,环状的,轮转的,周期性变化的

cyclic dispersion 见 cyclic fluctuation

cyclic fluctuation ①循环波动,循环变动率(指循环与循环之间的温度压力等的变动,亦称 cyclic variation,cyclic dispersion)②周期性波动,周期性变化

cyclic irregularity 周期性的不均匀度

cyclic loading 交变载荷,周期性发生的荷载

cyclic redundancy check (车用计算机控制系统数据通信中的)循环冗余校验法(简称 CRC,使用特定字符检测传输错误的一种方法)

cyclic stress 周期性(发生的)应力,交变应力

cyclic variation 见 cycle fluctuation

cycling 循环的,周期性的,交替的

cycling life test ①周期寿命试验,循环寿命试验(由某几种工况组成一个工作循环,连续重复该工作循环,测定某项性能指标下降到规定值时的该循环数,借以确定被测试件(器)的寿命指标。②(闪光器等的)闪烁寿命试验,闪光寿命试验

cycling pressure switch (车用空调系统的)循环压力开关(空调系统运转时,若蒸发器制冷剂压力低于某一规定值,如:175kPa 时,该开关断开离合器电磁线圈电路,当该压力高于某一值,如:310kPa 时,重新闭合)

cycling time 循环时间,周期时间

cyclo ①圆的,轮转的,旋回的,环(的)(=cycl-)②(载客的)三轮摩托车(=cyclo taxi,cyclopousse)

cyclo-alkyl 环烷

cyclo-butane 环丁烷

cyclo-hexane 环己烷

cyclohexyl benzthiazyl sulphonamide 环己基苯并噻次磺酰胺(天然橡胶的硫化剂,简称 CBS)

cycloid 摆线[在平面上一个动圆(发生圆)沿一直线(基线)作纯滚动时,此圆上一点的轨迹]

cycloidal drive with small teeth difference 摆线少齿差传动(指由摆线少齿差齿轮副,偏心元件及输出机构组成的摆线针轮行星传动)

cycloid(al) gear 摆线齿轮(齿廓为准确或近似的摆线的等距曲线形状的盘形或圆环形齿轮,以及齿廓为准确的或近似的摆线形状的圆柱齿轮,后者称摆线圆柱齿轮)

cycloidal gear pair with small teeth difference 摆线少齿差齿轮副(指由齿数差很小的摆线齿轮和针轮组成的摆线齿轮副)

cycloidal path embedded in the ground (车轮)沉入地面部分的摆线轨迹

cycloidal-pin wheel pair 摆线针齿轮副(由摆线齿轮和针轮组成的齿轮副)

cycloidal-pin wheel planetary drive 摆线针轮行星齿轮传动(由摆线齿轮-针齿轮副,偏心元件及输出机构组成)

cycloid curve 旋轮线(A 圆圆周沿 B 圆圆周无滑动地滚动时,A 圆圆周上任一点的轨迹)

cycloid pump 短幅直线型摆线内齿转子泵(转子泵的一种,以该摆线代替一般转子泵的外转子内齿的圆弧齿廓)

cyclometer 回转计,周期计,循环计数器

cyclone ①旋风②离心式分离器

cyclone air cleaner 离心式空气滤清器

cyclone combustion chamber 旋风式

燃烧室

cyclone scrubber 离心式洗涤机；离心式除尘器

cyclone separator 离心式空气粗滤器，离心式分离器

cyclone vane （空气滤清器的）旋风叶片

cycloolefin （或 cycloolefen）环烯

cyclo-olefin 环烯

cyclo-paraffin 环烷，环烷（属）烃

cyclo-pentane 环戊烷

cycloscope 转速计

cylinder air deflector （风冷发动机）汽缸冷却空气导流板（亦称 cylinder baffle）

cylinder arrangement 汽缸排列，汽缸布置

cylinder balance （多缸发动机）各缸（点火、功率、混合气分配等）平衡度

cylinder balance test 发动机平衡试验（使一缸或数缸断火后，测定发动机真空度与转速等的变化的方法来查明各缸技术状况的试验）

cylinder bank V 形发动机的半边（如 V-8 发动机的一排四缸）

cylinder barrel ①（特指空冷式发动机）汽缸外套，外缸套②缸筒

cylinder block 汽缸体，缸体（= cylinder body，指两个或多个汽缸铸成或焊成整体，或用螺栓联成一体的部件）

cylinder block flange recess 汽缸体上平面的汽缸套凸缘沉肩

cylinder block oil hole 汽缸体机油孔

cylinder block water distributor tube 汽缸体（水套）分水管，汽缸体冷却水分配管

cylinder bore （发动机）汽缸直径（指汽缸内孔的直径）

cylinder bore gauge 量缸表，缸径测定仪

cylinder boring and honing machine 汽缸镗（珩）磨床，镗缸磨缸机

cylinder boring bar ①（移动式）镗缸机②镗缸机镗杆

cylinder bush 汽缸套（见 cylinder liner）

cylinder-by-cylinder instantaneous torque feedback control 逐缸瞬时转矩（信号）反馈控制（根据发动机各缸做功冲程的瞬时转矩反馈信号，对汽油机各缸点火时刻，喷油量或柴油机各汽缸喷油时刻及喷油量作闭路控制，保证各缸输出转矩、功率均等并符合控制目标的要求，该反馈信息还可供车载诊断系统检测汽缸缺火等故障）

cylinder bypass control method （电子控制全液压动力转向系转向液压的）动力缸旁通控制法（其动力缸两室间装有一电磁阀控制的旁通通道，随着车速的增大，该电磁阀的开启度加大，于是动力缸的输出液压减小，转向盘转向加重）

cylinder cam 圆柱形凸轮，圆筒形（带槽）凸轮（= drum cam，barrel cam）

cylinder capacity （发动机）汽缸容积，汽缸排量（活塞从上止点至下止点所扫过的汽缸容积，亦称 cylinder displacement）

cylinder cast-in-pair 成对铸造的缸体，成对铸造的汽缸

cylinder center line space （各）汽缸中心线间距

cylinder charge 燃烧前进入燃烧室的新鲜混合气充量

cylinder clearance volume （内燃机）汽缸余隙容积（活塞在上止点时的汽缸容积，为汽缸的最小容积，亦称燃烧室总容积，压缩室总容积）

cylinder clothing 汽缸外罩（亦称 cylinder cap，cylinder head cover，cylinder cowl），

cylinder compression tester 汽缸压缩

压力表，汽缸压缩比测试仪
cylinder condensation 缸内凝结水
cylinder crack 缸体裂纹
cylinder cut-out 汽缸断火，(使)一缸断火
cylinder deck 缸体顶面（缸体与缸盖之接触表面）
cylinder-deglazing honer 汽缸去镜面珩磨机
cylinder diameter 汽缸直径，汽缸内径，缸径
cylinder end piece 汽缸体端盖（封盖汽缸体端面的零件）
cylinder end seal ①油缸端密封件 ②缸套下端水封圈
cylinder face 汽缸内表面
cylinder filling process 汽缸充气过程
cylinder fin 汽缸散热片，缸体散热片
cylinder firing frequency 汽缸点火频率，汽缸跳火频率（简称 CFF）
cylinder firing pressure (发动机)汽缸爆发压力
cylinder flange 汽缸凸缘，缸筒凸缘
cylinder foot 缸脚，缸体底边
cylinder frame 汽缸体机架（装在机座上，围住曲轴箱上部、支撑汽缸套及汽缸盖，并和汽缸、汽缸水套、汽缸体形成一体的部件）
cylinder front cover 发动机缸体前盖，正时齿轮盖
cylinder fuel-cut test 停缸试验（一缸或数缸停止供油，借以侧定多缸发动机继续运转能力及查明故障缸位和原因的试验）
cylinder gauge 量缸表（参见 cylinder bore gauge）
cylinder head 缸盖，汽缸盖（偶见称 cylinder cover）
cylinder head base 汽缸盖下层（指组合式汽缸盖的下部）
cylinder head bolt 汽缸盖螺柱（指将缸盖紧固于缸体的螺栓柱）
cylinder head gasket 汽缸盖（衬）垫片（指装在缸盖与缸体间密封燃烧室、冷却液和机油通道的密封件）
cylinder head hydraulic pressure test 缸盖水压试验
cylinder head joint ①缸盖衬垫（= cylinder head gasket）②缸盖接合面，缸盖平面
cylinder head nut 缸盖螺母
cylinder head ring gasket 汽缸盖密封环（装在汽缸盖与汽缸或缸套之间密封燃烧室的环形零件）
cylinder head stud 缸盖螺柱
cylinder head tester 缸盖检测器（测定缸盖是否渗漏）
cylinder head venturi 汽缸盖（涡流燃烧室的）喉管
cylinder head well 汽缸盖的火花塞凹窝
cylinder head with antechamber 带预燃室的汽缸盖
cylinder identification sensor 汽缸识别传感器（简称 CIS 或 CID sensor，向计算机控制模块提供汽缸识别信号，一般是当某一汽缸到达点火时刻，如：上止点前26°时，便向控制系统发出该缸信号的霍尔元件传感器，见 CMP）
cylinder injection system 缸内喷油系（燃油直接喷入汽缸内）
cylinder in line 直列式汽缸（= straight cylinder）
cylinder inside diameter 汽缸内径，缸径
cylinder iron 缸体铸铁
cylinder jacket 汽缸（水）套
cylinder leak（age）tester ①汽缸漏气测试仪（检测内燃机压缩冲程终了，进、排气门同时关闭时，燃烧室渗漏出的气体量）②汽缸渗漏测试仪（测试汽缸是否有油液或冷却

水漏入的仪器）

cylinder liner 汽缸套（由耐磨、耐蚀材料制成的筒形件，镶入汽缸孔内，作为汽缸的工作表面，有干式和湿式之分，亦称 cylinder sleeve，cylinder bush）

cylinder liner bottom gasket 汽缸筒底垫片，汽缸筒底部密封垫

cylinder liner puller 缸套拉器

cylinder load comparator 汽缸气压比较仪，汽缸负荷比较仪，汽缸气压表

cylinder offset 汽缸轴线偏移，汽缸偏置

cylinder oil 发动机机油，汽缸润滑油

cylinder on demand engine （工作缸数可变的）按需停缸式发动机（可根据汽车运行工况对发动机输出功率的要求改变工作汽缸数）

cylinder output checking 汽缸（输出）功率检测（多缸发动机分缸功率检测，=engine balance checking）

cylinder packing ring 缸套密封圈

cylinder passage ①缸口，缸孔 ②缸体的机油道、冷却水道

cylinder perpendicularity gauge 缸孔垂直度检测仪

cylinder plug gauge 缸径塞规

cylinder port （二冲程发动机）汽缸进、排气口

cylinder power （单一）缸输出功率

cylinder pressure 汽缸压力（如：汽缸内的压缩压力、燃烧压力、膨胀压力和负压）

cylinder pressure gauge 缸压表

cylinders cast-in-block 铸成一体的多缸缸体

cylinder scoring 拉缸（汽缸套、活塞和活塞环工作面因摩擦等原因拉伤而影响内燃机正常运转的现象）

cylinder set-up 汽缸布置（方案），汽缸的排列（=arrangement of cylinder）

cylinder side cover 缸体侧盖，缸体水套盖

cylinders in line 直列式缸体，直列式汽缸

cylinders in V-arrangement V形缸体，V形排列汽缸

cylinder sleeve 缸套，可更换式缸筒（压入缸体内的筒形件，=cylinder liner）

cylinder sleeve puller 缸套拆卸器

cylinder sleeve service tool 缸套拆装工具

cylinder spacer 汽缸体隔片（组合式汽缸体的一组汽缸体与另一组汽缸体之间的垫片）

cylinder sticking （内燃机）咬缸（活塞或活塞环与缸套互相黏结，咬住的现象）

cylinder stop 油缸（活塞）行程挡块

cylinder taper 汽缸（磨损成）堆面

cylinder-to-cylinder distribution （多缸发动机）缸与缸之间的（混合气）分配，各缸（混合气）分配

cylinder valve cover 气门室盖，气门机构盖

cylinder variation test 各缸工作均匀性试验

cylinder volume 汽缸容积（=volume of cylinder, stroke volume）

cylinder wall 缸壁（缸孔内壁）

cylinder wall drag 缸壁摩擦阻力

cylinder-wall pressure 缸壁压力

cylinder wall thickness 缸壁厚度

cylinder wear 缸壁磨损

cylindrial lantern gear 针轮（圆柱齿轮的一种，其轮齿由若干个轴线均匀分布于分度圆上并与齿轮轴线平行的圆柱销所构成）

cylindrical 圆筒形的，圆柱形的，圆柱体的

cylindrical base solid tyre 圆柱实心

轮胎（底部呈圆筒形紧固在轮辋上的橡胶实心胎）
cylindrical bearing 滚子轴承
cylindrical boss 圆柱形凸台；缸套凸台
cylindrical cam 圆柱凸轮（在一个圆柱上做出所要求的凹凸形状，= drum cam）
cylindrical discharge （高压喷油泵）圆柱形喷射雾束
cylindrical fuse 管筒式熔断器（熔丝装在陶瓷或玻璃管内）
cylindrical gear 圆柱齿轮（分度曲面为圆柱面的齿轮）
cylindrical gear pair 圆柱齿轮副（两轴线平行或交错的一对互相啮合的圆柱齿轮）
cylindrical spring 圆柱形弹簧
cylindrical thread 圆柱螺纹
cylindrical valve 筒形阀
cylindrical warm pair 圆柱蜗杆副（由圆柱蜗杆及其配对的涡轮组成的交错轴涡轮副）

cylindrical worm 圆柱蜗杆（= parallel type worm，指分度曲面为圆柱面的螺杆）
cylindrical worm gear 圆柱涡轮（与圆柱蜗杆相配的涡轮）
cylindro-conical helix 锥面螺旋线
cyliner head combustion chamber volume 汽缸盖燃烧室容积
cymograph 自记波长计、自记波频计（亦称 kymograph）
cymometer 频率计，波长计，波频计
cymoscope 检波器，振荡指示器
CYP （发动机）缸位（判别）传感器（cylinder position sensor 的简称）
CYS 见 critical yield stress
CYTRA （通用电气公司塑料集团新开发的汽车内部）亚光—免漆饰件用工程塑料的商品名（CYTRA 为丙烯—丁二烯—苯乙烯和聚对苯二甲酸丁二醇酯的共混物，经表面纹理模压后可产生丰富光彩的亚光效果，且成本低）

d ①日期（date 的简写）②日，白天（day 的简写）③十分之一，分（deci 的简写）④变形，失真（deformation 的简写）⑤深度（depth 的简写）⑥导数；派生的（derivative 的简写）⑦微分，差动（的）（differential 的简写）⑧美元（dollar 的简写）⑨剂量（dose 的简写）

3D 三维（three dimensions 的简写）

D-4 汽油直接喷射式四冲程汽油发动机（Direct Injection 4 Stroke Gasoline Engine 的简称，电子控制式汽油直接缸内喷射 4 冲程发动机的商品名。在低负荷下，通过对涡流阀开度的控制，在汽缸内形成强烈的涡流，汽油在火花塞临跳火前喷入缸内，形成整体混合比极稀的层状燃烧；高负荷时，涡流控制阀全开，进气阻力减少，汽油在进气冲程期间喷入缸内，形成均质混合气，即：空燃比随负荷的不同而在极稀混合比到理论混合气之间变化）

D ①柴油机(Diesel 的简写)②（自动变速器的）前进挡（Drive）的简写 ③驱动（Drive 的简写）④直流电动机的输出端（drive end 的简写）

D/A 数模转换，数字模拟转换（digital to analog 的简称）

da 十进制的（deca-）

DAA 数据存取装置（data access arrangement 的简称）

DAB 数字声频广播（digital acoustic-frequency broadcast 的简称）

DAC 数/模转换器，D/A 转换器（digital/analog converter 的简称，参见 A/D-converter）

DAC indicator （仪表板上的）下坡辅助控制系统指示灯（该灯亮表示 DAC 系统工作正常，闪光则表示系统未工作，见 DAC system）

Dacron-reinforced 聚酯纤维强化的

DACS 数据采集和控制系统（Data Acquisition and Control System 的简称）

DAC switch 下坡辅助控制系统开关（该开关处于接通位置时，DAC 系统才起作用）

DAC system 下坡辅助控制系统（downhill assist control system 的简称，电子控制模块根据车轮转速传感器和 G 传感器的信息确定车辆的行进方向和坡度），对各车轮实施制动，使下坡车速保持在前进 5～7km/h，后退 3～5km/h 的范围内，以确保安全。

DADA [美] 底特律汽车经销商协会（Detroit Automobile Dealer Assn 的简称）

DADD [美] 经销商反对酗酒驾驶（组织）（参见 Dealers Against Drunk

Driving)

Daewoo [韩]大宇公司

Daewoo Motor Co. 大宇汽车公司（韩国大型汽车公司之一）

DAF 达夫货车制造厂

DAIHATSU [日]大发（汽车公司名，日文ダィハツ的罗马字母拼音）

Dai hatsu Economical Clean up System- Lean burn [日]大发排气净化稀燃系统（由TGP及氧气催化转化器、EGR系统、空燃比控制系统、减速控制系统、点火时刻控制系统等组成，简称DECS-L）

daily inspection 每日检查，日常检查

daily maintenance 日常维护（旧称例行保养、每日保养）

Daimler-Benz Aktven Gesellschaft [德]戴姆勒-本茨股份公司（中国多简称奔驰公司）

Dakar Beige 达喀尔米金属漆（车身）

dam action 闸流作用（如：火花塞导体上预留小间隙，可增强火花）

damage ①损伤（指在超过技术文件规定的外因作用下，汽车或其零件的完好技术状况遭到破坏的现象），损耗，损失，破坏，摧毁，伤害；事故，故障②[复]损害赔偿费，赔款

damage speed 引起（机件）损坏的速度，破坏速度

damp 阻尼，减振，缓冲，衰减

dampening ball joint 阻尼式球节

damper ①减振器，阻尼器，缓冲器（吸收振动能量、减少振动的装置的统称）②消声器③节气门（参见damper）

damper circuit 阻尼电路

damper fluid 见 damping oil

damper fork （某些悬架的）减振器叉形支撑件

damper of friction 摩擦式减振器

damper piston 减振活塞（亦写作damping piston）

damper solenoid（valve） （减振等阻尼器件中由电子控制模块控制的变）阻尼（特性）电磁阀（该阀关闭时，减振液绕过主阻尼孔道而旁通，减振器件呈软阻尼模式，该阀开启时，减振液通过主阻尼孔，减振器件呈刚硬模式）

damper spring （离合器片上的）减振弹簧（亦写作damping spring, = torgue cushioning springs）

damper strut （独立悬架中，由弹性元件支承的）滑柱

damping ①阻尼（运动过程中，系统能量的消散，通常是利用机械摩擦或液体流过小孔吸收其能量）②起阻尼作用的，阻尼的

damping coefficient 阻尼系数（阻尼力与变形速度的比值，= damp coefficient，见 linear viscous damping coefficient, critical damping coefficient）

damping constant （材料的）阻尼常数 J（$J = \dfrac{D}{\sigma_o n}$，式中：$D$—单位阻尼能；$\sigma_o$—简谐正应力幅值；$n$—材料的阻尼指数，见 damping exponent）

damping control actuator 阻尼控制执行器（电子控制可变阻尼特性悬架系统中，由电子控制模块控制，改变阻尼器件阻尼力"damping force"的执行器，有旋转阀式"rotary valve type"和反压电效应式"reverse piezoelectric effect type"等多种）

damping control system （悬架的）阻尼控制系统（其主要功能是选择适合各种行驶条件的最佳阻尼力）

damp（ing）effect 缓冲作用，减振作用，阻尼作用（= deadening effect）

damping energy 阻尼能（材料在简谐应力下，一个周期内，由于材料内阻尼而消耗的能量，见 unit damping energy）

damping exponent （材料的）阻尼指数 n（$n = \dfrac{D}{J\sigma_o}$，见 damping constant）

damping factor 阻尼因素（在二阶线性系统的自由振动中，输出在最终稳态值附近的一对方向相反的连续摆动的较大幅值与较小幅值之比）

damping force 阻尼力（运动过程中引起系统能量耗散的力）

damping force characteristic 阻尼力特性（减振器的阻尼力与其活塞速度的关系特性）

damping force switching valve （三级阻尼可变式减振器的）阻尼力开关阀（控制减振器节流孔的开、闭及开口面积，借以改变阻尼力，实现"软"、"硬"、"中"模式变换的开关阀）

damping force switching valve （阻尼力可变型减振器的）阻尼力变换开关阀

damping of steering system 转向系阻尼（对转向角或转向盘转角运动的等价黏性阻尼，不包括转向轮与路面间的阻尼）

damping oil 减振液（液压式减振器等用油液，亦称 damping liquid 或 damping fluid）

damping orifice 阻尼节流孔

damping rate ①（汽车转向系）阻尼率，$\zeta = \dfrac{K_f + K_r l_2 + (K_f l_f + K_r l_r^2)m}{\sqrt{m l_2 K_f K_r l^2 (1 + Kv^2)}}$（m/s²），式中：$K_f, K_r$—前、后轮侧偏刚度之和，N/rad；$l_2$—车辆的转动惯量，kg·m²；$l_f, l_r$—车辆前后轮轴与重心间的距离，m；$m$—车辆质量，kg；$l$—轴距；$K$—稳定性因素；$v$—车速，m/s。亦称 damping ratio ②减振率（阻尼元件对能量的消耗率）

damping ratio 阻尼比（线性黏性阻尼系数与临界阻尼系数之比）

damping rubber 橡胶减振器，橡胶减振垫

damping slipper 拖板式减振器（支撑在链条传动、特别是顶置式凸轮轴链传动上的减振装置，用以减轻链条的周期性振动和颠动）

damping spring 阻尼弹簧，减振弹簧

damping torque 阻尼力矩（使可动部分停止摆动的力矩，其方向与可动部分的摆动方向相反，大小与摆速成正比）

damping torque coefficient 阻尼力矩系数（可动部分单位角速度的阻尼力矩）

damping transient 阻尼瞬变过程，衰减瞬变过程（= subsidence transient）

damping type anti-vibrator 阻尼式减振器（利用机械式流体摩擦阻尼限制振动振幅增大的减振器，亦称 damper）

damping valve 阻尼阀

damping vibration （物体在振动过程中不断克服外界阻力而消耗能量，振幅逐渐减小，最后停下来。这种振幅越来越小的振动叫）阻尼振动

dampness 潮湿；湿度，含水量

damp-proof 防湿的，防潮的

daN 10 牛顿（参见 decaNewton）

Dandelion metal 铅基白合金，铅基锑锡轴承合金（铅 72%，锡 10%，锑 18%）

danger 危险

danger of bottoming （车辆）托底的危险（车底碰到凸起物而使车轮抬起脱离地面的现象）

dangerous atmosphere 危险环境气

氛（含有可燃气体的浓度，已达到可点燃的程度，= explosive atmosphere）

dangerous critical injury （事故中）有（生命）危险的极限伤害

dangerous goods transportation inspecting and managing system 危险货物运输监管系统

dangerous severe injury （事故中）有（生命）危险重伤

danger warning 警告路标，危险警告（= warning against danger）

daNm 10 牛·米（参见 decaNewton meter）

daN/mm² 10 牛顿/毫米²（decaNewton/mm²，国际单位制的压力的选用单位）

DAP 邻苯二甲酸二丙烯酯，邻酞酸二丙烯酯 $[C_6H_4(COOCH_2CH:CH_2)_2]$（diallyl phthalate 的简称）

DAR 驱动桥传动比（见 drive axle ratio）

dark adaptation 暗（视觉的视觉）适应（见 scotopic vision）

darkfield 暗视场（= dark ground）

dark sensor （前照灯自动开关系统的）黑暗传感器

Darlington amplifier 戴林顿放大器（由两个集电极互相连接的三极管组成，其中第一个三极管的发射接第二个三极管的基级）

darting 驾车急驰，急驶；突然而急快的动作

DAS 驾驶员辅助系统（协助驾驶员控制车速及与前车或障碍物的距离等，driver assistance system 的简称）

dash board ①见 dash panel ②驾驶室仪表板（简称 dash，= fascial board, instrument panel）③车辆的前端部挡泥板

dashboard airbag 装在仪表板内的安全气囊

dash board cowl （轿车车身和长头货车驾驶室的）前围上盖板（车身风窗玻璃与机罩间的过渡段部分，亦称 cowl top panel）

dash board facing 仪表板护面

dashboard gearchange 仪表板式换挡（机构）（指换挡杆由仪表板伸出或装在仪表板内的换挡机构）

dashboard grab 仪表板上的把手

dashboard indicator （驾驶室）仪表板指示仪，仪表板指示灯

dashboard light 仪表板照明灯（= dashlamp, instrument panel lamp, dashlight, instrument cluster lamp）

dashboard mounted ①装在驾驶室前围板上的 ②装在仪表板上的

dashboard oil thermometer （驾驶室）仪表板上的机油温度计

dashboard radiator thermometer （驾驶室）仪表板上的冷却水温表

dashboard vent 仪表板上的通风口

dashboard ventilation hole （驾驶室）仪表板通风窗口

dash insulator ①（驾驶室）前围板隔热层 ②仪表板隔热板

dash light 仪表板灯（= dashboard light）

dash mounted 安装在仪表板上的

dash panel （轿车车身的）①前围板（发动机舱或前置行李舱与客舱之间的隔板，亦称 dashboard, toe board, = [美] bulkhead 及 firewall）②后围板（后置行李舱与客舱之间的隔板，= [美] bulkhead）

dash panel front brace （汽车车身）仪表底板前撑板条

dash post （驾驶室）仪表板立柱

dashpot 小孔式阻尼器（缸筒-活塞或缸筒-膜片组成的阻尼装置。其缸筒开有一小的排出孔，用于减缓与其活塞杆或膜片杆相连的部件的移动速度）

dash pushbutton ①装在仪表板上的（控制）按钮 ②装在（轿车）前围

板（轿车发动机舱或前置行李舱与客舱间的隔板）上的（控制）踏钮

dash side panel 前围侧板（= cowl side panel）

DASS 柴油添加剂自动添加系统（Diesel Additive Supply System 的简称）

data ①数据，资料②（在汽车电子控制系统中特指）源信息（发动机和整车的各种传感器，收集来的尚未经处理成逻辑化信息"logical information"的无序实时事实信息）

data access 数据存取

data acquisition 数据采集，获取数据

database 数据库（通常指可满足一给定用途或要求的系统化的数据集合）

data buses （车用计算机的）数据总线（指用于处理器内部传送数据和在存储器、处理器及外部设备之间来往传送数据的总线）

data collision （电子控制系统数据传输系统中发生的）数据冲突（指①两个和两个以上的数字信息同时争用一个设备或线路；②在数据传输系统中，在任一个给定瞬时仅能处理一个请求的设备上，同时发生两个或两个以上请求的情况；③两个不同数据信息项，争用同一个存储地址；④多个网络信息传输重叠发生在一个物理信道上等。这些都将导致数据被破坏）

data collision detection ①（数据）冲突检出②（数据）冲突检出信号（在汽车电子控制系统中指表示信息传输先后次序的标识符"identifier"简称"ID"，用来防止数据冲突）

data consistency 数据一致性（在汽车计算机控制系统中指由同一数字信号控制的多个执行器件的动作同步执行性，如：四个车轮的制动器同时动作等）

data decoding technique 数据译码技术（对以前已编码的数据进行逆操作，以变换数据）

data-drive analysis system 数据驱动分析系统（亦称数据流分析系统"data flow analysis system"，一种由数据而不是由指令来驱动程序执行过程的分析系统）

data entry keyboard 数据输入键盘

data field 数据字段（指一个数据库的任何已标明部分，一个数据库可包含一个或多个数据字段）

data input unit 数据输入装置

data link （计算机的）数据链路（指计算机系统中，发送和接收数字信号的电路，数据源与数据接收器之间的互联线路）

data link connector （车载式诊断系统的）数据线插座板（简称 DLC，一般位于仪表板下方，为各电子控制系统故障诊断数据的输出线的插座，按 SAE 的规定该插座必须有 16 个插口，并已对其中的 12 个插口的用途作了规定，如：第二行左起第 4 个插口，即 12 号插口，供 ABS 诊断数据输出用。将扫描检测仪或诊断数据读取装置的插头插入该插口内，即可读取故障诊断数据。美国政府规定从 1995 年 1 月起，原 Chrysler 公司的 Diag Test Connector，Ford 公司的 Self Test Connector，GM 公司的 ALDL 等术语，一律改用 DLC）

data-lock-out bistable circuit 数据锁定双稳态电路（指要求在其预备输入端建立并保持一个对于触发信号输入转换、不使输出改变状态的信号的双稳态电路）

data mining 数据挖掘（见 DM）

data（numeric）display unit 数据示装置

data-processing ①数据处理②数

处理的

data-standardizing formula （试验）数据标准化公式（将试验数据，按标准条件修正用的公式）

data stream 数据流（通过一个数据信道传输的所有数据。在车载式故障诊断系统中指所能检测的全部项目的数据）

data transmission 数据传输

data visualization 数据可视化

data-voice synchronous transmission （行车信息系统的）数据-语音同步传输（可在传输语音的同时传送数据）

datum axis 基准轴线，基准轴

datum hole 基准孔

datum level 基准面，零电平，基准水平

datum line ①基准线，基线 ②（齿条）基准线（指基本齿条的法平面与基准平面的交线，用于确定齿厚与齿距比例）

datum mark 基准点，水准点，（基准点）标高

datum plane （基本齿条或冠轮上的）基准平面（在该平面上，齿厚与齿距的比值为一给定的标准值，通常为 0.5）

datum point 基点，基准点，参考点，固定点

datum radius 零点半径（轮胎按规定充气后，从轮胎旋转轴中心到断面最宽点之间的距离）

datum surface 基准面

Davisson 戴维森（英国人 Robert Davisson，于 1873 年研究出第一辆使用有实用价值的蓄电池作为驱动动力的电动汽车）

day bus 昼行客车（以区别于卧铺客车）

day-cab 无卧铺的昼行货车驾驶室

day coach [美] 昼行客车（无卧铺等）

daylight 昼光，天然光（指直射阳光和天空散射光两部分组成的白昼光）

daylight factor 昼光因素（指车室内某给定平面的一点上天然光的照度与此刻车室外无遮挡水平面上扩散光照度之比）

daylight opening （汽车车顶的）天窗（简称 DLO）

daylight timing lamp 强光正时灯（白天室外亦可适用，= power timing lamp）

daytime fog （有）雾（的白）天

day time running light （汽车的）白昼行车灯（某些国家或地区规定白昼行车亦须打开行车灯，该灯通常使用发光二极管为光源，并多装在前照灯内）

dazzle 眩目（由于反差、光亮度和视角等因素干扰视觉的现象，= glare）

dazzle light（s） 汽车远光灯（= dazzle lamp）

dazzling effect （汽车前照灯）炫目作用，炫目影响

dB 分贝（见 decibel）

DBC ①下坡辅助制动控制系统（见 descent brake control system） ②动态制动控制（系统）（dynamic brake control 的简称，考虑制动过程中，载荷动态转移的电子防抱死制动系统）

DBCsystem 下坡辅助制动控制系统（见 descent brake control system）

DBCT 动态轴承腐蚀试验（dynamic bearing corrosion test）

DBL（method） 抗爆性边界线测定法（参见 detonation border line method）

dBV 伏特分贝（decibel volts 的简称，两个信号的相对强度单位，其数值为该两信号的电压比值的常用对数的 20 倍）

DBV system （美国福特汽车公司）点火推迟真空旁通系（由电控真空阀、点火延迟阀及止回阀组成，随气温和车速推迟点火提前角。delay bypass vacuum system 的简称）

DC ［美］①戴姆勒-克莱斯勒公司（Daimler Chrysler 的简称）②数据通信（data communication 的简称）③空气阻力系数（drag coefficient 的简称）④直流（电）（direct current 的简称）⑤死点（dead position）

DC-AC inverter 直流-交流转换器（如：将混合动力车驱动用电池的直流电流升压后转变为供驱动电动机用的三相交流电的转换器）

3D CAD 三维计算机辅助工业设计（指可绘出部件三维立体外形和内部形状的设计系统，为 3-dimension computer aided industrial design 的简称）

DC-DC converter 直流-直流变压器（如：将高压电池组的高压直流变换为传统照明、娱乐等电子系统所要求的 14V 低压直流的变压器，亦写作 DC-to-DC converter）

dc-firing 直流（脉冲）点火（指由直流脉冲信号引爆安全气囊）

DC generator 直流发电机（［美］简称 generator，=［英］dynamo）

DC generator regulation 直流发电机调节器（控制直流发电机输出的装置，由电压调节器、电流限制器和截流继电器组成）

DCH 双管路液压（制动）系统（dual circuit hydraulic brake system 的简称）

DCM 数据通信模块（data communication module 的简称）

DC motor idle speed control 直流电动机式怠速控制系统（简称 ISC，电子控制模块通过直流、可逆转电动机和齿轮驱动挺杆机构控制节气门怠速运转开度，借以控制怠速转速的系统，见 idle speed control）

D controller 微分控制器（controller with differentiating characteristics 的简称）

DC rim 见 drop center rim

DCS 见 deceleration control system

DC system 减速工况（强制怠速）空燃比控制系统（deceleration control system 的简称）

DCV （空燃比控制系统）减速工况旁通空气流量控制阀（deceleration control valve 的简称）

DCV carburettor 下吸式等真空度化油器（downdraft constant-vacuum carburettor 的简称）

Dd 直喷式柴油机（Direct Injection Diesel 的简称，日本五十铃公司的共用储油歧管高压直喷式柴油机的商品名。该柴油机使用美国卡特皮勒公司生产的共用储油歧管式直接喷射系统"HEUI"，详见 common rail direct-injection system②）

DDA Div 美国通用底特律阿里逊柴油机分公司（Detroit Diesel Allison Div 的简称）

DDB/Optical （C&C 公司推出的汽车局域网）音频系统数字数据光纤通信总线（Digital Data Bus/ Optical 的简称）

DDC （digital down converter 的简称，车用无线电通信系统接收到信息作 A/D 变换后进行数字变频、滤波和重采样）数字下变频器

DDEC 底特律柴油机电子控制系统（Detroit Diesel Electronic Controls 的简称，美国底特律柴油机公司开发的柴油机电子控制系统商品名，亦称 DD Electronic Controls）

DDM 驾驶座车门（控制）模块（driver door module 的简称）

DDR 诊断数据读取器（diagnostic data reader 的简称）

DDU 数字显示装置（digital display

unit 的简称)

DEA 柴油机分析仪(diesel engine analyser 的简称)

deacceleration fuel shut-off device 减速工况(强制怠速)节油器(发动机处于强制怠速工况时使怠速供油自动停止)

deactivation ①停止工作(停止运转,不再起作用)②惰性化,去活化(作用),钝化(作用),减活(化)(作用),惰性化(活化了的原子、分子或其他物质,回复到正常状态)

deactivator ①减活化剂(发动机润滑油用防氧化添加剂的一种)②发动机低速运转时进气通道通过断面缩小装置(以提高此时发动机进气流速,见 IMRChousing)

dead angle 死角(如:视野死区等)

dead axle 非传动轴,非驱动车桥

dead band ①(仪表)不灵敏区,不工作区②(数据传输中的)死区(指输出的模拟变量在输入模拟变量值的某一特定范围内为一常数)③(空气动力学中的)静带,死带

dead battery 放完电的蓄电池,电耗尽的蓄电池 (= discharged battery, rundown battery)

dead center [美]止点,死点(指活塞往复运动时,其顶面从一个方向转向反方向的转变点的位置,简称 DC)

dead-center indicator (活塞式发动机)止点指示器,止点标记

dead earth 完全接地,完全短路,直通地

dead (engine) start 冷车起步(见 standing start with dead engine)

dead head operation (汽车等的)空载行驶

dead head pressure (油泵)零流量压力

dead hole 盲孔,不通孔 (= closed hole)

dead joint 不可拆的接头

dead line 截止日期,期限,安全界线

dead load 恒载,静载,静负荷,静重,(结构)自重

dead man's handle 中断式安全装置(常装于电车控制器上,一旦驾驶员晕倒或其他原因松开操纵把柄时,电流立即切断,电车立即制动,现在也用于汽车上)

dead pass inspection pit 非通道式(汽车)检修地沟

dead pedal 某些车型上,位于离合器踏板左侧的搁脚板

dead-reckoning (车辆导行系统中使用的)车位推算法(由测定车辆已行驶距离的距离感传系统和测定车辆方向变化的方位传感系统输出的信号,经适当的软件处理后,确定车辆的实时位置。一般方位传感器使用固体电路磁通量阀门罗盘、陀螺系统或由一对转速传感器,左、右前轮各一个,组成的左、右轮转速差传感系统等)

dead space ①死角,死区②(特指二冲程发动机活塞下方供新鲜充量)预压缩的空间(亦称 crankcase air space)

dead stop 固定挡块,固定冲程限制器

dead time ①空载时间,停工时间②无效时间(由于惯性、齿隙、游隙等无效冲程而损失的时间)③时滞(指输入量产生变化的瞬间到仪器仪表等输出量开始变化的瞬间为止的时间,亦称死时)

dead volume 死区容积(在滤纸式烟度计中,取样探头进口到滤纸表面的所有容积)

dead weight ①固定负载,不变负载 (= dead load,指结构的总负载,即:结构自重与结构所承受的永久

负载之和）②（货车的）额定总装载质量 ③ 按质量计算运费的货物

deadweight capacity （车辆的）总装载质量吨位（简称 DWC，= deadweight tonnage，汽车的额定装载质量总吨位）

deadweight tester 活塞式压力传感器（测力活塞通过 O 形密封环等密封在测力缸内，作用于活塞的压力引起活塞位移，进而确定引起该位移量的压力值）

dead weight ton（s） ①（车辆的）总装载质量吨位，总载重吨位（简称 dwt 或 TWT，亦写作 deadweight tonnage，= deadweight capacity）②长吨，载重吨（= 2240lbs，参见 longton，weightton）③自重

dead wind 逆风（= head wind）

dead window 死窗（不能开启的车窗，= dummy window）

deaerate 除气，排气（从液压系统中排除空气），通风

deaerator 除气器，排气装置，空气分离器，油气分离器，脱氧器

dealer-installed 经销商加装的

dealership （汽车）代理商，销售商

deashing 除灰，脱灰，去灰分

debooster ①限制器，限幅器，减压器②（在动力转向系统中保证汽车驾驶员在操纵转向盘时有一定的路感和车轮能自动回正的）解助力装置

debugging ①排除故障，修正错误②（计算机等的）程序调整

debugging period 排除故障的时间

debus 从公共汽车上下来，从客车上下车，（美军）由载货汽车上卸下

decaNewton 10 牛顿（力的倍数单位，代号 daN.）

decaNewton meter 10 牛·米（国际单位制的力矩倍数单位，代号 daNm，10Nm）

decarburize ①脱碳②清除积炭（亦写作 decarburise，decarbonise，decarbonize，= decoke）

decarburizer 脱碳剂，除碳剂（= decarburiser，亦写作 decarboniser，decarbonizer）

DECAT 驾驶员节能意识训练（Driver Energy Conservation Awareness Training 的简称）

decay ①衰退，下降，减弱②（放射性元素的）衰变（指其原子核在放出某种粒子后，变成新的原子核）

decay state （防抱死制动系统的）减压工况（见 pressure drop②）

decay time ①（振动）衰减时间 ②衰变期（见 half life②）③（光亮度的）下降时间（指透过或反射的光亮度最大变化量的 90% 变化到 10% 时的时间间隔）

decelerate 减速

deceleration ①减速②减速度③减速力

deceleration-conscious apportioning valve 减速度感知式（制动）比例分配阀（见 inertia-controlled apportioning valve）

deceleration dashpot 减速缓闭器（减速时减缓节气门关闭速度的小孔阻尼器。如果节气门关闭过快，将引起混合气过浓而使发动机熄火，参见 dashpot）

deceleration fuel cut off 指电子控制式化油器或喷射系统，当发动机达到工作温度、节气门关闭、空挡、转速高于规定的怠速时，切断燃油供给的）减速断油

deceleration mode （电子控制汽油喷射系统的）减速模式

deceleration sensing proportioning valve 减速度感知式比例分配阀（见 DSPV）

deceleration signal （汽车的）减速信号

deceleration spark advance control 减速点火提前控制装置（在减速工况期间提前点火时刻的一种装置）

deceleration to idle 发动机转速降低至急速工况

decelerometer 减速度计（测量车辆制动时减速度的仪器）

decelration valve 减速阀［减速工况下开启，使附加空气流进入进气歧管，以防止回火（backfiring），见 antibackfire valve］

decentralize ①分散②疏散③分管

dechoker 阻风门开启装置

deci （国际计量标准词头）10^{-1}，十分之一（代号 d）

decibel 分贝［代号 dB，亦称 decomlog, logit decilit, decilog, decilu, 参见 bel①表示两个电功率或两个声功率 W_1，W_2 的比值的单位，$NdB = 10 \log_{10} \frac{W_1}{W_2}$；②表示在相同电阻下的两个电压或电流，两个声速或声压 p_1，p_2 的大小的比值单位，$NdB = 20 \log_{10} \frac{p_1}{p_2}$；③人耳能感觉到的振动或噪声大小，即响度的比较单位，$NdB = 20 \log_{10} (V/V_0)$，式中：$V_0$—基准响度；$V$—比较响度］

decigram 分克（= 1/10 克）

decilit 分贝（见 decibel）

decilog ①分洛（压力单位。用对数标度来表示压力的大小，主要用于低压）②分贝（= decibel）

decilu 分贝（decilogarithmic unit 的简称，= decibel）

decimal 小数的，十进位的，十进制的，小数

decimal-binary system 十进位-二进位制

decimal code 十进制（代）码（= coded decimal）

decimal point 小数点（to three places of decimal 小数点后第三位）

decimal system 10 进制（decimal 原于拉丁文 10）

decimeter 分米（十分之一米，代号 dm）

decision-making 决策

deck ①货车的货槽底板②客车的车身地板③轿车的车顶④汽缸体的上平面⑤平台，盖板，覆盖物，层

deck-and-half bus 一层半式公共汽车，一层半式客车（单层车厢，双层座位）

deck bridge 上承式公路桥（= top-road bridge）

deck chair （可折叠式帆布等）活动座椅

deck compartment （roadster 型双座敞篷车后行李舱盖开启后，以行李舱盖为靠背的）后座间（参见 roadster）

deck lid 行李舱盖（= [美] trunk-lid 或 [英] bootlid）

deck lid spoiler 装在行李舱盖上的导风板

deck panel 见 rear deck panel

deck trailer 平板挂车（= platform trailer）

declared power 标称功率（内燃机制造厂家宣布的标定有效功率）

declared speed （发动机的）标称转速（= rated speed 发动机发出标称功率时的相应转速）

declared working condition 标称工况（发动机发出标称功率时的工况）

decline 下降，倾斜；斜坡

declinometer 测斜仪，坡度仪

declutch （使）离合器分离，脱开离合器；离合器分开（= disengage the clutch, press down the clutch pedal）

declutchable flywheel 离合式飞轮

declutching lever 离合器分离杆，离

合器操纵杆

decoater ①（材料，零件等的）镀覆层清除器，漆层清除器 ②镀层（漆层）清除剂

decode 译码，解码（指翻译代码对已编码的数据进行逆操作，以转换数据，恢复其原来的形式或由阅读器等读出。参见 encode）

decoder ①解码器（将二进制数转换为 10 进制形式的装置）②译码器

decoke 刮除积炭，清除积炭；去焦炭，除焦（= decarbonize）

decomlog 见 decibel

decomp ①减压（= decompression）②减压装置（= decompressor）

decomp lever 减压杆，减压阀操纵杆（decompression lever 的简称，= relief lever）

decompress 减压

decompression valve 减压阀（参见 compression release valve）

decompressor ①减压器，减压装置 ②（特指柴油机或旧式汽油机为减轻起动阻力的手动汽缸）减压阀

decorate 装饰，修饰

decoration chrome plating 装饰性镀铬

decoration coating 装饰涂层，装饰漆

decorative rib （轮胎胎侧上凸起的）装饰（性）线（条）

decorative sidewall 装饰性胎侧（颜色不同于外胎表面其他部位的彩色胎侧）

decorative trim ring （装在车轮轮圈上的）装饰环

decrease speed （汽车）减速（松开加速踏板，= ease up on the gas, release the accelerator pedal, shut-off the gas）

decrement 减少，减少量

decremental hardening 局部淬火（= selective hardening）

DECS （日本）大发公司汽车节油排气净化系统（Daihatsu Economical Clean up System 的简称）

DECS-Lean burn （日本）大发汽车公司的稀燃节油排气净化系统（简称 DECS-L）

dedendum 齿根高（①圆柱齿轮指齿根圆与分度圆之间的径向距离；②锥齿轮指分度圆至齿根圆之间沿背锥母线量度的距离 ③圆柱蜗杆指齿根圆柱面与分度圆柱面之间的径向距离 ④环面蜗杆指分度圆与分度圆之间的径向距离）

dedendum angle （锥齿轮的）齿根角（指分锥角与根锥角之差）

dedendum circle （齿轮的）齿根圆（亦称 root circle，锥齿轮指根锥与背锥的交线，圆柱齿轮指其齿根柱面与端平面的交线）

dedendum flank （齿表面的）下齿面（位于分度曲面与齿根曲面之间的齿面）

de Dion joint 多迪奥联轴节（允许连接的轴作轴向滑动的联轴节，亦称滑柱式联轴节，= plunging joint 或 sliding-block joint）

de Dion tube 多迪奥驱动桥管状梁（见 de Dion axle）

de Dion type suspension 多迪奥式悬架（主减速器安装在车架或车身上，左、右车轮用刚性轴连接起来的悬架形式，见 de Dion axle）

de-energized 不通电的，不带电的，（切）断电（流）的，去励磁的，去能的

DEEP 发动机参数的动态测定（dynamic evaluation of engine parameters 的简称）

deep black 深黑（车身颜色）

deep-bowl-in-asymmetrical-crown piston 非对称型深（燃烧室凹）窝顶活塞

deep-chromed 厚镀铬层的

deep cycle battery 指在设计上可承受连续多次反复充、放电循环的蓄电池

deep cycling （指蓄电池）经反复完全放电和再充电

deep discharge 大量放电，急剧放电

deep-dished 深碟形的（活塞顶等）

deep-groove ball bearing 深槽式球轴承

deep-loading trailer 低车架挂车（= cranked frame trailer）

deep low gear 最低挡

deep-race bearing 深槽座圈轴承

deep ruby metallic （汽车车身的）金属光泽的深红色，深红宝石金属漆色

deep seat 软垫式座椅

deep see blue 深海蓝（车身颜色）

deep-skirted crankcase 长裙曲轴箱，长壁曲轴箱

deep vision surveying instrument 深度视觉测试仪（测试驾驶员在行车过程中判定汽车和两旁物体相对位置的能力）

deep-well rim 凹槽轮辋，深式轮辋，凹底轮辋（= drop base rim, well base rim, drop center rim）

DEF 柴油机排气过滤器（diesel exhaust filter 的简称）

defect ①缺陷（指汽车零件任一参数不符合技术文件要求的状况）②故障，损坏，损伤

defect detecting test 缺陷检查，探伤试验

defect detector 缺陷检查器，探伤仪（= detectoscope）

defectogram 探伤图

defectoscope 探伤仪（= defect detector）

defensive driving 安全驾驶，防肇事驾驶

DEFI 数字式电子燃料喷射系统（digital electronic fuel injection 的简称）

define 给…下定义；确定，规定，限定

definite-correction servomechanism 精确修正型伺服机构

deflagrable 易燃的，可速燃的

deflagrate 迅速燃烧，瞬时燃烧（伴随释放大量热量）

deflagration 快速燃烧，亚音速燃烧（火焰面以亚音速传播的燃烧）

deflamation 熄灭火焰

deflate 放气（如：给轮胎放气），减压

deflated tire 放了气的（轮胎）（参见 = blown out tire）

deflation valve 放气阀，排气阀

deflator 放（出空）气减（少）压（力的）装置，减压装置

deflect ①挠曲②偏转，偏斜③（光）折射

deflecting force 弯曲力，偏转力

deflecting plate 导流板

deflecting yoke ①致偏衔接②致偏线圈，偏转线圈③偏转系统

deflection ①偏转②挠曲，挠度③偏转角（= deflexion）④减小；变形量⑤（特指轮胎的）下沉量（按规定充气后，静负荷下轮胎断面高度的减量）

deflection angle ①偏角（曲线的切线与弦所形成的夹角）②（特指液力变矩器内油液的）偏转角（该角越大，输出轴的转矩便越大，取决于叶片角）

deflection curve 变形曲线，载荷-形变曲线；挠度曲线，垂度曲线

deflection factor 偏转因数，偏转灵敏度，偏移系数，变形系数

deflection limiting volume 变形极限区（见 DLV）

deflection movement valve （摆杆式减振器的）压缩（冲程）阀（在车桥与车架相互靠近的压缩冲程，该

阀在减振液的压力下开启）

deflection of crankshaft 曲轴弯曲

deflection of (the) spring 弹簧变形

deflection over steer 变形过度转向（变形转向角增加汽车过度转向量的变形转向，见 deflection steer）

deflection proportional amplifier 偏转型比例放大器

deflection ratio ①（轮胎的）下沉率（轮胎下沉量与断面高度的比率，亦称压缩系数）②（钢板弹簧的）压缩率（每压沉一英寸或一厘米所需的力的磅数或公斤数）

deflection shape of tire 轮胎变形形状

deflection steer 变形转向（作用于悬架与转向系统构件上的力或力矩，使构件变形而引起前轮或后轮相对于悬架质量的转向运动）

deflection steer angle 变形转向角

deflection steer coefficient 变形转向系数（指在轮胎接地面上作用于轮胎的力或力矩，每单位改变量所引起的变形转向角的改变量，该改变量可表征变形转向作用的大小）

deflection understeer 变形不足转向（变形转向角增加汽车不足转向量的变形转向，见 deflection steer）

deflectivity 可变曲性，可挠曲性；偏斜

deflectometer 挠度计，弯度计；偏转计

deflector ①（流体）导向叶片，导流板（= 美 baffle plate）②反射镜，反射器③挡板，护板，轮罩

deflector crown piston 见 deflector piston

deflector head （二冲程发动机配合楔形顶活塞使用的）半圆形燃烧室缸盖

deflector piston （横流扫气式二冲程发动机楔形部分起导流作用的）楔形顶活塞（亦称 deflector crown piston）

deflexion 挠曲，歪斜，歪曲（= deflection）

deflocculated graphite 悬浮于机油中的胶态石墨

defoam 去泡沫

defoamant 去泡沫剂，消沫剂（= defoaming agent）

defoamer ①去泡沫剂②除泡沫器

defog and defrost systems （汽车）防雾和防霜系统

defogger ［美］（汽车风窗玻璃或后窗玻璃的）除霜器，除雾器（美亦称 defroster，= 英 demister）

defogging 去雾；消除风窗玻璃上的雾气

deform 变形

deformable barrier （车辆碰撞试验中使用的）可变形障壁

deformable solid body （机械方法储能的）可变形固体（如：弹簧等）

deformation condition 形变条件

deformation drag 形变阻力

deformation ratio 变形比（变形后的尺寸与原尺寸）

deformation slip （弹性轮胎）变形滑摩（行驶中的轮胎传递驱动力受压变形，在行将离开地面而恢复原状时与地面的滑动摩擦现象等）

deformation zone 见 crumple zone

deformed rim 变形的轮辋，扭曲的轮辋

deformeter 应变测定仪，形变检测仪

default ①系统设定（当用户未作设定时，由计算机系统自动进行的设定）②系统设定值（= default value）

defroster （汽车风窗玻璃）除霜器（利用暖风或玻璃内埋设的电阻丝加热除霜。一般风窗与侧窗多用暖风，后窗多用电热，亦称 demister，defogger）

defroster system （窗玻璃）除霜系统，防霜装置（=demister）

defrosting windshield （装有除霜器的）防霜风窗玻璃

defuelling ①二次加注燃油②放出存油

defuzzification of output data 输出数据的解模糊化

defuzzifucation 指在模糊逻辑定速巡行控制中将输出的速度控制级别转换为模拟输出值的过程

de-gassing filter 尘-气滤清器（不仅能滤去固体杂质，也滤去气体，避免气阻等的内燃机燃油供给系的滤清器）

deglazer 汽缸搪磨机

degradated failure 劣化故障，退化型故障，渐衰失效，衰退性失效

degradation （性能）退化，（能量）衰减

degradation failure 衰退性损坏

degrease （表面）除油；脱脂，清除油

degreaser 脱脂装置，除油设备，去油垢器，脱脂剂，去油污剂

degreasing agent 去脂剂，去油污剂，洗油腻剂

degree ①度（温度、角度等的度量单位）②程度，等级，阶段③次，次数（数字），方次，幂④比例，比率⑤学位

degree Celsius 摄氏度（°C）

degree Fahrenheit 华氏度（°F）

30degree oblique left (right) hand impact test （汽车）左（右）侧30度角斜碰撞试验

degree of adjustment number 调整程度

degree of advance 提前度，提前角度（如：发动机点火及进、排气门开启等的提前角）

degree of atomization （燃料）雾化度

degree of compression 压缩比，压缩（程）度

degree of constant volume 等容度

degree of contamination 污染度

degree of curvature ①曲度，曲率②弧长所对的圆心角（英、美制）③曲线方程的幂数（方次数，指数）

degree of finish 粗糙度

degree of freedom 自由度（简称DF，=degree of liberty）

degree of hardness 硬度

degree of mixing 混合均匀程度

degree of saturation 饱和度

degree of saturation of specific humidity （湿度的）饱和度（相对湿度100%时的绝对湿度为饱和湿度X_s，某条件下的绝对湿度X与X_s之比$X/X_s=\phi$，称为饱和度）

degree of sensitiveness 灵敏度

degree of the temper （汽车用安全玻璃的）钢化度（指钢化玻璃中内应力的大小，一般用光弹仪测得的双折射光程差来表示）

degree of tortuosity ①扭曲程度②（撞车试验等造成的车辆）破坏性程度

degree of understeer 不足转向度（指前、后桥侧偏角差值与侧向加速度关系曲线上侧向加速度值为$2m/s^2$处的平均斜率，即：其纵坐标值除以横坐标值）

degree of valve lift 气门升起度（用与气门升程相对应的凸轮轴转角表示，即：升起度$=\partial d/\partial m$，式中：∂d—气门某一升起高度时的凸轮转角；∂m—气门最大升起高度时的凸轮轴转角）

degree wheel （装在曲轴上用于精确气门正时的）刻度盘

dehumidification 干燥（作用），脱水

dehumidifier 干燥器，干燥装置，干

燥剂（= dehydrator）

dehumidify 烘干，使干燥，脱水，去湿

dehydrate 脱水，使干燥

dehydration 脱水（作用），干燥（作用）

de-icer ①风窗玻璃除冰器②（由该除冰器喷出的）喷雾状除冰液

deicer-switch （风窗玻璃）除冰器开关

deicing properties 防结冰性能

deicing salt （道路）防冰冻用盐

de-ionized water 去离子水（除去各种杂质的纯净水，用于添加蓄电池）

delaminate 分层，成层

delamination 成层，分层，脱层（如：夹层玻璃胶合层与玻璃脱开的脱胶现象等）

delay 延迟，推迟，滞后，迟缓

delay angle 延迟角（如：柴油机的着火延迟角，相位延迟角等）

delayed-action linkage 延迟动作用连杆系

delayed burning period 滞燃期（在柴油机汽缸内从开始喷油到开始着火自燃的这段时间）

delayed ignition 点火延迟，延迟点火（= delayed firing, retarded ignition, retarding ignition, late sparking）

delayed relay 延时继电器；延迟继电器

delay firing 着火滞后，发火滞后；点火迟后

delay line 延迟线

delay nozzle 延时喷油器（针阀式喷油器的一种，在燃油主喷射前，有小股预喷射）

delay of ignition 着火落后期，（见 ignition delay）

delay time 延迟时间，滞后时间；（继电器的）延迟动作时间

delay valve （真空或液压系统中使用的）延迟阀（阀门的动作较控制信号推迟一定的时间）

Delco-Maranic brake （一种）浮钳盘式制动器（商品名，sliding caliper disc brake 的一种）

Delco Moraine ABS VI （通用公司雪佛兰"chevrolet"部的）德尔科·莫瑞恩 VI 型防抱死制动系统（该系统用于通用公司中、小型车辆，与其他系统相同，由车轮转速传感器、电子控制模块、带真空助力器的总泵及制动液压力调节器组成，所不同的只是其液力调节器由三部带电磁制动器的直流电动机，及其带动的三套球面螺杆-螺母机构和由该螺母推动的活塞-球阀机构组成。正常制动时，球阀被电动机通过螺杆-螺母-活塞顶开，制动液经该球阀由总泵流入车轮分泵。防抱死制动时，电动机反转，该球阀落座而关闭总泵与分泵间的油路。这时通过活塞的上、下位移，改变油缸容积，来调节与控制分泵液压。此外，总泵与分泵间尚有一旁通油路，由一电磁阀控制其开、闭。该阀一般情况下常闭，仅在 ABS 出现故障时开启，保证制动油液由总泵流至分泵实现正常制动）

delete 删除，除去，卸掉

deleterious 有害的，有毒的；有害杂质的

deliver ①（油泵等）泵出或输出（液体等）②将新车由生产厂开至销售点等

delivered air-fuel ratio 供给空-燃比（指实际供给汽缸的空燃比，而非理论空燃比）

delivery car 送货车，货物分发车（= delivery truck, delivery van）

delivery chamber ①排出室，输出腔②扩压腔（= discharge chamber）

delivery cone 输出喷嘴（= delivery nozzle）

delivery mileage only 新车仅从工厂到销售点的行驶里程

delivery orifice （水、燃油、机油的）输油孔

delivery pipe 输出管

delivery piping 输出管道，排水管路，输送管道系统

delivery pressure 出口压力

delivery range 输出流量范围

delivery ratio （二冲程发动机的）给气比［指在一个工作循环中，通过扫气孔（进气口）的充量与按进气管状态充满汽缸工作容积的充量的质量比，亦称扫气过量空气系数"excess air factor of scavenging"］

delivery side 输出端，输出侧

delivery speed （气体、液体）排出口速度，排出速度

delivery truck 送货汽车（参见 delivery car）

delivery type pump 分配式燃油喷射泵（= distributor type pump）

delivery unevenness （发动机各汽缸）供油不均匀度（平均供油量的最大偏差与平均供油量的百分比）

delivery valve （柴油机柱塞式喷油泵的）出油阀（出油阀偶件中作往复运动的零件，具有圆锥形密封面）

delivery valve assembly （柴油机柱塞式喷油泵的）出油阀偶件（由出油阀和出油阀座两个零件组成）

delivery valve gasket （柴油机柱塞式喷油泵的）出油阀垫圈（指出油阀紧座与出油阀座之间防漏密封垫）

delivery valve holder （柴油机柱塞式喷油泵的）出油阀紧座（以螺纹旋入喷油泵体或上体，固定出油阀座的零件，上端有螺纹及出油口，与高压油管组件相连）

delivery valve opening pressure （柱塞式喷油泵）出油阀开启压力（使出油阀克服其弹簧压力而升起的燃油压力）

delivery valve seat （柴油机柱塞式喷油泵的）出油阀座（出油阀偶件中的圆筒形零件，出油阀在其孔内作往复运动）

delivery valve spring （柴油机柱塞式喷油泵的）出油阀弹簧（装在出油阀上部，使出油阀在柱塞卸油时迅速回落并保持闭合状态的圆柱形螺旋弹簧）

delivery valve volume reducer （柴油机柱塞式喷油泵的）出油阀减容器（在出油阀弹簧上端，减少出油阀紧座腔室容积的零件）

delivery van （小型城市用）厢式送货汽车，轻型短程送货车（= delivery truck, delivery vehicle, delivery wagon, delivery car, motor delivery van, light van）

delivery volume （泵、抽气机、压气机等的）流量，排出容积

Delphi 德尔福汽车集团（Delphi Automotive Systems 的简称，见 ACG）

Delphi safety technologies 德福尔安全技术（见 ISS）

Delrin 汽车碰撞试验用假人主要关节垫片材料的商品名

delta configuration （交流发电机三个定子线圈的）△形接法，三角形接法（= delta connection）

delta metal δ-合金（铜、锌、铁合金）

delta P (flow) sensor 压差式（流量）传感器［通过测定流体流过某装置（如喉管等）前、后的压力差来确定其流量，亦称 differential pressure flow sensor 或 differential flowmeter］

delta-type engine 三角形发动机（= deltaic engine，相对于一根曲轴，汽缸布置成三角形的三缸或多缸发动机）

Delta-wound stator winding （交流发电机的）三角形接法定子绕组

deluxe （来自法语，简称 DL，= luxurious, sumptuous, elegant）普豪型，普通豪华型（指设备的质量与水平高于基本型，一般装有空调和制动防抱死系统的轿车）

DEM 数字式电子模块（digital electronic module 的简称）

demagnetization 退磁，消磁，去磁

demagnetize 退磁

demamd bus 传呼公共汽车，呼应公共汽车

demand ①要求，需要②要求通行（交通控制用语，要求绿灯信号，通行权）③需要量，消耗量④质询，询问

demand-actuated systems （新型运输系统中的）按需行驶系统，按需开动系统

Demand Responsive Transit 传呼公共汽车，（乘客可用电话呼叫，到乘客所在地接运并直送目的地，亦称 demand response transit system，简称 DRTS）

demarcation 边界，界限

demerit 短处，缺点；过失

demerit rating （汽车发动机燃烧和润滑产生的积炭结胶）脏浸程度评价指标（体系，分成 0~10 度，0 表示完全清洁）

demesh 分离；（齿轮）脱开啮合

demi-aircondition （车厢内）简易空调装置，部分空气调节装置（简称 demi-con）

demister （汽车风窗玻璃、后窗玻璃的）去霜、去雾装置（美称 defogger, defroster）

demodulation 解调（制）（将已调制信号还原为原状态）

demodulator 调解器

demonstration body 带玻璃橱窗的展览车车身

demonstration car 展览汽车，展示用汽车，样品车

demonstration engine 示范发动机，样机

demonstrator （特指）供销售商试驾驶并在用过一年或一年以内减价出售的轿车

demount 拆卸

demountable ①可拆的，可分开的（= detachable, removable, separable）②见 demountable body

demountable body ①可拆卸的车厢②（特指，带有可伸缩式支腿，便于落座在敞开式平板货车或专用的集装箱货车上，可自由停放的）独立式货箱或集装箱（简称 demountable，亦称 swap-body 或 swop-body）

demountable cylinder head 可拆卸式汽缸盖（= detachable cylinder head）

demountable rim 可拆式轮辋（= detachable rim，指可以拆开为 2~5 件主要零件的 2~5 件式轮辋）

demountable tanker carrier 背罐车（装备有机械手和液压系统，能实现自背自卸容罐的罐式汽车）

demulsibility （滑油等的）抗乳化性，乳化稳定性（指滑油从其乳化液中分离出来的能力。参见 demulsification number）

demulsification number （滑油类的）抗乳化值（一般用从乳化液中分离出一定数量的滑油所需时间的分钟数或 1/2 分钟数来表示抗乳化性能）

demulsifier 抗乳化剂（增加滑油等抗乳化性的添加剂，见 demulsibility）

demultiplexer 多路分解器（简称 demux，在多路复用传输通道的终端，接收多路复用器经单线输入的组合信号流，按时间或频率还原为原先的单个信号或数据并分配给相应的接收装置）

demux 见 demultiplexer

denatured alcohol 变性酒精（液压制动系部件清洗用，漆料的溶剂）

Denision motor 德尼森马达［一种柱塞（式）液压马达］

de Normanvile transmission 多罗曼威尔变速器（一种液压行星齿轮机构手动变速器，通过系统控制的制动带或外制动蹄对行星齿轮机构的外制动鼓施加约束来实现手动换挡）

Denovo tyre Denovo 轮胎（［美］Dunlop 公司生产的特种轮胎的商品名，爆胎或漏气后仍可以 50 英里/小时的车速行驶 100 英里）

deNOx cell 可分解 NO_x 的电化学电池

DENO$_x$ TRONIC system （波许公司的柴油机）NO_x（排放）选择性催化还原转化系统（商品名）

dense 浓的，密的，厚的，稠密，稠的

densify 增大密度，增加浓度

densi(to)meter 密度计；比重计，相对密度计

density ①密度（如：标准状态下的大气空气密度为 $1.225 kg/m^2$）②比重③（电场，磁场）强度④浓度，厚度

density separation （混杂物利用其各自）密度（的不同而实现）分离（的方法）

dent ①凹坑，凹槽；压痕②压凹，敲凹

dental formula differential 牙嵌式自由轮差速器（常用于通过性要求高的汽车）

dented leaf spring 凹形板簧

dent puller （车身板件）凹瘪拉器（将凹瘪处拉复原形）

dent resistance （金属板材的）抗撞凹性能（不易被撞击为凹坑的性能）

Denver boot ［美］见 wheel clamp

DEO 柴油机机油（diesel engine oil 的简称）

deoiling 去油

deoxidate 去氧，还原

deoxidation 去氧，还原（= deoxidization）

department 部门，部，司，局，处，科，室；系

Department of Energy ［美］能源部（简称 DOE）

departure angle 离去角（车辆支撑平面与切于静载车辆最后车轮轮胎外缘的平面之间所夹的最大锐角，位于最后车轴后方的任何固定在车辆上的刚性部件均在此平面上方，= descent angle，亦称后悬角［美］"rear overhang angle"）

dependability 可靠性

dependability level 可靠程度，可靠性水平

dependent failure 从属性故障，从属性失效（由其他元件故障而连带引起的故障，= associated failure）

dependent suspension 非独立悬架

dependent variable(s) 函数

depersonalized repair method 混装修理法（不要求被修复的零件或总成装回原车的修理方法）

depleted electrolyte 废电解液，废电液（= spent electrolyte）

depletion 损耗，耗尽；减少，减损

depletion mode (MOS transistor) 耗尽型（金属-氧化物-半导体晶体管）

deploy ①部署，调动②（有效地）利用，运用（electrically deployable 电动的牵引杆、拉钩等）

depolarization 去极（化）作用，（消）退磁（性），退极（性），消偏振（作用）（= depolarisation）

depolarize 退磁，去磁，消偏振；退极（化）

depolarizer ①去极化剂，退极化剂（一种氧化剂，用以消除电池阳极产生的氢氧，防止逆电流。如：干电池电解质中的过氧化锰）②消极化器③消偏振镜

deposit ①沉积（物）②电镀层，喷镀层，喷涂层③沉积，附着，喷，涂，镀薄层

deposit chamber 沉淀槽，沉淀室

deposit ignition 积炭点火（由积炭引起的表面点火"surface ignition"的一种，亦称 deposit-induced ignition，deposit induced runaway surface ignition 简称 DIRSI）

deposition 沉积，附着，涂，覆，镀

deposit of scale 水垢

deposit welding 堆焊（= built-up welding）

depowering 降低功率，减小功率，降低（发动机）强化度

depreciation ①减价，贬值②折旧③损耗④磨损，性能恶化

depreciation costs 折旧费

depreciation factor ①（减光）补偿率②照度补偿系数（照明设备维护系数的倒数，见 maintenance factor）③折旧率，折旧系数

depress 踩下，压低，降低，少

depressed centre car 低底板大型载货汽车（参见 well car）

depressed rib （胎面暗花纹条，轮胎胎面凸起花纹间的低陷肋条，= depressed running rib，sub-tread）

depression ①表面（特指地面）凹陷处，凹坑②（因气流受约束而形成的）低气压，稀薄度，部分真空③低于大气压的静压（如：表面在一定真空度下受到的低压）

depression tank 真空筒，真空容器

depression volume （旋转活塞）凹坑容积，转子工作面凹坑容积

depth 深度；高度；厚度；浓度，稠度

depth filter element 深滤型滤芯（指棉纱及各种纤维材料滤芯，杂质被阻挡在滤芯内部，以别于表面型滤芯，见 surface filter element）

depth of discharge （蓄电池的）放电程度（指尚存容量占总容量的百分比，简称 DOD）

depth of focus （金相显微镜）聚焦深度（指试样可摄最近的最远清晰面间距）

depth of housing 腔体高度（指腔体内孔的轴向尺寸）

depth of penetration ①渗透深度②（贯入计）贯入深度，贯穿深度

depth of root 齿根高（见 dedendum）

depth of (the) piston 活塞高度

depth of thread 螺纹深度

depth of tooth 齿高（圆柱齿轮指齿顶圆与齿根圆之间的径向距离，圆锥齿轮指齿顶圆至齿根圆之间沿背锥母线量度的距离）

derated engine 降低强化程度的发动机，降低额定功率的发动机

derating power ①减额功率（使发动机在稍低于持续功率的工况下运转，并调整喷油定时或压缩比，使最高燃烧压力与持续功率时相同，以降低油耗为目的，比持续功率值低一些的功率）②减载功率

deregister （报废车的）注销

derivation ①推导，推论②求导数

derivative ①变形，变种，改型，引申出来的形式；导出物，派生物②导数，微商③导出的，派生的，由…转化而来的

derive ①推导出，派生出②求导数

derived unit 导出（量测）单位

DERM 见 air bag (system) control module

Dermitron （一种）高频电流测镀层厚度法

derrick ①动臂起重机②起重臂，动臂，吊杆

derust 去锈，除锈
derv （高速）柴油机（道路）车辆（＝diesel engine road vehicle 的简称）
derv fuel 高速柴油机燃料，车用柴油机燃料（凡适合于作高速柴油机燃料的统称）
desaxe 轴线偏移，不同轴性，异轴性
desaxe engine 曲轴偏置式发动机（其曲轴轴线偏移至汽缸中心线的一侧，以增加做功冲程的转矩，减少活塞对缸面的侧向压力）
descale ①除去锈皮，清除氧化皮；去除水垢②缩小比例（尺）③降级
descaling 清除水垢，清除积炭；清除氧化皮
descending grade 下行坡度，下坡
descending stroke ①下行冲程，向下冲程②（一般指）进气冲程（＝downward stroke，inward stroke）
descent ①下降，降落②斜坡，坡道，下坡道
descent angle ①见 departure angle ②（对带摆动式两轴并装后桥悬架的车辆，指）摆角（即：悬架摆动时，后桥前、后轴的升、降角）
descent automatic engine braking （当电子控制模块根据发动机转速、车速及加速踏板位置信号判断，汽车在下坡时即自动起动发动机制动，并可根据坡道的陡、缓程度控制发动机制动的强度）
descent brake control system 下坡辅助制动控制系统（当下坡车速达到危险阈值时即自动制动减速，简称 DBC system）
descent test 下坡运行试验，下坡滑行试验；降落试验
desert buggy 沙漠用越野汽车
desert environmental test 沙漠环境试验
desert-grade gasoline 沙漠地区用汽油
desert vehicle 沙漠汽车（行驶于沙漠地的车辆）
desiccant ①干燥用的，除湿用的，除去水分的②干燥剂，除湿剂
desiccation 脱水，干燥，烘干，烤干，干缩化
desiccator ①干燥器，防潮器②干燥剂，吸湿剂
design ①设计②构造，结构
design capacity （道路的）设计通行能力（等于或略低于实用通行能力）
design criteria 设计规范，设计标准
designed-in cab crash protection 结构型驾驶室碰撞保护（功能）（当车辆发生严重的正面碰撞时驾驶室会沿着底盘上的轨道向后方移动。这时，驾驶室后壁作为相对挂车的碰撞压损区，以保护驾驶室前端各种设备、装置、操控件、仪表和驾驶人员）
designed test 特定条件下的试验，在人工控制条件下的试验
designed（useful）life 设计寿命（＝design life）
designer 设计师，设计人员
design feature 设计特点，结构性能
design for disassembly 拆卸性结构，拆卸性设计（指所设计的产品结构报废时可拆卸，修复的部件可拆下再生使用，简称 DFD）
design for finite life 有限寿命设计法
design hip point 设计臀点（指用于设计和测试车辆座椅用的人体模型的大腿和躯干间的枢轴点，亦简称 design H-point 或 H-point）
design（hourly）volume 设计（小时）交通量（美简称 DHV，＝英 design flow）
designing concept 设计理念（亦称 design idea）
design-it-yourself system 自行设计系

统（由用户自己进行设计的系统）

design life 设计寿命，计算寿命［=designed (useful) life］

design limit load 设计极限载荷，极限设计负载（简称 DLL）

design of interior （汽车的）内饰设计

design path （液力变矩器或耦合器等的）设计液流路线，设计流路，设计流线（指假想的平均有效液流的路径，作为确定叶片的位置角及入、出口半径等的基准）

design radii （液力变矩器等叶片的）设计半径（在设计流线与叶片的理论出口边交点处，所测得的半径）

design speed ①（汽车的）设计车速（在汽车总体设计时所确定的最高车速，与汽车实际测定的最高车速是两种概念）②（道路的）设计车速（保证汽车安全行驶，在道路的平曲线半径、纵坡视距等线形结构设计时所采用的车速）

design vehicle 设计汽车（为确定道路设计条件而使用的车辆。以其总质量、尺寸、行驶特性作为该种车辆，如：轿车、货车的代表值）

design weight 设计重量（设计汽车时确定的整车总质量的旧称）

desmodromic system 凸轮强制关闭式气门控制系统（与常规气门系统不同，气门的关闭不是靠弹簧压力而是由附加的凸轮或拉索机构强制关闭，其结构复杂，但控制精确，可消除气门跳振，简称 desmodromine，亦称 positive cam action type system）

desmodromic valve 见 desmodromic system

desoption 解吸，脱吸（指从物质中放出、排出，脱去吸附的物质，是 adsoption 的反义词）

desoxyribonucleic aid 脱氧核糖核酸（简称 DNA）

destance-measuring device 距离测量装置

destination ①（路程）终点，终点站，目的地 ②目标，目的

destination board （用图形、文字说明公共客运车辆线路、去向的公共汽车）路牌，站牌

destruction test 破坏性试验（= destructive test）

destructive pitting 破坏性点蚀

destructive readout 存储器等的破坏性读出（指使存储的信息从其读出的存储区消失的读出过程）

destructive test 破坏性试验（= destruction test）

desulfuration 脱硫，去硫，（= desulphurization）

desulphurize 去硫，除硫

desuperheat 过热后冷却，降温

det ①拆开的，分开的（detached）②零件，细目，详图（detail）③检波，检测（detection）④检波器，控测仪（detector）

detachable 可拆卸的，可分开的，可摘下的

detachable drop-sides 可拆卸的翻落式货箱侧栏板（亦简称 detachable-side）

detachable endless flange （3~5件式轮辋的）挡圈（可以从轮辋上拆卸下来的轮缘）

detachable endless taper bead seat ring （4~5件式轮辋的）座圈（可以从轮辋上拆卸下来的胎圈座）

detachable hard top 可拆卸式硬车顶（= removable hard top）

detachable head （普通的）可拆卸式缸盖（相对 block head 而言）

detachable spring flange （两件式轮辋的）弹性挡圈（可以从轮辋上拆卸下来的、能起锁圈作用的轮缘，见 lock ring）

detachable tray 可拆卸的底壳，可

拆式货车车厢底板

detachable valve seat 镶式气门座圈，气门座镶圈（= inserted valve seat, valve inserted seat）

detachable wheel rim 可拆卸式轮辋（有时指可从轮辋上拆下来的轮缘，如：挡圈、弹性挡圈等）

detachably-mounted 容易拆装

detachment 分开，分离，拆下，脱开

detail ①细节，细部；零件图，细部详图②详述，列举③（根据总图）拆绘零件图，分件设计；画细部图，细部设计

detecting means ①（控制系统的）检出部，传感部②检测方法，检测手段

detecting test （汽车）检测，检验（确定汽车技术状况或工作能力的检测试验）

detecting test station （汽车）检测站（[美] inspection station）

detection circuit 检波电路，探测电路，传感电路

detector ①检波器，探测器，传感元件②检出器（用以指示某种特定量或物质存在但无须提供量值的装置或器件）

detector cell （红外线气体分析仪的）检测室

detector of defects 探伤仪（= flaw detector）

detent ①棘爪，掣子，锁销，插销；止动块，止动器②闭锁，锁止③（钟表的）擒纵装置

detent ball and spring 弹簧碰珠，弹簧球珠（亦称 detent springs，由一小弹簧和弹簧顶压的铜珠组成）

detent pin 止销，止塞，止爪，掣销

detent torque 起动转矩，阻滞转矩（使未激励的静止永磁电动机转动所需的最小转矩）

detent valve 见 shift over-control valve

detergent ①洗涤剂，清洁剂（= cleaning agent, cleaning compound, detergent additive）②（特指机油或汽油内添加的可除去沉积物或使杂质处于悬浮状态以避免其沉附于机件表面的）清净分散剂③清洁的，含有清洁分散剂的

detergent-inhibitor 清洁分散-抗氧化剂（润滑油的添加剂）

deteriorate 变质，变坏，劣化；损坏

deterioration factor 衰退因素，劣化系数（在汽车使用过程中或进行耐久性试验时，每隔一定的运行时间测得的有关性能参数，如：有害物排放量、油耗等的变化程度，简称 DF）

determination ①确定，规定②定义

determination of direction and range 见 dodar

deterministic data 确定性数据（确定性物理现象的试验结果得到的数据，其主要特征是：物理量之间具有对应关系，变化规律可用明确的函数式描述，在一定精度范围内，可预测未来时刻的值。参见 random data）

deter rust 防锈

detonating velocity 爆震速度

detonating wave 爆震波

detonation 爆燃，爆震，亦称 detonation combustion 爆震燃烧（指汽油在燃烧过程中，末端混合气主火焰前锋面到达之前完成焰前反应，引起自燃，以极高速度传播火焰，产生带爆炸性质的冲击压力波，伴以尖锐的金属敲击声，故亦称敲缸"knock"）

detonation borderline（method） 抗爆性边界线测定法（简称 DBL.，汽油的道路辛烷值的一种测定法，1970 年左右美国 CRC 建立了修正边界法，测定汽油在道路上实际使用时的抗爆性。参见 road knock rat-

ing method)

detonation inhibitor 抗爆（震）剂，防爆剂

detonation-limit surface 爆燃极限点火角曲面（不致产生爆燃的最大点火提前角在发动机转速、真空度等变量所确定的空间坐标系中的坐标点所形成的曲面）

detonation meter 爆震测量仪

detonation sensor 爆震传感器

detonation suppressor ①防爆震剂，汽油抗爆添加剂②抗爆装置（= knock suppressor）

detonation suppressor system 防爆震系统，爆震抑制系统（根据发动机的转速及负荷的变化将点火时刻自动控制在不致产生爆震的范围内）

detoxed vehicle 见 controlled vehicle

detoxer unit 废气净化装置（口语）

detoxification （排气）净化，清除污染物

detoxify （废气）净化

detrimental impurity 污染性夹杂物，有害杂质（= inimical impurity）

detrition 磨损，摩擦损坏

detritus 碎屑，碎末；磨损产物

Detroit 底特律（美国的汽车城）

Detroit Automobile Dealer Assn ［美］底特律汽车经销商协会（简称 DADA）

Detroit Diesel Allison Div （美国通用汽车公司的）底特律阿里逊柴油机分公司（简称 DDA Div）

Detroit horsepower 广告马力（参见 advertised horsepower）

Detroits Big Three （美国汽车城）底特律三巨头（指通用、福特、克莱斯勒三大汽车公司）

Detroit Testing Laboratory ［美］底特律测试实验室（简称 DTL）

detruck （货车）卸货，卸车，把…从货车上卸下来

detrucking area 载货汽车卸货场

detrusion 剪切，剪切变形

detune ①（对发动机而言指）有意将功率调小（为了节油或更高的适应性）②消除谐振，解谐

detuned road-going version （指经调整、改装后功率较小但更适合道路上使用的）公路（竞赛）用变型（车）

detuning coupling 非线性转矩传动联轴节

deuteranopia 红绿色盲（= red-greenblindness）

Deutsch ACCUmotive Co 德国蓄电驱动公司（Dimlar 公司和 Evonik Industries 公司合资企业名，研发车用动力电池）

Deutsche Normen 德国标准（旧称德国工业标准 Deutsche Industrie Normon，简称 DIN）

devaporation 抑制汽化，防止汽化（作用）

developed horsepower 见 development horsepower

developed representation 展开图示法

development 发展，开发，研制

development ability （新产品、新技术等）开发能力，发展能力

development (al) test （新产品）研制试验，开发性试验

development engineer 开发工程师（开拓某一新的领域）

development horsepower （发动机的）发生马力，（简称 Dhp，= developed horse power，非标准术语，表示发动机所发出的功率，有时指发动机的有效功率，= brake power，有时指发动机的指示功率，= indicated power）

development of heat 发热，发出热量

deviate 偏离，偏斜，改变方向

Deviated state （车辆处于）偏离

（车道）状态

deviation ①控制偏差（=目标值，控制量）②偏差，偏移，偏向，漂移，偏转

deviation angle 偏角，交角（美称 intersecting angle）

deviation from intended lane （车辆）偏离预定车道

deviation from mean 对平均值的偏差

deviation in direction 方向偏差，方向偏离

deviation of reading 示值偏差

device 装置，机构

device-dependent 与设备有关的，和装置相关的

device-independent 与设备无关的

device to apply correction to braking force 制动力调节装置

Dewar flask 杜瓦真空瓶（夹壁式镀银玻璃瓶，夹壁之间抽成真空的保温真空瓶，由苏格兰物理学家 Sir James Dewar 发明，故名。）

dewatering ①脱水，除水②脱水的，除水的

dewax 脱蜡，除（去车身板件上的）蜡

DEWETRON 美国一家提供试验与检测设备的知名厂商名

dew point 露点（气体中含有能冷凝的饱和气冷凝为液体时的温度）

de-xenon system 直流氙光系统（一种高强光源）

dextrorotatory （亦写作 dextrorotary）①右旋螺纹的，顺时针方向的 ②（光传播的）右旋性（指线偏振光通过解厉时，迎着其偏振面沿顺时针方向旋转的性质）

dextrorsal 右旋螺纹的，顺时针的

dezincification 除锌（作用），失锌现象，锌的浸析

DF ①设计公式（design formula 的缩写）②测向，定向（direction finding 的缩写）③去雾（defogging 的缩写）④推入配合（drive fit 的缩写）⑤净化系数（decontamination factor 的缩写）⑥劣化系数（deterioration factor 的缩写）

DFC 见 digital frequency control

DF chart （车辆位置等的）无线电定向图（direction finding chart 的简称）

DFD 见 design for disassembly

DF (elastomeric) materials DF 合成橡胶材料（指耐热老化温度为150℃，耐油浸泡胀率最大为60%的橡胶材料，参见 type and class of elastomeric materials）

DFI 数字燃油喷射系统（Digital Fuel Injection 的简称，通用公司电子控制汽油喷射系统的商品名）

DFM 东风汽车公司（Dong Feng Motor Corporation 的简称）

D-front car 装 D 形风窗玻璃的汽车

DFT 可试验性能设计（design for test ability，指在装置或系统设计的初期便考虑对其以后的试验要求的设计方法）

DG ①（美国石油协会润滑油分类记号）轻型柴油机用润滑油②微分增益（differential gain）③圆盘研磨（disk grind）④双层玻璃（double glass）⑤双槽（double groove）

DGR 废气稀释比（dilute gas ratio 的简称，见 dilution ratio）

dhc 见 drophead coupe

DHE 数据处理设备（data handling equipment 的简称）

DHFC 直接（使用）氢（的）燃料电池（direct hydrogen fuel cell 的简称）

Dhp 研制马力（development horsepower 的简称）

DHV 设计（小时）流量（design hourly volume 的简称）

DI ①方向指示器（direction indicator

的简称）②柴油指数（diesel index 的简称）③分电器式电子点火系统（美国政府规定从1995年起带分电器的电子点火系统一律采用SAE推荐的统一名称distributor ignition，简称DI，取代各公司的术语，如：福特的TFI，通用的HEI等）

diac 两端交流开关（元件），双向触发（器）二极管，双向击穿二极管（＝bidirectional trigger diode）

diag ①对角线（diagonal）②图表，图解，曲线图（diagram）③图表的（diagrammatic）

diagcode 故障诊断码（diagnostic code的简称）

diagnosable switch （可）自诊断（电路是否断线或短路的微）开关

diagnose connector （汽车自诊系统的）诊断插座（亦称diagnostic connector，参见Scanner）

diagnoses diagnosis的复数

diagnosis 诊断（在不解体或仅卸下个别小件的条件下，确定整车或某系统技术状况，查明故障部位及原因的检查，一般使用电子仪器）

diagnostic analyzer 故障（诊断）分析仪

diagnostic code 故障诊断码（简称diagcode）

diagnostic expert system 故障诊断专家系统

diagnostic lane （汽车维修厂等的汽车）诊断车道，试车车道，检验车道

diagnostic link 诊断链路（汽车上的诊断系统的连接电路和连接线）

diagnostic parameters 诊断参数（供诊断汽车故障用的，表征汽车技术状况的参数，参见vehicle diagnosis）

diagnostic plug 故障诊断插头

diagnostic readout tool （自诊断系统）诊断读出工具（用于读出各种故障代码等的工具的通称）

diagnostic scope analyzer （故障）诊断示波分析仪

diagnostic sensor 诊断传感器

diagnostic service center （车辆）故障诊断与维修中心

diagnostic socket （汽车上插接车外）诊断（设备连接线的）插座

diagnostic station （汽车）诊断站

diagnostic testing 故障诊断试验（通过试验查明故障）

diagnotor ①诊断程序（包含诊断和编辑程序，以分析异常情况并指明隐含结果的程序）②诊断器

diagonal ①对角线；斜撑，斜构件②对角线的，斜纹的，交叉的

diagonal beam 斜梁，对角梁，对角撑梁

diagonal belt 见shoulder belt

diagonal brace ①对角撑②斜撑，斜拉条（亦称diagonal bracing）

diagonal control （车轮防抱死的）对角控制（用同一指令来控制车辆对角的车轮）

diagonal cut joint piston ring 见diagonal joint piston ring

diagonal distortion （车身等的）歪斜变形，歪扭，歪曲

diagonal flow 斜流

diagonal joint piston ring 斜切口活塞环（＝diagonal cut joint，obliquely cut，bevelled joint piston ring）

diagonal line 对角线

diagonally-braced frame 带X形加强梁的车架（＝cross braced frame）

diagonal(ly) split type dual-circuit brake system 对角线分路式双回路制动系（指"左前轮与右后轮"和"右前轮与左后轮"各有一条独立回路的制动系统，亦称braking force diagonal distribution type dual circuit brake system，有时diagonal用"×"形符号代替）

diagonal member 对角构件，斜构件

(diagonal beam brace 及 strut 等的通称)

diagonalply tire 见 diagonal tyre
diagonal pump 斜流泵
diagonal ribs (胎面的)人字花纹
diagonal strut 对角支撑,斜撑
diagonal tyre 斜交轮胎(指帘布层和缓冲层各相邻层帘线交叉,且与胎面中心线呈小于 90° 角排列的充气轮胎,亦写作 bias tyre)
diagram 图,图表,图解;简图,示意图;曲线图,特性曲线图
diagram of valve movement 配气相位图,气门冲程图(表示气门位移与活塞位移之间的关系)
diagram of wiring 布线图,配线图,接线图,线路图 (= wiring diagram)
diag test connector 见 DLC
diag-tester (故障)诊断器,诊断测试装置
dial ①表盘,指针盘,刻度盘②表盘式的,表盘的
dial couple caliper 千分表式卡钳(副尺为一千分表)
dial cylindergauge tester 缸径千分表检验器
dial depth gauge 深度千分表
dial gauge (可测量到 $\frac{1}{100}$ mm 或 $\frac{1}{1000}$ inch 的带测头和表头的百分表,千分表)
dial indicator 百分表,千分表;表盘式指示器
dialing ride system 应招客运系统(旅客可用电话向出租车中心站要车)
dial instrument 表盘式仪表
dial type switch 盘式旋钮型开关
diamagnetic ①抗磁性的,反磁性的②反磁性体,抗磁体
diameter ①直径②透镜放大的倍数
diameter ratio 内外径比

diameter run-out 径向跳动
diametral 直径的,沿直径方向的(亦写作 diametric 或 diametrical)
diametral pitch (齿轮)径节(圆周率 π 除以齿距的商,其值等于模数的倒数)
diametral plane (直)径面
diametral quotient 直径系数(圆柱蜗杆分度圆直径与轴向模数的比值)
diamond ①金刚钻,金刚石②菱形③菱形的,钻石的
diamonding (汽车前端或后端一角受到直线碰撞以致向后或向前位移,使车架或车身成)菱形变形
diamond interchange 菱形立体交叉口(四路相交的互通式立体交叉的一种)
diamond lens (前照灯的)钻石型配光镜
diamond plate (载货汽车车身等的防滑)钻石花纹底板,钻石花纹踏板,菱形花纹板
diamond-pyramid hardness test 维氏硬度试验(用金刚石压头测定硬度的试验)
diamond pyramid indenter (硬度试验用的)金刚石棱锥压(坑)头
diamond-shaped 菱形的
diaphragm ①膜,膜片②光阑;光圈③(涡轮机)导流板
diaphragm accumulator 膜片式蓄压器,膜片式储能器
diaphragm carburettor 膜片式化油器(无浮子式化油器,具有一个或两个供油膜片,因而可在任何角度下工作并且不受振动和加速等的影响)
diaphragm chamber 膜片室
diaphragm clutch 见 diaphragm spring clutch
diaphragm follower 由膜片驱动的从动件

diaphragm gasoline pump 膜片式汽油泵

diaphragm link 膜片杆（膜片推动式拉动、传递膜片运动的杆件）

diaphragm pneumatic actuator 膜片式气动执行机构

diaphragm-potentiometer 膜片式电位计

diaphragm pressure switch 膜片式压力传感开关

diaphragm spring （膜片弹簧式离合器的）膜片弹簧（对压盘施加压紧力的特殊结构的碟形弹簧，兼起分离杆作用）

diaphragm spring ring （离合器）膜片弹簧（钢丝支撑）卡环（亦称 fulcrum ring，由 inner 和 outer fulcrum ring 组成，卡装在膜片弹簧销孔的两边，成为膜片弹簧的工作支点）

diaphragm-spring（type）clutch 膜片弹簧离合器（现代手动变速器式车辆最常用的一种离合器，采用膜片式弹簧作为压紧弹簧，将从动盘紧压在飞轮与压盘之间）

diaphragm's screen 膜片罩板

diaphragm stack 膜片组

diaphragm stem 膜片杆，膜片连杆（=diaphragm link）

diaphragm（type）brake chamber 膜片式制动气室［以膜片作为承受并传递气压元件的制动气室，亦称 diaphragn-type servo-（air）motor］

diaphragm（type）pump 膜片（式）泵（如：借助膜片的往复运动将油箱内的汽油泵出的汽油泵）

diaphragm type vacuum sensor 膜片式真空传感器

diaphragm-tyre servo-motor 见 diaphragm-tyre brake chamber

DIA procedure 红外线区分检验法（differential infrared analysis procedure 的简称）

diathermance 透热性，传热性，导热性（=diathermancy）

diathermanous ①透热性，导热性 ②透热辐射的，导热的，热射线可以透过的，红外线可以透过的（亦写作 diathermal）

diathermic heating 高频电流加热

dibenzoyl disulphide 二苯甲酰二硫［$(C_6H_5CO)_2S_2$，发动机润滑油中的一种耐极压抗磨剂］

dibromide ethylene 二溴乙烯

DIC 驾驶员信息中心（参见 Driver Information Center）

dichroicratio 二色性比（液晶显示中，指在两个不同的方向上各向异性物质对光吸收程度之比）

dichromatism 二色眼，二色盲（色盲的一种，只能看出两种颜色）

dicky （亦写作 dickey）①（单排双座轿车的）额外的（备用）折叠式后座椅，（=美 rumble seat，亦称 dicky seat 或写作 dickey seat）②易碎的，脆弱的，不可靠的

diclorodifluoromethane 二氯二氟（代）甲烷，氟氯烷（制冷剂 12，用于空调系统）

DI diesel engine 直接喷射式柴油发动机（direct injection diesel engine）

die ①模具，锻模，冲模，铸模，压模 ②板牙；螺丝板 ③小的方立块形零件，小方块 ④冲模成形，模制成形

die-cast（ing） ①压铸，压模铸造 ②压模铸件

diecasting aluminum wheel 模铸铝合金车轮

die-cast rotor housing （转子发动机的）压铸缸体，硬模铸造缸体

die forging 模锻，型锻（=stamp forging）

dielectric absorption （电）介质吸收

dielectric（al） ①电介质，介质（指无须外界能源提供能量或仅提

供微量能量便能保持一稳定电场的任一固体、液体、气体物质，因而是绝缘体）②介质的，介电的，不导电的，绝缘的，非传导性的

dielectric anisotropy 介电各向异性（长轴方向介电常数与短轴方向介电常数之差）

dielectric bonding 高频焊接（= highfrequency welding）

dielectric breakdown test 绝缘击穿试验，电解质击穿试验

dielectric capacity 见 dielectric constant

dielectric cell technique 介电盒法（用连续测定废气的介电常数，来计算空燃比的方法）

dielectric constant 介电常数（在电介质中，点电荷间库仑力 $F = KQ_1Q_2/\varepsilon r^2$，式中：$K$—静电力恒量；$Q_1$，$Q_2$—两个点电荷电量；$r$—二者间的距离；$\varepsilon$—介电常数，其值随介质不同而不同，为表征物质绝缘性能的一个系数，亦称 dielectric coefficient 或 dielectric capacity）

dielectric oil 绝缘油，变压器油

dielectric resistance 绝缘电阻

dielectric strength 绝缘强度，电介质强度

die model 车身主模型（根据车身主图板、车身零件图和样板等所给出的尺寸和外形用优质木材制造的 1∶1 实体模型）

Diesel ［德］鲁道夫·狄塞尔（Rudolf Diesel，1858～1913 年，1892 年研制成燃烧柴油的压燃式发动机，即柴油机，其热力循环称为狄塞尔循环）

diesel ①柴油机（= diesel engine，亦称 oil engine，oil injection engine）②柴油车（泛指以柴油为动力的各种车辆，= diesel-engined vehicle）③柴油④柴油的⑤（汽油机熄火后）继续运转

diesel additive supply system 柴油添加剂自动加添系统（简称 DASS，根据发动机的工况要求，自动加添所需的添加剂）

diesel car 柴油机轿车（= diesel-engined passenger car）

Diesel cycle 狄塞尔循环（由绝热压缩、等压加热、绝热膨胀、等容冷却组成，亦称等压循环，"constant pressure cycle"）

diesel cycle methanol vehicle 狄塞尔循环甲醇汽车（使用全甲醇做燃料的柴油机汽车）

diesel-dope 柴油添加剂（用以改善柴油性能）

diesel-electric drive 柴油机-电机驱动（系统）（由柴油机驱动发电机发电，进而由电动机驱动汽车，这一动力系统的优点是柴油机可在最佳工况、转速下运转，无须变速机构，通常用于大型工程车辆或越野车辆）

diesel engine analyser 柴油机分析仪（简称 DEA，亦称柴油机燃烧分析仪）

Diesel engine automobile ①柴油机轿车（= diesel-engined passenger car）②（欧洲泛指）柴油车，柴油机汽车（= compression ignition engine automobile，diesel-engined vehicle）

diesel engine cut-off control 柴油机停机操纵件（柴油机停机装置的手操纵件）

diesel-engined 以柴油机为动力的，柴油机驱动的

2007 diesel engine emissions standards （美国环保局拟定的）2007 年车用柴油机排放标准（简称，07 diesel standards）

diesel engine exhaust deterioration 柴油机排气恶化（指其有害排放物超过正常排放量的状态）

diesel engine with air blast injection

空气喷射柴油机（利用高压空气喷射柴油的早期低速柴油机，亦称 air injection engine）

diesel engine with air cell 空气室式柴油机（带空气副室，燃烧粗暴，汽车上几乎不再使用，亦称 diesel engine with air chamber）

diesel engine with air cell and controlled turbulence 见 diesel engine with turbulence chamber

diesel engine with airless injection 无气喷射式柴油机（见 airless injection）

diesel engine with antechamber 预燃室式柴油机（间接喷射的分隔式燃烧室柴油的一种，由汽缸盖内的预燃室和活塞上的主燃烧室组成，二者之间相通的孔道截面积很小，且不与预燃室相切，在压缩冲程中，预燃室内形成强烈的紊流，而不是涡流，亦称 diesel engine with precombustion chamber）

diesel engine with direct injection 直接喷射式柴油机，直喷式柴油机（指无副室、燃油直接喷入唯一的一个燃烧室内的开式、半开式、M 过程的燃烧室等的柴油机，相对于间接喷射而言）

diesel engine with precombustion chamber 见 diesel engine with antechamber

diesel engine with solid injection 无气喷射式柴油机（见 airless injection）

diesel engine with turbulence (air) chamber 涡流室式柴油机（为间接喷射的分隔式燃烧室柴油机的一种，由活塞顶和汽缸之间的主燃烧室和汽缸盖内的涡流室组成，二者由一个或数个易于形成涡流的通道相通，喷油器装在涡流室内，压缩冲程中在涡流室中形成强烈的有组织的即受控的涡流，故名，亦称 diesel engine with turbulence, swirl-chamber diesel engine, diesel engine with air cell and controlled turbulence）

diesel engine with two opposed cylinders 双缸对置式柴油机

diesel exhaust filter 柴油机排气过滤器（简称 DEF，装于排气系统，过滤排气中的炭粒粉尘等）

diesel exhaust odor 柴油机废气臭味（odor 亦写作 odour）

diesel fuel 见 diesel fuel oil

diesel-fuel carbon 柴油残炭，柴油积炭

diesel-fuel dribbling 柴油自喷嘴滴漏现象

diesel-fuel fume 柴油气味，柴油恶臭（亦称 diesel fume 或 diesel odour）

diesel fuel grade 柴油等级（1-D 供低温使用，2-D 供常规使用）

diesel-fuel improver 改善柴油特性的添加剂（如：提高柴油十六烷值的添加剂）

diesel fuel oil 柴油，柴油机燃料油（包括轻柴油、重柴油，= diesel fuel）

diesel fuel particles filter 见 DPF

diesel-fuel R. C. engine 柴油转子发动机，柴油旋转活塞发动机

diesel-gas engine 柴油煤气机（双燃料发动机的一种，以煤气为主要燃料并用柴油压燃着火）

diesel-hydrostatic drive 柴油机-静液驱动

dieseling （汽油机）继燃（断开点火开关后继续运转的现象，= afterrun, post-ignition, running on）

diesel injection pump 柴油机喷油泵（机械式油泵，产生高压使燃油由喷射器喷嘴喷入燃烧室）

dieselize 装以柴油机，采用柴油机，柴油机化

Diesel knock 柴油机爆震，柴油机敲

缸（柴油机燃烧过程中发生爆震，速燃期的压力增长率过大，且压力上升产生不连续现象，使曲柄连杆机构强烈振动，而发出敲缸噪声，亦称 diesel rattle，参见 diesel roughness）

Diesel lndex 柴油指数［表示柴油着火性能的一种指数，常简写为 DI，$(= \frac{AC}{100}$，式中：A—柴油的苯胺点；C—柴油的 API 比重度。）柴油的柴油指数愈高，其着火性能愈好。参见 aniline point，API gravity］

diesel-methanol-isopropyl alcohol blends （柴油机等使用的）柴油-甲醇-异丙基乙醇混合燃油

diesel-motored 用柴油机作为动力的（= diesel-operated、diesel-engined、diesel powered）

（**diesel**）**nanoparticles** 纳米微粒物（柴油机排放的毫微米，10^{-9} m 级微粒物）

diesel number 柴油值，柴油标号

diesel odor ［美］柴油机排气气味（=［英］diesel odour）

diesel odor analysis system 柴油机气味分析系统（简称 DOAS，用于分析柴油机运行中放出的臭味）

diesel oil ①柴油，柴油机用燃料（= diesel fuel）②柴油机用润滑油

diesel particulate filter 柴油机废气（中的）微粒滤清器（装在柴油机排气管后，外形类似蜂窝状催化转化器，但无催化净化作用，仅将微粒机械滤除，亦称 diesel particulate filter）

diesel particulate-NOx reduction system 柴油机微粒（排放物）与 NOx（同时）净化系统（为一种多孔陶瓷载体型吸附、还原三元催化系统，废气由陶瓷载体的孔隙间通过时可使微粒物的数量同时减少，一般装在排气管或消声器内）

diesel pilot 引燃柴油（指双燃料发动机中，为了引燃用主要燃料而喷入的少量柴油，参见 dual fuel/ matural gasdiesel engine）

（**diesel**）**PM emission** （柴油机的）微粒物排放（PM 为 particulate matter 的简称）

diesel rattle 见 diesel knock

diesel roughness 柴油机工作粗暴（①指柴油机发生爆震时，工作粗暴②指柴油机即使不发生爆震，只要其燃烧压力升高率超过 0.5~0.6 MPa/deg，也会发生很响的敲缸声，称工作粗暴）

diesel smoke 柴油机排烟，柴油机烟尘（指悬浮于柴油机排气流中，遮蔽、反射、折射光线的微粒）

diesel sparking 柴油机的排气火花

diesel starting fuel 柴油机用的起动燃料

diesel turbo engine 涡轮增压式柴油机

diesel Wankel 汪克尔柴油机（柴油转子发动机，柴油旋转活塞发动机）

dieslization 装置柴油发动机，装用柴油发动机，柴油机化

diesohol 乙醇柴油（乙醇柴油混合燃料，ethyl alcohol-diesel blend fuel 的简称）

diester oil 由二元酸酯合成的润滑油

diesters （合成润滑剂中的）二元酸酯，双酯

diethylene-glycol 二甘醇（$OCH_2CH_2-OH_2$）（汽车发动机冷却系的一种防冻剂）

die welding 模焊

difar 定向及测距（direction-finding and ranging）

diff 见 differential

difference ①差别，区别，不同②差值

difference gauge 极限规

difference of front and rear slip angles

前、后车轮侧偏角差值（可表征汽车不足或过多转向特性）

difference of sideslip angles　侧偏角差（汽车稳态回转试验中，前、后桥综合侧偏角的差值）

different-diameter piston　异径活塞

differential　①差别②微分，差分③差速器（简称diff，能使同一驱动桥的左、右车轮或两驱动桥之间以不同角速度旋转并传递转矩的机构。前者称轮间差速器，inter-wheel differential，后者称桥间差速器，inter-axle differential）④差别的，差速的⑤微分的

differential amplifier　差分放大器（具有两个输入端，放大两个输入信号的差）

differential angle　（气门与气门座间的）座合面锥角的差角（二者相差的角度）

differential anti-skid sensor　差速器（电子防滑系的）车轮滑转传感器

differential axle　（驱动桥）半轴（=axle shaft，half shaft，wheel shaft）

differential bevel gear　差速器锥齿轮（差速器中的锥齿轮有：①由主减速器传动小齿轮驱动的从动冠轮；②差速器的行星小齿轮；③差速器的半轴齿轮等，若无特别说明，一般指①，见 differential crown gear）

differential bevel pinion　差速器行星（小）齿轮（一般简称 differential pinion）

differential box　差速器（外）壳，差速（器）箱

differential cage　（指驱动桥壳内的）差速器壳（由左、右两个圆形半壳组成，差速器的四个行星齿轮及两个半轴齿轮位于其中。主减速器传来的转矩经差速器壳传给十字轴至行星齿轮，再由行星齿轮分配给半轴齿轮，亦称 differential case，偶见称 differential housing）

differential capacitor　差动电容器

differential carrier　差速器前壳［指与整体式驱动桥壳的中央桥壳或可分式桥壳的左、右半桥壳垂直接装的喇叭形外壳。主减速器驱动（小）锥齿轮通过球轴承、差速器壳通过两侧的球轴承均支撑在该前壳内的轴承座上，为差速器外壳的主要组成部分，对双级主减速器，又称主减速器前壳］

differential case　见 differential cage

differential casing　差速器外壳［指差速器所在的那一部分桥壳，亦称 differential housing。由于主减速器与差速器实际上是一个不可分的总成，故又称 final drive casing "主减速器外壳"。它由整体式桥壳的中央外壳或可分式桥壳的左、右中央半壳和后盖及差速器或主减速器前壳（见 differential carrier）等部分组成］

differential circuit　微分电路

differentialcompound winding motor　差动复激式电动机（并激、串激绕组双重使用的电动机）

differentialcompound-wound　差复励绕的

differential cross　差速器的行星齿轮十字轴

differential crown gear　（指由主减速器主动锥形小齿轮驱动的）差速器主动冠轮（主传动从动锥轮，亦称 differential bevel gear，differential crown wheel，master gear，ring wheel，美称 ring gear，偶见美称 differential drive gear，见 crown gear）

differential device　差动装置，差速器

differential diesel engine　有单独传动增压器的柴油机

differential drive gear　见 differential crown gear

differential gas turbine engine　差速

燃气轮机（压气机、叶轮和输出轴用差速传动装置连接）

differential gear ①差速器，差速传动机构②（偶见美指）差速器半轴齿轮（=differential side gear 或 driven gear）

differential geared wheel reductor 差速型行星锥齿轮轮边减速器（亦称 bevel epicyclic hub reductor，由一套行星锥齿轮机构构成的轮边减速器，其减速比一般为2）

differential gear setting mechanism 见 differential limiting device

differential gear train 差动齿轮系，差动轮系

differential gear with self-locking device 自锁式差速器（=self locking differential, locking differential）

differential half-casing （独立悬架的断开式驱动桥的）差速器（左、右）半壳

differential Hall sensor 差动式霍尔元件传感器（由分开一定距离的两个霍尔元件组成，用作齿轮位置传感器等）

differential head 压力差，压头差

differential heating 不均匀加热，差温加热（使零件各部在热处理后有不同的硬度）

differential housing 差速器外壳（见 differential casing）

differential infrared analysis procedure （滑油的）红外线对比区别分析法，红外线区分检验法，（简称 DIA procedure）

differential input linear amplifier 差动输入线性放大器

differential interlock unit 见 differential limiting device

differential limiting-device 差速限制器（指各种防止单侧驱动车轮高速滑转、将左右轮的转矩差自动限制在规定值以下的装置，亦称差速锁，=differential locking device, differential lock 或 interlocking unit, 简称 diff-lock, 偶见称 differential gear setting mechanism, 常见的这类装置有机械式差速器锁、摩擦离合器、黏性耦合器及电子控制式转矩传感式差动限制器等，装有差速限制器的差速器称防滑差速器 limited slip differential, 简称 LSD)

differential linearity error 微分线性误差（线性模/数、数/模转换器的台阶宽或高度的实际值与理想值之差值）

differential lock control 差速锁操纵件（控制差速器锁止装置的操纵件）

differential locking-device 差速锁

differential locking factor 差速器锁止系数（慢转车轮的转矩与快转车轮的转矩之比，亦称 differential locking bias ratio, 简称 differential ratio)

differential locking jaw （牙嵌式）差速锁的牙爪

differentially-inflated tire sections （双腔轮胎）高低压充气内、外腔

differential master gear 见 differential crown wheel

differential mechanism ①差速机构，差动机构②差动机理

differential method of measurement 微差测量法

differential microphone 微分扬声器

differential (mode) input (output) impedace 差模输入（或输出）阻抗（指线性放大器的两输入端或两输出端之间的阻抗）

differential mode voltage amplification （差动输入线性放大器的）差模放大倍数（在规定条件下，输出电压变化与输入电压变化之比）

differential motion 差动，差速运动

differential motor 差绕电动机（简称 DM）

differential odometer （左、右轮）速度差转速表（可测出与记录左、右车轮的转速与里程差，借以推算汽车行驶方向变化的仪表，在汽车推算式导航系统中，用作汽车行驶方向传感器，见 heading sensor）

differential pinion shaft 差速器行星齿轮（十字）轴（亦称 differential spider，differential cross）

differential piston 差压活塞，差动活塞，异径活塞，台阶活塞，双径活塞（活塞具有两种直径，形成阶梯式，= stepped piston，two-diameter piston）

differential-piston engine 差动活塞发动机（亦称 differential-piston motor，stepped piston engine）

differential planet gear 差速行星齿轮

differential power divider 差速器的分动器（箱）

differential pressure 压力降，压差（如润滑系机油滤清器进口与出口之间的压力差）

differential pressure feedback EGR 见 DPFE

differential pressure flowmeter 差压流量计（见 delta P sensor）

differential pressure sensor 压差传感器（见 delta-P sensor）

differential pressure switch 压差开关（当压力差达到规定值时即接通或断开某一电路）

differential protection valve 见 anti-compounding valve

differential ratio ①见 differential locking factor ②（柴油机喷油嘴的）差动比（指喷油嘴针阀圆柱工作面直径与其锥面密封直径之比）

differential right casing 差速器右壳

differential ring gear 见 differential crown wheel

differential screw jack 差动螺旋式千斤顶，差动螺旋起重器

differential shaft 驱动桥半轴，差速器半轴

differential side gear 差速器半轴齿轮（亦称 differential driven gear）

differential slip modulation （左、右轮）滑差控制（指通过差速器的作用，以及调节制动力和驱动力等方法控制左、右轮不同的滑动程度）

differential speed sensor 差速器转速传感器（某些后轮防抱死制动系统的车轮转速传感器装在差速器内，用于监测差速器的输出转速，作为电子控制模块确定后轮是否趋于抱死的主要参数）

differential spider 差速器行星齿轮十字轴（= differential pinion shaft）

differential (spider) pinion 差速器行星（小）齿轮

differential spider pinion 差速器行星（小）齿轮（= differential pinion）

differential supercharging （发动机的）差动增压

differential turbine （行星齿轮）差速燃气轮机（压缩涡轮轴与太阳轮连接，动力涡轮轴和齿环连接，动力输出轴和中间行星齿轮连接，以提高汽轮机部分负荷时的效率）

differential valve in dual-line braking system 双管路制动系中的压差阀（双回路间压力差的传感器件，当系统中一条管路破损泄漏制动压力下降时，则在阀内形成压力差，推动柱塞移动，使警告灯点亮，提醒驾驶员停车检查）

differential winding 差动绕组

differential with selflocking device 自锁差速器

differentiating circuit 微分电路（亦称 differentiator 微分器，其输出函数与一个或多个变量的输入函数的导数成比例）

differentiation ①差别，区别 ②区

分,划分③分化,变异④微分法⑤不同的事物,不同的东西

differentiator 微分器(微分电路,其输出函数与一个或多个变量的输入函数的导数成比例,见 differentiating circuit)

diff-H 高度差(difference in height 的简称)

difficult country 通行困难的地区,崎岖不平的地区,丘陵崎岖地区

difficult terrain 难以通行的地面(地形)

diff jack 差速器举升器,差速器专用千斤顶

diff lock 差速器锁(differential lock 的简称)

diffuse annealing 扩散退火(把工件加热到高温,长时间保温,利用原子的扩散,从而消除或减少偏析现象)

diffused junction (半导体的)扩散结

diffuse field (声的)扩散场(指各个方向的声压均相等的区域)

diffuse lighting 漫射照明(指投射的光在任何方向上均无明显差别的照明)

diffuser ①(化油器的)喉管②扩压管,扩压器〔废气涡轮增压器压气机工作叶轮出口处,将气体的部分动能转变为压力能的有叶或无叶的固定通道装置〕

diffuse reflector ①(光或声)漫反射(光或声波在粗糙表面上的反射,取决于表面粗糙度尺寸与波长间的关系)②漫反射膜(产生漫反射的膜,如:用于反射型液晶显示者)

diffuser vane 扩散器叶片,(活动)喉管叶片;喉管片

diffuser wing curtain (活动喉管式化油器等)活动喉管翼片式叶片

diffuser wing curtain spring (活动)喉管叶片弹簧

diffusing air hole (化油器主供油装置中控制渗入空气流量的)空气量孔(= air-correction jet, 参见 air bleed)

diffusing lens (汽车前照灯的)配光镜,(亦称散光镜,散光玻璃,由透明玻璃压制而成,外表面平滑,内表面为凸透镜和棱镜组合体,其作用是折射和散射前照灯反射镜反射的平行光束)

diffusion ①扩散②漫射,散射

diffusion coating 扩散镀复层

diffusion coefficient 扩散系数

diffusion combustion 扩散燃烧(指燃料与空气边混合边燃烧,亦称 diffusive combustion)

diffusion combustion phase (柴油机燃烧过程中的)扩散燃烧期(燃油蒸气与空气混合后着火燃烧,火焰迅速扩散的时期)

diffusion flame 扩散火焰(指非预混的不均匀混合气燃烧火焰。扩散火焰由一层将燃料流与氧化剂流分隔开的放热反应区构成,即在扩散火焰中燃料和氧化剂被火焰面隔开,二者分别向该火焰面,即反应区扩散,形成混合气而燃烧,故名)

diffusion metallizing method 金属扩散镀覆法

diffusion rate of cars 轿车普及率(一般用每1000人拥有轿车数表示)

diffusion technique (半导体制造的)扩散工艺(将杂质原子扩散到半导体晶体中,形成P型或N型电导率区域的过程)

diffusor 见 diffuser

digger 挖掘机,挖土机

digger bucket 挖掘机铲斗,挖斗

digit ①数(字),位数(= figure)②手指,一指宽(约3/4英寸)

digital 数字的,计数的

(**digital**) **adaptive headlights** （数字式）适应性前照灯（系统）（该系统可根据道路和行驶条件等自动改变前照灯的光形"lighting pattern"）

digital adder 数字加法器（见 adder）

digital-analog decoder 数字-模拟译码器，数模译码器（简称 DAD，将数字数据转换成等价的连续变量的模拟计算装置）

digital brake model 制动器数字模型

digital caliper 数字读出式游标卡

digital circuit 见 digital integrated circuit

digital clock 数字显示式时钟

digital code 数字编码，数字代码（用0与1的集合表示的编码或代码）

digital computer 数字计算机（处理数字数据，即运用数字技术处理数据的计算机）

digital controlled 数控的，数字控制式的

digital dash （汽车的）数字（显示式）仪表

digital data 数字数据（指用数字表示的数据，有时带有特殊字符）

digital data bus 数字式数据总线（简称 d^2B，见 data bus）

Digital Data Bus/ Optical 见 DDB/ Optical

digital decoder 数字译码器（由逻辑元件组成，能按照输入信号组合选择一条或多条输出通道的电路）

digital display unit 数字显示装置（简称DDU）

digital EGR valve 数字式 EGR 阀（指不由发动机进气管真空阀而由电子控制模块直接通过占空比控制其开启时间，以调节废气再循环量的电磁阀）

digital electronic fuel injection 数字式电子控制燃油喷射系统（简称DEFI）

digital electronic module 数字式电子控制模块（简称 DEM，即：汽车电子控制系统的电子计算机）

digital feed forward （积极式噪声控制中的）数字前馈法（根据噪声源头的噪声波形由数字电路产生反噪声波形，使噪声在传播途中被抵消，见 antinoise）

digital filter 数字滤波器［是指一个数字运算过程和电路。对它输入一个数字序列，经过按一定要求（程序）的运算，变换成另一个数字序列输出，由此而达到提取有用信息的目的］

digital frequency control （车用收音机的）频率数字控制系统（可自动稳定或调节所选定电台的频率，简称 DFC）

digital fuel consumption meter 数字式燃油消耗计，数字式油耗计

digital fuel injection 数字式汽油喷射系统（美 Cadillac 公司的电子控制式双喷油器双节气门体汽油喷射系统的商品名，简称 DFI）

digital/graphic display （汽车仪表的）数字-图案显示

digital information 数字信息

digital integrated circuit 数字集成电路（指在输入端和输出端用数字信号工作的集成电路，亦简称 digital circuit）

digital knock control system 数字式爆燃控制系统

digital lean-burn controller （美国克莱斯勒公司稀燃发动机的）数字式稀燃控制器电脑（= digital lean-burn computer）

digital means 数字技术，数字方法

digital measuring instrument 数字式测量仪器（仪表）（指提供数字化输出或数字显示的测量仪器仪表）

digital model assembly 数字模型总

成，数学模型总成（指设计过程中零件及组件的设计及组装均由计算机软件来完成，无须绘制零件图、装配图等，简称 DMA）

digital process control 数字程序控制

digital processing 数字处理（指利用数字电子计算机进行试验数据的运算与分析）

digital readout 数字读出（简称 DIGRO）

digital road map 数字化路线（地）图（亦称 digitizing road map）

digital rolling simulation technology (Dunlop 公司轮胎设计、制造的) 数字滚动模拟技术

digital roughness control （柴油机的）数字式粗暴控制系统（通过调整喷油时刻，减少柴油机工作粗暴倾向的电子控制系统，见 diesel roughness）

digital shaft encoder 数字式（轴）转速编码器（计数一定时间内发生的转速脉冲信号，其精度取决于轴每转产生的脉冲信号数）

digital signal 数字信号（指离散的或不连续的信号，由二进制数码表示的信号）

digital signals interface 数字信号接口

digital simulation （电子计算机）数字模拟

digital simulation model 数字模拟模型，数学模拟模型

digital single point sensing system （安全气囊的）数字式单点碰撞传感系统（亦称 all-electronic single point sensing system 全电子单点碰撞传感系统，见 single point electronic sensing system）

digital speedometer 数字式车速表

digital tachometer 数字式转速表

digital-to-analog converter 数（字）-模（拟）转换器（简称 D/A 转换器，"DAC"，指：①将数字数据转换为以等价的模拟表示的一种功能部件②将数字值转换为与其成比值的模拟信号的装置）

digital torque indicator 数字式转矩指示器

digital torque wrench 数字式转矩扳手

digital type EGR (control) valve 数字式排气再循环（控制）阀（由动力控制模块直接操纵多个不同大小的废气回流孔开放和关闭的电磁阀，根据发动机运转工况的要求，使其中的一个孔或数个孔开启或关闭，以供给最佳数量的再循环废气）

digital type sensor 数字型传感器（可分为计数型和代码型两种，详见 counting type sensor 和 encode type sensor）

digital vehicle 数字车辆（计算机辅助设计中用纯数字化表现的车辆外形、结构、性能等）

digital vehicle control system 数字车辆控制（指数字车辆驾驶系统）

digit figure 数字，（数）位

Digi-Tire 数字滚动模拟技术子午胎（Dunlop 公司使用 digital rolling simulation 技术开发的公路用和泥泞地用子午胎的商品名）

digitize 数字化（指以数字形式表示非离散型数据及用数字表示物理量的模拟值）

digitized signal 数字化信号

digitizer 数字变换器，数字化仪器（可将图形成图像资料转换成数字计算机所要求的二进制数值输入的一种低速输入装置）

digit screen 数字化显示屏

DIGRO 数字读出（digital readout）

DIG Turbo 汽油直接喷射涡轮增压发动机（direct injection gasoline turbo-charging engine 的简称）

dihedral ①由两个平面构成的,二面的,V形的②二面角 (= dihedral angle)

dihydrochloride 二氢氯化物,二盐酸氯化物 [R·(HCL)$_2$]

dike ①障碍物②(路边的)防护栏③堤、坝④渠、排水道(= dyke)

dilatability 膨胀性,膨胀率;延伸性

dilatable 可膨胀的,可延伸的

dilatation coeffcient 膨胀系数

dilatation joint 膨胀缝,伸缩缝

dilatometer 膨胀仪

diluent ①稀释剂,溶剂(亦称thinner)②稀释的物质③稀释的,冲淡的

diluent ratio 稀释比

dilute ①冲淡,稀释②淡的,稀释的

diluted charge 稀释性充气(以达到稀燃的目的)

diluted exhaust 稀释排气(经过稀释的废气)

dilute gasoline engine 稀混合气燃烧式汽油机

dilution 稀释,冲淡;稀释度,淡化度

dilution air (在排放测试中)稀释废气用的空气

dilution ratio 稀释率,稀释比(指CVS容积与排气容积的比率,通常用稀释时的CO$_2$浓度除以经稀释后的CO$_2$浓度求得)

dilution tunnel 稀释风道(经清洁空气稀释的排气中的微粒物质的滤纸式定量采样装置,多与CVS装置结合使用)

dim ①(汽车)近光灯,前照灯的短焦距光束②暗淡的③使暗淡

dim-dip (汽车前照灯)近光

dimension ①尺寸,大小,外形尺寸②因次,量纲;维,度,元③确定尺寸

dimensional 尺寸的;量纲的,因次的;空间的,维度的

dimensional interchangeability 尺寸互换性

dimensional precision 尺寸精度

dimensional restrictions (汽车)尺寸限制

dimensional stability (在环境变化的影响下物体保持其外形不变的)尺寸稳定性

dimensional standard 尺寸标准(如:经过不断评价改进的汽车全尺寸模型,就成为原型车设计尺寸的标准)

dimensional tolerance 尺寸公差

dimension chain 尺寸链(零件图上的有关尺寸需按一定的顺序标注,这些尺寸彼此连接构成封闭式链,称为尺寸链)

dimensionless ①无因次的,无量纲的②无穷小量

dimensionless coefficient 无量纲系数,无因次系数

dimensionless speed 无量纲速率

dimension limit 尺寸公差;公差范围,公差极限

dimensions of the loading space (车箱)有效装载面积(可利用来装载的面积)

dimentional parameters of mobility 汽车机动性尺寸参数,汽车通过性尺寸指标(如:最小离地间隙、接近角、离去角、纵向通过角、转弯直径、转弯通道圆等)

2-Dimention computer-Aided Industrial Design 计算机辅助二维工业设计(参见2DCAD)

dimethyl benzene 二甲苯

dimethylether 二甲基醚(亦称二甲乙醚,简称DME)

dimethyl poly-siloxanes 聚二甲基硅氧烷(一种硅酮基制动液,参见 silicone brake fluid, polydimethyl siloxanes)

dim filament 见 dip filament
diminish 减少，缩小，削弱
diminution 减少，缩小，衰减
dim light （汽车前照灯的）近光灯，近光（= anti-glare light，[美] lowered beam，lower beam，low beam 及 meeting beam，passing beam，low passing beam，dimmed light，anti-dazzle light）
dimmer ①暗光控制装置（= dimmer control）②（前照灯）近光开关（= dimmer switch）
dimmer control （仪器及照明的）变光装置，暗光控制装置
dimmer glass 减光玻璃
dimmer lamp bulb 近光灯泡
dimmer switch （[美]汽车前照灯）近光开关（一般指脚踏开关，= dimming switch，dim switch，dipper switch，dipping switch，dip switch，beam deflector switch，foot operated onti-dazzles witch，pedal operated dip switch，简称 dipper）
dimmer-type room lamp 减光式车厢灯（该灯的开关与车门联动。开门时，门控开关闭合，该灯亮；关门时，门控开关断开，该灯仍亮 2~3 秒，然后开始减光，减光维持 3 秒左右后熄灭）
dimming button 变光（按钮）开关（亦称 dimmer button，beam switch button）
dimming filament （见 dip filament）
dimple 凹座，凹坑；铸件表面伤痕
dimple fracture （金属件）微凹断裂（由产生的微孔成核长大，相互连接而形成的断裂）
DIN 德国工业标准（Deutsche Industrie Normen 的简和）
dinging hammer （修复车身板件的）精敲平手锤
dingy 弄脏了的；无光泽的，暗淡的

dint ①凹痕，凹陷；印痕，压痕 ②压凹
dio 二极管（diode 的简称）
diode 二极管（只允许电流从一个方向通过的电子元件）
diode mounting plate （发电机硅整流器的）二极管安装板
diode transistor logic 二极管-晶体管逻辑（电路）[简称 DTL，指仅由二极管、晶体（三极）管构成的逻辑电路。一般多以二极管作为输入，实现"与"逻辑操作，再由晶体管电路反相输出，即实现正逻辑的"非与"操作或副逻辑的"或非"操作]
diopter ①窥孔，瞄准器②屈光度，屈光率单位（透镜焦点距离的倒数，凸透镜为正，凹透镜为负）
dioptra 一种测量高度及角度的光学仪器
dioptric adjustment ring （金属显微镜目镜等的）屈光调节环
dioxide 二氧化物
dip ①下垂，下沉②接通（前照灯）近光
DIP 双列直插式封装（dual in-line package 的简称）
dip angle 俯角，倾角，（汽车的）栽头角，前俯角（参见 front end dip）
dip brazing 浸浴铜焊，浸浴（硬）钎焊
dip calorizing 浸镀铝，浸铝处理
dip-coating 浸涂，浸渍涂敷，浸漆，热（浸）镀
dip filament （汽车前照灯的）近光灯丝（= dim filament，dimming filament，anti-glare filament）
dipole ①偶极，对称振子②二极（磁铁），双极点③偶极天线
dipole antenna 偶极天线（车用 VHF 和 VHF 系统的一种天线）
dipole modulation 双极调制（见

non-polarized return-to-zero recording)
dipole moment 偶极矩
dipped beam 见 dim light
dipped head-lamp 汽车前照灯的近光灯
dipper 见 dimmer switch
dipper switch 见 dimmer switch
dipping （将电器元件或材料等浸入液态绝缘物质或涂覆材料中，使之注入或涂覆绝缘物质或涂层的）浸渍法
dipping mirror 防眩后视镜
dipping switch 见 dimmer switch
dip seal 液封，液密（用液体密封）
dip sign （道路的）凹部地形警告标志，洼部警告标志
dip soldering 浸焊，浸浴（软）钎焊，浸溶锡焊（多用于电子元件、印刷电路板的锡焊，将其浸入溶化锡液中，立即取出）
dip stick 油尺，机油量尺，量油尺（= 美 oil gauge）
dip stick heater 电棒式预热器
dip stick opening （发动机）机油尺插孔，机油尺插孔
dip stick tube 机油尺插管
dip switch ①见 dimmer switch ②双列直插式开关（印刷电路板上的双列引线直插式开关，亦写作 DIP switch）
dip wire 暗线
dir 见 dealer
DIR 见 Distronic
direct ①直接的②指导，引导；校正，修正
direct access （存储设备的数据）直接存取方式（数据的存取权取决于数据的位置，而不必参考以前访问过的数据）
direct-acting shock absorber 见 telescopic shock absorber
direct acting vacuum servo 直接作用式真空助力器（利用发动机进气真空，直接增补驾驶员制动踏板力的装置）
direct action 直接作用
direct addressing mode 直接寻址模式（亦称 direct control 或 command mode，指车用主从式计算机系统的一种运转模式，主机对网络采用提示符控制来实现其输入/输出功能）
direct-axis ①纵向轴线②纵向的
direct bearing 导向轴承（如：离合器内的变速器第一轴轴头的轴承）
direct change 直接变速（指一般非远距离操纵的变速杆直接换挡，= floor change，floor shift）
direct combustion period ①（指柴油机燃烧过程中速燃期结束后，喷入汽缸的油雾遇到速燃期发生的火焰不经过延迟期便）直接燃烧（的）时期②（在此期间的燃烧可通过适当增减燃油的喷射量来控制，因此亦称为）控制燃烧期③（这时喷入的燃油在火焰包围之中，进行扩散燃烧，燃烧较慢，因而又叫作）缓燃期
direct-comparision method of measurement 直接比较测量法（将被测直接与已知值的同类量相比较的测量方法，如：用等臂天平测量质量）
direct cone clutch 正锥形离合器
direct connection of motor with transmission type parallel hybrid system 电动机与变速器直接连接型并联式混合动力系统（见 Twin hybrid system）
direct continuous sampling method 直接连续取样法（废气分析中，将部分排气直接连续取样并通入分析仪中的取样方法）
direct controlled fan drive 直接控制型风扇驱动装置（指由发动机电子控制模块根据发动机工况要求，直接控制风扇转速的驱动装置）
direct controlled wheel 直接受控车

轮（特指在汽车防抱死制动系统中，由车轮本身装备的传感器提供的信息，来调节其制动力的车轮，参见 indirectly controlled wheel）

direct control suspension 直接控制式悬架（Benz 的减振器的阻尼效果可根据路况和行驶条件自动调控的悬架的商品名）

direct control transmission 直接操纵式变速器（由手直接通过换挡杆完成换挡功能的手动变速器）

direct coupling ①直接联轴节，直接啮合②直接耦合（指电气件，如：放大器的前级输出通过电阻或直接连接后一级的输入端）

direct-cranking starter 直接驱动式起动机（指直接驱动飞轮的起动机）

direct cross wind （与运动方向成）直角（的）横向风（= quartering wind）

direct-current 直流（电）（只向一个方向流动的电流，简称 DC）

direct current luminescence 直接电流照明（汽车仪表等无附加灯光照明，而直接由数字或图像显示本身发光照明，简称 DCEL）

direct current shunt motor 直流并激式电动机，直流并励式电动机（其磁场绕组与电枢绕组并联）

direct damage 直接（由碰撞造成的）损伤

direct digital-readout dashboard （汽车的）直读式数字仪表板

direct digit control 直接数字控制（简称 DDC，指使用数字计算机同时对多个受控装置直接进行控制）

direct drive 直接（挡）传动，直接（挡）驱动（指发动机与变速器以相同的转速运转的直接挡驱动）

direct-drive clutch 直接挡接合器，直接挡离合器（= direct driving clutch）

direct drive transmission 直接挡变速器（最高挡为直接挡，即：输出转速等于输入转速的变速器）

direct-drive water pump （装在汽缸盖上的）直接驱动式（发动机冷却）水泵（不再像常规那样使用传动带和传动带盘）

directed beam 定向光束

direct fourth （变速器）直接（挡为）第四挡（口语）

direct fuel injection 燃油直接喷射（见 direct injection engine）

direct gasoline 直馏汽油

direct glare 直接眩光（由视野中的高亮度或未曾充分遮蔽的光源所产生的眩光）

direct glare 直接眩光

direct high （变速器）直接（传动）挡（指没有超速挡的变速器，直接挡为最高挡）

direct hitch 刚性牵引装置

direct hydraulic brake system 直接式液压制动系统（指无助力器的液压制动系统）

direct ignition system 直接点火系（简称 DIS，无分电器式点火系的一种，火花塞点火高压直接来自点火线圈的点火系，又可分为双火花塞同时点火式，即：一个点火线圈同时为两个汽缸的火花塞提供点火高压和单火花塞直接点火式，即：每一个火花塞上都直接装有一个点火线圈。后者又称 plug on coil ignition system，见 distributorless ignition system）

direct impact 正面碰撞，直碰

direct impingement 直接撞冲（加热）（燃烧产生的高温产物，以很高的速度直接撞击到需要加热的物体表面上）

directing point 基准点

direct-injection alcohol engine （燃油缸内）直喷式醇类燃料发动机

direct injection combustion chamber 直喷式燃烧室（各种开式或半开式燃烧室的统称，相对分开式的间接喷射式而言，燃料直接喷入燃烧室内）

λ = 1 direct injection combustion system 见 Stoichi D-4 system

direct-injection engine 直接喷射式发动机（①指直接将燃油喷入燃烧室内，而无预燃室、涡流室等副室的直喷式柴油机②指将汽油直接喷入汽缸燃烧室内，而不是喷入进气门前或副室内的火花点火式发动机，= direct injection spark ignition engine）

direct-injection PCCI engine 直喷式预混合充气压燃机（如：使用天然气-空气预混合气作为主燃料，由进气口吸入汽缸，经压缩后，将柴油直接喷入汽缸点燃）

direct-injection stratified-charge engine 直喷式分层充气发动机（由进气孔吸入稀混合气，然后将汽油直接喷入燃烧室内而在火花塞附近形成浓混合气区，电火花点燃后火焰扩散传播到周围的稀混合气区内的层状燃烧发动机，简称 DISC）

direct injection turbocharged aftercooled (diesel) 直喷式涡轮增压后冷（柴油机）（简称 DITA，指进气空气经增压后再行冷却，以进一步提高进气密度的直喷式柴油机）

direction 方向

8-direction adjustable electric driver seat 八方向可调电动驾驶座椅

directional balance 见 directional stability

directional capacity of tire 轮胎保持行驶方向的能力

directional characteristic 方向特性（指汽车行驶方向受到干涉或干扰时，系统的瞬态和稳态响应特性）

directional control （车辆的）方向控制，方向操纵（使车辆按所要求的行驶方向行驶的过程及性能）

directional cooling 定向冷却

directional coupler 定向耦合器

directional detector 单方向车辆检测器，单向车辆探测器（只感应单向行驶的车辆）

directional flow 定向（气）流

directional island 方向岛（为变更车辆行驶路径而设置的交通岛）

directionality 方向性；定向性

directional lighting 定向照明

directional luminous reflectance 光的定向反射能力，光定向反射率（指不完全扩散和不完全反射面的亮度与完全反射和完全扩散面亮度之比）

directional pattern （轮胎的）方向性花纹（轮胎上具有规定的旋转方向标记的胎面花纹，只有按标记规定的旋转方向安装，才能确保达到其胎面花纹的设计效果，如：良好的排水性和优异的抓地能力等）

directional pavement marking 路面导向标志，路面指向标志（在路面上绘制的方向线、箭头或符号，= directional roadway marking, directional carriageway marking）

directional properties 定向性

directional pull 与（运动）方向一致的拉力，定向拉力

directional reading 直接读数（指测试仪表等直接数显结果）

directional response characteristics （汽车的）方向（稳定性）响应特性（将汽车行驶方向对外力，如：操作转向盘、空气动力、地面不平等输入的响应特性。包括输入开始阶段的瞬态响应 transient-state response 和之后的稳态响应 steady-state response 两个阶段）

directional response pattern 方向响应特性模式（如：不足转向，过度

转向等)
directional roadway marking 见 directional pavement marking
directional separator 方向分隔带(对向交通的分隔带,即路中分隔带)
directional sign 指路标志,方向标志(指示路名或路线编号、距离、路程方向的标志, = direction sign)
directional signal 见 turn signal lamp
directional signal-canceller (汽车)转向信号熄灭器
directional signal indicator 见 direction indicator warning light
directional stability (汽车的)方向稳定性(指:①汽车行驶方向的可控制性②汽车在外力干扰下,保持既定行驶方向稳定的动特性,偶见称 directional balance)
directional stability during braking (车辆)制动时的方向稳定性
directional tagging 定向作用,导向作用,指向作用,方向示踪
directional tread pattern (对轮胎的滚动方向有规定要求的)定向胎面花纹
directional turn signal (汽车)转向信号灯(参见 traffic indicator)
directional valve 方向(控制)阀
direction-finder (无线电)探向器,定向仪
direction finding 探向,测向
direction finding chart (车辆位置)无线电定向图(简称 DF chart)
direction indicator (指一般位于汽车前、后方,左、右两侧的)转向信号灯(简称 DI,美称 turn indicator 或 turn signal lamp)
direction indicator control 转向指示器操纵件(转向指示信号的操纵件)
direction indicator switch 转向指示灯开关

direction indicator warning light (驾驶室仪表板上指明转向信号灯是否正常工作的)转向指示灯(亦称 directional signal indicator, direction indicator lamp, direction indicator light, direction indicator tell-tall 或 turn light indicator)
directionless 无方向的
direction meter (无线电)定向仪
direction of rotation 旋转方向
direction of travel 行驶方向(亦称 travel direction)
direction reverser 换向机构
direction road signs 方向路标,指路标志
direction sensor 方位传感器(用于电子导航系统测定汽车行驶方位的传感器,目前使用的有地磁式方位传感器、气流式方位传感器和车轮转角-轮速式方位传感器等)
direction signal 见 turn signal lamp
direction signal indicator 见 direction indicator warning light
direction traffic 定向交通(按方向分组的交通运输)
direction valve 方向阀
direction variable 方向变数
directive antenna (车用)定向天线
directive gain 方向获益,定向增益
directive wheel 导向轮
directivity 方向性,定向性,方向律
direct lighting 直接照明
direct liquid cooling type power module 直接液冷式动力模块
directly controlled wheel (根据车轮本身所安装的传感器的信号来控制防抱死的)直接受控车轮
directly proportional 成正比例的
direct methanol fuel cell 直接甲醇燃料电池(简称 DMFC,直接以甲醇作为燃料,以区别于甲醇重整燃料电池,见 MRFC)
direct method of measurement 直接

测量法（指直接用量具对被测量物进行测量，而不必对与被测量有函数关系的其他量进行测量的方法，如：用标度尺测量长度）

direct on-line processor 直接在线联机处理器

director ①导向器，导向装置 ②(车用液晶显示器件的)指向矢(表示液晶分子长轴平均方向的单位矢量)

director circle 准圆

director plate 导向板(指装在汽油喷嘴内的多孔板，以准确地形成所要求的喷射形状和质量)

direct pressure control valve 直接压力控制阀

direct proportion(ality) 正比(例)

direct ratio 正比

direct-reading instrument 直读式仪表

direct resistance heating 直接电阻加热(电流直接通过需要加热的物件)

directrix 准线

direct sampling method 直接采样法(将发动机排出的废气直接通入具有前处理功能的分析仪中的)

direct select 直接选择(如：使用装在多功能转向盘上的换挡拨片或按钮直接选择挡位)

Direct Shift Gearbox 见 DSG

direct shop (汽车)直销店

direct speed (变速器)直接挡 (= direct gear)

direct starting 直接起动，全电压起动(一种起动鼠笼式电动机的简单方法，以增大起动转矩, = on-line starting, full-voltage starting)

direct steering (无伺服机构的)直接操纵转向

direct straight through ditch 直通式(车辆维修)地沟

direct supply 直流电源，直接供电

direct vacuum servo (液压制动)直接真空助力装置

direct valve (无先导阀的)直接作动阀

direct-vision block 装在观察窗口上的玻璃块

direct water injection (发动机的)直接喷水法(直接将水喷入燃烧室中)

direct yaw-moment stabilization control system 横摆力矩稳定性定向控制系统(见 DYC)

dirt ①污泥，污垢 ②弄脏

dirt excluder 防尘器 (= dust excluder)

dirt guard 挡泥板 (= antisplash guard)

dirt-proof 防(灰)尘的，防污的

dirt reservation 灰尘沉积

dirt seal 防尘密封件

dirt shroud 防尘罩

dirt-track race 泥路赛车

dirt trap 集尘器，集污器，脏物收集器 (= mud trap)

"dirty" exhaust gases 未净化废气，脏废气，含有害物质的废气

DIS ①无分电器式点火系统(distributorless ignition system 的简称，美国通用、福特、克莱斯勒等公司原来对无分电器式电子点火系统的旧称，美国政府规定从1995年1月起，一律按 SAE J 1930 推荐的术语，将无分电器式电子点火系统称 electronic ignition system，简称 EIS 或 EI system) ②分电器式点火系统(按美国政府规定，从1995年1月起，一律按 SAE J 1930 推荐的术语，将有分电器的电子点火系统称为：distributor ignition system，简称 DIS 或 DI system) ③驾驶员信息系统 (driver information system 的简称) ④国际标准草案 (Draft International Standard 的简称)

disability 失去工作能力(如：车辆

报废）

disability glare 失能眩光（导致视觉功能和可见度降低的眩光）

disability glare factor 失能眩光因数（简称 DGF,指在指定照明设施下的可见度与它在参考照明条件下的可见度之比）

disabled ①（对车辆指）因损坏或故障而不能驾驶的②（对驾驶员）因手足伤残而无法工作的

disabled vehicle detection system 故障车辆（位置）检出系统（确定故障车辆在道路上的方位,以便救援）

disable input （集成电路的）禁止输入（阻止一个或多个规定操作继续进行的输入,亦称 inhibit input）

disable time （集成电路）禁止时间（指禁止点到终点之间的时间间隔）

disadjust 失调（的）

disalignment 错位,偏离中心线,中心线偏移,轴线不重合,未对准（中心）。不平行,不同轴,不同中心,不正

disappearing ash tray （座位上的）暗置（烟）灰盒

disappearing centre arm rest （车厢双人）座位中间的折叠式扶手

disassemble 拆开,分解,解体（=dismantle）

disassembly-and-assembly stand 拆装台

disassembly cleanliness 解体清洁度（用规定方法,从经过磨合的总成或整车解体后的规定部位采集到杂质微粒的大小、数量、轻重来表示）

disc ①圆盘②磁盘,光片（=disk）③（车轮的）轮辐

discal rotor （电磁缓速器的）盘形转子

disc brake 盘式制动器（制动力产生于与车桥固定的摩擦件和与车轮固定的一个或多个圆盘两侧面之间的摩擦式制动器,分为钳盘式和全盘式两大类）

disc brake calipers 盘式制动器卡钳

disc brake gauge （测量）制动盘（厚度、磨损和磨痕深度的）量具

disc brake rotor ［美］盘式制动器的制动盘（=brake disc）

disc brake with fixed caliper （固）定钳-盘式制动器（制动盘的两侧均装有制动钳,在整个制动过程中钳体固定不动）

disc brake with floating caliper 浮钳盘式制动器（只在制动盘的一侧装有制动钳,靠其本身的浮动产生制动压力的钳盘式制动器）

disc cam 盘形凸轮,偏心轮（=circular cam）

6-disc CD 六盘式 CD 机

discharge ①卸货,卸载②泵出,排出,流出；放电③输出流量,排出量④排出物

discharge angle （自倾车身）倾卸角

discharge capacity ①放电量,流量②通过能力,卸载能力

discharge chamber 排出室（参见 delivery chamber）

discharge cock 排放旋塞,放出旋塞,排放开关（=draining cock, blow-off cock, bib cock, purge cock, drain tap）

discharge coefficient 流量系数（=coefficient of flow,单位时间的流量）

discharge connection 输出接管,输出管接头,分配管接头

discharge current 放电电流

discharge cycle （蓄电池的）放电循环

discharged battery 电放完的蓄电池,电耗尽的蓄电池(参见 dead battery)

discharge fan 排风扇（参见 draft fan）

discharge filter 出口滤清器,回油滤

清器
discharge head lamp with auto leveling mechanism 具有高度（可随路况变化）自动调节机构的气体放电式前照灯
discharge hose （空调系统等的）排气软管
discharge indicator 见 battery discharge indicator
discharge of pump 泵的输出量，泵的排出量，泵的输出流量
discharge orifice angle （柴油喷嘴）喷孔角，喷口锥角
discharge pipe （泵的）输出管，（空调系统的）排气接管
discharge pressure （空压机的）排气压力（指压缩机在标准排气位置排出的气体的平均绝对全压力，= head pressure）
discharge rate ①（蓄电池）放电量，放电率②（泵等的）排出量，排出速率③（喷头的）喷（射）量
discharge side ①输出端②（空调系统指）由压缩机至膨胀阀的高压部分
discharge stroke （活塞泵）排出冲程
discharge temperature （压缩机的）排气温度（指其标准排气位置排出的气体的全温度）
discharge tester 放电试验器（如：蓄电池放电叉）
discharge voltage 放电电压
discharging ①卸货，卸载；放出，排出，倒空；放电②卸载的，卸货的；放电的
discharging of the brake ①从液压制动系中放出制动油液②液压制动系放气（从放气孔排出制动液内的气泡，= bleeding of the brake）
discharging test （蓄电池）放电试验
discharging tube 排出管，排水管，排气管

disc lathe （盘式制动器）制动盘专用车床
disclination 向错（指液晶分子取向在空间的不连续的现象）
discol （一种）抗爆燃油（醇50%，苯25%，烃类25%）
discolored bearing （由于润滑油质量不好或过热造成的）色泽变暗或过热变色的轴承
discolour 变色，褪色；脱色
discomfort 不舒适，不舒适性，不方便
discomfort glare 不舒适眩光（引起不舒适感，但不一定降低规定视觉功能或可见度的眩光，参见 disability glare）
discomfort in riding 乘车不舒适，乘坐舒适性差
disconnect 拆开，脱开，分离，切断，断开
disconnectable clutch 分离式离合器（亦称 disconnect-type clutch）
disconnector 断路器，切断开关；分离装置
disconnect switch ①断路开关，切断开关②（汽车乘员安全带和发动机起动机的）连锁开关（未系好安全带便不能起动）
discontinuity 不连续性，间断性，不均匀性，不均质性
discontinuous 不连续的，间断的，断续的
discount-priced minicar 廉价微型轿车
disc pad 盘式制动器的摩擦块
disc rating 金属盘标度（在滑油薄膜氧化试验时，用金属盘的清洁度表示滑油的高温抗氧化性能）
discrepancy within experimental error 在试验误差范围内的偏差
discrete ①不连续的，离散的②分立的，间断的
discrete coefficient 离散系数

discrete-component 分立元(器)件，单个元(器)件，单独元(器)件

discrete distribution 离散分布

discrete filter 离散滤波器

discrete Fourier transform 离散傅里叶变换（简称 DFT，用数字计算机进行傅里叶变换时，要将连续量转化为离散量，并采用离散傅里叶变换计算式）

discrete material 松散材料

discreteness ①离散，不连续性，分散性②目标的鉴别能力，目标相对于背景的显明度

discrete optimization 离散优化

discrete phenomena 离散现象

discrete solution 离散解

discrete valuation ring 离散赋值环（评价离散度用）

discrete variable valve lift 离散可变气门升程（气门升程离散变化模式可随所要求的发动机工况自动或手动改变）

discriminating gear device （变速器）挡位选择机构

discrimination （仪器仪表等的）鉴别力（指其对输入值微小变化的响应能力）

discrimination threshold 鉴别力阈（指可使仪器仪表产生一个可察觉响应的最小输入值，如：若使天平指针产生可见位移的最小负载变化为 90mg，则其鉴别力阈为 90mg）

disc sander （金属板件的）圆盘形沙磨机，圆盘打磨器（电动或气动，用于修理、焊接等之后及涂漆、钎焊等之前将表面打净或磨糙）

disc-shaped combustion chamber 盘形燃烧室

disc spring 碟形弹簧，盘形弹簧

disc type horn 盆形电喇叭（汽车用无扬声筒的电喇叭，亦称高频喇叭"high frequency horn"）

disc valve 盘形阀、片阀（旋转阀的一种，可给液体提供一弧形通路）

disc wheel ①幅式车轮（轮辋与板式轮辐永久性结合的车轮）②圆盘砂轮

disc wheel with flange openings 轮缘带孔的幅板式车轮

disc wheel with holes 带孔的幅板式车轮（亦称 spoked disc wheel）

disengageable 可拆开的，可脱开的，可分离的，可断开的

disengaged position （离合器）分离位置

disengage the clutch 使离合器分离，踩踏离合器踏板，松开离合器（= declutch, clutch out, depress the clutch pedal）

disengaging clutch 分离式离合器（= disconnectable clutch）

disengaging fork （离合器的）分离叉

disengaging gear ①从啮合中脱出的齿轮②分离机构

disengaging of clutch 离合器分离

disengaging yoke 分离拨叉

dish ①盘形零件，碟形零件②盘形的，中凹的

dished 碟形的，盘形的，中凹形的（亦称 dish-shaped）

dished-head piston 浅盆顶活塞，凹顶活塞

dished piston head 带燃烧室的凹形活塞顶

dish of wheel 车轮盘状辐板，车轮辐板凹度

DISI engine （燃油）直接喷射-电火花点火式发动机（direct injection-spark ignition engine 的简称）

disincrustant 除垢剂，积垢清除剂

disinflate 放气（如：轮胎放气）

disjoint ①拆散，分开，拆开；不连贯，不贯串；不相交②不相交的，不连贯的

disjunction ①分离，分开②（计算机的）逻辑加法，逻辑和（亦称 logical add，一种布尔运算，只有当每个操作数均为布尔值 0 时，其运算结果为布尔值 0，= inclusive-OR operation, OR operation "或操作"，"或运算"）③（电路）切断，断开

disjunctor 分离器；断路开关，开关

disk 见 disc

disk armature ①盘形电枢②盘形衔铁

disk brake 盘式制动器（端面受制动块总成压紧后起制动作用的圆盘形制动器）

disk brake pad 盘式制动器摩擦块（制动衬块）

disk brake squeal 盘式制动器（制动时发出的）吱吱响噪声

disk brake with fixed caliper 定钳盘式制动器（制动钳固定在制动器两侧且在其两侧均设有加压机构的钳盘式制动器）

disk cam 圆盘凸轮

disk clutch 盘式离合器

disk coupling 盘式联轴节

disk oil filter 圆盘叠片滤芯式机油滤清器

disk pack （计算机的）磁盘组（可换用的存储器）

disk parking brake 盘式驻车制动器

disk piston 盘式活塞

disk-shaped 盘状的，碟形的

disk spring 碟形弹簧

disk-type combustion chamber 盘形燃烧室

disk-type wave generator （谐波齿轮传动的）圆盘式波发生器（由圆盘偏心置于输入轴上的非积极控制式波发生器）

disk valve 圆盘阀，盘形阀

disk wheel 辐板式车轮（指轮辋与板式轮辐永久性结合的车轮，亦写作 disc wheel，= plate wheel, web wheel）

dislocate 使离开原来位置，使变位，弄乱位置，搞乱次序，脱节，使混乱

dislocation ①变位，错位；转换位置②叠差（指车用夹层玻璃胶合层黏结的内、外层玻璃互相偏移的现象）③关节脱出，脱节④断层⑤次序弄乱

dismantle 拆开，拆卸，拆散，（机器）解体，分解

dismantling from car to units 汽车拆成部件，汽车拆成总成

DIS Mod 无分电盘式电子点火系统控制模块（distributorless ignition system module 的简称，见 ICM）

dismount 拆除，拆卸，拆下

dismountability 可拆卸性

dismountablel amp （汽车的）可卸式（前照）灯（等）

disorder injection （柴油机）不均匀喷油（针阀最大升程不等，启喷时间也不等，致使各循环喷油不均匀的现象）

disparity ①不同，不等，不一致，不一样，差别②不相称，悬殊

dispenser ①分配器，分送装置；配量装置②（燃料）加油站，加油塔

dispensing equipment 分配油料的装置，配料设备

dispensing pump （加油站）量油泵

dispersant 分散剂（机油的一种添加剂，可使机油内的固态或液态杂质保持悬浮状态，以减少沉积和结胶，亦称 dispersant additive, dispersant agent）

dispersant oil （按配方制加有分散剂可防止结胶的）免结胶机油

disperse 分散，散射，散布；喷射，喷雾

dispersion ①离散，分散，扩散②偏差，标准离差（= standard devia-

dispersive muffler 扩散型消声器（使废气在曲折通道内绕行，以消耗废气能量，而降低排气噪声的消声器）

displace ①移位②取代，代替，置换③排出，排量

displaceable 可移动的，可转移的；可更换的，可置换的

displaced indicator diagram 以活塞位移为横坐标的示功图

displacement ①位移，平移②置换，取代③（容积式压缩机的）理想容积流量（指其第一级压缩元件在单位时间内所扫过的容积）④（泵等的）排出量，生产率⑤（发动机的）排量（＝缸径×冲程×缸数，表示一个汽缸每一进气冲程所能吸入的混合气的理论容积乘以缸数，亦称 capacity 和 swept volume）

displacement compressor 容积式压气机

displacement corrector 位移校正器

displacement factor 排量因数（主要用于美国的一项汽车性能指标，为发动机排量与主减速器减速比的乘积除以驱动车轮滚动半径与净重的乘积）

displacement for a displacement compressor 容积式压缩机第一级压缩元件在单位时间内所扫过的容积

displacement head 带工作容积的缸盖

displacement on demand type auto engine （通用公司的）按需（可变）排量型车用发动机（其排量即汽缸容积可根据行驶状况而自动变化，达到节油，减少排放的目的）

displacement transducer 位移传感器

displacement volume （发动机）汽缸工作容积，汽缸排量［指在一个工作循环内，一个汽缸的最大容积与最小容积（包括燃烧室容积）的差值，即活塞上、下止点之间所扫过的容积，单位升 L，亦称 cylinder capacity, swept volume, stroke volume, piston swept volume］

displacement volume of a single chamber （转子发动机的）单室排量（即旋转活塞的一个工作面与外旋轮线缸壁面形成的最大容积减去最小容积，＝chamber displacement）

displacer ①抽出器，排出器，压出器②（Stirling 发机动的）驱气活塞（＝displacer piston）③排出物，置换剂④平衡浮子

displacer piston ①（斯特林发动机的）泵气活塞，驱气活塞（简称 displacer，参见 Stirling engine）②排气式活塞（一种可减少泵气损失的活塞）

display ①显示②显示器

disposable battery 一次性电池（使用后即废弃，不能再充电）

disposable overalls 一次性（带前胸口袋与背带的）工作裤

disrepair 失修，破损

disrupt 断裂，破裂；碎裂，毁坏

disruption characteristic ①断裂强度，破坏特性②（电解质的耐压）击穿性能

disruptive discharge 击穿放电

disruptive distance 火花间隙，击穿间隙

disruptive load 断裂载荷，破坏性载荷

disruptive strength 击穿强度，介质强度，破裂强度

disruptive voltage 击穿电压（＝break-down voltage）

dissimilar metal contact corrosion 不同金属的接触腐蚀

dissipate ①消散，分散，弥散，散逸②消耗，耗尽，耗散③变稀，稀释

dissipating area （水箱等的）散热面积

dissipation factor 介质损耗因数
dissociate 分解,分离,游离,分裂
dissociation 离解(作用),分解,分裂,游离,解离
dissolubility 溶解度,可溶性
dissolution 分解,分离;溶解;融解
dissolved gum 溶解于燃油中的胶质(= actual gum, existent gum, performed gum)
dissolved impurities 溶解(了的)杂质,溶解(在其他介质中的)杂质
dissolvent 溶剂
dissolving capacity 溶解能力,溶解度
distance 距离,间隔
distance apparatus 遥测仪器,远距离量测装置
distance bar 限距杆,定距杆,间隔棒(= spacer bar)
distance between axles 轴距(见 wheel space)
distance between centers ①中心距 ②顶尖距
distance between centre lines 中心线间距
distance between fifth-wheel coupling pin and front end of towing vehicle 牵引座牵引销孔至牵引车前端的距离(从通过牵引座牵引销孔中心的垂线至通过车辆最前端点且垂直于车辆的支撑平面和纵向对称平面的两平面的距离)
distance between seats (客车)座间距
distance between side windows (车身)侧窗距
distance between skylight windows (客车)顶窗间距
distance between stops 停车站之间的距离
distance between tyres 轮距(亦称 wheel gauge,见 track)
distance bolt 定距螺栓,支撑螺栓
distance collar 隔圈,隔环,定距环
distance control 遥控,远距离控制(= distant control)
distance detection system for ahead vehicle 前车距离探测系统
distancee between shafts 轴间距
distance filament 远光灯灯丝(= distance-light filament)
distance gauge 测距仪(亦称 distance meter)
distance headlamp (汽车前照灯)远光灯(= long distance headlamp, far-reaching headlamp, high beam, distance lamp, distance light, bright light, upper beam, full head lamp beam, driving beam, far beam)
distance of run 冲程
distance of skid (车辆的)滑移距离
distance of towing attachment in front of rear of vehicle 牵引装置前置距[下列各点或面至车身后端点(不考虑后挡板铰链,销闩等)的距离:①球头式牵引装置,球的中心 ②插销式U形牵引装置,通过插销孔轴线且平行于车辆纵向时称平面的平面 ③拖钩式牵引装置,环形拖钩子午线断面(断面的中心线垂直于车辆支撑平面)的中心]
distance piece 隔件(指装于两零件间,使它们保持所需正确间距的隔离件"spacing piece",如:隔环"distance ring",隔套"distance sleeve",隔垫"distance spacer",隔管"distance tube",隔垫或隔圈"distance washer"等的统称)
distance recorder ①(车辆等的)行程记录仪,里程表 ②计距器
distance sensor (行程)距离传感器(用于汽车导航系统测定行驶距离,见 dead reckoning)
**distance short run-length communica-

tion （防碰撞系统等使用的）短行程距离通信（简称DSRC）

distance thermometer 遥测温度计

distance-to-empty 空箱距离（指燃油箱中剩余燃油尚能行驶的距离）

distance totalizer （行驶）距离总计表，总里程表

distance-type 遥控式的，遥测式的，远程式的，远距离操纵式的

distance-type of cooling thermometer 冷却系远距离温度计，仪表板装冷却系温度表

distant 远距离的，遥远的

distant collision 远距离碰撞，大冲击参数碰撞

distillate fuels 馏出燃料（在常压下，由石油中蒸馏出的燃料。一般指汽油、煤油等，而不包括粗柴油，但有时也包括轻粗柴油，参见 light gas oil）

distillation 蒸馏；蒸馏物，蒸馏液；馏分，馏出物；精华

distillation characteristics （汽油等的）蒸馏特性，分馏特性曲线，分馏曲线（表示温度与蒸馏量之间的关系，亦称 distillation curve）

distillation endpoint 终馏点（燃油完全蒸馏的温度）

distillationtest method 蒸馏试验法（测定液体燃料挥发性的一种方法）

distilled gasoline 直馏汽油（用分馏法生产的汽油，主要含饱和烃，抗爆性能较差）

distilled water 蒸馏水

distinction ①差别，区别②（显示屏等的）清晰度

distinctive ①有特色的，独特的，特别的②区别的，鉴别性的

distinguishing feature 特点

distorted surface 变形表面，翘曲面

distortion 变形；挠曲，扭曲，扭转，扭变；失真，畸变，偏差

distortion angle （转向中汽车车轮的）侧偏角（见 slip angle）

distortion inaccuracy 由于变形而引起的误差（如：由于热处理变形而引起的零件尺寸偏差）

distortionless 无变形的，无扭曲的，无歪曲的；无畸变的，不失真的

distortion test 挠曲试验

distr ①分配，分布（distribution 的简称）②分电器，配电盘（distributor 的简称）

distracted driving （处于）精神涣散（状态下的）驾驶

distress call 呼救信号，求救呼叫，遇险信号，肇事信号（= distress signal）

distribute 分布，分配，分发；配给，配置；分类，分级

distributed air bag sensing system 分布式安全气囊传感系统（见 multi-point electromechanical sensing system, air-bag sensing system）

distributed multi-node control system 分布式多网点控制系统

distributed weight 分布重量（分布质量的旧称，如：各个车轮所分担的车辆质量）

distributer type injection pump （柴油机）分配式喷油泵

distributing tank ①洒水车，喷洒车 ②沥青洒布车

distribution board 配电板（亦称 distribution panel）

distribution circle （摆线轮）分布圆（分布圆柱面与端平面的交线）

distribution cylinder （摆线轮）分布圆柱面（摆线轮理论齿廓平均齿高所在曲面）

distribution diagram 配气相位图

distribution diameter （摆线轮）分布圆直径（分布圆柱面和分布圆的直径）

distribution gear （凸轮轴上的）分电器（驱动）齿轮（= camshaft

timing gear, secondary gear)

distribution of weight on the chassis 底盘上的重量分配，底盘上的载荷分布

distribution piping 配油管道，配气管线

distribution pitch （摆线轮）分布圆齿距（指在摆线轮的一个端平面上，两个相邻而同侧的理论齿廓之间的分布圆弧长）

distribution surface （摆线轮或针轮的）分布曲面（确定摆线轮或针轮的齿轮尺寸及位置的基准）

distribution tubes （发动机冷却系内的冷却液）配流管（将冷却液分配和导向关键部位）

distribution valve 分配阀（= distributing valve）

distributive law 分配律

distributor ①（点火系）分电器（见 ignition distributor）②（传动系）分动箱 ③（涡轮机）导向装置 ④（沥青）洒布机 ⑤（交通流的）分流道路 ⑥（负荷）分配装置 ⑦分配者，发行者，批发商，经销商

distributor advance curve 分电器（点火）提前角曲线（发动机转速与提前角的关系）

distributor-and-contact-breaker unit 断电器与配电器总成（断电器和配电器制成一体的分电器）

distributor barrel （分配式喷油泵的）分配套筒（装在分配外壳内与分配转子配成一对的燃油分配偶件）

distributor base plate （断电器）底板（分电器体内安装断电器或点火信号发生装置的底板，分电器轴由其中心孔通过）

distributor body 分电器体（= 美 distributor housing）

distributor box ①分配器 ②配电箱 ③分动箱（= distributing box）

distributor brush 见 distributor rotor

distributor cam 分电器凸轮，断电器触点凸轮［装在分电器轴上带有凸缘的转子，周期地使断电器触点断与闭合，= contact breaker cam, breaker (point) cam］

distributor cap 分电器盖（由高绝缘材料制成，带有高压插座的盖子）

distributor case 见 distributor housing

distributor drive 分电器驱动机构

distributor fuel injection pump （柴油机的）分配式喷油泵

distributor (fuel injection) pump （多缸柴油机的）分配式喷油泵（具有一个分配转子或分配柱塞和与缸数相等的多个出油口，燃油依次被压出出油口，亦称 delivery type fuel injection pump）

distributor housing ①［美］分电器体（= distributor case）②（分配式喷油泵的）分配外壳

distributor ignition system with computer-controlled ignition advance 计算机控制点火提前（角）的分电器式点火系

distributorless ignition system 无分电器式电子点火系（无常规旋转分电器的电子点火系，简称 DIS 或 DLI）

distributor lower drive shaft casing 分电器下驱动轴外壳

distributor modulator 分电器真空控制装置（由转速传感器、气温传感器、电控真空放大器和三向电磁阀组成，用于控制分电器膜片的真空输入，参见 electronic distributor modulator system）

distributor moving contact plate 分电器活动触点板

distributor pickup mechanism （无触点式点火系装在分电器内的）点火信号发生装置（= ignition signal generating mechanism）

distributor point aligning tool 分电器触点校正工具

distributor rails ①高压线分配总管 ②共用进油歧管（见 common rail）

distributor reference pulse （分电器式电子点火系的）分电器基准信号脉冲（简称 REF，或 DIST，向电子控制模块提供发动机转速和曲轴转角位置信号）

distributor rotor ①（分电器）分火头（将点火线圈产生的高压电分配给分电器盖上的电极的带分电臂的转子，亦称 distributor rotor arm，简称 rotor arm，偶见称 distributor brush, distributor track）②（转子式分配泵的）分配转子（在分配套筒内做旋转运动，以泵油和分配燃油的零件）

distributor solenoid 分电器（点火时刻延迟）电磁线圈（参见 solenoid retarded distributor）

distributor timing control 分电器点火正时调节，分电器点火正时控制（= adjustment of timing, ignition control, spark control）

distributor tower 分电器（盖上的）高压插座（亦称 terminal tower。其中，位于分电器盖中央的点火线圈高压线插座，称为 centre terminal tower，位于分电器盖四周的火花塞高压线插座，称 outer tower）

distributor track 见 distributor rotor

distributor weight 分电器离心点火提前装置的离心块

district 段，工段，区域，地段，地区，市区

Distronic 雷达测距防撞控制系统（简称 DTR，该系统用于控制与前车的距离，并向驾驶者发送危险距离警报信号等）

disturbance 扰动，干扰（①广义指包括驾驶员各种操纵在内的一切影响汽车等原运动状态的力的输入。狭义指不必要的力，如：风力，路面不平等的输入②电子控制系统不希望有的信号或脉冲③通信系统不希望的噪声信号④同一光源的光被分成两束光，经过不同路径相互叠加，形成条纹的现象）

disturbance-elimination （无线电）干扰消除，射频屏蔽（= disturbance suppression, noise suppression, inference elimination, radio shielding）

disturbance force （对系统产生）扰动（的）力（亦称 disturbing force）

disturbance observer 干扰观测仪

disturbance response 扰动响应（由干扰性外力作用所引起的汽车响应，如风力、路面不平引起的汽车振动、位移等）

disturbance voltage 干扰电压（由电磁干扰在两个分开的导体的两点间产生的电压，亦称 interference voltage）

disturbed area 受干扰区

disturbing residual braking torque 干扰后效制动力矩（指制动控制装置和传能装置已放松后，依然存在的制动力矩）

disutrbing current 干扰电流

DI system 分电器式点火系统（distributor ignition system 的简称。美国政府规定从1995年1月起，凡使用分电器的点火系统，无论其点火时刻是否由电子电路控制均一律按 SAE 标准，称 DI system）

DITA 见 direct injection turbocharged aftercooled

di-t-butyl peroxide 二特丁基过氧化物［双$(CH_3)_3C-$］（一种专用汽油添加剂，可在燃烧室内的高压下，促进自由基的形成，以扩大稀燃失火界限，简称 dtbp）

ditch grade （汽车维修地沟）沟底坡度（便于清洗，避免积污）

ditching （液压系统阀的）振动

di-tert-butyl peroxide 过氧化二叔丁基（简称 DTBP，燃油十六烷值的提高剂）

dither arm 高频振动臂

dither motor 高频振动用电动机

DIU 数字输入装置（digital input unit，指在数据处理系统中，将数据送入系统的设备）

diurnal breathing losses 日换气损失（模拟一天环境温度变化燃油箱测得的燃油蒸气排放量）

divalent metals 二价金属（指化合价为 +2 的金属）

dive （车辆制动时）点头，栽头（见 brake dive）

divergence ①离散，发散（性）；散度，发散量②分歧，分支③偏离，偏差

divergent instability 发散不稳定性（给汽车一个小而短暂的扰动或控制输入时，汽车的运动响应总是增长的，而不是在工作点附近等幅或减幅摆动的汽车响应特性）

divergent modulation 发散性调节（液力变速器换挡滞后随气门开度增加而增加的换挡规律）

divergent steering 发散转向（指由于车辆发散不稳定性造成的车辆偏离所希望行驶方向的现象）

diverging lens 散光透镜，散光玻璃

diversification ①多变性，变化性②（公司生产的车型或产品等）多种多样性

diversify ①（企业或厂家）增加产品品种，研发新产品，扩大经营范围②多元化，多样化

diversion ①（因前方修路等原因而）改变行车路线②（液、气流等）改变流向

diversity ①分集，分散，分隔，多道②发散性，疏散性③不同，异样，参差异相，差异，多种多样性，异样性，变化④合成法

diversity antenna system 分集式天线系统［指在两个或两个以上的天线所接收的电波中，恒选择接收效果最佳的电波的接收系统，用于调幅（FM）收音机和车用电视系统］

divert （使液流、气流、车流等流往不同的方向）分流，转向，转变方向

diverter ①电阻分流器，分流电阻②转向器，换向器

diverter pole-generator 分流磁极发电机

diverter valve ①分流阀②见 air gulp valve

divide ①分，划分，区分，分开；除，等分②分度，刻度③分配，分摊

divide-by-N counter N 分频计数器（其中 N 代表任一具体数字）

divided 分离的，分开的；分度的，刻度的；等分的

divided Ackermann steering linkage 分段式转向梯形杆系（前轮为独立悬架所采用的一种转向梯形杆系）

divided axle ①断开式驱动桥，对开桥，对开轴②见 swing axle

divided back window 分开式后窗（参见 divided rear window）

divided bearing 对开式轴承，剖分式轴承

divided braking 分路式制动（指由两条或两条以上的回路组成的制动系统，其中一处失效，仍能部分或全部传递产生制动力的能量，= split braking）

divided chamber system 分开式燃烧室式（发动机）（= front chamber system, 见 divided combustion chamber）

divided chassis and body type （汽车的）底盘与车身分离式（结构，见 drive module 和 life module）

divided circle 分度圆（= graduated circle, graduated ring）

divided combustion chamber 分开式燃烧室（为涡流室式燃烧室、预燃室式燃烧室等的统称，燃烧室被明显地分为两部分，一部分由活塞顶面与汽缸盖底面组成，另一部分在缸盖或缸体内，二者以一条或数条通道相连接）

divided crank 组合式曲柄

divided crankcase 剖分式曲轴箱

divided device （铰接式客车机械连接装置的）等分机构（无论直线行驶或转向，均能使连接伸缩缝的中间框架处于主、副车相对夹角的等分位置）

divided gauge 刻度盘

divided highway 分隔带公路（中间具有分隔带的公路，如：分隔为上、下车道的公路）

divided piston rod 组合式连杆

divided propeller shaft 组合式传动轴（指一般后轮驱动的长底盘车辆用的由万向节连接并具有中间支撑的两节式传动轴，亦简称 divided propshaft）

divided rear window 分为两扇中间带立柱的后窗（= divided back window, twin rear window）

divided rim 对开式轮辋（由两个对开的零件，紧固在一起形成的有两个固定轮缘的轮辋）

divided road [美] 中间有分隔带隔开的道路（= 英 dual carriage way）

divided seats 分隔成多个单人座位的长座椅

divided (steering) tie rod 分段式转向横拉杆

divided-system hydraulic brakes 分路式液压制动器（= split-system hydraulic brakes, 见 divided braking）

divided type disk wheel 对开幅板式车轮（参见 disk wheel, divided wheel）

divided type rim 对开式轮辋（代号 DT, 见 divided rim）

divided ventilation 分道通风

divided wheel 对开式车轮（轮辋由两个用夹紧螺栓紧固成一体的对开元件组成，形成有两个固定轮缘的车轮，亦称 split wheel）

divided wing 分开式翼子板

dividend ①被除数②利息, 红利

divider 画线规, 分隔板, 分流管, 分配器, 分度器, 除数

divider calipers 分规, 等分卡钳

dividing ①分开, 分隔；划分；分割；分度②除法③分开的, 起划分作用的

dividing circuit 除法电路（进行除法运算的电路）

dividing wall 隔墙, 隔板, 间壁（= division wall, bulk head, partition wall, separating wall, division wall）

diving key 滑键

diving moment （使汽车头部下栽的）栽头力矩

divisional island 中央分割岛, 分车岛, 导向岛（参见 center island）

division-control multivibrator 分工况控制式多谐振荡器（根据发动机转速与进气空气流量的反馈数据来确定喷油脉冲特性的电子电路）

division line 分隔线（在无分隔带的道路上, 标明对向交通的分界线等）

divisor ①除数, 因子, 约数②分压器, 自耦变压器③（道路上的）分车带

divorced cementite 断离渗碳体, 不连续网状渗碳体, 网状渗碳体

diy 自己动手（维修车辆等, do-it-yourself 的简称）

D-Jetronic （德国波许公司 1967 年推出的）D 型电子控制汽油喷射系

统（商品名，采用进气管压力传感器输出的进气压力信号作为控制喷油量的主要参数的多点式汽油喷射系统，1973 年后改进为以吸入空气的质量流量作为控制喷油量的主要参数，称为 L-Jetronic，现在广泛应用）

DKM-125 单纯旋转活塞发动机-125（工作室容积为 125cc，参见 DKM）

DKM 单纯旋转活塞发动机（德文 Drehkolben motor 的简称，其运动部件只是围绕其自身的重心做等角速度运动，而自身不绕其他中心做行星运动，= SIM type engine，参见 KKM，SIM）

DKM Wankel engine 汪克尔单纯旋转发动机（活塞和缸体都绕同一固定轴旋转，无偏心运动，由旋转缸体输出功率）

DL1 见 distributorless ignition

DL 见 deluxe

D2L(brake) 见 duo two leading shoe brake

DLC 数据链路连接器（data link connector 的简称，如：连接车装诊断系统数据输出插座与扫描仪、解码器插座的带插接头的转接线等。见 data link connector）

DLI 无分电器式点火系统［distributorless ignition system 的简称，= DIS，指不用分电器分配点火高压，而由点火线圈直接向各缸火花塞供给点火高压的汽油机点火系统，目前有以下几种：①每个火花塞都由一个点火线圈直接供给点火高压的整体式"unit（ized）ignition type"②每两个火花塞同时由一个点火线圈供给点火高压的同时点火式"synchronous ignition type"③每四个火花塞由一个点火线圈通过二极管电路同时提供点火高压的二极管电路分配式"diode distribution type"］

DLL 设计极限载荷（design limit load）

DL pulley （取代汽车空调系统可变排量压缩机电磁离合器等的新型）减振和转矩限制型传动带盘（damper and limiter pulley 的简称，该传动带盘毂与压缩机轴间通过金属-断开型转矩限制结构"metal-breakage type torque limiter"传递转矩与减振结构分开，一旦转矩超过规定的安全值，转矩限制结构的金属臂件即断裂，于是传动带盘空转，避免压缩机受损。旧型 DL pulley 的减振橡胶件同时起转矩限制件的作用，其转矩限定值受工作温度影响，极不宜用于空调压缩机）

DLSC 直喷式分层充气发动机（direct-injection stratified-charge engine 的简称）

DLV （车辆等的坠落物防护结构及滚翻防护结构的）变形极限区，变形禁区（按 SAE J397a 的规定，当身高 188cm，体重 97.5kg 的操作人员坐在标准座位时的安全区，上述结构受冲击时，其挠曲等变形不得进入该区域内，deflection limiting volume 的简称）

dm 分米（=1/10m）

DM ①（美国石油协会润滑油分类记号）使用劣质柴油的柴油机用润滑油②脱氢混合物（dehydrogenated mixture 的简称）③设计手册（design manual 的简称）④发展里程碑（development milestone 的简称）⑤差绕电动机（differential motor 的简称）⑥驱动磁铁（drive magnet 的简称）

DMA 见 digital model assembly

DME 二甲基醚（亦称二甲乙醚，dimethyl ether 的简称，天然气、煤气等原料的合成燃料，具有高的十六烷值，良好的压燃着火性能，用作柴油机燃料时无微粒排放物，

NO$_x$ 排放可减少 20%—30%，是公认的清洁燃料）

DME direct injection system 二甲基醚缸内直接喷射系统

DME engine 二甲基醚发动机

DME spray mixture formation 二甲乙醚喷射式混合气形成（法）（将代用燃料二甲乙醚直接喷入燃烧室或高温-高压的定容积室内形成混合气的方法）

DMF （从1999年开始在重型货车上使用的）双质量飞轮（dual mass flywheel 的简称）

DMFC 直接甲醇燃料电池（direct methanol fuel cell 的简称）

DMFC 见 direct methanol fuel cell

DMFW 双质量飞轮（dual mass flywheel 的简称，装在不使用液力变矩器而使用离合器的发动机和CVT之间，利用装在两块飞轮盘即所谓的双质量飞轮之间的螺旋弹簧和黏性油液吸收发动机转速变化引起的转矩变动和低速振动等）

dmim 丝米（decimillimeter，= 10^{-4} 米）

D-model carburettor 见 double barrel carburet(t)or

DMPR damper 的简称

DMU 见 dynamic mockup

DNA 脱氧核糖核酸（desoxyribonucleic aid 的简称）

DNF （比赛车辆因事故被阻等而退出赛事时，宣布）未完成（did not finish 的简称）

DOAS 柴油机气（臭）味分析系统（diesel odor analysis system 的简称）

DOC 柴油机（排放物净化用的）氧化催化剂（diesel oxidation catalyst 的简称）

dodar 导达，（超声波定向和测距装置，determination of direction and range 的简称）

DOD of battery 蓄电池的放电率（指蓄电池已放电量占其容量安培-小时的百分比，depth of discharge of battery 的简称）

DOE ［美］能源部（Department of Energy 的简称）

6-DOF movement of vehicle 车辆的6自由度运动（DOF 为 degree of freedom "自由度"的简称，指侧倾、纵倾、横摆、横向移动、纵向移动、垂直运动）

2-DOF-vehicle model 二自由度汽车（数学）模型（亦称 bicycle model，用前、后两个车轮，类似自行车的结构来表示整车运动的数学模型，其中 DOF 为 degree of freedom 的简称）

dog bolt 铰接螺栓［= hinge (d) bolt］

dog bone drive 偏心连杆式传动（机构，将旋转运动由一轴传至另一轴、由两端带轴承并与偏心轮等结合的连杆组成，偶见用于顶置式凸轮轴取代其齿轮或链传动）

dog clutch 牙嵌式离合器（亦称 claw clutch，= dog coupling）

dog clutch for direct drive 直接传动的牙嵌式离合器

dog engaged constant mesh gears 牙嵌式啮合套式常啮合齿轮

dogging 夹住，钳住

dog (-) leg 狗腿（轿车车身后柱"C-pillar"接门槛板的下段，多呈〈形，故称）

dog leg section 四门轿车后侧板"rear quater panel"前缘沿车轮洞延伸到腰线的不规则外形部分

dog point （无头蜗杆的）止端

dog wheel 卡轮

DOHC 双顶置凸轮轴（double overhead camshaft 的简称，亦写作 dohc）

DOHC engine 双顶置凸轮轴发动机（double overhead camshaft engine 的简称）

do-it-yourself kit 由买主买回去自行装配的成套零件

dollar ①元（反应性单位。1元=缓发中子产生的反应性）②美元（代号$或$,简写d,1美元=100美分）

dolly ①（半挂车）停放支地架②小车,台车③（拖故障车用的）带轮拖架（被拖的前轮支撑在该架）④（钣金工用的）垫模,垫铁,铁砧,托模（亦称dolly block）

dolly block （钣金工用的）铁砧,垫块（简称dolly）

domain ①区域,范围②定义域③畴（如：磁畴和在液晶中液晶分子指向矢基本相同的微小区域等）

dome 球头帽,圆顶,拱顶,钟形罩

domed section wing 圆顶剖面翼子板

dome head cylinder ①半球形燃烧室汽缸,（=hemispherical-head cylinder,参见hemispherical combustion chamber）②半球形燃烧室发动机

dome head piston 球面顶活塞,圆顶活塞,凸顶活塞（=arched top piston,convex head piston,crown head piston）

dome lamp ①（[美]圆顶形）车内照明灯②顶灯（亦称dome light,=ceiling light）

dome nut 圆盖螺母

domestic 本地的,本厂的,本国的,国产的

domestically-made vehicle 国产车辆

Dong Feng Motor Group （中国）东风汽车集团（东风汽车工业联营公司1992年9月1日起的新名,英文名Aeolus Group,其中Aeolus为希腊神话中的风神"伊俄勒斯"）

donkey-engine ①绞车,绞盘,卷扬机②辅助发动机

donor car 取件用车（指用其部件来修配同型号的车辆或拼装其他车辆的旧车）

doodlebug ①[英]小型赛跑车②[口语]侦察车,战车

5 door 五门（轿车）（在四门轿车的基础上加有一个后门）

door-ajar warning lamp 车门未关妥的警告灯[=door-lock warning lamp,(door) ajar warning light]

door aperture protecting edge 门洞护条,门框护边

door beam 见side impact bar

door bottom 车门底（指车门包皮和门框二者的底部,有时亦指车门框带排水孔的门框窄的横底板）

door buffer 车门缓冲器,车门防振装置,车门软垫（亦称door bumper）

door capping 车门扣条（在车门内装饰板和风窗玻璃之间的型条）

door case 车门框（架）（=door frame）

door catch 门锁,门闩

door ceiling light switch （由车门开、闭控制的）车门顶灯开关（=door dome lamp switch）

door check arm 车门开度限位杆（简称door check,若使用拉条时称door check strap）

door (check) stop 车门开度挡块

door closing cylinder （气动或液压式车门关闭机构的）车门控制缸

door contact 门控开关触点（当门开启或关闭时,使门控灯或车门半开警报件电路接通或断开）

door control transmitter （遥控门锁的）门锁控制信号发射器（遥控门锁的开、关电子控制信号钥匙,亦称remote keyless entry transmitter）

door dome lamp switch 车门顶灯开关（见door ceiling light switch）

door engine 车门自动开闭装置

4 door hardtop （车门没有车窗框但有中柱的）硬顶四门轿车

3 door hatch back (body) 三门舱背式车身（轿车）（除左、右两个

车门外还有一个后背门的直背式车身，见 hatch back body)

5 door hatch back（body） 五门舱背式车身（轿车）（除左、右各两个车门外，还有一个后背门的直背式车身）

door lock de-icer ①门锁化冻液（一般用按压式喷雾器喷入锁内化冻）②（电热式）门锁化冻器

door lock remote control 门锁遥控机构；门锁遥控

door-lock warning lamp （车）门未关妥警告灯（= door-ajar warning lamp）

door mirror with camera assembly 装在车门外的后视镜（带摄像头总成）

door module （装在车）门内（的）附件总成（锁、玻璃升降机构、开关机构、门控灯开关等）

door-mounted side air bag （装在车门内的）门装式侧面安全气囊（除正面的安全气囊以外，防止乘员侧向碰撞的伤害的气囊）

door-mounted thorax side airbag 装在车门内的防躯体胸部侧面碰撞安全气囊

door-mounted tweeter （车内的）门装式高音喇叭

door open/closed sensor 车门开/闭（状态）传感器

door operating cylinder 车门开关操作缸

door pier 车门角柱

door pillar 车门立柱（车门前、后的车立直板件，还用于支撑车顶和加强整个车身，使之成一整体，亦称 door post，包括 A-pillar, B-pillar, C-pillar 前、中、后立柱，两门车无 B-pillar）

door pillar switch 门控灯开关（大多装在 A-pillar 的下部，故名）

door sash ①车门窗框（= door window frame）②装于车门腰部的装饰

door shock absorber 车门减振器，车门缓冲装置（= door bumper）

door shut 门上关后，从里、外均看不见的侧边，亦称 door shut face

door slam cycle test 车门开关碰击循环试验［车门开-关循环寿命（次数）试验］

door slam rig 车门开-关试验装置

door slam test 车门开-关试验（测定车门框架、门锁等的疲劳寿命）

door speaker 装在车门内的音响喇叭

door test 车门（加载）试验（如：测定车门全开及开启10°时加载后的挠度和永久变形）

door to door 门对门（运输）（指运输的货物由发货人的仓库门装货，直达运输到收货人的仓库门卸货）

door-to-door delivery truck 挨户送货汽车（例如送奶车，= multistop truck, multistop delivery truck, peddle truck）

5-door version 五门型（厢式车辆，左、右各两扇门加一扇后门）

door well 车门内腔（指门框和内、外板间形成的空间）

door（window）ventilation glass 车门前角窗玻璃（指前门前部可旋转供车厢内通风的角窗玻璃，亦称 anti-drift ventilation glass）

dopant （为获得所需的某种特性而向液晶内）添加（的材）料

dope ①添加剂②抗爆添加剂（特指芳香烃类燃油添加剂，用于规则允许的赛事）③加添加剂

dope can ①发动机起动（时将燃油注入汽缸内的）注油枪②加油罐

doped fuel 加有添加剂的燃油（的统称，例如：乙基化汽油，掺抗爆剂汽油，含铅汽油，含添加剂柴油）

doper 滑脂枪，黄油枪，加油枪

doppler effect 多普勒效应（当向一

运动的物体发射频率为 f_1 的电磁波时,由该物体反射回来的电磁波的频率 f_2 将随着其相对运动速度的变化而变化,f_2 与 f_1 差,称为 doppler shift "多普勒频移"。产生多普勒频移的现象称为多普勒效应。运用这一效应,可以测定相对行驶的车辆等之间的相对速度、距离、接近速度及可能发生碰撞的时间等,进而制成汽车防碰撞紧急自动制动系统等的传感器件)

doppler radar 多普勒雷达(运用多普勒效应的无线电探测和定位系统)

doppler radar automatic braking system 多普勒雷达自动制动系统

doppler radar collision avoidance system 多普勒雷达防碰撞系统

doppler ranging 多普勒(雷达)测距(简称 doran)

doppler shift 多普勒频移(见 doppler effect)

doppler speedmeter 多普勒车速表

doppler speedsensor 多普勒车速传感器

doppler velocity and position finder 多普勒测速及定位仪(简称 dovacp,或写作 DOVAP)

doran 见 doppler ranging

dormant mode 休眠模式(汽车电子控制系统的某些控制模块,在发动机点火开关断开后 30 秒,即进入电能消耗最少的休眠状态)

dormant window 天窗,车顶窗(= dormer)

dormobile 住宿汽车,野营车(dormitory "宿舍" 与 automobile 两词的组合词)

dosing system (喷油)剂量系统

DOT 4 特高性能的制动液的标号

DOT ①美国运输部(Department of Transportation 的简称)②英国运输部(Department of Transport 的简称)

DOT code 标在轮胎侧壁上表示生产日期的字母和数字

dot weld (ing) 点焊,填补焊

double ①成双的,二倍的;双重的,双联的;两用的 ②见 double trailer

double-acting engine 双动式发动机(指活塞的两头都工作的发动机,参见 single-acting engine)

double acting fuel supply pump 双作用式输油泵(活塞往复行程中,两个行程均输出燃油的活塞式输油泵)

double-acting gate 双动式门

double-acting (hydraulic) brake expander (液压制动系)双向作用式制动轮缸(= double-acting wheel cylinder)

double acting main control valve (气制动系的)双作用式主控制阀(亦称双腔气制动阀 "dual chamber air brake valve",由两个膜片或活塞构成两个工作腔,在单一的制动踏板动作操纵下分别控制两条独立回路的气制动阀)

double-acting pump 双动式泵

double acting reciprocating compressor 双向式往复压缩机

double-acting servo 双向伺服机构(在单向伺服机构中,依靠液压、气压或电磁等的作用实现工作冲程,而由复位弹簧等实现回松冲程。在双向伺服机构中,上述两项冲程都由液压等实现)

double-acting shock absorber 双向减振器(= two-way shock absorber)

double-acting solenoid 双作用电磁阀(同时操纵两个不同作用的阀门的电磁阀)

double-acting swash-plate Stirling engine 双作用活塞型旋转斜盘式斯特林发动机(每缸中仅使用一个活塞代替原来的压气和做功的两个活塞,一般由四个缸联成一个循环系

统，前一缸活塞除做功外，还起下一缸压气活塞的作用，用旋转斜盘机构将活塞的往复运动转变为旋转运动）

double-action shock absorber 双向作用式减振器

double amplitude 双幅，全幅（正、负峰间的幅度）

double angular bearing 双列向心推力球轴承

double-arm lever ①双臂杠杆②（特指离心式点火提高装置离心块滑销的）双臂（滑）销（导）孔板

double arm type suspension 双控制臂式悬架（见 5-link type suspension）

double-bank radial engine 双排星形发动机

double bank rotary engine 双缸转子发动机，双缸旋转活塞发动机

double-bar bumper 双杆保险杠

double barrel carburetor 双腔并动式化油器（由两个相同的单腔组合而成，分别同时各向一组汽缸供给混合气，有的共用一个浮子室，或阻风门等，亦称 twin barrel 或 twin chock carburettor, D-model carburetor）

double-bead tire 双胎圈轮胎（= dual-bead tire, twin-bead tire）

double-bear 双支点的，双支撑的

double bearing 双列轴承

double bell-shape flexspline （谐波齿轮传动的）双钟形柔轮（指其基本形状近似于单叶双曲面）

double belt 双层传动带

double-bend V 形的，双弯曲的，双弯式的

double-bent valve （轮胎的）双弯式气门嘴（嘴体杆部有两处弯曲的气门嘴）

double-bevel 双斜（面）的，K 形的

double-block brake 双蹄制动器

double bottom 见 double trailer

double cab （货车的）双排座驾驶室

double-cambered wing 双曲面翼子板

double cardan（universal）joint 双联十字轴型万向节（由两个十字轴万向节组成的准等速万向节）

double-cavity type toroid 见 EXTOID CVT

double chamber hydragas spring 双气室油气弹簧，双腔油气弹簧（有高压和低压两个气室。汽车空载时，仅低压室承载，在满载时，高低压室冈时承载。类似钢板弹簧悬架主、副簧的作用）

double check valve 双道单向阀（从两个不同的气压源交替向一个气压元件供气的部件）

double-choke （化油器）双喉管的

double circuit 倍增（器）电路

double circular arc gear 双圆弧齿轮［基本齿条的法向或端面可用齿廓由两段圆弧（或近似圆弧的曲线）组成，上半齿廓为凸弧，下半齿廓为凹弧的斜齿圆柱齿轮］

double combustion chamber 双燃烧室

double-cone bearing 双内圈双列圆锥滚子轴承

double cone clutch 双锥型离合器

double cone-cup chamber 双锥杯形燃烧室

double contact breaker 双触点断电器（= double-point breaker, two-point breaker, dual contact breaker）

double contact bulb ①双脚灯泡②双接点灯泡

double-contact plug 双脚插头（= two-pin plug）

double container car 双层集装箱

double crossbearer （货车底板的）并装双横枕梁

double-cup bearing 双外圈双列圆锥

滚子轴承

double-curvature windshield 双曲率风窗玻璃

double curved surface 双曲面

double-cylinder engine 双缸发动机

double-deck 双层结构；双层的，两层的，夹层的

double-deck（er）bus ①双层客车（具有上、下两层座位的客车 = two deck bus, double decker）②双层桥梁，双层结构

double-deck top covered bus 车顶封闭的双层公共汽车

double-declutch （换挡操作中的）两脚离合器［=［美］double-clutch(ing)，用于无同步器的机械式变速器操作］

double dial timer 双刻度计时器

double diameter cylinder 双直径缸

double diaphragm brake chamber 双膜片式气制动室

double-dipping headlamp 双近光前照灯（= double-dipping headlight）

double direction ring （双层球轴承中间的）双面座圈

double-disc clutch 双片式离合器

double-door 双门的

double drive 指具有两个驱动桥的车辆

double-drive bogie 双轴并装驱动桥

double-drive six-wheeled chassis 双后桥驱动的三桥六轮车底盘，双后桥驱动的三轴车底盘

double drop frame 双弯低架式车架（平板半挂车，其前、后轮部位较高，中部下降的台阶式车架）

double duty tractor 两用拖拉机，两用牵引车

double end blade （螺钉旋具中的）两用旋杆，双头旋杆

double-ended cold piston （布什发动机的）双头冷（做功）活塞（参见 Bush engine）

double-ended hot piston （布什发动机的）双头热（做功）活塞（参见 Bush engine）

double ender ①两头构造相同之物（如：双头扳手，两面锉刀，双头工具）②可双头牵引的汽车挂车

double-end（go-no-go）plug gauge 双端（通-不通）塞规

double-end rod cylinder 两端带活塞连杆的油缸

double-engined drive 双发动机驱动

double enveloping worm gear pair 环面蜗杆副

double exhaust manifold 双排气歧管

double face lamp 双面灯（光线自前、后两面射出）

double-filament（light）bulb 见 bifilar bulb

double-fire ignition 双火花点火（= two spark ignition, twin spark ignition, double spark ignition）

double flare （管件、特别的制动管的）双厚喇叭口管端（喇叭口壁的厚度为管壁厚的一倍，以确保连接牢固安全，故名）

double flat 弯折180°，折为两层

double fluid coupling 闭式循环液力耦合器

double-folding door （公共汽车等）双折式车门

double folium 双叶（形）线

double-fork lever 双叉杠杆

double-gap 双火花塞间隙的

double-geared drive 二级齿轮传动

double gear final drive 双速主减速器（具有两种减速比和一套换挡机构的主减速器，亦称 two speed final drive, dual ratio final drive）

double generation （外旋轮线的）双重创成法

double glass 双层玻璃（简称 DG）

double governor 双级调速器，双级限速器

double headed conical spring 双头锥形弹簧

double header 双牵引车头的汽车列车

double heading （汽车列车）双车头牵引

double helical gear 人字齿轮（= chevron gear, double spiral gear, herringbone gear, 一部分齿宽上为右旋齿，而另一部分齿宽上为左旋齿的圆柱齿轮）

double helical spring 复式螺旋弹簧

double hexagon socket 12插口插座（板）

double hook piston ring 活塞双刃口刮油环

double ignition 双源点火，双火花塞点火（参见 dual ignition）

double-impeller torque converter 双泵轮液力变矩器（具有连续排列的两个泵轮）

double induction system 双重进气系统

double jackknife door 双扇折门

double jaw joint 双万向节（准等速万向节的一种形式，由两个十字轴型万向节组成，= double universal joint, 参见 cardan joint）

double-jointed drive shaft 双十字轴型万向节传动轴

double-jointed vehicle 双节铰接式车辆

double-joint rear axle 双万向节后桥

double-joint swing axle 双铰接接头式摆动桥（见 swing axle, 按其悬挂元件，又可分为螺旋弹簧式"with coil spring", 横置板簧式"with transverse leaf spring"和纵臂扭杆式"with trailing arms and torsion bars"等多种）

double-lane change 双车道变换（指车辆由一车道变换到与之相邻的另一车道）

double layer winding 双层绕组

double lead wire 双股导线

double-level bridge 双层桥（参见 double-deck bridge）

double-lift cam 双升程凸轮，双头凸轮

double-line traffic 双车道交通（= two-lane traffic）

double lipped roller bearing 内外圈均带双挡边的圆柱滚子轴承（可承受少量双向推力）

double magneto ignition 双磁电机点火

double mechanical seal 双端面机械密封（由两对密封端面组成的机械密封）

double-motor drive 双电动机驱动（机构）

double offset universal joint 双偏心球笼式万向节（指内、外滚道是平直的可轴向移动的球笼式方向节，因采用内、外球形支撑面不同心，其内、外球面中心分别偏至万向节中心的两侧的偏心式保持架，即：不同心式球笼 "non-concentric cage" 而得名，亦称 plunging joint）

double over 折边，弯边，卷边

double overhead camshaft 顶置双凸轮轴（一根用于进气门，一根用于排气门，简称 DOC 或 DOHC, 亦称 twin overhead camshafts）

double overhead camshaft engine 顶置双凸轮轴发动机，双顶置凸轮轴发动机（简称 DOHC engine）

double-park 双行停车，并列驻车（如：将汽车停放在与人行道平行停靠的汽车旁）

double pass system ①（燃油等的）双级（滤清）系统②双通道装置

double piston（type）motor ①双活塞式发动机（= double piston engine）②汽缸对置式发动机

double-pivot steering 双主销式转向

机构（指汽车通用的转向机构，左、右前轮均绕其各自的主销回转）

double-plate bearing 两面带防尘盖的液动轴承（= double-shield bearing）

double-plate clutch 双盘离合器（在飞轮与压板中间装有两片从动盘）

double point breaker 双触点断电器（= double contact breaker）

double pointer pressure gauge 双针压力表

double pretensioner belt 双预紧器型乘员安全带

double-profile cam 双升程凸轮（参见 double lift cam）

double-purpose 两用的，双重目的的

double-range bearing 双列滚动轴承（= double-row bearing）

double-reduction final drive 双级主减速器（由两对齿轮组成的主减速器，通常为锥齿轮副与圆柱齿轮副）

double-reduction spur pinion 双级减速主减速器直齿小齿轮

double reduction thru-drive 双级贯通式主减速器（由两对齿轮-通常为圆柱齿轮副-锥齿轮副，或锥齿轮副-圆柱齿轮副组成的贯通式主减速器，见 thru-drive）

double reductor 两级减速器

double roller chain 双排滚子链（亦称 duplex chain）

double-roller wave generator （谐波齿轮传动的）双滚轮波发生器（在滚轮架上装有两个对称滚轮的波发生器）

double rotation brake （可反转式液力变矩器的）双向旋转式制动器（由行星架制动器 P 和太阳轮制动器 S 协同动作，实现导轮的双向旋转。起步时放松制动器 S，收紧制动器 P，行星齿系带动导轮与泵轮反向旋转，以加大转矩。当速比为 1 时，收紧制动器 S，放松制动器 P，于是导轮被固定而与泵轮同向旋转，见 single rotation brake）

double-row engine 双列（排）汽缸发动机

double-row radial thrust ball bearing 双列向心推力球轴承（亦称 double-row angular contact ball bearing，可同时承受径向和轴向载荷的双列角接触球轴承）

double（row）riveting 双排铆接

double runner rotor （液力缓速器的）双叶片转子

double-sandwich 双夹层，（由两种不同材料或同一材料横直相夹的）四层

double-sashed window 双框（上、下升降玻璃）窗

double-seal（ed）bearing 两面带油封的轴承

double-seam 双接缝

double-seated valve 双座阀

double-seator ①双排座轻型货车 ②双座轿车

double-semielliptic spring 椭圆形钢板弹簧

double-service 两用的，双用的，双效的

double-shaft drive 双轴传动

double-shield ball bearing 两面带防尘盖的球轴承（= ball bearing with double side shield, double-plate bearing）

double shift gearbox 双离合器型变速器（简称 DSG，= twin-clutch gearbox）

double-shut-off hose coupling 双自封软管接头

double-sided 双侧的，双向的，双边的

double-sided impeller 双面叶轮，双

面泵轮

double side port system （转子发动机的）双端面进气系统（主、副进气口都为端面进气的系统）

double side seals （转子发动机的）端面双道气封装置，端面双气封条（=dual side seals）

double side tipping 双侧倾卸，两边倾卸

double sliding door 双向滑动车门

double-slot piston ring 双槽活塞油环

double spark ignition 双火花点火（=two spark ignition, twin spark ignition）

double speed final drive 双级主传动（具有两种减速比的两挡主传动机构，亦称 double ratio final drive, double reduction final drive）

double spiral gear 人字齿轮（=double helical gear）

double spline 双列花键

double-staged turbine 双级涡轮机

double stage voltage regulator 双级电磁振动式（电压）调节器（通过两对触点的开闭控制发电机电压的装置）

double steering 双转向操纵装置

double sun roof 双天窗

doubles van 双节厢式挂车，双节厢式车身

double-swing door 双扇摆门，双开门（=double-wing door）

double taper faced piston ring 双锥面活塞环

double tee section 双T字形剖面，双T形断面，工字形断面

double-threaded screw 双头螺纹

double-thread worm 双头螺旋蜗杆（=two-thread worm）

double thrust bearing ①双向推力轴承（双面均承受轴上载荷）②双列推力轴承

double-tire wheel 双胎并装车轮（=dualtire wheel）

double-tone horn 双音喇叭（=dual-tone horn, two-tone horn, twintoned horn, twin horn set）

double toothed type coupling 双齿型联轴节

double track 双车道道路，双轨路，复线道路

double trailer 双挂车汽车引车（一般指加带一辆全挂车的半挂列车，亦称 double train, 简称 double）

double trailing arm type suspension 双纵臂式悬架（每侧车轮通过上、下两根纵臂与车架相连的独立悬架）

double-T section 工字断面，工字钢断面

double tube 套管

double-tube shock absorber 双筒式减振器（由两个同心的钢筒组成，外面的钢筒为储油筒，里面的钢筒为工作缸，亦称 twin-tube damper）

double tube telescopic damper 套管伸缩筒式减振器

double-tube tire 双腔轮胎，双内胎轮胎

double-turbine torque converter 双涡轮液力变矩器（具有连续排列的两个涡轮）

double-type 成双的，成对的；双向的，双面的

double underdrive 两级减速传动

double universal propeller shaft 双十字轴型万向节传动轴

Double VANOS （BMW的）双凸轮轴可变气门正时系统（商品名）

double variable valve timing 见 DV-VT

double-vee 双V形的，X形的，W形的

double V-engine 双V形发动机，W形发动机

double walled 夹壁的，双层壁的
double-walled piston 夹壁活塞
double wave (谐波齿轮传动)双波(指波发生器每一整转期间，柔轮齿圈中性层任一点上产生变形波的循环次数为2)
double way check valve 双进口单向阀(常指两个入口各在阀的一端，出口在阀中间的一种单向作用阀)
double-way tipper 双向(两侧)卸货的自卸汽车
double wheel 双胎并装车轮(= double tyre, dual tyre, dual wheel, duplex wheel)
double windshield wiper 风窗双刮水器
double wing door 双开门(= double swing door)
double-wiper rotor (点火系的)双触点臂分火头，双头分火头，双接触片分火头
double wire bulb 双丝灯泡
double wishbone arm type suspension 双A形控制臂式独立悬架(指上、下横臂均使用A形控制臂的双横臂式独立悬架，见wishbone)
double-wound 双股(线)的，双线绕的
doubling ①加倍；重复，重叠②加倍的，重复的，成双的
doughnut ①[美]汽车轮胎②环状物③环形室
doughnut coupling 环形联轴节(一般为橡胶制成的面包圈状挠性联轴节，如：用于传动轴前端接变速器的联轴节，亦称doughnut joint)
doughnut tyre (球形断面)低压轮胎(见balloon tyre)
Dovap 见Doppler velocity and position finder
dovetail ①燕尾形的②燕尾形零件
dovetail furrow 燕尾槽(= dovetail-groove, dovetail slot)

dowel ①(使两个零件间保持准确定位的)定位销(亦称dowelpin)②用定位销定位
dowel bolt 定位螺栓
dowel(ed) joint 暗销连接，定位销连接，定缝钉接合
dowel hole 定位销孔，键槽孔
dowel pin 定位销
dowel screw 双头螺钉
Dow metal 镁基铝合金
down cover 底盖(= 美bottom cover)
downdraft constant-vacuum carburetter 下吸式等真空度化油器(即下吸式活动喉管化油器，依靠喉管断面的变化保持喉管主喷嘴处在发动机各种工况下真空度接近相等，简称DCV carburetor)
down exhaust pipe 见down pipe
down-flow radiator 下流式散热器(由上、下水箱和连接二者的散热芯组成，热水由发动机缸盖出水口流入上水箱，散热后冷水由下水箱流出至汽缸体入水口)
down flow type converter 下流式转化器；(①排气向下方流动与催化剂接触的催化转化器，如：排气管内装式转化器②指双转化器系统中的第二个转化器)
down-folding gate 下折放式货厢后栏板
down force (高速行驶时利用导流板产生的空气动力)向下的压力(抵消空气动力浮力，使车轮紧压地面，提高其与地面的附着力)
down-grade ①下坡，降级②下坡的，降级的③降低…等级，使…降级
down grade against engine ①带发动机制动的下坡②发动机降级
down hill assist control system 下坡辅助控制系统(见DAC system)
down-hill axle (在坡道上汽车的)

下方车桥（居于坡道下方的车桥，即上坡时的后桥、下坡时的前桥）
down hill braking 下坡制动
down hill coasting （汽车）下坡惯性滑行，溜坡滑行
down hill retarder 下坡缓速器
down period （发动机的）停机期，（汽车）停车期
down pipe （down exhaust pipe 的简称，直接连接发动机排气歧管的废气系统的）前端管（件）（亦称 head pipe）
Down Pot 商务轿车（指具有商务车的实用性，又具有小轿车的快适性的一种新型区市用车辆）
down scale car 低档轿车（一般指价格低廉的经济型轿车）
down shift ［美］挂低速挡，降挡（由较高的挡位换到较低的挡位，［英］称 change down = downward change）
down shifting smoothness 换入低挡时的换挡平顺性
down shift inhibitor 防止自动脱入低挡装置（用于自动变速器）
down sized car 缩小型轿车，减小尺寸的轿车（主要指车身尺寸较原生产型缩小的车型）
down sizing （汽车等）减小尺寸，缩小尺寸，缩短尺寸
downspeeding 减速
down stream ①下流的，下游的，后段的；后置的②（交通）下游（指合流或分流后的主线公路下游段）③下降气流，顺流，顺流的
down stream injection （指将汽油喷至进气气流末端，一般是进气门处的）下流喷射
downstream O_2 sensor 下游传感器（装在催化转化器后方的 O_2 传感器，用于测试催化转化器净化处理后废气中的氧气含量）
down stream pressure （液压元件）下游压力，（阀）后压力
down stroke （活塞等的）向下冲程（如：直孔式发动机的进气和工作冲程，= descending stroke）
down take pipe 接在排气歧管后的第一根排气管
down-turned eye （钢板弹簧）下卷耳
downward（**s**） 向下的，下降的，下坡的，下方的
downwards angle of visibility 下视角（指驾驶员过眼点的 z 平面与眼点至风窗下缘的直线之间的夹角，见 z plane）
downward ventilation system （由车顶进气，车下排气，以防灰尘进入车身内的）下行式通风系统
down wash 气流向下的分流（特指运动中的车辆后面的向下气流）
dozer ①推土机②推土铲
DP 双相（钢）（dual-phase steel 的简称，其主要成分是 C 和 Mn，主要组织是铁素体和马氏体，为先进高强度钢的一种，见 AHSS）
DPA ①（柴油机）分配式喷油泵总成（distributor pump assembly 的简称）②数字时间（波形）分析（digital period analysis 的简称）
DPC 数据处理中心（data processing center 的简称）
DPDT 双刀双掷（开关）（double-pole double-throw 的简称）
DPF 柴油机（排放）颗粒过滤器（diesel particles filter 的简称）
DPFE 压差反馈式 EGR（differential pressure feedback exhaust gas recirculation 的简称。DPFE 传感器把循环废气进入进气系的量孔前、后取出的废气压力差信号，作为实际废气循环流量的信号，反馈给发动机控制模块"PCM"，由 PCM 根据当时所要求的废气循环量，对实际循环量进行修正。美国政府规定，从

1995年1月起,一律使用SAE推荐的DPFE这一术语取代福特公司的PFE等)

DPFE sensor 压差反馈(式)废气再循环传感器(differential pressure feedback EGR sensor 的简称,OBDII系统中监测EGR系统工况的传感器件)

DPF substrate 柴油机微粒排放物滤清器(滤芯)基体(DPF 为 diesel particulate filter 的简称)

DPI 数据处理设备(data processing installation 的简称)

D-pillar (旅行车车身等的)尾柱,D-柱(最后的立柱,位于车身后门的两侧,亦称 D-post, = rearmost vertical pillar)

DPNR (丰田公司轻型柴油货车用的)柴油机微粒物和 NO_x 排放(同时)减少系统 [diesel particulate and NO_x (simultaneous) reduction system 的简称]

DPR 柴油机微粒排放主动减少系统(diesel particulate active reduction system 的简称,商用车用微粒排放量超低减少系统的产品名)

DPR-cleaner 柴油机微粒排放物后净化处理器(diesel particulate rear cleaner 的简称)

DPST 双刀单掷(开关)(double-pole single throw 的简称)

3-D quantum ICs 三维量子集成电路(可集成 $20×10^9$ 个三极管)

draft ([美]= draught) ①拉,拖曳,牵引,牵引力,牵引阻力②通风,通过管道吸入空气,抽风气流;通风装置③草图,草案

draftless ventilation 非直吹式通风(= antidraft ventilation, draft-proof ventilation)

draft link (独立悬架)下摆杆,下悬架臂,下臂

draft resistance 牵引阻力

draft standard 标准草案

draft-type air-cooling 吸入式空气冷却,直吹式空气冷却

draft vehicle 牵引车(= towing vehicle)

drag ①(指离合器)不能彻底分离(亦称 clutch drag)②(指松开制动踏板后,制动器松放不彻底,继续保持的)制动拖滞(亦称 rubbing 或 brake drag)③(汽车行驶时,车身的)空气动力学阻力,风阻④(机油等黏性引起的运动)黏滞阻力⑤drag racing 的简称⑥拖曳,拉,牵⑦被拉之物

drag acceleration (车辆因行驶阻力,如:风阻等产生的)负加速度,减速度

drag area (汽车)风阻面积

drag bar 牵引杆,拉杆;连接杆(= draw bar)

drag car 短程加速赛用车(见 drag racing)

drag center (空气)阻力中心,风阻中心

drag chain 牵引链

drag coefficient ①风阻系数,空气阻力系数(= coefficient of air resistance)②(油液等黏性引起的)黏滞阻力系数

drag divergence 迎面阻力(发散导致的系数)增大

drag down 换入低速挡,挂低挡

drag foiler (装在货车身顶部的)导风罩(减少行驶时产生的迎面风阻)

drag force ①空气阻力,风阻②牵引阻力(等于负的牵引力)

dragging ①拖曳,牵引;刮平②摩擦,阻尼,拖滞③(离合器或液力传动分离不彻底引起的)缓慢拖滞转动④牵引的

dragging bucket (装载、挖掘机械等的)拖斗

drag link ①转向直拉杆（指非独立悬架转向杆系中连接转向摇臂和转向节臂的杆件、在某些结构中，连接转向接臂与中间摆臂，亦称 drag rod）②牵引杆，拉杆

drag link arm 转向直拉杆臂

drag link ball-joint 转向直拉杆球（头销）节

drag link body 转向直拉杆杆身

drag link end 转向直拉杆端头（= steering gear connecting rod end）

drag loss 由空气阻力引起的损失

drag of brakes 制动器（分离不彻底引起的）拖滞

drag racing 短程（1/4 英里）加速赛 [在专用赛道上，静止起步加速行驶 1/4 英里（500 米）的秒数计成绩的一种汽车赛事，每趟两辆，有多种级别，一般使用为此专门设计的赛车，见 dragster，有时亦使用改装车，见 hot rod。以美国举办的全美加速赛 "National Drag Race" 最负盛名，亦称 drag race，简称 drag]

drag reducer 见 drag spoiler

drag reducing cowling 减阻罩，导流罩

drag-reducing device （汽车的）空气阻力减少装置，导风减阻装置（根据空气动力学原理，设计出的导风装置，装于汽车上以减少空气阻力，= air drag reduction device, drag reducer，参见 drag-spoiler）

drag resistance （汽车行驶时受到的）空气阻力（包括迎面正压和后面负压，主要取决于车身的空气动力学外形，故又称车形阻力、外形阻力）

drag shoe 制动蹄片

drag spoiler 空气阻力减少装置（根据空气动力学原理，制成的各种减少空气阻力的车身附加板件或帘幕的总称，亦称 air drag reduction device, drag reducer; airfoil shield, air shield，根据安装部位及减阻原理的不同，有多种不同的名称）

dragster 1/4 英里短程加速赛赛车 [专门为上述赛事设计和制造的赛车，一般装有大功率的增压式发动机（位于底盘后部），极宽的后轮，使用降落伞制动，俗称 rail]

drag strip 1/4 英里短程加速赛跑道

drain ①排水管，排水道；（复）排水系统②（场效应晶体管）漏极③排出（将水排尽而）变干④（逐渐）消耗，流失

drain back 排回，回流

drain back passage （循环液体，如：机油等的）回流通道

drain cock 排放开关，放水阀，放油阀，放气阀，排污阀（亦称 drain tap）

drain contact （场效应晶体管的）漏（极）接点

drain oil unit 滑油排放装置，放油工具，放油装置

drain period 换油周期，换水周期

drain plug heater 放油塞加热器（以降低润滑油黏度）

drain terminal （场效应晶体管）漏（极）端子，漏极引出线

drain the transmission 从变速器放油

drain valve 排放阀，排污阀，放水阀

dramatic ①突然的②巨大的③引人注目的

Draper's equation （估算汽油机爆震频率的）杜雷波公式（$f_r = P_{mn} \times C/\pi B$，式中：$f_r$—爆振共振频率；$P_{mn}$—振动模式系数；$C$—汽缸内的气体的声速；$B$—汽缸半径）

draping ①覆盖②隔声，消声，减轻噪声

draught （= [美] daft）①进入车厢内的直吹气流②通风③拉，曳，牵引④从容器中汲取

draught bar 牵引杆,拉杆

draught excluder ①封闭阀,通风管路密封件②排除器③防尘器(=dust excluder)

draw ①拉,拖,牵引,拔出,抽出②拉制,拔制,拉丝③回火④制图,制定⑤驱动电器装置所需的电流量

drawability ①可拉延性,压延性能②回火性

drawback cylinder 复位油缸,反向冲程油缸

drawback temperature 回火温度

draw-bar 牵引杆,拉杆(特指双轴全挂车的牵引-转向架,亦写作drawbar,=draft bar,drag bar)

drawbar category 按牵引能力划分的(牵引车)等级

drawbar combination 货车-双轴全挂车列车(俗称drawbar rig)

drawbar coupling 牵引装置

drawbar efficiency (有效)牵引效率,(挂钩)牵引效率

drawbar force 有效牵引力,挂钩牵引力

drawbar frame 牵引架

drawbar height 牵引点高度,拉杆高度

drawbar hook 牵引钩 [= pull hook, tow (ing) hook]

drawbar horsepower 有效牵引功率,拖钩功率(=tow-rope horsepower)

drawbar length 牵引杆长度(牵引杆处于正前方位置时,垂直于车辆支撑平面的牵引杆销孔中心线至过牵引杆固定在全挂车上的连接销轴线,并垂直于车辆支撑平面的平面距离)

drawbar load 牵引载荷,牵引负荷

drawbar pin 牵引杆连接销

drawbar pin hole 牵引杆销孔

drawbar plate-brace 牵引杆加强角撑

drawbar pull (牵引车的)牵引杆拉力(简称DBP)

drawbar pull limit (汽车的)拖杆拉力极限,拖钩拉力极限(在不计空气阻力及加速阻力的条件下,汽车拖钩上能达到的最大拉力)

drawbar pull-slip curve 牵引力-滑移曲线

drawbar-pull-weight ratio (牵引车)挂钩牵引力与(车辆)重力之比

drawbar resistance 挂钩牵引阻力,有效牵引阻力

drawbar spring 牵引杆缓冲弹簧

drawbar stabilizer 牵引装置横向稳定器,拉杆稳定器

drawbar test 牵引试验(指使用适当的仪器,通过牵引的方法来测试汽车的行驶阻力和有关参数)

drawbar trailer (指由)牵引杆牵引的(前轮转向)双轴全挂车

drawbar train 全挂车列车(指由主车和牵引杆拖挂的全挂车列车)

draw coupling altitude (牵引车)拖挂连接装置高度(其中心距地面高度)

draw coupling reach (牵引车)后轴中心至拖挂连接装置末端距离

draw crack 拉伸(应力)裂缝

drawer 拔取工具,拉拔工具,带起子的锤

drawer-type glove box (驾驶室内)抽屉式手套箱

draw gear 牵引装置,车钩,牵引架

draw gear length 牵引架长(牵引杆处于正前方位置时,垂直于车辆支承平面的牵引杆销孔中心线至过全挂车前轴中心线且垂直于车辆支承平面的距离)

draw-in bolt 拉紧螺栓

drawing ①拖,拉,牵引②拉制③回火④制图,绘图⑤图样,图纸

drawing die 冲压模,拉伸模;拉丝模

drawing effect ①回火效应，回火作用②拉制效应，拉伸效应
drawing pump 吸入泵，抽出泵
drawing scale 制图比例尺，绘图比例尺（= draughting scale）
drawing vehicle （特指装备牵引设备的专用）牵引车（主要用于英国的正式术语）
draw spring 牵引缓冲弹簧
draw the spark 扩大火花塞的跳火间隙
draw tongue 牵引架（= pull tongue）
draw to scale 按比例绘制（图）
draw up 拧紧，紧固（螺钉）
draw up bead ring （轮胎外观缺陷）钢丝圈上抽（钢丝圈向胎侧部位上移的现象）
dray ①（原意为低平而无侧板的四轮载货马车，现在亦指）无拦板的低平板式四轮货车车身②运输农产品或酒类的车辆
DRB 诊断（结果）读出仪（diagnostic read-out box 的简称）
DRC 动态平顺性控制（系统）（dynamic ride control 的简称）
dream car 理想车，梦幻车（在设计汽车时的一种理想构思的车型）
3-D recognition technology （计算机控制系统的）三维识别技术
dress ①覆盖物②修饰，装饰；整理；修平，磨平（用磨等方法给粗糙表面、边缘等以正确形状）③道路复面，敷面
dresser 修整工具，修整器
Dresserator 汽油音速喷雾器（一种代替化油器使汽油雾化的装置，它以音速将汽油喷入一扩散器内，汽油被粉碎成极细小的微粒而与空气形成十分均匀的混合气）
dressing ①覆盖物；修饰，装饰②修整，整理，清理③（道路）表面处治
dressing burr 修整毛刺，打磨毛刺
dressing plate 校正平板，标准平板

dressing tool 砂轮修整工具（= truing tool）
dressing work 精整加工（如：研磨等）
drg 阻力，制动器，滞后，拉（drag 的简称）
DRGS 动态行车路线引导系统（见 dynamic route guide system）
DRI （车座等的）动态反应指数（参见 dynamic response index 的简称）
dribble 滴落，滴漏，渗漏
dribble pipe 喷油嘴溢油管
dribbling （喷油后，喷嘴）滴流，滴漏，渗漏（= after-dripping）
drier ①干燥器，干燥箱②干燥剂（= dehumidifier）③烘干炉，烤漆房（= drying oven）
drift ①漂流，漂浮，漂动②发展趋势③偏离，偏差④漂移（如：仪表零点漂移等）⑤变化（如：灵敏度变化等）⑥冲击⑦（汽车高速转弯时，若离心力大于轮胎与路面附着力，产生的向弯道外侧的）滑移⑧（赛车弯道驾驶技术）滑移转向（主动控制与利用上述滑移现象，实现赛车的弯道高速转向）
drift angle 偏移角，偏差角，滑角
drift compensating 零点漂移补偿
drift-free （仪表指针）无漂移的
drift start （试验或使用中）参数偏离起动
drift time （汽车）由高速挡换至低速挡时所需滑行时间
drill ①钻头，钻床②训练，练习，演习
drill bit 钻头
drilled 钻（有）孔的，钻有油孔的
drilled valvehead 带凹槽的气门头（供接装研磨工具用）
drink-holder （车上的）饮料杯架
drinking driver 饮酒驾驶员
drink meter （驾驶员）饮酒测定器

（测定呼气中的酒精浓度）

drip 滴，滴下，滴流，滴漏

drip cup 滴式油杯

drip feed ①点滴注油（润滑）②滴油器，滴液器

drip (-feed) lubrication 滴油润滑法

drip feed lubricator 滴油润滑器，滴油器，滴油杯（= drop oiler, feed oiler）

drip-feed oil pump 滴油润滑泵，滴漏式润滑油泵

drip guard rail （车身的）檐条（= cornice）

drip line 滴线

drip moulding （车顶周边的）流水槽，雨水檐槽（亦称 roof drip, drip channel, gutter channel, =［美］roof side drip rail）

drip pan ①集油盘②承屑盘，落屑盘

dripping ①滴下，滴落，滴漏②水滴，油滴

dripping test （滑油的）滴点试验（机油一滴一滴地滴落在高温钢板上，最后观测钢板上沉积物情况）

drip pipe 冷凝水泄出管，液滴集流管

drip-proof 防滴漏的，防滴式

drip rail 见 drip moulding

drip ring 滴油环，（轴承）环形滴油槽

drivability ①（对发动机指）操纵性（起动性，对加、减速的响应性，怠速运转平顺性及其他影响操纵、驾驶及可靠性的性能等）②（对汽车指）驾驶性能，运行性（一般指能用"好"、"坏"来评价的机动性，平顺性、加速性、起动与升温的快慢，以及操纵性和舒适性等车辆的使用性能）

drivability control system （车辆的）操纵性控制系统

drivable （指车辆）可驾驶的，可行驶的、可开动的

DRIVE （美国）汽车高效与节能研究和创新伙伴联盟［美国能源局 2011 年 9 月宣布将原自主汽车与燃油伙伴联盟（Freedom Car and Fuel Partnership）升级并更名为"Driving Research and Innovation for Vehicle Efficiency and Energy Sustainability"，简称"DRIVE"，是研究汽车技术发展的需求、目标和路线及对实现目标的过程进行评价的专家机构，勿与"drive"混淆］

drive ①乘车(出行)（= travel in a car 或 by car）②驾驶（汽车）③驱动④传动装置，传动系⑤（自动变速器的）前进挡（D）⑥通过邸园直达住宅的私人道路（=［美］driveway）

driveaway ①直驶交车(由车厂直接驾驶着买主所订购的车辆送交买车者的一种售车交货方式)②[动]乘车去，开着车走掉；驱逐，赶走

drive-away （汽车）起步

drive-away operation （汽车）起步运行，起步操作

drive axle （汽车的）驱动桥

drive-axle alignment 驱动桥定位

drive axle allowable input (output) torque 驱动桥标称最大输入（输出）转矩［指由制造厂规定的驱动桥的输入（输出）转矩］

drive axle efficiency 驱动桥效率（驱动桥输出转矩/驱动桥输入转矩比，即：驱动桥减速比乘以100%）

drive axle floatation 驱动桥漂浮（现象）

drive axle mass 驱动桥质量

drive axle maximum input torque 驱动桥最大输入转矩（按发动机最大净输出转矩，变速器最低挡及分动器低挡的减速比工况计算，不计传动效率，传到主传动输入轴上的转

矩)

drive axle pinion 驱动桥(差速器)主动圆锥齿轮

drive axle ratio 驱动桥减速比(指在不差速条件下,主减速器输入转速与车轮转速之比,简称 DAR)

drive axle with banjo housing 整体式桥壳驱动桥(见 banjo axle housing)

drive axle with two-piece split housing 二件可分式桥壳驱动桥(见 split axle housing)

drive back (将汽车)驶回,开回

drive ball (万向节的)传动钢球(如:球笼式万向节的钢球,球销式万向节的球环,球叉式万向节的钢球和定心钢球等)

drive belt 传动带

drive belt housing 传动带罩

drive bevel pinion 驱动小锥齿轮

drive (bevel) wheel of differential 见 differential crown gear

drive box [美]俗称,= transmission

drive-by noise level 汽车驶过的噪声(大小)等级

drive-by test (测定车外噪声等的)驶过试验

drive-by wire (电子)线控驾驶(系统)(指通过电子电路而不是机械系统来操纵和控制发动机及汽车的系统)

drive cam (凸轮传动中的)传动凸轮,驱动凸轮,主凸轮;驱动偏心轮(如:凸轮轴上的汽油泵偏心轮等,= driving cam)

drive chain 驱动链,传动链

drive circuit 激励电路,驱动电路

drive dick assembly (机械式调速器的)传动斜盘组件(由传动斜盘和推动轴承等组成,将速度传感部件的作用力传给油量调节机构的部件,如:齿轮拉杆)

drive down ①挂低挡,由高挡换低挡②降低车速,降低转速

drive efficiency ①驱动效率②(特指汽车的)驱动轮效率(表示驱动轮打滑的程度,即车轮每转一周时,汽车的实际移动距离与车轮按滚动半径计算的圆周的比率)

drive end (轴的)驱动端

drive end (bearing) bracket (发电机的)驱动端盖,前端盖[亦称 drive end hsg, drive (side) plate]

drive end cover 驱动端壳盖

drive end plate 驱动端盖板[= drive (side) plate]

drive fit 紧配合,密配合,打入配合(= driving fit)

drive flange 见 driving flange

drive friction plate 传动摩擦盘

drive front axle 驱动前桥(参见 drive axle)

drive gear ①主动齿轮②驱动机构,传动装置(= driving gear,偶见美指差速器从动冠轮)

drive gearbox 传动齿轮箱

drive handle (套筒扳手用的)棘轮扳手,(内四方、六方等螺母螺孔用的)扳手杆

drive idler gear 空转传动齿轮,中间传动齿轮

drive in [美]①免下车餐馆,路边餐馆(饭菜送入车内吃)②drive-in cinema 的简称③路边服务式的,露天营业式的

drive-in cinema 汽车电影院(汽车可进入场内,坐在汽车内看电影,= drive-in theater)

drive layout (汽车)发动机与传动系统的布置(形式)

drive line ①动力传动系统,传动系(= powertrain, power transmission,指从发动机输出轴到驱动轮的整个传动系统,[美]称 drive train)②(有时亦包括发动机在内的)驱动系统③(有时指)传动轴系(由

一个或多个可轴向滑动的传动轴总成组成的系统,能以固定或变化的角度传递转矩和旋转)

drive line drag 传动系旋转阻力(包括轴承摩擦、齿轮啮合、搅油损失等形成的阻力,= drive train drag,在有些文献的论述中包括车轮反馈的行驶阻力)

drive line efficiency 传动系效率

drive line layout 传动系布置,传动系设计

drive manner 驾驶方式,驾驶方法

drive master (汽车)自动传动装置(商品名)

Drive mode selector (汽车)行驶模式选择器[由驾驶者通过拨杆或按钮等选择行驶模式的装置。通常会标明可选择的行驶模式的数量,如:five mode drive selector,可选择5种模式。其中最低端为节油环保(Eco)模式。选择该模式时,节气门对加速踏板的响应度降低,即,加速踏板每单位行程的供油量相应减少到低限,达到节油环保的目的。最高端为运动S+(Sports+)模式,选择该模式时,可极大地提高节气对加速踏板的响应度,即,加速踏板每单位行程的供油量相应增加到高限,加速踏板一触即发,汽车强劲行驶。中间各挡节气门开度对加速踏板的响应度居中,见variable driving pattern system]

drive module ①互换式动力总成(指根据需要和条件可在同一型号的汽车上互换使用的带整套附件的电动机或发动机总成,拆下一套便可换上另一套) ②(在车身和底盘分离式电动汽车中指安装蓄电池、电动机、传动装置和悬架等的)底盘("行驶"的部分,底盘上面的车身称 life module,即乘员"生活"和"操作"的部分)

drive motor (电动汽车的)驱动电动机

driven engine 从动发动机,被动发动机(如:发动机制动时由车轮带动的发动机)

driven flange assembly (柴油机机械式喷油提前器)从动法兰部件(由从动法兰、飞锤销等组成,将驱动法兰的运动传给喷油泵凸轮轴)

driven friction disk 从动摩擦盘,被动摩擦盘

driven gear 从动齿轮

driven load 从动荷载,传动载荷(在机械动力传动系统中包括静载荷及动载荷)

driven plate (离合器)从动盘(亦称 clutch disc, driven disc, friction plate)

driven reverse gear (机械式变速器)倒挡从动齿轮

driven spur gear 从动圆柱直齿轮

driven wheel 从动车轮,被动轮,被驱动车轮

driven wheel of differential (主传动)从动冠轮(见 crown wheel)

drive-on type 驶上型(如:汽车驶上秤台的台秤)

drive-on type auto lift 驶上型汽车举升器(多用于轿车,先将汽车前、后轮直接驶到举升器上,然后举升器升到所需高度)

drive performance 驱动特性(特指正常旋转方向,正常功率流向,即:泵轮驱动时液力传动装置或液力变速器的特性)

drive pinion 传动(小)锥齿轮(特指主减速器驱动差速器从动冠齿轮的小齿轮)

drive pinion adjusting nut 传动(小)锥齿轮调整螺母

drive pinion shaft 传动(小)锥齿轮轴(一般该轴与小锥齿轮为整体件,一端为驱动差速器从动齿轮,

即冠轮的主动小锥齿轮,另一端为花键端)

drive pulley (传动带传动机构的)驱动皮带轮

driver ①驾驶者(= chauffeur, motorist, motor man)②(液力变矩器等的)泵轮(参见 impeller)③主动轮,传动件,驱动件④起子⑤将电能传递给下一级的固体电子电路⑥([美]俗称)日常使用的轿车

driver acceptance 驾驶者(对车辆或车辆的某系统的)接受程度

driver access authorization system 驾驶者进入车内认可系统(防盗系统的一种)

driver-adaptive (可自动适应各种行车条件和驾驶者驾驶风格的)驾驶者自适应式(汽车自动控制系统)

drive radial 驱动轮用子午胎(drive radial tire 的简称)

driver agent ①(对"驾驶者-操控系-动力系-行驶系-反馈系"组成的汽车闭路系统的性能、材料、结构进行各项计算、试验、建模时考虑的)驾驶者因素,驾驶者因子,驾驶者起的重要作用②驾驶者的代理人

driver aid 辅助驾驶仪(帮助驾驶者按规定条件驾驶的装置,如:在多工况试验时,指示驾驶员加速、减速、等速行驶的指示仪,亦称行驶监视仪)

driver aid information and routing system 汽车驾驶者辅助仪表、信息及导行系统

(driver and passenger) side knee airbag (驾驶员和乘员的)侧面护膝安全气囊

driver assistance system 驾驶员辅助系统(参见 DAS)

driver assist system 驾驶者辅助系统(新型的驾驶者辅助系统由①可监测、发送并显示脉搏、心电图和身体各部位骨骼肌肉动作等生理状态数据的驾驶者监测器 driver monitor ②装有360°影像摄取、处理数字摄像机,可监测发送并显示轮胎侧偏角"tire side slip angle",重力加速度、发动机转速、轮速和车轮转向角的车身监测器③上述监测数据的数字、图表、曲线显示设备等组成)

driver barrier panel (客车的)驾驶区隔板(亦称 driver partition,指车厢内分隔驾驶区与乘客区的板件)

driver behavio(u)r (驾驶员的)驾驶操作,驾驶动作

driver-behind-engine bus 长头客汽车(驾驶员座位在发动机后的客车)

driver-beside-engine bus 平头客车(驾驶员座位在发动机旁边的客车)

driver braking performance 驾驶员的制动操作能力(指驾驶员的制动反应灵敏程度、踩踏力等)

driver cab 驾驶室(= driver's cab)

driver-car collaboration 驾驶者-汽车(之间的相互)协调

driver circuit 激励电路,驱动电路

driver comfort 驾驶(员)舒适性

driver-controlled difference (汽车油耗等的)驾驶差别,驾驶员操作因素造成的差别

driver-controlled switch (液力自动变速器等的)驾驶员操纵开关

driver door (四门轿车的)前车门(= front door),(客车的)驾驶员车门

(driver) drowsiness alarm system (驾驶者)瞌睡警报系统

driver element 驱动元件,传动元件

Driver Energy Conservation Awareness Training (美国能源部的)驾驶员节能意识训练(课程,简称 DECAT)

driver-focused 以驾驶员为焦点的

（一切为了驾驶者考虑，以驾驶者为中心的）

driver-friendly 对驾驶者友好的

driver gear 传动齿轮，驱动机构

driver guide 驱动件的导向件（如：柴油机调速器中安装推力斜盘的传动导套）

driver habits 驾驶习惯

Driver-Information Center 驾驶员信息中心（简称 DIC）

driver-information system 驾驶员信息系统（装在仪表板旁，由选择开关、微型电子计算机、信息显示板及各种接线组成。美国 Cadillac 的 Trip Computer 就是其中的一种）

driver judgement time 驾驶员判断时间（驾驶员对某事态察觉后，考虑车速及交通条件，对该事态作出判断所需的时间）

driverless 无人驾驶的

driverless rubber-tired vehicle 无人驾驶轮式车辆

driver licencing 驾驶执照考发，驾驶资格考试与执照核发

driver load 驾驶者（肌肉体力）负荷（driver muscular load 的简称，指各种驾驶操作所消耗的体力）

driver load line 激励级负载线

driver-memory seat 驾驶者（体重、身高、坐姿、驾驶习惯等信息）记忆座椅

driver-model 驾驶者模型（模拟驾驶者认知/判断/操作驾驶行为的数学模型）

driver-monitoring system 驾驶者监视系统（见 Human Central ITS View Aid System）

driver nameplate 驾驶员名牌（如：公共汽车上标记的驾驶员姓名等的公示牌）

drive robot 驾驶（汽车的）机器人

drive rod 传动杆，驱动杆

driver-only-bus 无人售票客车，无售票员公共汽车（一般指自动售票公共汽车，工作人员只有汽车驾驶员一人）

driver-operated 驾驶员操纵的，驾驶员驾驶的（相对于汽车在 automated highway system 中自动驾驶而言）

driver-oriented 以驾驶者为本的

driver-over-engine 驾驶员座位在发动机之上（的车辆）

driver partition 见 driver barrier panel

driver perception reaction distance 驾驶员反应距离（从驾驶员觉察到要制动，到踩制动踏板的反应时间内车辆的行驶距离，简称 driver reaction distance）

driver perception reaction time 驾驶员觉察反应时间（简称 driver reaction time）

drive(r) plate 驱动盘（如：自动变速车辆上，用螺栓紧固在曲轴端接装变矩器的凸缘）

driver response logic 驾驶员反应逻辑（简称 DRL，汽车驾驶员接收信号后的反应规律）

driver response to cumulative vibration effect 驾驶员对累积振动效应的反应

driver response to needed directional corrections 驾驶员对必要的方向修正的反应

driver's awareness and attention level 驾驶者的清醒和专注程度

driver's behavior 驾驶者的操作行为特性

driver's cab panelling （货车）驾驶室前围板总成（一般指前围板及前围侧板和上盖板总成）

driver's cab rear window 驾驶室后窗

driver's certification 驾驶执照（= driver's certificate, driver's license, driving licence, driving license, operator's permit） (driver's) cognitive process （驾驶者对路况及驾驶中出现的各种情况及各种仪表、指示、警报信息的）认知过程

driver's compactment partition （客车）驾驶区挡板，驾驶区隔板（分隔乘客区与驾驶区的板件）

driver's environment （汽车）驾驶环境（包括座位的形状尺寸、操纵机构及仪表布置等驾驶员劳动条件）

driver's eye location 驾驶员的眼睛位置

driver's eye range 驾驶员眼睛活动范围，驾驶员眼睛位置范围（参见 eye ellipse）

driver's fatigue 驾驶员的疲劳（强度）

driver's fuel consumption 实际驾驶油耗（参见 customer fuel consumption）

drivership 驾驶技术，驾驶员素质

driver's instruction 驾驶员守则

driver size 驾驶员身体尺寸

driver's licence 见 driver's certification

driver's mental quality 驾驶员心理素质

driver's package ①（汽车的）驾驶室布置草图，驾驶室组合草图（草图包括座位、转向盘、加速踏板等，以及所有操作时所用控制机构的位置和车门布置等）②（汽车）驾驶室总成

driver's reach （汽车）驾驶员的操作（空间）范围，驾驶员驾驶动作所及（空间）范围

(driver's) resource for information processing 驾驶者（在行驶过程中）处理（各种）信息的智能

driver's seat 驾驶员座椅（亦写作 driver seat）

driver's seat back cushion 驾驶员座位靠背软垫

driver's seat with torsional suspension 带扭杆悬架的驾驶员座椅

driver's speed setpoint （定速巡行系统的）驾驶员选定的车速点

driver status monitor 驾驶者状态监测器（用于监测驾驶者在驾驶过程中知觉或注意力下降、醉酒、服用麻醉剂、疲劳、注意力集中于使用移动电话等状态，时酌情发出相应的警报）

driver steering performance model 驾驶者转向操控性能模型

driver's tension level （遇危急驾驶情况时）驾驶员的紧张度

driver's tool 随车工具（= chauffeur's tool）

driver stopping distance 驾驶员停车距离（从驾驶员认为有必要停车的瞬间起到车辆停止时为止汽车行驶的距离）

driver support system for lane-keeping 支持驾驶员保持行车路线的系统（亦称 lane-following assistance system，见 LKAS）

driver's view （车辆的）驾驶员视野，驾驶员视界

driver's working environment 驾驶员工作环境

driver torque 驱动力矩

driver training school 汽车驾驶培训学校（= autoschool）

driver-vehicle braking performance 驾驶员-车辆（系统）制动性能

driver viewing distance 驾驶员目视距离（指在行驶中，驾驶员眼睛所见到的距离点的水平距离）

driver vision 驾驶员的视线

driver vision aids and safety system 驾驶员视力支助和安全系统（用于提供夜间驾驶员清晰的观视图像）

driver zone （客车）驾驶区

drive screw 传动螺杆

drive shaft ①泛指一切传递转矩和

旋转的轴件②（=［美］propeller shaft，汽车上特指带有万向节传递转矩和旋转运动的）传动轴③（有时亦指驱动桥的）半轴

drive shaft absorber 传动轴减振器（安装在传动轴上吸收或缓冲振动，降低噪声的装置）

drive-shaft fuel injection pump 合成式喷油泵（带有自驱动凸轮轴的柱塞式喷油泵）

drive shaft housing 驱动桥半轴套管，半轴壳

drive shaft length 传动轴特征长度（指传动轴外端两万向节中心距。对中心距固定的传动轴指其公称尺寸。对中心距可变的传动轴指其允许的最大和最小长度）

drive shaft ringing （由于谐振引起的）驱动轴振响（特别是管状驱动轴）

drive shaft safety strap 传动轴安全带（防止轴脱落的金属带）

drive shaft sleeve 驱动轴套

drive shaft spline 驱动桥半轴花键

drive (shaft) tube 万向节驱动轴套管（= cardan tube）

drive-shaft tunnel 驱动轴通道（沿车身底板纵轴线凸起的半圆筒形部分，提供车身底板下容纳驱动轴的空间，= propeller shaft tunnel）

drive side of tooth （齿轮）工作齿面，啮合齿面

drive (side) plate （转子发动机的）驱动端缸盖，后端缸盖，后端盖，后缸盖（= drive end hsg, drive side hsg, drive end plate）

drive signal 驱动信号，控制信号，激励信号

drive sprocket axle 主动链轮轴，驱动链轮轴

drive station car navigation stand 驱动站型汽车导航台（一种可将驾驶者手机作为导航仪使用的汽车导航系统的产品名）

drive strap （离合器压盘的）驱动片（沿压盘圆周布置，用于传递离合器盖对压盘的压力，其中驱动片径向布置者称 radial drive strap，切向布置者称 tangential drive strap）

drive system ①驱动系②驱动体制，驱动类型（如：前桥驱动，后桥驱动，全轮驱动等）

drive-thru (vehicle washing equipment) 汽车驾驶穿过型（整车清洗装备）

drive tool 与套筒扳手一起使用的任一附件（包括套筒扳手加长柄等）

drive torque 驱动力矩（= driving torque）

drive traction ①驱动力，牵引力②（特指）驱动附着力，驱动抓着力（驱动车轮对地面的抓着力，驱动车轮与地面间的附着力）

drive train ［美］驱动系，驱动系统（指从离合器经变速器、传动轴到主传动和半轴的所有动力传递件，有时也包括发动机，亦称 power-train，= drive line）

drive train drag 见 driveline drag

drive train handler 驱动系装卸小车，驱动桥拆装运送车（可作为变速器举升器、差速器后桥壳等的拆装运送车）

drive train interlock belt system 驱动系-安全带互锁系统

drive unit ①驱动装置，驱动部分②（汽车列车的）牵引车，拖车，主车

drive way ①汽车路，车行道②私用车道（由私人住宅通往街道的汽车路）

driving ①驾驶，行车②驱动③主动的，传动的，驱动的

driving adhesion coefficient 驱动附着系数（在给定工作点下，驱动力系数所能达到的最大值，参见 driving force coefficient)

driving advisory system for forward obstacles 回避前方障碍物的驾驶指导系统

driving-age population 汽车驾驶适龄人口数（指按法规允许驾驶汽车的年龄的人口数）

driving and steering axle 转向-驱动桥

driving aptitude 驾驶适应性

driving away from rest 起步,起动

driving axle 驱动桥,驱动轴（亦称 living axle）

driving axle housing 驱动桥壳

driving beam （前照灯）远光（= high beam, distance light, main beam, up beam）

driving behavio(u)r （车辆）操纵性能,驾驶性能

driving bogle 双轴并装驱动桥

driving cam 传动凸轮,驱动偏心轮（参见 drive cam）

driving comfort 乘坐舒适性,驾驶舒适性

driving condition （指交通状态、路况和气候等造成的）行车条件,驾驶条件

driving cycle 汽车行驶多工况循环（测定汽车排放或燃料经济性的一组模拟实际行驶的标准工况,一般包括加速、减速、等速和怠速工况）

driving direction ①驱动方向②（车辆的）行驶方向

driving disk ①主动片,驱动盘②（特指机械式调速器的）传动斜盘

driving end ①（轴的）驱动端,主动端②套筒扳手杆端

driving end bearing bracket （电机）前端盖（指发电机、起动机驱动端支承电机转子的支承座）

driving fit 紧配合,轻迫配合,打入配合

driving flange ①（柴油机机械式喷油泵前器的）驱动法兰（将柴油机正时齿轮的运动传给从动法兰的部件）②（差速器主动圆锥齿轮轴连接传动轴的凸缘）驱动凸缘（= drive flange）

driving force 驱动力（由驱动力矩作用而引起的正的纵向力,参见 motive force）

driving force coefficient 驱动力系数（驱动力与垂直负荷的比值）

driving force curve 驱动力特性曲线（表示汽车行驶速度与各种挡位下的最大驱动力的关系,= constant power curve）

driving frequency 驱动频率（指驱动电流的频率）

driving gear 见 drive gear

driving habit(s) 驾驶习惯

driving lamp ①（辅助前照灯用的）聚光照明灯（= driving light, spot lamp）②前照灯（= head lamp）

driving lamp (equipped on root) （装在车顶上的）驾驶射灯

driving licence 见 driver's certification

driving link 传动杆件（拉杆、推杆等传动件）

driving link shackle 传动杆件的中间悬吊式支点

driving manipulators （车辆的）驾驶操作装置

driving mirror （汽车）行车后视镜,后照镜（= observation mirror）

driving mirror bracket 后视镜支架,驾驶后视镜支撑架

driving mode responsive type hybrid power steering system 行车模式响应型复合动力转向系（复合动力转向系的一种。行车模式"driving mode"指城区、农村、公路或冬季行车等,该系统可自动判别行车模式并据此确定转动转向盘所需的力的范围。在各范围内,转动转向盘

所需的力的细调"fine adjustment"，则取决于车速，车速越高，转向助力系统提供的助力越小。见 hybrid power steering system）

driving mode selector switch （复合动力车的）行驶模式选择开关（由驾驶员控制，目前生产的复合动力车"HEV"的该开关一般具有以下三种行驶工况挡位：①常规汽车"CV"工况，由发动机驱动；②电动汽车"EV"工况，由电动系统驱动；③复合动力车工况"HEV"，由发动机-电动机复合动力系统驱动）

driving performance ①（汽车的）驾驶性能，驾驶特性，操纵性能 ②（发动机的）运转特性，操纵灵敏性

driving position 驾驶位置（由与转向盘、各种操纵踏板、杆件的距离及驾驶座靠背角度等决定的驾驶员的落座位置）

driving power （汽车的）驱动功率（指汽车发动机经传动系实际传到驱动轮上克服道路阻力的功率，参见 road horse-power，驱动功率等于发动机额定功率减发动机附件消耗功率及传动系消耗功率）

driving range 可行驶距离（参见 vehicle range）

driving resistance （汽车的）行驶阻力（包括滚动阻力、加速阻力、转弯阻力、上坡阻力和空气动力阻力在内的汽车行驶过程中发动机输出动力所需克服的各种阻力的总称，亦称 total driving resistance，简称 TDR）

driving road wheel （汽车的）驱动车轮

driving safety （车辆）驾驶安全性

driving shaft 传动轴，驱动轴

driving simulator 驾驶模拟器

driving support system （智能运输系统"ITS"中广泛使用的）驾驶支持系统（如：前车距离探测系统"distance detection system for vehicle ahead"，车道偏离感测系统"lane departure detection system"等）

driving technique （汽车）驾驶技术

driving test ①（车辆）道路试验 ②（车辆）操纵性试验 ③汽车驾驶员行驶执照的考试

driving tire 驱动轮用轮胎［参见 drive (-wheel) tire］

driving tire traction 驱动轮胎牵引力，驱动轮胎与路面间附着力

driving torque 驱动力矩，驱动转矩（等于正的车轮转矩）

driving trailer 可操纵的（如：可转向的）挂车

driving (upper)(high) beam tell-tale 远光信号灯（表示前照灯远光接通的信号灯）

driving visibility 驾驶的能见度

driving voltage 驱动电压（使电器工作或液晶器件显示等所施加的电压）

driving wheel ①驱动轮，主动轮（= drivewheel）②转向轮（［英］旧称，= steering wheel）

driving wheel torque 驱动轮转矩

Drok upper cylinder lubricator 汽缸上部润滑器（仅在起动时自动对汽缸顶部喷注少量机油，预先润滑汽缸）

dromedary （［美］俗称，指带牵引座"fifth wheel"的半挂车牵引货车）

drooping （特性、性能的）下降，降低

drop ①滴②下落，下落物

drop arm 转向摇臂（将转向器输出的转向传递给杆系，如：使直拉杆直线运动的杆件，= steering arm，［美］称 pitman，pitman arm）

drop arm shaft 转向摇臂轴

drop arm stop collar 转向摇臂轴止动环

drop axle 垂梁式非驱动桥（指前桥梁的主要部分均低于车轮中心的梁式转向前桥等，亦称 dropped axle）

drop base rim 深底轮辋，凹底轮辋（参见 deep-well rim）

drop box 低输出轴式变速器（指输出轴低于输入轴的变速器，一般用于发动机的安装位置比传动轴高的货车，= drop gear①）

drop-center 中央凹下的

drop-center axle 中央凹下的梁式非驱动桥（其中央部分凹下，一般为了给传动轴提供空间，注意不同于 drop axle）

drop centre rim 深槽轮辋（= deep-well rim，主要用于轿车，其中部有一条环形深凹槽，以便于拆装外胎，在凹槽两侧与轮胎胎圈配合的台肩通常是倾斜的，代号 DC）

drop end （货车车厢能放下的）后栏板

drop engine speed 发动机降速

drop forged 模锻的

drop frame ①中凹式车架，低架式车架（= dropped frame, underslung frame, 参见 step-down frame）②可落地式的车架

drop-frame semi trailer 凹式车架半挂车，低车架半挂车；可落地式半挂车

drop-frame trailer ［美］凹式平板挂车（整个货台低凹，以降低载货重心高度，仅前、后车轴部位升高，以提供车轴安装空间，= 英 low loader，亦称 cranked frame trailer）

drop front axle 下凹式前桥（= dropped axle）

drop gear ①见 dop box ②降挡减速

drop head ①可收放的折叠式软顶 ②带可收放的折叠式软顶的敞篷轿车（= convertible）

drophead coupe 活顶轿车（单排、双座、双门、活顶）

drop-in engine 更换下来的发动机，从车上卸下来的发动机

droplet erosion 滴点（高速）冲蚀（湿气流对汽轮机叶的冲蚀等），液滴腐蚀

droplet evaporation model 油滴蒸发模型

drop oiler 滴油杯

dropped frame 见 drop frame

dropping point ①初馏点 ②（润滑脂）滴点

dropping resistor 降压电阻器

dropping type power steering (system) 见 speed reaction type power steering (system) ②

drop point ①（润滑脂的）滴点，滴点温度 ②画线针

drop-shaped 水滴状的，水滴形的（如：车身的流线型）

drop-side truck 车身侧板可以放落（以便装卸货物）的载货汽车（亦称 drop-side flat，因其货槽底板是平的，故名）

drop valve 吊阀；吊装式气门，吊式气门，上置式气门（= overhead valve, inverted valve, caged valve）

drop well 车身地板的凹下部分

drop window 下落式车窗

drowsiness degree （驾驶者的）瞌睡程度

drowsy driver warning system 欲睡状态驾驶员警告系统（亦称 drowsy driving warning system, drowsiness alar system）

DRP 德国专利（Deutsches Reichs-Patent 的简称）

DRS ①数据简化系统（data reduction system 的简称）②资料反应系统（data reaction system 的简称）

DRTS 传呼公共汽车系统（demand

drug ①麻醉品②（因服用麻醉品而）麻醉

drug box （客车内的）药箱

drum ①鼓，鼓形物②（特指）制动鼓

drum brake 鼓式制动器［摩擦力产生于与车辆固定部件相连接的部件（制动蹄）与制动鼓内表面或外表面之间的摩擦式制动器］

drum brake shoe 鼓式制动器蹄片

drum cam 鼓形凸轮（参见 cylindrical cam）

drum capacity （绞车的）转鼓容量（转鼓上卷绕的钢丝绳长度和钢丝绳的最大额定拉曳能力）

drum cleaning （零件的）旋转滚筒清洗

drum dispensing pump 桶装油料抽油泵（亦称 barrel dispensing pump，简称 drum pump，barrel pump）

drum drag brake （绞车的）转鼓制动装置，转鼓锚扣制动装置

drum hoist 转鼓吊车，滚筒式绞车

drum in disk brake 四轮盘式制动系统中增加的后轮鼓式驻车制动器

drummed gasoline 桶装汽油

drum roller bearing 鼓形滚柱轴承

drum type lubricating pump 筒式润滑泵

drum worm wheel 鼓形蜗杆涡轮

drunk driving 酒醉开车，酒醉驾驶

drunken ①不等螺距的，不等节距的②扭曲的③酒醉的，摇晃的

drunken driving 酒后驾驶

drunk·o·meter 酒气测定仪（根据驾驶员呼出的气体，测定体内的酒精含量）

drw 图纸，草图（drawing 的简称）

dry ①干燥，干燥状态；干旱的地方、季节②干的，无水的，干燥的

dry band-type brake 干（式）带式制动器

dry basis emission concentration （排气检测中的）干基排放浓度（指将排气试样冷凝除水后测得的排放浓度）

dry-batch truck 斗式车箱散装干料运输车

dry battery ①干电池②见 dry-charged battery，dry storage battery

dry bulb temperature 干球温度

dry cargo container 干货集装箱，通用集装箱（装运日用百货、五金电等件杂货）

dry-charged battery 干（极板）充电电池（指未保留电解液但极板已经充电的酸铅蓄电池，一般销售前储存均处于此种状态，临用前注液）

dry clutch with cerametallic facing 金属陶瓷衬面干式离合器

dry crankcase 干式曲轴箱

dry cylinder liner 干式汽缸套（= dry liner）

dry (-disc) rectifier 干片整流器，固体整流器

dry disk clutch 干盘式离合器，干（摩擦）片式离合器（亦称 dry plate clutch）

dry distillation 干馏，分解蒸馏

dryer 干燥器，干燥箱；干燥剂

dry friction ①干摩擦（摩擦面向无润滑剂）②干摩擦阻力

dry friction belt-force-limiter 干摩擦式（汽车乘员）安全带拉紧力限制器

dry gallon 干加仑（量干物体积的单位，在英国不分干、液，在美国干加仑较液加仑略大，参见 U.S. gallon）

dry galvanizing 干膜热浸镀锌法（金属件先浸入熔剂溶液中，然后取出干燥在金属件表面形成熔剂薄膜预镀层，金属件再浸入热浸镀锌槽，该薄膜便溶解于镀液中，在镀液中加入某些金属，如锡、铝等以

提高其流动性和镀层光亮度，参见 wet galvanizing)

dry gas ①干馏煤气②干气

dry gas engine 干馏煤气机

dry house 干燥室，烘干间

dry ice 干冰（固体二氧化碳，一种冷冻剂，大气压下，-75.5℃升华）

drying agent 干燥剂

drying of car after washing 洗车后擦（吹、风）干

drying oven 烘炉，烘箱，（车身）烤漆房

drying zone （洗车设备中的）烘干区，烘干间，干燥区

dry joint 接触不良的电接头

dry liner 干式汽缸套（= dry cylinder liner，dry sleeve）

dry lubricant ①干膜润滑剂（涂于被润滑表面后立即形成干膜，起保护与润滑作用，亦称 dry film lubricant）②固体润滑剂（= solid lubricant）

dry lubrication ①干润滑（指摩擦面间无液体润剂的状态）②固体润滑剂润滑

dry mass 干质量（不包括燃料和冷却液的底盘质量或整车质量，分别称为底盘干质量 chassis dry mass 或整车干质量 compete vehicle dry mass）

dry mixture ①干混合料②干混合气（不含液态燃油的混合气）

dryness 干燥度

dry parking turn （汽车或拖拉机的）在干燥地面上原地转向

dry point 终馏温度，干点

dry quart 干夸脱（参见 quart，美国量干物体积的单位，1 干夸脱 = 2dry pints = 1/8pecks = 1/32bushels）

dry running ability 干摩擦运转能力（无润滑油或缺润滑油的状态下的工作能力，= dry-run capability）

dry single disk friction clutch 干式单片摩擦离合器

dry skidding （汽车）在干燥道路上的滑移

dry sleeve cylinder 干缸套汽缸（冷却水不直接与缸套接触，[英] dry liner cylinder）

dry-sleeved 带干式汽缸套的

dry starting method （发动机的）干起动法（起动时，先不喷油，而由起动机带动发动机旋转至某规定转速后再开始喷油）

dry sump lubrication （发动机的）干底壳式润滑（底壳中不存滑油，其润滑系有两只油泵，一只将一单独的机油箱中的滑油压送到发动机的各润滑点，另一只将汇集到底壳内的滑油泵回机油箱）

dry type clutch 干式离合器（= dry clutch）

dry type compound belt 干式复合传动带（一种横 H 形拉力传动带，由左右两侧嵌有张力带的数百片高强度铝合金传力片"见 element"组合而成，其张力带由嵌有碳素纤维和聚酰胺纤维心线的耐热树脂材料模制成型，用于 1998 年五十铃公司推出供小型轻型轿车使用的干式-复合传动带式 CVT，耐热树脂材料本身具有良好的润滑性能，无须润滑液，故称干式，由多种材料制成，故称复合）

dry weight 自重，干重，净重（指不包括燃润料和冷却液的车重）

dry-wet basis calculation （废气成分分析的）干-湿基换算（干分析法和湿分析法测定结果的换算）

DS ①（柴油机排放微粒物中的）干烟（dry smoke 的简称）②（美国石油协会润滑油分类记号）高负荷、频繁起动、停机的柴油机用润滑油③爆燃传感器（detonation sensor 的简称，见 knock sensor）

DSC Ⅲ （宝马公司）Ⅲ型动态稳定性控制（系统）（dynamic stability control system Ⅲ 的简称。当电子控制模块测得汽车在转弯或在弯道行驶时方向偏离驾驶者的意图、转向不足时，DSC 立即降低发动机输出转矩，使汽车减速，并在必要时，对弯道内侧后轮施加制动，以增加车辆的转向角，转向过度时，DSC 在降低发动机转速，减少其输出转矩的同时，对弯道外侧前、后轮施加制动，以校正车辆转向角度，保证弯道稳定行驶，见 turn-rate control system）

DSC ①动态稳定性控制（dynamic stability control 的简称，当出现各车轮间牵引力不均衡时，该系统通过减少发动机输出转矩和对牵引力过大的单个或多个车轮施加制动的方法实现车辆的稳定性控制）②双离合器换挡式变速器（dual clutch shift transmission 的简称）

DSG 直接换挡式变速器［Direct Shift Gearbox 的简称，德国大众公司 2002 年推出的一种电子控制液压机械式双离合器齿轮变速器的商品名，亦称 dual clutch shift gearbox（双离合器换挡变速器），twin-clutch layshaft gearbox（双离合器中间轴型齿轮变速器）或 double shift gearbox］

DSM 驾驶员座椅（控制）模块（driver seat module 的简称）

DSM system （汽车电子控制系统中的闭路传感的）δ-Σ 调制系统（delta-sigma modulation system 的简称）

DSP ①数字信号处理（digital signal processing 的简称）②数据信号处理器（digital signal processor 的简称）③（丰田公司 sierra 轿车上安装的）5 音箱剧场效果立体声音响系统（的商品名，Digital Signal Processor 的简称）

dSPACE system dSPACE 系统（德国 dSPACE 公司开发的汽车电子控制产品开发、设计、测试和标定匹配的应用平台软件商品名，见 RCP 及 HIL）

DSPV 减速度感知式比例（分配）阀［deceleration sensing proportioning valve 的简称，亦称 inertia proportioning valve（惯性比例分配阀），可根据制动减速度改变后轮制动力分配比例］

DSRC （防碰撞系统等使用的）短行程距离通信；专用波段频道窄域通信（distance short run-length communication 的简称）

DSSS （公路车辆）安全行车支援系统（亦写作 DS-SS，driving safety support system 的简称）

DST （日本デンソー公司推出的便携式汽车）故障诊断器（商品名，功能齐全，适用于大型汽车维修企业，其简易版为商品名 DST-i）

DSTC （Volvo 公司的）动态稳定性及牵引力控制（系统）（dynamic stability and traction control 的简称，当汽车在弯道行驶、转向不足时，该系统对弯道内侧前轮施加制动，转向过度时对弯道外侧前轮施加制动，实现汽车的稳定转向，见 turn-rate control system。若弯道车速超过 40km/h，则同时对发动机输出转矩加以控制）

DTBP 见 Di-tert-butyl peroxide

D2T（brake） 见 duo two trailing shoe brake

DTC （诊断）故障代码（diagnostic trouble code 的简称，汽车车装式故障诊断系统中表示故障部位和性质的代码）

DTC system 动态牵引力控制系统（dynamic traction control system 的简称）

DTIA ［美］自卸车运输业协会（Dump Transport Industries Assn 的简称）

DTL ①二极管-晶体管逻辑（见 diode transistor logic）②［美］底特律测试实验室（Detroit Testing Laboratory 的简称）

DTM 数字地面模型（digital terrain model 的简称）

DTSw 双掷开关（double throw switch 的简称）

duad ①成对品，成双的东西②（一）对，（一）双

dual ①二（重）的，双的，双联的②复式的（通常指由两个不相同的部件构成的）③（由单车道路）改为双车道路

dual-acting 双向作用的（= double-acting）

dual-action tailgate 可放平或下垂的后栏板

dual-action telescopic shock absorber 双动套筒式减振器

dual advance distributor 双膜片真空点火提前分电器（参见 dual diaphragm vacuum advance distributor）

dual air bags 双安全气囊

dual air brake valve 见 dual air chamber brake valve

dual air conditioner system 双空调系统［指汽车的前、后部装有冷风器（蒸发器）的空调系统，以保证车内温度分布均一，提高后座的舒适性］

dual air management valve system （通用公司）双空气控制阀系统（由空气泵和换向阀及开关阀组成的二次空气喷射系统，用于装有双床式催化转化器的发动机。发动机升温期，空气由换向阀经开关阀喷入排气歧管，当达到工作温度后，空气经开关阀喷入双床式转向器的氧化床。节气门全开和减速工况时，换向阀将空气引入空气滤清器，以免转化器过热）

dual-ball-joint SLA front suspension 双球节长/短臂前悬架（SLA 为 short/long arm 的简称）

dual battery electric powerplant 复式蓄电池动力装置（如：用铅电池驱动，锌空气电池补充铅电池的电能等）

dual-bead tire 见 double-bead tire

dual beam headlamp （装有远光、近光）双灯丝（的）前照灯

dual-beam oscilloscope 双线示波器

dual bed catalytic converter （简称 dual catalytic converter, dual bed converter, 指排气净化器中的）双床式催化转化器（其中，具有一个还原或三效催化床和一个氧化催化床，二者分别装在各自容器内，排气先流经还原或三效催化床后再流入氧化催化床，在氧化催化床的前方设有供给二次空气的装置）

dual-bed monolith converter 整体式双催化床转化器

dual brake reservoir 双回路液压制动系统制动主缸的双储液室

dual braking system （汽车的）双路制动系（当一条制动线路发生故障时，另一条制动线路仍可发生作用，亦称 dual brakes）

dual breaker points 双触点式断电器

dual butt-butt side seals （转子发动机的）双道头对头端面气密封条装置，双道对接端面气密封条

dual cab （客货两用车等的）双车厢（前客厢和后货厢）

dual camshaft 指具有两个凸轮轴的发动机

dual carburetor ①双腔化油器（= two barrel carburetor, two throttle carburetor, dual throttle carburetor, double barrel carburetor, duplex carburetor）②双化油器（指一台多缸

发动机，装用两个化油器，如：V8型发动机，左右两列汽缸各用一只化油器）

dual carriageway 有中央分隔带异向行车的两车道道路（参见 divided road）

dual-catalyst system 双重催化系统，复式催化装置（使用两种催化床的系统。一种为氧化床，一种为还原床，用以降低排气中的碳氢化合物、一氧化碳和氮氧化物。此两种催化床可装在一个容器内，也可装在两个单独的容器内）

dual center-mounted exhaust outlets 双中置式排气尾管（双排气尾管装在车底后端的中央）

dual chamber air brake valve 双腔气制动阀（由两个膜片或活塞构成两个工作腔，分别用相同动作控制两条独立回路的气制动阀，简称 dual air brake valve，亦称 double-acting main control valve）

dual-chamber tire （无内胎式的）双层轮胎，夹层轮胎（外层穿孔后内层仍可支撑汽车行驶）

dual chamber vortical flow after burner （汽车排气净化系统中的）双室涡流再燃烧器，双室涡流二次燃烧器，双室涡流后燃器

dual-channel accelerometer 双通道加速度计

dual-channel frame 由两根槽形纵梁组成的车架

dual circuit air brake system 双管路气制动系统（简称 DCA，见 dual circuit brake system）

dual circuit brake system 双回路制动系统（由两条独立回路分别组成的制动系统，其中一条失效，另一条仍能部分或全部传递产生制动力的能量，简称 DCB）

dual clutch shift gearbox 双离合器型变速器（见 DSG）

dual coil four-plug ignition system 双线圈四火花塞点火系统

dual combustion cycle 沙巴特循环，混合循环（参见 Sabath's cycle）

dual compartment air brake chamber 双腔式气制动室

dual contact breaker 双触点断电器（＝double contact breaker）

dual control car 带两套驾驶系统的轿车（其中一套供教练员在紧急时使用）

dual controls ①双重控制②（有时特指）供驾驶教练员使用的第二套驾驶系统

dual-control training bus 双操纵装置的教练用客车

dual-cycle engine 混合循环发动机（＝combined-cycle engine）

dual damping actuator （阻尼可变式空气悬架的）软/硬双阻尼模式变换执行器

dual-density oil filter 具有两种不同密度滤清材料的机油滤清器

dual-diagonal ABS circuit system 对角线布置的双回路防抱死制动系统（前左轮与后右轮、前右轮与后左轮分别组成两条相互独立的防抱死制动回路，其中某一条回路发生故障，以致防抱死功能消失时，自动转为常规制动状态，而另一条仍可独立起防抱死制动功能）

dual-diaphragm, back pressure type EGR valve 双膜片背压型废气再循环阀（指以排气压力作为控制信号来控制再循环排气量的双膜片式废气再循环阀）

dual-diaphragm (vacuum advance) distributor 双膜片真空点火提前分电器（＝dual advance distributor）

dual drive 双联驱动，双联传动装置

dual drive six-wheeler 双轴驱动的三轴汽车

dual-drive tandem 并装双驱动桥

dual engine drive 双发动机驱动（指两台发动机与传动系组合的驱动）

dual exhaust system 双排气系统（如：V形发动机左、右两侧各有一套排气-消声装置，亦称 Twin exhaust system）

dual-flow damper 双流（速）型减振器

dual flush multi-directional nozzles （燃油喷射式转子发动机上的）双多喷孔喷嘴

dual-fuel conversion system （可分别使用两种燃料的双燃料发动机的）双燃料转换系统

dual-fuel engine 双燃料发动机（①指两种燃料同时进入发动机汽缸内燃烧做功的发动机，如：柴油-天然气双燃料发动机，天然气与空气混合气先进入汽缸，压缩后喷入柴油着火，同时燃烧做功；②指可分别使用两种不同燃料的发动机，= flexible fuel engine）

dual gear 二联齿轮，双联机构

dual harmonic gear drive 复式谐波齿轮传动（柔轮上的两个齿圈通过一个波发生器的作用，分别与两个钢轮啮合，以产生复合运动的传动）

dual headlamps 双前照灯

dual（hydraulic）solenoid valve（assembly） ①（某些后轮防抱死制动系统的）双电磁液压阀（总成）[装在主缸与轮缸之间。制动期间由电子控制模块根据车轮转速信号以一定的占空比控制制动液压，防止后轮抱死并将其滑移率保持在20%左右的制动液压调节装置。由一个隔离阀（或称输入阀）、一个快泄阀（亦称输出阀）和一个弹簧低压蓄压器组成] ②（一个阀体内装有两个可独立控制的电磁阀的）双作用电磁阀

dual ignition system ①双源点火系统（汽车发动机采用两种独立的电源点火，一种为蓄电池，一种为磁电机）②双火花塞点火（每缸内装有两只火花塞，分别由两套点火电路控制，但共用同一电源，亦称 two plug 或 two spark ignition system）③双触点点火系统（分电器具有两套触点，分别控制各自的点火线圈，两套触点交替断开，各向发动机的半数汽缸提供点火高压，亦称 twin ignition system）

dual ignition timing control device 双火花塞点火时刻控制装置，双火花塞点火正时装置

dual injection nozzle system 双喷嘴燃油喷射系统

dual in-line package 双列直插式封装（集成电路的一种封装形式，有两排直插式16到40条引线，简称DIP）

dual installation （轮胎的）双胎并装

dual-intensity switch 双亮度开关

dual-level deployment capability （乘员安全气囊的）双级膨胀能力，双级膨胀性能（可随碰撞强度的不同，而分别触发一级或二级充气源）

dual level system （汽车灯光系统，特别是制动灯、方向指示灯等的）双亮度系统（其灯泡可在高低亮度间变光）

dual LIN （汽车的）双线制本地互联网（主网点通过两条总线分别与两组从网点相连，见 LIN）

dual line braking system 双管路制动系统[指牵引车与挂车之间有两条或两条以上的制动管路（线路）连接，分别用于供能和操纵的汽车列车制动系统。注意：不同于 dual-circuit braking system]

dual-link strut type suspension 双（平行）连杆型（麦弗逊）滑柱式

悬架（左、右两侧均有两根平行的下横臂与车架或车身连接的麦弗逊滑柱式悬架）

dual load 双胎负荷（在规定的胎压下并装双胎的每一轮胎的对应负荷）

dual logic 双模式的，双逻辑（控制）电路

dual manifold system 双进、排气歧管系统

dual map lights with sunglass holder 带太阳眼镜架的双地图灯

dual-mass flywheel 双质量飞轮（由通过弹性减振元件连接成一体的主动盘和从动盘组成，其主动盘称为一级质量，装在发动机曲轴端，从动盘称为二级质量，接离合器并通过其外齿圈接起动机。这种结构可衰减发动机传来的扭振，并可隔离噪声，降低发动机怠速，减轻离合器从动盘质量，提高换挡平顺性，实现对传动系的过载保护）

dual master cylinder 双腔式制动主缸（指由两个工作腔和两个活塞组成，为双回路液力制动系供给液压的制动主缸，该两个工作腔和活塞一般在缸体内串联排列，各向一条回路供给液压，全称为：series dual-chamber brake master cylinder，= tandem master cylinder）

dual mixture induction system 双浓度混合进气系统

Dual Mode （美国的一种）两用式公共汽车（可在一般道路上行驶，亦可在轨道上行驶）

dual-mode adaptive cruise control system 双模式适应性定速巡行控制系统

dual mode muffler 双工况消声器（低速时废气通过一个通道，高速时废气同时通过两个通道，以减少排气阻力）

dual mode traffic system 两用式交通运输系统（指公路和轨道两用）

dual-mode vehicle 两用式车辆（可在普通路面及轨道上行驶）

dual mode 4 wheel steering system 双模式四轮转向系统（该系统具有运动"sport"和正常"normal"两种模式。运动模式可使汽车更富有运动车的快捷、灵活、机能性能，正常模式可使转向更为平稳。此外，倒车时可自动转为二轮转向）

dual mufflers （发动机的）双消声器

dual/multi-beam laser welding 双/多光束激光焊（①同时将两台或两台以上激光器的光束聚焦于同一焊接点，以提高总的激光能量；②将两束激光前后排列或平行排列实施焊接，以减少在厚板焊接，特别是铝合金焊接时容易出现的气孔）

dual oil seal （转子发动机等的）双级式润滑油封，双级油封

dual-output drop-gear box 双挡减速器

dual output-shaft motor 双输出轴电动机（具有两个转速不同的输出轴，其商品名为 Super Motor）

dual overhead camshaft ［美］双顶置式凸轮轴（=［英］twin overhead camshaft）

dual path turbine drive 双路涡轮驱动

dual-performance rear axle 双速后桥

dual-phase steel 双相钢（见 DP）

dual-piston engine 双联活塞式两冲程发动机（= twin-piston engine）

dual-piston floating caliper type disc brake 双活塞浮钳式盘式制动器

dual planetary arrangement 双行星单排行星齿轮机构（由互相啮合的内、外行星齿轮及中心轮、行星架和内齿圈组成。其内行星轮与中心轮啮合，外行星轮与内齿圈啮合）

dual-plug ignition system 双火花塞

点火系统

dual-pole variable reluctance sensor 双极式变磁阻传感器

dual power brake system (重型车辆使用的真空助力和液压助力并用的)双动力制动系统

dual powerplant 双动力装置,复合动力装置(参见 Volvo dual powerplant)

dual-pressure pump 双压泵,高低压泵

dual-pulley 双槽(V形)传动带盘

Dual-pump 4WD system (本田公司的前、后)双泵四轮驱动系统(商品名,可根据行驶工况,自动在两前轮驱动和四轮驱动间转换)

dual purpose catalyst 双效催化剂(具有两种作用的催化剂)

dual-purpose tread pattern (轮胎胎面的)混合花纹(其胎面中部为公路花纹,两侧为越野花纹,亦称)通用花纹

dual-purpose vehicle 两用车辆

dual range (auto shifting) indication system 双量程(自动换程)指示系统

dual-range gearbox 双挡区变速器(多用于四轮驱动车辆,有两套变速比,即:两段速比范围,一般一套高变速比用于公路行驶,另一套低变速比用于越野行车。结构上多采用主、副变速器组合形式)

dual range planetary reduction 双行星齿轮减速

dual-range unit 双级装置,双区间装置,双波段装置,双量程装置

dual-rate spring 双刚度弹簧(如:带副钢板的钢板弹簧)

dual ratio axle 双减速比驱动桥,双挡驱动桥(= two-speed axle, dual reduction axle, dual range axle)

dual-ratio carburetor (分层充气式发动机的)双混合比化油器

dual ratio control 两极调节,双极控制,双速比控制,双比控制

dual ratio final drive 见 double gear final drive

dual-ratio induction manifold (分层充气式发动机的)双混合比进气歧管

dual rears 双胎并装后轮

dual rectangular headlamp arrangement (四灯制车辆每侧)双矩形前照灯布置形式

dual reduction axle 双减速比驱动桥(= dual ratio axle)

dual rotation 双转子旋转(指单纯旋转活塞发动机的内、外转子都旋转,参见 DKM)

dual round sealed beam headlight arrangement (四灯制车辆每侧)双圆形密封灯丝前照灯布置形式

duals ①双轮胎②双排气管和双消声器(各供一列汽缸排气)

dual seat 双人座椅

dual side inlet ports 双端面进气口(转子发动机的主、副进气口都在端盖上)

dual side seals (转子发动机)端面双气封装置(= double side seals)

dual snorkel air cleaner 双吸气管式空气滤清器

dual solenoid-operated hydraulic valve (轻型货车后轮防抱死制动系统中使用的)双电磁阀控制式液压阀(该液压阀体内有一个后轮趋于抱死时阻止制动液进入后轮分泵从而防止后轮制动压力进一步增加的隔离阀,一个当后轮分泵压力即使保持不变仍临近抱死时开启,使后轮分泵压力快速释放的快泄阀,和一个存储快泄液压的活塞式储能缸)

dual space 并装双轮间距(指并装双轮的两个车轮的中心面间的横向距离,亦称 space between twin wheel)

dual spark ignition coil 双火花（塞）点火线圈（无分电器式电子点火系中同时直接向两个火花塞提供点火高压脉冲电流的点火线圈）

dual spark plug system 双火花塞系统（每一汽缸内装两个火花塞，以缩短火焰冲程，加速燃烧过程）

dual-speed power take-off 两挡取力器

dual spindle 双轴

dual stage front airbag 双级（起爆）式前安全气囊

dual thick of inner tube 内胎（胎身平叠后的）双层厚度

dual tire wheel 双胎并装车轮（= double tire wheel）

dual-tone horn 双声喇叭（= double-tone horn, two-tone horn）

dual-trace oscillograph 双线示波器

dual-tread tire 双花纹轮胎（胎面具有两种不同花纹的全天候轮胎，通常其内侧具有粗花纹，以增加在滑路上的转弯力，而外侧则呈光面或细纹，以便在干路面上产生最大牵引力）

dual two leading shoe brake 双向双领蹄式制动器（简称 D2L 式制动器，指制动鼓正、反向旋转时，两蹄均为领蹄的内张型鼓式制动器）

dual two trailing shoe brake 双向双从蹄式制动器（简称 D2T 式制动器，指制动鼓正、反向旋转时，两蹄均为从蹄的内张型鼓式制动器）

dual vision meter 双重显示仪表（指可显示实像和虚像的显示仪表，如：双重显示速度表"dual vision speed meter"，既可用指针或数字作"实像"显示，又可利用虚像作远视点放大显示）

dual-voltage fuel pump 双电压式燃油泵（起动及起动后 60 秒内，发动机转速超过 3300r/min/分及节气门全开等工况下燃油泵以蓄电池电压工作，而在上述工况以外的工况下运转时，燃油泵以 7～10V 电压工作，以降低油泵转速和噪声）

dual VVT-i 智能型双可变正时气门系统（亦简称 DVVT-i，dual variable valve timing-intelligent 的简称，= dual valve timing control，简称 D-VTC，指进、排气门二者的正时均可根据发动机工况要求连续可变的控制系统）

dual-wave band IR sensor 双波段（3～5μm，8～12μm）红外线传感器（IR 为 infrared "红外线"的简称）

dual-way check valve 双向止回阀，双通换向阀（以两个独立的气路交替向同一气压元件或向一条控制管路充气的单向阀）

dual wheels 双轮并装（车轴的每端装有两个车轮，= double wheels）

dual wheel spacing 并装双轮间距（并装双轮中心面间的距离）

dual zoon climate control （左、右或前、后）双分区（空调系统）的气候控制

Dubonnet suspension 杜鲍奈悬架（20 世纪 30～40 年代的一种前轮独立悬架，两端装有主销的前桥梁与车架刚性连接，转向节臂弹性支撑悬架臂，车轮装在悬架臂短轴上）

duck-board （辅于泥泞路上的）木板

duck joint 帆布挠性万向节（为挠性万向节之一种，参见 flexible joint）

duck tall 鸭尾形（车身尾部边缘像鸭尾一样向上翘起，用于减少高速时车身，特别是后部的空气浮力）

duct 管，管道；通道，通路；输送管，导管；沟，渠，槽

duc tboards 通风搁板（装在货车地板上，中间有格架或空腔的可拆卸式装货垫板，利于通风和排水等）

ducter 微（电）阻计（测微小电阻

的欧姆表）

ductile 可延展的，可锻的，可塑的，韧性的

ductile fracture （金属件的）延性断裂（伴随明显塑性变形而形成延性断口，断口面上具有细小凹凸，呈纤维状的断裂）

ductility 可延展性，可锻性，可塑性，韧性

ducting ①管道，管道系统②（缸体内润滑油道等的）孔道系统

DUET-EA 发动机-自动变速器二重奏［Duet-Engine Automatic Transmission 的简称，日本日产公司的发动机-自动变速器联合控制系统的商品名。发动机电子控制单元（ECU）和自动变速器电子控制单元（TCU）二者互通信息，共同实现最佳控制功能，如：变速时，自动变速器电子控制单元向发动机电子控制单元发出要求降低发动机输出转矩的信号，发动机电子控制单元收到该信号后切断3个汽缸（1，3，5缸）的供油，发动机转速下降，输出转矩降低，实现无冲击平滑变速和降低油耗］

DUET-SS 超声波悬架-转向二重奏［日本日产公司由一个电子控制模块同时控制弹性元件阻尼可变式悬架系和操舵力可变式转向系的联合电子控制系统的商品名，duet-supersonic suspension steering 的简称。该系统利用超声波声呐路面仪测定路面与车身间的间距及其变化，借以确定路面的平整度（坑凹和起伏程度）。电子控制模块：①根据路面状况及汽车制动、减速与否自动控制悬架的软、硬，即最佳振动衰减力；②根据车速自动调整转向盘的操作力。该系统可由驾驶员通过开关选择：①舒适模式（comfort mode），重视驱车轻快和乐趣，减振器柔和，转向盘操作轻便；②运动模式（sport mode），重视操作稳定性，减振器坚挺，转向盘操作较重］

dull 纯的，无光泽的，模糊的

dumb irons ①（汽车纵梁上的）副钢板弹簧支架（当主钢板弹簧负荷超过一定值时，副钢板弹簧的端部与车架纵梁上的此支架接触，副钢板弹簧开始承担负荷）②（有时亦指汽车纵梁上的）前桥钢板弹簧前端的支架

dummy ①（实体）模型，全尺寸模型（参见 buck）②（汽车碰撞试验等用的）假人

dummy coupling （气制动管的）密封栓，密封堵头（用于堵塞未拖带挂车的牵引车的挂车制动管接头）

dummy data （汽车试验）假人数据

dummy gauge 温度补偿应变片，无效应变片，平衡应变片

dummy load 仿真载荷

dummy test 模拟人（假人）试验（如：在汽车的撞击试验中利用仿制的假人，来试验驾驶员、乘员负伤情况）

dummy window 不能开启的车窗（＝dead window）

dump-bed 底卸式（＝dump-bottom）

dump body （自卸车的）倾卸车身

dump car 自卸汽车，自动倾卸载货汽车，自倾车（＝dump truck, tipper, tipper dumper, tip lorry, tipping car, tip cart, tipping lorry, tipping truck）

dump concrete truck 混凝土自卸运输车

dumper ①自卸货车（dump truck 的俗称）②倾卸器

dumper skip 自卸车车箱（＝dumping body）

dump height （自卸车）卸货高度

dump indicator lamp （自卸车的）倾卸作业指示灯

dumping angle （自卸车身）倾卸角

dumping device （自卸汽车）倾卸机构（=dumping gear, dumping mechanism）

dump ram （自卸汽车货箱）顶升油缸

dump trailer 自动倾卸挂车，自卸挂车（=tipping trailer）

Dump Transport Industries Assn [美]自卸车运输业协会（简称DTIA）

dump truck ①自动倾卸式载货汽车，自倾货车（=self-dumping truck, tipper truck, tipping truck, 参见dump car）②（有时特指建筑工地用的）小型前翻斗倾卸车（装料翻斗在驾驶室前）

dump valve ①放泄阀，快泄阀（如：油罐车放油的阀门）②（泛指各种）减压阀③（特指）挂车制动应急继动阀的控制阀（当挂车制动管路漏气或损坏时，使挂车制动应急继动阀"relay emergency valve"工作的阀件）

Dunlop Pirelli Union 邓禄普公司（意大利的一家轮胎公司，1990年世界市场占有率约6.5%）

duo duplex brake 见wedge-operater brake

duo leading-trailing shoe (drum) brake (assembly) 双向领从蹄式（鼓式）制动器（总成）（简称DS制动器，其轮缸两端各有一个活塞，制动时分别顶推一个制动端，故又称双向伺服式制动器"duo servo brake"。这种制动器的特点是无论制动鼓正、反转总有一个制动蹄是领蹄，一个制动蹄为从蹄，故名）

DUONIC 双离合器型变速器（为DUO"塔挡，二重奏，一对表演者"与BENZ对自动变速器的称呼"TRONIC"二者的组合词）

duo two leading shoe brake 双向双领蹄式制动器（制动鼓正向或反向旋转时，两蹄均为领蹄的内张型鼓式制动器，简称D2L式制动器，参见two leading shoe brake）

duo two trailing shoe brake 双向双从蹄式制动器（指制动鼓正向、反向转动时两蹄均为从蹄的内张型鼓式制动器，简称D2T式制动器，参见two trailing shoe brake）

duplex 成双的，成对的，双联的，双面的，双重的，双的，加倍的，复式的

duplex bearing 双排轴承，双联轴承（两个单列滚动轴承合装在一起）

duplex bus 可同时接收和发送数据的多路总线（亦称full duplex）

duplex carburetor 并联分动式化油器

duplex chain 复(式)链，双排链；双排滚柱链（如：正时链）

duplex induction system 复式进气系统

duplex wheel 双胎并装车轮（=double wheels）

duplicate (d) control 复式控制，复式操纵，双联控制

duplicate parts 备用零件，备件，修理用配件（=repair parts, reserve parts, replacement parts, service parts）

duplicating attachment 双套附件

duplicating device 双套装置，复式装置

durability 耐久性，寿命，使用期限，使用寿命（=longevity, working life, endurance, running life, length of life, fatigue life）

durability cobblestone road test （车辆）在卵石路面上的耐久性试验

durability driving schedule ①耐久性试验驾驶操作规程②可延长汽车使用寿命的驾驶操作规程

durability rating ①耐用性评价②额定使用寿命

durable 耐久的，经久耐用的，使用寿命长的

duralumin（**ium**） 硬铝，杜拉铝（商品名，含铜 3.5% ~ 4.5%，镁 0.4% ~ 0.7%，锰 0.4% ~ 0.7%，硅 0.7%以下的铝基合金，简称 dural）

duration of breaker contact 断电器触点（白金）接触持续时间

duration of breaking 断开（断路）持续时间

duration of charge ①（蓄电池）充电持续时间②燃料喷射持续时间③（汽缸）充气持续时间④装料持续时间

duration of heat release （燃烧的）放热持续期（从放热始点到放热终点的持续期，以曲轴转角表示）

duration of service （设备）使用年限，服役年限

duration of valve opening 气门开启持续时间（= valve opening duration）

durometer 杜罗硬度计（用小锥压头或粗针压头，压入橡皮等材料上，测定其硬度，= duroscope）

dusk sensor （前照灯自动开启系统的）黄昏传感器（当环境光线昏暗时即发出亮灯信号）

dust ①灰尘，尘埃，灰砂；粉尘，粉末，粉剂，粉屑②清除灰尘，集尘③把…弄成粉末④喷涂粉末于…上

dust bin （吸）尘箱，尘埃箱，垃圾箱（= dustbin）

dust boot 防尘套（多指由橡胶制成，用于减振器、制动主缸等）

dust cap 防尘盖（有时特指轮胎气门嘴咀上的小螺纹盖帽）

dust cart 垃圾车（= refuse collector, refuse collecting truck, garbage truck, garbage-removal truck, dust collector automobile）

dust counter 计尘器，量尘计（测定给定容积的空气中的尘埃微粒数）

dust excluder 防尘件（防尘罩、防尘板、防尘套、防尘密封件等的通称，亦称 dirt excluder, = 美 dust shield）

dust free ①不含灰尘的，无尘的②防尘的，抗尘污染的

dust lip （油封等的）防尘唇边，防尘突边

dust sheet （停放于车库或不使用的汽车的）防尘罩布

dust shield （特指盘式制动器中防止水、泥等污染制动盘内表面的）挡污板（亦称 splash shield）

dust tunnel 尘洞（试验汽车密封性能）

duty ①任务，责任②运转，运行，工作③负荷（状态），负载（状态）④功能，能率⑤税

duty cycle ①负载循环，运转循环；负载周期；运转周期②（在汽车电子控制系统中指频率保持不变的连续脉冲控制信号的）脉冲周期（一个脉冲前沿至下一个脉冲前沿所经过的时间，即：脉冲持续时间+脉冲停止时间，或通电时间+断电时间）③（当前面加有某百分比值时，表示连续固定频率控制脉冲的）占空比（指脉冲持续时间占脉冲周期时间的百分比值，如："90% duty cycle"，表示该连续控制信号中，通电时间，即脉冲持续时间占脉冲周期的 90%，称其占空比率为 90%）

duty（**cycle**）**control** ①（对）占空比（的）控制②（汽车电子控制系统的）占空比控制（方式，通过调制固定频率连续脉冲控制信号的占空比，即调制该连续脉冲信号占脉冲保持时间与脉冲周期的比值来实现控制的方式，如：电子控制喷油系统，电子控制化油器空燃比电磁

阀，电动汽油泵转速等的控制方式等）

duty cycle frequency ①（连续）脉冲周期的频率（每秒钟内的脉冲周期数）②负载循环频率（占空循环频率，电子控制模块以恒定不变的频率，如10次／秒使执行器件的电磁阀的电磁线圈电路断开与接地，电磁阀开启的时间长短决定于其电磁线圈每次接地时间，即通电时间的长短，每次通电时间与整个通-断循环时间之比称为负载比或占空比，通-断循环的频率，即每分钟通-断次数，称为负载循环频率或占空循环频率）

duty cycle injection 占空比控制式汽油喷射（通过调制喷油器电磁线圈的频率固定连续控制脉冲的占空比，即每一脉冲周期内的通电时间与脉冲周期的百分比值来控制喷油量，用于各种电子控制系统，如节气门体式喷油系等，亦称 duty factor 或 duty ratio injection）

duty (cycle) signal （电子控制系统的）占空比信号，占空比控制信号（见 duty control③）

duty-cycle solenoid 占空比（控制型）电磁阀（参见 pulse width solenoid）

duty factor ①利用系数②（汽车电子控制系统控制信号的）占空比（亦称 duty ratio, dwell ratio, 指频率固定的连续控制脉冲信号每一脉冲周期内，脉冲保持时间与脉冲周期的比值，或单位时间内，脉冲持续时间乘以脉冲频率与该单位时间之比，用%cycle表示，见 duty cycle）

duty free car 免税轿车

duty horse power 额定马力，捐税马力，报关马力（=rating horsepower, horsepower rating, taxable horsepower）

duty plate 性能标志板

duty ratio 占空比（负载比，见 duty cycle, duty factor, duty cycle frequency）

duty solenoid 占空比控制式电磁阀（由占空比信号控制其累计开、闭时间的电磁阀，见 duty control②）

DUVA 双电压式交流发电机控制系统（dual voltage alternator control system 的简称，可输出12V或24V两种电压的交流发电机控制系统）

DVD 数字（式）视盘，数字影碟（digital visible disk 的简称）

DVD language electronic navigation system DVD电子语言导航系统（其中 DVD 数字视盘为 digital video disc 的简称）

DVD roadmap DVD公路电子地图

3-D velocity measurement system 三维速度测量系统

dvicesium 类铯，钫 Fr

dvimanganese 类锰，铼 Re

dvitellurium 类碲，钋 Po

DVLA [英]驾驶员和汽车执照代理处（Driver and Vehicle Licensing Agency 的简称）

DVLC [英]驾驶员和汽车执照管理中心（Driver and Vehicle Licensing Centre 的简称）

DVOM 数字式伏-欧表，数字式电压-电阻表（digital Volt-Ohm meter 的简称）

D-VTC 见 dual VVT-i

DVV 双路真空阀，（double vacuum valve 的简称）

DVVT ①[日]大发可变气门正时（系统）（Daihatsu Variable Valve Timing 的简称）②双可变气门正时（进、排气门正时均可变，Double Variable Valve Timing 的简称）

DWC 总载重吨位（dead weight capacity）

dwell ①停留，停顿，保留，保持，闭合，闭锁，保压（及上述各项的时间，如：保持时间等）②（凸轮轮廓的）同心部分（及同心部分内其随动件的相应静止时间，= dwell time）③（在汽车电气电子系统中指线圈等的）通电时间，（触点的）闭合时间（= dwell time，dwelling period，及上述时间内曲轴或凸轮轴的相应转角，= dwell angle；如：分电器式点火系统的触点闭合时间及相应的凸轮转角。无断电器式点火系中功率三极管通导到截止的通电时间及相应的凸轮轴转角。电子汽油喷射系统喷油器电磁线圈的通电时间及相应的曲轴转角）④占空比（dwell ratio，见 duty factor）

dwell angle　①（用曲轴或凸轮轴转角表示的电磁线圈通电时间或触点闭合时间的）通电角，闭合角（如：点火线圈初级绕组通电时间内的曲轴或凸轮轴转角）②（凸轮轮廓同心部分圆弧的）圆心角

dwell angle closed loop control ignition system　闭合角闭路控制式点火系统［电子控制模块以点火线圈初级绕组的实际通电时间（闭合角）为反馈信号，对其根据发动机转速及进气管真空度确定的闭合角控制指令进行修正的闭路控制系统，可防止低速时通电时间过长，消耗电能和线圈过热；高速时通电时间过短，点火电压下降］

dwell angle control　闭合角控制，通电角控制（①指对闭合角大小的控制；②指通过对闭合角的控制来控制火花能量和喷油量等）

dwell map　通电角特性曲面，闭合角特性曲面（指点火线圈初级绕组最佳通电时间随发动机转速和进气管真空度而变化的三维特性曲面图，是电子点火控制初级绕组通电时间、火花能量的重要依据）

dwell meter　控制脉冲占空比测试仪通电角测试仪，闭合角测试仪（亦写作 dwell meter，= dwell tester）

dwell section　（发动机示波器基本波形中）断电器触点闭合段，初级绕组通电段，电磁线圈通电段

dwell-tach tester　发动机转速与触点闭合角测试仪

dwell test connector　（发动机自诊断系统的）通电角测试接口，闭合角测试仪插接座，汽油喷射喷油量控制脉冲宽度测试仪插接座，控制脉冲占空比测试仪插座

dwell tester　见 dwell meter

dwell variation　①（高速时）触点闭合期间断电器凸轮转角的变动量②（各种因素造成的）脉冲宽度、闭合时间及通电时间的变动量

DWS system　顿绿普车轮传感系统（Dunlop Wheel Sensing System 的简称。由于当胎压降低时，轮胎有效直径变小，要保持相同车速，转速必然增加，因此该系统利用制动防抱死系统已有的车轮速度传感器连续监控车轮转速，以确定轮胎是否漏气并发出相应的警报信号）

DYC　定向横摆力矩控制（direct yaw-moment control 的简称，利用左、右车轮不同的制动力或牵引力所产生的定向横摆力矩，使汽车的运动保持稳定的控制方法）

dyed gasoline　着色汽油（如：乙基化汽油等）

dye penetrant test　染色渗透试验（无损试验，确定表面裂痕位置）

dying-out　衰减，消失

dynaflow drive　（Buick 轿车采用的一种）液力自动变速传动装置（的商品名）

dynaflow torque converter　动液变矩器，流体动力变矩器，液力变矩器

dynam　动力学（dynamics 的简称）

dynamic　①动力，动态②动力（学）的，动态的（亦写作 dynamical）

dynamical instability 动态不稳定性

dynamical location （存储器）动态配置，动态分配

dynamically and statically balanced-crankshaft （经过）动平衡与静平衡（的）曲轴

dynamically balancing 动平衡

dynamical parameter 动力参数，动态参数

dynamical similarity （与实物间的）动力相似，动态相似，动力性模拟（风洞模型试验等）

dynamic analysis 动力学分析，动力学解析，动态分析，动力特性分析

dynamic axle weight 车桥动载荷（汽车运动时，车桥承受的实际载荷）

dynamic balance 动平衡（=running balance）

dynamic balancer 动平衡机，亦称 dynamic balancing machine）

dynamic balance test 动平衡试验（按标准规定，在动平衡试验机上，测定轮胎等旋转件在旋转中的动不平衡量）

dynamic binding light （汽车前照灯的）动态弯道转向照明（可自动跟随转向的方向照明）

dynamicbraking ①（汽车的）动力制动（利用发动机的动力产生反向转矩，如挂倒挡制动）②（电动机的）发电制动，再生制动（=regenerative braking）

dynamic braking weight 制动动载荷（由于制动作用，产生载荷转移，使后桥载荷移向前桥，此时车桥的载荷称为制动动载荷；制动动载荷是可供制动利用的有效载荷，故亦称车桥制动有效载荷"effective braking weight"）

dynamic breaking 在动载作用下的破坏，动载破坏

dynamic characteristic test of torque converter 液力变矩器动态特性试验（指在非稳定工况下液力变矩器的特性试验）

dynamic compliance 动态贴合性，（如：活塞环），动态柔量，动态顺从性，动柔度，位移导纳（参见 mechanical mobility，亦称 dynamic flexibility）

dynamic cornering fatigue test （车轮的）抗侧偏疲劳试验

dynamic coupling （谐波齿轮传动的）齿啮式连接（柔轮筒壁与输出连接盘以相同齿数的内、外齿圈构成同步啮合运动的连接形式）

dynamic curve 动态特性曲线

dynamic damper 动态阻尼器（通过附加质量产生阻尼作用）

dynamic damp type in-wheel motor 动态减振轮内驱动型电动机（呈环状，通过减振元件悬挂于车轮附件的车架部件，经挠性元件驱动车轮。这种结构既保留了常规轮内电动机驱动的优点，又避免了常规轮内电动机驱动簧下质量过大带来的诸多缺点）

dynamic deflection of suspension 悬架的动挠度（指汽车行驶时，在路面不平等冲击载荷的作用下悬架的变形值）

dynamic digital torque meter 数字式动态转矩测试仪

dynamic drive 动态驱动（液晶显示器的时间分割驱动方式，显示像素的两个对应电极上，同时分别施加扫描信号和寻址信号，参见 static drive）

Dynamic Drive （宝马新7系的）防侧倾系统（商品名）

dynamic effect of pressure waves （进、排气管内的）压力波动态效应（指排气管内因高压废气冲入激励和进气管内因活塞吸气激励而产生的压力波，在管内来回振荡产生

的惯性效应和脉动效应。充分利用该效应使正、负压力波重合，即正、负压力波谐振可提高排气和进气效率）

dynamic endurance test 动态寿命试验

dynamic equilibrium 动平衡，动态平衡

dynamic evaluation of engine parameters 发动机参数的动态测定（简称DEEP）

dynamic factor 动载系数，动态因数，动力因素（$D = \dfrac{驱动力 - 空气阻力}{汽车总质量}$，表示作用于单位汽车质量的克服道路阻力和使汽车加速的驱动力）

dynamic flexibility 动柔量，动柔度，位移导纳（= dynamic compliance）

dynamic flip-flop 动态触发器（无延迟双稳态多谐振荡器）

dynamic friction coefficient 动摩擦系数

dynamic hardness 冲击硬度

dynamic horsepower 动态功率

dynamic ignition timing 动态点火正时法（使用由第一缸点火脉冲控制的点火正时灯等，对在规定的条件和工况下运转的发动机的点火提前角进行动态调定，亦称 stroboscopic ignition timing，相对静态点火正时而言，见 static ignition timing）

dynamic load between wheel and road surface 车轮与路面间的动载（为其悬架弹性恢复力 F_r 与阻尼力 F_d 之和，即动载 $F_D = F_r + F_d = Ma$，式中：M—车轮承受的簧上质量，a—该簧上质量的垂直加速度）

dynamic load-deflection characteristic 动负荷挠曲特性（指构件等承受冲击等动负荷时的抗挠曲变形特性）

dynamic loaded radius （轮胎）动负荷半径（负荷行驶且倾角为零时，轮轴中心到支撑平面的垂直距离）

dynamic load transfer （汽车制动或加速过程中的）动态负荷转移

dynamic loudness compensation 动态响度补偿

dynamic loud-speaker 电动喇叭，电喇叭，电动（式）扬电器

dynamic magnifier 动态放大因子，共振放大因子［当强迫振动的频率 f_F 等于悬架质量的固有振动频率 f_N 时，在理论上悬架质量的固有振动的振幅 x_0 成为无穷大，即 $x_0 = y_0 / 1 - (f_F/f_N)^2$，式中：$y_0$—强迫振动的振幅，$1 - (f_F/f_N)^2$ 称为共振放大因子，参见 steady state vibration］

dynamic measurement 动态测量

dynamic meter 动态测力计

dynamic mixture formation 动态混合气形成，混合气动态形成（指层状充气或层状燃烧等汽缸内混合气的形成）

dynamic mockup 动态的（1:1）实物模型，动态全尺寸模型（简称 DMU）

dynamic parameter(s) 动态参数（①机械、车辆、设备工作或运动状态下的参数；②表示集成电路和元器件交流特性的电参数）

dynamic pressure 动压力［指匀速流动的气体当动能全部且无损耗（即等熵）地转换为压力时，所增加的那部分压力］

dynamic range ①动态范围（指汽车多路传输系统中一个系统或元件正常工作时，其最高电平信号与最低电平信号的比值，或者说用饱和信号与噪声等效信号之比表示的有用线性工作范围，通常用 dBV "伏特分贝" 表示）②动力学研究范围

dynamic read/write memory 动态（读写）存储器（指为了保持存储的数据，要对其存储单元重复施加控制信号的存储器）

dynamic register 动态寄存器

dynamic response 动态响应

dynamic response codes 见 service codes⑤

dynamic response index （车座等的）动态响应指数（用以评价汽车座位对乘员的动态响应特性）

dynamic rollover propensity evaluating test 翻车倾向的动态评价试验

dynamic roll-over test （车辆的）动态倾翻试验（指行驶倾翻试验）

dynamic route guide system 动态行车路线引导系统（简称 DRGS，根据道路交通情况的变化，不断实时提供到达预定目的地的最佳路线或绕行路线）

dynamics 力学，动力学，动力，动态（简称 dyn）

dynamic sampling 动态取样法，连续取样法（发动机排出的将部分废气连续吸出，同时泵入分析仪器的取样法，= continuous sampling）

dynamic scattering mode 动态扩散型（液晶显示方式的一种。在定向处理的液晶分子上加电压，使液晶分子产生混乱，液晶盒内各处的折射率不断变化，利用入射光的散射进行显示）

dynamic seal 动密封，动密封件（指一运动件与一固定件或两个相对运动的表面或零件之间的密封，参见 static seal）

dynamic shock absorber 动力减振器（通过弹性元件将一重物接装于振动系统，利用该重物在振动过程中产生的相位振动来减振的一种结构形式）

dynamic side force （汽车的）动态侧向力（指汽车运动状态下产生或受到的侧向力，如：弯道行驶的离心力等）

dynamic side-impact protection （车身的）动态侧面碰撞保护

dynamics of combustion 燃烧动力学，燃烧力学

dynamic spring rate 弹簧的动载刚度

dynamic stability 动态稳定性

dynamic steering headlight system 见 DynaView™

dynamic steering headlight system 动态转向前照灯系统（见 DynaView™）

dynamic stiffness 动态刚性，动刚度，位移阻抗（参见 mechanic impedance）

dynamic strength 动载强度（指动载下工作时，构件的强度）

dynamic structural response test 结构动态响应特性试验

dynamic supercharging 动态增压（指不使用机械增压，而利用进气气流自然动态特性，即：其动能或谐振使进气增压的方式）

dynamic system simulator 动态系统模拟装置

dynamic temperature 动温度［指匀速流动的气体中，当动能全部且无损耗地（即等熵地）转变为热能时所增加的那部分温度］

dynamic test 动态试验（指在动态下的试验：①现场使用试验；②模拟使用中实际运转条件的台架试验）

dynamic test stand 动态试验台

dynamic toe-in tester 动态前束仪，动态前束测试台（指前轮在滚动或转动状态下测定前束的各种设备）

dynamic torsional and beaming test （车辆等构架的）动载扭转及弯曲试验，动态弯扭试验

dynamic transfer characteristics 动力传递特性

dynamic type RAM 动态（型）随机存取存储器（见 RAM）

dynamic unbalance 动不平衡度（旋转件，如轮胎等在动态旋转中的不平衡度）

dynamic unbalance 动不平衡（旋转件在转动时产生的不平衡现象，如：跳动，振动等）

dynamic universal aligner ①汽车转向轮动态定位仪②汽车动态四轮定位仪③汽车动态万能试验台（可测定前轮横偏角、前束、主销纵倾、底盘输出功率、驱动力、车速、后轮横偏角、燃油消耗量、前后轮的行驶阻力、制动力、制动力差、加速度以及探测轮胎是否扎有铁片等）

dynamic vehicle simulation 车辆动态模拟

dynamic viscosity 动力黏度

dynamic visibility （汽车驾驶员的）动视界，动视野，动能见度，动可见距离，动可见范围

dynamic weight 动态重量（在车辆行驶中的质量，动态质量的旧称）

dynamic weight distribution （车辆）动态重力分配（在车速变动情况下车桥或车轮上的重力分配）

dynamic weighting 动态称重（在汽车行驶中称重，= in-motion weighing）

dynamic weight transfer （汽车的）动载荷转移量（指汽车运动时前、后桥载荷的变化量。如：汽车制动时，将有 ΔW_d 的载荷量，由后桥转移到前桥，即前桥动载荷 $\overline{W}_{fd} = \overline{W}_f + \Delta W_d$，后桥动载荷 $\overline{W}_{td} = \overline{W}_t - \Delta W_d$，式中：$\overline{W}_f$——前桥静载荷；$\overline{W}_t$——后桥静载荷）

dynamic wheel balancer 车轮动平衡机，车轮动平衡试验机（亦称 shimmy detector）

dynamic wheel demonstrator 就车型车轮动平衡机，就车作业式车轮动平衡机

dynamic wheel load 车轮动载荷（汽车行驶过程中速度变化时，车轮的动态载荷）

dynamo （直流）发电机（=［美］DCgenerator）

dynamo-battery ignition umit 发电机、蓄电池点火系统

dynamo coupling 发电机联轴节

dynamocradle 发电机支架

dynamo engine 发电用发动机（驱动发电机用，= engine for generator）

dynamo field coil 直流发电机磁场线圈

dynamo governor 发电机调节器（= generator regulator）

dynamograph 自记式测力计

dynamo-magneto 磁电机

dynamometer 测功器，测力计

dynamometer brake 测功机制动装置

dynamometer car 测功车（辆）（用以测试汽车的驱动功率，参见 dynamometer trailer）

dynamometer trailer 测功挂车（被测汽车用贴有应变片的拉杆牵引测功挂车，在挂车上装有吸收功率的加载装置，被测汽车行驶时，便可根据测出的牵引力计算出被测汽车驱动轮输出的功率，即牵引功率"tractive power"）

dynamometer-type instrument 测力计式仪表

dynamometric power 测功机马力，测功机功率（自测功机上测得的功率）

dynamometry 测力法，测功法

dynamo oil 电机油（发电机、电动机、鼓风机等高速轴承用油）

dynamo output control 发电机输出控制，发动机充电电流电压调节器

dynamo terminal 发电机接线柱

dynamotor ①发电机-电动机（指既可做电动机又可作为发电机的两用机，亦称共极电动发电机）②发电机电动机组（简称 DYNM）

dynastart(**er**) （20世纪20～30年代使用的）发电机-起动机（目前多用于二冲程摩托车发动机）

DynaView[TM] 动景（海拉公司开发的动态转向前照灯系统，"dynamic steering headlight system"的商品名，TM为商标"trade Mark"的简称。该前照灯系统左、右两侧的前大灯内都装有一个主照明灯和一个转向辅助照明灯"steering added lighting lamp"，后者由称为"Intelli Beam"的电子控制模块控制。当前照灯主灯点亮时，如果汽车转向，则Intelli Beam将根据车轮速度传感器的左右轮速度差信息点亮转向一侧的转向辅助照明灯，照亮弯道。汽车恢复直线行驶时，该灯自动熄灭）

dyne 达因（力的单位，简称dyn，1 dyne = 10^{-5} Newton）

DYNM 电动机-发电机（dynamotor的简称）

dyno 测功机,测力计,功率计（= dynamometer的俗称）

dynode 倍增器电极，二次放射极，打拿极（中间极）

dyotron 超高频振荡三极管，微波三极管

dystectic 高熔（点）的

EA 紧急救援［Emergency Assist 的简称，如：Ford 借助其车载多媒体通信娱乐互助系统 SYNC 提供的连接服务（SYNC connect），当发生碰撞事故，安全气囊爆开或油路中断时，该系统激并自动通过已与"SYNC"平台连接的智能手机（smart mobile phone）发出紧急呼救信号，将车辆位置和碰撞信息自动发给 Ford 紧急呼叫中心，建立车主、呼叫中心和当地救援部门三方通信，实现当地救援部门的紧急救助］

EAA ［美］电动汽车协会（Electric Auto Association）

eActive suspension 电子控制主动式悬架（electronic active suspension 的简称，可根据对前方路况的预测数据，通过相应的执行机构实时自动控制悬架的工况，以适应路况的变化，保证车辆的最佳行驶平顺性和操纵稳定性）

EAC valve ①电子控制空气控制阀（electronic air control valve 的简称，亦简称 EACV，日本本田公司发动机怠速转速控制装置的商品名。该装置由发动机电子控制模块控制的电磁阀组成。当节气门周边的空气通路因脏污而不畅通，以致发动机怠速转速下降到某基准值时，EACV 开启，空气经 EACV 进入进气歧管，使转速上升，以维持所要求的怠速转速；当开动空调或使用动力转向等耗电量大的系统而导致怠速不稳定或转速降低时，EACV 开启，进入进气歧管的空气量增加，使怠速上升或保持在所要求的范围内）②电动空气流量控制阀［electric air control valve 的简称，为美国通用公司发动机减速空气增补阀（见 air gulp valve）的别名，该阀起三个作用：正常的减速空气增补作用，即当进气管真空度迅猛升高时将增补空气输入进气管，以防混合气过浓；当空气喷射系统压力超过某规定值时，可将空气引回空气滤清器，起减压作用；由于它是由电磁控制的，可以由电子控制模块控制在任一所要求的工况下，增补或引出空气］

EAD 能量吸收装置（energy absorbing device）

EAE 乙烯/丙烯盐酸共聚物人造橡胶（ethylene/acrylic elastomer）

Eager Beaver （口语）载载质量为 2.5t 的水陆两用汽车

Eagle Eye 鹰眼（［美］Transportation Safety Technologies 公司的障碍物探测系统的商品名，见 obstacle detection system）

Eagle View⁺ 鹰视（一种车载 360°环景影像系统商品名，装有多个摄像

EAICV 见 puls air system
EAIR 见 air injection reaction system
EAIV 见 puls air system
EAP 电动空气泵（electric air pump 的简称）
ear ①耳状物，凸耳（= lug）②（特指）装在车身后（门）窗后的导风板（用以改善横风稳定性）
ear-clip-type （别在乘员耳朵上的）耳夹型的(人体信息传感器等)
early 早，早的，初期的，早期的；提前的，过早的［early ignition 早燃，过早点火，= premature ignition；early injection 过早喷射，提前喷射；early model 旧式，老式，初期形式（的），= old model，early stage；early opening 气门等的提前开启，= advanced opening；early timing 点火、喷油，气门开起等的正时提前］
early failure 早期故障（新车或大修车常常会出现因设计、材料、零件加工、装配工艺及调整作业等原因造成的各种故障，这些故障暴露于使用初期，故称。早期故障的发生期称早期故障期"early failure period"，早期故障发生部位称早期故障区"early failure region"）
early fuel evaporation system 燃油早期汽化（蒸发）系统，［简称 EFE system，直接对节气门体下方的进气歧管区域加热，以防止冬季节气门结冰，或在发动机热起升温期促进燃油汽化，以降低此时对混合气浓度的要求，改善发动机的操纵性和减少有害物排放。前轮驱动的 DFI 车采用废气加热，由水温控制的真空开关驱动 EFE 执行器（EFE actuator）开启或关闭 EFE 废气阀（EFE Valve），使废气在水温为 49℃ 以下时流入、49℃ 以上停止流入进气歧管的 EFE 通道 "EFE Passage"。后轮驱动的 DFI 车则采用电加热］
early warning radar 预警雷达
earth ①地，地面②土，土壤③接地（汽车上指电器或电路经导线或导体与汽车车身、底盘或发动机体连接形成回路，我国国家标准 GB 称搭铁，美称 ground）④搭铁线，搭铁件，地线⑤接地的，搭铁的［用此义时，= earthing 或 earthed，美相应称 grounding 或 grounded。如：earth bus bar 搭铁母线杆；earth brush 搭铁电刷；earth cable 搭铁缆线或数股单线的绞合线；earth conductor 泛指用电线或各种导体的搭铁线；earth conduit 搭铁（线的）导管；earth connection 搭铁点，搭铁连接；earth connecting contact 搭铁触点；earth cord（较细的）搭铁缆线；earth detector 搭铁引起的短路，漏电等的检测仪；earth electrode 泛指各种搭铁电极，特指火花塞侧电极；earth fault 搭铁故障：一是指搭铁线本身的故障，如：断线等，二是指因导线或元器件绝缘故障而引起的误搭铁漏电等；earth lead = earth cord，earth line 搭铁线路，有时指具体的搭铁线；earth plate 搭铁板；earth point 搭铁点；earth pole 蓄电池搭铁极桩；earth return 搭铁回路；earth strap 特指蓄电池的带接线夹的编织搭铁线；earth screw 搭铁螺钉；earth short-circuit test 用搭铁短路的方法来测试电路完好性；earth strip 搭铁扁线；earth system 搭铁系统；earth terminal E 接线柱：泛指各种搭铁接线柱，特指发电机或调节器搭铁电路的接线柱；earth wire 多指单根搭铁线］
earth-fixed axis system（X、Y、Z）地面固点坐标系（X、Y、Z）（固点在地面上的右手直角坐标系。原点为地面上的某一点，X 轴和 Y 轴位于水平面内，X 轴指向前方，Y 轴

指向左方，Z 轴指向上方。汽车运行的轨迹，常用该坐标系描述）

earth flax 石棉（= fossil flax）

earth-magneto gyro （测定车辆行驶方向的）地磁陀螺仪

earth(y)water 硬水（= hard water）

EAS ①废气后处理系统（exhaust after treatment system 的简称），②电子控制空气悬架（electronic air suspension）

ease ①容易，轻便；轻易程度；舒适，安逸（如：ease of access 接近容易程度，用于评价检修、维护的方便性；ease of control 操纵轻便；ease of ignition 易起燃性，易点燃性；ease of steering 转向轻便）②减轻，减弱，减速，使轻便，使舒适（如：ease off 放松，松开螺母等；ease the engine 降低发动机转速、负荷，减轻发动机的强化程度；ease up the gas 松开加速踏板，减速，= decrease speed）

easement ①（道路）通行权 ②平顺，方便 ③（车身内）使乘客舒适的装备

easement curve 缓和曲线，过渡曲线（半径逐渐变化的曲线 = transition curve）

easily 容易地，方便地（如：easily accessible seat 便于入座的座椅，easily detachable 易于拆卸的；easily controlling 容易控制的）

e-Assist （Mitsubishi 公司由 radar cruise control system, forward-collision mitigation brake system, lane departure warning system 等组成的）电子安全辅助系统（商品名）

east-west horizontal crankshaft 东西向水平横置曲轴，水平横置曲轴发动机（指发动机安装在其曲轴与汽车中心线水平直角交叉位置）

east-west layout （轿车发动机的）横向布置，横置式（亦称 transverse engine, 多见于前轮驱动轿车）

east-west transverse position 东西向横置位置，横置位置，横向位置（指与汽车的中心线水平直角交叉的位置）

EAS valve 电控空气开关阀（指排气净化系统中的空气流向控制开关阀，electronic air switching valve 的简称）

easy 容易的，简易的；轻便的，方便的；舒适的，平缓的，不陡的，缓坡的，微微倾斜的 [如：easy care 易维护；easy-change 易更换的，易换挡的（指变速器）；easy curve 平缓曲线；easy drive 不需熟练技术即可操作的简便驾驶装置，= fool proof drive；easy fit 松配合（为 easy push fit 轻推配合与 easy running fit 轻转配合, slide fit 轻滑配合等小间隙配合的通称）；easy grade 平缓坡度，easy gradient 平缓坡道，= flat gradient；easy off 易拆的；easy on 易装的；easy starting 易起动的；easy working 易于操作的，操作轻便的；easy repairing 易修理的；easy to install 易于安装，亦写作 easy-to-install 易于安装的]

Easy Access system （Lexus LX SUV 上装备的）易进出系统（汽车停车熄火后，该系统即自动将座椅推后并将转向盘退后，扩大驾驶区活动空间，以方便驾驶者进出）

easy release parking brake lever 驻车制动器易释杆（日产公司轿车装在中央控制台上的拨杆式驻车制动器解除开关的商品名）

easy-to-grip 易于握持的

EAT ①电子控制式自动变速器（见 electronic automatic transmission）②电动辅助增压器（electric assistant turbo 的简称，在涡轮增压器轴上加装的一台辅助电机，起动之初，该电机驱动增压器叶轮迅速运转，发

动机高速运转时，该电机发电，输入蓄电池）

E-AT 电子控制式自动变速器（"electronic-automatic transmission"的简称，该变速器在电子控制式自动变速器中最早实现五挡化）

E-4AT （富士重工研制的）电子控制式四挡自动变速器（的商品名，其D挡有"动力"和"经济"2种功能选择，全称为：全程电子控制4挡自动变速器"All Range Electro 4 Speed Automatic Transmission"）

EATC ①电子温度自动控制（electronic automatic temperature control 的简称）②时间与警报电子集中控制系统［Electronic Time and Alarm Control System 的简称，三菱公司时间与警报集中控制系统的商品名，通过智能接线系统（见 smart wiring system）互联的三个电子控制模块，集中控制警报装置、时间控制装置和电动车窗］

EATC module 电子自动温度控制模块（electronic automatic temperature control module 的简称）

EATX ①见 transaxle ②电子控制式自动变速驱动桥（electronic automatic transaxle 的简称）

EATXM 见 transaxle

EATX relay 电子控制自动变速驱动桥继电器（electronic automatic transaxle relay 的简称，点火开关接通，自诊断系统确认变速驱动桥电子系统无故障时，该继电器闭合，蓄电池向 TCM 及其控制的各电磁阀和压力开关供电）

EBA 紧急制动辅助系统（emergency braking assist 的简称，亦称 Emergency Brake Assistance）

EBCDIC 扩充二-十进制交换码（Extended Binary-Coded Decimal Interchange Code 的简称，一种由8位编码字符"0—9"10个数字，英文大、小写字母和符号组成的字符集，用于数字信息处理与通信系统设备间的信息交换）

EBCM 电子制动控制模块（electronic brake control module 的简称）

EBD system 电子控制制动力分配系统（electronic brake force distribution system 的简称，制动时由电子模块根据车辆载荷状态和因制动减速度引发的载荷转移，控制前、后车轮制动力。弯道制动时，同时控制左、右车轮制动力，使前、后，左、右车轮制动力最佳分配，确保车辆稳定）

EBG 见 ethanol blended gasoline

EBL 见 electronic back-up light

ebonite 硬橡胶，胶木（ebonite battery box 硬橡胶蓄电池壳，= ebonite battery jar; ebonite bush 胶木衬套; ebonite driver 胶柄起子; ebonite monoblock 胶木整体壳件）

EBP 见 exhaust back pressure

EBR 电子束记录系统（electron beam recording system）

EBS ①电子束扫描系统（electron beam scanning system 的简称）②电子控制制动系统（electronic brake system 的简称）③等效障壁速度（equivalent barrier speed 的简称）

EB system （一般指重型车辆使用的）电子控制制动系统［electronic brake system 的简称，亦简称 EBS，这类制动系统大都采用线控（by wire），以减轻驾驶员的劳动强度］

EBTC 电子控制制动-牵引力控制（系统）（electronic brake and traction control 的简称，由电子模块对制动力和牵引力做联合控制，既防止制动力大于附着力，以避免车轮抱死，又防止牵引力大于附着力，以避免车轮原地滑转，其控制模块称 EBTC module，简称 EBTCM）

EBTCM 电子制动-牵引力控制模块（electronic brake-traction control module 的简称，指带牵引力控制功能的 ABS 系统的控制模块。当通过驱动车轮转速传感器测得驱动车轮滑转时，该模块可控制制动压力调节器的相应电磁阀，对滑转的驱动轮施加制动或减小节气门开度，或向动力系统控制模块发出信息，减少点火提前角和/或挂高挡，借以减少驱动轮上的牵引力）

ebulliometer 沸点测定计

ebullition cooling 蒸发式冷却

EBW 电子束焊接（electron-beam welding）

EC ①弹性系数（elasticity coefficient 的简称）②电子计算机（electronic computer 的简称）③电子控制的（electronically controlled 的简称）④漆包的（enamel covered 的简称）⑤修正误差（error correcting 的简称）⑥电解腐蚀（electrolytic corrosion 的简称）⑦欧洲共同体（European Community 的简称）

ECA 福特公司动力系电子控制模块的旧称，见 Electronic Control Assembly

E-Call （车内）应急电话系统

eCall-equipped car 见 eCall program

eCall program "电子紧急传呼"规划 [European Commission 提出的一项安全规划，要求在欧洲出售的汽车全部装备可自动预测碰撞和在驾驶者无能力呼救的情况下发出紧急求救电话的系统（eCall）。装有这一系统的汽车称为 eCall-equipped car 或简称 eCall car]

EC-AT （马兹达公司研制的电子控制式自动变速器的商品名，electronic control-automatic transmission 的简称）

ECB2 第二代电子控制制动系统（electronically controlled brake system, second-generation 的简称，指线控式电子控制制动系统）

EC brake 耗能式制动器（energy consumption brake 的简称）

ECBS 电子控制制动系统（electronically controlled braking system 的简称）

ECB system （丰田公司用于丰田复合动力车"THV"的）电子控制制动系统（商品名，electronic control brake system 的简称，由带制动力分配装置"EBD"的常规"ABS"液压制动系统和牵引力控制系统"TRC"、车辆稳定性控制系统"VSC"，以及复合动力中前后轮驱动电动机的再生制动能量回收系统组成的综合电子控制系统）

ECB warning lamp 电子控制制动系统故障报警灯（该灯通过闪光模式表示电子控制制动系统故障代码，见 ECB）

ECC ①偏心的（eccentric 的缩写形式）②电化学浓差电池（见 electrochemical concentration cell）③电子控制化油器（electronically controlled carburetor 的简称）④电子气候控制（electronic climate control 的简称）⑤设备结构控制（equipment configuration control 的简称）⑥误差检验与校正（error checking and correction 的简称）

eccentric ①偏心的 ②偏心轮的 ③（转子发动机和某些旋转泵的）曲轴，（或起曲轴作用的）偏心件，偏心轮 ④偏心机构（的）

eccentric adjustment ①（利用）偏心件（如：凸轮等进行的）调整 ②偏心调整机构；凸轮调节机构

eccentric angle ①偏心角 ②（转子发动机的）主轴转角，偏心轴转角

eccentric axis 偏心轴，凸轮轴

eccentric base rim 槽底偏置式轮辋（指中心线与轮辐安装面不重合的轮辋，轮辋中心线位于轮辐安装面内侧、外侧或重合的车轮分别称：

内偏距"inset"、外偏距"outset"或零偏距"zeroset"车轮）

eccentric bearing （转子发动机的）偏心轴颈轴承，转子轴承（装在主轴的偏心轴颈即转子轴颈上）

eccentric birotor oil pump 偏心双转子式机油泵

eccentric cam ①偏心（凸）轮②偏心垫圈（起调节作用的垫片式凸轮，= cam washer 或 eccentric washer）

eccentric center 偏（心中）心

eccentric clamping ①偏心夹头，偏心自锁搭扣，偏心锁紧式夹箍②偏心夹紧，偏心固定

eccentric crankshaft-main-bearing type variable compression-ratio engine 偏心曲轴主轴承型可变压缩比发动机（电子控制模块通过执行机构转动偏心主轴承，可使压缩比在 8~16 间连续变化）

eccentric distance 偏心距

eccentric drive 偏心轮驱动，凸轮驱动

eccentric (driven) pump 偏心泵（由偏心件驱动的泵）

eccentric element 偏心件，偏心元件（①旋转轴线或运动支点不在其中心的元件的总称 ②少齿差行星齿轮传动中，支撑行星齿轮的构件，见 gear pair with small teeth differ-ence）

eccentric gear 偏心齿轮，偏心机构

eccentric headed adjusting screw （分电器断电器固定触点调节板端的）偏心（头）调节螺钉（转动该螺钉，可使调节板及固定在该板上的固定触点绕销钉转动，从而改变触点间隙）

eccentricity 偏心率,偏心距,偏心度

eccentricity of the output shaft （转子发动机等）输出轴的偏心距（常用 e 表示）

eccentricity tester 偏心距检查仪

eccentric journal 偏心轴颈（如曲轴的连杆轴颈等）

eccentric loading 载荷偏置，偏载

eccentric piston ring 偏心活塞环

eccentric radius 偏心半径

eccentric rod gear 偏心连杆机构

eccentric rotor bearing （转子发动机的）转子轴承，旋转活塞轴承，偏心轴轴承（即偏心轴上支承转子的轴承）

eccentric rotor chamber 见 eccentric swirl chamber

eccentric rotor movement （转子发动机的）转子偏心运动，旋转活塞偏心运动（指转子除绕本身质心自转外，还绕另一中心公转）

eccentric rotor pump 见 rotor-type pump

eccentric swirl chamber （间接喷射式柴油机分开式燃烧室的）偏心式涡流室（亦称 eccentric rotochamber 或 eccentric turbulence chamber）

eccentric turbulence chamber 见 eccentric swirl chamber

eccentric valve seat grinder （砂轮中心线与阀座偏心的）气门座磨削装置

eccentric wear ①偏心磨损 ②（轮胎）偏磨耗（指轮胎胎面中心线两侧出现不对称的磨损）

ECCS 见 electronic concentrated ergine control system

ECD ①能量转换装置（energy conversion device 的简称）②估计的完工日期（estimated completion date 的简称）③电子控制式柴油机（electronic control diesel 的简称）

ECDN DRIVEN IND （汽车仪表板上指示驾驶员省油操作的）经济驾驶指示灯（economically driven indicator 的简称）

ECDY 电涡流测功器（参见 eddy

ECE ①欧洲经济委员会（Economic Commission of Europe 的简称）②外燃机（external combustion engine 的简称）

ECECS 发动机电子集中控制系统（Electronic Concentrated Engine Control System 的简称）

ECE cycle 欧洲经济委员会测试循环（标准的欧洲汽车废气排放测试循环的通称）

E-CELL 电池

E-cell 电子定时模块（为汽车动力电子控制模块的附加件。由一银阴极和金阳极组成，点火脉冲电压经一电阻加在该模块上，在通电过程中，阴电极材料银不断被吸附于阳电极材料金上，当所设计数量的点火脉冲，即发动机运转一定的里程后，银电极便完全消失，该模块电路断开，于是给发动机电子控制模块 PCM 一个里程信息。这一信息供 PCM 调整其对发动机的控制参数，以补偿发动机机件磨损或性能变化等。如：Oldsmobile 和 Chevrolet 8 缸发动机电子控制模块上装的 E-cell 用于发动机的走合期。在走合期内 E-cell 通导，电子控制模块按走合期要求的各种标定参数对发动机进行控制，走合期后，E-cell 断开，电子控制模块将控制参数调整到适应正常运转的要求。因此该 E-cell 常称为绿色发动机标定器件 green engine calibration unit）

ECE 15 mode test cycle 欧洲经济委员会（和欧洲经济共同体，1970 年制订的冷起动）15 工况循环（测定汽车的排放质量，以后又用来测定燃料经济性）

ECE Regulations 欧洲经济委员会规程（见 ECE）

ECE test （排放的）欧经委员会测试（对一取样袋内收集的试样经稀释后测定发动机的排放质量）

ECE test cycle 欧洲经济委员会试验循环（如：大部分欧洲国家采用的 13 分钟模拟城市行驶工况排放测试法，包括较长时间的怠速和 35 英里/小时以下的低速工况，而不考虑公路常速）

ECF 欧洲旅居车旅行联合会（European Caravanning Federation 的简称）

ECGI （日本五十铃公司）电子控制汽油喷射系统（商品名 electronically controlled gasoline injection 的简称）

echelon parking 梯队驻车（指汽车一辆挨一辆以一定斜角紧对着路缘石的驻车形式）

EC Himati （丰田公司研制的装有自动变速器和电子控制液压式多片离合器，将驱动力分配给前、后车轮的）四轮驱动系统（的商品名）

Echo 回声（丰田公司的 1.3L 和 1.5L 型小轿车车名，该车多次入选世界十大小车和最安全小车称号）

echo ①回声，回音，回波，反射信号，波的折回，反应；仿效，重复 ②发出回声，波折回，反射，产生共鸣，模仿

echoed signal 反射信号

echoless chamber 消音室（参见 anechoic chamber）

echolocate ①回波定位 ②回波测距

echo pip （荧光屏）反射脉冲，回波

ECI 电（子）控（制）燃油喷射（electronically controlled injection 的简称，= ECCI）

ECI-MULTI 电子控制多点燃油喷射系统（商品名，Electronic Control Injection-Multipoints 的简称）

ECI-Turbo 电子控制燃油喷射涡轮增压式（发动机）

ECL ①发射极耦合逻辑（电路）（emitter coupled logic 的简称）②工程计算实验室（engineering computation laboratory 的简称）③设备元件明细表（equipment component list 的简称）

eclipsing effects 重叠效应

ECM ①电子控制模块（electronic control module 的简称，美国通用公司对其 CCC 系统中所使用的控制计算机的称呼。美国政府规定从1995年起发动机控制计算机一律使用 SAE 提出的标准术语 PCM）②有时亦作为 engine 或 emission control module 的简称

ECM-controlled air management system 电子控制模块控制式空气喷射系统（指将新鲜空气喷入发动机排气系统，如：排气歧管，以使废气中的 HC、CO 氧化，同时使 O_2 传感器和催化转化器快速升到工作温度）

ECM-controlled shift solenoids 电子控制模块控制的换挡电磁阀

EC module ①排放控制模块（emission controlled module 的简称）②发动机控制模块（见 engine controlled module）③见 ECM

ECO ①经济的（economic 的简称）②生态的（ecologic 的简称）③发动机检测（见 engine checkout）④工程更改指令（见 engineering change order）⑤乙烯化氧共聚物（见 ethylene oxide copolymer）

EcoBoost 节能动力 [Eco（生态、经济）和 Boost（促进、提高、增强）两词的组合。Ford 公司环保节能型发动机的商品名。如：用于该公司多款 SUV 的 3.5L 双增压 V 型 6 缸发动机]

ECO drive support system （汽车）节能型行驶支持系统（见 ECO MODE switch）

Eco-driving technique （驾驶者的）节能驾驶技术

eco-friendly technology 生态友好型技术

eco-hybrid truck ①节能型混合动力货车（economical hybrid truck 的简称）②生态环保型混合动力货车（ecological hybrid truck 的简称）

ecological damage 生态破坏（指对环境的破坏，就汽车而言，指排放对环境的污染）

ecological design 生态设计（指汽车等为了环境保护，降低排、放噪声等符合生态学要求的设计，简称 Ecodesign）

ecologically harmful 破坏生态的（对汽车指排放对环境污染的）

ecological protection 生态保护（指净化汽车排放等，保护环境的工作）

ecology 生态学（研究生物与其环境之间相互关系的科学）

ECO MODE switch （汽车可变行驶模式中的）节能模式开关（该开关闭合时汽车进入节能模式：发动机、空调、四轮驱动系统均在其电子控制模块的控制下按节能原则运转，ECO 亦写作 eCO）

ECO-motor （混合动力车等使用的）节能生态型电动机 [ecological-economical motor 的简称，指①具有行驶时输出动力的电动机和制动-减速时逆转发电、回收减速能量的发电机两种功能的二位一体机②具有减速时逆转发电的发电机（generator-alternator），停机后再起动时的起动机（starter）两种功能的二位一体机。通常用于怠速停机系统（idling stop system）③具有减速时逆转发电的发电机（generator-alternator），停机后再起动时的起动机（starter），行驶时输出动力的电动机（power motor）三种功能的三位一体机。在日产 S-hybrid 车上称：Sub motor-generator]

ECON （本田的）智能化辅助节能

系统（商品名，①可控制节气门，避免因过猛踩踏加速踏板而造成的燃油不必要的过多消耗②可自动根据车内气温调节空调制冷工况而节油等）

econ ①经济学（economics 的简称）②节约，节省，有效利用（economize 的简称）③省油器，节热器（economizer的简称）④节约，经济（学）（economy 的简称）

econobox 小型经济型汽车

economic（al） ①经济（上）的；经济学②节约的，节省的③（指车辆时）节油的（简称 ECD）

economical consumption of fuel 经济油耗（车辆以经济车速行驶时消耗的燃油量）

economical life of vehicle 车辆的经济寿命（新车开始投入使用到油耗及各种使用费用高到已不合算而需要更新的使用期限，即车辆能获得最佳经济效益的期限，一般以年或里程为计算单位，亦写作 economic life）

economically repairable 修理合算的（在经济性上修理是合理的）

economical mixture 经济混合气

economical operation 经济运行

economical speed （亦写作 economic speed）①经济车速（燃油消耗量最少时的车速）②经济转速（指内燃机在经济工况时的相应转速）

economical speed consumption of fuel 经济车速（时的）油耗

economical speed range （汽车）经济车速范围，（发动机）经济转速范围

economical yard sticks （可靠性评价中的）经济尺度（年维修费/购置费，维修费＋运转费/运转时间等）

economic characteristics 经济特性

Economic Commission of Europe （联合国）欧洲经济委员会（简称 ECE）

economic die 经济模，临时冲模，低熔点合金模（＝temporary die，参见 low melting point alloy die）

economic effect 经济效益

economic gear 经济挡（指在满足驱动轮牵引力要求的条件下，保证汽车高的经济性行驶的挡位）

economic performance 经济性能，经济性（对发动机，指其单位有效的耗油量，即有效比油耗或称有效油耗率的多少。对汽车指其百公里油耗的多少）

economic power 经济功率（内燃机在燃油消耗率较低经济的功率区运转时发出的功率）

Economic rationality 经济（上的）合理性

economic value 经济价值（＝commercial value）

economic working condition 经济工况（指在油耗率较低的功率和转速下运转的工况）

economizer ①（单腔或双腔并动式化油器中的）省油器（实际上是节气门全开、满负荷时的混合气加浓装置。由于有了这一装置，主油系可设计成在节气门部分开起的中、小负荷下提供经济混合气，达到省油的目的，因而称为省油器。一般有真空式和机械式两种）②（泛指一切采用控制燃油流量或空燃比的方法减少汽车油耗的）节油装置（＝economy device）

economy ①经济，经济学，经济性，节约，节省②（对汽车指）节油，油耗低

economy car 经济型轿车，省油轿车，节油轿车

economy competition 经济竞赛，经济竞争

economy cruising 经济巡行（指以稳定的经济车速行驶）

economy gear （经济行驶的）高挡位，高速比，（亦称 economy ratio）

economy index 经济指标

economy of fuel 节约燃油，节油；燃料经济性（= fuel saving, fuel eco-nomy）

economy of scale 经济规模（生产成本达到最低的年产量规模，如：有的经济学家认为轿车工业的经济规模，一般为年产 30 万辆）

economy running system （汽车）行驶节油装置，行驶节油系统，经济运行系统（简称 ERS）

economy shift mode 经济换挡模式（简称 ESM）

economy-size car 经济型轿车（一般指尺寸大小符合经济运行要求、车价低、油耗低、使用费用低的轿车）

economy test 油耗试验，（燃料）经济性试验

ECO(N) pattern 节能模式（economic pattern 的简称，= ECO MODE）

Eco Pro 生态保护（ecological protection 的简称）

E core coil 福特公司 EECIV TFI-IV 点火系使用的一种点火线圈，可输出 5000V 点火高压

Eco-Routing ①节能选线，选择节能路线②路线探索③在选定的路线上节能驾驶操作

eco-run 经济工况运行

Ecosystem 生态系统

ECOTEC ①生态技术（ecological technology 的简称，指符合生态保护要求的技术，亦写作 ECOTECH）②排放-油耗最佳化技术（Emission-Consumption Optimization Technology）③（通用公司 GM）节能技术（双凸轮轴气门可变定时 1.8L 汽油机商品名）

ECR 当量连续运转定额（equivalent continuous rating 的简称）

ECS ①发动机控制系统（engine control system 的简称）②误差校正伺服机构（信号）[error correction servo (signals) 的简称]③蒸气物污染控制系统（evaporative emission control system 的简称）④电子控制悬架系统（electronically controlled suspension 的简称）

ECT ①电子控制（汽油）喷射系统的简称（Electronic Controlled Injection 的简称，三菱公司单点式汽油喷射系统的商品名，见 single point injection system）②发动机特性试验仪（engine characteristic tester 的简称）③发动机停机定时器（engine cut-off timer 的简称）④电子控制式变速器（electronic controlled transmission 的简称）⑤发动机冷却液温度（engine coolant temperature 的简称）⑥发动机冷却液温度传感器（engine coolant temperature sensor 或 eng. coolant temp. sensor 的简称，美国政府规定从 1995 年 1 月起用 SAE 推荐的这一术语取代原各厂家自定的名称，如：Chrysler 和 GM 的 CTS 等）

ECT-i 智能型电子控制变速器（其中 i 为 with an intelligent control system 或 with intelligence，或 intelligent 的简称）

ECTL 发射极耦合晶体管逻辑（emitter coupled transistor logic 的简称）

ECTS （欧洲）生态城市运输系统（Ecological City Transport System 的简称）

ECT sensor 发动机冷却液温度传感器（engine coolant temperature sensor 的简称）

ECT switch 发动机冷却水温开关（engine coolant temperature switch 的简称，指由冷却水的温度控制的各种电路中的串联开关，如：当水温

高于某规定值时,即断开点火电源等)

ECU 电子控制模块(见 computer)

ECV 发动机零部件认证(鉴定)(engine component verification 的简称)

ECVT 电子控制式无级变速器(见 electro continuously variable transmission)

E-cycle E 循环(指车用计算机的数据处理、指令执行、反馈修正、结果存储等电子控制装置的控制循环)

ED ①电子设备(electronic device 的简称)②误差检测(error detecting 的简称)

EDA 电子(电路)设计自动化(electronic design automation 的简称)

EDC 柴油机电子控制(系统)(electronic diesel control 的简称)

EDC-C air suspension (宝马新 7 系列的)电子无级连续阻尼控制空气悬架(electronic damper control-continuous air suspension 的简称)

EDCS 柴油机电子控制系统(electronic diesel control system 的简称,由电子控制模块控制喷油时刻及喷油量)

EDCtransmission 电子控制双离合器变速器(electronic duel-clutch transmission 的简称)

EDDA [美]能源研究与开发管理局(Energy Research and Development Administration 的简称)

eddy ①涡流,旋涡 ②起旋涡,形成涡流,涡动,回旋

eddy axis 涡流轴线

eddy current (电)涡流(因电磁感应作用,在整块导体中产生的一种旋涡状感应电流,会导致导体发热而增加电能损耗,且具有削弱原磁场的作用。通常用增大涡流回路电阻的办法减弱涡流,但亦可用于测功和制动装置,吸收能量,产生制动力等)

eddy-current brake 涡流制动器(切割磁力线产生涡能,吸收汽车的动能,制动减速或测功)

eddy-current engine dynamometer 发动机电涡流测功机,[亦称 eddy current absorption dynamometer, 简称 eddy current(type)dynamometer, 发动机输出的功,全部转换成电涡流,随即转换成热能消耗掉的一种功率吸收装置,用以检测发动机输出功率]

eddy-current loss 涡流损失,电涡流损失

eddy current retarder (电)涡流缓速器(通过金属圆盘在电磁场中旋转而产生电涡流的阻力作用使汽车减速的一种机构,常用作汽车下坡时的辅助制动器,亦称 electro dynamic retardor 或简称 electric retarder)

eddy-current revolution counter 电涡流转速计

eddy current test 电涡流试验,涡流试验(将电涡流导入试件的一种无损试验)

eddy current transducer 电涡流传感器

eddy flow 紊流,涡流,旋流

eddy(flow)motion 紊流运动,涡流运动;涡流,旋流,紊流,湍流(=turbulent motion, eddying, vortex motion, whirling motion)

eddy-free front (流线型)无涡流车身前部

eddying ①涡流(的),湍流;②涡动(性),紊流度,涡流运动

eddy-resistance ①涡流阻力的 ②阻止涡流的

eddy zone 涡流区

EDFC 电控双燃料切换装置(elec-

edge ①边,棱;刀口,刀刃;肋,筋条;散热片;边界,界限 ②使锋利,开刀刃;装刀刃;镶边,嵌入;沿边移动

edge angle 边缘角,偏角,棱角

edge binding (车身底板地毯的)滚边带,包边带

edge brand 制作在制件边缘上的厂牌或参数说明等(如制动摩擦衬片边缘的厂标及型号等)

edge cam ①轴端凸轮(end cam) ②端面槽型凸轮(face cam)

edge conditions 边界条件,极限条件

edge filter 缝隙式滤清器(被滤清油液等通过大量滤件间的缝隙而得到滤清)

edge line 路幅边线,行车道外边线,路面边线(路肩与车道分界线上表示车道外边的标志线, = pavement edge line)

edge stone ①(道路的)边缘石 ②磨石

edge thickness coefficient (汽轮机叶片)边厚系数

edge thick offlap (轮胎)垫带两边缘的厚度(见 flap)

edge tone element 流振元件,哨音元件

edge-triggered (transition-operated) bistable circuit 边沿触发(转换工作)双稳态电路(有一个或多个转换工作输入端的双稳态电路)

edgewise weld (ing) 沿边焊接

edging ①修饰边缘,修边,去飞边 ②卷边,卷突缘

edible oil pump delivery tanker 食用植物油加油车(除具有食用植物油运油车的基本装置外,还设有泵油系统、工作仪表和操作装置,能自行加注食用植物油的罐式汽车)

EDIC 柴油机电控喷射系统(见 electronic diesel injection control system)

EDIS ①电子信息交换系统(electronic data interchange system 的简称) ②电子控制无分电器式点火系统(electronic distributorless ignition system, 见 EIS)

Edison base 螺丝口灯头(亦称 Edison screw 或 Edison screw lamp cup, 由爱迪生发明, 故名)

Edison battery 爱迪生(蓄)电池, 碱性(蓄)电池 [= alkaline cell, 亦称 Edison (storage) cell]

Edison socket 螺丝口灯座

EDL 见 electronic differential locking system

EDLC 双层电容器型蓄电池(electric double layer capacitor 的简称, 与常规铅蓄电池比较, 不仅充、放电快, 耐高压, 而且寿命长, 用于汽车减速能量频繁回收发电系统中, 可无损耗的瞬时存储回收电能)

EDM ①电火花加工(electric discharge machining 的简称) ②电子扩散率测定法(electron deffusibility measurement 的简称)

EDPC 电子数据处理中心(electronic data processing center 的简称)

EDPE 电子数据处理设备(electronic data processing equipment 的简称)

EDPS 电子数据处理系统(electronic data processing system 的简称)

EDR [美]汽车行驶数据记录仪(event data recorder 的简称, 指电子控制数字式汽车行驶记录仪)

E-drive (电动汽车的)电力驱动系统 [如: vehicle with E-drive (电动汽车)]

EDS 电子(控制)差速器锁止系统,(electronic differential locking system 的简称)

eduction 放出, 排出, 排泄; 析出

Edwardian car 爱德华时代经典车

(指英皇爱德华七世期间 1901—1910, 亦说指 1905—1918 年间生产的英国经典车)

EEA [美] 能源与环境分析公司(见 Energy and Environment Analysis)

EEC ①发动机电子控制(系统)(Electronic Engine Control 的简称,福特公司发动机电子控制系统的商品名,其后的罗马数字表示为第 n 代,如：EEC Ⅲ, 第三代 EEC 系统) ②蒸发排放物控制(evaporative emission control 的简称,为美国政府规定使用的 SAEJ1930 标准术语,取代原 Chrysler 的 EVAP, 通用, 福特的 CANP 等旧称) ③发动机电子控制中心(engine electronic center 的简称) ④欧洲经济共同体, 共同市场(European Economic Community 的简称, Common Market, 共同市场)

EECV (福特公司) V 型发动机电子控制系统(Electronic Engine Control V 的简称, 指装有 Ⅱ 型车载诊断系统 "OBDⅡ" 的发动机控制系统)

EE(ee) ①电机工程师(electrical engineer 的简称) ②电机工程(electrical engineering 的简称) ③电子工程师(electronics engineer 的简称) ④实验站(见 experimental establishment)

EEG 脑电波(图), 脑电波图(electroen-cephalogram 或 electroen-cephalography 的简体)

EEM system 发动机电子管理系统(electronic engine management system 的简称)

E-engine E 发动机(指内能不需要首先变成热的发动机, 如内燃机、汽轮机等)

e-3engine e-3 发动机(英国 Mayflower 公司推出的一种新概念的变压缩比和变排量发动机的商品名。该发动机的连杆与曲轴通过一可在水平和垂直方向移动的杆件连接, 借以实现活塞冲程长度, 即压缩比和排量的改变)

EEPROM 见 EPROM

EEROM 电可擦只读存储器(electrically erasable read-only memory 的简称, 指其存储内容可由电信号擦除, 亦称 electrically alterable read only memory, 简称 EAROM 或 electrically alterable ROM, 它类似 EPROM 或 EROM, 但后二者是用紫外光擦除)

EEV ①省油车(高效利用能源的车辆, energy efficient vehicle 的简称) ②(可适应)环境严格要求的车辆(environmentally enhanced vehicle 的简称)

EF ①应急设备(emergency facilities 的简称) ②等效焦距(equivalent focal length 的简称) ③排气风扇, 排风机(exhaust fan 的简称)

EFE(S) 燃油早期汽化(系统)(见 early fuel evaporation system)

eff ①效果, 效应(effect 的缩写形式) ②效率, 有效系数, 效能(efficiency 的缩写形式) ③有效的(effective 的缩写形式)

effect ①效果, 效应 ②引起, 实现, 达到 ③有效的(=effective)

effective ①有效的 ②实际的 ③现行的

effective angle of obliquity 见 angle of inclination

effective axle weight ①车桥有效载荷, 车桥动载荷(=dynamic axle weight) ②车桥有效制动载荷, 车桥制动动载荷(=dynamic braking weight)

effective brake 高效制动器

effective brake thermal efficiency 有效热效率(内燃机有效功的热当量与燃料热量的比值, 即燃料中的热

能转变为有效功的份额）

effective compression ratio （汽缸的）有效压缩比［内燃机进、排气口（门）全部关闭的瞬间的汽缸容积与汽缸最小容积之比］

effective cylinder volume 汽缸有效容积（指汽缸内可容纳工质的最大容积，＝汽缸有效工作容积＋余隙容积）

effective deflection （悬架等在规定载荷下的）实际变形量（而非理论变形）

effective diameter of bellows 波纹管有效直径（指波纹管波峰外径与其波纹凹谷底外径的平均值）

effective face width 有效齿宽（一对相啮合的齿轮在齿宽上相互搭接的宽度）

effective filter area （柴油机排烟测定用的滤纸式烟度计的）滤纸有效面积（指滤纸起过滤作用的那部分面积）

effective indicated mean pressure 有效平均指示压力（减去机械损失后的平均指示压力）

effective inertia mass （汽车的）有效惯性质量（即旋转运动质量折合为直线运动质量的当量质量和直线运动质量的总和）

effective injector pulse width 有效喷油（量控制）脉冲宽度（为基本脉冲宽度根据蓄电池电压、冷机起动、升温、怠速、加速等工况对喷油量要求进行修正后的实际脉冲宽度）

effective leakage path 有效泄漏通道，（实际漏失面积）

effective length 有效长度，实际长度（如：对滤纸式烟度计而言，有效长度指抽气容积减去死区容积除以滤纸有效面积的值，单位 m，是这种烟度计的一个重要参数）

effectiveness 效率，效能，效用，效果；有效性

effectiveness factor 效能因素（如：盘式制动器制动盘摩擦表面积与作用于制动块上的输入力之比）

effectiveness of performance 实际性能，性能效率；运行效率，操作效果

effective number of coils 螺旋弹簧的有效圈数（参见 number of spring coils）

effective optical path length （柴油机排烟测定用的光学式烟度计的）光通道有效长度（指在发光器与检测器之间穿过排气流的光束长度，并对由于密度梯度和边缘效应引起的不均匀度进行校正）

effective overlap period ①有效重叠期 ②（转子发动机的）气孔有效重叠（指进、排气孔的有效重叠度。在周边进气时，指三角活塞工作面凹坑前端到后端，通过旋轮线缸壁细腰处的名义密封线的时间）

effective piston swept volume 汽缸有效工作容积（在排气冲程中自进、排气门全部关闭瞬间至活塞运动到上止点所扫过的汽缸容积）

effective port area （转子发动机的进、排）气孔有效面积

effective power 有效功率（指发动机输出的功率，等于发动机的指示功率减去摩擦功率或机械损失功率，亦称 effective engine power, effective horsepower, net horsepower, actual horsepower 等，见 brake power）

effective retarding force （汽车的）有效减速力（一般指制动瞬间开始产生制动作用的实际制动力和其他外界阻力的总和）

effective rolling radius 有效滚动半径（指假想的刚性车轮以实际车轮的角速度和无侧偏滚动时的半径。由此可得出车辆的实际线速度。该半径特别是子午胎的实际半径，恒小

于轮胎未变形的外圆半径，即自由半径。有效滚动半径 $r = s/2\pi n$ (m)，n—车轮转动圈数，s—该转动圈数时轮轴中心的位移，简称滚动半径 rolling radius）

effective search range ①（灯光的）有效照射范围 ②（摄像系统的）有效摄像范围 ③（探测装置的）有效搜索范围

effective sectional area 有效截面面积

effective static deflection 有效静载变形量，有效静力下沉量（指悬架系统或轮胎在承受法向静载荷时产生的变形或下沉量，=悬架系统或轮胎承受法向静载荷时的静载荷量除以该系统或轮胎的刚度）

effective stroke （二冲程循环发动机的）做功冲程

effective summed horsepower （发动机的）总有效功率，总有效马力（简称 ESHP）

effective swept volume 实际扫气容积，有效扫气容积

effective throat 喉管有效截面

effective tire surface 轮胎（与地面）有效接触面积

effective value 有效值，均方根值（=root mean-square value）

effective weight 有效自重，实际自重（对车辆讲，指车辆整备质量，即车辆带全套装备，准备投入使用时的实际自重）

effective yield strength 有效屈服强度（表示塑性屈服对断裂试验参数的单向屈服强度的设定值）

effect of altitude 高度效应，高海拔效应

effect of synchronizing brake action （牵引车与挂车或各车轮）制动同步效应

efficiency ①效率，有效系数 ②效能，效果 ③能力，功能，性能 ④功效，实效，生产率，经济性

efficiency diode （高压整流用）高效二极管

efficiency factor 效率系数，效率

efficiency of brake 见 brake efficiency

efficiency of hydrodynamic converter 液力变矩器效率（=速比×变矩系数）

efficiency of supply ①供给效率 ②（柴油机喷油泵）供油系数

efficiency of (the) fan 风机效率（指风机传送给空气的有效功率与风机轴功率的比值）

efficiency of vehicle components 车辆（各）部件效率

efficiency test 效能测试，效能试验，效率测试

efficient ①有效的，有用的 ②高效率的，高效能的

Efficient Dynamicstechnology 高效快速反应技术（BMW 公司提出的其所有汽车研发部门遵循的行动纲领，简称 Efficient Dynamics 或 ED，目标是不断地降低汽车的油耗，其支柱是改善常规器件和最大限度地开拓电子器件）

efficient gas 废气（见 exhaust gas）

effort ①作用力，有效力，力量 ②努力，企图，尝试，成果，成就 ③工作（项目），研究（计划）

effortless operation 不费力的操纵（如：在电气、液压操纵中只需按下电钮或拨动开关）

effuser （扩散）喷管；收敛形进气道；风洞收敛道

effusion ①流出，溢出，喷出，渗出 ②喷发，喷射 ③渗透，隙透（指气体透过多孔壁的现象）

effusion cooling 喷射冷却，多孔蒸发冷却

effusion method （测定蒸气压力的）隙透法（利用气体透过多孔壁的效应）

effusion time (燃油、机油等流量测定时的)流出时间

EFI 电子汽油喷射系统(Electronic-Fuel Injection 的简称,福特公司节气门体单点式汽油喷射系统的商品名,见 single point injection system)

EFI-D 进气压力计量型电子控制汽油喷射系统[electronic fuel injection-Druek 的简称,Druek 为德文"压力"。应用进气管压力(进气歧管负压)与进气量成比例的原理,根据进气压力传感器测出进气压力,按发动机工况所要求的最佳空燃比算出每一循环的汽油喷射量]

E field 电场(electric field)

EFI-L 进气空气质量流量计量型电子控制汽油喷射系统(见 electronic fuel injection system Luft)

EFMS ①电子燃油控制系统(electronic fuel-management system 的简称)②电子燃油计量装置(electronic fuel-metering system 的简称)

EFP assembly 见 electronic foot pedal assembly

EFV 防过流阀(见 excess flow valve)

EFV 环境友好车辆(见 environmentally friendly vehicle)

EG 乙二醇(ethylene glycol 的简称)

E-gas ①(大众公司)电子节气门控制系统(商品名)②电子油门

E-Gas 电子控制油门

E-Gas (通用公司)电子节气门(商品名)

EGER 排气能量回收(exhaust gas energy recovery 的简称)

egg-crate grille 蛋篓形水箱护栅(由十字交叉的栅条构成,栅格略呈方形,亦见六角形者)

egg-shape piston (顶面凹窝断面呈 W 型,即:凹窝中央有一卵形凸起的)卵形顶活塞(该阀凸起的周边形成一圈凹环)

EGI ①(催化转化器快速起燃技术中的)废气点火(系统)(exhaust gas ignition system 的简称,使用火花塞在特定的燃烧区内,点燃冷机起动时,过浓可燃混合气废气中的 HC,以迅速加热催化转化器)②电子控制汽油喷射(electronically controlled gasoline injection 及 electronic gasoline injection 的简称)

egis 保护,掩护(= aegis)

EGI system 废气点火系统(exhaust gases ignition system 的简称,用于减少 HC,CO 排放)

EGOsensor 排气氧传感器(见 exhaust gases oxygen sensor)

EGP 排气压力(exhaust-gases pressure 的简称)

EGR 废气再循环,排气再循环(exhaust gas recirculation 的简称,指从排气管中引出一部分废气再经进气管道流回发动机汽缸的方法。由于废气中含有大量的惰性气体,可稀释新鲜混合气,使燃烧速度减慢,同时废气回流使燃烧过程中工质的热容量增加,即比热提高,二者均可降低最高燃烧温度,而有效地抑制 NO_X 的生成,减少排气中 NO_X 的含量和爆燃倾向,目前我国亦直接引用英语称 EGR)

EGR control module EGR 控制模块(电子控制式废气再循环系统的电子控制模块。根据发动机工况控制废气再循环量的电子电路模块,其中最简单者是由发动机水温、进气管真空度及变速器挡位等传感器输入信号控制的 EGR 继电器电路"EGR control relay")

EGR control solenoid EGR 真空通道控制电磁阀(简称 EGRC solenoid,该阀开启时真空进入 EGR 阀膜片阀真空室,EGR 阀开启,但 EGR 阀的开度由 EGRV solenoid 控制,见 EGR vent solenoid)

EGR control valve 废气再循环量控制阀，EGR 控制阀（EGR 系统中最主要的部件，由发动机电子控制模块通过电磁阀经真空膜片、气压膜片或直接控制该阀的开、闭和开度，以接通或关闭进入发动机汽缸的废气通路，或调节该通路的大小，简称 EGR valve 或 EGRV，我国称 EGR 阀）

EGR cooler EGR 冷却器（利用冷却水或冷风将废气温度控制在一定范围内，防止废气烧损回流废气流量控制阀等）

EGRC solenoid 见 EGR control solenoid

EGR diagnostic switch EGR 诊断开关（向电子控制模块报告 EGR 工作是否正常，有 thermal 和 vacuum-operated 两种）

egress 下车（从车内出来，上车见 entry）

EGR filter EGR 过滤器（用于过滤进入 EGR 系统的排气中的固体杂质）

EGR gas 再循环废气（在 EGR 系统中再循环的废气）

EGR port （发动机）废气再循环入口（exhaust gas recirculation port 的简称）

EGR/PR EGR 控制气压调节器（"EGR pressure regulator" 的简称，由 EGRP 和 EGRV 两个电磁阀组成，见 EGRP solenoid 和 EGRV solenoid）

EGRP solenoid （EGR pressure solenoid 的简称，福特 EEC 系统早期使用压缩空气膜片式 EGR 阀，以后为真空膜片式 EGR 阀所取代。EGRP 电磁阀的作用是断开或接通控制 EGR 阀的压缩空气）

EGR rate 废气再循环率（exhaust gas recirculation rate 的简称，再循环废气量与进气量或进气量加再循环废气量的质量比）

EGR shut-off solenoid EGR 真空通—断电磁阀（为福特公司使用的真空膜片式 EGR 阀真空通路的电磁阀，它只能接通或断开该真空通路，而不能调节其开度）

EGR shut-off solenoid with back-pressure transducer 带背压调节器的 EGR 真空通路电磁阀［为福特公司 EGR shut-off solenoid 的改进型，该阀装有一可通过改变真空强度从而改变 EGR 流量的背压调节器。当背压（即排气压力）低而进气管真空度高时，该调节器将空气孔开大，使进入 EGR 阀的真空度减弱，反之则将空气孔关小，进入 EGR 阀的真度空加强。这种 shut-off solenoid 不仅能控制 EGR 阀的开、闭而且可调节其开度］

EGR tolerance 废气再循环率容差，废气再循环率容许范围

EGR vacuum diagnostic control switch EGR 真空通断诊断开关（为一真空控制开关，装在 EGR 阀和 EGR 真空控制电磁阀之间的真空管道中，向发动机电子控制模块提供 EGR 阀的控制真空是否按电子控制模块指令的要求通、断的信息，亦称 EGR vacuum indicator switch）

EGR-vacuum modular （真空膜片式）EGR 阀的真空度调节器（根据发动机工况、进气管真空、变速器挡位、冷却水温等调节 EGR 阀膜片真空室的真空度，借以调节废气再循环量的装置的通称。一般由发动机电子控制模块，以脉冲形式发出的指令控制的电磁阀来控制真空通路的断和开，而开度由脉冲宽度控制，简称 ECR-VM）

EGR vacuum regulator （福特公司）EGR 阀真空调节器（为该公司所使用的真空膜片式 EGR 阀真空通路控制装置的一种，它取代了 EGRP/EGRV solenoid 系统。由电子模块控

制的电磁阀来控制 EGR 阀真空通路中的大气通路,从而接通、断开真空或调节其强度)

EGR-valve 见 VGR control valve

EGR valve position sensor EGR 阀位置传感器(简称 EVP sensor,向发动机电子控制模块报告 EGR 阀开、闭及开度信息,供计算空燃比、点火时刻,调整 EGR 量及诊断 EGR 阀故障之用,亦称 EGR valve lift sensor)

EGR valve temperature sensor EGR 阀温度传感器(为一热敏电阻,用于电子控制模块根据 EGR 阀的温度变化确认 EGR 的运转是否正常)

EGR VDC switch 废气再循环真空诊断控制开关(EGR vacuum diagnostic control switch 的简称,为一真空控制的电路开关。当有真空作用于 EGR 时,该开关闭合。如果在起动、怠速或任何其他使用 EGR 不应使用的工况下,该开关闭合,或在任一应使用 EGR 的工况下,该开关断开,则发动机控制模块立即点亮故障灯并输出相应的故障码)

EGR vent solenoid EGR 大气阀,EGR 泄放阀(该阀开启时,真空室与大气相通,真空泄漏,EGR 阀开度减小)

EGR venturi (aspirator controlled EGR 系统的) EGR 真空喉管(该系统空气滤清器内装有一吸气装置,当发动机真空度低时,一空气泵将空气泵到该装置的喉管区,产生真空,用以维持 EGR 的开度,当发动机真空度高时,空气泵断开,而由进气管真空供给 EGR 阀控制用真空源)

EGR-VM 见 EGR-vacuum modulator

EGR VS EGR 真空开关(EGR vacuum switch 的简称,指 EGR VSV 的控制电路的进气管真空度,即:发动机负荷传感开关)

EGRV solenoid EGR 大气阀,EGR 泄放阀(见 EGR vent solenoid)

EGR VSV EGR 阀的真空开关阀(EGR vacuum switch valve 的简称,为开、闭和调节 EGR valve 真空通路的电磁阀)

EGT 废气温度(exhaust gas temperatures)

EHB 电子控制液压制动系统(electronic hydraulic brake system 的简称。在该系统中,传统的直接控制制动主缸或助力器的机械式制动踏板已由具有踏板感觉模拟功能和驾驶者制动意图传感功能的电子踏板所取代,电子控制模块收到该踏板传递的驾驶者制动意图信号后,便向制动器液压执行器件发出制动指令,实现车辆符合驾驶者意图的减速或制动)

EHB system 电动液压制动系统(electrical hydraulic brake system 的简称)

EHC 电加热型催化剂(electro-heated catalyst)

EHC converter 电加热催化转化器(electrically heated catalytic converter 的简称)

EHL 弹性流体动力润滑理论(elastohydrodynamic lubrication theory)

EHN 见 ethyl-hexyls-nitrate

EHP ①有效马力(effective horsepower 的简称) ②电动马力(electric horsepower)

EHPAS 电子控制液力转向助力系统(electronic hydraulic power assist steering 的简称)

EHPH 电动马力小时(electric horsepower hour 的简称)

EHV 电动混合动力车(参见 electric hybrid vehicle)

EI ①电子(汽油)喷射系统(Electronic Injection 的简称,日产公司单点式汽油喷射系统的商品名,见

single point injection system 的简称）②排放量指数（emission index 的简称）③电子点火（electronic ignition 的简称）④电子喷射（electronic injection 的简称）

EIC 电子组合仪表板（electronic instrument cluster 的简称）

EICHC 电启动化学加热催化器（electrically initiated chemically heated catalytic converter 的简称）

eigen （字头）固有的，本征的［eigen frequency 固有频率；eigen mode（振动等的）固有模式；eigen vibration 固有振动；本征振动，eigen function 本征函数，特征函数］

eigenvalue 本征值，固有值（亦写作 eigen value，= proper value）

eight ①八 ②8 字形 ③八个一组 ④八缸发动机汽车 ⑤8 缸发动机 ⑥eight by ×（说明汽车时，by 前面的 8 表示该车的车轮数，by 后面的数字表示其中有 n 个车轮为驱动轮，如：8×4 指四轮驱动的 8 轮汽车）

eight-bit microcontroller 8 位微处理器（指字长为 8 位的微处理器，即：每一次处理 8 位一组的数据和指令，并且具有 8 位宽的内部总线和寄存器，亦写作 8-bit microcontroller，由于它成本低、能耗小，又具有足够的处理能力，在汽车电子控制系统中，多用来作为各种小型电动机的控制模块）

eight-cylinder engine 直列式八缸发动机，直列 8 缸发动机（= eight-in-line，straight eight）

"eight"（8）form driving test "8" 字形试验［评价汽车低速沿"8"字形曲线（双扭线）行驶时操纵力大小的试验］

eight-hour haul day 每天 8h 运输工作制，8h 运输工作日

eight-hour shift 8h 一班（制）

eight-in-line 直列八缸（指发动机或使用直列八缸发动机的汽车）

eight-in V V 形八缸（发动机或车辆）

eight pin header 八脚管座

eight-seater 8 座客车，8 座汽车

eight-seat van 8 座厢式客车，（俗）8 座面包车

eight shape 8 字形

eight-wheel（ed） 八轮（的），四轴的（汽车）

eight-wheeler （指两个转向桥和两个驱动桥的）四桥整体式货车［相对拖挂列车而言，亦称 eight wheel(ed) vehicle 或 four-axle vehicle］

EIN ①发动机出厂号码（engine identification number 的简称）②设备安装通知（equipment installation notice 的简称）

Einisil 渗碳化硅镀镍材料，硅镍复合渗镀层（见 CEM depositing process）

Einisil coating 硅镍镀层，镍-硅合金镀覆层（镀盖在转子发动机的旋轮线缸壁上，亦称 Einisil coating，nickel-silicon alloy coating。镀镍时，使碳化硅微粒悬浮于电解液中，在形成镀层的过程中，这些微粒分散渗入镍的基体中）

EIS ①电子点火开关（electronic ignition switch 的简称）②电子点火系统（electronic ignition system 的简称，美国政府规定从 1995 年 1 月开始使用 SAE 推荐的这一术语表示无分电器的电子点火系统，取代各公司自定的各种名称，如：chrysler 的 DIS，Ford 的 DIS，EDIS，GM 的 DIS，IDI，C^3I 等）③电动汽车（充电—通信）一体化系统，电动汽车—揽子化系统（Electric Vehicle Integration system 的简称，指近年提出的由电网和屋顶等太阳能发电装置双重向家庭供电，由无线通信系

统向电动汽车提供行车信息导行和控制家庭电源管理系统对电动汽车充电的一缆子系统，见 HEMS)

EISHC （催化转化器快速热起技术中的）电起动化学加热式催化转化器（electrically initiated chemically heated catalyst converter 的简称，首先经 3~4s 的电加热使催化器温度上升到 200℃，然后以甲醛为燃料，通过 2~3s 的自燃燃烧反应，使催化剂温度迅速上升到 400℃ 左右）

EI system 电子点火系统（electronic ignition system 的简称，美国政府规定，从 1995 年 1 月起，无分电器的点火系统，一律按 SAE 标准，称 EI system）

EI system using twin crankshaft position sensor 采用双曲轴位置传感器的电子点火系统，其中一个曲轴位置传感器用于产生点火和喷油同步信号（见 sync signal）

EJA 工程分析（engineering job analysis 的简称）

eject [动] ①喷射 ②推出，甩出

ejecta 排出物，喷出物，废物，渣

eject button （录放设备磁带或盘的）退出按钮

ejection ①抛出，喷出，射出，发射，抛出 ②排出物，抛出物，喷出物

ejection cylinder 推出油缸，喷油缸

ejection from vehicle （当发生事故时）乘客从汽车内甩出

ejection mechanism 自动抛出机构，自动拆卸机构，自动推顶机构

ejector ①喷射装置，（顶）推出装置，抛出装置 ②（柴油车制动系供能装置真空部分中的）喷射器 [指安装在柴油发动机的进气管路中，利用进气管高速气流形成的低压，将该装置中气室的空气吸出，产生真空度（负压）的部件]

ejector key 推顶键

ejector mechanism 工件自动拆卸机构，弹射机构

ejector nozzle 喷嘴，喷口

ekistics 人类聚生态学（= science of human settlements，研究人类居住的城市，区域生态环境）

EL ①弹性极限，弹性限度（elastic limit 的简称）②电致发光（electroluminescence 的简称）③高度（elevation 简称）④延长，伸长（elongation 的简称）

elaeometer 浮子式比重计

elapse 经过，驶过（时间，里程等），滑过，无声驶过

elastic 弹性的，有弹力的，有伸缩性的，灵活的

elastica ①弹力，弹性 ②橡胶

elastic aftereffect 弹性后效

elastically yielding bearing 弹性支撑轴承

elastic break-down 弹性破坏

elastic buckling 弹性拱曲

elastic clutch ①弹性离合器 ②弹性联轴节，柔性联轴节（= flexible coupling）

elastic coefficient 弹性系数（在弹性限度内，弹性体的弹力与其变形量的比值）

elastic collision 弹性碰撞（指碰撞前后，物体系统的动量和动能同时守恒，且恢复系数 $e = 1$ 的碰撞）

elastic component 弹性元件（指弹簧或气囊之类具有弹性的元件）

elastic constant 弹性常数（用应力的一次系数表示的应变成分的常数）

elastic coupling 弹性联轴节

elastic-damping type torsional vibration balancer 弹性-阻尼式曲轴扭振减振器（同时利用摩擦阻尼限制曲轴扭转振幅的增大和使用弹性摆运动时产生的惯性力来消减共振时的干扰力的减振装置，亦称复合

式减振器"composite damper")
elastic deformation 弹性变形（见 elasticity③）
elastic energy 弹性能（弹性变形所具有的形变能。在数值上等于外力使弹性体变形所做的功）
elastic failure 超过弹性极限的损坏
elastic fatigue 弹性疲劳
elastic force 弹力（发生弹性变形的物体力图恢复原状对与它接触物体产生的力）
elastic-frame vehicle 弹性车架车辆（泛指具有缓冲和能量吸收能力，或可伸缩能力的车架，或铰接式车架，或可扭转变形的车架等的车辆）
elastic grinding wheel 弹性砂轮（用橡胶类材料作为磨料黏合剂的砂轮）
elastic hardness 弹性硬度
elastic-hydrodynamic lubrication 弹性流体动力（动压）润滑（在汽车传动系中齿轮、滚动轴承等零件，受压时的接触为线接触或点接触，压强很高，而导致零件的弹性变形及润滑油黏度、油膜变化等问题，这类润滑称为弹性流体动力润滑，亦写作 elastohydrodynamic lubrication，简称为 EHL）
elastic hysteresis 弹性滞后
elastic impact 弹性冲击
elasticity ①弹性 ②弹性力学 ③弹性变形（在力的作用下变形的物体，在除去外力后能恢复原状的性质叫弹性，这种变形叫弹性变形，亦称 elastic deformation）
elasticity of demand 需求弹性（指运输需求随其他自变量变化而变化的程度，以运输需要量的变化率与自变量变化率之比"E"表示）
elasticity of engine 发动机（对燃油、使用条件等的）适应性
elasticity volume 弹性容量，弹性容积（指可变容积，可变容量）
elastic joint 弹性接合，橡皮联轴节，挠性接头
elastic limit 弹性极限（弹性材料不致产生永久变形的最大应力）
elastic modulus 弹性模量（指在弹性范围内物体的应力与应变之间的比例常数 $E = \sigma/\varepsilon$）
elastic nut 弹性螺母
elastic oscillation 弹性振动（在弹力作用下的简谐振动）
elastic pendulum-type torsional vibration balancer 弹性摆式扭转减振器（利用弹性摆运动时产生的惯性力消除共振时的干扰力，可消除曲轴系统原有扭转共振的装置，但又会形成新的弹性系统而在另一转速下产生新的共振，因而现代车用发动机多采用弹性摆和阻尼原理构成的复合式减振器，见 elastic-damping type torsional vibration balancer）
elastic potential energy 弹性势能（指物体发生弹性变形时，各部分之间存在弹力的相互作用而具有的势能）
elastic properties 弹性
elastic range 弹性变形范围，弹性范围
elastic reactance 弹性反作用力
elastic region 弹性区域
elastic resistance 弹性阻力
elastic response 弹性反应，弹性特性曲线
elastic-rim wheel 弹性轮辋车轮
elastic ring 弹簧垫圈，弹性圈
elastic strain 弹性应变（受力时，单位长度的弹性变形，伸长或压缩）
elastic strain energy 弹性应变能量
elastic stress 产生弹性变形的应力，小于弹性极限的应力
elastic support 弹性支架，弹性支座
elastic surface 弹性表面
elastic tire 弹性轮胎（= resilient

tire)
elastic vibration 弹性振动
elastic washer 弹性(簧)垫圈(=springwasher)
elastic wave 弹性波,弹性变形波
elastic wheel 弹性车轮
elastivity 介电常数的倒数,倒电容系数
elastohydrodynamic lubrication theory 弹性流体动力润滑理论(指考虑物体弹性变形引起的接触面积的改变、润滑油黏度在高压下的增大、高速下黏度阻力所占的比例增加等状态的润滑理论,亦写作 elastic-hydrodynamic lubrication,简称 EHL)
elastomer ①合成橡胶,人造橡胶(=synthetic rubber)②弹性体,弹性材料
elastomeric material (汽车用)弹性材料,橡胶材料(天然橡胶、再生橡胶、合成橡胶等的总称)
elastomeric vulcanizate 硫化弹性材料产品,硫化橡胶
elastomer test system 弹性材料试验系统
elastometer 弹性计,弹力计
elastometry 弹性测定法,弹力测定法
elastoplast 弹性塑料
elastoplastic(s) 弹性塑料,弹塑性的
elaterometer 气体密度计(=elatrometer)
elbow 直角弯头,肘状弯头,弯管,弯头;弯管接头;肘状物,(篷顶车篷架的)弓形上梁;(闭式车箱的)中梁弯头;座椅扶手
elbow bend 弯头,肘管,弯管(=elbow pipe)
elbow lever 弯肘杆
elbow rest (客车、轿车座椅上供乘客搁置肘臂的)肘靠(=armrest)
elbow room (车间内)肘可自由伸屈的空间

elbow-type combustion chamber L形燃烧室
elbow width 两肘紧贴躯干时的肘间宽度(用 W 表示,乘员座位的最小宽度)
ELB system 电子控制制动系统(electronic brake system 的简称,亦简称 ELBS)
ELCODE 奔驰车装用电子防盗系统的商品名(可防止盗贼进入车内开车)
ELC system 电子(车身)高度调平控制系统(electronic leveling control system 的简称)
elct 电子的(electronic 的简称)
ELD 场致发光显示(仪表)(electro-luminescence display 的简称,20世纪90年代末期开始用于汽车,见electroluminescent)
ELD 电气负载传感器(electrical load detector 的简称,用于监测汽车除空调和动力转向以外的各种电子控制或电动系统总耗电量的传感器。该传感器安装在汽车车身发动机舱的熔丝盒内,将汽车上述各负载电路的总耗电量变换为电信号送入发动机的电子控制模块,作为负荷变动时控制发动机转速、防止怠速运转不稳定的一个重要参数)
elderly driver 老年驾驶者
elec (tr) ①电的,电动的,带电的(electric)②电,电力,电气(electricity)
ELec-Trac 电子控制防滑转装置(美国 Aspro 公司的一种防驱动车轮滑转装置,根据滑转车轮与未滑转车轮之间的转速差值,通过逻辑控制电路等对滑转车轮施加制动力,使其转速降低,待越过泥泞区后,又自动恢复正常运转)
electric A. C. dynamometer 交流电力测功机(一种新型电力测功机,发动机带动的测功电机为交流电机,产生的交流电可直接输入电

网，参见 electric dynamometer）

electric actuated brake system 电动制动系统

electric actuator 电动执行器（指使用步进电动机、电磁阀、继电器、开关等元器件的执行器的总称，= electric actuating element）

electric air control valve 见 EAC valve

electric air switching valve 见 EAS valve

electrical actuation 电动，电驱动，电动执行

electrical air bag system 电控式（汽车乘员安全）气囊系统（指使用电信号引燃气体发生器，使气囊充气的安全气囊系统。当传感器输入的碰撞信号超过基准值时，电子控制模块发出点火指令，将点火剂引燃）

electrical analyzer 电器检测仪，电器故障分析仪

electrical and electronic sensing system 电气和电子传感系统

electrical arc welding 电弧焊接

electrical changing station （电瓶汽车的）电瓶更换站，换电（瓶）站

electrical charge 电荷（量）（= quantity of electricity，代号 Q，质子带最小的正电荷，电子带最小的负电荷，电荷的多少叫电荷量，其单位是库仑 C，见 coulomb）

electrical condenser 电容器

electrical conductance 电导（单位为西门子，见 siemens）

electrical conductivity 电导率（电阻率的倒数，见 electric resistivity）

electrical current sensor 电流（量）传感器

electrical four-post car lift 电动四柱汽车举升器

electrical generator 发电机

electrical grinding 电磨削（电化学反应和机械磨削相结合的一种复合加工工艺）

electrical hookup ①电耦合，电路耦合 ②试验线路，电路 ③线路图，接线图

electrical load detector 电气负载传感器（见 ELD）

electrical load（ing） 电力负载，电力负荷

electrically actuated convertible top 电动活动车顶

electrically assisted power steering （某些复合车上的）电辅助动力转向（用于复合动力系统中的内燃机停止运转时，提供转向助力）

electrically-charged 充电的

electrically conductive cloth 导电布

electrically controlled air horn （汽车的）电控气喇叭（指用电磁控制压缩空气通断的气喇叭，参见 air horn）

electrically controlled birefringence mode 电控双折射型（利用电压控制液晶双折射的显示方式）

electrically-energized 电控的，电操纵的，电激发的

electrically heatable safety glass interlayer 安全玻璃电热夹层

electrically heated catalyst converter 电加热型催化转化器（简称 EHC converter，利用电热的方法使催化剂快速到达起燃温度，即其工作温度）

electrically heated external mirror 电热式车外后视镜（防霜、雾）

electrically heated seat 电暖式座椅，电热式座椅

electrically induced alignment 电场感应取向（电子外加电场引起的液晶分子重新取向）

electrically noise environment 电噪声环境

electrically-operated door opener 电动开门器，电开门装置

electrically operated throttle kicker

电控式节气门顶开器（见 throttle kicker）

electrically polarized 电偏振的（简称 EP）

electrically-powered actuator （电子控制装置的）电动执行机构

electrically supercharged engine 电动进气增压发动机

electrical motor 电动机

electrical nut tightening tool 电动上螺母器，电动螺母扳手

electrical operation 电气作业（指对汽车电气设备所进行的清洁、检查、调整和润滑等项作业）

electrical panel 配电板，配电盘

electrical polishing 电抛光（一种在阳极表面及其附近通过电化学作用进行抛光的工艺）

electric (al) potential 电势，电位（符号 V, φ, 电场中某点的电荷的电势能与其电量的比值）

electrical propulsion 电力驱动，电力推动（简称 EP）

electrical pulse 电脉冲（偶称 electrical impulse）

electrical Q (Q_E) 电损耗

electrical resistance 电阻（见 ohm）

electrical retractor （汽车乘员安全带的）电动收紧装置

electric A. I. R. pump （由电子控制模块控制的）二次空气喷射反应系统的电动空气泵（见 air injection reaction system）

electrical sarting 电起动（用电动机带动内燃机曲轴旋转起动）

electrical screwdriver （一般指用于电气系统的小）电动螺丝起子

electrical spanner （小型）电动开口扳手（一般指两端扳口尺寸相同的双头扳手，其中一个扳口与扳手柄成 15°角，而另一个与手柄成 60°角）

electrical system （汽车）电气系统（汽车上的全部电器装置、设备和线路的总称，但在美国有时不包括点火系，= electric grid）

electrical traction vehicle 电动汽车，电力牵引车

electrical-type windshield wiper 风窗玻璃电动刮水器

electrical unit 电单位，电力单位

electric analogue 电模拟

electric and hybrid vehicle 复合电动车，混合电源电动车，双动力电动汽车，(= electric/hybrid vehicle, 简称 hybrid vehicle。①指装有内燃机发电机组和蓄电池两种动力源的电动车。内燃机发电机组经常在经济工况区工作，当行驶阻力小时，发出的多余电能充入蓄电池，待加速、爬坡时使用。在城市行驶，可只用蓄电池作动力 ②指内燃机和电动机两套驱动系统的车辆）

electric arc 电弧

electric-assisted choke 电热式自动阻风门（亦写作 electric assist choke, 使用电加热装置，可缩短阻风门关闭时间，减少在起动和暖机时 CO 和 HC 的排放量）

Electric Auto Association ［美］电动汽车协会（简称 EAA）

electric automobile 电动轿车，电动车

electric balance ①平衡电桥，惠斯登电桥 ②电秤；电子天平

electric brake ①电磁制器（亦称 electromagnetic brake）②电磁缓速器 (= electromagnetic retarder) ③（电动机的）电磁制动电路（利用电磁感应原理，在电源切断后，使电动机立即停止转动的电路）

electric brake away switch （挂车）脱钩时制动电开关

electric brake shoe stripper （旧）制动蹄摩擦片电动剥刮机

electric brazing 电加热钎焊，电热

硬焊料钎焊，电热铜焊；硬质合金电钎焊

electric bulb 电灯泡

electric camion 电动重型载货汽车，电动军用载货汽车

electric capacity 电容（量）

electric cell 光电管

electric choke 电控阻风门

electric cigar lighter 电点烟器

electric circuit 电路（指用导线将电源与负载连接起来构成具有一定功能的电流回路）

electric circuit safety device 电路保护装置（指电路断电器、熔断丝盒等防止电路过负荷的装置的总称）

electric conductor 导（电）体

electric connector 电路接头，插头，插塞，插座，接线盒

electric coolant pump 电动冷却液泵

electric cooling fan 电动式冷却风扇（以蓄电池为电源由电动机驱动的冷却风扇，多用于小型发动机或皮带驱动难以布置的前轮驱动车横置式发动机等，由冷却水温控开关控制其电动机停、转）

electric current 电流（电荷在导体内的定向移动形成电流）

electric DC dynamometer 直流电力测功机

electric delivery van 送货电瓶车，送货蓄电池车，电动送货车

electric discharge machining 电火花加工（简称EDM）

electric door opener 电动开门装置

electric double layer capacitor 双层电容器型蓄电池（见EDLC）

electric double layer capacitor 双层型电容器（电容器正、负极板间由中央隔板隔为两层，每层有一活性炭板及电解质）

electric double layer capacitor type rechargeable battery 双层电容器可重复充电蓄电池（将两块各重46公斤、由129个双层型电容器串联而成的电容器型"蓄电池"串接在一起，其最高电压可达346V，电容量140.6F,能量容量583wh,使用寿命10年或500.000km,又可用作为电动机-柴油机复合动力中型货车的制动能量回收和电动机驱动蓄电系统）

electric dynamic brake ①电力式制动器（利用电涡流进行制动，通常作为一种辅助制动器供车辆下坡缓速等用）②电力测功用制动器

electric dynamometer 电力测功机（当发动机带动测功电机的电枢旋转时，摆动式电机定子线圈的磁力线与电枢中电流产生的磁力线，形成电磁力矩，驱使电机外壳摆动，测出外壳的摆动力矩，即为发动机的输出力矩，用以计算输出功率。发动机带动的电机为直流电机者，称为直流电力测功机 electric D. C. dynamometer, 电机为交流电机者，称为交流电力测功机 electric A. C. dynamometer)

electric eddy current retarder 电涡流缓速器

electric-electric 电控-电动的

electric engine ①电力动力装置 ②电池动力装置（指电动汽车使用的燃料电池、太阳能电池、蓄电池等动力装置）③电动机

electric eye 电眼，光电元件，光电池

electric field 电场（存在于电荷周围的，对其他电荷有力的作用的物质形式）

electric field effect 电场效应（指电场物质特性的作用和影响）

electric field intensity 电场强度（=electric field strength, 代号E, 电场内某一点的强度为单位电荷在该点所受的电场力，单位为伏/米，牛/库）

electric filter 滤波器

electric fleet 电动车队

electric heating safety glass 电加温安全玻璃（可通电加热去除表面冰霜的安全玻璃，见 safety glass）

electric horn 电喇叭（= klaxon, 指电磁线圈激励膜片振动产生音响的喇叭）

electric/hybrid vehicle 参见 electric and hybrid vehicle

electric-hydraulic 电控-液压的（指由电信号或电器件控制而由液压元器件执行的）

electric impact tool 电动冲击工具，电动冲击式扳手

electric induction fan 吸入式电风扇

electricity 电，电学，电力，电流，电荷

electric leakage 漏电

electric linear discharge circuit （扫描激光雷达测距系统中的）线性放电电路

electric load detector 电器负载检测器（精确测定汽车发动机各种设备所需电气负载的负载传感器）

electric magnetic 电磁的，电磁力的（指由电磁元器件控制、操纵、驱动、执行的）

electric mirror （通常指装在车门外，可从车内调节的）电动后视镜

electric moment 电（力）矩

electric motor/pump 电动机驱动(液压)泵（electric-motor-driven pump 的简称，多制成一个整体）

electric-motor type seat belt pretensioner 电动机型安全带预收紧装置（由电子控制模块根据传感器信息判断碰撞临近或已不可避免时发出指令由电动机收紧安全带，无爆炸噪声而且可以调控）

electric motor vehicle 电动汽车，电力驱动汽车（由自身装载的电能储存装置供能，由电动机驱动汽车的统称，见 electric vehicle, electric driven vehicle, electro-mobile, accumulator vehicle, battery driven vehicle）

electric noise 电干扰，电气（设备中发出的）噪声

electric parking brake 电动驻车制动器

electric polarity 电极性

electric pole 电极

electric power compensation control system 电力补偿控制系统

electric power consumption （电）功耗（稳态时，电器在其工作范围内所需用的最大电功率）

electric powerplant ①电气动力装置，电力驱动装置，电力装置 ②发电厂

electric power steering 电动式动力转向（使用电动机驱动液压泵或直接驱动转向机构的动力转向的总称，无特殊说明时，一般指后者）

electric power take-off 电功率输出轴

electric pulse 电脉冲

electric rear drive 后轮电（动机）驱动（在某些复合动力车中使用电动机驱动后轮来补充汽油机-电力复合前轮驱动系统 "gas-electric front-wheel-drive system" 的不足）

electric rearview mirror 电动后视镜

electric remote-control 电力遥控，远距离电控，电力远距离操纵

electric resistance manometer 电阻压力计

electric resistance pyrometer 电阻高温计

electric resistance welding 电阻焊，接触焊

electric resistivity 电阻率（单位横截面积，单位长度的物质的电阻）

electric retarder 见 electro magnetic retarder

electric rheologic fluid 电磁流变液体（见 electrorheologic fluid）

electric rot 电腐蚀

electrics 电动车辆（= electric vehicle）

electric service 电器维护

electric servo 电动伺服机构

electric shematic 电路图（表示电气系统的布置、元器件位置、线路及电流等的原理图，亦写作 electrical schematic）

electric shift 电动换挡

electric sign ①灯光路标 ②电信号

electric soldering 电软钎焊，电锡焊

electric spark 电火花（由于分隔两端子的空气或其他介质材料突然被击穿引起带有瞬间闪光的短暂放电现象，亦简称 spark）

electric speed （混合动力车的）纯电动机驱动工况下的车速

electric standard 电气标准

electric start valve 电控起动（喷油）阀

electric stepless transmission 电力无极传动

electric strength 耐电强度

electric sunroof （轿车的）电动天窗（亦称 sunshine roof，简称 ESR）

electric suspension control system 悬架电控系统（ESC）

electric suspension system 电控悬架系统（简称 ESS，见 electronic suspension system）

electric symbol 电路图中用来表示电器件的符号

electric tachometer 电动转速表

electric taxi 电动出租车（用蓄电池、燃料电池等作为动力）

electric taximeter 电动计程表

electric tension 电压

electric test vehicle 电动试验车辆（简称 ETV）

electric top [美] 电动（车身）活顶盖（= power hood，由电动机操纵收放）

electric traction 电力牵引

electric traction control （汽车）牵引力电控系统（见 electronic traction control）

electric transmission 电力传动

electric transportation 电动（汽车）运输（简称 ET）

electric travelling crane 移动式电动起重机，移动式电动吊车

electric-type vulcanizer 电热型硫化器，电热补胎机

electric upsetting machine 电动镦锻机（多用于棒料一端镦粗的预成形工序）

electric valve grinder 电动气门磨床，电动磨气门机

Electric Vehicle Association [英] 电动汽车协会（简称 EVA）

electric vehicle commercialization 电动汽车商品化（简称 EVC）

electric vehicle lift 汽车电动举升器

electric vehicle propulsion system 电动汽车驱动系统（所有在汽车上存储电能和使用电能为汽车提供动力的部件和装置及其控制系统的总称）

electric vulcaniser 电热硫化器

electric wave 电波

electric wheel 电动车轮（参见 motorized wheel）

electric window 电动窗（其玻璃的升降由装在车门内壁或中央控制板上的按钮操纵电动机实现，美称 power window）

electric windshiled wiper 风窗玻璃电动刮水器

electric wire terminal 电线接头

electric wiring ①电气线路，电路 ②电气线路的敷设

electrification 电气化，使用电力；充电装置；充电，发电，感电（见

electrization）

electrified body 带电体

electrified vehicle 电动汽车［简称 EV，分两大类①全电池动力汽车（full battery electric vehicle）②电池-燃油混合动力车（fuel-electric hybrid powered vehicle，简称 hybrid）］

electrify ①通电，供电，充电 ②使…电气化

electrion 高压放电

electrization 电气化，使用电力，充电，发电，起电（= electrification）

electroanalysis 电解分析

electro anti-lock device 电子防抱死装置（用微处理器控制、调节制动力，防止车轮在制动时抱死的装置）

electrobrightening 电抛光（一种反向的电解淀积法）

electrochem cycle 电化学周期（蓄电池放电充电一次所用的时间）

electrochemical cell (NO_x-reducing) reactor 电化电池（NO_x 还原）反应器

electrochemical concentration cell 电化学浓差电池（简称 ECC）

electrochemical corrosion 电化学腐蚀（指不纯的金属或合金接触电解质溶液所发生的原电池反应，较活泼的金属原子失去电子而被氧化所引起的腐蚀，是最常见的金属腐蚀形式）

electrochemical equivalent 电化（学）当量

electrochemical mechanical machining 电化学机械加工（简称 ECMM）

electrochromic display (device) 电致变色显示（装置）

electrocircuit 电路

electro-cladding ①电镀层包覆的 ②电镀层，电镀保护层

electrocoated body priming 车身电泳法涂底漆

electrocoating （车身）电泳涂漆；电泳涂装（见 electrophoretic plainting）

electroconductibility 导电性；电导系数，电导率（= electro conductivity）

electro-constant 电化常数

electro continuously variable transmission 电子控制式无级变速器（简称 ECVT，由电子计算机控制的电磁离合器和通过改变传动钢带轮的有效半径来改变传动比的钢带传动无级变速机构组成，可实现从起步到最高车速间的连续无级变速）

electrocure process 电子束固化法，电子束硬化（用电子束照射加速涂层等硬化的方法）

electrode ①电极 ②（线圈的）铁芯 ③（电焊的）焊条

electrode adjusting tool （火花塞）电极（间隙）调节工具（用于扳弯或板直火花塞өл电极，以调节其间隙，通常与火花塞间隙检测表制成一体）

electrode cement 电极胶合剂，补电极胶，电极黏结剂

electrode chamber （转子发动机）火花塞腔

electrode gap （火花塞）电极间隙（= sparkplug gap）

electrode holders 电极夹，电焊钳

electrode plate （贴在燃料电池阴、阳电极外侧的）电极板

electrodeposited coating 电解沉积层，电镀层

electrodeposition 电（解）沉积（利用电解方法电镀金属或电泳涂漆等的统称）

electrode separator 蓄电池极板的隔板（防止正、负极板相互接触而造成短路）

electrode spacing 电极间距

electrodynamic (al) 电动力学的，

电动的
electrodynamic retarder 见 electromagnetic retarder
electrodynamic shaker （汽车寿命试验等用）电动振动器，电动加振装置（亦称 electrodynamic vibrator）
electrodynamometer 电力测功机，电测力计，电测功计
electroencephalogram 脑电图
electroencephalography 脑电流示波器
electro-fluidic actuator （汽车各种自动控制系统的）电控液（气）动型执行机构，电控流体型执行器（如电控液压阀或气压阀等）
electrofluorescence 电致发光，场效发光（= electroluminescence）
electroforming 电铸，电成型，电沉积
electrogalvanising ①电解镀锌 ②电镀
electrograph 电记录器，示波器；电刻器，电版机；电传照相（机），传真电报（机）；X 光照相
electrogyro ①电动陀螺（仪）②电子控制储能飞轮（由电子模块控制机械飞轮存储动力系统多余的能量，并在车辆需要时反输给驱动系统）
electro-heated catalyst converter 电加热型催化器（一种发动机冷起动时，电加热催化转化器，使催化器很快达到工作温度，简称 EHC）
electro heated oxygen sensor 见 heated oxygen sensor
electrohydraulic actuator 电控液压执行元件，电控液压执行器
electrohydraulic booster 电控液压助力器
electro-hydraulic controller 电（控）液（压）控制器
electrohydraulic forming 电水锤成型，水中放电成型（将储存的电能在水中放出，使产生冲击波而将工件压入模中）
electro-hydraulic limited-slip coupling 电控液压式防滑联轴节
electro-hydraulic power steering 电动-液压动力转向系统（其转向助力液压泵不是由发动机带动，而是专门的电动机驱动的车速响应式动力转向。电动机转向助力液压不受发动机转速与工况限制。高速时可产生手动转向的手感，低速时转向操作力十分轻快）
electrohydraulic pulse motor 电控液压脉动马达
electrohydraulic regulator 电控液压调节器
electrohydraulic servo valve 电控液压伺服阀
electrohydraulic shaker 电控-液压振动器
electrohydraulic suspension pressure control system 电子控制液压悬架的压力控制系统（由按照电子控制模块的指令，主动控制执行器液压和执行器液压因路面输入而产生波动时，对柱塞位移实现波动反馈控制的液压控制阀"pressure control valve"和执行器，即液力减振器组成）
electrohydraulic valve 电控液压阀
electro-hydraulic valve actuator 电控-液压式气门开闭执行机构（取代凸轮轴系统，用于无凸轮式发动机）
electrohydrodynamics instability （液晶的）电流体力学不稳定性（因电导率和介电常数的各向异性，一定强度的电场使液晶分子微扰不断增大的现象）
electro-hypress greaser 电动高压润滑装置
electro-illumination 电气照明
electro-induction 电感应（的）
electro-ionization 电离（作用）

electrokinetic potential　电动势
electrokinetics　电动力学
electrokymograph　电动转筒记录仪
electroless plating　化学镀（非电镀）
electrolines　电（场）力线
electrolock　电锁
electroluminescence　场致发光（将电场引至一介电的荧光物质而发光），电荧光，电致发光（= electrofluorescence）
electroluminescence display　①场致发光显示 ②场致发光显示板（亦写作 electroluminescent displays，简称 ELDs）
electroluminescent　场致发光的，电致发光的
electrolyser　电解槽，电解池，电解装置
electrolysis　电解，电解作用（指电流通过电解质溶液或熔化状态的电解质，使阴、阳两极发生氧化-还原反应的过程，即将电能转化为化学能的过程）
electrolysis liquid　电解液（= electrolyte）
electrolyte　①电解质（指在水溶液内或熔化状态下能导电的化合物）②电解液（电解质的水溶液）③（特指）（蓄电池）电解液，电液（= accumulator acid, battery acid, battery liquid）
electrolyte cooler　电解液冷却器
electrolyte pump　电解液泵
electrolyte tester　（蓄电池）电解液（浓度）测定仪（检测电解液浓度，从而测定其放电程度的装置）
electrolytic（al）　①电解的 ②电解质的
electrolytic bath　电解槽（亦称 electrolytic cell，由盛电解液的槽体和浸入电解液内的电极组成，通电时，完成电解作业）
electrolytic capacitor　电解质电容器（= electrolytic condenser）

electrolytic conduction　电解质电导率
electrolytic corrosion　电（解）腐蚀（简称 EC）
electrolytic deposition　见 electroplating
electrolytic dissociation　电离（作用），电解（作用）
electrolytic etching　电解浸蚀法
electrolytic galvanizing　见 electrogalvanizing
electrolytic grinding　电解磨削
electrolytic ion　（电解）离子
electrolytic isolation　电解分离，电解
electrolytic machining　电解加工（工件接直流电源正极，工具接直流电源负极。在工件和工具之间保持着 0.1~0.8mm 的间隙，其中有高速电解液通过。两电极之间通以低电压、大电流，工件表面与电解液接触处由于电化学反应发生溶解，溶解物被高速流动的电解液带走）
electrolytic phosphating process　电解镀磷法
electrolytic polarization　电解质极化（作用）
electrolytic polishing　电解抛光（将金属件置于特定的溶液中阳极腐蚀，形成光滑表面）
electrolytic protection　见 cathodic protection
electrolytics　电（解）化学，（水溶液的）电解学
electrolytic solution　电解液
electromachining　电加工
electromagnet　电磁铁，电磁体（代号 Mg）
electromagnet bearing　电磁轴承，电磁支撑
electromagnet core　电磁铁芯
electromagnetic actuator　电磁感应型执行机构（如：变压线圈、点火线圈等）
electromagnetic（al）field　电磁场

electromagnetic (al) gear 电磁传动机构，电磁联轴节

electromagnetically-operated 电磁控制的，电磁驱动的，电磁操纵的

electromagnetic (al) speed sensor 电磁式转速传感器

electromagnetic braking system 电磁制动系（指通过电能转化为电磁作用而使制动器动作的制动系）

electromagnetic clutch 电磁离合器（泛指任一种利用电磁力接合的离合器，如：空调系压缩机的离合器）

electromagnetic compatibility （电子设备对汽车等）电磁环境的适应性，电磁环境相容性（指汽车电气－电子系统对外电磁场干扰的适应度、耐抗度，简称 EMC）

electromagnetic control 电磁操纵，电磁控制

electromagnetic core 电磁铁芯（与线圈配合产生磁力的导磁零件，通常为线圈所包围）

electromagnetic environment （汽车的）电磁环境（指汽车范围内电场的强度）

electromagnetic environmental simulator 电磁环境模拟装置，电磁环境模拟室

electromagnetic flow meter 电磁流量计

electromagnetic fluid 电磁流体（简称 magnetic fluid，亦称 electric conducting fluid，指具有导电性的流体）

electromagnetic force 电磁力

electromagnetic fuel indicator 电磁式燃油指示表

electromagnetic fuel pump 电磁式燃油泵（一般指利用电磁铁与触点组合使柱塞往复运动而将燃油箱内的燃料泵出的燃油泵）

electromagnetic ignition 电磁点火

electromagnetic induced current 电磁感应（产生的）感生电流［注意区别于产生感生电动势的施感电流（inducing current）］

electromagnetic induction 电磁感应（闭合电路的一部分导体在磁场内做切割磁力线的运动时，导体中便会产生电流，这种现象叫电磁感应）

electromagnetic injector 电磁（控制）式喷油器（常用于汽油喷射发动机）

electromagnetic oil pressure indicator 电磁式（机）油压（力）表指示器（利用动铁芯与带电流的固定线圈之间的作用力而指示机油压力的指示器）

electromagnetic pickup 电磁式传感器

electromagnetic power brake 磁粉电磁制动器

electromagnetic radiation 电磁辐射

electromagnetic radiations emission 电磁有害辐射，有害电磁辐射

electromagnetic regulator 电磁（振动式）调节器（指通过触点开闭控制发电机电压的装置，亦称 vibrating type regulator）

electromagnetic retarder 电磁缓速器（电磁辅助制动器，利用旋转金属盘在磁场作用产生电涡流、磁滞等作用，吸收动能获得缓速效果的辅助制动装置，简称 electrodynamic retarder，亦称 electric retarder，偶见称 electric brake）

electromagnetic sensor 电磁传感器（利用电磁感应传感信息的元件）

electromagnetic shaker 电磁振动器

electromagnetic step motor 电磁步进电动机（由脉冲信号控制做步进运动的电动机）

electromagnetic switch core 电磁开关铁芯

electromagnetic temperature indicator 电磁式温度指示器（利用动铁芯与带电流的固定线圈之间的作用力而指示温度的指示器）

electromagnetic unit 电磁单位

electromagnetic valve 电磁阀（利用电磁力开启或关闭的阀）

electromagnetic variable cam phase mechanism （电磁式）可变凸轮相位机构

electromagnetic wave generator ①电磁波发生器（产生电磁波装置的统称）②（谐波齿轮的）电磁式波发生器（利用电力使柔轮齿圈产生变形波的波发生器，见 wave generator）

electro magnetism 电磁学

electromatic 电气自动的，电气自动式

electromechanic(al) 电动机械的

electromechanical actuator （汽车各种自动控制系统的）电控机械式执行机构，电控机械式执行器

electromechanical amplifier 电气机械放大器，电信号机械放大器

electromechanical analog computer 机电模拟计算机

electromechanical brake 电控机械式制动器

electromechanical flywheel 电动机械飞轮（由电动机通过机械传动带动的储能飞轮，可作为混合动力车的储能系统之一，其电动机电源来自发动机驱动的发电机或再生制动）

electromechanical parking brake 电动机械式驻车制动器

electromechanical power split device （全轮驱动汽车前、后轮的）电子控制机械型（如：电子控制的行星齿轮系）动力分配装置

electromechanical sensor 机电式传感器（如：安全气囊的惯性钢球触点式碰撞传感器，利用机械式惯性作用接通触点发生电信号）

electromechanical speed-sensitive power steering 电子控制机械式车速感应型动力转向（转向助力的大小与车速成反比）

electromechanics 机电学

electrometric(al) 电测量的，电测的

electrometric method 电测量法（如：用应变片、应变仪等来测车架的应力）

electro-mobile 电动车辆（参见 electric motor car）

electromotance 电动势

electromotive ①电动的②电动势的

electromotive force （电源的）电动势（符号为 E. 简称 e. m. f. 或 EMF，电源的电动势未接入电路时等于其两极间的电压，在闭合电路中等于内电压与外电压即路端电压之和）

electromotive vehicle 电动汽车，电驱动车辆，蓄电池汽车

electromotor 电动机

electro multivision 电子多图像系统（指通过各种图像实现与驾驶员和乘客通信的车载信息显示系统）

electron ①电子②电子合金（德国研制成的镁基铝合金的总称，较一般铝合金轻而强度高，在美国亦称 Dow metal）

electron carrier 电子载流子

electron current 电子流，电流（指自由电子在电场力作用下在导体内的定向移动，从而形成电流，但自由电子的移动方向与电流的方向相反，亦称 electron flow）

electronhole pair 电子空穴偶；电子空穴对

electronic acceleration sensor 电子加速度传感器

electronic active suspension 电子控制主动式悬架（见 eActive 3）

Electronic Active Torque-split 4WD （富士重工研制的）电子控制主动

转矩分配四轮驱动（系统）（商品名，在其电子控制式自动变速器后装有一个简称"MP-T"的电子控制多片式分动器，将驱动转矩分配给前、后车轮）

electronic aerosol analyser （柴油机排烟测定用的）悬浮微粒电子分析仪（使排气中的颗粒物带电而利用电阻变化测定粒度分布的仪器，亦写作 electronic aerosol analyzer）

electronic air control valve 电子控制空气控制阀（见 EAC valve）

electronic air suspension 电子控制式空气悬架系统（丰田公司研制的一种空气悬架系统的商品名，由传感器不断地检测车轮的上、下跳动状况，以实时调控空气弹簧的减振特性，使之始终处于最佳状态，提高乘坐舒适性）

electronically controlled and hydraulically operated by-wire brake system 电子控制、液压驱动、线控式制动系统

electronically controlled gasoline injection 电控汽油喷射（日本五十铃和日产）电子控制汽油喷射系统（的商品名，五十铃简称 ECGI，日产简称 EGI）

electronically controlled hydraulic solenoid 电子控制液压电磁阀

electronically controlled power steering 电子控制动力转向（可分为全液压式"full hydraulic"，全电力式"full electric"和混合式"hybrid"三大类）

electronic(ally)(fuel) controlled injection 电（子）控（制）燃油喷射［简称 ECI，20 世纪 70 年代开始用于汽油机，以后亦用于柴油机。由 PCM（power train control module 的简称）"动力控制模块"根据反映发动机和汽车工况的各种传感器的信息，指令喷油器将最佳数量的燃油在最佳喷油时刻或喷至各缸进气口处，或直接喷入缸内，或喷至发动机的进气歧管的节气门体内等］

electronically synchronized transmission assembly 电子控制同步变速器总成（换挡时，可控制离合器的分离、接合和变速器的同步装置，保证汽车平稳起步和换挡，发动机怠速运转时，使离合器自动分离，避免强制怠速工况的电子控制式机械变速器）

electronic analog display （汽车仪表的）电子模拟显示（指由电子系统传感与处理的结果由传统的模拟量显示方式来显示，以满足喜爱模拟式显示仪表用户的要求）

electronic "auto cruise" system （汽车）电子控制定速巡行系统（见 cruise electronic automatic transmission）

electronic automatic transmission 电子自动变速器（简称 EAT，车速和节气门开度等作为输入信号，经电子控制模块处理，向电磁阀发出变速指令，由电磁阀控制其离合器和制动器的液压回路，实现变速的自动变速器）

electronic brain 电脑（电子计算机，= electronic computer）

electronic brake and traction control (system) 电子制动力-牵引力控制（系统）（由电子控制模块控制车辆的制动力和驱动力，以防止车辆制动力过大车轮抱死或加速时牵引力过大车轮原地滑转的系统，简称 EBTC system，该系统的控制模块称 EBTC module 或 EBTCM）

electronic brake control module 制动（系统）电子控制模块（简称 EBCM）

electronic brake force distribution (system) （四轮）电子控制制动

力分配系统（由电子控制模块根据道路条件和制动减速度等，对前、后、左、右四个车轮的制动力作最佳单独控制与分配，简称 EBD）

electronic brake system　（重型车辆的）电子控制制动系统（简称 EBS，通常指重型运输车辆或特种车辆的电子控制制动系，见 brake by wire）

electronic bridge　（车身模型尺寸数据等的）电子测量桥

electronic building brick　积木式电子组件

electronic car　电子汽车（指大量使用电子控制装置的汽车）

electronic charging system　（高速公路用）电子收费系统（先进的电子自动收费系统，可在车道上的汽车不减速的条件下，自动记录通行时刻、通行里程，由银行结算通行费用）

electronic circuit　电子电路（一般指有电子元件的电路，参见 electric circuit）

electronic climate control　电子环境控制（指对汽车车内温、湿度等的控制，简称 ECC）

electronic collection of tolls on roads and bridges　路桥电子收费系统（ITS 的一个子系统）

electronic commutation motor　电子换向式电动机（使用电子换向器的电动机）

electronic commutator　电子换向器（交流电机用电子电路换向器，代替常规的电刷式换向器）

Electronic Concentrated Engine Control System　电子计算机发动机集中控制系统，发动机电子集中控制系统（用微型电子计算机集中控制汽油喷射、点火、废气回流、怠速排放等，因而得名，简称 ECECS，亦称 Engine concentrated control system，简称 ECCS）

Electronic Control Assembly　电子控制组件（福特公司对其动力系统电子控制模块的旧称，简称 ECA。美国政府规定 1995 年后，各厂均必须用 Powertrain Control module，简称 PCM，代替各厂家形形色色的商品名，我国译为"动力控制模块"或直接引用英文 PCM）

electronic controlled diesel　电子控制式柴油机［简称 ECD，指使用各种传感器测定发动机的工况（转速、节气门开度、进气空气压力、水温等），由电子控制模块对喷油（量）和燃油喷射时刻等作综合性控制，使发动机在最佳状态下工作的柴油机系统］

electronic controlled EGR system　电子控制式 EGR 系统，（根据发动机的运转工况，利用电子控制系统来控制再循环排气量的 EGR 系统）

electronic-controlled ignition system　电子控制点火系统

electronic controlled injection-multi　电子控制多点式燃油喷射（简称 ECI-multi，指每缸一个喷嘴的喷射系统）

electronic con trolled injection turbo　电（子）控（制）燃油喷射涡轮增压（发动机）

electronic-controlled leveling system　电子控制车身高度调平系统

electronic controlled suspention　电子控制式悬架（一般指由电子控制模块根据汽车行驶和载荷状况主动地控制与调节阻尼特性，即其：减振器或各类弹性元件的阻尼特性可变式悬架系统）

electronic-controlled test rack　电子控制试验台

electronic controlled transmission　电子控制式变速器（简称 ECT，为 EAT 的改良和发展型）

electronic control module 见 ECM ②

electronic control package 电子控制装置

electronic control unit 电子控制装置（简称 ECU，在美国政府规定按 SAE 的推荐使用 ECM 术语前，一些厂家对电子控制系统的车载电子计算机的称呼，见 PCM）

electronic data interchange system 电子信息交换系统，电子数据交换系统（简称 EDIS）

electronic data processing 电子数据处理

electronic diagnosis engine tester 电子发动机测试诊断仪，发动机电子故障分析仪（运用电子技术、计算机技术制成的发动机性能检测和故障诊断设备，= electronic engine analyzer）

electronic diesel injection control system 电子控制柴油机喷射装置（简称 EDIC）

electronic differential lock 电子差速锁（简称 EDL）

electronic differential locking system 电子控制差速器锁止系统（简称 EDL）

electronic distributorless ignition system 电子控制式无分电器式点火系统（简称 EDIS，见 EIS）

electronic 3-D model （设计阶段使用的）电子三维模型，计算机三维模型

electronic driver （无人驾驶车辆的）电子驾驶装置

electronic dual fuel cut 电子控制双燃油切换装置（简称 EDFC ①指柴油/天然气等双燃料发动机，两种燃料供给系统的电子控制切换装置 ②指可以切断两组不同缸数燃油供给的系统）

electronic dual valve speed-sensitive power steering 电子控制双阀车速感应式动力转向（其转向助力随车速而变，特点是使用两个液压阀，因而可使汽车在很宽的速度范围内获得最佳动力转向特性）

electronic EGR 电子控制式 EGR（见 linear EGR）

electronic-electric control system （四轮转向系统的）电子-电气控制系统（指由电子控制模块发出四轮转向指令，而由电动执行机构执行的四轮转向的系统，亦称全电动四轮转向系统 full-electric 4ws system）

electronic-electric control 4WS system 电子（控制）-电动四轮转向系统（由电子控制模块根据车速，前轮转向角和转向盘转动角速度等有关传感器的信息，控制一台步进电动机旋转量和旋转方向，并将电动机的旋转运动转变为推动车轮转向的直线运动，或者控制一台电磁型车轮转向执行器 "wheel steering electric actuator" 直接推动车轮按所规定的方向和角度转向。这类系统一般都可以同时保证汽车低速行驶时转向半径最小和高速行驶转向时的稳定性，以及对快速转动转向盘时的良好转向响应性）

electronic engine analyzer 发动机电子分析仪（电子控制的发动机测试设备，可测定发动机的转速、火花电压、点火正时、触点闭合角、真空度和废气成分等多项技术指标）

electronic engine control （福特车的）发动机电子控制系统（的商品名，由计算机对三元催化净化、汽油喷射、废气再循环量、点火时刻、发动机爆燃等进行综合控制的系统，简称 EEC。EEC 后面用罗马数字表示该系统属第几代产品，如：EECII 为装于 1979 年型部分福特车上的第二代发动机电子控制系统）

electronic engine cooling system 电子

控制发动机冷却系统

electronic engine management system 发动机电子管理系统（简称 EEM system，为某些厂家对点火、EGR、燃油喷射、定速巡航等发动机综合电子控制系统）

electronic espionage equipment 电子侦察设备

electronic fare payment system 电子支付系统，电子付费系统（ITS 的一个子系统，公路不停车电子收费系统中汽车的付费系统）

electronic foot pedal assembly 电子踏板系统［无机械传动杆系，仅使用电线将与踏板行程成正比的电位计（可变电阻）输出的电压信号传送给电子控制模块，简称 EFP assembly 或 EFPA］

electronic fuel injection ①（汽油机）电子控制喷油（系统的通称，简称 EFI 或 EFi。依据发动机转速、负荷、冷却水温、进气温度、排气成分等信号，运用电子控制系统控制喷油量、喷油时刻的喷油系统）②通用公司等早期的节气门体单点喷射系统"throttle body injection"的商品名，一般用其简称 EFI 或 TBI ③Cadillac 公司 20 世纪 80 年代使用的 Bendix 专利、专用模拟计算机控制的燃油喷射系统，也叫名，亦简称 EFI，以后为其 DFI（digital fuel injection 数字燃油喷射的简称）所取代 ④美国政府规定从 1993 年起一律用 SAEJ1930 推荐的 MFI 和 SFI 取代 EFI 和 PFI，见 MFI 和 SFI

electronic fuel injection-Druek 进气压力计量型电子控制汽油喷射系统（见 EFI-D）

electronic fuel injection Luft 进气空气质量计量型电子控制汽油喷射系统（简称 EFI-L，其中 L 为德文 Luft 的第一个字母，该系统使用空气流量计直接测定进气空气质量流量，并按此时发动机的转速，算出每一循环的汽油喷射量）

electronic fuel injection time 电子燃油喷射时间（指开始喷油到截止喷油时间）

electronic fuel-management system （克莱斯勒公司 1981 年轿车上使用的）电子燃油管理系统（商品名，用以代替化油器的电子控制供油系统，简称 EFMS）

electronic fuel metering system 电子燃油计量装置，电控燃油计量系统（一般电控燃油喷射系统都包括计量与控制系统，简称 EFM 系统）

electronic gas flowmeter ①电子气体流量计 ②电子汽油流量计

electronic gear-change control system 电子控制变速系统

electronic governor （柴油机的）电子调速器

electronic horn 电子喇叭

electronic-hydraulic automatic control system 电控液压式自动换挡系统（电脑依据车速、发动机负荷等信号，按预定的规律，选择换挡时刻，并向电磁阀发出换挡信号。其换挡的执行机构，仍为一般液压式）

electronic-hydraulic control system 电子液压控制系统（指由电子控制模块发出控制指令，而由液压装置执行指令的控制系统）

electronic-hydraulic control 4WS system 电子-液压控制四轮转向系统

electronic -hydraulic-mechanical (control) system 电子-液压-机械控制系统（指由电子控制模块发出指令，液压系统产生控制动力驱动机械系统执行指令的控制系统）

electronic-hydraulic-mechanism type 4WS system 电子液压机械式四轮转向系统（如：由提供转向助力的

液压系统和电子控制后轮转向方向及角度的步进电机转向相位控制系统"phase control system"两部分组成的四轮转向系统)

electronic idle-speed stabilizer （发动机）电子怠速稳定器

electronic ignition system 电子点火系统（按美国政府规定，以1995年1月起，分电器式电子点火系一律按SAEJ1930的规定，称电子点火系统"electronic ignition system"，简称EI system，而有分电器的电子点火系统，一律称distributor ignition system，简称DI system)

electronic instrument cluster 组合式电子仪表

electronic keyless entry 电子无钥匙自动车门锁（不用车门钥匙，而由电子系统遥控开、关车门)

electronic lean-burn system 电子控制稀燃系统（电子控制模块根据大气温度、节气门开度、冷却水温、发动机转速等变化参数，由电子电路自动控制燃烧稀混合气汽油机的点火时刻等，以达到节油和排气净化的目的)

electronic leveling control system （汽车）电子车身高度调平控制系统（由电子控制模块根据车身前、后高度传感器等的信息发出高度控制指令，而由执行机构通过前后油、气悬架将车身与地面的距离保持在恒定或最佳范围内，简称ELC system或ELCs)

electronic mail system 电子邮件系统

electronic management system （发动机）电子管理系统（简称EMS，某些厂家对发动机电子燃油喷射、电子点火、电控怠速、电控冷却系统等的统一电子控制系统的称谓，=engine electronic center)

electronic map 电子地图（汽车电子导行系统中的一部分，参见electronic navigation system)

electronic mirror 电子控制式防炫后视镜（夜间后方追随车的强烈灯光照射时，后视镜能自动转动角度，以免驾驶员目眩)

electronic navigation system （汽车的）电子导行装置，电子导航系统[早期的电子导航系统由车载计算机根据车速、行驶方向变化等信息算出车辆的位置，配合地图引导行驶方向。近年已来采用GPS（全球定位系统）导航系统，根据卫星信号算出车辆准确的经纬度，速度和方向，通过电子地图，向驾驶员提供导航信息]

electronic navigator （汽车的）电子导行器，电子导航器（指电子导航系统中的微处理单元，即电子控制模块，亦称trip computer)

electronic odometer （汽车的）电子车速里程表

electronic performance control 电子加速踏板控制器（简称EPC，当发动机转矩过大，车轮产生原地滑转时，控制加速踏板的位置)

electronic pressure-control solenoid valve （控制自动变速器内液压的）电子调压电磁阀（简称EPC solenoid valve，亦称variable force solenoid valve，简称VFS)

electronic production definition techniques （产品设计阶段的）电子计算机生产装配技术（根据计算机确定的产品及其全部组件的三维模型，研究该产品的装配方法、每一装配作业所需的空间及生产线旁所需的配件储备，并确定其生产效率、安全等的要求，简称EPD techniques)

Electronic Products Corporation [美]电子产品公司（简称EPC)

electronic programmed engine control 发动机电子程序控制（简称EPEC)

electronic programmed（或 **programming**）**spark timing** 电子程控点火正时（简称 EPST）

electronic regulator 电子电压调节器（由齐纳二极管或其他半导体器体控制的电压调节装置）

electronic revolution pulser （第五车轮等的）电子转数脉冲发生器

electronic ride control （汽车的）行驶平顺性电子控制系统（指由电子控制模块根据路面、载荷和行驶工况自动选择最佳阻尼特性的空气悬架式油气悬架控制系统）

electronic road-conditions senr 电子路况传感器

electronic road pricing 道路通行费自动征缴，道路自动收费系统（简称 ERP，指汽车缴纳道路通行费不必停车，不与收费者直接接触，而是在车辆通过时，由车辆自动识别系统，根据车辆总重定价，由中央电算中心，定期结算征缴）

electronic rotary type height sensor 电子旋转式高度传感器［用于测定汽车行驶时车轮相对车身垂直运动（下沉和反跳）的距离和速度］

electronic route guidance system （汽车）路线电子引导系统，电子导行系统（简称 ERGS，由美国运输部于 20 世纪 60 年代末提出，进行了小规模试验，以后又提出智能公路系统，发展到 20 世纪 90 年代的智能汽车运输系统，参见 IVHS、ITS）

electronics 电子学，电子仪器，电子设备，电子线路

electronic scales 电子秤

electronic-scan millimeter-wave radar 电子扫描微波雷达

electronic scanner ①电子扫描器 ②电子控制器 ③（汽车用）电子译码器

electronic screen 电子荧光屏

electronics data exchange system 电子数据交换系统

electronic servo 电子伺服系统，电子随动装置

electronic signpost 电子（交通）标志杆

electronic simulation 电子模拟

electronic simulator 电子模拟装置

electronic skid control 电子防滑控制（见 ESC）

electronic sound-insulation system （汽车客厢）电子隔声系统（由电子控制模块对车内所有的噪声进行分析，然后利用电子发声装置发出与噪声相位相反、波幅相同的声波，抵消噪声）

electronic spark advance 电子点火提前装置（由电子控制模块根据传感器输入的发动机转速、进入发动机的空气量、冷却水温等信号，选择预先存储在计算机内的适合发动机各种工况的最佳点火提前时刻，向点火器发出点火指令）

electronic spark control 电子点火控制（系统）（为通用公司 CCC 系统的一个子系统，它具有自己独立的控制模块，配合 CCC 的 ECM 工作，确定点火正时，因而亦称 electronic spark timing，当产生爆振时推迟点火时刻，简称 ESC。通用公司以后的一些系统也沿用此名）

electronic spark timing 电子点火正时（简称 EST，见 electronic spark control）

electronic speedometer 电子车速里程表

electronic speed-sensitive 4 wheel steering system 电子控制车速感应式 4 轮转向系（在低速区，即当车速低于某一规定值，如：35km/h 时，前、后轮转向方向相反，而在高速区，即高于上述规定值时，前、后轮转向方向相同）

electronics rear view mirror （汽车）

电子后视镜

electronic stability control system 见 ESC system

electronic starter repeat relay 电子控制起动机重复起动继电器

electronic steering 电子转向（系统）（根据转向盘操纵力传感器测得的驾驶员的操舵力的大小及方向，电子控制模块控制小型电动机驱动转向机等实现车辆转向的系统）

electronic stethoscope 电子听诊器

electronic suspension 电子控制式悬架（由电子控制模块根据车速传感器、转向盘转角传感器、制动踏板传感器和车身高度传感器等的输入信号，确定车辆的行驶状态和路面的变化，对车辆姿势和车身高度作最佳控制。车身高度通过电磁阀调整支撑车架、车身的空气弹簧的内压来控制，车身姿势通过装在空气弹簧上部的执行器增、减或开、闭减振器节流孔的通过面积来控制）

electronic suspension levelling system 电控悬架高度自动调平系统（简称ESLS）

electronic suspension system 电子控制悬架系统（简称ESS，电子控制车身高度调平系统 leveling system，自适应悬架系统 adaptive suspension system 及主动悬架系统 active suspension system 等的通称）

electronic switching system 电子开关系统（汽车上的一种简化配线系统，利用一根导线，采用时间分隔或频率分隔多路传输方式，按照一定顺序传送各种信号，简称ESS）

electronic tachometer 电子转速表（利用点火系统的脉冲信号或转速传感器工作的转速表工作）

electronic tag 电子标签（可装在汽车车窗上，发射出汽车本身特征信息码）

electronic throttle body injection （汽油机）电子节气门体燃油喷射（简称ETBJ）

electronic throttle control system-intelligent （日本本田公司）智能型电子节气门控制系统（商品名，简称ECTSi）

electronic ticketing system 电子售票系统

electronic time & alarm control system 见 ETACS

Electronic Time and Alarm Control System 电子定时与警报装置集中控制系统（见ETACS）

electronic toll and traffic management system 电子收费与交通管理系统（简称ETTM系统）

electronic toll collection systems （通行费）电子收费系统（简称ETCS，指高等级公路上，不停车收取通行费用的系统，为ATMS的子系统）

electronic torque split four-wheel drive system 电子控制转矩分配型四轮驱动系统

electronic traction control 电子牵引力控制（系统）（当传感元件测出因牵引力大于路面附着力而导致车轮原地滑转时，通过制动、降低发动机输出功率等减少车轮转矩等方法控制车轮滑转的系统，简称ETC）

electronic transmission control 电子变速控制（简称ETC，指控制自动变速器的系统或模块）

electronic trigger lug （无触点式点火系的）电子点火信号发生装置的转子凸齿或遮光片

electronic trigging 电子触发（如：点火线圈初级电路的半导体开关电路断开而在次级触发高压脉冲）

electronic tuning radio （车用）电子调谐式收音机

electronic valve ①电子管 ②电磁阀

electronic variable response turbo-

charging （柴油机的）电子控制可变响应涡轮增压充气系统

electronic variable shock absorber 电子（阻尼特性）可调式减振器（简称 EVSA）

Electronic Vehicle Associates ［美］电子汽车协会（简称 EVA）

electronic (vehicle) information center （汽车）电子信息中心［简称 E-(V)IC, 指由电子控制模块通过仪表板上的组合式电子仪表或风窗玻璃投影的抬头显示方式 HUD 向驾驶者提供：发动机温度、燃油量、各种警报信号、行驶距离、车速、油耗、车内外温度、剩余燃油可行驶里程等多种信息的电子系统的通称，源于某些公司产品的商品名］

electronic vehicle-location 车辆电子定位（由电子控制模块根据车速、转向、滑移等信息或卫星定位系统的信息，确定车辆的方位）

electronic wiper timing device 刮水电子定时装置

electron-mechanical package 电子-机械组件（指电子控制模块与电控机械执行机构等组装成一体的总成件，如：某些自动变速器中电子控制模块与电控液压换挡机构组成一体的总成件）

electron microscope 电子显微镜（简称 EM）

electron optics 电子光学，电（场）光学

electron ray 电子束，电子射线，电磁波

electron steering ①电子控制，电子操纵 ②电子转向

electron tube 电子管，真空管

electro-oculogram 眼球运动电位测定法，眼电图（简称 EOG）

electro-optical 电致发光的

electro-optical effect 电光效应（物质在电场作用下，光学特性发生变化的现象）

electro-optical signal 电-光信号（如：发光二极管等产生的电致发光信号）

electro-optical tubes 电（子）光（学）管（阴极射线管、电视显像管等的统称）

electropainting 见 electrophoretic painting

electropaint tank 电泳（涂装）槽，电泳（涂装）箱

electropercussive welding 冲击电焊

electrophoresis 电泳（现象）（胶体微粒在电场的作用下，在液体中的运动，正基组到阴极、负基组到阳极的现象，亦称 cataphoresis）

electrophoretic 电泳的

electrophoretic body-paint line 车身电泳涂装生产线，车身电涂工艺线

electrophoretic coating 电泳涂装［简称 electrocoating, = electrophoretic painting。又称 electrophoretic painting 一般指应用电泳过程给车身涂底漆，参见 electrophoresis。将清洁好待涂装车身金属部件或车身浸入盛有液态涂料的电泳槽中，待涂装件接负极（或正极）泳槽接正极（或负极），通电后在电场作用下，带正电（或负电）的涂料微粒便被吸附于呈负（或正）极性的涂装件上。其中，待涂装件接负极，因而带正电的涂料微粒吸附于呈负极性的工件者称为阴极电泳涂装 cathodic electropainting，而工件接正极，带负电的涂料微粒吸附于呈正极性的工件者称为阳极电泳涂装 anode electropainting］

electrophoretic primer 电泳涂装的底漆（层）

electro picker 电子开锁器

electroplate ①电镀 ②电镀品

electroplated coating 电镀层，电镀

覆盖层

electroplating 电镀（指应用电解原理在金属表面镀上一薄层某种金属或合金的过程，电镀时，镀件作阴极，施镀金属作阳极，共同浸入含有镀层金属离子的溶液-电解液中，接通直流电后，产生电解过程，作为阴极的镀件上便沉积一层阳极金属）

electropneumatic 电控气动的（简称EP，指用电信号操纵磁阀等控制气动执行机构完成某项操作或实现某项功能的）

electropneumatic actuator 电控气动执行器

electropneumatic horn 电动气喇叭（指由小型电动机驱动产生压缩空气的气喇叭，亦称compressor-operated air horn）

electropolarized 电（致）极化的

electropolish 电（解）抛光

electropositive 正电性的，阳电性的；金属的，盐基性的

electroprimer ①（静）电底漆涂覆装置 ②电动加油装置

electroprobe （试）电笔，电测针

electropyrometer 电阻高温计

electroresponse 电响应

electrorheological effect 电磁流变效应（通过在液体介质中极化的悬浮微粒可随电场方向及电量的变化而改变液体的黏度，从自由流动到完全固化，反应时间以 ms 计）

electrorheological fluid 电流变型流体（指悬浮有大量带极性的微粒、可产生电流变效应的液体。通过控制电场方向，可使其黏度在"自由流动"和"固态"间变化）

electrorheological valve 电磁流变阀（利用场致流变效应的电控阀门，用于液压系统）

electro-servo control 电动伺服控制（机构）

electro-slag welding 电渣焊

electrospark machining 电火花加工（利用电火花放电产生的高温对工件进行的刻蚀加工，简称electrosparking）

electrostatic actuator 静电式执行器式（利用磁致伸缩现象"magnetostriction"将电磁场能量转变为机械驱动力的微型执行器件）

electrostatic adherence 静电吸附

electrostatic coating 静电涂装

electrostatic deposition 静电镀覆，静电涂覆，静电沉积

electrostatic filter （粉尘，异味等的）静电过滤器

electrostatic micromotor 静电微型电动机

electrostatic painting 见 electrostatic spraying

electrostatic powder coating 静电粉末弥散涂装法（车身壳体的外面板件用粉末弥散法涂装，而凹腔处用阴极电泳法涂装）

electrostatic precipitator 静电沉淀器，静电滤尘器，静电除尘器

electrostatics 静电学

electrostatic spraying 静电喷涂（=electrostatic painting，指利用高压电场的作用，使从喷枪喷向工件的漆雾微粒带电并在电场力作用下迅速移向带异种电荷工件的表面而形成均匀漆层的方法）

Electro-Technical Laboratory ［日］电子技术综合研究所（简称 ETL）

electrotechnics 电工学，电气工艺学，电工技术

electrotester （汽车用）万能电气试验仪

electrothermal water temperature meter 电热式水温表

electrothermic 电（致）热的

electrothermics 电热学

electro-vacuum gear shift 电磁真空

变速装置（电磁阀控制的真空执行机构换挡）

electrovalve 电磁阀（见 solenoid valve）

electrowelding 电焊

electrowinning 电解沉积，电解冶金法，电积金属（法）

elec. vehicle 电动车辆，蓄电池汽车

elegant ①雅致的，优美的②格调高的，高尚的③一流的，极好的④漂亮的

elektron 一种镁锌合金

elem ①元素，要素（element 的简称）②基本的，初步的（elementary 的简称）

element ①元素，要素；单元，（组成）部分；元件，零件，构件②（蓄电池每一个单格电池的）正、负极板带隔板总成③（构成无级变速器钢传动带的）高强度钢片（亦称 block）

elementary 初步的，简单的，基本的

elementary combinatorial circuit 基本组合电路（指完成与、或、与非、与或四种基本的逻辑操作的组合电路。若干个基本组合电路连接或加上反相器，便可组合成多种非基本电路）

elementary composition 基本成分，主要组成（亦写作 elemental composition）

elementary diagram 原理图

elementary wave 基波，元波

elephant's ear type side access door （多功能车的）象耳型（宽大的）侧门

eleroterne ①铅锡合金电镀层②电镀铅锡合金薄钢板

eletroacoustilcs 电声学

eletronic fuel control system 电子燃油控制系统

elevate 提升，升高，举升，升运；增加，加大仰角

elevated (inner-city) highway （市内）高架公路（以缓解城市交通堵塞，一般高架公路允许车速较低，60~80km/h）

elevating capacity 起重能力，起吊能力，提升能力，举重能力

elevating gear 升降机械，举升装置

elevating platform fire truck 带升高平台的消防车

elevating screws 升降螺旋，升降丝杠，螺旋起重机

elevating stops 提升挡块，提升限位器

elevating truck 带举升平台的载货汽车（= elevating platform truck, elevator truck，这类汽车的车身称 elevator truck body）

elevation ①举升，提高，升高，升运②海拔高度，标高③正视图，纵剖面图

elevation (al) drawing 立面图（样）

elevation view 垂直剖面图；正视图，立视图

elevator 提升机，升运机，升降机，电梯

elevator cage ①（汽车等用的）升降吊笼②电梯格笼

elimination ①消除，除去，消去②（数学）消元法

elimination of hold-up 运输阻滞处理（货物运输过程中，因自然灾害、道路障碍等需要对货物做出不同处理的业务活动）

eliminator ①消除器②减振器③阻尼器

ell ①直角弯管，L 形短管②厄尔（长度单位，等于 45in）

EL lighting 场致发光照明（electroluminescent lighting 的简称，低亮度蓝-绿色光源，作为汽车液晶显示仪表等的背景照明）

Elliot axle 叉端式前桥,叉式前桥,叉式桥(= forked axle,见 Elliot type)

Elliot type ①(当说明前桥时,Elliot type front axle 是指其两端呈叉形,转向主销插入其上、下叉臂的主销孔中的)叉端式前桥,叉形前桥 ②[当说明转向节时,Elliot type steering knuckle(或 head)是指其与前桥的连接端呈拳形的]拳式转向节,拳形转向节(美国人 Sterling Elliot 发明,因而得名)

ellipse 椭圆,椭圆形

ellipsoid 椭圆体,椭圆球,椭圆面

ellipsoidal head lamp 椭圆形前照灯(= ellipsoidal headlight,指装有宽度大于高度的非圆形反射镜的前照灯,目前已取代了使用抛物线反射镜的前照灯)

ellipsoid head lamp 椭圆形前照灯(见 projector head lamp)

elliptical cam wave generator 椭圆凸轮波发生器(谐波齿轮的以椭圆作为凸轮基本廓形的积极控制式波发生器,见 wave generator)

elliptically polarized light 椭圆偏振光(两束线偏振光的电矢量相互垂直且具有恒定的相位差,该合成光束的电矢量的端点在与它们传播方向垂直的平面上,一般描绘出椭圆形轨迹,故名)

elliptical skirted piston 椭圆裙部活塞

elliptical steering wheel 椭圆形转向盘(不会挡住仪表板上的仪表和指示警告灯)

elliptic gear 椭圆齿轮(分度曲面是椭圆柱面或卵圆柱面的非圆齿轮)

elliptic polarization 椭圆偏振

elliptic spring 椭圆形钢板弹簧(指由两副半椭圆形弹簧扣合而组成的完整椭圆形的钢板弹簧,亦称 full elliptic,或 lenticular spring)

elliptic tire 椭圆轮胎,椭圆胎[断面呈椭圆形,较一般子午胎的胎压,可增加 3.6~5.4kg,因而可减少滚动阻力,节约燃油,安装这种轮胎的车轮称 elliptic(al) wheel]

elliptic trammel 椭圆量规

Elmillimess (一种)电动测微仪

Elnisil (coating) 硅镍镀层

Elnisil trochoidal surface (转子发动机的)旋轮线缸壁镍-硅合金镀覆面,硅镍旋轮线缸壁面,渗碳化硅镍层旋轮线缸壁面

ELR ①欧洲(重型货车发动机瞬态排烟浓度的)负荷响应(测试)循环(见 European Load Response cycle)②(安全带的)紧急锁紧式收紧装置(见 emergency-locking restractor)

Eltec 电子技术(electronic technology 的简称)

eltec sedan 电子化轿车,电子技术轿车

ELV 报废车(end-of-life vehicle 的简称)

ELV recycling rate 报废车可回收再生利用率(指其制作材料及构件可回收再生利用的比率)

ELV treatment system 报废车处理系统

EM ①电磁式的[见 electromagnetic(al)]②电动机械的(见 electromechanical)③应急维护(见 emergency maintenance)④工程手册(见 engineering manual)⑤发动机改型(见 engine modification)⑥膨胀金属(见 expanded metal)⑦实验备忘录(见 experimental memo)

EMA ①[美]发动机制造商协会(Engine Manufactures Association 的简称)②发动机维护场地(参见 engine maintenance area)③排放物测量装置(emission measurement apparatus 的简称)④甲基丙烯酸乙酯

(ethyl methacrylate)

E- Mail 电子邮件

e4MATIC (Benz公司) 通过4个车轮电动机控制转矩的电子控制四轮驱动系统 (商品名)

EMB ①电动机械式制动系统 (electro-mechanical brake system 的简称, 由电子控制模块按照传感器传送的驾驶者的制动意图, 控制电动机驱动车轮制动器) ②电磁制动器 (electromagnetic brake 的简称) ③见 energy management bumper

embedability 压入能力, 嵌入性 (如: 硬质微料嵌入软的减摩合金中的能力, 亦写作 embedibility)

embedded-case oilseal (橡皮) 包 (金属) 壳式油封

embedded control system (汽车发动机、变速器、防抱死制动系统等的) 内存式控制系统 (指按照予存在车载计算机内的控制软件完成自动控制程序的各总成控制系统, 简称 ECS)

embedded parts 预埋件, 嵌入件

embedded system (汽车电子控制系统中的) 嵌入式系统 (指插入到主系统中完成某种特定功能的专用系统)

embedded temperature detector 嵌入式温度传感器, 预埋式温度传感元件

embedding 灌封 (指采用能固化的树脂对电路、组件等的主体进行埋置的过程)

embedments 被嵌入的硬质微粒

emblem ①标记 ②符号 ③商标, 厂牌 (亦称 mark, insigne)

embossing 模压加工, 压花法, 滚花法, 轧花, 压纹, 浮雕

embossment ①浮雕, 浮雕装饰, 浮雕花样, 金属板件上打出的浮雕状凸起部分 ②浮雕花样的打出 ③浮雕细工

embowed 弯曲的, 弧形的

embrittle 使变脆, 脆比

embrittlement (指塑料或金属由于老化, 高温和使用不当而) 变脆, 脆化

embryo ①尚在设计阶段的产品, 尚在萌芽期的事物 ②尚在设计阶段的产品的, 尚在萌芽期的

embus 搭乘公共汽车; 使搭乘上客车, 把…装上客车

embussing point 公共汽车搭乘地点, 公共汽车站点, 客车站点

E/M button (显示仪表上的单位) 英/米制转换按钮 (其中 E/M 为 English system/Meter system 的简称)

EMC ① (汽车电子设备等对) 电磁 (环境的) 适应性, 电磁兼容性 (electromagnetic compatibility 的简称, 指电子设备防止电磁波干扰, 适应所处电磁环境的能力。提高电磁适应性的方式有绝缘体屏蔽和导电体屏蔽两种, 汽车大都使用后者) ②发动机维修中心 (engine maintenance center)

EMD 电动机驱动的 (electric motor driven 的简称)

EMER 危急, 紧急 (emergency)

emergency ①紧急情况, 危急状态; 意外事故, 不测事件; 事故, 故障, 应急, 急需, 备用 ②紧急的, 危急的, 应急的, 备用的; 救急的

emergency aid center sign 急救中心站标志 (为了紧急时的救援、通信、医疗服务而设置的各项中心站的指示标志)

emergency ambulance 紧急救护车

emergency brake control 应急制动器操纵件 (使车辆紧急减速或停车的装置的操纵件, 亦称 secondary braking control)

emergency brake system 紧急制动系统 (指主制动系产生故障时紧急使用的第二制动系统, 或任一可在紧

急情况下使汽车停车的系统，如：驻车制动系统等，=accident brake）

emergency break away valve 见 breakaway valve

emergency call box system 紧急呼叫系统（供急救、消防、警察等项目而设置在公路上的紧急无线电呼叫系统）

emergency control 紧急操纵机构（如：教练车教练员座上的操纵机构）

emergency cut-off receiver 紧急（情况下可自动）切断（的）（储气）罐

emergency decree 安全技术规程，安全法规

emergency door （客车的）安全门（=dead door, 指专为应急而设置的门）

emergency door clear width （客车车身的）安全门净宽（按安全门最大开启位置时，两门侧框之间的最小距离）

emergency door height 安全门高［抵靠上门框的Z平面（见Z plane）至出口处地板之间的距离］

emergency facility 应急装置，备用装置（简称EF，如：断电时使用的应急灯）

emergency feature （交通控制信号系统的）应急装置（异常情况下正常信号不能使用时，表示特别信号的继电器或其他装置）

emergency fuel tank 备用油箱，副油箱（=auxiliary fuel tank, fuel reserve tank）

emergency gear ①安全齿轮 ②应急机构，安全装置

emergency hammer 应急锤（供乘客在紧急情况下砸碎窗玻璃逃离车厢）

emergency hand brake 应急手制动器

emergency inflator （汽车轮胎的）急救充气罐（可给被扎破的轮胎紧急充气和喷入密封剂作临时性修补的压缩气罐）

emergency lighting 备用照明，应急照明（有时指应急照明设备）

emergency line tag ①（气制动系统）应急制动管路中的接头 ②备用管路标志

emergency-locking (inertia-real type) retractor （汽车乘员安全带的）（惯性卷筒型）紧急锁紧式收紧装置（简称ELR，指在一般情况下，安全带可任意拉长缩短，但遇紧急情况，汽车突然减速，便会立即馈死已拉紧的安全带）

emergency maintenance 应急维护，安全维护（简称EM）

emergency medical vehicle 医疗急救车（=ambulance）

emergency operation 应急运转（指机械、设备、系统在紧急状态或事故条件下的运转，如：发动机一缸或数缸熄火时的运转。应急运转功能称emergency function，应急运转模式称emergency mode，发动机电子控制模块为适应应急运转而调控的点火正时称emergency ignition timing，其具体的点火提前角称emergency ignition angle，应急运转控制系统称emergency control system）

emergency-parking brake system 紧急-驻车（两用）制动系统

emergency (pipe) line ①后备管路 ②应急管路（特指由牵引车给挂车传送应急制动所需能的专用管）

emergency response providers 快速反应系统，紧急响应服务系统

emergency service vehicle 技术救援车，抢险车，紧急救援服务车（备有牵引绞盘、起重吊车、修理机具等设备，可对损坏、失事、陷入困境的车辆提供技术服务和救援业

务，= recovery vehicle, rescue vehicle)

emergency set 抢修用成套工具，紧急情况备用装置（如：发电机组等）

emergency spare wheel 应急备用车轮-轮胎总成（这类备胎仅供应急之用，一般较小，以减少其占用的车内空间和载重量，车速大都限制在<80km/h的范围内）

emergency speed sign 紧急车速标志（如：在通过放射能污染区要求采用最大安全车速的指示标志）

emergency-steering avoid support system 紧急转向（障碍物）回避系统（根据微波雷达、激光扫描、CMOS摄像机、车速传感器等的信息，算出与突然发现或出现的前方障碍物或行人的距离和二者的相对速度已无法通过制动回避碰撞时，该系统可使车辆朝着无障碍物的方向紧急转向而避免事故）

emergency stop 紧急停车，紧急制动（emergency stop button 紧急制动按钮；emergency stop distance 紧急停车距离，紧急制动距离）

emergency stop signal （防止后车追尾碰撞，告诉后车驾驶者注意本车在紧急制动减速的高速闪光）紧急制动信号灯（简称ESS）

emergency switch height of emergency door （客车车身的）安全门应急开关高度（指安全门内侧应急开关把手上缘至最近地板之间的距离）

emergency transmitter 应急（无线电）发射机（装在车内，供驾驶员应急呼救等用）

emergency trip 紧急断开机构

emergency warning lamp 警告灯（指具有旋转光束的灯具，用于发出警告）

emergency windscreen 救急风窗玻璃（一般为尺寸和形状与原风窗玻璃相同并易于安装的透明塑料片，用于临时替换破碎的风挡玻璃）

emery 金刚砂，钢石粉，钢玉粉

emery cloth 金刚砂布，研磨砂布

E-metal 锌铝合金

EMF (e、m、f) 见 electromotive force

EMI 电磁干扰（electromagnetic interference的简称，如：EMI filter 防电磁干扰滤波器；EMI screening 或 EMI shielding 电磁干扰屏蔽）

Emile Lovassor 埃米尔·卢瓦瑟（法国人，与另一法国人Rene Panhard共同将德国人Daimler研制的汽油机汽车改进成发动机前置，通过离合器、变速器、链条传动差速器、后半轴，而由后轮驱动的汽车。1891年被法国科学院确认为第一辆现代汽车，并于1895年法国科学院正式将这一乘人的汽车定名为automobile。"auto"为希腊文"自身"，"mobile"为拉丁文"运动"）

EMIS 见 emission

emission ①排放物（简称EMIS，常用emissions指由汽车向外界环境排放的气体、微粒、噪声、电磁波等的总称，但习惯上指其中的有害污染物，= emission pollutants，包括排气排放物，蒸发排放物，曲轴箱排放物等）②（电磁波、电子等的）发射 ③放电（指电荷的释放过程）④（声、光的）辐射

emission abatement system 排放净化系统（汽车排放有害物消除系统）

emission analyzer （发动机）废气污染成分分析仪，废气有害物含量测定仪，排放分析仪

emission-based tax （机动车的）排放税

emission certification （汽车发动机的）排气污染鉴定（一般指新车型投入销售前由政府有关部门按排气污染法规进行的审批鉴定、排放认证）

emission concentration standard 排放浓度标准（用排放物的浓度来表示排放量限值的标准，其单位一般为 ppm 或容积百分比）

emission control ①（汽车）排放控制，排放净化 ②排气污染净化装置（= emission-control device）

emission control engine 低污染发动机

emission controlled module 排放控制模块（各种排气净化系统的电子控制模块，简称 E. C. module）

emission controller （汽车发动机的）排气净化系统电子控制电路，排气净化系统电子控制器

emission control system （汽车）排放物控制系统，排放净化系统（指汽车上为减少排气排放物、蒸发排放物等而安装的各种净化装置的总称，简称 ECS）

emission efficiency 阴极效率（见 cathode efficiency）

emission factor 排放系数（某种排放物在排放源的排放总量中所占的比例）

emission free vehicle 无污染车，零污排放车（= zero emission vehicle，一般指电动汽车及无 CO、HC、NO_x、SO_2 等排放的汽车）

emission index 排放率，排放指数（燃烧 1kg 燃料所排放出的污染物的质量，以 g/kg 表示）

emission level(s) 排气污染程度，（汽车的）排放水平（表示排放量的多少）

emission limit 排放限值（指对排气排放物中特定成分的排放量规定的界限值）

emission maintenance reminder light 排放维修指示灯（该灯亮表明排放超标，应对发动机或其排放控制系统进行维修和调整，简称 EMR lamp）

emission matching 排放平衡（指防止因采取某项净化措施以减少某种有害物排放而导致另一有害物排放量增加等）

emission measurement apparatus 排放物测量装置（简称 EMA）

emission of heat 热辐射，热发散

emission performance 排放特性（反映内燃机排放率和排放浓度指标的性能）

emission pollutants 排放污染物（汽车排放物中污染环境的各种物质，主要有一氧化碳 CO、碳氢化合物 HC、氮氧化物 NO_x 和微粒物 particulate matters 等）

emission rate （汽车）排放率（简称 ER，指有害物排出量）

emission regulation 排放法规（各国限制汽车排放物量的法规）

emission-related failure （发动机）与排放有关的故障（如：EGR 阀堵塞，而导致 NOx 增加等）

emissions figure （汽车发动机的）有害物排放量，有害物排放限值

emission spectro-chemical analysis 排放光谱化学分析（简称 ESCA）

emission standard 排放标准（为限制某种有害排放物的排放量，制订的容许极限量和检测排放量的方法等内容的法规文件）

emission test （发动机）排气试验

emission tube （曲轴箱通风系统的）曲轴箱废气输送管（将曲轴箱废气送至空气滤清器）

emissive capacity 发射能力，辐射能力，发放能力（= emissive ability）

emissive surface 散光面积，放射面（= emitting surface, emission surface）

emissivity ①发射率，发射系数 ②（热）辐射系数，辐射率，辐射能力

emitter ①（晶体管的）发射极

②（卡片穿孔机之类的设备中的一种时间脉冲）发生器 ③（泛指各种）发射体，发射区，发射器，辐射源，放射体

emitter-base 发射极-基极的

emitter-base junction （晶体管的）发射极-基极结

emitter coupled（**transistor**）**logic** 发射极耦合（晶体管）逻辑（电路）

emitter current （晶体管的）发射极电流

emitter injection efficiency 发射极注入效率

emitter-to-base voltage 发射极-基极间电压

emitting surface 发射面，发光面

EML 可扩充置标语言（Extensible Markup Language 的简称）

emmetropia （相对近视眼等而言的）正视眼，正常视眼；屈光正常

EM-motive （德国）电动车公司（Diamlar 公司与 Borsch 公司的一家合资企业，研发与生产车用动力电动机）

E-mobility 电动汽车（electric mobility 的简称，mobility 原意为：流动性，移动能力，此处泛指车辆）

emollient 润滑剂，软化剂

e-motor 电动机（electric motor 的简称）

EMPA service 发动机逐步分析维护法（见 Engine Maintenance through Progressive Analysis service）

empire 绝缘，电绝缘漆

empiric 经验的，实验的，以实验为根据的，以经验为基础的（亦写作 empirical）

empirical （以）经验（为根据）的，（以）实验（为根据）的

empirical equation 经验公式，实验公式（= empiric formula）

empirical injector constant 喷油器的实验常数（取决于喷油器的结构，是喷油器通电时间对喷油量的函数）

empirical tire model for non-steady state side slip properties （根据试验数据建立的）轮胎非稳态侧偏特性实验模型

emptier ①卸载器，倒空装置 ②倾卸式油罐车，倾卸式液罐车

empty ①空箱，空桶，空车，空的包皮 ②空的，未占用的；空载的，空车的；空洞的，无意义的 ③排空，倒空，卸空，使成为空的

empty container kilometrage 空箱里程（汽车载运空集装箱的行程）

empty-seat rate 空座率（指客车运输时，客车内客座无人乘坐率）

empty weight 空车重；皮重（= weight when empty）

EMR 电磁波辐射（electromagnetic radiation 的简称）

EMS ①发动机管理系统（engine management system 的简称）②（发动机）电子管理系统（见 electronic management system）③（复合动力车的）动力自动切换系统（energy management system 的简称）④电子控制悬架（electronic modulated suspention 的简称）

EmS 紧急开关（emergency switch 的简称）

EMT 高机动性载货汽车（expanded mobility truck 的简称）

emu ①电磁单位（electromagnetic unit）②电动势单位（electromotive unit）

emulsification 乳化，乳化作用

emulsified fuel 乳化燃料（用液面活化剂使燃料与水乳化。有水包油滴型或油包水滴型两种，后者使用较多，乳化燃料可显著减少排气中的 NO_x 和碳烟）

emulsifier ①乳化剂 ②乳化装置

emulsion 乳化液（两种流体未完全

混合的混合液,特指化油器中空气与未全气化的汽油的乳状或泡沫状混合液)
emulsion block 见 emulsion tube
emulsion cleaning (金属表面污垢的)乳化液清洗法
emulsion sludge 乳化沉淀物
emulsion type lubricant 乳状润滑油,乳化润滑油
emulsoid ①乳胶液,乳浊体 ②乳胶
enable ①允许,使能够,使实现,使成为可能 ②起动,启动,恢复操作〔如:enable input 集成电路的允许输入,指有效时允许一个或多个规定操作开始执行的输入信号;enable module 允许(中断)模块,指汽车电子控制系统中在执行期间的任何时刻都可被中断的模块;enable (enabling) pulse 起动脉冲,使动脉冲;enable (enabling) relay 起动继电器,指使某一系统或装置起动的继电器;enable (enabling) signal 车用电子控制系统的允许信号,指允许某一程序,或某一步骤开始执行或某一事件发生的控制信号〕
enamel ①搪瓷,珐琅,磁漆 ②上珐琅,涂磁漆,上彩色,使光滑
enameled 搪瓷的,珐琅的,上釉的,涂漆的,漆包的 (= enamelized, enamelled)
enameled cable 漆包线缆 (= enamel covered wire, enamel insulated wire)
enamel lacquer (纤维素)瓷漆 (= enamel varnish)
enantiotropic liquid crystal 互变性液晶(加热冷却过程中,相发生可逆变化的热致液晶)
enblock cast 单件铸造,整体铸造 (= monoblock cast, inblock cast)
encapsulation (电路和元器件等的)封装(指用保护介质包封电路和元器件等的通用工艺)
encased propeller shaft 管装传动轴,封装式传动轴,内装式传动轴 (= enclosed cardan shaft, enclosed propeller shaft)
enclosed body 厢式车身,闭式车身
enclosed-deck type body 闭式平板车箱
enclosed fuse 封闭式熔断丝,盒装式熔断丝 (= cartridge fuse)
enclosed-type cab 封闭式驾驶室
enclosure 外壳,机壳,机罩,箱,套,盒子,围栏,围墙,界限,附件,封入物,夹杂物,包围,包含,围绕,装入,篱栅
encode 编码(用一种代码来转换数据,即用一种信息表示方式转换成另一种信息表示方式,同时又要使它可以恢复成原来的形式)
encoder 编码器(①对数据进行编码的组合电路,有多个输入端和输出端,当一个输入端有信号输入时,输出端上就有一组相对应的信号输出 ②在微型电子计算机中将10进制数转换为二进制形式的装置)
encode type sensor 代码型传感器(又称 coder "编码器",为数字型传感器的一种,直接用数字代码表示所传感的物理量的检测器,每一输出代码相当于所传感的物理量的一定值,即:可对所传感的物理量数据进行编码的器件)
encroach ①侵犯(权利等) ②侵占(时间等) ③扩展(至某一新领域等)
end ①末端,终端;端头,端面,端壁;边缘,边界,界限,限度,极限,范围;终结,结束,尽头;目标,目的 ②竖直,竖立,端接;加尖端
end board ①(货车栏板式车厢的)后栏板 ②端板
end bracket 见 end cover plate
end clearance 端隙(如:活塞环开口间隙,轴的端部间隙等, = end

end

gap)

end coil （螺旋弹簧两端的）顶圈（仅起支撑作用，不参与能量吸收、释放和变形）

end cover ①（机械密封件中特指）密封端盖（指与密封腔体连接并托撑静环组件的零件）②见 end cover plate①

end cover plate ①端盖板，端盖（= end plate, end housing, end hsg, end casing, end plate, end bracket）②（转子发动机的）缸盖

end curtain （篷顶车）后篷

end cutting nippers 刻（剪）丝钳（= end cutter, end cutting pliers）

end door （车身）后门

end dump body 后倾（卸）式车身（= body tipped endways, rear dump body）

end dump truck 后倾卸式货车（= rear dump truck）

end elevation 侧视图

end face seal 端面密封

end fatigue 边缘处的疲劳（破坏）

end flange ①（转子发动机的）缸盖突缘，端盖突缘 ②（喷油泵等的）端面法兰

end flange mounted fuel injection pumper （柴油机的）端面法兰安装式喷油泵（安装面为垂直于凸轮轴轴线的带法兰平面的喷油泵）

end float ①（轴的）端隙，轴向游隙（= end play）②轴向浮动

end float misalignment ①（传动轴的）纵向窜位，轴向窜动（传动系统中两相互连接的传动轴，虽在一条直线上，但可沿轴向窜动）②上述窜动造成的中心错位

end gap 端隙（见 end clearance）

end gas 末端气（指燃烧室内，在燃烧过程中，火焰面未到之处尚未燃烧的混合气，亦称尾气）

end half-lap （车身木构件的）半端搭接

end housing ①端盖板 ②（转子发动机）缸盖（参见 end cover plate）

end hsg ①端盖板 ②（转子发动机）缸盖（参见 end cover plate）

end instr 敏感元件，传感器

end journal 轴尾的轴颈，端头轴颈

end junction ①端接头，端头连接件 ②（转子发动机的）端面密封接点，端面密封连接件；端面密封结

end lap 端搭叠

endless 无穷的，无限的，无边的；环形的，无端（头）的，循环的

endless belt conveyer 皮带循环输送机，环形皮带运输机

endless chain 环状链，无端链

endless flange ①环形突边，环状突缘 ②（车轮轮辋的）整体式轮缘（指轮辋上给轮胎提供轴向支撑的部分）

endless oil groove 闭合的（回线形）润滑油槽

endless taper bead seat ring （车轮轮辋的）整体式锥形胎圈座环（指轮辋上给轮胎提供径向支撑的部分）

endless track 环形跑道，环带；履带

endless-track vehicle 履带式车辆（= tracked vehicle, track laying vehicle）

end lift （更换轮胎，检修制动器等只需将汽车的前端或后端升起时使用的）单端举升器

end limit switch 终端限制开关（限制终端行程或由终端控制的开关）

end loading 从（汽车）后端装载

end nut 端螺母

end of conversion 转换结束，变换终了（简称 EOC）

end of delivery （高压油泵柱塞的）喷油终点

end of engagement （齿轮齿的）啮合终点

end office 终点站（简称 EO）

end of injection 喷油结束，喷油终点［简称 EOI，指喷油泵柱塞移至喷油终止（以针阀落座为标志）时的位置］

end-of-line （生产线，装配线，测试线等）终端（指位于终端的或最后的一道工序等）

end-of-line chassis dynamometer 下线底盘测功机（指汽车装配生产线上装配完毕，下线进行动力性、燃料经济性等性能测试用的底盘测功机）

end-of-line test stand （位于）生产线末端的试验台

end of run 行程终点，运程终端

end of test 试验结束，试验终了（简称 EOT）

end organ 传感器，灵敏元件

endoscope ①（机器内部零件的）远距离检验和摄影装置 ②非接触性间接检测装置（如：用来检验汽车车身等的封闭部分或内部零件的内窥镜、铸件等的内表面检查仪）

endoscope-based measurement system 基于远距离内测仪的测量系统

endothermic 吸热的，吸热反应的，内热的（= endothermal）

end plate scoring （转子发动机的）缸盖内壁刮伤，端盖刮伤

end play 端隙，轴向间隙，轴向游隙（= end float，指两个部件间的轴向活动量）

end plug （杆件、管件等的）端部螺塞

end point 终点，终端，边界点（亦称 ending point）

end point gasoline 终馏点汽油

end point of fraction 终点馏程

end point voltage 截止电压（= cut-off voltage）

end ring （轴端）卡环；（轴承）推力环

end shake 纵向振动，轴向振动

end slot （转子发动机转子）端面密封片槽

end-slot piston pin 端头带凹槽的活塞销

end speed zone sign 车速限制区间终止标志

end stop ①终点站 ②端点挡块

end temperature 终点温度，最终温度（如：压缩终了的温度）

end thrust bearing 轴端推力轴承

end-tip （向）后倾卸货的（亦称 end tipping，end-dump）

endurance 持久，持续，耐久性，耐用度，寿命，耐疲劳度，强度，抗磨度，持续时间，持续性

endurance bending test 弯曲耐久试验（弯曲疲劳试验）

endurance crack 疲劳裂纹

endurance failure 疲劳破坏（= fatigue failure）

endurance life 寿命，耐用期限（= endurance）

endurance limit 疲劳极限

endurance ratio 疲劳强度极限与（静载下的）抗断强度极限之比值

endurance road test(ing) （汽车）耐久性路试

endurance running 耐久性运转（试验），连续性运转（试验）

endurance strength 疲劳强度，疲劳极限

endurance tension test 拉伸耐久性试验，拉伸疲劳试验

endurance test 耐久性试验，寿命试验（= endurance trial，对发动机进行长期、耐久运转，考核零、部件的耐久性，可靠性及整机动力经济指标的稳定性所做的试验）

endurance torsion test 扭转疲劳试验

endurance trial 见 endurance test

enduring 耐久的，耐磨的，持久的，长寿命的

enduro ①(车辆的)耐力赛 ②耐力赛用车辆

enduro tyre 耐力赛用轮胎

endways 在长度方向上，纵向地；沿着轴向地；竖着地，直立地（=end wise）

end yoke ①万向节叉 ②前桥梁端叉形头（端头成叉形的部分）

energization-deenergization cycles (电磁阀等的)通-断电循环

energize ①激发，引起 ②增能，供能，施力 ③激磁，励磁

energized to run 通电使运行（简称 ETR）

energized to shut off 通电使停机（简称 ETSO）

energizing interval 励磁时间间隔（指对点火系初级进行充电所经历的时间，用曲轴或分电器轴的旋转角度来表示，＝dwell angle）

energizing signal 触发信号，翻转信号，激发信号，使动信号

energy 能，能量；精力，活力，活动力

energy absorber 能量吸收装置（简称 EA，=EAD，energy absorbing device，如：发动机测功用的电涡流功率吸收器）

energy absorbing 吸收能量的，能量吸收的［对汽车而言，这一用语主要说明具有吸收冲击能量的能力，以保护乘员，如：energy absorbing bumper system（碰撞）能量吸收式保险杠系统；energy absorbing frame（冲击）能量吸收式车架；energy absorbing front end（碰撞时冲击）能量吸收式（车辆）前部构造（指保险杠、驾驶室构件、转向盘柱等）；energy absorbing restraint system 能量吸收式乘员保护装置；energy absorbing reusable highway protective system 可重复使用的能量吸收型道路安全保护装置；energy absorbing roadside crash barrier 能量吸收式路边防撞护栅（护壁）；energy absorbing steering assembly 能量吸收型转向装置；energy absorbing（type）steering column 能量吸收式转向柱，可吸收碰撞能量的转向柱，一般为可压叠式转向柱、可压缩式转向柱，通过塑性变形或摩擦吸收冲击能量；energy absorbing tube 能量吸收式安全转向柱用的能量吸收管］

energy absorbing bumper system (车辆的)能量吸收式保险杠系统

energy absorbing U bracket (碰撞保护系统中的) U 型能量吸收护架

energy absorption test 冲击能量吸收试验

energy accumulating 存储能量的，储能的

Energy and Environment Analysis [美]能源和环境分析公司（简称 EEA）

energy assisted braking system 助力式制动系统（产生制动力所需的能量，除由驾驶员的体力供给外，还由另外一个或多个能源供给，如：真空助力制动器等，亦称伺服制动系"servo braking system"）

energy balance 能量平衡［如：供给发动机的能量与发动机产生（和损失）的能量之间的平衡等］

energy chamber (柴油机燃烧室的)空气室（参见 air-cell）

energy-conscious style of driving 节能驾驶方式

energy conservation ①能量储备，能源储量 ②能量守恒，能量不灭

energy-conserving 节能

energy consumption brake 动能吸收式制动装置，能量吸收式制动器（简称 EC brake）

energy consumption rate (汽车的)能量消耗率，能耗率（单位：MJ/km）

energy content 能量值，能的储量，含能量，发热量，热值

energy conversion 能量转换（指能量转变为另一种形式的能量或功）

energy crisis 能源危机

energy density ①（蓄电池等的）能量密度（每单位质量的储能量，单位，Wh/kg）②（电瓶等的）单位容积的电容量（Wh/L）③见 special energy

energy economy 节能

energy efficient vehicle 省油车（简称 EEV）

energy input 能量输入；输入能量

energy loss by wheel 车轮滚动的能量损失

energy management bumper 能量吸收式保险杠（简称 EMB）

energy management system ①能量控制系统 ②（复合功力车的）动力自动切换系统（简称 EMS）

energy monitor 能量监控器（如：混合动力车显示的蓄电池剩余电量、各种行驶模式下的前、后轮能量、转矩分布、剩余电量可行驶里程及能量不足警报等的监控屏）

Energy MXV8 （米其林公司生产的）V形胎面花纹节能环保"绿色"轮胎（商品名）

energy nozzle 喷头

energy of motion 动能

energy of position 位能

energy of recoil 反冲能，回弹能

energy of rotation 转动能

energy optimized 最佳节能的，能效最佳的

energy output 输出能量，能量输出

Energy Policy and Conservation Act ［美国］能源政策和保护法（美国1975年12月22日制定的一项法令，该法令规定，自1978年起的轿车平均油耗标准，凡达不到标准规定值的厂家，由国家征收罚金）

energy regeneration brake system 能量回收制动系统（如：混合动力车利用车辆动能驱动发电机发电，使车辆制动减速而将车辆动能转变为电能存储备用的系统）

energy-related hazard 能耗公害（与能耗有关的公害）

Energy Research and Development Administration （美国能源部的）能源研究和开发局（简称 ERDA）

energy reserve ①储备能量，能量储备 ②（特指汽车乘员保护系统等的）备用电源（蓄电池无电时自动紧急接通）

energy reserve module （安全气囊系统的）备用电源组件（汽车发生碰撞事故，导致蓄电池损坏或供电线路断开时，提供紧急电源）

energy saver 节能装置，节能器

energy-saving tire 节油胎（如：elliptic tire）

energy signal 能量信号（信号 $x(t)$，若满足 $\int_{-\infty}^{\infty} |x(t)|^2 dt < \infty$，则称为具有有限量信号，简称能量信号）

energy source 能源

energy storage spring 储能弹簧（利用压缩变形来存储气压或液压能量的弹簧）

energy storage spring brake 储能弹簧制动器［简称 spring brake，当制动液压或气压符合规定时，储能弹簧制动器室（energy storage spring brake chamber）内的弹簧被制动气压或液压压缩、储蓄能量。当制动气压或液压低于规定值时，弹簧伸展释放能量，通过杆件推动制动蹄或制动钳将车轮制动，避免车辆在制动气压或液压不足的情况下行驶，确保安全］

energy storage spring release mechanism 储能弹簧释放机构

Energy Supply and Environmental

Coordination Act ［美］能源供应及环境协调法（简称 ESECA）

energy supplying device 供能装置（能量供给装置的通称）

energy transfer ①能量传输 ②能量转换装置 ③（特指主要用于轻型轿车、摩托车等的由外线圈和在其中运转的转子构成的）点火系（如磁电机）

energy unit 能量单位（简称 EU）

enertial sensor type accelerator 惯性传感器式加速计

enertia type（mechanically actuated-electronic switching）impact sensor （安全气囊的）惯性式（机械驱动电开关式）碰撞传感器（车辆因碰撞而急剧减速时，重物在惯性力作用下，冲向触点，使触点闭合，而向电子控制模块发出碰撞信息或直接引爆安全气囊充气系统。一般按车辆正常行驶时固定重物位置的装置，分为 coil spring type"卷簧式"和 magnet type"磁铁式"等多种）

enfolding action 折叠作用（如转向时产生的切向力对轮胎的反复挤压-松释作用等）

engage 啮合；接合，连接，联结

engagement ①（齿轮）啮合（= mesh） ②接合 ③联结，连接

engagement interference 啮合干涉（齿轮副在啮合过程中，由于正确啮合条件不足，其中一个齿轮的齿面越出了所允许的运动界限，而出现在理论上穿越其啮合齿面的现象）

engagement sleeve 啮合套

engaging element （汽车液力变速器的）换挡元件（指通过分离或接合来换挡的元件，如：离合器，制动器等）

engaging friction cone （变速器、同步器的）啮合摩擦锥轮

engaging gear ①啮合齿轮 ②接合机构

engaging-in 啮入（轮齿从开始进入啮合至达到最大啮入深度的过程）

engaging-in region 啮入区（啮入过程经过的区域）

engaging-out 啮出（轮齿从最大啮入深度开始退出到脱离啮合的过程）

engaging-out region 啮出区（啮出过程经过的区域）

eng（ENG） ①发动机（engine） ②工程师（engineer） ③工程，工程学（engineering）

2012 engine 2012 年型发动机（指符合美国环保局 2012 年排放标准的发动机）

engine 发动机（一般指将液态或气态燃料的化学能转变为机械能的车用动力装置。在英国，motor 只表示电动机，但美国 motor 则表示一切类型的动力装置，包括内燃机。如：当表示常用的汽车内燃机时，engine 与 motor 是同义词。电动汽车的电动机称 electric motor，而车用外燃机，如：stirling 发动机，常称为 stirling machine 或 stirling engine）

engine accessory loss 发动机附件功率消耗（一般指装用风扇、发电机、液压泵等消耗的功率，及装用空气滤清器、消声器等使发动机功率受到的损失）

engine adapter 发动机适配器（指改装轿车将原厂发动机更换成不同型号的发动机时，新发动机与原厂变速器等的转接装置）

engine adjustment 发动机调节，发动机调校

engine air box （赛车用）发动机的进气箱（位于进气系统最前端的箱形进气口）

engine air intake system 发动机进气系统

engine air scoop 发动机兜（戽）形

进气口

engine analysis apparatus 发动机分析仪器（用以分析测试发动机各个系统的工作是否正常，诊断故障产生的部位及原因。早期这种仪器的功能单一，现代多采用电子技术并组合为多功能仪器，主要包括代码提取系统前端处理器、高速信号采集处理、故障诊断系统、排放测试系统、信息网络系统、显示系统等。= engine analyser）

engine-and-gearbox unit 发动机附变速器总成

engine automated design expert system 发动机自动设计专家系统

engine balance checking （多缸）发动机各缸功率平衡检测（通过停止一个或数个汽缸工作的方法的检测多缸发动机各个缸产生的功率，是否符合标准，以保证发动机运转的平稳性，特别是怠速平稳性）

engine bay （汽车的）发动机室（安装发动机的空间）

engine-bay catalyst converter 装在车身发动机室内的催化转化器（可装在靠近排气歧管，以加速起动时催化转化器的燃起，多见于前轮驱动，前置发动机汽车）

engine bench test 发动机台（架）试（验）

engine block （包括曲轴箱在内的）发动机汽缸体（指曲轴箱与汽缸或汽缸水套形成一体的构件）

engine block heater （发动机冷机起动用）缸体加热器（亦称 cylinder block header 或简称 block heater）

engine block stiffening rib （发动机）汽缸体上的加强肋

engine bonnet 发动机室罩（见 bonnet）

engine bonnet antichafing strip 发动机罩防松振垫带，发动机罩防松磨垫带

engine braking 发动机制动（利用发动机压缩阻力及摩擦力，吸收汽车动能的制动法，即：汽车带动发动机旋转，消耗汽车动能的一种辅助缓速法，这时要求有排气门关闭机构等）

engine braking power 发动机制动消耗功率（利用发动机制动时，发动机所吸收的功率。注意，勿与有效功率相混淆，见 brake horsepower）

engine breakdown 发动机故障，发动机损坏

engine breathing 发动机进排气，发动机换气

engine calibration 发动机标定（点火正时、空燃比、EGR 控制，最高转速、稳定怠速等运转参数的调整和设定，以获得所希望的结果）

engine calibration unit 发动机运行参数控制软件模块（一般为一插装式可编程只读存储器"PROM"集成块，直接插装于发动机电子控制模块的插座上，向电子控制模块提供针对所控制型号的发动机及变速器的特点，及该发动机所驱动车辆的尺寸、质量、传动比等的发动机运行参数控制量的软件。有的只供新车磨合期使用，有的可以更换，有的是永久性的，亦称 engine calibration assembly 等，因厂家而异）

engine capacity ①发动机排量（= engine swept volume，指发动机各汽缸工作容积之和）②发动机功率（= engine power，指发动机单位时间内所做功，即其输出功率）

engine carrier （维修场用的）发动机小车，发动机搬运车

engine characteristic map 见 engine map

engine characteristics 内燃机特性（指内燃机主要性能参数在一定条件下的相互关系，或随工况变化而变化的规律，常用曲线表示，称为

特性曲线)

engine characteristic tester 发动机性能测试台,发动机特性试验台(简称ECT)

engine checker 发动机检验仪

engine checkout system 发动机检验制度,发动机调试制度(简称ECO)

engine cleanliness ①(滑油对)发动机的沾污性 ②发动机的清洁性

engine clutch 发动机离合器(汽车发动机与变速器之间的主离合器)

engine clutch housing 发动机飞轮壳,发动机离合器壳

engine cold start control 发动机冷起动操纵件(使发动机易于冷起动的辅助装置的操纵件)

engine compartment (汽车的)发动机室,发动机舱(汽车上安装发动机的空间,亦称 engine bay)

engine compartment door (客车等的)发动机舱门

engine compartment mounted 装在发动机室(仓)内的

engine compartment rear bulk (车身)发动机舱后壁板

engine component verification 发动机零部件认证(鉴定)(简称ECV)

engine conditioning 发动机调整,发动机调校

engine conk 发动机运转中断,发动机产生故障

Engine Control Module 发动机控制模块(通用公司对其CCC系统发动机控制用电子计算机的称谓,简称ECM,美国政府规定从1993年起一律改用PCM)

Engine Control System (大发公司EF—VE型发动机的)发动机控制系统(商品名,简称ECS,由EFI—电子燃油喷射,ESA—电子点火提前,VVT—可变气门正时及ISC—怠速控制等的电子计算机综合控制系统)

engine control unit 发动机控制模块(简称ECU,PCM的旧称)

engine coolant heater 发动机冷却液加热器

engine coolant temperature indicator 发动机冷却液温度表(= engine coolant thermometer)

engine coolant temperature sensor 发动机冷却液温度传感器(简称ECT sensor)

engine coupled turbo-charger 发动机连接式涡轮增压器(指涡轮与发动机曲轴连接的涡轮增压器)

engine cover (后置式发动机轿车的)发动机罩(注意:英国的bonnet和美国的hood都只是指前置式发动机轿车的发动机罩)

engine crankcase force tester 发动机曲轴箱窜气测定仪(测试时该测定仪固装于曲轴箱机油加注口,同时将曲轴箱其他可能漏气的孔隙堵严,使窜入曲轴箱内的全部气体均由该测定仪排出,通过测定其排出压力算出窜气量及其变化规律,故名 force tester)

engine crankcase oil capacity 发动机曲轴箱机油容量

engine cross drive 横置发动机驱动

engine cut-off timer 发动机停机定时器(简称ECT)

engine cylinders opposed arrangement 对置汽缸发动机布置

engine cylinder volume 内燃机汽缸总容积(一台内燃机全部汽缸容积的总和,见 working medium volume)

engine data 发动机技术数据

engine-dependent 与发动机有关的,视发动机而定的,随发动机而变的

engine depression 发动机真空,发动机稀薄度(指活塞下行进气冲程在节气门下方进气歧管内所形成的

低压)

engine diagnostic connector 发动机诊断插座；发动机诊断接口(用于在发动机电子控制系统与发动机诊断分析仪之间形成接口，以读取发动机的有关数据以及存储在发动机控制系存储器中的故障代码等)

engine diagnostic package 发动机故障诊断包件，发动机故障分析装置

engine displacement 发动机排量(亦称 engine swept volume，= 汽缸工作容积×缸数，单位 cm³ 或 in³，见 piston swept volume)

engine dollars per horsepower 发动机每马力制造成本的美元数

engine drag 发动机运转阻力

engine drive 发动机驱动

engine-driven (直接由)发动机驱动的

engine driven blower 发动机驱动(式)压气机(指由发动机输出的动力驱动的进气增压器的压气机)

engine-driven supercharger 发动机驱动式增压器(指由发动机输出动力驱动的增压器以别于废气涡轮增压器，= gear-driven supercharger，geared supercharger)

engine dry mass 发动机净质量，发动机干质量(不包括冷却水、燃油、润滑油等质量)

engine dry weight 发动机干重(指不带燃料、冷动水、机油的发动机重，为发动机干质量 engine dry mass 的旧称)

engine dust test 在(人造)高含尘量条件下的发动机试验

engine dynamometer 发动机测功机(用于测定发动机的有效功率等)

engine ECU ①发动机电子控制模块(ECU 见 computer) ②(特指内燃机-电动机型混合动力车的)内燃机电子控制模块(见 power management ECU)

engine efficiency 发动机效率(指综合使用效率，包括油耗、维修费用、购置费用、发动机使用寿命等影响因素)

engine efflux 发动机的排气流，发动机排出的废气

engine electrical equipment 发动机电气设备

engine-electric drive 发动机-电动机驱动，发动机电力驱动(发动机带动发电机发电，再由电动机驱动汽车)

engine-electronic center 发动机电(子)控(制)中心(简称 EEC，参见 electronic management system)

2012 engine emission requirements (美国环保局拟定的)2012 年发动机排放要求

engine emission(s) 发动机排放，发动机污染排出物，发动机有害排出物(包括排气有害物、燃油蒸发有害物、曲轴箱排出气体有害物等)

engine emissions testing 发动机排放试验，发动机有害排出物试验

engine encapsulation 发动机封闭腔室(隔绝噪声装置)

engine endurance 发动机大修间隔里程

engineering analysis language 工程技术分析语言(简称 EAL)

engineering feasibility 工程可行性(通过样机研制，技术可行性论证后，进行小批量试制，同时对性能、结构等进一步改进，确定在工程上的可行性)

engineering plant 工程车(非货运或客运的专用车辆或挂车，如推土车、吊车等)

engineering plastics 工程塑料(指机械强度、耐热性、耐磨性很高的塑料，多用于汽车及电子机械等行业，更高强度、弹性、更好耐热、耐磨性塑料，称为超级工程塑料，

以前多用于航空工业，目前汽车工业亦开始应用）

engineering stress 工程应力（按照试样的原始横截面尺寸而计算的应力）

engineering tractor 工程机械用牵引车

engineering unit cost model 工程单位费用模型（工程单位费用估算模型，如：以运输生产全过程所需各项工程费用的估计值为依据建立的运输费用估算数学模型）

engine exhaust air pollutant emission 发动机排气中的大气污染物，发动机排出的大气污染物（简称 engine emission 发动机排放，见 emission）

engine fire wall （发动机舱与驾驶室间的）隔板（参见 fire wall）

engine flushing machine 发动机冲洗机

engine for different fuel 多种燃料发动机（= multifuel engine）

engine frame 发动机机架

engine friction horsepower 发动机摩擦功（主要指发动机各运动件的摩擦损失、泵气损失及气门机械耗功等）

engine front area 发动机正面面积

engine front cover 发动机前罩

engine front support bracket 发动机前支架

engine-fuel compatibility 发动机-燃油适应性，发动机对燃油的兼容性

engine gearbox unit 发动机带变速器总成，发动机变速器组

engine generator 发动机驱动型发电机，发动机发电机组

engine governed speed （调速器限制的）发动机额定转速

engine governor 发动机调速器

engine gross weight 发动机总重量（发动机总质量的旧称，指包括底架、散热器、传动装置以及不直接装在发动机上的机油冷却器、水泵等附件的发动机总质量）

engine gum 发动机结胶（汽缸内由润滑油中分解出来的胶质物）

engine heating device 发动机起动加热器

engine hoist 发动机吊车（将发动机吊出，吊入汽车发动机舱用的小型起吊装置）

engine hold-down bolt 发动机固定螺栓

engine hood 发动机罩（亦称 engine bonnet，指车身的发动机舱的盖板，= motor hood）

engine hour meter 发动机工作小时表（发动机运转工时自动记录仪表，供维修服务参考）

engine housing 转子发动机缸体，转子发动机机体（包括各缸的旋轮线缸体、端盖、中间隔板等）

engine-hydraulic drive 发动机-液压马达驱动，发动机液力驱动（发动机带动一个等排量液压泵产生的高压液流，进入一个变排量液力马达来驱动汽车）

engine idenfication codes 见 service codes⑥

engine identification number 发动机（出厂）编号（简称 EIN 或 engine number）

engine idling time 发动机怠速工作时间

engine idling timer 发动机怠速运转自动限时装置

engineimmobilizer 发动机（防盗）锁止机构

engine in situ 装在底盘上的发动机

engine installation angle 发动机安装角

engine in V-arrangement V 形（布置）发动机

engine knock 发动机敲缸，发动机爆燃（发动机爆振，见 knock）

engine knock sensor 发动机爆燃传感器（通过测定汽缸瞬时压力，缸体振动加速度等来感知爆燃）

engine lacquer 在发动机零件上的胶状沉积

engine layout ①发动机布置（指动机在车辆上的位置，如前置、后置、横置等）②发动机形式（指缸数及汽缸的排列方式，如：V形8缸等）

engine load sensor 发动机负荷传感器（节气门开度传感器，= throttle sensor，常用 potentiometer）

engine location 发动机布置（指其安装位置及方向）

engine lube system 发动机润滑系

engine lubricating oil 发动机机油（发动机润滑油，简称 engine oil）

engine maintenance area 发动机维护范围（简称 EMA）

engine maintenance center 发动机维护中心（旧称发动机保养中心，简称 EMC）

engine maintenance through progressive analysis service 发动机逐步分析维护法（按程序逐项分析，依据分析情况进行维护作业，简称 EM/PA service，相对于计划维护而言，亦称发动机视情维护法）

engine management system 发动机管理系统（简称 EMS。一般指汽油机电子控制系统，主要包括电子燃油喷射系统、电控点火系统等，= electronic management system）

Engine Manufacturers Association ［美］发动机制造商协会（简称 EMA）

engine map 发动机特性曲面图（发动机控制参数的三维曲线图，如：点火提前角随节气门开度和发动机转速变化的三维曲线图，= engine characteristic map）

engine mapping 发动机特性曲面的测定（特指相对于所选定的某两项发动机的独立变量，如：发动机转速、发动机负荷来确定发动机的某一项随变量，如：发动机各种转速和负荷下的最佳点火提前角，的三维特性曲面）

engine mapping data 发动机特性曲面测试数据

engine misfire 见 misfire

engine modification（s） 发动机改造（改进），发动机改型（简称 EM，一般指改变发动机特性，以提高功率、节油和排放净化）

engine motoring method 发动机马达法（参见 hot motoring method）

engine motoring test 发动机马达法试验（用其他动力带动发动机旋转进行的试验）

1 engine + 2 motor type hybrid vehicle 一台内燃机加两台电动机型混合动力车（如 VW 公司的 "Cross Coupe"，前部装有一台汽油直喷式涡轮增压发动机和一台 40 kW 电动机，后部装有一台 85 kW 电动机，可使用 "发动机驱动" "发动机加电动机驱动" 和 "前后两台电动机驱动" 等行驶模式。制动、减速时前后两台电动机同时逆转发电回收减速能量）

engine-mounted 装在发动机上的

engine mounting ①安装发动机的 ②发动机支座（车架或汽车承载构件上的发动机安装点）③发动机安装座垫（如：anti-vibration mounting，防振座垫，engine rubber mounting，发动机橡胶座垫等）

engine mounting bracket 发动机（本身的）安装托架

engine mounting in rubber 发动机橡皮座垫

engine mounting isolator/body elastic model 发动机支座隔振装置/车身弹性（数学）模型

engine mounts　发动机支座（由金属和橡胶制成的发动机在车架上的支撑件）

engine multi-tester　发动机多功能检测仪，发动机综合分析仪（＝engine multi-analyser）

engine nameplate　发动机名牌

engine net weight　发动机净重（发动机净质量"engine net mass"的旧称，指不包括油、水、底架，散热器及传动装置及其他不直接装在内燃机上的附件的内燃机质量）

engine noise　发动机（运转时产生的）噪声

engine number　发动机号码，发动机编号

engine octane number　发动机辛烷值（根据发动机燃烧室形状、压缩比、冷却效率等技术条件所能容许使用的燃料的最低辛烷值，使用低于该辛烷值的燃料时，发动机便会产生爆燃，简称 EON）

engine off　发动机停车，发动机熄火

engine oil　发动机用润滑油，机油（简称 EO）

engine oil filling cap　发动机润滑油加油口盖

engine oil level warning light　发动机润滑油液面警报灯，机油油量不足警报灯

engine oil pressure indicator　发动机机油压力表（显示发动机润滑系统中油压的指示器）

engine oil tank　①发动机机油箱　②运输机油的油罐车

engine oil temperature indicator　发动机机油温度表（显示发动机机油温度的指示器，＝oil thermometer）

engine operating condition　发动机工况，发动机运转工况，发动机工作状况

engine operating parameters　发动机运转参数（指节气门开度，进气压力，大气压力，发动机转速，发动机温度等）

engine-out　发动机排出的（如：engine-out particulate matter and unburned hydrocarbon emission 发动机排出的微粒物和未燃烧的碳氢化合物）

engine-out hydrocarbon　发动机排出的碳氢化合物（简称 EOHC）

engine out method　（发动机排放物的）机外（处理）法

engine output　发动机有效功率，发动机输出功率

engine output spectrum　发动机输出功率频谱

engine-out test　（底盘）断开或不带发动机的试验

engine overhaul　发动机大修（指将发动机完全解体，更换磨损件，镗缸，磨曲轴等恢复发动机原厂性能指标的修理）

engine overhaul kit　发动机大修包（指大修用全套配件，当 kit 前有定语时，指该定语所限定的配件的大修包，如：gasket kit 指大修用全套衬垫）

engine pack　带全套附件的发动机总成

engine parameter(s)　发动机参数（一般指其功率、油耗、转矩、排放水平、尺寸、性能等）

engine peak speed　发动机峰值转速，发动机最高转速

engine performance　发动机性能（按转速和载荷，表示输出功率、转矩、油耗、效率等发动机特性的总称）

engine performance analyzer　发动机性能分析仪

engine performance computer　发动机性能（检测用）计算机

engine pickling　发动机封存，发动机封藏

engine pit 发动机维修地沟

engine primer 发动机起动燃油加注装置

engine protecting plate 发动机护板

engine prototype and development 发动机样机与研制（简称EPD）

engine racing 发动机的高速空转，发动机飞车，发动机失控高速（= racing of engine）

engine rear mounting 发动机后支座

engine rear support member 发动机的后支撑件

engine rear support pad 发动机后支撑垫

engine rebuild（ing） 发动机大修（将某台发动机拆散，对零件清洗、检测，将可修零件加以修复，不能修的零件换新，然后按技术要求组装，完全恢复发动机的使用性能与寿命，这种方法修复的发动机称为rebuilt engine）

engine reconditioning 发动机修复，发动机大修（包括镗缸、研磨气门、磨曲轴、校正连杆以及组装、调试等工艺，参见 engine remanufacturing）

engine-related 与发动机有关的，发动机相关的

engine remanufacturing 发动机整修，发动机翻新（将多个相同的旧发动机拆散，对全部零件清洗、检测、分类，可修的修复，不可修的换新，然后将可用的零件，按技术要求组装成发动机，使每台发动机都完全恢复使用性能与寿命。这是一种批量整修发动机的方法，修复后的发动机称为 remanufactured engine，可在市场销售）

engine remotor 发动机遥控装置（发动机的车外操纵器，如：一名工人检修发动机时，使发动机起动、停止、加速、减速等用的遥控操纵装置）

engine renovation 发动机修复

engine responsiveness 发动机灵敏性，发动机响应性，发动机响应特性（= engine response, engine reaction, 指发动机对控制其工况的各种输入的响应灵敏程度）

engine restart switch （大型客车怠速停机系统的）发动机再起动开关（在怠速停机系统处于停机工况时，若根据当时的情况，空调系统等辅机必须由发动机带动运转，则可通过该开关再起动发动机。通常该开关位于转向盘柱的左侧，由驾驶者左脚控制）

engine retardation （用）发动机缓速

engine retarder 发动机缓速器（如：排气制动装置等，利用发动机内部阻力，对车辆产生制动、减速效果，是一种辅助制动装置）

engine revolution counter 发动机转数表，发动机转速表

engine rig test 发动机台架试验

engine rumble 发动机低频振动（由于发动机缸内最大燃烧压力出现过早，使发动机缸体等基础件产生低频振动，preignition是引起低频振动的主要原因）

engine runner 操纵发动机者

engine running 发动机运转

engine run up test 发动机加速试验（发动机迅速提高转速试验，发动机起动试验）

engine-scope 发动机示波器（由示波器和转速表、电压表等组成，主要用于检查点火装置等的性能，并可诊断发电机的故障及对发动机进行调节等）

engine screen 发动机屏蔽（用于隔离噪声，或对外界的电波干扰等）

engine's fundamental geometric characteristics 发动机的基本几何特征，发动机的基本几何特性

engine shield（ing） ①发动机罩 ②发动机屏蔽板

engine shorting-out 发动机某一缸或数缸缺火

engine size ①发动机尺寸 ② = engine capacity

engine skid plate 发动机油底壳护板

engine sludge 发动机油泥（机油氧化沉淀物）

engine snubber 发动机扭振减振器

engine solar oil 发动机太阳油，索拉油，粗柴油

engine souping ①加大发动机马力，提高发动机功率 ②调整混合气空燃比，使达到最高转速

engine space 发动机所占空间

engine specification tag 发动机说明牌，发动机说明卡片

engine specific weight ①发动机的规定质量 ②发动机每单位输出功率的重 ③发动机每单位排量的质量

engine speed governor 发动机调速器（简称 ESG）

engine speed limiter 发动机限速器（当转速升到某规定值时，即断开供油，直到降至规定范围）

engine speed map 发动机特性曲面（见 engine map 及 engine mapping）

engine speed overshoot 发动机转速过调（超过额定值）

engine-speed power take-off 与发动机同转速的功率输出轴

engine speed（sensing）**power steering** 发动机转速感知型动力转向（动力转向特性随发动机的转速而改变）

engine-speed-sensitive power assist （转向机构的）发动机转速感知式动力助力

engine speed sensor 发动机转速传感器（简称 ESS）

engine speed undershoot 发动机转速失调（低于额定值）

engine spinning 发动机高速空转

engine stalling 发动机过载熄火（由于负荷过大等原因，被迫熄火，停止运转）

engine stand （维修使用的）发动机支架

engine starting equipment 发动机起动设备

engine start preheating switch 发动机预热起动开关（发动机冷机起动电预热装置的通电开关）

engine stop 发动机停机，发动机熄火（多指操作不当或故障引起的熄火，简称 en-st）

engine stop device （指柴油机机械式调速器中的）停机机构

engine stopping by regeneration method 发动机能量回收停机法（停止喷油后利用起动机反转发电回收能量使发动机迅速停机）

engine stroke 发动机冲程

engine subframe （车身或车架支撑）发动机（的独立）底支架

engine sump 曲轴箱油底壳

engine sump well 发动机油底壳集油槽

engine supervisory system 发动机监测系统，发动机监视系统，发动机监控系统

engine support bracket 发动机支架（= engine bracket）

engine support cushion 发动机支座减振垫

engine suspension 发动机悬架

engine swept volume 见 engine displacement

engine tachometer 发动机转速表（目前使用的有电磁式 electromagnetic-type，发电机式 generator-type 和脉冲式 pulse-type 等多种）

engine technical requirements 发动机技术条件，发动机技术规范（工厂对发动机产品规定的多项重要性能指标、结构参数和特征）

engine telemetry 发动机遥测，发动机遥测技术（测定发动机内部温度、压力、油膜、损伤等）

engine temperature sensor 发动机温度传感器（注意：不是冷却水温传感器）

engine test at full load 发动机满负荷试验

engine test bed 发动机试验台架（= engine tester, engine test bench, engine test stand）

engine test-bench characteristics 发动机台架试验特性

engine test code 发动机试验规范，发动机试验标准

engine test facility 发动机试验设备

engine testing of lubricating oil 润滑油的发动机试验（通过发动机运转测试机油的各项性能指挥）

engine test panel 发动机试验控制台，发动机试验操纵台（简称ETP）

engine test procedure 发动机试验规程

engine time scale 发动机（电子控制系统的采样和控制动作的）时标（采样和控制动作的间隔时间，如：发动机瞬态运转参数采样的时标为 $30\mu s \sim 20 ms$）

engine timing 发动机正时（指调整发动机点火提前角与气门开、闭角等）

engine timing case 发动机正时齿轮箱

engine-to-alternator ratio 发动机-交流发电机转速比

engine tools 机修工具

engine torque control 发动机转矩控制器（当牵引力过大而使车轮产生原地滑转时，动力控制模块控制发动机转矩的执行装置）

engine torque sensor 发动机转矩传感器

engine tractive force 发动机牵引力

engine tractor （以）发动机（作为动力的）拖拉机

engine-transmission package 发动机-变速器机组，发动机带变速器总成

engine transporting car 发动机运送车

engine trouble 发动机故障

engine tuner 发动机调试仪

engine tune-up 发动机调试（通过使用各种测试分析仪器，对发动机的各个系统进行调校，使发动机的各项性能达到最佳指标或要求，亦称 engine tuning）

engine tune-up tester 发动机调试诊断仪（= engine analyser）

engine tunnel 发动机试验用的风洞（用来模拟车辆行驶时迎面空气流对发动机的冷却作用等）

engine type 机型，发动机形式

engine under cover （车身底板上的）发动机车底导流罩板

engine unit 动力装置；动力机组（= power supply unit）

engine up-shift speed （变速器）换入高挡时的发动机转速

engine vacuum checking gauge 发动机（进气管）真空度检查表，进气管真空表（亦称 engine vacuum tester）

engine valve 发动机气门

engine variables 发动机变量（转速、空燃比、增压器送气压力等）

engine varnish 发动机漆膜（发动机汽缸、活塞、活塞环上由于汽油燃烧和机油分解产品而形成的光亮的漆状硬膜）

engine vibration 发动机振动

engine wash ①发动机机洗（油底壳中注入洗涤剂，使发动机急速运转，用以清洗发动机）②冲洗发动机

engine water jacket 发动机冷却水套

engine water outlet 发动机出水管

engine wear 发动机磨损
engine weight 发动机重量（发动机质量的旧称）
engine-wise ①发动机安装方位 ②发动机旋转方向 ③与发动机转向一致的（简称EW）
engine with air cell 空气辅助室式柴油机（= air-cell diesel engine）
engine with antechamber 预燃室式发动机（= precombustion chamber engine）
engine with cylinders all in one piece 多缸整体式发动机（各汽缸铸成整体的发动机）
engine with direct injection 直接喷射式发动机（= direct-injection engine，对柴油机指无副室式的，对汽油机指汽油直接喷入汽缸内的）
engine with mechanical injection 机械式燃油喷射发动机
engine with open toroidal piston cavity 活塞顶部带环形燃烧室式的发动机
engine with opposed cylinders 对置汽缸发动机
engine with revolving cylinders 旋转汽缸发动机
engine with supercharger 增压式发动机（= supercharged engine）
engine with variable compression 可变压缩比发动机
engine yaw 发动机左右横摆（故障）
Engler's degree 恩氏黏度（°E）
Engler seconds 恩氏黏度秒数（流体恩氏黏度的单位，多用于欧洲大陆，指 $200 \times 10^{-6} M^3$ 的流体流过恩氏黏度计的时间秒数，= Engler number、Engler degree、Engler unit）
English heating test 润滑脂加热试验
English spanner 活动扳手，活络扳手
English system 英制
English thread 英国标准螺纹，威氏螺纹

English unit 英制单位
eng rm 发动机舱（engine room）
enhancement mode MOS transistor 增强型金属-氧化物-半导体晶体管
enlarged 放大的，扩大的，扩充的，增长的
enlargement of crankcase 曲轴箱裙部
enlargement of ring grooves 活塞环槽高（由于磨损造成）的扩大
Eno Foundation for Transportation [美]意那运输基金会
enriched fuel 浓缩燃料，富化燃料
enriched material 浓缩物，加浓物质
enriched water gas 浓化水煤气，浓水煤气（= carburetted water gas）
enriching device （可燃混合气）加浓装置
enrichment ①（特指混合气）加浓（提高混合气中燃油对空气的比例）②浓集，浓缩，使变浓
ENS （汽车）电子导行系统（electronic navigation system的简称）
en-st 发动机熄火（engine stop）
ensue ①（在某事件后）接着发生 ②因（某事件而）产生[如：the damage ensued（接着是损坏）；"in the ensuing time"（在随后的时间里）]
ensure 保证，确保
ent 入口（entrance）
entablature （机器部件的）支柱，上横梁（= entablement）
enterprise of vehicle maintenance and repair 汽车维修企业
entertainment controls （汽车车内设备的各种）娱乐性设施（如音响、影视等）操纵装置
enthalpy 热函，焓
enthusiasm （原意为人的热情、热心，现亦用于描述汽车发动机的）澎湃动力
4×4 enthusiast 四轮驱动车爱好者

entrained air 掺气，夹杂的空气（参见 aeration）

entrained droplet 夹杂（在气体中）的（液体）微滴

entrainment ①引开，输送，传输 ②带去，挟带，夹杂，③夹杂物（如：气流中悬浮的浮微粒、泡沫或液滴或液流中的气泡、微粒等）

entrainment rate （发动机的周围空气）吸入率，导入率

entrainment separator 液滴分离器，雾沫分离装置

entrainment trap 雾沫分离器，液滴分离装置，液滴捕集

entrance bias （液力变矩器叶片的）进口边斜角（指设计流线处的叶片进口边相对于轴平面的斜角）

entrance design radius （液力变矩器叶片单元等的叶片）进口设计半径（参见 design radial）

entrance discharge curve 入口流量曲线

entrance door 入口门；上车门

entrance velocity of whirl 入口涡流速度

entrant 赛车手（指参加赛车者）

entropy 熵（$dS = dQ/T$，式中 dQ 热变化量，T 绝对温度）

entropy diagram 熵图，熵-焓图

entruck 货车装货，把……装入货车，装入货车货箱

entry ①入口，门口，进口 ②进入，输入，引入 ③通路，通道，引入线

entry car 入门车（指新兴市场需求的经济车型）

entry/exit ease （汽车的）上/下方便性，进/出容易性（乘员自车门进出的容易程度）

entry height （客车）上下车高度，（车门）踏板高度

entry spin 进气旋转

entry-step height （客车或货车驾驶室门的）踏板高度

Entune 安顿［TOYOTA 公司新型车载信息系统（Toyota's information system）商品名］

envelope 蒙皮，外壳，外套，包装；机壳，机罩；包囊；包络线，包络面

envelope flame 包焰（混合气流速小于火焰传播速度）

envelope of a trochoid （转子发动机）旋轮线的包络线

envelope separator （免保养电池中使用的多孔塑料袋状）隔板

enveloping outer enclosure 外包络线

enveloping power of tire 轮胎（对路面不平度的）包容性能

enveloping worm 环面蜗杆（分度曲面是圆环面的蜗杆，旧称球面蜗杆或弧面蜗杆）

Enviroguard 环保（美国 Fleetguard 公司供 8-5 级货车使用的开式曲轴箱通风系统"open crankcase ventilation system"的商品名）

Enviroment Agency ［日］环境厅（简称 EA）

environment 环境，周围介质，外界条件

environment accelerated cracking 环境因素造成的加速缝裂（指腐蚀断裂，腐蚀疲劳，氢蚀致脆等）

environment-adapting headlamp 环境适应性前照灯（可根据行车环境，如市区、高速公路、雨天、雾天等自动调整照度）

environmental 环境的，周围的，外界的，外部的

environmental activity 周围介质的活动度

environmental coefficient 环境系数（表征环境变化造成的影响，如海拔高度时气压的影响等）

environmental compatibility 对周围环境的适应性

environmental condition （车辆或机

械，人员所处的）环境条件（所处周围的外界条件的总称）

environmental control unit 环境控制系统（简称 ECU，一般指温度、气压、湿度等的控制装置）

environmental demands 环保要求（环境保护对排放等的要求）

environmental effect 环境效应（指环境因素对车辆的影响）

environmental extremes 环境的极限条件

environmental factors 周围因素，外部介质条件，环境因素，外界条件因素

environmental hazard 环境公害

environmental impact （对）环境（的）冲击（如：汽车对环境的排气污染、噪声污染等）

environmental impact assessment 环境影响评估（简称 EIA）

environmental insulation 环境隔离（指隔离外界条件的影响）

environmental laboratory 环境人工模拟试验室（可再现汽车周围的使用环境和条件，可控环境条件试验室，亦称 environmental cabinet, environmental chamber。在这类试验室进行的试验称 environmental test，这类试验所使用的设备或设施称 environmental test facilities 或 environmental unit）

environmentally acceptable 环境可接受的（指对环境无污染、生态效应良好、降解率高者）

environmentally friendly liquid fuel 环境友好型液体燃料，对环境无害的液体燃料，对环境无污染的液态燃料

environmentally friendly vehicle 环境友好车辆（简称 EFV）

environmentally-oriented 与环境有关的

environmentally-sealed 与环境隔离的

environmental parameter 环境参数（表征环境条件的各种参数，如温度、湿度、风力、噪声等）

environmental pollution 环境污染

Environmental Protection Agency [美]环境保护局（简称 EPA）

environmental specification 对环境条件（如：气压、温度等）的规定

environmental stress 环境介质造成的应力

environment-conscious 有环境（污染）问题的，对环境污染有要求的

Envirox 一种燃油携带型催化剂的商品名

envision 展望

EO ①椭圆轨道（见 elliptical orbit）②终点站（见 end office）③技术指令（见 engineering order）④发动机机油（见 engine oil）⑤见 ergosphere origin ⑥异逻辑电路（见 exclusive-OR）⑦执行指令（见 executive order）

E-OBD Ⅱ 欧洲第二代车载式故障诊断系统（Europe-on-board diagnostic system Ⅱ 的简称）

EOC 转换结束，切换终了（end of conversion 的简称）

EOD 数据结束（end of data 的简称）

EOF 帧结束（end of frame 的简称）

EOHC 发动机排出的碳氢化合物（engine-out hydrocarbon 的简称）

EOHS 见 electrically operated hydraulic steering

EOI 喷油结束，喷油终止（end of injection 的简称）

EOL 使用寿命终了，寿命终止（end of life 的简称）

Eolys （罗地亚电子与催化剂材料公司研制的柴油添加剂型）微粒排放物过滤器再生催化剂的商品名，主要成分为铈土"Ce"，以添加剂的形式加入柴油，通过降低过滤器捕

获物—炭微粒的着火点和其燃烧温升来加速过滤器再生。据德国、瑞典等国家环保部门测试表明，Eolys与高效微粒物过滤器配合作用，柴油机的微粒物排放量可降低99%

EON 发动机辛烷值（engine octane number 的简称）

EOS ①电过载（electric overstress 的简称）②电光学系统（electro-optical system 的简称）③废气（中）氧含量传感器（exhaust oxygen sensor 的简称）

EOT 试验结束，试验终了（end of test 的简称）

EOTS 电子光学跟踪系统（electron optic tracking system 的简称）

EP ①搭铁板（earth plate 的简称）②发动机参数（engine parameter 的简称）③电偏振的（electrically polarized 的简称）④电力驱动（electrical propulsion 的简称）⑤电控气动的（electropneumatic 的简称）⑥终点，终端（end point 的简称）⑦工程项目（engineering project 的简称）⑧感应电位（evoked potential 的简称）⑨极限压力，超高压力（extreme pressure 的简称）

EPA ［美］环境保护局（Environmental Protection Agency 的简称）

EPA composite economy ［美］（按环保局城市-公路混合油耗标准测定的汽车）环保局混合经济性（用MPG 表示，= EPA'S composite city-highway fuel consumption value）

EP additive 极压添加剂（extreme pressure additive 的简称，用于提高润滑油膜承受超高压力的能力）

EPA highway cycle 美国环境保护局（颁布的）公路试验循环（用于测定汽车燃油经济性及排放的多工况试验循环）

EPA'S composite city-highway fuel consumption value ［美］保护局的城市-公路混合油耗标准（见 EPA composite economy）

EPAS system 电动助力转向系统（electric power assisted steering system 的简称）

EPB/APB 电子控制驻车制动器/主动式驻车制动器（electronic parking brake/active parking brake 的简称，由按钮操作，兼起防盗及各种辅助性制动作用）

EPC ①见 electrostatic power coating ②电子压力控制，电子调压（electronic pressure control 的简称）③［美］电子产品公司（Electronic Products Corporation 的简称）

EPCA ［美］能源政策与保护法（Energy Policy and Conservation Act 的简称）

EPC solenoid （电子控制式自动变速器的）电子液压控制电磁阀（根据电子控制模块的指令控制自动变速器主油路压力控制滑阀的电磁阀，electronic pressure control solenoid 的简称）

EPD 发动机原型与研制（engine prototype and development 的简称）

EPDM 见 ethylene-propylene-dimer rubber

EPD technique 见 electronic production definition technique

EPEC 发动机电子程序控制（electronic programmed engine control 的简称）

EP film 耐极压润滑油膜（= extreme pressure film 的简称）

EP gear oil 极压齿轮油（多用于变速器和主减速器等，可阻止高压下齿轮润滑油膜破坏、导致金属直接接触）

EPHS 见 electrically operated hydraulic steering

EPIC 见 exhaust port ignition cleaner

epichlorohydrin elastomers 氯甲代氧丙环（OCH_2CHCH_2Cl）弹性材料，表氯醇弹性材料

epicyclic 周转（圆）的，外摆线的

epicyclic gearbox 行星齿轮变速器（= planetary gearbox，美称 planetary 或 epicyclic transmission，指至少有一个轴线可转动的齿轮机构。由行星齿轮排、内齿圈、行星架和太阳轮组成，借助离合器和制动器控制上述元件的啮合和运动关系而实现速比变换）

epicyclic motion 周转圆运动（A圆沿B圆外周无滑动地转动时，A圆所做的运动。由于这一运动与行星绕太阳的运动相似，若将圆换为齿轮，则B圆为太阳齿轮、中心齿轮，A圆为行星齿轮，因此亦称为行星齿轮运动）

epicyclic single-planet helical gear 斜齿单排行星减速装置

epicycloid 外摆线〔旋轮线，在平面上，一个动圆（发生圆）沿着一固定圆（基圆）外侧做外切或内切滚动时，动圆圆周上任一点的轨迹。若该点在做外切的动圆之内，或作内切的动圆之外且与动圆固连，则其轨迹称短幅外摆线 curtate epicycloid，若该点在做外切的动圆之外，做内切的动圆之内并与动圆固连，则其轨迹称长幅外摆线 prolate epicycloid〕

epicycloidal 外摆线的

epidemic prevention vehicle 传染病防疫车

epidemiological approach 传染病学法（利用传染病学的方法，分析研究交通事故）

epitaxy 外延层，（晶体）取向接生

epitaxy technique 外延工艺（指在衬底上生长一层与衬底有相同或相近晶相的半导体材料的过程）

epitrochoid 长短幅圆外旋轮线（在三角转子发动机有关的术语中，可简称圆外旋轮线或外旋轮线）

epitrochoidal base circle 外旋轮线基圆（参见 epitrochoid）

epitrochoidal bore （转子发动机的）外旋轮线缸筒

epitrochoidal chamber （转子发动机的）外旋轮线工作室，工作腔（指外旋轮线缸壁与转子工作面形成的空间）

epitrochoidal engine 外旋轮线旋转发动机（指其腔室成外旋轮线形的旋转活塞式发动机，如：汪克尔三角转子发动机）

epitrochoidal generating point 外旋轮线创成点（参见 epitrochoid）

epitrochoidal path 外旋轮线轨迹（参见 epitrochoid）

epitrochoidal rolling circle 外旋轮线滚动圆（参见 epitrochoid）

epitrochoid generating radius （转子发动机缸体型线）长短辐圆外旋轮线创成半径

EP lubricant （耐）极压润滑剂（extreme-pressure lubricant 的简称，一般用于承受极高压力的运动摩擦件，如高性能齿轮系等）

epoxide 环氧化合物

epoxy ①环氧树脂（见 epoxy resin）②环氧树脂的 ③环氧树脂胶（= epoxy adhesive）

epoxy adhesive 环氧黏合剂，环氧树脂胶（简称 EA，亦称 epoxide cement，epoxy resin adhesive，简称 epoxy）

epoxy resin 环氧树脂（亦写作 epoxide resin，或简称 epoxy，其物理性质随硬化剂、硬化温度的不同而不同，一般硬化收缩率小，机械-电性质、溶剂性良好，黏接力强，常用

来做黏合剂）

epoxy-seal 环氧树脂封装的

EPR ①乙烯丙烯橡胶（ethylene propylene rubber 的简称，为乙烯和丙烯的聚合物）②工程部门要求（engineering part requirement）③发动机压力比（engine pressure ratio 的简称）④蒸发器压力调节阀（evaporation pressure regulator 的简称）

E-pretensioner 电子控制式（安全带碰撞前）预拉紧装置

E-program （汽车电子控制系统的）经济运行模式控制程序［economy (mode) program 的简称］

EPROM 可擦可编程只读存储器（erasable programmable read only memory 的简称，= reprogrammable read only memory，erasable read only memory，一种可编程的只读存储器，在正常使用时只能进行读操作，但其中的信息可使用紫外线辐射曝光擦除和再次编程。有的使用电信号擦除和编程，称电可擦可编程只读存储器，electrically erasable programmable memory，简称 EEPROM 或 electrically programmable read-only memory，也简称 EPROM）

EPS ①电动力转向（系）［electrical power steering (system) 的简称］②发动机性能控制（engine performance control 的简称）③电子控制动力转向（electronically controlled power steering 的简称）④蓄电（池）（electric power storage 的简称）⑤电源（electrical power supply 的简称）⑥应急动力源（emergency power supply 的简称）⑦多孔聚苯乙烯（expanded polystyrene）

EPS assistance 电动力转向助力（electric power steering assistance 的简称）

EP seal 乙烯丙烯密封件（ethylene propylene seal）

epsilon iron nitride surface 氮化 ε 铁表面

EPS motor 电动力转向（系）电动机（electrical power steering motor 的简称）

EPS system （全）电力转向系（electric power steering system 简称，其电子控制模块根据车速传感器、转向盘转矩和转向盘角速度传感器等的信息控制一台电动机通过传动机构提供最佳转向助力。全电力转向系又可分为齿轮助力型"pinion assist type"和齿条助力型"rack assist type"两大类）

EPT ①排气压力变换器（exhaust pressure transducer 的简称，装在某些 EGR 系统的进气歧管与真空调节器"VER"间的真空通路内，通过一膜片阀控制进入真空调节器"EVR"的真空。该膜片上方与节气门上方的真空孔相通，下方与 EGR 阀下方的排气管道相通。当发动机转速较低时，排气压力不足以使膜片阀关闭，由节气门下方来的真空经开启着的膜片阀消逸，不能进入 EVR，只有在规定转速下，排气压力足以将膜片阀关闭，进气管真空才能进入 EVR）②排气压力传感器（= exhaust pressure sensor，指将排气压力变为电信号输出的器件）

eq ①相等，等于（equal）②设备（equipment）③等效的（equivalent）④等式（eguation）

equal distance wear （轮胎的）等距磨耗（对不同轮胎在同一使用条件下行驶里程相等的单位磨耗进行对比）

equality-of-contrast photometer 等对比光度计

equalization 相等，均等；平衡，均衡；稳定，安定；调均，等化，补偿

equalize 使均衡，使平衡；使相等，

使均匀；补偿，调整

equalizer 平衡器件（起平衡、均衡、补偿作用的各种机构、装置、器件、部件的通称，如：①将驾驶员的控制力均衡地传给左、右车轮驻车制动器拉杆或拉绳的平衡臂②双轴并装车桥平衡式悬架中，使相邻两轴载荷成一定比例、保持平衡的平衡臂③车用立体声收音机的图像平衡器，多频音调均衡器④均衡电路，补偿电路⑤使曲轴保持动平衡块等）

equalizer bar (= equalizing bar) ①（悬架的）平衡臂（见 equilizer beam）②（泛指任一）起平衡作用的杆件

equalizer bar pivot 平衡臂摆动轴

equalizer beam ①平衡梁②（双轴并装式车桥平衡悬架中的）平衡臂（简称 equalizer，亦称 equalizer bar, equalizer rod, equalizing beam，使相邻两轴载荷成一定比例，保持平衡的构件）

equalizer circuit 补偿电路，均衡电路

equalizer turning radius gauge （汽车的）平衡型转弯半径测定仪（一种前轮的直前规型转角测定器，在测定器前装有车轮直前规，保证左右前轮处于直前位置驶入转角测定器，根据所测定的转角算出转弯半径）

equalizing gear 平衡机构（参见 balance gear）

equalizing spring （起）平衡（作用的）弹簧

equalizing (type) suspension （货车等双轴并装式后桥的）平衡悬架（可使相邻两轴和车轮的垂直载荷相等或保持平衡的悬架形式，有单钢板弹簧推力杆式，双钢板弹簧推力杆式和摆臂式等多种。详见 single-leaf-spring thrust-rod type equalizing suspension, two leaf-spring thrust-rod type equalizing suspension 和 swing arm type equalizing suspension)

equalizing valve 平衡阀

equal lay 等捻距，等绞距绞合（钢丝，绳索）

equal-loudness curves 等响度线（亦称 equal loudness contours，为声响测定仪器的设计基准，纵坐标表示声压级单位为 dB，横坐标表示频率，单位为周/s，图中用多条曲线表示纯音在不同频率时的声压级，这些曲线便称为等响度曲线。当某一声音的听觉响度与频率为 1K·Hz 的某纯音相等时，该音的响度级数即等于该纯音的音压级的分贝数，参见 loudness level）

equal power distribution 等功率分配（亦称 equal power split，指四轮驱动车辆中，分配给前、后轮的功率相等）

equal volume combustion 等容燃烧

equation 方程式；等式，公式

equation of motion （汽车的）运动方程（式）[$dE = (P - \sum R) dS$，式中：P—牵引力；$\sum R$—运动总阻力；E—动能；S—行驶距离]

equation of state 状态方程（一组表示系统状态与输入变量间的关系并含有状态变量一阶导数的方程式）

equatorial line （原意为地球上与南北极距离相等的赤道线，在汽车上指）轮胎胎面等分圆周线（轮胎的胎面与车轮过其旋转中心的垂直平面的相交圆）

equiangular 等角的

equicrural triangle 等腰三角形 (= isosceles triangle)

equidimension 等尺寸，等大小，同样大小

equidistant 等距（离）的

equidistant curve 等距曲线（在平面上，与既定曲线上各点的法向距离

处处相等的曲线，称为该既定曲线的等距曲线。若以该既定曲线上的各点为圆心，作一系列等直径圆，则这些圆内、外侧包络线也就是该曲线的等距曲线）

equidistant curve radius （转子发动机缸体型线）理论曲线的等距半径（即等于径向密封片圆弧半径）

equifrequent 等频率的

equilateral triangular rotor （转子发动机的）等边三角转子，等边三角旋转活塞

equilibrant ①平衡力，平衡者，均衡力，均衡物 ②平衡的，均衡的

equilibration 平衡，相称，均衡

equilibrium 平衡，均衡（复数为equilibria）

equilibrium about pitching axis 绕（汽车）纵倾轴的力矩平衡

equilibrium about rolling axis 绕（汽车）侧倾轴的力矩平衡

equilibrium diagram 平衡图，状态图，（合金的）金相图

equilibrium reaction potential （电化学反应的）最小反应电压

equilibrium reflux boiling point 平衡回流沸点（评定制动液等气障性的重要参数，测定方法：控制加热量使产生的蒸气冷凝后不断地定速、定量流回原混合液，测定其平衡沸点值）

equilibrium temperature 达到平衡状态时的温度

equilibrium value 平衡值，补偿值

equimolal ①等摩尔质量的（见molality）②等摩尔体积的（见molarity）

equimolecular 等摩尔分子量的

equip 装备，配备

equipage 设备，装备，成套设备

equipment ①设备，装备 ②工具，机具；装置，器械，仪器 ③（车身）附件（指装在驾驶室等处具有独立功能的总成，如：刮水器、门锁、门泵等，= body accessories）

equipment compatibility 设备互换性，设备兼用性

equipotential 等电位的，等电势的

equipressure cycle 等压循环

equiprobability 等概率，概率相等

equispaced 等间距的，等间隔的

equiv ①电化学当量（electrochemical equivalent 的简称）②当量，等效，等值，等价（equivalent 的简称）

equivalence ratio （混合气的）当量比（指空气燃料混合气中的实际燃料质量 m_r，与按化学理论计算，混合气中的氧气全部化合所需的燃料质量 m_t 的比值。$\dfrac{m_r}{m_t}=1.0$ 的混合气称为理论混合气，$\dfrac{m_r}{m_t}>1.0$ 的混合气称为浓混合气，$\dfrac{m_r}{m_t}<1.0$ 的混合气称为稀混合气）

equivalent ①当量；等效值；等价物；等效，等价 ②当量的，等效的，等价的 ③当量系统（在工程上常将复杂系统进行简化，简化后的系统与原来系统的效果相当，则称为当量系统，或等效系统）

equivalent barrier speed （车对车碰撞模拟试验中的）等效壁障速度

equivalent braking force 等效制动力率（美国SAE定义为：整车总制动力与总重之比,%。相当于我国常用的术语"制动减速率"或"制动强度",定义为单位车辆重力的地面制动力。GB5620.1—85定义为"制动因数" "braking efficiency factor"：总制动力与作用在车辆一个或若干个轴上的静载荷之比）

equivalent circuit 等效电路

equivalent concentration 当量浓度

equivalent emission 当量排放量（如：纯电动汽车的当量排放量便

是按提供其充电电量的发电厂在发电过程中的排放量来计算的)

equivalent g loading 以重力加速度g作为单位的等效载荷

equivalent inertia mass 当量惯量[在汽车底盘测功机上测试时,模拟汽车行驶时惯(性质)量的等效惯(性质)量,用惯性飞轮匹配。如日本规定试验汽车总质量为$1876\sim2125kg$的当量惯量标准值为$2000kg$]

equivalent input(output) capacitance (of a binary circuit) (二进制电路的)等效输入(输出)电容[作为二进制电路输入(输出)阻抗中的电容性成分,在数字信号波形上起等效分立电容器作用的电容]

equivalent length 当量长度,等效长度

equivalent load 等效载荷

equivalent noise method 等效噪声法(为噪声响度级的测定法,参见 stevens loudness level)

equivalent of cantilever spring 悬臂钢板弹簧的等效弹簧

equivalent priced distance 等值运距(指汽车货运中采用专用车辆运输与采用通用车辆运输时,其运输生产率或运输成本相等时的运输距离。等值运距包括生产率等值运距与成本等值运距两种)

equivalent representation 等价表示;等价表现

equivalent running time 等效运转时间,当量运转时间(在机器或零部件的耐久性和寿命计算中常常用当量时间的概念将在实际工作过程中的变动负荷折算成一不变的当量负荷,此时两者对机器或零部件耐久性的影响应相同)

equivalent shaft horsepower 等效轴马力,当量有效功率(简称ESHP)

equivalent steering angle 等效转向角(见 reference steering angle)

equivalent ton-kilometerage volume 换算周转量,当量周转量(客车附带载货或货车附带载客,按规定比例换算成统一的计量单位,中国规定:旅客周转量与货物周转量的换算比例是 10 人·km 等于 1t·km)

equivalent total displacement (转子发动机)整机当量排量,整机等效排量(由于三角转子发动机的主轴每转一转只有一个工作室做功,正好与两缸直列四冲程往复式发动机相同,因此从做功排量上看,一台单缸三角转子发动机等于一台每一缸排量与转子机单室排量相同的两缸直列式四冲程往复机。为了便于与四冲程往复发动机比较,转子发动机常采用整机等效排量。其计算方法:整机等效排量=单室排量×2×转子数,= equivalent displacement volume, 有时称 Wankel engines displacement, 参见 chamber displacement、chamber volume)

equivalent unit 等效单位,当量单位(简称EU)

equivalent value 当量值,等效值,换算值

equivanlent area of tubine nozzle (废气涡轮增压的)涡轮当量喷嘴面积(由喷嘴环出口面积与动叶轮出口面积所组成的一种折合面积)

Era 耐热耐蚀合金钢

erasable programmable read only memory 可擦可编程序只读存储器(用紫外线照射即可将存储的信息消掉,并可重新编程的只读存储器)

Erasable storage 可擦存储器(= erasable memory)

erase 擦除(在存储器中去除信息的过程)

ERDA [美]能源研究和开发局(Energy Research and Development

erection of engine 发动机安装

erection stress 安装应力，装配应力

erector ①（挂车的）升降架，举升器，安装架 ②安装工人，装配工人

erector transport vehicle 带起重设备的载货汽车；起重运输车辆

eremacausis 慢性氧化

ERF ① 见 electro-rheological fluid ②（英国）厄夫（汽车公司）

erg 尔格（能量或功的单位。1 尔格里 1 达因的力使物体移动 1cm 的功）

ergonomic 人体工程学的，符合人体工程学原理要求的

ergonomical design 人体工程设计（依据人体工程学原理和要求，对汽车的有关部位进行设计，如：对驾驶室、操纵机构、显示仪表以及座椅等等）

ergonomics 人机工程学，人体环境工程学，人机系统工程学〔研究劳动者与劳动环境之间的关系，就汽车领域而言，指研究与处理人体（乘员，驾驶人员）与其所乘坐或驾驶的汽车及汽车的控制与操纵之间的关系的科学，亦称 human factors，在美国多称 biotechnology〕

ergonomic seat 指符合人体工程学原理的（汽车）座椅

Ergonomics Research Society 人体工程学研究学会

ergosphere origin 驾驶员操作空间范围的几何平均值原点（简称 EO）

ERGS ①试验路线导向系统（experimental route guidance system 的简称）②（汽车）电子导航系统（参见 electronic route guidance system）

ERI 工程研究所（Engineering Research Institute 的简称）

Erichsen cupping test （板材的）爱氏冲盂试验

ERM 电子控制防翻车（系统）（roll-over mitigation system 的简称，见 RSC）

erode 腐蚀，磨蚀

EROM 可擦只读存储器（erasable read only memory 的简称，见 EPROM）

erosion 侵蚀（指生物、有机物和无机物的物理性质或所处状态引起或诱发的机械损坏或改变材料结构的现象）

erosion of electrodes 电极的烧蚀（如：火花塞电极的烧蚀）

ERP 道路电子收费（指道路通行费，由电子管理系统自动收取，汽车不必停车缴纳，electronic road pricing 的简称）

erratic 不规律的；反复无常的；不稳定的；移动的，漂游的；反常的；错误

error correcting 误差校正，修正误差（简称 EC）

error method 尝试法（见 trial and error method）

error of indication （仪器仪表的）示值误差〔仪器仪表示值减去被测量的（约定）真值〕

error rate 误差率

error sensor 误差传感器

error signal 误差信号（指示希望值与实际值之差）

ERS （汽车）经济运行系统（economy running system 的简称）

ERst 异常状态，错误状态（error state 的简称）

ERT （吸气歧管各汽缸的）等长度进气管（equal range tract 的简称）

ES ①节能装置（energy savings 的简称）②技术规范（engineering specification 的简称）

ESA 电子控制点火提前（装置）（electronic spark advance 的简称）

ESB ①电磁制动器（electromagnetic brake 的简称）②膨胀弹簧制动器（expansion spring brake 的简称）

ESC ①（Bosch 公司汽车）电子稳定性控制系统的商品名，electronic stability control 的简称，该系统根据有关传感器的信息确认车辆偏离驾驶人员意图的行驶方向时，而通过制动等方式修改，使车辆按驾驶员所操控的方向稳定行驶，防止汽车搭向滑稳等。三菱称 ASC，宝马称 DSC，奔驰称 ESP，保时捷称 PSM，日产称 VDC，本田称 VSA）②电子控制防滑装置（electronic skid control 的简称，防止制动时车轮抱死的电子控制系统，目前已不再使用这一术语，而普遍称 ABS "防抱死制动系统"）③电子控制悬架系统（electronic suspension system 的简称）④见 electronic spark control

ESCA 排放物光谱化学分析（emission spectro chemical analysis 的简称）

escalater 自动梯，自动升降机，自动电梯（= escalator）

escape 漏出，逸出；逸散，漏失；排放，排出

Escape Hybrid 福特公司一款混合动力运动型多功能轿车（SUV）的车名

ESCI 电子控制点火（electronic spark control ignition 的简称）

ESCS 电子悬架控制系统（electronic suspension control system 的简称）

ESC system（汽车）稳定性电子控制系统（electronic stability control system 的简称，指通过控制车轮的驱动力和制动力确保汽车不偏离规定车道、按驾驶者所要求的路线稳定行驶的电子控制系统，见 ESP。有时指 ABS、BA、ASR XDS、EDIC、TRSP 等与车辆行驶、制动稳定性有关的各个系统的总称）

E. S. C system（美国福特汽车公司的）电子控制点火提前系统（electronic spark control system 的简称）

escutcheon lamp 盾形铭牌、刻度盘等的照明灯

escutcheon plate 盾形商标牌，标牌，铭牌

ESCV 涡流电子控制阀（electronic swirl control valve 的简称）

ESD ①电火花检测器（electro spark detector 的简称）②静电放电（electro static discharge 的简称）

ESECA［美］能源供应及环境协调法（Energy Supply and Environmental Coordination Act 的简称）

ESF（Benz 公司的）安全概念车（名）

ESG 发动机调速器（engine speed governor 的简称）

ESHP ①总有效马力（见 effective summed horsepower）②当量轴马力（见 equivalent shaft horsepower）

ESI（汽车）电器维修信息（Electric Service Information 的简称，Bosch 公司为其汽车销售、维修店提供的电器维修资料手册名）

ESL 电控悬架高度调平系统（electronic suspension levelling system 的简称）

ESM ①膨胀弹簧制动器（expansion spring brake 的简称）②工程维修备忘录（engineering service memo 的简称）③工程技术标准手册（engineering standards manual 的简称）④试验性安全摩托车（experimental safety motorcycle 的简称）⑤安全试验机动车（experimental safety motor vehicle 的简称）

ESN 电子序列号（electronic serial number 的简称）

ESP ①电子控制稳定程序（electronic stability program 的简称，德国 Bosch 公司和 Mercedes-Benz 公司对汽车动态稳定性控制系统的称呼，=三菱公司的 ASC，丰田公司的 VSC，宝马公司的 DSC，保时捷公

司的 PSM。这一系统的电子控制模块通过车速、横向加速度和转向盘转角等传感器的信息，判定出现不利于车辆稳定性—稳定转向或稳定行驶的情况时，采用对相应车轮施加制动或降低发动机功率输出等方式，保持车辆的稳定行驶，参见 VSC, ASC）②节能产品（energy saving products 的简称）

ESP tractor-safety system 电子控制稳定性程序牵引车安全系统（Bendix 公司通过制动各个车轮和减低车速来防止汽车列车牵引车与挂车折叠，提供抗侧倾稳定性和校正横摆等的电子自动控制系统，ESP 为 electronic stability program 的简称）

ESP with brake assist 制动支持的电子控制稳定性程序（系统）

ESR 或（esr） 见 electric sun roof

ESS ①电子开关系统（参见 electronic switching system）②发动机转速传感器（见 engine speed sensor）③电控悬架系统（见 electric suspension system）④紧急制动信号灯（见 emergency stop signal）

ESSC ①欧洲（重型货车发动机排放的）稳态（13 工况测试）循环（European Steady State Cycle 的简称）②电子同步换挡控制系统（electronic synchro-shift control 的简称）

Essolube（日本标准石油公司制造的）润滑油（商品名）

EST 电子控制点火正时（electronic spark timing 的简称，一般是指发动机电子控制模块的点火正时功能）

ESTA 电子控制同步变速器总成（electronically synchronized transmission assembly 的简称）

estate car [英] 接站车（指具有后门的长方形车厢五门长头轿车。原来为接站或旅行时便于装、放较大件的行李，其车厢常为木制，亦有金属制，我国多称旅行车，简称 es-

tate，亦称 estate wagon, estewagon, 美称 station wagon）

ester 酯（R-CO O-R）

esterification 酯化作用；

ester oil 酯类合成机油

esthetic 美术的，美学的，美的，审美的（= aesthetic）

estimate ①判断 ②估计值，推定值，概算值，估价单 ③估计，估算，估价；评价

ESV（Experimental Safety Vehicle 的简称）试验性安全车（美国运输部 DOT 于 1972 年 2 月提出试验安全车计划，要求车辆以 50mile/h 迎面碰撞时确保乘员安全。为此包括美国在内的各主要汽车生产国均对车辆结构、强度及各种被动安全保护系统进行了试验，ESV 指的便是进行这项试验研究所专门设计、使用的车辆，其中轿车称 ESC, experi-mental safety car 的简称，客车称 ESB, experimental safety bus 的简称）

ESV energy management system 试验安全车能量吸收系统，试验安全车能量处理系统（指该车吸碰撞冲击能量以保护乘员的安全系统）

ET ①有效温度（effective temperature 的简称）②电动运输（electric transportation 的简称）③发动机试验台（engine tester 的简称）④排气温度（exhaust temperature 的简称）⑤超高温（extreme temperature 的简称）

ETA 估计到达的时间（estimated time of arrival 的简称）

ETACS 电子时间与警报控制系统（electronic time & alarm control system 的简称，是无钥匙进入系统、前照灯、刮水器、后视镜、警报系统、时间控制系统等的电子综合控制系统）

Etak Navigator Etak 导行系统（Etak 公司 20 世纪 80 年代在加利福尼亚推

出的第一代带有电子地图及推算法定位并由电子地图显示的汽车导行系统的商品名)

etalon ①基准,规格 ②标准量具,标准样件 ③光谱干涉仪 ④波光测定仪

etape ①日赛程(汽车拉力中,通常指一天的行程,是全赛程中的一个赛段。1个日赛程包括若干个特殊赛段,几个联络路段,以及几次聚集和休息,参见 rally) ②一日的行程 ③宿营地

ET-AT/S 马自达公司研制的电子控制自动变速器 EC—AT 的改进型

ETBI 电子控制节气门体汽油喷射(electronic throttle body injection 的简称)

ETC ①见 electronic throttle control ②见 electronic traction control ③见 electronic transmission control ④见 estimated time of completion ⑤见 European Transient Cycle

etch ①蚀刻,蚀刻剂 ②浸蚀,锈蚀,腐蚀 ③酸洗

etch pit 腐蚀斑点,锈蚀坑,腐蚀麻点,刻蚀凹坑

etch-proof 防腐蚀的,防锈蚀的

ETCS 电子收费系统(参见 electronic toll`collection systems)

ETCS-i 智能型节气门控制系统(丰田公司电子控制节气门系统的商品名,electronic throttle control system-intelligent 的简称)

ETDC 见 MSR

ETF ①发动机试验设备(engine test facilities 的简称) ②工程试验设备(engineering test facilities 的简称) ③环境试验设备(environmental test facilities 的简称)

ethanal 乙醛(见 aldehyde)

ethane 乙烷(C_2H_6)

ethanediol 乙二醇(见 glycol)

ethanol 酒精,乙醇(见 ethyl alcohol)

ethanol blended gasoline 酒精汽油(简称 EBG,将一定比例的酒精掺入汽油中,以提高汽油的抗爆性,= alcohol-gasoline,blend gasohol)

ethanol- butanol blended fuel 乙醇-丁醇混合燃料

ethanol-diesel blend fuel 乙醇-柴油混合燃料(简称 Ex-D, x 为某一数字,表示乙醇的百分比含量,如:E5-D,表示乙醇占5%,余为柴油)

ether 醚,乙醚(用于柴油机冷起动助燃液)

ether-air mixture 空气-醚混合气

ether-assisted start 用乙醚助燃的起动(柴油机冷起动)

ether fume 乙醚蒸气

etherified fuel 醚化燃料(20世纪70年代开发的一种非石油基燃料,见 MTBE)

ether spray priming system (柴油机的)喷醚引燃系统

Ethy ①四乙基铅 ②高标号四乙基铅汽油

ethyl ①乙基,乙烷基($CH_3CH_2—$) ②四乙基铅抗爆剂 ③含四乙基铅的汽油,乙基化汽油

ethyl alcohol 酒精,乙醇($CH_3CH_2 \cdot OH$,简称 alcohol,= ethanol)

ethyl alcohol-diesel blend fuel 乙醇柴油混合燃料(简称 diesohol)

ethylated gasoline 乙基汽油

ethylcellulose 乙基纤维素

ethylene 乙烯(C_2H_4),次乙基($—CH_2CH_2—$)

ethylene/acrylic elastomer 乙烯/丙烯盐酸共聚物,人造橡胶(简称 EAE,主要用于制造汽车密封件,具有良好的抗高温机油腐蚀性,可在 $-54℃ \sim +177℃$ 内正常工作)

ethylene chloride 氯化乙烯($CH_2CL \cdot CH_2CL$)

ethylene diamine 乙(撑)二胺,乙

二胺（[1,2] $NH_2CH_2CH_2NH_2$）

ethylene diffusion flame 乙烯扩散火焰

ethylene glycol 甘醇, 乙(撑)二醇（$HOCH_2CH_2OH$, 汽车防冻液的主要原料之一, = glycol, 简称EG）

ethylene glycol based antifreeze (汽车发动机用)乙二醇(甘醇)基防冻液

ethylene methyl acrylate 乙烯甲基丙烯盐酸（车用高性能人造橡胶的基料）

ethylene oxide copolymer 乙烯化氧共聚物, 环氧乙烷共聚物（简称EOC）

ethylene oxide epichlorohydrin (一种)车用人造橡胶（可在高温下保持良好的韧性）

ethylene-propylene-dimer rubber 乙烯丙烯(二聚物)橡胶（合成橡胶的一种, 为乙烯和丙烯的二聚物, 简称EPDM, 亦简称EPR）

ethylene propylene rubber 乙烯丙烯橡胶（= EPR）

ethylene propylene seal 乙撑丙烯密封件（简称EP seal）

ethyl fluid 乙基液（指含四基铅的抗爆液, 可减缓燃烧速率, 使燃烧压力升高线平缓）

ethyl gasoline 乙基汽油（指加有四乙基铅抗爆液的汽油, = ethyl petrol）

ethyl-hexyl-nitrate 乙基-己基-硝酸酯（简称EHN, 燃油十六烷值的增高剂）

ethylization 乙基化

ethylized fuel 乙基燃料, 乙基汽油, (加四乙铅的汽油, = leaded fuel)

ethyl nitrate 硝酸乙酯（$C_2H_5ONO_2$, 芳香无色液体, 柴油抗爆剂, 用来提高十六烷值）

ethyl petrol 含四乙铅汽油（= ethyl gasoline）

ETO 欧洲运输组织（European Transport Organization）

ETP 发动机转矩脉动模拟（engine torque pulsation simulation 的简称）

ETR ① 通电使运转（energized to run）② (空调)蒸发器温度调节器（evaporator temperature regulator）

ETS ①增强型牵引力控制系统（enhanced traction control system 的简称, 通过改变点火提前角和变速器挡位控制牵引力, 防止车轮滑转）②鉴定试验规范（evaluation test specification 的简称）③ (汽车碰撞)创伤伤害程度试验（experimental trauma severity 的简称）④废气涡轮增压器（exhaust-gas turbine supercharger 的简称）⑤驱动力电子控制系统（electronic traction system 的简称, 一般与ABC系统合二为一, 或成为ABS的一部分, 可自动感知车轮滑转状态, 并采取对滑转车轮施加制动或减少点火提前角、控制节气门、变速器换高挡等措施减少发动机输出转矩, 从而消除车轮因牵引力大于路面附着力而造成的滑转）⑥通用公司将具有通过减小点火提前角(或)变速器换高挡进行牵引力控制功能的系统, 也称ETS, 但它是Enhanced traction system 的简称, 即: 增强型附着力控制系统⑦电子控制转矩分配式四轮驱动系统（Advanced Total Traction Engineering System for All Electronic Torque Split 的简称, 日本日产公司四轮驱动汽车前、后轮驱动力分配系统的商品名。ETS的电子控制模块, 根据传感器输入的各种信号, 确定车辆的实际姿势并与此时转向盘位置下的标准姿势进行比较, 确定对车辆姿势的修正量及实现该修正量所要求的前、后轮驱动力比值。该系统可使车辆前、后驱动力的比值在0∶100到50∶50的范围

内连续无级变化,以保证车辆在各种行驶工况的条件下,保持转向盘转角的原转向姿势)

ETSO 通电使停机(energized to shut off 的简称)

ETTM system 电子交通管理及自动收费系统(electronic toll and traffic management system 的简称)

ETV 电动试验车辆(electric test vehicle 的简称)

E type multilink suspension E型多杆式(独立)悬架(日本马自达公司 1986 年开发的一种减振器、悬架弹簧紧凑布置在车身底板下的悬架形式商品名)

Eu ①能量单位(energy unit) ②熵的单位(entropy unit) ③当量单位(equivalent unit) ④安装设备(e-rection unit) ⑤铕(europium)

EU 欧洲联盟,欧盟(European Union 的简称)

eudiometer (气体燃烧时的)容积变化测定器,空气纯度测定管,测气计,气体燃化计

EUI (柴油机的)电子控制"喷油泵-喷嘴"一体式燃油喷射系统(electronic unit-injector injection system 的简称,每个汽缸均直接安装一个"泵-喷嘴"总成件的燃油喷射系统)

euphoria-driven(car) 驾驶起来特别愉快的(汽车)

EUP injection system 电子控制"泵-喷嘴"分体式燃油喷射系统(electronic unit-pump injection system 的简称,整台发动机使用一个喷油泵,喷油泵供给的高压燃油经高压油管分送到各缸喷油器的燃油喷射系统)

Euro 6 欧洲 6 排放标准,欧 6(将于 2017 年开始实施)

euro 欧元〔2002 年起欧盟成员国的货币单位,注意:欧元 e 为小写,勿与 E 为大写的 Euro(欧洲的、欧盟的)混淆〕

Euro Emission standards 欧洲排放标准(EuroⅠ,1993 年颁布,EuroⅡ, 1996 年颁布。EuroⅢ,2000 年颁布,该标准的排放限值为:颗粒物 0.05g/km,NO_x 0.5g/km,HC + NO_x 0.56g/km,CO 0.64g/km, EuroⅣ, 2005 年颁布,要求:颗粒物 0.025g/km,NO_x 0.25g/km,HC + NO_x 0.3g/km,CO 0.5g/km,目前已实施 EuroⅤ,要求更加严格)

EuroFOT 欧洲现场运行试验(European Field Operational Test 的简称,欧洲包括 Ford、BMW、Volvo 在内的 8 家汽车厂、12 所大学和研究单位、4 家支持机构参加,由汽车厂家和供应商提供 1500 辆小轿车和货车进行的现场安全评价活动)

Euromixcycle 欧洲混合循环(部分城市驾驶工况与部分公路驾驶工况的混合多工况排气污染测试循环)

EUROMOT 欧洲内燃机制造商协会(European Committee of Internal Combustion Engine Manufacturers' Association 的简称)

Euro NCAP 欧洲新车安全评价计划组织(European New Car Appraisal Plan 的简称)

European Caravaning Federation 欧洲旅居车旅行联合会(简称 ECF)

European Economic Community 欧洲经济共同体(简称 EEC,亦称欧洲经济共同市场 European Economic Common Market)

European Load Response Cycle 欧洲(重型货车发动机烟尘排放的)负荷响应(测试)循环(在规定的条件下迅速改变发动机转速和负荷,测定其瞬态烟尘排量,简称 ELR)

European Steady State cycle 欧洲(重型货车发动机排放)稳态(测试)循环(简称 ESC,包括发动机

可用转速范围内的13种工况，取加权值）

European Transient Cycle 欧洲（汽车发动机排放的）瞬态（测试）循环（整个测试期间转速和负荷不断变化，简称ETC）

European Transport Organization 欧洲运输组织（简称ETO）

European version （车辆等的）欧洲版（欧洲型，在欧洲销售的，在欧洲制造的，符合欧洲标准的等等）

europium 铕（Eu）

EUT 待试设备（equipment under test 的简称）

eutectic ①易熔的，低共熔的，共晶的，低熔的 ②易熔物质，低共熔混合物，共熔合金，共晶体，低共熔体 ③低共熔点（= eutectic point）

eutectic mixture 共熔点混合物（从溶液中同时析出两种以上结晶的混合物）

eutectic point 共熔点（混合物的共熔温度）

eutectoid ①共析体，不均匀共析体，共析合金，易熔质 ②共析的，共析混合的，共析体的

eutectoid structure 共析结构

EUV 超紫外辐射（extreme ultraviolet radiation 的简称）

EV 电动汽车（electric vehicle 的简称，一般指纯电动汽车，即：仅此高能源电池为动力的电动汽车）

ev 电子伏特（electron volt 的简称）

EVA ①一种聚烯烃塑料（ethylene vinyl acetate copolymers 的简称）②[美]电子汽车协会（Electronic Vehicle Associates 的简称）

EVAAP 亚洲太平洋电动汽车联合会（The Electric Vehicle Association of Asia-Pacific 的简称）

evacuate ①抽空，抽成真空 ②抽出，排出

evaluating test （对…的）评价试验（如：dynamic rollover propensity evaluating test 对动态翻倾特性的评价试验）

evaluation for noise 噪声的评定

evap ①蒸发（evaporation）②蒸发器（evaporator）

evaporate ①蒸发，挥发，汽化 ②脱水 ③浓缩 ④升华 ⑤逸散，消失，发散 ⑥（电子）发射

evaporation carburettor 蒸发式化油器

evaporation chamber 蒸发室，蒸发腔

evaporative condenser 蒸发式冷凝器

evaporative emission control system （燃油）蒸发排放物控制系统（减少燃油系蒸发损失和减少蒸发排放物对大气的污染的系统，亦称 vapour recirculation system。将蒸发排放物再直接送入进气系或暂时存入活性炭罐，适当时再送入进气系统的回收装置。一般由吸附燃油蒸气的活性炭罐，控制该罐与进气歧管连通的电磁阀或真空阀等组成。Chysler 公司简称 EVAP，福特与通用公司称 canister purge，简称 CANP。美国政府规定从1995年起一律使用 SAE 推荐的标准术语 Evap Emission Cont，简称 EEC）

evaporative emissions 蒸发排放物（从汽车的燃油系统，即燃油系、润滑系等处排放到大气中的燃油蒸气，有时包括整车涂料的溶剂蒸气）

evaporative leak detection system （燃料的）蒸发漏逸检测系统

evaporative losses （汽车的燃油）蒸发损失

evaporator 蒸发器（汽车空调系统中利用制冷剂蒸发吸收热量的热交换器）

evaporator core assembly （汽车空气调节装置等的）蒸发器芯子总成，

蒸发芯子总成，吸热芯子总成

evaporator-pressure regulator （汽车的液化石油气）汽化器-压力调节器（二者一般装在同一壳体内，用于使液化石油气气化并控制其压力）

evaporimetry 蒸发测定法

EVAP solenoid 蒸发排放物控制电磁阀（evaporative emission control system solenoid 的简称。当发动机起动后 PCM 进入闭路控制模式，冷却水温 >80℃，车速及发动机转速均在规定值以上时，PCM 使该电磁阀通电，该阀开启，储存在活性炭罐内的燃油蒸气便经该阀而被进气管内的真空吸入进气管。这一过程称为活性炭罐清除，故该电磁阀又称为活性炭罐清除电磁阀，见 CANP solenoid。当不符合上述条件时，该电磁阀关闭，燃油蒸气仍存储在活性炭罐内）

EVAP system 见 evaporative emission control system

evasive ability （汽车行驶时）闪避障碍物的能力；机警行驶的能力

evasive action （汽车的）避车动作（在紧急状态下汽车回避行驶障碍的动作）

EVC ①排气门关闭（exhaust valve closes 的简称）②电动汽车商品化（electric vehicle commercialization 的简称）

EVD 排气门积炭（exhaust valve deposit 的简称）

EVE 电动汽车工程（electric vehicle engineering 的简称）

even ①平滑的，平坦的，平整的；均匀的，均等的，相等的，一致的 ②偶数的，双数的

event ①事件，偶然事件 ②过程，现象，活动，作用 ③结果，终局 ④间隙，距离 ⑤（内燃机）冲程，动作

event-related distribution （软件模型的）事件相关分配

event test 破坏性试验

event triggered 事件触发的（用于说明通信协议。汽车电子系统中，指接受信息的精确时间未作规定，而是按随机事件触发的通信协议执行，参见 TTP/C）

eventual failure 最终破坏

even wear 均匀磨损

everlasting 永久（的），持久（的），耐久性，无穷（的），经久不变的，继续不断的

Everlube 一种低温润滑油（耐寒润滑油的商品名）

everyday car 日常用轿车（非豪华型轿车，普及型轿车的统称）

everyday check up （对汽车车况等的）每日例行检查

EV hybrid car 带内燃机/发电机组（向蓄电池充电以提高续航里程的纯）电动汽车

EVIC 见 electronic vehicle imformation center

EVIC Chrysler 电子控制车载信息娱乐中心（Chrysler vehicle information center 的简称，商品名，有时仅指该系统的显示-控制屏）

evidential breath test ①进排气验证试验 ②通风验证试验

EV mode （复合动力车的）电动车模式（electric vehicle mode 的简称，指仅由电动机驱动，以较低的，如 55km/h 以内车速安静行驶的运行模式）

EV-mode dash push button （复合动力车的）电动车模式踏钮（轻轻踩踏该踏钮，即可进入电动车"EV"行驶模式，供车辆在深夜等安静时刻驶入和驶出居民区）

EVO ①排气门开启（exhaust valve opens）②电子控制可变孔径（electronic variable orifice）

evoked potential （脑电波的）激发电位，感位电位，诱发电位（简称 EP）

evolute ①展开线 ②渐屈线，法包线 ③波形装饰 ④展开的

evolute profile splined joint 渐屈线花键接合

evolution car 进化车（指经过长期使用、参赛等不断改进的车型）

evolve ①逐渐形成，逐步发展 ②进化

EVP （公司，学会等的）执行副总裁（executive vice president 的简称）

EVP sensor 废气再循环阀位置传感器（EGR valve position sensor 的简称）

EVR ①见 EGR vacuum regulator ②见 external voltage regulation

EVRV 电子控制真空调节阀（electronic vacuum regulation valve 的简称）

EVS 电动汽车（国际研讨与）展览会（Electric Vehicle Show 的简称）

EVs 电动汽车（electric vehicles 的简称）

EVSA 电子（控制刚度）可变式减振器（electronic variable shock absorber 的简称）

EVT 电控连续变速器（electric variable transmission 的简称）

EW ①电动（车）窗（electric windows 的简称）②与发动机旋转方向一致（的），发动机旋转方向的（engine-wise 的简称）

e-4WD 电动式四轮驱动系统（日产公司的前轮由汽油机驱动，后轮由发动机驱动的发电机提供电源的电动机驱动的电子控制四轮驱动系统的商品名，由于不再使用后轮机械传动系统，不仅减轻车重，而且消除了后轮传动系统摩擦和传动损失。此外，还显著提高了车轮防滑控制性能）

EX ①试验过的，检查过的（examined，亦简称 EXD）②过剩，剩余（excess）③激励器，激磁机（exciter）④膨胀，扩张（expanding）⑤例，实例，例证（example）

exact fit 精确配合

examination of car 车辆检验，汽车审验，汽车检查

example 例，实例，例证，例题，范例，样品，样本

exanol 汽油轻馏分的聚合物

EX. B 排气制动（exhaust brake）

excavator 挖掘机，挖土机

excell tester （蓄电池的）单格电池充电状态检验器（测起动工作状态及非工作状态时的端电压）

excentric 偏心的

excentricity 偏心度，偏心率，偏心距

excentric shock absorber 偏心式减振器（＝excentric damper，或简称 excentric shock）

excess ①过量，过剩，过度，超过，超额 ②过量的，超过的，超额的，过剩的

excess air factor 过量空气系数，空气过量系数（＝实际空燃比/理论空燃比，亦称 excess air ratio，excess air coefficient）

excess consumption of fuel and oil （汽车）费油（指燃料的消耗超过技术文件的规定）

excess flow loss 溢流损失

excess flow valve 溢流阀，防过流阀（简称 EFV，一般液化石油气汽车的燃料供给系统中，在液化石油气瓶的排液阀处必须安装防过流阀，以保证安全）

excess force ①余裕力，余裕功率 ②（汽车的）后备功率，后备马力（汽车具有的驱动能力与行驶阻力之差，用来表示汽车的加速、爬坡、牵引等能力，亦称 excess power）

excess freight 超载货物

excess fuel device （为使混合气加浓

而)增加发动机供油量的装置(如起动加浓装置、阻风门等)
excess fuel limiter (柴油机喷油泵上的)过量燃油限制器
excess fuel limiter stop 过量燃油限制器断开器
excess voltage preventer 防超电压装置
exchangeable 可互换的
exchange diffusion (气体的)互相扩散,交流扩散,交互扩散(简称 EXD)
exchange engine 备用发动机,互换用发动机(一般指旧发动机修复后存库,准备换装于其他大修等车辆)
exchange of complete units (整套)部件总成更换
exchanger 交换器(如热交换器)
excide battery 铅蓄电池(糊制极板蓄电池)
excircle 外圆
excise tax [美]消费税(美国对汽车、备件、轮胎、汽油等征收的零售税)
excitation 励磁,激磁;激发,激励,刺激,扰动,干扰,激振
excitational equipment 激振设备(产生一干扰力或位移,使汽车或结构产生振动的设备)
excitation experiment 激振试验(将结构作为激振器的弹性负载,在激振器励激下产生强迫振动,从而确定结构的动态特性,如:固有频率、振型、刚度、阻尼及机械阻抗等)
excitation frequency 激振频率
excitation potential 激发电位
excitation winding 见 field winding
excite 激磁,励磁,激励,激发(如:在汽车电器中使电流通过磁场线圈等)
exciter ①励磁机;激发器,激励器 ②振荡器(亦写作 excitor)
exciter ring (变磁阻转速传感器的)激磁齿圈
exciting 励磁的,激励的

exciting current 励磁电流,激励电流(使线圈励磁的电流)
exclusive circuit 专用电路
exclusive guideway 专用导轨
exclusive-OR "异"逻辑运算(当 A、B 输入均为 1 或 0 时,输出 C 为 1,当 A、B 输入中有一个为 0 或 1,则输出 C 为 0)
exclusive pedestrian phase (交通信号中的)行人专用信号相
exclusive route 专营线路(由指定的运输经营者专门经营旅客或货物运输的线路)
exclusive transportation service 专营运输(由指定的经营者在特定的范围或条件内,专门经营的旅客或货物运输)
excursion ①偏差,偏移,偏离额定值 ②振幅 ③(短途)旅行,(集体)游览
excursion vehicle 游览车
EXD ①试验过的(examined) ②交互扩散(exchange diffusion 的简称)
ex-demonstrator 销售商用于展示的车辆
executive car 见 executive limousine②
executive-class sedan 行政首长级用双排座轿车
executive component 操作元件,执行元件
executive limousine ①华贵轿车,豪华轿车(中国标准,至少两排座,有 4 个或 4 个以上座位,前后排座间有隔板,有 4 个或 6 个侧门, = pullman saloon) ②商业首脑或行政部门主管官员乘用的大型大功率豪华轿车(亦称 executive car)
executive order 执行指令(简称 EO)
exempt vehicles 免税车辆(= tax exempt vehicle)
exergonic ①产生能量的 ②放能的,放热的,放热的
ex-Ford designer 福特汽车公司编外设计人员

EXH ①排气,废气(exhaust) ②展览,显示,陈列(exhibit)

exh 废气,排气(exhaust)

exhaust ①排出,排放 ②排气系统(= exhaust system) ③排出的废气(exhaust gas) ④排出的,排气的

exhaust advance angle 排气提前角(指膨胀冲程中,排气门开放的瞬时到活塞行至下止点的曲轴转角)

exhaust after-burner 排气后燃净化器(参见 exhaust air induce)

exhaust aftertreatment device 排气后净化处理装置(指废气自发动机排气门排出后进行净化处理的所有净化装置)

exhaust air induce 排气负压二次空气引入(利用排气脉冲负压将新鲜空气吸入排气系统,使废气二次燃烧,净化废气中的C、HC、CO等有害排放物,简称EAI)

exhaust analysis test (发动机)废气分析试验(指测定内燃机排放的废气成分及其含量的试验)

exhaust analyzer 废气分析仪

exhaust back pressure 排气背压(简称EBP或back pressure,指由于排气系的摩擦阻力和各种限制、拘束、阻碍排气的因素造成的对废气由发动机排出至大气的阻力;排气管出口处的废气压力,增压式柴油机,指涡轮后的压力)

exhaust back pressure sensor 排气背压传感器(亦称 exhaust back pressure transducer 或 exhaust back pressure transmitter)

exhaust blower 排气风扇,抽气风扇

exhaust box 排气消音器

exhaust brake (发动机)排气制动器(指通过限制、阻碍发动机排气气流的方法,增加发动机缓速效果的汽车缓速装置)

exhaust brake indicator lamp 排气制动指示灯

exhaust branch 排气歧管

exhaust calorimeter 排气热量计(测定发动机排气热含量的仪器)

exhaust cam 见 exhaust (valve) camshaft

exhaust camshaft 排气门凸轮轴(指顶置式双凸轮轴式发动机中开、闭排气门的凸轮轴,亦简称 exhaust cam, = exhaust valve camshaft 或 exhaust valve cam)

exhaust casing (利用高压废气直接压缩新气的气波增压器的)废气腔(= exhaust housing)

exhaust chamber 排气室(二冲程发动机排气系统中用于保持排气背压的腔室,亦称 exhaust chest)

exhaust channel (转子发动机的)排气孔道

exhaust control system 排气净化系统

exhaust cross-over intake manifold 废气横穿式进气歧管(该进气歧管内有一条由真空阀控制的废气横穿管道,冷机起动或低温运转时加热进气充量)

exhaust curve (示功图的)排气曲线,排气线(= exhaust line)

exhaust cut-out (排气缓速器的)排气阻断阀,排气节流阀(亦称 exhaust shutter valve, exhaust brake flap 或 muffler cut-out valve,装在消声器前的排气管内的阻滞排气气流流动的阀门。当需要发动机制动时,驾驶员操纵该阀门关闭,废气受阻,不再流向消声器排出,而产生缓速作用)

exhaust cycle 排气冲程,排气期

exhaust deflector 排气偏导器,排气挡板,排气导流板

exhaust detonation 排气爆燃噪声

exhaust dilution tunnel (柴油机排烟测定的)排气稀释风道(测定排气排放物中颗粒状物质质量的取样装置。用清洁空气稀释排气,使其按

一定流量流动。采集其中一定量于滤纸上,多与定容取样装置一起使用)

exhaust duration 排气持续期,排气持续角(指排气门开启到关闭所经历的曲轴转角)

exhausted cell 耗尽的电池,放完电的电池,用废的电池

exhausted gas 废气(发动机排出的气体,= exit gas)

exhaust emission control system 废气排放物控制系统,排气净化系统,废气净化系统(为减少排气排放物中有害成分的各种控制系统的统称,参见 emission control system)

exhaust emission(s) 废气排放,废气排放物(指发动机排气系统排到大气中的 CO、HC、NO_x、烟尘、SO_x 等的统称,= exhaust pollutants)

exhaust energy recovery 废气能量,回收,排气能量回收(主要包括热量、动能)

exhauster ①排尘器,抽风机,排气装置,排气通风机 ②利用部分真空卸散货(如:粉状货物)的装置

exhaust expansion ratio through turbine (废气涡轮增压的)涡轮膨胀比(涡轮进口气体静压与出口气体静压之比)

exhaust explosion 排气管爆燃(放炮)

exhaust extractor 废气抽出装置

exhaust fan 抽风扇,抽风机(draft fan)

exhaust flame damper 排气火焰消焰器

exhaust flap 排气阀

exhaust flow 排气流

exhaust fume 排烟,排出的废气

exhaust gas analyzer (发动机)废气(成分)分析仪,废气有害物含量分析仪

exhaust gas cleaners 排气清洁器(排气滤清器和排气净化器的总称,见 exhaust gas filter 和 exhaust gas scrubber)

exhaust gas composition 废气成分,排气成分

exhaust gas energy recovery 废气能量回收(简称 EGER,指排气热能、动能等的利用,如:废排气涡轮增压等)

exhaust gases 排气,废气(指从发动机排出的废气)= effluent gas

exhaust gas filter 排气滤清器(用机械、静电或其他物理方法除去废气中的固体微粒及油粒,水蒸气)

exhaust gas heater (汽车车厢的)排气预热式暖风器(利用废气热量加热暖风)

exhaust gas intake port (气波增压器)废气进口,排气流进口

exhaust (gas) oxygen sensor 废气含氧量传感器,排气氧传感器(废气流中的自由氧的数量可以直接反映混合气的空燃比,因此该氧传感器为任一种完善的发动机电子闭路控制系统必不可少的传感器之一)

exhaust gas purification (system) (柴油机的)排气净化系统[一般由EGR,废气净化器(见 exhaust scrubber),废气滤清器,(见 diesel exhaust filter)及(或)催化转化器等组成]

exhaust gas recirculation 见 EGR

exhaust gas recirculation/exhaust pressure regulation 废气再循环-废气压力调节(简称 EGR/EPR)

exhaust gas recirculation rate 废气再循环率(简称 EGR rate 或% EGR,有 EGR 时进气歧管中混合气的 CO_2 含量,减去无 EGR 时进气歧管中混合气的 CO_2 含量,再除以有 EGR 时进气歧管中混合气的 CO_2 含量)

exhaust gas recirculation valve 废气再循环阀(见 EGR valve)

exhaust gas recycle 废气再循环(= exhaust gas recirculation,简称 EGR)

exhaust gas sampling 废气取样法（废气取样分为直接取样、全袋取样和定容取样三种）

exhaust gas scrubber 排气净化器（指借吸附、吸收或化学作用除去排气中有害成分使其变为无害物的装置，简称 exhaust scrubber，见 exhaust gas cleaners）

exhaust gas sensor 排气传感器（测定排气中的氧含量的各种传感器的统称）

exhaust gas smoke cleaner （柴油机）排气黑烟滤清器

exhaust gas stator ①（气波增压器）废气进出口壳体 ②（燃气轮机）排气导流叶栅

exhaust gas temperature sensor 排气温度传感器（一般指装在催化转化器上，用于监测催化剂温度的传感器）

exhaust gas turbine supercharger 废气涡轮增压器（简称，exhaust gas turbocharger, ETS）

exhaust gear 排气装置，排气机构

exhaust-heated 废气预热的，利用废气加热的

exhaust-heated (open) cycle （燃气轮机）排气预热开式循环

exhaust heating 废气取暖（装置），排气加热（装置）

exhaust heat loss 排气热损失（指燃料热量中被废气带走的热量）

exhaust heat recovery device 废气热量回收装置

exhaust horn 排气喇叭（利用排气流发声）

exhaust hydrocarbon emission 废气中的 HC 排放（量）（专指排气管中排出的未燃 HC，不包括油箱、油管等处蒸发或泄漏出的碳氢有害物，即一般自排气中测出的 HC 有害物，= unburned HC emission）

exhaustion of the accumulators 蓄电池耗尽，储能器耗尽，储水器用尽

exhaustive ①消耗性的，会耗尽的 ②彻底的，详尽的，全面的

exhaust jacket 排气加热套，废气加热套（包覆于液加热体，废气从中流过）

exhaust jet 排气射流；废气射流

exhaust lag angle 排气迟后角（在排气过程中，从活塞行至上止点到排气门完全关闭的曲轴转角）

exhaust lay out 排气流程布置，排气线路，排气管道

exhaust lead 排气提前（排气门提前开启）

exhaust line （示功图中的）排气曲线

exhaust loss （发动机的）排气损失（废气带走的热量等）

exhaust main 排气总管

exhaust manifold （发动机）排气歧管（汇集各汽缸排出的废气并与后面的排气总管连接的废气管道）

exhaust manifold collar 排气歧管（管端的）安装凸缘，排气歧管安装法兰

exhaust manifold joint 排气歧管接头

exhaust manifold reactor 排气歧管反应器，排气歧管净化装置（将新鲜空气引入排气管，使 HC、CO 二次燃烧净化）

exhaust muffler 排气消声器

exhaust noise 排气噪声

exhaust note ①（排气管端产生的）排气声 ②排气特征

exhaust open 排气门开启（状态）（简称 EXO）

exhaust opening ①排气口，排气孔 ②排气门开度

exhaust oxidizer 废气氧化器（废气中的 HC、CO 氧化）

exhaust particulates 排气微粒（废气中各种固体微粒的总称，包括炭粒、烟炱，铅氧化物等重金属化合物等微粒）

exhaust phase 排气相,排气阶段,排气过程

exhaust pipe 排气总管(指内燃机,排气歧管或增压器废气出口与消声器之间的排气管)

exhaust pipe screening ①排气管隔热挡板(隔热层等,亦称 exhaust shielding)②排气管护罩

exhaust pipe yoke 排气管托架

exhaust piping 排气管路(布置)

exhaust plumbing 排气管道

exhaust pollutants ①见 exhaust emissions ②排气污染物(指排放物中对环境的污染物)

exhaust port 排气孔道,排气孔(①四冲程发动机指汽缸盖内的从排气门口到排气歧管之间的短孔道 ②二冲程发动机指汽缸壁上的将废气从汽缸排出至排气系的孔口)

exhaust port ignition cleaner 排气管点火废气净化系统(在排气管内设置第二火花塞,使废气中的CO、HC再燃烧,简称EPIC)

exhaust port liner 排气口衬套(为了使排气保持高温,便于其中的HC、CO继续燃烧而镶在排气口内的衬套。一般用耐高温合金或陶瓷制成)

exhaust pressure 排气压力(排气管内的废气平均压力,带废气涡轮增压器的指涡轮后的废气平均压力)

exhaust pressure controlled EGR system 排气压力控制式EGR系统(以排气压力作为控制信号来控制再循环的废气量的EGR系统, = exhaust pressure modulated EGR valve)

exhaust pressure pulsation 排气压力脉冲(排气形成的压力波)

exhaust pressure ratio 排气压力比(简称EPR)

exhaust pressure regulator 排气压力调节阀

exhaust products 排出的燃烧产物

exhaust-pulse scavenging 排气脉冲扫气(二冲程或增压发动机利用排气压力波的疏波部分,在排气口附近形成降压效应,使汽缸内的废气较多的排出的扫气方式,见 scavenging process)

exhaust purification 废气净化(指减少或消除废气中的有害成分, = emission control)

exhaust purifier 排气净化器

exhaust pyrometer 排气温度计,排气高温计

exhaust reheating 排气再热(用于排气净化)

exhaust residual percentage 残余废气百分率(指残余废气占汽缸内可燃混合气的容积百分比)

exhaust resistance 排气阻力,排出阻力

exhaust retarder 排气缓速器,排气制动器(利用阻止发动机排气的方法,增大发动机内部的运动阻力,而对汽车起缓速作用)

exhaust roar 排气噪声

exhaust scrubber (柴油机的)排气净化器(见 exhaust gas scrubber)

exhaust sensor 废气(氧含量)传感器(测定废气中的氧含量,借以确定混合气的空燃比以及发动机的燃烧状况,为三元催化净化系统的主要传感元件,现多称 O_2 sensor 或 oxygon sensor)

exhaust shroud 排气管罩,排气管屏板

exhaust shutter(valve) 排气阻流阀(exhaust retarder 中的主要部件,用以阻止排气流出的节流阀门)

exhaust side 发动机的排气门和排气歧管一侧

exhaust silencer 排气消声器(简称 silence, = muffler)

exhaust smoke (柴油机的)排气烟度(指柴油机排气被光束照射后吸收

光束的指标,或排气透过滤纸的染黑度,即:废气中相对的炭黑含量,简称烟度)

exhaust smoke density (柴油机等的)排烟浓度

exhaust smoke meter 排气烟度计

exhaust smoke opacity 排气烟不透明度,排气烟尘不透光度

exhaust solids 废气中的固体微粒(如:烟尘、粉尘)

exhaust stack 排气管,抽风管

exhaust stroke (四冲程发动机的)排气冲程(废气从汽缸内排出时相应的活塞冲程)

exhaust supercharger 废气涡轮增压器

4-2-1 exhaust system 4-2-1 排气系统(四缸发动机1、3缸和2、4缸的排气管先分别汇集连接至一根副排气主管,然后这两根副排气主管再汇集连接至一根排气主管)

4-1 exhaust system 4-1 排气系统(四缸发动机1、2、3、4缸的排气管全部汇集连接至一根排气主管)

exhaust system 排气系统(包括排气歧管、排气管、消声器、废气净化后处理装置。后处理装置如:催化转化器,排气再燃烧器等。此外,还包括废气增压器,以及监测、控制和利用废气的各种装置、支架、支座等)

exhaust tank 消声器;废气膨胀箱

exhaust temperature 废气温度,排气温度

exhaust thermal reactor 废气净化热反应器(见 thermal reactor)

exhaust timing 排气正时(指排气门开、关时刻或排气始、终点的控制或确定)

exhaust treatment 废气处理,排气处理(指排气净化,减少其有害物的任何措施)

exhaust tube 排气管,排出管

exhaust turbo blower 废气涡轮增压器的压气机(指由废气涡轮增压器的废气涡轮机带动的直接压缩新鲜空气的压气机部分,亦称 compressor wheel)

exhaust-turbocharged diesel engine 废气涡轮增压式柴油机

exhaust turbo supercharger 废气涡轮增压器(见 turbocharger)

exhaust turbo supercharging 废气涡轮增压充气,排气涡轮增压充气(利用排气驱动涡轮带动压气机增压充气)

exhaust valve ①(特指发动机的)排气门 ②(泛指各种)排出阀门

exhaust valve lifter ①排气门挺杆 ②(为减少起动时活塞压气阻力而设置的)排气门顶升机构

exhaust valve (lifting) cam 排气门(顶升)凸轮

exhaust valve regulator 排气门调节器

exhaust valve tappet clearance 排气门挺杆间隙(指排气门脚端面与其挺杆之间的间隙)

exhaust velocity 排气速度;排出速度,流出速度,出口速度

exhaust ventilation 排气通风,抽气通风

exhaust volume 排气容积

exhaust whistle 废气吹动的气喇叭

exhaust window 排气窗口

EXHST 废气,废物,用乏(exhaust 的简称)

EXH V 排气门(exhaust valve 的简称)

existent gum 溶于燃油的胶质(= dissolved gum)

existing 现行的,现存的(参见 existent)

exit ①出口,通道,太平门 ②(计算机的)退出(指终止或转移程序某一部分的执行指令或语句)

exit angle ①喷束锥角 ②出口角

exit bias (液力变矩器等的)出口斜边角(指设计流线型处的叶片出口边相对于轴平面的斜角)

exit design radius (液力变矩器等叶片单元的叶片)出口设计半径(见 design radial)

exit direction sign (高速公路的)出口方向标志(通常设置在减速车道起点,为驶离高速公路的驾驶员指示连接驶出匝道路线的名称、编号、目的地等)

exit door 出口门;下车门

exiting 从路上驶出;驶离(高速公路)

exit ramp marking 出口匝道路面标示,出口坡道路面标志

exit turn 转出,转弯驶出(从过境线转入匝道)

exit velocity of whirl 出口涡流速度

EXO 排气门开启(exhaust open 的简称)

exoenergic 放能的,放热的(= exoergic)

exoskeletal 无骨架的,无架的;整体承载外壳的,承载式的

exoskeletal structure 无架式结构,承载式结构

exoskeletal tanker semitrailer 无车架罐式半挂车

exostructure 外壳承载式结构

exotherm (因化学能量被释放出来而引起的)温(度)升(高)

exothermic 放热的,发热的,放能的(亦写作:exothermal)

exothermic reaction 放热反应

exotic ①外国产品,外来品种,外来语 ②外国制造的,外国来的,外国生产的 ③奇特的,稀有的

exotic performance car 特优性能轿车,高性能轿车

exp ①增大,膨胀(expansion) ②消耗性的(expendable) ③开支,费用(expense) ④有经验的(experienced) ⑤实验性的(experimental) ⑥指数(exponent) ⑦输出(export)

expandable polystyrene 可膨胀的聚苯乙烯(含有戊烷等挥发吹胀剂,当加热时可膨胀而塞满塑模)

expanded (cellular) rubber 海绵橡胶,多孔(泡沫)橡胶

expanded joint (管接头)扩口连接,扩口管接头

expanded metal 膨胀金属(简称 EM)

expanded mobility truck 高机动性载货汽车(简称 EMT)

expanded plastics 多孔塑料,泡沫塑料(见 aerated plastics)

expanded polystyrene 多孔聚苯乙烯,多孔塑料(简称 EPS)

expanded scale (仪表的非线性标度中的)扩展标度(标度范围内,不成比例的扩展部分占了大部分标度长度的标度)

expander ①膨胀器,扩张器,扩口器 ②(鼓式制动器的制动蹄)凸轮,(制动蹄)促动器

expander circuit 扩展电路(用来增加电路同等作用输入端的数量,而又不改变相连电路功能的辅助电路)

expander lever (鼓式制动器制动蹄)凸轮推杆(推动凸轮使制动蹄张开)

expander ring (活塞环油环的)涨圈(用于增加油环对缸壁的压力,以确保密封,多由数件零件组成,亦称 expander spacer)

expander spring 压缩弹簧,推力弹簧(= expanding spring)

expander type ring 带涨圈的活塞环

expanding ①膨胀,扩张,扩大,胀大;分解,展开,展成级数 ②膨胀的,胀大的,扩张的,扩孔的

expanding band brake 内张型带式制动器

expanding brake 内张式制动器(见

internal expanding drum brake)
expanding clutch 内张式离合器
expanding inside brake 内张式制动器（见 internal expanding drum brake）
expanding pulley 内张型可调式传动带轮
expanding wedge brake 楔形凸轮内张式制动器（= wedge brake, wedge-actuated brake）
expansibility 可膨胀性，可扩张性，可延伸性
expansible 可扩张的，可延伸的，可膨胀的，易膨胀的（= expansile）
expansion ①膨胀，扩张，扩展 ②延伸，碾轧，轧展 ③延伸率 ④展开，展成级数，展开式
expansion arc （转子发动机缸体的）膨胀区，膨胀段（指旋轮线缸体壁面对应于膨胀过程的弧段）
expansion bolt 膨胀螺栓
expansion brake 内张型制动器（见 internal expanding drum brake）
expansion cam （内张式制动器制动蹄的）张撑凸轮，促动凸轮
expansion coefficient 膨胀系数（物体温度升高1℃时，其体积的变化与0℃时的体积之比，亦见称 expansion factor，长度和面积的膨胀程度分别用线膨胀系数和面膨胀系数表示）
expansion coil spring 拉伸式螺旋弹簧（承受拉力的螺旋弹簧）
expansion combustion chamber （可变压缩比发动机的）可变容积燃烧室（简称 ECC）
expansion curve （示功图上的）膨胀曲线，膨胀线（= expansion line）
expansion element 膨胀元件（指热膨胀系数高的固体或液体受热后体积膨胀转变为膜片或其他弹性元件的往复运动促动件、执行元件等，如：expansion-element regulator，expansion element thermostat 等）
expansion-exchange stroke 见 expansion scavenging stroke
expansion fit ①热胀配合 ②（管接头）扩口配合
expansion gap （防止因）热膨胀（破损预留的）间隙
expansion joint ①伸缩接缝（钢轨，混凝土路面允许温度膨胀的接缝）②伸缩接头
expansion phase （转子发动机的）膨胀箱，膨胀过程
expansion pot 膨胀腔，膨胀箱（防止容器、管道或系统因其中所容纳的油、水、气等膨胀而破损所设立的附加容器或腔室）
expansion-proof 防膨胀（造成破损）的
expansion-scavenging stroke （二冲程汽油机的）膨胀-换气冲程（指混合气点燃后膨胀，使活塞向下移动至下止点，后期换气孔开启，开始换气的相应冲程，亦称 expansion-exchange stroke）
expansion stroke 膨胀冲程（亦称 power stroke，指"做功冲程"发动机可燃混合气点燃后膨胀推动活塞下行做功的冲程）
expansion stroke （四冲程发动机的）膨胀冲程（工质在汽缸内膨胀时相应的活塞冲程）
expansion temperature 膨胀冲程终了时的温度
expansion-travel test 弹簧的拉力-变形特性试验（确定弹簧拉力和变形间的关系）
expansion valve 膨胀阀（车用空调系统中位于冷凝器和蒸发器之间的流量控制阀，用于控制喷入蒸发器的制冷剂的流量）
expansion volume tank （thermal-expansion volume tank，或简称 expansion tank）①（指任何容纳由于气体、液体或其蒸气膨胀引起的溢流的容器，如：装在主油箱内，防止燃油受

热膨胀时溢出的)热膨胀箱 ②(特指发动机冷却系中由于沸腾而溢出散热器的冷却水在其中冷凝后再流回散热器的)冷凝箱

expansion wave 膨胀波(负压波)

expansive rivet 膨胀铆钉

expansivity 可膨胀性,可扩张性,可延伸性

expchange-compression stroke (二冲程发动机的)换气—压缩冲程(指二冲程发动机换气—压缩时相应的活塞冲程)

expectation ①期望,预期 ②期望值(见 expectation value)

expectation of life (根据概率统计算得的)平均寿命,概率寿命,估计寿命,概率使用期,计算出的工作期,估计使用期(= life expectation)

expectation value 期望值(指随机事件概率的总体平均值,简称 expectation, = expected value)

expendable 消耗的,消费的,易耗的,只供一次使用的

experiment 实验,试验

experimental safety motorcycle 试验性安全摩托车(简称 ESM)

Experimental Safety (Motor) Vehicle 见 ESV

experimental trauma severity (汽车碰撞)(外伤)伤害度试验(简称 ETS)

expert system 专家系统(指将某特定领域的专家的知识和经验输入电子计算机而持有与专家相同,或至少接近解决问题的能力的系统;一组模拟人类专家决策过程的计算机系统,用来解决通常需要专家才能解决的问题。至少要有:知识库,存储专家的知识;数据库,存放用户问题等;推理机,模拟专家的思维过程,利用知识库的知识,用推理策略去解决实际问题。另外有:解释程序,向用户解释为什么得出这样的结论及知识获取与提炼程序,用于增删修改知识库的知识,使之不断完善自然语言处理程序)

expert system generator 专家系统生成器(为建立专家系统而设计的一种软件开发工具,亦称 expert system shell)

expire (执照、证书、票据、卡等)过期,到期,不再有效

explanation program (专家系统)解释程序(见 expert system)

explicit ①明白的(明确的,明显的,清楚的) ②显的(显然的,显示的) ③必须直接付款的

exploded view ①(总成,部件)分解图 ②立体(三维)景象图

exploding primer (柴油)引爆添加剂

exploitation horse power 运行马力,工作马力,运行功率

exploratory development 探索性开发,技术可行性研制,试验性研制(如:研制几台发动机,在台架上或装车进行试验,证实某些新概念的技术可行性)

explosible mixture 可燃混合气(= combustible mixture)

explosimeter (气体)可爆性测定仪(通过测量空气中可燃气体的浓度,来测定其可爆性的仪器)

explosin proof tank 防爆式油箱

explosion ①爆炸 ②爆燃(= detonation, knock) ③早燃产生的强烈噪声 ④排气管放炮 ⑤(指发动机工质的)着火燃烧

explosion chamber ①(燃烧试验)燃烧罐 ②(发动机)燃烧室

explosion engine (使用轻油的)内燃发动机(亦称 explosion motor)

explosion in silencer 消声器放炮(= muffler explosion)

explosion of the combustible gases 可燃混合气的着火膨胀

explosion period 爆炸（时）期，燃烧期

explosion pressure 爆发压力，爆炸压力（指发动机燃烧室内的最高燃烧压力，= maximum combustion pressure）

explosion-proof 防爆的，抗爆的，防炸的（= explosion-safe）

explosion-safe 防爆的（= explosion-proof）

explosions per minute （发动机）每分钟爆发数

explosion stroke 爆发冲程，做功冲程

explosion turbine 爆燃式燃气轮机

explosive bonding 爆炸黏接（一种熔焊法，利用炸药的爆炸压力，使包覆材料冲击基体材料，在冲击点处产生金属材料的塑性流动而黏结在一起）

explosive combustion 爆炸燃烧（在发动机燃烧理论中，常分为并发式爆炸和渐近式爆炸，见 simultaneous explosion 及 progressive explosion）

explosive fuel vapo(u)r 易燃的燃油蒸气，易燃爆炸的燃油蒸气

explosive limits 爆发极限（可燃混合气能被点燃的混合比极限）

explosive loading （发动机中混合气燃烧时的）爆发载荷（爆发产生的压力）

explosive mixture 可燃混合气（= combustible mixture, inflammable mixture）

explosive rivet 炸药铆钉（一种半空心单面装压铆钉，将少许炸药自铆钉头部孔内装入空心底部，铆接时通电将炸药引爆，挤胀铆钉，铆紧构件）

exponent 指数，方次，幂

exponential distribution 指数分布（随机变量 x 的概率密度函数 $p(x)$ 为 $p(x) = \begin{cases} \lambda e^{-\lambda(x-\mu)} \\ 0 \quad x < \mu \end{cases}$ 时，则称该随机变量服从指数分布，记 $e(\mu, \lambda)$，式中，x 为随机变量的取值，λ、μ 为随机变量的分布参数）

exponent of adiabatic expansion 绝热膨胀指数

expose ①暴露，露出，外露；曝光 ②展览，陈列

exposed 暴露的，敞开的，外露的

exposed cardan shaft 开式十字轴万向节传动轴

exposed cords 露线（指车用轮胎的一种外观缺陷。exposed cords in tyre cavity 胎里露线，指胎里局部露出帘线的现象，俗称胎里掉皮。exposed cords in bead 胎圈露线，指该现象发生于胎圈）

exposure ①暴露 ②曝光，曝光量，曝光时间

exposure effect 大气暴露效应，大气影响效应

exposure knob （金相显微镜等的）曝光按钮，曝光旋钮

exposure limit 暴露极限（影响人的健康或安全的暴露时间界限）

exposure test 暴露试验（将被试物件露天以考验其受天气作用的影响和抗天气作用的稳定性，例如抗锈蚀、抗风蚀、抗盐蚀作用等，参见 weathering）

exposure time ①暴露时间（在汽车平顺性论述中，指人置于连续的振动环境中的时间）②曝光时间 ③暴露试验的时间

exposure time limit 暴露时间极限（指影响人的健康或安全的暴露时间界限，简称 exposure limit，见 exposure time①）

express ①快车，特快车；快件，快运 ②快速的，高速的，特快的 ③表示，表明，挤出，压出

express highway 快速公路（见 expressway）

Expresso(car) 特快(轿车)(美国克莱斯勒公司20世纪90年代轿车牌,装用2.0L,四缸,16气门132马力发动机,设有卫星导航系统)

express-up window regulator 快速式风窗玻璃升降器

express way ①[美]快速公路(相似于英国的motorway,多车道的快速交通干道,全部或部分出入控制,参见motorway) ②汽车专用公路(为全部或部分控制进入专供汽车行驶的各等级公路的总称,包括全部控制进入的高速公路"freeway"和部分控制进入的一级公路及二级汽车专用公路)

Expressway and Rapid Transit Authority of Thailand [泰国]高速公路与快速公共交通管理局(简称ERTAT)

expressway speed (汽车的)快速公路车速(指快速公路根据其设计标准,对在该路上行驶的汽车规定的车速)

exsiccative ①干燥的,除湿的,使干的,脱水的 ②干燥剂(=exsiccant)

ext dia 外径(external diameter的简称)

extended cab (货车的)加长驾驶室

extended-content 扩展的

extended-drain oil (允许延长换油周期的)长效润滑油

extended-reach(spark)**plug** 长形火花塞,长腿火花塞(=extended-core spark plug, long-reach plug,其绝缘体裙部加长,突出于壳体端面之外,因而吸收热量大,抗污能力强,绝缘体直接受进气冷却,不易引起炽热点火,电极伸入燃烧室内部空间,以增加与燃烧室壁的距离,我国称突出型火花塞,其产品型号第一个符号为汉语拼音字母T)

extended test 长期试验,延长试验

extended wheelbase 加长轴距

extender ①延伸杆,加长部分 ②延长器

extendible ①可伸长的,可延长的,可调长的 ②见extendible trailer

extendible portion ①延续部分,延伸部分,延长部分,扩张部分 ②延长绿灯时间,追响绿灯时间(交通感应信号控制系统中,车流增加时,在基本绿灯时间上追加的绿灯时间,参见initial portion)

extendible trailer 轴距可调长的或车身可加长的超长货挂车或半挂车(简称extendible)

extensibility 可延伸性,伸长率,膨胀率,延性,拉伸性,在张力作用下的形变程度

extensible 可伸长的,可延伸的,可延长的,可扩展的

extension ①伸长,伸出,扩展,延长,延伸,推广,发展,增加,增设,分设 ②伸出部分,扩建部分,延伸部分 ③延长期,扩建区,(可)扩展的范围,(可)延长的程度 ④范围,尺寸,(空间的)大小

extensional vibration 轴向振动(=longitudinal vibration)

extension instrument 附加仪表,外接仪表

extension ladder 伸缩梯(=extending ladder)

extension line for dimension 尺寸标注引出线

extension rim 加宽的轮辋

extension shoe (内张式制动器的)外张制动蹄

extension spring 拉簧

extensometer 延伸变形测定仪,伸缩计,伸长计

extention side 加长的(车箱)侧栏板

exterior ①外部,外表,外观,外形,外面 ②外部的,对外的,室外

的，外表的

exterior automotive（decorative）trim 汽车的外部装饰件

exterior color （车身等的）外部色彩

exterior-component wind noise （车身）外部件（如后视镜等引起的）风噪声

exteriority ①外表面，外形，外貌，外表 ②外在性，客观性（= externality）

exterior mirror （汽车装在车门外等处的）后视镜（= external mirror）

exterior panel （车身）外壁板

exterior template （车身）外廓样板，外形样板（供制作黏土模型等使用）

exterior trimming parts （车身的）外饰件（车身外部起装饰、美化与保护作用的零部件的总称，亦称 exterior trim）

exterior view 外视图，外表图，外貌图

external air（injection）manifold （空气喷射排气净化系统的）外装式空气喷射总管（装于发动机外侧，通过各缸的喷射分管将新鲜空气喷至排气门处，使 CO、HC 等二次燃烧净化）

external band brake 外带式制动器

external brake ①外带式制动器 ②外蹄式制动器

external cheek brake 外蹄式制动器

external circuit 外电路

external circular spline （谐波齿轮传动机构中的）外齿刚轮（即外齿轮）

external combustion engine 外燃机（简称 ECE，指燃料在发动机汽缸以外燃烧的发动机，如蒸汽机、stirling 发动机等）

external contracting drum brake 外收缩型鼓式制动器（指摩擦力产生于与车辆固定部件相连接的部件和制动鼓外表面之间的摩擦式制动器，见 externally acting brake）

external cooling 外部冷却（如：风冷）

external crack 外表裂纹，外部裂缝

external cycloidal gear 外齿摆线轮（指齿顶曲面位于齿根曲面之外的摆线轮，见 cycloidal gear）

external delivery point （液压系统与分置式油缸等相连接的）外接输出端

external diagnostic access 外部诊断设备（相对车载诊断设备和汽车电子系统自诊断系统而言）

external diameter 外径（= full diameter, outer diameter, outside diameter）

external dimensions 外形尺寸，外部尺寸

external earth 外搭铁（如：发电机磁场绕组的一端通过调节器后搭铁）

external EGR system 外废气再循环系统（指常规的由排气管引入废气的再循环系统，external exhaust gas recirculation system 的简称）

external filler valve with 80% cutoff （液化石油气汽车储液罐的）80%关闭型罐外加油阀（当液量加注至罐容积的 80% 时，该阀即自动关闭，停止进油，保证安全）

external gear 外齿轮（指齿顶曲面位于齿根曲面之外的齿轮）

external gearing 外啮合齿轮传动（见 external teeth）

external gear pair 外齿轮副（两齿轮均为外齿轮的齿轮副）

external gear-type oil pump 外啮式齿轮油泵

external-internal spur gear oil pump 内外啮合正齿轮机油泵

external knock sensor 机外爆振传感器（指装在发动机缸体外表面的爆

振传感器，易于拆装）

external limit gauge 外径极限规

external lock handle thumb button （汽车车门）外手柄车门锁按压开关

externally acting brake 外刹式制动器（具有外工作表面的鼓式制动器，外带式或外蹄式制动器，参见 external contracting brake）

externally fired 外燃（式）的

externally guided weight-loaded accumulator 带外导轨的重力加载式蓄力器

externally mounted calibration assembly （汽车动力系电子控制模块上）外加的插装式（发动机控制参数）标定模块

externally mounted mechanical seal 外装式机械密封（装于密封端盖或相当于端盖的零件外侧的机械密封件）

external micrometer 外径千分卡，外径侧微仪

external mirror （装在车身外部的）后视镜

external motion resistance （车辆）外部行驶阻力，外部运动阻力

external mounted headlamp （汽车的）外装式前照灯（整灯外露地装在车上的前照灯）

external performance 外特性（见 external characteristic）

external phasing gears （单纯旋转发动机的）外轴式相位（齿轮）机构

external pin wheel 外齿针齿轮（指齿顶圆柱面位于齿根圆柱面之外的针齿轮，见 pin wheel）

external planetary arrangement 外啮双排行星齿轮机构（由长行星轮、短行星轮、行星架、小中心轮及大中心轮组成）

external Q 外 Q 值，外品质因素

external sensor （安全气囊系统的）外置式碰撞传感器（指安装在安全气囊的控制模块以外的汽车碰撞区，如保险杠中心，前轮挡泥板，或车身侧板等区域内的机电式惯性传感元件。当安装于车前端时，亦称 front crash sensor 前碰撞传感器）

external sound penetrate （车身隔声不良造成的）车外声响透入车内

external split torque path type hydro-mechanic drive 外分流式液力机械传动（功率分流在液力变矩器外部实现）

external styling （汽车车身的）外部式样，外部造型（= exterior styling）

external support of flexible member （空气弹簧）挠性元件外支撑

external tank-type heater 外置水箱式加热器

external thread 外螺纹（= outside screw thread, male thread）

external transport 国外运输，涉外运输

external-type idle limiter 外装式怠速浓度调程限制器

external vane pump 外叶片泵（带叶片的椭圆形旋转活塞或偏心安装的圆形转子泵，见 sliding vane pump）

external voltage regulator 外装式电压调节器（简称 EVR）

external wave generator （谐波齿轮传动机构的）外波发生器（波发生器配置在柔轮齿圈之外者，见 wave generator）

externat characteristic (s) （发动机）外特性曲线，外特性（指汽油机节气门全开或柴油机喷油泵调节齿条固定在最大位置并带全部附件时的速度特性）

extinction 熄火（混合气燃烧中断），熄灭，消灭，衰减，消光，消声

extinction coefficient 衰减系数；消声系数，消光系数

extinguisher 灭火器，消火器，消除器（简称 EXT）

extra ①额外的，外加的 ②特大的，特佳的

extra air inlet 补充空气进孔，副进气孔

extra air valve 补偿空气阀（见 compensating air valve）

extra bus 特大型客车（如：铰接客车和双层客车等）

extra clearance period （红绿灯信号的）追加清尾时间（按照交通状况自动调节的绿灯时间）

extra coarse pitch thread 超粗牙螺纹

extracting tool 拉器（拆卸工具）

extraction ①抽出，排除，拔出，引出 ②提炼；精炼 ③抽出物，提取物 ④（数学计算中的）开方（法），求根（法）⑤摘要，精选（简称 extn）

extractor ①提取器，分离器，分离装置 ②拉器（轴承，衬套等的取出工具）

extractor fan 抽风机，抽风装置（= drawing fan）

extra current ①附加电流，额外电流 ②额外流量

extra-duty 超重型的，超重级的，超级的

extra easy maintenance brake 特易维护型制动器（简称 EEM brake）

extra fine thread 极（特）细螺纹

extra hard steel 超硬钢，极硬钢（含碳量约 0.70%，抗拉强度 700MPa 以上，拉伸 8% 以上）

extra-heavy duty ①超重载工况，极恶劣的工作（条件）②超重型的，特重型的

extra-heavy-duty take-off 供超重载条件下工作的功率输出轴，超重载功率输出轴

extra heavy off road vehicle 超重型越野汽车（中国规定：厂定最大总质量大于 24t 者）

extra heavy oil 超重油（分子量大，特别是黏度大的油类）

extra heavy semi-trailer 超重型半挂车（中国规定：最大总质量大于 34t 者）

extra high relay （电动机的）高速继电器（接通时，将串联于电动机电源电路中的电阻器短路，使电动机高速运转）

extra inner tube 备用内胎（= spare inner tube）

extra large size bearing 特大型轴承（外径超过 800mm 者）

extra light drive fit 特轻压配合，特轻打入配合

extra long wheelbase ①超长轴距（简称 XL WB）②超长载货汽车（的俚称）

extra low pressure tire 超低压轮胎 [指车轮上的载荷为最大容许值时，胎压仅 $(0.5 \sim 1.0) \times 10^{-1}$ MPa 的轮胎]

extraman 机械手

extraneous variable 随机变量（亦称 chance variable, random variable）

extraordinary rays （汽车液晶显示器件的）非寻常光线（指光线射入具有双折射性质的晶体时，分为两束，其中一束不遵守寻常的折射定律，在晶体内传播的速度随方向而异）

extrapolated unity-gain frequency （线性放大器的）外推单位增益频率（电压放大倍数的模与测试频率的乘积，亦称增益带宽乘积）

extrapolation ①推断（推论）②外推（法）

extra rim 备用轮辋

extras 外加的选购件（由生产厂按用户要求加装的或购后由车主自行加装的附件、装置等）

extra slack running fit 特松转动配合

extra soft steel 超软钢,极软钢(含碳量 0.03%～0.20%,抗拉强度 400MPa 以下,拉伸 25%以上)

extra traction 附加牵引力,辅助牵引力(如:四轮驱动的汽车挂上前轮驱动挡时增加的牵引力)

extra wheel 备用车轮(= spare wheel)

extreme ①极限,极限值,极端,极度 ②最末端的,尽头的,最后的;极限的,极度的

extreme boost 高压增压

extreme pressure 极限压力,极压(简称 EP,该术语一般指两个面之间的极高载荷,特别是齿轮传动润滑工况)

extreme pressure additive (润滑剂的)耐极压添加剂(简称 EP additive,亦称 extreme-pressure agent, EP agent)

extreme pressure lubricant 极压润滑剂(①石墨等固体润滑剂,= solid lubricant ②极压润滑油,指加有极压添加剂的滑油,可以在金属表面形成氧化物或硫化物薄膜,减轻在极大载荷下,油膜被破坏时,表面因干摩擦而造成的损伤,简称 EP lubricant)

extreme pressure transmission oil 极压传动系滑油(含有耐高压添加剂的,耐特高压变速器油)

extreme turn 极限转向(以最小半径转弯)

extreme value 极值

extremity of a segment 线段的端

extrinsic conduction 非本征导电,杂质传导(在半导体材料中,由于添加微量杂质而使材料具有的电气性能,= impurity conduction)

extrinsic semiconductor 非本征半导体(指加有微量铟 In、砷 As 等杂质的半导体)

EXTROID CVT (1999 年日产公司推出的)超级滚轮式连续无级变速器[商品名,EXTROID 为 Exceed(超越、领先)或 Excellence(卓越、优秀)的简称,EX 和 TOROID(环、环形面)的简称 TROID 的组合词,它的变速机构不是钢传动带和传动带轮,而是两对动力输入、输出盘(input-output disks)(以下称主-从动盘)和绕自身轴(trunnion)旋转的四个传力滚轮(power roller)。因此,这类无级变速器亦称 roller type CVT,其两对主、从动盘沿同一轴线安装,主、从动盘的相对一侧均为凹圆弧形环面(toroid),而在两对主、从动盘间形成两个环槽形空腔(double-cavity type toroid),因此这类无级变速器亦称 toroidal CVT, toroid transmission。其每个环槽形空腔内卡有两个传力滚轮,即:传力滚轮卡在主、从动盘之间。主动盘带动传力滚轮驱动从动盘旋转而输出动力。改变传力滚轮轴的倾斜角度即可改变传力滚轮在主、从动盘环面上的接触点至其轴线的距离,即主、从动盘各自的有效传力半径($R_i、R_o$),便可改变速比(R_o/R_i)。滚轮式无级变速器制造成本高,目前大多为钢传动带式连续无级变速器(belt-type CVT)所取代]

Ext W 备加线路,附加线路,分接线路,延长线路(extension wire 的简称)

exudation pressure 渗流压力,渗出压力

exurban driving 远郊区行车

eye ①眼,眼状物,眼孔 ②耳环,吊环,卷耳

eye-back distance 从乘员背部到眼睛的水平距离

eye bar 带眼杆件,带眼拉杆

eye blinking frequency (人)眨眼频

率（亦称 eye blinking rate）
eye bolt 有眼螺栓，环首螺栓，吊环螺栓
eye brow ①（孔等的）眉，眉边，翼边②前照灯外罩前缘；翼板
eyebushing 衬套
eye camera （获取驾驶者眼球活动及活动范围、速度等信息的）眼球摄像机
eye coupling bolt 孔眼头连接螺栓
eye height point setting 眼点（驾驶员坐姿时，瞳孔中心的位置，简称 eye point，E point）
eye hitch 牵引环（参见 ring-type hitch）
eye hole 观察孔，检查孔（= peep hole）
eye hook 带环吊钩，耳钩
eye irritation （柴油机废气引起的）眼发炎，眼刺痛
eye lens ①目镜 ②眼晶体
eyelet connector 带圆孔端的接线片，带圆孔接线片的接线端（圆孔套在接线柱上）
eyelet-hole ①小孔，窥视孔，观察孔，针眼，小眼，小环，铁环（= eye hole）②在…打小孔
eyelet pliers 打孔钳（该钳的一个钳口有一打孔柱，另一钳口有与之相配的柱孔）
eyelet terminal （电器连接件中的）眼孔式接线柱，孔式接头
eye level （驾驶员坐姿）眼睛高度
eyellipse （驾驶员的）眼睛椭圆 眼睛活动范围，（驾驶员眼睛的活动范围呈椭圆形，故称眼睛椭圆，= drivers eyerange）
eyellipse contour （驾驶员）眼睛活动范围轮廓线
eyellipse template （驾驶员的）眼睛活动范围基准图（用于设计驾驶室时，用于确定驾驶员对目标物的视线）
eye location 眼球位置
eye movement 眼球运动
eye nut 带环螺母，吊环螺母，环头螺母
eye of spring plate 弹簧钢板吊耳
eye piece 接目镜，目镜
eye point 见 eye height point setting
eye reach 视野（视力所及的范围）
eye slit 观察缝
eye tracking system 眼球跟踪系统（根据眼角膜反射映像等测出的眼球中心"瞳孔"的方位，确定与跟踪驾驶者视线的方向，用于智能驾驶安全支援系统、适应性前照灯系统等）
eye tracking system 眼跟踪系统（该系统可跟踪驾驶者头部及眼球运动位置，以及驾驶者眨眼频率，眼睛的开合度，视线的分散及凝视定位、暂停等，确定驾驶员的注意力与身体状况，以调整各种安全系统的有关功能参数和发出警告等）
eye turn（ing） 眼球转动
eye visible crack 肉眼可见裂纹
eye washer 孔眼清洗机，孔眼冲洗器
eye wash fountains 孔眼冲洗器（将水喷至孔眼处用于冲洗的喷水器）
EZ 电零点（electrical zero）
EZEV 当量零排放车（equivalent zero emission vehicle 的简称，见 equivalent emission）

F ①华氏(温)度(Fahrenheit degree 的简称) ②华氏温标(Fahrenheit scale 的简称) ③法拉(电容单位)(farad) ④磁场接线柱(field terminal 的简称)

F/A 燃空比(指可燃混合气中的燃料与空气的质量比,参见 fuel/air ratio)

fabric element ①纤维滤芯,织物滤芯 ②纤维(制)元件

fabric filter 纤维织物滤芯滤清器

fabric fuel tank 软油箱,软燃油箱

fabric light battery 纤维光电池,光纤电池

fabric-seal bearing 带织物油封的轴承(= lubri-seal bearing)

fabric tire 棉织物帘布层轮胎

fabroil gear 夹布胶木齿轮

face ①面,端面,外表面 ②仪表面,刻度盘 ③使面向,朝着,面对,面临 ④镶面,贴面,饰面 ⑤表面加工(如磨、刮、研等)

face bar 汽车保险杠(= bumper bar)

face cam 凸轮盘,端面槽形凸轮(= edge cam)

face centered cubic 面心立方(晶格)(简称 FCC)

face contact ①按钮开关 ②按钮接点 ③端压接触,面接触

face form (汽车碰撞试验等使用的)人脸模型,模拟人脸,人脸模拟件

face hardening 表面硬化,表面淬火(见 surface hardening)

face joint 端面接合

face leakage (密封件)端面泄漏

face-lift (车辆的)①翻新,修整 ②改变款式,变换车身式样、造型 ③增添新设备、新装置 ④改换内、外饰

face of piston ring 活塞环外表面(与汽缸的接触表面)

face recognition system 人脸识别系统

face runout 端面跳动

face seals ①面密封(装置) ②(转子发动机的)端面密封(装置)

face width of tooth (齿轮)齿面宽度(圆柱齿轮指齿轮有齿部位沿分度圆柱面的直母线方向度量的宽度;锥齿轮指轮齿沿锥母线度量的宽度)

face with stellite 用钨铬钴硬质合金堆焊表面

facia ①见 facia board ②带,饰带

facia board 驾驶室仪表板(= fascia panel, dash board, 简称 facia, 或 fascia, 亦称 instrument panel)

facial 正面的,表面的,面部的

facia panel ①仪表板(= dash board, switch board, dash panel) ②(车身)外壁板

facilitate ①使…便于实现 ②使…容易 ③促进 ④简化

facilities ①设备，设施 ②实验室，研究所，工厂，机关，机构

facility of access 易接近性，接近方便性（易于检查、维护、检修等）

facility request 设备要求（简称 FR）

facing front seat 面向前方的座位

facing-up ①滑配合 ②对研，配研，刮配

FACP 全自动计算机程序（fully automated computer program 的简称）

FAC PWR MON 设备的功率监控器（facility power monitor 的简称）

FAC PWR PNL 设备的电源板（facility power panel 的简称）

FACS 全自动阻风门系统（full auto choke system 的简称）

facs 设备，设施（facilities 的简称）

facsimile ①传真，传真通信 ②复制，影印（本）

factor ①因子，因数［若整数 a 能被整数 b（b≠0）整除，则 b 为 a 的因数］②（表示比例关系的）系数

factorial experiment 析因实验（分析因素的试验）

factorize ①因式分解，把…分解因子 ②把复杂计算分解为基本运算 ③编制计算程序（= factorise）

factor of air resistance 空气阻力系数

factor of evaporation 蒸发系数，蒸发率

factor of inertia 惯量系数

factor of proportionality 比例因子

factor of safety 安全因素，安全系数（= safety factor）

factory acceptance test 工厂验收试验，工厂认证检验（简称 FAT）

factory-adjusted 出厂调整的（指车辆出厂前调好并不得改变的）

factory-designed 厂家标定的，出厂标定的，工厂设计的，额定的

factory-engineered 4-wheel drive option 生产厂设计制造的选购型四轮驱动车（指标准的两轮驱动车型中可由用户选购的原厂家生产的四轮驱动型车辆，以区别于两轮驱动型车，销售后由改装厂改装成的四轮驱动车）

factory-filled 在出厂时已注满的（润滑或冷却系统）

factory-filled synthetic lube（新出厂时由）厂家添加的合成润滑油

factory-installed ①出厂时已安装好的（如：应用户要求出厂时已安装好的选购件等）②由制造厂调整确定好的（例如发动机的额定供油量）

factory-reconditioned 由（专业）工厂修复的

factory specification ①出厂技术条件，（制造厂规定的技术参数）企业技术规范 ②出厂说明书

fade 衰退①（泛指）机器丧失其原始性能，技术状态逐渐恶化 ②（特指）由于过热，水浸或其他原因造成制动器效能暂时降低的现象（见 heat fade，water fade）

fade-and-recovery test 衰退和恢复试验（确定制动蹄片发热或浸水时性能衰退和冷却或干燥后性能恢复程度的试验）

fade characteristics（制动器的）衰退特性（一般指制动器浸水或发热时效能保持能力的变化特性）

fade-free brake 抗衰退型制动器（制动效能在高温或水浸下保持不变）

fade-in 渐强，渐显（指示波器、收音机等的音响或图像逐渐清晰）

fade-out 渐弱，渐隐（指示波器、收音机等的音响及图像逐渐衰减）

fader（车用四喇叭音响系统中调节前、后喇叭音量平衡的）声响

调节器

fade resistance （制动摩擦材料的）抗衰退能力

fade-resistant 抗衰减的，抗衰退的

fade (stability) test （制动器的）衰退（稳定性）试验（汽车在高速重负荷或水浸下连续制动以测定由于发热或水浸而引起制动器效能的下降程度等）

fading range 衰退范围，衰减范围

FAFE 车队平均燃油经济性（fleet average fuel economy 的简称）

FAG （中国）第一汽车集团公司，一汽集团（China's First Auto Group 的简称）

Fahrenheit scale 华氏温标（代号°F，在标准大气压下，以纯水的冰点为32°F，沸点为212°F，冰点和沸点之间为180°F。1°F=5/9°C，华氏温标与其他温标的换算：5/9（°F－32）＝摄氏度°C，4/9（°F－32）＝列氏度°R，5/9（°F－32）＋231.15＝开氏度°K）

fail ①失效，失灵 ②破坏，损坏，故障，停止工作 ③衰退，衰减，变钝 ④受到破坏，出现故障，发生衰退出现衰减

fail close 出故障时自动关闭

fail open 出故障时自动断开或自动开放

fail-operational 故障运转的（在汽车电子系统中，指在部件发生故障的情况下，整个系统仍能继续安全运转的）

fail-passive 见 fail-safe

fail-safe 失效-安全的，故障-安全的（当个别元件或部分发生故障，失效时，后备系统即接替工作，系统或整机仍能安全运转并可保持基本功能的，亦称 fail passive）

fail-safe spring brake （货车或重型车辆气制动系统的）弹簧安全制动器（当气制动管路失效，以致制动气压不足时，便会在弹簧力的作用下自动制动的制动器）

fail safety 失效-安全性能（当个别元件失效时系统仍保持可靠工作的性能，亦写作 failsafety）

fail safe valve （电子控制液压悬架车身高度控制系统的）故障安全阀（当该控制系统发生故障时，该阀控制悬架的液压管路的流量，以避免此时车身高度的突然变化，亦写作 failsafe valve）

failsafe valve 故障安全阀（当某控制阀失效时，该阀自动顶替其作用的安全阀）

fail-silent 故障停止运转的（fail-operational 的反义词，汽车电子系统中指：出现故障后即停止运转。如：汽车防抱死制动系统，如果其电子控制系统发现故障，电子控制系统将自动断开，而由常规液压系统继续工作）

fail-soft 故障-疲软的（个别部件发生故障时，系统或整机虽能工作，但性能疲软或功能下降的）

fail tests （个别部件发生故障时，系统维持其功能的能力的）可靠性试验

failure ①失效（丧失规定的功能，对可修复者亦称故障）②不足，不能达到正常的或所期望的状态

failure analysis 故障分析，事故分析，破损分析，失效分析（简称-FA）

failure branch chart 见 failure tree

failure detection 故障检测

failure diagnosis 故障诊断

failure-free 无故障的

failure mechanism 故障机理，失效机理（指引起故障的原因，引起失效的物理、化学变化等内在原因）

failure mode 失效模式，故障模式（失效或故障的表现形式）

failure mode and effects analysis 故

障模式和影响分析

Failure Mode Effects Management 故障模式影响控制（电子控制系统的一种故障对策。无此项控制功能时，若传感器发生故障，以发动机控制为例，不是停机，便是导致发动机以无点火提前和固定空燃比运转。当具有此功能时，电子控制模块便可根据完好的其他传感器的输入，推算出故障传感器此时的应有输入值，从而保证某一个传感器发生故障时，仍可对发动机作最佳控制，简称FMEM）

failure rate 故障率（在规定的单位冲程内发生故障的概率，一般用作可靠性的量化指标）

failure stress 断裂应力

failure test ①可靠性试验（用来检查故障发生率的试验）②破坏性试验

failure tree 故障树（故障模式因果关系的分析图，图形像具有多个分支的树，故名，= failure branch chart, fault tree）

failure warning 故障报警的

failure wear (of parts) （零件自身）缺陷（造成的）磨损

fair ①博览会，展览会，交易会 ②相当好的，相当的，令人满意的，顺利的 ③清楚的，明晰的 ④外形平顺的，流线型的 ⑤使成流线型，使流线型化

fairing face 流线型表面

fairing panel ①流线型板件（指附加在车身突出处的流线型板件或整板可减少空气阻力的车身板件）②见front valance panel

fairlead ①（汽车）的天线导管 ②（缆索、试验仪表车的电缆线等的）导孔，导轮，引出管

fair running road surface 良好的路面，管理良好的路面，维护良好的路面

fairshaped 流线型的

fair visibility 良好的视野，良好的能见度（= clear visibility）

Fairway Metallic （车身的）金属光泽的浅色

fake car 冒牌轿车（市场上假冒名牌轿车的轿车）

Falex Test 润滑材料的耐极压性能试验

falling back （对汽车座椅，指）可下落的靠背，可翻转的靠背，可放下的靠背

falling dart test 落箭试验，飞镖试验（确定风窗玻璃承受尖头小刚体冲击能力的试验）

falling-drop shape 水滴状的

falling object protective structures （车辆的）坠落物防护结构（用于防护车辆操纵人员免受落下的砖石瓦块等砸伤，简称FOPS）

falling top 折叠式车顶（= collapsible top）

falling weight test 落锤冲击试验（用来测定材料的冲击韧性）

false bottom 活底，假底

false brinelling ①摩擦腐蚀 ②（滚柱、滚球、滚针等）在轴承滚动表面上形成压痕 ③虚假硬度

false front 散热器护栅（参见radiator false front）

false zero （仪表）不准的零位

FAME （包括植物衍生脂类在内的）脂肪酸甲基脂〔fatty acid methyl esters的简称，作为柴油的添加物或柴油的替代品，使用越来越广泛，有关标准规定在1、2、3类柴油中最多可添加5%（V/V），但第4类柴油不许添加〕

family (-sized) car 家庭型轿车（指适合整家人出行乘坐的轿车，一般为四门双排座轿车或带后门的四门轿车）

fan ①风扇，通风机，鼓风机 ②吹

风，通风，鼓风

fan and generator drive belt 风扇及发电机驱动皮带

fan-and-pump shaft bearing （发动机）风扇-水泵轴承

fan baffle 风扇防护板；风扇导流板

fan belt （发动机的）风扇皮带（指由曲轴前端的皮带盘带动风扇、发电机、水泵等的三角皮带或带齿皮带。当发动机使用电动风扇时，尽管该皮带只带动发电机、水泵而不再带动风扇，但仍沿用风扇皮带的称呼）

fan belt idler 风扇皮带张紧轮

fan belt tension gauge 风扇皮带紧度计

fan blade 风扇叶片（= ventilator blade，有时指整个风扇叶轮，= fan rotor，美称 fan impeller）

fan blade carrier 风扇毂

fan blast deflector （散热器）风扇气流折射板

fan blower 风扇式鼓风机

fan brake ①叶片式空气制动器 ②空气制动式测功器

fan clutch 风扇离合器（通常由恒温器根据发动机冷却水温自动接通或断开风扇驱动）

fan-cooled 风扇冷却的（= fan-cooling）

fan cowl 风扇罩（= fan housing, fan shroud）

fan delivery 风扇送风量

fan dynamometer 风扇式测力计，风力测功器（见 air friction dynamometer）

fan engine 风扇冷却发动机，风冷发动机

fanfare horn （指车用）高响度和声喇叭（电控膜片产生清晰而响亮的和声）

fan flywheel 风扇式飞轮，辐条式飞轮（= spoked flywheel）

fang bolt 地脚螺栓（= foundation bolt）

fan hub 风扇（叶片轮）毂（亦称 fan spider）

fan impeller 见 fan blade

fan in ①输入端数（指逻辑电路输入端的外部引线数）②输入

fanner 风扇，通风机

fanning 通风，鼓风

fanning effect ①（旋转零件造成的）风扇效应（引起空气流动的作用）②（通风机的）通风效果，通风作用

fan out ①输出端数（指逻辑电路输出端所连接的或可能连接的外部电路数）②输出

fan pulley bracket adjuster screw 风扇皮带轮托架调整螺钉（供移动皮带轮位置，以调整皮带紧度之用）

fan rotor 见 fan blade

fan shaft 风扇（叶片）轴（亦称 fan spindle）

fan shroud 风扇导风罩，见 fan tunnel

fan slip 风扇风压损失

fan spider 见 fan hub

fan spindle 见 fan shaft

fantail [口语] 水陆两用汽车

fantastic ①极好的，了不起的 ②奇异的 ③宜人的 ④富于想象的 ⑤（反应等）强烈的

fan tunnel [美] 风扇出风孔罩（= fan shroud）

fan-type engine 扇形发动机（相对于一根曲轴，汽缸布置成扇形的多缸发动机）

fao 全面精加工（finish all over 的简称）

farad 法（拉）（国际单位制的电容单位，代号 F，充入 1C 的电荷，板间电压升高 1V 的电容器的电容为 1F，1F = 1C/V = 1A·s/V，见 coulomb、volt，实际使用单位为微法

μF, 10^{-6}F 或皮法 PF, 10^{-12}F)

faraday 法拉第（电量单位 =96520C）

far beam （汽车前照灯）远光（ =high beam, distance light, full head lamp beam, bright beam, driving beam, long distance light）

FARE 减少（汽车）死亡事故实施方案（措施）（fatal accident reduction enforcement 的简称）

fare 运费，车费

fare box （公共汽车自动收费系统的）收费箱

fare register 运费计算器，票价计算器

far infrared ray 远红外线

far-infrared rays 远红外线（见 infrared rays，由于它的波长较长，能透过有机物质、高分子物质表层，深入物质内部，其辐射能量能被全部吸收，使物质分子、原子产生共振，而使物质的温度迅速上升，同时红外线碰到金属层时能产生反射、折射，所以常利用远红外线烘干车身油漆，以使油漆层可从底层先干，提高烘干质量）

farm-out 转交，移交，送去处理（如：送交修理或技术维护）

far reaching headlamp （汽车）远照距离照明灯（ = distance headlamp）

FARS （车祸）死亡事故报告系统（fatal accident reporting system 的简称）

fascia ①仪表板 ②饰带 ③腰线（绘制侧视图时，概括整个车身下部两侧的上边线线条， = waistline, belt line 或 door belt） ④［美］构成车身外装饰的一部分的板件（如汽车前保险杆下的装饰板，亦写作 facia）

fashion ①方式，方法，形式，式样，风格；型 ②制法，构造 ③流行的时新式样 ④形成，造作，铸成 ⑤使适合 ⑥最后加工，修饰，修整 ⑦改革，改变

fashionable style 流行式样，时髦形式

fashioned 流行式样的，时髦的

F. A. S. T. 摩擦鉴定分类试验（friction assessment screening test 的简称）

fast-acting 快速作用的，速动的

fast axle speed （双速驱动桥）高速挡

fast back ①（轿车车身的）斜背（指车身后部呈流线型斜面，以减少风阻） ②斜背式（轿车）车身 ③（各种）斜背式轿车（ = fast back car）

fast battery charger 见 fact charger

fast build state （防抱死制动系的）快速升压工况（见 pressure increase ②）

fast burn ①快速燃烧 ②（日本日产公司的双火花塞）高速燃烧系统（的商品名）

fast car 高速轿车

fast charger 快速充电机，（在短时间内以 40amp 或更大电流对蓄电池快速应急充电用。此外还可用来帮助发动机低温起动。一般为移动式的，使用交流电源，内部装有大容量的整流器、蓄电池诊断装置，以及防止电流过大和温度过高的自动开关等， = quick charger）

fast codes 见 service codes ①

fast colour 不褪色的颜色，不易褪色的颜色（ = permanent colour）

fast cornering （汽车等）急转弯，急转，快速转弯

fast coupling ①紧联合 ②刚性联轴节，常合联轴节 ③快速联轴节

fast cure polyesters 快速固化聚酯，速凝聚酯（以醇酸树脂为基料的一种造型材料，亦称 granular polyesters）

fast-curing 快速硫化的，快速固化的（ = fast-cure）

fast delivery van （送货到家的）厢式快速送货车

fasten 固定，紧固，夹紧，捆牢

fastener 紧固件（的通称）

fastening torque 紧固转矩

faster acting choke 速动阻风门

faster idler 怠速提速器（为了防止发动机怠速运转时汽车空调设备制冷能力下降或发动机熄火，而由空调开关控制的、自动提升发动机怠速转速的装置）

fast-fill valve 快速充气阀，快速充液阀

fast Fourier transform 快速傅里叶变换（简称 FFT，可用于对发动机噪声、振动作傅里叶解析，借以诊断发动机的故障，见 Fourier transform）

fast hitch 快速挂接装置（= quick hitch）

fast idle cam 快怠速凸轮（冬季发动机起动时，机油黏度大，发动机摩擦损失马力大，起动后的怠速运转时，需要较大的功率，节气门开度应大于一般怠速开度，该凸轮与阻风门联动，通过快怠速臂稍增加阻风门关闭时的节气门开度，简称 FIC，亦称 throttle cracker）

fast idle dashpot （装在具有自动变速器及空调系统的车辆上的日产 Z 系列发动机化油器的）快怠速节气门开度控制装置（简称 FIPot）

fast idle mechanism 快怠速机构（见 fast idle cam）

fast idle solenoid （与自动风门机构一起工作，当阻风门关闭时，自动将节气门稍许开大的）快怠速电磁阀

fast-idle speed 快（转）怠速（亦称 fast idling, 当发动机冷机起动时，暖机阶段的怠速应较热机时的正常怠速快一些，否则，汽车挂挡起步加速时，发动机会熄火或抖动，为此，有些化油器上装有快转怠速凸轮机构，参见 fast-idle cam）

fast ionization analyzer 氢焰离子化检测仪（简称 FIA，参见 flame ionization detector）

fast lane 快车道（一般设在多车道公路的外侧）

fast light-off lamda sensor 加速起燃式 λ 传感器（简称 FLS）

fastness ①坚固性 ②安定性 ③fastness to alkali 耐碱性，抗碱强度（= alkali fastness），④ fastness to light 耐光性，光照不褪色性 ⑤fastness to water 耐水性，抗水性

fast-operating 快速动作的，快速作用的（简称 FO）

fast preheating system 快速预热系统（见 quick preheating system）

fast-release 快速释放的，快速复位的（简称 FR）

fast-response 快速反应的，快速响应的

fast-return 快速返回的，快速回位的

fast rise ignition coil 高速升压点火线圈，速动点火线圈

Fast Start 快速起动（商品名，通用公司对其 C^3I, Type Ⅲ 的通称，见 C^3I）

fast-starting EI system 快速起动电子点火系统（该系统在起动机带动发动机曲轴旋转不到 120°，即 1/3 转时即开始跳火，故名）

fast thermocouple 小惯量温差电偶

fast to light （光照）不褪色的

fast traffic 高速交通，快速运输（= swiftly moving traffic）

fast wave （脑电波中的）速波（14Hz, 10～20μV 以上）

fat ①油脂（动、植物油）②润滑脂，润滑油 ③含脂的，多脂的 ④含沥青的

FAT 工厂验收试验（factory acceptance test)

fatalities ①死亡事故 (= fatal accident) ②(车祸)死亡率(以十万分之几计)

fatal lesions in 3 or more regions (车祸中乘员)身体3处或3处以上的致命伤

FAT DUCT CDEF 疲劳韧性系数 (fatigue ductility coefficient 的简称)

fatigue ①疲劳(指汽车部件长时间受交变载荷的作用,性能变坏,甚至断裂的现象)②使疲劳

fatigue debris 由接触疲劳引起的表面破坏物(碎片、破片)

fatigue-decreased efficiency boundary 疲劳降低工效界限(由于承受车辆振动而疲劳,引起人的工作能力和效率显著下降的暴露时间界限,参见 exposure time,亦称 fatigue-decreased proficiency boundary)

fat resistance 耐油脂性

fat spark 强火花

fatty acids 脂肪酸

fault ①缺点,缺陷,毛病 ②故障,损坏,失效 ③漏电,短路

fault clock 故障钟(用于记录故障所持续的时间)

fault current 漏电,故障电流

fault detecting 故障诊断[查明故障所在及原因,= fault finding, fault locating (着重查明故障部位和部件); fault tracing (着重根据征兆找出故障所在); 亦可写作 fault detection 和 fault localization 或 fault location,但此时更强调结果。fault detector, fault finder, fault locator, fault tracer 分别为完成上述故障诊断的装置和仪器。近年来,随着电子技术的进步,多采用不解体方法,通过各种传感元件或电子仪器查明故障,如同医生用各种医疗设备查明病情,于是原来仅用于医生看病的 diagnose 一词,被广泛用于
fatigue deformation 疲劳变形

fatigue ductility coefficient 疲劳韧性系数(简称 FAT DUCT COEF)

fatigue fracture 疲劳断裂(金属在循环载荷作用下产生疲劳裂纹扩展导致的断裂)

fatigueless 不致引起疲劳的,操作轻便的

fatigue life 疲劳寿命(指材料疲劳失效时所经受的规定应力或应变的循环次数)

fatigue limit 疲劳极限(指金属材料在规定次数重复的交变载荷作用下而不致破坏的最大应力)

fatigue loading 疲劳载荷(周期性或非周期性的动载荷,亦称循环载荷)

fatigue notch factor 切口应力集中系数,切口疲劳因数

fatigue pitting 疲劳剥蚀,疲劳穴蚀(对金属滚动部件表面造成蚀斑,剥蚀)

fatigue ratio 疲劳强度极限与(静载下的)抗断强度极限之比

fatigue resistance 见 fatigue strength

fatigue safety coefficient 疲劳(载荷)安全系数(简称 FSC)

fatigue shear test 剪切疲劳试验

fatigue strength (抗)疲劳强度(一般经受规定次数,如钢经受 10^6 次、有色金属经受 $10^7 \sim 10^8$ 次交变载荷作用而不产生破坏的最大应力,亦称 fatigue resistance)

fatigue strength coefficient 疲劳强度系数(简称 FAT STR COEF)

fatigue strength reduction factor (由于应力集中引起的)疲劳强度降低系数

fatigue stress 疲劳应力

fatigue-warning device 零件疲劳损坏警报装置

fatigue wear (表面)疲劳(引起的)磨损

表示汽车的不解体"故障诊断",见 diagnosis]

fault-free 无故障的,无缺点的

fault freedom 纠错能力(指汽车电子控制系统的某一部分软件或硬件出现错误时,系统通过软件或硬件自动纠错恢复正常的能力)

fault-indicating lamp 故障指示灯

faultless 无缺陷的,无故障的

faultless gear change 无冲击换挡,无损换挡(如使用同步器等)

fault location 故障定位(确定故障部位和性质)

fault memory 故障存储器(电子控制故障诊断系统控制模块内存储故障代码和有关资料的存储器)

fault rate 故障(发生)率,损坏程度

fault rate threshold 故障率阈值(指在规定的时间间隔内出现的故障次数,当该次数超过某规定值时,系统必须进行修理,亦称 fault threshold)

fault reader (汽车故障诊断系统的)故障读出器

fault-safety relay 故障保险继电器(当电子控制模块发现有可能导致控制系统误操作的重大故障时,控制模块即断开该继电器,中断向控制系统供电,停止该系统的功能)

fault scenarios 故障的情况(scenarios 意大利语:情况、状态、详情之意)

fault threshold 故障阈值(当系统的故障次数超过该值时,必须进行修复,排除故障)

fault time 故障时间(停机排除故障的时间)

fault to frame (电器)与车(机)架短路(的故障)

fault tolerance (汽车电子系统的)容错能力(指一个部件或多个部件发生故障时仍能正确工作的能力)

fault tolerance 容错性(指即使在一个或多个部件出现故障的情况下,系统仍能继续正常运行的性能)

fault trace 故障追迹(记录)(表征发生故障前、后及发生故障时的各种状态及其顺序)

fault tree analysis 故障树型分析法,故障树分析法,树枝图法(将汽车故障作为一种事件,按其故障原因进行逻辑分析,绘出树枝状图形,简称 FTA 法,亦写作 failure tree)

Faure type plate 富尔式极板(一般蓄电池采用的在铅锑合金铸制的栅板上涂以氧化铅粉末等的涂浆极板)

favo(u)rable wind 顺风(= favouring wind, following wind, leading wind, tail wind)

favo(u)rably situated 布置合理的,位置合适的

FAW (中国)第一汽车制造厂(First Automobile Works 简称)

FAW-Volkswagen Automotive Company (中国)一汽—大众汽车公司(中国第一汽车制造厂与德国 Vdkswagen AG. 的合资企业,1991 年 2 月正式成立, 开始生产, Santana, Jetta、Golf 等轿车)

fax 传真通信[facsimile 的简称,指经窄波(非视频)通信链路传送二维图文形式的数据通信方式]

faying face 接合面(= faying surface)

faying surface ①(耦合构件的)连接(表)面,接合(表)面(= faying face)②紧密贴合的表面

FB ①反馈,回授(feedback)②消防队(fire brigade)③运货单(freight bill)

FBC ①反馈控制(feedback control 的简称)②反馈控制式化油器(feed back carburetor 的简称)

FBC 燃油后备电路（fuel backup circuit 的简称，一般该电路包括在发动机标定软件包"calpak"内。当发动机电子控制模块的工作电压低于9V，PROM不工作或电子控制模块不能发出计算机控制脉冲"COP"时，该电路提供后备喷油控制程序，此时发动机属"带病"运转，并给出相应的故障码）

FBE 摩擦制动能量（friction braking energy 的简称）

FBHP 车身前部的铰链支柱（front body hinge pillar 的简称）

FBN 液压产生的噪声（fluid-borne noise 的简称）

FBP 干点（见 final boiling point）

F/Bumper spoiler （装在）前保险杠（上的）导流板（F/Bumper 为 front bumper 的简称）

FC ①燃料电池（fuel cell 的简称）②燃料消耗（量），油耗（量）（fuel consumption 的简称）③停止供油（fuel cut 的简称）

F-CAN 快速控制器局域网（F 为 fast 的简称，见 CAN）

FCC ①面心立方（晶格）（face-centered cubic 的简称）②装置控制台（facilities control console 的简称）③流体化催化裂化装置（fluidized catalytic cracker 的简称）④流体裂化催化剂（fluid crack catalyst 的简称）

FCDI system 铁磁谐振电容器放电点火系（ferroresonant capacitor discharge ignition system 的简称）

FCE bus 燃料电池大客车（fuel cell electric bus 的简称）

F-Cell 燃料电池（fuel cell 的简称）

FCEV 燃料电池电动汽车（fuel cell electric vehicle 的简称）

FCEV 燃料电池电动汽车（fuel cell electric vehicle 的简称）

FCEV（H） （丰田公司）高压氢型燃料电池电动汽车（商品名）

FCEV（M） 重整甲醇型燃料电池电动汽车

FCHV 燃料电池型复合动力车（fuel-cell hybrid vehicle 的简称，指由燃料电池提供电动机能源的内燃机-电动机复合动力车）

FCM 前方碰撞缓解（系统）

FCMB system 见 forward-collision mitigation braking

FCM system 见 forward-collision mitigation system

F1 control technology 一级方程式大奖赛车控制技术（见 formula③）

FCS [美]车队管理服务中心（Fleet Control Services 的简称）

FC solenoid 风扇控制电磁阀（fan control solenoid 的简称）

FCST [美]联邦科学技术委员会（Federal Council for Science and Technology 的简称）

FCT 见 full charge-state test

FCV 燃料电池车（fuel cell vehicle 的简称）

FCV 废气还流切断阀（见 full cut valve）

FCX （本田公司的）燃料电池车商品名（= fuel-cell vehicle，该车使用该公司最新研制的燃料电池堆，可在0℃以下起动，见 fuel cell stack）

FDBK 反馈，回授（feedback）

FDC （仪表板上的）燃油数据中心（fuel data center 的简称，集中显示瞬时油耗，平均油耗，剩余油量，剩余油量可行驶里程等与燃油有关的各种信息的仪表）

FDDS [美]联邦耐久性试验驾驶规程（Federal Durability Driving Schedule 的简称）

FDMA 频分多路复用存取（见 frequency division multiple access）

FDN 基础，地基（foundation）

Fédération Internationale de l'Auto-

mobile [法] 国际汽车联合会（简称 FIA，各国设有分会）

Fédération Internationale des Associations de Journalistes de l'Automobile [法] 国际汽车新闻工作者协会联合会（简称 FIAJA）

Fédération Internationale des sociétés d'Ingenieurs des Techniques de l'Automobile [法] 国际汽车工程师学会联合会（简称 FISITA. 1901年7月1日在法国成立，第25届年会1994年在北京举行，年会每两年举行一次，有26个会员单位）

Fédération Internationale du Sport Automobile [法] 国际运动车联合会（简称 FISA）

Fédération Internationale Motor-cycliste [法] 国际摩托车驾驶员联合会（简称 FIM）

FE 燃油经济性，燃料经济性（fuel economy）

Fe 铁（ferrum 的简称，= iron）

FEA ①[美] 联邦能源管理局（Federal Energy Administration 的简称）②有限元分析（finite-element analysis 的简称）

Fedearal bumper （符合美国）联邦（安全规程的）保险杠（要求能吸收5英里/小时车速碰撞的全部能量，亦称 five-mile-an hour bumper "5英里/小时车速保险杠"）

feasibility 可行性（feasibility analysis 可行性分析，根据投资、利润、技术条件等分析实现某种规划、设计的可能性；feasibility evaluation 可行性评估；feasibility check 可行性检验；feasibility study 可行性研究，研究某一新方案或设想能否实现；feasibility test 可行性试验）

feasible ①可实行的，可实现的，可行的，有可能的 ②合理的，有理的，可用的，合适的

feather ①滑键 ②加强肋 ③凸起，凸起部 ④羽状斑疵 ⑤（用楔形件）连接

feather in boss 轮毂滑键

feathering ①羽状磨损（轮胎的一种磨损形状，其胎面磨得很薄且边缘呈羽状飞边，亦称 feather wear）②很轻柔地踩下加速踏板或制动踏板

feather key 滑键，导向键（指圆头端面或方端面的平行工作面键，见 square key）

feather wear 见 feathering①

feature ①特征，特点，特性 ②装置，器件，部件 ③使…有特色，以…为特色 ④起重要作用

FEBIS 汽车前端障壁碰撞模拟（试验）（front end barrier impact simulation 的简称）

FEC 欧洲旅居汽车旅游联合会（European Federation of Caravanning 的简称）

Federal Durability Driving Schedule [美] 联邦耐久性试验驾驶规程（简称 FDDS）

Federal Emissions Tests [美] 联邦排放试验（法）

Federal Energy Administration [美] 联邦能源管理局（简称 FEA）

Federal engine （符合美国）联邦（排放标准并为 EPA 认证可在全美除加利福尼亚以外的各州使用的）发动机

federal exhaust emission test [美] 联邦排气有害物试验（法），[美] 联邦排放试验法

federal fuel-economy standards （美国）联邦（汽车）油耗标准，联邦燃料经济性标准

federal highway （美国的）联邦公路，国道

Federal Highway Administration （美国）联邦公路（管理）局（简称 FHWA）

Federal Motor Carrier Safety Administration （美国）联邦汽车货运公司安全管理局（简称FMCSA）

Federal Motor Vehicle Control Program [美]联邦汽车管理规程（简称FMVCP）

Federal Motor Vehicle Safety Standards [美]联邦汽车安全标准（美国联邦政府以法令形式规定的各汽车和汽车配件制造厂商出售的一切车辆及配件所必须遵守的最低安全技术要求。1968年1月1日起正式实施，以后年年增加新的内容，防止事故发生的安全性标准，编号由101开始，如：FMVSS121为对气制动系统的安全要求；发生碰撞后防止乘员受到二次冲击的安全要求由201开始编号；发生碰撞等事故后的安全要求从301开始编号，简称FMVSS）

Federal Specification [美]联邦政府规范（简称FS）

Federal Test Cycle for Exhaust Emissions [美]联邦废气有害排出物测试循环（对机动车辆）

Federal Test Procedure [美]联邦试验规程，联邦（汽车污染）试验规程（简称FTP，模拟典型运转工况的排放测试法）

Federal Test Procedure Cycles [美]联邦（机动车）多工况循环试验规程（简称FTP cycles）

Federal Urban Driving Cycle [美]联邦城市行驶工况循环（模拟汽车城市行驶工况，在底盘测功机上检测排气中有害物含量的多工况循环）

Federal version 联邦型（指符合美国联邦排放标准，但无须符合更严格的，如加利福尼亚州标准的汽车）

fee ①费，费用，税 ②交费，雇用，聘请

feeble current 弱电流，弱电

feed 供给，供应，供电，供油，供水

feedability （润滑油）易供给性（指容易进入摩擦表面的性能）

feed arrangement 供给装置，供电装置，送料装置，给水装置，供油设备

feedback 反馈 [①闭路控制系统不断将输出信号的控制结果作为输入信号，返回至控制系统与设定的控制目标值进行比较，以修正控制信号，使控制结果达到目标值的要求 ②闭路控制系统不断将输出信号的"一部分"作为输入返回，与目标输出值进行比较，实施自纠（self correcting），以消除或缩小偏差]

feedback characteristic 反馈特性

feedback (signal) amplifier 反馈信号放大器

feedback signal sensor 反馈信号传感器（亦称feedback transducer, feedback element，指反映控制结果信息的传感器）

feeder ①供给装置（送料，供料，进料，加料，给水，供油，供气等装置的通称）②馈电装置，馈电线，供电线

feeder cable 馈电电缆

feeder highway 支线路，公路支线

feeder street 支线街道（地方街道与主要街道或主要公路连接的街道）

feed forward control 前馈控制（根据预先设定的信号进行控制，如微机控制点火提前角，系根据发动机转速、进气真空度等信号，用查表法控制。简称F.F.C）

feeding system （油、气、液等的）供给系统

feeding transformer 馈电变压器

feed inlet 进气孔，进入口，吸气孔，吸入口（= inlet opening, induction opening, inlet）

feed line 供油管路，给水管道，进

给线，补给线，供料线路，供应导管，馈电线

feed mechanism 给水机构，供油装置，送料机构，输入装置

feed pump ①（泛指）输液泵，供液泵 ②（特指，将燃油从油箱中抽出并以一定压力和流量供给喷油系统的）供油泵，输油泵

feed stock 原料（= raw feed, original feed）

feed system ①（泛指）由泵、管道、阀门及其他构件组成的，以一定压力和流量供给液体的系统 ②（特指汽车燃油系中，将燃油从油箱抽出供给化油器或喷油装置的）供油系

feed through capacitor 旁路电容器

feel ①感觉，触觉，知觉 ②触，摸；感到，意识到，觉得，好像，以为，认为

feel cylinder 传感油缸

feeler ①塞尺，厚薄规 ②触头，探针

feeler gauge 厚薄规，测隙规（测隙片"feeler blades"和测隙线"feeler wire"的总称，指各种厚度的小间距或间隙，如：火花塞电极间隙，气门间隙等的量片或量线）

feeler inspection （用探针）触探

feeler microscope 接触式测微显微镜

feeler plug 测孔规，量塞，塞规

feeler strip 测隙片条（长条状测隙片，当频繁使用磨损时可适时切除一段继续使用）

feeler wire 测隙线，厚薄线（直径精确控制的量线，即：线状测隙规）

feeling evaluation 感觉评价（依据评价人员主观感觉进行的评价）

feeling of risk （乘客乘坐汽车时的）危险感

feel of the road 路感（汽车驾驶人员在驾驶时对路况的感觉）

feel servo mechanism 有反馈作用的伺服机构

feel test 感觉（感触）试验

FE engine 省油发动机（fuel-efficient engine的简称）

fee of permit 牌照税，执照税

FEEPROM 闪存式电可擦可编程只读存储器（flash electrically erasable programmable read only memory 的简称，亦写作 flash electrically erasable PROM）

feet （foot 的复数）①足，脚 ②英尺

FEI 见 fully electronic ignition

felloe 轮辋（= felly，一般称 rim，指车轮上安装和支承轮胎的部件，一件式轮辋包括槽底、胎座圈、轮缘等区段）

felt 毛毡［felt covering 毡套，毡罩；felt cylinder 毡筒芯；felt deadener 减振、防撞、隔音毡板；felt element 毛毡滤清器的滤芯；felt gasket 各种形状防漏毡垫；felt joint 带毡垫的接头；felt layer 毡（表、垫或夹）层；felt mat 或 felt pad 在外面的毡垫；felt metal case seal 毡芯金属壳密封（件）；felt（oil seal）retainer 毛毡油封的座圈；felt ring seal 毡密封环；felt underlayer 毡底层；felt washer 毡垫圈；felt wick 毡油绳］

FEM 有限元法（见 finite-element methods）

female ①凹形的，内孔的，阴的，母的（简称 f）②内螺纹的；管接头凹面垫圈

female adaptor ring 内螺纹过渡接头密封环（= female support ring）

female connector （电）插座

female dummy （试验用的）女性假人

female wrench 套筒扳手，（= box-end wrench）

FEMP 飞轮储能放能传动系统（flywheel energy management power plant 的简称）

femto- 毫微微，毫沙，尘，10^{-15}

fence type lane 路边栅栏式车道
fender ①[美]翼子板(遮盖车轮的)车身外板(= wing) ②挡泥板(fender board 的简称) ③导流裙板(装在车前端或后端,高度接近地面的导风板或压风板) ④挡板,护板,碰垫 ⑤(偶见指汽车)保险杠(= bumper) ⑥装在翼子板上的
fender apron (汽车)翼子板的后挡泥板(位于车轮后方,用橡胶板或金属板构成,亦称 fender flap, fender skirt, fender valance 或 mud apron, mud guard flap)
fender bender (汽车)翼子板矫正装置
fender bracket 翼子板托架
fender bumping hammer (车身)翼子板(凹陷部修复用的)敲出手锤,长头手锤
fender extensions 翼子板延长部分
fender flap 见 fender apron
fender lamp (汽车)翼子板灯,翼子板示宽灯,侧灯(= fender light, side lamp, marking light, side-marker lamp)
fender marker (在翼子板上的)宽度标志,边侧标志(= side marker)
fender mirror (汽车的)翼子板后视镜(装在翼子板上的后视镜)
fender-mounted 安装在翼子板上的
fender side shield 前翼子板侧板(见 valance panel)
fender skirt 见 fender apron
fender straightener 翼子板校直器,叶板整形机
fender support 翼子板支架
fender valance 见 fender apron
Fenton (bearing) metal 锌基轴承合金(锌80%,锡14.5%,铜5.5%)
FEP 氟基次乙基丙烯,氟化乙丙烯(fluoroethylene propylene 的简称)
Ferguson four-wheel drive 福格森四轮驱动(亦称 Ferguson four-wheel transmission,指通过一专门的黏液偶合差速器将驱动力的37%分配至前轮,63%分配至后轮的传动系统)
fermi 费米(米制长度单位,代号f,$= 10^{-13}$cm)
ferocious 强烈的,极度的,急剧的,猛烈的
ferodo 钢丝石棉板摩擦材料及这种材料制的摩擦片(= ferrodo)
Ferrari engine and transmission technologies 法拉利发动机与变速器技术
Ferrari S. P. A (意大利)法拉利股份公司(菲亚特控股)
Ferrari stability and traction control system (意大利)法拉利(跑车的)稳定性和牵引力控制系统
ferrel 见 ferrule
ferric 铁的,三价铁的
ferric chloride 三氯化铁($FeCl_3$)
ferric oxide 氧化铁(粉),三氧化二铁,西红粉(Fe_2O_3)
ferrimagnetic ①铁淦氧磁物,铁磁体 ②强磁性(的),铁磁性(的)(亦写作 ferromagnetic)
ferrite ①纯铁体,铁素体,α铁,自然铁;②铁淦氧(磁体),铁氧体;③(正)铁酸盐
ferrite cored coils 铁淦氧磁心线围
ferrite E' core (电磁线圈)E形铁氧体磁心
ferrite frequency meter 铁氧体频率计
ferritic alloy 铁氧体合金,铁淦氧合金
ferritic stainless steel 铁素体不锈钢
ferritic steel 铁素体钢
ferro 亚铁的、二价铁的,含铁的
ferro-alloy 铁合金
ferrodo 见 ferodo
ferroelectric material 铁电(体)材料,强电介质

ferromagnetic 见 ferrimagnetic

ferromagnetic material 铁磁材料（见 Barnett effect）

ferromanganese 锰铁，铁锰合金

ferromanganese steel 锰钢

ferro-nickel 镍铁，铁镍合金（铁 74.2%，镍 25%，碳 0.8%）

ferroresonant capacitor discharge ignition system 铁磁谐振电容器放电点火系（简称 FCDI system）

ferrosilicon 硅铁（合金），硅钢

ferrosteel 灰口铸铁（生铁、铸铁、废铁、废钢等混合炼成）

Ferrotic 渗碳化钛高铬合金钢（转子发动机径向密封片及旋轮线缸壁的喷镀层用材料）

Ferrotic apex seal （转子发动机的）渗碳化钛高铬合金钢径向密封片

ferrous ①亚铁的，二价铁的 ②含铁的

ferrous oxide 氧化亚铁，一氧化铁

ferrule 铁箍，金属箍，线圈管，套圈，套筒，环圈，（亦写作 ferrel）

ferrule-type compression joint 套箍式压缩密封管接头

ferrum 铁 Fe

ferry ①轮渡，渡口 ②浮桥 ③渡运，摆渡

Ferry 一种铜镍合金（铜 55%~60%，镍 40%~45%）

ferry charge 过渡费（对车辆通过渡口、桥梁、隧道或货物过渡倒装的费收）

fertilizer tanker 液体肥料槽车

FET ① field effect transistor 的简称 ② Federal Emission Tests 的简称

fetch cycle 检取周期（指计算机运行过程中，从主存读出一个操作数据或一个指令并将它写入控制寄存器或运算部件寄存器所需的时间）

FE Tire 有限元轮胎模型（finite element tire model 的简称）

FF ①前置发动机前轮驱动（front engine front drive 的简称）②触发器（flip-flop 的简称）③燃油流量（fuel flow 的简称）④全图，全像（full figure 的简称）

F. F. C 见 feed forward control

FFCS 燃油流量控制系统（fuel flow control system 的简称）

FF headlight 自由式前照灯（free-form headlight 的简称，= FF headlamp，指使用自由式反射镜的前照灯，见 freeshape reflector）

FF Midship （日本本田公司的）前中置发动机前轮驱动（front drive front midship engine 的简称，其发动机纵向布置于前桥上方，变速器接发动机后方，经传动轴将动力传给前轮驱动，这种布置使前、后桥载荷分配趋于合理）

FFT 快速傅里叶变换（fast Fourier transform 的简称）

FFT analyzer 快速傅立叶变换分析仪

FF/TOT 燃油流量总计指示器（fuel flow totalizer 的简称）

FFV 两用燃料汽车，可变燃料汽车（flexible fuel vehicle 的简称）

FF vehicle 前置发动机前驱动车辆（front engine front drive vehicle 的简称）

fgn 外国的，对外的（foreign）

F-head combustion chamber F 形燃烧室（排气门在缸体一侧，进气门顶置）

F-head engine F 型汽缸盖发动机（指进气门顶置，而排气门侧置的发动机，见 inlet over exhaust engine）

FHI （日本）富士重工（Fuji Heavy Industries 的简称）

FHP ①小马力（fraction horsepower 的简称）②摩擦功率（friction horsepower 的简称，亦写作 fhp）

FHP motor 小马力电动机（fraction horsepower motor 的简称）

FHWA 美国联邦公路管理局（Federal Highway Administration 的简称）

FI =fuel injection

FIA ①快怠速执行器（fast idle actuator 的简称）②国际汽车联合会（Federation Internationale de L'Automobile 的简称）③氢焰离子化检测仪，火焰离子化测定仪（flame ionization analyzer 的简称）

FIAJA 国际汽车新闻工作者协会联合会（Fédération Internationale des Associations de Journalistes de l'Automobile 的简称）

Fiala model （分析轮胎转弯力用的）Fiala 模型（轮胎分析模型"analytical tire model"之一）

FIAT ①菲亚特（车牌，Fabbrica Italiana Automobile Torino 的简称）②（意大利）菲亚特汽车集团（全称 Fiat Societapet Azioi；简称 Fiat，意大利最大的汽车企业，创立于 1899 年，年生产能力 200 万辆以上）

Fiat S. P. A （意大利）菲亚特股份公司

fiber 纤维；纤维板（亦写作 fibre）

fiber glass 玻璃纤维（=fibrous glass）

fiber glass-reinforced plastic 玻璃纤维强化塑料（缩写 FRP）

fiber glide bearing 纤维滑动轴承（一种自润滑轴承）

fiber grease 纤维状润滑脂

fiber heel （分电盘断电器触点臂与凸轮接触的）胶木（树脂纤维）顶块（=Bakelite heel）

fiber optic gyroscope 见 FOG

fiber optics 纤维光学，光导纤维术（=fibre optics，用极细的玻璃丝传输频率为 10^{14} Hz 的光脉冲信号的技术。玻璃丝起着引导光波的作用，它使光在其内壁上来回反射，使光能沿着弯路在很长的距离上被传送，且损耗极小，可代替电缆传递各种信息）

fiber-reinforced composite 纤维强化复合材料（简称 FRC）

fiber-reinforced plastic 纤维增强塑料，纤维强化塑料（简称 FRP）

fiber-reinforced thermoplastics 玻璃纤维强化热塑性树脂，玻璃纤维强化热塑料（加有 10%～40% 的短玻璃纤维，与一般热塑性塑料比较，抗拉强度、冲击强度、热变形温度显著提高，简称 FRTP）

fiber seal 见 fiber packing

fibre glass 玻璃纤维（=glass fibre，玻璃纤维经合成树脂黏合而成，固后成为质量很轻的高强度材料，可制作车身等的构件，亦称 glass reinforced plastic）

fibre glass body 玻璃纤维车身（指由玻璃纤维材料模制的整体式车身外壳）

fibre glass mat （修衬孔洞用的）玻璃纤维补垫

fibre-optic 光学纤维的，光导纤维的（见 fiber optics）

fibre-optical communication 光导纤维通信

fibre-optic cable 光纤电缆

fibre optic combustion pressure sensor 光纤式燃烧压力传感器（通过光纤将光源的入射光射向直接与燃烧压力接触的膜片，并由光纤将膜片的反射光传给光电元件，膜片传递的压力信号便由光信号转变为电信号，该传感器可小到装入火花塞内）

fibre optics 见 fiber optics

fibrous 纤维的

FIC 快怠速凸轮（fast idle cam 的简称）

FICD 快怠速控制装置（fast idle control divice 的简称，见 fast idle）

fictitious load 模拟载荷，假负载

fictitious power 虚功率

FID 氢焰离子化测定仪（用于测定废气中的 HC 含量等，flame ionization detector 的简称，亦称氢焰离子化分析仪 "flame ionization analyzer"）

fidelity ①逼真度，保真度，精确度 ②真实，正确

fidelity curve 逼真度曲线

fiducial error 引用误差（指仪器仪表的示值误差除以规定值。该规定值常称为引用值，如：仪表的量程或范围上限值等）

FIE 燃油喷射装置（fuel injection equipment）

field ①现场，工地 ②场，电场，磁场，引力场 ③活动范围，界，（领）域，（视）野 ④符号组，字段；信息组；代号组 ⑤现场的，实际使用的，在实际使用条件下的

field-alterable memory 信息组可变（换）式存储器，字段可换存储器

field amplifier 励磁电流放大器，磁场电流放大器

field assembly 现场装配

fieldate 军用数据处理系统

field-checking 现场检验，现场校验

field circuit 磁磁电路（交、直流电机中向激磁绕组提供励磁电流的电路，亦称磁场电路）

field coil （交、直流电机的）激磁线圈（由缠在铁芯或钢芯上的绝缘导线制成，通电后，形成具有强磁力的磁场，亦称磁场绕组，磁极绕组，= field winding）

field-collected data 现场收集的数据

field conditions 使用条件，现场条件

field-control motor 磁场可控式电动机，可调磁型电动机

field-control test 控制现场的试验；控制使用条件的试验

field core 磁场铁芯；励磁铁芯

field current 激磁电流（发电机工作时通过磁场绕组的电流，亦称磁场电流）

field data 现场数据（在现场使用中得到的观测数据）

field decay （发电机等的）磁场衰减

field density （磁、电）场强度，场密度；（磁）感应密度，通量密度

field development 在现场使用（或现场试验）中的改进

field diaphragm （金相显微镜等的）视野光阑（改变目镜中看到的物象的范围）

field dynamometer 室外测力计（= tension dynamometer）

field-effect transistor 场效应晶体管（简称 FET，①利用输入电压的电场控制输出电流的半导体器件，可起开关、振荡、放大作用；②一种源极和漏极间的电流受源极和栅极间电压的控制，从而可改变源极漏极间沟道的电导的半导体器件；③利用外加电场对半导体导电能力产生控制效应的晶体管）

field engineer 现场工程师，施工工程师

field failure 使用过程中的损坏，现场损坏

field feedback 用户（给制造厂的）反馈意见，用户反馈信息

field frame （安装直流发电机、起动机及小型电动机磁极的）机壳（本身也是磁路的一部分，旧称机座，外壳）

field in a data base 数据库中的字段（在数据库中可被访问的最小数据单位）

field intensity 场强度

field maintenance factor 现场维修率，使用维修率（简称 FMF）

field man ①现场工作人员 ②汽车销售指导员（由汽车制造厂派到各汽车交易场所，进行销售业务及技术指导）

field manual 使用手册（简称 FM）

field number (金相显微镜目镜等的)视野值(在透镜前形成的视野光阑物像的尺寸,mm)

field of view 视野(=field of vision)

field on a data medium(**or in storage**) 数据媒体(或存储器)中的字段(对字段均规定有其名称、长度、类型及起始位置)

field overhaul 在使用现场进行的大修,现场大修

field performance 现场工作性能,实际使用性能

field pole 场磁极

field-programmable gate array 现场可编程的门阵列(一种用户可编程的封装在一个芯片内的多个逻辑门组成的集成电路,简称 FPGA,用它可以迅速开发出用户所需的执行各种复杂的逻辑运算与操作的芯片,见 gate array)

field-programmable read-only memory 现场可编程只读存储器(在制作之后,每个存储单元的数据内容都可以修改的一种只读存储器)

field-proven 现场使用验证过的

field quenching diode 灭弧二极管

field-recorded 在使用现场记录下的

field relay 磁场继电器(用来自动接通与断开交流发电机磁场电路的继电器,旧称防倒流继电器)

field service ①现场维修,现场服务;②现场使用,实际运行

field strength (电、磁)场强度

field strength meter 场强仪,场强表(用于测定电、磁场的强度)

field terminal ①"F"接线柱(指发电机磁场接线柱或调节器的相应接线柱,旧称磁场接线柱)②(交通控制信号箱的)外来线接头

field test 现场试验,使用试验(简称 FT)

field-tested design (现场试验)考核过的结构(或设计)

field test support 现场试验支持条件(简称 FTS)

field variables 场变量

field warranty return 保用期内退换的产品

field winding 见 field coil

field winding shaft (交流发电机的)磁场绕组轴(美称 rotor shaft "转子轴")

field winding shaft ball bearing hub 交流发电机转子球轴承座孔

field winding terminal (电机)磁场绕组接线柱

field wireless van (厢式)无线电收发报车(=radio van)

fierce engagement ①(离合器等)猛烈接合,不平稳的接合 ②(齿轮)突然啮合

fierceness (离合器等)猛烈接合(现象)

fifth (机械变速器的第)五挡(=fifth gear, fifth speed,一般为速比最高的一挡)

fifth wheel ①牵引座(鞍式半挂牵引车拖挂装置的支撑转盘,亦称 fifth wheel coupling)②(车辆性能试验时的)五轮仪(由被试验车拖带的独立转轮,可高精确度地测定被试验车的车速及车速的变化)

fifth wheel coupling guide (半挂车牵引车)牵引鞍座的导向件(引导半挂车落座)

fifth wheel coupling hydraulic control (半挂车牵引车)鞍式牵引座(高度和升降的)液压控制(机构)

fifth wheel coupling mechanic control (半挂车牵引车)鞍式牵引座(高度和升降的)机械控制(机构)

fifth wheel coupling pin (半挂车牵引车的)牵引座牵引销

fifth wheel lead 牵引座前置距(有两种:一种计算长度用,指通过半挂牵引车牵引座的牵引销孔中心的

垂线至通过半挂牵引车最后轮轴线且垂直于车辆支承平面的平面的距离;另一种计算质量分配用,指通过牵引座的纵向摆动轴线的车轴支承面的垂面至通过半挂牵引车最后轮轴线的车轴支承面的垂面的距离

fifty-fifty 各半的,对半的,两半的,平分的

fifty-fifty power split 四轮驱动汽车前、后轮各50%的动力分配的传动模式

FIG ①配件,接头(fitting)②基础,地脚,地位(footing)

fig 图(figure 的简称)

figure ①图,图形,图解,图表,插图 ②形状,外形,轮廓 ③数字(指 0~9,如:double figure 两位数;six figure 六位数)

figured 图示的,图解的,带图案的,形象的,有花纹的

figured iron 型钢(= section iron, shaped iron)

figure-eight(shaped) 8字形的

figure of merit ①品质因素,质量因素,性能系数,优良指数,灵敏值,灵敏度值;最优值,优值 ②(特指)汽车视界评价参数(简称 FOM,FOM = 100 时,视界最佳,FOM = 0 时,视界不能满足行车的最低要求)

figure of noise 噪声指数

figuring of surfaces (车身等的)外表修琢工艺,表面修琢

fil ①灯丝(filament 的简称)②滤清器(filter 的简称)

filament ①丝,细线,游丝;纤维 ②(灯泡内的)灼热丝,灯丝(简称F)

filament cap (汽车前照灯丝的)配光屏(亦称 filament shield)

filament current 灯丝电流

filament line 流线,水条线

filament shield (前照灯的)配光屏(亦称 filament cap,安装于灯丝上侧或下侧,以获得所需配光特性的金属片,旧称屏蔽罩)

filbore 基础轴承

file ①锉,锉刀 ②文件 ③(计算机)外存储器,存储带,存储资料(信息)④行,行列,纵列

file communication system 文件通信系统

file crack 冷激裂缝,火裂(见 chill crack)

filled weight ①(车辆)湿重(见 wet weight)②罐车满载液体时的总重

filler ①加注口,油嘴,加油(水)口 ②漏斗,注入器,加料器 ③填料,充填物,垫片

filler cap ①(汽油箱)加油口盖(= gas cap, petrol locking cap, tank filler cap)②(水箱及其他一切液体容器的)加注口盖

filler gauge 测隙规(测量间隙大小用。由一组厚薄不同的钢片组成,将薄片插入间隙,测量间隙的尺寸,俗称厚薄规,亦称 feeler gauge)

filler neck restrictor 汽油箱加油管颈限径圈(防止加铅汽油注入使用无铅汽油的车辆的油箱加油管插头直径限制件,位于油箱加油口颈部)

filler piece 填隙片,垫片

filler pipe connecting hose 加油(水)软管接头

filler plug 加注孔螺塞

filler sealing plate (发动机散热器水箱盖内的)密封垫片

filler strip 嵌条

filler tube (燃油箱)加油口管(从加油口盖至油箱的油管,= filler neck 或 pipe)

filler wire ①焊丝,焊条(= filling wire, welding wire)②嵌填金属丝

(= filling wire)

fillet ①（内）圆角，倒角 ②饰带，装饰条 ③轮胎胎面凸起花纹间的低陷肋条，胎面暗花纹条（= subtread）④（成一定角度连接的两个零件间的）圆形接头 ⑤齿根过渡曲面（指位于可用齿面与齿槽底面之间的那部分齿面）

filleted corner 内圆角，圆角，过渡圆的角

fillet radius （内）圆角半径

fillets and rounds 内圆角与外圆角

fillet weld 角焊缝；填角焊，角焊（用于焊接相互垂直的焊件，焊缝呈三角形，焊件不开槽）

fill factor 占空因素

filling car 加油车

filling compound 填料（= filling material, filling element）

filling point 加油站，燃料加注站（= filling station, gas station, petrol filling station）

filling ratio （允许）加油率（油罐、油箱等都不应加满，加油率指实际加油量与容器容积之比，%）

filling station （汽车）加油站，加注站

film ①膜，薄膜 ②软片，胶片

filmatic bearing 油膜轴承

film coefficient of heat transfer 表面热传递率，热传递系数（单位面积、单位时间、单位温差的热传递量，亦称 surface coefficient of heat transfer，简称 coefficient of heat transfer，参见 heat transfer）

film condensation 膜状凝结，膜状凝聚

film conditions （润滑）油膜的状态

film-cooled combustion chamber （油）膜冷却燃烧室

film core （发动机散热器水箱的）薄片式散热芯

film integrated circuit 膜集成电路（元件和互连均以膜的形式在绝缘体基片表面上形成的集成电路，有薄膜 thin-film，厚膜 thick-film，多层膜 multilayer 等多种）

film lubrication 油膜润滑

film mixture 油膜混合（燃油被喷到燃烧室壁上形成油膜，利用壁温和压缩空气的热量及高速空气旋流的吹拂，使油膜快速蒸发形成油蒸气而与空气混合的一种混合方式）

film of lubricant 润滑油膜

film of rust 锈膜

film projection vehicle 电影放映车

film strength 油膜强度（指在边界的条件下，润滑油膜保持完整的能力）

film stripping test （油漆等）薄膜剥落强度试验

film varistor 膜式压敏（可变）电阻

filter ①过滤器（泛指各种滤清装置，如：滤波器、滤光器、机油滤清器等）②过滤用材料（简称 F）③过滤，滤清，滤掉（out）④渗入 ⑤把车子开入汽车队中（into）

filterability 可滤性，过滤性，滤过率（= filterableness）

filter-agglomerator 滤清器，（油泥）聚集器

filter bed ①过滤层，过滤床 ②滤清器壳体

filter bowl ①滤油杯（= filter glass）②滤清器壳

filter box 滤清器壳

filter capacity 滤清器的过滤能力

filter carton element 纸板滤芯

filter cartridge （滤清器）滤芯总成（见 filter element①）

filter case 滤清器壳体

filter cell 滤光室（NDIR 分析仪的组成部分。其中充满特种气体，以减弱干扰信号）

filter circuit 滤波电路

filter cloth 过滤布（参见 filtering cloth）

filter condenser 滤波电容器

filter disc 滤片

filtered pressure signal 经滤波处理的压力信号

filter element ①滤芯总成（滤清器中，由滤芯和支架组成的可更换组件，亦称 filter cartridge）②滤芯（指可阻拦、吸附、吸收或磁性分离燃油中杂质的部件，有金属网滤芯、毛毡或纸质滤芯、滤片等）

filter element scraper 滤芯刮垢片

filter element spring 滤芯弹簧（将滤芯压向滤清器内腔突缘或滤清器盖，以防止燃油漏滤的弹簧）

filter gauze 滤网（= filter screen）

filter glass ①滤油（玻璃）杯 ②滤色（光）玻璃

filtering ①过滤，滤清，滤波，滤光 ②（在主要车流停止时的）允许通行

filter loss 过滤损失（由于滤清器的阻力引起的损失）

filter membrane 滤膜（多孔材料制成的过滤用薄膜）

filter pack （填装在液压系统或滑润系统等有关部件或油道油液入口处的）过滤（材）料，滤垫，滤片，滤毡，滤网（等）

filter passband 滤波器通过频带

filter plate 滤片，滤板（滤芯的片状构件）

filter plugging （空气）滤清器阻塞，过滤器阻塞，滤网淤塞

filter screen 滤清器滤网，滤网（= filter gauze）

filter thin oil 机油精滤器，机油细滤器

filter type smokemeter 滤纸式烟度计［使一定量的发动机排气流过一张特制的白色滤纸，然后用光学手段评定其（染）黑（程）度并以其黑度作为评价烟度的参数，常用符号 R_B 表示。该烟度计不能作连续测定，参见 full-flow smokemeter］

filtration ①滤清，过滤，滤波，渗入，渗漏，渗透性 ②开进汽车行驶行列，插进汽车队伍 ③（在主要车流停止时的）允许转弯

filtration package ①（滤清器）可换滤芯 ②滤清器维修包

FIM 国际摩托车驾驶员联合会（Fédération Internationale Motor cycliste 的简称）

fin ①（泛指）各种片状物，鱼鳍状物 ②肋片 ③（特指发动机等的）散热片，冷却片 ④（装在车后端，改善方向稳定性的）垂直导风板

final 最后的，最终的，末级的，决定性的

final boiling point 干点（石油产品完全蒸发时的温度，简称 FBP）

final coating ①最后涂层；最后镀覆 ②上光漆，面漆

final control element ①调节元件，末控元件，末控器件 ②（控制系统）执行机构 ③执行机构的机械输出的第二级末级控制元件

final cost 成品价格，最后成本，商品价格，最终价格

final（discharging）voltage （蓄电池）放电终了时的电压

final drive 主减速器（通常位于驱动桥壳中部，将输入动力降低转速传给半轴及车轮的装置，当装有轮边减速器时，亦称中央减速器）

final drive casing 主减速器外壳（见 differential casing）

final drive housing = final drive casing

final drive ratio ①主减速器传动比（即：传动轴与车轮的速比）②驱动轮的最终减速比（指包括经变速器、副变速器，以及驱动桥主减速器等全部减速机构变速后，在驱动

轮上实现的最终减速比，= final gear ratio, final ratio)

final drive rear cover 主减速器壳后盖，差速器外壳后盖

final drive with（或 **and**）**differential assembly**（或 **unit**） 主减速器带差速器总成

final driving transmission 带主减速器及差速器的变速器（= transaxle）

final expansion pressure 膨胀终了压力

final gain characteristic 最终增益特性，终结增益特性

final gauge length 断后标距（试样拉断后断裂部分在断裂处对接在一起，使其轴线在同一直线上时的标距，见 gauge length）

final gear 见 final reduction gear

final gear ratio 主减速比（= final drive ratio）

final inspection 最终检查，出厂检视

final limit 终极限

final load 终负荷，最后负荷，最终负荷，最大负荷（如：测定硬度时，加于压头上的最大负荷值）

final pressure 最后压力，终压力

final product 成品

final project 最终方案

final rate of charge （蓄电池）终了充电电流强度，最终充电率；最终充电量

final ratio 主减速比（= final drive ratio）

final reading 末次读数，最终读数

final reduction gear 最终传动减速器。（汽车上无）轮边减速器时指主减速器"final drive"；有轮边减速器时指轮边减速器"wheel reductor"

final report 最后报告，总结报告（简称 FR）

final speed （传动系）终点速度，最终点速度

final speed of braking 制动终点速度（指减速性制动作用结束，车辆终止减速时的车速）

final (-stage) filter 最终级滤清器，精滤器

finance 财政，金融，收入，财源，资金（简称 F）

fin and tube radiator 管片式散热器，（由插装在多层冷却片中的大量冷却扁管组成 = gilled tube radiator, finned tubular radiator, flanged-tube radiator）

FINATA 国际运输商协会联合会（Federation Internationale des Association de Transporteurs et Assimiles 的简称）

find 发现；寻找，探索，探测；求出，求得，得知

finder 探测器，搜索器；定向器；测距器；选择器

findings ①（已得）数据，研究结果，调查结果，结论 ②附属，零件，附属品

fine ①细的，精细的，精加工的；成色好的，含量高的；优良的，美好的 ②使细密；使精细，精制；使变纯；使稀薄

fine adjustment 精（确）调（整），微调

fine boring 精镗

fine ceramics 精细陶瓷（汽车发动机零件的一种新材料，主要是由金属氧化物，金属碳化物等烧结而成，具有耐高温、耐腐蚀等特性，而且强度高，坚硬而不脆，亦可用作电器材料，保温材料等）

fine control 精密调节，微调控制（见 coarse control）

fine dotted line 细虚线

fine filter 精滤器，细滤器（= micronic filter）

fine fit 精密配合（相当于三级精度的配合）

fine "flour" abrasive 细粉磨料，研料

fine grain 细粒，微粒，细晶粒

fine-grained structure 细晶粒结构（金相）

fine hair ①绒毛 ②（安全夹层玻璃胶合层中黏附的）毛状黑物

finely disintegrated fuel 雾化燃料（= finely pulverized fuel）

finely-divided ①细碎的，细散的，粉碎的 ②细分的，细分割的

finely finished work 精密加工制品，精整加工制品，精加工制品，精制品

finely granular 细晶粒的，细粒状的

finely porous 微孔的（= fine-pored）

finely pulverized fuel 雾化燃料（= finely disintegrated fuel, finely subdivided fuel）

finely subdivided fuel 见 finely pulverized fuel

fine measuring instrument 精密测量仪器

fine mesh filter 细孔滤网滤清器

fineness ①精细，细度，细粒度 ②纯度，成色 ③精度，公差，粗糙度 ④长细比，径长比 ⑤精致，优良，美好，正确

fineness of atomization（亦称 fineness of pulverization）（燃料喷射的）雾化度

fineness ratio ①细度，径长比 ②长（度）厚（度）比，长（度）高（度）比

fine pitch 小螺距，细牙螺距

fine pressure 净压，吸入压

fine resolution 高分辨率（参见 high resolution）

fine wire 极细电线（如点火线圈的高压绕组用线）

finger contact （控制器内的）指形触点

finger control 手动调节，手控，指控

finger spring of seal 油封指状弹簧

finger-tip control ①按钮操纵，按钮控制，拨钮操纵，拨钮控制 ②按钮式操纵机构，拨钮式操纵机构

finger-tip rocker 手指状（气门）摇臂（= finger type rocker）

finger tremor （驾驶员等的）指尖颤抖，手指颤抖

finish ①完成，完工，结束；精整，精修，精整加工（精磨，研磨，抛光，珩磨等）②涂层，保护层，漆面；饰层 ③表面粗糙度

finish coat paint 面漆（= top coat）

finished blend 混成油（几种油品按一定比例，掺混制成的油）

finished diesel fuel 精制柴油，成品柴油（石油中间馏分的掺和物，见 middle distillate）

finished engine oil 精制（发动）机（滑）油，商品机油

finisher （车身的）装饰件（= trimming, molding）

finish heat treatment 最终热处理（决定机械零件使用状态下的组织与性能的热处理）

finishing allowance 加工留量；完工留量，精加工（公差）余量

finishing strip 装饰镶条，装饰条

finish lamp 竣工信号灯，操作完毕信号灯

finish mark 加工符号，粗糙度符号

finish rolling hardening 滚压强化（工艺）（在滚轮的压力作用下，金属表层冷作硬化，从而产生残余压应力的一种预应力强化法）

finite 有限度的，有限的；确定的，限定的

finite element analysis 有限（单）元分析，有限单元法（简称 FE analysis，见 finite-element methods）

finite-element methods 有限元法[简称 FEM，在汽车上主要用于车

身或大型构件,壳件结构计算。该法的基本思路是将复杂的结构看作是一有限单元所组成的连续弹性体,即:将任意形状的结构划分(或离散化)成有限多个只在有限个节点上相联的"基本单元",所有载荷与支承力均作为节点,以节点位移作为基本未知量并求得位移解,再依次确定各单元的内力与应力,而完成整个结构的计算]

finite-life design 有限寿命设计

finite life region (疲劳性曲线上的)有限寿命区

finned brake drum 带散热片的制动鼓

finned tubular radiator 片管式散热器(散热器芯子由水管及水管外的散热片构成, = fin and tube radiator)

finning ①加散热片;加筋条;加尾鳍②散热片(总体)(指发动机缸体,散热器,冷却等的散热片整体)

finny tail (轿车等的)翅尾,鳍形尾(车身后方的鳍状部分)

fin tube (散热器的)①薄片状水管②装有散热薄片的水管

FIP 国际保护行人联合会(International Federation of Pedestrians)

FIPG 就地成形式密封衬垫(formed-in-place gasket 的简称,指涂抹于密封处的液态或半液态密封材料黏合固化后形成的密封垫层)

FIPot 快怠速节气门开度控制装置(fast idle dashpot 的简称)

FIR ①设备安装检查(facility installation review)②设备干扰检查(facility interference review)③燃油表读数(fuel indicator reading)

fir ①冷杉 ②冷杉木

fire ①火 ②(发动机)起动,开始运转③点火,点燃(可燃混合气等)④着火 ⑤失火

fire an engine 起动发动机

fire annihilator ①(车载)灭火器②减振器,阻尼器 ③零化子

fire appliance ①消防设备 ②消防车(亦称 fire-fighting vehicle, fire engine)

fire assay (燃油等)燃点试验

fireball combustion chamber 火球燃烧室(瑞士防污染工业研究公司"Antipollution Industrial Research"工程师 May 研究成功的一种汽油机燃烧室,1981 年首次用于 Jaguar's 12V 型发动机,除了在顶置式排气门的下方具有一个小的浴盆形燃烧区以外,缸盖的其余表面,包括进气门区基本上与缸体上平面齐平,形成大的挤压面积,可产生强烈旋流,燃烧完全,热效率高,污染小,油耗低)

fire behaviour 着火性能(材料,部件或产品燃烧或暴露在火中发生的物理、化学变化,或仍保持原有性能)

fire bulkhead 见 bulkhead

fire engine 消防车,救火车(= motor fire engine)

fire equipment trailer (装有消防设备的)挂车

fire-escape trailer 带太平梯的消防挂车

fire extinguisher 灭火机,灭火器

fire extinguishing foam tanker 泡沫消防车(装备有水罐,泡沫液罐,泡沫液混合装置,空气泡沫-水两用枪,泡沫枪,用于扑灭油类火灾,或一般物资火灾的专用罐车)

fire-fighter truck 消防车(= fire truck)

fire-fighting turntable ladders 云梯消防车,云梯救火车(装备有可伸缩的云梯,利用液压传动机构控制其伸缩和旋转,用于扑灭高层建筑物的火灾和抢救人员)

fire gases ①可燃气体，易燃气体 ②燃气，燃烧着的气体

fire goods 易燃品

fire hazard 有火灾的危险性，易燃性

fire integrity 整体着火性（指在规定时间内的隔火结构元件，防火侧，防止火焰或热气穿透非暴露面的能力）

fire-new 全新的

fire point （燃料的）着火点，燃点（燃料上方的蒸气在空气中被点燃后，能够继续燃烧的最低温度，参见 flash point）

fire prevent system （汽车）防火系统（简称 fps，一般指发生碰撞事故时自动关闭电源、切断油路的安全防护装置）

fireproof ①耐火的，防火的，不燃的（简称 fp）②使具有耐火性，加装防火设备

fire pulse 点火脉冲

fire pump trailer 带消防水泵的挂车

fire resistance 耐火性（在标准耐火试验的规定时间内，元件、零件或结构满足所需的稳定性、隔热性、或其他规定的预期性能的能力）

fire-resistant 耐火的，防火的

fire ring （汽缸垫的）防焰环

fire safety 防火安全措施

fire service commanding car 消防指挥车

fire stability 对火稳定性（在标准耐火试验的规定时间内，承重或不承重的结构元件耐抗倒塌的能力）

fire stroke 燃烧冲程

fire switch （发动机的）起动开关（简称 FS）

fire test （油箱等的）防火试验，耐火试验

fire truck 消防车（= fire-fighter truck）

fire up 点火，生火，起火，（发动机）起动

fire wall ①隔火墙，防火壁 ②（货车驾驶室与发动机室间的）驾驶室前壁 ③前围板（美轿车发动机舱与客厢之间的隔板，= toe board, dash panel, dash board, bulkhead）

FIREX 灭火器（fire extinguisher equipment 的简称）

firing （汽油机）点火，（柴油机）着火（= ignition，指可燃混合气在汽缸内被点燃或压燃；firing circuit 点火电路；firing current 点火电流；firing end 点火端，指火花塞伸入燃烧室的部分；fire interval 点、着火时间间隔，指发动机相邻两次点、着火的间隔时间；firing in the silence 排气消声器着火；firing line 发动机示波器基本波形中的点火线；firing order 发动机各汽缸的点、着火顺序，如：6 缸发动机典型顺序为 1-5-3-6-2-4 等；firing point 点火时刻，= time of ignition, ignition point；firing stroke 做功冲程，= power stroke；firing section 发动机示波器基本波形的火花部分，由点火线 firing line 和火花线 spark line 两部分组成；firing temperature 着火温度，着火点，简称 FT；firing voltage 火花塞开始放电的点火电压）

firing threshold speed （安全气囊）点火门槛碰撞速度值（点火阈速度）

firm ①公司，厂商，商行 ②坚固的，稳固的；坚实的，结实的 ③使坚固，使稳固；压实，使坚实

firm acceleration 稳定加速

firm joint （内）（外）卡尺（卡钳的别称）

firm mode （可编程平顺性控制系统中悬架阻尼的）刚硬模式（在此模式下，减振器等对伸缩冲程的阻尼作用比柔顺模式大两倍，见 ride mode）

firm mode relay （空气悬架的）硬模式继电器

firm power 恒定功率，可靠出力

first ①第一；最初的，最早的；第一流的，最上等的；基本的，概要的 ②（变速器的）一挡（=first gear）

first aid 急救，事故抢救，急修，抢修

first aid kit 急救箱，急救药箱；（= first aid box, medical emergency case）

First Auto Group （中国）第一汽车集团公司，一汽集团（简称 FAG）

First Automobile Works （中国）第一汽车制造厂（1953年建厂，1956年投产，中国大型汽车企业之一，位于吉林省长春市，简称 FAW）

first coat 底漆；底涂层

first converter phase （两相，多元件液力变矩器的）第一变矩区，第一变矩器区（指液力变矩器在全部导轮元件固定不动、输出转矩与输入转矩之比值最大的状态下工作）

first cylinder spark plug cable 第一缸火花塞高压线

first dead center 上止点（=top dead center）

first fraction 初馏分（=overhead fraction）

first gear （变速器）一挡，头挡，最低挡（=bottom gear, first speed, starting gear，简称 first）

first lane 第一车道（多车道道路中，靠左行驶时为前进方向从左起的第一车道，靠右行驶时为前进方向从右起的第一车道）

first piston ①（发动机，多缸空压机等的）第一缸活塞 ②（串列式双腔制动主缸的）第一活塞（指由主缸推杆推动的活塞）

first rebuilding （发动机等的）第一次大修理，第一次整修

first speed 见 first gear

first stage filter 初滤器（第一级滤清器）

first stage gearset （变速器）第一挡齿轮组

first stage of impact 汽车碰撞的第一阶段（如：在摆锤碰撞试验中，碰撞的第一阶段为保险杠与摆锤碰撞面分离前的瞬间，参见 bumper ramping）

first step height （客车的）一级踏步高（第一级踏步上平面至地平面的距离）

first-to-last-axle dimension 汽车列车的总轴距（最前至最后车桥间的轴距）

first whirling speed （轴）一阶共振转速

fir-tree fastening （汽轮机叶片）枞树形根部固定方法

FISA 国际运动汽车联合会（法文 Fédération Internationale du sport Automobile 的简称）

fiscal horsepower 税制马力，税制功率（法国等国家对轿车征税制度，按特定的计算方法，计算轿车发动机的马力，称为税制马力，按税制马力的大小征税）

fiscal year 财政（会计）年度（简称 FY）

Fischer-MacMichael Viscometer 费-麦氏黏度计（用来测定胶合剂，密封胶剂，消声胶剂的黏度。将特制的柱塞插入旋转的试样中，根据试样对柱塞的摩擦扭力，测出试样的费-麦氏扭力黏度）

Fischer-Tropsch synthesis 费舍-特鲁普什合成法（将煤加氢，合成液体燃油）

fishhook maneuver （美国国家公路交通安全管理局规定用来测定车辆翻车倾向的）鱼钩形方向变换操作（使车辆按规定的速度向一个方向转一小圈，然后猛地向另一个方向急转弯）

fishhooks 鱼钩形曲线

fish plate 搭接板，鱼尾板，燕尾夹板，加强板，对接夹板

fishtail ①鱼尾槽，燕尾槽，鱼尾形喇叭口，扁漏斗；鱼尾状物，燕尾状物②鱼尾形的，燕尾形的

fish-tailing ［美］（汽车行驶时）鱼尾状左右摆动

FISITA ①国际汽车工程师学会联合会（1947年由法国汽车工程学会倡议，1948年创立，总部在巴黎，全称为 Fédération Internationale des Sociétés d'Ingenieurs des Techniques de l'Automobile) ②国际汽车技术学会联合会（Fédération Internationale des Sociétés des Techniques de l'Automobile 的简称）

fission ①裂变，分裂 ②使裂开，剥离

fissuration 龟裂，形成裂隙

fissure ①裂口，裂缝，裂纹，龟裂 ②使裂开，使龟裂

fit ①配合 ②跑合，磨合 ③装配，镶嵌 ④（两零件间的接触）面，配合面

fit a tyre 装配轮胎

fit joint 套筒接合

fit key 配合键

fitment ①设备②附件，配件（= fittings）

fit quality 配合等级，装配质量

fitted 配合好的，装配好的，安装的

fitter 装配工，修配工，钳工，镶配匠，修理工

fitting ①安装，装配，配合 ②管接头，连接件 ③配件，附件

fitting arrangement drawing 附件装配图

fitting body 管接头体

fitting line 装配线（模压在轮胎胎侧与胎圈交接处的单环或多环胶棱，用以指示轮胎正确装配在轮辋上的标线，旧称标志线，轮辋线，安装线，防水线）

fitting shop 装配车间，钳工工段，钳工间

fitting sleeve 接头套

fitting surface 配合面，装配面

fitting-up bolt 装配螺栓，接合螺栓

fit tolerance 配合公差（= tolerance on fit）

fit-up 修配，修合，配合；安装；装配

FIVA 国际旧式汽车联合会（Fédération Internationale des Voitures Anciennes 的简称）

five-bearing 五道主轴承的（曲轴）

five-bearing crankshaft 五主轴颈曲轴

five cylinder engine 五缸发动机

five-door 五门汽车（四个侧门，一个后门）

five-door version 五门型（车身）（指左、右各两个侧门，一个后门的车身）

five-gas engine analyzer 发动机五气分析仪（可测定排气中 HC, NOx, CO, CO_2 和 O_2 五种成分含量的废气分析仪）

five-link rear suspension 五连杆式后悬架（由两根纵臂、两根横臂和一根共用的横向推力杆控制每一个车轮的后悬架）

five-mile-an-hour bumber 见 Federal bumber

five-mile-per-hour crash test （汽车的）时速五英里碰撞试验

five-person car 五人座轿车（包括驾驶员）

five-piece rim 五件式轮辋（由轮辋体，两个挡圈，一个锁圈和一个座圈组成）

five-pinion planetary gear set 五（行星）轮型行星齿轮机构

five-ply 五层的（帘布层）

five-range transmission 五挡变速器（= five-speed gear box）

five-seat cabriolet 五座篷式轿车

five-seater 五座车，五座轿车

five-speed transmission [美] 五挡变速器（= five-range transmission）

five-star ratings 五星级

five-throw crankshaft （五缸直列式发动机用）五曲柄曲轴

five-tire car 五轮胎轿车（指通常带有备用轮胎的轿车，见 four-tire car）

five-valve head （装有三个进气门，两个排气门的）五气门式汽缸盖

five-volt reference 5 伏基准电压（除少数例外，汽车电子控制系统信息传输电路均采用 5V 电压为标准工作电压，该电压高到足以保证信息的可靠传输，又低到足以防止芯片上的微电路损坏）

fix ①安装；固定；定位，安装后的调整；确定，规定；凝固 ②（照相）定影

fixation 固定；安置；定位；凝固

Fix code 固定码（简称 FC）

fix-cycle light signal 固定周期的（彩色灯光）交通信号

fix-displacement pump 定排量泵

fixed 固定的；确定的；不变动的；定位的；凝固的

fixed attribute 固定属性

fixed axle 支重桥，非驱动桥（= solid axle，相对于驱动桥而言）

fixed bead seat （车轮的）固定胎座圈（一、二、三件式轮辋上给轮胎提供径向支承的部分，相对于四、五件式轮辋可从轮辋体上拆下来的胎座圈而言）

fixed-beam laser sensor 固定光束激光传感器

fixed bending light （相对于动态弯道照明而言的）静态转弯照明灯，固定式弯道照明（见 static cornering light）

fixed-caliper disk brake 定钳盘式制动器（见 disk brake with fixed caliper）

fixed caliper system （汽车盘式制动器的）固定式卡钳系统（指固定于制动盘两侧的固定式制动钳及其两侧的加压机构和管路）

fixed-cam brake 固定凸轮式鼓式制动器（凸轮轴固定在制动器底板上，因而两端的位移相等）

fixed-car moving-gantry car wash 车不动而洗车拱门移动式洗车装置

fixed-centre change gears 固定中心距变速齿轮系（变速时齿轮不作轴向滑动的常啮式变速齿轮系）

fixed centre distance 固定中心距

fixed condenser 固定电容器（相对可变电容器而言）

fixed constant velocity joint 定位式等速万向节（指球笼式万向节"Rzeppa 或 Birfield constant velocity"）

fixed contact （触点式断电器等的）固定触点

fixed control （车辆操纵稳定性运动特性控制方式中的）固定控制（转向系中的某些操纵点如转向轮、转向垂臂、转向盘的位置保持固定时的控制方式，参见 position control）

fixed coupling ①刚性联轴节，固定式联轴节 ②固定匹配，固定耦合

fixed cycle traffic light 固定周期交通灯光信号

fixed delay 基本延迟；基本阻车时间（车辆由于停车标志、信号等所引起的时间延迟）

fixed-displacement engine 固定排量发动机（指常规的活塞冲程及燃烧室容积固定的发动机，相对可变排量发动机而言）

fixed-displacement pump 定排量泵

fixed drawbar 刚性牵引装置

fixed drive 无差速驱动（指车辆驱动桥的左、右后轮间或四轮驱动式车辆的前、后驱动桥间无差速作用

的动力传动）

fixed drive shaft 万向节中心距固定的传动轴

fixed engine 固定式发动机（= stationary engine）

fixed extra clearance （比正常通过交叉口时间要长的）固定追加的通过（交叉口）时间

fixed flame front principle 固定火焰前锋原理，静止火焰前锋原理（在发动机燃烧室内，以一定的速度供给燃油和空气，可保持火焰前锋面基本上不动）

fixed flange （车轮的）固定式轮缘（指与轮辋制成一个整体的轮缘）

fixed front seal 固定式前座位（席）

fixed gate ①（栏板式车身货车的），固定式拦板 ②（汽车的）固定式挡泥板 ③固定式出入口，固定门

fixed-geometry tubocharger 固定几何形状式增压器

fixed guide vane ①（泛指各种）固定导流片 ②（特指变矩器的）导轮固定叶片

fixed-guideway transit 固定导轨快速客运，固定导线公共交通

fixed-head ①死顶双门单排双座厢式轿车（相对活顶车而言）②（与缸体铸成一体的）不可卸式缸盖

fixed hub 固定轴套，固定衬套

fixed ignition 固定点火（时刻）

fixed joint 轮端万向节，外端万向节（指前轮驱动车辆传动轴车轮一端的等速万向节，亦称 outboard joint）

fixed-length word （计算机的）固定长度字，定长字（指具有固定字节数或字符数的机器字或指字长固定的机器字，如：某控制模块，字长都采用32位二进制位）

fixedness 固定性，稳定性，凝固性，稳定性，耐挥发性（= fixity）

fixed object impact （汽车对）固定物（的）碰撞

fixed orifice 固定量孔，固定（小）孔

fixed part （被）固定件

fixed pedestal 固定支撑（座），固定（踩）踏板

fixed point （固）定点，不动点，不变点

fixed power take-off 独立式功率输出轴

fixed-programmed read-only memory 固定编程只读存储器（每个存储单元的数据内容在制造时已经确定，以后不能修改的一种只读存储器）

fixed ratio 固定比差，固定比率（如：相应价目运价与基本运价保持的固定比率）

fixed ratio braking system （前后车轮）制动力比固定式制动系（指无比例分配阀等制动力调节装置，因而在任何工况下前、后轮的制动力分配比例均不变化的制动系）

fixed-ratio transmission 固定速比式有级变速器

fixed restrictor ①固定节流孔，不变节流孔 ②固定的限制装置

fixed ring type labyrinth packing 固定环式迷宫油封

fixed setting method 固定安装法

fixed shaft transmission 固定轴式变速器（所有轴的旋转中心固定不变的变速器）

fixed shift points （自动变速器的）固定换挡点（指换挡滞后不随油门开度而变化的换挡规律）

fixed side 固定（车厢）侧栏板；固定侧板

fixed spark 不能调节提前角的定时点火

fixed spindle 固定轴，支承轴

fixed spring eye 钢板弹簧固定端卷耳

fixed steering control 转向盘转角固定控制（指汽车跑道试验的一种方

式，驾驶员将转向盘固定于某一转角，测定汽车受外力，如：横风等干涉时的响应特性）

fixed taper disc （CVT 主动传动带盘的）锥形固定盘（见 CVT steel belt puller）

fixed throttle（rack）characteristics （发动机）速度特性［当燃料供给调节装置，如：汽油机的节气门（throttle），柴油机的齿条（rack）位置固定不变时，发动机性能参数：转矩、功率、油耗等随转速的变化而变化的特性。该特性曲线，称速度特性曲线］

fixed-time 定时的，周期固定的，时间固定的

fixed-time testing 定时试验（工作一定小时后自动停止试验）

fixed timing 固定的（点火）正时

fixing part 固定件（起安装、定位固定结构作用的构件，亦称 stay retainer）

fixing rod 定位杆（如：后桥悬架系统的横向推力杆）

fix position 定位

FK LFT 叉式起重机，叉式举升器（fork lift）

flagging ①用石板等铺砌的路面，石板路 ②旗语

flagman 旗工，信号旗手（施工地点采用红旗或手动标志管制交通的人）

flagship 旗舰（对车辆而言指某一车型系列中的顶级车）

flagship model （厂家生产的车型中的）旗舰车（指最高级的车型，主打车型）

flag terminal 旗状接头（指与接线成90°的接线柱，形似旗帜，故名，通常用螺栓固定接线，主要用于大电流接头，如：蓄电池接线塔等）

flake graphite 片状石墨（= graphite flake）

flake white 碳酸铅白

flaking ①表皮剥落，表面剥蚀 ②穴蚀（= pitting）③薄片

flame 火焰

flame-blown 带着炽热的燃气流吹入的

flame cleaning （金属表明的）火焰清洁（法）（用火焰加热金属表面，以去除黑皮等，保持清洁）

flame contracting ring （车身暖气系统电点火燃气热风机的）聚焰环（使燃料的火焰聚集并朝一个方向喷出）

flame curvature 火焰曲率

flame cutting 气体火焰切割，气体切割（如：氧乙炔切割）

flame development angle 火焰展开角，火焰发展角（指点燃式发动机燃烧室内，从电火花开始出现到汽缸内10%或5%的可燃混合气燃烧完了的曲轴转角，简称 FDA，以代替难以量测的着火落后期，参见 ignition delay period）

flame engine 可燃气体发动机（= gas engine）

flame front 火焰前锋，焰锋（指由火花塞向四周传播的火焰的边锋）

flame front velocity 火焰前锋速度（指焰前锋面的扩张速度）

flame glow plug （点燃精确计量的少量燃油、产生一股火焰，以预热进气空气的）火焰预热塞

flame ignition combustion chamber 火焰点火燃烧室（一种燃烧稀薄混合气的燃烧室系统，由主、副燃烧室组成，先点燃副燃烧室里的浓混合气，再由副室喷出的火焰点燃主室的稀混合气，亦称 torch ignition combustion chamber）

flame ionization analyser 氢焰离子化分析仪（简称 FIA，在氢火焰中通入样气，产生的离子电流信号与每单位时间进入火焰的碳氢化合物

的质量流量成正比,通过测量此电流来确定碳氢化合物浓度的分析仪,亦称 flame ionization detector,简称 FID

flame kernel 火焰中心,火焰核心,焰核(指电火花点火开始经过一段时间出现的火源,即形成的火焰中心)

flameless 无焰的

flameproof 防火的,耐火的(= flame resisting)

flame propagation 火焰传播(在汽车发动机,指燃烧区或火焰前锋通过可燃混合气的传播)

flame quenching phenomenon (汽车发动机等的)火焰冷熄现象(燃烧室壁过冷,使火焰熄灭,不能完全燃烧的现象)

flame radius 火焰半径

flame resistance 耐火性,防火性

flame-resisting 见 flame proof

flame retardance 防火性,阻燃性能

flame sheet model 火焰面模型

flame shield 防火墙,防火隔板,防火罩

flame speed 火焰传播速度(flame propagation speed 的简称,= flame velocity,无特别说明时,指层流火焰前锋面在其法线方向相对未燃混合气的移动速度,因而常称法向火焰传播速度"normal flame propagation speed"或层流火焰传播速度"laminar-flow frame propagation speed",以别于表现火焰传播速度和紊流火焰传播速度)

flame speed factor 火焰速度系数(表征各有关因素,如:混合气运动状态、空燃比、燃烧室形状、压力对火焰速度的影响的系数)

flame stabilizer (燃气轮机的)火焰稳定器

flame stretch 火焰扩张,火焰扩展

flame tight 不透火的,防火的

flame travel 火焰传播距离

flame tube (燃气轮机燃烧的)火焰管

flame tube snout (燃气轮机)火焰管进口锥体

flame type ionization detector 见 flame ionization analyzer

flame velocity 见 flame speed

flame welding 气焊

flame zone 火焰带,火焰区,火焰范围

flammability limit (燃油空气混合气等的)可燃极限(见 flammability limits)

flammability point 燃点

flammability resistance 抗着火性,抗可燃性

flammability testing (材料等的)可燃性试验

flammable (fuel-air) mixture 可燃(燃料-空气)混合气(空燃比大于稀失火极限,小于浓失火极限的混合气,参见 misfire limit)

flammable limits (混合气组分的)点燃极限,可燃极限(有最稀、最浓两个极限,= flammability limits)

flange ①突缘,法兰,法兰盘,突缘盘;突缘的,带突缘的,带突缘盘的 ②(槽钢、角铁等的)股 ③(特指车轮的)轮缘(指车轮轮辋上给轮胎提供轴向支承的部分,如:flange edge radius 轮缘端部半径;flange height 轮缘高度;flange radius 轮缘半径,指轮缘弧状部分的半径;flange width 轮缘宽度,指轮缘端部与胎圈座圆角外边间的距离)

flange area ①突缘面积 ②(轮胎)紧贴轮缘的区域

flange beam 工字钢,工形钢梁,工字梁

flange bearing 带(止动)突缘边的轴承或(轴瓦)(= collar bearing,

可承受轴向推力）
flange-bolted 突缘螺栓固定的，突缘螺栓装配的
flange-cooled 散热片冷却的
flange coupling 突缘式联轴节，法兰盘式联轴节（= flanged joint, flanged coupling，由突缘盘通过螺栓连接）
flanged beam 工字梁（= I-beam）
flanged coupling 见 flange coupling
flanged cylinder 带突缘边的缸套 [= flanged (type) liner]
flanged lip 突缘边，法兰边缘（= flange edge）
flanged 12-point screw 带突缘的12方螺钉（12方螺钉头与螺纹杆之间本身有突缘）
flanged-tube radiator 片-管式散热器（= fin and tube radiator）
flangeless 无突缘的，无突边的
flange of oil piston ring 活塞油环刮油突边
flange pipe 带突缘的管子
flange sleeve （十字轴型双万向节传动轴前节传动轴花键端的）突缘套
flange tap （测量仪表的）突缘式接头
flange type puller 突缘型拉器（指卡住被拉出物的突缘进行拉拔作业的拉器）
flange yoke （十字轴式万向节的）突缘叉（具有突缘的万向叉，美称 companion flange）
flanging 折边，卷边，翻口，翻边，镶边
flank ①侧面，侧翼，侧腹 ②齿腹，齿侧面，齿根面
flank depression （转子发动机的）转子工作面凹坑，转子腹面凹坑（= rotor depression）
flank indicator ①侧面转向指示灯 ②车侧的示廓灯（参见 side indicator）

flank of cam 凸轮型面腹部（工作面）
flank profile 齿廓，齿形
flank radius （凸轮廓）工作面曲率半径
flanks 两侧车道（紧靠路边或人行道的车道）
flank wear 侧面磨损
flap door 下翻门（= fold-down door）
flap (= **flapper**) ①（指一边用铰链固定的平片状活门，用于单向关闭孔、口等的活板门的）活板，阀瓣，簧片，铰链板 ②可放倒的车栏板 ③挡泥板 ④（轮胎的）垫带（用于保护内胎着合面不受轮辋磨损的环形带）⑤水平横置的导风板，一般带有倾斜角控制与调整装置，用于引开气流，以免对汽车产生浮力 ⑥导风板可调节的后边板（用以改变导风板气流浮力或阻力）
flap hinge 活门合页
flap-up seat 向上折叠式座椅
flare ①（使端部向外扩张成）喇叭状 ②是喇叭状的孔、口或物 ③呈喇叭状的。如：flare angle 喇叭口张角；flare (d) coupling, flare fitting, flare joint 油管等的带喇叭口的接头；flared intersection 加宽式交叉口，漏斗式交叉口；flare nut 带喇叭管的连接螺母；flare nut spanner 带喇叭管的连接螺母用扳手，= line spanner；flare opening 喇叭口；flare tube 带喇叭口的管子；flaring tool （管子）扩口工具 ④突然燃烧，突然发出火焰，闪光（= flash）⑤闪光装置（= flashing feature）
flare board （货车）驾驶室顶篷上的遮阳板；防眩板
flash ①闪光，闪燃，突然燃烧；一闪，一亮 ②（特指摩擦面间的液膜突然由于摩擦热过大等原因而迅速汽化的）闪蒸现象 ③（驾驶人员）开启转向信号灯 ④（驾驶人员欲超

车或会车时提醒前车或对向车注意的）迅速反复开启前照灯随后立即关闭的闪光操作 ⑤闪存盘（一种速度比 EEPROM 电可擦可编程只读存储器快，可用于永久性存储并易于电重编程的新型存储器）⑥毛刺，飞边

flashback ①（发动机）回火（= flowback）②（起动时）发动机倒转（参见 back fire）

flash butt-welding 闪弧对接焊（电阻焊的一种，被焊着部分相互接触，通过电流，然后加压焊合）

flash coating ①薄镀（层），极薄镀（层）②光亮镀（层）（= flash plating）

flash control unit 闪存控制单元

flash disk 闪存磁盘

flasher ①闪光灯 ②闪光器（使信号灯闪光的装置，旧称闪烁继电器，闪光断续器，= flasher unit, flasher relay）

flash（er）lamp ①闪光灯（= blinker）②闪光灯灯泡（= flasher bulb, flasher indicator bulb）③（表示汽车要转向及回转方向等的）闪光信号灯（亦称 flashing signal, flashing indicator）

flashes per second 每秒钟闪光次数

flash glass 有色玻璃

flash gun （点火正时用）频闪枪

flash heat 快速加热

flashing ①（铸件）边缘毛刺，飞边，（轮胎胎面等处的）毛边 ②闪弧，闪光，放电，发火花 ③急骤蒸发 ④金属沉积镀层 ⑤防雨板，挡水板，防漏金属盖板 ⑥喷射 ⑦闪光的，闪烁的

flashing hand brake telltale 驻车制动的闪光指示灯（装在仪表板上；该灯闪，表示驾驶员驻车制动已拉上）

flash over 跳火，飞弧击穿（绝缘等，= jump over, flash over strength 火花击穿强度; flash over voltage, = breakdown voltage, 跳火电压, 击穿电压）

flash period 闪光持续时间

flash point （燃油等的）闪点（燃料上方的蒸气在空气中能被点燃而瞬即熄灭的最低温度，= flashing point, flash temperature, 有开式、闭式两种测定方法）

flash test ①发火试验 ②燃油闪点测定

flash welding 火花焊，闪光焊（电阻焊的一种）

flat ①平的，平整的，平坦的 ②（对蓄电池）指完全放电的（有时虽指部分放电的，但已不足以起动发动机或提供足够照明）③（对轮胎特指因扎破或气门漏气，而）完全放气的 ④（对发动机）指汽缸水平对置式的（flat twin, four, six, eight, 分别指水平对置式二、四、六、八缸发动机）⑤（球面上的）平面区 ⑥完全跑气的轮胎 ⑦（用油细砂子对漆面等作最后）抛光打磨 ⑧（无侧拦板和后栏板的）平板（式货台的）货车或挂车（亦称 float, platform lorry, platform truck）

flat angle 平角（180°，= straight angle）

flat area 平面面积

flat-band steel 带钢

flat bar 扁钢

flat base rim 平式轮辋，平底轮辋（简称 FB，指断面中部为平底的一种轮辋，主要用于安装客车和货车中尺寸较大、胎圈较硬的轮胎）

flat beam torque wrench 板式扭力扳手

flat bearing ①平面支撑 ②滑动轴承

flat bed ①平台，平底座，平板 ②平板车身，无拦板的车身（flat bed

trailer 平板挂车，= platform trailer; flat bed truck ［美］平板货车，= platform lorry，简称 flat bed truck）

flat belt 平（传动）带

flat belt chassis dynamometer 平带式底盘测功机（用活动平带模拟路面，替代通常用的滚筒，当汽车驱动轮在平带上旋转时，驱动皮带向后移动，而汽车保持不动，功率吸收装置与平带内齿啮合的齿轮连接，平带模拟路面更接近实际，但结构复杂）

flat bit tongs 扁嘴钳

flat-bladed screw-driver （常规的）平口起子

flat body = flat bed

flat bottomed 平底的

flat-bottomed land 平原地带

flat-bottom tappet 平底挺杆

flat-built (-tread) tyre 平胎面轮胎

flat countersunk (head) 平顶埋头的（如：平顶埋头铆钉、螺钉等）

flat-country test 平原地带试验（在平原地形下进行的汽车路试）

flat curve 平缓曲线

flat engine 卧式发动机，水平对置式发动机（= boxer engine, horizontally-opposed engine, horizontal engine, pancake engine）

flat face 平面

flat-faced cylinder head （无燃烧室的）平面汽缸盖

flat-faced moving barrier 平面型活动障碍物

flat face pulley 平面传动带轮

flat feeler gauge 片式测隙规，厚薄规，千分片

flat file 扁锉，板锉，平锉

flat flange joint 平面突缘连接，平面突缘接头，平法兰连接，平法兰接头

flat-floored 平地板的，平底板式的（车身等）

flat-four (engine) 四缸卧式发动机，四缸水平对置式发动机（每边一对汽缸。每边两个汽缸，或每边三个汽缸者分别称 flat eight, flat six）

flat frequency response 平坦频率响应曲线

flat fronted vehicle 平头汽车

flat fuse box 熔丝式保险盒（电路中防止电流过大造成事故的保险装置，装有低熔点的金属丝）

flat gasket 平垫圈

flat gradient 缓坡（= easy gradient）

flat head ①平头的，平头 ②（［美］指气门侧置式，即气门均装于汽缸体一侧的）平头发动机 ③（指盆形，碟形等顶面是平的，而不是楔形或球形的）平顶燃烧室

flat-head type 平顶型，平头型（如平顶活塞等）

flat horizontal surface 扁平面

flat hump 平峰（某些轮辋胎圈座的轮廓呈浅平驼峰状，用于卡住气压不足的轮胎的胎圈，防止胎圈被压进轮胎槽底，简称和代号 FH，见 flat pente）

flat key 平键

flatness 平面性，平直度

flat-out ①最大的，最高的，全速的 ②（指发动机）节气门全开运转，最高速运转的

flat-out acceleration 猛加速，突然加速，猛踩油门

flat pack ①扁平封装，扁平外壳，扁平组件 ②封装集成电路

flat pan ①平底盘 ②（发动机）平底油底壳

flat-panel display 平面型显示屏

flat pente 斜平峰（某些轮辋胎圈座的轮廓呈斜平驼峰状，用于卡住胎圈，防止胎胎气压不足时，其胎圈被压入轮辋槽底，与 flat hump 相比，其峰谷较斜也较宽）

flat piston 盘形活塞，扁平活塞（＝disk piston）

flat proof tyre 泄气保险胎，泄气安全胎（被扎伤、刺破而漏气或泄气后仍能可靠地行驶一定里程的各种安全胎的通称）

flat rack container 平架式集装箱（没有箱顶及两侧壁，具有加强的箱底、端壁和角柱，适于装重型机床，工程机械等重货）

flat rack folding container 折叠式平架集装箱（两端壁可折叠的平架式集装箱）

flat rate 按单位时间计价，按期付费，统一收费率，包价（收费制），普通费

flat ride （汽车）稳速、稳定行驶

flat rim 平轮辋，平底轮辋（＝flat base rim，简称及代号 FB）

flat roadway simulator 平路模拟试验机（＝flat-roadway test machine，用于测定和研究轮胎与路面间的作用力和力矩

flat saddle key 平鞍形键

flat seat ①平座 ②（一般特指用垫圈密封的）火花塞座面

flat-seated valve 平座阀，平座阀门

flat slope 缓坡

flat spot ①喘点（亦称 flat point，指化油器式发动机节气门猛然开放，进气气流剧增但出油迟后，造成短时间内混合气过稀而产生的加速时发动机瞬间转矩降低、加速滞后或转速下降的现象，亦称 flat stop）②轮胎的压平区（如制动抱死时，特别是赛车轮胎被压平的区域）③（轮胎长期停放形成的）平斑（＝flat spotting）④（轮胎的）平衬片

flat spring 片簧，扁簧，板簧

flat steel 扁钢

flat steel bar 扁钢条

flat steering-wheel hub 平转向盘毂

flat stop 见 flat spot①

flat tappet 平面挺杆（与凸轮接触的工作面为平面）

flatten ①弄平，展平，整平；弄直压扁 ②使失去光泽

flat thread 方形螺纹

flat-tip screwdriver 见＝flat-bladed screwdriver

flat tire 爆裂的轮胎，泄气的轮胎（＝blown-out tire）

flat-top(ped) 平顶的

flat-topped piston with machined eyebrows for valve clearance （顶置式凸轮轴发动机的）带机加工气门凹窝的平顶活塞

flat-topping 平顶（测量系统由于某些部分已饱和，失掉灵敏度造成的最大值，使超过它的数值均未能记录下来）

flat torque 均匀转矩（不管转速的变化，转矩的大小变化很小）

flat truck 见 flat-bed

flat tubular radiator 扁管式散热器

flat turn 大转弯

flat twin 双缸（水平）对置式发动机

flat two conductor cable （照明系用）扁平双导线电缆，双芯扁电缆

flatways 平面朝下与另一物接触着，平放着（＝flatwise）

flat width of inner tube 内胎的平叠宽度（内胎胎身平叠后的宽度）

flaw ＝defect

flaw detector 探伤仪（＝detector of defects）

flawless 无缺陷的，无裂痕的，无疵病的

flax ①亚麻 ②亚麻织物

flaxseed oil 亚麻子油

FLC 全负荷电流，满载电流（full-load current）

fld ①场（field 的简称）②流体，液体（fluid 的简称）

FLD 成形临界曲线圈（forming limit

diagram 的简称)

fleam 锯齿口与锯条面所成的角

fledgeling auto industry 幼稚汽车工业,年轻汽车工业(指汽车工业发展的初期)

fleet ①车队(指由一家公司或单位拥有的全部汽车,一般指货运车队)②(汽车厂家生产的多种品牌的)车族

fleet-average acceleration performance 车队平均加速性能

fleet average fuel consumption 车队平均燃油消耗量,车队平均油耗

fleet average fuel economy 车队平均燃油经济性(简称FAFE)

fleet-average inertia weight 车队平均惯量

fleet car 车队车(属于公司车队的汽车或供车队用的车辆,有别于私用车辆,一般为货车。特指其中由驾车里程长的销售代理人驾驶的带展示性质者)

fleet car field test 车队车使用试验

Fleet Control Services [美]车队管理服务中心(简称FCS)

fleet foreman 汽车车长,车队长

fleetline body 流线型车身

fleet maintenance mechanic [俗]车队维护技工,车队维修技工

fleet-maintenance soft package 车队维护软件包,车队维修软件

fleetman (载货)车队的驾驶、维修人员

fleet sales 车队用车批量销售(指将车辆成批地销售给公司供其组建、扩充或补充车队)

fleet service 车队服务(特指向专业公司拥有的车队提供的维修等服务)

fleet size (= total number of cars owned)车队大小,车队的车辆保有数,车队规模

fleet test ①(车辆)在汽车运输企业中的试验,使用性试验②(用同型号多辆车进行的)车队试验

Fletcher-Munson contours 等响度曲线,等音感曲线(= equal loudness curves)

flex ①花线,皮线,绝缘软线②使弯曲,挠曲,摺曲,拐折③挠性的,柔软的,活动的,灵活的,易挠曲的(= flexible)

flex arm suspension 挠臂悬架(后桥悬架结构的一种,由扭转挠性的后桥梁及支承后轮的挠性纵臂组成)

flex break 屈挠断裂(经挠曲试验或长期使用后的断裂现象)

flex cracking 挠裂

flex cycle 挠曲循环

flexer 挠曲试验装置

flex fatigue 弯曲疲劳,挠曲疲劳,耐挠曲疲劳(特性)(参见 bending fatigue)

flex-foil 柔性(金属)箔片

Flex Full-time 4WD (丰田公司用于小型轿车上的)柔性全时四轮驱动(系统)[商品名,该系统不是采用黏性耦合器,而是采用所谓的"三叶片式转子耦合器"(见 Rotary Tri-Blade Coupling)分配前、后轮驱动转矩的按需四轮驱动系统,见 on-time 4WD system]

flexibility ①柔(软)性,挠性,弹性②灵活性,机动性,适应性③(光的)折射性④(发动机的)韧性(指发动机在其整个转速范围内均呈现良好转矩特性,特别是优良的低速牵引能力)

flexibility agent 柔韧剂,增塑剂(= flexibilizer)

flexible ①可弯曲的,柔软的②可塑造的,有弹性的,可伸缩的③活动的,适应性强的,可变通的④具有韧性的(指发动机,见 flexibility)

flexible abrasive finishing ①软磨料抛光②预抛光,(擦光与抛光之间

的一道工序，采用软的无脂磨料，参见 finshing 及 polishing）

flexible-blade fan 挠性叶片风扇（其叶片角度可随转速而变，当车速提高时，叶片逐渐呈平直状，以减少风阻和摩擦损失）

flexible body 铰接式车身

flexible braided metal liner 弹性金属丝编织衬垫

flexible cable ①挠性电缆 ②软轴，软索

flexible cable system 软索驱动系统，软索系统（如：电动车窗玻璃的软索升降系统）

flexible can 见 flexible tin

flexible casing （机械传动用）挠性轴套管（亦称 flexible tube）

flexible contact 挠性触点

flexible control system （供汽车各种电子控制系统原型开发用的）多用途适应性控制系统（由控制系统所需的各种通用硬件和 CAN 通信接口等组成，只要加装软件，便能成为某一特定用途的控制系统）

flexible coupling 挠性联轴节［指仅用于两轴间只有小角度偏斜的传动的简单联轴节，一般通过连接两轴的弹性元件，如：橡胶块受压或夹布橡胶盘受拉来传递转矩，= elastic clutch, flexible（disc）joint］

flexible curtain （气垫车）挠性幕帘

flexible drive 挠性传动（如：转速表等传动用的套管钢索传动）

flexible duct 软管

flexible element 挠性元件（如：挠性万向节中用橡胶或夹布橡胶等弹性材料制成的中间传动元件，亦称 flexible member）

flexible facing （防碰，防撞的）软面

flexible file 挠性锉刀（如：可按车身面板弧度及曲面进行锉工作业的锉刀）

Flexible Format Audio system （车用）多制式适应型音响系统（可播放各种制式音响的多制式可转换型音响系统）

flexible fuel（engine）vehicle 可变燃料（发动机）汽车。多用燃料（发动机）汽车（简称 FFV, 指发动机结构不变，只是增加几种燃料供给系统。如：汽油机增加 LPG 燃料供给系统，成为可以单纯用汽油，亦可单纯用 LPG 作燃料的发动机驱动的汽车，即可用多种燃料的发动机的车辆）

flexible gear ①挠性连接传动（指皮带传动等）②（谐波齿轮传动中的）柔性齿轮，柔轮（在波发生器作用下能产生可控弹性变形的薄壁齿轮）

flexible gearing 挠性传动

flexible gear-shift lever 带球铰支撑的变速杆；挠性变速杆

flexible grinding 精整（参见 finishing）

flexible high-pressure fuel injection system （重型车辆柴油机的）柔性高压燃油喷射系统

flexible hitch 挠性挂接装置

flexible hose 软管

flexible joint （指用柔性材料，如：橡胶等传动的）柔性接头，挠性连接，挠性联轴节［如：flexible joint centring ring 柔性联轴节的定（中）心环；flexible joint cover 柔性联轴节的壳盖；flexible joint driver 柔性联轴节的传动元件，如：橡胶盘等；flexible joint front（rear）rubber plate 柔性联轴节传动元件的前（后）胶盘；flexible joint pilot sleeve 柔性联轴节的定（中）心衬套］

flexible lamp cord 电灯花线

flexible lighting （车内的）柔和光线照明

flexible machining centre 柔性加工中心（简称 FMC）

flexible manufacturing system 柔性制造系统，柔性生产系统（以适应多品种生产的要求）

flexible member assemble 挠性元件总成（挠性万向节的橡胶或夹布橡胶等弹性材料制成的中间传动元件总成）

flexible metallic conduit 金属蛇管，金属软管（= fexible metallic tubing）

flexible mounting plate 支撑件等的软垫（片）

flexible multi-body dynamics 柔性多体动力学

flexible oil (piston) ring （活塞）挠性油环（= flexline oil piston ring）

flexible outer mirror 柔性（支撑）外置式后视镜（当后视镜受到撞碰时，可变折，以免挂伤人或物件）

flexible pad 软垫（块）

flexible pavement 柔性路面

flexible pipe 软管

flexible progressive system （交通管理信号）弹性绿线系统，可变绿波系统（参见 progressive system）

flexible rack windscreen (windshield) wiper 柔性齿条式风窗玻璃刮水器（指执行机构由一根金属丝缠绕的挠性杆形成的简单齿条和与之啮合的驱动小齿轮组成）

flexible rear transverse beam 后桥挠性梁

flexible roller bearing 螺旋滚子轴承（= spiral roller bearing）

flexible rolling bearing 柔性滚动轴承，（简称）柔性轴承（专用于谐波齿轮传动中凸轮式波发生器的薄壁滚动轴承，其内外环的壁较薄，套装于凸轮上，能随不同凸轮形状而变形的轴承）

flexible rotor pump 柔性转子泵（转子叶片由柔性材料制成，紧贴泵壳内壁，由吸入区转入输出区时，叶片受压缩与壳贴的更紧）

flexible rule 卷尺

flexible safety barriers （道路的）挠性安全护墩

flexible sealing element 柔性密封元件

flexible shaft 软轴（如：车速里程表及转速表等的驱动挠性软索轴）

flexible skirt （气垫车）软围裙

flexible sleeve 软套，软垫套，软衬套

flexible strip 软垫条

flexible tank 软箱，软罐，囊

flexible tin （发动机冷却水箱恒温器的）感温器（如波纹管恒温器中的波纹管，石蜡恒温器中的橡胶伸缩软管，= [美] flexible can）

flexible tube 柔性管，软管（= flex-ible pipe）

flexible unit 通用设备，通用装置

flexible universal joint 挠性万向节（指由挠性元件总成连接两叉形元件组成的非等速万向节）

flexible valve seat insert 挠性气门镶座（用于风冷有色金属缸盖）

flexibly mounted engine 弹性支撑的发动机

flexile 柔性的，适应性强的（= flex-ible 常写作 flex.）

flexing ① 变曲，挠曲 ② 挠度 ③ （使…）弯曲的

flexing of piston ring ①活塞环（在汽缸内上下运动时由于汽缸的椭圆度和锥度引起的）收缩与张开 ②活塞环的挠曲

flexing resistance 抗挠曲阻力

flexitime 弹性工作时间（制）（工作时间由工作人员自己安排）

flex life 弯曲疲劳寿命

flexline oil piston ring 挠性活塞油环 [= flexible oil (piston) ring]

flexometer 挠度仪，挠曲计，曲率计，挠曲试验机

flex point （曲线的）拐点

FlexRay 柔光（BMW 公司开发的时间触发型车用具有故障容错能力的高速数据传输总线系统的商品名）

flex resistance （橡皮制品等的）抗挠损性能（指抗分层及挠裂等特性）

FlexRide 底盘多功能自适应性行驶系统（商品名，具有可识别 11 种不同的行驶工况，记忆车主的驾驶习性和风格，自动选定运动、标准和舒适三种行驶模式，以及随车速变化改变操纵能力等多种功能）

Flex 7 seats system （多功能车的）灵活（布置）7 座椅系统（如：可分别变换为 2，3，4，5，7 座，第三排可放到地板下，第二排可折叠向前放倒等）

flex steer 柔性转向（适应性转向的一种，可根据车速、转弯半径及转向力度等改变转向操纵力及转向速度等）

flexuose 锯齿状的，波状的，之字形的，多曲折的，弯弯曲曲的，多曲折的

flexural ①弯曲的（= flexure）②使产生弯曲的（= bending）

f/lg 焦距（focal length 的简称）

flicker ①不稳定的火焰 ②闪光，闪耀，闪烁 ③摇动，摇晃；颤动，摆动，脉动 ④抛掷器，搅动器

flickering lamp 闪光灯

flicker signal ①闪光信号 ②闪光信号灯

flick shift 按钮或拨杆式换挡

flinger 抛油环，抛油圈（见 oil flinger）

flip-chip ①倒装法，倒装片，倒装式；②反装晶片 ③倒焊法，叩焊

flip-flop 触发器（美指双稳态器件，英指单稳态器件，因此国际上已不推荐用此术语，而分别采用 bistable circuit、monostable circuit、trigger circuit 和 binary inverter 等术语）

flipper （轮胎的）胎圈芯包布（bead core flipper 或 bead bundle flipper 的简称，指包在钢丝圈和三角胶条外面的胶布，亦称 ply turn up）

flipper window 通风窗（= vent window）

flip socket （装于套筒板子方杆上的）锁球套筒，球销套筒

flip-top filler cap 快速开启的油箱（或水箱）盖（如：某些赛车或跑车上使用的轻轻一压再一转即可卸下的油箱盖）

flitch 增强件，补强件（指增加框架强度和刚度的构件，如支架横梁）

flitch plate ①条板，桁板，脊板 ②补强板

flivver ①廉价小汽车，廉价的小东西 ②失败，挫折

FLl 液面高度指示器（fluid level indicator 的简称）

float ①（泛指各种）浮在液面上的物体，如：浮筒，浮标 ②液面高度计量或控制系统的浮子件（如：燃油表的浮子）③（特指化油器的）浮子（空心金属或塑料筒件，或软木件，浮于化油器浮子室燃油液面，控制进油针阀，以维持所要求的油面高度）④平板货车或挂车（特指安装列队行进的彩车或展览车的展品或运送食品、饮料的平板车，亦称 flat）⑤（发动机气门在高速运转时）不停地跳振（倾向）

floatability 浮动性，漂动能力

floatable ①可漂浮的 ②可浮动的

float-and-valve 浮子带（针）阀

floatation ①漂浮性，浮动性 ②浮渡性能（轮胎行驶在松软地面上能防止沉陷的性能）

floatation area （雪地运动车的）漂浮面积（指最大总质量下，停放在刚性平面时，距离地面 76mm 水平面处，其履带和滑板表面支撑面积的投影）

floatation tire 高通过性的宽断面轮胎

flo a tation tyre 可在沼泽地浮行的越野轮胎

float charging 浮动充电（一种充电方式，使蓄电池永远与恒压电源相接，随时充电，以保持蓄电池经常处于完全充电状态，参见 floating battery）

floated disc clutch 浮盘式离合器［自（动）调（节）盘式离合器，一般指电磁操纵的离合器］

floater ①浮子，浮板，浮垫，浮动物 ②全浮式后桥（口语）

float feed 经浮子室供油

float gauge 浮子式液面计

floating ①漂浮，浮动，浮置 ②整平，抹光 ③漂浮的，浮动的，移动的，不固定的，自由转动的，铰接的，摆动的

floating action （组合式行星齿轮机构中某行星齿轮单元）空转，浮转（指在另一行星齿轮中，即另一列的内齿圈被制动，而由两单元共用的行星架输出增大的转矩时，该行星齿轮单元的全部元件皆无拘束地随着空转，对转矩增减不起任何作用的现象）

floating axle 全浮式半轴驱动桥（带全浮式半轴的驱动桥，= full floating axle 及 full floating axle shaft）

floating battery 浮充电池（组），浮（动）充（电）蓄电池（电源系统的发电机及蓄电池并联，可分担负荷。如：一般汽车电器系统，蓄电池永远与发电机连接，随时充电，一旦发电机损坏，蓄电池则可承担全部负荷，参见 float charging）

floating-bow top retention system （敞篷轿车）活动车顶的浮动式弓形撑杆系统

floating caliper （汽车浮钳盘式制动器的）浮式卡钳，浮动卡钳（指制动钳可平行滑动或绕一支承销摆动，即：是浮动的，且只在一侧内设有压力机构）

floating cam brake 浮动凸轮式制动器（指凸轮没有固定在其底板上，因而可对两个制动蹄施加相等的推力的鼓式制动器）

floating disc brake 浮盘式制动器（仅在制动盘的一侧设有加压机构的制动钳，而借制动盘的浮动对盘的另一侧产生压紧力使之制动的钳盘式制动器）

floating disc type output mechanism （行星齿轮传动中的）浮动盘输出机构（采用传递平行轴运动的浮动盘机构作为输出机构）

floating fulcrum 浮动支点（支点位置可移动，以改变输入与输出力臂比）

floating gate （数字电路电荷转移器件中的）浮置栅（一种无欧姆接触的电极，与半导体之间用绝缘层隔开，主要用于信号检测或再生电路中）

floating gudgeon pin 浮式活塞销

floating guide ring 浮动式导向内圈（多排式滚动轴承用，装在两排滚动件之间）

floating lever （柴油机调速器的）浮动杆，浮杆

floating line （水陆两用汽车）吃水线

floating oil filter （机油泵）浮式集滤器

floating piston 浮动活塞，自由活塞（见 secondary piston）

floating piston pin 全浮式活塞销（= full floating wrist pin）

floating plate （双盘离合器中两从动盘之间的）中间压盘（亦称 center plate, intermediate disc, floating disc）

floating point 浮点，浮动小数点

floating power engine mounting 发动

机的弹性支撑

floating region （数字电路电荷转移器件中的）浮置区（一种高导电特性而无欧姆接触的掺杂区，电荷包通过交叠栅或相邻转移栅经过该区进行转移，在检测或再生电路中，可作为电荷信号的传感器）

floating ring type labyrinth packing 浮环式迷宫油封

floating shoe （制动器）浮（动式制动）蹄

floating shoe slider （两）浮式制动蹄（下端的）支承滑板

floating shoe (slider) pivot 浮式制动蹄（下端的）支承滑板（的）销轴

floating shoe type brake 浮蹄式制动器（鼓式制动器的一种，其两个制动蹄的上端装有一双向作用的轮缸，下端各由一个可绕其共同支承销轴转动的滑板支承，二者可作相对滑动，即两制动蹄的下端均浮动地支承在滑板上，形成一个领从蹄式制动器。这种制动蹄称 floating shoe，其滑板称 floating shoe slider，滑板的支承销轴称 floating shoe slider pivot）

floating skirt piston 浮裙式组合活塞（由带有销座、活塞销槽的活塞头和可在活塞销上浮动的独立裙部两部分组成）

floating tire pad （汽车试验设备上的）①车轮浮式负载传感装置（一般为三轴向负载传感器，用空气轴承支撑，装在每只车轮下，参见 triaxial load cell）②车轮浮式支垫

floating triangle corner （转子发动机径向密封的）浮式三角角密封片（用弹簧装配的三片式径向密封片的两端角片）

floating type bearing 浮动轴承

float level ①浮子室油面高度 ②（确保所要求油面高度的）浮子调整 ③浮子水准

float meter 浮子式流量计

float needle (valve) 浮子针阀，浮子控制针阀

float of spare engines （车库和修理厂的）流动备用发动机

float-operated 由浮子控制的，由浮子操纵的

float pivot pin 浮子的销轴

float stocks （修理厂，车库等的）流动备用件

float suction control 见 float chamber suction control

float system 见 float circuit

float tank 有浮子的储液箱，浮子箱

float test 浮选试验，用浮子黏度计测定黏度

floc 絮片，絮状沉淀，蓬松物质，絮凝物

flocculating constituent 絮凝体，绒聚体，绒毛状组织

flocculation ①絮凝，絮结 ②絮凝体，絮结体

Flon 氟冷（类似氟氯烷的一种制冷剂，参见 freon）

flood ①大量涌出，泛滥 ②溢油（混合比过浓或汽缸内进油过多以致起动困难，产生的淹缸现象，产生这一现象的发动机称 flooded engine）

flood head lamp 强光前照灯

floodlight ①探照灯，泛光灯；强力照明灯（多装于警车，救护车上）②用泛光灯照亮；强力照明（见 flood lighting）

flood lighting 泛光照明，强力照明（指视亮度高于周围环境的照明）

flood lighting vehicle 照明车（装备有发电机、照明灯具、输电线路等装置，主灯通过液压传动，可升降、回转和俯仰，用于火灾现场、港口、码头、建筑工地及其他野外作业短期照明）

floor ①（轿车的）地板（亦称 floor

panel) ②（货车的）支承货物的底板（= load floor）

floor-based 装在地板上的，以地面为基础的

floor-beam （车身底板下的）横梁

floor-bearer （货车车身）底板枕梁

floorboard ①（汽车车身的）底板，地板，（货车货厢的）底板面板（= floor panel）②作车身底板的板料

floor board battery cover （车身）地板上的蓄电池检查盖

floor board covering （车身）地板护盖

floor carpet 地毯，地板铺覆物

floor change 落地式变速（方式）（指变速杆从驾驶室地板下伸出的方式，亦称 direct control，= floor shift）

floor console （轿车的）落地式控制台

floor covering 地板蒙皮，地毯

floor cross member （车身）地板横梁（= floor beam 指客厢底板的横向加强构件）

floor engine 安装在底板下的发动机，扁平型发动机，汽缸卧置式发动机（= underfloor engine, pancake engine）

floor front crossmember 车身地板前横梁

floor gear change 使用装在（车身）地板上的变速杆换挡（美称 floor shift）

floor height （客车车身的）地板高（度）（指通道地板上平面至地面之间的垂直距离，分别在前轴和后轴处测量）

floor-hopper truck 底卸式自卸汽车（车厢地板做成漏斗状，可从底部卸货）

floor jack 落地式举升器，落地千斤顶

floor level 地板高度，货厢地板的卸载高度

floor leveling control 车身高度调平控制装置，车身调平控制

floor line ①车厢地板离地高度；车厢平台卸货高度（= floor height）②地板线

floor load 车身地板载荷

floor mainside （厢式货车车架的）底板主纵梁

floor mat 车身地板上的橡胶等软垫或地毯

floor-mounted 装在（车厢）地板上的

floor pan ①轿车承载式车身底板，多呈线盘形（见 under body）②（泛指车身）底板（= floor）③（车身安装上面的）整个底板总成（= platform）

floor pan assembly （小客车承载式车身的）底板总成（= underbody assembly）

floor panel （车身）地板，底板（简称 floor）

floor rear crossmember （车身）底板后横梁

floor sheet （车身）地板用金属薄板

floor shift （[美] 驾驶室）地板上伸出的变速杆换挡 [= floor (gear) change，以别于转向盘柱上的变速杆换挡]

floor side member （车身的）后纵梁（在后轮部位的纵向加强件，= floor side rail, rear side member, rear floor side frame）

floor skid strip （车身）地板防滑条

floor time 停机时间

floor-to-cushion height 车厢地板至坐垫面的高度

floor trap handle 地板上的活门把手

floor truck 搬运小车，独轮手推车

floor tunnel 地板通道（指车身地板上凸起部分，主要是为了覆盖变速

器及传动轴，但同时有加强地板刚性的作用)

floor under cover 车身底板的空气动力学罩板

floor well (轿车)车身地板脚坑(供乘员放脚用，= fool well)

flop over ①触发器(触发电路，双稳态多谐振荡器，亦称 flip-flop)②(电视显示屏)图像上、下跳动

Flop/s 次浮点运算/每秒(单位，每秒钟内浮点运算的次数，可表征微处理器的能力)

flops 每秒的浮点运算数(floating point operations per second 的简称，微处理器的性能指标之一)

flotage ①浮力，漂浮 ②轮渡费(= floatage)

flotation ①漂浮性，浮动性(= floatation) ②(特指车辆的)浮渡性能(可操纵通过泥泞、沼泽或类似湿地的能力)

flotation kit 供汽车在水中浮渡的成套装备

flo-tester (散热器、水箱等的)流量检查器

flo-thru ventilation (车厢的)贯通式通风

Flotrol 一种恒电流充电机

flow ①流动，流出，流过 ②流(如：flow of fright 货流，指货物在既定时期内，沿运输路段一个方向上的流动量；flow of information 信息流；flow of lubrication 润滑油流)③流量，流出量 ④塑性流动，塑性变形 ⑤使屈服，使发生塑性流动

flowability 流动性

flow control ①流量调节，流量控制 ②(粉末的)流动控制

flow control method (电子控制液压式动力转向系转向助力的)流量控制法(其液压泵输出口处装有控制流量的电磁阀，汽车高速行驶时液压泵输出流量小，转动转向盘所要求的力变大，低速时液压泵输出流量大，转动转向盘所需的力变小)

flow control valve type crankcase ventilation system 流量控制阀型曲轴箱通风系统

flow counter 流量计，流量表[= flow instrument, flow meter, flow ga(u)ge, flow indicator]

flow divider valve (液压传动的)流量分配阀，分流阀(= flow dividing valve)

flow field 流场(指流体所涉及的范围)

flow friction 流体摩擦，液体摩擦(参见 fluid friction)

flow guide 导流板(车身上引导气流、减少空气阻力的板件，= air deflector)

flow improver additive (柴油等的)流动性添加剂，流动促进剂(提高流动性的添加剂)

flowing ①流动 ②流动的；连接不断的 ③平滑的

flow-interrupt valve 阻流阀，断流阀

flow line ①流线；流水线，气流线，金属变形线，晶粒滑移线，流量线 ②流动线路，流体管路 ③交通流线(特指沿最佳路径连接交通起点-终点的交通图标线) ④(车身)流线型线

flow line plan (交通)线流图(地图上表明某地区的交通流量、流向等交通状况)

flow line production 流水线生产，流水作业(= current production)

flow measurement orifice 流量测量孔，流量计量孔，量孔

flow method 流水作业法(各个工位按最佳工艺顺序依次连续排列成整个生产线，按规定的节拍进行流水式的作业，亦称 flow process)

flow nozzle 流量计喷嘴，测流喷嘴

flow off 流走，流出

flowout diagram 流出量图
flow path 流程，流动径迹，渗径
flow pattern 流型，流线谱，流线图
flow pipe 流管，送水管，排出管，输送管（道）
flow plan 流程图，输送线路图
flow point 流动点，流点（= pour point）
flow process chart 加工流程图，加工工艺卡
flow proportioner 流量比例调节器
flow rate ①流动速率，流速 ②（气体、液体的）消耗率 ③（单位时间内的）流量
flow-rate control valve type hydraulic suspension 流量控制阀型液压悬架（通过控制流量来控制阻尼力的液压悬架，以区别于通过控制液压来控制阻尼力的液压悬架）
flow-rate meter 流速表，流速计，流量计
flowrator 流量计，流量表
flow regulating valve 流量调节阀
flow resistance （稳态）流阻，流动阻力，流体阻力
flow restriction 节流，限流，约束流量
flow scheme 见 flow sheet
flow sensor 流量传感器，流速传感器
flow sheet 工艺流程图，流程图表，流向图，工艺卡片，作业图表，程序方框图，操作过程表，生产流程图解（= flow chart, flow diagram, flow scheme）
flow sight 流动观察孔，流体检查窗
flow stress 流动应力，屈服应力
flow structure observation technology （绕车身的空气动力学）气流结构可见化技术（亦称 flow visualization technology，见 streak line method, surface line method）
flow tank 沉淀池，沉淀槽

flow test （液体或气体的）流量试验
flow turning 分级旋转挤压（作业）（用旋转滚筒将金属毛坯逐步挤压到精加工尺寸，简称 floturning，原为商用名）
flow valve （液力变速器换挡控制系统的）流量阀（在换挡期间为接合的换挡元件快速供油）
flow velocity 流速
FLP 故障诊断仪表板（fault location panel 的简称）
FLS 快速起燃 λ 传感器（fast light-off lamda sensor 的简称，指冷机起动时，可迅速达到工作温度的 O_2 传感器，目前有两种：①安装位置靠近排气歧管，利用排气管热迅速升温 ②电加热）
FLT ①故障，缺点，错误（fault 的简称）②滤波器，滤纸，滤清器（filter 的简称）③满载转矩（= full-load torque）
FLU ①故障诊断设备（= fault location unit 的简称）；②终极限（上方）（final limit up 的简称）
fluctuate 波动，脉动，振荡，起伏，变动
fluctuating injection 波动喷油（每循环喷油时，针阀颤动，升程高度不规则，起落波动，导致喷油量波动的现象）
fluctuation rate （压力，温度等的）波动率，变动率，起伏率
fluctuations 偏差量
flue 烟道，暖风管
flue gas （指由燃烧区排出的）废气
flue-gas analysing apparatus 废气分析仪
fluent ①变量，变数 ②流畅的，无阻滞的 ③易变的 ④液态的
fluffy dust 毛状尘污
fluid ①流体（包括液体和气体）②流体的，流动的
fluid borne noise 液体传播的噪声

flu

(简称 FBN)

fluid brake　液压制动器（= liquid brake，指制动推动力来自液体压力的制动器）

fluid capacity　（油底壳，变速器，驱动桥，水箱，油箱等的机油，水或燃油的）容量

fluid chamber　液腔，液室

fluid clutch　见 fluid coupling

fluid computer　射流计算机（用射流元件制成的计算机）

fluid control valve　液压控制阀

fluid converter　液力变矩器（= torque converter，能改变所传递转矩的液力传动装置，其变矩比为速比的函数）

fluid-cooled　流体冷却的

fluid coupling　液力耦合器（液压传动装置的一种，仅能传递动力，但不能改变转矩，在所有的速比下，变矩比均相同，= fluid clutch, fluid flywheel, hydraulic clutch, hydraulic coupling）

fluid coupling phase　（两相式液力变矩器的）耦合相，耦合区相（指导向叶轮元件全部随泵轮同方向旋转，在输出转矩 Q_1 和输入转矩 Q 之比 $Q_1/Q = 1$ 的情况下工作，实际上起耦合器的作用）

fluid crack (ing) catalyst　流体裂化催化剂，液态裂解触媒（简称 FCC）

fluid curtain　（起隔热作用的）液体帘幕，水帘

fluid damper　液力减振器（= hydraulic damper）

fluid dirt level　液体脏污程度

fluid drive　①液力传动，液压驱动，流体传动　②液力耦合器（= fluid clutch）

fluid dynamics　液体动力学，流体力学

fluid-dynamics characteristics　流体动力学特性

fluid film　①润滑油膜　②（泛指各种）流体薄膜

fluid flow　流体流量，流体流动

fluid flow analogy　流体流动模拟

fluid flow regulator　（液压系统）流量调节器

fluid flywheel　液力飞轮耦合器（fluid coupling 的一种，指飞轮作为泵轮者，亦称 fluid-flywheel clutch）

fluid friction　流体摩擦；液体摩擦（= flow friction）

fluid gun　①注液器　②液体喷枪

fluid head　液体压头，液体系统压力（见 liquid head）

fluidic amplifier　射流放大器

fluidic leak detector　漏液检测器，渗漏检测器

fluidics　流控技术，射流学，流体学

fluidimeter　黏度计，流度计（= fluid meter）

fluid inlet angle　流体流入角

fluidised bed coating　（塑料）流化床涂层法（用空气吹拌塑料粉末，形成塑料粉末流，将已加热的工件置于粉末流中，工件表面黏附塑料粉末，然后固化形成涂层）

fluidity　①（流体如：机油等）流动性（指其容易流动的程度的特性）②（道路）交通流的连续性

fluidization　①流动化，流体化，液体化　②高速气流输送　③沸腾作用

fluidized bed decoater　流化床式漆层清除器（具有漆层或其涂复层的废旧零件或板料切碎后，置于悬浮在上升气流内的流态介质微粒中清除其原有的漆皮等，回炉再用，20世纪90年代末期采用的废料回收再利用技术之一）

fluidized catalytic cracker　流态触媒分解装置，流体催化裂化装置（简称 FCC）

fluid kinetics　流体动力学

fluid level gauge 液面指示器,液面表(＝fluid level indicator)

fluid level warning indicator (仪表板上指示制动系中的)制动液量过低的警报灯

fluid lever sensor 液面高度传感器

fluid link 液力传动节(液力传动系统中,单元组件的通称)

fluid lubrication 液体润滑

fluid mass 液体(亦称 liquid mass)

fluid mechanics 液体力学

fluid medium 流体介质,流质,流体

fluid meter (测油的)黏度计,流动度计(＝fluidity meter)

fluid motor 液动马达,液动机,液压马达(将液体压力变为旋转力输出的装置,亦称 fluid power motor)

fluid non-friction brake 非摩擦式流体制动器(利用流体压力产生反方向作用力实现制动的装置)

fluid oil 润滑油,液态油

fluid ounce 液盎斯[英制容积单位,代号 fl oz 或 fluid oz,在英国,1 fl oz(UK)＝1/20 pint＝28.41306cm³,在美国,1 fl oz(US)＝1/16pint＝29.57353cm³,见 pint]

fluid outlet angle 流体流出角

fluid oz 液盎斯(参见 fluid ounce)

fluid power motor 见 fluid motor

fluid power system 液压驱动系统,液力传动系统

fluid power transmission [美]液力变速器(指液力耦合器或液力变矩及与之耦合的定轴式或行星式齿轮变速器总成,＝fluid transmission, hydrodynamic transmission)

fluid reservoir 储液罐

fluid resistance ①流体流动阻力 ②(橡皮等的)耐非水流体的泡胀变质特性

fluid sealant 液体密封剂

fluid sensor 流体传感器(流体流量、温度、流速等传感器的通称)

fluid start (汽车的)液力起步(指利用动液或静液传动装置使汽车由静止状态起步)

fluid-tight 不渗透的,不透水的

fluid viscosity coefficient 流体黏滞系数(表示流体黏滞程度的物理量。定义为畸变应力与畸变时间之比)

fluon 聚四氟乙烯

fluorborate solution 氟硼酸盐溶液,氟硼酸盐电解液

fluorescence ①荧光(冷光的一种,电磁辐射物质在吸收其他辐射源辐射期间产生的可见光,如:荧光灯所发出的光),荧光性 ②发荧光

fluorescent 荧光的,发荧光的,有荧光性的

fluorescent lamp 荧光灯

fluorescent screen 荧光屏,荧光板

fluoride 氟化物

fluorinated elastomer 氟弹性材料(HK 橡皮材料,见 DF materials)

fluorinated silicone 氟化硅酮橡胶材料

fluorine 氟(F)

fluorine rubber 氟橡胶(合成橡胶的一种)

fluorocarbons 碳氟化合物,氟塑料(热塑性树脂)

fluorocarbon turbine 碳氟化合物汽轮机

fluoroelastomer 氟基弹性材料

Fluoro Ngliner 氟基尼龙衬套,氟基尼龙衬垫(商品名)

fluoroplastics 氟化乙烯树脂;氟基塑料

fluorosilicone 氟(聚)硅酮

fluorosilicone rubber 氟硅酮橡胶

flush ①液体射流,强压液流 ②液流冲洗 ③(特指机械密封的)冲洗(对于内装单端面机械密封,当被密封介质不宜做密封流体时,从外部引入与被密封介质相容的流体到

密封腔内,以改善密封工作条件的一种方法,起冲洗作用的外部流体称 flush fluid) ④(与周围的表面)齐平 ⑤齐平的,埋头的

flusher ①冲洗装置 ②喷洒装置 ③润滑油加注设备

flush fit 紧配合,打入配合

flush fitting sliding roof 嵌入式滑动车顶

flush floor type brake tester 平板式制动试验台

flushing oil 清洗油(如:清洗油底壳,机油道用的轻油)

flush mounted headlamp 嵌装式前照灯(装饰圈与配光镜外露,灯壳装在车身内的前照灯)

flush-mounted speaker 顺着车身内饰表面的轮廓齐平地嵌装于车身内壁的喇叭

flush type direction indicator 嵌入式转向指示灯(嵌入车身并于外表面齐平,= built-in direction indicater)

flute ①槽,沟,波纹 ②沟纹的;波纹的 ③开槽,刻槽,做出波纹

fluted nut 槽顶螺母,开槽螺母,花螺母(装撬口销用,= castle nut)

flutter ①跳动,振动,摇动,摆动,脉动,颤动 ②(飞轮)抖振 ③(转向轮)摆振(汽车在低速时,转向轮绕转向节主销的摆振,参见 shimmy) ④(汽车)振抖(汽车产生的技术文件所不允许的自身抖动现象) ⑤(示波)图像颤动 ⑥放音失真

fluttering 颤动;脉动,波动;扑动

flux ①(光,磁或电)通量(分别指单位区域中的光能密度,磁力线或电力线总数) ②助焊剂,焊药(在钎焊或熔焊中用来阻止氧化物生成,或溶解氧化物或其他有害物质的媒质) ③熔化,熔解

flux density ①气流密度 ②(磁,电)通量密度

fluxed electrode 涂药焊条(= flux-coated electrode)

fluxing temperature 熔解温度

flux linkage (电磁耦合器)磁链

flux meter 麦克斯韦计,通量计,磁通量计

flux path 磁力线通路

fly-ball governor 飞球式调速器(带球形重锤的离心式调速器,简称 ball governor)

flyer ①快车,快速公共汽车 ②飞轮 ③各种高速运动的机械装置 ④飞行器,飞机(= flier)

flyheaded screw 蝶形头螺栓,蝶形螺钉,元宝螺钉(= butterfly bolt, wing bolt, wingheaded bolt)

flying car 飞行汽车(空陆两用汽车)

flying dial gauge 连续式测厚千分表

flying duck 带有浮翼的水陆两用汽车

flying micrometer 快速测微仪

flying squad (公路上交通警察处理事故等问题的)紧急行动小组

fly lead 带接线端子的短引线

fly nut 蝶形螺帽,蝶形螺母

fly-over junction 上跨式立体交叉(指一条道路经跨线桥从另一条道路上方跨越的立体交叉,= flyover crossing 三层以上时称 multi-level junction 多层立体交叉)

fly-screen (摩托车上的)小风挡玻璃

fly start (汽车的)突然起动,猛起步

fly-under junction 下穿式立体交叉(= fly-under crossing,指一条路通过涵道从另一条路下穿过的立体交叉)

flyweight 飞重,离心重块(如:离心式点火提前机构中,能随发动机转速增加而在离心力作用下甩开的离心块)

flywheel 飞轮［具有一定质量的旋转圆盘，用于储存能量，发动机曲轴稳速运动的部件和离合器的主摩擦面，将发动机动力传给汽车的传动系。flywheel casing 飞轮壳，用于罩住飞轮的外壳，亦称离合器壳（= flywheel cover, flywheel housing）；flywheel clutch 飞轮离合器，即常规的以飞轮作为主动摩擦面的离合器；flywheel effect 飞轮效应，指飞轮旋转质量的惯性效应；flywheel end 曲轴的飞轮一端；flywheel horsepower 发动机的有效功率，指从发动机输出轴上即飞轮上测得的功率，一般称 brake power；flywheel generator 飞轮式发电机，小型摩托车上使用的小型交流发电机，其旋转磁场装在曲轴一端随曲轴旋转，同时起发动机飞轮的作用，故名；flywheel magneto 飞轮式磁电机，= flywheel type magneto, magnet flywheel，指用于小型汽油机作点火电源的磁电机，以其多极永磁转子作发动机的飞轮；flywheel hub 飞轮车毂，亦称 flywheel boss, flywheel nave；flywheel tim(ing) mark(ing) 飞轮上的点火正时标记；flywheel pilot flange 飞轮装配时，用来对正中心的导向突缘；flywheel ring gear，或 flywheel gear, flywheel gear ring, flywheel starter gear, flywheel toothed ring toothing 飞轮（与）起动（机起动小齿轮啮合的）齿圈（偶见称 flywheel rim）；flywheel turner 飞轮转动摇柄，由摇把和带卡钩的杠杆组成的手摇工具，在调整和维护作用中，用它卡住飞轮齿圈，可将飞轮转到所要求的位置；flywheel hybrid vehicle 飞轮复合动力车，指使用内燃机和飞轮储能系统（flywheel energy storage system 或称飞轮再生系统 flywheel regenerative system，利用飞轮转动惯量存储能量并释放使用的系统）组成的复合动力车辆，其发动机始终在稳定的经济转速下运转，输出恒定的功率，以便节能和排放干净，当行驶阻力小时，其多余的能量带动飞轮旋转，以借助其旋转质量惯性效应存储这一部分能量，当汽车爬坡等需要较大的功率而发动机所产生的恒定功率不足时，便通过飞轮储能传动系统（flywheel stored energy transmission system）与发动机共同驱动汽车，这一套储能放能传动系统总称为 flywheel energy management power plant，简称 FEMP "飞轮储能动力系统"，由动力控制模块 PCM 直接或通过飞轮能量控制模块 flywheel energy control module，简称 FECM，全自动控制］

flywheel absorber 飞轮减振器

flywheel battery 飞轮电池（20 世纪 90 年代初美国开发的一种新概念电池，实际上是以电枢转子起飞轮作用的电机。充电时电机作为电动机，在外充电电源驱动下，电枢高速旋转储存能量。放电时，电机利用飞轮"电枢"发电，实现机械能至电能转换。据称一次充电可供中型轿车行驶 600km）

FM ①磁极，场磁铁（field magnet）②现场手册（field manual）③现场修正，现场更改（field modification）④调频（frequency modulation）⑤减摩剂，摩擦改善剂（friction modifier）

F Matic 带手控模式的自动变速系统（Formula Matic 的简称，日本本田公司带手动控制模式的自动变速系统的商品名。该系统由常规的电子控制式自动变速系统及附加的手动变速加、减挡开关及挡位显示器组成）

FMC 柔性加工中心（flexible machining centre）

FMC （对车辆从发动机到车身及主要部件的）全盘改型（full mode change 的简称）

FMCEC ［欧洲］工程机械与起重设备制造商联合会（The Federation of Manufacturers of Construction Equipment and Cranes 的简称）

FMCSA ［美］联邦汽车货运公司安全管理局（Federal Motor Carrier Safety Administration 的简称）

FMEA 故障模式及影响分析（在某项系统或产品研制初期即对其预想的故障模式及该故障对性能的影响进行分析，以便使这类故障发生的可能性减至最小，从而提高该系统或产品的可靠性，Failure Mode and Effect Analysis 的简称）

FMEP 平均摩擦有效压力（friction mean effective pressure）

FMF 现场维修率（见 field maintenance factor）

FM MPX system 调频多路传输系统（frequency modulation multiplex system 的简称）

F-MPV 家用多功能车（Family-Multifunction Vehicle 的简称）

FMS ①柔性制造系统（见 flexible manufacturing system）②车隧管理系统（Fleet Management system 的简称）

FMVCP ［美］联邦汽车管理规程（Federal Motor Vehicle Control Program 的简称）

FMVSS ［美］联邦机动车安全标准（Federal Motor Vehicle Safety Standard 的简称）

FNP 熔点，熔化温度（fusion point 的简称）

FO ①快动作（继电器）（fast-operating relay 的简称）②点火顺序（firing order 的简称）③燃料油（fuel oil 的简称）

foam ①泡沫，泡沫状物，泡沫橡胶，泡沫塑料 ②海绵状的

foamed ceramic filter （柴油机用）多孔陶瓷滤芯过滤器（用于滤清排气碳烟）

foamed glass 泡沫玻璃，多孔玻璃

foamed-in wire harness process 泡沫塑料线束封装法（20世纪90年代末期出现的车用仪表电线封装技术，不用传统的线卡、线夹等固定，而用泡沫塑直接将多条导线封入仪表板等内）

foamed materials 泡沫材料，多孔材料［指高分子泡沫材料，有泡沫塑料 foam(ed) plastics, plastic foam 或 aerated plastics, 如: foam polyethylene 泡沫聚乙烯, foam polystyrene 泡沫聚苯乙烯等, 和泡沫橡胶 foam rubber, 如: foam neoprene 泡沫氯丁（二烯）橡胶两大类］

foam-filled tire 海绵轮胎（= cellular tire, 用高强性海绵代替压缩气体的轮胎）

foaming property 发泡（沫）性，泡沫生成特性

foam inhibitor 泡沫抑制剂（常用于润滑油中）

foamite 泡沫灭火剂，灭火药沫

foam retainer （滚动轴承的）多孔材料滚珠（柱）架，夹珠（柱）圈

foam shampoo 泡沫洗车剂，泡沫洗涤剂

focal-conic texture （液晶显示器用的）焦锥结构（胆甾相液晶中的螺旋轴呈不规则排列的结构，具有强烈的光散射）

focal distance 焦距（= focal length）

focal point ①焦点（= focus）②集中点，聚集点

focometer 焦距仪

focsia panel （驾驶室的）仪表板（= instrument panel）

focus ①焦点，焦距，中心点 ②聚焦，集中，以…为中心，聚束，对

光，调整焦距

focusing glass 聚焦镜，聚焦玻璃

focusing screw （汽车前照灯）焦点调整螺钉

focus（s）ing 聚焦，调整焦距，对光

focus（wheel）aligner 光学式车轮定位仪

fog ①雾 ②起雾，使朦胧不清

FOG 光纤陀螺仪（用于测定车身回转运动的角速度，fiber optic gyroscope 的简称，亦称 rate gyro）

fogbound 因浓雾所阻不能行车（的）

fog buoy 雾标

fog head lamp 防雾前照灯

fog horn 雾天音响信号喇叭

fog-lamp 雾灯（= fog light，亦称 adverse-weather lamp，指：装在汽车前面，发出可穿透雾、雨等的宽照射面近光，用于照亮道路的两侧或装在车后面的，与制动灯亮度相同的红色灯光）

fog light tell-tale 雾灯信号灯（装在仪表板上，供驾驶员了解雾灯是否点亮）

fog lubrication 油雾润滑

foil ①箔，金属薄片 ②装饰叶瓣 ③加装饰叶瓣

foil gauge 应变片

fold ①折叠，折合，重叠 ②折页 ③门扇 ④褶皱，起伏，皱纹

…fold… 倍（如：tenfold：十倍，hundredfold：百倍）

fold-away 可折叠的

fold crack 折叠裂缝，折合处裂缝（亦称 fold crevice）

fold-down door 下翻门（= flap door）

fold-down seat 下折叠式座椅

folded front radiator 折叠式前置散热器

folded rear-seat fixing hook 后座折叠后的固定钩

folder filter 多褶式滤清器

fold-flat seat backrest 可放平的折叠式座椅靠背

folding ①折叠式的，可开合的 ②折弯的，褶皱的

folding car （伞兵用）折叠式汽车

folding door 折叠式拉门（= jack-knife door）

folding down flat seat （靠背）可放平的座椅

folding seat 折叠式座椅（一般加座大多使用可折叠式座椅，故亦称加座椅，= additional seat）

folding soft roof （敞篷车的）可收折式软顶篷

folding strength 耐折强度

folding test （板材的）折叠试验（弯折180°）

folding top 折叠式车顶（= collapsible top，一般指敞篷车的可折叠式软顶）

folding top bow 折叠式篷顶的弧拱撑杆

folding top cover （篷顶式汽车的）可折式顶篷

follower ①从动件，被动件，随动件（特指直接由凸轮推动将动力传给有关零件，如：将动力传给气门的零件称 valve tappet "气门挺杆"）②（无线电）跟随器 ③复制器，复制装置 ④轴瓦，轴衬

follower ball joint 随动球节（见 steering ball joint）

follower gear ①从动齿轮 ②从动机构

follower pulley 从动传动带轮

following distance 后车距离，尾随车距

following edge 后沿，后边缘，下降边（= trailing edge, lagging-edge, back edge）

following too closely 后车跟前车距离过近（简称FTC，是追尾碰撞的

原因之一）

following wind 顺风 [= free wind, fair wind, tail wind, favo(u)rable wind]

follow me home （汽车）前照灯延时照明功能（关闭电源开关后，仍可延时照明一段时间，方便车主"回家"）

follow-on 下一代的，改进型的

follow-up ①随动系统（装置）；跟踪系统（装置）（简称 FU）；伺服系统 ②随动的，追随的，随后的，接着的，补充的

follow-up coil 螺线管，随动线圈

follow-up control system 随动控制系统，随动调节系统

follow-up injection （多段喷油式柴油机主喷射后的）后续喷射（亦称 after injection）

follow-up potentiometer ①反馈电势计，回授电势计 ②伺服系统电势计，随动电位计

follow-up theory 随动理论，伺服理论

follow-up valve 随动阀

folly proof drive ①傻瓜驾驶系统（运动神经迟钝的人亦能安全驾驶的操纵装置）②不需要什么技术的自动操纵装置

FOM ①性能系统 ②优良系数 ③汽车视野评价参数（参见 figure of merit）

FON 前辛烷值（fore octane number，指内燃机燃料中，蒸馏温度低于100℃的轻质组分的研究法辛烷值 "RON"）

food commodity based fuel 食用农产品基燃油（如用谷物为原料生产的乙醇汽油）

food container van 厢式食品运送车，食品集装箱运输车

food-handling truck 食品运输车

fool proof （亦写作 folly proof 或称 idiot proof）①有安全装置的，可防止错误操作的，确保安全的 ②极简单的，可由生手或任何人都能操纵的，傻瓜式的

fool proofness 运转可靠的安全装置

foot ①基脚，底座，最下部 ②支点 ③末尾，末位 ④英尺（英制长度单位，代号 ft, f, 1 ft = 12in = 1/3 码 = 0.3048m = 0.9144 尺）

foot board ①（上汽车的）踏脚板（= foot bar, foot plate）②搁脚板（= foot support）

foot brake 行车制动器（= toe brake，指由脚踏板控制的汽车主制动器）

foot candle 英制烛光（旧亮度单位，$= 1 \text{lumen}/\text{ft}^2 = 10.764 \text{lux}$）

foot change of the gear box 变速器的脚操纵机构，脚操纵变速机构（= foot gear control）

foot-control(led) 踏板控制的，脚操纵的（= foot-operated）

foot-crossing 人行横道，人行过街道

foot feed [美俚] 脚踏板控制（= foot control）

foot (headlamp) dimmer switch 前照灯近光的脚踏开关（= foot-operated antidazzle switch, foot-operated dip switch）

foot of bead （轮胎的）胎圈底（胎趾和胎踵的总称，见 bead toe, bead heel）

foot-operated 由脚控制的，脚踏控制的，脚操纵的

foot pedal pad 脚踏板垫（= pedal lining）

foot per second 英尺每秒（英制速度单位，ft/s, 1ft/s = 0.3048m/s）

foot per second squared (ft/s^2) 英尺每二次方秒（英制加速度单位，$1\text{ft/s}^2 = 0.3048\text{m/s}^2$）

foot-pound ①英尺-磅（英制功单位，$= 1.35 \text{N} \cdot \text{m}$，代号 ft-lb，即将 1 磅质量的物质，自地面垂直提升 1 英尺做

的功，= foot-pound force）②英尺-磅（英制单位的力矩单位，代号 ft-1b，即1磅力垂直作用于1英尺的力臂时的力矩，有时为了区别于功，称为 pound-foot，代号为 1b-ft）

foot-pound force 见 foot-pound②

foot powered 脚驱动的，足踏传动的

footprint area （轮胎等的触地）印痕面积，轮迹面积，触地面积（简称 footprint，亦称 contact area）

footprint aspect ratio 轮胎接地面的长宽比

foot print pressure （轮胎对地面）接触面压力，接触压强（= contact-area pressure）

footprint pressure distribution （轮胎的）印痕压力分布，触地压力分布

foot rest 搁脚板（汽车高速行驶，很少使用离合器时，供驾驶者左脚休息的踏板）

foot screw 地脚螺钉，地脚螺杆

foot space 腿脚活动空间（= leg room）

foot starter 脚踏起动机

foot step ①踏脚，脚蹬 ②台阶 ③梯级；立轴承，轴承架 ④脚步，步长

foot throttle 加速踏板（= accelerator pedal）

foot to head vibration 人体上下振动（沿人体脊柱方向的直线振动，参见 buttocks to head vibration）

foot valve 踏板操纵阀（= pedal operated valve）

foot warmer （驾驶员的）暖脚器

foot way ①人行道，步道，步径（在缘石线或行车道侧带线与路基边线之间，专供行人使用，= sidewalk）②小路

foot well （小客车地板）放脚坑（= floor well，指车身前围板底部的内凹部分，用于前座乘员和驾驶员搁脚和安装各种踏板）

FOPS 坠落物防护结构（falling object protective structure 的简称）

FOR ①燃油回路（fuel oil return 的简称）②快动作继电器（fast operating relay 的简称）

forage trailer 运饲料的挂车

forage wagon 运饲料的车辆

forbidding terrain 禁止通行的地面

force 力（国际单位制的代号为 F，单位为牛顿 newton，简称牛 N，CGS 制的单位为 dyne，英制的单位为 poundal，都是根据牛顿的 F = ma 定律导出的，即1单位的力使1单位的质量产生1单位的加速度）

force-air cooling 强制风冷

force-and-tone adjust screw （喇叭）音量和音调调节螺钉

force cell 测力传感器，测力计

force-circulation 压力循环，强迫循环

force control （汽车操纵性稳定性运动特性车辆控制方式中的）力控制（指对转向系施加力输入或限制时的汽车控制方式，与所需的位移无关，见 position control）

forced 强制的，强化的，加强的

forced circulation cooling 强制循环冷却（指用泵实现的冷却水循环冷却，亦称 forced feed cooling，见 pump-system water cooling）

forced damped vibration 强迫衰减振动，强迫阻尼振动

forced (down) shift ［美］（自动变速器节气门全开）强制换低挡（如紧急超车时，驾驶员猛踩油门，强制低挡阀起作用，使换挡阀向低挡方向移动，而实现的强制换低挡。实际上是由于人工干预，如将油门踩到底而造成的自动换挡机构的强制降挡，=［英］kick down）

forced downshift valve （自动变速器液力控制系统的节气门全开）强制换低挡阀（见 shift overcontrol valve

和 forced shift)
forced draught cooling 强制通风冷却
force-deflection characteristics (结构的)受力-变形特性,受力-挠曲特性,负荷挠度特性曲线
forced exhaust 强制排气(靠上升活塞或新鲜充量的推挤作用而将废气排出汽缸的排气过程)
forced-feed gun 压注式润滑枪 (= pressure gun)
forced-feed lubrication system 压力润滑系统
forced fit 压配合,紧配合 (= forcing fit, drive fit)
forced ignition 强制点火
forced induction engine 增压进气式发动机 (= super-charged engine, 指使用增压进气系统的发动机)
forced induction system (指使用增压器等的)强制进气系统,增压进气系统
forced locking device 强制闭锁装置,自动闭锁装置
forced lubrication 强制润滑(指由压力供油系统进行的润滑)
forced oscillations 强迫振荡,强迫振动
forced service ①强化工况下使用 ②(机器损坏后)被迫维修
forced torsional vibration 强迫扭转振动
forced undamped vibration 无阻尼的强迫振动
forced ventilation 强制通风 (= induced ventilation, positive ventilation)
forced vibrations 强迫振动,迫协振动 (= constrained vibration)
forced water cooling 强制循环水冷却 (= pump-system water cooling)
forced working (发动机)强化工作
force-elongation curve 拉力-伸长率曲线(拉伸力对伸长的关系曲线)
force feed gun 压注式润滑枪 (= pressure gun)
force-feed lubrication 压力润滑法 (= forced lubrication, 指由发动机驱动的机油泵通过发动机内的油道或外油管将机油压至各润滑点实现润滑的方法)
force field 力场
force fit 见 pressure fit
force-input device 加载装置
force limit device 负荷限制装置,作用力限制装置(亦写作 force limiting device)
force line 力作用线
forcemeter 测力计
force motor 执行电动机,作用马达
force of cohesion 黏聚力,黏性力,内聚力 (= cohesive force)
force of compression 压缩力 (= compressive force)
force plate 测力板
forcing fit 压配合,牢配合 (= forced fit)
forcing frequency 激振频率,扰动频率
forcing screw 拆卸工件的顶出螺钉
Ford [美] 福特(Henry Ford, 1863~1947年,原为钟表匠,1893年在 Detroit 市试制成一辆装用汽油机驱动的四轮车,采用自行车轮,故名 quidricycle,时速 20mile/h。1903年创建福特汽车公司,首先以新的设计思想,开发结构简单、省油、售价低廉的 T 型 Ford 普及型轿车。1913年创建世界第一条汽车流水生产线,到1925年生产量达200万辆,当时人称 Henry Ford 为汽车大王)
ford ①涉水 (fording capacity 车辆的涉水能力) ②浅滩,可涉水而过的地方
fordability (车辆)涉水能力(亦称

fordable depth (车辆的)允许涉水深度

Ford Cup 福特杯(一种黏度计,适用于测定稀胶合剂,密封胶剂的黏度,在具有一个特制小孔的杯内,盛入一定数量的试样,试样自小孔流尽的时间秒数则为福特黏度)

fording kit 供汽车涉水用的成套装备

Fordize 大量生产(按福特生产汽车的流水线方式,大批量生产产品)

Fordmatic 福特变速器,(一般指三个前进挡位,一个倒车挡位的汽车用变速器)

Ford Motor Company [美]福特汽车公司(创建于1903年,主要生产Ford, Mercury, Lincoln等牌号轿车)

Ford-o-matic transmission 福特车的一种自动变速器的商品名

Ford PAG Group 福特PAG集团(福特公司的高档车集团,旗下包括Aston、Jaguar、Land Rover、Martin等四大豪华品牌,以及原先的Volvo)

Ford's accident-avoidance system 福特公司的事故避免系统(该系统使用一台装在后视镜上方的摄像机并将所摄得的车流情况在仪表板内的屏幕上放映。当发现有其他车辆临近时,便会有绿色方框将该车框住,以引起驾驶者注意。如果发现该车已经对安全构成威胁,上述绿框变成红色,同时发出声响警告,并将安全带拉紧,以对付可能的碰撞,此外该系统还可以监视行人和自行车)

Ford type lug (蓄电池的)福特型接线板(由带螺栓、螺母的平接板组成的蓄电池接线棒和缆线之间一种特殊接线方式,亦称Fordtype terminal)

Ford viscosity 福特黏度(秒)(见 fording ability, ford trafficability)

Ford Cup)

fore ①前面,前部 ②前面的,前部的,在前的

fore-aft-and-cross steering linkage 带纵、横拉杆的转向杆系

fore-and-aft 前后方向的,纵向的

fore and aft acceleration sensor 前后方向加速度传感器(指纵向加速度传感器, = longitudinal acceleration sensor)

fore-and-aft grip (车轮或履带)沿全部接触长度上与地面的附着力,沿全部接触长度上与地面的抓着力

fore and aft G sensor 前、后方向加速度传感器

fore-and-aft shake 纵轴方向的平行振动

fore-and-aft shifts 纵向窜动,前后移动,前后窜动

fore-and-aft stability 前后稳定性,纵向稳定性

fore-and-aft tilt 纵向倾斜

fore axle 前桥,前轴(= forward axle, front axle)

forebody section 车身前部,(客车)前舱

fore carriage (全挂车)前转向架

forecast 预测,预报,预告,预定,展望

forecasting technique ①预测技术,预报技术 ②预告方法,预测法 ③预测技术装备

fore hand welding (气焊)左焊法,正手焊,前进焊

foreign ①外国的,涉外的(foreign-brand 外国厂牌的, foreign-built 外国制造的, = foreign made) ②不纯的,夹杂的,异(体)物的,外来的(foreign material 杂质,异物,外来物, = foreign matter, foreign substance, foreign object, 亦称 impurity substance; foreign-metal impurity 金属杂质, foreign particles 杂质微粒,

foreign object damage 落入异物而引起的损坏) ③外部的
forelock ①开口销,扁销,楔,栓 ②用开口销锁住
forelock bolt 带开口销的螺栓
forelocked bolt 用开口销锁住的螺栓
fore-octane-number 前辛烷值(见 FON)
foreside 前方
foresight Assistant (某些先进的导航系统的前方路况)预告功能(见 Predictive Power Management)
Forest air (function) (Infiniti M 系列空调系统的)森林飘香(功能)(商品用语,可自动切换,散发两种森林的芳香)
foresteerage 前轮转向
forest road 森林道路
forestructure (车身)前部骨架
fore-warming 预暖的,预热的(= preheating, preliminary heating)
forewarn system 预(先)警(告)系统(包括障碍物探测和防撞警报信息系统,可探测前、后、左、右的车辆,行人,静止物体等,向驾驶员传达预警信息)
forewheel 前轮(= front wheel)
forge 锻造;锻造炉;锻工车间;
forged aluminum wheel 锻造铝合金车轮
forge welding axle housing 锻压焊接桥壳(将方形钢环滚轧成桥壳的初始形状,然后锻压成半桥壳体,经修边后将两半桥壳体焊接成整体桥壳)
forging ①锻造 ②锻造的,锻工的 ③锻件
for hire (出租汽车)待租
fork ①叉,叉形件 ②分岔口,分歧点 ③分叉,分支,分歧,分流 ④做成叉形
fork arm 叉臂
fork ball end (离合器)分离叉球头支座
fork (ed) axle ①叉轴,叉端轴 ②叉端式前桥,叉式前桥(亦称 Elliot axle)
forked connecting rod (装两个活塞的)分叉式连杆
forked frame 叉形梁车架
forked rocker (arm) 叉形端摇臂(其叉形端控制两个气门)
forked tube 三通管
fork fuel control mechanism (柴油机)拨叉式油量调节机构(通过调节拉杆或调速杠杆上的调节拨叉拨动柱塞尾部的调节叉臂,使柱塞转动,以调节供油量的机构)
fork head 叉形头(例如连杆大头,变速器拨叉头等,= fork end)
fork lift truck 叉式装载机,叉车,铲车(可供集装箱装卸、堆码等作业之用,一般为前轮驱动,后桥动力输出操纵转向,起重叉架等,亦称 fork-lift, fork lifter, forklift loader, fork truck, chisel truck)
fork resistance tester (蓄电池)电压试验叉
fork wrench 叉形扳手
fork yoke (凸块式万向节的)凸块叉〔具有与中间连接元件的配合槽相配合的平面,并与输入或输出轴制成一体的叉形(头部)元件,其输入与输出端的凸块叉分别称 inner yoke 和 out yoke "内、外凸块叉",见 Tracta universal joint〕
form ①形式,形状,形态;外形,轮廓;方式,程式 ②模子,模板 ③形成,构成;产生;成形,仿形,造型,(模段,铸造)成型
formaldehyde 甲醛,蚁醛(HCHO)
formal test 正式试验,官方试验(指某种带官方性质的,或被公认有权威性质的试验机构所进行的试验,其结果带有法律权威的性质)
format ①板式,开本,格式 ②格

式，格式化（计算机中指：程序设计语言中的一种规定数据的字符表达形式的语言结构；对用于显示、打印输出或文卷的字符、字段、行等的规定排列方式和结构安排；数据单位的语法表示形式）

formation ①形成，构成，组成；成型，造型；建立，设立，组织，结构，构造；排列 ②道路路基面，路床面（包括路幅、路肩、人行道或自行车道等，但不包括填土方的边坡及其附属部分）

form drag 形状阻力（指置于流体中的物体运动时物体前后压力差所产生的阻力，因此亦称压力差阻力，形状阻力约占汽车空气压力阻力的60%，它直接与车身形状有关）

form drag coefficient 形状阻力系数（表征不同形状对形状阻力的影响程度）

"8" form driving test "8"字形车道行驶试验（评价汽车低速沿"8"字形曲线行驶时操舵力大小及操纵稳定性的试验）

formed-in-place 就地成型的（= formed-on-the-spot）

formed-in-place silicone type gasket 就地成型硅胶型密封垫（硅胶等材料的液体密封剂，装配时涂于密封处，即形成密封垫，简称 FIP gasket，= formed-on-the-spot silicone type gasket）

formed-plate accumulator （成）型（极）板式蓄电池

formed wire spring suspension （座椅的）成型钢丝弹簧悬架

former ①样板，成型量规；模型，模具；钣金工敲击成型用的木砧；成型刀具，成型设备（例如型材的成型轧辊）；靠模；（线圈）框架，骨架 ②从前的，以前的，在前的，早先的

formica 胶木，酚醛塑料板

form tolerance 零件外形公差

formula ①公式，方程式，计算式（简称f），结构式，化学式，分子式 ②配方，方案，准则 ③（特指一种汽车赛事的详细规则，我国直译为）方程式［如：formula I 指国际赛车联盟制定的被认为是世界冠军赛的顶级汽车大奖赛（我国称一级方程式大奖赛的）规则，简称F-1。按照F-1的规定，参加F-1大奖赛的赛车 V = 3.5L, P = 477.75 kW，见 Formula I race］

formula car （符合汽车赛规则的赛车，我国直译为）方程式赛车（见 formula③）

formula junior 准级赛车（指使用运动车或一般轿车总成，装配成的准级赛车，尺寸小于 formula car）

Formula Matic 带手控模式的自动变速系统（见 F Matic）

Formula One auto racing track 一级方程式赛车跑道（参见 formula Race）

Formula Race F-1 大奖赛（我国译为方程式赛车大奖赛简称方程式汽车大赛。国际赛车联盟规定大奖赛用车分为三个级别：发动机排量 V = 2L，功率 P = 124.95kW 为三级；V = 3L, P = 399.125kW 为二级；V = 3.5L, P = 477.75kW 为一级。Formula 1Race 指使用国际赛车联盟规定的一级赛车及其他有关规则进行的赛车，Formula 2 或 3race 则分别指使用二级或三级赛车并按相应规则进行的赛事。1950 年 5 月 13 日在英国银石赛车场，举行了第一次 F-1 大赛）

Formula 1-style shifting 一级方程式赛车型换挡机构

formula weight 分子量，（化学）式量

forthcoming model 新设计的形式，即将出现的形式，即将投产的

新形式

fortified tire 加强轮胎

FORTRAN （计算机）公式翻译编程语言，FORTRAN 语言（formula translation 或 Formula Translating system 的简称，一种为了用算术公式来表达计算机程序的编程语言，另一种主要为数值计算应用而设计的编程语言。FORTRAN 语言主要用于科学计算，工程技术及数学应用中）

forward ①向前的，前面的，前方的；提前的，预先的 ②［动］促进，助长；运送，转运

forward acceleration 前进加速度（质心加速度沿运动坐标系"moving axis system"的 x_0 轴方向的分量，取负值时加速度为减速度"deceleration"）

forward ageny 运输业（= forwarding business）

forward-and-rearward visibility （车辆）前后方视界

forward axle 前桥，前轴（= fore axle）

forward bias ①正向偏压，顺向偏压 ②加正向偏压，加顺向偏压

forward (brake) band （自动变速器的）前进挡制动带

forward brush lead （换向器）电刷前移（沿着旋转方向）量

forward bulkhead 见 front bulkhead

forward cab ①平头驾驶室（见 forward control cab）②前翻式驾驶室，前倾式驾驶室

forward-collision alert 前面碰撞警报

forward-collision mitigation brake system 见 forward-collision mitigation system

forward-collision mitigation system 前面碰撞减轻系统（简称 FCM system，亦称 forward-collision mitigation brake system，简称 FCMB system。监测前方车辆的距离和速度，当发现有碰撞危险时，即发出警报并自动减速或停车，以回避碰撞或减轻碰撞伤害）

forward conductance （晶体）前向电导

forward control (layout) cab （货车，大客车等的）前置式驾驶室（简称 forward cabnet，美称 cab over engine，或 cab-ahead-of engine，指位于发动机上方或前方的驾驶室，其中包括平头驾驶室及驾驶室在发动机上方的形式中的发动机部分突出驾驶室前部的短头驾驶室）

forward-control position of the driver 前置驾驶座位（驾驶座在发动机旁，= forward driving position, driver, beside-engine）

forward control truck 前置驾驶（式载）货（汽）车（如：驾驶室在发动机前方或上方的平头货车"cab-ahead-of-engine truck"，"cab over engine truck"，亦称"cab forward type truck"，见 forward cab①）

forward current rating 额定正向电流

forward curved blade （叶轮）前弯叶片

forward displacement ①前移距离，前进位移 ②（特指汽车碰撞时，乘员前移直到碰着障碍物或车身内饰的）前冲距离

forward drive 前轮驱动 [= front (end) drive]

forward driving position 前置驾驶位（= forward-control position of the driver 指驾驶位在发动机和前桥的前方）

forward efficiency （汽车转向系的）正效率（指转向摇臂轴输出功率与转向轴输入功率之比）

forward-facing seat （面向前方的）正向座椅

forward gear ①前进挡 ②前进挡齿轮

forward located depression （转子发动机的）前置凹坑（指转子工作面凹坑的位置偏向前方）

forward looking radar 前视探测雷达，前方侦察雷达

forward-mounted 前部安装的

forward movement 前进运动

Forward-obstruction warning system 前方障碍物警报系统（注意，勿与确认碰撞难以避免时即自动紧急制动以避免或减轻撞击强度的 collision mitigation system 混淆）

forward perception （汽车）驾驶员前方视野

forward position （变速杆）前进挡位置

forward-positioned gear-change lever 前置式变速杆（不装在驾驶座旁，而是向前移、装在仪表板上，驾驶者可自由地从左门或右门上车）

forward power 正向功率（指放大器或发电机的输出向荷载提供的功率）

forward rear axle （三桥汽车的）中桥

forward-reverse lever 前进-后退换挡杆，倒顺挡换挡杆

forward-reverse rocking cycle 汽车频繁地时而倒车时而正车行驶

forward-reverse switch 正反转开关

forward sensor （安全气囊系统的）车头传感器，前置传感器（一般装于汽车最前端，如：车头散热器护栅，用于首先测出车速因碰撞引起的突然异常猛降，而向控制模块发出碰撞信息的传感器）

forward shaft 前轴

forward shift ①前移 ②挂前进挡

forward shoe 见 leading shoe

forward speed ①前进车速（指质心速度沿运动坐标系 "moving axis system" 的 x_0 轴的分量，= forward velocity）；② （变速器的）前进挡

forward type ①平头型（汽车）②前进式

forward velocity 见 forward speed①

forward visibility （车辆）前方视野

fossil flax 石棉（= earth flax）

fossil fuel ①（煤，石油等）矿物燃料，化石燃料，古生物燃料 ②石油类燃料

fossil oil 石油，"petroleum" 的旧称

FOT ①车上交货运价（free on truck 的简称）②纤维光学阴极射线管（fiber optics cathode ray tube 的简称）

Foucault current 伏科电涡流，涡流（见 stray current）

foul ①污物，脏东西 ②弄脏的，污秽的 ③堵塞的，淤塞的 ④失效的 ⑤弄脏；堵塞，淤塞 ⑥（特指）火花塞积炭，结胶 ⑦妨碍，干扰

foul air 污染的空气，不干净的空气

fouled (spark) plug 积炭火花塞，污垢火花塞

foul electrolyte 废电解液，用过的电解液

foul gas 有害气体

fouling ①污染，脏污；污损（如火花塞积炭或结胶）②污染物 ③（仪表）读数不准

foul-proof 防（污物）堵塞的

foul valve 排污阀

foundation ①机座，底板，基础，地脚 ②出发点，基本原则 ③创立，建立，创办 ④根据

foundation bolt 地脚螺栓（= fang bolt）

foundation brakes ①主制动器（相对于汽车的辅助制动器而言）②（指除在被制动车轮内，随车轮旋转的部件以外的）制动机构 ③同②，但包括制动鼓

foundry(cast)iron 生铁，铸铁，铸造

用铁

fountain brush 喷水刷

"four" 四缸发动机（four cylinder engine 的简称）

four-axle rigid（truck） 四轴单体货车，单体四桥货车（区别于四轴的牵引车-挂车列车，简称 four-axle truck，见 rigid truck）

four-ball tester 四球试验机（测定润滑剂的减磨性）

four-banger ［美俚］噪声大的破旧四缸发动机老爷车（＝four-cylinder engine，六缸发动机称 six banger，余类推）

four-bar linkage 四连杆机构

four-bar linkage type suspension 四连杆式悬架（见 5-link type suspension）

four-barrel carburetor 四腔化油器（亦称 four-choke carburettor，指有四个腔体，各有一组喉管，四个腔分成相同的两组，每组中两个腔体内部构造作用不同，形成一个双腔分动化油器，参见 two-barrel duplex carburetor）

four-bar steering linkage 梯形转向杆系，四杆转向拉杆机构（＝Ackerman steering linkage）

four-beam headlamp 四灯芯式前照灯

four-bearing crankshaft 四（道主）轴承（式）曲轴

four-bladed fan 四叶片风扇（＝four bladed ventilator）

four-boss breaker cam （分电盘等的）四角凸轮，四楞凸轮，四棱凸轮

four-by-four（vehicle） 4×4 汽车（双轴全轮驱动车辆，×号前的数字表示全车的车轮数，×号后的数字表示驱动轮数，如：4×2 为四轮，即双轴，两轮驱动式汽车，余类推）

four-channel design antilock brake system 四回路防抱死制动系统（由四个车轮速度传感器和四个制动压力调节阀及其管路组成的防抱死制动系统，亦称 H-type ABS）

four-channel, four speed-sensors, four pressure-modulation-valves type antilock system ①（轿车的）四路、四速传感器、四压力调节阀型防抱死（制动）系统（每个车轮一个独立回路、都装有一个传感器和一个压力调节阀的四回路防抱死制动系统）②（6×4 货车或半挂牵引车的）四通路、四速传感器，四压力调节器型防抱死系统（两前轮和后四轮左、右两侧各有一套独立制动回路、传感器和压力调节器）

four-corner air suspension 全轮空气悬架，四轮空气悬架

four-cornered 四角的

four cycle ①四冲程循环（美，＝four stroke cycle）②四冲程发动机（＝four-cycle engine 的简称）

four-direction adjustable steering wheel 四方向可调式转向盘

four-directional adjustable hollow head rest 四方向可调空心头枕

four-door cabriolet ［美］四门敞篷轿车［指带可升起和放下的可折叠式软篷的四门带窗轿车，＝convertible sedan，英称 touring（car）或 tourer。注意 cabriolet 前后无说明词时一般指两门软篷活顶（敞篷）车］

four door convertible car 四门（车篷可折叠式敞篷的）活顶轿车

four-door hardtop saloon 四门硬顶轿车

four-door sedan ［美］四门轿车（轿车中最普遍和最典型的固定顶、四门、前、后两排座位，中间无隔断的厢式车型，一般称 sedan。sedan 前无特别说明时，即指四门 sedan，英称 saloon，亦称 four-door saloon，见 sedan）

four-gas analyzer 四气分析仪（如：可精确测定废气中 HC、CO、CO_2 和 O_2 四种成分含量的分析仪，亦称 four-gas engine analyzer）

Fourier（'s）analyser 傅里叶分析器，傅氏分析器（见 Fourie transform）

Fourier transform 傅里叶变换（是分析信号的一种数学工具，可以把时间函数转换为频率函数，即把信号从时间域转换到频率域上进行分析，从而可分析信号的频率结构及含量）

four-in-line engine 直列四缸发动机

four-lane road 四车道道路，四车道公路

four-level super crossings 四层立体交叉口

four-light（body） 有四个侧窗的车厢，四侧窗车身

four-light cabriolet 有四个侧窗的活顶轿车（一般为四门，见 four-door cabriolet）

four-link type suspension 四连杆式悬架（亦称 four bar linkage type suspension，见 5-link type suspension）

four lobe cam 四凸面凸轮

four-on-the-floor 变速杆装在车身地板上的四挡手动变速器

four-passenger body 四座车身

four-phase cycle （转子发动机的）四相循环（相当于往复式发动机的四冲程循环）

four phase single（two）stage torque converter 四相单（双）级液力变矩器（借助于单向轮、离合器或制动器改变变矩器叶轮在工作过程中的作用，从而改变变矩器的功能，变矩器可变更的功能的数称为相数，所谓四相指该变矩器可变更为变矩、耦合、直接传动等四种功能。安装在泵轮与导轮，或导轮与导轮之间的刚性连接的涡旋元件数称为级，刚性连接的数有两个的称双级，一个的称单级）

four-piece rim 四构件式轮辋（由轮辋体、两个可拆式挡圈、一个锁圈组成，或由轮辋体及可拆式座圈、挡圈和锁圈各一个组成）

four pin driven collar nut 四销孔突缘螺母

four piston linkage type fuel consumption meter 四活塞联动式油耗计

four-ply tyre 四层帘布层轮胎

four-point suspension 四点式悬架

four-pole 四极的

four-post car lift 四柱汽车举升器

four-race roller bearing 四排滚子式轴承

four-range 四区域的，四区间的，四区段的（如：仪表量程）

four-range transmission 四挡变速器（= four speed transmission）

four-roller ware generator （谐波齿轮传动中的）四滚轮波发生器（在滚轮架上装有四个滚轮的双波发生器）

four-rotor engine 四缸转子发动机

four-row 四列的，四排的

four-screw driver 四用螺钉旋具（可换螺钉旋具头的螺钉旋具的一种，具有四个可换的螺钉旋具头）

four-seater ①四座轿车 ②四座位的

four（4）-sensor，four（4）-channel ABS 四传感器、四通道式防抱死制动系统（其中，ABS 为 anti-lock brake system 的简称，指每一车轮均装有一转速传感器并由一个独立液压通道控制的防抱死系统）

four-sensor，three-channel ABS 四传感器、三通道式防抱死制动系统[指每一车轮均装有一转速传感器，两前轮分别由两条独立液压通道控

制，而两后轮则按低选原则（见 select-low），由一条液压通道同时控制的防抱死制动系统]

four-sensor, two-channel ABS 四传感器、两通道式 ABS（每一车轮装有一个转速传感器，但其两条液压通道呈 X 型布置，每条液压通道控制一个前轮和一个与之对角位置的后轮）

four sided rotor （转子发动机中的一种）四角转子，四角旋转活塞

four silent-speed gearbox 四速无声变速器，无声四挡变速器

foursome cabriolet 四座活顶轿车（见 four door cabriolet）

four-spark ignition coil 四火花点火线圈（由两个初级绕组和一个次级绕组组成）

four-speed all-indirect transaxle 无直接挡的四挡变速驱动桥（装有四个非直接挡的变速器的驱动桥）

four-speed box with gear-up top 带超速挡的四挡变速器

four-speed planetary transmission 四挡行星齿轮变速器（多在 Simpson 结构基础上加一个行星排组成，以提高燃料经济性）

four spring bogie 四弹簧悬架式并装双桥（指每一根桥由两架弹簧悬挂的并装双桥，见 four spring non-reactive 或 reactive suspension）

four spring non-reactive suspension （并装双桥的）非平衡式四弹簧悬架，非互动式四弹簧悬架（各弹簧的后端均与一反力杆联结，而各弹簧之间无互动作用，弹簧只承受垂直力和侧向力，制动、驱动及其反作用力由反力杆或称推力杆承受）

four spring reactive bogie 见 four spring reactive suspension

four spring reactive suspension （重型车辆并装双桥的）平衡式四弹簧悬架，互动式四弹簧悬架（各车桥均由右、左两架钢板弹簧悬挂，而前、后车桥相邻两弹簧由一称为平衡臂的中心枢轴摆杆连接，可使前、后两车桥载荷成一定比例。此时，钢板弹簧只传递垂直力和侧向力，驱动与制动及其相应的反作用力由推力杆承受）

four-square test 四方试验（通过作用于一对啮合齿轮的接触压力评定润滑油脂润滑性能的试验）

four-stage compressor 四级压缩机

four-stop-per mile driving cycle 每英里停车四次的行驶循环

four-stroke cycle 四冲程循环（含有进气、压缩、燃烧-膨胀和排气四个冲程的实际循环）

four-stroke engine 四冲程发动机（=［美］four cycle engine，活塞经过四个冲程完成一个工作循环的发动机）

four stroking （二冲程发动机的）四冲程着火（指怠速或整个运转中混合气过浓时二冲程发动机出现的每隔一个循环着火一次的不正常工况）

fourth ① 第四；四分之一 ② 第四的；四分之一的 ③ 四挡（= fourth gear）

four-throw crankshaft 四拐曲轴，四曲柄曲轴

four-tire car 四轮胎轿车（指使用被尖物刺穿或放炮漏气后仍能继续行驶的轮胎，不再需要备用胎，因此全车只有四个轮胎的轿车，参见 five-tire car）

four-valve engine 四气门发动机（指每缸有两个进气门、两个排气门的发动机）

four-valve head 四气门发动机汽缸盖

four-way 四通的（接头，阀门管道等），十字形的（交叉路口，扳手等），四个方向的（上、下、左、

右均可动,可调的等)

four-way emergency flasher 紧急事故四面闪光信号系统(= four-way hazard flasher)

four-way intersection (道路的)十字交叉,十字路口,交叉路口(两条道路的交叉点。当交叉角小于75°或大于105°时,称为 four-way oblique intersection 斜十字路口,斜交叉路口;当交叉角大于75°,小于105°时,称为 four-way right-angled intersection 正十字路口,十字交叉路口)

four-way stop sign (公路交叉路口处的)四向停车标志

four-way wheel wrench 见 wheel nut spider

four wheel alignment 四轮定位(指对两前轮和两后轮一起定位作业,亦称 all wheel alignment)

four-wheel antilock disc brake 四轮防抱死盘式制动器

four-wheel drift 四轮飘滑转向(指赛车转向技巧,即弯道转向时有意让四轮侧滑实现快速回转,简称 drift)

four-wheel drive 四轮驱动,(四轮车的)全轮驱动(简称4WD或FWD,亦写作 4×4)

four-wheel drive bogie 四轮驱动并装双后桥

four-wheel drive with constant power distribution 前、后轮动力固定分配式四轮驱动(指前、后轮动力分配比例不可改变的常规四轮驱动,亦写作 four-wheel drive with fixed power distribution)

four-wheeled timber trailer 四轮运木挂车,双轴长挂车

four-wheel garage jack 车库用四轮千斤顶,车库用四轮举升器

four-wheel separated ABS with high-pressure accumulator 带高压储能器的分体式四轮防抱死制动系统(由制动总泵带真空助力器、电子控制模块、包括一个电动机泵、一个压力开关和一个高压储能器的动力单元,以及三个电磁阀和四个分泵活塞的压力调节器及各车轮转速传感器等各自独立的分体式总成组成。当上述各独立总成都组合在一起,成为一个整体总成时,称为带高压蓄能器的整体式四轮防抱死制动系统"four-wheel integral ABS with high-pressure accumulator"。电动机泵用于保持蓄能器内的规定液压,在分体式中,高压储能器液压用于推动调节器活塞,而在整体式中高压储能器的液压用于取代真空助力器,增加驾驶者对总泵活塞的踩踏力)

four-wheel separated ABS with low-pressure accumulator 带低压储能器的分体式四轮防抱死系统

four-wheel steering system 四轮转向系统,(四轮汽车的)全轮转向系统(简称4WS系统。中、低速行驶转向时,后轮朝前轮相反的方向转向,以使转弯半径最小,提高车辆转向响应性,高速行驶转向时,前、后轮同方向转向,以保证车辆行驶的稳定性,可分为全机械式,电子液压、电子-机械-液压和全电子式等多种)

four zone air condition system 四区(域温度控制)空调系统(可分别对车厢内前、后、左、右四个区域的温度作独立调控的空调系统)

FP ①纸绝缘薄膜电容器(film and paper condenser 的简称)②竣工零件[finished piece(s) 的简称]③消火栓(fire plug 的简称)④摩擦功率(friction power 的简称)⑤燃油泵(fuel pump 的简称)

fp ①摩擦功率(friction power 的简

称）②供油泵，供给泵（feed pump 的简称）③闪点，起爆温度（flash point 的简称）④防火的，耐火的（fire proof 的简称）⑤英尺-磅（foot-pound 的简称）⑥冰点，凝固点（freezing point 的简称）

FPDM （电动）燃油泵驱动模块（fuel pump drive module 的简称，该模块根据动力控制模块"PCM"的占空比信号控制油泵转速，以满足在各种工况下对油泵最佳输油量的要求）

FP-ECU 汽油泵电子控制模块（fuel pump-electronic control unit 的简称，根据发动机转速、节气门开度、冷却水温、进气空气温度等传感器的信息，控制汽油泵电动机的开、停及驱动电压，以控制供油量及输油压力）

FPGA 现场可编程门陈列（field programmable gate array 的简称，一种可由用户实现程序编制的可编程集成电路，即可编程门阵列，见 field-programmable gate array）

FPLA 现场可编程逻辑阵列（field programmable logic array 的简称，一种可由用户自己在使用时通过烧断熔丝实现程序编制的可编程逻辑阵列）

FPRF 耐火的，防火的（fireproof 的简称）

FPS ①（汽车）防火系统（fire protection system 的简称）②英尺-磅-秒（foot-pound-second 的简称）

FPU 燃料净化设备（fuel purification unit 的简称）

FQCY 频率（frequency 的简称）

FR ①设备要求（facility request 的简称）②平均故障率（failure rate 的简称）③故障记录（failure record 的简称）④故障报告（failure report 的简称）⑤快速复原继电器（fast release relay 的简称）⑥励磁变阻器（field rheostat 的简称）⑦光测（flash ranging 的简称）⑧频率响应（frequency response 的简称）

fraction ①小数，分数，分式，比值，百分率②碎块，碎屑成分③组成④粒度组成，黏度级⑤馏分，分馏物（石油的分馏产物）

fractional ①分数的，小数的②部分的 ③分部的，分级的，分馏的 ④馏分的

fractional combustion 部分燃烧

fraction(al) horsepower ①小马力（小于 0.735kW 或 1 马力。常用于英国,北美工业界,简称 FHP）②小马力的

fractional load 部分载荷，部分负荷

fraction composition （燃油）馏分的成分，馏分

fraction defective 次品百分率（一批产品中有缺陷产品的比值）

fraction of an inch 零点几英寸

fraction ratio decimation filter 分数比抽取滤波器

fractography 金属断面检查法，金属断面的显微镜观察，断口组织试验（法）

fracture ①破裂，断裂，折断②裂缝，裂痕,断口，断裂面③使破裂，使断裂，使折断

fracture in shear 剪切断裂

fracture load by bending 挠折载荷，弯曲断裂载荷

fracture prediction technology 断裂预测技术

fracture stress 断裂应力（断裂开始时最小横截面积上的真实应力）

fracture toughness 断裂韧度（量度裂纹扩展阻力的通用术语）

fragile article 易碎品

fragility 脆性，易碎性，脆弱（= fragileness）

fragility factor 易碎指标，碰坏指标（电子设备的一种规定指标，防止

搬运等过程中摔坏。测试方法系采取摔落试验，测定所能承受的摔落速度值）

fragmentation test 破碎试验（指风窗玻璃破碎后，碎片对人的伤害性试验，用破碎后碎片的尺寸、形状、数量、分布状况来综合评价）

fraising ①铣切（活塞环槽等）②铰孔

frame ①机架（对发动机指装在机座上，围住曲轴箱上部支承汽缸水套，或汽缸体的零件）②车架③大梁④壳体；机壳⑤桁架，构架，刚架；框架，骨架⑥运件包（运输目的整体硬包装）⑦（数据传输和数据通信中的）帧（发送单位或数据单位）

frame alignment equipment 车架校正设备

frame altitude 车架离地高度（指货车车架上平面与车支承平面间的距离，= frame height）

frame-attached 固定在车架上的

frame bulkhead 车架横向加强板

frame car 车架式轿车（相对无车架的承载式车身轿车而言）

frame cylinder （铰接式车架的）转向油缸

frame extension 车架延长部分，大梁延长部分

frame free length （货车）车架自由长度（指车架装上驾驶室后总长中剩余的可"自由"配置的长度，即驾驶室后壁至车架后端面，不含拖挂装置的长度）

frame gauge （汽车）车架校正规，车架量规

frame geometry 车架几何形状

frame girder 见 frame rails

frame in data transmission 数据传输中的帧（指被起始和终止标志括起来并包括上述标志的一列连续的二进制位，参见 frame in SDLC）

frame in SDLC 同步数据链路控制中的帧（作为每条命令、每次应答及所有用 SDLC 规程传输的信息的载体的二进制位的组合，每一帧都有其起始和结束标志）

frameless 无架的

frameless glass （车身）无框架的风窗玻璃

frameless vehicle 无车架式车辆（包括无车架式轿车，客车和液罐车等，= frameless construction vehicle，亦称整体式车身车辆 integral body 和承载式结构车身车辆 load-carrying structure）

frameless window 无框窗（只有窗孔而无边框）

frame lift （汽车的）车身底架支撑式举升器（举升器的撑臂支撑在前后车轮间的车身底架上。汽车被举升时，其前、后桥不承受负荷）

frame member 车架构件

frame number 车架号码，车架编号

frame of triangular bridge-type construction 三角形桁架式结构车架

frame panel （底板式车架的）车架底板（指与车架制成一体的厚钢底板，见 platform type frame）

frame parallelism 车架平行度

frame press （汽车）车身-车架（校修）压力机

frame racking 车架扭曲

frame rails （一般指货车）车架（最外侧的两根纵）大梁（亦称 sill, frame side member, frame side rail, frame girder）

frame side member 见 frame rails

frame side rail 见 frame rails

frame-steered 腰扭式转向的（其前、后部分铰接，可作相对回转，以实现转向的 articulated frame"铰接式车架"）

frame straighter 车架校直装置，车架调校机

frame structure type body (轿车的)车架结构式车身

frame trap 燃气阻断阀(一般指位于由曲轴箱通往进气系的管道中,用于阻断被点燃的串缸气的阀门等)

frame turn-over hoist 车架翻转器(可使车架翻转180°的举升器)

frame weave 车架晃动,车架摆动,车架摇动(亦写作 frame weaving)

frame width 车架宽度(左纵梁外线至右纵梁外线)

frame with cruciform bearing X形撑梁车架(参见 X-type frame)

framework ①骨架,框架,构架,桁架,机架,机座 ②构架工程

framework crosspiece 构架的横构件

framework material (轮胎的)骨架材料(指构成外胎骨架的纤维织物和金属材料)

framework of body 车身骨架,车身构架

frame work type body (赛车等的)桁架结构式车身(整个车身为桁架结构,亦称立体构架型车身)

franchised dealer (汽车制造厂的)特许销售维修商(= authorized dealer)

frangibility 脆性,脆弱性,易碎性

frangible 脆弱的,易脆的

fray ①擦,磨,磨损,磨伤,擦断 ②磨损处

FRC 纤维强化复合材料(fiber-reinforced composite 的简称)

FRCP 设备的远距离控制台(facility remote control panel 的简称)

free ①自由的,不受约束的;松动的;独立的,单个的;任意的,随便的;畅通的,流利的,浮离的;空闲的,有空的;免费的,免税的 ②使自由,释放;解除,免除,使解脱;卸下,拆下;使空转,分离,放出

free acceleration engine tester 发动机无外载测功仪,发动机自由加速测功仪(在已知发动机运转件惯量的条件下,用自由加速测试法测算发动机功率)

free acceleration method (烟度测定的)自由加速法(在空挡无外载条件下,将柴油机由怠速急加速到最高转速的过程中,用烟度计测定排气烟度)

free access road 自由进入的道路,免费进入的道路

free beam 自由支撑梁,简支梁(= freely supported beam, simple beam)

free bearing 转向节轴承,铰链支撑(见 knuckle bearing)

free bend 自由弯曲(指在部件或试样两端部施压力,而不在最大弯曲点施加力,产生的弯曲)

free box wrench 活套筒扳手

free brake pedal travel 制动踏板自由行程(踩下踏板时,从踩板的原始位置开始到制动阀或制动主缸开始起作用为止,踏板所移动的距离)

free camber 自由弯曲度(如:未加荷重时弹簧钢板的自由状态弯曲度)

free carbon 游离碳

free cementite 游离渗碳体,过共析渗碳体

free clearance 自由间隙,浮隙,自由行程

free control 自由控制(对转向系不加任何约束的控制,参见 force control)

Freedom Car Partnership (2002年由美国总统提出的)自由轿车伙伴宣言(斥资120亿美元建立氢燃料研究奖励基金,鼓励氢燃料电池汽车的开发)

Freedom-drive (Jeep SUV 的)"自主驱动"系统(电子控制式自适应性四轮驱动系统的商品名,平时仅

前轮驱动,当电子控制系统测得前轮打滑时立即自动将50%的动力分配至后轮,实现"50/50"的四轮驱动)

freedom of movement 运动自由度(指运动体可自运动的方向,如两自由度,表示可在两个方向内自由运动等)

freedom of planetary gears 行星齿轮机构的自由度

free electron 自由电子

free-electron laser 自由电子激光,(其波长可以调节,可用来使某一物质增加或去掉电子,而改变其物质结构,形成新的物质)

free engine clutch 自由轮离合器,超速离合器(见 overrunning clutch)

free exhaust 自由排气(从开始排气到汽缸内的压力等于排气管内压力时为止的时间内的排气过程)

free expressway 免费快速公路,免费汽车专用公路(见 expressway)

free-fall velocity 自由落体速度,自由下落速度

free-field wedge 自由场楔(指无回声室内壁的楔形消声-吸声翅)

free-float flowmeter 浮子式流量计(= float-type flowmeter)

free-floating pin (可在活塞和连杆小头活塞销孔内自由转动的)自由浮动式活塞销,全浮式活塞销

free-flowing ①自由流动,自由流动状态 ②自由流动的,直流的,直通的,无阻碍的

free-flow operating speed 自由行驶车速(在不受其他交通影响时,驾驶人自由选定的车速,亦称 free speed)

free from acid 无酸的

free from contamination 没有污染的;无杂质的

free gap (活塞环)在自由状态下的间隙

free gear 自由轮,空转轮,浮滑轮(= free wheel)

free gyroscope (三)自由(度)陀螺仪

free-haul distance 免费运距,免费搬运距离

free jet tunnel 敞开式风洞,开口式风洞

free jet turbine 自由喷射式涡轮机

free lateral run-out (车轮和轮胎的)自由横向偏摆度(车轮和轮胎的中心平面,在自由状态下,相对车桥轴线的不垂直度,引起车轮和轮胎的动不平衡,行驶时,造成轮胎接地面蛇行,致使车身横向振动)

free length 自由长度(弹簧,如:气门弹簧,不受力时的长度)

free movement of the steering wheel 转向盘自由转动量,转向盘的空转量

free number of coils 螺旋弹簧自由圈数(指在工作中可沿作用力方向"自由"运动的圈数,等于从总圈数中减两端的各一圈,见 number of spring coils)

free of gear changing way 高速公路(见 free way)

free oscillations 自由振荡;自由振动

free passing 允许超车

free pedal travel 踏板自由行程(踩下踏板时,从其原始位置到踏板控制的机件起作用时为止的踏板行程)

free-piston 自由活塞式的

free-piston compressor 自由活塞式压缩机

free piston gas generator 自由活塞燃气发生器(亦称 free-piston gasifier)

free piston gas turbine 自由活塞式燃气轮机

free-piston (-type) engine 自由活塞

式发动机
free play 齿隙,空程,自由行程;空隙,自由间隙(美称 lash)
free play of clutch 离合器踏板自由行程(= clutch pedal clearance, free travel of clutch pedal)
free play of steering wheel 转向盘自由行程(转向轮在直线行驶位置时,转向盘的空转角度)
free play of tappet 挺杆自由间隙
free position 空挡(位置)
free power turbine 自由动力涡轮式(车用)燃气轮机(在这种燃气轮机中,动力涡轮与压气机-压气机涡轮之间无机械连接,即压气机轴与动力输出涡轮轴是分开的双轴式结构)
free radial run-out (汽车轮胎的)自由径向跳动,自由失圆度(指轮胎装在车轮上以后,在自由状态时,由胎面圆周测出的半径差值,是汽车行驶时,车桥上下振动的起因之一)
free radius (轮胎的)自由半径(指轮胎按规定充气后,在无负荷状况下直径的一半)
free-revolving engine 自由旋转式发动机(无限速装置,达到规定转速后自动切断燃油供给或指能直接加速到高转速的发动机)
free rise density 自由状态密度(在不受约束力条件下的密度)
free roadside assistance/recovery service 沿途免费救援/抢修(汽车)服务(站),(汽车的)沿途免费抢救(站)
free rolling 自由滚动的
free-rolling tyre ①平行环形花纹轮胎②从动轮轮胎,自由轮胎
free-rolling vehicle 滑行(中的)车辆(= coasting vehicle)
free rolling wheel 自由滚动车轮(在有垂直载荷的条件下,没有驱动力矩和制动力矩时的滚动车轮)
free-rotating valve 自由旋转阀(= free-turning valve)
Freerson (screw) driver 十字(形)螺钉旋具,十字槽(螺钉)螺钉起子
free (running) fit 自由配合,轻动配合
free running ①自由行程 ②无负载运转,空转 ③自由振荡,自激 ④不同步
free (running) frequency 自然频率,固有频率,自由振动频率(指物体不受周期性策动力时的振动频率,是由振动系统本身的特性决定的,亦称 free vibration frequency, natural frequency)
free-running sweep 不同步的扫描,自激扫描
free section 可拆部分
free service 免费服务,免费维修,免费救援
free shape 自由形状(指车身或前照灯反光镜等的形状只取决于发挥最佳性能的要求,即:何种形状能产生最佳性能,便取何种形状的设计方式)
free-sliding spline 滑动花键
free-space diagram 空间图,空间坐标图
free speed (汽车的)自由车速(指不受其他交通条件干扰下的车速,见 free-flow operating speed)
free state 自由状态
free steering control (汽车的)自由方向控制(车道试验法),松开转向盘(车道试验法)(指在汽车车道试验中,当汽车受到如横风等的外力干涉时,驾驶员撒手,松开转向盘,测试其瞬态与稳态响应,以评价其方向稳定性)
free-stream 自由气流,无旋涡气流,

未扰动气流,远前方的迎面气流,自由流线

Freestyle 自由风格(福特兼有运动型多用途车、微型厢式货车和轿车的特点的新型混合型"crossover"乘用车)

Free style door system (某些运动型轿车的)自由式车门系统[由四扇(每侧两扇)中央开启式车门组成,无固定后门的中柱,与常规的两门车比较后座乘员容易进出]

free tractive force (汽车的)剩余牵引力(在一定车速下,驱动轮上所能产生的最大牵引力减去在此车速下行驶时的滚动阻力、空气阻力后所余的牵引力,可自由地供爬坡、拖挂或加速等使用,故亦称自由牵引力和后备牵引力)

free travel 自由行程(指将踏板踩到它所控制的机构开始作用之前的空行程, = idle travel)

free-valve mechanism 自由气门机构(free-turning 或 free-rotating valve-mechanism 的简称,在气门开启时,气门弹簧不作用于气门,使气门可自由旋转)

free vibration 自由振动,固有振动(= natural vibration,指物体无策动力,即无周期性外力作用下的振动)

free water 非结合水,自由水

freeway 高速公路([美]全封闭,全部立体交叉,中间有分离带,全入口控制的免费多车道,并有车速限制的高级公路。在这种公路上行驶,车辆无任何障碍,通行无阻,即"free",故名,亦说在这种公路上可一路高速通行,无须换挡,因而是 free of gear changing way 的简称)

freeway in the sky 空中高速公路(美国宇航局和联邦航空局正在联合研究的"小型飞行器交通系统"的内容之一,给每辆飞行汽车指引安全飞行路线)

freeway management system 高速公路管理系统(系 1TS 的一项基础分支)

free-way network charge system 高速公路联网收费系统

freeway ramp 高速公路出入道

freeway ramp metering rates 高速公路入口车道通行量计算,高速公路入口车道额定通行量

freeway surveillance and control system ①高速道路监视管理制度 ②高速公路监视管理系统

free wheel ①自由轮,超越离合器(free wheel clutch 的简称,一种当被驱动件的转速超过驱动件的转速时,便使二者自动脱开或滑脱成空挡,不再传递转矩,即仅可单方向传动的单向离合器, = one way clutch。按其传动件的形式可分为 free wheel roller clutch "滚柱式自由轮离合器", free wheel spray clutch "楔块式自由轮离合器"等)②(特指旧时汽车上使用的)超速脱挡离合器(汽车下坡滑行等工况下,一旦传动系统转速超过发动机转速,该离合器便自动脱开发动机与传动系的连接,目的是为了节油,但目前大多数国家已严禁使用)③(行驶中)脱离路面的车轮 ④(车辆的)非驱动车轮

free wheel gear shift (自动变速器)自由轮离合器换挡(见 free wheel shift)

free wheel hub 自由轮式轮毂(①亦称 idling hub,指可任意切断或接通车轮驱动力的轮毂,某些分时四轮驱动汽车的前轮装有自由轮毂,车辆不需要前轮驱动时,可断开前轮驱动,亦称 free wheeling hud ②指非驱动轮可自由转动的轮毂)

free wheeling ①(发动机)空转,

无负荷运转 ②（汽车无发动机制动状态下的）自由滑行，惯性滑行的 ③自由轮作用，自由轮超越运转

free-wheeling-bub locking mechanism 自由旋转式轮毂的锁止机构（分为手动锁止"manual locking"和电动锁止"electric power locking"两种）

free wheeling hub 自由旋转式轮毂（①分时四轮驱动系统两轮驱动时作为从动轮轮毂，可自由旋转，四轮驱动时被锁死成为驱动轮轮毂，由半轴带动旋转②两轮驱动式车辆的自由旋转的从动轮轮毂）

free wheeling rectifier 削峰整流器（跨接于感应负载或半导体开关器电路，用来抑制负载断开时产生的峰值电压）

free-wheel lock 自由轮机构锁定器

free-wheel shift （自动变速器等的）自由轮换挡，单向离合器换挡（换挡时，有自由轮机构介入的转矩变换）

free-wheel vehicle 非轨道车辆

free wind 顺风（＝following wind）

free wrench 棘轮扳手

freeze ①冻结，结冰；凝固，凝结；②卡滞（[美]特指两个摩擦件由于过热和缺油而擦伤最终导致卡死或黏结，＝[英] seize）

freeze-frame data （在汽车电子控制系统或车载式故障诊断系统中处于）定格（状态）数据，（处于）冻结(状态的)数据，(处于）保持（状态的）数据（＝hold-mode data，如：车载式故障诊断系统将监测到的发生故障的时间和部位的代码及故障瞬间的状态记录下来，作为故障数据定格或冻结于，即：保持于freeze-frame 存储器内，供检修人员使用扫描解码器取出进行故障诊断）

freeze plug [美]见 core plug①

freeze point depressant 冰点降低剂，降凝剂

freezer car （泛指各种）冷藏车，冷冻车（＝refrigerator car）

freeze van 厢式冷藏车（参见 refrigerated van）

freezing ①冰冻，冻结，凝固②冰点 ③冰冻的，冻结的，凝固的 ④卡滞的

freezing point （＝freezing temperature）冰点，凝固点，冻结温度

freight ①货运，陆运②货物

freight car ①厢式货车（＝goods van, goods wagon）②厢式行李车（＝luggage van）

freight carrier ①货物运载工具，货车②货物运输公司

freighter （载）货（汽）车

freight flow 货流（在一定时期内，一定数量的货物通过公路运输沿某一方向移动所形成的物流，包括货物流量、流向和流时）

freight flow diagram 货流图（表示不同种别货物构成的货物流量和流向）

freight platform 平板货箱

freight space （汽车货箱的）载货空间

freight vehicle 货车（＝cargo vehicle）

French chalk 滑石，滑石粉，法国白（装内胎时撒在外胎内壁与内胎间）

french curve 云线板，云线规，云状规，曲线板，曲线规

French horsepower 公制马力（＝metric horsepower）

French standard thread 法国标准螺纹

freon 氟氯烷，氟利昂（$CHCl_2F_2$ 的商品名，一种制冷剂。无色、无臭的不燃性气体，对金属无腐蚀性，沸点为 -29.8℃。由于氟利昂会对大气环境造成危害，近年已不再使用，而改用无公害的新型制冷剂）

Freon-12 氟利昂-12（汽车冷气系统以往最常用的一种制冷剂，分子式为 $CHCL_2F_2$）

frequency ①频率 [= periodicity, 每单位时间内完成全振动或振荡或循环的次数，单位为赫兹（HZ），简称赫，见 hertz] ②单位时间内事件发生的次数

frequency allocation 频率分配（指将无线电频谱中可用频率分配给特定用户和用途，在用户之间干扰最小的情况下频率范围得到最大利用）

frequency analysis 频率分析（指测量频率，如：在声学中，用仪器测定一个作为频率函数的声音频带压强电平，借以确定其频率和频率范围或指将一周期性的函数分解为一系列的频率连续的谐波分量，进而求得其频谱的方法，因而也称频谱分析，谐波分析）

frequency band 频带，波段（= band of frequencies 两个界限频率之间的频率范围）

Frequency bandwidth 频带宽度，带宽（见 frequency range②）

frequency channel 频道（指按频带划分的传输信道）

frequency characteristics 频率特性（对汽车操纵稳定性而言，指以转向盘正弦指令输入频率为变量的响应特性，也可由不规则输入响应及瞬态响应求得）

frequency converter 频率变换器，变频器（= frequency transformer, frequency changer）

frequency coordination = frequency allocation

frequency counter 频率计

frequency-dependent 与频率有关的（随频率而变的，视频率而定的，取决于频率的）

frequency distribution ①频率分布 ②概率（密度）分布

frequency division 频分（指将一信道的频带再划分成若干较窄频带的过程，即：用一较宽频带生成多个窄频带，亦称频带分片）

frequency-divison multiplexer 频分多路复用器（简称 FDM，利用每个信号占用不同频率的方法，由一个公共通路传输两个或多个信号的多路通信装置，如：汽车电气和电子系统的单线系统）

frequency doubler （二）倍（增）频器（将输入信号频率乘以 2 的频率乘法器）

frequency drift 频率偏离值，频偏（亦称 frequency departure，指载波频率等偏离中心频率的数值）

frequency filter 频率滤波器

frequency function 频率函数，频数函数，分布函数

frequency limit 频率极限，频率范围

frequency modulated carrier 调频载波

frequency modulation 调频，频率调制（简称 FM，指按照信息信号的变化来改变固定振幅载波信号的频率的调制方式）

frequency modulation multipex system（简称 FM MPX system）调频多路复用系统（利用调频方式实现的多路复用系统）

frequency of accidents due to poor quality of service 货运质量事故频率（中国规定考核期内，百万吨公里货物周转量发生质量事故的次数）

frequency of current repair（of vehicle）汽车小修频率（单位行程的小修次数）

frequency of exiting force 激（振）力频率

frequency of natural vibration 固有频率，自然振动频率（= natural frequency）

frequency of occurrence （某事件）重复出现次数

frequency of unit (open loop) amplification （数字电路线性放大器）单位开环放大倍数频率（电压或电流开环放大倍数为1的频率，亦称单位增益带宽）

frequency range ①频率范围（指一个频带上、下限频率之间所包含的全部连续频率，= frequency limit）②频带宽度、带宽（指一个频带的上、下限频率之差，其单位用赫兹表示，= band width）

frequency resolution 频率分辨率（在谱图上显示不同频率下谱值的最小频率间隔，频率分辨率越高则频率的间隔越小，越能显示出谱形随频率的细微变化）

frequency response 频率响应（汽车对正弦波输入的稳态响应，求输出对输入的增益及相位特性等，可用转向盘转角、操舵力作为输入或指在线性系统中，输出信号的傅里叶变换与相应的输入信号的傅里叶变换之比。简称FR）

frequency-response analyzer 频率响应分析仪

frequency-response characteristic 频率响应特性（图）（为对数增益和相角以频率为函数的图解表示，通常用对数坐标表示）

frequency-response function 频响函数［系统输出（响应）与输入（激励）的傅里叶（Fourier）变换之比，常记作$H(\omega)$或$H(f)$。它表示线性系统的输入输出关系，是频率的函数］

frequency-response test （汽车的）频率响应试验（以各种频率进行周期性的操纵输入，用横摆角速度、侧倾角等对各种频率输入的响应特性进行评价的试验）

frequency scan button ①频率扫描按钮 ②自动调谐按钮，自动搜台按钮

frequency spectrum 频谱［物理现象的各成分或分量按其频率的大小依次排列成的频带，即：物理现象的频域结构。如：将一个复杂的振动分解为一系列简谐振动的叠加，这一系列简谐振动的频率连同相应的振幅的分布或排列，称为该复杂振动的（频）谱。周期性振动分解为基频和倍频的简谐振动，这种谱叫离散谱，非周期性振动，如脉冲的谱称连续谱，即：组成该脉冲的简谐振动是连续的］

frequency spectrum analyzer 频谱分析仪（将声振动转换为电振荡，光信号转换成电信号的换能系统，并在十分精确的水平上自动进行频谱分析。分析随机过程的频谱仪，一般由中心频率连续可调的窄带滤波器、平方器、平均器和输入、输出部分组成，用于动态信号分析。例如：汽车零部件的应力随时间变化过程的足够多的样本函数输入频谱分析仪，窄带滤波器可分离出各个谐波成分，由平方器算出平方值，经平均器对时间平均后，便可输出该随机过程的功率频谱）

frequency timedivision multiple access 频率时间分割多路复用存取（简称FTDMA，见FDMA "frequency division multiple access" 和 TDMA "time division multiple access"）

frequency tolerance 频率允许偏差，频率容限

frequency-to-number converter 频率-数字变换器

frequency transfer function 频率传输函数

frequency transformation 频率变换

frequency transformer 见 frequency converter

frequency valve （某些装有汽油连续喷射系统和催化转化器车辆上的燃

油分配器的）油量调节阀（该阀由电子控制模块根据排气氧传感器的信号发出的电压信号控制，连续调节燃油量，不断地按照发动机运转工况控制混合气的空燃比）

frequent 时常发生的，频繁的，屡次；习以为常的，常见的

frequcy-division multiplexing 频分多路复用，频分多路转接（将原信道的传输频带分割成若干较窄频带，每个窄频带构成一个个不同的信道，参见 time division multiplexing "时分多路复用"）

fresh air unit 新鲜空气导入装置，新鲜空气输送装置

fresh-air ventilation system （车厢内的）新鲜空气通风系统

fresh cadaver （供汽车碰撞试验用的）新鲜尸体（死后数日内采用特殊技术防止僵硬并注射一种相当于血液的液体，使外观及弹性和活人体十分接近，用来收集人体的碰撞伤害界限等有关数据）

fresh charge 新鲜充量（吸入的新鲜混合气）

fresh tar sign "注意新浇路面"标志（亦称 fresh oil sign，修理路面时，临时设置的警告标志，使车辆慢行，以免新浇的焦油沥青飞溅）

Fresnel lens 菲涅尔透镜（由一定数目的窄扇形镜片构成，与后视镜等联合使用，以增进汽车乘员的视野）

Fretecner Munson's curve ［美］福曼曲线，福氏曼氏等音曲线（纵坐标为音强，横坐标为频率，经过对一万人测试分贝量，描绘出的感觉上的声音大小，绘制等音曲线）

fretting 摩擦损伤，磨损，侵蚀，腐蚀；微振磨损

fretting corrosion （两接触表面摩擦而造成的）磨蚀，磨损（如振动结构中的机械接头）

friability 脆弱性，易碎性

friable 脆弱的，易碎的

frication-type self locking differential 摩擦式自锁差速

friction ①摩擦（两相互接触物作相对滑动）②摩擦力（两相互接触的物体，由于有相对滑动或相互滑动趋势而在接触面处产生的阻碍它们相对运动的力）

frictional 摩擦的，摩阻的，由摩擦产生的

frictional bearing 滑动轴承（＝plain bearing）

frictional clutch 摩擦离合器（指常规的机械摩擦式离合器）

frictional contact drive 摩擦接触传动

frictional failure 摩擦损坏

frictional ground force 地面摩擦力（指地面与车轮的摩擦力，＝车轮与路面的摩擦系数 × 路面对车轮的法向反力）

frictional ground reaction 道路摩擦反作用力（由于地面与车轮间的摩擦力而在汽车行驶时，地面对车轮驱动力产生的与汽车行驶方向相同的反作用力或在制动过程中，地面对车轮制动器制动力产生的与行驶方向相反的反作用力）

frictional horsepower 摩擦马力，摩擦功率（简称 FHP，指消耗于包括轴承在内的运动件之间的摩擦功率）

friction(al) loss 摩擦损失（因克服摩擦而消耗的功率）

frictional mechanical stepless transmission 摩擦机械式无级变速器，摩擦传动无级变速器（＝infinitely variable frictional transmission，指通过改变主、从动摩擦轮的直径比来实现无级变速的变速装置系统）

frictional resistance 摩擦阻力（指起阻力作用的摩擦力。注意，有时摩

擦力起推动力的作用）

frictional shock absorber 摩擦式减振器（利用减振器中做相对运动的元件间的固体摩擦力做功消耗振动能量以达到减振目的的一种结构形式）

friction(al) torque 见 friction moment

frictional torque 摩擦转矩，摩擦力矩（摩擦力与其作用半径的乘积）

friction ball joint 见 steering ball joint

friction bearing 滑动轴承（轴颈的支承面与轴颈间由润滑油膜润滑而相互滑动的轴承）

friction block 制动蹄摩擦片（块）

friction brake 摩擦制动器（靠摩擦力产生制动作用的制动器）

friction braking energy 摩擦制动能量（简称FBE）

friction clutch 摩擦离合器（依靠主、从部件间的摩擦传递动力的离合器）

friction coat 减摩涂层（提高表面光洁度，减少摩擦力的涂层）

friction coefficient 摩擦系数（$\mu = f/N$，即：摩擦力f与摩擦表面间的正压力N的比值，与表面的性质的粗糙程度有关）

friction cone （同步器等的）摩擦锥（指与同步器输入轴和输出轴制成一体的外锥面和与接合套花键毂成一体的内锥面，换挡时，在拨叉作用下，使内、外锥面接触产生圆周方向的摩擦力，促使输入轴和输出轴间的啮合件转速趋于一致，而平顺接合）

friction damper 摩擦减振器（见friction disc damper）

friction disc ①（离合器的）从动盘（= [美] clutch disc, [英] clutch plate, driven plate，指装在飞轮和离合器压盘之间，被压盘紧压传递与输出动力的离合器盘）②从动盘摩擦衬片（= disc facing [美], driven plate lining [英], clutch plate lining）

friction disc damper 摩擦盘式减振器（简称friction damper，旧时使用的利用摩擦材料盘吸收振动的装置）

friction drag ①空气摩擦阻力，摩擦风阻（指汽车行驶时，空气流与车身表面之间摩擦产生的空气动力阻力）②（离合器分离不彻底时引起的）缓慢拖带转动

friction force of steering system 转向系摩擦力（转向轮开始产生角位移时所必需的最小操能力，它不包括车轮与路面间的摩擦力）

friction gear(ing) 摩擦传动装置，摩擦传动（通过主、从动件间摩擦力传递动力）

friction head （液压管道）摩擦损失的压头

friction horsepower 摩擦功率（指克服机械或机械一流体摩擦所消耗的功率）

friction lining 摩擦片（制动器的制动衬片，离合器盘的摩擦衬片）

friction mean effective pressure 平均摩擦有效压力（简称FMEP）

friction modifier 减摩（添加）剂，摩擦改善剂（简FM，常用于润滑油中的减摩添加剂）

friction modifier （掺入机油、燃油内的）减磨改性剂，减磨添加剂

friction moment 摩擦力矩（= friction torque，指摩擦力与其作用半径的乘积，如：车轮制动器的摩擦力矩等于地面制动力与车轮半径的乘积）

friction of liquid 液体摩擦，流体摩擦（指两摩擦面间有液体，如润滑油膜时的摩擦）

friction of motion 动摩擦（= kinetic friction 指物体在运动过程中受到的

摩擦)

friction of rest 静摩擦(指两个相互静止接触的物体有相对运动的趋势时,在接触面处产生的阻碍相对运动的力, = static friction)

friction pad 见 brake pad

friction plate 离合器)摩擦盘,(一般指离合器的从动盘)

friction power (发动机的)摩擦功率(指发动机因内部各种摩擦而消耗的功率,制动功率+摩擦功率=指示功率,简称fp, FP)

friction resistance 见 frictional resistance

friction revolution counter 摩擦式转数计(亦称 friction tachmeter,通过一摩擦轮与被测件接触而测定其转速)

friction scrubbing apparatus (汽车车身的)摩擦刷洗装置,擦洗设备

friction shock absorber 摩擦式减振器(广义指利用摩擦吸收振动的减振器的总称;一般指使用摩擦零件,如摩擦盘等来吸收振动的减振装置)

friction start (汽车的)摩擦起步(利用摩擦元件实现车辆起步,即挂挡起步)

friction-stir welding (铁、铝等异种金属的)摩擦搅拌焊接(简称FSW)

friction stress (油膜等的)剪应力

friction tight 紧配合的(靠摩擦紧固的配合)

friction wear 摩擦损耗,磨损(一般简称wear)

friction welding 摩擦熔焊(借助摩擦发热的两表面在压力下熔合焊接)

fridge equipment 冷冻装置,制冷装置

frigid zone 寒带

fringe ①干扰带,干涉带;条纹;干扰边纹 ②边缘,界限,端 ③镶边,加边 ④附加的,边缘的,较次要的

fringe of fatigue scatter band (疲劳曲线图上)疲劳强度点散布带的边缘区

frit 釉料(半熔化玻璃状物质,研碎后用作釉,搪瓷,珐琅的基料)

frog cam 心形凸轮,凹槽形凸轮(= heart cam)

frog eye 蛙眼(1958~1962年生产的Austin-Healey Sprite 1系列轿车的绰号,因其前照灯突出于发动机罩而得名)

from stem to stern 从车头到车尾(指车全长)

front ①前面,前部,前方,前端(= frontend),锋面,波前,(特指轿车的)前座(= front seats) ②前面的,前方的,正面的 ③面对,朝向;附在前面,装饰在正面

front abstract-collision reducing brake system 前方障碍物碰撞减轻(自动)制动系统

front abstract detecting sensor 前方障碍物探测传感器

frontage ①正面,前面 ②正面的宽度

frontage road 侧道,辅助道路,服务性道路(与高速道路、高速公路或优先通行道路等邻接的平行侧道。一般只在特定地点与主要道路连接,供流入交通合流或流出交通分散, = frontage roadway, frontage street, service road, service roadway)

frontage street 辅助道路(参见 frontage road)

frontal area (汽车的)正面投影面积,正面迎风面积(估算的正面迎风面积=0.9×车身高×轮距,亦称 frontal projected area)

frontal collision (车辆的)正面碰撞,迎面碰撞(发生于两车或一车

与固定物之间，车前面受撞的碰撞）

frontal drag 正面阻力，迎风阻力（亦称 frontal resistance，指汽车正面投影面积所受到的空气阻力）

frontal electrode 正面电极（指普通型火花塞电极布置，其侧电极跳火面在中心电极的正对面）

front alignment 前轮定位（参见 front wheel alignment）

frontal impact 前面受撞（按受撞部位在汽车前面的两拐角之间，亦称 frontal crash，frontal end impact，见 collision 和 impact）

frontal projected area 正投影面积（汽车迎面投影面积）

frontal protrusion （车辆）前部外伸量（指前轴中心至保险杠的距离）

frontal resistance 见 frontal drag

front and/or rear fog light tell-tale 前和（或）后雾灯信号灯 ［表示前和（或）后雾灯接通的信号灯］

(front and rear) side curtain airbag （前、后的）侧面帘式安全气囊

front-and rear-wheel steer 前后轮转向（四轮汽车的全轮转向）

front apron 轿车车身前裙板（前保险杠下方，连接左、右前翼子板底端的板件，见 front valance panel）

front ash tray 前烟灰盒（指位于转向盘附近者）

front axle 前桥，前轴（指安装前轮的车轴或车桥。除前轮驱动和四轮驱动车辆外，前轮独立悬架的汽车已无此意义上的前桥或前轴，但仍可见文献中用"front axle"来表述前轮独立悬架总成和前轮支架系统，亦称 fore axle）

front axle aligning tool 前桥调准工具，前轮定位工具

front axle and rear axle split brake system 双管路制动系统（其中每一条制动管路均控前桥和后桥制动。注意：front axle/rear axle split brake system，则指一条管路仅控制前桥制动，而另一条管路仅控制后桥制动的双管路制动系统，二者含义是不同的）

front axle engaged/disconnect drive （分时四轮驱动系统的）前桥结合/分离装置

front axle final drive 前桥（驱动的）主减速器

front-axle pivot ①前桥半径杆中央枢轴 ②前轴（转向）主销

front axle propeller shaft （前桥驱动式或四轮驱动式车辆的）前桥传动轴

front axle radius arm 前桥半径杆（前桥悬架中连接车架与前桥梁，确保前桥相对于车架前后位置的附加杆件，见 radius arm）

front axle slip angle （汽车的）"前桥"侧偏角（将两只转向前轮的侧偏角，假想为前桥中点的一个车轮的侧偏角，称前轮侧偏角（见 slip angle)）

front axle steering knuckle 前桥转向节

front axle with inner steering knuckle 拳（形）端式前桥（前桥梁两端成拳形，见 reversed Elliot axle）

front axle with outer steering knuckle 叉（形）端式前桥（前桥梁两端叉形，见 Elliot type）

front baffle 见 radiator support

front-bank rotor housing （双缸转子发动机的）前缸体

front beam ①前横梁 ②前轴（工字）梁

front bench-type seat 前排长凳型座椅

front-biased weight distribution （车辆的）前端偏重的质量分布

front body ①（载货汽车车身的）驾驶室（=cab）②（轿车的）车

身前部（指客厢以前的车身部分）

front body hinge pillar 车身前部的（门）铰链支柱（简称FBHP，= A pillar）

front body overhang 车身前悬（前轮中心的横向铅垂面至车身最前端的水平距离，不包括保险杠及其附件，参见 front overhang）

front body shell （载货汽车车身的）前板件（驾驶室前方覆盖发动机和车轮的板件的总称，亦称 front sheet metal）

front box-pillar （轿车车身的）前立柱，前柱（=［美］A pillar）

front brake 前轮制动器

front brake drum with hub 前轮制动鼓带轮毂

front brake modulator 前轮制动压力调节器

front brake tube T-union 前轮制动管路三通接头

front bulkhead ①（轿车车身的）前隔壁板（隔开驾驶室与发动机室的板件，通常为车颈带仪表底板总成，亦称 forward bulkhead, scuttle bulkhead，我国称前围板，见 bulkhead）②客车驾驶员室与乘客室之间的隔板 ③（偶见指）散热器固定框（见 radiator support）

front bumper 前保险杠（现代轿车的前保险杠多与前导风板组合在一起）

front bumper bracket （汽车）前保险杠支架

front bumper height 前保险杠高度（保险杠最前部至地面的距离）

front bumper lower (upper) edge altitude over road surface 前保险杠下（上）边缘至地面的距离

front bumper shock absorber 前保险杠减振器

front bumper stone reflector 见 front valance panel

front bumper with built-in lamps 内置大灯型前保险杠

front center airbag （GM公司某些车型上安装的）前座中央安全气囊（发生碰撞事故时该气囊在前排座位之间胀开）

front coil suspension compression stroke buffer 前轮螺旋弹簧悬架压缩行程缓冲垫

front coil suspension rebound stroke buffer 前轮螺旋弹簧回升行程缓冲垫

front control plate （柴油机转子式分配型喷油泵的）前控制板（装在分配转子的凸缘上，与后控制板一起转动，可改变柱塞行程，用于调整最大供油量）

front corner marker lamp （装在挂车或半挂车前面边角上的）标志灯

front crash sensor 前碰撞传感器（见 external sensor）

front cross-member 前横梁（= front cross rail）

front differential （四轮驱动汽车的）前桥差速器

front directional （汽车的）前转向灯（的）

front disk/rear drum brakes 前轮盘式后轮鼓式制动系（目前，中、低档车的典型配置）

front door 前车门，（大客车）驾驶员车门（= driver door）

front dump 前卸，前方倾卸

front edge 前边缘（参见 advancing edge）

front elevation 前视图，正视图

front end 前端

front-end alignment equipment 前端校正装备，前端调校仪具（在汽车前端进行调校作业，如：前轮定位、前桥校直等所用装备及仪具的统称）

front end barrier impact simulation

test 汽车前端与障壁碰撞的模拟试验（简称 FEBIS）

front end cover （曲轴箱）前盖，前端盖

front end dip ①（汽车）栽头现象（如：制动时汽车后端升起，前端下栽的现象）②汽车栽头角（为汽车姿势角之一，汽车绕横向轴线前后簸动时，前端下栽的角度，= vehicle dip angle）

front（end）drive 前（端）驱动，前轮驱动（= forward drive）

front end housing （转子发动机的）前端盖，前缸盖，起动端缸盖

front-end impact = front impact

front end job 前桥维修作业（包括前桥校直、前轮定位、前轮平衡、轮胎充气等与前轮有关的维修作业的总称，= front end work, front end service）

front-end octane value （车用汽油的）头部馏分辛烷值〔以 R_{100} 表示，按英国标准方法（IP325）切取的 100℃ 以前的轻馏分，测出其研究法辛烷值，即所谓的头部馏分辛烷值，常用于表征发动机节气门全开加速时各缸之间汽油轻重馏分分配不均匀，头部馏分进入较多的远端汽缸发生爆燃的难易程度〕

front end panel （轿车车身等的）发动机罩前支撑板（发动机舱前端上部与左、右前翼板相联结的板件，亦可兼作发动机罩锁的固定板，= nose panel）

front-end ram （装在后倾卸式自卸汽车车身）前端（的）举升油缸

front end/rear head collision 追尾碰撞（后车车头碰撞前车车尾）

front end service 见 front end job

front end shirt edge （车身）前裙边

front end shop 前桥维修车间（包括前轮定位、前轮平衡等作业）

front end sill （车身底框的）前部端梁

front-end style 汽车头部式样

front-end volatiles 轻馏分，前馏分，头部馏分

front-end volatility （燃料）轻馏分挥发性，头部馏分挥发性

front end work 见 front end job

front engine front drive vehicle 前置发动机前轮驱动式车辆（简称 FF vehicle, = front-wheel drive vehicle）

front engine rear drive vehicle 前置发动机后轮驱动型汽车（即一般的后轮驱动式汽车等，相对于前轮驱动汽车而言，简称 FR vehicle, = front engine rear wheel drive vehicle）

front engine vehicle 发动机前置式汽车，前置发动机汽车（发动机位于驾驶区前方）

front engine（west-east） 发动机横向（西-东方向）前置

front entrance 车厢前部入口

front epicyclic gear （自动变速器的）前行星齿轮（机构）（相对其后行星齿轮而言）

front exit 前方出口，前门

front face 前脸，迎风面（指汽车的正面，主要包括保险杠、前照灯、散热器罩、商标、前风窗玻璃和后视镜等）

front fender 前翼（子）板（遮盖前车轮的车身外板，= front wing）

front fender apron 前挡泥板（= front mudguard, fender skirt, hood ledge, wheel apron, 指前轮内侧的挡泥板，亦即发动机舱的侧板）

front fender fin （车身）前扰流翅，前阻流压板（装在前翼子板附近，减小车身前端的空气浮力）

front fender liner （车身）前翼子板（内面的挡泥）衬板〔亦称 front wheel house inner panel（前轮口内挡泥罩板）〕

front fitting radius of semi-trailer 半

挂车前回转半径（指半挂车牵引销轴线至半挂车前端最远点的距离）

front floor crossmember （轿车车身）底板前横梁

front floor reinforcement （轿车车身）前底板加强件，前底板加强横梁

front foot corridor （客车等的）前座走道（宽度），前座通道

front frame ①前梁，前支架 ②（货车货箱）底板边梁（底板周围的加强件）

front glass 车厢前窗玻璃

front glass antenna 埋设在风窗玻璃内的天线

front grille （汽车车身的水箱）前护栅，前脸格栅

front guard frame ①前保险构架，前保险装置（如汽车前保险杠等）②（货车货箱的）货架（货箱前部支撑货物的构件）

front half bar (type) anticollision rack （越野车等的）半型防撞头架

front-heavy car 前重汽车（指前桥承受载荷超过汽车总质量50%的汽车）

front-hinged bonnet 前翻式（发动机）机罩（整个发动机罩的前端下方与车架前端铰接，机罩可翻向前方，便于发动机的维修）

front-hip-point 前臀点（指汽车乘员空间的人体基准原点——臀点的最前端位置，参见 hip point）

front hood (bonnet) control 发动机罩操纵件（打开发动机罩锁扣的手操纵件）

front license number plate bracket （汽车）前牌照板支架

front longitudinal （车身等的）前纵梁

front longitudinal extension （轿车车身的）底板前纵梁延长板

front lower body panel 见 front valance panel

front lower shroud 见 front valance panel

front main bearing 前主轴承

front main steering angle sensor （电子控制四轮转向系的）前轮转向角主传感器（指转向盘转向角传感器）

front-mounted 前悬挂的，前支撑的

front mounted double reduction final drive 前置式双级主减速器（装在桥壳前方的双级主减速器，见 double reduction drive）

front mounted flywheel 装在发动机前面的飞轮，前装式飞轮

front-mounted radiator 前置散热器

front mudguard 前挡泥板（见 front fender apron）

front nose section （轿车车身的）前端部（指构成轿车前端部的整体板件结构，包括散热器框板 "radiator grille surround"，左、右翼板 "wings"，前挡泥板 front apron 等）

front-obstruct-collision reducing brake system 前方障碍物碰撞减轻制动系统

front offset crash compliance test （车辆的）前面偏置碰撞合格认证试验

front of the engine 发动机前端（风扇端）

front outline 前视图，正视图，（如：汽车的前外形图，= front view）

front overhang 汽车前悬（前轮中心的横向铅垂面至汽车最前端，包括保险杠、挂钩等全部固装件的水平距离，注意与不包括保险杠及其附件的 "front body overhang" 不同）

front overhang angle 前悬角，接近角，前通过角（见 approach angle）

front packing strip （转子发动机三角转子的）前密封条（两个前密封条与径向密封片和弹簧件等构成转

子的角密封件总成)

front panel ①(轿车车身的)前脸板(指连接前翼子板并构成轿车前照灯和散热器框等的前脸面板,我国有关标准称散热器固定框,= radiator support, lamp support, shroud panel, front bulkhead, front baffle。由于空气经该板进入发动机舱因此亦称 deflector。当汽车前面无单独的前裙板时,该板件 = front apron)②前围板(货车驾驶室前部的护板,亦称 cowl) ③(轿车的)前围上盖板(见 cowl top)

front parking light (汽车的)前驻车灯

front pillar (轿车车身的)前支柱,(货车驾驶室的)前柱(支承顶盖,安装风窗玻璃与前门的立柱,= front standing pillar, front post, A pillar)

front pillar garnish moulding [美](轿车车身)前支柱的内装饰板件 (= [英] front pillar strap)

front pipe 前排气管(指从排气歧管至消声器的第一节排气管)

front position sensor 前轮(与车身间的相对)位置传感器

front power lift 汽车前端的动力提升机构

front power take-off (shaft) 前功率输出轴,前置功率输出轴

front propeller shaft 前传动轴(指万向节连接的双传动轴的前轴, front propeller shaft rear flange coupling 前传动轴后凸缘叉的凸缘套,该套通过花键与前轴端耦合,通过凸缘面与连接后轴的凸缘叉的凸缘面的螺栓紧固。front propeller shaft splines 前传动轴花键)

front pump (自动变速器液力控制系的)前泵(与发动机的转速成一定的关系,= input pump "输入泵")

front rack (车厢)前栏板栅板

front-rack slat 前栏板横栅条

front (rear) brake wheel cylinder (液压制动系)前(后)轮制动动缸

front/rear split type dual-circuit brake system 前、后桥独立双回路制动系统(指前后桥各有一条独立的制动回路的制动系统,亦称 brake force parallel distribution type dual-circuit brake system, 有时 parallel 一词用平行符号"//"代替)

front-rear torque ratio (四轮驱动车辆的)前、后轮转矩比

front/rear weight distribution (汽车)前后轴荷分配

front rim (组合式前照灯灯壳的)外装饰圈 (= [美] trim ring)

front roll center (汽车的)前侧倾中心(位于通过前轮左、右车轮中心的横向铅垂面内的侧倾中心,见 roll center)

front roll stabilizer 前(独立悬架)横向稳定杆(防止车身侧倾的杆件)

front roof bracket (轿车车顶)天窗前边框

front running light (汽车的)前运转灯,前工作灯(装在车前面,表示发动机正在运转的灯)

front screen 前风窗玻璃

front seat ①前排座 ②(货车驾驶室指与驾驶员座并排的)前座(注意: the front seats 指驾驶员座和与驾驶员并排的前乘员座)

front-seat-mounted side airbag 安装在前座椅内的侧面安全气囊

front seat test dummy 前座试验用假人

front shake 车头低频抖振(指汽车行驶时,车身前部产生的7~20周/s低频振动,使乘员产生不舒适感。在高速道路上以特定的高速行驶时,这种振动特别明显,产生这种

振动的主要原因为：非悬挂质量的强迫振动，通过悬架传至车身，引起车身抖动；非悬挂质量的振动传到发动机，引起发动机共振而产生车身振动)

front sheet metal 见 front body shell

front side 正面，前面

front side member 前纵梁（= front side rail, front side frame, 承载式车身前部的纵梁)

front silencer 前消声器（指双消声器系统的第一和主消声器)

front single-cross seat 前排长条座

front skirt panel 见 front valance panel

front span （车辆）外形前宽

front splash shield 前挡泥板

front spoiler 前导风板（指装在汽车前端的导风板或压风板，用于减少风阻或升力，改善车辆的操纵性、稳定性，地面附着力和节油)

front spring assembly 前（钢板）弹簧总成

front spring eye bushing 前钢板弹簧卷耳孔衬套

front spring fourth leaf clamp 前钢板弹簧第四片卡扣，前钢板第四片固定卡

front spring pad 前钢板弹簧橡皮垫块

front standing pillar （轿车车身的）前支柱（简称 A post, front pillar, 亦称 wind-screen pillar)

front strip （货车货箱的）底板压条（面板拼接处的压紧件)

front strut/rear multi-link suspension 前轮滑柱后轮多连杆式悬架

front sub steering angle sensor （电子控制四轮转向系的）前轮转向角副传感器（指直接测定前轮转向角的传感器，见 front main steering angle sensor)

frontsuspension cross member （车架或车身上）支撑前轮悬架的横梁

frontsuspension frame （麦弗逊型）前悬架下臂的盘状横梁（见 L type low arm)

front suspension shock absorber 前悬架减振器

front tipper 前倾翻斗车，前翻斗式矿车，前倾卸货手推车，前倾式卸车

front to rear body weight ratio （汽车的）前、后车重比

front torus （液力变矩器等的）泵轮（见 impeller 及 torus)

front track 前轮轮距

front-turn signal lamp 前转向信号灯

front underrun protection device （大型车辆的）防前方钻撞装置（简称 FUPD, = front underrun protector)

front valance panel （轿车车身的）前裙板（车身前下部连接左、右前翼板的横梁或外板，= lower front panel, front apron, front bumper stone reflector, front lower body panel, front lower shroud, front skirt panel, 偶见称 fairing panel)

front view 正面图，主视图，前视图

front wall （客车车身的）前围（由前围骨架，前围蒙皮，前围护板、风窗玻璃及所属车身附件等组成的部件, front wall frame 前围骨架，位于车身前端的骨架；front wall inner shield 前围护板 = front wall interior panel, 覆盖前围骨架内表面的板件；front wall outer panel 前围蒙皮 = front wall shin, 覆盖前围骨架的外表面的板件；front wall shirt rail 前围裙边梁位于前围骨架底边的横梁；front wall pillar 前围立柱前围骨架两侧起支撑顶盖及安装风窗玻璃的立柱；front wall shelf beam 前围横梁，前围骨架上搁置地板的横梁)

front-wheel ABS motor （通用公司德尔科·莫瑞恩Ⅲ型 ABS 中分别控制左、右前轮制动液压的两台）前轮 ABS 电机（见 Delco Moraine ABS

VI)

front wheel aligner 前轮定位工具，前轮定位仪（亦称 front wheel angle test）

front wheel alignment 前轮定位，前轮校准（= front alignment）

front wheel arch ①（小客车车身的）前轮轮口（指车身前部供前轮拆装与转向的开口，亦称 front wheel opening）②（大客车车厢内的）前轮罩板（亦称 front wheel hours）

front-wheel ballast weight 前轮压重块（某些特种车辆为了利用增加前轮负载的方法提高前轮附着力而使用的压载物）

front wheel bump travel 前轮跳动行程，前轮跳起高度

front wheel deflector （车身底板上的）前轮导流板

front-wheel drive 前轮驱动（简称 FWD 或 fwd）

front wheel feeding chamber （某些串列双腔式制动主缸的）前轮液压腔（双腔中向前轮制动缸供给制动液压的工作腔）

front-wheel gauge 前轮规，前束尺

front wheel guide device 前轮导向装置（指车辆测试时，为防止前轮横向滑移，装在底盘测功机滚筒两侧的导向挡轮和装在制动试验台前防止前轮驶偏的导轨、导板、导轮等）

front wheel house complete panel （车身的）前轮轮口内挡泥罩板总成（指前翼子板下的整块挡泥罩板，亦称 front fender liner，前翼子板衬板。有时该板由内、外两块组成）

front wheel house panel 前轮口侧板（即发动机舱侧板，亦称前挡泥板，见 front fender apron）

front-wheel hub 前轮轮毂

front wheel hub cap 前轮轮毂盖

front wheel locking mechanism 前轮锁止机构（底盘测功器、制动试验台等设备上用于防止汽车活动的装置）

front wheel oil seal felt washer 前轮挡油毡垫，前轮油（封）毡（垫）

front wheel position sensor 前轮位置传感器（装在前悬架与车身底板之间，向路敏悬架系统控制模块提供前轮相对车身运动及转速信号）

front wheel regularizer 前束调节器（参见 dynamic toe-in tester）

front wheel speed sensor 前轮转速传感器

front-wheel steer(ing) 前轮转向

front-wheel steering angle responsive type full-mechanical 4WS system 前轮转向角响应全机械式四轮转向系（全机械式四轮转向系的一种，其后轮转向的方向完全取决于前轮转角，但当前轮转向角小时，后轮转向的方向与前轮相同，而当前轮转向角大时，后轮向反方向转动）

front wheel tread 前轮轮距

front-wheel weight ①前轮载荷 ②前轮自重

front-wheel wobble 前轮（自激）摆动（绕转向主销的角振动）

front windshield (glass) 前风窗玻璃（= front screen, front windscreen）

front wing 前翼（子）板（车身遮盖前轮的外板，轿车多与车身制成一体，亦称 front fender, front wing panel）

front wing extension panel 前翼（子）板延伸板

front wing front panel 前翼子板前板

frost ①霜，霜冻 ②严寒期，严寒天气

frost burn 凝雾爆炸［液化天然气（LNG）汽车燃料系统中漏出的甲

烷在周围空气中凝聚、形成白色浓雾而引起的猛烈燃烧]

frost crack 冻裂（= frost shake）

frost damage （冷）冻（作用引起的破）坏

frosted focusing glass 聚焦毛玻璃，磨砂聚焦玻璃

frosted glass ①蒙上了白霜的玻璃 ②磨砂玻璃，毛玻璃

frost-proof 防霜冻的，防结霜的

frost removal （玻璃的）除霜器

frost shield 防霜罩，防霜板

froth ①泡沫，浮渣，渣滓 ②起（泡）沫，发泡

frothing oil 起泡沫的润滑油

froth rubber 泡沫橡胶

Froude brake 傅若德水力测功器 [= Froude (water 或 hydraulic) dynamometer, 一种能量吸收式测功器，由一套可以自由转动的转子和壳组成，转子和壳之间注入水，当发动机带动转子旋转时，形成旋流，对转子壳产生转矩，测出该转矩即可算出发动机的输出功率]

fro-wheel （汽车）前轮

frozen 冰冻的，结冰的，冻结的

FRP ①玻璃纤维强化的塑料（fiberglass-reinforced plastic 的简称）②纤维强化塑料（fiber-reinforced plastic 的简称）③回油管（fuel return pipe 的简称）

FRP/foam skin 玻璃纤维强化塑料（夹层）-泡沫塑料（内芯）（车身）外壳

FRTP 纤维强化热塑性树脂（fiber-rein forced thermoplastics 的简称）

frusto-conical 截头圆锥形的

frustum of a cone 圆锥载体

FR vehicle 前置发动机后驱动车辆（front engine rear drive vehicle）

F/R weight distribution （汽车）前后桥载荷分配比

f/s ①安全系数（factor of safety 的简称）②第一阶段（first stage 的简称）

FS ①安全系数（factor of safety 的简称）②可行性研究（feasible study 的简称）③（美国）联邦政府规范（Federal specification 的简称）④野战勤务；现场服务（field service 的简称）⑤发动机点火开关，起动开关（fire switch 的简称）⑥货物供应（freight supply 的简称）⑦频率标准（frequency standard 的简称）

FSI 燃油分层喷射（fuel stratified injection 的简称，汽油缸内直接喷射系统的一种，借以实现稀混合气分层燃烧）

FSR 故障保险继电器（failure safe relay 的简称，该继电器触点电路串联于系统的电源电路中，当电子控制模块测得发生有可能导致系统损坏的故障时，即停止向该继电器的触点吸合线圈供电，触点断开，系统停止工作）

FSS [美] 联邦规范和标准（Federal Specification & Standards 的简称）

FSW （铁、铝等异种金属的）摩擦搅拌焊接（friction-stir welding 的简称）

ft² 平方英尺，(英制面积单位。$1ft^2 = 144in^2 = 929.03cm^2 = 0.8361$ 市尺²)

FT ①一种炭黑的商品名（Fine Thermal 的简称，平均直径 $180\mu m$，表面积 $15.7m^2/g$）②现场试验（field test 的简称）③着火温度（firing temperature 的简称）④燃料装罐（fuel tanking 的简称）⑤不漏烟气的（fumetight 的简称）⑥功能试验（functional test 的简称）

ft 英尺（foot）

ft³ 立方英尺，英尺立方 [英制容积单位、体积单位。$1ft^3 = 1728in^3 = 7.4805u·s·gal$（液）$= 28.317$ litre $= 6.2305$ Imperial gal $= 0.7646$ 市尺³]

FTA ①故障树分析（fault tree analysis 的简称）②［美］联邦公共交通署（Federal Transit Administration 的简称，见 UMTA）③自由贸易区（free trade area 的简称）

FTCS 全轮牵引力控制系统（full-traction control system 的简称）

FTDMA 频率时间分割多路复用存取（见 frequency time division multiple access）

F terminal "F" 接线柱（指发电机等的磁场接线柱）

F TIRE （德国 Esslingen 大学 Gipser 教授开发的）柔性环轮胎模型（Flexible Ring Tire model 的简称，国际上仿真轮胎在短波不平路面上动特性的主流模型，亦称作 F tire）

F Tire 单挠性环轮胎模型［single flexible ring tire mode 的简称，沿胎面将轮胎分割成数百个小的挠性单元（flexible segment）进行分析］

ft.lb 英尺磅（参见 foot-pound，1ft·1b = 1.29 × 10^{-4} Btu = 3.24 × 10^{-3} kcal = 5.05 × 10^{-7} HPh = 5.12 × 10^{-7} psh = 3.76 × 10^{-7} kWh = 0.1383kgf·m = 1.355J）

ft-lbf 英尺-磅力（英制单位的能量单位，参见 foot-pound force）

ft.lbf/s 英尺磅力/秒（英制功率单位，1ft.1bf/s = 3.24 × 10^{-3} kcal/s = 1.29 × 10^{-3} Btu/s = 0.138kgf·m/s = 0.00182HP = 0.00184Ps = 0.00136kW）

ft/min 英尺/分（英制速度单位，1ft/min = 0.0167ft/s = 0.01136mile/h = 0.00508m/s = 0.01828km/h）

ft³/min 英尺³/分（英制容积流量单位。1ft³/min7.481u·s·gal/min = 28.3l/min = 0.0283m³/min）

FTP 美国联邦（排气污染）试验规程（Federal Test Procedure 的简称）

FTP cycles ［美］联邦试验规程工况循环（模拟典型行车模式测检排放是否符合联邦标准的多工况试验循环，Federal Test Procedure Cycles 的简称）

FTS ①现场试验后勤等保障（field test support 的简称）②功能试验规范（functional test specification 的简称）

ft/s 英尺/秒（英制速度单位。1ft/sec = 60ft/min = 0.6818mile/h = 1.097km/h = 0.3048m/s = 0.9144 市尺/秒）

F-type combustion chamber F 形燃烧室（指发动机侧置气门式燃烧室）

Fu 伺服系统，随动的（follow-up）

FUDC ［美］联邦城市行驶工况（Federal Urban Driving Cycle 的简称）

fue-air ratio dry 干燃空比（指柴油机进入汽缸的燃油量与充入汽缸的实际干空气量之比，亦称 dry F/A ratio）

fuel ①燃料，燃油②加装燃料，添加燃油

fuel accumulator 油压平衡器（波许 k-Jetronic 机械式连续汽油喷射系统中的喷油压力稳定装置，用于吸收稳定油压建立前，即刚起动时，油泵的初始压力脉冲并在发动机熄火后短时间维持油压，以防汽阻）

fuel acidity 燃油的酸度（中和 100mL 燃油中酸性物所消耗的氢氧化钾的 mg 数，以 mg HOK/100mL 表示）

fuel acid value 燃油的酸值（中和 1g 燃油中酸性物质所消耗的氢氧化钾 mg 数，用 mgHOK/g 表示。酸度与酸值均为表明燃油对机件的腐蚀性指标之一）

fuel additive 燃油添加剂（用以改变燃油品质，如：抗补剂，抗氧化剂等，简称 FA）

fuel-air mixture analyzer 燃油空气混合气成分分析仪，燃油空气混合气分析仪

fuel-air ratio (混合气的)燃/空混合比(英、美表示混合气稀浓程度的一种方法,简称 F/A,燃油质量与空气质量之比,等于 0.066 时,为理想混合比,小于 0.066 为稀混合比,大于 0.066 为浓混合比,为空燃比的倒数,参见 theoretical fuel-air ratio)

fuel-air weight ratio 燃料空气重量比

fuel-(and) vapor separator 油-气分离器(蒸发排放物控制系统中,防止液体燃油进入蒸发排放物储存装置的液体燃油收集器)

fuel atomizing 燃料喷雾,燃油雾化

fuel availability 燃料(有效)利用率

fuel backup circuit 喷油控制备份电路(见 TBB)

fuel bag 燃油囊,软油箱

fuel-based mass emission measurement procedure 排气有害物质的燃油计测法(根据燃油的成分及消耗量来推算排气有害物质的方法)

Fuel borne catalyst 燃油携带型催化剂

fuel cam 喷油(泵凸轮轴)凸轮

fuel cap 油箱加油管盖

fuel capacity 燃料箱容量

fuel cell ①燃料电池(指通过电化学反应将气体或液体燃料的能量转变为电能的装置)②油箱

fuel-cell bottom 在燃料箱中的沉淀物

fuel-cell car 燃料电池(驱动的)轿车(1996 年 5 月 14 日,由 Mercedes-Benz 公司在柏林展出世界上第一辆氢燃料电池轿车,将甲醇在车上通过一个专门的反应器,产生 H_2 和 CO_2,接着将 H_2 导入氢-氧型燃料电池,与空气中的氧反应,产生 H_2O 和电流,用该电流驱动车辆)

fuel cell power 燃料电池动力

fuel cell stack (多个燃料电池组合成的)燃料电池堆,燃料电池组(简称 FC stack)

fuel charge ①燃油加添量,加油量 ②充量(进入燃烧室的空气/燃油混合气)

fuel charger 加(燃)油泵,燃油泵,燃油加添泵

fuel choke 呛油(汽油机因供油过多,超过混合气可燃浓度范围,产生的熄火现象)

fuel cleaning machine 燃油供给系统清洗机

fuel clogging 燃油系堵塞,油路堵塞

fuel coarse filter 燃油粗滤器(滤除较大杂质)

fuel compartment (燃)油箱舱,油箱间,油箱室(安置油箱的舱室)

fuel computer 燃油消耗量指示器,油耗表(= fuel consumption indicator)

fuel conditioner 燃油处理器(具有滤清、油水分离等多种功能的综合处理装置)

fuel consumption 燃料消耗(量),油耗(量)[简称 FC,代号 B,fuel consumption average 平均燃油消耗量; fuel consumption gauge, fuel consumption indicator, fuel consumption meter 油耗计,油耗表; fuel consumption of 100km (汽车的)百公里油耗; fuel consumption per hour (发动机的)(每)小时燃油消耗量; fuel consumption quota (汽车的)燃油消耗量定额; fuel consumption standard 燃油消耗量标准; fuel consumption test, fuel consumption trial 燃油消耗量测定试验]

fuel consumption characteristics loops 万有特性(发动机各种主要性能参数相互关系的综合特性,为以转速为横坐标,平均有效压力为纵坐标画出的等功率、等燃油消耗率曲

线，并可根据需要增补速度特性、调速特性、推进特性等曲线。这些曲线统称万有特性曲线）
fuel contents gauge 燃油表，燃油存量表
fuel control barostat 气压控制式燃料供给调节器
fuel control helix 见 fuel control slot
fuel controller （柴油机等自动喷油量控制系统中的）喷油量控制器
fuel control mechanism 油量调节机构（柴油机柱塞式喷油泵中用以调节供油量，以适应柴油机负荷与转速变化的机构，分齿条式和拨叉式两种）
fuel control motor 喷油量控制电动机（用于柴油机等喷油泵齿条的自动控制）
fuel control relay 喷油量控制继电器（在柴油机等自动喷油量控制系中，向 fuel control motor 发送增、减油量信号）
fuel control slot 油量控制槽（喷油泵柱塞头部表面的喷油量和喷油终点控制边缘，通常呈螺旋槽形或斜槽形，亦称 fuel control helix）
fuel control solenoid 油量控制电磁阀
fuel control valve assembly （柴油机分配式喷油泵的）油量控制阀部件（由油量控制阀、连杆臂和拉杆销组成，用于调节供油量）
fuel conversion efficiency 燃料（能量）转换效率
fuel correction device 油量校正装置（柴油机在超负荷工作时，随着转速的降低，自动地稍增供油量，克服短期超负荷）
fuel cost 燃料费
fuel cut (device) 断油装置（目前汽车多装有电子控制自动断油装置，遇下列情况之一自动切断燃油供给：松开加速踏板，减速；下长坡；车速超过某规定的最高车速）
fuel data center 燃油数据中心（简称 FDC，置于仪表板或其附近的燃油数据显示装置，由驾驶员按压显示板上的各数据按钮，便会自动显示所需的数据）
fuel data inputs （电子控制模块的）燃油数据输入（指输入电子控制模块的油量信号等）
fuel data outputs （电子控制模块的）燃油数据输出（指电子控制模块通过 fuel data center 提供给驾驶员的瞬时油耗、平均油耗、余油可行驶里程及已使用油量等信息）
fuel delivery 供油量（燃油系统在一个工作循环内的供油量体积）
fuel delivery advance （柴油机的）喷油提前角（柴油机从开始喷油的瞬时到活塞行至上止点时的曲轴转角）
fuel-delivery characteristics 燃油分配特性，燃油供给特性
fuel delivery curve at constant speed （柴油机的）喷油泵等速喷油特性曲线（在转速固定的情况下，每循环喷油量随喷油泵调节杆位移量的变化规律，简称喷油特性）
fuel delivery curve at fixed rack （柴油机的）喷油泵等齿杆位置的喷油特性曲线（当喷油泵调节杆固定时，喷油量随油泵凸轮转速的变化规律）
fuel delivery law （柴油机的）喷油规律（喷油率随凸轮转角的变化规律，见 fuel delivery rate）
fuel (delivery) line 燃油（输送）管路（一般指从油箱至发动机内的油管）
fuel delivery per cycle per cylinder （柴油机的）单缸循环喷油量（一个工作循环内喷入一个汽缸的燃油量）
fuel delivery rate （柴油机的）喷油

率（单位凸轮转角内喷油泵的喷油量）
fuel dilution test （润滑油的）燃油稀释试验（在发动机运转中由于燃油进入润滑油中而引起的稀释）
fuel distance 燃料储备行程（车辆油箱加满燃油后所能行驶的里程）
fuel distributor （机械式汽油喷射系统中，根据发动机工况正确计量油量并将汽油送入各汽缸喷射器的）汽油分配器
fuel dope 燃油添加剂
fuel dragster 使用非汽油基燃料的短程（1/4 英里）加速赛用车
fuel dribbling （柴油喷油终点后由喷嘴漏出的）燃油残滴，燃油漏滴
fuel economizer 见 economizer
fuel economy ①燃油经济性，燃料经济性（简称 FE）②燃油消耗量（=fuel consumption）
fuel economy contest （汽车）燃油经济性竞赛，节油竞赛，节油赛
fuel economy of chassis dynamometer test cycle （汽车的）底盘测功机试验循环油耗
fuel economy of road test cycles （汽车的）道路试验循环油耗
fuel economy oil 节油润滑油，节油机油（指可减少燃油消耗量的机油，通常是采用降低黏度和添加减摩剂等方法）
fuel-economy penalty （超过美国联邦油耗标准而受到的）油耗罚款，燃油经济性罚款
fuel-efficient engine 节油发动机，省油发动机，燃料经济性高的发动机（简称 FE engine）
fuel-efficient research vehicle 节油研究车
fuel endurance 燃料（储有量）所允许的持续行驶时间
fuel equivalence ratio 燃料当量比（发动机燃油消耗量完全燃烧所需空气量与实际进入发动机的空气量之比值，为过量空气系数的倒数，参见 coefficient of excess air）
fuel evaporative emissions （发动机）燃油蒸发有害排出物
fuel excess pipe 多余燃油的排出管
fuel feed pump 燃料供给泵，供油泵
fuel filler door ①储油式车门，装油车门，车门油箱（将燃油充注在密封的车门内，利用车门当油箱）②加油管盖
fuel filler door opener 加油盖自动开启装置（坐在驾驶室内即可开、关燃油箱加油盖，加油时不必下车）
fuel filler flap 加油管盖板（必须将该盖板翻起，才能接近加油管盖）
fuel filler neck 加油管管颈（指油箱加油管的上端）
fuel filling column （汽车加油站等的）加油柱
fuel film 燃油膜
fuel filter heater 燃油滤清器的加热器（装在滤清器处的燃油加热器）
fuel fine filter 燃油精滤器
fuel-fired heater 烧油加热器（燃烧液体材料，加热风暖设备或发动机用的空气等）
fuel flow control system 燃油流量控制装置，燃油流量控制系统（简称 FFCS）
fuel flowmeter 燃油流量计
fuel-flow totalizer 燃油累积流量计
fuel flow transducer 燃油流量传感器
fuel flow trim 燃油流量调整，燃油量调节
fuel fouling ①油路堵塞，燃油淤塞 ②呛油（指汽油机在某种情况下，化油器浮子机构无法控制进入的油量，形成浮子室油面过高，出现溢油、混合气过浓现象）
fuel fraction constitution 燃油的馏分组成

fuel gage [美] 燃油表,燃油油量表(=fuel gauge)

fuel gas cell 气体燃料电池(氢气燃料电池,天然气燃料电池,CO燃料电池等)

fuel gauge 燃油表,燃油油量表(=美 fuel gage)

fuel gauge tank unit 装在燃油箱内的燃油表传感器总成

fuel gauge tester 燃油表测试器

fuel grade 燃油品级,燃油等级

fuel gravity tank 自流式燃油箱(依靠燃油本身的重力,由油箱流出,而不需要汽油泵抽油)

fuel-handing component ①(汽车)燃油系部件②(泛指)接触燃油的部件

fuel hand pump 手动燃油泵,手油泵

fuel head ①燃油面高度②燃料压头

fuel heater/water separation system (燃油系的)燃油加热/水分离系统

fuel-hole diameter 喷油嘴喷孔直径(=injection diameter)

fuel horsepower 燃料马力($L_f = BH_1/632.5$,式中:B—燃料消费量,kg/h;H_1—燃料的低发热量)

fuelie 以赛车用汽油作燃料的轿车(口语)

fuel induction 燃油吸入,进油

fuel inflow banjo (燃油滤清器的)进油口管节头(该节头带螺栓,呈鼓肚形,故名)

fueling 加油的,加注燃油的(fueling equipment 加油设备;fueling station 加油站;fueling vehicle 加油车)

fuel-injected 燃油喷射的,燃油喷射式的

fuel injection 燃料喷射(指在压力下将燃油喷入发动机进气管、进气门口,汽缸预燃室,或直接喷入汽缸内)

fuel injection advance angle 喷油提前角(从开始喷油瞬时,以喷油器针阀升起为标志,到活塞至上止点时,曲轴所转过的转角)

fuel injection (automatic) advance device (机械式喷油系统的)喷油(自动)提前器(转速变化时自动调整喷油提前角)

fuel injection beginning 喷油始点,喷油起点

fuel injection duration angle 喷油持续角(喷油始点至喷油终点之间曲轴的持续转角)

fuel injection end 喷油终点

fuel injection pattern 燃油喷雾形状

fuel-injection pressure 燃油喷射压力

fuel injection pump (柴油机)喷油泵(将燃油提高压力,经高压油管送至喷油器,定时、定量地喷入汽缸等处的装置)

fuel injection pump body (柴油机)喷油泵上体(分体式喷油泵的上部,用以安装喷油元件等零部件)

fuel injection pump cam box (柴油机)喷油泵下体(分体式喷油泵的下部,用以安装油量调节机构和凸轮轴等部件)

fuel injection pump housing (柴油机)喷油泵体(用以安装喷油泵全部零部件的壳体,分整体式喷油泵体和分体式喷油泵体两种)

fuel injection pump tester (柴油机等的)高压油泵试验台,喷油泵试验台

fuel injection rate (柴油机喷油泵的)喷油率,燃油喷射率(单位时间或单位油泵凸轮轴转角内喷入汽缸的油量)

fuel injection rate cure (柴油机喷油泵的)喷油率曲线(喷油率随油泵凸轮轴或曲轴转角的变化规律)

fuel injection retarding device (柴油机)供油提前角推迟装置(为了减少柴油机NO_X的排放,使燃油泵的

供油角随转速下降或供油量的增加而自动适当推迟的装置)

fuel injection starting compression pressure 喷油始点压缩压力（压缩过程中喷油开始时汽缸内工质的压力）

fuel injection system 燃油喷射装置，喷油系统

fuel injection valve 见 fuel injector

fuel injector 喷油器（指将喷油泵供给的定量的燃油喷至各喷油点，如：汽油机的节气门体、进气门口或燃烧室内，柴油机的开式或半开式燃烧室或燃烧室的副室内的装置。一般由燃油压力或电磁控制的针阀，针阀控制的带喷孔的喷嘴喷孔锥体等组成，亦称 fuel injection valve。有的柴油机的喷油器与高压油泵做成一个整体，一缸一个，称为泵-喷嘴总成"pump-and injector unit"，或"fuel injection unit"）

fuel injector cleaner ①燃油喷嘴清洁器（如喷嘴通针等）②燃油喷嘴清洗剂（如：喷孔去胶剂等）

fuel injector igniter 燃料喷射引燃点火器（压燃式可燃气发动机主燃料为可燃气体，使用喷入汽缸内的液体燃料引燃被压缩的可燃气体，见 igniter injector，duel-fuel engine）

fuel inlet 燃油进油孔；进油口

fuel inlet ball check valve 进油口球阀，进油口止回阀

fuel inlet fitting 燃油进口接头

fuel jet ①燃油射流 ②燃料量孔（限定燃油流量的定径孔，一般为拧装在燃油出口处的定径孔螺塞）

fuel knock resistance 燃油抗爆性（见 octane number）

fuel lag 供油迟后

fuel lead ①供油提前 ②油道

fuel leak 燃料泄漏，燃料渗漏

fuel-lean 稀混合气的，稀（混合气）燃（烧）的（fuel-lean engine 稀燃发动机；fuel-lean mixture 稀混合气，见 equivalence ratio）

fuel level 燃油油面高度［fuel level adjustment，油面高度调节；fuel level ga(u)ge 燃油表，油量表，= fuel level indicator；fuel level lamp 油量警报灯，= fuel level tell-tale，警报燃油已少到规定的数量；fuel level warning sensor 燃油液面报警传感器，燃油油面低于规定值时接通警报信号的装置，= fuel level transmitter］

fuel (-level) indicator ①油量表，燃油液面指示器 ②最低油位指示灯

fuel lid 油箱盖

fuel lift 加油（= fuel feed）

fuel make-up 燃料补给，燃料补添

fuel mass flow 燃油质量流量

fuel-metering device 燃油计量装置（亦称 fuel metering unit）

fuel-metering needle 燃油量针（控制量孔或喷油孔出流断面，从而控制供油量）

fuel mileage 燃油里程（［美］指每加仑燃油所能行驶的英里数）

fuel mixture 燃料空气混合气，可燃混合气（= combustible mixture）

fuel octane number 燃料辛烷值（燃料抗爆震特性的一种衡量指标，见 octane number）

fuel oil 重柴油，燃料油（一般指柴油等重燃油；特指燃烧炉内用的燃油）

fuel orifice ①喷油嘴孔 ②燃油量孔（见 fuel jet②）

fuel-oxidant mixtures 燃料-氧化剂混合液

fuel pacer system 燃油过耗警告系，耗油量过大警报系（由装在进气管内的真空开关和装在左翼子板上的警告灯等组成，当驾驶员操作不当，致使油耗超过实际需要时，警告灯即发出警报）

fuel particles 燃油微粒
fuel passage 燃油管道
fuel permeation test （油箱的）渗漏试验，渗油试验
fuel pin 喷油器喷油孔阀针，燃油针阀
fuel pipeline 燃料管路
fuel pipe union 燃油管管接头
fuel preliminary filter 燃油粗滤器
fuel pressure gauge 燃料压力表
fuel pressure pulsation damper 燃油压力脉冲平缓器（电子控制燃油系统中平缓供油压力脉冲的装置，结构类似于燃油压力调节器，见 fuel pressure regulator，但它不与进气真空接通，其作用相当于一个蓄液器，装在回油管上，位于燃油压力调节的后方，用来吸收因燃油喷射器开放-关闭而产生的压力脉冲）
fuel pressure regulator （电子控制汽油喷射系统的）燃油压力调节器（用于保持最佳油压，一般为膜片式，膜片的弹簧端接大气或发动机真空，另一端控制燃油喷射器进油道的溢油孔，当油压过高时，顶开膜片，多余的燃油从溢油孔流回油箱）
fuel primer pump 起动加油泵，起动油泵
fuel-proof 不透油的，耐油的
fuel pulsation 燃油脉动，燃油脉冲（油泵泵油时造成的燃油压力的波动）
fuel pump （从油箱将燃油泵出的）①输油泵（亦称 lift pump）②（柴油机的）高压（喷油）泵
fuel pump bowl 汽油泵滤杯
fuel pump lever 输油泵手驱动杆
fuel-pump module （装在燃油箱内的）燃油泵总成体（油泵、滤清器和压力调节阀等组成的一个整体式树脂壳总成）
fuel pump relay （电动）燃油泵继电器（根据发动机控制模块的指令接通和断开油泵，一般装在发动机室内、空调继电器旁）
fuel pump rocker arm 汽油泵摇臂（= fuel pump lever）
fuel pump switch 燃油泵断电开关（见 inertia fuel cutoff switch，亦称 fuel pump shut off switch，= fuel cut-off switch）
fuel-pump tappet 燃油泵挺杆
fuel pump test stand 喷油泵试验台
fuel pump test terminal （电动）油泵（通电）测试线接线柱（该接线柱位于发动机室或仪表板下，通过导线与电动油泵的动力线连接，只要将一电压表接入该接线柱，便可测定电动油泵是否通电）
fuel pump timing 喷油泵喷油时刻，喷油泵正时
fuel pump voltage signal wire （电动）油泵电压信号线（由电动油泵电源电路正极接发动机控制模块的信号线，当油泵通电源时，该线发出电压信号，供发动机电子控制模块判断油泵电源电路是否完好）
fuel purification unit 燃料净化设备（简称 FPU）
fuel-quality sensor 燃油质量传感器（通过运用近红外线光谱测定燃油的组分及分子结构，确定其质量好坏）
fuel quantity gauge 燃油油量表
fuel-quantity transducer 油量传感器
fuel rack test （柴油机柱塞式喷油泵）齿条在不同位置时燃油喷射量的试验
fuel rail （燃油喷射系统中，存储输油泵供给的燃油，保持所要求的燃油压力并直接或通过其各缸的支管供给喷油器燃油的）储油歧管（因其形状酷似一根长的横木，由多根细杆支撑的栏杆"rail"，故名。由于 rail 还有轨道的意思，不少人将

这一术语译为油轨）见 common rail direction-injection system

fuel rate 燃料消耗率

fuel regulator valve 燃油调节阀

fuel reserve tank 备用燃油箱，副油箱（见 emergency fuel tank）

fuel reserve warning lamp 燃油余量警报灯

fuel resistance （橡胶制品等的）抗燃油性，耐油性

fuel return pipe 燃油回流管，回油管（简称 FRP）

fuel-return valve (assembly) 溢流阀（总成）（由溢流阀体、弹簧和弹簧座组成，用于保持喷油泵油道中一定的压力）

fuel-rich 富油的，浓混合气的

fuel-rich engine 浓混合气发动机（一般相对稀燃发动机而言，指常规汽油机）

fuel-rich flames 浓混合气火焰

fuel-rich mixture 浓混合气（参见 equivalence ratio）

fuel sac （柴油机喷油嘴针阀与喷孔之间的）余油腔

fuel saving 节约燃料，节油

fuel-saving aerodynamics （汽车）节油空气动力学（研究汽车减少空气阻力以节油的空气动力学）

fuel saving design （汽车外形的）节油设计，节能结构

fuel saving measure(s) 节油测量法

fuel-saving techniques 节油技术

fuel segregation 燃油沉析

fuel sensitivity 燃油（爆燃）敏感度（一般，不饱和烃芳香烃的爆燃敏感度大，而饱和烃、链烷烃的抗爆燃敏感度小）

fuel sensor 燃油存量传感器，燃油面高度传感器（有时称 fuel sender 或 sending unit）

fuel servicing truck 带（燃）油罐的加油车

fuel shift switch 燃料转换开关（在两用燃料汽车中，两种燃料的转换开关，参见 flexible fuel car）

fuel shutoff knob （柴油机等的）断油按钮

fuel sieve 滤油网；燃油滤网

fuel specific gravity 燃油比重

fuel spray characteristic(s) 燃油喷射特性，燃油喷雾特性

fuel starvation 供油不足（由于油道堵塞、气阻或油泵故障造成的供油量不足以维持发动机正常运转的故障）

fuel storage stability 燃料长期储存稳定性（一般指储存期的抗空气氧化作用而保持性能不变的能力）

fuel strainer 滤油器，燃油滤网

fuel stratified injection 见 FSI

fuel supply advance angle （柴油机）喷油提前角（从开始供油瞬时，柱塞喷油泵以出油阀升起，分配式油泵以凸轮顶起滚柱为标志，到活塞行至上止点，曲轴所转过的转角）

fuel supply pump 输油泵（从油箱中吸出燃油并以一定压力和流量输入喷油泵的装置）

fuel supply rate （柴油机喷油泵的）供油率（单位时间或单位油泵凸轮转角内从喷油泵压出的油量）

fuel supply rate curve 供油规律（供油率随油泵凸轮或曲轴转角的变化规律）

fuel swirler 离心式燃油喷射器

fuel tank capacity 见 fuel tank volume

fuel tank check valve 燃油箱止回阀（防止箱内的液体燃油进入蒸发排放物储存装置）

fuel tanker 运油车，（燃料）油罐车（用于运输燃油，装有消电装置、通气阀、灭火器具等）

fuel tank filler cap 燃料箱加注孔盖，燃油箱加油口盖

fuel tank float type sensor 燃油箱浮子式油量传感器

fuel tank sender 燃油箱油量传感器，油箱油面高度传感器

fuel tank truck （燃油）油罐车（运油车，加油车的统称）

fuel tank volume 燃油箱容积（= volume of fuel tank, fuel tank capacity）

fuel-tight 不漏燃油的

fuel tolerance （发动机的）燃料裕度，燃料适应性（指发动机对燃料规格要求的宽严程度）

fuel transfer pump （柴油机等的）输油泵，供油泵

fuel validation test center 燃油鉴定试验中心

fuel vaporizer 燃料蒸发器，燃油汽化器

fuel vapor pocket 燃油蒸气泡

fuel vapo(u)r 燃油蒸气

fuel vapour lock （汽油）气封，气阻（简称 vapour lock, 因汽油蒸汽造成的油路阻塞）

fuel vapour pressure sensor 燃油蒸汽压力传感器（简称 fvps）

fuel vapour recirculation system 见 evaporative emission control system

fuel vapour storage (charcoal) canister 活性炭燃油蒸气储蓄罐（见 char-coal canister storage system）

fuel-viscosity variation 燃油黏度（随温度等的）变化

fuel-water emulsion 油-水乳化液，（发动机用）乳化油（指按一定比例将水掺入燃油中形成的油水乳状混合油，目的是节油和净化）

fugacity 挥发性，逸散性，逸散度

fugitive 一时的，短效的，易消失的

Fuji Heavy Industries Co., Ltd （日本）富士重工（业）有限公司

fulcrum 支点，铰接点（指杆件转动的支承，亦称 pivot point）

fulcrum ball 球铰的球头（球窝支承的球头）

fulcrum bearing 支点承座，支撑，刀口支撑，棱柱支撑（参见 knife bearing）

fulcrum pin 支点销（如转向主销）

fulcrum ring （膜片弹簧离合器膜片弹簧的）支承圈（位于锥式膜片弹簧两侧的钢丝支承圈，亦称 pivot ring, diaphragm spring ring）

fulcrum slide 支点滑板

full adder （汽车电子控制模块中的）全加器（亦称 three-input adder）

full adjustable seat 全调节式座椅（一般指高、低、前、后及靠背斜度均可调的座椅）

full advance （喷油、点火、气门开启等的）最大提前角

full-airwedge brake 全气动楔形制动器

full area wiping system （丰田公司气动）全面积刮水系统（将刮水器开关置于"高"挡，便可将刮水角度加到最大，有效刮除风窗玻璃大面积上的雨水）

full auto choke system 全自动阻风门控制系统（简称 FACS，见 automatic choke）

Full-auto Full-time 4D （日产公司研制的）全自动全时四轮驱动系统（一种黏性耦合器式全时 4 轮驱动系统的商品名）

full automatic vehicle 全自动车（智能型汽车，具有自动驾驶系统、卫星导行系统等装备的汽车，完全由电子计算机操纵，= intelligent vehicle, 参见 smart car）

full beam （汽车前照灯的）远光（= high beam, upper beam, driving beam, main beam, traffic beam）

full beam to dip switch （汽车前照灯的）变光开关（亦称 dimmer, 用以变换远近光）

full-boiling range reference fuel （试验用）全沸点标准燃油（在美国指 CRG 科学技术协作委员会配制的一种用于抗爆性要求试验的标准燃油，参见 antiknock requirement testing）

full boost 最大增压压力

full-bore running （汽油机）节气门全开运转

full-brake stop 满踏板行程紧急制动

full cab-over 平头型（汽车整个驾驶室在发动机的正上方）

full cabriolet ［美］篷顶四门轿车（4~7座，6窗，见 cabriolet）

full capping （轮胎的）全翻新，大翻修（指旧轮胎的胎面和胎肩等全面翻新）

full carbon wheel 全碳素纤维车轮（据称：其重量仅铝、镁合金车轮的 50%~75%）

full-cell stack 燃料电池组

full charge-state test 全充电状态试验（简称 FCT）

full-circle contact 全圆周上的接触

full closed crankcase ventilating system 全封闭型曲轴箱通风系统

full concealed wiper 全隐蔽式刮水器（不工作时，刮水片及刮水臂均处于隐藏位置）

full control of access （高速公路的）全入口控制（交叉口全部为立交，禁止与一切交叉道路平交）

full curve 实线曲线，连续曲线（参见 solid line curve）

full cut valve 节气门全开 EGR 切断阀（当节气门全开或开度在 55°以上加速时，与节气门连动的凸轮将该阀顶开，于是空气进入 EGR 阀的控制真空通管，EGR 阀在大气作用下断开废气还流，简称 FCV）

full-depth gear 全齿高齿轮（未作高度修正）

full depth tooth 全齿高，全高齿

full diameter 外径（= external diameter）

full Diesel 全柴油机，全压燃式发动机（指起动时全靠压燃点火的发动机，相对 semidiesel engine 而言，= diesel engine，一般简称 diesel）

full displacement position （变量泵）全排量位置

full door 到顶门（从车身底部到车身顶部）

full drive 用最快速度行车

full-drop window 全落式车窗，全程升降窗

full-duplex ①全双工（对通信电路，指两端能同时发送或接收数据的一种工作方式；对计算机，指可通过一条母线或通信信道同时向两个方向发送信息的能力，简称 duplex）②双向的，双工位的，双工的，双面的

full electric steering 全电力转向（系统）

full elliptic spring 椭圆形钢板弹簧（指由两架半椭圆形钢板弹簧一仰一扣地合在一起构成的整架钢板弹簧，因其似以一封闭的椭圆形，故名，见 semielliptic spring）

full film friction 全流体膜摩擦（指两摩擦面完全被流体膜隔开的摩擦状态，亦称 full film lubrication 全流体膜润滑）

full-flat able seat （靠背）可完全放平的座椅

full floating axle 见 fully floating axle shaft

full-floating axle shaft 全浮式半轴（指只传递转矩，不承受弯矩的半轴）

full-floating piston pin 全浮式活塞销（指可在连杆小头和活塞销座孔内自由转动的活塞销，仅限制其轴向移动，= full floating wrist pin, full floating gudgeon pin）

full flow heat exchanger 全流式热交换器（指全部流体都通过的热交换器）

full-flow oil filter 全流式机油滤清器（串联在主油道中，发动机全部循环机油均通过它滤清）

full-flow sampling 全流取样法（如：全流式烟度计的取样方式）

full-flow smokemeter 全流式烟度计（发动机所有汽缸或部分汽缸排出的全部废气都流过烟度计进行检测）

full fluid-film lubrication 全液膜润滑（指两接触面完全为连续的润滑油膜所隔开）

full fluid steering 全液压转向（转向盘不通过杆系而是通过液压系统和液压管道实现转向操控的系统）

full force feed lubrication 全压力润滑，全强制润滑

full-fresh oiling 全新鲜机油润油（指全过程均用新鲜机油润滑整个工作表面，用过的机油不再循环使用）

full front crash test （车辆的）前面全宽碰撞（全前面、非偏置碰撞）试验

full function trip computer 全功能行程计算机[亦称 full size basic trip computer，指车载的专用于获得有关行程信息的小型计算机，由功能选择键盘、中央处理器、显示装置和连接线路组成。所谓全功能是指其可提供信息项目较多的相对概念。一般全功能型可在行驶途中根据驾驶员按键选择提供燃油信息（瞬时油耗，平均油耗，空箱里程）、车速-里程信息（平均车速，目标平均车速，车速警报，目的地里程）、时间信息（已行驶时间，估计到达时间）、时钟信息（时间，日期闹铃时间）等]

full harness seat belt 捆绑式安全带（亦称 muti point seat belt 多点式安全带，4点，5点，6点式安全带均可称为捆绑式安全带）

full head lamp 远光灯（= long distance light）

full-height tooth 标准齿（未修正的，具有标准齿高的齿）

full house 指经过全面改造和加装全套设备，以发挥最高性能的发动机

full-injection turbine （液力变矩器的）导轮（= reaction turbine，一般称 reactor，指在液力变矩器泵轮和涡轮之间与壳体刚性连接或通过单向轮连接的导轮，它可以改变壳体内腔工作液的流动方向，给涡轮一个反作用力矩，而增大涡轮的输出转矩）

full keystone ring 全楔形环（环的上下两面都有斜度）

full-laden 满负荷的，满载的

full lap （货车车身木构件的）全搭接结合

full leather（upholster） 全真皮（座椅）

full LED headlight 全发光二极管前照灯（见 light emitting device）

full legal load 法定满负荷，法定满载荷

full-length contact 全长上的接触

full-life restoration 全寿命恢复（使修理的车辆恢复到原来的使用寿命）

full line 实线（参见 continuous line）

full load ①满载，满负荷（在规定条件下允许连续工作的最大负荷）②节气门全开工况（= wide open throttle，或其简称 WOT）

full load characteristic 全负荷特性，满负荷特性，外特性（见 external characteristic）

full-load cooling test （发动机）满负荷时（冷却系）冷却能力的试验

full-loaded 满负荷的

full load engine 按满负荷工作的发动机

full load enrichment 混合气的满负荷加浓

full-load fuel consumption （发动机）全负荷时的燃油消耗量

full load intermediate speed smoke characteristic （柴油机的）满负荷中间速度排烟特性

full-load life 全负荷寿命

full-load method （发动机烟度测定的）全负荷法（在台架上测定柴油机全负荷稳定运转时，不同转速下的烟度值）

full load performance curve 外特性（曲线）（在速度特性中，当燃料供给调节机构固定在全负荷位置时，试验所测得的速度特性曲线，即：在节气门全开时，发动机转速为函数的发动机功率、转矩、油耗等的变化特性曲线，亦称全负荷速度特性曲线，= external characteristics, full load characteristics, full throttle characteristics，柴油机亦称 full rock performance curve。发动机校正器起作用时的外特性曲线，亦称校正外特性）

full load power （发动机的）满负荷功率（指节气门开度最大或柱塞处于最大规定供油位置时的功率）

full load rated speed smoke characteristic （柴油机等的）满负荷额定转速排烟特性

full-load stall （液力变矩器等的）满载零速，最大负荷失速（现象）（指变矩器涡轮在达到所能拖动的最大负荷时而停止转动的现象）

full load stop 全负荷限制器（限制喷入柴油机汽缸内最大喷油量的装置）

full-load test 满负荷试验，满载试验

full-load torque 满载转矩（简称 FLT）

full-load trip 满载行程，满载运程

full lock （转向轮转到其锁止位置的）最大转向角（见 lock④）

full locking differential 全锁止式差速器（大多是在普通锥齿轮差速器基础上附加强制锁止机构——差速锁构成。当一个驱动车轮打滑时，通过电动、气动或机械操纵锁止机构，推动啮合套用锁销将壳体与半轴锁成一体，而使之失去差速作用）

full-lock skidding （车轮）抱死时的滑移

full-monocoque construction 承载式车身结构，独壳式车身结构（简称 monocoque construction，指无车架的整体结构形式的车身，亦称 unitary construction body 或 chassisless body）

full-open contact （两级式节气门位置传感器的）全开触点（亦称 power contact）

full-open throttle 全开节气门

full panel 板件总成（指由主板和各附加板件组成的车身某板件总成，如：轿车的前围总成由前围板、前围上盖板、前围侧板加风窗玻璃框组成等）

full pelt （汽车）全速（前进）

full pitch winding ①全节矩绕组，整节矩绕组 ②整节矩绕法

full plies （轮胎的）胎体层，帘布层（= carcass plies）

full-power circuit 全功率加浓装置（见 power system）

full power trial 全功率试验，全功率试车（简称 FPT）

full pressure system （指用油泵将机油从油底壳吸出并泵入发动机各润滑点的）全压力式润滑系统

full race cam 纯赛车（发动机用）凸轮（升程大，加减速度快，仅用于赛车）

full range throttle position sensor 全

ful

程式节气门位置传感器（简称 full-range TPS，向电子控制模块发送节气门从全闭到全开的各种开度信息，并可发送其开、闭速度，即快、慢信息）

full-range transmission 全变速范围的变速器，全程变速器

full-scale ①全尺寸的，原尺寸的，实物尺寸的，与原物一样大小的 ②全刻度的，满刻度的 ③完全的，全部的，完整的，未删节的 ④自然的，自然条件下的，真实的 ⑤全刻度值，满刻度值 ⑥足尺，实物尺寸

full-scale clearance 完全清零，全部清除储存信息

full-scale crash test 全尺寸(模型)碰撞试验，实物尺寸(模型)碰撞(试验)

full scale draft ①全尺寸草图，全尺寸设计图 ②（车身）主图板（表示车身主要轮廓和结构截面的图版。表示车身各零部件间的装配关系，各零件的结构截面，以及部件的运动轨迹校核，如：车门、行李箱盖等）

full-scale investigation ①实物研究，实物实验，②全尺寸模型研究

full scale model 实尺模型，原尺寸模型

full scale styling representation mock-up（汽车的）全尺寸造型模型（根据汽车内部和外部造形式样模型的主要尺寸制成的全尺寸模型，和实际汽车大小一样，供人们评价：外形、车门状况，视野状况，内部布置，操纵机构的位置，内部气流等。经过不断地评价改进，其各部主要尺寸就成为原型车设计的尺寸标准，参见 seating buck, prototype vehicle）

full scale wind tunnel test 整车风洞试验，全尺寸风洞试验（整车式全尺寸模型置于风洞中试验）

full-scope windshield 全景风窗玻璃（= panoramic windshield）

full service history（简称 fsh）全维修作业记录清单（指说明已对车辆进行过的全部维修作业的文件）

full-size car ①大尺寸轿车，大型轿车（= big car, large car）②（美特指美国轿车目录）最大型的轿车（如：Buick 的 LeSabre，Cadillac 的 Fleetwood，Chevrolet 的 Caprice，Lincon 的 Continental，Oldsmobile98 等长 213~235 英寸，六座大轿车）

full-size（d） 实际尺寸（的），全尺寸（的），原型（的），原大的，最大尺寸的，足尺的，实物大小的，真实的，全规模的，总容积的，满容量的

full size pickup 大型客货两用车

full skirt piston 全筒式活塞，筒式活塞，全裙式活塞（裙部未开缝的，有的装有裙部环，= full trunk piston）

full slide adjustment range（of seat）（座椅位置的）前、后滑动调节全程范围（mm）

full slipper skirt piston 围涎裙活塞（活塞主、副推力面有儿童围涎状裙，非推力面裙部被切除）

Fullspace 满空间（意大利 Merker 公司的旅居挂车的商品名）

full-stop braking distance（汽车的）停车制动距离（从施加制动力开始到完全停车，汽车所行的距离）

full-stop coasting-distance 滑行停车距离（不施加制动力，只依靠滚动阻力、空气阻力等，使滑行车辆由一定车速到完全停车的距离）

full-tank range 满箱里程（燃油箱加满后的汽车可行驶的里程）

full tapered bead seat rim 全斜胎圈座轮辋（简称 TB，指两侧胎圈座向中部成一定斜角的轮辋）

full throttle 节气门全开（美称 wide open throttle，= full bore）

full-throttle characteristics 见 full load performance curve

full throttle performance （自动变速器的）全油门特性（输入转矩和转速对应于发动机净扭矩曲线上的值时液力传动装置或液力变速器的特性）

full-throttle test （发动机）节气门全开试验，（发动机外特性试验）

full-time transfer case （全时四轮驱动用的）全时四轮分动箱（箱内装有差速器，允许前、后车轮以不同的转速旋转）

full time 4WD with center differential 带中央差速器的全时四轮驱动系（中央差速器亦称桥间差速器"inter axle differential，一般都装有锁止装置"）

full-time 4-wheel drive 全时四轮驱动（美，简称 full time 4 WD 或 full time drive，= permanent four wheel drive，指没有可断开某一车轿驱动装置的全四轮驱动式车辆，因而全部车轮在任何情况下，均为驱动轮，参见 part-time 4WD）

full trailer 全挂车（指其全部载重均由自身的车轮支承，仅由牵引车牵引并至少有两根车轴的挂车，见 semitrailer）

full trailer length 全挂车长（全挂车有包括和不包括牵引杆的两种长度）

full-transistor ignition system 全晶体管点火系（亦称无触点式晶体管点火系）

full trunk piston 筒式活塞，全裙（式）活塞（相对 slipper piston 而言，= full skirt piston）

full-type bearing without retainer 无保持架的全滚子或球轴承

full view ①全视图 ②全视野的，视野开阔的，全景的

full-view sunroof （轿车的）全景天窗

full voltage starting 全电压起动，直接起动（参见 direct starting）

full-wave rectifier 全波整流器（指利用二极管的单向导电性，由两个半波电路组合而成，在两个半波内都有输出电压，而且是同一方向，即可得到全波电流的变交流电为直流电的整流器）

full-width hub brake 全宽度轮毂制动器（制动鼓宽度等于轮毂宽度）

fully adjustable speed drive 无级变速传动装置

fully-articulated crash test dummy 全关节型（汽车）碰撞试验用假人

fully charged 充足电的；装满料的，充足气的；充满的

fully-constant-mesh 常啮合式（的）（全部齿轮均处于常啮合状态的，如：full-constant-mesh all spur gear transmission 前进挡的全部齿轮副都是直齿的常啮式变速器；full-constant-mesh all helical gear transmission 前进挡的全部齿轮副都是斜齿的常啮式变速器）

fully discharged 全放完电的

Fully Electrical Brake System 全电力制动系统（见 Brake by Wire System）

fully electrical brake system 全电控电力制动系统（见 brake-by-wire system②）

fully electronic ignition 全电子点火（指无分电器，由电子控制模块按最佳点火提前角曲面控制的点火系统，一般具有汽缸选择性爆燃控制、闭合角控制、数字式怠速稳定性控制等功能）

fully enclosed 全封闭的；密闭的，密封的，不漏气的

fully equipped engine 全附件发动机（发动机装有完成规定任务所必需的全部附件，除基础发动机所包括

的附件外，还包括涡轮增压泵、排气系、冷却系、起动机及排气净化装置，见 basic engine）

fully floating axle 全浮式后桥（指后桥半轴只传递转矩，而整个车重和轴向载荷由车轮轴承直接传给后桥壳）

fully inflated 充足气的

fully reclining turnable seat 靠背倾斜度可调到底的可回转式座椅

fully-sliding condition （车轮完全抱死时产生的）全滑移状态，全打滑状态

fully transistorized 全半导体化的，全晶体管化的

fully wrap-around rear window 全景视野后窗

fuly-recessed door handle 全凹式车门把手

fume （一般指气味强烈的）烟气或蒸气（常用复数）

fume consumer 窜缸气吸收装置（将从燃烧室窜入曲轴箱内的气体吸入进气系统的一种装置）

function ①函数（简称 F）②作用，功能，机能

functional addressing （汽车电子控制系统信息的）功能编址（用于与多个网点有关的信息。功能编址指给上述信息定址并按所定的功能址，将该信息发送至两个或两个以上有关的网点。如：运用功能地址，可将车速信息发送至要求车速数据的所有网点）

functional-block diagram 功能框图（按功能表示复杂集成电路内部基本单元结构的图，简称 functional diagram "方框图，框图"）

functional gradient material 功能梯度材料，功能模糊材料（日本发明的一种新型材料，这种材料一面是金属的，另一面则是陶瓷的，它不同于将金属板料和陶瓷板料贴到一起的复合材料，而是材料本身的分子结构，逐步由金属向陶瓷连续不断地变化，致使金属与陶瓷没有分界线，故称模糊材料）

functionality ①实用（性能符合设计目的），符合实际②（计算机或电子控制系统的）功能，功能范围③（产品的）设计目的，设计功能

functional superset 超级功能集（如：C 级多路复用网络被定义为 B 级和 A 级多路复用网络的超级功能集。作为超级功能集，必须具有能实现该集内的网络的全部功能的通信能力）

functional symbol （元件）功能符号

functional test ①功能试验，机能试验（简称 FT）②（电子控制系统自诊断系统的）自我功能测试（常称 Self-Test）

function block 功能块，功能部件，功能单元，亦称 functional unit，指能完成特定功能的硬件或软件，或由两者构成的实体。在汽车电子计算机系统指完成某一功能的硬件或软件或二者组成的模块，如：算术逻辑，运算单元，存储单元，控制模块，输入一输出接口等，其中的硬件称 function device 功能硬件）

function device 功能器件（简称 FD，完成某一功能的硬件）

function element （完成某一）功能（的）元件

function generators （多功能）函数发生器（一种多用电子信号发生器，可输出方波、三角波、正弦波等，其输出的模拟变量等于其输入变量的某个函数）

function of road surface roughness 路面平面度函数［路面相对基准平面的高度 x 沿道路走向 l 的变化 $x(l)$，亦称路面纵剖面曲线］

function plotter 函数关系记录仪

function-select keyboard 功能选

择键盘

function (sequential) matrix 功能时序表（一列有若干输入，并对每一输入组态给出可能的输出组态，而且可直接读出从每一特定的输入组态向任意其他输入组态转换时产生的输出组态的表）

function specification （车辆）功能说明，功能规格，使用规范

function table （指明数字电路的输入端和输出端上的数字信号值之间关系的）功能表（表中各列给出数字电路一个输入端或一个输出端上的数字信号值，表中各行给出各输入端上的数字信号的一组值，以及在各输出端上所产生的数字信号的结果值）

fundamental ①基本，主要成分 ②基波，一次谐波，基本谐波 ③基本的，根本的，主要的；原始的，固有的 ④基波的，基本频率的

fundamental frequency 基本频率，基谐频率，基频（= base frequency，任何一个以 T 为周期的复杂振动，可以分解为一系列简谐振动的叠加，这些简谐振动的频率等于系统的固有振动频率 ω 的整倍数，ω 称为基频，2ω，3ω 等称为 2 倍频，3 倍频等，统称倍频或谐频）

fundamental function ①基本功能，主要功能 ②本征函数，特征函数（= eigen function, proper function）

fundamental parts 基础零件（指汽车上成为总成装配基础的重要壳体件）

fundamental research 基础（性）研究

funnel ①漏斗，喇叭口，漏斗状物，喇叭形物 ②烟囱

funneled 漏斗形的，带漏斗的

funneling 路幅漏斗形缩小，车道数减少，路幅宽度变窄

"fun-of-driving-first" design idea （车辆的）"驾驶乐趣第一"的设计理念

fun vehicle 游乐车，休闲用车

FUP 熔点（fusible point）

furfural resin 糠醛树脂

furnace 炉

furniture van 厢式家具搬运车（= pantechnicon van）

furol ①重油，燃料油，渣油（用来铺路）②糠醛（$C_4H_3O \cdot CHO$）

furred radiator 水垢阻塞的散热器

furring ①水垢 ②蓄电池极板积垢

fuse ①熔断丝（简称 F，亦写作 fuze，旧称保险丝，一般为熔点低的或细小的金属丝或薄片，串联在电路的前端，当通过的电流、电压达到额定熔断值时，熔断丝即被烧断而对电路起保护作用。fuse alarm 熔断丝烧断警报信号；fuse block，亦称 fuse box 熔断丝盒。汽车电气和电子系统，往往将多条线路的熔断丝集中装在一个带有可卸式外盖的盒形容器内，称 fuse cylinder，亦称 fuse tube，为装有熔断片或丝、两端带有熔断丝接线端的玻璃或陶瓷管；fuse link，见 fusible link；fuse plug 插塞式熔断丝，熔断丝插头；fuse rating 熔断丝额定值，包括额定电流，额定熔断电流，额定工作电压，额定工作频率等，当无特别说明时，一般指额定熔断电流；fuse wire 熔断丝）②熔化 ③电器，电路等因熔断丝熔断而断路（如：fog lamp has fused，指雾灯因熔丝烧断而熄灭）

fused-salt high-temperature cell 熔盐高温电池（以熔盐作为电解质的电池）

fusibility 可熔性；熔度

fusible 可熔的，易熔的

fusible alloy 低熔点合金，易熔合金

fusible cone （测高温用的）熔锥（参见 pyrometric cone,）

fusible cut 熔丝断路器（亦称 fusible cut-out，不可复通式断路器的一种，由熔断丝烧断而断路）

fusible link ①（大电流）熔断丝（一般指熔断电流极大的熔断丝或熔断条，其额定熔断电流值为100A，300A 等。车型不同，这种熔断丝的安装方式与位置也不同。如：有的将电源电路按点火系、前照灯系、充电系分开，各设一个大电流熔丝，合装在一个熔丝盒内） ②（电流的）可熔断连接，熔丝连接 ③（可编程只读存储器或逻辑电路的）可熔断连接，熔丝连接（一种制作法，通过编制程序将某些熔丝连接的电路用大电流熔断，而未加大电路的熔丝电路仍保持接通）

fusible plug = fuse plug

fusible point 熔点（= fusing point, fusion point，简称 FUP，亦称 fusion temperature）

fusible safety vent （油箱等的）可熔安全孔（由易熔材料制成的孔塞，当箱内温度、压力升高到规定值时，该孔塞即被熔脱或冲脱，而防止油箱爆炸）

fusing current （熔断丝的）熔断电流（指可使熔断丝烧断的额定熔断电流）

fusion ①熔解，熔化，溶接，结合，合流，汇合，合成 ②（核）聚变（反应）

Fusion Hybrid FORD 公司一款中级复合动力硬顶四门轿车（sedan）的车名

fusion point 熔点，熔化温度（简称 FNP 或 fnp，见 fusible point）

fusion welding 熔焊（= fusing welding，简称 welding，指焊件基体金属熔化的气焊或电焊，以别于焊件金属不熔化的钎焊）

Futuristic （车辆的设计、结构等）极其现代的，极其新潮的，未来的

fuze 见 fuse

fuzzification of inputs 输入的模糊化

fuzzified data 模糊化数据

fuzzy control 模糊控制（不同于用精确数量进行的数字控制，而是按人的逻辑思维判断方法形成的模糊控制规则，用模糊量进行的控制。模糊控制规则的一般形式为："if A and B then C"，其中 A、B、C 均为模糊量。如在发动机转速模糊控制中，有三种模糊量：一为发动机输出转速与目标转速的差额 A。二为转速差额的变化率 B。A、B 一般取 8 个模糊量：负大"NB"，负中"NM"，负小"NS"，负零"NZ"，正零"PZ"，正小"PS"，正中"PM"，正大"PB"。这 8 个模糊量均不是精确值，而是一个范围。三为控制量 C，取 7 个模糊量：负大，负中，负小，负零，正小，正中，正大。当传感器测得的 A 与 B 为上述某一模糊量时，便可从储存在计算机中的控制表格中查出与之相对应的 C 的模糊量，而按该量进行控制。不过被控对象即发动机进行控制时，还需对 C 的模糊量进行"精确化"，以驱动执行机构）

fuzzy control rule table 模糊控制规则表

fuzzy logic design 模糊逻辑设计

fuzzy neural decoupled hybrid controller 模糊神经解耦控制器

fuzzy neural network 模糊神经网络

fuzzy programming 模糊编程（模糊逻辑程序的设计、编写和调试过程）

FWB 前轮制动器（front wheel brake）

FWD ①前轮驱动（front wheel drive 的简称）②四轮驱动（four wheel-drive 的简称）

fwd ①向前的，前面的（forward） ② = FWD

FWD/REV change-over mechanism (变速器的) 前进挡/倒车挡变换机构 (forward-reverse change-over mechanism 的简称)

FWD vehicle with motor drive rear wheel 带电动机驱动后轮的（内燃机）前轮驱动式汽车（简称 e-4WD，指在常规内燃机前轮驱动系统的基础上加装后轮电动机驱动系统的四轮驱动车辆）

GA 遗传算法（genetic algorithm 的简称，是一种借鉴生物界自然选择和自然遗传机制的随机化搜索算法，由美国 Michigan 大学 Holland 教授提出）

Ga 镓（gallum, 原子量 69.723）

gabarit(e) ［法］①外廓、外形尺寸 ②模型，样板 ③曲线板，曲线规

gabarite lamp 车宽灯，车身外廓标志灯

GAC ［美］通用联合汽车公司（General Automotive Corporation 的简称）

gag ①塞头，堵头 ②压板，压紧装置 ③堵塞，关闭（阀门）；(发动机)关车熄火 ④矫正，压平

gage 见 gauge

gage tolerance 量规公差

gage zero shift 仪表零位偏移

gaging nozzle （喷油泵）调校用喷嘴

gag press 矫正压床，矫正压力机

gain ①增加，增进 ②盈利 ③增益 ④增益系数（= gain factor，指信号通过放大器、扩音器、天线后幅度增加的程度；系统输出功率与输入功率之比；设备的输出信号与输入信号之比，通常用分贝 dB 表示）⑤获得；改进；增加；逼近，抵达；（钟表等）比正确时间走得快；赢得

gain characteristic 增益特性

gain control 增益控制，增益调节

gain factor 见 gain④

gaiter 波纹防尘罩（= boot 的简称②）

gal ①伽，10^{-2} m/s² （见 Galileo）②加仑（见 gallon）

GAL ①允许总负载，容许总载荷（gross allowance load 的简称）② = gal①

Galaxsee glass 盖克西玻璃（20 世纪 90 年代初盛行的一种隐蔽玻璃，作为车用风窗玻璃，外部看不见车内，含有稀土矿物质，呈深黄黑色）

gale 大风，风暴，八级大风（风速 17.2 ~ 20.7m/s, = fresh gale）

gale signal 大风信号，风暴信号

GALFAN 加尔防（一种含 5% 铝和稀土元素的锌合金热浸镀钢板的商品名）

Galileo 伽（利略）（重力加速度单位，= 10^{-2}米/秒², 简称 gal）

gall ①损伤，擦伤，磨破 ②咬死（如：滚动轴承滚子卡死）

gallery 走廊，通道

g-alleviation 加速度作用减弱，加速率变缓

galley 旅宿车内的厨房

galling ①（金属表面）磨损，擦伤 ②（两金属表面间因过度磨损而）咬住，卡滞 ③（齿轮）塑变，黏结

galling of liners 拉缸（指缸套擦伤）

gallium 镓（Ga）

gallium arsenate 砷化镓（GaAs，耐高温集成电路材料）

gallium arsenate crystal 砷化镓晶体（一种在磁场作用下，导电性变化的半导体材料）

gallon 加仑［英制容积单位，代号 gal，有英国加仑 gal（UK）和美国加仑 gal（US）之分。1 gal（UK）= 6/5gal（US）=4.54609L（升），1 gal（US）= 3.78541 L（升）。美国又有干、液加仑之分。在英、美，习惯上仍用加仑表示油耗，gallon per unit 指每单位里程油耗，该单位可能是小时，英里，百英里，吨英里等，如：gallon per hour 每小时油耗的加仑数，加仑/小时，简称 GPH；gallon per mile 每英里加仑数，加仑/英里，简称 GHM。1 gal（UK）/mile = 2.835L/km，1 gal（US）/mile = 2.352L/km］

gallonage ①加仑容积 ②加仑量，加仑数 ③按加仑计的燃油消耗量（如：每加仑燃油所能行驶的英里数等）

galloping （发动机运转不正常或其他原因造成的汽车车轮时而离地高速）疾驶，跳跃飞奔

gallows bit 双柱吊架

gallows frame 门式吊架，龙门起重架

G AL -SHIFT 全（方位）加速度 G 控制自动换挡（弯道行驶辅助系统，可预测弯道制动减速行驶时要求的动力，自动降到最佳挡位并根据所测出的前、后及横向加速度 G 实时变换或维持最佳挡位，确保车辆弯道平顺行驶）

Galvalume 嘉露维姆［一种热浸镀铝（55%）锌（43.4%）硅（1.6%）合金钢板的商品名］

galvanic ①电流的 ②电镀的 ③镀锌的

galvanic battery 蓄电池组，原电池组

galvanic cell 自发电池，原电池，一次电池（primary cell 的旧称，指化学能通过不可逆反应转变为电能，因而只能一次性使用，不可再充电的电池，亦称 galvanic element 或 primary element）

galvanic corrosion 原电池腐蚀，电偶腐蚀，电化学锈蚀，电蚀，（两种不同金属的接合件遇到某种电解液时，就会分别极化成阴极和阳极，形成原电池，产生腐蚀现象，即由于电位差引起的腐蚀现象）

galvanic protection 防自发电池腐蚀，防原电池腐蚀，防电化学腐蚀

galvanic skin response （人体）肌肤电流反应

galvanization ①电镀 ②（无特别说明时，一般指）镀锌 ③通以电流

galvanize ［动］①通电流于… ②电镀（包括热浸镀 hot-dip galvanization 和电沉积 electrodeposition）③（特指）镀锌（指用上述方法电镀锌或锌合金层防锈、防腐蚀）

galvanized coating ①电镀层 ②（无特别说明时，一般特指）锌（合金）镀层

galvanizing bath ①镀槽 ②镀锌（浴）槽

galvannealing 镀锌层扩散（退火）处理（工艺）［指将热浸镀锌钢板在 600～650℃下退火并在镀层锌合金熔点（450℃左右）保温一定时间，此后缓慢冷却至常温，目的是使镀层与基体金属表面间形成较厚的、含 γ 铁 21%～28% 的锌-铁合金层，即：所谓的 gamma layer 或 γ layer，以提高镀层在钢板上的附着强度］

galvano-chemistry 电化学

galvanolysis 电解

galvanomagnetism 电磁

galvanometer 电流表（测定电流大小及方向和电压的仪表）

galvanometer oscillograph ①示波器

式电流表 ②示波器（简称 oscillograph, = oscilloscope 或 gal scope, 各种波形显示电流、电压变化及其各项数值的仪器）

GALVND 经镀锌层扩散处理的 (galvannealed, 见 galvannealing)

galvo amplifier 电流放大器

game theory 博弈论，对策论，策略运筹学（运用数学分析方法，去选择最佳策略，亦称 theory of game）

gamma ①伽马（磁场强度单位，= 10^{-5} 奥斯特，简称 gm）②γ量，微克（$1\mu g = 10^{-6} g$）③（摄影）灰度（非线性）系数

gamma layer γ 铁-锌合金层（见 galvannealing）

gamma rays γ 射线，γ 辐射

gamut ①全量程，全范围 ②全音域

gang ①组、队，一组，一套，全套，路，路程 ②连接，同轴连接；组合成套，联合成组 ③同轴的，连接的

gang control 联动操纵，同轴控制，共轴调节

ganged 成组的，成套的，一组的，一套的，联动的，网轴的

gang way （客车座位之间的）通道，过道［亦称 aisle，gang way floor 通道地板；gang way rail 通道栏杆，出入口栏杆；gang way seat 过道（可收的）座椅］

gantry ①起重架，吊架，龙门架 ②龙门式起重机（= gantry crane, 亦称 gauntree crane, gauntry crane, frame crane）③（道路的）跨线桥 ④（挖掘机）臂架

gantry traveller 移动式龙门起重机

gantry truck 门式汽车吊（车）

gap ①间隙，缝隙，空隙 ②间距，区间，间隔 ③裂缝，裂口，缺口 ④放电器

gap acceptance （高速公路交通的）可合流车间距离

gap acceptance data （高速公路交通的）可合流的车间距离值，可合流的车间时间间隔值

gap adjustment 间隙调整

gap bridging 通路短路（导致火花塞不再跳火）

gap eliminator 间隙消除装置，消除间隙机构

gap frame C 形框架

gap gauge 间隙量规，隙规，厚规，千分规

gap of tooth 齿隙

gapper （美俚）厚薄规（= feeler gange)

gap seal ①（货车的）封隙帘（用柔软帘布制成，装在货车驾驶室和箱式车身之间的两侧面，密封两者之间隔，改善环绕该间隔气流的流动，以减少空气阻力，参见 AOA device）②间隙密封件

gap style 间隙形式（指火花塞电极的布型形式，如：标准型，多电极型，沿面型等）

gap type distributor 跳隙式配电器，间隙式分电盘

garage ①（停放汽车的）车库 ②汽车维修店，汽车维修行（除维修车辆外，有的还兼营配件和燃润料）③将汽车存进车库内，将汽车开进维修店维修

garaged ①停放在车库内的 ②已送往维修店维修的（广告中常简写为 gar'd）

Garage Equipment Association ［英］汽车车库设备协会（简称 GEA）

garage float 维修店的流动备用件

garage jack 维修店用千斤顶，轮式千斤顶，小车式千斤顶（= garage trolley jack, roller type jack, wheeled jack）

garage lamp （带金属丝护网的）安全灯，工作灯

garbage (-and-refuse) body 垃圾车车厢

garbage-removal truck 垃圾车（= dust cart, garbage truck, dust cart, refuse collecting truck, trash truck）[美] garbage wagon

garbage truck [美] 垃圾车（见 refuse vehicle）

garden seat （观光客车）车顶上的座椅

Gardner engine 加得纳尔发动机（润滑油试验用单缸发动机）

Gardner Mobilometer 加得纳尔滴度计；加纳尔黏度计，加氏黏度计（用来测定胶合剂和稀薄密封胶剂的黏度，将一只标准柱塞总成沉落在试样中，沉下 10cm 的时间，用秒数表示，称为加氏黏度）

Gardner viscosity 加得纳尔黏度，加氏黏度（参见 Gardner Mobilometer）

gargle pipe 排泄管，排放管；排出有害物质的管道

Garlock oil seal 加氏油封

garnet 石榴石（氧化硅与各种元素的化合物，密度大，硬度高，用于制作磨料）

garnet red 石榴红（车身颜色）

garnish ①装饰物；覆盖层；修饰件 ②装饰，添饰，覆盖，（车身的）内饰

garnish moulding （车身）装饰镶条

garnish rail （车门或门框等的）装饰条

garnish rim （灯头等的）装饰边框

garter spring 夹紧盘簧，箍簧，自紧（油封）圈簧

garter spring seal 带箍簧的油封

gas ①（包括空气在内的各种）气体 ②煤气，燃气，天然气，可燃气体 ③[美俚] 汽油（gasoline 的简称，=[英] petrol, motor spirit）④充气；供给煤气；踩踏加速踏板，加油

gas analyzer 气体分析器

gas-assisted 气压助力的，气动助力的（指利用压缩空气来增补人力的，亦称 air-assisted, air-boosted, gas-boosted）

gas at low heating value ①低热值煤气，贫煤气 ②稀可燃混合气

gas automobile 汽油车（= gasoline automobile）

gas bag 气袋，气囊

gas bomb 储气瓶，气瓶

gas-boosted 见 gas assisted

gas brazing 气焰硬钎焊，焰钎焊，氧气铜焊（见 brazing）

gas burner ①煤气喷灯，气割焊炬 ②（使用标准汽油而不用加有乙醇、氧化亚氮等混合油的）纯汽油发动机赛车（亦称 gasser）

gas can [美] 汽油壶，汽油桶，油油箱

Gas CAP [美] 汽油储备规划（Gasoline Conservation Awareness Program 的简称）

gas cap 汽油滤清器盖（= filler cap）

gas carbon 炭黑，烟黑，蒸馏炭（= retort carbon, 纯度高，用做电池、电弧灯的电极，电刷等）

gas carburization 气体渗碳（= gas carburizing，为目前工业生产中使用的主要渗碳方法。将工件置于渗碳炉内气体渗碳介质中，加热到一定温度并保温，使介质中的活性炭原子渗入工件表层，提高其含碳量以增加表面硬度，耐磨性和疲劳强度）

gas carburizer 气体渗碳剂（指气体渗碳炉内的气体渗碳介质，如：煤油等在渗碳炉内分解而析出的活性炭）

gas casing （气波增压器）废气进出口壳体（见 Complex pressure wave supercharger）

gas cavity 气孔

gas chamber （pressurized gas chamber 的简称）①（泛指各种用途的）压

缩气室②（特指某些单筒式减振器的）气压腔（该腔内充满压缩气体，由一个自由活塞"free piston"或称分隔活塞"dividing piston"将该气压腔与液压腔"hydraulic chamber"或称工作腔"working chamber"隔开。当减振器活塞处于伸张冲程时，自由活塞在气压腔内压缩气的作用下随工作腔油液的减少而上升，避免了工作油液的渗气和空穴现象）

gas-charged front struts 充气式前滑柱（悬架）

gas-charged shock absorber 充气式减振器

gas chromatograph 气相色谱仪［利用移动相（气体），通过固定相（充填剂）时，移动相所含成分被分离出来的作用，检测复杂混合气体中个别气体的仪器。在分析发动机排气时，常用来确定多种碳氢化合物中，个别碳氢化合物的浓度，简称 GC，气相色谱法称为"gas chromafography," 亦简称 GC］

gas chromatographic column 气相色谱分析柱（气相色谱仪中的毛细管，根据在其中被吸收的倾向，从混合气中分离与识别个别成分）

gas conductor 气体导电体，导电气体（气体电离后形成的等离子气体，见 plasma）

gas constant 气体常数

gas consumption rate 汽油消耗率，耗油率（每单位时间或里程的汽油消耗量）

gas control lever 节气门操纵杆（= gas throttle lever）

gas cutting 气割（= autogenous cutting）

gas cyaniding 气体氰化，气体碳氮共渗（为气体渗碳和氮化的综合，在气体渗碳炉内，同时滴煤油和液氨，在高温下分解为活性碳原子和氮原子，被工件表面吸收，而在表面形成 0.5~0.8mm 耐磨、抗疲劳、抗腐蚀，且具有较高淬透性的氰化层）

gas cylinder ①高压储气筒，高压气瓶，储气筒，煤气罐②汽缸（相对液压缸等而言）

gas damper 见 gas shock absorber

gas detector 漏气检测器（= gas leak tester）

gas/diesel (dual fuel) engine 气体燃料/柴油双燃料发动机（指用气体燃料作为主要燃料，将柴油喷入汽缸内辅助压燃点火的气体燃料柴油机。一般是在柴油机上增加一套气体燃料供给系统，当不用气体燃料时，仍可单独使用柴油，亦称 gas-oil fueled engine）

gas diffusion layer 气体扩散层

gas discharge 气体放电（气体电离后发生的导电现象）

gas discharge display 气体放电显示器（汽车仪表上使用的一种利用电离氖气发出的光组成字母、字符的元器件）

gas discharge headlight 气体放电式前照灯（指使用气体放电效应发光的气体放电灯泡 gas discharge lamp 的前照灯，亦称 gaseous discharge headlight，其发光部分为惰性气体、水银和金属卤化物组成的高压气体，在高电压下电离为等离子体，电流通过该电离气体而发光，在功耗接近的情况下，其光通量为卤素灯的 2~3 倍）

gas dome 气室（如：汽油箱中的供容纳汽油蒸气的区室）

gas duct 气道（发动机汽缸盖或汽缸体中的进、排气通道，= gas port）

gas eater ［美俚］油老虎（油耗量大的汽车）

gas eddy 气涡流

gas efficient car 省油轿车

gas-electric front-wheel-drive system （某些复合动力车的）汽油机-电动机前轮驱动系统（亦简称 gas-electric FWD system，见 electric rear drive）

gas electrode 气体电极（如：zinc-air 电池，以锌和空气作为电极）

gas engine ①可燃气体发动机，天然气发动机，煤气发动机 ②汽油机，汽油发动机（亦简称 gas eng，gasoline engine 的简称）

gaseous corrosion 气相腐蚀

gaseous-discharge bulb 气体放电灯泡（见 gas discharge headlight）

gaseous emission （排气中的）有害气体，气体排放物

gaseous flow 气流，气体流

gaseous-fuel(ed) vehicle 气态燃料车辆（燃用气体燃料如天然气、LPG 煤气、氢气等的车辆，= gas fuel vehicle）

gaseous fuel injection system 气体燃料喷射系统（一般指将电控汽油喷射系统的技术，引入天然气等气体燃料发动机的电控喷射系统）

gas exchange (process) （二冲程发动机的）换气过程［指从排气开始，经进气、扫气过程到进、排气门（口）全部关闭为止的整个工质更换过程，亦称 gas replenishment process］

gas exchange loss 换气损失（指整个换气过程所消耗的功率）

Gas F 气体滤清器（见 gas filter ②）

gas-filled bulb 充气灯泡（泡内充有氮、氩等不活泼气体保护灯丝）

gas-filled device （内部）充（有）气(体)的装置

gas (filled) photocell 充气光电管

gas-filled shock absorber 充气减振器（一种单筒式减振器，在 20 世纪 50 年代中期由法国特·卡尔朋发明。该减振器的工作缸由一自由活塞分隔成液压腔和充有压缩惰性气体，如氮等的气压腔两个部分，见 gas chamber②）

gas-filled tube rectifier 离子整流器；充气管整流器

gas-filter ①汽油滤清器 ②气体滤清器（特指为防止异物由废气净化系统各种负压取出管道进入进气管，而设在负压取出口处的滤清器，简称 Gas. F）

gas-fired heater ①气火焰加热器 ②汽油火焰预热装置

gas-fittings 煤气管接头

gas flow ①气流，气体流（在发动机中指空气燃油混合气流，废气流）②气流量

gas flow counter 气体流量计

gas fouling （火花塞等被）油污

gas fuel 气体燃料，可燃气燃料（= gaseous fuel）

gas gasoline 液化天然气汽油（机用燃料）

gas gauge 气体压力表；煤气（耗量）表；汽油（油量）表

gas generator (= gas producer) ①煤气发生炉（通过燃烧木炭、煤等固体燃料而生成可燃气体的装置，车载式煤气发生炉提供的可燃气可作为汽车用燃料）②（供燃气轮机动力涡轮起动用的）燃气发生装置（一般为一尺寸紧凑的简单型附属燃气轮机）③（燃气轮机的）燃气供给部分（包括压气机、压气机涡轮和燃烧室，起着向动力涡轮提供高压、高温燃气，驱动动力涡轮高速旋转的作用，亦称 gasifier）④（产生热的压缩气体，供给涡轮机工质的）两冲程压气机

gas generator turbine （燃气涡轮的）起动用燃气发生器（见 gas generator ②）

gas gouging 气体火焰割槽作业（=

flame gouging)

gas guzzler (美俚)油老虎(耗油量大的汽车)

gash ①齿隙 ②裂纹,裂口 ③划开,裂成深长的切口 ④多余的,备用的

"gas-hoarding" technique (德Robert Bosch 的)"汽油节约存储"技术(用于发动机节能系统,汽车滑行或遇红灯、堵车等原因而停车时,发动机自动熄火,处于静候状态,驾驶者只要操作有关按钮,发动机便可立即恢复运转)

gasholder 储气瓶

gas horsepower 以马力计的煤气或汽油能量

gasification 气化,气化作用,气体的生成

gasified fuel cell 气体燃料电池

gasifier ①燃气发生器,煤气发生器(= gas producer, gas generator) ②燃气发生装置(燃气轮机产生高温高压燃气的部分,见 gas generator ③)

gasifier speed (燃气轮机的)燃气发生器转速

gasifier turbine (燃气轮机的)压气机涡轮(见 gas generator③,= compressor turbine)

gasify 气化,使转化成气体

gas impermeability test 气密性试验

gas injector nozzle ①汽油喷射器喷嘴 ②气态石油气(或天然气)喷射器喷嘴

gasket ①垫,衬垫,垫圈,密封垫 ②(在发动机中主要指夹在两钢皮或钢皮面板之间的毡、软木或石棉材料组成的)可压缩型平面密封垫或金属片型平密封垫(用于要求气密,接合面防气、液渗漏,如:汽缸体与汽缸盖之间的缸垫、进、排气歧管与缸盖或缸体之间的密封垫,火花塞与缸盖间的密封垫等) ③装衬垫,密封,填实

gasket asbestos core 密封垫石棉芯,缸垫石棉芯

gasketed 装有密封衬垫的,带密封衬垫的

gasketing ①密封件材料,密封件型材(用以切制密封件) ②安装密封垫

gasket ring 密封环,密封圈(= sealing ring, joint ring, sealing washer)

gasket seal paste 衬垫胶,衬垫密封膏(亦称 gasket sealants,涂于衬垫两面,增加密封性能和安装时定位)

gas knock 燃油爆燃(由于汽油的辛烷值过低所引起的发动机的爆燃,= fuel knock)

gas laser 气体激光器(以气体作为工质的激光器,见 laser)

gas leak tester 气体漏泄试验器,漏气检验器(= gas detector)

gas-liquid chromatography 气-液色谱分析法(简称 GLC)

gas-loaded accumulator 气压蓄能器

gas measuring flowmeter 气体流量计

gas medium 气体介质

Gas Mileage Guide (汽车)油耗指南,油耗手册(根据美国能量方针和保护法,制造厂必须向用户提供的有关车辆燃料经济性的手册)

gas-mileage test 汽车里程油耗测定试验(测定每单位耗油量,如:每加仑汽油所能行驶的英里数)

gas mixer 气体混合器(气体燃料发动机中使空气和气体燃料混合,形成气体燃料-空气混合气的装置)

gas noise 气体噪声(如:充气电器装置中由于分子杂乱运动产生的气体电离噪声)

gaso 汽油(gasoline 的简称)

gasohol 酒精汽油(无特别说明时,指由 10%的酒精和 90%的无铅汽车

组成的车用混合燃料)
gas oil 气体油,瓦斯油(原油直馏时沸点低于煤油高于润滑油原料油的中间馏分,常分为轻气体油 LGO,催化裂化轻气体油 LGCO 和重气体油 HGO。用于制造油气或水煤气,故称为气体油、瓦斯油。现在主要用来作为柴油机燃料或燃料油或裂化汽油的原料,但有时仅指后者而不包括前二者。用来作为柴油机燃料时称为柴油, = diesel fuel)

gas-oil fueled engine 见 gas-diesel (dual fuel) engine

gasol 气体油,液化石油气(= LPG)

gasolene 见 gasoline

gasoline 汽油[美], =[英] petrol,指火花点火式内燃机用轻馏分碳氢化合物液态燃料,并写作 gasolene(旧体),俚称 gas

gasoline acidity 汽油酸度(指中和 100mL 汽油中酸性物质所耗的氢氧化钾 KOH mg 数,用 mg KOH/100mL 表示。中和 1g 汽油中的酸性物质所耗的氢氧化钾 KOH 的 mg 数称为酸值 acid value,以 mg KOH/g 表示,酸度和酸值是保石油产品不腐蚀容器和机件的主要指标)

gasoline additive 汽油添加剂(指提高汽油品质的抗爆剂、助燃剂等的统称)

gas(oline)-air mixture 汽油空气混合气

gasoline alarm 油面过低警报,油量不足警报信号

gasoline carrier 汽油槽车,油罐车,汽油储运装置

gasoline consumption per car 单车油耗(运输企业平均单车油耗)

gasoline container 汽油容器,汽油罐,汽油箱,汽油桶(= petrol container, jerry can, gasoline cistern, gasoline can)

gasoline-content gauge with float 浮子式汽油存量表,浮子式汽油表

gasoline corrosion test 汽油腐蚀性试验(包括铜片浸试验和含硫量、水溶性酸碱及酸度等测试,各国均规定有标准评定方法)

gas(oline) depot 汽油库(= petrol storage)

gasoline-depth gauge 汽油深度计,汽油液面计,汽油表(= petrol-depth gauge)

gasoline detergent 汽油清净分散剂(添加剂的一种,亦称 gasoline dispersant,为胺和具有表面活性的羧酸或磷酸等的衍生物,用以减少或消除汽油在燃料系部件上的沉积物)

gasoline direct injection engine 直喷式汽油机(汽油直接喷入燃烧室,而不是喷至进气门前方,简称 GDI 或 gasoline DI engine)

gasoline dispersant 汽油(沉积物)清净分散剂(见 gasoline detergent)

gasoline dope 汽油添加剂(= gasoline additive)

gasoline-driven [美]用汽油机驱动(= petrol-driven)

gas(oline)-electric car 汽油电动车(= petrol-electric car,由汽油机带动的发电机发电驱动汽车的电动机和蓄存多余电能的蓄电池及电子控制系统组成。其汽油机稳定在节油和污染少的经济区运转。当行驶阻力小时,发电机的多余电能由蓄电池存储,供阻力大或加速时使用。在市区行驶时可关闭汽油机,仅由蓄电池驱动,减少污染)

gasoline-electric hybrid vehicle (见 gasoline-electric car)

gasoline filler neck 汽油箱加油口管

gasoline filter 汽油滤清器(= gasoline seperator, petrol strainer, petrol filter, petrol trap, gasoline interceptor)

gasoline（fuel）injection 汽油喷射（1951 年德国 Robert Bosch 公司首先推出轿车机械式汽油喷射系统，目前是指由发动机电子控制模块"PEM"闭路控制的多点顺序喷射系统，将汽油喷至各缸气道进气门前方或直接喷入缸内，见 EFI）

gasoline gage （表示油箱内现有汽油量的）汽油表（= gas tank gage）

gasoline gage dash unit 汽油表头

gasoline "homogeneous" charge RC engine 均质充气汽油转子发动机（指充入均质混合器的转子发动机，区别于分层充气，或非均质充气式转子发动机）

gasoline induction period 汽油的诱导期（亦称感应期，指油样在标准钢筒内通入氧气后发生明显氧化前所经历的时间，该时间越长，汽油的安定性越好，美、英、德等国的有关标准均规定汽油的诱导期不应少于 240 min）

gasoline lead additive 汽油铅添加剂，汽油四乙基铅添加剂

gasoline-level gage 汽油液面计，汽油（油量）表（= petrol-level gauge）

gasoline lift pump （汽油）输油泵，供油泵（= gasoline feed pump, gasoline supply pump，指将汽油从油箱吸出输给汽油喷射系统的油泵，简称 gasoline pump）

gasoline-like alternative ［美］类汽油代用燃料（如：甲醇 methyl alcohol，乙醇 ethyl alcohol 等）

gasoline measure ①汽油加注量桶（如：每桶 3 加仑或 5 加仑等）②汽油计量单位

gasoline mileage tester 汽车英里油耗计（用来测定每单位容积或质量的汽油所能行驶的英里里程）

gasoline octane rating 汽油辛烷值标定；汽油辛烷值（见 octane rating）

gasoline oil 汽油（= gasoline）

gasoline olefinicity 汽油含烯度（指汽油中的烯烃 C_nH_{2n} 的含量）

gasoline-only vehicle 单汽油机车辆（相对于汽油机-电动机复合动力车"gasoline-electric hybrid vehicle"而言）

gasoline pipe 汽油管（一般使用铜管或钢管，但发动机和车身或底盘之间则亦使用耐油性良好的橡胶或尼龙软管，亦称 gasoline feed pipe）

gasoline power fraction 汽油功率成分（指汽油在规定的馏出温度下，馏出 50% 的馏分的 50% 馏出温度馏分，亦称汽油的主馏分）

gasoline（practical）gum 汽油（实际）胶质（指在规定条件下使油样蒸发至干的残留物，美、英、日、德的相关标准中均规定汽油的实际胶质≤5mg/100L）

gasoline precipitation test 汽油沉淀试验（用于测定汽油生成胶状物质或酸性物质等沉淀的程度，判定汽油的安全性及纯洁度）

gasoline-pressure gauge 汽油压力表

gasoline-proof grease 耐汽油的润滑脂

gasoline resistance 耐汽油性（抗汽油浸蚀的能力）

gasoline-rich crankcase vapor 含汽油蒸气多的曲轴箱气

gasoline sensitivity 汽油灵敏度（指同一汽油之马达法辛烷值和研究法辛烷值的差）

gasoline stability 汽油的安定性［指汽油抗氧化缩合、生成胶状或酸性物质、变色、变质的性能，通常用（实际）胶质（gasoline practical gum）和诱导期（gasoline induction period）两项指标来评定］

gasoline stand 加油站（= filling station）

gasoline startability 汽油起动性（指汽油的发动机起动性能，一般与其

10%馏出点，即汽油中轻馏分含量有关，10%馏出温度越低，汽油机在低温下便越易于起动）

gasoline substitutes 汽油代用品

gasoline sulfur test 汽油含硫量测定（为汽油的腐蚀性评定中的测试项目之一，各国均规定有标准的测试方法）

gasoline supply pump 汽油泵，供油泵（= gasoline lift pump）

gasoline tank capacity 汽油箱容积，汽油箱容量

gasoline tanker （运输汽油的）油罐车（偶见简称 gasoline tank）

gasoline tank gauge 汽油箱存量计，汽油罐油量表

gasoline tank settler 汽油箱沉淀槽

gasoline tax 汽油税

gasoline tetraethyl lead test 汽油（中）四乙基铅纯铅（含量）测定试验（简称 CTT，指测定四乙基铅汽油的纯铅含量，各国对汽车的四乙基铅加入量及其相当的纯铅含量均有明确规定，如：0.8g/kg 的四乙基铅加入量，相当于纯铅含量 0.36g/L）

gasoline tractor 汽油机拖拉机，汽油（机）牵引车（= petrol tractor）

gasoline trap 汽油分离器（= petrol trap, petrol separator, gasoline separator）

gas(oline) truck ［美］油罐车，汽油油罐车（=［英］petrol tanker）

gasoline-vapor and air mixture 汽油蒸气和空气的混合气，汽油-空气混合气

GASP 见 gas plasma panel

gas panel 见 gas plasma panel

gas pedal ［美］加速踏板（= accelerator pedal）

gas-permeable graphite paper 透气性石墨纸（制作车用燃料电池的部件）

gas per mile gauge 汽车英里油耗计（测定汽车行驶 1 英里的汽油消耗量）

gasping sound （发动机的）喘气声

gas plasma display 气体等离子体显示器

gas producer vehicle 煤气发生炉汽车（指直接将煤气发生炉装在汽车上产生煤气供应汽车燃料的汽车）

gas-proof 不透气的，不漏气的，防漏气的

gas prop （汽车行李舱盖、后车门等的）气压助力斜撑、气助力撑杆（指只要用手轻轻一推，就会在压缩空气的助力下将后车门等撑开）

gas replenishment process （二冲程发动机的）换气过程（见 gas exchange process）

gas sampler （汽车）排气试样采集器，废气取样器

gas saver ［美］省油器，节油装置

gas sealing agent （防止漏气的）气密封剂

gas sealing mechanism ①气密封机构，气密封装置 ②气密封机理

gas separation pressure 气泡析出压力（工作液体中，气体开始析出产生气泡时的压力，见 air separation）

gas separator 气体分离器

gasser ①汽油机汽车（俚语）②见 gas burner②

gas shielded (arc) welding 气体保护（电弧）焊（指使用惰性或非惰性气体，如：二氧化碳等对熔化极进行保护的电弧熔焊）

gas shock 充气式减振器（gas-assisted shock absorber 的简称，为单筒式减振器的常见结构形式，有 de Carbon 型和 Wood head-Munroe 型两种。前者在其工作腔下有一个为自由活塞所隔开、充满压缩气体的气压腔，后者工作腔内充以油-气乳化液，参见 gas chamber）

gassing ①气体生成 ②充气 ③放气 ④冒气,产生气泡,起泡

gassing current (蓄电池完全充电后仍继续充电时所产生的易燃易爆)气泡束,气泡流

gas soldering ①气(焰)钎焊(指用气体火焰作为热源的钎焊,最常用的是氧—乙炔钎焊) ②(偶见指)气焰熔焊

gas solenoid 气管电磁阀

gas spring ①气压弹簧,气弹簧(由夹有帘线层的橡胶囊充以氮气等制成,可分为囊式和膜式两大类) ②(特指空气弹簧式悬架中使用的以空气为介质的弹性元件)空气弹簧

gas station [美]加油站(= gasoline station, service station, [英]petrol station, filling station, filling point)

gas tank ①([美]汽车的)汽油箱(= [英]petrol tank) ②([英]汽车的)液化石油气箱或其他气体燃料箱 ③煤气罐、储气罐

gas (tank) cap 汽油箱盖,汽油桶盖

gas tanker 液化可燃气油罐车;汽油罐车

gas throttle lever 节气门操纵杆(= gas control lever)

gas tight 气密的(= air tight, 指可防止气体通过的,不漏气的)

gas (-tight) piston ring (活塞)气环,压缩环(简称 gas ring, 一般称 compression ring, 活塞环中起压缩密封作用者)

gas tight seal 气密密封(件)

gas tight thread 气密螺纹

gas-to-liquid fuel 见 GTL fuel

gas tongs 管钳(= pipe tongs)

gas transfer velocity 气体转移速度,燃气转移速度(如:在转子发动机内,由于工作室随着转子旋转,室内气体也随着转移的速度)

gas transport time (电子控制汽油喷射系统的)气流迁移时间(指从空气/燃油混合气形成开始到空燃比闭路控制系统的氧传感器产生传感信号为止的时间)

Gas Treatment 汽油清洁添加剂(一种燃油系清洗添加剂的商品名,加入汽油内可清除油路污垢,使油路畅通)

gas turbine 燃气轮机(由包括压气机、压气涡轮和燃室的高压高温燃气供给部分和包括将高温高压燃气的能量转变为高速旋转转矩的动力涡轮和减速机构的动力部分组成的发动机,分单轴再生循环、双轴再生循环和三轴再生循环式等。汽车上使用的主要是双轴式的,其动力由减速机构输出经变速器传给驱动车轮, = combustion gas turbine, 亦称 gas turbine engine)

gas turbine engined 以燃气轮机为发动机的,以燃气轮机为动力的(= gas turbine powered)

gas turbine hybrid bus 燃气轮机混合动力大客车(一般由燃气轮机和发电机-电动机组成的混合动力系统驱动)

gas-turbine wheel 燃气轮机叶轮

gas welding 气焊(= torch welding, 指使用氧乙炔火焰加热的熔焊,故亦称, Oxyacetylene welding, 目前逐渐为惰性气体保护焊所代替, 见 metal/inert gas welding)

gate ①大门,闸门,阀门;②门(a. 指门电路,可以实现基本逻辑运算的组合电子电路,通常只有一个输出端,一个或多个输入端,只有在它的输入端上出现某种特定的组合脉冲时,它的输出端上才出现脉冲,见 AND gate, OR gate, NOT gate 等, = gate circuit); b. 指提供上述电路的一种器件,即具有一个输出通道和一个或多个输入通道,

其输出通道的状态完全由输入通道的状态决定的器件；c. 指逻辑元件（= logical element，计算机逻辑运算系统中的最小构造单元，两个输入变量导致一个输出结果的开关元件）③（场效应管FET的）控制栅（即其输入端）④（特指手动机械式变速器变速杆的）王字或H形槽口换挡杆导板 ⑤（拦式货车的）货箱拦板（两侧的拦板称 side gate 边板，后部的拦板称 rear 或 tail gate 后板）

gate array 门阵列（一种封装在一个芯片内的多个逻辑门组成的集成电路芯片。在制造时可以将这些逻辑门按一定程序连接起来去执行某一项逻辑操作，因而可以作为标准产品使用。有的可由用户现场编程，去执行各种特定的复杂操作，后者称为现场可编程门阵列，见 field-programmable gate array）

gate change （手动或半自动变速器的）槽导换挡，槽导变速（如通常换挡时变速杆沿H形导程移动）

gate circuit 门电路（见 gate②）

gate control switch 门控开关（由门电路控制的开关，见 gate②，简称 GCS）

gate crossing （有安全栅栏的）交叉道口

gate electrode （场效应晶体管的）栅极（见 FET）

gate junction 栅极结（见 FET）

gateless gearshift 无导向槽板的换挡机构

gate lever 王字或H形导向板式变速杆

gate pulse 门脉冲，选通脉冲（使门电路接通或断开的脉冲）

gate region （场效应晶体管等的）栅极区（见 FET）

gate terminal 栅（极）端子，栅极引出线，（控制）门接线柱（见 FET）

gate turn-off thyristor 门控可关断晶（体）闸（流）管（门极控制开关，简称 GTO）

gate type lift 门式（汽车）举升器

gate valve 闸阀，阀门

gateway ①门道，通路 ②入口 ③门框 ④手段

gateway (server) 网关（服务器）（汽车局域网内的功能部件，通过网关实现各总线间的信息共享、各控制系统终端间的通信及协同控制和汽车局域网的内部管理等）

gate wing 门扇（两扇门中的一扇门）

gather ①前轮前束，前束（= toe in）②收集，采集，聚集，集合；渐增；逐渐获得

gathering 聚集，集合，会合，集聚，积累

gathering plates （机油粗滤器滤片的）清洁片，刮污片（gathering plate spinder 刮污片轴杆。转动该轴杆，刮污片便从各滤片间扫过，而除去污物）

Gathers 本田公司供用户选购的专用音响系统名

gather speed [动] 加速

gauge （= [美] gage）①（金属板等的）厚度 ②（轨间的）距离，轨距 ③（金属线等的）直径 ④（有关标准，规格等所规定的上述厚度、间距、直径等的）标准值（= standard measure）⑤量规，卡规，线规（等检测间隙，形状和尺寸是否符合规定的公差要求的工具）⑥测量仪表（如：仪表板上的机油表、水温表等，以及胎压表之类的带量具和表头的某一物理量的测量仪表）⑦限度，范围（= extent）

gauge block 块规块（指一套块规中的某一片规块，参见 block gauge）

gauged orifice 标准量孔（= calibrated orifice）

gauge length 标距（试件上测量应变部分的标志距离）

gauge of charge remaining in battery 电池剩余电量表

gauge of tyres （并装双胎的）两轮胎内侧间距（= wheel gauge）

gauge point 计量基准点

gauge pressure 表压力（指压力表的压力读数，在大气压力下，读数值为0）

gauge reading 量具读数

gauging fixture 测量用夹具

gauging head 测头，测量用塞规（= gauging plug）

gauntry crane 龙门起重机，龙门吊，门式吊车（= gantry crane）

gauss 高斯（磁通量的密度单位，代号 Gs，1Gs = 1maxwell/cm² = 10^{-4} T，参见 maxwell，tesla）

Gaussian distribution 高斯分布；正态分布（见 normal distribution）

gauze ①纱，纱布 ②滤网，线网，金属丝网 ③抑制栅极

gauze carburetor 油网式化油器（一种早期的化油器，吸入的空气经汽油流过的油网吸收汽油蒸气，见 wick carburetor）

gauze element 滤网，金属丝布滤芯

gauze filter 网式滤清器（mesh filter）

GAWR ［美］最大核定轴载重量（gross axle weight rating 的简称，指考虑到材料的强度，轮胎的承载能力等因素而核定的最大轴载质量，为 gross axle mass rating 最大核定轴载质量的旧称，但美仍沿用至今，= maximum axle laden weight）

Gay Lussac's law 盖-吕萨克定律（一定质量的气体，在压强不变的情况下，其体积与热力学温度成正比）

gaze direction（of a driver）（驾驶者的）注视方向（凝视方向）

GB ［中国］国家标准（汉语拼音 Guojia Biaozhun 的简称）

Gb 吉（磁通势单位，见 Gilbert）

G ball G球，惯性球（球形惯性质量，= inertia ball）

GBC （催化转化器快速热起技术中的）汽油燃烧控制（系统）（gasoline burner control 的简称，利用汽油燃烧的火焰使催化剂迅速热起至起燃温度）

G-Book （丰田公司的车装）资讯网络服务系统（商品名，内容包括现场直播导航系统、娱乐节目和安全资讯）

GC ①气体色谱仪（见 gas chromatography）②（公路路面）优质混凝土型（= good concrete）

GCC 海湾国家合作委员会（Gulf-Co-operation Council 的简称）

G-clamp G形夹具（状如G形的，借助螺纹拧紧力夹紧的夹具）

g/cm³ 克/厘米³（国际单位制密度单位，参见 t/m³）

GCM 汽车列车总质量（gross combination mass 的简称）

GC/MS 气相色谱-质谱测定法（见 gas chromatography/mass opectrometry 的简称）

GCS 见 gate control switch

GCW 汽车列车总重（gross combination weight 的简称）

gcwr 汽车列车（拖车加挂车）总重额定值，汽车列车额定总重（gross combination weight rating 的简称）

GDI engine 直喷式汽油机（见 gasoline direct injection engine）

GDL system 见 graduated driver licensing system

GDP 国民生产总值、国内生产总值（gross domestic product 的简称）

Ge 锗（germanium）

GEA [英]汽车车库设备协会（Garage Equipment Association 的简称）

gear ①齿轮 ②齿轮传动装置 ③机构，装置 ④（变速器的传动速比）挡，挡位

gear and pinion steering 见 warm and selector steering gear

gear back lash （齿轮）齿侧间隙，齿隙，侧隙

gear box 齿轮箱，变速器，变速箱（美称 gearcase 或 transmission，一般指手动变速器。gearbox imput shaft 变速器输入轴，变速器第一轴，将动力由离合器输入变速器的轴；gearbox output shaft 变速器输出轴，变速器第二轴，将动力由变速器输出的轴）

gearbox adapter 变速器座，变速器（与发动机间）过渡壳体

gearbox capacity ①齿轮箱（额定）能力，齿轮箱（最大允许传递）功率 ②齿轮箱滑油容量

gearbox countershaft cluster gear 变速器中间轴齿轮组

gearbox flange 变速器油底壳突缘（= transmission case flange）

gearbox forks 变速（器）（变速）叉

gear box gearshift mechanism 变速器操纵机构（使变速器齿轮变换啮合位置，产生变速作用的机构，包括发动机后置时的远距离换挡操纵机构）

gear-box input torque 变速器输入转矩

gearbox main shaft 变速器主轴，变速器第二轴（变速器的输出轴，[美] transmission mainshaft）

gearbox output 变速箱输出功率，变速器输出

gear-box output torque 变速器输出转矩

gearbox selector ①变速器换挡机构 ②变速杆

gearbox steering linkage system 变速器换挡机构杆系（见，= gear change linkage）

gearbox steering system 变速器换挡机构（见，= gear change mechanism）

gear carrier 行星齿轮架

gearcase [美]变速器，变速箱（= [美] transmission，[英] gearbox）

gear change 变速；换挡（美称 gear shifting 或 shifting）

gear-change by wire 导线换挡（指驾驶员通过转向盘柱上的选挡按钮和导线系统将选挡意图"通知"变速器电子控制模块，而由电子控制模块控制液压系统实现符合驾驶员意图的最佳换挡，不再使用换挡杆及其连接杆件的纯电子换挡系统）

gear change control housing 变速杆座；变速器操纵机构壳体；变速器换挡机构壳体（= selector rod housing, shifter housing）

gear change (hand) lever 手动变速杆，变速（操纵）杆 [= gear shift (ing) lever, gear control lever]

gear change mechanism 换挡机构（指由杆件及其连接件组成的实现变速器换挡操纵的杆系，因而亦称 gearchange linkage 换挡杆系。罕见有使用拉索实现换挡操纵者，称 gear change cable "换挡拉索"）

gear change selector shaft （变速器的）选挡拨叉轴，换挡拨叉轴，换挡轴

gear change shift fork 换挡拨叉（= gear shift fork）

gear change timing （自动变速器）换挡正时（指换挡过程中分离和结合件的作用压力随时间变化的相对关系进行的调节）

gear clasher （换挡）齿轮撞击试验装置

gear cluster ①齿轮组 ②（特指）变

速器中间轴齿轮总成（偶见称 cluster gear）

gear clutch 齿轮式离合器，齿套式离合器，齿套式接合器，内外齿离合器

gear (control) lever （驾驶员操纵手动变速器换挡的）变速杆，换挡杆（= gear change lever, gear stick, 美称 gear shift, shifter, shift lever）

gear differential 齿轮式差速器（通过各行星齿轮机构起差速作用的总成的通称）

gear down ①换低挡，挂上低速挡 ②开慢车，降低速度，减慢

gear drive （通过齿轮传递动力的）①齿轮传动 ②齿轮传动机构

gear-driven supercharger 机械驱动增压器（= engine-driven supercharger, geared supercharger）

geared-down speed ①（自动变速器）换入低挡时的发动机转速 ②经过齿轮箱减速的转速

geared engine 带减速器的发动机（= second-motion engine）

gear(ed) pump 齿轮泵（最简单的齿轮泵，如：发动机润滑系中使用的齿轮型机油泵"gear-type oil pump"，由两个齿轮和泵壳组成）

geared ring 齿圈（= gear ring）

geared speed ①（由发动机转速总传动比及驱动轮直径所导出的）汽车的理论车速 ②在每一挡位上汽车所能达到的最高车速（非首选的定义，参见 powered speed）③非直接挡车速

geared supercharger 机械驱动增压器（= engine-driven supercharger）

geared turbine 带减速器的涡轮机

geared-up speed ①（自动变速器）换入高挡时的发动机转速 ②经过齿轮箱增速的转速

gear face 齿轮端面，齿面

gear grease 齿轮润滑脂

gear hub 齿轮轮毂，齿毂

gearing ①齿轮传动（指传递动力的齿系）②（泛指）传动装置 ③（齿轮）啮合 ④齿轮的

gearing-down ①利用齿轮传动装置降低转速；减速传动（装置）②换低速挡

gear(ing) level 挂中速挡

3:2 gearing relationship 3:2 啮合比，3:2齿轮传动关系比（在转子发动机中，指转子的相位内齿圈的齿数与端盖固定相位齿轮齿数之比为 3:2）

gearing shaft 齿轮传动轴

gearing-up ①利用齿轮传动装置增加转速；增速传动（装置）②换高速挡

gear-jammer ［美俚］公共汽车驾驶员

gear knob 变挡按钮，换挡按钮

Gear knob 换挡杆的球头

gearless 无齿轮的，无齿轮传动装置的

gear lever interlock 换挡互锁装置

gear lever lock 变速杆锁

gear lock 变速器换挡机构锁

gear lubricant 齿轮油（简称 GL）

gear noise 齿轮噪声（指齿轮的啮合声，它是衡量齿轮质量的重要指标之一）

gear nut （蜗杆-螺母式转向器蜗杆-螺母传动副中的）蜗杆螺母

gear oil 齿轮油（汽车上指变速器和主减速器等使用的齿轮润滑油）

gear-on-gear pump 外啮合齿轮泵

gear pair 齿轮副［指由两个轴线相对位置不变，各绕其自身轴线转动，而互相啮合的齿轮组成的基本结构。gear pair with shaft angle modification（轴交角不等于两齿轮分锥角之和的）角变位锥齿轮副；gear pair with intersecting axes（两轴线相交的）相交轴齿轮副；gear pair with modified centre distance（名义中心

距不等于标准中心距的)角变位圆柱齿轮副;gear pair with non parallel, nonintersecting axes (两轴线不平行,也不相交的)交错轴齿轮副;gear pair with parallel axes (两轴线平行的)平行轴齿轮副;gear pair with reference centre distance (名义中心距等于标准中心距的)高变位圆柱齿轮;gear pair without shaft angle modification (轴交角等于两齿轮分锥角之和的)高变位锥齿变副;gear pair with small teeth difference 由齿数差很少的内齿圈,与行星齿轮组成的齿轮副]

gear puller 齿轮拉器(指具有两个或多个卡爪和压力螺杆、用于在拆卸作业中拉出齿轮、轴承、皮带盘等的齿轮拆卸器,亦称 gear withdrawer)

gear pump with pressure axial clearance 带轴向间隙压力补偿的齿轮泵

gear pump with pressure-dependent axial and radial clearance 轴向和径向间隙随压力变化的齿轮泵;带轴向径向压力补偿的齿轮泵

gear rack 齿条

gear range (自动变速器的)挡位[自动变速器典型的挡位有:驻车挡 p(park),倒车挡 R(reverse),空挡 N(neutral),前进挡 D(drie),低速挡 L(low)等]

gear ratio ①齿数比(指齿轮副中,大齿轮齿数与小齿轮齿数的比值)②传动比(指在齿轮副或齿轮系中,其始端主动轮与末端从动轮的角速度比值, = transmission ratio)

gear reduction ratio 齿轮减速比

gear reduction start (汽车的)减速式起动机(电枢的旋转力矩通过齿轮减速机构传给另一装有单向离合器的输出轴输出,见, reduction type stater)

gear rim 齿轮轮辋,齿轮轮缘(= rim of gear)

gear ring 齿圈(= geared ring)

gear roller (针齿轮的)针齿套(= ring gear roller,见 pin gear)

gear sector 扇形齿轮,齿扇

gear selector (特指自动变速器的)换挡杆(手动齿轮变速器的换挡杆一般称 gear lever)

gear selector indicator (自动变速器的)挡位指示器(一般装在仪表板上或换挡杆的导向槽板上,用字母或数字显示,自动变速器当前所选定的挡位)

gear set ①齿轮组,成套齿轮 ②减速器,变速器 ③(特指)传动系中的冠轮,直齿锥齿轮和差动齿轮总成

gear shift [美]换挡机构,换挡(见 gear change)

gear shift dome (变速器)换挡机构球盖

gear shift drum (摩托车的)换挡凸轮轴

gear shifter ①换挡拨叉 ②变速杆 ③(偶见)变速器

gear shifter shaft lock ball 换挡拨叉轴锁球

gear shifter shaft-lock spring 换挡拨叉轴锁弹簧,换挡拨叉锁球弹簧

gearshift fork arm (变速器)换挡叉臂

gear shifting diagram (变速器)换挡示意图,变速挡位图

gear-shifting display 挡位显示器(所换挡位或所在挡位的电子图形或文字显示装置)

gear shift(ing) fork 变速叉,换挡拨叉(= shift fork,位于变速器各挡位齿轮侧面,在变速杆系操纵下直接拨动齿轮,改变其啮合状态实现换挡、挂挡或空挡的叉形构件)

gear shifting without clashing 无声换

挡（=gear shifting without grating）
gear shift knob （按钮式变速系统的）换挡按钮
gear-shift lever （驾驶员直接用手操纵变换挡位的）变速杆，换挡杆（[俚]=gear lever, gear-change lever, gear stick）
gear shift lever ball 变速杆球头
gear shift lever knob 变速杆捏手
gear shift lever oil seal 变速杆油封
gear-shift lock 变速器换挡锁定器（=gear lock, gear-shift shaft lock）
gear shift pedal （摩托车等用）变速踏板，换挡踏板
gear shift rail 换挡拨叉轴
gear-shift shaft lock 变速器换挡锁
gear splitting ①齿轮开裂 ②（变速器）各挡传动比间隔
gear step 两相邻挡位的速比差
gear stick [俚]换挡杆（见 gear lever）
gears with addendum modification （径向）变位齿轮（指产形齿条的分度曲面与齿轮的分度曲面不相切的齿轮）
gear tester 齿轮检查仪；齿轮试验机
gear thickness gauge 齿厚规
gear tooth （齿）轮齿（指齿轮上每一个用于啮合的凸起部分）
gear-tooth calipers 齿轮齿规，齿轮齿游尺，齿轮齿游标卡尺
gear tooth comparator 齿厚比较仪
gear tooth depth gauge 齿高量规
gear tooth gauge 轮齿规，齿距规
gear tooth noise 齿轮啮合噪声
gear tooth vernier caliper 轮齿游标卡尺
gear train 齿轮传动系（=train of gears, 指实现某一给定最终速比或称总速比的一系列相互啮合的齿轮）
gear transmission ①齿轮传动 ②齿轮变速器
gear tumbler 齿轮换向器，换向轮
gear type motor 齿轮式液动机
gear wheel ①齿轮（=gear①）②大齿轮（常简称 wheel, 指齿轮副的两个齿轮中，齿数较多者，齿数较少者称小齿轮 pinion）
gear withdrawer 齿轮拉器（见 gear puller）
gear with equal-addendum teeth 等齿顶高齿轮（见 addendum）
gear with helical teeth 斜齿轮（指齿线，即齿面与分度曲线的交线为螺旋线的齿轮，无特别说明时，指斜齿圆柱齿轮，=helical gear 或 single-helical gear）
gear-within-gear pump 内啮合齿轮泵（内啮合指有一个齿轮是内齿轮的齿轮副，见 internal gear）
gear with tooth correction 轮齿修形齿轮（=gear with tooth modification, 指轮齿经过修形的齿轮。轮齿修形包括齿廓修形、齿向修形、齿端修薄和鼓形修整等，见 profile modification, axial modification）
GED 汽油机驱动的（gasoline engine driven）
gee-pound g 磅值（质量单位，=slug）
gel ①凝胶，胶状体，胶状物 ②形成胶体，胶凝，胶化
gel coat ①凝胶漆，凝胶涂料 ②凝胶树脂涂层（玻璃纤维增强塑料模制件的具有可上色的光滑表面的外层）
gel coat resin 凝胶树脂（制作凝胶树脂涂层用）
gel(l)ation ①胶凝作用，（凝）胶化（作用）②胶凝体 ③凝结，胶结，冻结
gelling drier 聚氯乙烯密封剂用的）促凝剂，速凝剂，快干剂
GEM ①通用电子（控制）模块

(general electronic module 的简称，某些汽车上使用的对多项功能进行控制的车用微型计算机，它可提供许多 BCM "车身控制模块" 所提供的控制功能，如：后窗与后视镜加热；刮水器时间间隔、速度和喷水控制；前照灯亮、车门半开、安全带未扣、钥匙未拔等声音警告；门控灯开关、点火开关断开后，信息中心、电动车门、车顶灯等的延时供电；蓄电池节能；四轮驱动的 4-2 轮驱动变换；后轮打滑时的前轮驱动控制；点动式车窗等等）②地面效应机械（ground effect machine 的简称，如：气垫车等）

Gemmer steering（**gear**） 蜗杆滚轮式转向器（亦称 Marles steering gear，或 hourglass worm and roller steering gear, waisted worm and roller type steering gear, helically cut waisted cam and roller steering gear，或 cam and roller steering gear，由一球面蜗杆和与之相啮合的凹面滚轮组成，滚轮通过滚动轴承支承在摇臂轴上，蜗杆所传递的转向盘轴的圆周运动通过滚轮带动摇臂而改变为摇臂的摆动）

GEN ①普通的，通用的，一般的；总的（general 的简称）②产生，引起（generate 的简称）③发电机（generator 的简称）

gene engineering 基因工程

general ①全面的，总的，普通的，一般的，通用的，平常的，非专门性的；简略的，概括的 ②总则，全体，一般

General Agreement on Tariffs and Trade 关税贸易总协定（简称 GATT，于 1996 年改为国际贸易组织，World Trade Organization，简称 WTO）

general arrangement drawing 总布置图

general arrangement plan 总体布置方案

general assembly drawing 总装（配）图（简称 gad）

general corrosion 整面腐蚀（指金属件整个表面腐蚀，以区别于点蚀 pitting）

general description 概述，一般说明

general design 总体设计

general electronic module 通用电子模块（见 GEM）

general engineering research 一般工程研究，通用工程技术研究（简称 GER）

general gas law 理想气体状态方程（$\dfrac{PV}{T}$ = 恒量，式中：P—压强，V—体积，T—温度）

generalizability ①可普及，可一般化，可推广 ②可概括，可归纳，可总结，可法则化

generalized management information system 综合管理信息系统（简称 GMIS）

general layout 总布置，总平面图

General Motor Corporation ［美］通用汽车公司（简称 GM，于 1908 年美国人 William Durant 以 Buick 汽车公司为核心组合 Chevrolet 等汽车厂，创建 General Motor Company，1916 年改现名，总部设于美国 Detroit 市，制造厂、装配厂遍布各地，为世界汽车工业的集团化、专业化开创了道路，年生产规模近 1000 万辆，居世界第一位，沃克斯豪尔 "Vauxhall" 是它在英国的子公司，欧宝 "Opel" 是它在欧洲的另一家子公司）

General Motors Europe 欧洲通用公司，通用公司欧洲公司（简称 GME）

general outline ①概要，总纲 ②总外形图，总外貌图，总平面图，总

布置图（＝general arrangement）

general overhaul （汽车）大修（亦称 major repair，指通过分解检查，更换或修理零部件、总成的方法，恢复汽车技术完好状态和完全或接近完全恢复汽车寿命的恢复性修理）

general proportions of car 汽车的外形尺寸

general-purpose 通用（的），多种用途（的），万能（的）（＝general service，general-utility）

general purpose car 多功能轿车（如：全轮驱动的北京切诺基轿车）

general purpose shop truck 通用修理（服务）车，通用修理工程车，多功能维修工程车

general purpose vehicle 通用汽车，多功能汽车（简称 GPV）

general-service 见 general-purpose

generate 产生，发生；引起，导致，造成，生成（＝produce）

generated teeth 产形轮齿（以范成法切出的轮齿，其齿面为切齿刀具的切削刃按照一定的运动条件，在实际空间中描绘的运动轨迹曲面族的包络曲面的轮齿）

generating angle （轮齿）压力角，（＝pressure angle，指齿面上任一点处的径向直线与齿面在该点处的切平面所夹的锐角）

generating capacity ①发电能力 ②装机容量

generating circle 发生圆，滚圆，母圆，创成圆（摆线轮的发生圆柱面与端平面的交线，参见 epitrochoid）

generating cone （锥齿轮的）基锥

generating curve 母曲线

generating cylinder （齿轮的）发生圆柱面（在基圆柱面上做纯滚动以形成摆线轮齿面的一个假想圆柱面）

generating line 母线，生成线，产形线

generating radius （外旋轮线的）创成（圆）半径（参见 epitrochoid）

generating set 发电设备，发电机组（见 genset）

generating unit 发电装备（全套发电装备，＝generating set）

generation ①代，世代，阶段；发展型 ②产生，引起，发展，发生，生成；加工，组成，制造，形成 ③范成，用范成法加工制造

generation gas 发生炉煤气（由车载式发生炉用木炭作燃料，产生的发生炉煤气成分，按体积计 N_2 65%，CO_2 1%，CO 34%；用无烟煤燃料的煤气成分 N_2 66%，CO_2 5%，CO 25%，H_2 3%，CH_4 1%，其低热值约 800～1000kcal/m^3，＝generator gas，producer gas）

generative fuel ①再生燃料 ②煤气发生炉燃料

generator ①发生器（指各种发生装置，如：煤气发生炉、信号发生器、射流发生器等）②（特指汽车用的任一种形式的）发电机（包括交流发电机和直流发电机）③（美仅指）直流发电机（＝DC generator，dynamo）

generator and starter armature tester 发电机及起动电机电枢试验器

generator-battery ignition system 发电机-蓄电池点火系统

generator charge gauge 发动机充电指示表

generator cutting rule 发电机切割法则（参见 generator effect）

generator effect 发电机效应（导体切割磁力线产生电动势，故亦称发电机切割法则，＝generator cutting rule）

generator field 发电机磁场

generator field coil 发电机磁场线圈

generator gas 发生炉煤气（指煤气

发生炉产生的煤气,以别于管道煤气)

generator monitor 发电机监测传感器(通过监测发电机输出电压测定发电机工况,实际上是一接在发电机供电电路上的导线,向电子控制单元输送其电压信号)

generator regulator 发电机调节器(见 regulator①)

generator set 发电机组

generator/starter 发电-起动电动机(发动机起动时起带动发动机旋转的电动机作用,而在停机时,由发动机惯性反拖起发电机作用回收能量,见 dry starting method、engine stopping by regeneration method)

generator-starter tester (汽车)发电机-起动机测试仪

generic ①未注册的,不受商标注册保护的②一般的,普通的(specific 的反义词)

generous size glove compartment (汽车仪表板上的)大尺寸手工具箱,大号的杂件箱

genetic algorithm 见 GA

Geneva International Motor Show 日内瓦国际车展(一年一度,始于1905年)

genset 发电机组(generating set 的简称,一般包括发电机、驱动发电机的发动机和各种控制仪表等)

genset engine 发电用发动机(用作发电机动力的发动机,generating engine 的简称,亦称 dynamo engine)

gentle 和缓的,平缓的;轻微的,轻度的

gentle acceleration 逐渐加速,缓加速

gentle start (汽车)平稳起步

genuine leather wrapped 真皮包复的

genuine spare part(s) 原厂配件(= original spare part)

geomagnetic 地磁的

GeoMessaging (公路沿途的)地理信息

geometry similarity 几何相似(几何形状、尺寸成同一比例,亦写作 geometric similarity)

geometric(al) 几何的,几何学的,几何图形的

geometric deflection (钢板弹簧)几何挠度

geometric displacement (三角转子发动机的)计算排量(见 cell swept volume)

geometric free camber of spring 弹簧自由状态时的挠度

geometric fuel delivery (柴油机柱塞式喷油泵)几何供油(指凸轮推动柱塞实现的供油。geometric fuel delivery beginning 几何供油始点,指凸轮使柱塞开始移动至关闭进油孔时的位置,以凸轮转角表示;geometric fuel delivery duration angle 几何供油持续角,指几何供油始点与几何供油终点间的凸轮持续转角;geometric fuel delivery end 几何供油终点,指凸轮使柱塞开始移动至回油孔开启时的位置,以凸轮转角表示;geometric fuel delivery stroke 或 geometric fuel delivery effective stroke 几何供油有效冲程,或几何供油冲程,指几何供油始点至几何供油终点之间柱塞的有效冲程)

geometric progression 几何级数,等比级数

geometric projection 几何投影法

geometry ①几何学 ②几何图形 ③几何形状,几何结构(当用于转向系和悬架系时,指构件之间的角度和直线关系及其在运转中的变动)

geothermal 地热的

German 德国的,德国人,德语的,日耳曼的(简称 G)

germanium 锗（Ge，原子量72.61）

German silver 锌镍铜合金（Cu40%～65%，Ni6%～35%，Zn15%～35%）

germedical paint 灭菌漆，防霉漆

gerotor (type) pump 转子泵，转子式油泵［由一带有四个或多个外齿的内转子主动件与带有相应数量的圆弧内齿（一般比内转子多一个）的外转子从动件组成，= rotor pump，外转子齿形以旋轮线代替圆弧者，称为旋轮线转子泵，= trochoid pump］

get away ①起步，开动，离开 ②（汽车赛用语）出发，开跑

get-you-home safety tyre 安全回家轮胎（一种无内胎轮胎，胎侧有左、右两气室，与主气室互不相通，分别充气，当轮胎某处被刺穿漏气时，汽车仍可安全驶回，因而可不用备胎）

GEV 地面效应车（如：气垫车，ground effect vehicle 的简称）

gf 克力（力的单位，= g-force，见 gramme force）

GFI 汽油喷射（gasoline fuel injection 的简称）

GFRP 玻璃纤维强化塑料（glass fiber reinforced plastics 的简称）

G, g ①重力加速度（acceleration of gravity）②重心（center of gravity）③千亿（giga）④克（gram）⑤栅极（grid）⑥重力（gravity）⑦搭铁（ground）

GG 气体发生器（gas generator 的简称）

GHE 温室效应（green house effect 的简称）

Ghia Connecta ［美］（福特）吉亚康尼克塔（Ford 汽车公司的电动汽车的商品名，在城市道路行驶一次充电可续航160km，车身由碳素纤维制造）

ghosted view 显示内部的透视图（= skeleton view）

gi ①加强筋；散热片 ②吉尔（见 gill）

gib ①榫，扁栓，夹条 ②吊杆，起重机臂（= gibbet）

giga 京，千兆，十亿（10^9，代号 G）

gigajoule 千兆焦耳（国际单位制的热量的倍数单位，代号 GJ，1GJ = 10^9J）

gigameter 百万公里（10^6km）

gigawatt 千兆瓦（国际单位制的功率倍数单位，代号 GW，1GW = 10^9W）

Gilbert 吉伯（磁通势单位 = 0.796 安匝，代号 Gb）

gill ①肋条，支骨，加强筋；散热片，波形板，百叶窗 ②吉耳（液量单位 = 0.25pint = 0.14L）③基尔（完成一次给定操作的时间单位）

gilled tube radiator 管片式散热器（= fin and tube radiator）

gills ［俚］可调式百叶窗

gimbal ①（多用复数，罗盘等的）平衡环，水平环，方向支撑环（由环状支架或称支撑环，及装在环上的四个各相隔90°的枢轴组成，其中每两个相隔90°的枢轴成一对，两对枢轴的连线均过环心并相互垂直。一对枢轴 A 用于将环装在支座上，另一对 B 则用于安装位于环内的要保持水平位置的装置，如：指南针等。环可绕枢轴 A 的连线转动，而装在环内的装置又可绕枢轴 B 转动，于是无论环支座如何倾斜，装在环中的装置均可在重心作用下保持水平，亦称 gimbal ring）②万向接头

gimlet ①（木工）手钻，木锥，螺丝锥 ②有钻孔能力的 ③用手钻钻，用锥子锥，穿透

gin ①三脚起重架，起重装置；绞车绞盘 ②打桩机

girder ①梁，桁（架），托梁 ②撑柱，撑杆 ③槽钢

girder frame 梁式车架

girder spanner 手柄与板爪成直角布置的可调扳手

girder steel 钢梁，工字钢

girdle ①环带，环形物 ②环绕，用带缠束

GIS 地理信息系统（geographic information system 的简称，用于汽车导航技术）

give way line 让车标线（交叉口处次要道路驶入车辆必须在让车标线前暂停，让主要道路驶入车先行通过）

GJ 千兆焦耳（见 gigajoule）

g/kWh 克/千瓦小时（欧共体用于评定货车发动机 CO、NO_X、HC 等排放量的质量度量单位）

G/L （车辆）总质量与装载质量之比，总重与有效载重之比（gross weight to pay load）

GL ①齿轮油（gear lubricant 的简称，美国 API 的齿轮油代号，分五级，用 GL-1、GL-2、GL-3、GL-4、GL-5 表示）②标距长度（gauge length 的简称）③玻璃，车窗（glass）④搭铁指示灯（ground lamp 的简称）⑤地平线（ground line 的简称）⑥华贵豪华型（Grand Luxe 的简称，比 CL 更为豪华的车型，见 CL）

glacier white 冰川白（车身颜色）

gladhand （牵引车和挂车的气制动系）软管快速（多管道）接头

glancing impact 制动时，由于惯性继续向前滑动而发生的撞车

gland ①（防止油、液从运动的轴、杆类零件上泄漏的）密封件，密封装置 ②（密封装置内的）密封填料，密封材料 ③（密封材料的）压盖，塞栓，封套（gland bonnet 轴端的密封盖；gland box 填料箱，填料函；gland cock 本身带密封件的旋塞；gland cover 密封压盖；gland nut 密封螺母，密封件的压紧螺母；gland packing 密封件内的填料；gland ring 密封填料函压环，密封环）

glandless 无密封的（如：对密封材料有腐蚀作用的各种液体用的无密封泵"glandless pump"）

gland nut 密封螺母

glare ①光滑明亮的表面 ②闪光，眩光，强光，刺目光（光学上特指强度超过人眼适应范围的光，如前照灯的正面）③发强光，闪光

glare effect 眩光效应，炫目效应，耀眼影响（汽车会车时，前照灯光对驾驶员眼睛的炫耀作用）

glare-free instrument module 不反光仪表组件

glare ice 薄冰（= clear ice）

glare proof inner mirror 防眩式车内后视镜

glare-proof mirror 防眩后视镜（其镜面为反射光较弱的低反射玻璃面，有手调和自动两种）

glare reduction techniques （汽车照明的）防眩技术

glare screen 眩光屏，遮眩板（使驾驶员不受对向车前灯眩光干扰的反眩设施，= glare shield）

glaring light 炫目灯光，眩光（灯）（= dazzle lighting）

glass ①玻璃，玻璃制品，玻璃纤维 ②镜，镜片 ③玻璃（车）窗，车窗玻璃板 ④镶装玻璃，用玻璃覆盖 ⑤磨光，抛光，使平滑如镜 ⑥反映

glass area （车身的）窗面区［①仅指其车窗的（玻璃）表面区 ②指车身腰线以上的整个区域，因为车窗玻璃都布置在腰线以上］

glass bowl ①（汽油滤清器的）玻璃杯壳 ②（汽油泵等的油污）玻璃沉淀杯 ③（泛指各种）杯状玻

璃件

glass bulb 灯泡

glass ceramics 玻璃陶瓷

glass channel [美]车窗玻璃槽（= window channel）

glass cleaner ①挡风玻璃刮水器 ②车灯玻璃擦洗器 ③玻璃清洁器

glass cloth ①玻璃砂布，玻璃砂纸 ②玻璃丝布（由无机玻璃经熔化，抽丝，纺织成布，在汽车用钢化玻璃中起增强作用）

glass-cloth epoxy laminate 浸透环氧树脂的玻璃纤维层压板（亦称 glass-fiber epoxy laminate）

glass cord 玻璃纤维帘线（= glass-fiber cord）

glass-core cable ①玻璃纤维芯导线 ②玻璃绳芯拉索

glass dimmer 滤光玻璃遮阳板

glass dish evaporation test 玻璃皿蒸发法（测量汽油中的实际胶质，= glass dish gum test）

glass dome （轿车车身的）透明车顶

glassed dial 带玻璃面的刻度盘，玻璃面表盘

glass electrode 玻璃电极

glass-fabric-reinforced polyester laminate 玻璃纤维强化聚酯层压板

glass-felt plastic 玻璃钢，玻璃纤维增强塑料（以玻璃纤维、布、带或毡为增强材料，以合成树脂为黏合剂，经过一定的成型工艺而制成的一种复合材料）

glass fiber 玻璃纤维（直径 $5\sim10\mu m$ 的单纤维，抗拉强度可达 $150\sim200kg/mm^2$，= fiber glass，作为层压塑料的增强材料，或声、电、热的隔绝材料，亦写作 glass fibre）

glass-fiber cord 玻璃索，玻璃纤维帘线（= glass cord）

glass-fibre belted radials 玻璃纤维带束子午线轮胎（见 radial type）

glass-fibre clad 玻璃纤维包覆的

glass-fibre moulder 玻璃纤维塑料造型机；喷射造型用玻璃纤维造模

glass-filled 玻璃填充的［如：glass-filled SMC（玻璃填充的SMC）可用来制作车用透明构件，见 SMC］

glass-filled nylon 玻璃纤维填充尼龙

glass frame 玻璃窗框

glass front 车身前部的风窗玻璃

glass gauge ①玻璃管液面指示器 ②玻璃量筒（带有刻度的液体容积量具）

glass holder 玻璃吸盘（吸住玻璃可将玻璃正确地安装至窗框上）

glasshouse [美俚]有盖汽车

glassification 玻璃化

glass laminate 安全夹层玻璃

glass lens （前照灯的）配光镜（指一个或一个以上光学单元组合获得所需配光特性的透镜，简称 lens）

glass mat 玻璃纤维垫，玻璃纤维板

glass oil cup 玻璃油杯

glass pack muffler （无阻流挡板，使用玻璃纤维包覆的多孔管以消除排气声的直通式）玻璃纤维填充消声器

glass paper ①玻璃纸 ②玻璃砂纸（表面有玻璃微粒层的打磨和抛光用砂纸）

glass partition （轿车分隔驾驶席与后席的）玻璃隔墙

glass peephole 玻璃观察孔

glass-PVB-glass material 玻璃-聚丁缩醛乙烯-玻璃夹层材料（其中 PVB 为 polyvinyl butyral 的简称）

glass regulations （对汽车车身和驾驶室用）玻璃质量规范

glass regulator 车窗玻璃升降器

glass reinforced 玻璃纤维强化的（指加有玻璃纤维丝、玻璃纤维织物或玻璃纤维帘布，以增加强度的。glass reinforced epoxy 玻璃纤维强化环氧树脂；glass reinforced filler paste 玻璃纤维增强填料，一般指加

有玻璃纤维丝的聚酯填料）

glass reinforced plastics 玻璃纤维增强塑料（简称GRP）

glass-reinforced polyester laminate 玻璃纤维强化聚酯层压板（简称GRP laminate）

glass-reinforced tire 玻璃纤维帘布层轮胎

glass remover 碎玻璃清除器（从车窗框架中清除碎玻璃的工具）

glass rim （窗）玻璃框

glass-run (channel) 风窗玻璃升降槽，车门玻璃导槽（门玻璃移动的导轨衬条兼作密封条）

glass-run weather strip 风窗玻璃（升降或移动）槽（的）密封条

glass screen 风窗玻璃

glass seal （火花塞的）导电玻璃密封（装在火花塞绝缘体内腔中部，连接其接线螺杆，即中央铁芯和中心电极的密封剂或密封件）

glass shield ①玻璃护罩②风窗玻璃

glass sphere 玻璃珠（颗粒状玻璃强化填料）

glass strip 窗玻璃密封镶条

glass tampering detector 风窗玻璃撞击传感器（汽车警报系统中探测玻璃正受到撞击或被击破的部件）

glass thread 玻璃丝

glass-topped piston （研究燃烧过程用的）玻璃顶活塞

glass tube 玻璃管

glass type main antenna （汽车分集式天线系统中的）玻璃型主天线（埋设在风窗玻璃内的主天线）（见 diversity antenna system）

glass weather strip 风窗玻璃密封条

glass wool 玻璃纤维棉（用于保温、防火、隔声、过滤、电绝缘等）

glass yarn 玻璃线

glassy cabin 玻璃车厢（指周围都是玻璃窗的超优视野车厢）

glaze ①釉料，瓷釉，珐琅（简称GL）②光泽，光滑③光滑面，光滑层（如：汽缸壁镜面）④上釉，涂釉，抛光，上光研磨

glaze breaker 镜面磨具（亦称deglazer，汽缸壁镜面等抛光面的磨削工具）

glazed ①结有薄冰的（路面等）②装有玻璃的③具有光滑，抛光表面的

glazer's body 运送玻璃板的车厢

glazing ①窗用玻璃，玻璃窗②装玻璃作业③上釉，釉彩，抛光④光辉，光泽

glazing floor (area) ratio 窗壁（面积）比（指车窗洞面积与壁面面积之比）

glazing machine 抛光机，上光研磨机

glazing strip （风窗玻璃或其他门、窗玻璃框的）玻璃安装条（一般为模制橡胶条，用于固定和密封玻璃）

GLC 气液色谱分析（gas/liquid chromatography 的简称）

gleaming ①反光的，镜面的，抛光的②微光的③闪光的

Gleason spiral bevel gear 格里森弧齿锥齿轮（锥齿轮的齿制有三种，美国的Gleason齿制，瑞士的Oerlikon齿制和德国的Klingenberg齿制，它们的齿廓形状都是近似球面渐开线的，而格里森制锥齿轮的产形冠轮上的齿线是圆弧的，因而形成的齿线呈圆弧形，故名）

Gleason tooth system 格里森齿制（指在格里森机床上用圆盘铣刀加工出来的曲线齿锥齿轮，具有圆弧形的节锥齿线，故又称圆弧齿锥齿轮）

GL-3 gear lubricant [美] GL-3级齿轮油（适用于手动变速器及载荷一般的锥齿轮减速器，见GL）

glider automatic 自动滑行机场（当

驾驶员松开加速踏板汽车处于减速工况时,自动断油熄火,而当驾驶员再踏下加速踏板时,又自动恢复供油的装置,亦称自动强制怠速节油器)

glider door 拉门,推拉门

global automobile production ranking 全球轿车(年)产量排序,世界轿车(年)产量序位

globalization 全球化

global kinetic parameters 地球的动态参数(如气温等)

global positioning system 全球定位系统(该系统由24颗卫星组成,在6条轨道上运行,每12小时绕地球一圈,连续不断发射位置和时间信号,覆盖全球范围,配合车上接收与导航系统,驾驶员可准确地确定自己的方位,并可选出最佳行车路线,简称GPS)

Global Road Safety Campaign Decade Plan (联合国2010年3月正式宣布的2011~2020年)道路安全行动十年计划(目的:确保道路交通安全,降低道路交通事故伤亡率)

Global Road Safety Week 全球道路安全周("道路安全行动十年计划"开展的宣传活动之一,见Global Road Safety Campaign Decade Plan)

Global Technical Regulation (由联合国专门的委员会主持美、日、德等23个国家和地区参与共同制定的)全球(统一)技术法规(简称GTR)

global vibration test 全系统振动试验(测定结构各元件共振频率的试验)

global warming 全球变暖

globe 球,球状物[globe bearing 球面轴承; globe cam 球形凸轮; globe cock 球形阀,球阀(= ball cock); globe holder 球形卡座,球形灯座; globe joint 球铰接,球关节; globe journal 球形轴颈; globe valve 球阀]

globoid ①球状体 ②球状的,球形的

globoidal worm 环面蜗杆(旧称"球面蜗杆"及"弧面蜗"此两词现均已停止使用。18世纪英国钟表制造者Hindley发明,因而亦称Hindley Worm,该蜗杆的中部直径小,向两端逐渐地对称加大,呈沙漏形,以增大接触面积,减少磨损,故又称沙漏形蜗杆"hourglass worm"。Hindley发明之初,环面、蜗杆轴向齿廓均为直线,故确切地说,Hindley worm是指直廓环面蜗杆,见Hindley worm)

globular 球形的,球面的,圆的,小球的

globular graphite 球状石墨,球墨

glocalization 全球-本地双重化(指汽车产业必须形成全球生产系统,通过全球化采购、生产和销售创立全球品牌;在本地区域范围内形成集群生产系统并在群落间形成紧密的多种协作关系)

glossy 光滑的,光泽的,发光的

glove box [美] (= glove compartment,汽车仪表板旁或下方的)手套箱,小工具箱,杂物箱(glove box catch,glove box fastener,glove box lock 小工具箱锁,手套箱锁扣; glove box cover 手套箱盖,= glove box lid; glove box lamp 手套箱照明灯)

glow 发光,白热,灼热(指无焰烧灼)

glow-discharge heating 辉光放电加热

glower plug 电热塞(①柴油机的,预热塞,= glow plug, glow tube, heating plug, heater plug,用于冷机起动时预热进气空气或燃烧室,一般为电热丝式 ②预热-助燃塞,和上述预热塞类似,但起动后在运转过程中,一直处于白炽状态,用于混合气引燃或助燃)

glow ignition 灼热点火（汽油机积炭，排气门等热点引起的混合气非正常点火，早燃现象）

glowing filament 白热灯丝

glow lamp ①白炽灯，辉光灯，灯泡（=bulb）②辉光放电管

glow plate ①（柴油机燃烧室内的）绝热衬里；炽热衬板 ②炽热板

glow plug 见 glower plug

glow plug filament 加热塞电丝，预热塞电阻丝

glow-plug ignition 电热塞点火

glow plug indicator 预热塞指示器（简称 glow indicator，与预热塞串联的电热丝指示器，当预热通电并达到预热温度后，该电热丝即发红，表示发动机已可起动，亦称 glow plug pilot）

glow plug/starter switch （柴油机的）预热塞/起动机开关（同时控制预热系通电和发动机起动的点火开关）

glow time （柴油机的预热塞）预热时间

glow tube 见 glower plug

Gls' vehicle ［美］多用途军用车

glue ①胶，黏结剂（如，制动蹄摩擦片的黏结剂）②胶合，黏接

glued wood 胶合板（=plywood）

glueing 上胶，黏接，黏牢

glue joint 黏胶连接

glug （质量单位）格拉格（一克的力能使一格拉格质量产生 $1 cm/s^2$ 的加速度）

glycerate 甘油酸盐

glyceride 甘油酸酯

glycerine 甘油，丙三醇（$C_3H_6O_3$，无色黏稠吸湿性液体，汽车上可掺入冷却水内作为防冻液材料）

glycol 乙（撑）二醇（$HOCH_2CH_2OH$）（俗称甘醇，见 ethylene glycol）；乙二醇（=ethanediol，防冻液的主要成分）

glycolal 乙醇醛（CH_2OHCHO）

glycol brake fluid 甘醇制动液，甘醇制动油，乙二醇制动液

glycol ether 乙二醇乙醚（$HOCH_2CH_2OC_2H_5$，防冻液主要成分之一）

Glyko metal 锌基轴承合金（锡5%，铜25%，锑4.7%，铅2%，锌85.5%）

glyptal lacquer 甘油苯二甲醇树脂漆，葛利弗塔漆，甘肽树脂漆

GM ①总经理（general manager 的简称）②［美］通用汽车公司（General Motors Corporation 的简称）③调速机用电动机（governor motor 的简称）④（浮体的）稳心高度（metacentric height）

g_m 或 Gm（低频）互导，跨导（low frequency mutual conductance）

GMC （美国）通用汽车公司（General Motors Corporation 的简称）

GM CADILLAC Seville car 通用凯迪莱克塞维利亚轿车（美国通用汽车公司 cadillac 部生产的豪华型轿车）

GMIS 统一化的管理信息系统（generalized management information system）

3.5G mobile broadband 3.5G 移动（电话）（网络）宽带

GMODC ［美］通用汽车公司海外开发公司（GM Overseas Development Co 的简称）

GM Truck Bus Group （美国）通用客货车集团（公司）

GND 接地，搭铁（ground）

GN/m^2 千兆牛顿/米^2（giganewton/meter^2，国际单位制的压力的倍数单位）

go ahead motion 前进运动

goal 目的，目标；目的地，终点

go-anywhere leisure vehicle 高通过性旅游车，越野旅游车

go-anywhere vehicle 越野车辆

(= off road vehicle)

GOA safety impact body （丰田公司的）全球顶级安全碰撞车身（GOA为 Global Outstanding Assessment 的简称，丰田公司根据世界上多个国家，如：美国、欧洲、澳大利亚、日本的安全标准独立研制的安全车身，能在碰撞时有效地吸收碰撞能量，并将其均匀地分散至车身各部分骨架，确保座舱的安全，据称可满足全球任一国家的安全标准）

go astern 后退，倒车

go-cart ①手推车（见 kart）②娱乐用的无车身一人座超微型汽车

Gogan hardness （摩擦材料）高氏硬度，高根硬度（规定直径的圆柱形压头，在一定的负荷下压入试样一定的时间，压头每压入 0.00025 in 为一度，用于测定制动蹄摩擦片，该硬度仅表示摩擦片的耐压能力，与其摩擦性及抗衰减能力无关。通常在检查摩擦片质量均一性时使用，根据所加的负荷及压头直径，分为 ABCD 四种刻度，分别用 GA、GB、GC、GD 表示）

go gauge 过端量规，通过规

goggles 护目镜，风镜（防止尘埃和强光）

go home 备用发动机（见"home going" motor)

going report 地面或地形的（可行驶性）状况报告

go-kart 微型赛车

gold ①金 Au ②金制的 ③金色的

gold bonded diodes 金键二极管

gold doping 掺金，金（的掺杂）扩散（将金杂质原子扩散到晶体中）

golden proportion （车身造型的）黄金比例

gold-plated ball （安全气囊的磁铁式惯性机电传感器中的）镀金惯性球（正常情况下，由永磁铁将该球吸住。当发生碰撞、受到因汽车减速度而产生的超过永磁吸力的惯性力的作用时，该球沿一管状通道弹出，将管道末端的点火机械触点闭合，安全气囊起爆）

gold wire pencil （在特制涂面的铝板上绘图用）金芯铅笔

Golf Blue-e-Motion （VW 公司 2013 年推出的）高尔夫牌环保电动汽车车名

go light 绿灯，可通行灯

gon 刚（= grade，度，平面角的单位，$1 \text{ gon} = \frac{\pi}{200} \text{rad}$）

gondola ①（运输混凝土的）有漏斗状容器的货车，带漏斗的挂车 ②悬挂式小型零件搬运箱（零件由侧面装卸）③敞篷车

goniometer ①量角仪，测角器 ②测向器无线电方位测定器

go-no-go gauge 过端-不过端量规，合格-不合格量规（用来检验产品是否合格的一种量规，它并不测定具体的数值，而只区分合格"通过"和不合格"不通过"两种情况）

good condition of vehicle （车辆）完好技术状态（指汽车完全符合技术文件规定要求的技术状态）

good lock (on a vehicle) （车辆的转向轮转到锁止位置时的）最大转向角度（该角度越大，说明该车转弯半径越小，见 lock④）

good mileage 每单位燃油能够行驶的里程较多，汽车燃料经济性较好

goodness 优良，优质；精华；优势；优良性，优质性，品质因数

goodness-of-fit test 拟合良好性检验（在数理统计中对统计假设可置信性的检验，如：对随机量分布规律的假设是否合理等）

goods 货物，车辆所运输的货物（相对乘客而言，= 美 freight③）

goods chassis 货车底盘（= 美 freight chassis，见 chassis）

goods road train 货车列车（指货车拖挂牵引杆式或中置轴式挂车组成的汽车列车）

goods traffic ①货运交通 ②货物运输业（美称 freight traffic）

goods transport（ation） 货物运输，货运［美称 freight transport(ation)］

goods van 厢式货车（= 美 freight van）

goods vehicle 货运汽车，货运车辆（= 美 freight vehicle）

good working condition 完好工作状态；良好工作条件

Goodyear 固特异（美国人，首创橡胶硫化法，1842 年初制成实心橡胶胎；Goodyear 公司生产的轮胎的商品名）

Goodyear Tire and Rubber Co. （美国）固特异轮胎橡胶公司

go off 起步，起动

goose neck ①（泛指各种）鹅颈状物；S 形弯管，S 形零件 ②（工作灯等的可调）挠性灯杆 ③（全挂车的）鹅颈形拖杆 ④（半挂车的）台阶式车架的前部

gooseneck type tanker 鹅颈式液罐车

goose test 见 service code⑤

gore sign （互通式立交的）主线分流点标志

gorge （涡轮、蜗杆）咽喉面（指其齿顶曲面上呈圆环状的那一部分齿顶表面，即齿顶圆环面）

gorgeous 华丽的（好看的，漂亮的，豪华的）

gorge radius 涡轮、蜗杆咽喉半径（指其齿顶圆环面，即咽喉面的母圆半径）

GOS 一般操作规程，通用操作规程（general operating specification 的简称）

go-side （极限量规的）通过端，合格端

goudron 渣油，减压渣油，残油

goudron highway 沥青渣油公路

gouge ①半圆凿，弧口凿 ②凿出的槽孔 ③用半圆凿凿槽 ④（边缘较为平缓因而可用加热使其收缩或用成形砧垫撑托锤击的方法恢复原形的车身板件上的）较大但平缓的凹陷

Gough-Joule Effect 高夫-焦耳效应（指处于拉伸状态的橡胶受热时收缩的特性，与大部分工程材料相反）

Gough's tyre characteristic diagram 高夫轮胎特性图，轮胎转弯特性图（V. E. Gough 将轮胎的转弯力，自回正力矩，气胎拖距，侧偏角与垂直负荷之间的关系，用一幅综合图来表示，亦称 tyre cornering characteristics diagram）

gouging abrasion 凿击磨损，撞击磨损

governed speed 受调速器限制的转速

governing 调整，调节，控制，操纵

government fleet 政府机关所属的汽车车队

government rubber 丁腈橡胶（acrylonitrile butadiene copolymer 丁二烯—丙烯腈共聚物，简称 GR-A）

government stimulated market 政府促进的市场

government test 国家试验，政府试验

governor ①调节器，控制器（泛指各种自动控制转速、位置、供给量等的装置和器件）②（特指柴油机的）调速器（限制和稳定柴油机最高和最低转速，或在柴油机工作的整个转速范围内均起作用，即保证其在每种转速下的稳定运转的装置）③（自动变速器的）速控阀（见 governor valve）

governor and rear pump gear （[美]

自动变速器输出轴上的）速控阀和后机油泵驱动齿轮（＝英 regulator and rear oil pump gear，见 governor valve③）

governor assist plunger 调速器助动柱塞

governor assist spring 调速器副弹簧

governor ball 离心调速器的飞球

governor control characteristics 调速特性（表示调速器作用前后柴油机的转矩、功率、油耗量等参数与转速之间的相互关系）

governor drive （发动机的）调速器驱动机构

governor fork 调速器杠杆的叉头

governor housing pressure （柴油机自动）调速器腔内压力（简称 housing pressure，指由压力调节器控制，作用于调速器弹簧活塞的压力，与作用于动力活塞的输油泵压力相互配合决定喷油提前或推迟）

governor hunting （柴油机）调速器速控波振（指调速器的速度控制波动，以致发动机周期性地发生短期转速过低或过高的波动）

governor plate 断电器底板

governor pressure （自动变速器液控系的）速控液压（指速控液压阀输出的调制液压，用于控制各换挡阀柱塞的位置，以实现自动变速器随车速度变化的自动换挡）

governor spring 调速（器）弹簧（与速度传感部件的离心力，或其分力相平衡的主弹簧）

governor（throttle）position valve （节气门）位（置）控（制）阀（自动变速器液力控制系统中由节气门开度控制的液压阀，该阀的输出压力用于控制液压系统的主调压阀或称主压力阀柱塞的位置，以实现主压力随节气门开度的自动变化，在电子控制自动变速器中为节气门位置传感器及相应的执行元件所取代）

governor valve ①（泛指各种控制或调节压力、流量等的）控制阀，调节阀 ②（气制动系统中控制空气压缩机压缩空气输出量的）控制阀 ③（自动变速器液压系统的）速控阀（由自动变速器输出轴上的一齿轮驱动的离心式液压阀，简称 GV，其输出液压称为 governor pressure，与液力变速器输轴转速成正比，因而与车速成正比，用来控制各换挡阀"shift valve"的工作位置，实现随车速变化的自动换挡。在电子控制式自动变速器中该阀已为变速器输出轴的转速传感器及有关执行元件所取代）

governor weights （离心式）调速器重锤（＝advanced weight）

governor with load sensing 负荷感知型调速器

GP ①一般用途的，通用的（general purpose）②几何级数，等比级数（geometric progression）

GP 吉普车（jeep, general purpose 的简称，一般指装载质量为1/4t全轮驱动的军用汽车

GPa 吉帕（国际单位制压力单位，$1GPa=98kgf/cm^2$）

gpf ①防毒气的 ②不透气的（gas-proof）

GPH ①加仑/小时（gallon per hour 的简称）②克/小时（见 gram per hour）

gpm （亦写作 GPM）①每分钟加仑数（gallons per minute 的简称）②加仑/英里（gallons per mile 的简称）

G point G 点（汽车座椅中心平面上，同靠背表面相切的垂线与座垫上表面的交点）

GP polystyrene 通用聚苯乙烯，一般用途聚苯乙烯

GPS 全球定位系统（见 global posi-

GPS -based 基于 GPS 的
GPS base receiver station fixed on the ground 固定在地面上的 GPS 基准接收站（亦称 reference station）
GPS -enable headlights dim GPS（信息）控制（变光的）前照灯（系统）（电子控制系统根据 GPS 的信息判断对向行驶的车辆临近规定的距离时，即相应关闭部分 LED 等发光元件，使前照灯减光或改变照灯射明区，做到既可让本车驾驶者看清前方路况，又可避免对方车驾驶者炫目）
g/psh 克/公制马力小时（发动机油耗率的米制单位）
GPS navigation GPS 导航
GPS rover receiver station fixed on vehicle 固定在车上的 GPS 流动接收站
GPS satellite constellation 全球定位系统卫星群（指 GPS 的 24 颗导航卫星形成的星群）
GPU 单位加仑数（gallon per unit 的简称，指以每小时、每英里或每吨英里为单位，汽车所消耗的燃油的加仑数）
gr ①传动比（gear ratio）②坡度；等级；梯度（grade）③格令（英制最小质量单位）；颗粒（grain）④克（gramme）⑤豪华的（grand）⑥重力（gravity）⑦磨，研磨（grind）⑧总的（gross）⑨搭铁，接地（ground）⑩组，类；集团（group）
grab (= grap, snatch, 作名词时 = grabbing) ①抓取，钳住 ②（一踩下制动踏板，制动器便）突然刹死 ③（一松开离合器踏板，离合器便）突然接合（以致车辆突然向前冲动）④（由于制动鼓变形或制动蹄片维护不良引起的）缓踩（制动踏板，制动器却）急刹（车的）现象
GRAB （汽车）爬坡能力，（最大）爬坡度（grade ability）
grabber 见 seat belt grabber
grab handles ①扶手，拉手，把手 ②（车门内侧的关门）拉手；（设在挂车尾部，供人力调动车位用的）把手
grab hook 起重抓钩
grab pole （公共汽车内）乘客扶手杆
grab sample 随机采样，非连续采试样，单采试样（如：用一密封的注射器在短时间内采集的废气试样，供成分分析用 = batch sample, non-continuous sample）
grad ①坡（gradient）②毕业生（graduate）③graduation 的简称
grad ability limit （汽车的）爬坡度极限（指汽车在等速爬坡时的最大爬坡能力，并写作 grade ability limit）
grade ①[美]坡，坡度，倾斜度（=[英] gradient）②等级，品位，级别；分类；分级，分等 ③程度；梯度 ④（砂纸的）粒度（美称 grit，用"目"表示，根据砂粒的细度对砂纸进行分类。"目"是指砂粒能通过的筛子的单位长度的孔数）⑤（砂轮砂粒的）结合强度 ⑥分类，分级；定坡度
grade ability 见 grade climbing ability
grade ability test （汽车）爬坡性能试验
grade angle 坡度角（坡路斜面与水平面的夹角）
grade-braking performance 坡道制动性能
grade-climbing ability 爬坡能力（= climbing ability, 简称 grade ability, 或 GRAB; 指汽车在良好的路面上以最低前进挡所能爬行的最大坡度，为汽车动力性指标之一。有的国家则规定用在常遇的坡道上能否

以一定速度行驶来表明汽车的爬坡能力，如：要求单车在3%的坡道上能以60km/h的车速行驶等)

grade climbing performance 爬坡性能 (= hill climbing performance)

grade-crossing (美·道路)平面交叉，平面交叉口 (= crossing at grade, 英称 level crossing, 相对立体交叉而言)

graded hardening 分段淬火 (= broken hardening)

grade line 道路纵剖面曲线

Grade 120M machine screw (美制)120M级机器螺钉(表示螺丝的抗拉强度为 120 000 lbf/in^2)

grade numbers (材料等的质量)等级编号，等级代号

grade of fit 配合等级

grade of slope 坡度，斜坡度 (见 gradient)

grade parking performance 车辆的坡路停车性能，坡道驻车性能 (见 on grade parking performance)

grade performance (汽车的)爬坡能力，登坡能力 (= grade-climbing ability)

grade profile (道路等的)坡度纵剖面

grader 平地机

grade ratio (公路的)坡度比(即升高与水平投影距离之比，如：1:40，即每40m水平距离中升高1m)

grade resistance 上坡阻力，坡度阻力 (指汽车重力平行于路面的分力)

grade resistance horsepower 爬坡阻力功率 (指克服上坡阻力所消耗的功率)

grade retard clutch (自动变速器内)自动缓速装置离合器(控制自动缓速装置的湿式多片离合器)

grade retarder ① (自动变速器内的)自动下坡缓速装置 ② (泛指汽车上使用的各种)缓速装置，缓速器 (见 retarder)

grade-separated interchange 道路立体交叉 (= grade separation)

grade-speed ability (车辆的)坡度-速度性能(以一定车速上坡的能力)

grade-up 上坡，升坡

gradient (美称 grade, 因此凡用 gradient 处均可用 grade) ① 坡(无特别说明时，一般指道路的纵坡, = slop) ② 坡度 (= degree of slope, 英美习惯上用坡高与坡底水平长度之比来表示，如：a gradient of one in nine, 9:1的斜度，但工程上一般用坡度角α，即：路面与水平角的夹角，或用坡度高 h 与底长 s 之比 $\frac{h}{s}$，即：α的百分率表示，一般小坡路坡度可近似认为 $\sin\alpha \approx tg\alpha$)

gradient board 坡度标牌

gradient capability 上坡能力，爬坡能力

gradienter 倾斜计，斜率仪，坡度仪

gradient interfering with view 妨碍视线的坡度

gradient of slope 斜坡的坡度

gradient resistance 上坡阻力，坡度阻力，爬坡阻力

gradometer 坡度测量仪

gradual braking 渐进制动(指在制动控制装置正常操作范围内，驾驶员能够运用控制装置随时增加或减少制动力，制动力与操作力按比例变化的制动作用，亦称 progressive braking)

gradual engagement 逐渐接合，平稳接合

gradual failure 逐渐损坏，渐变失效，可预测的故障(通过事前的测试、检验或监控可以预测到的故障)

graduated 分度的，带刻度的；分等

的，分级的，校正了的，经标定的
graduated circle 刻度盘，分度圈（=graduated ring）
graduated disk 刻度盘
graduated driver licensing system 渐进式驾驶许可制（简称 GDL system，分等级的驾驶许可制，不同等级的安全驾驶条件限制不同）
graduated tint 逐变色度（如：为了遮阳在风窗玻璃的顶边有一条色度逐渐由浅变浓的色带）
graduation ①分度，刻度，（一个刻度或分度的）值域 ②分类，分级 ③校正，标准，标定
graduation between seats 客车座间距（指前排座左边线至后排座后边线之间的距离，包括座椅和乘员活动空间）
graduation line 分度线，刻度线
graduation mark 分度符号，分度线，刻度线
graft copolymer 接枝共聚物（指在一聚合物的主链上连接有多个不同结构的聚合物的支链共聚物）
grain ①格令，英厘（英制的最小质量单位，代号 gr，$1gr = 64.8 \times 10^{-6}$ kg。英制的常衡、金衡、药衡都以 gr 为最小单位，1 常磅 1b = 7000gr = 0.453592kg,1 金衡磅 troy 1b = 1 药衡磅 1b apoth = 5760gr = 0.3732kg）②砂粒，晶粒；颗粒；粒度 ③（木材的）纹理；粗糙的面 ④［动］做成细粒；漆成木纹；使表面粗糙
grain alcohol 酒精，乙醇（=ethanol）
grain boundary 晶（粒边）界（=crystal boundary）
grain carrier 谷物运输车
grain coarsening 见 grain growth
grain composition 颗粒组成，晶粒组成
grained 细粒化的，使成粒状的；使成纹理的
grain extension 谷物运输车厢栏板接长（或加高）部分
grain fineness （晶）粒度；颗粒细度
grain growth （金属的）晶粒长大，晶粒粗化（钢是铁碳合金，由若干不规则的多面小晶粒组成，在高温下其晶粒有长大、变粗的趋势，而使制件的机械强度降低，亦称 grain coarsening）
grain hopper body 运送谷物的漏斗式车厢
grain sludge （发动机曲轴箱内的）粒状淤渣
grain trailer 运粮挂车
gram(me) 克（CGS 单位制的质量单位，代号 g 或 gr，原指 $1cm^3$、4℃水的质量，现规定为：保存在苏黎世的千克原器的质量的千分之一，参见 kilogram，作为质量单位，$1g = 0.001kg = 0.0353ounce$）
gram(me)-calorie 小卡，克卡（=gram calory, small calorie, small calory）
gramme force 克力（力的单位，代号 gf，使 1 克质量产生 1g 加速度的力，工程上常用 kgf，很少用 gf，$1gf = 10^{-3} kgf = 1gwt$，参见 gramme weight）
gramme weight 克重（重力的单位，代号 gwt，即 1 克质量的重力，$1gwt = 981dynes$，参见 gramme force）
gram-molecule 克分子（简称 mol）
gram per hour 每小时克数，克/小时（简称 GPH, gph）
Grand Luxe 见 GL⑥
Grand prix 国际汽车大奖赛（亦称 grands prix race，1906 年法国汽车俱乐部举办了第一次，为一种场地汽车赛，但国际赛车联盟只承认一级方程式赛车锦标赛才是汽车大奖

赛，方程式赛车有三个级别：排量 $V=2L$，功率 $P=124.95kW$ 为三级方程式赛车；$V=3L$，$P=399.125kW$ 为二级方程式赛车；$V=3.5L$，$P=477.75kW$ 为一级方程式赛车，1950年5月13日在英国银石赛车场，举行了第一次一级方程式赛车锦标赛，简称F-1大赛）

grand touring car 华贵轿车（亦称 Gran turismo，普通实用型轿车称为 touring car，以别于 sports car，而 grand touring car 则指那些不考虑经济性，专供要求高速、高加速性能及舒适性的用户生产的华贵型轿车。用这类轿车进行的赛事称为 grand touring race，国际运动法典将其列入附则 J 项 A 部第三组，并要求参赛车必须是连续12个月间最低产量500辆，至少两座的批量生产车，其参赛的发动机允许改造范围与列入同项部第二组的普通实用轿车相同。为了表明其车常"性能"的形象，这类车常简称GT，并标明在车身后面）

Grand Touring-injection 安装汽油喷射式发动机的华贵轿车（简称 GT-i）

grand touring race 见 grand touring car

granularity 粒度（如：金相组织晶粒的粗细度）

granular salt depositor （汽车的）盐粒撒布器（将粒状盐撒布在轻微结冰或积雪的路面上，促使其融化，借以防滑）

graph ①图表，曲线图，图解 ②用图表（曲线）表示，作曲线图

grapher 记录仪器，自动记录仪

graphic(al) 图示的，图解的，用图表示的，曲线图的

graphical procedure for determination of turning radius （汽车）转弯半径图解法

graphic chart 图表

graphic display （汽车仪表的）图像显示（用各种生动的图像显示有关值或部件、系统的状态等）

graphic display unit 图像显示装置

graphic equalizer （车用立体声声响设备的）图形均衡器（可分别调节从超重低音到高音的各种频率段的信号强度的装置，并配有动态图形实时显示各频段的强弱）

graphic instrument 自动记录仪，图示器

graphic model 立体模型，三维模型

graphic representation 图解表示法，图解法

graphics-based instruments 图案式仪表

graphic symbol 图例，图解符号，图示符号

graphite ①石墨（英指碳的自然形态，由于它的润滑性能，多用于制作滑动密封件、电刷固体润滑剂或滑脂的添加剂。美则指各种形态的碳，如：强化塑料的碳素纤维等）②涂上石墨，注入石墨

graphite apex seal （转子发动机的）石墨径向密封片

graphite-based material 石墨基材料（亦称 carbon-based material 碳素基材料）

graphite-brass composition 石墨-黄铜混合料（一种摩擦材料，用来制造制动器摩擦片等）

graphite brush （电动机或发电机的）碳刷，石墨电刷

graphite bushing 石墨衬套

graphite coated 石墨涂盖的，石墨涂覆的

graphited braided asbestos packing 石墨处理的编织石棉填料，石墨处理的编织石棉密封件

graphited oilless bearing 无油石墨润滑轴承（无须润滑油润滑的含石墨

的粉末冶金轴承)
graphite fiber reinforced plastics 碳素纤维强化塑料,石墨纤维强化塑料(简称GrFRP或CFRP,= carbon fiber reinforced plastics,为母体是树脂,与碳纤维的复合材料,高强度、高刚度,高耐蠕变性、耐蚀性、耐磨性,且抗振动衰减性良好)
graphite fibre 碳素纤维,石墨纤维(= carbon fibre,指纤维状石墨)
graphite grease 石墨润滑脂(加有石墨添加剂的润滑脂,用于钢板弹簧片,制动拉索,速度表软轴,汽油泵等处的润滑)
graphite washer 石墨垫圈
graphitic 石墨的,含石墨的
graphitic corrosion 石墨腐蚀(灰铸铁的一种选择性腐蚀"见 selective corrosion",其中的铁等金属元素先期腐蚀并脱落而仅剩下碳元素)
grass (heat) shield 草地隔热板(指装在汽车排气管、催化转化器等高温部件下方的隔热板件,防止汽车驶过草地时引起失火)
grass hopper spring 半椭圆形悬臂钢板弹簧(指仅中部和一端支撑固定而另一端呈悬臂状的半椭圆形钢板弹簧)
grass track race 草地赛车
graticulation 在设计图上画上方格,在方格纸上作图(以便放缩)
grating ①格,栅,栅状物 ②晶格,点格,点阵
grating of gears 齿轮噪声,齿轮(摩擦)发响
gravel bombardment 飞沙撞击(汽车行驶时道路上等飞起的沙砾对各种装置等的打击)
gravel gun 砾石枪(喷射碎石的装置,如:用碎石射击板件试样,以测定其抗破碎能力时用的喷石枪等)

gravimeter 比重计,重力计
gravimetric analysis 化学分离测重法(先用化学分析法将材料的组分分离出来,然后分别称出质量)
gravimetric efficiency (发动机充气的)质量效率(指实际充气量 m 与最大理论充气量 ma 的比率 m/ma%)
gravitational acceleration 重力加速度 $(g, 9.81 \text{m/s}^2)$
gravitational energy 位能,重力能
gravitational field (万有)引力场,重力场
gravitation constant 万有引力常数,万有引力恒量($F = G\dfrac{m_1 m_2}{r^2}$,式中 m_1, m_2 为两物体质量,r 为两者间的距离,G 便是万有引力恒量,其值为 $G = 6.67 \times 10^{-11}$ 米^3/千克·秒^2)
gravity ①重力,地心引力,万有引力 ②比重
gravity braking system (挂车的)重力制动系统(其制动力的能量来自挂车某一构件重心下降的重力作用)
gravity circulation 重力循环,自流循环(指依靠流体本身重力实现的循环)
gravity dump body 利用(货物)自重倾卸的自卸式车厢
gravity dumping 自重卸载,重力卸料
gravity feed (借助重力供给油、水及砂、粉或浆等的)重力供给(方式)(如:利用位置较高的油箱将汽油供给位置较低的燃油管路等)
gravity (feed) lubrication 重力润滑
gravity-feed spray gun 重力供给式喷枪(漆料等借重力由位于枪顶的高位容器流下,以减少压缩空气用量)
gravity flow 重力自流(靠重力自动流动 = flow by gravity)

gravity loading 自流式装载，依靠（物料）自重的装载

gravity lock 自落式闭锁装置，重力式锁定器

gravity petrol tank 重力汽油箱（利用重力作用供油，= gravity gasoline tank）

gravity-system water cooling 重力自流式循环水冷却系统，温差自流式环流水冷却系统（= natural water cooling, thermosiphon water cooling）

gravity tank truck 自流式油罐车，自流式油槽车

gravity vertical 重力垂线，重垂线

gray (pig) iron 灰口铸铁，灰口铁[含碳量大于2.06%的铸造用铁碳合金，因其断口呈暗灰色而得名，在汽车上一般用于制造发动机缸体、缸盖、飞轮、飞轮壳、进、排气管等、离合器压盘、变速器壳及盖、制动鼓及制动总泵、分泵缸体等，亦写作 grey (pig) iron]

GRD （密封环槽的）槽底直径（= groove root diameter）

grease ①润滑脂（指以脂肪酸钙、锂、钠皂为稠化剂，分散于矿物润滑油或合成润滑油中形成的一种具有塑性的油脂状润滑剂。一般加有抗氧、防腐、防锈、抗磨和抗压剂等添加剂，主要用于汽车轮毂、底盘及万向节等部件的润滑）②加润滑脂

grease additive 润滑脂添加剂（指改善润滑脂特性，如：黏温、抗氧化等特性所用的微量添加剂）

grease baffle 挡脂圈，滑脂挡板

grease box ①润滑脂杯 ②（零件之间）盛满润滑脂的空间

grease bucket pump （带储脂筒的）手动滑脂加注泵

grease cup （加装润滑脂的）滑脂杯（一般位于轴等的重要润滑点，有的依靠轴承件产生的摩擦热自然熔化流出，有的则靠挤压螺纹件，手动压出润滑）

grease fitting 滑脂加注嘴

grease gate 润滑脂充填口

grease gun 滑脂枪（亦称 lubricant gun，加注润滑脂的枪式手动泵或电动泵，亦称 grease squirt，或 grease pump）

grease gun nipple 润滑油嘴（装在各润滑点，接受泵入的润滑脂的单向阀嘴，亦称 grease fitting nipple，或简称 grease nipple）

grease monkey [俚]汽车维护工，汽车保养工，汽车维修工（原指加注润滑脂的工人）

grease pit （汽车保修场内的）润滑脂加注地沟

grease proofness 耐油性，油脂密封性

greaser ①加注润滑脂的工具，油枪 ②加油工

grease remover 脱脂剂

grease resistance 耐油脂性

grease retainer 润滑脂护脂圈

grease spots 油渍

grease way 润滑油道

greasy surface 油滑的表面，油腻的表面

great calory 大卡，千卡（= great calorie, large calorie, major calorie, kilo calorie）

greatest lower bound 最低下界，下极限界

green (automotive) vehicle 绿色汽车（一般指低排放、少噪声的低公害汽车，各国对电动汽车、太阳能汽车、氢气汽车、天然气汽车等统称为绿色汽车，又称环保汽车、清洁汽车等）

Green Book 天然橡胶规格说明书（美国橡胶生产者协会出版，国际商业通用）

green car 绿色轿车（指无公害或低

公害车辆)
green-crop trailer 运青饲料的挂车
green engine calibration unit 绿色发动机标定器件(见 E-cell)
green heat-insolating glass (车用)绿色隔热玻璃
greenhouse ①[俚]= glass area ②温室
green house effect 温室效应(指汽车等燃烧含碳能源,排放 CO_2,在空中破坏臭氧层引起温室效应,使大气温度变暖的现象)
green house gas 温室效应气体(主要指 CO_2 和氟利昂制冷剂产生的破坏大气臭氧层、使地球气温升高的气体)
green light ①(交通)绿灯 ②放行,准许通过
green light optimal speed (汽车赶遇各路口)绿灯(的)最佳行驶车速
green oil 高级石油,新鲜油,绿油(绿色的石油馏分)
green phase 绿灯信号相,通过相
green rot 绿蚀,绿锈(在渗碳气氛中,由于高温下形成碳化铬,在晶粒界处发生选择性氧化而造成的一种危害性极大的腐蚀作用)
green stage (树脂涂料或填料刚刚施用即出现的)硬化阶段(其固化过程的初始阶段,即已变硬,但尚未成固态)
Green Star 绿星(一种汽油添加剂的商品名,主要成分为经特别净化处理的煤油"kerosene",可减少 CO,HC 排放和降低油耗)
green straight-through area 直进绿灯箭头(这时,车辆只能直行前进而不能左右转弯)
green test (发动机)试运转,连续试验
Green test 格林试验(测定汽油中胶质的含量)
green traffic light 绿色交通信号,交通绿灯,交通放行灯
green tyre 未硫化的轮胎,生胎
Green Wave Advisory system 绿波支援系统(简称 GWA system,意图让车辆途经的交叉路口均为绿灯的运行支援系统)
Greney bronze 哥瑞内青铜(减摩轴承合金,75.8% Cu,9.2% Sn,15% Pb)
grey hound [美俚]长途公共汽车
GrFRP 石墨纤维强化塑料(见 graphite fiber reinforced plastics)
grid ①格子,栅格,栅架,栅条 ②(道路)网,(输电)网,(管道)网 ③(特指蓄电池的)极板(= grid plate,由铅锑合金栅架和涂在该栅架上的活性物质组成,正极板上的活性物质是二氧化铅 PbO_2,负极板上的活性物质是海绵状铅 pb,正、负极板形成电池的正、负极,置于硫酸水溶液电解液中,借助于氧化-还原反应而产生电流。免保养型蓄电池,亦称无须维护蓄电池多用铅钙合金或低梯合金作栅架,以减少析气量、耗水量和自放电) ④(电子管的)栅极(指电子管中具有网孔的控制电极) ⑤(计算机系统光符识别中的)(坐标)网格(两组相互垂直的平行线构成的一平面网格,用来指定或测量字符图像的位置)
grid-bias battery 栅极偏压电池(简称 G battery)
grid-controlled ignition (system) (坐标)网格控制式点火系统(指根据存储在控制模块只读存储器内的点火提前角随发动机转速和负荷或称进气管真空度而变化的点火特性曲面"ignition map"控制点火的电子点火系统)
grid cover 格栅护罩
grid current 栅(极电)流
grid filling 蓄电池极板的活性物质

（铅蓄电池正极板上的活性物质为二氧化铅 PbO_2，负极板上的为海绵状铅 Pb）

grid potentiometer　栅极电位计

grid shielding　栅极屏蔽

grid voltage　栅极电压

Griess reagent　格里斯吸收试剂，格里斯（脱氨基）试剂［如：测定废气中的 NO_x 含量时使用的吸收试剂，其配方如下：将磺胺酸（$NH_2C_6H_4SO_3H$）5g，注入 945ml 蒸馏水和 5mL 的醋酸溶液中，待磺胺酸溶解后再注入 50ml 的染色溶液。测定时，将试样引入该试剂中根据颜色变化深浅，用比色计即可确定 NO_x 的含量］

grill(e)　①格栅，网栅，格子窗 ②（特指汽车车身位于冷却水散热器正前方的）散热器护栅，散热器护罩（亦称 grille panel，用保护散热器并让冷却空气流通过，流入发动机室，有时简称 radiator grille）

grille guard　栅格保护装置，护栅

grille shutter　（车身前脸的）格栅护盖（以降低风阻）

grill guard　（越野汽车的）前防撞栏栅

grind　磨削，研磨，磨，碾碎

grinding abrasion　磨料磨损（较冲击磨损轻，参见 gouging abrasion）

grinding disc　砂轮，磨盘（= abrasive disk 或 abrasive wheel）

grinding finish　精磨，磨削的表面粗糙度

grinding-in　磨合，磨配，研磨

grip　①紧握，抓紧 ②夹卡，夹具，夹钳 ③螺栓连接中的钢板总厚度（螺栓头到螺母之间的距离）④紧扣；控制；（机器等的）煞住，扣住

grip brake　驻车制动器，手制动器

grip channel　（橡胶密封条等的）固定槽

grip nut　夹紧螺母，防松螺母，固定螺母

grip of the wheel　车轮对地面的抓着力（轮胎制造业对轮胎与路面的附着力的称呼，指由胎面和路面状态和性质决定的附着系数和轮胎对路面的压力的乘积，亦称 grip force。不少人将它等同于车轮与路面间的摩擦力）

gripping clutch　分离不开的离合器（= grabbing clutch）

gripping device　夹具，固定器，抓取器

gripping pattern　（轮胎）防滑花纹

gripping ring　卡环

grip roller freewheel　滚子式单向离合器

grit　①沙粒，沙砾，粗沙 ②（在结冰的路面上）撒沙砾，撒沙子，撒盐粒等 ③研磨，摩擦 ④发轧轧声 ⑤目，粒度

grit blasting　喷砂作业，喷砂清理，喷砂处理（用压缩空气将砂喷于金属铸件、板件或零件，以清除表面或间隙等处的异物或旧漆皮等）

grit number　（［美］砂纸的）目，粒度（见 grade④）

(600) grit paper　(600) 目砂纸

grom(m)et　（亦称 grummet，泛指各种镶嵌在金属件等孔边的橡胶或塑料制的）密封、绝缘或隔垫环（如：轮胎气门嘴的轮辋密封垫环），或织物、橡胶、塑料制品孔边的金属保护环（如：汽车用篷布拉索孔环等）

groove　①沟，槽（如活塞环槽，润滑油槽，螺纹槽）②切槽，开槽，挖沟

groove-and-fongue　槽-榫（连接）的

groove angle　槽角，凹槽角，齿槽角，坡口角（焊接）

groove bottom diameter　（活塞）环槽底直径（= groove root diameter）

groove coupling　（凸块式万向节的）

凹槽凸块（带有相互垂直的两个凹槽的半球形中间连接元件，亦称 leading floating yoke 后浮动叉块，见 Tracta universal joint）

grooved 开槽的，有槽的，带槽的

grooved center ball （球叉式万向节的）定心钢球（为该万向节定心并承受轴向推力、具有一个销孔的钢球，其销孔内的销使方向节的各元件保持为一个总成，见 Weiss universal joint）

grooved compression ring （活塞的）开槽式压缩环，开槽式气环（指开有环槽的气环，这种气环不仅起一般压缩环的作用，而且由于开槽，还可起一定的刮油环的作用）

groove depth 槽深；活塞环槽深

groove insert 镶式活塞环槽，活塞环槽镶套

groove of thread 螺纹谷，螺纹槽

groove pin hole （球叉式万向节球叉的）曲面槽销孔（其中心定位钢球的销的销孔，见 Weiss universal joint）

groove race （球叉式万向节主动叉和从动叉上的传动钢球的）曲面凹槽（装合后四个传动钢球被夹在主、从动叉的该曲面凹槽之间，见 Weiss universal joint）

groover root diameter （活塞环槽等的）槽底直径，槽根直径（简称 GRD）

groove wear （活塞）环槽磨损

groove weld 坡口焊缝；坡口焊

groove width 槽宽；活塞环槽宽

grooving ①切槽，开槽，刻槽；企口连接，凹凸榫接；电化学腐蚀沟槽 ②开口的，开槽的

grooving of the valve seat 在气门座上磨出的凹槽

gross ①总的，全部；整个的 ②粗的，大的 ③粗劣的 ④粗略地，大体上地 ⑤总数，总额，总计 ⑥罗（单位，=12打=144个，简称gr）

gross allowable load 允许总负载，容许总载荷（简称 GAL）

gross area 总面积

gross axle weight 见 gross axle weight rating

gross axle weight rating ［美］标定最大轴载重量（简称 GAWR，指所规定的轴载总重量，为标定最大轴载质量"gross axle mass rating" GAMR 的旧称，但在美国仍沿用至今）

gross brake horsepower （发动机）总制动功率，总有效功率（指示功率扣除基本发动机内部机械消耗功率）

gross calorific value 总发热量，总含热值，总卡值；高热值（参见 high heating value）

gross combination weight （最大装载质量下的）汽车列车总重，牵引车带挂车总重（为汽车引车最大总质量 gross combination mass 的旧称，但英美仍沿用至今，= gross train weight，简称 GCW，亦称 gross combined vehicle weight）

gross combination weight rating 汽车列车额定总重（简称 gcwr，额定分为厂定 manufacture's，和官定 authorized 两种）

gross contact area （轮胎的）总接地面积（包括胎面花纹沟槽部分的投影面积，亦称 contact patch, tire footprint gross area）

gross domestic product 国民生产总值，国内生产总值（简称 GDP）

gross dry weight 干毛重，干总重，（干总质量的旧称，对车辆而言，"干"指不包括燃、润料，工作油液和冷却液）

gross empty weight 空车总重（汽车空车总质量的旧称，但英美仍沿用至今）

gross engine output　见 gross power

gross head　总水头，总压头，总扬程（水头指流体，主要是液体单位体积的能量与该流体单位体积的质量比，用长度，如："英尺"、"米"来表示，为泵等所泵出的液体的能量的简便表示尺度）

gross heating value　总热值，高热值（= hight heating value）

gross horsepower　见 gross power

gross laden weight　总装载重量（总装载质量的旧称）

gross life　总使用期限，总寿命（自投入使用到最终报废前的使用寿命）

gross load　总载荷量，总装载量

gross load spring　（离心调节器）重块主弹簧

gross output value　总产值

gross payload　总有效载荷

gross power　总功率（指基础发动机只带有维持运转所必需的附件，如：水泵、发电机等所输出的校正有效功率，见 corrected brake power, net power, basic engine power, gross engine power, gross horsepower, gross engine output）

gross ton　①长吨，英吨（见 long ton）②总吨数（= tonnage）

gross torque　（发动机）最大转矩（指全负荷速度特性曲线上的最大转矩值，= maximum torque）

gross tractive effort　（地面对牵引车的）总推力（未扣除牵引车本身滚动阻力的总牵引力，切线牵引力）

gross tractive force　总牵引力（发动机在一定转速下，驱动轮可产生的最大牵引力）

gross trailer weight　挂车总重（简称GTW）

gross train mass　（汽车）列车总质量

gross train weight　汽车列车总重（指牵引车带全挂车及装载的总重，简称 GTW 或 gtw，见 gross combination weight）

gross vehicle weight　车辆总重，车辆总重量（简称 GVW，指在任意规定条件下车辆的总质量，如：厂定车辆总重量，含最大装载重量或不含最大装载质量的车辆总重量等。为车辆总重量 gross vehicle mass, GVM 的旧称，但英美仍沿用至今，并简称 gross weight）

gross vehicle weight rating　车辆的总重额定值，车辆额定总重（简称 gvwr）

gross weight　①全重，总重（简称 GW, = full weight, 为 gross mass, GM 总重量的旧称，但英美仍沿用至今）②gross vehicle weight 的简称

gross weight distribution　（车辆）总重量的分配（总质量分配的旧称）

gross weight-to-payload　车辆总重量与装载质量之比（简称 G/L）

ground　①地面，土地；场地 ②基础；理由 ③[美]搭铁，接地（代号 G 或 gr，= 英 earth，指电流经车架或发动机体形成回流）④建立，树立；打基础；上底色 ⑤碾碎了的，磨成粉的；研磨光的

ground based vehicle　陆地用车，陆用车辆

ground cable　搭铁线，接地线

ground circle　（齿轮的）基圆

ground clearance　（汽车的）最小离地间隙（指车辆底部低点与地面之间的距离，反映汽车无碰撞地通过地面凸形障碍的能力。严格定义为汽车中间区域内最低点到车辆支撑平面的距离，中间区域定义为平行于车辆纵向对称平面且与其等距离的两平面之间所包含的部分，两平面之间的距离为同一车轴上两端车轮内缘最小距离的80%）

ground clearance between axles　（多轴汽车的）轴间离地间隙

ground clearance control ①离地间隙控制（指电子控制悬架系统的汽车车身离地间隙自动控制功能或装置）②（有时特指装在油气悬架式轿车驻车制动器附近的）离地间隙控制杆（一手控小杆，用于在通过不平路段或更换车轮时，使车身升高，加大其离地间隙）

ground clearance diameter （车辆可通过的道路）最小横向拱度直径（小于该直径时车辆将被顶起而无法行驶）

ground clearance protecting border （车身侧壁的）离地间隙护边（板）

ground clearance sensor （汽车自动调平式悬架系统中使用的）离地间隙传感器

ground coat 底涂层

ground coat paint 底漆，(= prime paint)

ground communications 地面交通，陆路交通

ground contact （车轮）与土壤的接触，接地

ground contact area 接地面积（见 contact path）

ground contact force （轮胎）接地压力

ground contact point （汽车等的）车轮接地点

ground count 路上行车动态计数，路上观测统计（交通起-止点调查中，在道路各观测点上对全部车辆进行的实地计数）

ground crawling vehicle in the ocean 海（洋）底（行驶）车辆

ground drive system （水陆两用车辆）地面驱动系统

grounded ①接地的，搭铁的 (= earthed) ②安装，紧固在机壳上的（如：grounded ring gear 指固定在机壳内的内齿齿圈，roller bearing with outer race grounded 指外座圈固定在机座内的滚子轴承）

ground effect 地面影响，路面影响，地面效应，路面效应（如：地面对车辆的空气动力效应，特指气垫车十分接近地面时，地面对车的空气动力效应）

ground-effect lift force 地面效应升力（如：地面对气垫车的反作用浮升力）

ground effect machine 地面效应机械（气垫式运载机械的总称，指各种借助于地面和机械间封入的高压空气浮行的运载工具，简称 GEM, 亦称 ground effect vehicle。一般在陆地及水陆两地使用者称为气垫车 air car, hover car, hover-craft 或 air cushion vehicle）

ground effect vehicle 地面效应车辆，地面效应运载装置（简称 CEV, 见 ground effect machine）

ground electrode 搭铁电极，接地电极 (= earth electrode)

ground-grip tyre 抓地轮胎，大花纹轮胎，越野轮胎，高通过性轮胎

grounding ①［电］接地，搭铁 ②（由于离地间隙不足而造成的）车底碰触路面

ground lamp 搭铁指示灯，接地指示灯（简称 GL）

ground level 地平面；地平高度，地面标高

ground-level front-loading semi-trailer 前端落地式装载半挂车

ground-level loading trailer 底板可落地的平板挂车（见 trailer with detachable rear axle）

ground line ①地平线（简称 GL）②轴线；基线

ground line angles 车辆地面夹角（车辆的接近角，离去角和纵向通过角的总称，表示车辆通过凹凸不平的路面的通过性能）

ground line gradient 地面坡度，自

然坡度

ground loading capacity 地面承压能力

ground loop 接地环线，接地回路，接地电路

ground noise 基底噪声，本底器声，背景噪声

ground plane 车辆所停驻的水平（参考）地面

ground-plane forces 地面平面力系，地面力系

ground pressure （履带，车轮等的）对地压力，接地压力

ground speed ①（车辆的）行驶速度，车速 ②水陆两用车或气垫车的陆地行驶车速

ground speed relative to vehicle 相对于地面的车速

ground state 基态

ground-surface 路面的；地面

ground transportation 陆上运输

ground transport vehicle 地面运输车辆（简称 GTV，= land transport vehicle）

ground turbine 陆地车辆用燃气轮机，车用燃气轮机

ground wheel （半挂车）支地轮（参见 supporting wheels）

group ①组，类，群，族，系，组合，分组 ②分组，分类，组合，集合

group charging （蓄电池）成组充电

group drive 成组传动，集中传动（由一台发动机带动若干工作机构，或若干机械装置）

Groupe de Travail de la Sécurité de la Circulation （国际）交通安全工作组会议（简称 GTSC）

grouping ①部件装配图 ②分组，分类，成群，组合，配合；归并（统计）

group method 组合加工法

group of cables clamping ring 导线束卡环（将多根散导线卡箍成束）

group rapid transit 高速成批客运，快速公共交通（一般指新型的快速客运系统，如：cabintaxi 的 mass transit style, 简称 GRT）

group selective assembly 分组选法（将组成装配尺寸链中的零件公差按装配精度要求的允差放大若干倍，使之能按经济加工精度制造零件，加工后的零件经密度测量，并将其分成若干组，按对应的组进行装配）

group test 多车对比试验，多车试验

group valve 组合阀

growl （类似于横过金属格板所产生的）车轮轮胎胎面的低频噪声

growler ①液体的量测容器 ②（电机）转子试验装置 ③线圈短路测试仪（为具有两个可调极板的电磁装置，用于寻找线圈短路，进行磁化及退磁，armature tester 的俗称）

grown inner tube 内胎胀大（指内胎平叠宽度局部大于标准尺寸，以致充气后胎身局部胀大、鼓肚现象）

grown tyre 胀大（的）轮胎（指用过一段时间后，尺寸略有增大的轮胎）

GRP ①玻璃纤维增强塑料（glass reinforced plastics）②群，组（group）

grp 群，组，族，类（group 的简称）

GRP body 玻璃纤维强化聚酯车身（glass reinforced polyester body 的简称）

GRT 成批快速公共交通（参见 group rapid transit）

grub screw 无头螺钉，全螺纹螺杆

gruelling wear 破坏性磨损，极度严重的磨损

grummet 见 grommet

Gruzdev's coefficient of mass inertia （车辆）格氏转动惯量换算系数

gr wt 总重（gross weight）

Gs 高斯（磁通量密度单位，见 gauss）

G senser （车辆）加速度传感器

g sensor emergency locking retractor （汽车乘员安全带的）车辆减速度感知式紧急锁紧型收紧装置

G signal 凸轮轴转角信息（= camshaft angle signal）

GSR 皮肤电气反应（记录驾驶员驾驶期间生理过程的生理学指标之一，galvanic skin response）

GST （奔驰的）大型运动旅行车（grand sports tourer 的简称）

GST 消费税（购买商品及服务的税金，故称商品及服务税，Goods & Services Tax 的简称）

G-string 见 start up groan

GT ①燃气轮机（见 gas-turbine）②见 Grand Touring

GT-1 （宝马车系的一种）故障诊断仪（商品名）

GTBA 汽油级叔丁醇（gasoline grade tertiary butyl alcohol）

GT car 见 grand touring car

G-t characteristics （汽车的）加速度-时间特性（汽车行驶加速度 G 响应与踩踏住加速踏板的时间 t 之间的关系特性）

GTDi 汽油直喷涡轮增压（发动机）（gasoline turbo-direct injection 的简称）

GT engine 燃气轮机（gas turbine engine 的简称）

GTi 见 Grand Touring injection

GTL fuel 可燃气体合成液态燃料（gas-to-liquid fuel 的简称，指由天然气、煤气等可燃气体采用 Fischer-Tropsch 法合成的液体燃料，与液化气不同，在大气压力和常温下仍为液态，作为压燃机燃料其十六烷值高，硫和芳香族化合物含量低，但润滑性差）

GTL technology 气-液转化技术（gas-to-liquid technology 的简称）

GT race 华贵汽车赛（见 Grand Touring）

7G-Tronic Plus 增强型 7 挡电子控制自动变速器（Benz 公司原 7 挡电子控制自动变速器"7G-Tronic"的改进型，其中 Plus 为改进、优化、增强的意思）

GTSC （国际）交通安全工作组会议（Groupe de Travail de la Sécurité de la Circulation 的简称）

GTV 地面运输车辆（ground transport vehicle 的简称）

GTW ①见 gross trailer weight ②见 gross train weight

guarantee 保证，担保，保证性鉴定；承认，许诺

guarantee maintenance service （汽车的售后）保修服务

guarantee period 保证使用期，保用期（= guarantee time, guarantee life）

guaranty test 保用性（鉴定）试验，保证性鉴定试验（保证产品在保用期内符合规定技术条件的试验，= guarantee test）

guard ①防护；保护 ②挡板，护板，护罩，防护装置，保护器 ③给…装防护装置

guard bearing （功率输出轴的）外壳轴承

guard board （载货汽车车箱的）边板，拦板，护板

guarded (level) railway crossing 带栅栏的公路铁路交叉口

guard fence 护栏，护栅，安全栏栅（= safety fence）

guard frame （货车车箱的）货架（指货箱前拦板上部支撑货物的构件）

guard frame 护框（护栏，护架）

guard ring 保护环，护圈；挡油环，隔离环

guard tube 保护管，管状外罩（= protective tube）

guard wire ①金属丝防护网 ②屏蔽

金属丝网

gudgeon 轴,枢轴,耳轴,销轴,轴头

gudgeon pin ①活塞销(美称 piston pin, wrist pin,指活塞与连杆小头之间的连接销)②耳轴、枢轴、枢销(= trunnion)

gudgeon pin boss 活塞销孔座,活塞销孔凸台(= piston-pin boss,指活塞顶与活塞裙之间开有活塞销孔的内凸台部分)

gudgeon pin bush(ing) 活塞销衬套(= piston pin bush)

gudgeon pin circlip 活塞销锁环(= piston pin circlip,防止活塞销在活塞销孔内横向窜动的卡环,装在活塞销孔两端,见 floating piston pin)

gudgeon pin end (安装活塞销的)连杆小头

gudgeon pin lock screw 活塞销锁止螺钉

guest-host effect 宾主效应

Guibo coupling 盖波式联轴节(一种挠性环状联轴节)

guidance ①引导,制导,导航 ②控制,操纵,驾驶 ③导槽,导轨,导板

guidance cable (全自动运输车辆)导行电缆(埋设在路面下,控制车辆自动运行的缆线)

guide ①指引,导航,导向 ②控制,操纵,管理 ③导杆,导槽,导板,导向器,导向装置,路标 ④指南,手册,指导书

guide bearing 导向轴承(如:变速器第一轴,即变速器输入轴轴端的轴承,亦称 pilot bearing)

guide bolt 导向螺栓

guide bush(ing) ①导向衬套(= pilot bushing)②(气门)导管

guide clearance 导程间隙;导向部分的间隙

guide coat 指示涂层(车身上完第一层底漆在上第二层底漆之前或上完漆料后,喷在有缺陷处的、与周围漆层颜色不同的薄漆层,用来指示"该处有缺陷")

guided bend (材料力学性能试验中的)导向弯曲(用压杆对试样施力,使试样在规定的模型中得到一定形状的弯曲)

guide groove (车身板件中的)导槽(起导向或固定作用的带槽件)

guide hole 导向孔

guide lamp ①反光灯 ②聚光灯(= spot light)

guide mounting bracket (钢索)导架(汽车钢索式保险杠,固定在车架左右两端的导架,汽车碰撞时钢索在该导架上滑动)

guide seat (客车上的)导游(员)座椅

guide vane ①导流片 ②(变矩器)导轮叶片(见 guide wheel①)

guideway ①导行路,导向路,轨道道路,轨道 ②(全自动运输的)导轨道路 ③导沟,导轨,导向槽,导板

guideway-bus 导轨公共汽车,高架轨道客车

guide wheel ①(液力变矩器)导轮(= reactor,亦称导向轮,反应器,反作用叶轮,用来改变变矩器壳体内腔工作液体的流动方向,给涡轮一个反作用力矩,而增大其输出转矩)②(链条传动或皮带传动的)导轮,惰轮,张紧轮(= guide、idle 或 tensioner sprocket 或 pulley)③(履带的)导轮(履带最前方的大链轮)④(涡轮机的)导向叶轮

guiding 导向,定向,制导,导航;控制,操纵

guiding device 导向装置

guiding nut 导向螺母

guiding of traffic 交通指挥

Gulf coastal oil 海湾产石油,海湾原

油（= Gulf coastal crude）

Gulf Co-operation council　海湾（产油）国家合作委员会（简称 GCC 包括六个石油生产国：Saudi, Arabia, Kuwait, Oman, Qatar, Bahrein）

gulide bar　导杆（如：变速器换挡拨叉的滑动轴杆）

gullet　①齿槽 ②锯齿间隙 ③水槽，水道

gull wing door　鸥翼式车门（左、右车门与车顶铰接的，如：鸥翼向上翻开的上翻式车门）

gull wing opening type box van with tail/side lift　鸥翼开启式后/侧栏板起重运输车（用自身动力驱动液压装置，使货箱侧栏板或尾栏板开启、关闭和升降以起重货物的厢式货车）

gully　排水沟，檐槽

gully emptier　污水罐车，污水车

gulp capacity　吸气容量

gulp valve　（发动机的）补气阀（为进气管真空控制的膜片阀。当发动机处于减速或强制怠速工况时，在进气管真空作用下该阀开启，新鲜空气便被吸入进气管，使进气管真空度相应降低，以防此时混合气过浓，造成进、排气管回火和油耗过高。为了防止冷机起动时该阀开启，在该阀的真空控制通路中还设有一温控阀，当发动机温度低于规定值时，该温控阀可切断其真空通路，补气阀不再开启，而避免冷机起动时混合气过稀）

gum　①树胶，树脂，胶质物 ②［美］橡胶 ③（在燃油系或有关零件上由于燃油氧化而形成的）胶状沉积物 ④上胶，胶合，胶接

gum content　（燃油）含胶量

gum deposit　胶状沉淀物（= gum residue, 如：油箱内由于长期存油，在底板形成的稠黏状沉淀物）

gum elastic　天然橡胶（= caoutchouc）

gum-formation test　结胶试验（汽油中胶质状沉淀物生成试验，= gumming test）

gum inhibitor　（汽油）结胶抑制剂

gumlike material　（裂化汽油在储运过程中生成的）类胶物质

gummed (-up)　结胶的

gumming　结胶，涂胶，胶接，生成胶质状沉淀，（汽油中）胶质生成

gumming test　见 gum-formation test

gum-producing substance　致胶物质（促使汽油产生胶质的物质）

gum residue　见 gum deposit

gun　①（工具中形状如手枪的）喷枪，加油枪，铆钉枪；喷射器；喷雾器；润滑油泵，润滑脂加注枪等 ②猛踩加速踏板，猛加油

gun adapter　滑脂枪注油嘴

gunboat body　鱼雷型车身（= torpedo body）

gun-filled　用滑脂枪加注的

gunmetal　炮铜，锡锌铜合金，锡锌青铜（铜 90%，锡 10%，或铜 88%，锡 10%，锌 2%，或铜 88%，锡 8%，锌 4%，有时加微量的铅、镍）

Gurney flap　廓尔尼板（装于赛车后部垂直翼板尾边的空气动力导流板，在尾边产生低压，以发明人美国赛车手 Dan Gurney 命名）

gusset　角板，三角加强板，角撑板，加强板（指两构件连接处的平板型加强件，通常焊接或铆接于接合处）

gust velocity　阵风速度

gut　①油管内（或油罐内）加热用的水蒸气小管 ②剥除轿车的内饰；卸除消声器内的阻流板

gutter　①槽（指起导流、导向或固定作用的带槽或槽形的零件，如窗框的玻璃槽板等；零部件上的槽形部分，如轮辋上用以安装锁圈或弹性挡圈的定位槽。gutter tip 锁圈槽

顶；gutter groove 锁圈槽沟）②开沟，开槽

gutter channel （沿车身顶盖边及门前部的）流水槽，檐沿，檐边，雨檐，饰条（见 cornice）

guy ①拉线，牵线；拉条（固定物品的绳或杆）②用拉线等物稳定，加固

guzzling gas car 油老虎（油耗量大的轿车）

GV 见 governor valve

G valve 减速度阀（最简单的减速度控制阀是惯性式钢球控制阀。当汽车减速度达到某域值时，在惯性作用下，钢球离开阀座接通或断开电路、油路等，亦称 inertia valve 惯性阀）

G-Vectoring control 加速度矢量控制（指根据汽车进入弯道后产生的横向加速度率控制车辆减速，以防止汽车转向不足而驶出车道，见 Preview G-Vectoring control "加速度矢量预控制"）

GVTW 见 gross vehicle test weight

GVW 见 gross vehicle weight

GVWR 见 gross vehicle weight rating

GW ①千兆瓦（gigawatt）②总重量（gross weight）

GWA 绿波支援系统（见 Green Wave Advisory system）

gwt 克重（重力的单位 gramme weight）

gymkhana 一种美国汽车竞赛（在广场上用轮胎或其他标志围成竞赛路线，以驱车驶完该路线的时间长短决胜负）

gypsum 石膏

gyration （gyratory motion 的简称）①回转运动，回旋运动（指沿环形或螺旋形轨迹运动）②旋转（绕固定轴转动）

gyratory ①回转的 ②旋转的

gyratory intersection （道路）环形交叉

gyratory motion 见 gyration

gyratory system （道路交叉口）环形交通单向通行方式

gyro ①陀螺仪，回转仪（= gyroscope）②旋转，回转（= gyration）

gyro bus 飞轮储能客车（利用大质量飞轮的转动惯量存储发动机的剩余动力或汽车减速能量，待在行驶阻力高或加速工况中使用）

gyro-rotor 高速旋转转子；高速旋转圆盘

gyroscope ①回转仪，陀螺仪 ②（高速旋转的、应用陀螺效应起稳定作用或起储能作用的）大质量飞轮或圆盘系统

gyroscope wobbing （陀螺）旋进摆动（如：转向轮的摆振，见 gyroscopic action）

gyroscopic action 旋进（指绕自身轴线高速旋转的物体，在外力作用下，其自身轴线将绕另一轴线做回转运动的现象。绕自身轴线做高速回转的物体称回转仪 gyroscope。陀螺是最简单和最典型的回转仪，故上述现象又称陀螺旋进。汽车高速旋转的前轮便是一个"回转仪"。当车轮行经凹凸不平的路面时，在颠簸外力作用下，将产生陀螺旋进，结果是前轮摆振）

gyroscopically-controlled （用）回转仪控制的

gyroscopic compass 方向陀螺仪，回转罗盘（利用旋进效应制成的罗盘、指南针等）

gyroscopic effect ①回转仪效应，陀螺效应（指高速旋转的物体保持其自身旋转轴线空间指向固定，或尽可能不变的倾向，转速越高，该倾向越强，利用这一效应可制成指示固定方向的回转罗盘，方向陀螺仪或用大质量高速旋转圆盘制成的起稳定作用的陀螺仪、回转仪）②（陀螺）旋进效应（指陀螺旋进

所造成的影响，如汽车前轮的摆振 wobbling 等）
gyroscopic moment　回转力矩
gyroscopic movement　回转运动
gyroscopic torque　陀螺转矩（使旋转物体绕轴线产生运动的转矩，简称 gyro torque，参见 gyroscopic action）
gyroscopic wheel wobble　（汽车通过凹凸不平道路时）陀螺旋进引起的车轮摇摆（见 gyroscopic action, gyroscopic effect②）
gyro sensor　（测定汽车行驶方向的）陀螺传感器
gyro torque　见 gyroscopic torque

habitability 可乘坐性（客车和轿车的主观评价指标之一）

habitable compartment （客车的）座舱，乘客间（= passenger compartment）

HAC 坡道起动辅助控制系统（hill start assist control 的简称，防止车辆在上坡道上起动后溜）

hackie ［俚］出租汽车驾驶员

hackney 出租汽车

hackstand ［美］出租汽车停车场

HACV 热空气调节阀，热空气控制阀（见 hot air control valve）

Hadfield steel 奥氏体锰钢，高锰钢

HAF 一种炭黑的商品名（High Abrasion Furnace 的简称，平均直径 $24\mu m$，表面积 $77m^2/g$）

Hagen-Poiseulle's low 哈根-泊萧定律［直圆管内层流状态的流体的压力降与其黏度，管长，平均流速（即流量）成正比］

hahnium 𰿉（Ha，第 105 种元素，1970 年发现）

HAI 自动调温式空气滤清系统（见 hot air intake）

hail ①召唤（雇用出租汽车）②发出高声信号 ③冰雹

hair crack 发裂（指肉眼看不见的细微裂纹）

hair cross （目镜中的）十字线，叉线，瞄准线（= cross feed hairs，亦称 hair line）

hair felt 毛毡，油毛毡

hair line ①见 hair cross ②发线，极细的线，游丝 ③细缝，发状裂缝（= hair line crack，指由于材料中的应变或极大的温差而形成的细微裂纹，注意 crazing 指网络状细裂纹，而 hair line crack 一般指单条出现的细裂纹）

hair pin ①道路急转弯（原意为发夹，指如同发夹形的急剧转变，亦称 hairpin curve，hairpin turn）②急转弯的

hairpin road block 道路急转弯处的护石

hairpin spring 发夹形弹簧

hairpin valve 发夹状阀（如：自动变速器、自动控制系中的油路转换阀）

hair sealing fabric 坐垫衬里毛鬃织物

hairspring ①游丝，细弹簧 ②丝极 ③灯丝

hair-trigger ①微力触发器，发丝触发器 ②一触即发的

half-adder 半加器（简称 HA，= two input adder，具有两个输入端：加数 A，被加数 B；两个输出端：无进位 S，进位 C。A、B 为 0 时，S、C 均为 0；A、B 均为 1 时，S 为 0，C 为 1；A、B 中有一项为 1 时，S

为0，C为1）
half-and-half 等量，一半一半，两种成分各半，（两者）各半（的东西），一比一
half automatic ignition 半自动提前点火
half-axle 半轴（见 half shaft）
half axle tube ①半轴（套）管 ②（管状）半轴
half bearing （滑动轴承）轴瓦（= two part bearing）
half-blank ①半成品 ②半成品的
half-breadth 半宽（宽度的一半）
half cab （只能为一名驾驶员提供乘坐空间，偏于汽车中心线一侧或发动机侧面的）侧置单位驾驶室
half-cab truck 侧置单座驾驶室货车（= cab-beside-engine truck）
half-car vehicle model 半车模型（指分析和计算整车动力学性能用的前、后各一个车轮的简化模型）
half-cat ［俚］半履带机械
half charged battery 半充电（量）蓄电池
half clip 对开夹
half-cloverleaf 半苜蓿叶式（交叉口）（四路互通式立体交叉口中只保持两个象限的匝道）
half-deck coach 一层半客车（亦称 one-and-a-half decker coach，一层车厢两层座椅）
half dual space 半并装双轮中心距（双轮中心距的一半，见 dual space）
half-elliptic spring 半椭圆形钢板弹簧（见 semi-elliptic spring）
half front axle 前半轴（前桥驱动左、右两半轴的通称）
half gantry crane 单脚高架起重机
half-hard steel 中等硬度钢
half height open top container 半高式顶开集装箱（高度为通常集装箱高度的一半）

half keystone piston ring 单面梯形（活塞）气环（半楔形环 ①指环靠汽缸的一面有斜度，靠活塞环槽的一面无斜度 ②指环面的上半部有斜度，下半部无斜度）
half-killed steel 半镇静钢（见 killed steel）
half-life ①半寿命期，半使用期 ②半衰变周期，半衰期（指放射性元素的原子核有半数发生衰变所需的时间，亦称 half period，见 decay）
half mirror 半透镜，半透明镜，半反射镜，半透明膜
half-moon key 半月键
half-nut 对开螺母
half-octave analyzer 半倍（频）带分析器（见 octave bond analyzed）
half octave band filter set 半倍频带滤波器（见 octave hand filter）
half-period 半周期（= half life②）
half-power bandwith 半功率点带宽（用来表征频率特性曲线上凸峰所跨越的频率范围）
half rear axle 后半轴（后桥驱动左、右后半轴之通称）
half-selected element （汽车用液晶显示的）半选择点（指在多路驱动中，扫描电极和信号电极之一施加驱动信号的像素）
half-servo brake 单向自动增力蹄式制动器（不对称式）
half shaft （驱动桥）半轴（将差速器输出的转矩传给车轮的传动轴。因左、右各有一根，如同一根整轴被差速器从中截开成左、右各半，故名半轴，= differential axle，half axle）
half shaft spline shaft （前轮驱动-转向桥的）半轴花键轴（该轴一端为万向节，与半轴连接；另一端为花键端，驱动车轮，亦称 half axle spline shaft）
half-skeleton-type body 半骨架式车

身（承重载的部位采用骨架，而受轻载的部位则以蒙皮的加强筋来取代骨架）

half-speed ①半速（驱动件或被动件的转速为被动件或驱动件的一半，half-time）②半挡

half-speed shaft 半速轴（如四冲程发动机中转速为曲轴一半的凸轮轴）

half step type active shift transmission （混合动力系统电动机输出动力的）半挡型主动换挡式变速器（有一根装有各挡位全挡齿轮和一根装有各挡位半挡齿轮的两根输入轴，兼有转矩支援、再生制动和怠速超时停机等功能）

half-system failure 半系统故障（指双回路制动系统的一条回路发生故障）

half-time gear 半速齿轮（使速度减半的齿轮传动，如：四冲程发动机的凸轮轴齿轮）

half track ①半履带式的（指后轮为履带式，提供驱动力，前轮为轮式，控制车辆行驶方向和转向，= semitracked）②半履带式的车辆（= semitracked vehicle）

half turn 半周、半圈、半匝

half-wave rectifier 半波整流器

halfway ①一半路程；半程；半转；半圈；一半长度；一半距离、中途 ②中途的；中间的，不彻底的；不充分的

half wing 半翼板（翼板的可卸部分）

Hall Cl 霍尔集成电路，霍尔集成块 [霍尔元件（见 Hall generator 或 Hall element）产生的电压脉冲信号要放大，反向并转换成数字信号，这些电路组成的一个集成电路，再加上霍尔发生器，总称霍尔集成电路，有时霍尔集成电路不含霍尔发生器，仅指上述信号处理电路的集成块]

Hall effect 霍尔效应（亦称电磁效应 galvanomagnetic effect，当载流金属片置于一与其表面垂直的磁场中时，该金属片的两侧边将产生电势差 U_H，亦称霍尔电压"Hall voltage"，$U_H = R_H/D \cdot IB$，式中：R_H—霍尔系数，由金属片材料决定的常数；I—通过金属片的电流；B—磁场强度；D—金属片厚度）

Hall effect ignition system 霍尔效应点火系（指应用霍尔效应传感器向动力控制模块发送相对于活塞上止点位置的曲转转角信号和发动机转速信号，作为确定点火正时基准的电子点火系统）

Hall effect sensor 霍尔效应传感器（= Hall effect switch, Hall sensor, Hall transduser, 亦偶见称 Hall element, Hall generator, 曲轴位置和转速传感器的一种，一般装在分电器内，由霍尔半导体薄片，即霍尔元件，永久磁铁和一个随分电器轴同步旋转、带有与汽缸数相同的叶片的转子组成。每次一个叶片转过磁铁与薄片之间的狭小间隙都会使作用于该薄片的磁场强度发生急剧变化，于是，由于霍尔效应，薄片便发出一个供电子控制模块确定活塞位置和曲轴转速的电压脉冲信号）

Hall (effect) switch ①霍尔效应开关（亦称 Hall vane switch，指接通和断开霍尔效应的"开关"元件，如：霍尔效应传感器中的转子叶片）② = Hall effect sensor

Hall element ①霍尔元件（指霍尔效应传感器中的半导体材料薄片，亦称 Hall generator，见 Hall effect sensor；指该薄片与信号放大，反向及模变换等电路组成的集成块，见 Hall Cl）②（偶见指）霍尔效应传感器

Hall generator ①霍尔元件（一种半导体材料薄片，亦为 GaAs，= Hall

element，其输出电压与通过它的电流及与其垂直的磁场强度的乘积成正比，我国有人直译为"霍尔发生器"）②（偶见指）Hall sensor

Hall transducer 见 Hall effect sensor
Hall vane switch 见 vane switch
Hall voltage 见 Hall effect
halogen 卤族元素（简称卤素，位于周期表的 VIIA 族，包括氟 F、氯 Cl、溴 Br、碘 I、砹 At 五种元素）
halogen headlamp 卤素前照灯（指充有卤族元素，氯、溴、碘等的前照灯，可在不增加耗电量的条件下，增加灯的亮度，= halogen regenerative-cycle headlamp, halogen-cycle headlamp, 参见 halogen regenerative cycle）
halogen regenerative cycle 卤素再生循环（卤素前照灯内，钨丝的钨蒸气微粒与卤素在灯泡壁附近形成的化合物，在灯丝热区又分裂为钨原子和卤素原子，钨原子重新沉淀在灯丝上，卤素原子则又扩散到泡壁附近与钨微粒反应，这一循环称为卤素再生循环，因而加充有卤素的灯泡，亦称为 halogen regenerative-cycle lamp）
halo ring （环绕前照灯的 LED）光环，光轮
halt ①（暂停）小站，招呼站 ②站住，暂停 ③使停止，阻挡，拦截，阻拦
Haltenberger linkage ahead of axle 带中置转向摇臂的前置梯形转向杆系
halting 断续工作的（发动机），断续着火的（发动机）
halting point 停车站
halt sign 停车标志，停车信号
Hamlin switch 汉姆林开关（一种悬吊质量-摆锤式加速度传感开关，用于防止安全气囊、安全带等装置在低于规定加速度阈域内误动作的安全开关，取代早先使用的水银式开关，亦称 pendulum switch pendulum system）
hammer ①锤 ②锤击，敲打，锻造
hammer forging 自由锻，非模锻件
hammer form （车身零板件敲击成形作业中使用的）成型木砧（用于敲出所要求的形状）
hammer shock test 锤击振动试验（借助电子计算机中快速傅里叶变换的功能，利用脉冲试验原理和模态理论迅速测得结构动力特性、模态参数的一种试验）
hammer welding 锻焊（指不用焊条，仅借助于锻打，将工件已加热至一定温度的部位"焊"在一起并作光整加工的工艺，一般用气焊焊炬或锻工炉加热工件焊接部位）
Ha；mo "和谐"交通网络的简称（Harmonious Mobility Network 的简称，近年提出并已在某些国家和地区试行的人、车、路和公共交通最佳组合、和谐运行的新型通行网络，由①根据节能、环保原则，通过智能手机向出行者发布到达目的地的、包括合用私人车辆在内的最佳交通工具、驻车-停车位和路线的"和谐"交通网络导航服务"Ha；mo NAVI" ②向目的地距离在数千米以内的出行者提供共用超小型电动车的"和谐"交通网络车辆服务"Ha；mo RID"等组成）
Ha；mo NAVI "和谐"交通网络导航服务
Ha；mo RIDE "和谐"交通网络车辆服务
hamper ①阻碍物 ②妨碍，阻止，阻碍
hand accelerator 手动节气门，手拉油门
hand adjustment ①手动调整 ②手调装置
hand advance 手动提前点火，手控

点火提前（= manual spark advance）

Handa R&D Americas, Inc 本田公司北美研究与开发公司（本田公司在北美的基地）

hand banisters （双层客车楼梯）扶手

hand brake 手制动器（指用于操纵杆控制的制动器，如常见的驻车制动器。hand brake bracket 手制动器支架；hand brake control 手制动器操纵装置；hand brake drive rod adjusting fork 手制动器驱动杆调整叉；hand brake lever 手制动器拉杆，手制动器拉杆；hand brake on 手制动器已接合，手制动已拉紧；hand brake pawl rod 手制动棘爪拉杆；hand brake telltale 手制动接合指示灯；hand brake turn 手刹跑偏，手刹偏转，指车辆开始转向时，若猛拉后轮手制动器致使后轮抱死，而产生的车辆偏转 180° 的现象；hand brake warning light 手制动器警告灯，亦称 hand brake telltale，该灯亮表示手制动器已拉紧，汽车起步前必须将手制动器松开。在大部分新型轿车上单独的手制动警告灯已为多功能制动警告灯所取代）

hand bucket pump 手动桶式滑油泵

hand bumping tool set （校正车身外壳用）成套手工整形工具

hand choke control 阻风门手控装置

handed ①按规定的方向、端面或位置安装或装配的，不能互换的（= not interchangeable）②（被）传递的，交给的

hand fit 压入配合

hand-free communication 免提（电话）通信

hand-free operation 免提的，无须用手操作

Hand Free Profile （使用蓝牙技术的）车载免提电话设备协议子集

hand gear control 手操纵变速装置

hand governing 手（动）控（制），手调，人工调节（= manual adjustment, hand regulation）

hand-held data entry keyboard 轻便型数据输入按钮板，携带式数据输入按钮板

hand hole 检修孔，观察孔

handicapped person carrier 伤残者运送车（装备有特殊设备，专门运送坐在轮椅中的伤残者的厢式汽车）

handiness 易操纵性，操纵方便性；灵巧，灵便

handing of engine 发动机旋转方向

handing stability （汽车的）操纵稳定性

hand lay-up ①手工胶合，手工结合 ②（特指用手工将树脂材料刷或喷在模具上的玻璃纤维强化材料上，制造大型玻璃纤维强化部件或板件的）手工涂敷

handle ①手柄，把手，提手，拉手，手轮；扶手 ②（民用频段无线电用户的）代码名称（见 CB）③处理，应付 ④（特指车辆及其总成、部件对恶劣行驶环境、行驶条件，如：恶路、高速、长时间满负荷运行等的）承受和适应（能力）⑤运送；调度；控制，操纵 ⑥车辆（对驾驶人员各种操作，特别是对转向、保持所要求的行驶方向及回避障碍或在狭小空间内行车操作的）响应，（车辆的）操纵性（见 handleability）

handleability （车辆的）操纵性（亦称 handling 或 handling properties，车辆操纵稳定性中，操纵性指车辆及时而准确地执行驾驶人员转向操纵或指令的能力，而稳定性则指车辆受到外界干扰后维持或迅速恢复原行驶方向或状态的能力及响应特性）

handle-bar grip 手把柄

handle change 转向盘柱变速，转向盘柱换挡（变速杆装在转向盘柱上

的变速换挡方式)
handled 手操纵的
handle grip 手柄
handle knob ①捏手柄 ②按钮
handle lock nut 手柄锁紧螺母
handle position 手柄位置
handler ①近距离操纵机械手 ②装卸装置,输送装置 ③信息处理机,处理程序
hand lever brake 手动杠杆式制动器
hand lever shifter 变速杆
handling ①操纵,控制,驾驶 ②(机器)维护,维修 ③装卸,搬运,转运,输送 ④管理,经营 ⑤处理,对付 ⑥(特指车辆操纵稳定性中的)操纵性(见 handleability) ⑦用手握,拿,持
handling and storage characteristics 储运特性(如:汽油在储存运输过程中,抗氧化成胶等特性)
handling capacity ①装卸能力(装卸企业或装卸机械在一定时期内,所能完成的最大货物卸装量) ②搬运能力
handling characteristics ①(汽车的)操纵特性 ②(货物的)装卸特性(如:易碎性等)
handling loss 搬运损失,运输损失,装卸损失
handling maneuver [美]①(汽车的)转向动作(包括变更车道、躲避障碍、超车及改变行车方向等各项靠转向实现的动作,一般按其产生的离心加速度分为三级:离心加速度超过0.5g者称为高离心加速转向;在0.3~0.5g范围内者称为中离心加速转向;低于0.3g者称为低离心加速转向动作) ②转向操作,驾驶操纵,调动(= 英 manoeuvre, manoeuver)
handling of traffic 交通管理,交通指挥
handling operation ①装卸业务(从装卸受理到装卸完毕所进行的经营管理工作) ②装卸作业
handling package (悬架系统中的)以操纵性为重点的悬架总成(使用刚性较大的减振器和弹簧,粗大的防侧倾杆"anti-roll bar"等,以获得良好的操纵性和行车路线保持能力)
handling precision (汽车驾驶时的)操纵准确度;控制精度
handling quality (汽车的)操纵性,方向操纵性能(驾驶员对汽车方向控制性能及灵敏程度的总印象。如:在超车、紧急变更车道、闪避障碍物的转向操作中,驾驶员对汽车方向控制机构的轻便性、准确性、灵敏性等方面的总感觉)
handling radius 作用半径,工作半径,操纵半径(如:起重机动臂的回转半径)
handling stability (汽车的)操纵稳定性
handling test (汽车的)方向操纵性试验,车道变换性能试验,曲线行驶特性试验
handling time ①辅助时间(例如机器的维护时间) ②(数据,资料的)处理时间 ③(货物的)装卸时间
hand lubrication 手动润滑(法),人工润滑(法)
hand-luggage rack (客车的)手提行李用行李架
hand measurement 手量测
hand molding 手工造型(= hand moulding)
hand of rotation 旋转方向
hand of spiral 螺旋方向,螺纹方向
handrail (大客车登车阶梯等的)扶手
hand reach 手伸界限(指在拘束状态下坐姿的乘员和驾驶人员伸手所能达到的活动范围,亦称 hand

hand regulation 手动调节

hand reset 手动调零,手动复位,手动回零

hand semaphore signal 手动动臂信号(臂板升起或落下而发出信号)

hands-free 免提的,无须动手的,无须用手的(如:hands-free car phone 免提式车用电话)

hands-free keyless entry and startup system 免手操控无钥匙式进出车门和发动机起动系统

hand shaft (仪表的)指针轴(= hand spindle)

handshaker [美俚]手动变速轿车

hand skill 手艺,手工技巧

hand snips (车身板作用)手剪

hands-off (and feet-off) operation (汽车的)撒手(抬足)驾驶,撒手操作(指驾驶员撒开双手,不抓转向盘,不踩踏板汽车依靠自身的方向稳定性行驶)

hands-off speed (汽车的)撒手速度(指驾驶员双手离开转向盘时的稳定行驶车速)

hand start ①手起动(指手摇起动或用手动弹簧储能式起动器起动,见 recoil starter) ②手动起动装置(= hand starter)

hand starter 手起动装置(= hand starting arrangement,如:起动摇把、弹簧储能式起动器、绳索滑轮式手拉起动装置等)

hand starting button 起动按钮,手控起动开关

hand test (汽油)蒸发性的手掌法试验

hand throttle link cover bracket 手油门拉杆盖支架

hand throttle wire 手油门拉线

hand-trimmed 手工装饰的,手工修饰的,手工修整的

hand wheel 手轮,操作轮(包括与手轮作用相同的十字形手柄)

hand-wheel torque ①转向盘转矩,转向盘力矩 ②手轮转矩

handy 便于使用的,合手的,驾驶灵便的,容易操纵的,灵巧的,近便的,可携带的

handy reel lamp 带线卷盘的手提工作灯

hang ①斜坡,倾斜 ②下垂物,下垂状态 ③悬挂,安装,吊重

hange plate 车门铰链板(指车门铰链和车门板之间的加强板,用于将作用于车门铰链螺栓上的力分散到车门板的更大区域)

hanger ①吊杆,吊架,支架;悬架;吊钩,带环 ②(特指用瞄准仪检测车身是否变形而装在车身上的观测瞄准点的)安装件 ③吊装的,吊挂式的

hanger for inner tire 内胎挂架

hanger pin 吊耳销

hanging ①悬吊,悬挂,悬置,斜坡;[复]窗帘;工作吊架;顶盘,上盘,顶板 ②悬式的,悬空的,悬垂的,垂下的

hanging test 挂重法断裂试验(用悬挂重物来测定断裂强度)

hanging-up ①挂起,悬挂;中止 ②挂料,悬料 ③(单向阀)卡止,不回位

hang-on part 汽车车身的铰接件(如:发动机罩盖、车门等)

hang-on trim panel 悬挂式装饰板

hangover 低车身车(一种定制的变形车,带独立底盘,其地板升高,但车身却放低,看上去像是罩在底盘上的车身已放低到路面的高度)

hang up ①挂起,悬起 ②(气门)卡住 ③中止操作,拖延 ④车身中间被地面凸起物托起而不能行驶

hang-up diameter (车辆不能通过的)最小纵向拱度直径(指使汽车中间底部被顶住而失去通过性的最

小拱形障碍物与前、后两车轮相切点的外切圆直径）

hang-up failure of vehicle （通过性中的）汽车（被路面凸起物）顶起而不能行驶（由于是离地间隙不足引起的，故又称："汽车的间隙失效"）

haptic ①触觉的（由触觉引起的）②能触知的

HAR 美国联邦公路管理局公路咨询广播（highway advisory radio 的简称）

harbor lodge 汽车渡船的停泊码头

hard alloy steel 硬质合金钢

hard and fast rule 不许变动的规则，硬性规定，精确的标准

hard anodized coating 硬质阳极氧化镀层（指使用硬质阳极氧化镀覆"hard anodizing"的方法在铝和其他轻合金制件表面镀覆的高硬度耐磨氧化层）

Hardas process 硬质氧化铝膜处理法

hard board 纤维板，硬厚纸板（木板代用品）

hard borosilicate glass 硬质硼硅酸盐玻璃（耐火玻璃）

hard brake application 紧急制动，急剧制动（指猛踩制动踏板制动）

hard brake stop 紧急制动停车，急刹车

hard brittle material 脆性材料

hard chromium plating 镀硬铬，硬铬镀层（指结晶细密的高硬度的耐磨电镀铬层）

hard coal 无烟煤（=coal stone）

hard copper 硬铜，冷加工铜

hard core ①硬核心，硬核 ②（道路的）硬路基，碎石路基

hard-disc based 基于硬盘机的，由硬盘操控的

hard-disc NAVI 硬盘导航系统

hard-dry （指油漆层等已）干硬（到足以进行打磨和抛光作业）的

harden 硬化，变硬，淬硬，固化，硫化

hardenability （可）硬化度，（可）淬硬性，淬火性，硬化性，淬透性

hardenability band （钢的）可淬硬性带

hardenability characteristic （钢的）可淬硬性，可淬透特性，淬火特性，可硬化特性

hardenability limit （钢）淬透性极限，可淬硬性极限

hardenability of core （渗碳钢件的）内心淬透性

hardenability test 可淬性试验；淬透性试验

hardenability value 淬硬性指数；淬透性指数

hardened 硬化的，淬火的

hardened and tempered steel 调质钢（指专供调质处理的碳素结构钢如：30~45号钢和合金结构钢35SiMn6、40Mn、40CrV、40Cr等）

hardened face 淬火（渗碳）表面，硬化面

hardened glass 钢化玻璃（由氧化硅及一些氧化物熔化而制成的平板玻璃，再经淬火热处理）

hardened verge 硬路肩，经加固的路缘

hardener ①硬化剂，固化剂；淬火剂 ②母合金，中间合金

hardening ①（油漆，涂料层的）固化，硬化（=setting，指涂层变干硬或使其变干硬的工序或过程）②（钢制件的）淬火（=quenching，指将钢件加热到一定的温度得到奥氏体组织，经保温后快速冷却使组织变为马氏体的热处理工艺，使工件强化和硬化。钢件淬火后必须再及时进行回火处理，见tempering）③（橡胶的）硫化（=curing, vulcanizing，指高温加硫化使橡胶硬化）④（汽车用黏结剂，如：

环氧树脂，酚树脂的）固化（= setting）
hardening agent 淬火剂（= hardening compound）
hardening and tempering 调质（钢件淬火后硬度高，但塑性、韧性差，内应力大，必须经回火，消除上述不足，并促使残余奥氏体转变稳定组织才能使用，淬火后加高温回火，统称调质）
hardening babbit 硬质巴氏合金（低锡巴氏合金）
hardening crack 淬火裂纹（亦称 hardening flaw）
hardening furnace 淬火炉
hardenite 细马氏体（钢淬火后获得的一种高硬度铁碳合金组织）
hardest driver 工作条件十分艰苦的驾驶员
hard facing ①表面硬化，表面淬火 ②镀复硬质材料（作为硬表面）③（表面焊一层硬金属材料的）加焊硬面法
hardness 硬度（金属材料和塑料的硬度，指其抵抗局部变形，塑性变形，压痕和划伤的能力）
hardness change ①硬度变化 ②（材料老化前后的）硬度变化量
hardness-depth curve 硬度-深度曲线（材料硬度随深度而变化的曲线）
hardness penetration 淬硬深度
hardness scale 硬度计表盘刻度
hardness tester 硬度试验机，硬度计（= hardometer）
hard-packed snow 压实的积雪
hard pan 硬磐层，硬土层
hard pedal 踏板硬（指制动踏板等的踩踏阻力过大、过硬现象）
hard plug 热型火花塞（= hot plug，见 heat range）
hard-pumped 充足气的（轮胎）
hard-rubber 硬橡胶（= ebonite，指不含填料的硬黑炭橡胶化合物）

hard scope 袖珍式（肖氏）硬度计；微型硬度计
hard service 超（负）载工作，在恶劣条件下工作，超载使用
hard shoulder 硬质路肩，铺砌的路肩（= paved shoulder）
hard-sided caravan 硬壁旅居挂车（指装有可折叠的硬侧壁板的旅居挂车，见 caravan）
hard solder 硬焊料（指熔点 600 ~ 1000℃的高熔点，接合力强的钎焊焊料）
hard soldering 硬钎焊；铜焊（指用硬焊料进行的钎焊，其结合强度在熔焊与软钎焊之间，= brazing）
hard spots （材料）硬点
hard steel 硬钢（含碳量 0.5% ~ 0.7%，抗拉强度 600 ~ 700MPa，伸长 14% 以上，见 high carbon steel）
hard steering 转向沉重，转向盘重
hard stop 重踩制动，猛踩制动（= hard braking，指用力猛踩制动踏板，但不致使车轮抱死）
hard surfacing ①表面淬火，表面硬化 ②硬质面层
hard-to-machining 难以机加工的
hard top （相对 soft top 而言）①硬壳车顶（指金属或硬塑料制的刚性固定车顶，或可拆卸的硬顶板）②（无间隔的四门或两门）固定硬壳车顶轿车（= hard top saloon 或 sedan）③（单排双座或在前排主座后带有一排备用双座，相当于）带硬壳车顶的运动车（= sports car with a hard top）④（有时指）活动硬顶轿车（= hard top convertible，将硬顶取下，即成为一辆敞篷轿车）⑤硬路面道路 ⑥泛指一切硬的顶面
hardtop-cabriolet body 活动硬顶车车身（具有可以收起的活动刚性车顶盖的双门轿车车身）
hard top container 硬顶式集装箱

（顶开式集装箱之一种，箱顶用薄钢板制成，可用叉车或吊车装卸顶盖）

hardtop convertible 活动硬顶小轿车（车顶为金属或塑料制成，可收折或卸下，为硬顶车的一种）

hard top jeep 硬顶吉普车

hard top stand 硬顶支架（可垂直存放拆下来的硬顶的折叠式支架）

hard-to-reach place 难以拆装的地方，不易动手的地方，手不易伸到处

hard trim 硬内筛（指车身内部，如：仪表板等处的硬塑料筛面，相对于软皮包装的软筛面而言）

hard usage 不细心的使用，粗鲁的使用

hard ware ①金属构件，金属器皿，铁器，小五金 ②（计算机的）硬件，硬设备

hard water 硬水 [＝earth (y) water，指钙盐，镁盐含量较多的天然水]

hard-wearing 耐磨的，抗磨的

hardwiring 固化（指由制造厂直接将固定的程序写入计算机的可编程只读存储器或只读存储器内，如：汽车电子计算机控制系统的控制程序等）

hardwood 硬木

Hardy disk 哈代盘（形挠性联轴节）

hardy Spicer (constant-velocity universal joint) 哈代斯派士尔等速万向节（通常用于汽车传动轴的等速万向节）

H-armature H 型截面电枢，H 型电枢

harmless 无害的

harmonic ①谐波（指其频率与某一基频成整倍数的电磁波，机械振动波或声波）②谐（和）的

harmonically balanced crankshaft 得到完全平衡的曲轴（指一阶旋转惯性力，一、二阶往复惯性力及产生扭转共振的干扰力等，各种导致不平衡力均得到完全平衡的曲轴）

harmonic balancer 谐振平衡器（亦称 harmonic damper 谐振减振器，指各种利用旋转式摆动质量使简谐波叠加产生相消干涉的振动消减装置，如：发动机曲轴扭振的弹性摆式减振器和可完全平衡发动机一阶、二阶往复惯性力的兰彻斯特平衡机构等，见 Lanchester anti-vibrator)

harmonic cam 正弦运动凸轮，谐和运动凸轮（指凸轮轮廓曲线随时间按正弦或余弦规律变化的凸轮）

harmonic curve 谐波曲线（指按正弦或余弦规律变化的曲线）

harmonic damper 见 harmonic balancer

harmonic distortion （电子信号发生器）非线性畸变，谐波失真

harmonic frequency 谐振频率（谐频，与基频成整倍数的频率，见 harmonic vibration）

harmonic gear drive 谐波齿轮传动（由波发生器，柔性齿轮，刚性齿及轴入、输出轴等基本件组成。波发生器使柔性齿轮按一定变形规律产生可控周形性弹性变形波，并与刚性齿轮啮合来传递运动和力）

harmonic gear drive with contrate gear meshing 端面谐波齿轮传动（在波发生器作用下，柔轮与刚轮呈端面啮合，它们之间的变形波垂直于谐波齿轮传动的输出轴）

harmonic gear increaser 谐波齿轮增速器（输出轴转速大于输入轴转速的谐波齿输传动机构）

harmonic gear reducer 谐波齿轮减速器（输出轴转速小于输入轴转速的谐波齿轮传动机构）

harmonic generator ①谐波发生器，谐波振荡器 ②（谐波齿轮的）波

发生器（见 harmonic gear drive）

harmonic induction engine 谐波进气式发动机（亦称 tuned induction engine，指利用适当选择进气道长度，以便在某一所希望的狭小速度范围内能利用进气反射波改善容积效率的发动机，见 pressure wave supercharging②）

harmonic oscillation ①谐频振动（见 harmonic vibration）②（电磁波）谐频振荡，谐振（指无线电接收装置的输入电路固有振动频率调到与发射装置发射的载波频率相同时，出现的电磁共振。此时输入电路可获来外来频率相同的最大振幅的受迫振荡，从而获得最大能量由放大系统放大后输出。使输入电路发生谐振的过程叫调谐"tuning"或"harmonization"）③共振（指在受迫振动中当受迫系统的固有频率与外来强迫力的频率相同，即为倍频时，振幅最大的现象，当 harmonic 表示这一含义时 = resonance）

harmonic strain 简谐应变（由简谐应力产生的随时间按正弦或余弦规律变化的应变）

harmonic stress 简谐应力（按余弦或正弦规律变化的应力）

harmonious lines （车身）圆滑过度的曲线

harmonization 调谐（见 harmonic oscillation②）

harness ①线束；电线，电线束 ②电气配线 ③吊带，带状装置 ④（特指汽车乘员的）安全带系统（如：由两条肩带和两条臂带及中央锁扣组成的轿车儿童座椅安全带系统）

harrison type radiator 哈立逊式散热器（一种铜带制蜂窝状散热器）

harsh driving 胡乱开车，粗暴驾驶

harsh environment 恶劣环境，苛刻环境

harshness ①粗糙性 ②驾驶员动作的猛烈性 ③汽车行驶的不平顺性 ④车辆在垂直平面内的小振幅振动，车身跳动 ⑤（车辆的）行驶路面接缝噪声（参见 pavement-joint noise）

Hartridge smokemeter 哈特里奇烟度计

Harvard architecture （电子控制系统）哈佛结构（指程序和数据置于单芯片的两个分隔的区域内并且由两条分隔的总线平行传送的结构）

hasp 搭扣，搭钮

hastelloy 耐蚀镍基合金（一种高级燃气涡轮合金），耐盐酸镍基合金，耐热镍基合金

hatch ①舱口 ②货车或驾驶室与乘客室之间有壁板隔开的客车的驾驶室后壁上的小窗口 ③舱门

hatchback 舱门式后背小轿车（亦称 lift back，指带向上翻开的大倾斜变后门的掀背式轿车）

haul ①搬运 ②牵引 ③运距，运输量

haulage ①拖曳，拖运，搬运，运输，调动，输送 ②牵引力，拖力 ③运输方式 ④运程，行驶里程 ⑤拖运量，牵引量 ⑥拖运费；货车使用费

haulage company 运输公司

haulage truck 载货汽车，货车

haul distance 运程长度，运输距离，运距

haul fleet 货物运输车队，货运车队

hauling ability ①搬运性能 ②牵引性能

hauling capacity ①牵引能力 ②运输能力

hauling unit ①（一台）运输车辆，单位运输工具 ②牵引车 ③运土车

Havoline Dex-Cool （美 Texaco 公司生产的）乙二醇长寿有机型配方发动机防冻液（商品名，车上使用寿命可高达五年，储存期至少八年）

hawk eye headlights 鹰眼前照灯，

隼眼前照灯

Hayes transmission 海斯变速器（一种复曲面形无级变速器，通过在复曲面形环道内滚动且其主动环道与从动环道间的滚动直径比是可变的滚轮来实现变速。因其发明人 Austin Hayes 而得名，用于某些早期车辆）

hay trailer 运干草的挂车

hazard 危险，危害

hazard flasher 危险警告闪光器（汽车紧急停车时，避免其他车辆碰撞，使前后及左右两侧的闪光灯同时闪光的装置，亦称 four-way flasher "四向闪光器"）

hazard-free circuit 无危险电路，安全电路

hazard marker 危险指示标（设置在路上障碍物之前或急弯处，表示存在危险的标示）

hazard marking light 危险标灯（预告通行危险地点而配备的标灯）

hazardous location （交通）事故多发地点，危险地段（参见 traffic black spot）

hazardous materials 危险物品（易燃，易爆等物品）

hazard warning light 危险报警闪光灯（装在汽车的四角，车辆因故障或事故而停在公路上时，发出闪光警告信号，告诉其他车辆，"此处有车"）

hazard warning signal control 危急信号操纵件（由于车辆本身的紧急状况，对其他车辆将造成暂时的危险而发出警告信号操纵件）

hazard warning switch 危险警告闪光开关（= hazard light flasher switch，指汽车独立的危险警报信号灯开关，见 hazard warning light 或指可使汽车全部转向信号灯、驻车灯及尾灯，有的还包括前照灯均同时闪光，借以发出车辆处于危险状态或非正常停车位置的警告信号开关）

hazard warning system tell-tale （驾驶室内的）危急报警系统信号灯（该灯亮时，表示危急报警系统已接通）

hazard way light 险路信号灯

hazchem 危险化学品（hazardous chemicals 的简称，一般标在运输这类化学品的车上）

haze ①烟雾，薄雾；模糊，朦胧 ②使朦胧，变浑浊

hazing 模糊（如：因刮水器不良造成的风窗玻璃透明度下降而模糊不清）

H/B （轮胎的）扁平比（其断面高 hight 与公称断面宽 breadth 之比）

HBA 紧急制动辅助系统（hazard brake assist 的简称）

h bar 百巴（压力单位，hectobar）

HBC system 复合制动控制系统（Hybrid Brake Control system 的简称）

H-beam 工字梁

H$_2$ blends 氢气混合物

HBSS [美]汽车工程师学会人体生物动力学和模拟分会（The SAE Human Biomechanics and Simulation Subcommittee 的简称）

HBW 紧急制动提示系统（hazard brake warning 的简称）

H/C （烃的）氢碳比（hydrogen/carbon）

HC 碳氢化合物，烃（hydrocarbons 的简称）

HC 混合动力车（见 hybrid vehicle）

HCCI 均质充气压（缩着火）燃（烧）（homogeneous charge compression ignition 的简称）

HCCI combustion 均质充气压燃点火燃烧（homogeneous charge compression ignition combustion 的简称）

HCCI engine 均质充气压燃发动机

(homogeneous charge compression ignition engine 的简称)

HCEI 烃排放量指数（hydrocarbon emission index 的简称）

HC engine 高位凸轮轴发动机（high-camshaft engine 的简称，指凸轮轴位置高于曲轴，但并未装在汽缸盖内的发动机，可以使用较短的气门挺杆，有助于提高发动机的设计转速）

HCFB System 高压缩比快速燃烧系统（high compression fast burn combustion system 的简称）

HCG 重心的水平方向位置（horizontal center-of-gravity 的简称）

HCM 液压控制模块（hydraulic control module 的简称，旧称液压控制单元 hydraulic control unit，简称"HCU"）

HCMTS 高容量车用电话系统（参见 High Capacity Mobile Telephone System）

HCS 高碳钢（high carbon steel 的简称）

HC-SCR catalyst 碳氢化合物选择催化转化型还原催化剂（hydrocarbon selective catalytic reduction catalysts 的简称）

HC trap type catalyst converter HC 捕集型催化转化器

HCU ①液压（系）控制单元（hydraulic system control unit 的简称）②液力耦合件（三菱公司开发的黏性耦合器的商品名，hydraulic coupling unit 的简称，一般的黏性耦合器是利用硅油的黏性传递转矩，而 HCU 则是利用黏性油流过节流孔，产生黏性阻力传递转矩的，可传递的转矩大，耐热，只要改变节流孔尺寸，便可很容易地改变其性能）③（具有防滑转牵引力控制功能的防抱死制动系统 Tevers Mark Ⅳ 中的）液压控制总成（hydraulic control unit 的简称，由泵，电动机，加压电磁阀，减压电磁阀和隔离阀蓄液箱等组成的制动液压调节器）

HCV 温度控制阀（heat control valve）

HD ①重型，高负荷，高容量（的，heavy duty 的简称）②高频（的，high frequency 的简称）③高密度（的，high density 的简称）④高清晰度（的，high definition 或 high distinctness 的简称）⑤十六烷（hexadecane 的简称）

H/D 加热器-除霜器（heater/defroster）

HDAC 加热，除霜，空调总成（heater, defroster, air conditioning assembly）

HDC ①下坡（车速）控制（系统）（hill down control 的简称）②（汽车）下坡（自动）缓速控制（hill descent control 的简称）

HDD ①硬盘（hard disk 的简称）②驱动（hard disc drive 的简称）③高密度数据系统（亦写作 HDDS，high density data system 的简称）④测定撞车低头（观看的）显示系统（head-down display 的简称）

HDD navi 硬盘导航（系统）（hard-disk navigation 的简称）

HDEP 重型发动机平台（heavy duty engine platform 的简称）

HDI diesel engine 高压直喷式柴油发动机（high pressure direct injection diesel engine 的简称）

HDPE 高密度聚乙烯（high density polyethylene）

HDR 扶手（hand rail）

HDS 见 hill descent system

HDT 热变形温度（heat distortion temperature）

HDTV 高清晰度电视（high definition television 的简称）

HD unit 动液传动装置（hydrodynamic unit，见 hydrodynamic drive）

HE ①厚搪瓷，厚瓷漆（heavy enamel 的简称）②高效率（high efficiency 的简称）③人体工程学（human engineering 的简称）

He 氦（helium）

head ①头，头部，顶部，端部，车头，前部，突出部分 ②水头，压头，扬程，落差（gros head）③汽缸盖（cylinder head 的简称）④头部的，主要的，首席的

head aim corrector 汽车前照灯照射方位调整器（随着汽车姿势的变化，自动调整前照灯照射方位的装置，参见 vehicle attitude change）

head airbag 头部安全气囊

head board （货车车箱）前拦板

head bolt 汽缸盖螺栓，缸盖螺柱

head circle （齿轮）齿顶圆

head clearance 头顶空隙（指坐在座位上的乘员，头顶与车室顶棚之间的距离）

head combustion chamber 汽缸盖（内的）燃烧室

head coolant 汽缸盖冷却液

head cushion （座椅的）头枕

headed 具有镦粗头部的

head-end compression ring 第一道活塞压缩环，头道气环

head-end volume 活塞顶上的（燃烧室）容积

header ①头部，顶，盖（如：后窗顶盖）②（发动机散热器的）上水室，上水箱（header tank 的简称）③（[美]汇合水流、气流、液流的）集管（= 英 head pipe，如：汽车排气管系中，接在发动机排气歧管后的第一根管子。相对于排气管系中将废气排至大气的最后一根管子"排气尾管"而言，称排气首管。有单管型、双管型、Y 型和内装微型催化转化器等多种）④（货车或挂车的货台两端的）安全挡板（防止汽车起步、加速或制动时，货物移动）⑤（切除铆钉头等的）切头器

header bar （某些车型汽车发动机罩前端的）顶部撑条（当打开发动机罩后，该撑条支撑于风窗玻璃框的顶边。该撑条一般用薄钢板制成，且其支撑面形状与风窗玻璃框顶边弧度相吻合。美称 head bow）

header board ①前挡板，前面板 ②（货车或挂车车箱等的）前（栏）板（亦称 front board，当货车货箱前端装有货架时，指货架下部货箱的前栏板，参见 front guard frame）

header board outside panel （货车货箱的）前板外板，前拦板外板（前拦板外部的板件）

head(er) brace 车顶加强板，车顶撑条

header tank （散热器的）上水箱，上水室（简称 header）

head face 端面

head fall ①纵向坡度，纵向倾斜 ②水头下落

headform （汽车试验时使用的）人头模型，假人头

head-form test 人头模型冲击试验（测定撞车时风窗玻璃的抗人头冲击强度和对头的伤害程度）

head fuel fraction 燃油的初馏分

head gasket 汽缸盖衬垫，汽缸垫（cylinder head gasket 的简称）

head gasket volume 汽缸盖衬垫容积，缸垫容积（= 缸口面积×缸垫装配厚度）

head gear 顶齿轮（重型车辆变速器的中间轴减速齿轮副）

head hex(agonal) 六角头

head-impact degrading interior 头部冲击缓和型车身内室

heading ①方向，方位，朝向 ②（铆钉、螺栓）镦头；镦粗，镦锻 ③标题，项目

heading angle ①汽车方位角（指汽车纵轴在路面上的投影和地面固定

坐标系 X 轴间的夹角）②汽车的侧偏角（指行驶中汽车的纵轴线与其实际行驶方向的夹角，见 yaw angle ②）

heading change sensor （汽车行驶）朝向变化传感器（见 heading sensor）

heading die 镦粗模，锻模

heading joint 端接合，直角接合

heading sensor （汽车的）行驶朝向传感器［提供汽车的行驶方向及行驶方向变化信息的各种传感器件，如：固态磁通量（闸）门罗盘，左-右车轮转速差表，陀螺仪等，亦称 heading change sensor］

Head Injury Criterion （汽车碰撞事故中乘员的）头部伤害度评定基准，头部伤害度标准（简称 HIC）

headlamp 前照灯，大灯，头灯（指汽车正前面的主大灯）

headlamp adjusting screw 前照灯（光束中心离地高度及水平位置的）调节螺钉

headlamp aim(ing) （汽车）前照灯对光，汽车前照灯光束配光的调整（= headlight adjust, headlamp beam setting，指检验和调整前照灯远、近光束明暗截止线的分布特征，即其配光特性和光轴的方向）

headlamp aiming screen 前照灯配光屏（幕）

headlamp base 前照灯座

headlamp blinding glare （汽车）前照灯眩光

headlamp body 前照灯壳

headlamp bracket 前照灯座架［指货车或某些轿车的独立式前照灯，即不与车身轮廓线成一体的单独的前照灯（的）支座］

headlamp bulb （汽车）前照灯灯泡

headlamp case 前照灯壳

headlamp case-rim （汽车）前照灯边框（= bezel of headlamp）

headlamp concealment device 前照灯遮光装置

headlamp cover 前照灯护罩（不用灯光时，防止尘土污染或碎石击损前照灯的防护罩）

headlamp dim 前照灯灯光昏暗（故障）

headlamp dimmer （前照灯）变光开关

headlamp door 前照灯装饰圈（亦称 head lamp ornament，指前照灯前面周边用作装饰目的的圈形部件）

headlamp door latch 前照灯外罩（罩门）搭扣（锁闩）

headlamp flasher 前照灯闪光器（见 hazard warning switch②）

headlamp glass rim 前照灯玻璃边圈，前照灯玻璃框边

headlamp grid 前照灯护栅（亦称 headlamp guard）

headlamp insert 前照灯密封灯泡（= sealed beam lamp, sealed beam unit）

headlamp lens （汽车）前照灯散光玻璃

headlamp leveling motor 前照灯照射方向调整电动机

headlamp leveling system 前照灯（光轴上、下）自动调控系统（见 headlight levelling）

headlamp lighting range automatic regulator 前照灯射域自动调节装置（可根据车辆载重分布的变化引起车头倾斜、下沉或扬起时自动调整前照灯灯光射域，以保证最佳照明效果。由车身倾斜传感器，左、右前照灯射程调节伺服电动机及控制模块组成）

headlamp lower beam 前照灯近光

headlamp meeting beam 汽车前照灯会车灯光，前照灯近光

headlamp mounting panel 前照灯安装框板（方形前照灯的金属底板，点焊于轿车前脸部、邻接散热器护

栅板，为前照灯提供安装点）
headlamp reflector 前照灯反光镜
headlamp rim 前照灯框
headlamp shell 前照灯壳
headlamp support 前照灯支架
headlamp support tie rod 前照灯支座横拉杆，大灯支撑杆
headlamp tester （汽车）前照灯光测试仪（测定前照灯光束光轴的偏斜方向和偏斜量及发光强度的仪器）
headlamp testing aiming equipment 前照灯对光装置（见 headlamp aim）
headlamp upper beam 前照灯远光
headlamp visor 前照灯檐板（灯框外缘与配光镜之间的连接件，仅见于某些古典车）
headlamp wash wipe （由清洗液喷头和清洗刮片组成的）前照灯清洗装置
head land （活塞顶边至第一道活塞环槽顶边间的区域，称为活塞）顶岸（活塞承受最大热负荷的区域）
head length 人头部的前后长度，人体头部厚度
headless shoulder screw 无头有肩螺钉
headlight ①（汽车）前照灯，头灯，大灯 ②前照灯的光束，前照灯光
headlight adjust 汽车前照灯（光束）调整（指调整前照灯光束中心的照射方向，= headlamp aiming, beam setting）
headlight beam ①（汽车）前照灯光束 ②前照灯灯丝
headlight beam aiming control 前照灯光束对光操纵件（补偿车辆在不同载荷时对光束倾斜度的影响而对前照灯光束方向做垂直方向调整的操纵件）
headlight bracket 前照灯支架
headlight checking equipment 前照灯检验仪（用以检查光束投射方向及光强度）
headlight cleaner control 前照灯清洗器操纵件（控制清洗前照灯配光玻璃外表面的装置的操纵件）
headlight dazzle （汽车）前照灯眩光（= headlight glare）
headlight dipper（switch） 前照灯近光开关，前照灯变光开关（的统称，亦称 dip switch，包括脚踏式和手动按钮式、拨杆式等将远光变为近光的开关）
headlight flasher 前照灯闪光开关（一般为弹簧拨杆式开关，在弹簧作用下，将该拨杆压向下方接通位置，用手将该拨杆拨向上方使可断开前大灯电源，一松手拨杆又弹回，反复迅速向上拨动该拨杆，即可实现大灯迅速闪光，用以提醒对向车注意或向前车发出超车信号）
headlight levelling 前照灯光束自动调控系统（有驾驶员操纵与自动控制两种，当车头由于载荷等原因而下沉或上翘时，使前照灯光束保持正确位置的系统，亦称 headlamp leveling）
headlight main-beam indicator 前照灯远光指示灯（装在仪表板上，指示远光接通 = high-beam headlight indicator）
headlight on/off delay system 前照灯开灯及关灯延时系统（①关灯延时功能：只要设置这一功能，驾驶人员离开已停放到车位上并关断了前照灯开关的车辆后，前照灯仍能亮3分钟左右 ②自动开灯、关灯功能：通电后，电子控制模块根据装在仪表板上的光电元件传感器测得车外光线暗到规定值时自动将前照灯打开，而当光线亮到某规定值时，自动将前照灯关闭）
headlight pattern 前照灯光斑，前照灯照射区模式

head light protecting seal wire 汽车前照灯护套包线

headlight range dynamic adjustment 前照灯光照射距离动态调整功能（如：可随车速调整照射距离等）

head light retractor indicator lamp （自动伸缩式前照灯的）回缩指示灯（前照灯的罩板开启，前照灯伸出或前照灯缩回，罩板关闭时，该指示灯亮）

headlights beam switching control dimmer switch 前照灯变光开关（变换前照灯远光或近光的操纵件）

head light tester 前照灯灯光仪（见 headlamp tester）

headlight vertical aim control 前照灯光束垂直照射方向控制（装置）

headlight wiper control 前照灯刮水器操纵件（控制前照灯刮水器工作的操纵件）

head lining 车顶篷蒙里，车顶软衬里（= head liner，美称 roof lining）

head office 总公司，总部

head of pump 泵的扬程

head of water 水头，水压头

head-on-collision （汽车等的）迎面碰撞，正面碰撞（= head-on crash, head-on impact，指两汽车面对面直线碰撞）

head-on view 正视图

head(-on) wind 顶风，迎面风，逆风（= adverse wind, baffling wind, dead wind）

headpipe 见 header③

head pivot point （驾驶员）头的转动中心

head pressure 见 discharge pressure

head resistance 迎风阻力，迎面阻力

head rest （座椅）头枕（亦称 head restraint）

headrest-mounted rear-seat DVD system （装在前座）头枕后面的后座 DVD 系统

headroom 净空，净空高度（亦写作 head room，车内：座椅至顶篷的高度"headroom over seat"，乘员头顶至顶篷高度"headroom over occupant's head,"客厢通道地板至顶篷高度"headroom over aisle"；车外，指通过桥梁等障碍物时，车顶与桥底面间的最小间距）

head shop （发动机）缸盖维修间；缸盖综合维修台，缸盖综合修理机床

headsignal lamp 车头信号灯（指车头的转向和示廓灯等）

head torquing 汽缸盖的拧紧，汽缸盖的扭紧，汽缸盖的紧固

head trim （车内）顶篷衬面（= roof lining）

head-turned angle （驾驶员）头的转动角度

head-turned eye ellipse （驾驶员）头转动的眼睛椭圆（头部转动时眼睛活动位置的轮廓线）

head unit 上方的装置（如：车内可存取安装在其下方卡槽内手机的全部信息，并可对手机全部功能实施操控的、位于上方、与手机显示屏相同仅尺寸放大的显示屏）

head-up display 抬头显示（指将汽车有关信息的数字或图形投射到风窗玻璃区驾驶员平视的视野范围内，因此驾驶员无须低头看仪表，故名。简称 HUD，抬头显示系统由一般装在仪表板顶部的 HUD 控制模块，光学投射系统，高亮度真空荧光蓝-绿七段数字管和图像符号管等组成的信息源，与风窗玻璃制成一体的全息合成器及影像亮度、垂直位置调整和控制开关等组成。一般抬头显示投射的项目有车速表读数，带英/米制转换，转向信号灯指示，前照灯远光指示，燃油不足指示和有关警告等）

headway ①车头时距，车头时间间

隔（以车辆最前端为基准测定的，同一条车道上行驶的前后车辆头部通过某一定点的时间间隔）②（顶部）净空，净空高度 ③前进，行进；进展，进步；前进速度

headway distributions 车间距离的分布，车间间隔的组成

head wind/tail wind 逆风-顺风（简称H/T）

Health Effect Institute ［美］（汽车排放对人体）健康影响研究所（简称HEI）

heaped capacity ①车箱堆装容量 ②（铲斗）铲装容量

hearing loss 听力损害，听力损失

hearse 殡仪车，灵车，柩车

heart cam 心形凸轮

heart check 内部裂缝

heart wheel 心形轮

heat ①热，热量，热度 ②加热，预热，变热，发热

heat-absorbing glass 吸热玻璃（内含差色氧化物，具有吸热作用，多用于车厢门窗）

heat absorption capacity 热容量，吸热能力

heat abstraction 除热，散热，排热

heat accumulation 积热，聚热，储热

heat accumulator 储热器（= thermal accumulator）

heat addition 预热，加热，供热

heat ageing ①热老化（指材料因长时间暴露于热环境下，其机械与物理性质发生的退化）②抗老化试验（测定长期暴露于热环境下对其性质的影响）③加热时效处理

heat ageing test 热老化试验

heat alarm 过热警报，过热信号，温升报警信号

heat baffle 绝热板，隔热罩（= thermal baffle）

heat balance 热平衡［对车用发动机，指燃料燃烧所产生的热量消耗于做功，及各项损失的百分比，用图、表表示这种百分比时分别称heat balance chart（表）和heat balance diagram（图）］

heat balance test 热平衡试验（测定发动机所消耗燃料的热量转化为有效功，冷却水带走热量，废气带走热量，以及其他热量损失等所占的比例的试验）

heat battery 储热器（= thermoaccumulator，一种可在 $-29℃$ 的外界温度下，存储汽车停车前的余热达三天之久的器具，其储热介质为温度超过 $78℃$ 时由固态变为液态的盐基晶体，用于低温起动预热和乘员取暖）

heat-blocking action 隔热作用，绝热作用

heat booster 加热器

heat calculation 热平衡计算

heat capacitor 储热器

heat carrier 热载体，载热介质（= heat-carrying agent）

heat catalysis 热催化作用，热催化反应

heat change 热交换

heat check 热检测

heat chemical treatment 热化学处理，化学热处理（指将工件置于一定介质中加热和保温，使介质中的活性原子渗入工件表层，以改变其化学成分和组织，如：渗碳、渗氮、氰化等）

heat coil （柴油机等的）预热塞电阻线圈（= heating coil）

heat color （加热）火色（指工件加热到 $530℃$ 以上时会发生不同颜色的光线，称火色，借以判断其加热温度，如：暗红色：$650～730℃$，亮樱桃色：$800～830℃$）

heat compensator 热平衡器，热补偿器，热膨胀圈

heat conductivity 热传导率,热导率（参见 thermal conductivity）

heat conductor 热导体

heat consumption 热量消耗,热能消耗,耗热量

heat content 比焓,热函,焓,热容量,热含量（常用代号 H, h, 亦称 = enthalpy,工质的热动力特性, $H=U+pV$,式中 U = 内能, p = 压力, V = 系统的容积）

heat control valve ①（泛指各种）调温阀,节温阀,温度控制阀（简称 HCV）②（特指排气歧管内在发动机冷机起动或低温运转时,将部分热废气引入进气歧管废气穿越式加热道内促使燃油气化的）加热控制阀

heat convection 热对流（= thermal convection,指靠液体或气体流动来传热）

heat corrosion 高温腐蚀

heat cracking （金属）高温裂纹,热裂纹（一般呈细小而不规则形,如：制动盘上的热纹）

heat crossover （V 形发动机两排气歧管间的）热跨接管（从化油器区经过,以便在发动机热起运转期间加热化油器）

heat cure(d) 热补(的),热硫化(的)

heat dam [美]①（泛指各种）隔热板,隔热墙,隔热挡②（特指活塞上的）隔热环槽（或隔热镶嵌环）（用来减少热量从头部向其他部分的传递,带隔热槽的活塞,英称 slotted piston）

heat difference 温差

heat diffusion 热扩散（= thermal diffusion）

heat dispersion 热散射,热耗散,散热

heat distortion 热变形,热扭变（简称 HDT）

heat drop 绝热热降,热降（单位质量的水蒸气或其他气体在绝热膨胀时,所释放的和理论上可转变为机械功的热能,adiabatic heat drop 的简称）

heated air intake system 暖空气进气系统,预热空气进气系统（其空气滤清器进口处装有冷热空气调温装置,保证任何情况下都能将适宜温度的暖空气吸入进气歧管, = hot and cold air intake system）

heated air outflow （暖风系统的）热空气出口通路

heated and cooled seat 冷-热调控式座椅

heated and lighted mirror 加热与照明式后视镜（装有照明灯及电热丝的后视镜）

heated bitumen tanker 沥青运输车（装备有沥青储运容罐和沥青加温设备,用于运输沥青的罐式汽车）

heated door mirror 电热式车门后视镜

heated exhaust gases oxygen sensor 电热式排气（中含）氧（量）传感器（简称 HEGO sensor 或 heated oxygen sensor,见 oxygen sensor）

heated flame ionization detector (analyzer) 加热式氢火焰离子化检测器（分析仪）（为了防止水分或碳氢化合物在取样系统内凝结或吸附,而对检测器和检测器的取样系统加热的氢火焰离子化检测器,简称 HFID）

heated glass backlight （轿车车身的）电热型后玻璃窗

heated intake 进气预热（系统）（指对混合气进行预热,以易于起动和减少起动期间的有害物排放,以及保证低温平稳运转）

heated oxygen sensor 电热式氧传感器（与一般氧传感器工作原理相同,仅在其内部装有一电热件,以保持其足够的工作温度,简称

HO_2S)

heated power outside mirror 电加热式电动车外后视镜

heated rear window 加热式后窗玻璃（一般是在玻璃内夹有细的电热丝，用于清除玻璃车内表面的露珠，车外表面的霜，美称 heated backlight）

heated sample cell （分析仪的）加热型样品室

heated seat 电热式座椅

heated tanker 加热式液罐车

heated tool welding 热盘压力焊（将要焊合的工件压于一高温热盘上加压的压合熔焊）

heated total hydrocarbon analyzer 加热式全烃分析仪（可检测各种碳氢化合物）

heated windscreen 加热式风窗玻璃（指电热或暖风加热的风窗玻璃，以除霜和化雾）

heat efficiency 热效率（= thermal efficiency，指用于做动的那部分能量与燃料完全燃烧所释放的总能量之比）

heat elimination 散热、排热、清热

heat emission 热辐射（由物体沿直线向外射出的热传递方式）

heat endurance 耐热性

heat energy 热能（= thermal energy，指物体内部所有分子无规则运动的动能和分子间相对位置所决定的势能的总和，称物体的内能，简称热量，单位：焦耳 J，卡 cal）

heat engine/battery hybrid 热机/蓄电池复合动力汽车（采用热机/电机复合驱动系统的汽车，= heat engine electric hybrid vehicle，参见 heat engine/electric hybrid drive system）

heat-engined vehicle 热机车辆，装用热机作动力的车辆

heat engine/electric drive train 见 heat engine/electric hybrid drive system

heat engineering 热工学（= thermal engineering）

heat engine/flywheel hybrid 热机/飞轮复合动力汽车（采用热机及储能飞轮作为复合动力的汽车）

heat equivalent of mechanical work 功（的）热当量（指每公斤·米的功相当的热量，$A = \frac{1}{427} kcal/kg \cdot m$）

heater ①加热器，加热装置 ②预热器 ③热源 ④保温装置 ⑤暖气设备，采暖设备

heater air pipe （汽车暖气系统的）暖风管

heater button 预热器按钮

heater control ①暖风操纵件（控制暖风装置工况的操纵件）②加热器控制装置

heater core 暖气芯（电热式暖风系统指电热丝芯；水暖式暖风系统指冷却水热水与气流的散热器式热交换器，亦称 heater radiator）

heater/defroster 加热器-除霜器（简称 H/D）

heater-defroster-air conditioning assembly 加热器-除霜器-空调总成（简称 HDAC）

heater element 加热元件，加温器（= heating element）

heater fan 暖风鼓风机（= heater blower，一般为电动鼓风机。驱动此鼓风机的电动机称暖风电动机 heater motor）

heater flange （柴油机进气歧管）预热器凸缘（指将预热器装在进气歧管上的凸缘；偶见指进气空气的凸缘型预热元件，= preheating element）

heater plug resistor （柴油机等的）预热塞电阻器

heater switch ①加热器开关 ②暖风开关

heater winding 电热丝线圈

heat exchange 热交换

heat exchange cycle 热交换循环
heat exchanger 热交换器（将热量从一种介质传给另一种介质的装置，如：冷却水散热器便是一种将热由冷却水传给空气的热交换器）
heat exchanger core （冷气装置，散热装置等的）热交换器芯
heat expansion 热膨胀（= thermal ex-pansion）
heat fade 热衰退（如：制动器发热而造成的制动效果衰退现象）
heat-fast 耐热的
heat flux ①热流（亦称 heat flow）②热通量 ③热流量（flux of heat）
heat gain 热增益，热的增加量
heat gauge 量热塞，热感应塞，温度感应塞，温度计
heat gradient 热（量）梯度
heating alloy 合金电热丝
heating apparatus 加热器，加热装置，取暖装置，（= heating arrangement, heating device, heating equipment, heating installation, heating unit）
heating area 传热面积，加热面积
heating capacity ①热容量（= heat capacity）②加热能力
heating coil ①加热盘管，加热蛇形管（= heating spiral）②加热线圈
heating coil of cigar(ette) lighter 点烟器加热线圈
heating crack （受）热（龟）裂
heating current 加热电流
heating curve 加热曲线
heating cycle ①加热循环 ②加热周期
heat(ing) effect 热效应，加热作用（= thermal effect）
heating efficiency 加热效率
heating element ①加热元件；发热元件 ②散热片
heat(ing) generator 高频加热器（见 high frequency heating）
heating jacket 预热套，加热套

heating period ①升温期 ②加热持续时间
heating plug 预热塞（见 glow plug）
heating schedule 加热程序
heating space 加热空间，供暖空间
heating surface area 加热表面积
heating system 加热系统，暖气系统
heating torch 气焊枪（= brazing torch）
heating up period （发动机的）升温阶段，热起阶段，升温期，暖机期，热起期（= warming-up period）
heating-value （燃料的）热值，燃烧值（指燃料完全燃烧释放的热量）
heating ventilating and air conditioning (system) 采暖、通风与空调（系统）（简称 HVAC）
heat input 热量输入；输入热量
heat-insulated (ceramic) engine 绝热陶瓷发动机；绝热发动机（无冷却系，采用陶瓷顶活塞，带陶瓷覆盖层的缸套，带陶瓷隔热板的缸盖，陶瓷涂面的气门以及陶瓷涂层的排气歧管及进气孔等，并具有充分回收高温废气能量的装置，其热效率可高达52%）
heat insulation 绝热，隔热（= insulation against heat, thermal insulation）
heat insulator ①绝热材料 ②热绝件
heat interchange 热交换，热量交换
heat leak 热泄漏
heat load(ing) 热负荷
heat localization 热积聚（= heat accu-mulation）
heat loss 热量损失，热损失
heat meter 温度传感器；温度计
heat of combustion 燃烧热
heat of compression 压缩热
heat of evaporation 蒸发热，汽化热
heat of fusion 熔化热，熔解热（= melting heat）
heat of vaporization 汽化热，蒸发热
heat outlet washer 导热垫圈

heat output 热量输出,放热量,放热率

heat passage ①热传导 ②传热通道

heat path 热传导通路,热路

heat penetration 加热深度

heat-producing capability 发热量,热值

heat(-)proof 耐热的,防热的,隔热的,保温的,热稳定的,不传热的;难熔的

heat protecting screen 保温罩

heat prover 废气分析仪,排出气体分析器

heat pump 热泵(广义,包括所有的由高温物体采热和将热授予低温物体的装置)

heat quantity 热量

heat-radiation 热辐射(见 heat emission)

heat radiation pyrometer 热辐射高温计

heat range (火花塞的)热值(亦称 heat rating, heat value,是火花塞的热特性的评价指标,为用一组由小到大的数字来表示的比较值,如:1、2、3、4、5、6、7、8、9、10等,称为热值指数"heat range index",该指数越大,表示火花塞的吸热、传热和散热能力越强,即保持适当的温度,不致因其自身炽热点而引起混合气自点火早燃的能力越强。这样的火花塞称为冷型"cold",反之,热值指数越小,表明上述能力越差,称为热型"hot"。所谓冷型、热型是相对的,决定于火花塞绝缘体裙部的长短、电极的形状和材料等,热型火花塞用于低压缩比、低速、小功率发动机。冷型用于高压缩比、高速大功率发动机)

heat range reserve (火花塞的)热值裕度(指火花塞在不断增加热负荷的情况下,开始产生炽热点火,即达到其炽热点火始点的时间,用曲轴转角表示。其值可作为制造厂设定的点火正时中,不致发生早燃的提前增量)

heat ray 热线,(一般指红外线)

heat recover(y) 热回收

heat-reflecting function of windshield (汽车)风窗玻璃的热反射功能(一般在风窗玻璃夹层中夹有透明的金属氧化物薄膜,可反射肉眼看不到的红外线等,从而降低日晒对车内的影响)

heat regenerator 热交换式回收器,热再生器(= heat accumulator, regenerative heat exchanger)

heat regulator 热量调节器,温度调节器

heat rejection 排热,散热

heat release 热量析出,热量放出

heat release beginning 放热始点(汽缸内燃料着火后的放热始点,一般将放热始点、燃烧始点及着火始点视为同一时刻,以活塞到达止点前、后的曲轴转角表示)

heat release end 放热终点(指汽缸内燃料燃烧放热的终点,一般将放热终点与燃烧终点视为同一时刻,以曲轴转角表示)

heat release rate 放热率(燃料燃烧过程中单位时间或单位曲轴转角内放出的热量,其最大值称放热峰值"heat release peak value")

heat release rate curve 放热规律(曲线)(指描述放热率随时间或曲轴转角变化规律的曲线)

heat removal 热量排除,散热

heat-removing 放热的,除热的

heat requirement 需要的热量

heat-reserve combustion chamber 储热型燃烧室(分开式燃烧室的一种,其副燃烧室为经常保持高温的储热室,燃油喷入主燃烧室后,一部分由经通道进入副储热燃烧室,

遇该室内的高温而首先着火）

heat-resistance 抗热能力，耐热性，热稳定性，高温稳定性（= high temperature stability, resistance to heat）

heat-resistance test 耐热性试验，热稳定性试验

heat resisting steel 耐热钢（在高温下有足够的强度又不起皮的钢）

heat-retaining ①保热的，保温的 ②热保持，蓄热能力

heat-riser ①（进气）预热阀（为一装在排气歧管内的恒温弹簧控制的瓣阀。当发动机温度低时，该阀关闭，发动机排出的热废气被引向加热进气歧管，使进气得到预热，而改善发动机的冷机运转状况。当发动机温度升高后，该阀开启，废气不再流至进气歧管预热通道，亦称 heat riser valve）②（进气）预热套

heatronic molding 高频电热模塑法

heat run 热试（车）；发热试验，耐热试验

heat screen 隔热屏，绝热罩

heat sealing （热塑性塑料的）热封（如：塑料袋等封口）

heat-sensitive 热敏的

heat sensor 温度传感器

heat shield 隔热板，防热层，热屏蔽

heat shock 热冲击

heat shrinking 热缩敲平，热缩平整（工艺）（指用气焊焊炬加热车身金属板件局部凹陷处，并用板件修理用的专用手锤和成型砧垫等，将该凹陷处整平）

heat shrink tubing （汽车电线接头处用的）热缩型保护套

heat sink （通过传导和辐射将热散至大气的）散热装置，散热件（特指防止电子电路系统元器件过热的、带冷却散热片的罩、盖或底板）

heat sink test （发电机整流器二极管的）散热底座测试法（用电阻表通过底座搭铁散热片来测二极管电阻）

heat soak ①热烤，热浸（指长时间受高温作用或长时间处于高温环境中）②（热处理中的长时间加热保温作业）均热（使被加热件热透）

heat soak-back 热回放（零件等在较高的温度环境下吸收的热量在较低的温度下放出的现象）

heat soak-back temperature 热回放温度（参见 heat soak-back）

heat soak losses 见 hot soak losses

heat source 热源

heat spacer （石棉板等）隔热片

heat stability 热稳定性，高温稳定性

heat storage ①蓄热 ②蓄热器

heat stove （排气歧管的）热套（由薄钢板制成的，围在排气歧管外面而在排气歧管外壁与该套之间形成的热空间，其作用为：冷机时 ①从该空间将热空气引进空气滤清器，使空气进入发动机前预热 ②将该热空间内的热空气引入自动阻风门壳，控制其开闭）

heat stress 热应力（在高温作用下，因受热膨胀等原因而生成的内应力）

heat stretch 热拉，加热拉伸

heat test 发热试验，温升试验；加热试验，耐热试验

heat tint 热变色，回火色，氧化色（= oxidation tint）

heat-tolerant electronic control 耐热型电子控制系统

heat transfer 热传递（= transfer of heat, transmission of heat, thermal transmission, 指热从温度高的物体或物体的高温部分传到温度低的物体或物体的低温部分。热传递的方式有三种：传导，对流，辐射）

heat transfer fluid 传热流体（指将热量从系统的一部分传至另一部分的高比热的液体或蒸气）

heat transmission 热传导，传热现象（参见 heat transfer）

heat transport 传热，热传导

heat treatment 热处理（指对金属，主要是对钢材固态加热、保温和冷却以改善其机械性能。钢的热处理分两大类：一是中间热处理或预备热处理，目的是消除上一道工序的某些副作用，如：退火和回火；二是最终热处理，以达到设计性能，如：淬火和回火及表面热处理等）

heat treatment crack 热处理（所产生的）裂纹，淬火裂纹

heat treatment in vacuum 真空热处理（金属零件在真空度为 1.33～0.0001332Pa 的加热室中进行的淬火、退火、化学热处理等）

heat unit ①加热装置 ②热量单位，热单位（= caloric unit, thermal unit，参见 kcal，BTU）③绝热体，热辐射体

heat up time 加热时间

heat utilization ratio 热量利用率（在燃烧过程中某一瞬时放出的热量能转变为机械功的份额）

heat value ①（燃料的）热值（亦称发热量，单位燃料燃烧时释放的热量，= heat of combustion, thermal value，参见 caloric value）② = heat range

heat vulcanization 热硫化（= hot vulcanization）

heat-vulcanized 热补的，热硫化的（= heat cured）

heat wave 热浪，热（辐射）波

heave 鼓起，隆起；举起，提起

heavier-duty 加强型，加重型；繁重工况

heavies [俚] 重型载货汽车

heavily-padded 装有厚软垫的

heavily stressed 高应力的

heaving road 起伏不平的道路

heavy ①重的（指比重大的，质量大的）②重型的（指车辆等，= heavy duty）③（操纵起来）费力的、重的 ④大量的（= of great quantity，指车流等）⑤交通密度大的 ⑥困难的，繁重的 ⑦厚的（漆层等）⑧恶劣的，泥泞的（道路等）

heavy and bulky goods 长大、笨重货物（中国规定长度超过 6m，高度超过 2.7m，宽度超过 2.5m，质量超过 4t 中一个及一个以上条件的货物）

heavy-bodied oil 黏稠机油，高黏度机油

heavy castings 大型铸件

heavy dock 重型船坞，大型检修棚

heavy dump truck 重型自卸汽车（= heavy dumper, heavy tipper）

heavy duty ①重载工况，繁重工况 ②重型的，大功率的（= high duty, severe duty）③（设计能）承受重负荷的，可在恶劣环境下工作的

heavy-duty alternator 重型汽车用交流发电机

heavy-duty deep tyre 重型深纹轮胎

heavy-duty double leaf spring（重型汽车用由正、副两副钢板弹簧组成的）双重钢板弹簧

heavy-duty engine 重型发动机（供繁重工作条件使用的发动机；大功率发动机）

heavy-duty oil 重负荷滑油，重工况润滑油（在苛刻条件下使用的优质滑油的统称。指加有抗氧化腐蚀等添加剂的 MS 级汽油机滑油，DS 级柴油机滑油或加有耐特压添加剂的双曲线齿轮滑油等）

heavy-duty test ①重载试验 ②在重载（恶劣）工作条件下的试验

heavy-duty trailer tow package（主车的）重型挂车拖挂装置

heavy-duty truck [美] 重型载货汽车 [= camion, heavy (-duty) lorry,

heavy goods vehicle, HGV, heavy (motor) truck, heavy wrecker]
heavy-duty type 重型
heavy-duty vehicle 重型车辆 (= heavy vehicle)
heavy ends 重质尾馏分, 重质馏分
heavy foot 重脚快车 (俚, 指重踩加速踏板, 在节气门全开, 发动机全负荷工况下高速行驶)
heavy force fit 重压紧配合
heavy fraction fuel 重馏分燃料
heavy fuel 高黏度燃油, 重质燃油, 重柴油, 重油 (亦称 heavy fuel oil)
heavy-fuel engine 重油发动机
heavy fuel fraction 燃油的重馏分
heavy fuel rotating combustion engine 重油转子发动机, 重油旋转活塞发动机
heavy gas oil 重气体油, 重瓦斯油 (自残油中真空蒸馏出的油, 参见 long residuum)
heavy gauge ①大型量规 ②(板材的)大厚度, 大尺寸 ③(线材的)粗直径
heavy gauge metal (按英国标准线规规定的)厚级板材, 厚度大的金属板材, 厚(金属)板
heavy-going 难以通过的, 很难通行的
heavy grade 陡坡, 大坡度
heavy gradient ①陡坡 ②很大的梯度 (= steep gradient)
heavy ground 难以通行的地形
heavy handled 难以操纵的, 难以控制的, 难以驾驶的
heavy hauler 大吨位载货车, 重型牵引车
heavy hydrocarbon gases 重烃可燃气, 重燃气
heavy in section 大截面的
heavy insulation 加重绝缘, 强化绝缘
heavy load ①重负荷, 重载荷, 重负载 ②(对发动机指)持续高速高输出运转(状态)
heavy lubricating oil 黏稠机油, 高黏度机油; 重润滑油 (比重大于1)
heavy off-road vehicle 重型越野汽车 (中国规定最大总质量大于 13t 且小于或等于 24t)
heavy oil ①重柴油 ②黏稠润滑油, 高黏度机油
heavy partial overhaul 局部大修 (如: 发动机曲轴磨损量低于某规定值, 不拆卸曲轴修理发动机)
heavy pressure 高压(力)
heavy repair 大修 (= big repair)
heavy resurfacing 路面大修, 路面翻修
heavy roughing hammer (车身板件凹陷的)粗敲出重手锤
heavy seal coat (路面)加固的保护层
heavy section ①厚壁断面 ②重型型材
heavy semi-trailer 重型半挂车 (中国规定最大总质量大于 19.5t 且小于或等于 34t)
heavy stain (机油)湮点试验 (一种用专用试纸检查机油状况的方法)
heavy starting duty 恶劣起动工况, 恶劣的起动条件
heavy traction vehicle 重型牵引车
heavy traffic 繁忙的交通 (= dense traffic)
heavy-walled 厚壁的
heavy wares 重型设备, 重型车辆, 重型机械
heavy weight ①沉重的 ②大载重量(的汽车); 自重大(的汽车)
hectare 公顷 (米制面积单位, 1 公顷 = 100 公亩 = 10000m^2 = 2.471 英亩 = 15 市亩 = 90000 市尺^2)
hecto 百 (词头, 代号 h, 10^2)
hectobar 百巴 (压力单位, 代号

hbar, 1hbar = 10^2 bar = $10^7 N/m^2$ ≈ 0.646tonf/in^2 常用于工程界)

hectometre 百米

hectowatt 百瓦(特)

heel ①根部 ②(锥形齿轮的)大端 ③推力轴颈,枢轴 ④凸轮曲线的非凸起部分 ⑤(轮胎)胎踵(见 bead heel)⑥制动蹄的固定销端 ⑦断电器活动触点臂上的摩擦顶块 ⑧尾随,附从;装配;使汽车倾斜

heel bead wire (双钢丝边轮胎)胎边外缘钢丝(第一道钢丝圈)

heel block 垫块,垫板

heel board 踵板 ①指位于轿车底板的后座椅区盖板"seat well"前边缘、与车身等宽的竖立薄钢板横条,用于连接后座椅区盖板与车身底板,并增强二者的强度 = heel plate ②指车身前围板的下部

heel clearance angle 推土铲后角(参见 tool sliding clearance of dozer)

heel contact (锥齿轮啮合的)大端齿接触,齿根接触(齿轮啮合调节不当时产生的一种不正常啮合)

heel dolly 后跟形砧

heel end of tooth (锥齿轮)齿的大端

heel fit 重推配合(指相当于用手掌根推力推入配合。如:将活塞销装入销孔)

heeling 倾斜,偏转

heeling angle 倾斜角

heel of bead 见 bead heel

heel of tooth 齿根面

heel rest 搁脚板

heels 剩余物,残余,渣滓,结瘤,底结

HEF 高能燃料(high energy fuels)

HEGO sensor 加热型废气氧传感器(heated exhaust gases oxygen sensor 的简称)

HEI ①高能点火(见 high energy ignition) ②[美] (汽车排放对人体)健康影响研究所(Health Effect Institute 的简称)

HEI-EST 见 high energy ignition system with electronic spark timing

height adjustable flexible syntheticrubber skirt (气垫车)高度可调的柔性人造橡皮围裙

height-adjustable lumbar support airmat (座椅的高度调式)腰背部支撑气垫

height adjustable steering column 高度可调式转向管柱(指其长度或角度可调,以适应不同驾驶员)

height adjuster (车身)高度调整装置(如:调节扭杆弹簧安装角或调节空气弹簧空气压力以调节车高的装置)

height control ON/OFF switch (电子控制空气悬架系统的)高度控制通/断开关(该开关一般装在汽车后行李舱内,用于接通与断开电源与空气悬架系统电子控制模块间的电路。当对悬架系统进行维修或使用千斤顶举升车身或汽车被牵引时,均应将该开关置于 OFF "断开"位置)

height control sensor (车身高度自动调节系统的车身)控制高度(变化)传感器

height control switch (车身)高度控制开关(装在驾驶室仪表板区,用于选择主动式空气悬架的车身控制高度,分为高"HIGHT"和正常"NORM"两挡)

height-control valve (汽车空气悬架或气液悬架)高度控制阀(= height corrector valve)

height corrector (汽车空气悬架或油气悬架系统的)自动高度调整装置(亦称 height regulator, = automatic leveling control device)

height ga(u)ge 高度规,测高计,高度尺,高度游标卡尺

height hamper pitch control 悬架压缩冲程限位挡块（=bump stop）
height of camber 路拱高度
height of center of gravity above roll axis （汽车）相对于侧倾轴线的重心高度
height of center of mass 质心高度［由轮胎接地面到汽车质心的垂直距离为汽车质心高度；从轮胎接地面到簧上（簧下）质心的垂直距离为簧上（簧下）质心高度］
height of chassis above ground 车架离地高度（在轴距的中央位置，从接地面至车架上平面的距离，多轴车指最前、最后两轴中央）
height of couping face （半挂车）牵引鞍座结合面高度（指处于水平位置的牵引鞍座结合面主车辆支撑平面的距离）
height of drop 下落高度
height of gravitational center （汽车等的）重心高度（从接地面至汽车重心的垂直距离）
height of lift 举升高度，提升高度（=lifting height）
height of roll center （汽车）侧倾中心高度
height of seat of fifth wheel （半挂车牵引车）转盘高度（指转盘主销座中心至地面的距离）
height of suspension displacement limit （汽车）悬架位移极限高度
height of thread 螺纹高度，螺纹牙高
height of tooth 齿高
height of towing attachment （全挂车）牵引装置高度（指球头牵引装置的球头中心距叉销式U型牵引装置两内表面等距的水平面；拖钩式牵引装置的环形拖钩子午线断面等至车辆支撑平面间的距离）
height of valve lift 气门升程
height sensor （电子控制悬架系统中的）高度传感器
height to width ratio 高宽比
Hele-Shaw motor 径向活塞式液压马达
heliambulance 运送伤病员的直升机，直升救护飞机
helibus （作为公共交通工具的）公用直升机
helical ①螺旋线，螺旋面 ②螺旋线的，螺旋状的
helical angle 螺旋角
helical-band friction clutch 平卷簧式摩擦离合器
helical bevel gear 斜齿锥齿轮（指产形冠轮上的齿线是不通过锥顶的直线的锥齿轮）
helical blower 螺旋桨式通风机
helical coil 螺旋形线圈（亦称 helical winding）
helical conveyer 螺旋输送器
helical curve 螺旋曲线，螺旋线
helical cutter 螺齿铣刀
helical duct intake 螺旋进气道进气（指进入发动机汽缸内的空气，经过螺旋进气道的导流作用，在缸内形成涡流的过程）
helical flute 螺旋槽
helical gear 斜齿轮（一般指齿线为螺旋线的斜齿圆柱齿轮，亦称 single helical gear。注意：旧称"螺旋齿轮"一词，已停止使用）
helical gearbox 斜齿轮变速器
helical gearing 斜齿轮传动装置（=screw gearing）
helical gear pair 斜齿轮副（指由两个斜齿圆柱齿轮组成的斜齿圆柱齿轮副）
helical gear pump 斜齿轮泵
helical groove （高压泵柱塞控制喷油量的）螺线切口，螺旋槽（=plug helix, metering helix）
helical line 螺旋线
helically cut waisted worm roller steer-

ing gear 螺旋齿细腰型蜗杆滚轮式转向器（由螺旋齿细腰型蜗杆-滚轮副组成的转向器）

helical pitch 螺矩（①指相邻两螺纹或螺旋线的间距 ②胆甾相液晶内，沿螺旋轴的同向指向矢之间的最短距离）

helical port 螺旋进气道（亦称 helical duct，以一定的螺旋角将进气流引入汽缸，而形成强烈涡流）

helical rack 斜齿条（指齿线是倾斜于齿的运动方向的直线的齿条）

helical spline 螺旋键槽，螺旋花键

helical spline type actuator 螺旋花键式作动器，螺旋花键式执行机构

helical spool 螺旋槽滑阀

helical spring shock absorber 螺旋弹簧减振器

helical staircase 螺旋式楼梯，旋梯

helical surface 螺旋面

helical tooth 斜齿

helical worm gear （螺旋）涡轮

helicar （一种兼有轿车与直升机性能的）轿车型直升机，直升飞行轿车

helicoid ①螺旋面，螺旋体，螺圈 ②螺旋状纹的

helicoidal area 螺旋面积

helicoidal surface 螺旋面

helicoidal toothing 斜齿传动，斜齿啮合

helicoil 见 Helisert②

helicopter 直升机

heliocentric coordinates 螺旋心坐标

Helisert ①螺嵌（螺孔修复套的商品名，为一内、外面均带螺纹的螺套。如：当螺孔滑扣或磨损后，可先扩孔，切去旧螺纹，再切割新螺纹，选用尺寸适当的上述螺套拧入新扩的螺孔中，以代替原螺孔）②螺镶（防止螺纹连接松滑的镶圈，为断面呈菱形的金属丝螺旋形线圈，镶在两螺纹连接件的螺纹之间，将螺纹挤紧防松，亦称 helicoil）

helium 氦（He）

helium-filled bellow 充氦伸缩筒，充氦波纹筒

helium leak test 氦气加压测漏试验

helium-neon laser 氦-氖激光

helix ①螺旋线（螺旋线有圆柱与圆锥螺旋线两种，无特别说明时，helix 指圆柱螺旋线，即：动点沿圆柱面上的一条直母线做等速移动，而该直母线又绕圆柱面的轴线等角速旋转运动时，动点在圆柱面上的运动轨迹，= circular helix）②螺旋状物 ③螺旋状的

helix angle 螺旋角（指圆柱螺旋线或圆锥螺旋线的切线与通过切点的圆柱面直母线所夹的锐角）

helix angle tester 螺旋角检查仪

helix forming method 螺旋成形法（在切齿过程中，被切齿轮固定，圆铣刀盘除在旋转切削运动外，还借助专用凸轮使刀盘沿其轴线做往复运动，此两运动的组合即形成螺旋运动）

helix hand 螺旋方向

helix lead ①螺旋线升程，螺旋线导程（指圆柱或圆锥面上的一条螺旋线与该圆柱或圆锥面的一条直母线的两个相临交点之间的距离）②（柴油机柱塞式喷油泵的柱塞的）螺旋槽导程（指螺旋槽油量控制边缘在柱塞直径一周内沿轴线上升的距离）

helix line 螺旋线

helix of thread 螺纹螺旋线

helmet ①发动机罩；罩盖，防护罩，头盔，安全帽，（电焊）面罩，安全钢盔 ②给…装上防护装置

helmet connector （将锥形接线柱安装到蓄电池上的）盔状接头（亦称 helmet lug）

helmet shield 焊工面盔，工作帽，安全帽

HELP bumper 高能充气保险杠（high energy level pneumatic bumper 的简称）

HELP equipment 公路（事故）紧急无线电定位图示设备（Highway Emergency Locating Plan equipment 的简称）

helper ①副手，助手②辅助机构

helper spring 副钢板弹簧（= auxiliary spring，亦称 helper leaf，仅在重载下，主钢板弹簧压到一定程度时起作用）

helper spring stop bracket 副钢板弹簧限位托架

hemi ［俚］①半球形缸盖②半球形燃烧室缸盖（hemispherical head 的简称）③半球形燃烧室式发动机（见 hemihead engine②）④（泛指各种）半球形物

hemi-anechoic chamber 半消声室（指地板仍会反射声波的消声室，亦称 semi-anechoic chamber）

hemihead engine ①半球形缸盖发动机②半球形燃烧室发动机

hemisphere ①半球，半球形②（活动的）范围，领域

hemispheric(al) 半球面状的，半球状的

hemispherical combustion chamber 半球形燃烧室（顶置气门汽油机的一种燃烧室，横剖面呈半球形，由汽缸盖上的凹坑，配合活塞的凸顶形成，火花塞居中，进排气门左、右倾斜布置，两气门轴线夹角一般在 60°～75°）

hemispherical-head cylinder 半球形燃烧室缸盖汽缸（参见 dome head cylinder）

hemispherical lens 半球形透镜

HEMS 家庭能源管理系统（home energy management system 的简称，其管理项目之一是由无线网络控制，使用电网和太阳能发电提供的家用电源给电动汽车充电）

H engine H 形发动机（两对水平对置式汽缸共用一根中央输出曲轴的发动机）

henry 亨（利）［国际单位制的电感单位，代号 H，在电路中，电流变化率为每秒 1A（1A/S）时，产生的感应电动势为 1V，$e = -L\dfrac{di}{dt}$，e 为感应电动势（V）；L 为电感（H）；$\dfrac{di}{dt}$ 电流变化率，所以 1H = 1V · S/A，参见 inductance coefficient］

Henry Ford 亨利·福特（美国福特汽车公司的创始人，参见 Ford）

Henry meter 亨利计，电感计

hen tracking 微小的鸡爪形裂纹（如：巴氏合金表面的细小裂痕）

heptamethylnonane α-甲基萘

heptane 庚烷（C_7H_{16}，有 9 种异构体）

heritage （历史悠久的企业、厂家、院校等的）传统和特色

hermaphrodite calipers ①（盘式制动器）单边卡钳②定心划规

hermetic(al) 密封的，气密的，不透气的，密闭式的（= hermetically sealed）

herringbone 人字形的

herringbone frame 中央独梁半承载式车架（见 backbone frame）

herringbone gear 人字齿轮（亦称 V-toothed gear, double helical gear）

herringbone tooth 人字齿（亦称 double helical tooth）

hertz 赫（兹）（国际单位制的频率单位，代号 Hz，即每秒 1 个循环，$1Hz = s^{-1}$，参见 frequency）

Hertz contact 赫氏点接触（指齿轮、滚动轴承等摩擦副，在承受负荷时，使接触部分的材料变形，形成很小的接触面，同时产生接触应

力，这时的接触形式称为赫氏点接触，其变形称为 Hertz deflection，产生的应力称为 Hertz stress)
Hertz deflection （弧面接触应力）赫氏弹性变形（参见 Hertz contact)
Hertz stress 赫氏点接触应力（见 Hertz contact)
hesitate 犹豫
hesitation ①（汽车）加速停滞（指踩加速踏板时，汽车不能圆滑加速，且陷入熄火或失速状态，原因多为燃油系堵塞或点火时刻失调）②（汽车行驶时的）喘抖现象③（发动机断续缺火所产生的）喘气现象
Hesselman engine 赫色尔曼发动机（吸入空气，在压缩冲程后半期喷射燃油，然后用电火花点火，为瑞典 K. T. E. Hesselman 所发明）
hessian cloth 黄麻布（座位铺装用）
heterodox 不合于公认标准的，非正统的，异端的
heterogeneity ①杂质，异质，异成分 ②不均匀性，非均匀性，不纯一性，多相性；杂拼性，复杂性
heterogeneous 不均匀的，非均质的，异质的，各种成分构成的，多相的
heterogeneous population （统计研究对象的）不同类型总数
heterogeneous strain 非均匀应变
heteropolar step motor 异极式步进电动机，亦称 polarized magnetic circuit step by step motor 极化磁路步进电动机，是步进电机应用最广者）
HEUI 电子控制液压喷油系统（Hydraulic Electric Unit Injector 的简称，美国卡特皮勒公司共用储油歧管型高压喷油系统的商品名）
heuristic approach （计算机解题的）探索接近法
hexadecimal system 16 进制（base 16 system)

hexafluorobenzene 六氟苯
hexagon 六角形，六边形，六角体
hexagon(al) collar 六角形夹套〔套在螺钉起子上，以便用扳手卡住该夹套转动，增加转矩，一般用来拧出锈死或卡死的紧螺钉，亦称 hexagon(al) bolster〕
hexahedral 六面的，六面体的
hexane 乙烷（C_6H_{14})（汽油为多种碳氢化合物的混合液，但常以乙烷代表其成分，有 5 种异构体）
hexane emission 乙烷排出量；含乙烷有害排出物
hex bolt 六角头螺栓
H Exch 热交换器（heat exchanger 的简称）
hex drive tool 六方螺母旋具（= hex-nut driver)
hex key 六角键
Hex-socket head bolt 内六角圆柱头螺栓（= hexagonal-socket cylindrical-head bolt)
hex washer 六角（形）垫圈（片），六方垫圈
hex-washer head screw 六方头带垫螺钉，带垫六角头螺钉（垫圈与螺钉的六角头部制成一体）
hex wrench 六角扳手，六方扳手
hexyl alcohol 乙醇
HF ①高频（high frequency 的简称）②氟化氢（hydrogen fluoride 的简称）
HFC 高速风扇控制器（high-speed fan controller 的简称）
HFC134a 氢碳氟冷媒（对大气臭氧层无破坏作用的汽车空调系统用冷媒，分子式 CH_2FCF_3，沸点 $-26.3℃$，通常用 refrigerant 的第 1 个字母 R 代替 HFC，简称 R134a)
HFCV 氢燃料电池车辆（hydrogen fuel-cell vehicle 的简称）
HFE 人类工程学，人体因素工程学（human factor engineering 的简称）

HFEDS [美] 公路行驶燃油经济性测试程序（Highway Fuel Economy Driving Schedule 的简称）

HFET 公路燃油经济性试验法，分路行驶油耗测定法（Highway Fuel Economy Test 的简称）

HFID 加热式氢火焰离子化检验仪（heated flame ionization detector 的简称，= heated flame ionization analyzer）

HFM air flow sensor 热膜式空气流量传感器（HFM 为 hot-film-mass 的简称）

HFP （电子汽油喷射系统中使用的）高速油泵（high speed fuel pump 的简称）

HFRR 高频往复试验机（high-frequency reciprocating rig 的简称，柴油润滑性能的标准测试设备）

h. f. s 电暖式前座椅（heated front seat 的简称，多在广告宣传中使用）

HF welding 高频电焊（high frequency welding 的简称）

Hg ①汞，水银（mercury）②气压计的水银柱

H-girder 工字梁

HGV 重型货运汽车，大件货物运输车（heavy goods vehicle 的简称）

HGV driving licence 重型货车驾驶证，重型货车驾驶执照（HGV 为 heavy goods vehicle 的简称）

H（h） ①速度等级为"H"的轮胎（字母 H 标示胎侧，表示用于轮辋直径为 12in 时该轮胎最高设计车速为 195km/h，用于轮辋直径为 13in 以上时该轮胎最高设计车速为 130km/h，见 speed rating）②焓（enthalpy，heat content）③硬度（hardness）④水头，压头，落差（head）⑤高度（height，对轮胎，指其断面高度）⑥亨（电感单位 henry）⑦小时（hour）⑧氢（hydrogen）⑨磁场强度（magnetic field intensity）

HHGCB [美] 家用商品运输局（Household Goods Carrier Bureau 的简称）

HHS 见 hill hold system

HHV （燃料的）高热值（high heating value 的简称）

hiatus ①间断，中断②停滞

HIC ①（汽车碰撞事故中乘员的）头部损伤指数（head injury criteria 的简称，$= [1/(t_2 - t_1) \int_{t_1}^{t_2} a \cdot \mathrm{d}t]^{2.5} (t_2 - t_1)$，式中：$a$—试验假人头部质心处合成加速度；$t_1$，$t_2$—使 HIC 计算结果达到最大值的碰撞过程中的两个时刻，单位 s，HIC 值不应超过 1000）②（发动机）高温怠速空气补偿阀（参见 hot idle compensator）③混合集成电路（hybrid integrated circuit 的简称）

HICAS （日产公司）四轮转向系统（商品名，High capacity Active Controled Suspention 的简称，实际上是指 20 世纪 80 年代开发的电子控制四轮转向系统，其改进型称 super HICAS）

HIC Igniter Unit 混合集成电路点火器总成（hybrid integrated circuit igniter unit，见 hybrid integrated circuit 及 igniter）

HID ①高强度放电（high-intensity discharge 的简称）②氦电离检测器（helium ionization detector 的简称）

hidden 潜在的，隐藏的

hidden switch 暗开关（隐蔽式防盗开关）

hidden wiper 隐式刮水器（其停止位置低于正常可见区，故名，亦称 hideway wiper）

HID driving lamp （汽车的）高强度放电行车灯（HID 为 high-intensity discharge 的简称，菲利普公司氙气灯的商品名）

hide covering （座椅的）蒙皮，皮质蒙套

HID lamp 高强度放电灯（指水银蒸汽、卤素、高压钠灯等，high-intensity discharge lamp 的简称）

HIDS ［日本］本田智能驾驶员支援系统（Honda Intelligent Drive Support System 的简称，由协助驾驶员保持行车路线的车道保持支援系统和智能公路巡行控制系统中车间距离保持支援系统两部分组成，见 LKAS 和 IHCC）

hierarchical ①分级的（等级制的）②体系的（谱系的）③分层的（层次的）

hierarchical network （汽车电子控制系统的）分层网络（用专门设计的不同层次的控制模块执行各层次的处理和控制功能的主从网络系统，见 master/slave system）

hierarchy 科学分类（科，目等），谱系

hierarchy of types 类型谱系

HIF carburettor 水平整体浮子室式化油器（horizontal integral float carburettor 的简称，可变喉管化油器的一种，见 SU carburettor）

hi-fi 高保真度（high fidelity 的简称）

hi flow ceramic ball bearing turbo 高流量球轴承式陶瓷涡轮增压器（采用球轴承减少摩擦阻力，陶瓷合金减少转动惯量）

high 高的，高度的，高级的，高等的，高超的；高音的，尖锐的；高含量的；高色调的；强烈的，重大的

high-accident location 交通事故多发地点（参见 traffic black spot）

high accumulator （自动变速器行星齿轮机构液压系内的）离合器控制液压储能减振器（见 accumulator）

high-adhesion rubber 高附着力橡胶

high-alloy steel 高合金钢

high-altitude 高海拔的，高原地区用的

high altitude compensation sensor （海拔）高度补偿传感器［利用压力电阻效应"piezoresistance"将大气压（绝对压力）转变为电信号输出，以测定海拔高度。在发动机电子控制系统中用于修正因吸入空气的密度随海拔高度变化而产生的空燃料比误差］

high altitude compensator 海拔高度补偿装置（简称 HAC，随海拔高度变化修正空燃比的自动装置）

high angle 大角度（一般指接近90°的角度）

high-angle joint 大偏角万向节

high back chair 高靠背椅（一般指头枕与靠背合成一起的座椅）

high-ball ［俚］①（汽车）全速行驶 ②使汽车全速行驶的信号

high beam ［美］远光（= main bean，参见 long distance light）

high beam headlamp 远光前照灯（= distance headlamp，指四灯制装于内侧的一对远光单光束灯）

high-beam headlight indicator 前照灯远光指示器，前照灯远光指示灯（= headlight main-beam indicator, blue control lamp, beam indicator lamp，指装在仪表板上指示"远光灯开着"的小指示灯）

high blower engine 高增压发动机

high build filler （喷）厚底漆（以遮盖板件上的小凹陷）

high build galvanizing 厚层镀锌（工艺）

high burr （电机换向器表面呈）锯齿形磨损

high calorific value 高热值（见 higher heating value）

high camber ①大挠度，大拱度 ②大外倾角

high-camshaft engine 见 HC engine

high-capacity 大容量的；高生产率的，大载质量的；大功率的；高通行能力的

High Capacity Mobile Telephone System 大容量车用电话系统（美国电话和电报公司提供的一种较廉价的汽车用电话系统，简称 HCMTS）

high-capacity starter motor 高能起动电动机，高能起动机

high-capacity tyre 重型轮胎，高载重轮胎

high-carbon 高含碳量的，高碳的

high-carbon steel 高碳钢（简称 HCS，指含碳量 > 0.60% 的优质碳素结构钢，热处理后具有高的强度和良好的弹性，主要用于制造各种小型弹簧件，简称 high steel）

high centre rim （用于 CTS 车轮系统的）高中心轮辋（轮辋中心向外鼓起）

high chrome stainless steel 高铬不锈钢

high-chromium irons 高铬铁合金（无石墨铸铁，含有 15%~35% 铬，可耐 1 050℃ 的高温，同时耐磨耐腐蚀）

high-class 优质的，优等的，高质量的，高级的，高精度级的

high-class fit 一级精度配合

high-clearance carrier 离地间隙大的运输车

high-compression engine 高压缩比发动机

high-compression fast burn combustion system 高压缩比快速燃烧系统（指为了降低排放和油耗，采用稀混合气的一种燃烧系统，简称 HCFB system）

high-control (led) 高度可控的，高度可调的

high coolant temperature alarm system （发动机）冷却水高温警报系统（当水温传感器测得冷却水温超过某规定值时，即点亮警报灯并接通蜂鸣器，某些车辆还具有在发出上述警报 30~60s 后自动切断燃油供给停机的功能，称 automatic engine shutdown）

high-copper 高含铜量的

high crown panel 高拱曲板（指拱曲度很高的拱形板件）

high cruise 高速巡行（一般指发动机转速在 2500r/min 以上的车速下稳定运行）

high data transmission rate EI system 高数据传输率电子点火系统（亦称 high signaling rate EI system，其中，EI 为 electronic ignition 的简称，见 low data transmission rate EI system）

high deck body （货车的）高台货箱（常规的后置货箱，相对低台货箱而言）

high-definition television 高清晰度电视

high-density assembly 高密度装配

high-density polyethylene 高密度聚乙烯（一种汽车上使用的热塑性塑料，简称 HDPE，具有足够的强度，耐腐蚀，长期稳定性良好，质量轻，多用于制作油箱、保险杠等吹塑成型件）

high-drag body 空气阻力大的车身

high-dump wagon 高位倾卸车身

high duty 重负荷的（参见 heavy duty）

high-duty-cycle switching circuit ①高通-断循环率开关电路（指单位时间内接通-断开次数多的开关电路，如：闪光灯开关电路）②高占空比开关电路

high efficiency 高效率；高生产效率

high-end 高端的（最高一级的）

high-end coach 后部地板抬升成高台状的长车身大客车（一般指车身长 10m 以上，后部抬升，以提供后置式发动机的安装空间）

high-energy battery 高能（蓄）电池

（指供电动汽车用的新型电池，"高能"指比能量高，"高"也是相对的，一般，比能量达140w·h/kg，循环次数达800次才能算高能电池，种类繁多，如：钠硫电池，锌空气电池，各种燃料电池等）

high-energy coil 高能点火线圈［泛指各种可产生高的点火电压并且（或者）具有高的能量转换率的点火线圈］

high-energy fuel 高能燃料（简称HEF）

high-energy-ignition system 高能点火系统（简称HEI，最初为一种当时新型点火系的商品名，以后泛指可提供比旧式点火系统高的点火能量，即可提供大电流的高压点火脉冲的新型点火系统。"高"是一种相对概念，20世纪70年代的高能点火系统已经采用电子控制模块和电磁传感器式点火信号发生装置，但仍采用机械式点火提前装置，因而在20世纪80年代初70年代末开始出现电子点火提前控制时，还将由电子控制点火提前的高能点火系统专门叫作 high energy ignition system with electronic spark timing, 简称HEI-EST，到20世纪80年代中期至90年代，电子点火提前控制已相当普及，只要是电子点火系统"electronic ignition system"便全具有电子控制点火提前功能，已无须加以说明。20世纪90年代至今，电子控制点火已成为由动力控制模块PCM控制的发动机综合控制系统的一个子系统或一项控制功能）

high-energy level pneumatic bumper 高能级充气保险杠（简称HELP bumper）

high-energy plasma jet sparking plug 高能等离子流火花塞（见plasma jet ignition system）

high-energy rate forming （金属加工）高能快速成型法（如：爆炸成型，电水锤成型等，参见electro-hydraulic forming）

higher gangway width in driver's door 驾驶员门的通道宽大

higher heating value （燃料的）高热值（燃料燃烧生成的产物中的H_2O为液态时，其所释放的热量称高热值，= high heating value，简称HHV）

higher hydrocarbon 高分子烃

Highest Useful Compression Ratio 最高有用压缩比（Ricardo提出的一个术语，指特定燃料，在特定发动机内的可用压缩比的极限，达到此极限值后，若压缩比进一步提高，则产生突爆的损失，将超过提高压缩比之所得，简称HUCR）

high fidelity ①高度保真，高保真度，高度传真性 ②高度保真的（简称hi-fi）

high field (electron) emission 高电场（电子）发射

high finish 高精密的精整加工

high flash oil 高闪点机油（见flash point）

high flex cord ①高软索 ②高柔性帘线

high floor height （客车的）高地板高度（指通道两旁高地板上平面至通道地板上平面间的距离）

high flying highway 高架公路

high (-) frequency 高频（的）（3000~30000Hz，简称HF）

high-frequency heating 高频电流感应加热（指利用电涡流损耗和磁滞损耗加热工件的表层，多用于曲轴、凸轮轴、齿轮等的表面淬火作业）

high-frequency performance （晶体管等的）高频特性，高频性能

high-frequency pulsations 高频脉动

high-frequency semiconductor 高频

半导体（元器件），射频半导体（元器件）（指用于1GHz左右的高频系统的半导体元器件，如汽车移动通信和近距离障碍探测系统内使用的半导体元器件等）

high-frequency welding 高频焊接（简称 h. f. welding，亦称 dielectric bonding "高频黏焊"）

high gate cargo body （货车的）高栏板货箱

high gear ①高挡（指五挡变速器的4、5挡）②超速挡（= high range over drive gear, overs peed drive，指速比低于1 如：0.7,0.8 的挡位）

high-gear clutch 高速挡离合器

high-geared operation ①（汽车）挂高速挡行驶 ②（泛指）大速比传动

high-gloss black 强光泽的深黑色涂料（油漆，颜料等）；光亮深黑色

high-grade ①高级（的），优等（的），优质（的），高品位（的）②高质量（的），高坡度（的），陡坡

high heating value （燃料）高热值（= gross calorific value, high calorific value, gross heating value, total heating value, 见 higher heating value）

high heat rating type spark plug 高热值型火花塞（见 cold type spark plug）

high-humidity 高湿度的

high hysteresis tread 高阻滞力轮胎花纹

high impact polystyrene 耐高冲击力聚苯乙烯（简称 HI polystyrene）

high-impedance 高阻抗（的）

high-impedance digital volt-ohmmeter 高阻抗数字式电压-电阻表（简称 DVOM，标准电压电阻表的输入阻抗仅 10kΩ/V 左右，而 DVOM 则高达 10MΩ/V，其测量精度高，且适应于电阻高，但电压和电流却很低的电路）

high intensity (gas) discharge lamp 高亮度气体放电灯［简称 HID lamp，指水银蒸气，金属卤化物和高、低压钠蒸气灯等每瓦所产生的流明量（lm/w）比白炽灯高4倍以上的高亮度低能耗灯］

high intensity illumination system 高亮度照明系统

high intensity zone （前照灯灯光照射的）高亮度区，光斑的亮区

high-knock rating gasoline 高辛烷值汽油（= high octane gasoline）

high-land 丘陵地带，高地

high-lead down lifter （气门的）高速回位（液压）挺杆，高速回降（液压）挺杆

high-level delivery tipping trailer （带有货台举升装置，向高处自卸货物的）高位送货自卸挂车

high level frame 高架式车架，高车架

high level input current 高电平输入电流（对输入端施加高电平时，通过该输入端的电流）

high-level input voltage 高电平输入电压［用来表示二进制变量的两个值域中较高正值（或较高负值）的输入电压］

high-level language program 高级语言程序（指通用语言程序，如：ALGOL, COBOL, COGO, FORTRAN, PL/1, SIMSCRIPT 等都是高级语言）

high level output current 高电平输出电流（在规定输入条件下，使输出端处于高电平时通过该输出端的电流）

high level output voltage 高电平输出电压（在规定输入条件下，输出端处于高电平时的电压）

high level to low level propagation time 高电平到低电平传输时间（指输出向低电平变化时，输入脉

冲与输出脉冲上规定参考点之间的时间间隔）

high level to low level transition time 高电平到低电平转换时间（输出向低电平变化时，输入脉冲与输出脉冲上规定参考点之间的时间间隔）

high-level ventilation 高效的通风，良好的通风

high-lift air suspension axle （重型多轴载货汽车可变轴距的）可提升式空气悬挂车桥

high-lift cam 高升程凸轮（供赛车发动机用，以提高气门升程）

high-lift loader 具有高举升高度的装载机

high lift van 车厢举升式厢式货车（如：由地面向飞机客舱送货等而将车厢升至所需高度的厢式货车）

highlight ①重点，要点 ②珍闻 ③强光，辉亮部分，高光

highlight control （车身表面的）辉光控制，辉亮控制（保证车身表面的各个视面均能反射比例均匀的强光）

highlight line （车身板件大样图等的）辉光控制校核线（与车顶线等基准线成30°、45°、60°角的车身凸曲面切线，用以校核该凸曲表面是否符合辉光控制的要求，参见 highlight control，highlight method）

highlight method （车身外壳三维表面光滑度的）辉光线校核法（一组成不同角度但通过同一条线的平面切割该三维表面，这组平面与三维表面的相交线应成为一组平滑的曲线）

high-light-to-low-light ratio （明暗光线的）反差比（= contrast ratio）

high limit 高限，上限

high limit of size 上限尺寸

high limit of tolerance 上限公差

high load capacity solid tyre 高负荷实心胎（指负荷能力高于同规格橡胶实心胎的其他弹性材料实心胎）

high load enrich device （混合气）大负荷加浓装置

high-loader trailer 高货台挂车

high-load operation 高负荷运行，大负荷运转

high/low range gearbox 高/低挡区变速器（指主变速器前方或后方加装的具有高、低两挡的副变速器，可将主变速器挡位增加一倍）

high low type 垂直式

high-lug wide section pneumatic tire 深花纹宽断面充气轮胎

highly-mechanized 高度机械化的

highly oxidized 严重氧化的

highly polished 高级抛光的

highly volatile 高挥发性的，易挥发的

high mag 高电压永磁发电机（= high voltage magneto）

high manganese steel 高锰钢

high MAP 高进气歧管绝对压力（high manifold absolute pressure 的简称，指节气门全开或接近全开时，进气歧管真空度在 -2inHg 左右，此时其压力最高，接近大气压力，见 low MAP）

High Mecha Twin Cam （日本丰田公司的）无间隙齿轮传动双顶置式凸轮轴系统（商品名）

high mica ①高级云母，优质云母 ②电枢等的绝缘云母片过高（需要改整）

high-mirror finish 镜面状精加工，镜面抛光（= mirrorlike finish，mirror finishing）

high-mobility multipurpose wheeled vehicle 高机动性多用途轮式车辆（简称HMMWV）

high-mortality parts ①易损零件 ②极易导致整体破损或失去工作能力的致命性部件

high mounted brake light 高位制动

灯（指装在汽车后窗玻璃中部、上边缘或车身后围压流板的后边缘内第三制动灯，其安装位置高于常规制动灯，故名，亦称 high-mounted stop lamp）

high-mount interchange light 立体交叉高空照明

high nut 厚螺母

high occupancy vehicle 多乘客汽车（简称 HOV，指在一辆车中有多名乘客的汽车，如：公共汽车，合乘的小轿车，参见 occupancy）

high occupancy vehicle lane 高占有率车道

high octane gasoline 高辛烷值汽油（指研究法辛烷值在 95 以上的车用汽油）

high octane number component （燃油的）高辛烷值成分，高辛烷值组分

high-octane rating 高辛烷值

high-output engine 大功率发动机

high-pass 高通的（简称 hp）

high-pass filter 高通滤波器（频率高于基准频率的全部信号都可自由通过）

high penetration resistance （轮胎等的）高抗穿透性，高抗穿透能力（简称 HPR）

high performance capacitor type rechargeable storage device 高性能电容器型可再充电储能装置

high-performance header 高性能排气歧管（相对于常规铸铁排气歧管而言，指由铜管焊接而成的排气歧管，无急转弯，排气通道流畅平顺，虽强度较低，成本较高，但质量轻，还可省去常规排气歧管后面安装的排气总管）

high-performance metal-oxide-silicon device 高效金属氧化物硅半导体器件（简称 HMOS）

high polishing 镜面抛光

high potential 高电压（的），高位能（的）

high-power test （发动机在最大功率工况下的试验）大负荷试验，大功率试验

high-precision 高精度的，高度精密的

high-pressure car washer ①高压汽车清洗设备 ②高压街道清洗车

high pressure-charging （发动机进气增压技术中的）高增压（指增压压力 p_b 大于 0.25 MPa，小于 0.35 MPa 的增压）

high-pressure cut-out switch （车用空调系统的）高压断开开关（位于空调系统的高压侧，当制冷剂压力过高时，该开关断开压缩机离合器）

high pressure diesel type nozzle 高压柴油机用喷油嘴（一种用于柴油转子发动机燃油喷射的喷油装置）

high-pressure hot water jetting and washing machine 高压热水冲洗机

high-pressure hydrogen fuel cell vehicle 高压氢（350MPa）型燃料电池车

high pressure low flow system 高压低风量（空冷）装置；高压低流量系统

high pressure moulding 高压模制法（压力约为 980kPa 或更大）

high-pressure pump 高压泵

high-pressure relief valve 高压安全阀（一般装于液压或气压系统的高压侧，当压力超过某规定值时，该阀开启，使压力恢复正常，以保护系统免受过高压力造成的损坏）

high-pressure sewer flushing vehicle 高压污水管道冲洗车（装备有水罐、高压水泵、管路系统、卷管器和操纵装置，用于清理地下管道沉积物，亦可清洗机械表面）

high-pressure sodium lamp 高压钠（气）灯

high-pressure stage 高压级

high pressure turbo-charger 高压涡轮增压器（二级增压系统中的第二级增压器，由低压增压器传递来的空气被压缩至增压压力）

high pressure tyre 高压轮胎

high priced car 高价车

high-production 高生产率的

high-production engine 大功率发动机（=high-power engine）

high-quality 高质量的，上等的，优质的

high range ①大比例，大刻度，高灵敏度量程 ②（二进制信号的）高值域［二进制信号最高正（或负）电平范围，亦称 H—值域，该值域内的任意电平称 H—level "H 电平"或"高电平"］

high range lateral acceleration handling maneuver （汽车的）高离心加速转向，高横向加速转向（离心加速度超过 0.5g 的转向动作，参见 handling maneuver）

high range overgear 超速挡（= over drive gear）

high rate discharge tester （蓄电池）高放电率放电试验器（亦称 cell tester, excel tester, 在强电流放电下，测定蓄电池的电压降，借以简单推算起动机的起动转矩）

high ratio compact chamber 高压缩比紧凑型燃烧室（简称 HRCC）

high-reduction drive （汽车的）高降速比驱动，低速挡驱动

high-res 高分辨率的（high-resolution 的简称）

high-resistance 高阻的，高阻力的

high resolution 高清晰度，高分辨能力，高分解能力，高分辨率（= fine resolution）

high-resolution screen 高分辨率显示屏

high-response servo valve type hydraulic suspension 高速响应伺服阀型液压悬架

high-revolving 高转速的，高速的

high revs 高速（high revolutions 的简称，一般指发动机或其他旋转机械高速运转）

high-rise manifold 高位进气歧管（指安装位置比标准型高出发动机许多的进气歧管，以改善供油角）

high-road 公路干线，交通要道（= highway）

high roof body 高顶式车身

high-safety glazing 高安全度风窗玻璃

high-selective 高选择性的

high-sensitive 高灵敏的

high servo 高速加力，高速助力

high shoulder （弯道外侧）超高路肩

high-side ①空调系统的高压侧（指压缩机与膨胀阀或节流管之间，包括冷凝器的区段）②（泛指）各种高压、高速、高温、高载等区域

high-sided truck 高栏板货车

high side switching （汽车灯具的）高位开关电路（指电灯接在晶体管开关器件与共用搭铁之间，见 low side switching）

high-silicon cast irons 高硅铸铁（含硅 14%～17%）

high silicon molybdenum ferritic nodularcast iron 高硅钼铁素体球墨铸铁（耐高温，且在高温下膨胀小，多用于铸造排气歧管）

high-silicon piston 高硅铝合金活塞

high solid lacquer 速干漆，快干漆，硬漆（树脂等不挥发成分较多，光泽耐久）

high-sounding 高音的

high-speed-brake testing （汽车的）高速制动试验

high-speed camera 高速照相机

high-speed cinematography 高速电影摄影

high-speed circuit ①高速系;高速环路 ②(化油器)主供油系(= main metering system)

high-speed clutch 高速离合器;高速挡离合器,高速挡接合器

high-speed crash 高速碰撞

high-speed cruising 高速巡航

high-speed diesel engine 高速柴油机(一般指曲轴转速 $n > 1000\text{r/min}$,或活塞平均速度 $V_\text{m} > 9\text{m/s}$ 以上的柴油机)

high-speed divided highway 高速分隔带公路(有分隔带的高速公路)

high-speed energy wheel 高速储能飞轮

high speed expressway 高级快速公路(标准较高,大部分采用立体交叉)

high-speed film 高速影片

high-speed fuses 高速熔丝

high-speed governor 高速限速器(= maximum-speed governor)

high speed jet 主喷嘴,(化油器)主量孔(= main jet)

high speed machine tool 高速机床

high speed motion picture study 高速电影研究法(利用高速电影摄影,研究瞬间发生的现象等)

high speed needle 高速油针

high-speed operation 高速运转,在高速工况下工作

high-speed oscilloscope 高速扫描示波器

high-speed oval 汽车高速试验用的椭圆形跑道

high-speed passing 高速超车

high speed performance test 高速性能试验(在高速条件下,对性能进行的考核试验,如:轮胎的高速性能试验指在高速试验机上考核轮胎的高速耐久性)

high-speed photography 高速摄影术

high-speed plunger tire test (试验台加载)柱塞高速加载下的轮胎试验

high speed proving ground (汽车)高速性能试验场,高速性能测试基地

high-speed 4×4 radial tire 高速四轮驱动子午胎

high speed reverse 高速倒挡

high-speed score test 齿轮轮齿的高速擦伤试验

high-speed shimmy 高速摆振(转向轮在较高的车速 50~60km/h 下产生的强迫振动,见 shimmy)

high-speed steel 高速钢(指加有钨、铬、钒等元素的耐热合金钢,多用于制作高速切削工具)

high speed test circuit 高速试验用环形路道,高速试车环道

high-speed tire 高速轮胎(赛车用轮胎)

high speed tool steel 高速工具钢

high speed track (汽车)高速试验跑道

high-speed tractor 高速拖拉机;高速牵引车

high-speed traffic 高速交通(= express traffic)

high splitter 副变速器高挡

high spot 凸起点,突出部分

high stake rack truck 高栅栏货台货车,高栅柱货箱货车

high steel 硬钢,高碳钢(= high carbon steel)

high-stepping driver 爱开快车的驾驶员

high stiffness body 高刚度车身(具有极高的抗扭曲、弯曲、冲击强度的车身)

high-strain-rate 高应变率的

high-street 大街,主街道(= main street)

high strength low alloy steel 高强度

低合金钢(简称 HSLA steel, high-strength steel)

high strength structural adhesion 高强度结构胶

high stress environment (产生)高应力(的)环境

high-sulphur 高含硫量的,高硫的

high swirl port 强涡流进气孔(进气管走向稍呈螺旋,使进气冲程时进入缸内的混合气绕燃烧室圆周方向形成涡流,同时在进气孔下缘加有导流边,以增强这种涡流效果,简称 HSP)

high-talc 滑石;云母

high-tech 高科技的

high-temperature alloy 耐热合金

high-temperature circulation test (橡胶油管等的)高温运行试验,高温老化试验(在试样中,通入高温、高压油流,经过长时间的运行后,用压力法试验油管是否渗漏,用绕在心轴上的办法,观察油管表面有无裂纹,以确定其老化程度)

high-temperature detergency 在高温下(润滑油)的净化作用

high temperature flame ionization analyzer 高温火焰电离分析仪

high-temperature sludge 高温形成的机油氧化沉淀物

high-temperature stability 高温稳定性,耐高温特性

high temperature tempering 高温回火(加热至 500~650℃ 所进行的回火)

high-tensile 高抗拉强度的

high tension ①高(电)压 ②高压的(亦写作 high-tension,多用于说明点火系的高压电、高压线等)

high-tension circuit 高压电路

high-tension coil 高压线圈(点火线圈中向火花塞提供点火高压的次级绕组;点火线圈)

high-tension current 高压电(流)[= high-voltage current, 如:汽车上一般指点火线圈产生的高电压,电流值小的(数 mA)点火高压电流]

high tension line 高压线(= high tension lead)

high tension side 高压侧,次级侧(如:点火系的次级侧,变压器的高压侧等)

high tension steel 高强度钢

high tension terminal 高压接线头

high-test 经过严格试验的,适应高要求的

high-theft vehicle 防盗性好的车辆

high tilt cab tractor with sleeper 带卧铺的可向上翻起式驾驶室牵引车

high-tin babbit alloy 高锡巴氏合金(锡 83%~89%)

high torque (capacity) belt CVT (供 V 型 3.0~3.5l 发动机用的)大转矩(容量)型钢带无级变速器(见 CVT)

high torque drive 大转矩驱动,大转矩传动(简称 HTD)

high torque low-speed test (发动机)在低转速大转矩工况下的试验

high torque rise (发动机)提高转矩装置(如:柴油机的废气涡轮增压器等)

high-traction differential 高附着力型差速器(指锁紧系数和转矩分配系数大的防滑差速器。当一侧车轮滑转时,可通过强制锁死或自锁机构大幅度地增加另一侧未滑转的车轮的转矩,以充分利用另一侧路面的附着力)

hight speed idle gear (双级减速主传动的)高速(挡)中介齿轮

high-turbulence combustion chamber 强涡流燃烧室(简称 HTCC)

high vacuum 高真空(= perfect vacuum)

high-viscosity 高黏性的,高黏度的

high-volatile 高挥发性的

high-voltage 高电压的（= high-tension）

high voltage coil ①高压线圈（= high tension coil）②（点火线圈的）高压绕组，次级绕组（= high tension winding）

high voltage lay-out （点火系等的）高压线路的布置

high-voltage porcelain 耐高压瓷

high-voltage reserve 高压储备（指在给定时刻，所能提供的点火电压与所需的点火电压之间的差额）

high voltage surge 浪涌高压，高压浪涌

high voltage winding 高压绕组（亦称 secondary winding"次级绕组"，见 high tension coil②）

high volume low pressure system 高风量低压头（空冷）装置；高流（容）量低压系统

highway 公路，交通要道（原指比地面"高"的路，如：与马车驿道相比，故名）

Highway Advisory Radio （美国的）公路交通信息播音（一种利用无线电通信系统，随时播放公路沿线的交通信息，供驾驶员合理的选择线路）

highway carriers ①公路运输系统 ②公路运输公司 ③公路运输车辆，公路运载工具

Highway Code [英]公路法规，公用道路法规

highway communication system 公路交通通信系统

highway cycle 公路循环（模拟汽车在公路上行车的台架测试循环，由公路行车的各种工况组成，见 EPA highway cycle）

Highway Emergency Locating Plan equipment 见 HELP equipment

Highway Fuel Economy Driving Schedule 见 HFEDS

Highway Fuel Economy Test 公路燃油经济性试验（美国环境保护局 EPA 制定的公路行驶油耗测定法，简称 HWFET）

highway grade separation （公路）立体交叉（简称 grade separation）

highway hopper body 装运筑路材料用的漏斗式车箱

highway information system 公路信息系统

Highway Loss Data Institute [美]公路事故损失数据研究所（简称 HLDI）

highway merging 公路汽车合流（参见 merging）

highway patrol 公路巡警

highway performance （车辆）公路行驶性能

highway police operation 公路按章运行（指汽车在运行中按公路规章高速行驶）

highway-rail bus 公路有轨公共汽车（= road-rail bus）

highway regulations 公路交通规则，公路交通条例

Highway Research Information Service [美]公路研究信息服务处（简称 HRIS）

Highway Safety Act of 1966 （美国）1966年公路安全法（该法令对驾驶执照考核制度，公路设计、修建、养护等做出了规定）

highway skid resistance 公路防滑性

highway sleeper 公路卧铺客车（参见 sleeper bus）

highway speed （高速）公路汽车行驶速度

highway tire 公路用轮胎（花纹细而浅，花纹沟所占的比例小）

highway tonnage capability 公路承载能力（以车辆单桥载荷吨计）

highway tractor 公路用牵引车（= over-the-road tractor）

highway traffic control 公路交通管理，公路交通控制，公路交通指挥（简称HWTC）

highway tread patten （轮胎胎面的）公路花纹（指主要适用于铺装路面的胎面花纹）

high-wearing 强烈磨损的

high-wheeled 大车轮的，大直径车轮的

high yield 高产出率

hi-heat = high heat

HIJET CARGO （大发公司开发的）混合动力货车（商品名）

HIL 硬件在线仿真（hardware-in-the-loop simulation，指用dSPACE仿真车辆部件，通过I/O接口与控制器相连，利用各种测试手段对新研制的控制器产品进行全面、详尽测试以缩短测试周期，提高测试安全性和可靠性，见dSPACE）

Hilbet transform 希尔伯特变换（分析信号的一种数学工具，将一个实信号表示为一个复信号，由此研究实信号的包络，瞬时相位和瞬时频率）

hill (-climbing) gear （汽车变速器的）爬坡挡

hill climbing performance ①（汽车的）爬坡性能（常用在一定坡度的坡上爬一定里程所需的时间来表示）②（蓄电池汽车的）爬坡性能（常用充一次电后以一定车速，爬一定坡度的坡，能爬行的最大里程来表示，= grade climbing performance）

hill climbing resistance 坡道阻力，爬坡阻力，上坡阻力（= $W \cdot \sin\theta$，式中W为车重，θ为坡面与水平面夹角）

hill climbing test 爬坡能力试验，爬坡试验

hill-climb race 爬坡赛（山路赛车，按登上陡坡山顶的时间取胜负，为motor cross 的一种）

hill descent system 下坡（安全制动）系统（当下坡车速超过安全阈值时，即自动制动减速，简称HDS）

Hill hold 山抓（汽车山坡防滑坡装置的商品名，为一液压装置，与离合器踏板连动，起步时，即使松开制动踏板，制动器仍不松开，只有离合器踏板松开，制动才会松开。同类商品还有anti-creep system 等）

hill-hold function 坡道驻车制动功能

hill hold system ①阻止坡道（起步、换挡）滑溜、熄火系统（简称HHS）②坡道驻车系统

hill launch assist 坡道（起步）下滑阻止系统（简称HLA）

hillocky 多丘的（地带）、丘陵地带的

hillside tractor 坡地牵引车

hill sign （道路的）坡路标志

Hill start assist control system 坡道起动辅助系统（简称HAC或HSAC system，防止汽车在陡坡或滑溜的坡道上起步时，驾驶员脚由制动踏板换向加速踏板期间，汽车后退。当电子控制模块收到传感器送来的车轮起步中后退的信号时，即自动使车轮制动）

hilly 丘陵的，崎岖的

hilly area 山区

hilly cross country 丘陵不平地区

Himet 碳化钛硬质合金

hi-mu grip （轮胎）与泥泞路面的良好抓着作用

hind （指前后相对而言的）后面的，后部的，后边的，在后的

hind axle 后轴，后桥

hinder ①妨碍，阻滞②后方的，后面的

Hindley worm 亨得利蜗杆（直廓环面蜗杆，亦称AT-worm，轴向齿廓为直线的环面蜗杆）

hindrance to traffic 交通障碍物
hind wheel 后轮（=rear wheel）
hinge ①铰链，折页，合页，活动关节；枢纽，关键，转折点；铰接 ②给…装铰链，铰接
hinge angle brake （汽车列车制动或倒车时，主挂车）铰接装置回转角限制器，拖挂机构回转角限制器（防止折叠现象）
hinge axis 铰链轴
hinge bow （活动软顶逢的敞篷车顶逢的）主弓形支架，主弓形支杆（见 main bow）
hinged 铰链的
hinge(d) bolt 铰接螺栓（= dog bolt, link bolt）
hinged fender 铰接式挡泥板，活动挡泥板（= hinged mudguard）
hinged frame 铰接式车架
hinged pedal 铰支式踏板（下端与驾驶区地板铰链连接的踏板）
hinged quarter window 铰接式后边窗（由铰链铰接因而可以开启的后角窗，位于 B 立柱与 C 立柱之间。四柱式接站车"estate car"，则在 C 立柱和 D 立柱之间）
hinged seat 铰接式可翻座椅
hinged side 铰接式（车厢）侧栏板
hinged valve 瓣阀（= clack valve）
hinge eye 铰链枢轴孔
hinge face （亦写作 hinge facing，指车门框架的）铰链面（包括供安装车门铰链用的带铰链螺孔的加强板在内的车门框侧面板，注意它不同于 hinge panel）
hingeless 非铰接的，无铰链的
hinge of spring 钢板弹簧吊架，钢板弹簧吊耳
hinge panel 立柱铰链板（指点焊于 A 立柱或前翼子板后端，安装车门铰链用的金属板）
hinge pillar ①车身框架中支撑车门的铰链立柱（= hinge post，指立柱下段、支撑车门铰链的那一段，上段一般为风窗玻璃边框 ②有时指整个立柱，即 = pillar）
hinge pillar reinforcement 车身立柱铰链安装段的垂直加强板件
hinge pin 铰链销，关节销
hinge-point 铰链点，铰接点，折叠点，开合点
hinge post 见 hinge pillar
hinge shaft 铰链轴
hinge strap （车门）铰链
hinge tapping plate （车门）铰链螺孔板（在车门铰链立柱 hinge pillar 或车门框架上点焊有一薄金属板制的框盒，铰链的螺孔板便装在该框盒内，通过螺栓将车门铰链固定在此板上，该板可在框盒内移动，因此车门位置可在一定范围内调整）
HINO 日野（日本汽车公司名）
hip belt 见 lap belt
HI polystyrene 耐高冲击压力聚苯乙烯（high impact polystyrene）
hipped roof combustion chamber 斜坡屋顶式燃烧室，斜截头形燃烧室
hip point （作为汽车驾驶员上半身和下半身活动中心的）臀点（汽车驾驶员操作空间范围的人体基准原点，简称 H point "H 点"）
hiproom （车身内）座位处车身两侧壁间的空间（距离）（指左车门槛至右车门槛间的距离）
HIPS （汽车乘员）头部防撞保护系统（head impact protection system 的简称）
hip width of sitting passenger 乘员就座时的臀部宽度
hire ①租用；雇用；租金 ②（按时收费，在车库待客租用的）出租车 ③租借；出租，租用；雇用
hire car 出租汽车
Hi-Ref Coat （马兹达公司）（车身）高级涂装（的商品名，其漆面光滑艳丽，坚硬抗刮）

hire purchase （贷款购车分期还款的形式之一）租赁（指汽车注册登记车主为贷款购车人，付首期，最高贷款额为9期，即：首付+按揭）

H-iron 工字铁，工字钢

hi-roof 高顶汽车

hiss ①发嘶嘶声 ②啸声，嘘声，杂声，漏气声

hiss arc 响弧，啸声电弧

histogram （数理统计的频率）直方图，矩形图频率分布图；频率曲线；（统计），次数组织图

history ①历史，沿革 ②（机器技术状况、性能、工作情况的）过程记录，经历记载；历程 ③随时间变化关系的图解（曲线、函数）

hit 击中，碰撞

hit and miss governor 断火法调速器，断续法调速器

hit-and-run （汽车等）肇事逃逸，闯祸逃走的

hitch ①挂住，钩住，咬住，卡住 ②悬架装置，牵引挂接装置 ③简单的球-窝式连接节 ④带急冲的运动

hitch assembly 挂钩装置总成

hitch ball 见 tow ball

hitch bar （挂车）牵引杆，辕杆，拖杆（= tow bar）

hitch cylinder 液压牵引油缸，联结器油缸

hitch hole 牵引销孔

hitching force 拖挂牵引力，挂钩牵引力

hitch pin hole 牵引装置销孔，挂钩销孔

hitch point 悬架点，牵引点 ①挂车与主车的拖挂联结点 ②悬架装置下拉杆的联结铰链

hitech 高技术的，高科技的（hightechnique 的简称）

hi-tension cord （点火）高压线（一般使用电阻值均一，耐20000V以上高压，抗射频干扰的碳素纤维线）

Hi-test 高辛烷值汽油（指辛烷值在90～95左右的汽油）

hi-tilts ［口语］可向上翻起式驾驶室载货汽车

hit on obstruction 碰在障碍物上，撞在障碍物上

HK 努氏硬度值（参见 Knoop hardness number）

HLA 坡道（起步）下滑阻止系统（hill launch assist 的简称）

HLDI ［美］公路事故损失数据研究所（Highway Loss Data Institute 的简称）

HLL 高级语言（高级程序语言，high-level language 的简称）

HMI ①人-机接口（human-machine interface 的简称。在汽车上，指乘员与各种车载计算机控制系统和导航、信息系统之间的通信联络的人机对话界面）②高分辨率图像（high-resolution graphics 的简称）

HMMUV 高机动性多用途车（high-maneuverability multi utility vehicle 的简称）

HMMWV 高机动性多用途轮式车辆（high mobility multipurpose wheeled vehicle）

HMOS 高性能金属氧化物硅晶体器件（high-performance metal-oxide silicon device）

HMS ［韩］现代汽车服务公司（Hyundai Motor Service 的简称）

H-NDIR 加热型不分光红外线分析仪（heated nondispersive infrared analyser 的简称，见 NDIR）

hob ①滚齿刀 ②轮毂 ③衬套 ④滚齿

hob seal 轮毂油封

hob tap 标准螺丝攻,标准丝锥（= master tap）

hodometer 里程表，路程表，计距器

HOE 液压设备（hydraulically opera-

hog ①使向上拱曲,使中部起拱 ②不顾危险的开快车,横冲直撞 ③向上拱曲的 ④拱,拱曲物;软管,弯头,弯拱

hogging ①弯曲,扭曲,翘曲 ②挠度 ③凸起

hoist ①起重机,滑车组,起重葫芦;卷扬机,绞盘,绞车;举升器 ②吊起,绞起,提升

hoister ①起重机,卷扬机 ②起重机驾驶员

hoisting ①起重,提升 ②起重的

hoisting capacity 起重能力,起吊量

hoisting crane 起重机,吊车

hoisting depth 提升高度(如:自卸车车身的举升高度)

hoisting drum 卷扬机卷筒,绞盘鼓轮(= winch drum)

hoisting jack 举升器,千斤顶

hoisting magnet 起重磁铁(= lifting magnet)

hoist pump 起重液压泵

hold ①抓住,保持,把握,固定 ②把手,手柄 ③夹子,支持器

hold-all 工具袋,工具箱,帆布袋,杂物箱,手提包

holdback clutch 安全离合器

hold clutch (自动变速器的挡位)保持离合器

hold down ①按下,压下 ②握住,保持 ③压板,压紧装置

hold-down arm 安装臂,支撑臂,夹持臂

hold-down bolt 地脚螺栓,安装螺栓,固定螺栓

holder 把,柄,杆,夹,夹子;支持器,保持架;架,支架,托架;灯头;容器,盒,罐

holdfast 夹紧机构,夹钳;支架

hold-in coil 保持线圈(亦称 holding coil, = hold in winding, holding winding,指使某一部件或零件保持某种状态或位置的线圈或绕组,如:起动机电磁开关内的保持线圈。当电磁开关内的吸引线圈吸动铁芯使触点闭合,电磁开关处于工作位置后,吸引线圈即被短路,这时,由保持线圈使电磁开关保持在工作位置,即:保持电磁阀的活动铁芯处于吸合位置)

holding anode 保持阳极(汞弧整流器的辅助阳极)

holding brake 后备制动器,减速制动器(一种辅助制动器,一般装于变速器的输出轴上,当重型货车驶下长坡时使用,或者用于经常停车的公共汽车上,以减轻车轮制动器的磨损)

holding capacity 容积,容量,容载量,收容能力,保持能力

holding coil 见 hold-in coil

holding company 控股公司(拥有其他公司的股份,可以控制其他公司的公司,但不同于母公司,参见 parent company)

hold(ing) control 同步调整,同步控制

holding current 保持电流,吸持电流

holding device 夹具,夹持装置,吸持装置

hold(ing)-down clamp 压具

holding-up hammer ①圆边击平锤 ②铆钉抵锤

holding valve (液压系统的)保持阀(用于防止液压支撑的部件非正常移动或下滑,如:防止必须暂时保持在某升起位置上的挖土机挖斗下落等)

holding winding 见 hold-in coil

hold lamp 占线指示灯

hold mode (自动变速器的)挡位保持模式(挡位保持系统工作时,自动变速器不再自动变速,而保持在某一固定挡位不变的工作模式)

hold pressure 保持压力（指液压系统中保持所选工位不变，或某部件，开关等位置不变的压力。如：在自动变速器液压控制系统中，保持所选挡位不变，阻止所选挡位范围之外升挡的压力，此时亦称限挡压力）

hold regulator valve 限挡调压阀（限挡压力的调节阀，见 hold pressure）

hold system （自动变速器的）挡位保持系统（使自动变速器保持在某一挡位上，不再自动换挡变速）

hold time 保持时间（指保持某种状态、动作、信号、参数、挡位、电压、电流等不变的时间间隔）

holdup ①支撑，支持 ②举起 ③阻塞，障碍 ④停车；拦劫车辆 ⑤继续下去，持续

hole ①孔，洞，眼，坑 ②钻孔，打洞

hole angle 喷孔角（多孔喷油器的各喷孔中心线形成的圆锥角）

hole base system 基孔制 [= basis hole system, hole basis (limit) system]

hole carrier （半导体）空穴载流子

hole conductivity 空穴电导率

hole current （半导体中）空穴电流

hole cutting snips （在金属上切孔用的）剪孔钳

holed 带孔的，有孔的

hole density （半导体的）空穴密度

hole-depth indicator 孔深指示器

hole drill 螺孔钻，螺纹底孔钻

hole for the split pin 开口销插孔

hole gauge 塞规，内径规，孔规，内测微计

12-hole injector 12 孔喷油器

hole nozzle （柴油机的）孔式喷嘴（为闭式喷嘴的一种，不喷油时，其喷孔为针阀尖端所封闭，一般有单孔式和多孔式两类，多用于直接喷射式柴油机，它们与倒锥针式和柱针式喷孔的主要区别在于：其针阀端部不伸出于喷孔之外，因而喷孔仅为圆孔，不成环形，针阀只起封闭和开启喷孔的作用，而不影响喷孔的大小及油雾的形状，亦称 open type nozzle）

hole punch 冲头，冲孔机（用于在金属板材上冲孔）

hole saw 孔锯（在钣金件上锯孔用的孔形筒锯）

hole tolerance 孔径公差

hollow ①空腔，空穴；凹部，凹槽 ②空的，中空的，空心的，凹陷的 ③挖空，掏空；弄凹

hollow cone spray （燃油的）空心锥形喷束

hollow cooling ring groove-insert 空心冷却式活塞环槽镶圈，空心冷却式镶式活塞环槽

hollow crankpin 空心曲柄销，空心连杆轴颈

hollowing 钣金工的深拱敲击（作业）（指使用手锤或专用的锤，将钢板垫在深拱形砧垫上敲击成深拱形的板件）

hollowing block （深拱敲击作业用的木制）深拱形砧垫

hollow rivet 空心铆钉

hollow spots 凹部，凹坑

hollow steel spoke wheel 钢制空心辐条车轮

hollow valve stem 空心气门杆

hologram 全息摄影

holographic combiner （抬头显头系统中与风窗玻璃制成一体的）全息合成器（用在风窗玻璃驾驶员的平视区内呈现清晰、生动立体感强的全息数字或图像信息，见 head-up display）

home built 手工制作的，自己制造的，国产的

home bus 国产客车

Home Energy Management system 见 HEMS

home freight 回头运费

"home going" motor 备用发动机(意为主发动机出现故障时仍可用此机将车开回家 = "go home engine", "home going" engine)

home interview origin and destination survey 登门访问, (交通)起讫点调查, 交通起点-目的地调查

home-made ①自制的, 本国制造的 ②手工制作的

home market 国内市场

homeostasis 自动(调节)动态平衡

homeostatic mechanism 适应性机能, 同态性机能

homeotropic alignment (液晶分子的)垂面排列(在定向处理的基板表面处, 液晶分子垂直于基板面的排列)

home part 国产配件, 国产零件

home position 零位, 原始位置, 原来位置, 静止位置

home-theater surround sound system (车用的)家庭影院式环绕声系统

home-to-job transport 上下班运输

home-trade 国内贸易, 国内销售

home trailer 旅居挂车, 居住车(=house trailer)

homing action 回位, 还原作用

homochromatic after-image 同色余像, 同色残留影像(色彩与原物大致相同的余像)

homodyne 零拍, 零差; 自差法

homodyne circuit 零差式电路

homodyne detector 零拍检波器

homodyne solid-state Doppler radar 零差固态电路多普勒雷达

homofocal 共焦点的(同一焦点的)

homofocal headlamp 双丝灯双焦距前照灯(一种使用双灯丝灯泡, 具有拼装式双反射镜或一个两段式反射镜, 而形成长短不同两种焦距的前照灯, 其副反射镜, 或副反射面比主反射镜或主反射面的焦距短。亦称 bi-focal headlamp。其反射镜系统称为 bifocal reflector 或 stepped reflector, 见 bi-focal headlamp)

homogeneity 均匀性, 均质性, 一致性, 同一性, 均一性

homogeneous 同族的, 同类的, 相应的, 相似的, 类似的, 对等的, 同原的, 同种的, 同质的, 同性的, 均匀的, 均质的, 纯一的, 单一的, 一致的, (数)齐的, 齐次的, 同次的, 齐性, 齐次, 均匀

homogeneous alignment (液晶分子的)沿面排列(在定向处理的基板表面处, 液晶分子平行于基板面的排列)

homogeneous boundary condition 齐次边界条件

homogeneous-charge compression ignition combustion 均质混合气充气压燃点火燃烧(简称 HCCI combustion, 指均质混合气充气后压燃)

homogeneous charge engine 均一充气发动机, 均质充气发动机(指充气为均质的发动机, 区别于分层充气发动机的不均质充气)

homogeneous deformation 均匀形变

homogeneous stirred reactor 均匀搅动燃烧器, 均匀搅动反应器

homogeneous strain 均匀应变

homogeneous stress 均匀应力

homogeneous system 均匀系, 单相系(指组由单相组成的系统, 即该系统内任意物理上的微小部分的化学成分和物理状态与该系统的其他任意部分相同)

homogeneous tube 无缝管

homogenizing ①均质化 ②金属组织的均质化热处理(均质退火, 扩散退火)

homokinetic joint 等速万节向, 等速联轴节(见 constant velocity joint)

homologation (指权威部门或官方)认可,同意,批准

homologation requirement (国家)正式批准的(法规,标准等的)要求,确认的(规范的)要求

homologation test 鉴定试验(指对新设计或重大改进后的发动机进行的性能试验、耐久性试验和配套试验等各项试验,以考核其性能指标是否达到设计、改进要求,是产品的认可和准产试验)

homopolar motor 单极电动机

Honda Accord car 本田雅阁轿车(日本本田公司生产的中档轿车)

Honda Accure-Nsx sport car 本田阿库拉 NSX 运动车(日本本田公司生产的高级运动车,中置发动机,后轮驱动,装用 DOHC、铝制缸体、缸盖、钢质缸筒 V6 发动机,排量 2977mL,最大功率 198kW,最大转矩 233N·m,最高车速 270km/h,装有导航、防抱死、自动变速等控制系统)

Honda civic car 本田国民轿车,本田市民轿车(日本本田公司生产的轿车,装用 VTEC 系列 DOHC、汽油喷射发动机)

Honda FC STACK (本田 PCX 燃料电池车上使用的)本田燃料电池堆(见 fuel cell stack)

Honda hybrids 本田复合动力车(包括 hybrid Accord, Civic 和 Insight 等三种车型的复合动力车)

Honda Intelligent Driver Support System 见 HiDS

Honda Motors Co., Ltd. 本田技研公司(简称本田公司,创立于 1948 年,年生产能力约 190 万辆,为日本五大汽车公司之一)

Honda Multimatic 本田多挡自动变速器(商品名)

Hondanoid (日本本田公司生产的具有人类特点,外形像人的步行式机器人的商品名)本田类人机器人(该机器人最早型号为 P-1 型,1996 年推出了 P-2 型,1997 年又介绍了高 1.6m、重 130kg 的 P-3 型,据称可在 21 世纪投入使用)

Honda Prelude car 本田序曲轿车

hone ①珩磨(指抛光性精磨,特指对发动机汽缸,各种液压缸和气压缸镗缸后的镜面精磨) ②珩磨石,油石,极细的磨石 ③珩磨工具(特指珩磨缸面用的珩磨头,为一装有多片砂条的圆柱形磨头,装在磨缸机或搪磨两用机的磨杆上由磨缸机带动旋转)

honer ①珩磨机 ②珩磨头

honey car 污水抽吸车(参见 vacuum car)

honeycomb ①蜂窝状物,蜂窝状结构 ②蜂窝状的,多孔式的,网格式的 ③使成蜂窝状

honeycomb catalyst support (排气催化转化器的)蜂窝状催化剂载体(= honeycomb catalyst substrate,亦称 monolithic substrate "整体式载体",因整载体式载体均呈蜂窝状,故名,见 substrate③)

honeycomb cracks 网状裂纹,蜂窝状裂纹

honeycomb grill 蜂巢状栅格

honeycomb laminate 蜂窝状多层材料

honeycomb radiator core 蜂窝式散热器芯子

honeycomb structure 蜂窝结构

honey wagon [口语] ①旅居挂车上的活动厕所 ②垃圾车,粪车

honing 珩磨(见 hone)

honing head (磨缸机)珩磨头;珩刀架

honing stone ①磨石 ②(特指珩磨用的)磨条

honk ①汽车喇叭声响 ②揿喇叭,喇叭鸣叫

hood ①[美]发动机罩(=[英]bonnet) ②(活顶汽车的)可折叠、收拢的软篷(=[美]soft top,收合后即成为敞篷车)

hood air bag (碰撞中保护步行者的)发动机罩装安全气囊

hood anti-squeak strip 发动机罩防响垫条

hood bar (活顶汽车的可折叠)软篷的弓形支撑杆(亦称 hood bow,一般用钢管或薄钢板制成,旧称 hood stick)

hood lacing 发动机罩边橡皮软垫

hood ledge ①盖、罩的支撑边(周边突缘) ②(轿车车身的)前挡泥板(前轮内侧的挡泥板)

hood lift 发动机罩吊装工具

hood line (汽车)发动机罩轮廓线

hood louver air door 发动机罩通风道风门(一般由动力控制模块控制,当冷却水温和节气门开度到一定值时,该风门开启,新鲜空气进入发动机罩下空气滤清器区)

hood louvre 发动机罩通风孔道(=hood louver)

hood nose piece 发动机罩前脸

hood safety catch (发动机)机罩安全拉钩(防止发动机罩开跳的)拉钩(亦称 hood auxiliary catch hook, hood safety lock, hood secondary latch)

hood scoop [美俚]发动机罩上的风斗(经发动机罩引入额外的空气冷却发动机舱的通风斗)

hood shutters (发动机)机罩百叶窗

hood side panel 发动机罩侧板

hood side piece 发动机罩边板(=bonnet side piece)

hood strap 发动机罩(吊)带

hook ①钩,吊钩,钩状物;环,扣,箍;爪,夹,掣子,卡子 ②钩住,挂上,用钩联结,连接上(亦称 hook up)

hook block ①带钩滑车,挂钩滑轮 ②钩吊部件

hook bolt 带钩螺栓,钩头螺栓,地脚螺栓,丁字头螺栓

Hookean spring (指符合胡克定律,其应变与应力成正比的)虎克弹簧

hooked scraper 钩形刮刀

Hooke's coupling 虎克式万向节(即常用的十字轴式万向节,因варь明人而得名,由一个十字轴连接两个万向节叉组成的非等速万向节,=Hook's(universal)joint,或 cardan universal joint)

Hooke's law 虎克定律(弹性材料的应变与应力成正比,当应变开始不与应力成正比时的应力,称为弹性极限,参见 elastic limit)

Hooke's low shaft 虎克定律轴(一种转矩传感器,为装在发动机与测功器之间的驱动轴上,通过一应变仪电桥测出其扭转变形算出发动机转矩)

hook height 车挂钩高度(从地面至挂钩内底的高度)

hooking device 挂钩装置,牵引装置

hook joint 钩接(合)

hook joint ring (两切口端相互勾接的)勾接(密封)环(用于自动变速器的液力系)

hook rule 钩尺(用以测量突缘或圆形物直径,或测量卡钳、两脚规等的开度)

hook-spanner 钩形扳手(=pin wrench)

hook tooth 棘轮(=ratchet tooth)

hook type electrode (双侧电极式火花塞的)双钩式电极(在中央电极的两侧各有一个钩状侧电极)

hookup ①试验路线,接线图 ②电路耦合 ③挂钩,联系,连接 ④悬挂装置,联结器

hook-up cable 夹接缆线,钳接缆线

hookup lamp (位于大型半挂牵引车驾驶室后背左右的)半挂车夜间挂

接和脱挂作业用照明灯
hookup time （挂车的）挂接时间
hook wrench 钩形扳手
hoop ①环，箍，圈 ②扣箍
Hooper engine 胡帕式发动机（各种阶梯式活塞发动机的统称，见 stepped piston engine）
Hooper stepped piston engine 不等径台阶形活塞发动机（为双缸并联二冲程发动机，两个上部直径小、下部直径大的凸阶形活塞装在与之相对应的两个不等径汽缸内，汽缸的小直径部分有一个排气孔和一个由相邻汽缸大直径部分供给新鲜充量的进气孔，汽缸的大直径部分有一个新鲜充量进气孔和将新鲜充量输入相邻汽缸的输气孔。火花塞装在汽缸小直径部分的顶部，当某一缸活塞上行到上止点时，该缸所有的进、排气孔均关闭，新鲜充量被压缩在活塞小直径部分的顶面与汽缸盖内表面形成的燃烧室内为火花塞点燃而做功，当活塞下行至下止点的过程中，进、排气孔逐步开放，新鲜充量由此时向上止点上行的邻缸大直径部分经进气孔压入活塞下行的汽缸小直径部分，并将其中的废气用排气孔扫出，同时新鲜充量由进气孔进入该缸大直径部分，准备输入邻缸）
hoop-iron 带钢，窄带钢，铁箍
hoop stress 圆周切向应力
hooter 喇叭，汽笛
hop 跳动，跳振（特指车轮在路面与簧上质量间的上、下振动现象）
hop-off （自动风门等的）风门开始开启
hopped up engine 强化的发动机（= uprated engine）
hopper ①漏斗，装料车；斗仓 ②（自卸车的）底卸式车箱 ③底卸式自卸汽车，漏斗式车箱自卸汽车

hopper-bottom 底卸式的；漏斗式底部的
hopper-bottom grain truck 车箱底部卸粮汽车，漏斗式运粮汽车
hopper-shaped trailer 漏斗式车箱的挂车
hopper throat 料斗的卸货口
hop-up test （内燃机）强化试验（将各项技术指标，如：转速、功率、最高燃烧压力等提高到超过标定工况的数值，按规定运转时间进行的试验，以考核内燃机质量，可靠性和工作潜力）
horizon ①水平线，地平线 ②视界；视距 ③范围，前景
horizontal ①水平线，地平线 ②水平的，地平的；横的，卧式的
horizontal adjuster 横向、水平（方向的）调节装置（如前照灯光束的横向对光螺钉）
horizontal alignment 横向对正，水平校正
horizontal axis 水平轴线
horizontal brace 横拉条
horizontal centerline 水平中心线，水平轴线，横轴线
horizontal center-of-gravity 重心的水平方向位置（简称HCG）
horizontal component 水平分力
horizontal curve （道路的）水平方向曲线（表明道路方向变化）
horizontal cylinder 卧式汽缸
horizontal datum 水平基准，水平基准线
horizontal displacement 水平位移，横向位移
horizontal draft type 横向通风式，横吸式
horizontal engine 卧式发动机（指汽缸中心线平行于水平面的各种发动机，= flat engine，如：汽缸水平对置式发动机，= boxer engine；安装位置转90°的常规式直列式发动机）

horizontal force 横向力，水平力
horizontal frame 水平框架
horizontal illuminance 水平照度（水平面上一点的照度参见 illuminance）
horizontal keiretsu 横向系列（keiretsu 词意等于汉语的系列，指日本汽车工业集团的一种组织形式，各成员公司之间彼此拥有相对来说小额的股份，而且各集中于一家核心银行，这一组织形式可以使各成员公司的经营免受股市波动和控股企图的影响，而放手进行长远规划和致力于各项创新项目，这是日本汽车工业的一个关键性因素，见 vertical keiretsu）
horizontal light beam adjusting screw 前照灯光束水平位置调节螺钉
horizontal load 水平荷载，横向负荷
horizontally-opposed flat-four engine 水平对置卧式四缸发动机（汽缸水平对置于曲轴两侧）
horizontal outline 平面轮廓图（俯视轮廓图）
horizontal parallax 水平视差（简称 hp）
horizontal polarized component 水平偏振分量
horizontal power control spring （丰田 Harrier 车悬架上的）横向力控制弹簧（可减轻悬架上、下作用于减振器的横向力）
horizontal projection 水平投影
horizontal section 水平剖面
horizontal slot ①水平槽 ②横切口（如：活塞头与裙部之间的横隔热切口）
horizontal spindle 水平主轴，横轴
horizontal-spindle double-ended grinding machine for piston ring 活塞环卧轴双端面磨床（用两个砂轮的端面而同时磨削活塞环的双端面）
horizontal thrust 水平推力

horizontal travel 水平移动
horizontal-type compressor 卧式压缩机
horizontal valve 水平横置式气门，卧式气门
horn ①（汽车）喇叭（通常由电磁线圈、压缩空气或晶体管电路等激励膜片振动而产生声响）②操纵杆，机臂，悬臂
horn anvil 角砧
horn bar （转向盘上的）横杆式喇叭按钮
horn brush/slip-ring （装在转向盘中央的）喇叭按钮的电刷/滑环（喇叭电路的环状触点，由电刷和滑环组成，可保证转向盘作任意转动时均能可靠接触）
horn button 喇叭按钮（亦称 horn boss，horn push）
horn cable 喇叭线（= horn wire）
horn diaphragm 喇叭振动膜（= horn membrane）
horological gears （微型）钟表齿轮，（微型）时计齿轮
horse box 运马用的厢式货车或挂车（= ［美］horse van，［澳］foat）
horse power 马力（英制功率单位，代号 hp 或 HP，即每分钟做 33.00 英尺磅功的能力，1hp = 33.000ft·1b/min = 42.44Btu/min = 746W = 1.014ps = 76kgf·m/s = 0.178kcal/s）
horsepower characteristic 功率特性，马力特性（功率随某自变量而变化的特性）
horsepower hour 英制马力小时（功能单位，代号 HPh，hph，即 1 英制马力工作 1h 的功，1HPh = 1.014PSh = 0.7461kWh = 2.741 × 10^5 kgf·m = 2.684 × 10^6 J = 641.6kcal = 2543Btu = 1.984 × 10^6 ft·1bf）
horsepower input 功率输入，输入功率（马力）

horsepower output 输出马力；输出功率

horsepower per liter 升功率，升马力（发动机功率排量比，马力/升）

horsepower per unit of weight 单位质量的功率（马力）

horsepower rating 额定功率，计算功率；功率标定，马力标定（见 duty horsepower）

horsepower requirement 需用马力

horsepower screw ①功率调节螺钉（指废气涡轮增压系统废气旁通阀盖内的弹簧高度调整螺钉。拧紧或拧松该螺钉可调节废气增压压力，从而增、减发动机功率，故名）②（泛指）任一可直接或间接影响发动机输出功率的调整螺钉（如：化油器内的各种燃油或空气调节螺钉等，亦称 power screw）

horsepower spectrum 功率谱，马力谱

horsepower-weight factor 马力-质量因素（表示车辆总重与驱动马力之间的关系，用车重除以驱动力得出每单位质量的驱动马力值，单位：马力/磅，为动力因素或比功率的旧称，但英美仍延续使用至今，见 power-mass factor 或 power/mass ratio）

horseshoe 马蹄形，U形

horseshoe electromagnet 马蹄形电磁铁

horseshoe type thrust bearing 马蹄形止推轴承

horseshoe vortex 马蹄形旋涡（指行驶中的汽车车后涡流区内在两股涡流的旋涡间产生的空气动力旋涡，包括横涡和纵涡）

horse vehicle 运马用车辆

horticultural tractor 园艺拖拉机（= garden tractor）

Horton Diesel temp fan clutch 霍顿（型）柴油机温控风扇离合器（商品名，霍顿公司生产的由水温传感器控制气压开关接通或断开的风扇离合器，用于重型柴油车，亦称 Horton thematic engine fan）

HO₂S 加热式氧（含量）传感器（heated O_2 sensor 的简称）

hose 软管

hose balancer 平衡软管，软管平衡器

hose clamp 软管卡箍，软管夹子（= hose band，美称 hose clip）

hose connector (= hose connection, hose coupler, hose coupling, hose fittings, hose joint, hose nipple) ①软管接头（指接装在软管上的各种接头）②连接软管（指用来连接金属管的软管）

hose pinch-of pliers （修理冷却系时使用的）软管夹钳（将软管夹扁至不再流通，因此修理软管下游的部件时，无须将冷却系内水放干）

hose-proof enclosure 防溅渗外壳，防漏水壳罩（用软管冲洗时水不会漏渗入机器内）

hose reel set （汽车维修厂用供电、供油、供气等）软管卷轴，软管卷筒（一般拉出后，软管长度可稳定并可自动收回）

host ①许多（一大批）②主的（如：host processor 主处理机，host media 主介质）

hostile ambient temperature 有害的环境温度

host vehicle （相对于其他车辆而言的）本车（如：in front of host vehicle 指"在本车的前方"）

hot ①热的 ②通高压电的 ③强烈的，热烈的，厉害的

hot air control valve 热空气调节阀，热空气控制阀（缩写 HACV）

hot air engine 热空气发动机（参见 air engine）

hot-air heated 热空气加热的，（热）风暖的

hot air horn 热空气喇叭

hot air intake system 热空气进气系统（指自动调温式空气滤清进气系统，简称 HAI）

hot(-)air pipe 热气管

hot-air vulcanization 热空气硫化（hot air cure）

hot-air windshield defroster 风窗玻璃热风除霜器

hot and cold air intake system 冷热空气调温进气系统（参见 heated air intake system）

hot arc （转子发动机）热（弧）区，热（弧）段（指旋轮线缸体壁对应燃烧、膨胀相的弧段，= hot lobe, hot side）

hot-asphalt tanker 热沥青罐车

hot-bending test 热弯曲试验

hot-blast 热风，热压缩空气流，热空气喷流

hot-brittleness 红脆性，热脆性（= red brittleness）

hot-bulb ignition 热球点火，烧球点火，热面点火，灼热点火（一种称为半柴油机的点火方式，利用伸入燃烧室的热球点燃喷入燃烧室内的重油，= hot-tube ignition, surface ignition，用这种方式点火的发动机称热球式发动机"hot-bulb engine"或半柴油机"half diesel"）

hot cap 热补用胎面（轮胎热翻新所用的胎面）

hot cathode rectifier 阴极整流器

hot cell 高温试验室，高温室，热室

Hotchkiss drive 霍契凯斯传动（常规的双万向节传动轴后轮驱动系统，由传动轴通过前、后两个十字轴万向节分别连接变速器和驱动桥差速器总成，并由装在车桥上的半椭圆形钢板弹簧悬架支撑车身或车架，传递扭力和推力）

hot chloride bath （镀铁时使用的）热氯化亚铁镀槽，热氯化亚铁镀液

hot cleaner 高压热水洗车机，热水清洗装置

hot cleaning vat （蒸气或）热（水）（清）洗箱

hot-cold cycle 加热-冷却循环

hot-cold drift 温变偏差，温变误差，冷热误差（由于温度变化所造成的变化，误差、偏差等）

hot cold work （在临界温度下的）中温加工

hot crack 热裂纹（受热时形成的裂纹）

hot cure 热处理；热硫化，热固化，热补

hot curve 温度曲线（各种随温度而变化的变量的曲线的通称）

hot defroster （车窗）加热去霜器

hot desert test 在炎热沙漠条件下的试验

hot dip 热浴镀，热浸镀（将镀件浸入熔化的金属如：锌、锡等内，以获得表面镀覆层）

hot-dip alloying 热浸镀合金，热浴镀覆合金

hot dip aluminizing 热浸镀铝

hot-dipped galvanize 热浸电镀，热浴电镀（无特别说明时，一般指热浸镀锌）

hot -dip(ped) galvanized sheet steel 热浴镀锌薄板钢材

hot-dipped terne 热浸镀铅锡合；热浴镀铅锡合金薄钢板

hot-ductility 热延展性，热锻性

hotel bus 旅居客车（附有卧铺、烹调间、卫生间等设施的客车）

hot-engine 热机（指本身温度高，处于热态，相对于温度低的冷态发动机-冷机而言）

hot-engine sludge （发动机内的各种）高温残渣

hot-etching test （金相试样的）热酸蚀试验

hot film air flow meter 热膜式空气

流量计（亦称 hot film mass air flow sensor，见 hot wire air flow）

hot-flame （发动机燃烧过程中的）热焰（指冷焰，蓝焰反应后紧接着的热焰反应，是基于冷、蓝焰反应中聚集的热量及足够的活性分子浓度和自加速反应达到一定深度形成爆炸性的燃烧火焰）

hot-flame ionization detection 热氢焰离子化检测法

hot-foiling （用锡、铜等金属粉末或箔片装饰车身制品的）热包工艺

hot-forming 热模锻，热压成形

hot-gas engine 热气体外燃发动机（参见 Stirling engine）

hot-gas welding （塑料的）热气焊接（焊接厚的热塑性塑料薄板时，用喷管将经加热的惰性气体或空气吹到焊接处，同时将同质塑料的焊条送到焊接处）

hot-hardness 高温硬度

hot-hatch 高性能仓门式后背型汽车（= high-performance hatch back）

hot-head ignition 缸盖灼热点火（由于缸盖、燃烧室灼热部分引起的不正常早燃）

hot-heading 热镦

hot-high-pressure cleaning system 热水高压清洗装置

hot-idle （发动机过热或混合气过浓引起的）不稳定怠速（运转）

hot-idle compensator （发动机的）高温怠速空气补偿阀（发动机怠速时若由于发动机过热、混合气过浓而转速下降，则该阀在双金属片的控制下开启空气旁通管道，使空气直接进入进气管，获得适当的混合比，防止发动机怠速不稳定，简称 HIC）

hot-isostatic pressure machine ①等压加热（理论循环型）热机②（指各种在等压下高温作业的机械，如：用于烧结陶瓷件的）等压加热烧结机（简称 HIP）

hot-junction （热电偶的）高温接点，热接点（见 thermocouple）

hot-lobe （转子发动机缸体的）热（弧）区（参见 hot arc）

hot-melt strength 热熔强度（热塑性塑料在稍低于熔点时的拉展成形能力）

hot-metal 液态金属，熔融金属

hot-mixture ①致热混合气（指稀混合气，相对于浓混合气而言。浓混合气利用燃油的蒸发热会使进气温度降低，称为致冷混合气）②热混合气（指本身温度高）

hot-motoring method 热机马达法（用电动机驱动发动机测试摩擦功率，= engine motoring method）

hot-override switch 热断开关（当高于某一温度时，使某一工作回路断开）

hot-patch （内胎）热补胶片

hot-peening 高温喷砂处理

hot-plasticity 热塑性，热延展性

hot-plug ①热型火花塞（亦称 soft plug, hot running spark plug，见 hot spark plug）②（柴油机的镶块式结构涡流室的）绝热下半块（具有切向布置的通道与主燃烧室相连，在压缩冲程，空气顺该通道压入涡流室，在涡流室内形成强烈的压缩涡流，燃油喷入涡流室内遇热空气涡流而着火，火焰被裹在未燃烧的浓混合气的中心，又从该通道中喷入主燃烧室，在主燃烧室内形成二次涡流并与其中的热空气进一步混合而充分燃烧）

hot-potato 难以诊断的故障，棘手的问题，难处理的问题

hot-press 热压机（简称 HP）

hot-press molding （玻璃纤维强化塑料制件的）坯件热模压制法（在热钢模上使用压力机将坯件压制成型）

hot-riveted 热铆的

hot-rod ［俚］热杆（指加速赛，特别是四分之一英里加速赛用经特殊改装的大功率赛车）

hot-rolled thin steel sheet 热轧薄钢板

hot-rolling spring steel 热轧弹簧钢

hot-rubber 热聚合橡胶（在规定温度下进行聚合的苯乙烯-丁二烯橡胶，见 SBR）

hot running-in 热磨合（大修理发动机装配竣工，先经冷磨合，然后在台架上加载运转一定时间，以改善摩擦副的摩擦表面状态，参见 cold running-in）

hot-set ①热作加工用用具，热锻用具 ②热凝固，热固，热变定

hot-shaping 热成形，热锻压

hot-shift PTO 动力接合式取力箱（指通过液压，气动或其他动力挂接的取力箱 "power take off" 的统称，= power shift PTO）

hot-short 热脆性；热脆的

hot-shortness 热脆性，热脆（材料的高温脆化，亦称 red shortness）

hotshot 急驰汽车，快车

hotshot express 直达车，特快车

hot-side 热侧，热区［如：转子发动机的热（弧）段，= hot arc］

hot-soak 热烤，热浸（指受发动机，特别是发动机熄火后机身高温的烘烤，= heat soak）

hot-soak losses 热浸损失（= heat soak losses，从发动机停机瞬间算起，在规定时间内因机身热度烘烤而造成的燃油蒸汽排放量）

hot-space 热区

hot spark plug 热型火花塞（简称 hot plug，亦称 soft plug，指裙部长，因而受热面积大，传播距离长，散热速度慢，裙部温度较高的火花塞，见 heat range）

hot-spot ①热点，过热部位，过热点 ②预热面，预热区（特指发动机进气歧管与排气歧管之间的相互接触区，以便利用废气热量促进进气歧管内的燃油进一步气化）③汞弧整流器的阴极斑点 ④辐射最强处 ⑤前照灯主光轴照射中心点

hot-spot application （可燃混合气）缸面预热（见 hot pot②）

hot-spot beam （汽车前照灯的）高速车照明光束（直线高速行车时，发出的强光）

hot-spot illumination （汽车前照灯的）高速行车照明（汽车直线高速行车时，加大照明度，以确保安全）

hot-spot manifold 热面式进气歧管（利用排气自动加热新鲜混合气，见 hot spot②）

hot-spray-gun （涂料的）加热式喷枪

hot-spraying 加热喷雾，（特指加热喷漆，漆料在喷射前先行加热，以减低其黏度，因而无须溶剂稀释便可喷成雾状）

hot-spray paint heater 热喷漆加热器

hot-stall ①热车熄火（运转中，因温度过高造成气阻等原因熄火）②热机不能起动现象（由于高温引起压缩冲程途中缸内非正常热点的早点火而将活塞压回所致）

hot-start CVS test 热起动定容取样试验（见 cvs test）

hot-start enrichment 热机起动加浓（指发动机短暂停机后仍处于高温状态时再起动加浓。一般见于汽油喷射式发动机，由于发动机温度过高，燃油大量蒸发，以致由喷嘴喷出的燃油不足以形成所需空燃比的混合气。这时需适当加浓，加浓的方法有两种：一种是电子控制模块根据燃油温度传感器输入的油温信号适当增加喷嘴控制脉冲的宽度，即增加喷嘴喷油时间；另一种是通

过一个譬如装在冷机起动加浓阀电路内的热机再起动脉冲继电器"hot-start pulse relay"控制冷机起动加浓阀供油)

hot starting ①热机起动(利用暖气等设备,使冷却水、机油、发动机本身均达到某一规定的较高温度后,再行起动)②热机再起动(指发动机短暂停机后,当处于高温状态时的再起动。这时由于在停机期发动机高温使汽油蒸发,汽油蒸气聚积于从空气滤清器到进气歧管的进气系统内,亦常导致起动困难)

hot-start pulse relay 见 hot-start enrichment

hot-sticking 热黏结,热卡结(特指运动件由于高温而卡滞,如:活塞环被高温形成的结胶物卡死在环槽内)

hot-straightening 热矫正

hot-strength 高温强度,热强度

hot surface ignition 高温表面点火

hot-surface treatment 表面高温处理,表面热处理

hot-tear (铸件表面等的)热裂纹(间断性的枝状裂纹)

hot-tensile test 热拉伸试验

hot-test ①在加热状态下的试验,热态试验 ②(发动机的)运转试验(一般指新的或大修的发动机在排气、冷却、燃油系统均接装好以后,在规定运转条件下进行的试验室试验,亦称 hot testing)

hot-tire recap (operation) 轮胎热翻新(工艺)

hot-tube ignition 热球点火(见 hot-bulb ignition)

hot-tunnel climatic test (汽车)热风洞试验(人造热带气候的风洞试验)

hot-type plug 热型火花塞(hot plug,见 hot range)

hot-vulcanization ①(橡胶)热硫化②(轮胎)热补

hot-water heater 热水采暖装置,热水加热器

hot-water jacket 预热水套,热水套

hot-wave 热波

hot-wax flooding 热蜡填补法(德国大众公司发明的车身板件孔穴填补法,使用所谓的"热蜡填补器"hot wax flooding unit 将预热至60℃的无溶剂蜡即热蜡 hot wax 喷入孔穴内将孔穴补平。热蜡填补器由加热部分,浇蜡部分和供小孔穴用的滴蜡部分组成)

hot-weather trial 热带(适应性)试验(见 tropical trial)

hot-wire ①热电阻线 ②热线(见 hot wire air flow sensor)③(指)直(接)连(接蓄电池或与蓄电池直接连接的电路的某一部分的导)线,载电线(= current carrying wire)

hot-wire airflow sensor 热线式空气流量传感器(亦称 hot-wire airflow meter,装在发动机进气道内,直接测定进入发动机的空气质量。将一导线加热到一定温度并保持恒温,空气流过该热线时将带走热量,为了保持热线恒温必须有更多的电流流过热线,测出这部分增加的电流量,即可算出与之成一定比例的空气流量,有的用热膜代替热线,称 hot-film airflow meter)

hot-wire analyzer 热电阻丝型(废气)分析仪,热电阻丝型空-燃比测定仪(通过对废气中 CO_2 含量的测定来推算混合气的空燃比)

hot-wire anemometer 热线风速计(如:测量汽缸内充量的流速及流动方向用的)热线式气流速度仪

hot-wire element 热线元件(如:热线式空气流量传感器的电热丝)

hot-wire ignition 电热丝点火

hot-wire instrument 热线式仪表

hot-wire plug-in type air flow meter

螺塞式热线型空气流量传感器

hot wire rear window 热线式后窗（指玻璃内埋有细镍铬合金电热丝的后窗）

hot-wire type flasher 热丝式闪光器（以热丝热胀冷缩来控制继电器动作的闪光器）

hot-working 热加工

hour 小时（时间单位，代号 h）

hourglass worm 环面蜗杆（见 globoidal worm）

hourglass worm and roller gear 环面蜗杆滚轮式转向器（一种用环面蜗杆作主动件，用支撑于转向摇臂轴上的滚轮作为被动件的转向器形式）

hourglass worm and sector gear 环面蜗杆齿扇式转向器（用环面蜗杆作为主动件，用齿扇作为从动件的转向器形式）

hourly capacity ①小时生产率 ②小时功率 ③小时通行能力

hourly car yield （每）小时轿车产量

hour meter indicator lamp 计时表指示灯

12—hour rated power 12h 功率（指在标准环境条件下，以发动机能连续运行 12 小时的最大有效功率）

hours to failure 损坏前的工作总时数，完好工作时数

house-brand gasoline ①普通品种汽油 ②家用汽油

Household Goods Carrier Bureau ［美］家用商品运输局（简称 HHGCB）

house-to-house delivery van 沿街挨户送货的厢式送货车

house trailer 旅居挂车（= home trailer）

housing ①外壳，外罩，屏蔽套，护罩 ②（轴承）盖，（包装）箱 ③（转子发动机的）缸体；机架，支架，框架，机体，机座 ④卡箍，垫圈 ⑤槽，腔，凹部 ⑥房屋 ⑦蔽盖物

housing assembly 壳体总成（如：转子发动机的缸体总成，包括外旋轮线缸体、端盖等件）

housing box 轴箱，壳箱

housing cooling system （转子发动机的）缸体冷却系统

housing distortion ①壳体变形 ②（转子发动机的）缸体变形

housing of the fuel injection pump 喷油泵壳体

housing part ①壳体零件 ②（转子发动机的）缸体零件，缸体部件（指外旋轮线缸体、端盖、中间隔板等）

housing structure ①壳体结构 ②（转子发动机的）缸体结构

housing washer 推力（滚动）轴承外圈（与壳体接触的座圈，见 outer ring）

housing with two cylindric grooves （球笼式万向节的）双柱槽壳（内壁带有两个径向对置的轴向柱槽的部件，见 ball and trunnion universal joint）

HOV 多乘员汽车（high occupancy vehicle 的简称）

hovercar 气垫车（参见 hovercraft）

hovercraft 气垫飞行器（从飞行器内向下吹喷气，形成气垫，支撑飞行器本身，使飞行器能在距水面或陆地很近的距离上运动，如：气垫车"air cushion vehicle"，亦称 hovercar）

hovercraft seakeeping capability 气垫船海上行驶能力

hover-height （气垫车）腾空高度

hovering power （气垫车）腾空（消耗的）功率，（气垫车）腾空能力

hovertruck 货运气垫车

HOV exclusive lane 多乘员汽车专用道（HOV 见 high occupancy vehicle）

HOV priority signal 多乘员汽车优先信号（如：对公共汽车优先通过的信号，见 high occupancy vehicle）

hozzle hole area 喷孔面积（指喷孔的截面积）

H-pattern shift H 形换挡（指换挡杆按 H 形槽板换挡的操作，一般左上端为一挡，左下端为二挡，右上端为三挡，右下端为四挡）

4HP14 automatic transmission （德国 ZF 公司研制的轿车用）横置式前轮驱动四挡自动变速器（其中，4 表示 4 个前进挡，H 表示液压控制，P 表示使用 Ravigneaux 行星齿轮机构，14 表示最大转矩，见 Ravigneaux planetary gear set）

HPD 高功率密度（high power density 的简称）

HPh, hph 马力小时（horsepower hour 的简称）

HP·hp ①调和级数（harmonical progression 的简称）②高通（high pass 的简称）③大功率的（high power 的简称）④高压的（high pressure 的简称）⑤（剃齿刀具）增高齿顶（hip point 的简称）⑥水平视差（horizontal parallax 的简称）⑦水平面（horizontal plane 的简称）⑧马力（horse power 的简称）⑨热压机（hot press 的简称）

hp/hr/lb 马力/小时/磅（英制单位质量的储能能力）

H pipe H 形管（如：汽车双排气系的，由左右两根排气管及连接这两根排气管的中间平衡管组成的 H 形排气管）

HPI-TP common rail fuel system （Cummins 公司柴油机的电子控制）高压喷射、时间-压力型共用高压储油管式燃油喷射系统（high pressure injection time-pressure common rail fuel system 的简称。注意与 Cummins 公司的 PT 燃油喷射系统区别，TP 系统控制燃油喷射量的变量是 time "T"，而不是 PT 系统的 pressure "P"）

hp/litre 马力/升，升马力（发动机每升排量产生的马力）

H point H 点，臀点（hip point 的简称，指二维或三维试验假人上身躯干和大腿中心线的铰接交点，用于设计和测定座椅及乘坐区的舒适性等）

H point manikin 臀点试验假人

HPR 高抗穿透性（high penetration resistance 的简称）

HPX 高性能-四轮驱动车（丰田"Lexus"的概念车名，high performance and a 4WD 的简称）

HR 心跳速率（heart rate 的简称）

HRB [美] 公路研究委员会（Highway Research Board 的简称）

HRCC 高压缩比紧凑型燃烧室（high ratio compact chamber 的简称）

HRIS [美] 公路研究情报服务处（Highway Research Information Service 的简称）

HRS 热轧钢（hot rolled steel 的简称）

HR-sound system （车用）高保真音响系统（HR 为 high reality、high resolution 的简称）

HRSS （汽车车身）高刚性安全结构（high rigid safety structure 的简称）

HS 肖氏硬度值（见 shore hardness number）

HSA (C) 坡道起步辅助系统（见 hill start assist control system）

HSB headlamp 封闭卤素泡前照灯（halogen sealed bulb headlamp 的简称）

HSDI 高速直接喷射式（High Speed Direct Injection 的简称）

hsg 外壳，机座（见 housing）

HSHS （电动汽车的）智能家庭家电充电系统（Home Smart Home Sys-

HSIO 高速输入和输出（装置）（high speed input/output units 的简称）

HSLA steel 高强度低合金钢（high strength low alloy steel 的简称）

HSP 强涡流进气孔（high swirl port 的简称）

HSS 高强度钢（high-strength steel 的简称）

H/T 逆风-顺风（headwind/tailwind 的简称）

HT 高（电）压，高（电）压的（= high-tension 的简称）

HTCC 强涡流燃烧室（high-turbulence combustion chamber 的简称）

HT circuit 高压电路（在汽车点火线中亦称 secondary circuit "二次电路，次级电路"）

HTD ①大转矩传动（high torque drive 的简称）②大转矩传动用皮带（high torque drive belt 的简称）

HT lead 高压线（如：火花塞的高压线）

HTLS 低速大转矩（high torque, low speed 的简称）

HTRP 公路交通调度站（highway traffic regulation post 的简称）

HTS HC 捕集系统（hydrocarbon trapping system 的简称）

HTV 复合动力试验车（hybrid test vchicle 的简称）

H type ABS 四通道式防抱死制动系统（四个车轮都装有速度传感器，有四条液压通道，四套制动压力调节阀，各车轮独立调节的防抱死制动系统，亦称 four channel ABS）

H-type engine H 形发动机（汽缸按 H 形布置的多缸发动机）

hub ①毂，轮毂（通过轴承安装到轴上的车轮的中心部分，有的与轮辐制成一个整体）②接套，轴套 ③多条道路的交汇点

hub bolt 轮毂螺栓，车轮螺栓

hub borer 毂孔镗床

hub brake 轮毂制动器（制动鼓或制动盘直接安装在车轮轮毂上的车轮制动器）

hub cap ①轮毂罩（罩住整个轮毂及其轴承的端盖）②轮毂轴承盖（仅仅罩住外轮毂轴承的小端盖）

hub cap emblem 轮毂罩（上的）标记，厂标等

hub carrier 轮毂托架（独立悬架车辆支撑轮毂的部件，如：支撑前轮轮毂的转向节 "steering knuckle"）

hub centric fit （车轮的）轮毂定位销装配（指车轮装配时，不是靠螺柱定位，而且靠将轮毂上的定位销插入车轮盘上的精密加工定位孔定中心装配）

hub drive 轮边传动（见 wheel-hub drive）

hub dynamometer 轮边测力计（用来测定传递给车轮的转矩）

hub embellisher （轿车）轮毂装饰罩

hub extractor 轮毂拉器

hub flange 轮毂突缘

hub lock 轮毂锁（用于使全轮驱动汽车的前轮与前桥半轴接合和脱开的机构）

hub (nut) wrench 轮毂螺母扳手（通称 clip wrench）

hub odometer 车轮转数计（用来计测行驶里程）

hub planetary axle 带行星齿轮轮毂减速器的驱动桥，轮毂行星齿轮减速式驱动桥

hub plate （离合器的）从动盘盘毂（固定从动盘片带摩擦片的花键毂，安装于离合器毂或称变速器第一轴花键端上的盘形零件）

hub puller 轮毂拉器（由爪钳和滑动锤组成，将轮毂从车轮上拉出的专用拆卸工具）

hub ratio 轮毂减速比

hub reduction 轮边减速（器）（= wheel reduction）

hub-reduction gearing 轮毂减速机构（= wheel reduction gear，指装在轮毂内的减速机构，一般为行星齿轮机构，多见于重型车辆，用来增加传动速比，即挡位数，并减少半轴和差速器的扭转载荷）

hub sleeve 轮毂衬套

hub spacer 轮毂隔圈

hub stud 轮毂螺栓

hub-tip ratio （叶轮的）毂径与外径之比

hub yoke （四轮驱动车辆）前轮轮毂的万向节叉

HUCR 最高有效压缩比（Highest Useful Compression Ratio 的简称）

HUD 抬头显示（见 head-up display，车速等动态参数，显示在风窗玻璃驾驶员平视的位置上，驾驶员不用低头便可观看）

hue ①色，色彩，颜色，色调，色度 ②混合 ③形式，样子，噪声

HUF ［美］公路使用者联合会（Highway Users Federation 的简称）

huffer ［口语］①带涡轮增压器的发动机 ②涡轮增压器

hull plate ①（装甲汽车的）装甲板 ②（水陆两用汽车）外壳板

hum ①（电路）交流声 ②轮胎噪声（在平坦道路上直线行驶时产生的轮胎噪声）

human anatomy 人体解剖学（= anthropotomy）

human blood type B B 型人血

Human Centered ITS View Aid system 以人为中心的智能运输系统的观察辅助系统（该系统由以下子系统组成：观测车辆驾驶环境，如：路面状况和车间距离的车载传感系统"on-bound sensing system for detecting driving environment"；监测驾驶者生理信息，如：瞌睡程度"drowsiness degree"及脉搏等的驾驶者监视系统"driver monitoring system"；信息与警报显示系统"information and warning display system"；车间通信系统"inter-vehicle communication system"等）

human-control characteristics （运输工具的）驾驶操纵特性，人操纵特性

human discomfort （车轮振动噪声等引起的）乘员的不快感，不舒适感

human element accident 责任事故，人为因素事故

human endurance 人体承受持续工作的能力，人体耐力

human engineering 人体系统工程学，人类工程学，人体工程学［= ergonomics，研究人的动作等，以提高劳动效率。应用生理学、解剖学、心理学等方面的知识，研究机器、仪表、控制系统等的设计和布置，使人在操作时发挥最高效率，= human factors（engineering），美国常用 human factors 替代 ergonomics］

human error 人为误差

human factor ①主观因素，人的因素 ②见 human engineering

Human FEM model 人体有限元法模型（FEM 为 finite-element method 的简称）

human friendly vehicle 与人友好型车辆（指处处考虑以驾驶与乘坐者的方便、舒适、安全、省力等的主旨而设计的车辆）

human interface （各种自动控制装置和系统等的）人机接口（装置或系统与人的界面，联系和关系）

human-like test 拟人试验，类人试验（如：使用与人体十分相似的假人进行的碰撞试验等）

Human/Machine Interaction System 人-机互动系统

human machine interface computer

人机接口处理机（指在自动控制系统中向操纵人员显示主控机信息和输入操控指令的人-机界面处理终端计算机）

humanoid robot 类人机器人，人形机器人，步行式机器人

Human performance centre （赛车手的）体能训练中心

human response 人体反应

human sensitivity to vibration frequency 人体敏感的振动频率范围（人体最敏感的频率范围，即：忍受加速度最小的频率：对垂直振动为 4～8Hz，水平振动在 2Hz 以下。在 2.8Hz 以下的同样持续时间，水平振动容许的加速度值低于垂直振动，在2.8Hz 以上则相反）

human-size crash dummy （试验用）实际人体尺寸碰撞假人

human spine 人体脊椎骨

human survival limit 人的减速度生存极限（人的生命所能承受的减速度极限，一般为20g左右）

human tolerance ①设计汽车时考虑人体尺寸的变化范围 ②人体承受能力范围

human tolerance level 人体容忍碰撞强度，人体可耐碰撞强度（指汽车发生碰撞事故时，造成人体各种伤害的碰撞强度，一般分为志愿者允许撞伤强度，轻伤碰撞强度，中伤碰撞强度，重伤碰撞强度）

human tolerance test 人体忍耐力试验

human visceral resonance 人体内脏共振（行驶平顺性中考虑的问题）

humid 湿的，湿润的，潮湿的

humidification 湿润，湿润作用，弄湿

humidifier 增湿器，加湿器

humidifying tower （各种人工控制大气环境模拟试验室中使用的）加湿塔

humidifying ventilation 加湿通风，润湿通风

humidistat 湿度控制器，恒湿（度）器

humidity 湿度

humidity cabinet test （在人工控制的）湿度试验室内进行的试验，（在人工模拟的）高湿气候条件下的试验

humidity chamber 人工控制湿度试验室（可模拟各种大气湿度环境，如热带、亚热带高湿度环境等，供车辆或零部件进行耐湿性试验）

humidity control 湿度控制

humidity correction factor 湿度校正系数（根据大气湿度对氮氧化物排放量的测定值进行校正时所用的系数，此系数取决于吸入空气中所含水分的绝对量，简称 KH 系数）

humidity sensor 湿度传感器（利用有机高分子或陶瓷材料的电阻值等随大气中水蒸气的含量，即湿度而变化的特性，将湿度变为电信号输出的传感器）

humidity test 耐潮湿试验（如：将风窗玻璃试样置于密闭容器内的潮湿环境中，一定时间后按试样的外观质量和光学性能的改变状况来评价）

humidor 保湿器，保湿储藏

humming ①齿轮噪声（= 室 gear whine）②嗡嗡声；喇叭鸣声

hump ①山冈，凸处；隆起 ②（车轮轮辋胎圈座内边的）凸峰（防止轮胎气压不足时胎圈被压入轮辋凹槽内，按其形状有平峰 flat hump 和圆峰 round hump 之分）③曲线顶点，峰值 ④使隆起成圆形，急速移动

humping hammer （车身板件凹陷的）敲出手锤

hump mode 黏液耦合器的峰值工况（黏液耦合器的工况之一，亦称接合

工况，相对于耦合器片未相互结合时在黏液中旋转的黏液耦合工况而言，指耦合器片已完全接合，通过耦合器片间的机械摩擦传动转矩，因而传递的转矩可比黏液耦合工况时增加数倍，见 Viscous coupling）

hump rim 带凸峰的轮辋（详见 hump ②及 flat bump, round bump）

hump-type expander （活塞环的）波形胀圈

Hundredfold 一百倍

hundred weight 英担（英制常衡单位，代号 cwt，在英国 1cwt = 112b，= 5080g，在美国 1cwt = 1001b，= 4535g，= centum weight，见 avoirdupois weights）

hunter tune-in wheel balancer 车轮就车调试平衡器（将车桥顶起，该平衡器直接堆放在车轮下，带动车轮旋转，进行调试平衡作业）

hunting ①游车（指装有调速器或固定供油式发动机由于调速系统动力稳定性不好，或每循环喷油量不均匀，引起转速持续周期性地在一定范围内变化）②（混合气过浓引起的发动机）不平稳运转 ③（车辆行驶时的）摆动 ④（仪表指针）不稳定地摆动

hunting leak 测定泄漏点，测漏

hunting link （汽车的）驱动力传递杆件（如：车轴与车架或车身之间的推力杆，转矩套管等）

hunting tooth （齿轮上额外增加的一个）追齿（在一对啮合齿轮中的一个齿轮上多加一个齿，以保证相互啮合的不总是同一对轮齿，可减轻磨损）

hustle along 轿车在拥挤的车辆中曲折穿行

HV ①复合动力车（指使用两种或两种以上不同动力源，如"发动机＋电动机"等的车辆，hybrid vehicle 的简称）②维氏硬度值（参见 Vickers hardness number）

HV 混合动力车（见 hybrid vehicle）

HVAC 暖气，通风和空调（系统）（heating, ventilating and air conditioning 的简称）

HV battery 混合动力车驱动用蓄电池（混合动力车有两套蓄电池，一套为灯光、刮水、空调、无线电设施等供电的辅机电池，HV battery 专指另一套是为驱动电动机供电用的高压">200V"电池）

HV-ECU 见 power management ECU

HWA 热线风速计，热线式气流速度计（见 hot-wire anemometer）

H waves H 波，纵电波

HWFET 公路燃油经济性试验，公路油耗试验（见 Highway Fuel Economy Test）

HWTC 公路交通控制（管理）（见 highway traffic control）

Hyatt roller bearing 海特滚子轴承（与常规的滚子轴承相似，只是其滚子是空心的且开有特殊形状的通槽）

hybrid ①混合，混合型，复合式 ②混合的，混合型的，复合式的，复合式的 ③复合动力汽车（= hybrid car，指由两种动力装置驱动的车辆）

hybrid battery system 复式蓄电池系统，复式电瓶系统（铅电池和其他种类的电池并用的电瓶驱动系统）

hybrid body 双材料型复合车身（如：前部用铝合金，后部用钢板制成的拼合式小轿车车身）

hybrid circuit 混合电路（指两种以上不同类型的电路组成的电路，如：模拟电路和数字电路组成的电路；指将小型电路互连或采用不同工艺安装在一个基片上制成的电路；见 hybrid integrated circuit）

hybrid Coaster minibus （丰田公司的）考斯特复合动力小型客车

hybrid drive 双动力驱动，混合动力驱动，复合动力驱动（①指用两种不同的动力装置驱动，如：电动机和发动机分别驱动，或联合驱动，②指仅由一个电动机驱动，但使用两种不同的电池，如：常规电池与燃料电池等，亦称 hybrid propulsion）

hybrid engine ①双制发动机（指可按两种不同的工作原理运转的发动机，如：既可压燃点火，又可由火花点火的发动机）②（与其他动力装置一起共同驱动汽车的）双动力装置中的任一个（如：与电动—机械驱动系统一起运转的发动机）

hybrid film integrated circuit 混合膜集成电路（指至少包含一个密封或未密封的元器件的膜集成电路，参见 film integrated circuit）

hybrid fuel 复合燃料，双燃料（如：将一定量的煤粉与柴油混成煤浆，作为柴油机的燃料）

hybrid gasohol 汽油-酒精混合燃料

hybrid inflator （汽车安全气囊的）混合式充气装置（hybrid compressed gas and pyrotechnic air bag inflator 的简称，指利用电流引发雷管，使雷管周围的烟火炸药爆炸，加热压缩氖气筒内的氖气，氖气迅速膨胀而充入气囊。这种充气器使用两种充气源，故名。又由于它一般呈筒状，亦称 tubular inflator）

hybrid integrated circuit 混合集成电路（由半导体集成电路与膜集成电路的任意组合，或上述集成电路与分立元件的任意组合形成的集成电路，见 semiconductor integrated circuit 和 film integrated circuit）

hybrid integrated circuit igniter unit 混合集成电路点火装置（简称 HIC Igniter Unit）

hybrid petrol/hydrogen vehicle 汽油-氢混合燃料汽车

hybrid power steering system 复合式动力转向系（指由电动机驱动液压泵提供动力的液压动力转向系，转动方向盘所需力的大小由液压泵转速，即其输出来控制，与全液压型动力转向系的区别在于全液压型的液压泵是由发动机直接驱动的。故复合式动力转向系亦称电动液压动力转向系" electro-hydraulic power steering system"）

hybrid power system 复合动力系统，双动力系统；混合动力系统

hybrid propulsion 见 hybrid drive

HybriDrive propulsion system 混合动力驱动系统

hybrid solar car 太阳能复合动力汽车（指以太阳能电池为主要动力，在阴天夜间应用其他能源的动力，如：燃料电池等）

hybrid step motor 复合式步进电动机（指变磁阻式 variable-reluctance-type 与异极式 heteropolar type 的复合形式）

hybrid SUV 复合动力型多用途运动车（其中 SUV 为 sport utility vehicle 的简称）

hybrid test vehicle 复合动力试验车（简称 HTV）

hybrid vehicle 混合动力车（简称 HV，指由两种不同动力，如：内燃机和电动机等串联或并联驱动的车辆，见 serious HV, parallel HV）

HYD head 液压头（hydraulic head 的简称）

Hydragas suspension （车用）液压空气悬架，油气悬架（商品名，见 hydro-pneumatic suspension）

Hydraguide 液力转向装置（Gemmer 公司生产的液压转向助力装置的商品名）

Hydra-Matic （Chevrolet 的）四挡液力自动变速器（商品名）

Hydra-Matic transmission （通用公

司）海德拉-马梯克变速器（通用公司海德拉-马梯克部"Hydra-Matic Division"生产的电子控制自动液力变速器的商品名）

Hydramatic transmission 液压自动变速器（通用公司电子控制液压自动变速器的商品名）

Hydraseal 海卓密封型离合器（英国Lipe离合器公司生产的一种重型货车用密封型湿式离合器的商品名）

hydraudynamic clutch 见 fluid coupling

hydraulic ①液体的，液压的，液力的；水力的，水工的 ②液压传动装置

hydraulic absorber 液压缓冲器（指利用液压作用吸收与缓冲振动的装置，如：装在挺柱导套内或气门杆端部，用以消除气门间隙并起缓冲作用的液压组件）

hydraulic accumulator 液压蓄能器，（利用弹性元件或可压缩气体等存储液压源输入液压装置的通称；可以用于吸收液压的波动；存储有一定压力的油液，必要时迅速输出，使系统内的压力平缓上升或使系统保持稳定的高压等）

hydraulic accumulator power steering 液压储能式动力转向（系统内有储能器，使整个系统内经常保持高压）

hydraulic action 液压作用

hydraulic active suspension 主动式液力悬架（指可根据车身高度及前后、左右、上下方向的加速度传感器的信息，自动纠正车身姿势的液力悬架系统）

hydraulic-actuated clutch 液力操纵式离合器，液动离合器（由液力伺服机构来控制离合器的接合与分离）

hydraulic- actuated CVT-puller moving taper disc 液压执行件推动型连续无级变速器主动传动带轮的活动锥形盘（见 CVT steel belt puller）

hydraulic actuating cylinder 液压缸，液压执行缸

hydraulic actuator 液压执行器（由液压驱动完成某规定动作的装置，即将液体能量转换为机械能，执行某一规定动作的装置，可分为液压缸式和液压马达式，前者完成直线动作，后者完成摆动或转动动作等）

hydraulic actuator with pressure control valve （主动式液压悬架系统的）液压执行器带压力控制阀

hydraulic aerial cage 液压高空作业车（通过液压传动系统驱动臂架和臂端作业斗将作业人员和物具举升到一定高度进行高空作业的汽车）

hydraulic air servo 液压气动式增压器（由液压控制启动高压空气完成增压或助力作用，俗称油顶气）

hydraulically actuated wet disk type brake 液压驱动湿式盘式制动器

hydraulically actuated wet multi-plate clutch 液压驱动湿式多片离合器

hydraulically damped seat 液压减振座椅

hydraulically opened nozzle 油压开启式喷嘴（当输至喷嘴的油液达到规定的压力时，将喷嘴的弹簧加载式阀门顶开而实现喷油）

hydraulically operated clutch 液力驱动的机械式离合器

hydraulically operated equipment 液压控制的设备，液压驱动的装置（缩写HOE）

hydraulically powered booster （制动踏板）液压加力器

hydraulically-powered suspension leveling system 液力悬架车身高度自动调平系统

hydraulic amplifier 液压加力（装置）

hydraulic arm 液压机构工作臂，液

压臂，液压悬臂

hydraulic automatic control system　全液压自动控制系统（控制信号的产生和传递，控制点的选择以及控制动作的执行完全是由液压系统完成的）

hydraulic boost type ABS　液压助力式防抱死制动系统（见 ABS without vacuum booster）

hydraulic brake　液压制动器（见 hydraulic brake system）

hydraulic brake booster　液压制动系统的助力器（= hydraulic brake servo，指液压制动系中增补驾驶员施加在踏板上的踩踏力的部件，有利用负压助力的真空助力器"vacuum booster"和利用压缩空气压力助力的气压助力器"air booster"两种）

hydraulic brake drain tube　液压制动系制动液或空气的排放管

hydraulic brake filler　液力制动器制动液加注器

hydraulic-brake fluid　制动液

hydraulic brake intensifier　液压制动系的增压器（指增高制动管路液压的部件，有利用负压增压的真空增压器"vacuum intensifier"和利用压缩空气压力增压的气压-液压增压器，俗称气顶油"air over hydraulic intensifier"两种）

hydraulic brake servo (unit)　见 hydaulic brake booster

hydraulic brake with vacuum power　真空增压液压制动器（见 vacuum intensifier）

hydraulic braking system　液压制动系统（指管路内充满制动液，驾驶员的踏板通过制动主缸变为液压力传到各制动轮缸推动制动蹄而产生制动力矩的制动系统。这种制动系统中使用的制动器，装有由液压驱动顶开制动蹄的制动轮缸，称为液压制动器 hydraulic brake。有的液压制动系内装有增补驾驶员施于踏板上的力的真空助力器或气压助力器；有的装有增高制动管路液压的真空增压器或气压增压器）

hydraulic buffer　液压缓冲器，液压减振器（= hydraulic shock absorber）

hydraulic bumper cylinder　液力保险杠液力缸

hydraulic capstan　液压绞盘，液压立式绞车

hydraulic capsule　膜式水力测压器，液力薄膜测力计；液压传感囊，测力囊

hydraulic cell　液力测压计，液压传感器

hydraulic change (-) over　液力换向机构

hydraulic characteristic curve　液压特性曲线

hydraulic circuit　液压管路

hydraulic clutch　液力耦合器（亦称 fluid coupling，见 fluid flywheel）

hydraulic constant flow type power steering system　常流式液压动力转向系（汽车直线行驶时液压控制阀位于中间常开位置，油泵泵送的液压油不断地经回油油路流回油箱，即液压油处于常流状态，无助力作用。当转向盘向某一侧转动时，控制阀关闭回油油路并使油液流入助力油缸与转向盘转动方向相应的一侧，产生助力作用）

hydraulic constant pressure type power steering system　常压式液压动力转向系（汽车直线行驶时液压控制阀位于中间常闭位置，各油路均关闭，油泵不停地运转，通过液压储存器、稳压阀的作用，整个系统内保持恒定的高压。当转向盘向某侧转动时助力缸该侧的油路开启而产生助力作用）

hydraulic control　液力操纵，液压

控制

hydraulic control block 液压控制阀总成（见 control valve assembly）

hydraulic control systems 液压控制系统（指依靠液压机构自动或在人工控制下实现各项操作功能，如：液力变速器换挡功能等的系统）

hydraulic control valve 液压控制阀（①指由液压系统控制的阀门 ②指液压系统本身控制其工作油液压力、流量及流向的阀件）

hydraulic converter 液力变矩器（见 hydraulic coupling，它与液力耦合器的区别：在作用上，它能将输入扭矩变大或变小，但汽车上主要用于将转矩变大，转速变小；在结构上，在泵轮与涡轮之间增加了一个与壳体刚性连接或通过单向离合器连接的导轮，以改变壳体内腔工作液体的流动方向，给涡轮一个反作用力矩，而增大涡轮的输出转矩。为了扩大传动比范围并得到空挡和倒挡，需要在变矩器后加装一个辅助变速器，汽车上广泛使用的是行星齿轮变速器）

hydraulic coupling 液力耦合器（利用流体功能传递动力的装置，由带叶片的泵轮和涡轮组成，装在封闭的壳体，形成一个封闭的液力循环系统。发动机带动泵轮旋转，泵轮通过液流带动涡轮旋转，涡轮输出动力。若略去轴承密封件等的摩擦损失，则输入泵轮的转矩 M_B 等于涡轮输出的扭矩 B_T。即它不能将输入转矩变大或变小，见 hydraulic torque converter）

hydraulic cylinder 液压缸，液压油缸

hydraulic damper 液力减振器，液力阻尼器（指黏性液体通过小孔产生的节流阻尼来吸收振动的减振装置，= fluid damper, liquid damper, hydraulic shock-absorber, dashpot-type shock absorber）

hydraulic damping 液压减振，液力阻尼

hydraulic depth control （挖掘机悬架装置的）液压（挖掘）深度调节器

hydraulic diaphragm accumulator （用膜片分隔油、气的）膜片式液压储能器

hydraulic differential 液压差速器（差速器壳内有两排径向液压缸，液压缸的活塞支撑在半轴的链轮上，在壳体的中部有加装弹簧的可调滑阀。汽车直线行驶或车轮无滑转时，活塞不移动且与差速器壳一起转动，滑阀处于中间位置，当汽车转弯或一个车轮滑转时，快转的半轴开始相对壳体转动，活塞做往复直线运动，把油压到滑阀端面之下，滑阀移动并使油溢出。在溢油总管内安装一个远距离操纵阀，在关闭状态时阻堵住滑阀腔内的油，差速器连锁）

hydraulic drawbar control 牵引装置液压控制

hydraulic drive 液力传动（亦称 liquid drive，汽车的液力传动分为动液传动"hydrodynamic drive"和静液传动"hydrostatic drive"两大类，前者是以液体动能，后者则以液体压力能来传递能量或动力）

hydraulic dump truck 液压自动倾卸车

hydraulic dynamometer 水力测功机（指以水作为吸收功率媒介的吸收式测功机。发动机带动一位于充满水的外壳内的转子旋转，外壳支在两端的轴承座上，水与外壳间的摩擦转矩等于转子传给水的转矩，即发动机的输出转矩，通过测力器测出外壳在该转矩作用下的转动量，即可测定发动机转矩，进而根据转速便可算出发动机功率）

hydraulic elevator 液压升降机
hydraulic energy nozzle 液压喷头（见 hydraulic pressure spraying）
hydraulic engine 液动机，液压马达（见 hydraulic motor）
hydraulic engine mounting （汽车）发动机的液压支座
hydraulic expander （液压制动器中直接推动制动蹄张开的）制动轮缸（偶见称 hydrolic expander）
hydraulic fan 液力风扇（由发动机驱动的液力马达系统带动）
hydraulic floor jack 液压落地千斤顶，液压固定式举升器，车用液压固定举升器（= roll-a-car hydraulic jack）
hydraulic fluid ①（液压系统的）工作液 ②（液压制动系统的）制动液（= brake fluid，液压制动系中传动液压的油液，包括醇型制动液、矿物油制动液和合成制动液等多种）
hydraulic garage jack 车库用液力千斤顶，维修用液力千斤顶
hydraulic gear 见 hydraulic drive
hydraulic governor （燃油喷射系的）液压式调速器（具有液力伺服助力装置，以增加操作力的机械式调速器，参见 mechanical governor）
hydraulic head assembly （分配式油泵的）泵头总成（燃油的泵吸、计量、分配件总成）
hydraulic hitch 液压操纵的挂接装置
hydraulic hoist 液压式起重机，液压式举升器，液压式吊车，液压式起吊装置
hydraulic hood （活顶汽车的）液压顶篷（由液压系统撑开和合拢的活动顶篷）
hydraulic hose 液压系软管
hydraulic leak 液压系统的漏液
hydraulic lift 液压举升器（= hydraulic hoist）

hydraulic lifter 见 hydraulic valve lifter
hydraulic lock （液压阀、滑柱或转阀等）卡死现象
hydraulic lock clutch 锁止式液力离合器（由静止起步、加速时起液力耦合器的作用，而在其他工况下锁止，起机械离合器作用）
hydraulic main 液压总管
hydraulic mechanical efficiency 液力机械传动效率
hydraulic medium （液压系统的）工作液
hydraulic modulator （防抱死液压制动系统的制动）液压调节器（根据电子控制模块的指令增加或降低制动液压的装置，由电磁阀及其所控制的油路等组成）
hydraulic motor 液力马达，液压马达，液动机（一种用于静液传动中将液力变为机械力的装置。目前常见的是一种用高压油液驱动的多缸往复式或转子式动力装置，简称 hydromotor，亦称 hydraulic engine）
hydraulic motor safe stall pressure 液压马达的安全止动压力
hydraulic packing 液压填密，液体密封，水封
hydraulic pipe 液压管，输液管
hydraulic pipe bender 液压弯管机
hydraulic piston 液压（系统）活塞（如：液压制动系的真空增压器中置于低压与高压腔之间，根据压差产生增压压力的活塞）
hydraulic piston accumulator （用弹簧加载活塞分隔油、气的）活塞式液压储能器
hydraulic plate bender 液压弯板机
hydraulic power cylinder 液压缸（由缸筒-活塞-连杆系统将液压转换为机械运动的组件）
hydraulic-powered wiper motor 液压式刮水器的液力驱动器，液力式刮水器的液压马达

hydraulic power steering 液压式动力转向

hydraulic power take-off 液压驱动功率输出轴

hydraulic press 水压机，油压机

hydraulic pressure head 液压头，水压头

hydraulic pressure regulator 液压调节器，液压系压力调节器

hydraulic pressure spraying 液力喷雾（用液力喷头喷雾）

hydraulic pressure test 水压试验，液压试验（如：检查汽缸体等的渗漏，= hydraulic test）

hydraulic pump 液压泵（= hydraulic pressure pump，液压系统的动力源，提供具有一定压力的工作油液）

hydraulic pump motor （制动系统中将储液筒内的低压制动液抽出加压后泵入储压器或直接泵入 ABS 中的）电动液压泵（简称 pump motor，亦写作 pump/motor）

hydraulic ram 液压缸

hydraulic ratio changer 液压比变换装置，变换液压比装置（如：制动系防抱死装置中的自动减小后轮液压的比例分配阀等）

hydraulic reaction force control method （液压动力转向）液压反作用力控制法（利用液压反作用力机构产生的反作用力来控制转动转向盘所需的力的大小，反作用力的大小则取决于车速，见 hydraulic reaction force mechanism）

hydraulic reaction force mechanism （液压动力转向系中的）液压反作用力机构（由一液压反作用力控制阀"hydraulic reaction force valve"和液压反作用力室"hydraulic reaction force chamber"组成，车速升高，则反作用力控制阀输入反作用力室的液压升高，转动转向盘遇到的反作用力变大，转动转向盘所需的力增加）

hydraulic relay valve 液压继动阀（方向变换阀的一种，用于顺序控制回路中，自动接通与断开某一通路的阀件）

hydraulic resistance 液体阻力

hydraulic retarder （汽车的）液力缓速器（适用于装有液力变矩器的重型汽车，以液力变矩器的油液作为工作介质，利用液体的阻力，吸收能量而起制动作用，使汽车缓速行驶）

hydraulic riveter 液压铆钉枪

hydraulic road simulator 液压道路模拟装置

hydraulic rotary transmission 动液传动（= hydrodynamic transmission）

hydraulics ①水力学 ②液压机械，液压装置

hydraulic scissors jack 剪式液压千斤顶

hydraulic seal 液压油封

hydraulic seat leveler 座位的液力自动调平装置

hydraulic selector 液压换挡机构

hydraulic servo 液压伺服机构，液压助力器（亦称 hydraulic servo motor）

hydraulic servo ABS 液压助力式防抱死制动系统

hydraulic servomotor 液压伺服马达（指由液压执行机构及其液压供给控制装置组成的液压执行装置）

hydraulic servo steering 液压伺服转向，液压动力转向（指以液压为动力的转向系统，一般由转向盘操纵的液压控制阀，液压源（泵），推动转向摇臂的液压缸组成。来自液压源的液经控制阀按转向盘回转的方向、角度及快慢等流入液压缸相应的腔室内，推动摇臂实现所希望的转向，亦称 hydraulic power

hydraulic shock absorber 液压减振器（利用液体流动阻力迅速衰减车身振动的装置，= hydraulic buffer, hydraulic damper, dashpot-type shock absorber, oleo damper）

hydraulic shock ware 液力冲击波

hydraulic slip （液力变矩器的）滑差（液力传动输入和输出的转速差）

hydraulic-slip loss （液力变矩器的）滑差损失

hydraulic spring 液体弹簧（指以液体作为介质传递载荷的弹簧）

hydraulic spring type suspension 液体弹簧式悬架（以液体弹簧作为弹性元件的悬架）

hydraulic stabilizer （悬架系统的）液力稳定系（提高抗侧倾能力，亦称液压式横向稳定杆系）

hydraulic starter 液压起动马达（指用作起动机的液压马达，见 hydraulic motor，用液力马达实现的起动称液力起动 hydraulic starting）

hydraulic steering booster 液压转向助力器（由驾驶员通过转向盘操纵的一液压缸，该液压缸直接推动转向摇臂实现转向，起助力作用）

hydraulic steering pump 液压转向助力泵

hydraulic steering unit 液压转向装置（由液压泵、控制阀及助力缸组成，为目前汽车上采用最为广泛的转向助力装置。按其控制阀、助力缸的装配位置分为连杆型"linkage-type"、整体型"integral-type"和半整体型"semi-integral type"三种，按其作用性质又可分为液压助力"hydraulic booster"和液压动力"hydralic power"，即 hydraulic servo 液压伺服两大类）

hydraulic stroker （疲劳试验）液压加载油缸

hydraulic suspension 液压悬架（系统）（指以液体弹簧作为弹性元件的悬架）

hydraulic suspension seat 液压悬架座椅

hydraulic tappet 液压挺柱（= oil tappet，美亦称 hydraulic valve lift，或 hydraulic barrel，指利用液体不可压缩性传递往复运动的挺柱，见 tappet。一般由柱塞、柱塞弹簧、带单向阀的内缸筒和储油外缸筒组成，当气门和挺柱或摇臂间出现间隙时，在挺柱弹簧作用下挺柱会自动上升，始终顶住气门杆或摇臂推杆或摇臂，使之与柱塞同步上升，外缸筒内的油液经单向阀被吸入内缸筒填补柱塞上升形成的空间，因此这种挺杆可一直保持气门零间隙，而无须调整）

hydraulic test 水压试验；液压试验（= hydraulic pressure test）

hydraulic timer 液压式喷油（时刻）控制装置（指装在分配式喷油泵内，由输油泵的送油压力控制的喷油时刻控制装置）

hydraulic timing advance mechanism 液压式喷油提前器（执行机构为活塞式液压传动机构的柴油机喷油提前器）

hydraulic tipper 液压自卸车

hydraulic tipping gear 液压倾卸机构，液压倾翻机构

hydraulic tipping ram （自卸汽车）液压倾翻机构油缸

hydraulic tipping trailer 液力倾卸挂车，液压自卸挂车

hydraulic torque converter 液压变矩器（见 torque converter）

hydraulic torque converter driving wheel 液力变矩器主动轮（指由发动机带动的泵轮）

hydraulic torque meter 液力转矩计，液力测扭仪

hydraulic transmission ①液力传动；液压传动装置（= hydraulic transmission gear）②液力变速器（hydrodynamic 或 hydrokinetic transmission，指使用液力变矩器和行星齿轮变速器的变速装置，见 hydraulic converter）

hydraulic transmission fluid 液压传动（动液传动，静液传动）用油

hydraulic-vacuum (braking) system 液压-真空加力制动系统（利用发动机进气负压或专门的真空泵负压来提高制动管道液压或驾驶员制动踏板踩踏力的真空助力式液压制动系的总称）

hydraulic valve 液压阀（开、闭液压系统通路的阀门）

hydraulic valve lifter 液压式气门挺杆，液力气门推杆（见 hydraulic tappet）

hydraulic variable speed drive 液压变速传动（= hydraulic transmission）

hydraulic vehicle lift 汽车液压举升器

hydraulic vibrator 液力振动器，液力加振装置

hydraulic wave generator （谐波齿轮传动的）液动式波发生器（利用液力使柔轮齿圈产生变形波的发生器）

hydraulic wedge （修理撞凹的车身板件用的）液压楔形头千斤顶（其顶头成楔形，可插在被撞凹的板材的后面，在液压作用下将它们顶回恢复原形）

hydraulic wrench 液压扭力扳手，液力转矩扳手

hydrazine 肼，联氨（$NH_2 \cdot NH_2$，加水：$N_2H_4 \cdot H_2O$，成为一种新的液体燃料，将作为新一代燃料电池电动汽车的能源，可以和汽油一样，装在汽车的油箱内，其能量密度高，安全，组成成分只有 H 和 N，O，排放中 CO_2 为零）

hydrazine air fuel cell system 联氨空气燃料电池系统

hydride 氢化物，含氢化合物

hydroactive suspension 液气悬架（见 hydro-pneumatic suspension）

hydro-blasting （铸件的）水力清砂（用高压水冲刷）

hydro-boost brake 液压助力式制动器（通常是利用动力转向的动力源通过由制动踏板控制的液压缸增加对制动主缸的推力）

hydro-carbon 烃（泛指各种碳氢化合物，即碳和氢组成的化合物的总称）

hydrocarbon-air fuel cell 碳氢化合物-空气燃料电池（以空气中的氧化正极，以 HC 为负极的燃料电池）

hydrocarbon compound 碳氢化合物，烃

hydrocarbon emission （发动机）碳氢化合物排放（指由发动机排放至大气中的未燃烧或部分燃烧的碳氢化合物，简称 HC）

hydrocarbon fuel 碳氢燃料，烃类燃料（指汽油、柴油、天然气等烃类混合物液态和气态燃料。如：汽油为 4～11 个碳原子的烷烃、环烷烃、芳香烃和烯烃的混合物）

hydrocarbon gas 石油气，气态碳氢化合物；碳氢类可燃气；烃类可燃气

hydrocarbon-oxy-compound 含氧烃类化合物（指烃的含氧衍生物，如：醇 R-OH 等）

hydrocarbon plastics 碳氢塑料（指仅由碳和氢组成的单体聚合而成的树脂为基体的塑料）

hydrocarbon ratio of atomic number （燃油的）氢-碳原子比（指燃油中氢原子与碳原子数之比）

hydrocarbon reforming cell 碳氢化合物改质处理燃料电池

hydrocarbon response 碳氢化合物响应度（分析仪对各种碳氢化合物成分的响应程度。用 NDIR 时，用正乙烷为基准的输出比，即相对灵敏度表示；用 FID 时，则以丙烷指示值或碳数当量表示）

hydrocarbons monitor 碳氢有害排出物监测器

hydrocarbon-steam-air system 烃-水蒸气-空气系统（水蒸气转化制氢系统）

hydrocarbon trap 碳氢化合物捕集装置（捕集排气中的未燃烧碳氢化合物，送回进气系统，阻止其排入大气造成污染和节油的装置）

hydrocarbon trap catalyst and absorber system HC 捕集催化和吸收系统

hydrochloric acid 盐酸（HCL 的水溶液）

hydro-control unit 液压控制单元（防抱死制动和附着力复合控制系统中由各种电磁液压控制阀，液压泵，液压泵电动机及储液箱等组装成的一个硬件单元，简称 HCU）

hydrocracking 加氢裂化

hydrodynamic aided rotary shaft lip seal 流体动压式旋转轴唇形密封圈（密封唇后表面附有某种有规则花纹，能改变密封唇与轴的接触状态，可使通过唇口泄漏的流体返回被密封腔体内的密封圈）

hydrodynamic(al) ①动液的，液力的（指以液体的动能来传递能量的）②流体动力学的（指与流体运动所产生的力和力矩有关的）

hydrodynamic bearing 动液轴承（指该滑动轴承内承载压力的油膜是由轴颈在轴承内旋转时的油楔作用形成的，而不是由轴承外的油泵产生的，见 hydrostatic bearing）

hydrodynamic brake 动液制动器（即常规的液压制动器，= hydraulic brake）

hydrodynamic contour 流体力学外形（合乎流体力学要求的外形，或从流体力学的观点考虑的最佳外形，亦称流线型）

hydrodynamic drive 动液传动；动液传动装置（指 hydraulic drive 中完全依靠在封闭循环回路中的动液的作用来传递动力，即通过液体循环流动过程中，流体动量的变化来传递动力的传动装置，简称 HD unit = hydrokinetic drive）

hydrodynamic effect 流体动力（学）效应（指流体在运动过程中产生的各种力和力矩的影响和作用）

hydrodynamic lubrication 流体动力润滑（指润滑油膜是由两摩擦面的相对运动和存在于两相对运动面间的油楔作用而产生的）

hydrodynamic mechanic seal 流体动压式机械密封（密封端面设计为特殊的几何形状，利用相对旋转自行产生流体动压效应的机械密封）

hydrodynamic (modelling) theory 流体动力学模拟理论（交通工程学中，将车流比拟成流体，应用流体动力学的基本原理，从宏观上描述车流的运动规律，又称车流宏观理论）

hydrodynamic power transmission ①动压传动 ②液力变速器（= hydrodynamic transmission）

hydrodynamic retarder 液力缓速器，液力减速器（利用液力阻尼作用而获得减速作用的一种辅助汽车制动装置）

hydrodynamics 流体动力学（研究流体受力时所产生的运动及运动时所产生的力和力矩及其作用等）

hydrodynamic shift 液力换挡（指机械式变速器的液力换挡；液力变速器的换挡）

hydrodynamic torque converter 见 torque converter

hydrodynamic transformer 液力变矩器

hydrodynamic transmission ①动液传动，液力传动 ②液力变速器（指使用有液力变矩器的变速器，= hydrodynamic power transmission，hydraulic rotary transmission, hydrokinetic transmission，见 hydraulic transmission）

hydrodynamic unit 动液传动装置（指液力耦合器，液力变矩器等，简称 HD unit）

hydrodynamic unit charge pressure 动液装置的充填压力，动液装置的入口压力（使动液装置工作的外加压力，亦称液力变矩器充油压力）

hydrodynamic wedge 动液油楔，流体动力（学）润滑油楔（如：轴颈在轴承中旋转将油带至轴颈与轴承表面之间而形成的油楔，转速越高，油楔越来越厚，而使两摩擦面分开）

hydro-electric 电动-液压的，电控-液压的

hydro-extractor 脱水器

hydrofining 加氢精制（法）（加氢以改进产品，如：机油的质量）

hydroflated tire 充液轮胎，充水轮胎

hydrofoil (wing) amphibian 水翼式水陆两用车

hydroformer gasoline 临氢重整汽油（在具有一定压力的氢气中，将直链烃加热，通过触媒催化，转变为芳香烃而提高品质的汽油）

hydroform(ing) ①液压成形法 ②临氢重整（的）（在氢气或含氢气体的压力下加热使直链烃芳烃化）

hydrofuel 加氢燃料，加氢燃油（见 hydrogen enriched gasoline）

hydrogasoline 加氢汽油（= hydrogenated gasoline，见 hydrogen-enriched gasoline）

Hydrogen 3 （通用公司的）氢三型（氢燃料电池车的商品名）

hydrogen （H_2，无色气体，可从天然气、煤和水中制取，氢的稀薄燃烧极限很低，抗爆性好，火焰传播速率高，排气中有害物少，但密度低，仅 0.0898 克/升，因此需变成液体低温储存，或与稀土合金 Ln-Ni-Al 等反应成金属氢化物 M·H，装在发动机上利用发动机排气加热使氢析出，氢作为汽车代用燃料在技术上是可行的）

hydrogen RE 氢燃料转子发动机

hydrogen-air fuel cell 氢空气燃料电池，氢-氧燃料电池（= hydro-oxygen fuel cell，常温型燃料电池的一种，将氢注入负极，氧或空气导入正极，以氢氧化钾作电解液，当将电池的正负极接上外部电路时，电池因氢的氧化反应"$2H_2 + O_2 = 2H_2O$"所生成的热量直接变为电能，氢作为电池的燃料，故名）

hydrogenate ①加氢，用氢处理，使氢化，使还原 ②氢化物

hydrogenated fuel 氢化燃料，加氢燃料（= hydrofuel）

hydrogen attack 氢脆（见 hydrogen embrittlement）

hydrogen brittleness 氢（蚀致）脆、氢脆性（见 hydrogen embrittlement）

hydrogen-carbon ratio （烃的）氢碳比（H/C）

hydrogen-chlorin fuel cell 氢氯燃料电池

hydrogen cracking ①（烃类）加氢裂化（见 hydroform）②（金属的氢脆现象引起的裂纹）氢致裂纹（见 hydrogen embrittlement）

hydrogen cyanide 氰化氢（HCN）（发动机排出废气中的一种有害物）

hydrogen cylinder 氢气瓶，氢气筒

hydrogen desulphurization 加氢脱硫（法）

hydrogen embrittlement 氢脆性，吸氢变脆效应（在酸洗或镀覆工艺中，金属由于吸氢变脆，韧性或延伸率降低，= hydrogen brittleness）

hydrogen embrittlement torque （镀锌镀镉螺钉等的）氢蚀脆断转矩（指螺钉等镀锌镀镉过程中，因吸氢作用而变脆后，不致被拉断的最大转矩）

hydrogen engine 氢气发动机

hydrogen-enriched gasoline 加氢汽油（加氢燃油的一种，将少量的氢气加入汽油内，使汽油有可能在极稀的混合比下燃烧，借以减少废气中的HC、CO排量）

hydrogen FEMFC （以氢为燃料的）氢质子交换膜燃料电池（见FEMFC）

hydrogen flame ionization detector 氢火焰离子检测器（用来精确测定未燃氢化合物HC浓度的一种装置）

hydrogen fluoride 氟化氢，氟氢酸

hydrogen fuel cell 氢燃料电池（简称HFC，亦称氢-氧燃料电池"hydrogen-oxygen fuel cell"，将氢注入多孔质负极，将氧或空气导入多孔质正极，以氢氧化钾溶液作为电解液。当在电池外部接上电气回路时，电池内的氢经氧化反应所生成的热量直接变为电能）

hydrogen fuel cell car 氢燃料电池轿车（参见 fuel cell car）

hydrogen-fueled system 氢燃料系统（由氢存储系统，如：高压缩氢、液化氢、金属氢化合物等的存储装置，氢释放系统，如：将氢由高压缩液态或金属化合态中释放的系统和氢气-空气混合器，相当于化油器的作用，配制发动机不同工况所要求的氢-空气混合气等装置组成）

hydrogen-fuel engine 氢燃料发动机，氢气发动机（指以 H_2 为燃料的四冲程发动机，见 hydrogen）

hydrogen gas generator 氢气发生器

hydrogen gas injector （氢燃料发动机的）氢气喷射器

hydrogen nitrate 硝酸（HNO_3）

hydrogen nitride 氨（NH_3）

hydrogenous coal 褐煤（含水量较高的煤）

hydrogen-oxygen-carbon fuel cell 炭极氢氧燃料电池（以氢为燃料，用炭精作电极的燃料电池）

hydrogen peroxide 过氧化氢

hydrogen-powered vehicle 氢燃料汽车，氢动力车，氢汽车

hydrogen production and distribution system （氢燃料汽车的）氢气发生和分配系统

hydrogen-rich gas 富氢燃气

hydrogen safety sensor 氢安全传感器（用于测定氢在空气中的浓度，防止氢爆炸。一般氢浓度达4%～75%时，均有可能爆炸）

hydrogen safty sensor （氢燃料发动机汽车的空气）氢安全（浓度）传感器（通过测定热传导率，测定氢浓度，防止空气中氢浓度过高而引起爆炸）

hydrogen station （为氢燃料汽车加燃料的）氢燃料站

hydrogen sulphide 硫化氢

hydrogen-supplemented fuel 加氢燃油

hydrokinetic 流体运动学的

hydrokinetic transmission 见 hydrodynamic transmission

hydrokinetic type hydraulic transmission 动液式液力传动（= hydrodynamic transmission）

hydrolastic suspension 液压橡胶（弹簧）悬架（一种专利产品，由液压压缩锥形橡胶弹簧元件吸收振动的悬架系统）

hydrolysis 水解（作用），加水分解

hydro-master 液压能手（一种液压

真空助力器的商品名,见 hydraulic-vaccum braking system 和 vacuum booster)

hydro-master tester 液压助力器试验器(气压及液压系统的密封性及工作性能试验台)

hydromatic 液力传动,液压传动(系统)(商品名,= hydraulic transmission)

hydromatic transmission brake (液力传动系)行星齿轮变速器的制动器

hydro-mechanical transmisslon 液力-机械式变速装置,液力-机械传动

hydromechanics 流体力学,水力学

hydrometer 液体比重计(在汽车上①用于测量电瓶电解液比重,以确定其充电率 ②测量冷却液的比重,以确定其防冻能力等)

hydrometer syringe 液体比重计(用)吸液器

hydro-mixed clean car system 轿车发动机混氢净化系统(将供给发动机的汽油的一小部分输入氢气发生器中生成的氢气,再与汽油、空气形成混合气进入汽缸燃烧,达到排气净化的目的,同时又可节油)

hydro-motor 见 hydraulic motor

hydromount (发动机等的)液力支架,液压支座

hydro-peening 喷水清洗,冲洗

hydrophilic ①水(的)吸引力,水(的)吸力 ②水吸引附的,水抓附的,水吸住的

hydrophilic tread (汽车轮胎的)水吸式胎面(在水湿的路面不会打滑)

hydrophone 液振传感器(泛指各种置于液体中传递液体所传导的各种振动的传感器件,如:装在缸体冷却水套内的爆振传感器)

hydroplanetary transmission 带行星变速器的液力机械传动(见 hydraulic converter 和 hydraulic transmission)

hydro-planing [美](汽车在有水路面上高速行驶时产生的)浮滑现象,滑水现象,浮滑状态(这时形成水楔,使轮胎浮离地面,严重时失去制动作用,造成横滑,= [英] aquaplaning)

hydroplaning effect 浮滑效应,滑水效应(参见 hydroplaning)

hydroplaning speed (车辆)水滑速度,浮滑速度

hydropneumatic 油压气动的,液压气动的,液控气动的,液气的

hydropneumatic regenerative braking system 油气式再生制动系(制动时将汽车的动能回收储存于液压式储能器内,待加速或正常行驶时,输出驱动静液马达,再经传动轴驱动车轮)

hydropneumatic spring 液气弹簧(为空气弹簧的特例,通常充以氮气,引入液体作为传递载荷的中间介质。油和气由膜片隔开。液气弹簧气室压力比空气弹簧高 10~20 倍,体积小,质量轻,液体介质经阻尼阀可产生较强的阻尼,又具有非线性弹性特性,隔离振动与冲击的能力强)

hydro-pneumatic(spring type)suspension 液气(弹簧式)悬架,气液悬架(指以液体传递载荷,以气体,一般以氮作为弹性元件,即使用液气弹簧的悬架系统)

hydro power ①汽车车身修理用液压机具(由底座、液压缸和接装在液压缸上各处形状的一套压头及液压泵组成)②液力,液力源,水力

hydropulser 液压脉冲发生器(指各种产生液压脉冲的装置,如:查明汽车噪声源的试验中激发汽车以各种频率振动的脉冲液压加振系统的液压脉冲源)

hydrorefined 加氢精制的

hydro-rubber spring type suspension 橡胶液体弹簧式悬架(指以液体传

递载荷，以橡胶作为弹性元件的悬架形式）

hydrostatic bearing 流体静压轴承，静液轴承（轴颈-轴承间的压力由轴承内表面油槽中的机油形成的油膜承受）

hydrostatic chain driver 液体静压链驱动装置，静液链驱动装置

hydrostatic compensation 流体静压补偿，静液补偿（如：利用液体静压补偿摩擦件的磨损间隙等）

hydrostatic CVT 静液压式连续无级变速器（CVT 为 continuously variable transmission 的简称）

hydrostatic differential transmission 静液压分流传动（一部分功率由液压传递，其余由机械传动，分为输入分流式和输出分流式两类）

hydrostatic drive ①静液传动（指通过受压液体作为工作介质来传递动力。动液传动 hydraudynamic drive 与静液传动的基本区别在于，动液传动是通过液体的动能，即受压液体或带有压力的液体的运动来实现能量或动力的传递，而静液传动主要是通过液体的静压来进行能量传递。在静液传动中，液体流速一般不超过5m/s。车用静液传动系统是由发动机驱动液压泵使液体压力升高，受压液体驱动液压马达，亦称液动机输出动力，来驱动车轮，亦称 hydrastatic transmission）②见 hydrostatic motor

hydrostatic gauge 液体静压力计，静液压力计

hydrostatic gear 静液机构（一般指液压泵及液压马达等）

hydrostatic head 静液压头，静水头

hydrostatic mechanical seal 流体静压式机械密封（密封端面设计成特殊几何形状，利用外部引入的压力流体或被密封介质本身通过密封界面的压力降产生流体静压效应的机构密封）

hydrostatic motor 静（液）压马达（一种静液驱动装置，一般由旋转斜盘等机构组成，利用液压泵送来的高压静液的压力产生旋转运动，亦称 hydrostatic drive）

hydrostatic oil bearing 静液轴承（简称 hydrostatic bearing，指轴颈与轴承支承面间的油膜是由轴承内表面的油槽中的机油形成的一类滑动轴承）

hydrostatic power transmission 流体静压传动系，静液传动装置（见 hydrostatic drive）

hydrostatic pressure 静液压（参见 hydrostatic drive）

hydrostatic primary machine 静液马达主机，液压马达主机，液动主机（见 hydraulic motor）

hydrostatics 流体静力学，静液力学（研究流体在静态下的特性，特别是研究静液的压力传动）

hydrostatic steering 液力静压转向，液力静压转向系（一般指无机械转向杆系的全液力转向，参见 full fluid steering）

hydrostatic stored energy transmission system 静液压蓄能传动系（利用液压储能元件存储车辆制动、减速的能量，以及发动机的剩余功率，供正常行驶或需要大的驱动力时使用）

hydrostatic suspension 液-气悬架装置（见 hydro-pneumatic suspension）

hydrostatic test 流体静力学试验，静液压试验，水压试验

hydrostatic transmission 静液传动，容积式液压传动（详见 hydrostatic drive①）

hydrostatic vehicle 液体静压驱动车辆，静液驱动车辆（指由发动机驱动液压泵使工作油液压力升高，进而带动静压马达驱动的车辆）

hydrotreating 氢气处理，加氢处理

hydrous ethanol 含水乙醇，含水酒精

Hydro-vac （一种装于液压式制动系中的)真空助力器的商品名

hydrox cell 氢氧燃料电池

hydroxide 氢氧化物

hygrometer 湿度计,湿度表(= hygrograph)

hygroscopic character 吸湿特性,吸水性

hygroscopicity 吸湿性,吸湿度,吸水性

hygrostat ①恒湿器 ②测湿器

hypalon 氯磺酰化聚乙烯橡胶(= chloro-sulfonated polyethylene)

hypalon coated wiring 氯磺酰化聚乙烯合成橡胶包线

hyperacoustic 超声波的（指高于2000赫兹的机械波)

Hyperbar turbocharging system 海帕巴废气涡轮增压系统(法国人 Jean Melchior1970年发明的一种柴油机增压系统,由法 Hyperbar 柴油机公司获得专利,因而得名)

hyperbola 双曲线［平面内与两个定点的距离差的绝对值是常数（小于两定点间距离)的点的轨迹]

hyperbolic(al) 双曲线的

hyperbolic gear 双曲线齿轮

hyperbolic spiral 双曲螺线

hyperboloidal gear 双曲面齿轮（斜齿锥齿轮)

Hyper-CVT 超级-CVT（1997年日产公司推出的世界首套装用液力变矩器、可供 2000 cc 级轿车用的4挡；CVT 商品名)

hyper-elastic deformation 超弹性变形（在弹性极限之外的变形)

hyper-eutectic steel 过共析钢（指含碳量大于 0.8%,其合金组织为渗碳体加珠光体的钢组织结构)

hypermetropia 远视,远视眼(= hyperopia)

hypersonic 高超音速的（指超音速5倍以上者)

hyperstatic 超静定的

Hyper system 复合动力系统（商品名 Hyper 为 hybrid 和 performance 的复合词,由一台发动机和一台电动机组成,起步加速时二者同时驱动,制动时电动机变为发电机储能)

hyper-velocity 超高速的

hypocycloid 圆内旋轮线中的内摆线［指平面上,一个动圆（发生圆)沿一固定圆（基圆)内侧做纯滚动时,动圆上一点的轨迹,见 hypotrochoid]

hypocycloidal tooth 内摆线齿

hypoeutectoid steel 亚共析钢（指碳含量小于 0.8%,其合金组织为铁素体加珠光体的钢)

hypoid axle 准双曲面齿轮驱动桥（指使用准双曲面齿轮的驱动桥,详见 hypoid gear)

hypoid bevel gear 准双曲面锥齿轮(= hypoid bevel wheel,指一对轴线交错的锥齿轮副中的任一个,见 hypoid gear)

hypoid final drive 准双曲面齿轮主传动（见 hypoid gear)

hypoid gear 准双曲面齿轮（指一对轴线交错的圆锥形或近似圆锥形的齿轮副中的任一个齿轮,其形状及齿轮曲线与锥齿轮相同。但驱动小齿轮的轴线可以装在从动齿轮轴线的上方或下方。用于汽车驱动桥主减速器时,驱动小齿轮轴线多位于从动齿轮轴线下方,以降低传动轴位置,提高车辆高速行驶稳定性。由于两齿轮轴线不在同一平面上,故两齿法向周节虽然相同,但驱动小齿轮的端面周节较大,可得到较大的螺旋角,尺寸增大,刚性加强。加大驱动小齿轮的螺旋角,可使更多的轮齿同时接触,因而运转平滑,且齿面正压力减少。准双曲面齿轮啮合时,除滚动外,还有滑动,因而对润滑油有较高的要求。

其节面为一准双曲线旋体表面,故称准双曲面齿轮)

hypoid-gear and pinion 准双曲面锥齿轮副(见 hypoid-gear pair)

hypoid gear oil 准双曲线齿轮滑油,准双曲面齿轮油(简称 HP oil,参见 hypoid gear)

hypoid gear pair 准双曲面齿轮副(指一对轴线交错的圆锥形或近似圆锥形的齿轮)

hypoid oil 准双曲面齿轮油(简称 HP oil,指重负荷车辆齿轮油,由精制润滑油加入多种添加剂制成,具有极好的极压耐磨性,氧化安定性和防锈蚀性,用于工作条件苛刻的准双曲面锥齿轮主减速器等,相当于美国标准 API-GL-5,亦称 hypoid lubricant,简称 HP lubricant)

hypoid pinion 准双曲面齿轮副的小锥齿轮

hypoid pinion offset 准双曲面齿轮副传动中驱动小齿轮偏移量(指其轴线与大齿轮轴线的错开量)

hypotenuse 弦,斜边

hypothetic(al) ①假定的(假设的,假想的) ②有前提的

hypotrochoid 内摆线 [亦称内旋轮线, = hypocycloid,指在平面上一动圆沿固定基圆的内侧作纯滚动时该滚动圆圆周上的一点的轨迹。该滚动圆称创成圆(creating circuit),该点称创成点(creating point)。若创成点在创成圆圆周之外且与创成圆固连,则创成点的轨迹称长幅内摆线 prolote hypotrochoid 或 prolote hypocycloid。若创成点在创成圆内且与创成圆固连,则创成点的轨迹称短幅内摆线 curtate hypotrochoid 或 curtate hypocycloid]

hypotrochoidal engine 内旋轮线式(转子)发动机

Hyrastic suspension 高静压悬架(Austin 公司推出的一种不同弹簧和减振器而在每一个车轮上作用有一个特种橡胶制的大型缸筒,其中封入 18 大气压的不冻液特殊混合液,前后用 2 根钢管连接,依靠高压液体的前后移动,可自动地保持车身常处于水平状态)

hysteresis ①迟后,迟滞(指系统或系统单元的响应落后于输入信号强度增减变化的现象,或系统的输出变化落后于输入变化的现象) ②滞留影响(指两相关的物理量 x、y,x 的值到某一阶段后不再随 y 值的变化而变化,却仍受该阶段前 y 值变化的影响的现象) ③磁滞(现象)(指介质磁化到饱和点后,磁感应强度 B 不再随磁场强度 H 增加而增加,H 减小,B 随之减小,但 B 的变化总是落后于 H 的变化,这一现象称磁滞,参见 hysteresis loop)

hysteresis curve ①迟滞曲线 ②磁滞曲线(参见 hysteresis loop)

hysteresis damping 迟滞阻尼(当振动系统做简谐振动时,由材料内摩擦产生的阻尼。它在一个周期中的能量耗散与频率无关,与振幅平方成正比)

hysteresis loop ①迟滞环(描述在周期性变形过程中,材料连续应力—应变或力—位移况态的闭合曲线) ②磁滞回线(描述介质磁化达到饱和后,磁场强度 B 由饱和点 S 下降到零,并由零增大到反向饱和点,再由反向饱和点经零回到饱和点,S 的一次循环中磁感应强度的变化历程的两条曲线所形成的一个闭合曲线。磁滞回线包围的面积代表一个循环过程中单位体积铁芯内损耗的能量,称为磁滞损失 hysteresis loss,它最终将以热的形式消散)

hysteresis loss 磁滞损失(见 hysteresis loop)

hysteresis set 滞后变形;滞留变形

Hyundai Motor Company 现代汽车

公司（韩国三大汽车公司之一，1967年为小型组装汽车厂，1976年开始生产汽车，1993年生产已达125万辆，国内市场占有率达42.8%）

Hyundai Motor Service ［韩］现代汽车服务公司

Hy-wire （通用公司）氢燃料电池电动机驱动-线操控车（商品名，为Hydrogen与by-wire二词的组合词，该车的转向、加速、制动全部控制功能均集于面板两侧的手柄上）

Hz 赫兹（参见hertz）

I ①点火(ignition) ②强度(intensity) ③中间挡(intermediate speed) ④碘(iodine)

i (injection 的简称,在下列简称中表明该发动机是汽油喷射型的,如:GTi,EFi,1.6i 等)

IA ①输入轴(input axis) ②国际埃(波长量测单位,参见 international angström)

IAA 怠速空气调整(idle air adjustment 的简称)

IAATM 国际交通事故和交通医学协会(International Association for Accident and Traffic Medicine 的简称)

IAB 进气空气旁通阀(intake air bypass valve 的简称,多为一电磁阀,高速时该阀开启,以增加进气量)

IAC 怠速空气控制(系统)(idle air control 的简称,为了保证发动机低温快怠速热起或在怠速运转中,负荷变动如:接通空调、自动变速器挂挡,使用各种电器等情况下提高怠速转速,以防止发动机熄火,而将所要求数量的附加空气,绕过关闭位置的节气门,送入节气门后方的进气歧管内的系统,该系统由怠速空气通道,控制该通道通过断面的针阀及由电子控制模块控制的针阀步进电动机或电磁阀等组成)

IACF 国际汽车俱乐部联合会(International Automobile Club Federation 的简称)

IAC motor 怠速空气控制电动机(idle-air controlling motor 的简称)

IACV ①怠速空气控制阀(亦写作 IAC valve,怠速空气控制装置中控制怠速空气通道的针阀"pintle valve") ②进气空气(通路长度)控制阀(induction aircontrol valve 的简称,见 ACIS)

IAD [美]国际汽车设计公司(International Automotive Design 的简称)

IAE 国际人体环境工程协会(International Association of Ergonomics 的简称)

IAE [英]汽车工程师学会(The Institution of Automobile Engineers 的简称)

IAEA (联合国的)国际原子能机构(Intenational Atomic Energy Agency)

IAF 国际汽车联合会(International Automobile Federation 的简称)

IAI 国际汽车学会(International Automobile Institute 的简称)

IAM 国际机械师协会(International Association of mechanists 的简称)

IAME [日]汽车机械工程师学会(Institute of Automobile Mechanical Engineers 的简称)

IAQS (volvo 的)车厢内空气质量系统(Interior Air Quality System 的简称)

IAT (装在进气歧管或空气滤清器内的)进气空气温度传感器(intake air temperature sensor 的简称,美国政府规定从 1995 年起一律用 SAE 推荐的这一术语表示进气空气温度传感器,取代原 chrysler 的 CTS,Ford 的 ACT,通用的 MAT,ATS 等)

IATM 国际试验材料协会(International Association for Testing Materials 的简称)

IAT sensor 进气温度传感器(intake air temperature sensor 的简称)

IBC (美国著名的车辆预防性安全系统生产厂家 TWR 推出的)集成型制动控制系统(的简称,该系统不再使用真空助力装置,而由一台驱动的执行器根据电子控制模块发出的转数、转速和位置指令直接控制制动器。与常规的电子防滑制动系统"ESC"比较,IBS 不仅响应灵敏,而且体积小,重量轻。据称,该超高速无刷电动机可使 IBC 系统产生极高的制动压力升高率,车辆的减速度最终可达 1 G/<150 m-sec)

I-beam 工字钢,工字梁(= joist steel, flanged beam,简称 I)

I-beam axle 工字梁前桥,工字梁桥(整体式刚性车桥,= rigid axle)

I-beam rotor (转子发动机的)工字形截面转子,工字形截面旋转活塞(旋转活塞内部呈工字形截面,并有径向筋条,防止热变形)

IBEM (噪声源定位和分级的)逆边界方法(inverse boundary element me-thod 的简称)

Ibis white 朱鹭白(车身颜色)

IBM 离子束加工(ion beam machining)

IBMCo. [美]国际商用机器公司(International Business Machine Co. 一家世界闻名的计算机公司,其 PC 公司专门设计、生产、经营 personal computer)

IBOY 20×× 见 ITOY 20××

IBT 制动摩擦片初始温度(initial brake lining temperature 的简称)

IC ①(电子点火系统的)点火控制信号(ignition control 的简称,美国政府规定 1995 年起一律使用 SAE 推荐的 ignition control,表示电子控制模块输出的火花塞跳火控制指令脉冲信号,取代原 Ford 的 spout 和 GM 的 EST 等用语)②电感量-电容量(inductance-capacitance 的简称)③集成电路(integrated circuit 的简称)④中间电路(intermediate circuit 的简称)⑤内部连接(internal connection 的简称)

IC (乘员的)充气式护帘(见 inflatable curtain system)

ICA 防早燃添加剂(ignition control additive 的简称)

ICAS (日本)五十铃汽车排气净化系统(Isuzu Clean Air System 的简称)

I^2C bus I^2C 总线(一种用于集成电路器件之间连接的二线制总线,仅使用串行数据线 SDATA 和串行时钟线 SCLOCK 2 根线,就可构成多个主机和多个从机之间的数据通信连接)

ice ①冰 ②冰冻,冻结 ③用冰覆盖

ICE ①车内娱乐(设施)(in-car entertainment 的简称)②内燃机(internal combustion engine 的简称)

ice accretion 积冰

ice body 装运冰块用的车厢

ice building 结冰

ice-control rock salt (道路)防冰冻用岩盐

ice covering 表面结冰(如路面等)

ice-cream body 运送冰激凌用的车箱

ice crust 冰壳,薄冰层

ICE-electric hybrid ①内燃机-电动

机混合动力的 ②内燃机-电动机混合动力系统 ③内燃机-电动机复合动力汽车

ice engine oil 冷冻机用滑油

ice formation 结冰

ice-glazed 覆盖冰（霜）的

ice-gripping tread 用于冰结道路上的抗滑胎面

ICEI [美]内燃机研究所（Internal Combustion Engine Institute 的简称）

ice load-bearing capacity 冰层承压能力

ice nail （轮胎上的）冰地防滑钉

IC engine 内燃机（internal combustion engine 的简称）

IC engine spark arrester 内燃机火星捕捉器，内燃机排气火星消除器（消除排气中的火星，防止点燃附近的易燃物资）

ice-patch surface 结冰路面

ice point 冰点

ICE-powered 内燃机作动力的，内燃机驱动的

ice scraper 冰刮（从风窗玻璃和门、窗玻璃刮除冰、霜的塑料小刮具）

ice silver 水晶银（车身颜色）

ice tray （冷藏车冷冻系统的）冰盘

ICEV 内燃发动机汽车（Internal Combustion Engine Vehicle 的简称）

icing 结冰，冻冰（如：icing of throttle plate 因混合气温度过低而导致节气门上）

ICM ①点火控制模块（ignition control module 的简称，该模块根据动力控制模块的指令，在精确的时刻切断点火线圈初级电路，确保火花塞在最佳点火提前角跳火）②防盗系统控制模块（车辆防盗系统锁止装置控制模块 immobilizer control modula 的简称。旧称 ICU，为 immobilizer control unit 的简称）

icon 像（图像，插图）

iconoscope 光电摄像管，光电显像管，电子摄像管

IC regulator 集成电路调节器（利用集成电路开关特性控制发动机电压的装置，= solid state regulator, electronic regulator）

ICRV 进气调节旋转阀（intake control rotary valve 的简称）

ICS ①智能定速巡航系统（见 adaptive cruise system）②综合控制件（integrated control system 的简称，商品名，装在转向盘柱等上面的车内电子系统，如：音响、空调、导航等的组合式开关、按钮组件）

I&C systems 仪表与控制系统（instrumentation and control system 的简称）

I cycle 指令周期（指计算机中央处理器从主存储器中找到和取出一条指令并准备进行处理的系列步骤，instrument cycle 的简称）

ID ①电感放电（点火）（inductive discharge 的简称）②证实；识别；等同（identification 的简称）③导流通风（inducted draft 的简称）④内径（inside diameter 的简称）⑤标识符（identifier 的简称，见 collision detection②和 C^2D system）

IDAS 智能驾驶辅助系统（intelligent driving assist system 的简称，通常为安全车距保持、车道保持、后视影像、自动驻车系统等的通称）

IDB （汽车局域网的）智能数据总线（intelligent data bus 的简称，指 SAE 车辆网络委员会划分的汽车网络分类中传输速率最高的一类"D类网络系统"，D 类网络协议的传输速率为 250kb/s～400Mb/s）

IDB -C 智能运输系统数据总线（Intelligent transportation system data bus 的简称，基于 CAN 的控制用汽车局域网协议）

IDBRA 国际驾驶员行为研究协会（International Driver's Behaviour Research Association 的简称)

ID Code 识别码 (见 identification code)

ideal braking force distribution curve 理想(制动器)制动力分配曲线(指在任何载荷与轮胎-地面附着系数下,汽车在水平路面上制动时,前、后轴车轮均能同时接近抱死状态的前、后制动力分配曲线)

ideal car 概念车,概念轿车(理想型的轿车,不是正式生产的轿车,参见 concept car)

ideal compression ratio 理想压缩比 (见 ideal theoretical compression ratio)

ideal critical diameter 淬火理想临界直径(假定在冷却剂的冷却能力无限大的条件下,理想淬火时试件中心部分的50%成为马氏体的临界直径作为可淬火性的比较基准)

ideal cycle (发动机)理想循环(指经过适当假定,科学地抽象,简化并可用数学公式表达其热效率的热力循环,其工质为理想气体,工质的加热与放热是瞬时的并不计循环中的热损失)

ideal multi-stage compression 理想多级压缩(各级吸气温度及耗功相等时,对理想气体进行的等熵压缩)

ideal theoretical compression ratio (转子发动机的)理想压缩比(即转子工作面上没有凹坑时的压缩比,= ideal compression ratio)

identical ①完全相同的,完全一样的,完全相等的 ②同一的(同一个,同一种,同一轴等)

identical part 共用件(指同一系列不同车型均使用的相同总成和零部件,如:制动器、悬架等,见 shared component)

identification 识别,辨别,鉴别;认出,认明,查明

identification card ①标签,货物标牌,证件 ②身份证 (= identity card)

identification code 识别码(简称 I.D. code,指用数字、文字、符号或颜色等表示零部件的用途,安装部位,特征等的代码。其中,用数字表示的代码亦称 identification number, number code。用颜色表示的代码,亦称 identification colour 或 colour code,多用于表明电线等的用途或用在何处)

identification lamp 标志灯(特指装在大型车辆前、后顶部表明其特殊车型的标志灯组)

identification of modal parameter 模态参数识别(指根据振动测试数据经数学方法确定结构振动的模态参数,又称试验模态分析)

identification of position 位置的确定,定位(简称 IP)

identification sign 识别符号

identification tag ①识别标志 ②(车辆的)牌照 (参见 license plate)

identifier 识别标志,名称,名号,标志;鉴别器,鉴定用试剂;鉴定人,检验人

identify ①识别,鉴别,辨认 ②认为同一,使成为同一

identifying dye 识别染料(渗入汽油内区别汽油品种或添加剂的特点)

identity ①同一(性),完全相同,一致 ②恒等(式) ③本身、本体 ④身份,国籍

identity markings (产品的)识别标志(注明制造厂家,出厂日期等),出厂标记

IDI ①间接喷射(见 indirect injection) ②整体式直接点火(系)(见 Integrated Direct Ignition)

IDID 柴油机喷油器内部的沉积物 (internal diesel injector deposits 的简称,如:漆状沉积物化 lacquering)

IDI diesel engine 间接喷射式柴油发动机(见 indirect injection diesel engine)

idiot proof 傻瓜式（见 fool proof）

IDIS （Volvo 的）智能驾驶信息系统（Intelligent Driver Information System 的简称）

IDK system 车间距离保持系统（见 adaptive cruise system）

IDL ①怠速（idle 的简称）②怠速开关（idle switch 的简称）③怠速触点（idle contact point 的简称）④（驾驶者）驾驶合法性（评价）指标

idle ①怠速（指发动机在节气门关闭的情况下的正常稳定的低速运转，＝ idling）②怠速的 ③怠速运转

idle adjusting screw 怠速调节螺钉

idle air bypass valve solenoid 怠速空气旁通阀（的控制）电磁阀（见 solenoid-type idle air bypass valve）

idle air control 怠速空气量控制（由在怠速运转时，将附加空气送入节气门后方的旁通空气道，控制其通过断面的针阀及控制该针阀行程和位置的电磁阀或可逆转步进电动机组成。发动机电子控制模块根据工况要求，通过上述机构控制通过该通道的怠速空气量，以提高和稳定怠速转速）

idle arm ［美］（前轮独立悬架式轿车转向杆系中央连杆远离转向器端的）空转支臂（亦写作 idler arm ＝ idling lever，该臂的一端通过销孔与中央连杆端的回转支撑销连接，起支撑作用并保证中央连杆可做横向移动，该臂的另一端亦通过销孔装在车身上的一个带支撑销的托架上。在某些转向杆系中，该臂不仅起中央连杆一端回转支点的作用，而且还兼起将中央连杆的运动传给远离转向器一端车轮的转向节臂的作用，称随动臂"relay lever"）

idle capacity 备用容量，储备容量，备用电容，空用功率，备用能力，后备容量，后备功率

idle component ①无功分量 ②无功元件

idle component of current 无功电流（见 reactive current）

idle contact （节气门位置传感器的）怠速触点（简称 IdL）

idle discharge port （化油器）怠速喷口

idle (fuel mixture)(adjustment) limiter 怠速调整螺钉混合气浓度调程限制器

idle gear 惰轮，中介齿轮（指两齿轮间不改变该两齿轮的速比而使该两齿轮向着同一方面旋转的中间齿轮）

idle hours ①停歇时间，停工时间 ②（发动机）怠转时间

idle instability 怠速不稳定性

idle limiter 怠速限制器（为使怠速运转时排放的一氧化碳浓度低于一定水平而限制怠速油量的装置）

idle load compensator 怠速负荷补偿器（为一进气管真空控制的膜片式节气门，当发动机负荷增加时，该膜片在进气管真空作用下，使节气门适当开大，简称 ILC）

idle mixture adjusting screw 怠速混合气调整螺钉（一般该螺钉正对怠速燃油量孔，拧转该螺钉可改变怠速量孔出油量，从而调节怠速混合气浓度）

idle motion 空冲程，空转，怠转，无负荷运转，空载运行

idle odor 发动机怠速运转时的排气臭味

idle oil pressure 怠速时的机油压力

idle operation 空驶，空转

idle pulley 张紧轮，惰轮，中间轮

idler ①惰轮，中间齿轮（＝ idle gear，介于两齿轮间不改变速比，仅改变旋转方向）②（履带）间轮，导向轮 ③（传动带、链条的）

张紧轮

idler arm 见 idle arm

idle revolutions 空转

idler lever 惰轮操纵杆，传动带张紧轮拉杆

idle roller 空转液柱

idler pulley 传动带张紧轮，传动带导轮，中间传动带轮（= belt tensioning pulley）

idler reverse gear （齿轮变速器的）倒挡中间齿轮（亦写作 reverse idler gear）

idler shaft 惰轮轴，空转轮轴

idler spring （履带）导向轮张紧弹簧

idler sprocket （履带）张紧链轮

idle run(ning) 无负荷运转，怠速运转（= no-load run, unloaded running）

idler wheel ①（履带行走装置）导向轮，张紧轮 ②惰轮 ③（传动带）张紧轮

idle silence valve 怠速消声阀

idle speed （发动机）怠速（运转时）的转速（= idling speed）

idle speed control ①怠速控制（一般为发动机电子控制系统的一项控制功能，根据发动机、空调、动力转向等附件的工况，调控发动机怠速转速以防止怠速熄火、怠速过高、怠速不稳、怠速过低等，简称 ISC）②怠速控制机构

Idle speed control motor 怠速控制电动机（根据电子控制模块的指令通过控制节气门开度来控制怠速的可逆转型永磁电动机，简称 ISC motor）

idle speed control switch 怠速控制开关（节气门关闭时，该开关触点接通，向发动机控制模块发送"对怠速进行控制"的信号，节气门开启时，触点断开，向发动机控制模块发出"停止怠速控制"信号，简称 ISC switch）

idle speed control valve 怠速控制阀（简称 ISCV，发动机电子控制模块通过对该阀的开度来控制吸入的空气量，从而控制怠速转速）

idle speed emission standard （汽车）怠速排放量标准（限制汽车在怠速时排放 CO、HC 等成分排放量的标准）

idle speed solenoid 怠速电磁阀（作用：①保持节气门正确开度 ②点火断开后，使节气门密闭，以防继燃）

idle speed stabilizer （发动机的）怠速稳定装置（使怠速运转时转速稳定的装置，如：怠速调节螺钉，节气门怠速限位螺钉等）

idle sprocket spindle 张紧链轮轴

idle stability 怠速稳定性

idle stop ①怠速停车（指发动机怠速运转时挂空挡停车）②（防止怠速超时运转的）怠速超时停机系统（指停车怠速运转超过某规定时间即自动停机的系统）③怠速停机系统（= idling stop system，有多种，如：一种是松开加速踏板即自动停机，踩下加速踏板即自动起动。另一种新型的是，松开加速踏板临停车前，车速降到 9 km/h 时自动停机，操纵转向盘，发动机即自动起动。还有一种带减速能量回收功能，在停机的同时启动减速能量回收系统）

idle stop screw （化油器或喷油泵）怠速限位螺钉

idle stop solenoid ①怠速节气门增开电磁开关（发动机点火开关接通后怠速运转时，该开关可将节气门稍许顶开，增大节气门怠速开度，使怠速时有较多的空气吸入汽缸，混合气变稀而减少废气污染）②（有时指）节气门断火速闭电磁阀（用于装有自动变速器及其他怠速转速较高的发动机，在点火断开后，立

即将节气门关闭，完全切断燃油与空气的供给，防止点火开关断开后熄不了火而继燃，亦称 solenoid throttle stop, idle stop valve)

idle stop valve 见 idle stop solenoid②

idle stroke 空冲程

idle system （化油器）怠速系统（由怠速量孔、怠速空气量孔、怠速喷口、怠速过渡喷口、怠速调节螺钉和怠速油道等组成。当气门关闭，发动机怠速运转时，供给发动机维持稳定低速运转所需的混合气，亦称 idling circuit，参见 slow speed system)

idle time ①停歇时间，停工时间 ②（发动机）怠速运转时间（= idle hours）③空闲时间（指功能部件处于可运转状态但未使用的那段时间）

idle timer 怠速运转自动限时器（到规定的怠速时间后，该装置即可将发动机关闭熄火，以防怠速时间过长）

idle torque （发动机）怠速转矩

idle tracking switch 怠速跟踪开关（简称 ITS，控制节气门的一个开关。当节气门关闭，发动机怠速运转时，该开关开启，节气门开启时，该开关闭合。发动机电子控制模块根据该开关的信息确认节气门是处于开启或闭合状态，若处于闭合状态，便启动其怠速控制程序，见 idle speed control motor)

idle travel 空冲程（= free travel）

idle up (device) （电子控制式）怠速提高装置（如果发动机怠速运转时使用空调或动力转向，该装置可使发动机怠速转速提高 100～200 转/分。此外，冷机起动时，也可自动使发动机以较高怠速运转）

idle wheel 空转轮，惰轮

idling 怠速运转，空运转（见 idling speed）

idling adjustment 怠速调整，调节怠速装置

idling and low speed circuit 怠速供油系（= slow speed system）

idling characteristic 怠速特性

idling circuit 见 idle system

idling drag 怠速拖动（指装有自动变速器的车辆，当发动机怠速运转，变速杆挂前进挡，即"D"挡时的缓慢向前行驶，亦称 creep）

idling gear 空转轮，惰轮

idling gear shaft 惰轮轴，空转齿轮轴

idling lever bracket 转向杆系中央连杆空转支撑臂（在车架上的）回转托架（见 idle arm）

idling loss 怠速运转损失，空转损失

idling roller 导轮，（传动带）张紧滚轮，空轮滚轮

idling setting 怠速调整（= slow running adjustment）

idling shaft ①中介轮或中介齿轮的轴 ②中间轴，副轴（= countershaft, lay shaft）

idling speed （发动机）最低空载转速（在空负荷时能稳定运转的最低转速，简称怠速，= noload speed）

idling speed adjusting screw 怠速调节螺钉

idling speed delivery 怠速喷油量（指柴油机怠速工况下，喷油泵的循环喷油量）

idling speed test 最低空载转速试验，怠速试验（测定发动机最低空负荷时的稳定转速值的试验）

idling stability 怠速稳定性

idling stop system ①怠速停车（指车辆在发动机怠速运转状态挂空挡停车）②怠速熄火系统（美国规定从 2007 年起总重超过 14000 磅的大型柴油车都必须加装此系统：连续怠速运转超过 5 分钟，即自动熄火停机，以减少排放）

IDM 点火诊断监测器（ignition diagnosis monitor 的简称，用于诊断点火控制模块"ICM"的信号和监控火花输出"spout"信号的前沿和后沿。当"spout"信号出现问题时，"IDM"便通知动力控制模块"PCM"将一个故障判断码，"DTC"送入 PCM 存储器中）

i-DM 智能驾驶大师（intelligent drive master 的简称，教授驾驶者技巧、提高驾驶乐趣的软件和硬件设备）

IDP 国际驾驶执照（International Driving Permit 的简称）

I-Drive 智能驾驶系统（Intelligent drive system 的简称，全计算机控制式驾驶系统）

i-Drive （某几款宝马车中控台上的）组合操纵件（键、按钮、拨杆开关等）

IDS 智能驾驶系统（Intelligent Drive System 的简称）（欧宝 Opel 的）智能驾驶系统（通过电子控制系统，实现悬架、转向、制动间的联网，可根据驾驶者的要求，做出智能化选择）

i-DSI 智能型双火花塞系统（intelligent duel spark plug ignition system 的简称，双火花塞系统的一种，可根据发动机转速及负荷的变化调整和错开汽缸内两个火花塞的跳火时刻）

IE ①指标误差，系数误差（index error 的简称）②工业工程师（industrial engineer 的简称）③工业管理学（industrial engineering 的简称）

IEA 国际能源局（International Energy Agency 的简称，设在法国巴黎）

IEC ①国际电子委员会（International Electronical Commission 的简称）②综合环境控制（integrated environmental control 的简称）

IECEC ［美］跨学会能源保护技术会议（Intersociety Energy Conversion Engineering Conference 的简称）

IEE 环境工程师学会（Institute of Environmental Engineers 的简称）

IEEE 见 Institute of Electrical & Electronic Engineers

IEEE1394 （美）电气与电子工程师学会 1394（汽车局域网信息系统通信协议）

i-E Loop 智能减速能量回收系统（intelligent-energy-loop 的简称，"智能能量循环使用"的意思，马自达公司采用电容器型蓄电池存储减速时利用电动机反拖发电回收的汽车减速-制动能量的系统的商品名。据称频繁加减速工况下行驶时可节油 10%）

I-Eloop 制动能量回收系统的商品名

IETG 国际能源技术集团（International Energy Technology Group 的简称）

IF ①（英国）燃料学会（Institute of Fuel 的简称）②中频，中间频率（intermediate frequency 的简称）

IFAC 国际自动控制协会（International Federation of Automatic Control 的简称）

IFC 综合供油控制（Integrated Fuel Control 的简称）

IFE 瞬时燃油经济性（instantaneous fuel economy 的简称）

i-Four 智能化四轮控制系统［intelligent Four 的简称，日本丰田公司四轮驱动系统的商品名。该系统对汽油喷射、变速、防抱死、四轮驱动、四轮转向、空气悬架等实行综合协调控制，信息共享，传感器共用，使各个系统的性能得以提高，最大限度地发挥轮胎对地面的抓着能力。该系统还可自动判断路面状况，当车辆在滑路上行驶时，其性能指示灯（function indicator）将闪光，提示驾驶人员采取相应驾驶措施］

IFS 前轮独立悬架，独立前悬架 (independent front suspension 的简称)
IG 点火 (ignition 的简称)
I-gauge 工字形极限卡规
IGBT 绝缘门双极结晶体管 (insulated gate bipolar transistor 的简称，一种半导体开关元件)
IGFET 绝缘选通电路场效应晶体管 (insulated gate field effect transistor 的简称)
I-girder 工字梁 (= I beam)
ign-det 点火检验仪 (= ignition detector)
ignitable 可燃的，可着火的 (= ignitible)
ignite 点燃，点火；着火，发火
igniter injector 燃料喷射点火器 (见 fuel injector igniter)
igniter plug (柴油机起动的电点火) 引燃塞
ignitible 可燃的 (参见 ignitable)
ignition ①点火 (指火花塞跳点火花，点燃缸内混合气) ②着火 (指汽缸内一定温度和压力条件下，具有一定浓度的可燃混合气经过焰前反应，开始进入热焰燃烧的现象)
ignition accelerator (柴油) 着火加速剂，引燃添加剂 (为了改善柴油着火性能，缩短滞燃期，亦称 ignition promoter)
ignition advance 点火提前 (= spark advance, 指火花塞在活塞到达上止点前跳火，以活塞到达上止点前曲轴转角度数表示其提前的程度)
ignition (advance) lever 点火提前调整杆 (= ignition timing lever)
ignition advancer 点火提前装置 (= ignition governor, 一般指离心式或真空式点火提前机构，分别根据发动机转速或发动机负荷自动调节点火提前角)
ignition amplifier 点火放大器 (指电子点火系中点火信号放大电路)
ignition angle 点火角 (一般指点火提前角，即活塞到达上止点前，火花塞跳火花点火时起到活塞到达上止点止，曲轴所转过的角度，有时亦表示点火迟后角，点火延迟角，见 ignition retard angle)
ignition by compression 压缩点火，压燃 (= compression ignition)
ignition cable 点火线，点火高压线 (= ignition lead, 点火系中，从点火线圈到分电器，从分电器到火花塞等的高压线的通称)
ignition cam (分电盘) 断电器凸轮 (指使点火线圈初级电路触点闭合和断开的凸轮)
ignition cam dwell 断电器凸轮闭合角 (指触点闭合期间，凸轮的转角)
ignition capacitor 点火电容器 (①指常规分电器式点火系中，与断电器触点并联的电容器，其作用是: ⓐ当初级电流断开时可加速磁场消失，从而提高次级电压 ⓑ减弱断电器触点火花，延长触点使用寿命 ②指电容放电式点火系中储蓄点火电能的电容器，该点火系的充电电向向电容器充电到 400V, 点火时刻电容器向点火线圈一次绕组放电，而在二次绕组中感应出点火高压)
ignition capacity of an accumulator 蓄电池点火容量 (反复短时间放电容量)
ignition circuit 点火电路 (见 primary circuit, secondary circuit)
ignition coil 点火线圈 (点火系中产生火花塞跳火所需的高压电的感应线圈，由初级绕组和次级绕组组成)
ignition coil head 带高压线插座的点火线圈盖
ignition contact maker 触点式点火信号发生装置

ignition control 点火控制信号（简称IC，美国政府规定，从1995年1月起，发动机的电子点火控制信号一律使用SAE推荐的ignition control一词，取代以往各生产厂家的种种名称，如：通用公司的EST, electronic spark timing, 福特公司的spout, spark output 等，并规定使用SAE推荐的ignition control module一词表示点火控制模块，简称ICM，取代福特的DIS mod, 通用的C31mod及ignitor等）

ignition control additive 着火控制添加剂，防早燃烧加剂（防止灼热点火，简称ICA，参见 glow ignition）

ignition control lever 点火提前调整杆（= ignition timing lever）

ignition control module （电子）点火正时控制模块（简称ICM，根据发动机控制模块"PCM"的指令，准确地接通和断开点火线圈的初级电路，确定最佳点火正时，见ignition control）

ignition cover （转子发动机的）点火系外盖，点火装置外罩

ignition current 点火电流

ignition cut-out 点火断电器（传统点火系分电器的点火线圈初级电路的凸轮控制触点式开关）

ignition cycle （汽油发动机的）点火循环（发动机每次"起动-运转-关机"为一个点火循环）

ignition delay (period) ①（柴油机燃烧过程的）着火延迟期，着火落后期（指从燃油喷入汽缸内起到着火为止的期间，亦称燃烧准备期，= ignition lag）②（汽油机燃烧过程的）着火落后期（指从电火花跳火起到形成火焰中心即燃烧压力开始迅速上升为止的期间，亦称诱导期，= ignition lag）

ignition detector 点火检查仪

ignition diagnostic monitor 点火诊断监控线（为一根由点火线圈负极端接发动机电子控制模块的带20～22kilohm电阻器的导线，该电阻防止点火线圈高压损坏控制模块，电子控制模块根据该导线输入的信号，确认它所输出的点火指令是否已被执行及点火正时是否正确）

ignition disabler （汽车防盗系统的）点火阻止装置

ignition discharge wave form 点火放电波形（指火花塞跳火时观测到的次级电路的电压和电流波形）

ignition distributor （点火系）分电器（= current distributor, 接通与断开点火系的初级电路，使点火线圈次级绕组感生高压电，并按发动机要求的点火时刻和顺序将高压电分配给相应汽缸内的火花塞装置）

ignition dope 着火加速剂（如：在柴油中添加十六烷）

ignition due to compression 压缩点火，压燃（= compression ignition）

ignition energy 点火能量（指火花塞火花放电能量，为电火电流与火花电压乘积在整个火花持续时间的积分，为保证可燃混合气可靠点燃应不小于30MJ）

ignition failure ①点火系统故障，点火故障 ②缺火

ignition file 修整断电器触点等使用的锉（= contact file, points file）

ignition fluctuation 点火波动，失火波动（指有时着火，有时失火）

ignition glowing plug （燃料燃烧加热式暖风系统中的点燃燃料的）点火电热塞

ignition governor 点火提前机构（= ignition advancer）

ignition harness 点火高压线束

ignition improver （柴油机的）着火促进剂，点火促进剂（用于冷机起动，促进着火，消除冒烟）

ignition in dead center 上止点点火

ign

(=dead center ignition)

ignition index 点火正时标记(= timing mark)

ignition inhibitor 防止起动机误动的开关(或开关电路,亦称 neutral start switch)

ignition injection 引燃点火喷射(利用喷射液体燃料点火引燃,见 fuel injector igniter)

ignition interference 点火干扰(指点火系对电子仪器的干扰,点火造成的对无线电干扰)

ignition interval 点火间隔时间

ignition irregularities 点火不正常,点火不规则

ignition knock 点火爆震(由于点火过早,产生的爆震, = spark knock)

ignition lag 点火迟后; 着火滞后(见 ignition delay)

ignition lead 点火(电路导)线; 点火高压线(见 ignition cable)

ignition limit 着火极限,发火极限; 点火极限

ignition lock 点火开关

ignition loop (安全气囊的)引爆电路

ignition map 点火曲面(存储于发动机电子控制模块只读存储器中的多张最佳点火正时曲面,该曲面包括了在整个发动机工作范围内各种转速与进气管真空度下的最佳点火时刻,不是单一的曲线,而是由两个变量"转速、负荷"决定的点火时刻三维立体曲面,故名,亦称 ignition timing surface, ignition topography)

ignition marker lamp (发动机)点火开关指示灯

ignition-miss monitor 缺火监测器(向电子控制模块发送各缸点火时刻曲轴加速度及加速时间信息,借以确认某缸是否缺火)

ignition module 见 ignition control module

ignition nuclear 点火核(一般指柴油机内压燃着火点)

ignition order (发动机各汽缸的)点火次序

ignition oscilloscope 点火示波器(显示点火电压等随时间、曲轴转角变化的波形的点火系调整用示波器,一般为发动机测试仪的一个组成部分)

ignition output tester 点火输出电压测试表

ignition pattern 点火波形(指示波器按发动机点火顺序显示的点火系初级电路和次级电路的电压随时间、曲轴转角等而变化的波形)

ignition periscope 点火探视镜

ignition plier 点火系用手钳,点火电路用手钳

ignition plug 火花塞(= spark plug)

ignition point ①(燃料的)燃点,着火点,发火点(燃料受热后发火并继续燃烧的最低温度, = ignition temperature, 亦称 autogenous ignition temperature, firing point, 简称 IP) ②断电器触点(= contact breaker point)

ignition process ①点火过程(指火花塞跳火花点燃混合气的过程) ②着火过程(指燃料开始进入汽缸起,到开始着火所经过的全部物理化学过程)

ignition promotor 助燃剂(= ignition accelerator)

ignition quality (柴油的)着火性,着火品质(常用十六烷值表示)

ignition quality improver 着火性改进剂(改善柴油着火性的添加剂)

ignition radiation (发动机的)点火(电波)辐射

ignition range (混合气可)着火(的)浓度范围,可点燃的混合比范围

ignition retard ①发火延迟，着火（滞）后（见 ignition delay）②点火延迟（指火花塞在活塞到达上止点后跳火，一般用曲轴在活塞到达上止点后的转角度数表示，称点火延迟角）

ignition retarder 着火阻滞剂（作用类似 TEL 抗爆剂）

ignition retarding device 点火延迟装置（汽油机部分负荷时，延迟点火，延长燃烧时间，提高排气温度，降低 HC 排放量）

ignition scope （发动机）点火故障诊断示波器，点火检查示波器

ignition sequence （发动机）点火顺序（= ignition order）

ignition setting 点火正时调整

ignition shield ①（无线电收音机等的）防电火花点火干扰屏蔽罩 ②火花塞防干扰屏蔽罩（亦称 ignition shielding）

ignition signal generating mechanism 点火信号发生装置（见 distributor pickup mechanism）

ignition signal generator 点火信号发生器（分电器式点火系中向点火控制模块发送点火信号的电磁感应式传感器，由凸轮轴驱动的带凸齿的转子、永久磁铁及感应线圈组成）

ignition starting aid （冷机）着火起动辅助设备，柴油机冷机起动着火辅助设备

ignition starting compression pressure 着火始点压缩压力（指混合气着火始点时汽缸内的压力）

ignition switch 点火开关（指位于转向盘柱或仪表板上的接通与断开点火电源及汽车电器系统电源的钥匙开关并兼作起动机开关）

ignition switch cable 点火开关导线（= ignition lock cable）

ignition (-switch) key 点火开关钥匙（接通与断开点火开关的钥匙，一般兼作起动开关钥匙）

ignition system 点火系统（指由点火电源，点火信号发生装置，点火高压产生与分配装置，点火时刻控制装置，在汽缸内产生火花点燃混合气的装置等组成的整个系统）

ignition temperature ①着火温度（= ignition point，指在一定压力下，理论可燃混合气逐步加热到开始自行着火时的温度，即燃料的自燃点）②点火温度（火花塞跳火花时的混合气温度）③（燃油等的）闪点（见 flash point）

ignition tension 点火电压

ignition terminals 点火线圈接线柱

ignition tester 点火系试验仪

ignition time delay 点火迟后期，发火延迟期

ignition timer （点火）分电器（= current distributor）

ignition timing ①点火正时（指火花塞跳火时刻的确定、控制与调节 = spark timing, advanced ignition timing）②点火时刻（指火花塞跳火时刻，用上止点前曲轴转角度数表示）

ignition timing adjustment 点火正时调整

ignition timing control system 点火正时控制系统

ignition timing lever 点火提前调整杆 [= ignition (advance) lever, ignition control lever]

ignition-timing surface 点火正时曲面（适应某种要求，如：防爆，最大转矩，最佳油耗等的点火提前角在发动机转速、真空度、冷却水温等两个以上变量所确定的空间坐标系中的坐标点连成的曲面，= ignition map，亦称 ignition topography）

ignition toolkit 点火调整工具包（成套小工具，通常包括 3/16～7/16 英寸的 8 个开口扳手，一个小螺钉旋

具和一把触点锉刀）

ignition topography 见 ignition-timing surface

ignition transformer 点火变压器［在发动机点火系中称 ignition coil（点火线圈）］

ignition transistor 点火（系统用）晶体三极管（一般指用作点火初级电路开关的功率晶体三极管）

ignition trouble 点火系统故障

ignition voltage 点火电压（指火花塞电极的跳火电压，当前一般为3000V）

ignition voltage reserve 点火电压储备（在规定条件下，点火次级有效电压与火花塞需要电压之差）

ignition (warning) lamp 点火电路警报灯，灯火开关警报灯

ignition wave form 点火波形（发动机点火系诊断仪屏幕上显示火花电压、电流随时间变化的波形）

ignition wire 点火线，点火高压线，火花塞高压线

ignition wire rubber protecting cap 点火线橡皮保护盖

ignition wiring 点火系线路

igniton coil resistance 点火线圈镇流电阻（= ballast resistance，见 ballast ignition system）

ignitor 点火装置，点火器（①指在点火系初级电路中按照点火信号发生器或发动机控制模块的点火信号，断开点火线圈初级绕组电流的电子电路。美国政府规定，从1995年1月起，一律按 SAE 标准，称为点火控制模块"ignition control module"，见 ICM ②指安全气囊的触发点火器 ③指燃气轮机的起动点火装置）

ignitron ①点炎管，引燃管，放电管 ②汞弧半波整流管（用汞作为阴极，可进行大电流整流）

I-groove 平头槽，工字形槽

IGT 点火触发器，点火脉冲信号发生器（ignition trigger 的简称）

IHCC system 智能公路巡行控制系统（Intelligent Highway Cruise Control System 的简称。该系统除常规巡行定速控制功能外，还增加了公路高速行车时，与前车的车距维持支援功能"assistance function for keeping distance to fore vehicle"，通过微波雷达测定前车车速及行驶状况，以控制自身车速，保持车距。当车距小于某值时，通过减小节气门开度，必要时施加制动减速，以维持车距，而当车距大于某值时，该系统通过常规巡行定速控制手段提高车速，以保持车距，可完全免除驾驶者为保持车距而频繁地制动、加速操作，见 HiDS）

I-head ［美］I型汽缸盖，顶置气门式汽缸盖（见 overhead valve engine）

I-head engine ［美］顶置气门发动机，I型汽缸盖发动机（=［英］overhead valve engine，指进、排气门均装在汽缸盖内的发动机）

IHP 指示马力（见 indicated horsepower）

ihp-hr 指示马力小时（indicated horse-power-hour 的简称）

IIA 见 integrated ignition assembly

IIAE ［英］汽车工程师联合学会（Incorporated Institution of Automobile Engineers 的简称）

IIEC 跨工业排放物控制，行业间排放物管理（inter industry emission control 的简称）

IIHS ［美］公路安全保障研究院（Insurance Institute for Highway Safety 的简称）

IIR 异丁橡胶，异丁烯-异戊=烯橡胶（isobutylene-isoprene rubber 的简称）

I-iron 工字形铁

IIW 国际焊接学会（International Institute of Welding 的简称）

i-key 带防盗功能的卡片式遥控钥匙（商品名）

ILC ①怠速螺钉限制帽（idle limiter cap 的简称）②怠速负荷补偿器（idle load compensator 的简称）

ill-conditioned 情况欠佳的，条件较差的，情况恶劣的

illegal exhaust and noise （汽车）排放与噪声超标（指汽车在运行过程中产生的有害排放物和噪声超过技术文件规定的现象）

illegally assembled car 非法组装的轿车

illicit car （法律禁止使用的）非法轿车

illness 故障，损伤，毛病，异常

illuminance 照度（见 illumination）

illuminate 照明，照亮，照射；用灯装饰；说明，阐明

illuminated 照明的，装有照明的，加有彩饰的

illuminated car 彩车，花车

illuminated dial instrument 带照明的表盘式仪表

illuminated direction indicator (arm)（旧式汽车使用的）箭头式转向指示灯（= illuminated trafficator arm，简称 illuminated arm）

illuminated entry system 入口照明系统（装在车门下面板及车身地板乘员搁脚区等处在辅助照明系统，只要打开车门，便可照亮车门入口区域）

illuminated license plate 有灯光照明的牌照板（= illuminated number plate）

illuminated sign （由特设的光源照明的）照明式标志（相对于无照明的反光式标志而言）

illuminated trafficator 见 illuminated direction indicator

illuminated vanity mirror in sun visors 装在车内遮阳板内、带灯光照明的化妆镜

illuminating power 发光强度，光强（单位为坎德拉，代号 Cd 或 CD，见 candela）

illumination ①照，照明，照射 ②照度（一般指平面照度，单位面积上的光通量，代号 E，$E = d\phi/dA$，$d\phi$-光通量 lm，dA-面积 m^2，亦称 illuminance）

illumination control 汽车前照灯的变光控制开关（= dimmer control）

illumination photometer 照度计（简称 illuminometer）

illuminator ①照明装置，照明灯 ②发光体

illumine 照亮，照明

illustration ①插图，图表，图解 ②实例，例解，例证

ILS （汽车）内部照明系统（automotive interior lighting system 的简称）

ILSAC 国际润滑剂标准化与认证委员会（International Lubricant Standardization and Approval Committee 的简称）

ILSAC Certification mark 国际润滑剂标准化与认证委员会认证标识

IM ①脉冲调制（impulse modulation 的简称）②感应电动机（induction motor 的简称）③检验手册（inspection manual 的简称）④索引手册（index manual 的简称）

IMA （本田仅使用一台电动机的轻量的、紧凑型混合动力车的）整体式电动机助力系统（Integrated Motor Assist 的简称）

image ①图像 ②描绘，使……成像

image converter 图像光电变换器，图像光电变换管

image forming model （计算机影视的）成像模型

image fusion technique 图像融合技术

image information 影像信息
image method (汽车风洞试验的)镜像法,映像法
image projector type 幻影式照明法(如:驾驶室仪表板的间接照明)
image recognition 图像识别
image smoothing algorithm 图像平滑算法(主要有邻域平均法,中值滤波法,自适应平滑算法等)
IMAP 见 intake manifold absolute pressure
IMA system 见 integrated motor assist system
imbalance 失去平衡,不平衡,失调,不稳定(性)
imbed 嵌入,镶入,埋入(=embed)
imbedded 嵌入的,夹入的
imbibition 吸入,吸收,透入
IMC 见 inter metallic compound
IM240 chassis dynamometer IM240底盘测功机(IM240测试规程用底盘测功机,一种具有可变惯性质量,可根据被测试汽车总质量提供测功机负荷的实时测试设备)
IMCO system (美国福特汽车公司的)改良排气净化系(improved exhaust emission control system 的简称,包括恒温空气滤清器,使用稀混合气,节气门关闭时推延点火等项目)
IME [英]机械工程师学会(Institution of Mechanical Engineers 的简称,亦写作 IMechE)
IMEP 见 indicated mean effective pressure
IMF 国际摩托车联合会(International Motorcycle Federation 的简称)
IMI [英]汽车工业学会(Institute of Motor Industry 的简称,英国汽车工业管理人员的组织)
i-MID (Honda 某些车型上安装的)智能多媒体信息显示器(Intelligent Media Information Display 的简称)

IMII [日](通产省的)工业产品检查所(Industrial Manufactures Inspection Institute 的简称)
imitate 模仿,模拟;仿造,仿制
imitation ①模拟,模仿,仿真,仿造 ②仿造品,伪造品,赝品
imitation leather 假皮,人造革(=leather substitute, artificial leather, leatherette)
immac ①整洁的,洁净的 ②无缺点的,无瑕疵的(immaculate 的简称,说明书、广告等用语)
immalleable 不可锻的,无韧性的
immature failure 磨合期的损坏,早期损坏(=infant failure, infantile failure, early failure)
immerse 浸入,沉没
immersed method 水浸法(探伤,测漏,见 immersed test)
immersible 可浸水的,密封的,防水的
immersion 浸入;沉入,沉没
immersion test 浸入试验(以在水中是否形成气泡来检查密封性)
imminent failure 即将发生的损坏,即将发生的故障(=impending failure, oncoming failure)
immobile ①(本身)不能动的 ②不能(被)移动的
immobiliser ①(使发动机等停止运转的)停机装置,停车机构 ②(泛指各种使某物、某部件不能移动的)锁止装置,锁止件(等)
immobilization ①固定,不动,定位,降低流动性,缩小迁移率 ②(车辆)失去机动能力 ③(地面、路面)失去通过能力
immobilized vehicle 损坏的车辆,失事的车辆,封存车辆,停用车辆
immobilizer ECM (汽车电动防盗系统使车辆)停住不动的装置(vehicle immobilization device)的电子控制模块

immobilizing failure 车辆由于长期停放而引起的故障；致使车辆损坏不能使用的故障

IMMO II （通用公司某些车辆上使用的 SIEMENS 新一代滚动码）第二代防盗系统（商品名，ImmobilizerⅡ 的简称）

IMMO·SMART （通用公司）智能防盗系统（商品名）

immovable 不能移动的，固定的

immovable fitting 紧固配合

IMMU （防盗系统的发动机）锁止控制单元（immobilizing control unit 的简称）

immune 不敏感的，不受…的干扰；免除影响的，无响应的

immunity 免除，抗扰；钝感性，迟钝性，抗扰性，不敏感性，抗噪声度

immunization 钝化处理；免除，豁免；免疫

IMO （防盗系统中阻止发动机起动和汽车起步的）阻动装置（immobiliser 的简称）

IMO module 阻动器控制模块

IMP ①冲击，碰撞（impact 的简称）②（液力变矩器等的）泵轮（impeller 的简称）③冲量；脉冲（impulse 的简称）④综合监控台（integrated monitor panel 的简称）

impact ①冲击，碰撞；冲力 ②受撞（对被碰撞的一方而言，用于研究受撞时作用力的大小、方向、变形及受撞位置）

impact absorber 冲击能量吸收件，冲击能量吸收装置，缓冲器（如：装在汽车保险杠与保险杠支座之间、防止冲击能量传入车身内的冲击阻尼部件等）

impact-absorbing construction （可）吸收冲击能量的结构

impact absorbing energy 冲击吸收能量（指被冲击物受到冲击时产生的变形或断裂所吸收的能量）

impact accelerometer （汽车）碰撞加速度计；冲击加速度计

impact angle 受撞角度（指受撞车上的纵向对称平面与作用在该车上的主要力所在的铅垂平面之间的角度。该角度的测量以该车的纵向对称平面为基准，左、右均不超过180°）

impact break ①冲击断裂 ②（轮胎）冲击破裂

impact cushion 缓冲软垫，缓冲垫

impact damage 冲击（造成的）损伤

impact damper 缓冲器，减振器

impact driver 锤击式螺钉旋具，敲击式螺钉旋具（将手锤的冲击力，变为旋转螺钉旋具的转矩，= hammer driver, shock driver, impact screwdriver, hand impact screwdriver）

impact energy absorption device （碰撞）冲击能量吸收装置

impact fatigue 冲击疲劳（重复冲击载荷所导致的疲劳）

impact horn （汽车的常规膜片式）电喇叭

impact location 受撞位置（车辆受撞位置，由变形区所在部位确定）

impact pendulum test （在摆锤冲击机上做的）摆锤冲击试验

impact pipe 冲击能量吸收管（受冲击时，该管件可折叠而吸收冲击能量，是一种简单的缓冲装置）

impact point 碰撞点（简称 IP）

impact predictor （汽车）碰撞点预测器（简称 IP）

impact protection for the driver from steering control system 转向操纵系统对驾驶者碰撞的保护

impact resistance 耐冲击性；抗冲击强度，冲击韧性

impact resistance test 耐冲击试验（见 Charpy impact test, izod impact test, impact-tensile test 及 impact toughness)

impact screwdriver 锤击式螺钉旋具（亦称 hand impact screwdriver，将手锤的冲击力转变为转矩的螺钉旋具，见 impact driver）

impact sensor （汽车乘员保护系统的）碰撞传感器

impact simulation 碰撞模拟

impact simulator （汽车）碰撞模拟装置

impact sled （车身）碰撞试验滑轨

impact socket 冲击式套筒（指电动或气动冲击式套筒扳手的套筒，= impact wrench socket）

impact strength 冲击强度（材料在不致发生应变的条件下所能承受的最大冲击载荷）

impact stress 冲击应力（物体受冲击力作用所导致的物体内部之间的相互作用力称冲击内力，单位面积上的上述内力称冲击应力）

impact tensile test 冲击拉伸试验（试样在拉伸状态下承受冲击试验力的一种动态力学性能试验）

impact tester 冲击试验机

impact toughness 冲击韧度（指材料冲击试样缺口底部单位横截面积上的冲击吸收功）

impact velocity 冲击速度，撞击速度（= velocity of impact）

impact wrench （电动或气动）冲击式套筒扳手（= striking wrench，shock wrench，见 impact driver）

impact wrench socket 见 impact socket

impairment ①损害，损伤 ②削弱，减弱

impassability 不可通行，不能通过，无路可通

impassable 不能通过的，不能通行的

Impco [英] 帝国学院（Imperial College 的简称）

Impco evaporator [英] 帝国学院式蒸发器

impedance 阻抗（指电路中的电阻、电感和电容对流经它的交流电或变化的电流的总的阻碍作用，阻抗的单位也是欧姆，阻抗 $Z = E/l$，式中：E—电路两端的电压；l—流过该电路的电流）

impedance coil 扼流圈，电抗线圈（起阻抗作用的线圈）

impedance compensator 阻抗补偿器

impedance head 阻抗头（由一个压电式传感器和一个压电式速度传感器组合而成，用于原点阻抗测量）

impedance matching 阻抗匹配（在网络中，使负载或终端设备的阻抗与相连驱动设备或网络的阻抗相互匹配）

impede 妨碍，阻碍，阻止

impediment 障碍；障碍物

impel 推进，推动；强迫，迫使；刺激，激励

impeller ①（液力变矩器或耦合器的）泵轮（为液力变矩器等的主动叶轮单元，即动力输入单元，在发动机驱动工况下，吸收动力的叶轮，亦称 pump input member，driver 及 front torus）②（水泵等的）叶轮 ③（风扇等的）叶片轮 ④（废气涡轮增压器的）废气涡轮

impeller blade ①叶轮叶片，工作轮叶片 ②（变矩器）泵轮叶片

impeller channel （叶轮）叶片间通道（= impeller passage）

impeller channel velocity 叶轮通道流速

impeller clearance 叶轮与固定件之间的间隙

impeller disk （液力偶合器，液力变矩器）泵轮，工作轮

impeller passage 见 impeller channel

impeller pump 叶轮泵（如：叶轮式离心水泵）

impeller rim 叶轮轮辋

impeller torque （液力变矩器的）泵轮转矩

impending ①临近的，即将来临的 ②迫切的 ③吊挂的，悬吊（在顶上）的

impending braking 紧急制动

impending failure 即将发生的故障（损坏）（= imminent failure）

impending skid(ding) 紧急制动打滑，（车轮抱死引起的滑移）

impenetrable obstacle 不可通过的障碍

imperfect combustion 不完全燃烧（= incomplete combustion）

Imperial bushel 英国蒲式耳（英制容积单位，代号 UK bsh，1 英国 bsh 约等于 36 升，见 Imperial gallon，bushel）

Imperial gallon 英国加仑（见 gallon，英国容积单位的基本单位，代号为 imp gal，1963 年规定为密度 0.998859 克/cc 的蒸馏水，10 磅所占的容积。单位递进为 1gallon = 4quarts = 8pints = 32gills = 160fluid ounces = 1280fluid drams = 76800 minims. 1gallon = 1/2pecks = 1/8bushels = 1/64quart = 1/24sacks = 1/288chaldron）

Imperial quart 英国夸脱（英国容积单位，代号有时用 UK qt，见 Imperial gallon）

Imperial standard wire gauge 英国标准线规

impermeability ①不渗透性，不透性，密封性，水密性，气密性 ②不能通过性

impermeability test 抗渗透试验；密封性试验

impermeable ①不渗透的，不透的（= impervious）②不能通过的

imperviousness 不通；难入；不透…性；防…性（to）

impetus ①原动力，推动力 ②动量 ③推动，促进，激励

impg 见 impregnate①

imp gal 英国标准加仑（= 4.456L，见 imperial gallon）

impingement ①碰撞，冲击，打击，冲突 ②紧密接触 ③（雾点的）动力附着 ④水锤 ⑤（光线）射至（on…）

impingement attack 浸蚀，滴蚀，腐蚀

impingement cleaner 滤芯可清洗式空气滤清器（指由涂复黏性外层的棉线滤芯组成，所滤除的尘粒可以用清洗的方法从外层清除）

implate 包以金属皮

implement ①工具，器具，仪器，设备，装置，机具 ②供给器具装置；履行，执行；完成，实现；补充

implications of unreliability 不可靠性引起的后果，故障造成的后果

import ①输入，进口，进口商品，进口货 ②含义，意义，重要性 ③含有…的意思，意味着

imported vehicle 进口车辆

import licence (= import license) 进口许可证

import repairman 进口车修理商，进口车修理者，进口车修理工

imposed stress cycle 加载应力循环

impracticable 不能实行的，行不通的，不现实的

impregnate ①注入，充满，注灌，饱和，浸渍，刻蚀（简称 impg）②浸渍的，浸透的，饱和的，充满的 ③浸渍树脂

impregnated graphite apex seal （转子发动机的）渗（金属）石墨径向密封片

impregnating compound 渗入剂

impregnating material 浸渗材料（指渗入基体材料中的其他材料）

impregnation 渗透，浸渍，浸透，

饱和，注入
impression 印痕，压痕；印记
impression die forging 闭合模锻（= closed die forging）
imprint 印痕，印迹
improper 不恰当的，不合适的；不规则的，非正常的；不正确的，错误的
improve 改进，改善，增进
improver 添加剂，改进剂
impulse ①碰撞，冲击 ②冲量（= impulsion，两物体撞碰时，在撞击的瞬间彼此间产生一反作用力 F，该力与时间的乘积 $\int F dt$ 称为冲量，两物体中任一物体的冲量等于其动量的变化，即 $Ft = MV$）③脉冲 ④冲击的，脉冲的
impulse effect 脉冲效应
impulse response 脉冲响应（在一个输入上施加一个脉冲函数引起的时间响应）
impulse response function 脉冲响应函数 [传递函数的拉氏（Laplace）逆变换，或频响函数的傅氏（Fourier）逆变换称为脉冲响应函数。数值上它正好是系统在脉冲函数（δ-函数）激励下的响应。脉冲响应函数是在时域上描述线性系统传递关系的固有特性]
impulse signal 脉冲信号
impulse starter 冲击式起动机
impulse turbine 冲击式涡轮机（= velocity turbine）
impulse wheel speed sensor 脉冲式车轮速度传感器
impulsion ①冲击，碰撞，推动 ②冲量 ③推力；脉冲
impulsive 冲击的
impulsive welding 振动堆焊，电脉冲堆焊
impurity ①污染，沾染 ②不纯；杂质，掺和物，污染物

impurity conduction 非本征导电（见 extrinsic conduction）
IMRC housing 进气歧管通道控制腔（intake manifold runner control housing，亦称 deactivator。为一节气阀门机构，用于减小发动机低运转时的进气通道面积，以提高进气流速）
IMS ①智能制造系统（intelligent manufacture system 的简称）②累计里程传感器（见 inferred mileage sensor 的简称）
IMS 国际金相学会（International Metallographic Society 的简称）
IMS 智能记忆系统（如驾驶席等的 IMS，可自动存储驾驶者的体重、身高、坐姿、驾姿及与转向盘、各种控制件、踏板等的距离数据并自动保持或调整座席位置）
IM240 Test Procedure （美国联邦环境保护局"EPA"）IM240（汽车排放）测试规程（在原美国联邦测试规程"FTP"基础上提出的轿车和轻型货车的底盘测功机多工况模拟实时排放测试法，由加速、减速和等节气门开度等行驶工况组成，但不含冷起动工况，测试时间240秒）
IMTV 进气歧管进气量调控阀（intake-manifold turning valve 的简称，由电子控制模块通过电磁阀控制，当发动机低速运转时，该阀关闭，当转速上升到某规定值，如：3025～4650r/min 时，该阀开启，进气空气量增加）
IMU 惯性测量单位（inertial measurement unit 的简称）
in 英寸（英制长度单位，见 inch）
In 铟（indium）
in^2 平方英寸，英寸^2，（英制面积单位，为 square inch 的代号，1 in^2 = 645.16mm^2 = 0.00694ft^2 = 0.0058 市尺^2）
INA 不提供情报，不提供信息（in-

formation not available 的简称)
inaccessibility (检修,维护的)难接近性
inaccessible 难于接近的,难于达到的
inaccessible value 不可达值,不可及值
inaccuracy 不准确度、不精确性,误差,偏差
inaction period 不作用期间,停工期间,故障期间,故障周期,钝化周期
inactive component (of current) 无功电流(见 reactive current)
inactive molecule 非活性分子
inadaptability 不适应性,不适用性
in a pulsing fashion 以脉冲的形式
inattention 疏忽(注意力不集中,处于不注意状态)
in-axle speed-sensing system 车桥内车速传感系统(车速传感器装在桥壳内,便于保护)
"in axle" wheel sensor 车桥内轮速传感器,桥装轮速传感器(防滑制动系统的一项装置,由装在桥端的齿轮形定子和装在轮毂上转子组成)
INBD 见(in board)
in-bed trunk (pickup 车的)封闭式货仓
inblock cast 单体铸造,整体铸造(= integral cast, enblock cast, monoblock cast)
in board ①在船内的,在机内的 ②[美]在车内的(简称 INBD)
inboard brakes 远置式制动器(指制动器的安装位置靠近车辆中心线,其制动力矩由半轴传给车轮,参见 outboard brakes)
inboard shoe and lining (浮钳式盘式制动器的)内侧(油缸侧)制动块总成(由制动摩擦衬块及其背板组成,= inboard brake pad assembly)

inboard starter 回缩式(啮合)起动机(指起动机小齿轮朝起动机壳体方向移动而与飞轮啮合的惯性式或称邦迪克斯式起动机)
inboard universal joint 独立悬架式驱动桥)半轴内侧万向节
inbound traffic 入境交通
inbuilt 装入的,内装式的
inbuilt jack 固定式千斤顶,安装在固定地点的举升器(= built-in jack, permanent jack)
inbuilt luggage (与车身成一体的)车内行李舱
INC ①煅烧装置(incinerator 的简称)②进入的(incoming 的简称)③合并的(incorporated 的简称)④包括在内的,计算在内的(inclusive 的简称)⑤增加;增量(increase 的简称)⑥进气停止(inlet close 的简称)
incandescence ①炽热,白炽,灼热 ②白炽发光,炽热发光(物质在高温下发光)③白炽光,炽热光,闪闪发光的
incandescent bulb 白炽灯泡
incandescent dust cloud 发光尘云,炽热尘云(黄焰放射的微粒,主要是一种黑色碳粒)
incandescent (electrical) load (电热)白炽负载
in-car entertainment 车内娱乐性设备(如:收音、音响、影视设备等)
in-car internet access 车内互联网访问(功能)
in-car multimedia system 车内多媒体系统(见 multimedia system)
in-car phoning ①车内电话,车用电话 ②车内打电话
in-car test equipment 安装在车内的试验设备
inch ①英寸(英制长度单位,代号 in, 1in = 25.4mm = 0.762 市寸 =

1/12ft）②少量，少许 ③渐进；一步一步地前进；一点一点地测量，以英寸测量

in-chamber NO$_x$ control 燃烧室内 NO$_x$ 控制（法）（一般指废气回流等）

5-inch body lift spacer kit （可使）车身升高5英寸的垫块套件

10inch center pole impact test （汽车）254mm正中柱碰撞试验

inching ①发动机低速转动 ②缓慢施压；微调 ③平衡缓慢移动，微动，蠕动，点动，一点一点地移动

inching control 微调（节）

inch per second 英寸/秒，每秒英寸（简称 ips, in/s）

inch screw die 英制螺纹板牙

inch screw tap 英制螺纹丝锥

inch size 英制尺寸

2-inch suspension lift kit （可使车身升高的）2英寸的悬架提升套件（供改装越野功能用）

inch (system screw) thread 英制螺纹

2-inch up (or down) sus （改装车用可使车身比原车）升高（或降低）2英寸的悬架（sus 为 suspension 的简称）

inch water gage ①英制水表 ②英制水柱压力表 ③英寸水柱（压力单位，代号 in. W. G. 用水柱高的英寸数表示压力，使用时应有温度条件，如：在4℃时的水柱高，1in. W. G. = 0.00246 atm = 1.87mmHg = 0.0254 m. W. G. = 2.49×10^{-3} bar = 0.0361 1bf/in^2 = 0.0254kgf/cm^2）

incidence ①（光线的）入射 ②倾角，安装角 ③落下（的方式）④影响（的程度），影响（的范围）

incidence angle 入射角

incident ①事故，肇事 ②入射的

incident management system （事故）紧急救援管理系统，（ITS 的一个子系统，参见 intelligent transportation system）

incipient 起始的，开始的，初期的，刚出现的

incipient crack 初期裂纹，初发裂纹

incipient knock 初发爆震，轻微敲缸（= incipient detonation，指正在开始出现刚好能听到的轻微爆震）

incircuit 接入电路，接通

incity transportation 城市内运输

inclement weather 恶劣的天气，恶劣的气候

inclination 倾斜；倾角，斜度；斜坡，坡角；倾向

inclination angle ①（泛指）侧倾角，倾角，倾斜角，斜角 ②（对车轮，指）外倾角（为正外倾与负外倾的统称，见 camber angle）③（对主销，指）内倾（见 kingpin inclination）

inclination of ramp 坡道角（如：高速公路进出车道坡度角）

inclination of steering knuckle pivot 转向主销内倾角，主销侧倾（= king pin inclination, tilt camber）

inclination sensing module （车身）倾斜传感模块

incline ①倾斜 ②斜面，斜坡 ③倾斜角

inclined 斜的，倾斜的，有坡度的

inclined axial piston pump 斜置式轴向活塞泵

inclined bathtub combustion chamber 斜浴盆形燃烧室

inclined engine 斜置式发动机（[美] slant engine，指汽缸中心线与水平面有一定角度，但不是直角的发动机，亦称 sloper）

inclined joint 斜接，斜接缝

inclined parking arrangement （停车场）汽车斜角停车排列，斜向停车布置

inclined surface 斜面（= slope sur-

face, slanted surface)
inclined valve 斜置气门
incline level 坡度计，倾斜计
incline of front wheels 前轮外倾，前轮侧倾
inclinometer 测角仪，坡度仪（见 clinometer）
inclosed body 厢型车身（= enclosed body）
included angle ①夹角②车轮与主销夹角（主销内倾角与前轮外倾角的总和）
inclusion ①包括，包含②杂质，夹杂物，内含物
inclusive 包括的，包含的，计算在内的，包括在内的
incoherent scattering 非相关散射，杂乱散射
incombustibility 不燃性，防火性
incoming ①进入的新鲜可燃混合气，新鲜充量②正在进入的
incoming inspection （原料、半成品等）进厂（车间）检查
incoming side （齿轮）啮合面
incoming test ①（制件从协作企业运到工业厂时做的）进厂检验②（材料、零件、半成品入库时的）入库检验
incompatible ①不相容的，不协调的，不适合的，不能共存的，互斥的，性质相反的，不能融合一起的，有矛盾的②不相融，不协调
incomplete combustion 不完全燃烧
incomplete vehicle （RE5定义的）非完整车辆（指至少还需要进行一次进一步加工才能达到其设计和构造目的的所有车辆，见RE5）
incompressible 不可压缩的
Inconel 因科镍合金（镍铬铁耐蚀合金，极高的耐高温氧化性及耐盐类水溶液的腐蚀性能，80％镍，14％铬，6％铁，及少量的锰、硅或铜，亦称 inconel alloy）

inconel exhaust valve 镍铬铁耐热耐蚀合金排气阀
inconel X X 镍铬铁耐热合金（镍73％，铬15％，铁7％，钛2.5％，铝0.7％，铌1％，硅0.4％，锰0.5％，碳0.04％）
Incorporated Institution of Automobile Engineers ［英］汽车工程师联合学会（简称 I IAE）
incorporation ①结合，合并，加入，联合②公司，团体
incorrect timing 不正确的（点火）正时（点火过早或过晚）
increased shank （螺栓等的）加粗杆部（其无螺纹的杆部直径大于螺纹部分）
increase gear 超速挡，超速传动
increasing-amplitude test 应力振幅渐增的（疲劳）试验
increasing rates for decreasing distance 递进递减运价（在规定的一定里程范围内，随着运距递进相应提高运价率的运价）
increment ①增大，增加，增长，增益②增量，增值，增额
increment（al）load 附加载荷
incremental position sensor 增量型位置传感器（位置传感器分为两大类：增量型和绝对型。增量型指以相对设定的参照点或零点来测定位置的变化增量，如：以上止点为零点，按与曲轴转角成比例的脉冲数确定活塞在上止点前或后的位置等的传感元件，简称 incremental sensor，亦称 incremental transducer）
incremental ratio 增量比（= incremetary ratio）
incremental transducer 见 incremental position sensor
increment induction pickup 磁感应型增量传感器
incrust 结水垢，结水锈
incrustated substances 水垢

incrustation ①起硬皮，结垢，结水垢，结水锈 ②积炭；水垢，水锈，硬皮

incrustation of piston 活塞积炭

incrusting solids 水垢（覆盖）层

in-cylinder mixture strength 缸内混合气浓度

in-cylinder movie technique （发动机）缸内连续高速摄影技术

in-dash 6-CD changer 装在仪表板内的6CD盘自动换碟机

in-dash display 仪表板上的显示屏

in-dash gauge 安装在仪表板上的仪表

in-dash infotainment system （触摸式显示-操控屏装在驾驶室）仪表板上的资讯-娱乐-通信系统（见 infotainment system）

indefinite ①无限的，无穷的 ②不定的，未确定的，不明确的

indent ①锯齿形；刻痕，凹痕 ②刻成锯齿形，压（出）印痕，压凹痕

indentation 缺口，凹入，凹陷；锯齿状，刻痕，凹槽，成穴作用；压印，压坑（一般指较小的压痕或凹痕，如其他车辆的牵引杆等在车身上撞出的凹坑）

indentation hardness 压痕硬度（指在规定的静态试验力下将压头压入材料表面，用压痕深度或压痕表面面积评定的硬度）

indentation test 压痕硬度试验

indenter 压痕试验用的压入头，硬度计压头

independent 独立的，不相依赖的；单独的，个体的

independent failure 独立损坏（非从属性损坏，不是由于其他元件的损坏而引起的）

independent five-link rear suspension 五连杆式后轮独立悬架

independent front (-wheel) suspension 前（轮）独立悬架（简称IFS）

independent heating 独立式取暖装置（配有汽车发动机以外独立的动力装置）

independently controlled power take-off （单独操纵的）独立式功率输出轴

independently sprung wheels 独立悬架车轮（= independent wheel）

independent oiler （供单独润滑各部位用的）独立油嘴

independent power take-off clutch 独立式动力输出轴离合器

independent rear (-wheel) suspension 后（轮）独立悬架（简称IRS）

independent retarder 独立式缓速器（指其运作与主制动系，或称行车制动系无关，独立进行的缓速器）

independent suspension 独立悬架（指各个车轮各自独立的悬架系统，左、右车轮不连在一根车轴上，而是单独通过各自的悬架与车架或车身相连，因此每一车轮的上、下运动都不致影响其他车轮，其中前轮独立悬架"independent front suspension"，简称IFS，后轮独立悬架"independent rear suspension"，简称IRS，通称 knee action individual suspension）

independent suspension by guides and springs 带导向杆系和弹性元件的独立悬架（独立悬架的导向杆系指连接车轮与车架或车身的横臂、纵臂、斜臂及滑柱、摆臂等起控制车轮空间位置与运动的杆件，弹性元件则为螺旋弹簧、空气弹簧、气液弹簧等起减振作用的元件）

independent suspension by oblique arm(s) 斜臂式独立悬架

independent suspension by parallelogram 平行四边形独立悬架（导向杆系呈平行四边形的独立悬架）

independent suspension by swinging

arm（s） 摆臂式独立悬架［= independent suspension by control arm(s)，指通过横向、纵向或斜向布置的摆臂件控制车轮运动的独立悬架，摆臂亦称控制臂 control arm，横向布置者简称横臂 transverse arm，纵向布置者简称纵臂 trailing arm，斜向布置者简称斜臂 oblique arm］

independent suspension by trailing arm（s） 纵臂式独立悬架

independent suspension by transverse arm（s） 横臂式独立悬架

independent suspension by vertical guide（s） 带垂直导向杆件的独立悬架

independent suspension drive axle 独立悬架式驱动桥（指装用独立悬架车轮的驱动桥）

independent suspension lower support arm （双臂式）独立悬架（的）下臂

independent suspension wheel with knee action 膝动式独立悬挂车轮（见 knee action wheel）

independent suspension with torsion-bar 扭杆弹簧式独立悬架（由承受转矩的杆状弹簧作为弹性元件的独立悬架）

independent trailer 全挂车

independent variable 独立变量，自变数，自变量

independent wheel 独立悬挂车轮（= independently sprung wheels）

independent wheel torque control （电动车辆的）车轮转矩独立控制（通过对轮内电动机的单独控制，实现各车轮转矩的按需独立控制）

independing test 独立试验（指由与制造厂商无关的公正的试验机构所进行的试验，参见 official test）

index 索引，指标，指数，标志，符号，记号

index correction 仪表读数校正，仪表误差校正

index dial 表盘，刻度盘

indexed address 变址地址（按变址寄存器的内容进行修改了的地址）

indexed register 变址寄存器（其内容能在计算机指令执行前或执行期间加到操作数地址上的暂存器，亦称 index register）

index of quality 质量指标

index of refraction 折射系数，折射率（透明材料的入射角和折射角的正弦之比）

index registor 变址寄存器（其内容可用于在执行计算机指令时修改操作数的地址的寄存器）

index ring 刻度环，分度环

Indiana testing method for oxidation （润滑油）印第安纳氧化试验法

india rubber 天然橡胶，生橡胶，纯橡胶（= caoutchouc）

India rubber tube （天然）橡胶管（= rubber tubing）

indicate 指示，表示，显示，指出；简述，简要说明，做示功图

indicate an engine 绘制发动机示功图，录制发动机示功图

indicated diagram 示功图（见 indicator diagram）

indicated efficiency （发动机）指示效率（一般指示热效率，见 indicated thermal efficiency）

indicated heat specific consumption 指示热消耗率（按指示功率的热消耗率，千卡/马力小时或千卡/千瓦）

indicated horsepower 指示马力，指示功率（指以马力为单位的指示功率，英美沿用至今，简称 IHP）

indicated lateral acceleration 指示横向加速度（指装在簧上质量 y 轴上的加速度计的指示值，其值比侧向加速度大｜$g\sin\phi$｜，式中 ϕ — 车身侧倾角）

indicated mean effective pressure 平

均有效指示压力，平均指示有效压力（指一个循环中，工质所做的功与工作容积之比，即单位工作容积所做的功，但具有压力量纲，用活塞面积上假想不变的压力表示，kgf/cm^2，简称 IMEP，见 mean effective pressure 及 mean indicated pressur)

indicated power 指示功率（发动机单位时间内所做的指示功，单位 kW，亦称 indicated output）

indicated specific carbon monoxide 指示马力一氧化碳排放率（指示每马力的一氧化碳排放量，简称 ISCO）

indicated specific energy consumption 指示能耗率（发动机每千瓦指示功率每小时的能量消耗量，简称 ISEC）

indicated specific fuel consumption 指示油耗率（发动机每千瓦指示功率每小时的燃油消耗量，简称 ISFC）

indicated specific HC 指示马力碳氢化合物排放率（指示每马力的碳化氢排放量，简称 IS HC）

indicated specific NO emission 指示马力一氧化氮排放率（指示每马力的一氧化氮排放量，简称 ISNO）

indicated specific NO_x 指示马力氮氧化物排放率（指示每马力的氮化物排放量，简称 $ISNO_x$）

indicated thermal efficiency 指示热效率（燃料所含的热能在内燃机中转变为指示功的份额，以百分数表示，简称 ITE）

indicated work 指示功（在汽缸内完成一个循环，工质所做的有用功，常以 p-v 图的封闭面积表示，单位 kJ）

indicating calipers 指示卡规（带可显示测量示值的装置的系统）

indicating device 指示器，指示装置（如：量测仪器仪表内显示被测量值或它的有关值的装置）

indicating gauge 指示表，百分表，千分表

indicating instrument 指示仪器仪表（可显示被测量值或其有关值的仪器仪表，如：数字式电压表）

indicating needle （仪表等的）指针

indication ① 指示，表示，显示 ②（仪表）读数，示值 ③ 象征，迹象 ④ 标记，信号

indication error 示值误差，读数误差，指示误差

indicative mark 包装储运标志（为使存放、搬运适当，按规定的标准以简单醒目的图案和文字表明在包装物一定位置上）

indicator ①（泛指各种）指示器，显示器，指示仪表 ② 指标，指针，标记 ③（特指发动机的）示功器（测量汽缸内气体压力随曲轴转角和活塞冲程而变化的仪器，有机械式，气电式电子式等多种）④（汽车的）转向信号灯（= direction indicator, turn signal lamp）⑤（各种指示灯 = indicator light）

indicator arm （旧式汽车的）转向指示臂（见 arm for direction indicator）

indicator card （发动机）示功图（见 indicator diagram）

indicator-channel （燃烧室壁上专门为安装示功器用的）示功器通道

indicator cock ① 指示开关（如：液面玻璃管开关）② 示功器放水阀

indicator diagram （发动机的）示功图（由示功器描绘出的汽缸内的工质的压力随曲轴转角或汽缸容积而变化的曲线图形，根据该图可测定平均指示压力，可表明进、排气，点火，燃烧等现象，亦称 indicator card）

indicator lamp terminal ①（泛指各种）指示灯接线柱 ②（特指）充

电指示灯接线柱（简称 Lterminal）

indicator needle shaft 指针轴

indicator sending casing base 指示仪表壳体的底板

indicator sleeve 冷却水温表的水温传感头的壳体

indicator test 示功图测定试验

indicatrix 指标线，指标图，指示线，指示量，特征曲线

indices of handling operation 装卸作业指标（反映装卸作业量和工作效率的指标的通称）

indices of vehicle maintenance and repair 汽车维修指标（评价汽车维修工作的量标）

indicium ①记号，标记，象征②（贴在轮胎侧壁上的）编号签条（复数 indicia）

indifferent driving 不谨慎驾驶（＝careless driving）

indifferent equilibrium 随遇平衡

indirect address 间接地址（指存放地址的存储单元的地址）

indirect analog computer 非直接模拟型计算机（指函数型模拟计算机）

indirect clutch 间接传动离合器

indirect contact 间接接触

indirect controlled wheel 间接控制车轮（在汽车防抱死制动系统中，根据其他车轮的传感器提供的信息调节其制动力的车轮，参见 direct controlled wheel）

indirect damage 间接损伤（由于其他部位或部件受到直接撞击的撞击力传至非直接撞击件或部位所造成的损伤）

indirect drive （发动机）间接驱动（指发动机只作为原动力，而实际驱动是由发动机带动发电机发出的电力或液压泵产生的液力实现的，如：engine-electric drive）

indirect extrusion 逆挤（法），间接挤压（压力头的外径与装有被挤物的容器的内径相同，但压力头是空心的，模具装在压力头的内腔，当压力头向前推进时，被挤物则经压力头的空心，进入模具，因此被挤物的流动方向与压力头的运动方向相反，故名，参见 direct extrusion）

indirect gear 非直接挡

indirect heating ①间接取暖，间接供暖（利用中间媒介供暖）②间接式取暖设备（如：汽车的发动机热水暖气装置，利用发动机冷却水加热空气，然后用风扇将热风送入车箱供暖）

indirect injection ①间接喷射（简称 IDI，指将燃油喷入开式燃烧室副室中初步燃烧，然后混合气和燃气再通过联接通道喷入主燃烧室继续燃烧，简称简喷）②指将燃油喷至进气歧管内，或进气口外，即汽缸外

indirect-injection engine 间接喷射式发动机（简称简喷式发动机，美称 precombustion engine，一般指将燃油喷入分式燃烧室的副室的柴油机，不过近年来也指间接喷射式汽油机）

indirect lighting 间接照明

indirectly controlled wheel （汽车防抱死制动系统）非直接控制车轮（指其制动压力是根据其他车轮上的传感器信号来控制的车轮，见 directly controlled wheel）

indirect method of measurement 间接测量法（通过对与被测量有函数关系的其他量进行测量而得到被测量值的方法）

indirect noise 间接噪声（如：由轮胎作为直接或间接振动源并将该振动传至车身而产生的噪声）

indirect tire pressure monitor system 胎压间接监测系统

indirect welding 单面点焊

indium 铟 In（原子序数 49，原子量

114.818)

individual ①个人的,个体的,个别的,单独的,单一的;专用的,特殊的,独特的 ②个体,个人,独立单位,单体

individual cutout switch (各个车灯)独立开关

individual-cylinder engine 分置缸体发动机

individual-injection system 分缸喷油系统,各缸独自喷油系统(各个汽缸均配置有单独的喷油泵)

individual in-wheel-motor vehicle 单轮独立控制的轮内电动机驱动式车辆

individualistic 个性的,个体独特性的,独特特征的(如:车辆造型风格,设计风格或某种牌号的车辆具有的独特特色等)

individually adjustable chair (轿车)可单独调节的座椅

individually adjustable seats 单人可调整(多座)座椅

individual method of vehicle repair 就车修理法(汽车总成及主要零件经修理后装回原车或原机的修理方法)

individual own car 个人自用轿车,私人轿车

individual production 单件生产

individual throttle valve (每一个汽缸的进气管内都装有一个节气门的)独立节气门

individual transportation 单件运输(相对于 mass transportation 而言)

individual user (车辆的)个人用户

individual-vehicle pollutant control requirements (美国 EPA 对每辆车的)单车排放控制要求(相对公司平均废气有害物排出量而言,参见 CAEF)

individual wheel control (车辆防抱死制动系的)单轮独立控制(如:每一个车轮制动器的制动力各自独立进行的控制)

individual wheel torque control (各个)车轮单轮转矩控制(系统)

indivisibility 不可分性,不可分散性,不可分割性

Indolene 美国联邦试验汽油(CH 1.92,氢与碳比为1.92,一种专供汽车排放污染试验用的标准汽油)

indoor 室内的,内部的

indoor chassis rolls dynamometer 室内滚筒式底盘测功器

indoor lab test 实验室室内试验

indoor proving ground 室内试验场

indoor road tester (汽车)室内道路模拟试验装置;(如:转鼓道路模拟试验台)

indoor stroke 吸气冲程,进气冲程

indoor test 实验室试验,室内试验

indophenol method 靛酚试验法(废气中的氨含量分析法)

indraft 引入,吸入,流入,吸气

induce 感应;引起,激起;诱导

induced current 感应电流(见 electromagnetic induced current)

induced draft fan 吸风机,抽风机,抽气风扇

induced drag (汽车空气阻力中的)诱导阻力(汽车空气阻力分为摩擦阻力与压力阻力,诱导阻力是压力阻力的一种,为空气升力的水平分力和由于车身后面形成涡流区造成车身迎面与背面空气流静压不等而诱生的阻力,以及空气升力造成汽车浮升趋势所招致的动力性下降的等效阻力等的统称,其中由于涡流区的产生而诱生的阻力,称 vortex induced drag "涡流诱导阻力")

induced electric field (变化的磁场在其作用空间激发的)感生电场

induced electromotive force 感生电动势(简称 induced emf,又称感应电动势指电路元件在磁场中无相对

运动，仅仅是由于磁场随时间而变化引起的感应电动势。若电路的一部分在磁场中有相对运动而产生的感应电动势称动生电动势"induced electromotive force by relatively moving in magnetic field"）

induced traffic 诱增交通量（由于新增加或改良的交通设备而增加的交通量）

induced ventilation 强制通风（= forced ventilation）

inducer ①（压气机）进口段，导风叶轮 ②电感器

inducer flow area 进口通道面积

inducible property 可归纳的性质

inducing current 施感电流（见 mutual induction）

inductance ①电感，电磁感应（现象，= induction）②电磁感应系数［= induction coefficient，单位亨利，简称亨，代号 H，为自感系数（self induction coefficient）与互感系数（mutual induction coefficient）的统称。1H = 1V·A/S，即：电流变化量每秒 1 安，产生 1 伏的电动势，则其电感为 1 亨利］③电感线圈（= inductance coil）

inductance loop detector 电感回路式传感器［如：电感回路式（车辆）检测器］

inducted air 进气，吸气（= induction air）

inducted draft 引导通风，导流通风，导向通风，导流

induction ①（电-磁）感应 ②吸入，吸进；引入 ③（特指）将空气或混合气吸入汽缸（亦称 aspiration "进气"）④前言，绪论

induction air 进气，吸气（柴油机指吸入发动机或汽缸内的空气，汽油机则指已吸入发动机但尚未与燃油混合的空气，= induced air，intake air，suction air，inducted air）

inductional velocity 吸入速度

induction brazing 感应加热（硬）钎焊（利用电感效应产生的热量进行的钎焊）

induction coil 感应线圈（应用电磁感应原理产生感应电流或变换电压的线圈的统称，如：点火线圈，便是一种用来产生点火高压脉冲的感应线圈，亦称 inductance coil）

induction coil system 感应线圈点火系统

induction current 感应电流（= induced current）

induction field 感应（电、磁）场

induction hardened （采用高频或中频电流加热）（电）感应淬火的

induction heater （零件的）高频电流感应加热器

induction heating 高频电流感应加热

induction induced swirl 进气诱发涡流

induction manifold 见 intake manifold

induction motor 感应电动机，（亦称异步电动机 "asynchronous motor"）

induction motor controller 感应电动机式控制器（由转速随电源的电压而变化的电动机来驱动的控制器）

induction noise 进气噪声

induction opening 吸入口，进气孔

induction period ①（内燃发动机的）吸气过程，吸气期 ②（汽油生成胶质的）诱导期 ③（变压器油氧化试验的）感应期

induction period test （汽油的生胶）诱导期试验

induction phase （发动机的）进气相，进气过程

induction pipe ①（加装在发动机后置式跑车尾窗顶的）导风管（将风引入后置式发动机舱，以提高发动机进气效率）②吸气管，吸入管；进气管（一般指节气门与汽缸盖之间的进气管道，= suction pipe，in-

751

let pipe)

induction-pipe depression 进气管负压（进气管真空度）

induction port （发动机燃烧室的）进气孔（见 intake port）

induction pulsation 进气脉冲

induction ramming （发动机）进气系统的空气惯性压缩

induction stroke 进气冲程，吸气冲程（活塞下行，将空气或空气燃油混合气吸入汽缸内的冲程，= admission stroke, suction stroke, charging stroke, aspirating stroke, 美称 intake stroke）

induction system （发动机的）进气系统［一般指空气滤清器，进气管道进气预热器，进气歧管，进气增压器，进气门及其驱动装置等所组成的吸入空气和（或）将空气燃油混合气送入汽缸的整个系统，个偶见有人将化油器及汽油喷射系统也算作汽油发动机进气系统组成部分］

induction tachometer 感应式转数计，感应式测速仪

induction tract 进气管道

induction type pulse generator 感应式脉冲发生器（应用电磁感应原理产生脉冲信号的传感器件等，= magnetic pick-up）

induction valve 进气门，吸气阀；进油阀，吸油阀

induction velocity 诱导速度，吸入速度

inductive circuit 感应电路

inductive coupler 电感耦合器

inductive coupling 电感耦合

inductive discharge 电感放电［火花塞跳火放电过程中，击穿电极间隙的电容放电完成后，点火线圈铁心中心的剩余能量继续放电并维持一定时间（1~2ms），火花呈紫红色的放电，此时电极间电压仅数 KV，但对点燃混合气起重要作用的放电过程，亦称为电弧放电"arc discharge"；简称 ID］

inductive (electrical) load （电）感应负载

inductive ignition system 电感式点火系统（蓄电池向点火线圈的初级绕组供低压电，当切断初级电路时，靠电磁感应作用在点火线圈的次级绕组中产生高压电通过火花塞跳火，即：将初级能量先存储在点火线圈初级绕组内，而由次级绕组感生点火高压的点火系统）

inductive kick （点火线圈二次绕组的）感应高压脉冲

inductive (pulse) pick-up 电磁感应式传感器（应用电磁感应原理产生脉冲信号的传感器 = magnetic pick-up）

inductive reactance 感抗

inductive storage system （电子计算机）感应储存系统

inductive switching （汽车电系的）开关感应（如：感应装置断开时产生的负峰）

inductive transducer 电感式传感器，电感式变换器

inductive transient （汽车电系的）感应瞬变现象

inductive winding 感应线圈（= pick-up coil）

inductivity ①介电常数 ②感应性 ③诱导率 ④电容率

inductor 电感器，感应器，感应线圈（能在电流流过所产生的磁场中存储能量的电磁器件，即利用电磁感应原理产生电动势的器件）

inductor generator 感应式发电机

inductor winding 感应线圈

inductosyn 感应式传感器（不接触直接测量位置的传感器）

inductothermy 感应电热法

induration 硬化（作用），变硬，

固化

industrial 工业的，产生的，工业用的，工业生产的；工业高度发达的

industrial carrier 工业用输送机（指四轮龙门式吊运装置等）

industrial engine 工业用发动机；固定式发动机

industrial fleet 专为工业运输服务的汽车车队

industrial transport 工业运输

Industrial Transport Association [英]工业运输协会（简称ITA）

industrial truck 工业用货车（厂内运输用载货汽车）

Industrial Truck Association [美]工业用载货汽车协会（简称ITA）

industrial tyre 工业用轮胎，运输车用轮胎

industrial utility vehicle 工业用多功能车辆（厂矿通用运输车辆）

Industrial vehicle 工业用车辆

industrial wheeled equipment 轮式工程机械（按SAEJ297的规定，指装有下列作业设备的轮式拖拉机：造园，建筑，装载，挖掘，土壤保持，公路维护）

industry 实业，工业，产业

inefficient 失效的，无效的

inelastic 非弹性的，无弹力的

inelasticity ①非弹性，无弹性 ②无适应性

in-engine performance （火花塞等发动机内部的零件和装置的）机内性能，机内特性（如：对燃油经济性的影响，对空燃比失火极限的影响等）

inert 惰性的（指化学性质不活泼的）

inert air cathode （锌-空气电池等的）惰性空气阴极

inert arc welding 惰性气体保护电弧焊（见 inert-gas shielded-arc welding）

inert atmosphere 惰性气氛

inert constituents 惰性成分

inert gas（es） 惰性气体

inert-gas shielded-arc welding 惰性气体保护焊，惰性气体掩弧焊（电弧熔焊的一种，用一层惰性气体掩盖焊件熔池，以防止焊缝氧化，简称 inert arc welding）

inert gas shielded tungsten arc welding 惰性气体保护钨极电弧焊（简称 Tig weld, inert-gas-tungsten, tungsten inert gas welding, 使用钨电极的惰性气体保护电弧熔焊）

inertia ①惯性（指物体总保持静止或匀速运动的状态，直到其他物体的作用迫使它改变这种状态为止的性质）②惯量（指刚体的转动惯量，是刚体做旋转运动时，对其固定轴心的转动惯性的大小的度量，$I = \int_v r^2 \rho dv$，式中：ρ—密度，dv 是与轴心垂距为 r 的质元 dm 的体积，对于圆柱体或圆盘，$I = \frac{1}{2}mR^2$，式中：R—半径，m—质量）

inertia-actuated oil circulation method 惯性油液环流法，惯性甩动油液环流法（转子发动机转子液冷的一种方法）

inertia anti-lock device 惯性防抱死装置（采用惯性式传感元件感受车轮滑移情况并调节制动压力，以控制车轮在制动过程中抱死滑移的装置）

inertia balance 惯性平衡，动平衡

inertia ball 惯性球（如：飞球式无级变速器中的飞球）

inertia brake （汽车列车挂车的）惯性式制动器（牵引车制动时，挂车在惯性作用下继续前驶，利用挂车的这种前冲力驱动液压总泵来实现挂车制动的装置，亦称 overrunning brake）

inertia braking system 惯性制动系（指产生制动力的能是靠挂车惯性

inertia clutch 惯性式离合器（指依靠惯性结合的离合器，如：依靠驱动齿轮的惯性运动与飞轮齿环啮合的起动机的 bendix drive）

inertia coefficient 惯性系数

inertia-controlled apportioning valve 惯性控制（制动）比例分配阀，减速度感知（制动）比例分配阀（= deceleration conscious apportioning valve，利用惯性控制的球阀，来改变前后轮制动力比）

inertia-controlled ball 惯性控制式球阀（随车辆减速度的变化所产生的惯性作用来改变或切断制动液压通路的球阀）

inertia-controlled shock absorber 惯性控制式减振器

inertia cooling 惯性冷却，惯性冷却法（利用惯性力将冷却介质送至被冷却部位）

inertia couple 惯性矩，惯性力偶

inertia-coupled free-piston engine 惯性耦合型自由活塞发动机

inertia damper 惯性减振器

inertia disc 惯性盘（装在旋转轴上的飞轮状消声器，用于消减共振，从而减少某一特定频率带的噪声）

inertia drive starter （汽车发动机的）惯性式起动机（靠驱动小齿轮的惯性运动与飞轮齿环啮合的起动机，见 Bendix drive）

inertia effect 惯性作用，惯性效应

inertia force 惯性力；惯性阻力（= force of inertia）

inertia fuel cutoff switch 惯性控制式供油切断开关（当车辆发生碰撞，突发性急剧减速时，在惯性力作用下断开电动油泵电源，中断向发动机供油的开关，亦称 fuel cutoff switch，fuel pump shut off switch）

inertia governor 惯性调速器

inertia hammer 惯性锤（= slide hammer）

inertia lag 惯性滞后

inertia loading 惯性载荷，惯性负荷

inertia lock type 惯性锁止型（同步器）

inertia mass 惯性质量（物体惯性的大小用质量来表征，就是惯性质量，在一般情况与表征物体间产生万有引力的能力大小的引力质量的数值是相等的，统称为质量）

inertia measurement units 惯性式测定装置（指应用惯性作用测定车速及行车方向的装置，简称 IMU）

inertia navigation system 惯性式导行系统（指由加速仪和陀螺回转仪等可确定汽车速度和行驶方向变化的惯性器件组成的导行系统，多用来作为汽车行驶在高大建筑物区或山区卫星导行受干扰时的辅助系统）

inertia-oil bath type air cleaner 惯性油浴式空气滤清器

inertia pinion （惯性式起动机的）驱动小齿轮（见 Bendix drive）

inertia pressure 惯性（引起的）压力

inertia principal axis system 簧上惯性主轴坐标系（以簧上质心为原点，以簧上质量惯性主轴为坐标轴的右手直角标坐标系，该坐标系随同簧上质量一起运动和旋转）

inertia proportioning valve 惯性式比例分配阀（见 DSPV）

inertia proportion(ing) valve 惯性比例阀（根据汽车减速度的大小，调节前、后制动车轮制力的分配比例，以获得较佳制动性能的装置，简称 G valve，inertia valve）

inertia ramming 惯性增压，惯性压头

inertia reel （汽车乘员自动安全带收紧装置的）惯性卷筒（当车辆静止或平稳行驶时，安全带可轻易拉出

或收回，以保证乘员行动自如。一旦车辆发生碰撞或紧急制动而突然减速，乘员惯性作用下向前猛冲时，该卷筒立即将安全带锁死，防止乘员二次碰撞，使用这种卷筒的安全带称 inertia reel seat belt)

inertia resistance 惯性阻力

inertia-responsive 惯性反应的，惯性作用的

inertia safety belt 惯性式安全带

inertia-scavenging rotor cooling method （转子发动机的）转子惯性扫气冷却法，旋转活塞惯性扫气冷却法

inertia simulation （汽车）惯性模拟

inertia supercharging 惯性增压（充气）（利用进气的惯性效应或脉冲效应，来增加充气量，提高充量密度的技术）

inertia switch 惯性（作动）开关（由车速的突然变化驱动的开关，如：发生碰撞瞬间接通安全气囊点火电路的开关等）

inertia switch type safety fuel pump 惯性开关式安全燃油泵（当汽车发生碰撞时，该开关断开油泵驱动电路，使油泵停止供油）

inertia synchronizer 惯性同步器

inertia torque 惯性转矩

inertia type 惯性式

inertia type brake tester 惯性式制动试验台（用旋转飞轮模拟汽车平移质量的滚筒式制动试验台）

inertia (-type) starter 惯性啮合式起动机（= Bendix starter）

inertia valve 见 inertia proportion valve

inertia weights ①（传动系台架试验时作为模拟惯性载荷用的）惯性重块 ②（由于旋转件）转动惯量（造成的）重力 ③（汽车急加速或急制动时由于惯性作用引起的）转移车重

inertia welding process 惯性焊接法（利用储存在飞轮中的能量，当将两个零件用力压在一起时，通过结合面的摩擦，使动能转化为热能）

inert nitrogen carrier 惰性氮载体，惰性气体氮运载装置

inerts 惰性气体，惰性物质，惰性组分，不活泼物质

in-exhaust manifold three-way catalyst 排气歧管内置（废气净化）三效催化剂

inextensibility 非延伸性

inextensional deformation 非延伸性的形变，非伸缩形变

infant failure 早期损坏（亦写作 infantile failure, = immature failure)

infantry vehicle 步兵运输车辆，运兵车

infant safety seat （轿车的七岁以下）婴幼儿安全座椅（= baby seat)

inference engine ①（人工智能专家系统中的）推理机（指根据存储在知识库中的信息，应用推理原理，导出问题的结论的系统，亦称 inference machine) ②（计算机的）推理程序（按一个或几个搜索策略对知识库中的内容进行处理，推导出问题的结论的程序）

inference machine （专家系统）推理机（亦称 inference engine, 见 expert system)

inferior ①下级的，低等的，劣等的，低品质的，差的；次于，低于(to); 在下方的，下部的 ②下级，下属 ③次品 ④下附文字

inferior limit 下限，最小限度，最小尺寸

inferred mileage sensor 里程推断传感器（该传感器根据发动机的点火数，推断出发动机运转工时或里程，并通知发动机控制模块，后者据此及时改变有关的控制参数值，简称 IMS)

inferred-zero instrument 无零点仪表

(= suppressed zero instrument)

in (-) field 在现场；在野外；在工地

infiltrate ①渗透，渗漏 ②透过，过滤

infiltration 渗入，渗滤，渗透（作用），浸润，浸渍，渗入物，吸水量

infiltrometer 渗透计，透水性测定仪

infinitely-variable drive 无级变速传动装置（= continuously variable drive）

infinitely variable frictional transmission 无级变速摩擦传动（装置）（= frictional mechanical stepless transmission）

infinitely variable hydrodynamic transmission 无级液体动力传动器，无级动液变速器，无级动液传动器

infinitesimal 无穷小，无限小（的），极微小（的），极小量，微元

infinitesimal calculus 微积分

infinitesimal geometry 微分几何

infinity 无穷，无限，无穷大，无限大

inflame 燃烧，着火

inflammability 易燃性，可燃性，点燃性，燃烧性

inflammability limit 着火极限

inflammability test 可燃性试验

inflammable mixture 可燃混合气（= combustible mixture, explosive mixture）

inflatable curtain 充气式安全护帘（亦称 inflation curtain）

inflatable curtain system （简称 ICS，汽车乘员侧向碰撞保护）充气式帘系

inflatable occupant restraint system （汽车乘员的）充气式保护装置，充气式保护系统（简称 IORS，如：安全气囊等）

inflatable seat-belt system 充气式安全带系统（参见 air-belt system）

inflatable tubular structure head air bag 充气管式乘员头部保护气囊（可在正面、侧面碰撞和车辆翻滚时保护乘员头部，简称 ITS head air bag）

inflate 充气，打气，使膨胀，吹胀

inflated tire 充气轮胎

inflation control seams （安全气囊充气速度和充气特性的）控制接缝（见 tear seam）

inflation gauge 轮胎气压表，充气压力表

inflation hose 轮胎充气用软管

inflation pressure ①轮胎气压，胎压 ②（特指）充气内压 [轮胎在使用环境温度下，按标准规定所充入气（液）体的压力，不包括轮胎在使用中所增大的内压]

inflation pump 打气泵，充气泵

inflation valve （轮胎）气门嘴（= inner tube valve, tyre valve）

inflator ①充气泵，打气机，充气装置 ②（特指安全气囊的）充气器（一般位于折叠好的气囊的下方，充气器的核心是雷管，当汽车发生碰撞时，安全气囊的起爆传感器与碰撞判别传感器便相继接通而向雷管提供足够的点火电流，使雷管瞬间起爆点燃包在它周围的炸药，进而点燃固体燃料产生大量的高温高压氮气，经充气器内的散热元件和滤网冷却、滤清后充入气囊，使气囊在 30ms 内膨胀而保护乘员免受撞伤。有的充气器内有一个压缩氩气筒，当雷管通电引爆炸药后迅速加热氩气，急剧膨胀而充入气囊。有的安全气囊系统用加速度传感器取代起爆和判别传感器经安全气囊控制模块向充气器雷管供送它引爆所需电压的电流）

inflection point （曲线）拐点，回折点（亦写作 inflexion point）

inflexibility 非挠性，刚性

inflexible 不可弯曲的，非挠性的，刚性的，不可改变的

inflow 流入,流入量,吸入,吸入量,进气,进水,流入物

inflow curve 进气流量曲线

inflow port （油液等的）流入孔,进液孔,进油孔

inflow valve 进气门;进油阀

inflow wheel （液力传动的）向心式叶轮

influence ①影响,作用,效应 ②感应,感化

influence quantity 影响量（如：环境温度、被测交流电压的频率等影响仪器仪表示值的量）

influxion ①流入(量),注入,灌注 ②注入口

info 信息(information 的简称)

informal 不规则的,非正规的,非正式的

informatics 信息学

information 信息,数据,资料;新闻,报道,消息;报告,通知,查询,询问（简称 info）

information content 信息量

information fusion 信息融合,信息合成

information highway 信息公路（指大量发收信息的网络,20 世纪 90 年代各国都建设信息高速公路）

information sign 导向标志,指路标志,路标,信息标志

infotainment system （车载）资讯娱乐通信导航一体化系统

infrabar 低气压

infraction 破坏、不遵守（法律），违犯（交通规则）

infrared ①红外线的,红外的 ②产生红外线的,对红外辐射敏感的（见 infrared rays）

infrared absorption band 红外线吸收带

infrared analyzer 红外线分析仪,（一般指红外线废气分析仪,利用连续光谱的红光线等通过废气时,某些波长的红外线被吸收而产生的吸收光谱来分析和测定废气中有害物成分 CO 及 HC 等及其含量的仪器,亦称 infrared CO-HC analyzer, infrared emission analyzer, infrared exhaust gas analyzer, 简称 IRA）

infrared anti-collision technology 红外线防撞技术

infrared band 红外线频带

infrared detection unit 红外线探测器,红外线探头

infrared dryer 红外线烘干装置

infrared light emitting diode 红光线光发射二极管

infrared light ignition system 红外线激光无触点点火系统

infrared maser 红外线脉塞（见 maser）

infrared night vision system 红外线夜视系统

infrared obstruction detector 红外线障碍物探测器

infrared ray bulb 红外线灯泡

infrared rays 红外线（一种人眼看不见的电磁波。波长在 $0.25\sim3\mu m$ 者称为近红外线,波长在 $3\sim6\mu m$ 者称为中红外线,波长在 $6\sim1000\mu m$ 者称为远红外线, = ultrared rays）

infrared rays stand （可移动的）台式红外线烘干器

infrared remote control 红外线遥控器

infrared sensor 红外线传感器

infrared signal 红外线信号

infrared stereo camera 红外线立体摄像机

infrared temperature sensor 红外线温度传感器

infrared thermometer 红外线温度计

infrared trace 红外线扫描,红外线扫迹

infrared vision 红外线映像（技术）

infrastructure 基础设施，基础结构，基本建设

infringe ①损害，侵害 ②违背，侵犯 ③使…受到（不利的）影响

infusible ①难熔化的，不熔的 ②能注入的，能灌输的

in gear 啮合的，处于啮合的

ingredient ①（混合物的）成分，拼料 ②要素 ③配料；填充料

ingress 进入，入口，进路

ingress and egress 出入（汽车车道）

ingress/engress （客车等的）进-出，下-上（车），车站（旅客的）出入口

in-ground full hydraulic lift 地上全液压举升器

inhaust 吸入，吸气

inherent 内在的，固有的，特有的，先天的

inherent balance （发动机等本身结构决定的）固有平衡

inherent characteristic 固有特性

inherent damping in suspension 悬架固有阻尼

inherently safe 自身安全的，本身安全的

inherent reliability （结构）自身具有的可靠性

inherent resistance ①内在抵抗（力）②固有阻力

inherent stress 预应力，内在应力

inherent vice 固有缺陷，内部瑕疵

inherent weakness failure 本质失效（由于本身固有的弱点，缺陷而引起的失效）

inhibit 抑制，制止，防止，限制，阻止，约束

inhibited engine ①暂时停止工作的发动机 ②暂时封存的发动机

inhibited shift （自动变速器的）限制换挡（防手动换挡，在规定的运转条件下，自动限制手动换挡，如：在高速条件下自动防止手动换入低挡）

inhibition 抑制，遏制，制止，阻止，防止，禁止，阻滞，延缓，保护，约束

inhibitor 抑制剂（可防止或减缓某些不良化学反应的物质，如：机油的抗氧化剂，金属件的防锈剂等）

inhibitor effectiveness 抑制效能（如：防止燃料氧化的添加剂的抑制效能，防腐效能）

inhibitor valve 限制阀，限止阀

inhibitory action 抑制作用，阻滞作用

inhibitory coating 防护层，保护层

inhomogeneity ①不均匀性，不均质性 ②非同质性，不同族性

inhomogeneous coordinates 非齐次坐标

inhomogeneous distribution 不均匀分配

in-house design 国内用设计，国内用结构（为国内使用而设计的结构）

in-house styling input 室内造型输入（指一种新车型在工程设计前，输入计算机内的室内造型，作为工程设计的依据）

in-house test 实验室试验，室内试验

inimical impurity 有害杂质（见 detrimental impurity）

initial 初始的，原始的，初期的，预加的，起始的，首次的，起初的，基本的

initial adjustment 初调

initial air inlet （进入发动机的）主进气口

initial (boiling) point （分馏）始点；初沸点，初馏点

initial brake-lining temperature 制动摩擦片初始温度（简称 IBT）

initial charge 初充电，初次充电（新蓄电池第一次充电）

initial charging speed （汽车用交流

发电机等）充电始点转速（开始充电时的转速）

initial condition 原始条件，初始状态

initial control activity （新产品生产的）初期质量管理工作，（在新产品大量投产前，为了稳定产品质量，而对产品生产过程进行的质量控制、管理、改进等工作）

initial cooling 预冷（却）

initial cost ①初期投资，建造费，基建费 ②生产成本 ③创办费 ④原价（＝first cost, prime cost）

initial data 原始数据，原始资料（＝original data）

initial exhaust 先期排气[二冲程发动机从排气门（口）开启到进气门（口）开启的这段时间中排气的过程]

initial failure 初期损坏，刚开始的损坏

initial impact force 初始碰撞力

initialization mode （发动机电子控制模块的）起动控制模式（点火开关接通后，电子控制模块即进入该起动控制模式，向发动机提供12.8：13.2：1的浓混合气。若起动时发动机温度较高，则该模式在起动后数秒钟即停止而转入闭路控制模式，冷机起动时，要等发动机温度上升到某规定值后，起动模式才随之停止）

initial line 起始线

initial lube drain interval （新车）首次润滑油放油期（指首次换油里程）

initial oil drain 第一次更换润滑油

initial permeability ①起始磁导率，起始磁导系数，起始磁导性（磁化曲线的起始部分）②起始渗透性，初始透气率

initial phase 初始相，起始相位（简称IP）

initial pitting 初始点蚀，初始穴蚀

initial point 初始点，起始点（简称IP）

initial position 起点，零点，初始位置

initial speed 初速

initial speed of braking 制动初速度（制动时，汽车开始减速时的行驶速度，减速始点车速）

initial tension of spring 弹簧的预紧力

initial value 初值，始值

initial velocity 初速度，初速

initial wear 走合期的磨损，初期磨损

initiation combustion 发火，初期燃烧，起燃

inject 喷射，注射，注入

injected engine 燃油喷射式发动机（fuel injected engine 的简称）

injected-formative plastic 注射成型塑料（采用注射成型法加工成制品用的塑料）

injected fuel spray 燃油喷雾束

injection advance 喷射提前，喷油提前（指喷油提前到活塞到达上止点前，用开始喷油到活塞到达上止点期间曲轴转角度数表示其提前量）

injection advance device （发动机）喷油提前装置

injection advance lever 喷油提前角调整杆

injection air 喷射（的）空气，喷气

injection back pressure 喷油背压（喷油过程中汽缸内空气的瞬时压力）

injection carburation 汽油喷射汽化方式（指不用化油器，将汽油直接喷入汽缸内或进气歧管形成混合气）

injection carburetor 喷射式化油器（燃油加以压力，利用阀门控制喷射量）

injection characteristics 喷油特性,喷油规律(每循环过程中,喷入汽缸内的燃油量或喷油速率随曲轴转角或喷油泵凸轮轴转角的变化规律)

injection delay 喷油延迟(指实际喷油始点落后于喷油泵几何供油始点的时间,通常以凸轮轴转角表示)

injection density 喷射密度

injection diameter (喷油嘴)喷孔直径(= fuel-hole diameter)

injection duration 喷射持续角(指从实际开始喷油瞬间,即燃油实际开始喷入缸内的瞬间到停止喷油的曲轴转角)

injection hole 喷射孔,喷孔

injection interval (多缸发动机的)喷油间隔(通常用曲轴角度数表示)

injection lag 喷油延迟角(指出油阀升起瞬间到喷油器针阀升起瞬间所经历的曲轴转角,或供油提前角与实际喷油提前角的差值)

injection moulded 喷射成形的,喷射模制的,吹铸的

injection nozzle tester 喷嘴试验器

injection of ammonia (排气净化措施中的)喷氨处理

injection order 喷射顺序;喷油顺序

injection orifice 喷孔,喷油嘴喷孔

injection peak pressure 喷油峰值压力(喷油持续期内喷嘴压力室内的最大压力)

injection period 喷油期(指喷油始点至喷油终点及所经过的时间)

injection pressure 喷油压力(喷油持续期内喷嘴压力室内的燃油压力,该压力随时间或凸轮轴转角而变化,其最大值即喷油峰值压力)

injection process 喷油过程(燃油喷入燃烧室内的过程,包括喷射、破碎、雾化和扩散过程)

injection pulse-spectrum 喷射脉谱(喷油量控制脉冲宽谱)

injection pulse width 喷射脉宽(喷油量控制脉冲宽度)

injection pump 喷射泵,喷油泵(燃油喷射系统中,将一定压力的燃油供给喷油器的装置,见 injector ②)

injection pump barrel 喷油泵(柱塞)套筒

injection pump plunger 喷油泵柱塞

injection pump stroke 喷油泵柱塞行程

injection rating 燃油喷射率(若微小时间 dt 或微小曲轴转角 $d\theta$ 内的喷油量为 dq,则 dq/dt 或 $dq/d\theta$ 称为燃油喷射率)

injection starting pressure 启喷压力(喷油开始时,针阀腔内的燃油压力)

injection stream 喷射流

injection timing 喷油正时

injection-valve closing pressure 喷油阀关闭压力

injection-valve opening pressure 喷油阀开启压力

injection wear ①喷射磨损(如:喷嘴喷口的磨损)②喷油嘴零件的磨损

injector ①喷射器,喷嘴 ②(特指发动机的)喷油器(将一定压力的燃油喷入汽缸或进气道的装置)

injector balance test (发动机各缸)喷油器平衡试验(测试各缸喷油器的喷油正时及喷油量是否一致和是否符合规定要求的试验)

injector body 喷油器壳体(= nozzle body)

injector control circuit 喷油器控制电路(电子汽油喷射系统中,由发动机电子控制模块的喷油控制脉冲的始点和脉冲宽度控制的喷油器电磁线圈通电始点及通电时间的电路,即喷油始点及喷油量的控制

电路)

injector drain pipe 喷油器溢流管(回油管)

injector filter element 喷油器滤芯(装在进油接头内,滤除燃料的杂质)

injector-igniter combination 喷油-点火组合装置,喷油器-火花塞组合(如:转子发动机使用重油时的喷油-点火组合装置)

injector nozzle (喷油器的)喷油嘴(将高压燃油喷出雾化与空气混合形成混合气的装置)

injector orifice 喷油器喷孔

injector overflow 喷油器溢流孔(回油孔)

injector protrusion 喷嘴伸出量(直喷式柴油机和汽油机喷嘴端部伸出汽缸盖底平面或燃烧室壁面的长度)

injector sleeve (柴油机)缸盖喷油器安装孔密封套(防止燃烧室内的燃气等由该孔漏逸)

injector timing 喷油正时(指喷油时刻的确定、控制和调节)

injector valve 喷油器针阀

injurious ①损坏的,受伤的 ②有害的

injury criteria (交通事故的人员)伤害标准,伤害规准,伤害度

injury index (汽车碰撞事故中乘员的)伤害指标[如:head G peak (头部最大加速度)、max. rib deflection (肋骨变形量)、peak abdominal force (下腹最大受力)等]

injury-producing force (汽车碰撞时)引起乘员受伤的力

injury risk index (交通事故的人员)伤害风险指数(简称 IRI)

injury severity index (撞车等事故的人员)伤害度指数(简称 ISI)

injury severity score 综合伤害严重程度

injury threshold 致伤碰撞阈(汽车碰撞时使乘员造成伤害的碰撞强度范围,参见 human tolerance level)

inlet ①进口,入口 ②进气(水,油)口 ③进入,吸入,引入,输入 ④进气

inlet air solenoid 进气空气控制电磁阀(发动机冷机起动时,空气滤清器吸气管的大气阀门关闭,该阀开启,吸入经排气管预热的空气)

inlet air temperature sensor (发动机)进气空气温度传感器(电子控制燃油喷射系统中,测量发动机吸入的空气温度的传感器)

inlet and exhaust manifold bracket 进排气歧管支架

inlet angle 进气管道入口角

inlet branch 进口支管

inlet cam ①(凸轮轴的)进气凸轮(进气门顶升凸轮,进气阀凸轮,= inlet-valve cam, admission cam)②(顶置双凸轮轴中的)进气门凸轮轴凸轮

inlet camshaft (指顶置双凸轮轴式发动机的)进气凸轮轴

inlet channel 进气通道,进管道(如:汽缸盖内的进气道)

inlet close ①进气门关闭 ②进气停止(简称 INC)

inlet conditions 进口气流参数,进口液流参数,进气条件

inlet connection 进口接管,进气歧管进气管接头

inlet duct 进气道

inlet gas ①新鲜的可燃混合气充量 ②吸入的可燃气

inlet line (泛指各种)进气、进液的管道、软管或管路

inlet loss 进气损失,进口损失

inlet manifold 进气歧管(向内燃机各汽缸分配充量的进气管道,[美] intake manifold)

inlet manifold heater 进气歧管

预热塞

inlet-manifold pressure 进气歧管压力

inlet over exhaust engine 顶置进门、侧置排气门式发动机，F 型缸盖式发动机（简称 IOE engine，= F head engine，指进、排气门垂直布置于燃烧室侧的气门室中，一般排气门在下方，侧置，由汽缸体侧或上曲轴箱内的凸轮轴直接驱动，进气门在上方，顶置，由凸轮轴通过推杆和摇臂驱动）

inlet pipe 进入管，进气管，（指将新鲜充量输入进气支管或汽缸的管道），进水管（= suction pipe）

inlet port ①（泛指各种）进入孔，进液孔，进气孔（= 美 intake port）②（特指柴油机柱塞式喷油泵的）进油孔（在几何供油始点，柱塞所关闭的柱塞套上的油孔）

inlet porting （转子发动机的）进气孔布置，进气孔布置方式

inlet screen 进口滤网，进气滤网

inlet silencer ①（排气制动系中的）进气管消声阀（防止排气制动时，高压空气逆流出进气管，降低排气制动效率和产生噪声）②进气消声器（抑制进气噪声）

inlet spider （燃气轮机）进气口辐式导流栅

inlet stroke （四冲程内燃机的）进气冲程（进气门开启，排气门关闭，活塞下行，将新鲜充量吸入汽缸，= induction stroke）

inlet swirl vane 进口旋流叶片

inlet temperature ①（泛指各种气、液的）入口温度 ②进气温度（指内燃机、压缩机标准吸气位置的气体的全温度）

inlet tract （进气歧管通向各汽缸进气口的）进气支路，进气分支管

inlet triangle （叶轮）入口速度三角形（如：变矩器泵轮入口速度三角形）

inlet tube 进气管（道）

inlet valve ①进气门（开启和关闭空气或空气/燃油混合气进入汽缸的进气口的阀门，美称 intake valve）②进油阀，进液阀

inlet valve cam 进气门凸轮

inlet-valve seat 进气门座

inlet-valve spring 进气门弹簧

inlet velocity 进气速度；进入速度（= input velocity, intake velocity）

inlet velocity head 进口处的速度压头

inlet volume （气体，流体）进入容积

inlet water hose 进水软管

in-line canister purge solenoid 串联式燃油蒸气活性炭罐净化电磁阀（见 canister purge，指该阀串联在燃油蒸气活性炭罐与进气歧管的连接管道中，由发动机电子控制模块控制，开启时，活性炭罐存储的燃油蒸气即被吸入进气歧管内）

in-line cylinder arrangement 直列汽缸排列，汽缸顺列法，汽缸直列

in-line engine 直列式发动机（= straight-line engine，指具有两个或两个以上汽缸并呈一列布置的内燃机）

in-line fuel injection pump （柴油机的）直列式喷油泵（各柱塞偶件的轴线相互平行且位于同一平面内的合成式喷油泵，见 drive shaft fuel injection pump）

in-line power steering 整体式动力转向（指由转向机、控制阀和动力缸三者制成一体的动力转向机构，参见 offset power steering）

in-line production 流水线生产

in-line pump 直列多柱塞（喷油）泵

in-line quick coupling 串联式快速接头

in-line smoke meter 内装式烟度计

(= built-in smoke meter)

inline type 直列式

in-motion axle weight 动态车桥荷载（汽车行驶中测量的车桥荷载）

in-motion shifting 行驶中换挡

in-motion weighing 动态称重（量）（= dynamic weighing）

innards 内部结构，内部机构（= entrails）

inner ①内部，里面 ②内部的，内侧的，里面的

inner attachment face 内安装面（如：制动盘毂或制动鼓直接固定在轮毂上的安装面，= inner mounting face）

inner ball race （球笼式万向节）钢球的内滚道（指其星形套上的曲面凹槽）

inner band brake 内带外张式制动器

inner bead reinforcing strip （轮胎）胎圈内缘加强带

inner bearing cup shoulder （车轮的）内轴承座圈

inner brake 内胀式制动器（见 internal expanding brake）

inner brake shoe （位于制动鼓内的）内制动蹄（片）

inner carrier （可变压缩比活塞的）内活塞

inner case of seal 油封金属内圈

inner cone ①（火焰的）内锥，内层 ②（锥齿轮的）前锥面，前锥（指此齿轮小端端面的一个圆锥面，其母线与分锥垂直相交）

inner cone distance （锥齿轮的）内锥距（分锥顶点沿锥母线至前锥的距离）

inner cylinder 内缸筒（如汽车悬架的双筒式减振器的内筒）

inner dead 内止点，内死点（水平或垂直对置式发动机活塞的内止点，相当于直列式发动机的上止点，见 top dead center）

inner diameter 内径（= internal diameter, inside diameter, interior diameter）

inner drum （制动器，离合器的）内鼓

inner engine emission control 发动机排放的机内控制（指通过内燃机内部结构的改进，减少排气有害成分）

inner envelope of the epitrochoid 外旋轮线的内包络线（如：转子发动机中旋转活塞的周边外形曲线）

inner envelope rotor flank （转子发动机）内包络线转子工作面，旋转活塞内包络线型线工作面

inner fender 内挡泥板

inner flexible shaft （传动软索的）钢丝内芯（美称 inner cable 或 drive cable）

inner guide （弹簧）内导杆

inner headlight （四灯制前照灯中的左、右两个）内侧前照灯（一般为远光灯）

inner-hexagon spanner 内六角扳手

inner housing 内壳，内体壳（如：滚动花键球笼式万向节的、外圆柱表面上开有数条轴向滚动花键槽的钟形元件）

inner lens （车灯的）内置式配光镜

inner liner ①内部衬垫，内衬圈；轮胎衬里层 ②无内胎轮胎气密层（无内胎式轮胎胎里及其与轮辋胎圈座的接触面上的防透气胶层）

inner loop （互通式立体交叉中的）内转（插入）匝道，内环路，内侧道（如：在车辆左侧行驶的道路中，车辆需右转驶入另一与之立体交叉的道路时，所使用的内环匝道）

inner package （仪器仪表的）内包装，内层包装

inner planet gear 内行星齿轮（复式行星齿轮机构中与外行星齿轮及中

心轮啮合的行星齿轮)

inner race ①(滚动轴承)内座圈,内环滚道,内圈 ②(球笼式等速万向节的)星形套(在球形的外支撑表面上沿轴截面方向开有球槽并有内花键的环形元件,亦称 joint star member)

inner race with cylinder ball grooves (可轴向移动的球笼式万向节的)柱形滚道星形套(在球形的外支撑表面上沿轴向开有柱形滚道,因而可实现轴向移动,并具有内花键的环形元件)

inner rear wheel arch (轿车车身)后轮内罩板,后轮罩板

inner ring 滚动轴承内圈

inner ring rotor gear (转子发动机的)转子内齿圈,转子相位内齿圈,转子内正时齿圈(= internal timing gear, rotor annular gear)

inner ring with rib 有导向突缘的(滚动轴承)内圈

inner rotor ①(单纯旋转发动机的)内转子,旋转活塞(见 SIM)②(齿轮泵的)内齿轮

inner-rotor type electric wheel 内置转子型电动车轮(装在车轮内的电动机的转子位于定子绕组内腔经减速机构驱动车轮旋转,见 in wheel motor 和 outer-motor type electric wheel)

inner sill panel (车身)内门槛板(车门槛后的车身底板加强短纵梁板件)

inner sleeve 内套筒

inner space 内部空间

inner spiral angle (锥齿轮)小端螺旋角(其轮齿顶端齿线的螺旋角)

inner spring 内(圈)弹簧

inner spring seat 内弹簧座

inner steered angle (转向时)内侧车轮的回转角

inner stress 内应力

inner synchromesh disc 内同步啮合盘

inner tire shoe 轮胎衬带,轮胎内衬块

inner tube (轮胎的)内胎(= tire tube)

inner tube body (汽车轮胎的)内胎胎身(内胎不包括气门嘴及其胶垫的环形胶管)

inner tube deflation 内胎放气;内胎降压

inner tube valve 内胎气门嘴,(见 inflation valve)

inner-tube valve cap (轮胎)内胎气门嘴盖,内胎气门嘴帽

inner valve (轮胎气门嘴中的)芯阀,气门芯子(= valve core, valve inside)

inner valve spring 气门内弹簧(套在气门外螺旋弹簧中的内螺旋弹簧)

inner wheel path (转弯时)内轮轨迹

inner width 空隙,内腔宽度

inner wing panel 内翼子板(指装在发动机舱左、右两侧的翼子板)

inner wire ①内索,内线(装在挠性导管内的传动索)②内部导线

inner yoke (凸块式万向节的)内凸块叉(指驱动端,即靠发动机一端的凸块叉,见 fork yoke 及 Tracta universal joint)

innovation 革新,技术革新;新设施,新发明,新技术

innovative 采用新方法的,创新的,引进新思想的,具有创意的

Innovative Traction control system (本田公司的)创新型牵引力控制系统(本田公司研制的不采用差速器而是通过左、右两根驱动轴上布置的两个黏性耦合器传递和分配驱动转矩的四轮驱动系统的商品名)

inoculation cast iron 孕育处理铸铁,

变性处理铸铁，加孕育剂处理的铸铁（= Meehanite cast iron）

inoperative 不起作用的，不工作的，不生效的，无效的，无法使用的，不能再用的

inoperative period 非运行期，停机期

inordinate wear 异常磨损，过度磨损，不规则的磨损

inorganic 无机的，无机物的（一般指不含碳元素的，简称 inorg）

inorganic compound 无机化合物（一般指不含碳元素的化合物，但 CO，CO_2，NaCN 等少数含碳化合物也属于无机化合物）

inoxidable 不可氧化的，抗氧化的

inoxidizability 抗氧化性，耐腐蚀性

inoxidizing coating 防氧化涂层，防腐蚀覆盖层

in parallel 并联

in-phase ①同相的 ②同相

"in place" conditions 现场条件，现场状况

input ①输入；输入端，输入量（例如：输入电压，输入电流，输入电路，输入功率，输入信号，输入数据等）②供给，进给，进料

input amplifier 输入信号放大器

input axis 输入轴（简称 I.A）

input bias current temperature coefficient 输入偏置电流温度系数（输入偏置电流随温度的变化率）

input clamp voltage （数字集成电路的）输入钳位电压（在小微分电阻上足以限制输入电压幅度的输入电压）

input configuration （二进制电路的）输入组态（在给定瞬间输入端上低电平与高电平的组合，亦称 input pattern "输入图形"）

input cross talk attenuation （模拟信号开关电路的）输入串扰衰减（模拟信号开关电路一处于截止态通道输出电压与其在另一个处于导通态通道输出中产生的不需要电压之比）

input current 输入电流（通过输入端的电流）

input current operating range （线性放大器的）输入电流工作范围（使放大器功能符合规范规定的输入电流范围）

input data 输入数据

input drift （线性放大器的）输入漂移（为补偿输出的直流电压或直流电流因电源电压、时间、温度等的变化而引起的变化，所加的输入直流电流或直流电压的变化，亦称等效输入漂移"equivalent input drift"）

input flange 输入轴突缘

input horsepower 输入马力，输入功率

input impedance （模拟集成电路的）输入阻抗（指每一输入端或并联输入端到电参考点的阻抗；两输入端之间的阻抗）

input loading factor （双极型数字电路的）输入负载系数（一种用数字电路的一个规定输入端上的输入电流与被选作参考负载的特定电路的输入电流之比而得到的系数）

input modulator valve ①（防抱死制动系的）压力调节器输入阀（由防抱死制动电子控制模块控制的电磁阀，其数目与车轮制动轮缸数相等，即每一个输入阀控制一条轮缸的输入液压通路的开启与关闭）②（装在 ABS 压力调节器的各车轮分泵进油路中的）进油阀（由 ABS 控制模块控制的电磁阀，在正常制动和 ABS 升压阶段该阀开启，保压和降压阶段该阀关闭）

input offset current 输入失调电流（①为使线性放大器直流输出电压等于规定电平，通常为零，两输入端间所加的直流电流之差 ②为使接

口电路直流输出电压达到规定值，通过两个差动输入端之间的直流电流的差值）

input offset voltage 输入失调电压［为使线性放大器和接口电路等的直流输出电压等于规定电平（通常为零），在接口电路的差动放大器输入端之间所必须施加的直流电压和在放大器规定的输入和输出电路的差动放大器输入端之间所施加的直流电压］

input/output interface 输入/输出接口（在汽车电子控制系统中，将输入-输出设备与电子控制模块连接起来的硬件电路，最主要的是将各种传感器的模拟信号转换为控制模块所能接受的数字信号的输入接口和将控制模块各种数字指令转变为外部执行机构所能接受的模拟量的输出接口，简称 I/O interface，其主要功能为：地址译码，按控制模块送出的地址找到指定的外部设备；数据缓冲与锁止，使 I/O 接口与控制模块的 CPU 在数据传输速度上得到匹配；信息转换，如：模/数、数/模转换、信息电平高低转换、串行与并行传送方式转换等；提供时控与状态信息，如：设置时钟控制时序，以及将外部设备的运行状态信息告知控制模块等）

input pickup （发动机示波器等的）输入传感器，输入信号传感器

input pump 输入泵（参见 front pump）

input reduction type 3-shaft gear train CVT （日本大发公司 2006 年推出的汽车前进时发动机动力）减速输入（驱动带轮）式三轴型行星齿轮传动（的）连续无级变速器［发动机动力由液力变矩器经 CVT 的动力输入轴传至行星齿轮机构的太阳轮。挂空挡和驻车时，行星齿轮机构的前进挡制动器（forward brake）和倒挡离合器（reverse clutch）放松，行星齿轮自转，不传递动力。挂前进挡时，前进挡制动器将行星架锁死，动力由太阳轮经行星轮、齿圈传至 CVT 的驱动带轮，此时驱动带轮的旋转方向和发动机相反而转速降低，减速比为 1.492。挂倒挡时，倒挡离合器结合，行星齿轮机构锁死，动力直接由太阳轮传至齿圈，此时驱动带轮的旋转方向和转速均与发动机相同］

input regulation coefficient ①（电流调整器的）输入调整系数（在规定输入电压变化值下，输出电流的相对变化）②（电压调整器的）输入调整系数（输入电压规定的变化值下，输出电压的相对变化值）

input regulation range （电压调整器的）输入调整范围（对应于输入调整系数或输入稳定系数的输入电压范围）

input shaft 输入轴（指将动力引入机器系统或装置内的轴，如：通过离合器从动盘将发动机动力输入变速器的离合器轴"clutch shaft"）

input signal 输入信号（加到输入端的信号）

inputs of state （系统）状态的输入量（如：阻尼系统的状态输入量是外力）

input terminal （电路，电器的）输入端

(input) threshold voltage （输入）阈电压（一种当输入电压值超过它时，能改变输出逻辑状态的输入电压电平）

input torque 输入转矩，输入轴转矩

input transient recovery time （调节器的）输入瞬态响应时间（输入电压规定跃阶变化与输出电压或电流值最后一次进入包括输出电平最终值的规定电平范围瞬间之间的时间间隔）

input variable 输入变量（如：输入

到仪器仪表的变量)
input velocity 进气速度,入口速度(参见 inlet velocity)
input voltage 输入电压
input work 输入功
in-reservoir filter (油箱中的)浸入式滤清器
in running order 处于工作状态下,在运转中;完好的,准备进入工作的,处于运转准备状态的
inrush ①起动转矩,起动功率,起动冲量,起动电流 ②侵入,涌入,闯入,吸入
inrush current 起始电流(如:开关接通瞬间的电流)
inrush load 起动功率负载,起动冲量负载
in/s 英寸/秒 (inch per second)
INS 惯性导航系统 (inertia navigation system 的简称,该系统一般由3个加速表和3只陀螺仪组成,具有很高的精度和高速获取数据的能力,但会产生累计误差)
inscribed 内切的,内接的
insect deflector (风窗玻璃的)昆虫挡板 (=bug deflector)
insecure 不可靠的,不耐久的;不完全的,危险的
insecurity 不完全,不可靠,不安全因素,不安全事物
insensibility 不灵敏性,钝性,不敏感 (=insensitiveness)
inseparable chamber 整体式燃烧室,不可拆卸式燃烧室,不可分式燃烧室
insert ①插入物,嵌入物,镶入物 ②衬垫,衬套,轴套,轴衬,镶套,垫圈 ③嵌入式路面标志 ④插入,嵌入,镶入
insert bearing 滑动轴承轴瓦 (=renewable metal)
inserted guider 镶装式气门导管(镶在汽缸盖内的气门导管)
inserted joint (管端)套筒接头
inserted liner 镶入式缸套 (=insertion liner)
inserted sleeve 镶式衬套
inserted valve seat 气门镶座,嵌入阀座,气门座镶圈(亦称 valve seat insert, insert for valve seat,见 detouchable valve seat)
inserter 镶套压装工具,镶装工具
insert gauge 塞规
inserting slit 插装缝,插装槽,安插缝
insertion ①插入,嵌入 ②插入物,嵌入物,镶入物 ③衬垫,安置,存放
insertion gain 介入增益,插入增益(如:电路中插入一阻抗匹配变换器时,其分贝的增益)
insertion liner 镶入式缸套 (=inserted liner)
insertion loss 介入损失,插入损失(如:电路中插入一阻抗匹配变换器等时,其分贝的损失)
insertion piece 插入件,垫片
insertion spanner 镶接扳手
insert metal 滑动轴承轴瓦 (=renewable metal)
insert of seat 镶入式气门座圈 (=valve seat insert)
insert socket (套筒扳手的)嵌装式套筒
insert tread ①硫化轮胎用的可拆式胎面模具 ②镶装胎面
insert type multi-speed transmission 插入式多挡变速器 (=interpolation multispeed transmission)
in-service evaluation (对新型结构等的)使用鉴定,使用评价(在使用过程中进行的评价)
in-service failure 在作用过程中的损坏,在使用期内的损坏 (=service failure)
in service fuel economy 运行燃料经

济性，使用燃料经济性（= in-use fuel economy）

in-service test 使用试验，实用试验

in-service time （机器）作用时间，作业时间，使用时间

inset ①插入，嵌入，引入，加进 ②插入物，嵌入件，镶装件 ③（内偏距车轮的）内偏距（轮辐安装面到轮辋中心线的距离，inset distance 的简称）

inset dish wheel 内偏距车轮（指辐安装面在轮辋中心线外侧，即轮辋中心线在轮辐安装面内侧的车轮）

inset type multi-speed transmission 插入式多挡变速器（由主、副两套变速器构成，主变速器挡位间速比较大，副变速器插入其间，二者组成一多挡传动比系列）

inset valve seat 阀门镶座，气门镶座

inside ①内部，内面，里面 ②内部的，内面的，里面的

inside bevel (led) chromium piston ring 内倒角镀铬活塞环

inside bevel (led) piston ring 内斜面活塞环，内倒角活塞环

inside bevel (led) taper-face piston ring 内倒角锥形活塞环

inside brake cheek （鼓式制动器）外张式制动蹄（= internal expanding brake shoe）

inside calipers micrometer 内卡钳千分表

inside ceiling panel （车身）内顶板

inside clearance 内间隙，内余隙

inside (dial) indicator 内径千分表，内径测微指示器

inside diameter 内径（简称 ID, = inner diameter, internal diameter, core diameter）

inside door handle （从车内开、闭车门的）车门内手柄

inside door knob （从车内锁车门的）门内手柄按钮

inside lead gauge 内螺纹导程（螺距）规

inside liner （轮胎的）内衬层（在有内胎式轮胎的外胎胎里上的胶层）

inside panel （车身侧壁等的）内蒙皮，内壁板（= wainscoting）

inside primary coil （点火线圈的）内层初级绕组（简称 IP coil）

inside rear view mirror （车身）内部后视镜（= interior mirror）

inside thread 内螺纹（= internal thread）

inside tire （装在双胎并装车轮中之）内侧轮胎

inside view 内视图（如：车厢内部的视图）

inside wheel turning angle 内转向轮转向角（内转向轮轴与前桥的交角）

in-silencer type PM trap and catalyst converter （柴油车的）消声器内置型微粒排放物捕集和催化转化器（装在消声器内的排放物后处理净化装置的一种，将捕集到的 PM 在氧化催化剂作用下燃烧净化）

in-situ accessibility （汽车装置）就车检修的可接近性，就车检查的可及性

in-situ replacement 就车更换零部件（不拆卸总成）

in-situ test 现场试验

INSMAT 材料检验员（inspector of material）

insolation 日晒（暴露于阳光下）

insolubility 非溶性，不溶性

insoluble ①不溶（解）物质 ②不溶解的（简称 insol）

INSP ①检查（inspection）②检验员（inspector）

inspect and repair as necessary 按需检修（简称 IRAN）

inspection ①检查，检验，检测 ②检视（主要指凭感观和使用简单工具对车辆总成及零部件技术状况进行的检查）③监督，校对

inspection after running 运行后的检查

inspection certificate （产品的）检验合格证

inspection-classification 检验分类

inspection code 故障等检验规程，检验指导书

inspection cover 检查盖，检查孔盖

inspection door 观察孔，检视口，检查用窗孔（亦称 inspection hole，inspection opening，参见 access door）

inspection frequency 检测频率（每单位时期内的检验次数）

inspection hammer （故障）检查用手锤（用轻敲的方法检查螺栓、连接件等有无损伤或故障，亦称 test hammer）

inspection intervals 检查间隔（里程或时间）

inspection lamp socket （手提）工作灯插座，检查灯插座，行灯插座

inspection lot 质量检验中随机抽取的一批样品

inspection maintenance program （汽车的）检测维修计划

inspection manual 检测手册

inspection mirror 检视镜（用于检视汽车零部件的隐蔽部位）

inspection of goods 验货（根据运单，对运输货物的数量、尺码、特性、包装和存放地点等进行查验）

inspection pit 车辆检修地沟，维修地沟

inspection rack （汽车）检修台

inspired ①性能卓越的，品质优秀的 ②（与名词、形容词、副词联用表示…性质的，或在…方面优越的，如 aeronautically inspired cockpit 航空器般的优越汽车驾驶室）

instability 不稳定性

install 设置，安置；安装，装配

installation ①安装，装配，设置 ②整套装备，设备，设施 ③台，站

installed engine 装车发动机，装机发动机（已装在汽车上的发动机，装有所需要的全部附件，如：消声器、空气滤清器等）

installed height 装配高度（如：弹簧等装配就位后的高度）

installed net horsepower （发动机的）装车净马力，装机净马力（指扣除了各种附件损失，大气修正及全部附加耗损的净输出马力，= net horsepower）

installed net torque （发动机的）装车净转矩，装机净转矩（指扣除了各种附件损失，大气修正及全部附加耗损的净输入或输出转矩）

installed output （发动机的）装车功率（实际驱动汽车的最大功率，用于计算功率车重比等）

installed power （发动机的）装车净功率（扣除驱动附件后的净功率，= net power）

installer ①装配工 ②安装者

installing 安装，装配，设置，建立，安置

installing torque 安装转矩（指安装零件时拧紧其螺纹所施加的转矩）

installment plan ［美］①分期付款计划（购车分期付款，英称 hire purchase plan）②分批交货办法

installment purchase of cars ［美］轿车分期付款购销（= 英 hire purchase，见 installment plan）

instancy of ignition 点火瞬间，着火瞬间

instant 瞬间，时刻（时间上的某一）点

instantaneous acceleration 瞬时加速度

instantaneous angular speed 瞬时角速度（°/s）

instantaneous availability 瞬时有效度（汽车在某时刻具有或维持其规定功能的概率）

instantaneous axis 瞬时轴线

instantaneous brake power 瞬时制动功率（瞬时总制动力 F_f 与相应的瞬时车速 v 的乘积，$p_f = F_f \cdot v$）

instantaneous braking deceleration 瞬时制动减速度 $a\left(a = \dfrac{dv}{dt}\right)$

instantaneous center of turn 瞬时转向中心；瞬时旋转中心

instantaneous crankshaft position sensor 曲轴瞬时位置传感器（用于发动机瞬时转矩测定）

instantaneous cylinder pressure sensor 汽缸瞬时压力传感器

instantaneous direction （汽车行驶中的）瞬时方向

instantaneous displacement 瞬时位移（量）

instantaneous excitation test 瞬态激振试验（快速测试方法，宽频带激振试验技术）

instantaneous fuel economy 瞬时燃油经济性（简称 IFE）

instantaneous linear velocity 瞬时线速度

instantaneous piston speed 活塞瞬时速度（活塞在行程中某一点或曲轴某一转角时的速度）

instantaneous power 瞬时功率

instantaneous relay 瞬时继电器，速动继电器

instantaneous speed change 瞬时（转）速度变动率

instantaneous stress-strain curve 瞬时应力-应变曲线

instantaneous suspention center 悬架的瞬时中心（悬架压缩-回跳运动过程中某一点的几何投影中心）

instantaneous torque feedback control system （发动机的）瞬时转矩（信号）反馈控制系统（根据发动机瞬时转矩反馈信号，适时修正汽油机点火或柴油机喷油时刻的闭路控制系统）

instantaneous value of shear stress 切应力瞬时值（某一给定瞬时切应力的大小）

instantaneous welding of small areas （摩擦表面）微小面积在摩擦高温下的瞬时熔接

instant center 瞬时中心

instant getaway （汽车）起步加速

instant of the beginning of control device movement 控制装置开始作用时刻，控制装置作用始点

instant of the beginning of deceleration to be approximately stable （汽车制动过程中）减速度接近于稳定的开始时刻，减速度趋于稳定的始点

instant of the beginning of deceleration to decrease rapidly （制动过程中）减速度开始急剧减弱时刻，减速度急剧减弱始点（从这一时刻起减速度开始急剧下降，相当于制动踏板放松始点）

instant of the deceleration to begin （制动过程中的）减速度开始产生时刻，减速始点

instant of the deceleration to cease （制动过程中的）减速度终止时刻，减速终点

instant-setting characteristic 快速装配特性，快装特性，速调特性

instant spare 紧急备件（①指重要的急用备件 ②指在紧急情况下，可自动起作用的备件，如：轮胎扎破后，可立即自动充气和喷射密封剂，以应急的紧急充气器等）

instant start 瞬时起步，突然起步

in state of charge （蓄电池）有电状态

in-step 同步的，相位一致的

institute ①学院；研究院；学会，协会，学术会议 ②建立，设置，制定；开始，着手，创始

Institute of Automobile Mechanical Engineers ［日］汽车机械工程师学会（简称 IAME）

Institute of Electrical & Electronic Engineers （美）电气与电子工程师学会（简称 IEEE）

Institute of Fuel 英国燃料学会（简称 IF）

Institute of Motor Industry ［英］汽车工业学会（简称 IMI）

Institute of Road Transport Engineers ［英］道路运输工程师学会（简称 IRTE）

Institute of the Rubber Industry ［英］橡胶工业学会（简称 IRI）

Institute of Traffic Engineers ［美］交通工程师学会（简称 ITE）

Institute of Transport ［英］运输学会（简称 IOT）

Institute of Transportation Engineers 交通运输工程师学会（国际性学术组织，原名 Institute of Traffic Engineers，20 世纪 70 年代改称现名，简称 ITE）

Institution of Mechanical Engineers 机械工程师学会（简称 IME，或 I Mech E）

in stock 库存，存有

in-stream location ①（将仪器）安置在交通流中 ②置于气（水、油）流中

instroke 吸气冲程，吸入冲程

instruction ①指示书，说明书，须知，细则，规程，守则；通知，指南，指导，教导，教育，讲授 ②（计算机）指令

instruction address register （汽车电子控制系统的）指令地址寄存器（保存要执行的下一条指令的地址）

instructional car 教练车

instruction counter （汽车电子控制系统控制模块的）指令计数器（指出下条要执行的计算机指令的地址）

instruction monitor 指令发布器，指令显示装置（电子计算机-人工诊断系统中，由电子计算机根据作业程序向操作人员发布作业、工序等指令的装置）

instruction register 指令寄存器（汽车电子控制模块中存储要进行解释的指令的寄存器）

instrument ①仪器，仪表（简称 instr）②给…安装仪表

instrument(-board) clock （装在）仪表板（上的）时钟

instrument board compartment （汽车仪表板上的）手工具箱（glove compartment）

instrument case 仪表壳

instrument cluster ①仪表板 ②组合式仪表

instrument constant 仪器、仪表常数（仪器仪表的直接示值×系数=仪器仪表示值，该系数即为仪器仪表常数，当直接示值等于被测量值时，该常数为 1）

instrumented dummy passenger 装有各种测试仪器的试验用假人乘员

instrument error 仪器误差

instrument fascia bezel 仪表饰带（饰条）卡环

instrument gears 仪表齿轮，精密齿轮（见 miniature gears）

instrument glass 仪表玻璃

instrument head ①量测头，测量端 ②表头

instrument lag 仪表的滞后

instrument of ratification 批准书，批准文件

instrument panel ①（车身）仪表安装板，仪表底板 ②（风窗玻璃下

的）仪表板（= dashboard, dash panel instrument board, instrument carrier board 或 panel）

instrument panel bracket 仪表板支架

instrument panel crossmember （支撑）仪表板的横梁

instrument (-panel) lamp 仪表（板）照明灯［亦称 instrument (-panel) light, dashboard light］

instrument range 仪表量程，仪器量测范围

instrument reading 仪表读数

instrument test repair laboratory 仪器检测修理实验室（简称 ITRL）

instrument upper garnish 仪表装饰性护檐（仪表板上起装饰和安全防护作用的檐盖）

instrument with contacts 接触式测量仪器，带测试触头的仪表

insufficient 不足够的，不充分的，不适当的

insulant 绝缘材料，绝缘物质，绝缘电阻

insulate 绝缘，绝热，隔离，隔音，隔热

insulated canister （液化燃料的）绝热绝缘金属罐

insulated car 保温车

insulated return electrical system 绝缘回路电系（相对于车架搭铁回路而言）

insulated van 厢式保温车，绝热保温车，保温冷藏车（指装有隔热车厢，但没有制冷装置，短途运送冷冻货物的专用车辆，见 refrigerated van）

insulated wire 绝缘导线（= covered wire）

insulating 绝缘的，保温的，绝热的（指起绝缘、绝热作用的）

insulating cap （点火线圈的）绝缘盖

insulating material 绝缘材料

insulating strength 绝缘强度（以加在绝缘部分之间不致产生飞弧或通过绝缘材料的电流不超过某规定值的直流或正弦交流电压值来表征）

insulating tape 绝缘带，绝缘胶带

insulation ①（电）绝缘，绝热，隔音，隔离 ②绝缘体，绝缘材料

insulation against heat 绝热，隔热（= heat insulation）

insulation current 绝缘漏电流

insulation layer 绝缘层（指防止导电而涂覆的一层薄膜或设置的隔层）

insulation paste 绝缘胶

insulation resistance 绝缘电阻（指在仪表、仪器、电路等的绝缘件或绝缘部分之间施加规定的直流电压所测得的电阻）

insulation rubber ①绝缘胶（片、带、块、件等）②隔缘胶（指轮胎中贴在胎体帘布层之间的薄胶层）

insulation strip （将公路加速车道或减速车道与主行车道分隔开来的）隔离带，分隔带

insulation washer 绝缘垫圈（= insulating washer）

insulation workshop 保温车间

insulator ①（电）绝缘物，绝缘体，绝缘子 ②绝热体 ③隔声体 ④隔离物

insulator firing end （火花塞的）绝缘体的火花端（指伸入汽缸内的锥形端，= insulator cone, insulator nose, insulator tip）

insullac 绝缘漆

insurance 保险，保险费，保险单，安全保障，安全措施

insurance against all risks 全能保险（= all-risk insurance）

insurance against fire 火灾保险（= fire insurance）

insurance against responsibility 责任

保险

insurance against theft 失窃保险,盗窃保险

insurance certificate 保险凭证

insurance device 保险安全装置,保险机构(如:铰接式客车牵引机构万一失去连接功能时,仍能保证主、副车不脱开,以保障乘客、车辆安全的机构)

Insurance Institute for Highway Safety [美]公路安全保险学会(简称IIHS)

insurance of unexpected injury of passenger 乘客意外伤害保险

insure 保险,保证,保障,为…提供保证

insured transportation 保价运输(按保价货物运输办理运输承托手续,在发生货物赔偿时,按托运人声明价格及货物损坏程序予以赔偿的货物运输)

inswept ①流线型的,前端窄的 ②扫过

intact 完整的,无损伤的

intake ①进口,入口 ②吸入,引入,进气,进水,进油 ③吸入量,进风量 ④吸入道,进气管道

intake advance angle 进气提前角(四冲程内燃机从进气门开启到活塞到达上止点曲轴所转过的角度)

intake air 进气,吸气(= induction air)

intake air heater 进气空气预热器(= intake air preheater,指装在进气系统对进气进行预热的装置)

intake air mass flow sensor 进气空气质量流量传感器(直接测出进气空气流质量的热线式传感器等,亦称mess airflow sensor。由于汽车上已不再使用早期的进气空气体积流量传感器,故一般简称的 air flow sensor 空气流量传感器,均指质量传感器)

intake air restriction (柴油机等的)吸气阻气,进气阻力;进气节流

intake air temperature compensator 进气温度补偿阀(简称TTC)

intake branch 进气歧管

intake charge heating 进气充量预热(利用废气或电热加热进入进气歧管的新鲜充量)

intake control rotary valve 进气调节旋转阀(简称ICRV)

intake CO_2 W/EGR 有EGR时进气歧管中CO_2含量

intake CO_2 WO/ECR 无EGR时进气歧管中CO_2含量

intake depression 进气(管)真空,进气(管)负压(指进气管中形成的低于大气压的负静压)

intake duration angle 进气持续角(从进气门开启到关闭所经历的曲轴转角,即:进气提前角+180°+进气迟后角)

intake elbow 进气弯管,进气歧管的弯管;进入管弯管

intake filter 进口滤清器,入口滤清器

intake gas (内燃机进气冲程)吸入的空气(或)吸入的可燃混合气(= suction gas)

intake heater (发动机)进气预热器

intake lag angle 进气迟后角(四冲程发动机活塞自下止点行至进气门完全关闭所经过的曲轴转角)

intake manifold [美]进气歧管(= induction manifold, suction manifold,指连接化油器或节气门体和各汽缸进气孔的多分支型管件,即将进气或可燃混合气由节气门体或化油器引入各汽缸的总管,亦写作进气支管,但进气支管应该指进气歧管与各汽缸进气孔连通的分支管"runner of manifold 或 branch of manifold"更为妥切)

intake manifold tuning valve 进气歧

管调谐阀（见 IMTV）

intake manifold vacuum 进气歧管真空（指节气门至进气门之间的进气歧管内真空度）

intake manifold vacuum-meter 进气歧管真空度表

intake muffler 进气消声器

intake opening 进气口，吸入口

intake period 进气冲程，进气期，吸气期，充气期（= admission period, charging period）

intake phase 进气相，进气阶段

intake pipe preheating jacket 进气管预热水套

intake plenum ①进气系统集气室（见 plenum chamber）②（进气增压式发动机的）蓄气（压）室

intake port （［美］= induction port, inlet port）①（进气门所关闭，开启的）进气孔 ②（通向进气门的）进气孔道

intake-port fuel injection system （汽油喷至）进气孔口的汽油喷射系统

intake port time-area （转子发动机等的）进气口开启时间-面积图

intake pressure 进气压力（充量进入汽缸前的压力）

intake process 进气过程（充量进入汽缸过程）

intake resistance 进气阻力；进口阻力

intake silencer 进气消声器（为防止进气管内发生噪声，在进气管设置的部件）

intake silencer with wet air cleaner 带湿式空气滤清器的进气消声器

intake stroke （［美］四冲程内燃机的）进气冲程（活塞由上止点向下止点运动吸入新鲜充量的冲程）

intake swirl 进气涡流（在进气过程中采取措施，包括结构上的措施，使工质形成的基本上绕汽缸中心线旋转的涡流）

intake temperature ①进气温度（指充量进入汽缸前的温度）②入口温度

intake turbulence 进气紊流（进气过程中，汽缸内工质不规则的运动）

intake vacuum 进气真空（指发动机由于吸气而造成的进气歧管内低于大气压的压差值）

intake valve ①［美］进气阀，进气门（= inlet valve）②进油阀，进液阀

intake velocity 进气速度，进口速度（= inlet velocity）

intake volume 进气容积

intangible ①难以确定的，不能实现的，不现实的 ②不能肯定的因素 ③不现实性

integral ①整体，总体 ②积分（integral eguation 积分方程，definite integral 定积分，double integral 二重积分，indefinite integral 不定积分）③整体的，完整的，总体的；组成的，集成的；积分的，积累的，综合的；主要的；构成整体所必要的

integral ABS 整体式防抱死制动系统（指制动总泵与制动压力调节装置组成一体的 ABS）

integral body （轿车等的）承载式车身，整体式车身，单件式车身（= mono body, unite body, monocoque body, integral body and frame, body integral with frame, 指车身与车架成一体，无独立车架的结构形式）

integral bus 承载式车身客车

integral cam 整体凸轮（和轴制成一体的凸轮）

integral cast 总体铸造（指两个以上的组成部分一起铸造，= mono block cast, inblock cast, enblock cast）

integral counterweights 整体式平衡重（和曲轴制成一体的平衡重）

integral crankshaft 整体式曲轴（用整根钢料锻造，或铸造的整体曲轴）

integral curb （与路面）筑成一体的路缘石

integral cylinder head 整体式缸盖

integral flange of axle shaft 和半轴结成一体的突缘，整体式半轴突缘

integral front mounted splitter group 整体式前置副变速器（与相当于主变速器功能的传动装置组装在一个完整的体壳内的、与后置副变速器等效的传动装置）

integral fuel injection pump housing 整体式喷油泵壳

integral gearbox （装在发动机曲轴箱内的）整体式曲轴箱变速器（= integrated engine transmission）

integral gear rotor （转子发动机的）带齿整体转子，整体带齿旋转活塞（将转子和相位内齿圈铸成整体）

integral guide 整体式气门导管（指在缸盖内机械加工出的气门导管，相对于镶装式套管而言）

integral handle screw driver 固定手柄螺钉旋具

integral housing 整体式壳体；（特指）整体式后桥壳（= one-piece housing）

integral-hp motor 大于 1 马力的电动机

integral hub bearing 整体式轮毂轴承（车轮轴承与轮毂组成一体，形成一个总成，省去了轴承的专用内外圈）

integral implement 全悬架式农机具（= mounted implement）

integral intake 与汽缸体铸成一体的进气道

integral intake manifold 整体（铸造）进气歧管

integral key 花键

integral linkage power steering system （转向阀和油缸做成一体的）整体杆系式动力转向系统

integrally closed 整体封闭的

integrally feathered shaft 花键轴（= integral key shaft）

integral metal 整体滑动轴承，浇铸轴承（合金）

integral motor-generator 一体式电动机-发电机

integral moulded seat 整体模制座椅（指集成有三点式安全带的模制座椅）

integral number 整数

integral one-piece mainshaft （多缸转子发动机等用的）整体式主轴，整体式偏心轴

integral part ①整体件 ②整体件的一部分（如：cam lobe is an integral part of camshaft，凸轮的凸角是曲轴的一部分）

integral rear mounted gear group 整体式后置副变速器（与相当于主变速器功能的传动装置总装在一个完整的体壳后方，与内置变速器等效的传动装置）

integral rear trunk 布置在车身后部的行李舱（室）

integral sleeper 驾驶员卧室与驾驶室构成整体的驾驶室，位于驾驶室内的卧室

integral type ABS 整体式防抱死制动系统（指制动总泵与制动压力调节装置合并组成一个总成的防抱死制动系统）

integral type power steering 整体式动力转向器（其特点是液压泵、控制阀、动力转向缸等与机械转向器组成一体，位于转向盘柱管的下端，参见 linkage-type power steering）

integral water jacket 和汽缸制成一体的水套，整体式水套

integral with the shaft 与轴制成一体的

integrate alternator 整体式交流发电机（内装电子调节器的交流发电机）

integrated ①成一体的 ②集合的,汇集的 ③合计的,求和的,累计的 ④积分的

Integrated Brake Control 见 IBC

integrated brake wear and wheel-end temperature sensor 集成式制动器磨损和轮端温度传感器

integrated chassis control system 汽车底盘集中控制系统（指将独立的制动、转向、悬架等控制系统组合成由一组电子控制模块集中控制的一个统一的系统）

integrated circuit 集成电路（简称IC,指在电气上互连的若干电路元件不可分离地连接在一块完整基片上所构成的整体电路）

integrated circuit ignition unit 集成电路点火装置

integrated circuit memory 存储器集成电路（由存储单元组成,通常还包括：地址选择器、放大器等相关电路的集成电路）

integrated circuit microprocessor 微处理器集成电路［具有以下功能的集成电路：能按编码指令操作；能按指令接收供处理和存储的编码数据,并按指令对输入及存储在其寄存器和外存储器的数据进行算术逻辑运算,按指令发送编码数据等；能接收和（或）发送用以控制和描述微处理器集成电路的操作或状态的信号］

integrated collision avoidance system 综合防碰撞系统（自动驾驶系统的一个子系统,防止汽车前、后端与左右两侧与其他车辆相撞的智能系统,见 AVCS）

integrated diagnostic system 综（总）合式（车况）诊断系统,集成式诊断系统

Integrated Direct Ignition system 集成式直接点火系统（通用公司商品名,电子控制无分电器点火系的一种,由点火控制模块控制的点火线圈直接向火花塞输出点火高压,简称 IDI system）

integrated engine transmission 整体式曲轴箱变速器,（变速器在发动机的曲轴箱内,= integral gearbox）

integrated four-wheel antilock brake system with high-pressure energy-accumulator 带高压储能器的四轮整体式防抱死制动系统（制动主缸,泵电动机,高压储能器及其压力开关,电磁阀组等组合成一个总成的四轮防抱死制动系统。该系统不使用真空助力器,而由高压储能器经制动踏板行程控制的主缸柱塞推杆阀供给高压制动液推动主缸柱塞,实现增压助力）

integrated fuel control 燃油集中控制（使发动机在各种工况下的供油量都在最佳状态,以保证净化要求及燃料经济性等,简称 IFC）

integrated hydraulic system 集中液压系（制动、转向、离合器等机构共用的集中液压系）

integrated ignition assembly 整体式点火装置（日本电装公司生产的分电器型电子点火系的商品名,简称IIA,其点火线圈、点火控制模块和中央高压线均集成在分电器内,与分电器制成一体）

integrated microcircuit 集成微电路（指在电气上互连的若干电气元件不可分割的连在一起的微电路,在不会误解的情况下,可简称为集成电路"integral circuit",分为：半导体单片集成电路,半导体多片集成电路,薄膜集成电路,厚膜集成电路和混合集成电路）

integrated motor assist system （日本本田公司推出的）集成式电动机助

推系统（该系统用于小型轿车，加速时由电动机提供助力，减速时电动机起发电机作用，吸收并存储制动能量，简称 IMA system）

integrated retarder 整体式缓速器（指其运作与行车制动系有连带关系的缓速器，参见 independent retarder）

integrated silicon pressure sensor 集成电路型硅压电晶体压力传感器

integrated starter generator （混合动力车上使用的）集成式电动机/发电机，单体式电动-发电（两用）机（简称 ISG，起动时用作起动机，非制动-减速工况下由发动机驱动用作发电机，为蓄电池充电，减速、制动时由车轴反拖作为发电机发电，回收能源，在某些 HEV 上还作为汽车需要大功率驱动时与发动机一起驱动汽车的电动机）

integrated transportation system 一体化交通运输系统（简称 ITS，指将所有的交通工具、交通设施，以及使用交通工具、设施的人和物，进行统一规划，统一管理，统一组织，统一调配，达到整体优化使用，满足人们对交通的需求，陆、海、空、水运一体化）

integrating accelerometer 积分加速表，积分加速仪

integrating circuit 积分电路（见 integrator）

integrating flowmeter 累计流量计

integrating instrument 积分仪器仪表（通过一个量对另一个量进行积分以确定被测量值的测量仪器仪表，如：电度表）

integrating tachometer 累计式转数计

integration ①一体化②结合，综合③（产业的）集中④积分（integration by parts 部分积分法）

integrator 积分器，积分电路（指其输出模拟变量是输入模拟变量对时间或其他变量的积分，亦称 integrating circuit）

integrity 完整性，完全性，完善

integrity basis 整基（底）

integrometer 惯性矩面积仪

intellectual language network four-wheel alignmenter 智能语音网络四轮定位仪（具有语音提示功能）

intellectual property rights 知识产权（简称 IPR）

IntelliBeam 见 DynaView™

intelligence engine analyzer 智能发动机综合分析仪（具有故障诊断功能的微机控制发动机分析仪）

intelligence high beam function 见 smart headlamp

Intelligent and Innovative Vehicle Electronic Control System 创新型车辆智能电子控制系统（见 INVECS）

intelligent car 智能化汽车，智能轿车（指运用计算机技术、信息技术等使汽车能以最佳路线、最佳工况行驶，且能在自动公路上无人驾驶，自动行驶）

Intelligent catalyst （日本大发公司研制的排气净化用）智能催化剂（商品名，该催化剂具有"自己再生 self regeneration"机能，不仅可大量节约贵金属，而且可以确保排气净化。此项发明一经发表，受到世界各国汽车界注目，并获 2003 年度日本"自动车工学本年度""10 项最佳技术"奖，为两层结构，其下层为钯—$MFeO_3$ 催化剂，见 Pd-perovskite catalyst，上层为，Pt—Rh NO_x 还原催化剂）

intelligent control 智能化控制

intelligent co-pilot 智能（化）自动驾驶系统

intelligent cruise control （汽车）智能定速巡行控制（系统）

intelligent cruise system 智能定速巡

航系统（见 adaptive cruise system）

intelligent data bus 见 IDB

intelligent drive assist system 智能驾驶辅助系统［简称 IDAS，为 ACC（自适应性巡航系统）、Front Assist（正面碰撞预防辅助系统）、Lane Assist（车道保持辅助系统）、Park Assist（倒车入库、驻车辅助系统）、Rear Assist（后视影像辅助系统）等的统称］

intelligent drive master 见 i-DM

intelligent driver assistance system 智能型驾驶者帮助系统

intelligent duel spark plug ignition system 见 i-DSI

intelligent electric sunroof （轿车的）智能电动天窗

intelligent four 智能化四轮控制系统（见 i-Four）

Intelligent Highway Cruise Control (system) 见 IHCC

intelligent lighting 智能照明（技术）［可根据天气状况（雨、雾、晴等），车速、路况和交通状况改变前照灯光束的形状和强度，并可根据转向盘转角、转向信号灯及驾驶员视线方向改变前照灯照射方向，亦称 adaptive lighting］

intelligent lighting system 智能灯光照明系统（见 adaptive front-lighting system）

intelligent manufacture system 智能（化）制造系统（简称 IMS）

intelligent parking assist system 智能驻车协助系统（有多种类型，其中较先进者只要驾驶员根据后视摄像机提供的图像设定驻车车位和挂入倒车挡，电子控制模块将指挥电动倒车-转向机构自动完成整个驻车入位操作）

intelligent parking system 智能驻车系统

intelligent power module （混合动力车的）智能型驱动力控制模块

intelligent supervisory energy management system 智能型能量管理系统（一种供中型柴油机-电动机混合动力车使用，根据驾驶员的操作指令、排放要求和蓄电池充电状态，由电子计算机控制实现能量流"energy flow"连续最佳化算法的能量管理系统）

intelligent transportation infrastructure 智能交通设施（简称 ITI）

intelligent transportation system 智能（汽车）运输系统（简称 ITS，由交通安全系统，交通控制系统，出行者信息系统，道路引导系统，汽车自动驾驶系统，自动公路系统等组成的运输系统）

intelligent vehicle 智能化汽车，智能汽车（简称 IV，1989 年由欧盟组织开发，称 VITA 计划，1991 年由 Benz 公司推出样车，当时主要由装在汽车前后端及左右两侧的红外线摄像机，安装在车内的计算机、电子地图、光学感应仪器等组成，可自动选择最佳路线，操纵汽车行驶、停车、减速、加速、转向等，近年来功能与水平进一步提高，参见 ITS）

intelligent vehicle-highway system 智能汽车-公路系统（简称 IVHS）

Intelligent Weather Control System 智能化气候控制系统（可根据车外温度、日照程度及气候环境等对车内温、湿度作最佳自动调控，简称 IWCS）

IntelliLink infotainment system （GM 公司的）智能资讯娱乐系统（为该公司 Buick Enclave，Buick Encore 等车型的标准装置）

intended life 预定的使用寿命

intended load condition （汽车的）预计负载状态（指在厂家规定的车辆总重范围内，汽车可能出现的各

种负载状态和负载分布)

intended size 公称尺寸, 额定尺寸, 标称尺寸, 给定尺寸

intensification 强化, 加强

intensifier ①加强器, 放大器; 倍增器 ②增厚剂

intensify 增强, 强化, 加剧, 加厚

intensity 强度, 紧张程度, 密集度, 亮度, 光度; 强烈, 剧烈; (底片的) 明暗度

intensity coil 二次绕组, 二次线圈

intensity level ①强烈度, 强弱程度 ②(噪声的) 声强级, 响度级 (用声音大小的 ph 数表示, 见 phon)

intensity of bus runs 客车班次密度 (在单位时间内, 班线上发出的客车班次数)

intensity of combustion 燃烧强度 (每单位容积的混合气所放出的热量, 其常用单位 kcal/m³)

intensity of compression 压缩比, 压缩强度

intensity of current 电流密度

intensity of draft 牵引力大小, 牵引力强弱 (= intensity of draught)

intensity of illumination 照明强度

intensity of passenger flow 客流密度 (在单位时间内, 一定线路或区段上旅客向同一方向流动的人数)

intensity of pressure 压强 (指物体单位面积上所受的压力)

intensity of stress ①应力 (= stress, 物质内部每单位面积上抵抗作用力的力, 应力 = $\dfrac{作用力}{作用面积}$, 应力分两大类, 法向应力和剪切应力, 常用单位有 bar, hbar, MN/m², kN/m², bf/in², tonf/in², 参见 normal stress, shear stress) ②受力强度

intensity of the color 色素强度 (参见 absorbance of the color)

intensive test conditions 强化试验条件

interact 相互作用、相互影响、相互联系、互相制约、相互穿插、交相感应

interacting subsystem 相互作用的分支系统, 相互制约的辅助机构

interaction 相互作用, 相互影响, 相互联系, 相互制约, 交互作用, 交相感应, 干扰

interactive computing (多个企业共同使用的) 合用电子计算机系统; 联合 (电子计算机系统) 运算, 联合情报处理

inter-and-intraurban 城市间及城市内 (运输), 长途及市内 (运输)

interaxle 轴间的, 车桥间的 (亦写作 interaxial)

interaxle differential 桥间差速器, 轴间差速器 (= center differential 指并装双后桥的桥间差速器; 四轮驱动车辆的前、后桥间差速器)

interaxle lockable differential 桥间可锁式差速器

interaxle shaft 双驱动桥桥间传动轴

inter-bank angle (V 形发动机) 两列汽缸间的夹角

inter-bus communication system 客车内通信系统

intercar radio 汽车之间的无线电通信装置, 车间无线电通信装置

intercell link 蓄电池单格电池连接铅条

intercell partition 蓄电池单格电池隔板

intercept 截距

intercepted crossroad 横路交通截断型交叉路 (为了使主要道路交通能连续地通过交叉口, 而将交叉路横路的交通直接截断)

interceptor ①拦截装置, 拦截器 ②遮断 (光线的) 装置 ③扰流板 (亦写作 intercepter)

interchange ①互换, 交替, 交换, 轮换 ②道路互通式立体交叉, 道路

立体交叉枢纽

interchangeability 互换性,可交换性(指零件、部件、构件或总成在尺寸、功能、外形上能够彼此互相替换的性能)

interchangeable bearing 互换性轴承(指内、外圈等零件可互换的同型号可分式滚动轴承)

interchange of heat 热交换

interchanging of tires 轮胎换位

intercity bus 城市间客车,长途客车 (= intercity motor bus)

intercity trucking 长途货运 (= interurban trucking)

intercoastal 海岸间的(美国大西洋与太平洋海岸间的)

intercom (大型观光、游览客车等使用话筒、扩音器等设备的)车内通话系统

intercom 双向通信(intercommunication 的简称)

intercommunication 双向通信,对讲电话装置(汽车与汽车之间的通话装置,简称 intercom)

interconnected hydraulic suspension 互联式液压悬架(指前、后轮有管道互联、相互平衡的液压悬架系统)

interconnecting cable 中继电缆

interconnecting nut 中间连接螺母

interconnecting wiring diagram 接线图,布线图 (= interconnection diagram)

interconnection ①相互连接,互连,内连 ②横向过道,相互连接的通道

intercooled diesel engine 中冷增压柴油机

intercooler 中间冷却器,增压中冷器(实现增压空气中间冷却的冷却装置)

inter-cooling 中间冷却,增压冷却(①指对增压后的新鲜充量在进入汽缸前再由中间冷却器加以冷却,此时亦称后冷却, = after cooling ②指多级压缩之间的冷却)

inter-cooling level (进气增压的)中冷度(指经过中冷器前后空气的温度差与中冷器前空气温度的比值,以百分比表示,亦称 after-cooling level,见 inter-cooling)

intercooling stage (增压器)中冷段,中冷级

intercrystalline 晶粒间的,晶间的,沿晶界的

inter-cylinder fuel distribution characteristics (发动机的)缸间燃油分布特性

interdependent torsion bar (悬架的)互联扭杆

interface ①交界面,分界面;贴合面,接触面 ②连接体,连接装置 ③(电子计算机)接口(指起连接作用的系统、程序或设备的硬件和软件。特别是连接电信号互不相容的两个部分的硬件或软件,或二者兼有)④对接,接合,连接

interface integrated circuit 接口集成电路(指以其输入端和输出端连接电子系统中电信号互不相容的各个部分的集成电路)

interface logic 接口逻辑,界面逻辑

interfacial tension 界面张力,面际张力(分界面上的表面张力)

interfacial weld 摩擦面焊合(点)(摩擦表面因高温而引起的表面熔合点)

interfactory 厂间的,厂际的

interfere ①干涉,干扰,干预 ②抵触,妨碍 ③过盈

interference ①干扰,(光波、电波等的)干涉 ②(零件配合的)过盈 ③(齿的)啮合干涉,切齿干涉

interference angle ①干涉角 ②(汽车的)纵向通过角(见 ramp angle) ③气门座合面差角(气门座合面与

气门座座合面之间的斜角差，一般气门座合面成45°角而气门座座合面则为44°角，二者的差值1°）

interference elimination （无线电）消除干扰

interference filter ①无线电干扰滤波器 ②干扰滤光器（测定废气中有害成分的仪器，将厚度大致等于某种光波的薄膜组合起来，利用它所产生的干扰，只通过或反射特定波长光的滤光器，亦称 interferential filter）

interference fit 静配合，过盈配合，压配合

interference fringe 干涉条纹

interference generator 干扰（信号）发生器（用于器件的抗干扰性试验）

interference level 干扰电平，噪声级

interference locator 无线电干扰源探测器

interference pattern 光干扰图，干涉特性图，干涉图（案）

interference protection 防干扰

interference source （无线电）干扰源

interference suppressor （无线电）干扰抑制栅

interference trouble suppressing device 防干扰装置，干扰抑制装置（= interference preventer）

interferometer 干涉仪，干扰计

interfin space （风冷发动机汽缸的）散热片间距

interfin velocity （风冷发动机）散热片间的气流速度

intergranular ①颗粒状，晶粒状 ②颗粒间的，晶粒间的，晶界的（= intercrystalline）

interim standards （汽车废气有害含量等的）过渡性规定，过渡性标准，暂行标准

interior ①内部，内侧，国内，车内 ②内部的，国内的，里面的，室内的，车身内的

interior angle 内角

interior buck 车身内部的全尺寸模型

interior decoration （车身）内部装饰

interior diameter 内径（= inner diameter）

interior dimensions of body 车身内部尺寸

interior environment system 车内环境调控系统（车身内部的空气调节系统）

interior fittings 车身内部装饰件

interior head impact regulation 车内（乘员）头部碰撞法规

interior heater （车身）内部暖气设备

interior information guidance system （汽车的）内部信息导航系统（相对于卫星导航的外部信息导航系统而言，利用装在车上的惯性传感器、地磁传感器、汽车行程传感器、汽车方向传感器等的信息，实现行车导向的系统）

interior inspection tool 内腔检测工具，内部窥测器

interior light ①车内灯（光）②（特指）车内顶篷灯（= ceiling lamp）

interior light cable 车厢内电灯线

interior light switch ①（车身）内部灯光开关 ②（特指）车厢内照明顶灯开关

interior line 内部轮廓线，内部造型线

interior lining panel 内衬板

interior material （车身）内饰材料

interior mirror （装在风窗玻璃顶部中央附近的）车内后视镜

interior motion sensor （外人）闯入车内活动传感器（防打、砸型盗窃系统的传感元件）

interior noise ①车内噪声（传入车

内的道路噪声、机械噪声、排气噪声及风响噪声等的混合噪声）②内部噪声，厂（室）内噪声

interior noise level 车内噪声级，内部噪声级

interior plastic material 内饰用塑料

interior roof lamp door switch （车厢的）车顶灯车门开关（打开车门该开关即接通车顶灯电路）

interior roominess 车身内部宽敞度；内部宽敞性

interior space （车辆的）内部空间

interior styling （汽车车身的）内部造型（指座位、门框、仪表、转向操纵装置的式样位置，踏板的布置，乘坐室及地板的布置等）

interior trim color 内饰色彩；车身内饰色彩

interior trimming parts （车厢，驾驶室的）内装饰件（在车内部起装饰和防护作用的零件）

interlayer ①中间层，夹层，隔层 ②层间的

interleaf cushion spring （离合器从动盘）摩擦片间缓冲弹簧片（铆装在从动盘摩擦片上的波形弹簧片，使从动片具有轴向弹性而接合平顺，注意与"torsional drive spring"装在从动盘毂上的扭转减振弹簧不同）

interleaf friction （汽车钢板弹簧）板片之间的摩擦（力）

interleave ①交替（交织、交错、交叉、间隔）②交叉存取 ③隔行扫描

interleaves 钢板弹簧片间的减摩隔板（= interleave plate）

interlock ①连锁，互锁，联动，闭锁 ②连锁器，并锁装置（如：手动机械式变速器中防止同时挂上两个挡位的互锁机构）

interlock ball 互锁装置的锁定球

interlock circuit 互锁电路，连锁线路

interlocking ①互锁，连锁，闭锁 ②互锁的，联锁的，闭锁的

interlocking plunger 互锁销（亦称 interlock pin, interlock plug）

interlocking relay 连锁继电器

interlocking roller in striking rod （齿轮变速器换挡互锁机构）锁球的滑动顶销

interlocking signals 连锁信号

interlocking switch 连锁开关

interlock spring （变速器）互锁弹簧

interlock system ①连锁装置，连锁系统 ②连锁制

interlude ①中间时间 ②间隔的时间，间歇

intermediary shaft 中间轴，副轴

intermediate ①中间物，中间层 ②中间的，居中的，中立的，中间位置的 ③（美国轿车分级中的）中级（轿车）（指长 207～215 英寸的 5～6 座轿车，intermediate size car 或 intermediate car 的简称，一般其排量大于 2.5L，小于或等于 4L）

intermediate axle 中间轴，中间桥

intermediate axle left wheel brake tube 中桥左轮制动管路

intermediate base ①中间基（底）②中间轴距（前桥至中桥的轴距）

intermediate bearing 中间支撑

intermediate car 见 intermediate③

intermediate disc （双盘离合器的）中间压盘（双盘离合器中两从动盘之间的压盘，亦称 intermediate plate 或 interplate）

intermediate drive 中间传动

intermediate gasoline 中级汽油（研究法辛烷值在高级汽油和常规汽油之间，参见 premium gasoline）

intermediate gear ①（变速器的）中间挡（= intermediate speed, middle gear, 如：三挡变速器的二挡）②中间齿轮，惰轮

intermediate hold 中间挡（源于早

期前进挡只有高、中、低三个挡位的自动变速器用语，当前指变速杆导板上的"D2"挡位）

intermediate housing （简称，intermediate hsg 多缸转子发动机中各相邻缸之间的）中间缸盖，中间隔板（= center separation）

intermediate plate 见 intermediate disc

intermediate-pressure turbine 中压涡轮机

intermediate rod ①中央连杆（见 center link）②见 relay rod，track rod

intermediates 半成品，半制品

intermediate shaft （机械式变速器）中间轴，副轴（= counter shaft，lay shaft，secondary gear shaft）

intermediate shaft supporting bracket 中间轴支架

intermediate-size car 中级轿车，中型轿车（见 intermediate③）

intermediate speed ①中间转速（指最大转矩转速或60%额定转速二者中的较高者）②中间挡（见 intermediate gear）

intermediate steering arm （转向机构）中间转向臂

intermediate steering shaft 中间转向轴（连接转向盘柱与转向器）

intermediate stop （公共汽车等的）中途停车站，中途站

Intermediate Super Abrasion Furnace 一种炭黑的商品名（平均直径18μm，表面积129m²/g，简称ISAF）

intermediate wheel ①中速齿轮 ②中间挡齿轮 ③中间齿轮

intermittence 中断，间断；间歇性，周期性

intermittent 间歇的，中断的，断续的，脉动的，周期性的

intermittent angle 断续角，瞬时角（如：汽车在不平道路上行驶时，万向节瞬时夹角等）

intermittent brake power （标定功率中的）非持续功率（指厂方按用途和使用特点标定的15min，1h，12h连续运转的有效功率，亦称 intermittent rating power，见 declared power）

intermittent combustion engine 断续燃烧发动机（指常规汽油机、柴油机等）

intermittent contact 接触不良，间断接触，（电路故障）继续接触

intermittent current 脉动（脉冲）电流

intermittent cycle engine 间歇工作型发动机

intermittent-cyclic-combustion process 间断循环燃烧过程（如：一般活塞式内燃机的燃烧过程）

intermittent disconnection ①间歇性断电（电线连接松动等原因产生的电气故障）②断续性开脱

intermittent exposure 间歇暴晒（如：间歇暴露试验）

intermittent failure 间歇失效，间歇性故障（汽车出现故障后，不经修复而在一定的时间内，能自行恢复功能的故障）

intermittent fillet weld 间断填角焊缝（参见 fillet weld）

intermittent fuel injection ①间歇性喷油（指每循环中只喷油一次或数次，而不是连续不断喷油的系统）②间断喷油（不是每一工作循环针阀都升起喷油，而是每隔一、二个工作循环才升起针阀并喷油一次的不正常现象）

intermittent gear 间歇运动机构（如：一部分没有齿的齿圈，一部分无齿的齿条）

intermittent gross torque 发动机不带附件试验时的短时间最大转矩

intermittent ignition 间断着火（现象）（如：一些发动机在高速时间

断失火的现象)
intermittent operation 断续作业, 间歇工作, 间歇运转 (= discontinuous operation)
intermittent rating power 见 intermittent brake power
intermittent shock load 间歇冲击荷载
intermittent signal 闪光信号灯
intermittent visibility 经常变化的能见度; 断续的视野 (视野为车厢的某些部分所遮没)
intermittent wiper 间歇式刮水器 (不连续工作而是每间隔一段时间刮水若干次, 有间隔时间固定式和可调式两种)
intermittent wiping 刮水器的间歇擦拭 (间歇时间可以调节, 美称 mist action)
intermix 掺和, 混合, 搅拌, 重叠, 重复
intermodel surface transportation 地面运输联运, 陆路联运 (公路, 铁路等的联运)
Intermodel Surface Transportation Efficiency Act [美] 陆路联运效率法 (规) (1991年美国国会通过的一项规范公路、铁路等联运, 旨在提高运输效率的法案, 简称 ISTEA, 因与 ice tea 谐音, 故称"冰茶"法)
internal ①内部的, 里面的 ②国内的, 内政的 ③固有的
internal absorption factor 内吸收系数 (光束通过透明物体时, 从第一表面到达第二表面被吸收的光通量与离开第一表面时的光通量之比)
internal air injection manifold (二次空气喷射式排放控制系的) 空气内喷式歧管
internal and cylindrical centerless grinding for piston ring 活塞环内外圆无心磨床
internal band brake 内带外张式制动器
internal block brake 内蹄外张式制动器
internal cal (l) iper gauge 内径卡规
internal car noise 车内噪声 (指车内乘员感受的噪声)
internal cell resistance 蓄电池内电阻
internal characteristic (液力变矩器的) 内特性 (指液力元件工作腔中液流内参数之间的关系)
internal circular spline 谐波齿轮传动的) 内齿刚轮 (即内齿轮)
internal circulation 内循环 (指机器内部形成的闭合回路内的循环, 如: 内燃机冷却水的循环)
internal clearance (滚动轴承等的) 内部间隙, 内间隙 (轴承内、外环与球、滚柱等滚动件之间的间隙)
internal combustion engine 内燃发动机, 内燃机 (指燃料在发动机内燃烧的发动机, 如: 汽油机、柴油机、燃气轮机等简称 ICE, 或 combustion engine)
Internal Combustion Engine Institute [美] 内燃机研究所
internal-combustion piston engine 活塞式内燃发动机
internal combustion turbine 内燃涡轮机
internal courtesy light 门控车内灯 (当车门开启时灯光电路自动接通, 车门关闭时, 灯光自动熄灭, 故称礼貌灯)
internal current mirror element (电路) 内部电流传感元件 (亦称 internal current sensing element)
internal cycloidal gear 内齿摆线轮 (齿顶曲面位于齿根曲面之内的摆线轮)
internal damping 内阻尼
internal defect (铸件, 橡胶制品等的) 内部缺陷 (如: 气泡等)
internal diameter 内径 (= inner

diameter, inside diameter)

internal dimensions of the loading space （车箱，货台）装载容积的内部尺寸

internal drag 内部阻力

internal drowning 内部浸湿（如：氢氧燃料电池中在反应时生成的H_2O会吸附于炭精电极上，使电极受湿，称为内部浸湿）

internal earth 内搭铁（如：发电机磁场绕组的搭铁端与发电机壳相连接）

internal efficiency 内效率（理论功率与内功率之比）

internal EGR system 机内废气再循环系统（如：废气由排气门直接经通道进入进气门区，= internal exhaust gas recirculation system）

internal electrical conductive layer （废气氧浓度传感器中包覆固体电解质的）内导电层（亦称内电极，一般用铂，= inner electrode）

internal energy 内能

internal exhaust gas recirculation （进排气门重叠开启的）机内废气再循环

internal expanding drum brake 内张型鼓式制动器（如：靠位于制动鼓内的制动蹄张开产生的摩擦力制动的制动器，亦称内蹄外张式制动器，= expanding inside brake, inner expanding brake, inside expanding brake, 见 internally acting brake）

internal/external gear arrangement ①内外齿轮装置，内外齿轮机构 ②（转子发动机的）内外齿轮式相位装置（见 phasing gear）

internal-external gear clutch 内外离合器，齿套式接合器，齿套离合器（简称 gear clutch）

internal-external rotary pump 内外转子泵（一种旋轮线泵，在旋轮线型的外转子内装有旋轮线包络线型的内转子，二者在同一泵体壳内以同一方向旋转的转子泵，如：某些发动机的机油泵）

internal gauge 内径规

internal gear 内齿轮（指齿顶曲面位于齿根曲面之内的齿轮，如：annular gear）

internal gear clutch 内齿离合器，内齿接合器

internal-geared axle 内齿圈轮边减速式驱动桥

internal gear pair 内齿轮副（一个齿轮是内齿轮的齿轮副）

internal gear pump 内（啮合）齿轮泵（由一内齿轮及装在该内齿轮中并与之啮合的从动齿轮组成的齿轮泵，在内、外齿的非啮合空间装有一防止油液流回油泵进油侧的月牙形件）

internal gear tester 内（接）齿轮检查仪

internal graticule ①（阴极射线管的）内标度 ②内十字线，标线

internal groove 内槽

internal illumination 内部照明

internal keyway 内键槽

internal leakage （液、气在装置或系统内的）内部泄漏，内部泄漏量

internal leakage in steering control valve 转向控制阀内泄漏量（在额定工况下，单位时间内，阀内的液压油从高压腔向低压腔及向阀体外的总泄漏量）

internal limit gauge 极限塞规，内径极限规

internal lubrication 内部润滑（法）

internally acting brake 具有内工作表面的鼓式制动器（内带式或内蹄式制动器）

internally adjustable mirror 车内调节式后视镜（可在车内调节后视镜的位置和角度）

internally mounted mechanical seal

internally powered 由自带发动机驱动的

internal measuring instrument 内径量测仪器，内部尺寸测量仪

internal mirror （装在）车内（的）后视镜（= inside mirror）

internal motion resistance （车辆）内部运动阻力

internal operation ①内表面加工 ②内部操作

internal piloting 内部控制，内部引导，自控

internal pin wheel 内齿针齿轮（齿顶圆柱面位于齿根圆柱面之内的针齿轮）

internal point （攻螺丝的）定心孔

internal power 内功率（指示功率加上热传递和泄漏损失的功率）

internal resistance ①内部阻力 ②内（电）阻（相对外部电路电阻而言的电源内部的电阻，如：汽车蓄电池内极板与电解液之间的电阻，极板电阻，电解液对离子流的电阻，内部接线电阻等各种电阻形成的蓄电池内阻）

internals 内部零部件

internal splined shaft busing （柴油机分配式喷油泵的）内花键轴套（两端具有内花键的筒形零件，将花键轴的运动传递给调速器轴）

internal splined sleeve （柴油机分配式油泵的）花键套（具有内花键的固接前控制板和分配转子的零件）

internal styling （汽车车身的）内部造型；内部式样（= interior styling）

internal supporter tyre 内支撑轮胎（在外胎内腔中，靠近胎圈部位的轮辋上放置硬支撑物的充气轮胎）

internal taper 内锥度

internal thread 内螺纹（如：螺母的螺纹，亦称 female thread，= inside thread）

internal timing gear （转子发动机的）相位内齿圈，定时内齿圈，正时内齿圈（固定于转子上的定相齿圈，= inner ring, rotor gear）

internal torque 内转矩（汽车自身的传动系自至车轮的转矩）

internal traction force 内部牵引力，内牵引力（指车辆自身的动力系统产生的牵引力）

internal transport and transit （厂、矿等的）内部交通运输

internal-type idle limiter 内装式怠速浓度调程限制器

internal vacuum ①内部真空度 ②用真空吸尘器清扫车厢内部

internal vane pump 内叶片泵（见 sliding vane pump）

internal wave generator 内波发生器（谐波齿轮的波发生器置于柔轮圈之内者）

internal wheel 内齿轮

international angstrøm 国际埃（X射线，电磁波等波长的量测单位，代号 IA。1 IA = 10^{-10} m，导出来源于 15℃，760mm 水银柱压力下，镉 cd 放射线的波长为 $6438.4696 \times 10^{-10}$ m）

International Association for Accident and Traffic Medicine 国际交通事故和交通医学协会（简称 IAATM）

International Association for Testing Materials 国际材料试验协会（简称 IATM）

International Association of Ergonomics 国际人机工程学会（简称 IAE）

International Automobile Club Federation 国际汽车俱乐部联合会（简称 IACF）

International Automobile Federation 国际汽车联合会（简称 IAF）

International Automotive Institute 国际汽车研究会（简称 IAI）

International Auto Show 国际汽车展览会

International Business Machine 国际商用机器（电子计算机）公司（简称 IBM）

international candle （国际单位制发光强度单位）烛光（见 candle）

international car show 国际汽车展示会

international competitive bid 国际竞争性投标（简称 ICB）

International Driver's Behaviour Research Association 国际驾驶员行为研究协会（研究驾驶员的心理、生理、思维、动作等，简称 IDBRA）

International Electronical Commission 国际电子委员会（简称 IEC）

International Energy Agency 国际能源局（署）（简称 IEA，由北美、欧洲及太平洋地区的 23 个国家组成，应付能源危机）

International Energy Technology Group 国际能源技术集团（简称 IETG）

international exchange activity 国际（学术）交流

International Federation of Automatic Control 国际自动控制联盟（简称 IFAC）

International Federation of Pedestrians 国际保护行人（步行者）联合会（简称 FIP）

international haulage semi-trailer 国际货运（汽车）半挂车

international identity plate 国际通行牌照（板）（= international license plate）

International Motor-cycle Federation 国际机器脚踏车联合会，国际摩托车联合会

International Motor Show 国际汽车展（销会）（简称 IMS）

international nautical mile 国际海里（美国 1954 年规定为 6076.1033ft = 1.852km, = nautical mile）

international ohm 国际欧姆（电阻单位，1908 年规定，为 14.4521g 质量的水银，在融冰℃下长度为 106.3mm 时的电阻值。在 1948 年后逐步由绝对欧姆代替，1 国际欧姆 = 1.00049 绝对欧姆，见 absolute ohm）

International Organization for Motor Trades and Repairs 国际汽车贸易及修理组织（简称 IOMTR）

International Pacific Conference on Automotive Engineering 国际太平洋汽车工程会议（简称 IPC）

International Permanent Bureau of Motor Manufacturers 汽车制造商国际常设局（简称 IPBMM）

International Petroleum Commission 国际石油委员会（简称 IPC）

International Petroleum Company 国际石油公司（简称 IPC）

international practical temperature scale 国际实用温标（与摄氏热力学温标最为接近的实用温标，以下列六个基本固定点为根据来标定 -183℃以上的各种温度。在 101.325 kPa 下，氧的沸点为 -182.97℃，水的三相点为 0.01℃，纯水的沸点为 100℃，硫的沸点 444.6℃，银的凝固点为 960.8℃，金的凝固点为 1063℃）

International Radio Consultative Committee 国际无线电咨询委员会（简称 IRCC）

International Road Federation 国际道路联合会（简称 IRF）

International Road Transport Union 国际道路运输联盟（简称 IRTU）

international sales networks （汽车

的）国际销售网

International Science Organization 国际科学组织（简称 ISO）

international screw tap 公制螺丝攻

International Snowmobile Industry Association 国际雪地机动车工业协会，国际雪地汽车工业协会（简称 ISIA）

international standard atmosphere 国际标准大气压

International Standardization Organization 国际标准化组织（= International Organization for Standardization，简称 ISO，1947 年成立，设在日内瓦，制定各项标准的国际化组织）

international (standard) thread 国际标准螺纹，标准公制螺纹

International Steam Calorie 国际卡（见 International Table Calorie）

International Steam Table 国际水蒸气表（水蒸气热量等有关量的国际单位规定表，如：1BtuIT 国际英热单位 = 1055.06J；1CalIT 国际卡 = 4.1868J，见 joule）

international symposium 国际讨论会

International Table Calorie 国际卡（热量单位，国际水蒸气表规定的卡，代号 CalIT，1CalIT = 4.1868J）

International Texicab Assn ［美］国际出租汽车协会（简称 ITA）

international traffic 国际交通（至少通过一国国境的交通运输）

International Transportation Service 国际运输服务公司（简称 ITS）

International Transport Committee 国际运输委员会（简称 ITC）

international unit 国际单位

International Weights and Measures Congress 国际权衡会议

Internavi Premium Club 车载导航高级俱乐部（日本丰田公司车载导航系统的商品名，该系统具有语音识别功能，除了能用语音设定目的地外，还可由语音操控空调与车载音响，此外，该系统配备有车辆信息通信系统"VICS"）

Internet ①因特网（美国 ARPAnet 发展而成，原译为"互联网"，1997 年 7 月 1 日全国科学技术名词审定委员会，正式定名"因特网"。泛指由多个计算机网络相互连接而成的一个大网络）②互联网（是集局域网、广域网和高速数据传输服务的一种网络，采用 Internet 相关技术将基于计算机的基础网络结构与各用户连接起来的企业内部网络）

internet radio 互联网收音机

interpenetration 互相渗透，互相贯通

INTERPET 国际石油公司（International Petroleum Company）

interphone 内线自动电话，内部通信装置；对讲电话，互通电话；长途汽车内的内部服务电话

interplate （双盘式离合器两从动盘之间的）中间压盘［= intermediate (drive) plate］

interplay 相互影响，相互作用，作用和反作用，相互关系

interpolation-multi-speed transmission 插入式多挡变速器（其主变速器挡位间传动比较大，副变速器的传动比均匀地插入主变速器各挡传动比之间，两者共同组成一个连续的传动比序列）

interpole 整流极，极间极，附加极，辅助极，补极（设在直流发电机等的中性区、消除电枢反作用的小磁极，= commutating pole）

interpretation ①试验结果整理；资料分析 ②解释，说明 ③翻译（指口译）

interrupt ①切断，断开，中断，间断，阻止，妨碍，打扰 ②（汽车电

子控制系统的）中断任务（指在执行某一程序过程中，根据某一输入/输出装置的要求暂时中断该程序，转而去执行其他的优先任务，然后再重新恢复执行原程序）

interrupted 中断的，被打断的，被阻止的，不通的，断开的，间歇的

interrupted control method 断续控制法（如：电瓶车车速控制方法之一，改变半导体断续器的高频通断的接通时间，来改变电流的平均值，亦称 chopper method）

interrupted drive transmission 换挡时动力中断的变速器

interrupted injection 间歇喷射，断续喷射

interrupter ①断电器，断续器，断流器 ②（汽车电子控制系统的）中断，挂起（指当计算机执行某程序时，由于其他外部事件，将该原执行的程序暂停执行，即，"挂起"，转而去处理外部事件，然后再恢复执行原来的程序的动作方式）③阻碍物，障碍物

interrupter cam 断（分）电器凸轮；断续机构凸轮

interrupter contact 断续器触点，断电器触点

interrupter lever 断电器触点臂

interrupter point 断电器触点（见 make and break contact）

interruptible gas supply 断续供气，断续供油

interruption 中断，间断，中止，停止

interrupt service routine （汽车电子控制系统的）中断服务子程序（CPU 在收到某输入/输出设备的中断请求后，转而去执行另一个实现所要求的其他动作的子程序，完成该子程序后，又恢复执行原程序，简称 ISR）

interrupt unit ①中断部分，中断装置，中断系统 ②（自动诊断系统本身的）故障检测系统，故障警报系统（装置）

intersect 横断，横切；贯穿，相交，交叉

intersected country 地形复杂的地区，丘陵地区

intersecting angle ［美］交角，偏角（英国习惯称 deviation angle）

intersecting axis 交叉轴，交叉轴线，相交轴线

intersecting line 交线

intersecting point 交点，转角点（简称 IP）

intersection 交，相交，交叉；交线，交点；相交线；交会；交集，横断；横切，交切，交叉口，十字路口

intersection support （驾驶员辅助系统的）交叉路口支持（功能）（可根据摄像系统、雷达传感器等测得的交叉路口的车辆及通行情况，自动减速、制动或停车并向驾驶者发送必要的提示或警告）

intersection-type collision 交叉碰撞

interspace ①空间，空隙，间隙，间距，净空 ②留出空隙，留出间隔，填充…的间隙

inter-split torque path type hydromechanic drive 内分流式液力机械传动（指液力机械变矩器的输入功率在变矩器内部分流，然后经行星齿轮机构或固定轴式传动将功率汇流后输出，目的在于提高液力元件低速比时的变矩系数、高速比时的效率和扩大高效范围）

interstate common carrier hauling ［美］洲际货车运输，洲际货物运输（= interstate trucking）

interstate road ［美］洲际道路

intertooth space 齿沟，齿间隔，齿谷

intertown bus 长途客车，长途公共汽车，市际公共汽车（= intercity bus, interurban bus）

interunit compatibility 部件间相互适应性

interurban 城镇间的，长途的，市际的

interval 间隔，间距；时间间隔；区间，范围；间歇

interval dial 间隔自动定时转盘

interval fuel feed system 间歇供油系统

interval mileage of major repair 大修间隔里程（参见 major repair life）

interval operation 间歇运转（＝inter-mittent operation）

inter-vehicle communication system 车间通信系统（指汽车与汽车之间相互传递信息的系统，自动驾驶系统的子系统，见 AVCS）

inter vehicle short-range communication 车辆间短程通信（车辆间短距离内信息交换系统，用于防止碰撞等）

intervehicular distance 行车队列中汽车之间的间隔距离（＝vehicular distance）

inter-vehicular distance keeping system 车间距离保持系统（见 adaptive cruise system）

intervention ①插入 ②介入（干涉，干预，指在处理过程中中断或改变某一操作）③妨碍 ④修正（指对原定的数量、时间、程序等的改变）

intervention switch 应急保险开关

inter winding insulation （点火线圈）初级与次级绕组间的绝缘

in-the-block heating 用安装在汽缸体内的加热装置预热

intimate contact ①（运动件间缺润滑油时）直接接触 ②紧密的接触

in-time operation 定时操作（如：按照预先制定的时间表来决定交通信号系统红绿灯之间的时间关系）

intl 国际的（international）

INTLK 连锁装置，保险设备，安全开关（interlock 的简称）

INTMT 间断的（intermittent）

in-to-in tire width 两侧内轮轮胎内侧之间的宽度，轮式车辆车辙的内侧宽度

in-to-in track width 两履带内侧之间的宽度，履带车辆车辙的内侧宽度

in top（gear） 全速地，以高速挡

intoxicated 因饮酒过量而醉的（in-toxicated driver 酒醉的驾驶者，in-toxicated driving 醉后驾驶）

intoxication （饮酒过度而）醉（＝酒精中毒"alcoholic poisoning"）

intranet （汽车区域的）内联网

in-transit terminal 行车线路终点站

intrastate traffic ［美］州内交通

intricately shaped 形状复杂的

intrinsic accuracy 内在精度，原设计精度（＝intrinsic precision）

intrinsically safe circuit "i" 本质安全电路"i"（在规定条件下，正常工作或规定故障下产生的电火花和热效应均不致点燃规定的爆炸性混合物的电路）

intrinsic conduction 本征电导率，固有导电性，内禀传导性

intrinsic error 基本误差，固有误差（如：在参比条件下仪器仪表的示值误差）

intrinsic fatigue limit test 检验疲劳极限是否和额定值相符的试验，本征疲劳极限试验

intrinsic property 固有特性，本征特性

intrinsic semiconductor 本征半导体（亦称 proper semiconductor，指未添加锗 Ge、硅 Si、硒 Se 等，其固有电阻值随周围条件，如：温度、光、电压等而变化的半导体）

introduce 引进，引入；引导，介绍；引起，导致

introduced contaminants 外界杂质

introduction 引进,引入,传入,输入;引导,介绍,提倡,推广;引言,前言,绪言;入门,初步

introscope 内孔窥视仪,内壁检验仪,内壁显微镜,内部检视仪

intrusion in side impact 侧面撞入(指侧面碰撞时,主撞车辆撞入受撞车内)

intrusive ①插入的 ②侵入的 ③干涉的 ④妨碍的

intuitive 直观的,直觉的

intumescent 湿胀性的,泡胀性的,热胀性的(指在受热或水浸泡下会膨胀的)

"in use" consumption 实际行车油耗(=customer fuel consumption)

in use fuel economy 使用燃料经济性(=in service fuel economy)

in-use inspection (对汽车排气污染等的)使用中检查(以别于出厂审查鉴定)

in use maintenance and repair (汽车)在使用中的维护与修理

in-use performance 使用性能

in-use vehicle 在用车(投入使用的汽车,在中国指已经取得行驶牌照的汽车)

invalid 无用的,无效的,作废的;不能成立的(假设等)

invalid vehicle 专供残疾者使用的车辆

invar 因钢(一种铁镍合金的商品名,镍36%,铁63.8%,碳0.2%。热膨胀系数极小,多用于量具、仪表,亦称因瓦合金)

invariable ①不变量 ②不变的,无变化的(=invariant)

invar strut piston 带因瓦铁镍合金镶片的活塞,嵌因钢片活塞(见 invar 及 autothermic piston)

INVECS 创新型车辆智能电子控制系统(Intelligent and Innovative Vehicle Electronic Control System 的简称,日本三菱公司利用经验丰富的老驾驶员的知识对车辆进行综合模糊控制的系统的商品名。该系统通过各种传感器元件,了解道路的坡度、弯度、打滑程度等车外的环境因素和转向盘、加速踏板、制动踏板的操作等驾驶员的意图及发动机的转速,进气量和节气门开度等车内状况,根据系统内存储的老驾驶员的经验进行推断而实现车辆全运转区域的最佳控制。此外,该系统还具有"学习控制"机能和附加的手动换挡功能)

3-in-1 vehicle 三合一车辆(如:一拖两挂汽车列车等)

in-vehicle fuel economy measurement system 车装式燃油经济性测定系统,车载式油耗测定装置

in-vehicle information system 车内信息系统,车装式信息系统

In-Vehicle Multiplexing System 车内多路传输系统(见 IVMS)

inverse ①相反量,相反值;倒数 ②相反的,反向的,反相的,倒转的,倒置的,倒相的

inverse cam 反转凸轮

inverse current 反向电流;切断电流(如:电路断开时产生的自感电流)

inverse distance ①距离倒数 ②与距离成反比的数

inverse feedback 负反馈

inverse image 逆像,倒像

inversely proportional 反比例的

inverse network 倒量网络,回(归)路,反演电路

inverse path 逆路线(道路)

inverse perspective mapping 反转透视图法(简称 IPM,障碍物探测的识别方法)

inverse ratio 反比值,反比

inverse square law 平方反比律(指某物理量,如:光亮度随光源的距离而变化,并与距离平方成反比,

适用于任意发射波正面成球形的发射系统)

inverse-time 与时间成反比的

inverse voltage 反向电压,逆电压

inversion ①"非"门,"非"逻辑,"非"运算,求反(二进制运算中的求反运算,即:所有的1都变换成0,所有的0都换成1)②反向,反转③逆风④倒置,颠倒⑤转化,变换,转换⑥(电流)换流

inversion layer ①反型层(如:半导体 n 层,相对 p 层而言)②逆温层(其温度随高度而增加)

invert ①倒置,翻转,颠倒,转化,转回,反转,使方向②颠倒了的事物,管道内底③颠倒的,倒转的

inverted engine 倒置式发动机(汽缸在曲轴下方的发动机)

inverted flared nut 反喇叭口螺母

inverted rotary convertor 反相旋转变流器(如:在客车中用直流电动机将直流电变为交流电,供荧光灯使用的电源装置,inverter 的一种)

inverted semielliptic spring 倒置半椭圆形钢板弹簧

inverted tooth chain 逆齿链(一种无声传动链)

inverted T-slot 倒 T 形槽

inverted valve 顶置式气门(= drop valve)

inverted valve engine 顶置式气门发动机(参见 overhead valve engine)

inverted vee-engine 倒置 V 形发动机,倒 V 形发动机

inverted vee(slide)way 倒 V 形滑轨

inverter 变换器;倒相器;逆变器;反相旋转变流器;变流器;变换电路;转换开关;变频器;变压器

inverter circuit 反演电路,倒相电路,翻转电路

investigation ①研究,调查,试验②调查报告,研究论文

investment ①投资②授予③熔模铸造

investment casting 熔模铸造,蜡模铸造

invisible door hinge 暗门铰链(= concealed door hinge)

involuntary ignition 自燃着火,不按规定着火,失去控制的着火

involute ①渐开线[无特别说明的,指圆的渐开线,常用 involute to a circle,简称 involute,在平面上一条动直线沿一个固定圆(基圆)作纯滚动时,此动直线上一点的轨迹,见 prolate involute, curtate involute, spherical involute]②渐伸的,渐开的

involute cam 渐开线凸轮

involute curve 渐开线

involute cylindrical gear 渐开线圆柱齿轮(指端面上的可用齿廓是一段渐开线的圆柱齿轮,简称渐开线齿轮)

involute gear pump 渐开线齿轮泵

involute helicoid 渐开线螺旋面[一平面沿着一固定的圆柱面(基圆柱面)作纯滚动时,此平面上一条以恒定角度与基圆柱的轴线倾斜交错的直线在固定空间内的轨迹曲面]

involute helicoid warm 渐开线蜗杆(齿面为渐开螺旋面的圆柱蜗杆,其端面齿廓是渐开线,亦称 ZI-worm)

involute internal gear pair with small teeth difference 渐开线少齿差内齿轮副(由齿数差很少的内、外渐开线齿轮组成的齿轮副)

involute profile 渐开线齿廓(齿廓为渐开线)

involute serrations 渐开线花键(= involute spline)

involute spur gear 渐开线直齿圆柱齿轮

involute teeth 渐开线齿

involute tester 渐开线检查仪

involute tooth 渐开线（形）齿

involute worm 渐开线蜗杆

involve ①包，卷，卷入；包含，包括，含有 ②牵涉到，涉及 ③自乘，乘方

inward camber （前轮）负外倾（亦称 reverse camber）

inward-facing seat （客车等车身内）面向内的侧边座位

inward flange 内突缘

inward-flow turbine 向心式涡轮机（= centripetal turbine）

inwardly illuminated license plate 内部照明的牌照板

inward stroke 向下冲程（= descending stroke）

in-warranty failure 保用期内的损坏

in WG 英制水表（inch water gage）

13-in wheel （轮辋直径为）13 英寸（的）车轮

in wheel brushless dc electric motor （轮内直接驱动式电动汽车的）轮内无刷直流电动机

in-wheel drive system 轮内驱动系统（如：装在车轮内直接驱动车轮的电动机系统等）

in-wheel motor （电动轮式电动汽车与车轮轮毂制成一体的）轮内电动机（简称 IWM）

in working order 处于工作状态下，完好的，在运转中，处于运转准备状态的

I-O 输入/输出（input/output 的简称）

IOCS 输入输出控制系统（input-output control system）

iodine 碘 I，碘酊

iodine number 碘值

iodine penta-oxide method 五氧化二碘法（气体置换吸光度法，使样气与五氧化二碘反应，测定游离碘的吸光度，进而求得一氧化碳浓度的方法）

iodine (vapor) lamp 碘弧灯

IOE engine 见 inlet over exhaust engine

IOMTR 国际汽车贸易及修理组织（International Organization for Motor Trades and Repairs）

ion 离子（指失去电子的原子或得到电子的原子，前者带正电荷，为阳离子，后者带负电荷，为阴离子，带电的原子团亦称离子）

ion beam machining 离子束加工（简称 IBM）

ion conductivity 离子传导率

ion exchange fuel cell 离子交换燃料电池

ion exchanger 离子交换剂

ion exchange resin 离子交换树脂

ion gap plug 离子间隙塞

ionic 离子的

ionic conductivity 离子电导率，离子导电性，离子传导性（指传导离子的性能，如：在 ZrO_2 中混合 4mol% ~ 5mol% 的 Y_2O_3，便可使该陶瓷混合物成为良好的离子 O^{-2} 传导体，用作废气氧浓度陶瓷传感器中的固体电解质）

ionic current measuring method 离子流测量法（= ionic current technique，如：火花间隙的导电性的测试）

ionic dissociation 离解成离子，电离，离解

ionic mobility 离子迁移率，离子消失度

ion implantation 离子注入法（见 ion injection）

ion injection 离子束注入（将所选定的化学元素 N、C、B、Mo、P、Ar、Co 等在高真空中电离呈离子状态后，再利用高压电场加速到几十至几百电子伏特的能量，将上述离子汇聚成束注入待处理材料的表层中，使工件表层材料合金化，或注

入半导体晶体中，使该晶体中形成P型，N型或本征导电区，亦称ion implantation）

ionization 电离作用，离子化

ionization current sensing technique 电离电流传感技术

ionization detection plug 电离测定塞（监测燃烧室内可燃混合气的电离状态，以确定火焰的流向及传播）

ionization potential （气体的）电离电位，电离电势（达到电离电势时，给以足够的能量就可自气体的原子或分子中分离出电子）

ionization sensor （一般与火花塞组装在一起的）电离传感器（用于检测缺火和爆燃等）

ionize ①游离 ②电离，离子化（使成离子，见ion）

ionized air knife 电离喷气刀（一种清除制件尘积的装置，高速空气经电离后喷至被清洁表面，正、负子可消除尘积的电荷，尘积即由高速空气吹净）

ionized stratum 电离层

ion-nitriding 离子氮化（将渗氮零件装置在带有阴、阳极的真空装置内的阴极上，慢慢通入氨气等，并在两极之间加上500~800V电压，在高压电场作用下，零件周围的气体发生电离，产生高能量的氮离子，以极高速度冲击零件表面，使零件表面温度升高，并且氮离子被零件表面所吸收，经扩散而形成渗氮层）

ionomer 离子聚合树脂，离子交联聚合物，含离子键聚合物

ion-plating technique 离子镀覆技术（镀覆金属铬、钴、铁等，在800~1000℃温度下，离子化而进入被镀覆金属表面层，形成镀复层，这种镀覆技术，1963年由美国人发明）

ion sheath 离子镀层

IORS （汽车乘员的）充气式约束性保护系统（为inflatable occupant restraint system的简称）

IOS 仪表操作台（instrumentation operations station）

IOT [英] 运输学会（Institute of Transport的简称）

IP ①石油协会（The Institute of Petroleum）②定位（identification of position）③碰撞点（impact point）④吸气过程，诱导期（induction period）⑤初始点（initial point）⑥点火线圈内层初级绕组（inside primary）⑦中间压力（intermediate pressure）⑧交点（intersecting point）⑨初始相（initial phase）⑩碰撞点预测器（impact predictor）⑪燃点（ignition point）⑫铁管（iron pipe）

IP 仪表板（instrument panel的简称）

ip 指示功率（indicated power的简称）

IPB 附有图解说明的零件破损情况（illustrated parts breakdown）

IPBMM 汽车制造商国际常设局（International Permanent Bureau of Motor Manufacturers）

IPC 国际石油公司（International Petroleum Company）

IPC 国际石油委员会（为International Petroleum Commission）

IPC 太平洋国际汽车工程学会联合会（International Pacific Conference on automotive engineering）

I-P diagram （热工）焓-压图

IPHE （美国能源部推行的）氢-经济国际伙伴活动（国际合作开展氢燃料电池等的研究与应用，研讨氢能源对社会经济的影响等）

i-Pod, i-Phone interface （车内的）i-Pod，i-Phone（与车载导航、信息、娱乐系统连接的）接口（i-Pod, i-Phone分别为美国苹果公司生产的便携式多媒体接收播放设备-

平板电脑和移动电话）
IPR 知识产权（intellectual property rights）
ips ①英寸/秒（inch per second）②铁管尺寸（iron pipe size）
IPT 在生产过程中的试验（in-process testing）
IP-testing method ［英］石油协会试验法（其中，IP 为 Institute of Petroleum 石油协会的简称）
IR ①红外线（的）（infrared）②内电阻（interior resistance, internal resistance）
IRAN 检查并按需要加以修理（inspect and repair as necessary）
ira'ser 红外激光［infra-red amplification by stimulated emission of radiation（红外受激辐射放大）的简称］
IR drop 内电阻引起的电压降
IRE 无线电工程师学会（Institute of Radio Engineers）
IRF 国际道路联合会（International Road Federation）
IRHD 国际橡胶硬度标度（international rubber hardness degrees）
IRI （撞车等事故的乘员）伤害风险指数（injury risk index）
IRI ［英］橡胶工业学会（Institute of the Rubber Industry）
iridescent （随观察位置或角度不同而变换彩色光谱的）呈彩虹的,显晕光的,闪光的,闪色的
iridium 铱（Ir）
iridium tip spark plug （中央电极带）铱尖的火花塞
iris ①隔膜,膜片,隔板 ②（照相机）光圈 ③（眼球的）虹膜 ④虹,虹状物,彩虹,彩虹色
irising from tempering float glass （车用安全玻璃的）钢化彩虹（浮法玻璃淬火后表面出现的杂色现象）
iron ①铁,铸铁（一般含碳量 1.7% ～ 6.7% 的铁碳合金称生铁,铸造用的生铁称为铸铁。铸铁又可分为灰口铸铁、可锻铸铁、球墨铸铁、白口铸铁和合金铸铁等）②烙铁,熨斗 ③［美］撬胎棒（= tyre lever）④铸铁的,铁制的 ⑤熨平,压薄,压平；矫直
iron-air cell 铁-空气电池
iron ammonium sulphate bath （镀铁用的）硫酸亚铁铵镀槽,硫酸亚铁铵镀液
iron-base bearing 铁基粉末冶金轴承
iron base bushing 铁基粉末冶金轴套
iron-based fuel additive 铁基燃油添加剂（用于柴油机,以减少排气烟尘）
iron brass 铁黄铜,硬黄铜
iron carbide 碳化铁
iron-cased 装在铁壳里的,表面覆铁的
iron casting 铁铸件,铸铁铸造
iron cement 铁胶合剂
iron channel 槽钢,槽铁,U 型钢,U 型铁
iron-clad 铠装的,装甲的,金属覆层,包覆金属的
iron clamp 铁夹
iron constantan thermocouple 铁康铜热电偶（参见 constantan）
iron core 铁心,铁芯（一般指发电机、电动机、点火线圈及电磁铁等中为线圈缠绕的中心部分,磁力线容易通过,铁心因而可增强磁力。为了减少铁损,大多用多片硅钢片相互绝缘叠合而成）
Iron grey 铁灰（车身颜色）
iron hand 机械手
iron loss ①铁损（磁铁线路中由于交变磁通量造成的能量损耗）②金属烧损
iron oxide 氧化铁
iron oxide treatment 氧化铁膜处理

（将活塞环和冷激铸铁制成的气门挺杆等铸铁零件在含有水蒸气的气体介质中进行处理，使表面获得 FeO 或 Fe_3O_4 等氧化物的表面防护层，= oxide treatment）
iron pig 生铁
iron pipe 铁管（简称 IP）
iron pipe size 铁管尺寸（简称 IPS）
iron plating 镀铁，镀钢
iron rust 铁锈
iron shoe （制动器）铸铁蹄（片）
iron solder 铁焊料
iron sulfide film 硫化铁薄膜（防止刮伤的保护层，将钢或铸铁零件，如：活塞、活塞环等浸入苏打及硫的水溶液中，零件表面上即获得此种薄膜）
iron-tired 装铁轮的
iron-titanium hydride （氢气动力车存储氢气用的）铁钛氢化物（依靠化学键能，将氢气储存在干燥的铁钛金属粉末中，当发动机使用氢气时，只要利用发动机冷却液的热量，便可将氢气从铁钛氧化物中释放出来，见 metal hydride storage system）
iron-titanium hydride storage 铁钛合金氢化物储氢（利用铁钛合金在可逆放热反应中吸收氢气，而形成的铁钛氧化物储存氢气，供氢气动力车使用）
iron tyre 铁轮
iron weights （车辆试验时作为压载用）的铁块（或钢锭）
ironwork fault 铁件损坏
irradiate ①（用 X 射线、紫外线或日光、灯光）照射 ②发射，发出，放射 ③照耀、发光 ④发送（能量等）
irregular ①不规则的，不对称的，不均匀的，无规律的，参差不齐的；有凹凸的；非正规的，不合常规的 ②非正规的东西，不规则的东西
irregular flap （轮胎的）带身不正（垫带带身歪斜现象）
irregular ignition 不规则点火，点火中断，点火不均匀
irregular tank 异型汽油箱，异型燃油箱，非常规油箱
irregular terrain 不平地带，崎岖地带
irregular wear 不均匀磨损，不规则磨损（= uneven wear）
irremediable defect 永久性损坏，不能补救的损伤
IR remote control 红外线遥控（infrared remote control 的简称）
irreparable 不能修理的，不能恢复原有性能的，不可补救的
irreversibility 不可逆性，不可回溯性
irreversible 不可逆的，不可逆转的，不能倒置的，不能翻转的，不能倒退的
irreversible cycle 不可逆循环
irreversible steering gear 不可逆转向机构（= self-locking steering gear）
irreversible worm 不可逆转的（自锁）蜗杆
IRS 后轮独立悬架，独立后悬架（independent rear suspension）
IRT 红外辐射温度计（infrared radiation thermometer）
IRTE ［英］道路运输工程师学会（The Institute of Road Transport Engineers）
IRTU 国际道路运输联盟，国际公路运输联盟（International Road Transport Union）
IRU 国际无线电协会（International Radio Union）
isa （电阻用合金）锰铜
ISA ①美国仪表协会（Instrument Society of America）②国际标准大气（international standard atmosphere）
isacoustic curve 等响曲线，等响线

ISAF 一种炭黑的商品名（Intermediate Super Abrasion Furnace 的简称）

ISC motor 怠速控制电动机，（见 idle speed control motor）

ISCO 指示马力一氧化碳排放率，单位指示马力一氧化碳排放量（indicated specific carbon monoxide）

ISC switch 怠速控制开关（idle speed control switch 的简称，当节气门关闭时，该开关的触点闭合，向发动机电子控制模块发出"对怠速转速进行控制"的信号。当节气门开启时，上述触点断开，电子控制模块不再控制怠速转速）

ISCV 怠速速度控制阀（idle speed control valve 的简称）

ISEC 单位指示马力能耗率，指示马力比能耗（indicated specific energy consumption）

ISFC（或 isfc） 指示马力油耗率，指示马力比油耗，指示比油耗（indicated specific fuel consumption）

ISG 集成式起动机发电机（integrated start generator 的简称）

I-shape 工字形

I-shape armature I 形衔铁，I 形电枢

ISHC 指示马力碳氢化合物排放率，单位指示马力碳化氢排放量（indicated specific HC）

ISI ①（碰撞时）乘员伤害度指标（injury severity index 的简称）②国际钢铁学会（International Iron and Steel Institute 的简称）

ISIA 国际雪地机动车工业协会，国际雪地汽车工业协会，（International Snowmobile Industry Association）

Island grey 玄武灰（车身颜色）

island site 安全岛

ISNO 指示马力一氧化氮排放率，单位指示马力一氧化氮排放量（indicated specific NO emission）

ISNO$_x$ 指示马力氮氧化合物排放率，单位指示马力氮氧化物排放量（indicated specific NO$_x$）

ISO ①国际标准协会（International Standards Organization）②国际标准化组织（International Standardization Organization）③国际科学组织（International Science Organization）

isobaric ①等压（线）的 ②同量异位的

isobaric line 等压线

isobutane 异丁烷

isobutene 异丁烯（= isobutylene）

isobutene rubber （聚）丁烯橡胶

isobutylene-isoprene rubber 异丁烯-异戊二烯橡胶，异丁（烯）橡胶（合成橡胶的一种，为异丁烯和异戊二烯的共聚物，简称 IIR）

isocandela curve （汽车照明）等光光强曲线（在同一平面内光强度相等的各点的连线）

isochore 等容线，等体积线（亦写作 isochor）

isochromatic ①等色的，单色的，同色的 ②等色带，带色干涉带，等色线

isochronism speed governor 同步调速器

isochronous ①等时的，同步的，同谐的（亦写作 isochronal, isochronic）②定速控制（控制机器定速运转，而不受负载影响）

isocline planes 等斜平面

isoclinic ①等磁倾线 ②等倾斜的，等向的（亦写作 isoclinal）

isocyanate 异氰酸盐，异氰酸酯

ISO-DIS 国际标准化组织的国际标准草案（ISO Draft International Standard）

ISO Draft International Standard 国际标准化组织的国际标准草案（简称 ISO-DIS）

isoelectric 等电位的，零电位差的

isoenthalpic ①等焓线，等热函数 ②等焓的

isoentropic ①等熵线 ②等熵的

isoentropic change 等熵变化，绝热变化
ISO-FIX 国际标准化组织（儿童等）座椅在车上安装、固定的安全标准
isogonal 等角的
isohydric solutions 等氢离子溶液
ISO Information Network 国际标准化组织信息网（简称 ISONET）
ISO International Standard 国际标准化组织的国际标准（简称 ISO-IS）
ISO-IS 国际标准化组织的国际标准（ISO International Standard）
isolate ①绝缘，隔离 ②使离析
isolated value 孤值，游离值，离散值
isolation ①隔离，分离，游离，隔绝 ②绝缘，隔声 ③离析（作用），析出 ④查出（故障）
isolation booth 隔音室，隔热室
Isolation damper 隔振型减振器
isolation diode 断路二极管，隔离二极管
isolation method 隔离法，分离计算法
isolation mounting 隔振支垫，隔振装置，绝缘支座
isolation valve （ABS/ASR 液压系统的）隔离阀（亦称 isolation solenoid valve，用于保压和降压工况时断开总泵与车轮分泵间的液压通路）
isolator ①绝缘体 ②隔离装置，隔离件
isolux curve （汽车照明的）等照度曲线（在被测面上照度值相等的各点的连成的曲线）
isomer ①同分异物体 ②同质异能素
isomerization 异构化（作用），异性化，异性化处理
isometrical ①等角的 ②等容的，等体积的；等大的；同大的 ③等比例的，等距离的
isooctane 异辛烷（2、3、4—三甲基戊烷，测定燃油辛烷值时使用的辛烷值为 100 的标准燃油）
isoparaffins 异链石蜡，异链烷烃
isoparametric 同参数的，等参数的
isopentane 异戊烷
isophonic contour 等响度曲线，等音感曲线，等声强曲线（参见 equal-loudness curves）
isopiestics 等压线
isopleth ①诺莫图，列线图表（参见 nomogram 及 alignment chart）②等值线 ③等浓（度）线
isoprene 异戊间二烯，2-甲基丁二烯
isoprene type centerblock 异戊间二烯型中心框架
isopropyl 异丙基
ISO Recommendation 国际标准化组织推荐标准
isoscope 同位素探伤仪
ISO standard 国际标准化组织标准
ISO/TC104 国标标准化组织技术委员会 104（the International Standardization Organization Technical Committee 104）
ISO Technical Report 国际标准化组织的技术报告（简称 TSO-TR）
isothermal 等温的（亦写作 isothermic）
isothermal container 保温集装箱，绝热集装箱（指仅具有隔热性能而无冷冻设备的集装箱）
isothermal curves 等温线（= isothermal line）
isotope 同位素
isotopic tracer 同位素指示器（剂），示踪原子，示踪物
ISO-TR 国际标准化组织的技术报告（ISO Technical Report 的简称）
isotrope 各向同性，各向同性晶体，均质
isotropic 各向同性的，无向性的，均质的，迷向的，迷向
isotropy 各向同性（物质的性质不

因方向而异）

isovel(s) ①等速线 ②等容线，等体积线

ISO viscosity 国际标准化组织黏度（即运动黏度，单位厘泊 cst，= $10^{-6} m^2/sec$）

ISS ①（汽车碰撞事故中乘员的）伤害严重程度记分（目前广泛用于撞伤急救，injury severity score 的简称，ISS≥20 时应予急救）②（车辆）集成安全（控制）系统［Integration safety (control) system 的简称，美国 Delphi 公司，在 2000 年 SAE 世界年会上推出的一辆设计样车，集 50 余项安全技术，现大都已装车使用］③输入速度传感器（input speed sensor 的简称）④工业标准规范（industry standard specifications 的简称）

i-Start （按钮式一键起动）智能起动系统（Intelligent Start 的简称。通常，同一按钮亦一键停机）

ISTEA ［美］陆路联运效率法案（Intermodal Surface Transportation Efficiency Act）

I-steel 工字形钢

i-Stop ①智能急速停机系统（怠速停车时间超过规定值时即自动停机，踩踏加速踏板即可自动起动）②（见 i-Start）

Isuzu （日本）五十铃汽车公司

Isuzu Clean Air System （日本）五十铃汽车排气净化系统（简称 1. CAS）

IT ①信息技术（information technology）②点火正时（ignition timing）

ITA ①［美］工业用载货汽车协会（Industrial Truck Association）②［美］国际出租汽车协会（International Taxicab Association）③［英］工业运输协会（Industrial Transport Association）

ITARDA 交通事故研究与数据分析（Traffic Accident Research and Data Analysis 的简称）

ITC 国际运输委员会（International Transport Committee）

ITCS 智能运输控制系统（Intelligent Transportation Control System 的简称）

ITE ①运输工程师学会（国际学术组织，Institute of Transportation Engineer）②指示热效率（indicated thermal efficiency）

item ①项目 ②条款 ③零件，元件，物品

item description 项目说明

iteration method 迭代渐近法，逐次近似法，逐次逼近法，反复法，重复法，累接法

iterative process 重复过程，反复过程

ITI 智能运输基础设施（参见 intelligent transportation infrastructure）

itinerary ①行车路线，预定行程；旅行指南，旅行计划 ②旅行的，旅途中的

IT machine （汽车的）信息（传输）技术机器（指各种以车载式行车信息、导行信息系统为中心的硬件设备）

I-TOOA ［美］独立载货汽车业主－工作者协会（The Independent Truck Owner-Operators Association）

ITOY 20×× 20××年度国际货车（International Truck of the Year 20×× 的简称，欧洲 17 国媒体代表经评审从 20××年间推出的新车型中选出的当年最佳货车。选出的最佳大客车称 International Bus of the Year 20××,简称 IBO Y 20××）

ITRL 仪器检测修理实验室（instrument test repair laboratory）

ITRO 综合测试大纲（integrated test requirement outline）

ITS ①筒状（安全）气囊结构（inflatable tubular structure 的简称，常

用于 head airbag 和 side airbag) ②智能运输系统（Intelligent Transportation System 的简称，原称智能车辆-公路系统 Intelligent Vehicle-Highway System，简称 IVHS，1994 年改称 ITS，指"将先进的检测、通信和计算机技术综合应用于汽车和道路而形成的道路交通运输系统"。美国、欧洲和日本都在积极开展 ITS 研究与开发，其开发项目可分为：ATMS 先进的交通管理系统；ADIS 先进驾驶员信息系统；AVCS 先进的汽车控制系统；CVOM 营运车辆调度管理系统；APTS 先进的公共运输系统) ③国际货车展（International Trucking Show 的简称) ④国际运输服务公司（International Transportation Service) ⑤怠速跟踪开关（见 idle tracking switch)

ITS America 美国智能运输系统事务局（1990 年 8 月成立，联邦运输局 ITS 的咨询机关)

ITS head air bag 充气管式乘员头部保护气囊（见 inflatable tubular structure head air bag)

IV 智能化汽车（intelligent vehicle)

IVC 进气门关闭（inlet valve close 的简称，一般用于气门正时图等图表中)

IVD 进气门上的沉积物（intake valve deposits 的简称)

IVECO 依维柯（公司及车型名，为 Industrial Vehicle Company 的简称，该公司为意大利 Fait 集团的一个成员)

IVHS 智能车辆公路系统（intelligent vehicle highway system，见 intelligent transportation system)

IVMS ①车内多路传输系统［In-Vehicle Multiplexing System 的简称，日本日产公司轿车用车身电气设备的单线多路通信控制系统的商品名。该系统的主控制模块（IVMS computer) 通过一根导线与各局域分控模块（local control unit) 连接，实现主控单元与各分控单元之间的信息传输和指令传送。各个分控模块分别控制左、右、前、后电动车窗，电动车门锁，驾驶席座椅，车内照明等各种车身内的电气设备，不仅减少了大量连接导线，减轻了质量，而且减少了许多由于接线断、脱、松漏等造成的故障，可靠性显著提高］②车内多路通信网络（In-Vehicle Multiplexing System 的简称，日本日产公司轿车用单线多路传输控制系统的商品名。该系统由 IVMS 控制单元，五个局部控制单元、各种电器、传感器等组成。IVMS 控制单元与各局部控制单元之间用一根导线连接，传送各种信息和指令)

IVO 进气门开启（inlet valve open 的简称，一般出现于图表中)

ivory 象牙色的

IVT 无级变速器（infinitely variable transmission)

I-VTEC system 智能可变气门正时及升程电子控制系统（intelligent variable valve timing and valve lift electronic control system 的简称，由可变气门正时与升程控制系统和可变气门相位控制系统二者组合而成，见 VTC，VTEC)

IW 惯性重块，惯性平衡重（inertia weights)

IWCS 智能化气候控制系统（见 Intelligent Weather Control System)

IWD-EV 轮内（电动机）驱动型电动汽车（in-wheel drive electric vehicle 的简称)

I-4WD system 智能型四轮驱动系统（intelligent four wheel drive system 的简称，前、后轮的驱动动力可在30∶70～50∶50 间无级连续变化，各控制系统间信息共享、实现整体综合

控制)
IWM (装在车)轮内(的驱动)电动机(in wheel motor 的简称)
IWP 内轮轨迹,内轮印迹,内轮行迹(inner wheel path)
IWRC (绳索的)独立线束铁心(independent wire rope core)

Iyasaka (日本)弥荣公司(生产汽车检测设备等)
Izod impact test 艾氏冲击试验(用规定高度的摆锤对处于悬臂梁状态的缺口试样进行一次性打击,测量试样折断时的冲击吸收功)

J ①千斤顶（jack）②焦耳（国际单位制的功　能量单位，joule）

J1850 ［美国SAE（汽车工程师学会）提出的车身系统控制用］汽车局域网（协议，2000年以后已为CAN所取代）

JAAMA 日本（全国）汽车用品制造商协会（Japan Automobile Article Manufacturer Association）

jab 冲击，撞击

jack ①起重器，千斤顶②动力油缸，液压缸③用千斤顶举起，抬高

jack bar 千斤顶杆

jack bolt ①千斤顶螺栓②起重螺栓③调节螺栓，定位螺栓

Jack brake 见 Jacob's engine brake

jack cylinder 起重（机）油缸，举升（器）油缸

jack down 用千斤顶降下（物件）

jack engine ①辅助发动机②小型蒸汽机

jacket ①套，罩，护套，外壳，包甲②加套，复以外壳

jacket-cooled engine 水套冷却式发动机

jacket core 水套型芯

jacket drain cock 水套排水阀（＝jacket water cock）

jacketed cylinder 带冷却水套的汽缸；带冷却水套的缸体

jacketed wall ①双层隔墙；双层壁②带水套的汽缸壁

jacket heating （利用）水套加热，（进气管壁的）水套预热

jacket heat loss 由冷却水带走的热量损失

jacking ①用千斤顶举升②安置千斤顶③见 jack up

jacking bracket （车身底部的）千斤顶支座

jacking plate （车身的）举升垫板，举升凸耳（承载式车身等，本身具有供千斤顶等举升设备顶举的垫板　亦称 jacking pad，jack lug，jacking lug，见 body lifting jack）

jacking point （承载式车身底部为支撑千斤顶而加固的）支顶点，千斤顶支座，（亦称 jacking bracket，jack up point）

jack-in-the-box （俗）螺杆千斤顶（原义为一种玩具，＝jack-in-a-box）

jackknife （汽车列车产生）折叠（现象）（当牵引车与挂车不在一条直线时，由于制动、倒车等驾驶动作，使挂车绕牵引车连接点回转而与牵引车之间出现类似折叠式小刀的折合，即两车的夹角变小到90°或90°以下，成V字形的现象，亦写作 jackknifing）

jackknife door 折叠门（＝folding door）

jackknifing 见 jack knife

jack-knifing damper （铰接式车辆机械连接装置的）防折叠限位机构（限制主车和副车之间的最大水平转角，防止产生折叠现象，由限位元件和报警装置组成）

jack lever 千斤顶加力杆（= jack iron）

jack rabbit start （汽车）急速起步，猛冲起步（[美俚]指不惜离合器磨损和变速器振响，只求迅猛加速效果，亦称 stoplight drag）

jack shaft ①起重器轴 ②（两根传动轴之间的）中间轴（= intermediate shaft）③（分电器等）传递旋转运动的小轴

jack stand （修理汽车用的）可升降支架（一般支在车桥下，故亦称 axle stand）

jack up ①（汽车在转向过程中受到大的横向加速度作用，特别是悬架结构侧倾中心位置较高的车辆，车身向上）举升（的现象，亦称 jacking）②用千斤顶起（物件）

jack-up test of suspension 悬架举升试验（评价悬架举升特性的试验）

Jacobs engine brake 杰考伯斯发动机制动器（以厂名命名的大型车用柴油机电控液压机械式发动机排气制动系统，制动时切断供油，关闭气门，使发动机成为空气压缩机，以产生制动作用，简称 Jacobs brake 或 Jack brake）

JADA 日本汽车经销商协会（Japan Automobile Dealers Association, Inc.）

JAE [英]汽车工程杂志（Journal of Automotive Engineering）

jagged 锯齿状的，凹凸不平的，粗糙的，参差不齐的

JAIA 日本汽车进口商协会（Japan Automobile Importers Association）

JAIS 日本（汽车乘员）受伤简略分度法（Japan Abbreviated Injury Scale）

jallopy 破旧的汽车；老式车辆（= jalopy）

jalousie （水箱）百叶窗

jam ①阻塞，堵住不通 ②卡住，楔住，夹住 ③损坏，故障

JAMA 日本汽车制造商协会（Japan Automobile Manufactures Association）

JAMAIA 日本汽车用品工业协会（Japan Motor Articles Industry Association）

jamb （车厢）侧柱，门窗侧壁（亦写作 jambe）

jamb switch （车门或仓门）门窗侧框上的按压式开关（门控室内灯、行李舱灯等的开关，亦称 jam switch）

jammed 被卡住的，被楔住的，阻塞不通的

jamming ①人为干扰，电子干扰，接收干扰，干扰杂音，干扰噪声 ②堵塞，卡住，咬住，卡滞，楔住，夹住

jamming roller 压滚

jam nut 防松螺母，锁紧螺母，自锁螺帽（= lock nut, back nut, check nut, self locking nut, block nut）

jam welding 对接焊，对头焊接

JAP 日本汽车联合会（Japan Automobile Federation）

japan ①亮漆 ②给…涂漆 ③涂漆的

Japan 日本国（简称）

Japan Abbreviated Injury Scale 日本（汽车乘员）受伤简略分度法（简称 JAIS）

Japan Autobody Industrial Association 日本汽车车身工业协会（简称 JABIA）

Japan Automobile Article Manufacturers Association 日本（全国）汽车用品制造商协会（简称 JAAMA）

**Japan Automobile Dealers Association, Inc 日本汽车经销商协会（简称 JADA）

Japan Automobile Federation 日本汽车联合会（简称 JAP）

Japan Automobile Importers Association 日本汽车进口商协会（简称 JAIA）

Japan Automobile Manufacturers Association 日本汽车制造者协会（简称 JAMA）

Japan Automobile Research Institute, Inc 日本汽车研究所（简称 JARI）

Japan Automobile Standard Organization 日本汽车标准组织（简称 JASO）

Japan Auto-Parts Industries Association 日本汽车零件工业协会（简称 JAPIA）

Japan Electric Vehicle Association 日本电动汽车协会（简称 JEVA）

Japan Electronic Industry Development Association 日本电子工业开发协会（简称 JEIDA）

Japan Engineering Standard 日本工程标准（简称 JES）

Japanese Automobile Tire Manufacturers Association 日本汽车轮胎制造商协会（简称 JATMA）

Japanese Automobile Wheel Manufacturers Association 日本汽车车轮制造商协会（简称 JAWMA）

Japanese Council of Traffic Sciences 日本交通科学委员会（简称 JCTS）

Japanese Industrial Standards 日本工业标准（简称 JIS）

Japanese Industrial Standards Committee 日本工业标准委员会（简称 JISC）

Japanese lantern-type jacket tube （转向盘柱的）日本灯笼式柱管（受冲击式可像日本式灯笼折叠，吸收冲击能量，故名）

Japanese 10/11 Mode test cycle 日本 10/11 工况测试循环（日本对使用汽油和 LPG 燃料的总质量 2.5t 以下货车、10 座以下客车，1973 年起实行市区热起动模拟 10 工况法测定汽车排放，自 1975 年起又增加了冷起动模拟 11 工况法，测定汽车排放）

Japanese 4 Mode test cycle 日本 4 工况测试循环（日本 1966 年到 1972 年间对使用汽油或 LPG 燃料的总重量 2500 磅以下货车和 10 座以下客车，实行排放检测的工况法，1973 年起使用 10/11 工况法）

Japanese 6 Mode test cycle 日本 6 工况测试循环（1974 年起对客车和总质量 2.5t 以上货车实行排放检测的工况法）

Japanese Society of Mechanical Engineer 日本机械工程师学会（简称 JSME）

Japanese Standards Association 日本标准协会（简称 JSA）

Japan Gear Manufacturers Association 日本齿轮制造商协会（简称 JGMA）

Japan Industrial Vehicle Association 日本工业车辆协会（简称 JIVA）

Japan Industrial Vehicle Association Standard 日本工业车辆协会标准（简称 JIVAS）

Japan Machinery & Metals Inspection Institute 日本机械与金属检查学会（简称 JMI）

Japan Motor Articles Industry Association 日本汽车用品工业协会（简称 JAMAIA）

Japan Motor Industrial Federation 日本汽车工业联合会（简称 JMIF）

Japan Motor Wheel Company 日本车轮工业公司（简称 JMW）

japanning （特指日本亮漆）涂漆，涂漆层

Japan Science Council 日本科学委员会（简称 JSC）

JAPIA 日本汽车零部件工业协会（Japan Auto-Parts Industries Association 的简称）

jar ①振动 ②（刺耳的）杂声，噪声 ③容器，瓶，蓄电池壳 ④加目（电容单位，=1/900μF）

Jaray car 水滴型车身轿车（前端为圆球形，后端呈楔形，因发明人澳大利亚空气动力学家 P·Jaray 而得名）

JARI 日本汽车研究所（Japan Automobile Research Institute, Inc 的简称）

jar of water 水力冲击，水击

jarring motion 振动，震动，颤动

jarring table 振动（试验）台

JASO 日本汽车标准组织（Japan Automobile Standard Organization 的简称）

JATMA 日本汽车轮胎制造商协会（Japanese Automobile Tire Manufacturers Association 的简称）

Jatropha-derived bio-diesel 麻风树子（油提炼的）生物柴油（代号 J××；J40 为麻风子生物柴油含量为 40% 的油料。Jatropha 为一种落叶灌木或小乔木，原产热带美洲，现我国两广地区和云贵川等地均有栽植，其果实榨出的麻风油呈鲜黄色，印度、埃及等地已用来产生物柴油）

Java cotton 吉贝（印度尼西亚爪哇出产的一种木棉，见 kapok）

jaw ①夹具，虎钳 ②颚，颚板 ③游标尺 ④（虎钳，扳手等的）钳口 ⑤牙，爪，凸轮 ⑥（吊环，钩环上的）开口，孔

jaw brake 爪式制动器

jaw clutch 牙嵌式离合器，爪式离合器，颚式离合器

jaw couping 牙嵌式联轴节，爪盘联轴节

JAWMA 日本汽车车轮制造商协会（Japanese Automobile Wheel Manufacturers Association 的简称）

jaw vice 虎钳

jay-walking ［美］行人违章横越街路（不遵守交通规则乱穿马路或交叉口，不在规定的过街横道上穿过马路，这类行人被称为 jay walker）

JCTS 日本交通科学委员会（Japanese Council of Traffic Sciences）

JD 目测距离（judging distance）

JD power surver JD 功率检测（美国购买名牌汽车时，对汽车的一种检测）

Jeantaud steering 见 Ackerman steering

Jeep 吉普车［二次世界大战中美军使用的全轮驱动四轮小型敞篷越野车，由美国威利斯-奥弗兰公司生产，称为 general purpose car，简称 G. P. car。当时美国一种流行的连环画中具有非凡能力的魔术师 Engine the Jeep, Jeep 与 GP 同音，试车驾驶员就给这 G. P. 车取名 Jeep，厂家于 1940 年用 Jeep 注册为该车商标，俗称 bantam，中国北京汽车工业总公司 1983 年与美国汽车公司（AMC）合资成立北京吉普车有限公司，生产切诺基四轮驱动车，亦称北京切诺基吉普车 "Beijing cherokee Jeep"］

jeepable 吉普车可通过的，可通行吉普车的

jeep-ambulance 全轮驱动的救护车，吉普型救护车

jeep bridge 供轻型运输车辆用的桥梁

Jeep Commander 吉普指挥者（一种电动多功能、全轮驱动汽车的商品名，使用两套电驱动系统分别驱动前后桥。为减轻车重，采用塑料车身，20 世纪 90 年代末问世）

jeep-like vehicle 吉普类越野车

jeepney 吉普尼花车（菲律宾的一种

jeep–jet

小公共汽车，用吉普车改装而成，可搭客10人左右）

jeep-type vehicle 吉普型汽车（微型多功能越野车辆）

JEIDA 日本电子工业开发协会（Japan Electronic Industry Development Association）

jellied gasoline 胶凝汽油（凝固汽油）

jelly ①胶体，胶质，胶状物；糊状物，浆 ②使成胶状，凝结，使冷冻

jemmy 短撬棍（= jimmy）

jeopardize ①使陷入险境 ②危险

jeopardy 危险（通常用于 be in 或 place in jeopardy，表示处于或使陷于危险）

jerk ①（汽车等）突然前冲，猛然一撞 ②急推，急跳，急冲，串动 ③加速度变化率（m/s³, ft/s³）

jerk fuel injection pump （柴油机的）柱塞式喷油泵（柱塞偶件和出油口数量相同的喷油泵，柱塞偶件泵压的燃油分别从其对应的出油口输出）

jerkiness 带急跳（急冲）的运动

jerk pump （柴油发动机凸轮轴驱动的）直列式柱塞型喷油泵（的俗称）

jerk sensor 冲击传感器（测量位移的三阶导数的传感器，曾用作爆震传感器）

jerky ①不平稳的，颠簸的 ②（汽车加速时）窜动的，猛然一冲的

jerky feed 不平稳供给（如：猛然多供给一股燃油，供油时多时少）

jerrican （5加仑装）金属油桶，金属液体容器（= jerry can）

jerry 偷工减料的，草率的

jerry can ①汽油箱，汽油桶，汽油罐（= petrol can, gasoline can, gasoline container）②水罐，液罐（特指其容积为5加仑的大罐）

JES 日本工程标准（旧名，Japanese Engineering Standards 的简称，现用 JIS）

Jessop H40 捷索普H40耐热合金钢（碳0.25%，锰0.4%，硅0.4%，铬0.3%，钨0.5%，钼0.5%，钒0.75%）

jet ①射流 ②量孔 ③带量孔的喷嘴，喷口 ④喷气发动机 ⑤喷射，喷注，喷出 ⑥接点，接合焊接（= junction）

jet adjuster ①量孔调节装置（如：针阀等）②喷嘴（压力）调节装置（如：调节螺钉等）

jet atomizer ①喷雾器 ②喷嘴

jet bearing （斯特罗姆伯尔格式可变喉管化油器的）针阀式量孔喷嘴座（见 stromberg carburettor）

jet bore ①量孔 ②量孔直径

jet boundary 射流边界

jet calibration ①射流参数校准 ②量孔校准

jet calibration tester 量孔校准器（量孔流量计）

jet carburetor 喷雾式化油器

jet carrier （化油器的螺塞式）量孔座（量孔置于该螺塞内，便于拆装，亦称 jet head）

jet cleaner ①喷嘴清洁器，量孔清洁器，喷嘴通针，量孔通针 ②喷洗器，冲洗装置

Jet Controlled Super Lean Combustion （日本三菱公司的）喷流控制超稀燃系统

jet cooling 喷流冷却（如：喷液冷却，喷气冷却）

jet core （喷）油柱芯

jet dispersion （燃油）喷柱的雾化

jet-driven 喷气式的（用喷气发动机推动的，= jet-powered, jet-propelled）

jet efflux （喷气发动机的）喷流

jet flow 喷气流，射流（= jet stream）

jet-form 喷油柱形状

jet front 喷油柱前锋（jet head）

jet fuel 喷气发动机燃料

jet head 见 jet carrier

jet ignition 火焰喷射点火（等离子流点火 = plasma jet ignition, plasma arc ignition）

jet injector 喷油嘴，喷射器

jet mantle 喷油柱外层（= jet envelope）

jet mixing 喷射混合，喷流混合

jet needle 量孔针阀（= metering needle, metering rod, metering pin）

jet number （燃油）量孔尺寸编号（一般为号数愈大，流量愈多）

jet orifice 喷孔，喷口

jet-powered car 喷气式汽车

jet power ring 喷气功率环（装于火花塞座处，进气行程中将一部分空气经火花塞螺纹间隙引入燃烧室，起到节油、净化与提高功率的作用）

jet (propulsion) engine 喷气发动机 [= reaction (propulsion) engine]

jet pump 喷射泵

jet space ①喷嘴前空间 ②射流空间，喷雾空间

jet stem 喷嘴杆

jet stream ventilation 定向射流通风

Jetta 捷达（轿车牌名，德国大众汽车公司20世纪80年代初推出的一种普及型轿车，至今已发展多种升级换代车型）

jetted grid 喷射栅，喷流栅（置于进气道或进气门上流的栅状导向片，使气流产生所要求的旋涡）

jetter 抖动（跳动，在汽车电子系统中，指传输数字信号的各种不良变化，在显示屏上映像出现不符合要求的变形等）

jettisonable 可投弃的，可抛下的，可分离的

jet tube ①量孔喷管 ②（特指SU可变喉管化油器中的针阀式）主量孔喷管（主量孔装在该管内，见SU carburettor）

jet type mixer 射流式混合器

jet valve ①（特指某些稀燃发动机或层状充气发动机的）空气喷射阀（该阀紧靠常规进气门侧，由杆状阀门、阀体、阀体弹簧、带喷孔的阀座组成一个整件拧装在汽缸盖内，由进气门摇臂同步开启，空气由专门的通道经该阀直接喷向火花塞，形成强烈涡流）②喷射阀，射流阀

jet velocity 喷射速度，射流速度

jet well 量孔油槽，量孔油井

jet with transverse holes 带径向（横向）喷孔的喷嘴或量孔

JEVA 日本电动汽车协会（Japan Electric Vehicle Association）

jewel ①宝石 ②宝石轴承 ③把宝石轴承装进仪表内

jewel bearing 宝石（仪表）轴承

JFET 结型场效应晶体管，面结合型场效应晶体管（junction type field effect transistor 的简称）

J-flange J型轮缘（当前轿车轮辋最常见的轮缘形式，其高为17.3mm）

JGMA 日本齿轮制造商协会（Japan Gear Manufacturers Association）

JHFC 日本（推广氢燃料电池汽车的）实验认证计划（Japan Hydrogen Fuel Confirmation Project 的简称）

jib ①（起重机的）起重臂 ②（机械）铰辘 ③挺杆，臂杆，动臂，吊杆，支架 ④榫 ⑤夹具 ⑥横滑；改变方向

JICST 日本科学技术情报中心（Japan Information Centre of Science and Technology）

jig ①夹具，钻模；装配机具；样板，模板，模子，胎具 ②用夹具夹紧

jigging 颠振，振动

jigging table 振动（试验）台

jiggle ①轻摇，摇晃，跳动 ②减幅振荡变压器，可变耦合变压器 ③淘

簸筛，淘汰机，簸选机 ④盘车，辘轳 ⑤（车轮平衡器的）车轮不平衡度感传-放大装置

jiggle bars 突起人字形路带，凸人字形分隔带（阻止驾车横向撞入，= serrated strip，ramble strip）

jiggle jack 轻便千斤顶

jimmy 短撬棍

J-integral J 积分（围绕裂纹前缘，从裂纹的一侧表面至另一侧表面的线积分或面积分的数学表达式，表征裂纹前缘周围地区的局部应力-应变场）

JIS 日本工业标准（Japanese Industrial Standards）

JISC 日本工业标准委员会（Japanese Industrial Standards Committee）

jitney ①公共汽车（= bus，一般指票价低廉的公共汽车）②按灵活的行车时刻表，在一定线路上行驶的公共汽车 ③小型电动车（在火车站、汽车站、飞机场等地运送货物）④价格便宜的东西

JIT（system） 见 just-in-time system

jitter ①颤抖，振动，晃动 ②（信号，图像的）不稳定，跳动，起伏

JIVA 日本工业车辆协会（Japan Industrial Vehicle Association）

JIVAS 日本工业车辆协会标准（Japan Industrial Vehicle Association Standard）

JJD wheel 双 J 型轮缘双胎并装车轮（JJ double wheel 的简称，在由两个单独轮辋并装组成的一个双辐轮辋内装有两个独立的充气轮胎的车轮，其中一只轮胎跑气，另一只仍能支撑行驶）

J-K flip flop J-K 触发器

J/kgK 焦耳/千克·开氏度（国际单位制的比热单位。即每 1kg 物质的温度，每升高 1K，所需热量的焦耳数，水的比热，在英制中为 1Btu/16°F，在 CGS 制中为 1Cal/g°C，在 SI 制中为 4.1868kJ/kgK）

JMI 日本机械与金属检查学会（Japan Machinery & Metals Inspection Institute）

JMIF 日本汽车工业联合会（Japan Motor Industrial Federation）

JMW 日本车轮工业公司（Japan Motor Wheel Company）

JNCAP 日本新车评价纲要［Japan New Car Assessment Program 的简称，日本国土交通省和独立行政法人-日本汽车安全与车祸伤害人员救助机构（NASVA）联合实施的日本新车安全综合评价大纲，最高安全级别为五星级］

job ①工作，作业，工序 ②成品，成果 ③工件，零件

jobber machine shop 汽车零部件修复厂（一般这一类企业，还同时批发、销售新零部件）

jobbing ①小修理，零活，零星工作 ②单件生产 ③计件工作（按件付酬）

J-OBD Ⅱ 日本-第二代车载式自诊断系统（日本提出的"高度车载式故障诊断装置"，规定 2008 年 10 月以后生产的新车型和 2010 年 9 月以后继续生产的旧车型均须义务安装，诊断项目共 18 项，其中有关触媒劣化、发动机缺火、EGR、氧传感器和空燃比传感器及二次空气喷射系统 6 项的诊断结果，作为 readiness data 长期存储于诊断系统的故障数据存储器中，可供以后车检时查阅故障履历之用）

jockey wheel ①（履带行走装置）导向轮，张紧轮 ②（半挂车）支地轮 ③（正时皮带的）张紧轮（亦称 jockey pulley）

jog ①轻推，轻晃，微摇 ②凹凸不平处，粗糙面 ③缓慢进行，逐渐进展 ④（车辆）缓慢地颠簸着的行驶 ⑤（金相平衡图）等温线

joggle ①推动，摇动，晃动，颠簸 ②榫接，拼接 ③榫，榫舌

joggled ①折曲的，曲柄的 ②榫接的，拼接的，镶合的

joggling table 振动（试验）台

join ①连接，接合，结合 ②接合处，接合点，接合缝，接合面

joiner ①接合物 ②细木工

joinery 细木工车间；细木工；细木工技术，细木工行业；细木工制成品

joint ①联结，连接，接合，榫合，接缝，接头，接合点，榫头，铰键，关节，铰接头；（桁架）节点，结点 ②连接的，接合的

joint angle （球节，万向节，挠性节及各种关节等的）夹角，工作角

joint center （万向节的）十字轴 (= joint cross, joint spider)

joint coupling ①十字轴万向接头 ②耦接，电缆接头套筒

joint driver shaft （万向节联结的）被驱动轴，动力输出轴

joint driving shaft （万向节联结的）驱动轴，动力输入轴

joint dynamometer 万向节测力计（用来测定万向节传递的转矩）

joint face 接合面

joint flange 连接突缘 (= connecting flange)

joint hinge 连接铰链

joint homocinetique a 3 pivots 三销式万向节（由两个三销轴连接两个偏心轴叉组成的准等速万向节）

joint housing with outer races （球笼式万向节内支承球面上开有球槽，即带内滚道的）钟形壳（见 outer race③）

jointing compound 填封剂，油灰，腻子

jointing edge 接合边，合缝边

joint leakage 接头（处）泄漏

jointless 无接缝的，整体的

joint liner 接合面密封垫

joint loosening 接头松动，连接松动

joint of framework 构架的节点

joint of girders （车厢骨架或车架中）梁的节点

joint ring 密封垫圈，密封环 (= gasket ring, junk ring, sealing ring, sealing washer)

joint sleeve 连接套

joint splitting tool 球节拆卸工具 (= ball joint separator)

joint star member ①（万向节）十字轴 (= spider) ②（球笼式万向节）星形套（见 inner race②）

joint-stock company 股份公司

joint time-frequency analysis 时间-频率结合分析（获得频率-振幅随时间变化的三维频谱图）

joint tongue 榫舌，滑键

joint trunnion ①联结枢轴 ②（转子发动机的）角密封销，密封销

joint with three degrees of freedom 三自由度铰接

joint yoke 万向节叉

joist steel 工字梁（简称 jois, = I-beam）

jolt 颠簸，摇摆，振动

jolting ①颠簸，振动，摇摆 ②（特指）猛松离合器造成车身纵向反复振动

Jominy test 乔氏试验（用钢试棒端部淬火的方法来测定钢材的可淬硬性）

Josephon effect 约瑟芬效应（两个超导体之间的弱相互作用）

joule 焦耳（国际单位制的功，能量单位，代号 J，1 牛顿的力，作用距离为 1 米时所做的功，$1J = 1Nm = 1kgm^2/s^2$, $10^7 ergs = 0.10204 kgf \cdot m = 2.778 \times 10^{-4} kWh = 0.7381 ft \cdot 1b = 3.777 \times 10^{-7} PSh = 3.723 \times 10^{-7} HPh$；1948 年国际权衡会议采用 joule 为热量单位，1kg15℃ 水的比热为

4185.5J/kg℃ = 4.1855kJ/kg℃，1J = 0.0002389kcal = 9.48×10^{-4} Btu）
Joule cycle 焦耳循环
Joule's equivalent 焦耳当量（热功当量，参见 mechanical equivalent of heat）
jounce ①摇动，振动，颠簸 ②[美]车轮悬架弹性元件的压缩行程（= bump travel）
jounce and rebound 压缩和回弹（= bump and rebound）
jounce bumper （汽车悬架减振器或滑柱顶部的）压缩缓冲件（亦称 jounce buffer）
journal 轴颈，枢轴
journal bearing ①（发动机曲轴）主轴承（= journal metal）②轴颈轴承，轴承（多指滑动轴承）
journal bearing for axial load 轴向荷载轴颈轴承
journal bearing sleeve 轴颈轴承套
journal box 轴颈轴承箱
journal brass 轴颈铜套
journal bronze 轴颈青铜套
journal bush 轴颈衬套
journal collar 轴颈凸环
journalling sleeve 轴颈套筒，轴（颈衬）套
journal neck ①轴颈 ②轴颈上的环槽
journal packing 轴颈密封垫
journal pressure 轴颈压力
journal rest 轴颈支撑（轴承，轴套等）
journal sticking 抱轴（指轴颈与轴承互相黏结和咬住的现象）
journey ①旅行 ②旅程，路程，行程 ③移动，流动
journey's end （长途）旅行的目的地（旅程终点）
journey time （汽车）实际行驶时间，路程时间，旅行时间（指旅行需要的时间，包括路上停车及延误的时间，但在路外停车及延误的时间除外，= travel time）
joy ride 为好玩乱开车（不顾安全高速违章驾驶汽车，亦称 joy riding）
joystick control （有两个自由度，如：前-后，左-右，或前-后+左-右的）手操纵杆件
joystick type manipulator 飞机操纵杆式操纵机构
JPI 日本石油研究院（Japan Petroleum Institute 的简称）
JSA 日本标准协会（Japanese Standards Association）
JSAE 日本汽车工程师学会（Japanese Society of Automotive Engineers）
JSC 日本科学委员会（Japan Science Council）
JSME 日本机械工程师学会（Japanese Society of Mechanical Engineers）
J-turn （汽车的）J形转向，转向掉头（指汽车作180°转向）
jubilee truck （一种车身狭而深的侧卸式）小型侧卸货车，轻轨料车
jubilee wagon 小型厢式货车
judder ①（来自制动器或离合器总成的）低频振动 ②（离合器接合时的）抖动（见 clutch judder）
judging distance 判断距离（目测距离）（简称 JD）
juggernaut 巨型货车（俚）
jumbo tyre 特重型轮胎（巨型轮胎，特大车胎）
jump ①跳跃，跳动，跳起（特指气门振动时由凸轮上弹起的现象，见 bounce）②突增，猛增 ③跳变，突变 ④跨接 ⑤（薄板叠轧时的）折皱（缺陷）
jumper ①跨接线，跨接片，搭接片 ②（牵引车与挂车间的）跨接电缆 ③（两端带鳄口夹的）跨接缆线（美亦称 jump wire, jumper cable, = [英] jump lead, 见 jump start）
jumper head 牵引车和挂车间的电气

线路连接插头

jumper hose 跨接软管（如牵引车与挂车之间传送制动气压的软管）

jumper hose connections （牵引车与挂车之间的）制动跨接软管的可分式连接装置

jump gap distributor 有火花间隙的分电器

jumping start vehicle （给电池电力不足的车辆）搭接起动电源的车辆（见 jump start）

jumping (-up) test 镦锻试验（参见 up-ending test）

jump out （手动机械式变速器）掉挡（变速器在行驶中突然脱挡变成空挡）

jump out of mesh 脱离啮合

jump over ①跳过 ②跳火，产生火花（＝arc over, flashover, spark）③击穿

jump phenomenon ①跃变现象 ②跳跃现象

jump seat 折叠式活动座椅

jump spark 跳火花

jump-spark coil ①点火线圈高压绕组 ②点火线圈

jump-spark current 跳火电流

jump start 搭接起动（指车上蓄电池电力不足时，利用搭接缆线将其他车辆电力充足的蓄电池等接在本车电力不足的电池上起动车辆，亦称 jump starting）

junc-ring ①（车轮上紧压胎唇的）挡圈（＝side ring）②接合环，卡环，压环，挡环，锁环

junction ①接合，连接 ②接点，接合处，接头，节点 ③枢纽站；换车站 ④交叉点;（道路）交叉口（包括平交和立交，在美国称 intersection）⑤（半导体中的）结

junction block ①道路交叉口的拦路装置；道路交叉口交通堵塞 ②接线盒（＝junction box）③接线板

junction bulk-type field-effect transistor 体结型场效应晶体管

junction curve 过渡曲线，连接曲线

junction field effect transistor 面结型场效晶体管

junction laser 结型激光器

junction line ①中继线 ②接合线，连接线

junction marker 交叉路口指示标（表明交叉口、转向、线路方向、路名编号等的指示牌）

junction transistor 结式晶体管，面结型晶体管

juncture ①连接点，接合点，接缝，焊接点，交界处 ②中继线 ③结，接头

jungle jeep 丛林越野车

Jungner battery 杨格纳蓄电池（铁镍蓄电池，碱性蓄电池的一种）

junior [口语] 小尺寸的，轻型的

junk ①零碎废物，废料（废铜烂铁等）②旧废汽车，廉价汽车 ③碎片，金属片 ④（填缝隙用）绳屑 ⑤冒牌货

junked car 废旧轿车（在废旧汽车市场上出售的轿车，亦称 junked-auto, junk heap）

Junkers pump （柴油机等的）容克型喷油泵

Junkers water dynamometer 容克水力测功器（吸收式测功器的一种，其原理与傅汝德水力测功器相同，见 Froude water dynamometer, 只是后者的转子是利用半椭圆形空腔搅动水，而容克式则是由转子上的搅水棒搅水）

junk ring ①（内燃机的）活塞环槽镶圈（镶式活塞环槽，镶在活塞上形成活塞环槽）②（蒸汽机）活塞的密封软件函封圈

junk yard 废车场（废车放置场）

jury pump 备用泵，应急用泵

jury repairs 临时应急修理

just-as-good 代用的；可代用的；刚

合适的，刚好的
just critical 正好在临界状态下
just gap ［美］电极间隙，火花间隙（= air gap）
justify 证明…是正确的；说明…是有理由的；对…辩护；认为…是正当的；提供证据
just-in-time（system） 准时（制）（简称JIT，指日本丰田汽车公司20世纪60年代创立的一整套看板作业、按时供件等生产管理模式）
just size 正确尺寸
jute yarn ①黄麻，黄麻纱线 ②电缆黄麻包皮线
juvenile motor vehicle 儿童汽车（= boy motor vehicle）
juxtapose 并列，并置
JW 水套冷却水（jacket water 的简称）
JWL Standards 日本轻合金车轮标准（Japan Light Alloy wheel standards 的简称）

KΩ 千欧姆（kiloohm）
K ①容量；能力（capacity）②克拉；开金（carat）③阴极（cathode）④阴极射线管（cathode-ray tube）⑤赛璐玢，玻璃纸（cellophane）⑥百卡（centuple calorie）⑦常数（constant）⑧化学当量常数（constant of chemical equilibrium）⑨电离常数（ionization constant）⑩钾（kalium）⑪K介子（kaon）⑫开氏绝对温标（kelvin）⑬千（kilo）⑭千克［kilogram（me）］⑮千磅（kip）⑯节（kont）⑰化学反应速度系数（velocity coefficient of chemical reaction）
kadenacy effect 凯德纳西效应（二冲程发动机排气口突然开启，废气由排气口急速排出时，会产生以声速沿排气管传送的正压力波，其疏波部分，在排气口附近产生部分真空，形成降压效应，使缸内的废气能较多地排出，而改善排气，以其研究者法国人 Michael Kadenacy 命名）
KA（ka） ①千安培（kiloampere）②阴极（cathode）
kalium 钾 K（＝potassium）
kalium cyanide 氰化钾
KAM 见 keep-alive RAM
kamash alloy 锡基轴承合金（karmarsch alloy）
kamm-back 卡姆背式车身（20世纪30~40年代一种轿车车身形状的名称，亦称 Kamm-tail, Kamm-shape, 简称 K-back, K-shape, 其车厢顶面呈平缓的斜坡形，而背面突变为平直状，以减少旋涡形成，以德国空气动力学家 W. Kamm 命名）
kangaroo ［口语］装甲运输车
kangorooing （初学驾驶者，因离合器操作不当造成车辆）连续向前冲撞
kaon K介子
kapok 吉贝（一种木棉，作为缓冲填料，隔音材料，绝缘材料等，亦称 ceiba, ceiba pentandra, Java cotton, silk cotton, capoc）
Kapp line 卡普线（磁感应线，简称 KL, 每条卡普线 = 6000 麦克斯韦, 即：1 KL = 6000Mx）
Kapp method 卡普法（直流电机效率试验法）
karat 克拉（见 carat）
karl Benz 卡尔·本茨（1844~1929）（德国人，1879年将 otto 四冲程煤气机，改用汽油作为燃料，1885年将研制的转速 250r/min 小汽油机装在三轮车上，1886年1月26日专利生效，成为世界上第一辆汽油机动力汽车。所创建的 Benz 汽车公司于 1926 年与 Daimler 汽车公司

合并，为 Daimler-Benz 公司，中国称为奔驰汽车公司）

karman-swirl air flow meter 见 Karman vortices air flow meter

karman vortices 卡曼旋涡（流体流经障碍物时，在障碍物后产生的一系列有规则性的旋涡，旋涡的发生数与流体的流量成正比）

karman vortices air flow meter 卡曼旋涡式空气流量计（由置于进气通道内的涡流发生柱等组成，进气流流过涡流发生柱时，便在其后方产生一系列旋涡，利用超声波等测出该旋涡的数量，借以测定吸入的空气流量，亦称 karman-swirl air flow meter, karman vortices air flow sensor）

karmarsch alloy 一种锡基轴承合金，（锡85%、锑5%、铜1.5%、锌1.5%、铋1.5%；或铜12.5%、铅1.2%，其余为锡；或锑7%、铜3.7%，其余为锡。亦称 Kamash alloy）

kart ①卡丁赛车（亦称 Go kart 或 Go cart，原是一种底盘很低的游戏用小车，现是一种小型赛车，为由两轮轻便马车 cart 演变的商标名）②轻型敞篷货车（= light open carriage）

karting (= go cart racing) 卡丁车赛

kathode 阴极（= cathode）

K-b 键盘（key-board）

K-back 见 kamm-back

K-band frequency K 波段频率，K 波频

KC 千周波，千赫（kilocycle）

kcal 千卡，大卡（kilocalorie, kilogramme calorie）

kcal/m³ 千卡/米³（燃烧强度的单位，参见 intensity of combustion）

kcal/s 千卡/秒（热功率单位，1kcal/s = 3.968 Btu/s = 5.61HP = 5.7PS = 4187W = 427kgf·m/s = 3090ft·lbf/s）

50K (certification) test （催化剂的）5万英里耐久性鉴定试验

KCS 爆燃控制系统（knock control system 的简称）

KD 拆散的，解体的（见 knocked down）

KDC 散件组装轿车（见 knock-down car）

KDCL （货物）以拆散状态装车（见 knocked-down in car load）

KD export 散件出口（见 knocked down export）

KD operation 散（件组）装业务

KD plant 散件总装厂（见 knocked down plant）

keen draft ①强空气流 ②穿堂风，贯穿风

keep 保持，保存，保留；履行，遵守（规则等）；制止，抑制，妨碍；继续，维持，坚持

keep-alive memory 保持通电型存储器（必须保持续通电状态才能保存所存储的信息的计算机存储系统，如果断电，则所存储内容便会消失）

keep-alive RAM 保持通电型随机存取存储器（汽车电子控制模块中通过熔丝直接与蓄电池连接，在断开点火开关后仍保持通电状态的随机存取存储器，keep-alive random access memory 的简称，亦简称 keep-alive memory 或 KAM）

keeper ①夹头，保持器，定位件 ②锁紧螺母，止动螺母 ③（气门弹簧座）锁止 ④为保持磁力而吸附于马蹄形永久磁铁上的铁片

keep in good condition 保持良好状态

keeping steering force 保舵力（指为保持汽车某一运动状态时，而加在转向盘上的切向力，亦称 steering force for keeping a given control）

keep in order 保持秩序，保持有条

不紊
keep in touch 保持接触,保持联系
keep left (道路的)左侧通行,靠左行车(=keep to the left)
keep off median sign 路中分隔带禁止进入标志(指不准驶入路中分隔带停放车辆)
keep on the go 维持(机器)运转,保持(机器)处于工作状态
keep right (道路的)右侧通行,靠右行车(keep to the right)
keep right sign 右行标志(在靠右行车的国家和地区,表明路中有分隔带、交通岛、桥台等障碍物,必须从右侧通行的标志)
keep the distance 保持(某一)距离
keep the engine alive 保持发动机运转
keep traffic moving 保持交通畅通
keep up 支撑,支持,坚持
keep warranty in force 保单有效,保单生效
keg (一般指容量为10加仑以下的)小圆油桶,小油桶
kei (长不超过3.3m,宽不超过1.4m的)轻型轿车(来自日语轻"けい"的译音)
Keil Rheometer 凯氏压流计(测定胶合剂等黏度用,亦称 pressure flowmeter)
keiretsu companies (日本的)大型集团公司(日文系列"けいホつ"的译音,其特点是集团各公司间形成紧密的买-卖关系,即有生意或供需,首先在集团各公司间做)
KE-jetronic (博世公司推出的)机械-电子混合型汽油喷射系统(在原 k-jetronic 基础上增加了电子控制模块、多个传感器和电子控制电路。当电子系统失效时,机械控制部分仍能应急运行)
kelmet ①油膜轴承合金(含铅20%~40%的铜铅合金)②油膜轴承
Kelvin 开氏度(国际单位制的热力学温度单位,代号为K,一开氏度等于水的三相点温度的1/273.16。自1968年改变原来的代号°K为K)
Kelvin absolute scale 开氏绝对温标(代号K)
Kelvin bridge 开尔文电桥
Kelvin double bridge 开尔文双电桥
Kelvin rating 绝对温度值,开尔文温度值,开氏温度值(K)
Kelvin temperature 绝对温度,开尔文温度
Kelvin thermodynamic scale of temperature 开氏热力学温标[国际单位制的温标。自绝对零度开始到水的三相点为273.16度,到水的沸点为373.15度。参见 triple point of water,开氏温标代号为K,与其他温标的换算:$K - 273.15$ = 摄氏度°C;$9/5(K - 273.15) + 32$ = 华氏度°F;$4/5(K - 273.15)$ = 列氏度°R]
kennedy key 肯尼迪键(切向布置的双键)
kep 安全卡锁
kerb 路缘(石),侧石(= kerbstone,道路的一部分,沿路面或路肩的边缘设置,用以沟保持垂直或倾斜面,用以保护行车道并对驾驶人显示行车道的边缘,美写作 curb)
kerb capacity 见 curb capacity
kerb clearance circle 见 curb clearance circle
kerb feeler (车上的)路缘石传感器(以防擦碰缘石)
kerbing 将车辆放置在靠近人行道边缘
kerbing rid 见 curb rid
kerbside loading 由人行道边登上公共汽车(或其他车辆)
kerb (side) weight (汽车)整备质量(见 curb weight)

kerf ①切口，锯口，切缝（气割的），切槽 ②截断，切开，剪断，锯槽 ③（特指轮胎胎面花纹槽间的）连续细浅槽（用于减小噪声、散热，增加胎面的柔性和利于排除胎面附着的残留水分等，亦称 sipe）

kernel ①中心，核心，要点 ②核，模心，型芯撑 ③原子核 ④（积分方程的）影响函数核 ⑤模芯 ⑥（带电导体中）零磁场强度线

kerosene 煤油（［美］，亦写作 kerosine，为石油在 150～300℃温度范围内的蒸馏产品，相对密度0.75～0.85，主要成分为低辛烷值的链烷烃和异链烷烃。现在主要用作燃气轮机、煤油火花点火发动机及低污染柴油机等的燃料，在修理作业中，用作去脂熔剂及蒸气喷洗机的燃料，英写作 paraffin oil，早期用作灯油）

kerosene engine 煤油机（使用煤油的火花点火发动机）

kesternich test 耐蚀试验

Kettering ignition system 克德林式点火系（指最常见的由感应式点火线圈、断电器、电容器和蓄电池组成的点火系，由美国人 Charies Franklin Kettering 发明）

kevlar 聚芳酰胺纤维（用作轮胎帘线及这种帘线的胎体，亦称芳纶）

Kevlar-reinforced tire 芳纶强化轮胎

key ①钥匙，电键，电门，点火开关，按钮，扳手，键，楔，栓，销 ②关键，要害，秘诀，纲要 ③线索，索引，检索表 ④解答，题解，图例，答案 ⑤（油漆或填料层的）粗糙底面 ⑥接合，咬合，黏合 ⑦主要的，关键的，基本的

key board （电）键盘，电键板，开关板

key boss 键槽式轮毂

key buzzer 见 **key reminder buzzer**

key chime （警报装置发出的未拔）钥匙警报声

key code 钥匙密码

key-controlled switching 用钥匙控制的（起动及点火）开关

key diagram 索引图，解说图，原理草图，总图，概略原理图（= keydrawing）

key dimension 主要尺寸，基础尺寸，关键尺寸（= main dimension）

key drive 键传动，键控

keyed amplifier 键控放大器

key file 键锉（键槽或其他小件用的 100～150mm 长的各种形状的小锉）

key hole 钥匙孔

key inter-lock device （某些电子控制自动变速器换挡锁系统"shift lock system"中的）点火开关钥匙互锁装置［当点火开关钥匙置于关断位置时，转向盘和换挡手柄便被锁住"lock"，而当点火开关置于接通位置（包括点火 IG 和附件供电 Acc 位置）时，转向盘和换挡手柄才开锁，但只要换挡手柄未置于驻车挡位（P），点火开关钥匙，便不能从接通位置转到关断位置，因此要通过点火开关钥匙锁住换挡杆之前，必须将换挡杆置于驻车挡位］

key lamp 开关照明灯

keyless entry system （汽车车门或行李舱盖的）无钥匙开关系统（如遥控式或密码键式车门开关系统等）

Keyless Go （不用点火开关的）按键式起动

Keyless Smart Access （Lexus 的）无钥匙智能进出系统（只要将钥匙袋放在衣袋内，驾驶者便可以通过触摸车门把手锁门、开门和起动发动机）

key number 钥匙号码

key panel 键盘

key pin 键销

key plate 锁孔板

key point 要点，关键

KeyReader 钥匙读取器（读取宝马车便捷乘入系统的电可擦可编程只读存储器和遥控钥匙内存储的有关车辆及车况数据的装置）

key reminder buzzer 钥匙（未拔出）蜂鸣警报器

key spring （机械式变速器同步器）滑键弹簧（呈环状，亦称 insert spring）

keystone ①根本原理，基本点；要点，关键问题 ②拱心石，楔石

keystone piston ring 楔形断面活塞环（环的外圆面宽度大于内圆面宽度，断面呈拱石状）

keystone specification 主要技术规范，基本技术规范

key switch 电键开关，钥匙开关

key technology 关键技术

key terminal 枢纽站

keyway 键槽（= key base, key bed, key groove, key seat, key seating, key slot）

key wrench 套筒扳手

K-factor ①（转子发动机的）K 系数，形状系数（转子发动机的设计参数之一，$K=R/e$，其中 R 为转子中心到转子角顶的距离，即转子半径；e 为转子中心到主轴中心的距离，即偏心距）②（液力变矩器的）K 系数（$K=N_1/\sqrt{T_1}$，N_1 为叶轮转速，T_1 为输入转矩，亦称能容系数"capacity factor"）③（设备的）利用系数

K-flange 轿车车轮的）K 型轮缘（其高度为 19.3mm，目前已很少使用）

kg 千克，公斤（kilogram）

kg-cal 千克·大卡（kilogram calorie）

kg/cum 公斤/立方米（kilograms per cubic meter）

kgf 千克力（kilogram force）

kgf/cm² 千克力/平方厘米（米制压力，应力单位，称为工程大气压，$1\text{kgf/cm}^2 = 98.0665 \times 10^3 \text{N/m}^2 = 14.2231 \text{bf/in}^2 = 0.9807\text{bar} = 735.56 \text{mmHg} = 0.9678\text{atm}$）

kgfm 千克力·米（kilogram forcemeter）

kgf·m/s 千克力·米/秒（工程用米制功率单位，$1\text{kgf·m/s} = 9.81\text{watt} = 0.0133\text{PS} = 0.0131\text{HP} = 7.233\text{ft·lb/s} = 0.00234 \text{kcal/s} = 0.0093\text{Btu/s}$）

kg/l 千克/升（国际单位制的密度单位，见 t/m^3）

kg/m³ 千克/立方米（国际单位制的密度单位，kilogram/meter^3）

kgm ①千克（kilogram）②千克米（kilogram meter）

kgmt 千克·米，公斤·米（kilogramme meter）

K-GPS 运动型全球定位系统（Kinematic-GPS 的简称，普通汽车导行系统的 GPS 是通过来自四颗或四颗以上的定位卫星传输信号的时间差测定车辆的方位，其方位测定误差为 20m，而 K-GPS 则是利用来自各定位卫星的载波信号间的相位差"phase differences"来测定方位，是一种差分-GPS，它使用来自地面固定站的修正信息。这一系统由两个接收站组成，一个固定在车上的流动站，一个固定于地面的基准站，彼此间通过无线电通信。使用 K-GPS 技术测定车辆的实时位置称为 real-time-kinematic-GPS，见 RTK GPS）

kg/s 千克/秒（国际单位制的质量流量单位，kilogram/second）

KHN 努普硬度，努氏硬度（见 Knoop Hardness）

2K-H type planetary gear drive mechanism 2K-H 型行星齿轮传动机构（K 表示中心轮，H 表示行星架，2K-H 型表示由两个中心轮和一个行星架组成的行星齿轮传动机构）

K-H-V type planetary gear drive mechanism （其中V表示输出轴，K-H-V型表示由一个行星架H，一个中心轮K和一个输出机构组成的行星齿轮传动机构）

kHz 千赫兹（kilohertz）

Kia Motors Corporation 起亚汽车公司（韩国最早的汽车公司，创建于1944年，主要生产轿车、大客车、载货汽车、专用汽车）

kick ①反冲，反冲力，冲击，弹力，反应力，轴向压力 ②逆转 ③指针跳动 ④汽油的起动性 ⑤（石油产品的）初馏点 ⑥突跳，抖动，（发动机）猛地起动 ⑦［美］（塑料车身填料）开始硬化（= go off）

kick-back 逆转，反转，回跳，反冲（= kicking, 特指转向盘反冲，由于路面不平产生的冲击力传到转向盘上的现象）

kick-back test 反冲试验（评价汽车在坏路或凹凸不平路面上行驶时的保舵力、转向盘反冲大小的试验）

kick-back torque 反冲力矩，逆转转矩

kickback voltage 反冲电压（如来自电动机电感的反向冲击电压）

kickdown ①换低挡（= change down）②（自动变速器的）强制降挡（系统，=［美］forced downshift, 该系统在驾驶员将加速踏板踩到底时，自动将挡位降到比自动变速器所选定的挡位低的挡位，使汽车急速加速，简称CD）③下弯（倾）④自动跳合

kick-down (actuated) valve ①踏板前端控制阀（指主制动系气压不足时，制动踏板阻力很小，驾驶员轻轻一踩，便会将踏板一踩到底，这时，被踏板前端便将安全辅助制动系的控制阀压开）②（自动变速器的）加速踏板强制降挡阀（亦称detent valve, 当驾驶员猛踩加速踏板到底急加速时，该阀强制自动变速器液压系统的节气门控制阀移至降挡位置）

kickdown servo （汽车自动变速器的）强制降挡伺服机构

kickdown switch ①（加速踏板踏到底时自动变速器的）强制降挡开关 ②加速踏板控制开关（当踏板踩到底时与之联动或由进气真空控制的开关）

kicker cylinder 回位油缸，回程油缸

kick gear （摩托车）起动轴齿轮

kick of engine 发动机起动时的反冲

kick panel （轿车车身的）围在几个结构件之间的垂直扳件

kick-pedal （摩托车等的）脚踩起动踏板

kick plate ①（一般指）保护面板 ②（特指）车身门槛上的装饰板（= kick strip 或 scuff plate）

kick spring （摩托车）起动（蹬杆）复位弹簧

kick starter （摩托车）脚踏起动装置

kick stopper screw （摩托车）起动蹬杆止动螺钉

kick up ①扰动（= disturbance）②（汽车行驶中车轮遇到小石块等的）跳动现象 ③向上弯曲 ④急剧提高汽油辛烷值 ⑤公共汽车后排座位之间的空间（口语）⑥倾翻，翻倒

kickup frame （车桥处）向上拱曲式车架（为车桥、悬架提供安装空间，参见 upswept frame）

kickup of frame 车架（或承载式车身底板，为了给前、后悬架或前、后车桥提供安装空间而）向上拱曲的部分

kick-up part 车架后部为容纳车桥而向上拱曲的部分

kick-up pipe ①向上弯曲的管段

② (特指) (排气管系中从后桥上绕过的) 拱曲弯管 (一般位于双消声器式的后消声器前) ③ ([美俚] 指消声器后的) 排气尾管 (= tail pipe)

kick-up system (双腔分动式化油器) 副腔节气门的强制开启机构

kidney dolly (车身扳件不易接近的凹凸变形处敲整用的) 扁曲形砧 (逐渐向端部变薄并呈曲面的金属扳砧, 亦称 toe dolly)

kidney-shaped epicycloid 肾形外摆线 (当创成圆和基圆的半径相同时创成的外摆线, 见 epitrochoid)

kidney-shaped slot 肾形槽

killed steel 镇静钢 (脱氧钢, 炼钢过程中, 为了在钢水中脱氧, 加有一定量的强脱氧剂, 使钢水在钢锭模内凝固时不产生 CO 气体而保持平静, 用这种方法生产的钢的化学成分均匀, 焊接性好, 抗腐蚀性强)

killed (steel) wire (机械处理过的) 去弹性钢丝

killer 限制器, 抑制器; 断路器

killer driver 杀手驾驶员 (严重肇事驾驶员, 如: 酗酒开车的驾驶员)

kill switch (发动机的) 紧急切断点火开关, 紧急断火开关

killter [口语] 良好状态

kilo- 千 (英文冠词, 代号 k, $=10^3$)

kiloampere 千安培, 千安 (国际单位制的电流倍数单位, 代号 kA, 1kA = 1000A, 见 ampere)

kilobyte 千字节 (KB, 车用计算机存储容量单位, 一个千字节是 2^{10}, 即 1024 个字节, 例如 6KB 表示该计算机存储容量为 6144 字节, 见 byte)

kilobyte second 千字节秒 (①数据传输速率, 指每秒传输的千字节数 ②存储器利用率单位, 如一程序在某一处理阶段使用 10KB 存储器 0.2s。则称使用存储器 2 "千字节秒")

kilocalorie 千卡, 大卡, 公斤·卡 (热量单位, 代号 kcal, Cal, 工程界常用单位, 1kcal-1000calories = 1.558×10^{-3} HPh = 1.581×10^{-3} PSh = 1.163×10^{-3} kW·h = 427.2kgf·m = 4.186×10^3 J = 3.968Btu = 3090ft·lb)

kilog 公斤, 千克 (= kilogram)

kilogram 公斤, 千克 (国际单位制的质量单位, 代号为 kg, 等于一个国际公认的铂铱合金原器的质量, 该原器保存在巴黎附近的国际度量衡局。用作质量单位时, 1kg = 1/1000t = 2.2046 pound = 35.274 ounce = 1000g = 2 市斤 = 20 市两, 亦写作 kilogramme)

kilogram force 千克力, 公斤力 (MKS 单位制的力的单位, 代号 kgf, 使 1 千克质量的物体产生 1 个重力加速度 g 的力, 1kgf = 9.81 Newton = 9.81×10^5 dyne = 2.2046 lbf)

kilogram force-meter 千克力·米 (MKS 制的) (①力矩、转矩、弯矩单位 ②功、能单位, 代号 kgf·m, 1kgf·m = 9.81 N·m = 9.81J = 2.772×10^{-6} kW·h = 3.701×10^{-6} PSh = 3.649×10^{-6} HPh = 2.341×10^{-3} kcal = 9.29×10^{-3} Btu = 7.233ft·lb)

kilogram (me) calorie 公斤·卡, 大卡 (见 kilocalorie 及 great calorie)

kilogram (me) equivalent 公斤当量 (元素的公斤当量等于其公斤原子量除以原子价)

kilogram (me) -meter 千克米

kilohertz 千赫兹 (国际单位制的频率倍数单位, $= 10^3$ Hz, 代号 kHz)

kilojoule 千焦耳 (国际单位制的热量的倍数单位, 代号 kJ, 1kJ = 10^3 J = 0.2389kcal)

kilol 千 (公) 升 (= kilolitre)

kilom 公里，千米（=kilometer）

kilomega 千兆（10^9，代号 kM）

kilometer 公里，千米（代号 km，里程通用单位之一，1km=1000m=0.6214 mile=1093.6 yard=0.5396 nautical mile=2 市里=3000 市尺）

kilometer per hour 公里/小时（代号 km/h，速度单位）

kilometer speedometer （以公里计的）车速里程表

kilometrage 公里里程（以公里计的里程）

kilometre post 里程标

kilometre stone 里程碑（石）

kilonewton 千牛顿（国际单位制的力的倍数单位，代号 kN，1kN=10^3N）

kilonewton meter 千牛·米（国际单位制的力矩倍数单位，代号 kN·m，=10^3N·m）

kiloohm 千欧姆（国际单位制的电阻倍数单位，代号 kΩ，1kΩ=10^3Ω，参见 ohm）

kilopascal 千帕（国际单位制的压力倍数单位，代号 kPa，1kPa=1000pascal）

kilopond ［德］千克力（代号 kp）

kilosecond 千秒（国际单位制选用的时间倍数单位，代号 ks，1ks=10^3s）

kiloton 千吨

kilovar 千乏（无功功率的倍数单位，代号 kVAR，1kVAR=1000VAR，见 VAR）

kilovolt 千伏（国际单位制的电压倍数单位，代号 kV，1kV=10^3V，参见 Volt）

kilovolt-ampere 千伏安（国际单位制的视在功率倍数单位，代号 kVA，1kVA=10^3VA，见 apparent power）

kilowatt 千瓦（国际单位制的功率倍数单位，代号 kW，1kW=10^3W，1kW≈1.34HP=1.36PS=102kgf·m/s=737ft·lb/s=0.238kcal/s=0.947Btu/s）

kilowatt-hour ①千瓦·小时（MKS 制的功、能单位，代号 kW·h，kW-hr，1kW·h=3.6GJ=3.673×10^5kgf·m=1.36PSh=1.34HPh=859.9 kcal=3421 Btu=2.657×10^6ft·lb）②度（一般用来作为电能单位，1kW·h=1000W·h=3.6Gz）

kilowatt-hour meter 电（度）表，千瓦小时表

kind ①品种，种类 ②品质，性质，特性

kinding 点火，起燃，着火

kinding point 着火点（=kindling temperature）

kinematic inversion 运动模式转化，运动原理改变（如：转子发动机由单纯旋转式改型为行星旋转式，由旋转缸体改型为固定缸体等）

kinematic similarity 运动相似（如：两液力元件中液体的流动状态相似，则两者相应点的速度成比例且方向相同）

kinematics of machinery 机械运动学

kinematic support 活动支撑（如：被支撑物的位置不受热膨胀影响的支撑形式）

kinematic variables （汽车的）运动变量

kinematic velocity 运动速度

kinematic viscosimeter 运动黏度计（测定流体运动黏度所用的黏度计）

kinematic viscosity 运动黏度（代号 γ，流体的动力黏度与同温度、同压力下的该流体密度之比，国际单位制规定的单位为 m^2/s，CGS 单位制的单位为 cst，见 centistokes）

kinematic viscosity coefficient 运动黏度系数（见 viscosity index）

kinematic wave theory （交通工程

应用的）运动波理论
kinematic wobble （转向轮）行驶中摆振
kinemograph 转速图表；流速坐标图
kinemometer ①流速计，流速表 ②转速表，转速计
kinescope 电子显像管
kinetic-control 动态控制
kinetic energy 动能
kinetic energy recovery system （汽车的）动能回收系统
kinetic energy storage system （汽车制动能量回收系统中的）动能存储系统
kinetic friction 动摩擦（= friction in motion）
kinetic head 速头（表示运动流体具有的能量，= velocity head）
kinetic pressure 动压
kinetic pump 动力泵
kinetics 动力学
kinetic simulator 动态特性模拟器，动态模拟仪
kinetic viscosity 动力黏度（= dynamic viscosity，亦称 absolute viscosity "绝对黏度"，指相距 1cm 面积为 $1cm^2$ 的两液层，其中一液层以 1cm/s 的速度相对另一液层移动时，产生的剪切阻力称为动力黏度，若这个值等于 $1g/cm^2$，则液体的动力黏度等于 1p，见 poise "泊"）
kinetic wheel balancer 车轮动平衡机（= dynamic wheel balancer）
kineto-elastodynamic 运动弹性动力学
king bolt bush 转向节销衬套，主销衬套（= king pin bush）
king journal 主轴颈
kingpin ①转向节主销，转向主销（非独立悬架前桥转向轮转向时绕其运转的转向节轴或斜轴，亦称 axle pin, king bolt, steering swivel pin, steering pivot pin。对独立悬架的轿车而言，虽然已不使用主销，但该名词仍沿用至今，是指转向时前轮绕其运转的轴线，如：双横臂式独立悬架的上、下臂球节中心连线）②中心立轴 ③（半挂牵引车鞍座装置的）立轴，中枢轴
kingpin angle （转向节）主销倾角（包括主销正、负后倾和正、负内倾，见 caster 和 kingpin inclination，但一般指后者）
kingpin axis ①（非独立悬架前轮）转向主销轴线 ②（独立悬架前桥转向轮的）转向轴线（转向时，前轮绕其转动的轴线，如：双横臂式独立悬架转向节上、下球节的中心连线，亦称 steering axis, swivel axis）
kingpin axis inclination （独立悬架）转向轴线内倾（= ball joint axis inclination，相当于非独立悬架的主销内倾）
kingpin boss 转向节主销孔凸台
kingpin bush 主销衬套（= king bolt bush）
kingpin caster 转向主销纵倾（包括主销后倾，负后倾，即前倾。无说明时，一般指主销后倾，见 caster）
kingpin caster angle 主销后倾角（指转向主销中心线与过车轮中的铅垂线在车辆纵向中心平面上的投影的夹角，转向主销的上端向后倾，该角为正，称正后倾；转向主销的上端向前倾斜，该角为负，称负后倾）
kingpin centers distance 主销中心距（指左、右转向轮轴线与左、右主销轴线的两交点间的横向距离）
kingpin geometry （转向节）主销几何学，转向主销几何（指主销空间位置及其有关部件之间的几何学关系）
kingpin inclination （转向节）主销侧倾，（一般指主销内倾，主销内倾角，在过主销轴线或独立悬架前

轮转向轴线的横向垂直平面内，主销轴线与地面垂线之间的夹角>0，则称主销内倾，= inclination of steering knuckle pivot，亦称 steering-axis inclination，swivel-axis inclination，kingpin tilt)

kingpin offset 转向主销偏距（转向主销偏移距，指转向轮在直前位置时，主销轴线交地点与车轮中心平面的交地线之间的距离，亦称 scrub radius "磨胎半径"，其大小取决于车轮外倾和主销内倾量。当主销轴线与车轮中心平面的投影线在地平面相交时，该偏距为零。若在地平面下相交，该偏距为正值，若在地平面以上相交，该偏距为负值）

kingpin offset at the ground 转向主销轴线与路面之交点至车轮中心平面与路面的交线间的距离

kingpin offset at the wheel center 转向主销轴线与地面的交点和过车轮中心的垂线与地面的交点之间的距离

kingpin point steering 带分开式转向横拉杆的转向机构（= centre point steering）

kingpin spacing 左右转向节主销中心线接地点间距

kingpin steering assembly 主销式转向机构（转向节式转向机构、梯形转向机构总成，= steering knuckle type of steering，参见 Ackerman steering）

kingpin support assembly 转向节总成

kingpin (thrust) bearing 转向主销（推力）轴承

kingpin tilt 转向主销内倾（见 kingpin inclination）

Kingsbury thrust bearing 金斯伯瑞推力轴承

king size (d) 特大尺寸的，特大的

kink ①（软管、线索等）扭结，缠纽，绞结；结点，死扣 ②套索，铰链 ③弯曲，弯折，曲折 ④转折点

kinked ①（软管等）扭曲，扭结的 ②（车桥或车轮间制动力分配、比例、平衡等）失调（的）

kintal ①（一）百公斤（= guintal，亦称分担）②英担（[英]= 112磅，[美]= 100磅）

kip (s) ①千磅（= kilopounds）②旅店

Kirchoff's law 基尔霍夫定律（复杂电路中的电阻一般不是简单的并、串联，基尔霍夫定律由两个方程组组成，用于解复杂电路，其第一方程组说明任一多条支路相交的节点处电流强度的代数和为零；其第二方程组表明对任一闭合回路，电势降落的代数和为零，因此基尔霍夫定律亦称为基尔霍夫方程组）

kirkifier （一种）线性整流器

KIS 韩国工业标准（Korean Industrial Standard）

Kistler calibrator 凯斯特勒标定器

Kistler pick-up 凯斯特勒传感器

kit 成套（的零件、仪表或工具）

kit-bag ①旅行包，旅行袋 ②工具包，工具袋（参见 tool bag）

kit car 套件装配汽车（一种简易轿车，最早出现在 1957 年，Lotus7 型轿车，开始称为零件汽车，即 component car，用最便宜的成套零件组装，20 世纪 60 年代后则有专门批量生产出售的套件装配轿车）

kitchen truck 炊事车（供行军、旅行用的装在货车上的活动厨房，= kitchen vehicle）

kit form 成套散件形式（以成套的汽车零件，运往销售国组装成车的销售形式，即 CKD 的运销方式）

kJ 千焦耳（kilojoule）

K-jetronic （德国博世公司 1967 年推出的）机械式汽油连续（低压）喷射系统（商品名，燃油连续喷至各缸进气门前的进气道内，只要油

管内的压力大于喷油器针阀弹簧压力便连续喷油,其喷油量取决于由空气计量器中的气流压力传感板测定的吸入空气量)

KKM 行星旋转活塞发动机(德文 Kreiskolben motor 的简称,为 DKM 的发展形式。这种发动机的所有运动部件都围绕其自身的重心作等角速度运动,但至少有一个运动件,像行星一样,围绕一点沿圆形或近似圆形的轨道运转,= PLM type engine,参见 DKM,PLM)

KKM 2×300 双缸行星式转子发动机(单室排量为 300mL)

kl 千升(= kilolitres)

klaxon (原为电喇叭生产厂家名,现已为汽车用)电喇叭(的代名词,= electric horn)

KLCR 爆震极限压缩比(knock limit compression ratio)

klm 千米,公里(= kilometer)

KLSA 爆震极限点火提前角(knock limit spark angle)

km² 平方千米(面积单位,$1km^2$ = $1000000m^2$ = 100hectare 公顷 = 247.1acre 英亩 = 1500 市亩 = 0.3861 平方英里)

km ①千米,公里(kilometer)②千兆(kilomega)

km/h 公里/小时,千米/小时(国际单位制速度单位,1km/h = 0.2778 m/s = 0.6214mile/h = 54.678ft/min = 0.9113ft/s = 0.54knot)

K Monel K 镍铜合金(镍63%,铜30%,铅3.5%,铁1.5%)

kN 千牛顿(kilonewton)

kneading of traffic [口语]破坏交通秩序

knee ①(人体)膝部②弯头,肘节,弯管③角铁,角钢④膝形杆件,曲形支架、托架⑤(曲线的)弯曲处,拐点

knee action ①(汽车)独立悬挂的横臂或纵臂(类似于)膝关节的上下动作 ②膝动作用,膝形铰接动作

knee-action suspension 横臂或纵臂式独立悬架

knee action wheel 横臂或纵臂式独立悬架车轮(= independent suspension wheel with knee action)

knee air bag (保护乘员的)膝部安全气囊

knee bar (汽车乘员保护系统中的)膝部安全杠

knee bend 弯头,弯管接头,肘形弯管,管子弯头

knee bolster ①护膝垫板(一种能量吸收垫板,用于碰撞事故中保护乘员膝部,限制乘员腿部移动和身体下滑)②(汽车乘员保护装置中的)膝垫,膝枕(位于仪表板下方的冲击吸收防护板,发生正面碰撞时,可保护前座驾驶员或乘员膝部免受碰伤,亦称 knee impact bolster)

knee brace 膝形拉条,斜撑,角撑

knee bracket 膝形托架

knee brake 曲拐驱动带式制动器

knee-height 膝部高度的,高及膝盖的

knee impact protection device 防止撞车时乘员膝部被撞伤的各种装置的通称(亦称 knee protector,如:knee airbag 膝部安全气囊,knee护膝杆,knee blocker 膝挡,knee impact panel 膝部防撞板,knee pad 膝部防撞垫等)

knee-iron 角铁,角钢,耦铁

knee joint 肘节连接

knee of curve 曲线的转折处,曲线的拐点

knee of S-N-curve 疲劳曲线的转折处,疲劳曲线拐点

knee piece 弯管,肘管,弯头

knee pipe 曲管,弯管,弯头

knee restraint (汽车乘员的)膝部约束性保护装置(防止撞车时,膝

部前冲而碰伤的约束保护装置，如膝部安全带等的通称）

knee room （车内乘员的）膝部（活动）空间

knee table 可收放的小桌（工具车上的）

knee (-toggle) lever 肘节杠杆，曲拐杆，曲臂

knife bearing 刀口支撑，刃型支撑（= blade bearing, fulcrum bearing）

knife edge ①刀刃 ②支撑刀刃（如天平的支点）③刃状物

knife-edge bearing 刀形支撑

knife edge follower 刀形随动件

knife-edge load 刀刃荷载（线荷载）

knife switch 闸刀开关

knifing stopper （车身表面小凹坑和缺痕的）细填料

knight engine 耐特式滑阀配气发动机

KNK RTD CYL 为阻止爆燃而推迟点火提前角的汽缸（knock retard cylinder 的简称）

kN/m² 千牛顿每平方米（常用压力单位 $1kN/m^2 = 0.0102kgf/cm^2 = 0.145lbf/in^2$）

kNm 千牛·米（kilonewton meter）

knob ①按钮 ②球形手把，球形捏手 ③圆头突起物

knobby tire 凸块高花纹轮胎

knob control 按钮控制（= button control）

knock ①敲击，打击，撞击 ②敲击声，打击声 ③（发动机）爆燃，爆震（engine knocking 的简称，指汽油机在燃烧过程中，由于局部混合气完成焰前反应，引起自燃，以极高的速度传播其火焰，产生带爆炸性质的冲击波，发出尖锐的金属敲击声，亦称 detonation, ping, pinking, run away knock, spark knock。对柴油机称 diesel knock，指由于其燃烧过程的速燃期压力增长率过大，而导致即使不发生爆震，也会发生很响的敲缸声，我国汽车界多称这种情况为：工作粗暴，当敲缸严重时，亦称爆震）

knock analyzer 爆震分析器

knock characteristic ①爆震特性 ②（汽油的）抗爆特性

knock-compound 抗爆剂

knock control system 爆燃控制系统，爆震控制系统（如出现爆燃时，延迟点火等，简称 kcs，亦称 knocking evasion system）

knock detection 爆燃监测，爆震监测

knock down ①易于拆卸的，能拆卸的，拆散的 ②易于拆卸的装置 ③击倒，击落 ④拆卸，解体 ⑤（特指将车辆）拆为散件以便于运输

knock-down car 散件组装轿车（将散件运到某地，就地组装成的车，简称 KDC）

knocked down export 散件输出，散件出口（特指将汽车等以散件的形式出口，然后在输入国装成整车，简称 KD export）

knocked-down in carload （货物）以拆散状态装车

knocked down plant （汽车等的）散件装配工厂，散件总装厂（指设在输入国内将进口散件装成整车的工厂，简称 KD plant）

knocker ①燃料中的爆震成分 ②[美俚]车身板件（凹陷）拉器（= panel puller）

knock-free 无爆震的，抗爆震的

knock free power 无爆震功率

knock-free region 无爆震区（一般指使用各种浓度的混合气时，不发生爆震的功率区）

knock-fuel 抗爆震燃料（= anti-knock fuel）

knock hole 定位（销）孔，顶销孔

knock-in 敲入，打入

knock index （汽油的）抗爆指数（指汽油马达法和研究法辛烷值的平均值，美国规定它作为划分汽油等级的抗爆性指标）

knock inducer 爆震诱导剂（参见 tetralin）

knocking ①爆震，爆燃，突爆（见 knock③）②（轴承松旷产生的）敲击噪声 ③打击，敲击

knocking evasion system 见 knock control system

knocking limit compression ratio 爆燃极限压缩比（不致发生爆燃的最大压缩比，简称KLCR）

knocking of (the) piston 活塞敲缸（亦称 piston knock）

knocking sensor 爆震传感器（= knock sensor）

knocking simulation tool 爆燃模拟器

knock inhibitor 抗爆剂

knock intensity 爆震强度

knock (-intensity) indicator 爆震（强度）指示仪

knock limit 爆燃极限，爆燃界限（指对具体发动机而言，压缩比、点火提前角及所用汽油的辛烷值和其他运行条件与状态等不致发生爆燃的极限值）

knock-limited engine 采用抗爆措施的发动机

knock limit spark angle 爆燃极（界）限点火（提前）角（简称 KLSA）

knockmeter 爆震强度测定仪（亦写作 knock meter，一般指测定燃油辛烷值用的 CFR 发动机的附件，测定爆震强度的电气仪表）

knock noise 爆燃噪声

knock of crank 曲轴敲击声

knock-off ①敲落，敲击 ②停止工作，停机

knock-off cam 停机凸轮

knock off/on nut 敲击拆装式车轮中心锁紧螺母（亦称 knock on nut，或 spinner，早期英国 Rudge—Whitworth 公司为快速更换赛车车轮而推出的，只要用轮锤敲击，便可拆装的车轮中心自锁螺母，左螺纹者供左侧车轮使用，右螺纹者供右侧车轮使用）

knock-off wheel 敲击拆装式车轮（使用 knock-off/on nut 的赛车车轮，其轮毂带花键，呈锥形，与之配合的车轮中心内面亦为带花键的锥面，只要用软头锤敲击，便可快速拆、装其中心自锁螺母和车轮，亦称 knock-on wheel）

knock-off wire wheel 带快速拆装钢丝辐条的车轮（= knock-on wire wheel）

knock-on collision 对面碰撞，迎面碰撞，直接碰撞，对头碰撞（= head-on collision，central collision）

knockout ①打击，敲击 ②拆卸工具，顶出器

knock-out axle （低平板货车的）可拆式车桥（以便进一步降低平板高度）

knockout cylinder （拆卸用）顶出油缸

knock-pin ①定位销，锁止销 ②顶销，顶出杆

knock rating ①爆震率，爆震值 ②抗爆性测定 ③辛烷值（辛烷值的非正规名称，= octane rating）

knock rating method （车用汽油的）抗爆性评定法，辛烷值测定法（分为实验室法和道路法两类，都是用被测定的燃油与异辛烷和正庚烷的混合液标准燃油进行对比，参见 octane number，laboratory knock-testing method，road-knock rating method）

knock-reducer 抗爆剂，减震剂

knock resistance （燃油的）抗爆性

（用辛烷值表示，见 octane number）
knock resistant　抗爆的，阻爆（燃）的
knock sensor　爆震传感器（亦称 knocking sensor 或称 detonation sensor，利用压电晶体将爆燃时产生的 4～7kHz 的振动转换为电信号输出）
knock suppressor　①抗爆添加剂　②抗爆装置（= detonation suppressor）
knock tendency　爆燃倾向
knock test　爆震试验，抗爆试验
knock test engine　燃料抗爆性测试发动机，辛烷值测试发动机
knock value　抗爆值
knock wave　爆震产生的冲击波
knoop hardness number　努氏硬度值（简称 knoop number，努氏硬度计金刚石棱锥压头压痕单位投影面积承受的平均压力表示的硬度值，代号 HK，$HK = 1.4509 \frac{F}{d^2}$，式中：$F$—试验力，N；$d$—压痕长对角线长度，mm）
knot　①节（速度单位，代号 kn，每小时1海里，1knot = 1.51mile/h = 1.852km/h，见 nautical mile）②海里，浬（距离单位，代号 kt，约为1852m，同 nautical mile）③结，结节，纽结
knowledge acquiring and refining program　（专家系统）知识获取与提炼程序（见 expert system）
knowledge base　（专家系统）知识库（见 expert system）
known　已知的
knuckle　①关节，铰链，肘节　②万向接头　③转向节（steering knuckle 的简称）
knuckle arm　转向节臂（见 steering arm）
knuckle bearing　关节轴承（= balland socket bearing, free bearing, pivoting bearing）
knuckle centre　万向接头十字轴
knuckle joint　①铰链连接（可容许在一个平面内相对转动）②球节
knuckle joint end　球铰端头；球头
knuckle pin　①（独立悬架上、下横臂）球节中心连线　②（非独立悬架的转向节）主销（= king pin, knuckle pivot, steering knuckle pivot, steering swivel bolt, steering-yoke bolt, swivel pin）③铰链销
knuckle pin angle　主销倾角（主销内倾，主销后倾）
knuckle-pin center　转向主销轴线与路面的交点
knuckle pivot　[美] 转向节主销（= king pin, knuckle pin）
knuckle pivot center　转向节主销中心（线）
knuckle spindle　转向节轴，前轮轴（与转向节叉制成一体，安装前轮的短轴，= wheel spindle, wheel axle，亦称 stub axle）
knuckle support　（独立悬架）转向节支架
knuckle thrust bearing　转向节推力轴承
knuckle tooth　圆顶齿
knurled　滚花的
knurled piston　滚花修复活塞，压花修复活塞（活塞裙部磨损后，经压花胀大再用）
knurling type plating　细菱形花纹镀覆
KOEO　点火开关钥匙断开，发动机熄火（key off engine off 的简称，指在上述状态下，用诊断仪对汽车发动机等进行诊断）
KOER　点火开关钥匙接通，发动机运转（key on engine running 的简称，指在上述状态下，对汽车发动机等进行诊断）
konimeter　空气尘度计，尘量计（测定空气中的含尘量，= koniogravimeter）
Korean Industrial Standard　韩国工

业标准（简称 KIS）

Korean Society of Automotive Engineers Ins 韩国汽车工程师学会（简称 KSAE）

Kp ［德］千克力（参见 kilopond）

kPa 千帕斯卡，千帕（= 10^3 Pa，参见 Pa）

KPH 千米/小时，公里/小时（kilometer per hour）

KPI 转向主销倾角，转向主销内倾（见 kingpin inclination 的简称）

krinkle finish （制件表面，如气门摇臂盖表面的）最后皱面加工涂装（加工表面呈黑灰色耐磨皱皮，亦称 wrinkle finish）

Kritn 克瑞（气体质量单位，等于氢在标准状态下 1L 的质量，1 克瑞 = 0.0896 克）

KRT 阴极射线管（cathode-ray tube）

Krupp Junkers engine 克虏伯·容克型发动机（对向活塞式二冲程发动机，在同一缸内对向装用两个活塞，上活塞驱动扫气装置，下活塞完成做功循环，在两活塞顶间形成燃烧室）

kryoscope 凝固点测定计

kryptol ①碳棒，硅碳棒 ②粒状炭

krypton 氪（kr）

krypton lamp 氪灯（亦称 krypton filled lamp，充氪以延长寿命，增加亮度）

Krypton test 克瑞普顿试验（指使用由专利持有人克瑞普顿命名的仪器对内燃机进行的诊断和性能测试）

ks ①千秒（kilosecond）②闸刀开关（knife switch）

KS 爆振传感器（见 knock sensor）

KSAE 韩国汽车工程师学会（Korean Society of Automotive Engineers Inc.）

200 K samples per second 每秒 200 千次采样（亦写作 Ksamples，为采样次数的常用单位之一）

kt ①克拉（karat）②千吨（kiloton）③成套零件（工具）（kit）④节（knot）

3k type planetary gear drive mechanism 3k 型行星齿轮传动机构（指由三个中心轮组成的行星齿轮传动机构，k 表示中心轮，参见 2k-H 及 K-H-V type planetary gear drive mechanism）

K-type thermocouple K 型热电偶（K 指 Kelvin 开，绝对温标）

Kumm transmission 卡姆变速器（通过平传动带和可变直径式传动带轮调速的无级变速器）

kVA（KVa, kva） 千伏安（kilovolt-ampere）

KVAR 千乏（无功功率单位，kilovar）

kVIS 运动黏度（参见 kinematic viscosity）

kV（kv） 千伏（kilovolt）

kW 1024 字符（kilowords）

kW 千瓦（kilowatt）

kWh（kW·h, kW-h, kW-hr） 千瓦·小时（kilowatt-hour）

Kyanize 给木材注入升汞，用升汞溶液（给材料）防腐

L ①（自动变速器）低速挡（low）②螺旋线导程（lead of helix）③升（litre）④流明（国际单位制光通量单位，lumen）⑤豪华（型汽车，luxe）

La 镧（lanthanum）

lab 实验室，试验室（laboratory 的简称）

label ①标牌（标明汽车结构性能参数及使用特性的说明牌）②（挂在行李等上面的）标签③（用示踪原子）示踪

labelled compound 示踪化合物（含示踪原子化合物）

labile 易变化的，不稳定的，不安定的

labile oscilator 易变振荡器

labization （转向杆系和前轮悬架的）补偿弹簧（通常为扭力弹簧，在地面上的投影成Z字形，故亦称z-bar）

labor （指汽车发动机）因超负荷而吃力地运转（亦写作 labour）

laboratory 实验室，试验室（简称 lab）

laboratory crash simulation 室内碰撞模拟

laboratory engine 实验室用发动机

laboratory equipment 实验室设备

laboratory findings 实验数据，实验结果

laboratory investigation 实验室研究

laboratory knock-testing method （车用汽油的）抗爆性实验室评定法（实验室辛烷值测定法一般分为研究法和马达法，都使用单缸可变压缩比发动机进行测定。马达法的转速为 900r/min，进气温度预热到 150℃；研究法的转速为 600r/min，进气系统不预热。因此同样的汽油，其研究法辛烷值较马达法辛烷值高一些）

laboratory life 实验室试验寿命

laboratory octane number （车用汽油的）实验室辛烷值（用实验室辛烷值测定法测出的辛烷值的通称，见 laboratory knock-testing method）

laboratory procedure 实验程序，实验步骤

laboratory reliability test 实验室可靠性试验

laboratory-scale 试验规模的，试验用的，试制的，小规模的

laboratory shop 试制车间

laboratory simulation 实验室模拟

laboratory simulation test 实验室模拟试验（模拟使用条件的实验室试验，例如在人工气候试验室中进行试验）

laboratory testing rig 实验室试验设备

laboratory vehicle 车载试验室，流

动汽车实验室（指装有实验设备的厢式车辆）
labor-intensive 劳动力密集的
labouring 运转吃力的（美称 lugging）
labour-saving 省力的，节省劳力的
labyrinth box 迷宫式密封箱
labyrinth gland 迷宫式密封装置
labyrinth oil retainer 迷宫式挡油圈
labyrinth packing 迷宫密封，迷宫式密封件
labyrinth piston 带迷宫式密封的活塞
labyrinth plate 迷宫式密封板，迷宫式密封片
labyrinth ring 迷宫式密封环
labyrinth seal 迷宫式密封（利用离心力和迷宫式结构防止轴渗漏的非接触式密封件）
labyrinth sealing 迷宫式密封，迷宫式密封件（= labyrinth packing）
labyrinth-type excluder 迷宫式密封装置
labyrinth type mud excluder 迷宫式挡泥装置
lac 虫胶，虫漆
lace ①带，束带 ②花边，装饰带，缀合，编织
laced spring type flexible coupling 带簧式挠性联轴节
lace-on 用带子系紧的
laceration index （汽车撞车时，乘员的）皮肉划破伤害度（简称 LI）
laceration injury （撞车时乘员的）皮肉划破创伤
lacet S 形弯道，盘山道路
lacker surfacer 腻子，二道底漆（介于底漆与面漆之间的涂料，其作用为填补底漆微小的凹凸，使涂层光滑，提高面漆的附着强度，亦称 lacguer surface）
lack of alignment ①歪斜（中心线偏斜，轴线偏斜）②（车轮）定位不当
lack of balance 不平衡，失去平衡（亦称 lack of equilibrium）
lack of fuel 燃料不足，缺油
lack of power 功率不足，马力不足，乏力
lack of skill 技术不熟练
lack of space 缺少空间，空间不足
lack of water 缺水，水量不足
lacquer ①漆（pyroxyline lacquer 的简称，油料、树脂、颜料和各种添加剂组成的表面涂装用混合物）②（燃油和润滑油分解产物聚合而在发动机零件表面上形成的光滑）漆状沉淀，漆状胶结物 ③涂漆 ④漆层，涂漆层
lacquer build-up 积胶，结胶
lacquer coat 漆层，漆涂层
lacquer deposit 漆状沉积物（= varnish deposit）
lacquer enamel 磁漆（热固性色漆）
lacquerer （油）漆工
lacquer finish ①涂装作业，油漆作业，油漆涂装作业（= paintwork, body finish）②涂面漆
lacquer formation 漆状物生成，漆膜形成
lacquer-like product 漆状产物
lacquer putty 漆系腻子，漆基油灰
lacquer thinner （挥发性）油漆稀释用溶剂
lacquer varnish 亮漆，清漆
lac varnish 虫胶漆，亮漆，光漆（虫胶溶于酒精中的快干性涂料）
ladder ①梯子，楼梯 ②车箱栏板的接高部
ladder-and-X-brace frame 由两侧纵梁和 X 形横梁构成的车架
ladder truck 带梯子的货车
ladder type frame ［美］梯形车架（英称 ladder chassis，指两侧大梁由相距一定间隔的多根横梁连接，形如梯，故名，常用于客车，但现代

整体式结构中已淘汰，亦称 longitudinal frame）

lade 装载，装货，加载

laden 被装载的，装着货的，满载的

laden height 满载状态下的高度

laden in bulk （被）散装的

laden weight 满载量，满载重量（满载质量的旧称）

laden weight of a vehicle 车辆总重量（可行驶状态下车辆自重、乘员重及装载质量之和，车辆总质量的旧称）

ladies category race 女士赛

lading ①载重，荷重，荷载，货物 ②装载，装货，加载

lag ①滞后，迟滞，迟后（特指发动机气门在活塞到达上止点后关闭，用时间用曲轴转角度数表示）②变弱 ③卡住 ④错开，平移，偏置 ⑤防护罩，外罩，罩壳

lag bolt 方头螺栓

lag correlation 落后相关

laggage carrier （车内）行李架，行李搬运车（= baggage holder）

lagging ①滞后，延迟 ②套板，隔板，隔层 ③蒙皮，包皮，保温套，防护套 ④绝热层，保温层 ⑤刻纹 ⑥滞后的，慢的，凹凸不平的，粗糙的

lagging edge 后沿，后边缘（见 following edge）

lagging jacket 保温套

lagging material 保温材料，热滞材料

laggrangian interpolation coefficient 拉格朗日内插系数

LAG Process 雪崩式燃烧过程（LAG 燃烧过程，拉克燃烧过程，哥萨克燃烧过程，苏联科学院化学物理研究所 L. A. Gussak 等对所研制的火炬点火式汽油机燃烧机理的解释，运用 Semenov 的连锁反应理论，说明在燃烧室中形成的大量的活性原子团，然后喷入主燃烧室产生连锁反应的快速燃料过程，以研制者 L·A·Gussak 的名字、父名、姓氏的第一个字母命名为 LAG 燃烧过程）

lagrangian 拉格朗日算子

Lagrangian（polynomial）fit 拉格朗日（多项式）拟合（一种电子计算机技术，将一组数据点用内插法形成多项式曲线，要求将 N 个数据点形成一条 $N-1$ 次方的曲线，这项技术用于绘制分析仪的校正曲线，其特点是用内插法形成的曲线能精确地通过每个数据点）

laid-up 暂停使用的，拆开待修的

lake pipes （汽车车身侧面无实际用途的）装饰性管件（亦写作 lakes pipes）

lambda 希腊字母，大写 Λ、小写 λ 的读音，在汽车发动机中用来表示相对空燃比，见 normalized air/fuel ratio lambda

lambda = 1 closed loop control $\lambda=1$ 闭路控制（指发动机空燃比闭路控制系统，一般包括废气中氧含量传感器和三元催化转化器，电子控制模块根据氧含量传感器的反馈信息，将空燃比控制在 $\lambda=1$ 的范围内，以保证三元催化转化器的最佳净化效率和燃油经济性，λ 指可燃混合气的相对空燃比，见 lambda）

lambda control range λ 控制范围（指发动机空燃比闭路电子控制系统的相对空燃比控制范围，一般发动机为 $\lambda=1$，稀燃和稀混合气发动机为 $\lambda=1.4\sim1.7$）

lambda probe λ 传感器（见 lambda sensor）

lambda sensor λ 传感器，相对空燃比传感器（亦称 lambda probe，测定并向动力控制模块反馈发动机废气中的氧含量，供后者确定和控制

发动机可燃混合气实际空燃比的传感器，亦称 O_2 sensor, oxygen sensor)

lambda = 1 sensor λ=1 传感器（废气氧含量传感器中用得较多的一种，基本上是一个固体电解液氧浓度电池。当 λ=1 时，其电动势发生急剧变化，而 λ<1 或 λ>1 时，其电动势变化相当平缓，发动机电子控制模块根据其输出电压信号，对实际空燃比实施 λ=1 闭路控制，以保证三元催化转化器最佳的净化效果，可分为勒恩斯特型"Nernst type"和半导体型"semiconductor type"两种）

lambda sensor control window 氧含量传感器的（空燃比）控制范围

lambda system λ系统（废气氧含量反馈控制空燃比系统，的简称，该系统通常与三元催化净化系统合用，由氧含量传感器，即所谓λ传感器、电子控制模块及控制空燃比的执行机构组成闭路控制系统，见 lambda window）

lambda window λ区（指混合气的过量空气系数 α=1 或相对空燃比 λ=1 的狭窄区域，在该区域内，废气中的 CO，NOx 及 HC 排放最少，三元催化剂的效率最高，亦称 catalytic converter window）

lambert 朗伯（亮度单位，=1 流明每平方厘米）

lambertian surface （电场光学）完全散射面

lame ①损坏的，有缺陷的 ②（金属）薄板，薄片 ③使损坏，使不中用

lamella clutch 多片式离合器

lamellar ①薄板的，薄片的 ②多片的（离合器）③多层的，鳞片状的，层状的

lamellar fracture 层状断裂面

lamellar fuse 片状保险丝，片状熔丝，熔片，熔箔（亦称 foil fuse）

lamilla spring 钢板弹簧

laminar boundary layer 层流边界层（流体分子成层状流动的边界层）

laminar film 薄层，薄片，层膜

laminar flow 平流，层流，流线流（=stream-line flow）

laminar flow flowmeter 层流流量计

laminar heat transfer 层流中的热传导

laminate ①多层材料，层压材料，层压板 ②分层，成层，层压 ③制成层压薄板

laminated brush 叠片电刷

laminated coating 多层涂层，分层覆盖层

laminated core 叠片式铁芯

laminated flat torsion spring 多片组合式扭杆弹簧（亦称叶片扭杆弹簧，由若干片两端固定在四方孔套内的扁钢片组成）

laminated gasket 层合式垫片（如汽缸垫）

laminated glass 夹层玻璃（中间夹有高强度、高透明度塑胶膜的多层安全玻璃）

laminated iron cored coils 层叠铁芯线圈

laminated leaf-spring 多片式钢板弹簧

laminated piston ring 薄片组合式活塞环，多片组合式活塞环

laminated plastics 层压塑料

laminated plywood 多层胶合板，层板

laminated safety glass 夹层安全玻璃（由两片或两片以上的玻璃用一层或数层有机材料胶合层黏结在一起的安全玻璃）

laminated screen （汽车驾驶室的）夹层风窗玻璃

laminated shim 叠层薄垫，调整垫

片，层叠填隙片

laminated spring （汽车用的）钢板弹簧（见 leaf spring①）

laminated structure 层状结构，胶合板结构

laminated windshield（glass） 夹层风窗玻璃（用有机胶料将几层玻璃胶合而成，一旦破碎，碎片不易伤人，且光学性能符合风窗玻璃性能要求的高级夹层玻璃）

laminated wood 胶合板，叠层木板，层压板，叠层板，层板

laminating ①覆有特殊涂层的薄板 ②覆有特殊塑料膜面的膜压件

lamination ①分层，成层，叠层，叠合 ②薄层，薄板 ③层状结构 ④（构成磁场铁芯的）软铁薄片 ⑤沿圆周面的胎面波状花纹，（胎面的）周圈流水花纹

lamp aperture 灯孔（车身板件上的前照灯或尾灯的安装孔）

lamp bar ①灯架支杆，灯架撑条 ②灯架（指装在车头前方、用于支撑改装时新加装的强光灯具的支架，有的就是一根不锈钢杆）

lamp bayonet holder 卡口灯座（= bayonet base）

lamp black 炭黑，灯黑（= carbon）

lamp blackening 灯泡发黑（因灯丝金属蒸发，沉积于玻璃泡内壁）

lamp bracket ①车灯托架（lamp mounting bracket）②灯泡座

lamp bulb 灯泡

lamp cluster （装在同一个外壳内的）组合灯（如：在同一灯壳内装有制动灯、转向灯等的尾灯）

lamp cord 灯线

lamp drive module 灯光（电路）驱动模块

lamp-driven circuit 灯具开关电路

lamp driver 灯具开关装置

lamp failure sensor 车灯故障传感器（通过对灯泡电路电流值的检测，发出车灯不亮或断丝信号的传感器件）

lamp failure warning lamp （装在仪表板上的）车灯故障警报灯

lamp fitting 电灯附件（= lamp armature）

lamp fuse 灯用熔断丝

lamp glass 灯玻璃，前照灯配光镜（= headlamp lens, headlamp glass）

lamp lens 车灯玻璃，前照灯配光镜

lamp moulding （汽车）车灯玻璃嵌圈，前照灯配光镜边框（= headlamp glass rim, bezel of headlamp）

lamp mounting bracket 车灯安装支架（= lamp bracket）

lamp oil 灯油，煤油

lamp reflector 灯反射镜

lamp sealed beam unit （前照灯）密封式灯芯总成

lamp socket dimmer 前照灯灯座（内的远、近光）变阻器

lamp switch knob 灯开关钮

lamp unit （灯玻璃、灯芯与反射镜座封在一起成一整体）前照灯总成，灯总成（亦称 light unit）

lamp wire 灯线，灯丝

lamp wiring 灯光配线，灯光线路，灯光线

LAN 局域网（见 local area network）

Lanchester anti-vibrator 兰彻斯特减振机构（亦称 Lanchester balancer，以发明者 F·W Lanchester 命名，由曲轴通过中间齿轮带动的角速度与曲轴相等，而旋转方向彼此相反的两个齿轮及其重物所产生的离心力合力平衡发动机一级往复惯性力，进而通过上述两个齿轮带动的以二倍曲轴角速度旋转的两个齿轮及其重物所产生的离心力合力平衡二级往复惯性力的机构，但其结构复杂，一般平衡一级往复惯性力已足够，故很少使用）

Lancia S.P.A （意大利）兰西亚

股份公司（菲亚特子公司）
land access （公路的）进出口，进出口引线
land access road 引线道路，便道（交通量非常小，主要是地区性小路、乡镇道路、县级公路的辅助线等）
land-and-water 水陆两用的，两栖的
landau 半篷式轿车（车身后部为可收叠的顶篷，美多称 landaulet 或 landaulette）
landau-coupe 后部为可收叠式活顶篷的两门单排座轿车
landau-limousine 驾驶区与乘员区带隔壁的后部活顶式豪华轿车
landau-sedan 后部活顶式四门双排座轿车
land between grooves （活塞）槽岸，槽脊（两环槽之间的活塞外圆表面，见 land②）
land carriage 陆（上）运（输）
land conveyance 陆路运输工具
land cruiser ①（日丰田公司）四轮驱动越野车的商品名（见 Jeep）②长途公共汽车
land diameter 活塞环槽岸直径（活塞环槽之间的活塞外圆面直径）
land engine ①陆用发动机（陆上机械用，以区别于车用发动机）②农、林业机械用发动机
land implement 农、林用拖挂式机具
landing gear （半挂车与牵引车分离后，其前端的可收放或拆下的）落地支架
landing leg （半挂车与牵引车分离后其前端的）落地支腿（可收放式拆下，有时带有小轮可作有限移动，亦称 landing gear）
landing vehicle 登陆车辆
landline 陆上运输线
land locomotion soil characteristics 越野行驶时的土壤通过特性
land locomotive ①重型（指超过法定质量的）农、林用牵引车，农、林用拖拉机②农业机械用牵引发动机
land-mobile communication 车-地通信（指行驶中的车辆与车站等地面固定点间的无线电通信）
land mobile radio service 地-车无线电联系（车站等地面固定点与行驶车辆之间的无线电服务，简称 LMRS）
land of valve 阀门的锥面（阀门的密封面）
land Rover （英国 Rover 公司）四轮驱动越野车的商品名（见 Jeep）
landscaped thoroughfare 林荫大道；风景区干道，游览区道路
land speed 车速，（水陆两用汽车的）陆地行驶速度
land tractor 农、林业用牵引车，农、林业用拖拉机（有法定质量限制并不准在公路上行驶）
land transport 陆路运输，陆上运输（= overland transportation, surface transportation）
land vehicle 地面车辆，陆地车辆（= ground vehicle, surface vehicle）
lane ①行车带，行车道，车道 ②通道
lane capacity 车道通行能力（在不出现明显延滞的情况下，一条车道可以通行所规定车速的车辆的最大数目）
lane change （汽车的）变换车道，改变车道，换车道（如：由快车道换入慢车道）
lane change maneuvers test 车道变换操纵机动性试验（车道变换操作试验，通过驾驶员实践感觉来评价车辆变换车道时的操纵性）
lane-changing and passing performance 车道变换和超车性能

lane-control-capable vehicle 具有行车路线保持与控制能力的车辆［一般指具有"线路保持"（lane-keeping）或称"线路跟随"（lane-following）系统的车辆］

lane departure detection system 车道偏离感测系统

lane departure warning system 车道偏离警报系统（简称LDWS）

lane-directional control signal 车道通行方向控制信号

lane-following ①（汽车）车道跟随（指在驾驶中沿着车道行驶，不偏离车道）②（在自动驾驶系统中，指汽车）自动沿目标车道行驶（的能力）

Lane Keep Assistance System 见LKAS

lane-keeping assist torque （车道保持系统作用于转向系的）车道保持助力转向转矩（见LKAS）

lane keeping system 行驶车道保持系统（当根据摄像系统的信息确认车辆偏离预定车道时，电子控制模块即通过动力转向系统使车辆回到要求的车道行驶）

lane line ①车道分界线，路面分道线，车道边界线②［美］路面上的纵向警告、导向等标志线（＝英traffic line）

lane mark 车道标线，车道线

lane occupancy 车道占用率（车道交通量）

lane-off alarm （汽车在高速公路上高速行驶时）偏离（既定的）车道（时车道偏离警报系统发出的）警报

lane recognizing 车道认知传感器

lane separator （同向）车道分隔带，（同向）车流之间的分隔带

lane tracking performance 车道保持性能（跟踪所确定的车道行驶的性能）

lane-use control marking （在交叉口驶入引道处设置的）车道控制使用路面标志（为了补充车道指定标志，而设在交叉口进入部分的路面标志）

lane-use control sign （交叉口处）车道控制使用标志（指示该车道的允许行驶方向用的标志，简称lane-usesign）

langley 蓝勒（太阳辐射能通量单位，克·卡/厘米^2）

lanora air cell （某些形式的柴油机的）雷诺瓦氏空气室（位于汽缸盖内的狭长凹窝，垂直于汽缸轴线并在主燃烧室的对面，喷油嘴喷入的燃油一部分被聚在该凹窝中而产生类似于点火的效果，但严格地说，雷诺瓦氏空气室并不是预燃室。带有这种空气室的缸盖称Lanova head，这种燃烧室称Lanova combustion chamber）

lantern ①灯，提灯；信号灯，信号台②幻灯机③滚柱小齿轮，钝齿齿轮（不倒角）④润滑环

lap ①（涂）漆（＝lacquer）②研磨工具（＝lapper）③研磨剂，研磨膏（＝lapping compound）④重叠，搭接（＝overlap）⑤搭接边，搭接部分，重叠部分⑥（试验车道等的）一圈，（电缆等的）一圈⑦研配，研磨，研合，磨光⑧卷叠⑨在车道上跑一圈⑩（汽车乘员取坐姿时，腰至膝盖间的大）腿（上表）面

lap and diagonal belt （汽车乘员的）横跨大腿面并从肩部斜跨胸部的）三点式（整根）安全带（＝lap-and-shoulder belt，lap/shoulder safety belt）

lap belt ①横跨大腿面或臀部的两点式安全带②（组合式）腿-肩三点式安全带

lap-ended piston ring 叠口活塞环，

搭接切口活塞环
lap in cross-over position (滑阀)换向位置的重叠度
lap joint ①搭接，搭接头 ②（活塞气环的）搭接式切口
lap joint front axle 叠接式（可伸缩）前桥（＝lap style axle）
laplace transform 拉普拉斯变换
laplacian 拉普拉斯算子
lapped ①搭接的，重叠的 ②磨砂的（玻璃），研磨的
lap (ped) butt （端）搭接（＝overlap butt）
lapped finish 研磨加工，研磨的表面粗糙度
lapper ①研磨机，精研机（＝lapping machine）②研磨工具，研具，配研工具（＝lapping tool）
lapping ①搭接，重叠，覆盖 ②研磨，抛光 ③绕（线，带等）
lapping allowance 研磨加工留量
lapping compound 研磨剂，研磨膏
lapping finish 最后研磨加工，研磨精加工
lapping-in （一零件与另一零件）对磨，磨合
lapping liquid 研磨液
lapping rejects 磨屑，研磨屑
lap riveting 搭接铆（合），互搭铆接
lap room （车厢内座椅间的乘员）膝部（活动）空间
lap round window ①大围角（前后）风窗玻璃 ②（汽车）大曲面前（后）风窗玻璃
lap -sash seatbelt 横跨膝上的腰腹安全带
lap seam 搭接缝
lapse of time 时间迟差
lapse rate 温度（气压等）下降梯度，温度（气压）直减率
laps on a test track 在试验跑道上行驶的圈数

lap splice 互搭接头
lap style axle 叠接式车桥（＝lap joint front axle）
lap time （跑道上）跑一圈的时间
lap weld (ing) 搭接焊，搭焊
lap winding 叠线法；叠绕组；叠绕
lard 猪油滑脂（用猪油精制，攻丝套扣等作业使用）
large arrow sign 大箭头标志（急弯或危险的 T 形或 Y 形交叉口处指示转弯用的标志）
large bus 大型客车（中国规定车长大于 10m 的客车）
large calorie 千卡，大卡（＝great calorie, kilocalorie）
large-capacity 大容量的
large-capacity valve 大流量阀
large city bus 大型城市客车
large cross-section tire 大横断面轮胎
large displacement RC engine 大排量转子发动机（大排量旋转活塞发动机）
large-duty ①高生产率的 ②大型的
large intercity bus 大型长途客车
large mixed fleet 大型混合车队
large motor transportation enterprises 大型汽车运输企业（中国规定所有营运汽车全年完成换算周转量在 10000 万 t·km 及以上、车辆保有量在 600 辆及以上的汽车运输企业）
large private bus 大型自用客车（用于运送本公司职工上下班和其他公务）
large research safety vehicle 大型安全研究车（美国运输部在 RSV 小型轿车安全研究车的基础上，提出以 chevrolet 为基准的大型家用轿车的安全试验车，简称 LRSV，参见 research safety vehicle）
large-scale 大规模的，大型的，大尺度的，大量的，大批的，大比例尺的

large-scale experiment ①大规模的试验 ②放大尺寸的模型试验

large scale integrated circuit 大规模集成电路（简称 LSI, 亦写作 large scale integration circuit）

large-scale test ①大规模试验 ②大尺寸（大比例尺）的模型试验

large sightseeing bus 大型观光客车（用于运送乘客观光游览，视野开阔、乘坐舒适、设备齐全）

large size bearing 大型轴承（外径 180~800mm）

large-size（d） 大型的，大号的，大尺寸的

large tail end muffler 大口径尾管消声器

large-tonnage 大吨位的，大产量的

large truck fleet 重型货车车队

large（-volume）output 大量生产，大量输出

L-arm （某些麦弗逊滑柱型悬架的）L形下控制臂（= lower control Larm）

laser 激光（light amplification by stimulated emission of radiation 的简称，为可产生接近单色和高度相干光束）

laser altimeter 激光测高仪（测定地面平面度等）

laser and holographic inspection method 激光全息摄影检查法

laser anticollision technology 激光防撞技术

laser beam 激光束

laser diagnostics（for combustion process） （燃烧过程）激光诊断分析

laser doppler 激光多普勒移动速度测定仪（由激光利用多普勒原理测定移动速度）

laser doppler anemometer 激光多普勒风速仪（简称 LDA）

laser doppler velocimetry 激光多普勒测速法（一般用于速度、距离等测量，简称 LDV）

laser-electric arc compound welding 激光-电弧复合焊

laser fuel ignition 可燃混合气激光点火

laser gyroscope 激光陀螺仪（激光沿环形光路传播时，若使光学系转动某一角度，则激光左右两次通过环路的时间将产生差异。根据这一差值测定转角的陀螺仪称为激光陀螺仪，可分为环形共振器型的 ring laser gyroscope 和光纤干涉型的 optical fibre laser gyroscope 两大类）

laser hardening 激光硬化（工艺）

laser holographic measurement of vibration 激光全息测振 [指用激光做相干光源，运用全息照相技术测定机件的应力应变场（形变场）、振型、刚度、疲劳裂纹等]

laser holography 激光全息摄影（指利用激光的可干涉性，记录并再现物体的立体影像的技术）

laser-ignited engine 激光点火发动机（激光光束点火的内燃机）

laser-induced combustion 激光致生燃烧（由激光点燃的燃烧）

laser infrared ray 4 wheel（alignment）system 激光红外线四轮定位系统

las（er）ing 产生激光（的），激光作用

lasering heat treatment 激光热处理（利用高功率的激光束，对金属表面进行局部高速加热和高速冷却的热处理新工艺）

laser interferometer 激光干涉仪

laser lighting system 激光照明系统（亦称 lighting system based on laser, 荧光粉将激光二极管发射的激光转变为可见光，据称其光强度为 LED 的 1000 倍，但能耗仅为 LED 的 1/2）

laser machining 激光加工（激光的功率密度极高，其值可达 10^7~10^{11}

W/cm², 温度可高达万摄氏度以上, 任何坚硬材料都将瞬时急剧熔化和蒸发, 并产生强烈的冲击波, 使熔化物质爆炸式地喷射去除)

laser measurement system 激光量测装置 (如: 用激光干涉仪等量测画线板等的平直度)

laser metrology 激光计量学

laser optics 激光光学

laser processing 激光加工

laser quenching 激光淬火

laser radar 激光雷达 (在汽车上用于测定障碍物及其距离和接近速度等)

laser scanning inspection system 激光扫描检测系统

laser scoring 激光刻线, 激光刻制

laser surface treatment 激光表面处理

laser transmitter 激光发射器

laser velocimetry 激光测速法

laser weld 激光焊接 (亦称 laser beam welding, laser welding)

laser welder 激光焊接机 (亦称 laser welding apparatus, laser welding machine)

lash 空隙, 游隙, 余隙, 自由间隙 (=[美] free play)

lash adjuster 间隙调整装置 (如: ①齿轮配合背隙调整装置②制动蹄片与制动鼓间的间隙调整装置, = lash adjusting device)

lashing ①(捆绑用的)捆索, 绑绳, 链条②清除岩石

lashing eye 车上供绳索穿过或固定的带孔眼的捆绑用凸耳或凹缘

lashing hook 捆索挂钩, 牵引索挂钩

lasting 持久的, 长久的, 耐久的, 坚固的, 稳定的, 耐磨的, 固定的, 永存的, 延长的

lasting accuracy 持久精度

lasting quality 耐久性, 持久性

last station memory (车用收音机/电视机的)关机台位记忆装置 (开机时可自动接至该台)

last term 末项

last war car 战后生产的汽车 (post war car 一般指第二次世界大战后生产的汽车)

LATAC 横向加速度 (lateral acceleration 的简称)

latch ①闩, 插销; 搭扣, 挂钩; 碰销, 弹簧锁, 掣子, 棘爪, 挡器, 卡铁 ②(计算机)锁存器 (指由输入信号来控制置位和复位的双稳态电路, 它可维持某一位置或状态, 直到由外部手段将其复位到前一种状态) ③闩上, 栓上, 上插销; 封闭, 闭锁, 锁住

LATCH 儿童安全座椅的低位固定点和系带 (lower anchors and tethers for children 的简称, 美国联邦标准规定的儿童安全座椅固定方式)

latch clutch 掣爪式离合器

latch gear 锁销装置 (操纵棘爪或锁销的机构)

latch(ing) pillar 门锁立柱 (轿车车身构件中的 B 立柱或 C 立柱, 因车门闩碰板装在该立柱上, 故名)

late burning 后燃, 迟燃

late closing of valve 气门(延)迟关(闭)(= retarded closing of valve)

lated sparking 延迟跳火

late ignition 延迟点火, 点火迟后 (参见 full retard)

late injection 迟后喷射

late model 最新型 (= recent model)

latence 见 latency

latency ①等待时间, 等数时间, 取数时间 (指等待来自存储器的信息被送入运算单元的延迟时间, 亦称 latence) ②(计算机控制系统指令控制器的)等待时间 (指令控制器开始调用数据和实际开始传送数据

之间的时间间隔,亦称 waiting time)③潜伏,潜在④潜伏物,潜在因素

latent chemical energy　化学潜能

latent energy　潜能(如:势能,位能)

latent fault　潜在故障(已存在,但未暴露或未发现的故障)

latent heat　潜热(物质由固态变为同温度液态或由液态变为同温度气态所需的热量,有熔化潜热、液化潜热和汽化潜热之分)

latent heat of evaporation　蒸发潜热(亦称 latent heat of vaporization)

lateral　横向的(指垂直于速度矢量方向。注意:对车辆来说,"lateral 横向"与"side 侧向"是有区别的,前者指运动坐标系 y_0 轴方向,后者指汽车坐标系 y_0 轴方向。见 moving axis system 和 vehicle axis system)

lateral acceleration　横向加速度(质心加速度沿 y_0 轴方向的分量,见 moving axis system)

lateral acceleration at neutral steering-point　中性转向点横向加速度值(前、后桥侧偏角差与横向加速度关系曲线上,斜率为零处的横向加速度值)

lateral acceleration gain　横向加速增益

lateral acceleration model following control system　横向加速度(数学)模型追随控制系统

lateral adhesion coefficient　横向附着系数(在给定工作点下,自由滚动车轮横向力系数所能达到的最大值,参见 lateral force coefficient)

lateral adhesive force　侧向附着力(= lateral adhesion force,轮胎与路面的侧向附着系数与轮胎垂直载荷的乘积)

lateral area of a cone　锥的侧面积

lateral area of a cylinder　柱的侧面积

lateral axis　横轴,横轴线,y 轴线

lateral balance　(车轮等的)横向平衡

lateral bending　横向弯曲

lateral buckling　横向翘曲

lateral clearance　①侧向间隙,横空隙,侧隙 ②侧向净空(同向或对向行驶的两辆汽车的横向间距)

lateral control force　见 cornering force

lateral damping　横向(振动)阻尼

lateral deflection　横向挠曲,横向偏转

lateral deformation　横向变形

lateral edge of a prism　棱柱体的侧棱

lateral face　侧面,横向表面

lateral flexibility　横向挠性

lateral flexure　侧向挠曲,横向弯曲

lateral force　横向力

lateral force coefficient　横向力系数(横向力与垂直负荷的比值)

lateral force compliance camber　①(汽车的)横向力致生车轮侧倾现象(在横向力的作用下,由于转向机构、悬架系统等的柔性变形,使车轮产生侧倾或对原有的外倾角改变的现象) ②(车轮的)横力致生侧倾角(由于上述现象,车轮产生的侧倾角)

lateral force compliance camber coefficient　(汽车车轮的)横向力致生侧倾系数(即单位横向力使车轮产生的侧倾角,=侧倾角 deg./横向力 kg)

lateral force compliance camber steer　(汽车的)横向力致生车轮侧倾转向现象(由于横向力致生车轮侧倾而引起车轮转向角的改变现象,参见 lateral force compliance camber)

lateral force compliance effect　(汽车车轮的)横力致生效应(指汽车车轮的

在横向力的作用下，路面对车轮的反作用力，引起车轮的侧倾角等变化和悬架柔性变形的现象)

lateral force compliance steer (汽车的) 横力致生转向 (在横向力的作用下，由于悬架系统、转向机构、转向轮等的柔性变形，改变转向角的现象)

lateral force compliance steer coefficient (汽车车轮的) 横力致生转向系数 (车轮转向角的改变度与所受横向力之比，deg/g，即每产生1重力加速度 g 的横向力引起的转向角改变量)

lateral force of tire 轮胎横向力 (路面作用在轮胎上的力沿 Y' 轴方向的分量，见 tire axis system)

lateral force variation 轮胎横向力的变动 (简称LFV)

lateral grip (轮胎的) 横向抓着力 (指轮胎胎面与路面间的侧向附着力，决定轮胎在受到外来的方向性干扰影响时，保持其行进方向，或正常转向控制的能力)

lateral G sensor 横向加速度传感器 (亦称 left and right accelerating force sensor)

lateral impact 侧面碰撞，侧向冲击 (亦称 side crash)

lateral inclination 侧向倾斜，横向倾斜

lateral instability 横向不稳定性

lateral isolation sheet (液罐车液罐内的) 横隔板

lateral jerk 横向冲越，横向加速度率

lateral leaf-type stabilizer spring (车身) 侧向稳定板簧 (起横向稳定作用的钢板型弹簧)

lateral link 横拉杆，横向连接杆，横向撑杆，横撑

lateral load 横向荷载

lateral load transfer 荷载横向转移 (质量的横向转移，左、右轮间的荷载再分配)

lateral motion 横向运动

lateral oil seal (转子发动机) 端面油封 (= side oil seal)

lateral oscillations 横向振动，横向摆动 (= lateral vibration)

lateral plan 侧视图

lateral PNP transistor 横向PNP型晶体管

lateral pressure 横向压力

lateral rib 横肋

lateral rigidity 横向刚性

lateral road ①横道，侧路 ② (汽车悬架系统中的) 横向推力杆 (在车轴与车架或车身间横向布置的推力杆)

lateral rod (悬架装置的) 横向控制杆 (横向布置，确定左、右车轮位置，承受横向力作用的杆件)

lateral runout (车轮，制动盘，转子等的) 横向摆动 (见 waddle)

lateral section 横断面，横剖图

lateral shake 横向摇动，横向振动；车身横向低频振动

lateral slip 横向偏移量 (在侧滑试验台上测得的直行轮胎单位滚动距离的横向偏移量，用m/km，mm/m表示)

lateral stability 横向稳定性 (指车辆抵抗各种横向力的作用按驾驶方向前进的性能)

lateral stability boundary 横向稳定区域

lateral stabilizer 横向稳定杆

lateral stabilizer shock absorber 横向稳定减振器 (减少车身侧倾的稳定装置)

lateral stiffness ① (轮胎的) 横向刚度，横向刚性 [轮胎接地中心沿横向，即 Y' 轴方向 (见 tire axis system) 移动的单位增量，所对应的横向力的增量] ② (车身等结构

的）侧向刚度（抵抗侧向冲击的能力）

lateral thrush 横向推力

lateral tie-rod （独立悬架前转向轮转向拉杆系中，中央横拉杆两侧的）横拉杆

lateral tilt 横向倾斜

lateral velocity 横向速度（质心速度沿 y_0 轴的分量，见 moving axis system）

lateral vibration 横向振动（= lateral oscillations）

lateral view 侧视图，侧视

late release （绿灯）推迟显示，延迟关闭

later-model 新型的（= new-model）

late spark 延迟点火（= ignition retard, late sparking, delayed firing）

late timing 延时，延期，（特指点火、气门关闭、喷油时刻）延迟

latex 胶乳，橡胶乳液（天然橡胶原料）

latex sponge 海绵（状）橡皮

lath 板条（狭的平板）

latices 橡胶乳液（latex 的复数）

latitude ①纬线，纬度 ②活动余地，宽（容）度，范围

lattice ①格子，格栅，晶格，栅格，点阵，串列，网络，网络结构，支撑桁架，承重结构 ②做成格状，缀合

latticed 格状的，网格状的

lattice frame 格构桁架，格形骨架，格构架（亦称 lattice framework）

lattice point 格（子）点，阵点，网点

lattice structure 晶格结构，网格结构，格状结构，点阵结构

lattice translation vector 晶格平移矢量

lattice truss 格构桁架

lattice type frame 桁格构架式车架，网格桁架式车架（由上、下、左、右四根边纵梁及连接上、下纵梁的多根短竖直梁和横梁、斜梁组成，美称 trass construction type frame）

launch ①发射，起飞，弹射 ②创办，开办，发起

launcher vehicle 火箭发射车，自行式火箭发射装置

lava grey 火山灰（车身颜色）

law 规律，定律，法则，规则，守则，规程，法律

lawful driver 有执照的驾驶员

law of conservation of energy 能量守恒定律

law of dynamical similarity 动态相似法则（参见 dynamical similarity）

law of errors 误差律

law of highway transportation 公路运输法规（由国家机关制定的关于公路运输方面的规范性法律文件的总称）

law of the perfect machine 理想机械定律（输入该机械的功等于由该机械输出的功）

lay-by ①（干线道路）路侧停车带，备用车道 ②超车或避车车道

lay-days ①装卸时间（= lay time）②停工（停运）天数（= days out of service）

layer ①层，分层，层次 ②敷设机 ③涂层，焊层

layered structure 层状结构

layer metal 多层金属轴瓦（如巴氏合金轴瓦）

layer of carbon 积炭层

layer of scale 结垢层，水垢层，硬垢壳（= scale crust）

layer of solid lubricant 固态薄膜润滑层（固态润滑膜，由于极压添加剂与轴承表面反应，形成的一种极薄固态润滑层，掺有这种添加剂的滑油称为极限-压力润滑油）

layer short （线圈）层间短路

3 layers safety protection （日产公司

的）三重安全防护（理念）[即：通过信息防护（information protection system）、控制防护（control protection system）和碰撞防护（collision protection system）三道防护系统，确保车辆乘员安全]

layer structure 层状结构

layer thickness 层厚度（如镀层厚度、涂层厚度等）

laying-up 封存（汽车），搁置停用

lay length （绳索）捻距

lay of land 地形

layout ①布局，方案，草案，草图设计，设计方案，示意图 ②布置，安排，设计，规划 ③画线，画样，放样

layout circle 配置图

layout design 草图设计，图纸设计，电路图设计

layout plan 规划，设计，平面图

layover ①（公共交通）终点站停车处 ②旅行中途逗留时间

layrub coupling 雷鲁伯挠性万向节，（橡胶弹性元件挠性万向节，两轴的接合盘间夹有四块模制橡胶块，亦称 layrub joint）

lay shaft （位于变速器输入轴与输出轴之间并与之平行的）中间轴（通过齿轮组将输入轴的运动体给输出轴并提供其所需的速比，= intermediate shaft，美称 countershaft）

layshaft box 中间轴型齿轮变速器（= countershaft transmission，见 layshaft）

layshaft drive gear 中间轴主动齿轮

layshaft gear cluster （变速器）中间轴齿轮组（中间轴宝塔齿轮）

lay up ①扭绞，绞合 ②接头，接合处 ③敷层，成层，一层层地铺上去（如制作玻璃纤维强化塑料壳体时，将玻璃纤维编织层和树脂层一层一层地敷上去）

Lazy Locking （遥控车门）自动锁闭系统（商品名）

lazy pinion 空转小齿轮（惰轮）

lazy tongs ①惰钳，长柄钳（用来夹远处的物件）②（自由活塞燃气发生器的）同步机构

LB ①一种炭黑的商品名（Lamp Black 的简称）②救生艇（lifeboat）③轻型托架（light bracket）④（电话）占线（line busy）⑤本机电池（local battery）

lb 磅（英制质量单位，pound）

L-bar L 形不等边角钢

lb-cal 磅卡（英制热量单位，pound-calorie）

LBE 稀燃发动机（lean-burn engine）

lbf 磅力（pounds force）

lbf/in² 磅力每平方英寸（英制压力，应力单位，$1 \text{lbf/in}^2 = 0.0703 \text{kgf/cm}^2 = 6894.76\text{N/m}^2 = 0.06895\text{bar} = 51.715\text{mmHg} = 0.703\text{mW} \cdot \text{G} = 27.72\text{in.W} \cdot \text{G} = 0.068\text{atm}$）

lb/ft³ 磅每立方英尺（英制密度单位，$1\text{lb/ft}^3 = 0.00058\text{lb/in}^3 = 0.1606 \text{lb/imp gal} = 0.01205 \text{ton/yd}^3 = 0.01602\text{t/m}^3$）

lb-ft 磅·英尺（pound-foot）

lb/HPh 磅每英制马力小时（发动机油耗率的英制单位，$1\text{lb/HPh} = 447.8\text{g/PSh} = 608.6\text{g/kW} \cdot \text{h}$）

lb/imp·gal 磅每英加仑（英制密度单位，$1\text{lb/imp} \cdot \text{gal} = 0.0036 \text{lb/in}^3 = 6.228 \text{lb/ft}^3 = 0.07507\text{ton/yd}^3 = 0.09976\text{t/m}^3$）

lbm 磅（质量）（pounds mass）

lb. per sq. in. g. 磅每平方英寸（表压）（pound per square inch gauge）

lbt 磅推力（pounds thrust）

L-Cap 锂离子电容器型蓄电池（商品名）

LCA technique 寿命循环评估技术（life cycle assessment technique 的简

称)

LCC 寿命周期成本 (life cycle costs)

L-C circuit 电感-电容电路

LCD module 液晶显示模块 (liquid crystal display module 的简称)

LCFB (汽车碰撞试验用) 装有负荷传感器的固定障壁 (load cell fixed barrier)

LCL ①少于一车货物 (零担货, less than carload) ②局部的, 当地的, 本机的, 本车的 (local) ③控制下限 (lower control limit)

LCM 照明控制模块 (lighting control module 的简称, 指汽车照明控制计算机)

L-combustion chamber L 形燃烧室 (进、排气门侧置的汽油机燃烧室)

lcr (LCR) 低压缩比 (low compression ratio 的简称)

LCR meter 电感电容电阻测定计, 万用表

LCS 变换车道支持系统 (Lane Changing Support 的简称。变换车道时若雷达或摄像系统测得欲换上的车道上有车辆或其他障碍物时, 即发出声响和灯光警报)

LC vibrator 电感电容振荡器 (利用线圈电感和电容器电容产生电气共振的振荡电路, 用于点火正时灯等)

LCW AUTOMOTIVE (美) 林肯汽车厂 (Lincoln Works -Automotive 的简称)

LCX 同轴泄漏电缆 (参见 leakage coaxial cable)

LDA 激光多普勒风速仪 (laser doppler anemometer)

LDC ①下死点, 下止点 (lower dead centre) ②长途电话, 长途通话 (long distance call)

LDDS 车道偏离探测系统 (lane-deviation detection system 的简称)

LDPE 低密度聚乙烯 (low density polyethylene)

L/D ratio 长度与直径比

LDV ①激光多普勒测速法 (laser doppler velocimetry 的简称) ②激光多普勒速度计 (laser-doppler velocimeter)

LDWS 车道偏离警报系统 (lane departure warning system 的简称, 这类警报系统种类多, 一般都是使用各种传感元件持续跟踪检测白色车道标线, 一旦发现在驾驶者未发出转向、超车或改换车道指示信号的情况下汽车偏离原行驶车道时即发出声响-灯光警报。某些 LDWS, 当汽车在因修路而封闭对向车道以致在狭窄的单车道上双向行驶时, 可通过开关将其报警功能暂时关闭)

leach ①沥滤, 浸滤 (用水漂滤, 溶滤, 浸析, 浸出, 取) ②沥滤器

leaching reagent 浸出剂

lead ①导线 ②导管 ③导柱 (等引导件) ④铅 (Pb), 铅制品, 铅锤, 铅封, 汽油的含铅抗爆添加剂 ⑤导程 (螺栓等的螺纹的导程指相邻两螺纹顶间的距离, 圆柱螺旋线的导程指任一条螺旋线与该圆柱面一条直线的两个相邻交点之间的距离, 螺杆的导程即其每一转的升程, 或螺距) 螺距 ⑥引导, 导向 ⑦提前, 超前, 前置 ⑧ (汽车因转向系失调, 装载不均匀, 胎压不等等原因造成的) 行驶侧偏趋向 ⑨ (发动机进气门的) 提前开启 (角)

lead acid battery 铅酸蓄电池 (指以硫酸水溶液为电解液, 铅锑合金栅板和二氧化铅活性物质 PbO_2 制成的正极板, 铅锑合金栅板和海绵状铅活性物质 Pb 制成的负极板等组成的可充电式蓄电池, 目前汽车起动系、点火系的电源均为这种蓄电池, 亦称 lead and acid battery, 简称

lead battery)
lead-acid cell 铅酸单体电池（一般车用蓄电池由数个单体电池串联而成）
lead-acid cobalt battery 铅酸钴蓄电池
lead alkyl antiknock compound 烷基铅抗爆化合物，烷基铅抗爆剂
lead alloy 铅合金
lead and cadmium alloy （轴瓦用）铅镉合金
lead and lag （指气门的）提前（开启）和延迟（关闭）
lead angle ①超前角，提前角 ②导程角（圆柱螺旋线的切线与端平面之间所夹的锐角；对于斜齿轮是指分度圆螺旋线的导程角，对于渐开线齿轮是指基圆螺旋线的导程角）
lead-antiknock additive 铅基抗爆震添加剂
lead-antimony grid （铅蓄电池极板的）铅锑合金板栅（含锑 Sb 量一般为 5% ~7%，加锑是为了增加板栅强度和改善浇铸性能，将铅粉置于空气中氧化成氧化铅，加入一定的添加剂和硫酸溶液调和成膏状，涂于板栅上，干燥后，即为蓄电池的极板，简称 lead grid，亦称 lead grill）
lead-base alloy 铅基合金
lead base bearing alloy 铅基轴承合金
lead bath 铅浴，镀铅槽
lead bath quenching 铅浴淬火
lead-bearing gasoline 含铅汽油（= leaded gasoline, lead-containing gasoline）
lead brass 铅黄铜
lead bronze 铅青铜
lead-bronze bearing 铅青铜轴承，铅青铜轴瓦（含铅 15% ~20% 的铜合金，耐压，抗磨）
lead-cable automatic guidance system 引导电缆式自动导向系统
lead coating 镀铅层，铅覆盖层，铅包皮
lead-containing gasoline 含铅汽油（= leaded gasoline, lead-bearing gasoline）
lead-covered steel sheet 镀铅钢板
lead deposit 铅沉积（由蓄电池极板上离析出的或加铅汽油中分离出的铅微粒及铅化合物微粒形成的沉积物）
lead dioxide 二氧化铅（= lead peroxide）
leaded ①加铅的 ②铅包皮的 ③镀铅的
leaded fuel 加四乙基铅燃油，加四乙基铅汽油，加铅汽油（= ethylized fuel）
leaden sleeve 铅套，铅衬套
leader ①领导者，指挥者，（车队）首车 ②导管，导杆，导轨 ③丝杠，导螺杆 ④导程
lead error 导程误差（螺距误差）
lead ethyl 铅乙基，（二）乙基铅 [Pb (C$_2$H$_5$)$_2$]
lead fouling 铅沉积（见 lead deposit）
lead-free carbon brush （起动机用）无铅炭刷
lead-free electronic device 无接线的电子装置
lead-free fuel 无铅燃油（一般指无铅汽油）
lead-free gas 无铅汽油（[美] lead-free gasoline 的简称，英称 lead-free petrol）
lead-free plain bearing 无铅滑动轴承
lead gauge 螺距规（= lead tester）
lead glazing 铅釉（火花塞的一种故障，燃油中的铅盐熔化后，沉附于火花塞，凝固而形成黄色、褐色或绿色釉状层）

lead grill 见 lead-antimony grid
lead hardening 铅浴淬火
lead hole 导向孔（= pilot hole）
lead-in ①输入，引入 ②引入线，输入线
leading ①向前的，前面的，导向的，主导的，首要的，指导性的 ②超前，提前 ③乙基化，加铅 ④塞铅条 ⑤铅制品，铅条
leading angle ①（转子发动机转子尖端与缸面法线的）前面夹角，前夹角，超前夹角 ②提前角，超前角
leading arm ①前置臂，导臂，前臂 ②前推式纵臂（轿车前轮独立悬架纵向布置的控制臂，因该臂所支撑的前轮在其固定于车架的摆动枢轴点的前方，故名，参见后拖式纵臂 trailing arm）
leading auto company 在技术与产量上领先的汽车公司
leading axle 前轴，前桥
leading brake shoe 制动器领蹄，自紧制动蹄片（见 Leading shoe）
leading (comb) chamber ①（转子发动机的）前置燃烧室，转子工作面前置凹坑（指凹坑偏置前方）②（转子发动机的）燃烧室前部，转子工作面凹坑前端（指转子工作面凹坑的前部分）
leading curve （车辆转弯时）前导曲线（指前桥中心转向轨迹）
leading dimensions 轮廓尺寸，基本尺寸
leading edge ①（凸轮）上升面 ②（滑阀）工作棱 ③（叶片）前缘 ④（转子发动机径向密封片的）前棱 ⑤（刀具）前刃（= advancing edge）⑥（车身板件的）前边缘 ⑦（脉冲的）上升边
leading-edge scientific fields 领先边缘科学领域
leading features 主要特征
leading floating yoke （凸块式准等速万向节的）①前浮动凸块（指凸块式万向节中带有相互垂直的榫舌和凹槽的中间连接元件，故又称 tongue and groove coupling），②前浮动凸块叉（指具有与该凸块槽相配合的叉头的、与输入轴制成一体的叉形件，亦称 leading fork yoke，见 Tracta universal joint）
leading-in terminal 引入线端，引入接线柱
leading mark 方向标，标志
leading pedestrian phase 行人先走信号相
leading phase 超前相位
leading plug （转子发动机的）前置火花塞（装置在燃烧室火焰前部区域）
leading portion 前段，前部分，前导部分
lead (ing) screw 导螺杆，丝杠，推动螺杆
leading section （按运动方向的）前（端）
leading shoe 领蹄[=[美]primary shoe, forward shoe, 在领、从蹄制动器中, 当蹄张开时的转动方向与制动鼓旋转方向相同, 则称为领蹄, 领蹄具有增强制动蹄与制动鼓间压力, 亦即摩擦力的作用, 故亦称自增力蹄, 增力蹄(self-energizing shoe)。与之相对应的是从蹄 trailing shoe, 从蹄张开时的转动方向与制动鼓相反, 具有减弱制动力的作用, 故亦称减力蹄]
leading shoe and trailing shoe brake 领从蹄式制动器（鼓式制动器中的一种常见形式，具有一个领蹄和一个从蹄。两制动蹄的支撑点都位于蹄的同一端，亦写作 leading-trailing shoe brake）
leading surface 先导工作面（如：凸轮上的升高面或制动器中领蹄的表面）

leading wind 顺风 [= favo(u)rable wind]

lead-in wire 引入线

leadless ①无铅的（汽油）②无引线的

lead limit switch 行程限位开关

lead-lined accumulator box 衬铅的蓄电池箱

lead lining 铅衬板

lead loading 铅补（指用车身修理专用铅料填补车身板件上的凹坑和损伤）

lead monoxide 一氧化铅（PbO，亦称 lead oxide）

lead of cam 凸轮升程（凸轮转一周，随动件被顶起的高度，= lift of cam，cam lead 与 rise of cam 不同，rise of cam 指凸轮转任意角度时，随动件被顶起的高度）

lead of screw（thread）螺纹导程（螺旋转一周，螺纹件的移动距离，与螺距 pitch 不同，如三头螺纹的导程等于螺距的三倍）

lead-on ramps 引导半挂车牵引销插入牵引车转盘式牵引架销孔的导向件

lead-out 输出，输出线

lead-oxide ①氧化铅（铅蓄电池极板原料，= lead monoxide）②铅的氧化物

lead peroxide 过氧化铅，二氧化铅（PbO_2，= lead dioxide，铅蓄电池正极板上的活性物质）

lead pipe 铅管

lead-plated 镀铅的

lead plier 长嘴平口钳

lead pollution 铅污染

lead scavenger 铅携出剂，除（氧化）铅添加剂（将某些卤化物加入四乙基铅液中，待燃烧完毕后，可随废气将氧化铅携出燃烧室外）

lead sled 铅雪橇（20 世纪 50 年代美国流行的一种特制车身造型的俗称，叫雪橇是它的线条流畅，叫铅是说它要使用大量车身修补用铅才能造出其理想的光滑线条）

lead solder ①铅焊料②铅钎焊

lead sulphate 硫酸铅（$PbSO_4$，如铅蓄电池放电后，两极板上的活性物质与电解液发生作用，都会变为硫酸铅，充电后又恢复为原来的海绵状铅和二氧化铅）

lead susceptibility （汽油）对铅的敏感度

lead switch 磁控触点开关（密封玻璃管内装有两片金属薄片式触点片，在管外磁力作用下闭合而导电，为了防止触片氧化，玻璃管内一般充有氮气）

lead tester 导程检查仪，螺距规（= lead gauge）

lead tetraethyl 四乙（基）铅 [$Pb(C_2H_5)_4$]

lead-tin overplate （薄壁轴瓦的）铅锡表面层（与轴颈直接接触的巴氏合金减磨层）

lead-tin solder 焊锡，锡钎焊

lead tolerance （汽油中的）容许含铅量，美国 ASTM 规定不得超过 1.1g/L

lead valve 片阀，舌片阀（如：小型二冲程发动机曲轴箱中，随压力差自动开闭的片阀）

lead vehicle ①飞机牵引车②先导车

lead weight （平衡车轮用的）铅平衡重块

lead wire ①铅丝②引线，引出线，接头线

lead-wire check （轴承间隙等的）铅丝检测（法）

leaf ①页，张；叶片，瓣，叶瓣②薄板，薄片，薄的金属片，箔；弹簧片③（门窗）页扇，门扉④活门，节流门⑤（螺纹规的）螺纹片，塞尺片

leaf of spring 钢板弹簧片

leaf spacer (装在钢板弹簧片间的)隔片(钢板弹簧垫片)

leaf spring 钢板弹簧(①指由多片钢板组成的整架钢板弹簧,亦称 laminated spring) ②指单片式钢板弹簧(亦称 single leaf)

leaf spring bushing (汽车)钢板弹簧(卷耳孔内的)衬套

leaf spring eye 钢板弹簧卷耳

leaf spring rate test 钢板弹簧刚度试验(包括静刚度和动刚度两个试验)

leaf spring shackle 钢板弹簧吊耳(亦称 leaf spring hanger)

leaf spring sliding plate 钢板弹簧(滑动端的)支撑滑板(可更换的滑动支撑)

leaf spring sliding seat 钢板弹簧滑动座(钢板弹簧非吊耳滑动端的滑动支撑)

leaf spring U-bolt 钢板弹簧 U 形螺栓(骑马螺栓,亦称 leaf spring yoke)

leaf tin 锡箔(= tin-foil)

leaf-type spring 片簧,板簧

leaf-valve 叶片阀,片式阀,片阀(= flat valve)

leak ①泄漏,渗漏;泄放,泄流 ②渗漏处,泄漏处 ③漏出物 ④泄漏量

leakage area 泄漏面积,漏油(气)面积

leakage coaxial cable 同轴泄漏电缆(简称 LCX 电缆,沿着自动化公路敷设,传输汽车、道路之间连续出现的信息,如对汽车传达路上各种障碍等信息)

leakage current 泄漏电流

leakage flow ①泄漏流 ②泄漏流量

leakage loss 泄漏损失

leakage radiation 泄漏辐射

leakage rate 泄漏量(指密封装置中被密封流体在规定条件下泄漏的体积或质量)

leakage test 渗漏试验(密封性试验)

leak check 漏泄检查(密封性检查)

leak detector ①测漏仪 ②漏电指示器(如:短路指示器,测漏器)

leakdown rate ①(液压气门挺杆的)回降速度 ②(液压气门挺杆柱塞止回阀下油液的)回漏速度

leaker 漏油、漏水、漏气等的元件或制品

leak hole (喷油器的)溢油孔

leakiness (接头、连接件的)不紧密性,泄漏性

leaking ①渗漏的,漏出的,有漏隙的,易漏渗的(= leaky) ②透水性,渗漏,漏泄

leak-off pipe (喷油器等的)溢油管(亦称 leak off line)

leak pressure 泄漏压力(可导致泄漏的压力)

leak preventer 防漏剂

leakproof fit 密配合(防泄漏配合)

leakproofing material 防漏材料,密封材料

leak test (轮胎等的)气密性试验,渗漏试验

leak-tight 不渗漏的,密封的,无漏耗的,紧密的

leak-tight joint 紧密连接,水密连接,密封接合(= tight joint)

leaky valve 泄漏阀

lean ①倾斜,偏斜 ②坡度 ③使倾向于,使偏向于 ④使(混合气)变稀 ⑤稀的,贫的(混合气)

lean A/F sensor 稀空燃比(氧)传感器[废气氧含量传感器的一种,其输出电压信号可反映 $\lambda > 1$ 的稀混合气的实际空燃比。稀燃发动机所要求的空燃比,如:$\lambda = 1.4 \sim 1$ 的闭路控制分为勒恩斯特型(Nernst type)和限流型(limiting-current type）两类]

Lean Authority Limit Switch （美通用公司开发的混合气）稀薄极限控制开关［商品名，利用空气滤清器的温度真空开关（见 TVS）监控进气温度，防止冷机起动时混合气过稀］

lean-burn emission controlled engine 稀燃式排放控制发动机（指使用稀混合气以减少排气有害物的发动机）

lean-burn engine 稀燃发动机，稀混合气发动机（一般指使用空燃比 18∶1 以上的稀混合气的发动机，亦称 lean combustion engine）

lean burning ability （发动机的）稀燃能力，稀燃性能（指可燃用稀混合气的能力）

leanest fuel torque 燃用最稀混合气时的发动机输出转矩

lean flammability limit 稀混合气可燃极限，稀燃极限，稀燃界限（指发动机内维持火焰传播的最稀混合比极限，简称 LFL）

lean-homogeneous combustion 均质稀混合气燃烧

lean ignition limit ①稀混合气可点燃的最稀混合比极限②可点燃稀混合气的最低点火能量极限（使稀混合气达到最低点燃温度所必须提供的最小点火能量）

lean-in 向内倾

leaning ①倾斜度，坡度；倾向②贫，稀（混合气）③倾斜的，可倾的

leaning angle 倾斜角（= angle of inclination）

lean limit （混合气燃烧的）稀薄极限（参见 limit of inflammability）

lean metering 稀混合气调节

lean misfire 稀燃缺火（指使用混合气过稀时，不能点燃的现象）

lean misfire limit （混合气的）最稀失火极限，最稀点火极限

lean mixture 稀混合气（一般指 air-fuel ratio = 15～20，或 fuel-air ratio = 0.05～0.066 或 MS = 0.7～1，即在着火极限内的稀混合气，参见 poor mixture）

lean mixture limit （发动机的）稀混合气极限（指在该发动机中可以正常燃烧的混合气的最稀混合比）

lean mixture sensor 稀混合气传感器（当混合比稀于理论混合比时可向控制模块发送稀混合比信号）

lean mixture strength 稀混合气强度（简称 lean MS，见 mixture strength）

lean-out ①向外倾②使混合气变稀

lean position 使用稀混合气时的节气门开度

lean reactor 稀混合气反应器（稀燃排气净化反应器，用于稀燃发动机的废气余热二次燃烧反应 HC、CO 净化装置，不需要二次空气来补充氧气，参见 rich reactor）

lean stumble （由于混合气）过稀（而造成的发动机）不稳定运转（忽快忽慢）

learning control ①学习控制（不仅能检知和修正由于作为控制对象的零件或整机制造误差及使用老化等引起的控制特性的偏差，而且还可以检知控制对象工作环境、使用条件、运转模式乃至操作方式的变化，并确定与上述变化相对应的修正和控制模式。这一过程称为"学习"，学习过程中所确定的修正量称为学习修正量。如果每次所确定的学习修正量都能存储在控制系统的存储器中，以便在下一次同样的变化出现时，可根据该学习修正量进行修正性控制，则称该系统具有学习控制功能。具有学习控制功能的系统，能在环境与使用条件变化的情况下，仍保证系统的最佳控制）②（汽车计算机控制系统的）

学习控制（控制系统本身具有根据汽车运行条件的变化、机件磨损、系统性能变化、驾驶者操作习惯的不同等对以往的控制结果进行评价的功能，并在此评价的基础上对装置存储的控制数据或控制逻辑进行修正，以适应上述种种变化，保证控制目标值不致受到上述变化的影响。与一般自适应控制不同之处在于自适应控制的重点放在逐步适应新环境上，而学习控制则是具有"学会"并"记住"适应性控制的修正结果而在下一次的控制中直接使用能力，亦称学习能力"Learning ability"）

leased telephone line （呼叫出租汽车的）租车专用电话线

least-cost operation 最低费用运转，最低消耗运转

leather ①皮革（的），革制品（的），皮带（的）②用软皮擦③蒙皮，用皮革包盖

leather bucket 皮碗，皮涨圈（= leather cup）

leather cleaner （车身内饰）皮革及合成革制品洗涤剂

leatheret（te） 人造革

leather-grain （设备仪器等的全金属或塑料外壳的装饰性）皮革纹理表面

leather-metal case seal 皮革芯金属壳油封（金属外壳皮密封件）

leather sport seat 皮革跑车型座椅

leather substitute 人造革，假皮

leather top （活顶轿车等的）皮质车顶篷

leather-trimmed 皮革装饰的（车身构件等）

leather-trimmed wheel 皮革包覆的转向盘

leather washer 皮革垫圈

leather-wrapped 皮革包敷的，皮面的

leave angle 离去角，后悬角，后通过角（= real overhang angle，见 departure angle）

leaving home function （前照灯的）离家上车照明功能

leaving whirl velocity 出口处的涡流速度

LED 发光二极管（见 light emitting diode）

ledaloyl 铅石墨含油的合金（主要用作自润轴承）

LED day time running light 发光二极管白昼行车灯（见 day time running light）

ledebur bearing alloy 锌基轴承合金（锡17.5%，铜5.5%，其余锌）

ledeburite 莱氏体

ledge ①凸出部，架状突出物 ②凸耳，凸边，凸棱，横挡，壁架

ledge joint 搭接接合

ledgement ①展开图 ②横线条

LED headlights 发光二极管式前照灯

LED tail lamp 发光二极管式尾灯

Leeway ①（按自己所想的方式）采取行动或活动的自由度 ②（汽车行驶中承受的）风压，风压差，风压角（风压方向与行车方向的夹角）③（因风力造成的）行驶方向的偏差 ④时间上的损失，落后

leeway ①（活动）余地 ②可容许的误差 ③风压，风阻；风压角（固风压造成的侧偏角）④时间的损失 ⑤落后

left bank 左排，左边，左列（如从驾驶座看V形发动机缸体的左边）

left coil 左旋蛇管；左旋线圈；左旋绕组

left elevation 左视图

left flank 左侧面，左侧齿面

left half axle housing 左半桥壳

left-hand 左，左手的，左方的，左侧的，左旋的，左转的，靠左行驶的

left-hand air intake control lever （汽车通风系统位于转向盘左侧的）左侧新鲜空气或冷风开关及风量控制柄（美称 left side fresh air control lever）

left-hand control car 左转向盘车辆（左座驾驶车辆，用于车辆靠右行驶的国家，= left-hand drive car）

left-hand corner 左转弯（= left-hand turn）

left-hand crankshaft 左式曲轴（在直列六缸发动机中当第一缸在上止点时，从前端看，第三、四曲轴连杆轴颈在左侧，其点火顺序为 1-4-2-6-3-5）

left-hand drive （汽车等的）左座驾驶（车辆靠右行驶的国家，汽车的转向盘在驾驶室的左侧，简称 LHDR）

left-handed 左旋的，向左旋转的（反时针的，反时针旋转的，逆时针旋转的）

left-hand teeth （斜齿圆柱齿轮和涡轮或曲线齿锥齿轮的）左旋齿（指端面齿廓向反时针方向转过某一角度的齿）

left-hand-traffic 靠左行驶交通（车辆靠左行驶，转向盘装在驾驶室右侧，在英国、日本、澳大利亚、印度、新加坡等国实行）

left-hand turn 左转弯

left-in-place 留在原地的

left-lane 左车道（在多车道道路，一个方向行驶车辆的车道中最左侧的车道；若是右侧通行的双车道道路，也可指对向行驶的车道）

left-luggage office （车站）行李寄存处

left over ①剩余的，残留的 ②剩余物，残留，残留物

left-right staggered junction 左-右错位交叉口

left steering trapezoid connection 左转向梯形臂（连接转向横拉杆与左转向节）

left view 左视图

left-wheel ①汽车左转弯行驶，左转弯行走 ②左轮的

leg 腿，支腿，支柱

legal ①法律上的，法定的，合法的，正当的 ②法定权利

legal gain（in load-carrying capacity）合法超载量（法定允许超载量）

legal gross weight 法定车辆总质量（法律规定的最大允许车质量）

legal limit 法定极限（值）

legal load 法定荷载（法定装载质量）

legal periodical inspections （汽车的）法定按期检验（制度）

legal stopping ability 法定制动停车能力（一般指停车距离）

legal vehicle running weight 法定车辆运行质量（法律规定的车辆运行质量）

legend 图标符号，图例，符号表，代号

leg guard 乘员的腿部保护件（如：腿部防撞板等）

legibility 清晰性，易辨认性

leg injury 腿部伤害

legislation ①制定法律，立法 ②法律，法规，规范

legislative compulsion 法规强制

legislative control on safety 安全法规，安全管理规章

leg of frame ①框架的立柱 ②机架的支腿

leg power 踏力，踏踩（踏板的）力

leg reach （驾驶员的）腿操作空间范围

leg room （车辆）供驾驶员或乘客伸腿或腿活动的空间

legs of a right triangle （直角三角形的）勾股，（直角三角形的）两股

leg space （车内的）腿部活动空间

leisure car （业余）休闲用轿车（相对 business car 而言）

leisure vehicle 休闲车［指所有假日、空闲时间使用的汽车，如旅游车、休闲车等，相对商务车（business vehicle）而言，亦称 leisurecar］

Lemoine type 雷莽型（转向节）（转向节轴与主销构成一体，现已淘汰）

lemon 柠檬（俚，指有许多缺陷的次品新车或旧车）

lemon law ［美］柠檬法（保护汽车消费者权益的一项法令）

length ①长度 ②持续时间，期间，期限 ③区间，范围，程度

length-diameter ratio of spray orifice （喷油嘴）喷孔长-径比（喷孔长度与其直径之比）

lengthen 延长，加长，伸长，延伸

length mil 密耳，密尔（长度单位，1 mil = 0.001 inch = 0.025 mm，简称 mil，千分之一英寸，有时亦称 thou）

length of arc 弧长

length of common normal 公法线长度

length of contact 接触长度

length of fit ①配合长度 ②（螺纹）旋入长度

length of haul 运距

length-of-life test ①寿命试验（用以确定可使用期限）②使用期内性能检查试验（在整个使用期定期进行的技术状态观测试验）

length of operation 操作持续时间（作业的持续时间）

length of piston travel 活塞行程（= length of stroke）

length of sealing line 密封线长度

length of spark 火花长度（= spark length）

length of stroke （发动机）冲程长度（= length of piston travel）

length of track on ground 履带的接地长度

length of trailer field 挂车长度代号（在挂车牌号中表示长度的字号，如：美国 SAE 建议用"C"表示长度为 2.4～3 m）

length of travel 行程

length of warranty 保用时期，保用期限

length overall 全长，总长（简称 LOA）

length regulations 车辆长度法规（限制载货汽车或汽车列车总长度的规定）

length stop 纵向止动器

length-to-diameter 长度直径比（简称 L/D）

length travel 纵向位移

lengthways ①长度方向的，纵向的 ②在长度方向，在纵向（= lengthwise）

length × width × height （物体尺寸的）长×宽×高（简称 $L×W×H$）

lengthwise ①长度方向的，纵向的 ②在长度方向，在纵向

lengthwise angle 纵向折角（如球铰式机械连接的主、副车汽车列车，以过球销球心且垂直于主车支承平面的中心线为基准，副车绕过球心的横向中心线回转所形成的角度，亦称 longitudinal bending angle）

lengthwise movement 纵向运动

lengthwise seat 纵长座

lengthy test 长期试验，连续试验

Lenoir 里诺（法国人 Etienne Lenoir 于 1860 年研制成第一台可供实用的常压煤气机，为混合气不经压缩而点燃的煤气机，转速 100 r/min，功率 735～1470 W）

lens ①透镜，镜头 ②（汽车前照灯的）配光镜（由一个或一个以上光学单元组合起来获得所需配光特性

的透镜，旧称前照灯散光镜，=glass lens) ③ 带透镜的灯罩 ④（各种灯的）玻璃镜面

lens aberration 透镜像差，透镜失真

lens-end bulb 聚光灯泡

lens mounting rim 灯玻璃镜面边框

lentor (CGS 制的运动黏度单位) 伦托 (stoke 的旧名)

lenz's law 楞次定律（感应电流总要阻碍磁通量变化）

LEO （一种公制加速度单位）利奥 ($=10m/s^2$)

LEP ①大型电子设备控制板 (large electronic panel) ②最低有效功率 (lowest effective power)

Lepelletier planet gear set 列柏勒梯尔式行星齿轮组（以发明人 Lepelletier 命名的自动变速器用行星齿轮系，由一个单排行星齿轮组和一个附加连接的双排行星齿轮组组成，后者包括同尺寸的两个太阳轮，三个短行星轮，三个长行星轮，一个行星架和一个齿圈）

less-accident prone car 不易发生交通事故的轿车，安全性好的轿车（具有防止发生交通事故能力的轿车）

lesser-calorie 卡，小卡 (=small calorie)

lesser road 简易道路

less-in-demand 不常需要的，需求量少的

less-than-truck-load transportation 零担货物运输（简称 LTL）

let in ①放入，放进，嵌入 ②（离合器等）接合

leucoscope ①光学高温计 ②感色计，色光光度计

LEV 低排放汽车 (low-emission vehicle 的简称)

level ①水平，水平面，水平线，水平的 ②电平，电位 ③等级，级层能级 ④水平仪，水准仪 ⑤校平，使成水平

level angle 水平转角（如：在铰接式客车球铰式机械连接装置中，以过球头销球心的主车纵向水平线为基准，副车绕球头纵销轴线回转所形成的角度）

level control ①高度调平控制 ②液面控制 ③信号电平控制（简称 levecon)

level controller ①液面调节器，液面控制器 ②（车身等的）高度调平装置

level cross country 平野，平原地区

level crossing [英]（公路与铁路等的）平面交叉 (=[美] grade crossing)

level filler 液面控制加注孔（加注油液至该孔高度所决定的液面，若继续加注，油液将从该孔流出）

level gauge 液面计，水准仪（亦称 level indicator)

level ground 水平地面

leveling air-oil suspension （车身高度）调平液压-空气悬架

leveling cylinder 调平(机构)油缸

leveling device ①液面控制装置 ②(车身)高度调平装置

leveling handle 调平手柄

leveling jack 校平用的千斤顶，调平千斤顶

leveling sensor （车身高度调平系统中的)高度传感器（亦称 height sensor）

leveling warning switch （制动系)液量不足警报开关(制动液面低于规定值时,接通警报灯电源)

leveller ①校平器，调平器 ②电表 ③水平仪 ④矫直机，钢板矫平机

level line 水平线

level(l)ing 找平，置平；校平；整平；矫直，矫正；调整，调平，

调电平；水平测置；水准测量

levelling block 校平垫铁，水平校正块，调水平角楔块

levelling machine （板材）矫平机，矫直机，平整机

level (l) ing of local projections 局部突出物的整平

levelling screw 校水准螺钉，校平螺钉

levelling valve （汽车空气悬架或油气悬架系统的）高度调平阀（调整车身与各车轮之间的距离，使车身在任何动载情况下，均能保持规定高度和水平状态的气压或液压阀，亦写作 leveling valve）

level meter ①液位指示仪，油位指示器 ②电平表，电平指示仪 ③水平指示器，水平仪，水位仪

levelness 水平度

level of efficiency 效率等级，效率水平

level-operated input （数字集成电路的）电平工作输入（指只要保持在有效电平内就连续有效地引起激励的输入）

level plug 液面高度螺塞（如：变速器壳侧面加油面规定高度处的螺塞，当机油加到规定高度后，拧开该螺塞，机油便会从该螺孔流出）

level recorder ①电平记录仪 ②液面记录仪

level road horsepower 平路（行驶阻力）功率（包括克服滚动阻力、空气阻力的功率，一般按等速行驶计算，不包括克服加速阻力的功率）

level rod 水准尺

level sensor ①液位传感器 ②水平高度传感器

level shifter 电平转换器（指能对数字输入电压做出响应并能输出电平不同的数字电压或电流的集成电路，其输入与输出的电平不同，有一个或多个输出端）

level sight glass （显示液面高低的）液面观测玻璃（管）

level surface 水准面，平面，液面

level switch 电平开关，钳位电平转换开关

level track 水平试验跑道

level valve 液面高度指示阀（液面高度指示器的一种，当液面达到该阀高度时，油液即由该阀流出）

level warning switch 液面报警开关（感知液面高度，当液面高度低于某规定值时便会使液面警报器开启的开关装置）

lever ①杠杆，杆；杠杆比 ②手把，操纵杆 ③伸出长度 ④途径，工具，手段 ⑤用杠杆撬

lever actuation （用）杠杆使动，杠杆作动，杠杆执行

leverage ①杠系，杠杆系，杠杆装置，杠杆机构 ②杠杆传动，杠杆作用 ③杠杆臂长比，力臂比，杠杆效率 ④扭转力矩

leverage dolly 杠杆支撑的顶具（如：用来校正车身板件用的支撑杠杆顶头）

lever arm 杠杆臂

lever brake 杠杆驱动式制动器

lever change （使用）变速杆变速，变速杆换挡

lever connector （摇臂式减振器）摇臂（与车桥的）连杆件

lever control 杠杆操纵，杆系控制

lever crank mechanism 摆臂曲柄连杆机构，摆杆曲柄机构

lever fulcrum 杠杆支点

lever grease gun 杠杆式滑脂泵（枪）

levering bar （车身板件的校平）撬杆

lever jack 杠杆式千斤顶

lever starter ①手柄式起动机开关 ②杠杆式起动装置

lever stop 手柄行程挡块
lever switch 手柄式开关
lever transmission ①杠杆传动 ②变速杆换挡变速器
lever-type dial indicator 杠杆式千分表，杠杆式百分表
lever-type shock absorber 摇臂式减振器（通过固定在车架上的液力减振器伸出的摇臂来接受与传递振动的减振装置）
lever-type vacuum booster （装有反馈杆和反馈盘的）反馈杆真空助力器（见 reaction lever, reaction plate）
levitated vehicle 浮垫车，悬浮车，（用高压空气将车悬浮起来，离开路面的，常称为气垫车，用磁力将车悬浮起来离开轨道的，称为磁垫车或磁悬浮车，参见 magnetically levitated vehicle）
levorotatory （线偏振光的）左旋性（指线偏振光通过介质时，迎着光传播方向观察，其偏振面沿逆时针方向旋转的性质）
lewis hole 燕尾槽，鸠尾槽，吊楔孔
Lewis-Von Elbe bomb 利维-温埃伯弹（测试燃烧的球形弹，弹壳不膨胀，可记录弹内燃烧压力的变化）
Lexus 日本丰田公司生产的一款轿车名，我国原称凌志，后改称雷克萨斯
LFL 稀混合气可燃极限（见 lean flammability limit）
LFT （发动机）喷油量修正过迟（long-term fuel trim 的简称，指动力控制模块处于闭路反馈工况时，在超过连续两个行驶循环的时间后才进行喷油量修正。这时，OBD Ⅱ系统将点亮故障信号灯，见 SFT）
LFV 横向力的变动（见 lateral force variation）
LGP 低的对地面压力（见 low ground pressure）
lg tn 长吨（见 long ton）

LH ①潜热（见 latent heat）②左侧的（见 left hand）③液态氢 LH_2（见 liquid hydrogen）④下半部（lower half）
LHC 液态氢容器（见 liquid hydrogen container）
LH_2 car 液态氢轿车（使用液态氢作为燃料的轿车）
LHD ①装运卸（车辆的装载，运输卸货作业，load, haul, dump 的简称）②（汽车等）左座驾驶（left hand drive）
LHDS 激光钻孔器（laser hole drilling system）
L-head combustion chamber L 形燃烧室（气门侧置，燃烧室呈扁平形，位于缸盖凹坑内，大部分在气门上面，小部分在活塞上面，横剖面呈 L 形）
L-head engine [美] 侧置气门发动机，L 形汽缸盖发动机（指进、排气门均在缸体内并位于汽缸同一侧的直列式发动机，故英亦称 side valve engine）
LHM （法国某些雪铁龙汽车悬架系统使用的）绿色液压油（法文 Liquide Hydraulique Minerale 的简称）
LHR (engine) 低散热发动机（low-heat rejection engine）
LHT 靠左行驶交通（left hand traffic）
LHV ①（燃料）低热值（lower heating value）②液氢容器（liquid hydrogen vessel）
LI ①（汽车撞车时乘员的）皮肉划破伤害程度指数（laceration index 的简称）②荷载指数（见 load index）
Li 锂（lithium）
liabicity 责任（应负责任，义务）
liability insurance 责任保险
liable 有（法律）责任的，有义务

的；有…倾向的，易于…的

liaison engineer （技术）联络工程师（负责工程技术方面的联络、接待等工作）

LIB ①（汽油的）含铅异辛烷-苯值（lead isooctane-benzene 的简称，表征汽油表面着火倾向的一项指标，故亦译为：汽油的表面着火倾向值。此处的 lead isooctane 为含铅量 0.08% 的异辛烷，其 LIB 值为 0，benzene 为 LIB 值高达 100 的苯。用二者按不同体积混合比配制的混合液与汽油做表面着火倾向的对比性试验，以确定汽油的 LIB 值。常规汽油的 LIB 值在 50~75 的范围内）②锂铁电池（lithium-ion battery 的简称）

liberated heat 释放热（放出的热量）

liberation 解脱，解放；释放，放出，逸出，析出；游离

Liberation truck 解放牌货车

liberty mutual automotive crash simulator （汽车）任意相互碰撞模拟装置（自由相互碰撞模拟装置）

Library of Congress Science and Technology Division ［美］国会图书馆科学技术部

licence 执照，牌照（美写作 license）

licence lamp ［美］（汽车）牌照灯（license plate lamp 的简称，英称 licence light, registration plate lamp）

License bracket （汽车）牌照支架（= license plate holder, license support, number plate support）

licensed driver 有执照的驾驶员，考取执照的驾驶员

licensed pressure 注册压力（文件批准的最大压力）

license plate （汽车）牌照板，牌照牌（= license tag, identification tag, registration mark, 美称 number plate）

License plate character recognition 车牌字符识别

lid ①盖，罩（= cap），帽，顶 ②突缘，凸起

Lidar 光达，激光雷达［light detection and ranging（激光探测与测距）的简称，= laser radar］

lidar sensor 光达传感器（激光雷达传感器）

life 使用期限，寿命

life appraisal study 寿命评价研究

life belt 安全带

life between overhauls 大修间隔期（里程）

Life Breath 生之氛（日 Mazda 车内空气过滤系统的商品名，据称可滤除空气中的乙醛等有毒物）

life-certification test 寿命认定试验（检验与技术文件规定的寿命是否相符的试验）

life curve 寿命曲线（使用期限的特性曲线）

life cycle costs （汽车的）使用寿命期成本（主要包括燃料、轮胎等消耗费、维修费、购置折旧等成本）

life-cycle test ①循环荷载寿命试验，循环荷载耐久性试验 ②循环寿命试验（如：蓄电池的充-放电循环寿命试验）

life dispersion （疲劳）寿命统计数据的离散性

life expectancy （根据概率统计求得的）预期工作耐久性（预期寿命，概率寿命）

life-expectancy analysis （汽车等的）寿命预计分析，寿命估计分析

life expectation 预期寿命，概率寿命（= expectation of life）

life exponent 寿命指数（表示制件疲劳寿命与负荷关系曲线的幂指数）

life factor 寿命因数；耐久性系数

life forecast 寿命预报，寿命预测

life-guard design 乘员安全设计，乘员保护结构

life insurance 寿命保险（使用期限保险）

life length 寿命，使用期

life (-length) distribution 寿命的频率分布

Life module 指车身与底盘分离式电动汽车中装在底盘之上具有底板、座椅、驾驶操纵系统等的车身（即：乘员生活、操作的部分，见 drive module）

life requirements 寿命要求，耐久性要求

life-shortening 缩短寿命的

life-size model （汽车设计、试验等用的）真人尺寸（人体）模型（如：表示驾驶人员平均体重、高度、脚长等的模拟模型、用于研究座椅的舒适性等）

life-span 使用寿命，使用期限

lifetime lubrication 全寿命润滑（在制造时，采用一种润滑装置，可使部件在整个使用期限内不再需要润滑）

life uniformity design （产品各部件）等寿命设计

lift ①举升，提升，起吊 ②升程，扬程，水头，举升高度 ③举升器，升降机，电梯 ④举升力，升力，浮力 ⑤（失圆的车轮）最大半径与最小半径间的差值

lift axle 见 lifting axle

liftback 见 rear hatch (= hatchback)

lift check valve （升降机）升降止回阀

lift coefficient （升降机）升力系数

lift control lever （升降机）升降操纵杆

lift counter （升降机）举升计数器

lift cylinder 起重油缸，举升缸，举升油缸

lifter ①起重机，升降机，升降台，提升机构 ②（气门）挺柱，挺杆（美亦称 tappet，指压靠在凸轮上并在导套中滑动，将凸轮旋转运动转变为往复运动传递给气门推杆或摇臂或气门的组件）③凸轮 ④拆卸工具

lifter guide （气门）挺杆导管，挺柱导套

lifter roller （滚轮式）挺杆（的）滚轮（顶在凸轮上，使挺柱与凸轮作滚动接触，美称 tappet roller）

lift fan （气垫车）的升降鼓风机

lift force 上举力，升力，浮力（= lifting force）

lift gate ①［美］某些厢式车身轿车和小客车可向上开启并带有后窗的后门（=［英］lift tail gate）②（［美］某些箱式货车的）起重后门（由液压式电动控制，可下放到地平面，装卸货后再回升到货箱地板高度，便于装卸货物，=［英］tail lift）

lift hook 吊钩，起重钩

lifting 上升，提升，起重，举升

lifting axle （空载时）可提升离地面的非驱动副后轴（亦称 lift axle）

lifting cab 升起式驾驶室（进行维修作业时，可向上升起的平头货车驾驶室，而不是向前翻倾）

lifting capacity 提升力，起重力；起吊质量，举升能力（可举升高度与举升质量等）

lifting crane 起重吊车，起重机

lifting curve （凸轮）升程曲线

lifting eye bolt 吊环螺栓（= eye bolt）

lifting force 升力，举升力

lifting height 举升高度，提升高度（= height of lift）

lifting jack 千斤顶（= lifting screw）

lifting magnet ①起重磁铁 ②磁力起

重机（参见 hoisting magnet）
lifting motor 起重电动机
lifting movement 上升运动，举升运动
lifting platform ①（货车的）举升式货台，起重货台 ②（修理厂的）举升台，举行器
lifting platform take-up point （轿车的）举升支撑点（厂家标明的用举升装置举升轿车时，举升装置在轿车上的支撑点）
lift（ing）range 升举高度范围（举升行程）
lifting screw ①机械式千斤顶 ②千斤顶螺杆，举升螺杆
lifting sunroof （客车轿车的）举升开启式天窗
lift lace （窗框的窗玻璃）举升带
lift limiter 升程限制器（=lift stop）
lift linkage 提升机构杆系
lift master ①举升台 ②（汽车的）四柱式通用举升器，四柱多用举升器（商品名）
lift of cam 凸轮升程（参见 lead of cam）
lift off effect （电涡流测试中的探头）提升效应（指探头与被测试件间距离的微小变化都会导致测试输出信号的大幅度变化）
lift off tuck-in 某些结构形式的前轮独立悬架在汽车转向松开加速踏板时突然产生的前轮前张的趋向。如果为后轮驱动，便会出现转弯半径缩小的现象
lift of wheel 车轮提升高度（在其余全部车轮都不离开支撑地平面的情况下，车轴某一端车轮在可能提升的最大高度上，该车轮最低点离支撑地平面的距离）
lift-over height （货物装车时必须）提离（地面的）高度
lift pump 见 fuel pump
lift rack （维修诊断用的）汽车举升架，汽车举升台
lift sensor （喷油器喷嘴针阀）升程传感器
lift tail gate 见 lift gate
lift-the-dot fastener 搭扣（式），卡扣（式）（紧固件），碰销-锁孔式紧固件（=[美]snap fastener）
lift truck ①（汽车式）装载机，叉车 ②高架升降车
lift-type valve 升式阀
lift-up door 上升式活动门
light ①光线，光源，光学 ②（绘图中）明亮部分 ③灯，灯光，灯标 ④（汽车的）车窗 ⑤（色彩）淡的 ⑥光亮的，明亮的，发光的 ⑦不重要的，轻微的 ⑧轻的，轻载的，轻型的 ⑨（操作）轻便的 ⑩少量的，薄的
65% light-absorbing glass 光吸收率为65%的（车窗）玻璃
light-activation ignition 光照活性化着火
light adaptation ①眼睛对光的适应性 ②（特指）明适应（指人眼的明视觉的视觉适应，见 photopic vision"明视觉"）
light ageing 光致老化
light ag(e)ing test 光照老化试验
light air ①微风，风速1.6~5.0 km/h ②稀薄空气，高空大气
light aligner 光学式前轮定位仪
light-alloy casting ①轻合金铸件 ②轻合金铸造
light-alloy engine 轻合金发动机（指铝合金等轻金属合金发动机）
light alloy housing 轻合金缸体；轻合金壳体
light alloy wheel 轻合金车轮（一般为铝合金车轮）
light automobile crane 轻型汽车吊车（借助于安装在车上的小型吊车来完成装卸工作的货车）
light band 照明带

light barrier 光线阻挡件（如挡光板等）

light-based distance sensor 光基测距传感器（基于光学原理测定障碍物距离的传感器）

light beam （车灯等的）光线，光束

light bracket 轻型托架（简称LB）

light bulb 灯泡（简称bulb）

light bus 轻型客车（一般指乘员定额30人以上，10人以上的轻型载客汽车，中国国家标准规定为长度 >3.5m 且 ≤7m 的客车）

light car 轻型小轿车（小排量轿车）

light characteristic 照明特性

light chopper 斩光器（光线断续器，截光器）

light circuit 照明电路

light control switch 照明控制开关（灯光开关）

light degradation 光致退化（光作用引起的性能退化，光致衰减）

light diesel fuel 轻柴油

light distillate 轻馏分，轻馏出物

light distribution curve 光度分布曲线

light docking 小修理

light dope 轻微掺杂

light dragon 轻型火炮牵引车；轻型装甲牵引车

light drive fit 轻压配合（轻打入配合，亦称 light force fit）

light dump truck 轻型自卸汽车（中国国标规定的最大总质量≤6t者，参见 light truck）

light durability 光照稳定性（对光线照射影响的稳定性）

light duty ①轻载工况，轻工作（条件）②轻型的，小功率的（= low duty）

light-duty axle 轻载桥，轻载轴，轻型车辆车轴

light duty test 轻载试验，在轻工作条件下的试验

light duty truck 轻型货车（参见 light truck）

light-emitting device 发光装置（光发射装置，光束发射装置）

light emitting diode 发光二极管（光发射二极管，被激励时可发出可见光或红外线的半导体元件，简称 LED）

lightened valve 减轻型气门（指将所有允许减少的金属均磨去，以减轻质量的气门，用于高速发动机）

light engine ①发光器（产生照射光的装置的通称，如汽车的前照灯就是一种 light engine）②轻型汽车用发动机，小型发动机

lightening hole 为减轻构件质量而开的孔

light equipment ①照明设备②轻型设备

lighter ①打火机，点火器，引燃器（汽车上特指仪表板上的）点烟器②照明器③轻型运输机械

light excluding shutter （照相机等的）遮光门

light-fast 不受光线影响的

light flux 光通量

light-footed 轻踩加速踏板（的驾驶模式，以节油）

light fuel 轻燃料（易挥发性燃料）

light fuel fraction 燃油的轻馏分

light fugitive 不耐光的

light goods 轻货（轻泡货物，轻浮货物，中国国标规定为每千克质量的体积 >4dm³ 或每立方米体积的质量 <250kg 的货物）

light grade ①小坡度②低品位③低标号

light guide 光制导，光导

light hopper wagon 轻型漏斗车（如：轻型混凝土斗车）

light indicator 灯光指示器

lighting ①照明，采光 ②点灯 ③照明设备 ④起动，发射

lighting cable 灯线；照明系的电缆；照明线

lighting circuit 灯光电路，照明电路

lighting device 照明设备，照明装置（= lighting installation, lighting equipment, lighting facilities）

lighting dynamo 照明用发电机

lighting hours ①照明时间（lighting time）②照明小时

lighting pattern （前照灯的）光形（指前照灯光束投射到一平面或地面上时所形成的光斑的形状，即光照区的图形）

lighting regulations 汽车照明法规（确定汽车照明设备位置、质量和形式的规定）

lighting signal device 照明信号装置，灯光信号装置

lighting-up ①（行车）开灯 ②点燃，点火

lighting-up time （法令规定的前照灯）开灯时间

light intensity 光度，照度

light intermittent test 轻载间歇试验

light keying fit 轻迫配合

light/laden valve 荷载感知式制动液压控制阀

light lorry 轻型货车（= light truck）

light luggage 轻浮行包，轻泡行包（中国国标规定每千克质量体积超过 $4dm^3$ 的行包）

light measuring window （光学仪器等的）测光窗（如通过该窗测量曝光量和色温等）

light-metal alloy 轻金属合金

light-metal rim 轻金属轮辋

light military vehicle 轻型军用车辆

lightness contrast 明度对比（指视野中的目标和背景的主观亮度差别的评定，亦称 brightness contrast）

lightning generator ①光脉冲发生器 ②人工闪电发生器 ③照明用发电机

lightning protection 避雷（防雷击）

lightning rod 避雷针（= discharging rod）

light obscuration 暗度，光阻率，不透光率（见 opacity）

light off 燃起（催化转化器达到规定温度开始起作用）

light off-road vehicle 轻型越野汽车（中国国标规定最大总质量小于或等于 5t）

light-off temperature （指示灯的）熄灯温度（特指汽车排放控制系统的催化转化器转化效率达到某一给定值时的温度，如转化效率达到 50%时的250℃左右，在仪表板上用指示灯熄灭来表示，亦称起燃熄灯温度）

light off time 催化转化器催化剂的）起燃时间（从发动机起动到废气催化转化器达到工作温度的时间，简称 LOT）

light oil ①轻油，轻柴油 ②低黏度机油

light-on reminder 关灯提醒器（一般用声响信号提醒驾驶员车灯尚开着勿忘关闭）

light output 光能输出，光输出

light paste 软膏（= runny paste, thin paste）

light pencil ①光束 ②光笔（亦称 light pen）

light permeation type instrument ①（汽车的）泛光式仪表（内置照明光由透光的仪表板面后弥漫射出）②内照明式仪表（照明光源从仪表板背面发出）

light-pole collision （汽车）与路灯杆等发生的碰撞

light press fit 轻压配合

light pressure 光压（光的压力）

lightproof 不透光的，遮光的

light quantity 光通量
light repair 小修
light repair detachment ①巡回修理队 ②派遣的维修小组
light resistor 光敏电阻器
light running 小负荷运转，轻载运行
light running fit 轻转配合，轻动配合
light section ①薄壁断面 ②轻型型材
light semi-trailer 轻型半挂车（中国国标规定最大总质量小于或等于7.1t）
light sensitive 光敏的，光感的
light-sensitive vehicle detector 光感式测车器（光电车辆检测器，使用光电元件测定有无车辆通过及所通过汽车数的元件）
light shield （前照灯的）遮光罩（装在反射镜上遮挡发光体直射光的罩子）
light signal 灯光信号
light-sized 小尺寸的
light-spot 光点
light stability 光稳定性
light stiffening （橡胶）曝光硬化
light stock （轮胎）缺胶（指轮胎表面局部少胶的凹陷现象，俗称缺肉，明疤）
light stock of flap （轮胎）垫带缺胶（带边严重缺胶裂口）
light-tight 不透光的
light transmittance （车用玻璃的）透光度（$=\dfrac{\phi_t}{\phi_i}$，式中：ϕ_t—透过玻璃射出的光通量；ϕ_i—射入的光通量）
light transmitting fiber 光导纤维
light trigger （电子点火系中的）光-电触发器（光-电式点火信号发生器）
light truck 轻型货车（中国国标规定为厂定最大总质量大于1.8t且小于或等于6t的货车。英、美一般指总重3t以下且不需货车驾驶执照便可驾驶的货车，= light lorry, light duty truck, 其中带箱式车身者称 light van）
light type 轻型
light unit 见 lamp unit
light utility vehicle 轻型多用途汽车（是 jeep, pick-up, all-activity vehicle 等轻型多功能车的通称）
light valve ①防炫灯光控制阀 ②光阀（指外加电场、磁场、电子束等改变光传输特性的器件）
light van 轻型厢式货车（见 light truck）
light volatile fuel 易挥发性燃料
light volume adjustment filter 光量调节滤光镜（亮度调节滤光镜）
light watt （光通量单位）光瓦特
light-weight 轻质的，轻的，轻型的，轻便的，平均质量以下的
6 light window （**type car**） 六窗式轿车（指除了四个车门窗外，左、右后门柱后方还各有一个小三角窗的四门轿车）
lignite benzine 由褐煤中提炼的汽油，挥发性
ligroin（**e**） 里格若英（汽油和煤油间的一种石油馏分，称：粗汽油，石油醚，挥发油，= benzine）
ligthen ①照明，点灯 ②发光，闪耀 ③减轻，缓和，使轻松
likelihood ①相似性 ②似真，可能 ③可能发生的事物
likelihood-ratio test 似然比值检定
like-pole 同极（性）的
Lilliput car 微型汽车，微型车辆，微型轿车（= mini car, Lilliput 原意为英作家 Swift 小说《格里佛游记》中的小人国）
LIM ①直线感应电动机（linear induction motor） ②极限（limit） ③限

制器,限幅器(limiter)
limb ①肢,分支 ②零件,部分 ③电磁铁心 ④分度弧
limber ①(炮的)牵引车 ②柔软的,轻快的,敏捷的,易弯曲的,可塑的,有弹性的 ③可变通的
limbering-up operation 试验前的调试运转,试验前的练习运行
limber up period (正式试验前的)预试阶段,调试期,练习期
lime ①生石灰,氧化钙(CaO) ②碳酸钙($CaCO_3$) ③水垢(指水套、散热器等内壁的水垢,= scale)
lime deposit 碳酸钙沉淀物,水垢(亦称 scale,lime 或 lime scale)
lime-green 淡黄绿色的,酸橙绿色的(车身等)
lime stone base grease 钙基润滑脂(指以脂肪酸钙皂或12-羟基硬脂肪酸钙皂做稠化剂的润滑脂,耐水性良好,简称 lime grease 或 lime soap grease,耐水性良好,亦称 cup grease)
lime stone-sodium base grease 钠-钙基润滑脂(指以脂肪酸钠皂和复合钙皂做稠化剂的润滑脂)
limit ①极限,限度,极点;范围,区域 ②限制,限定,约束 ③极限值,极限尺寸
limitary 边界的,极限的
limitation ①限制,制约 ②极限,界限 ③局限性
limitcator 电触式极限传感器
limit-cycle 极限循环(计算机闭路控制系统的一种运作模式,其反馈信号仅在控制变量超出规定的上、下界线值时发送,被控制的变量在上、下极限间循环,使其平均值保持在某预定的值附近)
limit-cycle control 极限循环闭路控制[见 closed-loop (feedback) control system]

limit design(ing) 极限设计(极限强度设计,最大负载设计法)
limited 有限制的,受限制的,限定的,有局限性的
limited access highway 控制进入的公路(= controlled access highway)
limited company 有限责任公司(简称 Co. Ltd)
limited condition of vehicle 汽车极限技术状况(汽车技术状况参数达到技术文件规定的极限值)
limited current 极限电流
limited flow 限制流量(由流量控制阀所限制的流量)
limited operational strategy (汽车电子控制模块的)有限运转策略(简称 LOS,亦称 limited operational mode,limp home mode,backup mode 或 fail safe mode)有限运行控制模式(简称 LOS,指当电子控制模块发现有部件损坏时,立即中止正常运转模式而进入有限功能运转模式、故障安全运转模式,使受控系统继续运转,但只能维持一定的有限作用水平以保护其他部件并使发动机具有足够维持汽车驶至修理场地的操纵性。如果电子控制模块的中央处理器发生故障,电子控制模块将进入固定控制模式,在此模式下无点火提前及废气再循环,二次空气亦将排至大气)
limited-production 限量生产的,少量生产的
limited slip axle 带防滑差速器的驱动桥
limited slip differential 防滑差速器(简称 LSD,= controlled slip differential,通过锁止作用能防止驱动轮打滑的差速器,见 differential limiting device。常用的 LSD 有:cone clutched type 锥形离合器型的 hydraulic multi-disc clutch type 液压法式离合器型的,electronic-hydraulic

type 电控液压型的，automatic posifire looking type 自动强制锁止型的和 viscous clutch type 黏液离合器型的等多种）

limited stop bus 大站停车的快速公共汽车

limiter 限制器（①限制转速、行程、压力等的装置的统称②电子控制系统中防止变量超过规定极限的功能部件）

Limiter LSP （制动系的）感载式比例限压阀（LSP 为 load sensing proportional 的简称）

limit gap gauge 间隙极限规

limit gauge 极限量规

limiting availability 极限有效度（指时间趋于无限时，瞬时有效度的极限值，亦称稳态有效度）

limiting bearing temperature 极限轴承温度

limiting clearance 极限间隙（达到技术文件规定的极限状况的配合副间隙值）

limiting condition 极限状态

limiting current 极限电流（由电流限制装置控制的最大输出或输入电流）

limiting-current type lean air/fuel sensor 限流型稀空/燃比传感器（见 lean A/F sensor）

limiting device 限制器，限位器

limiting fatigue stress 极限疲劳应力

limiting force 极限力，限制力

limiting gradient 极限坡度

limiting lateral acceleration test ①极限侧向加速试验（测定汽车沿圆周行驶时所能达到的极限侧向加速度）②极限横向加速度试验（确定汽车沿圆周行驶时能达到的极限横向加速度）

limiting (limit) position 极限位置

limiting resolution （液晶显示的）极限分辨率（图像水平或垂直方向能分辨出的明暗交替条纹的总数）

limit (ing) screw 限位螺钉

limiting speed 极限车速（允许最高速度）

limit (ing) stop (per) 限位挡块，终点挡块

limit (ing) stress 极限应力，临界应力

limiting temperature 极限温度

limiting valve 限止阀，限制阀，限压阀（如：后轮制动液压限制阀）

limiting viscosity 特性黏度，极限黏度

limiting wear 极限磨损（零件已不能保持工作要求的磨损量）

limit load 极限荷载

limit of accuracy 精度极限

limit of adhesion 附着力极限（附着极限）

limit of audibility 能听度极限

limit of combustibility 可燃极限（可燃性界限）

limit of compression 压缩极限

limit of elasticity 弹性极限（比例极限）

limit of error 误差极限（最大允许误差，亦称 maximum permissible error）

limit of explosion （混合气浓度的）爆发极限（可燃极限）

limit of fatigue 疲劳极限

limit of inflammability （混合气的）失火界限（可燃极限空燃比，一般汽油混合气的稀可燃极限空燃比为 20:1，亦称 limit of misfire）

limit of profitable haul 有利运距极限

limit of proportionality 比例极限（弹性极限，比限，= proportional limit）

limit of sensibility 灵敏度极限

limit (of) size 极限尺寸

861

limit of sliding 侧滑极限（= skidding limit）
limit of stability 稳定性极限
limit of wear 磨损极限
limit of wheeled traffic （地面）轮式车辆可行驶性（通过性）极限
limit plug gauge 极限塞规
limit snap gauge 极限卡规
limit speed 极限速度
limit switch 限位开关（极限开关）
limit system 极限制（公差制）
limit thread gauge 极限螺纹规
limit thread snap gauge 极限螺纹卡规
limit value 极限值
limit visibility 能见度极限
limousine ①（4～9人乘坐的、四门、双排主座，中间加有一排副座，驾驶室与后座间有玻璃隔墙等，后座区宽敞豪华的）高级轿车（俗称 limo）②接送旅客的交通车
limp-home mode 慢行驶回模式（汽车的电子系统发生故障时，由备用电路应急运转，仍能以较低车速驶回车库等的运行模式）
limp-in mode 跛行模式 [亦称 limp-home (operating) mode, lamemode, 如：①自动变速器电子控制模块的跛行模式，当其自诊断功能测得系统产生危害行车安全的严重故障时，控制模块即解除对变速器的控制置并换入低功率运行模式 ②低出力控制模式（当电子控制模块收不到某一个重要传感器的信息或收到的信息超出正常范围时，将根据其他相关传感器的信息推算出的所缺的信息，对发动机进行控制，此时发动机虽继续运转，但功率将有所降低）]
LIN 本地互联网 [local interconnect network 的简称，在汽车上指本车网，亦称局域网（local area network），简称 LAN]

LIN （汽车的）局域互联网络（Local Interconnect network 的简称，为现有汽车局域网，如：CAN 提供辅助功能的串行通信总线网络，主要用于车门、车窗、转向盘、座椅、照明、空调、发电机等）
LIN bus LIN 总线 [一种低成本的串行通信网络。其最高传输速率为 20kb/s，在汽车的分布式电子控制系统中，作为汽车主总线网络（如 CAN）的辅助总线网络，用于对传输速度和实时性要求不高的场合，参见 CAN]
Lincoln Town Car [美] 林肯城市轿车（Ford 汽车公司生产的一种豪华轿车）
line ①线路，管路，管道 ②管 ③线，绳索 ④纹，痕 ⑤行，列，串，系列 ⑥生产线
line a bearing 浇注轴承，挂瓦
lineal 直线的，线性的
lineal element 线素
linear ①直线的，直线状的 ②长条状的，带状的 ③纵向的，沿线的 ④线性的，线性化的；一次的，一维的 ⑤长度的
linear absorption coefficient 线性吸收系数
linear acceleration 直线加速度
linear accelerometer 直线加速度计
linear actuator 直线性作动器，直线（动作）执行机构
linear ADC 线性 ADC [线性模拟-数字转换器（linear analogue-to-digital coverter）的简称，指有理想等宽台阶的模-数转换器]
linear amplifier 线性放大器（指输出信号是输入信号线性倍增的放大器）
linear averaging 线性平均（简单地把各样本的处理结果求和，再除以样本总数）
linear bearing 直线轴承

linear charge concept 线性增压充气方案（发动机高速运转区的增压输出降减，而改善常用的低速区增压特性的增压进气方案）

linear DAC 线性 DAC，线性数字-模拟转换器（linear digital-to-analogue converter 的简称，指有理想等高台阶的数-模转换器）

linear decrement 线性衰减量（率）

linear deformation 线性形变（变形）

linear dependence 线性相关，线性关系

linear dimensions 线性尺寸

linear displacement sensor 直线位移传感器（见 linear position sensor）

linear EGR 线性 EGR［电子控制式 EGR（electronic EGR）的别称，由电子控制模块根据发动机工况和反馈系统的信息，通过步进电机或电磁阀控制 EGR 阀的开、闭和开度，而将精确数量的废气输入进气歧管］

linear electric motor 直线电动机（简称 linear motor，相当于将常规感应式电动机的转子电枢和定子磁场展开成直线状，原转子的旋转运动变为直线运动，从而产生直线拉力或推力）

linear error 线性误差（如：分析仪的实际读数与在有效范围的上限和下限间的线性函数之间的最大偏差）

linear expansion coefficient 线膨胀系数（亦称 linear expansion factor）

linear fan clutch 线性风扇离合器（可根据通过散热器的空气流的温度，调整风扇驱动转矩，以获得最佳风扇转速的风扇离合器，亦称 linear fan coupling）

linear flow 层流，线流

linear friction 线性摩擦

linear function 线性函数，一次函数

linear induction motor 直线感应电动机（简称 LIM，= conventional linear motor，见 linear electric motor）

linear integrated circuit 线性集成电路（输出信号随输入信号的变化呈线性解析函数，即比例关系的集成电路）

linearity 直线性，线性度（对变量，指一次函数不偏离直线的程度；对控制系统，指对输入信号的响应不偏离直线的程度；对仪表，指校准曲线与规定直线的一致程度）

linearity error 线性度误差（如仪表，其校准曲线与规定直线间的最大偏差）

linearized theoretical models 线性理论模型，线形理论模型

linear load 线性荷载，单位长度荷载

linearly dependent 线性相关

linearly polarized light 线偏振光［光束的电矢量具有单一的振动方向，亦称平面偏振光（plane polarized light）］

linear material 线性材料（呈线性黏性阻尼特性的材料）

linear measurement 线性量测，直线测量

linear momentum 线动量（参见 momentum）

linear motion type seat 直线移动式座椅

linear-movement pickup 线性运动传感器

linear oscillator 线振荡

linear paper 方格纸

linear phase shift 线性相移

linear pitch （蜗杆等的）轴向节距

linear polarization 线偏振，平面偏振（= plane polarization 见 linearly polarized light）

linear position sensor 直线位移传感

linear potentiometer 线性电位计

linear programming 线性程序编制，线性规划

linear region 线性区（如：三极管的集电极电流恒正比于基极电流的工作区域）

linear regulation control law （车辆的）线性管理法规，线性控制管理法则

linear relationship 线性关系

linear scale 线性标度（标度中各分格间距与对应的分格值呈常数比例关系的标度）

linear sealing 线密封，（直）线性密封

linear shear apparatus 直线剪切装置，直线剪切机

linear shift control （连续无级变速器车辆的）线性（加速）换挡控制（指可让驾驶者在踩踏加速踏板加速的过程中感到发动机转速是随着加速踏板位置及车速的变化而自然流畅地变化的三者最佳配合的控制模式）

linear solenoid valve 直线型电磁阀（做直线运动）

linear (source) lamp 见 festoon bulb

linear source (of sound) 线声源

linear space 线性空间

linear speed 直线速度，线速度

linear speed sensor 直线速度传感器

linear strain 线应变（由外力引起的原始尺寸每单位长度的变化）

linear stress field 线性应力场

linear system 线性系统

linear TPS 直线式节气门开度传感器（linear throttle position sensor 的简称，装在节气门轴上的凸轮在节气门转动时顶压一传感柱塞，使该柱塞产生与节气门转角成比例的直线移动，将该直线移动转变为电信号输出的传感器件）

Lineartronic (Subaru) 带 6 挡手动拨片换挡模式的电子控制连续无级变速器（商品名）

linear type EGR valve 直线型 EGR 阀（控制 EGR 的流量的电磁阀，其开启度直接由动力控制模块通过脉冲宽度调制信号控制，开启度越大，废气再循环量越多）

linear type sensor 线性传感器（其输出电压与被传感值的变化呈线性关系的传感元件）

linear type throttle position sensor 线性型节气门位置传感器（见 throttle position sensor）

linear variable differential transformer 线性差动变压器（在汽车电子控制系统中指直线位移差动变压器式传感器，利用强磁性体芯子在线圈中直线移动，改变电感而引起线圈电流变化，而将直线位移量变为电压信号输出，简称 LVDT）

linear velocity 线速度

linear vibration 线性振动，直线振动

linear viscous damping 线性黏性阻尼（在振动中由大小与变形速度成正比、方向与变形速度相反的材料内阻尼力所引起的材料或部件的能量消散作用）

linear wiper system （汽车风窗玻璃的整幅横向）直进式刮水系统（其刮片臂的上、下两端分别装在风窗玻璃顶端和底端的导轨机构内，刮水时刮片由风窗玻璃的一端横向直进到其另一端，而不是常规的弧线运动）

line belt 传送带

line boring machine （缸体主轴承孔等的）直线镗削机，直线同心多孔镗床

line busy （电话）占线（简称LB）
line call-out specification 规格代号，代号规格（用简单字母或数字，来代表材料的技术规范，如2BC515橡皮，其中"2"代表质量要求代号；"B"代表耐热温度为100C；"C"代表耐油浸最大泡胀率为120%，"5"代表杜罗硬度值为50，"15"代表抗拉强度为1500kg/cm^2）
line capacity 作业线（生产）能力
line commutated inverter 线换向变流器（直流变交流的有源逆变器）
line connector 电线连接件（如：接线夹）
line contact 线接触
lined ①覆面的，饰面的 ②加衬的
line-departure warning system 离线警报系统（简称LDW system）
line driver （计算机控制系统的）线路驱动器（用于驱动大量负载的功率放大器）
line drop 线路电压降
line filter 管路滤清器（装在气压或液压管路中，起二次滤清作用的部件）
10-line grid 纵、横线条间距为10（如：10in或10cm等）的方格（纸等）
line-haul 固定线路货物运输
line-haul intraurban 城市内的定线运输
line loss 管路（阻力）损失，线路损失
line man's plier （电）线路工用手钳（电工手钳，剪丝钳）
linen ①亚麻布，亚麻布制品 ②亚麻布制的，亚麻色的
line of action ①（力的）作用线（= line of action of force）②（齿轮）啮合线（= line of contact）
line of centers ①中心连接线 ②连心线（如：在平行轴或交错齿轮副中两轴线的公共垂线）
line of communication 通信线路
line of contact ①接触线 ②齿啮合线（指瞬时接触线，即在某一瞬时内，两个相啮齿面所有接触点的连线）
line of curvature (on surface)（曲面上的）曲率线
line of demarcation 分界线，边界
line of equidistance 等距线
line-off 下线（汽车装配完毕离开装配线，= off line）
line of flow 流线
line of force ①力的作用线 ②磁力线（= magnetic line of force）
line of intersection （相）交线
line of magnetic force 磁力线（= magnetic line of force, line of magnetization）
line of motion 运动线
line of obliquity 斜线
line of parallelism 平行线
line of production 生产线
line of reference 参考线，基础（基）线
line of rupture 破裂线，断裂线
line of screw 螺旋线
line of shortest length 最短线
line of sight 视线，瞄准线
line-of-sight coverage 视距，视界，视野
line of slide 滑动线，滑移线
line of weakness 最小强度线
line (plane) of projection 投影线（面）
line pressure ①管道压力，输送管压力 ②（液压系统的）主压力（指液压系统中主油路的压力，如：液力变速器的换挡压力，它随发动机转速的升高而升高，为液压控制系统中的最高压力）③气压系统的工作压力
line pressure test （自动变速器的）

管道压力试验（测定各挡位下油泵输出压力，以检查油泵的工作状况和管路有否渗漏）

line production　流水作业，流水线生产

liner　①衬瓦，衬套，衬垫，衬里 ②轴瓦 ③汽缸衬套，缸套（cylinder liner 的简称，美称 sleeve）④车身衬里 ⑤覆面层，镶条 ⑥固定路线的运输车辆 ⑦直线规，画线工具 ⑧（车厢内的）装饰性软壁面

line rate　生产线的作业速度，流水作业线的生产速率

liner backs　缸套外表面

liner blank　汽缸套毛坯

liner bushing　衬套

liner coolant　（汽缸）衬套冷却液

line receiver　线接收器［指通过传输系统（传输线）与发送器耦合，其输入端以单端或差动方式接收电压或电流信号，输出数字电压信号的集成电路］

liner flange　①汽缸套凸缘 ②缸套凸缘高出（缸体顶面）高度

liner lead　汽缸套导向表面

liner neck　缸套凸缘颈（湿式缸套上定位环带）

liner of cylinder　汽缸套（=cylinder sleeve）

liner puller　缸套拉器（拆汽缸套工具，缸套拔出器）

lines　（汽车内饰材料的天然或人造）花纹

line segment　线段

line shafting　传动轴系

line-side storage　生产线旁的配件储备（装配线旁的总成配件储备）

line size　管子横断面尺寸（管路通道断面尺寸）

line spanner　见 flare nut spanner

line speed　线速度（直线速率）

line station　线路停车站

line-to-line lap　（滑阀）零重叠度

line trace　（试验车辆在某车速下转向的）行驶轨迹（评价转向特性）

line trace performance　（汽车的行驶）方向-线路跟随性能（指：①汽车"行驶方向-路线稳定性"，即沿规定的路线、车道行驶，不偏离车道的性能 ②汽车"转向顺应性能"，即其顺应驾驶者通过转向盘所要求的路线行驶的性能）

line transmitter　线发送器［指通过传输系统（传输线）与接收器耦合，其输入信号为单端数字电压，输出信号为单端或差动电流或电压的集成电路］

line-up　①（用途相同的）一批构件、装置、东西 ②（对汽车指）同一系列或车型的车辆（亦写作 line-up）

line up　①对准中心，调直，调整，校正，校直，调成一直线，排成一行，排队，使平直 ②序列，阵容，（同一用途的）一批东西，排列，排队

line voltage　线电压

lin expansion　线膨胀（=linear expansion）

lining　①衬垫，衬套，衬里 ②（制动蹄的摩擦）衬片 ③（浇铸的轴瓦）衬面 ④镀层，涂层，覆面层 ⑤上底漆 ⑥矫平，矫直

lining board　（车身骨架）衬板，内壁板

lining bond　摩擦衬片黏合剂（参见 lining cement）

lining break-in　摩擦衬片磨合

lining cement　（制动器、离合器摩擦片的）黏合剂（=lining bond）

lining dust　摩擦衬片磨屑（磨耗后形成的粉末）

lining fading　摩擦衬片（性能）衰退

lining glaze　摩擦片表面釉光化（摩擦片表面釉光状磨损）

lining life 衬里（衬垫、衬片、衬套等的）寿命（如：离合器、制动器的摩擦衬片的寿命，炉衬的寿命等，汽缸套寿命）

lining material 衬料，衬带（里、套等材料）

lining of car 车身衬里

lining pad 摩擦衬块

lining plate 衬板

lining ring 衬环，衬圈

linings total area （制动蹄、块及离合器盘等的）摩擦衬面总面积

lining stripper 衬面刮除器

lining surface 摩擦衬片表面

link ①链环，环 ②连接杆件 ③连接，接合 ④（汽车悬架系统中的）控制臂，推力杆，拉杆（等杆件， = suspension arm, suspension link, suspension rod）

linkage ①连接，联结，联系，连锁，联合 ②（由各种杆件、臂等组成的传力）杆系

linkage ball joint 杆系球节

linkage combined type power steering gear 整体式动力转向器（转向动力缸、转向控制阀、机械传向器组合为一个整体的动力转向器，亦称 integral power steering gear）

linkage geometry 杆系几何学，杆系几何结构

linkage guide 杆系中的导向件

linkage separate type power steering gear 半整体式动力转向器（动力缸与控制阀分离安装，而只有控制阀与机械转向器组成一个整体的动力转向器，亦称 semi-integral power steering gear）

linkage system （传力）杆系

linkage (type) power steering 杆系型动力转向（系统）（为目前广泛使用的动力转向系的一种，其基本特点是控制阀和动力缸等动力装置的构件都接装在转向摇臂以下的转向拉杆系中，亦称 offset power steering，参见 integral type power steering）

link arm 连杆臂

link ball 联杆球头，拉杆球头

link block ①连接滑块，导块 ②（转子发动机的）密封销

link block spring （转子发动机的）密封销簧

link bolt 铰接螺栓［= hinge（d）bolt］

link chain 片节链（无声链的一种）

link fulcrum 杆件的支点

linking bar 拉杆

link on 结合，连接

link ratio （传动杆系的）传动比（指杆系的输入移动量与输出移动量之比）

5-link strut type suspension 五连杆型滑柱式悬架（具有上、下横臂，上、下斜撑和一根横向推力杆的麦弗逊型滑柱悬架）

3-link suspension 三连杆式悬架［指每侧车轮由一个横向布置的控制臂与车身或车架连接，在两个车轮悬架之间还有一根横向布置的稳定杆，一共三个连接杆件，故名。但由于每侧车轮只有一根控制臂，又称单控制臂式悬架（single control arm suspension）］

link system of suspension 悬架杆系

link type seal ①连锁型密封装置，连锁密封 ②（转子发动机的）密封销型径向密封装置

5-link type suspension 五连杆式悬架（刚性桥的非独立式悬架①由支撑车架或车身的上、下纵向控制臂和一根横向推力杆、一根横向稳定杆及其两端与车架或车身连接的连杆五种八根杆件再加上螺旋弹簧-减振器总成组成的悬架系统 ②指由左、右、上、下纵向控制臂和横向推力杆等五根杆件外加螺旋弹簧-减振器

总成组成的悬架系统)
linoleum 亚麻油毡
linseed oil 亚麻仁油
lintfree cloth 无棉绒布
lip ①刀刃,唇,唇状物,(凸)缘 ②悬臂,支架 ③百叶窗片
lip angle 楔角,缘角
lip curb 缓斜路缘,唇状路缘(路缘面与斜面角度在60°以上,混凝土路面为改善排水条件及保护路肩而加厚的路缘)
lip opening pressure (密封唇式密封件的)密封唇部泄漏压力,密封唇口张开压力(指在被密封液体或气体压力下密封唇口离开轴表面并产生规定泄漏量的液、气压力)
Lipowitz's alloy 利波维兹合金(低温易熔合金,熔断丝等用,铅35.5%,锡10.2%,铋44.6%,镉9.7%,熔点70℃)
lip packing 唇形密封件
lipping 卷边
lip seal with garter spring 带箍簧的唇密封(带自紧圈簧的密封唇式油封,旋转轴的径向密封件的一种,防止漏油和尘污,统称 radial shaft seal)
lip temperature 边缘温度,端边温度
lip-type air drag reducer 唇形空气阻力减小装置(装在箱式货车车身的前壁,包覆其顶边及两侧)
lip-type seal with finger spring 带指状弹簧的唇状油封
lip-type seal with garter spring 带箍簧的唇状油封
lip-type seal with no spring 无弹簧的唇状油封
lip-type (synthetic rubber) seal (合成橡胶自紧式)唇状油封
liquation 熔解;熔融,熔析,液化
liquefaction ①液化作用 ②稀释,冲淡
liquefied ①液化的 ②稀释的
liquefied coal 液化煤(将煤加工成煤浆,可作为石油、天然气的代用燃料,一般2t煤浆相当于1t原油)
liquefied gas ①液化煤气 ②液化可燃气(= liquid gas)
liquefied natural gas 液化天然气(主要成分为甲烷,其沸点−161.5℃,低热值49.54MJ/kg,辛烷值RON, MON均为120,用作汽油机的代用燃料,简称LNG)
liquefied natural gas tanker 液化天然气罐车
liquefied natural gas vehicle 液化天然气车辆(使用液化天然气作为燃料的车辆,简称NGV)
liquefied petroleum gas 液化石油气(简称LPG,主要成分为丁烷,或丙烷,或二者的混合物,为石油精炼的副产品,沸点−5℃,饱和蒸气压力358.5kPa,低热值45.31MJ/kg,辛烷值RON94, MON90,用作汽油机的代用燃料,亦称 autogas)
liquefied-petroleum-gasengine 液化石油气发动机(使用液化石油气作为燃料的火花点火式发动机,亦称 liquid petroleum gas, gas engine,简称LPG engine)
liquefied petroleum gas vehicle 液化石油气汽车(所有使用液化石油气作燃料的车辆的通称,简称LPGV)
liquefied refinery gas 精炼液化石油气(简称LRG)
liquid ①液体,流体 ②液体的,流动的
liquid air 液态空气
liquid brake 液压制动器(= fluid brake, oil brake)
liquid-carburizing 液体渗碳
liquid car wax 液态车用打光蜡
liquid clutch ①湿式离合器,油浸离合器(= wet clutch) ②液力耦合器(= fluid coupling, hydraulic clutch)
liquid container ①液体容器 ②液体(货物)集装箱
liquid coolant 冷却液

liquid-cooled 液体冷却的，水冷的

liquid-cooled ac permanent magnet syncronous motor 液冷交流永磁同步电动机

liquid-cooled brake 液体冷却制动器

liquid-cooled engine 液冷发动机，水冷发动机

liquid coupling 液力耦合器

liquid crystal 液晶（具有双折射及其他晶体特性的流体）

liquid crystal cell 液晶盒（两极板之间夹有液晶的器件）

liquid crystal display device 液晶显示器（由液晶盒组成的平面型显示器，简称 LCD，亦称 liquid crystal indicator）

liquid crystal layer 液晶层（指两基板之间充填的液晶物质）

liquid crystal multivision display 液晶多图像显示（装置）

liquid crystal temperature range 液晶温度范围（液晶物质呈液晶态的温度范围）

liquid crystal touch panel 液晶触摸屏

liquid damper 油液阻尼器，液体缓冲器（= hydraulic damper, liquid shock absorber）

liquid dispenser 液体喷雾器（如：清洗风窗玻璃的喷水器）

liquid drive 液体传动（参见 hydraulic drive）

liquid film 液膜（液体的薄膜）

liquid-flow equation 液体流动方程

liquid flow sensor 流体流量传感器

liquid flywheel 液力飞轮（起液力耦合器或液力变矩器泵轮作用的飞轮）

liquid friction 液体摩擦

liquid-fueled vehicle 液体燃料汽车（指汽油、柴油、甲醇、乙醇等液体燃料）

liquid fuel inflator （汽车安全气囊的）液体燃料充气装置

liquid gallon 液加仑（美国常用的液体的容积单位，代号 lg，参见 U.S. gallon）

liquid gas 液化气体（= liquefied gas），密封垫（一般为管装液态密封剂，使用时挤出在需要密封处，可在室温下固化而成为密封垫）

liquid gas vehicle （使用）液化气体燃料（的）车（辆）

liquid head 液体压头（液压系统压力）

liquid hydrogen container 液态氢容器（简称 LHC）

liquid hydrogen Dewar （装）液态氢的夹层真空型绝热容器（Dewar 为以发明人苏格兰物理学家 Sir Jannes Dewar 的名字命名的真空夹层保温瓶 "Dawar ressel"、"Dawar flask" 的简称）

liquid level 液面水平，液面高度

liquid line ①液体管路 ②（空调系统的膨胀阀和储液-干燥器之间的高压）液态制冷剂管路

liquid-liquid heat exchanger 液对液式热交换器（全液体型热交换器）

liquid manometer 液体压力计（液柱压力计）

liquid metal cell 液态金属电池（使用阳极材料的熔盐做电解液，其阳极本身也可能是熔化金属，= molten electrolyte cell）

liquid metal contact 液体金属接点，液体金属触点

liquid methane 液态甲烷（简称 LM）

liquid methanol 液态甲醇

liquid nitrogen 液态氮（-196℃时沸腾）

liquid nitrogen engine 液态氮发动机（一个单位容积的液氮在大气温度、压力下可膨胀到 640 个单位容积的氮气，通过气马达输出这一能

量的装置,称为液氮发动机)
liquidometer ①液体流量计 ②液面计,液位计
liquid-operated 液动的
liquid packing 液体密封装置
liquid petroleum oil 煤油
liquid phase 液相
liquid propane engine 液化丙烷燃料发动机
liquid proportioner 液体比例混合器
liquid pump 液压泵
liquid quart 液夸脱(参见 liquid gallon)
liquid quench hardening glass (汽车用)液冷钢化玻璃(用液体做骤冷介质的安全钢化玻璃)
liquid reaction molding 液态化学反应成形法(塑料)
liquid resistance 液体阻力
liquid rotational molding 流体旋转造型,液态旋转成形(法)
liquid rubber 液态橡胶,液体橡胶
liquid shock absorber 液压减振器(= liquid damper)
liquid sodium 液体钠
liquid spring unit 液体弹簧装置
liquid state 液态
liquid tank 液箱,储液罐
liquid thermostat 液体节温器(液体恒温器)
liquid traction (涂在赛车轮胎上增加胎面与地面摩擦力,以提高牵引力的)增力液
liquid trailer 液罐挂车,油罐挂车
liquid trap 液体分离器,油分离器,水分离器
Liquid-vapor separator 液-汽分离器
liquid withdrawl (指液化石油气汽车从液化石油气箱底)取液供气(以免从箱顶抽出已成气态的液化石油气)
liquif(ic) ation 液化(作用),溶化,溶解,稀释
liquified gas tanker 液化气罐车
L-iron L形角铁(不等边角铁)
list ①表格,清单,目录,一览表 ②倾斜,侧倾,倾向性 ③狭布条(木条) ④边饰 ⑤列表,编目 ⑥镶边
listening rod 听诊棒
listening tube 听筒(见 speaking tube)
listen to the engine 用听觉检查发动机
list of spare parts (备用)零件清单,零件目录(= parts catalogue)
list price 出厂价(相对实际售价而言)
lite 轻的(light 的另一种拼法,多见于美国)
liter (公)升(容量单位=1000cm^3,亦写作 litre)
literal coefficient 文字系数(字母表示的系数)
literal equation 文字方程
literature 文献
liter capacity ①(以升计的)发动机排量 ②(发动机)升功率
liter car 升排量车(发动机排量为1000mL级的小型汽车)
litharge 一氧化铅(PbO,涂于蓄电池极板的活性涂料)
lithium 锂(Li)
lithium base grease 锂基(润)滑脂(指以脂肪酸锂皂或复合锂皂做稠化剂的润滑脂,美国、日本、西欧各国汽车用润滑脂一般都是通用的锂基滑脂,简称 lithium grease)
lithium-chlorine cell 锂-氯电池(= chlorine-lithium cell)
lithium-copper fluoride cell 锂-氟化铜(蓄)电池
lithium fluoride 氟化锂(LF)
lithium-ion capacity 锂离子电容器
lithium-iron battery 锂-铁电池
lithium-moist air cell 锂-湿空气电池

lithium-organic electrolyte cell 锂-有机电解液(蓄)电池

lithium-sulfur cell 锂-硫电池

litmus 石蕊(溶解于水和酒精,测试酸、碱的试剂,遇酸性呈红色,遇碱性呈蓝色)

litmus paper 石蕊试纸

litre 升(容积、体积单位,代号 L, 1964 年定为 1 liter = 1dm³ = 1000cm³。原义为 1kg 质量的水在其最大密度的温度时的容积等于 1.000028dm³; 1 liter = 10^{-3} m³ = 0.2642gallon = 61.03in³ = 27 市寸³ = 10^{-1} 市斗 = 1 市升,亦写作 liter)

Litronic bulb 光电子灯泡(light-electronic 的简称,一种氙气气体放电前照灯系统的商品名)

litter end 连杆小头(= connecting rod small end)

live ①活动的、活跃的、可变的 ②有效的、能起作用的 ③运转着的、正在使用的、能开动的 ④动力驱动的、传动的 ⑤充电的、带电的

live axle 驱动轴、驱动桥(= powered axle)

live axle housing flange 可分割式驱动桥壳对接凸缘

live circuit 有电压的电路、通着电的电路

live end 有效端、加压端

live engine 使用中的发动机(正在工作的发动机 = operating engine, service engine)

live fish carrier 活鱼运输车

live hydraulic system 有源液压系统(油泵独立驱动的液压系统,本身有独立液压源的液压系统)

live lever 活动杠杆(浮动杠杆)

live load 活荷重(移动荷载,实际工作荷载;动荷载)

lively vehicle 动力性能良好的车辆

live parking 不熄火停车

live power take-off 独立式功率输出轴

livery car (出租店的)出租轿车

live stock carrier 牲畜运输车(亦称 live stock transporter)

live stock container 牲畜集装箱

live stock trailer 牲畜挂车,运畜挂车

live wire ①带电导线,通着电的导线 ②(特指不经点火开关起动,而用一导线直接接蓄电池或其他情况下直接由蓄电池取电的)取电电线(亦称 hot wire)

L-jetronic system (德国博世公司)进气空气流量型电子控制多点喷射式汽油喷射系统(的商品名,其主要特征是以吸入发动机的空气质量流量和发动机转速作为控制基本喷油量的参数,有 LE-jetronic, L3-jetronic, LH-jetronic, LU-jetronic 等多种变型目前被广泛使用,其中, L3-jetronic 采用了数字技术,其电子控制模块直接装在空气流量传感器上, LH-jetronic 采用热线式或改进后的膜式空气质量流量传感器,以吸入空气的质量与发动机转速共同作为控制喷油量的主要参数)

LKAS (协助驾驶者保持行车路线的)车道保持支援系统(lane keep assistance system)的简称[由摄像型行车路线传感系统(camera type lane sensor system)将路宽、路弯曲度和车辆位置等告知电子控制模块,由控制模块精算出保持车辆沿行驶路线中央行驶所必需的转向盘转矩,同时监视驾驶者所施加的转向盘转矩,并通过电子控制动力转向电动机给予支援,达到该必需值,驾驶者可轻松自如地保持行车路线,见 HiDs]

LLC 长效防冻冷却液(long-life coolant)

L_{10} life 10% 余寿(产品使用达寿命储备的 90% , = B_{10} life)

lllium 依里乌姆合金（耐蚀镍铬合金，Ni 56%～62%，Cr 21%～24%，Cu 3%～8%，Mo 4%～6%，少量 Si、Mn、W、Fe，对硝酸、硫酸有极强的耐蚀性能）

lm ①极限（limit）②流明（国际单位制的光通量单位，lumen）③流明范围（lumen range）

l/min 升/分（国际单位制容积流量单位 1 l/min = 0.001m^3/min = 0.2642us. gal/min = 0.0353ft^3/min）

LML ①稀混合气可燃极限（lean mixture limit）②稀混合气失火界限（lean misfire limit）

LMRS 车站等地面固定点与行驶车辆之间的无线电服务，地-车无线电联系（land mobile radio service）

LMS （一个系统内的误差的）最小均方判据（least mean squares 的简称）

LNGV 液化天然气汽车（见 liquefied natural gas vehicle）

LOA 全长，总长（length overall）

load ①荷载，负荷（对发动机而言指驱动从动机械所消耗的功率和转矩的大小、本身所承受的机械应力和应力的大小、节气门开度大小）②装载物，货物 ③装载量，运量 ④发电量，用电量 ⑤（将软件）装入（计算机）

load afloat （水陆两用汽车）浮渡装载质量

loadage 装载量，载重；装载质量

load alteration effect 荷载变动效应（指由于加速、制动、转向等原因造成荷载动态转移时，对汽车转向、驱动系等的影响）

load and time sensor 负荷-时间传感器

load at failure 破坏荷载

load balancing mechanism 荷载平衡机构（使各部件均匀承受荷载的机构，如：能够补偿制造误差、使各行星齿轮均匀承受荷载的机构）

load base 货车前轮中心线至重心（或当荷载均匀分配时，至货箱的横向中心线）间的距离

load bearing ①承载，承重 ②承载负荷的，承载的，承重的

load-bearing frame 承载构架，承载车架（= supporting frame）

load box 负荷电阻箱

load bracket （车上的）载货架，载物架

load brake 超载制动器，超重制动器

load bucket capacity 装载机铲斗堆装容量

load capacity 承载能力，荷载能力，载质量，允许荷载，起重能力（= load carrying capacity）

load carrier 货物运输工具（如：运货汽车）

load-carrying 承载负荷的（承载的，承重的

load carrying ability 载重能力（起重能力，负载能力；容量）

load-carrying ball joint 承载球节（参见 loaded ball joint）

load-carrying capacity 承载能力，负载能力，载货容量，装载量（= load-carrying ability）

load carrying capacity test 承载能力试验

load-carrying covering 承载外壳

load-carrying element 承载构件，支撑构件（亦称 load-carrying member）

load carrying floor （货车的）承载地板

load carrying index （车辆）装载指数，功率利用指数（车辆有效装载质量和车速的乘积与额定功率之比）

load-carrying skin 承载蒙皮

load-carrying structure 承载结构

load-carrying unit （结构的）承载件

load-carrying vehicle ①起重车辆（如：前端装载机，汽车吊车等）②货运车辆

load cell （压电式）负荷传感器（测力传感器，测压计，测力计，= load-measuring cell）

load cell fixed barrier （汽车撞击试验用的）装有负荷传感器的固定障壁（简称 LCFB）

load characteristic 负载特性，荷载特性曲线

load coil 加载线圈（加感线圈）

load condition 荷载状态（负荷状况，负载状况）

load control 负载控制（荷载调节）

load-controlled power distribution 荷载控制式驱动力分配（亦称荷载感知式动力分配，根据汽车在行驶过程中荷载的动态转移和变化，分配前、后车桥及左、右车轮的驱动力）

load control lever （柴油机调速器的部件，将加速踏板的运动传递给控制齿条的）负荷控制杠杆

load curve 荷载曲线

load deflection 加载挠度，加载变形（荷载作用下的挠度）

load-deflection curve 荷载-变形曲线（= load-deformation curve）

load-deflection diagram 荷载-挠度曲线图（= load-deformation diagram）

load dependent brake 荷载控制式制动器（根据荷载大小及变动，改变制动力的制动器）

load dependent relay valve 负荷感应继动阀，载控继动阀

load diffusion 负荷传播，负荷扩散

load distance 运距，载运距离

load distribution ①（各车桥、车轮上的）荷载分布（= distribution of load）②（桥间或轮间的）荷载分配比

load distribution performance 负荷分布特性

load dividing dolly （并装双后桥汽车悬架的负荷）平衡架

load-dump testing 负载速断试验，（突然）卸载试验

loaded 负载的，载重的；加载的

loaded ball joint （前轮独立悬架的）承载球节（= load carrying ball joint）

loaded container kilometrage 重箱里程（汽车载运装货集装箱的行程，集装箱内不论装有多少货物均为重箱）

loaded kilometrage 重车公里（重车行程，载货或载客的工作车辆的累计行程，= loaded vehicle kilometer）

loaded length 在加载状态下的长度

loaded section of tyre 轮胎承载断面（负荷下的断面）

loaded section width （轮胎的）负荷下断面宽度（指轮胎按规定要求充气后，其在法向负荷作用下的断面宽度）

loaded state 受载状态，承载状态

loaded tire radius 承载轮胎半径

loaded-up condition 装载情况，（在装载状态下）负载状况，荷载状态

loaded vehicle kilometer 重车公里（汽车装载行驶的公里数，相对空车行驶里程而言，= loaded kilometer）

loaded work piece 负载工件

load equalization 荷载平衡

loader ①装载机，铲运机 ②传送带，输送器，装料-送料装置 ③见 volumer

load extension diagram ①荷载-伸长曲线（= load-elongation curve）②荷载-伸长曲线图

load factor ①荷载系数，负荷系数，

loa

荷载因素（最大强度和实际荷载的比值）②（交通）绿灯时间利用百分率 ③（汽车）载质量利用系数 ④（设备的）利用率，负载率（某规定时间内，设备的平均负载与设备最大容量之比）⑤里程利用率（车辆总行程中，重车行程所占的比率）

load factor of passenger 载客量利用率（指统计期内客运汽车实际完成的旅客周转量与客座设计可完成的周转量之比）

load floor ①（货车的）货箱地板 ②（轿车等的行李舱或行李区）地板 ③载货区的面积或装货区（= loading area）

load-free speed 无负载速度（空转速度）

load haul dump 装车，运输，卸车，装运卸（简称LHD）

load hook 起重吊钩

load impedance 负载阻抗（如：仪器仪表输出端连接的所有装置及连接导线的阻抗总和）

load in bulk 散装荷载

load increment 荷载增量

load index 轮胎的荷载指数（某些轮胎规格标记，如Alphametric制轿车轮胎规格标记中，用一组数字表示在厂家规定的使用条件和速度下，轮胎可承受的最大荷载，这组数字称荷载指数，如：88，145，157分别表示该轮胎最大负荷为560kg，2900kg、4125kg，简称LI，= load rating②）

load-indicating-type washer 荷载指示式垫圈（被螺母压紧时，可指示压力的大小）

load inflation quotient （轮胎的）荷载轮胎压力系数（荷载气压比）

load-inflation table （轮胎）负荷和充气压力关系表

loading ①装载（的），装运（的），加载（的），加料（的）②充电（的）③荷载，载重（车上装载的）货 ④填料，填充物

loading and unloading operation 装卸作业

loading area （车身）货箱面积，承载面积

loading area index 货箱面积利用系数（指货箱有效面积与汽车占地外廓面积"汽车的总长×总宽"之比值）

loading cam 加载凸轮机构，传力凸轮机构，驱动凸轮机构（如：由带斜槽面的主、从动凸轮盘和夹在二者之间的传力滚子组成的圆盘凸轮传力机构）

loading capacity ①（车辆的）装载能力 ②起重能力 ③荷载能力，承载能力（如：曲轴轴承承受燃烧压力的能力，亦称load-carrying capacity，load capacity）

loading chart 荷载分布图

loading condition 负载条件，负载状态

loading curve 荷载曲线，负载曲线

load (ing) diagram 荷载（分布）图

loading equipment （试验）加载设备，加载装置；（物料）装载设备

loading facilities ①装载设备 ②（试验）加载设备

loading factor 装载系数，储备系数，安全系数

loading frame （轮胎6维试验机等的）加载架（向被试车轮加载）

loading gauge 装载量测定仪

loading height 装载高度（汽车装货后的外形高度）

loading in bulk 散装，堆装

loading level 加载程度，负载程度

loading performance 加载性能（指内燃机加载过程的性能）

load (ing) program （零部件试

验)加载程序

loading rate 加载速率;负载率,载重率

loading sensing pressure limiting valve 感载限压阀(可感知汽车装载质量,并根据该装载质量自动改变限压作用起始点压力)

loading sensing proportioning valve 感载式比例分配阀(可感知汽车的装载质量,并根据该装载质量来调节前、后车轮制动工作压力的比例分配阀)

loading shovel 装载铲,(铲运机)铲斗

loading space 荷载容积,(车厢)有效装载空间

loading station ①(公共汽车的)上、下车站(passenger loading station)的简称 ②(货车的)装货站

loading surface altitude (货车)货箱底板的离地高度

loading test 负载试验(= load test)

loading/unloading volume 货物装卸量

loading-unload machine 装卸机械

loading weight (车辆)装载重量(装载质量的旧称)

loading wheel 承重轮

load (ing) zone 荷载作用区

load input 加载,加力

load insensitive device 对负载不敏感的装置

load-leveler shock absorber (车身荷载后)高度调平式减振器

load-leveling air suspension 载荷调平式空气悬架(可随载荷大小自动调控车身高度)

load-leveling hitch 带调平机构的悬架装置,带调平机构的挂接装置

load limiter 负荷限制器(如:限制安全带收紧力,防止乘员勒伤的装置)

load line ①荷载曲线,力作用线 ②(水陆两用汽车)吃水线

load losses (齿轮传动的)负荷损失(齿轮传动中齿面摩擦造成的功率损失,该项损失与负荷成正比)

load-measuring cell 负载传感器(利用压电效应或液力效应等测量负载的元件,按其结构设计可测定单向负载、多向负载或扭转负载,并能远距离显示或记录其测量结果)

load member 承载构件,承载件

load meter 荷载计,轮载测定仪,落地磅秤(称量载货汽车等用,亦写作 loadometer)

load on the axle 轴荷(轴上的荷载)(= axle load)

load overhang (货车装载长货物时)外伸长度(指货物从货车车箱后边缘向外伸出的长度)

load path 负荷传递路线,负荷作用路径

load-penetration curve (土壤)荷载-贯入曲线

load per unit length 单位长度上的荷载

load proportional brake control (system, device) 荷载比例制动控制(根据荷载比例分配前后桥制动力的系统或装置)

load proportion EGR system 负荷比例式 EGR 系统(按发动机负荷确定废气还流比例的废气再循环系统)

load range ①(轮胎等的)额定负荷(指所能承受的最大负荷,= maximum load, max load,轮胎的额定负荷常用从 A 到 N 的字母代码表示) ②荷载范围(制件或材料疲劳载荷中连续谷值与峰值或连续峰值与谷值的代数差。在恒载荷中,指最大负荷与最小载荷的代数差)

load rate 加载速度(单位时间内载荷的增加量)

load ratio 荷载比（指疲劳荷载每一循环中的两个荷载参数，如：最大与最小荷载，谷值与峰值荷载，荷载幅与平均荷载的代数比值）

load ration ①负载定额，负载额定，额定负载 ②（轮胎的）荷载指数（见 load index）③轮胎的额定负荷（标准规定的不同充气压力的对应负荷，亦称标准负荷，推荐负荷，设计负荷，包括最大负荷）

load regulation coefficient （电压调整器或电流调整器的）负荷调整系数（指其他条件不变时，在规定的输入电流或电压变化下，输出电压或输出电流的相对变化率）

load-relay 负荷继电器，负载继电器，过载断电器

load removal 卸载

load resistor 负载电阻（器）

load rest 托板，托座，支座，荷重座，支撑架

load/RPM point （发动机的）负荷/转速点（指喷油量与负荷/转速关系特性曲面中的每一点，亦称 operating point）

load saturation curve 负载饱和曲线

load sensing braking force metering device 载荷感知式制动力调节装置（= load sensing braking force control device）

load sensing governor 负荷感知式调速器

load-sensing height-adjusting rear air suspension system 感载高度调节式后空气悬架（当电子控制模块收到行李舱或后座载荷增加，以致后端车身高度降低信号时，即启动空气压缩机并开启后轮空气弹簧进气阀，直至后端升起到规定高度）

load-sensing limiter 荷载感知式制动液压限制阀

load sensing proportioning valve 荷载感知式比例阀（可随着汽车前、后桥荷载的变化，控制与调节前、后轮制动压力，以防止后轮先于前轮抱死而产生侧滑，简称 LSPV，亦写作 load sensing proportion valve）

load-sensing unit 测力元件（荷载传感元件）

load-sensing valve 负载传感阀，负载感知阀

load-sensitive brake 可根据负荷自动调节制动力的制动器

load-sensitive shock absorber 荷载感知式减振器，感载减振器

load sensitivity （对）荷载（的）敏感度

load sensor 负荷传感器（指用于测定所承受的外力的压力传感器）

load space 载货空间，载物空间

load space lamp （轿车）行李舱（盖控制的）照明灯（亦称 boot lamp）

load spectrum 荷载谱（汽车零、部件的实际载荷多数属随机荷载，通常把表示随机荷载统计特征的图形、数字表格、矩阵等统称为荷载谱）

load speed 负载转速（发电机达到额定电压及电流时的转速，= speed under load）

load stabilization coefficient （电压调整器或电流调整器的）负载稳定系数（指其他条件不变时，输出电压或输入电流的相对变化与规定输出电流或规定负载电阻的相对变化之比）

load stone 天然磁石（= natural magnet）

load-strain diagram 荷载-变形曲线图

load tension 由于荷载而引起的拉伸

load test 负载试验，负荷试验（= loading test, load trial）

load time 加载时间

load-time diagram 荷载-时间曲线图，按时间分配的荷载分布图

load transfer 荷载转移（=weight transfer，指制动引起的车重由后桥向前桥、加速引起的前桥向后桥及转向引起的内侧向外侧的转移）

load transfer path （车辆碰撞时的冲击）荷载传递路径

load transient recovery time 负载瞬态响应时间（负载瞬变过程持续时间）

load transient(s) 负载瞬变过程

load trial 负载试验（=load test）

load-up condition 装载情况（在装载状态下）负荷状态，承载状态

lobe ①突出部，凸台，凸座，凸角 ②（特指凸轮高出其基圆的）凸缘部分（=cam lobe）

lobed rotor pump 凸轮转子泵

lobe/flank ratio （转子发动机的）缸面弧数-转子边数比（如三角转子发动机缸体外旋轮线弧数为2，转子的侧边为3，其弧数、边数比则为2:3）

lobe of the rotor （转子发动机的侧边）转子工作面，转子凸面，旋转活塞工作面

lobe-type supercharger 双螺旋凸面转子容积式增压器

lo-boy ［美］低货台挂车（=low-bed trailer）

local ①近郊的，市内的，当地的，地方的 ②局部的，狭隘的，本机的，本身的

local action 局部作用

local area network 局域网（在汽车电子控制系统中，指某一主控模块系统内，主控模块与各传感器和执行器或分控模块之间的宽带双向单线多路复用数据通信网络系统，简称LAN）

local assembly 当地组装

local battery 局域电池（简称LB，亦称local cell，存在于电池内的金属杂质，主要是锑Sb，附着于极板并与极板间形成"电池"，即局域电池，局域电池两极间的短路电路是导致电池自放电的原因之一）

local contraction 局部收缩

local control 就地控制，就机控制，直接控制（相对远距离控制而言）

local controller 局部控制机（管制一个交叉口或两三个邻近交叉口信号的控制机）

local corrosion 局部腐蚀

local current 局域电流（如蓄电池内形成的局域电池的短路电流）

local deformation 局部变形

local effect 局部效应

local heating 局部加热

local highway 地方公路，地区公路

local homomorphism 局部同态（局部异质同晶现象）

Local Interconnect Network 见LIN

locality 地带，地区；地点，位置，所在地；场所，现场

localization ①本地化 ②定位，探测，位置的测定 ③局限（性），限制（在一区域内），局部化，集中 ④位置，部位

localize 定位

locally isomorphism 局部同构（类质同象现象）

local mixture strength 局部混合（气）强度

local pressure 局部压力（如发动机爆燃时，燃烧室局部产生的异常高压）

local probability of failure 局部故障概率

local road 地方道路，本地区道路

local section 局部剖面

local strain 局部应变

local stress 局部应力

local traffic (起讫点在同一个地区的)当地交通,本区交通,地方交通

"local traffic only" sign "禁止过境交通"标志(只准当地车辆通行的标志)

local transit 地方交通,当地交通,市内公共交通(一般指车速低、停车点频繁的区域性公共交通)

locate ①确定位置,判明位置②(固定于一定的位置上)布置,设置,安排;定线,放样;测位,定位

locating bearing 定位轴承

locating distance 安装距(锥齿轮分锥顶点至定位面的轴向距离)

locating dowel 定位凸销(= locating pin,如:轴承瓦片背面嵌入轴瓦座面内的凸榫,见 locating lug)

locating face 定位面(如:作为安装基准,确定锥齿轮轴向位置的平面)

locating joint 定位接头(= indexing joint)

locating lug 定位突块(缘),定位突销,定位榫(= locating pin, locating dowel)

locating notch 定位槽口

locating points (工件)定位点

locating screw 定位螺钉

locating sleeve 定位套

locating spring 定位卡簧(如盘式制动器中,将油缸固定在浮钳架上的钢丝卡簧)

locating stud 定位螺柱,定位销(= locating pin, positioning stud)

locating surface (工件的)定位面

locating tab 定位榫(销)

location ①配置,安置,布置,安装②探测,测定;测位,确定位置;(公路)定线 ③位置,位置,地点,场所,场地,现场部位 ④(车辆等的)出租(契约)⑤所在,部位;局部化,局限性

location bearing (轴向)定位轴承

location bolt 定位螺栓

location hole 定位孔

location of malfunction 故障部位诊断(确定发生故障的部位)

location of powerplant 动力装置的布置

location pin 定位销

location tolerance (相对)位置公差(= positional tolerance)

locator ①定位器,安装用定位销,锁止器②探测器,探头

lock ①锁,闩,止动器,锁定器②卡住,锁上,锁住,锁紧,锁定,闭锁,联锁 ③(交通)阻塞④(汽车转向轮转到锁止位置时的)转动量(用角度表示)

lockable 可锁上的,可锁住的,可闭锁的

lockable differential 可锁止式差速器,强制锁止式差速器(亦称locking differential, lock-up type differential,见 limited slip differential。当两驱动轮中有一车轮打滑空转时,通过手动操纵或自动控制锁止机构锁死,不再起差速作用,而使左右两车轮同步转动的差速机构)

lock actuator (独立于气动制动系,因而与制动气压无关的驻车制动器的)锁定机构

lock angle ①锁止角,最大角②(转向车轮的)最大回转角,最大转角(= angle of lock)

lock barrel (弹子锁)锁芯(= lock cylinder)

lock bolt 锁紧螺栓

lock brake chamber (气驻车制动器的)锁止式制动气室(用楔环等锁止件锁止制动气室推杆,使驻车制动器起作用的制动气室)

lock chain 防盗锁链(用于锁死转向盘或车轮,亦称 chain lock)

lock chamber （锁止式制动气室的）锁止腔（利用充气、放气过程使锁止机构起作用和放松的腔室）

lock cylinder （车门上）锁芯（圆柱形锁芯，亦称 key cylinder）

locked 关闭的，闭合的，锁住的

locked cone friction clutch 锁锥式摩擦离合器（= bevel cone friction clutch）

locked-in direct drive （液力变速机构）锁止（后）直接驱动

locked-in torque ①（闭式循环试验台中的）加载转矩 ②锁止转矩（液力变速器锁止直接驱动时的转矩）

locked transmission ①闭路传动系（封闭式传动系，发动机、变速器与主传动连成一整体）②被锁止的变速器

locked wheel （制动时，因制动力大于路面摩擦力而被）抱死的车轮

lock facing （车门上安）装锁（的表）面

lock groove （安装锁环、卡环、定位环等的）锁槽

locking angle 锁止角（如：最大活动角，车轮的最大转向角）

locking arm connector 锁臂式接线管［小电流电路用的小型接线器，由圆管形接线夹（锁臂）和管壳组成，用于组合式仪表等之类的窄小场合下所使用的电器件的接线］

lock(ing) ball 锁球［（拨叉等的）定位钢球］

locking ball 锁球，锁珠（如：变速器换挡轴的自锁及互锁机构的钢球）

lock(ing) bar ①锁杆，锁销 ②（车门上）装锁的横梁

locking circuit 保持电路（吸持电路，自保电路，强制同步电路）

locking clutch 锁止离合器（= lock-up clutch）

locking coefficient of differential 差速器的锁止系数（指两侧快、慢半轴转矩 M_1、M_2 相差的倍数 $K = M_2/M_1 > 1$，亦称 differential locking factor）

locking differential 见 lockable differential

locking dog 制动爪，销定爪

locking dowel pin 限位销（如：使离合器压盘传动和定位的销）

locking factor （防滑差速器的）锁紧系数（指两侧半轴转矩 M_1、M_2 可能相差的最大倍数 $K = M_2/M_1$）

locking gas cap 汽油箱锁盖

lock(ing) gear 锁定机构，闭锁机构，联锁机构

locking hub （非全时四轮驱动的）可锁断式前轮毂（通过轮毂内的离合装置可按需要手动或自动接通或断开传动）

locking key ①锁键，止动键 ②锁定开关，止动按钮

locking reel （汽车乘员安全带的）自动锁止式卷筒（当乘员因紧急制动或撞车而猛向前冲的加速度超过规定值时，该卷筒即自动锁死，将安全带卡住）

locking synchromesh 锁止式同步器（如：装有锁环或锁销的惯性式同步器，锁止件用来阻止接合套在换挡齿轮接近同步前继续前移而产生的冲击性啮合。目前手动式变速器均使用这类同步器，亦写作 lock synchromesh。因其同步啮合压力与换挡力成正比，故又称 proportional load synchromesh）

locking thread sealant 螺纹紧固件的防松剂（一般为厌氧型化学密封剂，涂于紧固件螺纹，防止松动）

lock(ing) wire （螺栓）锁紧铁丝

lock knob 门锁按钮

lock nut ①（拧在另一螺母上的）锁紧螺母，防松螺母（参见 jam

nut）②自锁螺母（见 self-locking nut）

lock of chamber （液化石油气发动机燃料系蒸发器的）停机燃料切断部件（发动机停机时，控制燃料流出）

lock-o-matic （一种）自动锁止式差动限制装置（商品名，由两组多片式摩擦离合器组成，加装在一般的差速器上，可自动限制差动作用）

lock on ①（开始）自动跟踪，跟踪②锁住，锁定（= lock onto）

lockout ①脱开，分离，切断②闭锁，关闭，锁定

lock-out circuit 保持电路，闭塞电路

lockout relay 锁止继电器，闭锁继电器，锁定继电器

lock piece 锁止件

lock pillar （车门等的）锁扣支柱（B支柱，车门锁碰板装在该支柱上，故名）

lock pillar closing plate （汽车车门）锁扣支柱的合接板

lock pin 锁销

lock plate 锁止板，锁板，锁片

lock position ①止点位置（如：活塞在上、下止点时的曲轴位置）②锁止位置

lock prevention brake 防抱死制动器（见 anti-blocking brake）

lock ring for piston pin 活塞销锁环

lock seaming （薄板构件）锁口接缝（卷边接缝，咬口接缝）

lock spring 锁簧，锁止弹簧

lock striker （车门锁或行李舱锁销孔）碰销（简称 striker）

lock test ①（起动机）制动试验（将起动机夹在虎钳或其他夹持装置上，并在其驱动齿轮上装一杆臂和弹簧秤，接通起动电源，测量其电流和力矩，二者都不应大于规定值，否则说明其线围短路或焊接不良）②（制动器的）抱死试验③拘束（束缚）试验，锁止试验

lock-to-lock turn （转向盘）从一极限位置转至另一极限位置

lock torque ①（车轮）抱死转矩②（起动机在规定条件下）全制动时的力矩（见 lock-test①）

lock-type hose coupling 锁紧式软管接头

lock-up ①（车轮）抱死（当制动力大于轮胎与路面附着力时，发生的现象亦称 block）②（液力变矩器的）锁止（运转模式，液力变矩器的泵轮和涡轮机械地结合成一体，以与发动机相同的转速旋转，消除在无须液力变矩时的动液摩擦损失，亦写作 lockup）③（起上述作用的）锁止机构（亦称 hold system）

lock-up clutch （液力变矩器的）锁止离合器（见 lock up②、③）

lockup cut off valve 锁止切断阀（指松开锁止作用的阀，如：在液力变矩器中，在换挡期间起自动松开其锁止离合器作用的阀或阀组）

lock up disc （自动变速变矩器离合器的）锁止盘（通过花键与变矩器涡轮连接的摩擦盘）

lock-up torque converter （可）锁止式液力变矩器（可通过电子控制系统或锁止离合器，将其泵轮和涡轮锁止成一体，直接传送转矩，以减少液力传动损失的变矩器）

lock up valve 锁止阀（如：在液力变矩器中，在调制压力作用下导致液力变矩器锁止的阀）

lock voltage （起动机的）制动电压（其全制动时的端电压，见 lock test①）

lock washer 弹簧垫圈（锁紧垫圈）

locomotion ①运动，移动，行走，行驶 ②行驶能力

locomotive （陆路）牵引车（指拖

挂多节挂车的拖车，一般除法规性文件外很少使用）

locus ①轨迹，轨线 ②（空间）位置，场所，地点，所在地

locus nut （带外螺纹的）镶孔螺母（通过其外螺纹拧入金属板件较大的螺孔中，以便使用直径较小的，即与该螺母内螺纹尺寸相同的螺纹紧固件）

locus of points 点轨迹

lodging vehicle 旅居车（= mobile home）

Lo-Ex Lo-Ex 合金（一种低膨胀合金，low-expansion alloy 的简称，为活塞用轻合金的一种，其成分为：Si 11.0% ~ 13.0%，Ni 1.0% ~ 2.5%，Cu 和 Mg 0.8% ~ 1.3%，微量 Fe，Mn，Ti，其余为铝。耐热，耐压，耐腐，耐磨蚀，目前用得最广）

Loftin-white amplifier 罗夫亭-怀特放大器（一种直接耦合的直流放大器）

log ①（未经刨削的）圆木，原木；大木料 ②值班记录，维修记录，（运行）日记 ③汽车里程表 ④（发动机等的运行）记录，履历表 ⑤对数符号，对数曲线图 ⑥行车日记，作记录，记录行驶工况

logarithm 对数

logarithmic decrement 对数衰减率，对数减缩率（指在单频衰减振动中，同侧两个相继的幅值之比的自然对数）

logarithmic nomal distribution 对数正态分布

log(arithmic) table 对数表

log body 原木运输车箱

log bunk （原木运输车上的）横向支撑（件）

logger ①记录器，自动分析记录仪 ②原木装载机，原木装运车（= logging vehicle）

logging arch 跨拱式运木车

logging transporter 原木运输车（亦称 logging vehicle）

logic 逻辑，逻辑学；逻辑部分，逻辑线路

logical "and" "与"逻辑，逻辑"与"（简称 and）

logical "and" component 逻辑"与"元件（执行"与"逻辑操作的元件）

logical calculus 逻辑演算

logical circuit 逻辑电路（亦写作 logic circit，指由触发器和各种逻辑门组成的电路，是数字电路的基本电路，广泛用于计算机控制系统）

logical combination of gear-solenoid states （电子控制自动变速器挡位变换的）换挡电磁阀工位逻辑组合，对四挡自动变速器只需要两个换挡电磁阀，五挡自动变速器只需要三个换挡电磁阀按一定的通-断 "on-off" 工作组合，便可实现全部换挡控制，如：

挡位	电磁阀1	电磁阀2	电磁阀3
1挡	on	on	on
2挡	on	on	off
3挡	on	off	off
4挡	off	off	off
5挡	off	off	off

logical component 逻辑元件

logical computer 逻辑运算计算机

logical constants 逻辑常量，逻辑常项，逻辑恒量

logic(al) decision （计算机）逻辑判定，逻辑判断（逻辑运算结果，指对问题的回答，只有是或否的选择过程）

logical IC 逻辑集成电路（logical integrated circuit 的简称）

logical "not" component 逻辑"非"元件

logical "or" component 逻辑"或"元件

logical sum 逻辑和

logical symbol 逻辑符号（表示运算符、函数或函数关系的符号，即代表某一逻辑算符的符号，亦写作 logic symbol）

logical unit 逻辑系统，逻辑部分，逻辑装置

logic analyzer 逻辑电路分析仪（用于测试逻辑电路工作是否正常）

logic circuit 逻辑电路

logic controller （防车轮抱死制动系等的）逻辑控制器

logic element 逻辑元件（计算机或数据处理系统中最小的构造单元，如与门和或门，= gate）

logic gate 逻辑门[将各种输入信号转变为一个特定数（0 或 1）输出的电路，亦称 logic circuit。车用微型计算机中使用的基本逻辑门有以下五种：与门（见 AND gate），或门（见 OR gate），非门（见 NOT gate），非与门（见 NAND gate），或非门（见 NOR gate）]

logic of modality 模态逻辑

logic probe （向示波器输入数字信号的专用）数据采集线

logic test 逻辑试验

logistic ①数理逻辑 ②后勤，后勤供应技术 ③逻辑的，对数的，后勤的 ④物流的（见 logistics）

logistic enterprise 物流企业（是一种多功能的货物运输企业，从事货物联运、仓储、装卸、分送、中转、加工、包装、通信等业务）

logistics 物流学，物流管理学（物流学是一门新学科，研究的内容是如何及时而又低成本地将原材料、货物、零部件按所要求的数量和质量运送到所需要的地点，若以制造商为中心，则 logistics = material management + physical distribution）

logistics centre 物流中心（一般指以交通运输枢纽为依托，经营社会物流业务的货物集散场所，是社会物流网络的结点，具备订货、咨询、取货、包装、仓储、装卸、中转、配载、送货等服务设施，搬运设备、通信设备、控制设备等）

logistics information exchange system 物流信息交换系统

logistics process 物流过程，货物运输、配送过程

logistic trailer ①后勤挂车 ②配货挂车

log manifold （指接装四个或四个以上的化油器的）异形进气歧管（其管状干区的每侧均有供安装化油器的座面）

log screw 方头木螺钉（参见 coach screw）

log truck 原木运输车（带长货挂车的载货汽车，= lumber truck, timber truck, 参见 pole trailer）

London type smog 伦敦型烟雾（工厂和家用煤炉产生的烟雾，原于英国伦敦市区，现泛指由亚硫酸气、煤烟、粉尘及雾和汽车排放等形成的烟雾）

long amplitude （制件或材料的）荷载幅[指荷载范围的1/2，即 =（最大荷载 - 最小荷载)1/2]

long and short arm suspension 长短臂式独立悬架（上臂短、下臂长的双横臂独立悬架，可保证车轮在垂直方向的变动对外倾角的影响最小）

long and short dash line 点画线

long and two-short dash line 双点画线

long arm 长臂（如长、短臂式悬架的下臂）

long-arm-short-arm linkage 长、短臂悬架杆系

long base cab （指前、后壁间距）长（的平头货车）驾驶室（因而有足够的空间可将驾驶座拉向后壁，上、下

车方便)
long base car 长轴距车辆
long bending(seat) switch (汽车乘员安全系统的)弯弓形(乘坐感知)开关
long block engine 长缸体发动机(一般指缸体比四缸或 V 形八缸发动机长的直列式六缸发动机)
long column 长柱(长度大于 20 倍直径的杆件)
long combination vehicle 长汽车列车,多挂car汽车列车
long-distance 长距离的,长途的
long-distance beam (前照灯)远光(= driving beam, far beam, high beam, main beam, traffic beam, upper beam, long distance light)
long-distance bus 长途公共汽车,长途客车
long distance haulage 长途运输,长途货运
long-distance passenger transportation 长途客运
long distance road race (汽车)长途道路竞赛
long-distance transport 远距离运输,长途运输(亦写作 long-distance transportation)
long-distance trucking fleet 长途货运车队
long-distance vehicle 长途运输车辆
long-drain oil (可长期使用、无须经常更换的)长效机油
long dual exhaust manifold (三菱公司 MIVEC 发动机上使用的)加长型双排气歧管(用以减少排气压力损失)
long-duration cyclic test 长期耐久性循环试验
long dwell cam (凸轮曲线)同心部分展开长度长的凸轮(无增量部分大的凸轮,如:气门或触点等闭合角大的凸轮,大闭合角凸轮)

longer-lived 使用寿命较长的(比较耐用的,使用期较长的)
longeron (车架)纵梁,大梁(亦称 longitudinal, longitudinal beam, longitudinal bearer, side member, main side member)
longeval 使用期长的,寿命长的(亦写作 longevous)
longevity 耐久性,寿命,长寿命
longevity test 耐久性试验
long-fibre grease 长纤维润滑脂(耐高温,多用于球轴承)
long flat nose pliers 长平头(口)钳,鸭嘴钳,尖嘴钳
long haul 长途运输;长途货运,长途距,长途程
long haul diesel 长途货车用柴油机
long-haul over-the-highway truck 公路长途货车,长途货运汽车
long-haul rate 长途货运价(中国指货物运距在 25km 及以上的汽车运价)
longitude 经度,经线
longitudinal ①大梁,纵梁,边纵梁(= longitudinal member, side member)②纵向的,经度的,经线的,轴向的,长度的
longitudinal acceleration 纵向加速度(汽车质心加速度矢量,沿 x 轴方向的分量,见 vehicle axis system)
longitudinal aerodynamic force coefficient (汽车的)纵向空气动力系数[运动坐标系(moving axis system)x_0轴方向空气动力分量的无量纲系数 Cx,定义为 $Cx = F_{ax}/q \cdot A$,式中:F_{ax}—空气动力在 x_0 轴上的投影;A—汽车正面投影面积;q—合成气流速度形成的动压]
longitudinal axis 纵轴,纵轴线
longitudinal bending angle (of truck tractor with semitrailer) (牵引车与半挂车之间的)纵向折角(见 lengthwise angle)
longitudinal cardan shaft (常规的)

纵向布置的十字轴万向节式传动轴
longitudinal clearance 纵向间隙
longitudinal crack 纵向裂缝,纵向裂痕
longitudinal damping 纵向阻尼(纵向振动减振)
longitudinal direction 纵向
longitudinal displacement 纵向位移
longitudinal engine (传统后轮驱动式车辆)纵向布置的发动机(亦称 north-south layout)
longitudinal expansion 纵向膨胀
longitudinal fiber 纵向纤维,经线
longitudinal floor beam (客车等的)地板纵梁
longitudinal force 纵向力(作用在汽车上的力矢量在 x_o 轴方向的分力,见 moving axis system)
longitudinal force of tire 轮胎纵向力(路面作用在轮胎上的力沿纵即 X' 轴方向的分量,见 tire axis system)
longitudinal frame 见 ladder type frame
longitudinal girder (车架的)大梁,纵梁(= side member, 亦称 longitudinal member, longitudinal beam)
longitudinal G sensor 纵向加速度传感器(亦称 fore and aft G force sensor)
longitudinal half-elliptic leaf spring 纵向布置的半椭圆形钢板弹簧(见 semi-eliptic leaf spring)
longitudinally-gilled cylinder 带纵向散热片的汽缸体(= longitudinally-ribbed cylinder)
longitudinally load 纵向负载
longitudinally mounted engine 纵向布置的发动机(平行于车辆纵向轴线)
longitudinal member 车架纵梁
longitudinal movement 纵向运动
longitudinal noise 纵向噪声
longitudinal oscillation 纵向振动

longitudinal overturned car 纵向滚翻的车
longitudinal plane of symmetry (汽车的)纵向对称平面(纵向中心铅垂面,汽车在直前位置时,通过左、右轮中点的铅垂面)
longitudinal projected area of vehicle 车辆的纵向投影面
longitudinal rail (车架)纵梁
longitudinal rib 纵向肋(如:纵向布置的散热片,加强肋等)
longitudinal rocket arm (悬架的)纵臂(纵向布置的控制臂, = trailing arm)
longitudinal rod (悬架系统的)纵推力杆(在车轴与车架或车身间纵向布置的推力杆)
longitudinal runner 纵梁
longitudinal seam 纵向接缝
longitudinal seat 纵向长座椅
longitudinal section 纵向剖面,纵向断面
longitudinal separation ①纵向间隔 ②纵向隔断
longitudinal shaft 纵轴
longitudinal slip ①纵向滑移(指轮胎与路面间沿车辆行驶方向产生的滑移) ②纵向滑移率[指:(车速 - 车轮切向速度)/车速 × 100%,见 slip⑥]
longitudinal slope 纵坡
longitudinal slot 纵向槽
longitudinal speed 纵向速度(质心速度沿 x 轴的分量,见 vehicle axis system)
longitudinal stability 纵向稳定性
longitudinal strain 纵向应变
longitudinal stress 纵向应力
longitudinal torsion bar suspension 纵置扭杆弹簧型悬架
longitudinal travel 纵向位移
longitudinal traverse 纵向移动
longitudinal vehicle axis 汽车纵轴线

longitudinal vehicle ground clearance 车辆纵向离地间隙

longitudinal velocity 纵向速度(汽车速度沿 x 轴的分量,见 vehicle axis system)

longitudinal vibrations ①纵向振动(对车辆,指沿平行于地面的前进方向的直线振动;对人体,指沿人体脊柱方向的直线振动) ②扩张振动(= extensional vibration)

longitudinal view 纵向视图

long-lasting 耐久的,长寿命的,经久耐用

long-life coolant 长效防冻冷却液(用乙二醇90% ~95%,防腐剂3% ~10%,水0 ~5%,和其他材料组成的防冻液,其更换期可延长到2 ~ 3年,简称 LLC)

long-life engine 长寿命发动机

long nose ①长头,长嘴 ②(特指为了减小前轮空气浮力,提高空气动力稳定性的)长鼻车身

long-nose cam 大升程凸轮

long nose pliers 长嘴手钳,(亦称 snipe-nose pliers)鹬嘴钳

long-oil varnish 长油性清漆(稠油漆)

long planet gear 长行星齿轮

long-radius curve 长半径曲线(平缓的曲线,长半径弧线)

long-range 远程的,长距离的;大范围的;广泛的;长期的,长远的

long range fog lamp 远程雾灯

long-reach plug 长腿火花塞(安装螺纹部分较缸盖螺孔长,因而可伸入燃烧室,见 short-reach plug)

long residuum 久沸残油,久沸渣油(石油在一个大气压下,分馏出汽油、煤油、粗柴油后所余的重油馏分。将久沸残油进行真空蒸馏,可馏出重粗柴油及精制轻重润滑油的原料油,其所余残油称为真空蒸馏残渣,见 short residuum)

long response time ①长响应时间 ②(继电器)长的动作时间 ③(仪表的)响应迟缓

long roof (汽车的)长车顶(车身)(指车顶长的车身造型)

long run test 长期试验,连续(长期)试验

long skirt type 长裙式(如为了提高发动机缸体与变速器的结合强度,而将缸体下部延长的形式)

long-stem nozzle 长杆喷油器(针阀芯比较长)

long-stroke engine 长行程发动机(汽缸行程缸径比大的发动机)

long-term 长期的,长远的;长久的

long-term behavio(u)r 长期使用的性能

long-term lubricant 长效润滑剂

long-term operating economy 长期运行经济性

long-term (run) test 长途行车试验,长期试验 (= long-time test)

long-term travel (家庭等的)长途旅行

long-term use 长期使用,连续使用,持续使用 (亦写作 long-term usage)

long-time count (交通调查中的)长时计数(运量观测中一日内连续八小时及八小时以上的计数)

long ton 大吨,长吨,重吨,英吨 (= 2240 磅 = 1016 千克,亦称 gross ton,weight ton)

long wave 长波

long-wave pitching track 长节距波形试验跑道

long-wearing 耐磨的

long wheelbase ①长轴距 (简称 LWB) ②长轴距的

look-ahead procedure 预测法,预计法

looking-glass symmetry 镜像对称

look-out angle 视角

lookout hatch 检视口,监视孔,观察窗

look-up table (计算机控制系统存储的)查阅表(表中存储有各种被控制量与各种变量的对应关系数据,如点火提前角与转速、进气管真空度的关系曲面等,当传感器输入某一信号时,即可将该信号转换为与某被控制量相关的值,亦称 look up chart)

loom 线束,电线束(= wiring harness)

loop ①圈,环,耳环,卡环 ②线圈,回路,环路;环形跑道,环形道路,绕行道路

loop aerial 环形天线(亦称 loop antenna)

loop battery (电动汽车中的辅助电源,向空调、音响设备等供电的)辅助蓄电池

loop checking system 回路校验系统

loop circuit 环路电路

loop curve 闭合曲线

loop distance 往返行程长度,往返运程长度,往返里程(= round-trip distance)

loop hole ①观察孔,观察窗 ②透光孔 ③透气孔 ④漏洞

loop line 环行线路(环线)

loop osciIograph 回线式示波器(振子式示波器)

loop road 环路,环线,环道;绕越道路,绕行道,迂回道(亦称 detour, diversion)

loop scavenging 回流扫气,还流扫气(进气口与排气口位于汽缸同一侧或两侧下方,使充量从进气口进入汽缸后冲向其对面的缸壁而向汽缸上部迂回,驱使废气从下方排气口排出的扫气方式,因扫气路线从汽缸下方经上方又回到下向,形成回流或还流,故名,亦称 backflow scavenging, reverse flow。)

loop service 环行运输(几辆车在一闭路环行道内运行)

loop turn 环形道,转圈圈,环形转弯

loose ①松的,宽松的,松动的 ②无束缚的,无拘束的,自由的 ③松开,放开,解开

loose-blade damping system (燃气轮机)叶根松装减振法

loose bush 活动衬套(可更换的衬套)

loose fit 松配合

loose goods 散装货物

loose gravel (path) 松碎石(路面)

loose-leaf shim (松紧度)调整垫片

loose material 疏松材料,(化学)不稳定材料

loosen 松开,使松动,使松弛

looseness ①游隙,间隙 ②不紧密性;松弛性,松动,松度,松散性,疏松

loosening of tread (轮胎)胎面的剥离(故障)

loosen the brake 放开制动(松开制动踏板,脱开制动,= release the brake)

loose packed 散装的

loose pivot 松铰接点

loose pulley 游轮,惰轮,空转轮

loose running fit 松转配合,松动配合

loose scale 疏松氧化皮,疏松水垢

loose side (传动带、链条等的)松边,非张紧边,非传动边

lopping ①(发动机)不均匀的运转,怠速时异常横摆 ②修剪

lopsided ①不平的,倾斜的 ②不对称的,不均衡的,不平衡的

lorry 载货汽车,货车(美称 truck,多指栏板式货车或平板式货车)

lorry-mounted 安装在载货汽车上的

lorry-mounted crane 汽车吊车（起重汽车）
lorry winch 货车绞盘
lorry with heat-insulated (refrigerated) van 冷藏（冷冻）货车[具有冷藏（冷冻）车厢的运货车]
lorry with platform body 平板货车（参见 flat bed truck）
Los Angelos smog [美]洛杉矶烟雾（光化学烟雾，1943 年秋，洛杉矶市天空经常出现一种烟云，致使人们发生疾病，植物枯黄，经过十几年的研究，发现这种污染大气的烟云主要是由汽车排放的 HC、NO_x 与大气中的 O_2 在太阳光下进行复杂的化学反应，生成的有害物质。此后，美国首先对汽车排放进行法规性的限制，故名）
lose speed 失去速度（不能保持速度）
loss ①损失，损耗 ②下降，降低衰减 ③亏损 ④烧损，烧蚀（金属）
loss angle 损耗角（简谐振动中，应变与应力的相位差角）
loss by radiation 辐射损耗，辐射损失
loss due to friction 摩擦损失
loss due to leakage 泄漏损失
loss factor ①损耗系数，损失率（参见 loss tangent）②损耗因子（材料或构件阻尼能力，即耗散能量的能力的一种量值：材料单位阻尼能与单位应变能之比；构件阻尼能与应变能之比）
loss free conditions 无损失条件
loss from suspension vibrations 悬架振动引起的损失
loss in efficiency 效率损失（功率损失，= loss in power，power loss）
loss in head 压头损失，压头降（亦称 loss of head）
loss in power 功率损失（= loss in efficiency，loss of power）
loss in voltage 电压降
loss in weight 重量损失（质量损失的旧称）
loss modulus of elasticity 损耗弹性模量（指复弹性模量的虚部）
loss of adjustment 失调
loss of control 失控
loss-of-drive failure 引起传动失效的故障[引起（车辆）不能开动的故障]
loss of life 寿命缩短（使用期缩短）
loss of mobility 机动性的丧失（失去机动性）
loss of steering way （车轮侧偏等引起的转向不足或转向过度，导致）车辆偏离所预定的转向轨迹
loss of tune 调准不当造成的损失
loss shear modulus of elasticity 损耗切变模量（复切变模量的虚部）
loss stiffness 损耗刚度（复刚度的虚部）
loss tangent 损失角正切值（作用在橡胶弹簧原件上的正弦力与由此引起的弹簧元件变形之间的相位角的正切，亦称损耗因素、阻尼因数、机械损失角正切，即 loss factor，damping factor，mechanical loss tangent）
lost motion 空行程，空程，无效行程，空载行程，自由行程[因构件间隙引起的空程称间隙空程（lost motion caused by clearance），因构件弹性变形引起的空程，称弹变空程（lost motion cause by elastic deflection）]
lot production 大批生产，批量生产（= series production）
lot tolerance percent defective （大）批量生产中容许的次品率（%）（简称 LTPD）
lot wax process 失蜡精密铸造法，熔模铸造法
loudness ①（声）响度（指听觉产

生的声音大小感，随声音的频率而变化，声强级相同的声音，频率不同时听感响度不同，用响度级 loudness level 来表示）②高声，大声

loudness contour 等响线

loudness level 响度水平（响度级）

loud pedal （俗）加速踏板（= accelerator pedal）

loud (-tone) horn 高音喇叭

lounge （车辆销售、维修店的顾客）洽谈室，候修室，休息室（亦称 ownership lounge）

louvcar 一种轮胎扎入铁钉等的检测装置

louver ［美］（= louvre）①散热器百叶窗 ②（车身的）通气窗，天窗，风窗 ③（发动机罩或行车舱盖上冲压出的）成排通风缝 ④通风孔，通气孔（= vent）

louver angle （管带式散热器波形散热片上的）通风槽隙的角度，百叶窗式翅片角度

louverd 带百叶窗式孔隙的

louver effect 百叶窗式孔隙效应（如：附在管带式散热器波状散热片上的百叶窗式翅片或孔隙，可提高散热片与空气间的热传导率）

louver panel 百叶窗式壁板

louver pitch （管带式散热器波形散热片上的）百叶窗式槽隙的宽度

low accumulator （自动变速器行星齿轮机构液压系）制动带伺服缸控制液的储能减振器（参见 accumulator⑤）

low-air warning （气制动系）气压不足警告信号

low-alloy (tool) steel 低合金（工具）钢

low and wide （汽车的）扁宽（车身）（目前流行的又低又宽的车身造型）

low-angle 小角度的（一般指小于 45°的锐角）

low antimony battery 低锑蓄电池（简称 low anti-battery，介乎常规的铅-锑电池与免维护的铅-钙电池之间的一种"少维护电池"，含锑量少，约3%左右，价格较铅-钙电池低廉）

low-ash oil 低灰分机油

low-aspect tire 低高宽比轮胎（宽断面轮胎，轮胎断面的高度与宽度之比较小）

low baking 低温烘烤（的）

low battery （接近）完全放电的蓄电池

low beam ［美］（汽车前照灯）近光（= dipped beam，指前照灯在汽车按有关法规交会车或尾随其他汽车行驶、市区行驶等情况下使用的近距离照明光束，亦称 passing beam）

low beam filament shield （前照灯的远-近光双丝灯泡中）近光灯丝的遮光屏，配光屏（用于欧洲式配光制前照灯泡，近光灯丝沿光轴移至焦点前方，其下方设此配光屏，使其光线只落在反射镜的上半部分而被反射成下倾光束）

low-bed trailer 低平板式挂车,低货台挂车［= deep-loading trailer, low loader, low deck trailer, low-body trailer, low-load(er) trailer, cranked frame trailer, 英称 low loader, 美俗称 low boy 或 lo-boy］

low-boiling 低沸点的

low bracket gasoline 低辛烷值车用汽油

low brake pedal （要踩得很低制动才开始起作用的）踏板过低现象（故障）

low brass 软黄铜

low built car 低（车身）轿车

low-built chassis 低底盘（= low height chassis）

low-cab-forward commercial truck 前置式低驾驶室商业运输用货车

low calorific value of fuel 燃料的低热值（每千克燃料完全燃烧放出的全部热量中，若扣除燃烧产物中水蒸气的潜热，称低热值，若不扣除上述潜热，称高热值）

low car 低车身（高速）小客车（= low-slung car）

low-carbon steel 低碳钢（指含碳量0.03%~0.3%的碳素钢）

low-cetane 低十六烷的

low chrome-structural steel 低铬结构钢

low clearance sign 高度限制标志（净高限制标志）

low-compression engine 低压缩比发动机

low-consumption engine 低耗油量的发动机

low control arm （双臂式独立悬架的）下控制臂，下（横或纵）臂

low coolant temperature switch 低冷却水温开关（当冷却水温低于某规定值时，该开关接通，向控制模块输出冷却水温低于规定值的信号）

low cost 低成本，低价，低费用

low country 低洼地，低地

low crown 横坡小的路拱，低路拱

low crown panel 小弧度车身板件，低弧面车身面板（如：大多数轿车的车门面板）

low cruise 低速巡行（一般指发动机在1200r/min左右时汽车的稳速行驶）

low-cycle fatigue 低周疲劳（指制件或材料在接近或超过其屈服强度的循环应力作用下，经10^2~10^5次塑性应变循环次数而产生的疲劳）

low-cycle fatigue test 低循环数的疲劳试验

low data transmission rate EI system 低数据传输率电子点火系统〔亦称low signalling rate EI system，其中EI为electronic ignition的简称，曲轴每转一转其曲轴位置传感器（CKP sensor）向电子控制模块发送3个前沿电压信号和3个后沿电压信号，凸轮轴每转一转其凸轮轴位置传感器（CMP sensor）只产生1个前沿电压信号和1个后沿电压信号。相对于曲轴每转一转，曲轴位置传感器向电子控制模块发送35个脉冲信号的高数据传输率电子点火系统而言，这种点火系统传感元件每秒钟内的数据传输量低，故名〕

low deck body 低台货箱

low density polyethylene 低密度聚乙烯（简称LDPE，质地较柔韧，多用做塑料薄膜和薄板）

low-down trailer 低车架挂车（= cranked frame trailer）

low-drag cowl 风阻小的前围板（参见cowl）

low-drag profile 空气阻力小的（车辆）外形

low-driving-resistance tyre 低行驶阻力型轮胎

low-duty 轻型的，小功率的（亦称light-duty）

low-duty-cycle switching circuit ①低通-断循环率开关电路（指单位时间内接通-断开次数少的开关电路，如前照灯开关电路等）②低占空比开关电路

low-emission technology 低排放技术（减少有害排放物技术）

low emission vehicle 低排放车辆（简称LEV）

lower ①下部的，下方的 ②劣等的 ③下降，低降，放低，降低

lower arm 下臂，位于下方的臂件（如双纵臂或双横臂式悬架的下纵臂或下横臂）

lower attachment ring （减振器的）

底部安装环

lower back panel (轿车)后端底板(=rear end panel)

lower ball joint (下悬架臂的、与转向节连接的)下球头节

lower beam [美](汽车前照灯的)近光(=meeting beam, passing beam, nondazzling light, dipped beam)

lower bearing ①位置较低的轴承 ②滑动轴的下半块轴瓦

lower block 见 open deck type block

lower bound(ary) 下边界,下界,低界,下境界

lower brass 下(黄铜)轴瓦

lower calorific value (燃料)低热值(=lower heating value)

lower chamber pressure (博世KE型电子控制多点式连续汽油喷射系统燃油分配器内的)下室压力(与上室压力共同作用,以调节喷油器的喷射压力)

lower change point 下变点,下限点(下临界点,如:碳化铁开始融入γ铁中形成奥氏体的温度)

lower class 下等(级),低级

lower combustion value 低热值

lower control-arm 下控制臂(指双臂式独立悬架的下横臂或下纵臂,=lower suspension arm)

lower control limit 控制下限(简称LCL)

lower control piston (气制动系的挂车制动分配阀中的)下控制活塞

lower crankcase 下曲轴箱(油底壳)

lower critical point 下临界点(参见lower change point)

lower cylinder bore wear 下止点附近汽缸壁的磨损

lower dead-center indicator 下止点标记(=bottom dead-center indicator)

lower dead centre 下止点(简称LDC,亦写作 lower dead center, = lower dead point, bottom dead centre)

lower density 低密度

lower deviation 下偏差(公差带的下限)

lower D post (轿车车身)下D柱,下后侧柱,下后支柱

lower extreme point 下端(点)

lower front panel 见 front valance panel

lower front wing (轿车车身的)前下翼子板

lower half 下半部

lower half crankcase 下(半部)曲轴箱(亦称 lower half of crankcase)

lower half main bearing 主轴承下瓦,曲轴轴承下瓦

lower header (散热器的)下(部储)水箱(下水室,=lower tank)

lower heating value (燃料)低热值(简称LHV, = lower heat value, net heating value, net calorific value, 见 lower calorific value of fuel)

lower hitch pin (悬架装置)下控制臂连接销

lower insulator gasket (火花塞)绝缘子下密封垫

Lower L-arm (某些悬架杆系中的)L形下控制臂

lower limit 下限尺寸,最小尺寸,下限

lower limit of variation 偏差下限

lower limit on the left 左下限

lower limit on the right 右下限

lower plastic limit 塑性下限

lower-powered 功率较小的

lower pull-rod end ①拉杆下端 ②(由调整套连接的上、中、下三节式拉杆的)下节

lower reaction rod (悬架的)下反力杠,下拉力杆(见 reaction rod)

lower-segment 下段(的)

lower side panel (engine hood)

（发动机罩）下侧板

lower sidewall ①（轮胎）胎侧下部（胎侧胶最薄部分）②下部侧壁

lower speed nozzle 低速喷嘴（= pilot running nozzle, slow speed jet）

lower suspension arm （双臂式独立悬架装置的）下悬架臂（下控制臂，见 lower control arm）

lower tension (piston) ring 低张力（活塞）环

lower tonneau panel （轿车车身）后翼子板外下侧板（亦称 rear wing side outer lower panel）

lower track wheel （履带行走装置）支重轮（= bogie wheel）

lower tube （冲击能量吸收式转向盘轴的部件）下能量吸收管（与转向盘组合，吸收冲击能量）

lower valve ①下置气门 ②（双腔气制动阀的）第二回路制动阀

lower variation of tolerance 偏差下调，公差下限

lower "wishbone" link （双A形臂式独立悬架的）下A形臂

lower yield point 下屈服点（当不计初始瞬时效应时，构件屈服阶段中的最小应力）

lowest continuous speed with load （发动机的）最低工作稳定转速（指燃料供给调节机构调到标定功率位置时，负荷下能连续稳定运转的最低转速）

lowest effective power 最低有效功率（简称 LEP）

lowest idling temperature （发动机）怠速运转最低温度

lowest ignition limit 最低点燃极限

lowest ring travel （发动机）活塞环刮缸行程的下止点（缸壁锥形磨损的最低点）

low-floor bus 低地板客车

Low-floor wagon （专门运输大型货车的）低地板铁路平板车（近年来货车尺寸越来越高，已很难用平板汽车之类的公路运输车辆运送，由汽车制造厂直接将新车开至用户交货地点成为新车配送的重要手段，但用户不满意，于是出现了可输送高4m的货车的铁路平板车）

low-flow radiator 低流速散热器（降低散热器内的冷却液流速以便降低冷却液温度，节约燃料，增长发动机寿命）

low-freezing 低凝固点的，低结晶温度的

low frequency 低频（率）的

low-friction 低摩擦系数的

low friction engine 低摩擦损失发动机（如：运动部件较少的转子发动机）

low fuel consumption 低燃料消耗（量），低耗油量，低油耗

low fuel indicator （燃油箱）低油面指示灯（当油箱油量少到规定值，如只能行车25~50英里时，该指示灯第一次点亮，发出低油量警报）

low-fuel relay 低燃油面信号继电器

low-g accelerometer 低g加速度计（1~2g）

low gear （变速器）低挡

low geared 挂低挡的，低速大转矩传动的

low-grade ①平缓坡道，平坡坡度 ②低等级的，次等的，低质量的，低品位的

low-grade car 低档轿车（一般指排量1L以下的普及型轿车）

low-gravity fuel 低比重燃料（轻燃料）

low ground pressure （履带、车轮等）低对地压力

low-hardenability steel 低淬透性钢

low head 低压头，低水头

low-heat rejection engine 低散热发动机（绝热发动机，简称 LHR engine，见 adiabatic engine）

low-height chassis 低底盘（= low-built chassis, low-loading chassis, low-level chassis）

low idling speed 最低空载稳定转速，最低稳定怠速转速

low land tyre 低湿地轮胎

low lead gasoline 低铅汽油（按美国 ASTM 规定，含铅量不多于 0.13g/L的汽油）

low-level 低级的，低标准的，低水平的，低标高的，低能的

low-level charge （数字信号的）低电平电荷（指在规定的数字信号低电平下已经注入所有势阱中的电荷）

low level input voltage （数字信号的）低电平输入电压（指二进制变量的两个值域中较低正值或较低负值的输入电压）

low-level output voltage 低电平输出电压（指在规定的输入条件下，输出端处于低电平时的电压）

low-level warning switch 低油面警告灯开关

low limit of size 尺寸下限

low limit of tolerance 公差下限

low loader ①低斗装载机（铲斗高度很低）②低货台货车（通常这类货车装有一可伸出的装货斜板或可放到地面上的起重后栏板）

low load Vickers hardness test 小负荷维氏硬度试验（试验力范围在 1.961~49.03N的维氏硬度试验）

low-low gear ratio （组合式变速器的）低挡传动比（最低传动比，其主、副变速器都挂最低挡时的速比）

low-low speed （组合式变速器）主、副变速器均挂低挡

low maintenance batteries 低维护蓄电池［简称 LM batteries，指在整个使用寿命期只需加添少量蒸馏水的蓄电池或完全无须加水且无加水口者称免维护蓄电池（maintenance free batteries），简称"M-F batteries"］

low manganese steel 低锰钢

low MAP 低进气歧管绝对压力（low manifold absolute pressure 的简称，指节气门关闭、发动机怠速时，进气管真空度最高可达 -18inHg 左右，此时其绝对压力最低，见 high MAP）

low-melting alloy 易熔合金

low-melting-point 低熔点的

low-molecular-weight 低分子量的

low nose high deck （汽车的）前低后高形（车身）（目前一种流行的楔形车身造型，nose 指汽车前端，deck 指汽车后窗或行李舱部位，见 deck panel）

low-oil alarm 低油位警报

low-pass filter 低通滤波器（频率低于基准频率的全部信号都可自由通过）

low passing beam （前照灯）近光（= dim light）

low-performance engine 低性能发动机

low phosphorus pig iron 低磷铸铁

low pivot swing axle （独立悬架式）低铰接点摆动式驱动桥（其差速器壳底通过一铰接装置固定于车架，由差速器壳一端或两端伸出的半轴及半轴壳可上、下摆动，其摆动的枢点与差速器壳底铰枢点处于同一高度，故名）

low-pollution combustion engine 低污染燃烧发动机

low pollution-high mileage car 低污染低油耗车

low-power（ed） ①小功率的，低功率的②装有小功率发动机的

low power objective 低（放大）倍（数）物镜

low -pressure accumulator/sump 低压储液箱/槽

low-pressure balloon tire （广泛用于轿车的）低压充气轮胎（指充气压力在 0.15～0.2MPa 的宽断面胎，缓冲性能好，行驶平顺，接地面积大，抗滑，牵引力大，制动性能良好，参见 balloon tire，doughnut tire）

low pressure charging 低增压（通常指充量增压压力≤0.15MPa 的增压）

low-pressure cut-out （汽车空调系统的）低压保护开关，低压断电器（设在空调系统高压回路中，防止压缩机在缺少制冷剂的情况下空转而遭损坏，当制冷剂压力低于某一设定值时，使触点断开，压缩机停转）

low pressure indicator （储气筒的）低压指示器（当筒内气压低于某一规定值时，即发出低压警报）

low pressure indicator diagram 低压示功图（指换气过程中，汽缸内压力随曲轴转角或汽缸容积变化的曲线图）

low pressure intake manifold injection 进气歧管低压喷油

low pressure line （空调系蒸发器出口至压缩机之间的）低压（气态制冷剂）管路

low-pressure pump 低压泵

low-pressure sodium lamp 低压钠（气）灯

low-pressure turbo-charger 低压涡轮增压器（二级增压系统的第一级）

low pressure warning switch 低压警报开关（当管路压力低于某规定值时，开启低压警报装置的开关）

low-price（d）auto car 低价轿车，廉价轿车

low-profile 薄断面的，轮廓（高度）低的，矮（形）的，低（外形）的，扁平的，高度小于宽度的

low-profile air cleaner 扁平的圆盘形空气滤清器（多直接装在化油器顶部）

low-profile head 低断面汽缸盖（薄型缸盖）

low-profile tire 扁平（轮）胎（= low section tyre，指高度≤70% 宽度的轮胎）

low quench combustion chamber 冷激面积小的燃烧室

low range ① 低量程 ② 低挡区 ③（二进制信号的）低值域（指二进制信号最低正电平，或最低负电平范围）

low-range gear ratio 低挡区传动比（副变速器接低挡时，主变速器各挡的总传动比）

low range lateral acceleration handling maneuver （汽车的）低横向加速转向运动（低离心加速转向，指在正常驾驶条件下的转弯、变更车道等运动，车速和转弯半径形成的离心加速度在 0～0.39g 范围内，见 handling maneuver）

low-range shift button （自动变速器的）低挡变换按钮

low-rank fuel 低级燃料，低品质燃料

low-rate suspension 低刚度悬架

low-μ road 低附着系数道路

low section height tyre （汽车用）扁平（轮）胎，低断面轮胎（指其扁平率，即其断面高度与宽度之比为 0.7～0.88 的充气轮胎，= low profile tyre）

low-servo （自动变速器的）低速挡自动液压控制装置

low-shear-strength film 低抗剪强度油膜

low side ①（空调系统的）低压侧（指制冷剂由膨胀阀节流降压后流经蒸发器蒸发吸收周围空气的大量

热量，降低车内室温，再沿管道流回压缩机的一侧。在某些结构中，蒸发器与压缩机之间还装有储液-干燥器）②（泛指各种系统的）低温侧，低压侧，低速侧（等）

low side switching （汽车灯具的）低位开关电路（指电灯接在电源与晶体管开关元器件之间，见 high side switching）

low-slung car 低车身高速轿车（= low car）

low-sounding 低音的

low-sounding horn 低音喇叭

low speed adjustment 低速调整

low speed circuit （化油器的）低速油系，低速系统

low-speed diesel engine 低速柴油机（一般指曲轴转速≤300r/min 或活塞平均速度≤6m/s 的柴油机）

low speed following system 低速追随系统（简称 LSF system，当前方行驶车辆的速度低于所设定的巡航车速时自动减速，并可以维持与前车安全距离的低速行驶）

low speed gear （变速器中的）低速挡齿轮

low speed high torque 低速大转矩（简称 LSHT）

low-speed input/output port （车用微处理器的）低速输入/输出接口（相对于高速输入/输出接口而言）

low speed nozzle 怠速喷孔，低速量孔（= idling nozzle, slow speed jet）

low-speed servo （踩踏加速踏板时强制换）低挡伺服机构（见 kick-down servo）

low-speed shimmy 低速摆振（转向轮在较低的车速 20~50km/h 下产生的以自激振动为主的振动）

low-speed stability 低速稳定性

low speed steering efforts test 低速大转角转向操舵力试验（评价汽车在停车场地停车过程中，或在城镇狭小街巷以低车速和前转向轮大转角行驶时的转向轻便性）

low-speed traction control 低速牵引力控制（系统）

low splitter 副变速器低挡

low spots 低点，凹部，坑点

low stagger blade 小倾角叶片（小安装角的叶片）

low stake rack truck 低栅栏货台货车

low-standard reference fuel 低标准参考燃料

low sulfur fuel ［美］低硫燃料（= low sulphur fuel）

low-tach 低速的，低转速的

low temperature activity （催化转化器的）低温活性（指在冷机起动后的升温阶段中，催化转化器的废气净化能力）

low temperature annealing 低温退火（将非淬火钢加热，一般为550~600℃以下的温度保温一定时间，通常以 3~4min/mm 计，缓慢冷却至低于200℃时出炉空冷）

low-temperature brittleness 低温脆性（亦称 low-temperature embrittlement）

low temperature carbonization 低温碳化处理，低温渗碳

low-temperature distillation 低温蒸馏

low-temperature fluidity 低温流动性

low temperature fouling （由于工作温度低而引起的火花塞）冷积炭，低温积炭

low temperature grease 低温滑脂

low temperature nematic liquid crystal 低温向列相液晶（低温下，保持向列相的液晶）

low-temperature oxidation 低温氧化

low-temperature properties 低温性能

low-temperature pumpability limit 可泵性温度下限

low temperature resistance 耐低温性，耐寒性

low-temperature stiffening （橡胶等的）低温硬化

low temperature tempering 低温回火（简称 low tempering，将淬火工件加热至 150～250℃的回火）

low-temperature test ①低温下进行的试验 ②耐寒试验

low temperature vacuum signal modulator 低温真空信号调制器

low tension battery 低压蓄电池

low tension breaker 低压断电器

low tension cable terminal （点火线圈的）低压线接线柱

low-tension capacitor discharge ignition 低压电容放电点火

low tension coil 低（电）压线圈

low-tension current 低压电流（指直流 750V 以下、交流实效值 300V 以下的电流）

low-tension ignition 低压（电火花）点火

low tension terminal 低压接线柱（如：点火线圈初级绕组接线柱）

low-tension winding 低压绕组

low tire indicator 胎压过低指示灯（当胎压低于某规定值时，该灯亮）

low traffic capacity （道路的）低通过能力

low tyre pressure sensing system 轮胎气压不足传感系统

low vacuum 低真空（= coarse vacuum, rough vacuum）

low-viscosity 低黏性的，低黏度的

low visibility 不良的能见度（= poor visibility）

low voltage circuit ①低压电路，低压回路 ②（特指变压器、点火线圈等的）初级电路（= low tension circuit）

low voltage tester 低压测试仪（用于检验汽车电器及线路接触不良、断线等故障）

low voltage winding 低压绕组

low-volume highway 低交通量公路，低通行量公路

low-volume vehicle 小批量生产的车辆

low-water alarm 水面过低警报（水量不足警报信号）

low-weight alloy body 轻质合金钢车身

low wheel speed sensor 低轮速传感器（①自动转向、弯道行驶、车道维持及稳定性控制等系统中向电子控制模块发送低车轮转速信号的传感器 ②可测出低转速的传感器）

low yield point 下屈服点（指不计初始瞬时效应时，试件屈服阶段中的最小应力）

lox trailer 运液态氧气的挂车（lox 为 liquid oxygen 的简称）

lozenge ①菱形，菱形面，菱形物 ②成菱形，菱形变形，歪斜变形，歪斜，歪扭，歪曲 ③菱形的

LP 润滑剂参数（lubricant parameter）

LP 线性规划，线性编程（序）（linear programming）

L Package （汽车的）驾驶室，驾驶区

LPG ①液化石油气（liquefied petroleum gas）②液态丙烷（liquid propane gas）

LPG engine 液化石油气发动机（liquefied petroleum gas engine）

LPG mixer 液化石油气混合器（燃烧液化石油气的汽车，LPG 经过蒸发调压器以气态流出，进入混合器与空气按一定比例混合，进入汽缸）

L-plug （转子发动机位于缸体短轴以上的）上位火花塞

LRC （车身高度自动）调平系统

(level regulation control system 的简称)

LR/CC solenoids （自动变速器的）低速倒挡/变矩器离合器电磁阀（low reverse/converter clutch solenoids 的简称）

LRC switch （丰田公司）凌志车行驶平顺性控制开关（Lexus ride control switch 的简称，装在驾驶室仪表板区，用于选择其主动式空气悬架的阻尼特性，分为运动模式"SPORT"和正常模式"NORM"两挡）

LRG 精炼液化（石油）气（liquefied refinery gas）

LR pressure switch （电子控制自动变速器的）低倒挡压力开关（换挡时将低倒挡液压信号反馈给电子控制模块）

LRSV 大型安全研究车（large research safety vehicle）

LSB ①最低有效位（least signification bit 的简称，在二进制中只有最低位权值的位，如1010中最右边的0，即为LSB）②线性转换器模拟分辨率值的单位符号（以它作为基本单位，用其倍数或约数来表示同一转换器其他模拟量的值，特别是表示模拟误差的值。例如："1/2LSB"指等于0.5倍模拟分辨率的模拟量）

LSC 豪华型运动车（luxury sport coupe）

LSD 防滑差速器（limited slip differential 的简称）

L-section ring （高性能二冲程发动机上使用的）L形断面活塞环（可利用燃气压力，提高活塞环对缸壁的压力，而增加密封性）

LSF 低速跟随（系统）（low speed following 的简称）

L-shaped combustion chamber L形燃烧室

LSHT 低速大转矩（low speed, high torque）

LSI ①大规模集成电路（large scale integrated circuit）②大规模集成化（large scale-integration）

LSIO 低速输入/输出（装置）（low speed input/output units 的简称）

LSPV 感载比例阀（见 loading sensing proprotioning valve）

LSUV 大型运动型多功能车（large sports utility vehicle 的简称，如：Volvo XC90、BMWX5、Lexus RX300、Porshe Cayenne 等）

LT circuit （点火线圈的）初级电路（low tension circuit 的简称）

LTD test 低温沉积物试验（low temperature deposition test 的简称，检验发动机机油的一种试验）

L-terminal 指示灯接线柱（indicator lamp terminal）

LTL 汽车零担（货运）（less-than-truck-load）

LTPD （大）批量生产中允许的次品率（lot tolerance percent defective）

3.6 ltr diesel 排量为3.6L的柴油机（其中 ltr 为 litter 的简称，说明书、广告等用语）

L-type low arm （新式麦弗逊型前轮悬架的）L形下臂（由盘状横梁支撑）

lube ①润滑油（lubricating oil 的简称，有时亦称 lube oil）②润滑（lubrication 的简称）

lubed-for-life bearing 终身润滑轴承（一次性润滑轴承，在使用中不需再加润滑剂）

lubed-for-life design 全寿命润滑设计（终身润滑结构，在整个使用寿命期无须添加润滑剂的结构设计）

lube oil cooler 润滑油冷却器

lube oil heater （油底壳）机油加热器

lube use rate 滑油消耗率

luboil 润滑油，机油（亦写作 lub-oil，lube oil 为 lubricating oil 的简称）

lub-oil consumption 润滑油消耗量，机油消耗量（指发动机每小时消耗的机油总量）

lub-oil pressure 机油压力（机油经滤清器后进入内燃机体主油道前的压力）

lubreel 润滑油脂自动加注软管卷筒（lubrication reel 的简称）

lubricant 润滑剂（润滑油，润滑脂，固体润滑材料的总称）

lubricant additive 润滑油（脂）添加剂

lubricant base （配制）润滑剂（的础）基（础）油（润滑剂基础成分）

lubricant carrier 润滑剂载体

lubricant film 润滑油膜

lubricant gun 润滑脂加注枪（= grease gun, grease pump, grease squirt, compressor gun）

lubricant parameter 润滑油参数（简称 LP）

lubricant separator 机油分离器 [油（水）分离器]

lubricant spectral analysis 润滑油光谱分析（确定在用润滑油中磨损微粒的化学成分及数量，用以诊断发动机摩擦副的磨损状态，并可确定是否需要更换新润滑油）

lubricated wear test 润滑条件下（摩擦表面）的磨损试验

lubricating compressor 压力润滑机

lubricating grease 润滑脂（亦称 lubricating paste）

lubricating hole 润滑油脂加注孔

lubricating jelly 凝胶润滑剂

lubricating motor （驱动）润滑油泵（的）电动机

lubricating oil dilution 润滑油稀释（指燃油或冷却水混入润滑油中，使其黏度降低、变稀的现象）

lubricating oil fine filter 润滑油精滤器

lubricating pit 润滑作业地沟（= lubrication pit）

lubricating pump 润滑油泵

lubricating ring 润滑油环

lubricating screw ①黄油枪 ②润滑（孔）螺钉

lubricating system 润滑系（简称 lube system 润滑系）

lubricating wick 润滑油绳

lubrication 润滑，润滑方法，润滑作业

lubrication adapter 油嘴，润滑脂加注嘴（亦称 lubricating nipple）

lubrication chart 润滑点说明图（= oiling chart, lubrication diagram）

lubrication failure ①润滑系统的故障 ②因润滑不良造成的故障

lubrication filler ①润滑油加油嘴 ②润滑油注油器

lubrication film 润滑油膜

lubrication oil pump 润滑油泵（亦称 lube oil pump）

lubrication oil strainer 润滑油过滤器，滑油滤清器

lubrication point （加注润滑油脂的）润滑点

lubrication pressure ①润滑压力（指润滑油路的压力）②（自动变速器液力控制系中的）润滑用液压

lubrication pressure regulation 润滑油路压力调节阀，润滑调压阀

lubrication reel 见 lubreel

lubrication system （发动机的）润滑系

lubricator （加注润滑油、脂的）润滑油嘴，加油嘴，黄油嘴

lubricator wick 润滑油绳

lubricity 润滑性质，润滑能力（指燃油、润滑油脂等在重载和边界条件下的润滑能力）

lubricity additive （机油）润滑油

性提高剂

lubri-seal bearing 带油封的轴承（=labri-seal bearing）

lubritorium [美] 汽车润滑站（从事加注润滑油、润滑脂等维护作业，亦称 lubritory）

lubro-pump 油泵

Lucas 英国鲁卡斯（汽车产品）公司

lucite 有机玻璃，2-甲基丙烯酸，透明塑料

lucite pipe 透明塑料管

Luder lines 吕德线（拉伸应变线，=stretch strain lines）

lug ①凸块，凸销，凸耳，凸榫，凸键 ②（越野轮胎上的）凸块式花纹 ③轮胎花纹（见 logging）

lug angle 轮胎花纹角（花纹中线与轮胎中心平面的夹角）

lug base 轮胎花纹根部宽度

lug bolt 带耳螺栓

lug down method （柴油机烟度测定的）加载减速法（将柴油机汽车安置在双滚筒底盘测功机上，使柴油机加速到最高转速，然后保持节气门位置不变，逐步加载，使发动机转速降低，测定 100 ~ 400r/min 范围内的烟度值）

lug down smoke characteristics （柴油机等的）加载减速排烟特性（参见 lugging）

lug-down test 加载减速试验（参见 lug down method）

lug fillet （轮胎）花纹筋条

luggage 行包（旅客随身携带或托运的行李、包裹，美称 baggage）

luggage accommodation ①行李舱，行李间 ②行李安置，行李安放

luggage boot （轿车的）行李舱，后行李箱（简称 boot，亦称 luggage compartment，美称 trunk）

luggage boot lamp 行李舱灯（当打开轿车后的行李舱盖时，能自动接通照明行李舱的一种小灯，亦称 luggage boot light，但严格说，light 是指照明灯光）

luggage capacity （轿车）可装行李的空间容量（并非单指后行李舱容积，很多轿车车厢内还设有专门的行李间，参见 trunk roominess）

luggage carrier extension （汽车）行李架的延长部分

luggage carrying capacity 行包承载能力（行李容量，= luggage capacity）

luggage compartment （客车的）行李间，（轿车的）行李舱，行李室（= baggage compartment, boot compartment）

luggage compartment lid 行李舱盖，行李舱门

luggage-down 因超载而减速的（发动机）（=stalled，见 lugging）

luggage grid 栅格式行李架（参见 baggage grid）

luggage hold 行李架（= baggage holder, luggage rack, parcel rack）

luggage ladder 行李梯（客车上车顶行李架的梯子）

luggage rail on top 车顶行李框栏杆（= top luggage rail）

luggage space （轿车后座后面的）行李舱

luggage trailer 行李挂车

lugging ①用力拉，用力拖，拖动 ②（发动机的）加载减速（美指节气门及挡位不变，拖载增加而减速的现象，= labouring）③（越野车等承受暂时性）超载（的）能力 ④车辆前、后方向急剧振动 ⑤起步操作不当，车辆串动（④，⑤两项同 jerk）

lug nut [美俚] 车轮螺母（= wheel nut）

lug pitch （轮胎）花纹节距

lug side （轮胎）花纹凸肋侧面

lug the engine （由于换挡不及时）使发动机处于低速过载下工作

lug-type chain 抓地齿型防滑链

lug type tread pattern 胎面横纹花纹，横向花纹（如：烟斗花纹，其牵引和制动力较大，且耐磨、夹石子少，但抗倾向力差，噪声大，适用于砂、石路面，简称 lug pattern）

lug width 轮胎花纹抓地齿宽度

Luk metal link chain （德国）Luk（公司的）金属片节链型［（无级连续变速器用）传动链（简称 Luk chain，在传递力的过程中承受拉力，称 pull type（拉力型），使用这一类传动链的 CVT 称 pull-type CVT 拉力型无级连续变速器］

lumbar support （汽车座椅靠背的）乘员腰部支撑机构（用以减轻长途乘车疲劳，其支撑强度可分挡调节）

lumber body 木材运输车身

lumber plank road 木板路

lumber truck 原木运输车（= log truck）

lumen 流明（国际单位制的光通量单位，代号 lm，即 1 烛光均一强度的点光源在一个球面弧度立体角内放射出的光通量。1 流明 = 1 烛光/球面弧度，1 lm = 1cd. sr. 所以 1 烛光点光源的总光通量为 4π 流明 "$4\pi \cdot lm$"，参见 steradian, candela）

lumen method 流明法（一种既考虑直射光通，又考虑反射光通的照明设计方法）

lumen range 流明范围

luminaire efficiency 灯具效率（灯具发射出的光通量与灯具内全部光源发射的总光通或流明之比，亦称 light output ratio of luminaire）

luminance 亮度（表面的亮度，即单位面积表面的发光强度，常用代号 L，表示表面的法向照度，单位 cd/m^2，参见 candela）

luminance contrast 亮度对比（指视野中目标和背景的亮度差与背景或目标亮度之比，对于均匀照明的无光泽的背影和目标，亮度对比可用目标和背影的反射率差与目标或背影反射率之比来表示）

luminance difference 亮度差

luminance factor 亮度因数（非自发光体表面上某一点给定方向的亮度与同一条件下全反射或全透射的漫射体的亮度比）

luminance ratio 亮度比（视野中任何两个表面的亮度之比）

luminescence ①冷光（非热能产生的光，如磷光、荧光，见 phosphorescence, fluorescence）②发冷光

luminosity ①亮度，辉度 ②发光度，光度，可见度 ③（眼睛等的）感光度，光感

luminous dial 发光表盘（荧光表盘，夜光表盘，= blackout dial）

luminous element 发光元件，夜光元件

luminous emittance 发光度（简称 H 或 h）

luminous flame 黄焰（见 yellow flame）

luminous flux 光通量［发光体在单位时间内发出的光波能量，即光波的流能密度，单位：流明（lm）见 lumen］

luminous intensity 光照强度，光照度，照度［指被照射物体每单位面积上接受的光通量的流明数，单位为勒（克斯）lx，见 lux］

luminous intensity distribution ①灯具的光照度分布 ②（特指汽车前照灯的）配光（即根据汽车行车要求所设计的前照灯光照度分布）

luminous paint 光亮漆

luminous power 发光能力，发光功

luminous signal 灯光信号
luminous transmittance 光透射比（物体透射的光通量与入射光通量之比）
lumpiness（of engine） （发动机的）迟钝性（不灵敏性，反应迟后）
lunar（rover）vehicle 登月车（月球车，月面车，亦称 lunan roving vehicle）
lurching ①受挫现象，（齿轮变速器换挡时汽车产生的）歇气（现象），喘气（现象）②摆动，横摆（特指车辆无侧倾地左、右摆动）③突然一歪，倾斜
lustre ①反射光；光泽，光辉 ②光滑的表面 ③光滑的，有光泽的（美写作 luster）
luton （车箱高度超过驾驶室且其上前端伸出在驾驶室顶上的）伸顶型箱式货车
lux 勒（克斯），米烛光（国际单位制的光照度单位，代号 lx，或 Lx，即每平方米的面积上有1流明的光通量。1勒=1流明每平方米，1Lx = 1 lm/m², 见 luminous intensity）
luxe 豪华（简称L，指汽车时，表示豪华型，但实际上指基本型或标准型，参见 CL, GL）
lux gauge （灯光的）照度计（以 lx 为单位测定表面照度的仪器）
Luxgen 纳智捷［台湾裕隆生产的一款SUV的车名，为 Luxury（豪华）和 Genius（智慧）的合成词］

luxurious interior （车身）豪华型内饰
luxury sport coupe 豪华型运动车（简称 LSC）
3.5L V6 and 6A 3.5升V形6缸内燃机和6挡自动变速器机组
LVDT 线性可变差动变压器（linear variable differential transformer 的简称）
LVFA 低速摩擦（测试）装置（low speed friction apparatus 的简称，用于测试自动变速器工作油液的摩擦系数与速度的关系特性）
LWB 长轴距（long wheel base 的简称）
L×W×H 长×宽×高（length × width × height）
Lx （lx）勒克斯（参见 lux）
lye ①（由木灰沥滤制成的强碱性）灰水，木灰水（清洗塑料等制品最有效）②强碱溶液（一般指氢氧化钾、氢氧化钠溶液）③沥滤液（指任何一种沥滤出的水液）
Lynch bridge 楞氏桥（用于量测塑料的电介质）
lyotropic liquid crystal 溶致液晶（因加入不同量的溶剂而形成液晶态的物质）
Lysholm 里谢尔姆型增压器［类似于罗茨型增压器的双螺旋凸缘面滚筒形转子机械式增压器，但其效率更高，亦称 Lysholm（twin-screw）compressor, twin-screw super-charger］

4M 生产四要素（指 man 操作者，machine 机器，method 方法，material 材料）

M20 甲醇20汽油（指含20%甲醇、80%汽油的混合油）

M ①磁粉探伤（magnaflux）②磁铁（magnet）③磁偶极矩（magnetic dipole moment）④磁矩（magnetic moment）⑤插入式的（male）⑥标记（mark）⑦质量（mass）⑧麦（磁通量单位，maxwell）⑨平均（值）（mean）⑩中（间），介质（medium）⑪兆（10^6）（mega）⑫兆欧（megohm）⑬经线，子午线（meridian）⑭浮体的稳定中心（metacenter）⑮微（10^{-6}）（micro）⑯话筒（microphone）⑰中（middle）⑱英里（mile）⑲最小（minimum）⑳导弹（missile）㉑模式，方式（mode）㉒模型（model）㉓调制器（modulator）㉔模块，模数（module）㉕克分子（mole）㉖分子量（molecular weight）㉗力矩（moment）㉘月（month）㉙电动机（motor）㉚弯矩（bending moment）

m ①质量（mass）②中午（meridiem，=noon）③米（metre）④英里（mile）⑤一毫（10^{-3}，milli）⑥百万（million）⑦分（钟）（minute）⑧质量克分子浓度（molality）

mΩ 毫欧（milliohm）
MΩ 兆欧（megohm）
5M 5挡手动变速器（5-speed manual 的简称）
M85 甲醇85汽油（指含85%甲醇、15%汽油的混合油）
M. a. 微安（培）（microampere）
MA ①甲醇（methyl alcohol）②混合放大器（mixed amplifier）③受调放大器（modulated amplifier）④机械效益（mechanical advantage）
MABT （可产生）最佳转矩的最小点火提前角（minimum advance for best torque 的简称）
MAC 多路访问，多路存取（multi channel access 的简称）
macadamized road 沥青碎石路（= tarmac①）
macadam pavement 碎石（砾石）路面
macadam road 碎石路
machine 机器，机械，设备，工具（= machinery）
machine base 机床座，机器底座
machine(-) building 机械制造（的），机械制造工业（的）（= machine manufacturing）
machine components 机械零件，机器零件
machine handling 机械化装卸（输送）作业（= mechanized handling）
machine hour 机械运转时间，机器

小时

machine language 机器语言（一种由计算机指令组成的、能够由控制模块或计算机直接执行或使用的二进制数据的人工语言，亦称computer language）

machinery ①机器（制造），机械（制造，装置，设备），机构 ②工具，手段，方法

machinery utilization 机器利用（率）

machine-shaping 机加工成型的

machine shop truck 修理（服务）车，修理工程车（= repair truck, shop truck, tool truck, workshop truck）

machine-shop van 厢式修理工程车

machine-spoiled time 机器故障时间，机械损坏时间

machine steel 机器钢（简称MS）

machine testing 在试验机上试验，机器试验

machine time 机器运转时间，机器作业时间，计算机时间

machine vision 机器视觉（亦称computer vision，指计算机视觉系统）

machine washer 平垫圈

machine work 机械加工，机加工，切削加工

machining allowance 机械加工余量

machining dimension 机械加工尺寸

Mach meter （测速用）马赫计，马赫表

Mach number 马赫数（在同样状态的介质中，流体流动速率或物体运动速率与声速之比值，简称Mach。Mach=1时，该流体速率等于声速；Mach<1时，为亚音速；Mach>1时，为超音速；当马赫数在5~10时，为高超音速）

Mack integrated powertrain （美国Mack公司的）集成式动力系（发动机、电子控制系、变速器、车架和悬架六套总成组成一个整体式系统）

MacMichael（M）viscosity 麦克米契尔扭力黏度，麦氏扭力黏度（参见Fisher-MacMichael viscometer）

Macpherson strut 麦弗逊式滑柱（麦弗逊式独立悬架的主要部件，由滑柱管身、外螺旋弹簧、上支杆、减振垫和上、下弹簧座及上、下支撑件、减振筒等组成，其上端通过轴承固装在车身发动机舱侧壁板的滑柱座内可作少许转动，下端固定在前轮转向节上，兼起上悬架臂和减振器的作用，有时简称strut）

Macpherson strut suspension 麦弗逊式独立悬架，滑柱连杆式独立悬架（= Macpherson type suspension，简称Macpherson suspension或strut suspension，由麦弗逊滑柱和下横臂组成，多用于前轮驱动的前桥独立悬架，某些车辆亦用于后悬架，亦称滑柱连杆式独立悬架，见strut and link type suspension）

Macpherson strut tower （轿车车身发动机舱侧壁板上的）麦弗逊滑柱支座（亦称suspension leg turret, shock tower，有的是一独立板件，点焊在发动机舱侧壁，即前轮内侧挡泥板上，有的则在该壁板上直接深冲压加工成型，用于支撑麦弗逊式悬架的麦弗逊柱上端）

macrography 宏观检查，肉眼检查，粗形（宏观，粗视组织）照相，低倍照相（图）

macromolecular 高分子的

macromolecule 高分子（分子量数在千以上的分子称高分子，如：合成橡胶、塑料、纤维等合成高分子化合物的分子）

macroperfection 宏观完整性

macroporous 大孔隙的

macroscopic observation 宏观观察

macrostrain 宏观应变（相对于微观应变而言，可测得任何限定标距上的平均应变）

MAD 计程式转鼓底盘测功机（mileage accumulation dynamometer）

MAF 空气质量流量（mass airflow 的简称）

MAF relay circuit 空气质量流量传感器继电器电路

MAF sensor ①进气空气流量传感器（manifold air flow sensor 的简称）②空气质量流量传感器（mass air flow sensor 的简称）

MAG ①期刊（magazine）②（仓）库，箱，盒（magazine）③镁（magnesium）④磁铁（magnet）⑤磁性的（magnetic）⑥磁（magnetism）⑦磁电机（magneto）⑧磁控管（magnetron）⑨量、大小（magnitude）⑩最大可用增益（maxium available gain）

Mag ①磁电机，永磁发电机（magneto 的简称）②磁的（magnetic 的简称）

mag ①磁电机（= magneto）②镁合金车轮（mag wheel，magnesium wheel 的简称，原指使用轻镁合金轮辋的车轮，现用来表示任一种使用特殊材料和结构的车轮）

mag-dynamo 永磁发电机，永磁直流发电机，磁电机（= mag-dyna, mag-dy, mag-dyno, magneto dynamo）

MAGFET 磁性金属氧化物半导体场效应晶体管（magnetic metal-oxide-simiconductor type field effect transistor 的简称）

magic eye 魔眼（一种前照灯自动变光器，它可根据来车的光线使前照灯自动减光或照射方向向下）

magic formula 魔术方程式（一种包括15种参数的汽车轮胎特性计算机模拟模型的名称）

maglev vehicle 磁力悬浮车（= magnetic levitation vehicle）

magna-check 磁力探伤（将铁粉等撒在被磁化的磁性材料制件上，根据铁粉的图纹来检查制件内部缺陷等，亦称 magna flux powder checker, magnet check）

magna flux 磁通量

Magna-glo ①（磁力探伤用的）磁性粉末，探伤用磁粉 ②磁粉探伤法

magnalium 镁铝合金

magneplane transportation system 磁力悬浮车运输系统

magnesium 镁（Mg）（工业用金属中最轻的一种，相对密度仅1.74，为铝的2/3，镁合金强度高于铝合金，可以高强度合金钢媲美。镁的弹性模量小，能吸收较大的冲击功，但抗腐蚀性差，纯镁机械性能差，不能制造机械配件，一般使用镁合金）

magnesium alloy 镁合金（见 magnesium）

magnesium fluoride 氟化镁（MgF_2）

magnesium spinel material 镁尖晶石材料（为镁氧化物结晶体，与铝尖晶石等均为陶瓷材料，在汽车上用作 O_2 传感器外侧电极的保护材料）

magnesium wheel 镁合金车轮（简称 mag wheel 或 mags）

magne-switch 电磁开关，磁力开关（= magnet-switch, magnetic switch）

magnet 磁石，磁铁（指永久磁铁）

magnet clutch 电磁离合器（electro-magnetic clutch 的简称）

magnet coil 电磁线圈

magnet coil tyre fan clutch （电动）冷却风扇的电磁线圈型离合器（由发动水温开关控制风扇电动机继电器的电磁线圈电流的接通与断开。水温低时，电磁线圈断电，风扇电动机开关断开；当水温达到某规定值时，线圈通电，电动机开关接通）

magnetic actuator 电磁型执行器（electromagnetic actuator 的简称，如电磁阀、步进电动机等）

magnetic after effect 磁后效应，剩磁效应

magnetic ageing 磁铁老化，磁性衰退（磁性物质在磁场作用下磁化，在去掉磁场后，由于磁畴的重新排列，使磁铁衰化）

magnetic（al） ①磁性的，磁铁的 ②（可）磁化的，能吸引的

magnetic alloy 磁性合金

magnetically controlled ignition 电磁控制点火

magnetically levitated vehicle 磁力悬浮车（参见 levitated vehicle）

magnetically triggered system 磁触发系统，磁电触发系统（如：无触点式电子点火系中的磁电式点火信号发生系统）

magnetic amplifier 磁放大器

magnetic-armature 动（磁）铁式的（由外部磁场控制磁铁芯位置的，= moving-iron）

magnetic attraction 磁力（磁吸引力）

magnetic base （千分表等的）磁性底座

magnetic bearing 磁力轴承

magnetic body 磁性体

magnetic brake 电磁制动器，磁力制动器

magnetic bubble storage （电子计算机的）磁泡存储器（亦称 magnetic bubble memory，或简称 bubble storage，bubble memory，一种非易失性固态存储器，由芯片上的细小极化磁性薄膜形成的磁泡表示"1"和"0"，来存储信息，优于 RAM，它无机械传动部件，故优于磁盘）

magnetic bypass 磁分路（见 magnetic shunt）

magnetic bypass plate 磁分路片（利用合金的磁组随温度变化的特性来调节电压的温度补偿零件）

magnetic card 磁卡

magnetic cassette reader 盒式磁带读出器

magnetic circuit 磁路（磁力线通过的线路）

magnetic clutch 电磁离合器（electromagnetic clutch 的简称）

magnetic clutch lamp 电磁离合器工况指示灯（当电磁离合器工作不良，造成主动件与被动件间转速比 <1时，该灯亮）

magnetic compass 磁罗盘

magnet（ic）conductivity 导磁性，磁导率

magnetic controlled transistor ignition system 磁控晶体管点火系统

magnet（ic）core 磁芯（电磁铁芯）

magnetic coupling 电磁联轴节

magnetic-coupling flowmeter 带磁性耦合器的流量计

magnet（ic）crane 磁力起重机

magnetic creeping 磁滞（现象）

magnetic cycle 磁化循环（磁化周期，充磁周期）

magnetic defectoscope 磁力探伤器

magnetic diode 磁场效应二极管

magnetic dipole moment 磁偶极矩

magnetic disc 磁盘

magnetic dispersion 磁泄漏

magnetic domain 磁畴（指在没有外磁场条件下，铁磁质中电子自旋磁矩形成的小自发磁化区，因各磁畴方向不同，对外不显磁性，只有受到外磁场作用时，外磁场越强，各磁畴排列越整齐，对外显示的磁性越强）

magnetic-drag 磁引力（一种非磁性良导体金属圆板与旋转磁铁接近时，由于在圆板内引起涡电流而产生的向磁铁旋转的方向曳引该圆板的力，汽车的电磁式车速表即利用该原理制成）

magnetic drag tachometer 磁感应式转速计，磁引力式转速表
magnetic (drain) plug 磁性（放油）塞（如：油底壳的可吸附金属磨粒的放油塞）
magnetic drum ①磁鼓 ②转鼓状磁铁分离器 ③磁力滚
magnetic-energy storage coil 磁能存储线圈
magnetic examination 磁力探伤检查
magnetic fan coupling 风扇电磁离合器
magnetic field 磁场（简称 mf，指磁体周围对置于其中的磁体或运动的电荷或电流产生力的作用的空间场）
magnetic-field intensity 磁场强度（在 MKSA 单位制中，单位为安培/米；在 CGS 单位制中，为奥斯特，参见 oersted，亦称 magnetic-field strength, magnetic intensity）
magnetic figure 磁场图形（磁力线图）
magnetic filter 磁性滤清器
magnetic flaw detecting 磁力探伤
magnetic flaw detector 磁力探伤器
magnetic flux 磁通量 [指通过某一断面积的磁力线的条数，简称磁通，其单位为韦伯，简称韦（Wb），见 weber]
magnetic flux density 磁通（量）密度，磁感应强度（代号常用 B）
magnetic flux test (ing) ①磁力探伤（利用磁力线变化检验）②磁流试验
magnetic flywheel 飞轮式磁电机 [= flywheel (-type) magneto]
magnetic force 磁力，电磁力
magnetic force line 磁力线（亦写作 magnetic line of force，指用来描述磁场分布的假想曲线，磁力线上各点的切线方向与该点磁场方向一致，而磁力线的疏密程度表示该处磁场的强弱，在匀强磁场内，磁力线是分布均匀、方向相同的平行直线。磁力线亦称磁感应线）
magnetic head 磁头
magnetic holding device 电磁夹具
magnetic ignition 磁电机点火
magnetic induction 磁感应（指磁性体在磁场中磁化的现象）
magnetic inductive speedometer 磁感应式车速里程表（利用磁感应原理指示车速，利用机械传递记录行驶里程的仪表）
magnetic inductive tachometer 磁感应式转速表
magnetic inductivity 磁导率（ = magnetic inductive capacity）
magnetic inspection 磁力探伤
magnetic inspection of crack 磁力探测裂缝，裂纹磁力探测
magnetic intensity 磁场强度（ = magnetic-field strength）
magnetic iron 磁铁
magnetic lag 磁（化）滞（后）（磁惯性）
magnetic levitation vehicle （轨道）磁垫车，磁力悬浮车（利用磁力的排斥或吸引，使车辆悬浮在轨道上行驶，简称 maglev vehicle）
magnetic loading 磁负载（单位：Wb/m^2）
magnetic material 磁性材料
magnetic-matrix switch 磁模开关
magnetic-mechanical 磁-机械的（简称 MM）
magnetic mechanical seal 磁力机械密封（用磁力代替弹簧力起补偿作用的机械密封）
magnetic moment 磁（力）矩
magnetic needle 磁针（如：指南针）
magnetic oscillograph 电磁振子式示波器
magnetic particle coupling 磁粉式离合器

magnetic particle display 磁粉显示（器）(利用磁场使磁粉按所要求的方向活动而实现数据、图像显示的无源显示器)

magnetic particle inspection 磁粉探伤，磁力探伤

magnetic pendulum 磁摆

magnetic permeability 导磁性，磁导率

magnetic pickup 电磁感应式脉冲电压发生器（在汽车电子控制系统中，用来作为发动机曲轴位置和转速传感器，有多种结构形式，但其共同点是利用一个与分电器轴同步旋转、带有与汽缸数相同的凸齿形的转子切割或改变永磁定子感应线圈的磁场，使通过感应线圈的磁通发生周期性变化而产生感应电压，以脉冲形式输出，有的直接利用飞轮代替转子)

magnetic pick-up device ①电磁拾音器 ②电磁传感器

magnetic pick-up tool （金属零件的）磁力吸拾器（利用装在长杆或软棍上的磁头从难以接近处找回和拾起螺母、螺栓等金属件的装置，简称 pick-up tool）

magnetic pole 磁极

magnetic position sensor 磁效应位置传感器（各种利用磁效应，如：variable reluctance 可变磁阻，hall effect 霍尔效应，inductive 电磁感应，magneto resistive 磁致变阻及 magneto strictive 磁致伸缩传感器等的直线和角度位置传感器的总称）

magnetic-powder clutch 磁粉离合器（磁力离合器的一种，它利用磁粉励磁后的电磁力来传递转矩）

magnetic powder method 磁粉探伤法（亦称 electromagnetic powder method）

magnetic powder transmission system （使用）磁粉离合器的传动系统

magnetic properties 磁性

magnetic-pulse controlled 电磁脉冲控制的

magnetic reactance 磁抗

magnetic recording head （磁带）记录头，录像磁头，录音磁头

magnetic remanence 剩余磁感应，剩余磁通密度

magnetic resistance 磁阻

magnetic ride active-damping shock 见 magnetic selective ride control package

Magnetic Ride Control（Cadillac 豪华型活顶双座跑车的）磁致流变型平顺性控制（系统）[据称该系统为世界上响应速度最快的悬架控制系统之一，四个车轮场装有车身相对位移传感器，其电子控制模块根据这些传感器的信息可在 1ms 内改变各个车轮悬架减振器的阻尼特性，比实时阻尼系统（real-time-damping system）要快 5 倍。减振器使用磁致流变型减振液（magneto-rheological fluid），其中悬浮的铁微粒几乎可在瞬间对电磁变化做出响应而改变阻尼特性]

magnetics ①磁学，磁力学 ②磁性元件（材料）

magnetic saturation 磁饱和（外界磁场的磁感应线即使再进一步增加，被磁化的磁性体的磁感应强度，即其磁通密度也不再增加的现象）

magnetic screw driver 磁性螺钉旋具

magnetic selection 磁选

Magnetic Selective Ride Control (suspension) package （通用公司 Chevrolet 的 F55 型）电磁选择平顺性控制型（悬架）总成 [该悬架系统使用所谓的电磁平顺性主动式减振器（magnetic ride active-damping shock），可由驾驶员根据眼前的路状即时选择确保行驶平顺性的阻尼模式]

magnetic sheath 磁感应屏蔽层

magnetic shield 磁屏蔽（利用磁感应线在介质的分界面上会发生折射的现象，用磁导体制成屏蔽外壳，阻止磁感应线，保护壳内的电器或电路免受外界磁场影响）

magnetic shunt 磁分路（主磁路的分支磁路，亦称 magnetic by-pass）

magnetic sound recorder 磁带录音机

magnetic spectrometer 磁谱仪（简称 MS）

magnetic speedometer 磁力车速表（在变速器主轴带动的永久磁铁旋转磁场的作用下，使非磁性、良电导体金属片内感生涡电流，该涡电流和磁力线相互作用产生与转速成正比的使金属片转动的力，用金属片的转动量表示相应的车速）

magnetic steel 磁钢（是具有高饱和磁感强度和高磁导率的磁性钢种）

magnetic storage （计算机）磁性存储器

magnetic substance 磁性体

magnetic sweeper 磁力清扫车

magnetic switch 磁力开关，电磁开关（= magne switch, magnet switch）

magnetic switch conductor 电磁开关接点

magnetic tape 记录磁带，磁带（简称 MT）

magnetic tape recorder 磁带记录器，磁带录音（像）机

magnetic testing 磁力探伤

magnetic thickness tester （镀层等厚度的）磁性测厚仪

magnetic transducer 电磁传感器

magnetic transistor 磁场效应三极管

magnetic transmission 磁力传动

magnetic valve 电磁阀（利用电磁力开启、关闭的阀门）

magnetic vector sensor 磁矢量传感器（利用铁磁体轴在传递转矩时，原来随机分布的磁畴会朝切线方向转动的特性制成的非接触式磁电转矩检测器件）

magnetic vehicle detector 电磁侦车器，电磁式车辆检测器（车辆通过速度与数量的电磁检测器）

magnetic wall thickness gauge 壁厚磁测仪

magnetized 被磁化的

magnetizing coil 励磁线圈

magnetizing current 励磁电流

magnet moving plate （电喇叭的）电磁活动片，电磁活动触片

magneto 磁电机，永磁发电机，磁石发电机（利用导体和永久磁铁相对运动而产生电动势的装置，有低压用和高压用的两种。目前主要用作摩托车等发动机的点火电源，= magneto generator，亦作 magnedo，= mognetodynamo）

magneto advance lever 磁电机点火提前角调节杆

magnetocaloric 磁致热的

magneto chemistry 磁化学，磁电化学

magneto coupling 电磁耦合器，电磁联轴节

magneto-dynamo 永磁发电机，磁电机（= magdynamo）

magneto electric pulse generator 磁电脉冲发生器

magneto electric tachometer 磁电式转速计（表）

magneto grease 磁电机滑脂（用于润滑磁电机轴承的耐热优质滑脂）

magneto hydrodynamical 电磁流体动力的（简称 MHI）

magneto hydrodynamic electrical converter 磁流体动力发电机（= magneto hydrodynamic generator，利用导电磁流体磁力线产生电能的装置，简称 MHD）

magneto ignition coil 磁电机点火线圈（磁电机感应线圈，= magneto

magnetomotive ①磁势 ②磁力作用的,磁动力的

magnetomotive force 磁通势〔亦称 magnetic motive force,封闭磁路周围磁场强度的线积分,简称 m.m.f. 或 MMF, $= \oint H \cdot dl = NI$,式中:H—磁场强度;dl—线元;N—线圈匝数;I—每匝内的电流量〕

magneto optics 磁光学

magnetoplasma dynamic generator 磁等离子流动力发电机(磁流体动力发电机的一种。利用等离子流切割磁力线而产生电能的装置,简称 MPDG)

magneto pole 磁极

magneto resistive effect 磁(致)阻(变)效应(导体或半导体电阻随所在磁场强度的变化而变化的现象,简称 MRE)

magneto resistive effect element 磁(致)阻(变)效应元件(应用磁阻效应的各种元件,如电位计、位移传感器、非接触式开关等)

magneto resistive effect sensor 磁(致)阻(变)效应传感器(简称 MRE sensor, 或 magneto resistive sensor)

magneto resistive sensitivity 磁致阻变敏感度(相对于磁场变化,电阻变化的大小)

magneto rotor 磁电机转子

magneto sensitivity 磁场敏感度(如:磁致阻变元件的电阻随磁场变化而变化的程度)

magneto starting accelerator 磁电机起动加速器(起动时使磁铁转子瞬时加速,保证产生足够高的点火高压,可靠点火,同时起动时使点火时刻延迟,防止汽油机反转的装置)

magneto stator 磁电机定子

magneto striction 磁致伸缩(现象),磁致变形(在磁力线变化作用下,材料晶体结构产生弹性收缩和膨胀变形的现象)

magneto strictive 磁致伸缩的,磁致变形的

magneto strictive actuator 磁致伸缩执行器,磁致变形执行器

magneto strictive linear displacement sensor 磁致伸缩效应式线性位移传感器(简称 magneto strictive sensor)

magneto strictive relay 磁致伸缩继电器

magneto strictive transformer 磁致伸缩式变换器(将电信号变换为机械运动的执行元器件)

magneto-type ball bearing 磁性球轴承

magnetron 磁控(电子)管

magnet sensor 电磁传感器

magnet shunt 磁分路

magnet steel 磁性钢,磁钢

magnetswitch 电磁开关(electromagnetic switch 的简称,用电磁力完成开关动作的装置,如:solenoid switch)

magnet type speedometer 磁铁式速度表

magnet valve 电磁阀(使用电磁线圈吸动衔铁开闭的阀门)

magnification 放大倍数,放大率,扩大,增加;放大,增大;伸缩(变换)

magnifier ①放大器,扩大器 ②放大透镜

magnitude ①大小,尺寸,量度,数量,数值,值积,幅 ②等级,数量级 ③重大,重要,巨大

magnitude comparator 数值比较器(对两数进行比较并给出比较结果 magnon 磁振子的组合电路)

magnus aja-dip (汽车零件的)摇式自动洗涤机

mag wheel 轻镁合金车轮（magnesium wheel 的简称，= mag, mags, 原指使用镁合金轮辋的车轮，现指任一种使用特殊材料和结构的车轮）

mAh/g 毫安小时/克（milliamp hours per gram，蓄电池的容量质量比，每克质量所能提供的毫安小时电量）

mahogany ①桃花心木，（硬）红木 ②赤褐色

mail carrier 邮件运输车（= mailtruck, postal delivery van, motor mail truck, mail car）

mail vehicle 邮车，邮政车（mail car, mail truck, mail van, mail wagon, motor mail truck, postal truck, mail bus, postal vehicle, post office vehicle, mobile post office 的统称）

main accumulator of hydraulic active suspension 主动式液压悬架系统（前桥和后桥悬架系统各有一个，其主要功能：存储油泵经多阀体输入的压力油液并保持所要求的油压，以便在需要时向执行器提供足够的压力油液；当发动机熄火时，提供足够的液压，保持车身高度）

main air bleed （化油器主油系的）空气补偿量孔

main air intake 主进气道，主进气口

main air reservoir 主储气筒

main air valve 空气主阀

main anode 主阳极

main bar （敞篷汽车软顶篷的）主弓形撑杆（亦称 main bow）

main beam 前照灯远光，前照灯远光灯丝（= long-distance beam, full beam, 美称 high beam, driving beam）

main beam filament 前照灯远光灯丝

main beam telltale 远光灯接通指示灯（亦称 main beam indicator）

main bearing ①主轴承 ②（特指）（发动机）曲轴主轴承（曲轴颈轴承）

main-bearing bridge 缸体上作为曲轴主轴承支撑的横隔板（亦称 main bearing panel）

main bearing cap （曲轴）主轴承盖

main bearing clearance 曲轴主轴承间隙（主轴颈与主轴承间的间隙）

main (bearing) journal （曲轴）主轴颈

main bearing lining 主轴瓦耐磨合金层，主轴承抗磨合金层

main bearing locating lip 曲轴主轴承瓦片定位凸唇

main-bearing oil seal 主轴承油封

main bearings aligning gauge （发动机曲轴）主轴承孔同轴度检测仪

main bearing shell 主轴承瓦

main-bearing stud 主轴承螺柱

main bearing wrench 曲轴主轴承螺母扳手（= bearing wrench）

main body entrance 车厢主要进口

main body entrance door 主车门

main bore ①主腔，主筒（如双腔化油器的主腔）②主孔径

main brake cylinder （液压制动系）制动主缸（= master brake cylinder, 亦写作 main braking cylinder）

main brake pedal 行车制动踏板（常用制动踏板，主制动器踏板）

main braking time 主制动时间（指制动力达到一定值后，基本保持不变的那段时间）

main brass 主黄铜轴承套

main brush 主电刷

main camshaft 主凸轮轴（指发动机内驱动气门的凸轮轴）

main casing ①主壳，主壳体 ②（单纯旋转发动机的）外壳体（指旋转缸体之外的固定壳体）

main centre floorpanel （轿车车身

的）中主底板

main choke tube 主喉管

main circuit 主回路，主油路，主线路，主电路

main circulating pump 主循环泵

main clutch shifting lever bracket 主离合器拨叉支架

main combustion chamber （分开式燃烧室的）主燃烧室（简称 main chamber）

main combustion period （内燃机的）主燃期（从汽缸内出现最高压力起到出现最高温度时为止的一段燃烧时间，以曲轴转角表示，等于速燃期与缓燃期之和，燃料的主要部分在主燃期内燃烧完毕）

main control logic 主逻辑控制电路，主控制逻辑

main dimension 主要尺寸，基本尺寸（= key dimension）

main discharge jet （化油器）主量孔

main discharge tube （化油器）主量孔喷管（= choke delivery tube）

main drive gear ①主传动齿轮，主动齿轮 ②主传动机构（简称 main drive, main gear）

main drive motor 主驱动电动机

main drive shaft ①主驱动轴，主传动轴 ②（特指）变速器第一轴（= clutch shaft）

main environments 主要的外界条件，主环境

main floor unit （轿车车身等的）主底板总成，前底板总成

main frame ①主机架 ②（汽车）底盘，主车架 ③总装配架 ④大型电子计算机，主机 ⑤（电子计算机内具有存储、算术逻辑功能及寄存功能的）中央处理器（= CPU, 亦称主板）

main fuel 主燃料（指内燃机同时燃用两种或两种以上的燃料时，每循环发热量较多的燃料）

main fuel filter 主燃油滤清器

main fuel tank 主燃油箱

main gallery （发动机汽缸体内的）主机油道

main gear 主传动

main gearbox 主变速器

main headlamp ①（汽车）前照灯（= head lamp）②（多前照灯制中的）主前照灯

main highway 公路干线，干线公路（= arterial highway, main-line highway, trunk highway, major highway）

main injection （柴油机喷油器的）主喷射

main jet 主喷嘴

main lamp switch 主灯开关，主照明开关（多挡多灯开关，可在不同挡位开apo前照灯、驻车灯、尾灯、仪表照明灯及室内照明灯，并可通过转动旋钮调节亮度）

main leaf (of spring) with bushing 弹簧钢板主片带衬套（= master spring leaf, top leaf of spring, main plate of spring）

mainline 干道，干线；主线

main-line highway 干线公路，干路；主要公路（= main-trunk highway）

main line pressure （液压控制系统的）主管路压力，管路压力（简称 main pressure）

main lubricating oil pump 主润滑油泵

main means of transport 主要运输手段

main member 主构件

main metal 曲轴主轴承瓦

main motion 主运动，主体运动

main motor 主电动机

main office 总公司，总部，主管部门

main oil conduit 主机油道，润滑油总管路

main oil distributing passage 主油道
main oil pressure line 主压力油道
main petal （双级簧片阀的）主簧片
main plane in collision 碰撞中（车辆的）主平面（①在两车正面或一车前面与另一车后面纵向碰撞中指两车的纵向对称平面②在一车垂直碰撞另一车侧面的碰撞中指碰撞车的纵向对称平面，受撞车过座椅基准点 R point 的横向铅垂平面）
main pole 主磁极，主极
main pressure regulator valve （液力变矩器控制系统中的）主调压阀（调节换挡元件工作压力的阀）
main propeller shaft （全轮驱动式汽车的）主传动轴（将动力传至分动箱的传动轴）
main relay 主继电器（一般指减轻主电路电源开关的负载的电源继电器）
main road ①（高速）干线，公路（=turnpike）②主干道路，公路干线
main routine （汽车电子控制系统的）主程序（= main program，指在一组相关程序中的主要程序，或在多个程序或子程序各层次中，运转时首先接受控制的程序。即可调用其他程序而不被其他任何程序所调用的程序）
main seal bar （转子发动机）径向密封主片，刮片
main servomotor 主伺服（液压）马达，主伺服电动机
main shaft （变速器）主轴（第二轴），输出轴，亦写作 mainshaft，= output shaft
main shaft bearing 主轴轴承
main shaft bearing cover ①（变速器）第二轴轴承盖 ②主轴轴承盖（= main shaft bearing cap）
main shaft of RC engine 转子发动机的主轴（转子发动机的偏心轴，转子发动机的输出轴，转子轴）

main shaft pilot bearing 主轴导向轴承（变速器第二轴导向前轴承）
main shaft speed （变速器的）第二轴转速，主轴转速
main shaft spline 主轴花键（段）
main sill 纵梁（亦称 main bolster, side sill）
main spring 主钢板弹簧
main spring leaf 主钢板弹簧片
main straight 干线直线区段
mainstream model 主流（车）型
main sun visor （双片式遮阳板系统中的）主遮阳板（可左、右转动的主板）
main supply switch 总开关
maint 维护，维修，保养（maintenance 的简称）
maintain ①维持，保持，保存，保留 ②（日常）维护，保养，维修
maintainability ①维修性（在规定条件下使用的汽车在规定的时间内，按规定的程序和方法进行维修时，保持或恢复到能完成规定功能的能力）②维修度（指在上述条件下进行维修时，保持或恢复到能完成规定功能状态的概率）③维修方便性，可维修性，维修性
main technical data 主要技术数据
maintenance 维护，维修（指为保持或恢复汽车能够完成规定功能的能力而采取技术管理的措施）
maintenance and service 维修与服务（简称 MS）
maintenance charge 维修费（= maintenance cost, upkeep cost, maintenance expense）
maintenance control report 维修管理报告（简称 MCR）
maintenance cycle 维修周期（指各项技术维护作业的间隔里程）
maintenance depot 维修场，检修所，维修站，维护站（亦称 maintenance station）

maintenance engineering order 维护技术规范，维护技术规程（简称 MEO）

maintenance equipment company ①维护设备公司，维修设备公司 ②（美军）维修连

maintenance expense 维护费（= maintenance charge）

maintenance-free battery 免维护蓄电池（极板栅架采用低锑合金或铅钙合金代替原来的铅锑合金，气体的析出电位提高，析气量、自放电和电液损耗显著减少，加上隔板及壳体结构上的各种改进，使蓄电池在使用过程中无须添加蒸馏水和补充充电）

maintenance free modification 免维护化

maintenance indicator system （汽车）维修指示系统（简称 MIS）

maintenance inspection 技术维护过程中的检查

maintenance instruction （汽车）维护规程

maintenance intervals 维护周期（维护间隔里程，= service intervals）

maintenance log （车辆）维护记录

maintenance manual 维护手册（简称 MM）

maintenance rate （车辆）非完好率（车辆总车日中维护、修理、待修车日所占比率，表示车辆不能使用的程度），维护率

maintenance, repair, operation 维护，修理，使用（简称 MRO）

maintenance test 维修适应性（方便性）试验

maintenance train 移动式维修工程列车（装在汽车列车上的维修车间）

maintenance truck 保修服务车（= service truck）

main thoroughfare （公路）主干道

main-trunk highway 干线公路（= mainline highway）

main venturi （化油器的）主喉管（在多层喉管中，指主喷油嘴所在的喉管）

MAIS 最大受伤简略分度值（亦称 max AIS，指受伤部位，各种损伤的最大 AIS 值）

major ①较大的，较重要的，较长的；主要的，重点的，多数的，第一流的 ②主科，专业科目；成年人 ③主修，专门研究

major adjustment 大调整

major air cell ①（涡流室式柴油机的）主燃烧室 ②主空气室

major axis ①（椭圆）长轴，长轴线 ②主轴，主轴线

major axis of cam 凸轮长轴（凸轮的最大径向尺寸）

major diameter ①（螺纹）外径 ②椭圆形的长径

major diameter of epitrochoid 长幅外摆线长轴（径）[$= 2(R+e)$, 式中：R—基圆半径与作外切纯滚动的发生圆半径之和；e—创成点至发生圆中心的距离，= major axis of epitrochoid，参见 epitrochoid]

major failure 严重失效，重大故障（导致汽车降低完成规定功能的能力的主要总成的严重失效或重大故障）

major filament （两丝灯泡的）大灯丝

majority carrier 多数载流子（如：n-型半导体中的电子，p-型半导体中的空穴）

major project ①重点研究课题 ②大型（工程）计划，重大项目

major repair （汽车）大修（用修理或更换零、部件总成，包括基础件的方法，恢复汽车的完好技术状况，功能指标的恢复性修理，= major overhaul, complete overhaul, rebuilding, major repair）

major repair life 大修间隔里程（大修出厂到下一次大修期间，汽车行驶的里程，= interval mileage of major repair）

major semi-axis 长半轴

major thrust face 主要推力支撑面（活塞裙部承受最大侧压力的支撑面）

major total 总计，主要统计值

major tune-up ①大调整，全面调试（特指每年或每两年进行一次的全面检修调整）②（为了提高输出功率而做的）重大改造，全面改造

major urban arterial highway 都市主干线

make-and-break cam （电路）通断凸轮（如：断电器凸轮，磁电机断电器凸轮）

make and break contact 断续触点（= breaker point, interrupter point, contact breaker point）

make and break device 断续装置，断电器

make-and-break ignition ①断电器点火 ②内燃机早期使用的使低压电路通-断产生自感火花的点火方式

make-and-break key 通-断开关

make-before break relay contact 常闭式继电器触点

makeover ①转让，移交 ②改造，改做，翻新 ③创造

maker 制造者，生产者（如：汽车制造厂，汽车制造公司）

maker option 生产厂装选购件（指用户选定而由生产厂家在生产线上组装好的非标准设备和装置）

make up ①成分，组成，构造，组织，编制 ②性格，特征，性质 ③补偿，补充 ④修理，装配，制作 ⑤接通，闭合

make up oil （液压系统闭式回路中）泄漏补充油（由专门的补油泵供给）

maladjustment ①调整不当，失调 ②不匹配，不协调，不适应，不一致性

malchaert's coefficient of efficiency of acceleration power 马氏加速功率利用系数（地面附着系数所能利用的最大理想功率与车辆实际装备功率之比）

malcolmizing case-hardening process 快速氮化表面硬化处理法

malcombustion 不正常燃烧

maldistribution 分配不均匀，分布不均，分布不准，分配不当

male ①外的，阳的，公的，凸的，插入式的 ②男性的

male adapter 外螺纹过渡管接头，外螺纹内管接头

male connector （电）插头，插销

male driver 男驾驶员

male flange 带凸台的法兰（突缘）（= tongued flange）

male friction cone （同步器）阳摩擦锥

male member （配合件的）凸件，公件

male-pipe 外螺纹管

male plug 塞，栓，螺塞

male screw thread 阳螺纹，外螺纹（亦简称 male screw, male thread）

male splines 轴花键，外花键

malfunction alarm 故障警报（信号）

malfunction indicator light 故障警报灯（简称 MIL，车载诊断系统装在仪表板上用闪光次数作代码，发出故障警报的指示灯，通用公司称 check engine lamp。美国政府规定从1995年1月起凡美国市场销售的汽车一律将该警报灯称为 MIL）

malfunction(ing) 故障，失灵

malfunction probability 故障概率

malleable ①韧性的，可锻的，可延展的 ②可锻铸铁（= malleable cast iron）

malleable casting 可锻铸铁铸件

malleable (cast) iron 可锻铸铁（由白口铸铁件经热处理、石墨化、退火处理，而得到一种有较高强度又有良好塑性和韧性的铸铁）

malleable pig iron 制造可锻铸铁用生铁，可锻铸铁用白口铸铁（碳 4.0%，硅 1.7%～2.1%，锰 0.2%～0.4%，磷＜0.1%，硫＜0.04%，铜＜0.18%，铬＜0.03%）

mA（ma, ua） 毫安（培）（milliampere）

man 手动变速器（manual gearbox 的简称）

management ①管理，处理，操纵，控制驾驶，经营 ②管理部门

management department of highway transportation 公路运输管理部门

management information system 管理信息系统（简称 MIS）

management technology 管理技术

manager 管理人，经营者，经理

managerial strategy （企业等的）经营策略，管理对策

man-auto 手动-自动（的）

mandate ①命令，指令 ②授权 ③委托管理

mandatory ①强制性的，必须遵循的，法定的，命令的，指示的 ②委托的 ③代理人，代办者

mandatory fitment（s） （法规等规定）强制性安装的设备，义务性安装的装置

mandatory test 强制性试验（法定试验，必须遵循的试验）

M and F 男女乘员（male-female occupation）

mandrel ①心轴，静轴 ②芯棒，型芯，芯子 ③冲子，顶杆（亦写作 mandril）

mandrel press 心轴压床，心轴压力机（亦称 arbor press）

maneuver ①策略，机动 ②（车队等的）调动，调遣 ③（汽车的）运用，操纵（＝maneuvre）

maneuverability 机动性，操纵性，灵活性（＝maneuvreability）

maneuvering performance 操纵性能，机动性能（亦称 maneuvering capability）

maneuver traffic 调度交通

man failure 人为损坏（由于操作不当引起的损坏）

manganese 锰（Mn）

manganese bronze 锰青铜（合金）

manganese-lithium battery 锰-锂电池

manganese phosphate treatment 磷酸锰溶液表面处理［以获得抗黏合拉伤的磷酸锰保护层（manganese phosphate coating）］

manganese steel 锰钢

manganin ①锰铜，锰镍铜合金（锰 12%，镍 2%，铜 86%；或锰 13%～18%，镍 1.5%～4%，其余铜，＝manganin alloy）②锰铜线（＝manganin wire，锰 13%，铜 87%）

man-hour requirement （单位产品）所需工时

manifestation 表明，表示，表现形式，现象，体现

manifold 歧管（如：进气歧管，排气歧管）

manifold absolute pressure sensor 进气歧管绝对压力传感器（简称 MAP sensor，使用空气体积流量传感器的汽油喷射系统中用来测定进气管壳空度的传感元件，近年来体积传感器已逐渐为空气质量传感器所取代，不再需要进气歧炭绝对压力传感器）

manifold accumulator effect （发动机）进气歧管的储效应（指驾驶员踩下加速踏板时，进入进气歧管的气流立即增加，但汽缸内的进气量却不能同步增加，以致部分进气"存储"在进气歧管内）

manifold after burner 排气歧管后燃室(设在排气歧管内的后燃器,见 after burner)

manifold air flow sensor 进气空气流量传感器(简称 MAF sensor)

manifold air injection 排气歧管空气喷射(向排气歧管内喷入空气,以便利用排气余热使废气内的 HC、CO 进一步燃烧,减少排放污染)

manifold air temperature sensor 进气温度传感器[一般装在空气滤清器内,测定进入进气歧管的空气温度,简称 MAT sensor,某些美国公司使用的术语,美国政府规定从 1995 年 1 月起一律改用 IAT(intake air temperature sensor)一词]

manifold catalystic converter 排气歧管内藏型催化转化器(催化床直接装在排气管腔内,简称 MCC)

manifold clamp 进、排气歧管夹

manifold depression 进气管中的真空度,进气歧管负压(指发动机进气歧管平均静压与其周围大气压力的差值,在自然吸气式发动机中,一般呈负压,而在增压式发动机中却呈正压,这一术语一般表示非增压式发动机进气歧管负压)

manifold film (发动机)进气歧管油膜,进气管壁油膜(附着于进气管壁的燃油膜)

manifold fitting 进、排气歧管接头

manifold gauge ①(发动机)进气管真空表 ②(发动机)排气歧管压力表 ③(检查汽车空调系统高、低压侧压力,加注或排放制冷剂,以及制冷系抽真空作业用的)歧管压力计(由低压表、高压表、基体和高、低压侧手动阀及连接高、低压工作阀和真空泵或制冷剂罐的三根接管组成,因其形呈歧状,故名)

manifold heat control valve 排气歧管加热控制阀(简称 manifold heat valve,指装在排气歧管或排气管上,控制废气流向化油器或进气管道加热套或加热管的阀门)

manifold heater 进气管加热器,进气管加热装置(用于改善发动机的冷机起动性能)

manifold injection ①(发动机的)进气歧管喷水法(将水喷射到进气歧管内,使之随进气气流进入汽缸)②进气管汽油喷射(将汽油喷入进气歧管,而不直接喷入各个汽缸内)③排气歧管喷水冷却(排气门)④排气歧管内喷入二次空气,以利用废气余热氧化废气中的 HC、CO

manifold injection system 进气管喷射系统(= suction pipe injection system)

manifold plate heater 进气歧管预热装置

manifold preheater valve 进气管预热阀(控制进气管预热介质,如废气、冷却水等的阀门)

manifold pressure 歧管压力(见 manifold depression)

manifold-pressure compensator (增压柴油机喷油量的)增压压力补偿器(指按照增压柴油机进气管压力来调节喷油泵供油量的装置)

manifold pressure gauge (发动机)歧管压力表

manifold reactor 排气歧管热反应器(设在排气管内利用废气余热,使废气中 HC 和 CO 进一步氧化的二次空气喷射式热反应装置)

manifold suction system 进气管(真空)抽吸型曲轴箱通风系

manifold tuning valve 进气歧管调节阀(简称 MTV,装在增压式发动机进气歧管的增压室中央,可根据发动机转速控制和调节进气量)

manifold vacuum 进气歧管真空,进气歧管真度

manifold vacuum (crankcase ventilation) system (= manifold suction system) 进气管真空(抽吸)型曲轴箱通风系

manifold vacuum purge line (蒸发排放物控制系统的)进气歧管真空清除管道(连接进气管与活性炭罐的吸气管道,利用进气管真空将新鲜空气及活性炭罐内残存的燃油蒸气吸入进气歧管,见 canister purge)

manifold wall wetting (进气)歧管内壁浸湿,进气歧管壁浸油(燃油附着于进气歧管内壁)

manifold (water) induction (发动机的)进气歧管吸水法(利用进气真空,将水滴与气流一并自进气歧管吸入汽缸内,见 direct water injection)

manikin (试验用的)假人,人体模特,人体模拟装置

manipulability ellipsoid forecast technique (驾驶者手臂)可操作(范围)椭圆形预测技术

manipulated variable (控制系统的)操作变量,控制变量

manipulation 操作

manipulator finger 机械手,机械手指

man-machine complex 人-机组合

man-machine interface 人-机接口,人-机界面(使用者与计算机之间通信和对话的各种硬件和软件系统)

man, machine, method, material 操作者,机器,加工方法,材料(生产四要素,简称4M)

man-machine system 人-机系统(①指劳动者与劳动机具相结合的有关系统。如:影响汽车驾驶员劳动的座位形式、尺寸,操纵机构、观测仪表的设计布置,驾驶室的光度、温度等;②指计算机与用户间的通信对话系统③将机器与操纵机器的人作为一个整体来考虑的系统)

man-made emission 人为污染物(如:CO、NO_x 等,以区别于自然污染物)

man-month 人-月,人月(计算单位,一人工作一月,简称 MM)

mano-contact 压力触点(如:油压控制的油压不足警报灯开关触点,制动液压控制的制动灯开关触点等)

manoeuvre (汽车的)驾驶操纵(特指操纵汽车绕过障碍物或在狭窄的空间内转弯等的技巧,美写作 maneuver)

manoeuvre ability ①(车辆)机动性,易操纵性,驾驶灵活性 ②机动性驾驶操作(包括紧急避让障碍物掉头、进入停车位置,驶出停车位置、倒车等,= 美 maneuver ability)

manoeuvre ability of automobile 汽车操纵性(驾驶机动性)

manoeuvring test (车辆车道变换)灵活性试验,机动性试验,操纵性试验

manometer 气压计,真空表

man power ①(作为功率单位的)人力(指一个人的体力在单位时间内所能完成的机械功,1人力普通等于1/10 马力)②人力(指一个人的体力所能产生的劳动能力)

manual ①手动的,手控的 ②手册,说明书,指南,细则 ③手动变速器(manual gearbox 的简称)

manual acting 用手操作的

manual adjustment 手调,手调节

manual advance device (柴油机等的)手动喷油提前器(根据柴油机转速变化,由手柄调整,使喷油泵供油始点提前的装置)

manual book 手册

manual brake 人力制动器(制动时所需的能量,完全由驾驶员的体力供给的机械式制动器和无助力装置的液压制动器)

manual control 手动操作,手工操纵,人工控制,手控(简称 M/C,= manual operation, physical operation)

manual controller 手动控制器(如:人工控制交通信号的控制器)

manual control panel 人工控制(开

关、仪表)板
manual-crank window 手摇升降车窗(亦称 manually operated window)
manual effort 操作力(如:操纵离合器、制动器时驾驶员的踩踏力)
manual-gantry vehicle washing equipment 手动式龙门型整车清洗装备
manual gearbox 手动机械式变速器
manual (gear shifting) transmission 手动换挡变速器 [= manually (gear) shifted transmission]
manual hub (分时四轮驱动式车辆前轮与驱动系统结合和分离的)手操纵切换装置(亦称 manual free wheel hub)
manual input device 人工输入装置,手动输入装置
manual locking free wheeling hub (分时四轮驱动系统的)手动锁止型自由旋转式轮毂(见 free wheeling hub)
manually operated 手操纵的,手动的
manual mode ①(CVT的)手动换挡模式(通常在CVT变速操纵机构上装有拨杆等手动换挡操纵件,驾驶者可按照自己的意愿手动换挡,CVT电子控制模块收到手动升、降挡"+、-"信号后,即向换挡控制装置"步进电机"发出指令直接换至相应挡位)②(各种自动控制系统的)手动模式
manual modulation valve 手动调节阀(简称MMV)
manual override 自动控制系统的超越手动操纵,手动超越控制(见 override linkage)
manual setting 手动调整,手调
manual shift ①(机械变速器的)手动换挡 ②(自动变速器的)手动选挡(= manual selection)
manual shift lever ①(机械变速器的)换挡杆 ②(自动变速器选择驻车,倒车,空挡,前进$_1$,前进$_2$,低速等挡区的)手动选挡杆
manual shift valve (自动变速器控制系统中由手动选挡杆控制的)手动选挡阀(亦称 manual selector valve,或简称 selector valve,控制工作油液进入驻车,倒车,空挡,前进$_1$,前进$_2$,或低速挡区的执行油路)
manual spark advance 手动点火提前,手控点火提前(= hand advance)
manual steering effort 手动转向力(驾驶员两手作用于转向盘上之力,= manual steering force hand force)
manual steering system 机械转向系统(完全靠驾驶员手力驱动的转向系)
manual steery gear 机械转向器(将驾驶员操纵的转向盘的转动变为转向摇臂的摆动,并按一定的传动比将转矩放大的机构)
manual switch 手动开关
manual transaxle 手动变速驱动桥
manual valve ①手控阀,手动阀 ②(自动变速器液压控制系的)选挡阀(由驾驶员通过杆系操纵的挡位或挡区范围选择阀,亦称 selector valve,简称MV)
manual version 手动变速型轿车
manufactory 制造厂,工厂
manufacture certification (由国家有关机关对新车排气污染等进行的)投产认证,投产鉴定
manufacturer ①制造者 ②制造厂,工厂(简称MFR)
manufacturer's certificate 工厂营业执照
manufacturer's guarantee 制造厂保证
manufacturer's maximum towed mass 厂定最大拖挂质量(制造厂根据牵引车的特性而核定出的拖挂质量)
Manufacturers of Emission Control

As-sociation [美]排气净化装置生产者协会（主要由生产催化转化系统的厂家组成，简称 MECA）

manufacturer's trials 制造厂试验，工厂试验

manufacture's performance ratings （汽车）制造厂家规定的（车辆）性能数据

manufacture's service manual 制造厂提供的（汽车）维修手册，使用手册

manufacturing-oriented 从事生产的，与生产有关的

manufacturing plant 制造厂

manufacturing systems engineering 制造系统工程（简称 MSE，20 世纪 70 年代后期，日本京都大学人见胜人教授运用系统工程的理论和方法，研究和处理产品的开发、规划、设计、制造、调试、管理、运筹、评价等整个制造过程的有关问题，以整体优化为目的的一门综合性软科学）

manufacturing tolerance 制造公差

manumatic transmission 半自动变速器（= semi-automatic transmission）

manure trailer 运厩肥的挂车，厩肥撒布挂车

man-vehicle interface 人车接口，人车界面（指人控制与驾驶车辆的各种操纵件：按钮、踏板、杆件、转向盘及汽车向人提供车速、转速、油耗、车况等信息的各种仪表，显示和警报装置及其相关软件等）

many-purpose 多用的，多用途的（= multi-purpose）

many-valued 多值的

map 曲面图，曲面［指随两项或两项以上的自变量的变化而变化的函数所形成的三维曲面，如：随发动机转速和进气管真空度变化的最佳点火提前角的三维曲面。在电子控制模块中，上述曲面的自变量和函数值是以查阅表（look-up table）的形式存储在存储器内的］

MAP and BP sensor 进气歧管绝对压力和大气压力传感器（manifold absolute pressure and barometric pressure sensor 的简称，二者装在一个外壳内的，亦称 B/MAP sensor）

map and direction-finding system 交通图及方位寻找系统

map-controlled ignition system 点火曲面控制式点火系统（亦称 mapped ignition system，由电子控制模块根据预存于存储器内的点火曲面所规定的各种转速和负荷下的最佳点火提前角来确定点火时刻的点火控制系统，见 ignition map 及 characteristic map）

map holder （驾驶室内的）地图夹架

MAPI [美]机械及联合产品研究所（Machinery and Allied Products Institute 的简称）

map light 地图小灯（亦称 map lamp，车厢内看地图、线路图等用的小灯）

map matching ①地图匹配（确定车辆在标有街道名称和地址名称的地图中的位置的相关技术）②（汽车全球定位等导航系统中的）地图叠合（将将汽车的实际行驶路线"叠合"在数据库存储的数字化地图上，通过屏显地图直观汽车的所在位置和行车路线）

map-matching software （导航系统的）地图叠合软件（可分为半确定性型和概率型两类，见 semideterministic map-matching software 和 probabilistic map-matching software）

map matching technology 地图匹配技术（简称 M.M.T.，指汽车全球定位导航系统中，采用的自动标示汽车在行车地图上的实时位置的技术）

map narration type navigation system

声音型导行系统（指用声音引导汽车行驶路线的导行系统）

map of operational lines 营运线路图（营运区域内班线和站点的示意图）

mapping ①绘制三维特性曲面图 ②三维特性曲面图（= characteristic map）

map pocket （汽车仪表板上的）地图箱，文件箱，文件袋［一般设在仪表板侧部，供装放小物件、路单、文件、手套等用，亦称手套箱（glove compartment、glove box）］

MAP sensor 进气歧管绝对压力传感器（manifold absolute pressure sensor 的简称）

mar ①损坏，毁坏，损伤，毁损，擦伤，划痕；障碍，缺点 ②微量分析试剂（micro-analytical reagent 的简称）

maraging steel 马氏体时效钢

Marcus 马尔库斯（奥地利人 Siegfried Marcus 1864 年曾将一台点燃式常压内燃机装在一辆四轮马车上，为后置后驱动，因无离合器难以起动，1875 年改进后的内燃机汽车仍存在维也纳博物馆中，1950 年曾在街上表演一次，车速 3mile/h）

margin ①边，缘，端 ②幅，界限，范围，极限 ③余量，裕度，储备值，安全系数 ④气门头边缘厚度（指气门顶表面至气门锥形座面间的距离）⑤收益

marginal bars 护栏

marginal check 边缘检验，临界试验（见 marginal test）

marginal data ①图例说明 ②边界数据

marginal stability 临界稳定性

marginal strip （车行道）路缘带

marginal test 边限校验，边缘试验（改变电子设备的某些工作条件，例如：改变电源电压、信号幅度、频率等进行试验，以检测和确定即将出现故障的界限，= marginal check）

marginal unit 临近损坏的元器件

marginal user 旧车转卖过程中最近的一个户主

margin capacity 备用容量

margin of energy 能量储备，后备能量

margin of safety 安全系数，安全储备（简称 MS，= safe margin）

margin of stability 稳定系数，稳定储量（= stability margin）

margin tolerance 公差范围

marine atmosphere 滨海区大气环境

marine blue （车身涂装的）海蓝色

marine exposure test 海洋性气候下的暴露试验（见 exposure test）

Mariotte's law 马瑞奥特定律（见 Boyle's law）

mark ①痕迹，斑点，污点 ②记号，标志，标牌（如汽车的车标，亦称 insignia, emblem）③（考试的）分数，点数 ④目标，目的物 ⑤标准（仅用单数）

marked capacity 额定生产率，额定容量，标定载（货）量（简称 MC）

marked guard 带警告标志的防护罩

marker （路面上指示交通用的）路标，标线，标示；标志，标志牌；路钉，路钮，标记（表示某段信息开始或终了的符号）

marker lamp 标志灯（亦称 markerlight，如：①表示公共汽车，装在前风窗玻璃上方的蓝紫色小灯 ②表示出租汽车的车顶灯 ③路标灯，信号识别灯 ④车辆的示廓灯）

market car 流动售货车（一般食品及日常用品等的流动零售汽车）

market for automobiles 汽车市场，轿车市场

market option 出厂前（用户要求厂方安装的）选购设备

market-oriented 面向市场的（市场定位的，市场取向的）

market quality information 市场质量信息（指用户对产品的评价）

market share （某一车型的）市场份额（市场占有率）

market truck 商品运输车

marking 打印，做记号，标记，记号，标识，印痕；画线，条纹；商标，路标

marking light ①标示灯 ②示宽灯（= fender lamp）

marking of freight transportation 运输标志（以文字、符号和图形等形式表示货物运输特性，装卸、运输、保管注意事项，收货、发货方名称和地址等）

mark of conformity （产品的）合格标志（证明产品符合相应标准或规范的标志）

Marles steering gear 球面蜗杆滚轮式转向器（亦称 hourglass warm and roller steering gear，指通过球面蜗杆滚轮传动副，将转向盘转动变换为摆动的转向器，Marles 为该转向器的专利权持有者）

Marles-Weller steering gear 蜗杆指销式转向器（亦称 warm and peg steering gear，指通过蜗杆指销传动副将转向盘轴转动变换为摆动的转向器，Males 和 Weller 为其专利权持有者）

marque （汽车的）牌名，（汽车的）商品名（如：Cadillac、Rolls-Royce 等）

marrow-meshed 带小孔的，小网格的，密的（滤网）

marsh buggy 沼（泽）地用汽车（湿地用车，沼泽地机动车辆，具有宽大的车轮或轮胎等泥泞地行驶装置，= swamp buggy）

marsh gas 沼气，甲烷（CH_4）

marsh land truck 沼泽地货车

marsh screw amphibian 沼泽地螺旋推进水陆两用车

marsh tire 沼泽地用轮胎（= water boggy tire）

marshy area 沼泽地，泥泞地，湿地（亦称 marshy Cand）

martempering 分级淬火（马氏体等温淬火，将工件加热到淬火温度，保温后先在温度略高于马氏体开始转变点的热浴中停留一段时间，待工件各部分与热浴温度一致，取出置于空气中，在缓冷条件下进行马氏体转变）

martensite 马丁体，马氏体（钢加热到 750~980℃，保温后快速冷却淬火所获得的高硬度体心立方格子微细针状组织，但共塑性、韧性差，必须经过回火处理）

martensitic steel 马氏体钢

MAS ①金属氧化铝半导体（metal alumina semiconductor） ②金属-氧化铝-硅（metal-alumina-silicon） ③军事标准化研究局（Military Agency for Standardization） ④毫安秒（milliampere second） ⑤混合气调节螺钉（mixture adjusting screw）

maser 脉塞（微波激射器，受激辐射微波放大器，microwave amplification by simulated emission of radiation 的简称）

Maserati 玛莎拉蒂（意大利的一家汽车制造厂名，20 世纪 80 年代初期推出世界第一辆双涡轮增压发动机汽车，1992 年推出 V6 跑车，时速 260km/h）

mask ①模板，型板 ②掩膜（光刻时使用按设计要求漏光、遮光或减光的膜片）③遮光屏，面具，面罩 ④（发动机进气门上的）导流屏 ⑤屏蔽 ⑥（计算机信息系统的）掩码

mask artwork 掩膜原图（制作光刻掩膜时用的原图）

masked inlet valve 带导流屏的进气门（亦称 screened valve）

masked inlet valve intake 导流屏进气（指进入汽缸的充量，在进气门导流屏的作用下在汽缸内形成强涡流的进气过程）

masked seat (cylinder) head 气门座导气屏式汽缸盖（指进气门座具有导气屏的结构，形成强涡流而实现稀混合气燃烧，简称 MSH，见 Jet Controlled Super Lean Combustion System）

masking ①杂音干扰现象（由于外音而使某音难以听到的现象）②遮蔽，掩蔽，阻碍，妨碍，遮涂，遮覆 ③[大量生产只读存储器（ROM）采用的]掩蔽法，掩膜技术（采用掩膜技术生产的 ROM 称 masked ROM）

masking compound 遮覆料（如喷漆时，涂在不需要涂漆部分上的遮覆剂，易于除净）

masking tape ①胶纸带（= gummed tape）②遮覆胶带（贴于不需要涂漆的表面）

mask of the inlet valve 进气门（头上的）导流屏

mask-programmed read-only memory 掩膜编程只读存储器（每个存储单元的数据内容在制造时采用掩膜已确定，其后不能修改的固定编程只读存储器）

masonite 绝缘纤维板，夹布胶木板

mass ①质量 ②物质 ③块，团；多数，大量，大部分，成批，许多 ④集中，集合，聚集，聚结，密集 ⑤大量的，大批的，大规模的

Massachusetts Institute of Technology （美国）麻省理工学院

massage function （汽车座椅的）按摩功能

mass air flow meter 空气质量流量传感器（可直接测定进气空气质量的传感器件，如热线式空气质量流量传感器、热膜式空气质量流量传感器等，亦称 mass air flow sensor，简称 MAF meter 或 MAF sensor）

mass analyzer 质谱仪

mass-burned fraction 燃烧率（指燃烧室内已燃混合气质量所占总混合气质量的比率，亦称已燃质量百分率，简称 MBF）

mass car 普及型轿车（大量生产的大众型轿车）

mass center 质量中心，质心

mass damper （装在前轮驱动车辆的半轴上的）质量型阻尼器（惯性式减振器，用于减轻或消除传动轴振动或摆振，通常为一可平衡或抵消上述振动的重物）

mass distribution ratio 质量分配比（如：前、后轴载质量分配的百分比）

mass-elastic characteristics （发动机的）质量-弹性特性

mass emission （排放有害物的）质量排放量（单位时间或每次试验期内排放出的污染物的质量，以 g/h 或 g/次试验为单位）

mass factor （汽车运动的）质量因数（即有效惯性质量 m' 和直线运动质量 m 的比值，常用 $r = \dfrac{m'}{m}$ 表示，一般货车的 r，在高速挡时为 1.09，在低速挡时为 2.5。见 effective inertia mass）

mass flow 质量流量

mass flow rate 单位质量流量，质量流量率

mass-flow rate perturbation 质量流量的波动

mass in running order （车辆）行车质量

massive 整体的，大块的，巨大的，笨重的，大规模的，大量的，结实的

mass moment of inertia 质量转动惯量（见 weight moment of inertia）

mass number 原子质量数（一个原子

核中中子和质子的总数,即原子量)
mass of vehicle 汽车质量(在任意荷载状态下,汽车的总质量)
mass per liter (发动机的)升质量(发动机每升排量所分摊的质量)
mass point 质点
mass-power ratio 质量功率比(内燃机净质量与标定功率的比值,旧称 weight-power ratio)
mass-produced car 大量生产的轿车
mass production 大量生产(批量生产,简称 mass pro, = quantity production, stock production)
mass rapid transit system 公共快速交通系统,公用快速运输系统(简称 MRT)
mass rate of emission standard (汽车的)质量排放标准(以单位行驶距离或单位运转时间内的排放质量来表示排放量限值的标准)
mass recirculation 质量再循环率(循环气量与消耗气量之比)
mass resistivity 质量电阻率(比电阻)
mass spectrometer 质谱仪,质谱分析仪
mass storage unit (计算机的)海量存储设备(亦称 mass storage device,见 mass storage system)
mass tone (车身油漆配色的)原色(指各种色漆和涂料的原色,即:不混以白色调浅,而保持漆面呈漆料的原色)
mass transfer ①质量转移,分子转移(分子通过对流或扩散的方式转移)②分子转移学(研究分子对流扩散等现象)③物质传递
mass transit engineering 公共交通工程(公共交通系统设计与管理、分析与评价,交通车辆及构造物的有关技术,公共交通政策及投资等问题)
mass transport phenomena 质量转移现象

mast 柱,柱状物(如:汽车的转向盘轴)
M-ASTC 三菱(公司)主动式稳定性牵引力控制系统(MITSUBISHI-active stability traction control 的简称)
master aluminium layout (车身板件等的)铝板大样底图(绘制在具有特殊涂层的薄铝板上,供照相复制大样图用)
master board 主控制(仪表)板
master bracket ①(曲线图上的)独立点②主支架,主托架
master brake cylinder 制动主缸(指在液压制动系中,将制动踏板踩踏力或其他助力或动力转变为制动液压力的部件,亦称 main brake cylinder)
master clutch 主离合器
master clutch brake (自动变速器行星齿轮机构的)主离合器制动器
master con rod (两冲程双活塞式发动机的)主连杆(master connecting rod 的简称,指直接与曲轴连杆轴颈铰接的连杆)
master controller 主控制器
master control program 主控制程序
master cup ①制动主缸皮碗②主皮碗
master cylinder 主缸(在液压系统中,通过活塞将各种机械力转变为工作油液压力的部件,如:液压制动系中的制动主缸)
master cylinder and pedal bracket 制动主缸和踏板的支架
master cylinder inlet valve 制动主缸进油阀
master cylinder main tube (液压)制动主缸主油管
master cylinder piston (液压系)主缸活塞
master cylinder piston push rod 主缸活塞推杆(直接驱动主缸活塞的杆件,简称 master cylinder push rod)

master cylinder piston return spring 主缸活塞复位弹簧

master cylinder piston travel switch （ABS 中向电子控制模块提供）制动主缸活塞行程（信息的）开关（器件）

master cylinder pressure sensor 制动主缸（输出）压力传感器

master cylinder reservoir air vent 液压制动主缸储液室通气孔

master cylinder reservoir cap （液力制动系）主缸储液室盖

master cylinder residual valve （液压制动系有补偿孔式制动）主缸残留阀（使液压制动系内保持一定残留压力）

master gauge ①标准规，校对规 ②总表（如总压力表等）

master layout ①总布置，总布置图 ②（车身板件等的）大样底图，大样原图

master lighting switch 灯光总开关（前照灯及示廓灯等的手动开关，亦称 main lamp switch）

master link ①主连接杆②履带闭合链节

master meter 标准仪表，基准电表，主表，检验表（指检测头与表盘分离式检测仪表的显示表头）

master-meter method 标准仪表比较检验法（以标准仪表检验同类仪表）

master model 母型，原模型（供复制模型用，亦称 master pattern, master mould, die model）

master note 主网点（在某些汽车环形网络或回路控制系统中可以启动所有数据传输的网络节点，见 slave node）

master plan 总体规划，总计划，总布置图，总体布置，总平面图

master power controller 主功率控制装置（简称 MPC）

master rod （星形发动机等的）主连杆（承装有其他连杆的主连杆）

master sequencer 主程序装置（简称 MS）

Mastershift ①高超型换挡控制（模式）（一种新型的节油型动力控制方式，电子控制模块以加速踏板位置作为驾驶者对汽车车速的要求信号，通过执行机构控制节气门开度和挡位选择，以实现最低油耗行驶）②绝妙方略（英 H·M Streib 和 R·Leonhard 于 1922 年提出的汽车动力系功能的分层控制策略的称谓。该方略的基本思路是增加一电子控制节气门系统，实现该系统与发动机电子控制系统、变速器电子控制系统之间的信息交换，将加速踏板的位置作为加速要求，即：对驱动车轮的转矩的要求，通过频繁换挡，使发动机在节气门全开、低速大转矩工况下运转，确保节油与优良的动力性能，据称这一方案可节油 5%～10%）

master-slave arrangement （数字集成电路中的）主从电路（由两个双稳态电路组成的电路，其中一个"从"电路再现另一个"主"电路的输出组态）

master/slave system （汽车的）主从（式电子控制）系统（由一主控制模块和与它相连并受它控制的多个辅助控制模块组成的电子控制系统）

master slice method 母片法（大量生产同一品种半导体集成电路的方法）

master spring leaf 钢板弹簧主片（= main leaf of spring）

master switch 总开关，主控开关

master to slave communication 主-从通信（汽车本地网络中主网点至从网点的数据传输，见 LIN）

master vac （原为一种）制动真空助力器（商品名）[现已逐渐变成装在制动踏板与制动主缸间的制动真

空助力器（vacuum brake booster）的代名词]
master valve 主阀（= main valve）
master window lift switch 风窗玻璃升降机构总开关
mastic joint 玛碲脂接缝，胶泥接缝
mastic seam sealant （接头或接缝处的）防水密封胶剂
mastic sound deadener 黏胶树脂隔声涂料（用于做车身底部外表面的隔声、防尘、防水涂层等）
mast jacket 轴柱外套管（如转向盘柱的套管）
MAT 进气空气温度传感器［manifold air temperature sensor 的简称，通用公司对进气空气温度传感器的称呼，美国政府规定从1995年1月起一律改称 IAT（intake air temperature sensor）]
mat ①地席，垫席，垫子，衬垫物，麻袋，（包装货物的粗糙）编织品；底板，罩面，面层②（指颜色）暗淡的，无光泽的③（指表面）不光滑的，粗糙的（亦写作：matt）
matched data 匹配数据
match（ed）joint （木构件等的）舌槽接合，企口接口，合榫；凹凸接头，雌雄接头（= tongue and groove joint）
matched pair 选配零件副
matching mark 对准标线，装配标记，配对标记
matching parts 配件，配合件
matching point ①配合标记②平衡工作点
matching surface 配合面
matching torque converter （与发动机）匹配的变矩器
mat coat 保护层，面层，罩面
mat-covered pavement 有保护层的路面
MATC system 三菱主动式牵引力控制系统（Mitsubishi active traction control system 的简称）

mate ①配合，装配；成对；连接，相连②配合物（一对中的一个）；接合面，拼合面；啮合件，啮合部分
mated gear 配对齿轮（一对齿轮中的任一个为另一个的配对齿轮）
mated pair 配合偶件，配合偶，配合副，配合对（如柴油机喷油泵的柱塞-套筒副）
material ①材料，原料，物质，物资②技术资料
material point 质点
materials handler 材料装卸机，材料堆垛机，材料吊运机
material specification 材料规范，材料规格，（复）材料技术条件（简称 MS）
material testing machine 材料试验机
Material Transportation Bureau ［美］（运输部的）材料运输局（简称 MTB）
mat glass 毛玻璃，磨砂玻璃
mathematical 数学的
mathematical analysis 数学解析，数学分析
mathematical expectation （数理统计）数学期望（值）
mathematical manipulation 数学处理（数学运算，数学变换，如：求导，积分，相乘等）
mathematical model 数学模型
mathematical modeling techniques 数学模拟技术（用数学方程表征各种过程、机构和系统等的技术）
mathematical statistics 数理统计（学）
mathematic approximation 数学近似法
mathematics 数学
math modeling 数学模拟，（用）数学模型（方法表述）
mating flank 相啮齿面（齿轮副中，两个相互啮合的齿面，互称为相啮齿面）

mating gear 配对齿轮（齿轮副中的两个齿轮互为对方的配对齿轮）

mating part（s） 配合件，相配零件

mating pinion 配对小齿轮

mating ring （水泵用的机械密封件的）密封滑环（一般用耐磨的氧化铝陶瓷材料制成）

mating surfaces 配合表面，接触表面

mating thread 配合螺纹

Matlab/simulink （目前汽车建模上普遍采用的）图形化软件名（为建模与仿真的技术平台，可直接在该平台上建立汽车及汽车系统模型，也可利用该平台进行二次开发）

matrix ①矩阵，方阵②真值表，母式③模型，阴模④母材，基体⑤（燃气轮机热交换器的）吸放热件⑥（在计算机中矩阵指）由输入线或输出线列阵形成的一种逻辑网络（其某些交点上用逻辑元件连接）

matrix adder 矩阵加法器

matrix afterburner 格板式后燃器，网格式后燃器

Matrix alloy 铋锑铅锡合金（铅28.5%，锑14.5%，铋48%，锡9%）

matrix analysis 矩阵分析

matrix display （液晶显示器件的）矩阵显示（由正交带状电极的交点组成像素进行的显示）

matrix encoded digital road map 矩阵编码数字化路线（地）图

matrix metal （粉末冶金中的）黏结金属

matrix plate 网格板

matrix table 矩阵表（按照严密数学规律和设计排成矩阵形的一组专用数值集）

MAT sensor 进气温度传感器（manifold air temperature sensor 的简称）

mat surface 无光泽表面

matter ①物质，物体（对 mind, spirit 而言）②实质，实体（对应 form）③理由，原因，根源④事实，事件⑤数量，内容⑥重要事项，重要性

mattress 垫

mat type oil clean 化学纤维压缩圆桶形滤芯机油滤清器（多用于柴油机）

mature technology 成熟技术，完善技术，完美工艺

Maxaret brake 防抱死制动器（的旧称，原用于飞机，后经改造移植于汽车，Maxaret 为其专利权持有人，现改称 anti-lock brake 或 anti-block brake）

max. chamber volume ①最大室容积②（转子发动机的）最大工作室容积，最大单室容积（参见 chamber volume）

max. flash temperature index 最高闪点指数（最大闪火温度指数）

maximal condition 最高条件

maximile （以英里计的）最高经济车速（= maximum economical speed in miles 的简称）

maximum （简称 Max.）①最大，最高，最多，极大，高峰，极点，最大值，极大值②最大（值）的，最大（限度）的，最高（额）的，最高（限）的，最多的，极大值的

maximum adhesion torque 最大附着转矩（由地面附着条件决定的驱动轮可能产生的最大转矩）

maximum（and）minimum speed governor （柴油机的）两速调速器，两极调速器（仅在发动机转速超过规定的最大转速和最低转速时起作用，而在发动机处于最高和最低转速之间时不起作用，亦称 R governor）

maximum angle of dumping 最大倾卸角

maximum annual hourly volume 年最大小时交通量

maximum authority 最大规定值,最高允许值(如:通用公司CCC系统中的怠速控制电动机所能提供的最高急速转速)

maximum authorized axle laden mass 允许最大轴载质量(车辆管理部门根据使用条件而规定的轴载质量)

maximum authorized laden mass 允许最大装载质量(允许最大总质量与整车整备质量之差)

maximum authorized mass of an articulated vehicle 铰接车允许最大总质量(车辆管理部门根据使用条件而规定的铰接车最大总质量)

maximum authorized total mass of train 汽车列车允许最大总质量(车辆管理部门根据使用条件而规定的汽车列车最大总质量)

maximum authorized weight (车辆)法定最大总重(最大允许总质量的旧称)

maximum boost horsepower (发动机)最大增压功率

maximum brake power 最大有效功率(在一定转速下,发动机产生的最大有效功率, = peak brake power, 见 brake power)

maximum centripetal acceleration 最大向心加速度(汽车在人为控制或固定控制条件下进行曲线运动时达到的向心加速度的最大值)

maximum combustion pressure (内燃机的)最高燃烧压力(燃烧过程中,汽缸内工质的瞬时最高压力)

maximum combustion temperature 最高燃烧温度(燃烧过程中,汽缸内工质的瞬时空间平均最高温度)

maximum continuous rating 最大连续功率(最大持续功率,简称MCR)

maximum continuous sparking speed 最高连续发火转速

maximum cruising power 最大巡航功率(最大持续功率 = continuous maximum power)

maximum cylinder volume 汽缸最大容积(活塞在下止点时汽缸的容积,等于汽缸工作容积与余隙容积之和)

maximum deceleration 最大减速度,最大负加速度

maximum deflection angle ①最大折射角,最大偏角,最大偏转角,最大偏斜角②[特指液力变矩器的工作油液由泵轮以高速冲击涡轮叶片时,其冲击叶片的入射速度方向与遇叶片后的反射方向间的夹角称折射角(deflection angle),此角在涡轮静止时最大,称]最大折射角(此时变矩器输出转矩达最大值)

maximum dimensions 最大尺寸

maximum feed stop lever 最大供油量限止杆

maximum flow 最大流量

maximum fording depth 最大涉水深度

maximum frictional force 最大摩擦力

maximum fuel adjusting screw (柴油机调速器燃油量控制齿条的)最大喷油量调节螺钉(喷油量齿条最大行程调节螺钉)

maximum full-load speed 满载时最高速度

maximum gather passengers 旅客最高聚集人数(一年中旅客发送量偏高的一定时期内,每天最大的同时在站人数的平均值)

maximum gradient 最大坡度

maximum grading angle of front end loader bucket 前端装载机铲斗前刃在地面上时的最大下倾角

maximum gross weight 最大总重

maximum ground contact pressure 最大接地压力

maximum height 最高高度

maximum idling speed delivery （柴油机）最高怠速转速供油量（在柴油机最高空载转速工况下，喷油泵的循环供油量）

maximum indicated lateral acceleration 最大指示横向加速度（汽车在人为控制或固定控制条件下进行曲线运动时，横向加速度计指示的最大值）

maximum internal dimensions of (goods vehicle) body （厢式货车）车厢内部的最大尺寸

maximum internal dimensions of rear body 汽车货厢的最大内部尺寸

maximum laden mass 最大装载质量（一般分为：额定最大装载质量，由厂家根据设计参数确定；允许最大装载质量，由主管部门根据使用条件确定）

maximum lateral acceleration 最大横向加速度（汽车在人为控制或固定控制条件下进行曲线运动时达到的横向加速度最大值）

maximum legal vehicle running weight 车辆法定最大使用重量（车辆法定最大允许质量的旧称，参见 operating weight）

maximum likelihood 最大可能性，最大似然性（简称 ML，= maximum likeliness）

maximum limit of size 最大极限尺寸

maximum load 最大荷载，最大负荷

maximum loading capacity 最大允许载质量（= maximum pay load）

maximum load per tyre 单胎最大负荷

maximum manufacturer's axle laden mass 厂定最大轴载质量（制造厂考虑到材料强度、轮胎的承载能力等因素而核定出的轴载质量）

maximum manufacturer's laden mass 厂定最大装载质量（厂定最大总质量与整车整备质量之差）

maximum manufacturer's total mass 厂定最大总质量（制造厂根据特定的使用条件，考虑到材料强度、轮胎承载能力等因素而核定出的最大总质量）

maximum manufacturer's total mass of train 汽车列车厂定最大总质量［牵引车与挂车（一辆或一辆以上）的最大总质量之和］

maximum mass borne by a fifth wheel for a semi-trailer 牵引座上最大质量（半挂车分配在牵引鞍座上的最大质量）

maximum mass of an articulated vehicle 铰接车最大总质量（牵引车与被铰接车的最大总质量之和）

maximum mean piston speed 活塞最高平均速度（简称 mmps，= 冲程 × 2 × 曲轴的分钟转数）

maximum noload (governed) speed 调速器控制的无负荷最高转速（指车用柴油机在空转时喷油泵在最大供油量位置，柴油机依靠调速器能自动控制的最高稳定转速，约为柴油机额定转速的 110%，亦称 maximum idling）

maximum non-proportional shear strain （制件扭断时其表面上的）最大非比例切应变

maximum output ①最大输出，最大输出功率②最大生产能力，最大生产率（= peak output）

maximum overall diameter in service （轮胎的）最大使用外径（轮胎经使用胀大后，所允许的最大外直径）

maximum overall length 最大全长，最大外廓长度

maximum overall width in service （轮胎的）最大使用总宽度（指轮胎经使用胀大后，所允许的最大总宽度）

maximum pay load （货车等的）最大容许载重（= maximum loading capacity)

maximum pedal travel 踏板最大行程

maximum permeability ①最大磁导率，最大磁导系数②最大渗透率，最大透气率

maximum permissible acceleration 最大允许加速度

maximum permissible concentration 最大容许浓度（简称 MPC）

maximum permissible gross laden weight （车辆）最大容许满载总重

maximum permissible load 最大容许荷载

maximum permissible speed 最大容许速度

maximum power 最大功率（指内燃机在规定时间内所能发出超过标定功率的最大有效功率）

maximum power speed （发动机发出）最大功率（时的）转速

maximum problem 极大（值）问题

maximum ratio 最大比例，最大比率

maximum revolution 最大转数

maximum rotating angle of pitman arm shaft （转向）摇臂轴最大转角

maximum scale value （仪器仪表的）标度终点值（标度终点标记所对应的被测量值）

maximum size 最大尺寸

maximum slope limited by lost of steering control （拖拉机、汽车等）丧失转向操纵能力限制的最大坡度

maximum-speed governor 最高速度限速器（= high-speed governor）

maximum speed in gears 各挡位下的最高速度

maximum speed of revolution 最高转速

maximum speed on cross-country 最高越野行驶速度

maximum speed test （发动机）在最高转速工况下的试验

maximum strain theory of failure 最大应变破坏理论（常用于脆性材料）

maximum stress 最大应力（简称 MS）

maximum swing angle of steering pitman arm 转向摇臂最大摆角

maximum tension 最大张力，最大拉力

maximum torque 最大转矩（如：内燃机全负荷特性曲线上的最大转矩值）

maximum torque spark timing 最大转矩点火正时（指发动机产生最大转矩时的点火时刻，最大转矩点火角，简称 MTST）

maximum torque speed 最大转矩转速（指发动机发出最大转矩时的转速）

maximum total mass 最大总质量（整车整备质量与最大装载质量之和）

maximum total mass of train 汽车列车最大总质量（牵引车与挂车最大总质量之和）

maximum towable mass 最大牵引质量（按车辆制造商规定的能被车辆牵引的最大质量）

maximum towed mass 最大拖挂质量[牵引车能够牵引的全挂车和（或）半挂车的最大总质量]

maximum transient speed （带有调速器的内燃机的）最高瞬时转速（指运转时，突然卸去负荷瞬时所达到的最高转速）

maximum transmission ratio 最大传动速比，最大传动比

maximum tyre load 最大轮胎负载

maximum useful rate 最大有效率,

最大应用率（简称 MUR）
maximum value 最大值，极大值
maximum water holding capacity （土壤）最大含水量，最大水分保持能力
maximum weight 最大重量（最大质量的旧称）
maximum weight and load capacities （汽车的）最大重量和装载量
maximum weight set by the manufacturer 制造厂规定的（在一定使用条件下的）最大重量（一般指最大总质量）
maximum width 最大宽度
maximum working pressure 最大工作压力
maximum working space 最大工作空间
maxium axle capacity 最大轴荷
maxium braking deceleration 最大制动减速度（最大可能的制动力作用下产生的减速度峰值）
maxium gradability of vehicle 汽车的最大爬坡能力（指汽车在良好路面上挂最低挡所能爬越的最大坡度）
maxium tyre capacity 最大轮胎荷载
maxmium current output 最大输出电流（如：交流发电机在额定电压时，其输出电流随转速增加至不再继续增加时的值）
max. permitted speed 最大容许速度
max. possible compression ratio ①最大可能压缩比②（转子发动机的）最大理论压缩比，最大压缩比（在转子工作面上没有凹坑时，达到的最大压缩比）
max-power-output speed （发动机的）最大功率转速
max. roll（angle） 最大侧倾角（maximum roll angle 的简称，见 roll angle）
max temp 最高温度

MAXUS （英国）大通多功能商务车（其品牌及知识产权已为我国收购）
maxwell 麦，麦克斯韦（磁通量的单位，代号 Mx，$=10^{-8}$ 韦伯，参见 weber）
Mazda 626 car 马自达 626 轿车（日本马自达公司 1992 年推出的普通型轿车，装用 DOHC 燃油喷射发动机，排量 1991mL，四挡自动变速，四轮 ABS 系统，最高车速 200km/h）
MAZDA Sentie Car 马自达森地亚轿车（马自达公司 1991 年产品，采用四轮转向系统，V6DOHC 发动机）
mazut 重油，黑油（＝mazout，masut）
mb 毫巴（＝mbar，见 millibar）
M-B car 奔驰（公司生产的）轿车（MercedesBenz car 的简称）
MBD 每日百万桶（million barrels a day，国际石油生产国计算石油产量的计量单位）
MBECS 汽车制动节能系统（通过回收制动时汽车动能达到节能目的，motor vehicle brake energy conservation system 的简称）
M·Benz hand held tester 奔驰（专用维修）手提式测试仪
MBF 已燃烧质量百分率（mass-burned fraction）
MBG 甲醇汽油（掺甲醇的汽油，methanol blended gasoline 的简称）
MBS ［美］客车学会（Motor Bus Society）
mbt spark timing （可生产）最佳转矩的点火正时（spark timing maintained at minimum for best torque）
M/C ①人工控制，手动操作（manual control）②混合气控制（mixture control）
MC ①机器（machine）②机器执照（machine certificate）③临界试验（marginal check）④标定容载量（marked capacity）⑤中心控制

(master control) ⑥微型电容器 (midget condenser) ⑦摩托车 (motorcycle) ⑧中小型的 (medium-compact 的简称)

MC 小改 (minor change 的简称)

MCA ①(日本)三菱汽车排气净化系统 (见 Mitsubishi Clean Air) ②多路存取 (multichannel access 的简称)

MCA-JET system 日本三菱喷流控制超稀燃系统 (Jet controlled super lean combustion 的商品名)

MCBSP 多通道缓冲串口 (multi-channel buffered serial port 的简称)

MCC 排气歧管内藏型催化转化器 (manifold catalytic converter 的简称,装在排气歧管内的小型催化转化器)

MCCC solenoid (电子控制自动变速器的)变矩器(锁止)离合器控制阀液压通路调节电磁阀 (modulated converter clutch control solenoid) 的简称[电子控制模块通过该电磁阀控制变矩器锁止离合器控制阀的液压通路,使变矩器离合器接合或分离(见 CCC valve)。所谓调节 (modulated), 是指电子控制模块根据发动机和汽车运行工况,以0~100%的占空比控制该电磁阀,使变矩器锁止离合器控制阀的液压在零~最大值间变化。锁止离合器在液压为0时完全松开,在最大液压时完全锁止,在二者之间时液压在>0, <max 间变化,亦称 TCCC solenoid]

MC centre 监测和控制中心,监控中心 (monitoring and control centre)

MCFC 熔融碳酸盐燃料电池 (molten carbonate fuel cell 的简称)

Mclead gauge 麦氏真空计 (一种测量高度低薄气体压力的压力计,因发明人而得名)

MCM 多片组装式模块 (multichip module 的简称,指由多个集成片组装成的一个控制模块)

MCN 多路复用通信网络 (multiplex communication network 的简称)

M-combustion chamber (柴油机) M 形燃烧室 (半分开式燃烧室的一种,多呈球形,故亦称球形燃烧室,其特点是喷入汽缸的燃油大部分随气流均匀分布在燃烧壁上,少量在燃烧室空间的燃油形成的混合气着火后,不断点燃由壁面逐层蒸发的燃油蒸气形成的新混合气,工作柔和)

McPherson strut type suspension 麦弗逊柱式悬架 (多用于小型轿车前轮的独立悬架的一种,由美国福特公司的 McPherson 发明,其柱的上端为外面套有螺旋弹簧的减振器总成,固定于车身,柱的下端通过臂件与前轴连接)

MC platform 中-小型(车)基础平台 (medium-compact platform 的简称,以该平台为基础,加装不同装置,设计制造各种不同牌号与型号的中-小型车辆)

MCR ①维修管理报告 (maintenance control report) ②主要更改记录 (master change record) ③最大持续功率 (maximum continuous rating)

MCS [美]汽车安全运输局 (Motor Carrier Safety)

MCS 多循环取样 (multi-cycle sampling)

MCT 金属氧化物半导体控制闸流管 (MOS-controlled thyristor 的简称)

MCU ①混合气调节装置 (mixture control unit) ②微处理器控制单元 (microprocessor control unit 的简称) ③微控制器 (microcontroller unit 的简称)

MCU-based ①微处理器控制的[指用单片机进行控制的,如: MCU-based speed control system (微处理器速度控制系统)、MCU-based light driver（微处理器灯光控制灯光开关系统）]②以微程序控制单元为基础的（microprogram control unit-based 的简称）

MCU-based lamp driver 微处理器控制器型灯具开关装置（其中 MCU 为 microprocessor control unit 的简称）

MCU lamp control 微处理器灯光控制（系统，指由一个电子控制模块对汽车灯光的开关电路、光强变换、开路检测、短路防护和诊断系统进行全面控制）

M curve 力矩曲线，弯矩曲线，力矩图，弯矩图（moment curve）

MCV 混合气调节阀（见 mixture control valve）

MD （发动机）可变排量（modulated displacement 的简称，可根据负荷要求改变工作缸数节油）

MDAI [美]汽车事故的多方面调查（multidiciplinary accident investigation）

MDB （汽车撞车试验的）活动式易变形障碍物，活动柔性壁障（moving deformable barrier 的简称）

MDB [欧洲新车安全评价试验（Euro NCAP）中使用的]可变形移动障壁（Moving deformable barrier 的简称）

MDBF 平均故障间隔里程（mean distance between failures）

MDE ①电子设备的积木化设计（modular design of electronics）②三菱可变工作缸数型可变排量发动机（见 modulated displacement engine）

MDL 最小检测范围（minimum detection limits）

MDS （发动机）多排量系统（multidisplacement system 的简称，可在高经济性的 4 缸运转和高动力性的 8 缸运转工况间平稳转换的 8 缸员动机）

MDV 最小检测值（minimum detection value）

MEA （燃料电池的）膜-电极组件（membrane-electrode assembly 的简称，燃料电池的阳极-质子交换膜-阴极三个部件用热压法制成一体的总成件）

meager 不足的，贫乏的，不充分的，量少的，无味的（亦写作 meagre）

mean ①平均（数），平均（值）（常用代号 M）；中项；中数；中间 ②中间的，平均的，普通的；下等的 ③意思是，意味着

mean absolute deviation 平均绝对偏差

mean absolute error 平均绝对误差

mean amplitude processing method （对机件荷载时间历程进行统计处理的）幅度均值计数法（除了对幅度计数外，同时还对相应的平均值计数）

mean availability （设备及仪器仪表的）平均有效度（在某个规定时间区间内有效度的平均值，见 availability②）

mean axis (of an ellipsoid) （椭球的）中（平均）轴

mean braking deceleration 平均制动减速度（制动过程中两个瞬时速度之差，与该两个瞬时的时间间隔的比值）

mean 0~100℃ calorie 均值卡（热量单位，代号 $cal_{(mean)}$，即 1 克纯水温度自 0℃ 上升到 100℃，所需热量的 1/100，1 $Cal_{(mean)}$ = 4.1897 joules，参见 calorie）

mean camberline （液力变矩器叶轮叶片的）平均曲弧线（叶片骨线，指叶片沿液流方向的截面形状的中线，即：与叶片剖面两边相切的一系列圆的中心轨迹）

mean carbon content 平均含碳量

mean consumption ①平均消耗

（量）②平均耗油量，平均油耗

mean crossings （疲劳荷载中的）平均交叉（荷载-时间历程在其给定长度内与具有正斜率或负斜率或两者都有的平均荷载水平交叉的次数）

mean distance between failures 平均故障间隔里程（简称 MDBF）

mean effective pressure 平均有效压力（简称 MEP，指折合到单位汽缸工作容积每工作循环所产生的有效功，用单位活塞面积上所受的假想不变压力表示）

mean effective value 平均有效值（均方根值）

mean fatigue stress 平均疲劳应力

mean indicated pressure 平均指示压力（简称 MIP, mip，指折合到单位汽缸容积每工作循环所做的指示功，用单位活塞面积上所受的假想不变压力表示）

mean level 平均水平，平均能级，平均电平（简称 ML）

mean life 平均（使用）寿命，（指寿命或无故障工作时间的平均值，亦称平均无故障工作时间，= mean time between failures，简称 MTBF）

mean line 等分线，中线，中心线

mean load 平均荷载［=（最大荷载+最小荷载）/2］

mean mechanical loss pressure （内燃机）平均机械损失压力（折合到每单位汽缸工作容积的每工作循环中的机械损失功，用活塞面积上假设不变的压力表示）

mean piston speed 活塞平均速度（亦称 average piston speed，指在标定转速下，曲轴每转活塞两个冲程中速度的平均值）

mean repair time 平均修复时间

mean running speed 平均行驶车速

mean sea level 平均海拔（高度）（简称 MSL）

mean specific heat 平均比热

mean speed 平均速度（= average speed）

mean spiral angle （螺旋伞齿轮）齿宽中点的螺旋角

mean square 均方（简称 MS）

mean-square deviation 均方差

mean square error 均方误差

mean-square error criterion 均方误差准则

mean square modulus 均方模

mean square value 均方值

mean strain 平均应变（一次应变循环中最大应变与最小应变的代数平均值）

mean stress 平均应力（应力循环中最大应力和最小应力的代数平均值）

mean technical speed （汽车的）平均技术速度（指按纯运行时间计算，车辆平均每小时行驶里程）

mean time between failures 平均无故障工作时间（简称 MTBF，指无故障工作时间的平均值，= mean life）

mean time between maintenances 平均维护间隔期，维护平均周期（简称 MTBM）

mean time between repairs 修理平均周期，平均修理间隔时间，修理平均间隔期（缩写 MTBR）

mean time to catastrophic failure 平均重大故障间隔时间（简称 MTCF）

mean value theorem 平均值（中值）定理

measurable quantity 可测的量（可以定性区别和定量确定的一种现象、物体或物质的属性）

measure ①量度，大小，尺度，尺寸，数量，质量②测量，测定，估计，估量，衡量③度量单位，度量标准④量具，量器，比例尺⑤计量办法⑥措施，手段，方法⑦程度，范围，限度⑧公约数⑨判断；调节，使均衡

measured 实测的，量过的，被测量的，作为测量对象的

measured error 测量误差（测定值与实际值之差）

measured value 测定值（通过测量仪器，将被测量参数与同一物理量的标准值比较，或者用事先经过标准校正的测量仪器进行测量，所得到的数值）

measure expansion 体（积膨）胀（度）

measureless 非常的，巨大的

measurement ①测量，计量，度量②测量法，测定法，度量制，衡制③测量结果④计量单位⑤尺寸，大小，量度，长度，宽度，高度，深度⑥容量，体积⑦（复数）规范

measurement accuracy 测量精度

measurement goods 体积货物（按体积或容量来计算的货物，= measurement cargo）

measurement point ①测量点②测试点

measurement range 里程，测量范围

measurement ton 容积吨（指按被测量的物质的容积或体积折算出的吨数，如：木材40ft³为1t，石材6ft³为1t）

measures and weights 权度，度量衡（= weights and measures，为 mass and measure 的旧称）

measuring accuracy 量测精度

measuring circumference （轮辋的）检验周长（采用专门的量具在胎圈座或其他特定部位测得的直径，一般用周长换算，用以保证标定直径，见 specified diameter）

measuring element 量测元件，传感元件

measuring float 计量浮子

measuring head 测（试）头

measuring instrument 量具，量测仪器，测量仪表（= measuring implement）

measuring jet ①量孔（计量喷嘴，= calibrated restriction）②可调量孔（= metering jet，metering orifice）

measuring load 测定荷载（测定时，对试件所加的荷载）

measuring pin ①量孔针阀②计量阀针（= metering pin）

measuring plate type air flowmeter 量板式空气流量计（测量片装在进气通道内，吸入空气的流体动力作用于该量片，使量片转动一定的角度，该角度转换为电信号输入至电子控制模块以用作进气空气体积流量信号）

measuring projector 轮廓投影仪

measuring range 量测范围，量程

measuring range higher limit 测量范围上限值

measuring range lower limit 测量范围下限值

measuring rim 测量用标准轮辋（用于检验其他轮辋的尺寸）

measuring surface （量测仪具的）测量面（指与被测定物接触的量头的工作面等）

measuring system 测量系统（= metering system）

measuring tape 卷尺

measuring transducer 传感器（= sensor，感受被测量、并按一定规律将其转换成电信号等价输出量的装置）

measuring vane type air flow sensor 量板式空气流量传感器［早期使用的空气体积流量传感器（volume air flow sensor）的一种］

MECA ［美］排放控制装置制造商协会（Manufacturers of Emission Control Association）

meca noise 机械噪声（指机械运转时内部产生的噪声）

meca-tro technology 机械-电子一体

化技术（mechanical-electronic technology 的简称）

mechanical ①机械的，机械制的，机动的，自动的 ②机械工程的，力学的，物理上的

mechanical admixture 机械杂质

mechanical advance ①机械式点火提前（机构，亦称 centrifugal advance，利用重锤离心力控制的点火提前机构）②机械效益（= mechanical advantage，简称 MA，指机械的有用阻力与动力之比，机械利益可等于或大于1）

mechanical aiming capability （汽车前照灯的）机械对光性能（用机械方法对光的能力）

mechanical analogue 机械模拟

mechanical arm （操作器）机械手

mechanical automation 机械自动化

mechanical balance 机械平衡（亦称 mechanical equilibrium）

mechanical brake 机械式制动器（指仅由踏板的踏力或拉柄的拉力通过机械杆系驱动的制动器）

mechanical braking transmission 机械式制动传动装置

mechanical breakdown 机械性损坏

mechanical breaker 机械断电器

mechanical centrifugal supercharger 机械离心式（进气）增压器

mechanical characteristics 机械性能

mechanical charger （由发动机曲轴驱动的）机械式进气增压器

mechanical checkout 机械校正（简称 mech c/o）

mechanical clearance 机械间隙

mechanical clutch （用机械驱动的）机械式离合器

mechanical comparator 机械比较仪

mechanical contact 机械接触

mechanical control fifth wheel coupling （半挂牵引车的）机械控制鞍式牵引连接装置

mechanical damage 机械损伤（硬伤）

mechanical draft 机械通风（强制通风）

mechanical drive system ①机械式传动系统 ②（特指电动汽车的由输出电动机功率的变速器、传动轴及差速器等机构组成的）机械传动系

mechanical duct controls （汽车通风与暖气系统的）机械式风道控制系统（由装在仪表板上的控制件通过拉索或拉杆操纵风门来实现暖风开关和风量的控制）

mechanical efficiency 机械效率（实际输出功率与理论输出功率之比或有用功与总功的比值，恒小于1，通常用%表示，如发动机的机械效率为其有效功或有效功率与其指示功或指示功率的比值）

mechanical efficiency of power transmission 传动系机械效率

mechanical-electrical transducer 机-电传感器（将机械量转变为电量的变换器）

mechanical energy 机械能

mechanical engaged drive stater 机械啮合式起动机（用机械方法将驱动小齿轮推出与飞轮齿圈啮合的起动机）

mechanical equivalent of heat 热功当量（指每卡热相当的机械功量，1卡=4.1855焦耳，4.1855焦耳/卡称为热功当量，亦称焦耳当量，Joule's equivalent）

mechanical expander （制动器的）机械式制动蹄促动器（一般为凸轮式）

mechanical expander slidable actuating lever （驻车制动器）机械式制动蹄促动器滑动促动臂

mechanical four-wheel brake 机械式四轮制动器

mechanical friction 机械摩擦

mechanical fuel injection 机械式燃

油喷射（如：博世公司的 K-Jetronic 型汽油喷射系统和一般的柴油机喷油系统）

mechanical galvanizing 冷作镀锌（用冷加工方法镀覆锌表面层）

mechanical governor 机械式调速器（应用飞锤等感应元件和机械式执行机构的离心式调速器）

mechanical hardware ①机件，机构 ②硬件

mechanical horn 机械喇叭（亦称 klaxon）

mechanical-hydraulic type steering mechanism 机械-液压型（四轮）转向机构（前轮的转向角信息通过机械方式传递至后轮转向液压执行机构的四轮转向机构）

mechanical hysteresis 力学滞后（在加力和卸除力的整个循环过程中，受力体所吸收的能量）

mechanical ignition timing 机械式点火正时（指离心式或真空式点火提前，相对于电子点火正时而言）

mechanical impedance 机械阻抗（使某个物体运动时，推动该物体所需的总力与所产生的速度之间的比值，即产生每单位速度所需的力，它包括两部分：一部分为真实运动阻力，代表着机械运动所做的功；一部分为虚拟运动阻力，它是不做功的，代表物体弹性变形所储的能量）

mechanical impedance analysis system 机械阻抗分析系统

mechanical impurities 机械杂质

mechanical injection 机械喷射（相对于电子喷射而言）

mechanical lock-type （用）机械（方法）锁止式

mechanical loss 机械损失，机械损失功率（如：汽油机内部零件的摩擦损失，泵气损失及驱动附件所消耗的功率）

mechanical loss tangent 机械损失正切角（参见 loss tangent）

mechanically actuated 机械驱动的（= mechanically driven）

mechanically controlled 机构控制的

mechanically operated inlet valve 机械推动的进气门（简称 MOIV）

mechanically propelled vehicle 机动车辆

mechanically scanned guidance system 机械式扫描导向系统

mechanically steered headlight 机械转动式前照灯（通过杆系供前照灯在水平方向绕其轴转动，以改变其照射方向）

mechanical mobility 机械导纳（机械阻抗的倒数，参见 mechanical impedance）

mechanical noise ①机械噪声 ②电子管中的喀啦声（简称 MN）

mechanical octane value 机械辛烷值（亦称 mechanical octane number，发动机结构的抗爆性评价值，即发动机结构对燃油辛烷值的要求）

mechanical operating system with separated auxiliary brake 主制动器与驻车制动器，独立型机械式制动传动杆系（制动踏板与驻车制动拉杆各自通过互相独立的传动杆系，将制动操纵力传给制动器促动器）

mechanical operating system with integrated auxilary brake 主制动器与驻车制动器共用型机械式制动传动杆系（制动踏板与驻车制动拉杆共用同一套制动传动杆系，将制动操纵力传给促动器）

mechanical oscillograph 机械示波器（用于测试橡皮材料等的机械性能）

mechanical parking 机械化驻车（场）

mechanical powered drive 机械动力驱动（如车辆用高能飞轮驱动）

mechanical properties 机械性能，力

学性质

mechanical reactance 机械反作用力（力抗，力阻抗的虚部）

mechanical reduction gear 机械减速机构（如齿轮减速装置）

mechanical remote control 机械遥控（机械式远距离操纵）

mechanical resistance 机械阻力（力阻）

mechanical retractor ①机械式收紧装置，机械式收缩装置，机械式拉紧装置②（特指盘式制动器卡钳摩擦片磨损间隙的）机械式补偿装置③（安全带的）机械式收紧装置

mechanical reversibility 机械可逆性

mechanical rotory expander （制动器的）机械转动式制动蹄促动件（通过凸轮转动将双蹄撑开）

mechanical rotory slidable expander （制动器的）机械转动-滑动件式制动蹄促动器（其转动凸轮沿制动器端滑动而将蹄撑开）

mechanical ruggedness 机械坚固耐用性

mechanical seal 机械密封（亦称 face seal，由至少一对垂直于旋转轴线的端面，在流体压力和补偿机构弹力或磁力的作用及辅助密封的配合下，保持贴合与相对滑动而构成的防止流体泄漏的装置）

mechanical sensor 机械式传感器（如：钢球式加速度传感器等）

mechanical servo 机械随动系统，机械伺服机构

mechanical servo brake 机械伺服式制动器（机械加力制动器）

mechanical slidable expander （制动器的）机械滑动式制动蹄促动器（如：楔形促动器相对于转动式而言）

mechanical specialities 机械特性，机械性能（简称 MS）

mechanical stability 机械稳定性

mechanical steering unit 机动转向加力的装置（一种通过两个摩擦离合器直接利用发动机的动力输出，进行转向加力的装置，目前很少使用，亦称机械式动力转向，= mechanical-type power steering）

mechanical stoppage 机械故障停车

mechanical strength 机械强度

mechanical stress 机械应力［一般称应力（stress），指固体或部件受外力作用时，在弹性力限度内，分布于截面积上的力和截面面积的比值，即单位面积上所承受的作用力］

mechanical supercharging （内燃机进气的）机械增压（相对于废气涡轮增压而言，指内燃机以机械方式驱动机械增压器进行的增压）

mechanical surface treatment 表面机械处理（表面清洗、抛光、研磨、喷砂等机械处理的总称）

mechanical system 机械系统，机械装置，力学体系

mechanical test (ing) 机械（性能）试验

mechanical tire inflator 机械动力驱动（的）轮胎充气泵

mechanical traction 机械牵引

mechanical trail （在结构上主销后倾所形成的）主销后倾距（见 caster ②注意：不同于因高速时弹性胎变形，使轮胎接地面中心逐渐后移而形成的轮胎拖距，见 pneumatic trail）

mechanical transmission ①机械（式）变速器（指通过齿轮或其他机械元件，来改变及保持速比与转矩比的变速器）②机械传动（系）

mechanical transport company （英军）汽车运输连（机械化运输连）

mechanical treatment 机械加工（冷加工）

mechanical-type power steering 机械式动力转向（装置）（亦称 mechan-

ical steering unit)
mechanical unit 机械单位
mechanical vehicle 机动车辆（= motor vehicle）
mechanical ventilation 机械通风
mechanical vibration 机械振动（指机械系统中运动量的振荡现象）
mechanical viscosity 机械黏度
mechanical 4WD system center shaft 机械传动式四轮驱动系统中间轴（将前轮转向动力传至后轮的传动轴）
mechanical wear 机械磨耗
mechanical work 机械功
mechanical wrench 机动扳手
mechanician 技工，机械技术人员，机械师
mechanics ①力学②机构学③机械系；机械（部分），机构，结构④技术细节，技巧，技术方法
mechanic's creeper （修理工在汽车底盘下进行维修作业时的）躺板（简称 creeper）
mechanics of bulk-materials handling 散装物资运输装卸机械
mechanics of materials 材料力学
mechanics of tire cornering 轮胎转弯力学（研究弹性轮胎受外来横向力时所产生的问题）
mechanics of vehicles 车辆力学
mechanic's stethoscope 发动机听诊器（亦称 soniscope）
mechanism ①机械，机构②机构学，结构方式③机械作用，作用原理，作用过程④机理，历程，进程
mechanism hysteresis time 机构滞后时间
mechanism of combustion 燃烧机理
mechanism of deposit formation 沉积物形成机理
mechanism of flame propagation 着火机理
mechanism of harmonic gear drive 谐波齿轮传动机构（由波发生器、柔性齿轮和刚性齿轮三个基本构件组成的传动机构，波发生器使柔性齿轮产生可控弹性变形，而与刚性齿轮啮合来传递运动和力的传动机构）
mechanism of ignition （混合气的）着火机理
mechanist 机工，技工，机械师
mechanized handling 机械化装卸作业（亦称 machine handling, mechanical handling）
mechanized parking garage 机械化（停）车库
mechanocaloric 机械致热的（用机械方法使温度产生变化的）
mechano-electronic transducer 机-电变换器（机-电换能器，机-电传感器，常指将机械量变换的电位号量输出的传感器）
mechanokinetic 机械动力的（如：储能飞轮等）
mechatranics 机械-电子一体化，机电一体化
mechatronic 机电一体化的
mechatro spark system 机械-电子式点火系统（简称 MS system）
mech c/o 机械校正（= mechanical checkout）
mechnanical key code （防盗系的）点火钥匙齿形码（简称 MK）
media ①中间②媒介，媒体，手段③中数（medium 的复数）
medial divider （公路、道路）中央分隔带（= central reserve）
medial friction ①（对向车流间的）交会阻力②均值摩擦力
medial island 交通岛（= center island）
medial strip （公路、道路）中央分隔带（= central reserve）
median driver 中等身材的驾驶员（按人体测量的数据，= average driver）

median lane 分隔带车道（位于分隔带中的变速车道，便利转弯车辆）

median speed 中间车速（速度累积分布图中各种车速按大小顺序排列时的中间值，即50%车辆所采用的车速）

Media Orientated System Transmission 见 MOST①

mediate friction （润滑油）层间摩擦（在两摩擦面间的润滑层间的摩擦）

medical emergency case 急救药箱

medical transport 救护运输（= ambulance transport）

medical vehicle 医疗车，救护车

medium ①媒介；介质；媒体，中间物；传导体 ②手段，方法 ③中间，中等，平均，中数（常用代号为 M）④染料的溶解液 ⑤中等的，普通的

medium alloy steel 中合金钢（合金元素≥5%～10%）

medium bus 中型客车（中国规定长大于7m且小于或等于10m）

medium-carbon steel 中碳钢（含碳量≥0.25%～0.60%）

medium city bus 中型城市客车

medium-duty axle 中型车辆车桥，中型车桥

medium (duty) dumper 中型自卸汽车（= medium dump truck，中国规定为最大总质量≤14t的自卸汽车）

medium-duty truck 中型载货汽车（参见 medium truck）

medium fit 中级精度配合（相当于三级精度配合）

medium force fit 中级压配合

medium-frequency （指频率300～3000kHz的）中频

medium-heavy duty ①中重工况，中重工件（条件）②中重型的，中重功率的（= moderate duty）

medium-heavy duty class 中等重型，中重级（英国载重8t左右的货车的等级）

medium intercity bus 中型长途汽车

medium knocked down 中挡散件组装（介于 CKD 和 SKD 之间的一种汽车就地组装成车的方式，简称 MKD）

medium-lived 中等使用寿命的

medium lorry 中型货车

medium-maintenance company （美军）中修连，中修-维护连

medium off-road vehicle 中型越野汽车（中国规定最大总质量大于5t且小于13t的越野车）

medium oil 中黏度机油

medium operating conditions 中等使用条件，平均使用条件

medium plastic surface 半塑性路面（如草地等）

medium pressure charging （内燃机进气）中增压（指增压压力0.15～0.25MPa的增压）

medium-pressure engine 中压发动机

medium private bus 中型自用客车

medium repair （汽车）中修（用更换或修复有限零、部件，恢复汽车完好技术状态和维持汽车寿命的平衡性修理）

medium scale integration 中规模集成电路（简称 MSI，指由100～1000个三极管构成的集成电路，或每一芯片上具有的10～100个门电路的半导体器件，但这只是一个相对概念，随着电子技术的发展，电路的集成度越来越高）

medium semi-trailer 中型半挂车（中国规定最大总质量大于7.1t且小于或等于19.5t）

medium sightseeing bus 中型旅游客车（用于载送乘客观光游览的视野开阔、乘坐舒适、设备齐全的中型客车）

medium size 中等尺寸

medium size bearing （外径80~180 mm 的）中型轴承

medium-sized motor transportation enterprises 中型汽车运输企业（中国规定所有营运汽车全年完成换算周转量在 2000 万 t·km 及以上至 10 000 万 t·km，车辆保有量在 600 辆以下的汽车运输企业）

medium speed diesel engine 中速柴油机（指工作转速在 300~1000r/min 或活塞平均速度为 6~9m/s 的柴油机）

medium steel 中碳钢（简称 MS，指含碳量在 0.30%~0.60% 之间的优质钢，强度高于低碳钢，多用于制造中型货车的曲轴、凸轮轴、曲轴齿轮、连杆、前桥工字梁、转向主销、钢板销等）

medium temperature tempering 中温回火（将淬火钢件加热至 350~450℃左右，经保温后空冷以获得回火屈氏体组织的热处理工艺）

medium truck 中型载货汽车，中型货车（中国规定为厂定总质量大于 6t，小于或等于 14t 的货车，= medium-duty truck）

medium type 中间型

medium wave 中波（波长 200~1000m 的电磁波，简称 MW）

Meehanite metal 密烘铸铁，孕育铸铁（用硅化钙 CaSi 及 $CaSi_2$ 孕育处理成的高硅铸铁，抗酸蚀，较一般铸铁拉伸强度高，亦称 Meehanite cast iron, Meehanite iron）

meet-homomorphism 保交同态

meeting ①会议，集合；会合，集合 ②合流点，交汇点 ③会车

meeting beam （汽车前照灯）会车灯光，（近光，= short-distance beam, lower beam）

meet the test of experiment 与试验结果相符的，获得试验证明，用试验证实

mega- 兆（词头，简称 M，10^6，用十进制表示为 1000000 当表示存储器的容量时为 2 的 20 次方 2^{20}，用十进制表示为 1048576，亦称 megalo-）

megabit 兆位（一兆个或称一百万个二进制单位，简称 Mbit）

megabyte 兆字节（简称 MB，一般用于表述计算机存储器容量的存储单位，= 2^{20} 字节，即：1 048 576 字节）

mega city 大都市，大城市

megacycle 兆周，百万周

megadiamond 大颗粒金刚石，大颗粒钻石

megagram 兆克（国际质量单位的倍数单位，代号为 Mg，$1Mg = 10^6 g$）

megahertz 兆赫（代号 MHz = 10^6 hertz）

megajoule 兆焦耳（国际单位制的热量的倍数单位，代号 MJ，$1MJ = 10^6 J$）

megalo- 兆（词头），特大（mega）

megamega- 兆兆（词头，代号 MM，= 10^{12}，根据国际单位制的规定，用 tera 代替 megamega，如：兆兆米不用 MM，而用 Tm）

megameter ①兆欧表，高阻表 ②大千米（= 1000 千米）（简称 MM）

meganewton 兆牛顿（国际单位制的力的倍数单位，简称 MN，$1MN = 10^6 N$）

meganewton-meter 兆牛·米（国际单位制的力矩的倍数单位，简称 MNm，$1MNm = 10^6 Nm$）

megaohm 兆欧姆（国际单位制的电阻倍数单位，代号 MΩ，$1MΩ = 10^6 Ω$，参见 ohm）

mega-scale 百万（标度）级的

megasecond 兆秒（= 10^6 秒，简称 Ms）

Mega-Storage Capacity 特大容量级电容器型蓄电池（一种供混合动力车减速能量回收发电系统使用、可

快速存-放电的特大容量锂离子电容器型蓄电池的商品名）

megavolt-ampere 兆伏安（国际单位制的视在功率倍数单位，简称 MVA，$1MVA = 10^6 VA$）

megawatt 兆瓦（国际单位制的功率倍数单位，简称 MW，$1MW = 10^6 W$）

megger ①携带式绝缘测试器（一种内部带有手摇发电机、测定绝缘电阻的仪具）②高阻表，兆欧表（megameter 的简称）

meg (-) ohm 兆欧 MΩ（$1MΩ = 10^6 Ω$）

MEI ①技术细则手册（manual of engineering instructions）②金属工程研究院（Metals Engineering Institute）

Meissner effect 麦斯南效应（材料超导电状态的一种特性）

melamine 密胺，三聚氰酰胺［$C_3N_3(NH_2)_3$，= cyanuramide］

melamine-formaldehyde resin 三聚氰胺（甲醛）树脂（为热固性树脂的一种，有良好的机械强度、硬度、耐热品性、耐热性、耐溶剂性）

melamine plastic 密胺塑料，三聚氰胺（甲醛）塑料

Melinex 聚酯薄膜纸（参见 Mylar）

melt fluidity （塑料等的）熔融流动性

melting heat 熔化热，熔解热

melting ice 正在融化的冰

melting-in 熔挂法（亦称 burning-in，一般指滑动轴承上减摩合金的浇挂法）

melting point 熔点（亦称 melting temperature，在一定压力下，通常指大气压下，固态与液态或液晶态平衡时的温度）

melting zone 溶化层，溶区

meltometer （测熔点用）高温温度计，熔点计

MEMA ［美］汽车和设备制造商协会（Motor and Equipment Manufacturers' Association）

member ①组成部分，构件，部件，元件②成员，成分③（汽车车架的）纵梁，横梁柱，架（及任一空心构件）④（液力耦合器、液力变矩器的）叶轮（指由单排或多排导流叶片组成的工作轮：泵轮、涡轮、导轮的总称，有多排叶法的叶轮亦称为刚性连接的多元件叶轮）⑤元件［a. 指液力变矩器中带有多排叶片的叶轮的刚性连接的每一排叶片，如一个由单排叶片的泵轮、双排叶片的导轮和三排叶片的涡轮组成的变矩器称（三叶轮）六元件变矩器；b. 行星齿轮机构的太阳轮、内齿轮、行星轮等的总称］

membership function 幂函数（函数 $y = x^a$，称幂函数，其中 y 为自变量，a 为常数，$a \in R$）

membrane ①膜片（= diaphragm）②薄膜（= film）

membrane-electrode assembly （燃料电池的）膜-电极组件（简称 MEA，指用热压法制成的阳极、阴极和质子交换膜组件）

membrane filtration insolubles procedure （滑油）非溶解物质薄膜过滤法（简称 MFI procedure）

membrane filtration test （滑油等的）薄膜过滤试验

membrane horn switch 膜片式喇叭开关

membrane keyboard 膜式键盘（一种触摸薄膜式键盘）

membrane-type 膜片式，膜片型的

membrane waterproofing 防水膜，防水层

MEM-CAL （通用公司 P4 型动力控制模块上的插接式）存储-标定芯片（将可编程只读存储器和发动机标

定软件包合成一个芯片直接插装在其动力控制模块上，为 memory-calpak 的简称）

memoir 纪要，（学术）报告，论文，学会论文集

memory （电子计算机）存储器（可存储和读出各种程序和数据的器件，由存储单元组成，通常还包括地址选择器、放大器等的集成电路，亦称 storage，但不包括 storage 中的外部存储器，如磁盘、软盘、磁带等。在汽车电子控制系统中使用只读存储器存储各种控制程序，使用可编程只读存储器存储特定的整车和发动机的调整数据，及特殊要求的控制程序，使用随机存取存储器存储各种传感器的输入信息、中央处理器的处理过程中需要暂存的信息或处理结果等，见 ROM, PROM, RAM）

memory access time 存储器存取时间（将一个字送入或读出存储器所需的时间）

memory address register 存储器地址寄存器（处理机中存放正在被访问的存储单元的地址的寄存器）

memory alloy 记忆合金［亦称形状记忆合金（shape memory alloy），可分为单程效应型（one way effect type）和双程效应型（two-way type）两种。前者当受热温度升到某阈值时，可恢复其本来形状，后者除上述热复原外，在遇冷温度降到某阈值时，也可恢复原来形状。此外，形状记忆合金在受到拉伸负荷时，可伸长10%，一旦卸去该负荷，又可恢复原状。常见的记忆合金有 NiTi-、CuZnAl-合金等］

memory back-up 存储数据备份（指将存储信息复制在不断电的非易失性存储器内备用）

memory bus 存储器总线（将二进制数据送入和送出存储器的电路。存储器包括三条总线：地址总线，以及 CPU 与存储器间的数据存入线和取出线，一般这三条总线分时共用一条总线）

memory button 存储式操纵按钮（可将驾驶员的要求存储于存储器内的电动座椅、电动后视镜等的操纵按钮）

memory capacity 存储容量（亦称 storage capacity，存储器中可存储的数据总量，以二进制位、字节、字符、字等的数量表示）

memory cell 存储单元

memory codes 见 service codes④

memory device （电子计算机）存储器

memory expansion mother board 存储器内存扩充主板（供插装存储容量扩充件的带插装槽的主板）

memory expansion option 存储器容量扩充选购件（指插入扩充主板内的容量扩充件）

memory master time control 自动计时控制（装置）

memory package （记忆转向盘柱高度、角度，座椅位置，后视镜位置的）存储软件包

memory property （计算机）存储性能

memory storage capacity （电子控制系统）存储器的存储容量［存储器可容纳的数据总量，可用二进制位、字节、字符、字或其他的数据单位来度量，如：128K（ilo）bytes，指其存储容量为128千字节，每1千字节"1 kilobyte" = 1024字节］

memory-stored control （电子计算机）存储装置控制

memory system ①存储系统（简称 MS）②记忆系统（可存储并自动再现驾驶人员各项要求，如座椅高度、转向盘管柱倾斜度等系统）

mend a puncture 内胎补洞，补胎（=patch an inner tube）

M-ENG 多发动机的（multi-engined）

M-engine M燃烧室发动机（柴油机的一种，见M-combustion chamber）

meniscus ①（毛细管内液体的）弯月面，新月形（由于表面张力，毛细管内的液体沿管壁周围的高度比中心部分高，而形成的中凹形曲面）②凹透镜

mental stress （驾驶人员的）精神压力（心理压力）

mental workload 精神负担（指驾驶员驾驶中精神紧张造成的负担）

MEO ①维护规程（maintenance engineering order）②发动机大修（major engine overhaul）

M. E. P. ①平均有效压力（亦写作MEP，mean effective pressure的简称）②工程实践手册，施工手册（manuals of engineering practice的简称）③发动机端板（motor end plate的简称）

Mercedes Benz ［德］奔驰公司（德国Daimler Benz公司的子公司）

merchant steel 商品钢

mercurial ①水银的，汞的，含水的，似汞的②易变的，灵活的，活泼的

mercurial barometer 水银压力计（=mercury manometer）

mercurial gauge 水银计（水银压力计、水银温度计的总称）

mercuric compound 水银化合物，汞化合物

Mercury 墨丘利（水神，商神，美福特公司轿车名）

mercury 水银，汞（Hg）（相对密度13.59，熔点 –38.832℃，沸点356.7℃）

mercury-arc lamp 水银萤灯，汞弧灯（=mercury vapor lamp，高亮度气体放电灯的一种）

mercury-arc rectifier 汞弧整流器（=mercury vapor rectifier）

mercury column 水银柱，汞柱（1大气压=760mm水银柱）

mercury contact 水银接点，水银触点

mercury cooled valve 水银冷却气门（一般用于排气门，气门中空，内装一定量的水银）

mercury-free 不含水银的，无汞的

mercury manometer 水银压力计，水银气压计（=mercurial barometer）

mercury pool valve ①汞弧整流管②汞池阴极，汞阴极装置

mercury switch relay 水银开关继电器

mercury thermometer 水银温度表

mercury vapor 水银蒸气，汞气

merge ①汇合，组合，插队，合并，归并，（汽车等）驶入队列②吸收，溶解，融合；消失

merging 合流（同方向的两股车流汇合成单一车流的过程）

merging end 合流端，汇合端（交通岛或路幅与路幅之间中间地带的尖端，即交通合流处）

merging process （高速公路的车辆）合流过程

merging traffic sign "合流交通"标志（交叉口前方有合流交通的预告标志）

meridian ①子午线，子午圈（指通过地球极轴的理想平面 meridian plate 子午面，与地球表面相交的圆）②高潮，顶峰③顶点的

meridian curve of a surface of revolution 回转面的子午线（经线）

meridian tyre 子午线轮胎（现多称 radial tyre）

meridional contour （涡轮）子午线剖面轮廓

meridional plane 子午（平面）（子午线断面）

merit ①长处，优点；价值 ②指标，准则，标准

merit rating ①质量评定，质量评价指数；优点评价，优点评分 ②发动机清洁度评价指数（指发动机被燃烧和润滑中所产生的积炭和结胶污染的程度，用数字 0~10 表示，10 表示完全清洁，参见 demerit rating）

merits and demerits 优点和缺点，优缺点（亦称 merits and drawbacks, merits and faults）

merry-go-round ①旋转，急转 ②旋转升降装置，盘旋式升降机（如高层停车场用的汽车升降机械）③环形的

MESFET 金属半导体场效应晶体管（metal semiconductor field effect transistor 的简称，由 GaAs 半导体制成的高频半导体器件）

mesh ①网眼，筛孔 ②网状结构，网状组织，网状物 ③相互啮合，相互咬合

mesh analysis 筛析，筛选

mesh drive （使起动机驱动小齿轮与飞轮齿圈接合的）啮合驱动装置

mesh filter 网式滤清器，滤网（= gauze filter）

meshing 啮合，咬合；搭住，结网

meshing backlash （齿轮的）啮合背隙（轮齿在啮合过程中，两非啮合齿面间的间隙，可分别从法向或圆周方向度量）

meshing bevel gear 啮合锥齿轮

meshing drive （驱动起动机小齿轮与飞轮齿环相互接合的）啮合驱动装置

meshing engagement 啮合

meshing point 啮合点

meshing spring （起动机的）啮合弹簧（装在起动机单向离合器上，当拨叉推动驱动小齿轮与飞轮齿环啮合时的中间缓冲弹簧）

meshing zone （齿轮）啮合区

mesh interference （齿轮轮齿的）啮合干涉（指由于制造、安装误差，或齿变形导致任一齿面越出所允许运动界限，而在理论上穿越其相啮齿面的现象）

mesh jacket 网状套，罩网

mesh screen 筛目，滤网，金属丝网

mesh type 网格型（转向管柱，汽车前方碰撞时，可利用网格管柱段变形吸收冲击能量）

mesh type DPF （三菱公司的）筛网状柴油机微粒排放物滤清净化器（其前端装有氧化催化剂，燃烧微粒排放物中的悬浮油粒，后端捕集并燃烧炭粒，最后排出 H_2O 和 CO_2，见 DPF）

mesopic vision 中间视觉（眼睛适应亮度介于明视觉和暗视觉范围之间时，由视网膜的锥体和杆体两种细胞同时起作用的视觉）

message centre （汽车自诊断系统在仪表板上的）信息中心[一种多项显示器，其典型的信息是：normal（正常），tailgate open（后门未关），door ajar（车门半开），lamp out（灯未关），washer fluid low（冲洗液不足）等，亦称 system scanner]

metacenter （浮力的）定倾中心，稳定中心

metacentric height （浮力的）定倾中心高度，稳心高度（简称 GM）

meta-gasket 金属制密封垫，金属片型密封垫

metal ①金属 ②减摩合金，轴承合金 ③滑动轴承，轴瓦

metal-air cell 金属-空气（蓄）电池

metal and rubber press fit surface of seal 油封的金属橡胶压配合表面

metal apex seal （转子发动机的）金属径向密封片

metal arc cutting 金属电弧切割

metal arc welding 金属电弧焊接
metal armor 金属装甲（金属护甲）
metal armoured cable 金属铠装电线
metal asbestos gasket 金属石棉衬垫（如：发动机汽缸盖使用的用软钢片做芯，中间为石棉橡胶材料，外面再包敷软钢片的缸垫）
metal backing （镀层的）金属底层
metal bath 金属浴
metal bellows mechanical seal 金属波纹管机械密封（补偿环的辅助密封为金属波纹管的机械密封）
metal-bellow-type accumulator 金属波纹管型储油筒
metal belt fastener 金属带扣
metal-bonded-case oil seal 金属壳式油封
metal-bonded iron insert （铝活塞）渗铝铸铁镶式环槽
metal brush 金属电刷
metal-cased rotary shaft lip seal 外露（金属）骨架旋转轴唇形密封圈（骨架外围不包覆橡胶的唇形密封圈）
metal cased rotary shaft lip seal with minor lip 有副唇外露骨架旋转轴唇形密封圈（有副唇，骨架外围不包覆橡胶的唇形密封圈）
metal-cased seal 带外露金属壳的油封，带（外露）金属骨架的油封
metal case hardening 金属表面强化处理，金属表面硬化处理
metal catalyst ①金属载体催化剂（以金属件作为载体的催化剂）②金属催化剂（贵金属，铂、钯、铑及普通金属，铜、铬、镍、钴作工件材料的催化剂的通称）
metal catcher 金属杂质分离器，金属收集（接受、吸收、捕集、俘获）器
metal ceramics ①金属陶瓷②金属陶瓷学（= metallized ceramics）
metal cleaner ①金属制件表面去垢剂，金属制件清洁剂②金属制件清洁器，金属制件清洗装置
metal clearance 滑动轴承与轴间的机油间隙（亦称 bearing clearance、oil clearance）
metal-cloth filter 金属丝布滤清器
metal coat 金属涂层，金属包覆层
metal conduit 金属导管
metal-containing addition （铸件中的）金属（成分）添加剂
metal-cord tire 金属丝帘布层轮胎（钢丝帘布层轮胎，= wired type tire）
metal covering 金属壳，金属盖
metal deactivator 金属钝化剂（燃油、润滑油的添加剂）
metal debris 金属末，金属碎片（零件磨损产物）
metaldehyde （低、多、四）副醛[$(CH_3CHO)_n$ 且 $n=4,6$ 的聚合物，112~115℃左右升华，能与空气均匀混合，随之再结晶，对空气流具有良好的跟随性，反光性高，可用于使进气流及汽缸内的气流可见化的示踪剂]
metaldehyde approach （低、多、四）副醛法[使用 $(CH_3CHO)_n$ 且 $n=4,6$ 的聚合物作为可见化示踪剂来测定高温气体的流动]
metal deposition 金属镀覆（金属电解沉积）
metal dust 金属粉末
metal electrode ①金属电极②金属焊条
metal electro-sparking work 金属电火花加工
metal fatigue 金属疲劳
metal filler 金属填料，金属填补料，填隙合金（见 filler metal）
metal film resistors 金属薄膜电阻器（在瓷棒外表沉积一层金属薄膜，其电阻值的大小可在两端之间划螺旋槽来控制）

metal finisher 金属制作精加工,(车身钣金构件等的)精修饰工
metal flexible hose 金属软管
metal fluoride 金属氟化物
metal foil 金属箔,金属薄膜
metal foil sensing element (空气质量流量传感器的电热型)金属热膜传感元件(电子控制模块根据维持该薄膜在进气空气流中达到的规定温度值所需的电流量确定进气空气的质量流量,千克/秒)
metal foil sensing element 金属箔膜传感元件
metal galvano (cermet) resistors 金属陶瓷电阻器
metal-gate (场效应晶体管的)金属栅
metal graphite gasket 金属石墨衬垫(软钢外皮和内芯间压装有膨胀石墨的缸垫等)
metal grill 金属栅栏,金属网格
metal halide lamp 金属卤化物灯
metal halogenide cathode 金属卤化物阴极(如:在汽车用无水电解质蓄电池、锂-氯化铜电池中,使用有机物质做电解质,活性金属锂做阳极,金属卤化物氯化铜做阴极, = metal halide cathode)
metal harness ①金属电线导(套)管(= metallic conduit) ②金属线束,导线束
metal headform (汽车安全试验用时的)金属人头模型
metal hose 金属软管
metal hydride storage system (氢燃料汽车的)金属氢化物储氢系统,粉末金属化合型储氢系统(参见iron-titanium hydride)
metalic tire 胎面硫化时嵌入金属物的轮胎
metal-impregnated amorphous carbon 金属浸渍无定形碳(= metallized carbon, 亦称 metal-impregnated electrographite)
metal inert gas arc welding 金属惰性气体保护电弧焊(简称 MIG welding)
metal-inert-gas (shielded-arc) welding 金属焊条电极惰性气体掩弧焊,金属焊条惰性气体保护焊(简称 MIG welding, 亦写作 metallic inert gas welding)
metalization [美]金属喷镀(英写作 metallization, 见 metalizing)
metalizing [美]金属喷镀(英写作 metallizing, = metal spray, metallization, 一般使用熔点为 1000℃ 以下的金属丝电弧或高温燃气熔化后由高压气体喷至零件表面形成镀覆层,汽车上多用于修复汽缸、曲轴等磨损表面)
metalled ①用金属色覆的 ②碎石路面的
metalled road 碎石路
metallic 金属的,含金属的,金属性质的
metallic additive(s) (机油中的)金属类添加剂
metallic arc welding 金属极(电)弧焊
metallic asbestos yarn 金属芯石棉线
metallic belt (无级变速器 CVT)的金属传动带(由左、右两侧卡装有 9~12 层厚 0.2mm 的马氏体时效处理的高强度薄钢叠成的两条带圈"含镍 18~25 的 maraging steel ring set"上的 300~400 片称为 element, 亦称 block 的单片组合而成)
metallic bond 两种不同金属层的黏结或烧结
metallic braid 金属编织带
metallic cab 金属制驾驶室
metallic carbon brush 金属石墨电刷(一般由金属粉与石墨粉混合制成,特点是电阻小,摩擦系数小)
metallic character 金属特性

metal（lic）coating 金属喷涂（法），金属喷镀（层），金属镀层
metallic compound 金属化合物
metallic conduit （保护绝缘电线的）金属导管（见 metal harness①）
metallic contact ①金属表面接触 ②金属触点
metallic disk brake pad 盘式制动器的金属（摩擦）衬块（由铁、铜等金属粉，掺入石墨粉等固体润滑材料压制或烧结而成，耐磨、抗振、由于掺有石墨粉，因而又称半金属衬块，semi metallic disk brake pad）
metallic filament 金属灯丝，金属丝
metallic filament lamp 金属丝灯
metallic finish 金属漆面（亦称 metallic paint，指在漆料中加有细小的、不同尺寸的反光金属薄片的面漆涂层，由于这些薄片随机无序地排列，从不同角度观察时，呈缤纷异彩的光泽）
metallic friction material 金属粉末烧结摩擦材料
metallic graphite carbon 金属石墨（电刷）（见 metallic carbon brush）
metallic lacquer 金属漆（掺有铝粉等的车身涂料，涂层呈金属光泽）
metallic luster 金属光泽（亦写作 metallic lustre）
metallic mold（mould） 金属型
Metallicon 金属喷镀法（亦写作 metallikon，原为金属喷镀法商标名，现已成为许多地方，如日本等对金属喷镀的通称，= metal spraying，亦写作 metallikon）
metallic oxide 金属氧化物
metallic packing 金属密封填料，金属密封垫片
metallic paint （可发出金属光泽车身）金属漆
metallic paint 金属漆（掺配有金属粉末的漆料，色彩鲜亮，硬度高，多用于车身涂装）
metal（lic）pattern 金属模（型）
metallic segments in the distributor cap 分电器盖扇形金属片触点（分电盘盖分缸触点）
metallic-silicone compound 金属硅酮化合物
metallic soap 金属皂（高脂肪酸、树脂酸等一元羧酸 R·COOH 和钙、铝、铜、铅等二价或三价金属的盐类，一般不溶于水而溶于苯，主要作为润滑剂、防水剂、干燥剂）
metallic sodium 金属钠
metallikon 金属喷镀（见 Metallicon）
metal liner （发动机汽缸的）钢衬套，金属缸套
metal lining ①（非电解）镀覆金属 ②金属衬垫
metallization ①金属化②（使具有导电性的）导体化③金属喷镀，敷覆金属，喷涂金属粉
metallize ①敷覆金属（薄）层 ②［美］金属喷镀③电镀金属④真空镀敷金属薄膜⑤浸渗金属，浸渗金属化合物
metallized carbon 渗金属碳，金属渗渍石墨（在高压下将金属或合金渗入碳的孔隙中，= metal-impregnated amorphous carbon, metallized graphite, metal-impregnated electrographite）
metallized ceramics 金属陶瓷（= metal ceramics）
metallized paint 金属涂料（金属含量多的涂料，具有导电性，常涂于阴极金属构件，以减少阳极金属件的自发电池腐蚀）
metallized plastic 渗金属塑料
metallizing ［美］金属喷镀（= metal spraying）
metallo- 金属的
metallo-detergent 金属去垢剂
metallographic（al） 金相的，金相学的

metallographic examination 金相检验 [= metallographic test, 亦称金相分析 (metallurgical analysis)]

metallography 金相学, 金属学

metalloid 类金属(的), 准金属(的), 金属似(的)(指具有金属的某些性质, 又具有非金属的某些性质的物质, 如硼、硅、锗、砷等)

metalloscope 金相显微镜 (= metallurgical microscope, 亦写作 metaloscope)

metalloscopy 金相显微(镜)检验(亦写作 metaloscopy)

metallurgical bond 金属键

metallurgical technology 金属工艺学

metal matrix composites 金属粉末烧结复合材料 (简称 MMC$_s$)

metal mesh 金属滤网, 金属丝网 (亦称 wire mesh)

metal mold casting 硬模铸造, 金属模铸造 (将熔化的金属浇入用金属制成的铸模中以获得铸件)

metal monolith (催化转化器催化剂的) 整体式金属载体 (亦称 metal monolithic substrate, metal support, monolith metal design, metal monolith catalyst, 一般为在催化反应中呈惰性的热稳定性含铁、铬或铝的合金, 制成呈蜂窝状整块)

metal o-ring seal 金属 O 形密封环

metal oxide film resistors 金属氧化物薄膜电阻器

metal oxide semi-conductor 金属氧化物半导体 (见 MOS)

metal-oxide-semiconductor fieldeffect transistor 金属氧化物半导体场效应晶体管 (简称 MOSFET)

metal-oxide-semiconductor integrated circuit 金属-氧化物-半导体集成电路 (简称 MOSIC, 指以金属-氧化物-半导体场效应晶体管为基本有源元件构成的集成电路)

metal-oxid-semiconductor random access memory 金属-氧化物-半导体随机存取存储器 (简称 MOSRAM)

metal-oxygen cell (battery) 金属-氧(蓄)电池 (一般使用碱溶液做电解质, 一个电极为金属, 一个电极为氧气, 其缺点是气体作为电极的结构尺寸太大)

metal particle 金属微粒

metal polish 金属抛光剂, 金属抛光磨料; 金属磨料抛光

metal-powder 金属粉末

metal powder parts 金属粉末零件, 粉末金属零件

metal preservative compound 金属制件保护剂 (喷于各种金属制作表面防锈、防腐蚀等)

metal press fit surface of seal 油封的金属压配合表面

metal pulverization 金属喷涂

metal rectifier 金属整流器 [固体整流器, 亦称 dry type rectifier, 干片式整流器, 指利用半导体整流作用的各种整流器。如: 硒整流器 (selenium rectifier)、锗整流器 (germanium rectifier)、硅整流器 (silicon rectifier) 等]

metal resilient coupling 金属弹簧联轴节

metal road 碎石路(面)

metal-rubber support 金属-橡皮支座

metal sheet 金属板

metals-joining process 金属件连接法

metal skin 金属皮

metal slap 发动机敲缸声, 发动机爆燃声

metal spacer 金属隔片

metal spray by plasma 等离子电弧金属喷涂

metal spray gun 金属喷枪

metal spraying by electric-arc 金属电弧喷涂 (将电弧熔化的金属用高速气流喷敷于零件表面, 形成表面

喷镀层，亦称 metallizing by electric-arc

metal spring type suspension 金属弹簧式悬架（钢板弹簧、螺旋弹簧、扭杆弹簧等金属弹簧做弹性元件的悬架的总称）

metal-strengthened tire 金属加强轮胎（采用金属丝帘布层和胎面嵌入金属物等方法提高轮胎耐磨性）

metal surface treatment 金属表面处理

metal tire stud （轮胎）金属抓地齿

metal-to-metal brake 金属对金属的制动器（指全金属蹄片式制动器或全金属卡钳式制动器）

metal-to-metal clutch 金属与金属接合的离合器（全金属离合器）

metal-to-metal contact 金属与金属件的直接接触

metal-to-metal seal 金属环式接触密封件，全金属密封件

metal transfer 金属转移（如断电器触点由于金属转移，正侧凸起，负侧凹陷）

metal wool 金属棉，钢丝棉（如空气滤清器滤芯，= steel wool）

metal working 金属加工（亦写作 metalworking，金属冲、锻、铸压成型加工的总称）

metalworking spoon （车身板件修复用工具中的）钣金勺（亦称 body spoon）

metal-zeolite-type catalyst 金属-沸石型催化剂

METAPOR F100 AL 麦踏波（一种透气、透水的微孔铝材的商品名，由70%~90%的铝粉和10%~30%的环氧树脂制成，外形似铝，但比铝轻37%）

meta-stable output configuration ［数字集成电路中的时序电路（sequential circuit）的］亚稳态输出组态（指施加适当的激励之后，仅在有限的时间内存在的输出组态，亦称 meta stable output pattern 亚稳态输出图形）

meteorological conditions 气象条件

meterage ①计量，量测②测量费，量表使用费

meter calibration 仪表标定

meter candle 米烛光（见 lux）

meter constant 仪表（校正）常数，校正常数，计数器常数

meter creeping 仪表表针漂移现象

meter dial 仪表刻度盘

metered fuel charge 计量供（燃）油

metered injection （燃油等的）计量喷射，定量喷射

metered lube dispenser 润滑油（脂）计量加注器

metered orifice 量孔

meter full scale 仪表满刻度范围（仪表最大量程）

meter glass 量杯

meter hand 仪表指针

meter-in circuit with spill-off 带溢流道的进油计量油路

metering ①测量②测定（燃油供给量的）计量

metering error 计量误差

metering helix （柴油机柱塞式喷油泵柱塞上的控制与计量喷油量的）螺线切口

metering-in control system ①（液力传动）进油计量调节系统②（柴油机喷油泵）控制进油的计量方式

metering injector 计量喷油器

metering jet 量孔，剂量量孔；出油量孔（亦称 measuring jet, metering orifice, metering port）

metering needle 量针（= jet needle）

metering oil pump 滑油计量泵，计量油泵

metering-out control system ①（液力传动）出油计量调节系统②（柴油机喷油泵）喷油计量控制系统

metering pin 量针（= measuring pin）

metering pin valve 计量针阀

metering plunger （柱塞式喷油泵在凸轮的顶推下产生喷油压力和计量喷油量的）计量柱塞

metering plunger cam 计量柱塞凸轮

metering rod ①油尺，量油杆②（喷嘴）量针（见 jet needle）

metering rod jet 针阀量孔（= needle jet）

metering section ①计量流体通过断面②量测断面③计量部分

metering system ①计量系统，测量系统②统计系统，记录系统③统计制度，计量制度（参见 measuring system）

metering unit 计量装置

metering valve ①计量阀②（前盘式-后鼓式制动器液压制动系的）节压阀（装在前轮盘式制动器液压管道内，在后轮鼓式制动器制动液压上升到足以克服制动蹄复位弹簧拉力之前，该阀延缓前轮液压的上升速度，以保证后轮鼓式制动器与前轮盘式制动同时起作用）③（柴油机转子式分配泵的）计量阀，喷油量控制阀（由调速器控制、精确计量喷油量的供油阀）

metering valve sensor （柴油机电子控制系统的）喷油量控制阀传感器（向电子控制模块发送喷油量控制阀开度信号的可变电阻式传感器，简称MVS）

meter-kilogram 米·千克（= kilogram-meter）

meter, kilogramme, second, ampere system 米·千克,秒,安培制（简称 MKSA system）

meter(metre) ①米（国际单位制的长度单位,代号为 m,等于氪 Kr^{86} 放射橘红色光的波长 1650763.73 倍,约为 3 尺,或 39.37in）②量表,测量仪表③节奏,拍子；周期性④使用仪表量测⑤计量供给（燃油等）⑥液体流量计量或控制装置

meter multiplier 仪表量程倍增器

meter needle 仪表指针

meter panel 仪表板

meter per second squared 米每平方秒,米每二次方秒（m/s^2,加速度单位）

meter rule 米尺

meter screw 米制螺纹,公制螺纹

meter sensitivity 仪表灵敏度

meter system ①公制,米制②仪表系统,仪表装置,量测系统

meter taper 公制锥度（规）

meter water gage ①米制水表,米制水柱压力表②米水柱（压力单位,用水柱高的米数表示压力。使用时应有温度条件,如在4℃时的水柱高多少米。代号 mW·G。1mW·G = 0.0968atm = 1.4223lbf/in^2 = 39.5inW·G = 0.0981bar = 73.556mmHg = 0.1kgf/cm^2 = 9.8 × 10^3 N/m^2）

methacrylate resin 甲基丙烯酸酯,异丁烯酸酯树脂

methane 甲烷,沼气（CH$_4$,可用作汽油机的代用燃料）

methane equivalent 甲烷当量（用于计测排气碳氢化合物含量）

methane fuelled engine 沼气发动机

methane value （表示气体燃料抗爆燃性的）甲烷值

methanol 甲醇（CH$_3$OH, 旧称 methyl alcohol, 无色透明液体,类似酒精,但有毒,一般 8~20g 失明, 30~50g 致死,可用做燃料、溶剂、酒精变性处理,亦为防冻液的主要成分之一等）

methanol aqueous solution 甲醇水溶液（小型车燃料电池用燃料）

methanol blended gasoline 掺甲醇汽油,甲醇汽油（简称 MBG,可显著提高抗爆性,缸内积炭少,排气较干净,但其与汽油互溶性差,汽

中甲醇含量超过5%，遇低温或水易分离为两相，且甲醇在低温下不易起动，高温下又容易出现气阻，热值亦相应降低，见 methanol gasoline）

methanol fuel-cell system 甲醇燃料电池系统

methanol-fueled car 甲醇（燃料）轿车（简称 MFC 亦称 methanol powered car）

methanol-fueled engine ①甲醇燃料发动机，甲醇发动机②甲醇点燃式发动机（methanol-fueled spark ignition engine 的简称，甲醇为燃料，电火花点火）

methanol gasoline 甲醇汽油（一般用 Mx 表示汽油中掺入甲醇的百分比，如：M3、M5、M15、M85、M90 分别指掺有 3%、5%、15%、85%、90% 的汽油，M100 指全甲醇）

methanol-hydrogen engine 加氢甲醇发动机（甲醇中加氢可促进充分燃烧，尾气无须净化处理）

methanol-hydrogen reformer 甲醇-氢重整器（裂化甲醇，使生成 H 和 CO 作为燃料电池汽车的能源或直接送入发动机燃烧）

methanol reforming fuel cell 甲醇重组燃料电池（简称 MRFC，甲醇重组产生氢气并经处理除去 CO，以免电池催化剂中毒，实际参与电池反应的仍为氢气）

methanol reforming technique 甲醇重整技术（亦称 methanol catalyst reformation technique、methanol cracking technique，利用发动机废热，以钯或铜锌催化剂，使甲醇分解为 H 和 CO 后送入汽缸。压缩比为 10:1 时，其热效率比汽油高 30%～40%，HC 排放量仅占汽油的 1/10，但 CO 排放较汽油多）

methanol vehicle 甲醇汽车（以甲醇作燃料的车辆）

methanol-water mixture 甲醇-水混合液（一种抗爆液）

method 方法，方式，手段；整理，整顿；条理，秩序，规律，顺序

method of calculating 计算方法（= method of calculation）

method of least squares 最小二乘法，最小平方法

Method of Test for Vapor Pressure of Petroleum Products 石油产品雷德蒸气压力试验法（见 Reid Method）

method of trial 试探法

method of vehicle maintenance and repair on universal post 汽车维护与修理的定位作业法（相对于流水作业法而言，指在一个全能工位上完成全部汽车维修作业的方法）

methodology 方法学，方法论；研究法，分类法

methyl 甲（烷）基（CH_3-）

methyl alcohol 甲醇（CH_3OH）（methanol 的旧称，防冻液主要成分之一，亦与汽油混合成甲醇汽油）

methylated 变性的，甲基化了的，加入甲醇的

methylated alcohol （掺入甲醇后的）变性酒精（亦称 methylated spirit，有毒不能饮用，用做清洁剂）

methylene blue method （碱性）亚甲蓝法 $[(CH_3)_2N]_2C_{12}H_6NS(OH)$（废气中的硫化氢含量分析法）

methyl ester 甲酯

α-methyl naphthalene 1-甲基萘（亦写作 α-methyl naphthalene，$C_{10}H_7$-α-CH_3，燃点高、滞燃期长，评定柴油十六烷值时以纯 α-甲基萘的十六烷值为 0，纯十六烷的十六烷值为 100，二者按不同比例混合而获得十六烷值从 0 到 100 的标准油）

methyl nitrate 硝酸甲酯（CH_3ONO_3）（芳香中性液体，有挥发性，可提高

柴油的十六烷值）

methyl pentene polymer 甲基戊烯聚合物，甲基戊酮聚合物

Methyl tertiary butyl ether 甲基叔丁基乙醚（20世纪70年代后期，欧洲广泛使用的一种汽油掺和燃料，掺和量一般为5%~10%，既为燃料的一种组分，又是提高辛烷值的抗爆剂，以代替铅抗爆剂，简称MTBE，姆特比抗爆剂）

metre ①米 ②测量仪表（=meter）

metre to the power minus one 负一次方米（m^{-1}）

metric ①米制的，公制的 ②度量的，测量的，量规的（亦写作metrical）

metrical instrument 计量仪器

metric atmosphere 公制大气压

metric coarse thread 公制粗牙螺纹

metric engine 公制发动机，米制发动机（采用米制尺寸的发动机）

metric fine thread 公制细牙螺纹

metric horse power 公制马力，米制马力（=75kg·m/s=0.986horse power=735.5watts。法文cheval vapeur,cavallo vapore,cavalos vapor,简称CV;德文pferdestärke简称PS）

metric nylon fastener 米制尼龙紧固件

metrics 度量指标（如度量爆振强度的频率、振幅、时间等）

metric system 公制，米制

metric (system) thread 公制螺纹（螺距以mm为单位、顶尖角为60°的螺纹）

metric tire 米制轮胎，公制轮胎（米制尺寸轮胎）

metric ton 公吨，法吨（亦称tonne，代号t，等于1000千克，为国际单位制的质量单位。1公吨=0.9842long ton=1.1023 short ton=2204.6 pound=2000市斤=20市担）

metric units 公制单位

metro driving ［美］市区驾驶，市区行车（=英urban driving）

metrograph 汽车速度计，车速表

metrology inspection vehicle 计量检测车（装备有砝码箱、检测仪器、工作台和宣传设施。用于衡器鉴定、计量器具检测及计量知识宣传的厢式汽车）

metropolitan 都市的，大城市的；首都的

metropolitan-type 都市型，都市型的

MF ①密胺甲醛（melamine formaldehyde）②主馈（电）线，干线（main feed）③机械滤波器（mechanical filter）④微法拉（μF，microfarad）⑤微型胶卷（microfilm）⑥多焦点的，多焦距的（multifocal）⑦多频（multifrequency）⑧倍率，放大率（multiplying factor）

mF 微法拉（μF，millifarad）

MF battery 免维护蓄电池（maintenance-free battery）

MFC 甲醇（燃料）轿车（methanol-fueled car）

MFDCS 多功能显示和控制系统（multifunction display and control system）

MFG 制造（的），生产（的）（manufacturing）

MF headlight 多焦点前照灯（multifocal headlight的简称，指装有多焦点反射镜的前照灯）

MFI ①熔融流动指数（表示熔融流动性，melt flow index）②多点式汽油喷射（multiport fuel injection或multipoint fuel injection的简称，每缸一个喷油器，但两个、三个或四个喷油器为一组，视发动机型号而异，每组喷油器用一根电线与电子控制模块连接，因而电子控制模块每发出一个喷油信号，同一组的各个喷油器均同时喷油一次，故名，

参见 SFI)

MFI procedure (滑油)非溶解物质薄膜过滤法(membrane filtration insolubles procedure)

MFJ 日本摩托车联合会(The Motorcycling Federation of Japan)

MFM 改进调频制(modified frequency modulation 的简称)

MFR ①制造商,制造厂,制造者(manufacturer) ②多频接收机(multifrequency receiver)

M100 fuel 纯甲醇燃料(= pure methanol)

M85fuel 85%甲醇燃料(含85%甲醇,15%汽油)

MFV 多功能车(multi-functional vehicle 的简称)

Mg ①电磁铁(electromagnet) ②镁(magnesium)

MG ①电动—发电一体机(mator & generator 的简称) ②一种旧式英国跑车(商品名,MorrisGarges 的简称)

mg 毫克 [milligram(me)]

MG-ECU 见 motor-generator electronic control unite

Mg/m³ 兆克每立方米(国际单位的密度单位的倍数单位,megagram/meter³)

mH 毫亨利(参见 millihenry)

MHD ①磁流体(动)力学的(magnetohydrodynamical) ②磁流体力学(magnetohydrodynamics)

MHD (Smart 车的)微型混合驱动系统(亦写作 mhd, micro hybrid drive 的简称,可根据行驶工况和路况自动停机和重起发动机,据称可节油30%)

MHD generator 磁流体动力发电机,磁等离子流动发电机(利用一种导电等离子气体流过横向磁场而产生电能的装置,= magnetohydrodynamic generator, magnetoplasmadynamic generator)

MHH 金属氢化物(metal hydride)

mho 姆(欧)(电导单位,欧姆的倒数)

MH$_x$ car 金属氢化物轿车(指采用金属氢化物储氢装置的轿车,如 FeTiHx 型氢气车,加热氢即可释放,氢气用完后,可重新充入,见 iron-titanium hydride)

MHz 兆赫(见 megahertz)

MI (车载故障诊断系统的)故障指示器(malfunction indicator)

MIC [美]摩托车工业委员会(Motorcycle Industry Council)

MIC 机械组合仪表板(指各种由电子电气控制的指针式仪表板,mechanical instrument cluster 的简称)

mica condenser 云母电容器(由云母薄片与锡箔交互叠合而成)

mica insulation 云母绝缘

mica sheet 云母板,云母片

mica spark(ing) plug 云母火花塞

mica under-cutter (电机换向器云母绝缘片修整刀)

mica washer 云母垫圈

micell(a) 胶囊,胶束,胶(质)粒子,胶态分子团,晶子,微团,巢(橡胶纤维及其他复杂物质的单元结构)

micelle micella 的复数(= macellae)

Michelin 米西林(公司)(法国著名的轮胎公司,1990年的世界市场占有率已达29%,全钢丝子午线轮胎开发者)

Michell(thrust)bearing 米歇尔式(推力)轴承(为推力轴颈轴承,其推力垫支撑推力肩或轴颈,在其相对运动表面间的油楔作用下,推力垫稍许倾斜,这样形成的润滑状态可以造成很低的摩擦系数,从而减少轴承内的动力损失)

micom 微型电子计算机(见 Micro computer)

MICR 磁性墨水文字读出器（magnetic ink character reader）

micro ①微米，百万分之一，10^{-6}；测微计，千分表（常用 μ 作为代号）②微型的，微观的，显微的

microactuator 微型执行器

micro-adjustment 微调

microampere 微安（国际单位制的微电流单位，代号 μA，过去用 M.a 或 μa，$1\mu A = 10^{-6} A$）

micro-analytical reagent 微量分析试剂（简称 mar）

micro-assembly 微型组件

microbabbit main bearing 细晶粒巴氏合金曲轴主轴瓦

microbar 微巴（压力单位，代号 μb 或 μbar，$1\mu b = 10^{-6} bar = 1 dyn/cm^2$）

microbial corrosion 微生物腐蚀

microbiological deterioration 微生物引起的变质

micro-bus 微型客车（载客 10 余人的小型客车，= minibus）

microcar 微型汽车

microcell 微电池，微电池对

micro chip ①微硅片②微型集成电路片，微型芯片

microcircuit 微电路［具有高密度等效电路元件和（或）部件，亦可作为独立件的微电子器件，可以是微型组件或集成微电路］

micro computer 微型电子计算机［简称微机（micom），由中央处理器（CPU）、输入/输出（1/0）接口和存储器（memory）三个功能单元组成，一般做在一块或数块大规模集成电路（LSI）板（芯片）上。在汽车上用作控制发动机、传动系、制动、转向悬架、空调等的车载计算机，称为 electronic control module 电子控制模块，见 ECM］

microcomputer controlled engine 微型电子计算机控制式发动机［指由车载式微型电子计算机，在汽车上称动力系控制模块（powertrain control module）对空燃比、点火正时、喷油时刻、排气净化等进行综合控制的发动机］

micro computer control system 微型计算机控制系统

Microcomputer Preset Driving Position System 微机预置驾驶位置系统（将驾驶者要求的与乘坐和驾驶操作有关的位置信息，如座椅位置、转向盘位置、安全带长度、后视镜位置等输入微机，只要该驾驶员坐上座位，上述输入的要求便可自动实现的系统）

micro controller 微控制器（亦写作 microcontroller，指控制用的单片微型计算机）

microcontroller-based electronic control module 以微控制器为基础的电子控制模块

microcracked chromium 带微裂纹的镀铬层

microcrystalline wax 显微结晶蜡

micro electronics 微电子学，微电子技术

microencapsulated powder 粉粒包覆黏结铁粉（见 microencapsulation）

microencapsulation 铁粉微粒包覆黏合技术（使用聚合物黏结剂将铁粉微粒包覆并黏结压制成型。在汽车上的用例有代替常规的点火线圈层叠铁芯的微粒黏合铁粉成型铁芯，这种铁粉铁芯的饱和磁通密度要比常规的层叠钢片铁芯低 10%）

microfarad 微法（拉）（电容的常用单位，等于 10^6 法拉，代号 μF，$1\mu F = 10^{-6} F$）

microfiche （记录数据或资料的）小卡片

microfilm 微型胶卷，缩微胶卷（简称 MF）

micro-finished surface 微精加工表面

microflaw 显微裂纹，发裂纹

microgalvanic cell ①微电池，微电池对②微原电池，微自发电池［如蓄电池内的局域电池（local cell）］

micro（gas）turbine （美国 Capston 公司生产的）微型燃气轮机［其结构紧凑，尺寸小巧，各国生产的燃气轮机混合动力大客车（gas turbine hybrid bus）多采用该机作为动力］

micrograph 显微照片，显微传真

microhardness instrument 显微硬度计（用显微镜观测压痕的硬度计，亦称 microhardness tester）

microhardness test 显微硬度试验

microheater 微型加热器，小型加热器

microhenry 微亨利（国际单位制的电感分数单位，代号 μH，1μH = 10^{-6}H，见 henry）

microindicator 测微指示器，指针测微器

micromachine 微型机器（运用产生静电及超导现象的迈斯纳效应微米的机械）

micromachined accelerometer 微加工型加速度计（可直接装在印刷电路板内）

micromachining 微加工（工艺）（指通过化学刻蚀的方法在硅片或其他半导体材料上制造传感器、执行器等器件的加工工艺）

micromechanical valve 微型阀门（见 microvalve）

micrometer ①微米（美写作 micrometre，亦简称 micron，国际单位制的长度分数单位，代号 μm，以往曾用 μ 或 micron 表示微米，1μm = 10^{-6}m = 39.37×10^{-6}in，我国工厂中习惯用的长度单位"丝"或"道"，1 丝 = 1 道 = 0.01mm = 10μm）②千分尺，测微计（测量外径、内径、厚度等尺寸的精密仪具，一般测量精度为 1/100mm）

micrometer calipers 千分卡尺，千分卡规，千分测径规；螺旋测径器

micrometer depth gage 深度千分尺，深度千分卡规

micrometer dial 千分刻度盘，微米刻度盘，测微表

micrometer gage 测微规

micrometer screw calipers 测微螺纹卡尺

micrometer with dial gauge 带表千分尺

micrometer with vernier 游标千分尺

micrometric timing adjuster 正时微调装置

micromicro- 微微（词头，一般用 μμ 作为代号，1μμ = 10^{-12}，见 pico-）

micromicrofarad 微微法拉（为电容的常用单位，代号为 μμF。现国际单位制用 picofarad 代替 micromicrofarad，同时代号用 pF 代替 μμF）

micromodule 超小型器件，微型组件（简称 MM）

micron ①微米，见 micrometer②百万分之一（10^{-6}）③微子（直径为 0.2~10μm 的胶状微分子）

micronic filter 微米级滤清器（指可滤除微米级微粒的精滤器）

micron micrometer 千分尺，微分表

micron order 精密级，微米级

microphenomenon 微观现象

microphone ①（扩音器等的）话筒 ②（声级计等的）测声头（指将声波变换为等价电波信号输出声-电变换装置）

microphysical property 微物理（学）特性

micropoise 微泊（流体黏度单位，常用于气体，代号 μp 为 10^{-6}p。20℃时的空气黏度为 181μp，见 poise）

microporous chromium 多孔镀铬层

microporous plastics 微孔塑料，细

泡沫塑料

microporous rubber 多孔性橡皮（简称 mipor）

microprocessed automatic air conditioner （车用）微处理器控制自动空调系统

micro processor 微处理器［在汽车电子控制系统中，作为微型电子计算机的中央处理器（CPU），由算术逻辑运算器（ALU）、累加器（AC）和控制器（controller）等组成，此外还包括一组寄存器（register）。中央处理器是整个控制系统的核心，它通过接口（interface）接收多种传感元件的信息，对控制所需要的各种参数进行处理、运算和逻辑判断，向各种受控设备发出指令］

microprocessor chip 微处理器芯片

microprocessor controlled car 微机控制轿车（一般指微机控制点火、喷油、变速的轿车）

microprocessor controlled clutch 微处理器控制式离合器

microprocessor control system 微处理器控制系统（微机控制系统）

microprocessor control unit （福特公司的）微处理器控制系统（简称 MCU，商品名，由电子控制模块控制发动机混合比、点火时刻等）

microprocessor spark timing system 微处理机控制点火正时系统（简称 MSTS，见 mapped ignition system）

microscope ①显微镜 ②微观（= mike②）

microscope camera 显微照相机

microscopic asperity 微观平面度，显微粗糙度

microscopic test ①金相试验 ②显微试验，显微镜分析

micro seal 微隙密封件（防以微米计的微小间隙渗漏气体或液体的密封件）

microsecond 微秒（代号 μs，$1\mu s = 10^{-6} s$）

microsize grade 微粒级（一般指直径 $1 \sim 10 \mu m$ 的粒子）

microstrain 微观应变（与金属原子间距可相比的任何标距上的应变）

microstructure 微观组织，显微结构，显微组织

micro swirl 微涡流（指运动范围和尺寸小均微小的涡流）

micro (-) switch 微动开关，微型开关

microtechnic 精密技术

microvalve 微型阀（micromecha-nical valve 的简称，指用化学刻蚀等半导体器件工艺和半导体材料制作的电子电路器件使用的微型阀门器件）

microvan 微型客车（可乘坐6人）

microwatt 微瓦（代号 $\mu W = 10^{-6}$ watt，参见 watt）

microwave 微波（波长在 1mm 和 30cm 之间，频率为 0.3×10^{12} 到 $10^9 MHz$ 的电磁波）

microwave band 微波波段

microwave doppler speed sensor 微波多普勒效应速度传感器

microwave heating 微波加热（一般频率限制在 $900 \sim 2450MHz$，以防产生无线电波干扰）

microwave integrated circuit 微波集成电路（指在微波频段工作的集成电路，简称 MWIC）

microwave oven 微波炉

microwave propagation 微波传播

microwave radar 微波雷达传感器（如：测定汽车前、后方车辆、障碍物及路况的微波雷达发射和接收系统）

micro-wave radar 微波雷达

microwave sensor 微波传感器（利用微波雷达测距、测速及视线死区的传感器件的通称）

microwave switching tubes 微波开

关管

micro-wave type inter-vehicle distance warning device 微波（雷达）型车间距离警报器

MICS （日本）三菱（公司的）智能驾驶座系统（商品名，该系统不仅可调整座椅本身位置，而且在调好位置后，有关附件如后视镜等可随之自动调到与之相适应的最佳方位，Mitsubishi Intelligent Cockpit System 的简称）

mid 中间（的），中央（的），中部（的）

mid and dual-temperature switches 中温和双温度开关（福特公司 MCU 系统中由"中温度开关"和"低-高双温度开关"两个开关组成的发动机冷却水温传感开关。双温开关在 13℃时接通，113℃时断开，中温开度在 53℃时接通。当这两个开关都未接通时，电子控制单元判断：水温低于 13℃，当中温开关断开而双温开关接通时，表明水温在 13～53℃之间；当中温开关与双温开关均接通时，表明水温在 53～113℃之间；当中温开关接通而双温开关断开时，表明水温超过 113℃）

midband frequency 中波频率

mid beam （汽车前照灯中的）中光灯，中光

midbed （带二次空气喷射的双床式三效催化转化器的前还原催化床与后氧化催化床之间的）中间床［亦称 mixing chamber（混合室），二次空气喷入该室中，与前还原床流出的废气混合，增加其氧含量，再进入后氧化床进行氧化反应］

mid-boiling point （燃油等的）中馏温度（中馏分沸点，燃油等馏出 50% 时的温度）

mid-carbon steel 中碳钢（指含碳量在 0.30%～0.60% 之间的优质钢）

mid-continent crude ［美］中部原油

middle ①中间，中部，当中 ②中间物，媒介质；中等物品 ③正中的，中级的，中等的，中央的，中间的 ④放在正中位置，处于中心位置

middle axle differential case 中（间）桥差速器壳

middle bearing 中间轴承

middle circle of toroid 圆环面的中性圆（圆环面的母圆圆心绕轴线做旋转运动时，在中间平面上的轨迹，见 toroid）

middle cone （锥齿轮的）中间锥面，中锥（其母线通过齿宽中点，并与分锥垂直相交的假想锥面）

middle distillate 中间馏分（石油蒸馏时，沸点较汽油高、较久沸残油低的馏分，一般指煤油、粗柴油等，常作为商品柴油的原料）

middle-eastern crude 中东原油

middle floor cross member （承载式车身）底板（加强）横梁

middle-grade car 中档轿车

middle lane 中间车道（如六车道的道路中，路中线车道与路边车道之间的车道）

mid (dle) percent curves 50% 曲线

middle plane 中面，中间平面（= mid plane）

middle point 中点

middle position 中间位置

middle scale integrated circuit 中规模集成电路（指由 100～1000 个左右的元件集装在一片晶片上的集成电路，简称 MSI）

middle standing pillar （轿车车身侧壁）中柱（中间立柱，亦称 center pillar, B-pillar）

mid-engine ①发动机中置式轿车（发动机位于客舱中部或后部的轿车）②发动机中置式客车或货车（发动机位于前、后桥之间，车身底板下面）

mid engine (north-south) 发动机

纵向（北-南方向）中置
mid-engine racing car （发动机位于前、后桥之间的）中置发动机赛车
mid-front powertrain layout （汽车）动力系统的中前位布置（指发动机位于前桥后方的布置形式）
mid-gear ①中间挡，中挡②中间齿轮，中（央）齿轮（如主减速器中的驱动小齿轮，亦称 middle gear）
midget car 微型轿车（= lilliput car, minicar, minibody car, cycle car）
midget condenser 微型电容器（简称 MC）
midget truck 微型货车
mid-mounted power take-off 前后桥中间部位的功率输出轴（轴间功率输出轴）
mid plane of toroid 圆环面的中间平面（圆环面的对称平面，它包含中性圈，并与轴线相交）
mid-point 中点
mid range ①中馏分（燃油）②中列数③（变速器的）中间挡位，低挡与高挡间的中间挡区
mid-range lateral acceleration handling maneuver （汽车的）中等横向加速转向运动（指离心加速度在 0.3～0.5g 范围内的避开障碍物等的转向运动，见 handling maneuver）
mid-range speed ①中间速度②中间挡
mid-range torque （发动机）中速转矩（指发动机以中速运转时的转矩）
mid section 中间截面，中部剖视
midship engine （安装在驾驶员座后，后桥前的）中置式发动机（亦称 mid-ships engine，= central engine）
midship engine rear drive type 发动机中置后轮驱动型
midship engine vehicle 发动机中置式汽车（发动机装在驾驶座后，后桥前，多见于跑车）
midship-mounted under floor engine 安装在前、后桥间车厢地板下面的发动机
midship mounting 中间支座，中间支撑，中间支架（如：传动轴的中央支撑）
mid-side wall 胎侧中部（确定轮胎的最大宽度）
mid-size car （美国轿车分类中的）中型轿车（指 compact car 与 full-size car 之间的各种轿车，但对欧洲等美国以外的国家，实际上指如 Audi 100/200、BMW 7 系列、Mazda 626、Mercury cougar、Pontiac 600、Volvo 740/940 等大型轿车）
mid-size truck 中型货车（最大车辆总重：8t）
mid-value 中值
midway deflection 中点挠度（如：调整风扇传动带等的紧度时，用规定大小的力按压两皮带盘间皮带的中点，该点的下垂距离）
MIG 金属惰性气体保护电弧焊（welding metal inert gas arc welding 的简称）
mighty vac （发动机检测用）手动真空泵（一般带有真空表，可确认其真空负压值）
migration ①移动，徙动，迁移，流动②移位，进位③（电泳涂装中，漆料微粒的）吸附（于车身）
migratory stain 接触污染（移附污染，如橡皮与有机涂料相接触时的污染，涂料移附于橡皮上）
MIG welding 金属焊丝惰性气体保护焊（metal inertia gas welding 的简称）
mike ①扩音器（microphone 的简称）②显微镜（microscope）③千分表（= micrometer）④测微（见 miking）

miking 测微(用千分卡规等测微量具测量)

mil ①角密耳(angular mil) ②(英里)里程(mileage) ③军事的,军队(military) ④百万(million) ⑤毫弧度(milliradian) ⑥密耳(英制长度单位,1mil = 1/1000英寸) ⑦毫升(volume mil)

MIL (装在汽车仪表板上的)故障指示灯(malfunction indicator light 的简称,按美国加州大气资源局的规定,凡1994年以后生产的轿车、轻型货车和中型车辆,仪表板上必须安装可以自动警告汽车动力系统任一部件影响排放的故障的指示灯)

milamine panel 密胺塑料板,三聚氰酰胺塑胶板(用做客车车身内侧壁衬覆材料等)

MI lamp 故障指示灯(见 MI)

mild-duty 轻型的,轻载的,轻负荷的,在轻载、轻负荷条件下运转的

mildew-resistant paint 防霉漆

mild steel 软钢,低碳钢(简称 MS,为含碳约 0.1% ~ 0.25% 的热轧钢的统称,但这一术语现在已不大使用,而多用具体的名称或标号表示具体的钢种)

mild steel pin (火花塞的)软钢芯杆(连接火花塞外端高压线接线螺母和内芯气密封剂或密封件的导电芯杆,亦称接线螺杆)

mile 英里(= statute mile, 1mile = 1.6093km = 1760yards = 0.8695nautical mile = 3.2187市里 = 4828市尺。按英美陆程长度递进表, 1mile = 880fathoms = 1760yards = 5280feet = 5280 × 12inches)

mile² 平方英里(英制面积单位, 1平方英里 = 2.59平方千米 = 295.01公顷 = 640英亩 = 3885.63市亩)

mileage ①英里里程数②汽车的英里行程数(指汽车已行驶的总英里数)③按里程计算的运费④汽车消耗一加仑燃油所行驶的平均英里里程(单位:英里/加仑)

mileage accumulation dynamometer 计程式(底盘)测功机(汽车驶上试验台后,测功机可自动累计汽车车轮在转鼓上的转数和转速及其里程,简称 MAD)

mileage between overhauls (汽车)大修间隔里程(英里)

mileage bogey 车辆试验规定的标准行车英里数

mileage chart (以英里计)行车里程图

mileage clerk 汽车(英里)里程统计员,汽车(英里)里程登记员

mileage-controlled lubrication 由车辆行驶(英里)里程控制的自动润滑

mileage counter (英里)里程表(= mileage recorder、mileage indicator、odometer)

mileage influence on …行驶里程对…的影响

mileage inspection 行驶一定(英里)里程后的检查

mileage life 以(英里)里程计的寿命

Mileage Marathon (壳牌石油研究从1939年开始定期举办的)长途行车节油竞赛

mileage tester (英里)里程油耗计[汽车燃料经济性测试装置,测定汽车消耗 1gal 或 1L 燃油,所行驶的(英里)里程数]

mileage/ticket price table (英里)里程票价表

mile/h 英里/小时(英制速度单位, 1mile/h = 88ft/min = 1.467ft/s = 0.869knot = 0.447m/s = 1.609km/h = 3.218市里/h)

mile meter (用英里计数的)里程表,里数计(亦写作 mileometer,

美称 odometer)

mile per gallon 英里/加仑（汽车油耗英制单位，简称 MPG，参见 miles per gallon)

milepost （英里）里程碑，里程标

miles per gallon （汽车燃料经济性的一种英美单位）每加仑燃油所行英里数（简称 MPG)

miles-per-gallon meter 加仑里程计（测定每加仑燃油所行驶的英里里程)

miles per hour 每小时英里数（车速单位，简称 mph)

24000 miles test 24000 英里路试（汽车的一种标准路试)

miles to empty 用空里程（指到汽车燃油箱存的油量用空所能行驶的英里里程)

milestone ①（公路上的）里程标，（英里）里程碑②（历史上的）重大事件

military ①军事的，军用的，陆军的，陆战的（简称 mil）②军队，陆军

military amphibian 军用水陆两栖汽车

military automobile road 军用公路（= military highway)

military characteristics 军事特性

military-designed vehicle 军用车辆（= military vehicle)

military fighting vehicle 军用战斗车辆，战车

military land transportation 陆上军运

military lubricant 军用润滑剂

military motor transport 军用机动车辆运输

military motor vehicle 军用机动车辆

military ratings (of oil) ［美］（机油的）军用分类

military relays （极端恶劣环境使用的）军用继电器

military specifications 军用规范（简称 MS)

military standard (s) 军用标准（简称 MS)

military utility tactical truck 军用轻型战术车（0.25~2t 级)

milk tanker 奶罐车（装备有卫生防腐蚀的奶罐、保温装置和吸排管路系统，用于运输牛奶，亦称 milk tank vehicle)

milky surface 乳白镀层（电镀时电流密度过低或镀液浓度过高而形成的无光泽镀层)

mill ①碾压，碾磨②铣，铣削③铣刀（= milling cutter）④铣床（= milling machine)

mill board （汽缸垫金属片之间的）石棉板

milled head 滚花头（美称 knurled head)

milled helicoid worm 锥面包络圆柱蜗杆（亦称 ZK-worm，指齿面为锥面的包络曲面的圆柱蜗杆)

milled nut 周缘滚花螺母

milled screw 滚花头螺钉

Miller cycle 米勒循环（R. H. Miller 提出的一种有效压缩比小于膨胀比的循环，可提高热效率，减少废气排放，动力性高，油耗低)

Miller cycle gasoline engine 米勒循环汽油机（日本马兹达公司于 20 世纪 90 年代研制的采用进气增压和加大进气冲程的凸轮工作角等方法实现米勒循环的汽油机)

milli 毫（词头，代号 m, 10^{-3}），千分之一

milliampere 毫安培，毫安（国际单位制的电流分数单位，代号 mA，$1 mA = 10^{-3} A$，见 ampere)

milliampere meter 毫安表

milliard 十万万，十亿（= 10^9)

milliarium ［英］距离单位（= 1.48 千米 = 0.92 英里)

millibar 毫巴（压力单位，代号 mbar 或 mb，$1\text{mb} = 10^{-3}\text{bar} = 10^2\text{N/m}^2 = 10^3\text{dyn/cm}^2$。常用于气压量测）

millibar-barometer 毫巴气压表

millicron 毫微米（10^{-9} 米）

millidegree 毫度（$=10^{-3}$ 度）

millier ［法］千千克，公吨

millifarad 毫法拉（国际单位制的电容分数单位，代号 mF，$1\text{mF}=10^{-3}\text{F}$，参见 farad）

milligal 毫伽（$=10^{-3}$ 伽，重力加速度单位，参见 galileo）

milligamma 毫微克（$=10^{-9}\text{g}$）

milligram（me）毫克，公丝（$=10^{-3}\text{g}$，代号 mg）

millihenry 毫亨利（国际单位制的电感分数单位，代号 mH，$1\text{mH}=10^{-3}\text{H}$，参见 henry）

millilambert 毫朗伯（亮度单位 = 1/1000 朗伯）

millilitre 毫升（容积单位，代号 ml，或 mL，等于 cm^3，$1\text{mL}=1/1000\text{litre}=0.027$ 立方市寸 $=0.061\text{in}^3$，美写作 milliliter）

millimeter 毫米（1/1000 米，代号 mm，亦写作 millimetre）

milli（meter）-wave radar 毫米波雷达［多用汽车各种安全系统的前、后及左、右两侧移动或固定障碍物的探测雷达，近年来除了上、下、左、右平面方向的二维毫米波探测雷达外，又出现了还可探测上、下方向的 77 GHz 波段三维毫米波扫描探测雷达（three-dimensional milli（meter）-wave scan radar）］

millimetric 毫米的

millimicron 毫微米（10^{-9} 米，代号 mμ）

millinewton 毫牛顿（国际单位制的力的分数单位，代号 mN，$1\text{mN}=10^{-3}\text{N}$）

milling ①铣，铣削，铣削加工②铣的，铣削的，铣削加工用的

milliohm 毫欧姆（国际单位制的电阻分数单位，代号 mΩ，$1\text{m}\Omega=10^{-3}\Omega$，参见 ohm）

million ①兆，百万（$=10^6$，简称 mil）②大众，群众③百万的④大众的

milliradian 毫弧度（平面角单位，代号 mrad，$1\text{mrad}=10^{-3}\text{rad}$，简称 mil）

millisecond 毫秒（国际单位制的时间分数单位，代号 ms，$1\text{ms}=10^{-3}\text{s}$）

millivolt 毫伏（国际单位制的电压分数单位，代号 mV，$1\text{mV}=10^{-3}\text{V}$，见 volt）

millivoltmeter pyrometer 毫伏计式高温计

millivolt test 毫伏电压（降）试验

milliwatt 毫瓦（国际单位制的功率分数单位，代号 mW，$1\text{mW}=10^{-3}\text{W}$）

mill-type cylinder 大型油缸

Milner's Theory 米尔勒理论（根据概率统计预测在变应力状态下工作的零、部件的概率寿命的理论）

mimetic 模仿的，拟态的

MIMO 多输入多输出的（multi-input, multi-output 的简称）

min ①最小的（minimum）②较小的，次要的（minor）③分钟（minute）

MIN （车辆）型号识别码（vehicle model identification number 的简称）

min chamber volume （转子发动机的）最小工作室容积（见 chamber volume）

mine-haul truck 矿石运输车

mineral ①矿物，矿质，无机物②含矿物质的，无机的

mineral binder bond 无机黏结剂

mineral black 石墨

mineral compound 无机化合物

mineral oil 矿物油

mineral solid lubricant grease 固体矿质润滑脂

mine truck 矿用货车

Mini ①（英国 Sir Alec Issigonis 于 1959 年设计的一种前轮驱动的著名）微型轿车 ②（以后泛指各种类似的前轮驱动轿车、乘员不超过 4 人的）微型轿车（亦写作 mini，又 minicar）③小型的，小规模的，缩小的

miniature ①缩影，（缩小的）模型，微型 ②小型的，缩小的，小规模的，微小的，袖珍的 ③使小型化，用缩图表示

miniature bearing 微型轴承（外径小于 9mm）

miniature bore cylinder 小缸径油缸，小缸径汽缸

miniature bulb ①小电灯泡（电珠，= miniature lamp）②小球

miniature gears 微型齿轮（的统称，包括三大类：①小功率齿轮，英国指用于 750W 以内者 ②仪表齿轮，亦称精密齿轮 ③时钟齿轮，计时齿轮）

miniaturised circuit element 微型电路元件

miniaturization 小型化，微型化

miniaturized data acquisition unit 小型数据采集系统（简称 Mindau）

mini body car 微型轿车（= mini car）

mini-bus 小型客车（一般指载客 12～20 人或长度小于或等于 3.5m 的小型客车）

Minicar 小型轿车（简称 mini，一般指发动机排量小于或等于 1L，乘员不超过 4 人的前轮驱动轿车）

mini catalytic converter （装在排气管内的）微型催化转化器（见 header③）

minicomputer 微型电子计算机（简称微机）

miniframe （汽车车身或车架上附加的）小支撑架，小安装架（如：某些车辆车身上的隔声、隔振型可拆式悬架支撑架，见 suspension sub-frame）

Minilite 镁合金车轮（原为 Derek Power 为微型汽车设计的镁合金车轮的产品名，现泛指各种镁合金车轮）

min. illumination 最小光照度

mini lube （汽车用）小型滑脂加注器

minim ①量滴，咪[英制最小容积单位，英国咪较美国咪略小，1 英国咪 = 1/76800UK gallon = 0.003612in³ = 0.960754 美国咪；1 美国咪（液）= 1/61440US gallon = 0.003759in³ = 0.0616mL，见 imperial gallon，liquid gallon]②微小；一滴，一点，一笔

minimum ①极小；最小值，最小限度，最低点，极小量，极小值 ②最低的，最小的，最少的

minimum advance for best torque 最大转矩最小点火提前角（汽油机调整点火提前角的正确原则，即将汽油机调到能输出最大转矩时的最小点火提前角，简称 MBT 或 MABT）

minimum authority 最低规定值，最低允许值（如：通用公司 CCC 系统怠速控制电动机，当节气门杆位于怠速止动螺钉止动的位置时，其主量孔量杆所限制的最低转速）

minimum clearance 最小间隙

minimum cylinder volume 汽缸的最小容积（指压缩冲程活塞到达上止点瞬间的汽缸容积，见 compression volume）

minimum design weight 最小设计重量（最小设计质量的旧称）

minimum detection limits 最小检测范围（简称 MDL）

minimum detection value 最小检测值（简称 MDV）

minimum diameter of thread 螺纹最小直径

minimum dual spacing （并装双胎）两胎中心线间的最小距离

minimum ground clearance of rear axle 后桥最小离地间隙

minimum horse power 最小马力

minimum interference ①最小公盈 ②最小干涉

minimum-jolt zone （汽车前后车桥间的）最小颠簸区

minimum movable space 最小活动空间（轿车车身内驾驶员和乘客所需占用的最小空间）

minimum negotiable radius （车辆能通过的）最小弯道半径

minimum non-passing sight distance 最短停车视距（从驾驶员看到道路前方10cm高的障碍物的瞬间起到使车辆停止所行驶的距离，= stopping、sight distance）

minimum oil film thickness 最小油膜厚度（简称 MOFT）

minimum operating speed 最低工作转速（如：在规定条件下，点火系统正常工作的发动机最低转速）

minimum performance criterion for brake system 制动系统最低性能标准

minimum phase shift network 最小相移网络

minimum problem 极小（值）问题

minimum road clearance （汽车车身的）最小离地间隙（亦称 minimum ground clearance 或 ground clearance，指车辆中间区域的最低点至地面的距离）

minimum scale value （仪器仪表的）标度始点值（标度始点标记所对应的被测量值）

minimum size 最小尺寸，下限尺寸

minimum spark advance for specified torque （能达到）额定转矩的最小点火提前角（简称 MST）

minimum spark ignition energy 火花点火（所必需的）最低能量

minimum specific fuel consumption （内燃机）最低燃油消耗率

minimum speed 最低速度

minimum speed in gears 各挡位下的最低车速

minimum steady running speed 最低稳定工作转速（发动机在全负荷工作时能稳定运转的最低转速）

minimum transient speed （带有调速器的内燃机的）最低瞬时转速（指其运转时，突加负荷，瞬时所达到的最低转速）

minimum turning clearance inner radius 车身内侧最小转弯半径（汽车以最大转向角转弯时，车身最内侧部位的回转轨迹半径）

minimum turning clearance outer radius 车身外侧最小转弯半径（汽车以最大转向角转弯时，车身最外侧部位的回转轨迹半径）

minimum turning diameter （汽车的）最小转弯直径（指汽车外侧前轮的最小转弯直径）

minimum turning diameter between walls （汽车的）壁间最小转弯直径（指汽车车身轮廓最外点的最小转弯直径）

minimum turning diameter test 最小转弯直径试验（保持转向盘转角在最大位置并以极低车速行驶，测定汽车最小转弯直径的试验）

minimum turning inner radius 内侧轮胎最小转弯半径（汽车以最大转向角转向时，最内侧轮胎接地面中心轨迹的半径）

minimum turning path 最小转弯轨迹（车辆以最大转向角度转弯时，车辆某定点的轨迹）

minimum turning radius 最小转弯半径（车辆以最大转向角转弯时，外

侧前轮轨迹的最小半径)

mining vehicle 矿用车辆

mini pickup 小型客货两用车,小型皮卡(特指载重质量半吨上下,带敞式货槽和轿车式驾驶室、外形尺寸、质量、性能、燃油经济性等均与小型轿车相仿的客货两用车)

mini-rotary viscometer 微型旋转式黏度计(1979年美国ATMA提出,用来测定多级机油泵送特性的仪器)

mini-SAE conference [美]小型汽车工程师学会会议

mini spare wheel 缩小尺寸备用车轮,缩小尺寸备胎

Ministry of Education [美]教育部(简称MOE)

Ministry of Transport ①[日]运输省(运输部) ②[英]运输部(简称MOT)

mini-truck 微型货车(中国规定,其厂定最大总质量小于或等于1.8t的货车)

minium control speed 最低控制速度(①指所控制的最低速度 ②指控制系统不再起作用的速度低限,如:汽车低于某速度时,防抱死系统不再起作用,该速度称防抱死的最低控制速度)

minium delivery per cycle per cylinder 最小循环喷油量(一个循环中,喷入发动机每一个汽缸中可保证发动机稳定运转的最小油量)

minium(ite) ①红铅(粉),红丹,铅丹(四氧化三铅 Pb_3O_4) ②朱色

mini van 小型厢式客车;轻型客车(=[英]people carrier)

mini watt 微小功率

minlon 矿物纤维强化聚酰胺,矿物纤维强化尼龙(在汽车上用做合金车轮的轮辋装饰等)

min-max governor 两极调节器,两极调速器

minor adjustment 小调整

minor air cell ①(涡流室式柴油机的)涡流室 ②小空气室

minor axis (of an ellipse) (椭圆的)短轴,短轴线

minor axis of cam 凸轮短轴(凸轮最小的径向尺寸)

minor axis of epitrochoid 外摆线的短轴(见 minor diameter of epitrochoid)

minor diameter ①螺纹内径 ②椭圆形的短径

minor diameter of epitrochoid 外摆线短轴(径) $[=2(R-e)]$,式中:R—基圆半径与滚动圆半径之和;e—创成点至滚动圆中心的距离。= minor axis of epitrochoid,参见 epitrochoid]

minor diameter of thread 螺纹内径(= root diameter of thread)

minor engine overhaul 发动机中修(更换发动机汽缸-活塞组的零件)

minor engine repair 发动机小修

minor failure 小故障(指汽车在运行过程中能及时排除并不影响总成完成基本功能的故障)

minor filament (双灯丝前照灯中的)近光灯丝

minor highway 次要公路,辅助道路,支路(= minor road, subsidiary road)

minor injury 轻伤

minority carrier 少数载流子(如:N-型半导体中的空穴,P-型半导体中的电子)

minor repair (汽车)小修(用更换或修理个别零、部件的方法,恢复汽车工作能力的运行性修理,= current repair,参见 major repair)

minor semi-axis 短半轴

minor thrust face (活塞裙部承受)最小侧压力的支撑面

minor tune-up ①小调试,部分调试

②（为提高发动机等的性能而进行的）小改革，小改造，部分改造，部分改革

mint ①巨大，巨额，大宗②崭新的，新造的，完好的，完美的③创造，新造，造出

minus ①负，负数，负量；负号（-）②减的；负的，阴的（= negative）③减去；失去，少掉

minus back-pressure EGR (control) valve 负背压排气再循环（控制）阀（发动机高速运转时，排气脉冲负压降低，使得膜片室与大气相通的控制阀孔关闭，于是只要有真空供给膜片室，EGR阀便相应开启）

minus camber ①（车轮）内倾，负外倾②负外倾角（偶见于独立悬架前轮）

minus caster 主销负后倾，主销前倾（= negative caster）（指从侧面观察，转向主销向前倾斜，多见于使用扁平低压轮胎的轿车。高速行驶时，由于胎面变形，使轮胎接地面中心逐渐向后移动而使轮胎后倾距增加，相当于主销后倾加大，主销后倾过多，不仅造成转动转向盘所需的转矩增加，转向操作困难，而且会导致前轮摆振。为了抵消上述现象，高速轿车常使主销前倾，即负后倾一定角度）

minus earth 负极搭铁，负极接地

minus effect 不良效果，副作用，反效果

minus head differential 负水头差（评价燃油泵性能时，表示从油箱至油泵的高度）

minus ion generator 负离子发生器

minus lap （进、排气门）重叠关闭（指排气门关闭至进气门开启之间，进、排气门同时关闭期，用曲轴转角表示，亦称进、排气门重叠，相对于进、排气门重叠开放而言，见 pluslap）

minus load control （底盘测功机的）减载控制（测试时，逐渐减少功率吸收装置的加载量）

minus plate 负极板，阴极板

minus projections 极微小突出部分

minus screw ①左旋螺纹［= minus thread, lefthand (ed) thread］②一字槽头螺钉

minute ①分（时间单位，1小时的六十分之一，简称 min）②分（角度单位，1度的六十分之一）

minute bonder （制动蹄摩擦片）快速黏接器

minute crack 微细裂缝

minute irregularities 微小不平整处

minuteness 精密，精确，微小，详细

15-minute rated power 15min 功率（在标准环境条件下，发动机能运转15min的最大功率）

MIP ①平均指示压力（mean indicated pressure）②方法改进程序（methods improvement program）③最小冲击脉冲（minimum impulse pulse）

mipor 微孔橡皮（micro-porous rubber 的简称）

MIPs 百万指令每秒（汽车电子控制系统每秒钟执行指令的百万单位，millions of instructions per second 的简称，亦写作：MIPS）

MIRA ［英］汽车工业研究协会（Motor Industry Research Association）

mirror 镜，反光镜；（汽车上一般指）后视镜

mirror bracket 镜架

mirror face 镜面（亦称 mirror surface）

mirror field of view 后视镜视野（驾驶员坐在驾驶座位上，从后视镜中观察到的范围）

mirror light 后视镜（照明）灯

mirror-like finish 镜面抛光（= mirror finish, highmirror finish, mirror polish)

mirror placement （后视）镜的布置

mirror reflectivity characteristics 后视镜反射特性

MIS ①（汽车）维护指示系统（maintenance indicating system）②管理信息系统（management information system）

misadjustment 失调（不准确的调整，错误的调节，该调而未实施的调节）

misadministration 管理不当

misaligned 不对准（直线）的，不同轴线的，不同心度的，失调的

misaligned wheels 前轮定位失调的（车辆外倾、前束等调整不当）

misalignment ①失调，不同心，不同轴线，（车轮）定位不当②（因碰撞等事故造成的各种类型的）车架损坏，车架歪斜（的统称）③不对正，错开，不在一条直线上

misapplication 误用，错用，不正确应用，使用不正确

MISAR 迈塞（汽车发动机的微处理机控制传感和自动调节系统，美Delco Remy公司研制和生产的Microprocessed Sensing and Automatic Regulation的简称）

miscellaneous ①各种各样的，混杂的，多方面的，杂项的②其他

miscellaneous charges for passenger transportation 旅客运输杂费

misdetection 误测，误检，误侦查

misfire （发动机）缺火（失火，混合气点火后不燃烧或火花塞不跳火，亦写作 miss fire，简称 miss）

misfire cycles （发动机的）缺火循环数

misfire limit 缺火极限（指不能点燃着火的燃料-空气混合比。混合气过稀不能着火的混合比称为 lean limit，混合气过浓不能着火的混合比称为 rich limit）

misfit ①配合不良，错配②不相配合的零件，错配件

mishap 损坏，破损，破坏，折断，断裂（= break down, breaking down）

mismatch 失配（配合不当，不匹配，零件错配）②失谐，不重合，未对准

mis-operation 误操作（误动作）

misplacement 错位

miss ①遗漏，漏失，错过②失火，缺火（= misfire）

miss detector （发动机汽缸）缺火传感器（测出汽缸内混合气未着火的传感元件，misfire detector 的简称）

missed gear （汽车）换挡不当

missile-component trailer 运火箭（导弹）的挂车（= missile transporter trailer）

missile launching vehicle 火箭（导弹）导弹发射车

missile maintenance van 厢式火箭维修服务车，导弹维护工程车

missile transporting truck 火箭运输车

mission ①（汽车的）变速器（transmission 的简称）②任务，使命

mission computer 自动变速器变速控制计算机

mission housing 变速器壳

miss starting-acceleration inhibiting system 误起步加速抑制系统（简称 MSAI，车辆以低于 10 km/h 的车速行驶或起步时，若驾驶者在未发现前方有障碍物的情况下，加速踏板踩踏量超过规定值，该系统将发出警报并自动限制发动机输出功率，以抑制急速起步或急加速）

mist action [美] 风窗玻璃刮水器（按预定的间隔，一般为 2 ~ 40s 的）间断刮拭（因这类刮拭模式多

用于小雨、雪、雾天或风窗玻璃被其他车辆溅污，故名，=［英］intermittent wiper control）

μ mist fuel injection system （喷出的油雾粒径可小到5μm的）微细燃油（油雾）喷射系统

mist separator 湿气分离器，油雾分离装置

mist spray 喷雾

misuse failures 误用故障（使用错误造成的损坏，因滥用而产生故障）

MIT （美国）麻省理工学院（Massachusetts Institute of Technology 的简称）

miter angle 45°角，斜角

miter gear ①等径锥齿轮，等径直角相交锥齿轮②等径直角相交锥齿轮传动（传动比=1:1，亦写作 mitre gear，见 miter wheel）

miter joint ①斜接口，斜接头，斜（面）接合，斜角连接②（活塞环）斜切口（= diagonal-cut joint，angle joint）

miter valve 锥形座面阀

miter wheel ①等径锥齿轮，等径直角相交锥齿轮（两轴相交成直角，可互换的一对锥齿轮，亦写作 mitre wheel，= miter gear，wheel miter）②锥齿轮（= bevel gear）

MITI ［日］通产省（国际贸易和工业部，The Ministry of International Trade and Industry 的简称）

mitre ①成45°角斜接，斜接面，斜接规；斜榫，斜接缝；45°角；45°接合，45°角接口②斜接，成45°角接，做成斜的（亦写作 miter）

Mitsubishi Clean Air ［日］三菱汽车排气净化系统（的总称，简称 MCA）

Mitsubishi Colt Car 三菱小马轿车（日本三菱公司的 Colt 1600 型普及型轿车，装用直列4缸 SOHC，16气门，发动机排量1597mL，最高车速179km/h）

Mitsubishi intelligent & innovative valve timing & lift electronic control system 见 MIVEC

Mitsubishi Lancer car 三菱枪骑兵轿车（日本三菱公司轿车，装用直列4缸 DOHC 发动机，排量1834mL，压缩比8.5，最大功率107kW，最大转矩270N·m，最高车速211km/h）

Mitsubishi Mirage VIEV6 Car 三菱海市蜃楼 VIEV6 轿车（日本三菱公司生产的普通型轿车，装用 DOHC 发动机，排量1597mL，最大功率107kW，最大转矩147N·m，最高车速185km/h）

Mitsubishi Motors Corp 三菱汽车公司（创立于1970年，年生产能力约132万辆，由日本三菱重工业股份有限公司与美国克莱斯勒公司合资的汽车制造企业，为日本五大汽车公司之一）

Mitsubishi SBM 三菱汽车公司 SBM 子公司（拉力赛车开发与维修专业工厂，从事拉力赛车设计、材料加工、组装、维修）

MIVEC 三菱智能-创新型气门正时和升程电子控制系统（Mitsubishi intelligent & innovative valve timing & lift electronic control system 的简称）

MIVEC 三菱创新型气门正时与升程自动控制系统（Mitsubishi Innovative Valve Timing and Lift Electronic Control 的简称，利用两种不同凸轮工作角，按发动机工况需要改变气门开闭时刻和升程的自动控制系统）

mixed amplifier 混合放大器（简称 MA）

mixed cycle engine 混合循环发动机（参见 combined-cycle engine）

mixed dielectric capacitor 混合电介质电容器（由塑料薄膜及纸混合制成）

mixed film friction 混合膜摩擦（亦

称 mixed film lubrication 混合膜润滑，指摩擦面间同时存在流体摩擦和边界摩擦的摩擦或润滑状态）

mixed fleet 多种车辆的混合车队

mixed-flow 混流式（的）［指轴流式与径流式二者混合形式的，即流体既沿轴向流动又沿径向流动，如 mixed-flow compressor（混流式空气压缩机）、mixed-flow impeller（混流式涡轮）、mixed-flow pump（混流式泵）等］

mixed flow compressor 混流式压气机

mixed-in-transit 在运输过程中拌和的

mixed lighting 混合照明（一般照明与局部照明组成的照明）

mixed liquid crystal 混合液晶（不同液晶的共溶点混合物）

mixed loading 混装（在同一车内装载不同种类的货物）

mixed potential 混合电位（自发电池电偶在总氧化反应和总还原反应相等时的电位）

mixed signal （数字与模拟信号的）混合信号

mixer ①混合器，混合装置，拌和装置，搅拌机②（汽车上指液化石油气发动机使液化石油气汽化后与空气混合组成混合气，并装有节气门根据发动机的负荷控制该混合气供给量的）混合器（偶指化油器）

mixer-lorry （混凝土）拌和车

mixing chamber 混合室（①化油器及燃气轮机燃烧器中，燃油与空气相混合形成混合气的腔室②双床式三效催化转向器的中间床，二次空气与从前催化床流出的废气的混合室，亦称 midbed）

mixing-cup temperature 混合平均温度（按体积计算的平均温度，= bulk temperature）

mixing device 搅拌装置，混合装置

mixing device of (the) gas producer 煤气发生炉搅动装置

mixing feed 混合供给（如二冲程发动机燃料与润滑油混合吸入方式）

mixing period （发动机）混合气形成期

mixing ratio 混合比（如：混合气燃油与空气的质量比，亦称空燃比）

mixing space 混合空间，混合区，混合腔

mixing value （煤气发动机等的）混合阀（混合煤气与空气）

mixing zone （混合气）混合区

mix truck 水泥混凝土搅拌车（= agitator truck）

mixture ①混合物（指两种或两种以上不同气体、液体或固体粉末、微粒等的混合物，以别于化合物）②（在内燃发动机中特指燃油与空气的）混合气

mixture adjustment 混合气调节

mixture adjust screw 混合气浓度调节螺钉（简称 MAS）

mixture chamber 混合室（= mixing chamber）

mixture composition 混合气组成，混合气成分

mixture-compressing engine 压缩混合气式发动机［指火花点燃式发动机（spark-ignition engine）］

mixture concentration 混合气浓度（混合气中燃油的含量，见 mixture strength）

mixture control knob （一般指装在仪表板上的化油器）阻风门拉钮（= choke knob）

mixture control screw （通过调节燃油通过断面来控制出油量借以调节混合气浓度的）混合气调节螺钉

mixture control solenoid （美国通用公司 CCC 系统中使用的）混合气控制电磁阀（由电子控制模块控制的电磁阀，通过一量杆按一定占空比

改变单位时间内化油器主量孔的通过断面积,借以控制混合气的空燃比,简称 M/C solenoid)

mixture control system ①混合气控制系统(控制与调节混合气供给量及混合比的系统的通称) ②(特指汽油机减速时,防止混合气过浓的)混合气浓度调节器(节气门关闭减速时,利用减速时进气管真空使连接节气门两侧的空气通路开启,将空气引入节气门后方)

mixture control unit (博世 K-Jetronic 机械式低压连续汽油喷射系统的)混合气调节器(简称 MCU,由空气流量传感器及该传感器的气流传感板控制的燃油量分配器组成,可根据吸入汽缸的空气量将组成混合气所需的燃油量分配给各缸的喷油器)

mixture control valve 混合气调节阀,混合气浓度控制阀(简称 MCV,车辆减速时,在进气歧管负压作用下开启,将新鲜空气直接引入节气门后方,以防混合气过浓,HC 排放增加)

mixture cycle (内燃机的)混合循环(由绝热压缩、定容加热、绝热膨胀和定容放热四个过程依次组成的理想循环)

mixture cylinder (配对汽缸发动机的)(浓)混合汽缸(见 paired-cylinder engine)

mixture density ①混合气浓度 ②混合物密度

mixture distribution 混合气(按汽缸的)分配

mixture equivalence 混合气当量比

mixture formation process 混合气形成过程

mixture heater (发动机)混合气预热装置

mixture homogeneity 混合气均匀度

mixture indicator 可燃混合气的成分指示器

mixture lubrication (二冲程汽油机的)混合(气)润滑(将汽油与机油按一定容积的混合,以这种混合油作为燃料,同时起到润滑运动件的作用)

mixture optimum 最佳混合气

mixture preheater valve balancing weight 混合气预热阀配重

mixture ratio ①(混合气的)混合比(混合气中,燃料与空气的质量比,英、美常用 air-fuel ratio 或 fuel-air ratio 来表示,欧洲常用 mixture strength 表示) ②配料比

mixture ratio of fuel to oil (采用混合润滑的二冲程发动机的)燃油-机油混合比(指汽油与机油的容积比)

mixture response curve 混合气响应曲线(表示采用加浓混合气抗爆时输出功率增益与燃料消耗的关系,一般用抗爆后的输出功率与燃料消耗率的曲线说明)

mixture robbery 抢气(多缸发动机因进气歧管布置不当而引起进气流相互干扰,从而降低充气量的现象)

mixture strength 混合气强度(亦称 mixture concentration, 表示实际混合气稀浓程度的一种方法, 简称 MS = $\frac{实际燃油/空气混合比}{理论计算燃油/空气混合比}$, MS = 1 表示实际燃油/空气混合比等于理论燃油/空气混合比, 称为理论混合气强度; MS < 1 表示实际燃油/空气混合比小于理论燃油/空气混合比, 称为稀混合气强度; MS > 1 表示实际燃油/空气混合比大于理论燃油/空气混合比, 称为浓混合气强度, 参见 theoretical fuel-air ratio)

mixture temperature 混合气温度

mixture turbulence 混合气紊流

mixture volume 混合气的体积,混

合气容积

Mizarprinto type flying car （美国加州 AVE 集团 1973 年推出的）飞行汽车（的名称）

MJ ①胶泥接缝（mastic joint）②兆焦耳（megajoule）

MKD 中间级散件组装（medium knocked down 的简称，为介于 SKD 和 CKD 之间的就地组装方式）

m·kgf·s 米·千克力·秒单位制（为米制单位制的一种，常用于工程技术界，基本单位为米·千克力·秒。力是基本单位，而质量是导出单位，1 千克力指 1 千克质量的物体产生 $1g$ 加速度的力，等于重力）

MKSA system 米制单位制，公制单位制，米·千克·秒·安单位制[与 MKS 制同，只增加一个电学基本单位安培（A），我国在 1959 年正式推行，为 metre、kilogramme、second、ampere system 的代号，= metric system]

ML ①（美国石油协会原来的润滑油分类记号），指一般常用工况下工作的汽油机用润滑油 ②机器语言（见 machine language）③材料单位（material list）④极大似然性（maximum likelihood）⑤平均水平（mean level）

ml ①毫朗伯（millilambert）②毫升（millilitre）

MLIT （日）土地、基础设备、运输、观光部（Ministry of Land, Infrastructure, Transport and Tourism 的简称）

MlMO feedback control system 多输入-多输出反馈控制系统（MlMO 为 multi-input multi-output 的简称）

MLP sensor ①见 MVLPS ②手柄位置传感器（manual lever position sensor 的简称）③手动换挡杆位置传感器（manual lever position sensor 的简称，亦写作 MLPS）

500 mL single-rotor Wankel engine 500ml 单缸汪克尔转子发动机（指单工作室排量为 500ml 的单缸三角转子发动机，见 Wankel engine's displacement）

MM ①美国石油协会润滑油分类记号（指长距离运行车用汽油机用润滑油）②磁-机械的（magnetic-mechanical）③保修手册（maintenance manual）④人-月（man-month）⑤制造手册（manufacturing manual）⑥兆米（megameter）⑦微型胶卷（microfilm）

mm 毫米（millimeter）

Mm 兆米（megameter）

MMC ［日］三菱汽车公司（Mitsubishi Motor Corporation）

MMCo ［美］汽车维修公司（Motor Maintenance Company）

MMCS 三菱多信息显示系统（商品名，Mitsubishi multi communication system 的简称，该系统通过位于中央控制板上的显示屏显示：行车地图与行车导行路线、音响设备控制状态、电视图像、剩余燃油量等有关信息，并可存入与显示个人有关信息）

MM design conception （本田公司提出的汽车）"人占用空间最大化，机器占用空间最小化"的设计理念（MM 为 man maximum、mechanism minimum 的简称）

MME 机械工程硕士（Master of Mechanical Engineer）

mmf ①磁动势，磁通势（magnetomotive force）②微微法拉（$\mu\mu F$, micromicrofarads）③旋轮线距 1mm 的转子发动机（1mm from trochoid engine 的简称，指实际缸壁曲线距理论旋轮线为 1mm，参见 equidistant curve radius）

mmHg 毫米水银柱高[常用压力单位，使用时应有温度条件，如在 0℃时的水银柱高 1mmHg(0℃) = 0.0136mW・G = 0.535in・W・C = 1.31 × 10^{-3} atm = 1.333 × 10^{-3} bar = 0.0193lbf/in^2 = 133.332N/m^2 = 1.36 × 10^{-3} kgf/cm^2]

MMI 多媒体信息系统（multi-media information 的简称）

MMIC 单片式微波集成电路（monolithic microwave integrated circuit 的简称，指将微波发射器与接收器二者制作在一块基片上的微波雷达集成电路）

m^3/min 立方米/分（国际单位制容积流量单位，1m^3/min = 1000l/min = 264.17 u. s. gal/min = 4.4028u. s. gal/s = 35.315ft^3/min）

'M' motor 一种低功率低速步进式电动机（常用于仪表）

2mm-project （20 世纪 90 年代美国三大汽车公司与密西根大学等共同投巨资建立的）2mm 工程［指从系统的观点出发，采用车身制造综合误差指数，即 6 倍均方差（6σ）来控制车身制造质量，并用一整套确保汽车制造尺寸偏差最小化的技术和流程，达到汽车车身密封、噪声、外观、寿命等制造偏差水平在 "2mm" 所代表的极小范围以内］

mmps 活塞最大平均速度（maximum mean piston speed）

MMPV 微型多功能车（mini multi-purpose vehicle 的简称）

MMT ①地图匹配技术（map matching technology 的简称）②（一种在市场上作为汽油辛烷值增强添加剂出售的）锰基化合物（有节油效果，但会增加 CO、NO_x 等的排放和堵塞催化转向器部件）

MMV 手动调节阀（manual modulation valve）

mN 毫牛顿（millinewton）

MN 机械噪声（mechanical noise）

Mn 锰（manganese）

MN 兆牛顿（meganewton）

MN/m^2 兆牛顿每平方米（meganewton/$meter^2$，国际单位制的压力倍数单位）

MNm 兆牛顿・米（meganewton-meter）

MNOS ①金属-氮化物-氧化物-半导体（metal-nitride-oxide-semiconductor 的简称）②金属-氮化物-氧化物-硅（metal-nitride-oxide-silicon 的简称）

MNOS memory 金属氮化物-氧化物-半导体存储器（一种靠栅区氮化砖 Si_3N_4 中的静电荷来编程的电可擦只读存储器）

Mo 钼（molybdenum）

moan 呼啸声，类似呼啸的噪声，类似呜咽的噪声（频率为 100Hz 左右持续不断的低频噪声，如轮胎行驶中的低频噪声）

mob ①汽车②移动式（= mobile）③汽车商店，流动售货车（美国一种直接开到买主家门口的 mobile shop 的俗称）

mobile ①运动物体，活动装置②［美］汽车的通称③活动的，机动的，可移动的，流动的，动态的；灵活的，轻便的，可携带的；多变的，易变的；汽车的

mobile aircraft landing stairs 机场客梯车（装备有液压式舷梯，供乘客上、下飞机用的机场专用汽车）

mobile analyzer 移动式分析器

mobile animal epidemic control van 畜禽流动防疫车

mobile bee-keeper 养蜂车

mobile boiler 锅炉车

mobile canteen 流动餐车

mobile cleanser 移动式清洗机

mobile clinic 流动诊所

mobile crane 自行式起重机（装有自行动力的轮式或履带式起重机械的通称，轮式称 wheel crane，履带式称 crawler crane）

mobile crime investigation vehicle 刑

事勘察车

mobile device ①（泛指各种）可移动的装置 ②（车载式）移动通信、信息装置

mobile device interface （车载式）移动通信设备的接口（如：iPod、iPhone 等的接口）

mobile drain unit （维修厂、车库更换机油用的）移动式放油装置

mobile emissions test laboratory 流动式排放实验室

mobile engine 车辆（等移动机械）用发动机

mobile environment monitor 环境检测车

mobile epidemic control vehicle 防疫监测车

mobile equilibrium 动态平衡

mobile family-planning clinic 计划生育车

mobile gas [美]车用汽油

mobile generating set 移动式发电设备（发电车）

mobile grease （由润滑油做基础油与脂肪酸金属皂稠化剂和必要的添加剂制成的有一定流动性、适宜于用润滑脂抢注入润滑点的）汽车底盘用润滑脂（亦称 chasis grease）

mobile ground anchor vehicle 地锚车（装备有可回转的吊臂、钻地锚及辅助装置，用于固定钻机、修井机等作业机械及各种井架、高塔绷绳的专用汽车）

mobile highway 移动式公路（由铝板等连接而成，哪里公路坏了，就运到哪里救急）

mobile home 旅居住车（指装备有床位等生活设施的挂车，＝ mobile quarters，motorised caravan，lodging vehicle）

mobile laboratory 移动实验室

mobile launcher 自行式发射装置

mobile library 流动图书馆

mobile liquid 流动性液体（低黏度液体）

mobile load 活动荷载，动载

mobile loudspeaker 宣传车（喇叭车）

mobile lubrication system 移动式润滑装置

mobile lubrication truck 机油油脂加注车

mobile maintenance and support equipment 移动式维修设备

Mobil engine maintenance through progressive analysis laboratory （美国）Mobil 石油公司的发动机累进分析维护法实验室（依据对发动机润滑油的定期连续累进分析资料，确定发动机的维护周期、维护项目等的实验室，简称 Mobil EM/PA lab）

mobile nondestructive testing laboratory 无损检验工程车，流动无损试验车

mobile oil [美]汽车发动机润滑油[车用机油（engine oil）的统称，源自美国 Mobil 公司的商品名]

mobile phone ①手机，便携电话机，移动电话机；（＝ cellphone, mobile telephone）②汽车电话（特指功率及通话时间均大于一般移动电话的汽车专用无线电话）

mobile phone prep （车上的）手机插座（大多带 USB 和充电接口）

mobile photographic studio 摄影车

mobile post office 邮政车，流动邮局（＝ post office vehicle, mail vehicle）

mobile proving ground 流动试验站（＝ mobile test centre）

mobile quarters 住宿车，旅居车

mobile radio unit 移动式无线电台

mobile repair-shop 流动修理站

mobile shower bath 淋浴车（供野外工作人员淋浴的厢式汽车）

mobile showroom 流动展览室（展览车）

mobile source emission factors 流动源排放因素（简称 MSEF，指来源于机动车辆等的废气、噪声污染排放因素）

Mobile Source Enforcement Division ［美］（环保局的）机动车辆污染源强制管理工作部（简称 MSED）

mobile sources 机动车辆（污染、噪声等）源

Mobile Source Testing Laboratory ［美］（环保厅的）机动车辆污染源试验所（简称 MSTL）

mobile store 售货车

mobile test centre 流动试验中心，流动试验站（= mobile proving ground）

mobile test stand 移动式试验台架

mobile tire inflation unit 移动式轮胎充气装置

mobile toolbar 自动工具架（= self-propelled tool bar, powered tool-frame, self-propelled tool frame）

mobile-transport truck （供）机动性运输（的）载货汽车（简称 MTT）

mobile TV receiver 汽车用电视接收机

mobile two-way radio 移动式双向无线电台（供民用频带通信用的收/发两用车载电台）

mobile unit 活动作业车（指以车辆为独立作业场地的专用车，如：流动服务车、活动诊所车等）

mobile unit truck 流动作业车（如：电视摄制车等）

mobile welding workshop 移动式焊接车间（装有焊接装备的车辆）

mobile workshop 流动修理车间（修理工程车）

mobile X-ray clinic X 射线流动诊所（用于 X 射线诊断的厢式汽车）

mobility ①机动性，灵活性，能动性，机动性②浓度③迁移率

mobility circle 导纳圆

mobility over unprepared terrain 无路地面通行能力（指汽车在额定荷载下能以足够高的平均车速通过各种坎坷不平地段、无路地带和克服各种障碍的能力）

mobility test （车辆）机动性试验

mobiloil 车用机油（= mobile oil）

mobilometer 浓度计，黏度计

mobus 客车（= motorbus, motorcoach）

mocab 出租汽车（motor cab）

mocar 轿车（= motor-car）

Mocca anthrazit 摩卡棕（车身颜色）

mockup ①全尺寸实物模型（如：1:1的汽车模型，同实物等大的研究用模型；样品）②制造模型（汽车）③全尺寸模型的，模型的

mock-up cabin 驾驶室模型

mock-up test （1:1的）实物模型试验

modal ①最普通的，最常见的，典型的（在观测中出现的频率最高的）②模式的，方式上的，形式的，模态的，形态的

modal analysis （振动的）模态分析（根据振动试验所取得的数据用数学的方法确定结构振动的模态参数，建立结构动态数学模型，见 modal analysis test、modal parameter）

modal analysis test （振动的）模态分析试验（为取得模态分析用的数据而对试件或结构的某特定单位或多点施加激振载荷的振动试验）

modal parameter 模态参数（利用系统主模态的正交性进行坐标变换，可使物理坐标下的方程组变换为模态坐标下的彼此独立的方程，每一个方程相当于一个自由度的动态方程而使求解简化。模态坐标下的各广义刚度矩阵，广义质量矩阵、广义阻尼矩阵及振型矩阵和各阶固有频率等统称为模态参数，见 mode of vibration）

modal speed 典型车速，最多用车速，最常见车速（车速调查所得到的车速频度分布中，频度值最高的车速）

modal system 模态系统

modal truncation 模态截断

modal value 众数（出现频率最高的值，最常见的值）

mode ①形式，手段，方式，方法，样式②模，模式（常用代号为M）运转模式，运行工况（如：加速、减速、等速、急速等）③（统计学上的）众数

mode bench test 多工况台架试验（在底盘测功机台架上，汽车按规定的多工况循环来模拟道路行驶测定排放、油耗等）

mode change 汽车换型（将已生产的汽车换成新设计的型号生产）

mode changing switch 模式转换开关（如：多行驶模式混合动力车的模式按钮式变换开关）

10mode cycle 10工况循环（日本测定汽油机燃油经济性及排气有害物含量的一种运行循环，模拟城市行车的运行工况）

11mode cycle 11工况循环（日本测定燃油经济性及汽油车排气有害物含量的一种运行循环，模拟汽车自郊外驶入市区的运行工况）

5-mode drive selector 见 drive mode selector

2ModeELC （三菱公司的）两模式电子控制自动变速器（商品名，有动力与经济两种可供选择的换挡模式）

mode enable switch 工况选择开关，工况接通开关（如：用于选择试验工况等）

10mode fuel consumption 10工况燃油消耗率（用10工况循环测出的燃油经济性）

model ①模型②型号（用字母、数字等表示产品形式、规格的符号）

model analysis 模型分析

model armature （黏土模型等的）模芯，模架，模基

model-based 基于（数学）模型的（分析、研究、开发、计算等）

model building 建模，创建数学模型

model cam 样板凸轮，标准凸轮

model car 模型车

model change （汽车等的）改型（亦称 model changeover）

model designation 车型简介（用文字或数字等对车型的名称、豪华等级、是否为汽油喷射、发动机排量、驱动形式等作的简短说明）

model experiment 模型试验

model following control system 仿型控制系统（如：四轮转向的仿型控制系统，预先设定汽车对驾驶人员转向操作及行车状况的最佳响应模型，预存于电子控制模块。在实际转向过程中，以行车状况及转向操作为输入，电子控制模块从预存中选出最佳的转向模型，向前、后轮发出转向指令，确保汽车实现模型所设定的最佳转向）

model following sliding control （适应性四轮转向车辆的基准）仿型滑移控制（系统）

model following velocity control method （基准）仿型速度控制法[控制系统根据基准模型（reference model）来控制车辆的加、减速度]

model launching 新型号投产，样机投产

modelling ①模式，模式化，模型化，造型，成型②模型制造，模型试验③模拟（试验）④建（立数学）模（型）

modelling bar （缩放仪）比例杆

modelling light 立体感灯光

modelling tool 模型法

modelling transportation technology

运输模式化技术；运输模拟技术
model machine 样机
model matching theory （数学）模型适配理论
model number 型号（序数）
model of a quadric 二次曲面模型
model scale （数学）模型的规模（用网点和网络数量表示的模型的大小）
model support （风洞里的）模型支架
model test ①模型试验，样机试验 ②（产品）定型试验 ③（过程的）模拟试验
Model T Ford （美国）福特公司早期生产的T形轿车（20世纪20年代的世界名车之一）
model-to-model versatility （各种附加装置或电子控制系统的）对各种不同车型的通用性，多车型适用性，车型多用性，异车型通用性（= model-to-model coverage）
model wind tunnel test 模型风洞试验（将按比例缩小的汽车模型在风洞试验）
model year 车型年，年型（简称MY，通常一种新年型车的生产开始于前一年的夏季，汽车生产厂停产，改变生产线以适应下一年型车的变化的停产期后，如：model year 2002，2002年型可能是在2001年夏季停产期后的10月生产的）
modem 调制调解器（对信号进行调制调解的功能部件，可使数字信号经模拟系统传输）
mode of freight transportation 货运形式，货运模式
mode of passenger transportation 客运形式，客运模式
mode of vibration 振动模态（= pattern of vibration，N个自由度的振动系统有N个固有振动频率，每一个固有振动频率系统具有的确定振动形态称为振动的主形态或主模态，简称模态）
moderate duty 中型的，中等功率的，中等负荷的，中载的，在中等条件下运转的（介于heavy-duty与mild-duty之间的）
moderate gale 疾风（七级风，= near gale）
moderate injury （汽车碰撞事故中乘员的）中等程度伤害，中等伤害
moderate injury level 中等伤害碰撞强度（指汽车碰撞时，使乘员产生不致永久伤残而可痊愈的伤害的碰撞强度，参见human tolerance level）
moderate operating conditions 不繁重的使用条件（如在硬路面上汽车行驶速度不大于65km/h）
moderate speed 中等速度，中速（简称MS）
moderator 减速器，阻滞剂，缓化剂
mode regulator （发动机等的）工况调节器
modern ①现代的 ②时新的，新式的
modernization 现代化
modernize 使现代化，使成现代式；用现代方法
modern motor spirit 现代车用汽油（见motor spirit）
mode select switch （电子控制系统）模式选择开关
mode servomotor （系统运转）模式转换伺服电动机
13-mode test cycle （车用柴油机的）13工况（排放物台架测试）法
mode transducer （振荡）波形变换器，波型传感器
modifiable 可调节的，可修改的，可修正的，可改变的
modification ①改进，修改，改善，改装，改建，修正，改型，调整 ②变质处理，孕育处理 ③限制，减轻，缓和
modification kit 成套改型零件（改

型工具，改型附件）

modification of consignment 变更运输（对已托运或已起运的货物，变更到达地点或收货人等的业务活动）

modified alpax 变质硅铝合金（= modified silumin）

modified borderline technique （测定汽油道路辛烷值的）修正边界线技术

modified car 改良车，改造车

modified cast iron 孕育铸铁

modified engine 改良发动机（相对于常规发动机而言，在结构等方面有所改革）

modified McPherson strut suspension 异型麦弗逊型悬架（①没有常规麦弗逊型悬架的上控制臂②螺旋弹簧不套在滑柱上，单独装在车架与下控制臂之间，车身的重量由下球节支撑）

modified result 经修正、换算的（试验）结果

modified silumin 变质铝硅合金（又称变质硅铝明，一种新的活塞材料，= modified alpax，见 silumin）

modified uniontown method （测定车用汽油道路辛烷值的）连点修正法（简称 MUM，亦称 modified uniontown procedure，与连点法基本相同，只是在每种车速下，需要调整点火提前角，使爆震达到可听见的最低爆震级，而连点法则不改变试验汽车的点火提前角，见 uniontown procedure）

modifier 改善剂，改良剂；调节剂

modifying agent 改质剂

modular ①模数的，模的，系数的，比率的②由标准件组合的（按标准尺寸或标准件组成的，以易于各件之间的相互连接或排列）

modular air strut （自动高度调平式空气弹簧悬架系统中，与空气弹簧制成一体的且刚度和高度）可调式空气弹簧滑柱（亦称 selflevelling suspension strut）

modular bus body 标准件组合式客车车身

modular cab 标准件组合式驾驶室（亦称 modular cabin）

modular cast iron 球墨铸铁

modular component assembly （用）标准零、部件组装的总成

modular construction 单元结构，积木式结构

modular design 典型结构，组件结构；积木化设计

modular final drive 标准件组合式主传动器（积木式主传动器）

modular pulse converter 组合式脉冲转换器（装在排气歧管后端将汽缸排出废气的脉动压力变为较为稳定的压力的串接式部件）

modular pulse converter supercharging 组合式脉冲转换增压（介于定压增压与脉冲增压之间的一种增压方式。在每一汽缸出口排气歧管处设置渐缩管，排气汇入一直径不大的排气总管后进入涡轮增压器，其作用是将排气的脉冲能量转换为较为稳定的压力进入涡轮）

modulate ①调节，调整②变换③调制，调幅，调谐

modulated coverter clutch control solenoid 见 MCCC solenoid

modulated displacement engine 可变排量发动机（如：三菱公司的工作缸数可变的发动机，简称 MDE）

modulated pressure （自动变速器液力控制系的）调制压力（指直接或间接由转速或发动机负荷调制后的主油路压力）

modulated strategy （福特公司 EEC-VI 系统的）调制工况（指发动机冷机起动、过热和在高海拔地区运转时，为保持发动机输出功率，电子

控制模块实施的补偿控制)

modulating valve 液压调制阀,调节阀

modulation ①调整,调节,变换②调制,调谐,缓和

modulation distortion 调制失真

modulation valve ①调节阀②(ABS系的)制动压力调节阀(根据电子控制模块的指令调控制动压力,防止车轮抱死,亦称 brake modulator, pressure modulation valve) ③(液力变速器中的)主油路压力调节阀*(见 modulator②)

modulator ①调幅器,调节器,调制器,(压力)控制阀,(压力)调节阀(常用代号 M) ②(自动变速器液压控制系统中调节主油路压力的节气门阀的)真空调制器(由进气管真空控制的一个膜片阀,将节气门开度变化引起的进气管真空度的变化转变为膜片的位移,借以推动与之相连接的节气门阀,以调节主油路压力) ③见 modulation valve②

modulator pressure (自动变速器控制系统的进气管)真空调制压力(亦称 vacuum modulator pressure,指由进气管真空度,即节气门开度调控的主油路压力,为发动机的转矩信号)

modulator strategy (发动机电子控制系统的)调节性控制模式(指在冷机起动、发动机过热、高海拔地区行车等要求电子控制模块对发动机的基本运行参数控制量作较大修改,以保证发动机良好操纵性的各种工况下的适应性控制模式)

modulator valve ①(自动变速器中调节主油路压力的真空控制式节气门阀,见 throttle valve) ②见 EGR VM

module ①模块[指由若干元件组成、能完成一定功能的组合电路(electronic control module)的简称]②模数,系数,比率,因素③基本流量单位(=100L/s)

module displacement 可变排量,可变排量控制(指根据发动机负荷,改变发动机工作缸数等,以改变量的可变排量方式)

module displacement engine 变缸可变排量式发动机(采用改变工作缸数变排量的发动机,简称 MDE)

module fuel pump assembly 模块式燃油泵总成

module of gear 齿轮模数(齿距除以圆周率 π 所得的商,以毫米计)

modulous cementite 球状渗碳体

modulus 模量(应力与相应应变的比值)

modulus in shear 切变模量(亦称 shear modulus,指切应力与切应变量呈线性比例关系范围内,切应力与切应变之比)

modulus of elasticity 弹性模量(杨氏模量,弹性物体在虎克定律的弹性范围内,正应力与线应变的比值,= elastic modulus,见 Hook's law)

modulus of resilience 回跳模数(回弹模量)

modulus of rigidity 刚性模数,刚性模量

modulus of torsion 扭转(弹性)模量

modus operandi 运用方式,工作方式,运用法(= way of doing)

MOFT 最小油膜厚度(minimum oil film thickness 的简称)

mogas [美]车用汽油(mobile gas 的简称)

mohair (车厢内蒙布用)安哥拉细山羊毛或其织物

Mohs hardness 莫氏硬度(材料的一种硬度指标,数值越大,越硬,如:铁的莫氏硬度值为 4.5,铝为 2.9,石墨为 1～2)

Mohs' scale number 莫氏硬度值
moist air 湿空气
moistener 加湿器
moistness （潮）湿度
moisture absorption 吸湿
moisture absorption test 吸湿性试验
moisture capacity 湿度（亦称 moisture content）
moisture content change with depth （土壤）含水量随深度的变化
moisture control （车内）湿度控制器（如车内加湿器）
moisture eliminator ①干燥器②干燥剂
moisture percentage 含水量百分率
moisture-resistant 防潮的，耐潮湿的，抗湿的
moisture sensitivity 湿度敏感性
moisture separator 水气分离器
moisture tester 湿度计
moisture test（ing） ①湿度测定②在湿气作用下进行的试验
moisture trap 除湿器
MOIV 机械驱动式进气门（mechanically operated inlet valve）
molal 摩尔质量的，质摩的（见 molality）
molal concentration 摩尔质量浓度（= molality）
molality 摩尔质量（质摩，一摩尔物质的质量称该物质的摩尔质量，单位为克/摩，为 6.02×10^{23} 个物质微粒的总质量，见 mole）
molar 摩尔体积的，体摩的（见 molarity）
molar behavior （驾驶操作中的）宏观动作（指转动转向盘、踩踏制动踏板等手、足动作，见 molecular behavior）
molar concentration 摩尔体积浓度（= molarity，每一升溶液中溶质的克分子数）
molarity 摩尔体积，体摩（1 摩尔物质占有的体积，标准状态下 1 摩尔任何气体所占的体积均设为 22.4 升，这一体积称气体摩尔体积）
molar ratio 克分子比，克分子浓度（= mole ratio）
molar solution 体积摩尔溶液，体摩溶液
molar volume 摩尔体积（= molal volume，见 molarity）
molar weight 摩尔重量（= molal weight，摩尔质量的旧称，见 molality）
mold ［美］铸模，涛铸用模（= 英 mould）
mold commutator （将换向器片埋在绝缘体中制成的）模压换向器
molded brake lining 模压制动器摩擦衬片（见 moulded facing）
molded case of seal 油封的模压成型外壳
molded headlinig 整体式成型（车身）顶棚（模压装饰板成型的整体式车身内顶棚）
molded headlining （轿车车身的）整体模制成型内饰顶篷
molding ①造型（法），制型，翻砂，制模，模压②模制零件，压制件，塑造物，铸件③倒角④嵌条，线条（= moulding）
mole ①摩（尔）（国际单位制物质的量的单位，代号为 mol，过去称克分子量为 mol，现在 mol 的定义是一个包含的结构粒子数与 12×10^{-3} 千克碳^{12} 的原子数目相等的物系的物质量，使用摩尔这个单位时，应指明结构粒子是原子、分子、离子，还是其他粒子或这些粒子的特定组合体）②分子（molecule 的简称）③克分子（gram-molecule 的简称）④分子的（molecular）⑤克分子（量），摩尔（见 mole）⑥克分子浓度（mole concentration 的简称）

molecular adhesion 分子间附着力

molecular behavior （驾驶操作中的）微观动作（指构成驾驶操作宏观动作中，手、足的肌肉运动、腺分泌等，参见 molar behavior）

molecular heat 分子热（物质的比热与其分子量的乘积）

molecular number 分子序（数），（分子内）原子序数和

molecular-scale 分子级的（指所涉及的空间规模小到分子一级）

molecular volume 摩尔体积（= molar volume）

molecular weight 分子量（分子的相对质量，等于一个分子中各原子的原子量的总和，没有单位）

molecule ①分子②微点，微小颗粒（简称 mol）

moleculus 分子常数（一摩尔的理想气体在0℃和1大气压下，每单位容积中的）分子数

mole mixture ratio 摩尔混合比（以摩尔数计量的混合比）

mollerize 钢渗铝（对钢件渗铝）

Mollier chart 莫里尔蒸气图（用来计算蒸汽机或制冷循环效率的图表，= Mollier diagram，焓熵图）

molten carbonate fuel cell 熔融碳酸盐燃料电池（简称 MCFC）

molten carbonate process 碳酸盐溶液法（排气中的铅及其他微粒的净化方法）

molten electrolyte cell 溶盐电解液电池（见 liquid metal cell）

molten mass 熔体，熔融物质（= fused mass）

mol wt 分子量（molecular weight）

molybdenum 钼（Mo）

molybdenum coating 镀钼层，镀钼

molybdenum disulfide [美]二硫化钼（MoS_2，英写作 molybdenum disulphide，黄色粉末，作为减磨剂加入润滑材料）

molybdenum disulfide grease 含二硫化钼的润滑脂（见 moly grease）

molybdenum disulfide (MoS_2) shot peening 二硫化钼粉末喷渗（一种2002年后采用的新减磨技术。将平均直径为 $11\mu m$ 的 MoS_2 粉末以 900kPa 的高压喷至零件表面，如活塞裙，在此时产生的高压下，MoS_2 粉末渗入表层，并在表层形成 $6\mu m$ 厚的再结晶减磨层，简称 MoS_2 shot peening）

molybdenum-faced piston ring 镀钼活塞环（= moly-coated piston ring）

molybdenum spray 钼喷涂，喷钼（如转子发动机缸壁的喷钼处理）

molybdenum steel 钼合金钢，钼钢

moly-filled piston ring 带充填二硫化钼槽的活塞环

moly grease 含二硫化钼的润滑脂（molybdenum disulfide-grease 的简称）

molykote dry bonded lubricant 钼化物黏性干润滑剂

moly ring coating 活塞环镀钼，活塞环镀钼层

moment 力矩（= moment of force）

moment arm 力偶臂，力矩臂

momentary 瞬息间的，瞬时的，顷刻的，短暂的，刹那的

momentary overload ①瞬时超载，短时间过载②瞬时超载时所受到的荷载

moment balance 力矩平衡（亦称 moment equilibrium）

moment of deflection 弯曲力矩（= moment of flexure，bending moment）

moment of inertia 转动惯量（某物体绕一定轴线旋转的转动惯量，$I = mk^2$，式中：m—物体的质量；k—回转半径）

moment of inertia of steering system 转向系转动惯量［转向系的运动部件和转向轮换算为绕转向轴线（或

主销）旋转的旋转体的等价转动惯量]

moment of momentum 动量矩，角动量（为一矢量，指一物体的角速度与该物体绕转轴的转动惯量的乘积，亦称 angular momentum）

moment of sparking 点火时刻（= ignition point）

moment of torque 转矩，力矩

momentum 动量（物体的质量与其速度的乘积）

momentum-driving （汽车的）动量驾驶，惯性驾驶（加速-滑行驾驶法）

momo ①单的 ②单声道的（monophonic 的简称）

MON 马达法辛烷值（motor octane number 的简称）

Monel(metal) 蒙乃尔合金，蒙乃尔高强度耐蚀镍铜（锰铁）合金，蒙乃尔高强度良延性抗蚀合金（镍68%，铜28%，锰1.5%，铁2.5%；或铜26%~32%，镍64%~69%，少量锰、铁，因其开发者 Monel 而得名）

monikrom cast iron 铬镍钼合金铸铁

monitor ①监控器 ②监控程序 ③（从用户中选出的对试制车的）试驾驶或试乘人 ④监控，监测，监管

monitor display 监控显示器

monitoring and control centre 监测和控制中心（监控中心，简称 Mc-centre）

monitoring around sensor （汽车防碰撞系统的）周边（障碍物）监测传感器（亦称 peripheral monitoring sensor）

monitoring resistor （安全气囊碰撞传感器内的）故障监测用电阻器（与传感器触点并联，由安全气囊控制模块供给微量电流经该电阻器，如果控制模块的电路或传感器出现短路或断路，或接地时，该电流便发生变化，控制模块发现这一变化，将立即点亮仪表板上的安全气囊警报灯）

monkey screw wrench 活扳手（亦称 adjustable spanner, monkey wrench, 简称 monkey，从侧面观察，这种扳手形似猴状，故名）

mono- [词头]单一的，单一

monoblock （全部汽缸均铸成一个整件的）整体式缸体

monoblock battery 整体蓄电池，单壳蓄电池组（若干单电池装在一个壳内）

monoblock cast 整体铸造（= en-block cast）

monoblock construction 整体结构

mono body 承载式车身，整体式车身（= integral body）

monocar 单座轿车

monochlorodifluoro-methane 一氯二氟-甲烷

monochromatic 单色的

monochromatic lamp 单色车灯（指不亮时其表面与车身同色，点亮时则可射发白光或有色光）

monochrometer 单色仪（单色光镜）

monoclinic system 单斜晶系，单斜系

monocoque 硬壳式结构，承载式结构（亦称 unitary construction, frameless body, stressed-skin body, unitary body, unitized body, single-unit body, mono body, integral body, 指车身为一整体的无车架式结构）

monocoque car 整体式车身轿车（= unitized car）

monocoque construction （结构应力全部由车身壳板承受的轿车的）承载式车身结构，独壳式（车身）结构（车身外壳板不仅受剪切应力，而且承受弯曲应力的无车架式车身结构，亦称 monocoque body construction, monocoque skin construc-

tion，见 monocoque body）
monocoque shell 承载式车身外壳
monocrystalline silicon 单晶硅（= single crystal silicon）
monocular region 单眼可视区，单眼能见区
mono fuel vehicle 单燃料汽车（只有一套燃料供给系统，只能使用一种燃料的汽车，以区别于 dual fuel vehicle 或 flexible fuel vehicle）
monogram （表示车辆商标等的）图案化组合字（一般由公司或个人名的各部分的头一个字母组成）
Mono-Jetronic （德国博世公司的）单点低压型节气门体汽油喷射系统（商品名，其喷射压力仅0.1MPa）
mono-lever operation 单操纵杆控制，单杆操纵，单杆控制
monolith ①整块材料，整块，单片 ②（常用来表示催化转化器中催化剂的）蜂窝状整体式陶瓷载体（亦称 monolithic substrate）
monolithic ①单片（指在一片半导体晶片上制作的集成电路）②整体的，整块的，单块的，单片的
monolithic block 整体式缸体（指汽缸、缸体、曲轴箱铸造在一起的发动机缸体）
monolithic catalyst 整体催化剂
monolithic construction 整体式结构，整体构造
monolithic integrated circuit 单片集成电路（全部元件制作在一块半导体芯片上的集成电路）
monolithic microwave integrated circuit 见 MMIC
monolithic substrate （催化转化器催化剂的）整体式载体（有陶瓷和金属的两种，结构一般是蜂窝状的）
monomer 单体，单分子物体，单基物，单元结构
mono multi 单稳多谐振荡器（monostable multivabrator 的简称，当有触发脉冲作用时，电路从稳态翻转到另一暂稳态，保持一段时间后又回到稳态）
monophase 单相，单相位（亦写作 single phase）
monoplunger pump 单柱塞泵，分配泵（= distributor type pump, delivery type pump）
monopole 单极，单极的
mono purpose 单用的，单一用途的
monorail car 单轨轨道车辆
monorotor engine 单缸转子发动机
mono-side structure （车身的）整体侧架式结构
monospace car 单厢式轿车
monostable circuit （数字集成电路中的）单稳态（触发）电路（亦称 monostable trigger circuit，指只有一个稳定输出组态的时序电路，但习惯上指除稳定输出组态外，至少还有一种亚稳态输出组态的时序电路）
monostable multivibrator 单稳多谐振荡器（一种能将信息保存一段固定时间的电路，该时间的长短取决于电路元件的特性）
monostable trigger circuit 单稳触发电路（见 monostable circuit）
monotone horn （汽车的）单声喇叭（只有一个声调的单只喇叭）
monotopic liquid crystal （相对可逆变的）单变相液晶
monotube damper 单筒式减振器（亦称 monotube shock absorber，= singletube shock absorber）
monotube type 单筒式（如：既作外壳又是缸筒的单筒式减振器）
monovalent element 单价元素，一价元素
monoxide 一氧化物（的通称）
Monroney sticker （贴在待销售的新车风窗玻璃上的）背胶粘贴标签（美国联邦政府规定凡在美国境内

出售的汽车，必须在风窗玻璃上粘贴具有下列内容的说明标签：厂家建议的零售价，所有可由厂家安装的选购件，由最后总装点或进口口岸到销售点的预定运价，以及美国环保局的燃油经济性评定。此外，所有的经销商会在风窗上另贴一张标签，列出在经销店加装的附件的清单及其他费用)

mon-slip differential 防滑差速器

monsoon grey 季风灰（车身颜色）

monster engine 巨型发动机（一般指小轿车用的大功率发动机）

Monte-Carlo method 蒙特-克罗法（用数学模型代替实际系统进行试验的一种数字仿真法，通过大量数学模拟试验，得出某事件出现频率或随机变量的平均值作为问题的解）

mood ①氛围，气氛 ②（驾驶者的）情绪，心情

moon dune buggy 月面沙丘汽车（宇宙航行员在月球上使用的汽车）

Mooney viscosimeter 穆尼黏度计（用一钢片盘埋在所测黏性材料中，以低速旋转，量测这些材料的剪切应力）

Mooney viscosity （表征未硫化橡胶等黏性材料的剪切应力的）穆尼黏度

moonlight blue 月光蓝（车身颜色）

moon roof 轿车车顶上的天窗（一般指材料为强化玻璃者）

moorse chain （美式）无声链

moped 机动自行车，助力脚踏车（有动力装置助力的脚踏车，所装动力一般不大于 50mL 的汽油机或功率小于 0.6kW 的电动机。日本等国家都不将其列入机动车范围内管理，为 motor assisted pedal cycle 的简称，有时讹称 mopet，morpet）

MOPTARS 多目标相位跟踪和测距系统（multi-object phase tracking and ranging system 的简称）

moquette （车室内壁蒙装、坐垫、地毯等用）短毛绒织物

morning thickness （衬片等摩擦材料受液露浸湿增厚，以摩擦系数异常增大的）晨厚（现象）

Morse's cone 莫氏圆锥

Morse standard taper plug gage 莫氏标准锥度塞规

Morse test 发动机一缸断开检查试验（多缸发动机，每次断开一缸，依次测定各汽缸在发动机总输出功率中的份额，诊断故障部位）

mortality （汽车事故等造成的）死亡人数，死亡率

mortality equation 折旧方程

mortise ①榫眼，笋眼，凹（凸）榫，槽，沟，孔 ②开榫眼，用榫眼接合（亦写作 mortice）

mortise (d) and tenon (ed) joint （木车身构件的）榫眼及榫头接合，雌雄榫接头 (= mortise joint)

MOS 金属-氧化物-半导体（metal-oxide-semiconductor 的简称，指制作场效应晶体管之类的元件的材料与结构，以 MOS 场效应晶体管为例，它由掺杂较少的 P 型硅片做底衬，在底衬上制成两个掺杂较多的 N^+ 型区做源极"S"和漏极"D"，在 S 和 D 极间的 P 型底衬硅片上覆盖一层二氧化硅 SiO_2，在其表面上涂一层金属铝做栅极"G"，因而栅极与其他电极和硅衬片之间是绝缘的，由于它是由做电极的"金属"，做绝缘层的"氧化物"和做衬片及 S，D 极的"半导体"三种材料构成，故名金属-氧化物-半导体，亦称 metal-oxide-silicon)

mosaic crack 龟裂，网裂

MOS capacitor 金属-氧化物-半导体电容器

MOS circuit 金属-氧化物-半导体电

路，MOS 电路（指由 MOS 器件组成的电路，功耗低，面积小，适合组成大规模及超大规模集成电路，亦称 MOS integrated circuit）

MOS dynamic random access memory MOS 动态随机存取存储器［随机存储器中最重要的一种，利用栅极与基底间的寄生电容存储信息，以 MOS 管做地址选择开关，为了补偿 P-N 结漏电造成的存储电荷（即数据）的丢失，必须周期性地充电。单元结构简单，密度高，耗电低，多用于大容量存储器］

MOSFET 金属氧化物半导体场效应晶体管（见 MOS field effect transistor）

MOSFET bridge circuit 金属-氧化物场效应晶体管桥式电路（如：控制动力转向电动机旋转方向的桥式电路）

MOS field-effect transistor 金属-氧化物-半导体场效应晶体管，MOS 场效应晶体管，MOS 管（简称 MOS transistor，MOSFET，一种高输入阻抗，低开关速度及低功耗的半导体器件，其源极和漏极间的电流由输入源极和栅极间的电压的电场作用控制，该电场的大小改变源极漏极间沟道的电导，故名。见 MoS 及 field-effect transistor）

MoS₂ shot peening （摩擦表面的）二硫化钼粉末高压喷渗（处理）（如：以 900kPa 的高压将平均直径 11μm 的 MoS₂ 粉末喷至活塞摩擦表面，利用此时产生的热量，使 MoS₂ 粉末渗透入活塞表层，形成 6μm 大小的再结晶层的减摩技术）

MOST ①（汽车）多媒体用传输通信系统（Media Orientated System Transmission 的简称，由 20 余家汽车制造商和 50 家汽车配件制造商共同制定的汽车局域网多媒体系统传输网络，在汽车局域网内最多可连接 64 个节点，使用一根光纤最多可传送 15 个频道的非压缩音频数据）②金属氧化物半导体晶体管（metal-oxide semiconductor transistor 的简称）

MOS transistor 金属-氧化物-半导体晶体管（见 MOS field-effect transistor）

most severe injury degree 最大伤害度，最重伤害度

MOT ①［日］运输部，运输省 ②［英、美］原运输部（Ministry of Transport 的简称，现称 Department of Transport，简称 DOT）

MOT certificate 运输部检测合格证（见 MOT test）

motel 汽车旅馆（motor hotel 的简称，公路沿线，供驾车人住宿并可保管所驾车辆的旅店）

mother oil 原油（= crude oil）

motif 动机（参见 motive②）

4 Motion （大众汽车公司）四轮驱动系统（商品名，可根据路面附着条件，将驱动力按需分配给每一个车轮，确保每一个车轮都具有最佳的牵引力和抗侧滑能力）

motion 运动，移动，运转，运行

motion-characteristic equation 运动特性方程

motion-dependent resistance force 随运动而变的阻力，运动产生的阻力，运动阻力

motion-impeding 阻碍运动的

motion of translation 线性运动，平移运动（平移，平动）

motion resistance due to mass inertia 惯性阻力（车辆加速时由质量惯性引起的运动阻力）

motion resistance due to vegetation 指植被对车辆产生的运动阻力

motion-resistance force 运动阻力

motion-resistance-force characteristics （汽车的）行驶阻力特性，运动阻

力特性

motion resistance statistical evaluation （车辆）运动阻力的统计评价

motion shaft 动轴（相对于固定轴、死轴而言，一般指传递动力的旋转运动轴，如：齿轮传动系的①主轴，main shaft；②中间轴，副轴，lay shaft，countershaft 等）

motion sickness 晕车（由于低于1Hz的振动引起乘员恶心、呕吐等病理现象）

motion sickness frequency range 晕车频域（使乘员产生恶心、呕吐等晕车现象的频域，大致低于1Hz的频率范围）

motion thread 传动螺纹

motion transmissibility 运动的传输率，运动传递的速比（如：轮毂速度与轮胎接地面速度之比）

motion weighing （车辆）行驶中过秤，驶过（地秤）称重

motion works （机构的）运动件

motivate 推动，诱导（= motive③）

motivation ①动机，动因，目的（促使某项行为，某项运动的）原因 ②激发，刺激，推动，动力 ③机能

motivation constant （驾驶员）反应诱导常数

motive ①具有动力的，驱动的，原动的，发动的，引起运动的，移动的，活动的，不固定的 ②动机，动因；主题，主旨，要点；特色（= motif）③提供动力，推动；诱导，刺激（= motivate）

motive force 原动力，推动力，驱动力，牵引力（= driving force, motion-promoting force, propelling power）

motive means 动力装置，使动装置（使…产生运动的装置）

motive power 驱动功率，推进力

motive-power battery 动力型电池（= traction-type cell）

motive power machine 动力机械

motive unit 牵引车

motocar 轿车（一般写作 motor car，简称 car，美亦称 automobile）

motocross ①越野的（= cross-country）②陡坡恶路摩托车赛（美称 scramble）

motocycle 摩托车（一般写作 motorcycle）

motogas 车用汽油（= motor gasoline）

motometer 汽车仪表（= motor meter）

motor ①电动机（= electric motor）②发动机（= engine）③轿车（英国的非正式称呼，= motor car, automobile）④机动的，由发动机驱动的 ⑤驾驶汽车，用汽车搬运，乘汽车旅行 ⑥起动（发动机）

motorable road ①适于汽车行驶的道路，②汽车公路

motor-actuated CVT-puller moving taper disc 电动机推动型连续无级变速器主动传动带轮的活动锥形盘（见 CVT steel belt puller）

motor analyser 发动机诊断仪（= engine analyser）

Motor and Equipment Manufacturers Association （美国）发动机和汽车设备制造者协会（简称 MEMA）

motor assisted 4WD system of FF vehicle （发动机前置前轮驱动车辆的）电动机帮助型四轮驱动系统（只在必要时，利用电动机驱动后轮实现四轮驱动，见 FF）

motor bandit [美]车匪（乘汽车行劫的盗匪）

motor benzene 车用苯

motor benzine 车用轻质汽油（亦写作 motorbenzine）

motor benzol 车用粗苯

motor braking 发动机制动（= engine braking)

motor bus 客车 (= mobus)

Motor Bus Society [美] 大客车学会（简称 MBS）

motor cab 出租轿车 (= mocab, taxi cab)

motor cade [美] 汽车行车列队（汽车的长蛇阵, = autocade, motorkeid)

motor-car ①[英] 小轿车（美称 automobile, 简称 car, 亦写作 motocar) ②（铁路火车）车厢

motorcar accessories 轿车附件

motorcar alternator 车用交流发电机

motor caravan 旅居汽车（机动旅居车，自带动力的旅居车, = motorized caravan, self-powered caravan, 美称 motor home)

motorcar dry weight 汽车干重（不计冷却水及燃油的汽车净重）

motor car exhibition 汽车展览会 (= automobile exhibition)

motor carrier 汽车运输公司（一般指货运公司）

Motor Carrier Safety Status Management System 见 Safe stat

motorcar show 汽车展览会 (= automobile exhibition)

motor-(car) works 汽车工厂 (= automobile works)

motor club 汽车俱乐部 (= automobile club)

1 motor + 2 clutch (type hybrid system for FF vehicle) 1 台电动机 + 2 套离合器（型发动机前置前轮驱动汽车用混合动力系统，其起驱动与减速能量回收发电作用的电动机通过两套离合器直接与发动机和 CVT 连接，即：发动机→离合器 1→电动机→离合器 2→CVT。平时行驶无须发动机加力时发动机熄火，离合器 1 断开，离合器 2 接合，汽车由电动机单独驱动，或者制动减速时 CVT 反带电动机逆转给蓄电池充电。当加速或上坡行驶需要更大的驱动力或驱动电动机的蓄电池电力不足时两套离合器同时接合，发动机参与驱动）

motor coach 客车（一般指长途或观光大型客车）

motor-coach sleeper 带卧铺的长途客车，卧铺客车

motor controller 电动机控制器（在电动汽车中，用于控制电动机的转速和转矩，此外还具有限制最大电流，实现发电制动，正转、反转、空转及起动大转矩控制和过载/过热保护等功能）

motor control method （电动力转向系转向助力的）电动机控制法（可分为电流控制法和电压控制法两种，见 motor current control method, motor voltage control method)

motor convoy 护卫汽车（护送汽车，警卫汽车）

motor court 汽车旅店（汽车旅行者停车住宿休息的地方, = motor hotel, motor inn, motor lodge, motel)

motorcraft 福特公司生产的各种型号的交流发电机总成的商品名

motor crane 汽车吊（车）(= autocrane)

motor current control method （电动力转向转向助力的）电动机电流控制法（电子控制模块根据车速传感器的信息控制电动力转向电动机的电流，从而控制其输出的转向助力转矩）

Motorcycle Industry Council [美] 摩托车工业委员会（简称 MIC)

motorcycle with side-car 带跨斗的摩托车

motor cycling 乘骑摩托车

motor-cylinder block （汽）缸体

motor delivery van 厢式送货汽车（见 light van)

motor-dom 汽车行业，汽车界，汽车业（包括汽车设计、制造销售、使用、维修界及从业人员）

motor-driven doorlock （汽车的）电动车门锁

motor-driven-to-linear motion 电机驱动的线性运动

motor-drive pump 电动泵

motor drome 汽车场，汽车比赛场，试车场

motor dynamometer 电力测功机（= electric dynamometer）

motored engine （试验时）由电动机带动的发动机（被拖动的发动机）

motored vehicle 汽车，机动车

motor efficiency 电动机效率（指电动机消耗的电能与产生的机械能之比，用%表示）

Motor Equipment Manufacturers' Association （美国）汽车设备制造者协会（简称 MEMA）

motor-fan ①汽车爱好者，汽车迷 ②电动风扇

motor fire brigade vehicle 灭火车，消防车（亦称 motor fire engine, fire engine）

motor flusher 洗车机（车辆冲洗装置）

motor fuel 车用燃油

motor gasoline 车用汽油（= motor petrol）

motor generator 发动机-发电机组（指由发动机带动发电机发电的机组，= motor-generator set, motor-dynamo，简称 motor gen）

motor-generator arc welder 发动机-发电机组电弧焊机

motor-generator electronic control unite （混合动力车的）电动机-发电机电子控制模块（简称 MG-ECU，亦称 power management computer，通过 CAN 与混合动力车的主电子控制模块联结，根据其指令控制发电机和电动机及直流升压、降压变压器和交-直流、直-交流变换器）

motor/generator revolution sensor 电动机/发电机转速传感器（Inoue 公司称之为 resolver）

motor generator system （复合动力车的）电动机-发电机系统

motor grader ①轮式平地机（= power grader）②刮板式扫雪车

motor hearse 殡仪车，灵车（= cold wagon, cold cart）

motor highway 公路（= motoring highway）

motor hoist 电动提升机，电动葫芦

motor-home ［美］机动旅居车，旅居汽车（= 英 motor caravan）

motor hood 发动机罩（engine hood）

motor horse box （载货汽车的）运马车厢

motor hotel 汽车旅馆（简称 motel, = motor inn）

Motor Industry Research Association ［英］汽车工业研究协会（简称 MIRA，创立于 1946 年，研究汽车事故调查、声学、人类工程学以及汽车工业中有关的污染、噪声、道路、风洞试验等）

motoring ①驾驶汽车，乘坐汽车，开车，坐车②驾驶汽车或乘坐汽车游乐、兜风、运动③驾驶汽车的，汽车驾驶人员的，汽车的④用发动机带动⑤用电动机带动发动机空转，磨合运转⑥用电动机带动发动机空转测定机械损失（= motoring test①）⑦用汽车搬运

motoring breakdown 倒拖法（用电动机拖动发动机旋转，用于测量发动机摩擦功消耗和磨合等）

motoring condition （汽车的）行驶状态，汽车运行状态

motoring connoisseur 汽车评论家

motoring draw-test 电动机拖动试验

(见 = motoring test)

motoring highway 公路 (= motor highway)

motoring indicator diagram （内燃机的）拖动示功图（内燃机不喷油或不点火，由外力拖动时的示功图）

motoring machine （大修后用其他动力驱动发动机的）发动机磨合台

motoring map 公路交通图

motoring method 马达法，拖动法（一般指用电动机驱动发动机进行各种测试的方法，如测定汽油辛烷值的马达法）

motoring plug 火花塞

motoring test ①（发动机的）电动机拖动空转试验（用电动机拖动发动机空转，以测定其机械损失）②（直流发电机的）电动机试验（将电流输入直流发电机内，使发电机作为电动机回转，以此时的状况，判断其机能）

motor inn 汽车旅馆（见 motor hotel）

motor insurance 汽车保险 (= automobile insurance)

motorised caravan 旅居汽车，机动旅居车

motorist 汽车驾驶人，汽车驾驶员 (= driver)

motorists hotel 汽车旅馆（见 motor court）

motorized power cylinder 电动液压动力缸

motorized trailer 带动力的挂车（挂车自身装有发动机，在特殊情况下可自己行走，长途运输时则用牵引车拖挂或利用铁路平板车托运，见 piggyback transportation）

motorized troop 摩托化部队，机械化部队

motorized wheel 电动车轮（指内部装有电动机的车轮，见 motorized wheel drive）

motorized wheel drive 电动车轮驱动，轮内电动机驱动（指内燃机-电动机复合动力车驱动方式的一种，内燃机发电，然后由装在车轮内的电动机直接带动车轮转动）

motorkeid 汽车列队行车（见 motorcade）

motor ladder ①车顶行李架梯②（消防车用）机动伸缩梯

motorless 无发动机的，非机动的

motor licence 汽车执照

motor lifting hook 发动机起吊钩 (= engine lifting hook)

motor light （美国石油学会原来使用的机油分类中的）轻负荷汽油机用机油（简称 ML）

motor live time 汽车寿命

motor loop 液压马达回路，液动机回路

motorlorry （载）货（汽）车 (= auto truck, motor truck, 简称 truck)

motorlorry workshop 修理工程车

Motorloy 摩托乐意（一种汽油添加剂的商品名，主要成分为锡，另外配合8种金属粉，用以清除积炭和填覆活塞、缸筒、气门等摩擦表面，达到提高发动机使用寿命和性能的目的）

motormaker ［美］汽车制造商，汽车制造厂

motorman ［美］驾驶员 (= motorneer)

motor mechanic 汽车维修工 (= car mechanic, auto-repairman)

motor meter ①电动机型电度表（积算式电流表的一种，装有一只电动机，其转速与所接线路内的电流量成正比，因而电动机主轴的累计转数与该线路所消耗的电量成正比）②汽车仪表

motor method （测定汽油抗爆性的）马达法（为实验室辛烷值测定法之一种，参见 laboratory knock-testing method）

motor mix 乙基液（车用汽油的抗爆剂）

motor moderate （美国石油学会 API 原来的机油分类中的）中负荷汽油机用机油（简称 MM）

motor number 发动机号码，发动机编号（= engine number）

Motor octane number （汽油的）马达法辛烷值（在 CFR 发动机上用马达法测定的燃油辛烷值，简称 MON，见 octane number, motor method 及 research octane number）

motor oil ①电动机用滑油②发动机滑油，机油（= engine oil）

motor-omnibus 客车（= omnibus, motor bus, bus）

motor-paced race 跟在领头车后的竞赛

motor passenger vehicle 客运车辆

motor pedicab 机动三轮车，小型三轮汽车

motor petrol 车用汽油（参见 benzine）

motor plant 汽车制造厂

motor-polo ①机动车球赛（一种乘机动车的击球赛）②汽车集中调度场（= auto-polo, motor pool⑥）

motor-pool ①战备车队②战备车辆基地③备用车队④备用车辆基地⑤［美］汽车停车场⑥汽车集中调度场

motor-powered 用发动机作动力的，装有发动机的（= engine-powered）

motor-powered vehicle 机动车辆，机动车（简称 MPV）

motor pump 机动泵，电动泵

motor race 汽车竞赛，赛车

motor-race track 赛车跑道（= speed way）

motor racing fan ［美］赛车迷

motor rally 汽车拉力赛

motor regeneration 电动机能量再生运转（如：电动机制动能量回收发电运转）

motor relay 电动机继电器

motor repair trade 汽车修理行业

Motor Report International 国际汽车通报（期刊）（简称 MRI）

motor road 机动车路，公路

motor road test 汽车路试

motor rotating angle sensor 步进电动机转角传感器

motor-scooter ①低座小摩托车②［美］汽艇

motor severe （美国石油学会 API 原来的机油品质分类中的）重负荷频繁起动、停机的汽油机用润滑油（简称 MS）

motor severe process （美国材料试验学会 ASTM 对美国石油学会 API 原机油分类中的）MS 油的发动机程序试验（方法的总称）

motor-show 汽车展览（会）

motor skinner ［美］汽车驾驶员

motor speed ①电（动）机转速②发动机转速

motor spirit 车用汽油（英国对火花点燃式发动机用轻质液态碳氢化合物燃油的统称，= petrol, gasoline, motor fuel, benzine, 现代车用汽油多为几种石油产品的掺和物，如直馏汽油、裂化汽油、异构物、苯，以及酒精，以满足辛烷值等的要求）

motor sprinkling machine 洒水车（= motor water car）

motor squadron 汽车队

motor stall torque 停机转矩（指在规定条件下，发动机所能保持的最大转矩）

motor starter ①汽车（发动机的）起动机②电动机（的）起动器③电流调节电阻器

motor starting characteristic 发动机起动性能

motor station 汽车站

motor steering 汽车转向（= motor turning）

motor stethoscope 发动机听诊器

motor street washer 街道冲洗车

motor support bottom cover 发动机支座底罩

motor-sweeper 道路清扫车

motor-tank truck 罐车[= tank(-body) truck]

motorteria [美]顾客自己取货的食品杂货车

motor three wheel 机动三轮车（= three wheeled vehicle）

motor tilter 自动倾卸汽车，自卸汽车，自卸车（= dumper car, dumper truck, dumper, tip car, tipcart）

motor tire 轿车轮胎

motor traction ①（公共）汽车运输（事业）②汽车的牵引力

motor traction control （内燃机-电动机复合动力车的）电动机牵引力控制（系统）（当车辆遇冰、雪等滑路而前轮或后轮路面附着力突然发生变化时，其驱动力分配系统将在瞬间做出反应控制驱动力，保持车辆稳定）

motor tractor （一般指空车质量在7370kg以内的）牵引车（美多称truck/tractor）

motor-traffic 汽车交通

motor transportation enterprises on exclusive lines 专线汽车运输企业（在指定的专线上，从事客、货运输的汽车运输企业）

motor transport enterprise 汽车运输企业

motor transport vehicle 运输车辆（运输用机动车辆）

motor trend's car 代表发展趋向的汽车，发展趋势代表车

motor trip （乘）汽车旅行

motor truck 载货汽车，货车（机动运货车辆的统称，= automotive truck 简称 truck）

motor truck for refuse collection 垃圾收集车

motor truck road 公路，汽车干道，公路干线

motor truck scale [美]汽车磅，汽车地秤

motor truck with livestock rack 牲畜运输车

motor type precrash belt retractor 电机型安全带碰撞前（自动）收紧装置（测得汽车有可能发生碰撞时由电动机预先将安全带收紧）

motor type subantenna （汽车分集式天线系统中的）电动（伸缩型）副天线（见 diversity antenna system）

motor tyre casing 汽车轮胎外胎

motor van 厢式货车

motor vehicle ①汽车（中国定义是由动力装置驱动，具有四个和四个以上车轮的非轨道无架线的车辆）②机动车辆（指不在轨道上行驶并装有橡胶轮胎的所有自带动力装置驱动的车辆，如轿车、货车、客车、各种特种车辆和摩托车等）

motor-vehicle accident 汽车事故，车祸

motor-vehicle accident death 汽车事故死亡（事故发生后一定时间内，因事故造成的死亡，日本规定24小时内，美国规定12个月以内）

motor-vehicle accident injury 汽车事故致伤，车祸致伤（按美国规定，因车祸致伤，在12个月以内应由肇事者负责医治）

motor vehicle cassation 车辆报废

motor-vehicle chassis 汽车底盘，机动车底盘

motor vehicle exchange 机动车交易所

Motor-Vehicle Information and Cost Saving Act of 1972 （美国1972年）汽车信息及节约费用法令（该

法令要求汽车制造厂家设计和生产保障乘员安全的车辆,并对减轻伤害的保险杠、油耗标准、自动诊断系统、汽车仪表等作出规定)

motor-vehicle inspection ①机动车辆检验②(特指)机动车辆审验(由政府部门根据各种安全和车辆法规对车辆进行的审核性检测,简称MVI)

motor-vehicle inspection station 机动车检测站,汽车检测站

motor vehicle length 汽车长度(汽车前后最外端突出部位之间的距离)

Motor-Vehicle Manufacturers Association (美国)机动车制造商协会(简称MVMA)

motor-vehicle non-traffic accident 路外汽车事故,非道路交通事故(指在道路以外的场所发生的行车肇事)

Motor Vehicle Program [美](国家公路交通安全管理局的)汽车规划部门(简称MVP)

motor-vehicle registration and titling 机动车辆登记注册

motor vehicle-related fatality 汽车肇事死亡,车祸死亡

Motor Vehicle Safety Standard [美]汽车安全标准(简称MVSS)

motor-vehicle tax 汽车税,机动车辆税

motor-vehicle traffic accident 机动车交通事故

motor vehicle wheel space 汽车轴距

motor voltage control method (汽车转向系电动转向助力的)电动机电压控制法(电子控制模块根据车速传感器的信息,控制电动机的输入电压,从而控制其输出转矩)

motor-wag(g)on 厢式货车

motor washer 洗车机(车辆清洗装置)

motor water car (街道)洒水车(= sprinkling truck, street flusher, street washer)

motorway [英]高速公路(= [美] free way,指带中央分隔带的多车道高速汽车专用干线,全封闭,主体交叉,具有少数出入口)

motor winch 由车辆发动机驱动的绞盘,机动绞盘

motor winding 电动机绕组,电动机线圈

Mo-town [美]汽车城节奏的(指一种节拍强而另一种慢的节奏和布鲁斯舞曲,汽车城指美国底特律城)

Motronic ①(博世公司1979年首次推出的)发动机综合电子控制系统(商品名,由一台电子控制模块对喷油时刻、空燃比、点火、点火正时、怠速、排放等进行统一控制的一体化数字系统)②内燃机电子技术,发动机电子技术

MOT test (汽车的)运输部检测[由英国、美国原运输部,现称 DOT,授权汽车维修场对两年以上的全部汽车进行的一年一度上路许可检测,相当我国的机动车年检,其检测项目包括转向、悬架、制动、车轮和轮胎、安全带、喇叭、排气系统(含排放),以及整车结构]

mottle cast iron 杂晶铸铁,马口铁,麻口铁

mottled patterns (in tempered glass plates) (车用钢化玻璃的)应力斑,应力花纹(反射光线时,从玻璃表面看到的干涉图形)

mould (浇铸用)铸模(美称 mold)

mould ability (金属与塑料的)可模铸成型性

moulded facing ①模压成型衬面材料(以石棉纤维为主,混以橡胶或合成树脂在压模内加热成型的磨料材料,用于制动器离合器片等)②粉末烧结合金模压成型衬面材料(亦称

moulded lining　模压(制动蹄)摩擦片

moulded plastic compound　模压塑性材料,模压塑料

moulded type ignition coil　塑封型(闭磁路)点火线圈(见 closed magnetic circuit ignition coil)

moulded work　模塑品

moulding　①模铸件,模压件,模型制器(= moulding article)②嵌条(= insertion strip)③装饰性边框,装饰条④铸造,模铸,造型,模压(均可写作 molding)

moulding article　模塑制品,模铸制品(特指喷射模铸、模压成型塑料制品,亦称 moulding part)

mould pressing　模压

mouldproof　防霉的,防潮致霉的

Moulton hydragas suspension　牟尔顿油-气弹簧悬架(由液压传递载荷,而由通过膜片与液压隔离的气囊弹簧元件吸收载荷的油-气弹簧悬架。同侧前、后悬架的液压系统互相连通,以减少侧倾,简称 hydragas suspension)

Moulton suspension　牟尔顿悬架(英 Leyland 公司生产的以发明人 A. Moulton 命名的液压-橡胶弹簧悬架与油-气弹簧悬架的总称)

mount　①架,座②(显微镜的)检镜板③(车身的)边饰④安装,装配,镶上,把…固定在…上⑤(数量等)增加,增高⑥测定,确定,规定

mountable curb　斜式缘石(容许车辆驶上的缘石)

mountain cork　(亦称 mountain cloth, mountain flax, mountain leather)石棉

mountain country　山地,山区(亦称 mountainous country, mountainous district, mountainous terrain)

mountain driving　山区行车,山区运行

mountain highway　山区公路

mountain sage　山艾色(车身颜色:呈灰绿色)

mountain test　山区试验,山地试验

mountain test course　山区试验路线

mount bracket　支架,固定架,安装架,托架

mounted smoke meter　外装式烟度计(烟度计的工作部位布置在发动机排气管路尾端, = end of line smoke meter)

mounting　①安装,装配②支撑(件),支架,支座,支撑物,托架

mounting block　装配台,安装台,装配架,安装架

mounting eye　固定孔,安装孔(如:外壳上供穿过紧固螺栓的孔或带孔凸缘)

mounting flange　安装凸缘,装配突缘

mount(ing)gum　支座橡胶软垫

mounting plate　安装板,安装座板,安装底板

mounting rate　(设备、附加装置等的)装着率

mounting ring　安装环,安装圈(环形安装座)

mount insulator　支座隔振垫(如垫在发动机支座与车身或车架间的减振软垫或液压减振垫)

mouse-style controller　鼠标型控制器,鼠标型操纵件

mouth　口,出口,入口,出入口,喇叭口;开口处;输入端,输出端,进气管

mouth of the tongs　钳口(= jaw of the tongs)

movable　可动的,活动的,可移动的,移动式的

movable air compressor　移动式空(气)压(缩)机

movable anode　可动阳极

movable bearing　活动支架,活动支撑

movable capacitor plate 可变电容器的活动板

movable contact 活动触点，活动接头，移动式触头，滑动式触点

movable crane 移动式吊车，移动式起重机，桥（式）吊（车）

movable fit 动配合，松配合

movable-floor trailer 活底挂车（见 moving-floor trailer）

movable foot pedal 可调式踏板（位置可调整的踏板，相对于一般汽车上的位置固定的踏板而言）

movable license plate 可动型（车）牌照板

movable load 活动荷载，动载

movable steering wheel （汽车的）可调式转向盘（其位置可以调整）

movable vane 活动叶片（亦称 movable blade）

movable vane axial-flow pump 叶片角可调式轴流泵

movable weight（of distributor）（分电盘）活动配重块

movement control ①交通调度，行车调度 ②运动控制

move off （汽车由静止到开动）起步

mover ①运动件，运动的物体 ②原动机，发动机 ③[美]搬运公司

moving armature 动衔铁

moving axis 动轴

moving axis system （汽车的）运动坐标系 (x_0, y_0, z_0)，（固定在汽车上的右手直角坐标系，原点在汽车质心，x_0 轴为汽车的纵向对称面与通过汽车质心的水平面的交线，沿汽车的主运动方向指向前方；y_0 轴垂直于纵向对称面，水平指向左方；z_0 轴垂直于 x_0 和 y_0 平面，指向上方）

moving barrier 活动障碍物（汽车撞车试验用，如：装在轮式底盘上，以规定的速度运动，模拟汽车碰撞）

moving-base car-following automobile simulator 活动台基跟随前车式汽车驾驶模拟装置（用于模拟研究高速公路上的车辆和驾驶员的关系）

moving bridge crane 移动式桥式起重机，活动桥式吊车

moving cell （自动化运输系统的）动单元，运动单元

moving chamber （转子发动机的）动工作室，移动型工作室（在一个热力循环中，工作室随着转子工作面旋转移动，区别于往复式发动机的固定工作室）

moving coil type 活动线圈型（指仪表，将装有指针的可动线圈置于固定式永久磁铁的磁场中，利用可变电阻获得随温度、压力、液面高度等变化的电流通过该线圈时，便可将上述变化量转变为线圈的移动量，借以指示上述各变量的变化值）

moving contact 活动触点（如：起动机电磁开关的活动触点）

moving contact arm spring 活动触点臂弹簧

moving core type 活动铁芯型（亦称 moving iron type，见 moving-magnet）

moving deformable barrier （汽车撞车试验的）活动式易变形障碍物（活动柔性壁障，简称 MDB）

moving flat road （轮胎三维试验机的）活动路面平板（代替路面，被试验的车轮支撑在该平板上，试验时该平板可按要求前、后运动）

moving floor body 带活动地板的车厢

moving-floor trailer 活底挂车（带有推送货物的活动底板或底板装有传送装置的挂车，= movable-floor trailer）

moving force 驱动力，牵引力（= motive force）

moving iron （电磁开关等的）动铁

芯，活动铁芯（见 magnetic-armature）
moving load 活动荷载，动载
moving magnet ammeter 动磁式电流表
moving magnet fuel indicator 动磁式燃油表指示器
moving magnetic oil pressure indicator 动磁式机油压力表指示器
moving magnetic temperature indicator 动磁式温度表指示器
moving-magnet（type） 动磁式，可动永久磁铁式（指利用可变电阻等获得的随温度、压力、液面高度等变化的电流量通过一固定线圈，将上述变量转变为线圈中的可动永久磁铁的位移量，以指示上述变化值的各种仪表，亦称 moving core type）
moving object detection （车外）移动物体探知（功能）
moving parts 运动部件（= movable parts）
moving picture car 电影放映车
moving plate （电喇叭的）振动膜片（亦称 vibrating diaphragm）
moving road （传送带式的）活动道路
moving stud （电磁控制齿轮移动式强制啮合型起动机的电磁开关活动的铁芯端部与拨叉连接的）推柱（其长度可调，以调整驱动小齿轮与飞轮齿环的啮合位置）
moving table 活动工作台
moving taper disc ［连续无级变速器（CVT）主动传动带轮的］锥形活动盘（亦称 movable disc，见 CVT steel belt puller）
moving van 家具搬运车，搬家车（= furniture van, removal van, pantechnicon）
moving velocity 行驶速度，移动速度

MPa 兆帕（压力单位，$= 10^6$ Pa，见 pascal）
MPC ①一种炭黑的商品名（Medium Pressing Channel 的简称，平均直径 $25\mu m$，表面积 $120m^2/g$) ②最大允许浓度（maximum permissible concentration 的简称）③主功率控制装置（master power controller）
MPG 每加仑燃料行驶英里里程（miles per gallon 的简称，亦写作 mpg）
MPG lean cruise （福特公司的 EEC IV 系统的）低油耗稀混合气定速巡行（汽车定速行驶中，当达到某规定车速时，电子控制模块使发动机脱离闭路控制而转为使用稀混合气，以达到节油目的）
mpg-meter 加仑英里里程表（燃油消耗量表）
80-mpg super car 80 英里/加仑超级车（每加仑汽油可行驶 80 英里的超级高效车）
mph ①英里/小时（miles per hour 的简称，亦写作 MPH）②偶尔指每小时米数（m/h, meters per hour 的简称）
mphps （加速度单位之一）每秒每小时英里数（miles per hour per second 英里/小时/秒）
MPI 多点燃油喷射（multi-point injection 的简称）
M-process（combustion）**chamber** M 型燃烧室（德国 Meurer 首创，在活塞顶部形成，燃烧室呈球形，属半开式燃烧室的一种，燃油在燃烧室内实现油膜混合燃烧）
mps ①活塞平均速度（mean piston speed 的简称）②米每秒（meter per second 的简称，亦写作 m/s）
MPT 多片式离合器型四轮驱动前、后桥转矩分配控制分动箱（multi-plate transfer 的简称）
MPU 微处理器（microprocessor unit

MPV ①多用途汽车，多功能汽车（multipurpose vehicle）②发动机驱动车辆，机动车辆（motor-powered vehicle 的简称）

mrad 毫弧度（见 milliradian）

MRE ①磁致阻变元件效应元件（magneto resistive effect element 的简称）②阻磁元件（magneto resistive element 的简称，如霍尔效应等传感器中隔断磁力线的元件）

MRE sensor 见 magneto resistive effect sensor

MRFC 甲醇重整燃料电池（methanol reforming fuel cell 的简称。甲醇 CH_3OH 经重整生成 H_2 和 CO，净化处理除去 CO，将 H_2 作为燃料输入燃料电池，因此实际上是一种氢燃料电池）

MRI 国际汽车通报（期刊）（Motor Report International）

MRO 维护，修理，使用（maintenance, repair, operation）

MRT 公共快速交通系统（mass rapid transit system）

m^2/s 米²/秒（国际单位制的运动黏度单位，参见 kinematic viscosity）

m^3/s 立方米每秒（国际单位制容积流量单位，$1m^3/s = 60m^3/min = 60000L/min = 15850$u.s.gal/min $= 211.89ft^3/min$）

m/s 米/秒（国际单位制速度单位，1m/s $= 3.6$km/h $= 2.237$mile/h $= 196.86$ft/min $= 3.281$ft/s）

MS ①（美国石油协会原润滑油分类记号）频繁起动、停止的汽油机用润滑油②机器螺钉（machine screw）③机器钢（machine steel）④磁谱仪（magnetic spectrometer）⑤磁存储器（magnetic storage）⑥主开关（main switch）⑦维修和使用（maintenance and service）⑧生产现状（manufacturing status）⑨安全系数（margin of safety）⑩主程序装置（master sequencer）⑪总机（master station）⑫主控开关（master switch）⑬材料规格（material specification）⑭最大应力（maximum stress）⑮均方（mean square）⑯机械特性（mechanical specialities）⑰中碳钢（medium steel）⑱存储系统（memory system）⑲公制，米制（metric system）⑳军用规范（military specifications）㉑军用标准（military standards）㉒中等速度（moderate speed）㉓改进总结（modification summary）㉔容模溶液（molar solution）㉕软钢（mild steel）㉖机器已检查（machinery surveyed）㉗混合气浓度（mixture strength）

ms ①质谱仪（mass spectrometer）②兆秒（megasecond）③毫秒（millisecond）

MSAI 见 mis-starting-acceleration inhibiting system

MSAPC ［美］（环保局）机动车辆污染源大气污染控制办公室（Office of Mobile Source Air Pollution Control）

MSD ignition 多火花点火系统（multiple-spark discharge ignition）

MSDS （汽车修理车间使用的各种化学品的）材料安全数据表（Material safely Date Sheet 的简称）

MSE 制造系统工程（manufacturing systems engineering）

MSED ［美］（环保局的）机动车辆污染源强制管理部（Mobile Source Enforcement Division）

MSH 导气屏式汽缸盖（见 masked seat head）

MSI 中规模集成电路（见 medium scale integration）

MSIS 微处理器控制式点火正时系统（microprocessor spark timing system 的简称）

MSL 平均海拔（高度）（mean sea level）

MSR 发动机（制动的）阻滞转矩调节（系统）（德 VW, BMW 等用语，德文 motor schleppmoment regulation 的简称，= 英文的 engine drag-torque control，简称 EDTC）

MS System 机械电子式点火正时控制装置（mechatro spark system）

MST 额定转矩最小点火提前角（minimum spark advance for specified torque）

MSTL [美]（环保局的）机动车辆污染源试验所（Mobile Source Testing Laboratory）

M&S tyre 泥雪路面轮胎（亦称 mud and snow tyre, M + S tyre）

M + S tyre 泥-雪轮胎（mud and snow tyre 的简称，一种深花纹胎面的冬季用轮胎）

MT 磁带（magnetic tape）

MTB [美]（运输部的）材料运输局（Material Transportation Bureau）

MTBE 甲基叔丁基醚（见 methyl tertiary butyl ether）

MTBF 平均故障的间隔时间（mean time between failures）

MTBM 平均维护（作业）间隔时间（mean time between maintenances）

MTBR ①平均修理间隔时间（mean time between repairs）②更换平均间隔期（mean time between replacements）

MTCF 平均重大故障间隔时间（mean time to catastrophic failure）

MTG 甲醇汽油，加甲醇的汽油（methanol-to-gasoline 的简称）

MTL 机械试验丛书（Mechanical Testing Library）

MTREC （日本本田公司的）多节气门高响应发动机控制系统（multi throttle responsive engine control system 的简称，商品名）

MTT 机动性运输载货汽车（mobile transport truck）

MTTF 平均初次出故障时间（mean time to failure）

MTTR 平均首次修理前时间（mean time to repair）

MTV （发动机）进气总管通路调节阀（manifold tuning valve 的简称，位于进气总管通路的中央，由发动机电子控制模块通过真空马达控制其开、闭。当发动机转速低于 3008 r/min，或高于 4288r/min 时，该阀关闭，进气通道被分为左、右两路各向一排汽缸供气。当发动机转速在 3008～4288r/min 之间时，该阀开启，左、右两路合并成一路）

MTV 进气歧管调节阀（manifold tuning valve 的简称）

M-type highway 混合交通公路，M 型公路（M 是 mixed 的简称，指各类道路交通工具混合行驶的公路）

mud ability 泥地行驶能力，泥地通过能力

mud and snow pattern 雪泥花纹（适宜于泥泞与冰雪路面上行驶的胎面花纹）

mud-and-snow tyre 泥雪路面轮胎（简称 M&S tyre）

mud-and-stone deflector 泥-石挡板

mud baffle 挡泥板

mud bath （车辆试验用）泥槽

mud box 沉淀箱

mud chamber pit 滤清器油污沉淀槽

mud cock 排污旋塞（= sludge cock）

muddy ground 淤泥地，泥泞地

muddy road 泥泞道路

muddy terrain 泥泞地带，泥泞地面

mudflap （汽车的）挡泥帘（橡胶或维尼龙材料制的挡泥软帘，mudguard flap 的简称，亦称 mud apron）

mud guard ①挡泥板（= antisplash guard，美称 fender）②（车轮后吊挂的橡胶制）挡泥帘

mudguard bracket 挡泥板撑架

mudguard lamp 翼子板灯（= fender

lamp, wing lamp)
mud performer 泥地高通过性车辆
mud shield of output shaft 输出轴挡泥护罩
mud terrain tyre 泥地轮胎
mud wing 挡泥翼子板（= splash wing, 多指货车后轮的挡泥板）
muff ①衬套，套筒②保温套
muff coupling joint 球销式万向节（= pin and ball trunnion type universal joint, pot joint, trunnion joint, 一种由允许轴向滑动的自承式非等速万向节，见 ball and trunnion universal joint）
muffled steel sheet with plastic plate 塑料包覆钢板
muffler ①消声器（= sound deadener）②汽车的排气消声器（美称 exhaust silencer 或简称 silencer, 有时指两级消声器的主消声器，参见 resonator）
muffler bracket 消声器支架
muffler cut-out valve （排气制动时）消声器断流阀，消声器截流阀
muffler-exhaust system tool 排气系及消声器维修工具
muffler explosion 消声器放炮（= explosion in silencer）
muffler resistance （发动机的）消声器排气阻力
muffler shell 消声器外壳
muffler tail pipe 消声器尾管
muffling 减音，消声，隔声
mule pulley 惰轮，传动带张紧轮（= idler, belt tightening pulley）
MuLS 多层层状充气（式发动机，multi-layer stratified 的简称）
Multec injector （多点式汽油喷射系统用的）复合技术喷油器（商品名，Multiple Technology injector 的简称，其工作电压低，响应迅速，喷雾良好，用电磁线圈铁芯的球形端头取代传统喷油器的喷针）

Multec system （发动机）综合控制系统（Multiple Technology system 的简称，商品名，由一套车用计算机共用一套传感器通过各自的执行元件对喷油量、点火时刻及排放等做一体化综合最优化控制）
mult-function 通用的，多功能的，多用途的，多作用的
multi- （词头）多
multiaxial stress state 多轴应力状态
multiaxis loading 多轴向荷载（多方向荷载）
multi-axle trailer 多轴挂车
multi-axle truck 多轴货车
multiball type combustion chamber 多球形燃烧室
multibank engine 多列汽缸发动机
multi-barrel carburetor 多腔化油器（= multithroat carburetor）
multi-battery hookup 多台蓄电池的连接（指两台或两台以上的蓄电池并联或串联成一个整体电源）
multibelt tension gauge （发电机、风扇等的）多传动带紧度测量仪具（两根或两根以上单行传动带拉紧度测量用的测力表）
multi-blade blower 多叶片式鼓风机（指三个叶片以上者）
multibladed tread （提高抗滑能力的）多沟槽胎面
Multiblock （德国 Krone 公司挂车车厢内的）通用货物捆绑系统（的商品名）
multi body dynamics model 多体动力学模型（一种计算机数字模拟模型，用于新车研制和操纵性、稳定性研究）
multi-body occupant dummy （撞碰试验用）多器官乘员假人
multi-bucket loading machine 多斗式装载机
multi-cable plug 复线插头
multicarbide 多元碳化物，复合碳

化物

multi(-)channel ①多通道的，多频道的，多信道②多通道法（指先将一个信号的频谱分成几个可独立传送的频带然后再合成的方法）

multichannel 多路的，多频道的，多信道的，多通路的

multi-channel data acquisition system 多通道数据采集系统

multichannel potentiometer-type recorder 多路电位差计型记录器

multichannel recorder 多路记录器，多线记录器

multichip integrated circuit 多片集成电路（指由两块或多块半导体芯片组成的集成电路）

multichip microcircuit 多片微电路（由两个或多个半导体芯片上的电路所组成的微型电路）

multichip module 见 MCM

multi-circuit braking system 多回路制动系（指两条或两条以上回路组成的制动系，若其中有一条失效，仍能保证一定的制动能力）

multiclearance labyrinth packing 多隙式迷宫油封

multi-colo(u)r(ed) 多(颜)色的，彩色的

multi-combustion chamber 多腔燃烧室

multicompression 多级压缩

Multicon 多引脚插接系统（multi-connector system 的简称，如：供挂车电气接线的13插孔插座系统）

multicone friction clutch 多锥摩擦离合器

multicone synchronizer 多锥面同步器

multi-connector plug 多头插销

multicontact switch 多触点开关

multi-cycle sampling 多循环取样（简称 MCS）

multi cylinder camshaftless fuel injection pump 多缸分列式喷油泵（指不带自驱动凸轮轴的多缸柱塞式喷油泵）

multi-cylinder engine 多缸发动机（指具有两个或两个以上汽缸的发动机，对单缸发动机而言）

multi-cylinder fuel injection pump 多缸喷油泵（具有多个出口，供多缸发动机用的喷油泵）

multi-decker sandwich of alternating layers of ice and snow 冰雪交错形成的多层地面

multi-degree-of-freedom suspension 多自由度悬架

multidiameter shaft 多直径段轴，变径轴（一根轴上有大小不同的直径段）

multidimensional 多维的

multidirectional 多方向的，多向的

multidirectional injector 多喷孔異向喷油器

multidisciplinary accident investigation [美]汽车多项违章事故调查（简称 MDAI）

multi-disc limited slip differential 多片式（摩擦离合器）防滑差速器（亦称 multi-disc self-locking differential "片式自锁差速器"）

multi-disc wet clutch 多片湿式离合器

multi-display ①多项显示的，多信息显示的②多项显示监控仪表，多信息显示装置

multi-effect 多效的，多效应的

multi-electrode spark plug 多电极型火花塞

multi-element amphibian 多节水陆两用车

multi-energy plant 多种能源动力装置

multi-engine ①多缸发动机②多发动机的

multi-engined 多发动机的（简称

MENG)

multi-entry pump 多进口泵（亦称 multi-inlet pump，指同一泵轴上并联有两个或两个以上的泵轮，同时泵吸两股或两股以上液流的多路泵，但一般是两路）

multi-eyes 复眼，多眼（自动公路系统中行驶的车辆上安装的激光雷达、摄像头和多种传感器等信息获取装置的总称）

multifarious 多样性的，多方面的，种种的，各种各样的，千差万别的

multi-focal 多焦距的，多焦点的（简称MF）

multi-focal headlight 多焦点前照灯（具有多焦点反光镜的前照灯）

multiform function ①多值函数②多种功能

multifuction steering column lever 装在转向盘柱上的多功能操纵杆（如：可控制刮水/冲洗器，近光，转向信号灯，车道变换等）

multifuel engine 多种燃料发动机（=engine for different fuels，omnivorous engine，指可以使用一种以上的燃油的内燃机）

multifuel Wankel 多种燃料转子发动机，多种燃料旋转活塞发动机，多种燃料汪克尔发动机

multi-function control stalk 多功能操纵杆，多功能控制杆

multi-function display 多功能显示屏

multi-function display and control system 多功能显示控制系统（简称MFDCS）

multi-function indicator display 多功能显示屏（可由按钮或遥控器控制，显示汽车各有关信息、电视节目、导行地图和路线指示等的显示屏）

multi-function steering wheel 多功能转向盘（装有多种控制与操纵按钮、开关、拨杆等）

multi-function switch 多用途一体式组合开关

multi-function test stand 多功能试验台，综合试验台（参见 comprehensive test stand）

multigang switch 多联开关

multi-gap plug 多（跳火）间隙火花塞（亦称 multigap spark plug）

multigauge 多用量测仪表

multigrade 多品位的，多级的

multigrade oil 多级油（亦称 multi-viscosity oil，指用低黏度基础油加入高分子聚合物调制而成，可同时符合高温和低温两个黏度等级，具有优良的起动性、低温泵送性、热机起动性和燃料经济性，如：10W—30，10W—40，15W—50，20W—50等机油，其中，××W表示低温黏度等级，—××表示高温黏度等级）

multigroove friction clutch 多槽式摩擦离合器

multi-groove valve stem 多环槽气门杆

multi-hole nozzle （有两个以上喷油孔的）多孔喷嘴

Multi-H type floor panel 多H形（车身）底板（由多根纵梁和横梁，如：四根纵梁和五根横梁组成的多H网格状车身底板）

multi-ignition ①多火花塞点火（=multi-plug ignition）②多（跳火）间隙火花塞点火（=multi-gap plug ignition）③多火花点火（=multi-spark ignition）

multijet spray 多嘴喷雾

multi-jet spray nozzle 多孔喷嘴（=multi-jet nozzle，multi-hole nozzle，multi-orifice nozzle）

multikey shaft 多键轴

multilane freeway 多车道高速公路（一般指四车道以上的高速公路，=multiple lane freeway）

multilayer film circuit 多层膜电路（绝缘膜或间隙隔开的多层膜互连电路）

multi-leaf spring 多片式钢板弹簧

multilegs intersection 多路交叉口（= compound intersection）

multi-level and multi-factor test 多因素多水平试验

multi-level junction 多层立体交叉口（= multiple-bridge intersection）

multilift 多头起吊装置，多功能吊车

multi-line braking system （汽车列车的）多管路制动系统（指牵引车与挂车间有多条管路，分别用于供能或操纵的制动系统）

multi-line transmission device 多管路传动装置，多管路传导装置（如：多管路制动系统中的多管路制动气压或液压传动系统）

multi-link independent rear suspension 多连杆式后轮独立悬架（使用多杆件控制车轮位置的后驱动轮独立悬架系统的通称，如：three-link，four-link，five-link rear suspension 等，亦简称 multi-link type suspension，multi-arm rearsaspention 多连杆式悬架，一般指 4 连杆或 4 连杆以上的悬架形式，而且大多是在采用双 A 形臂结构的基础上增加各种控制倾倾、车轮跳动等的杆件，一般用于后轮）

multi-location maintenance 多位维护，多点维护

multiloop servo system 多路伺服系统

multilpe-cord tire 多帘布层轮胎

multilple crossing 多路交叉口

multi-luber （汽车底盘的）多点自动润滑系统（驾驶员在驾驶室内通过按钮操纵，= auto luber）

multimeasurement device 万能量测仪具（多项测仪）

multimedia 多媒体（功能）（如：计算机将声音、画面、动态影像合为一体的功能）

multimedia workstation 多媒体工作站（如：计算机控制的车况监测和通信系统等）

multimeter 万用表，多用表（指多项、多量程测量仪表，在汽车电子-电气设备检测中，一般指多量程的电流-电压通用测量表）

multimodal transportation networks 复式运输网（多种运输形式的运输网）

multi-mode operation ①多项操作，多项作业 ②多模式操作，多模式运转

multimotored （装用）数个发动机的

multination enterprise 跨国公司，多国公司

multi-nozzle fuel injection system 多喷嘴燃油喷射系（指每汽缸均有一个喷嘴的喷油系统）

multiobjective decision 多目的决策，多目标决策

multiobjective optimizing model 多目的优化模型，多项最佳化模型

multipass forced-flow cooling system 多通道强制冷却系统（多通道压力冷却系统）

multipass performance （土壤）多次通过性能

multipass sinkage （土壤）多次通过下陷量

multi path interference 多路干扰（指接收调频信号的同时还会收到建筑物和山丘等反射的反射波，二者相互干扰，而发生杂声和失真的现象）

multipath signal 多路传输信号

multipath traffic assignment probabilitic model 多线交通分配概率模型

multi P. C. D wheel 多螺栓孔分布圆直径式车轮（指该车轮有多个不同直径的螺栓孔分布圆，因而可安

装在不同的轮毂上，见 pitch circle)
multiphase ①多相②多相的
multi-phases signal intersection 多相位信号交叉路口
multipiece camshaft 多件组合式凸轮轴
multipiece oil cooled piston 组合式油冷活塞
multipiece piston（steel oil control）ring 多片组合式活塞（钢刮油）环（一般由上、下刮片及隔片和弹簧涨圈等3～4件组成，质量小，因而惯性小、张力大，即使缸壁磨损亦可保持良好的气密与刮油性能）
multipiece rim 多件式组合轮辋（两件及两件式以上的组合式轮辋的总称，如 two-piece, three-piece, four-piece, five-piece rim等）
multi-plate brake 多片式制动器
multi-plate clutch 多片式离合器（= multiple-plate clutch，美称 multiple-disc clutch）
multi-plate steering clutch 多片式转向离合器
multi-plate transfer （四轮驱动汽车的）多片摩擦离合器前、后桥转矩分配型分动器（简称MPT）
multiple access 多路访问，多路存取（简称 multiaccess，指多个用户或多种装置同时访问一个计算机系统并互不干扰地执行各自的程序）
multiple-axle drive vehicle 多桥驱动式汽车
multiple-axle trailer 多轴挂车
multiple-band receiver 多波段接收机，多波段收音机
multiple barrel injection pump 多缸喷油泵（把各缸的泵芯装在同一壳体内）
multiple bay （汽车维修场用）多功能支架，多功能工位
multiple（beam）headlamp （汽车的）多光大灯，多光前照灯（指带远、近光等的前照灯）
multiple belt drive 多传动带并装传动（如：用2～3根较窄皮带代替一根宽皮带驱动风扇、发电机等）
multiple-bridge intersection 多层（立体）交叉口（由两层或三层以上的立体交叉所组成，一般用于多层交通，各交叉道路可直接相互连接，= braided intersection, multi-level junction）
multiple carburetor 多联化油器（= compound carburetor）
multiple casing 多壳式
multiple circuit brake system 多管路制动系（制动管路分成两组以上，分别将制动液压或气压传递给各组的制动器）
multiple coil ignition 多（高压）线圈点火
multiple compartment lamp （车辆的）（由一个或一个以上的共用构件，如外壳或透镜，将两个或两个以上的独立发光区连在一起，发出同一灯光信号的）多光信号灯
multiple-contact relay 多触点继电器
multiple correlation coefficient 多重相关系数（= coefficient of multiple correlation）
multiple-cylinder 多汽缸（的）
multiple discharge（ignition）system 多火花点火系统（多次放电跳火的点火系统）
multiple disk brake 多盘式制动器
multiple disk clutch 多片式离合器（= multi-plate clutch）
multiple draft 多机牵引
multiple electric motor type antilock brake system 多电动机（控制）式防抱死制动系统（利用电动机带动的执行元件控制各液压通路的降压、升压和保压的防抱死制动系统）
multiple electrode spark plug 多电极

火花塞

multiple excitation experiment 多点激振试验[用一组激振器在结构的多个部位同时施加激振力。通过调节各激振力的幅值、相位、频率及施力部位（常称适调）使结构作单阶纯模态振动（主振动）的一种试验方法]

multiple exhaust 多管排气

multiple-expansion engine 多级膨胀发动机（蒸气或其他工质顺序在尺寸逐步加大、压力逐步下降驱动同一曲轴的两个或两个以上的汽缸内逐级膨胀的发动机）

multiple-expansion piston engine 多级膨胀活塞发动机

multiple (hole) nozzle （柴油机的）多孔式嘴喷（孔式嘴喷的一种，见 hole nozzle）

multiple intersection 多路交叉口（参见 compound intersection）

multiple keys 花键

multiple lamp arrangement （车辆灯光信号的）多灯同（信）号（指在车辆的每一侧用两个或两个以上的独立信号灯表示同一信号）

multiple-lane road 多车道道路（= multilane road）

multiple lip seal 多唇密封

multiple network （汽车电子控制系统的）多路通信网络系统

multiple network architecture 多网络结构

multiple-party occupancy （公共运输工具的）伙用，共用，公乘（如目前的公共汽车，见 single-party occupancy）

multiple-piston rotary pump 多活塞旋转泵

multiple-plate clutch 多片式离合器

multiple plug system 多火花塞点火系统（一个汽缸有两只以上火花塞）

multiple-plunger pump 多柱塞泵

multiple-point welding 多点焊

multiple-purpose diesel motor 通用柴油机（适应多种用途的柴油机）

multiple-purpose tester 万能测试器（多用途测试工具）

multiple range gates 多阶门，多域门

multiple range transmission 多挡区变速器（将整个变速范围分成若干挡区的副变速器，例如高、低挡副变速器）

multiple-rotor Wankel engine 多缸汪克尔转子发动机，多缸汪克尔旋转活塞发动机

multiple-runner turbine 多级涡轮机（= multistage turbine）

multiple sampling 多次取样

multiple sensors 多重传感器（如：汽车碰撞与安全气囊起爆传感器一般使用 3～5 个传感器，实现多点传感 "multipoint sensing"）

multiple slip aligner （汽车的）多用式侧偏试验台（可测定前轮侧倾、前束、侧偏值等的滚筒试验台）

multiple-spark discharge ignition 多次火花放电点火（多火花点火，简称 MSD ignition）

multiple-spark (ignition) coil 多火花点火线圈[用于无分电器的静态高压分配式点火系统，为双火花点火线圈或四火花点火线圈等的通称，不用分电器而采用高压分配电路，将各线圈产生的高压脉冲分配给相应的两个或四个缸火花塞，简称 multi-spark (ignition) coil]

multiple-speed gearbox 多挡变速器

multiple spline hub 花键轮毂

multiple spline shaft 多键轴，花键轴

multiple spring 复式弹簧

multiple-stage 多级式（的），多层的，多段的

multiple-stage planetary gear train 多级行星齿轮系

multiple-(start) screw thread 多头螺纹,多线螺纹

multiple-storey garage 多层车库

multiple-thread (ed) worm 多头螺纹蜗杆,多线螺纹蜗杆（参见 multithread worm）

multi (ple) -throw crank shaft 多曲柄曲轴

multiple-unit 多元的,复合的；多发动机的,多机组的,多动力装置的

multiple vee-belt drive 多条三角传动带传动（= multiple-strand drive）

multiple-wheel drive 多轮驱动

multiplex address/data bus 多路地址/数据总线

multiplex communication system （单线）多路复用通信系统（指用一条传输线同时传送多条信息的通信方式,见 multiplexer）

multiplexer （单线）多路复用器,（单线）多路转换器[将同时从许多终端接收的低速输入数据或信号,转换成一个高速数据或信号流并通过一个通道（即单线）输出的装置,在其输出单线的终端由一个多路分解器"demultiplexer"将该高速信号流分解,还原为原低速数据或信号,分配给相应装置。高速流数据或信号传递方式分为：时分多路复用和频分多路复用两种,见 time division multiplexer 及 frequency division multiplexer]

multiplexing control system 多路传输控制系统（单线多路复用控制系统）

multiplexing network 多路复用网络

multiplex stereo 多声道立体声

multiplex technology （单线）多路复用技术（用一根导线向多种复用器设备供电,或对多种设备进行控制,或传输多个信号的技术）

multiplex wiring system 单线多路复用电路系统

multiplication ①增加,增多,倍增,倍加,放大,按比例增加②乘法,相乘,乘积

multiplication current （雪崩）倍增电流

multiplicator ①乘数,系数,因数②乘法装置,倍增器,放大器,扩大量程装置（= multiplier）

multiplier linkage 加力杆系

multiplying factor 放大系数,倍数,乘数,倍率（= X factor）

multiply tyre 多层（帘布）外胎,多帘布层轮胎

multipoint electromechanical sensing system （安全气囊的）多点机电式传感系统（亦称 distributed air bag sensing system 分布式安全气囊传感系统,相对于单点式电子传感系统"single point sensing system"而言,指由两个或四个分布在汽车的各碰撞挤压区前沿的机电式碰撞判断传感器"crash discrimination sensor"和一个装在起诊断、储能和变压作用的电子控制模块内的附加保险传感器"arming sensor"组成的传感系统,后者用于防止气囊在非碰撞时的误起爆。相对于无外装式传感器,只在客舱内的电子控制电路中装有一个加速度传感器的 single-point electronic sensing system,或称 central air bag system 而言）

multi-point fuel injection system 多点式汽油喷射系统（简称 MFI,亦简称 multiport fuel injection system, MPI;原来相对于中央单点式节气门体汽油喷射系统而言,指每一汽缸进气口处装有一喷油器的汽油喷射系统,亦称 port fuel injection system;但目前按 SAEJ1930 的规定,仅指每缸一个喷油器,将汽油喷至进气门孔附近的喷射系统中,视发

动机型号不同，每两个、三个或四个喷油器为一组，用一根控制电线与电子控制模块连接，因而电子控制模块每发出一个喷油信号，同一组的各个喷油器均喷油一次的喷油系统，见 SFI）

multi-point injection methanol fuel engine 甲醇燃料多点喷射式发动机

multi-point LPG liquid fuel injection system 多点式液化石油气液态燃油喷射系统

multipoint temperature monitor 多点温度监测器，多点温度计

multipolar machine 多极式电机（具有四个以上磁极的发电机或电动机）

multipolar synchro 多极同步机

multiport fuel injection 见 multipoint fuel injection system

multi-position switch 多位开关

multiprocessing 多重处理（指由一台计算机或电子控制模块同时执行两道或多道计算机程序或指令序列）

multiprocessor 多处理机（共用一个主存储器和外部设备的两台或两台以上各自独立执行程序，相互间可实现通信的处理器组成的控制用计算机或控制系统）

multiprocessor system 多处理机系统（由两台以上独立执行程序，有各自的控制对象，共享公用主存和外部设备，相互间通过互联网络实现通信的中央处理机组成的系统）

multi-pull brake 多次拉动式制动器（指带棘轮机构的驻车制动器，需要拉动多次才能全制动，故名）

multipurpose 万能的，通用的，万用的，多用途的，多功能的

multipurpose display 多用途显示屏（供导航、车况信息通信以及电视等使用）

multipurpose grease 多用途润滑脂

multipurpose mover 多用途车辆

multipurpose oil 多用途润滑油

multipurpose passenger vehicle 多用途乘用车，多功能乘用车（简称 MPV）

multipurpose trailer 多用途挂车，万能挂车

multipurpose vehicle 多用途车（简称 MPV，如：pick-up）

multirange receiver 多波段收音机

multirange transmission 多挡变速器（= multispeed gear box）

multiratio variable drives 多速比可变传动

multi-reed cage （两冲程发动机进气系统的）多片式簧片阀，多瓣式簧片阀（见 reed valve）

multi-reflector rear combination lamp 多反光镜型后组合车灯

multi-reflector type headlamp 多重反射镜型前照灯

multirib belt （发电机、风扇等的）多肋型传动带，多槽形传动带

multi-road pass construction （车身碰撞时受力）多路分散传递结构

multi-roll bearing 滚针轴承，滚柱轴承

multi-row 多排的，多列的，多行的

multi-segmented steel pusher belt ［无级连续式变速器（CVT）的］推力型多节式钢传动带

multi-sell compound 发泡材料（如：发泡橡胶、发泡塑料等多孔复合材料）

multi-spark ignition 多火花点火（指火花塞每次点火不只是跳一次火花，而是连续发出多次火花点火）

multi-speed drive 多级变速传动

multi-speed gear box 多挡变速箱，多挡变速器（= multiple range transmission）

multi-speed motor 多速电机

multispeed power take-off 多挡取

力器

multispeed transmission 多挡变速器

multispherical combustion chamber 多球形燃烧室（缸盖上由多个球面组成的燃烧室，可加大进、排气门尺寸和将火花塞布置在燃烧室中间）

multi-spindle 多轴（的）

multi-spindle nut-runner 多头螺母扳机，多扳杆螺母拧紧机

multispot electronic fuel injection 多点燃油喷射

multi-spot weld machine 多焊头点焊机，多头点焊机

multistable circuit 多稳电路

multistage active turbine 多级冲击式涡轮机

multistage catalyst converter 多级催化转化器（一般指前置催化转向器和主催化转化器串联成一体的转化器）

multistage centrifugal compressor 多级式离心压缩机

multistage centrifugal pump 多级离心泵

multistage compression refrigeration system 多级压缩冷冻系统

multistage converter 多级液力变矩器（插在液力变矩器其他叶轮元件之间的涡轮元件称为级，级数是指其中刚性连接的涡轮元件数，多级液力变矩器，是指该变矩器具有两个或两个以上的刚性连接的涡轮元件，参见 member④，⑤）

multistage filtering 多级过滤

multistage gas turbine 多级式燃气轮机

multi-stage injection （柴油机压电晶体式喷油器等的）多段喷射［用得较多的是每做功冲程三段喷油：预喷（pre-injection）、主喷（main injection）和后喷（after-injection），但最多可分9段喷油。多段喷油可避免常规的每循环1次喷油造成的喷油量多，燃料在高温高压下急速燃烧，噪声加剧和 NO_X 增加的缺点，见 piezo injector］

multi-stage power window 多段升降型电动车窗

multistage pump 多级泵（泵的"级"是指在同一泵轴上串联安装的泵轮或其他泵压元件，如"两级"和"三级"，是指同一轴上串联有两个和三个泵轮，"多级"是装有两个或两个以上的泵轮的通称，多级泵亦简称 multiple pump）

multistage reaction turbine 多级反击式涡轮机

multistage reciprocating compressor 多级往复式压缩机

multistage turbine 多级涡轮（机）（= multiple-runner turbine）

multi-stage waste gates （废气涡轮增压器的）多段式废气泄放阀（以保证废气增压压力适应发动机各种工况的要求）

multi-start 多头（螺纹）的，多线（路）的，复线（螺纹）的

multi-start worm 多头螺纹蜗杆

multistep cone pulley 多级（皮带传动）塔轮

multistep control servo mechanism 多级控制的伺服机构

multistop body 多停车点式客车车辆的车身（在设计上要求能确保驾驶人员和乘员快速上下车）

multistop delivery 多点分送货物

multistop delivery truck ①包裹投送车（= package delivery truck）②送货上门车（= door-to-door truck, door-to-door delivery truck, peddle truck）

multistorey car park 多层停车场

multi-strike ignition 多次火花点火

multi-suction pump 多吸口泵，多进口泵（见 multi-entry pump）

multi-terrain monitor （越野车等装

有360°摄像头的）全周边障碍物监控器

multi-tester 多功能检测仪，多用试验台

multithread worm 多头蜗杆，多线蜗杆

multi-throat carburetor 多腔化油器（＝multibarrel carburetor）

multitone（d）horn 多音喇叭

multitrace oscilloscope 多线示波器

multi-trailer vehicle 多节挂车列车

Multitronic 手动/无级变速一体式变速器（商品名）

multitubular radiator 多管式散热器

multitude ①许多,大量②多倍③集,组④许多的,众多的,大量

multiunit 多组件的,多部件的,复合的,多重的

multiunit rotary engine 多缸转子发动机,多缸旋转活塞发动机

multi-unit truck combination 多节挂车的货运汽车列车

multiunit vehicle 多节铰接式车辆,多节挂车列车

multiuse recreational vehicle 多种用途的游乐车（简称 MURV）

multivalve ①多（电子）管的②多阀门的,多气门的

multi-valve combustion system 多气门燃烧系统（指内燃机每缸有两个以上的气门,如：四气门,有两个进气门,两个排气门,进气充足,排气干净）

multivalve engine 多气门发动机（指每个汽缸多于两个气门的发动机）

multivalve unit of hydraulic active suspension 主动式液压悬架系统的多阀体（该阀体内集成有：①保持液压稳定的主减压阀"main relief valve"②将油泵输出后经滤清的油液送至液流控制阀的主液道止回阀"main check valve"③发动机熄火时关闭主液道,而发动机起动时逐渐开启主液道防止液压突升的液流控制阀"flow control valve"④液压超过规定值时开启,低于规定值时关闭,并在发动机熄火时保持稳定液压的液压先导控制阀"pilot controlled valve"⑤当电子控制系统发生故障时,引导液压通路,防止车身高度突然变化的安全阀"failsafe valve"）

multi-variable control system 多变量控制系统

multivariant quality inspection 多参数的质量检查

multi-variate analysis 多变量分析

multi-vibrator 多谐振荡器

multiviscosity oil 多级润滑油（见 multigrade oil）

multivoltage management system （重型货车或牵引车等电路的）多电压控制系统（指 24～12V 或 12～24V 的转换系统,供对要求不同电压的设备或工况使用,最简单的是 12V 蓄电池的串联并联切换系统,目前已采用 12～24V 或 24～12V 电子控制调控系统）

multi vortex stratified combustion system 多涡流式层状燃烧系统（简称 MVCS）

multiway connector 多孔插座,多头插销,多引脚接线器

multiway intersection 多路交叉口（＝compound intersection）

multiway power seat adjuster （汽车）座椅的电动多项调节装置,电动座椅多项调节装置（一般可对座椅的高低、前后及斜倾等多项要求进行自动调节）

multiwheeled vehicle 多轮汽车,多轴车,多桥车（一般指两桥以上的汽车）

multi-wheeler 多轴汽车

multi-zone temperature regulation （汽车分区温控空调系统的）多区域温度调节

mult-spark（ignition）coil 多火花

点火线圈 [见 multiple-spark (ignition) coil]

municipal fleet 市政（服务）车队

municipal transport 城市运输 (= municipal transportation, city transport)

Munsell chroma 孟塞尔色品

Munsell system 孟塞尔（色标）系统

Muntz metal 四-六黄铜（锌铜合金，锌40%，或35%~45%，其余为铜，亦称60-40 copper zinc alloy）

MUP 连点修正法（见 modified uniontown procedure）

MUR 最大有效率（maximum useful rate）

Mural 用喷枪在车厢外壁上喷绘的各种彩画或图案

murderous test 特别恶劣工作条件下的试验

MURV 多功能游乐车（multiuse recreational vehicle 的简称）

muscular energy braking system 人力制动系（= manual brake）

mushroom button 菌形按钮

mushroom cam 菌状凸轮

mushroom tappet 菌形挺杆（= mushroom type follower, mushroom type plunger）

mushroom-type 菌形的，蘑菇形的，伞形的（= mushroom-shaped）

mushroom-type lifter 菌形凸轮随动件（如：菌形气门挺杆，= mushroom-type valve lifter）

mushroom-type plunger ①菌形柱塞 ②菌形挺杆（= mushroom tappet）

mushroom valve 菌形气门，菌形阀

mushroom valve stem （杆端墩粗的）菌式气门杆

Muskie law 马斯基法（美国联邦政府1963年颁布的防止空气污染的"大气清洁法" Clean Air Act 的俗称，美参议院议员 Edmon Muskie 为其提案人，故名）

mu split 路面打滑（因道路摩擦系数过低或突然变小而造成的制动或转向滑移现象，亦写作 μ split）

Mustang （福特）野马（跑车名）

mutual action 相互作用

mutual-inductance 互感（系数）

mutual induction 互感，互感现象（指放在一起的两个线圈，当其中一个线圈有电流通过时，由于电磁感应作用，而在另一个线圈内产生感应电动势的现象）

mutual inductor 互感线圈，互感装置（包括具有一定电感的两只感应线圈）

mutually exclusive 互不相交；互不相容的，互斥的

mutual overtaking （汽车的）相互超越

mutual repulsion 相互排斥

MUX ①多路（multiplex 的简称，在一个通道上，通过时分或频分传输多个信息流）②多路转接器（multiplexer 的简称，可同时从许多终端接收低速输入数据，然后转换成高速数据流并在一个通道上传输的装置，其输出端的分路分解器又将高速流数据转换为一系列低速输入数据输出。其通道分为时分多路或频分多路方式）

mV ①毫伏（millivolt）②毫瓦（milliwatt）

MV 手动阀（manual valve）

MVA 兆伏安（megavolt-ampere）

MVCS 多涡流式层状燃烧系统（multivortex stratified combustion system）

MVI 汽车检查，汽车检测（motor vehicle inspection）

MVLPS （自动变速器的）手动（选挡）阀杆位置传感器（亦简称 MLP sensor, manual valve lever position sensor 的简称）

MVMA [美] 汽车制造者协会（Motor Vehicle Manufacturers Association)

MVP [美]（国家公路交通安全管理局的）汽车规划部门（Motor vehicle progam）

MVS 喷油量计量阀传感器（见 metering value sensor）

MVSS [美]汽车安全标准（Motor Vehicle Safety Standards）

M10W 90%的甲醇加10%的水（以体积计）[90（volume）percent methanol and 10 percent water 的简称]

MW ①中波（medium wave）②兆瓦（megawatt）③微瓦（microwatt）④微波（microwave）⑤分子量（molecular weight）⑥最有价值的（most worthy）

mW G 米制水表（meter water gage）

Mx 麦（磁通量单位，见 maxwell）

m-xylene 间二甲苯

MY 年型（见 model year）

my-car driver 驾驶自己车的人员，自车驾驶人（亦称 owner driver）

MyFord Touch infotainment system 福特触摸屏式多媒体互动系统（商品名，2013年生产的多款福特车上均装有此系统，简称 MyFord Touch）

Mylar 密拉薄膜（聚酯薄膜纸，聚酯薄膜板，密拉薄膜板，美国产 polyetheleneterephthalate polyester film 的商品名。具有极好透明度及电性能的强劲膜片，亦称 Melinex）

Mylink （雪佛兰上使用的）车载信息系统（商品名，一般都附带导航功能）

MYM 万米，十千米（myriameter）

myopia 近视，近视眼

N ①毫微，纤 10^{-9}（nano）②负的，阴极（negative）③空挡（neutral）④牛顿（力的单位）（newton）⑤氮（nitrogen）⑥正交，法线，标准（normal）⑦当量浓度（normal concentration）⑧北（north）⑨北极（north pole）⑩数字编号（number）⑪尼龙（nylon）

N/A 自然吸气，非增压（发动机）（natural aspirate）

NA 阿伏伽德罗数（$=6.023\times10^{23}$，Avogadro number 的简称）

Na 钠（sodium）

N/A 不装备，不提供（not available 的简称）

NAA [美] 全国汽车协会（National Automobile Association）

NAAA [美] 全国汽车拍卖协会（National Auto Auction Association）

NAAD [美] 全国汽车经销商协会（National Association of Auto Dealers）

NAAQS [美] 国家环境空气质量标准（National Ambient Air Quality Standard）

NAASVA 国家汽车安全与车祸受害者救助机构（National Agency for Automotive Safety &Victims'Aid 的简称）

NaBH₄ hydrogen-storage system 硼氢化钠储氢系统（NaBH₄ 是一种无毒、不自燃、无污染环境的廉价化合物，在常温下与水混合为液态，氢存储其中。无须加压和冷却，只要加入适应的催化剂，便可将高纯度氢分离出来，供应燃料电池。据称在试验车的燃料箱中加入204.4L NaBH₄ 水溶液，可保证试验车行驶483km）

NACA 全美航空咨询委员会（National Advisory committee for Aeronautics 的简称）

NACA duct 全美航空咨询委员会（开发的空气动力学外形薄型）风屏（常见于跑车等的发动机罩，供通风、冷却发动机等，亦称 air scoop）

NACC [美] 全国轿车商会（National Automobile Chamber of Commerce）

nacelle ①护罩，流线型外壳，（轿车车身或长头货车驾驶室的）流线型前围上盖板②客舱，机舱

NADA 全美汽车经销商协会（National Automobile Association）

NADART [美] 全国汽车经销商协会退休信托基金会（National Automobile Dealers Association Retirement Trust）

NADCF [美] 全国汽车经销商公益基金会（National Automobile Dealer's Charitable Foundation）

NAE [美] 国家工程院（National Academy of Engineering 的简称)

NAFA [美] 全国车队管理者协会(National Assn of Fleet Administrators Inc)

NAGS [美] 国家汽车用玻璃规范(National Auto Glass Specification)

NAH (汽车 NVH 测量中应用的)近场声全息(技术)(Near-field Acoustical Holography 的简称,见 NVH)

NAHSC 全美自动公路系统基金会(参见 National Automated Highway System Consortium)

NAIAS 北美国际汽车展(North American International Auto Show 的简称)

NA-IDI 自燃吸气式非直接喷射式(发动机)[natural aspirate-indirect injection (engine) 的简称]

nail ①钉子②钉钉子

nail-catcher 起钉钳(亦称 nail extractor, nail puller)

naked ①开启的,无遮蔽的,不保护的;裸露的,不绝缘的②清除外皮的,除去外壳的

naked wire 裸线(= bare wire)

n-alkyl chain 正烷基链

NAMBO [美] 全国客车驾驶员协会(National Association of Motor Bus Operator)

name ①名称②命名,取名

name of parts 品名,零件名

name plate 铭牌,产品型号牌

name plate rating 铭牌(功率的)标定值

NAND element 与非元件(见 NAND gate)

NAND gate 与非门(逻辑电路的一种,将非门接在与门上,呈正输入-输出关系或将与门接在非门上,呈负输入关系组成,二者都是两个输入均为 1 时,输出为 0,若有一个输入为 0,或两个输入均为 0 时,输出为 1,亦称 NAND logic gate 或 NOT and gate, = NAND element)

NAND operation "与非"逻辑,"与非"运算(三个命题全部为真时,结果为假,至少有一个命题为假,则结果为真的逻辑运算)

Nanjing Automobile Works (中国)南京汽车制造厂(简称 NAW)

nano 毫微,纳($=10^{-9}$,简称 n 或 N)

nanoammeter 毫微安培计

nano and micro relief 粗糙度,微观平面度

nanometer 纳米,毫微米($=10^{-9}$ 米,简称 nM)

nanometer 毫微米,纳米($=10^{-9}$ m)

nanoparticle emission 纳米级微粒排放物

NanoPro Tech (Bridge Stone Tire Co. 的材料)纳米处理技术(通过对材料分子结构的设计,控制材料的细微组织结构,以达到使材料产生必要的特性的技术的总称,是该公司的核心技术之一)

NanoScission (美国 Primed Precision Materials 公司研发的制作电动汽车用锂铁电池电极原料——粉状结晶锂粒等的)纳米剪切法(取代旧的研磨法,据称可节约成本 ≥60%,且提高品质,缩短制作时间)

nanosecond 毫微秒,纳秒(简称 nanosec)

nanotechnology 纳米技术

nanowatt IC 毫微瓦集成电路

NAO 非石棉类有机材料(non-asbestos organic 的简称)

NAPA [美] 全国汽车零部件协会(National Automotive Parts Association)

NAPCA [美] 国家大气污染控制局(National Air Pollution Control Agency,现改为环境保护局)

naphtha ①粗挥发油（石油和煤焦油蒸馏获取的低沸点碳氢化合物的混合物，亦称石脑油）②重质汽油（注：150～220℃温度下馏出的汽油）

naphthene 环烷烃（如：环己烷"C_6H_{12}"，环戊烷"C_5H_{10}"等分子式为C_nH_{2n}的碳氢化合物的总称）

naphthenic oil 环烷基润滑油（使用环烷烃为基础油制成的机油，与石蜡基机油比较，其低温流动性较好，氧化沉积物较软）

naphthenic ring 环烷环

napier 奈培（电信功率比值单位，见 neper）

napier ring L形断面气环，L形断面压缩环（亦称 Dykes type compression ring）

Napier's logarithm 纳氏对数，自然对数（John Napier 英口数学家，对数发明者）

NAPS-Z （日本）日产公司Z系列发动机排气净化系统的总称（每缸使用两个火花塞点燃稀混合气，以提高燃烧效率，减少 CO，HC 排放）

narrow-band 窄频带，窄带

narrowband noise 窄频带噪声

narrow-band wave analyser 窄频带波分析仪

narrow base tyre 窄基轮胎（轮辋宽度与轮胎断面宽度比为0.70以下的普通断面轮胎）

narrow bridge sign 窄桥标志（桥宽不足6m的窄桥标志）

narrow curve ①急弯，险弯，陡弯 ②小曲率半径弧线，锐曲线

narrow cut 窄馏分（初始沸点与终沸点间温度相差小，即沸点范围窄的石油馏分，亦称 narrow boiling fraction）

narrow-faced and double bevelled oil control ring 上、下双倒角窄面刮油环，上、下双斜边窄面油环

narrow-faced top bevelled oil control ring 上倒角窄面刮油环，上锥面窄面油环

narrow face ring 窄面活塞环（指与汽缸壁接触面窄的活塞环）

narrow gap 窄间隙，窄隙

narrow-gauge 窄轨的，窄轨距的

narrow gear stepping 窄速比挡位间隔，窄速比间距

narrowing 变窄，收缩

narrow-mouthed 窄口的

narrow range ①窄范围，窄幅度，窄值域，窄量程，窄波段，窄区间 ②窄速比间距（指各挡位速比间相隔的幅度很小）

narrow road drive assist system 狭窄道路行车帮助系统（简称 NRDA system，用车内屏显或路面投影显示狭窄道路障碍物及推荐行驶路线或推荐转向盘转角的方式，帮助驾驶者越过狭窄路段）

narrow slit 窄缝

narrow stepped transmission ［美］各挡间速比差距小的）窄速比变速器（＝narrow stepped gear box）

narrow-track tractor 窄轮距牵引车［亦称 narrow（-gauge）tractor］

narrow tube 小直径管

narrow-type bearing 窄系列滚动轴承

narrow type oil ring 窄型油环（指宽度小的油环，在涨圈的压力下可紧贴缸套表面，而改善刮油性能）

narrow-type 4×4 radial mud tire 四轮驱动窄型泥泞地用子午胎

narrow V-engine 窄式V形发动机（指两排汽缸间夹角小于60°的V形发动机）

NAS ［美］国家科学院（National Academy of Science）

NASCAR ［美］全国普通轿车赛车协会（National Association for Stock Car Auto Racing，该协会称的

"stock car"指美国大众级主流轿车,轴距为120英寸,排量7 000CC以下的在市场上销售的大量生产型普通轿车)

NASS [美]国家交通事故取样系统(National Accident Sampling System)

NATA [美]全国轿车运输协会(National Automobile Transportation Association)

natatorial 浮水的,游泳的

NATEF [美]全国汽车技术人员教育基金会(National Automotive Technicians Education Foundation)

national 国家的,国有的

National Academy of Science [美]国家科学院(简称NAS)

National Accident Sampling System [美]国家交通事故取样系统(简称NASS)

National Air Pollution Control Agency [美]国家大气污染管理局(简称NAPCA,现改为Environment Pollution Agency环境保护局,简称EPA)

National Ambient Air Quality Standard [美]国家环境空气质量标准(简称NAAQS)

National Assn of Fleet Administrators' Inc [美]全国车队管理者协会(简称NAFA)

National Assn of Truck Stop Operators [美]全国载货汽车站工作者协会(简称NATSO)

National Association for Stock Car Auto Racing 全美普通汽车赛车协会(见NASCAR)

National Association of Auto Dealers 全美汽车销售商协会(简称NAAD)

National Association of Motor Bus Operator [美]全国客车驾驶员协会(简称NAMBO)

National Auto Auction Association [美]全国汽车拍卖协会(简称NAAA)

National Automated Highway System Consortium 全美自动公路系统基金会(成立于1994年,其目的在于通过发展智能公路技术来促进运输安全与效率,简称NAHSC)

National Automobile Association [美]全国汽车协会(简称NAA)

National Automobile Chamber of Commerce [美]全国轿车商会(简称NACC)

National Automobile Dealers Association Retirement Trust [美]全国汽车经销商协会退休信托基金会(简称NADART)

National Automobile Dealers Charitable Foundation [美]全国汽车经销商公益基金会(简称NADCF)

National Automobile Transportation Association [美]全国轿车运输协会(简称NATA)

National Automotive Parts Association [美]全国汽车零部件协会(简称NAPA)

National Automotive Technicians Education Foundation [美]全国汽车技术人员教育基金会(简称NATEF)

National Bureau of Standard [美]国家标准局(简称NBS)

National Capital Transportation Agency [美]国家首都运输局(简称NCTA)

National Committee of Uniform Traffic Laws and Ordinances [美]统一交通法规条例全国委员会(简称NCUTLO)

National Crash Severity Study [美]全国汽车碰撞严重程度研究会(简称NCSS)

national defence highway 国防公路

national defence standard [日]防

卫厅标准（简称 NDS）
national design award 国家设计奖
national driver register 国家驾驶员注册（登记）（简称 NDR）
national economy 国民经济
National Electric Code ［美］全国电气规程（简称 NEC）
National Electronic Injury Surveillance System ［美］国家电子伤害监视系统（专门用于监视交通事故的伤害设施，简称 NEISS）
National Energy Development Policy Act ［美］国家能源开发保护法（为了保护能源，贯彻能源开发、使用等政策的法规，简称 NECPA）
National Environmental Research Center ［美］（环保局的）国家环境研究中心（简称 NERC）
National Federation of Vehicle Trades ［英］全国汽车贸易联合会（简称 NFVT）
National Freight Corporation ［美］全国货运公司（简称 NFC）
National Fuel Gas Company ［美］国家可燃气体公司（简称 NFGC）
National Highway 国有公路，国道
National Highway Safety Act ［美］国家公路安全法
National Highway Safety Advisory Council ［美］国家公路安全咨询委员会（为国家公路交通安全管理局 NHTSA 的咨询机构，简称 NHSAC）
National Highway Safety Bureau ［美］国家公路安全管理局（简称 NHSB）
National Highway Traffic Safety Administration ［美］国家公路交通安全管理局（简称 NHTSA）
National Independent Truckers' Unity Council ［美］全国独立汽车货运工作者联合委员会（简称 NITUC）

National Institute for Automotive Service Excellence ［美］全国争取汽车维修质量优秀协会（由美国汽车保修界各方面人士组成的非营利性组织，简称 NIASE）
national(ity) plate 国家牌照（全国通用牌照，= national tag）
National Lending Library for Science and Technology ［英］国立科学技术租赁图书馆
National LEV program 全美低公害车计划（National low Emission Vehicle program）
National LP-gas Association ［美］全国液化石油气协会（简称 NLPGA）
National Lubricating Grease Institute ［美］全国润滑脂学会（简称 NLGI）
National Maximum Speed Limit ［美］国家汽车最高车速限制规定，国家最高车速限额（简称 NMSL）
National Motor Freight Traffic Association ［美］全国汽车货运交通协会（简称 NMFT）
National Motor Vehicle Safety Advisory Council ［美］国家汽车安全咨询委员会（简称 NMVSAC）
National off-Road Race Association ［美］全国汽车越野赛协会（简称 NORRA）
National Oil Fuel Institute ［美］国家石油燃料学会（简称 NOFI）
National Petroleum Association ［美］全国石油协会（简称 NPA）
National Petroleum Council ［美］国家石油委员会（简称 NPC）
National Petroleum Refiners Association ［美］全国石油炼制商协会（简称 NPRA）
National Police Agency ［美］国家警察署（简称 NPA）
national road 国道，国有公路

National Safety Mark 国家安全标记（加拿大交通安全法规，规定进口车按加拿大的汽车安全标准检验合格者，必须加上"枫叶标记"，称为国家安全标记）

National Science Foundation ［美］国家科学基金会（简称NSF）

national setting 国别设定

national standard 国家标准

national standard thread 国家标准螺纹

National Technical Information Service ［美］国家技术信息服务处

National Traffic and Motor Vehicle Safety Act ［美］国家交通与机动车安全法（简称NTMVSA）

National Traffic Policy Study Committee ［美］国家交通政策研究委员会（简称NTPSC）

National Transportation Safety Board ［美］国家运输安全委员会（简称NTSB）

national version factor 国别系数（如：按不同国别根据基本保修周期确定保修周期的修正系数）

native ①本国的，本地的，地方的 ②天生的，天然的，原来的

native copper 自然铜

native metal 自然金属，天然金属

natrium 钠（Na）

natrium cooled valve 钠冷却气门（一般用于排气门，气门制成中空，空腔内装以熔点为97℃的金属钠，在气门工作温度下钠液化，当气门往复运动时，钠液上、下流动，将气门头的热量经气门导管传给冷却水，=Sodium cooled valve）

natrium sulfur battery 钠硫电池

NATS 日产防盗系统（Nissan Anti-thief System的简称）

NATSO ［美］全国载货汽车站工作者协会（National Assn of Truck Stop Operators）

natural ①天然的，自然的；固有的 ②实物的 ③正常的，普通的

natural abrasive 天然磨料

natural ag(e)ing 自然时效，自然变质，自然老化

natural air draught 自然通风，自然气流（美写作natural air draft）

natural alloy iron 天然合金铸铁

natural aspirated engine 自吸气式内燃机，非增压内燃机（=non-supercharged engine，指吸入汽缸前的空气或混合气未经压气机压缩的内燃机，仅带扫气泵而不带增压器的二冲程内燃机亦属此类，简称NA或N/A engine）

natural aspiration 自然吸气（靠活塞从上止点向下止点移动时，汽缸内形成的真空度而吸入新鲜充量，简称NA或N/A）

natural capacity 固有电容

natural circulation 自然循环（对流循环）

natural condition test 自然条件下的试验

natural convection 自然对流

natural cooling 自然冷却，对流冷却

natural crack 自然裂纹，天然裂纹

natural (draft) ventilation 自然（抽吸式）通风

natural frequency 自然频率，固有频率［自由振动的物体或系统，在单位时间（秒）内振动的循环数，见free vibrations，频率的高低决定于物体或系统本身的弹性及惯性或称本身的质量和刚度］

natural gas 天然气（分为干性和湿性两大类，前者指煤田或沼泽地产生的以甲烷"CH_4"为主要成分的可燃气体，后者指石油井等产出的由乙烷"C_2H_6"，丙烷"C_3H_8"等碳氢化合物构成的可燃气体）

natural gas engine 天然气发动机

natural gas filling station 天然气加

气站（为天然气汽车添加压缩天然气的站，一般备有将天然气压缩到25.3MPa的压气设备，及销售压缩天然气的计量装备）

natural gas liquid 液化天然气（简称LNG，= liquefied natural gas）

natural gasoline 天然汽油，无添加剂的汽油

natural gas powered vehicle 天然气汽车（简称NGV）

natural head 自流压头

natural homomorphism 自然同态

natural ignition engine 自燃着火发动机（不装用点火装置，依靠空气的压缩热使燃料达到自燃点而着火燃烧的发动机的总称）

naturalistic driving behavior （驾驶者的）日常驾驶方式，日常驾驶习惯，自然的驾驶动作

natural language processor （专家系统的）自然语言处理程序

naturally air-cooled engine 自然空气冷式发动机（指不用风扇等强制通风的风冷式发动机）

naturally aspirated engine 自然吸气式发动机（非增压式发动机）

natural magnet 天然磁铁

natural oscillations 固有振荡，自由振荡；固有振动

natural oxide film （铝等金属表面的）自然氧化膜（亦称natural oxide skin "自然氧化皮"）

natural parameter 特性参数

natural period 自然周期，固有周期（自然频率的倒数，即自由振动的物体或系统每一个振动循环所需的时间，见natural frequency）

natural resonance 自然谐振

natural road 天然（土）路

natural rubber 天然橡胶（简称NR）

natural scale ①自然量，固有量，固有数②实物大小，自然比例尺

natural seasoning 自然时效，自然干燥

natural ventilation 自然通风，自然换气

natural vibration 自然振动，自由振动（= free vibration）

natural water cooling 重力（温差）自流式水冷却（= gravity-system water cooling）

natural wear 自然损耗

natural weathering 自然风化（测定材料抗腐蚀性能的露天自然腐蚀试验）

nature ①自然界；自然状态，原始状态②本性，性质，特质，特征，类型

nature of soil 土壤特性，土壤性质

nautical fathom 海英寻（英、美长度单位，简称naut. fa，在英国1海英寻=6.08英尺，在美国1海英寻=6.086英尺，见nautical mile）

nautical mile 海里，浬（英、美海程长度单位，简称naut. mi或n. mile，地球纬度1/60的距离，随着纬度的不同而不同，英国海里1UK nautical mile = 6080ft = 1853.18m，国际海里1 international nautical mile = 1852m）

nave ①毂，轮毂（= hub）②（对开式车轮及辐板式车轮的）轮辐

nave face （对开式车轮及辐板式车轮）辐板的安装面（用轮毂螺栓紧固于轮毂上的装配平面）

nave plate ①轮毂罩（= hub cap）②（对开式车轮及辐板式车轮的）辐板

NAVI-5 （日本五十铃公司的）新型先进智能自动变速器（商品名，new advanced vehicle with intelligence的简称，"-5"表示5挡，如果是6挡，则写成NAVI-6。NAVI为机械变速器，只是换挡杆操作和离合器控制改由车载计算机控制液压机

构来进行。由于不使用液力变矩器,油耗不致增加,在大型车上亦可使用,此外,它还能切换成手动变速操作)

navigate 导行,导航,引导

navigational computer (汽车)导行计算机

navigation system 导航系统,导行系统(指使用汽车方位和车速传感装置及卫星全球定位系统"GPS",精确确定汽车所在位置,并通过显示屏向驾驶者指示汽车实时位置及到达目的地的路径等信息的行车路线引导系统)

Navigation System Timing and Ranging/Global Position System 授时与测距导航系统/全球定位系统(见 NAVSTAR/GRS)

Navigator (美·林肯)导航者(豪华型多用途跑车,5.4L,230马力)

navigator ①领航员,领路员(如:坐在赛车助手座上的领路员) ②导航设备,导行设备,导行系统

Navi (software) package (汽车电子系统)导航软件包(汽车导航电子控制系统的程序(软件包,如:其 24G 集成电路芯片和外壳)

Navlab (美国匹兹堡的卡内塞麦偏大学和休斯敦的哈里斯郡都会运输管委员联合研究课题名)自动行驶研究(该课题作为阶段成果于1997年在美国展出,轿车、客车上安装自动行车装置后可在非自动公路上自动行驶)

NAVSTAR/GPS 授时与测距导航系统/全球定位系统(Navigation System Timing and Ranging/Global Position System 的简称,为一般常用全球定位系统"GPS"的全称,由21颗工作卫星和3颗备用卫星组成,分布在相互夹角为60°的6个轨道平面上,同时位于地平线以上的卫星数目随时间和地点不同可为4~11颗,这一布置可保证在地球上任何位置同时观测到至少4颗卫星,最多可达11颗卫星,可实现精确导航和定位的目的)

navy blue colour 海军蓝,深蓝色,藏青色

NAW 南京汽车制造厂(中国)(Nanjing Automobile Works)

NBC (丰田公司的)新基础车(New Basic Car 的简称,丰田公司作为发展各种新车型的基础平台车)

NBFU [美]国家火灾保险业者委员会(National Board of Fire Underwriters)

NBR 腈基丁二烯橡胶(nitrile butadiene rubber)

NBS ①[美]国家标准局(National Bureau of Standard) ②[英]新标准线规(New British Standard)

NBS standard reference gases [美]国家标准局标准参比气体(用于废气分析仪的标定)

NBS test [美]国家标准局试验

NC ①噪声标准,噪声允许极限(noise criteria) ②常用的(normally closed 的简称)

NCAP (美国国家公路交通安全局2004年拟定的)新型小轿车鉴定大纲(New car Assessment Program 的简称)

NCCO 纳米级排放物氧化催化转化器(nanometer-catalytic converter-oxidation 的简称)

NC curve 噪声容许极限曲线,噪声评定标准曲线(noise criteria curve)

NCD [美]无索赔折扣优惠(No Claim Discount 的简称,指保险公司对刚过去的一年无索赔记录的车主可获得一定百分比的折扣优惠,如两年或两年以上无索赔则每年可多加 10% 折扣等,最高 NCB 为60%)

NCEO 新概念发动机润滑油(new

concept engine oil，如：各种合成型机油）

n-channel metal-oxide semiconductor 见 NMOS

n-channel MOSFET N 沟道金属氧化物半导体场效应晶体管（简称 n-channel transistor，见 MOS、MOSFET）

NCM 氮氧化物排放控制模块 [NO_x-control module 的简称，加装在波许公司发动机综合电子控制系统（见 Motronic）上的数字电路点火控制模块，用于改善点火正时特性，以减少 NO_x 排放]

NCO 数字控制振荡器（numerical controlled oscillator 的简称）

NC PEP 数字控制性能评价程序（numerical control performance evaluation program）

NCS 消声系统（noise cancellation system 的简称）

NCSS [美] 全国汽车碰撞严重程度研究会（National Crash Severity Study）

NCTA [美] 国家首都运输局（National Capital Transportation Agency）

NC threads 美国粗螺纹（National coarse thread sizes，见 Seller's thread）

NCUTLO [美] 统一交通法规与条例全国委员会（National Committee of Uniform Traffic Laws and Ordinances）

NCUTLO （美）国家交通法律统一委员会（National Committee on Uniform Traffic Lows and Ordinance 的简称）

NCV value 正常燃烧速度值（normal combustion velocity value 的简称）

2nd cut file 细锉（= second cut file）

2nd-generation DPF 第二代柴油机（排放）微粒滤清器（见 catalyzed DPF）

NDI 非破坏检验方法（non-destructive inspection method）

n-dimensional (vector) space n 维（度）（矢量）空间

NDIR 不分光式红外线分析仪（non-dispersive infra-red analyser 的简称，指不用棱镜或衍射光栅分光，而用气体滤光器或选择性检测器对排气中的 CO、CO_2、NO_x 和 HC 作选择性分析的检测仪）

NDR [美] 国家驾驶员注册（National Driver Register）

NDS ① [日] 防卫厅标准（national defence standards） ②（由变速器换挡杆控制的）空挡驱动开关（neutral drive switch 的简称，变速器挂空挡时，该开关接通，变速器挂前进挡或倒挡时，该开关断开，借以向电子控制模块提供变速器挡位信息，供电子控制模块控制发动机怠速转速等）

NDT 非破坏性试验，无损试验（non-destructive test 的简称，指超声波、X 射线、染色渗透等不致造成破坏的测试方法）

2nd-4th gears pressure switches （电子控制自动变速器的）2-4 挡压力开关（换挡时，将 2-4 挡液压信号反馈给电子控制模块）

NDUA 非分光紫外线分析仪（non-dispersive ultraviolet analyser 的简称）

Nd：YAG laser Nd：YAG 激光器（固体激光器的一种，可输出波长 $1.06\mu m$ 的脉冲和连续激光，最大输出功率达 10kW，其激光可通过光纤传输）

Ne 氖（neon）

near-coastal exposure 在接近海滨气候条件下的暴露（试验）

near constant velocity universal joint 准等速万向节（输出轴与输入轴的瞬时速度比仅在二者夹角为设计值时等于 1，而在其他夹角值下近似

等于 1 的万向节）

near-destructive test 断裂界限试验

near failure 接近于损坏，接近于破坏的极限

near gale 疾风（七级风，风速 13.9～17.1m/s，= moderate gale）

Near infrared ray 近红外线

Near miss ①接近目标，但不理想 ②（车辆）幸免碰撞，险些碰撞

near-obstacle detector 近距离障碍物探测器（用于汽车倒挡行驶防撞系统）

near side （道路上的汽车）靠近路边的一侧（亦写作 nearside，靠右行的国家指汽车的右侧，靠左行的国家指汽车的左侧，简称 NS，N/S，如：在英国指左侧，= left side，见 offside）

nearside wheel （并装双轮的）内侧轮

near-term 近期的

near ultimate load 接近极限的载荷

neat ①纯好的，未掺杂的，未加任何添加剂的②整洁的，整齐的③简洁的④精致的

neat gas burner ①天然气燃烧器（= natural gas burner）②液化石油气燃烧器（= LPG burner）③气体燃料简易燃烧器（只用一个喷嘴，引出煤气燃烧）

neat's foot Oil 牛脚油（从牛脚骨中提炼出的淡黄色不挥发性油，汽车业用来作为使革制件保持柔软的护革油）

Nebraska test 美国内布拉斯加农业大学拖拉机试验场进行的拖拉机试验（带官方法规性质的试验）

NEC ①[美] 全国电气规程（National Electric Code）②数字电磁编码（numerical electromagnetics code 的简称）

NECAR 纽卡，新车（德国奔驰公司 20 世纪 90 年代末研制的氢-空气燃料电池无排放车的商品名，该车巡航车速为 90km/h，最高车速 110km/h，不加添燃料可行驶 250km）

necessary torque curve 必需转矩曲线

necessitate 使…需要，以…为条件；迫使，要求，使成为必要

neck ①颈，轴颈；颈状部，直径缩小部位；颈状孔口，环槽，喉管，颈状喷管②截面收缩，颈缩

neck airbag 颈部安全气囊

neck breaking speed 危险速度

neck bush 轴颈衬套

necked ①带颈的，颈状的②带环槽的③收缩的，拉细的

necked-down section 收缩断面

neck injury 颈部伤害

neck journal 轴颈（= neck of shaft）

NED Di （日本）日产（公司）生态型（汽油）直接喷射系统（商品名，Nissan Ecology Oriented Performance Direct Injection System 的简称，该系统通过进气涡流，特殊的活塞顶形状，汽油直接缸内喷射，实现低负荷时整体混合比 40∶1 的超稀层状燃烧，高负荷时，理论混合比的均匀燃烧，节油、净化，且具有足够的动力，用于该公司的 VQ30DD 发动机）

NEDPA [美] 国家能源开发保护法（National Energy Development Policy Act）

needle ①针，针状物②箭头，指针③（滚针轴承的）滚针（细长的针状滚子）④（量孔、阀孔、喷孔等的）针阀（针状锥形头阀杆）

needle bearing 滚针轴承（= needle rollerbearing，quill bearing）

needle-bearing universal joint 带滚针轴承的万向节

needle bush（ing） 无内圈的滚针轴承

needle deflection （测量仪表）指针

偏转

needle-flame test 针形电位跳火试验（模拟评估失火危险程度的试验）

needle gap （点火试验用针状电极放电器的）跳火间隙

needle indicator 指针式指示器

needle jet ①针阀量孔（利用阀针等调节油量的量孔，量针油孔 = metering rod jet），②量针喷嘴（由量针控制通过断面）

needle/jet rubbing wear 量针-量孔磨损

needle lift 针阀升程（①指喷油器等的针阀升起的高度随时间变化的瞬时值；②针阀最大升程的简称，即：该词条一般指针阀的最大升程）

needle lubricator 针孔润滑器，针孔油枪

needle magnet ①磁针，针状磁铁（石）②指针式仪表用的磁铁

needle -motion sensor （喷油嘴）喷针移动传感器（向电子控制模块发送喷油始点信息）

needle-pointdischarge 针尖放电

needle regulation （喷油嘴）针阀调整

needle roller rocker arm 滚针轴承式摇臂（使用滚针轴承的气门摇臂机构）

needle shell-type bearing 带冲压外圈的滚针轴承

needle stroke 针阀行程

needle thermocouple 针形热电偶

needle valve 针阀（= needle-point valve，控制流量的针形阀门）

needle valve seat hermetic test device 针阀座气密度试验器

needle-valve shock absorber 针阀式减振器

negative ①阴性的，负的，否定的，消极的②负数，负值③阴电，阴电极，负电极

negative acceleration 负加速度（减速度）

negative back pressure (modulated) EGR valve 负背压（控制式）EGR 阀，负背压（控制式）排气再循环量控制阀（在 EGR 阀膜片中央有一个常闭式控制阀，当发动机转速较低时，排气系统的负脉冲使该控制阀开启，EGR 阀关闭。当发动机转速上升到规定值时，排气负压脉冲减弱，控制阀关闭，这时，只要膜片上方通入真空，EGR 阀便开启，亦称 negative randucer EGR valve，见 positive back-pressure valve）

negative booster 降压器，减力器

negative brush 负极电刷

negative burner 发动机排气碳氢化合物含量氢焰-离子分析仪的）阴极燃烧器

negative camber ①车轮外倾，车轮内倾（指车轮平面向内倾斜，亦称 minus camber，见 camber）②车轮负外倾角，车轮内倾角（车轮内倾后，其中心平面与中心平面接地线的垂直平面间的夹角）③（车身壁板的）内曲面④负凸度，负挠度

negative carrier 负电荷载流子（电子载流子）

negative caster （亦写作 negative castor，指转向节）①主销负后倾，主销前倾（沿汽车前进方向，转向节主销轴线的交地点，落在车轮中心对地面投影点之后，见 caster）②主销前倾角，主销负后倾角（= negative caster angle）

negative caster offset 转向主销前倾后置量（转向主销轴线与路面交点至车轮与路面接触中心纵向垂直平面的距离，详见 caster）

negative catalysis 负催化（作用）（缓化作用）

negative-channel metal-oxide-silicon

device　N沟道金属氧化硅半导体器件（电子载流子金属氧化硅半导体器件，简称NMOS）

negative characteristic　负特性（下降的特性曲线）

negative charge　负电荷

negative crystal　负晶体（寻常光的转换速度小于非寻常光传播速度的晶体，如方解石）

negative damping factor　负阻尼系数

negative diode　负极二极管（引线为负极，外壳为正极，管壳底一般有红字标记）

negative direction　反向

negative electricity　负电，负电荷

negative electrode　负电极，阴极

negative emission　负排放（指发动机排气管排出的废气比发动机吸入的空气还要清洁，据称日本本田公司20世纪90年代末生产的ZLEV型发动机已在大城市十字路口的条件下做到这一点）

negative going (input) threshold voltage（数字集成电路特性）负向（输入）阈电压（输入电压下降时的输入阈电压，见input threshold voltage）

negative ground　负极接地，负极搭铁（如：蓄电池的负极与车体相连接，亦称negative earth）

negative impact　负面影响，不良影响

negative kingpin offset　转向主销负偏距（见kingpin offset）

negative lift　①（空气动力中的）负升力，负浮力，负扬力，向下的力（指可增加车辆对地面的接触压力，从而提高稳定性，可减少牵引力损失的向下的力）②负升程③负上升，下沉

negative load condition（发动机的）负载荷状况（被驱动状态，如利用发动机制动时）

negative logic　负逻辑（低值域用"1"表示，高值域用"0"表示的逻辑）

negative number　负数

negative offset　①转向主销负偏距（negative kingpin offset的简称，亦称negative scrub radius，见kingpin offset）②车轮内偏距（见negative wheel offset）

negative offset steering　负偏距转向（机构）（转向主销呈负偏距的转向/悬架系统）

negative off tracking（汽车列车转向）负偏离轨迹（指最后轴中心的转向轨迹，在最前轴中心的转向轨迹之外，与一般情况相反）

negative overall height of the spring　钢板弹簧负全高

negative peak　负峰值

negative plate group（蓄电池的）负极板组，阴极板组

negative plate unit pole bridge（蓄电池）负极板组的汇流排

negative pole　负极，阴极

negative-positive-negative transistor　NPN型晶体三极管

negative power　①负幂②负动力，阻力

negative pressure　负压力（负压，低于大气压力或1 013.250kPa，或101.3kPa的压力）

negative proton　反质子，阴质子，负质子

negative ratio（轮胎胎面花纹的）底/面比（指花纹底面积与胎面面积之比。一般汽车轮胎该比率为30%～40%，越野车轮胎大于50%，亦称sealand ratio。该比值大者，称开式花纹"open pattern"，该比值小者称闭式花纹"closed pattern"）

negative rear-axle steering　后轴反向转向

negative scrub radius　负磨胎半径，

转向主销负偏距（见 kingpin offset，负磨胎半径多见于发动机前置前轮驱动式轿车）

negative spark 负极跳火（指高压电的负极接火花塞中心电极，火花塞侧电极为正极搭铁，呈高压正电位，电子由中心电极飞向侧电极而产生的火花）

negative spring camber 钢板弹簧负挠度

negative suction head 负吸水头，压水头，（亦称 suction lift）

negative temperature coefficient thermistor 负温度系数热敏电阻（温度越高，其阻值越小的热敏电阻，简称 negative temperature thermistor，NTC thermistor）

negative terminal 负极接线柱，负极接线桩（亦称 negative terminal post）

negative thread 阴螺纹，内螺纹

negative transducer EGR valve 负背压控制式 EGR 阀（见 negative back pressure EGR valve）

negative understeer 负不足转向，过度转向（= oversteer）

negative voltage-current characteristic （断电器断电时的）反向电压电流特性

negative wheel offset 车轮内偏距（简称 negative offset，亦称 inset，指轮辋中心线位于轮辐安装面内侧的车轮，轮辋中心线与轮辐安装面间的距离，简称 negative offset）

negligible 可忽略的，可略去不计的

negotiable curves between obstacles 障碍物间可通行的弯道

negotiate 克服（困难），越过（障碍）

negotiate the corner 拐弯

negotiation capability （车辆）越（过）障（碍物的）能力

NEI 噪声等效密度（noise equivalent intensity）

Neidhart cushion 奈氏缓冲器（奈氏软垫减振器，瑞士人 H. J. Neidhart 在 1947 年发明的一种软垫缓冲件，由分别固定于车架与车桥上的内外方形框件，及装在两框之间的四块橡胶件组成亦称 Neidhart spring）

neighborhood EV 邻里型电动车（美指一次充电行程短，只能在邻里间等附近区域行驶的单座两轮或四轮超小型低速电动车）

NEISS ［美］国家伤害电子监视系统（National Electronic Injury Surveillance System 的简称）

nematic-isotropic phase transition （液晶）向列相-各向同性相转变（随温度上升，向列相液晶转变为各向同性液晶的相转变）

nematic liquid crystal 向列相液晶（分子长轴大致按一定方向排列，分子重心随机分布的液晶）

nematic with positive dielectric anisotropy N_p 液晶（分子长轴方向介电常数小于短轴方向介电常数的液晶）

NEO Di 日产生态型直接喷射系统（Nissan Ecology Oriented Performance Direct injection system 的简称，日本日产公司汽油直接喷入汽缸内的喷射系统的商品名。低负荷时，少量汽油在压缩冲程中喷入进气冲程形成的强横向空气涡流中，在特殊浅盘状活塞顶的压缩下，喷入缸内的汽油仅在火花塞附近形成超浓混合气，点火后火焰迅速向四周空气层中扩展而实现整体空燃比为 40:1 的超稀混合气层状燃烧，以降低油耗。高负荷时，多量的汽油在进气冲程中喷射，在整个汽缸内形成理论混合比的均质可燃混合气，点火后实现常规的均质燃烧，以确保所要求的功率）

neodymium 钕（Nd，亦称 neodym）

neodymium permanent magnet 钕永久磁铁

neon 氖（Ne，稀有气体元素，空气中的含量约为0.0012%的惰性气体，充入密封的玻璃管内，加以高电压时，发出红色光，用于制作点火高压测试仪等）

neon bulb 霓虹灯泡，氖管，氖灯泡（= neon lamp, neon indicator, neon light, neon tube）

neon timing light 氖光正时灯（检验点火正时用）

neon type spark plug tester 氖光式火花塞试验器

Neoprene 氯丁二烯橡胶（聚氯丁橡胶，美国DuPont化学公司开发的合成橡胶的商品名，其性能可与天然橡胶媲美，且耐油性好，广泛用来制造密封垫、衬垫、油封等，亦称chloroprene gum）

neoprene based rubber 氯丁基橡胶

neoprene sponge 氯丁乙烯海绵（聚氯丁泡沫橡胶）

neoprene synthetic rubber 氯丁合成橡胶

NEO VVL 日产生态型可变气门升程及正时机构（Nissan Ecology Oriented Performance Variable Valve Lift and Timing 的简称，日本日产公司的发动机高、低速运转时气门升程及开、闭时刻自动控制切换系统的商品名）

NEPA [中] 国家环境保护局（National Enviromental Protection Agency）

neper 奈培（亦称napier，电信或声音的功率比值单位，亦称衰减单位，代号Np，常用于欧洲大陆国家，以代替bel。奈培是以自然对数的方式表示两功率的比值，如功率由 P_2 衰减到 P_1，其差别比较用 nNp 表示，因 $P_1/P_2 = e^{2n}$，所以 $n = 1/2\ln P_1/P_2$，1Np = 8.686dB，见 decibel）

neptunium 镎（Np，旧称錼）

NERC [美]（环保局的）国家环境研究中心（National Enviromental Research Center）

nerf bar [美] 汽车前保险杠护杠（一般指由一横梁支撑，从前端下方水平延伸并向上弯曲的一对镀铬钢管护杠）

Nernst 勒恩斯特（亦译内恩斯特，全名：Nernst Walther Nermann，德国物理学家，化学家，1920年诺贝尔化学奖得主）

Nernst equation 勒恩斯特等式（$U_L = RT/4F \cdot \ln(p''_{O_2}/p'_{O_2})$，式中：$U_L$—氧传感器无负荷输出电压；$R$—气体常数；$T$—绝对温度；$F$—法拉第常数；$p''_{O_2}$—空气的氧分压；$p'_{O_2}$—废气中的氧分压）

Nernst's heat theorem 勒恩斯特热定理，（亦称）能斯脱热定理（当任一均匀系统的绝对温度达到零度时，其自由能量的温度系数和比热等于零，见 homogeneous system）

Nernst type exhaust gas sensor 见 ceramic exhaust gas sensor

Nernst type lean A/F sensor 勒恩斯特型稀空燃比传感器（可测出 λ > 1.05后输出的电压信号微小变化的氧传感器，供稀燃发动机电子控制模块对其所要求的稀混合气空燃比作闭路控制，见 Nernst equation）

nerve fiber 神经纤维

Ne signal 曲轴转角信号（= crankshaft angle signal）

nest ①承窝，座②成套，一套；组合件，成套件③槽，孔④定位圈⑤（齿轮）组，宝塔齿轮⑥放入（支撑）；支撑在座内；安装入；敷设，套用，叠垒

nestle 坐落，紧贴，贴附，紧靠，挨靠

nest spring 双重螺纹弹簧，复式盘簧

net ①网；网状物，网状组织，网络

②净的（常用代号为 n），纯净的，纯粹的③净得，获挣收益④用网捕获，编造网络；成网状

net brake power test 净有效功率试验（指全附件发动机，在节气门全开条件下，测试各种转速下的输出功率，见 fully equipped engine）

net caloric value 净热值（低热值，= lower heating value, net calorific value, net heating value）

net contact area 净接触面积（如：轮胎的净接地面积，指胎面花纹的实际接地面积，即扣除花纹凹槽后的接地面积）

net efficiency 净效率，有效效率（对汽车发动机或电动机，指输入的能量或动力中有百分之多少转变成了有用的机械或电气动力，见 thermal efficiency）

net engine horsepower 发动机净马力（以马力计的发动机净功率）

net head 净水头，有效水头（指总落差减去管道摩擦损失等的有效落差）

net lift ①净升程，有效升程（如凸轮升程减去气门系统间隙后的气门实际升程）②有效扬程

net load 有效载荷，净荷重

net of curves on a surface 曲面上的曲线网

net positive suction head 有效吸水头（有效吸升位差，有效吸升力）

net (power) output （发动机）净输出功率（有效输出功率，带全部附件的输出功率）

net sectional area 有效截面面积

net theoretical work 净理论功

net thrust 净推力

net time （完成某一工序的）纯耗费时间

net tolerance 净公差

net ton ①净吨，短吨（= 2000 磅，多用于美国，亦称美吨，= short ton）②净吨位，净装载吨数

net torque/maximum total mass ratio 比转矩（发动机净转矩与汽车或汽车列车厂定最大总质量之比）

net type steering column 网格型转向管柱（一种部分做成网格状的转向柱管，当人体胸部撞到转向盘上的冲击力超过允许范围时，网格部分被压缩产生塑性折叠变形，吸收冲击能量，减轻冲击对驾驶员的伤害）

net volume 净容积

network ①网；网状物，网状组织，网状系统②网络（指有三个或三个以上的网点支持通信的系统，或称用通信线连接数据站、网点形成的资源共享系统）③电路④电网，道路网，广播网⑤网状图表，计算图表⑥使成网状

network access 网络访问（使用通信网络网点传输信息）

network analogue 网络模拟

network characteristic 网络特性曲线

network display 网络显示器（指车上安装的可连接互联网、导航和音频、视频及交通流信息系统等的综合显示屏）

network element 网络单元（网络的构成单元，主要有连线和节点）

networking ①联网技术②网络服务

network interface unit 网络接口部件

network intrude detect system 网络入侵检测系统（简称 DIDS）

network node 网点（计算机网络中的点、站或终端，该处有一个或多个功能器件与传输线连接，如：在汽车电子控制系统多路复用网络中的 engine node, driver door node 等）

network service ①网道运输（在交叉密布的多站网络上运输）②网络服务

network structure 网状组织，网状结构

network topologies 网络拓扑结构（网络的网点和链路的连接模式或布局结构）

Net Wt 净重（net weight）

neural cell 神经元（见 neuron）

neural (cell) state 神经（元）状态 [神经元恒处于两种状态之一：①neutral state，沿其轴突（axon）不发放冲动（a spike）②emitting state，沿其轴突（axon）发放冲动（a spike）]

neural lamp 勒思斯特灯（氧化钍白炽灯）

neural net （生物型计算机系统中模仿人类神经网络行为的）人工神经网络（见 artificial neural net）

neuron 神经元 [= neural cell，神经系统的组成细胞，当刺激加于其树突（dendrite）时，接收离子电流；当进入其中的电流电位累加至某一定值时即发出一作动电位，即：冲动（spike）。单个神经元结构极其简单，但海量神经元构成的网络系统所能实现的行为极其丰富多彩]

neutral ①（汽车变速位置的）空挡，空挡的②中间的，中性的（既非酸性亦非碱性的），中和的；不带电的

neutral axis 中性轴，中性轴线

neutral density filter 中性滤光器（见 neutral filter）

neutral drive switch 空挡起动开关（简称 N/D switch 或 NSW，变速器挂挡时，该开关断开起动机电路，因此必须挂空挡发动机才能起动）

neutral equilibrium 随遇平衡，自然平衡（当一物体的重心在该物体受外力推动时，始终处于原所在高度或外力除去后即可恢复原有高度，则该物体处于自然平衡状态，亦称 neutral balance）

neutral filter 中性滤光器（不改变所通过光线的色品，通过这种滤光器的全部颜色都一致减弱，所通过光线的能量的频谱分布不变，= neutral density filter）

neutral flame 中性焰

neutral gas ①化学计算的燃烧产物 ②惰性气体，中性气体

neutral indicator lamp （变速器）空挡指示灯

neutralization 中和（作用），抵消；使失效，抑制；平衡，中立（状态）

neutralization number 中和值（表示机油或燃油的酸、碱度）

neutralizer 中和剂，缓冲器（= neutralizing agent）

neutral layer of flexspline's toothed ring 柔轮齿圈壁厚中性层（设定柔轮齿圈段，平分齿根至柔轮内壁距离所在的曲面）

neutral line 中性线（如：①交流发电机中，与流过磁场绕组和电枢绕组的电流所感应的磁力线成直角的线；②受弯曲力矩作用的梁的横断面上拉伸应力至压缩应力间应力为零的点的连线）

neutral line of lateral force 横向力中性线（横向力中性点的集合，见 neutral point of lateral force）

neutral oil 中性润滑油

neutral point ①空挡②中心点③中性点

neutral point of lateral force 横向力中性点（横向力垂直作用在车辆纵向对称平面上时，汽车不致产生横摆角速度的着力点）

neutral position ①（变速器的）空挡位置，空挡②中性位置，中立位置，中间位置

neutral programming language 中性编程语言（指人-机皆识的第四代编程语言）

neutral stability 中性稳定性（对指

定工作点而言，扰动或控制输入有短暂改变时，汽车运动响应将保持在接近于但不能达到由工作点所规定的运动状态）

neutral start switch （发动机的）空挡起动开关（发动机只有在挂空挡时，起动电路才能接通的安全开关，亦称 neutral drive switch）

neutral steer （汽车的）中性转向（特性）（亦写作 neutral steering，在车速一定而改变横向加速度时，若名义转向角的斜率等于阿克曼角的斜率，该汽车的转向特性称中性转向，即在侧向力作用下，前、后桥侧偏角相等的车辆的转向特性。中性转向特性的汽车，直线行驶时，受侧向力作用后，汽车将沿与原方向成某一角度的直线方向斜行，而在转向盘转角保持不变的圆周运动时，车速增加，汽车将沿与原圆周成同心圆的轨迹行驶，简称 NS）

neutral steer line of lateral force 横力中性转向线（横力中性转向点的集合，见 neutral point of neutral steel line）

neutral surface 中性面（梁等物件承受弯曲力矩而作用有垂直应力时，其内部不产生垂直应力的面，即不受拉伸或压缩的面）

neutral switch （变速器）空挡开关（①发动机起动电路中的变速器不挂空挡，发动机便不能起动的安全装置，亦称 neutral safety switch；②向电子控制模块发送变速器是否处于空挡位置的传感开关）

neutral terminal （发电机的）N 线接线柱，零线接头（交流发电机中性点的接线柱，简称 N terminal）

neutral turn （履带式车辆的单侧履带）脱挡转向（一侧履带驱动，一侧履带空挡实现的转向）

neutron （原子核中不带电荷的）中子（简称 n）

New British Standard（Imperial wire gauge） 英国新标准线规（帝国线规）（简称 NBS）

new candle 新烛光（见 candela）

new car delivery service 新车交接检修，新车交接检验，新车交货服务

new car releasing meeting 新车发表会

new comer 新车，新产品，新结构，新材料（等的泛称，可用来表示一切新出现的事、物、人）

new concept engine oil 新概念机油（指完全用化学方式配制合成的润滑油，简称 NCEO）

newel （双层公共汽车）螺旋梯的中柱

new fashioned 新式的

new -gen 新一代的

new-generation 新一代（的）

new mode 新模式，新式样，新形式

new-old-stock part 旧车型的库存新配件（指一般已不再生产的原有库存，尚未用过的旧车型正品配件，简称 NOS part）

new process 新工艺，新工序，新规程（简称 NP）

newspaper van 送报汽车

Newton ①牛顿（代号 N，国际单位制根据牛顿定律 $F=ma$ 导出的力的单位，1N 为使 1kg 质量的物体产生 $1m/s^2$ 加速的力。$1N = 1kg \cdot m/s^2$，1newton = 0.102kgf = 10^5dyne = 0.2248 1bf）②牛顿（英国科学家，1642~1727 年）

newton automatic clutch 牛顿自动离合器（一种弹簧加载飞重式离心力控制的自动离合器，无须离合器踏板，达到规定转速后自动接合）

Newtonian fluid 牛顿流体（指剪切应力 τ 与剪切速度 dv/dy 之间的关系式：$\tau = \eta dv/dy$ 成立的流体，式中：v—x 方向的流速；y—垂直于 x

的坐标；η—黏度。其中黏度 η 与 τ 和 dv/dy 的大小无关，仅与温度和压力有关)

newton meter 牛·米（国际单位制的力矩、转矩、弯矩单位，代号 Nm，1Nm=0.102kgm）

Newton's alloy 牛顿合金（一种铋铅锡易熔合金，铋50%，铅31.2%，锡18.8%，熔点95℃，亦称 newton metal）

Newton's laws of motion 牛顿运动定律（即运动三大定律：①在不受外力作用下，动者恒动，静者恒静；②具有 m 质量的物体受外力 F 作用时，产生加速度 a，其关系为 $F=ma$；③作用力等于反作用力）

new-treaded tire （胎面）再生轮胎，翻新轮胎（=renewed tire, renovated tire, retreaded tire）

NExT Combustion （日本）日产（公司）精密调控燃烧方式（商品名，Nissan Exqisitely Tuned Combustion 的简称，低负荷时采用超稀混合气层状燃烧，中、高负荷时采用常规均质混合气燃烧，用于该公司的 VQ30DD 型发动机，见 NEo Di）

next exit sign 下一个出口标志（高速公路上预示前面有支路可驶出的标志，通常标有距出口的里程）

next-gen 下一代的（next-generation 的简称）

NFC （信息的）近域（无线）传输（功能，如：只要将具有此功能的车钥匙在具有此功能的智能手机上晃一下，就能将该钥匙上传给手机显示，near field communication 的简称）

NFCC ［美］全国货运公司（National Freight Claimant Corporation）

NFGC ［美］国家可燃气体公司（National Fuel Gas Company）

NF threads 美国细螺纹（National Finethread Sizes）

NFVT ［英］全国汽车贸易联合会（National Federation of Vehicle Trades）

NGL 液化天然气（natural gas liquid, =LNG）

NGV 天然气汽车（natural gas vehicle）

NHA(A) IAC （美）国家公路事故与伤害分析中心（National Highway Accident and Injury Analysis Center 的简称）

n-hexane 正乙烷

NHRA 全美热棍车协会（National Hot Rod Association，见 hot rod）

NHSB ［美］国家公路安全局（National Highway Safety Bureau）

NHTSA ［美］国家公路交通安全管理局（National Highway Traffic Safety Administration）

Ni 镍（nickel）

NIAE test 英国国立农业工程研究所进行的拖拉机试验（带官方法规性质的试验）

NIASE ［美］全国汽车维修质量创优协会（National Institute for Automotive Service Excellence）

nib 尖，尖端，尖头，尖劈，尖楔，突边，突出部

nibbed 有尖端的

NIC 网卡（network interface card 的简称）

Nicasil （铝缸体表面的一种）镍-硅镀层（用于德 Audi-NSU 公司的转子发动机）

Ni-Cd cell 镍-钙电池（nickel-cadmium cell）

niche ①壁龛（修车地沟内放灯用）②适当的场所，恰当的位置③将…放在恰当位置

nichel plating ①镀镍②镀镍层

nichrome 镍铬合金

Ni Chrome glow strip 镍铬预热片（装于转子发动机缸体或端盖的一

定位置上，类似柴油机的预热塞，作为火花塞的辅助点火装置）

nichrome wire 镍铬合金线（以镍铬合金为主体的合金线，阻值高，耐高温，用做电热器等的电阻丝，为了降低成本，改善加工性，有的加有25%左右的铁）

nick ①刻痕，缺口，V形小刻痕；裂缝；凹隙 ②做刻痕，刻V形缺口；截入

nickel ①镍（Ni）②镀镍

nickel alkaline battery 镍碱性蓄电池（以氢氧化镍为正极板和使用碱性电解液的蓄电池的总称）

nickel alloy 镍合金

nickel alloy central electrode （火花塞的）合金中心电极

nickel bronze 镍青铜（镍5%~8%，锡5%~8%，锌1%~2%，少量磷）

nickel-cadmium（alkaline）battery 镉镍（碱性）电池（用氢氧化镍和5%~30%的铁粉活性物质为负极板，氢氧化镍粉末活性物质为正极板，密度为1.20~1.23的氢氧化钾加少量氢氧化锂溶液为电解液的碱性电池，内阻小，电流大，充电循环寿命高，亦可快速充电，可用做汽车的起动电源或电动汽车的动力源，亦称nickel-cadmium cell，简称Ni-cdcell）

nickel chrome cast iron 镍铬铸铁

nickel-chrome molybdenum steel 镍铬钼钢

nickel contamination 镍污染

nickel dam （轴瓦巴氏合金与铝青铜法之间的）镍层

nickel-hydrogen battery 镍氢电池（一种可再充电的无污染蓄电池，1984年荷兰Philips公司研制成功）

nickel hydroxide 氢氧化镍

nickelic 镍的，含镍的（= nickelous）

nickel-iron alkaline cell 镍-铁碱性电池

nickel-iron battery 镍铁蓄电池（正极板有氢氧化镍和镍粉活性物质，负极使用纯铁粉，电解液为氢氧化钾溶液的碱性电池，亦称neckel-iron cell，简称NiFe battery，亦读作nife battery，可大电流放电，用做电动汽车的动力源）

nickel-metal hydride battery 镍-金属氢化合物Ni/MH蓄电池（以镍或镍基为正极板，金属氢化物为负极板的镍碱性电池，可快速充电，能量密度高）

nickel oxide 氧化镍

nickel plating 镀镍（亦称nickel coating nickeling）

nickel-silicon alloy coating 镍-硅合金镀覆层（= Einisil coating）

nickel-silicon carbide coated housing （转子发动机的）镍-碳化硅镀覆缸壁

nickel-silver（metal） 镍银（镍铜锌合金）

nickel-supplemented fuel 含镍添加剂的燃料

nickel-zinc battery 镍-锌（蓄）电池（正极板为氧化镍，负极板为锌，电解液为氢氧化钾溶液的碱性电池，亦称nickel-zinc cell）

nicotine-resistant 耐尼古丁的（车厢内部装饰材料）

NICS （日产公司电子）进气控制系统（商品名，Nissan Induction Control System 的简称，其进气通道，即进气歧管长度可变）

NICS 日产进气道长度可变控制系统（Nissan Intake Control System 的简称）

Ni/Cu composite center electrode （火花塞）镍/铜复合中心电极

NIDS 网络入侵检测系统（network intrude detect system 的简称）

Niemann Test 尼曼试验（齿轮油的一项试验）

nife battery 镍铁电池（NiFe battery 的读音）

Night blue 夜光蓝（车身颜色）

night coach 夜间（卧铺）客车

night driving 夜间行车，夜间驾驶（亦称 night travel, night trip）

night-road illumination 夜间道路照明

nighttime meeting 夜间会车

nighttime pedestrian accident 夜间行人（碰撞）事故

night vision safety mirror 夜间安全后视镜（防炫目）

night vision technology （应用红外线热成像技术实现夜间行车观察的）夜视技术

Ni-hard 镍铬冷硬铸铁（一种含镍的耐磨铸铁，碳 3.3%～3.5%，硅 0.75%～1.25%，镍 4.5%，铬 1.5%，其余为铁）

NIISAC [美] 国家公路安全咨询委员会（National Highway Safety Advisory Council）

Nikasil coating 一种渗碳化硅镀镍层

Nikolaus A. Otto 尼柯拉斯 A. 奥托（德国物理学家，1602～1686年，见 otto cycle）

nil ①零，无 ②零的

NILS 尼尔司（VW 公司的一人乘小型电动汽车名）

nimble 敏捷的，迅速的

nimble handling （车辆的）操控敏捷轻快

nimbleness 敏捷性，轻快性，机敏性

nimonic "镍莫尼克"（一种用在燃气涡轮机中的耐热合金）

nine-bearing crankshaft 九道轴承曲轴（九主轴颈曲轴）

ninepoint dynamometer test （测功机）九点试验（参见 qualifying point）

niobium 铌 Nb（旧称 columbium "钶"）

nip ①夹，箝，挤，咬，剪 ②（松动的钢板弹簧两相邻簧片中间的）间隙

nipped inner tube （安装不良，被外胎）夹皱的内胎

nipper pliers 剪钳，手钳（简称 nippers，亦称 cutting nippers, nipping pliers）

nipple ①乳头状突起物（如：滑脂加注嘴，轮毂钢丝辐条张紧度调节螺帽）②管接头（带外螺纹的短管接头）③螺纹接套

Nippondenso 日本电气设备公司（日文"日本电装"的读音）

Ni-resist cast iron 耐蚀高镍铸铁（Ni14%，Cu6%，C3%，Cr2%，Si 1.5%；热膨胀系数在 $16\sim18\times10^{-6}/℃$ 以下。柴油机等的镶式活塞环槽多使用这种铸铁制造）

Nishboric suspension system 自动转向摆杆式悬架系统（商品名，通过一摆杆使后轮在车辆转向时向着与前轮转向相反的方向转过一定角度的悬架系统）

Ni-speed 高速镀镍法（采用高沉积率以控制硬度及内应力）

NISSAN 日产（日本汽车厂名：日文"ニッサン"的读音，我国亦按音译尼桑）

Nissan Anti-Pollution System （日本）日产公司汽车废气净化系统（的总称，简称 NAPS）

Nissan Bluebird car 日产蓝鸟轿车

Nissan Cocoon L Wagon 日产蔻肯 L 旅行车（日产公司推出的家庭用车，3 排 6 座，后座可动，装有导航系统）

Nissan Ecology Oriented Performance Direct injection system 日产生态型直接喷射系统（见 NEO Di）

Nissan Figaro car 日产费加罗轿车（日本日产公司1991年推出的微型轿车，装用SOHC涡轮增压发动机，排量387mL，最大功率56kW，自动变速，可折叠式软车顶）

Nissan Valve Control System 日产气门控制系统（见NVCS）

Nissan Variable Induction System 日产可变进气系统（其进气道长度可随发动机转速及工况而变化，简称NVIS）

nit 尼特（表面亮度单位，等于每平方米1新烛光）

nital 硝酸乙醇腐蚀液（相对密度1.42的浓硝酸5mL和95%的乙醇100mL相混合，常用于金相试样表面侵蚀"nital etch"）

nit obsn 夜间观察（night observation的简称）

nitrate ①硝化，用硝酸处理②硝酸盐，硝酸根

nitric acid 硝酸（HNO_3，无色透明液体，溶点-41.3℃，沸点86℃，比重1.52，其水溶液为强氧化剂）

nitric oxide emission （废气中）氮氧化物（NO_x）排放

nitric oxide emission index （发动机的）氮氧化物排出量指数（简称NOEI）

nitridation 渗氮硬化

nitrided hardening 渗氮硬化（处理）（= nitrogen hardening）

nitrided steel 渗氮钢

nitriding 渗氮，氮化法（将氮原子渗入钢件的表面，增加其硬度、耐磨性、疲劳强度和耐腐蚀性等，汽车工业上采用的渗氮法有：气体渗氮、离子氮化和气体碳氮共渗等）

nitriding steel 氮化钢（专用于渗氮热处理的特殊合金钢）

nitrile 腈（R.CN）

nitrile butadiene rubber 腈基丁二烯橡胶（简称NBR或nitrile rubber，可在-54~+149℃下正常工作，主要用来制造汽车的密封件）

nitro 硝基甲烷（nitro-methane的非正规简称）

nitrobenzene 硝基苯（亦写作nitro-benzol，燃油添加剂，有毒）

nitrocellulose 硝化纤维素，硝化棉（由强硫酸、强硝酸混合液处理纤维素生成的硝酸酯，$N=10.7\%$~11.5%的低分子量者用做汽车硝基漆的原料，而$N=11.8\%$~13.5%者，用做炸药）

nitrocellulose lacquer 硝化纤维漆

nitrogen 氮（N_2）

nitrogen carrier gas 载氮气体

nitrogen compound 氮化合物，氮化物

nitrogen-filled 充氮式

nitrogen-filled (hydraulic) accumulator 充氮式（液压）蓄压器

nitrogen generator （安全气囊的）氮气发生器

nitrogen hardening 渗氮硬化处理（= nitrided hardening）

nitrogen oxides 氮氧化物，氮的氧化物（一般用NO_x表示，为汽车排放的各种氮氧化物的总称）

nitrogen-shielded arc welding 氮保护电弧焊

nitroglycerin(e) 硝化甘油，甘油三硝酸酯［化学式$C_3H_5(ONO_2)_3$，无色油状极易爆炸的液体］

nitromethane-oxygen mixture 硝基甲烷-氧气混合气

nitro-tech treatment （钢铁制件的）渗氮处理，氮化处理（表面硬化工艺，= nitrogen hardening）

nitrous oxide (injection) system 氧化亚氮（喷射）系统（由控制按钮、电磁阀、高压氧化亚氮瓶、喷嘴和管道组成，在按钮控制下，将高压氧化亚氮喷入进气歧管，快速引入附加能量，使发动机动力猛

升，氧化亚氮-90℃的低汽化温度可使空气/燃油急剧冷却，而抑制爆燃并可降低因负荷增加而引起的应力，氧化亚氮 N_2O 亦称一氧化二氮，笑气）

NITUC ［美］全国独立汽车货运工作者协调委员会（National Independent Truckers' Unity Council）

nium 铝（aluminium 的简称）

NLGI ［美］国家润滑脂研究所（National Lubricating Grease Institute）

NLR （汽车安全带）非锁紧式伸缩装置（non-locking retractor）

N/m² 牛顿每平方米（国际单位制的压力、应力单位，参见 pascal；$1N/m^2 = 0.10197 kgf/cm^2 = 0.145 \times 10^{-3} lbf/in^2 = 10^{-5} bar = 7.5 \times 10^{-3} mmHg = 0.102 \times 10^{-4} mW.G$）

Nm 牛顿·米（Newton-meter 的简称，力矩单位）

NMFTA ［美］全国汽车货运交通协会（National Motor Freight Traffic Association）

NMHC 非甲烷碳氢化合物（Non-methane hydrocarbons 的简称）

NMHCE 非甲烷类碳氢化合物当量（nonmethane-hydrocarbon equivalent 的简称）

n. mile 海里（nautical mile）

N/mm² 牛顿每平方毫米（newton/millimeter²，国际单位制的压力的选用单位）

NMOG （发动机排放物中的）非甲烷有机气体（non-methane organic gases 的简称美国联邦环境保护法规规定 2003 年以后汽车"NMOG"的排放只许有 0.06g/mile）

NMOS N 沟道金属氧化物半导体（指由 P⁻型硅片制成的 MOS 器件，通电时产生负电荷载流子，即负电荷载流子在其源极与漏极间流动，negative-channel metal-oxide silicon device 的简称）

NMOS inverter NMOS 反相器（由两个 NMOS 三极管组成的、输入"1"产生"0"输出、输入"0"输出为"1"的非门电路）

NMOS transistor N 沟道金属氧化物半导体晶体管（n-type metal oxide semiconductor transistor）

NMSL ［美］国家汽车最高车速限制规定（National Maximum Speed Limit）

NMVSAC ［美］国家汽车安全咨询委员会（National Motor Vehicle Safety Advisory Council）

No ①数，数量（如 No of seats 座位的数量）②号数，号码，第…号（number 的简称）

NO 北方，北方的（north 或 northeern 的简称）

noble gas 稀有气体（惰性气体）

noble metal 贵重金属，稀有金属

noble-metal catalytic agent 贵金属催化剂（指铂、钯、铑或钌做工作材料的催化剂）

noble potential （金属的）高电位，惰性金属电位

NO Claim Discount 见 NCD

no-clearance tappet （气门的）无隙挺杆（如液压挺杆等，见 zero lash tappet）

no-clutch （日式英语）自动变速车辆

no-coil ammeter 无线圈式电流表，无线圈式安培计

no-constant 不固定的，非固定的，无固定的

nocturnal vision 夜间视力，夜间视觉

nodal 节点的

nodal point 结点，交叉点；节点（见 node）

nodding action 上、下点动（如：点头似的摆动）

node ①交叉点，结点，结，节，波节，节点，交点，中心点，轨迹交点（= nodal point）②分支③网点（指在网络中，一个或多个功能部件与信道或数据线路互连的一个点，在网络拓扑结构中，分支的端点，亦称 network node）

node of net 网点（指在网络中，一个或多个功能部件与信道或数据线路互连的一个点）

node of vibration 振动结点（= vibration node point）

Node position detection technology 节点位置探测技术（简称 NPDT）

No.1-D grade of diesel fuel oil 1-D 级柴油

no-draft ventilation ［美］非贯通式通风，非穿堂式通风（= no draught ventilation，指非直接将空气通入的通风方式，如：通过汽车行驶时产生的吸引作用，由侧窗将空气吸入的通风方式）

nodular graphite cast iron 球墨铸铁，球铁（简称 nodular cast iron，或 nodular iron，= ductilecast iron, spheroidal graphite iron，指基体中的石墨呈球状的铸铁，一般是在铸铁水中加入球化剂，如稀土镁和墨化剂，如硅铁制成。铁素体球墨铸铁具有较高的塑性和韧性，球光体球墨铸铁具有较高的强度和硬度）

nodular steel casting 球化钢铸件，球化铸钢件

NOEI 氮氧化物排放指数（nitric oxide emission index）

no extra cost 无额外收费，无另加费用

no-failure life 无故障使用寿命（无故障的工作期限）

NOFI ［美］全美石油燃料学会（National Oil Fuel Institute）

no fire threshold speed （安全气囊）不致点火的碰撞速度阈值（不点火阈速度）

no-glare 防炫目，防耀眼（= anti-dazzle）

no-glare back window 防炫后窗

no go light 禁行灯（如：十字路口的红灯）

no-go side （极限量规的）非通过端（= no-go end）

no-horn 禁止鸣号（交通管理用语）

noise 噪声，杂音

noise abatement 噪声消减，噪声抑制（= noise attenuation, noise cancellation, noise reduction, noise alleviation）

noise analysis 噪声分析

noise audiometer 噪声仪

noise barrier 吸声板，消音屏（为了使空气传播的响声衰减而设置在音源与受音点之间的隔音屏板，亦称 noise barrier panel）

noise blanker 噪声消减装置，消声器

noise brake （制动鼓变形，与蹄片接触不良，因而制动时）发出噪声的制动器

noise bridge 噪声桥（指将噪声源的噪声传导出去或传导噪声的部件、构件或总成件）

noise cancellation system 消声系统（简称 NCS，见 anti-noise system）

noise characteristic 噪声特性

noise condenser 防杂声干扰电容器（如：与直流电机输入-输出端并联，用来吸收换向器火花所产生的高频电波，以防止对无线电造成杂声干扰的电容器）

noise control 噪声控制

Noise Control Act of 1972 ［美］1972年噪声管制法规（美国1972年将各州制定的噪声标准，加以统一制定的联邦噪声标准法）

noise cover 隔声罩，消声罩，消声盖

noise criteria 噪声标准（简称 NC）

noise cycle （噪声源的）噪声重复循环（如：四冲程发动机内为曲轴每两转重复一个噪声循环）

noise density 噪声强度

noise dispersion （噪声频谱中）噪声（声压级的）离散性（其最大声压级与最小声压级的差值范围）

noise elimination 消除噪声

noise eliminator 噪声消除器，消噪器（亦称 noise suppressor, interference suppressor，指吸收火花塞、直流发电机、电动机换向器、点火线圈等发生的高频电波，以防止无线电波受到干扰而产生噪声的各种装置，如：大阻值电阻、电容器、屏蔽线和屏蔽件等）

noise emission 噪声排放，噪声污染

noise equivalent flux density 噪声等效通量密度

noise equivalent intensity 噪声等效密度（简称 NEI）

noise equivalent signal （数字集成电路电荷转移器件电路特性中的）噪声等效信号（使输出功率增加到无输入信号或无照射时的两倍所需要的输入信号或照射功率的方根均值）

noise filter 静噪滤波器

noise-free 无杂音的，无噪声的，安静的

noise-generating surface 噪声引发路面（如：试验悬架噪声的不平路面等）

noise immunity 抗噪声性，抗噪声度

noise-induced hearing loss 噪声导致的听觉丧失

noise-inducing vibration 噪声导生振动（噪声诱生振动）

noise inside body 车内噪声

noise insulation factor 隔声系数（声音通过隔壁前后的声压差）

noise intensity 噪声强度

noise interference 噪声干扰

noise killer 噪声抑制器，噪声消除器，消声器

noiseless 无噪声的，无干扰的，无声的，静的

noiseless drive 无声传动

noiseless run（ning） 无噪声运转（＝quiet running）

noiseless shift（ing） 无声换挡（＝silent shifting, quiet shifting）

noise level ①噪声度，噪声级，声压级（以分贝"dB"为单位）②噪声电平，杂音电平，干扰电平

noise-level tester 声级计，声量计（以分贝"dB"为单位表示声量的大小）

noise main frequency range 噪声的主频率范围

noise margin 噪声容限

noise-measuring meter 噪声测量表，噪声计 [＝noise (level) meter]

noise-monitoring equipment 噪声监测装置

noise nuisance 噪声危害，噪声公害，噪声干扰

noise of exhaust 排气噪声

noise of suction 吸气噪声

noise outside body 车外噪声（如：道路噪声等）

noise peak 噪声峰值

noise pollution 噪声污染

noise-pollution (level) meter 噪声公害测定仪（指噪声级测定仪，简称 NPL meter）

noise power 噪声功率（与声强级"SPL"平方成正比）

noise proof 防噪声的，隔声的，抗噪声的

noise propagation 噪声的扩散，噪声的传播

nois equivalent 噪声等值信号，噪声等效功率，等效杂波

noise rating number 噪声额定值，噪声评定值（国际标准化协会规定的噪声容许值评价方法中使用，简称 NR number）

noise reduction ①噪声的消减 ②（特指消声器等的）减音量，消声量（简称 NR，亦称 attenuation，单位为分贝，NR = SPL′ − SPL，式中：SPL′—消声处理前的声压级；SPL—消声处理后的声压级，亦称 noise abatement 或 Att）

noise-reduction coating 消声涂层

noise remover 噪声抑制装置，消除噪声设备

noise sensor 噪声传感器

noise shield cover ①隔声罩，噪声屏蔽罩 ②防噪声干扰屏蔽罩（防噪声对汽车电子控制系统及无线电波干扰的屏蔽罩板）

noise silencer 消声器

noise source 噪声源

noise source location 噪声源定位

noise spectrum 噪声频谱

noise spot 噪声引起的干扰斑点

noise suppression 射频屏蔽（见 disturbance elimination）

noise suppressor ①噪声抑制器，无线电干扰抑制器（见 noise eliminator）②消声器，隔声器

noise trap 噪声截集装置（如：消声器）

nois frequency 噪声频率

noisiness 噪声度，噪声量，噪声特性

noisy 吵闹的，有噪声的，有干扰的，嘈杂的

noisy gear 噪声大的齿轮

no king pin type steering system 无主销式转向装置

no-lead gas 无铅汽油（未加含铅抗爆剂的汽油）

"no left turn" 禁止左转（道路标志）

no-live load 固定载荷，静载

no-load 空载，无负荷（对发动机，指无功率输出的运转状态）

no-load characteristic test 空载特性试验（测定内燃机空载时，燃油消耗量随转速变化的试验）

no-load curve 空载特性曲线（内燃机空转时，其燃油消耗量随曲轴转速变化的特性曲线）

no-load jet 怠速量孔（= idling jet）

no-load losses performance （液力变速器的）无负荷损失特性，寄生损失特性 [= parasitic losses performance，指输出轴空转时，液力变速器输入转矩（功率）与转速关系的特性]

no-load operation 怠速运转

no-load power loss （次级线圈）无负载时的功率损耗（初级线圈的铜损和铁损）

no-load return trip 空驶回程

no-load saturation curve 空载饱和曲线（= no-load curve）

no-load setting 无负荷调整（在无外载条件下，调校发动机点火系、燃料系、进气系等）

no-load speed 空转速度，无载荷速度

no-load steep acceleration mode 无负荷急加速工况

no-load terminal voltage 无负载端电压

no-load test 空载试验，无负荷试验

no-load voltage 空载电压（不供电时的电源电压，亦称 no-load tension）

nomenclature （学科的）命名法，术语

nominal 名义的，公称的，标称的

nominal aspect ratio （轮胎的）名义高宽比（轮胎安装在理论轮辋上的断面高度与断面宽度的比率，见 aspect ratio）

nominal capacity ①额定功率，标称功率，名义功率②标称容量，名义容量，额定容量③额定生产率

nominal engine speed 发动机额定转速（亦称 rated engine speed）

nominal pressure 公称压力，标称压力，标定压力，额定压力，名义压力（= rated pressure）

nominal rolling radius （轮胎）名义滚动半径

nominal sealing line 名义密封线（指转子发动机的转子工作面和外旋轮线缸壁短轴处的理论密封线。这里没有真正接触，而有必要的运动间隙，只是气流的一种潜在密封线，限制气流窜动）

nominal size 名义尺寸，公称尺寸（亦称 nominal dimension）

nominal steering angle 名义转向角（由转向盘转角与转向系角传动比计算而得的转向轮转角）

nominal stress 标称应力，名义应力（不考虑孔、沟、圆角等几何不连续性所产生的影响而按简单理论计算的净截面上一点的应力）

nominal tire bearing surface 轮胎名义接地面积

nominal value 公称值，名义值

nominal voltage 标称电压（指汽车电气系统的名义电压，亦称 basic system voltage）

nominal volume 额定容积，公称容积

nominal working pressure 额定工作压力

nomogram 列线图，诺谟图（= alignment chart, nomograph, nomographic chart）

nom rock (arm) ratio 名义摇臂比（指一般顶置气门摇臂传动的名义尺寸比，气门开启高度 = 凸轮升高度×名义摇臂比）

non-acid 不含酸类的，非酸性的，无酸的（free from acid, acidless）

non adjustable 不可调的

non-air-pump system 非（二次）空气喷射型排气净化系（指通过对燃料、燃烧等的改进，减少排气有害物生成的前处理净化系统，参见 AIR system）

non-alignment diagram 非列线图

nonane 壬烷 [$CH_3(CH_2)7CH_3$, 常温下为蜡状固体, 石油和天然气的主要成分]

nonaqueous electrolyte battery 无水电解质蓄电池

nonautomotive 非汽车的，非车用的

nonautonomous system 非自控系统

nonbalanced 非平衡的，无压力补偿的

nonbraked trailer 无制动挂车

non-catalytic reduction 非催化型还原转化（将还原剂引入废气中，与排放中的有害氧化物间化学还原反应而生成无害物排出的净化方式）

non-centre point steering 非中心点转向（= divergent steering）

non-circular gear 非圆齿轮（分度曲面不是旋转曲面的齿轮，其齿轮副啮合过程中，瞬时角速度按某种既定的运动规律而变化，如椭圆齿轮）

non-clashing gear set ①变速器常啮合齿轮组②带常啮合齿轮的变速器③带同步器的变速器

non clutch transmission 无离合器式变速器

non-coherent 无黏聚力的，不黏聚的，松散的，不附着的，无黏性的（= noncohesive）

noncombustible ①不燃的，不能燃烧的②不燃物

non-compensated magnetic vehicle detector 非修正式电磁车辆检测器（见 compensated magnetic vehicle detector）

noncomputer-controlled function 非计算机控制功能（汽车各系统中不由计算机控制的各种功能）

non-concentric 偏心的，不同心的

non-concentric cage （球笼式万向节的）偏心保持架（内、外球形支承表面不同心）

non condensing gas cycle ECE 非冷凝气体循环外燃机（其中 ECE 为外燃机"external combustion engine"的简称）

non-conductive 非导体的（绝缘体的）

nonconductor 非导体，绝缘体，电介体

non-congealable oil 防冻机油

nonconstant velocity universal joint 非等速万向节（当两轴夹角大于零时，输出轴与输入轴的平均角速度比等于1，但瞬时角速度比不断变化的传动万向节）

non-contact ①非接触（式）的 ②无触点的（= noncontact-point）

non -contact charging system 见 wireless charging system

non-contact copying measurement 非接触仿形测量

non-contacting mechanical seal 非接触式密封，受控模式机械密封（流体动压和静压式机械密封的总称）

non-contacting position sensor 非接触型位置传感器

non contacting test equipment 非接触型测试设备

noncontact torque sensor 非接触式转矩传感器

non-continuous braking system 非连续式制动系（汽车列车的制动系，既不是连续式，又不是半连续式，见 continuous braking system, semicontinuous braking system）

noncontinuous sampling 非连续采样 [= batch (type) sampling]

non-conventional engine 非常规发动机（如：斯特林发动机、蒸汽机等正在发展中的发动机）

non-corrodibility 抗（腐）蚀性（= rustless property）

non-corrosive grease 无酸腐蚀润滑脂（= acid-free grease）

non-countable 不可数的

noncountersunk style 非埋头型

nondangerous moderate injury 无（生命）危险的中等程度伤害

nondangerous severe injury 无（生命）危险重伤，无生命危险的严重伤害

non-dazzling 不炫目的，防炫的（= anti-dazzling）

nondestruction test 无损试验，非破坏性试验

non-destructive bit-by-bit arbitration （汽车多重控制和处理系统使用优先权管理的）非破坏性逐位判优

non-destructive inspection 非破坏性检验，无损探伤，无损检测（= nondestructive testing，简称 NDI，如用 X 光、激光、磁粉等对零部件内部缺陷和损伤的检验）

non-detachable 不可拆卸的，不可拆开的，不可脱开的

non-detonating fuel 抗爆震燃油（= antiknock fuel）

non-diathermal 不透热（辐射）的（亦写作 nondiathermic）

non-dimensional coefficient 无量纲系数

nondirectional tire tread design 无方向性的胎面花纹结构

nondispersive infrared analysis 不分光红外线分析法（在测定能吸收红外线气体浓度的装置中，不用棱镜或衍射光栅分光，而用气体滤光器的分析方法，一般用来检测发动机排气中的 HC，CO，CO_2 等，简称 NDIR）

nondispersive ultraviolet analysis 不分光紫外线分析法（在连续测定能吸收紫外线气体浓度的装置中，不用棱镜或衍射光栅分光，而用干涉滤光器得到选择性，再用光电管检测的分析法，可测出发动机排气中的 NO_x，简称 NDUA）

nondriving axle 非驱动桥

non-drying oil 不干性油（在空气中不致干枯而形成树脂状薄膜的油，如：牛脚油、花生油、橄榄油等）

non-ECM emission control 非电子控制型排放控制（装置，如：曲轴箱强制通风阀、无 EGR 阀的机内废气再循环装置等；其中 ECM 为 electfronic control module 的简称）

non-electrolyte 非电解质（在水溶液中，不易电离为离子，即：其水溶液不导电的物质）

non-engine-related 与发动机无关的

nonequalizing differential 不等转矩差速器

non-equilibrium 不均衡的，不平衡的

nonesterified vegetable oil 非酯化植物油

non -EV 非电动汽车（指内燃机汽车等）

non-exhaust valve engine 无排气门式发动机（如：常规的二冲程发动机）

nonfade lining 抗衰减衬片（耐高温、水湿等的摩擦衬片）

non-fatigue failure 非疲劳性破坏

non-ferrous alloy 非铁合金，有色合金

nonfilling slot-type bearing 不带装球切口的球轴承

non-flammable 不燃的，不易燃的，无焰的（亦写作 nonflammable）

non flammable fiber 阻燃纤维

non flammable fuel 无焰燃料

non flammable mixture 不可燃混合气（指空燃比小于稀失火极限或大于浓失火极限的混合气，参见 nis-fire limit）

non-floating axle 非浮式半轴（亦称 plain axle，其内端支撑在差速器上，即其轴承装在内端上，由桥壳支撑，外端亦由装在半轴壳内的轴承直接支撑，这种结构要承受分配在后桥上的全部车重，并承受转矩和弯矩）

non-fluid oil 非流动性润滑油（如：滑脂）

non-fogging 防雾的，不起雾的

Non food related ethanol 非食物原料乙醇

non-forced circulatory lubrication 非压力循环润滑

non-fossil fuel 非石油类燃料

nonfouling spark plug 防污染火花塞

non-freezable oil 防冻机油

nonfreezing solution ①防冻剂，防冻液 ②添加有防冻剂的冷却水

non-fuel efficient 不节油的，燃油经济性差的，费油的，油耗高的

nongasoline fuel 非汽油燃料（一般指代汽油燃料，如：酒精、氢气、甲醇等）

non-glare glass 防炫玻璃（= anti-glare glass, nondazzling glass）

non-glare headlamp 防炫前照灯（= anti-glare headlamp）

non-glare mirror 防炫后视镜（= antidazzle mirror）

non-hardening 不变硬的，不硬化的

nonhomogeneous charge engine 非均质充气发动机（如：柴油机和层状充气式汽油机）

nonhydrocarbon fuel 非碳氢化合物燃料（非烃类燃料）

nonhygroscopic 不吸湿的（不吸水的，不吸潮的）

non -independent suspension 非独立悬架（亦称 rigid axle suspension，指

将车身或车架支撑在一根整轴或整根车桥上的悬架形式)
non-inductive 非感应的,非诱导的
noninflammability 不可燃性,不着火性
non-inflatable tyre ①非充气轮胎②免充气轮胎
non-insulation brush 非绝缘电刷
non-integrated ABS 非整体式 ABS (指制动氧化氮主缸、制动液压调节器和助力器等分别为独立总成的 ABS,见 integrated ABS,亦称 add on ABS)
non-interchangeable bearing 非互换性(滚动)轴承(内、外圈不可互换)
non-interconnected local controller 非互连式局部控制器
non-intercooled 无中间冷却的,非中冷式的
non-intersection speed controller 非交叉口地段车速控制器(公路非交叉口车速控制装置,如:限速标志,车速测定装置等)
nonintrusive ①无妨碍的②非干涉的(无干涉的)
nonius ①游标②游标卡尺,带游标的量具,带副尺的量具(原于法语,亦称 vernier calipers, slide calipers)
nonknocking fuel 抗爆震燃油(= antiknock fuel)
nonleaded gasoline 无铅汽油(不含乙基铅抗爆剂的)
non-linear and time variable system 非线性时变系统(随时间而变化的非线性系统)
non-linear fuzzy logic 非线性模糊逻辑
non-linear integrated circuit 非线性集成电路(输出信号随输入信号的变化呈非线性解析函数关系的集成电路)

non-linearity 非线性
non-linear material 无线性参数的材料(如:电阻值与温度无线性变化关系的材料)
nonlinear scale (测量仪表的)非线性标度(标度的各分格间距与分格值呈非常数比例关系的标度,如:对数标度,平方律标度)
nonlinear suspension 非线性悬架
non-linear system 非线性系统
non linear transformation 非线性变换
non-linear viscous damping 非线性黏性阻尼[振动中,由振幅与变形速度的某次幂(不等于1)成正比,方向与变形速度相反的材料内阻尼力引起的材料能量耗散作用]
non-load friction 空载摩擦
non-load sensing limiter 非载荷感知式制动液压限压阀,非载荷感知式限压阀(见 limiting valve)
non-load voltage 无负载电压,空载电压(停止送电时的电源电压。如:铅蓄电池的空载电压,与极板大小无关,每一单电池约为2V, = no-load potential)
non-locking retractor (乘员安全带的)非锁紧式伸缩装置(简称 NLR)
non-lubricating 无须润滑的(机器在使用期间不需要定期润滑的)
non-magnetic material 非磁性材料(不产生磁感应的物质,一般指铁、钴、镍、钆、镝等铁磁质和铝、锰、铜、银、铅等弱磁质以外的物质,但钢中也有非磁性钢)
nonmeasurable defect 测量不出的缺陷
non-metal 非金属的
non-methane hydrocarbons 非甲烷碳氢化合物(除甲烷以外的碳氢化合物,简称 NMHC)
nonmethane organic gas 非甲烷类有

机气体（大气烟雾的主要成分，简称NMOG）

non-misting 不起雾的，不起蒙的，不模糊的

non-motor-vehicle fuel 非车用燃料

non-muscular energy braking system 全动力式制动系（产生制动力所需的能量，不需驾驶员的体力供给，见manual brake）

non-Newtonian fluid 非牛顿流体[指剪切应力τ与剪切速度D之间的比例关系不成立的流体的总称，按D与τ的函数关系可分为以下三大类：①纯黏性流体"pure viscous fluid"，$D=f(\tau)$；②时间关系流体"timedependent fluid"，$D=f(\tau,t)$；③黏弹性流体"viscoelastic fluid"；$D=f(\tau,s)$，式中：t—时间；s—剪切应变]

NO_2-NO converter NO_2-NO 转化室（二氧化氮转化为一氧化氮）

non-operative 不工作的，无效的，不动作的

non-operative vehicle-days 停驶车日

non-oxidizing 抗氧化的，不氧化的

non-parametric test 非参量性的测试

non-penetrated 不通的，不贯穿的，盲的

non-periodic function 非周期函数

non-petroleum-based fuel 非石油基燃料

non-plane motion 非平面运动（曲面运动）

nonplated piston ring 无镀层的活塞环

non-pneumatic tire 非充气轮胎

non-poisonous 无毒的

non-polarized return-to-zero recording 非极化归零制记录法（车用计算机系统二进制数的一种返回基准的记录方式。以未磁化状态代表1，而以磁化状态代表0，或反之，以前者代表0，后者代表1，亦称双极调制 dipole modulation，见 polarized return-to-zero recording）

nonpolluting coating 防污涂层，无污染涂层

non-polluting fuel 无污染燃料（燃烧时不产生HC，NO_x，CO等污染大气的燃料，如：H_2等）

non-poppet valve engine 无气门式发动机

nonpowered axle 非驱动桥，非驱动轴（不传递驱动力的从动桥，从动轴）

nonpower shift （自动变速器等的）非驱动换挡，中断驱动换挡（指在中断动力传递的状况下换挡，见power shift）

non-precious 非精密的，非贵重的，非珍贵的，廉价的

non-pressure charging 非增压式充气（自然吸气）

Non Profit Organization （民营的）非营利性团体

non-reactive suspension （并装双轴车桥或多轴悬架中的）非平衡式悬架（驱动和制动转矩及振动负荷不由双轴或其悬架间的杆系平衡，而由各自的机械杆系平衡的悬架系统）

non-recoverable 不可回收的，一次性使用的

non-reflecting finish 钝光精整加工，表面无光泽的精整加工（= dull finish）

nonreflective road sign 非反光路标（亦写作 non-reflexive road sign）

non-refuelling 不加油的，不再加油的

non-relevant failure 非关联失效（如：在解释试验结果或计算可靠性特征量的数值时，不计入的失效）

non-removable metal 不可拆卸式滑动轴承，固浇式滑动轴承（减摩合

金直接浇铸在机体轴承孔表面上）

nonresinous oil 不含树脂性物质的润滑油

non-resonance type detonation sensor 非共振型爆燃传感器

nonreturn flow 单向流动

non-return valve 止回阀，单向阀（= check valve, back valve）

non-reusable 一次性的，不可重复使用的

non-reversible 单向式的，不可逆的，不可反转的（= irreversible）

non-right-of-way vehicle （在交叉路口等处）非（具有优先）通行权的车辆

nonrigid 非刚性的

non-road engine emission values 发动机非道路排放值（指实验室试验取得的发动机排放值）

non-rotating clutch case 离合器固定壳

nonrunner vehicle 有故障的车辆，失修的车辆

non-rusting 防锈的，不锈的，抗蚀的

non-rust steel 不锈钢

nonsaponifying oil 非皂化润滑油

non-saturating 非饱和的，不饱和的

nonscheduled 不定期的，不按计划的

nonscheduled maintenance 非计划性维护，不定期维修（如：按需维修）

nonsealed fluid coupling 非密封式液力耦合器（变量液力耦合器）

non-sealing 非密封性的，不密封的，无密封件的

non-self-priming pump ①起动时要灌水的离心式水泵 ②起动时要注油的离心式油泵

non-self-supporting universal joint 非自承式万向节（需要其他外部机构支撑的万向节，如：装于转向车轮的凸块式和球叉式万向节）

nonsensitive 不敏感的

nonseparable 不可拆开的，不可分开的

non-separated 非分离的

non-serviceable ①（在设计和结构上）不允许改装或大修后重新装配的（部件或装置）②使用寿命不长的（部件或装置）③不能使用的

non-servo brake （固定支撑销领、从蹄结构的）非伺服型鼓式制动器

non-shatterable glass 防碎玻璃，不碎玻璃

nonsizing 防卡滞的，防黏附的，防黏附磨损的，抗擦伤的，抗拉伤的

non-skewed spray 非斜孔喷射（指喷油器喷口不偏离喷油器中心线的喷射）

non-skewed type injector 非斜孔喷射型喷油器（指喷口不偏离喷油器中心线的喷油器，见 skewed type injector）

nonskid ①不滑动的，防滑的 ②防滑装置

nonskid braking 无滑移制动（如：车轮不抱死制动）

non-skid chain （轮胎的）防滑链条

nonskid device 防滑装置（antiskid device）

nonskid pattern （轮胎）防滑花纹

nonskid relief depth （轮胎）不打滑的最小花纹深度

nonskid road surface 不打滑的路面

nonskid tire 防滑轮胎（= antiskid tire）

nonskid tire life 轮胎的打滑前寿命（轮胎工作至花纹磨光引起打滑前的使用期限）

nonskid tread （轮胎的）防滑胎面，抗滑胎面（= nonslip tread）

non-skid wear （轮胎的）不打滑磨损（指轮胎磨耗至花纹磨光前的磨损或轮胎正常滚动下的磨损）

nonsliding vane pump 叶片不滑动的油泵

non-slip 防滑的,限滑的,无滑动的

non-slip differential 防滑差速器,防滑转差速器(见 no-slip differential, no-spin differential, limited slip differential)

nonslip drive 无滑动传动,无滑差驱动(=1:1 drive,如:驱动轴与从动轴之间采用摩擦离合器时,离合器摩擦片没有打滑,则驱动轴与从动轴的转速为1:1)

non-slip shaft (万向节传动的)非滑动轴

nonslip tread 防滑胎面(=nonskid tread)

nonsludging oil 防氧化结胶润滑油,氧化稳定油

non-smoking ①不准吸烟的 ②无烟的,不产生烟尘的

non-sparking hammer 无火花手锤(指敲击时不会产生火花)

nonspill coupling 自封式管接头

nonspill truck body 供运输散装物料用的高栏板车箱

nonspill type airvent (油箱的)不漏油式通风孔

non-stage transmission ①无级变速 ②无级变速器,无级变速装置

nonstandardized 非标准(化)的

non-stationary 非固定的,非稳定的,不固定的,不稳定的

nonsteady heat transfer 非稳定热传导

non-steerable 非转向的(如:非转向轮,非转向桥)

non-stop (中途)不停(的),不间断的,直达的

nonstop bus 直达公共汽车,直达客车

non-stress-carrying part 非承载件,非受力件

non-stressed skin (承载构架式轿车车身的)非受力外壳(板),不受力外壳板(亦称 non-structural skin)

nonstructural safety device (汽车的)非结构性(乘员)安全装置(指安全皮带、安全气囊等不作为汽车结构一部分的安全装置,相对保险杠等结构性安全装置而言)

non-supercharged engine 非增压式发动机(自然吸气式发动机,直接从大气压下吸气的发动机,相对增压式发动机而言,=normally aspirated engine)

non-surging spring 抗颤振(气门)弹簧(高速运转时不会产生因共振而剧烈颤振的气门弹簧,如不等距弹簧、双重弹簧等,=surging dispatch spring, variable pitch spring)

non-symmetric 不对称的,非对称的(=non-symmetrical)

nonsynchronized 不同步的,非同步的

nonsynchronized mode 非同步运转模式(如:节气门体式汽油喷射系统按固定的时间间隔,如12.5毫秒,喷油器喷油一次,而不与汽缸点火同步,见 synchronized mode)

non-tapered key 非锥形键

non-throttling (pintle nozzle) injector 非节流(针阀)型喷油器

non-toxic fuel 无毒燃料

nontraditional 非传统的,非常规的

non-transitive 非传递的

non-uniform acceleration 非等加速度(变加速度,=variable acceleration)

non-uniform approach 非均匀趋近

non-uniform charge engine 非均质充气发动机(分层充气发动机=stratified charge engine)

non-uniform combustion 不均匀燃烧,非均质燃烧

non-uniformly preheated gas 不均匀预热气体

non-uniform rotary motion 非匀速旋转运动（变角速度旋转运动，非等速旋转运动）

non-uniform scale 非等间距标尺

non-unloading compressor 不卸压式压气机

non-usable 非可用的，不可用的，无用的

non-user accident 非（车辆）驾驶者（责任）事故

non-vent cap 无通气孔道的罩盖（密封盖）

non-vibrator coil 无振（子）线圈

non-volatile 非挥发性的

non-volatile memory system 非易失性存储系统，长存式存储器（断电后存储的信息不会消失的存储系统，简称 NVM）

non-working flank （齿轮轮齿的）非工作面

non-woven carpet material 无纺地毯材料（车内装饰用）

non-zero digit 非零位

NO·O₃ reactive cell NO-O₃ 反应室（一氧化氮和臭氧反应，生成激发态二氧化氮的反应室）

No Over Taking 禁止超车

no-parking 禁止驻车（禁止停放车辆）

no passing ①禁止超车，不准超车（= no overtaking）②禁止通行

no-passing barrier 禁止通行的拦路障

no-passing line ①禁止超车线②禁止通行线

no-passing zone ①禁止超车区②禁止通行区

no-pitching 无纵倾（车辆前端无仰头低头的振动）

NOR ①或非（一种逻辑运算符号，当所有命题为假时，才为真，若至少有一个命题为真，则结果为假，= not-or）②既不是…，也不是…（如：P NOR Q，表示既不是 P，也不是 Q）

NOR circuit "或非"电路（只有当所有输入为 0 时，输出才为 1 的逻辑电路）

Nordberg key 圆键（= round key）

NOR element "或非"元件（见 NOR gate）

no-resonant intake duct 非共振型进气道（其管道壁具有多孔材料，以消减进气噪声）

NOR gate "或非"门（= NOR element，指完成"或非"布尔运算的逻辑元件，即：有两个输入、一个输出的逻辑运算元件，只有当两个输入均为 0 时，输出为 1；当有一个输出为 1，或两个输入均为 1 时，输出为 0）

no right turn 禁止右转（道路标志）

norm 定额、定量、限额；标准、规格，规范，准则

normal ①正规，正常；常态；标准②法线，垂直线③正交，正态④正链的（不带支链的，如：正庚烷）⑤当量浓度的⑥平均的，普通的；中性的⑦正交的，垂直的；法线的

normal-air 标准空气

normal angle 法angle

normal axis 法向轴线

normal back lash （两齿轮的工作齿面相互接触时的）法向侧隙（指其非工作齿面间的最小距离）

normal base pitch （渐开线斜齿轮的）法向基圆齿距，法向基节（构成两个相邻同侧齿面的渐开线螺旋面的起始线间的法向螺旋线的弧长）

normal base thickness 法向基圆齿厚（渐开线斜齿轮基圆螺旋线在一个齿的两侧面的渐开螺旋面起始终之间的弧长）

normal brake application 正常制动

normal (brake) stop 正常制动停车

normal braking state 正常制动工况（多用于描述防抱死制动系的非防抱死工况）

normal butane 正丁烷（C_4H_{10}，见 butane）

normal cetane 正构十六烷，正十六烷（在高温高压下，会迅速地形成过氧化物，所以滞燃期限小，不易引起发动机的燃烧粗暴，因此评价柴油的着火性时，正十六烷作为十六烷值为100的标准油，其分子式为$C_{16}H_{34}$，参见 cetane method）

normal chordal tooth thickness 法向弦齿厚（一个齿两侧齿线间的最短距离）

normal circular pitch 法向周节

normal combustion 正常燃烧（对汽油机而言，指火花点火后，火焰以每秒10m以下的速度向四周传播，全部混合气均匀完全燃烧的状态）

normal combustion period 正常燃烧期（指缓燃期，汽缸内出现最高压力到出现最高温度时为止的一段燃烧时间，以曲轴转角表示）

normal combustion velocity 正常燃烧速度（简称NCV，指混合气在静止状态下相对于未燃气体的燃烧速度）

normal component 法向分力，法线分量

normal concentration 标准浓度（克当量浓度）

normal condition ①正常条件，常规条件，常规情况，正常情况②标准状态（0℃，101.325kPa）

normal cone （锥齿轮的）法锥

normal (control layout) cab （货车等的）长头驾驶室（发动机位于驾驶室前方）

normal control vehicle ①长头车（美称 cab behind engine，驾驶室在发动机后面的货车或大客车）②常规驾驶的车辆（指非自动驾驶）

normal crest width 法向齿顶厚（斜齿一个齿两侧齿顶圆螺旋线的法向螺旋线位于齿顶内面的弧长）

normal cross section 法向断面，正剖面，横截面，垂直断面

normal diametral pitch 法向径节（圆周率除以法向齿距所得的商，为法向模数的倒数）

normal direction 法线方向，垂直方向

normal discharge curve 正规流量曲线

normal distribution 正态分布（正常分布，常态分布，高斯分布）

normal docking 正常修理，计划修理

normal equation 标准方程式，正规方程式

normal force 法向力（垂直力，正交力）

normal function ①正规函数②常规功能

normal helix 法向螺旋线（指在同一圆柱面上相交，且在任一交点处，各自通过同一交点的切线都互相垂直的两条螺旋线，互为对方的法向螺旋线，两者的螺旋方向相反，螺旋角互余）

normal heptane 正庚烷［CH_3(CH_2)$_5CH_3$］（作为内燃机燃料，最容易产生爆燃，因而在测定燃油抗爆性时，用做辛烷值等于0的标准油）

normal hexadecane 正十六烷（= normal cetane）

normal hexane 正己烷（C_6H_{14}）（汽油代表性成分之一，用于不分光型红外线HC测定仪样气室内进入的样气）

normal horsepower 额定马力（标称马力）

normal inflation （轮胎）额定充气压力（轮胎正常充气压力）

normal inspection 常规检查，常规检测

normality ①常态，标准状态，标准性质②正规性，正常性③当量浓度，规定浓度④垂直

normality condition 正规状态，正常条件

normalization ①标准化，规格化，规范化，正规化，正常化②校正，取准③正火（见 normalizing）

normalized ①规格化的，归一化的，标准化的；常规的②正（过）火的

normalized air/fuel ratio lambda 相对空燃比 λ（亦称空燃当量比"stoichiometrical air/fuel ratio, λ = 实际空燃比。当 λ = 1 时，表示混合气的实际空燃比等于理论空燃比；λ > 1 时，为稀混合气；λ < 1 时，为浓混合气）

normalized rms acceleration 标准均方根加速度（国际标准组织提出的标准三维振动加速度，其中 rms 为 root-mean-square "均方根" 的简称）

normalized tire force coefficient 轮胎侧偏刚度系数（亦称 cornering stiffness coefficient，自由滚动的轮胎的侧偏刚度与垂直负荷的比值）

normalizing ①（使）正规化，标准化，规范化②正火（将钢加热到高于临界温度 Ac₃ 或 Acm 30～70℃，保持一定时间，达到完全奥氏体化或均匀化，然后在自然通风的空气中冷却，以细化晶粒，提高强度、韧性，改善切削性，或为淬火创造条件）

normalizing condition ①正规条件，归一条件②正火状态

normal jet ①标准气动量规②普通喷嘴，标准喷嘴

normal line 法线

normal load ①正常载荷，额定载荷，标称载荷②法向载荷，垂直载荷

normally aspirated engine 非增压式吸气发动机，自然吸气发动机（亦称 naturally aspirated engine，指无增压常规活塞式发动机，见 non-supercharged engine）

normally closed contact 常闭触点

normally closed solenoid valve 常闭式电磁阀（无控制信号、不通电时，其阀处于关闭位置）

normally closed valve 常闭阀

normally open contact 常开触点

normally open solenoid valve 常开式电磁阀（无控制信号、不通电时，处于开启位置）

normally open valve 常开阀

normal mixture 标准混合气（指理论混合气，含有可使混合气中的汽油完全燃烧所必需的空气量的汽油空气混合气，即空气-汽油的质量比为 14.7∶1 的混合气）

normal mode ①标准模式②（电子控制式悬架的）正常模式

normal module 法向模数，法面模数（如：齿轮的法向模数，为法向齿距除以圆周率 π 所得的商，以毫米计）

normal octane 正辛烷［$CH_3·(CH_2)_6·CH_3$，分子量较大，且无分支的饱和链烃，抗爆燃性差，辛烷值 -17］

normal operation 正常运转（= normal running, normal working, regular operation）

normal paraffin(e) 正（链）烷属烃

normal pitch 法向齿距（斜齿轮分度圆柱面上，两相邻同侧齿面间齿线法向螺旋线的弧长）

normal pitch diameter （锥齿轮的）法向节圆平均直径

normal plane ①垂直面，法向面②（齿轮的）法平面（指垂直于轮

齿齿线的平面)

normal plane(of a space curve) (空间曲线的)法(平)面,(挠曲线的)法面

normal position 正常位置

normal power 常用功率(指内燃机从效率和寿命考虑,能经济运转的常用功率)

normal pressure 正常压力,标准压力

normal pressure angle ①法向压力角(过齿线上的任意点处的径向直线与齿面在该点处的切平面所夹的锐角,若该任意点所在范围扩大到整个齿面,则称任意点的法向压力角"normal pressure angle at a point")②基本齿条的法向压力角(又称"齿形角")

normal probability curve 正态变量概率分布曲线,高斯曲线

normal profile 法向齿廓(齿面被法平面所截的截线)

normal profile angle 法向齿形角

normal random variable 正态随机变量

normal rated power 额定功率

normal revolution ①正常转数②正转

normal running conditions 正常运转状态,正常运转条件

normal-running fit 转动配合

normal-running spark plug 通常型火花塞,普通型火花塞

normal running temperature 正常运转温度

normal section 正剖面,横截面,正截面

normal shear 垂直剪切力

normal solution ①当量溶液②规定溶液

normal space 正规空间,规定空间

normal space width (斜齿轮的)法向齿槽宽(一个齿槽内,两侧齿线的法向螺旋线位于该齿槽内的弧长)

normal speed 正常速度,规定速度

normal state 正常状态,标准状态

normal strain 法向应变

normal stress 法向应力(垂直于力作用平面的应力分量,即:每单位截面面积上,抵抗法向作用力的力,分拉伸应力或压缩应力,常用代号 δ 或 f,常用单位 kN/m^2,kgf/cm^2,lbf/in^2 等并规定拉应力为正,压应力为负,见 intensity of stress)

normal surface 垂直面,正交面,法面

normal temperature 标准温度,规定温度

normal test ①正态性检验(鉴别数据幅值的概率分布是否服从正态分布)②常规试验,标准试验

normal thrust 垂直推力

normal to a curve ①曲线的法线 ②垂直于某曲线的

normal to a surface ①曲面的法线 ②垂直于某曲面的

normal tooth thickness 法向齿厚(斜齿轮齿线法向螺旋线在一个齿的两侧齿面之间的弧长)

norm of fuel consumption 燃料消耗定额

norol ①汽车坡道停车防滑机构②无滚子的

NORRA [美]全国汽车越野赛协会(National Offroad Race Association)

north ①北,北方,北部(代号N);北半球②北方的,北部的;位于北面的;朝北方的

North American model 北美型(汽车)

north pole 北极,北磁极(代号N)

North-south crank shaft 南、北向曲轴,纵向曲轴(纵置式发动机,纵向布置发动机,指发动机安装在汽车纵向位置)

Northwestern University Transporta-

tion Center Library ［美］西北大学运输中心图书馆（简称 NT）

Norton gear 诺顿齿轮（三星齿轮）

Norton type gear（box） 诺顿齿轮箱（只有一个传动齿轮的三星齿轮箱）

no-rust 防锈的，免锈的

NOS 见 new-old-stock part

nose 端，尖端，前端，突出部，管口

nose circle （轴）端圆

nose cone （汽车车身空气动力学附加装置中的）前锥（指装在厢式货厢前板处的凸锥形附件，用以改善气流特性，减小空气阻力）

nose-dip 汽车点头（如：制动或前轮载荷增加时车头的下倾现象 = nose-dive，nose-down）

nose end 孔端，管口端，端

nose fairing （汽车）车头流线型外罩（头部减小阻力装置）

nose fin 前鳍（前稳定板）

nose heavy （汽车载荷分配的）前重现象

nose of cam 凸轮鼻端（凸轮尖）

nose panel （轿车）发动机罩端板（= front end panel）

nose piece ①喷嘴，管口，接头②（显微镜上）换镜头用的旋转盘，物镜座盘

nose protector （汽车）车头防护罩（装在汽车前端防止飞石、路屑等损坏发动机罩和挡泥板的黑色软塑料罩，可见于在美国坏路上行驶的车辆，亦称 nose bra）

nose-up 汽车扬头（如：汽车起步急加速等驱动力突然增加、前轮载荷减少时，车头向上扬起的现象，亦称 nose lift）

nose weight （被牵引汽车的）前端质量（指被牵引车辆压在牵引车牵引点中心的垂直质量）

nose wheel 前轮

no-sky line 天空视见线，遮挡天空线（驾驶座上某点能直接看见和看不见天空的分界线）

no-slip drive 无滑动传动

no smokers box （轿车烟灰盒处为）不吸烟者（设置的）小物件盒

no spark 无火花

no-spin differential 防滑（转）差速器，防空转差速器（亦称 limited slip differential，no slip differential，non spin differential，指通过各种自锁装置或人为锁止机构防止驱动轮滑转，增大其锁止系数，将左、右车轮的转速差限制在一定范围内，直至使左、右驱动轮转速完全相等的差速器）

no standard （对某项指标等）无标准（无规定，标准中无规定值，未制定标准值，简称 NS）

No-stead state side slip properties （轮胎的）非稳态侧偏特性

no step bus （便于老人及残障乘客上、下车的低车身）无（台阶）踏板大客车

no-stop charging system （收费点的）不停车收费系统（见 electronic toll collection system）

no stopping 禁止停车

NOT "非"（一种逻辑运算符，当命题为真时结果为假，命题为假时结果为真）

notability ①知名度②知名，著名③著名的人、车等

NOT-AND 见 NAND

NOT-AND element 见 NAND element

NOT-AND gate 见 NAND gate

notation ①记号，记法，符号，用法；标志，注释②符号表示法，标志法，计数法，计数制

notch back ①（后窗接近垂直，与后行李舱盖间夹角大的三箱式轿车身的）凹背，折背，梯背②凹背式（轿车）车身（= notch back body）③凹背式车身轿车（＝notch back car）

notch back body 折背式车身（轿车）（普通的三箱式车身轿车，由于后面有行李舱，从客舱至行李舱车身背部有一阶梯状过渡，故名，亦称梯背式"ponton type"）

notch（back）couple （后窗接近垂直，与后行李舱盖间夹角较大的）凹背式两门一排主座箱式轿车

notch bar bending test （材料）切口试棒弯曲试验

notch bar impact test （材料）切口试棒冲击试验

notch bar pull test （材料）切口试棒拉伸试验

notch bar test （材料）切口试棒试验（用来测定冲击韧性的试验，在试验时给切口试棒以突然的冲击，同时测定试件断裂所吸收的能量）

notch board 凹板，（楼梯的）搁板

notch brittleness 缺口脆性，切口脆性

notch-cut type piston ring 边角切割型活塞环［①指内圆面上边角倒成斜面的内倒角气环，称 inner 或 inside bevel（ed）compression ring, inside bevel taper-face ring；②指内圆面上边角切割成台阶状内沉肩活塞气环以上①，②两种活塞环均统称 torsional compression ring 或 twist compression ring。在活塞除做功冲程以外的上、下冲程中，上述活塞环会产生扭曲，而与汽缸壁和活塞环槽形成线接触，密封性良好，且具有良好的刮油作用；③指内圆下边角倒角或切割成台阶形的气环，称 reverse torsional tape-faced compression ring, taper-faced reserve twist compression ring 或 reserve torsional internal stepped ring；④指外倒角活塞环，即：外圈上边角倒角成斜面的气环；⑤外沉肩活塞环，即外圆面下边角切割成台阶状的气环，亦称刮油型气环，带刮油刃口型气环，称 scraper compression ring, under cut type ring, wiper compression ring, 或外扭曲型气环，称 outside twist（或 torsional）compression ring］

notched section ①齿弧（带齿的弧形零件）②切口部分，切槽部分

notched type bearing 带装球缺口的球轴承（＝ball bearing with filling slot）

notch effect （由于阶梯、油孔、键槽等造成断面局部急剧变化以致应力集中的）凹缺效应（切口效应，缺口效应）

notch embrittlement 由于切口引起的脆性增大

notch filter 陷波滤波器（频率特性曲线下凹的滤波器）

notch plate 扇形棘轮板

notch toughness （钢的）缺口韧性（冲击韧性）

notch wheel 棘轮（＝ratchet wheel）

notchy （由于离合器未完全分离而引起的换挡）不平顺（齿轮轻微撞击）

NOT circuit "非"电路（输入为0时输出为1、输入为1时输出为0的计算机逻辑电路）

NOT element "非"元件（见 NOT gate）

Noteworthy ①显著的；明显的②值得注意的③重要的

NOT gate "非"门（实现"非"运算，即输入为1输出为0、输入为0输出为1的逻辑元件，＝NOT element）

not-go end 不过端，止端

not-go gauge 止端规，不过端量规，不通过规

no thorough fare 不收通行费，免费通行（路标）

noticeable wear 明显磨损，显著磨损

notice board 布告牌

not off-vehicle charging capacity 见 Not OVC cap

no-torque shift （自动变速器）转矩中断换挡

not ovc cap （电动或混合动力汽车蓄电系统的）无车外充电能力（指不具有利用车外电源充电的能力，not off-vehicle charging capacity 的简称）

"no transmission" characteristic （发动机等）未经传动装置减速的特性曲线

no turn 禁止转弯（路标）

no-turn shuttle hauling 无掉头的往返运输（环形线路运输）

novel 奇异的，新奇的，未出现过的，新的

novel type 新型

Nover ratio 车轮转数与行驶里程的比值，车轮转速与车速的比值

novolak resin 合成酚醛树脂，酚醛清漆树脂

no-voltage condition 无电压状态（零电压状态）

NO$_x$ 氮氧化物（oxides of nitrogen）

NO$_x$ absorber （重型车辆柴油机排放控制系统中的）NO$_x$ 吸收装置

NO$_x$ concentration signal NO$_x$ 浓度信号

NO$_x$-control module 氮氧化物控制模块（见 NCM）

NO$_x$ control system （排气）NOx 控制系统

NO$_x$ converter NO$_x$ 转化器，氮氧化物转化器（利用催化反应将 NO$_x$ 还原为 N$_2$ 和 O$_2$ 的转化器）

NO$_x$ emission downstream after-treatment NO$_x$ 排放下游后处理（2000 年以后发展的 NO$_x$ 净化技术，无须采用因避免燃烧温度过高而推迟点火时刻等减少缸内 NO$_x$ 生成措施，可提高发动机效率，节约燃油）

noxious 有毒的，有害的

noxious emission 有害排放（物），有毒排放（物）

noxious gas 毒气，有害气体

NO$_x$-selective electrode NO$_x$ 选择性电极

NO$_x$ sensor NO$_x$ 传感器（废气中，氮氧化物含量传感器）

NO$_x$ storage-reduction catalyst NO$_x$ 存储-还原催化剂

NO$_x$ storage reduction catalyst converter NO$_x$ 储存式还原催化转化器（由作为载体或载体涂层的氧化铝中的铈、铁等非贵重金属等短时间存储 NO$_x$）

NO$_x$ storage-reduction catalyst converter ［柴油机排放后处理系统（DPNR）中的］NO$_x$ 吸附-还原催化转化器（见 DPNR）

NO$_x$ system （发动机的）NO$_x$ 净化系

NOx trap NOx 捕集器，NOx 滤集器（= NOx filter）

NO$_x$ wet chemical analysis method NO$_x$ 湿化学分析法（应用化学试剂及光电比色分析排气中 NO$_x$ 含量的方法）

nozzle 喷管，喷嘴，喷头，喷口

nozzle angle 喷嘴角（喷口喷射角，喷嘴安装角）

nozzle body （喷嘴）针阀体（装在喷油嘴内，其头部有一个或多个喷孔的圆筒形零件，针阀在其腔孔中作往复运动）

nozzle bore ①喷油嘴孔②喷（油）嘴孔径

nozzle closure 喷口隔板

nozzle dribbling 喷油嘴滴油（喷油结束，指喷嘴针阀关闭后，因密封不良或针阀颤振使少量燃油滴出的现象）

nozzle erosion （柴油机等的）喷嘴烧蚀

nozzle flow characteristic 喷嘴流通特性（喷孔有效面积随喷油器针阀升程的变化规律）

nozzle head 喷嘴头

nozzle holder （柴油机）喷油器体（指安装喷油器各零、部件的体壳）

nozzle holder cap 喷油器（螺）帽

nozzle holder tube （柴油机汽缸盖安装喷油器体的部位中的）喷油器体安装孔套管

nozzle hole cone （多孔喷油嘴的）喷孔锥体，喷锥（多孔喷油嘴各喷孔中心线为母线所形成的锥体）

nozzle hole cone angle 喷孔锥角（指喷孔锥体的锥角）

nozzle hydrokinetic characteristics 喷嘴流体动力特性，喷嘴液力特性（指喷油器的喷油压力随喷油量或喷油速率的变化规律）

nozzle inclination 喷油嘴（安装）倾角

nozzle needle 喷嘴针阀（= valve needle, needle valve, nozzle pin, nozzle pintle）

nozzle needle seat 喷嘴针阀座

nozzle of air supply 空气喷嘴，空气喷管

nozzle opening 喷嘴开度（喷嘴开启截面）

nozzle opening pressure （喷油嘴）针阀开启（所需的）压力

nozzle orifice 喷孔（喷油嘴的喷孔，= nozzle hole）

nozzle protrusion 喷嘴伸出长度，喷嘴突出长度

nozzle restrictor （装在具有催化转化器的车辆的油箱加油管颈口内的）加油枪直径限制器（装有催化转化器的车辆不能使用加铅汽油，按规定含铅汽油的加油泵的加油枪直径较大，在油箱加油口颈内装上限制器后，可防止误加含铅汽油）

nozzle ring （燃气涡轮）喷嘴环，环状喷嘴

nozzle solenoid 喷嘴电磁阀（控制喷油嘴针阀的开、闭）

nozzle spray direction 喷嘴喷射方向

nozzle tester 喷嘴（性能）试验器

nozzle throat 喷嘴喉部

nozzle tip 喷油嘴喷头（见 spray tip）

nozzle valve 喷嘴针阀

nozzle wrench 喷嘴扳手

Np ①奈培（见 neper）②镎（neptunium）

NP 新工艺，新工序（new process 的简称）

NPA ①［美］全国石油协会（National Petroleum Association）②［美］国家警察署（National Police Agency）

NPC ［美］国家石油委员会（National Petroleum Council）

NPDT 见 Node position detection technology

NPL meter 噪声级测定仪［见 noise pollution (level) meter］

NPN Darlington transistor NPN 型达林顿复合晶体管

NPN transistor NPN 型三极管（在 NPN 型三极管中，电子从发射极流向集电极，电流由集电极流向发射极，其符号箭头向外）

NPO 见 Non Profit Organization

NPPS 新型程序控制式动力转向（系统）（商品名，New Progressive Power Steering 的简称，由电子控制模块根据车速、路面传给悬架系统的作用力等调控转向液压的动力转向系统）

NPRA ［美］全国石油精炼商协会（National Petroleum Refiners Association）

NPSH 有效吸升水头（net positive suction head）

NR ①天然橡胶（natural rubber）②噪声比（noise ratio）③噪声消减（noise reduction）④非电抗性的，不起反应的（nonreactive）⑤正规雷达（normal radar）

NRDA system 见 narrow road drive assist system

NRN 噪声额定值（亦写作 NR number noise rating number 的简称）

NRS 后轮非独立悬架（nonindepended rear suspension 的简称，= rear rigid axle suspension）

NRV （芬兰 Nokia 集团公司的伙伴公司）诺基鞍轿车轮胎公司 Nokian 生产的轮胎的商品型号名（这种型号轮胎的特点是胎面两侧呈不对称单向放射花纹，由一条偏位的排水槽隔开，具有优异的弯道稳定性和抗湿路浮滑性）

NRZ 不归零（non-return-to-zero 的简称）

NRZ-1 不归零按 1 记录（non-return-to-zero change-on-ones recording 的简称）

NRZ-O 不归零按 0 记录（non-return-to-zero change-on-zeros recording 的简称）

ns 纳秒（毫微秒，= 10^{-9} 秒，nanosecond 的简称）

NS ①见 near side ②无标准（参见 no standard）

NSC ［美］国家安全委员会（National Safety Council）

NSF ［美］国家科学基金会（National Science Foundation）

Ns/m² 牛顿秒每平方米（newton·second/meter², 国际单位制的流体动力黏度单位，参见 coefficient of viscosity, 1Ns/m² = 10 泊，见 poise）

NSTB ［美］国家运输安全委员会（National Transportation Safety Board）

NSU Motorenwerke AG （德国）纳苏发动机工厂

NSU/wankel engine 纳苏汪克尔转子发动机（简称 Wankel engine，亦称 NSU/Wankel RC engine）

NSW 空挡起动开关（neutral start switch 的简称）

NTC thermistor 负温度系数的热敏电阻（negative temperature coefficient resistor 的简称，温度越高，其阻值越低）

NTEA ［美］全国载货汽车装备协会（The National Truck Equipment Association）

N terminal 零线接线柱（见 neutral terminal）

NTIS ［美］国家技术信息中心（National Technical Information Service）

NTMVSA （美）国家交通与机动车安全法（National Traffic and Motor Vehicle Safety Act）

NTPSC ［美］国家交通政策研究委员会（National Traffic Policy Study Committee）

NTSB ［美］国家运输安全局（National Transportation Safety Board）

NTSEL 国家交通安全与环境试验室（National Traffic Safety and Environment Laboratory 的简称）

N-type region （P-N 结等的）N 型区

N-type semiconductor N 形半导体［指加有砷（As）等微量元素而在半导体内产生众多带负电的电子的非本征半导体］

N-type semiconductor material N 型半导体材料［指在纯半导体材料（如硅）中掺入微量五价杂质元素使半导体内自由电子数远多于空穴数，主要靠电子导电，即：自由电子是多数载流子的半导体］

nuclear ①原子核的，核的 ②有核的，核心的，中心的（= nuclear, nucleary）

nucleator （柴油等的）低温流动性改善剂

nuclei 核 nucleus 的复数

nucleus ①核，核心 ②原子核，晶核 ③有机化合物的原子团，环 ④核心程序

nucleuses 核 nucleus 的复数（亦称 nuclei）

nuisance vibration 有害的振动

null ①零，零位，空 ②零的，不存在的；无效的，无用的，无益的，无价值的；没有特征的，空的

nullify 废弃，取消，作废；使等于零，使⋯为零；使无效；变得没有价值

nullity ①无效 ②全无，无 ③无用之物，废物 ④零度，零维

null line 零线

null method of measurement 零位测量法

null point 零点（= zero point）

null setting 调零，调零装置

null shift （仪表）零点偏移

number ①（汽车等的）号码，号码牌，第⋯号（通常在数字前加 No.）②数，数字，数目，数量

number designation 数字标号，号码牌

number display （仪表的）数字显示

numbering 编号，编码

number of plies （轮胎的）层数（指外胎胎体帘布层的实际层数，注意与层级不同）

number of revolution per minute 每分钟转数

number of revolution per unit of time 单位时间转数

number of seats （车内）座位数（= seating capacity）

number of speeds （变速器）挡位数，挡数（= number of steps of speeds）

number of spring coils 螺旋弹簧圈数（有总圈数 total number of coils，有效圈数 effective number of coils 及自由圈数 free number of coils 之别。总圈数指卷簧一端至另一端的实有圈数；有效圈数指计算卷簧弹簧特性时，按照载荷和变形的关系而不考虑材料弯曲及底圈的影响等而确定的计算用圈数；自由圈数指从总圈数中减去上、下两端末圈后的圈数）

number of stages 级数，阶段数，台阶数，挡数

number of starts 螺纹头数（如：双头螺纹、三头螺纹等）

number of taper 锥度级数

number of threads per centimetre 每厘米螺纹扣数

number of turns ①（线圈的）圈数，匝数 ②转数，回转数

number of wave 波数（如：谐波齿轮波发生器转一整转期间，柔轮齿圈中性层任一点上产生变形波的循环次数）

number of whitworth thread cut 惠氏螺纹头数

number plate 牌照（美称 license plate）

number-plate lamp 牌照灯（number plate illuminating lamp 的简称，亦称 number plate light, registration plate lamp，美称 license plate lamp）

number plate support 牌照（板）支架（= license bracket, number stay, license plate holder）

number transfer bus 数字传送总线

numeral 数字（的），数的

numeral order 编号次序

numerator ①分子（对分母而言）②计数器，信号机，示号器

numerical 数字的，用数表示的，数值的，数量的，表示数量的

Numerical analysis model 分析模型

Numerical assessment 数学计算评价

numerical calculation 数值解，数值计算

numerical coding 数字编码

numerical control device 数（字）控（制）装置

numerical indication 数字指示

numerical order 号数，序号

numerical resolution （接口集成电路的）数字分辨率（表示台阶总数所需的数位个数）

numerical simulation 数值模拟，数学模拟

numeric display unit 数字显示装置

numeric fied calculation （电磁式执行机构）磁场参数电算法

nursing tube 供给管道，输送管道

Nusselt number 努塞尔数（热对流损失计算中的一个重要的无因次参数，记号 Nu）

nut 螺母

nut-and-lever steering gear 螺母曲柄销转向机构（见 warm and nut steering）

nut-and-sector steering gear 螺母扇齿式转向机构（见 worm-and-sector steering gear）

nut-and-sleeve flaring fitting 螺母-套管扩口式管接头（三元件液压管卡套式管接头）

NUTCL [美]西北大学运输中心图书馆（Northwestern University Transportation Center Library）

nut cracker 螺母破碎器（利用破碎的方法，取下锈死的螺母，亦称 nut splitter）

nut driver 螺母旋具（亦称 nut spinner, socket driver）

nut end （螺柱拧装的）螺母（的一）端

nut insert 螺孔塞（用于需要螺纹紧固而不能攻螺孔的薄板件）

nut lock bolt 螺母锁紧螺栓

nut locking device 螺母锁紧装置

nut lock washer 螺母锁紧垫圈（亦称 nut-lock ring）

nut retainer 螺母锁片

nut-runner （电动或气动）螺母旋具，螺母板具

nut seat 螺母支撑面，螺母座面

nut spinner 螺母旋具（手动、电动、气动螺母板具的总称，亦称 nut driver）

nut starter 螺母夹具（在窄小部位夹持螺母就位的工具）

N/V 发动机转速与车速之比（ratio of engine rpm to vehicles peed 的简称）

NVCS 日产气门控制系统（Nissan Valve Control System 的简称，日产公司通过使凸轮轴转动一定角度，改变凸轮轴相位，借以改变进气门开、闭时刻的电子控制系统的商品名。其电子控制模块根据发动机转速、节气门开度、吸入空气量及冷却水温信号确认发动机工况，通过可变气门正时电磁阀用上述方法改变凸轮轴相位而使进气门在高速大负荷工况下迟开迟闭，而在低、中速大负荷工况下早开早闭，以提高发动机充气效率，亦称 Nissan Valve timing control system，日产气门正时控制系统，简称 NVTCS）

NVH 噪声、振动、颠簸（noise, vibration, and hardness 的简称）

NVH standards 噪声、振动、粗糙标准（国际汽车世界，在 20 世纪 90 年代中期，为了环境保护提出的新标准。NVH 是使乘员感觉不适的三大问题：noise, vibration, harshness 的简称）

NVM 非易失性存储器（nonvolatile memory 的简称）

NVRAM 非易失性随机存取器（non-volatile random access memory 的简称）

nylon 尼龙（酰胺纤维）

nylon bush 尼龙衬套（用做整体式滑动轴承时，耐用且无须润滑，运转无噪声，故亦称 silence bush）

nylon carcass 尼龙帘线胎体（胎体 "carcass" 指由一层或数层帘布与胎圈 "bead" 组成整体的充气轮胎的受力结构）

nylon gear 尼龙齿轮（将粒状尼龙原料装入模型内压制而成，制造容易，耐磨）

nylon hammer 尼龙锤（带尼龙锤面的软面锤）

nylon nut 尼龙（制）螺母

nylon sliding roof 尼龙滑动车顶

nylon sunshine roof 透明尼龙车顶

nylon tyre 尼龙帘线轮胎

O ①振荡器（oscillator）②涂氧化物的（oxide-coated）③氧（oxygen）

OA ①1加法器（one adder）②输出轴（output axis）③总的，外廓的（尺寸等）（overall）

OAC [美]海外汽车俱乐部（Oversea Automotive Club）

oad ①外形尺寸，轮廓尺寸，总尺寸（overall dimension 的简称）②橡木

oak block 橡木垫块

oak panels 橡木镶板

OAL 全长（overall length）

OASIS [美]联机汽车服务信息系统（On-Line Automotive Service Information System 的简称，直接与汽车制造厂家连线，询问汽车维修与故障诊断问题的计算机网络系统，该系统较 Service Bay Diagnosis System 更为完善）

OAT sensor 车外气温传感器（outside air temperature sensor 的简称）

OBC 车装电子计算机（on board computer）

OBD 车装诊断系统（On-board diagnostic system 的简称）

OBD -I 第一代车装式自诊断系统（指1993年前各种车型自成体系、互不通用、种类繁多的自诊断系统）

OBD II 第二代车装诊断系统（第一代 OBD 没有统一的标准，通信接口和通信协议因生产厂家而异，使用时要采用不同的诊断设备，不同的诊断插头，十分不便，为此美国 SAE 通过一系列标准规定了位于仪表板下方的统一的16针脚诊断插座及统一的五位标准故障代码的车装诊断系统，OBD-II 只要用一台仪器便可对任何一种车辆进行诊断与检测。美国联邦大法污染防治法规定1996年后在美国出售的汽车都必须符合 OBD-II 的要求）

OBD system 车装诊断系统（on-board diagnostic system 的简称）

OBE （汽车无线通信、导航、娱乐系统的）车载机（on-board equipment 的简称，装在车内的接受、显示、发送、控制设备的统称）

OBHP-HR 实测制动马力小时（observed brake horsepower-hour）

object glass 物镜，接物镜（亦称 objective lens）

objection ①缺陷，缺点②异议③妨碍，障碍，反对的理由

objectionable 有异议的，不能接受的；不能采用的，不适合的

objective ①客观的②物镜③目标，目的④任务

objective evaluation ①（对车辆性能的）客观评价（指使用仪器、设备的测试评价）②（汽车平顺性

object line 可见轮廓线（外形线）
object marking 交通固定障碍物标志（如：安全岛、树木、岩石、桥台等的标志，亦称 obstruction marking）
oblate 扁球形的，扁圆形的
oblique 斜的，倾斜的；斜交的；偏离水平线的；偏离铅垂线的
oblique angle 斜角
oblique arm （独立悬架的）斜臂（斜向布置的控制臂）
oblique collision （汽车）斜向碰撞
oblique cone 斜（圆）锥
oblique course 斜向，斜向移动，斜向路线
oblique crank (shaft) web （曲轴的）斜曲柄臂
oblique crash （汽车与汽车或与障碍物的）斜向碰撞（亦称 oblique collision, oblique impact）
oblique crossing （道路的）斜形交叉
oblique cylinder ①斜柱②斜置汽缸，斜置液压缸
oblique drawing 斜视图
oblique gap 斜间隙，斜隙（如：斜切口活塞环的斜接口间隙）
oblique intersection 斜交交叉口（剪刀式交叉口，锐角交叉口，= skew intersection, scissors junction）
oblique line 斜线
oblique line of view 斜视线
obliquely cut piston-ring 斜切口活塞环（= diagonal cut joint piston ring, bevel joint piston ring, oblique gap piston ring）
oblique plane 斜面
oblique side collision （车辆）侧面斜向碰撞
oblique tooth gear 斜齿齿轮
oblique wind 斜风
oblique windshield 斜风窗玻璃（= slanted windshield, starting windscreen）
obliquity ①倾斜度，坡度②倾斜，斜交③平行度，垂直度
obliquity of the connecting rod 连杆倾斜度
obliquity of the wheels 前轮外倾（= wheel camber）
obliquity of wheels 车轮的平行度，车轮斜倾
oblong ①长方形的②椭圆形的③伸长的，拉长的
oblong ground clearance （汽车的）地面拱度纵向通过间隙（亦称 longitudinal vehicle ground clearance, 指汽车两桥间最低点与地面障碍物纵向拱度间的距离，该距离由轴距、车轮直径及障碍物坡度角等决定，表征汽车不被卡住而顺利通过障碍物的能力）
oblong hole ①椭圆形孔②长方形孔
OBM system of engine/vehicle emission control equipment 发动机/车辆排放净化设备的车载式管理系统（OBM 为 On Board Management 的简称，一般是指发动机/车辆排放净化设备的车载式诊断系统，= OBD system of engine/vehicle emission control equipment）
OBRIS 车载动态路况信息系统（on-board dynamic road information system 的简称）
obscure ①遮蔽，弄暗，使模糊不清②黑暗的，模糊的，含混的，不清楚的
observability ①可见性，可观察性②视野性
observation ①观察，观测②概述，简要的评述
observation (al) check 外部检查，目测检查

observation coach 观光客车（亦称 observation bus, sightseeing bus）

observation mirror 后视镜（= rear view mirror, driving mirror, rear reflection mirror, retrospection mirror）

observation roof panel 可打开的车顶板

observations 观察结果，观测值；观察报告

observation slit 观察缝

observation window 观察窗，观测孔

observed 被观察的，观测到的

observed availability 实测有效工作时间，实测（有效）利用率

observed brake horsepower （用马力表示的）实测有效功率（见 corrected power）

observed brake horsepower-hour 实测有效马力-小时（简称 OBHP-HR，见 corrected power）

observed brake power 实测有效功率（发动机在实际运转状态下所测定的输出的有效功率，参见 brake power）

observed data 观察数据，试验数据

observed drawbar horsepower （以马力为单位的）实测有效牵引功率

observed efficiency 实测效率，观测效率

observed mean failure rate （汽车）平均故障率的观测值（指汽车在规定的观察冲程内，故障发生次数与累计冲程之比）

observed mean life 实测平均寿命

observed mean repair time 实测平均修复时间（修复时间的总和与修复次数之比）

observed power 实测功率（在实际运转的大气条件下，所测出的发动机实际产生的功率，亦称观测功率，见 corrected power）

observed reading 观测读数（测量值）

observed reliability 可靠度的观测值（①对于不可修复的产品是指直到规定的时间区间终了为止能完成规定功能的产品数与在该时间区间开始时刻投入工作的产品数之比②对于可修复产品是指一个或多个产品的无故障工作时间达到或超过规定时间的次数与观察时间内无故障工作的总次数之比）

observed result 观察结果

observed value 观测值，实测值

observer 观察员，（试验）观测员

obsolescence ①陈旧，老化，折旧 ②报废，废弃，淘汰

obsolescence value 折旧剩余值

obsolete 陈旧的，废弃不用的，淘汰的；退役的（机械）

obsolete auto 废旧汽车，报废车辆，陈旧汽车

obstacle 障碍，障碍物

obstacle approximation 障碍近似（障碍模拟）

obstacle avoidance （行车中）回避障碍物

obstacle avoidance test 绕障碍物试验（汽车在直线行驶中绕过前方障碍物后回到原来行驶路线的试验，用最高车速、横摆角速度响应等进行评价）

obstacle belt 障碍地带

obstacle classification of vehicle-slope-elevation 车辆-坡度-升高障碍分类

obstacle (-climbing) capability （车辆）通过障碍物能力，越障能力

obstacle crossing 越障（超越障碍，通过障碍物）

obstacle detection system 障碍物探测系统

obstacle dynamic crossing 动态越障

obstacle-height to wheel-diameter ratio 障碍高度与车轮直径比

obstacle negotiation 克服障碍（物）

obstacle of vibration 振动危害，振

动干扰

obstacle overcomeability 通过阻碍物的能力

obstacle performance (车辆)越障性能

obstacle profile 障碍物轮廓尺寸

obstacle quasi-static crossing 准静态越障

obstacle race 越障竞赛

obstacle spacing (试验跑道上的)障碍物间距

obstruction approach marking (路面上的接近)障碍物警告标志

obstruction guard (汽车头前的)护栏,排障器

obstruction lamp 障碍物标志灯

obstruction marking 交通障碍物标志 (= object marking)

obstruction of traffic 交通阻塞

obstruction period of traffic ①阻车时间(交叉口红灯时间)②交通阻塞期

obstruction spanner 越障扳手(用于不易接近处的弯环状扳手)

obstructive 妨碍的,阻塞的,阻碍的

obturate 闭塞,阻塞,塞住

obturator 密封零件,密封装置,气密装置,塞子,密封件,填充体,紧塞装置,闭塞器

obturator piston ring 活塞密封环(指气环、压缩环)

obtuse angle 钝角

OBU 车装式组件,车装式装置(on-board unit 的简称)

obviate 排除,消除,避免,事前预防

OC ①氧化催化剂(oxidation catalyst)②开式燃烧室(open chamber)③机油消耗量(oil consumption)④顶置式凸轮轴(overhead camshaft)

occasion 时机,机会;诱因,近因;理由;必要,需要;场合,时刻

occlusion ①堵塞②封闭③遮断

occupancy ①占有率,占有期间,占用,占领,居住(期间)②(交通统计中指车辆在时间和空间上占用道路的比率)占用率(空间占用率指某瞬间,长度为 s 的路段上有长度分别为 l_i 的数个车群时,则该路段的占用率 $O_s = \Sigma l_i/s$,时间占用率指若干车群占用某段道路的时间分别为 t_i,则在时间 T 内,该路段的时间占用率 $O_t = \Sigma t_i/T$)

occupant ①乘客,乘员②占有者,占用者

occupant behavior analysis model 乘员行为分析(数学)模型

occupant crash protection system 乘员碰撞保护系统(简称 occupant protection system,或 OCP system)

occupant position detection system (汽车)乘员体位测定系统(测定乘员入座后坐姿高度及体态和身体各部分的方位、尺寸等,供乘员安全研究,简称 OPDS)

occupant position electrostatic capacity sensor 静电容式乘员位置传感器

occupant protection in interior impact (汽车)乘员的内饰件碰撞保护

occupant restraint system 乘员约束性保护系统(如:安全带等发生碰撞时,限制乘员身体前冲等,以避免二次撞碰的保护装置)

occupant-seat interface pressure distribution 乘员与座椅接触面上的压力分布

occupant sensing vision system 乘员观测系统(通过摄像装置观测乘员在车内的位置、坐姿、身体各个部位的状态等)

Occupational Safety and Health Administration [美](汽车)乘员安全与卫生管理局(简称 OSHA)

occupation coefficient 占用系数

occupation efficiency 占用率

occurrence ①事故，事变，事件 ②发生，出现，产生

occurrence of spark 火花的产生，火花形成

occurrences spectrum 频数谱（如：在疲劳载荷中用较低和较高带值之间的每一特定载荷范围内所发生的特定载荷参量，如峰值、范围等的次数表示的谱载荷成分）

OccuSense （座椅的）乘坐感知系统（商品名，向安全气囊控制系统发送座椅是否坐人的信息，源于 occupant sense 一词）

OCR 光（学字）符识别（技术）（optical character recognition 的简称）

OCR font 光（学字）符识别字体

OCR reader 光（学字）符阅读机

OCR scanner 光（学字）符扫描仪

OCS 氧化催化转化系统（oxidizing catalytic converter system 的简称）

octagon 八边形，八角形（的）

octagonal 八边形的，八角形的，八面的

octal system 8进制（使用 0～7 共 8 个数字和逢 8 进 1 的计数方法）

octane 辛烷（C_8H_{18}）

octane adjustment rod （分电器上的）辛烷值调节杆（改变点火提前角，消除爆燃）

octane booster 辛烷值增强剂（一种抗爆燃添加剂的商品名）

octane corrector 辛烷值校正器

octane enhancer 辛烷值提高剂，抗爆剂

octane index 辛烷值指数，抗爆指数（马达法与研究法辛烷值的平均值。美国材料试验标准 ASTM 和联邦汽油规格均采用该数值作为划分汽油等级的抗爆性指标）

octane number （汽油的）辛烷值（表示汽油的抗爆性，简称 ON，亦称 octane rating，octane value。当汽油试样在专门试验发动机中试验出的抗爆性与由异辛烷和正庚烷按一定比例组成的标准燃油相同时，该汽油试样的辛烷值，即等于该标准燃油中异辛烷所占的体积百分比，异辛烷的抗爆性定为 100，正庚烷为 0，辛烷值分为研究法辛烷值"RON"，马达法辛烷值"MON"与道路法辛烷值"RDON"等三种）

octane number requirements （对汽油的）辛烷值要求值（指发动机正常运转要求汽油具有的最低辛烷值，简称 octane requirements 或 ONR）

octane promoter 抗爆剂

octane quality （用辛烷值表示的汽油）抗爆性

octane rating 辛烷值（见 octane number）

octane requirement increase 辛烷值需求增势（发动机要求辛烷值增加的现象，如发动机工作一段时间后，由于缸壁过热等原因，其所要求的辛烷值有增加的趋向，简称 ORI）

octane selector 辛烷值选择器（根据汽油的辛烷值，调节点火提前角的装置）

octane unit 辛烷值单位

octane value （见 octane number）

octangular 八角的，有八角的

octant 八分仪，八分圆（圆周的八分之一），八分体，八分区；卦限

octave 倍频程，倍频带，八音度（当上、下限频率比为 2^n 时，两频率间的频段称为 n 倍频程。当 $n=1$ 时称倍频程，当 $n=1/3$ 时称 1/3 倍频程）

1/3 octave ①1/3 倍频 ②1/3 倍频的

1/3 octave acceleration 1/3 倍频加速度

octave analyzer （汽车噪声等的）倍（频）带分析器（octave band analy-

1/3 octave band 1/3 倍频带

octave band filter unit （汽车噪声）倍频带滤波器（= octave band filter set, 简称 octave filter）

octave band level 倍（频）带级

octave band sound pressure level 倍频带声压级

octave filter 倍频带滤波器（亦称 octave band filter set）

1/3 octave value 1/3 倍频值

Octoid form 奥克托形（用直边齿廓的平面锥齿轮或用具有直线刀刃的刀具加工出来的圆锥齿轮的齿廓曲线，是近似的球面渐开线）

octoid gear 8 字啮合锥齿轮（亦称 involute bevel gear "渐开线锥齿轮"，其产形冠轮的齿面形状为平面的锥齿轮，因其齿轮副在球面上的啮合线的完整形状是 8 字形的封闭曲线，故名）

octuple space 八维（度）空间

ocular ①目镜，目镜的②视觉上的

ocular dominance （视力的）单眼支配性（指大多数人的视力都在一定程度上受一只眼睛的支配）

ocular estimate 目测（法）

ocular proof （车祸的）目击证据

OCV （MAZDA 可变气门正时系统的）油压控制阀（oil control valve 的简称，电子控制模块根据发动机工况的要求，通过该阀控制可变气门正时机构的工作油压，调节进气凸轮轴及曲轴相位，优化气门正时，提高发动机动力性和经济性）

OD ①外径（亦写作 od, outside diameter）②操作指南（operation's directive）③原设计（original design）④外廓尺寸（outside dimensions）⑤超速挡（overdrive, 亦写作 O/D）⑥起点和终点（origin and destination）⑦全程，起点到终点（origin to destination）

odd ①奇特的，特别的②奇数的，单数的③个别的，零散的

odd firing engine （按规定的顺序每缸依次单独点火的）逐缸点火式发动机

odd-lane road 奇数车道公路（具有奇数车道、无分隔带的双向公路）

oddments shelf （车厢或行李舱内的）零散杂物搁板（亦称 oddments tray, = parcel shelf）

odd number 奇数

odds and ends ①无用的零件，无用的部分②废铁，零星废料，零星杂物

odd thread 奇数螺纹

odd-toothed 奇数齿数的

ODI ①[美]故障车辆调查办公室（Office of Defect Investigation）②机油更换周期（oil drain interval）

O/D off indicator 超速挡断开指示灯

O/D off switch 超速挡断开开关

odograph 里程表

odometer [美]里程表，车速表，转速表，里程仪，自动计距仪，测距仪（= mileage counter, mileometer）

odometer disc supporting bracket 里程表表盘支架

odometer drive 里程表驱动机构

odontoid 齿形的，齿状的

odontoid belt 齿形传动带

odontometer 渐开齿轮公法线测量仪

odor 见 odour

odor absorbing device 臭味吸收装置

odour （美亦写作 odor）①气味（= smell, 香味、臭味、异味多种气味的统称）②（特指柴油机的）臭气（柴油机排气散发出的一种特殊刺激性的气味。臭味强度与燃料性质和燃料种类、运转工况有关）

odour components （柴油机消除排气）臭气组件

odour evaluation system （废气）臭气鉴定装置

odour filter 臭味过滤器，臭味滤除器

odourless 无臭的，没有气味的

odour-producing compound （柴油机排气）臭味生成化合物

odour test 气味试验（如：对汽油味或驾驶室内油气味的测定）

ODS of rolling tire 滚动轮胎的运转变形形状（其中 ODS 为 operational deflection shapes 的简称）

OD solenoid （自动变速器的）超速挡电磁阀（overdrive gear solenoid 的简称）

OD survey 起终点调查，OD 调查（origin and destination survey）

OE 对置汽缸发动机（opposed-cylinder engine）

OECD 经济合作与发展组织（Organization for Economic Cooperation and Development，1960 年在法国巴黎成立）

OE（M） （制造厂的）原装设备 [original equipment (manufacture) 的简称]

OEM 原厂配件，原装设备厂家制造的（original equipment manufacturing 的简称，如：原车制造厂提供的配件等）

Oerlikon spiral bevel gear 摆线齿锥齿轮（产形冠轮上的齿线是长幅外摆线的锥齿轮）

Oerlikon tooch 奥林康型齿制（指在 Oerlikon 机床上加工出来的曲线锥齿轮，具有延伸外摆线的节锥齿线，与 Gleason 齿制的区别仅是加工机床、刀具和加工方法不同）

oersted 奥（斯特）（CGS 单位制的磁场强度单位，代号 Oe，当半径为 1cm 的单圈导线圈，通过 1 个绝对安培的电流时，线圈中心产生的磁场强度为 $2\pi \cdot$ Oe，所以 1Oe = 1CGS 绝对安培/2π 厘米，在国际单位制中采用安培/米为磁场强度单位，1Oe = 1000/2π 安培/米，见 abampere）

off ①（表示距离）在远处，去远处，离开②（水、电油路）断开，停止③（从车上）下来，出来，在（车、路）等以外④（在英国指车辆）右方的（= the right side，见 near side）

offal 废料，废物，碎屑，垃圾，次品

off-beat concept 非传统的概念，新概念；新设计，新结构

off-beat form 不规则的形式；非常规结构

off-board 车外的，车下的，非车载式的，非车装的（亦称 off-car）

off center [美] 中心不正，偏离中心，偏心（= 英 off centre）

off-centered 偏离中心的，不平衡的，不对称的

off-center lane movement 不等量车道车流分配（在多车道公路上，按照上、下行交通量的变化，在不同时间内把车道对上行和下行交通作不等量的分配，亦称 unbalanced lane movement）

off-centre 偏心（= off-center）

off-chip 芯片外的，不在同一芯片上的

off-chip memory （与微处理器不做在同一块芯片上的）片外存储器

off-course deviation （无人驾驶汽车等的）离线偏差，线路偏差

off day 预防修理日，停车检修日

off-design 非设计的，偏离设计的

offer 提供，提出，提议

offering ①用品，作品②（车上供乘员和驾驶人员娱乐消遣的）产品

off front wheel ①（左置转向盘的）右前轮②（右置转向盘的）左前轮

off-gauge ①不合标准的，不合格的，

等外的（=offgrade）②不均匀厚度，超差

off-grade 次（品），不合格（产品），等外的

off-highway 越野的，非公路用的（=off-highroad, off road）

off-highway truck 越野载货汽车，越野货车[=off(-the)-road truck]

off-highway utility vehicle 多用途越野车（亦简称utility vehicle）

off hind wheel ①（左置转向盘的）右后轮②（右置转向盘的）左后轮

office 政府机关；办公室，局，处，科；职务

office car 机关用轿车

Office of Defect Investigation [美]故障车辆调查办公室（简称ODI）

Office of Mobile Source Air Pollution Control （美国环境保护局的）机动车辆大气污染管理办公室

office-on-wheels 车上办公室（指带移动通信设备和打印设备的公务车）

official 官方的，正式的

official acceptance test 官方鉴定试验，正式验收试验

official gazette 政府公报

off (-) line ①（汽车装配完毕）离开装配线，下线（=line-off）②脱离主机单独工作的，脱机的，线外的，外线的，离线的

off-line acceleration 越野（行驶时的）加速性能

off-line computer 离线计算机

off-line control 离线控制

off-line repair 离开作业线的修理（单车就车修理）

off-line simulation on computer 计算机离线模拟

off load 卸（下负）荷，卸（去负）载（=unload）

off-loading 卸货，卸载，卸荷

off-normal position 不正常位置

off-on servo 接通-断开伺服系统（如：继电器伺服机构）

off peak 非峰值的

off-peak hour 非高峰期（指客货运量较少的时期，相对于高峰期而言，参见peak-hour）

off-peak time （交通）非高峰时间

off period 断开时期

off plumb 不垂直的（=out of plumb）

off position ①非操作位置，关闭位置，断路位置；非工作状态，关闭状态②非正常位置，离开正常位置，偏位

off-rating 非标准状态，非标准条件；超出额定值

off-road 在道路之外的，在无路情况下的，越野的，非道路的（=off-highway）

off-road capability 越野性能

Off-Road Challenge （汽车）越野挑战赛

off-road driving 路外行车，野地行驶，越野行车

off-road driving techniques 越野驾驶技术

off-roader 供在无路地区行驶的车辆，非道路车辆，越野车辆

off-roaders 越野驾驶爱好者

off-roading adventure sport genre （驾车）越野探险运动（genre为法语：种类，形式）

off road modification （对车辆进行的）越野改装

off-road payload ratio 越野行驶时有效载荷与车辆总重的比值

off-road performance 越野性能

off-road terrain 无路地带（野地）

off-road tire 非道路车辆用轮胎，越野轮胎

off-road vehicle 越野车辆，非道路车辆（=all-terrain vehicle, cross-country vehicle, go-anywhere vehicle, road-free vehicle)

off-season 非季节性的（淡季，闲季）

offset ①抵消，弥补，补偿，对消 ②偏位，偏心，偏置，偏移 ③偏心量，偏距，偏移距（如：主销偏移距，见 kingpin offset；准双曲线齿轮副的轴线偏置距；车轮轮辐安装面与轮辋中心线之间的偏距）④失调，不重合 ⑤分支，分岔 ⑥调整偏差 ⑦剩余差值，残留误差 ⑧残余变形，永久变形 ⑨偏置的，偏心的，偏离的，横向移动的 ⑩补偿的

offset angle 偏置角，偏角，偏斜角

offset cab 侧置式驾驶室（偏置于汽车中心面一侧的驾驶室）

offset cam 偏位凸轮，偏置凸轮（凸轮基圆中心偏离所顶的挺杆的中心线，可使挺杆旋转，防止偏磨）

offset choke valve 偏轴式阻风门（转轴偏离阻风门中心）

offset coefficient 偏移系数

offset coil spring （麦弗逊式独立悬架中）偏置式螺旋弹簧（①螺旋弹簧的中心线相对于滑柱中心线向车身外侧偏移 ②螺旋弹簧独立地安装在滑柱以外）

offset collision （汽车的）偏置碰撞（见 collision offset）

offset connecting rod 偏心连杆，偏置式连杆（连杆的中心线不在连杆大头中心，而沿曲轴连杆轴颈中心线偏移，可在不加大汽缸间距的条件下，增大轴承面积，简称 offset con-rod）

off-set construction 偏移结构，偏位结构

offset crank mechanism 偏置曲柄连杆机构（偏置汽缸，曲轴中心不在汽缸中心线上，从前方看曲轴中心偏置左侧，以减轻缸壁及轴承的磨损，＝ offset cylinder）

offset crankshaft 偏置式曲轴（指曲轴中心线与汽缸中心线不相交的曲轴布置形式）

offset cylinder 偏置汽缸（见 offset-crank mechanism）

40% offset deformable barrer impact test（汽车）40%偏置变形障壁碰撞试验

offset direction 偏离方向，偏移方向

offset distance 偏移距（指偏置的两部件中心线间的距离）

offset driveline 偏置的传动系统（偏置于车辆对称纵轴）

offset frontal collision 两车前面偏（置碰）撞（见 collision offset）

offset intersection 错位交叉口（交叉道路中一条道路的中线在交叉口处错开）

offset method ①偏装法 ②（测定屈服点）残余变形法，永久变形应力测定法

offset of hypoid gear 双曲面小齿轮（中心线相对大齿轮中心线的）偏移距

offset of tooth trace （斜齿锥齿轮产形冠轮的）齿轮偏移量（冠轮齿线至冠轮轴线的最短距离）

offset of wheel 车轮的偏置量（双轮并装式车轮中每一车轮相对于双轮对称平面的偏移量）

offset-phase twin-plug ignition system 双火花塞相差点火系统（每一汽缸内的两个火花塞按不同的点火时刻点火）

offset pipe 偏置管，迂回管

offset piston 偏置活塞，偏心活塞（指活塞销中心偏离活塞中心线，一般销偏向活塞推力面一侧）

offset piston pin 偏置活塞销

offset point ①（模/数变换或数/模变换）失调点

offset power steering 拉杆型动力转向系统（见 linkage power steering，

1059

inline power steering,指加力作用于转向摇臂的动力转向系统)

offset shaft 偏心轴

offset socket wrench 弯头套筒扳手

offset tappet (气门机构的)偏位挺杆,偏置式挺杆(挺杆的中心线偏离凸轮中心,借以防止挺杆局部偏磨)

offsetting ①偏移,偏置,移位,变位②偏心距③斜率,倾斜度,不均匀性

offset twin (曲轴连杆轴颈布置成180°的)对置双缸发动机

offset wheel 外偏距车轮(亦称 outset wheel,指轮辋中心线位于轮辐安装面外侧的车轮)

offside ①远侧(简称 O/S = far side)②后面,反面③(道路上的汽车)远离路中心的一侧(靠左行的国家指汽车的左侧,靠右行的国家指汽车的右侧,见 nearside,英国指)右侧 (= right hand)

offside door (左转向盘汽车指车身)右侧门②(右转向盘汽车指车身)左侧门

offside of bearing 轴承的润滑油出口边

offside overtaking 远侧超车(见 offside)

offside tank ①(左转向盘汽车的)右侧油箱②(右转向盘汽车的)左侧油箱

off-side wheel ①(并装双轮的)外侧轮②见 off front wheel, off rear wheel

off-size 尺寸不合格,非规定尺寸

off-state output current (数字集成电路的)截止态输出电流(亦称 high-impedance-state output current 高阻态输出电流,指在规定输入条件下使输出端处于截止态,即高阻态时通过该输出端的电流)

offtake ①排气管,排气口;排污口;泄水处②支管,支线③扣除,减去

off-test 未经检验的

off-the-car type 离车式(检验设备)(如:将车轮拆离汽车进行检验的车轮平衡仪"off-the-car balancer",相对 on the car type 而言)

off-the-highway ①在公路之外的,在无路情况下的②越野的,高通过性的,非公路用的

off-the-line 离线的(下线的;离开生产线的)

off-the-road requirements (对车辆)越野性能要求

off-the-road test (车辆)越野性试验

off-the-road time (汽车运输的)路外时间(指在完成某一运程所需的总时间中汽车处在运程路外的时间,如:宿夜的停歇时间等)

off-the-road tyre 越野轮胎(非道路用轮胎,高通过性轮胎)

off-the-road vehicle 非道路用越野车辆

off time 断开时间,停歇时间,停机时间

off track (汽车或列车转向时,最前轴中心的转向轨迹和最后轴中心的)①转向轨迹偏离(= off tracking)②转向轨迹偏离距离(= off tracking distance)

off tracking characteristics (汽车)转向轨迹偏离特性(见 off track)

offtracking distance (汽车)转向轨迹偏离距(亦称 offtracking value,见 off track)

off-vehicle 车外的,非车上的,非车载式的,非车装式的

off-vehicle automatic test equipment 车外自动检验设备(非车载式自动测试装置)

off-vehicle charging capacity 见 OVC

off vehicle starter motor check (将起

动机从车上拆下进行的）车外起动机（故障）检查

OFT 油膜厚度（oil film thickness 的简称）

Ogalloy 含油轴承合金（铜 85%～95%，锡 8.5%～10%，石墨 0～2%）

4+O gearbox 带超速挡的四挡变速器（=four-speed with overdrive gear）

3+O gearbox 带超速挡的三挡变速器（=three-speed gearbox with overdrive）

OHC 顶置式凸轮轴（亦写作 ohc，over head-camshaft 的简称）

OHC engine 顶置凸轮轴式发动机（over head-camshaft engine）

ohm 欧（姆）（国际单位制的电阻单位，代号 Ω，如果导体两端的电压为 1V，通过的电流是 1A，这个导体的电阻便是 1Ω，即：$1\Omega = 1V/A$，见 volt，ampere）

ohmage 欧姆值（欧姆电阻，欧姆阻抗）

ohmammeter 欧（姆）安（培）计（亦称 ohmer，ohme meter）

ohmic 欧姆的，电阻的

ohmic drop 电阻电压降

ohmic losses 欧姆损失（电阻损失，由内阻和接触电阻产生的 I^2R 热损失）

ohm meter 欧姆米（Ωm）

ohmmeter-diode tester 欧姆-二极管测试表

OH（oh） 见 overhang①

OHV 预置气门（overhead valves 的简称）

OHV engine 预置气门式发动机（overhead valve engine 的简称）

OICA 世界汽车组织（法文 Organisation Internationale des Constructeurs d'Automobiles 的简称，英文为 International Organization of Motor Vehicle Manufacturers，成立于 1919 年，总部设在巴黎，全球汽车制造业唯一的国际组织和代表，由世界各国汽车制造商组成，会员遍及全国，包括中国、美国、英国、德国、法国、意大利、日本、韩国、俄罗斯、印度、巴西等主要汽车生产国在内的 43 个国家和地区）

oil ①油（植物油或矿物油）②润滑油，机油③润滑，加油

oil-absorbing 吸油的

oil-absorbing coating 蓄油涂层，吸油镀覆层

oil additives 机油添加剂

oil analysis and service equipment 润滑油分析及维护装置

oil-and-moisture trap 油水分离器（亦称 oil and water separator，如：制动系中将压缩空气中的油、水等杂质分离、滤清的器件）

oil atomizer 喷油器，油雾喷射器

oil baffle 挡油圈，阻油环，挡油板

oil ball check valve 机油泵单向球阀（机油泵止回球阀）

oil-based gas 油基天然气（指天然气与石油同期形成，在油田附近的气田产的天然气）

oil basin 油盘，（发动机）油底壳

oil bath ①油浴②油槽，油池

oil bath air breathing 油浴式滤清器通气管

oil-bath clutch 油浴式离合器

oil-bath lubrication 油浴润滑（如轴等浸入油中实现润滑的方法）

oil bath (type) air cleaner 油浴式空气滤清器（=oil-type air cleaner，oil-wetted air cleaner，oil bath air filter，air filter in oil bath）

oil-bearing structure 油垫层结构

oil-block 被油（污）堵塞

oil borne abrasion 油中杂质或机油本身劣化引起的磨损

oil brake 液压制动器

oil breather pipe （发动机曲轴箱的）机油通风管（利用车速超过 20 英

里/小时的抽吸作用形成的稀薄度将曲轴箱内的串缸气或机油蒸气排出车外的抽气管,美称 road drift tube)

oil bucket pump 移动式润滑油加注器,手动加油泵

oil buffer 油压缓冲器(油压减振器)

oil burner 费油车(油耗过大的车)

oil cabinet ①(机油分配机构的)储油室②(集中润滑系统的)机油箱

oil can ①运油车②(加)油罐;(机)油罐,(机)油壶,机油加注壶③(车身板件上的)浅凹陷

oil can crasher 废油桶压扁机(将废弃的油桶压成铁片,以便于处理)

oil capacity 机油容量

oil catcher 挡油盘,护油圈,集油器,集油盘

oil catch ring 挡油环,护油圈;离心集油环

oil change at regular intervals 定期更换机油(= periodic oil change)

oil change indicator light 机油更换指示灯

oil change period 换油周期(机油更换间隔里程)

oil changer 换机油器,机油更换器(一般用电动油泵将发动机油底壳内的机油吸入一透明容器内检查,若需更换,则吸出全部废机油,并用轻油清洗油底壳后,注入新机油的装置,亦称 oil merchandiser)

oil-change reminder 换油提示装置

oil channel 润滑油道

oil check 滑油检验(指与滑油有关的各项检验作业,如:检查油面及油压等)

oil churning (齿轮等箱内的)滑油搅动

oil circuit 油路

oil circuit breaker 油路开关(油路断路器)

oil circulation gauge 机油压力表(= oil pressure gauge)

oil circulation system 机油循环系统

oil clarifier 机油滤清器(= oil cleaner)

oil clearance 润滑(油)间隙,油层间隙(指滑动轴承与轴颈间充满滑油层的间隙,亦称 bearing clearance)

oil clutch 湿式离合器(= oil-running clutch)

oil coaxing 机油伪蚀(由于机油劣化等原因,造成轴承表面产生细小伤痕的现象)

oil cock ①放油阀,机油开关,机油阀②(检查油底壳油面高度的)油面检查开关

oil collecting tray 集油盘

oil collector 集油器,润滑油收集器

oil-collector tank (干底壳润滑式发动机的)机油汇集箱

oil column 油柱(指液压系统中充满封闭管筒的油液,起到刚体柱件传动压力的作用)

oil combination splash and pressure system 机油飞溅和压力润滑复合系统

oil condenser 注油电容器(提高纸质电容器的防湿性)

oil conduit 机油管道

oil connector 机油道接头,油管接头

oil consumption 润滑油消耗量,机油消耗量(简称 OC,发动机机油的消耗量,一般按燃油消耗的百分率计算,如:某车的机油消耗量为汽油消耗量的1%等)

oil-consumption rate 润滑油消耗率,机油消耗率

oil content 含油量

oil control 润滑油调节,机油控制,刮油

oil-control ability (油环等)控油能力,滑油控制能力,刮油能力

oil control orifice valve （发动机缸盖与汽缸间的机油管道内的）机油控制孔阀

oil control (piston) ring 活塞（刮）油环（= oil scraper piston ring，简称 scraper ring 或 oil ring）

oil control valve ①油量控制阀②油路（开、闭）控制阀③（利用油压实现某项控制的）油压控制阀

oil control valve 机油控制阀（简称 OCV，由机油压力控制阀门的开、闭）

oil-cooled 油冷的（用机油冷却的）

oil-cooled engine 油冷却发动机（用油冷却汽缸和汽缸盖等零件的内燃机）

oil-cooled rotor （转子发动机的）油冷式转子（油冷式旋转活塞）

oil cooler bypass valve 机油冷却器旁通阀（当机油温度超过某规定温度时，该阀开启，使机油通过机油冷却器，防止机油温度过高。反之，当机油温度低于规定温度时，该阀关闭，机油不再通过冷却器，以免机油温度过低，亦称"机油温度控制阀"oil-temperature-controlling valve）

oil crises 石油危机（世界性石油危机，第一次由 1973 年中东战争引起，第二次由 1979 年伊朗事态引起）

oil crust 油垢，油垢层；机油积炭层

oil cup 润滑油杯

oil cushion 液压减振器（= oleo damper）

oil cut-off valve 断油阀

oil cylinder 油缸

oildag 石墨润滑剂，胶体石墨

oil damage 机油浸蚀，机油致损（由机油污损腐蚀、浸泡造成的橡胶制件的损坏等）

oil damper 油液阻尼器，油减振器

oil deflector 导油环，挡油圈，挡油板（见 oil slinger①）

oil degradation 油液降解，油液的递降分解，油液老化

oil-delivery 供油的，输油的

oil demand 润滑油需要量

oil deposit 机油形成的积炭；机油沉淀物，油泥

oil-derived 机油产生的，机油造成的，源于机油的

oil detergent 机油的清净分散（添加）剂（用于将机油劣化产生的胶质和酸性不溶物从活塞、缸壁等金属件表面移走，溶解或分散于机油中，以保持零件表面清洁）

oil diagnosis 机油诊断，滑油质量检测（通过对机油的分析、检验来诊断发动机等的损伤和故障）

oil dilution 机油变稀，机油稀释

oil dipper （飞溅润滑的）油匙（如：连杆大头上的匙状突起物，随着曲轴连杆轴颈的旋转，将机油甩起，实现飞溅润滑）

oil dip rod 量油尺，机油油位尺，机油尺（= oildipper rod, oil lever dip stick, gauge rod, oil depth gauge）

oil disc 甩油盘（见 oil flinger）

oil-dispensing pump 机油分配泵

oil distributor 机油分配器（将机油泵输出的机油分配至各润滑点及油路的装置，亦称 oil dispenser, oil-dispensing equipment）

oil dosing 机油计量的，机油定量的

oil drag loss 油膜摩擦损失，机油黏滞（造成的）损失

oil-drain ①油类流出口，放油孔，排油口②放油的，排油的

oil drainage 放油，排出（机）油，放油装置

oil drain canal 放油通道（亦称 oil drain duct）

oil drain cock 放油阀，排油开关（亦称 oil drain vale）

oil-drain interval 滑油更换期，换油

周期（简称 DOI，= oil-change period）

oil drain pan 放油盘，接油盘（用于接盛由发动机等放出的废机油等）

oil-drain period 滑油更换期（= oil-drain interval）

oil drain plug 放油塞

oil dropping ①（气门杆、气门导管磨损或油封不良造成的）机油滴缸（机油滴漏入燃烧室）②滴油

oil-drowned 浸入油内的，没入油池的，浸入油浴的

oil duct 润滑油道

oil duct closer 润滑油道塞

oil duct hole （曲轴）润滑油道喷油孔

oil dynamic viscosity 润滑油动力黏度（见 dynamic viscosity）

oiled 加了润滑油的，用油浸透的

oiled earth road 油土路（用铺路油类或沥青处理过的土路）

oiled gravel road 沥青碎石面层的道路

oil-efficient 省油的

oil-electric engine 柴油机-发电机机组

oil embargo 石油禁运，石油停止供应

oil emulsion 机油乳化油，乳化机油

oil engine ①石油类液体燃料发动机（以别于 gas engine）②重油发动机（= heavy oil engine，早期为火花点火式）③柴油机（= diesel engine，compression-ignition engine）④煤油机，轻油机（用煤油或轻油做燃料的化油器式点火发动机，一般为农用、船用小型内燃机，构造、使用简易，但热效率低）

oil-engined bus 柴油机客车

oiler ①加油器，注油器，油杯，加油壶，涂油机②加油工，润滑工③运油车④柴油车，柴油发动机

oil-exporting nations 石油输出国

oil extractor ①机油分离器（见 oil separator②）②（转子发动机的）冷却油道（= phased oil extractor）

oil extractor casing 机油分离器壳体（美称 oil extractor housing）

oil extractor valve 机油分离器的抽油阀

oil face 油面

oil feed(ing) 供油，加注滑油

oil field body 石油野外钻探车车身，油田（用车）车身

oil filer bypass valve 机油滤清器旁通阀

oil-filled 充满油的，充油的，机油充填的

oil-filled ignition coil 油浸式点火线圈

oil-filled working space 充油的工作容积

oil filler ①加油口②加油器，加油管

oil film 润滑油膜

oil film conductivity 润滑油膜导电性

oil film critical thickness 润滑油膜临界厚度（保持液体润滑的最小油膜厚度）

oil film strength 油膜强度

oil film test 润滑油油膜（强度）试验

oil film thickness 油膜厚度（简称 OFT）

oil-film viscosity 油膜黏度（简称 OFV）

oil filter 机油滤清器

oil filter body 机油滤清器壳体

oil filter cartridge （机油滤清器）滤芯及滤芯筒总成

oil filter element central tube 机油滤清器滤芯中心管

oil filter element cup 机油滤清器滤芯盘

oil filter neck 机油滤清器进油孔颈

oil filter outlet pipe 机油滤清器出

油管
oil filter screen 机油滤网
oil filter shaft lock washer 机油滤清器滤芯轴锁紧垫圈
oil filter tell-tale 机油滤清器警报灯（表示机油滤清器堵塞的信号灯）
oil-fired gas turbine 使用液体燃料的燃气轮机
oil flame 油焰
oil flinger 甩油盘（亦称 oil disk, oil slinger, 为浸入机油中的旋转圆盘，靠离心力将机油甩出并经油路引至轴承或其他需要润滑的表面，目前这种润滑方法已少见）
oil foam （空气混入形成的）机油泡沫
oil foaming 机油起泡，（机油形成泡沫的）乳化现象（导致流动性变坏，润滑能力下降，甚至发生油路气阻，影响供油）
oil foaming inhibitor 机油抗泡沫添加剂（= antifoaming additive）
oil fog lubrication 油雾润滑 亦称 oil mist lubrication）
oil fouled 被机油污染的，被机油弄脏的，油污的
oil fouling 污染机油的
oil-fuel injector needle-valve （柴油机）喷油器针阀（柴油喷嘴针阀）
oil-fuel mixture (method) 机油-油混合（润滑法）（将一定比例的机油掺入燃油中，使机油随着燃油进入汽缸，进行润滑）
oil-full pressure system 全压力机油润滑系统
oil gallery 润滑油道（汽缸体内的机油通道及其入口孔等）
oil gas 石油气（= petroleum gas）
oil gasification （柴）油的气化
oil gauge ①机油压力表（= oil pressure gauge）②机油油量表（= oil level gauge）③油尺，油面高度尺（= oil stick）
oil gauge cock 机油面高度检查开关，油面开关（= oil-level cock）
oil gauge glass 润滑油油面玻璃显示装置
oil gauge rod 油面测杆，油尺
oil gear motor 液压马达，流动机（亦称 oil motor, 以液压作为动力液的驱动装置，即将液压转换为机械驱动力，带动旋转件或移动件做功的装置，对比电动机，建议定名为"液动机"）
oil grade （按黏度分的）机油等级
oil groove （润滑）油槽（如：滑动轴承上的油槽）
oil grooved bushing 带油槽的轴套
oil grooves on piston 活塞裙（表面上刻制的细小机）油槽（以留存机油，增加活塞裙与缸壁间的润滑）
oil guard 挡油器
oil gun 注油器，注油枪
oil gun nipple 润滑油脂注射器油嘴
oil hammer 油锤作用，油击作用（在液压管道内产生的高压波作用）
oil hardening 油液淬火，油淬
oil header ①机油分配歧管②机油集油头
oil heater ①机油预热器（用于冬季降低黏度、增加流动性）②燃料油预热器（提高油温，促进燃烧）③（与发动机运转无关，单独烧煤油或汽油的汽车）油暖气炉，油暖风炉
oil hole 润滑油孔，注油孔
oil hydraulic pump 液压泵
oil -hydraulic tuber throttle 油-液管路的节流阀（控制油-液的流量）
oil identification mark 润滑油品质认证标志
oil-immersed 浸入油浴的，浸入油池的，浸油的
oil-immersed clutch 油浴式离合器，湿式离合器（亦称 wet clutch）
oil-immersed multiplate disk brake

油浴式多片盘式制动器
oil-immersed solenoid 油浴电磁阀
oil immersion （橡胶制件）油浸，油泡
oil immersion test 油浸试验
oil impregnated metal 含油轴承合金
oil indicator ①机油压力表（＝oil pressure indicator）②机油油位表（＝oil level gauge）③量油尺（＝oil dip stick）
oil indicator light 机油压力（过低）指示灯
oiliness ①（含）油性，润滑性②油质，油气
oiliness tester 油性试验器
oil-in-gasoline lubrication 混合油润滑（法）（发动机机油掺在汽油中，一起进入汽缸＝petrol lubrication, mixture method lubrication）
oil (ing) bushing 含油衬套（＝oilite bushing）
oiling chart 润滑图表（＝lubrication chart）
oiling up （火花塞等）黏油，油污
oil injection engine 柴油机（＝diesel engine）
oil injection lubrication 机油喷射润滑
oil inlet pipe union 进油管接头
oil intake tube （机油泵）进油管
oil interceptor 阻油圈，挡油环，挡油器
oil-in-water dispersion 油在水中弥散
oilite （多孔）含油轴承合金，石墨青铜轴承合金
oil jack 油压千斤顶，液压举升器
oil jet ①喷油射流②喷油嘴③机油喷射
oil-jet cooling 机油喷射冷却
oil jet plug 喷油塞（装在润滑油道上，带喷油孔，将润滑油喷至润滑点的塞状喷头）

oil kinematic viscosity 机油运动黏度（见kinematic viscosity）
oil leak 润滑油泄漏，漏机油（＝oil leakage）
oilless bearing 不加油轴承（如：自动润滑、石墨润滑、含油轴承等不需再加注滑油、滑脂的轴承，＝oilless metal）
oil level 油面高度
oil level cock 油面（测量）开关（＝oil gauge cock）
oil level control ①油面控制②油面控制机构，油面控制装置
oil level dip stick 油面指示尺，油面标尺，量油尺（＝oil dip rod，亦称bayonet gauge）
oil level gauge ①机油油面表，机油油量表，机油表（＝oil indicator）②机油油面高度量尺（＝oil level stick）
oil level indicator 油面高度指示器，油位指示器
oil level sensor 机油油面高度传感器（亦称oil sender, oil level transmitter）
oil level warning sensor 机油油量报警传感器（向控制模块或警报灯发出油面高度低于规定值信号的传感元件）
oil level warningtell-tale 机油油面警报灯（表示机油油面低于或高于规定油面的信号灯）
oil life index 机油寿命指标，机油使用期指标（亦称oil charge period index，包括其运动黏度变化率、开口闪点、水分、总酸值增加值、铁含量、正戊烷不溶物含量等，当上述指标不符合规定值时，表示机油使用期已到，应予更换）
oil line ①油管，油道②油路系
oil loss via piston ring 活塞环窜油损失（指机油经活塞环与缸壁间隙窜入燃烧室造成的损失）

oil loss via valve guides 气门导管窜油损失（指机油经气门杆与导管间隙窜入燃烧室造成的机油损失）

oil low temperature fluidity 机油的低温流动性（由机油的倾点、低温黏度和边界泵送温度三项指标表示）

oil main line 主油管，主油道

oil manometer 油压计，机油压力表

oil merchandiser 机油更换器，换机油器（= oil changer）

oil-metering pump 润滑油计量泵

oil mist 油雾

oil mixer ①滑油搅拌器②（二冲程发动机等使用的滑油-燃油）混合燃料搅拌-加注机

oil module (with a complete plastic housing) （带全塑料外壳的）机油（控制）模块（装在汽油直接喷射型发动机上，控制发动机机油的循环、滤清、冷却、压力以及曲轴箱通风等的电子控制拱堤）

oil-moistened air filter 油浸式空气滤清器

oil motor 油马达，液压马达，液力马达，液动机（见 oil gear motor）

oil nozzle 喷油嘴

oil-out 放油的，出油的，排油的

oil outlet （机油）出油口，出油管道

oil outlet temperature 出油温度，排油温度

oil overflow valve 机油溢流阀

oil pan [美] 发动机油底壳（= oil sump, 简称 sump）

oil pan gasket 油底壳衬垫（= sump gasket）

oil pan heater 油底壳预热器，机油盘加热器

oil pan tray （下曲轴箱）油底壳（= crankcase oil tray）

oil passage 油道

oil pickup ①（连杆）油勺，甩油勺②（从油底壳内将机油吸入粗滤器的）吸油管（亦称 oil pick-up pipe）

oil pipe union 机油管接头

oil-pressure adjusting screw 油压调节螺钉

oil pressure adjusting valve 油压调节阀

oil-pressure brake-lamp switch （制动）液压（控制式）制动灯开关（亦称 oil-pressure stop lamp switch, pressure stop light switch, 指制动时由制动管路液压控制的制动灯开关）

oil-pressure damper 油压阻尼器（= hydraulic damper）

oil pressure gauge 机油压力表（= oil circulation gauge）

oil pressure indicator lamp 机油压力指示灯

oil pressure regulating valve 机油压力调节阀（亦写作 oil pressure regulator valve, 用于防止发动机润滑系的机油压力超过规定值）

oil pressure relief valve 机油压力减压阀（= oil relief valve）

oil pressure retention （滑油的）油压保持能力（油压不随温度等变化的能力）

oil pressure sensor 机油压力传感器（亦称 oil pressure pickup, oil pressure transducer, oil pressure transmitter）

oil pressure stabilizer （机）油压稳定器

oil pressure switch 机油压力开关（油压开关，如：将油压变换为膜片位移，使触点闭合或断开的开关装置，简称 OPS）

oil-pressure switch type fuel pump 机油压力开关式燃油泵（燃油泵继电器触点并联一机油压力开关，在发动机正常运转工况下，如果燃油继电器出现故障，燃油泵仍可由机油压力开关获得电压，保持正常

工作)

oil pressure warning tell-tale 机油压力警报灯(表示发动机润滑系统油压不足的信号灯,亦称 oil pressure warning lamp)

oil print 油斑(用专用纸检查机油质量的评价标准)

oil proof 不透油的,不渗油的,防油的,抗油的,耐油(腐蚀)的

oil pump 机油泵,油泵

oil pump body 机油泵壳体(= oil pump case)

oil pump body cover 机油泵盖(= oil pump cover)

oil pump cam (驱动)机油泵(的)凸轮

oil pump capacity 机油泵泵油能力,机油泵流量

oil pump carrier 油泵托架

oil pump cover 机油泵盖(= oil pump body cover)

oil pumping ①泵送机油②(活塞环)窜油(指过量的机油经磨损的活塞环窜入燃烧室)

oil pumping ring 泵油环(= oil pumper,指磨损过度的活塞环,会使过量机油窜入燃烧室,等同一油泵,故名)

oil pump motor 油泵电动机

oil pump pressure relief valve ball 油泵减压阀的阀球

oil pump regulating valve 油泵调节阀

oil-pump safety valve 机油泵安全阀

oil pump screen 油泵滤网(= oil pump strainer)

oil pump shaft gear 机油泵轴齿轮

oil purifier 机油净化器(机油再生用,见 oil separator①)

oil quantity indicator 油量指示器

oil quench(ing) 油淬火

oil radiator 机油散热器

oil radiator connecting hose clamp 机油散热器连接软管夹

oil radiator inlet hose 机油散热器进油软管

oil radiator locking valve 机油散热器封闭开关

oil radiator valve 机油散热器开关阀

oil rail (活塞组合式油环的)环形刮油件(见 oil ring rail)

oil raising (燃烧室)窜油(指机油经活塞缸汽缸壁间窜入燃烧室)

oil release valve (机油)减压阀,溢流阀(指机油压力调节器中,油压超过某规定值时,机油由该阀溢出,使油压降低,以调节油压的阀门,亦称 oil relief valve)

oil relief ①溢流,溢流阀,溢流孔 ②液压气门挺杆体的进油孔区(该区域直径较小,形成凹形,故亦称 recessed area of hydraulic lifter body,发动机主油道中的压力机油从该凹区经进油孔进入液压挺杆,充满柱塞内腔及其下面的高压腔)

oil reservoir (储)油罐,(储)油槽;油容器

oil resistance 耐油性,抗油性,对油的稳定性

oil-resisting 耐油的,不怕油的

oil-retaining property (润滑面)保持润滑油的能力

oil return hole 回油孔

oil return line 回油管路

oil return pipe 回油管

oil return slots (活塞油环)排油槽,回油槽

oil ring (活塞)油环(oil control ring, oil scraper piston ring 的简称)

oil ring expander (组合式)油环(的)胀圈(使油环紧贴缸壁)

oil ring groove (活塞)油环环槽,油环回油槽

oil ring rail (三件和四件式组合)油环(的上、下)环形刮油片(简称 oil rail,上刮油片称 top rail,下

刮油片称 bottom rail，该上、下刮油片亦称 scraper ring，或简称 scraper)

oil ring spacer （组合式）油环（的）隔圈，撑环（将上、下刮油片撑隔开的匚形断面件）

oil-running clutch 湿式离合器（= oil clutch)

oil saving 节油的

oil scavenging pump 排油泵，回油泵（干式曲轴箱底壳润滑系统中，将流过发动机的机油送回外置式机油箱、进行循环的机油泵）

oil scoop （连杆的）油勺

oil scraper nose 刮油片的刮油边

oil scraper piston ring 活塞刮油环，活塞油环（= oil control ring，或简称 oil ring)

oil scraper ring ①（3~4件组合活塞油环的）刮油片（简称 scraper，见 oil ring rail) ②活塞油环

oil screen 机油滤网（机油泵进口滤网）

oil seal 油封

oil seal lip 油封件的唇部

oil seal remover 油封拆卸工具

oil seal ring 油封环，封油环

oil seal rubbing speed 油封摩擦速度（油封与配合面之间的相对滑动速度）

oil-seal torque 油封阻力矩，油封摩擦转矩

oil seal washer 挡油环，油封圈

oil separation filter 机油滤除器（见 oil separator②）

oil separation in grease 润滑脂的脱油（现象），润滑脂中的滑油分离（现象）

oil separator ①机油净化器（分离机油中的杂质，使机油再生的净化装置，亦称 oil purifier) ②机油分离器（滤除和截留压缩空气或曲轴箱通风气中的机油等的金属滤网等，亦称 oil extractor, oil separation filter, oil trap)

oil shale 油页岩

oil shield 护油罩，挡油盘

oil shock ①石油冲击②油压冲击，油击

oil shock absorber 液力减振器

oil shock of 1973 1973 年石油（危机造成的）冲击

oil siphon 油虹吸管（亦写作 oil syphon)

oil site 润滑点，润滑部位

oil skin 油布，防水布

oil skipper 油匙，油勺，油甩

oil slick （水面上的一层）浮油

oil slinger 甩油环，抛油圈（装在轴上的，利用离心力将油甩回，防漏，亦称 oil thrower, oil deflector)

oil sludge 机油油泥（机油变质生成的黏稠泥状物）

oil smog （机油燃烧引起的）淡蓝色烟，机油烟雾

oil smoke 机油窜入燃烧室形成的排烟

oil-soaked 油浸的，饱含油的，充满油的

oil space 油室，油腔

oil spit hole 喷油小孔（如：连杆小端将机油喷至活塞内腔的小孔）

oil splash gear 飞溅式润滑用齿轮

oil splash pan 飞溅润滑集油盘

oil-spot test 机油质量的渍点法试验（在专门的纸上印上油斑，根据油斑形态来鉴定机油质量）

oil spray 机油喷射（如：机油经曲轴连杆轴颈与其轴承间的间隙喷甩至汽缸壁）

oil spray cooling 机油喷射冷却（如：机油从连杆小头油孔喷入活塞内腔冷却活塞）

oil sprayer 油雾喷射器，机油喷管，机油喷口

oil spray lubrication 机油喷溅润滑（用喷溅方法将机油送至摩擦面进行润滑的方法）

oil stability 机油（性能）稳定性
oil stone 油石
oil stopper （装在曲轴正时齿轮端的）挡油环，挡油圈
oil storage capacity （滑动轴承材料等的）储油能力，润滑油存储能力
oil storage tank 储油箱
oil strainer 机油滤清器（多指机油泵入口前的细金属丝网滤清器）
oil suction bell （机油泵）进油喇叭口
oil suction pipe 吸油管
oil suction screen assembly 机油吸头滤网组件
oil suction screen casing 吸（机）油头滤网罩
oil sump ①曲轴箱油底壳（美称 oil pan）②油槽③机油沉淀池
oil sump baffle （发动机）油底壳隔板
oil sump capacity 机油盘容量，油底壳容量
oil sump strainer 油底壳内机油集滤器
oil supply system 供油系统
oil syphon lubricator 虹吸加油器
oil syringe 滑油加注器，注油器，油枪
oil tank ①机油箱，机油罐②运送机油的油罐车
oil-tank bottom 机油箱底部，润滑油箱底
oil tank car 油槽汽车，油罐车
oil tanker ①油罐车，油槽车（= oil tank truck, oil tank trailer）②油船，油槽船
oil tank vent filter 机油罐通风管滤器
oil tappet （气门的）液压挺杆（= hydraulic tappet）
oil tar 柏油，焦油，煤焦油
oilte bushing 含油衬套 [= oil (ing) bushing]

oil temperature gauge 机油温度表
oil temperature regulator 机油温度调节器（当发动机机油温度超过规定值时，自动使机油流过机油冷却器的装置）
oil temperature sensor 机油温度传感器，油温传感器，亦称 oil temperature pickup, oil temperature transducer, oil temperature transmitter）
oil tempering 油浴回火
oil test 机油试验（技术维护时对机油状况的检查）
oil test engine 油料试验机（试验机油等性能的专用发动机）
oil thermometer 油温（度）计，机油温度表
oil thickening 机油变稠，机油稠化
oil thief ①取油样器，简易抽油机②窃油贼
oil through 通油孔；油（的通）道
oil thrower ①甩油装置，抛油器；挡油圈②油雾喷嘴
oil thrower ring 挡油环，甩油圈
oil tight 油密的，不漏油的，油封油密，油密性
oil tight test 油密封试验
oil-to-air cooler 空气冷却式机油冷却器
oil-to-air heat exchanger 机油-空气热交换器（用做空气冷却式机油散热器、油加热式热风装置）
oil total acid number 机油的总酸值（简称 oil TAN）
oil total base number 机油的总碱值（简称 oil TBN）
oil-to-water heat exchanger 油-水热交换器
oil trap 机油收集器，机油分离器（见 oil separator②）
oil-type air cleaner 油浴式空气滤清器（= oil bath air cleaner, oil wetted air cleaner）
oil vane servomotor 叶片式油压伺服

机构

oil viscosity classification 机油黏度分类法（一般采用美国汽车工程学会 SAE J300 规定的按机油在规定温度下的最高黏度分级，不同黏度等级的机油适用于不同的使用温度范围）

oil viscosity index 机油黏度指数

oil viscosity-temperature characteristics 机油的黏（度随）温（度而变化的）特性（机油黏度随温度变化越小，其黏温特性越好，即黏度指数越高）

oil warning lamp 机油压力警报灯（机油压力低于规定值时，该灯亮，亦称 oil warning light）

oil-water separator 油水分离器

oil wax mixture 油、石蜡混合物

oil way 油道，油路（美称 oil passage，发动机或其他机械中润滑油的压力油道或油路）

oil wedge action （轴承等的）油楔作用（轴承内的滑油随着轴的旋转而楔入轴承的接触面，使轴浮起，形成液体摩擦）

oil whip ①机油起泡，润滑油起沫 ②润滑油由轴承内甩出

oil wick （润滑）油芯，油绳

oily 含油的，多油的，似油的，油性的，涂有油的，加油润滑的，油基的

oily elements 油污的零件，油污元件

OJT 在职培训（on the job training）

OK meter （装在仪表板上的）故障报警仪（商品名，发动机冷却水、蓄电池电解液等不足，制动摩擦衬片磨损超过规定值时，其警报灯亮）

OLASIS 在线汽车维修信息系统（On-line Automotive Service Information System 的简称）

old fashioned 旧式的，老式的，过时的

Oldham coupling 十字滑块联轴节，十字榫槽联轴节（可容许所连两轴的中心线不对准。该节有两突缘，其相对面上都有十字形径向槽。两突缘之间有一浮动盘，该盘两面具有与两突缘的径向榫槽相对应的十字形径向榫舌，相互装配在一起）

old model 早期形式，老（形）式，旧形式，旧式（= early model）

old-model car 老式轿车

Oldsmobile Navigation/Information system （见 Oldsmobile's Guide-star）

Oldsmobile's Guide star （通用公司）"奥丝莫尔"牌汽车导航装置（20世纪90年代的一种著名的车内导航系统，其导航软件可通过电子地图指明方向来描绘路线，驾驶人运用小键盘上简单的菜单式指令能选择到达目的地的最佳线路，亦称 Oldsmobile Navigation/Information System，为美国首次由用户选购的车装导行系统）

olefin 链烯烃，烯族烃

olefin compound 烯烃化合物

olefine （链）烯（烃），乙烯系（C_nH_{2n} 的别名，= ethylene）

olefin hydrocarbon （链）烯烃

oleic acid 油酸

oleo damper 液压阻尼器，液压减振器，液压缓冲器（= oleo buffer, oleo cushion, hydraulic buffer, hydraulic shock absorber）

oleo-pneumatic suspension 液压空气悬架，油气悬架（= hydropneumatic suspension）

oleo resin 松节油，松脂油（亦称 terebene, turpentine）

oleo shock absorber 液压减振器（= oleo damper）

Olin type air cushion （汽车座椅的）欧林型气垫

olive colour （车身油漆中的）橄榄色，黄褐色，黄绿色

olive oil 橄榄油
OLTBI 开环控制节气门体汽油喷射系统（open-loop throttle body fuel injection system 的简称）
O&M 使用与维护（operation and maintenance）
OMB （美国联邦）管理与预算办公室（federal office of Management and Budget 的简称）
ombrometer 雨量计
Omega Drive 奥米加传动装置（由液力耦合器和液力变矩器组合的一种自动变速装置商品名）
OMFS ［美］最佳米制紧固件系统（Optimum Metric Fastener System）
Omission ①省略（省去，删除）②遗漏（疏忽）
Omnibus ①客车，公共汽车（= motor bus，简称 bus）②总括的，混合的；公用的，多用的，多项的
omnibus for town service 城市公共汽车，城市客车
omnibus train 客车列车
omnibus with rear entrance 后侧上车的公共汽车（后侧开门的客车）
omnibus with side entrance 侧面上车的公共汽车（侧面开门的客车）
omnidirectional 全向的，无定向的，不定向的
omnidirectional tilt switch 全方向倾斜开关（用于翻车传感器，当车辆向任一方向的倾斜度超过规定值，如22°时，该开关接通，向电子控制摸或警报系统发出警报信号）
omnivorous engine 多种燃料发动机（= multi fuel engine）
OMR 光学符号读出器（optical mark reader）
ON 辛烷值（octane number）
on a level 在同一水平上，在同水准线上
on and off road tire 道路-越野两用轮胎（花纹较普通花纹粗，通常在胎面中间为适合公路行驶的菱形或纵向锯齿形花纹，而在两边为横向块越野花纹）
on-and-off the highway vehicle 公路和越野两用车辆
on board ①装在车上（= aboard）②装在仪表板上
onboard bar （豪华轿车的）车内酒吧
on-board battery charger （电动汽车的）车载式蓄电池就车充电器（美国 Delphi 公司的新产品名，可以使常规民用电网的交流电直接为电动汽车蓄电池充电）
on-board central computer 车载式中央电子计算机
on-board charger 就车充电器（利用外部电源对装在车上的蓄电池充电的装置）
on-board charging （蓄电池的）就车充电
on-board computer 车载电子计算机（装在车上的控制用计算机，简称 OBC，各汽车生产厂家使用形形色色的名称称呼其车载计算机。美国政府规定，从1995年起在美国销售的车辆一律使用美国汽车工程学会推荐的术语 electronic control module "电子控制模块"，如：控制发动机的车用计算机称动力系控制模块 "powertrain control module"，车身系统控制用车载计算机称车身控制模块 "body control module" 等）
on-board data acquisition computer system 车载式（运行、车况）数据采集计算机系统
on-board data base （汽车电子控制系统的）车装（式）数据库
on-board emission measurement system 车载排放检测系统
on-board (gasoline) vapor recovery 就车汽油蒸气回收
on-board hydrogen source （氢气汽车的）车载氢气源（装在车上产生

氢气的装置)
on-board knock control 车上爆燃控制(相对于提高汽油辛烷值等非车上爆燃控制而言,如:延迟点火,以消除爆燃的系统等)
on-board microcomputer 车载式微型电子计算机[指车用微型计算机。由于生产厂家不同,对车载式微型电子计算机有各种名称,常见的有 automotive computer, ECU (electronic control unit,电子控制单元),ECM (electronic control module,电子控制模块)和 CPU (central processing unit,中央处理器等)。为了统一术语,美国政府规定,从1995年1月起车载微型计算机一律称控制模块"control module",如:控制发动机的车用微机称 powertrain control module,见 PCM]
on-board NOx system 车载式NOx检测系统
on-board PM monitor 车载式微粒物监测仪
on-board refueling vapor recovery 车载式燃油蒸气回收(装置)(简称 ORVR)
on-board sensing system 车载传感系统
on-board unit platform for automotive telematics 汽车无线电通信系统的车载机平台(亦写作 automotive telematics on-board unit platform,简称 ATOP)
on-call stop 传呼车站(按乘客要求停的车站)
on-call traffic 传呼运输(系统,指随叫随到交通系统)
on-center handing (汽车方向稳定性中的)直线行驶能力(指在转向盘居中、无驾驶操作修正的条件下,汽车保持直线行驶的能力,亦称 straight-line handling)

once through lubrication 一次性润滑(指润滑油不循环的润滑系统)
on-chip 集成电路块上的,基片上的,芯片上的
on-chip (microcontroller) memory (与微处理器做在同一芯)片上(的)存储器
oncoming driver 迎面车辆的驾驶者
oncoming failure 即将发生的故障(损坏)(= imminent failure)
oncoming traffic 对向运输,对向交通;对向交通流,对向车流(= opposing traffic)
oncoming vehicle 迎面(驶来的)车辆
on corner 在转弯处
on-demand codes 见 service codes②
on-demand operation 按要求直达运行(如:专车直达客运)
on-demand stop 招手停车(根据乘客要求停车)
on-demand 4WD 按需四轮驱动系统(on-demand 4 wheel drive 的简称,其前桥和后桥间通过一黏性耦合器相连接,平时仅前轮为驱动轮,当前轮打滑空转而转速超过后轮时,在黏性耦合器的作用下,自动将转矩传给后轮,于是前、后轮同时成为驱动轮,故这种驱动形式亦称黏性耦合器式四轮驱动"viscous coupling type 4WD",参见 viscous coupling)
on-display type 屏显型
one-and-a-half decker coach 半双层旅游汽车,一层半旅游大客车,一层半游览大客车(见 half-deck coach)
one and a half ton truck 一吨半载货汽车,$1\frac{1}{2}$t货车(亦写作$1\frac{1}{2}$ton truck)
one and half box 见 one box
one-axle semitrailer 单轴半挂车

one bank cylinder block engine 直列式发动机（亦称 one-row cylinder block engine, in-line cylinder engine）

one body car audio （轿车的）整体式组合音响

one box ①单厢（式车身），一厢（式车身）（指发动机室、客厢和行李舱均在同一厢室内，彼此无隔挡的车身）②单厢式轿车（亦称厢式轿车，写作 1box。有的厢式轿车前面带突出的车头，有人称之为 one and half box，或写作 1.5box）

one box vehicle 单厢式车辆

one -CHANGES 一充（Suzuki 减速能量回收发电系统的商品名）

one chip microcomputer 单片微型计算机，单片机（指在一块集成电路芯片上装有中央处理器、存储器及输入、输出接口电路和必要的周边元器件，具有一般微机基本功能的微型计算机，亦称 microcontroller）

one cylinder shutoff test （测试多缸发动机状况的）单缸熄火法

one degree of freedom 一个自由度

one-dimensional 单维的，一元的

one-dimensional fuzzy controller 一维模糊控制器

one direction thrust bearing 单向推力轴承

one-end lift 单端举升器（仅举升车辆的前端或后端）

one-filament bulb 单丝灯泡（= single filament bulb）

one flank gear rolling tester （齿轮）单向啮合检查仪

one -grade parking performance （车辆的）坡度驻车性能（指车辆制动系统，包括行车制动、驻车制动，保持车辆停驻在坡面上的能力，= grade parking performance）

one-gun washer 单枪洗车机（单喷头清洗机）

one -highway load 公路行驶装载量（在公路上行驶时规定的车辆装载量）

one -highway motor vehicle 公路汽车（以区别于 off-highway motor vehicle）

one-hole injection nozzle 单孔式喷嘴

one hour rated power （内燃机的）1h 功率（在标准环境条件下，内燃机能连续运转 1 小时的最大有效功率）

one-in-ten sampling 十取一抽样

one-lane road 单车道道路

one-lever control 单杆控制

one-liquid hardening 单液淬火（将工件加热到淬火温度并使其组织奥氏体化，在水或油等单一淬火介质中一直冷至室温的方法）

one-man bus 单员公共汽车（指只有驾驶员一人而无售票员等乘务人员的公共汽车，车门开关由驾驶员远控，票资由乘客投入票费箱内）

one man per engine basis 一人一机制（修理或拆装时一名工人包一台发动机的工作法）

one-man top （敞篷轿车的）一个人即可张开和收拢的车顶篷（现多改为自动操作）

one-mile advance sign （在高速公路的交叉口前一英里设置的）一英里前置标志

one-off 单个生产的汽车或备用配件

one-phase 单相的

one-piece 整体的，不可拆的

one-piece apex seal （转子发动机的）单片式径向密封片（整片式径向密封片）

one-piece camshaft 整体式凸轮轴

one-piece construction 整体式结构

one-piece crankshaft 整体式曲轴

one-piece cylinder 整体式油缸，整体式汽缸

one-piece housing ①整体式车桥壳（= banjo housing, banjo axle casing）

②整体式壳体（= unitized housing）
one -piece rim 整体式轮辋（一件式轮辋）
one -piece rotor shaft （多缸转子发动机用的）整体主轴（整体偏心轴，整体转子轴）
one -piece screen 整体式滤网（单滤网）
one -piece steel (piston) ring 整片钢制活塞环
one -piece wheel 单件式车轮（整体式车轮）
one plane type （齿轮啮合位置的）单面式
one -point hitch 单点挂接装置（= single-point hitch）
one -pole 单极的
one -post lift （汽车的）单柱式举升机
one -quarter elliptic spring 1/4 椭圆形钢板弹簧
one -rank 单列的，单排的（= one-row）
one -rotor engine 单缸转子发动机
one -seater car 单座轿车
one sensor-one channel ABS 一传感器，一通道式 ABS（只有一个传感器和一条后轮制动液压通道，仅控制后轮制动力的防抱死制动系统，亦称后轮防抱死制动系统，见 RWAL brake system）
one -shield bearing 一面带防尘圈的轴承（= single-shield bearing）
one -shot lubricating system （车辆底盘）集中润滑系统（one-shot chassis lubrication system, central chassis lubrication system）
one -sided confidence limit （数理统计）单边置信度界限
one sided heating 一侧加热（单侧加热，单边加热）
Onesiphore Pecqueur 法国人，差动装置的发明者

one -stage torque converter 单级变矩器
one start screw 单头螺纹
one -tenth value thickness 1/10 厚度值（减弱一个数量级的厚度）
one third octave band filter 1/3 倍频带滤波器
one -thread worm 单头螺纹蜗杆
one -throw crankshaft 单曲柄曲轴
one -time load 一次性载荷
one -time operation 一次有效利用，只能使用一次
one -tone horn 单声喇叭（= single-tone horn）
one-touch closing sunroof 一触即闭式天窗
one touch switch ①点触式开关 ②单手柄（操作式）开关
one-touch type power window 一触式电动车窗（按压一按钮，玻璃便一次升降到底的电动车窗）
one -track 单线行驶的；单线的，单轨的，单车道的
one -tube shock absorber 单筒式减振器
one -turn radiator cap 一扣式水箱盖（一转即可拧紧的散热器盖）
one -way clutch 单向离合器，自由轮离合器（仅一个旋转方向传递转矩，而反方向允许自由转动的机构装置的总称，亦称 overrunning clutch, unidirectional clutch）
one -way element （单向离合器）单向传力元件（如：滚子、卡块、棘爪、摩擦盘等）
one -way haul 单向运输，单程运输
one -way radio 单向无线电通信
one -way ratchet clutch 棘爪式单向离合器
one -way restricted zone 单向通行限制路段
one -way road 单行道路

one -way roller clutch 滚子式单向离合器

one -way seal hose coupling 单向自封软管接头

one -way signal 单向信号（只有一个方向的信号装置）

oneway sprag clutch 楔块式单向离合器

one -way transition sign （设置在单向通行路段终点的）单向通行解除标志

one -way valve 单向阀（止回阀，逆止阀，= back valve, check valve, nonreturn valve）

one year warranty 一年保用，一年保修期

on-grade parking performance （车辆的）坡度驻车性能（指车辆制动系统，包括行车制动和驻车制动系保持车辆停驻在坡面上的能力，= grade parking performance）

on-highway load 公路行驶装载量（在公路上行驶时规定的车辆装载量）

on -line ①联机，联线的，在线的，主机控制的②在线的，在生产线上的，在生产线内的③与基准线一致

on -line computer 联机计算机（在线计算机）

on-line control 在线控制

on -line maintenance 在线维修

online mult media 在线多媒体技术（一种基于宽带互联网的应用技术，可以在网上发布图像流、声音流等动态信息。当宽带允许时，这些信息可以是实时的）

on -line repair 在线修理（流水线修理）

on load 负荷状态，负荷中

on -location test ①现场试验②就车试验（如：发动机在不从汽车上卸下的情况下的试验，= on-the-spot test）

on -off control 通-断控制

"on-off" cycle "接通-断开"循环

on -off fan clutch 断开-闭合式风扇离合器

on -off servomechanism 开关式伺服机构

on -off signal 开关信号（接通-断开信号）

on -off switch 通-断开关

on -off valve 通-断两位阀

ONO SOKKI Automatic Engine Testing System （日本）小野测具公司发动机自动试验台

on period （电路等的）接通期

on position ①工作位置，接通位置，闭合位置，接合位置②就位，在正规位置上，在正确位置上

on -position of a relay 继电器的工作状态（接通位置）

ONR 要求辛烷值（Octane number requirement）

on -ramp 高速公路进口车道，高速公路入口

on -road driver-aid services 途中驾驶员辅助装置（为驾驶员提供交通信息等驾驶员途中支援服务）

on-road driving performance （越野车辆等的公）路上行驶性能

on -road vehicle 道路车辆（包括各种客车、货车、公共汽车、机动车等在道路上行驶的车辆）

on -screen work 屏幕作业（指计算机设备、绘图及模拟等作业）

on -site test 现场试验

OnStar 安吉星（含碰撞自动求助、故障紧急求援、安全保障、导航、车况检测、全音控免提电话等六大类14项专属服务的车载信息服务系统的商品名）

On-Star system 安吉星系统（美国Cadillac牌轿车上安装的卫星信息通信导航服务系统的商品名。该系统包括：碰撞自动求助系统，紧急

救援系统，安全防盗保障系统，导航系统，车载式车况检测系统和全音控免提电话等）

on the car type ①就车式②不解体式（检验仪表等设备，相对 off the car type 而言）

on-the-car wheel balancer 就车式车轮平衡机（车轮不从车上拆下直接装在车上进行平衡作业）

on-the-go adjustment 行驶中调整（不停车调整）

on-the-ground test （汽车的）试验场试验

on-the-road test （车辆的）道路试验（非越野性试验）

on-the-spot repair 就地修理，在使用地点修理

on-the spot test 安装条件下的试验（= on-location test）

on turn 在转弯处，在弯曲处

on-vehicle 装在车上的，在车上进行的，就车的

on-vehicle alternator output test 交流发电机（装在车上进行的）就车输出试验

onward 前进的，向前的，进步的

onward type 平头型（汽车）（= cab over type, forward type）

on-way clutch 单向离合器

OOP 错位（指不在适当位置，out of position 的简称）

ooze 渗透，渗漏，泄漏

oozy glass 毛玻璃，磨砂玻璃（= clouded glass）

opacimeter 不透明度仪，浑浊度仪（测量液体中悬浮微粒含量的仪器）

opacity 不透光度，不透光率（由光源传来的光中不能到达观察者或仪器接收器的那部分，用百分数表示，亦称 light obscuration，不透光度 = (1 − T) × 100%，式中：T—透光度，见 transmittance）

opal glass 乳白色玻璃

op amp 运算放大器（= operational amplifier）

opaque ①不透明的，含糊的②（对光、热等）不传导的，非导体的③无光泽的，颜色晦暗的④迟钝的

opcode （电子控制系统机器指令中的）操作码（operating code 的简称）

OPDS 见 occupant position detection systems

OPEC 石油输出国组织（Organization of Petroleum Exporting Countries）

Opel 欧贝尔汽车公司（Adam Opel，原为 Daimler Benz 公司成立的分公司，1939 年被美国通用汽车公司收购）

open-air motoring （汽车）敞篷行驶（指将可敞开的车顶打开，在敞篷下行车）

open-air parking 露天停车（场）

open air sensor 车外气温传感器

open-air top 敞顶，敞篷

open belt 开式传动带（指驱动轴与从动轴相互平行的轴间传动带）

open body ①（轿车、客车的）敞篷车身②（货车的）栏板式车身

open-box truck 敞篷货车

open cab 敞篷驾驶室，敞开式驾驶室

open car 敞篷轿车

open cardan shaft （带两个十字轴形万向节的）开式传动轴

open-center hydraulic system （控制阀滑阀在中间挡位时，整个系统内全部油路相通的）中间挡位油全开式液压系统

open center loop booster 中间挡位油路全通式液压助力缸，常流式液压动力转向助力缸（当控制阀滑阀处于中间挡位时，助力缸活塞两侧均为压力相等的低压，油液各自形成环路汇合后流回油箱）

open center of slide valve （可使全

部油路相通的）滑阀中间挡位
open-center slide valve 中间挡位油路全开式滑阀（处于中间挡位时全部油路均相通的滑阀）
open-center tire 非封闭花纹轮胎
open chamber 开式燃烧室（指无副室，仅由活塞顶与缸盖间形成的一个整体空间燃烧室，直喷式柴油机多采用开式和半开式燃烧室，二者的区别仅在于开式燃烧室没有明显分隔只有很小的挤气面积，而半开式有较大的挤气面积，且活塞顶多呈球形，ω形等深凹坑，开式和半开式燃烧室在柴油机上又称直喷式燃烧室）
open choke 固定式喉管
open circuit 开路，断路，线路断开
open circuit fluid coupling （无内隔环的）开式回路液力耦合器
open circuit ignition 开式电路点火（指一次电路常开，只有在点火时闭合）
open-circuiting 切断，断开（电路）
open-circuit system ①（液压）开式系统②（电）开路系统
open circuit test 开路试验（空载试验）
open circuit voltage ①开路电压（电路处于断开状态的电压）②（继电器等的）断开电压，断路电压，断电电压
open-class race 公开赛
open cockpit vehicle 敞露驾驶式车辆（指无驾驶室而驾驶员座位及各种驾驶操纵装置均敞露在外的车辆）
open coil glow plug 双电极型电热丝式预热塞（亦称 open element glow plug, wire glow plug）
open combustion chamber 开式燃烧室（指在活塞顶型面与汽缸盖底面之间，中间没有明显分隔的燃烧室，见 open chamber）

open control 开路控制（指计算机闭路反馈控制系统按开环模式实施的控制，即其开路控制工况。如：起动时或急加速时，计算机只根据存储的数据对此时所要求的浓混合比作开路控制，而不考虑 O_2 传感器的反馈信息，亦称 open-cycle control, open loop control）
open cooling 开式冷却法（指：①冷却水箱与大气相通的冷却方式；②借助于自然空气流的空气冷却法）
open cycle 开式循环（指在热力发动机中，工质不循环使用，作过功的工质，在每个循环后都排出机外）
open cycle gas turbine engine 开式循环燃气轮机，开式燃气轮机（指其工质-空气从大气中吸入，继而随同燃烧产物一起又排入大气的燃气轮机）
open-deck cylinder block 敞顶式汽缸体（顶面敞开而由缸盖封盖的缸体）
open deck type cylinder block （由上、下两半组成的）组合式汽缸体（上面的一半称 upper block，下面的一半称 lower block）
open depot 露天仓库
open-door tell tale （汽车）车门未关指示灯，车门未关警报灯（亦称 open door warning light）
open driver's seat 露天驾驶员座
open-ended control 开路控制（无反馈控制，见 open control）
open-end（ed）spanner 开口扳手（亦称 open end wrench）
open end hole 透孔，穿孔，通孔（＝through hole）
opener 开启工具的通称
open exhaust 自由排气
open flame 明火
open fuse 裸露式熔断丝（相对 en-

closed fuse 而言)

open heating 明火加热

opening ①孔，口，开口，切口，缝隙② (扳头的) 开口，钳口③开启，打开，开启度，开度，开启着的，打开的

opening amperage 开路电流值，断路电流值（如：充电继电器断开时，由蓄电池流出的逆电流值）

opening angle 开启角（如：用曲轴或凸轮轴转角等表示的气门开启时间）

opening angle of emergency door (客车) 安全门开启角

opening cam 开启凸轮，顶开凸轮

opening force 开启压力（使阀等开启的压力）

opening line 开线（指外露的门、发动机罩等覆盖件的边界线）

opening of spanner 扳手钳口，扳头开口度

opening of spring 钢板弹簧挠度

opening overlap (进、排气门) 重叠开启，开启重叠

opening port area (发动机等的) 进、排气口的开口面积

opening pressure (阀门等的) 开启压力

opening pressure surge (液压油路) 开启时的压力冲击波

opening ramp (凸轮轮廓线中为防止气门初速度过高、产生强烈冲击噪声和磨损的) 上升缓冲段（将半径小于理论基圆的实际基圆与凸轮轮廓曲线基本工作段圆滑联结的过渡曲线段中的上升过渡曲线段）

opening shock 阀门开启时的冲击

open-jawed spanner 开口扳手

open load 开路负载

open load bed (栏板式车身的) 敞式货台

open-loop catalytic converter 开环式催化转化器（无氧传感反馈信号的催化转化系统）

open loop control 开路控制（①指只根据被控制量与各种变量的函数关系和事先确定的控制目标，按照各种变量的传感元件输入的信息对被控制量进行控制，而没有或不根据控制结果的反馈信息与控制目标作实时比较并根据该比较结果对被控制量作实时修正的控制模式，见 open control②见 open-loop mode②)

open-loop cut-off frequency (线性放大器) 开环截止频率（指开电压放大倍数的模减少到低频值的 $1/\sqrt{2}$ 时的频率）

open-loop mode ① (电子控制系统的) 开路控制模式 (见 open-loop control) ② (发动机特性测试中的) 固定负荷及固定测功机载荷模式 (指在发动机某一固定节气门开度和测功机某一固定载荷的条件下，使发动机转速稳定，测取该固定转速下的转矩、油耗、功率和油耗率等的速度特性测试模式，亦称 position mode)

open-loop sensing 开路传感（电路）

open-loop signal-conditioning circuit 开路信号处理电路

open loop voltage gain 开路电压增益

open nozzle (柴油机) 开式喷油嘴 (= open type nozzle，指无阀的喷油嘴)

open out 打开，开启，敞开；断开

open parking ground 露天停车场

open pattern (轮胎的) 宽槽花纹 (亦称 open profile)

open propeller shaft (带两个十字轴型万向节的) 开式传动轴

open rack vaporizer (利用海水热量使液化天然气气化为天然气的大型) 管架式气化设备

open railway crossing 没有栅栏的公路-铁路交叉道口

open side container 侧开式集装箱（除后端开门外，其一侧或两侧壁可以全开）

open-side cylinder block 侧开式汽缸体

open side type 侧（边）敞（开）式

open sipe （轮胎花纹凸面上的）横切细纹，横断细纹（以增加抓着力）

open splice 接头开裂（如：轮胎胎面、胎侧、气密层、内衬层、内胎等的接头裂开、脱开的现象）

open sports car 敞篷跑车，敞篷运动车

open symmetrical differential 普通型对称式差速器（普通非防滑型圆锥行星齿轮差速器 open symmetrical bevel planet-gear differential 的简称。"对称"是指其左右半轴齿轮尺寸相等）

open system 开放（型）系统（①指遵守国际标准化组织规定的标准，因而可以与遵守相同标准的其他系统互联的数据处理系统，相对于封闭系统 closed system 而言 ②指不对其资源进行保护的系统）

open system interconnection 开放型系统互联（指开放型系统遵照国际标准化组织的标准进行互相联网的方法和模式。国际标准化组织规定的这一模式为由 7 层网络功能组成的开放系统通信协议）

open the engine full out 节气门全开

open the throttle wide 加大节气门开度

open-tire wheel 带宽槽花纹轮胎的车轮

open-top box body 无顶箱式车箱

open top container 顶开式集装箱（在箱顶开门，以便吊装货物）

open-topped 无盖的，顶部开口的

open-top trailer 敞篷挂车

open to traffic 允许（车辆）通行，（车辆）可通行，交通开放

open tourer 敞篷观光车，敞篷游览车

open transport network 见 OTN

open type bearing 非密封式（滚动）轴承（本身没有密封件，见 sealed bearing）

open-type liquid cooling system 开式水冷系统（水箱盖中没有蒸气-空气阀，冷却系统通过水蒸气引出管与大气一直相通）

open type lorry with canvas cover 带帆布篷的栏板式货车

open type nozzle （柴油机的）开式喷嘴（在喷孔处没有封闭燃油孔道的零件，喷油器的内腔与燃烧室一直相通，用于燃气轮机等连续喷射燃油的燃烧装置，简称 open nozzle, = hole nozzle）

open (up) the engine 加大节气门开度（使发动机加速，= open the motor, step on the accelerator）

open voltage test 开路电压试验（如：在蓄电池电路断开的情况下测定其电压）

open washer 开口垫圈，C 形垫圈，弹簧垫圈

open wire 裸线，照明（= bare wire）

opera light [美] ①（装在轿车车身中柱上的装饰性）门控灯（车门开启时，该灯亮）② = opera window 汽车后座门上的小窗

operand （计算机控制系统的）操作数，运算元（简称 OP, OPD）

operate 操纵，控制；运行，运转；开动，使运转，使动作；起作用；使用，经营，管理

operate at full throttle 在节气门全开工况下运转（满负荷运转）

operating angle 工作角，运转角（如：万向节夹角等）

operating cam 操作凸轮，工作凸轮（一般指由手柄式踏板操作的凸轮。

有时指蹄鼓式制动器将制动蹄顶开的凸轮)

operating characteristic ①经营特点,营业特征②工作特性,运行特性,操作特点,使用特性

operating controls (汽车的)驾驶操纵装置

operating cost per mile (汽车)每英里的运行费用

operating current 操作电流,工作电流(如:继电器等电磁装置的吸动电流)

operating cylinder 动力油缸,操纵油缸

operating data 运行数据,运行资料,工作记录,运行记录,生产数据,操作记录(= operational data)

operating fork (离合器)分离叉(离合器中推动分离轴承,使离合器分离的部件,亦称 clutch release fork, withdrawal fork)

operating fork ball-end 分离叉球头支座

operating fork return spring 分离叉复位弹簧

operating frequency 工作频率,运转频率

operating gear 操纵机构

operating influence 工作条件影响(由工作条件变化造成的影响)

operating instruction 使用说明书,操作规程,业务规章,工作须知,使用指南(= service instruction, working, instruction)

operating lever ①操纵杆②起动摇把③(离合器液压式操纵机构的)分离杆(接受液压缸推杆推力,使离合器分离的杆件)

operating life 运行寿命,工作寿命,使用寿命(①指从启用到失效累计运行的时间、次数、里程、小时等②指有效工作时间的统计值)

operating life data 使用耐久性数据,使用寿命数据

operating maintenance 日常维护,例行维护,运行维护

operating manual 操作说明书,使用手册

operating mode ①工况,运转方式,运转模式②控制方式,操纵模式

operating parameter 运行参数

operating pedal 操作踏板,控制踏板

operating period 使用期(从启用到失效所经过的日期)

operating piston (自动变速器中变液压为机械力和机械运动用于驱动离合器、制动器油缸的)工作活塞

operating pressure 工作压力,作用压力

operating pressure range (压力传感器的)工作压力范围(输出符合规定要求的最大和最小工作压力之间的压力区间)

operating radius 作用半径,运行半径

operating range ①作用范围,工作范围②作用距离,有效距离,实际距离,运行区域(如:汽车运输的运行半径,营运区域;汽车的可行驶里程,行驶距离,见 vehicle range)

operating repairs 日常维修,运行期间的检修,运行修理

operating sequence 操作程序

operating speed 运转速度,使用速度,营运车速,运行速度(如:汽车的实际行驶车速)

operating temperature range (传感器的)工作温度范围(指其输出能符合规定要求的最高和最低工作温度间的温度区间)

operating tension 工作电压

operating turnaround 运输周转时间,作业循环时间,运转周期,作业周期

operating valve 操纵阀

operating variables 运行变量（运行过程的变化因素）

operating voltage 工作电压

operating wall temperature 工作壁温（如：汽缸壁工作温度）

operating weight 工作重量，运行重量（对车辆而言，通常指加满燃料、冷却水、润滑油、工作油等液体，并带备胎、随车工具等全部附属装备以及装载客货和驾驶员的重量，= running weight, service weight, working weight，为运行质量的旧称）

operation ①动作，操作，运转②工作，作业，使用，运用③工作过程，工序④运算步骤，运算过程⑤操纵，控制（机器）⑥（机构的）开动，起作用⑦效果，效力；有效范围

operational amplifier 运算放大器（简称 opamp，具有两个输入端和一个输出端，闭环时完成数字运算功能的放大集成电路）

operational analysis 运行分析，使用分析

operational data 使用数据，运转数据，工作数据，运算数据（= service data）

operational delay 运转延迟（如：交通组成因素间互相干扰引起的延迟）

operational efficiency 使用效能，工作效率（= operating efficiency）

operational feasibility 实施可行性，实用可能性，使用可能性，可实现性，工作可行性

operational flexibility （车辆等的）运行灵活性（运行机动性，操作适应性）

operational life 使用寿命

operational order ①操作命令，运算指令②操作次序

operational readiness 技术完好状态，备用状态

operational reliability 工作可靠性，操作可靠性，运行可靠性

operational repair 运行修理（汽车小修）

operational sequence 运行程序，操作步骤

operational speed 营运速度（车辆在线路上工作时间内的平均速度）

operational suitability 操作适应性

operational test ①操作试验②运转试验（工作状态下进行的试验）

operation mode 运转模式，工作模式（亦称 operation strategy 或简称 strategy）

operation parameter 使用参数，运行参数，操纵参数

operation requirements 操作要求，运转要求（简称 OR）

operation route 营运线路

operation's direction 操作指南，操作指示（简称 OD）

operation sequence control ①操作序列控制，工序控制②运算程序控制

operation specifications 操作规范

operations research 运算研究，运筹学（简称 opsear-ch, OR）

operation variables （发动机等的）运行变量（如：点火时刻、混合气浓度、进气量、喷油量等影响其运行工况的各种可变参数）

operative limits 极限工作条件（仪器仪表、装置、设备能经受且不致造成损伤或性能永久性降低的规定工作条件，亦称 limiting operating conditions）

operative symbol 运算符号

operator adaption 操作人员适应性（= operator adaptation）

operatorless device 自动装置，无人管理装置

opera window 汽车后座门上的小窗

ophthalmography 眼球运动角膜反

射测定法

ophthalmology 眼科学，眼科医学

opinion 意见，看法，主张，见解

opportunity 机会，时机，可能

opposed-cylinder (-type) engine 对置汽缸式发动机，对置式发动机（在曲轴的两侧汽缸呈180°对向布置的发动机，亦称 boxer engine，或 flat engine，两缸者称 flat twin，四缸者称 flat four 等）

opposed 4 piston aluminum caliper 对置四活塞式铝合金制动钳（一种新型盘式制动器的制动钳结构，钳的两侧各有一对轮缸和活塞，这两对活塞相互对置，制动时间同时动作，以增加制动力，多用于富车）

opposed-piston engine 对置活塞式内燃机（在同一汽缸内装有两个，同时向相反的方向运动的活塞，燃烧室在该两活塞顶面之间，亦称 opposed-type engine）

opposed vehicle 对向（行驶的）车辆

opposing traffic 对向交通，对向车流（= oncoming traffic）

opposite 矛盾的，对立的，相反的

opposite angles 对顶角（= vertical angle）

opposite (engine) rotation （发动机）反转，倒转（从输出端看为顺时针旋转）

opposite flank 异侧齿面（齿轮轮齿的左、右侧齿面互为异侧齿面）

opposite forces 反向力

opposite hand view 镜像

opposite lock 反锁（指向前轮转向相反的方向转动转向盘，以抵消过度转向作用。如：当由于右转弯过猛而导致后轮侧滑时，向左转动转向盘）

oppositely directed 反向的

opposite side 对边

opposite sign 异号，反号

opposite vertex 对顶

opposition 对立，对置，反对，障碍物

oppsite-phase ①反相位的，反相的 ②反方向的，反面的

OPS ①机油压力传感器（oil pressure sensor 的简称）②多孔氧化硅（oxidized porous silicon 的简称，用作传感元件的吸湿性介电质）③乘员坐姿感知系统 ④模拟可视倒车入库、驻车影视图像

opsearch 运筹学（= operations research）

opt ①选择，挑选 ②可选用的

opt 选择；两者取一，挑选（option 的简称）

Opti Air technology ［美］（Fleetguard 公司新型）空气滤清技术（的专利登记名）

optic(al) 光学的，光导的，视觉的，视力的，眼睛的

optical activity 光学活性（指某些分子或晶体具有的旋光性，见 rotatory polarization）

optical and ion current measurement （发动机燃烧状况的）光学摄影和离子流观测技术（燃烧火焰从加有直流电压的电极间通过时会产生与火焰强度相应的离子流，使用 X 光等光学摄影技术拍摄布置在燃烧室各测试点的火花塞型离子探测头电极间的离子电流量的变化，借以测定燃烧室内混合气燃烧状况的技术，见 ion prob）

optical angle encoder （光学式曲轴转角位置测定传感器的）光学角度编码器

optical axis 光轴（汽车前照灯的主光轴，指灯光最明亮的照射光向）

optical bench 光具座

optical bevel protractor 光学斜角规

optical card reader 光学卡片读出器

optical check 光学检查（指使用光学仪器或目视检测）

optical communication 光通信（指用光导纤维替代传统电线传送电信号的通信系统）

optical comparator 光学比较仪，光学比较器

optical crankshaft position sensor 光学式曲轴位置传感器

optical deviation 光学偏移（用通过玻璃观察远处的一个点时该点的真实方向与表观方向间的夹角表示）

optical direction and ranging 光雷达，光学定向和测距

optical distortion （汽车风窗玻璃等的）光学失态，光学畸变，光畸变（在玻璃表面上取两个点 M, M'，通过 M, M' 的视线间距为给定值 ΔX，则 M 和 M' 点处测定的光学偏移 a_1 和 a_2 的代数差 Δa 称为 MM' 方向的光畸变 "optical distortion in a given direction MM'"，即：MM' 方向的光畸变 $\Delta a = a_1 - a_2$，以逆时针方向的偏移为正，顺时针方向为负，见 optical deviation）

optical distortion at a point M M 点的光畸变（指以 M 为起点的所有 MM' 方向的光畸变的最大值）

optical distributor 光电（点火信号发生式）分电器

optical doze-warning system 光学式（驾驶员）打盹警报系统

optical-electric field sensor 光-电式场强度传感器

optical emission spectroscopy 光发射频谱分析

optical encoder 光学式编码器（利用光-电变换对数据进行编码的装置，可用于汽车转速、位置、开度等传感系中将光传感信号翻译成电子控制模块能接受的代码）

optical fiber 光导纤维，光（学）纤维（指在光通信中使用的高容量、低损耗的传输光信号的光学纤维，亦称 optical waveguide fibre）

optical fiber gyro （测定汽车行驶方向的）光纤陀螺仪（见 laser gyroscope）

optical fibre laser gyroscope 光纤（干涉型）激光陀螺仪（见 laser gyroscope）

optical filter-photo-multiplier combination 光学滤波照相放大组合仪

optical flat 光学平玻璃，平晶

optical grating 光栅

optical indicator 光学指示器，光指示器

optical instrument 光学仪器

optical karman vortices air flow meter 光学式卡门旋涡空气流量计

optical log 光学测程器

optically 用光学方法，光学上（地）

optically coupled 光偶合的，光学偶合的

optical maser 光脉塞（光学微波激射器，光受激辐射微波放大器，光激射器，见 maser）

optical measurement 光学测量

optical model 光学模型，影像模型

optical obscuration 不透光度（见 opticity）

optical parallel （检查两平面平行度的）光学平行仪

optical path 光径，光路

optical path shifting knob 光径变换按钮，光（学通）路变换按钮

optical path shifting prism 光径变换棱镜，光路变换棱镜

optical phase shift sensor 光学式相移传感器

optical plumb 光测垂线

optical projector 光学投影仪

optical pyrometer 光学高温计

optical range 光学测距

optical scanner 光学扫描器

optical sensor 光电式传感器（将光明暗变化转换为电信号的传感元件，一般由发光二极管、光电管及旋转遮光件等组成，如：曲轴转速、位置及点火信号传感器等）

optical simulation 光学模拟

optical smokemeter 光学式烟度计（使用光学手段直接测定排烟特性的烟度计）

optical spectroscopy 光谱仪

optical speed and distance sensor 光学式速度和距离传感器

optical system 光学系统

optical torque meter 光学式转矩（测定）仪

optical torsion strain sensor 光学式扭转应变传感器（亦称 optical twist sensor）

optical transistor 光敏晶体管

optical trigger 光学触发装置，光电触发器（如：汽车电子点火系的红外线光电触发器）

optical twist sensor 光学式扭转传感器

optical velocity sensor （车载式）光反射式速度传感器（由光发射和接收部分组成。如：将光射至地面，根据其反射时间等确定车速的传感器件）

optical warning control （汽车的）光警告操纵件（如：驾驶员控制前照灯发出光警告的操纵件）

optical-write-in mode 光写入型（利用光信号调制外加电压，而将光信号变为脉冲信号、电压信号或显示图像等）

optic axis 光轴

optic fiber CAN communication network 光纤 CAN 通信网络（以光纤为传输介质的 CAN 通信网络）

optic nerve 视神经

optics 光学

optic test 用光学仪器检查

optimal 最佳的，最优的，最恰当的，最适宜的

optimal control 最优控制（根据受控对象的动态特性，选择一种容许的控制参数，使受控对象处于所希望的状态运行并获得最佳的性能指标）

optimal load 最佳载荷（最经济装载质量）

optimal stochastic control 最优随机控制

optimatic 光学式高温

optimeter 光学比较仪，光电比色计

optiminimeter 光学测微计

optimization 最优化，最佳化

optimization of braking force distribution 制动力分配最佳化（制动力最佳分配）

optimization point 最佳点，最优点

optimize 使最佳，使最佳化（亦写作 optimise）

optimizing vehicle utilization 车辆最佳运用

optimum ①最佳的，最优的②最佳值，最佳点，最优状态，最佳条件，最佳，最优

optimum body deformation control 最佳车身变形控制（指尽量抑制碰撞时车身乘坐区变形，以减少对乘员的冲击）

optimum comfort angle （座椅靠背等的）最舒适角度（最佳舒适角）

Optimum Metric Fastener System [美] 米制紧固件最佳体系（简称 OMFS）

optimum MS 最佳混合气强度（参见 mixture strength），混合气优化浓度

optimum seeking method 优选法

option ①选择②选购③选购件（按用户要求而供应）

optional at extra cost 加价选购的（收取附加费用可选择供应的）

optional equipment 选购设备

optional extras 任选附件（亦称 optional fitment）

optional gear ratio 选定传动比（供用户选定的变速器或主传动器传动速比）

optional parts 选购件（亦称 optional units）

optional test 选择性附加试验（应用户要求而进行的附加试验）

opti-spark distributor （通用公司）光电点火信号分电器［商品名，该分电器上装有由发光二极管、带两组通光槽的传感盘和光电管组成的发动机转速和汽缸识别（哪一缸处于上止点位置）信号发生器，供电子控制模块测定发动机转速，触发燃油泵电路；测定各组（或各缸）喷油器的喷油时刻，计算点火提前角，发出各缸点火指令并根据曲轴转速的微小变化，精调点火和喷油时刻］

opti-spark ignition system 光电点火信号式点火系（通用公司商品名，其点火信号由一凸轮轴带动的遮光盘与发光二极管和光电管组成）

opti-spark sensor disk 光电式点火信号传感器遮光板（由凸轮轴带动，具有按一定间距布置的通光槽口，当其槽口转过发光二极管与光电管之间时，光电管即向电子控制模块发出发动机转速、曲轴位置或点火信号）

opto-electronic ignition system 光学-电子点火系统（光控电子点火装置）

opto-electronic materials 光电材料（电致发光、光致发电的材料的通称）

opto-electronic pickup 光电传感器，光（学）电子传感器

opto-electronic trigger signal 光电触发信号

OPUS 振荡传感式点火系统（无触点式半导体点火系统的别称，见 oscillating pickup ignition system）

OR ①运行记录（operation record）②运行报告（operational report）③操作要求（operation requirements）④运筹学（opsearch）⑤外半径（outside radius）⑥过载继电器（overload relay）

orange light 橘黄色灯光

orber ①次序，顺序，程序②命令，指令，指示③规则，规程④等级，阶，次⑤状态，情况⑥种类，目，族⑦订货，订货单，订单⑧整理，安排，调配，处理，管理

orbit ①轨道，轨迹②活动范围③沿轨道运行，环绕，绕…作圆周运动，使进入轨道运行

orbital motion 轨道运动

orbital path of charge （转子发动机的）进气相轨迹（由外旋轮线缸壁的形状决定）

orbiter 轨道运动件（如：汽车的静液压变速器用可变容积轨道泵的星形泵芯，该泵芯，亦称 spider 按轨道作波状运动）

orbiting charge （转子发动机内）沿轨道运动的充量（沿轨道运动的新鲜混合气充量，其切线速度影响火焰传播速度）

orbiting motion 轨迹运动，轨道运动

orbit period 轨道运动周期（经轨道一周的时间，= orbit time）

OR circuit 或门电路［逻辑电路的一种，在所有的输入信号中只要有任一个是 1（Hi），便输出 1 的电路］

orderly ［口语］（街道）清扫车，清洁车

order of firing 点火顺序，点火次序，发火次序

order of magnitude ①数量级②按大小、多少、快慢、长短等数值的度

量③绝对值的阶，绝对值的大小

order of march （汽车队的）行驶顺序

order of traffic 交通秩序

order tracking ①（故障诊断中的）顺序跟踪法②（噪声分析中的）频阶跟踪法

order-type 序型，顺序型

ordinal ①顺序的，按次序的，依次的；属于某科的②序数

ordinary 普通的，寻常的

ordinary ground 普通地形

ordinary steel 普通钢

ordinate ①纵坐标②竖标距，纵距③有规则的，正确的

ordnance vehicle 火炮牵引车

ore(-hauling) truck 矿石运输车

OR element "或"元件（或门电路元件，见 OR circuit）

organic 有机的

organic binder bond 有机黏结剂

organic chemistry 有机化学

organic compound 有机化合物（简称有机物，指含碳元素的化合物，但 CO，CO_2，碳酸盐等除外。组成有机物的元素除碳外，通常还有氢、氧、氮、磷、卤素等）

organic electrolyte 有机电解液，有机电解质

organic fluid 有机流体（工质）

organic friction material 有机耐磨材料，有机摩擦材料

organic impurities 有机杂质

organic lining 有机材料摩擦衬片

organic oxide 有机氧化物（如排气中的酮、醛类等含氧的有机化合物）

organic peroxide 有机过氧化物

organic Rankine cycle （发动机）有机工质朗肯循环

organic solvent 有机溶剂

organo additive 有机添加剂

organo-manganese compound 有机锰化合物（见 organo-metallic compound）

organo-metallic antiknock 有机金属化合物抗爆剂（见 organo-metallic compound）

organo-metallic compound 有机金属化合物 [指碳原子直接与金属原子键合的有机化合物，如四乙基铅 $Pb(C_2H_5)_4$ 等，简称 organo-metal]

organ type pedal （通过跟部的铰链固定在车身底板上，并以铰链轴为中心的）铰接式踏板

OR gate circuit 或门电路（一种实现"或"运算的门电路，亦称 OR logical gate，OR gate，见 OR operation，有两个或两个以上输入端，一个输出端的逻辑电路，当两输入端中的任一个或全部为 1 时，输出端为 1）

ORI 辛烷值需求增势（octane requirement increase）

orientate 定向，定方位

orientation ①定向，定方位，定位，校正方向②方位，方向，方向性，倾向性

oriented crystal bearing metal 定向结晶轴承合金（指表面呈单一方向锐角晶粒结构的滑动轴承合金，其结晶谷间饱含机油，可形成可靠的表面油膜，多用于高速轴承）

orifice 孔，口（如：量孔，流孔，节流孔；喷嘴，喷口）

orifice coefficient 孔口流量系数，量孔流量系数

orifice differential 小孔节流压力差

orifice plate （孔板式喷油嘴的）孔板（具有喷孔的圆板形零件，见 orifice plate nozzle）

orifice-plate flowmeter 孔板式流量计（简称 orifice meter）

orifice-plate nozzle 孔板式喷油嘴（指针阀座面采用平面密封，喷孔在平板上的喷油嘴）

1087

orifice plug 带计量孔的螺塞
orifice port （液体流通的）小孔，细孔
orifice restrictor 节流孔板
orifice spark advance control 小孔真空点火提前装置（指由节气门区的小孔引出真空控制点火提前角的装置，简称 OSAC）
orifice tube expansion valve （车用空调系统的）节流孔管式膨胀阀（由节流孔控制制冷剂流量）
origin ①（坐标的）原点②（计算的）起点③起源，原因，由来
original ①原始的，固有的，原来的；原装的②原物，原文
original car 原型车，非变型车
original crack size 原始裂纹尺寸
original data 原始数据（=initial data）
original design 原设计，原结构（简称 OD）
original drawing 原图
original feed 原料（=feedstock）
original inspection 初步检查
original life （新车）固有寿命（第一次大修前的使用寿命）
original record 原始记录
original shape 原样
original size 原始尺寸
original (spare) part(s) 原厂配件 [=genuine spare part(s)]
original specification 原始技术条件
original styling model 原车身造型模型，原车身式样模型
original tread （未经翻新的）原（始）胎面
origin and destination survey （旅客出行调查中的）起、终点调查
originate 引起，发生，起源，首创，创始，开始，出现，发明，创作
originating firm 制造厂，生产厂
originating traffic 始发交通
origin-destination matrix （城市道路）起、终点矩阵
origin-destination study （交通）起讫点调查，起点-目的地的调研（简称"O and D"study）
origin of coordinates 坐标原点
origin of force 力原点
origin-to-destination 起点到终点（的），全程（的）（简称 OD）
O-ring O 形密封圈，O 环（O 形断面橡胶密封环，用于保持运动件的气密、水密、油密等，汽车多用来作为油封，亦称 O-ring gasket, O-ring packing, O-ring seals）
OR logic gate 或门（亦称 OR gate, 指任一输入是 1 或两个输入均为 1 时输出为 1，否则输出为 0 的逻辑电路，见 OR gate circuit）
ornament ①装饰（件），饰品（如：前照灯的装饰圈）②（生产厂家或车型的）徽标（牌）
ornamental 装饰的
ornamental glass 装饰玻璃
ornamental hub cap 装饰性轮毂盖
ornamental radiator cap 镀镍水箱盖，覆盖有装饰层的水箱盖
ornamentation ①装饰，修饰；装饰品②装饰技术③汽车散热器上装的车徽（见 radiator emblem）
oroide 阿罗依德合金（一种铜、锌、锡合金，呈黄金色，车室装饰品及镀覆用材料）
OR operation "或"逻辑，"或"运算（亦称 disjunction，一种布尔运算，只有每一操作数都具有布尔值 0 时，其结果才具有布尔值 0，=logical add）
orthicon 正摄像管，正析像管，直线性光电显像管（=orthiconoscope）
orthiconoscope 正析像管（简称 orthicon）
orthocenter 垂心
orthodox 传统的，正常的，正统的，传统的；一般认为正当的，习俗

的，惯例的；通行的，通用的

orthodox car 传统汽车，普通汽车

orthodox production tooling 用传统生产工具加工

orthodox test 正规试验法（= ortho-test）

orthogon 矩形，长方形

orthogonal ①正交的，垂直的，直角的，矩形的 ②正交，直交

orthogonal level transducer 液面式垂直度传感器，水平式垂直传感器

orthogonal test design 正交试验设计（安排多因数试验方案的数学方法。运用"正交表"来设计试验方案，并按数理统计方法分析试验数据，以减少试验次数）

orthograph 正视图

orthographic ①直线的，直角的 ②用直线投射的，用直线画的 ③正视的，正交的

orthographic design interpretation （车身造型设计草案的）正投影图样说明（指设计草案的整体布置草图，见 package drawing）

orthographic drawing 正投影图

orthographic projection 正投影，正交射影

orthographic view 正视图

orthometric drawing 正视画法

orthopaedic technology 整形技术，矫形技术

orthorhombic structure 斜方晶结构，正交晶结构

ortho-test 正规试验法，标准试验法（= orthodox-test）

ORVR 车载燃油蒸气回收（装置）（on board refueling vapor recovery 的简称，如：储存燃油系产生的蒸气，再送回发动机燃用的活性炭罐等）

Os 锇（osmium）

OSAC system （[美] Chrysler 的节气门区真空孔引出的）孔真空点火提前控制系（一种 NO_x 控制系，orifice spark advance control system 的简称，根据节气门区的真空度，即发动机负荷的变化调节点火提前角，减少 NO_x 排放的系统）

OSAC valve （节气门区真空孔引出的）孔真空点火提前控制阀（orifice spark advance control valve 的简称）

OS characteristic 过渡转向特性（oversteering characteristic 的简称）

oscillate ①振动，摆动，振荡 ②示波

oscillating arm 见 swing arm ③

oscillating axle （一种独立悬架）摆动桥（见 oscillating drive axles 和 swing axle）

oscillating axle shaft （独立悬架）摆动式半轴

oscillating cam 摇臂（见 rocker cam）

oscillating circuit 振荡电路（亦称 oscillation circuit 或 vibrative circuit，一般指由电容器和线圈组成的闭路电路，利用电容器充-放电和线圈的电磁感应，在电路中产生往复流动的振荡电流）

oscillating control servomechanism 振荡控制伺服机构

oscillating curve 振动曲线

oscillating dipole 振动偶极子

oscillating drive axles 摆动式驱动桥（一种独立悬架断开式驱动桥，左、右桥壳及半轴可绕桥中心件上、下摆动，以提高整车通过性、平顺性及操纵稳定性）

oscillating load 波动的载荷（= oscillatory load）

oscillating motor 摆动（式油）马达，摆动油缸（见 oscillatory motor）

oscillating movement 摆动，摆振（= oscillatory motion）

oscillating pickup ignition system 振荡传感型点火系（无触点式点火系的别称，简称 OPUS，一般指由定

时转子、产生电火信号的传感器组件和点火信号整形、放大的电子模块等取代断电器触点及其凸轮的电子点火器）

oscillating piston pin （固定在连杆小头的）半浮式活塞销

oscillating pump 摆动泵

oscillating tooth （活齿行星齿轮传动机构中的）活齿［与内齿圈或针轮啮合，并能在活齿架的孔中作往复或回转运动的构件，有滚珠（ball）活齿、滚子（roller）活齿、推杆（rush rod）活齿和组合（compound）活齿等多种］

oscillating tooth carrier 活齿架［活齿按圆周方向分布在其孔（或槽）中并能在其孔中作往复和滚转运动的盘架］

oscillating tooth gear 活齿轮（由活齿和活齿架组成的齿轮）

oscillating tooth gear drive mechanism with small tooth difference 活齿少齿差齿轮传动机构（由齿数差很少的内齿圈与活齿轮组成的齿轮副和偏心元件组成的传动机构）

oscillating tooth gear pair 活齿轮副（由内齿圈与活齿轮组成的齿轮副）

oscillating type 摆动式，摇动式（如：固定于连杆小头内，而可在活塞销座孔内摆动的半浮动式活塞锁）

oscillating warning lamp 摆动式警告灯（灯芯按某一固定角度摆动的警告灯）

oscillation ①振荡，振动，波动，脉动，颤动，来回摆动②示波③振幅

oscillation amplitude ①振（荡）幅（度）②摆（动）幅（度）

oscillation at a point ①在一点上的振荡②在一点上的振幅

oscillation constant 振荡常数

oscillation counter 振荡计数器

oscillation cycle 振荡周期，振动周期（亦称 oscillation period）

oscillation frequency 振荡频率

oscillation generator 振荡发生器，振荡信号发生器（= oscillar）

oscillation in the pitch mode （汽车）纵倾型振动

oscillation in the roll mode （汽车）侧倾型振动

oscillation node 摆动结

oscillation period 振荡周期

oscillation pickup 振荡传感器

oscillator ①振荡器，振（动）子②断续器，振荡信号发生器，振荡器（= oscillation generator）

oscillatory circuit 振荡电路

oscillatory discharge 振荡放电

oscillatory hop （车轮等的）跳振（亦称 oscillatory jumping）

oscillatory instability 振荡不稳定性（给汽车一个小而短暂的扰动或控制输入时，汽车的响应振幅总是增大的，且在工作点附近来回摆动的汽车响应特性）

oscillatory load 波动载荷（= oscillating load）

oscillator(y) motion 摆动

oscillatory motor 摆动（式）液压马达（亦称 osillating motor，swing motor 或 oscillating actoator，指其输出轴在360°范围以内作往复回转摆动的执行器。将流体能量转变为机械转矩，有叶轮式和活塞式两大类）

oscillatory system 振动系统，振动装置

oscillector 振荡频率选择器

osciliation damping 摆动阻尼，振荡衰减

oscillight 显像管电视接收管

oscillistor 半导体振荡器

oscillogram 示波图，波形图

oscillograph 示波器，示波仪

oscillograph (ic) tube 示波管

oscillograph vibrator （光线）示波

器振子
oscilloprobe 示波器测试头
oscilloscope ①示波管②示波器
oscilloscope record （故障诊断仪等的）波形记录，示波图，波形图（亦称 oscilloscope pattern）
oscilloscope test （汽车发动机的）示波器试验
oscmium 锇（Os）
oscp 示波器（oscilloscope 的简称）
O₂ sensor 氧传感器 [= oxygen sensor, 亦称 λ-sensor 或 lambda sensor, 测定废气中氧含量的传动器，用于三元催化转化空燃比控制系统，目前用得最多的有氧化锆（ZrO_2）传感器与二氧化钛（TiO_2）传感器两种，前者将废气中氧分子含量转换为电压的变化输出，后者则是转化为电阻变化，但它与电子控制模块相接的负极也同样是电压变化。氧传感器的工作温度范围 300～850℃，氧传感器的正常输出信号电压随混合气成分的不同在 300～800mV 之间，亦说在 100～800mV 或 100～900mV 之间变化，其中 450mV 或 450～500mV 称为闭路控制模式的固定点"set point"，或称参考电压值"refrent value"，中心电压值"centre value"等。当氧传感器的输出电压或其负极电压为 450mV 或 450～500mV 时，表明可燃混合气的空燃比在理论空燃比范围内，超过该值时表示混合气变浓，低于该值时表示混合气变稀，电子控制模块根据氧传感器的信号及时增减喷油量，调节空燃比，将它限制在理论空燃比附近，即 λ = 1.0～1.05 附近。三元催化转化空燃比控制系统一般装有 1 个、两个或三个氧传感器，有的按顺序称为第一、第二氧传感器"O_2 senser 1, O_2 sensor 2"或按位置称为左、右氧传感器"O_2 sensor right 或 left"，

第三个大都是附加的辅助氧传感器"auxiliary O_2 sensor"]
O₂ sensor checker （确认氧传感器功能是否完好的）氧传感器检测仪
OSHA ［美］（汽车）乘员安全与卫生管理局（见 Occupational Safety and Health Administration）
O₂ S heater （加热型）氧传感器的加热装置（O_2 sensor heater 的简称）
OSI 开放（型）系统互联（见 open systems interconnection）
osmotic pressure 渗透压力，渗透压强，浓差压
OSS ①输出速度传感器（output speed senser 的简称）②输出轴转速传感器（output shaft speed sensor 的简称）
Oss sensor 输出轴转速传感器（output shaft speed sensor）
OTC 臭氧运输委员会（见 Ozone Transport Commission）
OTC monitor （美国）Owatonnd Tool 公司出产的汽车电子系统故障诊断-解码仪
Otg 车外温度计，车外大气温度表（outdoor 或 outside temperature gauge 的简称）
OTIS 顶置屏显式行车信息系统（overhead travel information system 的简称，由 PCM，BCM 等提供下列数据，在 OTIS 的显示屏上显示：①车内外温度②平均油耗③瞬时油耗④已行驶时间⑤已行驶距离⑥剩余燃油尚能行驶的距离。此外 OTIS 还显示行车地图）
OTN 开放型传输网络（open transport network 的简称，一种基于光纤技术建立的传输系统，可在广阔的地域上快速、可靠传输语音、数据、视频等不同类型的信息，只要符合其相关标准设计接口卡的设备都可毫无限制地互联，是一种灵活的支持多协议的开放式传输网）

OTO 外廓尺寸（见 out-to-out）

OTS 机油温度传感器（oil temperature sensor 的简称）

Otto [德] 奥托（Nicholas August Otto 1832～1891 年。1862 年制成一台二冲程常压煤气机，1864 年与工程师 Langen 合作创建世界第一个内燃机制造厂，1876 年研制成四冲程点燃式煤气机，整体紧凑，热效率高，为内燃机汽车的发展创造了条件）

Otto cycle 奥托循环（等容循环，等容加热循环，由绝热压缩、等容加热、绝热膨胀、等容排热组成，亦称 constant volume cycle，见 Otto）

Otto cycle thermal efficiency 奥托循环热效率 $[=1-(1/\varepsilon^{k-1})$，式中：$\varepsilon$—压缩比；$k$—工质气体绝对指数]

Otto-engined car 汽油机轿车

ounce 英两,盎司[质量单位,常衡中：代号 oz，1 oz = 0.0625 磅 = 28.35 g = 0.567 市两 = 0.076009 磅（金、药）= 0.912 英两（金、药）；金、药衡中：1 英两（金、药）= 1/12 磅（金、药），1 英两（金、药）= 1.09714 英两（常）= 0.83326 磅（金、药）= 0.068525 磅（常）= 31.0873 克，参见 avoirdupois weight 及 troy weights]

out ①（线路的）输出，出口 ②外部的，外表的；断开的，脱离的

outage ①排出孔，排气孔，出口 ②损漏，泄漏，漏损量，储运中的损耗 ③在工作中的停顿，中断，停机，运转中断；停电；断火 ④（发动机关闭后）油箱内的剩余燃料 ⑤（油罐、油槽内为了液体膨胀的）预留容积

out amplifier 输出放大器

outboard 外部的，外面的，车外的

outboard brake 外置式制动器（指装在轮毂上或靠近轮毂的制动器，相对 inboard brake 而言）

outboard (coil) spring and damper assembly （某些赛车在车身外的）外伸式（螺旋）弹簧-减振器总成

outboard component 车外附件（如：后视镜等突出车身外的附件）

outboard contre pente （车轮轮辋轮廓的）凹陷（简称 CP，指轮辋轮胎圈座呈凹形）

outboard flat hump （车轮轮辋轮廓的）平峰（简称 FH，指轮辋轮胎圈座呈平缓凸边形）

outboard flat pente （车轮轮辋轮廓的）平陷（简称 FP，指轮辋轮胎圈座呈平缓凹陷形）

outboard round hump （车轮轮辋轮廓的）圆峰（简称 RH，指轮辋轮胎圈座呈圆峰状凸边）

outboard support 外伸支架，托架，悬臂支架

outboard universal joint （独立悬架车桥的）半轴外侧万向节（与车轮连接的万向节）

outbound traffic 出境交通，外向交通

outburst 爆发，突爆

outcome ①结果，后果 ②产量，输出（量）③出口，排气口

outcoming signal 输出信号

outdated 旧式的，过时的，陈旧的

outdoor 室外的，露天的

outdoor exposure test 野外暴露试验

outdoor temperature gauge 室外温度计，车外温度表（简称 otg 亦称 outside temperature gauge）

outdoor weathering test 室外（大气条件作用下的）自然老化试验，室外自然时效试验

outdrive 超越；超车

outer-band brake 外带式制动器

outer bearing 外轴承

outer brake 外蹄式制动器，外带式制动器

outer bulb （气体放电灯的）玻璃灯泡，玻璃泡（亦称 outer envelope）

outer case of seal 油封（金属）外壳

outer casing ①外壳②外胎

outer circular road 外环路（在郊区环绕城市的道路）

outer clutch drum （转向）离合器外鼓

outer cone （火焰的）外锥，外层

outer cone distance （锥齿轮的）外锥距（指其分锥顶点沿分锥母线至背锥的距离）

outer connection （立体交叉左转弯的）外接匝道

outer cover ①外胎②外套，外罩

outer covering 蒙皮，外部涂层

outer cylinder （双向作用筒式减振器的）外缸筒

outer dead centre ①外顶点，外止点②（水平对置式发动机，偶尔也用于表示单缸发动机的）上死点，上止点

outer diameter 外径（简称 OD，= external diameter）

outer drum （制动器、离合器等的）外鼓

outer electrode ①（火花塞的）侧电极，接地电极（= earth electrode）②（分电器盖内的）旁电极（= outer terminal）

outer extremities 外形尺寸极限，轮廓极限

outer face 外端面

outer flexible tube （操纵索的）柔性外套管

outer guide （弹簧）外导管

outer head light （四灯制双前大灯中的）外侧前大灯

outer housing 外壳

outer jacket 外套筒，外套，外壳套，外壳

outer oil seal （转子发动机的）外油封（常用"O"形密封环，装在转子侧面，内油封的外方）

outer panel （客车车身）蒙皮（亦称 skin，最外层的板件）

outer planet gear 外行星齿轮（复式行星齿轮机构中与内齿圈和内行星齿轮啮合的行星齿轮）

outer race （滚动轴承）外座圈，外圈（亦称 outer ring）

outer roof bow 车顶外部弧拱

outer rotating body （单纯旋转发动机的）旋转缸体（见 SIM）

outer rotor （位于）外侧（的）旋转体（如：①内、外转子式旋轮线机油泵的外转子②电动机位于定子之外的外转子③单纯旋转发动机的旋转缸体等）

outer rotor type direct drive in-wheel motor 4WD 外转子式轮内电动机直接驱动型四轮驱动

outer rotor type electric wheel 转子外置型电动车轮（轮毂内的电动机转子位于定子绕组之外，直接驱动车轮旋转，见 inner rotor type electric wheel）

outer rubber cable （电线的）橡胶外套管

outer separator ①外分隔带（限制进入干道和服务性道路之间的分隔带）②外隔套，外隔板

outer shaft 外轴

outer shield 外部保护，屏蔽，遮挡件（如：外罩，外壳，外板，铠装等）

outer sill （轿车车身和货车驾驶室的）门槛（亦称 side sill，轿车车身侧部连接前、中、后柱的下边梁；货车驾驶室车门下方地板侧部的边梁）

outer skin 外蒙皮，外壳

outer spiral angle （锥齿轮的）大端螺旋角（其齿线在齿轮大端的螺旋角）

outer stay 外撑条，外拉条
outer steered angle （转向时）外侧车轮的回转角
outer steering lock （转向圆）外侧车轮最大转角
outer support 外支架
outer terminal （分电器盖内的）旁电极（每一个旁电极与一个火花塞相连接）
outer tire 外侧轮胎（＝outside tire）
outer tower （分电器盖上的火花塞高压线）插座（每缸一个，与分电器盖内的旁电极对应，因呈塔形，故名）
outer tread 胎面，胎面外层
outer valve spring 气门外弹簧
outer wrap 外壳，外罩，外层，包覆物，外裹层
outer yoke （凸块式万向节的）外凸块叉（见tork yoke）
outfit ①（成套）设备，装备，装置，仪器，用具，备用工具，附属装置，备件②供给，准备，配备
outflow 流出，外流；流出物
outflow conditions 出口气流参数，出口液流参数；流出条件
outflow resistance 流出阻力
outflow wheel （液力传动的）离心式叶轮
outgoing ①卸任的，离职的②向外的，离开的，离境的③换掉的，不再用的
outing vehicle 游览车
outlast the life of car 超过汽车的规定使用寿命
outlet ①排气，排出，输出②排气口，排出口，出口，排出管③引出线，引出端④出口接管⑤电源插座
outlet angle 出口方向角，排出管道斜角，排水道斜角
outlet branch 排出支管
outlet cam （凸轮轴）排气门凸轮
outlet cock 出口开关，排放开关

outlet connection 出口接管
outlet elbow 排出管弯管
outlet fitting 出口接头
outlet hole 排出孔
outlet (hot) air bonnet （暖风）出风口盖
outlet manifold 排出歧管（如：排气歧管）
outlet pipe 排出管
outlet side 排出侧，排出端
outlet slots blind （发动机冷却系节温器的）旁通阀（冷却水温升高时，关闭通向水泵的旁通孔道，亦称 bypass valve）
outlet tank （发动机冷却系横流式散热器的）出水箱（相当于下流式散热器的下水箱）
outlet temperature 排气温度，出口温度
outlet triangle （叶轮）出口速度三角形（如：变矩器涡轮出口速度三角形）
outlet union 排气管联管节，输出管联管节
outlet valve ①排气门，排气阀②排出阀，排出门
outlet velocity 出口速度；排出速度，流出速度（＝output velocity）
outlet water hose 出水软管
outlier ①脱离本体的，驶出车群的，脱离大多数的（事、物）②（试验测定值中的）废值，离散值③分离物，离层
outliers ①脱离本体的，驶出车群的，脱离大多数的（事、物）②（试验测定值中的）废值，离散值③分离物，离层
outline ①外形，轮廓②草图，略图；示意图，平面图③大纲，提纲，概要
outline drawing 外形图，轮廓图
outline of tooth 齿外形，齿廓
outmove 在速度方面超过于…，在

速度方面优越于…

out -of-action 不能工作的,不起作用的,无法使用的,不能运转的(= inoperative, out of operation, out of service)

out -of-adjustment 失调的

out -of-alignment 未对准的(如:不同轴的,偏斜的,定位不当的)

out -of-balance 不平衡的,失去平衡的

out -of-balance force 不平衡力

outof center 离中心的

out of control 失控,操纵失灵

out -of-date 过时的,落后的,陈旧的,旧式的,老式的(= out-of-fashion outmoded,不流行的)

out -of-flat ①平面度,不平直度 ②不平的,不平直的

out -of-gas (汽车等)汽油用完,燃料用尽

out -of-gear 脱离啮合的(亦称 out-of-mesh)

out -of-line 偏移的,不在同一直线上的

out -of-phase ①异相②异相的

out of plumb 不垂直(的)(= off plumb)

out -of-position 位置不正确的

out -of-position occupant 离座乘员(指不在乘坐位置或常规乘坐位置上的乘员)

out of repair 失修

out -of-round 失圆的

out -of-service inspection 停运检查,停机检查(暂停使用以供检查)

out -of-service time 非营运时间,非工作时间(如:汽车停驶、封存或送交修理等时间)

out -of shape 失去正确(几何)形状的

out -of-sight 在视野之外的

out -of-size 失去正确尺寸的,失去尺寸精度的,超出尺寸公差的

out -of-step ①不同步的,不合拍的 ②失调,时差,不合拍

out of (the) reach 达不到的

out of tolerance 超出公差范围以外

out of tune 失调,调整不当,调整不良

out of whack (运转)失常

output ①产品,产物,产量②输出,出产,传出(热量),输出值③输出功率④(电路的)输出端,输出信号,输出电流⑤工作容量,工作能力,生产能力,运输能力⑥生产率,生产效率⑦(电子计算机的)计算结果

output amplifier 输出(信号)放大器

output ballast resistor 见 ballast resistor

output characteristics 输出特性(曲线)

output circuit with drive stage 带驱动级的输出电路

output coefficient (功率)输出系数

output configuration (of binary circuit) (二进制电路的)输出组态(亦称 output pattern,指在给定瞬间,输出端上低电平和高电平的组合)

output current 输出电流

output current drift (线性放大器的)输出电流漂移(在其他条件不变时,输出电流的变化量)

output current operating range (线性放大器的)输出电流工作范围(使放大器功能符合规范规定的输出电流范围)

output data 输出数据

output disable time (集成电路特性中的三态输出的)输出禁止时间(指三态输出从规定的有效低或高电平转变为高阻态,即:截止态时,在输入和输出电压波形上规定

参考点之间的时间间隔）

output driver （电子控制系统控制模块中的）输出驱动器（微处理器发出的执行信号，如：喷油指令时，是先将指令发送至输出驱动器，然后由输出驱动器向执行器，即喷油器的电磁阀继电器发送一个接地信号，于是喷油器开始喷油。控制喷油器的输出驱动器称 injector driver "喷油器驱动器"）

output efficiency 输出效率

output element 输出件

output enable time （集成电路特性中的三态输出的）输出允许时间（当三态输出由高阻态，即截止态转变到规定的有效高或低电平时，在输入和输出电压波形上规定参考点间的时间间隔）

output energy 输出能量

output equation 输出方程（在现代控制理论中，状态变量不一定都是可见值，但输出量必须是能观察到的响应值，状态变量与输出量之间的函数关系称为输出方程）

output expander 输出扩展电路

output flange 输出轴突缘（out put shaft flange 的简称）

output governor 输出功率调节器

output impedance 输出阻抗

output-input ratio 输出输入比

output loading capability （双极型数字电路的）输出负载能力（亦称 output loading factor "输出负载系数"，指某一个规定输出端的最大输出电流与被选作参考负载的特定电路的输入电流之比）

output loading factor 输出负载率，输出负载系数（见 output loading capability）

output mechanism 输出机构

output modulator valve （ABS 压力调节器的通向蓄油器的回油路内的）出油阀（由 ABS 控制模块控制的常闭式电磁阀，在正常制动和 ABS 保压和升压阶段，该阀关闭，降压阶段该阀开启）

output noise voltage 输出噪声电压（指电压调节器输出端上仅由器件产生的噪声电压）

output per day 日产量，日生产能力，日生产率

output per litre （发动机的）升（输出）功率

output power 输出功率（＝power output）

output pulsation 输出波动，输出脉冲

output pump 输出泵

output rate 产量，生产率（＝productive rate）

output resistance 输出电阻

output shaft 输出轴（如：变速器的第二轴）

output shaft flange 输出轴法兰，输出轴突缘

output shaft speed sensor 输出轴转速传感器（简称 OSS）

output signal 输出信号

outputs of state （系统）状态的输出量（如：阻尼系统的状态输出量是位移）

output speed 输出速度

output terminal 输出接线柱，A 接线柱

output torque 输出转矩，输出轴转矩

output transient overshoot voltage （电压调节器的）输出瞬态过冲电压（在任一外加规定阶跃变化后，瞬态输出电压峰值与输出电压最终稳定值之差）

output variable 输出变量

output velocity 出口速度（＝outlet velocity）

output voltage 输出电压

output voltage drift 输出电压漂移

（在其他条件不变时，输出电压的变化量）

output voltage operating range （线性放大器的）输出电压工作范围（放大器功能符合规范规定的输出电压范围）

output voltage swing 输出电压摆幅

out race ①（球笼式万向节的）钟形壳（其一端为花键短轴，另一端为内表面开有纵槽形钢球滚道的钟形件，joint housing with out race 的简称）②（球轴承的）外圈 ③外跑道

out rear wheel arch （轿车车身）后轮外罩板

outrigger ①悬臂梁，支架，托架 ②（起重设备的）动臂，悬臂 ③汽车试验时的防翻装置（常用复数）

outrigger bracket （装在货车纵梁外侧面上的）梁外撑架，外撑架，车身底板纵枕梁架（用于支撑车身底板纵枕梁，并将车身质量传至纵梁外侧面，简写 outrigger）

outrun 超越，超过，胜过

outset ①开关，开端，开始，最初 ②外偏距（见 outset wheel）

outset wheel 外偏距车轮（指轮辋中心线位于轮辐安装面外侧的车轮，其轮辐安装面至轮辋中心线的距离称外偏距，亦称 outset dish wheel）

outside ①外部，外表，外观，极端 ②外部的，外观的，外表的；室外的；极端的，最大限度的

outside air 外界空气

outside appearance 外形，外观，外表，外貌

outside band brake 外带内紧式制动器

outside broadcasting van 广播车

outside calipers 外卡钳，外卡规，外圆卡尺

outside circle （齿轮）齿顶圆；外圆，外周圆

outside cone 外圆锥，（锥齿轮）齿顶锥

outside connecting rod 外连杆

outside diameter 外径（= external diameter）

outside dimensions 外部尺寸（简称 OD）

outside door handle 车门外把手

outside door panel 车门蒙皮（= door skin）

outside drawing 外视图，外形图

outside edge 外缘

outside engine noise （发动机）机外噪声

outside excitation 他激（= separate excitation）

outside frame 外框架

outside gauge 外径量规

outside micrometer 外径千分尺

outside-mounted brake 安装在车轮外侧的制动器

outside pitch line length （齿轮）外周节直线长度

outside race （滚动轴承）外（座）圈

outside radius 外半径（简称 OR）

outside real-view mirror 外后视镜

outside real-view mirror adjustment control 外后视镜调节操纵件（控制外后视镜调节装置的操纵件）

outside real-view mirror electric heater control 外后视镜电加热器操纵件（控制外后视镜电加热器工作的操纵件）

outside screw thread 外螺纹（= external thread）

outside shell 外壳

outside shoe brake 外蹄式制动器

outside spark gap 外火花间隙（用来防止火花塞电极间积炭引起的短路）

outside surface 外表面

outside tire （装在双轮胎车轮的）外侧轮胎

outside view 外观图，外形图

outside wheel turning angle 外侧转向轮转向角（外转向轮轴与车辆前轴的交角）

outsized vehicle 特大型车辆，超重型载货车辆（= oversize vehicle）

out spider （燃气轮机）排气口辐射式导流栅

outstanding features 显著的特征，突出的特点

outstrip ①超过，超越②优于；胜速

outstroke （发动机）排气冲程

outtake 排气管，排出管；通风的，排气的，抽气的

out-to-out 外廓尺寸，全长，全宽，外到外（简称OTO）

out-to-out tire width 两侧车轮轮胎外侧之间的宽度（轮式车辆车辙的外侧宽度，= outside-to-outside tire width）

out-to-out track width 两边履带外侧之间的宽度（履带式车辆车辙外侧宽度，= outside-to-outside track-width）

outward ①外部的，外形的，表面的；向外的，外出的，外来的；客观的②外部，外形，外表

outward camber （汽车的）车轮外倾，车轮外倾角（简称camber）

outward flange 外突缘，外法兰

outward-flow turbine 离心式涡轮（机）

outward sign 外部征兆，外部信号

outworn 磨损的

oval ①椭圆的，卵形的②椭圆；椭圆场地，卵形弧，卵形物，卵形线

oval cam 椭圆形凸轮

oval countersunk rivet 椭圆埋头铆钉

oval fillister-head screw 凹槽椭圆头螺钉

oval flange 椭圆突缘

oval-ground skirt （靠模）磨削的（活塞）椭圆形裙部

oval head valve 椭圆头气门

ovality 椭圆度，椭圆性，卵形度

ovalization 变成椭圆形，不圆

ovalizing deflection 椭圆变形

ovalizing stress （薄壁管）椭圆变形的应力

oval-section piston 椭圆形活塞（简称 oval piston，见 cam ground piston）

oval side rail （X形车架的）椭圆形断面纵梁，椭圆形断面大梁

OVC cap （电动汽车或混合动力汽车蓄电系统的）车外充电能力（off-vehicle charging capacity 的简称，指具有利用车外电源充电的能力）

oven 炉，焙箱

oven ag(e)ing test 炉内加热老化试验；炉内时效试验

overage 过多的，过剩的，超出的，逾龄的，超过正常使用期限的；陈旧的，过老化的；经人工时效的

overage equipment 陈旧设备，超过使用期的设备

overall diameter 最大直径；外直径，外形直径，外直径，外径

overall dimensions 总尺寸，最大尺寸，外形尺寸，极限尺寸，临界尺寸，轮廓尺寸

overall efficiency 总效率（理论功率与轴功率之比）

overall gear ratio 总传动比，总速比（如：汽车发动机转速与驱动车轮转速比）

overall heat transfer coefficient 热通导系数，热通导率（设固定壁面间两流体的温差为 Δt，所通过的热量为 Q，则热通导系数 $K = Q/\Delta t$，亦称 overall heat transmission coefficient）

overall height 总高，全高，外廓高度

overall length of trailer 挂车全长（带牵引杆）

overall projected vehicle area 车辆

总投影面积

overall size 轮廓尺寸，外廓尺寸

overall steering ratio 转向系总传动比

overall test 总体试验，综合试验，总试验

overall (travel) speed 综合车速（路段内车辆总行程除以总时间所得之商，总时间包括行车及停车时间）

overall travel time （汽车）总行驶时间，总旅行时间（包括道路上的停车及受阻时间，但不包括路外停车及受阻时间）

overall understeer （汽车的）总不足转向量，不足转向总量（车辆和轮胎的各种参数，引起的不足转向的总量，= total understeer）

overall view 全貌，全景

overall width 全宽，外形尺寸宽度，总宽度

overall width at center line of front axle （车辆）在前桥中心轴线平面（即过前桥轴线而垂直于地面之平面）内之全宽

overall width at center line of rear axle （车辆）在后桥中心轴线平面（即过后桥轴线而垂直于地面的平面）内之全宽

over-all yield 总产量

over-and-under controller 过度和不足两极控制器

overarm ①横杆，横臂 ②悬梁，悬臂

overaxle pipe （从车桥上方绕过的）拱形排气尾管，拱形管（亦称 kick-up pipe）

overbalance ①失去平衡，不平衡 ②使失去平衡，超出平衡

overbending 过度弯曲

overbored engine （修理后）具有加大尺寸的汽缸的发动机

overbore kit （修理用）加大尺寸的成套汽缸套、活塞和活塞环

overbridge 跨线桥（天桥，过街桥）

overburden ①超载 ②使超载

overcar aerial 车顶天线（= overcar antenna, top aerial, top antenna, roof aerial, roof antenna）

overcenter 超出中心

overcenter multiple-disc wet power-take off clutch 动力输出轴的偏心自锁常开多片湿式离合器

overcharge ①超载，过载，过负荷 ②过量充电，过量充气

overcharge life-test （蓄电池的）过充电寿命试验（在规定条件下，反复过充电，试验蓄电池的耐久性）

overcompensate 补偿过度

over-cooled 过冷的

over correction 过调量，过度修正（量）

overcrank protection divice （起动度运转）过度运转保护装置（当起动机连续运转超过某规定时间，如30秒时，该装置即自动断开起动机电路）

overcrank thermostat （起动机）过驱动保护装置的恒温器（当起动机因运转时间超过规定值而温度上升时，恒温器将起动机电路断开）

over-crossing （立体交叉的）上跨交叉

overcure 过度硫化

over-current 过量电流（超过允许值的大电流）

overdamped 过度阻尼的

over discharge 过度放电（指蓄电池放电电压降到规定电压以下，仍继续放电）

over-distance 超远（超过规定距离的）

overdrive ①（汽车的）超速行驶（指挂高速挡后，汽车以高于直接挡的速度行驶）②超速挡（$i=$ 输出转速/输入转速 >1，亦称 over-top gear）③装在主变速器和后桥间实现超速挡行驶的副变速器④挂超速挡,挂超速挡行驶⑤负担过重,使用过度

overdrive automatic switch off 超速挡自动脱开开关（一般装在加速踏板下,当将加速踏板踩到底时,该开关接通,加速挡脱开,自动转入主变速挡工作）

overdrive axle 超速传动轴

overdrive case 变速器超速挡箱

overdrive gear （变速器）①超速挡②带超速挡的变速器③超速挡传动

over drive gear pressure switch （电子控制自动变速器的）超速挡压力开关（换超速挡后,将超速挡液压信号反馈给电子控制模块,简称O/D pressure switch）

overdrive gear ratio 超速挡传动比（= overspeed gear ratio）

overdrive indicator（light）超速挡指示灯（挂上超速挡后,该指示灯亮,脱开超速挡时发亮的指示灯,称 overdrive off indicator light）

overdrive lever ①超速挡换挡杆②超速挡拨叉

overdrive manual switch off 超速挡手动脱挡杆,超速挡手动脱挡开关

overdrive manual switch on 超速挡手动挂挡开关,超速挡手动挂挡杆

over-drive relay 超速挡继电器（自动变速器中控制超速挡电磁阀的继电器）

over-drive select swith 超速挡选择开关（指接通超速挡继电器电流的开关,一般装在变速杆上）

over-drive selenoid （自动变速器内的）超速挡电磁阀（控制超速挡油路通断的电磁阀）

overdrive top gear （汽车变速器的）超速挡（见 overdrive②）

overdrive transmission 超速挡变速器（最高挡位为输出转速高于输入转速的超速挡的变速器。超速挡可装在变速器内,亦可在主变速器后加装一超速挡副变速器）

overestimate 估计过高,评价过高

over exposue ①曝光过久,过度曝光,感光过强②暴露过度,过度暴露

overfill limiting valve （燃油箱的）燃油加注过满防止阀（燃油加注量限制阀）

over-flood 流量过大,流出量过多

overflow ①溢流②溢流孔

overflow alarm 溢流警告信号

overflow hose 溢流软管

overflow tank （密闭式冷却系散热箱的）溢水箱,溢流箱（其作用为暂时集存从散热器溢出的水或水蒸气,发动机变冷时再送入散热器内,= surge tank）

overflow tube 溢流管（= overflow pipe）

overflow valve 溢流阀

overfreight 超载（超过规定装载量）

overfueling （给汽缸）供油过多,混合气过浓

overhang ①伸出部,突出部,悬臂②伸出量（特指：a 汽车的最前端点或最后端点与前轴或后轴中心线的距离,分别称前悬或后悬,简称OH, oh, 见 front overhang, rear overhang; b 装载的货物超出车身后端的长度,亦称 load overhang）③外伸,悬置,悬架

overhang beam （起重机）动臂,悬臂梁

overhanging ①悬臂的,悬架的,悬垂的,外悬的②悬臂长度,伸出量

overhanging pendant switch 外伸悬垂式按钮

overhanging spring ①上置式钢板弹簧（装在车架上的钢板弹簧）②悬臂式钢板弹簧［见 cantilever（type）spring 及 guarter elliptic spring］

overhanging support 外伸支架，托架，悬臂式支架

overhang of towing attachment （汽车的全挂车）牵引装置悬伸（量）

overhang wheel 外伸轮，悬臂车轮（如：捷克斯柯达独梁式货车的后轮）

overhaul ①[美]解体检修（通过解体、清洗、检验、修理、装配、调整、试验等作业，使汽车恢复规定性能，类似我国的大修，＝英国的 unscrew）②仔细检查，彻底检查 ③超过运输免费标准

overhaul distance ①（汽车的）大修间隔里程②超过免费标准的运距

overhauled 经过大修的，经过解体检修的

overhaul instruction 大修作业规程，大修作业指南

overhaul life 大修寿命（大修间隔里程，参见 overhaul period）

overhaul period 大修间隔期（车辆的大修间隔里程，大修周期，＝time between overhauls, overhaul life）

overhaul yardage 以立方码计的运输量

overhead 高架的，架空的，头上的，上跨的

overhead bridge 天桥

overhead cam belt 顶置式凸轮轴驱动带

overhead cam design （发动机的）顶置凸轮轴结构

overhead camshaft ①顶置凸轮轴（简称 OHC, OC, 装在气门上方，汽缸盖上的凸轮轴）②顶置凸轮轴结构

overhead console 头顶控制台（位于车厢顶篷驾驶者头顶区域的装有按钮、旋钮等的副控制台）

overhead drive 上置驱动，上置式传动装置（如：蜗杆置于涡轮上方的传动）

overhead electrode （火花塞）侧电极（＝side electrode）

overhead entrance 顶部入口（例如装甲车、坦克车等）

overhead exhaust valve 顶置式排气门

overhead fingertip reach 车厢地板至乘客向上伸直的手臂指尖的距离

overhead fraction 初馏分（＝first fraction）

overhead grasping reach 人手抓握高度（手臂向上伸直后手掌可抓握的高度范围）

overhead hoist rails 高架起重轨道

overhead hose reel set （维修厂润滑用）吊式加油软管卷筒总成

overhead inlet valve 顶置式进气门

overhead obstruction 限制运输车辆外形高度的架空障碍物

overhead parcel rack （客车的）车顶行李架

overhead passage way 高架通道（①指城市道路上的横跨天桥等②泛指高架道路）

overhead requirement 内务要求（指计算机控制系统用于系统自身运转而不是用作业所需的时间、硬件、软件和操作）

overhead rocker gear 顶置式气门摇臂机构

overhead type vehicle 平头车（＝cab-over-engine vehicle）

overhead valve 顶置式气门（吊装气门，简称 OHV, 参见 drop valve）

overhead valve engine 顶置式气门发动机，顶置式气门式发动机（指气门置于汽缸上部，气门头朝下的发动机＝inverted valve engine, overhead type engine, overhead-poppet engine, 简称 OHV engine, 美称 I-head engine）

overhead valve timing 顶置气门配气

机构，顶置式气门正时机构
overhead weld（ing） 仰焊
overhead worm 上置式蜗杆（蜗杆置于涡轮之上，= overslung worm）
overheat ①过热（指温度超过规定值的上限）②使过热
overheat bit 附加位（在计算机和通信技术中，指不是用于传递信息，而是专供控制或错误检测用的一位）
overheat control （防）过热控制
over heat indicator lamp 过热警报灯
overheating ①过热②特指火花塞过热而产生的自点火现象
overheat test 过热试验（在温度超过规定工作温度上限的条件下进行的试验）
overhight 超高（超过规定高度）
overhung 悬臂的，外伸的，悬架的，吊挂的，悬垂的
overhung mounting 悬臂式支撑
overinflated tyre （充气压力超过规定值的）充气轮胎
overladen 超载的，过载的
overland 陆上的，陆地的；地面的
overland obstruction （水陆两用车辆的）陆上障碍物
overland service （水陆两用汽车）陆地运行（亦称 overland operation）
overland vehicle ①越野车辆，高通过性车辆②陆地车辆
overlap ①搭接，重叠②重叠度，重叠量③搭接部分④（进、排气门的）重叠开启，重叠关闭
overlap angle 重叠角（如：进、排气门重叠开启或关闭期间曲轴的转角）
overlap arc （齿轮啮合的）纵向作用弧（指分别包含同一条齿线各一个端点的两个轴平面所截取的分度圆弧长）
overlap butt 搭接（= lap butt）
overlap period 重叠期
overlapping gate （电子电路电荷转移器件的）交叠栅（相邻电极交叠且彼此绝缘的一种转移栅，见 transfer gate）
overlap ratio （齿轮啮合的）纵向重合度（指其纵向作用角与齿距角的比值）
overlap shift （自动变速器换挡过程中）各挡搭接换挡，重叠换挡（指在换挡过程中同时有一个以上的挡位的转矩传递元件短时间啮合的换挡，即在短时间内有一个以上的挡位啮合的换挡）
overlap valve （液力变速器控制系统的）重叠阀（指在换挡期间，使分离和结合的换挡元件，在短时间内均处于部分接合状态的阀）
overlay ①（多层结构的）表面层，涂复层，覆盖层②外罩③涂，镀，覆盖④堆焊
overlaying welding 堆焊（= built-up welding）
overload ①超载，超重（现象）②超负荷（指发动机超过其满负荷"full lood"的负荷）③过量充电④使超载，使负担过重⑤在过载时断开的
overload ability 超负荷能力，超载能力（亦称 overload capacity）
overload characteristics 超载特性
overload clutch 超载离合器（当超载时自动分离的安全离合器，亦称 overload coupling, release clutch）
overload coupling 超载联轴节（见 overload clutch）
overload failure （由于）超载（造成的）损坏（亦称 overload breakage）
overload force 超载力
overload friction clutch 防超载式摩擦离合器（超载后即开始打滑）
overload indicating system 超载指示系统（超载警报系统）
overload light 过载信号灯

overload margin 过载定额，超载极限，超载余量

overload plug 防过载螺塞（= overload stud）

overload power output rating 过载额定输出功率，允许短时间超载运转的额定功率（= overload rating）

overload protection device 防超载装置

overload relay 过载继电器（简称 OR，= current breaker，当电流超过规定值时，切断电流的装置）

overload release 超载松脱安全器

overload relief valve 超载安全阀

overload shearing clutch 超载切断式离合器

overload spring 过载弹簧（如：载重超过某规定值时起作用的副钢板弹簧，参见 auxiliary spring）

overload stud 防过载螺柱（承受可能出现的过载荷，防止其他元件过载荷，= overload plug，thrust plug）

overload test 超载试验，过载试验

overload trip ①超载自动断开装置 ②超载行驶

overload wear 过载磨损

overlubricate 过量润滑（供给过多的润滑油）

overmaintenance （因机械磨损超过允许限度而造成的）工作量过大的技术维护

overmotoring 装用功率过大的，超过需要的发动机（亦称 overpowering）

overpass ①（立体交叉的）上跨交叉；上跨路，跨线桥，跨线路，上跨道（亦称 overcrossing）②上跨，越过

over pin （节圆直径滚柱测量法用）滚柱

over pin dial 跨针测齿厚仪

overplate ①覆盖层，表面镀层 ②盖板

overplated alloy bearing 镀有减磨合金层的轴瓦

overpressure ①超压，超高压 ②（传感元件可能承受的不致使其输出特性发生永久性变化的）最大规定压力

overpressure control 超压控制，限压控制

overpressure resistant 耐超高压的

overpressure stop 超高压防止装置，超高压防护装置

overprime 起动时燃料加注过多

overrange ①超出额定的界限，超出正常的界限 ②过量程的

overrange protection 防止超出调节范围的装置

overrate ①估计过高，评价过高 ②额定值确定过高，定额过高 ③超过额定值

overreach ①伸得过长 ②超过，渡越 ③延长动作（时间）④普及

over recovery （制动效能）过恢复（热量或水对制动效能的衰退影响消失后，制动效能恢复到大于衰退前的现象）

overregulate 调节过度，过调节

overrich （可燃混合气体）过浓的

over-richness （混合气的）过浓，过浓度

over ride 超控，超程

override linkage 超越控制杆系（指另一套可使基本控制杆系等失效或绕过基本控制杆系进行控制的联动或附加杆系，如：与制动踏板联动的节气门附加控制杆系，踩踏制动踏板时，加速踏板杆系即失效，而使节气门自动关闭）

override pressure 超增压力（见 pressure override）

overrider （汽车保险杠）护杆（美称 humper guard，指装在保险杠两侧的短垂直杆件，防止与其他车辆挤碰时，两车保险杠相互挂卡）

override type ①超越式（见 override

overriding ①占优势的，基本的，压倒的，主要的，重要的，首要的 ②超越，仪器过载

overriding clutch 超越离合器

overrun ①超过，超出，越程，超速（指速度或转速超过规定值，或被驱动方转速或速度超过驱动方）②挂车的车速超过牵引车③（发动机）强制怠速（发动机起制动作用，节气门关闭，由车辆惯性反过来带动发动机旋转，见 overrunning condition）

overrun brake （挂车的）防撞击主车制动器

overrun control valve （涡轮增压系统压缩机吸气道与出气道之间的连通管的）强制怠速控制阀（当节气门关闭，汽车不脱挡滑行，发动机处于强制怠速工况时，该阀开启，出气道输出的压缩气经该连通管又返回吸气道，并由吸气道进入压缩机作短路循环，以保证节气门重新开启，该阀关闭时，增压滞后时间最短）

overrun coupling ①超越式联轴节（被驱动方超过驱动方时，自动打滑）②见 overrun fluid coupling

overrun cut-off ①（发动机）强制怠速工况燃油切断装置（亦称 overrun shut-off, = deceleration fuel cut-off, 节气门关闭，车辆通过传动系反拖发动机运转时切断燃油供给）②超速断油装置（当发动机转速超过某规定值时，切断燃油，以降低其转速，亦称 overrun fuel cutoff）

overrun fluid coupling 超速液力耦合器（亦称 auxiliary fluid coupling, 用于发动机强制怠速运转工况的辅助液力耦合器）

overruning clutch drive starting motor 单向离合器驱动式起动机（使用滚柱式、棘轮式、摩擦片式等单向离合器，一旦发动机起动，转速超过起动机时，便可自动脱开或打滑，从而防止起动机电枢损坏的驱动装置的起动机，旧称超越离合器驱动式起动机）

overruning trailer brake 挂车超速制动器（当挂车速度超过牵引车时，即自动制动，亦称 overrunning type of trailer brake）

overrunning ①（发动机的）超（过规定的最高转）速运转 ②飞车，飞速

overrunning brake ①发动机制动 ②（当挂车车速超过牵引车时起作用的挂车）超速制动器

overrunning clutch 单向离合器（亦称 one way clutch, overrun clutch, free engine clutch, free-wheel clutch, 指只能从一个旋转方向传递转矩，而另一个方向则可自由旋转或打滑的离合器或耦合装置）

overrunning condition 强制怠速状态，发动机制动工况（= engine braking condition, 一般指节气门关闭，车辆由于惯性反过来带动发动机时的工况）

overrunning force （发动机熄火车辆不脱挡滑行时）车轮传给发动机的力

overrunning sprag clutch 楔块式单向离合器（= sprag clutch）

overrun regeneration （某些混合动力车发电-电动两用机的）强制怠速工况能量回收功能（不仅可以在汽车制动-减速时逆转发电回收能量，而且可以在任何情况下只要变速器未挂空挡而车辆处于强制怠速工况时均逆转发电回收能量）

overrun shift （液力变速器的）超限换挡（指在短时间内，节气门开度小于行驶阻力所要求的开度而发生的提前升挡）

Oversea Automotive Club ［美］海外汽车俱乐部（简称 OAC）

overseas-built 国外制造的

overshoot ①（脉冲波形）尖峰，过冲；过冲量 ②过调节，过调量，调节过量，调节过度，调节量过大 ③（汽车阶跃响应试验的）超调量[在阶跃响应试验中，横摆角速度响应的最大值与稳态值之差和稳态值的比值 $\sigma = (r_{max} - r_0)/r_0 \cdot 100\%$，式中：$r_{max}$—横摆角速度响应最大值（°）/s；$r_0$—横摆角速度响应稳态值（°）/s；$\sigma$—横摆角速度超调量，%，见 step response test]

overshoot factor （线性放大器电路特性的）过冲系数（指输入信号阶跃变化之后，输出信号电平相对于最终稳定值的最大偏差与输入信号阶跃变化前后输出信号稳定值之差的绝对值之比）

oversight 疏忽

over-simplification 过简，过度简化

oversize ①加大的（修理）尺寸 ②尺寸过大，超差；带加工裕量的尺寸

oversize bearing 具有加大（修理）尺寸的轴瓦

oversized ①加大尺寸的，加大修理尺寸的 ②尺寸过大的（大于负荷所要求者）

oversize parts 加大（修理用）尺寸零件

overslung 悬于上方的（亦写作 over slung）

overslung frame （装在悬架上的）上悬式车架

over slung type suspension 上置钢板弹簧式悬架（钢板弹簧安装在车架上的悬架形式，见 overhanging spring）

overslung worm 上置式蜗杆（= overhead worm，指安装位置在涡轮上方的蜗杆）

overslung worm transmission 上置蜗杆式传动装置（指蜗杆位于涡轮上方的涡轮—蜗杆传动）

oversnow train 雪地列车（= snow train）

oversnow vehicle 雪地车辆（= snow-going vehicle）

overspeed ①超速（指超过规定的转速或速度）②使超速，使高速运转，超速驾驶

overspeed device 限速器（= speed limit device）

overspeed drive 超速传动，超速挡驱动，超速驾驶（简称 overdrive）

overspeed gear ratio 超速挡传动比（亦称 overdrive gear ratio）

overspeed governor （燃料喷射系的）超速限制器[当发动机转速超过规定的最高转速时，通过机械方式或电动方式切断燃油或（和）空气供给的限速器]

overspeeding 超速行驶，超速运转（指超过规定的速度行驶或运转）

overspeed protection ①防超速装置 ②超速保护（装置）

overspeed signal 超速信号

overspeed test 超速试验

overspeed trip ①超速自动断开机构 ②超速行程

oversquare engine 超方型发动机（径超程发动机，活塞行程小于缸径的发动机）

oversteer 过度转向（特性）（作等速圆周行驶的汽车，若其后较的侧偏 δ_r 大于前轮的侧偏 δ_f，即：$\delta_r > \delta_f$，则称为过度转向）

oversteering car 具有过度转向特性的轿车

overstrain 过度应变，应变过度

overstress 应力过度，过度应力

overstroked engine 长行程发动机（行程缸径比大于1的发动机）

overtaking-prohibited 禁止超车

overtaking vehicle 超车的车辆（= passing vehicle）

over temperature protection system 过热保护系统

over-temperature sensor （当温度超过某规定值时发出传感信号的）超温传感器

over temperature warning system 过热警报装置（当热反应装置的温度超过控制范围时发出警报的装置）

overtension ①过应力，超限应力 ②电压过高 ③紧张过度

over-the-road fuel economy （汽车的）道路燃油经济性（实际行车燃油经济性）

over-the-shoulder belt （汽车乘员的）跨肩安全带

overthin 过度稀释，过稀

overtighten 过度拉紧，过度拧紧

over-top gear 超速挡（见 overdrive ②）

overtorquing （螺纹连接）用过大的转矩拧紧

over-traction 驱动力过大（指驱动力大于轮胎与路面的摩擦力，是导致车轮原地滑转的原因）

overtravel 行程过大，超行程（超越规定的极限行程）

overturn 翻过来，翻转，翻车

overturning couple 翻倾力偶，翻转力矩，倾覆力矩（= overturning moment）

overturning immunity test 抗侧翻试验

overturning limit angle 侧倾极限角［在整车整备质量状态下，用侧倾台向左（或向右）倾斜汽车，直到相反侧的全部车轮离开侧倾台面或车轮开始滑移时，侧倾台面与水平面间所夹的锐角］

overturning moment 翻倾力矩

overturning moment distribution 翻倾力矩分配（翻倾力矩在前、后悬架间分配的百分比）

overturning moment of tire 轮胎翻转力矩（由路面作用在轮胎上的力矩矢量，使轮胎绕纵向轴旋转的分量）

overturning test （运输车辆）翻倾试验，倾翻试验

overvoltage 电压过高，超电压，过电压（电压高于规定值）

overwater operation （水陆两用车辆或气垫车辆）在水面上的行驶（亦称 overwater service）

overwater performance （水陆两用车）水面行驶性能

overwater speed （水陆两用汽车或气垫车的）水面行驶速度

overweight ①过重，超重，超额 ②超重的，超载的，超额的，装载过多的

Owen bridge 欧文电桥（一种交流惠斯通电桥，用来测定层叠铁心感应器中电感的负载系数）

owner 所有者，物主，车主

owner-driver 车主驾驶员，自驾车驾驶员（亦称 my car driver）

owner's handbook 车主手册（随车提供的用户手册）

own frequency 固有频率

own position information sensor （导航系统中的车辆）自身位置信息传感器

own weight 自重（= sole weight）

oxalate 乙二酸盐，草酸盐，草酸酯

oxalic acid 乙二酸，草酸

oxidant ①过氧化物（的总称，源于法语，简称 Ox，大气污染成分之一，由汽车排出的 NO_x、HC 在阳光作用下光化学作用而生成，大部分为 O_3）②氧化剂

oxidate （使…）氧化

oxidation 氧化（作用）（亦写作 oxydation，指物质所含元素失去电子或电子偏离的化学反应）

oxidation and decarbonization （钢

件的）氧化与脱碳（氧化是指钢件表面与加热介质中的氧或氧化性气氛作用形成氧化铁 FeO 的过程；脱碳是指钢表面层中的碳被氧化，而使表层含碳量降低的现象）

oxidation catalyst 氧化型催化剂（促进碳氢化合物和一氧化碳氧化为水蒸气和二氧化碳的催化剂）

oxidation failure （由于）氧化（而引起的）损坏

oxidation film 氧化膜（= oxide film）

oxidation-inhibited oil 抗氧化润滑油（含抗氧化剂的润滑油）

oxidation inhibitor 抗氧化添加剂，抗氧化剂

oxidation reaction 氧化反应

oxidation-reduction catalyst 氧化-还原型催化剂（可同时促进 HC 和 CO 氧化及 HO_x 还原催化剂）

oxidation resistance 抗氧化能力

oxidation-resistant steel 抗氧化钢（不锈钢）

oxidation sludge 氧化（沉）渣

oxidation stability 氧化稳定性

oxidation stability with heat （润滑油的）热氧化稳定性

oxidation test 氧化试验

oxidation tint 氧化色（热变色，回火色，= air tint, heat tint）

oxidation treatment 氧化处理（将钢铁零件放在饱和蒸汽或化学溶液中加热到适当温度，使其表面生成一种均匀致密且与基体材料牢固相结合的氧化薄膜，以防止锈蚀及增加零件表面光泽和美观的方法）

oxidation under high pressure （在）高压（下）氧化

oxidation zone 氧化区，氧化带

oxidative breakdown 氧化分（离）解

oxide 氧化物

oxide blacking 氧化发黑工艺（将钢制品置入硝酸钠及亚硝酸钠等碱性氧化剂中，在高浓度和 130~150℃ 温度下，钢制品表面会产生一种装饰性的黑色氧化膜层）

oxide cermets 氧化金属陶瓷合金

oxide coating 氧化层，生成氧化膜

oxide conversion 耐蚀氧化膜强化过程（对铝及铝合金表面的自然氧化膜进行强化，增大其耐腐蚀性）

oxide film 氧化膜（= oxidation film）

oxide film resistor 氧化薄膜电阻器

oxide finish 氧化表面处理

oxide-insulator （场效应晶体管的）氧化物绝缘体

oxide layer 氧化层

oxide of nitrogen 氮的氧化物，氧化氮（NO 与 NO_2 等的总称，简称 NO_x）

oxide patch 氧化斑点

oxide skin 氧化皮（表面氧化层）

oxidize （使…）氧化

oxidized piston 氧化处理的活塞

oxidized porous silicon sensor 多孔氧化硅（湿度）传感器（在多孔氧化硅片的两面沉积金属电极，而制成的以多孔氧化硅片为电极间介电质的电容器型湿度传感器，该电容器的电容随多孔层吸收的水分量而变化，即：可将含水量—湿度变为电容信号输出）

oxidized product 氧化产物

oxidizing action 氧化作用

oxidizing agent 氧化剂（= oxidizer）

oxidizing atmosphere 氧化气氛，氧化环境

oxidizing catalyst 氧化催化剂（促进 HC, CO 与氧化合而生成 H_2O 和 CO_2 的催化剂）

oxidizing catalytic converter 氧化型催化转化器（简称 OCC，使用氧化催化剂和输出二次空气，以加速废气中 CO, HC 氧化反应而生成 H_2O, CO_2 的催化转化器）

oxidizing flame 氧化焰

oxyacetylene 氧乙炔，氧乙炔的
oxy-acetylene welding 氧-乙炔焊
oxyacid 含氧酸，羟基酸
oxy-catalytic scrubber （排气的）氧化催化转化器
oxydant 含氧化合物（汽车排气的光化学烟雾中的 O_3，RCHO，$RONO_2$，RCO_3NO_2 等氧化力极强的物质的总称）
oxydation 氧化（作用）（= oxidation, oxidization）
oxydation inhibitor 抗氧化剂，氧化阻缓剂
oxydizer 氧化剂
oxygen 氧 O_2
oxygen-abundant 富氧的，氧气过多的（如：稀混合气等）
oxygen-added argon-shielding gas laserwelding 加氧氩保护气体激光焊
oxygenant 氧化剂
oxygenate ①用氧处理，(使)氧化，用氧饱和，充氧 ②富氧燃料（一般用 oxygenates，= oxygen-enriched fuel）③抗爆燃剂（= aiti-knock additives）
oxygenated compound 氧饱和化合物
oxygenated fuel 含氧燃料，充氧燃料[如：甲醇($CH_3(OH)$)，乙醇($C_2H_5(OH)$)等]
oxygenated gasoline 含氧汽油（指含有一定数量的氧化合物，如：乙醇，甲基叔丁基醚"MTBE"等的汽油。通常是在汽油中加入10%的含氧化合物，以实现稀混合气燃烧和减少 CO 排放）
oxygenated hydrocarbon 氧饱和烃
oxygen-bearing 含氧的
oxygen bomb ①氧弹（一种由不锈钢抗腐蚀材料制成的耐高压弹性容器，在量测燃料的热值时，将一定的燃料放入弹性容器内，弹壁上有通入氧气的接头，也有引入点火系统的装置，亦称 bomb calorimeter）②（高压）氧气瓶，氧气筒
oxygen bomb calorimeter 氧弹热值测定器
oxygen bottle 氧气瓶
oxygen correction 氧校正（根据柴油机排气中氧的浓度对碳氢化合物检测器读数进行的校正。一般在氧浓度超过2%时才进行校正）
oxygen corrosion 氧腐蚀，氧化腐蚀
oxygen-deficient 氧气不足的（如：浓混合气）
oxygen-enriched 增氧化，富氧的
oxygen feedback system 氧传感器反馈控制系统（简称 O_2 feedback system，美克莱斯勒公司发动机电子控制系统的商品名，根据氧传感器反馈信号控制空燃比）
oxygen grabber 夺氧剂（指链烯烃等在不饱和状态下，迫切需要吸收氧气成为稳定的化合物，可作为着火阻滞剂）
oxygen interference 氧干扰（如：氧气中含氧浓度的变化对分析仪测定成分浓度的反应值的影响）
oxygen ion conductor 氧离子导体
oxygen residual 残留氧含量，氧残留量
oxygen richer （三菱公司的）富氧空气发生器（可向车厢内提供含氧量25%~30%的空气）
oxygen-rich exhaust 富氧废气（排气中含氧较多）
oxygen sensor 氧传感器（检测排气中氧浓度的传感器，亦称 O_2 sensor, lambda sensor 或 λ sensor, oxygen-probe）
oxygen sensor heater 氧传感器加热器（氧传感器要在一定温度下，如 >300℃ 才能正常工作，目前大部分氧传感器都加有一电热元件，可在发动机起动后20~30秒钟内，将氧传感器加热到工作温度）

oxygen sensor monitoring system 氧传感器（性能）监控系统

2oxygen sensor system 双氧传感器系统（在三效催化转化器的前、后均装有 O_2 传感器。催化器前安装的 O_2 传感器响应性高，用于进行基本空燃比控制，催化器后的 O_2 传感器作反馈控制，用于修正由于各种传感器和部件的误差造成的空燃比偏差）

oxygen sensor system thermo-switch 氧传感器馈式电子控制汽油喷射系统的冷却水温开关（向电子控制模块提供冷却水温信号）

oxygen sensor warning light 氧传感器（失效）警报灯

oxy-hydrogen gas 氢-氧混合气（如：氢-氧焊使用的氢氧混合气，铅蓄电池充电时产生的极易爆炸的氢-氧混合气等）

oxy-hydrogen welding 氢氧焊

o-xylene 邻二甲苯

oxynitride 氮氧化物

oz 英两，盎司（ounce 的代号：①英制常衡质量单位，= 28.3487g = 1/16lb，用 oz 表示②英制金、药质量单位，1/12lb = 31.0873g，其中药衡用 oz apoth 或 oz ap 表示，参见 apothecaries weight，金衡用 troy oz 表示③英制液量单位，= 1/160gal）

ozonator 臭氧发生器（亦等作 ozonizer）

ozone 臭氧（O_3，三个氧原子结合而成的氧分子，大气中的 HC 和 NO_x 在强日光下或火花放电等所生成的极不稳定的气体物质，极易分解为 O_2 和 O，其中 O 为极强的氧化剂，对橡胶制品等危害严重）

ozone chamber 臭氧（作用下的）材料老化试验室

ozone cracking 臭氧破损（指弹性材料在臭氧环境下经受循环应力时在机械疲劳极限前产生的破裂等损坏）

ozone-NO chemiluminescence method O_3-NO 化学发光法

ozono sphere 臭氧层

P ①页（page）②（自动变速器的）驻车挡，驻车（Parking）③部分，零件（Part）④过去的（Past）⑤每（per）⑥磁导（permeance）⑦吩（响度单位）（phon）⑧磷（phosphorus）⑨微微（10^{-12}, pico）⑩品脱（$\frac{1}{2}$夸脱$=\frac{1}{8}$加仑, pint）⑪齿距，螺距（pitch）⑫板，板（屏）极（plate）⑬泊（黏度单位，poise）⑭极距（polar distance）⑮（磁、电）极（pole）⑯正的，阳的（positive）⑰功率，动力（power）⑱（静）压力（pressure）⑲单位面积的压力（pressure per unit area）⑳质子（proton）㉑原型的，样机（prototype）㉒泵（pump）㉓（轮胎侧壁上表示该）轮胎最大设计使用车速为150km/h或95 mile/h的字母（详见 speed rating）

p/a 助力的，动力的（power-assisted 的简称）

Pa ①帕（pascal）②镤［prot（o）actinium］

PA 聚酰胺［polyamide 的简称，其商品名为 nylon（尼龙）］

PAB （车辆的）乘客安全气囊（passenger air bag 的简称）

PACE （美《Automotive News》设立的）汽车供应商杰出贡献奖（Premier Automotive Supplier's Contribution to Excellence 的简称，该奖项已成为美国及在世界范围内意义重大的权威认证）

pace notes 赛程提示（汽车拉力赛，根据赛前对赛程路况的勘查，拟定的各路段最佳车速及避开险情的措施等，比赛中，由副驾驶员通过头盔通话器向驾驶员提示）

Pacific Area Standards Congress 太平洋地区标准会议（简称 PASC）

pacity smokemeter （测定柴油机排气消光度的）消光烟度计

pack 包捆，部件，组合件，机组，夯实，压紧，渗碳剂，包装

package ①封装，密封，装箱，打包，装配②组件，插件，机件标准部件，单元，一组，一束，成套设备，外壳，封壳，盒，密封装置③程序包，软件包

package drawing ①（汽车车身设计草案的）总装草图，组装草图（表示车身各主要尺寸，及汽车各主要机构和乘员等在车内位置的三面或四面正投影草图，为设计草案的图样说明部分，= basic packing, base package）②总成装配图，总装草图

package option 成套选装件

package tray （汽车仪表板杂物箱下放置小物件、地图、书报等的）搁物盘

package truck 零担货车,零担货运汽车

package weight ①成套(机组,总成,部件的)重量②包装重量,包裹重量

packaging ①外包装②包装材料③包装作业④(汽车车厢内部空间)布局和容量

packaging density 封装密度

packed gland (泵轴的)密封填料函,密封填料盒,填料式密封装置(亦称 stuffing box)

packet wireless data communication network 分组无线电数据通信网络[指以分组的形式进行数据传输和交换的网络。分组(packet),亦称"信包"或"包",是数据传输和交换的基本单元]

packing cup (保持滑动部分气密性的杯状橡胶、毛毡、皮革制的)密封杯

packing drag (液压缸的)充液阻力(指将全部外力除去或平衡后,推动活塞所需的压力值)

packing factor (货车货箱的)容积利用系数

packing for transportation 运输包装

packing washer 密封垫圈(= sealing washer)

packless 无衬垫的,无填料的,未密封的,未加封的,无包装的,未填实的,疏松的

PACV (排气负压)脉冲二次空气(吸入系统中的)止回阀(pulse air check valve 的简称)

PAD [美]国防部石油管理局(Petroleum Administration for Defence)

pad ①衬垫,软垫,垫块,减振垫,缓冲垫(如:悬架杆件与车架间的缓冲胶垫)②(机器上的)把手柄(= small tool-handle)③(盘式制动器制动钳的)摩擦衬块④(装在路面上,由汽车触动的一种)信号传感装置(参见 vehicle actuated signals)⑤填装,填充,填实⑥加垫

padal stop 踏板限位块

padded 装有衬垫的,软垫包装的,软包的

padding disc (预压缩式二冲程发动机,装在曲轴箱内,以提高预压缩比,增加输出功率的)垫盘

paddle ①桨,桨状物,②(用于打击、搅拌、涂敷、抹平的各种)桨形工具(如:焊料抹子 solder paddle)③(拨杆式变速的)拨杆

paddle boxed rear wheels (厢式车身)被侧壁板遮盖住的后轮(= panel boxed rear wheel)

paddle shaft 叶轮轴

paddle shift (拨动式)桨片状换挡杆

paddle wheel 叶轮,径向直叶风扇轮

paddling the lead (车身板件凹坑修复中的)填铅(作业)(用于车身修理,用铅料填平凹坑并磨光)

paddock ①汽车等待比赛的停车场,临时停车场地②汽车制造厂的专用维修厂

pad retainer (pin) (盘式制动器)摩擦衬块固定销

pad wear indicator (盘式制动器)摩擦衬块磨损指示器(当磨损尺寸达到某规定值时,埋在摩擦材料中的金属片露出,与制动盘接触,而发出警告声响,或者造成电路断线或短路,而发出灯光警告信号。前者称为声响式 audible type,后者称为电气式 electric type)

PAF (排气负压)脉冲(二次空气吸入系统的)空气供给装置,pulseair feeder 的简称

PAFC 磷酸燃料电池(phosphoricaid fuel cell 的简称)

pagoda (-style) roof (德 Mercedes-Benz SL 硬顶轿车的)塔式车顶

PAH 聚芳香烃（poly aromatic hydrocarbons 的简称）

paint ①油漆，涂料②上油漆，涂装

paint adhesion test 漆料黏着（性）试验

paint booth 喷漆房，喷漆室

paint checking 漆皮龟裂

paint colour matching （修补车身漆面的）漆色选配作业（根据漆料色样和专门的拌和配色装置，必要时使用光谱分析仪选配与原车身漆色完全相同的漆料）

paint dipping 浸浴涂漆

painting line （车身）涂装线，上漆生产线

paint oven 烤漆烘箱

paint refinishing （二手车等的）重新油漆作业，重新涂装作业

paint streaming 颜料流线（风洞试验时，将 TiO_2 白粉用油酸和液状石蜡拌和后，涂滴于车身模型的表面，根据该颜料的流线来确定车身表面上的气流状态）

paint stripper （除去旧漆层用的）除漆液，除漆剂

paint work 油漆作业，涂装作业（亦写作 paintwork，= lacquer finish，varnish finish，body finish）

pair ①一对，一双②使成对

P-AIR （排气负压）脉冲（吸入）二次空气反应器（pulse air induction reactor 的简称，亦写作 PAIR，见 PAIR system）

pair-cast cylinder 汽缸成对铸造式缸体

paired-cylinder engine 配对汽缸发动机（一种稀混合气燃烧式层状充气发动机，一个汽缸吸入正常的浓混合气，另一个配对的汽缸吸入空气，而其压缩比浓混合气汽缸高很多，冲程相位角却滞后约30°。当浓混合气缸压缩终了点燃着火时，空气缸还继续压缩，高压空气自两缸顶部通道窜入浓混合气缸，增大紊流强度。当空气缸的活塞到达上止点后，开始下行时，浓混合气缸内的高压燃气冲入空气缸内，推动其活塞下行，此时两缸同时做功。这种新型发动机可降低燃料消耗，减少 NO_x，CO 等排气污染）

pair glass （风窗用的）双层安全玻璃

PAIR system （二次空气反应装置中的）脉冲空气系统（pulse air system 或 pulsating air system 的简称，利用排气脉冲负压，经单向进气阀，将新鲜空气引入排气系，使废气中 HC，CO 等氧化反应的净化系统，亦写作 P-AIR system）

palatable 可接受的，符合要求的

palid 铅基轴承合金（铅82%～90%，锑5%～11%，砷4%～7%）

Palio 派力奥（轿车牌名，意大利 Fait 20 世纪90年代产品，为三门、两厢、溜背式，有1.5L 和1.6L 两种16气门，多点燃油喷射发动机供用户选择，车身长3.74m，宽1.6m）

palium 铝基轴承合金（铜4.5%，铅4%，锡2.6%，镁0.6%，锰0.3%，锌0.3%，余为铝）

palladium 钯(Pd)（在汽车上用作催化转化器的贵金属氧化催化剂）

palladium-coated pellets （催化转化器中使用的）涂钯颗粒

palladium contact point 钯触点

palladium copper 钯铜合金（钯70%，铜25%，镍<1%，余为银）

pall away ①跑偏②拉出

pallet ①平板架，货架，板台②垛码盘，托盘，装货托板，集装盘③制模板④抹子，刮铲，抹灰刀⑤棘爪，擎子⑥锤垫⑦小车

palletized body 托板化运输车厢

pallet lorry ①托盘式货车②垛码货台式货车（带有可供堆集货物成垛的货台，一般装卸采用叉式载运车，

货台为双层底板,装卸叉可以插入)③码垛车(美称 pallet truck,其结构与作用与叉车相同,只是提升与运送货车的装置不是双叉,而是平板式托盘)

palm button 按钮开关,开关按钮

palm coupling 推压式接头,推压式联结器,推压式联轴节

palm fit (掌心)推压配合

palm test 汽油挥发性的手掌法试验

palse converter 脉冲转换器(装在排气歧管后端,使汽缸排出的废气的脉动压力在进入废气涡轮前变为较为稳定的压力的部件)

PAM 脉冲幅度调制,脉幅调制(见 pulse-amplitude modulation)

PAN ①过氧乙酰硝酸盐,过氧乙酰硝酸酯,硝化过氧乙酰(RCO_3NO_2, peroxy-acetylnitrate,亦称 X compound,汽车光化学烟雾成分,对人体、植物均有毒)②聚丙烯腈(poly-acrylonitrile)

pan ①盘,槽,盆②(各种)盆、盘形件(如:发动机的油底壳)

Panaroma 电动全景天窗(商品名)

pancake engine 卧式发动机(= flat engine, floor engine, under floor engine,多用于客车)

pancake synchro 扁平同步机(北美多用此名,英国用 slag synchro)

pane ①窗玻璃②方框③(螺母)棱面

panel ①板,配电板;仪表板;护板②(由金属板制成的各种)板件(如车身面板)③(由塑料模压、模铸而成的各种)板件(如:汽车内的各种装饰板)

panel assembly 仪表板总成,板件总成

panel board ①仪表板②车厢外嵌板,车身面板;墙板,壁板,镶板③控制板,操纵板④配电盘

panel body (汽车的)厢式车身(= van body)

panel(-body) truck 厢式载货汽车(= closed truck, wagon truck)

panel bonding 板件黏结(一种新型车身板件工艺,用黏结剂取代点焊)

panel-boxed rear wheel (厢式车辆)被侧壁板遮盖住的后轮(= paddle boxed rear wheel)

panel contour 车身板件外形(指无任何损伤的新制成的车身板件原形)

panel cutter 切板机(一般指车身修理作业中使用的旧板件气动切割机具)

panel defrost door (客厢)前围板上的除霜暖风门

panel floor 车身地板,车身底板

panel lamp 仪表板照明灯

panelled rear body 板式后备厢式(货车)车身

panelling ①镶板,车身板件的镶装②车身板件总成③塑料模制的装饰板

3-panel panoramic mirror 3 镜式全景后视镜(左、右两侧加装凸镜,以消除盲区的后视镜)

panel patching 车身板件修补,车身板件补片修补

panel puller (车身)板件凹陷拉器(美称 knocker)

panel spacer (车身)内外壁间衬条、隔板

panel strainer (车厢)板件加强肋

panel strip (车身壁板)嵌条

panel switch 仪表板开关

panel test 分段试验

panel tray 仪表板

panel-type frame 槽钢车架(由两条槽钢纵梁和几条横梁组成,发动机舱以后的部位装有车身底板。有时用 X 构件梁代替横梁,这时英国称为 cruciform frame)

panel van (驾驶室与货箱构成一整体的)厢式货车(亦称 root van,参见 van)

pan -European 泛欧洲的,全欧洲的

panhard rod 潘哈德杆(后桥与车身之间横向布置、起定位作用的横拉杆,用于防止横摆,亦称 track bar, transverse rod)

panhard rod mounting box 潘哈德杆(在后桥上的)箱形安装支架

panic alarm 紧急警报

panic stop 紧急制动停车,急制动

pannier (原意为驮在牲口两侧装货的驮筐,在汽车上指装挂在车身任一侧外方的)货箱,油箱,工具箱(等)

panoramic all-glass roof 全景式全玻璃车顶

panoramic glass sliding roof with four panels 四块全景玻璃滑动天窗式车顶(由四块玻璃板组成,后三块板可向后滑动开启,第一块板可斜着竖起,起导风板的作用)

panoramic imaging technique (数字摄像与互联网技术相结合的)全景图像技术[全景图像指大于双眼有效视觉(约水平 90°,垂直 70°)或双眼余光视觉(约水平 180°,垂直 90°)乃至 360°完整场景范围的图像,全景图像技术能够以 360°的旋转方式获得一个场景的图像,同时可以控制观察全景的方向,可左可右,可近可远,如:可以从车内或车外转一圈来浏览一辆汽车的构造]

Panoramic tilt/slide electric sunroof 电动(可)斜撑/滑动式全景天窗

panoramic view side minor (供驾驶员)全景侧视镜,宽视野侧视镜

panoramic visibility 全景视野

panoramic windshield 全景风窗玻璃(亦称 full-scope panoramic wind shield, panorama windscreen, windshield, scenaramic windshield, superscenic windshield, sweep-sight windshield, wrap around type windscreen, wraparound windshield)

pantasote top (敞篷轿车)带有折叠装置的车顶篷

pantavalent 五价的

pantechnicon van 厢式家具运送车(=furniture van)

pantograph ①比例绘图器,缩放仪,放大尺②导电弓,架式受电弓(亦写作 pantagraph)

pantograph jack (可伸缩的)菱形架式千斤顶

paper ①纸②论文

paper cartridge air cleaner 纸芯空气滤清器(简称 paper air cleaner)

paper condenser 纸质电容器(指用纸做绝缘体的电容器)

paper driver 有证无技术的驾驶者

paper(-element) filter 纸芯滤清器

paper facing 浸胶纸质摩擦衬面

paper filter element 纸滤芯

paper gasket 纸垫

paper packing 纸质填封材料,纸质衬垫,纸质填封件

paper washer 纸垫圈

par 同等,等价,平价,平均,标准,常态

parabola ①抛物线②抛物面反射装置

parabolic 抛物线的,抛物面的

parabolically sprung balance bogle 抛物线形弹簧平衡式双轴并装车桥

parabolic antenna 抛物面天线

parabolic dish 抛物面(反射器)

parabolic distribution 抛物线分布

parabolic headlamp 抛物线形前照灯(=paraboloid headlamp)

parabolic point 抛物点

parabolic projectivity 抛物性射影

parabolic reflector 抛物面反光镜(如:旧式前照灯的反光镜,光源位于焦点,而形成平行的反射光线)

parabolic spring 抛物线形钢板弹簧(一种中部向上突起的汽车钢板弹簧,由 1~4 片两端渐渐变薄的钢板

组成,亦称 taper leaf spring)
paraboloid 抛物面
paraboloidal coordinates 抛物面坐标
paraboloid of revolution 回转抛物面
parachute drag (赛车的)降落伞制动
paradigm 范例,示例,示范
paraffin-base oil ①石蜡基石油(= paraffin base petroleum)②石蜡基润滑油,链烷基机油(指以链烷烃为基础油的机油,其倾点高,但黏/温特性好)
paraffin content 石蜡含量
paraffin(e) ①石蜡(白色半透明蜡状固体,比重约0.9,熔点45~65℃,沸点300℃的烷属烃,C_nH_{2n+2} 的混合物,有天然品,但主要为石油分馏产物)②链烷烃③[英]煤油
paraffin engine [英]煤油发动机
paraffin hydrocarbons 烷(属)烃,石蜡族烃,链烷烃,饱和链烃
paraffinic 石蜡族的,链烷烃的,烷烃的
paraffin oil [英]煤油(= kerosine)
paraffin paper 石蜡纸(用做电容器,以及点火线圈二次绕组线间的绝缘物)
paraffin scale 粗石蜡(= white scale)
paraffin series 烷烃族,烷烃类(一般分子式为 C_nH_{2n+2} 的碳氢化合物)
paraffin wax 石蜡
parallax ①视差(a.观察点横向移动时,视野内的静止物体产生视觉上的相对运动现象,离观察者比凝视点近的物体好像向相反的方向移动,而比凝视点远的物体则好似向相同的方向移动; b.对速度完全相同,但与观察者距离不同的两物体的运动速度产生的视觉上的差别)②倾斜线
parallel ①平行线②平行的③并联的④平行于,相当于,使同时进行

parallel addressing 并行寻址(以同时提供多个地址的方式选择存储区)
parallel alignment 平行度校正
parallel angle 平行角
parallel-arm suspension 平行臂式(独立)悬架
parallel-axis gears 平行轴齿轮系
parallel beam 平行光束
parallel bearing 滑动轴承(= plain bearing)
parallel bumps (试验跑道上)平行布置的人造凸起障碍物
parallel circuit 并联电路(= shunt circuit)
parallel computer (具有多个运算器,能作并行操作或并行处理的)并行计算机
parallel connection 并联
parallel curves 平行曲线
parallel dielectric constant (液晶分子)长轴方向介电常数
parallel disposition viscous coupling type (常时四轮驱动车)黏性联轴节平行布置式轴间防滑差速器
parallel dual-chamber air brake valve 并列式双腔气制动阀(两个工作腔的轴线呈平行排列的双腔气制动阀)
parallel electric conductivity (液晶分子)长轴方向电导率
parallel-faced type of gauge 平行面规
parallel faces 平行面
parallel flow 平行流
parallel flow engine 轴流式燃气轮机
parallel-flow heat exchanger 轴流式热交换器
parallel-flow turbine 轴流式涡轮(机)
parallel force 平行力
parallel gauge 平行规
parallel-gear drive ①圆柱齿轮传动

②平行四连杆传动

parallel helical gear pair 平行轴斜齿（圆柱）齿轮副

parallel hop （汽车）簧上质量的上下垂直振动

parallel-hybrid diesel-electric system 并联式柴油机-电机复合动力系统

parallel hybrid drive type vehicle 并联复合动力驱动型车辆（指在公路行驶时，由内燃机驱动车辆行驶并带动电动机作为发电机运转向蓄电池充电；在市区行驶时，由蓄电池向电动机供电驱动车辆运行；当上坡或在其他需要最高功率行驶的工况时，由内燃机和电动机共同驱动车辆；减速制动工况中，车轮反带发电机发电给蓄电池充电，见 series hybrid system）

parallel hybrid vehicle 并联式混合动力车（亦称 parallel hybrid electric vehicle，汽车主要由内燃机驱动行驶，起步、加速等工况时电动机同时参与驱动，以增加动力。当制动或减速时汽车带动电动机逆转发电，回收汽车动能）

paralleling 并联

paralle link type suspension 平行臂式悬架（由两根平行布置的长短不等控制臂支撑的后轮悬架。当悬架受压缩时可使该后轮向内侧偏转某一角度，形成前束以保证车辆的方向稳定性）

parallel interface 并行接口［指同时完成若干个二进制数据位（通常为一个字节）的传输的接口］

parallelism 平行（度），平行（性）

parallel key 平行键，平键，滑键，导向键（亦称 feather key）

parallel leaf spring type suspension 平行纵置板簧式悬架（左、右各一架板簧与车架平行，做纵向布置的悬架形式）

parallel line 平行线

parallel link strut 双平行臂-滑柱式悬架（由双平行纵臂或横臂与滑柱组成的独立悬架，参见 parallel link type）

Parallel Link Strut (type suspension) 平行连杆-滑柱(式悬架)（日产公司研制的由两根控制臂和一个滑柱组成的一种前轮驱动式轿车后轮悬架的商品名，利用两根平行布置的横向控制臂杆，形成一平行四边形框架，控制后轮使之向内侧偏转某一角度，形成前束，以提高汽车的稳定性）

parallel link type ①双平行臂式（悬架）（指上、下控制臂平行布置的双横臂或双纵臂式独立悬架，前者亦称 double wishbone armtype）②平行连动式（风窗刮水器）（指由杆系连动驾驶座和位于座前的左、右刮水器平行刮动）

parallel link type suspension 双平行横臂式悬架（见 two transverse rocker arms type suspension）

parallelogram 平行四边形

parallelograming test （车架）抗平行四边形变形试验

parallelogram (linkage) steering system 平行四边形杆系转向机构（指具有转向摇臂和随动臂的梯形拉杆转向机构）

parallelogramming deflection （车架的）平行四边形变形

parallelogram steering linkage 平行四边形转向杆系（指梯形转向杆系）

parallelogram suspension 等长双横臂式（独立）悬架（指由同一长度且平行的上、下控制臂组成的双横臂式独立悬架，车轮上、下运动时，外倾角不会发生变化，不致引起车轮摆振，多用于赛车）

parallel operation 平行作业并行操作，并列运转，并列运算

parallel parking 顺列式驻车（平行于道路纵列停放车辆，车头方向和道路交通方向相同）

parallel pin 平销

parallel planes 平行平面

parallel plate condenser 平行片电容器

parallel polarizer 平行偏振片（偏振方向相互平行的两偏振片）

parallel presentation of information 信息并行传送（几个数据沿各自的通道或总线同时传输）

parallel processing 并行处理技术（多个算术运算同时进行的计算机处理技术，见 serial processing）

parallel real-time stereo vision system （可同时直接观看到一个或两个以上项目，如：车道和障碍物等的）平行实时立体电视显示系统

parallel reflective index （液晶分子）长轴方向折射率

parallel roller bearing 圆柱滚子轴承（= cylindrical roller bearing）

parallel rule (r) 平行规

parallel-series battery switching 蓄电池并-串联接通（法）（蓄电池型电动车的车速控制方法之一。通过改变各单个蓄电池的并-串联方式，控制电流，以控制电动机转速）

parallel shaft drive gear pair 平行轴传动齿轮副

parallel steer 平行转向，平行转向机构（指转向时，两转向轮转动的角度相同）

parallel trailing link suspension 双纵臂式（独立）悬架［用上、下纵臂将车轮（或车轴）与车架（或车身）连接起来的悬架形式，亦称 double trailing arm type suspension］

parallel twin 直列双缸发动机，并列双缸发动机

parallel-type worm 圆柱蜗杆（= cylindrical worm）

parallel valves （气门杆身平行布置的）并列式进、排气门

parallel waves 平行波

parallel working 平行作业

parallel wound motor 并绕电动机，分激电动机，并激电动机（= shunt wound motor）

parameter ①参变数②参量③母数④特性值⑤（确定汽车发动机等运转工况的）参数（如冷却水温、发动机负荷、空燃比，点火提前角，转速等）⑥（根据基底时间、劳动力、工具、管理方法等的）生产预测法

parameter adjustment control 参量调节控制

parameter drift-out 参数偏离（规定范围）

parameters for technical condition of vehicle 汽车技术状况参数（评价汽车使用性能的物理量和化学量）

parameter-transformation 参数变换

parameter value 参数值

parametric amplifier 参量放大器（用于微波的低噪声放大）

paramount ①头等的，最高的，至上的，首要的，卓越的②最高；主要，首要

paraphernalia ①附件，附属设备；零星器具②随身用具，随车工具

parasite current 寄生电流

parasite suppressor （无线电）干扰抑制栅

parasitic 寄生的，附加的

parasitic current 寄生电流（在汽车上，指点火开关断开后仍然流动的下列电流，如：电子控制模块的待机电流、收音机选台信息等的存储用电流，或钟表等运转所需的电流等，亦称 parasite current）

parasitic drag 寄生阻力（干扰阻力，汽车行驶时空气压力阻力的一部分，是由车身表面的突起或突出

部分,如:后视镜、天线、挡泥板、车门把手、悬架导向杆、驱动轴等零部件凸出于气流中,引起气流干扰而产生的阻力)

parasitic horsepower (以马力计的)寄生功率

parasitic loss 附加损失,杂项损失,寄生功率损失(如:发动机的附件损失)

parasitic oscillation 寄生振荡

parasitic power 寄生功率

parasitic reactance 寄生电抗

parasitic reflection 寄生反射

parasitic resistance 寄生阻力

parasitic thermoelectromotive force 寄生温差电动势

parcel (delivery) van 包裹运送车,小件货物运送车

parcel rack (客车车身内的)小件行李架(亦称 parcel shelf, parcel tray)

parent company 母公司(拥有几个自己投资的附属子公司,不同于控股公司,参见 holding company)

parent metal ①底层金属②母材③基(焊)料

parent vehicle 母车(①指安装机构、系统等的基础车辆②指改型或变形车的原型车)

parity ①均等,同位,类似,相同②(在计算机和通信技术中的)奇偶(法),奇偶(性)

parity bit 奇偶校验位(表明一组二进制数内所有"1"的个数,包括奇偶校验位是预先设定的某一奇数或偶数)

parity check 奇偶检验(检查所接收或处理的一组二进制数与附加的奇偶校验位所预置的奇、偶数是否一致的一种冗余校验法)

parity checking unit 奇偶校验装置,奇偶校验器(亦称 parity checker)

parity generator/checker 奇偶发生器/校验器(既能产生又能检验奇偶位的组合电路)

park ①停车场②(停车场上的)全部汽车③停放汽车④(自动变速器选挡杆的)驻车挡(简称P)

park and ride centre 停车-乘车中心(拥有停放车辆设施,如:停车场的公共交通枢纽站。乘客可驾驶自己的轿车至此中心,停放车辆后转乘公共交通车辆)

Parkarizing (钢铁表面的)磷酸盐覆膜防锈法(以开发该加工法的公司名命名)

ParkAssist 倒车入驻辅助系统(商品名,通常指由倒车雷达、倒车障碍物警报器、倒车摄像系统或倒车防撞自动停车系统等组成的自动倒车入驻安全系统。无倒车摄像者商品名称ParkSense,有倒车摄像者商品名称 ParkView。VW的一款驻车辅助系统,当驾驶者减速寻找车位驻车时其超声探测系统可按车长自动寻找驻车空位,并可在驾驶者挂入倒车挡位后自动转向入位)

Park Distance Control 驻车距离控制(系统)(简称PDC,通用公司倒车雷达警报系统商品名)

park distance control 入驻倒车距离控制(简称PDC)

parkerization 磷化(保护膜防锈)处理

parkerization lacquer paint 磷化清漆涂料

parkerize 磷化保护膜防锈处理(= parkerise,因发明者而得名)

parking 停放汽车,驻车

parking and starting supporting system (狭窄空间车辆)驻车与起步支援系统

parking apron (建筑物四周的)停车场地

parking area ①停车区,停车场(= parking lot, parking place, park-

ing space）②停车面积，驻车面积
parking assist system 驻车辅助系统
parking ban 禁止停车
parking brake 驻车制动器，手制动器（亦称 handbrake，side brake）
parking brake control 驻车制动器操纵件
parking brake holding power 驻车制动器停车能力（指汽车在坡道上停车时，驻车制动器保持汽车不动的能力）
parking brake indicator lamp 驻车制动指示灯
parking braking system warning tell-tale 驻车制动系警报灯（表示驻车制动器还未松开的信号灯）
parking capacity 驻车容量，停车容量（停车场等车辆停放场所所能容纳的最大车辆数）
parking forbidden （此处）禁止停车
parking heater （汽车于冬季驻车时，由发动机以外的热源供暖，使驾驶室、客车保持温暖的）停车暖气装置
parking lamp 驻车灯
parking lane 停车道，驻车道
parking leg （半挂车的）停放支架
parking light 驻车信号灯（亦称 parking lamp，表示该车在此停驻，一般前驻车灯为白光，后驻车灯为红光，有的车上仅装侧驻车信号灯）
parking limitations 驻车限制条例
parking line 停车线，驻车线（表示驻车场地的边界线）
parking lock （停车时锁定汽车的）防盗锁（亦称 parking interlock）
parking lot （道路以外的）停车场地，停车场，停车区，停车地段，停车地点，驻车场地（= parking area，美指地面露天停车场）
parking meter 驻车收费计时表
parking restriction 限制停放车辆，停车限制（道路上禁止或限制在某个时间内或某段空间内停放车辆）
parking shaft 驻车轴（指驻车制动力所作用的车轴）
parking sign 驻车标志（说明驻车方法、时间，或"不得驻车"及"不得停放重型车辆"等的标志）
parking space limit marking （停车场）驻车车位界线的地面标志（停车场地车位界线）
parking sprag 驻车制动器，驻车制动装置（如：①驻车时，将自动变速装置输出轴固定，防止转动的装置，见 braking lock pawl；②自动变速器的驻车挡"P挡"）
parking stall （驻车场地的）停车车位（一辆汽车在停车场所占用的地位）
parking ticket ①违章停车通知单（驾驶员到交通管理部门，接受处罚）②停车证，驻车收费票据
parking torque （汽车以极低的车速行驶或停止行驶时转动转向盘所需的）转矩
parking turnover rate 停车场车位利用率，驻车场停车面积利用率（一定时间内驻车车位的利用次数）
park/neutral switch （自动变速器）驻车挡/空挡开关（向电子控制模块发送自动变速器是否挂挡的信息的开关式传感器，简称 P/N switch）
park pilot front & rear 前、后驻车导向雷达
park relay 风窗刮水停动继电器
ParkSense 见 ParkAssist
park tractor 停车场上车辆移位用牵引车
Parktronic （Mercedes-Benz 公司的）自动驻车辅助系统（商品名，根据前保险杠侧得超声传感器在 ≤35km/h 的车速下的信息，找到适合车身长度的平行停车位和驾驶者挂入倒车挡、意欲驻车时该系统即

自动启动，通过仪表盘指示正确的转向盘转动方向和角度，并通过中央显示屏发出视频、音频倒车入位指示）

parktronic system ①（奔驰车）倒车入库障碍物探测系统（商品名）②电子驻车辅助系统③驻车（中）倒车防撞系统（商品名）

ParkView 见 ParkAssist

parkway ①禁止货车等重型车辆通行的林荫大道（如：连接公园的公路，风景区内禁止重型车辆通行的快速游览公路）②干线道路中心或两侧的绿化带

parlo(u)r coach 设备豪华的客车

paronite parts 石棉橡胶制零件

part ①部分，份额②零件，部件③分开，分成几部分

part-flow smokemeter 非全流式烟度计（仅一部分排气通过烟度计检测）

partial 部分的，不完全的，局部的

partial (-admission) turbine 部分进气式汽轮机

partial air lift vehicle （在松软地面上行驶时可减小车轮对地面压力的）半气垫式车辆

partial assembly drawing 零件装配图，装配分图

partial auxiliary view 局部辅助视图

partial balancing 部分平衡

partial burn limit 不完全燃烧极限

partial charge-state test 部分充电状态试验（简称PCT）

partial circulating operation 小循环运行，部分循环运行

partial clover 部分苜蓿叶式（道路枢纽），不完全的四叶式（交叉口）（在苜蓿叶式互通式立体交叉的四象限中只有一处、两处或三处有匝道设施）

partial combustion 局部燃烧

partial control of access 部分出入限制（主要道路交叉均为立交，但允许少数次要道路以平交连接）

partial dismantling 局部拆卸，局部解体

partial distillation 局部蒸馏，分馏

partial engagement ①（离合器）部分接合，非完全接合②（轮齿）部分啮合

partial enlarged view 局部放大视图

partial failure 局部损坏（局部丧失工作能力，局部故障）

partial flow 分流，部分流，局部流

partial-flow filter 分流式滤清器（= bypass filter）

partial-flow sampling 部分流取样法（如：选择发动机排气中具有代表性的部分，流过烟度计）

partial general view 局部总装图，局部全视图

partial lean burn system 局部稀燃系统（层状燃烧的一种，在火花塞附近的浓混合气区点火，火焰向稀混合气区传播，而完成整个燃烧过程，简称PLBS）

partial load 部分负载，部分负荷（发动机无负荷和满负荷之间的工况）

partial load characteristics （发动机的）部分负荷速度特性（曲线）（亦称 partial throttle characteristics,指燃料供给调节机构固定于部分负荷时，转矩、功率、油耗等随转速而变化的特性曲线）

partially combusted 部分燃烧的

partial opening （节气门）部分开放（亦称 partial throttle）

partial oxidation mixture （高压缩比汽油机等在火花塞跳火前已有）部分氧化的混合气（因而跳火后混合气迅速燃烧）

partial oxidation reaction 部分氧化反应

partial pressure ①分压，分压力，

分压强（组成混合气的各种气体成分，单独占有与该混合气相同的体积和温度时所具有的压力，若混合气的成分全部为气体，则混合气的压力，即总压力等于各气体成分分压之和）②局部压力

partial redundancy 部分容损元件制（在一系统中，一定数量的某些特定元件发生故障后，不致影响整个系统的工作，如：某系统中有 m 个元件，只要其发生故障的元件不超过 n 个，该系统就可正常工作，称为"n-out-of-m" partial redundancy）

partial reinforced glass （风窗用）区域钢化玻璃，部分强化玻璃（亦称 zoned tempered glass，指分区控制钢化程序的钢化安全玻璃，一旦破坏，总体上仍能符合安全玻璃对断裂碎片的要求，同时又提供一个不妨碍驾驶的视区）

partial skirt piston 滑裙式活塞（亦称 slipper skirt piston 或 slipper piston，指为了缩短活塞顶面至曲轴中心的距离，使用短连杆和将活塞销座下面的部分裙部切去，防止活塞碰及曲轴平衡块）

partial teardown 部分解体，局部解体

partial throttle acceleration 节气门部分开启加速（简称 PT accel）

partial throttling 部分节流，节气门部分开启

partial vacuum 局部真空

partial variation 局部偏差，局部变动

partial zero-emission vehicle （美国加利福尼亚州推出的）部分零排放车（简称 PZEV）

participate ①参与，参加 ②有关系，分担，共享

particle ①颗粒 ②质点 ③粒子 ④微料 ⑤极小量

particle and odour filter 柴油机排气微粒和异味滤清器

particle counter 粒子计数器

particle filter （柴油机排气）微粒过滤器

particle size 微粒尺寸，粒度（指用某种方法测量出的微粒最大长度名义尺寸，不含任何几何形状的意义，一般用微米表示）

particle size distribution 粒度分布

particular ①特点，特色 ②细节 ③特殊的，个别的，详细的，显著的，某种的，某个的

particular case 个别情况，特别情况；特例

particular tare 实际皮重（= real tare）

particulate ①微粒（指各种微小的固体物质或悬浮于空气中液态微粒）②粒子，微粒

particulate catalyst 颗粒状催化剂（亦称 pellet catalyst，一般指用颗粒状热稳定惰性物质为载体的催化剂）

particulated lead （废气等中的）铅微粒，铅化物微粒

particulate emission 微粒排放物（排气中各种固体微粒的总称，如：铅氧化物等重金属化合物，烟炭，炭粒等）

particulate filter （柴油机的）排气微粒过滤器

particulate filter oxidizer 排气微粒过滤器燃烧室

particulate ignition temperature 微粒燃烧温度

particulate matter ①微粒物，微粒（= particulates）②（特指发动机的）微粒排放物（排气中各种固体微粒的总称，通常包括铅氧化物等重金属化合物，烟灰和炭颗粒等）

particulates emission （排气中的）微粒排放，微粒状排出物

particulates emission control technique

（发动机）微粒状排出物净化技术

particulates emission limit value 微粒排放限制值

particulate trap （柴油机排气）微粒捕集器（简称 PM trap）

particulate trap oxidizer 微粒捕集燃烧器（简称 PTO）

parting face 分离面，分拆面，分割面（亦称 parting plane）

parting flange 分开面的突缘（如：上、下曲轴箱的分开面的突缘）

parting line 分开线，分界线，分割线

partition 分隔，隔开

partition chromatography 分隔式色谱法

partition coefficient 分隔系数（气相色谱仪被测定物质，在液态和气态中的浓度比例）

partitioned radiator 分段式散热器

partition panel 隔板（= partition board）

partition panel frame 隔板骨架

partition panel lining 隔板衬里

partition wall 隔壁，隔板，隔墙（= party wall，dividing wall）

partition window 隔壁窗（如：驾驶室与后车厢之间的隔壁窗）

part load ①（发动机）部分负荷（节气门部分开启）②部分载荷

part-load cylinder cutout system 部分负荷闭缸节油系统（发动机部分负荷运转时，使一个或数个缸停止工作，达到节油目的，简称 PCC）

part-load fuel consumption （发动机）部分负荷时的燃料消耗量

partly 部分地，局部地

partly open （节气门、阻风门等的）部分开启

partner comfortable seat 助手席舒适座椅（日产公司轿车上，靠背可放倒，座椅可斜躺等的助手席座椅的商品名）

partnership ①合作关系，合作伙伴②合营公司

part number minimization （设备、机器）零部件数量的最少化

part off 分开

part (-open) throttle ①部分开启节气门②节气门部分开启（指除节气门全开和全闭以外的各种开度）

part out ①拆散②［美］将旧车拆散取出可用件作为备件

parts 零件（简称 pts）

parts assembly drawing 零件装配图

parts caddie 零件手推搬运车（亦写作 caddy）

parts carrying truck 零件运送货车（= parts delivery truck）

parts catalogue 零件目录，配件目录（= spare parts list）

parts cleaner 零件清洗机

parts cleaning tank 零件清洗槽

parts cleanliness 零件清洁度

parts consumption 零件消耗量

parts cooperative 汽车配件购销合作社（近年来在美国出现的一种由独立经营的保修厂、车库、汽车零售商组成的合作组织，合作社直接从制造厂采购零件，然后分销给成员单位，以避免中间商的盘剥，亦称 buying group）

parts depot 零件仓库

parts distribution shop （汽车）零件零售店

parts drawing 零件图

part sectional view 局部剖面图，局部剖视图（= semi-sectional view）

part (s) number 零件编号（简称 p/n 或 PN）

parts per billion 十亿分之几（简称 ppb）

parts per hundred million 亿分之几（简称 pphm）

parts per million 百万分之几，百万分率（简称 PPM，ppm）

parts per million carbon 百万分率碳

（以甲烷为当量基础测定碳氢化合物的克分子容积，再乘以 10^{-6}，简称 ppmC）

parts washer 零件清洗机

part throttle characteristics 部分负荷特性（发动机转速保持不变，燃料消耗量、燃油消耗率等参数随部分负荷变化的关系曲线）

part throttle fuel economy （发动机）部分负荷（下的）燃油经济性

part-throttle knock 节气门部分开启时的爆震

part-throttle operation （发动机在）节气门部分开启下运转，部分负荷下运转

part throttle shift 部分节气门开度换挡（指在节气门部分开启位置下的换挡，即节气门全开以外的任一节气门开度下的换挡）

part through type 分流式（= bypass type）

part-time (transfer) case 非全时四轮驱动分动箱（指可由两轮驱动变换为四轮驱动的分动箱）

part-time 4WD 分时四轮驱动（part-time 4wheel drive 的简称，指通过分动器可实现全轮驱动与两轮驱动模式切换的驱动系统，平时为两轮驱动，必要时切换成全轮驱动）

part-track vehicle 半履带车辆（= half-track vehicle，亦称 part tracks）

partway 部分行程，部分路程

party wall 隔墙，隔板（= partition wall）

PAS ①动力转向（power-assisted steering 的简称）②脉动空气控制电磁阀（pulse air solenoid 的简称，见 pulse air system）

PASC 太平洋地区标准会议（Pacific Area Standards Congress）

pascal 帕（国际单位制的压力及应力单位，代号为 Pa，即每平方米承受 1N 的力，$1Pa = 1N/m^2 = 1kgm/s^2m^2$，见 newton）

Paschen's law 帕邢定律（在等温条件下，气体的击穿电压只是气体压力 p 与两平行电极板间距离 d 的乘积的函数）

PASDM 乘员安全气囊诊断模块（passenger air bag system diagnostic module 的简称，亦称 ASDM，见 air bag control module）

Paser 500 帕赛尔 500（一种火花塞电晕放电装置的商品名，由装在各缸高压线桩上的感应套组成，各缸点火之前，先在火花塞上进行一次电晕放电，使周围的混合气电离化，以提高混合气的着火性能）

PASM "保时捷"汽车的主动悬架管理系统（Porsche Active Suspension Management 的简称）

pass ①经过，越过，（检验）通过，传递，消逝 ②通道，小路 ③通行证，护照 ④免票 ⑤及格

passable 可通过的，可通行的

passage area 通道面积，通过面积

passage hole 通孔，通路孔

passage of heat 导热通道，热传导，导热（= heat transfer, thermal transmission）

passage period 通过时间，通过期

passageway 通路，通道

Passat （德大众汽车公司产）帕萨特牌轿车

passband 通频带

pass beam 见 passing beam

pass-by ①让车线，旁路，绕行道 ②绕行，超车

pass-by noise 过车噪声（车外噪声，按中国标准，测量汽车左、右两侧，距汽车中线 7.5m，离地 1.2m 处的噪声，测定时以发动机额定转速的 3/4 转速，用 3 挡或 2 挡车速行驶）

passeger compartment-mounted 装在客舱内的

passenger 乘客，旅客

passenger accommodation 乘客舱，乘客室

passenger air bag shutoff switch （座椅无成人乘坐时断开其安全气囊的）乘客安全气囊断开开关

passenger and child seat sensing device （汽车座椅上的）成人-儿童传感装置（体重超过12kg则判定为成人）

passenger car （小）轿车，小客车［用于载送少量人员及其随身物品且座位布置在两轴之间的四轮汽车，亦称 passenger automobile, 简称 automobile; motor car, 简称 car。我国1988年国家标准定名为"轿车"，在我国，自古以来将人抬的叫"轿子"，马拉的就叫"轿车"。现代沿用这一术语，将机动的小型载人车辆叫小"轿车"，小字往省略叫"轿车"，十分贴切。1999年后我国标准改名为"小客车"，作为客车，以区别于货车（truck），因载客较少，称"小客车"，也较妥切。不知何故2002年我国标准竟改名为"乘用车"，理由是乘用国际通用的车辆类型分类，那么"bus"就不"乘用"了吗？国际上英美将小轿车称为"motor car"简称 car, 美国也称为"automobile"，德国称为 limousine, 日本的标准术语称为"自动车"（"止礼也，将bus称为'乘坐自动车'，偶见日文文献中称'乘用车'，但不知道'乘用车'这三个汉字名称来自何方？"）］

passenger-car chassis 轿车底盘

passenger car diesel 轿车（用）柴油机

passenger car equivalent （客车、货车的）标准轿车当量（在实际道路条件和交通条件下，每辆货车或客车以标准轿车为单位的换算值）

(passenger car) pass-by noise （小客车的）驶过噪声

passenger-carrying chassis 客运车辆底盘

passenger-carrying vehicle 客运车辆（包括客车、轿车）

passenger car trailer 客运挂车

passenger car-trailer combination 轿车-挂车列车

passenger compartment （客车的）车厢，（轿车的）客厢（驾驶区与乘客区的总称，亦称 passenger cell, habitable compartment）

passenger compartment integrity （客运汽车撞车时）乘客车厢的完好程度

passenger compartment sensor （安全气囊系统的）客厢传感器（装在座椅后方，用于测报车速的突然下降，供安全气囊控制拱堤，判断是否发生碰撞及是否应立即点火起爆的依据之一）

passenger-compartment ultrasonic transmitter and protection system （汽车防盗系统的）客厢超声波发射-保护系统（由装在车身内的超声波发射器向车内防盗保护区：车门、中央门锁、行李舱盖等处发射超声波，形成超声波场"ultrasonic field"，当有异物或人体进入时即发出警报）

passenger door ①（四门轿车的）后车门（= rear door）②（客车的）乘客门

passenger-driver communication telltale 乘客与驾驶员联系信号灯（如：表示乘客要求和驾驶员通话的信号灯）

passenger flow 客流（在一定时间内，一定数量的旅客沿公路的某一方向，乘坐汽车或其他客运工具，实现位移所形成的人流。客流包括旅客流量、流向和流时）

passenger handling capacity 客运

能力

passenger-kilometer 人千米（客运计量单位，简称 passenger-km）

passenger-miles-per-gallon 人-英里/加仑（每加仑燃油所能完成的以人-英里为单位的客运量，客运燃料经济性的计算单位）

passenger number fluctuation factor 旅客波动系数［一年中最繁忙的运输季（月）度旅客运量与各季（月）度平均运量的比值，即旅客运输在时间上的不平衡程度］

passenger-oriented design 面向乘员的设计（指车上对乘客关心、为乘客着想的各种设计）

passenger rating （客车）乘客定额，载客定员

passenger ride （旅客）出行乘车

passenger seat ①客位（运输企业营运客车供旅客乘坐的座位）②乘客的座椅

passenger services 客运业务，客运工作，旅客服务业务

passenger service vehicle 客运车辆（简称PSV）

passengers hold （汽车的）可乘坐人数

passenger-side air bag 乘员侧面气囊（防止汽车侧面碰撞时乘员受伤的安全气囊）

passenger space 容纳乘客的空间

passengers quantity 乘客数量

passenger transportation management 客运组织，客运管理

passenger transportation network 客运网

Passenger Transport Authorities ［英］客运管理局（简称PTA）

passenger transport schedule 客运行车时刻表

passenger turnover 旅客运输周转量，旅客周转量（单位：人·千米"p·km"）

passenger van 厢式客车

passenger vehicle 客运车辆

passenger zone （客车车厢中的）乘客区

pass/fail limit 可通过的极限（值）（如：ISO规定油料添加剂颗粒可通过滤清器的极限值为460μm）

passibility 可通过性

passible 可通过的，允许通过的，合格的

passimeter ①自动售（车）票机 ②火花塞间隙规③内径规，间隙规

passing ①超车的；通过的，合格的；通行的，过往的，经过的②当前的，目前的③偶然的，短暂的④超车，超越⑤经过，通过，合格，及格

passing ability ①通过能力②超车能力

passing bay 让车道（供汽车超车的道路加宽处）

passing beam （汽车前照灯内的）超车闪光信号灯系（见 passing lamp）

passing beam tell-tall 超车信号接通指示灯（见 passing signal indicator）

passing circuit 无（电）源电路

passing danger time 超车过程中的危险时间（指超越车辆与被超车辆并列行驶的时间）

passing gear （自动变速器的）超车挡（为了超车加速踏板猛踩到底时，强制降挡机构将原挡位降低一挡后的挡位称超车挡）

passing lamp 超车（信号）灯（超车时专用的闪光信号灯）

passing light 超车灯光（指利用前照灯远光灯短时间闪光，以促使被超越的前车驾驶员注意的信号灯光，亦称 passing signal, passing signal light）

passing loop ①绕行道②（交叉口）环行道

passing maneuver 超车动作，超车

驾驶,超车操纵

passing performance testing (汽车的)超车性能试验

passing place 让车道,避车道(路幅局部加宽便于超车、让车用的车行道)

passing sight distance (可)超车视距(指驾驶员在距离路面 1.20m 的高度能确认道路上 1.20m 高的物体的顶点的最大距离,或汽车驾驶员在开始超车后见到迎面开来的汽车时,无须紧急减速,可安全轻易完成超车动作的最小视距)

passing signal indicator 超车信号指示灯(仪表板上告知驾驶者"超车信号已接通"的指示灯,亦称 passing beam tell-tall)

passing time 超车时间(汽车通过某一距离所需的时间)

passing topography capacity (车辆的)恶劣地形通过能力

passing track 超车道,越行道

passing vehicle 正在超车的车辆(= overtaking vehicle)

passivate 钝化

passivating action 钝化作用

passive ①被动的,消极的②(化学)钝态的,不活动的③无源的

passive car safety devices 被动式汽车乘员安全装置(见 passive safety)

passive circuit 无源电路(本身无电动势或其他电源)

passive component 迟钝态元件(见 passive element③)

passive display 被动显示(指本身不发光,通过调节控制或反射外界光进行显示的装置)

passive element ①被动元件,从动部件②无源元件(对电路功能起电阻、电容、电感或它们组合作用的元件)③迟钝态元件,不活泼元件(如:膨胀系数小的热敏元件,亦称 passive component)④不活泼元素

passive entry system 被动进车系统[简称 PE system,指使用 smart key(聪明钥匙)的车门自动开、闭系统。车主随身携带该钥匙,无论装在何处,走近自己的汽车车门便会自动开启,离开后车门即自动关闭]

passive front-seat automatic restraint system 被动式(汽车)前座乘员自动保护系统(见 passive safety)

passive metal 惰性金属,有色金属

passive muffler 消极式消声器(指利用吸收、扩散和反射的方法消耗废气能量,降低排气噪声的消声装置,见 absorptive muffler, dispersive muffler, reactive muffler)

passive noise control 消极式噪声控制(指:①通过改进结构设计,使机构运转保持良好平衡、对称,借以减小振动和噪声;②使用吸声和刚性材料来减小噪声强度等消极噪声控制方法)

passive passenger-recognizing system 乘员被动识别系统(简称 PPR system,电子控制模块利用乘员体重、身高、眼球运动等传感器,识别乘员体重、身高,动态的系统,以控制诸如安全气囊爆炸力、座位及悬架软硬度以及前照灯灯光照射方向等)

passive reflector (雷达波等的)无源反射器

passive restraint 被动式乘员安全装置(见 passive restraint system)

passive restraint readiness indicator 乘员被动式约束保护装置准备状况指示器

passive restraint system (汽车乘员的)被动式约束性保护系统(指只能在撞车时对乘员加以约束防止乘员发生二次撞击受伤,但不能防止撞车的装置,一般指安全气囊、安全带等)

passive restraint tell-tale 被动约束性乘员保护装置警报灯（一般指安全带、安全气囊等乘员被动性、约束性保护装置不能充分起作用时的警报指示灯）

passive safety （汽车的）被动安全性（指只能在汽车事故发生时，防止二次冲击、保护乘员免受伤害，减少事故损失，但不能防止撞车事故发生的安全保护，如：安全气囊，安全带、保险杠等）

passive safety feature 被动安全装置（如：安全气囊、安全带及能量吸收式转向盘柱等）

passive suspension 消极式悬架（指一般的常规弹簧悬架，以区别于可自动调节车身高度和阻尼特性的 active suspension"积极式悬架"）

passive switch 被动开关，消极开关

passive system 被动系统

passive (valve) seal 消极式（气门）密封件（如：O 形密封环）

passive 4 wheel steering 被动式四轮转向（指后轮无专门的转向控制机构，在低速时不参与转向，而高速行驶时，利用悬架的作用力控制后轮转角而实现的四轮转向）

pass-key 通行钥匙（美国通用公司 1998 年以后生产的车型带遥控钥匙的电子控制防盗系统商品名）

pass-light （前照灯的）近光灯（亦称 pass beam）

PASS-LOCK 通行锁（美国通用公司 1996 年及 1996 年以后生产的某些车型带遥控钥匙的电子控制防盗系统的商品名）

pass the test 通过试验

pass with care sign "谨慎超车"标志（设置在禁止超车路段终点的禁止超车解除标志）

password code （车门遥控开关等的）口令密码，开关密码

paste ①糨糊，膏剂（如：涂在蓄电池极板栅架上由氧化铅粉、添加剂和硫酸溶液调和成的膏状活动物质）②胶合，黏结

pasted plate （蓄电池）膏状活性物质型极板（如：将氧化铅粉与添加剂和硫酸溶液调和成膏状，涂在栅架上制成的极板）

past-sale service 售后服务

pat-car （警察）巡逻车，（高速公路管理）巡视车（patrol car 的简称）

patch ①补片（修补轮胎的胶补片，修补金属器皿的金属补片、补丁）②碎屑，斑点③衬板（车身上起衬垫或增强作用的板件）④临时性的线路⑤瞬暂接触面⑥修补，临时性修补

patchboard 接线板，转插板，转接插件；接线盘，配电盘

patch test method 滤膜（色度比较）测试法（流体清洁度的一种测试方法，按规定的条件使被测流体通过测试滤膜，然后将该滤膜与标准滤膜作色度比较，以判定流体的清洁度）

patch work 修补工作（如：轮胎、路面的修补作业）

patent ①专利，专利权②取得专利权③专利的

patent application 专利申请

patent office 专利局

patent protection 专利保护

patent specification 专利说明书

path ①路径，途径（如：声径，光径，通路，电路，流路，道路）②（线圈）分支③路线，轨迹，轨线，路程，行程

path finder （汽车行驶路线的自动）导行器，自动导行装置（参见 Advanced Driver Information System）

pathline 路线，流线

path of contact 啮合线

path of parallel wheel motion 平行车轮（中间点的）运动轨迹

path (pace) notes (拉力赛车时的)路情提要(指在赛车前车队工作人员在对路线查勘、路线情况的记录的基础上给出的建议,如:某一转弯以什么样的车速及方法通过等,由赛车的副驾驶员通过头盔中的通话器随时向主驾驶员通报)

path-velocity-time recorder 行程、速率、时间记录仪

patial pressure sensor (气体)分压传感器(如:废气氧含量传感器,便是一种利用空气与废气中氧分压比测定废气中氧含量的传感器)

patial throttle characteristics (内燃机)部分负荷速度特性(曲线)(见 partial load characteristics)

patrol car ①警察巡逻车②高速公路管理用巡视车(简称 pat-car, = cruise car, 美亦称 squad car)

patrol maintenance 巡回维护,巡回维修

patrol wagon [美]囚犯车(= police wagon)

pat's 专利(权)(patents 的简称)

PATS 被动式防盗系统(passive anti-theft system 的简称)

pattern ①图,图像,曲线②(天线)方向图,图案,花样,花纹③模型,模式,样式,样品④规范,制度⑤典型,榜样⑥晶格,结构⑦喷漆直径(喷嘴喷出的圆锥状涂料在一定距离处的直径)⑧(轮胎)胎面花纹⑨模仿,摹制⑩以图案装饰,构图⑪规律

pattern analysis 图谱分析,图像分析,模式分析

pattern assembly 模型总成

pattern dislocation (轮胎)花纹错位(指花纹偏离设计位置的现象)

pattern edge (胎面)花纹边缘

patterned heat 局部加热

patterned sheet 带花纹的金属板

patterned tire 胎面有花纹的轮胎

patterned tread (具有)花纹(的)胎面(相对于 smooth tread 而言)

pattern noise (轮胎)胎面花纹噪声(指汽车行驶中胎面花纹凸棱撞击路面和胎面花纹凹槽内的空气先被压缩,后又被释放而产生的爆破声等形成的噪声,亦称 tread noise)

pattern of vibration 振动模式(= mode of vibration)

pattern panel ①(车身修理用的)非原厂制造的板件②原厂制造的已不再生产的旧型车车身修理用板件

pattern recognition 模式判别(指电子计算机对外界事物与现象的判别和认知,可分为听觉信息处理判别和视觉信息处理判别两类。前者将声响输入计算机后,对其频率等进行分析而得出判别结果,后者是用摄像机将诸如文字、图形或人、物等的图像输入计算机,由计算机对其明暗、轮廓等的信息进行处理而得出判别结果)

pattern select switch 模式选择开关(亦称 pattern selector switch, 详见 program selector)

PAU 动力吸收装置(power absorption unit)

pause ①暂停;中止,停止;中断;间歇②(发动机)缺火(= misfire)

pausing wiper (风窗玻璃的)间歇式刮水器

PAV 直扣轮胎(见 Pneu Accrochage Vertical tire)

pave 砌石块路面(比利时石块路面,汽车强化试验道路之一)

paved shoulder marking 路肩铺装标志(表明与行驶车道有别的硬路肩的标志,多以斜影线表示)

pavement ①路面,铺砌层地面,护面,铺面②铺地材料,铺道③人行道

pavement crown 路面拱顶

pavement design 路面设计,路

面结构

pavement edge line 路面边线（= edge line）

pavement ends sign 路面铺装终止标志（表明由已铺好路面的路段改变为未铺路面或铺装低劣路段的预告标志）

pavement irregularity sensitivity 路面不平敏感性（路面不平扰动输入时，汽车的响应程度）

pavement irregularity sensitivity test 路面不平敏感性试验（考察汽车在高速行驶时，承受路面干扰保持直线稳定行驶的能力）

pavement joint noise 路面接缝噪声（路面噪声的一种，指车轮驶过路面接缝时，以振动的形式传给车身，而在车内产生的噪声，参见 road noise）

pavement loading （由于车辆行驶而引起的）路面载荷

pavement skid test 路面抗滑性能试验

pavement stripe 一段路面，路段

pavement width transition marking 路面宽度变化路段标志，车道数变化路段路面线标

pawl ①（棘轮）掣子 ②扣住

pawl and ratchet mechanism 棘爪棘轮机构

pawl clutch 棘爪式离合器，棘掣式单向离合器

pawl lever 棘爪杆（如：手制动杆）

pawl pin （棘轮）掣子销

pawl stop 棘爪式止动

pawl washer 棘爪式垫圈

pawl wheel 棘轮（亦称 ratchet wheel）

pay-as-you-board bus 上车付费的公共汽车（= pay-as-you-enter bus）

pay-as-you-enter bus 在车厢入口处付费的公共汽车（= pay-as-you-board bus）

paycube （货车货箱的）有效装载容积

payload ①有效载荷，有效负荷（汽车厂定最大总质量减去整车整备质量）②仪表舱

payload capacity 有效载荷，（车身的）有效容量

payload fraction （货车）有效装载（质）量与车整备质量之比（亦称 payload-weight ratio）

payload kilometrage of loaded vehicle 重车有效运载里程［载货或载客的工作车辆，按吨位或客位与重车行程乘积计算的重车吨（客）位公里数，亦称 loaded vehicle ton (seat) - kilometer］

payload ratings 额定载重，额定有效载重

payload ratio 有效载荷比（有效载荷与车辆总重的比值）

payload weight distribution 有效载重在车桥上的分配

payload-weight ratio 载重-自重比

pay mass （货车的）装载质量，计费质量

pay weight 收费质量，计费重量

pay yards 按立方码计的（车厢）有效容积收费

pb ①动力制动器（power brake 的简称）②铅（plumbum, lead）

PBD 聚丁二烯（polybutadiene）

PBN 苯基-β 萘基胺（phenyl-betan-aph-thylamine）

PBS （车辆的）基本性能标准（performance based standard 的简称）

PBTP 聚丁烯对苯二酸烯（polybutylene terephtharate 的简称，车用塑料的一种，亦简称 PBT）

pbw 重量比份（按重量比所占的份额，parts by weight, = pbwt）

PBX switch board （车场等用的）专用（电话）交换机，小交换机（=

private branch exchange switch board）

PC ①个人计算机（personal computer）②（车轮的）螺栓孔分布圆（见 pitch circle）

PCA （美国环保署排气法规中的）产品适应性鉴定（production compliance auditing）

PC/ABS 聚碳酸酯/丙烯腈-丁二烯-苯乙烯（Polycarbonate/acrylonitrile butadiene styrene 的简称）

PCB ①聚氯联苯（polychlorinated biphenyl）②印刷电路板（printed-circuit-board）

PC-based design expert system 以个人计算机为基础的设计专家系统

PC-based local area network 以个人计算机为基础的局域网

PCC ①［美］（汽车货运协会的）个体运输者会议（private carrier conference）②（发动机）部分负荷闭缸系统（part load cylinder cut-out 的简称，当发动机部分负荷运转时，部分汽缸停止工作，部分汽缸在经济区运转）③性能概念车（performance concept car 的简称）

PCCI engine 预混合充气式压燃机（premixed charged compression ignition engine 的简称）

PCD ①节圆直径（见 pitch circle diameter）②（车轮）螺栓孔分布圆直径（见 pitch circle diameter②）

PCEV 燃料电池（纯）电动汽车（fuel cell electric vehicle 的简称）

"P-channel" metal-oxide-silicon device P 沟通金属氧化物硅半导体器件（正电荷载流子金属氧化物硅半导体器件，简称 PMOS）

PCI 预燃室喷射（prechamber injection）

PCM ①（汽车的）动力系控制模块（发动机控制模块，指汽车发动机电子控制系统的电子计算机，以前各厂家使用不同的名称呼该计算机，如：通用公司称 ECM，福特公司称 ECA，克莱斯勒公司称 SMEC。为了统一这一术语，美国政府规定，从 1995 年 1 月起各厂家一律使用 SAE J1930 推荐的术语 PCM）②（电子自动变速器的）挡位控制模块（见 power control module）③脉码调制（见 Pulse-code modulation）④脉冲控制调制（见 Pulse control modulation）⑤含水量百分比（percentage of moisture）

P cock ①小开关（pet cock）②起动注油开关（priming cock）

PCS （Lexus 的）碰撞预防系统（pre-collision system 的简称，用于减轻不可避免的碰撞事故中乘员的伤害和车辆的损坏程度，由微波雷达探测汽车行进前方的障碍物，其电子控制模块首先根据车速、转向盘转角和横摆率等数据确定碰撞可否会避免，如果算出碰撞已不可避免，该系统立即收紧前排座的安全带并启动制动助力装置，以增加制动力，降低车速，减缓碰撞力度）

PCSDM （安全气囊系统装在）客厢（仪表板下方，乘员座椅下方等处的）传感器/诊断模块（passenger compartment sensor/diagnostic module 的简称，见 ASDM）

PC-SOL 活性炭罐清除控制电磁阀（purge control solenoid 的简称，见 purge valve）

PCT 见 partial charge-state test

PCTA 预燃室式涡轮增压后冷柴油机（precombustion chamber turbocharged after cooled diesel 的简称）

PCTFE 聚氯三氟化乙烯（poly-chlorotrifluoroethylene）

PCU （混合动力车"HV"的）电力控制装置（power control unit 的简称，亦称 motor-generator ECU，简称 MG-ECU，按照 HV power management ECU 的指令实施下列控制：

①由升压变压器将驱动用蓄电池的200V直流电压升至500~650V直流电压②由直交流变换器将该高压直流变换为三相交流驱动电动机③由交直变换器将发电机发出的三相高压交流电变换为高压直流电④由降压变压器降低该高压直流电的电压供HV蓄电池和空调等设备及蓄电池充电用⑤起动电动机/发电机及电力控制装置冷却器等)

PCV 曲轴箱强制通风（见 positive crankcase ventilation system）②预燃室进气门（prechamber valve 的简称，预燃室式层状燃烧发动机中供浓混合气吸入预燃室内的气门）③压力控制阀（pressure control valve 的简称）④燃料电池（电动）车（见 fuel cell vehicle）

PC valve 压力控制阀（pressure control valve 的简称）

PcV value PcV值（密封件端面比压 Pc 与密封端面平均滑动速度 V 的乘积）

PCV valve 曲轴箱通风量控制阀（positive crankcase ventilation valve，一般为电磁阀"solenoid valve"）

PD ①中径，分度圆直径（pitch diameter）②计划部门（plans division）③极间距离（polar distance）④电位器，变压设备（potential device）⑤电位差（potential difference）⑥电动的，动力传动的（power driven）⑦初步设计（preliminary design）⑧防护性延迟（preventive detention）⑨生产部门（production department）⑩传动带轮传动（pulley drive）⑪多普勒脉冲（Pulse Doppler）⑫脉冲宽度（pulse duration）⑬瞳孔中心距（pupillary distance）⑭货物配送（physical distribution）

Pd ①钯（palladium）②已付的，付讫（paid）

PDC 入驻倒车距离控制系统（parking distance control 的简称）

PDCA 计划-实施-检查-改进（plan-do-check-action，20世纪50年代初美国戴明首先提出全面质量管理循环 PDCA cycle）

PDF 概率密度函数（probability density function 的简称）

PDI 交车前检验（predelivery inspection 的简称）

PD indicator 压差指示器（pressure difference indicator 的简称）

PDM ①脉冲密度调制（pulse density modulation 的简称）②产品数据管理（product data management 的简称）

PDP 容积泵（变容泵，活塞泵，见 positive displacement pump）

Pd-perovskite catalyst （日本大发公司研制的具有自己再生机能的汽车催化转化器用）钯—$MFeO_3$（$LaFe_{0.95}Pd_{0.05}O_3$）催化剂（见 intelligent catalyst）

PD radar 脉冲式多普勒雷达（pulse doppler radar 的简称，指能够测量发射频率和所收到的目标反射频率之间频移并据此确定目标的接近速度和距离的雷达，具有很强的抑制固定目标或移动目标产生杂波的能力）

PDS 程序控制驾驶系统（见 Programmed Driving System）

PDSmethod 苯酚二磺酸法（见 phenol disulphonic acid method）

PE ①性能评价（performance evaluation）②外围设备（peripheral equipment）③允许误差（permissible error）④光电的（photo-electric）⑤聚乙烯（polythene）⑥预估，预先评价（preliminary evaluation）⑦压力元件（pressure element）⑧概率误差（probable error）

peak ①峰值，②波峰，尖峰

peak amplitude method 峰值振幅法

(最大振幅法)

peak brake power 发动机峰值有效功率(在发动机转速范围内,所能发出的最大有效功率,不同于 maximum brake power,对于商用柴油机来讲,maximum 及 peak brake power 都在通常使用范围以外,参见 peak power engine speed)

peak clipper 峰值削波器(峰值限幅器)

peak coil current (点火)线圈的峰值电流(指其初级绕组中流过的峰值电流)

peak combustion temperature 峰值燃烧温度,最高燃烧温度

peak contact 齿尖接触

peaked-head piston 凸顶活塞(亦称 peaked-roof piston)

peak efficiency 最高效率

peak engine (特性曲线中转矩随转速变化急剧,产生有效转矩的转速范围狭窄的)峰形转矩曲线发动机

peaker 脉冲修尖电路

peak factor 峰值因素(任一交变波的最大波幅与其均方根值之比,参见 rms value)

peak friction force (轮胎与路面间的)最大摩擦力,峰值摩擦力

peak hour traffic 高峰小时交通量(在一条道路上或车道上连续一小时内通过的最大交通量)

peak (ing) transformer 脉冲变压器(= pulse transformer)

peak inverse voltage 反向峰值电压(简称 PIV)

peak load 峰值负载(①恒值载荷的最大载荷②疲劳载荷中作为时间函数的一阶导数从正号变至负号处的载荷)

peak load conditions ①(汽车运输客货量)高峰期②最大负荷状况

peak output 峰值输出(最大输出 = maximum output)

peak performance 峰值功能(最佳性能)

peak power 峰值功率(简称 PP)

peak power engine speed (发动机)峰值(有效)功率转速(发动机发出峰值有效功率时的转速,参见 peak brake power)

peak pulse voltage 脉冲峰压(脉冲峰值电压,峰值脉冲电压)

peak revs 最高转速,峰值转速

peak smoke opacity characteristic (柴油机的)峰值排烟不透明度特性(峰值烟浓度特性,峰值排烟浓度特性,峰值排烟特性)

peak-to-average ratio 峰值与平均值之比

peak-to-peak ①正负峰间值,极大到极小(简称 PP)②(振摆或脉冲的)全振幅,双振幅

peak-to-peak noise 正负峰间值噪声

peak torque 高峰转矩,峰值转矩

peak torque speed (发动机的)峰值转矩转速(发动机产生最大转矩时的转速)

peak-to-valley ratio 峰值-谷值比

peak traffic flow 高峰(时间)交通流量(特定状况下的最大交通量,简称 peak traffic)

peak voltage 峰值电压,最大电压

peaky ①尖峰的②转矩特性曲线呈尖峰状的(指转矩特性曲线陡直的发动机,仅在狭小的转速范围内,才能产生足够的克服外界阻力的转矩,在不换挡的情况下,克服外界阻力的转矩增加能力很弱,行驶中必须频繁换挡)

pear curve 梨线

pearl curve 珍珠线

pearlite 珠光体(铁素体和渗碳体组织的机械混合物,含碳量平均0.8%,强度较高,硬度适中,有一定塑性)

pearlitic iron 珠光体铸铁

pearl mica coating （轿车车身的）珠光色云母漆面（将涂复二氧化肽层的云母研成细片混入涂料中制成，涂在车身上其漆膜呈珍珠闪光故名）

pearl white （车身颜色）珍珠白

pebble tread 卵石路面行驶用（轮胎）胎面

peck ①配克（英制容积，体积单位。在英国用于液体和干物，在美国只用于干物。1 peck = $\frac{1}{4}$ bushel，1英国配克 = 554.84in³，1美国配克 = 537.605in³ = 8.718L）②凿孔，用尖头工具凿孔

peculiar 独特的，特有的，特殊的

pedal 踏板，踩踏板

pedal-actuated 踏板驱动的（= pedal driven）

pedal backward movement preventing construction （碰撞时）踏板后移防止结构（避免踏板后移碰伤驾驶者下肢）

pedal brake 踏板（控制式）制动器，行车制动器

pedal clearance ①踏板离地间隙（指踏板踩到底时，与地板间的距离）②踏板自由行程（= free travel of pedal，pedalfree play）

pedal contact 踏板控制式触点

pedal control 踏板控制，踏板操纵（= pedal drive，treadle drive）

pedal curve 垂足曲线

pedal-displacement 踏板位移量，踏板位移距离，踏板移动距离

pedal effort 踏板力（= treadle effort，指踩踏板所用的力，亦称 pedal force）

pedal extension 踏板接长部

pedal feel （驾驶者的）踏板感（如：踏板软绵或过硬等）

pedal free auto choke 与加速踏板位置无关的全自动阻风门（简称 PFAC）

pedal gear change 踏板换挡，脚踏变速（装置）

pedal grip 踏板（防滑）踏面（如：踏板的橡皮踏面）

pedal hole lower covering 踏板孔底盖

pedal jack 脚踏式千斤顶（参见 foot-operated jack）

pedalless 无踏板的

pedal lever seal （离合器等的）踏板密封套（防止尘埃、水分等沿踏板杆件进入驾驶室的密封件）

pedal line 垂足线

pedal-operated dip switch 踏板变光开关（= dip switch）

pedal operated valve 踏板操纵阀（足控阀，脚控阀，= foot valve）

pedal panel （汽车车身的）踏板区底板（装制动踏板、离合器踏板、加速门踏板处的底板，= toe board，toe board panel）

pedal play 踏板自由行程，踏板空程

pedal position-sensing switch 踏板位置传感开关（向电子控制模块发送踏板踩踏信号）

pedal pulsation （ABS系统制动时，制动）踏板脉动

pedal ratio （制动）踏板比（指制动踏板行程与制动主缸活塞行程之比或踏板至支点的长度与汽缸推杆至支点的长度之比）

pedal release system 踏板松脱系统（当汽车碰撞冲击力超过某规定值时，制动器、离合器等的踏板会自动松脱，以避免驾驶人员脚、腿受伤，简称PRS）

pedal reserve 踏板行程余量（车身地板至踏板下面之储备距离）

pedal stroke sensor 踏板行程传感器（亦称，pedal travel sensor 传感踏板行程及踏板踩踏速率）

pedal surface 垂足曲面

pedal transformation 垂足变换
pedal travel gauge 踏板行程测量器
pedal triangle 垂足三角形
peddler ①（美俗）沿途各站都停的慢车（=pedlar）②流动商贩
peddle truck 挨户送货汽车（=door-to-door delivery truck）
pedestal ①底座，支座，台，台座，柱脚 ②轴承座，轴承台，轴架 ③基础
pedestrain detection technology 行人探测技术
pedestrain-impact-energy absorbing construction （汽车的）行人碰撞能量吸收结构
pedestrian ①行人，步行者 ②徒步的，步行的
pedestrian actuated controller （信号的）行人引发控制器（由行人探测器引动的自动信号控制器）
pedestrian actuated signal 行人引发信号（由行人探测器引动自动信号控制器发出的信号）
pedestrian airbag 行人安全气囊（装在汽车上的、撞到行人时即自动胀开、保护行人的安全气囊）
Pedestrian airbag system 行人（安全）气囊（在行驶中，当装在前保险杠后的碰撞传感器测得已有行人临近车头时，立即引爆发动罩下前端的安全气囊保护行人）
pedestrian barrier 行人护栏
pedestrian clearance interval 允许行人过街时间（从"允许行人过街"信号开始到"不许过街"信号出现之间一段时间）
pedestrian-controlled 由行人控制的
pedestrian crossing 人行横道（=cross walk）
pedestrian crossing sign 人行过路标志，人行横道标志
pedestrian detection, recognition and braking system 行人探测-认知和制动系统
pedestrian detector 行人感知器，行人探测器（通常为按钮感知器，设置在过路横道附近）
pedestrian guard rail 行人护栏（为行人安全设置的栏栅）
pedestrian injury reducing body （碰撞时）行人伤害减轻型车身
pedestrian island （交叉口处）行人安全岛，路中避车岛（在美国称 refuge island）
pedestrian motor vehicle traffic accident 行人与车辆碰撞事故（简称 pedestrian accident）
pedestrian phase 行人信号相（分配给行人交通的信号相）
pedestrian protection （汽车的）行人保护（系统，装置或技术）
pedestrian protection airbag 行人保护安全气囊（简称 PPA）
pedestrian protect system （汽车的）行人保护系统（简称 PPS）
pedestrian way 人行道
pedimeter 踏力计（测定制动踏板踩踏力的装置，=pedometer）
pedlar （美俗）慢车（每站都停的公共汽车，参见 peddler）
PEEC （卡特皮勒公司的）柴油机可编程电子控制系统（programable Electronic Engine Control 的简称）
PEEK 聚醚酮醚（polyether etherketone 的简称）
peeling 起鳞，剥落，脱皮
peel strength 撕裂强度
peel test 剥离试验（如：两黏接件的黏接强度试验）
peel tyres （驾驶汽车时）突然加大节气门开度
peen ①锤顶（锤的非锤击面端）②用锤顶端敲击，锤击，锤击修理车身板件 ③用小锤轻打使钢材表面硬化 ④喷丸处理（=pean, pene, pein）

peen plating （金属粉末）扩散渗镀法

peep 吉普车（美俚，=jeep）

peephole 检查孔，观察孔

peerless 无比的（无双的）

peerless alloy 镍路高电阻合金（镍78.5%，铬16.5%，铁3.0%，锰2.0%）

PEFCs 聚合物型电解液燃料电池（polymer electrolyte fuel cell 的简称）

peg ①销，销钉②（循环球-曲柄销式转向器中的）曲柄销③（蜗杆指销式转向器中的）指销（亦称 stud）④用销固定

peg and worm steering 蜗杆指销式转向机构（= peg-and-worm steering gear cam and worm steering, worm and peg steering, peg and worm lever steering）

peg wire 锁止钢丝，防松钢丝（= locking wire，防止螺母或螺栓松动）

PE headlight 多椭圆形反射镜气体放电灯泡式前照灯

pein 锤顶；锤击，喷丸（参见 peen）

pellet 小球，丸

pelleted substrate 颗粒状载体（催化排气净化装置中，一种具有鹅卵形、串珠形、小圆柱形或小球形的催化剂载体）

pelletized form （小）丸形；（小）球形，粒状

pellet-type catalytic converter 颗粒状载体型催化转化器（早期使用的催化转化器，目前多使用整体蜂窝状载体催化转化器）

pellet-type thermostat （散热器）子弹形石蜡节温器（其工作元件为封闭在其子弹型感应头体内、83℃时熔化成液体、体积急剧膨胀的特种石蜡）

Peltier effect 珀尔贴效应（电流通过两个非同类金属接触处的放热现象）

Peltier electromotive force 珀尔贴电动势

pelvic restraint belt 骨盆（部位）安全带，腰安全带（见 lap belt）

pelvis injury （碰撞事故中人体）骨盆伤害

PEM 质子交换膜（proton exchange membrane 的简称，燃料电池使用的聚合物电解质膜，不传导电子，但却是离子、质子的良导体）

PEMFC 质子交换膜燃料电池（proton exchange membrane fuel cell 的简称）

PEM fuel cell 质子交换膜燃料电池（proton exchange membrane full cell 的简称）

pen 笔，笔头

penalty test 补充性试验（正常试验所得结果不满意时所做的补充试验）

pencil ①束，簇②记录头，铅笔

pencil-type glow plug 铅笔型预热塞（亦称 sheathed-type glow plug, 封装在导热绝缘陶瓷内的电热丝型套管预热塞）

pencil-type injector 笔式喷油器

pencil (type) spray （燃油的）直柱形喷雾束

pen container 牲畜集装箱（装运活牲畜、家禽等，亦称圈栏集装箱，顶部可遮阳光，侧壁能开启，备有饲料槽等）

pendant ①吊挂，悬置，悬挂物②钩环，挂钩，吊架③悬吊式操纵台

pendant control box 悬垂式控制盒（悬吊式按钮开关盒）

pendant (control) switch 悬垂式控制开关，悬挂式按钮开关

pendant signal 悬垂式信号装置（如：悬挂在路幅上的信号机）

pendant type pedal 悬吊式踏板，吊装式踏板（= suspended type pedal）

pendular motion 摆动（= pendulum motion）

pendulous absorber （利用反相振动来消减曲轴、特别是柴油机曲轴振动的）反相减振器（亦称 pendulous damper）

pendulum 摆，摆动体

pendulum bearing 摆动支座

pendulum controlling ①摆锤控制 ②摆锤控制的

pendulum damper 见 pendulous absorber

pendulum gear 钟摆机构

pendulum stability 悬摆稳定性

pendulum-type 摆式的，摆动式的

pene ①锤顶 ②锤击 ③喷丸（参见 peen）

penetrable 可渗透的，可穿透的，可贯入的

penetrablility 渗透性，贯入性，可穿透性，透明性，透明度

penetrant ①渗透剂 ②渗透的

penetrant method （超声波探伤的）穿透法

penetrant nondestructive test 穿透法非破坏性试验（如：利用超声波、X光、γ射线等进行的测定和试验）

penetrate 渗透，穿透，贯穿

penetrating oil （松动锈死零件用的）渗透油

penetration-resistant glass 抗穿孔玻璃

penetrator （硬度计）压头

penetrometer number 针入度值，针入黏度值

penetrometer viscosity ①针入黏度，针入度 ②穿透度，刺度

penny weight 本尼威特（英钱，英、美金衡制单位，代号 dwt, pwt, 1 dwt = $\frac{1}{20}$ 金衡盎司 = 24 grain = 4.5552 g）

penople carrier 小型厢式客车，小型面包车（=[美] miniran）

Pensky Marten's Closed Cup Method 宾斯克-马丁密封杯（石油产品闪点）测定法，宾-马氏闭式闪点测定法

Pensky Marten's Closed Tester 宾斯克-马丁密封式（石油产品闪点）试验器，宾-马氏闭式闪点仪

pentane 戊烷（C_5H_{12}，有三种同分异构体，为汽油组分）

Pentastar 五星（Chrysler, Jeep 等使用的 3.6L V 形 6 缸顶置双凸轮轴可变气门正时 24 气门汽油机商品名）

pentasulfide 五硫化物

pent-crown piston 见 penthouse

penthouse （指单面靠墙搭建的）斜屋顶式棚舍[pent-roof 指这种棚舍的斜顶，用来说明燃烧室形状时：①指斜屋顶形燃烧室，为楔形燃烧室的一种 ②用来说明活塞顶时，如 pent crown piston，指斜（屋）顶形活塞，楔形顶活塞的一种 ③亦指四气门式的屋脊形燃烧室，每面两个气门，火花塞位于中央的类半球形燃烧室]

penthouse for motor car 停（汽）车棚

pentode 五极管

pent-roof combustion chamber ①楔形燃烧室，斜屋顶形燃烧室 ②半球形燃烧室，屋脊形燃烧室（见 penthouse③）

people's car 人民车，大众车（一般指小排量的廉价车）

peptization 胶溶（作用），分散（作用），解胶（作用），反絮凝（作用），塑解

peptize 胶溶（使成为胶体溶液，使成为溶胶，塑解）

PERA 英国生产工程技术研究协会（Production Engineering Research Association of Great Britain）

perambulator 测距仪，间距规

perbunan 丁腈橡胶，别布橡胶（见 NBR）

Perbury drive 泊伯瑞连续无级变速器（滚轮传动型无级变速器的一种，见 toric transmission）

perceive ①知觉，察觉，发觉②看见，听见③了解，领悟

perceived （人体）可感知的，可察觉的，可感觉到的

perceived intensity 知觉强度

perceived noise level 感知噪声级（用于评价活塞发动机或喷气机的噪声）

percent 百分数，百分率（%），百分比

percentage 百分数，百分率，百分比

percentage articulation 百分清晰度

percentage elongation 延伸百分率

percentage error 误差率（百分比相对误差）

percentage inclination （用百分比表示坡度的）倾斜率，坡度率

percentage of ash 含碳量百分比

percentage of burned fuel 燃烧百分率（累计燃烧率，指燃烧过程中某瞬时前已燃烧的燃油量占循环喷油量的百分数）

percentage of contraction 收缩百分率

percentage of film taken off （过滤液体用的滤膜的）滤膜萃取率（滤膜浸在洁净的 NY120 溶剂油后的失重百分率）

percentage of heat release 放热百分率（累计放热率，指燃烧过程中某瞬间前已放出的热量占循环喷油量总低热值的百分率）

percentage of mechanical handling 机械装卸作业百分比值

percentage of moisture 含水量百分比

percentage test ①（组成物含量、成分的）百分比测定②百分比抽样试验（在一组制品中抽出一定百分比的试样进行试验，= per hundred test）

percent by volume 体积百分比，容积百分比

percent by weight 重度百分率

percent content 百分率含量，含量百分率

percentile ①百分位，百分额，百分范围（如：a man of 95th percentile height 该人的身高在 95% 的人的范围内）②按总额百等分布的间隔

percentile curve 用百分数表示的分配曲线

85-percentile speed 85% 车速（道路交通中，指 85% 的交通车辆低于此车速，15% 的交通车辆高于此车速）

percent of grade 坡度百分比

percent of pass 合格率，通过率（%）

percentum 百分数，百分比（= percent）

perception ①感知，知觉②洞察力，理解力

perception-reaction time （驾驶员行车时）感知反应时间

perch ①（人的）安全位置②杆，棒；支垫，支座③杆（= pole, 英国的长度单位，1 perch = $16\frac{1}{2}$ feet, 但在爱尔兰 1 perch = 21 feet）④放置，搁下

perch bolt 汽车钢板弹簧 U 形螺栓（= spring centre bolt）

perchoroethylene 过氯乙烯，高氯乙烯（用以清洗零件表面油污的一种溶剂）

percolate 渗透，渗滤

percolation ①渗滤，渗透，渗流②浸出，浸透③呛油现象（化油器浮子室的汽油在夏季因受发动机罩

下高温作用而汽化，由各喷嘴渗漏到化油器腔筒及进气管内，导致混合气过浓，将发动机呛死或造成停车后再起动困难）

percolator 渗滤器，渗流器

percussion 冲击，撞击

percussion test 撞击试验，击穿试验

percussion wave 冲击波（= shock wave）

percussion weld ①冲击焊 ②冲击焊缝

perfect ①完全的，无缺点的，熟练的，理想的②使完全，完成

perfect combustion 完全燃烧（= complete combustion）

perfect elastic body 理想弹性体

perfect field 完全域（体）

perfect fitting 完全配合

perfect fluid 理想液体（= ideal fluid）

perfect gas 理想气体

perfect lubrication 完全润滑

perfectly diffused scavenging 完全混合扫气（假定新鲜充量进入汽缸的瞬间即与废气完全混合，而形成均一的混合气排出的扫气过程，= scavenging with perfect mixing）

perfectly stirred reactor 全搅动反应器（全搅动燃烧器）

perfectly stratified scavenging 完全层状扫气（在换气过程中，废气与新鲜充量始终分为两层而不混合，直到废气完全排净，汽缸完全被新鲜充量充满且新鲜充量亦无损失的理想换气过程，亦称理想扫气"perfect scavenging"）

perfect vacuum 完全真空

perfluoro plastic 高氟塑料

perforate 打孔，钻孔，穿孔，打眼

perforated basket 筛孔（在水槽中清洗小零件用）

perforated metal band excitor （一种传感器的）栅孔金属带激励环

perforated plate type atomizer 孔板式喷雾器

perforated tube 多孔管，带孔管（亦写作 perforates 如：消声器内的多孔管）

perforation ①打孔，穿孔②孔，眼，孔洞

perform 履行，实行，执行，完成

performance ①（运转）性能，特性（曲线），操作效能，表现②运行，执行，实行，履行，完成，作业，操作③作业效率（= 额定工时/直接作业用的实际工时%）

performance analysis 性能分析

performance based standard （车辆的）基本性能标准（简称PBS）

performance-boosting 性能强化的

performance car 高性能车

performance characteristics 工作特性

performance chart 性能曲线图，工作特性图（如：由测功机测得的发动机输出功率、转矩、油耗随发动机转速而变化的曲线图，亦称characteristic curve, performance diagram, performance figure）

performance correction curve 性能修正曲线

performance depreciation 性能恶化

performance estimation 性能预测，性能估计，性能评估

performance evaluation 性能鉴定，性能评定，性能评价（简称PE）

performance figure ①性能指标；质量指标，质量指数②性能图解，特性图③性能数据，性能数字

performance for anti-diesel knocking 抗柴油机爆燃性能，抗柴油机粗爆性能

performance for anti-knocking 抗爆性能

performance number ①特性值，性能值②（英国石油学会提出的表示

汽油抗爆性与发动机功率关系的)抗爆功率比(指辛烷值高于 100 的高级汽油和辛烷值为 100 的异辛烷,在无爆燃的条件下,所能发出的最大功率之比,用% 来表示,简称 PN)

performance parameter 性能参数

performance predication method (车辆的)性能估算法,性能预测法

performance prediction 性能预测

Performance Rod (日本本田公司)高性能滑柱式独立悬架(商品名)

performance rod (连接身车底面左、右悬架支撑杆支座的)车身横支杆(提高车身结构刚度,有的用于固定车身前围板)

performance simulation 性能模拟

performance test 性能试验,特性试验

performance-to-weight ratio 性能-重量比

performance-tuned suspension 性能可调控式悬架

per-hundred test ①(含量)百分比测定②百分比抽样试验(= percentage test)

pericycloid 外摆线(指滚动圆沿基圆的外侧作外切或内切的纯滚动时,动圆上任一点的轨迹,见 epicycloid)

peridic damping 周期阻尼(亦称 under damping "欠阻尼",指阶跃响应出现过冲的阻尼)

perimeter 周边,周围,周长;圆周

perimeter alarm (汽车防盗系统的)周边报警器

perimeter frame (轿车车身的)边框型车架(中间无横梁,车身安装在由两边纵梁和两端横梁组成的框架结构上,亦称 periphery frame)

perimeter protection (对汽车的)周边保护(指对汽车车门、行李舱、发动机罩驾驶室等汽车周边构件的状况进行的检测与维护,参见 volumetric protection)

perimeter-type frame 框形构架

period ①周期②时期,期间,阶段③时间,间隔,时代

periodic (al) ①周期的,定期的,定时的,间断的,间歇的,断续的,循环的②高碘的

periodic change 周期变化

periodic charge (蓄电池)定期充电

periodic current 振荡电流,周期电流

periodic duty 周期性负载工况,周期负载,循环作业

periodic exiting force 周期性激(振)力

periodicity ①频率(参见 frequency)②周期性

periodic maintenance 定期维护(按技术文件规定的间隔行程或时间进行的维护)

periodic motor vehicle inspection 汽车定期检验,汽车定期检测(简称 PMVI)

periodic oil change 定期更换机油

periodic one-way sign 定时单向通行标志(单向通行路每日某一定时间改变通行方向用的标志)

periodic oscillations 周期性振荡

periodic preventative maintenance inspections 计划预防维护检验

periodic preventive ①定期预防的②定期预防措施

period of acceleration 加速期,加速期间

period of braking 制动期,制动期间

period of parts accelerated wear 零件的加速磨损期

period of parts normal collaboration 零件的正常运转期,零件的正常工作期

period of valve opening 气门开启期

periodogram 周期图

period regulation 定期调整

peripheral 周边的，圆周的，外表面的

peripheral cam 圆周凸轮

peripheral clearance ①轮缘间隙（工作轮与导轮间的空隙）②周边间隙（如：旋转件周边与壳壁间的空隙）

peripheral component of velocity 切向分速度

peripheral driver （数字集成电路的）外围设备驱动器（能对数字输入电压做出响应，并能输出驱动电压或电流的数字设备与外部非数字设备的接口集成电路）

peripheral equipment 外部设备，外围设备（简称 PE）

peripheral exhaust port （转子发动机外旋轮线缸体上的）周边排气孔

peripheral flow air cooling system 环流风冷装置（转子发动机的一种冷却系统，散热叶片沿外旋轮线缸体外壳排列，冷却空气沿外壳周边流动）

peripheral force 圆周力，切向力（＝circumferential force）

peripheral inlet port （转子发动机外旋轮线缸体上的）周边进气口，周边进气孔

peripheral intake （转子发动机的）周边进气

peripheral jet ①切向射流，周边射流②（气垫装置底部）分布在周边的喷口

peripherally ported 周边开口的（二冲程汽缸）

peripheral magnetic voltage （电磁阀磁路的）周边磁感应电动势（闭合磁路周围的磁场强度的线积分，$V_\mathrm{m}=\oint H\cdot\mathrm{d}s$，式中：$H$—磁场强度。按安培定理，等于磁通势，见 magnetomotive force）

peripheral mixture （空气与燃油的）周边混合（指燃油被喷到燃烧室周边近壁处，有相当数量的燃油在燃烧室壁上形成油膜，而在燃烧室周边，其燃油蒸气与空气边混合边燃烧的混合方式）

peripheral monitoring sensor 见 monitoring around sensor

peripheral port （转子发动机）周边进、排气口

peripheral-port（RC）engine 周边进气式（转子）发动机

peripheral pressure 圆周压力

peripheral primary inlet port （转子发动机的）周面主进气口，周面主进气孔（主进气口在缸体内周面上）

peripheral pump 周流泵（非容积式离心径流泵的一种，如：impeller pump 叶轮泵、turbine pump 涡轮泵。流体在泵壳内旋转的叶轮或泵轮产生的离心力的作用下，沿泵壳内圆周面流动，并由该圆周面上的出口甩出）

peripheral ratio 周缘速比

peripheral secondary inlet port （转子发动机的）周边副进气口，周边副进气孔（副进气口在外旋轮线缸体上）

peripheral stress 边缘应力，圆周应力

peripheral support circuit （微型电子计算机的）外围支援电路（外部辅助电路）

peripheral velocity 圆周线速度，圆周速度（＝peripheral speed, circumferential velocity）

peripheral vision 周边视觉（将目标偏离主视线并在中央视野以外观看的视觉）

peripheric sealing （转子发动机的）周边密封（指径向密封片与缸壁之间的密封）

periphery 周边，周线，边缘，圆周，圆柱体表面，外围，外缘，周围，外周，周边

periphery efficiency 周边效率

periphery frame 见 perimeter frame

periscope-type rear view mirror 潜望镜型后视镜

peristaltic pump 蠕动泵（泵内壁由柔性材料制成，利用内壁的蠕动挤压所泵的流体）

peritectic structure （金相）共析组织

peri-trochoid （作为三角转子发动机缸体腔壁理论型线的）双弧长、短轴短幅外摆线 [为短幅外摆线 "curtate epicycloid" 的特例，亦称 epitrochoid，在平面上一动圆（发生圆）沿一固定圆（基圆）的外侧作外切纯滚动时，若该动圆的半径正好是基圆半径的1/2，则动圆半径上的一点（称创成点）的轨迹为一封闭双弧长、短轴短幅外摆线，亦称双弧长、短轴短幅外旋轮线，其长轴 = 2 ($R+e$)，短轴 = 2 ($R-e$)，R-基圆中心至动圆中心的距离，称创成半径，e-创成点至动圆中心的距离，称偏心距，见 curtate epicycloid]

peri-trochoid housing 三角转子发动机缸体（其内腔为三角转子发动机工作室，见 peri-trochoid）

perlite 珠光体（= pearlite）

permafrost 永久冻土

permalloy 坡莫合金（强磁性铁镍合金，透磁合金，具有高透磁性及低磁滞损失的特性。原指含镍78.5%，铁21.5%，现在也指加入其他元素如铜、铬、锰等的合金）

permanence 永久性，持久性，稳定度，安定度

permanence condition 不变条件

permanent 永久的，不变的，固定的，常设的

permanent deformation 永久变形，残余变形

permanent filter element 永久性滤芯（可清洗的滤芯）

permanent flow 稳定流

permanent four-wheel drive 常四轮驱动

Permanent International Association of Road Congress （联合国）常设国际道路会议协会，简称 PIARC

permanent joint 不可拆连接

permanent load 永久荷载，固定荷载

permanently-attached hydraulic jack 固定安装在车上的液压举升器（车装式液压千斤顶，= built-in hydraulic jack）

permanent magnet 永久磁铁

permanent magnet alternator 永磁交流发电机

permanent magnetic pulse generator 永久磁铁式脉冲发生器（用做转速或曲轴转角、凸轮轴转角传感器等）

permanent magnet suspension system 永磁体悬浮系统

permanent output 持久输出功率，长时间运转输出功率

permanent repair 小修，日常修理

permanent seal cooling （发动机的）长效密封式水冷却法（一种改良的压力式水冷法，另外加装有一套辅助散热器及水箱，供冷却水蒸发、膨胀时使用。一般都加有防冻剂等添加剂，使用期间不再补充加水）

permanent set 永久变形

permanent shear stability index 永久剪切稳定性指数 [简称 PSSI，表示车用发动机机油的增黏剂剪切稳定性的一种方法，PSSI =（剪切前黏度 - 剪切后黏度）/（剪切前黏度 - 基础油黏度）]

permanent side walls （敞篷车）车

厢固定侧壁
permanent slip 固定的滑移（必定要产生的滑移，如：液力变矩器将发动机输出转矩转换为自动变速器输入转矩的过程中，其泵轮与涡轮间的滑移）
permanent speed change 转速稳定变动率
permanent universal joint 不容许轴向移位的万向节
permanent way 轨道
permeability ①渗透性（指液体、蒸气或气体透过人造橡胶或天然橡胶一类固体材料的能力）②磁导率系数，磁导率
permeability apparatus 透气率测定仪（=permeability meter）
permeability test 渗透性试验
permeability to air 透（空）气性，透（空）气率（=air permeability）
permeability to heat 热导率，热导性（=permeability of heat）
permeable 可渗透的，可透过的，可穿透的，渗透性的
permeameter 渗透性试验仪，渗透仪，磁导计
permeance 磁导（磁路的磁阻的倒数，见 reluctance）
permeate 渗入，渗透
permeation 渗透（作用），穿透（作用）
permissible 容许的，许可的
permissible acceleration amplitude 容许加速度幅度
permissible clearance 容许间隙（见 limiting clearance）
permissible error 允许误差
permissible level of noise 容许噪声级
permissible load 容许荷载
permissible maximum weight of a vehicle 最大允许车重（道路所允许的，可行驶状态下车辆自重及其最大装载量之和）

permissible play 容许自由行程，允许间隙
permissible tolerance 容许公差
permissible variation 容许偏差
permissible wear 允许磨损（小于极限磨损，尚能保持技术文件规定的工作能力，并受经济因素制约的汽车零件磨损量）
permissible wear groove （盘式制动器摩擦衬片上的）容许磨损量标槽（当磨损到该槽底时，表示已到允许磨损极限）
permit 允许，准许
permitted rim 允许轮辋（指除标准轮辋外，尚允许使用的轮辋）
permittivity 电容率，介电常数
permutation ①排列②置换，交换，互换，变更，取代③重新配置
permutator 转换开关，变换器
perovskite chemical compound $MFeO_3$ 类化合物（指"$CaTiO_3$"中的 Ca，Ti 被其他元素置换的化合物）
peroxide 过氧化物
peroxide-destroying inhibitor 过氧化物分解剂（滑油防氧化剂的一种）
peroxide reaction 过氧化反应
peroxy-acetylnitrate 过氧乙烯硝酸酯，硝化过氧乙烯，过氧乙烯硝酸盐（RCO_3NO_2，汽车排放光化学烟雾成分之一，对人体、植物都有害，简称 PAN）
perpendicular ①垂直的，正交的，成直角的②垂直，正交，竖直③垂线，垂直面
perpendicular bisector 中垂线
perpendicular dielectric constant （液晶分子）短轴方向的介电常数
perpendicular electric conductivity （液晶分子）短轴方向电导率
perpendicular line 垂直线
perpendicular lug space （轮胎）花纹块法向间距

perpendicular movement　垂直运动

perpendicular reflective index　（液晶分子）短轴方向折射率

perpendicular space　正交空间

perpetual　不间断的，一直的，永久的

perpetuate　①（使）永存，维持 ②不间断的，永久的，永恒的（= perpetual）

per second　每秒（简称 ps）

persistence　存留，持久性

persistence of vision　视觉暂留

persistent　持久的，持续的，不断的

personal　个人的，私人的

personal breakdown cover　（车辆保险用语）含人身伤害（保险）

personal car　私人轿车，个人用轿车 （= personal automobile）

personal computer　个人计算机（简称 PC 机）

personal equation　个人在观察上的误差

personal factor　人为因素

personality　①个性 ②符合个人喜好的式样、颜色等

personality　（原指人的个性，现亦用于形容汽车的）特点，特性

personalized car　人性化轿车

personalized number plate　（英、美等国一种由车主姓名第一个字母或整名或专用职业等代号组成的）私人车牌（车牌内容由车主支出一定费用后自己选定，而与主管部门统一规定的格式不同）

personalized repair method　（车辆的）个人包修法

personal noise monitor　（测定人所受到的环境噪声的）携带式噪声监测器（注意：不是测定人的噪声）

personal radio　个人无线电通信（指无须取得无线电通信许可证的个人用无线电通信，如：日本规定为使用 900 MHz 频带的调频电波，输出功率在 5W 以内者，车对车通信距离为 2~5km）

personal rapid transit　快速个人公共交通（一般指新型的快速客运系统，如 cabin taxi 的 taxi style，简称 PRT）

personal transportation　个体运输（指个人乘坐轿车等出行，相对于乘坐公共汽车、大客车等出行的群体运输而言）

personal vehicle　乘用车（car 与 bus 的总称）

personal vehicle system　自动驾驶系统，智能汽车系统（= autonomous driving system，简称 PVS，日本 Nissan 公司，自 1987 年起开发的系统，为研究汽车自动驾驶基本功能）

personal weight distribution　体重分布（如：人体质量作用在座椅和靠背上的压力分布）

personnel　人员，全体人员

personnel restraining device　乘员约束性安全装置（如：安全带等）

personsal luggage　随身李行，小件行包

perspective　投影的，透视的

perspective drawing　透视图（亦称 perspective view）

perspex　①聚 2-甲基丙烯酸酯（polymethyl methacrylate，简称 PMMA）②塑胶玻璃

perspex headlamp cover　前照灯的塑腰玻璃罩

perturb　使紊乱，干扰

perturbation　扰乱，紊乱，波动

pervade　蔓延，弥漫，渗透，普及，充满

perveance　（电子管）电导系数

pervious　可透过的

PES reflector　多椭圆面反射镜

PES headlight　多椭圆面前照灯

PET　聚对苯二甲酸乙二醇酯（polyethylene terephthalate 的简称）

pet cock 小旋塞，小开关（简称 P cock）

PETP 对苯二酸酯化聚乙烯（polyethylene terephthalate）

petrochemical 石油化学的

petrochimical ①石油化学的②（以石油为原料的）石油化学产品

petroil 汽油机油混合油（petrol-oil mixture 的简称，用于二冲程发动机）

petroil mixture dispenser （加油站专为二冲程汽油发动机配制好的）汽油—机油混合油加注装置（简称 petroil despenser）

petroil（mixture）lubrication （二冲程发动机的）汽油机油混合油润滑方式（将机油按一定比例混入汽油中，随可燃混合气进入发动机）

petrol ①[英]汽油（亦称 motor spirit, petroleum spirit, 美称 gasoline 或 gas）②给……加汽油

petrol-air mixture 汽油空气混合气

petrolatum oil 凡士林油，液状石蜡，防锈油

petrol barrel 石油桶（[美]1 桶 = 42 gallon = 158L）

petrol bowser 汽油罐车（= petrol bulk lorry, petrol tanker）

petrol bus 汽油机客车（= gasoline bus）

petrol capacity 汽油（箱）容量

petrol consumption tax 燃油消费税

petrol-depth gauge （油箱内的）汽油深度计，油量计（= gasoline depth gauge）

petrol economiser 节油器，省油器

petrol-electric 汽油机-电机的（=[美] gas electric, 指汽油机发电、电动机驱动的）

petrol-electric generating set 汽油机发电机机组

petrol engine 汽油机（美称 gasoline engine）

petroleum ①石油②石油产品

Petroleum Administration for Defence [美]国防部石油管理局（简称 PAD）

petroleum-based energy 石油能源

petroleum gas 石油气（石油开采及提炼时的副产品，一般包括乙烷 C_2H_6，丙烷 C_3H_6，正丁烷 $n-C_4H_{10}$，异丁烷 $i-C_4H_{10}$，乙烯 C_2H_4，丙烯 C_3H_6，正丁烯 $n-C_4H_8$，异丁烯 $i-C_4H_8$，戊烷 C_5H_{12} 等组成，可在高压或低温下变成液体，称为液化石油气，用做汽车燃料，简称 LPG，见 liquefied petroleum gas）

petroleum naphtha 粗挥发油（旧称石油；石脑油，汽油与煤油之间沸点为 120~180℃ 的馏分）

petroleum tank ①原油罐②运输石油的油罐车

petroleum type hydraulic oil 石油类液压油（石油制取的液压油，以别于合成液压油）

petrol（feed）pipe 汽油管，汽油输送管

petrol feed pump 汽油（供给）泵[亦称 petrolift（er）]

petrol filler ①汽油加注口，加汽油漏斗②加注汽油工具（= gasoline filler）

petrol filler box lid （汽车车身的）汽油箱加油孔盖板

petrol filling station 加油站（简称 filling point）

petrol filter 汽油滤清器（参见 gasoline filter）

petrol gauge 汽油表（= gas tank gauge）

petrol-injected 汽油喷射的（简称 PI）

petrol-level gauge 汽油液面高度计（= gasoline-level gauge）

petrol lift 汽油泵

petrol line 汽油管路（= petrol feed

pipe, gas line)
petrol motor car 汽油车（= gasoline automobile）
petrol-powered lorry 汽油动力货车（汽油机货车）
petrol pump 汽油泵（美称 gas pump）
petrol sediment bulb 汽油沉淀杯
petrol service station 加油站（美称 gas station）
petrol storage 汽油库（= petrol store-house, gas storage, gas storehouse, petrol depot, gas depot）
petrol strainer 汽油滤清器，汽油滤网（= gasoline filter）
petrol tank 汽油箱
petrol tanker 汽油油罐车（美称 gas tanker, gas truck）
petrol vapo(u)r 汽油蒸气
PETS 踏板行程开关（pedal travel switch 的简称）
petticoat 喇叭口软管
petticoat rim 深凹式轮辋，深式轮辋
pet trailer 宠物挂车（专门装运狗、猫等宠物）
Peugeot S. A 标致汽车集团（法国规模最大的汽车生产集团，创立于 1896 年，1987 年从业人员 16.1 万人，生产能力为 220 万辆左右。1980 年由标致、雪铁龙、太保三家公司组成）
pewter ①锡基合金（的通称）②铅锡合金，铅锡合金制品
PFAC 全自动阻风门（pedal free auto choke 的简称）
PFD （发动机微粒排放物检测的）部分流稀释取样法［Partial Flow Dilution sampling 的简称，首先按比例抽取排气，然后稀释其中的一小部分，使用重差过滤器收集其中的微粒排放物，亦称 BG3 technology（BG3 技术），所使用的一套设备称 BG3 system（BG3 系统）］
PFE EGR （排气）压力反馈式电子控制废气再循环系统（pressure feedback electronic EGR 的简称）
PFE sensor 压力反馈型 EGR 流量传感器（pressure feedback EGR sensor 的简称，某些 EGR 系统，利用该传感器测定进入进气歧管的再循环废气压力，作为实际的 EGR 流量信号，反馈给动力控制模块，与目标流量值进行比较，借以对控制指令进行必要的修正）
PFI 进气口燃油喷射（多点式汽油喷射，port fuel injection 的简称，见 multi point fuel injection）
PFM 脉冲频率调制（pulse-frequency modulation）
PF (pf) ①微微法拉（picofarad）②光面，素面（plain face）③测位仪（position finder）④功率因数（power factor）⑤准备设施（preparing facility）⑥强制通风机（pressure fan）⑦脉冲频率（pulse frequency）⑧粉化燃料（pulverized fuel）
PFS （蒸气排放物控制系统的）清除流量传感器（purge flow sensor 的简称，见 purge valve）
PG 试车场（proving ground）
PGM ①可编程的（programmable）②程序控制的（programmed）
PGM-CARB 本田公司研制的电子控制式化油器［商品名，program (m) ed carburetor 的简称］
PGM - DSFI 程序控制双喷油器顺序燃油喷射系统（programmed duel sequential fuel injection system 的简称，每缸有低速、高速两个喷油器。节气门开度 < 50%、发动机转速 < 5500r/min 时仅低速喷油器喷油，节气门开度 > 50%、发动机转速 > 5500r/min 后高、低速两个喷油器同时按点火顺序逐缸喷油）

PGM-Fi 程序控制汽油喷射系统（Programmed-Fuel Injection 的简称，日本本田公司独立研制的所谓速度-密度型"speed-density type"汽油喷射系统的商品名。电子控制模块根据所测出的吸入空气量和预先存储的该车速下的最佳空燃比，决定汽油喷射量）

pH ①pH（代表溶液中氢离子浓度的负对数，pH = $-\log$ [H$^+$]，= $-\log$ of hydrogen ion concentration，见 pH value）②响度单位"口方"（见 phon）

ph ①每小时（per hour）②响度单位"口方"（见 phon）

phaeton 活顶游览汽车（原指二马四轮轻便马车）

phaeton body 四门活顶轿车车身（敞篷式四门车身，设双排座中间无隔断，带有可折叠式的软篷，车门上的玻璃不能升降，但易于连同窗框一起拆卸）

phantom black 幻影黑（车身颜色）

phantom line 虚线，想象线

phantom view ①显示内部的透视图 ②部分剖视图

phase ①（发展）阶段，时期，局面 ②相（如：物体的化学和物理性质完全相同的各部分或形态称为同相，反之，物理、化学性质不同的各个部分或形态称为异相，如水的气相、液相、固相）③相位（指从基准点开始测得的振动或周期性波形的某瞬间的位置值，或以360°为一循环，用角度表示的该瞬间点与基准点间的距离）④（液力变矩器的）相（数）（指其可用单向离合器、离合器或制动器等实现的功能或工况变换数，如：双相型液力变矩器，指该变矩器可变换为变矩器和耦合器两种功能或工况）

phase accumulation algorithm 相位累加算法

phase advancer 进相机（= advancer）

phase angle 相位角（见 phase③，对传动轴，则指同一根传动轴两端万节叉的相对转角）

phase-average measurement of periodic flow 周期性变动（非稳态）流的相位平均测定

phase control theory 相位控制理论

phase conversion （交通）信号相变换

phase converter 变相器，变相机，相位变换机

phase-correcting stage 相位校正级

phase correction capacitor 相位校正电容器

phase corrector 相位校正器，相位校正线路，相位移补偿器

phase cross-over 相位交错

phased dual ignition 相移双火花塞点火（在一个燃烧室内有两个火花塞，发火时间有一定的曲轴转角差）

phase-delay 相位滞后（①在频率响应试验中，横摆角速度响应相位与操纵输入的相位之差 ②在通信技术中，正弦波通过传输通道上的两点时由于其相位变化所表现的时间滞后）

phase detector circuit 相位测定电路，相位检测电路

phase deviation 相位移（亦称 phase displacement）

phase diagram 相图，状态图，平衡图，相位图（表示化合物及其混合物以及溶液等相互间的平衡关系图。如：表示金相的铁碳平衡图等）

phase difference 相位差

phase distortion 相位失真（指：①由系统的非线性相位/频率特性引起的失真或畸变 ②在传输系统的指定频率范围内，各频率成分中最

大传输时间与最小传输时间之间的差异)

phased oil extractor (转子发动机转子内的) 冷却油定向分配装置,相位冷却油道 (控制冷却油流的方向,简称 oil extractor)

phase in ①(分阶段)引入,纳入 ②进入一定位置(阶段,相位)

phase indicator 相位计,相位指示计

phase lag 相位滞后

phase lead 相位提前

phase line 相线,相位线

phase-locked loop circuitry 锁相电路(锁定电台频率,以保证频率最大稳定性的电路,简称 PLL circuitry)

phase margin 相位余量,相位补角,相位余裕角,相位余有角,允许相位畸变

phase meter 相位计,相位表(测定同一频率下的两交流值间的相位差)

phaser ①相位计,相位器,移相器 ②(自由活塞发动机)活塞同步器

phase resonance 相位共振,相位谐振

phase response 相位特性曲线,相位响应曲线

phase-reverse operation 换相运转,变相运转 (如:车辆低速行驶转向时,前、后轮朝不同方向转动,而高速行驶转向时,换成朝相同方向转动的四轮转向系运转模式)

phase-reversing 反相的,换相的(亦称 phase-rotation)

PHASE sensor 相位传感器组(日本日产公司 VQ 系列发动机用的电磁式曲轴转角传感器组的商品名。通常,汽缸识别、曲轴位置和汽缸上止点前基准信号均由一个光学式曲轴转角传感器发送,VQ 型发动机的该传感器组用于获取曲轴转角、转速及汽缸判别信号,由产生汽缸识别信号的相位传感器 "phase sensor",产生上止点前信号的汽缸基准点传感器 "reference sensor" 和产生汽缸位置转角信号的位置传感器 "position sensor" 组成,起着常规曲轴转角传感器的作用,但传送的信息更为精确)

phase-shifted sequence (双火花塞点火系的两个火花塞) 相移顺序 (点火,亦称 phased dual ignition)

phase shift trigger 移相触发器

3-phase slide-and-fold roof 三段式滑动-折叠活顶(小轿车)

phase synchronism 相(位)同步

phase transformation 相变(亦称 phase transition)

phase velocity ①相位速度,相速 ②波的传播速度,波速(见 wave velocity)

phasing control 相位控制(如:凸轮轴的相位控制指对进、排气门开、闭时刻及叠开角的控制)

phasing gears 相位齿轮,定相齿轮,(指转子发动机中装在转子上的内齿圈和装在固定缸盖上的小齿轮,通过这对齿轮的齿数比,控制转子的运动,确定热力过程的相位)

phasing-out model 淘汰型

phasing overlap (转子发动机的) 气孔相位重叠度

phasing voltage 定相电压

PHE 可编程高能点火系(programmable high energy ignition system 的简称)

phenate (苯) 酚盐,石碳酸盐 (C_6H_5OH,为汽车发动机用滑油的金属盐系分散净化剂的一种)

phenol (苯) 酚,石碳酸 (C_6H_5OH)

phenoldisulphonic acid method 苯酚二磺酸 $[C_6H_5(OH)\cdot(SO_3H)_2]$ 法 (用于分析排气中 NO_x 含量,该法较为烦琐。按 SAE 的推荐,现多改

用格里斯试剂法，参见 Griess reagent）

phenol-formaldehyde resin 苯酚甲醛树脂（亦写作 phenolic formaldehyde resin）

phenolic 苯酚（C_6H_5OH）的，酚醛树脂的

phenolic fiber-glass laminate 浸透苯酚树脂的玻璃纤维层压板

phenolic foam 苯酚泡沫，酚醛泡沫（塑料）

phenolic inhibitor 苯酚抑制剂（润滑油用的一种抗氧化剂）

phenolic resin 酚醛树脂（亦写作 phenol resin，= phenolics）

phenolics 酚醛塑料（酚醛树脂制成的各种热固性塑料，强度高，尺寸稳定性好，良绝缘体，= phenol resin，phenolic resin）

phenomenon 现象（复数 phenomena）

phenoxy 苯氧基（C_6H_5O）的

phenoxy resin 苯氧基树脂

phenylene diamine 苯二胺

PH（E）V ①并联式混合动力电动车（parallel hybrid electric vehicle 的简称，见 parallel hybrid drive type vehicle）②插入式混合动力电动车（见 plug-in hybrid electric vehicle 的简称）

phillips（head）（screw）driver 梅花（形）槽（螺钉）头旋具，粗十字（形）槽（螺钉）头旋具（亦称 plus driver）

pH meter pH 计（氢离子计，酸碱度计）

phon 叻（响度级单位，代号 p，简称 pH 或 ph）

phone ①电话②送受话器，耳机

phon meter 响度级计（亦写作 phonometer）

phonon 声子（晶体点阵振动能的量子）

phosgene gas 光气，碳酰氯（制冷剂 R-12 等接触火焰时产生的有毒气体）

phosphate 磷酸盐，磷酸酯

phosphate coating 磷酸盐保护膜防锈处理

phosphating 磷化处理（钢、铁件置于磷酸盐溶液中处理，使其表面获得一层呈微亮灰色或暗灰色，厚 $5\sim15\mu m$ 的磷酸盐结晶防锈薄膜）

phosphatize 用磷酸或磷酸盐处理，磷酸盐化

phosphonate 磷酸盐

phosphor 磷光体（能发射磷光的物质的总称）

phosphor-coated anode 荧光物质镀覆的阳极

phosphor copper 磷铜

phosphorescence ①磷光性（某些物质在除去激发能源后仍能继续发光 0.1 毫微秒以上的能力）②磷光（光学上指磷光性产生的光，化学上指白磷在空气中缓慢氧化时所能见到的绿色光辉）③发磷光，磷光现象

phosphoric acid 磷酸 H_3PO_4

phosphoric acid fuel cell 磷酸燃料电池（简称 PAFC）

phosphor screen 荧光屏

phosphorus ①磷（P）②磷光体

phot 辐透（厘米烛光，照度单位，=1 流明/厘米^2）

photion 充气光电二极管

photistor 光敏晶体管

photoactive 感光的，光敏的

photo bioreactor system 光照植物反应器（美国 Algae Tec 公司研制的不再使用粮食类谷物而使用藻类与 CO_2 光照反应生产植物乙醇技术使用的日光照射反应装置）

photo cell 光电管，光电池（受光照射产生电流或电动势的固态光敏元件，其电流、电压特性是入射光的函数，= photoelectric cell）

photo-cell adapter （柴油机滤纸式烟度计中，应用光电元件将滤纸的反射光量变为电信号以确定滤纸染黑程度的）滤纸黑度光电检测器

photo-cell scanning 光电（管）扫描

photochemical 光化学的（如：日光照射下引起各种化学变化的）

photochemically reactive hydrocarbons 光化学反应碳氢化合物（指排放到大气中光照下产生化学反应的碳氢化合物，为形成光化学烟雾的主要物质，参见 Los Angelos smoke）

photochemical smog 光化学烟雾（汽车排气中的 NO_x，HC 等受到强烈太阳光的紫外线照射引起化学反应而生成的白色或紫色烟雾，主要成分为 O_3，RCHO，$RONO_2$，RCO_3NO_2 等，为汽车排气公害之一）

photoconductive cell 光导管，光导元件（亦称光敏电阻，受到照射的光线越亮，其电阻值越小，通过的电流越大，在汽车上用于各种光控系统，如：前照灯随外界光线强弱而自动点亮或减光，关灯控制系统中使用的硫化镉 CdS 元件的外界亮度传感器等）

photoconductive detector 光敏电阻，光电管指示器，光电导探测器

photoconductivity 光电导性（如：硒等材料在光线影响下，其电导性能变化的特性）

photoconductor ①光电导体（电导能力随照射光的强度而变化）②导光材料，导光体

photo-coupler 光耦合器（由发光二极管与光电二极管或光电晶体管相对布置组合而成的装置。发光二极管将输入的电信号转变为光，再由光电管转变为电信号输出）

photocurrent 光电电流

photodecoder 光电译码器（将光源变为电子脉冲信号，信号调制后可再现光源）

photodetachment 光电分离，光致分离

photodiode 光电二极管（指光电变换二极管。当光电二极管加反向电压时，反向电流很小，仅数 μA，但此时 PN 结在光照下，该电流将随光照强度的增加而增加）

photoelastic coating 光弹涂层（测应变，亦称 photostress coating）

photoelasticity 光弹性（学），光致弹性

photoelasticity measurement 光弹性测定（法）

photoelasticity stress analysis 光弹应力分析（利用具有特殊光学性质的透明材料做模型，施加相应的荷载后，在偏振光的照射下，根据模型产生的光学效应来测定其应力分布）

photoelastic material 光弹材料

photoelastic plastic 光弹塑料

photoelastic stress analysis 光弹性应力分析，光弹应力分析［亦称 photoelastic（stress）study］

photoelastic stress pattern 光弹应力图形

photoelastic technique 光弹技术

photoelectric 光电的（简称 PE）

photoelectrical velocity measure equipment 光电测速设备

photoelectric cell 光电管，光电池（见 photo cell）

photoelectric colorimeter 光电比色计

photoelectric colorimetry method 光电比色法（利用光电效应测量有色溶液等的透光强度，求得其含量的方法）

photoelectric control 光电控制

photoelectric detector 光电检测器

photoelectric effect 光电效应（见 photo effect）

photoelectric follow-up 光电跟踪系

统，光电随动系统

photoelectric measurement Karman vortices air flow meter 光电计量（型）卡尔曼涡流空气流量计（见 Karman vortices air flow meter）

photoelectric switch 光电开关

photoelectric transducer 光电变换器（光电变换式传感器，亦称 photoelectric sensor）

photoelectric type steering sensor 光电式转向传感器（由发光二极管及与之配套的光电二极管组成，向电子控制模块发送转向盘转角及其转动速度信号）

photoelectroluminescence 光电场致发光（用光或其他电磁能产生电流，然后由电流引起场致发光）

photoelectrometer 光电计

photoemission 光电放射，光电发射，光电子发射

photoemissive element 光电放射元件（如：光电管，光电池）

photoengraving 光刻技术（= phototoetching）

photoexcitation 光致激发，光激，光励

photo-field-effect transistor 光控场效应晶体管（简称 photo-FET，见 field-effect transistor）

photogrammetric 摄影测量的，摄影制图的

photograph car 摄影车

photographic analysis 拍照分析（法），摄影分析（法）

photographic traffic survey 交通摄影调查，交通摄影鉴定，交通照相观测

photography 摄影，照相术，图像拍摄

photoionization 光致电离

photolithography 光刻蚀法，光刻技术（利用曝光、显影、刻痕等技术，在晶片上制作出所需图形的技术）

photomagnetoelectric effect 光控磁电效应

photometer 光度计，发光强度计（见 candela）

photometric 发光强度的，测定光强度的

photometric test （汽车灯等的）发光强度试验（按 SAE 的规定是将光度计置于距离灯头一定尺寸，如18.3m 等处测定其发光强度的新烛光数）

photomicrograph ①显微照相②显微照片

photomicrographic device 显微照相的装置

photomodulator 光调制器

photomultiplier 光电倍增器（如：光电倍增管）

photon 光子（光电子，光量子）

photopic adaptation 光适应性（= light adaptation）

photopic vision （人眼的）明视觉（指高于数 Cd/m^2 亮时，由视网膜的锥体细胞起作用、能辨认很小细节和有颜色感的视觉）

photorectifier 光电检波器，光电二极管

photoresist 光敏抗蚀剂，光致抗蚀剂（光刻技术中使用的一种特殊有机材料，在二氧化硅膜全面感光时，可使已感光部分易溶于有机药品）

photoresistance 光敏电阻

photoschmitt trigger 光电施米特触发器（见 schmitt trigger）

photosensitive 光敏的，感光的

photosensitive cell 光电管，光电池

photostress 光弹应力（photoelastic stress 的简称）

photoswitch 光控继电器，光控开关

photo synchro-selector 摄影同步选择器

photosynthetic 光化合作用的

photo-transistor 光敏三极管，光电三极管（将光能变换为电流的半导体元件，当其基极受光照射时，便有电流流通）

photo-trigger （无触点式点火系统的）光电触发器（光电式点火信号发生器）

phototron 矩阵光电管

phototube 光电管（指利用光照产生光电子的真空管，可将光变化转变为电流变化，如：前照灯会车时的自动减光器）

photovaristor 光敏电阻器

photovoltaic 光电的

phthalic acid 酞酸，苯二酸（$C_8H_6O_4$，无色，熔点 196～199℃，用于制作涂料，亦称 futar acid）

PHV （家电）插座（充电）式混合动力（电动）车（plug-in hybrid vehicle 的简称，亦写作 plug-in hybrid electrical vehicle，简称 PHEV。以丰田推出的 Prius 牌 PHV 和 HV 为例，比较二者的不同。PHV 装有比 HV 容量大得多的锂离子蓄电池组，并可使用普通 220V 或 110V 家用 AC 电源插座充电。用 220V 和 110V 的充满电时间仅分别为 90 min 和 180 min。PHV 在市区以中、低速行驶时，仅由蓄电池供电，电动机驱动，即：纯电动车模式行驶。当蓄电池电量低于 30% 或汽车需要较大的功率时，内燃机自动起动带动发电机发电，给蓄电池和电动机供电，仍由电动机驱动车辆行驶。此时，可看作是串联式混合动力车模式行驶，即："series hybrid vehicle drive mode"。当汽车上坡或高速行驶时，内燃机通过变速-传动装置参与车轮驱动，给电动机加力。此时，可看作是并联式混合动力车模式行驶，即："parallel hybrid vehicle drive mode"。制动减速时，车轮带动电动机反转发电，给蓄电池充电，回收汽车惯性能量。PHV 的纯电动车模式可行驶 24.4～26.4km，车速可高达 100km/h，而 HV 基本上没有纯电动车行驶模式）

pH value 酸碱值，pH 值（表示溶液中氢离子 [H^+] 浓度的负对数，即，pH = -lg [H^+]；pH = 7，溶液呈中性，pH > 7，溶液呈酸性，pH < 7 溶液呈碱性）

physical ①物理的②物质的③体力的

physical acoustics 物理声学，波动声学

physical address 物理地址（指硬件标识的实际存储器中的地址，或直接寻址的二级存储设备中的地址）

physical analogue 物理模拟

physical analysis 物理分析

physical change 物理变化

physical distribution 物资流通，货物配送（又称物流，指从生产厂家生产的产品，配送到用户手中的物资流动，简称 PD，参见 logistics）

physical distribution industry 物流业

physical operation 人力操纵，体力操纵（式）（指单凭驾驶员手或足的力进行操纵，而无助力装置加力的驾驶操作，参见 manual control）

physical test （相对于计算机虚拟系统试验等的）实体试验

physical vaporous deposition 物理气相沉积法（简称 PVD 法，在 1.33×10^{-4}～1.33Pa 的真空下，通过真空蒸镀、溅射或离子镀渗等方式，在工件表面沉积高硬度膜的方法）

physico-chemical 物理-化学的

physics 物理（物理学，物理性质，物理意义，物理现象，物理过程）

physiological 生理的，生理学的

physiological comparison of seat comfort 座位舒适性的生理学比较

physiological effect 生理效应

physiological response （汽车驾驶员

的）生理反应

physiologlcal data （驾驶人员等的）生理数据（如：血压，脉搏，生理疲劳程度等）

PI ①针入度指数，贯入度指数（penetration index）②塑性指数（plastic index）③汽油喷射的（petrol-injected）④圆周率（圆周长与圆直径之比，亦写作 pi，= π）

piano wire 钢琴丝（高碳钢线，用做螺旋弹簧、间隙规等）

PIARC （联合国）常设国际道路会议协会（Permanent International Association of Road Congress）

pick ①选择，挑选，摘取 ②加速 ③汽车中途上人 ④十字镐，锄

pick and finishing hammer （车身板件的）小凹陷敲出手锤

pickle brittleness 酸蚀脆性（= acid brittleness）

pickling ①酸浸，酸洗（= acid pickling）②浸渍，刻蚀

pickling oil 防锈油

pick-off （导航陀螺仪）脉冲传感器

pick out 选择，挑出

pickup ①轻便客货两用车（pick-up truck 的简称，俗称皮卡，指采用轿车底盘和驾驶室与货槽栏板组成的客货两用车。货槽系敞篷式，驾驶性能与轿车相同，载重一般为 $\frac{1}{2}$ t）②汽车的急加速能力 ③加速 ④摩擦件（如：轴承与轴颈间由于润滑不足而产生的黏结现象，严重时导致卡滞）⑤传感器，发送器，敏感元件，拾波器，拾音器，（光电管）受光元件，（邻近电路引起的）干扰 ⑦（继电器的）灵敏度 ⑧读出，读音，拾波，拾起 ⑨（汽车在途中）接收乘客 ⑩搭便车者 ⑪摄像管

pickup arm 传感臂，拾取臂

pickup body 轻便客货两用车车身（亦写作 pick-up body）

pickup box 轻便客货两用车的敞篷货箱

pickup brush 集电刷（= collecting brush）

pickup calibration 传感器校准，传感器标定

pickup camper 轻型客货车野营车（用轻型客货车改装的帐篷野营车）

pickup coil ①拾波线圈 ②传感器的电磁感应线圈

pickup element 拾感元件，拾音元件，传感元件

pickup hitch 自动挂接装置

pickup hole ①（压力）测量孔 ②通气孔 ③取样孔

pickup lag 加速迟缓（指发动机对加速踏板的踩踏响应迟缓）

pick-up module （电子点火系）点火信号发生模块，点火脉冲信号发生装置（亦称 pulse generator）

pickup of engine 发动机加速性

pick-up pipe 吸油管

pick up screen （机油泵的）吸滤器，吸油头滤网

pickup/sending unit （信息）传感与发送装置

pickup speed 加速

pickup sweeper 清扫车

pickup time ①（汽车）起步加速时间 ②（继电器等）始动时间

pick-up-truck 轻便客货两用车（见 pick-up）

pickup tube 摄像管（= camera tube）

pick up type brake tester 减速度计式制动试验台

pickup voltage 始动电压，吸引电压，接触电压；拾音电压，拾取电压，传感电压

pico- 微微（词头代号为 p，乘幂 10^{-12}，根据国际单位制的规定，用 pico 代替原用的 micromicro，如微微米，不用 μμ 也不用 pm）

picofarad 微微法拉（为电容的常用

单位，代号为 pF，1pF = 10^{-12} F，见 farad）

PI controller 比例-积分控制器（proportional-integral controller 的简称）

picosecond 微微秒（代号 μμs，= 10^{-12} s，简称 ps）

PI cruise control 比例-积分法定速巡行控制（见 PI speed error control）

pictorial diagram 实物形象图

pictorial report 附有图表的报告，用图表说明的报告

pictorial view 示图，插图

picture ①图，图片，照片，画面 ②用图表示

picture-processing system （电视摄影的）图像处理系统

PID control 比例-积分-微分控制 [proportional-integrating-differential control 的简称，在汽车实时控制中，总会有外界干扰和系统本身参数的变化，使系统的控制产生一定的偏差，为此除了按偏差的比例对控制过程进行调节外，还考虑偏差的积分，以克服余差，同时考虑偏差的微分，克服惯性滞后，即所谓的 PID 控制，其控制算式为：$P = K_p(e + \frac{1}{T_i}\int edt + T_d \frac{de}{dt})$，式中：$P$—系统控制量；$K_p$—比例系数；$T_i$—积分时间常数；$T_d$—微分时间常数；$e$—偏差，$e = u - y$，$u$ 为输入；y 为输出。P，I，D 可单独使用，也可组合使用，但微分形式很少单独使用]

piece 片，块，件，个

piece goods （按件托运和承运的）成件货物

piece of work 工件

piece production 单件生产

piece-to-piece (s) manufacturing variation （组合件的）零件累积加工误差

1 piece wheel 整体式车轮，单体式车轮（指轮辋与轮辐制成一体的非组合式车轮）

2 piece wheel 两件式组合车轮（指由轮辋和轮辐板二件组装成的车轮）

3 piece wheel 三件式组合车轮（指由一个轮辐板和左、右两个轮辋件组装成的车轮）

piedmont 山麓的，在山麓的

pier ①码头 ②桥台，桥墩 ③支柱

pierce 刺穿，戳穿，穿孔

piezo ①压，压力（指加压、施压，如：piezocaloric 加压生热的，压热的，piezochemistry 高压化学，piezomagnetic 压磁的，piezometer 压力计，piezometric 测压的）②压电的（指在压力下产生电变化的，如：piezolighter 压电点火器，piezoquartz 压电晶体，piezoelectric 在压力下产生电流的，piezoresistive 在压力下电阻变化的等）

piezo actuator 压电式执行器（利用压电效应的执行器件，施加一定值，如：500V 的高压，执行元件伸长 50μm，而将阀门顶开）

piezoceramic 压电陶瓷（材料）（将一高电压加于陶瓷材料上两电极间，同时将其加热到高于居里点温度，然后逐渐冷却，电极间的陶瓷材料将呈现压电特性）

piezoceramic accelerometer knock sensor 压电陶瓷加速度仪型爆震传感器（用压电陶瓷作为传感元件将爆震引起的振动加速变为电信号输出并借以确定爆震强度）

piezoceramics 压电陶瓷（piezoelectric ceramics 的简称）

piezocrystal 压电晶体（可将机械压力转变为电信号，或将电信号转变为机械压力的晶体，piezo-electric crystal 的简称）

piezoelectric 压电的（可在机械应力下产生电动势或在电压作用下产生

机械应力的）

piezoelectric accelerometer 压电式加速度计

piezoelectric activity 压电活性，压电性，压电作用

piezoelectric actuation 压电效应型执行器（利用在电压作用下变形的压电元件制成的执行器）

piezoelectric ceramic material 压电陶瓷材料（见 piezoceramic）

piezoelectric ceramic ring 压电陶瓷环（一种垫圈式压电传感器）

piezoelectric coefficients（*d* and *g*）压电系数（*d*—每一单位面积中每一单位应力释放的电荷；*g*—电极的每一单位面积，每一单位应力产生的电场）

piezoelectric constant 压电常数

piezoelectric crystal 压电晶体（见 piezocrystal）

piezoelectric effect 压电效应

piezoelectric effect type road (condition) sensor 压电效应型路面（状况）传感器（传感器的压电晶体元件装在减振器活塞杆上，将路面平面度产生的轴向冲击力变化变为电信号输出）

piezo electric element 压电元件（可直接将压力转变为电信号的原件，多用做传感器或执行器）

piezoelectric film 压电（硅）膜膜片（以电压变化形式输出承受压力时的应变信号）

piezoelectric gauge 压电计，压电仪

piezoelectric ignition system 压电晶体点火系（利用压电晶体受压产生高压脉冲点火）

piezoelectricity 压电现象，压电学，压电性

piezoelectric knock sensor 压电式爆震传感器

piezoelectric measuring system 压电量测系统

piezoelectric modulus 压电系数

piezoelectric pickup 压电传感器

piezoelectric pressure gauge 压电式压力计

piezoelectric pressure sensor 压电型压力传感器

piezoelectric quartz 压电石英，压电晶体

piezoelectric ring transducer 环型压电传感器（简称PPT）

piezoelectrics 压电学，压电装置，压电体

piezoelectric sensor 压电传感器（利用压电晶体元件将压力变为电信号的传感器）

piezoelectric sensor type TEMS 压电传感器型丰田电子调控悬架系统［丰田电子调控悬架系统的一种（见 TEMS），利用压电晶体传感器实时地将汽车行驶状态的信息传给电子控制模块，借以调控减振器的减振特性，使之达到最佳工作状态。如：当汽车越过凹凸不平路面时，可立即将减振器从"硬"态转换成"软"态，以适应行驶平顺性的要求］

piezoelectric strain gage 压电应变仪，压电应变片

piezoelectric transducer 压电式变换器，压电式传感器

piezoelectric transition 压电跃变（简称PZT）

piezoelectric type vacuum sensor 压电（晶体）式真空传感器

piezo-electric vibrator 压电式振动器

piezo element 压电元件（压电晶体制成的各种元件）

piezoid （压电）石英片，石英晶体

piezo injector 压电晶体式喷油器（利用压电元件在加电压后可瞬间形变的特性，来开、闭喷油器喷油嘴，用于汽油缸内直喷式发动机可实现每一做功行程的多段喷油，见

multi-stage injection)

piezo injector （柴油机的）压电式喷油器

piezomagnetic 压（电）磁的

piezometer 压电晶体型压力计，压强计，微压表（测定压电效应产生的电量，借以求出负荷或压力值的仪器）

piezoquartz 压电石英，压电晶体

piezo resistance effect 压敏电阻效应（指半导体和导体受到外来压力时，其电阻发生变化的现象）

piezoresistive ①压敏电阻的②压阻现象的

piezoresistive accelerometer 压敏电阻式加速度计

piezoresistive silicon diaphragm type pressure sensor 压敏电阻硅膜片型压力传感器（利用该膜片两侧压力差引起的膜片电阻值变化来测定压力或真空度的传感元件）

piezoresistive strain gage 压敏电阻型应变仪，压敏电阻应变片，应变片型压力传感器

piezoresistor 压敏电阻器，压电电阻器（= piezo resistive device）

PIF 等离子体感应炉（plasma induction furnace）

piggyback operations 驮背运输作业，背负式集装运输作业（见 piggyback transportation）

piggyback torque amplifier handle （螺钉旋具等手工具的）外套式加力手柄，手柄加力套（套装在原手柄上，加长直径以增大转矩）

piggyback trailer （驮运）联运挂车（既是汽车挂车又可直接开上火车平板车台上驮运，参见 piggyback transportation）

piggyback transportation 驮运联运（TOFC 联运方式的俗称，由牵引车拖挂装货挂车进行短途运输，长途运输则利用铁路平台车直接驮运装有货物的汽车挂车，见 piggyback trailer）

pig iron 铸铁，生铁（含碳量3%~5%）

pigment ①颜料，色素②（橡胶）填充料

pigmented resin 加颜料的树脂

pig-tail ①抽头，引线，引出线（如：电机电刷的引出线，= pig-tail wire 或 wire pigtail）②输出（端），引出（端）

pig-tail end 小端（如：螺旋弹簧的小直径端）

pig-tail wire 引线，引出线（= pig-tail）

pig tin 锡块，块锡

pike ①十字镐，尖嘴②收费高速公路（turnpike 的简称）③（公路）收费站（= toll gate, toll pike 的简称）

pilar jack 柱式千斤顶（亦称 tower jack）

pile ①桩，立柱②堆，垛，堆垛③堆集，结集④积炭层

piling 堆积物，沉积物（如：触点上的金属沉积）

pill 丸，小球，珠

pillar 柱子，支柱，立柱（车身骨架中竖置的构件，如：车顶与车身底框构件间的立柱，从前向后，依次分别称为 A-, B-, C-, D pillar "A 柱，B 柱，C 柱和 D 柱"或"前柱，前中柱，后中柱，后柱"，一般车身只有前、中、后三根立柱）

pillar brace 车身主柱角撑

pillar bracket （转向盘）柱支架，（转向盘）柱撑架（= post hanger）

pillared hard top 带中立柱的硬顶（轿车）

pillar industry 支柱工业

pillar less saloon 无中立柱的四门硬顶轿车（= pillarless hard top）

pillar light （装在车身）中柱（上的）门控灯（开车门时，该灯亮）

pill box [英]微型汽车的俗称
pillion 机器脚踏车上的后座（摩托车后座）
pillow ①枕，枕块②轴承座
pillow ball （转向拉杆系和悬架系使用的）球-环节（一侧的杆件固定于中央开孔的钢球孔中，该钢球装入一与另一杆件或支撑件固定的环状球座内）
pillow block 轴承座，支座；枕状支座（如：传动轴中间轴承的支座，前轮独立悬架上、下臂的支点座）
pilot ①导航员，领航员②导向件，定位件（决定机器某些总成、组件部位位置的部件）③（液压机构）先导阀④小规模试验性质的生产⑤引导
pilot-actuated 先导阀作动的
pilot area （汽车行车线路）自动导航区域（指行车线路自动导航系统的作用区域）
pilot bar 导向杆
pilot batch 试验批量
pilot bearing [美]导向轴承（= spigot bearing，如：变速器输入轴在曲轴飞轮端的导向轴承）
pilot bush (ing) 导向衬套（= guide bushing）
pilot car sign 先导车标志（在道路施工或大中修工作地点，控制单向通行交通的导向车后部装配的标志）
pilot cell ①控制元件②指示电池
pilot choke 先导系统节流阀
pilot circuit ①导频电路②（液压）控制油路
pilot control ①（液压机构）先导阀控制，伺服阀控制②导频控制
pilot-controlled actuator （使用一个或多个附加能源将输入信号变换并放大为输出信号的）伺服控制式执行器

pilot-controlled check valve （主动式液压悬架系统的）先导控制式压-止回阀（当液压超过规定值时，该阀开启；液压低于规定值时，该阀关闭。此外，当发动机停止运转时，该阀起止回阀作用，使系统液压保持在规定的范围内）
pilot engine ①辅助发动机②试验性发动机，样机
pilot factory 小规模试验件工厂
pilot fuel 引燃燃料（参见 pilot ignition fuel）
pilot hole 定位孔，导向孔（如：拧入自攻螺钉前，冲出的导向小孔，亦称 lead hole）
pilot ignition engine 引燃式发动机（双燃料发动机的一种，引燃燃料先着火，再利用火焰点燃另一种主体燃料，多以柴油等作引燃燃料的气体燃料发动机或醇类、植物油等代用燃料压燃机）
pilot ignition fuel 引燃燃料（指在柴油机中使用醇类、植物油等代用燃料时或在气体燃料发动机中，喷入不高于每循环总发热量20%、首先着火、引燃主燃料的柴油或其他燃料）
piloting 引导
pilot injection ①引燃喷射（见 ignition injection engine）②预喷射（在燃油至喷射前，先喷入汽缸内少量燃油）
pilot investigation 试点调查
pilot jet ①引燃油束②导流射流，导向喷流③起动喷嘴④（固定量孔式化油器怠速油系的）进油量孔⑤（位于节气门下游的）起动加浓量孔
pilot lamp 信号灯，指示灯
pilotless 无人驾驶的，无人操纵的
pilot light 导向灯，指向灯，指示灯，信号灯，监视灯，度盘灯（= pilot lamp, indicator light）
pilot line [制动管（线）路中的]

操纵管（线）路，控制管（线）路（指将制动能由一个控制装置，如制动阀传至另一控制装置，如：继动阀的管、线路）

pilot model 试选样品

pilot model inspections 示教模型检查法（维修人员培训方法）

pilot motor 伺服电动机，辅助电动机

pilot-operated absolute valve （汽车空调系统蒸发器输出压力的）针阀控制式绝对调节阀（由活塞-气囊组件控制的针阀精确地调节输出压力，以防止蒸发器芯过冷而冻结，简称 POAvalve，其作用与 suction throttling valve 相同，但控制精度更高，故称 absolute "绝对"）

pilot poppet （液压）控制提升阀

pilot pressure 先导压力

pilot shaft （装配时供零件定位、对中用的）定位轴（事后拆掉）

pilot sleeve 导向套筒

pilot spool 先导滑阀

pilot spray （某些柴油机喷油系统在主喷油前的）引燃喷油，点火喷油

pilot stage 先导级

pilot studies 探索性研究

pilot type proportional electromagnetic control valve 先导型比例控制电磁阀（由电子控制模块控制的小电磁阀，用于按比例控制主阀柱塞的液压入口的孔径，借以控制主阀柱塞的位移量，即其工位）

PIM ①进气歧管（绝对）压力（pressure of intake manifold 的简称）②永磁体（permanent magnet 的简称）

PI method 比例-积分控制法（见 proportional-integral control action）

pin ①销，销轴，（轴）颈，枢轴②用销子固定③插销，插头，插针

pin-and-ball trunnion-type universal joint 球销式方向节（见 ball and trunnion joint）

pin-and-cylinder electrical connector 插销-插套式电连接器

pin bearing 滚针轴承

pin bolt 销，销钉，带（开尾）销螺栓

pin boss 活塞销孔座（piston-pin boss 的简称）

pin bushing 活塞销衬套（= piston pin bushing）

pinch 夹住，夹紧

pinch adjustment （夹紧装置的）夹力调整

pinch-off （场效应晶体管）夹断（效应）

pinch-off seal 压紧密封

pin connection 销连接

pin drift 拔销器（销的拔卸工具 = pin punch，pin extractor）

pine tree 松木

pin fit 销配合

ping ①桃红色②[美]爆震，爆燃，敲缸（亦写作 pinging，英称 pinking，= detonation）

pin gear 针齿轮，针轮（见 pin wheel）

pin gear shaper 针齿轮刨齿机

pinhole ①销孔，针孔，小孔，小直径孔②（铸件）针孔状缺陷③（由于溶剂中水分蒸发或空气逸出而在涂层或漆层表面形成的）细小气泡（群）

pinhole boundary 针孔边界

pinhole grinder 销孔磨床，磨（活塞）销

pin-hole type output mechanism （少齿差行星传动的）销孔输出机构（由圆柱销将行星齿轮的运动传给输出轴盘的输出机构）

pin-holing corrosion 针孔形腐蚀，针孔形锈蚀

pinion 小齿轮（指齿轮副的两个齿轮中，齿数较少者，如：差速器的

pin

主动齿轮）

pinion and ring gear set （汽车主减速器的）驱动齿轮和冠形齿轮副

pinion assist type electronic power steering system 转向器助力式电子控制动力转向系统（指助力电动机装在转向器侧，通过减速齿轮将转向动力传给转向器的动力转向系，见 electronic power steering system）

pinion barrel （主传动的）主动齿轮壳

pinion cage ①行星轮架，行星架②差速器壳

pinion drive 齿轮传动（= gear drive）

pinion drive flange （差速器）小齿轮驱动（轴）突缘

pinion drive shaft 小齿轮传动轴

pinion file 锐边小锉

pinion frame 行星齿轮架，差速器行星齿轮架

pinion gear 主动齿轮，小齿轮（= pinion）

pinion gearing 小齿轮传动装置

pinion guide 滑动齿轮导向轴

pinion rack 齿臂，齿板，齿条

pinion shaft 小齿轮轴

pinion shimming 用垫片调整主动锥齿轮

pinion stop 小齿轮轴向位移挡块

pin-jointed track （履带板由）销轴铰接的履带

pin key 销键

pinking ［美］爆震，敲缸（亦称 pinging，= knocking）

pinkle ①（洗金属用的）淡酸水，稀酸液②泡在（盐水或醋里），（金属）浸泡在稀酸液中

pinnacle nut 六角槽顶螺母

pinning ①阻塞，闭合，销住，锁住 ②上开口销，销连接；支撑

pin-out diagram （标示微控制器、电子控制模块等集成块的）插脚功用图（在图的四周标明每一插脚的功用）

pinpoint ①针尖，极尖的顶端②精确的方位点，定点，精确决定位置 ③（多孔镀铬的）点状孔隙（简称 PP）④（电子电路插头的）插针，针脚⑤精确定位的，极精确的，细致的，详尽的⑥针尖的，极微小的

pinpoint test （电子电路插头）针脚测试，插针测试（指分别对多脚插头的每一针脚进行测试）

pinpoint welding 摩擦表面接触点间由于局部高温而引起的瞬时熔接

pin rocker bearing （在枢轴上的）摆动轴承，摆动支座（= rocker bearing, swing bearing）

pin roller （测量齿厚或节圆直径用）滚柱

pin-shaped side seals （转子发动机）密封销型端面气封装置

pin slider caliper disc brake 浮钳式盘式制动器（制动时，制动钳在导销套上滑动而对制动盘产生压紧力的盘式制动器，亦称 floating caliper type disc brake，简称 PS type caliper brake）

7-pin socket 7 插脚插座

pin socket 柱式插座，针孔式插座

pin spanner 叉销扳手，带销扳手（带槽的圆形螺母用，= pin wrench，亦称 book spanner）

pin synchronizer 锁销式（惯性）同步器（指通过在同一圆周上相互间隔均匀分布的若干锁销与定位销来连接接合套与两摩擦锥环，依靠摩擦锥环与摩擦锥盘间的摩擦实现同步换挡的同步机构）

pint 品脱（英制容量单位，代号 Pt，1 pint = $\frac{1}{8}$ gallon，在英国 1 pint ≈ 0.57 litre，见 Imperial gallon，在美国 1 pint 约等于 0.47 litre，见 U. S. gallon）

pintaux nozzle (柴油机的)副孔型轴针式喷嘴[即带辅助喷孔的轴针式喷嘴,当喷油泵转速及喷射压力较低时,燃油主要由辅助喷孔喷出,转速升高后,燃油主要由主喷孔喷出,与轴针式喷嘴比较,其起动性等较好,主要用于 Comet 直喷系统]

pin terminal ①柱式插头②接线柱

pin test (塑料管)的扩口试验

pintle ①铰链销,枢轴②针栓;针阀,轴针

pintle chain 套接链,扣针链

pintle hook 销栓挂钩,拖车挂钩

pintle nozzle (柴油机的)轴针式喷嘴(闭式喷嘴的一种,其构造特点是针阀体上有一个较大的喷孔,针阀下端的轴针部分伸入此孔中,喷油时,针阀升起,使喷孔成圆环形狭缝,喷出的油雾呈空心状,亦称 pintle (-type) atomizer)

pintle-shaft-armature assembly (电磁阀的)阀头-阀杆-衔铁总成

pintle-type of fuel injector 轴针式喷油器(指带轴针式喷油嘴的喷油器,见 pintle nozzle)

pintle valve 针阀(亦称 pin valve, needle valve)

pin type spike (雪地用轮胎的)销型防滑钉

pin wheel 针轮,针齿轮(亦称 pin gear,一种圆柱形或圆环形齿轮,其轮齿由若干个轴线分布在同一圆周上并与齿轮轴线平行的针齿销"gear pin"或称"ring gear pin"组成,有时包括针齿销套"gear roller"或称"ring gear roller")

pinwheel housing 针齿壳(安装针齿销的壳体)

pin wrench 钩形扳手,叉销扳手(= pin spanner, hook spanner)

PIO 并行输入/输出(parallel input/output 的简称)

pioneering technology 领先技术,先进技术

PIP ①(电子点火系曲轴位置传感器向电子控制模块发送的)(曲轴)位置与转速信号脉冲(position indicator pulse 的简称,控制模块根据该信号确定点火时刻,故又称点火位置信号)②仿形式点火传感器(见 profile ignition pickup)

pip ①记号,标记,②(荧光屏上的)尖头信号脉冲

pipe ①管件(参见 tube),管道②管道运输

pipe bend 弯管,管道弯头,管道弯曲部分

pipe boom (起重机的)管型起重臂

pipe branch 支管

pipe-carrying trailer 运管件的挂车

pipe choking 管道堵塞

pipe coil 螺旋形管,蛇管,盘管

pipe cushion 管式减振器

pipe fitting ①管路装配工作②管子配件,接管零件(如:弯头等管系附件),管接头

pipe frame 管式构架(= tubular frame)

pipe-laying tractor 铺设管道用牵引车

pipeline ①管道运输系统,管道输送线②管路,管线③用管道运输,为…装管道

pipeline system 管路系统

pipeline within a MPU 微处理器中的管线技术(流水线技术,指在前一条指令全部处理完之前,就同时开始执行下一条指令,以提高处理速度,或微处理器中由若干部分同时处理若干条指令)

pipe still 管式蒸馏器,管式散热器

pipe-stringing truck (管道铺设时)沿线分发管件的专用载货汽车

pipet 球头吸管(亦写作 pipette)

pipe thread 管螺纹(参见 V-thread)

pipette 球头吸管（利用橡皮球的作用，吸注液体的器具，如：吸注蓄电池液用的球头吸管等，亦称 pipet，squirt，syringe）

pipe ventilated 管道通风的（= duct ventilated）

piping ①管系，管道布置，导管系统（= pipework）②尖声（管鸣声）

PIP sensor 发动机转速与曲轴位置传感器（profile ignition pick-up sensor 的简称，该传感器为-霍尔效应开关。由霍尔效应元件、永久磁铁及由曲轴或分电器带动的隔磁叶片轮组成，向电子控制模块发送发动机转速、曲轴位置信号，故亦称曲轴位置传感器，= crankshaft position sensor，CKP sensor 或 CP sensor）

PIP signal （由）发动机转速与曲轴位置传感器（发出的）信号（告诉电子控制模块哪一缸的活塞正处于上止点前多少度，如 10°，按规定的点火顺序，下一个点火该轮到哪一缸或哪一组缸的信号）（见 PIP sensor）

pique （车室内筛用的）楞花棉布

PIR 插入式继电器（plug-in relay 的简称）

pirani gauge 皮拉尼真空（压力）计（测真空度用的电阻管式传感件）

pirani test 皮拉尼试验（电子管灯丝元件的试验）

PI speed error control 比例-积分（法）车速误差控制［proportional-integral (method) speed error control 的简称，用于汽车稳速控制，由比例增益电路产生与设定车速和实际车速差成比例的信号 P，由积分增益电路产生车速误差的时间积分的信号 i，根据 P + i 修正实际车速］

pistol-grip handle （手）枪把形手柄

pistol-like 手枪形的，手枪式的

piston 活塞

piston acceleration 活塞加速度

piston accumulator 活塞式蓄压器，活塞式储能器

piston angle （转子发动机的）旋转活塞转角

piston area 活塞面积（指以活塞名义直径，即以缸径为直径的活塞面积）

piston baffle 活塞折流顶

piston balancing （各缸）活塞的平衡（各缸活塞按质量选配）

piston barrel 活塞筒体（亦称 piston body）

piston bearing （三角转子发动机的）活塞（偏心轴）轴承

piston blast engine 活塞式鼓风机

piston blower 活塞式压气机

piston bolt 活塞螺栓

piston bore 汽缸孔径，缸径

piston boss ①活塞顶部凸台②活塞销孔座

piston-boss bushing 活塞销衬套

piston bottom 活塞裙部（= piston skirt）

piston brake chamber 活塞式气制动室（通过活塞将气体压力变换成驱动制动器的机械力的部件）

piston bush 活塞衬套

piston cap （由与活塞不同的材料制成的、装在活塞顶面以延长其使用寿命的）活塞顶盖

piston chamber （方向阀）滑阀腔

piston charging pump （二冲程发动机的）活塞式充气泵

piston clearance ①活塞顶间隙（活塞位于上止点位置时，活塞顶与缸盖底面间的空间）②汽缸工作容积（活塞面积 × 行程）③活塞与缸壁间隙（活塞最大直径与汽缸内径之差值）

piston clearance gauge 活塞间隙塞片规，活塞间隙量规

piston collapse 活塞（裙部因过热和

冲击应力而被）压瘪

piston combustion bowl 活塞（顶）燃烧室（指活塞顶上的凹坑与缸盖形成的燃烧室）

piston compression height 活塞压缩高度（活塞销中心与活塞顶间的垂直距离）

piston compressor 活塞式（空气）压缩机

piston controlled type 活塞控制型，活塞控制式（如：二冲程发动机中，由活塞开闭扫气孔等）

piston cooler 活塞冷却（机油）喷嘴

piston coverage area （内燃机燃烧室）活塞顶产生挤压作用的面积，活塞（顶）挤压面积（= piston squish area）

piston crank mechanism 活塞连杆机构，曲柄连杆机构（将活塞的往复运动通过连杆传递变为曲轴的旋转运动的机构）

piston crown 活塞顶，活塞顶部（亦称 piston head）

piston crown contours 活塞顶外形，活塞顶部轮廓

piston crown valve recess 活塞顶上的气门凹窝（防止顶置式气门开启时碰及活塞）

piston cup （液压缸）活塞皮碗

piston cup expander （制动分泵）皮碗胀簧

piston damper 活塞式阻尼器，活塞式减振器

piston depth 活塞高（度）

piston diaphragm （由真空或气压推动活塞运动的）活塞膜片

piston displacement ①活塞位移②活塞排量（汽缸的工作容积，= cylinder capacity）

piston drive 活塞驱动

piston driver 活塞杆

piston end position 活塞终点位置

piston engine 活塞式发动机（容积式发动机，指在每一个循环内，一定容积的工作气体在汽缸内膨胀，而推动活塞运动的发动机，= positive-displacement engine；常指活塞在缸内作往复运动的往复式活塞发动机，= reciprocating engine）

piston engine capacity 活塞式发动机工作容积

piston engine cycle ①活塞发动机循环（指热力循环，有 Otto cycle, Diesel cycle, Rankine cycle 等）②活塞发动机冲程（指冲程、二冲程等，2-cycle = 2-stroke, 4-cycle = 4-stroke）

piston expander 活塞裙扩张器（用特制内外小滚轮将裙部夹住滚压，使裙部扩张，以修正活塞与缸壁间的间隙值）

piston extension screw （串列式双腔制动缸主缸第一活塞和第二活塞之间的）活塞行程限制螺钉

piston eyebrow 活塞顶（避免撞碰气门）的凹窝

piston filler gauge 活塞（与缸壁）间隙量规（活塞间隙千分片，活塞间隙厚薄规）

piston force 活塞上的压力

piston friction 活塞摩擦

piston gas seal （三角转子发动机的）活塞（三角端部）气密封件

piston gear （三角转子发动机）活塞齿轮

piston grinder 活塞研磨机（用于研磨活塞外圆）

piston groove 活塞环槽（= piston ring groove）

piston groove cleaner 活塞环槽清洁器，活塞环槽积炭油污刮除器

piston head 活塞顶部（= piston crown）

piston heater 活塞加热器（一般为电热油浴加热装置，用于轻合金活

塞和连杆组件的拆装作业)

piston insert ①镶式活塞环槽,活塞环槽镶套 ②活塞顶部镶块 ③活塞裙部镶片

piston inserter 装活塞工具

piston knock 活塞敲缸声

piston land 活塞环槽岸,活塞环槽脊(活塞顶部除活塞环槽以外的部分)

piston lifter (Stromberg 式可变喉管化油器活塞室底座上的)活塞行程调节销(用于调定其活塞的自由行程,以控制混合气的浓度范围)

piston major thrust face 活塞(对缸壁的)高推力面(见 piston thrust force)

piston mass 活塞质量

piston minor thrust face 活塞(对缸壁的)低推力面(见 piston thrust force)

piston motor 活塞式液压马达,活塞式液动机

piston oval-grinding machine 活塞椭圆磨床

piston packing ring (油缸)活塞密封圈

piston pin [美]活塞销(= gudgeon pin, wrist pin)

piston-pin-bore 活塞销孔

piston-pin boss 活塞销孔座(活塞销孔凸台,= gudgeon pin boss, pin boss, piston boss)

piston pin boss hole 活塞销座孔

piston pin bushing 活塞销衬套(= pin bushing)

piston pin bushing reboring machine 镗活塞销衬套孔机

piston-pin button 活塞销端盖(防止活塞销突出后擦伤缸壁,亦称 piston pin cap)

piston pin circlip 活塞销(开口)卡环

piston pin drift 活塞销冲子

piston pin end cap 活塞销端盖

piston pin extractor 活塞销拉器

piston pin hole 活塞销孔

piston pin hole reamer 活塞销孔铰刀

piston pin knock 活塞销敲击声

piston pin locking screw 活塞销锁紧螺钉

piston pin lock ring 活塞销锁环

piston pin offset 活塞销偏置(活塞销的轴线稍许向活塞低推力面一侧偏移,以减小活塞销在上、下止点改变运动方向时对缸壁的敲击)

piston pin set screw 活塞销止动螺钉(亦写作 piston-pin setting screw)

piston pin snap ring 活塞销锁环

piston pin tool 活塞销维修工具

piston pin with taper bore 两端带锥孔的活塞销

piston play 活塞(与缸壁间的)间隙

piston pneumatic actuator 活塞式气动执行机构(一种直线运动机构,用压缩空气推动汽缸内的活塞,行程可调,用作执行机构)

piston position 活塞位置(指活塞在其上、下冲程中,距上止点的位置,用曲轴转角度数表示,如:上止点前 10°,指活塞处于曲轴尚须转 10°才到达上止点的位置)

piston-pressure diagram 活塞-压力图

piston pump 活塞泵

piston push-rod (弹簧-气压-活塞式制动气室的)活塞推杆(当制动管路压力低于某规定值或断开时,活塞在弹簧压力下推动推杆将制动器制动)

piston-rack (摆动油缸)活塞-齿条机构

piston return spring 活塞复位弹簧

piston ring 活塞环

piston ring back clearance 活塞环背

隙（活塞环内表面与环槽底面的间隙）

piston ring breakage 活塞环断裂

piston ring carrier 活塞环槽镶座（=ring carrier）

piston ring cast iron 活塞环用铸铁

piston ring chamfering 活塞环倒角

piston ring clamp 活塞环夹钳（活塞环安装钳）

piston ring compressed gap 在压缩状态下活塞环的端隙

piston-ring compressor （将活塞带装入缸筒时用的）活塞环压缩器

piston ring cylindricity light slit test 活塞环正圆度光隙检验（利用压缩后活塞环的外圆表面与标准座圆间的漏光程度来检验活塞环正圆度）

piston ring end gap 活塞环端隙（活塞环切口间隙，简称 piston ring gap，=piston ring end clearance）

piston ring ends 活塞环端头

piston ring expander 活塞环撑张器，活塞环扩张器（=piston ring tongs, ring pliers, ring spreader, ring squeezer）

piston ring face 活塞环外表面（与汽缸的接触表面）

piston ring filing tool 活塞环切口修整器

piston-ring flutter 活塞环颤动（活塞环工作时在环槽内的一种振动现象）

piston ring free gap 在自由状态下活塞环的端隙

piston ring gap in bore 活塞环在汽缸内的端间隙

piston ring gauge 活塞环量规（①量环径②量张力）

piston ring grinding machine 活塞环磨床

piston ring groove 活塞环槽

piston ring groove resizer 活塞环槽修理工具（活塞环槽恢复到应有尺寸的工具）

piston ring gumming 活塞环结胶

piston ring inserter 活塞环安装夹钳（用于将活塞装入汽缸）

piston ring joint 活塞环切口（活塞环端隙）

piston ring land （活塞环槽之间的）槽岸，槽脊

piston ring mounting and removing tool 活塞环拆装工具（见 piston ring putting in and out tool）

piston ring pin 活塞环定位销

piston-ring pliers 活塞环安装钳（将环撑开，以便装入活塞，亦写作 piston ring plyers）

piston ring putting in and out tool 活塞环拆装工具（=piston ring mounting and removing tool, piston ring-tool）

piston ring radial thickness 活塞环径向厚度

piston ring remover 活塞环拆卸工具

piston ring removing pliers 活塞环张口钳（拆卸活塞环钳具，活塞环撑张器，=piston ring expander, piston ring tongs）

piston ring removing tool 卸活塞环工具

piston ring scraper 活塞环积炭刮除器

piston-ring side 活塞环侧平面

piston-ring side clearance 活塞环侧隙（活塞环沿高度，即其上平面或下平面与环槽侧面的间隙）

piston-ring slot 活塞环槽

piston-ring spreader 活塞环拆装工具

piston ring steel-type apex-seal （转子发动机的）活塞环钢质径向密封片

piston ring sticking 活塞环胶结，活塞环卡滞

piston ring stop （某些二冲程发动机

压入环槽内的）活塞环止动销（防止活塞环转动，确保活塞环切口处于正确位置）

piston ring superfinishing machine 活塞环外圆超精加工机

piston ring tension 活塞环张力，活塞环弹力

piston ring tension scale 活塞环弹力测定器

piston ring tightener 活塞衬环

piston ring tongs 活塞环张口钳（= piston ring removing pliers）

piston ring tool 活塞环拆装工具（= piston ring remover）

piston ring travel 活塞环行程

piston ring type sealing arrangement 活塞环型密封装置

piston-ring width 活塞环宽度（高度）

piston rocking （活塞与气缸壁间隙过大，在上、下止点活塞改变运动方向时，碰击缸壁而产生的）活塞敲缸声（亦称 piston slap, piston side knock）

piston rod 活塞杆（如：内燃机中的连杆）

piston rod end 连杆小头（= connecting rod small end）

piston rod nut 连杆螺母（= connecting rod nut）

piston rod packing （活塞）连杆密封件

piston scraper ring 活塞（刮）油环

piston scuff 活塞（表面）擦伤

piston seal （液压缸等的）活塞密封件

piston seizure （由于过热或润滑不良等原因造成）活塞卡缸，活塞抱缸（活塞卡死，以致发动机突然停机）

piston separator （蓄压器）分隔活塞

piston side knock 活塞敲缸声（见 piston rocking）

piston size 活塞尺寸

piston skirt 活塞裙部（活塞销以下的部分）

piston skirt clearance 活塞裙间隙（活塞裙部与缸壁的间隙）

piston skirt expander 活塞裙部扩张器（简称 skirt expander）

piston skirt expanding （用扩张器、外表面滚花或从内面向外敲击等方法）扩张活塞裙（使其直径变大）

piston skirt slot 活塞裙槽，活塞裙切口

piston skirt thrust face 活塞裙部推力面

piston slap 活塞敲缸（声）（见 piston rocking）

piston slide valve 活塞式滑阀

piston slipper 活塞拖鞋式裙部（活塞销孔座以下的非受力面被切除）

piston speed 活塞速度

piston spring 活塞弹簧（液压或气压系平衡活塞运动的弹簧）

piston squish area 活塞顶挤压面积（= piston coverage area）

piston stopper （液压制动主缸的）活塞（行程）挡圈

piston stop washer 活塞止动挡圈（起液压主缸的液压活塞等返回非工作位置时的限位挡圈和单向球阀顶杆的挡圈的作用）

piston stroke ①活塞行程（活塞运行的上、下两止点之间的距离）②冲程

piston supercharger 活塞式增压器

piston-swept volume 活塞排量，汽缸工作容积（= displacement volume，活塞面积与行程的乘积）

piston throttle 活塞式节流阀

piston thrust 活塞（对缸壁）的侧向推力

piston thrust surface 活塞推力面（亦称 piston thrust force surface, 当曲轴顺时针方向旋转时，从发动机

后端观察，活塞在压缩冲程中的右侧，在做功冲程中的左侧分别对缸壁产生推压力，前者对缸壁的推力较低称 piston minor thrust face，后者对缸壁的推力较高称 piston major thrust face）

piston top 活塞顶（= piston crown）

piston top land 活塞顶岸（第一循环上方的岸面）

piston travel 活塞行程（= travel of piston）

piston travel switch （制动总泵的）活塞行程开关（向电子控制模块发送活塞行程信息，供故障检测用）

piston type brake valve 活塞式制动阀

piston type damper 活塞式减振器

piston type fuel supply pump （泵油元件为活塞的活塞式输油泵）

piston-type pressure gauge 活塞式压力计

piston type rotary pump 活塞式回转泵，旋转活塞泵，转子泵

piston type sampler 活塞式取样器

piston-type shock absorber 活塞式减振器

piston (type) valve 活塞式滑阀，活塞式气阀

piston underside pump scavenging （十字头式柴油机中的）活塞底泵式扫气（以其活塞下部空间为压缩室，利用活塞下行，使空气产生一定压力而实现扫气的方式）

piston-valve type two cycle engine 活塞进、排气孔阀式二冲程发动机（由活塞在其冲程过程中，开启和关闭进、排气孔，即兼起进、排气孔阀门的作用来实现进气和排气的二冲程发动机）

piston varnish 活塞表面的漆状沉积物，活塞表面（形成的）漆膜

piston velocity 活塞瞬时速度，活塞速度

piston vice 活塞台钳

piston wall 活塞侧壁

piston wear 活塞磨损

piston wick （真空助力器等的）活塞润滑油毡圈

piston with 带…的活塞（如：with articulated skirt 带铰接式裙部的活塞，with combustion chamber 顶面带燃烧室的活塞，with flame plate 带挡火板的活塞，with mixture cooling, oil-jet cooling, oil-spray cooling, 混合气冷却、机油喷射、机油飞溅冷却式活塞等）

PI system 汽油喷射系（petrol injection system）

pit ①（汽车的）维修地沟，维修地槽②（汽车比赛时的）加油站，轮胎修理处③（金属表面的）凹痕，凹坑，麻点，缩孔，砂眼④均热炉⑤使成凹坑，使有缩孔，起凹点

PIT 产品改进试验（= product improvement test）

pit area ①维修地沟区②维修地沟面积

pitch ①间距②螺距（相邻螺纹相同点上测得的轴向距离，单头螺纹的螺距即其导程，= lead）③齿距（齿轮某一既定曲面上，一条给定斜线被两个相邻同侧齿面所截取的长度）④倾斜，斜度，斜坡，高跨比，矢高⑤（汽车）纵倾，俯仰振动（指汽车簧上质量绕汽车坐标系 x 轴的角振动，见 vehicle axis system "汽车坐标系"）⑥程度（= degree）⑦投掷，投掷的距离⑧（声音的）高、低度⑨沥青⑩（翻车事故时，乘客被）摔出（车外）

pitch acceleration （汽车）纵倾加速度（见 pitch⑤）

pitch angle ①（锥齿轮）节圆锥角（维齿轮轴线与节锥母线间的夹角）②前轮外倾角③（车身）纵倾角（簧上质量质心为原点的汽车坐标

系 x 轴与地面固定坐标系 X-Y 所夹的锐角)④螺距角

pitch arc (齿轮)节距弧

pitch axis (汽车的)纵倾轴(通过俯仰振动的不动点且与汽车坐标系 y 轴平行的轴,参见汽车坐标系"vehicle axis system")

pitch base 齿轮的基圆节距

pitch circle ①节圆(圆柱齿轮的节圆,指其节圆柱面与其端平面的交线。锥齿轮节圆,指其节锥与背锥的交线)②(汽车车轮的)螺栓孔分布圆(指过其各螺栓孔中心连线所形成的圆,或各螺栓孔中心所在的圆,简称 PC)

pitch circle diameter ①(齿轮)节圆直径②(车轮)螺栓孔分布圆直径(简称 PCD)

pitch coal 沥青煤,烟煤

pitch cone (锥齿轮)节圆锥面,节锥(在相交轴齿轮副中,锥齿轮的节曲面,见 pitch surface)

pitch cone angle (锥齿轮)节锥角

pitch cone radius (锥齿轮)节锥半径

pitch control ①(汽车的)纵倾控制,俯仰控制②节距调节(机构),节距控制③(车身)色调控制

pitch control during braking (主动式悬架的)制动时纵倾控制(亦称 nose dive control,增加前悬架控制压力,减小后悬架控制压力)

pitch curve (齿轮的)节线(啮合曲线)

pitch cylinder 节圆柱面(指平行轴齿轮副中的圆柱齿轮的节曲面,见 pitch surface)

pitch diameter ①(螺纹)中径②(齿轮)节圆直径(简称 PD)

pitch diameter of thread 螺纹中径

pitch error 节距误差

pitch-free ride 无纵倾振动(无俯仰振动)的行驶

pitch frequency (车辆)纵倾振动频率,俯仰振动频率

pitch gauge 节径规,螺距规,螺纹样板

pitch gear 径节制齿轮

pitch helix 节圆螺旋线(斜齿轮的节圆柱面与齿面的交线)

pitch indicator ①螺距测量仪②(车辆)纵倾指示器,俯仰角指示器

pitch inertia 纵倾惯量(车辆在纵向平面内绕过重心的横向轴的转动惯量)

pitching ①扔出,投掷②布置(场面等)③调节④(机器的运动件)咬住⑤(汽车绕过重心横轴)纵倾,俯仰运动⑥倾斜的,陡的

pitch(ing) damper (车辆)纵倾角振动减振器,俯仰减缓器(用来缓冲车辆在纵向平面内绕重心轴的角振动)

pitching moment 纵倾力矩(作用在汽车上的力矩矢量使汽车绕以其质心为原点的汽车坐标系 Y_0 轴旋转的分量)

pitching moment coefficient (空气动力的)纵倾力矩系数(指空气动力形成的纵倾力矩的无量纲系数,$= \dfrac{T_P}{P_{air} \times A \times B_w}$,式中:$T_P$—纵倾力矩;$P_{air}$—气流速度形成的动压;$A$—汽车正投影面积;$B_w$—轮距,亦称仰俯力矩系数)

pitching moment of inertia of vehicle 汽车簧上质量纵倾惯性矩(汽车簧上质量绕汽车坐标系 x 轴,簧上惯性主轴坐标系 η 轴或纵倾旋转的惯性矩,参见 vehicle axis system, inertia principal axis system 及 pitch axis)

pitch input (路敏式悬架系统的车身)纵倾输入(由动力控制模块"PCM"根据节气门位置、车速、传动系挡位及汽车加速时车速变化率,算出车身仰起信息,而由汽

车减速时车速变化率,算出车身俯冲信息,并作为纵倾输入,传送至路敏悬架系统的电子控制模块"RSS module")

pitch line 节线(齿条的节平面与端平面的交线)

pitch number 节数

pitch of base circle (齿轮)基圆节距,基节

pitch of boom (起重机)起重臂的倾斜角

pitch of holes 孔间中心距

pitch of screw (thread) 螺距

pitch of strand (绳索)股的螺距

pitch of tread design 胎面花纹间距

pitch of worm 蜗杆螺距

pitchout (汽车行驶中的)突然转弯(动作)

pitch plane 节平面(平行轴或相交轴齿轮副中,垂直于公共轴平面并与两齿轮的节曲面相切的平面)

pitch point 节点(一对相啮合齿轮的两节圆的切点)

pitch radius (齿轮)节圆半径

pitch ratio 螺距-直径比

pitch-stabilizer damping (车辆)纵倾稳定器阻尼率,俯仰稳定器阻尼率

pitch-stabilizer spring stiffness 纵倾稳定器(俯仰稳定器)弹簧刚度

pitch surface 节曲面(在齿轮副中的任一个齿轮上,其配对齿轮相对于该齿作回转运动时的瞬时轴的轨迹曲面)

pitch system 径节制

pitch tester 节距检验器

pitch thread 齿节螺纹

pitch time (流水线等的)节拍时间,间隔时间

pitch tolerance (螺纹)螺距公差,(齿轮)齿距公差

pitch variation tyre 变间距胎面花纹型轮胎,非均匀性胎面花纹轮胎(用以降低轮胎行驶时产生的噪声)

pitch velocity 纵倾角速度(俯仰角速度,簧上质量绕其质心为原点的汽车坐标系 y 轴旋转的角速度)

pitch vibration 俯仰振动,纵倾振动(绕汽车过重心横轴的角振动)

pitchy 沥青,用沥青覆盖的;多树脂的

pitchy road 柏油路,沥青路

pit corrosion 点蚀,穴蚀

pit in (竞赛中)赛车驶入加油、换胎、抢修场地

pit jack 维修地沟用(汽车)千斤顶

pit lift 维修地沟用(汽车)举升器

pitman ①连接杆,连杆②摇杆转向垂臂,转向器臂

pitman arm [美]转向摇臂(将转向器的力和运动输出给转向直拉杆的摆臂, = drop arm, steering gear arm)

pitman arm shaft 转向摇臂轴,转向臂轴(亦称 cross-shaft, = rocker shaft, sector shaft "齿扇轴")

pitman arm steering gear 转向摇臂式转向机(见 worm and lever steering gear)

pitman head ①转向摇臂球头②连杆头,连接杆头

pitometer 皮托管测压器,皮氏压差计

Pitot flow meter 皮托管式流量计

Pitot tube ①皮托(流速测定)管(法国 Pitot 发明,简称 Pitot,为一种 L 形双重管)②皮托静止管(= Pitot static tube)

Pitot tube type 皮托管式(化油器主喷嘴,利用 pitot tube 原理, = plain tube type)

pit road 赛车场供赛车出入加油、换胎、抢修场地的道路

pits ①(穴蚀造成的表面)麻点②(赛车道上停下来维修、加油、换轮胎等的)维护点

pitsaw file 半圆锉
pitscale 地磅
pit stop 赛车停在维护点加油、换胎或修理等
pitted surface ①（金属）疲劳点蚀表面②有小坑凹的路面
pitted valve 点蚀的气门，穴蚀气门
pitting ①凹痕，麻坑，锈斑，（金属）点蚀穴蚀，表面麻点状腐蚀②局部锈蚀，剥蚀，锈痕③（焊接）烧熔边缘④（耐火材料的）软化，腐蚀
pitting and piling （断电器一对触点间产生的）剥附蚀损（由于高温气化或电容器容量不当造成的其中一个触点剥落的金属附着于另一个触点上的蚀损现象）
pitting corrosion test （抗）点蚀试验
pitting cracking 点蚀疲劳裂纹
pitting factor （金属表面）穴蚀因素（最深的蚀点深度与按质量损失算出的平均穴蚀深度之比）
pitting fatigue 点蚀接触疲劳
pitting fatigue life 表面点蚀疲劳寿命，表面穴蚀疲劳寿命
pitting of (breaker) points （断电器）触点烧损点蚀
pit type plating 多孔电镀（如：保持油膜、减少磨损的多孔镀铬）
pitwork （汽车维修）地沟作业
PIV ①反向峰值电压（peak inverse voltage）②PIV 型无级变速（装置）［positive infinitely variable (gear)的简称］
pivot 枢轴（指旋转件绕之旋转，摆动件绕之摆动的支撑轴，如：转向主销，控制臂支撑销轴，仪表指针中心轴等）
pivotal ①中枢的，枢要的，中心的，全局的② 枢轴的
pivot (al) joint 主销连接，枢轴连接
pivotally attached 铰接的

pivot angle 摆动角，转动角
pivot axis ①枢轴，枢轴线，旋转轴线②（汽车非独立悬架转向轮的）转向主销轴线，转向主销中心线（= kingpin axis）③（汽车独立悬架转向轮的）转向轴线（亦称 steering axis，指独立悬架上、下控制臂与转向节上、下臂连接的两球节中心连线，车轮转向时绕该连线回转，亦称 swivel axis。在某些文献中仍习惯上沿用 kingpin axis 表示该连线）
pivot bolt 主销，枢轴
pivot centre ①转动中心，旋转轴心；摆动轴心②转向节主销轴线与路面交点
pivoted 绕轴线摆动的，在轴上转动的，装在枢轴上的
pivoted axle flies 摆动桥（见 swing axle）
pivoted float 铰接式浮子，摆动浮子
pivoted shoe brake 支撑销蹄式制动器（蹄片支撑销固定在制动底板上的鼓式制动器）
pivoted ventilation window 枢轴式通风窗
pivot end 尖头，顶端，尖端
pivot (ing) beam 枢轴梁，翘板梁
pivoting bearing 转向节轴承（= knuckle bearing）
pivoting motion type seat 摆动式座椅
pivot journal 枢轴颈
pivot pin ①枢轴（= pivot）②转向主销（亦称 swivel pin, knuckle pin, = kingpin）
pivot pin bush ①枢销衬套②转向节销衬套，主销衬套（= steering swivel bush, king pin bush, king bolt bush, steering knuckle bush）
pivot point 枢轴点，旋转中心点，支点（如：气门摇臂支点）
pivot ring （膜片式弹簧离合器的）

支撑圈（位于推式膜片弹簧两侧和拉式膜片弹簧外端的弹簧钢丝支撑圈，亦称 fulcrum ring, diaphragm spring ring）

pivot shaft 铰销，枢轴（亦称 pivot spindle, pivot stud）

pivot suspension 枢轴支撑式悬架

pivot turn 原地转弯，原地掉头（= pivot steering, spot turn）

pivot type side slip tester 回转式侧偏试验台

pi-wren 管子钳（pipe wrench 的简称）

Pkm 人-千米（passenger-kilometer）

PL ①驻车锁（parking lock）②产品责任法［见 Product（s）Liability Law］

placard 说明牌，布告，告示

placard pressure 公告压力（如：厂方规定的轮胎充气压力等）

place ①地方，场所，地点，位置，位②安置，配置

placement 方位，部位，位置，布置，安排，布局，有规则的分布和排列

placement of signs 路标的布置

place name sign 地名标，地名牌

placing distance （圆锥齿轮）分度锥母线总长

plain ①平原②平的，平坦的③普通的④简单的，明白的

plain-and-ball bearing 由滑动轴承和球轴承组成的复合轴承

plain ball 普通钢球（相对于高级钢球而言）

plain bearing （与轴颈工作面接触的）滑动轴承（亦称 parallel bearing, 多指轴瓦或轴套式滑动轴承）

plain bearing fatigue 滑动轴承疲劳

plain bending 平面弯曲

plain brake drum 光制动鼓（无散热片的制动鼓）

plain combustion chamber 圆柱形燃烧室（指仅仅由活塞顶平面与缸盖平面之间的空间形成的燃烧室）

plain country 平原地区

plain cut-out 熔断丝

plain disc wheel （无孔或无槽的）整板辐板式车轮

plain drifting 转向漂动，转向滑漂，转向漂移

plain eyebolt 普通有眼螺栓

plain face 光面，素面（简称 PF）

plain fit 普通精度配合（相当于三级精度配合）

plain hole 光孔

plain metal ①普通金属②滑动轴承（= plain bearing）③滑动轴承轴瓦

plain nave 辐板式轮毂

plain nut 普通螺母，常规螺母

plain pattern tread 光胎面（= smooth tread）

plain pin 平销

plain piston ring 平活塞环，平气环（断面呈矩形的最常用的压缩环）

plain round nut 普通圆螺母

plain screw 普通螺钉

plain shaft 普通轴，光轴

plain snap gauge 卡规，普通外径规

plain stem （螺栓或螺钉的）无螺纹（的）杆身（部分）

plain taper sunk key 普通锥形埋头键

plain total enclosure 普通全封闭式机壳，简单全封闭式机壳

plain tri-metal bearing 三金属轴瓦，三层金属滑动轴承

plain tube type 皮托管式（参见 Pitot tube type）

plain type 简单型，简易式，普通式，平式

plain valve head 平气门头

plain washer 平垫圈

plain wheel 普通砂轮

plan ①计划，规划，草案，方案，平面图，示意图②定计划，订规划

planar 平面的，平的，在同一平面内的；二维的，二度的

plan area 平面面积

planar laser-induced 平面激光诱发的

planar oxygen sensor 平面型氧传感器（相对于套筒型氧传感器 thimble type oxygen sensor 而言，其传感芯件呈平面形）

planar point of a surface 曲面的平点

planar solution 平面解

planar technique 平面工艺（指采用掩膜、金属化、光刻技术等在底衬上制造元、器件和电路的过程）

Planck's constant 普朗克常数（简称 H 或 h）

plan-do-check-action 计划-实施-检查-改进（为全面质量管理中的一项措施，简称 PDCA）

plane ①平面②刨③平的

plane angle 平面角（= linear angle，两条直线组成的角）

plane axiom 平面公理

plane bearing 滑动轴承

plane bevel gear 平面锥齿轮（指节锥角 γ = 90°的圆锥齿轮，相当于直齿圆柱齿轮的齿条）

plane configuration 平面构形

plane curve 平曲线（大曲率半径曲线）

plane deformation 平面变形

plane diagram 平面图（亦称 plane figure）

plane harmonic motion 平面谐运动

plane kinematics 平面运动学

plane motion 平面运动

plane of action ①作用平面，作用面②（平行轴渐开线圆柱齿轮副的）啮合曲面

plane of a flat pencil （平）线束的面

plane of bending 弯曲平面，弯曲面

plane of datum 基准平面（指三维正交坐标系中的 z-水平面，y-铅垂面，x-垂直于 y, z 平面的平面）

plane of flexure 挠曲平面，挠曲面

plane of fracture 折断面

plane of gravity 重心面

plane of load 载荷平面，载荷面

plane of perspectivity 透视平面

plane of polarization 偏振（平）面（与线偏振光电矢量的振动面相垂直的平面）

plane of projection 投影平面，射影面积

plane of reference 参考面，基准面，基（础）面

plane of rotation 旋转平面

plane of rupture 断裂面

plane of symmetry 对称平面

plane of weakness 薄弱截面

plane-parallel 平行平面的

plane plate 平板

plane polarization 平面偏振（波的偏振被限制在一个平面内，= linear polarization）

plane reflection 平面反映

plane strain 平面应变

plane stress 平面应力

plane surface 平面

plane symmetry 平面对称

planet 行星齿轮

planetary ①行星（式）的，由于星作用的②行星齿轮的③轨道（式）的

planetary beval gear drive with small teeth difference 锥齿少齿差行星齿轮传动（由锥齿少齿差齿轮副、周向限制机构和曲拐元件组成的齿轮传动）

planetary cage 行星齿轮箱

planetary carrier 行星齿轮架（planetary gear carrier, planetary pinion carrier 的简称，行星小齿轮的支撑架）

planetary cluster pinion 塔轮式行星齿轮（行星齿轮组，复式行星齿

轮，如：自动变速器的组合式行星齿轮机构中使用的在同一根轴上具有两个行星齿轮的行星塔轮，= compound planet gear）

planetary double reduction final drive 行星齿轮式两级主减速器（由一对锥齿轮和一套行星圆柱齿轮减速机构组成的两级减速器）

planetary gear 行星齿轮（在行星齿轮传动中作行星运动的齿轮，亦称 planet-wheel, planetary pinion, cryptogear, 见 planetary gearset）

planetary gear apparatus 行星齿轮装置（机构）

planetary gearbox 行星齿轮变速器（= epicyclic gearbox，由行星齿轮机构组成的变速器）

planetary-gear bub drive 行星齿轮轮边传动

planetary gear carrier 行星齿轮架（见 planetary carrier）

planetary gear differential 行星齿轮差速器

planetary gear drive mechanism 行星齿轮传动机构（由一个位于中央称为太阳轮的外齿轮，一个位于外圈的内齿圈和在太阳轮与外齿圈之间并与二者相啮合的若干个等间距布置的，叫作行星齿轮的小齿轮及支撑这些小行星齿轮的行星架组成的齿轮系，在汽车上用于自动变速器、差速器等，亦称 planetary gear system）

planetary gear drive with small teeth difference 少齿差行星齿轮传动（指由少齿差齿轮副、偏心元件和输出机构组成的行星齿轮传动，见 gear pair with small teeth difference, eccentric element 及 out put mechanism）

planetary gear group ①行星齿轮组 ②行星齿轮副变速器（用行星齿轮传动的副变速器）

planetary gearing 行星齿轮机构，行量齿轮装置

planetary gears connected in three-freedom (type) transmission 串联式三自由度行星齿轮机构（式）变速器

planetary gears in changeable connection with three-freedom (type) transmisson 换联式三自由度行星齿轮机构（式）变速器

planetary gear train 行星齿轮系（指至少有一级行星齿轮传动机构的若干齿轮副的组合）

planetary gear transmission ［美］行星齿轮变速器（= epicyclic gearbox）

planetary gear-type torque-split mechanism （四轮驱动车前、后轮的）行量齿轮型转矩分配机构

planetary hydrodynamic transmission 行星齿轮式液力变速器（采用行星齿轮机构的液力变速器）

planetary inter axial differential 行星齿轮型轴间差速器（四轮驱动车辆，前、后桥间的行星齿轮型差速器）

planetary involute gear drive with small teeth difference 渐开线少齿差行星齿轮传动（由渐开线少齿差内齿副、偏心元件和输出机构组成的行星齿轮传动）

planetary motion 行星运动

planetary pinion （一般位于太阳轮与内齿圈间的）行星（小）齿轮（= planetary gear）

planetary pinion carrier （行星齿轮机构的）行星架（见 planet carrier）

planetary reducer 行星减速齿轮装置，行星齿轮减速器

planetary reduction gear 行星减速齿轮机构

planetary rotation engine 行星式旋转活塞发动机，行星式转子发动机

planetary rotation machine 行星式旋

转机(其运动件除绕自身重心作等角速度运动外,至少有一个运动件作行星运动,简称 PLM,参见 KKM)

planetary train 行星齿轮传动系

planetary transmission ①行星传动②行星齿轮变速器(美,= epicyclic gearbox)

planetary wave generator 行星式波发生器(谐波齿轮传动波发生器内配置有行星传动构件者)

planetary wheel ①行星齿轮②装有行星减速器的车轮

planetary wheel reductor 行星圆柱齿轮式轮边减速器(由一套行星圆柱齿轮机构构成的轮边减速器)

planet cage 行星齿轮机构壳体

planet carrier 行星齿轮架,行星架(可绕行星齿轮组中心轴线旋转并支撑各行星齿轮的构件)

planet motion 行星运动

planet pinion 行星齿轮,游星齿轮

planet pinion gear 行星小齿轮

planet spider (十字形)行星架

planet wheel 行星(齿)轮(= planetary gear,亦称 planet pinion, planet pinion gear,在行星齿轮组中,由行星架支撑,与太阳轮和外齿圈啮合的小齿轮)

planet wheel carrier 行星齿轮架

plane washer 平垫圈

plan form ①平面图②上视图(如:从上方俯视汽车所见的汽车轮廓图)

planimegraph 面积比例规,缩图器

planimeter 面积仪,求积仪,测面仪

planing 刨,刨削,整平,修平

planish 刨平,压平,敲平,磨平,碾平,弄平

planishing hammer (车身板件凹凸的)敲平锤,敲平手锤(简称 planisher,亦称 panel hammer)

plank ①厚板(厚5~15cm,宽>23cm),镶板,板条,跳板;支持物,基础②辅以厚板,在…上铺板

plankbed car 平板(货)车

plank body 木板车厢

plank road 木板路

planned dispatching 计划调度

planned life 计划寿命,设计寿命,预计寿命

planned maintenance 计划维护,计划检修,计划维修

planned transportation 计划运输

planning 规划,计划

planning study (按)计划研究,规划研究(简称PS)

planning transportation 规划运输,计划运输

plano-convex 平凸的

plan of site 总布置图

plan of work 工作计划,运行作业计划

planometer 平面规,测平面仪

plano-polyhedral angle 棱顶多面角

plans division 计划部门,计划局,计划处(简称PD)

plant ①工厂,车间②装置,设备,机组③植物④种植,播种

Plante type plate 普兰特式(蓄电池)极板(铅极板)

plant factor 设备利用率,设备利用系数

plant load factor 设备、装置的负载系数(负载率)

plant-manufactured 工厂制造的

plant pest control vehicle 植物病害控制车,植物病害治理车

plant seeds inspection van 种子检测车

plan view drawing 平面图

plasma 等离子区,等离子体(气体电离后分解成正、负离子和自由电子,而成为导电体,若由中性粒子和带正电粒子、带负电粒子,即正

负离子和电子组成的导电气体总体上呈电中性时,该导电气体称为等离子体)

plasma arc 等离子弧(使气体通过电弧形成高温电离气体流,用以切割、焊接、熔化金属等)

plasma arc ignition system 等离子弧点火系(参见 plasma jet ignition system)

plasma arc welding 等离子(气体)电弧焊

plasma carburising process 等离子流渗碳法

plasma-deposited ceramic coating 等离子体沉积陶瓷复层(亦写作 plasma-deposited cermet coating, plasma deposited metallic coating)

plasma display 见 plasma panel

plasma induction furnace 等离子气体感应炉(简称 PIF)

plasma jet ignition system 等离子流点火系(在小的副燃烧室中点燃且离子化的高温气体火焰,喷射到主燃烧室中点燃其中的稀混合气)

plasma panel 等离子体显示屏(= gas panel,指由充气平板和装在该板内的电极格栅组成的显示屏,电极格栅通电后,气体电离而发光,显示图像、文字或数字并在断电后仍可保持较长时间,使用这种显示屏的显示器称 plasma display)

plasma spray 等离子喷镀

plasma tron 等离子管(等离子流发生器)

plaster-model method 石膏模型法(设计燃烧室的一种方法,原由美国 chevrolet 厂的一位设计师采用)

plaster theorem 砌墙定理

plastic ①塑料(= plastics)②塑料制的,可塑的

plastic bearing 塑料轴承

plastic-bodied car 塑料车身轿车

plastic body ①塑性体,塑胶体②塑料车身,塑料车厢

plastic bronze 塑性铅青铜(轴承铅青铜,铜63.6% ~ 67.7%,铅26.6% ~ 30.1%,锡4% ~ 5.6%,镍0.1%,锌0.1% ~ 1%)

plastic cement 塑胶(塑料黏结料)

plastic cohesive soil 黏塑性土镶(= plastic clay)

plastic deformation 塑性变形(指固体受到应力超过其弹性极限时产生的尺寸和形状的永久性改变)

plastic engine 塑料发动机(指除燃烧室、排气歧管、活塞、缸套、气门等承受大的机械和热负荷的部件外,其余部件,如汽缸体、进气歧管、气门室盖、水泵壳、油底壳等均使用塑料制的发动机)

plastic filler method 塑料间隙规测定法(见 plastic gauge)

plastic filter 塑料芯滤清器

plastic flow 塑性流动

plastic foam 泡沫塑料(亦写作 foam plastics)

plastic fuel tank 塑料油箱

plasticimeter 塑性计

plasticine model 油泥模型(车身设计中常采用油泥敷在木质骨架上雕塑而成汽车模型)

plasticiser 增塑剂(塑料和橡胶等的柔性增加剂)

plasticity 塑性(指材料断裂前发生不可逆永久变形的能力,常用的塑性判据是伸长率和断面收缩率)

plasticity chart 塑限图

plasticity coefficient 塑性系数

plasticity index (土的)塑性指数

plasticity test 可塑性试验

plasticity theory 塑性理论(= plastic theory)

plasticization 增塑,塑化,塑炼

plasticizer 增韧剂,增塑剂,柔韧剂(亦写作 plasticiser)

plastic lead 塑性铅(环氧树脂与铅

粉末混合物用于修铺铸件缺陷）

plastic lens 塑料透镜（如：汽车的塑料灯玻璃）

plastic limit 塑性极限

plastic metal 高锡含锑轴承青铜（锑约10%，锡约80%，其余为铜）

plastic monoblock 塑料整体（壳）件

plastic optical fiber 见POF

plastic optic fiber 塑料光纤（简称POF）

plastic range （金属材料等的）塑性区

plastic refractory 塑性耐火材料（可涂覆在制件表面）

plastics 塑料（指以一种或数种高分子聚合物为基本成分的材料的总称）

plastics-bodied car 塑料车身轿车

plastics-coated 塑料覆面的（塑料涂覆的钢件等，起美观防锈作用）

plastic slip 塑性滑移

plastics molding 塑胶造型（法），塑料模压（法）

plastic soils 塑性土壤

plastic/steel laminate 塑料-钢层板，塑料-钢层板制件

plastic strain ratio 塑性应变比（金属板件轴向拉伸到产生均匀塑性变形时，宽度方向的真实应变与厚度方向的真实应变之比）

plastic surface ①塑性路面②塑性表面

plastic theory 塑性理论（= plasticity theory）

plastic working 塑性加工，压力加工

plastic yield 塑性屈服，塑变值，塑流点，塑性变形，塑性流动

plasti-gauge 塑料间隙规（将塑料细圆棒夹在轴颈与轴承间，用规定转矩扭紧，然后拆下，用专用量具量测圆棒压扁的宽度，即可精确测定间隙，亦写作 plastigage）

plastisol 塑料溶胶，增塑溶胶

plastisols （聚氯乙烯为原料的）热固性黏结剂（适用于大尺寸的汽车配件，特别是受热部件）

plasto-elasticity 弹塑性力学

plastometer 塑性计

plate ①板，板件（如：电容器板，蓄电池极板，垫板，检查板，信息板，离合器盘等平的圆形、方形、矩形板件）②（特指：装在商用货车上标明法规限定的该车的使用与装载条件的永久性）标牌③电镀

plate active material （蓄电池）正、负极板活性材料（正极板栅架上的二氧化铅，负极板上的海绵状铅）

plateau ①平稳状态，稳定状态；稳定时期，停滞时期②曲线的平坦段③坪，平台④高原（复数 plateaus 或 plateaux）

plate base （蓄电池）极板栅架

plate bearing test 平板载荷试验（承载板载荷试验，测定土的承载能力）

plate brake tester 板式制动试验台[分动板式（moving plate type）和静板式（static plate type）两种]

plate cam 平板凸轮

plate circuit 阳极电路，板极电路

plate clutch 盘式离合器

plate connection bus ①（蓄电池各）单格电池（间的）连接片②（蓄电池）极板连接母线

plate coupling 盘式联轴节，盘式耦合器

plated ①电镀的②复合金属板的③（工作表面）镀有耐磨层的（如：plated liner 镀有铬等耐磨层的汽缸套，plated ring 镀铬等的活塞环）

plated beam ①用板材加强的（箱形截面）梁②叠板梁

plate disc brake 盘式制动器

plated weight （地方或全国性现行法

规所允许的车辆或其单轴装载的最大总重)标示重量(见 plate②)

plate exchanger 薄片式热交换器

plate fin type radiator 薄板散热片式散热器(指发动机使用的冷却水管由多层薄金属片孔中穿过的散热器)

plate frame (蓄电池)极板栅架边框

plate friction lining (离合器盘等的)摩擦衬面,摩擦片

plate gauge 板规,样板

plate girder (由弯曲、铆接或焊制成的)薄板梁

plate glass 平板玻璃

plate grid (蓄电池的)极板

plate group 一组板件(如:多片式摩擦离合器的一组摩擦盘,蓄电池的一组正、负极板等)

plate guard 护板

plate-in type cylinder head gasket 板材补强式汽缸垫(指在缸垫的燃烧气体密封部分及其周边用金属板或非金属板补强的缸垫)

plate iron 厚铁板

plate link 平板链节

plate load (离合器接合时,离合器弹簧等的)压盘上的力

plate lock washer 锁紧垫片

platen ①(在金属板件上压制凸点、浮雕等的)压板 ②台板

plate-pasting technique (蓄电池极板等的)栅板涂膏技术

plate separator 隔板(＝baffle separator)

plate shackle 片式吊耳

plates of datum (三维正交坐标系中的)基准平面(指其 zero Z plate, zero Y plate 和 zero X plate:基准水平面,基准纵向铅垂面和基准横向铅垂面)

plate spring 钢板弹簧,片弹簧

plate strap (蓄电池单格电池同极性的各个极板的)联结横板(各极板焊接在该横板上,形成相互并联的正、负极板组,正、负极板组的联结横板分别与单格电池的正、负接线柱连接,亦称 connecting strap)

plate support (蓄电池壳底部的)极板支架

plate-type battery 极板(式)蓄电池(为常规车用阴极板、阳极板的铅酸蓄电池)

plate type guard 护板

plate-type sliding throttle 平板式滑动型节流滑阀

plate valve 平板阀,片状阀

plate varnish (转子发动机的)缸盖内壁漆膜

plate washer 板垫圈,平垫圈

plate wheel 辐板式车轮(＝disc wheel)

plate work 钣金工工作

platform ①站台,平台,货台 ②(货车等的)载货平板,货箱地板 ③(客车等的)上车台阶板 ④(雪地用轮胎的)磨损界限标志(通常当雪地用胎胎面磨损达到50%时,即失去其冰雪地抗滑性能,为此在其胎面花纹沟深50%处设有四个判断其磨损界限的标志,为了醒目起见,其胎侧具有该四点的指标)

platform and stake body 带可拆栅栏板的平板车箱

platform balance 台秤

platform body (无侧壁与顶的)平板车身

platform capacity ①(货车)货台装载量 ②站台通行能力 ③工作台生产能力

platform car 平板式载货汽车,平板车

platform development (以计算机系统作为)平台(进行的虚拟)开发(设计、试验等)

platform dimensions 平板货台尺寸
platform floor 车厢底板，货厢底板
platform for jumping （汽车越野赛路线中的）跳台
platform frame （一种轿车车身的）平板型底板（由加强的平板构成的底板结构，车身由螺栓紧固在该底板上，如：德大众公司甲壳虫轿车）
platform height （平板车）装货平板（离地）高度
platform scale 台秤（地磅，地秤，=weighbridge）
platform semitrailer 平板式半挂车（=flat bed semitrailer）
platform tent 车厢篷布，货厢篷布
platform tools box （载货汽车）货台工具箱
platform top bow （载货汽车）货台的弓形篷杆
platform trailer 平板（全）挂车（=flat-bed trailer）
platform truck [美] 平板式载货汽车（亦称 flat-bed truck，=platform lorry）
platform type frame （车架与车身底板制成一体的）盘式车架，半承载式车架（参见 tray type frame）
platform without stake 四边无栅柱的平板（车）货台
platina 粗铂，天然铂
plating ①（车身）面板 ②镀金属，电镀 ③电镀层
plating solution 镀液
platinum 铂，白金（Pt）
platinum alloys 铂基合金
platinum catalyst （催化转化器中使用的）铂催化剂（氧化催化剂）
platinum-coated pellets （催化转化器中使用的）涂铂颗粒（氧化催化剂）
platinum electrode （火花塞等的）白金电极

platinum-rhodium thermocouple 铂铑热电偶
platinum sparking plug 白金电极火花塞（一般指中心电极为白金制的火花塞）
platinum tippet spark plug 白金镶尖火花塞（指中心电极和侧电极端部焊有白金片的火花塞，与一般火花塞相比，其中心电极较细，耐蚀性强，可使用10万公里而无须维护，但不能含铅汽油，其绝缘体的波形部分有五条蓝色带，以资识别）
platinum tip spark plug （中心电极带）铂尖（的）火花塞（其上端有5道蓝条标记）
platinum wire resistor 铂线电阻器
platoon 排，组，队（如：前后以一定间隔在车道上成群行驶的车群，=wave）
platooning ①（汽车）车群跟车行驶（模式）②（在自动驾驶系统中，指）车群中跟车行驶性能（即在自动驾驶行驶中，与前车、两侧汽车保持安全距离的能力）
platooning (on highway) system （公路行车）排队系统（使公路行驶的车辆保持规定的安全车距的雷达测距与车速控制系统）
play ①间隙，游隙，间距，窜动量，空程，自由行程（亦称 free play，=lash）②（机器的）开动，作用，动作 ③表演，起…作用
play adjustment 间隙调整，自由行程调整
playback （磁性记录带的）重现，重放，放音，放像
playback head 放音磁头，放像磁头
playback speed 再现速度，读出纪录的速度，回放速度
play detector （动态）间隙检查仪（20世纪80年代欧洲出现的一种动态间隙检查仪具，整车在前后、左右振动状态下，检查汽车转向、悬

架系统的间隙,较静态检查更为方便、准确)

play for expansion 膨胀缝(伸缩缝)

play motion 自由行程

play of valve 气门间隙

PLBS 局部稀燃系统(partial lean-burn system 的简称)

pleasure car 游乐车,游乐轿车

plenum ①充满,充实,空间充满物质(vacuum 的反义)②压力通风系统,强制通风,进气增压③(发动机)进气通路,进气通道④(进、排)气流⑤充有高于外面的压力的空气或气体的容器⑥增压的,强制通风的,加压的

plenum chamber ①(指其内的空气或气体压力高于其外界气压的)高压气室,压气室②充气室[汽油喷射发动机进气系中连接节气门体(或进气管道)和进气歧管(或缸盖进气道)的合金铸造腔体]③(汽车车身通风系统位于前围上盖板与前围板之间的)通风气室(车室内的新鲜空气或暖气由该室提供)

plenum intake manifold 增压式进气歧管

plenum ventilation 压力通风,强制通风

pliability 柔韧性(可挠性,易弯性,可塑性,受范性,能适应性)

pliability test 韧性试验(弯曲试验)

pliable ①可弯的(易弯的,柔软的,柔顺的)②易受影响的,能适应的

pliers 钳子(亦写作 plyers,各种手钳的总称)

plies (轮胎的橡胶)帘线层(ply 的复数形式)

plinth 柱础,底座

PLM ①行星式旋转活塞机(planetary rotation machine)②脉冲宽度调制(pulse length modulation)

PLM design 行星旋转式装置,行星旋转式发动机设计(参见 PLM)

PLM(le)3:2RC engine 3:2 交衔啮合(外)行星旋转式发动机(相位机构速比为 3:2)

PLM(li)3:2engine 3:2 交衔啮合(内)行星旋转式发动机(相位机构速比为 3:2)

PLM(sli)2:3engine 2:3 滑移啮合(外)行星旋转式发动机(相位机构速比为 2:3)

PLM(type)engine 行星旋转式发动机(参见 PLM)

PLM Wankel RC engine 行星旋转式汪克尔三角活塞发动机,行星旋转式汪克尔转子发动机(即目前常见的转子发动机)

plot ①曲线图,图表②绘制曲线图

plot method 磁粉探伤法(= magnetic powder method)

plug ①塞、螺塞,旋塞,塞头②塞规③电插头,电插销④火花塞(spark plug 的简称)⑤(汽车轮胎气门芯的)芯体

plug and play device 即插即用型装置(如:货运车队的远程诊断系统,只要将无线远程诊断器的插头插入车载式诊断系统的插座内,就可将车辆行驶和技术状况的各项数据发给维修站或管理部门,实现远程故障诊断、维修服务和路边支援,并可实现驾驶者与车队调度-管理部门间的双向无线通信)

plug-board 插座板,插座式转接板

plug cleaner 火花塞清洁器

plug cock 螺塞开关,柱塞开关,柱塞阀

plug connector 插座式连接器,插塞接头,插杆接头

plug contact 插头

plug fuse 熔断丝塞

plug gap 火花塞间隙(指火花塞电极间的间隙)

plug gap gauge 火花塞间隙规（有线规、球规和片规等多种，用于测量火花塞中央电极和侧电极间的间隙）

plug gapping 火花塞电极间隙调整

plug gauge 塞规，内径规

plugged （泥污）堵塞了的

plugged piston ring （泄油槽）堵塞的油环

plug helix 螺线切口，螺旋槽（参见 helical groove）

plug hole ①螺塞孔②火花塞孔③橡胶塞孔

plug-in ①插装，插入②插装件，插头式零件③组合式的，插入式的，插上的，带插头的，接点的

plug-in assembly ①插入式总成，插入式组件②插入式组装

plug-in capacity （混合动力车等的动力蓄电池通过家用电插座直接用插销）插入充电功能

plug-in coil 插入式线圈

plug-in HV （家用电源）插座充电式混合动力车（见 PHV）

plug-in instrument 插入式仪表

plug-in pump 插入式整体油泵

plug-in switch 插头开关，插销开关

plug-in-unit 插头，插入部件

plug jet 气动测头，气动塞规

plug lead 火花塞（的）高压线

plug on coil ignition system （无分电器式点火系统中的）单火花塞-线圈式直接点火系统（direct ignition system 的一种，每一火花塞上均装有一个点火线圈的直接点火系统）

plug pipe tap 塞状管丝锥

plug-proof 防堵塞的

plug receptacle 插座

plug reversing （电动机的）插头反接（使电动机倒转）

plug seat （汽缸盖上的）火花塞安装座

plug spanner 火花塞（专用）扳手

plug switch 插头开关

plug terminal 火花塞接线头

plug tester 火花塞试验器（用于检测火花强度）

plug thread gage 螺纹塞规

plug valve 塞阀，旋塞，锥形阀，锥形旋阀

plug vent channel （蓄电池）电解液注入孔塞中心的通气孔道

plug voltage （点火系统的）火花塞电压

plug wetting 火花塞冷湿（指冷机时，燃油蒸气遇低温火花塞而冷凝且附着于其表面的现象）

plug wrench 火花塞扳手

plumb ①铅锤，测锤，线铊，垂线；垂直②垂直的；公正的；完全的，绝对的③用铅锤检查（是否垂直），测量；探测使垂直；垂直地悬挂着④铺设管道⑤灌铅（以增加质量）⑥用铅封⑦到达…的底部

plumbago 石墨

plumb bob 铅锤

plumb-bob technique 铅锤测量技术

plumbing ①管道系统，管道装置②液压系统管路③铅锤测量④同轴连接⑤管道，管道工程，管道装设⑥波导设备，波导管⑦客车卫生间内的抽水马桶（一般加定冠词 the）

plumbing connection 管道连接

plumbing system 管系，管道系统

plumbism （由于使用含铅汽油等排气铅污染引起的）慢性铅中毒

plumb line 铅垂线，垂直线，准绳

plumbum 铅（Pb）（= lead）

plummet ①铅锤②垂直落下，骤然跌落

plunge cut 全面进给法，全面进刀法，切入（式）磨削，横向进给磨削

plunge-jointed half shaft 插装式半轴，插接式半轴，插入连接式半轴

plunger ①柱塞②（电磁铁的）插

棒式铁心③（波导管）短路器④锁芯⑤推杆

plunger and barrel assembly 柴油机喷油系的柱塞偶件（由柱塞形柱塞套筒两零件组成，柱塞在柱塞套筒内往复运动而泵压燃油）

plunger arm （柴油机柱塞式喷油泵的）柱塞调节臂（装在柱塞尾部，带动柱塞转动，以调节喷油量的臂状零件）

plunger barrel 柱塞套筒 C 如：柱塞泵的柱塞在其中往复运动的缸筒，= plunger bushing

plunger control sleeve （柴油机喷油泵）柱塞控制套（上部安装调节齿圈，下部有直槽带动柱塞转动的套筒，注意与 plunger control-sleeve gear 的区别）

plunger control-sleeve gear （柴油机喷油泵的）柱塞控制齿套（其上部有齿与调节齿杆啮合，下部有直槽带动柱塞转动的套筒。它的作用与控制套筒装上调节齿圈后相同）

plunger door contact 车门顶杆式开关（= door switch）

plunger elevator 液压举升器，柱塞式升降机

plunger gear 喷油泵柱塞齿轮

plunger helix （喷油泵）柱塞螺旋槽

plunger leather 柱塞皮封

plunger lower helix （喷油泵）柱塞螺旋槽下线

plunger principle 柱塞式（防抱死制动控制系统，由电子控制柱塞元件调控制动压力，以区别于早期的阀门式控制方式）

plunger pump 柱塞泵（亦称 force pump，一般指由柱塞往复运动泵压油液的装置）

plunger return spring 柱塞复位弹簧

plunger switch 顶杆开关

plunger type (metering) pump 柱塞式计量泵

plunger type pressure regulator 柱塞式压力调节器

plunger-type solenoid 柱塞式电磁阀

plunger type vacuum booster 反馈柱塞式真空助力器（指用反馈柱塞取代反馈杆和反馈盘的真空助力器，见 reaction plunger）

plunger upper helix （喷油泵）柱塞螺旋槽上线

plunging constant velocity (universal) joint 可轴向移动的等速万向节（允许沿轴向相对移动的各种万向节的通称，如：可轴向移动的球笼式等速万向节，球销式万向节等，简称 plunging joint）

plunging tripod joint 三球销万向节（见 tripod universal joint）

pluonium 钚（pu）

plural 复数的，两个以上的，多元的，多数的

(plural) real-time-kinematic-GPS 见 RTK GPS

(Plural) RTK-GPS on vehicle 车载式（多元）实时运动型全球定位系统（plural real-time-kinematic-GPS on vehicle 的简称，用于测定汽车绕其坐标系 x，y，z 轴的回转角速度及其位置和姿势的 6 自由度实时全球卫星定位探测系统，详见 K-GPS）

plus ①加，加上，加的，加号②正，正的，正号③阳，阳性的④标准以上的，比同等产品等配置高的、尺寸等略大的⑤附加物，附加件

plus camber （车轮）正外倾，外倾（指车轮上方方向外倾斜，见 camber）

plus caster 正后倾（转向节主销中心线的上方向后方倾斜，见 caster）

plus driver 十字螺钉旋具，十字头起子（= phillips driver）

plus earth 正极接地，正极搭铁

plush ①长毛绒，丝绒（车身内筛材料）②长毛绒的

plush ride (悬架和减振器的)柔顺模式(见 programmable ride control system)

plus ion 阳离子(指带正电荷的原子或原子团)

plus lap (进、排气门)正重叠,叠开角(指进、排气门同时处于开启状态的时间,用曲轴转角表示)

plus mesh 筛上,(颗粒)大于筛孔

Plus Suspension 顶级悬架(商品名,德大众汽车公司高性能车上使用的前轮带滑柱、后轮带扭杆弹簧的纵臂式独立悬架)

plus thread 右旋螺纹,正螺纹[= right-hand (ed) thread]

ply ①(汽车在两地之间)来回行驶②层,片③(绳)股④(轮胎的橡胶)帘布层⑤叠,叠加

plyers 手钳(各种手钳的总称,亦写作 pliers)

plying taxi 野鸡汽车(美国一种未参加一定组织、私人拉客货的汽车)

ply mouth 顺风(一种轿车的商品名,美国克莱斯勒公司产品)

ply rating 层级(简称 PR,尼龙线或钢丝线,轮胎规格的一种表示法,表示该轮胎可承受相当于多少层棉帘线的负荷,如 9.00-20-12PR,表示该轮胎可承受相当于12层棉帘线的负荷,而不是实际层数,见 number of plies)

ply separation (轮胎)胎体分层

ply separation resistance (胎体)抗分层剥离的强度

ply separation test (轮胎帘布层的)抗脱层试验,分层试验

plysteer (由于轮胎帘布层不对称而导致的汽车)胎体失衡偏转

plysteer force (克服轮胎帘布层不对称造成的胎体失衡效应,使轮胎保持直线行驶所需的)胎体失衡平衡力

ply turn-up (轮胎的)胎圈芯包布(见 flipper)

ply-wood 胶合板,层(压木)板(= veneer sheet)

PM10 尺寸小于10微米的微粒

P/M ①粉末金属(powdered-metal)②预防性维护,预防性检修(preventative maintenance)

PM ①微粒物(particulate matter 的简称)②调相(phase modulation)③故障预防维护(preventive maintenance)④脉冲调制(pulse modulation)

P-metric (轿车轮胎的)公制规格标记(如:P155/80R13,P-轿车,155-断面宽度,in,80-高宽比,R-子午胎,13-轮辋直径,英寸)

pm-ification truck 具有净水设备的汽车(= water purification truck)

PMLFFC 无贵金属的液态燃料电池(precious metalless liquid feed fuel cell 的简称,如:用 $N_2H_4 + H_2O$ 为燃料的燃料电池)

PMMA 聚甲基丙烯酸甲酯,聚甲基异丁烯树脂,聚甲基丙烯树脂,有机玻璃(polymethyl methacrylate 的简称)

PM motor 永磁电动机(permanent magnet motor 的简称)

pmnp impeller blade (液力变矩器的)泵轮叶片

PMOS P沟道金属氧化物半导体(指空穴载流子金属氧化硅半导体器件,P-channel metal-oxidesilicon device 的简称,亦称 P-typeMOS)

PMOS transistor P型金属-氧化物-半导体晶体管(P type metal oxide semiconductor transistor 的简称)

PM reduction system (排气中)微粒物减少系统(particulate matter reduction system 的简称)

PM scheduling 预防维护图表作业(法),编制预防维护作业计划

(Preventive maintenance scheduling 的简称)

PM trap 见 particulate trap

PMVI 汽车定期检查（periodic motor vehicle inspection）

PMVR 原动机（prime mover）

PN ①零件编号［亦写作 p/n, part(s) number 的简称］②抗爆功率比值（见 performance number②）③可塑性指数（plasticity number）④请注意（please note）⑤节目预告（program notice）

PNA 个人导航支援（系统）（personal navigation assistant 的简称）

PND 个人导航装置（personal navigation device 的简称）

PN-dB 用分贝表示的感知噪声级（perceived noise decibels 的简称，见 perceived noise level）

PN diesel （日本 MAZDA 公司生产的）直列四缸，1.7L 家用轿车柴油机（商品名）

Pneu ①气动的（= pneumatic）②气动力学（参见 pneumatics）

Pneu Accrochage vertical tire （米其林"Michelin"公司 1999 年投入市场的）直扣气胎（一种双层安全胎，据称该胎破损后仍能以 80km/h 的时速行驶 200km。这种轮胎不是靠气压而是通过机械锁扣系统固定在轮辋上，故名，简称 PAV）

pneudraulic 气动液压的（pneumatic hydraulic 的简称）

pneumatic ①气动的，风动的，气力的，气压的，压缩空气操纵的；有空气的，有气体的，可充气的，装有气胎的②充气轮胎，装气胎的车辆

pneumatic accumulator 气压蓄能器，气压蓄压器

pneumatic actuator 气动执行器，气压执行器

pneumatic all-terrain amphibian 充气轮胎高通过性水陆两用车

pneumatically actuated 气动的

pneumatically controlled 气操纵的，气压控制的

pneumatic（ally）-tyre 装充气轮胎的

pneumatic analog computer 气动模拟计算机

pneumatic analogue 气动模拟

pneumatic atomizer 气动喷雾器

pneumatic automatic 气压自动装置，气压自动机械

pneumatic brake 气压制动器（= air brake）

pneumatic brake air compressor 气制动用空（气）压（缩）机

pneumatic buffer 气体缓冲器；气垫减振器（= air-cushion shock-absorber, air buffer, 见 pneumatic shock absorber）

pneumatic bumper 充气保险杠，气胎保险杠

pneumatic caulking tool 风动捻缝工具

pneumatic circuit 气动回路，气动管路

pneumatic clamp（ing） 气动卡具，风动卡具

pneumatic clutch 气动离合器

pneumatic control 气动控制，气动操纵

pneumatic controller 气压式控制装置，气动控制器

pneumatic cushion 气垫，气垫式缓冲器

pneumatic (cylinder) piston 气动缸活塞

pneumatic digital computer 气动数字计算机（流控数字计算机，指信号的发送、信息的存储都靠气流压力的变化和流动来实现的一类计算机）

pneumatic discharge vehicle 气动卸

1181

货式货车
pneumatic door opener 气动车门开关装置
pneumatic drive ①气动，风动（= air-operated drive）②气动装置
pneumatic elastic wheel 充气式弹性车轮，充气式弹性轮
pneumatic elevator 气动升降机
pneumatic engine 压缩空气发动机，气动机（各种以压缩空气为动力，即把压缩空气具有的能量变换为机械能的原动机总称，包括气动涡轮机、气动马达等，亦称 compressed air engine）
pneumatic fuel-pump 气动燃油泵
pneumatic gauge 气流千分仪，气压测微器（压缩空气通过某间隙时的流量、流速及背压均随间隙大小而变，测出上述三个参数中的任一个值，即可确定该间隙的大小，按此原理制成的测微装置的统称）
pneumatic governor （燃油喷射系的）气动式调速器（真空调速器及气压调速器的总称，见 vacuum governor 及 air governor）
pneumatic horn 气动喇叭，气喇叭（= air horn）
pneumatic hose 气动装置软管（压缩空气软管）
pneumatic hydraulic 气动液压的（由压缩空气压力推动油液执行的，简称 pneudraulic）
pneumatic jack 气动千斤顶，气动举升器
pneumatic lapper 气动研磨器，气动研磨机，气动研磨工具
pneumatic-mechanical wastegate （废气涡轮增压系统的）气动-机械式废气旁通减压阀（废气压力超过某规定点时该阀开启）
pneumatic motor 气动马达，气动机
pneumatic nut runner 气动螺母扳手
pneumatic panel 配气板

pneumatic piston motor 活塞式气动马达（常用于连续旋转机械，见 radial piston motor）
pneumatic power drive 气力传动，气力驱动，气动
pneumatic power shift 气动换挡
pneumatic preselection gear change control mechanism 气动预选换挡机构
pneumatic pump 气压泵
pneumatic pyrometer 气动高温计
pneumatic remote control system 气动远距离控制系统，气动遥控装置
pneumatics ①气动力学，气体力学 ②气动装置，风动装置 ③充气轮胎，气胎
pneumatic scrubber 气动洗涤机，气动擦洗装置
pneumatic seat 气垫座椅（空气悬架座椅）
pneumatic servo system 气动伺服系统
pneumatic shock absorber 气动减振器，气垫缓冲器，气垫避振器（= air-cushion shock absorber，pneumatic buffer，air damper，air buffer）
pneumatic shot blasting machine 喷丸处理机
pneumatic spring 空气弹簧
pneumatic spring pressure sensor 空气弹簧压力传感器
pneumatic starting device （柴油机）压缩空气起动装置
pneumatic steering unit 转向气动助力装置，气动转向加力装置（= air-power steering unit）
pneumatic suspension 空气悬架，气垫式悬架，空气弹簧式悬架（亦称 air suspension，指以空气或气体弹簧为弹性元件的悬架装置，= air spring type suspension）
pneumatic test 管件气压试验，管道漏气试验，气压试验

pneumatic timing system 气动正时系统

pneumatic tipping device (自卸车)气动倾卸装置(亦称 Pneumatic gear)

pneumatic tire 充气轮胎,气胎(亦写作 pneumatic tyre,简称 tyre)

pneumatic tool 气动工具,风动工具

pneumatic-tracked vehicle 气胎履带车辆,轮胎-履带复合式车辆(一般前轮为充气轮胎车轮,后端为履带驱动)

pneumatic trail ①气胎拖迹(现象)(滚动的充气轮胎在外来侧向力的作用下,产生侧偏角和转弯力。若转弯力的合力在接地面上的着力点落在车轮中心在地面上的投影点的后方,而且随着侧偏角的增大,着力点逐步后移,则这种现象称为气胎拖迹。见 cornering force)②气胎拖距(指产生上述现象时,转弯力合力作用点与车轮接地中心间的距离。气胎拖距和转弯力,形成一力矩,力图使车轮平面与滚动轨迹相重合,减小侧偏角,称为自回正力矩"self-aligning torque")

pneumatic transport 气动(管道)运输

pneumatic type valve 气动阀(气压阀和真空阀的统称)

pneumatic tyre cover 充气轮胎外胎

pneumatic tyre expander 气压张胎器

pneumatic wave generator (谐波齿轮传动的)气动式波发生器(利用气动力,使柔轮齿圈产生变形波的波发生器)

pneumatize 气动化

pneumotransport 气动运输(管道内利用气力推动进行运输)(= pneumatic transport)

PN junction PN 节(指使用一定的方法使 P 型半导体和 N 型半导体紧密结合在一起,而在二者交界面上形成的一层带 +、-电的空间电荷区,亦写作 p-n junction,见 semiconductor)

PNP PNP 型(晶体管)(positive-negative-positive transistor 的简称)

PNPN diode PNPN 二极管(具有两个独立的发射极,一个共同的集电极的双极管结构的半导体器件)

p-n-p transistor p-n-p 型晶体三极管

PNR 油泵额定噪声值,油泵噪声额定值(pump noise rating)

P/Nswitch (自动变速器)驻车挡/空挡开关(park/neutral switch 的简称,挂空挡或驻车挡时,该开关闭合,向控制模块发出变速器挂空挡/驻车挡信号)

POA valve 见 pilot-operated absolute valve

pocket ①袋,囊,匣,兜,壳,套,罩②穴,窝,坑,凹(如:转子发动机转子上形成燃烧室的凹窝)③(铸件)砂眼④袖珍的,小型的

pocketed oil (齿轮泵)齿间困油

pock markings 麻点(金属件表面的一种缺陷)

pocky 有凹坑的,斑斑点点的

pod ①容器,箱②(安装仪表、量具的)卡座,承座,承窝③(插装件,如:钻头上的)纵槽,插装槽

POD system 被动式乘员识别系统(passive occupant distinguishing system 的简称,该系统可识别座椅上有否乘员及乘员体重、身高及在座位上的具体位置,使安全气囊的释放作智能化选择,以保护儿童和防止膨胀力过大而伤害乘员,以及避免空座释放等)

POEM 合成橡胶软垫的最佳设计法(procedure for optimizing elastomeric mountings)

POF 塑胶光纤(plastic optical fiber 的简称,用丙烯树脂作为核心材料,通信速度高、成本低,具有很

强的抗震和弯曲特性,在汽车上得到广泛应用)
pogo stick (一种带有弹簧的)水准尺
point ①点,站,尖,尖端②触点(多写作 points)③(刻度盘的)刻度④时刻,瞬间⑤特点,特征⑥强调,指向,表明
point angle 顶角,锥尖角
point arm 触点臂,断电器臂
point bounce 触点回跳(反跳,跳动)
point breaker arm 断电器活动触点臂
point by point method 逐点测定法,逐点计算法
point-by-point test 逐点测试
point circle 齿顶圆(= addendum circle)
point contact 点接触
point-contact diode 点接触二极管,点接触整流管
point corrosion 点腐蚀
point-curve transformation 点线变换
point design 关键结构,关键设计(解决关键问题的设计感结构)
point diameter (螺纹的)前端直径
point drift (仪表、仪器等的)点漂(在规定工作条件下,对应一个恒定输入在规定时间内的输出变化,见 drift)
pointed ①尖的,尖角的,尖锐的,尖顶的②有所指的③突出的,显然的
pointed bolt 尖端螺栓
pointed cam 尖形凸轮
pointed corrosion 斑点腐蚀,麻斑腐蚀
pointed radiator V形散热器
pointed shell 散热器前罩,水箱前脸
pointed tooth 尖顶齿
pointer 指针,指示器
pointer stop (仪器)指针挡销
point file 触点锉
point follower (车速自动控制系统的)路边控制点跟踪装置
point gap 触点间隙
point gauge 点规,测针,针形水位计,量棒
point gearing 点啮合
point hardening 局部淬火(= local hardening)
point imperfection 疵点
pointless ignition 无触点点火装置(= breakerless ignition)
point load 点荷载,集中荷载
point of accumulation 聚点,集点
point of action 作用点
point of application 施(力)点,着(力)点
point of condensation 凝(聚)点
point of contact ①接触点②切点
point of emergence (光线等的)出射点
point of engagement 啮合点
point of fixation 凝视点,注视点(视野中,眼睛集中观察的一点或目标)
point of fracture 断裂点
point of fusion 熔点(= temperature of fusion)
point of ignition 点火时刻(= time of ignition)
point of incidence (光线等的)入射点
point of inflection (曲线)转折点,拐点
point of intersection 交叉点,交点
point of load 荷载点
point of measurement 量测点
point-of-measurement addressing 量测点寻址
point of neutral steer 中性转向点
point of observation (目视)观察点(指左、右眼转动中心的连接基线的中点)

point of oscillatory discontinuity 振动间断（不连续）点

point of pivot on road 转向主销轴线延长线与路面的交点

point of reference 基点，参考点，水准点，控制点

point of support 支点

point of tangency 切点（亦称 point of tangent）

point of transition 过渡点，转折点

pointolite 点光源

point particle 质点

point pressure 点压力

4-point racing harness （某些赛车手戴的）四点式安全带（系统）

point resistance test 触点阻抗试验

3-point seat belt 三点式安全带（由肩部和腰下横带组成，作用于肩及左、右两侧大腿根部三处的乘员安全带）

2-point (seat) belt 两点式（座椅）安全带（指两点式安全臀带）

points gap 触点间隙

12-point (socket) wrench 12角套筒扳手

point source 点音源，点声源，点光源，点热源，点辐射源

point source of light 点光源

point spectrum 点谱，离散谱

point station 停车站，停车点

point support 触点支座，触点臂支座

point toothing 点啮合

point-to-point speed 点间速率（直线运动速率，平移速率）

point type throttle position sensor 触点式节气门位置传感器（见 throttle position sensor）

point welding 点焊，凸焊

point welding machine 点焊机

poise ①泊（流体的动力黏度单位。代号P，即在流体内相距1cm的两平行层之间，具有1cm/s的相对运动，其剪切力为$1g/cm^2$时的流体黏度。泊的因次为$g \cdot cm^{-1} \cdot s^{-1}$，克·厘米$^{-1}$·秒$^{-1}$。因$1dyn = 1g \cdot cm/s^2$，所以$1P = dyn \cdot s \cdot cm^{-2} = 10^{-1} Nsm^{-2}$）②平衡，平静③砝码，秤锤④使平衡，使质量相等；过秤，称质量

poised 平衡的

Poiseuille flow 泊萧流（由法国科学家 Poiseuille 提出的温度与黏度的关系导出的非压缩性黏性流体的层流，见 Hagen-Poiseuille law 和 Poiseuille velocity distribution）

Poiseuille velocity distribution 泊萧流速分布（指圆管内非压缩性黏性流体的流速呈抛物线形分布）

poison ①毒，毒药，毒物②抑制剂③弊病，害处④使中毒，毒害⑤弄坏（机器等）；损害，伤害，沾污，弄坏⑥有毒的，放入毒物

poisoning （特指催化转化器的）催化剂中毒（铅、磷或硫等有害物质沉积在催化剂表面，削弱或消除催化剂催化转化能力的现象）

poisonous 有毒的，毒性的，有害的

poisonous exhaust composition 废气有害成分（废气中对人体有害的NO_x、HC、CO 及醛类、铅化物、硫化物和微粒物质等的统称）

poisonousness 毒性

Poisson distribution 泊松分布

Poisson period 泊松周期

Poisson's ratio 泊松比（轴向应力与轴向应变呈线性比例关系的范围内，材料受拉伸时，每单位长度的横向收缩，对每单位长度的纵向伸长之比，或定义为在该范围内，横向应变与轴向应变之比的绝对值。泊松比 v，杨氏弹性模数 E 和刚性模数 G 的关系为 $v = \frac{E}{2G} - 1$）

poke ①拨，推，戳，穿，刺，放置②（俗）动力（power）③加速度

poke weld 手动挤焊（亦称 poke push weld, poke welding, push welding）

polar ①极线，极性，极面②磁极的，极性的，极坐标的，极线的，级化的

polar additive 极性添加剂

polar axis 极轴

polar coordinate(s) 极坐标

polar crystal 极性晶体

polar curve 极坐标曲线,（配）极（曲）线

polar diagram 极坐标图

polar distance 极间距离，极距（简称 PD）

polarimeter 偏光计，偏振计，极化计，旋光计

polarimetric 测定偏振的，测定旋光的，测定极化的

polariscope 偏振光镜，偏光镜，偏光仪，旋光计

polarised light 偏振光，偏光

polarity ①极性②偏光性③配极（变换）

polarity effect 极化效应

polarity of electrode 电极极性

polarity of transformer 变压器绕组极性

polarity reversal 极性反向，极性颠倒

polarity sign 极性符号

polarization ①极化（a. 产生极性和致极性增强的过程；b. 电流通过蓄电池时，其正、负极板表面电极电位因电流通过极板、隔板、电解液所产生的压降，电解液中形成的离子密度差和极板上形成的电荷的积累对电化学反应的阻碍作用而产生的"移动"）②极化强度③偏振，偏振光（使自然光通过某种晶体薄片后只剩下沿某一方向振动的光，叫偏振，这种晶体薄片叫偏振片，只沿某一方向振动的光叫偏振光）④配极变换，两极分化

polarization analyzer 检偏振（光）镜

polarization cell 极化电池

polarization curve （金属的）极化曲线，极化强度曲线（原电池腐蚀中，根据氧化和还原反应说明金属电位与原电池腐蚀电流之间的关系曲线）

polarization photometer 偏光光度计

polarization property of reflected light 反射光的偏振特性

polarization resistance 极化电阻（蓄电池因极化而形成的内阻部分）

polarization switch 变极开关（极性转换开关）

polarization vector 极化矢量

polarize ①（使）偏振（使光波等按一定模式振动）②（使）极化（使产生极性）③（使）两极分化

polarized ammeter 极化电流表，双向电流表（零刻度在中央）

polarized beam 偏振光束

polarized electromagnetic ammeter 极化电磁式电流表（利用动铁芯与通电流的固定线圈和固定的永磁磁铁之间作用力而工作的电流表）

polarized head light system （汽车的）偏振光前照灯系统

polarized light 偏振光，极化光

polarized return-to-zero recording （车用计算机系统用一个磁化方向表示零、另一个磁化方向表示 1 的一种二进制数）极化归零记录法[简称 RZ（P），见 non-polarized return-to-zero recording]

polarizer 偏振器，偏振片，起偏镜（将自然光变为偏振光的平面透镜）

polarizing 极性的确立

polarizing angle 偏振角

polar molecule 极性分子

polar moment of inertia 转动惯性极矩，惯性极矩（物体绕垂直轴旋转

polarogram 极谱图（自极谱仪中取出的电流-电压曲线，电流波的高度与某一种物质的浓度成比例）

polarograph 极谱记录器，极谱仪（用于化学分析的一种仪器，记录出极化电极的电流-电压特性，称为极谱图，见 polarogram）

polarography 极谱法，极谱学

polaroid 偏光器，偏光片（原为一种人造偏光片的商品名，现指各种起偏光作用的镜片，见 polarization ③）

polaroid camera （金相显微摄影用的）波拉罗伊德照相机（一种拍照后随即冲洗的照相机，波拉罗伊德为该照相机的商品名）

polar radius of gyration 回转极半径

polar silver 极地银（车身颜色）

pole ①柱，棒，极，竿（通常指在10英尺以上的圆形杆）②极，地极，电极；磁极③杆（英、美长度单位，1 pole = $16\frac{1}{2}$ ft = $5\frac{1}{2}$ yd，有时称为 perch 或 rod）

pole carriage ①长货运输②运输管材的车辆

pole changer 换极开关，换极器，极性变换器

pole-changes 极变换

pole collision （汽车与电线杆之类的）杆状物碰撞

pole core 磁极（起动机等的磁场绕组的铁芯件，= pole piece）

pole distance 极距

pole doily 见 pole trailer①

pole drill and erection truck 钻孔立柱车（装备有钻孔装置、起重装置、拔柱机、卷扬装置、操纵装置和梯子，用于电力、电信工程挖掘柱坑、立柱、拔柱等作业的专用汽车）

pole face area 磁极端面积

pole lift 柱式举升器

pole of pole coordinates 极坐标的极点

pole piece （各种形状的线圈软铁芯件，如）极爪，极片，极板，极靴（等的通称，= pole core）

pole pitch 磁极间距（360°除以磁极数）

pole plate （蓄电池）极板

pole rotor and field winding （由极爪和磁场绕组构成的电机）转子总成（= rotor assembly）

pole sat infinity 无穷远极

pole shoe 极靴（电机磁场绕组的靴形铁芯）

pole shoe spreader （防止拆卸和紧固极靴固定螺钉时极靴变形而插入的）极靴撑件

pole trailer ①长货挂车，管式挂车，长件挂车（一种专门用来装运棒料、管件、梁件等长货件的无货箱挂车，通常车架由一根管状长轴制成，利用伸缩套管、移动车桥、改变牵引杆长度等方法来调节轴距或车长，以适应装运不同长度货件的需要，亦称 pole dolly 或 carriage）②牵引杆式全挂车（指通过一根与挂车转向轴连接的圆形截面长拖杆牵引的全挂车）

pole-trailer bar 管式挂车牵引杆，长货挂车牵引杆

pole trailer with telescopic tubular pole 带伸缩中央套管的长件挂车（参见 pole trailer）

pole transporter 管材运输车，长货运输车（具有敞开式长货架和管材固紧装置，用于运输各类管材等）

pole winding 磁场线圈

police 警察

police car 警察用车，警车

police interceptor 警用截击车

police licence plate 警车车牌

police wagon 囚犯车

polish ①抛光剂②抛光
polished chrome 光滑镀铬
polished surface 抛光面，精加工面
polisher 抛光机，光磨机，抛光机具；抛光剂；抛光工
polishing 抛光
polishing composition 抛光剂（亦称 polishing compound, polishing cream, polishing paste）
polishing wax 抛光蜡
polish up 修饰；改善
pollen filter 花粉过滤器（某些高级轿车内装用此件，以防乘员花粉过敏）
pollutant 污染物
pollutant emission sensor 有害排放物（指 HC, CO, NO_x 等）传感器［目前尚无理想的实用产品，一般是在催化转化器出口加装第二氧传感器"second oxygen sensor"，作为代用品，用以测定转化器和（或）第一氧传感器是否老化］
pollution 污染
pollution charge system 污染收费系统（国家对排放污染物征收排放费的系统）
pollution control 污染控制，污染对策，污染净化
pollution control system 污染控制系统
pollution-free 无污染的，无公害的
Pollution Tax 大气污染税（国家为防治环境污染所征之税）
polonium 钋（Po）
polyacetal 聚缩醛类（树脂）
polyacrylates 聚丙烯酸酯（类）
polyacrylic polymer 聚丙烯聚合物
poly-acrylonitrile 聚丙烯腈（汽车排放光化学产物之一，简称 PAN）
polyamide 聚（酰）亚胺（热塑性塑料的一种，耐热，电性质稳定，不易燃），聚酰胺树脂，聚酰胺纤维，耐纶，尼龙（= nylon）

polyaryletherketone （一种）高温模塑聚合物
polybutadiene 聚丁二烯
polybutadiene rubber 聚丁二烯橡胶（一种胎面橡胶，与天然橡胶相比，耐磨、耐低温、耐热老化，简称 BR）
polybuteleneterephthalate 聚丁烯对苯二酸酯（简称 PBT）
polycarbonate 聚碳酸酯（简称 PC，在宽温度范围内具有高的韧性和强度，良好的电性能与阻燃性能，用做喷射模塑、真空模塑件等的原料）
polycarbonate plastics 聚碳酸酯塑料
poly cell approach 多单元法（构成大规模集成电路的一种方法）
polychloroprene 聚氯丁烯，氯丁橡胶
polychlorotrifluoroethylene 聚氯三氟化乙烯（简称 PCTFE，其性质与聚四氟乙烯相似，但较易加工，见 PTFE）
polycrystal 多晶体
polycrystaline 多晶体的
polydimethyl siloxanes 聚二甲基硅氧烷（= dimethylpoly siloxanes，是一种无毒聚合物，焙烧时只生成二氧化碳、水和固体二氧化硅）
polydyne cam profile 高次方动力凸轮轮廓
polyellipsoidal headlight 见 PE headlight
polyester 聚酯（热固性塑料，韧性高，抗天气腐蚀性强，用做玻璃纤维强化塑料车身和部件）
polyester fibres 聚酯纤维
polyester powder coating 聚酯粉末涂料，聚酯漆粉
polyester resin （不饱和）聚酯树脂
polyester resin cure 聚酯树脂固化处理
polyether-polyester elastomer 聚醚-

聚酯弹性材料
polyethersulfone 聚醚砜（一种耐高温热塑性塑料）
polyethylene 聚乙烯（简称PE）
polyethylene oil 聚乙烯润滑油
polyethylene terephthalate polyester film 聚乙烯对苯二酸酯聚酯膜片，密拉薄膜片（见Mylar）
polyfoam 泡沫塑料
polyformaldehyde 聚甲醛（简称POM，制造汽车仪表板用）
polyfunctional 多功能的，多重（性）的
polyglass 苯乙烯玻璃（塑料）
polyglass tire 聚合玻璃纤维帘布层轮胎
polyglycol 聚乙二醇［乙烯和（或）丙烯醚的聚合物，用做合成润滑油或液压油］
polygon 多边形，多角形
polygonal 多边形的，多角形的
polyimide plastic 聚酰亚胺塑料
polyisobutene 聚异丁烯（= polyisobutylene）
polyisobutylene 聚异丁烯
polyisobutylene rubber 聚异丁烯橡胶
polyisoprene 聚异戊二烯；聚-2-甲基丁二烯［1，3］合成橡胶
polylol 多元醇（= polyol）
polymer 高聚物，聚合物，聚合体［亦称polymeride，指由较小的化合物（单体）分子互相结合而成的分子量较大的化合物］
polymer alloy 由两种或两种以上不同聚合物的混合物
polymer electrolyte fuel cell 聚合物型电解液燃料电池（简称PEFC）
polymer gasoline 聚合汽油
polymer hydrolysis process （化学）聚合物水解工艺（一种塑料再生的工艺）
polymeric coating 聚合物涂层，聚合物涂覆层
polymeric thickener （润滑油）聚合稠化剂
polymeride 聚合物，多聚物（= polymer）
polymerization 聚合（作用），聚合反应［指分子量较小的化合物（单体）分子相互结合成为分子量较大的化合物的反应，亦写作polymerisation］
polymerize 聚合成，缩合，使聚合，叠合
polymer whisker 高分子须晶（一种像人的胡须一样的细长的高分子结晶，如：直径1～3μm，长度10～15μm的聚氧化甲烯单晶体，富于弹性，又很轻）
polymethacrylate 聚甲基丙烯酸酯
polymethyl methacrylate 甲基丙烯酸甲酯，有机玻璃（简称PMMA）
poly-n-butene 聚正丁烯
polynuclear aromatic hydrocarbon emission （汽车发动机的）多环芳香族碳氢化合物排出物，汽车排气中的多环芳香族碳氢化合物
polyol 多元醇（= polylol）
polyolefins 聚烯烃类
polyolester （由多元醇与脂肪酸反应而制成的）合成润滑剂
polyphase ①多相②多相的
polyphase circuit 多相电路
polyphase torque converter 多相变矩器（见phase④）
polyphenylene oxide 聚苯氧化物，聚苯撑氧（简称PPO，耐冲击强度高，热稳定性及尺寸稳定良好，阻燃性强）
polyphenylene sulphide 聚苯撑硫（一种新型塑料，耐高温，耐酸，耐碱）
polypropylene 聚丙二醇酯（聚丙烯热塑性塑料的一种，简称PP）
polypropylene bumper 聚丙二醇酯

保险杠
polysilicon 多晶硅
polysiloxane 聚硅氧烷
polystyrene 聚苯乙烯（高频绝缘材料）
polysulfide 多硫化合物
polysulfide rubber 硫化橡胶
polysulfone 聚砜（耐热、不易燃的透明树脂，机械强度高，为热塑性树脂的一种）
polysulphide rubbers 硫化橡胶，硫合橡胶
polysulphone 聚砜（类）（= polysulfone）
polytechnic 多工艺的，多种科技的
polytechnic college （综合性）工（业）学院
polytetrafluoroethylene 聚四氟乙烯，特氟隆（简称PTEE，其商品名为teflon。掺入发动机机油内，使摩擦件表面形成一种很薄的坚韧油膜，以减轻磨损，减少动力损失，节约燃油，见teflon）
polytetrafluoroethylene bearing （无须润滑的）聚四氟乙烯滑动轴承，特氟隆轴承
polythene 聚乙烯（= polyethylene）
polytropic change 多变变化，多变过程（理想气体压力p和容积V变化的普遍规律，即：$pV^n=C$，式中n—多变指数；C—常数，亦称polytropic process）
polytropic efficiency 多变循环效率
polytropic expansion 多变（指数）膨胀
polytropic exponent 多变指数（见polytropic index）
polytropic exponent of compression 压缩多变指数（在压缩过程中，反映工质与缸壁等的热交换、工质漏失，以及工质比热变化的一个指数）
polytropic exponent of expansion 膨胀多变指数（在膨胀过程中反映工质与缸壁等的热交换、工质漏失，以及工质比热变化的一个指数）
polytropic index 多变指数（亦称polytropic exponent，polytrope index，见polytropic change）
polytropic index of compression 压缩多变指数（实际压缩过程中反映工质状态变化的瞬变指数）
polyurethane 聚氨基甲酸（乙）酯，聚氨酯，聚亚胺酯（简称PUR）
polyurethane foam 聚氨基甲酸乙酯泡沫（塑料，用于制作防音隔热材料、软垫及滤清器、滤芯等）
Polyurethane part 聚氨酯零件
polyurethane resins 聚氨酯树脂，聚氨基甲酸乙酯树脂
polyurethane rubber 聚氨基甲酸乙酯橡胶，聚氨酯橡胶
polyurethane-wrapped filter 聚氨基甲酸乙酯泡沫塑料卷滤芯滤清器
poly-v belt 聚乙烯V形凸脊传动带（摩擦面上有多条纵向V形凸脊的传动带，poly-v为商品名，亦写作poly vee belt。这种传动带一般都较长，盘旋于各个传动带盘间，如蛇状，故亦称serpentine belt）
polyvinyl 聚乙烯（有机化合物$CH_2=CH-$基的聚合物）
polyvinyl acetate 聚醋酸乙烯酯（简称PVA）
polyvinyl chloride 聚氯乙烯（简称PVC）
polyvinyl chloride acetate 聚氯乙烯-醋酸乙烯醋
polyvinyl fluoride sheet 聚氟乙烯板材，聚氟乙烯薄膜材料
POM ①聚合物材料（polymer material的简称）②乙缩醛（聚甲醛）塑料（polyoxymethylene的简称，= acetal）
pommel ①球头形构件，球形模头，球形冲垫，球形砧，球端，圆头；

(压出）柱塞②打，击
pomping brake 点刹制动（在滑路上制动的踏板踩踏技术，反复点刹，以防车轮抱死，人工防抱死制动技术）
pond 池塘
ponding 积水成池
Pontiac Division （美国通用汽车公司）旁蒂克部
pontoon ①浮筒，浮桥，浮船，趸船②用浮桥渡（车），架浮桥于…③（水下工程用）沉箱
pontoon trailer 运浮桥的挂车
pontoon-type body （轿车的）折背式车身（= notch back body，有发动机舱、客厢、后行李舱等三厢，故又称 three box 或 three compartment type body "三厢式车身"）
Pony 小马驹（韩国现代汽车公司 1976 年第一次推出自行开发的微型轿车牌名。车身由意大利汽车设计师乔治·雅罗设计，发动机、传动系由日本三菱汽车公司提供的图纸）
pony car 小型跑车，小型运动车（如：火鸟 "firebird"，卡玛洛 "camaro" 等）
pony engine （起动大柴油机用的）小起动发动机，小起动机
pony-size 小型的，小尺寸的
pool ①水坑，水池，槽②放置处，场③联营，联合，组合④集中备用的物资，备用物资储存处⑤统筹；合办，集中管理，集中控制；把…集中起来⑥采掘
pool burning 液面燃烧
pool-cathode rectifier 汞弧一阴极整流器
poor 贫瘠的，稀薄的（混合气），劣质的，贫穷的，不良的，低下的
poor adherence 附着不良，附着性差，附着力小
poor-cold-starting 冷机起动不良的
poor contact 接触不良
poor efficiency 低效率（= low efficiency）
poor fuel consumption 高燃油消耗量，高油耗
poor gas ①贫煤气②稀可燃混合气
poor handling 操纵性不良
poor mixture 稀混合气（= weak mixture, rare mixture, lean mixture）
poor movement of air and fuel （发动机）空气与燃油进量不足
poor-quality 劣质的
poor road 不良道路，坏路
poor starting 起动不良
poor stop 制动不良（以致制动距离延长）
poor visibility 低能见度，不良的视野（= low visibility）
poor weld 不良焊缝
pop 爆裂，噼噼啪啪响
pop back （化油器）逆火，回火，放炮（见 back fire）
popper 按扣型紧固件，按扣（亦称 snap fastener，美称 lift-the-dot fastener）
poppet ①菌形阀，提升阀（= poppet valve）②托架，支架③（制动系真空增压器控制阀中的）真空阀-空气阀体④（弹簧加载的）锁珠，定位珠（用于固定两个部件间的相对位置，如：变速器中换挡机构的互锁钢球以及门、盖件的碰珠等）⑤菌形的
poppet nozzle （中央多点式汽油喷射系统的）提升阀式喷油嘴（每一喷嘴直接向每缸进气道喷油，其头部有一止回阀，在汽油压力上升起，而将喷孔打开，喷出汽油）
poppet return spring （制动真空增压器控制阀内的）真空阀-空气阀体复位弹簧（制动踏板松开后将该阀体压回空气阀关闭、真空阀开启的位置）

poppet valve 菌状气门［由气门头、气门杆和带有密封座面的气门盘（阀盘）组成的零件，用于开放和关闭汽缸进、排气口，= puppet valve，亦称 mushroom valve］

poppet valve type hydraulic self sealing coupling 菌阀式液压自封接头

popping （化油器回火等发出的）砰砰，噼噼啪啪（一类的破裂声）

popping back 进气歧管回火（亦称 blowback，= explosion in the intake manifold）

popping in carburettor 化油器放炮，化油器回火（= back firing in carburettor, popping-back）

popping of injector 喷油嘴喷射声

pop rivet 膨胀铆钉

popular 大众的，人民的，风俗的，普及的，流行的

popular car 廉价轿车，普及型轿车，大众车

popularization ①大众车②普及化，通俗化

Popular Science ［美］大众科学（杂志）（简称 PS，每期内容都有关于汽车的评价试验报告，见 PS rating-test）

popular small car 普及型小轿车

population ①人口②保有量，总数

population average （按总人口或车辆数计算的）总平均值，人均（拥有车辆）数，人平均值

population parameters 总体参数（全部采样数据的表征值）

population variance （数理统计）母体的方差（离散值），总体的方差（离散值）

pop up 能弹出的（隐蔽件或闭合件，收合件）

pop-up headlight 能弹出的隐蔽式前照灯（见 concealed headlight）

pop up steering wheel 可收折式转向盘（便于驾驶者出入）

porcelain 瓷器，瓷料

porcelain bushing 瓷套管

porcelain core 瓷芯（如：火花塞）

porcelain enamel ［美］搪瓷（= vitreous enamel）

porcelain engine 陶瓷发动机（绝热发动机）

porcelain insulator 瓷质绝缘体

porcelain spark（ing）plug 瓷火花塞（= stone plug）

porch ①大门内停车处，入口处，门廊，走廊②（脉冲）前沿

pore 细孔，微孔

pore ratio pressure curve （土壤）孔隙比与压力关系曲线

pore size of filter element 滤芯孔眼尺寸

pore-solids ratio 孔隙率

pore volume 孔隙容积（= porosity volume）

porosint 多孔材料

porosity ①多孔性，松孔性②空隙率，孔隙率（物体中孔隙的总和占该物体体积的百分比）③（铸造件的）缩孔性④（金属件中的）细孔，气孔

porosity test 空隙率试验，孔隙率测定

porosity volume 孔隙容积（= pore volume）

porous 多孔的（见 pory）

porous bearing 多孔（材料滑动）轴承

porous bronze 多孔青铜合金（呈多孔状的烧结青铜合金，用作汽油滤清器滤芯等）

porous ceramics 多孔陶瓷

porous chrome（plated）piston ring 多孔镀铬活塞环

porous chromium plating 多孔镀铬，松孔镀铬（呈多孔或网状细纹镀铬层，有助于保持润滑油，改善润滑性能）

porous cooling 多孔冷却

porous metal ①多孔金属；烧结金属②含油轴承瓦片

porousness 多孔性，渗透性

porous spot 松孔（铸件缺陷），疏松部位

porous surface 多孔表面

Porsche 3008 Hybrid 4 保时捷4模式混合动力车［前轮柴油机驱动，后轮电动机驱动，有4种行驶模式可供驾驶者选择（①auto mode：由电子控制模块根据各种传感器的信息从前轮驱动、四轮驱动、电动机驱动等模式中自动选用最佳的驱动模式②sports mode：柴油机和电动机同时驱动，汽车以最大功率行驶③ZEV mode：仅由电动机驱动行驶，当驱动用蓄电池电量低于50%或长时间连续加速时，柴油机起动带动发电机给蓄电池充电④4 WD mode：柴油机和电动机同时驱动四个车轮，与sports mode不同之处在于其转矩分布随车速而变，后轮分布的最大转矩为40%］

Porsche SC system 保时捷层状充气系（Porsche stratified-charge-chamber system，由Porsche公司研制成功，具有三个单独的燃烧室，主燃烧室引入稀混合气，副燃烧室引入浓混合气，在副燃烧室内有一小的点火室，火花塞置于该小室内，以便易于点火并形成焰核，参见stratified charge）

Porsche-type synchromesh 保时捷式同步啮合技术（利用胀开式同步环产生的摩擦力实现同步啮合的技术）

port 窗，孔，口（如：油泵出入口，进、排气孔）

portable air compressor 移动式空气压缩机

portable alignment gauge ①携带式前轮定位仪，携带式前轮定位器②携带式校直仪

portable CO analyser 手提式一氧化碳分析仪

portable computer 携带式计算机

portable console 轻便型控制仪表板，携带式控制台

portable counter 携带式计数器

portable electric tool 手提式电动工具

portable exciter 移动式激振器

portable fire extinguisher 手提式灭火器

portable garage 移动式汽车库

portable gasoline measuring device 移动式汽油计量器（加油用），手提式量油器

portable heater 携带式加热器

portable hydraulic jack 手提式油压千斤顶（轻便式液力千斤顶）

portable jib crane 移动式旋臂起重机

portable lamp 携带式手提灯，行灯，工作灯

portable pneumatic tool 移动式气动工具

portable power ①移动式液压校正器（带有各种工作头的液压泵，用以校正车身板件等）②移动式动力源，移动式动力机械

portable spotlight 移动式聚光灯

portable test set 手提式成套试验仪器和工具

portable (test) tachometer 携带式测速仪，轻便转速表

portable tire changer 携带式轮胎拆装器

portable type crank grinder 轻便曲轴磨床

portable vibration meter 手提式振动仪

portable weld gun 手提式焊枪

portable wheel alignment board 移动式车轮定位板（功能类似侧滑台

por

"side slip tester")

portable wheel balancer 移动式车轮平衡检验设备（就车式车轮平衡仪，由车轮驱动盘、闪光灯和传感器等三部分组成）

portage ①运送，搬运，运输②货物③运费④水陆联运

port air （转子发动机中输出）排气孔处的二次空气（借以促使废气中 CO，HC 氧化）

portal 入口，桥口，隧道口，洞口，门架

portal jib crane 龙门吊车（见 gantry crane）

portal-to-portal travel 门到门运输

portal-type implement carrier 拱式高离地间隙自动底盘

port area 孔口面积，进、出口面积，通道面积（如：二冲程发动机的扫气孔面积）

port arrangement （转子发动机的）进排气口布置，进排气孔布置方式

port bar （二冲程发动机较大的）排气口（防止活塞环蹦入而设置的）隔条（亦称 port bridge）

port closing sensor （柴油机喷油泵柱塞偶件中柱塞完全关闭柱塞套进油孔的）进油孔关闭点（相应于喷油泵名义喷油始点）传感器

port deposit （气口配气发动机）进、排气口积炭

ported vacuum advance 孔口真空控制点火提前（由节气门区真空孔输出的真空控制的点火提前，简称 PVA）

ported vacuum controlled EGR system 孔口真空控制式 EGR 系统（由节气门区真空孔的真空度直接作用在 EGR 阀上，以控制再循环废气量）

ported vacuum signal （由节气门区的小孔输出的）小孔真空信号，真空孔真空信号

Port EGR + Port Opening-Closing Valve Mechanism 孔式 EGR + 孔开关阀机构（EGR 机构的一种，其再循环的废气由排气歧管各缸汇合处引出，经汽缸盖与进气歧管结合面的调节孔进入进气管，该调节孔由电子控制的阀门开、闭，以调节再循环废气量，简称 Twin Port system）

port engine （无气门，而由活塞控制进、排气口开放和关闭的）气口式发动机

portfolio （公司或企业提供的）系列产品，系列服务

portfolio ①（公司或厂家提供的）系列产品，系列服务②（证明资历的）作品、照片资料

Port Fuel Injection 进气孔汽油喷射系统（简称 PFI，每缸一个喷油器，汽油喷至进气孔前方的汽油喷射系统，亦称 multipoint fuel injection，简称 MPI "多点式汽油喷射"。按 SAEJ1930 的规定，不再使用 PFI 这一术语，而改为：①其中，按每缸点火顺序各喷油器依次独立喷油者，称 sequential fuel injection，简称 SFI "顺序汽油喷射系统"。②每三个或四个喷油器联成一组，分组同时喷油者，称 multiport fuel injection，简称 MFI "分组式进气孔喷射系统"。进气歧管在形状、长度、通过断面上经匹配，以获得最大容积效率者称 tuned port injection，简称 TPI "调配式进气道汽油喷射系统"）

porting ①进排气孔道布置②研磨孔穴（如：打磨汽缸盖内的进、排气孔，以减小气流阻力）

porting arrangement （气门）进排气孔排列；（二冲程发动机）气口排列，气孔排列

porting diagram ①（气口配气式发动机）气口配气相位图，气孔开闭时刻曲线图，气孔正时图（见 port-timing, = port timing diagram) ②气口面积（随曲轴转角）变化图

port injection 进气孔汽油喷射

port-install 卸货港装配，卸货港安装（指出口车辆教件，运到目的港口后再安装成车）

portion 部分，一份，分配

port leak valve （转子发动机中将）二次空气（送入催化装置的）控制阀

portless brake master cylinder 无补偿孔制动主缸（通过进油阀关闭储油室油路而产生油压的主缸）

portless type 无进油孔式

port liner 排气孔管衬套（保持废气高热，促进废气再燃烧净化，同时可降低缸盖温度的特殊不锈钢铸衬套）

port opening overlap period （发动机的）进、排气孔重叠开启期

port opening sensor （柴油机喷油泵柱塞偶件中柱塞开启柱塞套回油孔的）回油孔开启点（相应于喷油泵的名义喷油终点）传感器

port-power （汽车车身修理等用）轻便型液压机具，移动式液压机具（由底座、液压缸和安装在液压缸上的各种形状的压头及液压泵组成，portable power 的简称）

port's angle-area diagram （转子发动机的）进气孔开启角度-面积图

port scavenging 气孔扫气（通过汽缸壁上的进、排气孔扫气）

port sealing （转子发动机的）进、排气孔密封

port size （进、排）气孔尺寸

port time-area diagram （发动机的）进、排气孔开启时间-面积图

port timing 进、排气孔开闭正时（指由活塞开、闭的进气口、排气口及扫气口等的开、闭时刻，通常用上止点前后的曲轴转角表示）

port-type injection （转子发动机的）进气孔式喷油，（喷嘴装在进气孔道内，燃油自进气孔喷入）

port-type timing 滑阀配气的正时，气口开关的正时（见 timing of port events）

port valve 滑阀

pory ①多孔的，疏松的，有气孔的②能渗透的，可透气的，能渗水的（= porous）

pose ①造成，引起，产生，构成（问题，困难，风险，危险，挑战等）②质询，提问③摆好姿势④姿势

posh car （英俚）最漂亮的轿车，豪华轿车

position ①位置，场所，姿势②配置，安置

positional cylinder 定位油缸（多位油缸）

positional error constant 位置误差常数

positional tolerance 位置公差（= location tolerance）

position and power-law mode （发动机性能测试中的）固定节气门开度、调整测功机荷载模式（如：在速度特性测试中使节气门开度固定，改变测功机荷载以制取规定转速下的转矩/速度特性曲线的测试模式）

position and speed mode （发动机性能测试中的）转矩/速度特性曲线制取模式（固定节气门开度，测试不同转速下的转矩/速度特性曲线）

position control 位置控制（对转向系中的某些操纵点，如：转向轮、转向垂臂、转向盘施加位移输入或限制时的控制方式，与所需的力无关）

positioned 定位于，位于

positioned weld 定位焊，暂焊（用于定位）

positioner ①位置调节器，位置控制

器，定位装置②控制阀的反馈装置，反馈放大器③胎具，夹具

position error 位置误差

position estimation 定位，位置测定（＝positing）

position feedback signal 位置反馈信号

position finder 测位器，测位仪（简称PF）

position finding 定位（确定位置，寻找部位）

position fixing （测）定位（置），定坐标

position indicator 位置指示器，定位仪

positioning 定位，调位，位置控制，换位；配置，固定位置的装置

positioning dowel 定位销

positioning force （电磁线圈对衔铁的）定位力

positioning groove 定位槽

positioning stud 定位螺柱（locating stud）

position mode （发动机性能测试中的）固定节气门开度及固定测功机荷载模式（见 open-loop mode②）

position of crank shaft 曲轴位置（指以曲轴转角度数表示的各缸活塞在其冲程上止点前、后的位置，如：上止点前10°，上止点后50°等）

position of driver 驾驶员位置，驾驶员姿势

position of towing attachment 牵引装置的位置

position output ①位移输出（对应输入信号产生的位置变化或位移形式的输出）②（表示位置、转角及其变化的）位置输出信号（如：曲轴转角输出信号）

position sensor 位置传感器（汽车电子控制系统中，发送运动件所在位置或位置变化的传感元件，亦称 position transducer）

position servomechanism 位置伺服机构

position set pin 定位销

position switch 位置开关

position system （车辆等远距离测定的）定位系统

position tolerance 位置公差（指位置对基准所允许的变动余量）

position transducer 位置传感器（见 position sensor）

positive ①实在，确实；正数；正面；正像，阳极②确实的；肯定的；积极的；绝对的；断然的；证实的；确定的③阳性的；正的；正面的；完全的④刚性的（连接）；固定的（比率）

positive acceleration motion 加速运动

positive after-image 同色残留影像（见 homochromatic after-image）

positive angle 正角

positive back-pressure EGR (control) valve 正背压排气再循环（控制）阀（发动机高速运转时，在排气正压作用下膜片室与大气相通的控制阀孔关闭，只要控制用真空供给膜片室，EGR 阀便开启，即：高速时，排气压力使该阀关闭，膜片在进气歧管真空作用下，使 EGR 阀开启）

positive blower 压力通风机

positive brush 正极电刷

positive cable 正（极）导线，阳极线

positive camber ①（正）外倾（从正面看，车轮中心平面向车身外侧倾斜）②（正）外倾角（车轮中心平面外倾时与铅垂面间的夹角，见 camber）③（钢板弹簧等的）正弯度，正挠度

positive camber offset 车轮外倾主销偏移距（车轮外倾时，车轮中心平

面接地线与主销轴线接地点间的距离，亦称正磨胎半径"positive scrub radius"）

positive-carrier semiconductor 正电荷载流子半导体，正载波载流子半导体，空穴半导体，正调制载波半导体

positive caster ①（转向）主销正纵倾，主销正后倾（沿汽车前进方向，主销轴线的交地点落在车轮中心地面投影点之前）②主销后倾角（见 caster）

positive caster offset 主销后倾拖距（见 caster offset）

positive charge 正电荷

positive clutch 非摩擦离合器，刚性离合器（如：dog clutch）

positive collector grid （排气 HC 含量氢焰离子分析仪的）正极集电栅

positive control 直接操纵，强制控制，可靠控制

positive cooling 人工冷却，强制冷却

positive coupling 刚性联轴节

positive crankcase ventilation system 曲轴箱强制通风系（简称 PCV system，该系统通过一抽吸管经机油分离器、火焰隔阻器和强制通风流量控制阀将窜入曲轴箱内的燃气及机油蒸气等抽入进气歧管并将新鲜空气送入曲轴箱，= positive crankcase ventilator）

positive crankcase ventilation valve 曲轴箱强制通风系流量控制阀（简称 PCV valve）

positive damping 正阻尼

positive deviation （向增量方向的）正向偏离，正向偏移

positive displacement compressor 容积式压气机（指往复式或旋转式活塞、叶轮、滚轮等压气元件直接压气的压气机）

positive-displacement engine 容积式发动机，正排量式发动机，活塞式发动机（指往复式或旋转式活塞发动机等）

positive displacement flowmeter 容积式流量计（= volumetric flowmeter）

positive displacement hydraulic motor 容积式（液压）马达

positive displacement pump 容积泵（依靠泵壳内腔及与之接触的运动件间产生的密闭空间的移动和变化，将液体由吸入侧压至输出侧的泵，如：柱塞泵，活塞泵等）

positive draft 人工通风，强制通风

positive drive 强制传动，确切传动，啮合传动（区别于在传动中会打滑的皮带传动）

positive driven supercharger 机械驱动的增压器

positive electrode 阳电极；阳极，正极

positive engagement brake 刚性接合式制动器，强制啮合式制动器（一种驻车制动器，在汽车处于静止状态时，通过车辆本身的不旋转部件强制啮合，以阻止车轮旋转）

positive film 正片（相对于底片"negative film"而言）

positive gearing 强制传动，刚性传动

positive-going (input) threshold voltage 正向（输入）阀电压（输入电压上升时的输入阀电压）

positive-going input threshold voltage 正向输入阈电压

positive governing 直接调节，强迫调节，直接控制，直接操纵

positive ground 正极搭铁，正极接地

positive ground system （车辆电器设备）正极搭铁系统，正极接地系统

positive guide seal （由卡簧紧固在气门杆上的）气门导管（间隙）正压型密封环

positive hole 空穴
positive ignition 强制点火，电火花强制点火（= spark ignition）
positive integer 正整数
positive ion 正离子（带正电荷的离子）
positive lock control 任意定位装置，任意锁止装置，任意位置控制装置（如：用 Bowden 软锁，可将阻风门控制在任意位置）
positive-locking differential 强制锁止式差速器（= full locking differential）
positive logic 正逻辑（高值域用"⊥"表示，低值域用"0"表示的逻辑）
positive lubrication 压力润滑（法），强制润滑（法）（= forced lubrication）
positively charged particles 带正电荷的粒子（质子）
positively controlled 强制控制的，强制变速的
positively oriented curve 正定向曲线
positive motion 强制运动，确动
positive-negative-positive（transistor） ①PNP 结②PNP 型（晶体管）
positive number 正数
positive offset ①主销正偏移距（见 kingpin offset）②车轮的外偏距（亦称 outset，指轮辐安装面位于轮辋中心线的外侧时，二者的间距）
positive offset steering 主销正偏移距转向（指主销轴线延长线与地面的交点在轮胎接地面中心或车轮平面的内侧时的转向几何布置）
positive opening 强制开度，强制开启
positive overall height of the spring 钢板弹簧正全高
positive plate （蓄电池）阳极板
positive plate unit pole bridge 正极板组连接横板

positive pole 正极，阳极
positive post （蓄电池的）正极接线柱
positive potential 正电势，正电位，正电压，正压
positive pressure 正压力
positive reaction 正反作用（力）
positive rear-axle steering 后轴（与前轴）同向转向作用
positive rotation 正旋转
positive scrub radius 正磨胎半径（简称 positive scrub，见 positive camber offset）
positive semi-definite 正半定
positive sequence 顺序
positive-shift drive 带接合机构的起动驱动装置
positive side switching 正极接通（指负极固定接地，而开关元件设在正极端）
positive sign 正号
positive spring camber 钢板弹簧的自由拱度（= positive spring opening）
positive temperature coefficient （电阻的）正温度变化系数［指到达一定温度（居里点）后，在一定的温度范围内，电阻值与温度成正比，即电阻值随温度的升降而增减］
positive temperature coefficient heater 正温度系数电热丝，正温度系数电热器（简称 PTC heater）
positive temperature coefficient thermistor 正温度系数热敏电阻（简称 PTCT）
positive terminal 正极接线柱
positive thread 阳螺纹
positive traction differential 无滑差牵引差速器，无滑差牵引差速装置
positive translation 正平移
positive twist 正扭
positive type semiconductor P 型半导体（电流的多数载流子是空穴的半

导体)

positive valve gear 强制式阀门机构

positive ventilation 强制通风(= forced ventilation)

positive wire 正极导线(引线)

positraction 强制牵引

positron 正电子,阳电子

possibility 可能性

possible 可能的

possible capacity ①可能通行能力(在实际的道路条件和交通条件下,车道或道路的某点一小时能通过车辆的最大数) ②可能(达到的)能力,能力

possible cause (故障等)可能的原因

possible slope (车辆可克服的)极限坡度

post ①站,台 ②柱,杆,桩(如:车顶和车门的支柱,蓄电池的接线桩,接线柱) ③邮局,邮件 ④在⋯后

postal delivery van 邮件投递车,邮件分送汽车(= mail truck)

4-post alignment lift 四柱式定位用举升器,四柱式调校用举升机

postal vehicle 邮政车

post-catalyst (装于)催化转化器后的,催化转化器后方进行的,催化转化器后方发生的

post catalyst O₂ sensor 催化转化器后置式氧传感器,催化转化器下游氧传感器(装在催化转化器后面的氧传感器)

postcrack stage (疲劳)裂缝后的试验期(或使用期)

post-crash 碰撞后的

postcrash fire 碰撞后(引起的)火灾

posted capacity 路标上标明的(路面、桥梁等)承载量

post-estimation system 后评价系统[如:驾驶员节能驾驶操作(eco-driving operation)的后评价系统是使用录像系统配合车辆油耗记录系统,实时记录驾驶者的操作对油耗的影响,供事后评价使用,以提高其驾驶操作技能]

post-fade performance (制动器)衰退后的性能

post hanger 转向柱吊架(= pillar bracket)

post heating (电热塞在发动机起动后为防止升温期燃烧不完全而排蓝烟或缺火的)起动后加热,后加热

post ignition ①(汽油机)后期点火(指在电点火后发生的自点火) ②继燃(现象)(汽油机断开点火开关后,由于发动机过热、积炭等原因,继续点火燃烧的现象, = dieseling)

postion indicator pulse (曲轴位置传感器发送的)曲轴转角位置信号脉冲(见 PIP①)

postive crystal 正晶体(指寻常光的传播速度大于非寻常光传播速度的晶体,如:水晶)

postless steering 无转向柱的转向机构

post office vehicle 邮政车(可办理邮寄业务的邮件运输车,参见 mail vehicle)

postpone 推迟,延期

post processor 后处理器

post production service 生产后维修(简称 PPS)

post reaction 后反应,后期反应

postscript 附录,附言(= post scriptum,简称 PS)

post-start (发动机)起动后的,起动后发生的,起动后实行的

post-start enrichment program (发动机电子控制模块的)起动后(混合气)加浓程序(以改善怠速运转质量和对节气门的响应)

post-stressed 后加应力的

post-tensioned 后加拉力的
post-test-inspection 试验后检查,试验后的检测
post tie bar （货车侧栏板）中柱拉杆
postulate 假定；必要条件，基本要求；假设前提，公理，基本原理
postulated conditions 假定条件
posture ①姿势，姿态，形势②取…姿势，以…姿态
posture adjustment （汽车座椅等的高低、倾斜程度、前后位置等）姿势调整
post vintage car 第一次世界大战与第二次世界大战间（1931～1939年）生产的汽车
post war car 战后汽车（第二次世界大战后生产的汽车，= last war car）
post-weld heat treatment 熔焊后的热处理，焊后热处理
pot ①瓶，罐，壶，坩埚，熔埚，缸，筒②减速缓冲器（见 dashpot）
potash soap 钾皂（亦称软肥皂"soft soap"）
potassium 钾（代号 K，= kalium）
potassium dichromate 重铬酸钾
potassium hydroxide 苛性钾，氢氧化钾（KOH）
potassiurn cyanide 氰化钾（KCN，= kalium cyanide，白色粉末状，剧毒，0.15g 即可致人死亡）
potential ①势，位，电势，电位，位能，电压（见 voltage）②潜力，潜在能力，潜在性能，可能性③势差的，位差的，潜在的，可能，可能达到的，可能出现的
potential barrier 位垒,位(势)障壁
potential compression ratio 可能达到的最大压缩比（最大理论压缩比，在转子发动机中指转子工作面，没有凹坑时的压缩比）
potential corrosion 电位差引起的腐蚀

potential device 电位器,变压装置,变压设备
potential difference ①位能差,势能差,位差②电位差
potential drop 电位降,电压降;位能降,势能落差
potential energy 位能,势能
potential flow 势流;位流,潜流
potential function 位(势)函数
potential gum （石油等的）潜在胶质
potential heat energy 潜在热能
potentiality 可能性,潜力,潜能
potential leakage path 潜在泄漏通道（可能存在的漏气或漏油通道）
potential obstacle （道路前方的）潜在障碍物
potential output 潜在输出功率
potential problem 潜在问题,可能发生的问题
potential traffic flow 潜在交通流量（可能达到的最大交通流量）
potential well （数字集成电路电荷耦合器件的）势阱（在施加于转移栅上电压的控制下,电荷耦合器件的半导体中形成的、用于限制任何可能存在的可移动的电荷的最小势垒）
potentiometer ①电位计,电位差计,电势计②分压器
potentiometer slider 电位器滑触头,电位器滑臂
potentiometric optical pyrometer 电位计式光测高温计
potentiometric sensor 电压计式传感器（将物理量变换为电压输出的传感元器件）
potentioresister 精密电阻器
potentiostat 稳压器,电压稳定器,恒势器
pot flywheel 盆形飞轮（轮缘或外圈延展呈盆、碗状以容纳离合器总成）
pot galvanize 熔锅镀锌,热浸镀锌
pothole （路面）凹坑,凹窝车印

potholed road 坑洼不平的道路

pot joint （可轴向移动的）球销式万向节（＝muff coupling joint，见 ball and trunnion universal joint）

pot life 储放时限，（胶黏剂等的）适用期

pot-shaped hole （路面）凹坑，坑洼

pot-shaped solenoid 罐状电磁阀（短柱状衔铁在电磁线圈内移动，外壳呈罐形）

potting compound （封装电子零件等以防潮、防振的）封装剂

pot-type piston 杯形活塞

poultry carrier 家禽运输车（车箱为栅栏式结构，并装备有家禽运输周转箱、食料槽，用于运输鸡、鸭、鹅等家禽）

pound ①磅（英制重量单位，1963年规定的英国标准磅为0.45359237kg，美国磅为0.4535924277kg，代号1b）②镑（英国货币单位，代号£）③货物堆存处④危险地位⑤称…的重量⑥捣碎，捣成粉；乱敲；乱打，连续不断地打⑦围起来，包装起来

poundal 磅达（英尺磅秒单位制的力的单位，代号pdl，即使1磅的质量产生1英尺/秒² 加速度的力，1poundal = 0.138255 newton; 32.2 poundals = 1pound-weight）

pound-calorie 百度热单位，磅卡（工程常用英制热量单位，代号 lb-cal 亦称 centigrade heat unit,代号CHU，即1磅的水，自0℃上升到100℃所需热量的1%，1lb-cal = 1.8Btu）

pound-foot 磅-英尺（英制单位的力矩单位，代号 lb-ft，见 foot-pound ②）

pound-force 磅力（英制单位的力的单位，代号 lbf，即1磅重量的物体产生1g重力加速度的力，亦称 pound-weight，英制中国际公认的重力加速度 g 为32.1740ft/s²，所以 1bf = 32.2poundals = 4.4482newton = 0.4536 kgf）

pounding 碰撞，敲击，敲击声

pounding of vehicle 车辆的颠簸

pounds per brake horse-power per hour （英制燃油消耗量单位）每马力小时磅（LB/bhp/H）

pounds per square inch 每平方英寸磅（英制压力单位，磅/英寸²）（简称 psi）

pounds per square inch gauge 表压磅每平方英寸（简称 psig）

pour ①浇口②浇铸，倾注

pour a bearing 浇铸（巴氏合金）轴瓦

pour-depressant additive （油料等的）倾点下降剂（见 pour point depressor）

poured joint （路面）填充接缝，灌注接缝

pouring 浇铸，浇注；倾泻，淋出，源源输送

pouring defect 浇铸缺陷，铸造缺陷

pouring orifice 注油口

pouring temperature 浇铸温度

pour (ing) test 流动性试验，倾点试验；固化点（流动点）试验

pour point （油料等的）倾点，流动点（指在试验条件下，试样能流动的最低温度，亦称流点，＝ flow point）

pour point depressor 倾点下降剂（使油料倾点下降的添加剂，见 pour point）

pour point test 倾点试验

powder ①粉，粉末②碾成粉末，撒粉

powder adhesion 胶粉

powder clutch 磁粉离合器（在驱动件与从动件的窄隙间装有铁粉，当电流通过驱动件上的线圈时，铁粉磁化，于是从动件被吸附而与驱动件接合）

powder coating method 粉末敷涂法，

粉末静电涂装法，干粉静电涂漆法（利用静电涂覆法将漆粉均匀涂覆于车身表面经加热处理后形成光泽、耐用漆层的方法，又称 dry painting, powder coating process）

powder compacting　研末压制（= powder compression）

powder consolidation　粉末固结

powdered　粉状的

powdered bearing　粉末冶金轴承，粉末压制轴承

powdered coal　粉煤，煤粉（= pulverized coal）

powder (ed) emery　金刚砂

powdered fuel　固体粉末燃料，粉状燃料

powdered-iron core　铁基粉末冶金芯

powdered parts　粉末冶金零件

powder filler　粉末状填料

powder forging　粉末锻造（法）

powder gap　（磁粉离合器的）铁粉间隙

powder-metal bushing　粉末冶金轴套

powder metal hybrid model hydrogen storage system　（氢燃料汽车的）粉末金属混合式储氢系统（参见 iron-titanium hydride）

powder metallurgy magnet　粉末冶金磁铁（由金属氧化物粉末压缩成形，高温烧结后磁化而成）

powder metallurgy part　粉末冶金零件，粉末烧结零件（简称 P/Mpart）

powder metal type　金属粉末冶制的

powder pressing　粉末压实（成型）

powder rolling　粉末辊轧，粉末轧制

powder technology　粉末成型工艺

powder weld deposition　粉末堆焊

powdery　粉的，粉状的；容易变成粉的；满是粉的

powell's Magic Angle　鲍威尔魔角（指内燃机做功冲程上止点后15°角。为了获得最大转矩增量，应使汽缸压力波峰值出现在该角附近，由美国人 Powell, J. David 提出，故名，简称 Magic Angle）

power　①功率[每单位时间内所做的功，国际单位制的功率单位为瓦（W），即每秒完成1焦耳的功，1 W = 1 J/s，其倍数单位为千兆瓦（GW）、兆瓦（MW）、千瓦（kW）。在新国际单位制中功率的代号为 P，而旧单位制为 N，如：柴油机的功率，在新国际单位制中采用千瓦（kW），而不用马力，1千瓦 = 1.36 米制马力 PS = 1.341 英制马力 HP]②乘方，幂③动力，机力；能力④装上发动机；接装动力源，给⋯以动力，用动力驱动

power absorbing trailer　功率吸收挂车（指牵引试验用负荷车、测功挂车、带有测功加载装置的专用负荷车）

power-absorption equipment　（试验装置中的）功率吸收设备（如：测功器）

power-absorption fan　（发动机试验用）功率吸收风扇，空气制功器

power-absorption unit　（测功器等的）功率吸收装置（简称 PAU）

power-actuated　机动的，动力驱动的

power-actuated top　动力操纵的活动式（折叠式）顶篷

power adjustable pedals　功率可调式（加速）踏板（踏板单位行程所对应的功率变动量可调）

power adjusting needle　（化油器）功率量孔调整针阀（= jet needle）

power amplification　功率放大

power amplifier　功率放大器

power and propulsion system　（运输工具等的）动力和驱动系统

power antenna　动力天线（用电动机驱动伸出、缩回的汽车天线）

power assistance pump for steering　转向加力泵，转向助力泵

power-assisted brake 助力式制动（系），伺服式制动（系）[亦称 energy assisted brakes, servo brakes, 指利用气压（正压或负压）增加驾驶者制动踏板踩踏力的制动系统，亦写作 power-assisted braking system]

power assisted shift transmission 加力换挡变速器，助力换挡变速器（指通过使用液力、气力或电力来完成或协助人力换挡的变速器）

power-assisted steering 助力转向（简称 PAS，利用液压、机械或其他动力助力以减轻驾驶者作用于转向盘上的操舵力，同时又保持一定程度的路感的转向系）

power-assisted steering with reversion to manual operation 可回复到全人力操纵的助力转向

power balance 功率平衡（汽车行驶的每瞬间，发动机发出的功率始终等于传动系损失的功率与全部行驶阻力所消耗的功率）

power board 配电板

power booster （增加制动踏板对制动主缸压力的液力或真空）助力器

power boosting 功率增大；动力助力的，动力加力的

power-boosting capacity 功率提高能力

power brakes ①（测功机的）测力制动器 ②（汽车的）动力制动（系）（亦称 non-muscular energy braking system，指产生制动的能源来自气压、液压等供能装置，驾驶人员踩踏制动踏板的力很小，仅起"开关"作用，如：全液压制动系、气制动系等）③（有的文献中亦指增加驾驶者制动踏板踩踏力的）助力制动（系），伺服制动（系）（= servo brake）

power broom 机动路刷，机动刷路机

power bypass jet （化油器）省油器量孔（见 power jet②）

power cam 动力凸轮，驱动凸轮

power CAN （大众公司用于汽车驱动系统的）动力 CAN（其通信速率为 500kb/s，主要连线对象为发动机控制、防抱死制动、防滑转、动力转向系统、安全气囊系统、自动变速器、电子差速锁及组合仪表等对传输速度和实时性要求较高的控制系统，见 CAN）

power capability （可能产生的）功率，功率容量

power cepstrum 功率倒频谱[功率谱取对数称为功率倒频谱。功率倒频谱的正根号值称为幅值倒频谱，简称倒频谱，常记作 Cn（g）]

power certification 功率鉴定

power characteristics 功率特性，动力特性

power circuit 动力线路，电源电路

power circulation 功率循环（无轴间差速器的全轮驱动汽车，在行驶中，传动系寄生功率 parasitic power 的循环现象）

power cleaner 气动吸尘器，气动清扫器，电动除尘器，电动清洗装置

power closing （车门、窗等的）动力关闭系统（automatic power closing system 的简称）

power clutch cylinder 离合器动力缸

power connection 接电源，电源接头，电源接线，动力接头

power constant 功率常数

power consumption 动力消耗，功率消耗，电能消耗，耗电量，耗能量

power-consumption characteristics （发电机等）耗用功率特性，耗功特性

power-consumption curve 功率消耗曲线

power control ①功率控制，功率调节 ②起动杆

power controlled clutch 动力操控型离合器，加力操纵式离合器

power controller 功率调节器，功率控制器（控制、调节电动机、发动机等的输出功率）

power control module （电子自动变速器的）挡位控制模块（控制挡位和换挡的计算机，简称 PCM。注意：勿与控制发动机动力系统的 powertrain control module 混淆）

power control unit 见

power convertible soft top （敞篷轿车的）电动活动软顶篷

power convertion 功率换算（如：将发动机额定功率换算到某一海拔高度地区工作时所能发出的功率值）

power correcting 功率校正（指将发动机实测功率校正到标准大气状况下发生的功率）

power cost 能源费用，燃料费用，动力费用

power curve 动力曲线，功率曲线

power cut-off 断开电源，（发动机）熄火

power cut-off switch 电源总开关（亦称 battery master switch）

power cycle 功率循环

power cylinder ①（助力系统的）加力缸，助力缸 ②（伺服系统的）伺服缸，随动缸，动力缸

power delivered coupling 传动联轴节

power demand 所需功率，功率需求

power-density spectrum 功率密度频谱

power disk brake 动力式盘式制动器，助力式盘式制动器

power dissipation 功率消耗，功率耗散，功率损失

power distribution ①（驱动桥左、右车轮或四轮驱动汽车前、后桥间的）动力分配（驱动转矩分配）②电力分配，配电

power distribution trailer 配电挂车

power divider 分动器，分动箱（= torque divider，指将变速器-传动轴输出的动力分送到前、后驱动桥，或前、中、后驱动桥，或中、后驱动桥的齿轮机构，亦称 power transfer）

power dividing 功率流分配，功率分流

power dividing transmission 功率分流传动（液力变矩器与机械元件和齿轮传动组合的一种传动装置，输入功率一部分经过变矩器，另一部分则通过机械元件输出）

power door lock with remote keyless entry 动力门锁及无钥匙遥控开锁

power-drawn 动力牵引的

power drift （后轮驱动汽车转弯或弯道行驶时，因驱动力过大，后轮抓着力下降而使汽车急速转向的）加力侧滑现象（亦称 power slide, power glide。赛车时，用作弯道高速转弯的驾驶技术）

power driven 动力驱动的（简称 PD）

power-driven road vehicle 道路上行驶的（一般）机动车辆（的统称）

power-driven two wheeled trailer 双轮式动力驱动挂车（带有驱动桥的挂车）

power driven vehicle 动力驱动车（如：电动车、机动车等用于道路或非道路行驶，至少装有两个车轮的各种自驱动车辆）

power economy 动力节约，能源节约

powered 装有发动机的，有动力装置的，（产生）动力的，机动的，供电的，动力操纵的，补充能量的

powered and steering axle 转向-驱动桥（如驱动前桥）

powered axle 驱动桥，驱动轴（汽车的驱动轴，亦称 live axle）

powered door mirror 电动车门后视镜（通过电动控制可任意改变装在车门区的后视镜角度并可在窄路或入库时将后视镜收起）

powered rack and pinion steering unit 齿轮-齿条式动力转向机构

powered speed 实际驱动车速（指从发动机转速、传动比及车轮直径导出的理论车速中扣除各种损失，如：空气阻力，滑移损失等的每挡位下的实际车速，见 geared speed）

powered tailgate （载货汽车的）机动式后栏板，起重式后栏板，液压式后栏板

powered toolframe 自动底盘（= mobile toolbar）

powered wheel ①（轮内装有电动机的）电动驱动轮 ②驱动轮（= power wheel）

power efficiency 有效功率效率

power-electro deposition 粉末涂料电泳涂装

power engineering 动力工程

power enrichment （发动机电子控制系统的）功率加浓工况（为开路控制模式之一，当节气门全开、进气歧管真空度接近零时，控制模块发出混合比加浓指令，直至节气门开度变小转入闭路控制）

power-enrichment system （化油器）加浓装置，省油器装置（= power system）

power estimation 动力估计，功率估计

power event （发动机）做功冲程

power factor ①功率因数（简称 PF 或 pf，交流电路中，有功功率对视在功率的比值，等于电动势与电流的相位差角 θ 的余弦，cosθ。见 active power 及 apparent power）②（汽车）动力因素（表征汽车动力性能的指标，$D = \dfrac{F}{G}$，式中：D—动力因素；F—汽车驱动力；G—汽车总重，即：汽车用来克服道路总阻力和使汽车加速的汽车单位重量的驱动力）

power factor capacitor 功率因素计偿电容

power factor correction 功率因素校正，功率因素补偿

power factor indicator 功率因素指示表

power factor meter 功率因素测定表，功率因素表

power factor regulating relay 功率因素调节继电器

power failure ①供电事故，断电 ②动力中断，动力装置的故障

power failure feature ①（交通信号系统的）非常用装置（断电后维持信号灯继续运行的应急设备）②备用动力装置（动力装置发生故障后的应急动力装置）

power failure indicator 停电指示灯，动力故障指示器

power feed system （化油器）主配剂装置，主量孔供油系（= main metering system）

power flow ①能（量）通量（指动量等的通过、传递量）②功率通量 ③动力流程，动力流线（如：汽车的正常动力流线是发动机-变速器-传动轴-驱动桥-驱动轮）

power flow diagram 功率流示意图

power fluid （流体传动）工作油液，工作液体

power-folding 电动折叠（式）的[如 mirror（后视镜）、seat（座椅）等]

power frame 自动底盘，机动车架

power-frame tractor 自动底盘牵引车

power fuel 动力用燃料，发动机用燃料

powerful 强有力的，大马力的，大

功率的

power gain 功率放大（系数），功率增益

power gas 可燃气体；气体燃料

power gate lift truck 后栏板动力起重-举升式货车

power glide 加力侧滑（见 power drift）

Powerglide 希波莱汽车自动变速器的商品名（由液力变矩器与行星齿轮机构组成）

power governor 功率调节器

power grader 自行式平地机（见 motor grader）

power grease feeder 电动注脂器，电动黄油枪

power-grip drive belt 不打滑的传动带（如：带齿传动带等）

power-grip tyre 高附着性轮胎，抓地花纹轮胎，越野轮胎

power gun 气动滑脂枪，机动黄油枪，电动滑脂枪

power-handling capability （自动控制电路的）输出能量与驱动力控制能力

power head rest （汽车座椅的）电动头枕（可向上、下、左、右移动，调节位置）

power hood （敞篷车的）电动顶篷（美称 electric top）

power hot ①（汽车紧急起步时，加速踏板猛踩到底）驱动力增长过猛、过大现象②（因而导致的）驱动轮滑转、弹跳现象

power house ①动力站，动力室，动力厂②（指）动力装置，发动机（亦写作 powerhouse）

power hydraulic system 液压系统（对制动，指液压制动系）

power input 功率输入，输入功率

Powerise system （德国 Koblenz 公司生产的发动机舱盖、后行李舱门等的机-电-气动型）动力开关系统（商品名，按键遥控，可让门、盖开启、关闭或停留于任意开度）

power jack （带）动力（的）举升器

power jack knifing （汽车列车的）高驱动力折叠（由于牵引车驱动轮转矩过高导致驱动轮质地滑转而造成的汽车列车牵引车与挂车间的折叠现象）

power jet ①（化油器）功率量孔，主量孔（= main jet）②（化油器）加浓量孔，省油量孔（亦称 economizer jet, power bypass jet, power jet valve, power valve, step-up jet）

power jump function 功率跳跃函数

power kerosene 发动机用煤油

power lead 电源线，馈电线（= supply lead）

power level ①功率级，功率值，功率水平②（噪声等的）能量级

power leveling system （车身高度等的）动力调平系统

power lifter 动力举升设备，动力升降机构

power liftgate （小客车向上翻开的）电动鸥翼式车门

power line switch 供电线开关，输电线开关

power loader 动力驱动的装载机

Power Lock 动力锁（一种多片离合器式防滑差速器的商品名）

power locking free wheeling hub （分时四轮驱动系统的）电动锁止型自由旋转式轮毂（见 free wheeling hub）

power loss 功率损失，能量损失

power loss lamp （汽车仪表板上的）功率下降警报灯（亦称 check engine light，当发动机控制模块发现某重要故障而按低出力模式控制发动机运转时，该警报灯发亮，见 limp in mode）

power machine 动力机械

power management ECU （混合动力车的）动力管理电子控制模块［亦称：混合动力车电子控制模块（HV-ECU），该 ECU 通过多路传输系统（CAN）与 engine ECU, skid control ECU, air con ECU, battery ECU 等联成局域网，根据内燃机节气门、喷油和点火系及变速器、加速踏板、起动开关等传感器的信息，对混合动力车的内燃机、电动机、制动及制动能量回收和发电机、蓄电池、空调等进行全面控制。ECU 见 computer］

power margin （发动机）后备功率，功率储备

power mass ratio 比功率（发动机净功率与汽车或汽车列车的最大总质量之比）

power meter 功率表，马力表

power meter control panel 功率测量控制仪表板

power mirror 电动后视镜

power mixture radio （混合气的）功率混合比（发动机可发出最大功率的混合比，约为12.5空燃比）

power mode 功率型，功率模式（指追求动力、加速度而不考虑经济性的运转模式或工作模式，相对于经济型，经济模式"economy mode"而言）

power module 动力模块（亦称 power board, Chrysler 公司早期多点式汽油喷射系统中由逻辑模块"logic module"控制，通过接地电路接通点火线圈一次绕组和汽油喷射器并向逻辑模块提供电源的集成电路模块，以后后者与逻辑模块合二为一，称为 single module engine control module 简称 SMEC module）

power moon roof （轿车车顶上的）电动天窗

power MOSFET 功率金属氧化物半导体场效应晶体管（见 MOSFET）

power number （汽车的）功率指数（汽车驱动轮的输入功率与汽车总质量和车速的乘积之比）

power nutsetter 电动螺母扳手

power-off ①（发动机）停车，断开发动机，切断电源（的）②（关闭节气门）功率下降

power-off coasting （汽车）关掉动力滑行，断开发动机滑行（如：空挡滑行）

power-on ①开动发动机（的），接通电源（的）②节气门开大，功率增加

power operated 动力驱动的，机动的

power operated control 动力控制（如：助力控制，电动控制，机动控制，气动控制，液动控制）

power-operated window system 动力操纵车窗系统（如：电动车窗系统）

power-operated wrench 电动扳手

power output 功率输出，输出功率

power output density （蓄电池等的）输出功率密度（车辆每单位质量的输出功率，单位，W/kg）

power output per liter 升功率（发动机每升工作容积的有效功率）

power output shaft 功率输出轴，动力输出轴

power pack ①（汽车等的）动力部分（指发动机等）②电源箱，电源部分（指变压器、交-直流变换器等组成的电源装置）

power package 动力机组，动力组，动力装置，动力源

power pack section （积木式车辆的）动力部分

power panel 配电盘，电源板

power parking 有升降机的停车场

power per cylinder （发动机）单缸功率（多缸内燃机中平均每个汽缸发出的有效功率）

power performance ①（发动机）动力性能（反映发动机功率、平均有效压力及转矩、转速等动力指标的性能）②（汽车的）动力性能（反映汽车最高车速、最大加速能力和最大爬坡度等动力指标的性能）

power per piston area 单位活塞面积功率（折合到单位活塞面积上的有效功率）

power phase （转子发动机的）做功相，工作过程

power piston 动力活塞（①斯特林发动机的做功活塞，见 Stirling engine；②借助流体压差产生推力的活塞，亦称 power plate piston，如：制动助力装置、制动主缸、活塞式制动气室的工作活塞等）

powerplant 动力设备，动力装置（如：发动机组，带离合器、变速器的发动机总成）

powerplant characteristics 动力装置特性，发动机特性

powerplant emissions 动力装置排放到大气中的污染物

powerplant module 发动机组，动力机组

powerplant suspension 发动机悬架

powerplant weight 动力装置的重量

power producing characteristics （发动机的）动力特性，动力输出特性，功率特性

power proportioning 功率的按比例分配，动力的按比例分配（如：各车轴或各车轮间的动力的按比例分配）

power pulses 功率波动

power rack and pinion steering gear 助力式齿条齿轮式转向机器

power-raised ladder 动力升降梯

power range 功率范围

power rating 额定功率，额定功率标定

power relay 电源继电器

power reserve 储备功率，后备功率（内燃机最大功率与标定功率的差值）

power robbing 损耗功率的

power roller 见 EXTROID VT

power seat （靠背斜度、座椅高度等均能电动调节的）电动座椅

power semiconductor 功率半导体

power sensor 功率传感器

power set 动力装置，发电机组

power setting ①机动调节（非手动调节）②功率调节（调功率）

power shift ①（自动变速器等的）动力换挡（指在不中断动力传递的状况下换挡，见 nonpower shift）②（机械变速器的）伺服换挡，动力换挡，助力换挡

power shifted speed 动力换挡速度（指自动变速器，功率流不间断换挡时的车速）

power shift independent power take-off 动力遥控独立式取力器（由机械、液压或其他形式的动力遥控，并可在不切断功率流，即不影响汽车传动系正常动力传递和换挡的情况下独立地断开和接合功率输出轴或齿轮的取力机构，简称 power shift PTO）

power-shift transmission ①动力换挡变速器②助力换挡变速器，负载换挡变速器（可在不切断功率流和带负载的情况下换挡）

power slide 见 power drift

power source 电源，动力源

power source ECU 动力源电子控制模块（在混合动力汽车中指收到起动信号后向内燃机、电动机等发出起动指令、接通其电源的电子控制模块）

power spark 强火花

power spectral analysis 功率谱分析

power spectral density 自功率谱密度，功率谱，自谱［若时间函数 x

(t) 的自相关函数 $R_x(r)$ 存在，且 $\int_{-\infty}^{+\infty} |R_x(r)| \, dr < \infty$，则 $R_x(r)$ 的傅氏变换 $S_x(f)$ 即定义为自功率谱密度，可简称自谱或功率谱，亦称 power spectrum density，简称 PSD]

power spectral density analyzer 功率谱密度分析仪（简称 PSD analyzer）

power spectrum 功率频谱，功率谱

power speed curve （发动机的）功率速度曲线，速度特性曲线

power split 动力分配，动力分布

power split device ①（四轮驱动车辆前、后轮间的）动力分配装置 ②（复合动力车的发动机输出）动力（在驱动车辆和驱动发电机间的）分配装置

power spring 动力弹簧，储能弹簧（如：钟表等用的发条）

power-steering ①助力转向（power-assisted steering 的简称）②全动力转向（如：completely hydraulic or pneumatic steering system，简称 PS，在这一类转向中，驾驶员操纵的转向盘仅用于控制转向动力系统，而由动力系统的动力来驱动转向机构实现车辆转向，因此在这一类转向中，道路与驾驶员间无机械反馈，即操纵转向盘时无路感，只有先进的电子控制动力转向系统才加装有路感模拟功能）

power steering anticipate switch （Cadillac 轿车数字式汽油喷射系统中使用的）动力转向液压预控开关（当动力转向液压达到某预规定值时，该开关断开，电子控制模块收到此信息后即加大节气门开度，以支持发动机因此增加的负荷，简称 P/S anticipate switch）

power steering computer （根据车速、转向盘转动的速度、角度和路况等调节动力转向系输出的转向力的）动力转向计算机（动力转向控制模块 "power steering control module" 的俗称）

power steering (fluid) pressure switch 动力转向液压开关[简称动力转向开关，PS（F）PS，用于可变工作缸数发动机控制系统，当动力转向系工作时，为防止发动机因负荷增加，以致急速下降或停机而增加工作缸数的压力开关]

power steering gear valving 动力转向器液压控制阀系

power steering hydraulic pump 动力转向液压泵（简称 power steering pump）

power steering oil 动力转向油液（动力转向系工作油液，亦称 power steering fluid）

power steering rack 转向助力系齿条，转向助力齿条机构

power steering signal （动力转向开关向发动机电子控制模块发出的）动力转向信号（见 power steering switch）

power steering switch （通用公司 PFI 系统中使用的）动力转向开关（当动力转向液压高到影响发动机怠速运转时，该开关接通，于是电子控制模块通过怠速空气控制组件，增加怠速空气旁通进气量并推迟点火，以保证稳定怠速运转，某些系统还同时断开空调离合器）

power steering system response characteristic 动力转向系灵敏度特性（动力转向系响应特性，指在油泵流量为定值时，系统压力与转向盘转角之间的关系）

power steering with (vehicle) speed-dependent assistance 车速响应式动力转向[亦称 (vehicle) speed type power steering，转向助力随车速而变，车速越高，转向助力越小，转向盘越重]

power storing capacity 储能能力

power stroke ①（内燃机的）做功冲程，工作冲程（亦称 firing stroke）②（悬架装置）油缸提升冲程

power sunroof （轿车等的）电动天窗

power supply ①供电，动力供应 ②电源，动力源

power-supply change-over 动力变换，动力源变换，动力供应变换

power supply unit 动力装置，动力机组，发电机发动机组（见 engine unit）

power surplus （发动机）后备功率，功率储备

power switch button 动力开关按钮（电源开关按钮）

power-switch type regulator 功率开关型调节器

power system 动力系统

power take-off ①动力输出②动力输出器，取力器（简称 PTO，指由曲轴或变速器取出动力驱动发电机、泵及停车驱动车外设备等的装置）

power take-off cover （变速器的）取力孔盖

power take-off drive 取力器驱动

power take-off dynamometer 取力器测功器（测定取力器传递的转矩或通过取力器测定发动机功率）

power take-off horsepower 动力输出轴功率，取力器功率

power take-off lever 动力输出接合-分离杆，取力器接合-分离杆（= power take-off shift lever）

power take-off opening （变速器的）动力输出孔，取力器孔（= power take-off hole）

power take-off shaft 动力输出轴、取力轴（简称 PTO shaft）

power take-off shifter arm 动力输出器拨叉臂（取力器接合-分离拨叉臂）

power take-off speed 动力输出器转速，取力器转速

power take-off system 动力输出系，取力系，取力机构

power take-off trailer ①（装备有发电-电动机组或其他动力装置的）动力输出挂车（供野外作业或无动力情况下提供动力之用）②由变速器取力装置驱动的（带驱动桥的）挂车（见 PTO-driven trailer）

power take-off valve 动力输出开关（取力器开关，取力器阀）

power take-off washer 由功率输出装置驱动的清洗设备，由取力器驱动的清洗机

power tardy brake （大型柴油机汽车发动机制动的）制动加力机构（与发动机制动系统共同工作，其作用是发动机制动期间活塞上行时，使进气门关闭，活塞下行时使进气门开启，借以增加排气制动效果）

power test （发动机）功率测试，功率试验，测功试验，测功

power tilt mechanism （倾斜角可变式转向柱的）电动倾斜机构（调整倾斜角度的电动机称 tilt motor）

power timing lamp 强光正时灯（= day light timing lamp, power timing light）

power tire pump 电动轮胎充气泵，机动轮胎充气泵

power to bulk ratio （内燃机）单位体积功率（内燃机的有效功率与其外形尺寸"长×宽×高"所表示的体积的比值）

power tool 机动工具（电动、液动、气动等工具的总称）

power top （由电动油泵液压驱动或电动机驱动的汽车）电动折叠式车顶

power-torque characteristics （发动

机等的）功率转矩特性（功率和转矩随转速而变化的特性）

power-torque diagram （发动机的）功率-转矩特性曲线，功率-转矩图（功率转矩随着转速变化的特性曲线）

power-to-volume ratio 发动机功率-容积比（功率与排量之比，单位容积的功率）

power to weight 单位车重功率（kW/t）

power (to) weight ratio （汽车的）功率-重量比（车重与功率的比值，用 kg/ps 表示，为汽车质量与功率比"kg/kw"的旧称，但英、美仍在使用）

power traction 动力牵引

power train ①传力系，传动系（亦称 drive train，指离合器-变速器-传动轴-主减速器-半轴等整个传动装置的总称）②（有时指）发动机加变速器总成

powertrain control module ①发动机控制模块（简称 PCM，= engine control computer，美国政府规定，从 1995 年 1 月起美国生产的车辆一律采用 PCM 取代原通用、福特和克莱斯勒公司等对发动机控制计算机的术语 ECM，ECA，SMEC，SBEC 等）②（许多汽车将其自动变速器的控制模块 TCM 合并到 PCM 内，此时 PCM 既控制发动机又控制变速器，称）动力控制模块

powertrain grade braking 传动系坡道减速制动（通过自动挂低挡使下坡的车辆减速，以防制动器过热）

power train management system （通用公司 Allante 轿车的）发动机电子控制系统（商品名）

powertrain matching （汽车的）动力传动系匹配（选配发动机尺寸、变矩器、传动系速比、换挡程式及驱动桥等）

power transfer ①分动器（动力分配装置，亦称 torque transfer，见 power divider）②动力传递装置，动力传输系统

power-transfer clutch （接通前桥驱动机构的）分动箱离合器，分动器离合器

power transistor 功率三极管

power transmission ①动力传输，功率传递②传动系，动力传动装置

power-transmission system 动力传递系统，传动系统

power truck 动力车（如：装有发电机组，提供电动力源的车辆）

power trunk-lock （轿车车身）后行李舱盖动力锁

power-tuning （发动机的）最大功率调整（重点在于使发动机产生最大功率和最好的加速性能，而将怠速平稳和节油放在次要地位的调整作业）

power turbine 动力涡轮（①驱动输出轴的涡轮）②指某些发动机上安装的由废气驱动，将废气"动力"反馈至曲轴或驱动轴的废气能量回收涡轮

power understeer （前轮驱动车辆容易发生的）加速不足转向（指汽车弯道行驶时增加驱动力导致前轮地面抓着力降低而造成的不足转向）

power unit ①（ABS 的）动力单元（通常与压力调节器一起装在发动机舱内，由一台电动机带泵、一个高压储能器和储能器的压力开关型传感器组成。高压储能器由电子控制模块控制）②（泛指）动力部分

power valve ①省油器量孔，加浓量孔（= power jet）②省油量孔阀（= power jet valve，economizer valve）③增力阀，动力阀（某些化油器中使用的真空控制单向球阀式或与节气门连动的特定超负载运转

下的混合气加浓阀)

power vent outlet 强制通风出口(车厢内由鼓风机等送入的冷、暖风等的出口)

power wagon (牵引试验用)负荷车,测功车

power washer 动力清洗机,电动清洗机

power waste 功率损失,能量损耗(= waste of power)

power-weight spectrum (车辆)功率-总重相关统计谱

power wheel 电机驱动车轮(轮内装有驱动电机, = powered wheel)

power window 电动车窗(美称 electric window,指由电动机使风窗玻璃自动升、降或开、闭的车窗,一般有无级式"stepless tyre"和一触式"one-touch type"两种)

power window lock-out switch 动力车窗锁止阀(将各动力车窗的开关锁死,这时只有驾驶员控制的总开关可开、闭车窗)

power window regulator 电动风窗玻璃升降机构(由电动机、涡轮蜗杆传动等组成控制玻璃升降)

pozidriv 波日德里夫螺钉起子(八面棱螺钉旋具)

PP ①峰值功率(见 peak power)②正负峰间值(见 peak-to-peak)③(多孔镀铬层的)点状气隙(见 pinpoint)④塑料制品(见 plastic product)⑤聚丙二醇酯(见 polypropylene)⑥动力装置,发动机(见 powerplant)⑦抗压的,耐压的(见 pressure-proof)⑧概率规划法(见 probability plan method)⑨采购件的(见 purchased parts)⑩推拉式的(见 push-pull)

PPA 行人保护安全囊(Pedestrian Protection airbag 的简称)

PPATIS 便携式先进的旅行者信息系统(Portable ATIS 的简称,见 ATIS)

ppb 十亿分之几(parts per billion)

PPC 见 predictive power management

pphm 亿分之几(parts per hundred million)

PPM 见 predictive power management

PPMC 百万分率碳(以甲烷为当量基础,测定 HC 化合物的摩尔容积,再乘以 10^{-6},为 parts per million carbon 的简称)

PPM(ppm) ①百万分率,百万分之…(parts per million)②周期性永久磁铁(periodic permanent magnet)③生产计划会议(production planning meeting)④脉冲相位调制(pulse phase modulation)

PPO 聚苯撑氧,聚氧苯(polyphenylene oxide)

PPR system 乘员被动识别系统(详见 passive passenger recognizing system)

PPS ①每秒周期数(periods per second)②每秒脉冲数(pulse per second)③生产后维修(post production service)④聚苯(撑)硫(poly phenylene sulfide 的简称,一种新型车用塑料)⑤(汽车的)行人保护系统(pedestrian protect system 的简称)

PPT ①调制试验(preparation test)②试制性试验,生产前试验,预备试验(preproduction test)

ppt 沉淀(物)(precipitate)

PPV 压力保护阀(见 pressure protection valve)

PQC 产品质量控制(production quality control)

PR (轮胎帘线层的)层级(见 ply rating)

PRA [美]公路管理局(旧称)(见 Public Roads Administration)

practicable 可行的,实用的

practical 实际的,实践的,实用的,

事实上的
practical application 实际应用
practical capacity 实际通行能力，实际交通容量（在实际的道路和交通条件下，行车密度不致造成不合理的延滞或使驾驶操作受到不合理的拘束时，道路及其车道某指定点每小时所通过的最大车辆数）
practical cycle （内燃机的）实际循环（指工质为实际混合气，以燃烧加热和排气放热，并计及各种热力损失的实际工作循环）
practical driving condition 实际行车条件
practical duty 实际荷载，实用功率
practical efficiency 实际效率（actual efficiency）
practical engine-torque limit 发动机转矩实用极限（可实际应用的最大发动机转矩）
practicality ①实物 ②实例
practical life 实际使用寿命
practical unit 实用单位
practice 实践，实行，实施，惯例，实习
practice driving 训练性驾驶
practice ground 练习场地，实习场地，操作实习场
practise 实行，实施，练习，训练
Prandtl number 普兰托数（在热交换计算中使用的无因次值，等于等压比热×黏度/热导率）
P-range （自动变速器的）驻车挡（与空挡"N-range"不同，驻车挡是将输出轴锁死，而使驱动轮固定不动）
praseodymium 镨（Pr）
PRC （汽车）行驶平顺性程序控制系统（见 programmed ride control）
PRC module 可编程平顺性控制系统电子控制模块（programmable ride control module 的简称）
PRC system ①程序控制平顺性（控制）系统（programmed ride control system 的简称，由电子控制模块根据行驶条件和运转工况控制悬架减振器的软"plush"、硬"firm"模式，以适应行驶平顺性的要求）②（福特车等的）可编程平顺性控制系统（programmable ride control system 的简称，汽车的前、后轮滑柱式悬架和减振器的阻尼特性由 PRC 系统自动控制，确保在各种行驶条件下均提供良好的行驶平顺性和操纵性）
preacceptance inspection 验收前检查
preadmission 预进气
pre-alloy method （陶瓷合金零件的）合金粉末烧结法（使用预定成分的合金粉末烧结成形的方法）
preamplifier 前置增幅器，前置放大器
preassemble 预装配，预先装配，预先安排，预装
preassembly selection 装配零件预选分组
pre-assy 预装配
Preats bypass type element 普瑞兹型旁通式滤清器芯（混合有钛酸钾等助滤剂的菊花状滤纸滤芯）
prebreak-in 磨合前，预磨合期
preburnish check 磨合前的检查试验
preburnish effectiveness test 磨合前的效能检验
pre-buy 提前购买
pre-catalyst 装在催化转化器前的，催化转化器前方的，催化转化器前进行的
pre-catalyst converter 预催化转化器（装在主催化转化器前的，体积仅为主催化器的 10%～30%，但催化剂量约为常规转化器的三倍）
pre-catalyst O_2 sensor 催化转化器前置氧传感器，上游氧传感器（亦称 pre-catalyst lamda probe，装在催化转化器前方的氧传感器）

precautions 预防措施

precede 领前,居前,在先,在…之上,优于

precedence 领先,优先,优越性,优先权

preceding 以前的,上述的

preceding vehicle (在)前方(行驶的)车辆

precess 使进动,产生进动现象(见 gyroscopic action)

precession ①前进,先行,进行,领先②(陀螺仪现象的)进动(参见 gyroscopic action)

precession axis 旋进轴线(旋转物体的轴线产生进动现象回转时所绕的轴线,见 gyroscopic action)

precession velocity 旋进速度(见 gyroscopic action)

prechamber 预燃室(precombustion chamber 的简称,通过一个或几个通道与主燃烧室相通的副室,燃油喷入该室,形成极浓的混合气,部分燃烧产生高压而将已燃和未燃的燃油及其混合气经通道喷入主燃烧室,与其中的空气进一步混合,完成燃烧过程。一般预燃烧室占燃烧室总容积的3.5%~4%,以往预燃室仅用于柴油机,近年来亦见指某些汽油喷射式发动机,亦称 antechamber)

prechamber compression ignition engine 预燃室式压燃发动机

prechamber injection 预燃室喷射(指将燃油喷入预燃室内,简称 PCI)

prechamber torch ignition engine 预燃室式火炬点火发动机(具有主、副燃烧室,主室内为稀混合气,副室即预燃室很小,一般为总燃烧室的2%~10%,其中为易于点火的浓混合气,装有火花塞,点燃之后,火焰自副室喷入主室点燃稀混合气,见 LAG process)

prechamber valve 预燃室气门(简称 PCV)

precharge time 预充电时间(指充放电到预定工作电平时间)

precheck 预先校验,预先校验

precious metal 贵(重)金属

precious metalless liquid feed fuel cell 见 PMLFFC

precipitate ①沉淀物②沉淀,凝结

precipitation hardening 沉淀硬化(金属或合金沉淀析出新的金相而导致增加硬度)

precipitation tank 沉淀槽,沉淀箱

precipitation treatment 时效硬化,人工时效(老化)处理

precipitator 沉淀器,沉淀剂

precise 精密的,准确的,精确的,正确的

precise adjustment 精密调整(亦称 precision adjustment)

precise control 精密控制

precise gauge 精密量规

precise instrument 精密仪器

precision 精确,精密

precision accuracy 精度

precision bearing 精密轴承(一般指瓦片式滑动轴承,如曲轴主轴承和连杆轴承,亦称 insert bearing)

precision bearing metal 见 precision metal

precision casting 精密铸造,精密铸件

precision-docking ability (公共汽车等的)精确停靠站位能力

precision gauge block 精密块规

precision insert bearing 轴瓦式精密滑动轴承(由挂有耐磨合金层的上、下钢瓦片组成的滑动轴承,如:曲轴主轴承和连杆轴颈轴承)

precision instrument 精密仪器

precision-machined 精密机械加工的,精加工的

precision-machined surface 精加工平面

precision measuring instrument 精密量测仪器

precision metal 精密轴承瓦片（如：曲轴主轴承衬瓦等滑动轴承衬瓦，亦称：renewable metal, insert metal, replaceable metal）

precision of measurement 测量的精密度（测定值的密集性和重复性，称为测量的精密度，用来描述测量值在某范围内离散状况的一个定性概念，随机误差越大，测定值就越离散，测量的精密度便越低）

precision positioning 精密定位

precision test 精密度检验

precision tolerance 精确裕度

precleaner 粗滤器

pre-cleaner with dust bowl （某些空气滤清器进气管前端的）带集尘杯的预滤清器（dust bowl 亦称 dust cup）

preclude 排除，消除，妨碍，阻止，预防

pre-collision sensing method （汽车的）碰撞预感法（碰撞预测法）

pre-collision sensor 碰撞预测传感器（碰撞预感器，撞前传感器）

pre-collision system 见 PCS

precollision warning system 撞前预警系统（多指夜间行车安全系统，使用雷达和红外线技术探测前照灯照射范围以外的行人或障碍物）

precombustion chamber 预燃室（见 prechamber）

precombustion-chamber engine 预燃室式发动机（一般指预燃室式柴油机，预燃室式压燃机，= prechamber engine, engine with antechamber；近年来亦指预燃室式或副室式层状燃烧汽油机，参见 stratified charge engine）

precombustion engine ［美］预燃式发动机（指带预燃室的间接喷射式发动机，= 英 indirect injection engine）

precompressed 预压（缩）的

precompressed air （经）预压缩（的）空气

precompression 预压缩，预（加）压（力）

precompression chamber （二冲程发动机位于活塞下方的混合气）预压缩室（亦称 pumping chamber）

precompression ratio 预压缩比

precomputed 预先计算的

precondition ①先决条件，前提 ②预处理

pre-control 预先控制，预控制

pre-converter vehicle 在实施新车强制性安装催化转化器标准之前生产的车辆

precooler 预冷器（在燃气轮机中指工质开始压缩前降低温度的热交换器）

precooling 预冷

precorrection 预先校正

precrack stage 产生（疲劳）裂缝前的阶段（或使用期）

precrash safety system 撞前安全系统（当通过横摆率传感器、车速传感器和前方障碍物传感器等测得碰撞不可避免时即酌情发出警报或启动各种安全系统，如：收紧安全带、紧急制动等，以减轻碰撞造成的伤害）

pre-crash sensing technology 碰撞预警传感技术

predecessor ①（同一车型的）前一代产品（如：对全新的 2004 年型第二代 TOYOTA Prius 而言，1997 年首次投放日本市场的第一代 Prius 便是它的"predecessor"）②（某职位的）前任

pre-delivery inspection （修竣）交车前检验

predelivery test （车辆出厂）提交用户前的工厂试验

predetective power-train control 见 predictive power management

pre-determined 预定的，预先确定的

predetermined mileage （载货汽车的）预定行驶里程（如：大修间隔里程等）

predetermined selection （防抱死制动系控制模式的）预定选择，预选（以预先选定的一个车轮的信号或整组车轮瞬时速度平均值信号来控制该组车轮制动力的防抱死系统）

predetermined value 预定值

predict 预言，预告，预示，预测

predictability 可预测性

predictable 可预测的

predicted value 预测值，预计值

prediction 预报，预测

prediction accuracy 预测精度

prediction interval 预测范围

predictive ①预测的［如 predictive model（预测模型）、predictive power（预测能力）］②前瞻的

predictive power management (BMW 汽车的）动力预测管理（系统）［亦称 predictive power-train management 简称 PPM，或称 predetective power-train control，简称 PPC。该系统可根据 GPS 智能导航系统等对前方路段、地形的预测信息，自动控制发动机工况和传动系统的挡位等，如：导航系统的预测协助（Foresight Assistant）功能获得前方路段坡道的坡度、弯道的半径及其限制车速等，动力预管理系统据此对行驶至该路段时发动机的输出功率和变速器的挡位作最佳自动控制］

predictor 预报器（参见 prognosticator）

predominate 占优势，居支配地位

predry 初步干燥，预干燥

pre-engaged Bendix starter 邦迪克斯-预啮合式起动机

pre-engaged type (starter) drive 预啮合式（起动机）驱动装置（指在起动之初，起动机尚未带动驱动小齿轮转动时，该小齿轮已与飞轮预先啮合的起动驱动系统）

pre-evaluation test 预备性鉴定试验，预评估试验

pre-expansion chamber （消声器内）废气预膨胀室

prefab garage （预制件）装配式简易车库（prefabricated garage 的简称）

prefabricated building elements trailer （建材）预制件运输挂车

pre-fade performance （制动器）衰退前的性能，衰减前的性能

prefailure life 损坏前的寿命，发生故障前的使用期限

preferable ①比（to…）更好的（更可取的）②优越的③较好的

preference road 优先通行道路（= major highway）

prefetch 预取装（预先从存储器中取出一批数据并存入暂存器待用）

prefill ①预先填充，预先充填②预先加油，预先加注油液，预先加液

prefill valve 预（先加）注（油、液等的）阀门

prefilter 预滤清器（前置滤清器，粗滤器）

prefix ①首标，词头，放在标号前的字母或数字等②放在前头，附加标题

preflame 预焰，预燃

preflame reaction 焰前反应（一般指燃油进入内燃机燃烧室后，在高温高压下，碳、氢分子与氧分子间产生的一系列氧化反应，由冷焰、蓝焰等阶段组成，直到出现热焰并形成爆炸性燃烧前的全部化学反应过程）

prefocused lens 预聚焦透镜（定焦

距式透镜)
prefocus plate (固定在前照灯灯头上的)定焦盘(保证灯丝在规定焦点位置的座盘)
preformed gum 溶解于燃油的胶质(＝dissolved gum)
preformed part 预制件
pregnant-mother and her-unborn-baby safety seatbelt 孕妇和胎儿安全带
pregreased service lift 更换润滑脂前的使用寿命
preheat 预热
preheated and hot spot system (转子发动机的)预热与局部加热系统(对汽缸的冷弧区加热)
preheated catalyst converter 预热式催化转化器(在起动发动机前先对催化剂进行预热,使之达到生效温度,以免从废气中吸收达到工作温度所需的热量而延迟其废气催化转化起点时间)
preheater 预热器
preheater adjusting valve 预热器调节阀
preheating chamber 预热室
preheating indicator 预热(塞工况)指示灯(亦称 preheat indicator)
preheating of fuel-air mixture 可燃混合气预热
preheating timer 预热定时器(如:柴油机预热塞通电时间及电流量控制电路等,亦称 preheat timer)
preheating zone 预热区
pre-IF 前置中频放大器(＝pre-intermediate frequency amplifier)
preignition ①早燃(混合气在火花塞点火前自行着火的现象)②过早点火(火花塞在正常的点火期以前点火的现象)③早期点火(亦称 premature ignition,在电点火以前发生的自点火)
preignition chamber 预燃室(＝precombustion chamber)

preignition process (柴油机喷油后)着火前的理化过程
preinjection ①提前喷射②预喷射
pre-injection (多段喷油式柴油机主喷射前的)预喷射
preliminary 初步的,预备的
preliminary compression 预压缩
preliminary design 初步设计(简称 PD)
preliminary evaluation 预估,预先计算,预先评价(简称 PE)
preliminary filter 粗滤器(＝rough filter)
preliminary heating 预热
preliminary test data 初步试验数据
preliminary trial 初步试验
preload 预加应力,预紧度,预加负荷
preload adjuster 预紧度调节器,预载调节件(如:预载度调节螺钉等)
preloaded bearing 经预紧的轴承
preloaded rubber bushing 带预紧度的橡胶衬套
preloaded seat belt (汽车乘员的)预紧式安全带(亦称 preloaded safety belt)
preloader 预紧器,预载装置
preloading 预加应力,预紧,预加载
preloading shim 预紧调节垫片
preload spring 预压力弹簧,预压紧弹簧,预加载弹簧,加压弹簧
preload test 预荷载试验,预加荷载试验
pre-lube (给…)预先添加润滑油(预先对…进行润滑)
prelubracator 发动机临起动前,由电动泵将机油压至主要部件做润滑循环的)预润滑系统
prelubricated bearing 预加润滑剂的轴承(＝prepacked bearing)
PREM 高级车用汽油(premium mo-

gas)

premature ①过早的，不到期的；未成熟的，提前的 ②过早发生的事物

premature explosion 过早的爆燃

premature failure 过早的损坏

premature ignition 早燃，过早点火（＝preignition，premature firing）

premier car company 第一流的轿车公司（名列前茅的汽车公司）

premium brand 名牌，驰名品牌

premium engine oil 高级机油（高级发动机润滑油）

premium gasoline 高级汽油（在美国指研究辛烷值为100左右的汽油。94左右的称为常规汽油，此外还有：超高级"super premium"，中间级"intermediate"，低级"sub-regular"汽油之分）

premium-grade 高级的，优质的

premium mogas 高级汽车用油（简称PREM，＝premium gasoline）

premium-quality 优质的，高级的

premiun L package 高级L级轿车

premixed charge 预混合充量（指进入发动机汽缸的可燃混合气是在进入汽缸前混合形成的，参见dual fuel natural gas/diesel engine）

premixed charged compression ignition engine 预混合充气式压燃机（简称PCCI engine）

premixed-charge engine 预混合充气式发动机（如：化油器式汽油机，以区别于可燃混合气在汽缸内形成的压燃式发动机和汽缸内直接喷射式）

premixed flame 预混合火焰

pre-mixing combustion 预混合燃烧（指在着火或点火前，燃料与空气已预先混合成气相的可燃混合气）

premixing compression combustion technique 预混合压燃技术（柴油机压缩预先混合好的柴油空气混合气实现着火燃烧，可同时减少PM和NO_X的柴油机排放前处理技术）

pre-mixing phase 预混合期（如：柴油机燃烧过程中喷入汽缸内的燃油被压缩冲程产生的热量加热而气化、与空气混合的时期）

pre-mix method （陶瓷合金的）预混合烧结法（预先将各种合金成分与纯铁粉或低合金铁粉混合，通过烧结法使合金元素扩散而形成合金烧结制件的方法）

premix ratio ①预混合比 ②（转子发动机亦指）燃油/滑油预混合比

premuffler 前置消声器（串联两个消声器时的第一个称前置消声器）

preoiler 预润滑装置

preoiling 预润滑

pre-opened play of steering control valve 转向控制阀预开隙（阀在中间位置时，阀台肩相对于阀体台肩之间的轴向间隙或角度）

pre-operational test 交付使用前的试验

pre-operation maintenance 用前维护，出车前维护

pre-operative control 预定位控制

preoptive control 预选控制（＝pre-selective control）

prepacked bearing 预加润滑脂的轴承（＝prelubricated bearing）

prepaint 上底漆

preparation 预备，准备，预先加工

preparation test 调制试验，预备试验（简称PPT）

preparative treatment （表面）预加工，预处理

preparatory input terminal （数字集成电路的）预备输入端（指施加数字信号后能改变电路对其他输入端上的信号的响应，但不直接引起电路输出组态变化的输入端）

prepare 准备，预备，配制

prepay ①预先付款 ②预先付款的

prep chart （汽车等的）预防维护图表，维护图表；计划图表

prepeening （表面）预冷作硬化

pre-polishing 预抛光

preponderance （影响力、重要性、数量等）占优势，占上风，（比其他的）大、多，重要

preprepared 事先准备好的，提前准备好的

preproduction 试生产

preproduction model 试制模型，样机

preproduction test 试制性试验（生产前试验，简称 PPT）

preproduction vehicle 预生产车，原型车（参见 mockup, standard production vehicle）

pre-programed ①预（先）编（制）程（序）的，按预先编制的程序控制的②预先编制的程序所规定的，预定的

preprogramed automatic test 程序控制自动台架试验

pre-programmed A/F ratio system 空燃比预程序控制系统

preprogrammed look-up chart （电子控制模块内存储的）预编程序控制查阅表（以表格的形式存储的各种传感器的输入值与被控制量之间的对应关系数据，供查寻，以确定最佳控制量。如：根据发动机转速、负荷、水温等传感器的输入从该表格中查找出与之相对应的最佳点火提前角等）

preprogrammed spark advance schedule （发动机控制模块中储存的按预先编制的程序所规定的各种条件决定点火提前角的）预编程点火提前角数据表

preproved 经过初步试验的，经初步验证的

Prepurchases inspection 售前检查

pre-reaction 预反应

pre-recorded 预先记录的，预先录制的，预录的

pre-refrigeration 预冷（对冷藏集装箱式冷藏车储藏冷藏物之前的预降温作业）

prerequisite ①先决条件，前提②先决条件的，必须预先具备的，必要的

pre-routing （路线）预导航

pre-safe system （Benz 公司的车辆）预安全系统（由雷达探测、音像预警系统和当碰撞不可避免或临近撞前自动触发，以保护乘员的各种结构和装置，以及安全隐患提示设施组成）

presbyopia 远视眼，老花眼

preselectable position control 预选式位置控制

preselected engine rotational speed range 发动机预选转速范围（亦称 preselected engine speed window）

preselection 预选

preselection switch 预选开关

preselective control 预选操纵，预选控制（= preoptive control, preselector control）

preselective gearbox 预选换挡变速器［指带半自动换挡机构的常规齿轮变速器。在换挡前预先选定挡位，然后踩踏离合器或附加的换挡踏板，即可实现换挡，亦称 preselector gearbox, preselective transmission, 其换挡机构称 preselection gear shift (ing) control mechanism］

preselector （变速）预选机构

preselector mechanism （变速挡位等的）预选机构

presence detector 存在感知器（测定在公路等处有无行人或车辆的感传装置）

present ①现在的，目前的，在场的②交出，提出

presentation ①说明（介绍）②文献

（报告书，文章，论文等）③提出，表示④外观（形式）⑤图像（影像）

present-day 现代的，现在的，当前的，当前使用的

preservation 保护，保存，防腐

preservative coat 防护层

preserve 保存，保藏，保持，维持

preserver 保护装置，安全装置

preset ①给定程序的，预先调准的②预先调定，预调，初调，预先定位，按预定程序工作

preset adjustment 预调整

preset air pressure inflator （汽车轮胎的）预定气压充气装置（当胎压达到预定的压力值时，即自动停止充气）

preset parameter 预定参数

preset regulation 预调

preset spring 预加力弹簧

preset switch (ing) point 预定的开关点（如：温控开关预定的闭合温度等）

preset torque-wrench 预定转矩扳手

press button 按钮 (= push button)

press-button control 按钮操纵，按钮控制

press-button switch 按钮开关

press cure 加压硫化，加压固化

press door 车门窗框与车门一起整体冲压车门

pressed exhaust pipe 冲压制排气管

pressed lining 压制衬带，压制衬垫，压装衬料，压装衬片

pressed on 套压的，压装的

pressed-on solid type 压装式实心轮胎（指硫化后压装在轮辋上的非黏结性实心轮胎）

pressed seat 冲压座椅

pressed-steel affair 钢材冲压制品

pressed steel body 钢板冲压车身

pressed steel frame 钢材冲压车架

press fit 压配合，过盈配合（亦称 drive fit, force fit)

press fit diode 压装二极管

pressing clip 压紧夹

pressing plant ①压件厂，冲压厂，锻压厂②（在汽车制造中指冲压车身板件的）轿车车身制造厂

pressometer gauge 压力计，测压计

press polish 加压抛光

pressure ①压力，压强［单位面积上所受的压力，国际单位制的压力单位为帕"Passcal"，简称 Pa, $1Pa = 1N/m^2$，因帕（Pa）太小，一般选用千帕（kPa），$1kPa = 1kN/m^2$，在欧洲常用 bar 或 hbar，在英、美常用 lbf/in^2，$tonf/in^2$］②压，压迫，强制

pressure above the atmospheric 正压（高于大气压力的压力，相对负压而言）

pressure accumulator 压力储蓄器，储压器（如：带高压储能器的制动防抱死系统中的充氮膜片室或球形制动液压存储器）

pressure-actuated 压力促动的，压力使动的，压力操纵控制的

pressure-actuated valve 压力作动阀

pressure amplification factor 压力放大比，增压比（各种压力控制件的输入压力与输出压力之比）

pressure and flow limiting valve 压力与流量限制阀

pressure and time fuel injection system 见 FI fuel injection system

pressure angle （齿轮等的）压力角（过齿面或端面齿廓上的任意点处的径向直线与齿面或齿廓在该点的切平面所夹的锐角）

pressure at nozzle end 嘴端压力（指喷油器总成进油口端管内的燃油压力）

pressure-atomizing fuel nozzle 高压喷油嘴（高压燃油喷嘴）

pressure at pump end 泵端压力（喷

油泵出油口端管内的燃油压力)

pressure-balanced valve 压力平衡阀(利用弹簧压力与输出压力的平衡作用,使输出压力稳定在所调定的范围内,一般用作压力调节阀、限压阀或稳压阀等)

pressure below the atmospheric 负压(低于大气压力的压力,相对于高于大气压的正压而言)

pressure bleeder (液压系统排除空气用的)加压式排气器,压力式排气装置(如:在一定的压力下将制动液压入主缸,同时拧开轮缸的排气螺钉而将空气排出制动系)

pressure blower 高压鼓风机

pressure boost 压力放大,压力增大,增压

pressure build-up 压力建立,压力形成,压力产生

pressure cabin 加压室(室内压力高于大气压)

pressure cap 压力盖(指带压力阀和真空阀的散热器加水口盖)

pressure capsule 密封膜盒式压力传感元件(亦称 bellow type pressure sensor)

pressure cap tester 压力盖(开阀压力)测定器

pressure casting ①压铸,压力铸造 ②压铸件

pressure cell 压力传感元件(如:压力感传器,测压仪,压力室,压应力计)

pressure chamber 压力室,压力腔

pressure characteristics 压力特性

pressure-charge compressor (发动机)增压进气压缩机

pressure coefficient 压力系数

pressure coil (发电机输出电压控制其磁场电流的触点式调节器的触点)控制线圈

pressure compensated control 压力补偿控制(一般指利用压力信号来操作补偿装置的控制方式, = pressure-compensation control)

pressure compensated flow control valve 压力补偿流量控制阀

pressure-compensated gear pump 带压力补偿的齿轮泵

pressure compensator 压力补偿器

pressure component 分压力,压力分量

pressure connection 压力管接头

pressure contacting hole 压力传导孔(传递压力信号的孔道)

pressure contact welding 压力接触焊

pressure-control 压力控制的(为 pressure-controlling "控制压力的"和 pressure-controlled "由压力来控制的"二者的通称)

pressure control circuit 压力控制回路(为压力遥控回路、可变压力回路、压力缓冲回路、压力开关回路、压力保持回路、卸压回路、压力平衡回路、减压回路、增压回路、压力补偿回路、冲击消除回路等各种与压力有关的控制回路的总称)

pressure control restriction (液压管路中安装的)节流式压力控制件(如:控制管路通道孔径的电磁阀等)

pressure control servo valve 压力控制伺服阀(参见 servo valve)

pressure control spring 压力控制弹簧(如:调节制动比例阀开始起作用点的压力弹簧)

pressure control valve ①压力控制阀(各种与压力有关的控制阀的总称) ②(某些制动系中,用于防止后轮制动力过大而抱死的后轮制动)压力控制阀(简称 PCV)

pressure control valve type hydraulic suspension 压力控制阀式液压悬架(通过控制液压来控制阻尼力的悬架,以别于通过控制流量来控制

阻尼力的液压悬架）

pressure converter 压力变换器，压力转换器（将一种流体的压力变换为另一种流体的压力，或将压力变为电信号，或将压力变为运动件机械位移等装置的通称）

pressure curve 压力曲线

pressure cycling switch （车用空调系统低压侧的）压力循环开关（当制冷剂压力低于规定值时，该开关断开，空调压缩机离合器分离）

pressure decay 压力下降

pressure-dependent 取决于压力的，随压力而变的，与压力相关的

pressure-dependent brake force proportioning valve 感压式制动力比例（分配）阀（亦称 pressure sensitive brake force proportioning device, pressure-proportional brake contour device, 简称 proportioning valve, 指前、后轮制动回路的输入、输出压力等值增长到调节起始点压力以后，便使后轮制动回路输出压力与输入压力的比值按小于 1 的比例增长的部件）

pressure difference 压力差的，压差（简称 PD）

pressure differential 压力差的，压差的

pressure differential meter 差压式流量计

pressure differential sensor 压力差式压力传感器（亦称 differential pressure sensor, 膜片式可变电阻压力传感器的一种，膜片一侧通大气压，一侧通所测压力，由二者压力差决定传感器输出）

pressure differential switch 制动压差警报灯开关（见 pressure differential warning valve）

pressure differential warning valve 制动压差警报阀（指双回路制动系中，由于泄漏等原因有一回路的制动液压低于某规定值时，即两回路的压力差超过规定值时，该阀将装在仪表板上的压差警报灯开关触点接通，亦称 pressure differential switch）

pressure distributing valve 压力分配阀（亦称 pressure dividing valve）

pressure drag （汽车行驶时遇到的空气动力阻力中的）压力阻力（指车身表面受到的空气动力正压力的合力在行驶方向的分力。压力阻力又可分为形状阻力、干扰阻力、内循环阻力和诱导阻力。其中，由于车身迎面和背面的空气压差造成的形状阻力，约占总空气阻力的 60%）

pressure drop ① 压力降，压降 ② （防抱死制动系统工况之一的）减压（当制动器趋于抱死或车轮的滑移率达到设计规定的数值时，降低制动管路的压力，亦称 decay state "减压工况"）

pressure element 压力元件（简称 PE）

pressure-energized seal 受压自紧密封件

pressure equalizer for twin tyres 并装双胎胎压平衡器

pressure equalizing passage 压力平衡通道

pressure excess 压力增量，剩余压力

pressure excursion 压力偏离额定值，压力偏离规定值

pressure exerted by masses 质量压力（①指质量加、减速运动产生的惯性压力；②指质量产生的静压力）

pressure exploration 压力分布测定

pressure fan 强制通风机，压风机；增压风扇（简称 PF, = blast fan, blown-down fan, forced-draft fan）

pressure feed 压力供给

pressure feedback control 压力反馈控制

pressure feedback EGR （排气）压

力反馈式废气再循环系统(简称 PFE,该系统由一个称为 PFE 传感器的元件将排气压力变为电信号反馈给发电机控制模块,借以修正废气再循环量)

pressure feedback (EGR) sensor 废气再循环排气反馈压力传感器(简称 PFE sensor,向电子控制模块反馈排气压力信号,借以修正废气再循环量的传感器件)

pressure feed lubrication 压力润滑

pressure flowmeter 加压流量计(一种特制的流量计,用于测定黏结胶剂、密封胶剂、缓冲胶剂的黏度,使一定数量的试样在压力下通过特定的量孔,用流过时间的秒数表示试样的黏度)

pressure-flow system (气流或液流的)压力输送系统

pressure fluctuation 压力波动

pressure fluid 压力油(液压系统的工质,工作液体)

pressure-formed 压制的,压力成形的

pressure gage dash unit 仪表板上的压力表总成

pressure gain 压力放大(系数),压力增益

pressure gas 压缩可燃气(= pressurized gas)

pressure gas producer 压力式煤气发生炉

pressure gauge 压力表,压力计(亦写作 pressure gage)

pressure gear pump 齿轮压力泵

pressure governor 压力调节器

pressure gradient 压力梯度

pressure gradient control valve 压差控制阀,优先阀(保证主要管路达到一定压力后,才向辅助管路供压的控制部件)

pressure gun 压力式润滑枪(= force-feed gun)

pressure head 压位差,压头(以流体的高度来表示的该流体具有的压力能量,$= p/\gamma$,式中:p—流体压力;γ—该流体比重。当该流体为水时,一般称为水压头或水头)

pressure heat treatment 压力热处理(综合利用形变强化及相变强化,将压力加工与热处理操作相结合的一种工艺方法)

pressure hold ①保压,保持压力(指将压力保持在规定的规范内)②(防抱死制动系统工况之一的)保压(指制动主缸输出的管路压力不再增加,也不再降低,而维持某一定水平的制动工况,亦称 hold state "保压工况")

pressure holding circuit 压力保持回路(多用于要求长时间保持一定工作压力的系统)

pressure increase ①压力上升,压力增加②(防抱死制动系统工况之一的)升压(使制动管路压力恢复增加的工况,亦称 build state 升压工况)

pressure indicator 压力表

pressure intensifier 压力变换器(参见 pressure transducer)

pressure intensity 压强

pressure jump 压力跳跃(压力突变)

pressure limit 压力极限

pressure limiting valve ①限压阀(液压或气压、机油压力或燃油压力系统中任一种将压力限制在规定范围内的部件)②(特指制动系统中制动力调节装置的)限压阀(使某一回路中的压力达到规定值后,即不再随压力源供给压力波动,而保持压力不变的部件,或限制制动系作用压力始点的部件)

pressure line ①(齿轮)压力线②压力管路

pressure line filter 安装在压力管路

上的滤清器
pressure loss 压力损失，压力降
pressure loss factor 压力损失系数，压头损失系数
pressure loss in duct （压缩空气流过）管道（的）压力损失（简称管道损失）
pressure loss in steering control valve 转向控制阀压力降（指该阀处于中间位置时油液流经该阀的节流损失）
pressure lubrication system 压力润滑系统
pressure maintaining valve 稳压阀
pressure modulating piston （防抱死制动系液压调节装置中的）液压调节活塞
pressure modulator （制动防抱死系统中的）制动压力调节器（根据制动控制模块的指令调控制动管路压力的装置）
pressure modulator valve ①（柱塞式防抱死制动控制系统中由电子控制模块控制的）制动压力调节器中的电磁阀②（阀门式防抱死制动控制系统中指）制动压力调节器（= pressure modulator，亦称 ABS actuator）
pressure of explosion 爆发压力
pressure oil 压力油
pressure oil tank 压力油箱
pressure-operated 压力操作的，压力驱动的
pressure-operated valve 压力作动阀
pressure oscillation 压力振荡
pressure oscillation damper 压力振荡阻尼器（= pressure pulsation damper）
pressure override （安全阀等的）压力超增（安全阀全开达到额定流量时的压力与开启压力之差）
pressure pad 压紧垫片，压紧凸台
pressure piping 压力管道

pressure plate ①侧壁压板，压力板（利用背压作用防止高压时齿轮泵、叶片泵及齿轮式马达、叶片式马达等容积效率下降的侧面密封板）②（盘式制动器制动衬块）背板（亦称 back plate）③（离合器）压盘（传递压紧力、离合器结合时将从动盘紧压于飞轮的主动摩擦盘）
pressure plate spring （离合器）压盘弹簧（为一组螺旋弹簧或一个膜片式弹簧，通过压盘将从动盘紧压于飞轮）
pressure probe 压力探头（压力测头）
pressure profile 压力分布图
pressure-proof 耐压的，抗压的（简称 PP）
pressure-proportional 与压力成比例的
pressure proportional brake control device 感压式制动力比例分配阀（见 pressure-dependent brake force proportioning valve）
pressure protection valve （气压系统的）压力保护阀，气压保护阀（简称 PPV，气压管路损坏或漏气时，防止气压下降的保护性阀门。如：当牵引车与挂车之间的跨接软管漏气时，可保护牵引车制动系气压的挂车制动保持阀"trailer braking protection valve"）
pressure pulsation 压力脉动（一般指液压系统在稳定工作条件下输出压力的周期性变化，而不包括由于非正常因素造成的过度的压力变动）
pressure pulsation damper 压力脉动阻尼器（= pressure oscillation damper）
pressure purger 减压装置，减压阀（= pressure relief valve）
pressure ratio 压力比（如：增压器出口压力与进口压力比的增压比）

pressure ratio control system 压力比控制系统

pressure ratio detector 压力比传感器，压力比检测器（根据压差检测压力比的传感装置）

pressure reducing valve 减压阀（= pressure-relief valve, pressure reducing valve, pressure reduction valve, pressure-reductor valve）

pressure regulating valve 压力调节阀（简称PRV，亦写作 pressure regulator valve）

pressure regulator 压力调节器，压力调节装置（将压力保持在规定范围内的装置，如：限制最高压力的压力调节阀等）

pressure-relief valve 减压阀（= pressure reducing valve，在规定的压力下开启，防止压力超过规定值）

pressure-relief vent 减压孔，卸压孔

pressure reservoir 压力罐，储压筒

pressure responsive device 压力响应装置（如：压敏元件，压力传感器）

pressure-responsive valve 压力-响应阀（压力-响应开关）

pressure ring ①压缩环，气环 ②压力环（传递压力或推力的环状部件）

pressure rise rate 压力升高率（内燃机在燃烧过程中，单位曲轴转角或单位时间内汽缸内工质的压力升高量，简称压升率）

pressure rise ratio 压力升高比（内燃机燃烧过程中最大爆发压力与压缩冲程终点压力之比）

pressure-sensing device 压力传感器

pressure-sensing window 感压型车窗（车窗在关闭过程中，触及手指时，只要压力超过某规定值，即停止关闭动作，以防夹伤）

pressure sensitive adhesive 感压胶黏剂

pressure-sensitive brake force proportioning device 感压式制动力比例分配阀（见 pressure-dependent brake force proportioning valve）

pressure-sensitive capacitor 压敏电容器

pressure-sensitive diaphragm 压力传感膜片，感压膜片

pressure-sensitive element 压力传感元件

pressure sensitive grids type sensor （测定一定面积上的压力及其分布用的）格栅式压力传感器（如：豪华型轿车座垫上测定乘员乘坐压力及其分布，以便由反馈控制模块提供附加支撑气压，保证乘坐舒适的3600个触点组成的压力传感器）

pressure-sensitive paper 感压纸

pressure (sensitive) pickup 压力传感器

pressure-sensitive resistor 压敏电阻器

pressure sensitives 压敏材料（对压力敏感的物质）

pressure sensitive valve 感压阀（压力传感阀）

pressure-sensitive variable capacity 压力感应式可变电容器（活动电容器片复合在压力膜片上）

pressure-sensitive vehicle detector 感压式车辆检测器，压感侦车器（设置在路幅内，通过车辆的压力来测定路过车辆的侦车器）

pressure sensitivity 压力敏感性

pressure sensor 压力传感器（将压力变为电信号输出的器件，亦称 load cell）

pressure-setting plug （减压阀等的）压力调节螺塞，调压塞

pressure sinkage 压力下陷，静载下陷

pressure snubber 压力波阻尼器

pressure solenoid （控制）压力

（的）电磁阀（pressure-controlling solenoid 的简称）

pressure spring ①压缩弹簧，压紧弹簧（如：对离合器压盘施加压紧力的弹性零件）②调压弹簧（如：压紧力可通过螺钉等调节的阀门等的开启压力调节弹簧）

pressure spring screw （调压弹簧的）压紧力调节螺钉

pressure stage 压力级

pressure switch 压力开关（如：装在储压器内，当压力达到某规定值时，该开关接通向电子控制模块发送有关控制信号，如停止向储压器内输入液压等）

pressure switch circuit 压力开关电路（指利用压力达到某规定值时断开或闭合的压力开关来接通或断开电磁阀、继电器等执行元件的控制电路）

pressure system 压力系统

pressure tank 压力箱，压头油箱

pressure-temperature compensated flow control 温度-压力补偿流量控制阀

pressure-temperature compensating type flow control valve 压力-温度补偿型流量控制阀

pressure-temperature sensing system 压力-温度传感系统

pressure test 压力试验（在加压状况下的试验或测定压力）

pressure tester ①（检验水箱等使用的）加压测试器②（测定气压、液压等用的）压力测定器

pressure-tight 不泄压的，耐压密封的

pressure-time diagram 压力-时间曲线图

pressure time histories 压力随时间的变化关系曲线

pressure transducer 压力变换器（各种可将压力变换为其他物理量的装置的通称。当作为压力传感元件、将压力变为电信号输出时，称为压力传感器"pressure sensor"）

pressure transmission 压力传播，压力传送

pressure treatment （木材防腐的）压力处理，压力蒸炼

pressure tube 压力管（压力输送管）

pressure tubing 压力管道系统（如：压缩空气管道系统）

pressure turbine 反作用式涡轮机（= reaction turbine）

pressure type carburetor 压力型化油器（装在增压器与进气歧管间，通过化油器的空气为增压空气）

pressure type cooling ①（内燃机的）压力式冷却，闭式冷系（指散热器加水口上装有压力型散热器盖，使水循环系统与大气不直接相通，而保持高于大气压力的恒压水冷却方式）②减压式冷却法（冷却系压力保持在 30～50kPa，使沸点降低，防止过热，提高冷却效率）

pressure type radiator cap 压力型散热器盖（发动机闭式冷却系统带压力-真空阀的组合式水箱加水口盖。当冷却系内水温升高、压力超过某规定值时，压力阀开启，放出部分蒸气，使压力回落。当水温降低形成负压时，真空阀开启，吸入外界空气或膨胀箱内的冷却水）

pressure type thermometer 压力式温度计（利用气体或液体的压力随温度而变化的现象制成的流体温度计）

pressure unit ①压力感传器②增压器

pressure-vacuum relief filler cap （水箱或油箱的）加注口压力-真空安全阀盖（同时装有减压排气阀和真空进气阀的安全阀盖）

pressure valve 压力阀（指在规定压力下开启的阀门。其作用为：使密闭容器或系统内的液压或气压保持

相对稳定。若将其开启压力调到某较高值,则可起到提高密封容器或系统内气压或液压的作用,如:闭式冷却系统压力式散热器盖内的蒸气压力阀)

pressure valve spring 压力阀弹簧

pressure-versus-crank angle diagram (描述发动机工作循环的汽缸)压力-曲轴转角图

pressure-volume diagram 压容图,压力-比容图,P-V 图 [亦称 pressure-versus-volume diagram,描述发动机工作循环的汽缸压(力)-容(积)图,简称 P-V diagram]

pressure warning sensor 压力报警传感器(压力超出规定范围时,接通或断开报警信号的装置)

pressure washer (利用高压空气或高压水流等冲洗的)压力清洗装置,压力冲洗机

pressure washing 压力冲洗

pressure-wave propagation 压力波的传播

pressure wave supercharger 压力波增压器

pressure-wave supercharging ①寇姆普列克斯排气压力波增压(见 complex exhaust pressure wave supercharger) ②谐波进气增压(通过适当选择进气管长度,使在一定的转速范围内活塞吸气作用在气门处形成的膨胀波在进气管开口端形成的向气门反射回的压缩波到达气门时,气门正好处于开启状态,借以提高进气终了时的进气压力而实现的进气增压,亦称 harmonic induction, ram-pipe supercharging, tuned induction)

pressure welding 压力焊接

pressure zone 压力区

pressurization 加压

pressurize 增压,加压,对…施加压力

pressurized air 压缩空气

pressurized cabin 加压舱

pressurized container vehicle 带有压力卸货装置的集装箱运输车辆

pressurized cooling system 压力式冷却系(①指由水泵加压冷却水循环的冷却系;②指散热器加水口上装有压力-真空阀的闭式冷却系,压力阀一般调到高于大气压力,使冷却系内有一定的蒸气压力,以提高冷却液沸点)

pressurized crankcase 密闭式曲轴箱,加压式曲轴箱(如:无通风孔或通风孔关闭,箱内气压高于大气压力)

pressurized gas 压缩可燃气

pressurized mould 密封铸模,配压铸模(防止熔融金属漏出模外,所以使用密封铸模,或在铸模外加适当压力,平衡受压熔融金属对铸模的压力)

pressurized reservoir 压力容器

pressurizing pump 加压泵,压力泵(加压用泵)

press-welding axle housing 冲压焊接桥壳(钢板冲压成上、下两半壳体,再组装焊接成整体的桥壳)

presswork 冲压制品,压制件

press working 压力加工

pre-start-up check 起动前检查

prestige car (多年一直生产的)豪华名车(如:Rolls-Roys 等)

prestone 普列斯通(一种低凝点液体乙二醇防冻液剂商品名,由乙烯、乙二醇混合而成)

prestress ①预拉伸,预应力(简称 PS) ②预加应力于…,施加预应力

prestressed 预(加)应力的

prestressed road 预应力(混凝土)道路

prestressed (steel piston) ring (钢制)预应力活塞环(将活塞环张开,使活塞环外径表面受压缩,然

后镀铬，这种活塞环装入汽缸后，钢环镀铬层临界面上的应力为零，可提高环的疲劳强度）
prestressing 预加应力，加预应力
prestroke ①顶隙，余隙（见 top clearance）②预行程（如：柱塞式喷油泵柱塞从开始移动到关闭进油孔位置所行的距离）
prestroke actuator （电子控制柴油机燃油喷射系统的）预行程执行器
presumption 假定，推测，设想，预定
presumptive error 预定误差
presuppose 预想，推测，预先假定；先需有…，先决条件是…，以…为必要条件；含意；包含着
presure-sensitive switch （正、负压力达到规定值时接通的）压力传感开关
preswirl combustion chamber 涡流预燃室（指兼有涡流燃烧室和预燃室结构特点的一种燃烧室）
pre-tension ①预拉力，预张，预紧，预应力，预加载②要求
pretension and force limited mechanism （安全带的）预紧和收紧力限制机构
pretensioner 预应力装置，预加载装置；预张紧装置
pretest conditioning 试验前的调整（作业）
pretested 初步试验过的
pretest inspection 试验前的检查（作业）
pretightness of bearing 轴承预紧度
pre-timed controller 预定时间控制机（如：预定周期交通信号控制机）
pre-timed signal 预定周期式信号（如：预定时间的交通信号）
pre-torque 预加转矩，预转矩
pretreatment 预加工，预处理
pretrigger 预触发器

pre-trip inspection 出车（前）检查，行车前检查
pretty 相当的，很多的，十分恰当的，巧妙的，漂亮的
prevail ①克服（over）②流行，盛行③占优势
prevailing ①流行的，盛行的，一般的，普通的②主要的③占优势的，超过的④有效的，显著的
prevailing driving conditions （发动机）①主要工况，常见工况②当前工况
prevailing torque fastener 超转矩紧固件（多指 prevailing torque nut）
prevailing torque nut 超转矩螺母（用于在螺母与螺杆螺纹间形成过盈配合，实现过盈的方法为：将全金属螺母扭至变形或在螺纹间加装尼龙挤压件）
prevailing wheel load 车轮经常荷载（车轮最常承受的荷载量）
prevalent ①流行的，盛行的；一般的，普通的②占优势的
prevent 预防，防止，阻止；保护（from），避免，不使用，不采用
preventer ①防护器，防护设备，安全装置，保险设备②预防措施，安全防护法③防…剂
prevention of accidents 事故预防（＝accident prevention）
preventive ①预防法，预防措施，预防剂，预防药物②预防的，阻止的，防止的
preventive detention 防护性迟延，保护性阻滞（简称 PD）
preventive inspection 预防性检查
preventive maintenance 预防性维护
preventive maintenance inspection 预防性维护检测
preventive maintenance on schedule 计划预防性维护
preventive maintenance program 预防性维护计划

preventive maintenance scheduling （车辆）预防性维护图表作业法（简称 PMscheduling，根据预编制的图表，车辆定期按一定作业项目进行维护）

preventive repairing 预防修理

preventive servicing 预防维修（有计划地按期进行检查维修）

prevent water creep 防止渗水

preview 展望，展望；预习，预检，预测

Preview G-Vectoring control 加速度矢量预控制［指在汽车进入弯道前即根据前方弯道的曲率推算出可能产生的横向加速度，而在车辆进入弯道前预先控制车辆减速，以防止汽车转向不足而驶出车道，见 G-Vectoring control（加速度矢量控制）］

preview point 预测点［观察者至预测点的距离称 preview distance（预测距离）］

prewar car 战前型车（第二次世界大战前生产的车）

pre-yield strain 屈服点前的应变

pri ①原始的，初级的（primary）②个人的，私用的（private）

PRI 塑性保持指数（plasticity retention index 的简称）

price 价格

price current 定价表，价目表

price (-) list 货价单，价目表，价目单，定价表（= price catalogue）

price-to-performance ratio 价格-性能比

pricing system 收费系统

prick punch mark 定中心点

1 p rim 一件（整体）式轮辋（= one piece wheel）

primal 最初的，原始的，主要的，根本的

primarily 首先，起初，主要地，根本上

primary ①原始的，原有的，原来的，本来的②初步的，第一阶段的，初级的③基本的，首要的，主要的，居第一位的④（对发动机点火系，指其）低压电路的，初级电路的（如：primary winding "点火线圈初级绕组"）⑤（对发动机平衡，指）一阶的，一级的（即随曲轴转角或曲轴角速度、曲轴转速而变化的。随 2 倍曲轴转角或 2 倍曲轴角速度、2 倍曲轴转速而变化的，称二级的，二阶的 "secondary"）

primary actuated tachometer （发动机的）低压信号转速表（指从初级点火线路取得转速信号的转速表，简称 primary tachometer）

primary air 一次空气，初级空气，主空气

primary air inlet 主进气口

primary air tank ①（某些车辆制动系的）总储气筒（存储由空气压缩机泵入的压缩空气，保持恒压，向各制动管路的分储气筒供气）②（汽车列车的）主储气筒（指牵引车制动系的储气筒，以别于挂车制动系用储气筒）③（对带后轮弹簧制动气室的车辆指）行车制动系储气筒（以别于弹簧制动器用储气筒）

primary annulus （行星变速器）一级齿圈

primary barrel （双级式化油器的）初级腔，低中速腔筒（在发动机低速、中速时起作用）

primary battery 原电池组（见 primary cell）

primary brake shoe 制动器领蹄（见 primary shoe）

primary cable （点火系）低压导线，低压线

primary carbon 伯碳（原子）

primary cell 原电池，一次电池（指只能将化学能转变为电能的不可逆

一次性电池,即不可再充电的电池)

primary chamber ①(在位置或排序上的)第一室②(在作用上的)主室③(两级装置的)初级室(如:液化石油气发动机的初级减压室)

primary characteristic (液力传动装置的)原始特性(指液力传动装置的变矩比、能容系数和效率三者与速比关系的特性)

primary circuit 初级电路(指蓄电池点火系中相对于感生高压的次级电路而言的低压电路,由蓄电池、点火开关、断电器或点火信号发生装置、点火线圈初级绕组等组成)

primary clearance 初始间隙

primary clock 母钟

primary coat 底漆,底涂层,结合层,底层(= prime coat)

primary coil (点火线圈)一次绕组(低压电流通过的绕组,其电线较粗,圈数较少,一般线径 0.8~1.3mm,200~250 圈)

primary colour 底层漆色,底层颜色,底漆色

primary compression ratio (二冲程发动机利用活塞下行压缩曲轴箱内的充量,而活塞下部曲轴箱压缩空间内形成的压缩比)预压缩比

primary cost 生产成本,初期费用(参见 first cost)

primary couple 一阶力偶,一级力偶

primary creep 第一阶段蠕变(蠕变加速段)

primary cup (制动液压缸)第一皮碗,主皮碗(见 secondary cup)

primary current 初级电流(指初级电路流经点火线圈)一次绕组的电流

primary diaphragm ①(串列式双腔气制动阀)第一(工作腔的)膜片②(液化石油气发动机蒸发器的)初级(减压室)膜片③(双膜片真空点火提前机构的)点火提前膜片(亦称 advance diaphragm)

primary diaphragm hook (液化石油气发动机蒸发器)初级减压室膜片拉钩(当初级减压室压力超过规定值时,膜片拉钩拉动膜片阀杆将膜片阀关闭)

primary drive 初始传动

primary failure ①首次损坏②独立失效(独立故障,故障的产生与其他部件无关,即:不是由于另一部分或部件的故障引起的)

primary feedback signal 主反馈信号

primary filter 初级滤清器,粗滤器

primary flywheel 主飞轮

primary force (由于发动机旋转质量不均匀和往复质量往复运动,在发动机转速下产生并随曲轴角速度及转角变化的、使发动机失去平衡、产生摆振的)一级往复(或旋转)惯性力,一阶往复(或旋转)惯性力(参见 primary, primary couple)

primary function 主要任务

primary gasoline 高级汽油,[美]指辛烷值为 90~95 的汽油)

primary gear (变速器)第一轴传动齿轮

primary highway 干线公路,公路干线,主要公路

primary industries 第一产业,(包括农业、矿业等)基础产业

primary inlet port (转子发动机的)主进气口,主进气孔,一级进气孔(= primary stage port,见 two stage induction system)

primary jet (化油器等的)主喷嘴,主量孔

primary key (汽车的电源)总开关

primary line of sight 主视线(观察点和注视点间的连线,见 point of

observation)

primary magnetic field （点火线圈的）初级绕组磁场

primary member 主构件

primary oil filter 机油粗滤器

primary operating characteristics 基本使用特性，基本工作特性

primary pattern （示波器的点火系）初级电路图形

primary piston 第一活塞（亦称 first piston，串列双腔式制动主缸中，由主缸推杆推动的活塞）

primary pulley 主动传动带轮（①传动带式传动系统中的驱动轮，亦称 driving puller 轮②见 CVT steel belt puller）

primary pump （液力变速器液力传动系统的）前油泵（亦称 front pump 或 input pump，与发动机有固定传动比关系的油泵）

primary (reciprocating inertia) force 内燃机（往复运动件惯性质量的）一次往复惯性力，一阶往复惯性力〔沿汽缸轴线，随曲轴转角（即曲轴每转一周）按余弦规律变化一次的不平衡力〕

primary reference fuel （测定汽油辛烷值、柴油十六烷值的）基本参比燃油，标准燃油（分别称为标准汽油、标准柴油，如：用90%的异辛烷与10%的正庚烷掺和，就得到辛烷值为90%的标准汽油）

primary regulator valve （自动变速器液压控制系统的）主调压阀（亦称 main pressure regulator valve，用于调控油泵的输出压力，即控制系统主油路的压力）

primary road 主要公路，干线公路

primary route 公路干线，一级路线

primary safety design of vehicle 第一安全设施（车辆的基本安全设施指防止碰撞、翻车等的安全措施，如：制动、转向等各个方向的安全设计，帮助驾驶员避免肇事）

primary seal ①（串列双腔制动主缸）第一活塞油封②（一般机械的）主密封（指由一对密封环的密封端面所构成的密封环节）

primary sealing area ①第一密封面（如：第一道活塞环与缸壁接触的密封面）②主密封面（如：活塞环与缸壁密封面，转子发动机径向密封片与旋轮线缸壁之间的密封面，见 secondary sealing area）

primary shaft （变速器）第一轴（亦称 clutch shaft）

primary shaft bearing （变速器）第一轴轴承

primary shoe （制动器）领蹄（张开时转动方向与制动封旋转方向相同的制动蹄，亦称 leading shoe，forward shoe）

primary side 初级侧，一次侧，低压侧

primary signal face （交通控制信号中的）主信号面，第一信号面

primary spool 主滑阀

primary stage port 主进气口（= primary inlet port）

primary state highway [美]州级干线（参见 state highway）

primary structure component 主要结构件，主构件

primary supply voltage （点火系）初级供电电压（初级接线端的直流电压）

primary surface 基面

primary surge tank （为了在整个发动机的转速范围内均能获得最佳充气效率，某些发动机在进气歧管内设有利用进气压力波提高充气效率的两个脉动效应室中的）低速区脉动效应室（见 surge tank③）

primary tangent （切线分割法中的）主切线（如：与某曲线两端点 AB 连线近似平行且与该曲线相切的直

线，参见 master tangent)
primary technical maintenance 一级技术维护
primary terminal （点火线圈）初级绕组接线柱
primary throttle valve （双腔分动式化油器的）主（腔）节气门（简称 primary throttle)
primary valve ①（在位置或排序上的）第一阀②（在作用上的）主阀③（两级系统或装置的）初级（部分的）阀门，一次阀（如：液化石油气发动机蒸发器初级减压室膜片控制的燃料入口开闭阀，其阀杆称 primary valve lever)
primary vision area 主视区（指风窗玻璃正对驾驶员的区域）
primary voltage ①原电压②初级（线圈）电压
primary V-pulley （连续无级变速器"CVT"的）驱动轮（亦称 primary pulley, drive pulley. V 表示其传动带楔槽呈 V 形，该驱动轮由左、右两侧的锥面盘组成，其中一侧的锥面盘可在液压控制下向内、外滑动，借以改变其工作半径，从而改变驱动轮与从动轮间的速比）
primary winding （点火线圈的）初级绕组
prime ①最初的，原始的；首要的，根本的，主要的；最好的，第一流的②初期，最初③精华部分，全盛时期④（数）质数，素数，质元素，素元素⑤涂底漆⑥加注，注入（起动燃油等）
prime coat 底漆层，底镀层，底涂层，底覆盖层结合层（= primer coat)
prime cost 生产成本，出厂价格，进货价格，原价（= net cost, factory cost, cost of production, first cost, initial cost)
prime lacquer （上）底漆

prime mover ①原动机，发动机②原动力③牵引车（简称PMVR）
prime mover truck 牵引车（= towing truck)
prime number 质数，素数
prime paint 第一道漆，底漆，底层漆料（= ground coat paint)
prime power 原动力
prime pump 起动（注油）泵
primer ①为某项动作做准备的装置的总称（如：起动注油泵、导火线、始爆器、雷管等）②底漆
primer coat 底涂层，底镀层（= prime coat)
primer fluid 起动液，起动燃油（= starting fluid)
priming ①（发动机启动前预先）加注起动燃油②起爆药，点火药（剂）③打底漆
priming can （润滑）加油罐，注油壶；（水泵）起动注水罐；起动液罐
priming charge ①初充电（新蓄电池第一次充电）②（发动机）起动加注燃油
priming cock ①（柴油机）起动注油开关②（水泵）起动加水开关(亦称 priming cup)
priming color 底漆色
priming composition ①点火剂，起火剂②起动注液，起动液③配料，辅助剂④底漆配料，底漆料
priming cup ①起动注油杯②起动注旋塞（见 primary cock)
priming device （发动机输油泵起动）给油装置
priming lever （油泵的手动）起动注油杆，起动燃油加注杆
priming of battery 蓄电池加注酸液
priming paint 底漆
priming pump 预先加注燃油的手动泵（排除柴油机燃油系低压油路内混入空气时使用）

primitive 原始的，朴素的，基本的
primitive form 基本形
primitive road 天然土路，未改善的土路
principal ①主要的，基本的，重要的，第一的②主题，主梁，资本
principal axis 主轴，主轴线
principal axis of ellipse 椭圆的主轴
principal axis of quadric 二次曲面的主轴
principal branch 主页，主枝，主分支（机构等）
principal centers of curvature 主曲率中心
principal character 主特征标，主特性
principal curvature of a surface 曲面的主曲率
principal direction 主方向
principal direction of curvature 主曲率方向
principal force 主要力，主力（如：在发生汽车碰撞时，指碰撞瞬间作用在受撞车上使其变形和移动的最大合力）
principal inertia axis （汽车簧上质量）惯性主轴（亦称 inertia principal axis）
principal normal stress 法向主应力
principal part 主部，主要部分，主要零件
principal plane 主（平）面
principal plane of stress 应力主（平）面
principal radius of curvature 主曲率半径
principal representation 主表象，主表达式
principal section 主剖面，主截面，主断面
principal section of a quadric 二次曲面的主截面
principal strain directions 主应变方向，应变基本方向
principal supply road 主要供应线路
principal tangent 主（要）切线
principal theorem 基本定理
principal value of an integral 积分的主值
principle 原理，原则，定律，法则，方法，因素，组成部分
principle layout 总布置图
principle of virtual displacement 虚位移原理
principles of design 设计原理，结构原理
principle stress 主应力（主平面上的正应力）
prinicipal wire bundle 主（电）线束
print 印刷，印染，印痕，痕迹
print (ed) circuit board 印刷电路板（简称 PCB）
printed gasket 印刷密封垫（在基材上用印刷工艺生产的橡胶密封垫）
print (ed) motor 印刷式电动机（由印刷电路构成的直流微电机，其电枢的导体"印制"在绝缘盘上，直接与电刷接触，一般用来作伺服电动机）
printed wire （印刷电路板上的）印刷配线，印刷导线
printed (wiring) board 印刷（电路）板
printer 印刷机，印器器，打印器，（计算及测试结果的）打印装置
printout 印出，打印输出
priority ①优先权②优先性（如：对于强调加速性的车辆来说，加速性比经济性更重要，设计时必须优先考虑加速性能）
priority control strategy （汽车电子计算机控制系统的）优先控制策略，优先控制模式（如：高速行驶时，汽车 ASR/ABS 优先考虑横向附着力，而不是牵引力）

priority lane (高速公路的)优先车道

priority permit sign 优先通行标志

priority valve (液力变速器控制系统的)先导阀(设置在换挡阀或继动阀之前,起稳定主油路压力作用)

priority vehicle warning light (装在拥有优先行驶权的车辆顶部的)优先行驶警示灯(如:警车、急救车等的车顶闪光彩灯)

prior operation 准备作业

prior probability 先验概率(= probability apriority)

prise off 撬出(= lever off)

prism 棱柱(体)(如:三棱镜、三棱体、棱晶)

prismatic 棱镜的,棱柱的,棱镜分析的

prismatic plastic reflector 塑料多棱形反光镜

prison van 囚车

Prius 普锐斯(丰田公司推出的系列混合动力车商品名。目前有Prius HV、Prius PHV和Priusα三种车型)

Privacy (in the professional driver's workplace) (装有车主监控职业驾驶员工作态度的信息系统的大型货车驾驶室内驾驶人员的)隐私

private bus 自用客车(团体客车,非营业性客车)

private car ownership 自用轿车车主,私人轿车车主

Private Carrier Conference [美](汽车货运协会的)个体运输者会议(简称PCC)

private enterprise 私营企业

private fleet 私人经营的汽车运输车队(= privately-operated fleet)

private garage 私人车库

private lock 保密锁(需用特殊方法才能开启)

privately-operated fleet 私人经营的汽车运输队(= private fleet)

privately-owned bus company 私营客运公司

private motor car 自用轿车,私有轿车,私人轿车

private parking garage 私用停车库

Private Truck Council of America, Inc. [美]私人载货汽车委员会(简称PTCA)

private view 预展

PRNDL 自动变速器选挡杆挡位代号,依次分别表示park"驻车", reverse"倒挡", neutral"空挡", drive"前进挡", low"低挡")

PRO 泵性能试验用参考油(pump ability reference oil)

PRO-acoustic sound system (日产公司轿车)普罗音响系统(商品名,后音箱采用反射结构,与前音箱直接声混合可产生丰满音响效果)

probabilistic design 用概率计算方法进行的设计

probabilistic system 概率系统

probabilitic map-matching software 随机型地图叠合软件(特点是所涉及的车辆不一定要在限定的路线或道路网内行驶,无论在何处均可确定其位置,参见 semi-deterministic map-matching software)

probability 或然率,概率,几率

probability correlation 概率相关

probability current 概率流量,几率流量

probability curve 概率曲线

probability density analyzer 概率密度分析仪(幅值统计分析仪,用模拟法获取信号的概率密度分析专用仪器)

probability density curve for moisture content 含水量概率密度曲线

probability distribution 概率(密度)分布

probability distribution function 概率分布函数

probability of (equipment) failure (设备)故障概率

probability of error 误差概率

probability of "go" or "no-go" performance 通过或不能通过性能概率

probability of non failure 无故障概率

probability of survival 幸存概率

probability paper (统计计算用)概率图表纸,概率坐标纸

probability plan method 概率规划法(简称PP,综合应用概率论和线性规划来确定营运车辆最佳使用寿命、更新期的方法)

probability sampling 概率取样法

probable value 概值

probe ①探针,探头,探测器;取样针 ②试样;模型 ③穿刺;刺探;探查,清查

probe car (供性能测试等用的)样车

probe data 观测数据(如:车流量等的路边观测数据)

probe inspection 取样检查,取样检测

probe temperature 取样温度

problem 问题,难题

problematical 有问题的,可疑的,疑问的,不能预知的,悬而未决的,未定的,或然性的

problem component 故障部件,有问题的元件

proc 学报,会刊,会议论文集(见proceedings)

PROCC (美国福特汽车公司的)发动机程序控制燃烧(系统)(programmed controlled combustion system 的简称)

procedure 过程,步骤,程序,方法,工艺过程

procedures for sampling terrain values 地面值采样程序

process ①过程,流程,工序,步骤,工艺(规程),作业,操作 ②加工,处理,生产,使经历某一过程 ③经过特殊加工的

processability 加工性能,成型性能

process annealing (生产过程中的)中间退火(临界温度下低温退火)

process automation (生产)过程自动化

process average fraction defective 在生产过程中次品的平均百分率

process characteristic 过程特性

process control system (生产,工艺)流程控制系统,过程控制系统

process description 生产过程说明

processed information 已经整理过的数据(经处理的信息)

processed oil 成品油

processed surface 已加工表面

process flow 生产流程(= production flow)

process gas 生产(过程中产生的)废气,工业废气

process industries 制造工业,加工工业

processing ①(信号、数据等的)处理 ②加工 ③过程

process(ing) engineer 工艺工程师,工艺师

processing method using peaks and valleys 峰谷值计数法,峰谷值处理法(对机件的实测荷载时间历程进行统计处理的一种方法)

processing technique 生产技术,制造工艺

process of production 生产过程

processor ①处理器(a. 在计算机中指解释并执行指令的功能单元,处理器中至少包含一个指令控制器和一个算术与逻辑运算器; b. 在终端或其他处理装置中指翻译并执行指令的功能单元; c. 指能进行数据操作的设备或系统,如:数据处理器

或中央处理器）②处理程序（指能实现编译、汇编和翻译等功能的计算机程序，如编译程序，就是一种语言处理程序）

process simulator 程序模拟器

process specifications 操作说明书，程序说明书（简称PS）

process step 工序，工艺步骤

process variables 过程变量（过程的变化因素）

PROCO ①程序燃烧（programmed combustion）②程序燃烧发动机（programmed combustion engine）

Procon-ten （奥迪公司开发的）正面碰撞驾驶人员安全系统（的商品名，该系统利用汽车发生正面碰撞时发动机的相对位移，拉动一钢索将转向盘从驾驶人员身边拉开，同时将安全带拉紧）

PROCO-powered car 程序燃烧发动机汽车

procurement ①取得，获得；斡旋，达成②（政府的）订货，采购，征购

prod ①刺，戳，激励，推动②探针，试棒，量杆，锥子③生产的（produced）④产物，乘积（product）⑤生产，制品（production）

prod (magnetizing) method （磁粉探伤的）双头通电磁化法（圆棒电极磁性探伤法，亦称作 prod method，magnetizing）

produce ①生产，制造，产生，引起②产品，产量，成果

producer ①生产者，制造者②煤气发生炉，③发生器

producer furnace 煤气发生炉（亦称 gas generator，使固体燃料不完全燃烧，生成以 CO 为主的可燃气体发生装置。旧时因汽油短缺曾作为车载装置向发动机提供汽油的代用燃料，我国汽车界习惯上称它所生成的可燃气为煤气，或发生炉煤气）

producer gas 发生炉煤气（= generation gas，见 producer furnace）

producer gas engine 发生炉煤气发动机

producer gas generator ①煤气发电器（用发生炉煤气发动机驱动的发电机）②煤气发生器

producibility 易生产性，易制造性

product ①产品，制品②结果，成果③乘积

product developer 产品开发人员

product improvement 产品改进（简称 PI，依据市场需要，改善产品，如提高燃料经济性，降低生产成本等）

product improvement test 产品改进试验（简称 PIT 或 PI）

production ①生产，制造②产量，产品③批量生产的

production capacity 生产能力

production car 产品车（大量生产的车辆）

production-car race 生产车赛车（指使用批量生产、在市场出售的汽车进行竞赛）

production code number 产品编号（= series number）

production compliance auditing 产品适应性鉴定（指美国环保厅排气法规中规定的一种鉴定，简称 PCA）

production conformity 产品质量对法定标准的符合性

production control test 批量产品的质量控制性检测试验

production downtime 生产（被迫）停顿时间

production efficiency 生产效率

production engine 成品发动机，产品发动机（已成批投产的发动机，正式投产的发动机）

production flow 生产流程（= process flow）

production line 生产线，装配线

production model 生产车型，批量生产的车型

production parts 成批生产的零件

production per hour 每小时生产量

production personnel of motor transportation enterprise 汽车运输企业的生产人员

production planning 生产规划

production possibility 生产可能性

production process 生产过程

production program 生产计划，生产大纲

production prototype 投产原型，投产样品

production quality control 产品质量控制，产品质量管理（简称 PQC）

production quota 生产指标

production rate per hour 每小时生产率

production-release design 标准结构，标准设计，已通过生产的设计

production requirement 生产要求

production sample 产品样品

production specifications 生产技术条件

production targets 生产指标

production test 批量产品的试验，生产性试验

production test cell （新制造的发动机或其他产品的）生产性试验室

production tolerance 制造公差

production tooling 工艺装备，加工设备

production-type test 产品定型试验（见 production typical test）

production validation 许可生产，批准生产

production variations （发动机尺寸等制造中产生的）生产误差

production vehicle 投产车，成批生产车，产品车（正式成批生产的车辆）

production verification 批量生产合格证（简称 PV）

production verification specification 生产验证规范，生产验证技术条件（简称 PVS）

productive rate 生产率（= production rate, output rate, productivity rate）

productivity of autotransportation 汽车运输生产率（表示车辆利用效果的综合指标。一般指单位时间内车辆或车吨位完成的运量或周转量）

product line 产品系列（亦称 product range）

product of inertia of sprung mass about x and z-axis 簧上质量对 x 轴和 z 轴旋转的惯性积

product representation ①乘积表达（式）②产品描述，产品说明

product sign ①乘号②产品标志，产品代号

Products liability 负产品质量的责任，对产品质量负责

product(s) liability law 产品责任法［美国20世纪60年代、日本20世纪90年代制定的因产品缺陷造成人身伤害、财产损失时，可向生产者（厂家）提出损害赔偿的法律，简称 PS 法］

product styling 产品外形设计，产品形象设计，产品外形

product verification test 产品质量评价试验，产品质量检验试验

profession adaptability of driver （职业）驾驶（员）适应性（指驾驶员能够适应时刻变化的交通环境安全驾驶的生理、心理状态）

professional driver 职业驾驶员

professional driving competence 职业驾驶（员）资格（指从事职业驾驶员所必须具备的条件，如知识、技能等条件）

professional-grade 专业级的

professional racer ①职业赛车手

②专用赛车

proficient ①熟练的，精通的②专家

profile ①轮廓，断面，剖面，侧视图，轮廓设计②曲线图③纵断面，纵断面图

profile angle 齿形角，齿廓角

profile depth （轮胎的）胎面花纹深度（= tread depth）

profiled extrusion material 挤压成型材料

profile diagram 轮廓图

profile displacement 齿廓位移（直齿圆柱齿轮的齿形修正位移）

profile drag （汽车行驶的空气阻力中直接与外形有关的）形状阻力

profiled spring carrier 曲面钢板弹簧支架

profiled wiper （前照灯的）仿形刮水器（根据前照灯等外形表面特制的刮水器）

profile error 形状误差（如：齿形误差）

profile flow 翼型线流

profile ignition pickup sensor 仿形式点火信号传感器（福特公司使用的霍尔元件曲轴转速和位置传感器的商品名。电子控制模块按其传送的信号确定点火顺序与点火时刻，简称 PIP sensor）

profile meter （表面粗糙度）轮廓仪

profile modification 齿廓修形（指有意识地微量修削齿廓，使之偏离理论齿形）

profile of tooth 齿形，齿廓

profile outline 外形轮廓图

profile projector （轮廓曲线）光学投影仪

profile ratio （轮胎的）高宽比（轮胎断面高度与断面宽度的百分比，亦称 aspect ratio）

profile shaft 特形轴

profile shifted gear 交变齿轮，变位齿轮

profilometer ①轮廓曲线仪，轮廓仪，外形曲线测定仪②（道路）纵断面测绘仪③机械表面精测器，表面粗糙度测定仪，表面粗糙度轮廓仪④（地表）验平仪，自记纵断面测绘仪（= profilograph）

profit 利益，好处；利润，盈利

prognosticator 预报装置，预测器（= predictor）

program ①大纲，提纲，计划，方案②程序

program clock 程序控制时钟

program composition 程序编制

program-controlled running （发动机等的）程序控制运转

program control unit （汽车电子控制系统的）程序控制器（简称 PCU，= program controller，中央处理器中控制计算机指令的执行及其执行顺序的单元）

program counter （汽车电子控制系统的）程序计数器（= 指令计数器 instruction counter，指出下一条要解释的指令的地址）

program design 编制程序，程序设计（确立和规定某个程序的功能及其结构的过程）

programed test equipment 程序控制的试验设备

program (ing) unit （计算机语言中的）程序单位，程序段

program loading fatigue test 程序（控制）加载疲劳试验

programmable 可编程序的，可编程的（用来说明：①功能可通过编制程序来改变或建立的系统、装置、机构、控制器以及执行器、终端等；②可由用户使用编程器来编程的；③不是在制造时调整，而是由用户来调整的微机设备）

programmable automobile speed control system 车速程序控制系统

programmable diagnostics 程序控制

诊断

programmable logic array 可编程序逻辑阵列（简称 PLA，在其制成后可断开或接上内连线，以完成特定逻辑功能的集成电路）

programmable read only memories with erasable contents 可擦可编程序只读存储器（见 EPROM）

programmable readonly memory 可编程只读存储器（见 PROM）

programmable ride control system 可编程平顺性控制系统（由电子控制模块根据转向传感器、制动传感器、车速传感器、节气门开度传感器等的信号，确认车速、节气门开度、汽车侧向加速度、制动管路压力等超过预定值时，即通过执行器使悬架和减振器转至刚硬模式加大刚性。其他情况悬架和减振器回到柔顺模式，以保证车辆在各种行驶条件下都有良好的行驶平顺性和操纵性，亦称 programmed ride control system 程序变换式平顺性控制系统，均简称 PRC system）

programme 程序；大纲，方案，计划（=program）

programmed ①（按预先编制的）程序控制的（=program controlled）②按预先编制的程序规定的

programmed calibrations 预先编制的控制程序中规定的控制参数（如：点火提前角，燃油喷射量，怠速转速等）

programmed carburetor system （日本本田公司的）程序控制化油器系统（商品名，简称 PGM carburetor system，由电子控制模块根据水温、进气压力、转速等控制最佳空燃比）

programmed combustion 程序燃烧（方式）（美国福特公司研究发展的一种汽油喷射式层状燃烧方式，简称 PROCO）

programmed combustion engine 程序燃烧发动机（简称 PROCO engine 或 PROCO）

Programmed Driving System 程序控制导行系统（德国西门子公司试验的车辆行驶路线导行系统，由地面中心电子计算机通过车内的显示装置指引驾驶员选择最佳行车路线。简称 PDS）

programmed durability cycle （产品寿命试验）程序加载循环

Programmed-Fuel Injection 程序控制汽油喷射系统（见 PGM-Fi）

programmed instruction （人工-自动诊断等系统中向操作人员指示作业程序、工序等的）程序指示，程序指令

programmed nonvolatile memory 程序控制长存式存储器

programmed ride control 行驶平顺性程序控制（系统）（简称 PRC。仪表板上装有"软"、"硬"两挡悬架减振器模式选择开关，PRC 电子控制模块可根据驾驶者所选定的模式，通过电动执行机构调整减振器的阻尼特性。此外，当遇到紧急制动、急转弯、节气门开度超过 90% 或车速超过 132.8km/h 时，PRC 模块会发出指令，自动选择或改变减振器模式）

programmed self-steering system 程序控制自动转向系统（简称 PSS，1992 年法国雪铁龙汽车公司展出的 ZXAURA 轿车，当转弯行驶时，后轮能自动跟随前轮转向，以保证转弯时的通过性、操纵稳定性，该车系世界首次装有这种系统）

programmed spark advance 程序（控制）点火提前

programmer ①程序员（设计、编写、调试计算机程序的人员）②程序控制器 ③编程器（PROM programmer 的简称，亦称 programmer

program (me) selector （汽车电子控制系统的）控制程序选择件 [用于选择不同的控制程序，借以实现不同的控制模式。如：丰田 Camry 轿车仪表板上的电子控制自动变速器的换挡模式选择按钮开关 "pattern selector (button) switch" 就是一种控制程序选择开关。当该开关置于 "NORM" 位置时，按正常程序控制换挡模式，当按下该开关置于 "PWR" 功率位置时，便改为按功率程序控制换挡模式，即升挡或降挡车速或发动机转速均比正常换挡模式时高，以充分发挥汽车的动力性能]

programming 程序设计，程序编制

programming control 程序控制

programming language 程序设计语言（目前汽车计算机控制系统使用的程序设计语言多为 assembly languages 和 high-level languages）

program number （计算机）控制程序号（如：Cadillac 轿车空调的控制程序共有 101 种，分为 0~100 号，电子控制模块根据对车内气温与驾驶者所选定的温度的比较并考虑外界温度的影响，确定空调控制程序号，并按该程序控制风机速度、风门开度和制冷强度等）

program override （越过正在执行的自动控制程序而进行的）①人工操纵，手动控制②手动选择（另外的）控制程序

program parameter 程序参数

program selector 程序选择器

program test ①（计算机）程序校验，程序调试②程序（控制的）试验

progress 进步，发展

progress chart 进度表，进度图表

progress expectation research 预期性发展研究，远景发展研究

progression ①级数，数列②前进，渐进，进行，发展③一系列，连续④（曲线所表示的函数随自变量的）变化

progression jet （化油器的低-高速）过渡量孔（亦称 bypass hole）

progressive ①渐次的，渐进的，累进的，递增的②顺序联动的，顺序作用的③先进的

progressive-action test 递增加载试验（= progressive trial）

progressive analysis 累进分析法，逐步分析法

progressive approximation 逐步近似法（= successive approximation）

progressive assembly 流水线装配

progressive average 累加平均（= progressive mean）

progressive brake 渐进作用式制动器（制动力矩与踏板上的作用力成比例）

progressive braking 渐进制动（平稳地逐渐增加制动踏板力的平稳制动）

progressive carburettor 多腔分动式化油器（见 compound carburettor）

progressive characteristics （悬架刚度随荷载增加的）递增特性

progressive crack 扩展性裂纹

progressive damage 扩展性损坏

progress (ive) elongation 渐增性延伸

progressive error 累积误差，积累误差

progressive explosion 渐进式爆发燃烧（可燃混合气由外界火源点燃，围绕火花先形成燃烧火核，火焰前锋以一定的速率不断前进，参见 explosive combustion）

progressive failure 逐渐损坏

progressive linkage 顺序联动式控制杆系，依次联动式拉杆系

progressive(ly wound) valve spring （各圈间）变间距气门弹簧

progressive method 顺序法，渐进法

progressive pitting 扩展性点蚀

progressive power steering 递增式动力转向（日本丰田公司车速响应式动力转向"speed reaction type power steering"的商品名，车速越低，转向动力越大，转向盘越轻，车速越高，转向盘越重，以保证安全，简称 PPS）

progressive-rate suspension 刚度递增悬架（其刚度随荷载增加而成比例增大，简称 progressive suspension）

progressive ratio 速比

progressive spring 变刚度弹簧（其刚度随挠度而增加）

progressive swerving behavio(u)r （汽车）渐进偏转特性

progressive system （交通控制信号）绿线系统（所确定的绿灯始终可保证按规定车速在该信号系统所在线路上行驶的车群尽可能不停车地通过各交叉路口；有 simple progressive system 与 flexible progressive system 之分，前者称为简单绿线系统或固定的绿线系统，一天之内只有一种固定绿灯开闭时间，后者称为弹性绿线系统或可变绿线系统，其绿灯开闭时间一天之内有两种以上，可随交通状况而变。simple progressive system 又称 limited progressive system）

progressive transmission ①无级变速器（= stepless transmission）②顺序换挡式变速器（见 progressive type transmission）

progressive trial 逐步加载试验（= progressive-action test）

progressive type transmission 顺序换挡式变速器（变速杆按倒、空、1、2、3挡等顺序直线移动）

progressivity ①前进性，累进性，渐进性，递增性，进行性，进步性②（汽车转向速比的）渐变性（可变速比式转向机构）

progress of fatigue 疲劳损坏的扩展过程

progress of material wear 材料磨损过程

prohibit ①禁止②阻止，防止，制止

prohibitive overload 不容许的过载

prohibitory road sign 禁令性路标

project ①计划，方案②项目③题目④对象⑤草图⑥投射，放映，把…投影在…上（on），射出，发射

projected area ①投影面积②（轮胎的）印痕面积（指轮胎在规定的内压及静载下，胎面行驶面压在硬质平面上的投影面积，见 contact area）

projected-core spark plug （绝缘体）突出型火花塞（亦称 projected insulator nose spark plug 或 projected nose type spark plug，指绝缘体裙部突出在壳体端面之外的火花塞，亦称 projected nose type spark plug）

projected frontal area 正面投影面积

project engineer 项目主管工程师

projecting shaft ①悬伸轴，悬臂轴②轴的伸出部分

projection ①投影，投影图②凸出，凸出部分③计划，设计

projection drawing 投影图

projection line 投影线

projection screen 映像屏，投影屏，放映屏

projection type display 投影型显示

projection weld(ing) 凸焊，多点凸焊

projection weld machine 凸点电阻焊机，凸焊机

projective area of vehicle in direction of travel 车辆（按行驶方向的）正面（投影）面积

projective geometry 投影几何

projector ①探照灯②发射器③投射仪，投影仪④设计者，计划者⑤（画法几何）投影线

project organization 设计机构，项目编制

projector head lamp 聚光灯式前照灯（使用椭圆形反射镜和凸透镜式灯玻璃的前照灯，其光源布置在一次焦点上，反射镜反射的光在二次焦点上聚光并通过前面的凸透镜向路面折射，可有效地利用反射镜的反射光，且向上照射的光线少，可起到防炫作用，亦称 ellipsoid headlamp）

project study 专题研究，方案研究，项目研究

prolate cycloid 长幅摆线（在平面上某圆沿一直线无滑动地滚动时，该圆外并与该圆固连的一点的轨迹）

prolate epicycloid 长幅外摆线（在平面上一动圆沿一固定圆的外侧做内切或外切的纯滚动时，位于做外切的动圆之外或做内切的动圆之内并与动圆固连的一点的轨迹）

prolate hypocycloid 长幅内摆线（在平面上，一动圆沿一固定圆内侧作纯滚动时，在动圆之外并与动圆固连的一点的轨迹）

prolate involute 延伸渐开线（平面上一直线沿一固定圆作纯滚动时，与圆心同居于直线的某一侧并与直线固连的一点的轨迹）

proliferation 迅速扩大，快速增长，激增，扩散，繁殖

prolongation 延长，延期，延伸部分，延长部分

prolonged expansion （发动机燃烧气体的）持续膨胀

PROM ①行星式旋转活塞机（见 rotating piston machines similar to PLM）②可编程只读存储器（见 programmable read-only memory）

Prometheus 欧洲交通最高效率和空前安全纲要（Program for European Traffic with Highest Efficiency and Unprecedented Safety 的简称，本意为希腊神话中取天火给古人的普罗米修斯，其名正好与该纲要的简称吻合）

promethium 钷（Pm，第 61 号元素）

prominent 凸出的，突起的，著名的，杰出的，卓越的

promising 有前途的，有希望的，期望的，远景的

promote 促进，发扬，助长，发起，创立，提升

promotion 促进，加速，增进，助长；发起，倡议；开办，创建；提升；支持

promotions （车辆销售中的）促销活动（＝promotion activities）

promotor ①促进剂，加速剂，助触媒②加速器，激发器③发起人，创办人，促进者（＝promoter）

PROM pins （发动机电子控制模块的插装式）可编程只读存储器的插脚针

PROM socket 可编程只读存储器插座

prone 对…有倾向的（to）

Pron(e)y brake 普罗尼制动测功器（利用固体摩擦来消耗动力的最简单的吸收式测功器，由安装在曲轴或飞轮上的制动鼓及作用于该鼓上的制动带、弹簧秤、台秤等组成）

prong contact ①插销接触，插头接触，插接②插头触点

proof ①证明，证实②防…的，耐…的

proof by induction 归纳证明（法）

proof ground 试验场，试车场（＝testing ground）

proofing ①证实，验证②防护剂，涂防护剂③试验④防护

proof load ①（构件不致损坏的）

最大安全负荷②校验负荷，试验负荷，检验负载

proof pressure 保险压力（液压缸等不致产生损坏的最高压力）

proof strength 保证强度（弹性极限强度）

proof stress 弹性极限应力

proof test 校验，检验，可靠性试验，试用试验，验证试验

prop ①刚性支架，辅助支架，支柱，支杆，支持构件②支持，在下方用支架支住

propagate 传播，扩散，波及，增殖

propagation delay （信号等的）传递延迟，传播延迟，传递滞后

propagation delay time 传输延迟时，传输延时

propagation error 传输误差

propagation function 传播函数

propagation of error 误差的传播

propagation speed 传播速度（亦称 propagation velocity）

propane 丙烷（C_3H_8，液化石油气的主要成分，常温下为气体，加压易液化，无色，无臭，重为空气的1.5倍，发热量 $95488.7 kJ/m^3$）

propane-acid process 丙烷-酸法（精制润滑油）

propane-air mixture 丙烷-空气混合气

propane coach （发动机用丙烷作燃料的丙烷燃料客车）

propane-enrichment test （稀混合气浓度的）怠速丙烷加浓测试法（亦称 propane-enrichment idle fuel mixture check，简称 propane mixture check 或 test）

propane gas torch 丙烷喷灯（检查汽车冷气系统是否漏气的装置。该灯火焰遇制冷液的蒸汽后立即变色）

propane-powered vehicle 用液化丙烷为燃料的车辆

propel 推进，推动

propellant ①推进剂②推进的③火药④火器燃料

propellant-servicing vehicle 火箭燃料油罐车（= propellant tank vehicle，propellant truck）

propellant trailer 火箭燃料罐挂车

propeller 叶轮，推进器

propeller flowmeter 叶轮式流量计

propeller pump 叶轮泵

propeller-shaft （汽车）传动轴［带十字轴型万向节者亦称 cardan shaft，带万向节（含十字轴型万向节）者亦称 universal-joint shaft，一般指前置发动机后轮驱动式车辆动力装置和差速器之间带万向节的长驱动轴，简称 proshaft，美称 drive shaft］

propeller shaft center support 传动轴中间支承

propeller shaft housing 传动轴管［= cardan shaft housing，propeller (shaft) tube］

propeller-shaft intermediate bearing 传动轴中间轴承（亦称 propeller-shaft centre bearing）

propeller shaft joint 传动轴联轴节

propeller shaft shifting sleeve 传动轴滑套

propeller shaft tube 传动轴套管（= cardan tube）

propeller shaft tunnel （车身地板的）传动轴管状盖板（在万向节轴上方，车厢地板的管状凸起部，多见于轿车）

propeller shaft turning wrench 传动轴扳手

propelling energy 驱动能，推动能

propelling force 推进力，牵引力（= traction force，tractive power，motive force，propulsive force）

propelling rod 推力杆

propelling thrust 推动力，推进力，牵引力

propensity 倾向

propenyl 丙烯基（$CH_3CH:CH_3CH:CH-$）

proper 适合的，适当的，恰当的，特有的，专门的，固有的，本来的，正确的

proper function 特征函数；常义函数

proper head lamp （与其他车型的前照灯无互换性，专为某种车型独特设计的）专用型前照灯

properly seated 良好落座的，座面良好贴合的

proper mixture ratio 适当的混合比

property ①性能，特性，性质 ②财产，资产

property class number （打在公制螺栓头端面上表示其硬度或强度的）硬度级值（该数值越大，硬度越高）

property damage 财物损失（交通事故中可要求赔偿的财产损失，人身伤害及死亡不在其中）

property-determination test 定性试验

proper value 特征值

proper vibration 固有振动，自然振动

proportion 比，比例，部分，分量，（复）大小（长、宽、高），按比例分配

proportional ①比例的，按比例的 ②（数字的）比例量，比例数

proportional actuator （电子控制装置的）比例执行机构（输出与输入呈一定比例）

proportional control 比例调节，比例控制，线性控制（输出与输入呈线性关系）

proportional control action 比例控制动作（作用）（指输入与输出间具有连续的线性关系的控制作用）

proportional controller 比例调节器，线性调节器

proportional control system 比例控制系统

proportional counter 比例计数器

proportional curve 比例曲线，缩尺曲线

proportional divider （按）比例分配器，比例规

proportional error 相对（比例）误差率

proportional gain ①比例增益（由于比例控制作用引起的输出变化与输入变化之比）②比例放大

proportional-integral control action 比例-(加)积分控制动作（作用）（简称 PI，亦称 proportional plus integral control action，指比例加积分控制动作，如：汽车定速巡行控制系统"cruise control system"便是由比例加积分控制作用来修正实际车速与选定车速之间的误差的，见 PI speed error control）

proportionality factor 比例因子，比例常数

proportional limit 比限（= limit of proportionality）

proportional load synchromesh （同步啮合压力与换挡力成正比的）锁止式同步器（见 locking synchromesh）

proportional plus derivative controller 比例加微分控制器（产生比例加微分控制作用的控制器）

proportional (plus) differential control action 比例（加）微分控制作用（动作）

proportional plus integral controller 比例加积分控制器（产生比例加积分控制作用的控制器）

proportional plus integral plus derivativecontroller 比例加积分加微分控制器（产生比例加积分加微分控制作用的控制器，见 PID）

proportional sampler 比例取样器

proportional sampling 比例取样法，比例取样（如：根据发动机的进气量，按一定比例采集少量排气的取样法）

proportional scale 比例尺

proportional sensitivity 比例灵敏度，相对灵敏度

proportional solenoid 比例型电磁阀（指在加装的弹簧的作用下，其衔铁的行程可作为电流的函数来调节，即与电流成正比）

proportioner ①比例器，比例装置 ②（制动系统的）比例分配阀（控制后轮制动力，以防止后轮抱死或先于前轮抱死，见 proportioning valve）

proportioning 按比例定量，使成比例的

proportioning pressure regulator 比例式压力调节器

proportioning pump 比例计量泵

proportioning valve 比例（分配）阀（输入与输出压力等值增长到调节起点压力后，使输出压力值按小于1的比例增长的部件，如：装在后轮制动管路内控制后轮制动液压的比例阀，制动液压达到某规定值时，前轮制动液压的增量不变，而后轮液压的上升值则由该阀控制按一定比例减少，使前、后轮制动力的分配合乎或接近理想要求，前、后轮附着力被充分利用，且防止后轮先于前轮抱死，简称 P valve）

proportioning valve and bypass valve 与旁通阀制成一体的比例分配阀（其旁通阀用于管路破损时提供旁通通路）

proportion of ingredients 成分比例

proposal ①提议，建议 ②（厂家推出的）样车，新型车，新产品（等）

propose 提议，建议，打算，计划，推荐，提出

proposition 建议，主张，陈述，命题，讨论题，定理

proprietary ①专有的，特有的，独占的，有专利权的，（属于个人）所有的 ②所有权的，所有人

proprietary articles 专利品，专卖品，专利项目

proprietary design 专利设计（取得专利权的设计）

proprietary name 专利商标名

proprietary test 使用具有专利权的试验方法进行的试验

proprotionality 相称，比例，比值

propshaft （汽车）传动轴（见 propeller shaft）

prop shaft brake 传动轴制动器（中央轴制动器）

propuksin-torque proportioning （前、后轮或左、右车轮间的）驱动扭矩比例分配

propulsing-torgue （车轮的）驱动扭矩

propulsion ①推进，驱动 ②推进力，推力

propulsion motor/generator （复合动力车的）驱动电动机/发电机（该驱动电动机在汽车制动时被反拖起发电机的作用，将汽车的动能转变为电能向蓄电池充电）

propulsion power 驱动功率；驱动力

propulsion source 动力源

propulsive coefficient 推力系数，牵引力系数

propulsive efficiency 牵引效率

propulsive effort （驱动轮上的）驱动力（切线牵引力）

propulsive force ①原动力，推力，推进力，运动动力 ②（地面对车辆）的推力，切线牵引力（= propelling force）

propulsive power （汽车赖以行驶的）牵引力，驱动力

propulsive thrust 切线牵引力,驱动力。(行走机构)推进力

prop up 撑住,顶起,撑起,支撑,撑开

propyl 丙基

propylene 丙烯($CH_3CH:CH_2$);甲代乙撑;丙邻撑(CH_3CHCH_2-)

Prosmatic system (本田公司)电子控制自动变速器(商品名,亦写作 prosmatic system)

prospect 远景,前途,展望

prostand (摩托车的)折叠式停车支架

protactinium 镁(Pa)(= protoactinium)

protanopia (一种)红绿色盲(不能分辨红绿色,而且红色的相对光感较正常人弱)

protect 保护,防护

protecting 保护的,防护的

protecting cap 帽状保护罩(如:气门嘴护帽)

protecting cover 防护盖,护罩,防护套(= protective cover)

protecting device for inflating tire 轮胎充气保护装置,充气轮胎安全装置

protection 保护,防御;保护装置,保护措施,保护设备,护照,通行证

protection by metallic coating 用金属镀层保护

protection by oxide film 用氧化薄膜保护

protection by paints and lacquers 用涂料和漆保护

protection moulding 车身外部的防护性装饰条(见 moulding)

protection of pedestrains 行人安全措施

protection pressure 保护压力(由压力保护装置所维持的某一稳定压力)

protection pressure device (制动系的制动)压力保护装置(当某一制动装置或附件损坏后,可使其他部分制动装置仍维持一定制动压力的装置)

protection spring latch 弹簧护卡,弹簧锁卡

protection valve 安全阀

protective agent 防护剂(如:抗氧化剂)

protective atmosphere 防护气氛

protective coating ①保护涂层,防锈层②涂覆保护层等

protective earth(ing) 保护性接地,安全搭铁

protective film 防护膜,保护膜

protective finish 保护性加工(如:覆盖保护层)

protective shift control 安全换挡控制(防止误换挡的控制装置)

protector washer 保护垫圈,护垫,护圈(串列双腔式制动主缸中位于第一活塞及其油封间、用于支撑与保护油封的护圈垫)

protect rib (轮胎胎侧的)防擦线(亦称 kerbing rib,横凸在胎侧上部、保护胎侧不被擦伤的环形凸起胶棱)

protoactinium 镁Pa(第91号元素)

protocol 调查报告草案

proton (原子核中带正电的)质子(简称P)

proton exchange membrane fuel cell 质子交换膜燃料电池(简称PEM-FC,为了成为下一代汽车动力源的燃料电池,按其燃料和反应过程可分为三类:①hydrogen PEMFC 氢质子交换膜燃料电池,简称H-PEMFC ②methanol reforming fuel cell 甲醇重组燃料电池,简称MRFC ③director methanol fuel cell 直接甲醇燃料电池,简称DMFC)

prototyping platform 原型开发平台

prototype ①原型，样机，样板，样车，样品②足尺，模型，全尺寸模型，设计原型，模型机③典型，范例，标准，模范④实验性的，全尺寸模型的

prototype stage 原型阶段

prototype test 样机（品）试验，（机器设计的）原型试验

prototype vehicle 原型车，样车

protracted break 由于长时间受应力的作用而发生的破裂

protractor 量角器，分度规；半圆规

protruck 普罗赛车（一种在统一规格的底盘上，安装 V8 发动机和纤维增强塑料制客货两用车型高架车身的专用赛车）

protrude 凸出，伸出

protruding burrs 飞边，毛刺

protruding-core spark plug 芯部伸出的火花塞（亦称 projected-core spark plug）

protrusion ①突出，伸出②凸出部分，伸出部分

proud ①凸出于、高出于…之上②凸出于、高出于…之上的

prove (out) 试验，验证，证明

proven dependability 经过考验的可靠性

prove-out vehicles （在成批生产前生产的）小批试验性的车辆

proving ground （汽车）试验场（= testing ground）

provisional 临时性的，暂定的（亦写作 provisionary）

provisional license 临时许可证（如：临时驾驶证）

provisional weight （可卸除的）临时重量

prow 突出的前端（如长头车的车头）

prowl car 警备车，警察巡逻车

proximate analysis 近似（的）分析

proximate calculation 近似计算

proximity ①接近②邻近，附近，近程③接近度④近似⑤（金属的）接触溶积（在直接接触的两金属面间，金属自一个金属面上溶解析出，而沉积在另一个金属面上）

proximity beacon （一般设在关键性交叉路口或其他重要路边、通过短程无线电、微波或红外线信号向路过车辆内的接收器传送其所在位置或其他信息的）导航信号标柱

proximity effect 邻近效应

proximity radar 见 proximity warning indicator

proximity warning indicator （障碍物）接近警报器（当车辆接近障碍物时发出警报信号的探测装置，如障碍物接近探测雷达 "proximity radar"）

proximity (warning) sensor （可探测到其他车辆或障碍物）临近（的）传感器

proximi-valve 非接触式阀，邻近阀

PRS 踏板松脱系统（见 pedal release system）

PRT 高速个人客运（参见 personal rapid transit）

PR transducer 压力转换器（pressure transducer 的简称，将压力转换为电信号输出的器件，用作电子控制系统的压力传感器时，= pressure sen-sor）

PRV 压力调节阀（pressure regulating valve 的简称）

Prévention Routière Internationale ［法］国际交通事故预防委员会（国际的一个非营利的道路安全委员会，简称 PRI）

pry 撬杆，撬棍（= pry bar）

PS ①德制马力，公制马力（德语 Pferdestarke 的简称，IPS = 0.735 kW. 见 Cheval. vapeur 及 metric horse power）②皮秒（picosecond）

③（零）件，片（参见 pieces）
④规划研究（见 planning study）
⑤聚苯乙烯（见 polystyrene）
⑥［美刊］大众科学（见 Popular Science）
⑦附言，又及（见 postscript）
⑧助力传向（见 power-assisted steering）
⑨电力供应（见 power supply）
⑩预（加）应力（见 prestress）
⑪操作说明书（见 process specifications）
⑫伪造的，假的（见 pseudo）
⑬拉线开关（见 pull switch）

PSA （法）标致汽车集团（Peugeot sA 的简称）

P/S anticipate switch 动力转向预控开关（power steering anticipate switch 的简称，亦称 P/S switch，为一液压控制的电路开关，当动力转向压力超过某规定极限值时，该开关断开。点火开关接通后，蓄电池的电压经该开关送到发动机电子控制模块。如果怠速期间该开关断开，发动机电子控制模块接线柱上的该信号电压将降为0，于是发动机电子控制模块将加大节气门开度，以支持增加的发动机负荷）

PS car test 美国大众科学杂志（Popular Science）（组织的）轿车评价试验（试验项目包括燃料经济性、加速性能、制动性能、控制与操纵性能、舒适性、低噪声、宽敞性、视野、上下方便性等10项，见 PS rat-ings）

PSD 功率频谱密度（power spectrum density）

PSE （控制中央门锁等的）气动系统装置（pneumatic system e-quipment 的简称）

pseudo ①伪造的，假冒的，赝，伪 ②准的，拟（似）的

pseudo-stable ouput pattern （时序电路的）伪稳定输出图形（亦称 pe-sudo-stable output configuration "伪稳定输出组态"，指产生或维持它的激励被非激励的输入组态代替后，则不再继续存在的输出组态）

PSh 马力·小时

PSHEV 见 series-parallel hybrid drive type electric vehicle

psi 磅/英寸^2（pounds per square inch）

psia （英制）绝对压强（1bf/in^2）（pound per square Inch absolute）

PS idle up control valve 动力转向怠速提高阀（PS 为 power steering 的简称。装有动力转向系统的车辆在发动机怠速运转期间转向，该阀可提高发动机转速，以保证驱动转向机构所要求的动力，防止发动机怠速熄火）

psig （英制）表压（1bf/in^2）（pounds per square inch gauge 的简称）

PSK 移相键控（phase-shift keying）

P-skeleton of a complex 复合形的 P 维（度）骨架

PSM 保时捷稳定性控制系统（Porsche Stability Management 的简称，汽车弯道转向稳定性控制系统的商品名，当弯道转向出现转向不足时，对弯道内侧的前、后车轮施加制动，而当转向过度时，则对弯道外侧的前、后轮施加制动，若制动尚不能校正汽车行驶方向，则控制发动机扭矩，以保证车辆稳定转向。这一系统还配有自动锁紧式差速器。此外，若该系统处于关闭状况，遇紧急情况急制动时，该系统也会自动启动）

PS meter 功率表，马力表

P-S-N fatique curve 概率疲劳曲线（表示某给定概率 P 时的疲劳曲线。P 为破坏概率，S 为试件的疲劳强度，N 为疲劳寿命）

psophometer 噪声计

PSP 动力转向压力开关（power steering pressure switch 的简称，亦写作

puwer steering pras. sw. 美国政府规定从1995年1月1日起，一律以这一术语表示汽车动力转向压力开关，而取代福特公司使用的 psps，通用公司使用的 pssw。当动力转向液压超过某规定值，如 400～600 PSI 时，该开关闭合，此时电子控制模块将提高怠速转速，以补偿所增加的发动机负荷）

PS ratings 美国大众科学杂志轿车评分（根据轿车试验报告进行的评分，采用五级分制试验项目：燃料经济性，加速性能，制动性能，控制与操纵性能，舒适性，低噪声，宽敞性，视野，上下方便性等 10 项）

PSS 程序控制自动转向系统（见 Pro-grammed Selfsteering System）

PS serviceability ratings （美国）大众科学（杂志）汽车维护方便性评价（标准）（评价项目. 检查冷却水、机油等液面；检验发动机火花塞、分电盘、饥油滤清器等；曼侠水箱软管；更换前照灯、尾灯、停车灯等的灯泡；检查熔断丝；装卸备胎；更换皮带。根据进行这些项目的难易程度评价车辆维护的方便性）

PS type brake coliper 浮钳式盘式制动器的浮钳（pin slide type disc brake caliper 明同称）

PSV ①客运车辆（passenger service vehicle）②公用运输车辆（public service vehicle）

PSW ①（节气门等处于）大开度位置（触点式）传感器（position sensor-wide 的简称，向电子控制模块提供全负荷工况信息）②位置开关（position switch 的简称）③停车挡开关（parking switch 的简称）④压力开关（pressure switch 的简称）⑤电压开关

psychological 心理的。心理学的

psychology 心理学，心理

psychophysical effects of transportation 运输的心理、生理效应（指运输工具噪声、排出有害物、事故伤害、乘坐舒适性及驾驶. 操纵特性等对驾驶与乘坐人员心理、生理的影响）

psychophysiological measurement 生理心理检查，生理心理诊断

psychotechnic test 工程心理学试验

psychrometric chart 空气湿度图

psy～hrometer 湿度计（干湿球湿度计，干湿计）

PT ①节气门部分开启（part throttle）②纸带（paper tape）③光电管（phototube）④压缩空气输送管（pneumatic tube）⑤切点（Point of tangeney）⑥电源变压器（power transformer）⑦压力试验（pressuretest）⑧验收试验（proof test）

Pt ①品脱（英制容量单位，pint）②铂（platinum）

PTA ①[美]公共运输协会（Public Transport Association）；②[英]客运管理局（Passenger Transport Authorl ties）

PT accel 缓加速（节气门部分开启加速，partial throttle acceleration 的简称）

PT-AFC pump （Cummins 公司柴油机的）压力-时间、空燃比控制式喷油泵（pressure- timing air-fuel control pump 的简称）

PTC 正温度系数（见 positive tempera ture coefficient）

PTCA 美国私人载货汽车委员会（PdsateTruck Council of America, Inc）

PTC thermistor 正温度系数黝电阻（positive temperature coefficient thermistor）

Pterminal ①继电器接线柱（relay terminal）②正极接线柱

PTFE 聚四氟乙烯（polytetrafluo-ro-ethylene）

PTFE-lined seal 聚四氟乙烯衬面油封

PT fuel injection system 压力-时间控制式燃油喷射系（pressure and time fuel injection system 的简称，喷油量由燃油压力和量孔开启时间来控制的柴油机喷油系，用于美国康明斯系列柴油机）

P-T fuel pump assembly 压力-时间喷油泵总成

PT fuel system （Cummins 公司柴油机的）压力-时间燃油喷射系统（pressure-timing fuel system 的简称，以 pressure 为喷油量控制变量的机械式共用高压储油歧管型燃油喷射系统）

PT injector 压力-时间控制式喷油器

PT inner electrode （ZrO_2 氧传感器的）内层铂电极（内层的多孔铂导电膜，见 ZrO_2 tube）

PTO （亦写作 pto）①见反面，见下页（please turn over）②动力输出装置，取力器（power take-off）

pto coupling 动力输出轴联轴节

pto-driven trailer 动力输出轴驱动的挂车（挂车本身有驱动桥，亦称 power take off trailer）

pto horsepower （以马力计的）动力输出装置功率

p-to-P （正负）峰间值（从最大值到最小值，peak-to-peak 的简称）

pto power 动力输出轴功率，动力输出装置功率

ptotoeffect 光电效应（photoelectric effect 的简称，由光照引起电导率变化的现象）

PT outelectrode （ZrO_2 氧传感器的）外层铂电极（外层的多孔铂导电膜，见 ZrO_2 tube）

PTP 对等网络技术（peer to peer 的简称，指不同 Pc 用户之间不必经过中继设备直接交换数据或服务的技术，每个人都可以直接连接到其他用户的计算机，进行信息交换，不需要连接到服务器上浏览与下载，使网络上的沟通更容易、更直接）

pts 零件（parts）

PTS 踏板行程传感器（pedal travel sensor 的简称）

PT system 压力-时间（控制）

P-type highway 小轿车专用道路（passenger car type highway，专门按小轿车设计的道路，禁止货车通行）

P-type material P 型（半导体）材料（指加有铟 In 等微量元素而在半导体内空穴密度远超过电子密度，因而空穴成为电流多数载流子的非本征半导体材料）

P-(type), = P-type semiconductor region （P-N 靖等的）P 型区

Pu 钚（plutonium）

pubdle lamp （车门开启时照亮门槛用的）车门槛照明灯

public ①公共的，公众的，公开的 ②公众

public-address truck 广播车（= sound truck）

publication ①发表，公布，出版。发行 ②出版物，刊物

public automobile 公用轿车

public bus 公共汽车

public car station 公共汽车站，电车站，长途客车站

public conveyance 公共运输，公共交通

public garage 公用车库

public highway 公用公路，公路（= traffic way）

public nuisance 公害

public parking area 公共停车场区

public parking garage 公共停车库

public passenger transport 公共客运

Public Roads Administration ［美］

公路管理局（旧称，简称 PRA）
public service 公用事业
public service vehicle 公共客运车辆，公共汽车（一般指专业运输公司的载客量为 12 人或 12 人以上的出租或收费客车）
public transit 公共交通（行驶一定线路，经过指定的停车点，包括公共汽车、有轨或无轨电车、火车，也包括班机、班轮）
public transport 公共运输（区别于工厂、企业自有车辆的运输，= com-mon transport）
Public Transport Association 公共运输协会（简称 PTA）
public transportation systems 公共运输系统（= mass transportation systems）
public utilities （城市）公用设备，公用服务事业（如公共汽车公司等）
public vehicle traffic 社会车辆（非企业自身的车辆）运输，公用运输
public works vehicle 公用事业车（如邮政车，警车，通信车等）
Puch engine Y 形连杆式 U 内燃机（双缸单室式内燃机 "split-single" 的变形，将原来的两根铰接式连杆改成 Y 形连杆，见 U-engine）
puckering 起皱（= wrinking）
puddle （汽车越野赛线路中的）泥水坑
puddle welding 堵焊，边孔焊（亦称 plug welding）
puddling 捣成泥浆
puffs 皮皮法拉（picofarad，见 farad）
Pulair shutoff valve 排气负压二次空气截止阀（通用公司 CCC 系统中使用的排气负压脉冲空气控制阀，亦称 exhaust air induction control valve "排气脉冲吸气控制阀"，简称 EA-ICV。该阀由电子控制模块控制的真空膜片控制，仪在发动机热起工况时开启，利用排气脉冲可在吸入新鲜空气传废氧中的 HC，CO 等氧化）
pull ①拉，拖，牵引；扯开，拔除；吸收，吸引；获得 ②牵引力，拖力；引力 ③把柄；拉绳
pull action cylinder 拉力油缸
pull back bar 回位拉杆
pull back spring 复位弹簧
pullback weight 平衡重（= balance weight）
pull button 拉钮
puller 拉器（拆卸器，亦称 puller tool，pulling tool）
puller system （校正弯曲车架等使用的）拉力装置
pulley ①滑车，滑轮 ②传动带轮
pulley block 滑车组，滑轮组
pulley drive 传动带传动（简称 PD，= belt drive）
pulley extractor 传动带轮拉器
pulley groove 传动带轮上的传动带槽
pulley ratio 传动带传动比，传动带传动变速比（从动轮 – 驱动轮有效直径比）
pull hook 牵引钩（= drawbar hook）
pull-in ①拉入 ②（汽车）驶入路边或备用停车道
pull-in-and-slide window 拉滑式车窗
pull-in coil 吸引线圈（在电磁开关内，吸动铁芯，使触点闭合的线圈，亦称 pull-in winding，closing coil）
pulling ability 拉曳能力，牵引能力
pulling force 拉力，牵引力（= pulling power）
pulling jack 拉力千斤顶
pulling lever ①拉杆 ②（支点在中间或可嗣，一端受拉，另一端起推动作用的）摆杆（可改变力作用方向

的杠杆，美称 swivel lever)

pulling. off device （陷入泥潭中的车辆的）拉出装置

pulling relay coil 继电器吸合线圈

pull-in torque 牵入转矩，同步力矩，牵入同步力矩（步进电动机）

pull-in winding （起动电机开关内的）吸合线圈

pullman-limousine （驾驶区与后座区之间有隔栏的）大型豪华轿车（亦称 pullman saloon, executive limousine, saloon with divider）

pull off （汽车）驶离公路停车，驶离道路停车

pull-off coupling 拉脱式软管接头

pull-off spring 拉簧（一般指用于使气压或液压推动的工件，如制动蹄等回到非工作位置的复位拉簧）

pull out 牵出，拉出；汽车驶离车站，汽车驶出交通线；汽车驶离路沿

pull-out ashtray （座位上）推拉式烟灰盘

pull-out hand brake 手拉式驻车制动器

pull-out seat 拉出式座椅（备用座椅）

pull-out spot 路边停车坪，路侧驻车点

pull-out torque ①牵出转矩②临界过载力矩（如：同步电动机的失步转矩，感应电动机在额定电压及频率下运转时能发出的最大转矩）

pull-over （电机在运转时，出现转子与壳体接触擦磨的不正常现象，一般称为）扫膛（故障）

pull rod 拉杆

pull roke （油缸）活塞杆拉回行程

pull side （传动带或传动链的）紧边（拉力边，拉力面）

pull-slip evaluation of vehicle 车辆的牵引力-滑转率曲线评价

pull switch 拉线开关，拉钮开关，拉出式开关（简称 PS）

pull tension gauge 牵引力计，拉力计，张力计

pull test ①拉伸试验②拉力试验，牵引力测定

pull the lever （操纵者）将操纵杆拉向自身，拉近操纵杆

pull tongue 牵引架，拖杆（= draw tongue）

pull type 拖挂式的，牵引式的

pull type belt 通过拉力来传递动力的）拉力型传动带

pull-type clutch 拉式离合器（指分离时，分离轴承被拉离飞轮的离合器，相对于常规的、分离时分离轴承被推离飞轮的推式离合器 "push-type clutch" 而言）

pull type CVT 拉力型无级连续变速器（指使用拉力型传动带的CVT）

pull-up ①停车；刹住，停住②吸引；拉起③张力

pull-up torque （感应电动机）最小起动转矩

pull wire 牵引索，索引线，拉紧线，拉索，传动索

pull wire guide collar 拉索导套

pulpwood body 运输纸浆原材的车厢

pulsair system （通用公司）排气负压脉冲二次空气吸入系统[商品名，见 pulse (air) injection system]

pulsate ①脉动，波动，（有规律的）跳动，振动②脉动的，脉冲的

pulsating air intake 脉动进气

pulsating current 脉冲电流

pulsating flow gas turbine 脉动式燃气轮机

pulsating load 脉动荷载

pulsating movement 脉动

pulsating pressure 脉冲压力

pulsating stress 循环应力，脉动应力

pulsation ①脉冲，波动②交流电的角频率

pulsation damper 脉动平缓器（如消除油泵供油中的脉动或脉冲现象的平缓装置）

pulsation effect 脉动效应（亦称 pulsating effect）

pulsation error 脉动误差

pulsation-free 无波动的，平稳的

pulsation loss 脉动损失

pulsation welding 脉冲焊（接触焊）

pulsator ①脉动器，振动器，脉动试验机，振动试验机，脉冲振动机（= agitator）②液压拉伸疲劳试验机③蒸气双缸泵④（电子汽油喷射系统中连接油泵与汽油管并隔离油箱总成的机械振动和油压脉动的）脉动消除装置

pulsatron 双阴极充气三极管

pulse ①脉冲②脉动③加以脉冲信号，通以脉冲电压，发出脉冲

pulse 脉冲发生器，脉冲装置

pulse air check valve （排气负压）脉冲二次空气（系统中的）止回阀（简称 PACX，见 pulsair system）

pulse airfeeler （排气负压）脉冲（二次空气吸入系统的）空气供给装置（简称 PAF）

pulse air induction (reactor) system （排气负压）脉冲二次空气吸入反应系统 ［见 pulse (air) injection system］

pulse (air) injection system 排气负压二次空气吸入系统（亦称"pulse air induction reactor system, pulsating-air system，商品名：Pulsair system，简称 P-AIR，利用排气脉冲产生的负压将新鲜空气吸入排气管，使废气中的 CO、HC 氧化而减少其排出量的系统，新鲜空气在负压作用下经一止回阀吸入排气流中，该止回阀称 air check valve, pulse air check valve 或 exhaust air induction control valve，简称 EAIV"）

pulse amplifier 脉冲放大器

pulse amplitude 脉冲幅度（①无特别说明时指脉冲的最大瞬时值②脉冲的宽度、大小，但应加上平均"average"，瞬时"instantaneous"峰"peak"，均方根"rms"等形容词具体限定共意义）

pulse amplitude modulation 脉冲幅度调制

pulse-code modulation 脉码调制（简称 PCM）

pulse control modulation 脉冲控制调制（简称 PCM）

pulse converter supercharging 脉冲转换器增压（在废气涡轮前装有脉冲转换器，使涡轮进口处的排气脉冲压力近于稳定的增压）

pulse corrector 脉冲校正电路

pulse damper 脉动衰减器，脉冲阻尼器（= pulsation damper）

pulsed attenuator 脉冲分压器，脉冲衰减器

pulsed-doppler radar 脉冲调制多普勒雷达系统（简称 PD radar）

pulse delay fall time 脉冲下降延迟时间，下降时延

pulse delay rise time 脉冲上升延迟时间，上升时延

pulse delay variable resistor （间歇式风窗刮水系统中控制刮水停歇时间的）可变脉冲延时电阻器

pulse-detecting circuit 脉冲检测电路

pulsed laser beam 脉冲激光光束

pulsed laser power 脉冲激光功率

pulse Doppler radar （脉冲）多普勒雷达（见 PD radar）

pulse drop 脉冲衰减

pulse duration 脉冲宽度（脉冲持续时间，亦称 pulse length, pulse width, 指脉冲波形的上升和下降曲线；即前沿和后沿在半幅度点"half-amplitude points"间的时间间隔）

pulse duration modulator 脉冲宽度

调制（指随输入信号调整脉冲的宽度，简称 PPM，见 pulse width modulation）

pulse EGR 脉冲式废气再循环

pulse electrochemical finishing 脉冲电化学光整加工（简称 PECF）

pulse electrochemical mechanical machining （零件表面的）脉冲电化学机械加工（简称 PECM）

pulse exhaust manifold （内燃机）脉动排气管（容积较小，聚集某几个汽缸排出的废气，呈脉冲状输出的排气歧管）

pulse flow performance 脉冲流特性，波动流特性

pulse-forming network 脉冲形成电路（亦称 pulse former, pulse shaper）

pulse frequency ①脉冲频率②（驾驶员等的）脉搏（数）

pulse full time 脉冲下降时间

pulse generator ①脉冲发生器②（特指电子点火系）点火信号发生装置（亦称 pick-tip module）③（泛指各种随发动机曲轴、凸轮轴或变速器轴旋转而切割磁场产生脉冲电压信号的车速、转速、轴位置等的）脉冲式传感器

pulse input running test 脉冲输入行驶试验（汽车驶过凸块或凹块的平顺性试验）

pulse length modulation 脉冲宽度调制（简称 PLM，见 pulse width modulation）

pulse-manifold assembly 脉冲式进气歧管总成

pulse modulation 脉冲调制［简称 PM，为脉冲幅度调制（PAM）、脉冲宽度调制 PWM 和脉冲位置调制（PPM）的总称］

pulsemotor 步进电动机（亦称 step by step motor, stepping motor）

pulse overlap 脉冲重叠

pulse packet 脉冲群

pulse per revolution 每一转的脉冲数

pulse radar 脉冲式雷达

pulse repetition frequency 脉冲重复频率

pulse response 脉冲响应（特性曲线）

pulse response test 脉冲响应试验（如：以脉冲形式进行操纵输入，用横摆角速度、侧倾角等评价汽车响应特性的试验）

pulse ringing 脉冲瞬变

pulse ripple 脉（冲波）动

pulse rise time 脉冲上升时间

pulse separator 脉冲分离器

pulse sequence 脉冲串，脉冲列

pulse sequential type fuel injection 脉冲顺序汽油喷射（按各汽缸点火顺序，在规定的时刻，将汽油喷至进气孔附近或直接喷入缸内，喷油量决定于脉冲宽度）

pulse-shaping circuit 脉冲整形电路

pulse signal 脉冲信号

pulse signal interface 脉冲信号接口

pulse time 脉冲时间

pulse timing 脉冲计时

pulse totalizer 脉冲计数器

pulse transformer 脉冲变压器（= peak transformer）

pulse trigger 脉冲触发器

pulse triggered bistable circuit 脉冲触发双稳态电路

pulse tubo-charging 脉冲涡轮增压（废气涡轮增压的一种，进入废气涡轮增压器的废气压力呈脉冲状态）

pulse type sensor 脉冲型传感器（见 counting type sensor）

pulse vacuum hublock system 脉冲式真空轮毂锁系统（利用发动机进气歧管真空来控制的前轮毂与分时式四轮驱动车前桥半轴结合和脱开的机构，简称 PVH system）

pulse wheel 脉冲盘（电子点火系统点火脉冲信号发生器中带凸齿等的圆盘，其齿切割或隔断磁路，而产生点火脉冲信号，亦称 pulse generating wheel）

pulse width 脉冲宽度（见 pulse duration）

pulse width command 脉冲宽度指令（利用脉冲宽度表示的指令，如根据脉冲宽度确定喷油量的电磁阀开启时间长度指令）

pulse width control map （电子汽油喷射系统决定喷油器通电时间的）脉冲宽度控制曲面（由脉冲宽度随发动机负荷、转速、空燃比而变化的特性曲线构成的三维特性曲面图）

pulse width modulated alternator 脉冲宽度调制型交流发电机（简称 PWM alternator，可随发动机负荷和蓄电池充电状态控制发电量。下坡等发动机制动或减速时发电量最大）

pulse width-modulated power signal 脉冲宽度调制功率信号

pulse width modulating solenoid valve 脉冲宽度调制式电磁阀（简称 PWM solenoid，或 PWM valve，由脉冲宽度，即通电时间长短来控制其开启时间的电磁阀，亦写作 pulse width modulated solenoid，简称 pulse width solenoid）

pulse width modulation 脉（冲）宽（度）调制（简称 PWM，亦称 pulse duration modulation，简称 PDM，pulse length modulation，简称 PLM，①指通过改变脉冲上升沿和下降沿在脉冲幅度 50% 处的时间间隔，产生所要求的频率和占空比的波形的控制脉冲信号②用两种不同宽度的脉冲分别表示信息位"1"和"0"的二进制信道编码）

pulse wiper system 间歇式风窗刮水器系统（刮水器每运转一周停歇 0~25 秒）

pulsometer 脉冲计，脉搏表，脉动表

pulverization ①金属喷镀②喷雾，雾化③磨碎，碾碎。研末，粉末化

pulverization earburettor 喷雾式化油器

pulverized coal 粉煤，煤粉（=powdered coal）

pulverized coal engine 煤粉发动机

pulverized fuel ①雾状燃料②粉末燃料（亦写作 pulversed fuel）

pulverizer ①喷雾器，喷嘴②粉碎机

pulverizer 喷雾，碾碎

pulverizing technology 粉末化技术，碎粉技术

pump ①泵②泵送

pumpability 泵送性能，泵送特性（如：发动机油底壳内的机油，通过机油泵泵送到各润滑部位的性能，机油低温起动的一项重要指标）

pumpability reference oil 泵送性能试验用参考油（简称 PRO）

pump accumulator of hydraulic active suspention 主动式液压悬架系统的输油泵—（高压—稳压）储油筒总成

pump adjustment screw 泵调节螺钉

pumpage 泵流量（抽吸能力）

pump-and-injector unit 连泵喷油嘴总成（高压油泵与喷嘴制成一体）

pump-and-injector-unit-control rack 连泵喷油器的供油量控制齿条

pump-and-injector-unit follower 连泵喷油嘴推杆

pump-and-motor-displacement control （静液压传动的）泵和马达排量控制

pump blade ①泵的叶片②（变矩器）泵轮叶片

pump body 泵体

pump bypassing 泵的旁路、旁通阀

pump capacity 泵容量，泵流量
pump check valve 泵止回阀
pump circulation 泵循环（压力循环，强制循环，泵唧循环）
pump control rack （柴油机）喷油泵（齿杆式喷油量调节机构的）调节齿杆（该杆上有齿与调节齿套式齿圈啮合，其轴向位置由调整器控制）
pump cooling 泵循环水冷（强制冷却）
pump delivery 泵流量，泵生产率
pump discharged pressure 泵输出压力
pump displacement （活塞）泵的排量
pump drive 泵的驱动机构
pump duty ①泵的生产率，泵的输出量②泵的运转工况
pump efficiency 泵效率（驱动能量与输出之比）
pump-fed lubrication （由油泵给油实现润滑的）强制润滑（=forced feed lubrication）
pump frequency 活塞或柱塞泵的工作频率（如曲轴每转泵油次数，柴油机高压油泵供油频率）
pump impeller （液力变矩器等的）泵轮。
pumping action 泵唧作用，泵送作用
pumping braking 点刹制动（操作，以防止车轮抱死）
pumping chamber ①（二冲程发动机的）预压缩室（见 precompression chamber）②（活塞或柱塞式油泵的）泵腔，泵室
pumping cylinder 泵缸
pumping element spacing （柴油机）柱塞式喷油泵缸心距（指其相邻两柱塞偶件轴线间的距离）
pumping loss 泵气损失（消耗于进、排气上的发动机功率）

pump (ing) plant 泵站
pumping plunger 泵油柱塞
pump island （加油站安装）加油泵柱的岛形凸台
pump jet 加速（泵）量孔（=accel-crating pump jct）
pumpless diesel engine 无（喷油）泵式柴油机
pump lift 泵的扬程（泵的压头高度）
pump/motor assembly 泵带电动机总成（简称 pump/motor）
pump noise rating 油泵额定噪声（油泵噪声额定值，简称 PNR）
pump of constant delivery type 定量泵
pump of variable delivery type 变量泵
pump output 泵生产率（泵流量）
pump output power 泵的输出功率（由泵传给所泵送的流体的能量）
pump plate （冷却系变速风扇中的）泵盘
pump plunger cylinder （油）泵柱塞缸
pump powered hydraulic brakes 液压泵驱动式液力制动器
pump primer 泵起动注液装置（指水泵或油泵等吸入管道内无水或无油时，利用手柄操作等将其中注满油或水，以排除气阻等，使泵能以始动的装置）
pump regulator pressure 泵的调节压力（调节器控制的输出压力上限）
pump relay （电子控制喷油系的）电磁泵继电器（控制泵动作的继电器）
pump rotor 泵芯（指泵轮轴，泵轮及轴承，密封件等其他旋转件组成的离心泵转子总成）
pump's air 空气泵输送的空气，泵入的空气
pump seizure 泵卡死，泵卡滞

pump shaft 泵轴
pump spacer 马达式燃油泵的泵体
pump stick 泵卡滞（如喷油泵柱塞卡死）
pump stroke 泵行程
pump suction tube 油泵吸油管
pump-system water cooling 水泵强制循环冷却（＝forced water cooling, forced circulation cooling）
pump unit 泵机组
pump up ①（液压式气门挺杆的）泵升现象（高速时气门不能完全落座，而被液压式挺杆微微顶起的现象）②泵出，泵送
pump valve 泵阀
pump vane 泵叶轮，泵轮
pump wheel ①（离心）泵叶轮②（变矩器）泵轮
pump with automatic valves 带自动控制阀的（液压）泵
punch ①冲模，冲头，冲孔机②冲孔，冲压
punching pressure 冲击贯入压力
punching voltage 击穿电压
punch through 击穿现象，穿通现象（如晶体管发射极或集电极的空间电荷区向基区侵入现象）
puncture 戳穿，刺破，扎破，穿孔（俗称 punc）
punctured float 渗漏的浮子（＝leak-ing float）
puncture-proof tire 防穿孔轮胎（胎面有很高的抗穿孔强度，或穿孔后能自动黏合的轮胎，＝trouble-proof tire, puncture-sealing type, self-seal-ing）
puncture resistance 抗穿刺强度，抗穿孔强度
puncture-resistant 防刺破的（轮胎等）
puncture-sealing tire 胎面穿孔时自动封合的轮胎（＝self-sealing tire）
puncture test ①（轮胎）穿孔试验②（绝缘体）击穿试验
punishing start 在艰难工况下起动
punishing stress 疲劳破坏应力
punishing test 补偿性试验（普通试验结果不满意时所做的补充试验）
punt chassis 中央独梁式底盘（＝backbone chassis）
pupil ①（小）学生②瞳孔，光瞳
pupillary distance （在既定凝视点上的左右）瞳孔中心距（简称PD）
puppet valve 菌状阀（多用于内燃机的进排气门，由凸轮直接或通过摇臂-延杆机构等顶开，由弹簧复位，＝poppet valve，简称poppet）
PUR 见 polyurethane
purchase ①起重装置（特指滑车等）②购买
purchase block 起重滑车
pure 纯的，无杂质的，清洁的
pure bending 单纯弯曲（＝simple bending）
pure electric vehicle （相对混合动力车而言的）纯电动汽车［简称 pure EV，亦称 full battery electric vehicle（全蓄电池供电电动车）］
pure EV sports car 纯电动跑车，纯电动运动车
pure front impact 纯前面受撞（指作用于受撞车辆前面的主要力相对于该车纵向对称平面的夹角不大于45°）
pure gas-turbine engine 纯燃气涡轮发动机（指无冷却器和预热器的燃气涡轮发动机）
pure hydrocarbon 单一的烃，单一碳氢化合物
puremethanel fuel 纯甲醇燃料（＝M100fuel）
pure oscillation 正弦波振荡
pure rear impact 纯后面受撞（指作用在受撞车辆后面的主要力不大于45°该车纵向对称平面的夹角不大于45°）
pure rear impact 纯后面碰撞（指作

1257

用于受撞车辆后面的主要撞击力与该车纵向对称平面的夹角不大于45°)

pure rolling wheel 纯滚动车轮

pure rubber rotary shaft lip seal 无骨架旋转轴唇形密封件(纯橡胶制的供旋转轴用的唇形密封圈)

pure slip 纯滑移,纯滑动

pure sound 纯声,纯音(= pure tone)

pure stress 单一应力,单向应力

purfying rate 净化率(指在安装排放净化系统前后某种排放物降低的比率 $R = (1 - B/A) \times 100\%$,式中:$A$ 装排放净化系统前某种排放物的浓度,B 装排放净化系统后,某种排放物的浓度)

purge ①排污,除去杂质,净化,提纯②(用空气等)吹洗、吹净③清除、扫荡④(特指将蒸发排放物控制系统的活性炭罐存储装置中存储的蒸发排放物,吸入或释放到发动机进气系统的)清除(过程)

purge cock [美]放泄塞。排污开关,清洗螺塞(= drain plug, drain tap, discharge cock)

purge control valve ①清除阀(见 purge④及 purge valve①)②(控制活性炭罐蒸发排放物清除孔开启与关闭的清除阀的膜片上方进气歧管真空通路的)控制阀(为一个由电子控制模块控制的电磁阀,该控制阀开启时,真空进入上述膜片上方,膜片升起带动清除阀将清除孔开启)

purge hose (燃油蒸发排放物控制系统中,连接活性炭罐与进气歧管的)清除软管(存储在活性炭罐中的燃油蒸汽经该管输入进气歧管)

purge line 连接活性炭(罐和进气歧管的)清除管道

purge port ①清污孔,排污孔②(特指蒸发排放物控制系统活性炭罐内存储的蒸发排放物随吸入的空气一起进入进气管的)清除孔(该孔的开闭及开度由清除阀控制,见 purge valve 及 purge control valve)

purge switch (燃油式汽车暖风系统主开关断开后,仍使鼓风机短时间旋转以)清扫暖风机内的热气的自动开关②(使起动机开关在发动机运转时不起作用的)安全开关

purge tank 驱出机器及管道内的污物、水分等用的压缩空气存储箱

purge valve ①清除阀(蒸发排放物控制系统中,用来将存储在活性炭罐中的蒸发排放物释放到发动机进气系统的清除孔的真空膜片控制的阀门或电动阀门,亦称 purge control valve)②排气阀,抽气阀③清除阀,排污阀

purging medium 清洗介质(清洗剂)

purify 纯化,净化,提纯,精炼

purifying 净化(特指减少有害排放物的工作)

PU-RIM 反应-喷射成形聚氯基甲酸乙酯(制品)(reaction injection mold-ed polyurethane 的简称)

purity ①充气纯度(纯空气扫气后汽缸内实际留有的纯空气与量与残留废气量的比值)②纯度,纯净,纯正,品位,纯化

Purkinje effect 普尔钦效应(在微光下,人眼转为对光谱的蓝色端最敏感)

Purkinje phenomenon 普尔钦现象(见 Purkinje effect)

purple ①紫色②紫色的③染成紫色,使成紫色,变紫

purpose 目的,用途,作用

purpose-built washing equipment 专用清洗设备

purpose made 特制的,按要求订制的

purposive sampling 特定目的抽样

pursuance 进行，实行，从事
pursuit-type vehicle 尾随车辆（竞赛时跟随在赛车后面的服务车辆）
push 推
push action cylinder 推力油缸
push and pull lever type accelerator-brake manipulator system 推-拉杆式加速-制动操纵装置（向前推加速，向后拉减速，拉到底制动）
push and pull switch （电气等的）推拉式开关
push bar ①推杆（如：行车制动与驻车制动共用同一个鼓式制动器时，在推臂的作用下，顶开另一制动器的顶杆）②踏板
push broom 推式路刷
push button 按钮开关（= press button, thrust butter, 亦称 push switsh）
push-button door handle 按钮式车门把手
push-button drive 带按钮操纵的传动
push-button starter 按钮式起动电机（由驾驶员通过按钮操纵电磁开关，再由电磁开关操纵起动电机开关）
push button switch 按钮开关
push-button tester 按钮式测试仪
push cart ①推动式试验车（本身无动力装置而由外力推动的碰撞试验车）②手推车
push caterpillar 履带式顶推拖拉机（带顶推装置）
pushdown storage 下推存储器（后进先出式存储器，下一个要取出的项目就是仍存在存储器中最后，即最后存入的最先取出去"后进先出" last-in, first-out 存入的项一个）
pusher ①推压件，推压工具，顶推机构，推杆，顶具（如：衬套拆卸用顶推件）②（将车辆等顶推出坭坑的）顶车（等）
pusher axle ①［英］驱动轴 ②［美］非驱动轴（如：双轴并装后桥中的 pusher axle，美指其被驱动的前轴，而英却指其后驱动轴）
pusher dozer 顶推（推土）机，助铲（推土）机（用推土机对铲运机进行助铲）
pusher tandem 只有后轴是驱动轴的并装双轴后桥
push（er）type CVT 推力型无级连续变速器（见 VDT belt）
pusher type fuel pump 潜液式油泵（submerged pump 的一种，如：装在燃油箱燃油层内的电动油泵，无气阻之虞）
push fit 推入配合，密配合
push grade 极陡的上坡（需要用顶推机协助爬坡）
pushing force 推力
push out ring （密封件中的）撑环（撑开 V 形圈等辅助密封圈使之起密封作用的零件）
push-pull 推挽式的，推拉的（简称 PP）
push-pull control cable 推拉式操纵软索（Bowden wire）
push-pull light switch 推拉式车灯开关
push rod 推杆（传递推力的杆件，如：①制动主缸推杆，推动主缸第一活塞的推杆②离合器操纵机构中的分离推杆③气门推杆，亦写作 pushrod，将运动由挺柱或凸轮从动件传至摇臂的零件）
pushrod actuated coil-over shock 外套螺旋弹簧的推杆式减振器（如：MacPherson strut）
pushrod bushing 推杆衬套
pushrod engine （带推杆的）顶置式气门发动机（= overhead valve engine）
push rod tube 气门推杆导管（= valve-tappet tube）
push-roke （油缸）活塞杆推出行程
Push Start 按键式起动

push starting 推车起动（亦称 hump start）

push switch 按钮开关（见 push button）

push tractor 顶推拖拉机，助推拖拉机（= bank tractor）

push type clutch 推式离合器（见 pull-type clutch）

push type grease gun 推压式滑脂枪

push understeer （后轮）推力（致生）不足转向（某些大功率后轮驱动式车辆，当后轮驱动力过大时，即使方向盘转角较大，也会出现的在后轮强大驱动力推动下，前轮转向不足的现象）

push welding 手动挤焊（= poke welding）

put 放，置，叙述，说明，提出

put back ①返回，向后移，倒退，回驶，开回原地，放回原处②阻碍，阻止，推迟

put-e side impact 纯侧面受撞（指作用在受撞车辆侧面的主要力相对于该车纵向对称平面的夹角在45°~135°范围内）

put-ification 提纯，净化，精炼

put in first gear 挂上一挡，（挂一挡 = put in first speed）

put into operation 投入运转，投入使用

put on 装上，放上，戴上，把…放在…上，增加，添加；把…施加于；开动，推动，使运转；推进；拉紧；显示

put onthe air 充气

put on the brake(s) 施加制动，踏下制动踏板（= apply the brake）

put out of service 停止起作用，停止服务，停止工作（= put out of action）

putrifict 滤清器，净化器，清洗装置，清洗设备，提纯器，精制设备

putty ①油灰，腻子，研磨膏②用油

灰抹缝（或填塞）

put up the shutters 关闭（散热器）百叶窗

PV ①批准生产，生产合法化，投产鉴定（production validation）②生产合格证，批量生产许可证（production verification）

PVA ①聚醋酸乙烯酯（polyvinyl acetate）②聚乙烯醇（polyvinyl alcohol）③孔真空控制提前（见 ported vac-cam advance）

P valve 比例阀（见 proportioning valve）

PVC ①聚氯乙烯（polyvinyl chloride）②聚乙烯取芯管（polyvinyl corer）

PVC insulating tape 聚氯乙烯绝缘胶带

PVC seam sealing 聚氯乙烯接缝密封剂

PVC underbody treatment 车身底部面聚氯乙烯处理（防行车时砂、石刮伤及防腐蚀）

PVC underseal 车身底面的聚氯乙烯保护涂层（亦和 PVC underseal coating）

PVdF 聚偏二氟乙烯（polyvinylidene fluoride）

P-V diagram P-V 图，压力-容积图（pressure-volume diagram）

PVF 聚氟乙烯（polyvinyl fluoride）

PVH system 脉冲式真空轮毂锁系统（见 pulse vacuum hublock system）

PVS 生产验证规范（production verifi-cation specification）

PV valve PV 值（亦写作 PV valve 如：密封流体压力 P 与密封端面平均滑动速度 V 的乘积）

PW 电动车窗（power window 的简称）

P&Wkey 圆形端面滑键（pratt and whitney key 的简称）

PWM 脉冲宽度调剂（见 pulse

width-modulation)

PW motor 永(久)磁(铁)式电动机

PWM solenoid 脉冲宽度调制式电磁阀(pulse-width modulated solenoid valve 的简称)

PWM speed control (电动机等的)脉冲宽度调制速度控制(法)

pwt 英钱(英美金衡制单位,见 pen-nyweight)

P-xylene 对二甲苯

pycnometer 比重瓶,比重管,比重计

pylon ①支架,悬臂②标柱,标杆;定向塔③定向起重机④一种涂有黑黄色条纹的橡皮圆筒形标志(一般用于公路施工工地,或作为赛车路线标记)

pylon course slalom test 用圆筒形标志,pylon④,作为障碍物摆放成蛇行、蛇形行驶试验(评价转向时的随从性、收敛性、转向力大小、倾斜程度和避免事故能力的典型方法)

pyramid 棱锥(体),角锥(体),锥形体

pyrena 芘,嵌二萘($C_{16}H_{10}$,多核芳族化合物,废气 HC 排放物中的有毒致癌成分)

pyrex glass 硼硅酸(耐热)玻璃

pyridine 氮苯,吡啶(C_5H_5N)

pyrite (天然)二硫化铁(FeS_2),黄铁矿

pyro ①(词头部分)热,火,焦②邻苯三酚(pyrogallol 的简称.一种强还原剂)③烟火(技术)

pyroelectric ①热电的②热电物质

pyroelectric crystal 热电晶体

pyroelectric effect 热电效应

pyroelectrics 热电体

pyroferrite 热电铁氧体

pyrology 热工学

pyrolysis 热解(作用)(高温分解)

pyrolysis zone 热分解区,高温分解区

pyrolytic carbon film resistor 热解碳膜电阻器

pyrolytic stability 耐高温分解稳定性(耐热损伤强度)

pyrometer 高温计,高温表,高温热电偶(参见 thermoelectric couple)

pyrometer couple 高温计热电偶

pyrometric cone 温熔锥(塞氏测温锥,= fusible cone, Seger cone)

pyroscove 辐射式高温计

pyrotechnical actuator (安全气囊和充气式安全带的)火药式充气装置(亦称 pyrotechnical inflator, pyrotechnical gas generator)

pyrotechnically activated seat belt retractor (汽车乘员)安全带的火药式驱动收紧装置(亦称 pyrotechinc driver seat belt tightener)

pyrotechnically activated seat beltretractor 烟火药爆胀驱动型安全带收紧装置

pyrotechnic gas generator 烟火气体发生器(汽车乘员安全气囊的一种充气装置,利用烟火药爆燃产生气体充填气囊)

pyrotechnic seat belt pretensioner 燃爆烟火型安全皮带预收紧装置

pyro type 烟火式(见 pyrotechnic gas generator)

pyroxylin(e) lacquer 硝化纤维清漆,硝基清漆

PZEV 部分零排放车(partial zero-emission vehicle 的简称,仅某项或几项污染物零排放)

PZEV 见 partial zero-emission vehicle

PZT ①环型压电传感器(piezoelectric ring transducer)②压电跃变(piezo-electric transition)

Q ①库仑（电荷、电量单位，见 coulomb）②质量因数（见 quality factor）③数量（见 quantity）④热量（见 quantity of heat）⑤夸脱（1/4加仑，见 quart）⑥季刊（见 quarterly）⑦四开本（见 quarto）⑧问题（见 question）

QA ①象限角（quadrant angle）②质量保证（quality assurance）③快速的，速动的（见 quick-acting）

Q alloy 镍铬合金（铬15%~19%，镍66%~68%，其余铁）

qb 高速断路器，速断（quick break）

"Q"-brand of antiknock compound "Q"级抗爆剂，"Q"类抗爆剂

QC 质量控制（quality control）

QCD 质量管理科，质量控制科（Quality Control Division）

QCF 质量控制表格（quality control form）

QCM 质量控制手册（quality control manual）

QCO ①质量管理官员（quality control officer）②质量检验机构（quality control organization）

QCS 质量控制标准（quality control standards）

QCSEE "低噪声-清洁-短途"试验发动机（"Quiet-clean-shorthaul" Experiment Engine）

QD ［美］快件运输（quick dispatch）

QDM （本田公司的电子控制自动变速器的）四路驱动模块（quad driver module 的简称，指根据发动机控制模块有关信号、变速器输入轴和输出轴转速信号及节气门开度信号、换挡杆挡位信号及制动信号等来控制，A，B换挡电磁阀"shift solenoidA，shift solenoidB"，变矩器锁止离合器电磁阀"torque converter clutch solenoid"和变矩器锁止离合器的锁止液压的脉冲宽度调制电磁阀"PWM solenoid"等四路电磁阀的电子控制模块）

Q-engine Q发动机（指燃料的化学能转变为热能并传给一定的工质，由该工质去完成循环的各种发动机，如：蓝肯循环发动机、斯特林循环发动机等）

Q factor 品质因素，质量因素，Q值

Q-meter 品质因素计，优质计，Q表

Q-percentile life 可靠寿命（给定的可靠度所对应的时间）

qt ①数量（quantity）②夸脱（quart）③静的，低噪声的（quiet）

QTP 鉴定试验程序（qualification test procedure）

QTS ①鉴定试验规范（qualification test specification）②石英调谐系统

(quartz tuning system)

quad 四边形（见 quadrangle）

quad-camshaft 方凸轮轴（指每缸四气门的凸轮轴，似成方形，故名）

quad driver module 见 QDM

quad headlight 方形前照灯

Quadra-drive 全时四轮驱动（商品名，=full-time four-wheel drive）

Quadra-Lift air suspension 全轮可控空气弹簧悬架（亦简称 Quadra-Lift）

quadrangle 四边形（简称 quad，特指正方形或长方形）

quadrangular ①四边形的，四角形的，方形的②四棱柱

quadrant ①象限，1/4 圆周，1/4 圆，90°弧②四分仪，象限仪③扇形体，扇形座④扇形齿轮，齿扇（= toothed segment, rack circle, segment rack）⑤（变速器变速杆的）换挡挡位导板

quadrasteer 四轮转向系统（商品名，=4 wheel steering system）

quadratic ①二次（的），平方的，方形的，象限的②二次方程式，二次项

Quadra Trac（带后轮电子限滑差速器型的）四轮驱动系统（商品名）

quadrature ①求面积，求积分②平方面积③转相差，90°相位差④正交

quadrature component 正交横轴分量，90°相移分量

quadric crank mechanism 摆杆曲柄连杆机构，四连杆机构

quadrilateral ①四边形，四边形物②四边的，四角的，四方面的

quadruple-expansion engine 四级膨胀式发动机（蒸汽等工质顺序在四个尺寸逐步加大，压力逐步降低的汽缸内膨胀驱动同一曲轴，参见 multiple-expansion engine）

qualification ①熟练，技能，条件，资格②鉴定合格性，合格证书③执照，资格证明书（如：driver qualification 作为驾驶员的资格）

qualification test 质量鉴定试验，鉴定试验；资格考试，合格检验

qualification test specification 质量鉴定试验规范（简称 QTS）

qualifying examination（资格）检定考试

qualifying point 质量控制点

qualitative analysis 定性分析

qualitative assessment 质量评定

qualitative governing（发动机的可燃混合气）质量控制，变质调节（亦称 qualitative control，指通过改变空燃比来调控发动机功率，即通过改变混合气的质量而不是通过改变其数量来控制发动机功率等）

qualitative metallurgical analysis 定性金相分析

qualitative test 定性试验

quality 质量（产品、过程或服务满足规定要求或需要的特征和特性的总和）

quality assurance 质量保证

quality assurance engineer 产品质量（管理）工程师

quality booster 改善质量的添加剂

quality car 高级轿车，名牌轿车，质量优良的轿车

quality coefficient 质量系数

quality control 质量控制（为保持某一产品、过程或服务质量所采取的作业技术和有关活动），质量管理（简称 QC）

quality control officer 质量管理官员（简称 QCO）

quality control organization 质量控制机构，质量管理组织（简称 QCO）

quality control standards 质量控制标准，质量管理标准（简称 QCS）

quality control system（产品）质量管理系统，质量控制系统

quality factor 品质因数，质量因素，

Q 值（简称 Q factor）
quality factor for a material 材料品质因数（正比于单位应变能与单位阻尼能之比）
quality index 质量指标，质量指数
quality management 质量管理（对确定和达到质量所必需的全部职能和活动的管理）
quality of fit 配合等级
quality rebuilding 质量复原修复
quality requirements 质量要求
quality retention rating （橡胶等的）质量稳定性评价标准（指橡胶制品经过户外老化后，其抗拉强度等特性所应保持的最低程度）
quality specifications 质量标准，质量说明书，品质规格
quality supervision 质量监督（根据政府法令或规定，对产品、服务质量和企业保证质量所具备的条件进行监督的活动）
quantification 定量，数量化，以数量表示
quantitative analysis 定量分析
quantitative control （发动机的可燃混合气）数量控制，变量调节（亦称 quantitative governing，指通过改变混合气的供给量来控制发动机功率，而不是通过改变其空燃比，见 qualitative governing）
quantitative data 数量数据
quantitative determination 定量测定，量化测定
quantitative evaluation 定量评价，定量评估
quantitative index 数量指标，定量指标
quantitative performance 量化特性（指可用数量级表示的特性）
quantitative test（ing） 定量试验，定量（分析）测定
quantity ①量，数量②参量
quantity of fallen dust 降尘量（指 $1m^2$ 面积的工作台面，24 小时内降落的浮游粒的质量）
quantity of flow 流量
quantity of heat 热量
quantity of state 状态量（见 thermodynamic function）
quantity-produced 大量生产的，连续生产的
quantized signal 量化信号（具有量化信息参数的信号）
quantizer 数字转换器，编码器，量化器，量化装置，脉冲调制器
quantum ①量子②（定）量，（定）额③总数，总计④时限
quantum effect transistor 量子效应三极管
quantum electronics 量子电子学
quarry tipper （石）矿用自卸车
quart 夸脱（英制单位的容积单位，代号 Q_t，或 qt。在英国无干、液之分。1qt = 1.1365litre = 1/4 英加仑。在美国干夸脱与液夸脱不同，1dryqt = 1.1012litre，1liguidqt = 0.94633litre。但量酒液等用 requted quart 作单位。量酸溶液等仍用 Winchester quart）
quarter ①1/4，一刻钟，一季度，[美] 二角五分②方位，方向③地区，市区，街道④（轿车车身的）后部分，后侧部，后侧区（包括后支柱至后窗及行李舱之间的整个侧部组件，见 rear quarter panel）⑤象限⑥夸特（质量单位。1 夸特 = 28lb [英国]，1 夸特 = 25lb [美国]，见 avoirdupois weights，英制容量单位。1 夸特 = 8bushels [英国]，见 Imperial gallon）⑦分为四份，四等分
quarter bend 90°曲管，直角弯头
quarter-circular turn 直角转弯，转过 90°（= quarter turn）
quarter elliptic spring 1/4 椭圆形钢板弹簧（相当于半个常见的半椭圆形钢板弹簧，其基体部分固定于车

架或车身,而末端支撑车轿)
quartering ①四分法,四分取样法,四等分,四开②成直角的③从车后侧向(吹)来的(风)
quartering machine 曲柄轴钻孔机
quartering wind 后侧向风(= direct cross wind)
quarter light 边窗(见 quarter window)
quarter light break (轿车)侧窗开度限位器
quarter light reinforcement 后侧角窗加强板,后边窗加强板,角窗加强板
quarterly ①季刊(简称 Q)②季度的,每季的,一季一度的③每季地,一季一次地
quartermaster corps [美]后勤部队,军需部队,后勤运输部队
quartermaster truck 军需后勤运输车
quarter panel (轿车)顶盖后侧板(顶盖后侧面转角处的外板)
quarter rail (连接木制货车厢式车身侧立柱与横顶梁的)角梁
quarter size 1/4 缩尺
quarter turn 直角转弯(= quarter-circular turn)
quarter turn belt 直角挂轮传动带,直角回转带,半交叉传动带
quarter window (轿车车身后部侧面或前门窗主玻璃前方,后门窗主玻璃后方的)角窗,三角窗,侧窗(亦称 quarter light)
quarter window glass ①(轿车)后侧窗玻璃(在后顶盖侧板上的角窗玻璃)②(轿车)后角窗玻璃(a. 后三角窗玻璃;b. 后车门固定玻璃)
quartz 石英,水晶
quartz accelerometer 石英加速度计
quartz chronometer 石英钟,石英计时计

quartz crystal 石英晶体
quartz crystal clock 石英晶体时钟
quartz force transducer 石英测力传感器
quartz glass 石英玻璃
quartz grey 石英灰(车身颜色)
quartz halogen lamp 石英玻璃泡卤素灯(灯泡内充有卤素元素的钨丝灯)
quartz iodine lamp 充碘石英灯(卤素前照灯的一种,以石英为灯泡玻璃的充碘钨丝灯)
quartz pressure transducer 石英压力传感器
quartz sand 白砂,硅砂,石英砂(= silver sand)
quartz transducer 石英传感器
quartz tube 石英管
quasi-direct methanol fuel cell (基于混合聚合物膜电解质的)半直接甲醇燃料电池,准直接甲醇燃料电池
quasi-direct numerical simulation 准直接数字模拟
quasi-hydrodynamic lubrication 半流体动力润滑
quasi-periodicity 拟周期,准周期
quasi-stability 准稳定性,似稳态
quasi-static strength test 准静态强度试验,类似静态强度试验
quasi-stationary state 拟稳状态
quasi-steady-state torque (发动机的)准稳态转矩(指发动机运转平均转矩值)
quasi-steady-state torque feedback control (发动机的)准稳态转矩反馈控制(以准稳态转矩信号进行反馈控制的闭路系统)
quaterfoil crossing 四叶式(道路)交叉
quater-mile time (汽车起步后的)1/4 英里行驶时间
quaternary alloy 四元合金
Quattro (Audi 车的)全时四轮驱动

系统（商品名）
queen post 双柱架，木桁架副柱
quench ①抑制②使急冷③使熄灭④淬火⑤（特指内燃机可燃混合气燃烧过程中，当活塞顶与汽缸盖间的间隙最小时，间隙处面容比增大，与缸盖内表面接触的部分燃气热量急剧散失而温度下降的）激冷（现象，有利于抑制爆燃，但会导致不完全燃烧而增加 HC，CO 排放）
quench aging 淬火（后自然）时效
quench area （燃烧室的）挤压面积
quenched steel 淬硬钢
quench effect 冷激效应（汽油机燃烧室壁面某部分的冷却程度较大，导致该部分混合气温度较低，影响燃烧火焰传播。在离火花塞远处组织适当冷激反应，有利于防止爆燃）
quench fluid 阻封流体［当用单端面机械密封件密封易结晶或危险的介质时，在机械密封件的外侧（大气侧）设置简单的密封件，如衬套密封、填料密封、唇形密封件等，在两种密封件之间引入其压力稍高于大气压力的清洁中性流体，以便对密封件冷却或加热并将泄漏出来的被密封介质及时带走，以改善密封工作条件的方法，称为阻封"quench"，阻封流体指起阻封作用的外部流体］
quench hardening 急冷硬化，淬硬
quenching ①淬火②（由于温度较低的燃烧室壁面所引起的火焰前峰）熄火现象，猝熄③抑制，激冷，冷却，浸渍④遏止，阻尼，减振
quenching area 激冷面积，激冷区，冷熄区
quenching bath 淬火槽，冷却槽
quench (ing) crack 淬火裂纹，淬冷龟裂，骤冷裂纹
quenching diameter 熄火直径（火焰通过圆管传播时造成熄火现象的管径）
quenching distance 熄火距离（火焰经过两平行壁面间传播时引起熄火的壁面间距）
quenching distortion 淬火变形
quenching phenomenon 骤冷现象
quenching stress 淬火应力
quench interference （排放检测中的）熄光干扰（排气中的大量 CO_2 在化学发光分析仪反应室中与激发态 NO_2 碰撞，会使激发态 NO_2 失去分子能量，光强降低，使测定结果偏低的现象）
quench motor 燃烧室结构会导致激冷的发动机
queue ①等候的车列或人列，排队，行列，排列，队列，长列②排队等候
queue arrangement 停车站台设备
queue assist （车载系统的）排队等候（工况下的）辅助（功能）（指车载系统在车辆低速行驶，乃至完全停车的情况下仍能继续工作的性能）
queu(e)ing theory 排队论，排队理论
queue model 排队模型（指应用排队论的方法求解排队问题的数学模型）
quick-acting 快速的，速动的，高速动作的，灵敏的
quick (action) triple valve 快动三通阀
quick and easy 快速而方便的
quick-break switch 速断开关
quick change adapter 快速接头
quick change gears 快速换挡机构
quick charger 快速充电机，快速充电器（= fast charger）
quick-connect terminals 快速连接接（线）头
quick-cure tube gum 快速硫化内胎

补胶

quick-curing 快速硫化（的）

quick demountable rim 快卸轮辋（= quick detachable rim）

quick detachable 可快速拆卸的

quick disconnect couplers 快速脱开联结器，快脱挂钩（装置）

quick-disconnect coupling 快速拆卸式联轴节，快速拆装式耦合器

quick dispatch ［美］快件运输，快速发运，快运（简称QD）

quickest route 最快线路，特快线路

quick fittings 快速接头

quick-heat system 快速加热系统，快速暖机系统，快速暖风系统

quick hitch 快速挂接装置（= fast hitch）

quick index (ing) 快速检索

quick-learn （电子系统的）快速学习（功能）

quick-lift cam 急升凸轮，快升凸轮，速升凸轮

quick lube automotive center ［美］汽车快速润滑中心（除加注机油、齿轮油及各润滑点滑脂外，还进行调整、紧固、清洗等作业，亦称快速维护中心）

quick operated 快速动作的，快速操作的

quick preheater system 快速预热系统（亦称fast preheating system，由热起时间短的低压陶瓷电热塞和可根据水温传感器等的输入信号控制通电时间的预热时间控制器组成）

quick preset torque wrench 快速预调式转矩扳手

quick-release valve 快放阀（如：气压制动系中的快速放气阀）

quick-response 快速响应的

quick response transducer 快速响应传感器

quick return 快速返回，快速回位

quick sand 流沙

quick service 快速检修，快速维护；快速服务

quick take up master cylinder 快速充液式制动主缸（亦称fast-fill master cylinder）

3R （资源有效利用的）3R 原则（Refuse 减少废弃物的产生，Reuse 旧料、旧件直接再使用，Recycle 旧件、旧料回收加工后再使用）
Ra 镭（radium）
R134a 氢碳氟制冷剂（见 HFC134a）
rabbet ①榫头；槽口，槽舌；半槽边，启口缝②开槽口子；嵌接；槽舌接合，槽口接合
rabbet joint 槽舌接合；半槽接合；企口接合
rabble ①长柄耙②搅动
rabbler 铲子；刮刀
RAC ［英］皇家汽车俱乐部（Royal Automobile Club）
race ①竞赛，比赛②轨道，跑道（滚动轴承座圈）滚道③（滚动轴承内、外）座圈④急流，激流⑤超速运转，疾驶⑥使空转
race an engine 使发动机高速空转
race cam 竞赛汽车发动机用凸轮（升程高，开闭急速，开阀时间长）
race car 赛车
race course 跑道，竞赛车道，赛车行驶线路（亦写作 racing course）
race data 汽车竞赛资料
race engine 竞赛汽车发动机
race-proved 在赛车上试验过的
racer ①赛车，比赛用车②参加（速度）比赛者，赛车手
racer camshaft 赛车用凸轮轴（一般的结构特点是：气门升程大，速开速关、早开迟关，以提高发动机性能，供赛车使用）
race ring 滚道，座圈，轴承（内、外）圈
race rotation 空转
Race tech 赛车技术
race track ①赛车跑道②轴承滚道
race way ①（球节的）球头销座，②（轴承圈）滚道③电缆管道④输水管，水管
RAC horsepower （英国）皇家汽车俱乐部马力（按一定公式由缸数和缸径计算的损税马力）
racing ①竞赛，比赛②（发动机无负荷）空转；超速运转③疾驰的，高速的；竞赛的
racing body 赛车（型）车身
racing carburettor （竞）赛车化油器
racing (car) engine 赛车发动机
racing (car) tyre 赛车用轮胎
racing circuit 环形赛车跑道，环形赛车道
racing click （赛车或某些常规轿车使用的）光面轮胎（胎面无花纹，以最大限度地增加胎面与地面的接触面积，增加干路面上行驶时的附着力）
racing driver 赛车驾驶员，赛车运动员（=sporting driver, racer②）

racing of engine 发动机高速运转
racing of the engine 发动机（在）超速（状态下工作）
racing speed ①（液力变矩器的）空转转速（指在规定的输入转速下，涡轮无负荷而自由空转时的输入转速）②（发动机无负荷的）空转转速
racing team 赛车的驾驶和维修组
racing track 赛车跑道
racing-type foam-filled rubber fuel cell 赛车型泡沫橡皮燃油箱
rack ①栅，架，搁物架，行李架，支架，台架②齿条，齿轨③放在架上，装架④推榨，压榨⑤转动，振动⑥用齿条传动
rack-and-gear drive 齿条-齿轮传动（=rack-and-pinion drive）
rack-and-gear jack 齿条-齿轮（传动式）千斤顶（=rack-and-pinion jack, rack-bar jack, rack jack）
rack-and-pinion (-gear) steering gear 齿条齿轮式转向器（简称 rack steering gear）
rack and pinion mechanism 齿条-齿轮（式传动）机构
rack assist type EPS 转向机齿条助力式电动转向机构（rack assist type electric power steering 的简称，对齿轮-齿条式转向器的齿条施加转向动力的电动转向机构，亦简称 REPS）
rack bar 齿条（=toothed bar）
rack-body truck 栏板式车箱载货汽车
rack circle ①扇形齿轮，齿扇②圆形齿轮③平面锥齿轮（参见 quadrant）
rack driven 齿条传动的
rack entrance height 行李架入口高度（行李架入口处至顶盖护板之间的距离）
rack fuel control mechanism （柴油机柱塞式喷油泵的）齿杆式油量调节机构（通过调节齿杆与调节齿套或装在控制套筒上的调节齿圈啮合，使柱塞转动以调节供油量的机构）
rack scale （柴油机喷油泵控制齿条的）齿条位置调整器，齿条标尺
rack width 行李架宽度（与行李架外缘相切的 Y 平面至侧围护板之间的距离）
RACS ［日］道路车辆与通信系统（Road Automobile & Communication System）
rad ①弧度（见 radian）②拉德（见 radiation absorbed dose）③散热器（见 radiator）④基；根；重要的（见 radical）⑤无线电（见 radio）⑥无线电报；X 光照相（见 radiogram）⑦电报报务员（见 radio operator）⑧半径，辐射线（见 radius）⑨根源（见 radix）
radar 雷达（无线电探测和定位装置，radio detecting and ranging 的简称）
radar anti-collision technology 雷达防撞技术
radar bag initiator 雷达（控制的）安全气囊触发器
Radar-based system 基于雷达的操控系统
radar beamwidth 雷达射束宽度
radar brake controller （汽车用）雷达制动控制器（当两车的距离小到预定的最危险距离时，自动使车辆制动和使发动机怠速运转）
radar braking system 雷达（控制的）制动系统
radar collision 雷达防撞（装置）
radar coverage 雷达探测区
radar cruise control system 雷达巡航控制系统（亦称 active cruise control system，简称 ACC system，由雷达探测前方车辆的速度和相隔距离。当前方无车辆时，巡航系统以

常规方式按设定的车速行驶,与加速踏板的位置无关。当前方有车辆时,可随前方车辆加速、减速或停车,以保持与前方车辆设定的安全距离。此外当发现前方有可能发生碰撞的障碍物时即向驾驶者发出警报或强制制动减速、停车,以回避碰撞,减轻伤害)

radar detection sensor 雷达探测传感器

radar directed 雷达导向的

radar dish 雷达天线反射器,(截)抛物面天线

radar display 雷达显示

radar echo 雷达回波

radar electronic scan technique 雷达电子扫描技术(简称 REST)

radar fix 雷达定位

radar guidance 雷达导向,雷达导行

radar horizon 雷达探测范围

radar image demonstration system 雷达影像显示系统

radar imaging information 雷达影像信息(由雷达系统产生的三维影像信息,供驾驶员观察视线以外区域的路况和夜间路状)

radar pencil beam 雷达锐方向射束

radar range ①雷达测距②雷达作用距离,雷达有效区

radar ranging 雷达测距

radar scope 雷达屏,雷达示波器

radar sensor 雷达传感器

radar truck 雷达车(亦称 radar vehicle)

radar vehicle detector 雷达侦车器,雷达式车辆探测器

radar warning system 雷达警报系统

radial ①光线的,射线的,辐射的,放射的②半径的,径向的(指垂直于轴、汽缸、车轮等中心线的)③星形的(指发动机汽缸布置)④子午胎(radial ply tyre 的简称)

radial acceleration 径向加速度

radial acting hydrodynamic mechanical seal 径向作用流体动压式机械密封(能在径向形成具有抵抗泄漏作用的流体动压分布的流体动压式机械密封,亦称 positive acting hydrodynamic mechanical seal)

radial angular contact ball bearing 向心推力球轴承(亦称 angular ball bearing, radial-thrust ball bearing,指能同时承受径向和轴向荷载的球轴承)

radial antifriction bearing 向心滚动轴承

radial arm 旋臂,径向臂

radial axle box (内部装有)径向轴承(的)箱(形部件)

radial backlash 径向侧隙(一对齿轮,其工作状态下的中心距与无隙啮合状态下的中心距之差,称为径向侧隙。其值等于圆周侧隙的一半除以啮合角的正切所得到的商)

radial balance (车轮等的)径向平衡

radial bearing with snap ring (为了防止轴承轴向移动而)带卡环的径向轴承

radial blade 径向叶片(放射状叶片)

radial brush 径向电刷

radial cam 径向凸轮

radial capacity 径向荷载量,径向荷载能力

radial clearance 径向间隙(亦称 radial play)

radial component 径向分力

radial compressor 星形空压机(绕位于中央的曲轴呈径向布置的多缸往复活塞式小型空调用空气压缩机)

radial cracking 径向裂口(轮胎经试验或使用后,胎侧胶、胎肩胶或帘布层局部出现基本垂直于车轮旋转轴的裂口)

radial（cylinder）engine 星形发动机（绕位于中心的曲轴径向布置的多缸发动机）

radial deflection 径向变形量（构件的任一点在径向方向产生的变形量）

radial displacement 径向位移

radial divisor （车身外形线的）径向分割绘制法

radial double mechanical seal 径向双端面机械密封（沿径向布置的双端面机械密封）

radial equilibrium 径向平衡

radial face 径向面

radial flank 径向齿侧

radial-flow compressor 径流式压缩机（指离心式压缩机）

radial flow turbine 径流式涡轮（机）

radial flow type converter （废气净化系统的）径流式（催化）转化器（排气呈放射状或向心状流动与催化剂接触，催化剂布置成多层的同心圆形的催化转化器，见 catalytic converter）

radial flux type motor 径向磁通式电动机

radial force variation （承受负荷的轮胎旋转时在其一定半径上产生的）径向力的变动（简称 RFV）

radial forging machine 径向锻造机（利用分布在毛坯横截面周围的两个以上的锤头，对毛坯进行同步和对称的锻击。在锻造过程中，毛坯做轴向移动的同时，还做旋转运动）

radial inflow turbine 径流向心式涡轮（机）（= radial inward-flow turbine）

radial internal clearance （滚动轴承等的）径向内间隙（内、外圈间的径向移动量，参见 internal clearance）

radial inward-flow gas turbine 向心径流式燃气轮机

radial inward-flow turbine 向心径流式涡轮（机）（= radial inflow turbine）

radial lip sealing 径向凸缘密封

radial load 径向荷载

radially straight impeller blade 工作轮直线径向叶片

radial manifold converter （废气净化系统的）径流式排气歧管（催化）转化器（装在排气歧管内的径流式转化器，见 radial flow type converter）

radial motion 径向运动，沿径运动

radial multiple-piston type of pump 径向多活塞式泵（星形活塞泵）

radial packing strip （三角转子发动机三角转子的）径向密封条

radial pin coupling 径向销连接（输入件与输出件以径向孔和圆柱销连接的形式）

radial piston motor 活塞式星形发动机（多缸往复式发动机，各缸呈辐射状排列，连杆大头都接到共用的曲轴上，现在工业上这种发动机多为气动机，而航空发动机则为内燃机）

radial piston pump 径向活塞泵（星形活塞泵）

radial piston pump with exterior admission 外圆进油的径向活塞泵

radial piston pump with interior admission 内圆进油的径向活塞泵

radial piston transmission 径向活塞式（液压）传动

radial play 径向间隙

radial plunger pump 径向柱塞泵

radial ply 径向帘布层，向径线层

radial-ply-rigid-breaker tire 带刚性缓冲层的子午线轮胎

radial ply tyre 子午线轮胎（胎体帘布层帘线与胎面中心线呈90°角或接近90°角排列，以带束层箍紧胎

体的充气轮胎）
radial pressure 径向压力
radial rib 径向肋
radial road 辐射路，放射式道路（从都市繁华商业中心向周围地区辐射的主要道路）
radial roller bearing 向心滚子轴承
radial seal 径向密封，径向密封件
radial slots 径向槽，径向缝
radial spherical roller bearing 径向球形滚珠轴承
radial spoke 径向轮辐
radial stiffness 径向刚度（如：车轮中心与轮胎接地平面间垂直距离的单位增量，所对应的轮胎垂直负荷的减量）
radial strain 径向应变
radial street 辐射街路，放射式市区道路（从都市繁华商业中心向周围地区辐射的主要街路）
radial stress 径向应力
radial symmetry 径向对称
radial thickness 径向厚度
radial-thrust ball bearing 向心推力球轴承（见 angular contact ball bearing）
radial turbine 径流式涡轮（废气径向流入、轴向流出涡轮工作轮的涡轮）
radial turbocharger 径流式涡流增压器（= radial turbo blower, radial turbo-supercharger）
radial vaned impeller 径向叶片的叶轮
radial vector 径向矢量
radial velocity 径向速度
radial wall thickness （密封环等的）径向厚度
radial weight （车轮的）径向荷载
radian 弧度（为国际单位制的辅助单位，用来度量平面角，代号为 rad，1 弧度为圆周上等于该圆半径的一段弧所对圆心的角，2π rad = $360°$，1rad = $57.2958\cdots°$，$1° = 0.0174532925\cdots$ rad = $\pi/180$rad）
radiance ①发光度，发光，光亮度，光辉②面辐射强度［常用单位：瓦/（单位立体角·米^2）］
radian frequency 弧度频率（以弧度表示的角频率，$2\pi f$）
radian measure 弧度，弧度法
radian per second 弧度每秒（rad/s）
radian per second squared 弧度每二次方秒（rad/s^2）
radiant ①光源，热源②放射的，辐射的
radiant energy 辐射能
radiant heat 辐射热
radiant heater 热辐射式供暖器，热辐射式加热器
radiant heating 辐射热供暖，辐射热取暖
radiate 发射（热，光），放射，辐射；散发，传播；照射，照明，（道路的）辐射状布置（由中心向各方伸展）
radiated ignition interference （发动机）点火电磁辐射干扰
radiated noise 辐射型噪音
radiated power 辐射功率
radiated sound field 辐射声场
radiating 辐射，放射，扩散，发射，传播
radiating capacity 辐射量；辐射能力
radiating fin 散热片（亦称 cooling gill, radiating gill, radiating rib）
radiating flange 散热凸缘，（凸缘状散热片）
radiating pipe 散热管
radiating surface 辐射面，散热面
radiation ①发射（热，光）②辐射（能量以机械波、电磁波或粒子形式发射或传播）放射③照射，照明④辐射状排列
radiation absorbed dose 拉德（吸收

辐射剂量单位，=每1g组织吸收10^{-5}J能量，简称rad，亦称roentgen absorbed dose）

radiation damage 放射线伤害（指生物体被放射线照射后，细胞内引起电离现象使细胞变化，如遗传因子变化，致生白血病、白细胞减少等）

radiation density 辐射密度

radiation effect 辐射作用；放射作用

radiation hazard 放射线破坏（指物质被放射线照射后，引起构造和性质的变化，见 radiation damage）

radiation heat 辐射热

radiation loss 辐射损失

radiation of heat 热辐射（= thermal radiation, calorific radiation）

radiation of sound 声辐射

radiation resistance coefficient 辐射阻系数

radiation-safe 防放射性的，防辐射的

radiation shielding 辐射屏蔽

radiation source 放射源，辐射源，照射光源

radiation stability 辐射稳定性，散热稳定性

radiation test ①辐射试验（如：用紫外线照射一定时间后风窗玻璃透光度的降低和变色程度来评价耐光性能）②耐光试验（确定安全玻璃耐光照作用的性能试验。将试样经紫外线辐照一定时间，按其透光度的降低和变色程度来评定）

radiation value 辐射值，辐射系数，放射系数

radiative 放射的，辐射的，发射的

radiator ①散热器②辐射体，放射源，辐射器③发射天线

radiator air passage 散热器（散热片间的）风道

radiator apron 散热器保温套（= radiator cover）

radiator bar （车架的）散热器支撑横梁

radiator bearer 散热器支架

radiator blind 散热器的卷轴式保温帘（美称 radiator shade）

radiator blind roller 散热器卷帘的卷轴

radiator bottom tank 散热器的下水箱（亦称 radiator bottom header, radiator lower tank, 指下流式散热器"down-flow radiator"的出水箱"outlet tank"）

radiator brace 散热器支架角撑

radiator bracket 散热器支架

radiator bumper 散热器缓冲护栅

radiator cap 散热器水箱加水口盖（= radiator filler cap, radiator screw-cap, radiator locking cap）

radiator cap tester （汽车）散热器水箱盖（密封性能）测试器

radiator-cap thermometer 散热器盖温度计

radiator cement 散热器渗漏修补胶（= cement for radiator leaks）

radiator cleaner 散热器清洁器，散热器清洗装置

radiator cleaning compound 散热器清洗剂

radiator clip 散热器（软管）夹箍（= hose clamp）

radiator coil 冷却器蛇管，散热装置蛇管

radiator connection 散热器水箱进出水管接头

radiator coolant heater （利用）散热器冷却水（的）加热器

radiator cooling tube 散热器（芯的）冷却管

radiator core 散热器芯（亦称 radiator cell, radiator centre, radiator element）

radiator core fin 散热器芯散热片（亦称 radiator air fin, radiator fin）

radiator core guard 散热器芯护罩
radiator core section 散热器芯子单元
radiator core tube 散热器水管
radiator cover （冷天装的）散热器暖套，散热器保温罩（＝radiator cosy, radiator cowl, winter front, radiator muff, radiator apron）
radiator drainage valve 散热器放水阀
radiator drain cock 散热器放水旋塞（亦称 radiator draw-off cock）
radiator drain outlet elbow 散热器放水弯头
radiator emblem （装在散热器上的）车徽（＝radiator trademark, radiator monogram, ornamentation）
radiator expansion tank （发动机闭路冷却系统的）水箱膨胀箱（亦称 radiator recovery tank，当发动机闭路冷却系统的水温升高，冷却水膨胀时，散热器加水口压力盖内的压力阀开启，一部分冷却水经压力盖溢流管"overflow pipe"流入膨胀箱内。当发动机水温降低时，压力盖内的真空阀"vacuum valve"开启，膨胀箱内的冷却水又被吸回散热器，见 radiator pressure cap）
radiator-fan 散热器风扇
radiator fan relay 散热器风扇继电器
radiator fender 散热器护栅
radiator filler 散热器加水口
radiator filler cap 散热器加水口盖（＝radiator cap）
radiator filler gun （汽车）散热器水箱加水枪
radiator flap 散热器百叶窗活动片
radiator flap handle 散热器百叶窗活动片操纵手柄
radiator flush （高压液流）冲洗散热器
radiator frame 散热器框架

radiator grill （汽车的）散热器护栅 [亦称 radiator grate, radiator grille, radiator false front, radiator front, radiator shield, radiator (stone) guard]
radiator grill control 散热器护栅操纵件（打开散热器护栅锁止机构的操纵件）
radiator grille （汽车）散热器前面罩（位于前围上供散热器通风或起装饰作用的构件）
radiator hood cover （冷季用）散热器发动机保温套
radiator hood ledge 散热器上的发动机罩支撑边
radiator hose 散热器软管
radiator hose clamp 散热器软管夹箍
radiator hose connection 散热器软管接头
radiator inlet pipe 散热器冷却水进水管
radiator inlet tank （散热器的）进水箱（横流式散热器的进水箱位于散热器芯的一侧，而下流式散热器，则位于其散热芯的上端）
radiator leak 散热器泄漏，水箱漏水
radiator leak preventive 散热器防漏剂（＝radiator leak preventer）
radiator level 散热器液面高度
radiator locking cap 散热器锁盖（＝radiator cap）
radiator mascot 散热器装饰品（＝radiator ornament）
radiator monogram 散热器（上的）厂标（＝radiator emblem, radiator trademark）
radiator of sound 声源，声辐射器，扬声器
radiator ornament 散热器装饰件
radiator outlet pipe 散热器排水接管，散热器出水口
radiator outlet tank （散热器的）出水箱（经散热器芯冷却后的冷却

水汇集于该水箱流出，经软管流回发动机缸盖，下流式散热器该水箱位于散热器底部，称 bottom tank）

radiator outlet tube 散热器出水管

radiator overflow pipe 散热器溢流管（亦称 radiator overflow tube）

radiator pad 散热器安装垫块

radiator panel （汽车车身的）散热器框板

radiator plug 散热器塞盖，散热器注入口盖（= radiator filler cap）

radiator pressure cap 散热器（加水口）压力盖（由压力阀和真空阀组成，当散热器内的水温和压力升高时盖内的压力阀开启，真空阀关闭，散热器内的水蒸气或热冷却水经溢流管排至膨胀箱，而当发动机水温和压力降低，盖内的压力阀关闭，真空阀开启，膨胀箱内的冷却液又被吸回散热器）

radiator pressure cap rating 散热器压力盖额定值

radiator pressure cap sealing washer 散热器盖密封垫圈

radiator repair cement 散热器渗漏修补胶

radiator repair materials 散热器维修材料

radiator rim 散热器框架

radiator roller blind 散热器卷帘

radiator screw cap 水箱螺纹盖，水箱螺盖（= radiator cap）

radiator sealing compound 散热器密封剂

radiator service 散热器检修，水箱维护

radiator shutter 散热器百叶窗（亦称 radiator damp, radiator screen）

radiator shutter control 散热器百叶窗操纵件（用以控制百叶窗开度，以改变散热器冷却风进风面积）

radiator side screen 散热器边框

radiator stay 散热器撑条

radiator stone guard 散热器（防石）护栅（= radiator grill, radiator screen, radiator false front）

radiator strainer 散热器加水滤网

radiator support 散热器支架（散热器固定框）

radiator testing equipment 散热器试验装置

radiator testing wind tunnel （发动机）散热器试验风洞

radiator thermometer （发动机冷却系）散热器水温表（= water temperature indicator, engine cooling thermometer）

radiator thermostat 散热器恒温器

radiator tie rod 散热器撑杆

radiator top tank （散热器）上水箱（指下流式散热器中位于散热芯顶的进水箱"inlet tank"，热水由汽缸盖流出后，进入该水箱）

radiator under cover （车身的发动机）散热器车底导流罩板

radiator warm keep covering 散热器保温罩

radiator with detachable sections 可拆分段散热器，分段拼装散热器（指散热器芯子由几段拼装，可以分段拆散，= sectional core radiator）

radical ①基，根，原子团②根部，基础③基本原理④根，根式，根号⑤基本的，根本的；固有的，本来的，重要的，主要的，最初的，彻底的，原子团的，基的

radical principle 基本原理

radii radius 的复数

radio ①无线电；无线电报；无线电话；无线电广播；射电；收音机；X 射线（= X-ray）②高频的，射频的；放射的；射电的③发送无线电；无线电广播；用 X 光拍照

radioactive materials packaging 放射性物质，放射性材料

radioactive tracer 放射性示踪物

radio aerial 无线电天线，收音机天线

radio alert system （道路）无线电警报系统

radio communication 无线电通信

radio communication system tell-tale 无线电话信号灯（表示管理中心要求和驾驶员通话的信号灯）

radio controlled 无线电控制的，无线电遥控的，无线电操纵的

radio detected wear 用放射性同位素测定的磨损量

radio detector 无线电检波器，无线电探测器

radio-diagnosis 放射诊断（如：用X光检查）

radio diffusion van （厢式）无线电广播车

radio direction finder 无线电探向器

radio-dispatched delivery car 用无线电话调度的送货汽车

radio disturbance ①无线电干扰②无线电通信失调

radio-equipped 装有无线电的；装备有无线电装置的

radio examination X射线检验（=X-ray examination）

radio fixing 无线电定位，无线电定向测位（=wireless fixing, 亦写作 radio range fix）

radio frequency 无线电频率，射频（可分为：①超低频 VLF30kHz 以下②低频 LF30～300kHz③中频 F300～3000KHz④高频 HF3～30MHz⑤甚高频 VHF30～300MHz⑥超高频 UHF300～3000MHz⑦超超高频 SHF3～30GHz⑧特超高频 EHF30～300GHZ）

radio-frequency carrier signal 射频载波信号

radio frequency heating 高频电流感应加热

radio-frequency interference 无线电频率干扰，射频干扰

radio frequency isolation 射频屏蔽（简称 RF isolation，RFI）

radio-frequency plumbing 射频波导管

radio-frequency sputtering （为使二硫化钼等固体润滑剂与摩擦表面牢固结合而采用的）射频喷涂；射频喷镀

radio goniometer 无线电测向计，无线电方位计，无线电罗盘

radiography X光照相，射线照相，X光探伤

radio-guided 无线电导向的

radio-interference 无线电干扰

radio interference eliminator 无线电干扰消除器，无线电干扰抑制器（亦称 radio frequency suppressor, radio interference suppressor）

radio interference filter 无线电干扰滤波器（==radio interference eliminator）

radio interference suppression condenser （收音机）防无线电干扰电容器

radioisotope 放射性同位素

radio-labelled 放射性同位素示踪的

radiolocator 无线电定位器

radiometallography X光金属照相，射线金相学

radio navigator system 无线电导航系统

radio noise suppressor （无线电）噪声干扰抑制栅

radio patrol car 无线电巡逻车

radio plier （修理）无线电（用的）手钳，无线电工用手钳

radio positioning technology 无线电定位技术

radio receiver 无线电接收机

radio receiver controls 收音机操纵件［收音机开关、音量、调谐、波段选择等的旋（按）钮］

radio set 无线电设备，无线电台，收音机

radio shielded cable 无线电波屏蔽电缆，屏蔽电缆

radio-shielded spark plug cap 防电波干扰的火花塞屏蔽罩

radio shielding 射频屏蔽（= disturbance elimination）

radio-shielding cap （车装）收音机（的）屏蔽（干扰）罩

radiotechnics 无线电技术

radio telecontrol 无线电遥控

radiotelegram 无线电报

radiotelemetering ①无线电遥测②无线电遥测的

radio telemetry system （发动机的）无线电遥测系统（见 engine telemetry）

radio transmission 无线电传输

radio truck 无线电收发报车

radio-TV interference 对收音机和电视机的干扰

radio van （厢式）无线电收发报车（= field wireless van）

radio vector 定向无线电射束，无线电制导射束

radio wave 无线电波，射电波（电信）

radium 镭（Ra）

radius ①半径；半径范围②辐射线③轮辐；车轮辐条（复数 radii）

radius-changeable (tyre) puller 半径可变型传动带轮（一般由一固定锥形盘和一活动锥形盘组成，通过推动活动盘改变两者的间距以改变带轮的传动半径）

radius gauge （测量零件内、外圆角用的）曲度规，曲率规，圆角规，半径规，R 规，圆弧样板

radius leaf （悬架的）单片钢板弹式半径杆

radius link 半径杆（见 radius rad）

radius of action 作用半径，活动半径

radius of bend 弯曲半径

radius of convergence 收敛半径

radius of curvature 曲率半径

radius of flute of tooth 齿底半径

radius of gyration 回转半径

radius of relative stiffness （混凝土路面的）相对刚度半径

radius of rounding 圆角半径

radius of torsion 挠率半径，扭转半径

radius of turn (ing circle) 回转半径，转弯半径（= turning radius）

radius rod 半径臂，半径杆（悬架中一端固定于车桥，一端铰接于车架，用于保持车架与车桥呈直角布置，承受推力或转矩的杆件，允许车桥绕半径杆在车架上的支点上、下摆动某一角度，亦称 radius arm, radius bar, radius link, radius stray, torque arm, torque rod）

radius-rod drive 半径杆驱动（用半径杆将车轮的驱动力传给车架，亦称 radius arm drive）

radius stray 半径杆（见 radius rod）

radius to curb （汽车避开界石的）最小回转圆半径（见 curb clearance circle）

radius-to-eccentricity ratio （转子发动机的转子）半径-偏心距比（常用 R/e 表示，亦称形状系数 K，其中 R 为转子半径，即转子中心到顶角端的距离，e 为偏心距）

radius vector 位置矢量，向量径，（辐向）矢径，动径，向径，辐

radom(e) 雷达天线罩，天线屏蔽屏；整流罩，屏蔽罩

radon 氡（Rn）

RADOP 多普勒雷达（radar Doppler 的简称）

rad/s 弧度/秒（国际单位制的角速度单位，radian/second）

rag ①抹布，擦布；毛刺，飞边②去

毛刺；压滚花
ragged 凹凸不平的，外形参差不齐的；粗糙的，不完全的，未做好的；不协调的，紊乱的，不规则的
ragged edge of detonation 爆震临界边缘
rag top [美]带可收合的软顶篷和后窗的敞篷车（亦写作 ragtop，英称 soft top）
rail ①轨（轨道，钢轨）②栏杆（横挡，围栏）③横杆（横梁）④（电子控制燃油喷射系统向各汽缸喷油器供给稳定高压燃油的）共用储油歧管（见 common rail）⑤一种赛车的俗称（见 dragster）⑥梁（车身骨架中水平设置的构件，亦称 beam）
rail bar 栏杆支柱
rail bond 轨端导电接头（电气轨道为减少钢轨连接端的电阻，采用焊接连接）
rail car 轨道车辆
rail contact ①轨道接触②轨道触点
railed side 栏杆式（车厢）侧栏板
rail impact 纵梁碰撞（正面碰撞在汽车车架的纵梁上）
railing 栏杆，扶手；围栏，栅栏
rail joint bar （连接钢轨用的）鱼尾板
railless 无轨的
railless line 无轨道路（如：公路）
rail rapid transit 轨道快速运输，轨道快速公共交通
railroad advance warning sign 铁路道口预警标志（亦称 railroad crossbuck sign）
railroad crossing 公路与铁路的平面交叉（= railroad grade crossing, railway crossing）
railroad crossing angle 铁路道口交叉角（铁路与公路的交叉角）
railroad ties test （车辆）枕木跑道试验（车辆在铁路枕木构成的特种试验道路上进行颠簸试验）
rail vehicle 轨道车
rail vehicle transportation 轨道车辆运输（简称 rail transport）
rain backscatter 雨滴后向散射
rain channel 雨水槽，檐边（= cornice）
rain detector type automatic closing system （轿车、客车天窗的）雨水传感器型自动关闭系统
raindrops sensing wiper 雨滴传感式刮水器（装有雨滴强度和频度传感器，可根据雨量大小自动控制刮水器刮片动作次数）
rainfall ①下雨②降雨量
rainfall simulator 降雨模拟装置
rain flow method 雨流（计数）法（①对机件的实测荷载时间历程进行统计处理的一种方法②一种故障筛选分析法）
rain gutter 雨水排水沟，排雨檐槽
rainproof 防雨
rain proof instrument 防溅式仪器仪表（能防止雨水溅入的仪器仪表）
rain proof performance limit for buses 大客车防雨密封性限值
rain rail （车顶两侧的）雨水檐槽
rain-repellent polymer coatings 聚合物防雨涂层
rain sensor 雨滴传感器，雨量传感器（简称 RS）
rain-sensor-operated 雨传感器控制的（自动风窗、雨刮等）
rain switch 雨水（传感器控制的）开关
rain test 人工淋雨试验（车身密封性的试验）
rain tight 不漏雨的，防雨的
rain tyre 在多雨地区公路上行驶用的轮胎，雨季用轮胎
rain visor 遮雨板，雨檐板（亦写作 rain vizor, = rainvisor）
raised 高出来的，凸起的；升起的，

提高的

raised apex lands 转子角顶凸岸（指某些转子发动机的转子角顶安装径向密封片处两侧的加高部分，用以改善密封和气流特性）

raised control tower 交通（指挥）岗亭

raised curve （道路）外侧超高曲线

raised face 凸面

raised power take-off 装在较高部位的功率输出轴，高位取力器

raised rear fender 翘尾后翼板

raised separator 突起（高出路面）的分隔带

raised-tread tyre 高花纹轮胎

raising block 垫板，垫块

rake 倾斜，坡度，倾斜度；倾角，坡度角

rally ①收集；重整，集合，集队，集会，集结②汽车拉力赛（汽车集队长途连续行驶的比赛）

rally car ①集中强化试验用车（见 rally test）②拉力赛用车

rallyist 拉力赛车手

rally team （汽车）拉力赛车队

rally test 集中强化试验（汽车在各种恶劣条件下，集中进行不停车的连续行驶试验）

RAM ①（排气净化用）快速反应排气歧管，（rapid action manifold）②随机存取存储器（random access memory 的简称，可随时写入、读出和更新数据的存储器，断开电源，所有存储的数据便全部消失。在汽车电子控制系统中，用于暂时存储传感器输入信息、计算的结果或经常变换的程序等，供中央处理器调用。分为使用触发器存储信息的静态型"static type"和信息存储于存管的栅极电容上的动态型"dynamic type"两种，后者集成度高，每单片面积存储容量大，但必须每2ms对电容充电一次，并要外加刷新电路"refresh circuit"）

ram ①夯，撞锤，冲头，锤体，（压力机）压头，（压力泵）柱塞，推杆，顶杆，（牛头刨）滑枕，动力油缸，作动筒；（发动机进气）冲压管②维护与修理（repair and maintenance 的简称）③工作报告与备忘录（reports and memoranda 的简称）

ram air （汽车在无风的静止空气中行驶时，经风斗或各种开口孔、隙冲入车内具有一定动能的）冲击风（可用作冷风系统的风源或某些发动机进气系统的增压进气空气源）

ram air supercharging ①正压波脉冲增压（见 ram charging）②冲击风增压（见 ram air）

ram arm 液压缸摇臂，油缸摇臂，油缸臂，液压缸柱塞臂

ramble strip 凸人字形分隔带（见 jiggle bars）

ram charging ①正压波脉冲增压进气（发动机在进气冲程中，因活塞的吸气作用在进气管的气门端产生一负压，这个负压力波在进气管内以音速传播，到进气管的开口端形成正压力波，向进气门口反射，因此，只要恰当地选择进气管长度，使反射回的正压力波峰值恰好在进气门关闭前到达进气口，便可形成一股增压脉冲，而使进气量增加，亦称 ram air induction, ram air supercharging, ram pipe supercharging）②（利用汽车行驶中的）迎面风压增压进气

ram compression ①（利用汽车行驶中的）正面风压压缩（进气）②正压波脉冲压缩（进气）

ram cooling 迎风冷却

ram drive cylinder 柱塞传动油缸

ram duct ①（带涡流进气门的双进气门发动机中的非涡流）冲击风气道（见 ram air）②（长度经恰当

ram–ran

选择，可实现反射正压波脉冲增压的）增压进气道（亦称 ram pipe, 见 ram charging）

ram guide 滑枕导轨

ramification ①分枝，分叉；支脉，支流；②细节③门类④衍生物⑤结果，后果

ram induction engine 正压波脉冲增压进气发动机（见 ram charging）

ram intake manifold 正压波脉冲增压进气歧管（见 ram charging）

rammer ①夯，撞锤，型砂捣碎锤②压头，冲头③冲压，压实，捣固

ramming ①锤击，冲击；打夯，夯实②（空气）惯性压缩；速度头

ramp ①斜面，斜坡，坡道，斜台②装卸用的跳板③（支撑汽车前端或后端，以便进行车下作业的）撑具④（举升汽车的）举升台（如：二柱式举升台"2-post ramp"，四柱式举升台"4-post ramp"）⑤（互通式立体交叉的）连接匝道，匝道，进出坡道；引道⑥（高度不同的道路间的）连接坡道，（从一水平面到另一水平面的斜路或坡路，如：多层停车场中，汽车可驶上驶下的）盘形斜道

ramp angle 纵向通过角（当分别切于静载车轮前后轮胎外缘且垂直于汽车纵向垂直平面的两平面交于车体下部最低部位时，车轮外缘两切面之间所夹的最小锐角，该角为车辆可以超越的最大角度）

ramp approach 引道坡

ramp breakover angle ①高速公路进出引道通过角②纵向通过角（离地间隙角，SAE J689：轿车，旅行车，半吨货车的通过性能评价指标之一，前、后桥间车身底部最低点至前、后轮接地中心连线相交的外角，该角越大，离地间隙越大，通过性越好，见 ramp angle）

ramp control （高速公路等的）出入口匝道控制

ramped floor 倾斜地板（= slopping floor）

ramp entrance （高速公路，城市道路等的）匝道入口

ram piper 见 ram duct②

ram pipe super charging 正压波脉冲增压（见 ram charging）

ramp metering 驶入匝道车流调节（在高速公路驶入匝道上，为了配合主线交通状况对匝道驶入交通的驶入间隔或驶入交通量进行的调节）

ramp response 斜坡响应（一个输入量的变化斜率从零跃增到某有限值引起的时间响应，见 time response）

ramp response time 斜坡响应时间（从施加斜坡输入开始，到输出量保持在输入值乘静态增益减去输出量一阶稳态偏差之值的规定允差带内所需的时间）

ramp terminal （匝道与行车道连接的部分的总称）匝道终点，连坡终点，匝道枢纽（有驶出、驶入匝道终点之分，驶入匝道终点具有加速车道和合流区，驶出匝道终点具有减速车道和分流区）

ramp waveform 斜坡波形

ramp way ①坡道②（一般公路与高速公路相连接的）引道，匝道

ram tester 夯锤冲击试验机

ram (-type) cylinder 柱塞式动力油缸；液压升降器油缸，液压升降油缸，顶升油缸

ram-wing vehicle 升降翼汽车，冲翼车

ranch wagon （农牧场用）客货两用小客车（车后座位可翻倒，车身后部可作为货舱、行李舱）

r and m ①修理与维护（repair and maintenance）②工作报告与备忘录（reports and memoranda）

random ①随便的，任意的，不规则

的；（数理统计）随机的，偶然的 ②随机过程，随机取样

random access 随机存取

random-access memory 随机存取存储器（简称 RAM，允许按希望的顺序在任一地址单元存取的一种存储器）

random array 无规则排列，概率配置，随机排列

random crack 不规则裂缝，杂乱裂纹

random data 随机性数据（随机物理现象的试验结果得到的数据。其主要特征是：物理量之间没有确切的对应关系；变化规律不可能用确定的函数式描述；不可能确切预测未来时刻的值，只能用统计方法估计某给定值出现的概率，见 deterministic data）

random distribution 随机分布

random error 随机误差（在同一被测量的多次测量过程中，其变化是不可预计的测量误差）

random event 随机事件，偶然现象（＝random occurrence）

random excitation experiment 随机激振试验（以随机信号经功率放大对结构实施的激振试验）

random failure ①偶发故障，随机故障（指初期故障期以后至磨损故障期之前的时期内偶然产生的故障，亦称 chance failure）②偶然失效（由于偶然因素发生的失效）

random-failure period 随机故障间隔期

random-geometry-technique 不规则形状技术（指用任意形状之器件装配微型结构的技术）

random input running test 随机输入行驶试验（汽车在随机不平的路面上行驶时的平顺性试验）

random inspection 随机抽样检验

randomization 随机化；（产品或数值的）不规则分布

randomized program test （模拟）随机（负荷的）程序试验

random load 随机荷载

random loading 随机荷载（疲劳荷载中，峰值荷载和谷值荷载及其序列是随机出现的一种谱荷载）

random loading fatigue test 随机加载疲劳试验

randomness 随机性，偶然性，不规则性

random noise ①随机噪声②（自动化控制的）无规则微分急剧变化

random number 随机数

random occurrence 随机事件

random order 随机顺序（任意的次序，概率均等的次序）

random ordered loading 随机有序荷载（疲劳荷载中，利用特殊随机程序化方法，由一批不同的峰值荷载和谷值荷载构成荷载序列的谱荷载，通常同样重复有限长度的谱荷载序列）

random process 随机过程

random road-surface undulations 路面随机平面度（路面随机粗糙度，不规则的粗糙度，非常态的平面度）

random sample 随机样本（随意抽取的样品）

random scattering 随机分布

random sequence 随机顺序

random signal 随机信号（不规则信号，偶然信号）

random surface profile （地面）随机表面形状

random test ①随机性检验（在于鉴别试验数据中是否混杂周期成分）②随机试验，随机测试

random trial-and-error test 随机试凑试验（随机边试边改试验、随机渐近校正试验、随机试探试验、应变试改试验、随机逐次逼近试验）

random variable 随机变数（无规则变数，= chance variable）

random waveform 随机波形（任意波形）

range ①范围②幅度，限度③量程，行程，路程④区域⑤（作用）距离，作用半径⑥（变速的）挡区⑦（变化的）幅度

range ability ①幅度变化范围，量程范围，幅度②（汽车）运行距离，运距

range change ①（重型汽车带副变速器、分动器等的机械变速器的）挡区变换②（自动变速器的）换挡（换高、低速前进挡、空挡、倒挡、驻车挡等）

range conversion ①量程变换②挡区变换

range-cutoff function （雷达）有效距离截止功能，有效距离截止作用

rangeextender ①（电动汽车等的）行驶里程延长装置（如：在蓄电池式纯电动汽车上加装的"汽油机-发电机"充电系统在行驶过程中不断给电池补充充电，以延长其一次充电可行驶里程）②（泛指）可延长、扩大各种工作范围、量程等的装置

range extension ①量程的扩大②范围的伸展

range finder 测距仪（亦称 ranger）

range finding 测距，测定范围

range of action of the vehicle 车辆最大行驶半径

range of engine speeds 发动机的转速范围

range of headlamp （汽车）前照灯照射范围

range of measurement 量程（测量范围，= measuring range, measurement range，由上、下限所限定的一个量的区间）

range of spring （钢板）弹簧变形限度

range of stability 稳定性限度

range of strain 应变范围（一次应变循环中最大和最小应变的代数差）

range of stress 应力（循环）幅度，应力（循环）范围

range of stress-intensity factor 应力强度因子范围（一次循环中的最大与最小应力强度因子的代数差）

range on a tank of gas （汽车）满箱汽油的行驶里程

range (only) radar 测距雷达

range performance （蓄电池汽车等的）续航（里程）性能，储备里程性能（指一次充电后汽车可行驶的里程）

range-rate technique 距离-速度测定法，距离-速度探测技术

range resolution 距离鉴别力，距离分辨能力

range scale 量程刻度，距离刻度，距离度盘

range selector ①（副变速器高、低挡）变速杆②（自动变速器）速比范围选择器，选挡杆

range sensor 测距传感器

range shift ①副变速器换挡（高低挡、加力挡）②（自动变速器）工作范围变换，选挡

range-splitter （重型汽车变速器上附加的、带两套或两套以上不同速比的齿轮组，因而可成倍增加变速挡位的）多挡副变速器

range switch 量程选择开关，范围转换开关，波段开关，换挡开关

range system 测距系统

range-tracking 距离跟踪的

range unit 测距装置

ranging 调整范围；测距；距离修正

ranging circuit 测距电路

ranging computer 测距计算机

rank ①占首位，占第一位②排列，分类，评定③等级高于④位于⑤队

伍，行列，秩序，顺序，等级，地位 ⑥臭气难闻的，剧毒的，极坏的 ⑦秩

rank correlation 秩相关

Rankine cycle 朗肯循环（蒸汽机的一种复合循环，将水泵至锅炉加热蒸发，绝热膨胀，冷凝器冷凝至原始状态，我国亦译兰肯circle）

Rankine-cycle engine 朗肯循环发动机

Rankine scale 兰金温标（以华氏温标为基础的绝对温标，即兰金温度 = $F°+459.69$，水的冰点为 $491.69°$，沸点为 $671.69°$）

ranking test 分级试验，评价试验

rape oil 菜籽油（亦称 rapeseed oil, colza oil, 可用作代油燃油）

rapid ①快的，迅速的 ②（斜坡）陡的

rapid-acting ride control system 见 RCS

rapid action manifold 快速反应式（排气）歧管（废气中有害排放物在排气管中产生快速反应而转化为无害物）

rapid ascent 陡坡

rapid break-in 快速磨合

rapid combustion period （柴油机燃烧过程的）迅速燃烧期，速燃期（指从开始着火，即从着火延迟期结束时起，已喷入汽缸内的燃料迅猛燃烧，缸内温度和压力爆发性地上升的时期，以曲轴转角表示）

rapid convergence 快收敛

rapid determination 快速测定

rapid indexing 快速分度；快速分度法

rapidly tunable model 可迅速调整的（数学或物理）模型

rapid movement 快速运动

rapid prototyping technique 快速原型制造技术（简称 RP 技术，是综合 CAD、CAM、激光技术、精密伺服驱动技术、新材料等技术发展起来的高新技术。其原理是将计算机内的三维实体模型，进行分层切片，得到各层截面的轮廓，按此信息，用计算机控制激光器将材料切成片状，形成具有微小厚度的片状实体，再用黏结、烧结或其他理化手段，使逐层堆积成一体，即制成所设计的样件，1988 年美国 3D system 公司推出第一台成型机，缩短了汽车新产品开发周期）

rapid rail system 快速轨道运输系统

rapid-release valve （气制动系内的）快速放气阀（= quick-release valve）

rapid seating 座面快速磨合

rapid test 快速试验

rapid tool steel 高速工具钢

rapid transit series 快速运输系列，高速运输系列（简称 RTS）

rapid transit vehicle 快速运输车辆

rapid travel profilometer 路面平面度快速测定仪，路面轮廓快速测定仪

rapid undisassembly cleanliness 快速不解体清洁度（用规定方法，如：色度比较法，测定的经磨合而不解体的总成或整车的清洁程度）

rapid-varying 快速变化的

rapping 敲击

rare ①稀少的，稀有的，罕见的 ②稀薄的，稀释的

rare earth catalyst 稀土催化剂（用稀土元素，如：镧和铈，做活化材料的催化剂）

rare earth element 稀土元素〔亦称稀土金属 rare earth metal, 简称稀土 RE，是元素周期表第Ⅲ族副族包括镧（La）、铈（Ce）、镨（Pr）、钕（Nd）等 15 个镧系元素及与镧系元素密切相关的钪（Sc）和钇（Y）两个元素，共 17 个元素的总称〕

rare-earth/iron alloys 稀土铁合金

(高磁致伸缩性材料，用作磁致伸缩式执行元件)

rarefaction wave 稀薄波，负压波，稀疏波，疏波

rarefied 变稀薄的

rarefied air 稀薄的空气

rare gas ①稀有气体；惰性气体 ②稀薄的气体

rare-metal couple 稀有金属温差电偶

rare mixture 稀混合气（＝poor mixture）

RAS 见 remote access server

rasping road surface 引起车辆颤动的粗糙路面

raster 光栅［是能等宽，等间距地分割入射液前的、具有大量，⊕mm几十至几千条平行等宽、等距狭缝（刻线）的平面玻璃或金属片，利用多缝衍射原理使光发生色散，分辨为光谱的光学元件］

raster displacement grating sensor 光栅位移传感器（对光栅相对移动所形成的莫尔条纹信号进行处理，而获得光栅相对位移量）

raster display 光栅显像

raster generator 光栅发生器

raster pattern 光栅图谱

raster scan 光栅扫描（技术）（通过整个显示空间内逐行扫描来产生或记录显示图像的技术）

ratchet-and-pawl mechanism 棘轮-棘爪机构（亦写作 pawl-ratchet mechanism）

ratchet drive 棘轮传动

ratchet type clutch 棘轮式单向离合器（靠驱动棘轮的惯性运动与飞轮齿环啮合的离合器）

ratchet wrench 棘轮扳手（带棘轮的扳手）

rate ①率，比率，比值；速率，变化率；生产率；流量②等级，程度③标准，定额值④价格，费用⑤评价，评定，估价，估计⑥认为，列为⑦定等级，定定额；定运费

rate action 速率作用（速率对控制系统等的影响）

rate addition 运价加成（对某些条件下或有特殊要求的运输，规定的价外加成率）

rate control 速率控制

rated ①额定的②标定的③规定的④票面的，计算的，设计的；适用的

rated boost 额定增压

rated brake power 标定功率（厂方标定的有效功率，见 declared brake power）

rated capacity ①（蓄电池的）额定容量②（发动机的）标定功率③（设备等的）额定生产率

rated current-carrying capacity 额定载流容量

rated engine speed 发动机额定转速

rated fuel delivery （柴油机喷油泵的）标定供油量（相对于所配套柴油机在标定工况下喷油泵的循环油量）

rated horsepower （以马力为单位的发动机的）标定功率（见 rated brake power）

rated passenger capacity 载客限额，额定载客人数

rated payload 额定有效荷载

rated power 标定功率（制造厂根据具体用途规定，在额定的转速下，发动机应输出的有效功率，见 gross power）

rated power take-off engine speed 额定功率下的发动机转速

rated speed of car tire 轿车轮胎的额定速度（指轮胎可使用的最高车速，美共分 14 级，用英文字母表示，单位为"km/h"，F-80，G-90，K-100，L-120，M-130，N-140，P-150，Q-160，R-170，S-180，T-

190，H-210，V-240，W-270，如：S-180，表示该轮胎可使用的最高车速为180km/h）

rated spring capacity （汽车）弹簧额定负载量（设计汽车弹簧时的根据，按 SAEJ 274 的规定，每副汽车弹簧的额定负载量应等于或大于汽车满载时，弹簧上质量和弹簧下质量，对于该弹簧的最大荷载）

rated tonnage (seat) 吨（客）位，额定吨（客）位（对车辆规定或核定的载货标定吨位或载客标定客位）

rated value 额定值（= rating value）

rated voltage 额定电压（额定运行时的端电压。对发电装置，6V 系统为 7V，12V 系统为 14V，24V 系统为 28V）

rated wear 额定磨损量（指在规定使用寿命内的磨损量，即到不能使用时为止的可磨损量）

rated working pressure 额定工作压力（如：设计动力转向系时所规定的限制压力）

rate for special purpose vehicle 特种车辆运价，专用车运价（罐车、冷藏车和其他专用车运输特定货物的运价）

rate gyro 见 FOG

rate limitation 速率限制，比率限制，定额限制，费用限制，运价限制

rate-making standard 计价标准（对计算汽车运价的计费装载量、计费里程、运价单位和基本运价等的统一规定）

rate meter 测速计，速率计，计数率，测量计

rate of acceleration 加速度率，加速率

rate of actual loading 实载率（= utilization factor of payload or seats，载重、载客量利用率，全部工作车辆完成的主车自载换算周转量占总行程装载质量的比重，反映总行程装载质量的利用程度）

rate of adequacy of original records 原始记录完备率（原始记录表已记录的表数与规定记录表数的百分比）

rate of attenuation 衰减率

rate of braking 制动强度，制动强烈程度

rate of burning 燃烧速率

rate of camber change 车轮外倾角变化率

rate of caster change 车轮主销后倾角变化率

rate of change 变化速率，变化率

rate-of-change sensor （能测出变量每一瞬间值的）瞬态变量传感器

rate of charge （蓄电池）充电率，充电量，充电电流强度

rate of closure to other vehicle （行驶中）接近其他车辆的速率

rate of combustion 燃烧率；燃烧速度

rate of compliance inloading and unloading 装卸质量合格率（抽样检查装卸质量合格车次与抽查总车次的比率）

rate of consumption 消耗率

rate of contact material loss 触点材料损耗率

rate of container transport 集装箱运价（运输集装箱的价格）

rate of curve 曲率（曲线斜率）

rate of damage of goods 货损率（考核期内，货物运输中的货损吨数与货运量总吨数的比率）

rate of dangerous goods 危险品运价

rate of data signalling 数据传输率（亦称 data transfer rate）

rate of decay 衰退率

rate of depreciation 折旧率

rate of discharge ①（蓄电池）放电

（放电电流强度）率 ②排出速率，流出速率

rate of empty container　空箱运价（汽车运输集装箱空箱运价）

rate of explosion　（混合循环等容过程中的）压力升高比，等容压力比（最大压力与最小压力之比）

rate of flame propagation　火焰传播速率

rate of flow　①流速，流量率（单位时间内的流量）②车流率，交通流率

rate of freight compensation　赔偿率（货运质量事故实际赔偿金额与货运营业收入总金额的比率）

rate of fuel consumption　燃料消耗率（特指汽车在无弯道、平坦的铺装路面上，以固定车速，如：日本规定的60km/h行驶所测得的燃油消耗率）

rate of grade　坡度，斜率

rate of handling　装卸费率（计算货物或集装箱装卸费的单位价格）

rate of heat exchange　热交换率

rate of heating　①加热速率 ②发热速率（亦称rate of heat production）

rate of heat release in cylinder　（发动机）汽缸内的放热速率（单位时间内混合气在缸内燃烧反应所放出的热量）

rate of load application　加载速率，加载速度

rate of loaded container　重箱运价（汽车运输集装箱重箱和不对流空箱的运价）

rate of loss in accident　事故损失率（指统计期内因企业责任事故造成的直接损失金额与总行程或营运收入总额之比，是评价责任事故严重程度的指标）

rate of lubricating oil consumption　润滑油消耗率（汽车单位时间或距离等所消耗的润滑油，或者单位容积或质量的润滑油所能使用的行车里程或时间等）

rate of luggage compensation　行包赔偿率（行包责任赔偿金额与行包营业收入的千分比）

rate of on-schedule runs　客车正班率（客车正点班次与计划班次的百分比）

rate of on-time runs　发车正点率（客车正点发车班次与总班次的百分比）

rate of outflow　流出速率，流出速度

rate of pressure rise　压力升高速率

rate of pressurization　①增压速率 ②气密程度

rate of qualified vehicle maintenance　车辆维护质量合格率（指车辆维护竣工后，经检验部门鉴定合格的车辆数与全部维护车数的比例）

rate of regular transport of luggage　行包正运率（行包正运件数与发送件数的百分比）

rate of regular transport of passenger　旅客正运率（旅客正运人次数与发送总人次数的百分比）

rate of reliability　行车准点率（指统计期内准点行车次数与全部行车次数之比）

rate of revolution　转速（= rotative speed, rotative velocity, rotary speed）

rate of rise　①升高率，增长率 ②（曲线的）斜率（亦称rate of slope）

rate of roll　（汽车）侧倾率（亦称roll rate，指一定向心加速度下单位向心加速度的侧倾角）

rate of slope　①坡度 ②（曲线的）斜率

rate of speed　速度变化率（加速度或减速度）

rate of stops at fixed busstops　定站停靠率（客车实际停靠站数与规定停靠站数的百分比）

rate of strain 应变速率，应变率
rate of tension 张紧度
rate of traffic flow 交通强度，交通流率，行车密度，车流率
rate of trailer provision 挂车配比（在一定时期内，挂车配备数量占可以拖挂挂车的主车数量的比率，反映挂车配备程度）
rate of travel 相对移动量，行驶速率
rate of traverse 横动速率
rate-of-turn gyroscope 角速度陀螺仪
rate-of-turn record 转速记录器
rate of utilization of trailer 拖运率（指挂车所完成的周转量与拖-挂车合计完成的周转量之比，用来表示拖车动力的利用程度）
rate of wear 磨耗率，磨损率；磨耗速度；磨耗程度
rating ①额定值，额定，标定值，标定（功率，性能，能力，容量，负荷，生产率）；（额定的）参数，特性，规格；税率，工资率，运费率；等级，级别②额定值的标定，确定，测定，鉴定；估价，评价，评定，计算
rating axle capacity 额定车桥荷载能力（考虑材料强度、轮胎负荷能力因素，由制造厂所规定的车桥荷载能力）
rating data （机器）额定技术特性，额定数据（如：额定功率，额定生产率等）
rating formula 赋税功率的计算公式；额定功率公式
rating horsepower （以马力为单位的）标定功率（= duty horsepower, rated horsepower, horsepower rating）
rating method 额定法，标定法，测定法
rating plate 技术规格标牌
rating value 额定值，标称值

ratio 比，比值，比率，传动比
ratio arm 比率边，比率臂
ratio changer 比率变换装置，比率变换器（泛指各种改变比例的装置，如：变速器、液压制动系中，改变前后轮制动力分配比例的装置等）
ratio-changing-device （前、后轮制动液压、气压）比例变化装置
ratio control ①比例调节②（混合气的）混合比控制
ratio coverage 变速范围，速比范围
ratio error 比率误差
ratio flow controller 流量比控制器
ratio gear ①变速齿轮②变速齿轮机构
ratio governing （可燃混合气的）混合比调节（= ratio control）（见 qualitative governing）
ratiometer 比例表，比率表，比值计，比率计，比例尺
ratiometric （按）比率的，（按）比例的，（按）比率表的
ratiometric error （传感器等的）比率性误差（指因电源电压变动造成的输出误差，其差值与电源变化率成正比，亦称 ratiometricity error）
ratiometric sensor （电压或电流）比率式传感器（指传感器的工作电压与其参考电压值相同，因而其输出值恒与参考电压值成一比率关系）
rational ①合理的，有理的，合法的；理性的，纯理论的②有理数
rational transportation 合理运输（根据取得较佳经济效益的原则，选择合理的线路、车型、营运形式和组织方式的运输）
ration truck 口粮运输车
ratio of compression 压缩比
ratio of cornering radius 转弯半径比（汽车稳态回转试验中，质心瞬时转弯半径与初始转弯半径的比值）
ratio of engine rpm to vehicle speed

发动机转速与车速之比（简称 n/v）
ratio of expansion 膨胀比
ratio of greater inequality 优比
ratio of heat capacities 热容量比
ratio of less inequality 劣比
ratio of mixture 混合比（如：混合气的空燃比）
ratio of nozzle hole length-nozzle hole diameter 喷孔长径比（喷孔长度与其直径的比值）
ratio of number of teeth （一对齿轮）齿数比
ratio of oil to gasoline ①机油汽油混合比②机油汽油耗比
ratio of pressure rise 压力升高比［最高燃烧压力与压缩终点压力（不着火时）的比值］
ratio of revolutions 转数比，传动比
ratio of similitude 相似比
ratio of slope 坡度值，坡率；边坡斜度
ratio of specific heat 绝热指数，比热比值（＝定压比热 c_p/定容比热 c_v）
ratio of speed 速比
ratio of sprung mass to unsprung mass （汽车）簧上质量与簧下质量比
ratio of straight pass length to by pass length 直通线路长度与迂回线路长度之比
ratio of stroke to diameter （发动机活塞）行程缸径比
ratio of tire stiffness to suspension stiff-ness 轮胎刚度与悬架刚度比
ratio of torque to weight （发动机）转矩与车重之比值
ratio of turning radii 转向半径比［指在转向盘转角一定的条件下，作等速圆周行驶，以车速极低，侧向加速度为0时的转向半径 R_0 与其他某一车速下的转向半径 R 之比；R_0/R，作为表示汽车稳态响应的一个参数］

ratio-test 比率检验法，检比法
rat tails ①（铸件的）老鼠尾（缺陷，指铸件表面上凸出了多余的金属）②天线水平部分与引下部分的连接线
rattle ①咔嚓声，爆炸声，响度，急响器②使发出咔嚓声，咔嗒作响，发出爆炸声③使迅速移动，振动，扰乱
rattle trap ①破旧汽车②连接处不牢的
rave （载货汽车或挂车）底板边梁（底板周边的加强件，亦称 floor frame）
rave hook （帘式侧壁货箱式货车）底板边梁上的挂环
Ravigneaux planetary gear set （自动变速器用的）拉维格尼奥赫型行星齿轮机构（由两个不同直径的太阳轮，三个长行星齿轮，三个短行星齿轮，以及一个行星架，一个内齿圈等组成，通过离合器、制动器、单向离合器等锁止该行星齿轮机构的不同组件，而获得不同速比，动力由齿圈传给输出轴输出）
raw 生的，原状的，未加工的，未制炼的；未熟的；粗的，生硬的；未经训练的
raw exhaust gas （未经处理的）原废气
raw feed 原料（= feed stock）
raw material 原（材）料，材料
ray ①光线，射线，辐射线②放射，辐射，照射
raybesto(s) 一种胶压石棉（用作制动蹄片、离合器片等的摩擦材料）
Ray-bond （一种）环氧树脂黏结剂（的商品名）
Rayleigh distribution 瑞利分布［当连续随机变量的峰值 x_p 之概率密度函数 P_R 有形如 $P_R(x_p) = \dfrac{x_p}{\sigma^2}$

$e^{(-x_p^2/2\sigma^2)}$时，则称x_p符合瑞利分布]

Rayleigh equation 瑞（雷）利方程（式）（表示每人产生黄色光感所需的红-绿色比）

Rayleigh's law of scattering 雷（瑞）利散射定律（当一传导介质的导质的平均尺寸小于入射能量的波长时，入射通量的散射部分与波长的四次方成反比）

ray of light 光线

ray of spark 火花射线

rayon ①人造丝，人造丝织品 ②人造纤维，黏胶纤维

rayotube pyrometer 全辐射高温计

ray-proof 防辐射的

RBDS 无线电广播数据系统（Radio Broadcast Data system 的简称）

RBR （汽缸）相对窜气率（relative blowby rate）

RC （转子发动机的）旋转燃烧（rotating combustion）

RCA 影音输入接口

RC carburated engine 化油器式转子发动机

RCCC [美]有照运输业者协会（Regular Common Carrier Conference）

RCCI engine 反应控制压缩点火式发动机（reactivity controlled compression ignition engine）

RC1-1920 engine （美国莱特公司）RC1-1920 型转子发动机（RC 为型号，1 为转子机缸数，1920 为单室排量单位：立方英寸）

RC-2 engine 双缸旋转活塞内燃机（见 rotary combustion engine, two-rotor）

RC engine 旋转活塞内燃机，转子发动机（rotary combustion engine 的简称）

RCL 见 cone index

RCL engine dynamics 转子发动机动力学，转子发动机力学

R-clip 固定夹（retainer clip 的简称）

RCP 快速控制原型制作（rapid control prototyping 的简称，利用 dSPACE 的万能电子控制模块功能，将控制算法快速地通过 dSPACE 的各种 I/O 接口直接控制车辆部件，利用 dSPACE 软件进行交互调试，反复试验找到理想的控制方案）

RC-powered car 转子发动机汽车，旋转活塞发动机汽车

RCS 快速响应行驶平顺性控制系统（rapid-acting ride control system 的简称）

RC spark ignited coordinated injection engine 火花点火燃油喷射转子发动机

RC stratified charge system 转子发动机层状充气系统（转子发动机分层充气、燃烧系统）

RCTL ①阻容晶体管逻辑（resistance capacitance transistor logic 或 resistor-capacitor-transistor logic 的简称）②电阻耦合晶体管逻辑（resistor-coupled transistor logic 的简称）

R-curve R 曲线（裂纹扩展阻力值与稳态裂纹扩展量的关系曲线）

R&D 研究和发展规划，研制计划（research and development planning）

RD 残余变形（residual deformation）

RDAT 研究和开发验收试验（research and development acceptance test）

R&D firm 研究及开发公司，研制公司（research & development firm）

RdON （汽油的）道路法辛烷值（见 road octane number）

R&D planning 研究和发展规划，研制计划（research and development planning）

RDS 无线电数据系统（radio data system 的简称）

3rd/4th speeds striking rod （机械式

变速器的) 3/4 挡拨叉轴
REA 转子发动机 (rotary engine) (汽车) 追尾碰撞 (事故) (rear end accident)
reach ①达到……; 伸到, 延伸, 扩展到; 和……得到联系; 得到; 交给②(手脚)向前伸出③对……起作用, 影响④作用范围, 影响范围, 有效范围⑤到达距离; 工作半径, 手脚所能达到的限度⑥汽车的一次行程, 运行限距⑦(火花塞)拧入长度(从密封垫到螺纹端的距离)⑧(火花塞)伸入燃烧室的长度
reachable 可以达到的
reach of a crane 起重机动臂伸出量; 起重机工作半径
react 反应, 反作用; 反抗, 反攻; 再做, 重演
reactance ①电抗②电抗器, 电抗线圈③反应性
reactance amplifier 电抗耦合放大器
reactance capacity 电抗量
reactance coil 扼流圈, 电抗线圈
reactance coupling 电抗耦合
reactance factor 电抗因素, 无效功率因素, 无效因素
reactance function 电抗函数
reactance-grounded 电抗接地的
reactance integral 电抗积分
reactance modulation system 电抗调节方式
reactance multi-ports 电抗多口网络, 电抗多端对偶网络
reactant (化学)反应物
reactant ①反应物, 反应物质②试剂③成分, 组分
reaction ①反应, 反作用②反力, 反作用力③反动, 反冲; 反馈, 回授
reaction bar 转矩杆(见 torque arm)
reaction-bonding process (热)反应烧结化合法(如: 将制成一定形状的 Si 粉置于氮气 N_2 氛围中烧结, 在高温作用下产生下述反应: $3Si + 2N_2 = Si_3N_4$, 而生成蜂窝状多孔氮化硅块)
reaction chamber 反应室(进行化学反应等的腔室, 如: 燃烧室)
reaction component 虚数部分, 无功部分(= reactive component, imaginary component)
reaction cycle 反应周期
reaction distance (汽车制动的)反应距离(制动时, 驾驶员自接收信号, 将脚从加速踏板移动到制动踏板所需的时间, 称为驾驶员反应时间 "reaction time", 在此时间内汽车所行驶的距离称反应距离)
reaction force 反作用力
reaction gear (三角活塞转子发动机)主轴齿轮, 反动齿轮
reaction-injection moulding (塑料制件的)反应-喷射成形(法)(将两种塑料喷入金属模内, 这两种材料在金属模内混合, 起化学反应, 立即膨胀, 充满金属模腔而成形的方法, 目前已使用这种方法制造保险杠等塑料构件, 简称 RIM)
reactionless 无反应的, 惰性的
reaction lever (制动真空助力器的)反馈杠杆(将人力和真空作用力传至反馈盘的杆件)
reaction mechanism 反应机理
reaction member ①反应元件, 反作用构件②(液力变矩器的)导轮 (= reactor, guide wheel 或 stator) ③悬架内任一承受荷载或作用力并产生反作用和为其他构件提供正确位置的部件
reaction muffler 反射型消声器
reaction of bearing 支撑反力, 轴承反力
reaction plate ①(制动真空助力器的)反馈盘(承受反馈杠杆传来的人力和真空作用力, 并给出相应的

伺服力的元件)②(自动变速器行星齿轮机构多片式离合器的)固定盘,反作用盘(一般与变速器壳作固定连接, = stationary plate)

reaction plunger (制动真空助力器的)反馈柱塞(承受与踏板力相应的反力,控制负压信)

reaction pressure 反作用压力

reaction principle 反作用原理

reaction product (化学)反应产物

reaction (propulsion) engine 喷气发动机[= jet (propulsion) engine]

reaction ring (径向柱塞泵的)内凸轮环

reaction rod (悬架的)反力杆(亦称 reaction arm,装于前、后桥车轮附近与车架之间的杆件,利用对驱动、制动转矩的反作用力防止车桥发生扭转,亦称转矩杆、扭力杆"torque rod, torque arm")

reaction servomechanism 有反馈作用的伺服机构

reaction thrust 反推力

reaction time 反应时间(①从刺激开始到观察者开始做出反应的时间②外部或内部信号输入系统、装置或部件做出响应性输出的时间③化学反应的时间)

reaction time of braking device 制动器反应时间,制动器协调时间(中国定义为在紧急制动时,从制动踏板开始动作至制动力达到规定值的时间,如:总质量<4t的汽车,制动协调时间应≤0.33s)

reaction time of driver 驾驶员反应时间(如:从驾驶员接到的制动信号起,到驾驶员将脚踩上踏板为止所经过的时间)

reaction torque 反转矩,反作用转矩(= reactive torque)

reaction turbine 反力式涡轮机(亦称 pressure turbine, full-injection turbine)

reaction type brake tester (测定制动力的)反力式制动试验台

reaction (type) muffler 反射式消声器

reaction water (化学)反应(中生成的)水分

reaction wheel 反作用轮(如:液力变矩器中的导轮)

reaction zone 反应带,反应区

reactivation 恢复活动,使复活,再生

reactive ①反应的,反作用的;反动的,反冲的②电抗的,无功的,无效的

reactive cell (亦称 reactive chamber)反应室(如:使一氧化氮与臭氧反应产生激发态二氧化氮的反应槽)

reactive circuit 反馈电路,电抗电路

reactive coil 扼流圈,电抗线圈

reactive current 无功电流(交流电流与电动势的相位差为90°的部分,亦称 idle component of current, inactive current, wattless component of current, quadrature component of current, reactive component of current)

reactive exhaust manifold 反应式排气歧管(加大容积的排气歧管,以加强对废气中的HC、CO的排气热氧化反应)

reactive factor 无功功率因素(交流电路中,无功功率与视在功率的比值,参见 reactive power, apparent power, 等于电压和电流相位差角的正弦)

reactive force 反作用力

reactive link type double wishbone armrear suspension 反力杆式双A形臂后悬架

reactive metal 活性金属

reactive muffler 反射式消声器(利用谐振、共鸣将噪声能量向噪声源反射,借以降低噪声)

reactive power 无功功率,无效功率

(亦称 reactive volt-amperes，在交流电路中，有效电流、有效电压与它们之间的相位角差的正弦的乘积，即无功电压与电流或无功电流与电压的乘积，单位为乏，"var"，volt amperes-reactive 的简称，参见 reactive power)

reactive sputtering 反应气体阴极溅镀法（一种溅镀技术，在溅镀保护气氛中，引入参加反应的气体，即可与阴极材料表面形成一种化合物。如：喷涂硅时引入氮气，则可形成四氮化三硅"Si_3N_4"）

reactive torque 反作用转矩（= reaction torque）

reactive valve 反应阀，反作用阀（如：动力转向系统中，反应路况而使驾驶员产生转向盘"路"感的阀门，一般装在分配阀中段）

reactive voltage 无功电压，无效电压（在交流电路中与电流的相位差为90°的电压部分，亦称 reactive component of voltage）

reactivity 反应性，反应率，反应能力；反作用性；活动能力，活化度，活化性，电抗性

reactivity controlled compression ignition engine 反应控制压缩点火式发动机（简称 RCCI engine）

reactor ①（排放物控制系统中的）热反应器（见 thermal reactor）②电抗器（电抗线圈，扼流线圈）③（液力变矩器中的）导轮（亦称 guide wheel, reaction member，其作用是改变液流方向，给涡轮一个反作用转矩，使涡轮的输出转矩为泵轮转矩和导轮反作用转矩的向量和。导轮是固定不动的，或只能向涡轮旋转方向转动，故亦称 static reaction member 或 stator）

reactor blade （液力变矩器的）导轮叶片

reactor torque （液力变矩器的）导轮转矩（指工作液流经导轮转变流动方向后给涡轮的反作用力矩，$M_R = \gamma\theta/g\ (v_R r_R - v_P r_P)$。式中：$\gamma$——工作液体密度；$\theta$——工作液体流量；$v_R$, v_P——导轮、泵轮叶片出口处绝对速度的圆周分速度；r_R, r_P——导轮、泵轮中间出口处的作用半径）

readability 可读度，易读性，易辨认程度

read cycle time （存储器的）读周期（一个读循环起止的时间间隔）

readily 现成地

readiness ①容易，迅速②愿意③准备，备用，准备状态

readiness for operation 工作准备状态

readiness review （安装完）启用前检验

reading ①读，阅读②（仪表）读数

reading device 示读装置，读数装置，刻度盘

reading duration 读出期，读出时间

reading error 读数误差

reading lamp （车内）阅读灯（供阅读照明用）

reading microscope 读数显微镜

reading telescope 读数望远镜

readjustment ①更正，校正，校准②重调，再调整

read-only memory 只读存储器（简称 ROM，在正常操作期间其存储内容只能读出不能修改的一种存储器）

read-out ①读出（数据）②数字显示装置

read out instrument 数字显示仪表

read/write cycle time （存储器的）读写周期（存储器读出及新数据写入这一循环起止的时间间隔）

read/write memory 读写存储器（每个存储单元可通过输入适当的电信号来选择的一种存储器。其存储的

数据或是在适当的输出端上读出，或者根据另外适当的电输入信号而改变）

ready 有准备的，准备好的，准备就绪的；现成的，现有的；轻便的，简便的，易于……的；迅速的，立即的

ready-mixed concrete truck 混凝土搅拌-运送车（= concrete mixer car，简称 remi-con car）

ready state 待用状态（一切准备完善，等待使用状态）

reagent 试药，试剂

reagent grade 试剂等级

reaging 再老化，反复老化

real ①有效的，客观的，实际的，真实的，现实的，真正的 ②实在的东西，现实

real life emergency handling performance 真实突发事件的处置性能

real physical vehicle prototype 车辆的实体原型（real physical vehicle prototyping 是指车辆实体原型的设计制造）

real-time 实时的

real-time all-digital spectrum analyzer 实时全数字频谱分析仪

real time analysis 实时分析（信号分析速度达到信号的采集与分析结果几乎同时完成的程度时，称为实时分析）

real-time behavior 实时性

real-time control system 实时控制系统

real-time damping control （悬架的）实时阻尼控制（指随路况对悬架减振元件的阻尼作实时控制）

real-time damping system 实时阻尼系统（见 road-sensing suspension system）

real-time data transmission system 实时数据传输系统

real-time-dynamic traffic assignment 实时动态交通分配（理论）（用于解决动态和随机的交通流量在各路段和交通路口的分配问题）

real-time frequency spectrum analyzer-averager 实时频谱分析-平均仪

real time machine 实时计算机

real time method 实时法

real time operation 实时运算，实时工作，快速操作

real time route guidance system 实时导航系统（加拿大的一种驾驶员信息系统的商品名，见 ADIS）

real time simulation 实时模拟

real time sound level analyzer 实时声级计

real-time traffic advisory system 实时交通咨询系统

real-time traffic information 实时交通信息

Real time 4WD （本田公司研制的）实时四轮驱动系统（商品名。当前轮滑转时，可通过黏性耦合器，适当地将驱动转矩分配给后轮）

real-world 现场的，实际使用的（如：real world testing 实用试验，现场试验）

ream ①令（纸张的计数单位，1 令 = 500 张）②绞孔，扩孔，修整……的孔（out）

reamed 绞孔的，扩孔的

reamed bolt 精制螺栓（亦称 reamer bolt，精密配合螺栓）

reamer ①绞刀，锪钻，扩孔钻，扩孔器，绞床（= rimer）②绞孔，扩孔，扩大……的孔

reappear 再出现，再现

reapportion 再分配，重新分配

reappraisal 重新评价，重新鉴定

rear ①后部，后面，后方，尾部，后端；背后 ②后面的，后方的，尾部的；背面的，背后的

rear acoustical parking system 声响

警报（型）倒车入驻系统
rear axle （亦称 back axle）①（汽车的）后驱动桥（包括主传动、差速器、桥壳及左、右半轴在内的整个总成）②（驱动后桥的左、右）后半轴（将驱动力由差速器传给左、右后轮的传动轴，亦称 axle shaft）③（汽车的梁式或轴式）后从动桥
rear-axle casing 后桥壳（亦称 rear axle housing）
rear-axle casing cover 后桥壳盖
rear-axle gear ratio 后桥传动比，后桥减速比
rear-axle overhang of a towing vehicle 牵引车后悬（指牵引车后轴中心线至挂钩销栓的距离）
rear-axle shaft 后桥半轴
rear-axle shaft housing bushing 后桥壳衬套
rear-axle spring seat 后桥（钢板）弹簧座
rear-axle steering 后桥转向，后轮转向（= rear-wheel steering）
rear axle sway-bars system 驱动后桥的（独立）稳定杆系（左、右车轮直接与车架连接的多根杆件组成的防侧倾稳定杆系）
rear-axle switch 后桥开关（当后桥有一个车轮悬空，即完全不承受荷载、抬升离开地面时，该开关断开，发出汽车趋于翻车警报）
rear-axle tie-rod 后桥加强（拉）杆
rear-axle tube 后桥半轴套管
rear-axle whine 后桥噪音
rear axle with pair of torque reaction-rods 带双转矩杆的后驱动桥（桥左右两端均装有与车架连接的上下两根转矩杆及连接板组成的转矩杆系）
rear-axle yaw 后桥横摆（后桥非悬架质量绕其重心之垂直轴线的角振动，= yaw-motion of the rear axle）

rear-bank rotor housing （两缸转子发动机的）后缸体（指后一缸的外旋转线缸体）
rear batch （仓背式车身可向上开启的）后门（亦称 liftback）
rear bench-type seat 长凳式后座椅（= back bench type seat）
rear blind （轿车）后窗帘幔
rear body offset （货车）后车桥中心与货厢底板纵轴线的水平距离
rear body overhang 车身后悬（最后端的车轮中心的横向铅垂面至车身最后端的水平距离，不包括保险杠及其附件，见 rear overhang）
rear bogie （三轴汽车）双轴并装后桥
rear boot 后行李舱
rear box-bracket with pillar （轿车车身）后箱形托架带后支柱
rear brake 后轮制动器
rear brake modulator 后轮制动压力调节器
rear bulkhead （轿车车身等的）后隔板，后隔壁板（通常为车身的后座靠背板，= rear squab panel，同时起后横隔板即后壁板的作用，将后行李舱或后置式发动机舱与客舱分隔）
rear bumper height 后保险杠高度
rear bumper upper（**lower**）**edge altitude over road surface** （汽车）后保险杠上（下）边缘离路面高度
rear cam （汽车的）后方摄像机（rearview camera 的简称）
rear collision 后面碰撞（发生在两辆车或一辆车与固定障碍之间，一辆车后面受撞，另一辆车前面受撞，或两辆车均后面受撞的碰撞）
rear combination lamp 车后组合灯
rear compartment lid 后行李舱盖（= rear trunk lid）
rear control plate （柴油机分配式柱塞泵的）后控制板（装在分配转子

上,与前控制板一起转动可改变柱塞行程,用于调整最大供油量)

rear corner window 后角窗

rear crash warning system 后方碰撞警告系统

rear deck panel 后围上盖板(轿车车身后窗下的盖板, = rear window lower panel)

rear defroster 后窗除霜器

rear detecting and ranging system (汽车的)后方障碍物探测和测距系统(由发射器发射超声波脉冲,根据接收器收到反射超声波信号所需的时间,确定车辆后端离障碍物的距离,并酌情发出警报信号。当汽车入库等倒车需要监视后方的情况时,挂上倒车挡,该系统即开始工作)

rear diffuser (某些车辆装在车身后方底面用于消散排气管道系统和齿轮箱机油冷却器热量的)后散热器

rear directional lamp (汽车的)后转向灯

rear door ①(两门轿车的)后门(= passenger door)②后门(四门车的后部车门)

rear drive vehicle 后轮驱动汽车

rear dump ①(自卸车辆的)后卸(货物由车身后部卸出)②后卸式自卸车辆(= rear dumper, rear-dumping vehicle)

rear-dump body 后倾卸式车身(= end-dump body)

rear edge swing-out (四轮转向车辆转向时,车辆)后缘偏摆(现象)(偏离车辆前缘轨迹)

rear elevation ①后视图 ②(车身)后端抬升(= back elevation, end elevation)

rear end 后端

rear-end collision speed reduction brake system 防追尾碰撞制动系统(当根据车速及与前车间距判断有追尾碰撞危险时即自动制动减速)

rear end impact collision 追尾碰撞(后车车头碰撞前车车尾, = rear end impact, rear end accident, 简称 REC)

rear end panel (轿车车身)后围板(亦称 lower back panel, rear skirt panel,行李舱盖或后置发动机罩下方连接左右翼板的外板)

rear-end ratio (汽车的)后桥主降速比,后桥主减速比

rear end roll steer (汽车)后悬架侧倾转向(指后悬架系统侧倾引起的前、后轮转向角的变化)

rear-end stop lamp 后制动信号灯

rear end upper panel (轿车车身的)后围上板

rear-engine(ed) vehicle 发动机后置式车辆

rear engine/rear drive 后置发动机-后轮驱动(简称 RE/RD)

rear entrance 后部入口(= back entrance)

rear exit 后方出口;(车厢)后门

rear-exit bus 后门下车式客车

rear-extension 向后延伸的

rear face 背面

rear-facing seat (旅客面向后方的)向后座

rear fends [美](汽车车身的)后翼子板(英称 rear wing, tonneau panel)

rear-fin stabilizer 稳定尾翼(= tail-fin stabilizer)

rear fitting radius of semi-trailer towing vehicle 半挂牵引车后回转半径(半挂牵引车牵引座销孔中心至牵引车后端最远点间的距离)

rear foot brake 后轮行车制动器

rear foot corridor (轿车等的)后座走道(宽度)

rear/front steering angle ratio (四轮

转向车辆的）前后轮转向角比
rear gate （货车）后板（栏板式货箱后部的栏板，亦称 tail gate）
rear gate inside board 后板内板（后板内侧护板）
rear gate outside panel 后板外板（后板外侧护板）
rear gate side post 后板侧柱（后板两侧的立柱）
rear helper spring assembly 后副钢板弹簧总成
rear-hinge door 铰接式后车门
rear-hip-point 后臀点（指汽车乘员活动空间的人体基准原点——臀点的最末端位置，参见 hip point）
rear hood (boot) control 行李舱盖操纵件（打开行李舱盖锁止机构的手操纵件）
rear impact 后面受撞（是指车辆受撞部位在其后面的两拐角之间）
rear impact headrest inflator （发生）后面碰撞（时，座椅）头枕的充气器
rearing （行驶中由于轴荷再分配引起的）车辆翘头，车身后坐
rear kick up （车身造型的）后翘式（车身顶盖后段边缘升高，偏离整体轮廓线）
rear knee room （车身内）后座乘员膝盖至前座背面的空间（距离）
rear lamp 后（车）灯，尾灯（亦称 rear light）
rear light frame 后窗框架（= rear window frame）
rear loading vehicle 从后方装货的货车
rear longitudinal （轿车车身）后纵梁（亦称 rear longeron, rear sill）
rear main bearing 后主轴承
rear main spring leaf assembly 后主钢板弹簧总成
rear main steering angle sensor （电子控制四轮转向系的）后轮转向角主传感器（指装在后轮转向机处的转向角传感器）
rear marker 车辆后部的厂标
rearmost end 最后端
rear mounted double reduction fine drive 后置式双级主减速器（装在桥壳后方的双级主减速器）
rear-mounted engine 后置发动机
rear mounted flywheel 后装式飞轮（装在发动机后端的飞轮）
rear mounted gear group 后置副变速器（附装于主变速器后端的副变速器）
rear-mounted power take-off 后置功率输出轴，后置式取力器
rear-mounted radiator 后置散热器
rear-mounted transmission （装在车身后部的）后置式变速器
rear mounting of engine 发动机后置（= rear engine location）
rear object detection park assist 车后障碍物探测驻车辅助（系统）
rear overhang 后悬（分别过车辆后轴两轮中心和车辆最后端点，包括牵引装置、车牌及固定在车辆后部的任何刚性部件且垂直于 Y 和 X 平面的两平面之间的距离
rear overhang angle 后悬角，离去角，后通过角（见 departure angle）
rear panel 后挡板，后栏板
rear park assist 倒车入库、驻车辅助系统
rear passenger （轿车的）后座乘客
rear-perfect weight distribution （车辆的）后端偏重（型）重量分布（如：前桥承重 46%，后桥承重 54%，亦称 rear-biased weight distribution)
rear pillar 后柱（轿车车身后部支撑顶盖的立柱，亦称 rear post，C pillar）
rear platform board chain 货箱后拦板挂链

rear position sensor 后轮（与车身间的相对）位置传感器

rear pump （自动变速器液力控制系的）后油泵，输出泵（与变速器输出轴有固定传动比关系，亦称 output pump）

rear quarter centre panel assembly （轿车车身）后侧板中梁板总成（连接左右后侧板并构成后窗底框边）

rear quarter panel （轿车车身的）后侧板（常与后翼板成一整体，包括车身后支柱至车身后段及行李舱之间的整个区域，但有时仅指后窗与后门窗间的角板；或当后翼板为一单独构件时，仅指后翼板上面的侧板；或当车身顶板的两侧有窄边向下延伸而形成后窗框时，仅指该窄边窗框下面的侧板）

rear-quarter window 后座侧面三角窗

rear radius of truck tractor contour 半挂牵引车后端轮廓半径（指牵引转盘支承销中心至车架后端最远点的距离）

rearrangement 重新整理，重新安排，重新布置，重新排列；调整，调配，移项，变位

rearrangement of load （在车厢内）货物重新布置

rear reflecting mirror 后视镜（= rear reflection mirror, 亦称 rear view mirror, observation mirror）

rear reflector 后反光玻璃，后反光镜

rear roll center （汽车的）后侧倾中心（其位置由后悬架系统的结构和几何形状确定，见 front roll centre, roll center）

rear roof bracket 车顶后支架

rear running light （汽车发动机的）后运转灯（装在车身后部，表示发动机正在运转的灯）

rear scope （装在汽车后窗上的）后视镜

rear screen （汽车的）后窗玻璃

rear seat 后座（双排座驾驶室中后排的座椅）

rear-seat entertainment system （轿车）后排座（音像视频）娱乐系统

rear seat heelboard （轿车车身）后座踵板（后座底板前边及主底板加强板, = rear seat heelboard panel）

rear seat pan （轿车车身）后座盆形底板

rear-seat shelf panel 后窗台板（后座椅后边的搁板，简称 rear shelf, shelf panel）

rear (seat) squab （轿车车身）后座靠背

rear side housing （转子发动机的）后缸盖（后端盖、驱动端缸盖）

rear signal lamp 车后信号灯（装在车后的转向、车宽、制动、倒车等各种信号灯的总称）

rear-signal system （汽车）后部灯光信号系统

rear sill 后纵梁（= rear longitudinal）

rear single-cross seat 后排长条座椅（= back bench-type seat, rear bench type seat）

rear skirt rail （客车车身的）后围裙边梁（位于后围骨架底边的横梁）

rear span （车辆）外形后宽

rear spoiler ①后导流板（装在货车车身后方和三厢轿车后行李舱盖后方，两厢轿车车顶后边缘的整流板件，用于在汽车高速行驶时，减少尾部产生强涡流所形成低静压区造成的空气阻力中的形状阻力，利用空气动力产生的向下的压力，使车轮紧贴路面，以消减空气浮力所造成的牵引力损失）②后扰流板（装在车身后部附加空气动力学装置，用以改善汽车高速行驶时的稳定

性、减小风阻,如:升力及使后窗清洁)

rear spoiler with LED high-position brake lights 带发光二极管式高位制动灯的后导流板

rear spring 后悬架弹簧

rear spring boot 后悬架弹簧护套

rear squab panel (轿车车身支撑后座靠背,并隔开客舱及后行李舱或发动机舱的)后隔壁板(简称 rear squab, squab panel, = rear bulkhead)

rear standing pillar (轿车车身的)后支柱(= D post)

rear-steered semitrailer 后轮转向半挂车

rear steering actuator (电子控制四轮转向系中的)后轮转向执行机构(见 rear-wheel actuator)

rear steering angle (四轮转向系的)后轮转向角

rear-steering car 后轮转向车

rear steering gear (电子控制四轮转向系的)后轮转向机构(= rear steering actuator)

rear sub steering angle sensor (电子控制四轮转向系的)后轮转向角副传感器(指装在后轮处直接测量后轮转向角的传感器)

rear tandem suspension with rocker-beams 带摆臂的双轴并装后桥悬架

rear tipping trailer 后倾式自卸汽车

rear-to-front weight transfer (制动时)荷载由后轴向前轴的转移

rear track 后轮轮距

rear tractor clearance radius of semi-trailer 半挂车间隙半径(牵引销轴线至半挂车鹅颈部分圆柱面或其他向下突出部分表面的最近点在 Y 平面上的水平距离)

rear transaxle (变速机构及差速机构等装在后桥壳内的)后变速-驱动桥

rear turn signal lamp 后转向信号灯

rear tyre 后轮轮胎

rear tyre deflector (车身底板上的)后轮导流板

rear underride device (汽车的)车尾防钻撞装置(见 underride)

rear underride guard (汽车的)车尾防钻撞护栅(或护板)(见 underride)

rear under-run protection 防(止后车)钻(入前车)底装置(简称 RUP)

rear vehicle monitor system 见 RVM

rear view 后视图,背视图(= back view)

rearview camera 后视摄像头

rearview mirror 后视镜(= observation mirror, 多指车内后视镜)

rearview mirror attached TV camera 装在后视镜上的电视摄像头

rearview mirror bracket 后视镜支撑

rear vision area 后视野(指驾驶员借助后视镜,通过后窗的能见范围,亦称 rear visibility, back visibility)

rear wall (客车车身)后围(= back wall, 由后围骨架、后围蒙皮、后围护板、后窗玻璃及所属车身附件组成的总成)

rear wall frame (客车车身)后围骨架(位于车身后端的骨架,亦称 rear wall skeleton)

rear wall inner shield (客车)后围护板(覆盖在后围骨架内表面的板件,亦称 rear wall interior panel)

rear wall outer panel (客车)后围蒙皮(覆盖在后面骨架上外表面的板件,亦称 rear wall skin)

rear wall shelf rail (客车)后围搁梁(后围骨架上搁置地板的横梁)

rearward ①在后方的,向后方的,在后部的 ②后方,后部 ③向后方,

在后部，在后方

rearward-facing seat （面朝后的）后向座位

rearward operation 倒车；倒退操作，倒退行程

rearward perception 驾驶员后方视野

rear wheel 后轮（= back wheel）

rear-wheel ABS motor （控制两后轮制动液压的）后轮 ABS 电动机（见 Delco Moraine ABS Ⅵ）

rear-wheel actuator （四轮转向系中的）后轮转向执行机构（一般为机械式转向器、转向液压缸或电动机三类，亦称 rear steering actuator）

rear-wheel ballast weight 后轮配重块

rear wheel bump travel 后轮跳起高度

rear wheel drive 后轮驱动（简称 RWD）

rear wheel drive-engine situated transversely behind rear axle 位于后桥后面的横置式后轮驱动发动机

rear wheel feeding chamber （某些串列双腔式制动主缸的）后轮液压腔（双腔中向后轮制动缸供给制动液压的工作腔）

rear wheel flexible brake tube 后轮制动（器）软管

rear-wheel followed steering 后轮随动转向

rear wheel position sensor 后轮位置传感器（装在后悬架与车身底板之间，向路敏悬架系统提供后轮相对车身运动及车轮转速和后悬架高度变化信号）

rear wheel slip angle 后轮侧偏角

rear wheel speed sensor 后轮转速传感器

rear-wheel steering shaft 后轮转向轴（在机械式四轮转向系中，将前轮转向运动传给后轮的传动轴，亦称 center steering shaft）

rear-wheel steering suspension system 后轮转向悬架系统（当汽车驶入弯道或转向时，后轮悬架在所受离心力等外力的作用下，其一专门的摆臂将使后轮向着弯道外侧的方向偏转某一角度，汽车迅速实现转向）

rear-wheel weight ①后轮荷载②后轮自重③后轮（作用于地面的）总重

rear window （车厢）后窗（美称 back window, back light）

rear window central pillar （客车）后窗中立柱（后窗框架中部的立柱）

rear window cross sill （客车）后窗框下横梁（后窗框下部的横梁）

rear window (demisting and defrosting) electrical-heater tell-tale 后窗（防雾、除霜）电加热器指示灯（装在仪表板上，表示后窗加热器已接通）

rear window frame ①后窗框（= rear light frame）②后窗框架（供安装后窗玻璃用的框架）

rear window glass 后窗玻璃（货车驾驶室后部的窗玻璃，客车后围上的窗玻璃，亦称 back light）

rear window header crossbar 后窗框上横梁（后窗框架上部的横梁）

rear window louver 后窗护网

rear window lower panel （轿车车身）后围上盖板（位于后窗下面，= rear deck panel, upper back panel, rear waist panel）

rear-window sun curtain 后窗遮阳帘

rear window washer control 后窗玻璃洗涤器操纵件（控制后窗玻璃洗涤器工作的操纵件）

rear window wiper control 后窗玻璃刮水器操纵件（控制后窗玻璃刮水器工况的操纵件）

rear windshield （车身的）后窗玻璃

rear wing 后翼板
rear wing side outer lower panel 后翼板外下侧板（亦称 lower tonneau panel）
rear wing side outer rear panel 后翼板尾端外侧板
reason ①理由，原因；道理，情理，理性②推理，论证，说理
reasonable 合理的，有理的；适当的
reasonless 不合理的
reassembly 重新装配
reattachment 重新附着（如：气流剥离后重新附着车身表面）
Reaumur scale 列氏温标（以纯水在标准大气压下的冰点为0℃，沸点为80℃的温标，列氏度的代号为°R，$1°R = \frac{5}{4}℃$）
Reaumur thermometer 列氏温度计（在标准大气压下，纯水的冰点为0°R，沸点为80°R）
rebabbitt a bearing 重浇轴承合金，重（新）浇巴氏合金轴承
rebalancing 重新平衡
rebore kit ①供镗孔后的汽缸用的成套活塞和活塞环②供镗缸用的成套工具
reboring ①重镗孔，再镗孔②磨损汽缸的重新镗缸③经过重镗后的汽缸的孔径
rebound ①反弹，反跳②（悬架的）回弹（指悬架受压缩后的伸长行程，一般该行程的终点多超出其静止状态下的高度）
rebound action 回弹作用（弹性体或汽车上的各种能量吸收系统，受压或碰撞后的反作用）
rebound bumper 回跳缓冲器
rebound characteristics （汽车等碰撞时的）回弹特性
rebound clip ①（防止多片式钢板弹簧因回弹而散片的）回弹夹②（钢板弹簧的）回跳夹
rebound hardness 回跳硬度
rebound movement valve 摆杆式减振器的）回弹行程阀（减振器受压后回弹时该阀开启，见 deflection-movement valve）
rebound performance 回弹性能，回跳性能
rebound resistance （减振器）伸张行程（回弹行程）阻力
rebound stop 悬架回弹限位器（亦称 rebound check）
rebound test ①回弹法硬度试验（肖氏硬度试验，见 scleroscope hardness test）②（悬架的）回跳试验
rebound travel 回跳行程（亦称 rebound stroke，如：肖氏硬度试验的回跳行程，悬架弹簧的回跳行程，减振器的伸张行程等）
rebound valve （减振器）伸张（行程）阀
rebuild 重建，再建，改造，改建，翻新，大修
rebuildability 大修方便性（如：发动机缸套、气门座圈等是否容易更换的性能）
rebuilder 修旧厂，大修厂
rebuild kit 修复机器用的成套零部件
rebuild part 再生零件，修复件，修旧件（亦称 rebuilt component）
rebuilt truck 经过大修的货车
reburnishing 重新打磨，重新抛光；再磨合
rebush 更换衬套，更换轴瓦
recalculation ①重新计算，再核算②单位换算
recalibration 重新校准；重新标定
recall 召回（收回，撤回）
recall switch 回复开关（如：回复自动信号机操作的手动开关）
recap ①翻新胎（胎面翻新的轮胎，= recapped tyre）②将旧轮胎的胎面

翻新，轮胎翻新
recapper 轮胎翻新机
recapping （轮胎）翻新（更换已磨损胎面胶和两胎肩胶的翻新方法）
recapture energy underdeceleration 减速（时利用汽车惯性驱动电动机反转发电以）回收能量
recede ①向后倾斜，后退②退回③缩减，降低④失去重要性
receding side 退出侧
receipt ①收到，接收，接受②收据③签收，开收据
receive 接受，遭受，收到，容纳；承受
receiver ①容器，储器，储气筒，储槽②承架，底座，支架③接收器，接收装置④收报机，收音机⑤（电话）受话器⑥接受者，收件人
receiver area 接收面积（指可收到信号的面积范围）
receiver unit 接收装置；收音装置；受话装置
receiving antenna（亦称 receiving wire 或 aerial） 接收天线
receiving cone ①装料斗，进料喇叭口②进气喇叭口
receiving electrode 沉积电极
receiving inspection 验收检验
recent development 最新发展，最新技术
recent model 现代形式，最新型，新式（= late model）
recent trends 当前趋向
receptacle ①容器，接收器，储器②储藏所，仓库③插座，插孔
reception sensitivity （信号的）接受灵敏度
reception test 验收试验
recess ①凹入处，凹进部分，凹口，凹座；沉肩②切退刀槽，作沉肩，开凹槽
recess angle （齿轮的）渐远角
recessed headlamp 凹座前照灯（凹入车身前脸的前照灯，= built-in headlamp）
recessed head screw 槽头螺钉，凹头螺钉（如：头部有六方形旋具槽的内六方头螺钉）
recessed head screws 十字槽螺钉
recessed piston combustion chamber 活塞顶凹窝燃烧室
recessed-type handle 可压缩式转向盘柱（撞车受力后，转向盘柱可压缩，以免驾驶员胸部受伤，= collapsible steering post）
recessing 开（凹）槽，切槽
recess in rotor （转子发动机的）转子工作面凹坑（= rotor depression）
recession angle 移角（后悬架纵臂后端的垂线与轮轴中心垂线的夹角。当纵臂呈水平布置时该角度为0，抬高前端该角为正值增大）
recharge 再充电；再装载，再装料
rechargeable battery 可再充电的蓄电池
rechargeable battery type hybrid engine 13 mode exhaust gas test method 可充电蓄电池型复合动力发动机13模式废气试验法（日本运输省规定的标准试验法）
rechargeable energy storage system （车载式）可再充储能系统（简称RESS，指不仅可存储能量，还可利用汽车发动机带动的发电机或/和非车载电源提供的能量不断补充的储能系统，如：蓄电池、电容器和电动飞轮系统等）
recharge time （蓄电池的）重新充电（所用）时间
recharging control system （蓄电池等的）重复充电控制系统
recheck 复检，重新检查，再核对，再核查
recheck level 复检液位，复查油位
recheck test 复查试验（耐久试验后，为检查内燃机各项技术经济指

标与耐久试验前对比的稳定性的试验，见 steadiness test）

recipe 配方，制法，技术方法；秘法，诀窍

reciprocal ①往复的；相互的，交互的；互易的，倒换的，互换的；倒的，反的 ②倒数；互逆

reciprocal metre 每米负一次方米，m^{-1}

reciprocal observation 对向观测

reciprocal relation 互易关系，互反关系

reciprocate 往复，来回，作往复运动；交替，互换（位置）

reciprocating ①往复，往复运动，前后转动，上下移动；往复式发动机（= reciprocating engine）②往复的，往复式，摆动的，上下移动的

reciprocating ball （循环球式转向机构中的）循环球

reciprocating bearing 允许轴作旋转和往复运动的球轴承（= ball reciprocating bearing）

reciprocating inertia force 往复惯性力[指往复运动质量在不均匀运动中所产生的力，方向与该质量加速度方向相反，大小等于该质量与加速度的乘积。在发动机中一阶或称一级（first-order）往复惯性力是曲轴转角的余函数，即按简谐规律随曲轴转角变化的力，而二阶或称二级（second-order）往复惯性力是2倍曲轴转角的余函数，即按简谐规律随2倍曲轴转角变化的力]

reciprocating (internal combustion) engine 往复式内燃发动机

reciprocating pump 往复泵，活塞泵

reciprocating seal 往复运动密封件

reciprocating-type supercharger 往复式增压器

reciprocation 往复，往返，互换，往复运动

reciprocity 相互作用，相互状态；相关性，相互性；互换性；互易性，可逆性

reciprocity principle 可逆性原理，互换性原理

recirculated oil 循环润滑的润滑油

recirculating ball-lever and peg steering gear 循环球-曲柄销式转向器（具有曲柄销-销座传动副的循环球式转向器）

recirculating ball-rack and sector steering gear 循环球-齿条齿扇式转向器（具有齿条、齿扇传动副的循环球式转向器）

recirculation 再循环，封闭循环，重复循环；回流，逆环流

recirculation pump （排气净化）废气再循环泵

recirculation rate （排气净化）废气再循环量百分比，废气再循环率（%）

recirculation zone 再循环区，回流区

reckless driver 不遵守交通规则的驾驶员，不注意行车安全的驾驶员

reckon ①计算（数量、里程、方位、成本等）②推算

reckoning system 勘察系统，位置判断系统

reclaim ①将（旧废件等）回收（修复）；（废油等）精制，（旧胎等）翻新 ②改正，翻造，再生，修复，重新使用

reclaimed rubber 再生（橡）胶

reclaimer 再生装置，回收设备

recleaning 再清洗；重新清除；再净化

reclining adjuster （座椅靠背的）倾角调节器（亦称 tilt adjuster）

reclining angle 倾斜角

reclining back 倾斜式靠背

recoat 重镀，重涂，重漆，重新覆盖，重新涂装

recode 重新编码

recognition ①辨别②识别③认出

recoil ①反跳,跳回,倒退,反冲,反撞,产生反作用,产生反冲力②重绕

recoil of spring 弹簧复弹

recoil spring 缓冲弹簧

recoil stop (弹簧)回弹限位器(亦称 recoil check)

recombination 复合,再化合,再结合,重新组合

recommendation ①推荐,推举,介绍;建议,劝告②推荐书,介绍信

recommended route (导行装置向驾驶者)推荐的行驶路径

recommended standard 推荐标准

recondition 修理,修复,翻新,复原

reconditioned parts 修复的零件

reconditioning dimensions 修理尺寸

reconditioning facility 保修设备,修理设备,保修机具

reconditioning work 修理作业

reconnaissance vehicle 侦察车

record ①记录,记载②登记卡,记录本;记录数据,资料,记录曲线,记录磁带,录音带,唱片;档案,履历

record chart 记录图表(= recording chart)

recorder 记录器,记录装置;录音机

recorder/player 录-放两用机

recording bus 勘测工程车,自动记录仪表车(= recording car)

recording device 记录装置(记录仪器仪表内记录被测量值或其有关值的装置)

recording psychrometer 自计湿度计

recording speed indicator 速度记录显示仪

recording tachometer 记录式转速计,自动记录式转速计;自记式转数表

recording viscosimeter 记录式黏度计

record paper 记录纸

recover 收回,回收;重新发现;找到;赔偿,补偿,补救;改装,再生,利用(废料);恢复,恢复原状,重新装盖

recovery ①收回,回收②恢复所用的时间,恢复期③恢复;还原④再生;(废物)利用;矫正

recovery accessory (事故车)营救设备

recovery characteristics (弹性体的)复原特性;恢复特性

recovery curve 恢复过程曲线

recovery equipment ①修理工具,救援设备②(特指)将在公路途中发生故障的车辆拖运至修理厂等的施救设备

recovery factor ①回复系数②回收率

recovery of elasticity 弹性恢复

recovery service (汽车发生故障等后的)抢修,救援

recovery test 性能恢复试验(如:制动器受高热后工作能力恢复程度的试验)

recovery tractor 牵引损坏车辆用的牵引车

recovery vehicle 技术救援车(= emergency service vehicle)

recreational activity 休闲活动,游乐活动

recreational vehicle ①[美]野营车(=[英]camper,供旅行野营居住的厢式机动车,多备有起居室和炊饮设备)②休闲游乐车(简称RC,越野驾驶游乐用车辆)

recreation vehicle ①[美]旅行野营车(见 camper)②休闲游乐用车(简称 RV,指主要用于越野驾驶游乐用的车辆)

Recreation Vehicle Industry Association [日]游乐车工业协会(简

称 RVIA)
recruiting 补充,恢复原有性能,复原,养护,保养
recrystallization 再结晶,重结晶作用
recrystallizational annealing 再结晶退火(将经冷变形后的钢加热到再结晶温度以上,一般在 650～700℃,保温适当时间,出炉空冷)
recrystallization welding 冷压焊接,冷压再结晶焊(将要焊接的两表面清理干净后,紧密对接并施加压力,使两对接面上的原子互相结合重新结晶,亦称 cold pressure welding)
rectangle ①长方形,矩形②直角
rectangular 矩形的;长方形的,正交的,直角的,成90°的,矩形断面的
rectangular headlamp (汽车的)方形前照灯
rectangular hyperbola 等轴双曲线,直角双曲线
rectangular orifice 矩形喷孔
rectangular parallelepiped 长方体,矩体,直角平行六面体
rectangular prism 矩形棱柱,直角棱镜
rectangular section ring 矩形断面(活塞)环
rectangular triangle 直角三角形 (= right-angled triangle)
rectangular tube 矩形截面的管件
rectangular wheel 矩形"断面"车轮(指轮宽大于轮径的超扁车轮)
rectangular wire 矩形断面金属丝,扁电线
rectenna (电动汽车无线微波充电系统的微波)接收天线和整流电路总成
rectifiable ①可求长的②可校正的③可整流的
rectification ①整流,检波②精馏,净化③矫正
rectified current 整流电(流)
rectifier ①整流器,整流管②检波器,检波管③精馏器④矫正器
rectifier circuit 整流电路(将交流电变为直流电)
rectifier diode 整流二极管
rectifier meter 整流表
rectifier photocell 整流光电管
rectifier valve 整流管(亦称 rectifier tube)
rectifying grille (气流的)整流栅
rectilineal 直线的,直线运动的,直线组成的,用直线围着的 (= rectilinear)
rectilinear stiffness 拉压刚度(弹性体所受的拉、压外力的增量与其所产生的位移的增量之比)
recuperation ①复原,恢复②回收,再生③同流换热(法),换热作用,余热利用,余热回收④弥补损失
recuperative gas turbine 废气预热式燃气轮机,回热式燃气轮机
recuperative heat exchanger 热回收式热交换器
recuperative system 同流节热法,同流换热系统,回热系统
recuperator ①热交换器,回热器,蓄热器②回收装置,废油再生器
recure tire 胎面经硫化翻新的旧胎
recurrence of failure ①故障的复发②故障再现
recurrent ①复现的,再现的,反复发生的,周期发生的②(数学)递归的,循环的
rec-vehicle 改良车,改造车,改型车,改装车
recyclability ①(材料的)可再生性能,可再生性(指材料破损、老化等后经处理可再生使用的性能)②可重复使用性
recycle 再循环,回收,重复利用,再生(如:旧轮胎等的再生)

recycled coolant 再生冷却剂
red alert 红色警报（紧急警报）
red brass 红（色黄）铜（低锌黄铜）
red brittleness 热脆（性）（见 hot brittleness）
red check ①红色（渗透）探伤②红色渗透探伤剂（为一种红色渗透液，涂于零件表面，借以检查表面裂纹等损伤）
red delay portion 红灯信号延迟时间
redesign 重新设计，改型设计
Red Flag Act 红旗法（1865年英国颁布红旗法，限制蒸汽机汽车的车速，在市区内不超过2mile，在城市之间不超过4mile，并征收高额养路费等，使之难与马车竞争，制约了蒸汽机汽车在英国的发展）
red-green blindness 红绿色盲（= deuteranopia）
red hardness 红硬性（在红热状态下保持硬度的性能）
red heat 红热，赤热
redirect 改变方向，改变线路，改变车道
redistribution 重新分配，再分配；再分布
red lead 铅丹，红铅油，红丹，红丹粉（四氧化三铅 Pb_3O_4）
red light ①红灯（亦称 red lamp，如：停车灯，危险信号灯）②红色灯光，红光
red-light runner （触犯交通规章的）闯红灯者
red line 红线，（仪表盘）红刻线（表示最大或最小允许值界限）
red oil 红油（甘油三油酸酯，十八烯酸）
redox cell 氧化还原电池
red oxide 铁丹（氧化铁）
redox reaction 氧化还原反应
redraw 重新绘制
red reflection belt （某些轿车车尾的全宽）红色反光带
red reflector 红色反光镜
red-short 热脆的
red shortness 热脆（性）
red soil 红土
reduce ①减少，减小，缩减，降低；（断面）收缩，减轻②（数学）简化，约分，通分，换算，折算③还原，脱氧④整理，处理（数据）
reduced characteristic equation 简化特征方程
reduced characteristic function 约简特征函数
reduced comfort boundary 降低舒适界限（使人感到不舒适的暴露时间界限，见 exposure time）
reduced-maintenance 少维护的，少保养的，易维护的（指需要维护工作量少的）
reduced mobility passenger 行动不便的乘者（指活动能力衰弱的乘车人）
reduced order model 缩小次元模型
reduced pressure ①降低的压力②换算压力③对比压力（流体的绝对压力与其临界绝对压力之比）
reduced product ①（化学）还原产物②（数学）归纳积
reduced scale 缩小比例尺
reduced tariff 减税；减费
reduced temperature 对比温度（液体的热力学温度与其临界热力学温度之比）
reduced unit 折合单位
reduced viscosity ①换算黏度，温度折合黏度②下降的黏度
reduced visibility ①下降的能见度②受限制的视野
reduced volume 换算容积，对比体积
reduce in scale 缩小比例
reducer ①减压器，减压阀②减速器③减振器④渐缩管，变径接头⑤还

原剂⑥（底片）减薄剂⑦（合成瓷漆的）稀释剂

reducer LSP （制动系的）感载式比例减压阀（LSP 为 load sensing proportional 的简称）

reducible 可约的

reducing ①减小的，缩减的，减少的②还原的③渐缩的，缩径的④简化的，折合的⑤减少，缩减；还原；渐缩

reducing agent 还原剂

reducing atmosphere 还原气氛

reducing branch 缩径支管

reducing elbow 缩径弯头

reducing flame 还原焰

reducing gearbox 减速齿轮箱，减速器壳

reducing gear train 减速齿轮传动系

reducing joint 缩径（管）接头

reducing socket ①缩径球窝②缩径插座③缩径臼状管接头

reducing tee 渐径 T 形管

reducing valve 减压阀

reductant ①还原剂（= reducing agent, reducer）②试剂

reductase 还原酶

reducting flame 还原火焰（气焊中乙炔过剩的焊焰）

reduction ①减小，缩减，缩小，降低，减速；降低速比（指降低转速，增加转矩）②还原（反应，物质得到电子，所含元素化合价降低的化学反应）③缩径⑤简化⑥折合，变换

reduction box 减速箱

reduction catalyst 还原型催化剂（一种加速氮氧化物与一氧化碳、游离氢 H_2 或碳氢化合物起化学还原反应的催化剂。化学还原反应的理想生成物为氮气、二氧化碳和水，亦称 reducing catalyst）

reduction coefficient of rotating mass 旋转质量的换算系数（用于将车辆旋转质量的惯性阻力换算成平移质量的惯性阻力）

reduction formula 换算公式，归约公式

reduction furnace 还原炉

reduction gear ①减速挡②齿轮减速传动③减速齿轮

reduction gear apparatus 齿轮减速装置，减速传动装置

reduction gearbox 减速器，减速齿轮箱

reduction (gear) ratio 减速比，降速比

reduction of air resistance 空气阻力减小

reduction of area 面积缩小，断面收缩，断面缩减率

reduction of operation 运算，换算

reduction of wind resistance 风阻（力）减少

reduction range 减缩范围

reduction rate ①减速比②减少率③收缩率

reduction reaction 还原反应

reduction (type) starter 减速型起动机（亦称 gear-reduction starter, 指本身带齿轮减速机构的起动机，其输出转矩可增大数倍）

reduction valve 减速阀，减压阀

reductive ①还原的②简化的，缩减的③还原剂，脱氧剂

reductor ①减速器，减压器，减振装置②还原剂③缩放仪④变径管⑤电压表的附加电阻

redundancy ①（安全等的）余裕度②多余物，如：多余信息，多余部分，多余度等③过多，重复④超静定，静不定⑤（计算机）冗余（指通过编码后，信息长度得以减少的度量；在信息传输中，在不丢失基本信息的条件下，毛信息中可删除的内容）⑥冗余系统（并行地使用两套或多套系统部件，以提供错误

检测与校正能力,这种系统称为冗余系统)⑦备用系统或部件(当主系统或部件出现故障时,仍能保证正常运行的后援系统或部件)

redundancy signal ①(安全控制系统的)重复的保险信号②冗余信号

redundant ①冗余的,多余的,过多的②超静定的,静不定的

redundant circuit 备用电路

redundant sensor 备份传感器(当主传感器发生故障时,能自动接替主传感器完成原传感动作的后援传感器)

redundant structure 静不定结构,超静定结构

red warning triangle 红色警报信号三角

Redwood visco(si)meter 雷氏黏度计(工业用流出型黏度计的一种,在规定条件下,测定50mL试液流出的时间,其秒数即雷氏黏度值,称Redwood second 雷氏黏度秒,主要用于英国)

red zone (汽车仪表上的)红区(如:转速上显示发动机转速已超出允许最高转速的红色速带区)

reed ①弹簧片,平弹簧②(簧片式阀门中的)簧片③衔铁,振动片④钢材表面夹杂有非金属而引起的缺陷⑤在⋯上装簧片

reed contact 簧片式触点

reed frequency 簧片振动频率

reed relay 簧片式继电器

reed switch 簧片开关,笛簧触点开关

reed valve 簧片阀,舌簧阀

reefer ①冷藏车②冷藏车厢,冰箱③短罩

reel ①卷轴,卷筒,绕线筒,(磁带,纸带,影片)卷盘;绞盘,绞车;卷尺,带尺,皮尺;一卷,一盘(磁带,纸带等)②卷,绕

reeling 滚压,压平;卷绕,绕线;摇丝,绕丝;划槽;压花,压纹;矫直;摇晃,震颤

reel off 从卷轴上抽出,从卷轴上放出

reel on 卷上,绕上(亦称 reel up)

reel truck 电缆敷设车(= wire truck)

reel valve 簧片阀

re-engage 重新接合;重新啮合

re-engagement 重新接合;重新啮合

reengineered ①翻新的②重新设计、制作的(= rebuilt engine)

re-engining 更换发动机

reexamine 再次审查,重新审核

refabricated tyre retreads 再生式修补用胎面

reface ①重修表面,修理外观,修面②研磨(气门)③更换摩擦片

refacer 表面整修器,光面器

reface the clutch 更换离合器片,修磨离合器片

refacing (表面)重新研磨,重新磨光

referee test 仲裁性试验

reference ①参考,参照,查阅,咨询,询问②基准,基点,标准,依据,坐标,标记,读数起点,起始条件③参考文献,参考资料,说明书,附注④证明书,证明人⑤提到,论及,涉及,引用⑥职权范围,审查范围⑦注明资料来源⑧标准的,参考的,基准的,参照的

reference addendum 分度圆齿顶高(齿顶高,如:在涡轮上,是指分度圆与齿根之间的径向距离。对于具有径向变位的圆柱涡轮,其分度圆齿顶高之值等于节圆齿顶高与径向变位量的代数和)

reference area ①参考面积②基准面,起始面

reference axis 坐标轴,坐标轴线,基准轴,基准轴线,参考轴,参考轴线,读数轴线

reference book 参考书，参考用工具书，手册

reference car 概念车（concept car 的同义词）

reference cell 参比室（NDIR 分析仪的组成部分。其中通常充满空气，有时用氮气为检测器提供参比信号）

reference center distance （齿轮副的）标准中心距（两齿轮分度曲面相切时的中心距）

reference circle ①（简谐运动的）参考圆②分度圆（圆柱齿轮的分度圆柱面与端平面的交线。对于锥齿轮，其分度圆锥面被一个垂直于轴线的平面所截，其截线为一个圆。锥齿轮在此圆上的齿距为给定值时，此圆就称为分度圆。通常，分度圆被指定为分锥与背锥的交线）

reference conditions 基准条件，参考条件

reference cone 分度圆锥面（锥齿轮的分度曲面，简称分锥）

reference cone apex （锥齿轮）分锥顶点（分度圆锥面的顶点）

reference count 参考读数，基准计算

reference cylinder ①参照柱面②分度圆柱面（圆柱齿轮的分度曲面）

reference cylinder sensor 基准汽缸传感器（向控制模块发送基准信息）

reference data 参考数据

reference diameter 分度圆直径

reference dimensions 参考尺寸

reference diode 参考二极管（恒压二极管，用作参考基准）

reference fluid （试验时作为比较用的）标准油液，参考油液（如：reference fuel 参考燃料，标准燃料等）

reference frequency 参考频率，基准频率

reference gauge 检验量规，标准量规

reference helix 分度圆螺旋线（斜齿轮和圆柱涡轮的分度圆柱面与齿面的交线）

reference instrument 标准仪表（在标定仪器时作为比较标准）

reference level ①参考水平面，水平基点②参考电平，标准电平

reference line 参考线，零线，基准线

reference mark 参考刻度，零点，参照符号，基准标制，准线

reference model （作为控制基准的）参照（数学）模型

reference operating condition 参比工作条件（为仪器仪表性能试验或保证测量结果能有效地相互对比而规定的工作条件）

reference optical sensor 光电式基准信号传感器

reference performance characteristic 参比性能特性（在参比工作条件下达到的性能特性）

reference pitch 分度圆齿距（如：在涡轮的中间平面上，两个相邻的同侧齿廓之间的分度圆弧长，称为分度圆齿距。它等于配对环面蜗杆的分度圆环面母圆上齿距的名义值）

reference plane 参考平面，基准面

reference point 参考点，基点

reference position 参考位置，起始位置

reference rod 测杆

reference sensor 基准传感器（如：向电子控制模块提供发动机曲轴转速和活塞位置信息的曲轴位置传感器便是确定点火与喷油时刻的基准传感器，它发出的信号称为 reference pulse，简称 REF 或 REF pulse）

reference settling time （乘法 DAC 的）基准建立时间（基准电压阶跃变化时的瞬间与模拟输出信号最后

一次进入其最终值附近规定的误差带内时的瞬间之间的时间间隔)

reference signal characteristics（of a multiplying DAC） （乘法 DAC 的）基准信号特性

reference slew rate （乘法 DAC 的）基准转换速率（随着基准电压大的阶跃变化，输出信号变化的固有极限速率）

reference sound power 基准声功率（见 sound power level）

reference standard 参考标准

reference steer angle （汽车的）基准转向角，参考转向角（常用单位为 deg/g，使汽车产生一个重力加速度 g 的侧向力所引起的汽车转向角 deg，而其他原因，如：车轮外倾等引起的汽车转向角，都折算为基准转向角，称为等效转向角 equivalent steer angle）

reference surface ①（齿轮的）分度曲面（齿轮上的一个约定的假想曲面，齿轮的轮齿尺寸均以此曲面为基准而加以确定）②参考面，基准面，基面

reference system 参考系统（基准系统）

reference table 参考表，换算表

reference temperature 参考温度（起始温度，基准温度）

reference test 参考试验（基准试验）

reference test bar 测试杆 (= reference test rod)

reference test block 标准试块

reference time 基准时间

reference toroid 分度圆环面（指涡轮或蜗杆的分度曲面）

reference-value scale（of a quantity or property） （量或特性的）参比值标度（对于给定量或特性而言，由规定方法所确定的并为公认的一组值）

reference voltage 基准电压（如：为控制调节器而与反馈读出电压进行比较的电压）

refill ①再加注，再装满，再灌满②再装品，新补充的东西

refiller 加注装置（如：加油器，加水口，加油嘴等）

refiltered oil 经过滤的回收油

refine 精制，精炼，提炼；改进，改善；变纯，净化，清扫，清洗，澄清

refined oil 精炼油

refined steel 优质钢，精炼钢

refinement 精制，精炼，精加工；提纯，净化；清扫，清洗，清除；精致的产品，经过改进的装置（设计）；精细，精巧的程度

refine the grain （热处理）使晶粒细化

refining solvent （选择性的）精制溶剂

refinish 返工修光，整修……的表面

refit 修理，整修，重新装配；改装

refitted truck 改装货车（一般指用货车底盘改装的特种用途的货车）

reflect ①反射，反光②折回，弹回；反映，反响③有影响，有关系

reflectance ①反射，反射能力②反射率，反射系数

reflected glare 反射炫光（由视野中光泽表面的反射所产生的炫光）

reflected image 反映像

reflected pressure wave 反射压力波

reflecting coating 反光涂面，反光涂层，反光镀层

reflecting mirror 反射镜

reflecting power 反射能力

reflecting surface 反射面

reflection ①反射，反光②反射波，反射物③反射作用④折射，偏转

reflection coefficient 反射系数（亦称 reflection factor 反射率，被反射的光通量与入射光通量之比）

reflection time 反射时间

reflective area 反光面积，反射面积
reflective devices 反射装置，反光装置
reflective road sign 反光性路标
reflective type display 反射型显示（液晶盒在背面或背面电极配置反射膜，用显示屏调节控制外界光进行显示的方式）
reflectivity 反射能力，反射性
reflector 反射镜（具有反射面的光学零件）
reflector button 反光路钮，反光路钉
reflector frame outrigger 反照镜伸出支架
reflectorized paint （路面标志用的）反光涂料，反光油漆
reflectorizing (glass) beads （交叉路口安全标线的）反光玻璃珠
reflector lamp 反光灯
reflector marker 反光标志，反射路标（用反光涂料做的路侧标示）
reflector sign 反光标志（在车灯照射下反光，便于识别）
reflex ①反射，反光，反照；反射作用 ②反射的，折转的
reflex light 反光灯（本身不发光，反射照射光的灯具）
reflex-reflective material （汽车等后部、侧部反光器用）反光材料，反射材料
reflex reflector （装在车后及车侧的）反光器（本身无光源，依靠反光镜片反射光线的反光装置）
reflex reflector lens 反光器镜片，反光镜片
reflex silver 反射银（车身颜色）
reflux valve 回流阀
reform ①改革，改造，改良，革新 ②重作，改编，改造；重新排列组合
reformed methanol fuel cell vehicle 重整甲醇燃料电池车

reformer 重整炉（①裂化粗汽油、提高汽油辛烷值的改质炉，= reforming furnace ②裂化碳氢化合物气体与水蒸气反应产生氢气的装置）
reforming ①改造，改良；重整 ②碳氢化合物的裂化（提高汽油的辛烷值等）
reforming furnace 裂化汽油炉（见 reformer①）
reformulated gasoline 改质汽油，重整汽油（经改质处理，品质提高的汽油）
REF pickup （克莱斯勒公司发动机电子控制系统的）基准传感器（reference pickup 的简称，装在分电器上的霍尔元件传感器，分电器轴每一转产生与汽缸数相同并对应各汽缸的脉冲信号，向电子控制模块提供发动机转速与曲轴位置信号，与其他有关传感器信息一起用于确定喷油和点火时刻）
REF pickup signal 基准传感信号（reference pickup signal 的简称，如：由霍尔效应或光电式传感器发送至电子控制模块的发动机转速和曲轴位置信号，用于确定点火和喷油顺序及点火线圈初级电路闭合时间和喷油脉冲宽度）
REF pulse 基准信号脉冲（reference pulse 的简称，见 reference sensor）
refracting prisms 折射棱镜
refraction ①折射，屈射，折光 ②折射作用，折射度
refraction angle 折射角
refractive index 折射率（真空中光速与介质中光速之比），折光指数
Refractoloy 一种镍基耐热合金（碳 0.03%，锰 0.7%，硅 0.65%，铬 17.9%，镍 37%，钴 20%，钼 3.03%，钛 2.99%，铝 0.25%，铁 19%）
refractometer 折射计，折光仪，屈光度计

refractoriness 耐火性,耐熔性,耐热度

refractory ①耐火材料(= refractory material)②难驾驶的车辆③耐火的,耐熔的,耐热的,高熔点的④难控制的,不易处理的

refractory alloy 耐火合金

refractory ceramics 高温陶瓷

refractory clay 耐火黏土(= fire clay)

refractory lining 耐火衬里

refractory protection 防火装置,耐火防护设备

refrence cylinder 分度圆柱面(如:圆柱蜗杆的分度曲面)

refresh ①刷新,更新,翻新;恢复,小修②(蓄电池)重新充电

refresh circuit 刷新电路(为防内容丢失,而读出并重新写入动态 RAM 中的内容的电子电路,见 RAM)

refresh time interval (动态存储器的)刷新间隔时间(使动态存储单元的电平恢复到起始电平的连续信号起点的时间间隔)

refrigerant ①制冷的,冷冻的②制冷剂,冷冻剂

refrigerant fluid (冷冻装置的)制冷液

refrigerant oil 制冷压缩机油(空调系统压缩机的专用润滑油)

refrigerate 制冷,冷冻,冷藏

refrigerated body 冷藏车身

refrigerated container 冷藏集装箱(内壁装有隔热材料,箱内或箱外装有冷冻机,箱内温度可在 -18~20℃之间调节)

refrigerated goods 冷冻货,冷藏货,冰冻货

refrigerated vehicle 冷藏车,冷冻车(指装有隔热车箱,并装有制冷设施,用于长途运送冷冻物品的专用汽车,见 insulated van。这种车名称较多,如:refrigerated truck, chill car, car icer, freeze van, cold van, cold storage truck, freeze car, refrigerator van, refrigerating van)

refrigerated wind tunnel 冷风风洞

refrigerating capacity 冷冻能力,制冷能力,制冷生产率

refrigerating effect 冷冻作用,制冷效应

refrigerating unit 制冷装置

refrigerating vehicle 冷藏车(= refrigerator vehicle, refrigerated van, refrigerator car)

refrigeration 制冷,冷冻,冷却,制冷

refrigerator 制冷器;冰箱;冰冻机

refrigerator semi-trailer 箱式冷冻半挂车

REF signal 基准信号(reference signal 的简称)

refueling ①中途加油②添加燃油(简称 rfl)

refueling emission (汽车)加注燃油时的排放物(如:加油时排放的 HC)

refueling loss 燃油加注损耗

refueller 加油车(除具有运油车的基本装置外,还设置有泵油系统、工作仪表和操纵装置,可将油库中的油料吸入本车油罐,并能给飞机或其他机械设备加注油料,参见 fuel tanker)

refuelling depot 加油站,加油点,亦称 refuel(ling) station

refuel stop ①加油停车②添加燃料的停车时间

refuge island (行人过街)安全岛(= pedestrian island)

refuse ①废物,废品,渣屑,垃圾②拒绝③再熔化,重新熔化④无用的,不合格的,报废的,废料的

refuse collecting truck 装卸式垃圾车(以本车装置和动力配合集装垃圾的定型容器,如:垃圾桶等,自行

将垃圾装入、转运和倾卸的自卸式汽车，仅能自卸者，称 refuse tipper, refuse dumper）

refuse collector 垃圾车（= dust cart）

refuse oil 废油

refuse packer 带液压实装置的垃圾汽车

refuse packer trailer 带垃圾压实装置的垃圾运输挂车

refuse removing car 垃圾清扫车

refuse vehicle 垃圾车（垃圾收集和压实车辆，亦称 dust cart, 美称 garbage truck）

refuse wagon 箱式垃圾车

reg 注册，登记（registration 的简称，亦写作 rego，说明书、广告等用语）

regain ①收回，收复，回收②回到，返回

Regal 瑞加尔（一种用于橡胶、涂料、塑料工业的油炉炭黑的商品名）

regap 重新调整间隙（如：重调火花塞电极间隙）

regassing 加油（中途加油）

regen braking 见 regenerative braking

regenerate ①再生，更新，复原，还原②回收，回热③反馈，回授④革新，改革⑤再生的，更新的；革新的，改造的

regenerated rubber 再生橡胶（指利用废橡胶制品和生产中的边角料做原料，经处理加工后具有一定生胶性能的弹性材料）

regeneration 再生，更新；恢复；还原；脱硫；回收，回热，交流换热，蓄热；正反馈，正回授

regeneration under braking 制动（时利用汽车惯性能量反向驱动电动机发电等方法实现的）能量回收

regenerative afterburner 再生式后燃器

regenerative and hydraulic brake system（内燃机-电动机混合动力车的）再生-液压（双重）制动系统

Regenerative and hydraulic braking forces optimum distribution control（混合动力车的）电动机反转发电动制动和液压制动间制动力的最佳分配控制

regenerative apparatus 回收装置，再生装置（物质或热能回收、再生装置的总称）

regenerative braking 再生制动，能量回收式制动（制动时将汽车的动能转变为电能或飞轮的动能等存储起来，供汽车行驶时使用，简称 regen braking）

regenerative cooling 回收冷却法（利用低温介质回收热量，以冷却高温区或工质的方法）

regenerative cycle gas turbine engine 再生回热循环式燃气轮机（包括工质的连续压缩、回热加热、燃烧、膨胀和回流冷却的热力循环，见 regenerator）

regenerative fuel cell 再生式燃料电池

regenerative heat exchanger 再生式热交换器，蓄热式热交换器（带有中间载热介质的热交换器，= heat regenerator）

regenerative heating 再生加热，废热回收加热

regenerative particulate filter 再生式微粒物滤清器

regenerative resistance（电动机由汽车反拖逆转发电时产生的）再生发电阻力（为电动汽车的制动力）

regenerator ①热回收器，回热器（如：将废气带出的热量收回利用的装置）②交流换热器

regen system（减速能量等）再生回收系统（regeneration system 的简称）

Regie des Usines Renault　雷诺汽车集团（创立于1898年，法国最大的国有汽车生产企业，生产能力200万辆以上）

regime　制度；状况，状态，工况；方式，方法；领域，范围；规范

region　区域，地区，地带；部位，区段；领域，范围

Regional Bureau of Motor Carrier Safety　（美国加利福尼亚州）地区汽车安全局，地区机动车辆安全局（简称RBMCS）

regional motor transportation enterprise　区域汽车运输企业（在一定的经济区域、行政区域内从事汽车运输的企业）

region enclosed by a curve　曲线所包围的域

region of engagement　啮合区

region of no relief　平原地区

register　①（自动）记录仪器，计数器②（计算机）寄存器（由可接收、储存和取出信息的双稳态电路组成的电路，在汽车电子控制用计算机中，用于暂时寄存CPU该时刻正在处理的数据的小容量存储器件，包括：存储算术逻辑运算器输出的瞬时中间运算结果的累加器"accumulator"，在执行计算机指令时修改操作数地址的变址寄存器"index register"，存放要解释的指令或要执行的下一条指令的地址的指令寄存器"instruction register"，暂时存储正在执行的指令代码的程序寄存器"program register"和保存下推存储器"pushdown storage"，当前存入的数据项的地址的栈指针"stack pointer"等）③调节阀门，调温器，调气器④定位，对正⑤登记，注册，挂号⑥交付托运⑦（自动）记录，显示，指示⑧记数，存储⑨对齐，对准（with…, = line up with）

register calipers　指示卡规

registered tonnage　注册吨数；登记吨位

registered trademark　注册商标

register file　寄存器文卷（作为数据或指令的临时存放处的一种多位寄存器组，亦称堆栈"stack"）

registration　①登记，注册，挂号②（自动）记录③登记证④仪表读数，显示值⑤对准，定位⑥（图像）重合，对齐

registration mark　（汽车）牌照板（= license plate）

registration-mark lamp　牌照灯（亦称registration mark light, = number-plate light）

registration number origin and destination survey　录号起止点调查（记录车牌号的出发地与目的地的交通调查）

registration of vehicles　车辆管理（办理车辆注册登记、制发营运标志及控制车辆的布局、数量的增减和车型与车种的构成等管理工作）

registration plate　牌照

regression analysis　回归分析（法）

regrind　重磨，重新研磨

regrindable　可磨修的，可按修理尺寸研磨的

regroover　胎面花纹翻新机

regrooving of worn tyre　磨损轮胎的胎面花纹翻修

regulable　可调整的，可调节的

regular　①规则的，有规律的；正规的，常规的，正常的，标准的，通用的，普通的，习惯的；照例的，一般的；等边的，对称的；合格的，正式的；有系统的，整齐的，正规的（公共汽车等的）老乘客②（公共汽车等的）老乘客

regular bus　定班客车，客运班车（指城镇间、城市间的定时、定点运送旅客的客车）

1313

regular checking 定期检查,常规检查

Regular Common Carrier Conference [美]有照运输业者协会(简称 RC-CC)

regular engine oil 常规车用机油,普通发动机滑油

regular false method 试位法

regular fuel super car (使用)普通燃油(的)超级车

regular gasoline 普通汽油(指辛烷值为 80~90 的汽油,亦称 regular-grade gasoline,见 premium gasoline)

regularity for change of technical condition of vehicle 汽车技术状况变化规律(汽车技术状况与行驶里程或时间的关系)

regular line obstruction 班线阻滞(由于自然灾害、交通肇事等原因,使班车线路不能畅通)

regular line speed ①正常生产线速度,正规生产线速度(特指新产品经过试验性生产后的正式投产的生产速度)②客运班车线路(平均)车速

regular motor-oil 一般汽油机润滑油(相当于美国 ML 级润滑油, = regular engine oil,见 ML)

regular operation 正常运转,常规运行(= normal operation)

regular overhauling 定期大检修

regular production 正常生产,正规生产(特指新产品试制成功后正式投入的正常生产,以区别于试验性生产)

regular reflection 单向反射,规则反射,镜面反射

regular service conditions 正规使用条件,标准工作条件,一般运行条件

regular service route 班车线路,班线(营运客、货汽车按规定的班次、站点、时间运行和停靠,并已开办班车运输的线路)

regular size 正规尺寸,标准尺寸

regular (specular) reflection 规则(镜面)反射(遵守光学的镜面反射定律、无漫射的反射)

regular thumb screw 对称翼形螺钉

regulate ①调整,调节,校准②管理,限制,控制,管制③使整齐,使有规则

regulated crossing (进行)交通管制(的)交叉路口

regulated power supply 稳压电源

regulated variable 调节变量

regulating apparatus 调整装置,调节器

regulating characteristic 调整特性(曲线),调节特性(= adjusting characteristic)

regulating mechanism 调节机构,调速机构(= regulating organ)

regulating nut 调节螺母

regulating resistance 可变电阻,可调电阻

regulating resistor 调节电阻(如:电磁振动式调节器中,当触点接面时串联在磁场绕组中调节激磁电流的电阻)

regulating voltage 调节电压(电压调节器控制的电压)

regulation ①调整,调节,校准②控制,稳定,管理,管制③规章,规则,规程,条例④调整率 ⑤规定的,正式的,正常的,普通的

regulation characteristics 调节特性(功率、转矩、燃油消耗率等主要性能参数随混合气成分、点火时间或喷油时间等各项调节参数改变而变化的关系,其曲线称为调节特性曲线)

regulation of highway transport industry 公路运输行业管理(对公路运输行业事务的管理工作)

regulation repair 定期修理(按规定

时间或里程间隔进行的修理）
regulation size 常规尺寸，普通大小
regulator-rectifier 调节-整流装置
regulator tester （汽车发电机）调节器试验装置，调节器检验器
regulator valve 调节阀（如：曲轴箱通风系中的通风量控制阀 "PCV valve"）
regulatory sign 交通管制标志
rehabilitation 修复，恢复，复原，修理，重建，改建；整顿，休整
reheat ①再热，重新加热②（汽轮机）二次加热，中间再热③预热
reheat a /c（air conditioner）system 预热式空调系统
reheater 再燃器，再加热器（如：发动机工质两级膨胀之间重新加热的装置）
reheating 再热，重热，二次加热
reheating and regenerative cycle 重热回热循环，再热再生循环
reheat stage （燃气轮机）再热级
reheat temperature （汽轮机级间）再热温度
reheat treatment 二次热处理（如：回火、正火、调质等）
Reid Method 石油产品雷德蒸汽压力试验法（将石油产品，如：汽油，装入一密封的、称为测定弹的容积内，使弹内汽油与空气的容积比为1：4，测在37.8℃时汽油蒸汽对弹壁的压力，此压力称为雷德蒸汽压，亦称 Reid vapour pressure test）
Reid vapor pressure 雷德蒸汽压（在37.8℃下，空气汽油比为4：1时，在密封容器中测定的汽油蒸汽压，简称 Rvp）
reimbursement 赔偿，偿还，补偿
reinforce ①加强，加固；加（钢）筋②加强物，加固物，增强材料
reinforced hose 强化软管（用金属丝加固的橡胶管）

reinforced joint 加筋接缝，补强接合
reinforced plastic/foam 强化塑料皮层/泡沫塑料内芯（的夹层结构）
reinforced plastics 增强塑料，强化塑料（一般指用玻璃纤维或硅酸铝等加强的塑料）
reinforced plate 加固板
reinforced polyurethane 强化聚氨基甲酸乙酯（一般加添玻璃纤维）
reinforced reaction injection molding 强化反应注射成型；强化反应喷射成型（简称 RRIM，在反应喷射成形的原料中加有强化剂，以减少其线膨胀系数，提高耐热性，见 reaction injection moulding）
reinforced rib ①加强筋②螺纹钢筋
reinforced seal 带加强材料的密封件
reinforcement ①加固物，加强件（辅助加强主要承载零件或结构而增设的局部增强强度和刚度的辅助构件，亦称 stiffener）②加强，加固，补强③（焊缝）加厚
reinforcement bumper 加重保险杆，加强保险杆
reinforcement impact safety evolution 见 RISE
reinforcement of flexible member （空气悬架）挠性元件加强帘布层
reinforcer ①加固件，加强件②增加材料③强化剂，增强剂
reinforcing agent 增强剂
reinforcing fiber 强化纤维，加强纤维
reinforcing plies （轮胎的）加强帘线层
reinforcing steel 钢筋
reinspection 复查，复验（重新检验）
reinstalled 重新安装的，重新装配的
reinstatement 复原，修复，恢复原状
reject ①废弃，抛弃，排除，除去

②干扰，衰减③废品，废弃物，下脚料

rejectable quality level 不合格质量基准（简称RQL）

rejected heat 排出的热量

rejected material 废品，废料

rejection ①报废，剔除，排除，排斥，抛弃②抑制，阻止，干扰，障碍③衰减④废品，废物

rejection of car 汽车报废

rejector ①抑制器，拒收器②带阻滤波器③陷波器，陷波电路④杂音分离器⑤掺杂物分离器

related parts 相关零件，配合件

relation ①关系，联系，关系式，关系曲线②比率，比例关系

relation between design parameters and performance 设计参数与性能间的关系

relation between vehicle weight and nominal ground pressure 车重与名义接地压力的关系

relation of equivalence 等价关系

relationship ①相互关系，相互联系②关系曲线，特性曲线③关系式

relative ①相对的，相关的，相应的；比较的，成比例的；有关系的，有联系的，关联的②有关的事物，相对物，相关物

relative accuracy 相对准确度

relative air speed 相对气流速度，相对风速

relative articulation 相对（声）清晰度

relative bandwith 相对带宽（滤波器上、下限频率差与中心频率之差）

relative blowby rate （汽缸）相对窜气率（简称RBR，见blowby）

relative charge 相对充气量 $\left(=\dfrac{实际汽缸充气量}{汽缸排量\times 大气密度}\right)$

relative clearance volume （压缩机）相对余隙容积（某级的余隙容积与该级压缩元件行程容积的比值）

relative contrast 相对对比率（百分对比度）

relative contrast sensitivity 相对对比感受性［指作业在阈642度时的亮度对比值的倒数与背景亮度的关系，用一个在很高的漫射照明（通常为$100cd/m^2$）下得到的对比敏感度值的百分率表示，简称RCS］

relative coordinate 相对坐标（可用另一可编址点来标示某一可编址点位置的坐标）

relative cylinder charge 发动机汽缸的相对充气量（见relative charge）

relative deformation 相对变形

relative density 相对密度（= specific gravity）

relative displacement 相对位移

relative eddy 相对旋涡

relative efficiency 相对效率

relative elongation 相对伸长（参见relative deformation）

relative emission index （发动机有害物）相对排放量指数

relative error 相对（比例）误差（率）［绝对误差除以被测量的（约定）真值］

relative extremal 相对极（值）曲线

relative flow 相对流动

relative frequency 相对频率

relative humidity 相对湿度（空气中实际所含水蒸气密度和同温度下饱和水蒸气密度的百分比，也就是实际水蒸气压强和同温度下饱和水蒸气压强的百分比，简称RH）

relative movement 相对运动

relative position sensor （车身）相对位置传感器

relative pressure 相对压力

relative resolution (of a linear ADC or DAC) （线性ADC或DAC的）相对分辨率（模拟分辨率与实际的

或标称的满度范围之比)
relative speed 相对速率
relative steering wheel displacement 转向盘相对转动量(汽车以极低车速回转,当质心的转弯半径为 10m 时,转向盘的转动量)
relative theory 相对论
relative uniform convergence 相对均匀(一致)收敛性
relative viscosity 相对黏度
relative wear resistance 相对耐磨性
relative wind 相对风(指相对于汽车行驶方向和速度的外界气流)
relative wind velocity (汽车空气动力学)相对风速(车辆的速度向量 v 在 $X-Y$ 平面内投影的反向)
relaxation method 逐次近似法,叠弛渐近法,张弛法
relaxation oscillator 弛张振荡器,弛豫振荡器
relaxed stress 松弛应力(应力松弛试验中任一时间试件上所减少的应力,即初始应力与剩余应力之差)
relaxing of spring 弹簧的松弛
relax(**relaxation** 的简称) 弛张,弛豫,张弛;松弛,放松;减轻,缓和,削弱,衰减;卸荷,卸载
relay ①(电路中的)继电器(由电磁线圈控制的开关元件)②(通信技术中的)中继站(点到点的接收和重新发送站点)③中继装置(任一种由控制信号或某种激励操纵的机械、电力、液压、气动执行和开关器件的通称)
relay and quick release valve (气制动系)继动快放阀(具有继动和快放阀两种功能的部件)
relay armature 继电器衔铁
relay block 继电器盒(继电器和熔丝等组装成一体,并置于块状外壳内的器件)
relay box (汽车用的)中继变速器,半挡变速器(主变速器挡位数不变,在其前端或后端再增加的一个仅具有两种传动比的副变速装置,如:可将主变速器的四个挡位变为八个挡位的变速装置)
relay connection 中继电器连接
relay contact 继电器触点(亦称) relay contact point
relay coupled 断电器耦合的
relay cylinder 继动油缸
relay emergency valve (挂车制动的)紧急制动阀(简称 RE valve,见 trailer braking emergency valve)
relay lamp [美]多见于大型长车侧面的辅助转向信号灯(英称 intermediate direction indicator lamp)
relay piston ①(真空助力器等装置中的)伺服活塞(亦称 servo piston) ②继动活塞;转换活塞
relay point 转运站,中继站
relay rod ①中央连杆(见 center link) ②[美](直接与转向垂臂连接的)转向横拉杆(亦称 intermediate rod)
relay terminal (硅整流交流发电机定子线圈的)继电器接线柱(= stator coil terminal)
relay-type recorder 继电器式记录器
relay valve 继动阀(①在液力变速器控制系统中,指接收信号阀的换挡信号使换挡元件接合或分离的阀 ②在气制动系中,指由于气制动阀输出气压的作用,能使制动气室直接从储气罐获得所需气压的部件)
relay winding 继电器线圈
releasable connection 可拆连接
release ①释放,解除,放松,放开;脱扣,脱钩,脱开,分离;卸压,解压;放出,析出,排出 ②释放装置,松脱装置,脱扣装置;断路器,排气装置
release arm (离合器踏板至分离叉间的传动杆系中的)分离臂(将杆系中的横轴转动变换成摆动的臂

release arm rod (与离合器传动杆系中的分离臂连接,将该臂的摆动传给分离叉的)分离臂杆

release bearing (离合器)分离轴承(见 clutch release bearing)

release bearing and sleeve assembly (离合器)分离轴承和分离套筒总成(分离轴承与分离套筒组成的装置)

release bearing assembly 分离轴承总成(由离合器分离拨叉直接推动的带叉槽的分离盘和分离轴承等组成,亦称 throw-out bearing assembly)

release bearing oil tube 分离轴承滑油管

release cam 释放凸轮

release clutch 超载离合器(见 overload clutch)

release cock 减压开关,减压阀;放泄开关;放泄阀

release collar (离合器分离轴承的)分离套筒(亦称 release sleeve)

release curve (制动)松放曲线

released energy 释放出的能量(= let loose energy)

release handle 放松手柄,释放手柄

release hitch 带脱钩防止器的牵引装置

release hook 带脱钩防止机构的牵引钩

release lever (离合器)分离杆(能绕中间支点转动,使压盘分离或接合的杠杆,亦称 release pad)

release lever adjusting screw (离合器)分离杆调整螺钉(装在分离杆上用以调整离合器间隙的螺钉)

release lever axle (离合器)分离杆轴

release-lever gear ratio (离合器压盘)分离杆传动比

release lever plate (离合器的)分离盘(将离合器分离轴承的旋转运动传给分离叉的部件)

release lever screw (离合器压盘)分离杆调节螺钉

release lever support 分离杆支座(离合器上安装分离杆的支座)

release lever support bracket (离合器压盘)分离杆支架

release plate with thrust bearing (离合器分离叉推动、带环形槽的)分离叉拨盘带推力轴承(总成)(亦称分离轴承总成 "release bearing assembly")

release pressure of brake shoe assembly 制动蹄放松压力(使制动蹄松放所需的压力)

releaser 排除器,释放装置,松开装置

release relay 释放继电器,复原继电器,话终继电器

release rod 分离推杆(机械式离合器操纵机构中传递运动的推力杆件,亦称 operating rod)

release rod adjusting screw 分离推杆调整螺钉(装在分离推杆上,用以调整离合器踏板自由行程的螺钉)

release signal 复原信号,释放信号

release sleeve (离合器的)分离套筒[套在变速器轴承盖管状延伸部分的零件,对(离合器的)分离轴承的轴向移动起导向作用]

release spring 复位弹簧,分离弹簧(双盘离合器中使中间压盘脱离接合位置的弹簧)

release the (accelerator, clutch, brake) pedal 松开(加速器、离合器、制动器)踏板

release thrust bearing 分离轴承(作用在分离杆上,使离合器分离的轴承)

release time ①(继电器)断开时间 ②(制动)松开时间(从松开制动踏板到制动力消失的时间,亦称 release brake time)

release valve 放泄阀（如：气制动系的放气阀）

release yoke （离合器）分离轴承及分离套筒（总成的旧称）

releasing agent 防黏剂，脱膜剂，分型剂

releasing cam 释放凸轮，放气凸轮，排放凸轮

releasing device 脱钩装置，脱开装置，分离机构，释放装置

releasing of brake 制动器松开

releasing spring 释放弹簧，卸载弹簧，松脱安全弹簧，复位弹簧

re-leather the brakes 更换制动器摩擦片（= reline the brakes）

relevant 有关的，相关的；适当的，切合的；成比例的，相应的

relevant failure 关联失效，相关失效

relevant value 相关值

reliability ①可靠性（广义可靠性是指产品在其整个寿命周期内完成规定功能的能力，它包括了狭义可靠性和可维修性。狭义可靠性是指产品在某一规定时间段内发生失效的难易程度）②可靠度（完成规定功能的概率）

reliability assessment 可靠性评定

reliability certification 可靠性认证

reliability coefficient 可靠性系数

reliability compliance test 可靠性验证试验（为确定汽车的可靠性特征量是否达到所要求的水平而进行的试验，亦称 reliability audit test，reliability certification test，reliability demonstration test）

reliability control 可靠性控制，可靠性管理

reliability design review 可靠性设计评审

reliability determination test 可靠性测定试验（为确定可靠性特征量的数值而进行的试验）

reliability goal （所要求的）可靠性指标

reliability index 可靠性指数

reliability level 可靠性水平（可靠程度）

reliability, maintainability, safety and human factors （汽车的）可靠性，易维修性，安全性及人体适应性（简称 RMSH，参见 human factors engineering）

reliability of service 使用可靠性

reliability performance measure 可靠性量测（简称 RPM）

reliability proofing cycle 可靠性试验循环

reliability trial 汽车的长距离运行可靠性试验

reliability yardstick(s) 可靠性评价基准，可靠性尺度

reliable 可靠的，无故障的，（使用）安全的

relief ①减荷，卸荷，减载，降压，溢流，释放，解除，消除，松弛；②浮雕花纹，凸纹，凹凸 ③凸起的，起伏的

relief area 非摩擦区域，非接触区

relief cam 减压凸轮

relief circuit 减压回路，卸载回路，溢流油路

relief cock 降压开关

relief driver 助理驾驶员，换班驾驶员，副驾驶员

relief fitting 减压装置

relief road 间道，辅助道路，分担交通的道路，高峰分散路

relief sprue 除渣减压冒口，冒口，补助浇口

relief valve 减压阀（= pressure reducing valve, pressure relief valve, reduction valve）

relief valve ball 减压阀钢球

relieve ①减轻，减荷，卸载；降压，

减压，放气②分离，脱开，释放③救援，救济④替换，换班

relieve the stresses 消除内应力

relieving 减轻，减荷，卸载；降压，减压；分离，脱开，释放

relign ①重新排列，重组②重新校整③改组，改编④重新定位

reline ①更换（摩擦）衬片，更换（轴承）衬套，更换（车身）衬里②重浇轴瓦（亦称 remetalling）③重新画线

reline a bearing 重浇轴承合金，重新挂瓦（= remetal a bearing）

reliner （摩擦）衬片更换机，换衬器（亦称 relining machine）

reline the brakes 换装制动器摩擦片（= re-leather the brakes）

reline the clutch 换装离合器摩擦片

relink 重新连接，重新接线

reload 再装载，再装货，重新加载

reloader 化油器的一种加浓装置（保证冷态发动机能平顺地加速）

relocation 重新安置，重新布置，变换位置，改变位置，重定位置，易位；重新定线，（道路）改线

reluctance 磁阻（亦称 reluctancy，磁路中的阻抗，即磁路中的磁动势除以磁通量，见 magnetomotive force，flux）

reluctance switch 磁阻开关

reluctivity 磁阻率

reluctor （无触点式电子点火系点火信号发生装置中用来改变磁路的磁阻而使其传感线圈产生电压脉冲，即点火信号的）磁阻转子

reluctor type sensor 变磁阻型传感器（通过磁阻变化，在感应线圈内感生电压脉冲，亦输出该脉冲信号的传感元件，亦称 variable reluctance type sensor）

relugging 花纹块翻新（仅翻新局部胎面花纹块的方法）

remagnetizing 重新磁化，重新起磁

remainder 剩余物，残余部分；余项，余数；余部，余额

remainder heat loss 余项热损失（由燃烧发出的热量除去转化有效功、排气损失、冷却热损失以外的难以确切计量的损失，如：燃烧不完全和热辐射等热损失的统称）

remaining stress 剩余应力（应力松弛试验中试件在任一时间上所保持的应力）

remaining value 剩余价值

remaining velocity 剩余速度（指减速后尚有的速度）

reman 整修，旧修；整修业，旧修业，大修（remanufacturing 的简称）

remanence ①剩余磁感应②剩余磁通密度③顽磁性④剩磁（= residual magnetism）

remanent 残余的，剩余的，残留的

remanent magnetism 剩磁，残余磁性（= residual magnetism）

remanent strain 残余应变

reman part 整修部件，整修零件，旧修零件（亦称 remanufacturedcomponent）

reman shop 整修工厂，大修厂

remanufacture ①废料再生，旧料重制②废料再生工艺③（汽车或发动机的）大修

remanufactured-vehicle business 汽车修理业，汽车大修业

remanufacturing （制造厂）重新加工；重新制造，大修

remanufacturing machinery （汽车）大修用机器与设备（总称）（一般不包括轮胎翻新设备）

remarkable 值得注意的

remedial work 小修作业，维修作业

remedy 补救，修理，修补；校正，纠正

remelting 重熔化，再融化；回熔化

remembering function （控制模块的）记忆功能（如：可记住驾驶员调好的座椅高度、位置和角度，感

觉最舒适的温度及所调到的电台、电视台等)

remetal a bearing 重新挂瓦,重新浇注轴承合金 (= reline a bearing)

remi-con car 混凝土搅拌-运送车 (ready-mixed concrete car 的简称)

remnant 残余(物),残痕,余烬,零料

remodel 重新塑造,改型,改造,重建,重装

remold tire (胎面)翻新轮胎 (= remould tire,指将旧胎面切除,重新装新胎面胶,经硬化处理的旧胎)

remote 遥控的,远程的

remote acceleration sensor 遥感式加速度传感器

remote access server 远程访问服务 (简称 RAS)

remote central door locking system 遥控中央门锁系统

remote communication network 远程通信网络

remote console 遥控台,远距离控制仪表板

remote control ①遥控②遥控装置

remote-control rear-door opener (五门式车辆的)遥控式后门开启器

remote control relay 远距离控制继电器;遥控式继电器

remote control starter 遥控式起动机

remote control theft protection controller 遥控防盗控制器

remote control transmission 远距离操纵变速器(需要通过转换机构才能完成换挡功能的手动换挡变速器)

remote cycle change (交通信号等的)遥控周期变更装置

remote dial flowmeter 远距离刻度盘式流量计

remote electronic starting (control unit) 电子遥控起动控制装置 (简称 RES)

remote end 远端(如:轴的远端)

remote engine starter system (由安装在点火开关钥匙柄内的车门开关及起动-停车信号发生器和装在车上的遥控车门锁及遥控起动-停车装置组成的)发动机遥控起动系统

remote flashing relay 遥控闪光继电器

remote gear (box) control 变速器遥控,变速器远程操纵机构

remote handling 遥控,远距离操纵

remote keyless entry system 遥控无钥匙开门系统

remote keyless entry transmitter 见 door control transmitter

remote linkage power steering system ①(转向控制阀和动力缸)分置式动力转向系统②杆系遥控式动力转向系统

remotely controlled (受)遥控的,(被)远距离操纵的 (= remotely operated, remote-operated)

remotely controlled vehicle 遥控式车辆

remote measurement 遥测,远距离测量(亦称 remote metering)

remote mounting capability (液压、电气元件)遥置能力,分置能力

remote(-operation) cylinder ①远距离操作式油缸②外置式油缸

remote parameter control (汽车室内振动台模拟实际振动试验的)远程参数控制(其模拟点与加载点不在同一点上,而是以模拟点的振动参数控制加载点的驱动信号)

remote pendant 遥控板(装遥控按钮等的控制板)

remote pendant control 遥控板控制

remote pick-up ①(公路安全等用的)远距离电视摄像②远距离传感

remote possibility 极小的可能性

remote power cylinder (动力转向系

的）分置动力油缸

remote pressure control circuit 压力遥控系统，压力远距离控制系统

remote probability 低的概率

remote reading 遥控读数，远距离读数，遥测显示，远距离量测记录

remote-sense alternator （车用）遥感式交流发电机（由遥感系统根据所感知的蓄电池仓内的温度自动控制交流发电机调节器的调定电压，即发电机的输出电压，以确保蓄电池的最佳充电效率）

remote sensing 遥感，远距离传感

remote servicing 遥控操作，远距离维护

remote shift linkage 远距离换挡杆系，远距离变速连杆机构

remote signal 遥控信号，遥测信号

remote speed adjustment （发动机的）远距离（控制的）转速调节

remote start （汽车的）遥控起动

remote tire pressure sensor 遥测式胎压传感器

remote unlocking （汽车后行李舱盖的）遥控开锁功能

remote valve 远距离操纵阀，遥控阀

remoulded car 改造的汽车；改装的汽车；改型汽车

remoulding 全翻新（更换已磨损胎面胶、胎肩胶和胎侧胶，使轮胎具有"新胎"外观感的翻新方法）

removability ①可移动性②可拆卸性

removable ①可拆卸的②可移动的（见 demountable）

removable cylinder head 可拆式汽缸盖

removable gear lever 换挡杆，变速杆（美称 removable shift lever）

removable hard top 可拆卸式硬车顶（= detachable hard top）

removable metal 滑动轴承轴瓦（= renewable metal）

removable rim 可拆卸式轮辋（= detachable rim）

removable traction device 可拆卸的防滑装置（如：防滑链）

removable tread 活胎面（由一个或数个有钢丝等骨架材料构成的可以更换的胎面，= replaceable tread）

removal 移动，迁移，搬开，调动；拆除，除去，卸去，排除；放出，排出

removal data （零、部件，总成的）更换记录

removal of faults 排除故障

removal van 搬家车（美称 moving van）

remove 取去，拆去，卸下，除去，取消，排除，清除，清理，搬开，调动，迁移，移动，移置，切掉，锉去，磨掉，切削

remove flaw 清除缺陷，消除裂纹

remover ①拆卸工具，清除工具，拔取设备，清理设备②脱漆装置；脱漆剂，脱膜剂③（为渗漏检验用的）洗净液④搬运工具

remove slag 去渣

remove the play 消除间隙

Renault ［法］雷诺（汽车集团）（全名 Re gie Nationale des Usines Renault，创立于1898年，二战后由于前业主与纳粹"Nazis"的关系，1945年收归国有，是法国最大的汽车公司，年产量占法国全国产量的45％以上，1980年以后，陆续出售股份给私人，1996年国有股份由52％降为46％，走向私营）

Renault-American Motors 雷诺-美国汽车公司

render ①再现，重发，再生，表现，表达，使反响，归还；给予，移交，汇报，翻译，复制，描绘，提出，提供，使行，行使，执行，放弃，使…变成，使…变得，炼油，提炼②抹灰，粉刷，打底

Renesis （日本马自达公司研制的）新一代13B—MSP转子发动机的商品名（为rotory engine和genesis的组合词，该机用于该公司新一代RX—8型跑车。其特点是进、排气口都在侧面，而且采用有三个进气道的所谓组合可变进气系统"combined variable intake system"，怠速时，只有第一进气道进气，转速达到3750r/min时第二进气道开放，转速升至6250r/min时，第三个辅助进气道进气，而当转速升到7250r/min时，进气系统中的一阀门开启，使进气管长度缩短，进一步加大进入的空气量，该机还采用线控节气门系统）

RENESIS（MAZDA） 新一代转子发动机商品名(由rotary engine和genesis两词的简词组成，1.3L，184kW/8500r/min，216N·m/5500r/min）

renew 更新，更换，复原，恢复；翻新，再生，修复；重建，重做

renewable 可更换的，可更新的，可复原的，可翻新的，可修复的；可回收的，可再生的

renewable bearing 滑动轴承轴瓦（= renewable metal）

renewable energy 更新能源（主要指代替煤、石油等一次能源的太阳能、风能、水力能、地热能、生物能等）

renewable filter element 可换新的滤芯

renewable metal 滑动轴承瓦（减磨合金浇铸在轴瓦的基片上，= replaceable metal, insert metal, insert bearing, renewable bearing, removable metal, precision bearing）

renewal 更换，更新；恢复，修复；大修，翻新；重建，重做

renewal of facing 更换衬面，更换摩擦片

renewal of oil 换油，更换润滑油

renewal of parts by metal pulverization 旧（零）件金属喷镀修复（法）

renewals 修复件

renewed tyre 翻新轮胎（亦称renovated tire, new treaded tyre）

renovate 革新，改造，改建；恢复，翻新，修复；再制，重制

renovation project 技（术）改（造）项目

rent ①租金②出租；租用③裂缝，裂隙

Rent-A-Car 租赁汽车（见U drive-it-car）

rental charge 租赁费；租车费

rental fleet 出租汽车车队

rent automotive transportation 包车运输，租车运输

renter-car 租车人个人驾驶的租赁汽车（= rent-a-car）

reoiling 加添润滑油

repack ①重新包装，改装，再装配，换填料，拆修②加润滑脂，用滑脂润滑，换润滑油

repacking of bearing 轴承重新加油；更换轴承润滑油

repainting 重新喷漆，重新涂装

repair 修理（对汽车或总成的失效零部件进行机械加工或换新件修复），修补，修复；校正，矫正，修正，改正

repairability 可修理性

repairable 可修理的，可修复的，可修补的；可弥补的，可纠正的

repair and maintenance （汽车等的）修理和维护，维修（简称ram, r&m, r and m）

repairation ①修理，修复②修理工程，维修工作

repair creeper 躺板（在底盘下修车时使用，一般装有小轮，简称creeper）

repair depot 修理厂，修理所，修理

基地（= salvage depot）
repair gum 补胎用胶片，补胎橡胶
repair of malfunction 故障修理（相对于计划预防检修而言，即出现故障后再进行修理的一种维修方式，参见 preventive servicing）
repair on technical condition 视情修理，按需修理
repair part(s) 修理用配件（= spare parts, replacement parts, service parts, duplicate parts, repair pieces）
repair rate ①修理频率，检修频率 ②修复率（修理时间已达到某个时刻但尚未修复的设备、装置，在该时刻后的单位时间内完成修理的概率）
repair rubber-plug （无内胎轮胎）补胎塞
repair-shop truck 修理工程车（亦称 repair truck, machine shop truck, tool truck）
repair size 修理尺寸（零件磨损表面经过修理，形成符合技术文件规定的大于或小于原设计基本尺寸的基本尺寸）
repair tag （挂在发动机总成上说明需要修理的）修理标签
repair test 修理（大修）后的试验
repair time 修理时间，修复时间（从故障诊断到恢复规定功能所需时间，即：故障诊断时间、管理时间与实施修理时间之和）
repair tower （装在汽车底盘上的）修理塔（修理电车线路、路灯等用的修理高架塔）
repair welding 补焊
repaste （蓄电池极板）重涂活性物质
repeatability 重复性，再现性
repeatability error 重复性误差（在全测量范围内和同一工作条件下，从同方向对同一输入值进行多次连续测量所获得的随机误差）
repeatability of measurement 测量重复性（在相同测量方法、相同观测者、相同测量仪器、相同场所、相同工作条件和短时期内重复的条件下，对同一被测量进行多次连续测量所得结果之间的一致程度）
repeated bending stress test 弯曲疲劳试验
repeated compression test 压缩疲劳试验，交变压缩试验
repeated direct stress test 拉伸疲劳试验（= repeated tension test, repeated tensile stress test）
repeated (dynamic) stress test 交变应力下的（动态）疲劳试验
repeated impact bending strength 循环冲击荷载下的弯曲疲劳强度
repeated impact tension test 在交变冲击拉力下的（动态）疲劳试验
repeated impact test 冲击疲劳试验
repeated load 周期性荷载，反复荷载
repeated stresses 交变应力
repeated stress failure 交变应力引起的疲劳损坏
repeated tensile load 反复拉伸荷载，周期性拉伸荷载
repeated test 重复性试验；疲劳试验
repeated torsion test 扭转疲劳试验
repeated transverse stress strength 横向疲劳强度，抗横向重复应力强度
repeated use 反复使用，多次使用
repeat skin 重皮（轮胎各表面的胶层局部重叠分层的现象，包括内胎接头和轮胎气门嘴胶垫边缘的重皮）
repel ①拒绝，排斥 ②推开，弹回 ③防，抗
repellent ①排斥的；防水的；弹回的 ②防水布；防护剂；排拒力
repeller ①反射极 ②弹回装置 ③导流

板④（变矩器）导轮

repetition ①重复，反复，循环（出现）②再现，再显示③副本，拷贝，复制品

repetition interval 重复周期，循环周期（= repetition period）

repetition test 重复加载卸载试验

repetition work ①批量生产，成批生产②仿形加工

repetitive 反复的，重复的

repetitive (cyclic) load 重复（循环）荷载

repetitive manufacturing 大量生产，成批生产

repetitive timing circuit 循环定时电路

repetitive transportation 重复运输（货物运达卸货地后，又重新运回起运地的运输）

replace 调换，更换，替换，置换，取代；放回原位，复原，复位，移位，归还

replaceable 可代替的，可更换的，可调换的，可复原的，可放回原处的

replaceable-element filter 滤芯可换式滤清器

replaceable metal 滑动轴承轴瓦（= renewable metal）

replaceable tread 可更换胎面（= removable tread）

replacement ①更换，替换，调换，替代，取代，置换，交替作用②复位，复原；归还③替换件，代替物，备件

replacement engine 备用发动机，互换用发动机

replacement life （易损件）更换前的使用寿命

replacement parts 备用零件，修理用配件（= duplicate parts）

replacement test 允许更换故障零件的试验

replacement value （备件）更换价值

replacer 更换（损坏零件）用的工具，拆装工具

replenish ①再装满，再添足，再充电②补充，装添；加强

replenishment ①补充，添补；（再）充满，（再）装满②容量

replica ①复制品，拷贝，副本②供修理用的非原厂生产的车身板件③原厂恢复生产的已中断供应的作为配件的车身板件（亦称 reproduction panel, pattern panel）

replicate ①复制，精确仿制②再现，得出同样的（试验结果等）

replica test 重复性试验

reponse time 响应时间（如：在阶跃响应中，输出信号达到稳定值的特定范围的时间）

report 报告，报告书

reports and memoranda 工作报告及备忘录（简称 ram, r&m, r and m）

repowering 更换发动机；更换动力装置

represent ①代表，表示，表现，体现，显示②描绘，描述，说明，阐述

representation 表示，表现；描述，描绘；表示方法；说明，建议；显示，图像；（数学）表达式；标本

representative ①表示的，表现的②有代表性的，典型的，象征的③代表，典型；样本，样品，标本

representative method of sampling 代表性抽样法

representative sample 有代表性的样品

repressuring gasoline 加压（加丁烷）汽油

reproduce ①再生产，再制；复制；再现②仿制，模拟，靠模

reproducibility of measurement 测量再现性（测量复现性，当各次测量是在改变测量方法、观测者、测量

reproducibility 仪器、场所、工作条件和时间的条件下进行时，同一被测量的各测量结果之间的一致程度)

reproducibility of tests 试验结果的再现性，试验结果的重复性

reproducible 可复制的，可再现的，可重复的，可复验的

reproduction of traffic accident 交通事故再现

reprogram 重新编程

reprogrammable read-only memory 重复可编程只读存储器（可不止一次地修改每个存储单元数据的一种现场可编程序只读存储器）

REPS 见 rack assist type EPS

repulsion 推斥，斥力

repulsion (start) induction motor 排斥式感应（起动）电动机

reputed quart 称号夸脱（见 wine gallon，1 称号夸脱 实际上等于 0.56 Imperial quart)

request 要求，请求，申请；需要

require 要求，请求，申请；需要

required gear （变速器中的）所需挡位

required horsepower 所需功率

required spark plug voltage 火花塞要求电压（在规定的条件下，使火花塞电极间隙跳火必须加在火花塞接线柱上的电压，亦称 required ignition voltage)

requirement （必要的）条件，规格；要求；需要量，需要的装备，必需品

requisite ①必需的，必要的，需要的 ②必需品，必要条件，要素

rerating （功率、载质量等）额定值的重新规定

RE/RD 后置后驱动（后置发动机-后轮驱动，rear engine/rear drive 的简称）

re-ring 更换活塞环

reroute 道路改线，重定路线

rerun ①再开动，重新运转，重新运行 ②重新试验；重新处理 ③（计算机）重算程序

resample ①再取样，重新抽样 ②重新采取的试样

rescue ambulance 医疗急救车

rescue vehicle 技术救援车（= emergency service vehicle)

rescue work 救险作业，救援作业

rescure vehicle （越野比赛中发生被阻陷事故时的）救援车

research ①研究，调查，探索 ②科学研究工作

research activity 研究活动，研究工作

research and development acceptance test 研究和开发验收试验

research-and-development test （新产品）研制和开发试验

research engine 供试验研究用的发动机

research engineer 研究工程师

research institute 科学研究所

research method （测定汽油抗爆性的）研究法（为实验室辛烷值测定法的一种，见 laboratory knock-testing method)

research octane number （汽油的）研究法辛烷值（用研究法测定的辛烷值，简称 RON，见 octane number; research method)

research project engineer （主管某一课题研究的）项目工程师

research safety vehicle 安全性能研究车（简称 RSV，1973 年美国运输部拟定了对安全车的具体目标要求，并以 3000lb 级微型轿车为达到此目标的研究车，具体由 Ford、Volkswagen 等公司承担此项研究任务）

reseat ①更换新座，更换气门座 ②修整、重磨阀座，研磨气门座

reseater 阀座修整器，气门座修整工具

reseating of valve seats 气门座重新研磨；更换气门座（阀座）（= valve reseating）

reservation ①保留②预定③保留物

reserve ①保留，保存；储藏，储存，储备，备用，准备②储备物，储金，保存物，备用物③储藏量，储量，裕量④备用的，储的，预备的，多余的

reserve alkalinity 储备碱度（冷却液中用以抗腐蚀和中和酸值的碱金属盐添加剂的浓度）

reserve capacity ①后备量，储备能力②后备功率③（蓄电池的）储备容量（指蓄电池按所规定的条件能维持以 25A 的电流放电的时间，分）

reserve coefficient of clutch 离合器后备系数（离合器可靠地传递发动机转矩的程度）

reserved old series of tyre 保留生产轮胎（准备淘汰而暂时允许生产的轮胎）

reserved road （用作某种专用运输的）保留道路，备用道路

reserved seats 预备座位，备用座位

reserve fuel tank 储备油箱，副油箱

reserve fund 公积金

reserve parts 备（用）件（见 duplicate parts）

reserve tractive ability 储备牵引能力

reserve tractive force 后备牵引力（简称 res tractive force, res t force）

reserve tractive horsepower 后备牵引功率（指发动机净功率减去水平道路行驶阻力功率，以马力为单位，简称 res tractive hp, res t hp）

reserve travel 行程裕量（如：制动踏板踩到最大行程后与车身地板之间的间隙）

reserve vacuum tank 真空存储箱（用作真空控制装置的真空源）

reservicing 重新维护，重复保养；重新维修调整

reservoir stopper 储液箱（加液口）塞盖

reservoir capacity 油箱容量，容器容量

reservoir for condensation 冷凝箱

reservoir pressure gauge 储气筒压力表

reset ①重置，重新安置，重新设置，重新配置②重新调整，再调节，重调；重新调零；复位，复原③重镶，重嵌，重装，重磨

reset action 重新装配，重调作用，复位动作，回零动作

reset a spring 重调、校正弹簧弹力

reset button （仪表等的）归零按钮，复位按钮，重复起动按钮

reset condition 原始状态，复位状态

reset-set flip-flop 置"0"置"1"触发器，复位置位触发器，R-S 触发器（简称 RS flip-flop）

reset switch 转换开关

resettable fuse 自动回接熔断丝（切断电源后，又可自动恢复接通）

reset the clutch 重调离合器

reset time 复位时间，清除时间；调零时间

resetting ①重置；复位；调零②（气门）研磨③重新沉淀

reshape 重新修整，重新整形

reshaper （车身）整形工具

reshipment ①（货物的）重装②重新装运，转运，转载

residual ①残余的，剩余的，残留的②残余，剩余③（数字）残数，残差，残余误差（测定值与算术平均值之差，= RM.S error）

residual attenuation distortion 剩余衰减畸变

residual austenite 残余奥氏体

residual capacity ①剩余运力（指运输高峰期间与非高峰期间运输企业所提供的运力之差）②剩余能力

residual charge 剩余电荷，剩余充电量

residual compressive stress 残余压应力

residual deformation 残余变形，残留变形

residual elasticity 剩余弹性，弹性后效

residual error 残差（测量列中的一个测得值 a_i 与该列的算术平均值 $\bar{a}$ 之差，则残差 $v_i = a_i - \bar{a}$）

residual field method （磁粉探伤的）剩磁法

residual fraction 残余馏分

residual fuel ①残余馏分燃料，渣油燃料②残余燃油，残油

residual gas 残余废气（换气过程结束后残留在汽缸内的废气）

residual gas ratio 残余气体系数，残余废气比（见 scavenging efficiency）

residual heat 余热，残热

residual-heat type heater 余热式暖风系统（利用汽车发动机冷却水或废气余热采暖的暖风系统）

residual induction 剩余磁感应，剩磁值

residual magnetism 残余磁性，残磁，剩磁（= remanent magnetism, remanence）

residual microphone 残余噪声传感器（亦称 residual noise sensor）

residual noise 残余噪声（经消声处理，如：反噪声波抵消后残余的噪声）

residual oscillation 残余振幅，残余振荡

residual pressure 残余压力（如：供油结束后，高压油管中残存的燃油压力）

residual products 副产品，剩余产物，残油

residual sinkage 残留沉陷量（车辆通过后的轮迹深度）

residual strain 残留应变

residual strength 剩余强度（如：裂纹面积忽略不计时含裂纹试件所能承受的最大标称应力）

residual tension stress 残余拉应力

residual valve 残留阀（使液压制动系内保留一定残留压力的阀门）

residue ①残渣，滤渣，余渣，残油②残余物③残基④残数，余数（亦称 residuum）

residues of combustion 燃烧残余物，燃烧产物

resilience 弹跳，回弹，弹性，回弹性；弹力，恢复力，斥力；回弹能量；变形能，弹性能；弹性变形；冲击韧性；回弹物（亦写作 resiliency）

resilience test 弹性试验

resilient 有弹性的，有回弹力的，弹性的

resilient adhesive bonding 韧性黏结剂黏接，冶性黏结剂黏接

resilient coupling ①弹性连接②弹性联轴节

resilient mounting 弹性支撑，柔性支撑

resin ①树脂，树胶；松香②树脂状沉淀物③涂树胶，用树胶处理

resin acid 树脂酸（= resinous acid）

resin-bonded 树脂黏结的

resin content 树脂含量

resin-cored solder 松香芯软钎焊锡条

resin formation （燃料中）树脂状沉淀物的生成（亦称 resinification）

resin-free 无树脂状沉淀的

resin intake manifold 树脂材料进气歧管

resin mould 合成树脂模制成形（如：用石棉及其他材料和树脂模压而成的制动蹄摩擦片）

resinous ①树胶的，树脂（质）的②含树脂的，从树脂中获得的

resin-pigment ratio （油漆）树脂颜料比

Resin Transfer Molding （CFC 材料的）树脂倒模法（将树脂注入碳素纤维织物坯料加热加压固化成型，见 CFC①）

resist ①抵抗，反抗，阻挡，阻碍；耐受，承受；抵制，反对 ②保护层，保护膜③抗蚀剂，防腐剂

resistance ①抵抗，反对；抵制②阻力③电阻④抗…性，耐…性

resistance box 电阻箱

resistance brazing 电阻加热硬钎焊

resistance bulb 变阻泡，测温电阻器

resistance butt welding 电阻对接焊

resistance-capacitance time constant 电阻电容时间常数

resistance coil 电阻线圈

resistance decrement 电阻衰减量

resistance due to acceleration 加速阻力

resistance due to climbing 上坡阻力，登坡阻力，爬坡阻力（亦称 resistance due to grade）

resistance force 阻力（= resisting force）

resistance head （液压管道）阻力压头

resistance heater 电阻丝加热器

resistance of exhaust 排气阻力

resistance of motion 运动阻力；行驶阻力（亦称 resistance to motion）

resistance of shock absorber 减振器阻尼（特性）

resistance of spark gap 火花隙电阻

resistance seam welding 电阻缝接焊

resistance spot welding 电阻点焊，接触点焊

resistance strain gauge 电阻应变计，电阻应变片

resistance thermometer 电阻式温度计

resistance to abrasion 耐磨性

resistance to acids 耐酸（性）

resistance to ag(e)ing 抗老化性，耐老化性

resistance to alkalis 耐碱（性）

resistance to bending 抗弯能力

resistance to cold 耐寒性，耐冷性

resistance to corrosion 抗腐蚀性

resistance to curbing （轮胎）对路边石摩擦的耐磨性

resistance to deformation 变形阻力

resistance to displacement 位移阻力

resistance to effect of heat 耐热性

resistance to emulsification 抗乳化作用

resistance to evaporation 抗挥发作用

resistance to flow 流动阻力

resistance to foaming 防泡沫性

resistance to heat 耐热性

resistance to impact 耐冲击性；冲击韧性

resistance to indentation 抗压痕强度

resistance to lateral bend 抗横（侧）向弯曲的强度

resistance to motion 运动阻力；行驶阻力

resistance to penetration （土壤）贯入阻力

resistance to pit corrosion 抗穴蚀性

resistance to pressure 耐压性

resistance to salt 耐盐性，抗盐性

resistance to shear 抗剪强度（= resistance to shearing stress）

resistance to shock 耐振性

resistance to sparking 火花击穿电阻

resistance to suction 吸入阻力，进气阻力

resistance to thermal shocks 耐热冲击性，耐激热激冷性能（= spalling resistance）

resistance to torsion 抗扭强度

resistance to water 耐水性

resistance to wear 耐磨性

resistance to weather 耐受天气自然作用的能力，天气作用稳定性，抗风蚀暴露性（参见 weathering）

resistance-type electric strain gauge 电阻应变仪，电阻应变测量计，电阻式应变片

resistance type fuel gauge 电阻式燃油油量表，电阻式油耗计

resistance-type oxygen sensor 电阻型氧传感器 [如：二氧化钛型氧传感器（TiO_2 oxygen sensor），利用二氧化钛材料的电阻值随废气中氧含量的变化而变化的特性来测定氧的含量，故名]

resistance-type suppressor 电阻型抑制器

resistance welding 电阻焊，接触焊

resistance winding 电阻绕组，欧姆线圈

resistance wire 电阻丝，电阻线（亦称 resistor wire）

resistant 抵抗的，反抗的；耐久的，坚固的；稳定的；抗…的，耐…的

resistant metal 耐蚀金属

resistant to corrosion 耐腐蚀的

resistant to oil 耐油的

resistant to rust 抗锈蚀的，耐锈蚀的

resistant to tarnishing 抗锈蚀的，表面抗变色、失去光泽、晦暗的等

resister ①抵抗剂②电阻器（亦写作 resistor）

resisting force 阻力（= resistance force）

resisting moment 阻力矩

resistive cord ①电阻式高压点火线（见 resistor ignition wire）②（包有耐高压橡胶绝缘层和维尼龙外皮的）点火高压线（= high tension cord）

resistive (electrical) load 电阻负载

resistive plug 电阻型火花塞 [见 resistor (type spark) plug]

resistive transducer 电阻式变换器，电阻式传感器

resistivity ①电阻率，电阻系数，比电阻②抵抗性，抵抗力

resistor 电阻器

resistor-capacitor-transistor logic 电阻-电容-晶体管逻辑，阻容晶体管逻辑（电路，简称 RCTL，见 DCLT）

resistor coil 带附加电阻的点火线圈

resistor ignition wire 电阻式高压点火线（线内装有电阻，其作用与电阻型火花塞相同，见 resistor plug）

resistor (spark) plug 电阻型火花塞（中央电极中装有电阻，可减少高压电涌的数量，其阻值一般为 3～10kΩ，用于抑制火花塞产生的电波噪声。以降低所引起的静电放射，减少对无线电的干扰，并可减轻电极的腐蚀，亦称 resistive type spark plug, resistive plug）

resistor transistor logic 电阻-晶体管逻辑（电路，简称 RTL，见 DCLT）

resizing tool 尺寸修复工具（如：用挤压加工等方法恢复磨损零件使用尺寸的工具，= resizer，如：knurling tool）

resleeve 换汽缸套

re-sleeving plant 缸套换镶设备，镶套设备

resolute design 变通设计（指汽车总体设计中，主要总成可以改用其他形式总成，而不影响总体布置，如 Audi 100 可用 2.0L、四缸发动机，亦可用 2.6L、六缸紧凑型发动机）

resolution ①分辨率，分辨力，清晰度②分解，溶解，重新溶解③解析④解决⑤变化，转化⑥可分辨的最小读数

resolution capability 鉴别能力，分辨能力，析像能力

resolution of ADC ADC 的分辨率

(指 ADC 能够区分数值相近的模拟输入量的程度)

resolution of DAC DAC 的分辨率（指 DAC 能够给出数值相近的模拟输出量的程度）

resolution of forces 力的分解

resolution rate（**of an impulse wheel speed sensor**）（脉冲式车轮速度传感器的）分辨率（车轮旋转一周传感器所发出的脉冲数即每一脉冲所传感的转角度数）

resolution time （集成电路的）分辨时间（施加在同一输入端上的一个输入脉冲的终止到下一脉冲的开始之间的时间间隔）

resolve ①分解，溶解②解体，拆卸③分析，解析，解答，解决④分辨，判定

resolve into components 分解成分力

resolver 分解器；解析装置，求解仪；溶剂

resolving ability 鉴别力，分辨能力，解算性能

resolving power ①（光学系统的）析像能力，解像能力（指分清观察空间十分接近的两点的影像的能力）②解析能力，分析能力，分辨能力

resonance ①共振（见 steady state vibration）②谐振（电磁共振 electromagnetic resonance 的简称，如：电视机等的输入回路的固有振荡频率调到电视发射台发射的载波频率相同时，输入回路产生的最大振幅的变速振荡）

resonance amplitude 共振振幅

resonance chamber （发动机进气系统的）谐振室

resonance conditions ①产生共振的条件②共振状态

resonance frequency 共振频率（激励的频率与系统的固有频率相重合时的振动，称为共振。发生共振时的强迫振动频率，称为共振频率，为频率特性的峰值频率）

resonance intake tube supercharging 进气管谐振增压

resonance level 共振级，共振能级

resonance peak 共振峰值（Mp 值）

resonance point 共振点

resonance potential 共振电势

resonance test 共振试验

resonance type detonation sensor 共振型爆燃传感器

resonance vibration 共振振动，共振（= resonance, resonant vibration, 见 harmonic vibration③）

resonant 共振的

resonant combustion chamber （燃气轮机的）共振燃烧室，共振燃烧器

resonant disc （电喇叭的）共鸣板

resonant fatigue test 共振条件下的疲劳试验

resonant flip-flop 共振触发器

resonant noise 谐振噪声

resonant operation 在共振状态下工作

resonant peak level （汽车频率响应试验中的）共振峰水平

resonant speed 共振速率

resonant tester 共振（疲劳）试验机

resonate ①（使产生）共振②（使）谐振（调谐）③（使）共鸣

resonator ①共振器，共振箱，共振腔②共振片③谐振器，谐振箱，谐振腔（在汽车内燃机进、排气系统中，利用进、排气管内压力波来回振荡，产生谐振的动态效应以提高进、排气效率和降低进、排气噪声的装置）④（有时指双消声器系统中的）第一消声器

resonator exhaust system 带谐振消声器的排气系统

resonator-type silencer 谐振式消声器

resorcin(ol) 间苯二酚，苯间二酚，

雷琐辛（$C_6H_4(OH)_2$）
resource ①资源②储藏③物资④设备⑤手段；方法，对策，智谋
resource allocation 资源分配（为完成控制功能，而对电子控制系统硬、软件的分配）
resourceful ①资源丰富的②机智的
respace 重新隔开
respect ①关系，关联，方面②（着眼）点，考虑，重视，遵守
respiration rate （驾驶员等的）呼吸速度，呼吸速率，换气率
respond ①回答，响应，反应（= response）②应付③承担责任，负责，赔偿，履行④（结构）对称
response ①回答，答复②响应，反应③响应特性（曲线）④灵敏度
response characteristic 响应特性（在规定条件下，输入量与相应输出量的关系特性）
response characteristics （对控制、输入或信息的）响应特性
response control 响应控制
response curve for N cycles N 次循环响应曲线
response frequency 响应频率（rad/s）
response function 响应函数
response of the automobile to random road input 汽车对随机道路（平面度）输入的响应
response of vehicle （车辆的）响应特性
response pressure （限压阀的）响应压力（指其开启压力）
response range 响应范围，灵敏度范围
response to multi-axis vibration 多轴（多向）振动响应
response to steering （对）转向（操作的）响应
response transform 响应变换式
responsibility ①响应性（亦称 responsiveness）②可靠性③责任，义务
responsible 负责的，有责任的，可靠的，可依赖的，对…负责的，是造成…原因的，决定了…的，造成了…的（for）
responsive 应答的，（表示）回答的；响应的，反应的；敏感的，灵敏的，反应迅速的
responsive time 响应时间［输入信号由某值突然变到另一值时，共输出信号达到最终值的某一百分数时（一般为 90%）所需时间，亦称 response time］
resprayed body 重复喷漆的车身
RESS 可再充储能系统（见 rechargeable energy storage system）
REST ①雷达电子扫描技术（radar electronic scan technique 的简称）②节流阀；扼流圈；阻位器（restrictor 的简称）
rest ①座，台，架，托，垫，枕，支柱，支架，刀架，中心架②静止，停顿③其余（的人），其他，剩余部分④支撑在，搁在，放置在（…上）
rest and information area sign 休息与问询处标志（在出入控制的高速公路上标明路旁设施，如：休息处所、问询中心等的标志）
restart 重新起动，重新发动，再起动
rest bar （驾驶员）搁脚板
rest base 架底
rest halt ①休息站（指拉力赛的两个日赛程之间的夜间休息，赛车停放在封存点，车上人员都去睡觉）②休息时间（当一个日赛程过半的时候，在某地等候所有的赛车聚齐的时间），参见 etape，parc ferme）
restitution ①恢复，回复，复原②（变形体）复原原性能③归还，偿还，赔偿
rest mass 静质量

restoration 修复，修理，修补，翻修，整新；恢复原状，恢复原位，还原，再生；回收

restoration of parts by electrical sparking 电火花加工修复零件

restoration of parts by press 压力加工修复零件

restoration of worn out parts by steeling 镀铁修复磨损零件

restorative spring 复位弹簧（迫使部件复位到初始位置的弹簧）

restore ①复原，回复，恢复，修复，再生，重建，翻修②还原，去氧③把电再接通，重新起动④拉紧⑤提高，增加⑥归还，交还

restored energy 回收（的）能量

restored life 修复后的使用寿命

restore to a serviceable condition 修复至可用状态

restoring force 恢复力，回复力

restoring moment 恢复力矩，回复力矩

restoring time （转向盘）回正时间（从松开转向盘的时刻起，到所测变量回复到初始零线的时刻为止的一段时间间隔）

restoring worn parts 旧件修复，修复磨损零件

restractive horsepower （以马力为单位的）后备牵引功率（= reserve tractive horsepower）

restrain 抑制，制止，遏制；限制，约束，制约

restrained beam 约束梁（两端固定的梁）

restrainer ①限制器②抑制剂③酸洗缓蚀剂（参见 retarder）

restraining harness （汽车乘员的）拘束性安全装置（如：安全皮带等，= safety harness）

restraint ①制止，约束，节流，禁止，阻止，限制②限制器，限动器③（汽车乘员）限制性保护装置（如：安全带等）

restraint survival distance 避免乘员撞车伤亡的安全拘束距离（简称 RSD）

restrict 限制，限定，约束；节流，节制，禁止

restricted air bleed carburetor 受制渗气式化油器

restricted passing sight distance 限制超车视距

restricted speed signal 速度限制警戒信号（= restricting signal）

restricted-speed way 限制行车速度的道路

restricted stopping sight distance 限制停车视距

restricted traffic 受管制的交通车流

restricted view 受限制的视野

restricting signal （速度）限制信号

restriction ①限制，节流，约束②节流阀（= restrictor），缩口③干扰；流体阻力

restriction screw 带螺纹的针阀（如：尖头节流螺钉）

restrictive flow regulator 节流式调节器

restrictive sight distance 限制视距，约束视距

restrictor ①节流阀②扼流圈③限流器④定位器，限位器（简称 REST）⑤限制器（如：装在使用催化转化器的汽车加油管口处、防止大口径的含铅汽油加油枪插入的口径限制件，以保证只有无铅汽油的小口径加油枪才能插入加油）

restyle 重新造型，改型，更新式样

result ①结果②结果是…，得出…结果

resultant ①合力，合量，合成矢量②（化学反应）产物，生成物③合成的（如：resultant vector "合成矢量"，resultant velocity "合成速度"），综合的，总的；结果的，有

结果的
resultant acceleration 合成加速度
resultant air velocity vector 合成气流速度（环境风速与相对风速的向量和）
resultant current 合成电流
resultant force 合力（= composite force）
resultant gear ratio 总齿轮比
resultant law 结合分布律
resultant movement 合成运动
resultant pitch 合成节距
resultant quantity 合成量
resultant stress 合成应力
result of a measurement 测量结果（由测量所得到的被测量的值）
RESUME/ACCEL button （装在轿车转向盘上的变速巡行控制系统）复位（恢复原设定车速）/加速按钮
resume switch （定速巡行控制系统的）复位开关（按压该开关，可使车速恢复到原设定车速）
retail ①零售的，零卖的 ②零售，零卖
retail motor trader 汽车零售商
retail price 零售价格
retail sale 零售
retain ①保持，保留，保有，残留，维持 ②夹持，卡住，挡住，顶住，拦住
retained accessory power （点火开关断开后的）附件维持电源（当点火开关断开后，电子控制模块可立即接通该电源一段时间，如：10min，供电动窗、后行李舱盖及电动天窗等附件用电）
retained austenite 残余奥氏体
retainer ①保持器，夹持器 ②（滚动轴承滚动件的）保持架 ③定位器，限位器，止动器，掣爪，锁片，挡板 ④护圈，座圈，隔栅
retainer clip 固定夹子，弹簧卡子，防松夹子，固定弹夹（简称 R-clip）
retainer lock 锁片，锁环，锁销（亦称 cotter）
retainer of seal device 密封装置的传动座（用于与轴或轴套固定并直接带动旋转环转动的零件）
retainer pin ①（转子发动机的）角密封片定位销，密封销 ②固定销，保持销，锁销，卡销，定位销，挡销
retainer ring ①锁环，卡环；护圈 ②滚动轴承保持架（= retaining ring）
retainer seal 护圈密封件
retainer spring 扣紧簧，定位弹簧，保持弹簧
retainer with balls 球轴承保持架带球组件
retaining ring of headlamp 前照灯灯圈
retaining ring of rim 轮辋挡圈
retaining snap ring 弹簧卡环
retaining spring 定位弹簧，止动弹簧
retaining steering effort 保舵力（作用于转向盘维持转向盘转角不变的力）
retaining valve 止回阀
retaining washer 弹簧垫圈，锁紧垫圈
retapping 重攻螺纹
retard ①减速，减慢 ②延迟，推迟，延缓 ③阻滞，停滞，滞后，迟后 ④（特指）点火延迟（指推迟点火提前，即：减少点火提前角）
retardation ①减速作用，缓速作用 ②推迟，延迟；阻碍，阻止，阻滞，阻滞作用
retardation angle 滞后角，迟延角，迟后角
retardation coil 扼流线圈
retardation curve 减速曲线，缓速曲线

retardation efficiency 减速效能，缓速效能

retardation of linearly polarized light 线偏振光延迟（一束线偏振光射入双折射晶体后，分裂为两束线偏振光，由于传播速度不同，两者之间存在的延迟现象）

retardation test （车辆）滑行减速试验（测定车辆的滚动阻力等）

retard button 减速按钮，缓速按钮

retard control of spark advance 点火提前延迟控制（指根据工况要求，推迟点火提前角的控制，用于减少暖机过程中的废气有害物排放，加速催化转化器的催化剂升温，过热时保护发动机及断油后恢复供油时，降低自动变速器变速时的冲击等）

retard diaphragm （双膜片真空点火提前分电器的）点火延迟膜片（亦称 secondary diaphragm）

retarded 缓速的，延迟的，缓慢的

retarded closing of valve 气门迟闭（= late closing of valve，一般指气门在止点后关闭）

retarded combustion 延迟燃烧，延缓燃烧，缓慢燃烧

retarded force 减速力，制动力，阻滞力

retarded injection timing control system 推迟喷油时刻控制系统（为减少排气中的氮氧化物而推迟喷油时刻的控制系统）

retarded injection timing with load 负荷控制的推迟喷油时刻（为控制氮氧化物，随负荷改变而推迟喷油时刻）

retarded injection timing with speed 转速控制的推迟喷油时刻（为控制氮氧化物，随转速改变而推迟喷油时刻）

retarder ①缓速器（亦称第三制动器，减速制动器，如：排气制动器，涡电流制动器等）②（阻滞化学反应的）迟缓剂，阻滞剂，减速剂，抑制剂（= retarder thinner, restrainer）③硫化迟缓剂④延迟线圈

retarder by combustion engine 发动机缓速装置（利用发动机制动使车辆产生缓速作用的装置）

retarder by electric traction motor （汽车的）电机缓速装置（利用车辆惯性通过车轮等带动电动机发电而产生减速作用的缓速器）

retarder control valve 液力缓速器控制阀（控制液力减速器充油和放油的阀）

retarder thinner （塑料）迟干稀释溶剂（加入涂料中使涂层干燥迟缓，亦称 retarder）

retarding ①减速，缓速，延迟，推后②（发动机）延迟点火，推迟喷油，延迟气门关闭

retarding characteristic 滞后特性，延迟特性，减速特性

retarding force 减速力，缓速力

retarding torque 缓速力矩，减速力矩

retard stop ①（分电器真空膜片等的）点火延迟行程限制件②（离心式点火提前装置的）最大点火延迟角限制器

retempering ①再次回火②改变稠度

retention ①保存，保管；保持，维持，保留，阻挡，抑制，隔离②保持力，把持力

retention potential （滤清器）积垢容量，积尘容量

retention screw 紧固螺钉，止动螺钉

retentivity ①保持性②顽磁性，剩磁

retest 重新试验，再试验

reticular 网状的；网状组织的，网状结构的

reticule ①交叉丝，十字线，标度线，分度线，刻线②标线片，分划

板（= reticle）
reticule alignment 十字线对准，标度线校准
retighten 重新拉紧，重新拧紧
retiming 重新调整点火、喷油或气门正时
retina （眼睛的）视网膜
retinal illuminance 网膜照度（光刺激作用在视网膜上的照度）
retire ①收回（成本）②报废③更换轮胎
retired car 报废轿车
retirement ①退役，报废，注销②收回成本
retog ①（重新）施加（接通，接入，给予，加上电压、电流等）②再触发
retorque 恢复拧紧力矩，重新拧紧螺栓
retracing spring 复位弹簧，回位弹簧（= return spring）
retract 缩回，缩进；收缩，收回，退回，撤回；回程，退回
retractable 可伸缩的，收缩的，可缩回的
retractable hard top 可缩进的硬车顶，可伸缩的硬车顶
retractable head lamp 可收合式前照灯（可降低空气阻力，改善流线型，亦称 movable head lamp，分为收合后仍可见的半隐式和全隐式两种）
retractable rear spoiler （装车身后端的）可伸缩式后导流板
retractable rear spoiler （车身的）可收合型后导风板（当车速超过某规定值，如 97km/h "60mph" 时，该板自动升起一定角度，利用风阻的向下分力，使车轮紧贴路面）
retractable spring bumper damper （汽车）弹簧回缩式保险杠冲击吸收装置
retractable wheel 伸缩轮

retracting stroke 返回行程，回位行程
retracting transformation 收缩变换
retraction stroke （柴油机喷油泵出油阀的）卸载行程（与卸载容积相对应的出油阀行程，亦称减压行程）
retraction volume of delivery valve （柴油机喷油泵）出油阀卸载容积（从喷油泵出油阀卸载环带的下边缘盖住出油阀孔起到出油阀落座瞬时所扫过的容积，亦称减压容积）
retractor ①收缩装置②（安全带的）收卷器，收紧装置，拉紧器
retractor collar 分离套
retractor device （汽车乘员安全带的）收卷器，收紧装置，拉紧器
retraining 重新训练
retread ①翻胎（翻新或修理轮胎胎面），修补轮胎②翻新胎，修补过的轮胎，（旧胎的）新胎面
retreadability （轮胎的可）翻修性，可翻修能力
retreaded grooving 翻新胎面刻花（在翻新后的无花纹胎面上刻制花纹的工艺）
retreaded tyre 翻新轮胎（经翻新后能继续使用的轮胎）
retreat 重新处置，重复处置，重新加工
retrieval ①（可）取回，（可）收回②（可）修补，（可）恢复③（数据、信息的）检索、取回
retriever ①（在公路上）运输履带式机械用的平板挂车②救援车，救险车
retroaction 反作用；逆动
retrofitting ①（机械设备的）改装，改型，翻新改造②（汽车出厂后）加装（或改装）新部件
retroreflector ①反光镜②反射器③反抛器
retrospection mirror 后视镜（= ob-

servation mirror）

return ①返回，回动，回位，复位；归还，偿还，回答，回收，复原，再现，反射（信号）②返回的，回程的，重现的，报答的

returnability ①可回收性，可返回性，多次使用的可能性②回正性（汽车转弯时，松开转向盘后汽车恢复直线行驶状态的性能）

return ability test 转向回正性试验

return bend U形弯管（= U-bend）

return factor 回程系数（一定时间内，同一线路上回程与去程货物运量的比值）

return-flow combustion chamber （燃气轮机）回流式燃烧室

return flow restriction valve 回流限制阀

return flow wind tunnel 回流式风洞

returning rate of major repair （汽车）大修返修率（某统计时间内，大修出厂后回厂返修的车辆数与大修出厂车辆数的比值）

return line filter 安装在回油管路上的滤清器

return loss 回程损耗

return mechanism 回行机构

return passage 回流通道

return path 回程线路（= return lead）

return port 回流孔

return pressure null shift 回程压力的零点飘移

return pump 回油泵，回流泵

return shock 反射冲击波，反冲击

return speed 回程速度

return spring 复位弹簧，回位弹簧

return stroke 返回行程，回位行程（亦写作 return of stroke）

return-stroke time 返回行程时间

return wire （双线电路中的）回路导线，回路电线

reusability 重复使用可能性

reusable 可重复使用的

rev ①（发动机）旋转，转数（revolution）②倒退，后退（reverse）

revalving 更换气门

revamp 修补，修理；换新，刷新，翻新，整修，改进，部分地再装备

rev counter 转速表（= tachometer）

reveal ①显示，揭示②表明

reverberant cavity （试验汽车电子设备等的）混响腔，反射腔，混响室，反射室，回响室（= reverberant chamber 或 room，室壁可产生大的回声或反射声，进行噪声破坏试验）

reversal ①颠倒，相反；反向，换向；反转，逆转，倒转；反向行驶，倒车，倒退，反行程；撤销，废弃②反向（疲劳负载中，荷载作为时间的函数的一阶导数改变符号处。恒幅循环荷载中，反向次数为循环次数的两倍）

reversal load 交变荷载，反向荷载（= reversed load）

reversal of load 荷载反向

reversal of stroke 反行程

reversal valve 换向阀，可逆阀

reverse ①相反②倒退，倒车（美称 back up）③回动装置，回动齿轮机构④相反的，颠倒的，倒过来的，回程的，逆转的，倒车的，可逆的，转向的，反面的，废弃的，撤销的⑤使倒退，挂倒车挡⑥换向

reverse Ackermann steering geometry 反阿克曼型转向几何布置（转向时外轮转角大于内轮转角）

reverse-acting control valve 反作用控制阀

reverse bend test 交变弯曲试验

reverse bend test of metals 金属反向弯曲试验［将试样一端夹紧，在规定半径的圆柱形表面上进行90°的重复反向弯曲，检验金属（及覆盖层）的耐反向弯曲能力的试验］

reverse bias ①反向偏压，逆向偏压

1337

②加反向偏压，加逆向偏压
reverse camber ①（车轮的）负外倾，车轮内倾，车前轮内倾角（= inward camber, minus camber）②（弹簧等的）负挠度，反挠度
reverse caster （前轮定位的）负主销后倾，主销前倾
reverse check 倒挡锁定机构，倒挡锁止机构（= reverse lock）
reverse clutch （行星齿轮变速装置中的）倒挡离合器
reverse converter shuttle valve （自动变速器的）倒挡阀（该阀用于切断或接通倒挡伺服缸的油压通路，以脱开或挂接倒挡）
reverse coolant flow（cooling system）（发动机的）冷却水逆流式（冷却系）（经散热器散热的冷却液先流入汽缸盖，再流进汽缸体）
reverse current 逆电流，反向电流
reverse current cutout （发动机充电）逆流断电器
reverse-current relay 逆流继电器
reverse curve S形曲线，反（向）曲线
reverse curve sign S形急弯标志（亦称 reverse turn sign）
reverse-curve windshield 凹面风窗玻璃
reversed charge （蓄电池的）逆充电（指由于接线错误或断电器等故障造成的蓄电池反向充电）
reversed clutch 回动式离合器（其输入轴和输出轴在同一侧，多见于发动机横置式小型轿车）
reversed cone clutch 锥顶朝向发动机的）反向锥形离合器，反锥面离合器
reverse direction 逆向，反向
reversed load 交变荷载，反向荷载（= reversal load）
reversed offset wheel 内偏距车轮（亦称"inset wheel", 指轮辋中心线位于轮辐安装面内侧的车轮）
reverse drive 换向传动，倒车传动，逆向行程
reversed side 反面，背面
reversed stress 反向应力，交变应力
reverse efficiency 逆效率（如：转向轴输出功率与摇臂轴输入功率之比）
reverse electromotive force 反电动势（指电动机旋转时，产生的与电枢电流方向相反的电动势，转速越高，该电动势越大，导致电枢电流减少）
reverse Elliot axle 拳端式前桥，拳式前桥，拳式桥（反叉形端前桥）
reverse Elliot type steering knuckle 反拳形式转向节（转向节连接端成叉形，而转向桥工字梁端成拳形，见 Elliot type）
reverse feedback 负反馈
reverse flow 反向流动，回流，逆流
reverse flow combustion chamber （燃气轮机）逆流式燃烧室
reverse (flow) scavenging 回流扫气（见 loop scavenging）
reverse flushing 反向冲洗
reverse gate 变速杆倒挡定位槽
reverse gear ①倒挡齿轮②倒挡传动③倒挡（= reversing gear）
reverse gear ratio 倒挡传动比，倒挡速比
reverse gear-shift fork （变速器）倒挡拨叉
reverse gear sliding shaft bearing bracket （变速器）倒挡齿轮滑动轴轴承支架
reverse gear striking rod （机械式变速器的）倒挡拨叉轴
reverse gradient 反向坡度
reverse idle gear bearing 倒挡中间齿轮轴承
reverse "L" lower control arm （悬架的）反"L"型下控制臂

reverse-lockout valve （自动变速器的）倒挡锁止阀（该阀可防止汽车在非停止状态下挂上倒挡，即仅仅在汽车停止或基本上停止的状态下，手动变速杆处于倒挡时，该阀才允许液压输入倒挡伺服缸内）

reverse movement 逆动，反转运动，倒退运动

reverse parking warner 倒车入库警报器（利用超声波反射测距，探测障碍物的存在和距离，并发出相应警报信号）

reverse phase 反相（位）

reverse piezoelectric effect 反压电效应（施加一定电压时，元件产生伸张变形等）

reverse piezoelectric effect type damping control actuator 反压电效应式阻尼控制执行器（压电型执行器"piezo actuator"的一种，由装在减振器活塞杆内的压电晶体元件组成。加上500V的高压，利用反压电效应，压电晶体元件将伸长$50\mu m$，推动一柱塞将一减振液通旁通阀顶开，于是阻尼力减小，实现"软"减振模式。当无高压信号时，压电晶体元件缩回原尺寸，旁通阀关闭，阻尼力增大，实现"硬"减振模式，该旁通阀亦称阻尼力开关阀"damping force switching valve"）

reverse power take-off 可换向的功率输出轴

reverser 换向开关，换向器；逆转机构，换向机构

reverse rod 倒挡杆（自动变速器中连接控制杆与倒挡选挡机构的杆件）

reverse rotating torque (of steering gear)（转向器）反驱动力矩（转向盘处于自由状态时，使摇臂轴转动的力矩）

reverse run (ning) 反转，回转，倒转；回程

reverse servo （自动变速器的）倒挡伺服机构，倒挡伺服缸（为一液力缸，其活塞通过杆系控制行星齿轮系的倒挡制动器，借以改变输出轴的旋转方向而形成倒挡）

reverse sliding gear axle 倒挡滑动齿轮轴

reverse speed ①倒挡速度②（变速器）倒挡

reverse steering （汽车的）交变转向（当低于某一车速时，为 oversteering 或 understeering，超过该车速后，变为 understeering 或 oversteering，见 understeer 及 oversteer）

reverse stop 回动锁止装置

reverse stroke 返回行程，回程

reverse the direction 改变方向，换向

reverse turn ①倒车转弯，倒车掉头 ②反转

reverse twin gear 倒挡双联齿轮，倒挡塔轮

reversibility 可逆性；可反向性，可逆转性，可换向性

reversible center path （道路）允许掉头的中央地带

reversible change 可逆变化

reversible diaphragm piston type pneumatic spring 双向膜片活塞式空气弹簧

reversible drive 可换向的传动，可逆转的传动；可逆传动装置

reversible electric servomotor 正反转伺服电动机

reversible engine 可逆转发动机（亦写作：reversing engine）

reversible exothermic reaction 可逆放热反应

reversible flow sign （用于可变向车道上的）改变车道通行方向标志

reversible key 预热-起动双向钥匙

reversible lane 变向车道（在每天一定时间内可变更行车方向的车道）

reversible one-way street 变方向式

单行路（每天在一定时间内，只允许某一方向单行，另一时间内则只允许相反方向单行）

reversible process 可逆过程

reversible pump 可逆转泵，双向泵

reversible ratchet handle ①可逆式旋柄②可逆式棘轮式手柄

reversible ratchet magnetic screwdriver 可逆式磁性螺钉旋具

reversible reaction 可逆反应

reversible sleeve piston type pneumatic spring 双向筒形活塞式空气弹簧

reversible starter-generator 起动-发电两用机（既可用作电动机又可逆转为发电机）

reversible table 可翻转的工作台

reversible thermodynamic reaction 可逆热力（学）反应

reversible transformation 可逆（反）变换

reversible unit （维修用）周转总成（预先储备的汽车总成，用来替换维修中不可用的总成）

reversing arrangement 换向装置

reversing bleeper 倒车蜂鸣式警报器（挂倒挡时，自动发出声响警报，美称 back-up alarm）

reversing clutch 换向离合器，反向离合器

reversing commutator 电流换向器（电流方向转换器）

reversing dog 回动止动挡块，逆转止动块

reversing gear ①反向齿轮②换向机构，逆转机构，回行装置，回动装置③倒车挡，倒挡齿轮

reversing light 倒车灯（= backing light）

reversing radar 倒车雷达

reversing switch 换向开关，反向开关

reversing test 换向试验［可反转的内燃机（组）进行正、反交替换向运转的试验，以测定其换向压力、换向时间，或离合器接排与脱排转速等，以测试换向机构的可靠性和灵活性］

reversing turbine 可逆转式涡轮机

reversing valve 换向阀，回动阀

reversion 反转，反向，倒转，逆行，转换，颠倒；恢复，复原，退回

reversion characteristic （金属的）恢复特性，回复特性

reversion test （煤油）变质试验（用过氧化铅检查煤油颜色的稳定性，以检查煤油在储运过程中是否变质）

rev-happy engine 高转速发动机

Revigeaux mechanism 拉威挪结构（单行星排与双行星排组合成的复合式行星机构）

revise ①修正，改正，校对②改变③修订版

rev limit 转速极限

revolution ①旋转，回转②转数

revolution alarm （发动机）转速警报器

revolution counter 转速表（显示发动机工作转速的指示器）

revolution drop 转速降低，转速下降

revolution-meter 转数计数器，转速表（简称 revmeter, 亦称 revolution counter, revolution indicator）

revolution per minute 转/分（简称 rev/min, 旋转频率单位，每分钟的转数，代号为 r/min）

revolution per unit (of) time 单位时间转数（代号 N）

revolve （使）旋转，转动，运转；循环，周期地出现

revolving-armature type 旋转电枢型（电机）

revolving-core type 旋转铁心型（电压表或电流表）

revolving crane 回转式起重机

revolving cylinder engine 旋转汽缸式发动机
revolving drum 转鼓，滚筒
revolving magnetic field type 旋转磁场型
revolving table 回转工作台
revolving valve 旋转滑阀，旋转阀，转阀
revolving window 旋转窗
Revue Technique Automatic ［法］汽车技术评论（杂志），轿车技术评论（杂志）（简称 RTa）
Revue Technique Carrosserie ［法］车身技术评论（杂志）（简称 RTc）
Revue Technique Diesel ［法］柴油机技术评论（杂志）（简称 RTd）
revving down ［口语］减速，使…降低转速
revving up ［口语］加速，加快转速
reweighing 重新称重
rewind button （照相机等的）倒片按钮
rewinding 重绕，重卷
reyn 雷恩（英制动力黏度单位，≈1/68950 泊）
Reynold number 雷诺数（Re，表示管道内流体惯性力与分子黏性力之比值，$Re = uD/v$。式中：u—流速；D—管长；v—动黏度系数）
Reynold's analogue 雷诺数模拟
RF ①径（向）流（radial flow）②射频（radio frequency）③测距仪（range finder）④整流器（rectifier）
RFC ①雨林挑战赛（Rainforest challenge 的简称）②再生型燃料电池（regenerative type fuel cell 的简称）
RF carrier 射频载波（radio frequency carrier）
RFD 可靠性故障诊断（reliability failure diagnostic）
RFI ①无线电频率干扰，射频干扰（RF interference 或 radio frequency interference 的简称，电磁辐射所引起的干扰，如：无线电信号对汽车电子设备的干扰）②射频屏蔽（radio frequency isolation 的简称，亦称 RF isolation）
rfl 添加燃油（＝refueling）
rfs 不管零件外部尺寸如何，不考虑零件的大小（regardless of feature size）
RFV 径向力变动（radial force variation）
R governor 两极式调速器（见 maximum-minimum speed governor）
RGS （汽车）导行系统（参见 routes guidance system）
RH ①右手（的），右向（的），右边（的），右侧（的）（right-hand, right）②相对湿度（relative humidity）③变阻器（rheostat）④洛氏硬度（＝Rockwell hardness）
Rh 铑（见 rhodium）
RHDR 右方向驾驶（right hand drive，亦简称 RHD）
rhenium 铼（Re）
rheological fluid multi-plate clutch 流变黏液型多片式离合器
rheological properties 流变特性
rheology 流变学（研究物体流动与变形，特别是固体的塑性流动、黏弹性的学科）
rheometer ①电流计②流量计
rheostat 变阻器，可变电阻（器）（改变电阻，借以调节电路电压或电流的装置，有电阻式和晶体管式两种。前者利用可变电阻改变电路的电压，后者则是周期性地接通或断开电路，以调节电压）
rheostat arm 变阻器滑动臂
rheostatic 可变电阻的；电阻可变的，变阻式的
rheostatic braking 变阻器控制的电制动
rheostatic control 变阻控制（＝resistance control，如：通过改变电阻

控制转速等)

rhodium 铑(Rh,铂族中的银白色惰性金属,原子序数45,原子量102.90550,用于热电偶,以及作为排放控制系统中的催化转化器的催化剂)

rhombic drive (斯特林发动机的)菱形驱动机构

RHT 见 right hand traffic

rhysimeter 流体流速测定计

rhythmic corrugations ①(道路)有规则的波状起伏,有规则的搓板现象②有规律的波纹,规律性波纹

rhythmic purr 和谐声调(指调整好的多缸发动机发出的排气声等)

rib ①肋,棱;肋条;肋材;加强肋;拱肋,拱棱;凸肩②(轮胎胎面)纵向花纹条③加肋,用肋加强

RIB 加肋的,用肋加强的(见 ribbed)

rib arch 扇形拱,肋拱

ribbed 呈肋状的,加肋的,用肋状物支撑、加强的

ribbed brake drum 带(散热)肋片的制动鼓(= finned brake drum)

ribbed cylinder 带加强肋的缸筒;带散热片的汽缸

ribbed edge 带加强肋的边缘

ribbed rubber (垫在车身地板等上面的)肋状橡皮,波状橡皮垫

ribbed tube 加肋管(= rifled tube)

ribbon ①带;带状物②钢卷尺③条板带锯

ribbon cable ①带状电缆,扁电缆②扁索,带状绳索

ribbon tape ①卷尺,皮尺②窄带材,窄板材

ribbon wire 纱包线

rib of piston 活塞(筒腔内的)加强肋

rib stiffener 加强肋(亦称 reinforced rib)

rib-tread tyre 肋(条形花)纹轮胎,纵向折线花纹轮胎

rib type tread pattern 纵向折线型胎面花纹

Ricardo ①李卡图(英国内燃机设计师)②(英国以李卡图命名的)李卡图内燃机研究所

Ricardo comet (combustion) chamber 李卡图氏设计的彗星型涡流式燃烧室

Ricardo comet V swirl chamber 李卡图彗星V形涡流燃烧室

Ricardo head 李卡图型缸盖(挤压式燃烧室缸盖的一种,主要用于侧置气门发动机,见 squash type)

Ricardo's-squish 李卡图-挤压法(利用活塞运动挤压混合气,使其在燃烧室内产生乱流)

Ricardo's turbulent head 李卡图紊流式汽缸盖(侧置气门式燃烧室,在活塞顶与缸盖燃烧室顶壁之间形成较薄的气层,其面积称为挤压面积)

Ricardo type 李卡图式(燃烧室,见 Ricardo head,为挤压式燃烧室的一种)

rich 富的,浓的,稠的

richen (up) 加浓(混合气等)

rich idling setting 怠速加浓调节

richly tailored (在车身修饰)装潢精美的

rich metering 浓混合气调节

rich (misfire) limit 浓(混合气失火)极限

rich mixture 浓混合气(一般指 air-fuel ratio = 10~15, fuel-air ratio = 0.06~0.10, MS = 1~1.5,在着火极限内的浓混合气)

rich mixture strength 浓混合气强度(= rich MS,见 mixture strength)

rich reactor 浓混合气反应器(指使用浓混合气的常规发动机利用废气余热使排气中的 CO、HC 等进一步氧化反应的装置,反应器工作温度较高,并需要引入二次空气,以补充所需的氧气)

rich running (发动机)浓混合气

运转

ride ①(汽车的)行驶平顺性,乘坐舒适性②乘,骑,乘车,搭车;行驶,航行③浮,浮动④安放在…上,跨在…上,搭在…上

ride clearance ①(汽车行驶中车身的)最小动载离地间隙②(行驶时汽车钢板弹簧的)最大允许动载挠度③(行驶中汽车悬架的)最大允许压缩行程

ride comfort (汽车行驶)平顺性(避免汽车在行驶过程中所产生的振动和冲击使人感到不舒适、疲劳,甚至损害健康,或使货物损坏的性能,平顺性是舒适性"comfort"的主要内容之一)

ride-comfort criteria (运输工具的)行驶平顺性标准,乘坐舒适性标准

ride comfort evaluation (车辆)行驶平顺性评价,乘坐舒适性评价

ride comfort index 乘坐舒适性指数

ride comfort indices summation 乘坐舒适性指数总和

ride control 行驶平顺性控制

ride control shock absorber 行驶平顺性控制式减振器(可调阻尼式减振器)

ride control signals 行驶平顺性控制信号

ride down effect 减撞效应[汽车碰撞中乘员运动能量通过安全带等拘束装置为车身变形所吸收称为 ride down(减撞)。ride down 效应越大,乘员在车内的移动量(displacement)越小,得到的保护效果越佳]

ride down effects 车损效应,车损效果(碰撞时利用车身破坏来达到消减碰撞能量、减少乘员伤害的效果)

ride feeling performance (汽车行驶时乘坐人员感觉的)乘坐舒适性,行驶平顺性

ride-frequency 平顺性频率(乘坐舒适与否的评价参数之一,弹簧上质量自由振动频率,一般轿车为 70～80Hz/min,愈低愈舒适)

ride harshness ①行驶平顺性恶劣;行驶不舒适性②(行驶时)汽车车身在垂直平面内的小振幅振动③行驶时悬架过硬

ride height ①(汽车车身的)行车高度(汽车装货或载人后的高度,装载高度)②(汽车的)离地间隙(= ground clearance)③(汽车车身的)行驶高度

ride meter (车辆的)乘员振动分析仪,乘坐舒适性分析仪

ride mode (可编程平顺性控制系统中的悬架阻尼)柔顺模式(正常行驶模式,相对于刚硬模式而言,见 firm mode)

rid-engineering 行驶平顺性工程(学)

ride of vehicle 汽车的行驶平顺性,汽车的乘坐舒适性

rideograph ①(测量路面行驶平顺的)测振仪,平整度测定仪②(汽车)行驶平顺性测定仪(= ride meter)

ride performance 行驶平顺性

ride quality (车辆的)乘坐平顺性与乘坐舒适性质量

rider ①座,座席②乘车的人③(加固车身等的)斜撑

ride rate 悬架有效刚度(一定荷载状态下,簧上质心与地面间垂直距离的单位增量所对应的轮胎垂直负荷的减量)

ride the brake (行驶中)①缓制动,半制动(指制动踏板不踩到底)②制动器分离不彻底,形成制动拖滞现象

ride the clutch ①行车时脚一直踩在离合器踏板上②脱挡(踩离合器)滑行③不换挡利用离合器操纵行驶

ride transfer characteristic (车辆)行驶振动传递特性(车辆行驶平顺性、乘坐舒适性评定参数之一)

ridge line 分水岭线,山脊线

ridge reamer (切除因磨损而在汽缸套内圆顶部形成的凸肩的)缸口绞刀

riding ①乘车,驾车,驾车行驶②乘车的,乘坐的,行驶的

riding capacity 乘员定额

riding characteristics 行驶平顺性

riding comfort 乘坐舒适性,行驶平顺性

riding grade (路面)行车(质量)等级,(路面的汽车行驶平顺性评价等级)

riding public 公共交通车辆的乘客

rifle brush 螺旋状刷(如:油孔清洁用)

rifled tube ①加肋管(= ribbed tube)②内螺纹管,有镗线的管

rifle file 螺线锉,触点锉

rig ①装备,装具;装备齐全的汽车(如:有旅游生活设备的汽车),成套设备;台,试验台;索具,支架②装配;临时赶造(up),安装,悬架,调整;控制

rig body 带石油钻井安装设备的专用车厢

rigging pin 装配销

rigging screw 拉紧螺杆

right angle 直角

right-angled (成,有)直角的,正交的

right-angled bend ①直角转弯,直角弯曲②直角弯道③直角弯曲部

right-angled intersection 十字交叉,十字交叉路口(参见 four-way intersection)

right-angled monogram 直角列线图;直角诺谟图

right-angled triangle 直角三角形(= right triangle, rectangular triangle)

right-angle intersection 直角相交,直角交叉

right-bank 右部,右列,右侧部分(如:V形发动机缸体的右列)

right circular cone 直立圆锥

right circular cylinder 直立圆柱

right cone 直锥

right conoid 正劈锥曲面

right driving 右侧行车

right elevation 右视图

right flank 右侧齿面(一个观察者从齿轮上被选作观察基准的那个端面看过去,当被观察的那个齿的齿顶朝上时,位于右侧的齿面,称为右侧齿面)

right-hand 右的,右手的,右方的,右侧的,右旋的,右转的,靠右行驶的

right-hand component 右手坐标分量,向右分力

right hand control car 右转向盘车辆,右座驾驶车辆(用于靠左行驶的国家, = right hand drive car)

right-hand corner 右转弯

right-hand crankshaft 右侧(置)式曲轴(在直列六缸发动机中,当第一缸在上止点时,从前端看,第三、四连杆轴颈位于右侧,其点火顺序为1-5-3-6-2-4)

right hand drive (汽车的)右座驾驶,右转向盘驾驶(指道路交通左行国家汽车转向盘在驾驶室右侧,简称 RHDR)

right-handed nut 右旋螺母

right-handed rotation 顺时针旋转(= right-handwise, clockwise rotation)

right-hand mounted fuel injection pump 右机泵(观察者面对柴油机自由端,安装在柴油机右侧的喷油泵)

right-hand rotation 右转(从内燃机输出端看曲轴顺时针方向旋转)

right-hand teeth 右旋齿(对于斜齿圆柱齿轮和圆柱蜗杆,当观察者沿齿轮分度圆柱面的直母线方向看过去,轮齿上远离观察者的任意一个端齿廓,相对于接近观察者的任意一个端面齿廓,按顺时针方向转过

一个角度时,此轮齿就称为右旋齿。对于曲线齿锥齿轮,当观察者从锥顶朝大端看过去,轮齿上的背锥齿廓,相对于中间锥面上的齿廓,按顺时针方向转过了一个角度时,此轮齿也称为右旋齿)

right-hand traffic 靠右行驶交通(车辆靠右行驶,转向盘装在驾驶室左方,如:中国、美国、法国、德国、俄罗斯、意大利、蒙古、朝鲜等国)

right-hand turn 右转弯,向右旋转(= right turn)

right helicoid 正螺旋面

right lane 右车道

right-lay rope 右旋钢丝绳

right of priority 优先权

right-of-way ①(绿灯信号授予的道路交叉口)通行权;道路通行权;通过他人土地的权利;筑路权②道路用地;已筑有道路或将来要建设道路的公有地(简称 ROW 或/R/W)

right steering trapezoid connection 右转向梯形臂(连接转向横拉杆与右转向节)

right-to-left interchangeability 左、右方零件互换性

right to left side vibration 人体左右振动(沿人体左右方向的横向直线振动)

right triangle 直角三角形

right turn lane 右转车道

rigid ①刚度②刚性的③固定不动的,固定连接的④严格的,严密的

rigid axle 整体梁式车桥(= beam axle)

rigid axle suspension 整体梁式车桥非独立悬架(用一根整轴将左右车轮连接起来,并通过悬架与车架或车身相连的悬架形式,亦称 nonindependent suspension)

rigid barrier full frontal impact test (汽车)刚性障壁正面碰撞试验

rigid body ①刚性车厢②刚体

rigid body aligning torque steer (汽车的)整车回正力矩偏转(汽车全部车轮产生的回正力矩,企图使整个汽车偏转的现象,这种偏转效应一般都很小,而且常常是不足转向效应)

rigid cardan 刚性十字轴万向接头

rigid coupling ①刚性连接(具有刚性的连接形式)②刚性联轴节

rigid design 刚性结构

rigid drive axle (装有非独立悬架的)整体式驱动桥(非断开式驱动桥的半轴套管和主减速器壳均与桥壳刚性相连成为一个整体)

rigid dynamics 刚体力学

rigid fit 紧固配合(= tight fit)

rigid frame 刚性车架,刚性构架

rigidity gear 刚性齿轮(刚轮,工作时始终保持其原始形状的齿轮)

rigidity index 刚度指数

rigidity modulus 刚性模量,刚性模数

rigid joint 刚性连接

rigid pipe 刚性管(相对固定的零件之间,可保持永久形状的连接管)

rigid plastic 硬质塑料

rigid PVC 硬聚氯乙烯(无或少增塑剂的聚氯乙烯)

rigid test 在恶劣工作条件下的试验

rigid-type bearing 非自动调心滚动轴承

rigid (type) construction 刚性结构

rigid vehicle 单车(相对于汽车列车而言,单独的车辆,即:既不是汽车列车中的牵引车,也不是挂车,如:rigid truck,指不带挂车的单个货车)

rigid wheel 刚性车轮

rigor 苛刻,严格,苛刻条件,严格要求,精确,精密,严密,严重(= rigour)

rigorous data 精确数据

rig result 台架试验结果

rig test 台架试验

RIM (塑料制件的)反应-喷射成形

法(见 reaction-injection moulding)

rim ①(任何圆形物的)外缘(外边、周边、边框等)②(汽车车轮中指)轮辋(车轮上安装与支撑轮胎的部件)

rim beat 轮辋外缘(亦称轮缘,= rim flange)

rim bolt 轮辋螺栓

rim brake 轮辋制动器(作用于轮辋的制动器)

rim bruise (of a tyre) 轮辋造成的轮胎损伤

rim bruising (车轮的)轮辋撞伤,轮辋碰坏

rim center line 轮辋中心线(指轮辋垂直平分面上且通过其中心的垂线)

rim center section 轮辋体中段

rim clamp 轮辋紧固夹

rim clearance (并装双胎间的)轮辋间距,轮辋间隙

rim clinch 轮辋锁圈

rim contour 轮辋(截面)轮廓

rim cross-section 轮辋剖面

rim cut ①(轮胎的)轮辋切损,钢圈切伤(指胎压不足,驶过障碍物或高速行驶时,轮胎被轮辋切伤的故障)②轮辋断裂

rim diameter 轮辋直径

rim expander 轮辋拆卸工具

rim fit 轮胎在轮辋上的配合

rim gearwheel 齿圈(亦称 ring gear,见 internal gear)

rimless 无框的(前照灯等)

rim lock ①弹簧锁②轮辋锁圈

rim lock ring groove 轮辋锁圈槽

rimmed steel 沸腾钢(炼钢时加入一定量的锰,使钢水中保留有一定量的氧,钢水在钢锭模内凝固过程中形成CO气体逸出而产生"沸腾"现象)

rim nut 轮辋螺母

rim of flywheel 飞轮齿圈

rim of headlamp 前照灯灯圈(= headlamp glass-rim, bezel of headlamp)

rim profile 轮辋外廓

rim pry bar slot 轮辋(卸轮胎用)撬棒槽

rim pull (汽车的)路面牵引力(在轮胎与路面间测定的或根据发动机输出转矩与发动机—车轮间的传动比算出的牵引力)

rim remover 轮胎拆卸工具

rim section 轮辋断面

rim serrations 轮辋滚花

rim slip test 轮辋错动试验(评价轮辋错动难易程度的试验)

rim socket spanner 轮辋套筒扳手(= rim socket wrench)

rim spacer 并装双胎间的可拆式轮辋隔圈

rim speed 轮辋速度;轮缘速率

rim tool 轮辋拆装工具

rim 5° tyre mounting surface 轮辋5°轮胎安装面

rim width 轮辋宽度(= width of rim)

rim with removable flange 外缘可拆式轮辋

rim with removable side ring 边圈(挡圈)可拆式轮辋

rim wrench 轮辋螺母扳手

ring ①环,圈,箍,环状物②卡环,涨圈③环形电路;回路④环绕,卷绕,装环,装圈

ring belt 活塞环带(由活塞环槽和环岸构成的活塞环槽区域,亦称 ring-bend)

ring-belt temperature 活塞环带温度

ring bolt 环(头)螺栓,环端螺栓,带环螺栓(参见 eyebolt)

ring carrier 活塞环槽镶座(= piston ring carrier)

ring chamber 环形室,环状腔

ring clamp 夹箍,环夹

ring collector 环形集电器

ring compressor (将活塞装入汽缸时使用的)压环器

ring cup (液压缸的)皮圈(副皮碗,亦称 secondary cup)
ring cyclide (圆)环面
ring discharge 环形喷嘴
ring dynamometer 环形测力计,测力环
Ringelman's smoke chart 任格尔曼排烟浓度表(用于测定柴油机排烟浓度等)
ring expander (装在活塞环与环槽之间的弹簧)涨圈(使活塞环紧贴缸壁)
ring gage 环规
ring gap 活塞环切口间隙(活塞环端隙)
ring gear ①齿圈(任何大直径的环状齿轮,包括内齿圈、外齿圈,如:飞轮齿圈)②冠轮(冠状齿轮,见 crown wheel)③(差速器)从动冠轮(见 differential crown gear)
ring groove 环槽;活塞环槽
ring groove bottom 活塞环槽底
ring groove carbon remover 活塞环槽积炭清除工具
ring-groove pounding 活塞环对槽的冲击
ring-groove side 活塞环槽上下面
ring header 集电环,环形集电器
ring insertion 镶环,环形镶入物
ring job 活塞修复与换装新活塞环作业
ring laser gyroscope 环形激光陀螺仪(见 laser gyroscope)
ring lock 锁环
ring-lubricated bearing 油环润滑轴承(= ring lubricating bearing, ring-oiled bearing)
ring packing 环形密封件,密封环
ring radial wall thickness 环径向厚度,环径向壁厚
ring resilience (密封)环弹性,圆环弹力;圆环弹性变形;圆环回跳现象
ring ridge (汽缸表面的)活塞环脊(指活塞位于上止点时活塞环以上的汽缸壁面区磨损时,该区域形成凸台或凸脊,修理时必须除去)
ring road 环路,环形道路,环行道路
ring-shaped 环状的
ring-shape flexspline 环形柔轮(柔轮的基本形状呈环形者)
ring side area 活塞环上、下平面面积
ring spreader 活塞环胀圈(装在油环后面的弹性胀圈, = piston ring expander)
ring squeezer 活塞-活塞环总成装入汽缸时用的卡箍
ring surface 环面
ring travel shoulder (汽缸内孔上端)活塞环行程终点的磨痕凸肩
ring-type hitch 环式牵引装置,牵引环(= eye hitch)
ring valve 环形阀
ring width (活塞)环宽度(指环的轴向厚度)
rinse ①涮洗,漂洗,漂涮,洗净 ②冲洗,(用清水)涮;涮掉(out),灌入(down)
rinser 冲洗器,漂洗机
rinsing arch (洗车设备中的)淋洗龙门,涮洗龙门
Rio Declaration on Environment and Development 里约环境与发展宣言(亦称地球宪章,见 UN Earth Summit)
ripple amplitude 波纹幅值
ripple current 波纹电流(加在直流电上的弱交流电)
ripple finish 皱纹(罩面)漆,皱纹面饰
ripple frequency 波纹脉动频率
ripple rejection ratio (电压调节器的)纹波抑制比(输入纹波电压—峰值与输出纹波电压—峰值之比)
ripple(s) ①波浪状路面,搓板路面 ②波纹形,卷曲,波纹,皱纹 ②使成波浪状,波动

ripple time （线性放大器）脉动时间（对输入信号电平的阶跃变化，斜坡时间的终点与输出信号值最后一次进入包括输出信号最终值规定电平范围的瞬间之间的时间间隔）

ripple tolerance （线性放大器的）脉动容差（包括输出信号最终值的规定电平范围）

ripple voltage 脉动电压，波纹电压

ripple wave of tyre 轮胎的驻波状变形（见 standing wave of tyre）

RISE （汽车）碰撞安全强化技术解决方案（reinforcement impact safety evolution 的简称，见 zone body）

rise of a carriageway 车行道前后两点间的高差

rise of cam 凸轮升程，凸轮顶升高度（= cam rise, lead of cam）

riser ①（车身）地板高台，（地板在后座处的抬高部分）凸台②高起物

riser bar （整流子的）整流片（= seg ment）

rise time 上升时间［如：阶跃响应，当零开始的输出信号从到达最终稳态值的规定小百分数（如：10%）的瞬时起，到第一次到达该稳定值的规定大百分数（如：90%）的瞬时为止的时间］

rising edge 上升边（缘）（= advancing edge）

rising force 上升力

rising gust 一阵上升气流

rising rate suspension 升刚度悬架（指其弹性元件的刚度随荷载的增加而成比例地增高。如：当悬架被压缩时，其刚度随之增高）

rising rate valve system （可变阻尼式减振器的）节流阻力提升阀系统

risk 风险，危险

rival ①竞争者；对手；匹敌者②对抗的，竞争的③对抗，竞争

riverbed 河床（常常被选为越野赛车场）

riverine utility craft 河滩、沼泽地带用气垫浮行车辆（简称 RUC）

river simulator for amphibian tests 水陆两用车辆江河模拟试验装置

rivet 铆钉

rivet buster 铆钉截断器，铆钉铲

rivet clipper 铆钉钳

rivet connection 铆接，铆钉连接（= rivet bond）

riveted frame 铆接车架；铆接构架

riveting gun （风动或电动）铆钉枪（= riveter）

riveting hammer 铆钉锤

riveting machine 铆钉机

RKE module 遥控无钥匙（开门）出入模块（remote keyless entry module 的简称，该模块接收手持式遥控器发出的锁门或开锁密码信号，使相关继电器通电，让车门或行李舱门自动开锁或上锁。某些车型该模块与 BCM 构成一体）

RL （汽车底盘测功机等的）道路（行驶）阻力（模拟）加载（road load 的简称）

r&m ①修理和维护（repair and maintenance）②工作报告与备忘录（reports and memoranda）

RMA 橡胶制造商协会（Rubber Manufacturer's Association 的简称）

R mag 右旋磁电机

RMCS ［美］（加利福尼亚州的）地区汽车运输安全局（Regional Bureau of Motor Carrier Safety）

RMOD-k 德 Anhalt 大学 Oertel 教授开发的系列轮胎模型名

rms 平方根，均方根（root mean square）

RM. S error 标准误差，均方根误差（root mean square error 的简称）

RMSH 可靠性、易维修性、安全性及劳动者适应性（reliability, maintainability, safety, and human factors）

RMS value 均方根值（root mean

square value, = effective value)

road ①路, 道路②路得（英美面积单位 1 road = 40 sq. pole = 1/4 acre）

road-ability 路用性能（①对车辆,指其对路况的适应性、方向稳定性、行驶平顺性、克服路障的能力等②对轮胎,指其路面抓着力、方向保持能力及路况适应能力等）

roadable 可在公路上驾驶的,道路上可通行的

road adherence （轮胎的）路面附着力（= road adherency, road adhesion）

road-adhesion coefficient 道路附着系数

road agent （沿公路劫车的）车匪（亦称 highway man）

road-and-rail access 公路-铁路引道

road antiknock performance of car 汽车的道路抗爆特性（指汽车在道路上行驶时发动机本身的抗爆能力,可用其所要求的汽油辛烷值来表征）

road antiknock performance of fuel 燃料的道路抗爆性

road-bank elevation 路面横向倾斜,（弯道）超高（= roadside elevation）

road bay ①让车道②路面板分块

road beacon 筑路或修路用的标志灯（表示正在施工）

roadbed 路基, 路床; 路基（表）面; 路槽底（面）

road bend 道路转弯处, 弯道

road block ①路障, 道路行驶障碍物②交通警察设置的活动栅栏

Road Board 公路局

road book （某地区的）交通指南,交通路程便览

road border 路边, 路肩

road breakdown ①（车辆）途中损坏, 途中故障②道路损坏

road brightness 道路照明度

road broom 扫路机

road builder ①筑路机②筑路工作者

road camber 路拱（亦称 road crowning）

road capacity 道路通过能力

road carpet 路面表层

road circuits 环形交叉口, 环形口, 公路环道

road clearance （车辆）离地间隙（指汽车底盘前后桥、传动系的最低点离路面的距离, 为评价车辆通过性的参数）

road closed sign "此路不通"标志

road condition judgment logic 路面状况判断逻辑

road conditions 路况

road congestion 道路阻塞, 交通阻塞

road craft （驾驶员应有的）道路知识及驾驶技能

road crossing 交叉路口, 公路交叉口

road crust 路面表层, 道路铺面, 道路硬面

road curve 道路弯道, 道路曲线

road debris 道路上的碎石

road depression 道路上的凹陷处

road discipline 公路交通规则

road ditch 道路边沟, 排水沟

road diversion 绕行道路

road draft (tube type) system 行车气流抽吸（管）型曲轴箱通风系

road environment information 道路环境信息

road facility 道路设施（一般指安全通信设施）

road fatalities 道路交通事故死亡人数

road feel(ing) 路感（行车中, 驾驶员从转向盘和踏板及各种操纵杆件中感觉到的道路通过车轮及车辆运动产生的反馈信息）

road film （附着于车身, 车底的）道路污秽层

road fork 道路分岔口
road-free vehicle 越野汽车（= off-road vehicle）
road fuel consumption 道路燃料消耗量（汽车运行燃料消耗量）
road geometry information 道路几何信息（指车辆所在道路位置，道路对车辆的几何尺寸关系、道路弯道、交叉口等的几何尺寸等，供智能公路系统自动控制车速、转向及减速、制动等的参照信息）
road grade 道路坡度
road grader 平路机，平地机
road grip （轮胎或履带的）路面抓着力
road guard 道路护栏，道路防护物
road-handling capacity 道路通行能力
road haulage industry 公路货物运输业，汽车货运业
road head 路尽头
road hog ①乱开汽车②乱开汽车的人③乱停车；乱停放的车辆；乱停车的人
road hoggish （为汽车、摩托车等驾驶员服务的）路旁旅店（= road house）
roadholding （汽车的）道路保持能力（汽车操纵稳定性 handing 的一种非专业性说法）
road-holding ability ①（车辆的）方向稳定性，车道保持能力，方向操纵能力，方向控制稳定性②（轮胎的）路面抓着能力及车道保持能力（表示轮胎与路面间附着力的大小和轮胎的抗侧偏能力）
road-holding property （汽车）操纵稳定性
road horsepower （汽车）道路马力（指汽车在道路上行驶时，其驱动轮所输出的功率）
road house 公路两旁供旅客休息的酒店旅馆

road hump 路面隆起凸包
road illumination 道路照明
road inclination 道路坡度
road-induced vibration 路面不平激起的振动
road inequalities 道路的平面度（亦称 road irregularity）
road junction 道路交叉点，道路枢纽
road-knock rating method （车用汽油的）道路辛烷值测定法（通常有三种：联点法、联点修正法和边界法。它们都是在特定的行驶条件下直接在汽车发动机上采用异辛烷、正庚烷标准混合油的对比法，确定汽油试样的辛烷值。见 octane number, road octane number, uniontown procedure, modified uniontown procedure）
road knock test 道路爆震试验
road laws 公路交通规则
roadless 无路的
roadlice 小汽车，微型汽车
road load ①道路负载（由滚动阻力等道路阻力形成的车辆行驶负载）②道路行驶阻力模拟加载量（在底盘测功机上检测汽车性能时，模拟道路行驶阻力的加载量）
road-load input （车辆行驶中）道路（对悬架、车身系统等产生的）负荷输入
road load performance （液力变速器）道路负载特性（输出转矩一定或输出转矩和转速对应于车辆行驶阻力特性曲线上的相应值时，液力传动装置或液力变矩器的特性）
road load power 道路行驶（阻力）功率（克服滚动阻力、爬坡阻力、加速阻力等行驶功率）
road louse ［美］福特小汽车
road machine 筑路机械
road maintenance fee 养路费
road map 道路地图（一般专指汽车

驾驶员使用的道路图、路线图、交通图）

road marking 路面标示，路面标线，路标（除交通标志外，为了对交通的管制、警告、指导等目的，在路面、缘石、道路中或其邻近的物体上，以线条、图形、符号、文字、颜色表示的说明等，= traffic marking, pavement marking, carriageway marking）

road-metal 铺路碎石

road mixer 筑路拌料机

road narrows sign 路幅缩狭标志（在双车道公路中路幅突然缩狭，为了减速安全错车使用的警告标示）

road network 道路网

road noise ①（泛指各种）道路噪声②（特指汽车在不平的路面上行驶时，由于）路面干扰引起的车内噪声（即车轮受到的干扰，以振动的形式传至车身，而在车身内形成的噪声，亦称 road roar, road rumble, body rumble）

road obstruction 路障

road octane number （车用汽油的）道路辛烷值（简称 RdON，亦称 road octane-value，表示汽油在汽车实际道路上行驶时的抗爆性，更有实际意义，但测量费时、费事，故用实验室辛烷值近似地表示：$RdON = b_0 + b_1 RON + b_2 MON$，其中 b_0、b_1、b_2 系数由试验研究确定，参见 RON，MON，road-knock rating method。此外，实践证明，马达法和研究法辛烷值的平均值可近似地表示汽油的道路法辛烷值，故美国材料试验标准"ASTM"及联邦汽油规格已用上述二者的平均值，作为汽油等级的抗爆性指标，称：抗爆指数，见 antiknock index）

road operation test 道路运行试验，道路试验

road out 模拟道路的装置

road pavement 路面

road performance （汽车的）道路性能（主要指加速性能、最高车速、爬坡性能及方向稳定性等）

road performance of fuel 燃料道路性能（指燃料在汽车道路行驶中的实际使用性能）

road plane 道路平面（指车辆所停驻的参考平面）

road pressure 道路行驶胎压（在道路上行驶时的胎压）

road race 道路竞赛（在公路上进行的汽车竞赛）

road-rail bus 公路-铁路两用客车（= highway-rail bus）

road-reation-responsive hydraulic power steering 路面反力响应式液压动力转向（可根据所测定的路面对转向盘的反作用力，自动调整转向助力，亦称路面反作用力感知式液压动力转向 "road-reation-sensitive hydraulic steering" 及路面反作用力因变式液压转向 "road-reaction-dependent hydraulic steering"）

Road Research Laboratory （英国）道路研究试验室

road resistance 道路阻力，道路行驶总阻力

road roar 路面噪声（见 road noise）

road roughness random input 道路平面度的随机输入

road roughness tester 路面平面度测定装置

road rumble 路面噪声（见 road noise）

road salt （道路）防冰冻用盐

road scraper 铲运机，刮路机

road sense （驾驶员的）路感

road-sensing suspension system 路敏式悬架系统（简称 RSS system，该系统根据传感器输送的车身垂直加速度、车轮与车身间的相对位置、

车轮转速及车速、汽车纵倾等信息判断通路状况及行驶模式,以控制悬架的阻尼特性及车身高度,提供良好的行驶平顺性和操纵性,亦称实时阻尼系统"rear time damping system")

road service system 道路故障车救援系统,路上保修系统,沿路汽车救援系统

road shocks 路面(不平)冲击

roadside 路边,路旁地带,路侧地带(道路行车道的外侧及邻近地带的通称)

roadside assembly 路旁组合标志(设在路旁标志柱上的多标志牌)

roadside breakdown 汽车(在中途)故障

roadside communication unit 路边通信装置,路旁通信装置

roadside computer (自动公路系统信息实时处理及通用的)路边计算机

roadside control unit 路边控制装置(行车线路自动控制导行系统,装于路边、十字路口控制车地间通信、处理道路交通情报等的装置)

roadside elevation (弯道)超高,路面横向倾斜(= road-bank elevation)

roadside repair (车辆停在路边)途中修理

roadside sign 路侧标志(在道路侧设置的标志)

roadside signal 路边信号(由路边交通指挥或信息系统向车内接收系统发出的信号)

roadside survey 路边观察,路边测量;路边观测资料

roadside verge 路肩

road signal 道路标志

road simulation dynamometer 道路模拟底盘测功机

road simulator 道路模拟装置,道路模拟机

road simulator for vehicle 车辆(测试)用道路模拟装备(如:底盘测功机等,模拟道路的滚筒等)

road simulator test 道路模拟装置试验(如:在底盘测动机上试验等)

road slab 路面板

road snow clearing by exhausted heat energy (汽车)废气热能道路积雪清除(系统)

road speed 道路车速(公路行车速度)

road splash (在湿路上行驶时)路面飞溅的泥水

road spring (汽车)悬架弹簧

road sprinkler 道路洒水车(= road sprinkling truck)

roadstead 停泊所,抛锚处

roadster 单排座双门敞篷轿车(后部常备有翻转可作座位的行李舱门)

road structure detecting system (车辆上的)道路建筑物探测系统(该系统运用激光雷达扫描可准确地识别道路建筑物和前面行驶的车辆,用于防止高速行驶的车辆与道路前方潜在障碍物碰撞的自动制动系统)

road surface condition detecting system (车装式)路面状况测定系统(使用装在车上的摄像与屏显系统测定路面状况)

road surface condition monitor 路面状况监测器

road surface-embedded guide-nail (智能公路系统中的)路面导向钉

road surface input (来自)路面(的)输入

road surface meter 路面仪(实测并记录路面随机平面度的仪器)

road-surface roughness 路面粗糙度,路面平面度

road sweeper 扫路机

road tank car 油罐车(= road tanker)

road telltale 道路信号装置

road test （道）路试（验）（考核经济性、动力性、可靠性及耐久性等而在不同道路上进行的整车试验）

road-test car ①道路检验车（用以检查道路的质量）②道路试验车，路试用车

road test cycle 道路多工况试验循环

road test method （烟度测量的）道路试验法（汽车在坡道上加载行驶，使柴油机转速达到75%~100%最高转速范围内，用烟度计测烟度值）

road test mileage 路试里程耗油率

road test simulation （室内）道路试验模拟

road time ①（汽车运输的）路上时间（指在完成某一运程所需的总时间中汽车在路上运行的时间，包括实际行驶的时间和等红灯等临时停车时间）②（汽车队）沿道路的通过时间

road toll 道路通行费，过路费

road traffic 公路运输，道路交通

road traffic accidents statistics 道路交通事故统计（简称RTAS）

road traffic noise 道路交通噪声

road train ①（路上行驶的）一支车队②汽车列车（多指大型货车拖挂若干挂车组成的汽车列车）

road transport 公路运输，道路运输

road transport information/intelligent vehicle-highway system 道路交通信息/智能汽车-公路系统（简称RTI/IVHS）

road transport system 道路运输系统

road travel 公路运行，道路行车；公路旅行

road tunnel 公路隧道，地下道路，地下公路

road turn 道路弯道，弯路

road-tyre adhesion 道路-轮胎间的附着力，轮胎对地面的抓着力

road tyre contact 轮胎与路面的接触

road tyre interface 路面与轮胎之间的接触面

road upkeep 道路养护

road-use tax （车辆的）道路使用税

road-use vehicle 公路用车辆（行驶于公路的车辆，又称road vehicle）

road wander 车辆在道路上来回摆动（由于方向把握不良或车辆的方向稳定性不良）

road wave 道路的波伏平面度

roadway 车行道；公路（= carriageway）

roadway flusher （道路）洒水车（= watering car, water truck, sprinkler truck, motor sprinkling machine, street flusher, street flusher truck, street washer, motor water car, motor street washer, motor flusher）

roadway gate 道口栏珊，拦路木

roadway lighting system 道路照明系统

roadway sign 道路信号，公路标志

road wear 道路磨损，路面磨损

road weight 车辆的运行重量（见operating weight）

road wheel 车轮

road work ahead sign "前面道路施工"标志

road worthiness ①（车辆的）道路适应性②（道路的）车辆行驶适应能力

road worthiness test （汽车及部件的）道路适用性试验，道路适应性试验

road worthy 适用于道路的，能在道路上行驶的

ROB CAD 机器人式计算机辅助设计系统（robot computer-aided design的简称，为一系列计算机辅助生产工程系统的组合，可同时进行设计、模拟、最优化处理和自动化及

非自动化生产的离线编程等)

robe-cord 车内手握带,车内手拉吊带

Robert Hooke 罗伯特虎克(英国人,与 Cardan 同一时代,同样发明了十字轴万向节,所以英国有时称十字轴万向节为 Hookes joint)

Robertson(screw)driver 内方(螺钉)旋具(= Canada screw driver)

robot ①机械手,机器人②自动操纵的③自动交通信号(= automatic traffic signal)

robotary 机器人(集合体)

robotics ①自动机械手,(人工操纵的)自动手②机器人,拟人化自动机械

robotistic ①机器人的②(人工操作)自动机械手的③拟人化自动机械的

robot pilot 自动驾驶装置,机器人驾驶员

robot tractor 无人驾驶自动控制拖拉机;无人驾驶自动牵引车

robust ①耐用的②结实的(坚固的)③可在恶劣环境下保持完好状态和正常运转的

robustness 牢靠性(坚固性,耐久性,强度)

rock crawling(sport) (汽车)爬岩运动(一种新兴的汽车赛车,将巨石堆垒在指定赛场,插上小旗,作为比赛路线标杆。其特点是可在市区内举办)

rock crystal 水晶,石英

rocker actuator 摇臂式作动器,摇臂式执行器(参见 valve arm)

rocker arm 摆臂,摇臂(绕端部或中部支点摆动或摇动的杆件的通称,如:①气门机构的摇臂,= valve rocker arm②摆臂式减振器内的摆臂"rocker arm"③悬架系统的控制臂,= control arm④蜗杆指销式转向器内的指销臂,= peg arm, stud arm 等)

rocker arm bracket ①摇(杆)臂支架②摇臂座(支撑摇臂轴的零件)

rocker arm oil trough 气门摇臂油槽

rocker arm ratio 摇臂传动比(指一般顶置气门机构的摇臂传动比,= 气门开启高度/凸轮升程)

rocker arm shaft 摇臂轴(支撑摇臂并允许其自由摆动的零件,简称 rocker shaft)

rocker arm way 摇臂导轨

rocker compensating gear 气门摇臂间隙补偿装置

rocker panel 车门槛板(= sill panel)

rocker shaft ①(气门)摇臂轴②转向摇臂轴(转向器输出轴,转向摇臂装于该轴上,= pitman arm shaft, sector shaft,美亦称 cross shaft)

rocker shaft bracket 气门摇臂轴支架

rocker shaft spacer spring 气门摇臂间隔弹簧

rocker switch 翘板开关

rocker type shock absorber 摇臂式减振器(亦称 lever type shock absorber)

rocket engine 火箭发动机(喷射式发动机)

rocket fuel 火箭燃料

rocket truck 火箭运载车

rocket turbine 喷射式燃气轮机,反作用式涡轮发动机(= reaction turbine)

rock guard 挡石防护罩(= stone guard)

rock haul truck 石料搬运(汽)车,石料运输车

rocking motion ①摇动,摇摆动作②(转子发动机径向密封片的)颤动

rocking shaft (发动机的)摇臂轴

rock oil 石油

rock rails (越野车等的)防飞石围栏

rock tar 石油,原油,石焦油

Rock-Trac 一款机械分时四轮驱动系统的商品名

Rockwell hardness 洛氏硬度(在初始试验力及总试验力先后作用下,将金刚石圆锥或钢球压头压入试样表面,经规定保持时间后卸除主试验力,用测量的残余压痕深度增量计算硬度值的一种压痕硬度,初始试验力为29N,总试验力为147N,294N或441N)

Rockwell superficial hardness number 表面洛氏硬度值(用表面洛氏硬度标尺刻度满量程值与残余压痕深度增量之差计算的硬度值)

rock wool 石棉

rocky soil 石质土

rod ①(细长的)棒,杆,连杆,量杆②杆(= pole,英美长度单位,1 rod = 16$\frac{1}{2}$ feet = 5$\frac{1}{2}$ yard = 5.0292m) ③鲁莽、高速开车

rod aerial 杆状天线(亦称rod antenna, staff aerial)

rodbearing 连杆轴承(①指曲轴连杆大端轴颈轴承,= big-end bearing 或 crankshaft connecting-rod big-end bearing) ②指连杆小端衬套,活塞销衬套,(= connecting-rod small-end bearing, piston pin bearing)

rod boring machine 杆式镗床

rod cap 连杆轴承(下端)盖

rod control 杠杆机构控制,杆系控制,杆件控制,操纵杆控制,拉杆控制

rod crack ①纵裂纹②连杆裂纹

rodding the radiator (将散热器上水箱和/或下水箱拆去)用通条清除散热器芯(管道内的水垢、锈蚀等)

rod end (液压缸或气压缸的)活塞连杆端

rod end coupling 活塞连杆端接头

rod-end volume (油缸)活塞后方容积(活塞连杆后端的容积)

rod float 流速测定浮棒(= velocity rod)

rod fork connection (杆系)杆件间的叉形接头

rod gear 杠杆传动;拉杆传动

rod guide 拉杆导轨

rod head (转向)拉杆接头

rod iron 铁条,铁棒,元铁

rod jaw 叉杆

rod journal (曲轴)连杆轴颈

rod magazine 棒料送进器,棒料给进附件

rod pin U形夹销(= clevis pin)

rod reading 标尺读数

rod test (土壤的)探杆取样检查

rod tin 锡棒料(= bar tin)

rod yoke (油缸活塞)连杆连接叉

Roentgen 伦琴(①剂量单位,在1mL空气中生成正负电荷各为一静电单位的X射线或γ射线的剂量) ②X射线(= X-rays)

Roentgen rays 伦琴射线,X射线(= X-rays)

Roesch (type) rocker 罗斯(型)(气门)摇臂(其凹窝形断面的中部压装在带调整螺母的半球形支垫上摇动,而不装在摇臂轴上,亦称ball-type rocker)

R&O hydraulic fluid 防锈抗氧化液压用油,防锈防氧化液压油(在高度精制的石油系基油中加有防锈剂 rust preventives 及抗氧化剂 oxidation inhibitors。R,O分别为防锈剂、抗氧化剂的简称。亦称R&O type hydraulic oil)

ROI 投资回报(return on investment 的简称)

rolamite sensor (安全气囊的)滚子-

卷簧式碰撞传感器（惯性式机电传感器的一种，由卷簧控制惯性质量—滚子的位置）

roll ①卷，卷筒 ②滚翻 ③隆隆声，持续轰鸣声 ④（汽车车身）侧倾（vehicle roll，指汽车车身绕其侧轴线的侧向摆动，簧上质量产生侧倾和侧倾角的变化，见 roll axis 及 vehicle roll angle）

roll-a-car hydraulic jack （汽车用）固定式液压举升器（= hydraulic floor jack）

roll acceleration （汽车绕侧倾轴的）加速度

roll angle 见 vehicle roll angle

roll axis 侧倾轴线（连接前、后侧倾中心的直线，见 roll center）

roll-back top 后卷式软车顶

roll bar ①（乘员座位上方一般用钢管材制成的）翻车保护杆（亦称 roll-over bar，多见于敞篷越野车或赛车等）②（悬架系统的）抗侧倾稳定杆（见 anti-roll bar）

roll bellows 筒形气囊

roll brake （底盘测功机的）滚筒制动器

roll cage 翻车保护架（乘员座位上方的框架结构，翻车时保护乘员安全）

roll camber ①（汽车的）侧倾轮倾现象（指簧上质量侧倾及悬架系统几何形状的变形导致车轮外倾角改变的现象）②（汽车的）侧倾轮倾角（指由于上述现象，导致的车轮外倾角）

roll camber coefficient （汽车的）侧倾轮倾系数（指簧上质量每侧倾1°而引起的车轮外倾角的变化量）

roll camber steer ①（汽车的）侧倾轮倾转向（簧上质量侧倾引起车轮外倾角变化，而使汽车产生偏行的现象）②（汽车的）侧倾轮倾转向敏感度（即产生1个重力加速度的侧向力，所引起的簧上质量侧倾度，使车轮产生的外倾角变化引起的汽车转向角（deg/g）

$= \dfrac{\text{左右两轮的平均侧倾角 (deg)}}{\text{簧上质量侧倾角 (deg)}} \times$

$\dfrac{\text{簧上质量侧倾角 (deg)}}{\text{横向加速度} (g)} \times \dfrac{\text{外倾刚度}}{\text{比转弯力}}$,

见 camber stiffness, cornering power）

roll center 侧倾中心（簧上质量不产生侧倾的横向力的作用点，该点在通过同一轴两车轮中心的横向铅垂面内，前、后轴的侧倾中心简称前、后侧倾中心）

roll compliance 侧倾增益度（见 roll gain）

roll control （汽车主动悬架系统的）侧倾控制（当横向加速度传感器测得汽车在弯道行驶中因惯性而产生侧倾时，电子控制模块即发出指令，提高弯道外侧车轮悬架的控制液压，减少弯道内侧车轮悬架的控制液压，以消除或减轻侧倾）

roll couple （汽车的）侧倾力偶

roll damper （汽车的）侧倾阻尼器，车身横向角振动减振器

roll damping （车身）侧倾阻尼

roll damping coefficient 侧倾阻尼系数（C_φ, Nms/rad）

roll door 装在滚道上的拉门，带滚子的拉门

rolled off the line （汽车）下线（指新制造的汽车，完成了全部生产工艺过程，而离开组装调试生产线）

rolled section steel （车身等用的）轧制（异）型钢（材）

rolled sheet 轧制板材

roll effect （汽车的）侧倾效应（指汽车车身在横向力的作用下，向一侧倾斜时，由于转向拉杆、摇臂等的支点联件产生运动而改变转向角的效应，亦称 roll steer）

roller 滚轮（如：与凸轮轴的凸轮接触，在滚轮衬套上滚动的筒形零

件)

roller bearing with spiral rollers 螺旋滚子轴承(= roller bearing with wound rollers)

roller bench 滚筒式试验台架

roller blind cable (散热器的)卷帘拉索

roller bump rig (汽车的)滚筒式振动试验台

roller cage 滚子轴承(的滚子)保持架(亦称 roller holder)

roller cam follower 滚子式气门挺杆

roller cam steering gear 蜗杆滚轮式转向器(亦称 worm and roller steering gear, 由转向盘轴带动的蜗杆和与蜗杆啮合的滚轮带动的摇臂组成)

roller carrier of harmonic gear 谐波齿轮滚架(波发生器中支撑滚轮用的构件)

roller contact timer 带滚子触点的分电器

roller cup 锥形滚子轴承外圈

roller free wheeling 滚子式单向离合器, 滚子式自由轮传动(亦称 roller clutch)

roller inner race assembly (滚子轴承)滚子内圈总成

roller joint 球节, 球销节(= ball joint)

roller lifter 滚子式气门挺杆, 滚子式凸轮从动件(亦称 roller follower)

roller mat conveyor (地板上装有滚柱, 以便推移重笨货物的箱式货车或挂车)推货滚柱系统

roller mobile machinery shop for special purpose 轮式专用机械(如: 平地机、推土机、挖掘机等工程机械)

roller oscillating tooth 滚子活齿(采用滚子作为活齿, 见 oscillating tooth)

roller pin 滚轮销(装在挺柱内, 支撑滚轮和滚轮衬套的圆柱套)

roller race plate (滚子泵滚子的)滚板(呈弯月形, 泵腔内的容积随滚子沿滚板的滚动而变化)

roller rocker arm 滚子式摇臂(减少摩擦)

roller shaft (蜗杆滚轮式转向器的)滚轮轴

roller tappet 滚子式(气门)挺杆(亦称 roller foot lever, roller lifter)

roller thrust (ring) bearing 滚子推力轴承(亦称 roller step bearing)

roller (type) brake tester 滚筒式制动试验台

roller type chassis dynamometer 滚筒式底盘测功机

roller type CVT 见 EXTROID CVT

roller-type freewheeling clutch with polygon cam 带多边形凸轮的滚子式单向离合器

roller-type jack (车库用)带滚轮的千斤顶(见 garage jack)

roller-type overrunning clutch 滚柱式单向离合器(靠装在单向离合器滚道内的滚柱楔紧时传递力矩的离合器)

roller (type) pump 滚子泵(亦称 roller-cell pump, 容积泵的一种, 依靠泵腔内容积的变化而产生泵吸作用)

roller-type wave generator (谐波齿轮)滚轮式波发生器(以滚轮及滚轮架为基本构件组成的波发生器)

roller-vane pump with semicylindrical sealing members 带半圆柱形密封元件的滚子叶片泵

roll frequency (车身的)侧倾频率(车身绕侧倾轴的角振动频率)

roll gain (汽车的)侧倾增益度(产生1个重力加速度g的横向力作用下, 弹簧上质量相对于弹簧下质量产生的侧倾角, 单位为 deg/g, 亦称侧倾随变度、侧倾率、侧倾敏感

度，见 roll susceptibility, roll compliance）
roll inertia 车辆绕过重心的侧倾轴的转动惯量
roll inertia principal axis （汽车）侧倾惯性主轴
roll inertia principal axis 侧倾惯性主轴（指汽车簧上质量绕之旋转的汽车坐标系 x 轴，簧上惯性主轴坐标系的 ξ 轴或侧倾轴，见 vehicle axis system, inertia principle axis system, roll axis）
rolling ①（车辆等的）横摇，侧倾，翻滚；滚动，滚压，碾压，压平，压碎，碾碎；垂直面倾斜；颠簸，起伏；隆隆声，轰鸣 ②可滚动的，转动的，旋转的；起伏的，周而复始的
rolling bridge 开式桥（船通过时中间可开启，让开航道）
rolling cam ①滚动凸轮（断面轮廓可保证凸轮工作面与跟随件间纯滚动）②回转凸轮（做旋转运动的凸轮）
rolling cart 工具车（车间内装运工具等的小车等）
rolling circle ①滚动圆 ②（齿轮）基圆（= base circle）
rolling circumference 滚动周长（如：在规定的条件下，轮胎每滚动一周所行驶的距离）
rolling code （防盗系统的）滚动式密码（相对固定密码 fixed code 而言的，可滚动变换的密码）
rolling contact 滚动接触
rolling (contact) bearing 滚动轴承（= rolling-element bearing，滚子轴承、滚针轴承与球轴承的总称，亦称 antifriction bearing）
rolling contact fatigue （轴承等的）滚动接触疲劳
rolling country 丘陵地区
rolling diaphragm seal （斯特林发动机）卷动膜片式油封
rolling distance 滚动距离
rolling element （滚动轴承的）滚动元件
rolling-element fatigue 滚动件的疲劳（破坏）
rolling fluid transporter 运送液体的罐车
rolling friction 滚动摩擦
rolling ground 丘陵地带，丘陵地形
rolling home 活动住房；住房挂车，旅游居住挂车
rolling hotel 汽车旅店（= hotel car）
rolling instability （簧上质量相对于侧倾轴的）横向侧倾不稳定性（指由于悬架过软，使车辆簧上质量在高速行驶中转向时，车身簧上质量产生很大的侧倾和横向角振动）
rolling land 丘陵地（形）
rolling loss 滚动损失
rolling moment 侧倾力矩（作用在汽车上的力矩矢量使汽车绕运动坐标系 X_0 轴旋转的分量）
rolling moment arm 侧倾力臂（在静止状态下，簧上质心到侧倾轴的铅垂距离）
rolling moment of inertia of sprung mass 簧上质量侧倾惯性矩（簧上质量绕 x 轴、ζ 轴或侧倾轴旋转的惯性矩，见 vehicle axis system, inertia principal axis system）
rolling radius （轮胎）滚动半径（轮胎滚动周长除以 2π 所得的数值）
rolling resistance 滚动阻力（包括轮胎在路面滚动时的变形阻力、路面变形阻力及摩擦阻力等，注意不要与 roll resistance 混淆）
rolling resistance coefficient 滚动阻力系数（滚动阻力与垂直负荷的比值）
rolling resistance horsepower （消耗于）滚动阻力（上的）功率

rolling resistance machine （轮胎等的）滚动阻力测定装置，滚动阻力测试机

rolling resistance measuring machine 滚动阻力测量机（简称 RRM）

rolling resistance moment 滚动阻力矩（由路面作用在轮胎上的力矩矢量，阻止轮胎绕旋转轴旋转的分量）

rolling road 滚筒式试验台架

rolling speed ①滚动速度②轧制速率

rolling start 牵引起动

rolling stock average age 车辆平均使用寿命

rolling surface 滚动表面

rolling terrain 丘陵区，丘陵地带

rolling test 滚动试验（如：将包装件的每一面按规定顺序在坚硬、平整的水平面上进行翻滚动的能力和包装对内装物保护能力的试验）

rolling toilet 汽车盥洗室，活（移）动厕所

rolling topography 起伏地形

rolling tyre force characteristics （汽车的）滚动轮胎作用力特性（指轮胎所受的各作用力与横偏角、垂直负荷、充气压力等的关系，见 cornering force）

rolling tyre moment characteristics （汽车的）滚动轮胎作用力矩特性（指轮胎所受的各种力矩与侧偏角、垂直负荷、气胎拖距等的关系，见 tyre self-aligning torque）

rolling vehicle 轮式车辆

rolling velocity 滚动速度

roll moment arm （汽车的）侧倾力矩力臂（指横向力使汽车侧倾的力矩臂，即横向力着力点至侧倾轴线的垂直距离，参见 roll axis）

roll-off skip loader 车厢可卸式汽车（装备有液力拖吊装卸机构，能将专用的车厢拖吊到车上或倾斜一定角度卸下货物，并能将车厢卸下，可一车配置多个车厢使用，用于运输散装货物或垃圾的自卸式汽车）

roll off the assembly line 驶出组装线，（驶）下（组装）线

roll-on roll-off car carrier 轿车滚装运输车（指运送轿车的滚装运输车，让用户可购得行驶零公里的新轿车）

roll-on roll-off seaborne traffic （汽车的）滚装海运（由牵引车将半挂车直接拖上轮船海运，到达目的地后，又由牵引车直接从船上将半挂车拖走）

roll-on/roll-off ship （车辆）直接驶入的滚装船

roll opposite forces type brake tester 滚筒反力式制动试验台

roll-out tray （拆装总成用的）移动底架

roll-over ①（汽车）倾翻，翻车（事故）②翻转，转台

roll-over accident 翻车事故

roll-over air bag 翻车（时保持乘员头部等的）安全气囊

rollover check valve （油路）翻车防漏阀（一种装在汽油滤清器进口前的止回阀，当汽车倾翻后，即自动关闭，防止汽油泄漏）

roll-over error (of an ADC with decimal output and auto-polarity)（有十进制输出和自动极性转换的 ADC 的）极性转换误差（当转换到正、负极时，对同一接近满度模拟输入值的输出读数值之差）

roll-over guard （汽车的）翻车安全架

roll-over mitigation system 防翻车系统（简称 ROM，当根据有关传感器的信息确认导致车辆翻倾的趋向已达到预定的阈值时，即向发动机和制动系统发出减速指令，避免翻车）

roll-over overhead rail （敞篷车、赛

车等的高度超过驾驶员头部或跨越驾驶员头部上空的)翻车保险,翻车护栏

rollover propensity 翻车倾向

roll over protective structures （车辆的）滚翻防护结构,侧翻防护结构（防止车辆滚翻时乘员受伤,简称 ROPS）

rollover resistance test 抗翻车（性能）试验（= anti-rollover test）

rollover (safety) valve （燃油箱的）翻车安全阀（翻车时封死燃油出口,防止燃油外泄）

rollover sensing system 翻车传感系统（由测定汽车倾斜,后轮抬升和纵、横向加速度等传感器组成,当判定汽车有翻车趋向时,即开启翻车保护装置或采取制动,使发动机熄火等减速措施）

rollover sensor 翻车传感器（当车身向任一方倾斜超过某阈值时,该传感器即发出警报信号,见 omnidirectional tilt sensor 和 rear-axle sensor）

roll-over stabilization control 翻滚稳定控制（见 RSC）

roll-over stand 翻转式装配架

roll oversteer(ing) 侧倾过度转向（由于侧倾导致的增大汽车过度转向,或减小汽车不足转向的趋势）

roll-over test （运输车辆的）翻车试验

rollover valve 防翻车漏油阀（防止翻车事故时,燃油供给管路漏油的安全阀）

roll rate ①侧倾率,单位向心加速度的侧倾角 ②侧倾刚度（见 roll stiffness）

roll rate of autobody 车身侧倾度（车身侧倾角与侧向加速度关系曲线上,侧向加速度值为 $2m/s^2$ 处的平均斜率,即：纵坐标值除以横坐标值）

roll rate wave （汽车车身绕纵向侧倾轴线的）侧倾率曲线波形

roll-resistant （车辆的）侧倾阻力

roll resonance （汽车车身绕侧倾轴线的）侧倾共振

roll response 侧倾响应（在操纵输入或外部扰动输入时,汽车的侧倾运动响应）

roll restrictor （汽车）侧倾限制器,侧倾稳定器

roll restrictor valve （汽车）侧倾限制阀

roll-sensitive driving seat suspension 侧倾感知式驾驶员座椅悬架装置（侧倾危险警报系统的一种,当车辆侧倾角度达到可能引起倾翻的危险点时,座椅悬架系统可使驾驶员产生剧烈摇晃,借以对驾驶员发出警报）

Rollsock(seal) （斯特林发动机活塞杆的）橡胶油封,卷动膜片式油封

Rolls Royce ［英］劳斯莱斯（名贵轿车牌名,生产该车的 Rolls Royce 公司,由工程师 Henry Royce、投资商 Charles Stewart Rolls 合作筹建于 1904 年,到 1994 年共生产高贵轿车 16 万辆,1998 年 7 月由德国大众公司 Vokswagen 收购兼并,常简称 Roller）

roll stability （汽车）抗侧倾稳定性（见 road stability）

roll stability on side slope （车辆）在侧坡上抗侧倾稳定性

roll stand （移动式保修设备和机具的）滚轮式支架,滚轮式支座

roll steer coefficient 侧倾转向系数（悬架侧倾角单位变化量所引起的转向角的变化量）

roll steer effect （车身）侧倾的转向效应（侧倾引起的前、后较驶向角的变化）

roll stiffness （汽车的）侧倾刚度

(①侧倾1°所需的侧倾力矩值。单位：N·m/(°)，亦称 roll resistance ②指前、后悬架抗侧倾刚度之和)

roll stiffness of suspension 悬架抗侧倾刚度（见 suspension roll stiffness）

roll subsidence mode 侧倾衰减模式

roll susceptibility 侧倾增益率（见 roll gain）

roll-type speedometer tester 滚筒式车速表试验台

roll understeer(ing) 侧倾不足转向（增大汽车不足转向，或减小汽车过多转向的侧倾转向）

roll-up sunshade （车窗的）遮阳卷帘

roll velocity 侧倾角速度（簧上质量绕 X 轴旋转的角速度）

roll vibration （汽车）侧倾振动（绕质心纵向轴线的角振动）

roll warning device 侧倾警报装置，横向倾翻警报装置（当车辆绕侧倾轴的摇动车达到可能引起倾翻的危险值时，该装置即向驾驶人员发出警报，及时减低车速，减小转弯角或采取必要的预防措施）

roll welding 滚压焊

ROM ①只读存储器（read only memory 的简称，专供读取所有存储永久性数据的存储器件，一旦制成，不能再存入新的信息，切断电源，存储的信息也不会消失。在汽车控制用计算机中用来存储控制程序、特性曲线、特性数据与调整数据等，供中央处理器读出调用）②旋转活塞式机械（rotating piston machine，如：旋转活塞式发动机、压气机等）③防翻车系统（见 roll-over mitigation system）

Roman bronze ①罗马锡青铜（改良型锡青铜，铜 58%～60%，锰 0%～2%，铁 1%，铝 1.1%，其余锡）②罗马青铜（铜 90%，锡 10%）

romance car 游览汽车，观光汽车（指通道两侧都为面向前方的双人座椅的大客车）

Roman pewter 铅锡合金，白镴（铅 30%，锡 70%）

Roman vitriol 硫酸铜

RON 研究法辛烷值（见 research octane number）

roof （车厢）顶盖（由顶盖骨架、顶盖蒙皮、顶盖护板、顶窗及所属车内附件等组成的部件）

roof aerial 车顶天线（over car aerial）

roof and shroud upper panel 车身顶盖带前围上盖板（指车顶板和风窗框及前围上盖板为一整构件的结构）

roof binding 车顶边缘压条

roof board （汽车）车身顶板

roof bow ［美］（厢式车身）车顶拱架，车顶拱形横梁（＝英 roof stick）

roof box 车顶箱（加装在车顶上的装物箱）

roof crash resistance 车顶碰撞保护

roof cross rail 顶盖横梁（亦称 roof cross member，指汽车顶盖的横向加强梁）

roof drip 车顶流水槽（上边梁或顶盖外部两侧沿全部门窗上边的流水槽，亦称 roof drip channel, roof side drip rail, gutter channel）

roof drip moulding 车顶排水檐槽（＝gutter channel，亦称 cornice）

roof frame 顶盖骨架（位于车身顶部的骨架，亦称 roof skeleton），（车身的）车顶框架

roof handrail height 顶盖扶手高（扶手中心至地板之间的距离）

roof lateral cross member 车顶横梁

roof light 顶篷灯（亦称 roof lamp, ceiling light）

roof line 车顶（轮廓）线条

roof lining （美·客车车身的）车顶衬里（=英 head lining）

roof load 车顶荷重，车顶荷载

roof mark lamp （装在汽车）车顶（的）标志灯

roof-mount air-deflector 车顶上装置的导流罩（减小空气阻力）

roof-mounted air drag reduction device 安装在车顶上的空气阻力减少装置

roof-mounted luggage rack 车顶行李架

roof outer panel 顶盖蒙皮（覆盖在顶盖骨架外表面的板件，亦称 roof skin）

roof panel （车身）顶盖板

roof panel cross member 顶盖横梁

roof panel top 顶盖（客厢或驾驶室顶部的盖板）

roof rack 车顶（可拆卸式）货架

roof rail ①顶盖梁（汽车顶盖的加强构件，一般指车身侧部框架中，顶盖两侧纵向加强构件，如：上门框、车门上框等）②车顶行李架

roof-shaped combustion chamber （汽油机的）屋脊形燃烧室

roof side rail 车顶边纵梁（=cantrail）

roof slat 车顶板条

roof spoiler （两箱车及箱形车装在车顶后端的）车顶导流板（见 rear spoiler）

roof stick （厢式车身的）车顶横条，车顶横撑条，拱条（美称 roof bow）

roof stick carline （木制厢式货车车身的）横梁条，拱梁

roof surface 齿根曲面（包含齿轮各个齿槽底面的假想曲面）

roof trim panel 车顶内衬板

roof ventilation 车顶通风（通风口在车顶）

roof washer （客车）车顶清洗设备

roof window 顶窗（顶盖上的通风窗）

room-dry 室内风干

room index 室形指数（在计算时，用来表示房间几何特征的数码或代号）

roominess （车身内的）宽敞度，宽阔程度

room light 车内灯，室内灯（亦称 room lamp, interior light, tonneau light）

room temperature 室温，车厢内温度

room temperature liquid crystal 室温液晶（液晶相温度范围在室温内的液晶）

room temperature vulcanising 室温硫化，室温硬化（简称RTV）

roomy 尺寸大的，宽敞的，广大的，宽大的，广阔的

roomy car 车身内部宽敞的轿车

root angle 齿根角，根圆锥角（根锥角，锥齿轮轴线与根锥母线之间的夹角。轮齿位于根锥角之外）

root circle 齿根圆（对圆柱齿轮，指其齿根圆柱面与端平面的交线。对锥齿轮，指根锥与背锥的交线。对于圆柱蜗杆，指齿根圆柱面与端平面的交线。对于环面蜗杆，指齿根圆环面的内圆。对于涡轮，指齿根圆环面与中间平面的交线。对摆线轮，指齿根圆柱面与端平面的交线）

root cone 齿根圆锥面（根锥，锥齿轮的齿根曲面）

root contact 齿根接触

root cylinder 齿根圆柱面（如：摆线轮、圆柱齿轮的齿根曲面）

root diameter ①螺纹内径②（齿轮，花键）齿根圆直径

root diameter of splines 花键齿根圆直径

root diameter of thread 螺纹内径（=minor diameter of thread）

root distance 齿根距离

root mean square 均方根值（进行某项测试时，各测试值的平方相加，除以测试次数，再开方，即：$=\sqrt{a^2+b^2+c^2+\cdots+n^2/n}$，简称 rms，亦称 root-mean-square value, effective value)

root-mean-square criterion 均方根（误差，判别）准则

root relief 修根（齿廓修形的一种：指在齿根曲面附近对齿廓形状进行有意识的修削）

root surface 齿根曲面（包含齿轮各个齿槽底面的假想曲面）

root toroid 齿根圆环面（在涡轮或环面蜗杆上，与齿槽底面相切的圆环面）

root trailer 运根茎作物（如：萝卜等）的挂车

root van 整体式厢形货车（驾驶室与货厢制成一体，= panel van）

rope brake ①绳索制动器（利用绳索的拉力或摩擦力制动）②绳索制动式测功器（测定 7.35kW 以下的小型发动机有效功率用的一种最简单的吸收式测功器。由缠在滑轮上的绳索等组成）

rope drive 钢索传动（= cord drive, 亦称 rope transmission）

rope gearing 钢索传动装置

rope pulley 绳索轮，绳索滑车

rope seal （曲轴上使用的）细绳式油封

rope tourniquet ①捆索，捆带，绷带（= tourniquet, tightening flap）②轮胎捆带（= tyre band, 当无内胎轮胎充气时，用以捆缚轮胎使胎缘与钢圈密着）

ROPIMA 旋转活塞机（= rotary piston machine 的简称）

roping hook 车箱栏板滚绳钩

ROPS （汽车）滚翻防护结构（= roll-over protective structures 的简称）

rose joing 一种专利球窝型联轴节

Rose's alloy 罗斯易熔合金（铅铋锡易熔合金，作熔断丝等用，亦称 Rose's metal）

rosette ①插座，接线盒 ②套筒

rosette gauge 多片式电阻应变仪

rotameter 转子流量计，转子流速仪

rotary ①［美］转子发动机（= rotary engine）②［美］环行交叉路口（= round-about）③轮转（印刷）机 ④旋转的，轮转的，循环的；环行的

rotary abrasive tester 旋转式磨料磨损试验机

rotary abutment pump 外啮合凸轮转子泵

rotary actuator 转动式执行器

rotary adjustable torque driver 转矩可调旋转式（螺钉）旋具

rotary air engine 旋转式热空气发动机（用空气作工质，驱动旋转式膨胀器的开口循环外燃机，见 air engine, = rotary hot-air engine）

rotary balance 转动平衡

rotary barrel throttle 旋转滑套式节流阀

rotary-block radial pump 旋转缸体式径向柱塞泵

rotary blower 转子式压气机

rotary bucket-type flowmeter 旋转勺状叶片式流量计

rotary combustion 旋转燃烧（指转子发动机的燃烧）

rotary connection 旋转连接，旋转接触装置

rotary converters 旋转变流器，旋转整流器

rotary diesel 柴油转子发动机，压燃式旋转活塞发动机（亦称 rotary diesel engine）

rotary displacement compressor 转子（容积）式压气机

rotary displacement pump 旋转式容积泵

rotary distributor 旋转式分配器

rotary drum 滚筒，转鼓

rotary dumper 侧倾自卸货车（见 side dumper）

rotary encoder 转速编码器（用于直接测定车轮转速等）

Rotary Engine Anti-Pollution System （日本东洋工业公司的）转子发动机排气净化系统（的总称，简称 REAPS）

rotary engine bearing 转子发动机主轴轴承

rotary engine combustion cycle 转子发动机燃烧循环

rotary engined car 转子发动机轿车，旋转活塞发动机轿车

rotary expander cam （鼓式制动器制动蹄机械式促动器）旋转式开张凸轮（制动时同时将左、右制动蹄撑开的 S 形凸轮等）

rotary flow （流体的）环流（状态）

rotary flowmeter 旋转式流量计

rotary heat exchanger 旋转式热交换器

rotary hot-air engine 旋转式热空气发动机（见 rotary air engine）

rotary hydraulic motor 旋转式液压马达，旋转式液动机

rotary idle speed control valve 旋转式怠速控制阀（简称 rotary ISC valve）

rotary intersection 环形交叉口，转盘式交叉口（交叉口中央设置较大的环岛，以交织代替穿切车流，围绕中心环岛做一个方向运行的导流式交叉口，= traffic circle, traffic roundabout）

rotary island （环形交叉的）中心岛，环形交通岛（= central island）

rotary-piston compressor type super charger 旋转活塞（空气）压缩机型（进气）增压器

rotary piston machine 旋转活塞机，转子机（旋转活塞式发动机、泵及压缩机的总称，简称 ROPIMA）

rotary-piston steam engine 旋转活塞蒸汽机

rotary plug valve 旋转柱塞式滑阀

rotary pneumatic actuator 旋转式气动执行器（如：旋转式气动马达，见 pneumatic motor）

rotary position coder 转角编码器，旋转位置编码器（亦称 rotary position encoder，将转向盘转角传感器的模拟信号转变为数字编码输出的编码器）

rotary-powered 转子发动机驱动的，旋转活塞发动机驱动的

rotary pulverizer ①旋转式喷雾器（如：将燃油等喷成雾状的旋转机件）②旋转式粉碎机

rotary pump 转子泵；旋转活塞泵

rotary road brush 旋转式扫路机，旋转盘刷式扫路机（亦称 rotary power broom, rotary sweeper）

rotary scraper 旋转式刮土机

rotary seal 转动运动密封件

rotary shaft lip seal 旋转轴唇形密封圈（具有柔性唇，通常有一金属骨架支承的，靠密封刃口施加给轴的径向力，防止泄漏的密封圈）

rotary shaft oil seal unit 旋转轴油封组件

rotary signal 旋转信号灯

rotary spool 转动滑阀（亦称 rotary slide valve）

rotary switch 旋转开关，旋钮开关

rotary table 回转工作台，旋转平台

rotary throttle valve 旋转式节流阀

rotary TPS 旋转式节气门开度传感器的简称，将节气门轴的转动通过一旋转式可变电阻变为电信号输出的传感器件）

rotary transducer 旋转运动变换器（如：将旋转运动变为电信号输出

的转速传感器)

rotary transformer 直流电动机-发电机组变压器(一种用低压直流电源的直流电动机驱动发电机发出高压直流电的机组,亦称旋转式直流变压器)

Rotary Tri-Blade Coupling (丰田公司的Flex Full-time 4WD中的)三叶片转子式耦合器(其结构与黏性耦合器类似,在其充满硅油的体壳内,有一个三个叶片的转子和一个多片式离合器,当前、后车轮间出现转速差时,三叶片转子开始旋转,搅动壳体中的硅油,使多片式离合器接合,开始传递转矩,直到前、后轮转速相等时为止)

rotary truck 转子发动机货车

rotary type height sensor 旋转型(车身)高度传感器

rotary type steering pressure control valve (液力转向系的)旋转式转向液压控制阀(由旋转式阀芯和带进、出口的阀体组成,阀芯相对于阀体转动而改变通向转向动力缸的液压线路、流量和压力)

rotary valve type damping control actuator 旋转阀式阻尼控制执行器(电子控制悬架系统阻尼器件中的内装式电动机根据电子控制模块的指令转动旋转阀,改变减振液阻尼孔径,以实现"软、中、硬"等阻尼模式)

rotary valve type steering control valve 转阀式转向控制阀(转阀相对于阀体转动的转向控制阀)

rotary vane 旋转叶轮

rotary-vane internal combustion engine 旋转叶片内燃机(叶片装在偏心转子上的轴向槽内,可在槽内作径向滑动)

rotary vane type actuator 回转叶片式执行器

rotary vane type pump 回转叶片式泵

rotary vane-type shock absorber 旋转叶片式减振器

rotary viscosimeter 旋转式黏度计(= rotational viscosimeter)

rotated tyre pad (汽车试验设备的)回转式车轮荷载传感垫(一种可回转的车轮浮式支垫,装有测量车轮所受转矩、侧向力等的传感器)

rotating bar fatigue test 试棒回转的弯曲疲劳试验(= rotating beam fatigue test)

rotating beacon 旋转型警报灯光信号装置,旋转警报信号灯(亦称rotating warning lamp)

rotating bending 旋转弯曲(如:旋转轴的弯曲)

rotating bevel gear 转动锥齿轮(作平面回转运动的锥齿轮)

rotating combustion (转子发动机的)旋转燃烧(燃烧区随转子沿着旋转线缸壁转移,简称RC)

rotating converter 旋转变(电)流器

rotating cylinder ①回转油缸②转动柱体

rotating drum 转鼓

rotating electrode (分电器)旋转电极

rotating filter 旋转式滤清器,离心式滤清器

rotating guide vane 可转动的导流片

rotating housing (单纯旋转发动机的)旋转缸体(= outer rotor,见SIM)

rotating housing (DKM) engine 旋转缸体式单纯旋转活塞发动机(见DKM)

rotating (magnetic) field 旋转磁场

rotating mass inertia factor 旋转惯量换算系数

rotating multipole magnetic field 多极旋转磁场

rotating-part(s) inertia factor 旋转件转动惯量换算系数 [= mass inertia factor for rotating part(s)]

rotating piston (转子发动机的)旋转活塞,转子

rotating piston machine 旋转活塞机(简称 ROPIMA, ROM, 包括 SROM 及 PROM 两大类)

rotating piston machines similar to PLM 行星旋转活塞机(指具有往复运动件的行星旋转活塞机,简称 PROM,见 PLM)

rotating piston machines similar to SIM 单纯转动活塞机(指具有往复运动件的单纯旋转活塞机,简称 SROM,见 SIM)

rotating plane-vector 平面旋转矢量

rotating plate (自动变速器行星齿轮机构多片式离合器的)摩擦片(亦称 friction plate)

rotating pole-piece 旋转极靴

rotating ring (机械密封的)旋转环(动环,随轴做旋转运动的密封环)

rotating seal 转动式密封件

rotating shaft seal 旋转轴(合成橡胶型)密封件

rotating torque of steering gear 转向器转动力矩(摇臂轴空载时,使转向轴转动的力矩)

rotating valve 回转阀,旋转阀门

rotating vane pump 转子叶片泵

rotating wobble plate 旋转斜盘(= swash plate)

rotation(al) energy 转动能

rotational step motor 旋转式步进电动机

rotational viscosimeter 旋转式黏度计(= rotary viscosimeter)

rotation axis ①旋转轴线②旋转轴

rotation direction sensor 旋转方向传感器

rotation dynamometer 旋转式测力计(测定旋转转矩用)

rotation group 旋转群

rotation of axes 坐标轴的旋转

rotative speed 旋转速度,转速[亦称 rotary speed, rotation (al) speed ratative velocity, rate of revolution]

rotatory polarization 旋光性(线偏振光在介质中传播时,其偏振面发生旋转的现象)

rotodip process (汽车车身的)旋转式浸渍涂漆法

Rotoflex joint 旋转挠性节(一种六角形橡胶环形专利万向节的商品名)

rotor 转子(指任一种绕本身轴线旋转的部件或组件,如:①转子发动机的三角活塞②起动机和直流发电机的电枢总成③交流发电机的旋转磁场总成④液力变矩器的旋转叶轮⑤盘式制动器的制动盘⑥燃气轮机的涡轮⑦轴流式压缩机的叶轮⑧分电器式点火系分电器的分火头⑨无分电器式点火系中的正时转子等)

rotor acceleration (转子发动机等的)转子加速度

rotor angle (转子发动机的)旋转活塞转角,转子转角

rotor annular gear (三角活塞转子发动机)转子内齿圈

rotor apex (转子发动机的)转子角顶,旋转活塞角顶

rotor apex epitrochoidal path (转子发动机的)旋转活塞角顶外旋轮线轨迹,转子角顶外旋轮线轨迹

rotor arm (分电器的)分火头(亦称 distributor rotor, 将点火线圈产生的高压电分配给分电器盖上的各缸火花塞电极触点的转子)

rotor arm metal segment (分电器)分火头的金属触片

2-rotor automotive engine 汽车用双缸转子发动机

rotor bank (转子发动机的)转子数,缸数

rotor-bearing （转子发动机的）转子轴承，旋转活塞轴承

rotor-bearing oil seal （转子发动机的）转子轴承油封，旋转活塞轴承油封

rotor blade 转子叶片，旋转的工作轮叶片

rotor case 转子壳体；（转子发动机的）旋轮线缸体，缸体（= rotor casing, rotor hsg）

rotor casting （转子发动机的）转子铸件，转子铸造毛坯

rotor cavity ①（转子发动机的）转子工作面凹坑（= rotor recess，与转子缸体内壁形成燃烧区）②（转子发动机的）转子内部空腔，转子内腔

rotor center （转子发动机的）旋转活塞中心，转子中心

rotor c. g. （转子发动机的）转子重心

rotor chamber （转子发动机的）汽缸（旋轮线缸壁与两端盖形成的整个空间，转子位于其内）

rotor combustion chamber 转子发动机燃烧室，旋转活塞发动机燃烧区（即三角转子旋转时，其工作面凹坑与旋轮线缸壁间形成的容积不断变化的进气-压缩-燃烧-排气空间，见 rotor face cavity）

rotor contour （转子发动机的）转子外形曲线，转子周边曲线，三角转子周边曲线，三角旋转活塞外形曲线，三角活塞周边曲线

rotor cooling （转子发动机的）旋转活塞冷却；转子冷却

rotor-cooling induction system （转子发动机的）转子冷却式进气系统（新鲜充量通过转子，对转子进行冷却后再进入汽缸内）

rotor cooling oil 转子冷却油；旋转活塞冷却油

rotor distributor fuel injection pump 转子式燃油喷射分配泵（由柱塞泵油，转子配油的分配式喷油泵）

rotor-drive （转子发动机的）旋转塞驱动装置，转子驱动系统

rotor eccentricity （转子发动机）转子偏心距

rotor-end cover oil seal （转子发动机的）转子-端盖油封装置（指转子与缸盖间的滑油密封系统）

rotor end housing （转子发动机的）端盖，缸盖

rotor face （转子发动机的）转子工作面，旋转活塞工作面；转子周面，旋转活塞周面

rotor face cavity （转子发动机的）转子工作面凹坑（指形成燃烧区的凹坑，亦称 rotor combustion pocket, rotor combustion recess, rotor depression, rotor face recess, rotor face tub, roay pocket recess, rotor recess）

rotor flank ①（转子发动机的）转子周面，转子工作面 ②（转子发动机的）转子侧面，转子端面

rotor flank contour （转子发动机的）转子工作面轮廓线，转子周边曲线，旋转活塞周边外形线

rotor gear （转子发动机的）转子齿轮，转子内齿圈，旋转活塞内齿圈，转子相位齿圈

rotor gearing ratio 转子发动机的速比，转子相位齿轮啮合比，转子相位机构速比（指转子上的相位内齿圈齿数与固定的相位齿轮齿数之比）

rotor groove （转子发动机的）转子密封槽（转子上装密封元件的槽）

rotor guidance （转子发动机的）转子导动装置（减轻转子的振动）

rotor housing 转子发动机缸体（简称 rotor hsg, = rotor case, rotor housing）

rotor inertia 转动惯量

rotor inertia cooling （转子发动机

的）转子惯性（油）冷却法（转子内腔利用惯性力甩动冷却液）

rotor internal cavity （转子发动机的）转子内腔，旋转活塞内腔（冷却液、冷却油或冷却风通过其中）

rotor journal （转子发动机的）偏心轴颈，转子轴颈

rotor orbit （转子发动机的）转子运行轨道

rotor peripheral face （转子发动机的）转子工作面，转子周边面（简称 rotor face）

rotor-piston （转子发动机的）旋转活塞

rotor pitch 转子节距

rotor pocket （转子发动机的）转子工作面凹坑，转子燃烧凹坑

rotor radius （转子发动机的）转子半径，旋转活塞半径

rotor sealing system （转子发动机的）转子密封系统，旋转活塞密封系统（装在旋转活塞上全部密封装置的统称）

rotor side （转子发动机的）旋转活塞侧边，旋转活塞端面，转子侧面，转子端面

rotor side oil seals （转子发动机）转子端面油封装置，旋转活塞端面油封

rotor's leading apex （转子发动机的）转子的前角顶（沿转子转动方向看,指转子工作面最前面的角顶）

rotor speed 转子旋转速度；（转子发动机的）转子自转速度

rotor squish action （转子发动机的）转子挤压作用（由于转子的运动及转子工作面凹坑的位置、形状等不同,把工作室内的气体挤压成不同程度的紊流）

rotor's trailing apex （转子发动机的）转子的后角顶（沿转子转动方向看,指转子工作面最后面的角顶）

rotor timing gears （转子发动机的）转子正时齿轮机构,转子相位齿轮机构

rotor-to-crankshaft speed ratio （转子发动机的）转子对偏心轴的转速比,转子-主轴速比

rotor-type oil pump 转子式机油泵

rotor wheel （涡轮机）工作叶轮；转子

rotor width （转子发动机的）旋转活塞宽度,转子宽度,转子工作面的宽度

rotor width-engine generating radius ratio （转子发动机的）转子宽度对创成半径的比值

rotor winding 转子线圈

rouge ①铁丹,红丹粉,红铁粉,过氧化铁粉,三氧化二铁（Fe_2O_3）②涂红丹粉

rough air 扰动气流,冲激气流

rough approximation 粗略近似,大致接近

rough burning （发动机）粗暴的燃烧,不均匀的燃烧（亦称 rough combustion）

rough calculation 概算,粗略计算

rough copy 草图,草稿（=foul copy）

rough cross-country track 不平的越野试车道

rough-cut file 粗齿锉,粗纹锉,粗锉（=rough file）

rough deposit 粗糙镀层（见 rough surface ②）

rough engine 运转不平稳的发动机

rough estimate 粗略估计,近似估计

rough file 粗锉（=rough cut file,见 coarseness of file）

rough filter 初滤器,粗滤器（=coarse filter, preliminary filter）

rough fit 粗配合,低精度配合（相当于四级精度配合）

rough gas 粗滤煤气（=roughly-cleaned gas）

rough going 在凹凸不平的路面行

车，在崎岖不平的地区行车

rough ground 不平地面

rough idle 怠速不良，不稳定(的)怠速(运转)

roughing value 表面粗糙度指数

rough machining 粗加工

rough material 原料

roughness ①(柴油机等在运转过程中，即使不发生爆震，当其缸内压力增长率 $dp/\Delta\varphi$ 大于 $0.5\sim0.6$ MPa/deg 时，产生的)工作粗暴(声，亦称 roughness noise)②汽车在平路上行驶时，轮胎产生的100Hz以内的连续振动和噪声③(表面的)粗糙度，平面度④凹凸不平⑤粗糙部分⑥近似，忽略

roughness height (加工表面)平面度高度

roughness meter 路面粗糙度测定仪，路面平面度测定仪

roughness on tyre cavity 胎里凹凸不平(胎里表面局部高低不平的现象)

rough package drawing (车身设计方案的)总体布置示意(草)图

rough plan 设计草图，初步计划

rough road input (汽车平顺性和操纵性中的)路面凹凸不平的道路对车辆行驶、悬架系统、车身等产生的输入

rough-road simulator for wheeled vehicles 轮式车辆不平道路试验模拟装置

rough road tester (汽车的)恶劣道路试验台(由各种断面的滚筒组成，模拟各种恶劣道路)

rough rule 粗略规定，粗略标准，粗略近似法

rough surface ①粗糙表面，粗糙面②粗糙镀层(镀液中的固体浮游物进入镀层形成大量的小凸瘤，= rough deposit)

rough survey 草测，初步观测，初步调查

rough terrain 不平地带，崎岖地区

rough test 粗略的检查，初试

rough test track 特殊铺设的不平路面试验跑道

rough-track test (汽车)在崎岖不平的跑道上的试验(模拟坏路)

rough tuning 粗调(= coarse tuning)

rough use 恶劣条件下的使用

rough weight 毛重

roulette ①转迹线(当第一曲线沿第二曲线无滑动地滚动时，随第一曲线运动的任一点的轨迹和任一线的包络线。其中任一点的轨迹线又点转迹线，任一线的包络线又称线转迹线。点转迹线为旋轮线、摆线等的总称，故又称一般旋轮线)②滚花，压花，在…上面滚压连续点子③滚花刀具，压花刀具

round ①倒圆(角)，做圆，弯成圆圈②环绕，环行③圆形，球形④环行路；一圈，一周，一次，一轮⑤圆形的，圆的；完全的；整数的；巨额的⑥循环地；回转地，转着地；在周围；在附近

roundabout ①包围着的，广泛包含的；转弯抹角的，迂回的；走远路的②圆形物③环形交叉路口(= rotary intersection, traffic circle)

roundabout crossing 环形交叉路口，转盘式交叉(口)，环形交叉(= traffic circle)

roundabout route transportation 迂回运输，绕道运输(不按最短线路运送旅客和货物的运输，简称 roundabout transportation)

roundabout way 绕道，绕远道

round bar 棒料，圆钢

round beam torque wrench 圆杆式扭力扳手

round column 圆柱

rounded bead toe (轮胎)胎趾圆角(胎趾端部呈圆形的现象)

rounded pattern 花纹棱角呈圆形[胎面花纹块（条）的棱角不饱满，呈圆角的现象]

rounding off ①圆滑过渡，修整，使成圆形 ②舍入

roundness ①圆度 ②圆形，球形 ③球度 ④完整，圆满 ⑤无零数

round nut with lateral notches 侧向凹口圆螺母

round piece (of work) 圆形（工）件

round-the-clock dependability 日夜连续工作的可靠性

round thread 圆形螺纹

round trip ①环行运程，封闭路线的运程；往返一次 ②来回旅程的

round-trip distance 往返里程（= loop distance）

roundup ①集拢 ②综述

round vortexing 环形涡流

round wire gauge 圆线量隙规（亦简称 round gauge，断面呈圆形的钢棒间隙量规，钢丝间隙量规，如：火花塞间隙量规）

route-indicating signal 指路标志，路线标志（亦称）route indicator

route marker 路名或路线编号标志，指路牌（指路标志的一种，设置有路名或路线编号及有关联络路线的指路牌）

routes guidance system （汽车）导行系统（简称 RGS，指车载定位系统、卫星导行系统、车载通信系统、车载先进的驾驶者信息系统，及与公路沿线蜂窝通信系统相连的视听终端等的总称，见 GPS, ADIS IV, AVDS, ENS）

route sign 路线标志（表示路名或路线编号的方向类标志中的一种，表示已接近路口或弯曲路段，也有说明与其他路线的交叉及路线等级的）

routine control 常规控制，常规调节

routine inspection 例行检查，常规检验，定期维护

routine maintenance 例行维护，日常维护

routine quality control 例行质量管理

routine replacement 例行更换，常规更换

routine road test （汽车）常规路试

routine servicing 例行维护，例行维修

routine test ①出厂检验（为确认产品是否符合出厂要求，在出厂前对每一产品所进行的试验）②例行测试；常规试验

ROW 道路通行权（right of way）

row engine （单）列式发动机

row equivalent 行等价

3-row seats mini van 三排座小型厢式客车

row width 行距

Royal Automobile Club [英] 皇家汽车俱乐部（简称 RAC）

royal road 捷径，近路（= shortcut）

RP 循环电动泵（recirculation pump motor 的简称）

RPA （通用公司研制的）倒车（入库）辅助系统（reverse parking aid 的简称，倒车超声波雷达报警系统的商品名。当电子控制模块根据装在后保险杠上的超声波发射和接收系统的障碍物反射信息，确认障碍物的距离已在设定的报警范围内时，即通过蜂鸣器或指示灯发出报警信号。该系统还具有自诊断功能）

rpm ①可靠性量测（reliability performance measure）②转/分（revolution per minute）

rpm-dependent 与转速有关的，取决于转速的，随转速而变的

rpm indicator 转数表，转速表（= speed indicator）

rpm -regulated flap （通过调节进气管道通过断面来控制发动机转速的结构中的）瓣形转速调节阀

R point R 点（设置的座椅基准点，人体躯干线和大腿中心线的铰接交点。位于 R′点上方 75mm 处）

R' point R′点（R′点在座垫上表面的垂直投影点，距 G 点的水平距离为 100mm）

R' point height R′点高（R′点至地板表面的高度）

RQL 不合格质量基准（rejectable quality level）

RR ［英］罗尔斯-罗伊斯汽车和飞机发动机公司（Rolls-Royce）

R(Réau) 列氏温标（见 Réaumur scale）

RRC (system) control module 可编程平顺性控制系统的控制模块（programmable ride control system control module 的简称）

RRI 国际交通事故预防委员会

RRM 滚动阻力测量机（rolling resistance measuring machine）

RSA （催化转化器快速热起，亦称快速起燃技术中的）浓混合气起动和二次空气喷射（richer start and secondary air injection 的简称，指起动时使用浓混合气，保证起动平稳，但废气中有较多的 HC、CO，为此将二次空气喷入排气和催化转化器系统，实现二次燃烧，既减少了 HC、CO 排放，又可使催化转化器迅速加热到起燃温度）

RSC ①翻滚稳定控制（roll-over stabilization control 的简称，电子控制模块根据陀螺回转仪传感器检测到的汽车在行驶中侧倾的加速度和角度信息，估算到汽车有发生翻滚事故的可能性时，立即起动汽车的动态稳定和牵引力控制系统，通过减少发动机输出功率和调节车轮制动力，使汽车从非稳定状态恢复到稳定状态）②坚固型运动车（丰田公司一种单排座双门厢式跑车的概念车名，Rugged Sport Coupe 的简称）

RSD ①（安全带等拘束性安全装置）避免乘员撞车伤亡的安全拘束距离（restraint survival distance）②道路模拟底盘测功机（road simulation dynamometer）

RSE 后排娱乐系统（rear seat entertainment 的简称）

RS flip-flop RS 触发器（置"0"置"1"触发器，reset set flip-flop 的简称）

rsidual stress relieving 消除残余应力

RSL 适当规模集成电路（right scale integration）

RSP system （Bendix 公司的）抗侧倾稳定性程序系统（roll stability program 的简称，在进入弯道和回避障碍物等转向操控中，通过对各车轮进行制动，使车速减到侧倾临界值）

RSS 路敏悬架（road sensing suspension 的简称，该悬架系统可根据道路和驾驶条件的变化控制悬架减振器件的阻尼特性）

RSS module 路敏悬架（电子控制）模块（road sensing suspension electronic control module 的简称，该模块安装在行李舱的电子器件隔间内，内装三个微处理器，分别控制速敏转向"SSS"、车身高度调平"ELC"和路敏悬架"RSS"，该模块具有很强的系统自诊断能力）

RSS system 见 road sensing suspension system

RSU 路边设施（road side unit 的简称）

RSV 安全研究车（research safety vehicle）

RSV governor （柴油机的）变弹簧张力式全程调速器（机械式全程调速器的一种，调速弹簧的张力可随加速踏板的位置而改变的全程式调速器）

RSW 电阻点焊（resistance spot welding 的简称）
RT ①室温（room temperature）②研究性试验（research test）
RTA 道路交通事故（road traffic accident 的简称）
RTD ①（路敏悬架的）实时阻尼系统（real-time damping 的简称）②（美国各州）地区运输厅，地方运输局，地方运输管理区（Regional Transit District）③电阻式温度传感器（resistive temperature detector 的简称）
RTL/IVHS 道路运输信息/智能汽车公路系统（road transport informatics/intelligent vehicle-highway system 的简称）
R Tire 刚性环轮胎模型（rigid ring tire model 的简称）
RTL 电阻-晶体管逻辑电路（resistor transistor logic 的简称，见 DCTL）
RTS ①道路交通系统（road traffic system）②快速运输系列（rapid transit series）
RTV ①退回售主（returned to vendor）②室温固化的，室温硫化的（room temperature vulcanized）
RTV sealants 室温固化型密封剂
RTV silicone rubber 室温硫化硅酮橡胶
Ru 钌（ruthenium）
RUB 橡胶，合成橡胶（rubber 的简称）
rub ①摩擦，擦净，擦光②擦伤，磨损，磨耗③研磨
rubbed surface 摩擦面，磨损面，磨光面
rubber ①橡胶（指生胶硫化后的橡胶）②橡胶的③摩擦物，磨石，磨光器
rubber air seal ①橡胶气密封②橡胶气密封件
rubber-and-metal bearing 橡胶-金属轴承

rubber bag tank 橡胶囊式容器
rubber-bellows mechanical seal 橡胶波纹管机械密封（补偿环的辅助密封为橡胶波纹管的机械密封）
rubber bud ring 蕾形橡胶密封圈（截面像花蕾的橡胶密封圈）
rubber buffer 橡胶缓冲器（= rubber damper）
rubber-bushed torque rod 橡皮衬套扭力杆
rubber car fender （汽车）橡胶挡泥板
rubber carpet 橡皮地毯，地板橡皮铺面
rubber coupling 橡胶联轴节
rubber covered rotary shaft lip seal 内包骨架旋转轴唇形密封圈（骨架被橡胶包粘的唇形密封圈）
rubber covered rotary shaft lip seal with minor lip 有副唇内包骨架旋转轴唇形密封圈（有副唇，骨架被橡胶包粘的唇形密封圈）
rubber cup 橡胶碗
rubber cushion 橡胶软垫
rubber damper ①橡胶减振器（由一个具有一定转动惯量的圆环通过橡胶与曲轴等旋转件连接而产生弹性—阻尼效果的减振器）②橡胶扭转振动阻尼器
rubber diaphragm （油气弹簧的）橡胶膜片
rubber D ring D 形橡胶密封圈（截面为 D 形的橡胶密封圈）
rubber drum ring 鼓形橡胶密封圈（截面为鼓形的橡胶密封圈）
rubber engine mounting pad 发动机橡胶座垫
rubber-faced flat valve 带橡胶阀面的平板阀
rubber fender 橡胶挡泥板（= rubber mudguard）
rubber flooring （车身地板的）橡皮铺面板（亦称 rubber floor mat）

rubber foams 泡沫橡胶，多孔橡胶
rubber gaskets 橡胶密封垫（用于两个静止表面间的片状密封件）
rubber hill ring 山形橡胶密封圈（截面呈山形的橡胶密封圈）
rubber hose connection 橡胶软管接头
rubbering in 垫胶压整（工艺）（薄板制件常经液压机等模压成形后，为了消除皱皮等缺陷，在制件与压模间加垫氯丁橡皮片等，再次加压的最后精整工艺）
rubber insulation tape 橡胶绝缘带
rubberized breaker cord （轮胎）橡胶帘线缓冲层
rubberized cord plies 橡胶帘布层
rubber jar 硬橡皮容器，硬橡胶外壳
rubber J ring J形橡胶密封圈（截面为J形的橡胶密封圈）
rubber-like 橡皮状的；具有弹性的
rubber-lined 橡皮衬里的
rubber L ring L形橡胶密封圈（截面为L形的橡胶密封圈）
rubber-metal mounting of engine 橡皮-金属发动机支座
rubber-mounted suspension 橡胶弹簧式悬架
rubberneck bus [美俗] 游览客车，观光客车
rubber nipple 橡胶接头套（如：用来保护点火线接头的橡皮套）
rubber O ring O形橡胶密封圈（截面为O形的橡胶密封圈）
rubber plinth （后灯的）橡胶支座
rubber plug 橡皮塞
rubber press fit surface of seal 油封的橡胶压配合面
rubber protecting cover 橡皮保护盖
rubber rectangular ring 矩形橡胶密封圈（截面为矩形的橡胶密封圈）
rubber ring packing 橡皮填密圈，填密橡皮圈，橡皮密封环

rubber-sealed valve （无内胎式轮胎）带橡胶密封的气门嘴
rubber shackle block 钢板弹簧吊耳销橡皮衬套
rubber shock absorber 橡胶减振器
rubber shoe ①橡皮履板②橡胶轮胎（俚称）
rubber sleeve 橡皮套
rubber solution 橡胶溶液
rubber sponge 橡皮海绵，多孔橡胶
rubber spring shackle 带橡胶衬套的钢板弹簧吊耳
rubber spring type suspension 橡胶弹簧式悬架（以橡胶弹簧作为弹性元件的悬架形式）
rubber studded tyre 加装橡皮防滑钉的轮胎
rubber suspension system 橡胶弹簧式悬架系统（使用橡胶作为弹性元件的悬架系统。一般结构为悬架控制臂一端接车轮转向节，另一端通过由橡胶块等制成的弹性元件装在车架或车身上）
rubber-swelling test 橡皮泡胀试验（为评价燃油供给系统中橡皮或类似橡皮零件对汽油的适应性，用特种液体进行的泡胀试验）
rubber-swelling test fluids 橡皮泡胀试验用液（美国材料试验协会ASTM为了试验汽油供给系统的橡皮零件对汽油的适应性，所规定的一些专门试验用油液）
rubber torsion spring seat suspension 橡胶扭转弹簧座椅悬架
rubber-tracked vehicle 橡胶履带车辆
rubber universal joint 胶块式万向节（两轴间通过橡胶块传递转矩的柔性万向接头）
rubber U ring U形橡胶密封圈（截面为U形的橡胶密封圈）
rubber varnish 橡胶清漆
rubber vibroinsulator 橡胶防振装

置，橡胶防振垫，橡胶软垫
rubber V ring　V形橡胶密封圈（截面为V形的橡胶密封圈）
rubber washer　橡皮垫圈
rubber weather-strip　橡皮风雨条，橡皮防漏垫带
rubber window channeling　车窗玻璃橡皮槽
rubber W ring　W形橡胶密封圈（截面为W形的橡胶密封圈）
rubber X ring　X形橡胶密封圈（截面为X形的橡胶密封圈）
rubber Y ring　Y形橡胶密封圈（截面为Y形的橡胶密封圈）
rubbing block　（机械式触点臂与凸轮接触的）顶（擦）块（如：断电器触点臂上的顶块）
rubbing contact-material　摩擦接触材料
rubbing paste　抛光膏
rubbing plate　摩擦板，（自动倾卸汽车底架上供支撑车身用的）车身承板
rubbing strip　防擦条（为防止擦伤和轻微碰撞而装在车身腰线上的橡胶或塑料条）
rubbing surface of end cover　（转子发动机的）缸盖摩擦面（端盖内侧面）
rubbing varnish　耐磨清漆
rubbish disposal truck　垃圾处理车
rubidium　铷（Rb）
rub off　擦掉
rub rails　（汽车车身外部防擦伤的）防擦伤挡条（亦称 rub strip）
ruby glass　红宝石玻璃，红玉玻璃
ruby paper　红宝石纸，红纸（在透明聚乙酯对苯二酸酯树脂薄膜表面又被覆一层不透水银灯光的红色薄膜，用于制作光刻技术中的掩模原图）
RUC　河滩沼泽地多用途气垫浮行车辆（riverine utility craft）
rude edge-arrissing　粗磨边（倒棱，经粗加工的玻璃边缘，手摸有粗糙感但不会造成割伤）
Rudge hub　罗奇轮毂［赛车等使用的中央锁紧式快速拆装罗奇螺母（Rudge nut）的专用轮毂］
Rudge nut　罗奇螺母（见 Rudge hub）
rudimentary　①根本的，基本的，基础的②初步的，开始的③未成熟的，原始状态的，不先进的（＝rudimental）
Rudolf Diesel　鲁道夫·狄塞耳（1858～1913年，德国技师，于1897年发明柴油机）
Rudolph Ackermann　鲁道夫·阿克曼（英国人，梯形转向机构的发明者）
rugged cargo-hauling reliability　（货车）崎岖不平道路条件下的货运可靠性
rugged country　崎岖不平地区
ruggedness　强度，坚固性，稳定性，耐用性，耐振性，耐久性，坚固，结实
rugged terrain　起伏不平地区，崎岖地带
rugged vehicle　在繁重工作条件下使用的车辆
rule of thumb　经验法则，经验方法，靠目力估计，靠经验估算，大约计，概测法，大约估计，近似计算，手工业方式（＝rule-of-thumb method）
ruler　①直规，直尺，规尺，画线板②管理者
ruling　①画线，刻度，（用尺）量度，划出的线②管理，支配，统治；裁决③统治的，支配的，主导的，主要的，流行的，有力的，优势的④平均的（价格等）⑤画线用的，刻度的
ruling grade　（道路）限制坡度，控制坡度，最大纵坡

rumble ①音调低沉的低频噪声（如：发动机，特别是柴油机因压力增长率过高而产生的工作粗暴声，汽车在平路上行驶时，轮胎产生的连续低频振动噪声）②［美］老式轿车后部的无篷加座（= rumble seat，英称 dickey seat）

runabout ①小功率轻便轿车②轻便敞篷轿车，敞篷小轿车（= light uncovered wagon）③单排双座折叠式软篷轿车（= light roadster）

runabout crane 活动吊车，轻便起重机

run away 飞车，超速，过速（指内燃机对转速失去控制后，转速急剧上升超过最高允许转速并达到危险程度的现象）

runaway knock （发动机）失控性爆燃（指发动机在稳定转速和负荷条件下产生的越来越强烈的连续爆震）

runaway speed 失去控制的转速，飞车转速

runaway surface ignition 失控性表面点火［发动机汽缸内零件表面炽热点（不包括积炭）引起的异常点火现象，随发动机温度升高而加剧］

runaway velocity ①（燃气轮机中气流脱离叶轮的）溢出速度②（内燃机失去控制的）飞车速度

run down ①降速，减速，渐停，慢下来，变弱，用尽，逐渐变坏，减价，减少工作②查出，找出，查对，追究…的根源③过目，浏览④沿…而行，与…相撞，撞倒

run down battery 电耗尽的蓄电池（= dead battery）

run-down equipment 磨损了的设备

run down revolution （制动时）车轮的停止转数（台架制动试验时制动力作用始点至车轮完全停止的转数，根据该转数，可计算出制动距离）

run dry 干运行，无润滑油运行

run-flat tyre 泄气保用轮胎（由于外部尖物穿刺或自身放炮以致完全泄气时仍能保证汽车继续平稳行驶一定距离的轮胎）

run hot 运转发热，运转过热

run idle 急速运转，无负荷运转

run-in 磨合，走合（美称 break-in, wear-in，使新的或大修后的发动机、汽车在小负荷、低速下运转一定的时间或里程，以保证轴承和各种摩擦件完好配合。注意 run-in 为及物动词）

run-in time 磨合期，走合期；试运转期

run-in wear 走合期磨损

run mode （喷油系统等的）运转工况（由开环和闭环两种工况组成，见 open loop mode 和 closed loop mode）

runner ①滚子，转子；叶轮②雪橇滑板（与地面滑动的部分）③（汽车等的）驾驶员；（汽车等商品的）推销员④（液力变矩器的）从动叶轮，涡轮⑤（机器的）操作者⑥（发动机进、排气歧管接汽缸的）进、排气分支管

runner blade （液力变矩器的）涡轮叶片

runner torque （液力变矩器的）涡轮转矩

running balance 动平衡（= dynamic balance）

run(ning) board （车门口的）登车板踏脚板，脚蹬板

running-board lamp （车身两侧）踏脚板灯

running brake 行车（脚）制动器

running clearance 运转间隙（如：转子和缸盖间在运转时的间隙）

running condition 运转状态，使用状态，工作状态，运转条件，使用

条件,工作条件

running drum tester 转鼓试验台(汽车在室内进行行驶性能试验的专用设备,以转鼓模拟路面,汽车驱动轮置于转鼓上运转,并通过对转鼓施加不同负荷,模拟汽车的实际行驶阻力,以测定汽车行驶性能等)

running fit 转动配合,动配合

running free 空转,不加负载的运转,(汽车)空驶

running gear (汽车的)行驶机构(running gear 有多种解释:①传动、转向和悬架机构系统的总称②车身以下的车轮、车桥、主减速器、转向杆系等非悬架机构③车轮、车桥和悬架系统,=under carriage of vehicle④车架、悬架、车桥和车轮)

running ground 流沙地

running hours 运行时间,运转时间,行驶时间

running idle 怠速运转,无负荷运转,空转,空驶(=running no-load)

running-in 走合,磨合(总成或机构组装后,逐步改善零件摩擦表面几何形状和表面层物理机械性能的运转过程,run in 的名词,美称 breaking in, wearing in)

running-in free type piston-ring cylinder-liner assembly 免磨合型活塞环—缸套组件

running in maintenance 走合期维护(走合期间进行的维护作业,见 running-in)

running-in oil 磨合期用润滑油

running-in period 磨合期,走合期

running-in speed (汽车)磨合期的行驶速度,(发动机)磨合转速

running-loss control (对)运行(中产生的)损耗控制(如:回收燃油蒸气等)

running-loss emission 运行(中产生的)损耗性排放(如:燃油蒸发损失排放等)

running losses 运行损失(如:汽车按规定的试验规范运转,在此期间内排放的燃油蒸气量)

running maintenance 运行维护,日常维护,例行维护

running no-load 无负荷运转

running order 运转状态,工作状态;运转程序,工作顺序

running performance 运行特性,运行性能

running recorder 运转记录器,运行(时间,行程等)自动记录仪

running repair 日常维修,临时修理,小修(=temporary repair)

running resistance 行驶阻力(包括滚动阻力、空气阻力、爬坡阻力、加速阻力)

running resistance curve 汽车行驶阻力特性曲线(表示车速与行驶阻力之间关系)

running route 行驶路线,运行路线

running service 例行技术(保养)维护

running shed 车辆维护场

running speed ①行驶车速(一般指平均运行速度,以实际行驶时间除以全程距离)②运转速度,运行速度

running surface ①(道路的)路面(=road surface)②(滚筒试验台等的)滚筒面③工作面

running temperature 工作温度,运转温度

running test 运转试验;道路试验;行车使用试验

running test stand (汽车)运行试验台架

running time 运转时间,工作时间,行车时刻,运行时间,行驶时间

running time only (扣除停机后的)纯运转时间

running torque of starter 起动机转矩（起动机在不同负载及转速时的力矩）

running unload 急速运转（= idle running）

run off roadway 汽车驶出路外

run on 熄不了火（故障）（汽油发动机断开点火电路后，由于燃烧室内的灼热点点火，而继续运转的现象，亦称 after running, dieseling, auto ignition）

run on the rim （轮胎跑气后的）靠轮辋行驶

run-on tire （漏气）继行轮胎（安全气胎的一种，与专用轮辋合用，轮胎爆破或漏气时胎圈不会脱出，仍可保证汽车安全行驶一段距离）

run-out ①径向跳动，径向摆动②偏摆（如：车轮、制动鼓、齿轮等的中心平面与轴的中心线不完全垂直，转动时产生的摆振）③偏心率④用完，结束，到期⑤跑出，突出⑥停止运转，消退⑦流出，溢出，溢流⑧用坏，磨损

runout compensator 偏摆补偿器，摆动量补偿装置

run out of gas 汽油用完，汽油耗尽

run-through ①扎穿，刺穿，戳穿②穿过，贯穿③浪费，耗尽④遍达，普及到，遍及

rupture 破裂

rupture of tyre 轮胎破裂，轮胎爆破

rupture pressure （仪表、仪器的）破坏压力（由试验所确定的仪器仪表爆裂时的压力）

rupture test 破坏性试验

rupturing stress 破坏应力，断裂应力（= rupture stress）

rural atmosphere 野外环境，野外大气环境

rural district 乡村，农村

rural driving 乡村道路行车（= country driving）

rural truck 农用载货汽车

rush ①猛冲，飞奔，急冲，猛进，冲击②急需的，紧急的，急速的，突击的，繁忙的

rush hour(s) 交通拥挤时间，交通高峰时间

rush-rod oscillating tooth 推杆活齿（采用推杆作为活齿，见 oscillating tooth）

rust cement 防锈膏，防锈胶

rusted 生锈的

rust-free 不锈的，无锈的

rust greases 防锈润滑脂

rust inhibitor ①（冷却液，燃、润料的）防锈蚀剂（防止钢、铁零件，如：缸体水套、轴承、齿轮等锈蚀的化学添加剂，亦称 rust inhibiting additives）②（保护短期停用存放的机器、设备等的）防锈剂，防锈油（亦称 rust preventer, rust preventive）

rustless property 抗锈蚀特性（= stainless property, non-corrodibility）

rust preventive ①防锈剂（= rust preventer, rust-resisting compound, rust inhibitor）②防锈措施，防锈法

rust preventive packaging 防锈包装（亦称 rustproof packaging）

rust removal 除锈

rust remover ①除锈剂②除锈器

rust stable 耐锈蚀的

rust test 锈蚀试验

rusty 生锈的

rusty spot 锈斑

rut 车辙，压痕，凹槽，沟，沟槽

rutile 二氧化钛，金红石

RV ［美］休闲车（recreation vehicle 的简称）

RV governor （柴油机的）机械式全速调速器，机械式全程调速器（见 variable speed governor）

RVI ［美］休闲游乐车协会（Recreation Vehicle Institute 的简称）

RVIA ［日］休闲游乐车工业协会（Recreation Vehicle Industry Association 的简称）

RVM 后方车辆监测系统（rear vehicle monitor system 的简称，后保险杠左、右两端装有雷达，可测到后方临近车辆并在后视镜上发出频闪图像警报）

Rvp 雷德蒸气压（Reid vapor pressure）

RWAL 后轮防抱死（制动系统）（rear-wheel antilock 的简称，多用于轻型货车，防止制动时质量转移造成的后轮抱死）

RWD 后轮驱动（rear wheel drive 的简称）

Rzeppa universal joint 球笼式万向节（用一组钢球连接星形套和钟形壳组成的一种自承式等速万向节，钢球位于星形套和钟形壳轴向截面上的曲面凹槽内并由保持架保持在等速平面内，以发明人 A·H·Rzeppa 命名，亦称 Rzeppa constant velocity joint）

S-5 (对汽车货运配载系统的)五项要求(Service 对货主、车主服务,Speed 快速运转,Space-saving 节约装载空间,Scale-control 库存调度要方便,Safety 安全,=5S)

S ①西门子(siemens 电导单位) ②次级的(secondary) ③分激绕组(shuntwound) ④声测(sound ranging) ⑤南方(south) ⑥南极(south pole) ⑦速度(speed) ⑧运动车(sport car) ⑨稳定性(stability) ⑩应力(stress) ⑪开关(switch)

SA ①(美国 API 滑油分类中的)轻级 A 类(滑油)(适用于小型轻量级汽油机和柴油机,无特定的性能要求,一般不加添加剂,见 service class) ②截面面积(sectional area) ③半自动的(semiautomatic) ④旋转轴(spin axis) ⑤标准大气压(standard atmosphere)

Saab-Scania AB (瑞典)萨伯-斯堪尼亚公司(我国亦称绅宝公司)

Sabaru CVT Sabaru 电子控制型连续无级变速器(Sabaru-electronic control continuously variable transmission 的简称,日本 Sabaru 公司 1987 年推出的世界第一台电子控制连续无级变速器的商品名,用于小排量汽车,亦称 E-CVT)

Sabathé cycle 沙巴特循环(等容循环和等压循环的混合循环,由绝热压缩、等容加热和等压加热,绝热膨胀、等容放热组成的循环,亦称等容等压循环,复合循环 dual combustion cycle, = composite cycle)

Sabathé cycle engine 复合循环发动机(按复合循环工作的发动机,见 Sabathé cycle)

Sabre [美]马刀(通用汽车公司 Buick 厂生产的轿车名,1989 年、1990 年为美十佳轿车,用 Nissan 公司发动机,排量 1.8L,涡轮增压,最大功率 99kW,最高车速 208km/h)

sac ①袋,囊,气袋,液袋 ②(柴油机闭式喷油嘴喷孔前的)针阀下腔(当该腔内由喷油泵泵入的燃油压力超过针阀弹簧压力时,将针阀顶升,该腔内的燃油由喷孔中喷出)

SACA 美国蒸汽机汽车俱乐部(Steam Automobile Club of America)

saccadic movement (眼光)扫动(指眼睛由一凝视点向另一凝视点的突然移动)

sack ①包（英制容量单位，1 sack = 3 bushels，见 imperial gallon）；一包；一袋②装进袋内

sac volume 针阀压力室容积（喷油器针阀关闭后其下方至喷孔上方的容积，简称压力室容积）

SACVT ［英］气垫车技师学会（Society of Air Cushion Vehicle Technicians）

saddle ①鞍，鞍形物②座，座面（任何部件上安装和紧固另一部件的平面或凹面，如：非独立悬架车桥梁上的钢板弹簧座面，曲轴主轴承座）③（曲线的）凹谷

saddle clamp （钢板弹簧）U 形螺栓

saddle function 鞍式函数

saddle-shaped 鞍形的

saddle tank 凹形油箱，鞍形油箱（一般装于后桥上方）

saddle tractor （半挂车的）鞍式牵引车

SAE ［美］汽车工程师学会（Society of Automotive Engineers）

SAEA 澳大利亚汽车工程师学会（Society of Automotive Engineers-Australia）

SAE categories of communication systems ［美］汽车工程师学会通信系统分类［美国汽车工程师学会将车用电子控制装置通信系统分为三级，A 级（class A）用于低速网络，B 级和 C 级（class B，class C）用于高速网络，但 B 级无严格的安全要求，C 级有严格的安全要求］

SAE Computer Application Committee 美国汽车工程师学会计算机应用委员会

SAE Engine Test Code 美国汽车工程师学会发动机试验规范

SAE horsepower 美国汽车工程师学会马力（由 SAE 提出的下列公式计算的额定马力：$\dfrac{(缸径)^2 \times (缸数)}{2.5}$，用于注册登记，并不用来准确地确定实际有效马力，亦称 rated horsepower）

SAEHP 按美国汽车工程学会标准测定的马力（SAE horsepower）

SAE Motor Truck Rating Committee 美国汽车工程师学会货车评价委员会

SAE of China 中国汽车学会（= Society of Automobile Engines of China）

SAE rating 美国汽车工程师学会（发动机总有效马力的）测定标准（该标准规定在总有效马力的测试中，使用不带发电机、机油泵、燃油泵、水泵和排放控制系统等附件，而只装有维持运转所必需的总成的裸发动机，因此其测定值高于实际装车使用时的有效功率）

SAE SP ［美］汽车工程师学会专刊（Society of Automotive Engineers-Special Publications）

SAE standard ［美］汽车工程师学会标准

SAE standard air temperature 美国汽车工程师学会标准大气温度（该学会规定的标准大气温度为 60°F，常用以修正在测功器上测试出来的发动机性能数据等）

SAE standard barometric pressure 美国汽车工程师学会标准大气压（该学会规定 29.92inHg 为标准大气压，常用以修正实验室实际测出的发动机性能数据等，使之成为可对比性的数据）

SAE standard conditions 美国汽车工程师学会标准大气状态（为修正发动机在测功器上测试出来的性能数据等，美国汽车工程师学会规定的标准大气状态；标准大气压 = 29.92in Hg；标准大气温度 = 60°F）

SAE Technical Board 美国汽车工程师学会技术委员会

SAE transaction ［美］汽车工程师学会论文集

SAE viscosity 美国汽车工程师学会机油黏度，其黏度分级如下：

黏度级	100℃时的运动黏度 (mm^2/s)	
	最大	最小
0W	3.8	—
5W	3.8	—
10W	4.1	—
15W	5.6	—
20W	5.6	—
25W	9.3	—
20	5.6	<9.3
30	9.3	<12.5
40	12.5	<16.3
50	16.3	<21.9
10W/30	9.3	

SAF ①一种炭黑的商品名（Super Abrasion Furnace，平均直径 $14\mu m$，表面积 $134m^2/g$）②［美］战略空军（Strategic Air Force）③安全、保险（装置）（safety 的简称）

safe 安全的，可靠的，保险的，妥当的

safe allowable load 安全许可负载，安全负荷，容许荷载

safe allowable stress 安全容许应力

safe approach speed 安全接近速度（critical approach speed）

safe bearing load 轴承容许荷载

safe-conduct 通行证

safe curve speed （汽车的）弯道安全（行驶）速度

safe demostration 安全驾驶示范，安全驾驶示教，安全驾驶图解教学

safe driving support system 安全驾驶支持系统

safe fast road 安全快速道路

safeguard ①防护，保护，保险②（机构的）保护罩，安全装置，保险装置

safe guard bow 弓形护杠

safe-guard system 安全防护系统（简称 SGS）

safe load capacity 安全荷载量，安全承载量

safe maneuverability （汽车的）安全操纵性能，安全驾驶性能

safe margin 安全系数，强度储备（亦称 margin of safety）
　safe noise level 安全噪声级

safe operating area （电压及电流等的）安全运用区域

Safe pre-set distance （雷达巡航控制系统根据车速自动设定或由驾驶者设定的与前方障碍物间的）预置安全距离

safe range of stress 容许应力范围，容许应力限度

safe speed of rotation 安全转速

Safe Stat 汽车货运公司安全状况管理系统（Motor Carrier Safety Status Management System 的简称，美国联邦货运公司安全管理局研发的自动化数据驱动分析系统，见 date-drive analysis system）

safe stopping distance 安全制动距离

safety ①安全（措施），保险（装置）（简称 SAF）②安全性，可靠性③保安，保护④防护器材

safety-accented 以安全为重点的，特别强调安全的

safety air cushion （汽车乘员的）安全气垫

Safety Alert Seat system （Cadillac 的）安全警报椅系统（当遭遇险情时座椅振动以警告驾驶人员）

safety alert symbol 安全惊叹号（提醒人们注意小心谨慎操作等的惊叹号图案符号）

safety angle 安全角，换向重叠角（用于电子整流线路中，= commutation angle）

safety automobile system 安全轿车系统（安全装备完善的车辆）

safety belt 安全带（限制乘员突然移动的缚紧装置，亦称 seat belt）

safety belt interlock system 安全带互锁装置，安全带连锁系统

safety belt with two-way lock 双向锁紧式安全带

safety bolt 安全螺栓，保险螺栓

safety brake 保险制动器，安全制动装置

safety braker （液压制动系）安全阻振器（一种消除制动系管道中液压脉动的装置）

safety bumper （汽车）保险杠

safety cab 安全驾驶室（具有防撞结构及装置，防止乘员在撞车、翻车时受伤）

safety cage 安全栅

safety car 安全汽车（指碰撞时，乘员不致遭受重大伤害的轿车）

safety cell （汽车的）安全舱（作为一个结构单元，防碰撞、防挤压的乘员乘坐空间）

safety chain of full trailer 全挂车安全链（连接牵引车尾部与挂车前部之保险链，一旦挂车拖挂装置损坏脱挂时，可以拉住挂车）

safety chassis 安全底盘（如：低架、低重心底盘）

safety check system （汽车的）安全检查系统（如：润滑油面、前照灯、制动系等与运转和行车安全有关的自动检查、警报系统）

safety coefficient 安全系数

safety cylinder （液压制动系）安全缸（可自动封死渗漏制动液的管道，以保证其他车轮可正常制动）

safety double glass 安全夹层玻璃

safety driving assistant system 安全驾驶辅助系统（如：防止车辆间碰撞的短程信息交换及警报系统等）

safety factor of bead ring strength （轮胎）胎圈钢丝圈强度安全倍数（钢丝圈强度与钢线圈在标准规定最高充气压力作用下所受张力的比值）

safety factor of cord strength （轮胎）帘线强度安全倍数（帘线强度与胎冠部位帘线在标准规定最高充气压力作用下所受张力的比值）

safety fence 安全护栏（= guard fence）

safety frame （驾驶室的）安全护架

safety fuse cutout 熔丝安全断电器（= electric fuse）

safety glass 安全玻璃（由无机材料或无机与有机的复合材料所构成的产品，当其应用于车辆时，可以减少车祸中严重伤人的危险，同时对其可见性、强度和耐磨性都做了一定规定）

safety glazing test （安全）玻璃冲击碎裂试验

safety hubs 安全轮毂（装于后桥，防止车桥断裂事故中，车轮脱离汽车）

safety locking bolt 安全自锁螺栓

safety operation 安全驾驶，安全操作，安全运转

safety override 安全超越装置（电子控制系统中一种因安全原因而中止某机构工作或某项功能作用的装置）

safety performance 安全性能

safety rating （汽车等的）安全级别

safety reflective glass 安全反射玻璃（玻璃表面镀有金属或金属氧化物薄膜，具有一定反射能力的车用安全玻璃）

safety relay valve 安全继动阀（在行驶过程中，制动软管或膜片等的破损，发生漏气时能自动关闭破损管路，以防止压力下降的阀门）

safety research vehicle 安全研究车（简称SRV）

safety rim 安全轮辋（一般指两侧胎圈座有突峰的轮辋，遇爆胎时，突峰将轮胎紧卡在轮辋上，可阻止轮胎胎圈卷进轮辋槽底）

safety sensor （装在驾驶区的安全气

囊控制模块中最后判断是否发生严重碰撞而必须引爆气囊的)安全传感器(亦称 arming sensor, 一般与控制模块内的单通道电子减速度计串联)

safety (software) package (汽车电子系统)安全软件包(汽车安全电子控制系统的程序的软件包,如:其 24G 集成电路芯片和外壳)

safety (spark) gap 安全(火花)间隙(与火花塞两极并联的用来防止火花塞电极短路的火花间隙)

safety specification for motor vehicle's operating on road 机动车安全运行技术条件

safety standard 安全标准(以保护人和物的安全为目的制定的标准)

safety thermal-relief valve 高温减压安全阀

safety tread 安全防滑胎面

safety tyre 安全轮胎(一般指被异物刺穿后仍能保证汽车稳定行驶一定距离的各种轮胎)

safety valve 安全阀(如:防止气压系统的压力超过某一个规定数值的阀)

safety valve set pressure 安全阀调定压力,安全阀作用压力

safety vehicle 安全汽车(指具有各种乘员碰撞保护装置、能量吸收装置,车身耐冲击性好,翻车、碰撞肇事时,可保证乘员生命安全的被动安全系统和可预防碰撞、翻车及保证车辆稳定行驶的主动安全系统的车辆)

safety washer 防松垫圈

safety wire (螺栓)防松锁紧铁丝

safety zone 安全地带,安全区域

sag ①(在压力或重力下)下垂,垂弛;弯下;下沉②下垂度③凹部(道路纵断面上两个相邻坡段所形成的洼凹部)④凹下去;(梁等)压弯下来;沉下去

sag curve 挠度曲线,垂度曲线

sagging 弛垂,挠曲,垂度

sag of belt 皮带弛垂

sag test (密封胶剂等材料的)下垂试验(测定密封胶等在零件上保持涂覆位置的能力)

SAI (非独立悬架转向轮转向主销或独立悬架转向轮的)转向轴线内倾(steering axis inclination, 见 kingpin inclination)

sail-center 风帆中心(汽车各部分受空气力的合力作用点)

SAL ①维修记录(service action log)②符号汇编语言(symbolic assembly language)

S(A)LA independent suspension system 长短臂独立悬架系统 [short (and) -long arm independent suspension system 的简称]

salamander wool 石棉;石棉纤维

sale 销售,出售

sales agency 销售经纪商

sales and service center 销售及维修中心,销售服务中心

sales engineer 销售工程师

salient 凸出的,突起的,显著的

salient feature 特色,特征,显著的特点,卓越的优点

saline ①盐水,咸水②含盐的,咸的,盐性的

salinity test 盐分测定法,咸度试验,含盐量测定

salinometer 溶解盐分测定计,盐液比重计,含盐量测定计

saloon ①(双排座,硬顶,双门或四门,前后座间无隔断的)普通轿车(saloon car 的简称,美称 sedan)②(客车的)乘客区

saloon car 普通轿车(见 saloon①)

saloon coach 厢式客车

saloon landaulette 敞篷四门轿车,活顶四门箱式轿车(车顶可向前后折叠敞开,驾驶员与乘客间没有隔

栏)
salt 食盐,盐类
salt atmosphere 含盐的气氛(= salt-laden atmosphere)
salt bath quenching 盐浴淬火
salt-cooled 盐浴冷却的,钠盐冷却的
salt-cooled (exhaust) valve 金属盐冷却式(排)气门(= salt-filled exhaust valve)
salt corrosion 盐腐蚀
salt environment 含盐的周围介质,含盐的周围环境
salt-fog test 盐雾腐蚀试验(见 salt-spray test)
salt-laden atmosphere 含盐气氛(salt atmosphere)
salt solution method 盐分法,盐水浓度法(水流量测定法的一种,在水管或水路的上流,注入一定量的既知浓度的食盐水等,而在下流取出少量的试样,根据试样中的盐分浓度,求出水流量的方法)
salt spraying 盐溶液喷射
salt spray test 盐雾试验(①指在充以雾状氯化钠溶液的试验室内,评定承受大气腐蚀能力的试验②用喷射盐雾的方法检查金属材料或零件的抗腐蚀能力, = salt-fog test)
salt spray testing 喷盐试验(对铝板胶合车身接缝处的一种质量试验)
salt spreader (大型货车等的)撒盐器,盐粒撒布器(融雪防滑用)
saltus ①中断②急度,急转
Saltzman method 梭尔·茨曼法(B. E. Saltzman1954 年首先提出的化学分析方法,用来测定废气中 NO_x 含量等)
salvage ①(在事故的损失中)抢救的财货或获救的财物②(付与抢救财货者的)援救费③(加工后可再利用的)废料,废件
salvageable component 可修件

salvage crane 救援起重机,救险吊车
salvage depot 修理场(所)(= repair depot)
salvage facility ①(肇事车辆)救济装备,救援设备②(肇事车辆等的)救护机构
salvage lorry 救济车,救险车(= breakdown lorry, wrecker)
salvage plant ①(事故或故障车辆的)营救设备,救援车,②(特指)拖运事故或故障车辆的急救车
SAM ①座椅调节控制模块(seat adjustment module 的简称)②信号采集和执行模块(signal acquisition and actuation module 的简称)③二次空气管理(系统)(second air management 的简称)④独立存储器(stand along memory 的简称)
samarium 钐(sm,原子量150.4,原子序数62)
sample 样品,试样,抽样
sample-and-hold circuit 采样与保持电路(在汽车电子控制模块中检测和存储模拟信号瞬时值的电路,如:感知某传感元件输出的瞬时电压值,在较长时间内予以存储,如: 20 微秒,读出应用,也是将模拟信号转变为数字信号的第一步, = sampling hold circuit)
sample car 样车,样品汽车
sample cell (红外线气体分析仪的)气样室
sample collector 取样器,样本采集装备
sampled analog data 抽样模拟数据
sampled-data model 采样数据模型,抽样数据模型
sample distribution 样本分布,子样分布,抽样分布
sample filtering 抽样过滤(从全部混浊液中用规定方法抽取部分有代表性的样液进行过滤的方法)

sample fraction defective （抽样检查时的一批试样中的）样本缺陷产品的百分率，子样中的次品百分率
sample piece 试样，样件
sampler 试样采取器，采样器，取样器
samples taken at random 随机选样
sample survey 样品鉴定
sample test 抽样试验
sample traffic survey 抽样交通调查
sample unit 样本中的一个样值（= sampling unit）
sample variance （数理统计）样本的方差（离散值），子样的方差（离散值）
sample workplace 样件，试样
sampling 采样，取样，抽样
sampling analysis 采样分析，取样分析
sampling bag （排气）取样袋（采用 CVS 法或全袋取样法时，收集排气样气的袋子）
sampling basic number 抽样基数（在抽样检查时，供选择的最小产品数量以保证抽样的随机性）
sampling control system 采样控制系统（在控制系统中，采样指将连续时间信号转变为脉冲信号或数字信号的过程，汽车计算机数字控制系统便是一种典型的采样控制系统）
sampling detector 抽样用检测装置（如：在交通调节主控制器中，为了取得必要的车流量数据情报而使用的检车器）
sampling factor 抽样因素（亦称扩大系数，抽样率的倒数）
sampling fraction 抽样率，取样率（实际调查数占调查对象总数的比率，亦称 sampling rate）
sampling inspection 抽样检查，抽样检验
sampling location 取样部位
sampling probe （排气）取样头（如：插入发动机排气管中采集废气样本的插管，亦称 sample probe）
sampling procedure 取样程序
sampling rate 抽样（检查）率，取样率（见 sampling fraction）
sampling servomechanism 采样伺服机构
sampling test 抽样试验（从批量中随机抽取的一定数量试样的试验）
sampling time 采样时间（采样过程中检出被测量的时间）
sampling tolerance 抽样公差（在取样检查时用来评价总体用的对样本规定的公差范围）
sampling unit 样本中的一个样值，样本中的一个单元（如：产品的抽样检查中抽出几个产品作为样本，其中一个产品即为样本中的一个单元）
sampling without replacement 无退还抽样
sampling with replacement 有退还抽样
sand ①砂②撒砂，填砂③用砂纸打磨
sand-asphalt protective coat （路面的）砂沥青保护层
sandbag 沙袋垫（车身板件敲击成形用）
sand ballast 充砂压载物，充砂配重
sand belt （砂纸、砂布等制成的）打磨带，抛光带
sand-blast apparatus 喷砂设备，喷砂机（亦称 sand blast equipment, sand blaster）
sand blast cleaning 喷砂清理，喷砂清除
sand-blast type spark plug cleaner 喷砂式火花塞清洁器
sand blister 砂泡，砂疤（砂粒嵌入轮胎表面橡胶层的一种故障）
sand blower 喷砂鼓风机
sand cap 防尘罩，防砂罩

sand cleaner （清除火花塞积炭等用的）喷砂清洁器

sand-cored water jacket passage 砂芯铸空的水套通道，砂型铸造的水套通路

sand course 沙地试验路线

sand drift 流沙，流沙堆，沙丘

sanded ①撒上沙的（道路）②喷砂清理的③用砂布或砂带打磨的

sanded packed snow 撒砂的压实积雪

sander ①喷砂机，喷砂器②打磨器

sander-filer （车身板件的）砂磨-锉修两用机

sand grains 砂粒

sand-gravel road 砂砾路

sand hole （铸件）砂眼

sand inclusion （铸件）夹砂

sanding equipment （路面）撒沙设备

sanding ice covering （路面）冰层上撒沙

sanding vehicle ①运砂车②（道路养护用）撒砂车

sand load 砂配重

sandpaper ①（金刚）砂纸②用砂纸打磨

sand rim 沙地型轮辋（供沙土地行驶用的加宽轮辋）

sandshoe （挂车在松软或不平地面上停车时用的）撑脚

sandstorm 沙尘暴

sand tire 沙地行驶用轮胎

sandwich 夹层，层状结构（亦称 sandwich laminate）

sandwich construction 夹层结构（亦称 sandwich structure）

sandwich panel 层板

sandwich switch （汽车乘员安全带系统警报装置的）夹层结构型（乘坐感知）自动开关（乘员坐下来以后，利用乘员体重压缩夹层使触点闭合而输出乘坐信号）

sandy area 多沙地区

saponification number 皂化值

Sapper 工兵，工程兵

Sapphire ①蓝宝石②宝石蓝（车身颜色）

sapphire fiber optic temperature sensor 蓝宝石光纤温度传感器（可承受4000℃的高温，精度达0.2%/1000℃，用于检测爆震和火焰前锋传播等）

SAR ①扫气比（scavenged air ratio）②扫气面积比（scavenged area ratio）

sarface vaporiser 表面型化油器（早期使用的依靠空气流经过较大面积的汽油表面使汽油气化而形成空气—汽油混合气的化油器，亦称 surface carburetor）

SAS ①二次空气供给（secondary air supply）②怠速（混合气浓度）调整螺钉（slow adjust screw）③（驾驶者）睡眠警报系统（sleep alert system）

sash ①框，窗框②上、下拉动开闭的窗子

sashless door 无窗框车门（车门上方只有玻璃而无门窗框）

SAT ①自回正力矩（self aligning torque）②饱和（saturate）③系统验收试验（system acceptance tests）

satellite ①卫星②行星齿轮③（泛指各种位于）转向盘周围的控制件或控制板

satellite bronze supporting washer 行星轮支撑铜垫

Satellite data 卫星（定位系统发布的）数据

satellite differential 行星轮式差速器

satellite dish 锅式卫星信号接收天线

satellite gears 行星齿轮

satellite-monitored positioning system 卫星监测定位系统（亦称全球定位系统，汽车导行系统的重要组成系统，可测定汽车实时位置、方向，

显示在电子地图上。参见 electronic-navigation system, global position system)

satin ①缎（子）②如缎子般光泽的

satin finishing 抛光，研光，擦亮

satisfactory 令人满意的，良好的

sat-nav 卫星导航（satellite navigation system 的简称）

SATP 自回正力矩刚度（self-aligning torque power 的简称，亦称 aligning torque stiffness 或 aligning stiffness，如：轮胎侧偏角单位增量所对应的回正力矩增量）

saturant ①饱和的，浸透的②饱和剂，浸渍剂

saturate ①使…饱和，使…浸透②饱和的，浸透的③（复数）饱和物

saturated air 饱和空气（在某温度下空气和液态水平衡共存状态下的空气。此时的空气中含有水蒸气态的水分，应称为饱和湿空气"saturated moist air"）

saturated humidity ratio 饱和绝对湿度（饱和湿空气的绝对湿度）

saturated logic circuit 饱和逻辑电路

saturated pressure 饱和压力（同一物质的气相和液相或固相平衡共存时，该系统压力称为饱和压力。饱和压力值随温度而变）

saturated solution 饱和溶液

saturated steam 饱和蒸汽（= saturated vapor）

saturated steel 共析钢

saturate the way 道路饱和（达到道路的最大行车密度）

saturating signal 饱和信号，极限信号

saturation current 饱和电流

saturation curve 饱和曲线

saturation effect 磁性饱和效应

saturation flow ①饱和流量②饱和交通量

saturation flux density 饱和磁通密度

saturation induction 饱和磁感应强度，饱和磁化强度（某一材料的磁力线密度已达到饱和程度，即使进一步增大外界磁场强度，磁力线密度亦不会有明显增加，亦称 saturation magnetization）

saturation input signal（for digital signal applications）饱和输入信号（对于数字信号，指为填满势阱所要求的输入信号或照射功率）

saturation output signal（for digital signal applications）饱和输出信号（对于数字信号，指由满势阱所产生的输出信号）

saturation point 饱和点

saturation pressure 饱和压力

saturation signal（for analogue signal applications）饱和信号（对于模拟信号，能够以规定的线性度，在输入和输出之间转移的最大输入信号或最大照射功率）

saturation temperature 饱和温度

saturation voltage 饱和电压

saturator ①饱和剂②饱和器

saturn 洒特，洒脱（1992 年美国通用汽车公司推出的小型轿车牌名，自 1987 年开始开发，耗资 35 亿美元；Saturn 一词系 20 世纪 50 年代美国的火箭名，美国宇航员就是用这一火箭，第一次登上月球的）

saucer washer 碟形垫圈（= cupped washer）

sauter mean diameter 索特平均直径（简称 SMD，在一次喷射中，全部油滴体积的总和与全部油滴表面积的总和的比值）

SAV ①运动型多功能车［Sports Activity Vehicle 的简称，为 SUV 的另一种称呼，但与 SUV 相比，更注重路上（On road）行驶性能，亦称 drive's SUV］②空气喷射阀（shot air vale 的简称）

save ①节省，节约②储存，贮存③援救

saving fuel 节约燃料，节油

saving in energy 节省能量，节能

saw ①锯②锯开

SAW 表面声波（技术）（surface acoustical wave 的简称，利用晶体反射的特定形式的无线电波，作为自身标志信号，用于识别汽车的电子标签等，参见 electronic tag）

S-AWC 超级全轮控制系统［Super All Wheel Control System 的简称，可根据车上安装的各种传感器传递的路况、车况和行驶状况的信息，自动变换前、后车轮和左、右车轮的驱动力，以便对车辆的运动作全面综合控制，即：可①通过电子控制离合器（electronic control coupling）实现四轮驱动（4WD）或两轮驱动（2WD）②通过制动系统、左右轮间主动式差速器（active differential）和电动转向系统（electro-power steering）控制左右轮驱动力和制动力而实现汽车的主动式横摆控制（active yaw control）和左、右轮间主动式差速控制（active differential control），以保证车辆具有良好的弯道行驶方向跟随性（line-trace performance），直线行驶和变换车道的操控稳定性，以及低 μ 路面上的通过性。此外，可通过S-AWC模式选择开关（S-AWC drive-mode selector）选择以下四种行驶模式：①平时仅前轮驱动，节能，遇打滑路面时自动转为四轮驱动，确保汽车稳定行驶的全轮驱动节能模式（AWC ECO mode）②根据路况和行驶条件自动调控四轮驱动力的标准四驱模式（Normal 4WD mode）、（AWC Normal mode）③适应雪地等滑溜路面行驶要求的雪地模式（SNOW mode）④发挥最高通过性能的四轮驱动锁定模式（LOCK mode）］

sawtooth oscillator 锯齿波振荡器

sawtooth thread 锯齿波纹

sawtooth wave 锯齿波（简称STW）

sawtooth wear （轮胎表面的）锯齿形磨损

Saxomat auto-clutch 沙霍玛特自动离合器（德国沙克思公司研制成的一种利用离心力的自动离合器的商品名）

Saybolt furol viscometer 赛波特重油黏度计（美国测量重质油料黏度用的黏度计，将60ml的重油，加热到210°F，流过黏度计标准孔口的秒数，即为该油料的黏度秒）

Saybolt seconds 赛氏黏度秒（用赛波特黏度计测定流体黏度时，一定数量的流体流出的秒数，表示该流体的黏度）

Saybolt universal viscosimeter 赛波特通用黏度计

Saybolt universal viscosity 赛波特通用黏度（单位为秒，用赛波特通用黏度计测定的黏度）

SB ①（美国API滑油分类中）轻级B类（滑油）（适用于轻负荷下工作的汽油机，含有少量添加剂，具有抗氧化、防腐蚀等性能，见 service class）②二次（蓄）电池（见 secondary battery）③检修报告（见 service bulletin）④边频带（见 sideband）⑤单偏包线（见 single braid）⑥油污清除剂（见 sludge breaker）⑦固体（见 solid body）⑧声源方位（见 sound bearing）⑨防溅挡板（见 splash block）⑩标准碳酸氢盐（见 standard bicarbonate）⑪填（料）函（见 stuffing box）⑫开关板，交换机（见 switch board）⑬开关箱，配电箱（见 switch box）

Sb 锑（antimony）

SBC system 电子传感式制动控制系统（Sensotronic Brake Control System 的简称，一种由制动踏板踩踏力传

感器将驾驶者的制动意图信息传送至电子控制模块的线控式制动系统的商品名)

SBDS 维修间诊断系统(service bay diagnostic system 的简称)

SBR ①苯乙烯—丁二烯橡胶(styrene-butadiene rubber 的简称,为目前合成橡胶使用最多的一种,为苯乙烯—丁二烯共聚物)②选择性信标雷达(selective beacon radar)

SBT ①拉伸弯曲试验(stretch bend test)②表面组织喷丸处理的(shot-blast-textured)

SBV 海底车辆(sea bottom vehicle)

SBW 见 steering by wire

SC ①(美国 API 滑油分类中的)轻级 C 类(滑油)(适用于客车和货车汽油机,具有防沉积、防腐蚀性及较高的润滑性,service class)②砂型铸造(sand casting)③比例尺,标尺(见 scale)④清除;扫气(scavenge)⑤螺钉,螺旋(screw)⑥海岸(sea coast)⑦自检验(self check)⑧顺序(sequence)⑨程序控制(sequential control)⑩短路(short circuit)⑪信号中心(signal center)⑫信号调节(signal conditioning)⑬可控硅(silicon control)⑭单触点(single contact)⑮平滑的外形(smooth contour)⑯太阳能电池(solar cell)⑰固体电路(solid circuit)⑱控制技术要求(specification control)⑲抽查(spot check)⑳标准条件(standard condition)㉑标准电导率(standard conductivity)㉒铸钢件(steel casting)㉓存储能力(storage capacity)㉔层状充气,分层燃烧(stratified charge)㉕补充合同(supplemental contract)㉖后勤(供应)部队(supply corps)

scab ①瑕,疵,眼孔;铸件的表面黏砂②拼接板③凸块④结疤;拼接;铸型冲刷

scabland 崎岖地,劣地

scalar ①标量,无矢量,无向量②标量的,无矢量的③梯状的,分等级的

scalding 用沸水清洗

scale ①刻度,刻度盘;尺度,标度,度数;比例尺,标尺(简称 SC)②规模,比例,程度,等级③记数法;换算④金属氧化皮,锈皮;水垢⑤废料⑥按比例制图⑦约略估计⑧换算⑨起氧化皮,去垢

δ-scale δ-规格

scale beam 天平梁(= beam of balance)

scale car 称量车,计量车

scale-coated 积有水垢的

scale crust 水锈层,水垢

scaled-down 缩尺的,按比例缩小的

scale deposit 水垢

scale design ①缩尺设计(指利用缩尺图及缩尺模型对设计方案作进一步研究、讨论、修改)②缩尺结构

scale distance 标距

scale division 标度分格(任何两个相邻标度标记之间的标度部分)

scale down 按比例缩小,缩小比例

scale down vehicle parameters 缩尺汽车参数(供模拟用的按比例缩小尺寸的汽车的各项参数)

scaled plating 鳞片状镀层

scale drawing 比例图

scaled-up 按比例放大的

scale effect ①尺寸效应(尺寸大小对发动机等设备性能的影响)②(应用数学中的)标度效应;比例效应,缩尺效应

scale factor 比例因素,标度系数,标度因子,比例换算系数

scale flaking 表皮脱落,鳞片剥落

scale formation 水垢的形成;氧化皮的形成

scale handling 清除氧化皮,清除水

垢（亦称 scale removal）

scale illumination 刻度盘照明，刻度照明（= dial illumination）

scale incrustation 水垢

scale length 标度长度（在给定的标度上，通过所有最短标记中点的线段在始末标度标记之间的长度）

scale mark 刻度线，标度标记（指示装置上对应于一个或多个确定的被测量值的标度线或其他标记）

scale model 缩尺模型（按比例缩小的模型）

scale-model test 缩尺模型试验

scale numbering 标度数字（标在标度上的整组数字，它对应于标度标记所确定的被测量值，或只表示标度标记的数字顺序）

scale off ①片状剥落②敲掉水锈或氧化皮③按比例量出尺寸

scale-of-ten circuit 十进制电路

scale of two 二进位制

scale optimization 规模最佳化，规模优化

scale out 超过尺寸范围

scale platform 地秤平台

scaler ①（电子）计数器，换算装置②除水垢剂

scale range 标度范围（由标度始点值和终点值所限定的范围）

scale representation 缩尺模拟

scale solvent 除锈溶剂，水垢溶剂

scale spacing 标度分格间距（亦称 length of a scale division，沿着表示标度长度的同一线段上所测得的任何两个相邻标度标记中心线之间的距离）

scallop wear （轮胎）沟槽形（成块剥落）磨损

S-CAM 摄像机传感器[著名汽车安全系统生产厂家 TRW 推出的第三代摄像机用传感元件（video camera sensor）的商品名]

S-cam brake S 形凸轮制动器（制动时直接作用于制动蹄，使蹄张开紧压制动鼓工作面的制动蹄促动器为 S 形凸轮）

scan ①扫描，扫掠②浏览，搜索

scanatron 扫描管

scandium 钪（Sc）

SC and RA [美] 特种运输车辆与装备协会（Specialized Carriers and Rigging Association 的简称）

Scania 斯堪尼亚（瑞典 Saab 集团的一个汽车厂，生产重型汽车、客车等）

Scanner （美国 Snap-on 公司汽车电子控制系统故障）综合扫描仪（商品名）

scanner ①扫描器，扫描机构②析像器③多点测量仪，巡回检测装置④（读取汽车自诊断系统故障代码的）解码器

scanning electron microscope 电子扫描显微镜

scanning electron microscopy 电子扫描显微检查法

scanning laser Doppler vibrometer 激光多普勒扫描振动仪（简称 SLDV 或 scanning LDV）

scanning laser radar 激光扫描雷达（简称 SLR）

scanning mechanism ①扫描机构，扫描器②解码器

scanning mobility particle sizer （空中）流动微粒物扫描式尺寸测定仪（用于测定公路周边大气中排气微粒尺寸分布等）

scan (ning) speed 扫描速度

scan rate 扫描速率（对一系列模拟输入通道的采样速率，以每秒输入通道数表示）

SCAP (S) 硅（膜片式）电容器型绝对压力传感器（silicon capacitor absolute pressure sensor 的简称）

scar ①刀痕，瘢痕，裂痕，伤痕；痕迹②擦伤，留下伤痕，留有痕迹

scarcity (能源、物资、资料等)短缺,不足,稀少

scarf welding 斜面焊接,斜口搭接焊,嵌接焊

scarlet ①鲜红色,猩红②鲜红色的,猩红的

scatter band (曲线图上点的)离散带,点分散布区域

scatter band limit (曲线图上试验点的)离散带界限

scattered fleet 分散(在广大地区)使用的车队

scattergram (试验结果)分布图

scattering 分散,散射,离散

scattering light 散射光

scatter propagation 散射传播

scatter shield 防止汽车行驶时砂石撞击的保护罩(如:赛车的离合器罩)

scat type clutch 斯卡特式离合器(一种磁粉离合器的商品名,single coupling automatic transmission type clutch 的简称,见 powder clutch)

scavenge ①清除,打扫②(发动机)扫气

scavenge air ①(柴油机在换气过程中由进气门进入的)扫气空气(= scavenging air,将汽缸内的废气扫出排气门的空气)②扫气空气量(=总进空气量-实际充气量)

scavenge area 扫气面积(如:扫气孔面积)

scavenge blower 扫气泵,扫气装置

scavenged air ratio 扫气比(指发动机每循环通过扫气口的新鲜充量与理想充量之比,理想充量是指在一定的进气温度和排气压力下,充满整个汽缸的新鲜充量,简称 SAR,亦称 scavenge ratio,简称 SR)

scavenge filter (发动机干油底壳式润滑系回油路中的)机油滤清器(在流回机油箱之前滤清其中的金属微粒和杂质)

scavenge flow (发动机)扫气气流

scavenge oil 废机油

scavenge oil pump (自动变速器的)回油泵(使壳体中的油液返回油箱的抽油泵)

scavenger 清洁剂,净化剂(如:①防积炭添加剂②四乙基铅抗爆剂中防止在发动机燃烧室生成氧化铅和硫酸铅的卤素元素等)

scavenger circuit 换油油路,清洗回路

scavenging ①清扫,清除②扫气(如:二冲程发动机利用新鲜充量将废气驱出汽缸的扫气)③扫气用的新鲜空气(= scavenging air)

scavenging air receiver 扫气箱(二冲程柴油机扫气口前储气的箱形部件)

scavenging by blower 扫气泵扫气(借助于扫气泵将空气压力升高,而实现扫气的方式)

scavenging duct 扫气通道(亦称 scavenge trunk)

scavenging duration 扫气持续期(扫气过程持续的时间,以曲轴转角表示)

scavenging efficiency 扫气效率,换气效率(换气终了后,汽缸内留有的新鲜充量的质量 Q_c 与此时汽缸内全部气体,即残留废气加新鲜充量的质量 Q_n 的比值,即:$\eta = \dfrac{Q_c}{Q_n}$)

scavenging engine (强制)扫气式发动机

scavenging machine 扫路机

scavenging period 扫气(时)期

scavenging port 扫气口

scavenging port area (扫)气口开度(二冲程内燃机扫气口开启的程度随时间变化的瞬时值。亦常把气口最大开度简称为气口开度)

scavenging pressure 扫气压力[扫气时进气门(口)前的充量压力]

scavenging process 扫气过程〔在二冲程或增压内燃机中，在进、排气门（口）同时开启时，利用新鲜充量，将汽缸内的废气从排气门（口）驱赶出去的过程〕

scavenging pump （任一种将不需要的废液、废气、悬浮杂质或污秽从系统中排出的）排出泵（亦称scavenge pump，如：①换气泵，扫气泵 ②干油底壳式润滑法中，将机油抽回油箱的回油泵，亦称scavenge plunger，见 dry sump lubrication）

scavenging stroke 扫气冲程，扫气过程

scavenging utilization efficiency 扫气利用系数〔亦称 trapping efficiency，指在一个工作循环中，实际留在汽缸内的充量与经过进气门（口）充量的质量比值。扫气利用系数与扫气系数互为倒数，见 coefficient of scavenging〕

scavenging with perfect mixing 完全混合扫气，完全扩散扫气（理论上的发动机的一种极限扫气形式，新鲜混合气进入汽缸后瞬间即与废气完全混合，而形成均一混合气排出缸外，= perfectly diffused scavenging）

SCB 〔英〕高速公路管理局（Speedway Control Board 的简称）

SCBC 智能型城市行驶制动支持系统（smart city brake support 的简称，在风窗玻璃上端装有雷达传感器，在市区行驶，如车速在 4~30km/h 的范围内检测前方车辆，当测出与前方车辆有碰撞的危险时，若驾驶者仍未踩踏制动踏板，该系统即自动制动车辆，以避免碰撞）

SCC 安全概念车（safety concept car 的简称）

scceleroting ability 加速性能

scenaio （规定试验过程及试验操作等的）试验大纲（意大利语，原意为电影剧本、剧情概要）

sceondary spring 副钢板弹簧

Scetre 〔美〕别克帝王（通用汽车公司 Buick 厂生产的普通型轿车，V6发动机，排量 3.5L，最大功率184kW）

schedule ①目录；一览表；时间表，进度表，计划表；日程；工艺过程，规范；制度；预定计划，程序，大纲 ②制定规范，制定时间表；编写进度表；预定，计划

schedule control 按图表控制

scheduled major overhaul 计划大修

scheduled oil sampling 机油定期抽样分析法（机器内的润滑油，定期取样分析、诊断机器内各部件的磨损情况，简称 SOS 法）

schedule table 调度表

schematize 用图解表示，图解示意

scheme ①设计，方案，计划，图表，线路图 ②编制计划，制订方案

Schering's bridge 西林电桥(用于测量塑料的绝缘性能)

Schlieren method 施利仑法（用于高速气流的观察、燃烧及爆发现象的摄影等的暗线照相法、纹影法）

schmatic diagram 示意图，简图，原理图（亦称 schematic drawing）

Schmitt trigger 施米特触发器（将模拟信号转换为数字信号）

Schnürle scavenging （二冲程发动机的）回流扫气（德国人 Schnürle 发明，见 loop scavenging）

school bus 学校客车，校用客车（按专门规定的设计标准制造的运送学生的客车）

school crossing sign （设置在学校区行人横道前的）学生过街标志

Schottky barrier 肖特基势垒（金属与半导体间具有非线性阻抗的界面层）

Schottky-barrier diode chip 肖特基势垒二极管片，片状肖特基势垒二

极管

Schrader valve （气密封系统）弹簧加载式止回阀（在一定压力下该阀才单向开放，如：汽车空调系统的轮胎气门式维修阀）

SCI 串行通信接口（指信息或数据一个接一个地或连续通过该接口输入或输出，serial communication interface 的简称）

scintillation spectrometer 闪烁谱仪（简称 SS）

Scirocco "热风"牌轿车（德国大众汽车公司 Volkswagen，1975 年开始生产，销路极广，scirocco 为德文中的意大利语源词，schirokko，原意指地中海中常刮的西南热风）

scission ①分裂，分离，裂开②切断，剪断③裂变

scissors-like 剪刀形的，剪刀状的

scissors-type jack 剪式千斤顶

S-class（**car**） 豪华级（轿车）

sclerometer 回跳硬度计，肖式硬度计（通过量测自一定高度落下的菱尖重物在金属材料等表面上的回跳高度，确定该材料的硬度，= scleroscope, Shore hardness tester, Shore sclerometer）

scleroscope hardness test 肖氏硬度试验（亦写作 scleroscopic hardness test）

SCM 单片式微处理器（single chip microprocessor 的简称）

scoch block （车轮的）垫楔木（防止车辆在斜坡上下滑）

SC-OFF （定速巡航系统的）车速控制-断开（speed control-off 的简称）

SC-ON （定速巡航系统的）车速控制-接通（speed control-on 的简称）

scoop ①铲斗，铲斗车②汽车车身前围上盖板上的）风斗（收集和引导外界空气供通风、冷却用的通风孔、口）

scoop loader 斗式装载机

scoop shovel 铲斗挖掘机

SCOOT 开环补偿优化技术（英国交通与道路研究所 TRRL 在 20 世纪 70 年代中期开发的一种实时操作的自适应交通控制系统，Split Cycle Offset Optimization technique 的简称，根据车辆到达交通路口的信息，实时调整绿信比等参数）

scope ①场所②出口③目标④视野，眼界，范围⑤观测设备⑥指示器，显示器⑦示波器，阴极射线管⑧分野，辖域

scope analyzer 示波分析器

scope screen 示波器屏幕

score ①（表面）擦伤，刻痕，记号②[复] 许多，记数，理由，根据③二十④画线器，画线用两脚规

SCORE 见 Supplier Cost Reduction Effort

scored surface 擦伤面

scoring 刮伤（摩擦表面沿滑动方向形成宽而深的刮痕的现象）

scoring resistance 抗擦伤能力

scoring susceptibility （表面的）易擦伤性

scoring test （齿轮等啮合面间的）擦伤试验，（润滑油等的）抗擦伤试验，划痕试验

scotopic adaptation （视觉）暗适应（力）（= dark adaptation）

scotopic vision 暗视觉（当眼睛适应低于 10^{-3} cd/m^2 亮度时，主要由视网膜的杆体细胞起作用的视觉。暗视觉只有明暗感觉而无颜色感觉）

scotopic vision 暗处视力，暗处视觉（指在很微弱的光线下的视力）

Scotsma's sixth 下坡脱挡滑行（一般指货车，美称 Mexican overdrive）

Scott volumeter 斯可特容量计（测量粉末散装密度的装置）

Scot type clutch 斯考特磁粉离合器

scour ①擦到，擦光，擦净；冲刷；扫清；洗刷；洗涤；清除；打磨

②腐蚀，烧蚀③去锈；扫除；洗涤④刮伤，擦伤，刻伤

scouring ①擦洗，冲洗，洗刷②腐蚀③刮伤，擦伤，划痕，刻痕（如：轮胎胎侧式胎面擦伤）

scout carrier 侦察车，勘探车

scout vehicle 巡逻车

SCP 标准共用协议（美国汽车工程师协会标准"SAE J1850"规定的网络通信协议，近年来已为 CAN 取代）

SCR ①可控硅整流元件，可控硅整流器，可控硅（Silicon Controlled Rectifier 的简称）②选择催化还原（selective catalytic reduction 的简称）

scram ①紧急关闭②紧急制动

scrap ①废料，切屑②废弃，报废

scrape 刮痕，刮削，擦伤，擦痕

scrape against 擦过（= scrape past）

scrape away 刮掉，擦去，挖空（= scrape off, scrape out）

scraped car 报废车

scraper ①（活塞）油环（= oil control ring）②刮刀③铲运机，刮土机

scraper ring 刮油环，油环（简称 scraper, = oil control ring, oil scraper ring）

scraper seal 带刮片的密封圈

scraper-type loading machine 刮板式装载机，刮板式装货机

scrape the ing 刮轴瓦，刮瓦

scrapped age 汽车报废年限，汽车报废寿命

scrapped parts 报废零件

scrap value （设备等的）废旧价值（达到规定有用年限后的价值，亦称 second hand value, salvage value）

scratch hardness 刮测硬度，刮痕硬度

scratch hardness tester 刮痕硬度计

scratching 擦伤（摩擦表面沿滑动方向形成细小擦痕的现象），刮痕

scratch oil test 刮擦法油膜强度试验

scratch-pad（memory） 便笺式存储器，高速暂存存储器

SCR converter 选择性催化还原转化器（selective catalytic reduction converter 的简称）

SCR downstream aftertreatment device（装在排气尾管内净化 NO_X 的）选择性催化还原下游后处理器（见 SCR）

screen ①滤网，网，筛子②挡板，遮板③百叶窗，帘子④屏幕，荧光屏⑤（车厢内各区间的）透明隔板⑥空气偏流板，导流板⑦窗玻璃（如：后窗玻璃 "backlight glass"，风窗玻璃 "windscreen"）⑧（交通调查）流向线交织图⑨筛选，筛分⑩遮蔽，屏蔽

screened condenser 屏蔽电容器，防干扰电容器

screened housing 保护壳，屏蔽罩，隔离室

screened ignition cables 屏蔽点火高压电线

screened resistance 屏极电阻

screened spark（ing）plug 屏蔽式火花塞〔= shielded spark（ing）plug, shrouded spark（ing）plug〕

screened valve 导流屏式气门（= masked valve）

screen glass 风窗玻璃（= windshield glass）

screening 筛选（为了检测并剔除潜在的失效，对一批生产的全部产品所做的检验或试验）

screening test 筛选试验（为选择具有一定特性或剔除早期失效的产品而进行的试验）

screen perforation 网状孔，网孔

screen pillar 风窗玻璃立柱

screen printing ①丝网印刷（通过细目丝网将某种材料涂覆在基板上的印刷工艺）②漏模印刷

screen printing technique 丝网印刷

工艺（把浆料通过丝网压印到基片上形成膜的淀积过程）
screen protected enclosure （机器的）筛网形保护罩，筛网形安全罩（防止手指等接触内部机件）
screen side body truck 有固定顶篷，但侧面为金属网状的箱式载货汽车
screen velocity 通过网筛状物（如：散热器的百叶窗）的空气流速
screen washer 窗玻璃清洗器（如：windshield washer）
screen wiper 窗玻璃刮水器
screw ①螺钉②螺旋桨；螺旋状物体③用螺钉拧紧；拧紧；扭转
screw-and-nut steering gear 螺杆螺母式转向机（= screw-and-double nut steering gear, worm-and-double nut steering gear, worm-and-nut steering gear）
screw bolt 螺栓
screw brake 螺旋制动器
screw bushing 螺纹衬套（带螺纹的衬套）
screw cap ①螺纹盖②螺旋头
screw clamp 螺纹夹，螺旋夹紧装置
screw clip 螺纹夹，螺纹夹箍
screw driver ①螺钉旋具（螺丝刀，螺丝起子）②［美俚］不能把车开直的人，开车蛇行的人
screw driver cap 扳手帽（具有装卸气门芯作用的防护帽）
screw driver for hexagon insert bits 六角套筒螺钉旋具
screw driver for recessed head screws (with double offset) 双弯头十字槽螺钉旋具
screw driver for slotted head screws (with double offset) 双弯头一字槽螺钉旋具
screw driver slot （螺钉头上的）起子槽，旋具槽
screw driver with flared sides 夹柄螺钉旋具

screwed hole 螺纹孔
screwed joint 螺（纹套）管接头，螺栓接头
screw (ed) plug 螺纹塞，螺塞
screw extractor 断头螺钉取出器
screw eye 螺纹孔
screw fastener 螺纹紧固件
screw fastening 螺纹紧固
screw feed grease cup 螺盖加压给油式滑脂杯
screw gauge 螺纹规（= thread gauge）
screw gauge for taper thread 锥形螺纹量规
screw gear 螺旋齿轮，螺旋齿轮传动
screw helicoid 阿基米德螺旋面（动直线以恒定的角度与一条固定的直线相交，并沿此轴线方向作等速移动时，又绕此轴线作等角速的旋转运动，此动直线在固定空间内的运动轨迹称阿基米德螺旋面）
screw-in thread mounted type 螺纹安装式（如：螺纹安装式喷油器）
screw jack 螺旋千斤顶
screw nut 螺母
screw of cross recessed head 十字槽头螺钉
screw-pitch gage 螺距量规
screw plug gauge 螺纹塞规
screw pressure lubricator 螺旋压力（加油）润滑器
screw wheel 涡轮（= worm wheel）
screw with diamond knurls 菱形滚花头螺钉
screw with internal serrations 内多角螺钉
screw with straight-line knurls 直线滚花头螺钉
screw wrench 活动扳手（= adjustable wrench）
screwy 螺旋形的
scribe 画线

scriber 画线器,划针,划片具
scribing calipers 内外卡钳
scribing compasses 画线规
scribing tire 胎面上有中心线的轮胎(使前束容易调整)
scroll ①涡卷,涡卷形物件(如涡形管等)②旋涡③涡状的④(液力度矩器叶先的)色角(设计流线与叶先进、出口边变点处的两个轴平回倾夹的角)
scroll area (废气涡轮增压器的)涡轮废气通道横截面积(该面积 A 与该通道中心与涡轮轴中心距离 R 的比值 A/R 越小,增压器特性越呈低速型)
scroll case 蜗壳
scroll compressor 涡旋式(制冷)压缩机(用于汽车空调系统)
scroll cover (水泵、风扇等的)螺旋形壳盖
scroll end type 两端卷耳型(钢板弹簧)
scrub 擦洗,擦净,洗涤,洗刷,清洗,洗涤
scrubbing ①刮擦,擦伤②擦洗
scrub radius 磨胎半径(指转向轴线或转向主销轴线延长线落地点与车轮接地面纵向中心线间的距离)
scrub wear (胎面)啃胎磨损,擦地磨损;摩擦磨损
scrutineering ①(仔细)检查,彻查,审查,复查②(赛前)检车(拉力赛比赛前由法定检车人检查所登记的赛车安全设备是否合格,并对赛车上的有关设备贴上封条,防止非法修,检查其技术改装是否符合允许的范围等,亦称 scrutinizing)
SCS ①稳定燃烧系统(stabilized combustion system)②防滑系统(slip control system)③稳定性控制系统(stability control system 的简称)

SCS system 转速控制真空点火提前系统(speed-controlled spark system 的简称,亦称 speed sensitive spark advance control,作用与 TCS system 相似)
scuffed tire 胎面擦伤的轮胎
scuffing ①(带卷边部的)折皱变形②(齿轮等)咬接、划伤现象③表面产生塑性变形④刮伤,拉毛,擦伤,擦伤造成的磨损
scuffing of cylinder bore 拉缸
scuffing temperature 摩擦面擦伤临界温度(超过此温度即易发生胶合、咬接等现象)
scuffing test (摩擦面)擦伤试验
scuff resistance 抗擦伤性,耐刮伤性
scuff resistant coating 防擦伤、咬死的覆盖层
sculptural 雕刻的,雕塑的,刻蚀的
scum cock 放浮沫旋塞(= foam cock,参见 surface blow off cock)
scum rubber 泡沫橡胶
scupper 溢流口,排水口
S curve ①S 形弯道②S 形曲线
scuttle ①天窗,孔窗,窗孔,小窗②(轿车客厢和长头货车驾驶室及前排座乘员的)腿脚区(位于客厢或驾驶室前下方与发动机舱相隔)③(有时亦指)前围上盖板(scuttle panel 的简称,见 cowl③)
scuttle bulkhead (轿车车身的)前围板(见 bulkhead②)
scuttle-mounted 装在(轿车车身)前围上盖板上的(见 cowl③)
scuttle panel 前围上盖板(见 cowl③)
scuttle section (车身的)前围上盖板总成(指风窗立柱—前围上盖板,发动机舱与客厢或驾驶室间的隔板总成)
scuttle ventilation 前围上盖板通风口(亦称 scuttle ventilator, = cowl ventilator)

SCV 涡流控制（进）气门（swirl control valve 的简称，丰田公司汽油直接喷射、双进气道发动机汽缸的副进气门。高、中速运转时开启，在汽缸内形成纵向涡流，燃烧均质混合气，低速运转时该副进气门关闭，仅主进气门开启，在汽缸内形成横向涡流，实现使用空燃比为 30～40 的超稀薄混合气的层状燃烧）

SCVAC solenoid 控制车速的真空执行机构的真空通路控制电磁阀（该电磁阀控制通向真空式车速控制执行机构的真空通路，speed control vacuum control solenoid 的简称）

SCVNT solenoid 控制车速的真空执行机构的大气通路控制电磁阀（speed control vacuum vent solenoid 的简称，该电磁阀控制通向真空式车速控制执行机构的大气通路）

SD ①（美国 API 滑油分类中的）轻级 D 类（滑油）（适用于货车汽油机，性能较 SC 级优良，见 service class）②半径（semi-diameter）③施工详图，加工图（shop drawing）④滑动门（sliding door）⑤点火延时（spark delay）⑥火花放电器（spark discharger）⑦专门任务（special duty）⑧结构细节（structural detail）⑨标准偏差，标准离差，（平）均（平）方偏差（standard deviation）

SDC³ 富士重工的动态底盘控制概念（Subaru Dynamic Chassis Control Concept 的简称，使用高强度材料实现车身的高刚度和轻量化，确保汽车优异的操控性和行驶稳定性）

SDIMEP 平均指示有效压力的标准偏差（standard deviation of indicated mean effective pressure 的简称）

SDLC 同步数据链路控制（IBM 的一种通信线路规程，synchronous data link control 的简称）

SD screw 自攻螺钉（= self-drilling screw）

SDV 点火延迟阀（spark delay valve）

SE ①（美国 API 滑油分类的）轻级 E 类（滑油）（适用于客货车汽油机，质量较 SD 级高，参见 service class）②二次发射，次级发射（secondary emission）③维修设备；服务装置（service equipment）④声响效应（sound effect）⑤特殊设备（special equipment）⑥标准差（standard error）⑦系统工程（system engineering）

Se 硒（selenium）

SEA （构造物内振动能量传递、振动强度等的）统计能量解析法（statistical energy analyses 的简称）

sea bottom vehicle 海底车辆（简称 SBV，亦称 seabed work vehicle）

sea-going parking garage 汽车海运船；汽车渡（海）轮；（大型）海轮（上的）停车场；海上停车场

seal ①密封②封口，加封，嵌缝③密封件④铅封

sealability 可密封性

sealant ①（无内胎轮胎）气密层②密封材料，密封剂，衬垫涂料③密封流体（密封端面直接接触的高压侧流体。它可以是被密封介质本身、经过分离或过滤的被密封流体、冲洗流体或隔离流体）

seal area 密封区，密封面积

seal around pedal 踏板杆密封护套

seal band （密封件的）密封环带（较窄的那个密封端面外径 d_1 与内径 d_2 之间的环形区域）

seal bellow adaptor 波纹管座（轴向联结并定位波管的零件）

seal boot 防尘密封套

seal cartridge 密封衬套

seal casing 油封壳，密封箱，密封壳体

seal chamber 密封腔体（直接包容密封腔的静止壳体）

seal coat 密封面层，密封涂层，密封覆盖层
seal cover cap 密封盖
seal durability 密封件耐久性，密封件使用寿命
sealed 密封的，封口的，铅封的
sealed ball bearing 密封式球轴承
sealed beam headlight 封闭式前照灯（使用封闭式灯光组成的前照灯，其配光镜、反射镜和灯丝熔合密封成一个不可拆式光学整体件，亦称 sealed beam unit）
sealed beam unit 封闭式灯光组（配光镜、反射镜和光源熔合密封的不可拆的光学组件）
sealed bearing （在制造厂已加满润滑脂，然后密封，在使用期间无须润滑的）密封式轴承
sealed cap 密封盖，闭式盖
sealed cooling （system）闭路冷却（系）（见 closed cooling system）
sealed crankcase ventilation 封闭式曲轴箱通风（简称SCV）
sealed fluid coupling 封闭式液力耦合器
sealed-for-life vane pump 终生密封式叶片泵
sealed housing method for evaporative emission determination 密闭室测定蒸发排放物法（简称SHED，指在密闭室内测定汽车全部蒸发排放物的方法）
sealed medium 被密封介质（需要加以密封的工作介质）
sealed mounted 密封安装的
sealed-off 脱封，拆封的
sealed package 密封包装
sealed plug 封闭式电热塞（= sheathed plug）
sealed vehicle 车身密封的车辆
sealer ①密封件，密封器②密封胶剂
sea level 海平面
sea level engine 低海拔用发动机

sea-level horsepower 海平面功率
seal face 密封端面（密封环在工作时与另一个密封环相贴合的端面，该端面通常是研磨面）
seal friction loss 密封件摩擦损失
seal head （密封件的）补偿环组件（由补偿环、弹性补偿元件和副密封等构成的组合件）
seal in 封入
sealing article of rubber 橡胶密封件［用于防止流体从被密封装置中泄漏，并防止外界灰尘、泥沙以及空气（对于高真空而言）进入被密封装置内部的橡胶零部件］
sealing cap 密封帽（有密封作用的防护帽）
sealing compound 封口胶，密封膏，密封剂
sealing element 密封件
sealing lip （油封等密封件的）密封唇，密封边
sealing load 密封压力（密封垫的压紧力）
sealing strip of rubber 橡胶密封条（与接触物体表面产生接触压力起密封作用的条形密封件）
seal interface 密封界面（一对相互贴合的密封端面之间的交界面）
seal ring 密封环（机械密封中其端面垂直于旋转轴线且相互贴合并相对滑动的两个环形零件均称密封环）
seal sticking 密封件黏结（现象）
seal strip 密封条
seal swell 橡胶密封件（因受油、液浸泡而）膨胀
seal's wiping action （转子发动机的）径向密封片刮扫作用（指刮扫外旋轮线缸壁）
seal tip epitrochoidal path （转子发动机的）径向密封片顶端外旋轮线轨迹（指密封片与缸壁接触点的外旋轮线轨迹）

seal tip sliding velocity （转子发动机的）径向密封片尖端滑动速度，刮片尖端滑速度（相对于旋轮线缸壁）

seal tip wear （转子发动机）径向密封片尖端磨损

seal weld 密封焊

seal with metal shell 带金属外壳的油封

seal with U packing U形垫密封

seam ①缝；接缝；裂缝②裂开口，生裂缝；生皱纹

seamed pipe 有缝管（相对无缝管而言）

seamless ①无缝的②无中断的（指无中断、连续对接乘坐汽车、火车、飞机等不同类型的交通工具到达目的地，如 BMW 公司提出的 Seamless Intermodal Routing Service "选择最合适的各种不同的交通工具无停滞地对接到达目的地的出行路线选择服务"）

SEA model 统计能量分析模型（SEA 为 statistical energy analysis 的简称，预测复杂结构、特别是其高频区的噪声和振动的有力工具，广泛应用于大型壳状结构，近年来引入汽车工业，对车身的振动与噪声进行分析，21 世纪初，开始试用于发动机结构早期设计分析）

search 搜索，探索，调查，（计算机）觅数，检索

search engine 搜索引擎（从数据库或计算机网络，特别是互联网检索文件或数据的计算机软件）

searchlight 探照灯，聚光灯

searchlight vehicle 探照灯车（装有探照灯的车辆）

seashore freeway 沿海岸的高速公路（＝bayshore freeway）

seasonal maintenance 季节性维护（为使汽车适应季节变化而实施的维护）

seasonal oil change 季节性换润滑油

season cracking 老化开裂，自然开裂，风干裂缝，季裂（如：冷加工的黄铜管等在存放或使用中多产生这类裂纹）

seasoning 时效，时效处理，干燥处理，老化

Seat （西班牙）西特（公司、德国大众控股）

seat ①座椅，座位②座（支承或座合面，如：气门座，轴承座、钢板弹簧座等）③（活塞环与汽缸壁的）贴合面

seat adjustment control 座椅调节操纵件（调节座椅相对于车体作线位移或角位移机构的手操纵件，如：座位调节手柄"seat adjusting handle"）

seat adjustment motor 座位移动电动机（驱动座位移动机构的电动机）

seat angle ①（气门座等的）工作面锥角②（钢板弹簧）座角（＝spring seat angle）

seat armrest height （座椅的）肘靠高度

seat back ①座位靠背②（车身）后座靠背板（＝squab）

seat belt 安全带（将乘员约束在座椅上的安全装置，亦称 safety belt）

seat-belt anchorage （汽车乘员）安全带栓扣，安全带固定装置

seat belt grabber 安全带防松装置

seat belt guider 安全带导向件

seat belt pretensioner 座椅安全带预紧装置（亦称作 seat belt pre-tensioner）

seat belt pretensioner and force limiter 安全带的预紧和收紧力限制装置

seat belt pre-tensioning function （乘员）安全带预紧功能

seat belt tensioner （汽车乘员）座椅安全带收紧装置

seat belt utilization detector （汽车

用）安全带戴挂检查仪（检查安全带是否挂牢的传感器）

seat belt warning tell-tale 安全带警报灯（警告某个乘员的座椅安全带没有挂好的信号灯）

seat bottom channel 载货汽车车厢两侧可放下和撑起的长条木板椅的槽形底梁

seat box 座椅下面的箱子

seat buck ①（汽车）车身内部造型的全尺寸实物模型②汽车座位式样的全尺寸实物模型（亦称 seating buck）

seat-capacity （客车）客座容量，座位数

seat central plane 座椅中心平面

seat cutter 气门座修整刀具，气门座口绞刀（= seat reamer）

seated ①落座的②座面贴合的

seated knee level （汽车车身、驾驶室等的乘员）坐膝高度

seat guide rail 座椅导轨（= seat rail, seat track）

seat heater 座椅取暖器，座椅加热器

seat height 座椅高（在座椅中心平面上，座垫上表面最高点至地板的高度）

seat hing 可翻转座椅的铰链

seating ①落座，（阀门，密封面）座合②（阀门）密封面，支撑面③研磨（密封面）

seating accommodation 座舱，乘坐室，客舱，客厢

seating arrangement 座位布置

seating force （气门等的）座合压力，座合力

seating height of the insulator （火花塞）绝缘体裙部长度

seating reference point （人机工程学的）（乘员）坐姿基准点，座椅参考点（简称 SRP）

seating rim （灯玻璃的）座圈

seating space 座椅布置间隔

seating surface 支撑面，贴合面，座面

seat-kilometer 客（座）公里

seat lift adjuster switch 座椅升高调节开关

seat-mounted side airbag 装在座椅上的（防）侧面（碰撞）安全气囊

seat pan （轿车车身安装座椅的）盘形底板（见 front floor pan, rear floor pan）

seat pan load cell 座椅底板负荷传感器（测试汽车平顺性等特性时安装于座椅底板处，简称 SPLC）

seat pillar 座椅立柱

seat reamer （气门）座绞刀，气门座修整绞刀

seat recess 镶气门座的沉肩

seat-tire frequency ratio 座椅-轮胎振动频率比

seat upholstery 座椅蒙皮饰物

seat warmer （汽车）座椅取暖器；座椅加温器

SEBS 苯乙烯-乙烯-丁烯-苯乙烯（styrene-ethylene-butylene-styrene 的简称，苯乙烯系热可塑性弹性材料，具有橡胶般的弹性、易于成型、耐天候、耐水、耐酸碱）

seclusion 隔离

second ①第二的，二等的，第二次的②秒（= 1/60）③弧（度）秒（= 1/3600 弧度）④（流体黏度单位）秒（见 Saybolt seconds 及 Redwood risco meter）

second ①秒②第二③次等的，劣等的，从属的，辅助的

secondary 第二的，二次的；从属的，副的；补充的；辅助的；次等的，次要的，次级的；再生的，二代的

secondary air 二次空气（①在燃气轮机燃烧器中一般是先导入较少量的空气进行燃烧，称为一次空气。

此后为了使燃烧完全而导入的空气称为二次空气。二次空气由一次燃烧区后部的多个小进气孔缝导入 ②在排气净化系统中，则指送入排气管、后燃器或双床式催化转化器等的新鲜空气，促进废气中的 HC、CO 氧化）

secondary air control valve 二次空气控制阀（根据发动机的运转工况，控制二次空气进气量的阀）

secondary air distribution manifold 二次空气分配歧管（将二次空气分配到各个排气口的歧管）

secondary air diverter valve 二次空气转换阀（为了防止汽车减速时排气管放炮，在减速时立即暂时中止供给二次空气，并将它排到大气或者送入进气总管的阀门，见 secondary air switching valve）

secondary air injection relief valve 二次空气喷射减压阀（限制喷射空气最大供给压力的阀。通常与二次空气泵或二次空气转换阀组成一体）

secondary air injection system 二次空气喷射装置（将二次空气喷入排气系统的整套装置）

secondary air injection tube 二次空气喷射管［一种附加在排气歧管或汽缸盖（体）排气道内的管子，此管将二次空气分配歧管来的空气射向排气阀附近］

secondary air pressure sensor 二次空气压力传感器

secondary air pump 二次空气泵（用以供给二次空气的泵）

secondary air supply 二次空气供给系统（指废气后处理净化系统中，供给新鲜空气促进废气中 HC、CO 氧化的系统，简称 SAS）

secondary aluminium 再生铝

secondary available voltage 次级有效高压（在规定的条件下，在火花塞连接处可以利用的最小电压）

secondary axis ①副轴②副轴线

secondary balance （曲轴）二级惯性力平衡装置

secondary barrel （化油器）次级腔

secondary battery 蓄电池，二次（蓄）电池（放电后可多次充电使用的电池总称，＝secondary cell, storage battery）

secondary brake 第二制动器（指除行车制动器以外的各种制动装置，如：驻车制动器，缓速制动器，应急制动器，气压系气压不足时的弹簧安全制动器，发动机制动器等各种辅助制动装置）

secondary brake shoe （鼓式制动器的）第二蹄（指摩擦面朝向汽车后方安装的制动蹄。若该蹄张开时的转动方向与制动鼓正向旋转时的旋转方向相反，则亦称从蹄"reverse 或 trailing brake shoe"）

secondary brake system 第二制动系统，副制动系统，紧急制动系统（＝emergency brake system）

secondary breakdown voltage 二次击穿电压

secondary cable （点火系）次级线，高压线

secondary carbon 仲碳（原子）

secondary carburetor 次级化油器，二级化油器（两级化油器在高速、大负荷下参加供油的第二级，亦称 secondary side，见 two-stage carburetor）

secondary cell 二次电池，蓄电池（放电后可以重新充电的电池总称，＝storage battery，英国亦称 accumulator）

secondary circuit 二次电路，次级电路（如：发动机点火系中的高压电路）

secondary clearance 二次间隙，副间隙

secondary coil 次级线圈，高压线圈

secondary controller (在主控制机控制下的)二级控制机,副控制机

secondary creep 第二阶段蠕变(蠕变恒速段)

secondary crush zone (车辆碰撞中的)二次挤压区

secondary cup (串列双腔制动主缸中,由液压推动的)第二活塞的皮碗(secondary piston cup 的简称)

secondary current (点火系的)次级电流(点火线圈次级绕组感生的高压点火脉冲电流)

secondary diagonal 次对角线

secondary diaphragm ①第二膜片 ②推迟膜片(见 retard diaphragm)

secondary earth 次级接地,次级线圈搭铁

secondary (emergency) braking control 紧急制动器操纵件(使车辆紧急减速或停车的装置的操纵件)

secondary emission ratio 二次发射系数

secondary failure ①第二次的损坏 ②二次性(从属性)故障(由于另一部件失效引起的失效)

secondary filter 次级滤清器,细滤器

secondary flame front 第二火焰前锋,副火焰前锋(出现在汽油发动机表面点火继燃现象时,见 post ignition)

secondary flow 引射流,感应流,副流,二次流(圆筒器中的流体作回转运动时,除了同心圆主流的流体以外,在容器底面产生半径方向的流线,这两股流合成而形成向着中心的螺旋流,此时,半径方向的流称为副流或二次流)

secondary flywheel 副飞轮,辅助飞轮

secondary focal point 次焦点

secondary fuel filter 燃油次级滤清器,燃油细滤器

secondary gear ①(凸轮轴上的)分电器(驱动)齿轮(= distribution gear) ②凸轮轴正时齿轮(= camshaft timing gear)

secondary gear shaft (变速器)中间轴(= intermediate shaft)

secondary idle-hole 怠速过渡油孔(= bypass idle-hole)

secondary image 副像(指透过玻璃观察时,远处的光源被看成明亮的本像连着至少一个略暗的影像的现象。这种影像或幻影是虚像,常见之于夜间透过玻璃观察一个与周围环境相比非常明亮的物体,如:迎面驶来的汽车的前灯)

secondary image separation (车窗玻璃产生的)副像分离

secondary inertia 二次惯性的,二级惯性力

secondary inertia force (发动机)二级惯性力

secondary injection 二次喷油(①在喷油过程,第一次喷油即主要喷油后,针阀已落座,由于油路中的压力振荡和针阀落座反弹等引起针阀第二次开启而少量喷油的现象 ②在喷油泵下一个工作循环开始之前又出现一次不需要的燃油喷射现象)

secondary inlet port (转子发动机的)副进气口,副进气孔(参见 two stage induction system)

secondary lithium-sulfur battery 二次锂硫蓄电池

secondary machining (粉末冶金制件等的)二次机械加工

secondary outage voltage 次级输出电压(在规定的条件下,高压电源输出端可利用的电压)

secondary piston 第二活塞(如:串列双腔式制动主缸中,由液压推动的活塞)

secondary pulley ①(传动带式传动

系统中的）从动轮（亦称 driven pulley）②见 CVT steel belt puller

secondary（reciprocating inertia）couple ①发动机二级往复惯性力矩（二级往复运动惯性力对质心的力矩，随二倍曲轴转速变化，使发动机失去平衡、绕水平方向或垂直方向与曲轴成 90°角的轴线振动）②（在所涉及的内部中有两个或两个以上往复惯性力矩时的）第二力矩

secondary reciprocation inertia force （发动机往复运动件惯性质量产生的）二次往复惯性力（二阶往复惯性力为旋转矢量。沿汽缸轴线，随 2 倍曲轴转速即曲轴每转半周，按余弦规律变化一次的曲轴轴线任一平面内的不平衡力）

secondary road 次要道路（= by road）

secondary safety design of vehicle 车辆的第二安全设施（指车辆碰撞时，防止乘员受伤，保护乘员安全的措施，如：驾驶室等的抗撞设计，乘员安全带、安全座椅等装置，= passive safety design）

secondary seal 副密封（由能够伴随补偿环做轴向移动并起密封作用的弹性零件与相关零件所构成的密封环）

secondary sealing area 第二密封面，副密封面（如：常规发动机活塞环与环槽之间的密封面，转子发动机径向密封片与转子角顶密封片槽之间的密封面，见 primary sealing area，有时也指第二道环与缸壁间的接触面）

secondary seat 副座

secondary shield 二次屏蔽，二次遮蔽

secondary shoe ①［美］（鼓式制动器的）从蹄（指其张开时的转动方向与制动鼓旋转方向相反的制动蹄，从车前方观察是领从蹄式制动器中的第二个蹄片，故称 secondary）②（双蹄式鼓式制动器的）第二蹄（指按汽车行进方向的后蹄，其蹄片一般较前蹄——第一蹄长）

secondary signal 第二信号，次级信号

secondary squish velocity 副挤压速度；二次挤压速度（如：转子发动机中，转子工作面凹坑的气体挤压速度）

secondary stage port （转子发动机的）副进气口、副进气孔（= secondary inlet port）

secondary stress 次级应力，副应力

secondary sun gear （行星变速器）第二排太阳轮；第二级行星传动太阳轮

secondary terminals （点火线圈）次级绕组接线柱

secondary venturi （双重喉管化油器中与大喉管同轴线的）小喉管（亦称 auxiliary venturi）

secondary vibration 簧下质量的振动（指不由悬架承载的质量的据动，= unsprung mass vibration）

secondary voltage 次级（绕组）电压

secondary voltage rise time 次级电压上升时间（在规定的条件下，次级电压从某一值上升到另一值所需的时间，以 μs 表示）

secondary winding （点火线圈的）次级绕组（一般使用直径很细的导线缠绕 20～30 圈）

secondary winding impedance 次级绕组阻抗

secondary wires （点火系次级电路中的）高压线

second-best 次好的，仅次于最好的，居第二位的

second car 副车，第二轿车（一般指具有 2～3 辆轿车的家庭中专门为

采购生活用品等用的轿车)
second-class roads ①二级道路②次要道路
second clutch 第二离合器
second converter phase (两相、多元件液力变矩器的) 第二变矩相, 第二变矩器相 (指液力变矩器在第一导轮元件随泵轮同方向旋转, 而其余导轮元件固定不动的情况下工作, 输出转矩与输入转矩之比仍大于1, 但较第一变矩相小, 参见 first converter phase)
second cut (锉刀的) 细锉纹
second cut file 细锉 (简称 2nd cut file, 参见 coarseness of file)
second derivative control 按二阶导数控制 (如: 按加速度控制)
second gear (变速器) 第二挡
second gear torque 第二挡转矩
second generation 第二代
second-generation analog merging controller 第二代模拟型 (交通) 合流控制机
second generation anti-skid braking system 第二代防滑制动系 (指考虑路面状态的防滑制动系)
second generation electronic engine control system (福特公司的) 第二代发动机电子控制系统 (简称 EECII, 该系统由微型电子计算机控制, 根据进气温度、进气管压力、大气压力、节气门开度、冷却水温、曲轴位置及废气氧传感器的信号控制空燃比、二次空气量、点火正时、怠速等)
second-hand car 旧车, 二手车
second harmonic 二次谐波
second lane 第二车道 (多车道道路中, 靠左行驶时为前进方向从左起的第二车道, 靠右行驶时为前进方向从右起的第二车道)
second law of motion 第二运动定律 (即牛顿第二运动定律, $F = ma$, F 为力, m 为质量, a 为加速度)
second line of seal 第二道密封线, 辅助密封线
second 10, 000 miles test 第二个一万英里行车试验 (一种规定的汽车路试)
second-motion engine 带减速器的发动机 (= geared engine)
second order lag element 二次滞后 (控制) 元件
second order transfer function 二阶传递函数
second oxygen sensor 第二氧传感器 (亦称后置氧传感器、下游氧传感器, 装在催化转化器的出口端, 见 pullutant emission sensor)
second parts 旧件
second piston land (第一道和第二道活塞环槽间的) 第二槽岸
second-ring groove 第二道活塞环槽
second sealing system (转子发动机的) 副密封系统, 第二套密封系统
second speed (变速器) 第二挡, 二挡
second-stage gear set (变速器) 二挡齿轮组
second stage of impact 汽车碰撞的第二阶段 (如: 在摆锤碰撞试验中, 碰撞的第二阶段即保险杠与摆锤碰撞面分离后保险杠回跳的阶段, 见 bumper lift)
sec Red. Ⅰ 雷氏Ⅰ型黏度秒 (seconds Redwood Ⅰ)
secret code 密码 (简称 SC, 亦称 secret key, 简称 SK)
section ①剖面, 断面, 截面②部分; 段, 地段; 区段
sectional area 截面面积 (简称 SA)
sectional arrangement drawing 装配剖视图, 剖面总装图
sectional automation 分段自动化
sectional casing 组合式外壳, 分段式壳体

sectional core of radiator 拼合型散热器芯子，组合式散热器芯子，分组的散热器芯子

sectional core radiator 分段拼装式散热器（= radiator with detachable sections）

sectional drive ①分段传动，分段驱动，分节驱动②多电机驱动

sectional flywheel 组合式飞轮

sectionalized tractor 组合式拖拉机，积木式拖拉机

section (al) plane 截面，断面

sectional rim 分段轮辋

sectional test track （铺设不同路面的）分段式试验跑道

sectional type inner tube 分腔式内胎

sectional type multi-speed transmission 分段式-多挡变速器（主变速器挡位间速比较小，副变速器有高低两挡）

sectional view 断面图，剖面图（亦称 sectional drawing, section drawing）

section gap 交通流间隔，车群间隔

section height （轮胎）断面高度（轮胎按规定充气后，外直径与轮辋名义直径之差的一半）

section line 剖面线

section modulus 截面模数

section steel 型钢（亦称 sectional steel, section iron, figured iron）

section width （轮胎）断面宽度（轮胎按规定充气后，两外侧之间的最大距离，不包括标志、装饰线和防擦线所增加的宽度）

sector ①扇形（扇件，如：扇形齿轮，扇形板等）②区段，部分

sector arm 扇形臂

sector conductor 扇形导体（= conducting sector）

sector for hand brake lever 驻车制动杆扇齿（驻车制动杆限位扇形齿板）

sector gear 扇形齿轮

sector of circle （圆的）扇形（部分）

sector shaft ①（齿条—齿扇式转向器的转向）摇臂轴（Pitman arm shaft 的一种）②扇形齿轮轴

sector worm 扇形蜗杆

secular change 经年变化，长年变化，缓慢变化，长期变化

secular equation 特征方程（= characteristic equation）

secure ①取得，得到，紧固，牢置②可靠的，牢靠的，安全的，保证的

Securi-lock （汽）防盗系统（商品名）

security 安全，可靠，保证，担保

security code （安全）保险码（简称 SC）

security control 安全控制，安全管理

sedan ［美］（带中柱，固定车顶，车门带窗玻璃框，前、后排间无隔壁的）三厢式四门轿车（=［英］saloon。见 4 door hardtop 和 pillared hardtop）

sedan-cabriolet 四门篷顶轿车

sedan delivery body 安装在轿车底盘上的送货用厢式车身

sedan-landau 车顶后部为活动顶篷的四门轿车

sedan landaulet 敞篷活顶四门小型轿车（=［英］saloon landaulet）

sedan-making plant 轿车制造厂

sediment 沉积物，沉渣，残渣

sediment and water test （柴油等的）机械杂质和水含量试验

sedimentation 沉淀，沉积，沉降

sedimentation bowl 沉淀杯，沉积滤杯（= sediment bulb, settling bowl, sediment cup）

sediment chamber ①沉淀室，沉淀腔（亦称 sediment trap）②沉淀盘

(= sediment pan)

sedimenter 沉淀杯，沉淀装置

sediment incrustation 积垢

SEEC 富士汽车排气净化系统（Subaru Exhaust Emission Control）

SEEC-T engine 富士汽车排气净化发动机（Subaru Exhaust Emission Control Technique engine）

seeded driver 种子车手（汽车拉力赛中，这一资格一般给以前取得过好成绩的车手，在比赛起步时，享有处于前排位置的权利，参见 rally）

SEED rally 大学生汽车改进经济性设计竞赛（Student Engineered Economy Design rally）

SEEE 安全，经济，节能，环保（Safety，Economy，Energy，Environment）（S3E）

seeing distance 视距（= sight distance）

seek 寻找，探测，发现，企图，调查，勘查，探索

seepage ①渗，渗漏渗透②渗滤

see-thru 透明的（see-through 的简称）

SEFI （福特公司的）电子控制式顺序燃油喷射系统（的商品名，sequential electronic fuel injection 的简称，见 SFI）

SEGAS 连续汽化（见 sequential gasification）

Seger cone 塞氏测热熔锥，塞格测温锥（见 pyrometric cone）

segment ①圆弧与弦间的面积②扇形板，整流子片③轴瓦

segmental arc 弧段

segmental gear 扇形齿轮（= segment gear，toothed segment）

segment bearing 多片瓦轴承

segment die 组合模，可拆卸模

segment display 段显示（用笔画组合进行的显示）

segmented cell 分段式电池

segmented current collector 分段式集电装置

segmented mica 换向器云母片

segment electrode 段电极（笔画形显示电极）

segregation ①隔离（或分离）措施②车流分道行驶（如：segregation of divese traffic 不同类型的车辆分道行驶；segregation opposed streams and turning traffic 对向车流和转弯的车辆分道行驶；③分凝，凝离④离析性）

segregator 析离器

seismic ①地震的②振动的（如：seismic mass 振动质量）

seize ①（滑动接触的两零件由于高温或缺油表面熔合、黏结而突然）卡死②（上述原因卡死造成的零件表面）拉伤，擦损（亦称 seize up，seizure）

seized piston 咬死了的活塞

seizing 咬死，卡住，卡滞，抓住

seizing of piston 活塞卡缸，活塞咬缸，活塞拉缸

seizing of piston ring 活塞环咬死

seizure ①咬黏（两摩擦表面因黏附和材料转移发生损坏、进而导致相对运动中止的现象）②见 seize

SEL 故障停机警告灯（自诊断系统发现有较严重故障，如：机油温度、冷却水温度等超过安全值时，发亮并伴有蜂鸣警报，提示驾驶人员发动机将自动减速并将在规定时间如 30 秒后停机的警告灯，以便车辆驶往安全停车点，stop engine light 的简称）

sel-dynamo 起动-充电两用电机（多用于机动二轮车，简称 sel-dy）

select 选择

selected class 所选类，所选定的级别

selected element （液晶显示）选择

点（在多路驱动中，扫描电极和信号电极同时施加驱动信号的像素）

Selec-Terrain （越野车的）不同地域和路况条件下最佳驱动和悬架减振模式的选择系统

selection by wheel （ABS 控制模式中的）车轮选择（指根据预先选定的某一个车轮的抱死信号来实施防抢死控制的 ABS）

selection high 高选控制（指防抱制动系统根据最后一个抱死的车轮的抱死信号来实施防抢死控制，亦称 select-high）

selection-low 低选控制（指防抱制动系统根据第一个抱死的车轮的抱死信号来实施防抢死控制，亦称 select-low）

selective assembly 选择装配，选配

selective beacon radar 选择性信标雷达（简称 SBR）

selective catalytic reduction 选择性催化还原（简称 SCR）

selective compartments side dumping 可选择的车箱分格侧向倾卸（可使车箱的某一部分侧向倾卸）

selective corrosion 选择性腐蚀（选择性的局部腐蚀）

selective exclusion sign 车种限制标志（在某道路及路段上，禁止特定车种或行人通行的标志）

selective fit 选择配合，选配合，选配

selective gear shifting 选择式换挡（= selective gear shift）

selective gear transmission 选择换挡式齿较变速器

selective hardening 选择性局部淬火（= selective quenching）

selective heating 选择性局部加热

selective interchangeability 选择互换性

selective lever （变速器）换挡杆（亦称 select lever）

selective reflection 选择性反射（光反射与波长有关的现象）

selective sampling 选择性采样

selective traffic enforcement program [美] 特定交通法规（强制）实施规程（简称 STEP）

selective 4WD 选择式四轮驱动（富士公司的分时四轮驱动系统的商品名，见 part-time 4WD）

selectivity 选择性，选择能力

selectivity control 选择性控制

selector ①选择装置，选择件（执行选择、挑选任务的装置、机构或机件的通称，如：变速器的挡位选择机构，或挡位选择机构中的某一机件。有的文献将变速器推动拨叉轴滑动的拨杆称为 selector，其拨头称 selector rod）②选择器，选择开关 ③（自动或半自动变速器的）选挡杆，变速杆变速器

selector bar （变速器）换挡拨叉杆（= gear shift bar）

selector button （变速）选择按钮（开关）

selector control lever （装在仪表板或转向盘上的各种）选择控制杆

selector fork （机械式变速器各挡位滑动齿轮或接合齿套的）挡拨叉（美称 shift fork，shift arm）

selector mechanism （机械式变速器的）变速操纵机构，变速机构（由驾驶员操纵的变速杆、变速器内的拨杆、拨叉总成等组成，通过拨动相应挡位的滑动齿轮或接合齿套，同步器等使各挡位齿轮啮合而实现换挡变速的机构）

selector rod （机械式变速器的）①换挡拨叉轴（安装拨叉的滑竿，亦称 selector bar，selector rail，shift rail，shift fork shaft，shift fork shaft，shift rod，striking rod）②（某些机械式变速器拨动换挡拨叉轴的）拨杆拨头（见 selector）

selector rod housing 变速器换挡机构壳体（= gear change control housing）

selector switch 选择开关

selector valve ①（泛指各种）选择阀②（自动变速器的）挡位选择阀，挡域选择阀（参见 manual valve）

select shift 选择换挡（相对于换挡杆顺着固定轨道顺序换挡而言的按钮换挡等）

Select-Shift （Ford）6挡手自一体变速器（商品名）

select terrain （某些SUV具有的）行驶地区模式选择（功能）

selenic photoelectric cell 硒光电管

selenium 硒（Se）

selenium cell 硒（质）光电管，硒（光）电池

selenium rectifier 硒整流器（= seletron）

selenizing 硒化

self-acting （系统或机构本身）自动的

self-acting clutch 自动离合器（如：达到某规定转速即自行离合的离合装置）

self-acting control 自动控制（指无须外力做功而自行控制的）

self-acting intermittent brake 自动间歇（防抱死）制动器

self-acting seal 自紧密封件

self-acting trailer coupling 挂车的自动联结器，自动拖挂装置，自动挂钩

self-acting travel 自动行程

self-acting valve 自动阀（如：当真空或压力达到某规定值时即自动开启或关闭的阀门）

self-action 自动，自作用

self-activation 自激活，自活化

self-actuated 自行的，自激的，自动的

self-actuating brake 自增力式制动器（= self-energizing brake）

self-adaptive fuzzy control 自适应模糊控制

self-adjustable shock absorber 自动调节式减振器（阻尼力可随使用条件，如：道路平整度、荷载的变化而自行改变的减振器）

self-adjusting apex seal （转子发动机转子）自调式径向密封片

self-adjusting brake 自调间隙型制动器

self-adjusting serpentine belt accessory drive system 自调式蛇形传动带附件传动系统

self-adjusting tappet 自调间隙式（气门）挺杆（如：液压挺杆）

self-aligning 自动定位的，自动找正的

self-aligning double-row ball bearing 双列自动调心球轴承

self-aligning effect （汽车转向轮等的）自回正效应

self-aligning rear axle suspension 摆式高度自调多轴后桥悬架

self-aligning release thrust bearing 自动调心式分离轴承（自动消除离合器旋转轴线与分离轴承的同轴度误差或角度偏差的轴承）

self-aligning torque （汽车转向轮等的）自回正力矩（使转向轮自动返回中间位置的力矩）

self-aligning torque power 见SATP

self-balancing instrument 自动平衡式计量器，自动平衡量测仪（自动进行零位法量测的各种仪具的通称）

self bias 自给偏压，自动偏移，自偏置，自偏流

self-bleeding （液压系统）自动排（出）气（体）

self-braking 自动制动，自行制动的

self-cancelling 自动取消（的），自

动抵消（的）

self-cancelling trafficator 自熄式转向指示灯（转向盘转回直前位置后，转向指示灯自动熄灭，亦称 self-cancelling direction indicator）

self capacity 固有电容，自身电容

self-centering 自动定心的，自动回中的，自调中心的

self-centering brake 自行调心式制动器，自动调心制动器（制动蹄不直接装在轴销上，而是用杆件连接成浮式，制动时制动蹄与制动鼓自然同心）

self-centering steering 自动回正转向机构（松开转向盘后，转向轮自动回正）

self circulation （密封的）自循环（法）（利用密封腔内泵效装置使密封流体形成闭合回路以改善密封件工作条件的方法）

self-cleaning oil filter 自洁式机油滤清器

self-cleaning temperature range （火花塞的）自洁温度范围

self-closing 自动闭合，自闭合，自动接通（简称 SELF CL）

self-closing valve 自动关闭阀（如：发生事故时自动切断油路的阀门）

self-combustible 会自燃的，易自燃的

self-combustion 自燃

self-compensating 自动补偿的

self-contained 装在一个容器或机壳内，自身装备齐全，无须辅助与配套设备，即可独立完成某项工作

self-control type （指无须电子控制模块发出指令由执行元件控制）器件本身即可自行控制的（如：self-control type heater plug）

self-co(u)lored 本色的，天然色的

self diagnosis 自诊断（在汽车电子计算机控制系统中：指计算机对其自身及其所控制的系统的故障进行检测和定位的过程，由电子控制模块按照诊断程序 diagnostic program 对整个系统进行跟踪性监测。当发现系统的任一硬件及硬件间的接线发生异常时，便会自动通过仪表板上的故障指示灯发出故障警报闪光信号，常用闪光次数显示故障性质及部位代码，同时可存储故障信息，以备维护时读取）

self-discharging trailer 自卸（式）挂车（= self-emptying trailer, self-unloading trailer）

self-discharging truck 自动卸货车

self-drilling screw 自攻螺钉（简称 SD screw，亦称 self-drilling tapping screw）

self-drive car （租来）自己驾驶的汽车

self-dumping truck 自动倾卸式货车（= dump truck）

self-energizing brake 自增力式制动器（= self-actuating brake）

self-equilizing suspension system 自平衡悬架系统，自补偿悬架系统

self excitation 自激发，自激，自激磁，自励磁

self-excited dynamo 自激电机（亦称 self exciter, self-exciting dynamo）

self-excited vibration 自激振动（= selfinduced vibration, self-sustained oscillation）

self-expanding piston ring （不用胀簧衬环的）自胀式活塞环

self-extinguish 自动灭火，自身熄火

self fastening safety belt 自动拉紧式安全带

self filling windscreen washer （汽车用）自充水式风窗玻璃洗涤装置（自动收集风窗玻璃上流下的雨水或洗涤液，经过滤清，充入洗涤液储存器中）

self-forced ventilated 自动通风的

self-hardening steel 自淬硬钢，空气

淬硬钢（如：高速切削钢等含 Ni、Cr、Mo、Mn 的合金钢。由高于变态点的温度开始置于空气中冷却，不经淬火，即可硬化）

self-holding 自动夹紧的

self ignition ①（可燃混合气）自燃（无直接火花或火焰点火而自燃）②（火花点火式发动机）继燃（断开点火电路后仍继续运转的现象，亦称 auto-ignition, dieseling, running-on）

self-ignition engine 压燃式发动机（= compression ignition engine）

self-ignition point 自燃点（亦称 self-ignition temperature）

self-increasing skidding moment （汽车制动时的）自增侧滑力矩（两后轮抱死时，汽车的惯性力成为前桥的推力。倘若汽车的荷载分配中心不在纵向中心线上，惯性力就会形成一个绕前桥中心回转的力矩，促使后轮侧滑，汽车偏转，该力矩称自增侧力矩，亦称自增偏转力矩"self-increasing turning moment"）

self-indexing starter 自动定位式起动机（带盘式离合器的四极四刷式起动机）

self-induced emf 自感电动势（电路本身电流变化而产生的感应电动势，参见 mutual inductance）

self-inductance 自感（电路中本身电流变化而产生自感电动势的现象，自感单位为 henry，参见 mutual inductance）

self-induction coil 自感线圈

self-inflating air pressure system （轮胎的）自动充气系统

self-learning function （电子控制系统的）自学功能（可根据本身的记忆或经验来修改程序及控制量，以适应计算结果或环境变化的要求的功能）

self-level（l）ing air suspension 自动高度调平式空气弹簧悬架（每一个悬架空气弹簧内的气压都可按照要求自动升降，以保证汽车在各种荷载和道路条件下其质心的纵横轴线均处于规定高度的平面上）

self-level（l）ing devices for headlamps （汽车）前照灯高度自动调平装置

self-level（l）ing shock absorber （车身高度）自动调平式减振器

self-level（l）ing suspension 高度自动调平悬架（亦称 automatic level control suspension）

self-level（l）ing twin headlamps （汽车）自动调平式双前照灯

self-lifting system ①（泛指各种）自动提升系统；自力举升系统 ②（特指多轴重型汽车重载车轮的）自动升降系统（满载时将该车轮放至地面，空载时将该车轮提起与地面脱离）

self-loading vehicle 自动装货式汽车

self-locking differential with dog clutch 自动离合式自锁差速器（采用啮合式离合器的自锁差速器，亦称 automotive positive locking differential）

self-locking differential with slide ring and radial cam plate 滑环—径向波状凸轮曲面板式自锁差速器（亦称 gearless differential）

self-locking differential with sliding and radial cam plate 凸轮滑块式自锁差速器（由内外凸轮和滑块构成的自锁差速器）

self lock（ing）nut 自锁螺母

self-locking steering gear 自锁转向装置，不可逆式转向器（= irreversible steering gear, irreversible steering assembly）

self-lubricant bearing alloy 自润滑型轴承合金（含油轴承合金，如：金属粉末，经混匀、压制、烧结成型，浸入一定温度的润滑油中而制

成的含油减摩合金材料)
self-lubricating property (石墨等材料制成零件的) 自润滑性能,自润性
self-measuring tank 自计量式(油)箱
self-metering oil system 滑油自计量系统
self-mounting tyre chain 自装式轮胎防滑链
self-moved 自行运动(的),自动推进的,自行的
self-moving vehicle 自动车(亦称 self-propelled vehicle,即:汽车。Dyke's汽车百科全书的定义为自带动力驱动的车辆。中国早期称汽车为自动车,日本至今仍称汽车为"自动车")
self-oil(-)feeder 自行加油设备,自动加注滑油器
self-oiling 自动加注滑油的,自行润滑的(=self lubrication)
self-opening 自动开启的
self-operated control 自动控制(操作部分动作所必需的能量,直接由控制对象取得而进行的控制)
self-oscillating system 自激振荡系统
self-parking wiper 自动回位式刮水器(无论在何位置上停止使用,都能自动回到底位的风窗刮水器)
self-piercing rivets 自钻铆接(简称 SPRs, Henrob公司开发的一种车身构件连接新工艺,其特点为无须预先钻孔,自钻铆钉在压力下穿过上、下工件,在下工件底部凹模作用下,头部分开并弯曲,形成一个高强度连接)
self-potential 开路电压,自势,自位
self-powered 自带动力的
self-pressurized hydrostatic mechanical seal 自加压流体静压式机械密封(以被密封介质本身作为加压流体的流体静压式机械密封)

self-priming (起动时) 自动加注起动燃油的
self-priming pump 自吸泵(指能够自动实现初吸,即自动将进液管段吸成真空,而实现无加液抽吸的液压泵)
self-priming tank (可自动调节液面高度的)自动充油油箱
self-propelled 自动推进的,自行的,(简称 sp 或 self-prop)
self propelled chassis 自行底盘(亦称 mobile (tool) carrier, mobile toolbar, self propelled toolframe)
self-propelled crash test 用自身发动机驱动的汽车碰撞试验
self-propulsion point 自驱点(汽车挂车行驶性能曲线上挂钩牵引力等于零的一点)
self-protection circuit of auto electronic equipments 汽车电子设备的自保护电路
self-recording unit 自动记录装置(简称 SRU, 亦称 self-registering instrument)
self-recovery winch 车辆自救用绞盘
self-rectifying alternator 自整流式交流发电机
self regeneration 自己再生(机能)
self-regulating 自行调节的,自身节的(指机构的本身具有某种调节能力的,如: self-regulating vane-type oil pump "自身调压式叶片油泵",该油泵内具有限压阀,可使油泵的输出压力不受驱动转速的影响而保持在规定的范围内,这里主要强调油泵本身的这种调压能力,与"自动调节"在意义上有所差异)
self-regulating fuel pump 自行调压输油泵
self-regulation 自调节,自行调节
self-resonant frequency 自共振频率
self-restoring 自动复原的,自动复

位的,自动恢复原状的
self-retention 自锁
self-return 自动回位
self-righting effect (车轮的)自动回正效应,自动回正作用(= trailing effect)
self-seal inner tube (刺破后可自动密封补漏的)自封式内胎(= puncture-proof tube)
self-service 顾客自理(的),无人售货(的),自我服务(的)(如:自我服务式加油站、洗车机、无人售票公共汽车等)
self-servo action (制动蹄的)自增力作用,自助势作用
self-servo synchronizer 自动增力式同步器
self-shifting transmission 自动换挡变速器,自动变速器
self-stabilizing effect in braking (汽车)制动的自稳定效应(指在制动过程中①全部车轮均未抱死时的抗侧滑能力②前轮抱死,但后轮仍处于滚动状态时,若某干扰力使此时推动汽车前行的惯性力的方向偏离汽车纵轴线,而使汽车绕垂直轴线偏转某一角度 β,则该干扰这时产生的与纵轴垂直的分力将产生一使该初始角 β 减小的稳定力偶,让汽车维持稳定的运动状态)
self-stabilizing steering 自稳定转向系(前轮爆胎或产生严重制动滑移时仍能自动保持汽车直线行驶方向)
self-starting 自起动的(指本身装有起动装置的)
self-starting motor (汽车上的)起动电动机(亦称 self-starter, starter motor, starting motor, starter)
self-steering 自行隋动转向的
self-steering axle 随动转向桥(随主车自动转向的挂车车桥,或随前转向轮自动转向的后桥,亦称 self-tracking axle)
self-steering mechanism 自行随动转向机构(不是由转向盘控制转向,而是随着牵引力自行转向的后桥或挂车的转向机构,亦称 self tracking mechanism)
self-supporting universal joint 自承式万向节(不需要其他外部机构支撑的万向节)
self-supporting vehicle bodywork 承载式车身
self-sustained oscillation 自励振动,自激振动(不是与本系统的运动无关的外力引起的振动,而是由本系统的运动状态引起的振动,= self-excited vibration)
self-sustaining 自身支持的,自身承当的,自生的,自给的,独立的
self-synchronous 自动同步的(简称 selsyn)
self-tapping screw 自攻螺钉
self-test input connector 自诊断输入插座
selft-generating 自发的,自生的,无外加激励的条件下,本身可产生输出信号的
self-tracking bogie (多轴挂车后部)自行随动转向桥(见 self steering mechanism)
self-transit rail and road car 自动变换公路-轨道两用车(简称 Sta-RR car)
self-travelling 自(身)(移)动,自(动)行(进)
self-tuning engine 自调发动机(一般指能够自动调准到最佳燃料经济性、最佳运行工况、最佳污染净化的发动机)
self-unloading wagon 自卸车,自卸挂车
self-unloadinng trailer 自卸挂车(= selfdischarging trailer)
self-used vehicle 自用车辆

self-wiping contact 自洁（电）触点（带擦刷动作的摩擦接点）
Seller's coupling 塞勒联轴节
Seller's drive 塞勒传动
Seller's screw thread 塞勒螺纹（美国标准螺纹，螺纹尖角为60°，或将60°螺纹的高度切去一半形成的平顶螺纹，亦称 U. S. standard screw thread，简称 U. S. S. screw thread）
Seller's taper 塞勒锥度
selsyn motor 自动同步电动机
selsyn train 自动同步传动装置，自动同步齿轮系
SEM 电子扫描显微镜（scanning electron microscope）
SEMA [美]专用设备制造商协会（Speciality Equipment Manufacturers Association 的简称）
semaphore-type traffic indicator 动臂信号式交通指示器，横杆式交通指挥信号装置（= semaphore-type trafficator）
semblance 外观，外形，外表，样子
semi- （词头）半
semi-active suspension 半主动式悬架（指悬架元件的弹簧刚度和减振阻尼系数二者中只有一项可调的悬架，一般为阻尼系数可调式，将阻尼分为两级或三级，可由驾驶者选择或根据有关传感器信号由电子控制模块自动选择）
semi-anechoic chamber 半消声室（见 hemi-anechoic chamber）
semiautomatic gearbox 半自动变速器（指具有自动换挡的机械变速器，亦称 semiautomatic transmission）
semi-automatic headlamp beam switch 半自动前照灯远、近光开关（可由驾驶者选用自动或手动控制的远、近光开关）
semi-automatic mechanical transmission 半自动机械变速器（由手动杆件选定挡位，而由自动机构使所选定的挡位齿轮啮合的变速装置）
semiautomatic transmission 半自动液力变速器（部分换挡功能是自动实现的液力变速器）
semiautomatic welding 半自动焊接，半自动熔焊（一般指焊条的喂送、电弧长度的调节、保持等由机械自动控制，而焊条沿焊道的移动由手工控制的熔焊作业）
semiaxis 半轴（= semiaxle）
semiballoon tire 半低压轮胎
semi cab-over 短头型（汽车驾驶室的一半在发动机上方，一半在发动机后方）
semi-centrifugal clutch 半离心式离合器（利用飞重增加盘的接合压力，以防止高速和大转矩时打滑的干式单片式离合器）
semicircular key 半圆键
semi-closed-cycle 半闭合循环
semi-closed loop (operation mode) （某些节气门体喷油系统的）半闭路（控制模式）（当汽车以高速稳速行驶时，电子控制模块实行开路稀燃控制模式，混合比控制在16:5，同时电子控制模块将定期地转为闭路控制，以监控发动机的各项运行参数，如：发动机水温、点火正时及车速等，只要各项运行参数仍在规定范围内，又会回到开路稀燃控制，控制模式如此不断地在开-闭路间切换）
semiconductor 半导体（电导性能处于导体与绝缘体之间的物体的通称）
semi-conductor assisted ignition system 半导体辅助点火系统（由断电触点控制基极电流的半导体点火系统）
semiconductor chip hybrid integrated circuit 半导体芯片混合集成电路（一种含有一个或多个未封装的半导体器件的混合膜集成电路）

semiconductor device 半导体器件（基本特性是由于载流子在半导体内流动的器件）

semiconductor element 半导体元件

semiconductor integrated circuit 半导体集成电路（简称SIC）

semiconductor laser 半导体激光器

semi-conductor lighting 半导体照明（使用半导体材料灯的照明技术）

semiconductor spark plug 半导体火花塞（绝缘体裙端由半导体材料制成或裙部端面覆盖有半导体材料的火花塞）

semiconductor strain gauge 半导体应变计（片）

semiconductor type lambda = 1 sensor 半导体型 $\lambda = 1$ 氧传感器（用 TiO_2、$SrTiO_3$ 等氧化物半导体材料制成的 $\lambda = 1$ 氧传感器，见 lambda = 1 sensor）

semi-continuous braking system 半连续制动系（具有下列全部特征的汽车列车制动系：①驾驶员可在其座位上，使用单一动作平缓地直接操作牵引车的制动控制装置，以及间接操作挂车制动控制装置②牵引车与挂车所用制动能至少由两种不同的能源供给，能源之一可以是驾驶员的体力③牵引车与挂车应同步，或以匹配的相位进行制动）

semi-crawl vehicle 半履带式汽车（后端为履带驱动，前端为车轮转向，雪地用者将前轮为撬板）

semideterministic map-matching software 半确定型地图叠合软件（其特点是设定所涉及汽车仅是在限定的路线或道路网内行驶，其任务是确定汽车在该路线或道路网的何处）

semi-diameter 半径（= radius，简称SD）

semidiesel engine 半柴油机，半压燃机（指由电热装置点火的压燃式内燃机，如：热球式柴油机，见 hot-bulb engine）

semi-diode 半导体二极管

semi-direct lighting 半直接照明 [将照明灯具60%~90%的发射光通直接投射到工作面上（假定工作面是无边界的）的照明]

semi-down draft carburetor 斜吸式化油器（= slanting carburetor）

semi-drop center rim 半深式轮辋

semi-elliptical leaf spring 半椭圆形钢板弹簧（指由多片呈弧形的弹簧钢板叠合、螺栓紧固而成的非独立悬架中最常见的弹簧形式，其特点是最上面的一片最长，其两端通过吊架式支架与车架连接，尔后逐片变短，最下面的一片最短，装在车桥上，整架弹簧构成一根等强度的弹性梁，因其形状近似一椭圆形的一半，故名，亦称 half elliptic leaf spring。近年来亦出现单片式整体呈半椭圆的钢板弹簧）

semielliptic cantilever spring 半椭圆形悬臂钢板弹簧（见 cantilever spring）

semielliptic scroll spring 双弯头半椭圆形钢板弹簧

semiempirical relationship 半经验公式

semi-exclusive pedestrian vehicle phase 行人-行车半专用信号显示（车辆不得横穿人行横道，但可沿着与人行横道平行的方向及不横穿人行横道的其他方向行驶）

semi-fast back car 半快背式轿车（后高与行李舱的外形线不连续，二者间形成明显的转折）

semi-finished 半成品的

semi-finished nut 半精制螺母（指侧面不做精加工，而仅仅座面精加工的螺母）

semi-flat rim 半平式轮辋（半深式轮辋）

semiflexible 半挠性的
semi-floating axle 半浮式驱动桥（亦称 half-floating axle，其半轴的内端，即差速器端不支撑车重；外端，即车轮端支撑车重并承受推力）
semifloating piston pin 半浮式活塞销
semi-fluid 半流体的，半流动性的，半流质的
semi-fluid friction 半液体摩擦，半流体摩擦
semi-forward control cab 短头驾驶室（居于长头驾驶室与平头驾驶室之间）
semi-forward control vehicle 短头车（发动机的一部分伸进驾驶室内的货车或客车）
semi-fuel cell 半燃料电池
semi-guided bend 半导向弯曲（在试样的弯曲部位直接施加力得到的弯曲）
semi-hermetic type 半密闭型，半密闭式
semi-indirect lighting 半间接照明（假定工作面是无边界，将照明灯具 10%~40% 的发射光通直接投射到工作面上的照明）
semi-integral body 半承载式车身（车身骨架与车架采用刚性连接结构形式的车身，亦称 semi-monocoque body）
semi-integral type power steering 半整体式动力转向（系）（控制阀与转向器成一体，但助力缸则与之分离）
semi-killed steel 半镇静钢
semi-knocked down 半散装，部分散件组装（一种销售方式，不是将汽车全部拆散为零件，运到销售地组装成车，而是将部分未拆散的总成及部分零部件，运到销售地组装成车，简称 SKD，见 completely knocked down）
semiliquid 半流体的，半液态的
semi-locking differential 半自锁式差速器
semi-manufactured products 半成品
semi-metallic 半金属材料的（如：由有机材料与铁粉等制成的制动蹄用摩擦材料的）
semimounted 半悬架式
semi-open combustion chamber 半开式燃烧室（燃烧室在某种程度上被分为两部分，其一部分在活塞顶或汽缸盖的凹坑内，另一部分在活塞顶面与汽缸盖底面之间，两者之间有较大的喉口相连通的球形燃烧室、ω 形燃烧室、活塞顶内燃烧室等的统称）
semi-orthogonal coordinates 半正交坐标
semioscillation 半周期振荡
semi-passive seat belt （汽车乘员的）半被动安全带
semipermeability ①半磁导性②半渗透性、半透气性
semi-permeable 半渗透性的
semipneumatic tyre 半充气轮胎，大气压轮胎（如：海绵软垫轮胎，亦称 semisolid tire 半实心轮胎）
semiportable 半移动式的，半携带式的
semi-product 半成品
semi-rigid pipe 半刚性管（相对固定的零件之间，不能保持永久形状的连接管）
semirigid suspension 半刚性悬架
semi-rotary pneumatic actuator 半旋转式气动马达，半旋转式气动机
semi-round key 半圆键
semi-sealed beam headlamp 半封闭式前照灯（采用半封闭式灯光组的前照灯）
semi-sealed beam unit 半封闭式灯光组（配光镜与反射镜密封，灯泡可

以更换的光学组件)

semi-slipper skirt piston ①半滑裙式活塞(指活塞销孔座下方非受力面的裙部部分切除,其底边呈凹形的活塞)②半围涎裙活塞(活塞非推力面的裙部短,推力面的裙部长,形成半围涎状裙)

semisolid 半固态(的),半固体(的)

semi-sphere 半球(形的)

semispherical combustion chamber 半球形燃烧室

semi-station wagon 半旅行车(指车身后背介于普通折背式和客货两用式旅行轿车之间,亦称半接站轿车,简称SSW)

semisteel 半钢(的)[指低碳铸铁(的),高强度铸铁(的),类钢铸铁(的)]

semi-tracked vehicle 半履带式车辆

semi-trailer 半挂车(前端由牵引车支撑的挂车,简称stler)

semitrailer brake connection 半挂车(与牵引车的)制动系连接件

semi-trailer fifth wheel coupling altitude 半挂车(的牵引车牵引转盘)支撑点至地面的高度

semi-trailer length 半挂车长(分别过半挂车车身最前端点或牵引销轴心线和半挂车车身最后端点且垂直于Y和X平面的两平面之间的距离)

semi-trailer supports spacing 半挂车停放支撑点间距(脱离牵引车靠支架停放时,其前端支架落地中心与半挂车间的距离)

semitrailer tractor 半挂车牵引车(半挂车拖车,承受半挂车的前部分负载的牵引车,亦称semi-trailer towing vehicle)

semitrailer wheel base 半挂车轴距(亦称semitrailer wheel space,单轴半挂车指转盘中心销至车轴中心线铅垂面间的距离;多轴半挂车的第一轴距同上,其余轴距见 wheel base)

semi-trailer wheel space 半挂车轴距(见 semi trailer wheel base)

semitrailer with detachable rear-axle 后轴可拆半挂车

semitrailing arm (悬架的)半纵臂(指斜臂,= oblique arm)

semi-trailing arm type suspension 半纵臂式悬架(亦称单斜臂式悬架"single oblique arm type suspension",该臂一端与轮毂连接,另一端通过两个支点经橡胶衬垫与车架梁连接,且该两个支点的连线与车轴成一定夹角,即斜向布置,横向刚度较高)

semi-trailing type suspension 斜臂式悬架

semi-trailling arm type suspension 单斜臂式悬架(= single oblique arm type suspension,每边车轮通过一根斜臂与车架或车身相连的一种独立悬架)

semi-transistor ignition system 半晶体管点火系(仍使用断电器触点的晶体管点火系,但触点通过的电流很微弱,实际上只起点火时刻控制信号的作用)

semitranslucent 半透明的(= semi-transparent)

semitransparency 半透明性(= semi-transparence)

semi-used 半旧的(半新的,用过一段时间,仍可继续使用的)

semivulcanized 半硫化的

semiwater gas 半水煤气(H_2,CO,CO_2,N_2等的混合气体,其热值较低,约$125 Btu/ft^3$)

SEMM 智能能量综合管理系统(Smart Energy Mix Manager 的简称)

SEN 传感器(sensor 的简称)

sender 发射机,发信机;发送器信

号输出装置，发送装置（亦称 sending unit）

sender unit 开关式传感器（将温度、压力或转速、位移等物理量转变为电信号接通警报灯或驱动某种仪表的传感件）

sense ①方向②感觉③意义，观念，读出，判断力，灵敏

sense amplifier 读出放大器（对规定输入电压范围内的信号做出响应，并能输出数字电压的集成电路。它通常具有差动输入端和单端输出端，也可以包括一个选通端，及用来调整输入电压范围的输入端）

sense of orientation 定向，指向

sense of present （对车辆外观、形状等的）观感

sense recovery time 读恢复时间（将存储器从写状态转换到读状态，并输出获得有效数据信号所需要的时间间隔）

sense-reversing 逆向的

sensibilization 敏化（作用）（指增加敏感度）

sensible heat （物体的）显热

sensing ①感觉，感触②感传，检测

sensing element 敏感元件，传感元件

sensing equipment 传感装置

sensing head 传感头，感应头

sensing spring 传感弹簧

sensing time 传感时间（指传感器从接受传感量到发出传感信号可需的时间）

sensing unit 传感元件，传感器（亦称 sensor, sensitive element, sensitive member）

sensitive 灵敏的，敏感的，反应迅速的

sensitive film 高感光胶片

sensitive to heat 热敏的（对热敏感的）

sensitivity （亦称 sensibility, sensitiveness）①（仪表，控制系统的）灵敏度（指对输入响应的灵敏程度）②敏感度，敏感性；对…的敏感性，敏感度（如：汽油的抗爆性敏感度 "gasoline sensitivity to detonation"，指研究法辛烷值与马达法辛烷值的差值，敏感度小的汽油更能适应汽车在不同工况下对抗爆性的要求，欧美一般规定该值不大于8 或 10）

sensitivity analysis 灵敏度分析

sensitivity calibration 灵敏度校准

sensitivity control 灵敏度控制

sensitivity drift 灵敏度漂移

sensitivity index 灵敏指数

sensitivity to acceleration 对加速度的敏感性

sensitivity to disturbance 对扰动敏感性

sensitivity to light （感）光（灵）敏度

sensitized photocell 光敏电池

sensor interface circuitry （汽车自动控制系统的）传感器接口电路

sensor range 传感器的传感范围

sensor signal 传感器信号（由传感器供给的信息）

sensotronic brake control （Benz 公司 21 世纪初首次在其 SL500 型上采用的）电子传感制动控制（商品名，为 brake-by-wire "线控制动"系统，由装在制动踏板上的传感器将驾驶者的踏板力度和踩踏速度信息传给控制模块，控制模块的脉冲指令经"导线"驱动液压执行机构，实现车轮制动）

sentential calculus （语）句演算

Sentry Key （汽车）防盗哨锁（商品名）

separable ①可分的，可拆的（= demountable）②能区分的，能划分的

separable bearing 可分式（滚动）轴承（内、外圈可分离）

separable carrier-type axle housing 可分式桥壳（与主减速器壳分开制造而用螺栓连接在一起的桥壳，亦称 split axle housing）

separable rim 组合式轮辋，可拆式轮辋

separate ①分离，分隔②分离的

separate air conditioning system 分离式空气调节装置，分离式空调机（指压缩机与冷风机分离装配的空调系统，以便将噪音大的压缩机与车身客舱隔开）

separate combustion chamber 分隔式燃烧室

separated 可隔离的，单独的，另外的，分开的，分离的

separated ABS 分离式防抱死制动系统（指制动总泵和制动压力调节装置分别为独立总成的 ABS）

separate design type ABS/ASR system with brake intervention using stored energy 使用存储能量进行制动干预的分体式 ABS/ASR 系统

separated exciting 他激（磁式），他励（磁式）（利用外部电源对发电机励磁，亦称 separated excitation, outside excitation）

separated four-wheel antilock brake sys-tem with high-pressure energy accumulator 带高压储能器的四轮分体式防抱死制动系统（指制动主缸带真空助力器、ABS 控制模块、压力调节器带动力单元分别为独立的总成，安装于不同部位由管道相连的四轮防抱死系统）

separated four-wheel antilock brake sys-tem with low-pressure energy accumulator 带低压储能器的分体式防抱死制动系（制动主缸与真空助力器、制动压力调节阀等分别为独立的总成，由管道相连）

separated fuel injection pump housing 分体式喷油泵体（以上、下分体形式出现的喷油泵体）

separate drive 分别传动，单独传动

separated turning lane 分隔式转弯车道

separate frame （非承载式车身的）独立底架（亦称 separate chassis, 见 space frame）

separate grade crossing 道路立体交叉

separately cast cylinder 分铸汽缸

separately controlled 独立操控的，分别控制的

separate power take-off 独立式功率输出轴

separate type ABS 分离式防抱死制动系统（指制动总泵与制动压力调节装置分别为独立总成的防抱死制动系统）

separate type linkage power steering 分体式联杆型（液压）转向动力装置（联杆型转向加力装置的一种，见 linkage-type power steering, 其液压泵、控制阀和动力缸分别为独立的总成，而且接装在不同的位置上，见 combined type linkage power steering）

separate voltage reference chip 单独的电压参考值芯片

separate washer 隔离垫圈，隔环

separating point 分离点

separating strip （车道间）分隔带，分车带

separating tank 沉淀槽，沉淀箱

separating wall 隔板，隔墙（= dividing wall）

separation ①分离，分隔②（工作油内的气体以气泡的形式）析出（见 air separation）③（汽车高速行驶时，汽车后部车身表面空气附着层内的气流反向流动，由此产生的紊流区域，使附着层与车身表面产生）剥离（的现象）④（空气动力流的）紊变（由层流变为紊流的现

象）⑤脱层（轮胎各布层、胶层或部件之间的黏着面部分脱开的现象）

separation bubble （紊流）剥离气泡层（参见 separation③）

separation distance control system （公路行车）车间距离控制系统（可在无须驾驶者干预的情况下，自动将道路上行驶的车辆的车间距离保持在某规定的安全范围内）

separation resistance 抗剥离强度

separation test （轮胎帘布层的）脱层试验

separator ①隔离件，隔离物（隔垫、隔板、隔套等的总称）②分离器（指各种清除油液中的悬浮微粒、水分等的分离装置，如：离心式分离器、过滤式分离器等）③（道路上的）分隔带，分车道设备④分离符，分隔号，分离号

separator balls （无保持架轴承中的）分隔球

separator codes 见 service code③

seperating plate （蓄电池）隔板

septum 隔壁，隔片，隔膜，膜片

sequence ①顺序，次序，工序；序列，系列；数列；系，族，类②排列程序，定序，程序设计，使程序化

sequence-controlled computer 顺序控制式计算机，时序计算机（为任意顺序计算机与连续顺序计算机的总称，见 arbitrary sequence computer 和 consecutive sequence computer）

sequence of operation 操作顺序

sequencer 定序器，顺序控制器（确定工序、程序、指令等执行顺序，信息、数据排列顺序，信息存取顺序的装置或电路）

sequence switch 顺序开关（控制信号发送与接收顺序的开关元件）

sequence valve 顺序阀（在具有两个以上分路的液压回路中由回路的压力控制各分路工作顺序的阀，亦称 sequencing valve）

sequencing control 顺序控制（亦称 sequential control，按规定的顺序进行的控制，简称 SC）

sequencing effect （不同数值荷载的作用）顺序的影响

sequential 序列的，相继的，继续的，连续的，顺序的

sequential (digital) circuit 时序（数字）电路（在其输入端上至少存在一种数字信号组合，对应于这一数字信号组合，输出端上存在一组以上的相对应的数字信号组合的数字电路）

sequential fuel injection system 顺序喷油系统（根据汽缸的工作顺序，逐缸单独喷油）

sequential gasification 连续气化（指汽油在进入化油前与水一同输入一种改质处理装置中，同时将空气和一部分已经改质的气体燃料 $CO_2 + H_2$，反馈输入该装置中燃烧放出热量，使汽油和水产生化学反应，变成改质气体燃料 $CO_2 + H_2$ 的过程，简称 SEGAS）

sequential number 序号，编号，系列号（亦称 serial number）

sequential range gating technique 顺序测距选通技术

Sequential Spot Shift Transmission （Fort 的）顺序换挡式运动型手自一体变速器（商品名，简称 SSST）

sequential transmission 顺序换挡式齿轮变速器

sequential turbo-charging 相继涡轮增压（柴油机装有多台涡轮增压器，能按照转速的变化部分地停止或恢复工作，可在各种工况下改善柴油机的性能）

serial ①连续的，顺序的，序列的，串行的，串联的，排成一系列的②成套，系列；丛书

serial access memory 串行存取存储器（存储区只能按设定顺序存取的一种存储器）

serial accumulator 串行累加器

serial addressing 串行寻址（以连续提供每个地址位的方式选择存储区）

serial communication interface 串行通信接口（简称 SCI，指按位串行方式传递数据的通信接口）

serial data bus 串行数据总线（按顺序一次只传输一位数据，现在车载网络一般都采用这种总线）

serial data format 串行数据格式（指串行数据的排列或布局，见 serial data）

serial input/output 串行输入输出（法）（串行输入输出，简称 SIO，数据输入电子控制模块或电子控制模块向外围设备输出是经过一条线路逐位传递的）

serial interface 串行接口（①按位串行方式传递数据的接口②每次只支持对数据的一位进行处理的接口，见 parallel interface）

serial number of bus run （客车）车次，（班车）车次

serial presentation of information 信息串行传送（几个数据位沿单一通道或总线连续传输）

serial processing 串行处理技术（按顺序或相继执行两个或两个以上的操作的计算机处理技术）

serial production 成批生产，批量生产

serial transmission （汽车电子控制系统中信息的）串行传输（法）（按一定顺序连续或间隔地经一条数据线路进行传输，而不是同时传输）

seriation 系列化（将同一品种或同一形式产品的规格按最佳数列科学排列，以最小的品种满足最广泛的需要。它是标准化的一种形式）

series ①串联②系列；组③级数④成批的⑤串联

series circuit 串联电路

series coil 串联线圈（亦称 series connection coil）

series drive 串联驱动

series dual-chamber brake master cylinder 串列双腔式制动主缸（双回路液力制动系供给液压的制动主缸，由两个工作腔组成，活塞依次排列）

series dynamo 串激式（直流）发电机

series excitation 串激

series hybrid drive type vehicle 串联式混合动力车（亦称 series hybrid electric vehicle，简称 SHEV，其内燃机仅驱动发电机发电给驱动用蓄电池充电，汽车由电动机驱动行驶。和其他形式的混合动力车一样，当制动或减速时汽车带电动机逆转发电，回收汽车动能）

series 3 lubricating oil （通过美国 Caterpillar ID 及 IG 发动机试验确定的）系列"3"高级润滑油

series motor 串激电动机

series-parallel circuit 串联-并联电路（简称 SP circuit，指由串联与并联部分组成的复合电路）

series-parallel hybrid drive type vehicle 串联-并联式混合动力车（亦称 parallel-series hybrid electric vehicle，简称 SPHEV 或 PSHEV，为串联式与并联式驱动的组合方式，起步或低速行驶时汽车仅由电动机驱动。汽车正常行驶时由内燃机和电动机共同驱动。当制动或减速时汽车带动电动机逆转发电，回收汽车动能）

series parallel motor 串并联电动机（= compound motor）

series-parallel switch 串并联转换开关

series peaking 用串联法使频率特性的高频部分升高

series production 连续生产,大量生产,成批生产(参见 lot production)

series regulation 串联式电压调节,串联式电压调节装置

series resistance 串联电阻

series running 串联运转

series winding 串联线圈(如:串联在发电负载电路中,反映发电机输出电流大小的线圈)

series-wound 串激的,串绕的

series-wound DC motor 串激直流电动机(=series DC motor)

serpentine cooler 蛇形冷却管,蛇形管冷却器

serra ①锯(=saw)②锯齿状

serrate ①锯齿形的(=serrated)②切成锯齿状;铣成细齿

serrated joint 细齿连接,三角齿花键连接(亦称 serration joint)

serrated nut 细牙螺母

serrated shaft 三角形细齿花键轴,锯齿形花键轴(=serration shaft)

serrations ①锯齿(形),细齿②细齿花键连接③三角花键,细齿花键④锉刀花纹

S3ERSV 安全、经济、节能、环保研究车(Safety Economy Energy Environment RSV 的简称)

service ①使用,工作,服务②保养,检修,维修

serviceability 维修方便性,保养维护方便性;适用性,耐用性;操作性能,功能;使用能力,服务能力,使用可靠性,使用的舒适程度

serviceability rate 完好率,(车辆的)技术完好率(全部营运车辆的总车日中完好车日所占的比率,=technical serviceability rate of vehicle)

serviceable condition 可以使用状态,完好状态

serviceable life 使用寿命

serviceable vehicle days 完好车日(每天在用营运车辆中技术状况完好,不经过维护和修理即能参加运输的车辆数量的累计)

service action log 维修记录(简称 SAL)

service adjustment 维修性调整

service-and-inspection lane 供车辆技术维护和检查用的停车道

service application 使用申请,装机申请(书),维护申请(书)

service area ①(公路沿线提供休息和供应及维修服务等的)服务区 ②有效作用区,有效范围

service bay 维修间,维修台

Service Bay Diagnosis System [美]诊断服务系统(与底特律、密西根各大汽车制造厂连线的电子计算机网络系统,用于回答各地维修服务人员有关维修和故障诊断的问题)

service behavio(u)r 使用性能(=behaviour in service)

service bill 维修费用单,维修费用清单,维修费用账单

service brake 行车制动器,脚制动器,主制动器(以别于驻车制动器、紧急制动器和缓速器)

service brake pedal centre 行车制动踏板中心(行车制动踏板表面对称中心。当采用铰支式踏板时,指踏板表面中心线上距足后跟点 200mm 处的点)

service braking control 行车制动器制动操纵件(控制行驶车辆减速或停车时所使用的制动系统的操纵件,如:制动踏板)

service braking system warning telltale 行车制动系警报灯(警报灯亮时,表示可能有以下一种或几种情况:①在制动系统中某处压力不足②制动衬片过量磨损③防抱死制动系发生故障④液压制动液量不足⑤制动能量储存不足)

service bulletin （汽车生产厂家发布的新车新结构等最新维修资料的）维修公报

service car 修理工程车，技术服务车

service center 中心服务站，（汽车）维护中心，服务中心，救济中心

service check ①性能检验，性能校核②使用前检验（校核有关部分是否符合规定）

service class （美国 API 滑油分类中的）汽油机油（用于轿车和轻型货车的汽油发动机，通常简写为 S，下分若干类，分别按其品质由低至高用 SA，SB，SC，SD，SE，SF 等表示）

service code 故障码［亦称诊断故障码 diagnostic trouble code，简称 DTC。电子控制模块通过各种监测器对其控制的各种装置的输入和输出电路的电压等有关参数进行监控，当发现所监控的参数高于或低于规定值范围时，即认定该电路出现故障，以两位数字的代码表示该故障的部位并存储于控制模块的存储器中，可使用诊断设备从汽车的故障诊断数据总线读取。一般故障代码分为以下 6 种：①快速码（fast code），用于汽车总装线出厂诊断，其特点是闪现十分迅速，使用一般诊断设备不易读取②按需码（on-demand code，亦称硬代码 hard code），表示在自诊断取码作业进行中正存在着的故障③分隔码（separator code），只在进行自诊断取码开始之初出现，一般为"10"，表示按需码已完备，接下来便可输出④存储码（memory code），亦称 intermittent codes 或 continue codes "中间码或继续码"，代表在汽车正常运转中曾监测到的故障，但在诊断取码时已不存在⑤动态响应码（dynamic response code），仅出现于自诊断取码作业中发动机运转区段，为"10"，告诉检测人员必须在 15s 内将加速踏板踩到底并使之回升，在此期间内电子控制模块将对节气门开度传感器、进气歧管绝对压力传感器、叶片式空气流量传感器或空气质量流量传感器等进行诊断并显示诊断结果，此项检测亦称 goose test⑥发动机识别码（engine identification codes），此代码对诊断人员无意义，它仅用于向装配车间的出厂检测设备提供发动机汽缸数信息，如：20 表示 4 缸，30 为 6 缸，40 为 8 缸等］

service conditions 使用状况，使用条件

service conductor 引入线（= service wire）

service contamination ①使用过程中被污染或弄脏（= contaminated）②使用中产生污染或弄脏它物（= contaminating）

service creeper （在车下进行维修作业时使用的）躺板，维修用车下躺板（= repair creeper）

service data 运行数据，维护资料，技术资数，维修数据，业务资料（= operational data）

service direction （汽车）运行方向，营运方向（一般用 up 上行，down 下行表示）

service door clear width 乘客门净宽（车门在最大开启位置时车门两侧，包括车门扶手之间的最小距离）

service door height 乘客门高（第一级踏步板上平面至抵靠上门框的 Z 平面之间的距离）

service dynamo 辅助装置用发电机（如：照明用发电机）

service engine 使用中的发动机（= live engine）

service engineer 运用工程师

service failure 使用期内的损坏（=

in service failure)

service-free life 免维修使用期，无维护使用期

service-free reliability 不加维护情况下的使用可靠性，免维护的可靠性

service garage ①带维修场的车库，提供维修服务的车库②（汽车）维修厂、维修店

service hatch 检修窗孔，维修孔

service indicator （车辆需要）维修的指示信号

service instruction 服务指南，服务须知，业务规章，业务须知，服务细则，使用细则（参见 operating instruction, operator's hand book）

service interruption 停车；停运；服务中断

service interval （用里程表示的）使用寿命

service intervals 技术维护周期（= maintenance intervals）

service island 运输企业中划分出来专供汽车维修用的地区

service kit （汽车维修等部门使用的）维修包，维修工具箱，维修材料箱（内装常用的汽车维修救急材料及手工具等，简称 SK）

service lame ①维修作业线，检修作业线②维修车道

service lamp 便携式手提灯，工作灯

service life 使用寿命，使用期限

service light 故障警报灯（见 service soon light, service now light）

service line ①维修作业线②（从牵引车接到挂车的）制动控制管路

service load 使用荷载，使用负荷，工作荷载，工作负荷

service load spectrum 使用负荷频谱

service man 修理工，维修工，技术服务人员，技师，机械师

service manual （操作，使用，维护）规程，使用维修手册，使用说明书，维修说明书

service ML oil （美国 API 制定的发动机油性能分类中的）ML 级机油（motor light 的简称，指轻负荷发动机用机油）

service MM oil （美国 API 制定的发动机油性能分类中的）MM 级机油（motor moderate 的简称，指中等负荷发动机用机油）

service MS oil （美国 API 制定的发动机油性能分类中的）MS 级机油（motor severe 的简称，指重工况发动机用机油）

service network 服务网点，维修网点，维修网络

service now light "立即检修"故障警报灯（当自诊断系统发现必须紧急引起驾驶员注意的严重故障，应立即进行检修时，该警报灯亮，见 service soon light）

service pit 检修地沟

service point 维修点（汽车拉力赛参赛车队的维修人员，可在所安排的维修点，对赛车进行加油、检查、换胎、维修，见 etape, scrutineering, pace notes）

service project 维修计划；维修项目

servicer ①服务车②燃料加注车，加油车

service rack incline （汽车）维修台坡道，洗车台坡道

service reminder indicator （汽车部件、总成或系统应进行）维护的提醒指示器

service sign 服务设施标志（高速公路沿线，表明有汽车修理、食堂、专为汽车旅客开设的旅馆等商业服务设施的标志）

service-simulated conditions 模拟（的）使用条件

service simulating test 使用模拟试验

service soon light "尽快检修"故障警报灯（自诊断系统发现必须引起驾驶员注意，但还不那么紧急的故

障时,该警报灯亮,见 service now light)

service-tested 经过使用考验的
service time 使用期限;(技术)维护时间
service trial 运行试验,运转试验(=service test)
service truck 维修服务车(=maintenance truck)
service validation 使用鉴定(根据使用情况做出的评定)
service valves (空调系统供加注制冷剂,排除水分,用压力表进行各项测试用的)维护作业阀
service volume 适应道路服务水平的通行能力(在一定的道路服务水平下每小时能通过的最大交通量,多车道公路为单向交通量,双车道或三车道公路则为双向交通量)
service wear 使用性磨耗,运行磨损
service weight 运行质量(=operating weight)
service wire 引入线
servicing depot (汽车)维修厂
servo ①伺服(a.指根据反馈信号修正执行误差的闭路控制;b.指按照规定的比例关系,由小的作用力或输出控制大的作用力或输出的增力控制) ②伺服系统(或机构)(servo system 或 servo mechanism 的简称) ③伺服的 ④伺服机构的 ⑤伺服(机构)控制的(servo-controlled 的简称)
servo action ①伺服作用,随动作用 ②助力作用,加力作用
servo action of brake shoe 制动蹄的伺服作用(指在鼓式制动时,制动过程中若制动蹄张开时的转动方向与制动鼓的旋转方向一致,则由于蹄鼓之间的楔紧作用而产生较大的摩擦力的现象,见 due-servo brake, uni-servo brake)
servo actuator 伺服执行机构,助力执行机构

servoamplifier 伺服放大器
servo-and-power brake 伺服式动力制动器
servo-assisted brake 助力制动器,加力制动器,伺服式助力制动器
servo-assisted steering gear 伺服加力转向机构
servo braking system 伺服制动系(产生制动力的能是由驾驶员和一个或几个供能装置共同供给的制动系,亦称 energy assisted braking system "助力制动系")
servo clutch 伺服离合器(当松开加速踏板时,该离合器使传动系与发动机脱开,且同时控制燃油系中断供油。当再踏下加速踏板时,该离合器自动接通传动系。若此时变速器处于较低挡位,则可借助汽车的惯性起动发动机,是一种节油装置)
servo connection 伺服连接
servo-controlled 伺服控制的
servo coupling 继动接合套,伺服连接器
servo cylinder 助力缸,伺服缸(如:制动系中的真空助力缸"vacuum booster")
servo diaphragm 伺服膜片(助力膜片,亦称 boosting diaphragm)
servo drive 伺服系统传动装置,伺服驱动装置(=slave drive)
servohydraulic actuator 液压伺服执行机构
servohydraulic cylinder 液压助力缸,液压伺服缸
servohydraulic rotary motor 液压伺服旋转马达
servo-hydraulic test bench 液压伺服式试验台架
servo indicator (表示试验结果的)伺服型指示器(试验设备检出的电压输出经放大后驱动伺服电动机,

由该伺服电动机转动指针的指示器）

servo link 伺服传动杆件
servo-lubrication 集中润滑，中央润滑
servo-magnet 伺服电磁铁
servo-manometer 伺服压力计
servo-mechanism tester 伺服机构试验仪
servo motion 伺服运动，伺服动作
servo motor 伺服机构（起伺服助力作用的机构的通称，见 servo。如：①伺服电动机②膜片式制动气室 "diaphragm type servo-motor"，= diaphragm type air brake chamber③活塞式制动气室 "piston type servo-motor"，= piston type air brake chamber④真空助力器 "vaccum servo-motor"，亦称 vacuum brake servo ⑤液压式助力器 "hydraulic servo-motor"）
servo motor cylinder （活塞式）制动气室活塞（见 servo motor④）
servo motor diaphragm （膜片式）制动气室膜片（见 servo motor②）
servo motor for gas flow control （液化石油气汽车的）石油气流量控制用伺服电动机
servomotor torque constant 伺服电动机转矩常数（停转转矩/控制电压）
servomotor valve 伺服电动机控制阀
servomotor velocity constant 伺服电动机速度常数（= 空载转速/控制电压）
servomotor viscous friction 伺服电动机黏滞摩擦（≈ 停转转矩/空载转速）
servo-operated 伺服作动式的，助力式的
servo piston 伺服活塞（助力活塞，亦称 boosting piston）
servo piston plate （制动系真空助力缸的）盘状助力活塞
servo-potentiometer 伺服电位计，伺服分压器
servopump 伺服泵
servosimulator 伺服模拟机
servo-slave cylinder piston rod （气制动系平板活塞式真空助力器的）助力缸活塞杆
servo stabiliser for vehicle wheels 汽车车轮伺服稳定器（汽车车轮的防滑制动器）
servo-steering 助力转向
servo system 伺服系统（指使用液压、气压、电子执行伺服功能的系统，亦称 servo mechanism 伺服机构）
Servotronic steering speed-related control （Cadillac CTS Coupe 型轿车的）车速感应式电子控制助力转向系统（商品名）
servo-unit 助力器，伺服机构，随动机构，伺服单位，伺服机械
servo valve 伺服阀（如：控制伺服气室气压的阀）
set ①一套，一组集②装置，机组③凝固，硬化④定化，调整（指调到某规定的标准值）
SET 储能变速器（见 stored energy transmission）
setback ①壁的凸出部分②向后运动，退步③逆流，逆转④将指针拨回，后缩
setback (front) axle 后移式前桥（指位置后移至驾驶室后部的平头式货车前桥）
setback line （道路两侧的）建筑限制线，（房屋）收进线
set bolt 定位螺栓，紧定螺栓
set collar 定位圈，定位环，定位套，固定轴环
SET/DECEL button （定速巡行车速控制系统的）车速设定/减速按钮（按压该按钮，汽车减速，松开时所减至的车速，即为新的设定车

set

速)

set hammer 击平锤,堵缝锤,压印锤

set key 定位键

setover ①偏置,偏距②超过位置,过调

set pin 定位销

set point ①凝固点,塑性变形点②控制点,检查点③规定点,给定点,给定值,额定值,选定点,(控制系统对控制变量目标值的)设定点④调整点,调定点

set point value ①选定点值,选定值,规定值,调定值,设定值②凝固点值

set pressure 预定压力,预置压力

set screw 紧定螺钉(用于把零件固定于轴或轴套上的螺钉)

setscrew nut 定位螺母;止动螺母

set-speed button 速度选择按钮(= speed set button)

set switch 设立开关(如:定速巡行控制系统的巡行车速设定开关)

setting ①安置,装置,放置,装配②调整,调节,调定,固定,定位③画线④凝固,凝结,硬化⑤下沉;沉淀,沉降⑥(固定用)框架;(旋钮等的)调整位置⑦开动;起动,启动⑧定位螺钉,调整螺钉⑨镶嵌(物)

setting accelerator 促凝剂,凝固剂

setting accuracy 定位精度,调节精度,对准精度

setting point ①凝固点,凝结点②调整点

setting-point additive (机油)抗凝添加剂

setting pressure 设定压力,给定压力

setting tank 沉淀池,沉淀箱

setting time ①凝结时间,凝固时间②调整时间,定位时间

setting-unsetting device (汽车某些系统的)启用-关闭装置

setting up ①固定,调定,装配,安装,装置②凝固,凝结,硬化,固化

setting-up piece 固定垫片;调节垫片

setting-up procedure 调整顺序,装配顺序

setting value 给定值,设定值

settle ①沉淀②解决③结算④降落,下降⑤稳定

settled grease (出现)分层(现象的)润滑脂(分解变质的润滑脂)

settled sludge 沉渣,沉积淤泥

settling bowl 沉淀杯(= sediment bowl)

settling time 建立时间[从输入信号阶跃变化起,到输出信号偏离最终稳态值不超过规定允差(如:1%)时的时间]

settling time to steady-state ramp (乘法DAC的)稳态斜波建立时间(基准斜波电压起始时的瞬间与模拟输出值最后一次进入输出斜波最终值附近规定的误差带内时的瞬间之间的时间间隔)

set to zero 调到零位,调零,回零

set up 配置,装工具,布置,创立,设立,建立;装配,组装,竖起;装备,设备,配套,组合,调定;计划,方案,准备,(工艺过程的)安排,(问题等的)编排;构成,构造,组织,机构,体系;总体布置

set up procedure 准备程序,准备过程

set-up sheet 装配图表,装配(工艺)卡

set-up time (数字集成电路特性的)建立时间(从规定的输入端加上需保持的信号开始,到另一输入端上接着发生规定的有效转换之间的时间间隔,即:两个输入信号之间能

保证数字电路正确工作的实际最小时间间隔)

set-up-zero instrument 无零点仪表(=suppressed zero instrument)

SEV 气垫车(surface effect vehicle 的简称)

seven-bearing crankshaft 七轴承曲轴,七主轴颈曲轴

seven by nineteen cable 七股十九丝钢索绳

seven conductor connector 七线接头

seven-seater car 七座轿车

severance 切开,隔离,断绝,切断,割断

severe duty ①重载工况②重型的(=heavy-duty)

severe(-duty) test 重载试验;在重(恶劣)工作条件下的试验;苛刻条件试验

severe injury (汽车发生碰撞事故时,乘员的)重伤

severe injury level 重伤碰撞级(指汽车碰撞时,使乘员产生重伤至死亡的碰撞强度级)

severe jolt 强烈振动,剧烈颠簸

severe service conditions 困难的运行条件

severe wear 严重磨损(如:黏附磨损)

severity index 人体受冲击的剧烈程度指数(简称 SI)

severity of braking (汽车)制动强度,制动剧烈程度

sever switch 换通开关(接通或切断通向挂车制动气路的开关件)

sewage disposal 污水处理,废水处理(=sewage treatment)

sewage gas (污水、垃圾)沼气

sewing ①缝纫,缝合②(塑料)熔合③缝制品

sex differences 性别差异

SF ①半成品的(semi-finished)②剪切力(shearing force)

sf ①自馈(电)(self-feeding)②平方英尺(square foot)

SFC ①横向力系数(sideway force coefficient)②燃料消耗率,比油耗(special fuel consumption, specific consumption of fuel, 亦写作 sfc)

SFC clutch 固定磁场线圈型电磁离合器(stationary field coil clutch)

SFI 顺序燃油喷射(按点火顺序逐缸单独喷油, sequential fuel injection 的简称)

SFM clutch 固定磁场电磁离合器(stationary field magnetic clutch)

SFRs 专用暂存器(special function registers 的简称)

SFT (发动机)短时喷油量修正(short-term fuel trim 的简称,指动力控制模块"PCM"可在不超过两个行驶循环的短时间内,对喷油量进行修正。此时,OBDII 系统不当作故障处理,亦写作 short-term FT)

sg ①(变速器)滑动齿轮(sliding gear)②比重(specific gravity)

SG 火花塞间隙(spark gap)

SGS 安全防护系统(safe-guard system)

shackle ①(钢板弹簧)吊耳(连接钢板弹簧卷耳与钢板弹簧支架的构件)②U 形钩③钩环,挂钩④钢丝绳夹头,卡子

shackle angle (钢板弹簧)吊耳倾斜角

shackle bolt ①吊耳销②连接夹板销

shackle bracket (钢板弹簧)吊耳支架

shackle link ①U 形牵引钩,V 形钩②(钢板弹簧)吊耳

shackle pin ①钩环销②(钢板弹簧)吊耳销

shade ①遮阳板,遮光罩②阴影③色调

shaded area ①阴影区②划剖面线的区域,剖面线区

shade line 阴影线
shadow nodes 影子网点（时间触发协议结构中的一种网点，它接收输入信息，但只要其他两个网点正常工作，它便无任何输出，而一旦其他两个网点中的一个发生故障，它立即占用失效网点的时间分割多路存取时隙并产生输出信息）
shaft adapter 传动轴接头，动力输出轴过渡接头
shaft alignment 轴位对准，轴定位，轴位校准
shaft angle 轴交角（轴角，在相交轴齿轮副中使两轴线重合，或在交错轴齿轮副中，使两轴线平行，从而两齿轮的旋转方向得以相反时，两轴线之一所必须旋转的最小角度，称为轴交角）
shaft arm 轴臂，柄臂
shaft basis system 基轴制（= basis shaft system）
shaft casing 轴壳
shaft collar 轴颈圈，轴环
shaft coupling 联轴节
shaft drive 轴传动
shaft-drive type CVT mechanism 轴传动型无级连续变速器（这种CVT不是通过传动带而是通过两端带有锥形工作面摩擦轮的中间轴在驱动轮与从动轮间传递动力）
shaft eccentricity （转子发动机的）主轴偏心距
shaft end 轴端
shaft gear 传动轴齿轮
shaft hole 轴孔
shaft horse power （以马力为单位的发动机）有效功率（简称shp，= brakepower）
shafting 轴系；轴材
shaft(ing) bearing 轴承
shaft(ing) bracket 轴架
shaft journal overlap 轴颈重叠度（曲轴主轴颈与曲柄连杆轴颈重合的程度）
shaft key 轴键
shaft-mounted drive 变速机构与传动轴组成一体的传动系统
shaft neck 轴颈
shaft of hammer 锤柄
shaft pin 轴销
shaft pinion 传动（轴）小齿轮
shaft power 轴功率，轴输出功率，输出（ ）功率，有效功率，= brake power，见 shaft horsepower）
shaft power of compressor 压缩机轴功率（压缩机驱动轴所需要的功率，它等于内功率加上机械损失功率，但不包括外传动，如齿轮或皮带传动损失的功率）
shaft seal 轴密封件
shaft shoulder 轴（凸）肩
shaft straightener 轴矫正装置
shaft tip 轴端
shaft whirl ［美］（驱动轴，如：曲轴等高速旋转时产生的）弦振（亦称 shaft whirling，=［英］shaft whipping，指整个轴身产生如弦乐弓弦般的谐振）
shaft with key way 带键槽的轴
shaft work （输出）轴功（输出轴做的功）
shake ①振动，振荡，抖动 ②（汽车车身等的）低频振动（一般指 20～60C/s 的振动）③摇振（车轮失圆或不平衡引起的车身垂直振动和侧倾振动）④裂纹，裂缝，裂口 ⑤片秒，百分之一微秒（时间）
shake down ①（新设备）试运转，（新方法的）试用，（新工艺的）试验 ②缩减，衰减振动 ③试运转的，试行的，试验性的，临时性的
shake(-down) test ①振动试验 ②新工艺试验
shakeproof washer 防松垫圈，防振垫圈（防止因振动而引起螺母的松动，亦称弹簧垫圈"spring

washer")

shaker ①振动机,振荡器,摇动器,抖动机构,摇动筛,振子②动圈式电磁型振动和疲劳试验机

shake road (车辆)颠簸试验道路

shake table 振动(试验)台

shaking 振动,摇动,颤动

shaking a car to destruction 汽车破坏性振动试验,汽车加振破坏(试验)

shaking appliance 振动装置,加振设备,摇动机构

shaking of steering 转向操纵机构振动,转向盘抖振

shale gasoline 油页岩汽油

shale(rock) 油页岩,油母岩

shallow ①浅的,浅薄的,浮浅的,薄层的②浅的器具;浅凹处③使变浅;使减弱,减小

shallow fording 浅水涉渡

shallow oval indentation (活塞顶上的)浅椭圆形凹窝

shallow slot 浅槽

shallow water splash pool 试车浅喷水池(试车场检查车身密封性用的浅喷水池)

shammy(leather) 麂皮,油鞣革(= chamois)

shampoo spray arch (洗车设备中的)洗涤剂喷射拱门

Shanghai Volkswagen Automobile Corporation 上海大众汽车公司

shank ①躯干,柄②(螺纹紧固件从头部支承面至螺纹间的无螺纹的光)杆部

shank-type bevel pinion 带轴锥齿轮

shape ①形状,模型,形式②成形,选形,按模型或样板制造

shaped iron 型钢(= figured iron)

shape distortion 变形,外形损坏

shaped wire 成型的线材

shape factor 形状系数,外形系数(如:汽车外形对风阻力的影响系数)

shape of stress cycle 应力循环形式

shaper ①成形机;整形机;恢复正确几何形状的整修工具②脉冲形成电路,整形电路③牛头刨床

shape steel 型钢

shape-V thread V形螺纹,三角螺纹

shaping plate 型板,样板

shaping without stock removal 非切削成形,无屑成形

share ①(市场占有)份额②分派,分担,均分,共用

shared responsibility (与其他部门或人)共同分担性责任(见 sole responsibility)

share parts (丰田公司的)部件共享(技术)(使用通用部件,生产多种不同车型,参见 share platform)

share platform (丰田公司的)底盘共享(技术)(指设计制造出数种通用底盘,在每一种通用底盘上生产多种不同车型,以增加车型品种,降低生产成本)

sharp ①尖的,锐利的②急剧的,剧烈的③陡的④清晰的

sharp bend 急转弯(= sharp turn),锐角弯曲

sharp climb 陡坡

sharp corner ①锐角,尖角②急转弯,急弯道

sharp curve ①急弯,急弯道②曲率半径小的曲线

sharp cut-off ①突然截止②急剧停车

sharp decline 陡下坡,陡坡

sharp edge 锐边,尖棱

sharp highway junction 成锐角的公路交叉点

sharp highway turn 公路急转弯处

sharp incline 陡坡(= steep incline)

sharply-changing road conditions 激烈变化的路况

sharply turning 急转向(亦称 sharp

steering)
sharpness ①清晰度②急剧度③锐度
sharpness of turn 转弯急剧程度
sharp pounding 强烈的冲击，猛烈颠簸
sharp thread 三角螺纹（= V-thread）
sharp turn 急转弯（= hairpin turn, tight turn）
sharp worn 剧烈磨损的，磨损成尖头的
shatter crack 细裂纹，微裂纹，发裂
shatterproof 不碎散的，耐振的
shatterproof glass 防碎玻璃，安全玻璃（= splinterproof glass）
shave 剃，刮
shaving ①剃齿，修毛刺②[复]铁屑，切屑③车身整饰（指按照用户的要求，卸去轿车车身前、后端的镀铬装饰件，以获得仅由车身漆面本身光泽得到的流畅光洁的车身外形效果的一种车身改装作业，亦称nosing, decking）
SHD 重型专用汽车（special heavy duty）
shear ①剪切，剪断②剪切应力；（复）剪床，剪刀
shear bolt 抗剪切安全螺栓
shear breakdown 剪切破坏
shear crack 剪裂，剪应力裂纹
shear deformation parameter 剪切变形参数
shear degradation 剪切强度的逐渐下降（退化）
shearing adhesion 黏着抗剪强度，抗剪黏着力
shearing clutch 剪切销式安全离合器，断销式安全离合器（超载时，销即剪断）
shearing failure 剪切破坏
shearing force 剪切力（简称 SF）
shear(ing) load 剪切荷载
shearing resistance ①剪切阻力②抗切割性（轮胎在行驶中具有耐尖锐物切割的性能）
shearing section 剪切断面
shear(ing) stress 剪切应力
shear(ing) test 剪切试验
shear modulus 剪切模量（亦称 **shear modulus of elasticity** "剪切弹性模数"切变模量（切应力与切应变之比值）
shear pin 剪断式保险销
shear pin bush 剪切销衬套
shear plane 剪切面
shear stability （滑油等的）剪切稳定性
shear-stable 耐剪切的，抗剪切的
shear strain 切应变，剪切变形
shear strength 剪切强度，抗剪强度（缩写 SS）
shear stress 切应力（剪切于力作用平面内的应力分量）
shear test 剪切试验（用静拉伸或压缩力，通过相应的剪切工具，使垂直于试样纵轴的一个横截面受剪，或相距不远的两个横截面对称受剪，测定其力学性能的试验）
shear theory 切变理论
sheath ①外皮，蒙皮，护套，钢索包皮；外壳，（壳）层；皮膜，涂料②装上护套，包上外皮，包装（= sheathe）③正电压电极，阳极电子管，屏标④（电缆的）铠装
sheathed cable 铠装电缆
sheathed plug 封装式预热塞（= sealed plug）
sheathing wire 铠装线（金属护皮电线）
sheave ①滑轮，绳轮，带槽滑轮，三角皮带轮；牵引盘②捆住，束
sheave block 滑车组
sheave pulley 滑车，滑轮
shed ①[美]有盖汽车②车库，车棚；库房，堆栈③放出（光、热等）；（车

胎)脱皮;泻落(水滴等);扔掉,放弃;脱落,摆脱,卸载,卸料
SHED 密闭室测定蒸发排放物法(见 sealed housing method for evaporative emission determination)
shedding (附着泥土)自动清除
sheet ①张,片②金属薄板③卡片,表,图表
sheet aluminum 铝板
sheet asbestos 石棉板
sheet brass 黄铜薄板
sheet copper 紫铜板,紫铜片,铜皮,薄铜板
sheet gasket 密封垫片
sheet gasketing 密封用的薄板材料
sheet gauge ①薄板(厚度)量规②厚薄规,量隙片
sheet iron underguard 车身底部保护铁板
sheet metal fastener 薄铁皮紧固器,铁皮卡子,铁皮卡箍
sheet metal gauge 金属板规
sheet metal screw 金属板件用螺钉,金属薄板用螺钉
sheet-metal water jacket 用金属板材制成的水套
sheet molding compound 模压塑料板材(简称 SMC,供模压成型板件用的板材)
sheet number 图表编号,卡片编号
sheet packing 填密片,片状密封件,密封垫片
sheet steel 薄钢板
shelf 格;架子,搁板,(电键)盘(复数为 shelves)
shelf ageing (橡皮等)搁置老化
shelf corrosion 储存腐蚀,搁置锈蚀
shelf life 存放寿命,搁置寿命(指材料、溶液等能不变质存放的时间, = storage life)
shelf panel ①后窗台板(汽车客舱后座靠背上部与后窗连接的板件)②搁板

shelf test 搁置试验,放置试验,存放试验
shelf time 库存期限;库存延续时间
shell ①(对开式滑动轴承的)轴瓦②薄壳件③壳,外壳,套,罩④外环(指液力变矩器叶轮上循环圆的外壁)
shell bearing 轴瓦式滑动轴承(如:曲轴主轴承)
shell casting 壳形铸件,壳形铸造,薄壳铸造
shell construction 薄壳结构,壳体结构
shell hardening 表面淬火(= surface hardening)
shelling 脱层,层层剥落
Shell Mileage Marathon 壳牌油耗马拉松(壳牌石油公司组织的一种汽车油耗英里行程的长途竞赛,1939年开始,一种消遣性的活动,评价标准按每加仑燃油行驶的英里或吨英里计算)
shell selected fuel [美]壳牌石油公司精选燃油(简称 SSL)
shell(type)baffle 迷宫式障板,同心杯形障板
shell(type)construction 薄壳结构
sheltered location 掩蔽场所(为防止直接暴露在日晒、雨淋或其他降落物以及风吹中,无空气温度、湿度控制的场所)
sherardizing 扩散镀锌,粉镀锌法
SHEV 见 series hybrid drive type vehicle
shield ①罩,(干扰)屏蔽装置②保护,遮蔽,屏蔽(= screen)
shield bearing 防尘轴承
shielded arc welding 保护电弧焊,掩弧焊
shielded bearing 带防尘圈的轴承(= bearing with side plate)
shielded-ignition wiring 屏蔽的点火高压线

shi

shielded room 屏蔽室（具有金属壁，可隔绝室内外的射频波，用于汽车电子设备电磁环境适应性试验等）

shielded spark(ing) plug 屏蔽式火花塞(= screened spark plug)

shielded welding ①气体保护焊②药皮电焊条焊接

shielded wire 屏蔽电线 (= screened wire)

shield gas （气体保护焊使用的氩等）保护气体

shield glass 驾驶室风窗玻璃

shielding angle 遮光角（保护角，光源最边缘的一点和灯具出光口的连线与通过裸光源发光中心水平线之间的夹角）

shielding harness 屏蔽电缆，屏蔽导线束；铠装电缆

shielding technique 屏蔽技术

shift ①换班，轮班②［美］换挡③移动，位移，漂移

shift actuator （电子控制自动变速器中按照电子控制模块的指令执行换挡操作的）换挡执行器

shift bar ①变速杆，换挡杆②开关杆

shift-by-wire control （自动变速器的）线控换挡

shift characteristics 见 shift map

shift circuit 移相电路，移位电路

shift collar ①（常啮合式齿轮变速器的）换挡齿套（由换挡拨叉拨动，沿花键轴轴向移动与相应挡位齿轮啮合而获得不同的速比）②（起动机驱动齿轮拨叉的）拨环（在拨叉的拨动下，克服啮合弹簧缓冲力推动驱动齿轮与飞轮齿圈啮合的带拨叉槽的环形件，见 shift lever③）

shift comfort 换挡操作舒适性

shift control valve （CVT 液压系统根据驱动轮和步进电机的行程差控制驱动轮液压管道压力及流量，以控制驱动轮活动轮移动量的）无级变速控制阀

shift-conversion catalyst （分子结构）移置转化催化剂

shift cycling 换挡循环（指汽车行驶中出现的节气门开度不变时，自动变速器自动升挡后车速降低又降挡，降挡后车速升高又升挡，而在两相邻挡位间来回不必要的循环换挡的现象，可用改变节气门开度或挂低挡等方法避免）

shifted indicator diagram 移相示功图，变位示功图（示功图的相位移动 90°，上止点移至中央的示功图）

shift efficiency 工班效率（平均每工班完成的工作量，如：装卸工的工班效率 = 装卸量/装卸工班数（吨/工班））

shifter bar 变速杆 (= gear shift bar, selector bar)

shifter collar ①换挡啮合套，（变速器同步器）啮合齿套②（离合器）分离套，分离环

shifter cylinder 换挡油缸；换挡缸

shifter fork ［美］换挡拨叉（亦称 shift fork，= 英 selector fork）

shift feeling 换挡手感（用力大小，换挡时齿轮啮合是否顺畅，换挡杆行程长短等）

shift fork shaft cover 换挡拨叉轴盖

shift from fast to slow 从高速挡换到低速挡

shift from low to fast 从低速挡换到高速挡

shift gate （变速杆的）换挡导板

shift hysteresis （自动变速器）换挡滞后（同样节气门开度下，升、降挡的换挡点的车速之差）

shift indicator 挡位指示器（供驾驶员选择换挡范围的装置）

shifting ①移动，位移②［美］换挡 (= 英 gear change)

shifting coupling 换挡耦合器（用于液力机械式有级自动变速器中，借助于工作油的充入和排空来实现接合与脱开，代替摩擦式离合器，以完成由一个挡位换到另一个挡位的自动换挡动作，并使换挡过程更为柔顺）

shift(ing) down （由高挡）换入低挡，挂低挡

shift(ing) lock system （自动变速器）换挡锁止系统（当换挡手柄置于驻车挡位置，断开点火开关时，换挡锁电磁阀"shift lock solenoid"和钥匙互锁电磁阀"key interlock solenoid"断电，二者的铁芯移动，将转向盘和换挡手柄锁住）

shifting mechanism 换挡机构

shifting shock 换挡冲击

shifting spanner 活动扳手（= adjustable spanner）

shifting tester 换挡机构试验装置

shifting yoke 变速齿轮换挡拨叉（= shifting fork）

shift knob （按钮式换挡系统的）换挡按钮

shift law memory 换挡规律存储器（在微处理机中，存储动力性、经济性等最佳的换挡规律的可编程序只读存储器，亦称 shift schedule memory）

shift lever ①[美]（齿轮变速器的）变速杆（= gear shifting lever, speed change lever, gear control lever, shifter, gear lever） ②（自动变速器中连接换挡手柄拉索"selector lever cable"和控制阀体手控选挡阀"manual shift valve"的）选挡拉杆 ③（起动机上拨动驱动小齿轮与飞轮齿环啮合的）拨叉

shift light indicator 换挡提示灯（用于手动换挡的机械变速器，装在仪表板上。当电子控制模块根据发动机转速、负荷和水温信息确认应挂入高一级挡位时，便使该灯发亮，以提示驾驶者适时换挡）

shift logic （汽车变速机构的）换挡逻辑

shift map （电子控制自动变速器的）换挡特性图［指其各换挡点与加速踏板位置决定的节气门开度（发动机负荷）和变速器输出转速决定的车速之间的关系特性三维曲面，亦称 shift characteristics］

shift mode selecting switch 换挡模式选择开关（亦称 shift mode selector switch，装在仪表板上，供驾驶者选择自动变速器的不同换挡模式，如：正常"normal"或功率"power"模式，后者强调加速性能，其换挡点的发动机转速高于"正常"模式规定值；运动"sport"或经济"economic"模式，前者强调节能，后者强调动力）

shift-N （自动变速器的自动）换空挡功能（shift neutral 的简称，踩踏制动踏板时间超过某规定值，如：3s 后，即自动接空挡的功能）

shift number 换挡次数

shift overcontrol valve （自动变速器液力控制系的）节气门全开强制降挡阀（当节气门处于最大开度时，该阀可自动地强制降挡，由机械或电气方法操纵，亦称 wide-open throttle kick-down valve, detent valve 或 forced downshift valve）

shift pattern 变速杆各挡位置图

shift pattern generator 换挡指令发生器（是由逻辑电路组成的逻辑控制器，根据挡位指示器、车速传感器和发动机负荷传感器输入的电信号，选择在该工况下自动变速器的最佳挡位，向换挡控制机构发出换挡指令的装置）

shift point （自动变速器的）换挡点（由车速和节气门开度所决定的换挡时机）

shift range 换挡区（如：两挡式分动箱和组合式机械变速器的高、低速挡区，自动变速器前进挡区等）

shift register 移位寄存器（借助适当的控制信号，能够在相邻的保持一定次序的双稳态电路之间传送信息的寄存器）

shift schedule of optimum dynamical characteristic conditions 最佳动力性换挡规律（指着眼于使汽车获得最大加速度、最大爬坡能力和超越加速性能，提高平均行驶车速的换挡规律）

shift schedule of optimum fuel-economy characteristics 最佳燃油经济性换挡规律（指使汽车获得最小燃油消耗量，着眼于节约燃油的换挡规律）

shift shock 变速器（换挡时产生的）冲击（手感）

shift sleeve 啮合套（使齿轮与轴连接以传递动力的装置）

shift smoothness 换挡平顺性（指换挡过程中转矩传递的扰动程度）

shift solenoid （电子控制自动变速器的）换挡电磁阀（简称SS）

shift timer 换挡时间自动记测仪

shift timing （自动变速器电子控制系统控制的）换挡时刻

shift tower 挡位指示器，选挡器（= shift indicator）

shift valve （自动变速器液力控制系的）换挡阀（该阀以车速和节气门开度为输入信号自动控制行星齿轮系各离合器、制动器的液压流路，改变齿系的啮合关系而变换速比，亦称 change valve, coupling valve, relay valve, shuttle valve）

shim ①垫片②楔形垫块③用垫片调节

shim action 粗调，粗略调节，用垫片调整

shimming 用垫片调整；加垫片

shimmy ①汽车前轮摆振，转向轮摆振（不平衡等引起的绕转向主销的自激低幅机械振动）②汽车摆头（因前轮摆振引起的左右摇摆）③摆动，摆振；跳动，颤动，摇摆（= shimmy motion, wobble）

shimmy damper 摆振阻尼器（= shimmy damping device）

shimmy detector ①前轮摆动测定器②车轮动平衡试验机（= dynamic wheel balancer）

shimmy motion 汽车摆头（参见 shimmy）

shimmy-proof 防（转向车轮）摆振的

shimmy stop 转向轮抗摆头装置

shim washer 间隙调整垫圈

shine ①发光，发亮；磨光，擦亮②光泽

shipping-and-storage box 供运输和保存货物用的运输箱

shipping charges [美]货物运输费用，运费

shipping container ①船舶运输用集装箱②运输用集装箱

shipping data 装运数据（如：装箱尺寸、质量等）

shipping density （车、船）装货密度

shipping shock （汽车电子装置等的）装运振动，装运碰撞

shipping weight （车辆的）运输质量，装运质量，起运质量（装运空车时，除汽车的整备质量外，通常包括少量的燃料、油、水等，以供运输过程中短时间的开动用）

shm 简谐运动（simple harmonic motion 的简称）

shock ①冲击，撞击，振动②减振器（shock absorber 的简称）

shock absorber （悬架系统中的）减振器（消减振动的装置，亦称 shock damper，或 damper）

shock absorber bumper （汽车的）冲击吸收式保险杆

shock absorber durability test 减振器耐久性试验（在一定的强化条件下进行室内台架试验，在较短时间内获得接近于实际使用情况时产生的性能变化、磨损和损坏等资料）

shock absorber fluid 减振器油液（亦称 shock absorber oil）

shock absorber friction disk 减振器摩擦盘

shock absorber gear performance test 减振器特性试验（将减振器一端固定，另一端作简谐运动或近似简谐运动时，记录减振器两端相对位移与阻力关系的试验）

shock absorber intake valve 减振器进油阀（为一止回阀，减振器伸张冲程中，活塞上行，储油腔中的减振液经该止回阀进入工作缸下腔）

shock-absorber lever 减振器臂

shock absorber link bushing 减振器杆衬套

shock absorber relief valve 减振器卸荷阀（减振器在压缩冲程和伸张冲程中限制油压和阻尼力，使之不超过一定限度的阀）

shock absorber with variable damping force 阻尼力可变型减振器

shock absorbing circuit 冲击吸收回路，减振回路

shock attenuation device 减振装置，缓冲设备

shock bending test 冲击弯曲试验

shock burst （轮胎）爆破，冲击破裂（＝burst, blow out）

shock chamber 激冷室，骤冷室

shock chilling 激冷，骤冷

shock-cooled 骤冷的，激冷的

shock damper 减振器，阻尼器，缓冲器

shock diffuser 振动渗滤器

shock driver 锤击式旋具（＝impact driver）

shock eliminator 减振器，冲击缓冲器

shocker ①冲击器，振动器，激振机 ②减振器（俚，＝shock absorber）

shock Fourier spectrum 冲击傅里叶谱［频域上用冲击函数的傅里叶变换"$F(u(t))$"，描述冲击特性，$F(u(t))$称为冲击傅里叶谱或冲击频谱］

shock-free 无冲击的，无振动的（＝shockless）

shock insulator 隔振装置（亦称 shock isolater）

shock loading test 冲击荷载试验

shock loss 冲击损失，激波损失

shock mitigation 减振；缓冲

shock pads 减振垫，（轮胎等的）缓冲层，防振填料（＝shock plies）

shock ply 缓冲层，防振层

shockproof packaging 防振包装

shockproof steering gear 防冲击振动的转向机构（不使冲击传至转向盘）

shock reducer 减振器，缓冲器

shock resistance 抗振能力，抗冲击性能

shock-resisted complex steel sheet 减振复合钢板（一种防噪声材料，将具有黏弹性的高分子树脂夹在两层钢板之间组成）

shock sensitive 对冲击敏感的，不耐振的，怕振的，不耐冲击的

shock spectrum 冲击谱（冲击最大响应谱的简称）

shock stop pin 减振销

shock strength 抗冲击强度，抗振强度

shock stress 冲击应力

shock strut assembly 减振器滑柱总成

shock table 冲击试验台，振动试验台

shock test 冲击试验，振动试验
shock wave 冲击波，振波（= percussion wave）
shoddy ①次品，低质量产品②假的，伪造的，劣质的③长弹毛，软再生毛，再生布
shoe ①支撑垫块，支撑枕座②制动蹄（见 brake shoe）③履（带）板，履，靴
shoe block （制动）蹄块，蹄片
shoe brake 蹄式制动器（= block brake, check brake）
shoe contact pressure 制动蹄片接触压力
shoeless track 无履板式履带
SHO engine 特高输出功率发动机（福特公司 special high-output engine 的简称）
shoe pivot 制动蹄支承销（亦称 shoe anchor pin）
shoe plate 履板（亦称 shoe sole）
shoes expander mechanism 蹄片张开装置（鼓式制动器中使制动蹄片压向制动鼓的部件）
S-hook S形（挂）钩
shoot hole 喷焰孔，喷射孔，（转子发动机等的）火焰射出孔（指火花塞小室和燃烧室相通的小孔）
shooting 发射，射击；探查
shooting brake 接站车，旅行车（estate car 的旧称）
shooting space （转子发动机的）喷焰空间（指火花塞电极至燃烧室之间的空间）
shop assembly 工厂装配，车间装配
shop car ①流动售货车②厂内小型运输汽车
Shore hardness number 肖氏硬度值（用冲头弹起的高度和规定高度的比值与肖氏硬度系数的乘积表示的硬度值）
Shore hardness test 肖氏硬度试验（将规定质量及形状的金刚石或钢球冲头从一定高度落到试样表面上，用测量的冲头回跳高度计算硬度的一种动态力硬度试验，亦称 scleroscopic hardness test）
Shore hardness tester 肖氏硬度计（亦称 Shore sleroscope, Shore sclerometer）
shortage of fuel 缺油
short and long arm suspension system （轿车用的）长短臂独立悬架系统（上臂短、下臂长的双横臂式独立悬架，简称 SALA suspension）
short base 短轴距（short wheel base 的简称）
short base cab （仅一排驾驶与助手座的）窄型平头驾驶室
short-bonnetted type vehicle 短头型载货汽车
short-chassis car 短底盘小轿车
short-circuit braking （电机）短路制动
short circuit(ing) device 短路装置
short-circuit output current 短路输出电流（在规定的条件下，当输出端与地或其他规定电位短路时，通过该输出端的电流）
short-circuit protection 短路保护
short-circuit stable network 短路稳定网络
short circuit test 短路试验（在短路情况下进行的试验，对短路故障的检查）
short city hauling 市内短途运输
short-coming 缺点，缺陷
short connector 短路接线器（= short circuit device）
short conventional tractor 常规型短头牵引车
short(-)cut 简化，捷径，近路（见 royal road）
short-cut calculation 简化计算
short dash line 短虚线
short-distance beam （前照灯）近

光 (= dipped beam, lower beam, meeting beam, passing beam)

short distance hauling 短途货运

short-distance passenger transportation 短途客运

short-distance vehicle 短距离运输车辆，短途运输车辆

short-duration torque 短时间作用转矩

shorted load protection （电器的）短路负载保护

shorter process ①火焰表面硬化（= flame hardening）②（一般指用时较短的）快速工序，快速工艺过程

shortest confidence interval 最短置信节，最短置信区间

short fiber grease 短纤维润滑脂

short-haul diesel engine 供短途运输使用的柴油机

short-haul truck 短途货运汽车

shorting-out of plug 使火花塞短路

short interval GPS data 短周期 GPS 数据

short-life test 短寿命制件的耐久性试验

shortness ①脆性②不足，缺少③简，短，低，矮

short-nose plier 短鼻钳

short oil 短油（聚合程度小的油）

short-order test program 临时试验大纲

short planet gear 短行星齿轮（外行星齿轮机构中与长行星齿轮和小中心齿轮啮合的行星齿轮）

short-pulse radar sensor 短脉冲雷达传感器

short-range design 近期计划，近期规划

short-reach plug 短型火花塞，短腿火花塞（安装螺纹部分较缸盖螺孔短，见 long-reach plug）

short run production 小批生产，短期生产

short sensing and implementation system 短路传感及处理系统

short stroke engine 短行程发动机（行程缸径比接近1的发动机）

short supply 缺乏，短线（供应），短缺

short teeth 短齿，矮齿（= stub teeth）

short-term ignition cutout method （防滑转牵引力控制系统的）短期中断点火法（可实现发动机输出转矩的高速响应减少，且无须增加新硬件设备）

short term travel 短途旅行；短行程，短程

short (time) count 短时计数（通常指数小时以内进行的交通量调查）

short time rating ①（发动机）短时间工作额定功率②短时间工作功率的标定

short-time test 快速试验；强化试验（用加大负荷、高转速或加快磨损等方法进行机器的快速强化试验，以便短时间内较快地获得试验结果，简称 short tast）

short toe contact （锥齿轮）偏向小头的接触印痕

short to ground 接地短路（指电路中某一点接地形成的短路）

short ton ［美］短吨（= 907kg，简称 sh. ton）

short to positive 正极短路（如：点火线圈各匝间短接）

short-travel valve 短行程阀，短行程气门

short wave receiver 短波（sw）收音机

short wheelbase chassis 短轴距底盘

shot ①弹丸，小珠②金属内的硬夹杂物③（发动机起动时）少量燃油的射注④射，注，射束⑤损坏的，

破旧的

shot air valve (发动机强制怠速工况)空气喷射阀(控制混合气浓度,简称SAV)

shot-bag test 霰弹袋试验(确定安全玻璃在大的易变形的物体冲击下是否具有某种最低强度的试验)

shot-blasting 喷砂;喷金属丸,喷丸处理,喷砂清理

shot-blast-textured 表面组织喷丸处理的(汽车用冷轧钢板等,简称SBT)

shot cold activated hardening 冷激喷丸强化(用直径为0.4~2mm的冷激铸铁丸或钢丸以很高的速度50~70m/s,多次冲击零件已加工面,以形成冷硬层)

shot hanger blast 连续喷丸清砂

shot of oil (少量)机油的射注

shot peening 喷丸处理,喷丸(冷作)硬化(= shot-ball peening, shot blasting)

shot peening coverage 喷丸范围,喷丸区域,喷丸率(用喷丸区面积百分比表示,为喷丸效率指标)

shotpin 止销,制动销,锁销,挡销

shot-proof glass 防弹玻璃

shot-proof tire 防弹轮胎(= bullet-proof tire)

shot-welding 点焊

shoulder 肩,肩部(如:①胎肩,胎冠与胎侧之间的部分②轴肩,直径加大起支撑或推力面作用的部分③路肩,行车道外侧与路缘石之间的部分)

shoulder belt (汽车乘员安全带的)肩带

shouldered shaft 带肩轴

shoulder elevation (机械手的)臂关节弯曲件

shoulder eyebolt 轴肩上的带眼螺栓

shoulder harness (安全带的)肩带及其附件

shoulder indicator (装在车辆)前方上部的转向指示灯

shouldering ①肩,台②承受,承担

shoulder-located cylinder liner 带肩台的汽缸套,带凸缘的缸套

shoulder of spindle 轴肩

shoulder of tire 胎肩(轮胎肩部)(= tyre shoulder)

shoulder pitch 路肩斜度

shoulder point 肩点(汽车驾驶员手操作空间范围的原点,简称SP)

shoulder room (小轿车车厢的)肩部宽度(指乘客坐在座椅上时,从其肩部高度上测得的车厢内的宽度。由于乘客身高不同,将左、右车窗下沿高度,定为坐姿肩高,亦称 shoulder space)

shoulder screw 有肩螺钉

shoulder slope 路肩坡

shoulder support seat 肩撑式座椅(汽车转弯时,其肩撑可防止肩部横向滑动)

shoulder width (乘员)肩宽

shoulder work ahead "前面路肩施工"标志

shovel ①单斗挖掘机②铲子,挖斗

shovel bucket 挖掘机铲斗(亦称 shovel dipper)

shovel car 铲运车(车前端装有液压机构升降的铲斗等,利用车前进的推力将物料铲入斗中、升起运走)

shovel crawler 履带式挖掘机;履带式铲土机

shovel loader ①(铲)斗式装载机,铲车(= front end loader,俗称 shovel truck)②挖掘-装载机(一种前端带装载斗,后端带反铲挖掘斗的装载机)

show 展示,显示,指出,示出,说明,证明

showcase ①(产品)陈列柜②显示(某项优点)

showcase and testing ground 展示试

验场地，展销试用场地（一般指设在新车型开始销售地区的展销演示场地）

shower cooling 淋浴式冷却，喷洒式冷却

shower head 喷水头，喷头

showing room 陈列室，展厅（亦称 showroom）

shp 轴功率（shaft horsepower 的简称）

shrinkage 收缩，收缩性，收缩量

shrinkage allowance 收缩留量，收缩容许量，预留收缩量

shrinkage cavity （收）缩孔（= shrinkage hole）

shrinkage crack 缩裂，收缩裂纹（见 check crack）

shrinkage limit 收缩极限

shrinkage ratio 收缩比，收缩系数

shrinkage stress 收缩应力（= shrink stress）

shrink fit 冷缩配合，热胀配合，热压配合

shrinking hammer （车身板件深拉伸凹陷等的）热缩敲平手锤（其一端带凸方格平面，用于加热缩敲）

shrink on 热套，红套

shroud ①屏板，屏蔽，遮板；罩；幕，护套，套筒，壳，护壳 ②覆盖，遮蔽

shroud and dash panel assembly （轿车车身的）前围上盖、板带仪表板总成（= cowl and dash panel assembly）

shrouded impeller 密闭式叶轮，有外壳的叶轮

shrouded spark(ing) plug 屏蔽式火花塞[= screened spark (ing) plug]

shroud(ing) ring 箍圈，护圈

shroud upper panel （小轿车车身的）前围上盖板（= cowl upper panel）

shrunk fit 烧嵌，热嵌配合

shrunk-in liner 热压入式缸套

shrunk-on 热套的，红套的

sh. ton 短吨（见 short ton）

shudder ①抖动（颤动）②（特指液力机械工作油液在其摩擦系数 μ-速度 v 关系特性中 $d\mu/dv$ 为正值时产生的）黏滑现象（油液在沿工件流动的同时，部分黏附于工作壁面等，= stick-slip phenomenon）

shunt ①分路，分流，分激；并联 ②分激器，分路器；旁通道 ③（汽车）开往侧线，驶入会车支路 ④碰撞 ⑤撞车（特指追尾碰撞，即：后车撞击前车后部）

shunt circuit 并联电路

shunt compensation 并联补偿

shunt connection 并联

shunt(ed) excitation 并激

shunt feed 并联馈电

shunt feedback 并联反馈

shunt generator 并激发电机（亦称 parallel wound generator, shunt wound generator, 磁场绕组与电枢绕组并联，故名）

shunt(ing) resistance 并联电阻

shunt lead 分路线，并联线

shunt motor 并激电动机（亦称 parallel wound motor, shunt-wound motor）

shunt path 分路，分流电路

shunt peaking 并联电路升高法，并联建峰（用并联法使频率特性的高频部分升高）

shunt-regulated amplifier 并联调节放大器

shunt resistor 并联电阻器

shunt winding （电磁振动式调节器的）并联线圈（指直接或通过电阻并联接到发电机正负极两端，反映发电机端电压高低的线圈）

shunt-wound ①并激绕组 ②并激绕组的

shut 关,闭,切断

shutdown (发动机)熄火,关闭

shutdown alarm 故障停机警报信号,故障停车警报信号

shutdown feature 停止装置;断开装置;切断(电流)装置

shutdown signal 停车信号,停机信号,关闭信号,断开信号

shutoff ①关闭,切断,断路,停止 ②截流阀,关闭器

shutoff head 停止压头,停断压头(用压力表示的泵水量为零时的水泵扬程)

shutoff the gas 断油减速(见 decrease speed)

shut off threshold of smooth running (发动机)平稳运转停止阀(指维持发动机平稳运转的最低转速)

shutoff wrench 自动断开扳手(达到规定的转矩后,即自动切断动力源)

shutter ①百叶窗②挡风板,节气门,操纵门,蝶形板活门,闸门,闸板③断路器④(霍尔效应传感器转子上的)阻磁片(亦称 shutter blade)⑤快门,光栅,光栏⑥装上百叶窗,关闭百叶窗,关闭快门

shutter blade ①百叶窗片②(霍尔效应传感器等转子上的)阻磁片,斩磁片(简称 shutter)

shutter thermostat control (散热器)百叶窗恒温器控制;百叶窗的恒温操纵机构

shutter type blade (各种变磁阻型传感器转子上的)隔磁叶片(见 shutter wheel)

shutter wheel (霍尔效应传感器等的)隔磁叶片轮(带隔磁叶片的转子)

shutte (three-way) valve 梭动柱塞式三通阀(阀筒的两端各有一个入口,中央有一个由梭动柱塞控制的出口,柱塞总是被压向输入压力较低的一侧,而使较高的压力由中央出口输出)

shuttle ①短途穿梭运输工具,短途运输车,往复运输车;穿梭运动,往复运动②(交通工具)周转,(往复运输的)单程,单程运输的货物③往复式的,往返的,穿梭式的

shuttle armature type 电枢移动型(汽车起动机)(见 rushmore type)

shuttle bus 郊区公共汽车(=suburban bus)

shuttle dumper (在狭窄的,如:山洞等场地使用的,可双向行驶并具有可供双向驾驶的回转式驾驶座和驾驶操作系统的)双向行驶自卸车

shuttle gear shift 来回换挡(指①来回频繁换挡②在倒挡与前进挡间来回变换)

shuttle loop transit 往复环形运输,闭路往复运输(简称 SLT)

shuttle traffic 往复行车,穿梭交通

SI ①受伤程度指数(severity index)②火花点火(spark ignition)③国际单位制(System International d'unitès)

Si 硅(silicon)

SIA [法]汽车工程师学会(Societe des Ingenie de l'Automobile)

siamese ①双连的,连体的(指两个相同部件整体连在一起的,如:siamese cylinder bores 指中间无水套相隔,缸壁直接相连的连体汽缸,siamese exhaust pipes 指全长连在一起的两根排气尾管,siamese valve ports 指进、排气管道的两个相邻的进、排气门孔等)②双连件,联体件

sibling (原意为同胞兄弟姐妹或同科同属生物,对汽车指)同一品种的车型

SIC ①半导体集成电路(semiconductor integrated circuit)②硅集成电

路(silicon integrated circuit)③介电常数,电容率(specific inductive capacity)

SiC-DPF 碳化硅型柴油机微粒排放物滤清器(以碳化硅为滤芯基体,SiC 的热稳定性和抗腐蚀性良好,但抗热冲击性较差,且成本较高)

sick engine 带病发动机(有故障的发动机)

sickness 病,疾病;故障

SiC varistor 碳化硅可变电阻

SID 汽车侧面碰撞试验用假人(side impact dummy 的简称)

side ①边,侧面,侧壁,边板,山坡,方面②旁侧的,侧面的,侧向的(见 lateral)

side acceleration 侧向加速度(质心加速度矢量沿 y 轴方向的分量)

side acceleration sensor 侧向加速度传感器

side adaptive airbag 自适应性防侧面碰撞安全气囊(①置于车身两侧室内,如:座椅靠背外侧,发生侧面碰撞时直接保护乘员②置于两侧车门内,临碰撞前膨胀,增加车门抗撞击强度。这类气囊大部由波纹状薄金属材料制成空心梁状,爆发时高压燃气将其撑开,顶住车门,对抗撞击)

side aerodynamic force coefficient 侧向气动力系数

side air bag (汽车的)侧面安全气囊

side assist system (Audi 的)侧向辅助系统(转换车道或并线时若后方有车辆驶近,后视镜上的 LED 警报灯将不停闪光,提醒换道或并线有危险)

side-attached 侧面连接的,侧面悬挂的,侧面加装的

side-band 边频带,边带(简称 SB)

side beam 边梁,侧梁,大梁(见 side member)

side-bend specimen 侧向弯曲试验用试样

side board (货车车身)侧栏板(=side panel②)(栏板式货车车身的)侧栏板

side body 车身侧部(客厢及车身前、后部侧面部分的总称)

sideboom 侧置起重臂

side branch resonator (内燃机进、排气系统作为闭口端的)旁支谐振箱(见 resonator)

side-by-side test 总成的成对试验(如:成对变速器的功率闭路循环试验等)

side-by-side valves 侧置气门(=side valves)

side-by-side vehicle wheels 并装车轮(两车轮并装在一起)

side car ①(摩托车的)挎斗,边车②带挎斗的摩托车

side(-) chain (聚合物分子结构中的)支链,侧链

side clearance 侧面间隙,侧隙(任何部件或物体的侧面与另一部件或物体,或任一点、面间的距离,如:对汽车而言,指直线行驶或转向时,其左、右两侧与障碍物之间的距离。在论述汽车的通行和转向通道宽度时,指能保证汽车直线行驶或转向时汽车车身左、右两侧最外点不致碰到障碍物的最小通道侧隙)

side clutch 侧边离合器,副离合器

side collision 侧面碰撞(发生在两辆车之间,一辆车侧面受撞,另一辆车前面或后面受撞的碰撞)

side column 侧柱,边柱

side combination lamp 车侧组合灯(在车侧的几种不同用途的灯组装在一起)

side combustion seals (转子发动机的)端面气封装置,端面燃气密封

装置

side control 侧控制（指同一侧几个车轮的制动力由同一个指令控制）

side cover ①侧盖，边盖，端盖 ②（转子发动机的）缸盖

side crank 曲轴端曲柄

side curtain （篷顶车）侧篷；侧帘，侧挡帘

side-curtain air bag system 帘幕式侧面安全气囊

side cushion 肘垫，扶手

side deflector （装在货车车身上的）侧导流板（降低空气阻力）

side discharging car 侧倾自卸车，侧（边）卸（货）车（= side dump car, side tip car, side-tipping dump car）

side door beam （轿车车身的）侧门梁（车身侧面的加强件，吸收横向碰撞能量，保护乘员）

side door container 侧门式集装箱（除后端开门外，在侧壁中部还开一个侧门，以便装卸内部货物）

side-draft carburetor 平吸式化油器（空气由侧向吸入的水平腔式化油器）

side draft (on the drawbar) （挂钩上的）牵引力侧向分力

side-dump truck 侧卸式自卸汽车，（侧面卸货的自卸汽车，= side-tip truck, side dumper）

side effect 边界效应，副作用

side electrode （火花塞）侧电极（= overhead electrode, 即其搭铁电极）

side elevation 侧视图

side engine vehicle 发动机侧置式汽车（发动机位于汽车的侧面）

side entrance 车厢侧面入口

side-entry combustion chamber 侧方进气燃烧室

side exit 侧向出口，(车厢)侧门

side face of piston ring 活塞环两端面

side feed type injector 侧面进油式喷油器

side flap 可放倒的（货车）侧栏板

side flasher 装在车身两侧的闪光灯（如：车侧方向指示灯）

side force 侧向力（如：作用在汽车上的力矢量沿 y_0 轴方向的分量）

side force of tire 轮胎侧向力（车轮外倾角为0°时，为保持侧偏角，由路面作用在车轮上的侧向力）

side-force reaction 侧向反作用力

side fork lift 侧置式叉车，侧置叉式铲车

side-friction brake 侧面摩擦式制动器（如：盘式制动器）

side gate inside board 边板内板（边板内侧护板）

side gate outside panel 边板外板（边板外侧护板）

side gate side post 边板侧柱（边板两侧的立柱）

side gears 差速器的半轴齿轮（亦称 differential side gear）

side guard （装在货车两侧前、后轮区，防止其他车辆从侧面钻撞或伤及摩托车手等的）车侧护栅

sidehill 山坡（= hillside）

sidehill operation （车辆）在横坡上作业

sidehill road 山坡道路

side housing-antidrive side （转子发动机的）非驱动端缸盖，起动端缸盖，前端盖

side housing-drive side （转子发动机的）驱动端缸盖，后缸盖

side impact 侧面受撞（指车辆受撞部位在车的同一侧上的前面拐角和后面拐角之间）

side impact air bag 侧面碰撞气囊（轿车受侧面碰撞时，防止乘员受伤的安全气囊，见 SIPS）

side impact bar 防侧撞梁（装在车

门框结构内的加强梁，防止发生侧面碰撞时伤及乘员）

side impact dummy 汽车侧面碰撞试验用假人（简称 SID）

side-impact head air bag 侧面碰撞头部安全气囊

side impact protection system （小轿车）侧面碰撞防护系统（简称 SIPS，指小轿车受侧面碰撞时，防止乘员受伤的车身结构及防侧撞安全气囊、安全座椅等）

side impact test （汽车的）侧面碰撞试验

side indicator 车侧指示灯（如：侧面转向指示灯、示廓灯，= flank indicator）

side inlet port ①（转子发动机的）端面进气口，端面进气孔（进气口在端盖上）②侧进气孔

side-intake and peripheral exhaust ports （转子发动机的）侧面进气和周边排气孔（指进气口设在缸体盖而排气孔设在缸体圆周面上）

side-intake and side exhaust （转子发动机的）侧面进、排气（结构）

side knock ①活塞敲缸，活塞松动 ②横向冲击，侧向敲击

side lamp （汽车等的）侧灯（一般指装在车身前左方、右两边角的示廓小灯）

side lift 侧置提升器（安装在侧栏板上的举升机构）

side light ①侧灯灯光（指侧灯发出的灯光，而不是指侧灯）②侧向照明③边窗

sideline ①旁线，横线②（公路的）侧道

sidelines of science 边缘科学，边缘学科

sideling 斜的，斜向一边的，倾斜的

side load （车身）侧壁荷载，侧向负荷

side loader 侧式装载机

side loading fork truck 侧向装载的叉式装载机，侧向装载的叉车

side loading refuse collector 侧倾式废料收集车，侧倾式垃圾车

side loading vehicle 侧向装载的载货汽车

side marker 侧边标志，宽度标志 (= fender marker)

side member （汽车车架）大梁，侧梁，边梁，纵梁 (= longitudinal side bar, side beam)

side-member flange 车架纵梁（槽钢）的股，车架边梁翼边

side minder 侧向探测器（装在车尾两侧，利用雷达或红外传感装置，扫描车后及两侧障碍物等的一种预防事故装置）

side monitor （汽车的）侧面（路况）监测器 (= side minder)

side-mounted power take-off 侧置功率输出轴

side-object detection system （汽车）侧面障碍物探测系统（车侧障碍物雷达探测系统，当障碍物与车侧的距离接近某危险值时，即向驾驶员发出警报）

side oil seals （转子发动机的）端面油封

side on collision （汽车）侧面碰撞

side-opening rear deck （汽车的）侧开式后行李舱盖

side oscillation 侧向摆动

side overturned car 侧向翻倒的车辆

side panel ①（小轿车、大客车车身的）侧板②（栏板式货车车身的）侧栏板 (= sideboard)

side panel assembly （小轿车车身的）侧板总成（由前、中、后支柱，门槛板、侧架顶梁板及后边窗加强板等组成）

side-parking 路旁停车，路边驻车

side-parking lamp 侧停车灯

side pavement 人行道 (= side walk)

1443

sidepiece 边部构件,边件
side pillar (车身骨架的)侧柱
side plank (车身)侧壁外面板(= side panel)
side play 侧隙
side port (转子发动机)端面进排气口,侧孔,侧壁孔
side-port engine 端面进气(转子)发动机
side pressure of piston 活塞侧压力
side primary inlet port (转子发动机端盖上的)端面主进气口
side protection in sheet metal for engine 发动机侧挡泥板,发动机边护罩板
side radiator 侧置式散热器
side rail ①纵梁(= side member) ②车内两侧扶手
side rake 侧向(横向)倾斜,侧向(横向)坡度角
side reaction 侧向反作用力
side scuffing 侧面擦伤
side sealing strip (转子发动机的)端面气封条
side seal spring (转子发动机的)端面气封条弹簧,气封条弹簧
side secondary inlet port (转子发动机端盖上的)端面副进气孔
side shake ①(车身)横向摆振 ②(轴承的)端隙,轴向间隙(= end play)
side sill 门槛(车身侧部联结前、中、后柱的下边梁,亦称 rocker panel, sill panel)
side skid 侧滑
side-skidding characteristics (汽车的)抗侧滑特性
side skirt of body 侧裙板(位于货车货箱底板下方两侧的裙状空气动力学附加装置,用于减小空气阻力)
side skirt of fender 翼子板侧裙
side skirt rail (客车车身的)侧围裙边梁(位于侧围骨架底的纵梁)

side slip ①侧滑(滑向一边) ②(车轮)侧偏(侧向偏出)
side-slip angle (轮胎)侧偏角(指轮胎接地中心的行进方向与车轮中心平面方向间的夹角,= slip angle)
side slip angle observer 侧偏角观测器(由于侧偏角传感器"side slip angle sensor"很贵而且很难安装在车上,因此多使用根据转向盘转角、横摆率和车速来推算车身侧偏角的观测器)
side slip angle of vehicle 整车侧偏角(亦写作 vehicle's slip angle,指汽车受横向力作用,如:转向时,汽车重心的运动方向与汽车纵轴方向间的夹角)
side slip angle relative to air 相对风速的侧偏角(汽车行驶中,若相对空气速度与汽车 x 轴成一定角度时,汽车在 y 轴方向受该风速的侧向力分力作用,所产生的侧偏角)
side slip sensor 侧偏传感器
side-slip speed 侧偏速度
side slip tester 侧偏测试台(测定车轮侧偏的板式或滚筒式测试台)
side-slip velocity 侧偏速度
side slope 边坡,侧坡
side splitter 侧导流板(装在箱式货车车箱侧面底部的侧裙板,用于减小气流分离形成的空气阻力)
side spoiler (轿车车身)侧向气流稳定板(装在车身两侧下边,防横风,亦称侧裙板 "side skirt panel")
side stabilizer 侧向稳定杆
side stand (起重车辆或摩托车等可伸缩的)侧撑
side strip (道路)路边分隔带,路缘带(平行于行车道沿着人行道的长条形地带,未铺面层,往往种植草皮或灌木,亦称 margin verge)
side support air mat (座椅靠背上)侧面支撑气垫
side sway 横向摇摆

side-sway eliminator ①防横摇装置，防横摇杆②横向摆振（横向角振动）减振器

side sweep 车身侧面轮廓线

side throw （车厢的）横向摇晃

side thrust of piston 活塞侧向推力

side-thrust reaction 侧向反作用力（= side force reaction）

side tip car 侧（向）倾（卸）车（= side discharging vehicle, side dumper, side tipping dump car, side tip truck）

side-tipping dump trailer 侧卸挂车，侧向倾卸挂车（亦称 side-tipping trailer）

side tire scrubbing 胎侧擦伤

side-to-side adjustment 横向（位置）调整，横调

side-to-side vibration applied to the human body 作用于人体的左右振动（作用于人体的左右方向的直线振动）

side travel 侧向位移，横向移动（= cross travel）

side turn signal lamp （装在车身侧面的）车侧转向信号灯

side valve ①侧置气门②侧置气门式发动机（sided valve engine, side-valve type engine 的简称，指气门及气门机构装在缸体内汽缸的侧面，亦简称 svengine。进、排气门装于汽缸同一侧者，美称 L head，分装于汽缸两侧者称 T head）

side-valve drive 侧置气门驱动机构（如：侧置凸轮轴）

side valve head 侧置气门汽缸盖

side valve timing (mechanism) 侧置式气门正时机构（包括曲轴、凸轮轴正时齿轮、凸轮轴、气门挺杆及气门总成）

side velocity (v) 侧向速度（v）（质心速度沿 y 轴的分量）

side view 侧视图

Side View⁺ 侧视（一种接通转向灯后便可将转向侧的路况及环境影像实时显示于车内屏幕上的安全系统的商品名）

side view mirror （汽车的）侧视镜

side visor （车身）侧窗窗帘

sidewalk line 人行道线

side wall ①（客车车身的）侧围（由侧面骨架、侧面蒙皮、侧面护板、侧窗及所属车身附件等组成的部件）②（轮胎的）胎侧（胎肩至胎圈之间的部分）

sidewall body 带侧壁板的车身

sidewall flexing （轮胎）侧壁的挠度

side wall frame （客车）侧围骨架（位于车身两侧的骨架，亦称 side wall skeleton）

side wall inner shield （客车）侧围护板（覆盖在侧围骨架内表面的板件，亦称 side wall interior panel）

side wall outer panel （客车）侧围蒙皮（覆盖在侧围骨架外表面的板件，亦称 side wall skill）

sidewall panelling （车身的）侧壁板，侧壁镶板，侧壁板件

side wall pillar （客车）侧围立柱（侧围骨架中支撑顶盖安装侧窗且延伸至腰梁下方的支柱）

side wall rubber （轮胎的）胎侧胶（指胎侧外帘布层上的胶层）

side wall shelf rail （客车）侧围搁梁（位于客车基准 Z 平面附近，并用于搁置地板的纵梁）

sidewall stiffness （轮胎的）胎侧刚度

sideway floating 横向浮动

sideway force coefficient （车轮）侧向力系数（侧向力与垂直荷载的比值，简称 SFC）

sideway skid resistance 抗侧滑能力

sideways overturning （汽车等）侧向倾翻

sidewind force 侧向风力（= cross windforce）

side window 侧窗（美，= 英 quarter light）

side window handrail height 侧窗扶手高（扶手中心至最近地板之间的距离）

side window pillar （客车车身的）侧窗立柱（位于腰梁上供安装侧窗及支撑顶盖的支柱）

side window wiper control 侧窗玻璃刮水器操纵件（控制侧窗玻璃刮水器工况的操纵件）

side windshield （客车车身的）侧窗玻璃

side wind stability （汽车行驶中的）横风稳定性（在侧向风作用下，保持原行车路线的能力）

side wing （赛车上的）侧翼板（两块翼型部件，向前倾斜，与相对气流成负迎角。安装在驾驶室两侧。底面是负压区，顶面为正压区，可有效地产生向下方的作用力）

sidewise skidding （车轮）侧滑

sidewise tipping 侧向倾卸

siding machine 边缘修整机

SIE 工业工程师学会（Society of Industrial Engineers）

siemens 西门子（国际单位制导出的电导单位，亦称 mho，代号 Ω^{-1}，或 S，即欧姆的倒数，1S =1A/V）

SI engine 火花点火发动机（spark ignited engine 的简称）

sieve analysis （固体粉料等的）筛分测试，筛选测定，筛析（利用筛选确定粒度的方法）

sieve mesh 筛眼，筛孔（= sieve open-ing）

sieve method 逐步淘汰法，筛选法

sift 筛分，筛选，细查，栋选，挑选

sight ①视力，视界，视距，视野 ②目测，观测；视距 ③意见，见解 ④瞄准，照准 ⑤瞄准器；观察孔

sight distance 视距，能见距（= seeing distance，visibility distance，vision distance）

sight feed 可用直接观察方法监视的供给（如：滴油润滑）

sight gauge 目测计

sight glass ①仪表玻璃 ②观察窗玻璃 ③滴油杯

sight line 视线（从目标物到驾驶员眼睛椭圆的切线）

sight reading chart 操作指示图表（如：仪表板上可供边看边操作的变速杆挂挡位置图）

sightseeing bus 观光客车（= observation bus）

sight shield （汽车保险杠和车身前脸之间的）屏蔽板，遮蔽板（作为装饰板，使保险杠与车身看起来连成整体，看不到缝隙）

sight triangle （交叉口）视距三角形（两条交叉的道路上，接近交叉口的车辆驾驶员相互间观望的视线及各自视距形成的三角形）

sign 记号，符号，信号标记，征象，标志，预兆

signal 信号（载有由一个或几个参数表示的一个或几个变量的信息的物理变量）

signal acquisition 信号采集

signal ahead sign "前面有信号"标志（在交叉口信号200m前看不到该信号处设置的预告标志）

signal amplification 信号放大

signal charge 信号电荷（表示信号的电荷量）

signal conditioning 信号调制，信号处理（简称 SC）

signal control （交通）信号控制（用交通信号进行交通控制）

signal converter （将模拟信号变换为脉冲信号的）信号转换器

signal diaphragm-type vacuum booster

单膜片式真空助力器

signaled crossing 有信号管理的交叉路口，信号化交叉路口

signal generator 信号发生器

signal grid 信号栅极，调制电极，控制栅（极），调制电极

signal harness connector （控制系统）信号线束插接件

signal head ①信号器，多面信号器（可向一个或几个方面显示信号）②信号机头总成（包括机头在内的信号发光装置及光学装置的总称，=signal head assembly）

signalized intersections （公路的）信号化的交叉路口，信号自动控制的交叉路口

signal lamp 信号灯（亦称 signal lantern, signalling lamp）

signal level 信号电平

signal line （真空、气、液等信号的）信号管道，信号通道

signal rotor 信号转子（如：无触点式点火装置的点火信号发生器的变磁阻转子，斩磁转子，遮光转子等）

signal roundtrip time delay 信号往返时间滞后

signal-seeking radio 自动搜索信号的无线电接收机

signal-to-noise ratio 信噪比（信号与噪声的比，在测量中，信噪比越高，测量越可靠）

signal valve （自动变速器的）信号阀（受速控压力和油门压力的作用，对继动阀发出换挡信号的阀）

signal view （路标或灯光）信号的可见度

signature PIP （福特轿车用5.0L顺序汽油喷射式发动机的曲轴位置传感器发出的）点火缸序信号（其曲轴位置传感器隔磁叶片轮上有一个隔磁叶片较其他窄，该窄叶片通过霍尔元件与永磁元件的间隙时产生一窄脉冲信号，告诉电子控制模块下一个该轮到第二缸点火）

signboard 路标，标志牌，信号板

sign for uphill traffic lanes 上坡车道标志

significance level 显著性水平

significance test 显著性检定（=test of significance）

significant figure 有效数（字）

significant surface 有效面，有效表面

signing separators （车道）分隔带，各种行车道分隔标记

sign paddle 手动标志牌（由人工操作，控制交通的标志牌，如：停车、开动、减速牌等）

SIL （噪声的）谈话干扰级（speech interference level）

silage extension 青储料运输车箱栏板加高部分

silage trailer 运青储料的挂车

silastic 硅橡胶

silchrome steel 硅铬钢（亦称 silicon-chromium steel）

silel cast iron 硅铸铁（硅5%~6%）

silence cabinet 隔音室

silencer 消声器（美称 muffler）

silencer chamber 消声器腔，消音室

silencer-filter type air intake 带消声-滤清器的进气口

silencing unit 消声单元（起消声作用的结构部分）

silentbloc bearing （一种）橡胶金属防振支垫（的商品名）

silentbloc rubber bushing 橡胶金属减振消声衬套

silent chain 无声传动链

silent door furniture 车门消声装置，车门消声填充材料，车门消声设备

silent fan 无声风扇

silent gear 无声齿轮，无声齿轮机构

silent-mesh gearbox 无声啮合变速

器，无声换挡变速器
silent-running engine 无噪声发动机
silent shift（ing） 无声换挡（= noiseless shift）
silent speed 无声行驶速度
silent third 无声的第三挡（亦称 silent third speed, quiet third）
silent third-and-forth gearbox 第三、四挡带同步器无声换挡的变速器
silent tire 无声轮胎
silent-travel coachwork 隔音良好的客车车身；行驶时无声的客车车身
silhouette （车身或内符等的）轮廓，外形
silica 二氧化硅（SiO_2，= silicon dioxide）
silica gel filter （氧化）硅胶滤清吸湿器（用于滤除气体中的水分）
silica glass 石英玻璃
silica sand 硅土砂
silicate bond 硅酸酯黏结剂
silicate flux 水玻璃熔剂，硅酸盐焊剂
silicate scale 硅酸盐水垢
silicic acid calcium 硅酸钙
silicon 硅（Si，旧称矽）
silicon accelerometer 硅膜式加速器仪（传感器）
silicon-aluminum alloy 硅铝合金（摩擦系数极低；20世纪90年代末，奔驰公司用于制作缸套、活塞与缸壁，摩擦阻力可降低45%）
silicon bronze 硅青铜
silicon capacitive absolute pressure sensing element 硅膜电容式绝对压力传感器（简称SCAP sensor）
silicon carbide 碳化硅，金刚砂（= carborundum）
silicon chrome-steel 硅铬钢，亦称 silicon-chromium steel
silicon controlled rectifier 可控硅整流元件，硅（可）控整流元件，可控硅整流器（简称SCR，= thyristor）
silicon control rectifier chopper 硅可控整流器断续器，可控硅断续器（简称SCR chopper）
silicon diaphragm pressure sensor 硅膜片式压力传感器
silicon diode checker 硅二极管性能检验仪
silicon dioxide 二氧化硅（SiO_2）
silicone brake fluid 硅酮制动液（主要成分为高分子材料聚二甲基硅氧烷，不吸收水分）
silicon(e) fluid 硅酮液，硅流质（具有很高的热膨胀系数，装在感温盒内可使盒的热膨胀特性曲线近于直线）
silicon(e) fluid damper 硅酮液减振器（亦称 silicone oil damper 硅油减振器，在减振元件间充以高黏度硅油，以增强阻尼效果的减振器）
silicon gate （电子载流子金属氧化物硅半导体器件的）硅栅
silicon grease 硅脂，硅润滑脂
silicon integrated circuit 硅集成电路（简称SIC）
siliconizing 渗硅
silicon-manganese spring steel 硅锰弹簧钢
silicon nitride 氮化硅（Si_3N_4，具有良好的耐热冲击性和热及化学稳定性，为制造柴油机微粒排放物滤清器滤芯基体的优良材料，但以往其制造成本高，目前已有人研制成功成本相对较低的热反应烧结化合法，见 reaction-bonding process）
silicon nitride ceramics 氮化硅陶瓷
silicon oil filled fan clutch 硅油风扇离合器
silicon on sapphire 硅-蓝宝石（技术），硅-蓝宝石集成电路，蓝宝石硅片（简称SOS）
silicon photo transistor 硅光电晶体管

silicon rectifier 硅整流器

silicon resin 硅树脂（为热固性树脂的一种，耐热、耐寒，化学稳定性及电性质良好）

silicon rubber 硅橡胶

silicon solar cell 硅太阳电池（由薄硅晶片制成的将光能转变成电能的器件）

silicon steel plate 硅钢片（亦称silicon steel sheet）

silicon strain gage 硅应变仪

silicon symmetrical switch 双向可控硅，硅对称开关

silicon transistor 硅晶体管

silicon wafer 硅片（= chip）

silicon wafer diaphragm (type) MAP sensor 硅片膜片（型）进气空气压力传感器

silk 丝

silk cotton 吉贝木棉（见 kapok）

silk screen method 丝网漏印法（厚膜电路印制布线的一种方法）

sill ①底边纵梁，框架结构的底梁，车身底梁（亦写作 cill，如：门框板的底边梁，用于支撑门柱和构成门槛或与车门底边闭合）②基石，基木③梁（纵横梁的总称）

sill closing plate （汽车前翼板下端的）门槛接合板

sill crossbar 车门门槛横梁

sill facing panel （车身）门槛镶面板

sill frame side member 车架纵梁（= longitudinal member of frame, = frame side member）

sillicon-based gasket-sealing compound 硅基衬垫密封剂

sillimanite [美] 硅线石（= fibrolite），硅酸铝（Al_2SiO_5，用于陶瓷耐火材料）

sill panel 车门槛板（= rocker panel）

sill strip （车身）门槛梁，窗槛梁

silo memory （汽车电子控制系统电子控制模块的一种）先进先出（first input-first output）存储缓冲区

silt-covered 淤泥覆盖的

SILTO pump （柴油机的）希尔托型喷油泵（分配式喷油泵的一种，为法国人 P. Bessie're 设计，法 SILTO 公司生产，故名，现主要用于法国和日本生产的某些柴油机上）

silumin 铝硅合金，铝硅明合金，高铝硅合金（硅 11%~14%，铝 86%~89%）

silver ①银（Ag）②银器，银制品，③银制的，银质的，似银的，含银的，镀银的

silver-alloy brazing 银合金硬钎焊

silver-cadmium battery 银镉蓄电池（亦称 silver-cadmium cell）

silver copper 含银铜合金

silvered 镀银的，敷银的（亦称 silver-faced）

silver solderingl 银焊料软针焊

silver wire pencil 银芯铅笔（在特制涂面的铝板上绘图用）

silver-zinc battery 银-锌蓄电池

SIM ①转向指示灯控制模块（steering indicator module 的简称）②单纯旋转机（Single Rotation Machine）

SIM engine 单纯旋转发动机，单纯旋转活塞发动机（见 DKM）

SI/metric units [法] 国际单位米制

simi-forward control layout cab （货车、客车等的）短头驾驶室（发动机的一部分伸出驾驶室外）

similar curves 相似曲线

similar electric system （供模拟机械系统的）相似电气系统（见 similar system）

similar figures 相似（图）形

similarity ①相似（性），类似，相像②类似物，相似之点

similar system 相似系统（两个物理系统，虽有不同的物理外貌，却有

同一类型的数学模型或传递函数,则该两系统称为相似系统)
simple band brake 简单带式制动器
simple beam ①单光束②简支梁(= single supported beam)
simple bending 单纯弯曲,纯弯曲(= pure bending)
simple bundle 简单丛
simple cycle gas turbine engine 简单循环燃气轮机(只包括工质的连续压缩、燃烧、膨胀的简单热力循环)
simple distillation 简单蒸馏(作用)(如:当易于挥发的物质中含有不易挥发的成分时,一次简单蒸馏二者即可完全分离)
simple gas-turbine cycle (无热交换器的)简单燃气轮机循环
simple harmonic motion 简谐运动(简称 SHM,凡是某个物理量随时间按正弦或余弦规律变化,就说该物理量在作简谐振动,或简谐运动)
simple harmonic motion cam 简谐运动凸轮
simple harmonic vibration 简谐振动(任一物理量随时间按正弦或余弦规律变化,称该物理量作简谐振动)
simple intersection 简单交叉口,四路交叉口(两条道路相交的交叉口)
simple planetary arrangement 单排行星齿轮机构
simple square crossing 正十字交叉路口
simple tangent 单切线
simple tone 纯音(指单频率的声音,= pure tone)
simple version 简图
simplicial mapping 单纯映象
simplicity 简单,单纯,轻便
simplicity of operation 使用简便性

simplification 简化
simplified wiring system 简化配线系统(简称 SWS。由信号发生装置、控制装置和信号接收装置组成,只使用一根供电线和一根信号线,即可完成现有汽车电气设备复杂线路的全部工作)
simply connected manifold 简单连接型(进排气)歧管
simply uniformly convergent 简单均匀(一致)收敛
Simpson mechanism 辛普森机构(由齿轮参数完全相同的两个简单行星排组成的变速器,其中两个太阳轮共件,后行星排的行星架与前行星排的齿圈共件)
SIM (sle) 2:3 engine 2:3 滑移啮合(外)单纯旋转发动机(指相位齿轮速比为2:3)
SIM (sli) 3:2 engine 3:2 交衔啮合(内)单纯旋转式发动机(指相位齿轮速比3:2)
SIM type engine 单纯旋转发动机(指活塞和缸体都围绕同一固定轴旋转的发动机,= SIM engine)
simulated atmosphere 模拟气氛
simulated conditions (人为的)模拟条件,模拟状况
simulated diagram (重现实际过程的)模拟图
simulated environment test 在模拟环境下的试验(如:模拟寒带、热带、高温、高湿等环境)
simulated gradient test 坡道模拟试验(模拟自动变速器在上坡、下坡和侧倾情况下工作可靠性试验)
simulated service test 模拟现场使用条件下的试验(亦称 simulated field test)
simulated supercharging test 模拟增压试验(采用外部风源,使内燃机进、排气压力等模拟其规定的增压内燃机情况的一种试验方法)

simulated suspension (试验台的)模拟悬架

simulated use (在试验时进行的)模拟使用

simulating tractive performance 模拟牵引特性

simulation and dynamic programming 模拟和动态程序编制

simulation design 模拟设计；模拟结构

simulation laboratory test 实验室模拟试验，室内模拟试验

simulation language 模拟(用)语言

simulation mode analysis 模态分析(解决汽车结构设计中振动问题的主要方法，模态分析可直观地显示结构的动态特性，取得各阶模态参数，指出结构存在的问题，为改进结构设计提供依据)

simulation model 模拟模型

simulation module of auto performance 汽车性能仿真模块(用于嵌入高级汽车仿真器，见 ADVISOR)

simulation of road condition 道路条件的模拟

simulation study 模拟研究

simulation test 模拟试验(模拟试验可分为两类：一类指用缩尺模型或某种数字模型、电学模型进行的模拟试验；另一类指在再现的使用条件下进行的模拟试验，如：模拟高温、高湿的环境，模拟汽车的道路荷载等，=simulating test, simulative test)

simulative fatigue test (使用缩尺模型的)模拟疲劳试验

simulator ①模拟器，模拟装置②模拟物，模拟品

simultaneity of transportation product 运输产品同时性(指运输产品的生产与消费过程同时发生的特性)

simultaneous 同时发生的，同时做的

simultaneous explosion 并发式爆炸(均质混合气的成分及温度达到一定程度时发生自燃，各处同时发生急速的放热反应，见 explosive combustion)

simultaneous ignition 同时点火

simultaneous PM and NO_x reduction system (柴油机排放后处理系统中的)微粒排放物和 NO_x 同步净化系统

simultaneous system 同步系统(如：同步交通信号系统，联动信号系统的一种，一条道路上的所有信号在同一时间显示出同一的色灯信号)

sine 正弦

sine-acting engine 单动式发动机，单向作用式发动机(如：常规活塞式发动机，气体压力仅作用于活塞的一面，故称单向作用式，=trunk engine)

sine bar 正弦规，正弦板，正弦尺(测定角度或斜度的精密量具，与块规配合使用)

sine curve 正弦曲线

sine waveform 正弦波形

single 单一的，单独的，单式的，选出，挑选

single-acting cylinder 单向作用油缸

single-acting cylinderical cam 单动圆柱偏心轮

single acting fuel supply pump 单作用式输油泵(活塞往复冲程中，只有一个冲程输出燃油的活塞式输油泵)

single-acting hydraulic shock absorber 单动液压减振器

single-acting pump 单程泵，单动泵(指往复式泵中，各缸中的活塞或柱塞仅一端起作用，曲轴每转一转各产生一次抽吸、泵压冲程)

single-acting reciprocating compressor 单动式往复压缩机

single-acting shock absorber 单向减

振器

single air management valve system (通用公司) 单空气控制阀系统（由空气泵和一个换向阀组成的二次空气喷射系统。发动机升温期，换向阀将新鲜空气喷入排气歧管，使废气中 HC、CO 氧化，并使 O_2 传感器和催化转化器迅速升温。当发动机水温达到65℃时，电子控制模块控制换向阀将空气引入空气滤清器或大气）

single anchor brake 单支撑销式制动器（指两个制动蹄都绕一个支撑销或支撑轴转动的鼓式制动器）

single-and-multi-start worm 单头-多头蜗杆

single arm type suspension 单控制臂式悬架（见 3-link type suspension）

single-axis hitch 单轴挂接装置，单轴牵引装置

single-axle chassis dynamometer 单桥式底盘测功机（仅前桥或后桥在测功机上，即：前后桥不能同时在测功机上）

single-axle trailer 单轴挂车

single-axle truck 单轴后桥式（载）货（汽）车（以别于双轴并装后桥式货车）

single axle weight （汽车）单轴轴载重量（单轴轴载质量的旧称，相对双轴并装车桥而言，单轴各车轮传给路面的质量之和。前者称双轴轴载质量，如：中国规定：最大总质量在42t以上的汽车引车，单轴轴载质量不大于14t，双轴轴载质量不大于28t）

single-bank rotary engine 单缸转子发动机

single-bar bumper 单保险杠

single barrel injection pump 单体喷油泵（泵内只有一个柱塞偶件的泵）

single-bead tire 单胎边轮胎

single beam headlamp 单灯丝前照灯（只装有一根灯丝的远光，或近光前照灯）

single bed converter 单床式转化器（容器内只有一种催化床，即：氧化床或还原床的催化转化器，见 **dual-catalyst syst**/**single-belt accessory) drive system** （发动机的）单传动带附件驱动系统

single-bend valve 单弯式气门嘴（嘴体杆部有一处弯曲的气门嘴）

single bevel groove 单斜槽

single block ①单滑轮滑车②单块结构，整体结构

single braid 单编包线（简称 SB）

single-bucket loading machine 单斗式装货机

single bump （试验跑道上）单一的凸起障碍物（激起车轮的一次跳动）

single-butterfly throttle body 单蝶形阀式节气门体

single cab 单排座型客货两用车（亦称 single-row, two-seated pick-up）

single camshaft chain drive 单凸轮轴的链传动装置

single-cast cylinder 整体铸造式汽缸

single-chamber air brake valve 单腔气制动阀（由一个膜片或活塞构成的一个工作腔，用单一动作仅控制一条回路的气制动阀）

single-chamber brake cylinder 单腔制动主缸

single chamber displacement （转子发动机）单室排量（参见 chamber displacement）

single chamber hydragas spring 单气室油气弹簧，单腔油气弹簧（筒式空气弹簧的一种变形，一般以氮气气囊作为弹性元件，而在氮气与活塞之间引入油液作为中间介质。油气弹簧的工作缸由气室、油液和起减振作用的阻尼阀组成）

single-channel frame 槽形纵梁式车架

single chassis unit 单车（相对汽车列车而言，即不带挂车的载货汽车等），单底盘车

single check valve 止回阀（简称 check valve）

single-chip computer 单片机（美国 Gilbert Hyaft 1968 年申请专利，指仅由一片大规模集成电路构成的微机，或微处理器）

single-chip MCU 单片式微程序控制单元（single-chip microprogram control unit 的简称）

single-chip programmable digital signal processor 单片式可编程数字信号处理器（亦写作 single-chip programmable DSP）

single-circuit braking system 单回路制动系（传能装置仅由一条回路组成制动系统。若其中有一处失效，便不能传递产生制动力的能）

single circuit hydraulic brake actuating system 单回路液压制动器促动系

single coil ignition 单线圈点火

single-column 单柱的

single combustion chamber 单燃烧室，整体式燃烧室

single conductor system 单导线系统

single contact 单触点的

single contact lamp base 单触头的灯座（如：螺丝灯头）

single control arm suspension 见 3 link suspension

single coupé 双门单排双座厢式轿车

single-crystal piezoelectric accelerometer 单晶压电（晶体）加速度仪

single crystal quartz 单晶石英（用作单晶压电型加速器传感器中的传感元件）

single-crystal silicon 单晶硅（= monocrystalline silicon）

single curved surface 单曲面

single cut （锉刀的）单纹

single-cycle failure 单循环加载下的破坏，简单应力循环下的破坏

single cylinder camshaftless fuel injection pump 单缸分列式喷油泵（指用于单缸或多缸发动机一个汽缸的单缸分列式喷油泵，见 unit fuel injection pump）

single-cylinder engine 单缸内燃机（只有一个汽缸内燃机，简称单缸机）

single-cylinder engine test 单缸（发动机）试验（多缸机研制过程中，一般先在其单缸机上进行的各种性能或零部件结构考核等的试验）

single cylinder fuel injection pump 单缸喷油泵（只有一个出油口的喷油泵）

single-cylinder research work 单缸（机）研究工作（指一般发动机燃烧理论等研究工作先采用单缸机进行研究）

single cylinder test engine 单缸试验发动机，试验用单缸机

single cylinder type caliper （浮钳式盘式制动器的）单缸式制动钳（亦称浮动式制动钳"floating type caliper"）

single-deck bus 单层客车（亦称 single-decker, single-decker bus）

single direction thrust ball bearing 单向推力球轴承

single-disc clutch 单片式离合器（= single-plate clutch）

single drive ①单一传动（如：单条传动带传动，单链传动，单万向节传动等）②单桥驱动

single drive axle 单驱动桥（汽车）

single-ended amplifier 单端放大器

single-ended input impedance 单端输入阻抗（每一输入端到电参考点的阻抗）

single-end tenoning machine 单头燕尾榫开榫机

single end wrench 单头扳手

single engagement coupling (只用单个挠性元件连接两轴端的)简单挠性联轴节

single excitation experiment 单点激振试验(通过对结构上某一适当部位施加激振力而激发结构振动的一种激振试验方法)

single exhaust system 单排气系(相对双排气系而言,见 dual exhaust system)

single-faced signal lamp 单面信号灯

single failure 单一性故障

single-filament bulb 单丝灯泡(= one filament bulb)

single-file traffic 单车道交通

single final drive 单级主传动

single flow 单流

single-friction-surface clutch 单面摩擦式盘式离合器

single gap plug 单极火花塞,单间隙火花塞

single-groove 单槽的

single head straight socket wrench 单头直柄套筒扳手

single helical gear 单线螺旋齿轮

single hole nozzle (柴油机的)单孔式喷嘴(见 hole nozzle)

single hook piston ring 单刃口活塞环

single ignition 单火花塞点火

single jet carburetor 单量孔化油器

single joint coupling shaft 单万向节传动轴(只有一个万向节的传动轴)

single-joint swing axle 单铰接式摆动桥(两侧摆臂均绕一个铰接点摆动)

single joint swing axle with two coil springs (中央)单铰接接头,双螺旋弹簧式摆动桥(见 swing axle)

single-lane 单车道的

single-layer 单层的

single leaf spring 单片式钢板弹簧(由一片钢板弹簧组成的弹簧悬架)

single-leaf-spring type equalizing suspension (货车双轴并装后桥的)单钢板弹簧推力杆式平衡悬架(双轴共用一架钢板弹簧,起平衡臂"equalizer beam"的作用,其两端各通过一吊架或滑座与一后轴相连接,中部通过心轴亦称平衡轴"trunnion shaft"及其支架与车架铰接,只传递垂直力和侧向力,而驱动力和制动力及其相应的反作用力矩由两端分别与两后轴和心轴支架,亦称平衡轴支座"trunnion base"铰接的两根推力杆"thrust rod"承受)

single-level fatigue test 等幅应力疲劳试验

single lever control 单杆控制,单杆操纵

single-lever roller-mounted stud steering gear 曲柄销安装在滚子轴承上的曲柄单销式转向机构

single LIN (汽车的)单线制本地互联网(主网点通过一条主线与各从网点相连,见 LIN)

single-line braking system 单(线)路制动系[牵引车与挂车之间的制动管(线)路仅由一条管子(线)连接,该管(线)子既作供能也作操纵之用的制动系]

single load 单胎负荷(在规定气压下,单胎使用时的对应负荷)

single load level test 单一负荷条件的试验

single master cylinder and selector valve brake system 单腔主缸及选择阀制动系统

single mechanical seal 单端面机械密封(由一对密封端面组成的机械密封)

single network architecture 单网络结构

single oblique arm type suspension 单斜臂式悬架（用一根斜臂连接车轮与车架或车身的悬架形式，亦称 semi-trailing arm type suspension）

single-opening jet 单孔喷油嘴

single over-head camshaft 单顶置凸轮轴，顶置单凸轮轴（简称 SOHC）

single-party occupancy （公共运输工具的）包乘（由个人或同目的的几个人包用）

single permanent flywheel 单片式定惯量飞轮

single phase 单相（参见 monophase）

single-phase AC equipment 单相交流设备

single phase converter 单相液力变矩器（指只有一种功能，即仅起改变所传递的转矩的作用的变矩器，见 phase）

single phase motor 单相电动机

single piece apex seal （转子发动机的）整片式径向密封片

single-piece rim 整体轮辋（亦称 one-piece rim，相对于多件式轮辋而言的单件整体轮辋）

single-piece screen 整体式滤网

single-pin track 单销（单铰链）式履带

single-piston floating caliper disc brake 单活塞式浮钳型盘式制动器

single plane crankshaft （各连杆轴颈布置在同一平面内，即：彼此相隔180°转角的）单平面曲轴

single planetary gear train 单排行星齿轮系（单级行星齿轮系，由一级行星齿轮传动机构的若干个齿轮副的组合）

single-plate ball bearing 单面带防尘圈的球轴承

single-plate clutch 单片式离合器（= single-disc clutch，只有一片从动盘的干式离合器）

single plunger distributor fuel injection pump 单柱塞式分配泵（一个分配柱塞同时起泵油和配油作用的分配式喷油泵）

single-ply 单层的

single point electronic sensing system （安全气囊的）单点式电子传感系（只在其电子控制模块中安装一个碰撞传感器的传感系统，多使用能够确定冲击方向和强度的压电元件型减速度计，亦称中央传感系统"central air bag sensing system"）

single-point hitch 单点挂接装置（= one-point hitch）

single point injection system （电子控制式）单点式（汽油）喷射系统（指整个发动机只在进气歧管节气门的上方装有一个或两个电磁喷油器，将汽油直喷入进气气流中，经进气分支管分送至各汽缸，喷油器在结构上的布置相似于化油器。简称 SPI system。不同公司生产的单点式汽油喷射系统，有各自的商品名，如：波许公司称 Mono-Jetronic，通用公司称节气门体喷射系统"throttle body injection system"，简称 TBI，福特公司称中央汽油喷射系统"central Fuel Injection"，简称 CFI）

single-point suspension 单点悬架装置

single pole ①单极（简称 SP）②单柱，单杆

single pole double throw switch 单刀双掷开关

single-pole variable reluctance sensor 单报式变磁阻传感器

single post (auto) lift 单柱式（汽车）举升器

single-purpose road 专用道路

single-ratio drives 单速比传动（如：电动汽车的变频交流传动所使用的

单速比齿轮减速机构）
single-reduction axle 单级减速式驱动桥
single reduction final drive 单级主减速器（由一对齿轮所构成的主减速器，通常采用曲线齿的锥齿轮副）
single reduction thru-drive 单级贯通式主减速器（由一对锥齿轮所构成的贯通式主减速器）
single-rivet(ed) joint 单行铆接
single-roller cam steering gear 蜗杆单滚轮式转向机构（= cam-and-single-roller steering gear）
single rotation brake 单向制动器（仅制止一个方向的运动或转动的制动装置，如：液力变矩器导轮的单向离合器"one-way clutch 或 freewheeling clutch"等）
single rotation engine 单纯旋转发动机（指活塞和缸体都只围绕本身重心旋转的发动机，= SIM engine）
single rotation machine 单纯旋转机（其运动部件只是围绕自身的重心作等角速运动，而不作行星运动，简称 SIM）
single-rotor rotary-combustion engine 单缸转子内燃机，单缸旋转活塞内燃机
single row 单列，单排
single-row angular contact ball bearing with split outer race 双半外圈（外圈径向剖分式）单列向心推力球轴承（= split outer race bearing）
single-row ball bearing 单列球轴承
single-row cylinder arrangement 直列式汽缸
single-row deep-groove ball bearing 单列深槽球轴承
single-row grooved ball bearing 单列有槽球轴承
single-row radial ball bearing 单列向心球轴承
single-row radial engine 单列星形发动机（轴向仅一列汽缸的星形发动机，见 radial engine）
single-row roller bearing 单排滚子轴承
single-row self-aligning roller bearing 单列自动调心球面滚子轴承
single-row snap ring ball bearing with shield 带止动环和防尘圈的单列向心球轴承
single screw thread 单螺纹，单头螺纹
single-seater ①单座汽车 ②单座驾驶室
single serpentine belt 单条蛇形皮带（用单根皮带替代传统的多皮带驱动）
single shaft turbine engine 单轴燃气轮机（涡轮轴和压气机轴是同一轴，该轴直接连接输出轴或通过齿轮系统连接输出轴）
single-shield bearing 一面带防尘圈的滚动轴承（= one-shield bearing）
single shut-off hose coupling 单向自封式软管接头
single siamese side inlet port （转子发动机的）单孔双分式端面进气孔（在多缸转子发动机的中间隔板上，只开一个端面进气孔，供相邻两缸使用）
single-sided disk brake 单面带摩擦衬片的盘式制动器
single side seal （转子发动机的）单道端面气封装置，单条端面气封条
single signal 单信号（简称 SS）
single silk-covered wire 单丝包线
single-skinned body 单层蒙皮的车身
single-skin panel 单层板
single-span beam 单跨梁
single-spark ignition coil （无分电器式电子点火系统直接装在各个火花塞上、仅向该火花塞提供点火高压的）单火花（塞）点火线圈
single-speed power take-off 单速功

率输出轴

single-spring mechanical seal 单弹簧式机械密封（补偿机构中只包含有一个弹簧的机械密封）

single-spring non-reactive suspension （由纵向推力杆和一架钢板弹簧组成的双轴并装驱动桥的）非反力式钢板弹簧平衡式悬架（其钢板弹簧反扣安装，作为一个弹性平衡杆，两端分别与双轴并装驱动桥的一个轴连接，中部通过平衡轴支座与车架铰接，只传递垂直和侧向力。驱动和制动力及其反作用力由推力杆承受，亦称 dual-axle 或 two-axle balanced suspension，bogie balanced suspension，参见 two-spring non-reaction suspension）

single-stage 单级的

single-stage centrifugal compressor 单级离心式（空气）压缩机

single-stage centrifugal pump 单级离心泵

single-stage compression refrigeration system 一级压缩冷冻系统

single-stage compressor 单级压缩机

single-stage converter 单级液力变矩器（液力变矩器的级数是指插在其他叶轮元件之间的刚性连接的涡轮元件数，单级指这样的涡轮元件只有一个）

single-staged turbine 单级式涡轮机

single-stage-single-sided centrifugal compressor 单级单向入口离心式压气机

single-stage three-element torque converter 单级三元件变矩器（指由泵轮、涡轮及一个刚性连接的导轮三个元件组成的变矩器）

single-stage type through drive axles （双后桥并装驱动车辆的）单级型贯通式驱动桥（多采用双曲线齿轮驱动，利用其轴线偏移可由一根传动轴由中桥贯通至后桥）

single stage voltage regulator 单级电磁振动式电压调节器（通过一对触点的开闭控制发电机电压的装置）

single-start thread 单头螺纹，单线螺纹

single-start worm 单头螺纹蜗杆，单线螺纹蜗杆，单螺线蜗杆

single-state harmonic gear drive 单级谐波齿轮传动（由一个波发生器、一个柔轮和一个刚轮组成的传动）

single steady speed method （烟度测定的）单稳定车速法（将柴油机汽车安置在双滚筒式底盘测功机上，加载加速使发动机稳定在最高烟度的转速下，用烟度计测定其烟度值）

single stroke 单冲程

single supported beam 简支梁（= simple beam）

single sweep 单相扫描

single teethed type coupling 单齿型联轴节

single test ①单件试验 ②单一的试验

single throat carburetor 单腔化油器（= single barrel carburetor）

single throttle body fuel injection system 单节气门体燃油喷射系统

single throw crankshaft 单拐曲轴

single-thrust bearing 单列推力滚动轴承

single tie rod type ackermann geometry 单横拉杆型阿克曼梯形转向机构（我国称整体式梯形转向机构，见 steering tie rod 及 Ackerman geometry）

single tire 单轮胎

single-tone horn 单音喇叭（= one tone horn）

single-track car line 单向行车道

single-track vehicle 单辙车辆（如：摩托车，自行车）

single trailing arm type suspension

单纵臂式悬架（用一根纵臂将车轮与车身或车架连接的悬架形式）

single transverse rocker arm type suspension 单横臂式悬架（亦称 single swing arm type suspension，由一根横向布置的控制摆臂及一架减振器连接车轮与车架的悬架）

single trip 单程，单行程

single tube telescopic damper 单筒伸缩式减振器（亦称 single-tube shock absorber）

single-U groove 单 U 形槽

single-unit car 整体式车身小轿车（= unitized car，亦称 single-unit body car, monocoque body car）

single (unit) truck 单车（不带挂车的载货汽车）

single value 单值

single-valved ①单电子管的②单阀的

single-vehicle output 单车产量（在一定时期内，每辆车平均完成的换算周转量）

single venturi （化油器）单喉管

single-V groove 单 V 形槽

single way ①单向②单车道

single-wheel bump 单轮跳动

single-wheel load 单轮荷载

single(-wing) door 单扇门

single wire bulb 单丝灯泡

single-wire random lay （多路复用网络）单线随机布置（指多路复用网络的传输媒体由随机布置在汽车所有其他电路线束中的单根导线和公用回路组成，公用回路可能是车架或一根公用地线）

single wire system 单线制（利用车体金属部件作为电气回路的接线方式）

singly 各自地，独自地

singular 单一的，唯一的，特别的，非凡的

sink ①下沉，降低，埋入②（热工循环的）冷源

sinkage ①沉陷，下陷②沉陷量，下陷量

sinkage due to static load 静载沉陷量

sinking 下陷，下沉

sink key 埋头键（见 sunk key）

sink temperature （热力循环）冷源温度

sino-foreign cooperative auto enterprise 中外合资汽车企业

SINOPEC 中国石油化工公司（中国石化公司）（China Petro-chemical Corporation）

sinter ①粉末冶金，烧结，烧结物②（铁的）锈皮

sinter coating 烧结涂层（见 fluidised bed coating）

sintered alloy 烧结合金

sintered bearing metal 烧结（滑动）轴承（用减摩）合金

sintered bronze 烧结青铜件（青铜微粒热压成型的多孔件，多用做滤芯）

sintered gears 粉末冶金烧结齿轮

sintered metal substrate 金属粉末烧结材料基体（用于柴油机排放微粒滤清器等）

sintered part 烧结零件（金属粉末加热或加压，或同时加压加热烧结成的零件）

sintered polycrystalline diamond 烧结多晶体金刚钻，烧结多晶体金刚石

sintered powder metal lining 粉末冶金烧结金属摩擦衬片

sinter forging 烧结锻造（法）

sintering （金属陶瓷）烧结

sintering furnace 烧结炉

sintering temperature 烧结温度

sintering test 烧结试验

sinuous 蛇形的，波状的，起伏的，曲折的，弯曲的

sinusoid 正弦曲线

sinusoidal 正弦（曲线）的，正弦波的
sinusoidal output 正弦波输出
sinusoidal vibration 正弦振动
sinusoidal wave 正弦波
SIO controller 串行输入输出控制器（serial input/output controller 的简称，其基本功能是作为串行到并行或并行到串行的转换器/控制器）
sipe （轮胎胎面花纹）细缝（见 tread sipe）
siphon action ①虹吸作用②化油器怠速量孔溢油现象
siphon gauge 虹吸压力计，虹吸气压计
siphon pipe 虹吸管（= siphon tube）
SIPS （车身）防侧向碰撞结构（side impact protection system）
siren horn （消防车、救护车等用的）警笛，警报器
sirocco 热风
SIR system 辅助充气式（乘员）约束型安全系统（supplemental inflatable restraint 的简称，安全气囊、安全气帘、充气式安全带等充气式约束型安全装置的总称）
sister block 双滑轮，双滑车
sister hooks 姐妹钩，安全钩，双抱钩
SIT 自燃温度（spontaneous ignition temperature）
sit 坐，位于，坐落；安装，安放，搁置
site 地点，位置，部位，地段，地区
site assembly 现场装配
site engineer 现场工程师
site-plan 总平面图，总设计图；总布置的；总计划
site-tipper 工地用自卸汽车
sitting elbow height 乘员取坐势时的肘部高度
sitting eye level 驾驶员坐态时眼睛高度

sitting height 乘员取坐势时座椅面至头顶的高度
sitting knee height 乘员取坐势时的膝高
situated 位于…的，坐落在…的，布置在…的
situation 处境，形势，情况；位置，场所
SI units 国际单位制，公制（Systeme International Unites）
six ①六②六缸发动机（six-cylinder engine）③六缸发动机汽车（six-cylinder car）
six airbags system 六安全气囊系统
six-bearing crankshaft 六道主轴承的曲轴
six bladed fan 六叶风扇
six-cylinder car 六缸发动机汽车
six-degree-of-freedom control 六自由度控制
six-element gyroscope 六元素陀螺仪（又称六元素动态摆动记录仪，汽车操纵性、稳定性的基本测试仪器之一，由电动机驱动自由陀螺以 22500γ/min 高速旋转，作为基准面，记录基准面与保持面的相对运动，借以测定车辆的纵倾、侧倾、横摆角及角速度）
six-in-line engine 六缸直列发动机
six-ply tire 六层帘线轮胎
six-point seat belt 六点式安全带
six-point top attachment system （敞篷轿车）活动车顶的六点式撑装系统
six-seater 六座车
six-sided head 六角头
six-sided nut 六角形螺母
sixteen-cylinder 十六缸（发动机）
sixteen-cylinder car 十六缸发动机汽车
six-way adjustable driver's seat 六方向可调式驾驶座椅
six-wheeled vehicle 三桥汽车（一般

指具有一个前桥和两个双胎并装车轮中、后桥的三桥、六轮、十胎货车，亦称 six-by，six-wheel car，six-wheeled lorry，six-wheeler，six-wheel truck，six-wheel vehicle，其中两中、后桥的四个双胎并装车轮为驱动轮者称 six-by-four vehicle，全轮驱动者称 six-by-six vehicle，亦称 six-wheel drive vehicle）

six-wheeler trailing axle 三桥汽车的从动尾桥（仅中桥为驱动桥，后桥为从动桥）

sizable 相当大的，大小相当的

size 大小，尺寸；规模

size contraction （断面）尺寸缩小

size down 由大到小的逐个排列，渐次弄小

size effect 尺寸效应；比例效应

size marking 尺寸标记

sizer ①分粒机（分选机）②尺寸测定仪

size range 尺寸范围，尺寸系列

size reduction 尺寸缩小，缩减尺寸

sizes of tire prints in the ground 轮胎接地印痕尺寸

sizzle （汽车在光滑路面上行驶时，车轮与路面摩擦发出的类似于油炸食物时的）嘶嘶声

SK ①样品箱（见 sales kit）②维修材料箱（见 service kit）③草图，图样设计（见 sketch）④路面摩擦系数值（见 skid number）

skates 滑座，滑轨，滑动装置

SKD 半散装，部分散件组装（semi-knocked down 的简称）

skeletal ①骨架的，轮廓的②提纲式的③（垫有坚固的横梁或枕木以运输集装箱或其他箱式货物用的）半挂或全挂车底盘

skeleton ①构架，骨架；轮廓，梗概，草图，略图，纲要，计划②基干的，骨干的，原理的，纲要的

skeleton construction body （客车等的）骨架结构型车身（车身负荷全部由其构架承受，车身外壳板、内外蒙皮仅起饰面作用，见 stressed skin construction body）

skeleton drawing 轮廓图，草图，原理图，示意图，结构图（= skeleton layout，skeleton sketch）

skeleton framework 骨骼，构架

skeletonless body 无骨架式车身（为了减轻车身自身重量，利用各蒙皮板互相连接时所形成的加强筋来代替骨架的作用）

skeleton pattern 轮廓模型，示意模型，原理模型，构架模型

skeleton-skirt piston 骨架式裙部活塞

skeleton structure 骨架式结构

skeleton view 显示内部的透视图（= ghosted view）

skeleton wheel （大型非道路车辆，农用拖拉机等外轮缘上带钢制抓地齿的）钢制车轮（亦称 hollow drum wheel with steel lugs）

sketch ①草图，略图，简图，图样设计，设计图（简称 SK）②概略，大意，纲领

sketch design 草图设计，方案设计

skew 斜的，歪的，倾斜的

skew angle 斜（交）角（如：两直线交叉时，其锐角交叉角的余角）

skew-axes gears 偏轴齿轮系（指双曲面齿轮系，亦称 skew-axis gear，skew bevel gear，hypoid bevel gear，hypoid gear，skew bevel wheel，skew bevel wheel）

skew distribution 不对称分布

skewed surface 斜表面，扭曲表面

skew frequency distribution 偏斜频率分布

skew intersection 斜交叉口（= oblique intersection，skew crossing）

skew joint 斜接（= bevel joint）

skew line 偏斜（直）线

skewness ①误差度,偏差度②斜度,倾斜度,歪斜度③非对称性④失真,畸变

skewness index 偏差指数,误差指数

skewness of spot speed 点速度误差(瞬间速度的误差,点速率误差度)

skew quadrilateral 挠四边形,歪斜四边形

ski bob 雪橇车

skid ①(车轮)滑移(= slipping movement,指车轮制动力大于轮胎与路面附着力时,车轮抱死不转,而相对路面产生的任一方向的滑动,其滑动方向取决于汽车质心在各种外力作用下的运动方向。注意与车轮驱动力大于轮胎与路面摩擦力时,轮胎相对于地面原地空转的滑转"spin"相区别)②(木制或钢制的停车时垫在车轮下防滑溜的)三角垫③(便于举升或承载重物时用的)平木垫板,托盘,托板

skid coefficient of friction 滑动摩擦系数

skid control actuator (制动)防滑执行机构

skid-control computerized braking system 计算机控制防滑制动系统

skid control system for hydraulic brake 液压制动防滑系统

skid depth ①滑道深度②胎面防滑花纹深度(见 tread depth)

skid detector 车轮滑动检测器

skidding 滑移

skidding accident 滑移(引起的)事故

skidding behavio(u)r (车辆)抗滑性能

skidding collision (汽车)滑移碰撞

skidding distance (制动)滑移距离,拖印距离(从全部车轮抱死时起到汽车完全停住时止的距离)

skid(ding) force (造成车辆)滑移(的)力

skidding limit (车轮的)滑移极限,(取决于轮胎与地面的附着力,= limit of sliding)

skidding-resistance 防滑的,抗滑的

skidding tire 滑胎(如:不能防止汽车滑移的光面轮胎)

skid ECU ①(一般指 ABS,TRC 等系统中根据相应传感器的信息判断车轮处于打滑状态或在 ABS 中根据相应传感器的信息判断驾驶者意欲实施紧急制动时分别向制动执行机构发出减、增制动力指令的)防滑电子控制模块②(在混合动力车中指:除上述功能外,还对制动系统实施包括再生发电制动在内的全面调控)制动(力的)电子控制模块

skid frame 滑橇式底架

skid hazards (汽车)滑移造成的险情

skid-mounted 安装在滑橇上的

skid number 路面摩擦系数值(根据美国试验与材料协会规定的方法,使用两轮挂车在40km/h 的初速下制动时所测出的路面摩擦系数,简称 SK。$SK = \dfrac{F}{a\left(W - \dfrac{H}{L}F\right)} \times 100$。

式中:F—摩擦力;W—试验挂车静重;H—挂钩高度;L—挂车轮距;a—系数,挂车的一个车轮抱死时 $a = 1/2$,两个车轮同时抱死时 $a = 1$)

skid-off-the-road accident 车辆滑出道路的事故

skid pad (测试汽车操纵稳定性的)滑溜广场(地面光滑平整的方形或圆形汽车动态试验广场,用以测试操纵稳定性,如:进行受控滑移、横向加速度试验等,美称 vehicle dynamic area,亦写作 skidpad)

skid pad roadability test (汽车的)滑溜广场稳定性试验(= skid pad testing)

skid plate ①滑板②（任一种装在车身底面，阻挡、防止砂石等损坏擦伤机件的）护板（当特指发动机油底壳的防擦伤护板时，= sump guard）
skid prevention （汽车）防滑
skid-proof 防滑（动）的，抗滑的
skid-proof step 防滑阶梯
skid-resistance （路面对轮胎等的）滑动阻力
skid-resistance requirements （对道路等的）防滑要求
skid-resistance tester （轮胎）抗滑移试验装置
skid-resistance trailer 测定防滑性能用的挂车
skid-resistance tread 轮胎防滑胎面
skid resisting property （道路或轮胎的）防滑性能
skid ring ①（轮胎）防滑链，防滑环②轮辋挡圈，轮辋压圈
skid-ring tyre 带防滑环的轮胎
skid steer （履带式车辆的）滑移转向，（制动某侧的履带，车辆绕该侧回转的转向方式，亦可作 skid steering）
skid test 滑移试验
skid tester 滑移测试台
skid (test) trailer 侧滑试验挂车
skid tread depth （轮胎的）花纹滑移深度（轮胎花纹磨损至开始打滑时的深度）
skill 熟巧，技能，技艺
skilled 有经验的，（技术）熟练的；需要技能的
skim 在水面滑行，掠面而过，滑过
skimmer ①气垫车②刮路机③撇浮渣用具，撇沫器
skimming wear 擦地磨损，滑移磨损（如：轮胎制动时在地面上滑移造成的磨损）
skimobile 履带式雪地汽车
skin 车身覆盖件（覆盖在车身骨架表面上的板件，亦称 cover panel）
skin breakage 表面破坏；外壳破坏
skin capacity （人体对振动的反应所产生的）集肤电流量
skin covering of the surface 表面薄皮层，表皮层，表皮
skin decarbonization 表面脱碳（= surface decarbonization）
skin effect 集肤效应；表皮作用
skin friction 表面摩擦（一般指汽车行驶时周围空气与车身表面产生相对运动中由于空气黏性与车身表面间的摩擦）
skin-friction coefficient 表面摩擦系数
skin-friction force 表面摩擦力
skin friction temperature 摩擦面表层温度
skin-hard 表面硬化的，表面淬硬的，表面冷作硬化的
skin hardening 表面渗碳；表层硬化
skin hardness 表面硬度
skin line 车身轮廓线（= body line）
skin of paint 油漆层，涂装层
skin panel 车身外壳板
skin simulant （汽车试验假人等使用的）人造皮肤，模拟人皮（= skin simulator）
skin stress 表面应力
skin-to-skin 紧贴地，紧靠地
skip ①跳，跳跃②急速由一地转移到一地③可以从垃圾运输车上卸下的废料桶，垃圾桶
skip car 翻斗（小）车
skip loader ①使用可装卸的垃圾桶装运垃圾的运输车②翻斗式装载机
skip lorry 翻斗货车
skipping （发动机）缺火，熄火，不跳火
skip shift （变速器）跳挡（指非相邻两挡间换挡，如：由二挡换到四挡）
ski rack （车内）行李架（= bag-

gage carrier)

skirt ①裙,裙状物(如:活塞裙,绝缘子外裙,罩裙,厢式货车车身侧板的裙板)②车身裙部(车身腰线以下表面部分的总称)③位于…的边缘,和…接界,给…装防护罩,沿…的边界而行,绕过…的边缘

skirted fender (汽车车轮的)挡泥片,挡泥裙

skirt end of piston 活塞的裙端

skirt expander 活塞裙部扩张器(= piston skirt expander)

skirt member 底边梁,底边条(亦称 skirt rail,见 skirt)

skirt of body 车身裙部(腰线以下的车身表面部分的总称)

skirt relief (活塞)裙部切口

skirt ring (活塞)裙部环

skirt ring groove 活塞裙部的环槽

"skirt" side shroud (履带推进水陆两用车)"裙式"侧罩

skirt slot 活塞裙缝槽

skive ①刮削,切削,切割②研磨

ski vehicle 雪橇车辆(用雪橇代替车轮的雪地车辆)

Skoda Auto (捷克)斯柯达汽车公司(现为德国大众公司的子公司)

SKYACTIV technology 天效技术(日本 Mazda 公司推出的一系列革新技术的商品名,采用这一技术的汽油机、柴油机、变速器、底盘和车身分别称:SKYACTIV-G、SKYACTIV-D、SKYACTIV-DRIVE、SKYACTIV-CHASSIS、SKYACTIV-BODY)

Skycar (美国工程师保罗·莫勒研制的)飞行汽车(名,保罗·莫勒于2002年制成的世界上第一辆真正意义的飞行汽车"Skycar M400",能载4人,使用普通汽油可连续飞行1400km不加油,具有自动飞行控制系统、卫星导航系统,只需简单培训便可驾驶)

sky component of day light factor 采光系数的天空光分量(在室内给定平面上的一点,直接接受来自假定天空亮度分布的天空光照度与该天空半球在室外无遮挡水平面上的天空光照度之比)

skyhook damper 天钩减振器(汽车车身的跳振减振器,一种被动式减振器"passive damper"。根据装在车身上的垂直加速度传感器测出的车身上、下方向加速度,借以算出车身的绝对上、下速度,由一压力控制阀产生与该绝对速度成比例的阻尼力,限制车身的跳振,并改善车轮与地面的贴附)

skyhook damper control 见 bounce control

Skyhook suspension system 天钩悬架系统(一种电子控制悬架系统的商品名,该系统根据相关传感器输入的路状和车身振动信息,以1/1000s的速度对悬架减振系统的软硬程度作连续无级调节,可确保车辆在各种路面上行驶均十分平稳,如挂在天上一样,故名)

skylight 天空光(太阳光经过大气层时,因空气分子、尘埃和水蒸气等的作用形成的天空扩散光)

skylight window (客车或轿车的)天窗(车身顶上,可推开或拉开的透明窗,简称 skylight)

skylight window length 顶窗长(顶窗开启时,两边窗框之间在 Y 平面上的距离)

skylight window width 顶窗宽(顶窗开启时,两边窗框之间在 X 平面上的距离)

sky parking 立体停车,高层建筑停车

slab ①(平)板,(原)片;铁块,石板,钢板②铺石板,把…分成厚片,厚厚地涂抹

slab rubber 板状橡皮,橡胶板

slab synchro 扁平式同步机（见 pancake synchro）

slab zinc 锌锭

slack ①空隙，间隙，松弛（部分）②备用部分③轨间距离，轨距④静止不动，停止流动，熄火⑤淡季，休息时间⑥渣屑⑦松动的，疏松的；迟滞的，缓慢的；弱的；风化的；漏水的；微热的

slack adjuster ①松紧调节装置②间隙调节装置（亦称 lash adjuster 或 lash adjusting device，如：液压制动器制动鼓上的调整凸轮、调整螺钉或调整齿轮，气制动制动气室推杆和凸轮轴之间的调整臂总成等调整制动衬片与制动鼓工作面之间的间隙，以补偿制动衬片磨损的装置）

slack-free 无间隙的

slack hours （交通流等的）低峰时间

slacking （连接件）松动，弛垂

slack off 变弱，放松

slack of the steering wheel 转向盘空转量，转向盘自由行程

slack running fit 松转配合，松动配合

slack side 传动带松边，传动带从动边，传动链松边

slalom ①弯曲道路②弯曲道路上的驾驶比赛，穿桩驾驶比赛，障碍

slalom course 弯路，弯曲路线，Z 字形路，Z 字形坡道

slalom test 蛇行试验（汽车在一定间隔的标桩间蛇行，并用蛇行穿桩的最高车速、操舵力、横向加速度、横摆角速度响应、转向盘转角等来评价汽车的机动性、响应性和操纵稳定性的试验）

slam ①（猛）关（车门，窗，盖等）；撞击②砰的声响

slam lock 碰锁，弹簧锁

slamming 使劲关，砰地关上

slam(ming) fixture 冲击（试验用的）夹具

slamming the brake 紧急制动

slant 倾斜，歪斜的

slant angle （汽车车身后窗的）坡度角

slanted slot inclination angle （喷油泵）斜槽倾角（斜槽形油量控制槽与柱塞圆柱工作面轴线的夹角）

slanted squish area （某些发动机燃烧室的）倾斜型挤压区

slanted windshield 倾斜风窗玻璃（亦称 oblique wind-shield, slanting windshield, sloping wind-shield）

slant engine ［美］斜置式发动机（= inclined engine）

slant height 斜高

slanting back （车身）倾斜的后部，流线型（车身）尾部（= sloping back）

slanting carburetor 斜吸式化油器（混合气出口向下倾斜，= semi-down draft carburetor）

slanting set valve 斜置（座）阀

slant nose 斜头型（车身）（向前倾斜式的车头造型，可以减小运动阻力）

slap 拍掌声，拍击声，敲击声（如：①汽车制动时发生的敲击声②活塞等产生的敲打声，频率 10Hz③车轮驶过路面板块接缝或其他不平处时，轮胎产生的拍击声）

slash lubrication system 飞溅式润滑系（亦称 splash feed system，如发动机油底壳飞溅润滑系）

SLA suspension 长/短臂型悬架（short/long arm suspension 的简称）

slave axle 从动桥，随动桥

slave cylinder ①从动油缸②（液压系统中，将主液压缸输入的液压转换成推动机件运动的机械力的执行油缸。如：液压制动系统的轮缸，液压式离合器操纵机构中将主缸产生的液压变为推力传递给分离机构

slave cylinder piston (将工作缸内液力传至工作缸推杆的)工作缸活塞

slave cylinder piston return spring 工作缸活塞复位弹簧(工作缸活塞动作后使其恢复原始位置的弹簧)

slave cylinder push rod 工作缸推杆(直接传递工作缸活塞推力的杆件)

slave engine 被拖动的发动机(见 motored engine)

slave kit 全套辅助工具,全套伺服工具

slave node (汽车电子控制网络中的)从网点(接受主网点传来的数据或在主网点启动下相互传输数据的下一级网点,见 master node)

slave relay 随动继电器

slave-robot 机器人的

slave unit 从属装置,伺服装置

slave valve 随动阀

SLCT 突然变换车道试验(sudden lane change test)

sledge car 雪地汽车,机动雪橇

sledge hammer ①手用大铁锤,锻工用大锤②用锤敲击,猛击,锻炼③用大锤敲击的,猛烈的,重大的,致命的

sleek (车身外形)流线型的,表面光滑的

sleep alert system (驾驶员)临睡唤醒系统,瞌睡警告系统(由小型摄像系统监视驾驶员眼皮及头部的运动状态并输入计算机,当上述运动频率、速率、幅度达到瞌睡状态时,即由电脑控制发出警告声,或将冷风直吹眼部或向脸部直喷冷水等,简称 SAS)

sleeper bedding 卧铺车的卧床

sleeper bus 卧铺客车(备有睡眠设备的客车,= sleeping bus,简称 sleeper)

sleeper cab ①有卧铺的货车驾驶室②有睡铺的长途客车驾驶室

sleeper cab tractor 驾驶室内有睡位的牵引车

sleeper cab with bed 带卧铺的驾驶室

sleeper coach 带有卧铺的长途客车

sleeper pot (货车驾驶室顶部的)卧铺舱(亦称 top sleeper)

sleeper test track 枕木试验跑道(见 railroad ties test)

sleeping policeman (防超速)横挡(路面上拱起的或横置于路面上的低缓鼓包,用于防止超速行车,美称 speed hump)

sleep mode (电子系统的)休眠模式(降低能耗,亦称 sleep state)

sleep state 见 sleep mode

sleet 夹雪雨(夹带冰雹或雪的雨),冻雨

sleeve ①袖,袖状物②(光盘等的)硬纸套③[美]汽缸衬套(= 英 cylinder liner)④(汽车上多指各种精密配合的长度大于直径镶在孔中或套在轴上的)衬套,衬管,套管,套筒(如:半轴套管,离合器分离套,连杆小头衬套,轮毂衬套,滑动轴承套等。若直径大于长度,则多称 bush)⑤套筒阀(见 sleeve valve)⑥(套在两个圆柱形零件外将二者连接起来的)外套管

sleeve assembly 缸套总成,衬套总成

sleeve cap 电线的端套

sleeve connector (导线的)插塞式套管接头

sleeve coupling 套筒联轴节

sleeve half-bearing 轴瓦式滑动轴承

sleeve joint 套管连接

sleeveless engine 无汽缸套的发动机

sleeve nut 套筒螺母

sleeve pin 套筒销

sleeve port ①套筒孔②缸套孔

sleeve ring 缸套密封环

sleeve (type) bearing 滑动轴承,轴

套式滑动轴承
sleeve-type clutch 套筒式离合器
sleeve-type engine 滑套式发动机（= sliding sleeve engine）
sleeve valve 套筒式滑阀（= sliding-sleeve valve）
sleeve valve 套筒阀（装在活塞与缸壁之间，开有进、排气孔的筒状滑套，发动机运转时，该滑套转动或摆动，其进、排气孔按规定的相位和时刻分别与缸壁上的进、排气孔相通，而实现发动机的进气和排气过程，简称 sleeve）
sleeve valve engine 套筒阀式发动机（见 sleeve valve）
sleeve valve type hydraulic self-sealing coupling 套管滑阀式液压自封接头
sleeve yoke 带（花键）套筒的万向节叉
slender 细长的，细的，单薄的
slenderness 细长度
slenderness ratio 细长比，长径比，长粗比（如：卷簧的自由长度与其平均直径之比，亦称 slender proportion）
slenderness ratio of column 柱的长径比
slender piece 细长工件
slew ①（任一物体绕垂直轴线的）回转，旋转 ②（汽车制动时由于各车轮制动力差异产生的）偏转
slewing ①回转，摆转 ②摆转的
slewing circle 回转圆，转动圆
slewing crane 转动式起重机，回转式起重机
slewing journal 旋转轴颈
slewing ring （支撑平旋转体底平面，如：汽车起动机或挖土机机身底平面的）转盘（亦称 slew ring）
slew rate (**digital**) （线性或乘法 DAC 的）（数字）转换速率（即：maximum rate of digital change of output "数字输出变化的最大速率"。指数字输入代码的变化引起模拟输出值大的阶跃变化时，模拟输出值固有的极限变化速率）
SLH 自锁式轮毂（self-locking hub 的简称）
SLI battery 起动-照明-点火用电池（= starting-lighting-ignition cell）
slice 薄片，片，切片；份，部分
SLICK 车宝（美国的一种汽油添加剂商品名，为聚四氟乙烯胶体溶液，可在汽缸壁面、活塞表面形成一层聚四氟乙烯薄膜，减轻缸壁、活塞的磨损，并提高密封性）
slick pattern tire （赛车用胎面无花纹的）光面轮胎（在干燥路面上可获得最大附着力）
slick road condition 滑溜的路面状态
slicks 光面轮胎（适合于沥青路面、表面无花纹的轮胎，用于拉力赛汽车）
slide ①滑座，导板，导轨 ②滑动，滑移
slideable 可滑动的，滑动式的
slide-air suspension （可变轴距多轴重型载货汽车的）滑动式空气悬架
slide arm 滑臂
slide bar 导杆；滑块，滑竿；滑动接触式汇流条
slide bars 导杆（起链条减振和导向作用的部件）
slide bars of chain drive 链传动导杆（起链条减振和导向作用的部件）
slide block 滑块
slide block type output mechanism 十字滑块输出机构（采用传递平行轴运动的十字滑块机构作为输出机构）
slidec 滑线变压器，滑线电阻调压器（亦写作 slidac）
slide caliper(s) 游标卡尺，滑动卡规（= sliding calipers, slider calipers, slide gauge, nonius calipers,

指各种带副尺的卡尺)
slide face 滑动面
slide fastener 拉链(=zig fastener)
slide fit 滑动配合(=sliding fit)
slide gauge 滑尺,游标卡尺
slide gear 滑动齿轮
slide guide 滑动导轨,滑轨(亦称 slide rail)
slide hammer 惯性锤(=inertia hammer)
slide-in camper (轻便货车上装用的)抽屉式旅游帐篷
slide joint 滑动接头(=sliding joint)
slide-key drive 滑键传动装置
slide plate 滑板
slider ①导块,导瓦②滑块,滑板,滑座③滑尺,游标④滑动触点⑤(连续无级变速器"CVT"的驱动盘"drive pulley", "primary pulley", 的)位置传感件
slide rail of chain 链条张紧导轨(压靠在链条上,调节链条张紧度的导向部件)
slide rheostat 滑动触点变阻器
slide ring ①滑环②(转子发动机端面密封用的)滑动密封环(=sliding ring)
slide-roll ratio 滑移率(制动时滑动量与滚动量之比,亦称 slip rate,见 slip)
slider type suspension 滑动式悬架
slide shaft 滑动轴
slide shoe 滑块
slide-side door (车身的)侧拉门
slide spline 滑动花键
slide steering 单侧制动的滑动转向
slide switch (电气等的)滑动式开关
slide valve 滑阀
slide-valve engine 滑阀式发动机(=sleeve-valve engine)
slide way 滑槽,滑道,滑轨

sliding ①滑动的,滑转的,滑过的②(车轮)滑移(车轮不转,相对地面滑动或车轮中心的直线速度大于车轮的圆周速度,=slip)③(车轮)滑转(车轮不前进,仅原地旋转或车轮圆周速度>0,而车较中心的直线速度=0,=spin)
sliding armature starter 电枢滑动式起动机(依靠电枢移动,来实现驱动齿轮与飞轮齿圈的啮合与分离)
sliding axle 滑动轴
sliding bar 滑竿
sliding bearing (容许零件做轴向移动的)滑动轴承
sliding block 滑块
sliding-block joint 滑块式联轴节,多奥迪式联轴节(允许轴相对轴向滑动的万向节,亦称 de Dion joint)
sliding calliper ①(盘式制动器的)滑动式制动钳,浮动型制动钳(亦称 floating calliper, moveable calliper, moving calliper)②卡尺,滑动卡尺,游标卡尺(=slide callipers)
sliding cam ①滑动凸轮(凸轮工作面与跟随件间有相对滑动)②直线运动凸轮(凸轮件往复运动等)
sliding change drive 滑动变速传动
sliding clamp 滑动夹头,滑动锁夹
sliding cone clutch 滑动锥体离合器,滑锥离合器
sliding contact ①滑动接触②滑动触点
sliding control 滑动控制
sliding coupler 滑差耦合器(利用液体的黏性或油膜的剪切来传递动力的装置)
sliding coupling ①滑动齿套,滑动齿套式联轴节,滑动联轴节②(变速器同步器的)滑动啮合齿套③带滑叉的万向节,可轴向滑动的万向节
sliding dog ①(常啮式机械变速器换挡的)接合啮套(装在变速器主

轴的花键毂上，由换挡拨叉拨动的内花键滑套，换挡时，该齿套将空套在主轴上的所换挡位的齿轮的花键齿圈与主轴花键毂套合成一体，而改变传动比）②（同步器式机械变速器的同步器的部件）接合套（亦称 synchromesh sliding sleeve，见 synchronizer）③（任一种形式的轴向）滑动（的）牙嵌式离合器

sliding dog clutch 滑动牙嵌式离合器

sliding door （箱式车身的）滑动式车门

sliding fastener 拉链

sliding fifth wheel （牵引车上的）可滑动式（半挂车）鞍式牵引座（前后位置可调以适应不同长度的半挂车支撑主销位置和轴荷分布）

sliding fit 滑动配合（= slide fit）

sliding friction ①滑动摩擦②滑动摩擦阻力

sliding gauge 游标卡尺

sliding gear （变速器）滑动齿轮（简称SG）

sliding gearbox 滑动齿轮换挡变速器

sliding gear collar 滑动齿环，滑动齿套，滑动齿圈

sliding gear counter shaft transmission 滑动齿轮副轴式变速器（通过齿轮轴向滑动，改变与其啮合关系，借以变换速比的副轴式变速器）

sliding gear starter 齿轮移动式起动机（靠电磁开关推动安装在电枢轴孔内的啮合杆，使驱动齿轮移动而与飞轮齿环啮合的起动机）

sliding gear transmission 滑动齿轮变速器（多数挡位靠齿轮轴向滑动与另一齿轮相啮合而获得不同传动比的机械变速器，亦称 clash gear transmission）

sliding guide 导轨，滑动导轨

sliding hub （同步器）接合套

sliding jack 装在滑轨上的举升器

sliding joint 可轴向移动式联轴节（亦称 plunging joint, slide joint, slip joint, 各种允许被连接的轴作轴向滑动的联轴节的总称，如：可轴向移动的球笼式等速万向节，见 plunging constant velocity joint）

sliding key 导向键，滑键

sliding pair 滑动副

sliding part of interlocking unit 互锁装置的滑动件

sliding pillar type suspension 烛式悬架（滑柱式悬架，指车轮可沿主销轴线方向移动的悬架形式，亦称 candle type suspension）

sliding plate 滑板（如：钢板弹簧的可更换的滑动支撑）

sliding resistance 滑动阻力

sliding ring 滑动密封环（= slide ring）

sliding roof control 滑动车顶操纵件（用来开闭车身活动顶盖的手操纵件）

sliding-roof lock 滑动式活顶车厢的车顶锁定装置

sliding saddle 滑动座架

sliding sash 滑动窗框

sliding seat 滑动座（如：钢板弹簧的滑动支撑）

sliding selector shaft 换挡拨叉轴

sliding shoe 滑动式（制动）蹄

sliding side door 滑动（开、闭）式侧门

sliding sleeve engine 套阀式发动机，滑套式发动机（= sleeve-type engine）

sliding-sleeve valve 滑动套阀（= sleeve valve）

sliding socket joint 滑动套筒接头

sliding spline （允许万向节传动轴传递扭矩时轴向移动的）滑动花键（亦称 slip spline）

sliding spool 滑阀

sliding stability （汽车的）抗滑稳定性

sliding sunroof （客车、轿车的）滑动开启式天窗

sliding surface of piston 活塞滑动面

sliding tandem （重型货车间距可变的）可滑动式并装双桥（双桥间的位置可轴向移动，以适应荷载分布）

sliding tappet 滑动挺柱（具有底平面，并与凸轮作滑动接触的挺柱）

sliding test 滑动试验

sliding throttle valve 滑动式节流阀

sliding trailing axle （重型多轴载货汽车的可变轴距的）滑动式尾桥

sliding universal joint 带滑动花键的万向节（= slip universal joint, universal slip joint）

sliding vane compressor type super charger 滑动叶片式（空气）压缩机型（进气）增压器

sliding vane pump 滑动叶片式偏心转子泵

sliding vector 滑动矢量

slight 轻微的，少量的，细长的，脆弱的

slight sag 轻度弛垂

slim 细长的

sling ①吊环，链钩，起吊装置 ②吊起

sling cart 吊装车，吊搬车，装有吊链的运货车

sling chain 吊钩链

sling dog （钩索两头的）吊钩

slinger ①（将发动机油底壳内的机油抛至润滑面上的）甩油装置（如：曲轴甩油匙等）②（装在轴上将油液，特别是润滑油沿径向甩出，以防止流向油封的）挡油盘，甩油圈

sling-psychrometer 吊挂湿度计

slingshot 弹弓（[美] 1/4 英里加速赛用，车身细长，车桥和车轮重量均极轻的轻型赛车名）

slip ①滑动（两接触表面相对移动的总称）②（离合器）打滑（= clutch slip, 指离合器从动盘与飞轮间滑移）③车轮滑移（汽车行驶中车轮制动力大于轮胎与路面附着力时，车轮抱死引起的车轮轮胎沿路面向前或向一侧的滑动，= wheel skid 或 wheel slide）④车轮滑转（指汽车驱动力大于轮胎与路面附着力时，车轮原地不动的空转，= wheel spin）⑤（弹性轮胎在横向力的作用下产生的）侧偏（指车轮中心平面的方向侧向偏离轮胎接地中心行进方向的现象，= side slip）⑥（液力变矩器的）滑差（指其输入转速与输出转速的差值，可用输入转速的百分数表示）⑦（车轮制动时的）滑移率 = （车身瞬时速度 − 车轮瞬时速度）/车身瞬时速度 × 100%，车轮完全抱死时，= 100%，车轮完全自由转动时，= 0%）⑧允许滑动量（允许轴向滑动的长度）

slip angle （轮胎的）侧偏角（汽车行驶时，轮胎在横向力的作用下产生弹性变形造成的车轮中心平面的行进方向与车轮中心平面方向间的夹角，亦称 side slip angle, distortion angle 或 angle of deviation）

slip angle force 侧偏阻力，转弯力（= cornering force）

slip angle frame （轮胎六维试验台的）侧偏角架（用于形成被测试轮胎的侧偏角，参见 cornering force）

slip-angle steering （汽车的）侧偏角转向（指汽车在侧向力作用下，前后弹性车轮产生侧偏角，使行车方向发生的变化，见 slip angle）

slip band 滑动带，滑动区

slip board 滑板

slip clutch 打滑式安全离合器（超载时即打滑，= slipping clutch）

slip coefficient ①（土壤）剪切变形系数 ②（履带，车轮）滑移率（见

1469

slip)

slip controlled lock-up clutch torque converter 防滑锁止离合器型变矩器

slip control system 防滑控制系统（如：车轮防抱死控制系统）

slip counter 滑移率计

slip engagement 滑移啮合

slip fan 滑转式风扇（用液力耦合器等驱动，高速时打滑，风扇转速下降，以减少动力损失、噪声、磨损，并可防止发动机过冷）

slip fit 滑（动）配合（=slide fit）

slip-fit liner 滑配式缸套

slip gauge 精密度量用的标准块规

slip gear 滑动齿轮（=sliding gear）

slip-in bearing 瓦片式轴承，轴瓦轴承（=insert bearing, precision bearing）

slip indicator 车轮滑移指示灯（装在组合仪表内，车轮打滑时该灯亮，DAC系统工作时，该灯闪光）

slip indicator lamp 打滑指示灯（当汽车因牵引力大于车轮与路面附着力，导致某一个或两个车轮滑转，整车侧滑或转向中前、后轮出现过强侧滑，以致车辆失去方向稳定性，致使牵引力控制系统或车辆稳定性系统起作用时，该指示灯闪光，以警告驾驶员。见 TRC 和 VSC）

sliping braking adhesion coefficient 制动滑移附着系数（指制动时产生滑移的轮胎—路面附着系数）

slip joint （轴间传递驱动扭矩并允许两轴间作轴向位移的）滑动联轴节（=sliding joint）

slip joint coupling ①滑节；滑动接头②可轴向移动的花键连接

slippage 滑动，滑移（量），滑转，打滑，侧滑

slippage phenomenon （柔软的）跳齿现象（因超载或设计制造不当，在啮合中柔轮齿从刚轮齿中滑脱的现象）

slipped thread 已滑牙的螺纹

slipper ①滑块，滑动件②游标

slipper block （钢板弹簧的）滑动座（亦称 sliding seat，钢板弹簧后端的滑动支撑，当弹簧承载变形时，其后端可在该座上前、后滑动）

slipper bracket 有滑动支撑面的支架（如：没有卷耳的钢板弹簧的托架）

slipper-dip process （汽车车身的）滑动式浸渍涂漆法（简称 slipper-dip）

slipper (ended) spring （钢板弹簧主片制成卷耳通过支架销和支架与车架做固定连接，而后端由可拆式滑板或滑动座支承的）滑座式钢板弹簧

slipperiness 滑溜状态

slipper pretensioner （滚子链条的）滑动式预紧装置（用于消除因装配公差和磨损产生的松弛）

slipper pump ①（滑动）叶片泵（=vane pump）②滑块泵（见 slipper type pump）

slipper (-skirt) piston 滑裙式活塞（亦称 full-slipper skirt piston, partial skirt piston，指为了减轻重量，减少摩擦，将活塞销座孔下方非受力面的裙部全部切除的活塞，多用于短行程发动机，参见 semi-slipper-skirt piston 及 full-skirt piston 或 full trunk piston）

slipper type pump ①滑块式油泵（滑动叶片泵的变形，不同点只是用厚度较大的滑块代替叶片）②滑动叶片泵（参见 sliding vane pump）

slippery ground 滑溜路面，滑地

slippery layer （下雨后，路面上雨水与尘土等形成的）滑溜层

slippery-road braking 滑路制动

slippery when wet sign （道路上的）

"小心路湿打滑"标志

slipping 滑移

slipping area 滑移面,滑移区

slipping braking adhesion coefficient 制动滑移附着系数(在给定工作点下,车轮抱死时,制动力系数的数值,见 brake force coefficient)

slipping of belt 传动带打滑

slipping of brake 制动器(蹄片)打滑

slipping of (the) clutch 离合器打滑,离合器滑转

slipping torque 滑动转矩(引起车轮打滑时的驱动轮转矩)

slip pipe 滑动伸缩管

slip-plate type side slip tester 滑板式侧偏试验台(亦称滑板式侧滑试验台)

slip-pole (type) trailer 滑竿式长货挂车(后桥可在轴式车架上滑动,见 pole trailer)

slip rate 滑移率(①制动时,路面与胎面间的相对速度和行驶速度的比值②驱动时,路面与胎面间的相对速度与轮胎圆周速度的比值)

slip resistance 滑移阻力

slip-resistance symmetrical differential 防滑型对称式差速器(Slip-resistance bevel planet-gear symmetrical differential 的简称,指加装有一侧打滑时的半轴锁紧装置的普通对称型圆锥行星齿轮差速器)

slip ring ①(发电机)滑环(亦称集流环"collector ring")②(离合器)分离推力环

slip-ring circuit breaker 滑环断路器

slip-sensing torque distribution system 车轮滑转感知扭矩分配系统(如:后轮驱动车辆的防滑差速器系统和全轮驱动车辆的前后轮扭矩分配桥间差速器系统,可根据各驱动车轮或驱动桥间打滑程度的不同分配扭矩,即按比例增加不打滑车轮上的扭矩,以充分利用路面附着力)

slip shaft (万向节传动的)滑动轴

slip shaft yoke (十字轴式万向节的)花键轴叉(指带花键轴的万向节叉)

slip sinkage (车轮)滑转下陷,滑转下陷量

slip spline 滑动式花键

slip streaming ①尾流(汽车行驶时气流在其尾部形成的低压涡流区,亦称 wave)②贴尾行驶(指后车紧跟在前车后方行驶,以便利用前车尾流减小空气阻力)

slip test ①侧滑试验②滑动试验③(泵的)负载特性试验

slip threshold setpoint 滑转阈值设定点(= spin threshold setpoint)

slip threshold switch (防滑转系统的)滑转阈开关(汽车在砂或碎石路上行驶时,提高防滑转系统滑转控制阈的开关件)

slip torque 滑转扭矩(驱动桥的最大附着扭矩,指驱动轮滑转时的扭矩,等于驱动桥额定桥荷能力和最大附着系数以及车轮滚动半径三者的乘积)

slip universal joint 带滑动花键的万向节(= sliding universal joint)

slip yoke (十字轴式万向节的)滑动叉(指带滑动花键套的万向节叉,见 yoke of cardan universal joint)

slit 缝隙,切槽

slit nozzle 缝形喷口喷嘴

slit-skirt piston 裙部开槽的活塞

slitting 切口,开槽,切缝,纵切

slit type disk rotor 切槽式制动盘

SLMP technology (新型锂铁电池应用的)稳定锂金属粉技术(stabilized lithium metal powder technology 的简称,可给系统提供独立的锂源,打破了所有的锂均须来自阴极的限制,因而锂铁电池可使用非锂阴极材料,增强抗过充电能力且可

以使用高性能的新型阳极,电池的容量显著提高)

slope 边坡,斜坡面;坡度,斜度

slope angle 坡度角

slope coefficient (特性曲线等的)斜率

sloped curb 斜坡式路缘(缘石面与垂直面成 20°~60°角较陡斜坡)

slope index 坡道阻力指数(坡道角之正弦)

slope length 坡长

slope of curve ①曲线斜度②弯道斜度

slope of repose 休止角

slope of thread 螺纹斜度

slope performance (车辆)爬坡性能

sloper 斜置式发动机(见 inclined engine)

slope signal (速度曲线等的)斜率信号(如:dv/dt 等)

slopes statistical evaluation (车辆行驶地面的)坡度统计评价

slope time (集成电路线性放大器的)斜坡时间(指 rise time 和 fall time "上升时间和下降时间",对输入信号电平阶跃变化,延迟时间的终点与输出信号值第一次通过接近最终值规定电平瞬间之间的时间间隔)

sloping back (车身)倾斜的后部(= slanting back)

sloping curb 斜坡路缘石

sloping floor 斜地板(= ramped floor)

sloping part of S-N curve 疲劳曲线的倾斜部分

sloping radiator 斜置式散热器

sloping side 斜边

sloping test track 带坡度的试验跑道,坡道试验跑道

sloping valve 斜置式气门

sloping windshield 斜风窗玻璃(= slanting windshield)

sloppiness 潮湿,泥泞

sloppy 湿透的,泥泞的

slosh ①(液面)晃动②(因晃动而产生的)泼溅声③软泥,泥泞,雪水

slot ①槽,狭槽,键槽②开槽,开缝

slot atomizer 缝隙式喷(油)嘴(亦称 slot nozzle)

slotted 槽的,有槽的,开缝的,切槽的;有裂痕的

slotted circular nut 槽顶圆螺母,带槽圆形螺母

slotted core 开槽铁心(如:一般直流电机电枢铁心)

slotted frame 带维修槽孔的车架(便于通过槽孔进行前轮定位调整等)

slotted headless set screw 带槽无头定位螺杆

slotted head screws 一字槽螺钉

slotted oil piston ring 开槽活塞油环

slotted piston 裙部开槽的活塞(亦称 slit-skirt piston,美称 split skirt piston,一般指其裙部开有通槽,用于防止活塞受热变形)

slotted piston skirt 开槽式活塞裙

slotted screw 带起子槽的螺钉(一般指普通的单槽螺钉,亦称 slotted top screw)

slotted screwdrivers 凹槽螺钉旋具

slotted valve head 带槽的气门头(供插接研磨工具用)

slot washer 开口垫圈

slot width 槽宽

slough 泥坑,泥潭,洼地

sloughy 泥泞的,沼泽状的

slow-acting 慢动作的

slow adjust screw 怠速(混合气浓度)调节螺钉(简称 SAS)

slow axle speed (双速)驱动桥的低挡

slow battery charger 蓄电池的低速充电机(相对快速充电机而言)

slow brake release 制动缓慢松开

slow build state (防抱死制动系的)慢速升压工况(见 pressure increase②)

slow combustion 低速燃烧,缓慢燃烧

slow-drive zone (车辆)慢行区

slower-moving track (履带车辆转向时的)慢速侧履带

slower traffic keep right sign "慢车靠右行驶"标志(在多车道的道路中,指示低速车辆靠右侧车道行驶的标志)

slow moving load sinkage 低速运行的沉陷量

slow-speed engine 低速发动机(= low speed engine)

slow-speed governor 低速限速器,怠速限速器

slow speed system ①低速系②(化油器的)怠速油系(= idle system, idling circuit, idling and low speed circuit)

slow speed test 低速试验(简称 slow test)

slow-up traffic 减速车流

slow wave (脑电波中的)徐波(8Hz,25μV 以下)

SLR 激光扫描雷达(scanning laser radar 的简称)

SLS ①自动调平悬架(self-leveling suspension 的简称)②悬架高度调平系统(suspension leveling system 的简称)③选择性局部激光烧结(= selective laser sintering)

SLT ①固体逻辑技术(solid logic technology)②环形往返运输(shuttle loop transit)

sludge 油泥(润滑油、脂本身氧化或燃烧与半燃烧产物,如:未燃烧的 HC、炭粒、氧化物和醛聚合物等沉积而形成的浓稠状物质)

sludge binder 油泥胶质(固态油泥和漆状物中能被丙酮溶解的部分)

sludge breaker 油污清除剂(简称 SB)

sludge deposit 泥浆状沉积物

sludge digestion sewage process 菌致分解污水处理法(利用厌氧细菌使污水分解,产生可燃性气体)

sludge formation 沉淀物的形成

sludge pan 沉淀池

sludge proof (机油)防沉淀的,耐氧化的

sludge trap (一般多指平面底壳式发动机润滑系中,防止油泥随机油循环的)油泥沉集阱(亦称 sediment trap)

sludgy 污泥的,泥泞的

sluggish response 迟缓响应

slug relay 缓动继电器,延时继电器

slund load 并联负载

slurry ①泥浆②油水乳化液③膏剂

slush ①雪泥,半融化的雪地②稀泥③软土④污水⑤机油

slush casting ①空壳铸造,空心件铸造②空壳铸件,薄壳铸件

slush guard 挡泥板(= antisplash guard)

slushing compound 防锈油膏,防蚀油膏,抗蚀油脂,抗蚀润滑剂

slushing grease 抗蚀润滑脂

slush metal 易熔合金,软合金

slushy road 泥浆道路

SLV 超豪华(汽)车(super luxury vehicle 的简称)

S/M 表面积-质量比(surface-to-mass ratio)

small articles box (车厢内的)小文件箱,小物品箱

small batch production method 小批生产法

small-bore engine 小缸径发动机

small bore piston 小直径活塞

small-bore utility engine 小缸径通用发动机

small calorie ①克卡（gram calorie）②小卡

small car 小（尺寸）轿车（= compact car）

small car-derived van 小型轿车改装的箱式货车

small diameter workpiece 小直径工件

small displacement engine 小排量发动机

small end （连杆）小头（connecting rod small end 的简称，指连杆的活塞端）

small end bush(ing) （连杆）小头衬套

small gross 小罗（= 10 打 = 120 个）

small-hole gauge 小孔规

small internal gear 小内齿圈（组合式行星齿轮机构中，与小行星轮啮合的内齿圈）

small light 小灯（一般指汽车前照灯的近光灯）

small lot production 小批量生产（= small scale production）

small-power motor 小功率电动机

small-scale experiment ①小规模的试验②缩小尺寸的模型试验

small scale integrated circuit 小规模集成电路（简称 SSI。指 70 到 100 个左右的三极管等电路元件集装在一片硅晶基片上的集成电路）

small scale production 小量生产，小批量生产，小规模生产

small-scale specimen ①缩尺样品，缩尺模型②小尺寸试样

small screw jack 小型螺旋起重器，小型螺旋千斤顶

small serial production 小批生产

small set pavement 小方石（铺砌）路面

small signal 微弱信号

small size bearing 小型轴承（内径 10mm 以下）

small sun gear 小太阳轮，小中心齿轮（外行星齿轮机构中与短行星齿轮啮合的中心轮）

smart car ①漂亮汽车（俗）②智能汽车（= intelligent vehicle，并无明确的定义，一般指自动控制水平高的汽车，亦指装备有自动驾驶系统，不必由人操纵可在自动公路上行驶的车辆，见 automatic vehicle control system 近年来，随着通信—信息技术的飞速发展出现了新一代智能汽车亦称）Connected coos 见（omeeted）

Smart emergence call 智能紧急呼叫

Smart for two electric drive Smart 电动汽车（Smart 原为德国奔驰公司生产的二人乘名牌小型内燃机轿车，"Smart for two electric drive" 为在该小轿车基础上研制的二人乘电动小轿车，使用锂离子电池，一次充电行程 140 km，最高车速 120 km/h）

Smart headlamp （汽车的）智能前照灯［可根据雷达、摄像系统的信息，改变发光强度、照射范围和照射点。这类前照灯使用大量的（如：100 个）发光二极管（LED）密集布置成矩形、圆形或其他形状作为光源，其中任一个或任一组发光二极管均可独立点亮或关闭，因此只要改变点亮的发光二管的数量或部位，即可改变前照灯的亮度、照射范围以及照射范围内任一局部的明暗度，如：当雷达等测得前方有对向行驶的车辆时，即可将照射该对向车所在区域内的 LED 关闭，以免该车驾驶者炫目，而照射范围内的其他区域仍照度不减。此项功能称为：智能远光功能（intelligence high beam function）。此外，智能型前照灯还具有聚光（灯）照

射功能（spotlight function），如当雷达等测得在前照灯照射范围以外有行人或其他可能导致车祸的障碍物时，智能型前照灯在继续保持原照射范围的同时，另外向该行人或障碍物射出一道持续或频闪的聚发光束，提示驾驶者注意]

smart key　智能（车门）钥匙（车主无论将钥匙装在何处只要随身携带，无须按压按钮，走近自己的汽车，车门便自动开启，离开后车门即自动关闭。该钥匙还可扩展多项功能，如：在车外开关车内照明灯、发动机起动-停机按钮、调整座椅和后视镜角度、开关空调、调台等，以及提供行驶距离、轮胎气压、车辆技术状况等多种信息，而使汽车电子控制系统更为简约）

smart peripheral　（汽车电子控制系统的）智能型外围设备（指智能型输入输出设备，后备存储器，通信设备，调制调解器，各种执行机构，中间机构和传感器件等）

smart phone　智能（型）手机

smart phone interface　（汽车仪表板上的）智能手机接口

Smart, Safe Research Vehicle　（福特公司的）智能、安全研究车（见 S^2RV）

smart seat　智能（防盗）座椅（驾驶者离开车辆车门上锁或按下遥控开关后驾驶座会自动前移，其靠背下倾紧贴转向盘，其他人无法开车，以达到防盗目的）

smart traffic signal control system　智能型交通信号控制系统（ITS 的一个基础分支，亦称智能型交通信息管理系统，= intelligent traffic signal management system，近年来随着通信—信息技术的飞速发展，出现了下一代智能汽车，亦称 connected car，见 connected）

smart window　（德尔福公司的）智能车窗（2004 年开始大量生产使用的红外线非接触式车商玻璃控制系统的商品名，在玻璃关闭过程中只要有 4mm 以上的障碍物，便会自动停止，不会发生夹伤手指等事故）

smart wiring system　智能线路系统（简称 SWS，指用一根单线传送多重信息的多路传输系统）

smash　碰撞，砸坏，使破碎

smash up　①撞车②猛撞

SMC　模压（成型制品）用复合板材（sheet moulding compound 的简称，由上、下塑料薄膜裹覆的聚酯树脂、玻璃纤维、填料等辅助材料制成的复合材料板材，用来作为油底壳、隔热板、车身外板、托架、横梁等模压成型件的原材料，与钢板相比，重量轻，刚度高，隔热免锈，生产周期短）

SMC part　模压成型复合材料板件（sheet-module composite part 的简称，如：用复合材料板模压成型的车身板件等）

SMD　①（电子系统中的）表面安装装置（surface-mounted device 的简称）②表面安装技术（surface-mounted technology 的简称）

smear test　①涂色斑点（印迹）试验（按接触斑点来检查轴承、齿轮等配副的贴合状况）②机油质量的斑点法试验（在专用纸上印上油斑，根据油斑状态和颜色来鉴定机油质量）

SMEC II　（克莱斯勒公司的）单模块式发动机控制器（single module engine controller 的简称，按 SAE J1930，应称为 power train control module 动力系统控制模块）

smectic liquid crystal　层状相液晶（分子长轴方向一致，并且分子重心的排列位置呈层状结构的液晶）

S meter　信号强度计（信号强度指示仪，S 为 signal 的简称）

SMG 手动连续换挡变速器［商品名，sequential manual gearbox 的简称，只要用手指拨动转向盘上的桨状换挡杆或前、后推动身旁的换挡杆，便可实现挡位连续升降的计算机控制液压换挡变速器（compute controlled -hydraulically shifted transmission）］

SMI 标准量测仪器（standard measuring instruments 的简称）

smith anvil 锻砧，铁工砧

smithery 锻工工作，锻工车间

Smith's chart 史密斯圆图（输电线阻抗图）

Smithsonian Institution Science Information Exchange ［美］史密斯索尼安科学情报交流所

smog 烟雾，光化学烟雾（smoke 烟与 fog 雾两词的复合词，1943 年 9 月美国洛杉矶市上空出现由汽车废气中的 HC 和 NOx 在阳光紫外线作用下，发生光化学反应而产生烟雾状物笼罩城市上空，酷似英国伦敦的 smoke 和 fog，因而称为 Los Angeles Smog "洛杉矶烟雾"，smog 亦因而得名）

smog-control device 烟雾控制装置

smog-forming ability 光化学烟雾生成能力（= smog-forming reactivity, smog-forming potential）

smog-forming emission 形成烟雾（公害）的排放物

smoke 烟，烟尘

smoke abatement 消烟法，除烟法

smoke black 烟黑，炭黑

smoke chart 烟色浓度图，烟色图

smoke color 烟色

smoke control （柴油机）排烟控制

smoke density ①排烟浓度②烟浓度，烟密度

smoke diagnosis （发动机）排烟诊断（根据排烟成分等确定发动机的技术状况）

smoked lens lamp 烟膜玻璃罩灯（指玻璃罩蒙有一层烟膜、表面发黑或呈深灰色的汽车后组合灯等，玻璃做黑的方法除烟膜法外，还有玻璃着色法和表面涂色法等）

smoke emission （柴油机的）排气烟尘（指悬浮于排气流中，遮蔽、吸收、反射、折射光线的各种微粒）

smoke filter 排烟滤清器

smoke-free 无烟的

smoke index 烟度单位，烟度指数（= smoke unit）

smoke intensity 烟度

smokeless combustion 无烟燃烧

smokeless exhaust 无烟排气

smokeless fuel 无烟燃料

smoke limit characteristics 冒烟极限特性（柴油机排气烟度超出法规允许值时的功率随转速改变的关系，即在柴油机运转转速范围内，调节喷油泵的调节机构，测取各转速下排气烟度超出限值时的功率等参数所绘的曲线）

smoke limited power （柴油机的）排烟极限功率

smoke limit power 冒烟极限功率（柴油机等在某一转速达到某一功率时，如再继续增加喷油量将因空气不足或燃烧不完全而急剧冒烟到不允许的程度，这时的功率称冒烟极限功率，简称极限功率）

smoke measurement at free acceleration 自由加速烟度测量法（测量柴油机车辆排气烟度的一种方法。发动机从急速工况将油门踏板迅速踩到底，维持数秒钟后迅速松开，在加速过程中测量排气烟度）

smoke measurement at full load 全负荷烟度测量法（柴油机在全负荷稳定运转时测量烟度的方法）

smoke meter 烟度计（柴油机排烟浓度的测定装置，一般分不透光式

和滤纸式两种，不透光式又分全流式和部分流式两种，滤纸式只有部分流式)

smoke opacimeter 不透光式烟度计，不透明排烟浓度计（通过测量柴油机排气不透光度，来测定其排烟浓度，能连续测定，但不能区分排气中的黑烟、白烟、蓝烟）

smoke performance （柴油机的）排烟特性

smoke point 烟点

smoke-producing agent 发烟剂

smoke rating 排烟浓度额定值

smoker package （车上的点烟器、烟灰盒等）烟具

smoke sheets 烟片（橡胶）

smoke-suppressant additive （柴油机）消烟剂（烟度抑制添加剂）

smoke test cycle （柴油机）排烟浓度试验循环，排烟浓度测试循环（按 SAE J35 的规定，该循环由怠速、加速、额定转速运转、加载减速、中间转速运转、卸载等工况组成）

smoke tester （柴油机的）排烟浓度测定仪，烟度仪

smoke tunnel 烟流型风洞（利用烟流使流过车身或其部件的气流可见化）

smoke unit 烟度单位（亦称 smoke index "烟度指数"，用滤纸式烟度计测量发动机排气烟度时，表示滤纸染黑程度的数字，常用符号 R_B，见 filter type smoke meter）

smoke volatility index 烟发散指数

smokey quartz color （车身外壳的）烟晶色

smoking character 排烟特性

smokin' wheels 车轮冒烟赛（每年在关岛举行一次，从小型摩托、高通过性全地域车到全轮驱动多功能车、专用赛车等各种车辆汇集一场的大规模越野赛的称谓。该赛事从儿童摩托车赛开始，然后依次为成人摩托车赛、全地域车赛 ATV、专用赛车赛 buggy 等，各进行三个回合)

smokless air bag 无烟安全气囊

smooth ①光滑的，平滑的，平坦的，平稳的②弄平，弄平滑

smooth acceleration 平稳加速

smooth chrome 光滑镀铬，装饰镀铬

smooth combustion 平顺燃烧，稳定燃烧

smooth contour 光滑外形，平滑外形（简称 SC）

smooth curve 平滑曲线

smooth deceleration 平稳的减速

smoothed edge-arrissing 细磨边（经细加工的玻璃边缘，手摸有滑腻感但不透明）

smooth engagement （离合器，制动器）平稳接合

smooth engine 运转平稳的发动机

smoother ①平路机②修光工具③平滑滤波器④校平器

smooth finish 光洁加工，光面修整，最后修光

smooth idling 平稳的怠速运转

smoothness ①平滑度，平整度②平稳性，平顺性

smoothness of pick-up 接合平顺性（如：发动机与传动系接合的平顺程度）

smoothometer （道路）平面度测定仪

smooth operation 平稳运转，稳定运行，平静运转（= smooth running, quiet run）

smooth running shut-off threshold （发动机）平稳运转截止阈（指发动机平稳运转最低转速点）

smooth shifting 平稳换挡

smooth side 光滑面

smooth surface 光滑表面，平滑表面

smooth tread 光胎面（亦称 plain pattern tread，没有胎面花纹，或仅有两条用以测量胎面磨耗深度的窄沟的胎面）

SMPV 紧凑型多功能车（compact multi purpose vehicle 的简称）

SMR （电动车、混合动力车等高压电路的）系统主继电器（system main relay 的简称，接通、断开动力蓄电池高压电路的继电器，起着保护高压电路和防止发生漏电事故的作用）

smuggled car 走私轿车

smut ①污物，污点 ②燃烧污染物（未燃炭、灰、硫酸等），煤炱，积烟，片状炭黑 ③污染，弄脏，使变黑

SMV 低速车辆（slow-moving vehicle）

SN ①锡（tin, stannum）②卫生方面的（sanitary）③路面摩擦系数值（见 skid number）

snail 平面螺旋，平面螺旋线凸轮，涡形轮

snail cam 涡形凸轮（如：制动蹄片间隙调整凸轮）

snail-pace traffic 蜗行交通（由于堵车和拥挤而造成的十分缓慢的交通流）

snake ①蛇行（弯弯曲曲地行驶）②拖出来，拉上来 ③（发亮的）斑点；清除管道用的铁丝

snaking ①蛇行运动 ②（挂车）摇摆或甩动

snap ①紧压 ②揿钮，夹子，钩扣 ③折断声 ④急变，速动；容易的工作，易解决的问题；少量 ⑤咬住 ⑥（突然）折断 ⑦急速的，突然的 ⑧装扣门的，易扣住的

snap-acceleration 猛加速，急加速

snap(-) action ①（阀等的）速动（指阀件等迅速地从一个工位转移到另一个工位，在控制信号和动作间没有延时或很少延时）②快动作，快速；瞬时作用 ③快速动作的，迅速的，速动的

snap connector ①（电器中接线用的）弹簧卡紧式快速插装接头 ②（任一种用于机械、液压或气动系统中的）弹簧卡装式接头

snap coupling 快速联轴节，自动联结器

snap fastener 卡装式紧固件

snap fitting ①卡扣装接件，快速装接件，卡扣接头，快装接头 ②卡扣装接的，快速装合的

snap fixing 卡簧固定，卡扣固定

snap gauge （外）卡规

snap hammer 圆边击平锤，铆锤，抵锤

snap head rivet （半）圆头铆钉

snap-in anchor 揿压式卡夹，快速夹卡，卡夹

snap jet 气动量规，气动测头

snap lock 碰锁，弹簧锁，弹簧搭扣

snap piston-pin ring 活塞销弹簧卡环

snap ring 卡环（起轴向限位作用的零件）

snap-ring bearing 外圈带止动环的球轴承（= ball bearing with shoulder ring in outer race）

snap-ring expander 卡环扩张器，卡环拆装器（= snap-ring remover）

snapshot timing light 搭线式正时灯（发动机运转状态下，只要将该正时灯的搭线夹夹住第一缸高压线，即可发出闪光）

snap switch 快动开关

snarl 交通阻塞，交通混乱

snatch block 紧线滑轮，扣绳滑轮

snatching 窜动，抖撞（见 bucking）

snatch phenomenon 前窜现象（汽车等行驶和发动机等运转中突然加速一下的现象，见 bucking）

S-N curve 应力循环次数-疲劳曲线

（见 stress-number of cycles to failure curve）

S-N curve for P% survival P%存活率的S-N曲线（在各应力水平下拟合P%存活率疲劳寿命的曲线。它是所期应力与P%母体能尚存的破坏循环数之间关系的一种估计量。P可以是50，95，90等）

Snellen index 斯奈仑指数（视觉分辨力，被测试者与正常视力者能看清规定物体的距离比）

Snell's law 斯奈尔定律（折射定律：一定频率的电磁波射入任一对已知介质时，其入射角正弦与折射角正弦的比值为一常数）

snifting valve 吸气阀，进气阀

snips 铁丝剪，铗子，剪刀

snorkel （发动机空气滤清器的）加长型进气管（schnorkel或schnorkle的简写，原意为游泳潜水时用的呼吸管）

snorkel device （车辆涉深水时防止进水的）加长型进、排气管

snout （软管等的）嘴

snow barrier 挡雪墙

snow blockage 雪封（积雪堵塞交通）

snow breaker 除雪机

snow-cat 雪地履带式车辆

snow chain 雪地（车轮）防滑链

snow covering 雪覆盖层

snow-driving capacity 雪地行驶能力

snowed-up terrain 积雪地区

snow fence 雪障碍物

snow-going vehicle 雪地车辆（= oversnow vehicle）

snow gripper （装在汽车车轮上的）雪地防滑爪

snow guard 防雪板，防雪栅，雪栏

snowmobile ①雪地运动车（按SAE J33的规定，特打总质量不超过450kg，由雪橇板转向，履带驱动的雪地竞赛车辆或雪地儿童游乐车辆）②雪地用汽车，雪地用机动车辆

snowmobile industry 雪地汽车工业，雪地汽车产业（从事雪地汽车开发生产、销售的行业）

Snowmobile Safety and Certification Committee ［美］雪地汽车安全与鉴定委员会（简称SSCC）

snowpacker 雪地运输车

snow scraper 刮雪机

snow shovel 雪铲

snow sprocket 雪地履带车驱动链轮

snow sweeper 扫雪车

snow tire 雪地行驶用轮胎

snowy road surface 积雪路面

SN ratio 信噪比（signal to noise ratio的简称，亦写成S/N。信号大小与噪声大小的比值，单位用dB分贝表示，该比值越大，噪声越不明显）

snub ①制动减速（指用制动的方法使车减速）②减振，缓冲③减声

snubber ①减振器，缓冲器②［美］（汽车悬架系统的）缓冲块（英称bump stop或buffer stop，指在冲击荷载下避免刚性撞击和弹性元件产生过大变形而使用的橡胶块或其他弹性体的行程限制或回弹阻尼装置）③（泛指）行程限制器④减声器

snubber chain 止动链（= stop chain）

snubber type shock absorber 弹性件式减振器（如：使用橡胶做阻尼元件的减振器）

snub braking 减速制动

snub test （制动器的）减速制动试验

snug fit 适贴配合，滑动配合

snug washer 内藏（隐置）垫圈

soak ①浸湿，浸泡，泡②吸收（液体等）③浸透④热起（加热，而使整体达到某一稳定的温度，亦称

warm up，如：对发动机指起动后经短时间运转，包括远离汽缸的部件在内的整个发动机均达到其工作温度）⑤湿机（指热机停止运转后，在发动机余热的烘烤下，汽油蒸汽充满进气系统或继而冷凝于进气系统管壁的现象，亦称 hot soak）

soak condition ①（发动机）热起状态 ②（发动机）湿机状态（见 soak）

soaking-in ①吸入，渗入 ②电容器电荷增值

soaking-out ①渗出 ②漏电 ③剩余放电

soak（ing）time ①热起时间（起动后发动机全部零件均达到工作温度所需时间）②（干荷蓄电池的）液浸时间（指其注入电解液后到可使用状态所需的时间）

soak period ①（发动机）热起期 ②（发动机）湿机期（见 soak）

soak up oil by saw-dust 用锯屑吸尽污油，锯末吸油

soap bubble leak detection （肥）皂泡检漏（亦称 soap-suds test 肥皂泡密封性试验）

soapstone 滑石粉，滑石（= steatite）

soar ①急剧上升，猛增 ②上升高度

SOC ①（蓄电池的）充电率，充电状态（state of charge 的简称）②单片式（微控制）系统（system of chip 的简称，以 32 位或 64 位等高性能微处理器为核心的多变量、多任务的综合协调控制单元，其软、硬件集成在一块芯片上，为汽车用第三代嵌入式控制单元，如：集成化"ABS/ASr/ACC"综合控制模块、混合动力车的动力综合控制模块等）

Society of Air Cushion Vehicle Technicians ［英］气垫车技师学会（简称 SACVT）

Society of Automotive Engineers ［美］汽车工程师学会（简称 SAE）

Society of Automotive Engineers-Advances in Engineering ［美］汽车工程师学会的先进技术丛书（简称 SAE-AE）

Society of Automotive Engineers of Australasia 大洋洲汽车工程师学会（简称 SAEA）

Society of Automotive Engineers of China 中国汽车工程学会（简称 SAE-China）

Society of Automotive Engineers-Special Publications ［美］汽车工程师学会专刊（简称 SAE-SP）

Society of Automotive Engineers Thread 美国汽车工程师学会标准螺纹

Society of Motor Manufacturers and Traders 汽车制造商和销售商学会（创立于 1902 年，旨在促进英国和国外汽车工业的发展，活动内容有各种机动车辆及其部件和附件的制造和贸易）

Society of Petroleum Engineers ［美］石油工程师学会（简称 SPE）

Society of the Plastic Industry Inc ［美］塑料工业学会（简称 SPI）

socioeconomic 社会经济的

Société des Ingénieurs de l'Automobile ［法］汽车工程师学会（简称 SIA）

sock 敲击，撞击，敲打

socket ①球窝 ②插座，灯头，灯座 ③白状管接头 ④（套筒扳手的）套筒

socket and spigot joint （管端）套筒接合；插承接合；窝接，球窝节

socket joint 球铰接，球关节，球窝接合

soda ①碳酸钠，碳酸氢钠，苏打 ②氢氧化钠；氧化钠

soda ash 苏打灰，（钠）碱灰，纯碱，无水苏打，无水碳酸钠

soda bath ①盐浴（见 salt bath）②苛性钠等溶液（用于零件脱脂清洗）

soda lime glass 钠钙玻璃

sodalye 苛性钠，氢氧化钠（= caustic soda）

sodium 钠（Na）

sodium-air battery 钠-空气电池

sodium azide 叠氮化钠（氧化反应产生的安全气囊爆发时所需的充填气体）

sodium base grease 钠基润滑脂

sodium bicarbonate 碳酸氢钠（$NaHCO_3$）

sodium carbonate 碳酸钠（Na_2CO_3）

sodium cavity （排气门杆）装冷却钠盐的中空部分

sodium chloride 氯化钠（食盐，NaCl）

sodium-cooled (exhaust) valve 钠冷却（排）气门（亦称 sodium-filled exhaust valve，指杆部中空，内装有钠冷却剂的排气门，简称 sodium valve）

sodium hydroxide 苛性钠，氢氧化钠（NaOH）（= caustic soda）

sodium lamp 钠弧灯

sodium nitrate （亚）硝酸钠（$NaNO_2$）

sodium pentasulfide 五硫化钠

sodium phenolate （苯）酚钠（C_6H_5ONa）

sodium phosphate 磷酸钠（Na_3PO_4）

sodium silicate 硅酸钠（水玻璃，Na_2SiO_3）

sodium-soap grease 钠皂润滑脂，钠基滑脂

sodium-sulfur (secondary) battery 钠-硫（二次）电池（亦称 sodium-sulfur cell，以高温熔融状的硫黄为正极，及高温熔融多硫化钠或金属钠为负极，由离子通导的陶瓷电解质隔开，其化学反应式为 $2Na + S \rightleftharpoons Na_2S$）

sodium valve 见 sodium-cooled (exhaust) valve

sodium vapor light 钠汽灯

SO_2 emission SO_2 排放（二氧化硫排放）

SOF ①（柴油机排放微粒物中的）悬浮油粒（suspension of fuel 的简称）②帧起始（start of frame 的简称）

SOFC 固体氧化物燃料电池（solid oxide fuel cell 的简称）

SOFIS 完美与最佳的燃油喷射系统（Sophisticated and Optimized Fuel Injection System 的简称，日本日产公司的商品名。该系统的特点是不仅按常规根据空气质量流量、发动机转速、节气门开度等输入信号，而且还考虑喷入进气门前方的汽油在进气管和进气孔内壁的附着量及空气流量传感器所测定的空气量完全吸入汽缸的时间迟后等对空燃比的影响而实现对喷油量的最佳控制）

soft bronze 软青铜

soft bumper fascia 保险杆软罩

soft cast iron 软铸铁

soft ductile material 软韧性材料

soften ①软化，使软，弄软，使柔和②低温处理，退火

softener ①软化剂②软水器

softening temperature 软化温度

soft-faced hammer 软面锤（锤头用软金属覆面的手锤）

soft/firm relay （阻尼可变式空气悬架的）软/硬（阻尼）模式变换继电器

soft going 在松软地面上的行驶

soft hammer 软锤（用铅、铜或白合金制成的软质金属锤）

soft-land trailer 松土路挂车，高通过性挂车

soft magnet 软磁铁（暂时磁铁）

soft metal ①软金属（铅，锡，铝，

铜等)②（轴承用）减磨合金

soft mode （可控阻尼特性悬架的）软模式（阻尼力小）

soft mode relay （空气悬架的）软模式继电器

soft mount 软支座

softness 柔软度，柔软性，柔和性，平顺性

soft nitriding 氮化变软法

soft pencils 软铅笔（用符号B表示，B字越多铅笔芯越软）

soft plug 热型火花塞（见 hot plug ①）

softpressure tube （汽车行人保护系统装在前保险杠上的冲击压力）减压软管

soft shoulder sign "路肩软弱"标志（表示路肩未铺装，行车驶出路面有危险的警告标志）

soft soap 软肥皂（钾皂，= potash soap）

soft soil mobility 软土机动性（车辆在软土地上行驶的机动性能）

soft soil performance （车辆）软土通过性能

soft-solder 软钎焊（指锡焊等）

soft spot （材料）软点

soft steel 软钢（低碳钢）

soft sticky clay 胶黏土

soft-surface road 松软路面道路

soft temper 软化回火

soft tire 软胎（充气不足的轮胎）

soft tissue （人体）软组织

soft top ①（敞篷轿车的）折叠式软车顶②带折叠软顶的敞篷轿车

soft top cab 软顶驾驶室

soft top container 软顶式集装箱（顶开式集装箱之一种，箱顶用篷布制成，边缘有索孔，以备由绳索拉紧）

software （电子计算机）软件（指与数据处理系统的操作有关的计算机程序、过程、方法、规划、协议及有关文件等信息系统中一切非硬件部分，见 hardware）

software-based crash avoidance and mitigation system 基于软件的碰撞回避和减缓系统（由计算机软件对摄像机等拍摄的影像进行实时分析，当确认在当时的相对车速和车间距条件下有发生碰撞的危险时，即酌情向执行机构发出减速、制动或转向的指令）

software quality control （对）软件（的）质量控制

software support 软件支持

soft water 软水

soft wood 软质木材，软木

SOH （state of health 的简称）①（人员的）健康状态②（机器、设备的）技术完好状态

SOHC 单顶置凸轮轴（single overhead camshaft）

sohc design 采用先进技术的设计（sophisticated design 的简称）

soil 土壤，土

soil-asphalt road 沥青稳定土路（亦称 soil-bituminous road）

soil bearing capacity 土壤承载能力

soil bin test 土槽试验（土槽是一种专门供试验车辆的轮胎、履带或工程机械、农业机械的工作装置与土壤相互作用关系的试验设施，在土槽中可以进行轮胎、履带的滚动阻力、附着性能等试验）

soil capacity 土壤耐压力，土壤承载能力

soil-cement road 水泥稳定土路

soil coefficient of external friction 土壤外部摩擦系数（外部摩擦阻力与垂直压力的比值）

soil coefficient of internal friction 土壤内摩擦系数

soil compaction resistance 土壤压实阻力

soil constant 土壤常数

soil crust 土壤硬表层

soil effective stress 土壤有效应力（垂直于单位面积的颗粒间的平均压力）

soil external frictional resistance 土壤外部摩擦阻力

soil-mobility characteristics 土壤的通过特性

soil-pressure cell 土壤压力传感器

soil primary shear surface （与车辆前进方向平行的）土壤主剪切面

soil propelling force 土壤推力（车辆在松软地面上行驶时，驱动轮对地面施加向后的水平力，地面随之发生剪切变形，相应的土壤抗剪强度便构成土壤对车轮的推力）

soil resistance force 土壤阻力

soil slip 滑坡，坍方，土滑

soil surfaced road 土路（简称 soll road）

soil trafficability （车辆的）软地通过性

soil-wheel interaction 土壤-车轮相互作用

sol ①可溶解的（soluble 的简称）②溶液（solution 的简称）

solar car 太阳能轿车（＝solar powered car，以太阳能电池为动力源的电动轿车）

solar cell 太阳能电池（简称 SC，＝solar battery）

solar control film （车窗的）防晒隔热膜

solar energy 太阳能

solar energy reflecting glass 日光反射式玻璃（可反射日光中的长波，减弱日光直射的辐射热，多用于轿车后窗玻璃，可分为喷涂金属膜的直接反射式和利用光波干涉原理的干涉反射式两种）

solar oil 太阳油（灯用煤油，＝gas oil）

solar panel （装在车身顶面等处的）太阳能发电板

solar-powered race car 太阳能动力赛车

solar regenerative fuel cell system 太阳能再生式燃料电池系统

solar sensor 日照传感器（将阳光照度变换为电气量输出的器件）

solar-tinted glass （车窗的）有色遮阳玻璃

solder ①软钎焊焊料（熔点低于 $450°C$ 的钎焊焊料，如：铅锡合金焊锡）②软钎焊（被焊接件不熔化，而仅依靠焊锡等软焊料将工件焊接在一起）

solderable 可钎焊性，可低温焊接性能

soldered seam 软钎焊焊缝

soldering iron 钎焊用烙铁

soldering liquid 焊水，焊液，（钎）焊（用）酸（＝soldering acid, soldering water, soldering fluid）

soldering machine 钎焊机

soldering material 焊料，焊剂，焊锡，钎料（＝solder①）

sole ①底基，底座，座板，底部，垫板②单一的，唯一的

sole bar ①车架纵梁②底部边梁（＝side sill）

solebar angle （客车车身底部结构）纵梁角铁

Solectria E-10 （美国）Solectria 公司生产的 E-10 型蓄电池动力客货两用汽车（其一次充电行驶里程为 130km，最高车速为 100km/h）

solenoid ①螺旋线管②电磁线圈③（螺旋管式）电磁开关（＝solenoid switch）④（螺旋管式）电磁阀（＝solenoid valve）

solenoid actuated relays 电磁继电器（螺线管电磁线圈控制的继电器）

solenoid-actuated valve 电磁控制阀（亦称 solenoid-operated valve，简称 solenoid valve 或 solenoid）

solenoid actuator (电子控制模块控制的螺旋线圈型)电磁阀式执行器

solenoid-and-plunger 带铁心的电磁线圈

solenoid brake (螺旋线圈控制的)电磁制动器

solenoid clutch (螺线管)电磁(线圈控制式)离合器

solenoid coil 螺线管(圆筒形电磁线圈)

solenoid control circuit 电磁阀控制电路(控制电磁阀通、断电的电路)

solenoid controlled vacuum valve 电磁(控制的)真空阀

solenoid controlled valve 电磁(线圈控制的)阀

solenoid effect 线圈的电磁铁作用

solenoid injector (柴油机的)电磁阀式喷油器

solenoid-operated plunger (螺线管)电磁线圈控制的柱塞

solenoid-operated vacuum control valve (由)电磁阀操纵(其真空输入通路的膜片式)真空控制阀

solenoid-plunger type pressure modulator (ABS系统的)电磁阀—柱塞式制动液压调节器(由每一条制动回路的一个电磁阀和每一个轮缸的一个柱塞阀体组成,如:三回路四轮ABS系统中的调节器具有三个双作用电磁阀、四个柱塞阀,其中一个电磁阀控制左、右后轮共用回路的两个柱塞阀体,另两个电磁阀分别控制左、右前轮两条独立回路的两个柱塞阀。四回路制动系统则每一个车轮的柱塞阀都由一个单独的双作用电磁阀控制,而构成四条独立的制动回路)

solenoid regulator valve (自动变速器控制系)电磁阀调压阀(调节通往电磁阀工作液体压力的阀)

solenoid retarded distributor 电磁线圈控制式点火推迟分电器(节气门关闭时推迟点火时刻,为CAS系的一部分)

solenoid shift starter 电磁啮合式起动机(发动机起动时依靠螺线管电磁力使驱动齿轮与飞轮齿圈啮合,起动后利用超速离合器与齿圈分离, = overrunning clutch drive starting motor)

solenoid switch 电磁(线圈控制的)开关

solenoid throttle stop 电磁式节气门关闭器(防止发动机点火断开后继续燃烧的节气门断火速闭电磁开关,见 idle stop solenoid)

solenoid type idle air bypass valve 电磁阀(控制式)怠速空气旁通阀(为一电磁阀控制的柱塞阀,怠速运转中,节气门关闭的状态下,节气门前方的空气可通过该阀绕过节气门而进入节气门后方,其开启度由电子控制模块根据发动机运转条件的要求通过占空比控制,可在不动节气门的情况下,控制发动机的怠速转速)

solenoid type idle air control device 电磁阀式怠速空气控制装置(亦写作 solenoid type IAC,见 IAC)

solenoid-type parking lock (自动变速器的)电磁阀控制型机械驻车锁止器

solenoid vacuum switch 真空通路电磁开关

solenoid valve 电磁阀

solenoid valve pairs for compressed air increase/reduction (气制动 ABS 的)制动气压升/降调节用电磁阀副(由根据控制模块的指令开启/关闭提高或降低制动气压管路的两个电磁阀组件)

solenoid valve type antilock brake system 电磁阀(控制液压)式防抱死制动系统

solenoid winding 电磁线圈
sole plate 基础板，底板，地脚板，履带板
sole weight 自重（=own weight）
solid ①固体，实体②固体的，固态的，坚固的，实心的，整体的
solid angle 立体角（以立体弧度为单位，从某一点看的某一面的立体角，等于该面在以该点为圆心的球面上的投影面积除以该球面的半径平方，见 sr）
solid angle of cone 锥体的立体角（以锥体的顶点为球心作球面，该锥体在球表面截取的面积与球半径平方之比）
solid apex seal （转子发动机的）整片式径向密封片
solid arguments 有充分根据的论点
solid axle ①（汽车的）整轴，整桥（如：非独立悬架梁式车桥）②实心轴
solid axle suspension 整轴式悬架（亦称 rigid axle-suspension，指用一根整轴将左、右车轮连接起来，该整轴通过悬架与车身或车架相连，因而每一侧车轮的垂直运动都会传至另一侧车轮的非独立悬架"non-independent suspension"，参见 independent suspension）
solid bar apex seal （转子发动机的）单片式径向密封片，整体式径向密封片
solid bearing 整体式滑动轴承（轴套式滑动轴承，=bush bearing）
solid body 固体
solid borne sound 固体传播声
solid carburizing 固体渗碳
solid case （滚动轴承）整体保持圈
solid (-cast) cylinder head 整体铸造式缸盖（=integral cylinder head）
solid chromium 硬镀铬层
solid circuits 固体电路（指①在一块材料上通过熔结、掺杂、蚀刻、切片并使用必要的跨接线而生产的一种半导体网络电路②做在半导体晶体中或通过腐蚀或沉积做在基片上的三维空间超小型电路）
solid coal fueled engine 煤粉燃料发动机（=coal fueled engine）
solid conductor ①单根导线；实心导线②固态导电体
solid coupling 刚性联轴节
solid crankshaft 实心曲轴
solid disk brake 实心盘式制动器
solid drawn pipe 无缝（钢）管（=solid drawn tube）
solid electrolyte 固态电解质
solid enclosure 整体式外罩
solid figure 立体形
solid film lubricant 固体薄膜润滑剂（=solid lubricant）
solid friction 干摩擦，固体摩擦（指两物体接触并作相对运动时，接触面完全干燥条件下产生的摩擦）
solid-friction clutch 干摩擦式离合器
solid fuel 固体燃料
solid fueled engine 固体燃料发动机（如：煤粉作为燃料的内燃机）
solid full-width apex seal （转子发动机的）整片式径向密封片
solid head （连杆）不可拆开的小头
solid height of spring 螺旋弹簧的压合高度（螺旋弹簧压至各圈并合时的高度，螺旋弹簧最小高度）
solidification 硬化，凝固（作用），固化
solidification point 凝固点，凝结温度，固化点（见 solid point, solidification temperature）
solidified 凝固的
solidify 凝固，硬化
solid injection （目前常规的柴油机和汽油喷射式发动机靠燃油本身的压力喷射的）油压喷油（相对于早期靠压缩空气压力喷油的气压喷油

"air injection"而言，亦称 airless injection）

solidity ①固态，固体，固体性②硬度，硬③坚固，坚牢，稳固④确实⑤体积⑥立体，立体性

solid jaw 整体卡爪，固定爪

solid lifter （气门的）刚性推杆，刚性挺杆（相对液力挺杆而言的常规挺杆）

solid line 实线

solid line curve 实线曲线，连续曲线（= full curve）

solid logic technology 固态逻辑技术（指使用微电子电路作为现代计算机系统中的基本元件的技术，简称SLT）

solid lubricant 固体润滑剂

solid lubrication ①固体润滑，固态润滑②固态薄膜润滑（见 layer of solid lubricant）

solid of revolution 旋转体

solid oxide fuel cell 固体氧化物燃料电池（简称SOFC）

solid pattern 整体模型

solid phase welding 冷压焊接（= cold pressure welding）

solid point 凝点，凝固点，固化点（见 cloud point，我国的柴油牌号，是根据凝点命名的，如：20号柴油，表示其凝点应低于 −20°C）

solid reciprocating engine 固体燃料往复式内燃机

solid retainer （滚动轴承）整体保持架

solid rivet 实心铆钉

solid roller bearing （实心）滚子轴承

solid rubber ①硬橡皮，硬质橡胶②实心橡皮，整块橡皮

solid rubber tyre 实心橡胶轮胎

solid shaft 实心轴

solid skirt piston 裙部无开槽的活塞

solid solution strengthening 固溶体强化作用

solid-state ①固态的（指无运动件，由各种半导体元器件，或集成电路组成的）②固态电路

solid-state charger 半导体充电设备

solid-state chip 半导体基片，半导体片

solid-state chopper control 固态电路（光、磁、电路）断续控制

solid-state circuit 固态电路，固体电路（一般指半导体电路，见 solid circuit）

solid-state component 固态元件（依靠对固体中的电或电磁现象的控制来工作的各种元件，如：晶体管，氧铁体磁芯等）

solid-state control 固态控制装置，晶体管控制装置

solid-state device 固态器件（指无运动零件，无电热丝及无真空间隙的电流控制装置。所有的半导体器件都是固态器件，但固态器件不一定都是半导体器件，如：变压器）

(solid-state) flux-gate compass （固态元件）磁通量（闸）门罗盘

solid-state grounding switch 晶体管（电路型）接地开关

solid-state ignition system 固态器件点火系（电子点火系，如：无分电器式点火系，= distributorless ignition system, electronic ignition system）

solid-state logic system 固体逻辑电路系统（使用固体电路的逻辑电路）

solid-state oscillator 固体电路振荡器，半导体振荡器

solid-state physics 固态物理学（研究包括半导体在内的固体的结构和性质的物理学分支）

solid-state relay 固态继电器（使用固态半导体元器件的继电器）

solid-state sensing device 固态传感装

置

solid-state technique　固体电路技术，半导体技术

solid-state V8　（福特公司研制的）电子计算机控制V型8缸发动机（商品名）

solid-state (voltage) regulator　固态电压调节器

solids test　（胶合剂等的）固态物质含量试验

solid tire　实心轮胎（亦写作 solid tyre）

solid tyre base width　实心轮胎基部宽度（实心轮胎加强层基部的宽度）

solid urethanes　固态尿烷（聚氨基甲酸酯树脂）

solid waste　固体废料，整体废品

solid wheel　整体式车轮

solid wire　①单股线，单根线②实心线

solo running　单车行驶，单车运行（指不带挂车）

solubilization　增溶溶解，增溶化，助溶解（作用），增溶解（作用）

soluble　①可溶解的②可以解决的

soluble friction modifier　可溶性减摩剂

soluble fuel cell　可溶性燃料电池

solution　①溶液，溶解，溶体②解答，解决方法

solution of urea in water　尿素水溶液（喷入废气中作为 NO_x 还原剂，用于 NO_x 的选择性催化净化系统）

solution temperature　溶解温度

solve　①解决，解答②溶解

solvent　①溶剂②有溶解力的

solvent cleaning　（用）溶剂清洗（金属表面的油脂）

solvent degreasing　溶剂除油

SONAR　声呐（声波导航和测距系统，sound operation navigation and ranging 的简称，亦写作 sonar)

sonar pinger　声呐脉冲发生器

sonar pinger sensor　声呐脉冲探测器

sonde　①探测器，探测装置②探棒，探针

sone　宋（响度单位，声压级为40dB的1000Hz的纯音的响度为1宋）

SONH　（丹麦B&K公司推出的）统计优化近场声全息（技术）（用于汽车NVH测量，Statistically Optimal Near-field Acoustical Holography 的简称）

sonic　声音的，声波的，声速的

sonic after burner　音速（废气）再燃烧器

sonic analyzer　声波分析仪，声波探伤仪，声频故障仪

sonic boom　声震，声爆（剧烈的声响）

sonic carburetion　声速化油，声速雾化（燃油喷出后进入声速气流中，而形成良好雾化的过程）

sonic carburetor　声速化油器（一种活动喉管化油器，利用喉管的几何形状，通过断面的变化，使喉管中混合气的流速在发动机的各种工况下均保持声速，保证燃油的雾化良好，分配均匀，简称 sonic carb）

sonic controlled EGR system　声速控制式EGR系统（以声速喷嘴控制再循环废气量）

sonic detector　声呐（声波定位器）

sonic-idle carburetor　声速怠速化油器（美国福特公司生产的一种稀燃化油器，具有怠速时声速喷射系统）

sonic leak tester　声波测漏仪（用于测试制动管系及轮胎等是否漏气并查明漏气点）

sonic speed　声速

sonic test　噪声试验

sonic throttling　（采用缩小孔口或管道某段通过截面积的方法，使流过该处的流体的流速提高到声速

的）声速节流

sonic wave 声波（见 sound wave）

soot 碳烟（燃烧过程中燃油在高温和局部缺氧条件下脱氢并裂解，并被析出，后经聚合、浮游并附有复杂的高分子有机物的黑灰色固体微粒）

soot carbon 炭黑

soot deposit 烟炱沉积，烟灰沉积

sooted 烟灰的，积炭的，熏黑的

soot formation 积炭的形成（= carbon formation）

sooting of the spark plug 火花塞积炭

soot reduction technique （柴油机排气）烟尘减少技术

soot suppressant 烟垢抑制剂，积炭抑制剂，防积炭添加剂

soot suppression 积炭抑制作用，烟垢消除作用

sooty 积炭的，积垢的，烟灰的

sophisticated 高级的，尖端的，完善的，成熟的，精益求精的，采用了先进技术的，需要专门操作技术的，复杂的，富有经验的，老练的

Sophisticated and Optimized Fuel Injection System 完美与最佳的燃油喷射系统（见 SOFIS）

sophisticated design 先进设计，尖端设计，采用先进技术的设计（简称 sohc design）

sophisticated equipment 先进的尖端设备

sorbite 索斑体，索氏体（亦写作 sorbitic matrix）

sorbitic pearlite 索氏珠光体

sorption 吸着作用，吸收作用

sort 种类，类别，分类，选分，挑选

sorter 分类装置，分类机，分级机

SOS ①安全观察站（safety observation station）②国际通用船舶呼救信号，无线电呼救信号（save our ship）③润滑油定期采样分析（scheduled oil sampling）④同步轨道卫星（synchronous orbit setellite）

sound ①声，声音 ②发声 ③坚固的，完善的

sound-absorbing 吸声的

sound-absorbing padding 吸声衬垫

sound absorption ①消声，吸声 ②消声能力，吸声能力 [面积 S，吸声率为 a 的材料，其吸声能力 $A = a \cdot S$]

sound absorption coefficient 消声系数（吸声率，$a = (1 - R)/In$, In 为射入的声能，R 为反射的声能，= acoustic absorption factor, acoustic absorption coefficient, acoustic absorptivity）

sound absorption materials 吸音材料，消声材料

sound arrester 防音装置，隔音装置，吸音器，消声器

sound-attenuating system 消声系统

sound baffle 隔音板，消声板

sound barrier 声垒，音障

sound bearing 声响方位，声源方位（简称 SB）

sound box ①共振箱，共鸣器 ②吸音箱

sound buzzer 蜂鸣器

sound condition ①调声 ②完好状态（= good condition）

sound damper 消声器（亦称 sound deadener, silencer）

sound-deadened 消声的

sound deadening material 消声材料

sound duct 音管，喇叭的音管，扩音管（= trumpet）

sound effect 声响效应，音响效应（简称 SE）

sound energy 声能（指声波所传播的能量，即：介质质元因有振动速度而具有的功能与因发生变形而具有的弹性势能之和，并随时间作周

期性变化)

sound-energy density 声能密度(指声场介质单位体积传播的声能)

sounder ①发声器②探测器,测探器

sound field 声场(声能的分布范围)

sounding ①发声②探测

sounding tube 听诊器

sound-insulated 隔声的

sound-insulated chamber 隔声室

sound insulating material 隔声材料(＝sound proofing material)

sound intensifier 扩音器

soundintensity 声强(指单位时间内通过垂直于声波传播方向的面上的一点的声能)

sound intensity level 声强级(简称 sound level)

sound intensity technique 声强技术,声强法(是一种噪声测试技术,1992年国际标准化组织正式将声强法定为用于测量汽车、发动机等机器的声功率的国际标准方法)

sound level calibrator 声级标定仪

sound-level meter 声级计,声强计(＝phon meter, sound meter)

sound localization (噪声等)音源测定;声定位

sound locater 声波定位器,声呐(＝sound radar)

soundloudness 声响度(由声强决定的人听到的声音的强弱)

sound measurement ①声波测距(法)②音源标定

sound oscillations 声振荡

sound pollution 噪声污染

sound power 声功率(指声源在单位时间内辐射出的总的声能量,单位:W)

sound power level 声功率级[声功率也可以用dB(分贝)表示:$Lw = 10\lg (W/W_0)$ (dB),式中:W_0—基准声功率 "reference sound power"; W—所计算的声功率]

sound pressure 声压

sound pressure level 声压级(简称 SPL, $SPL = 20\log_{10} P/P_0$ (dB)。式中:P—所测定的某声压的实测值;P_0—基准声压的实效值,＝0.0002μbar 或 $2 \times 10^{-5} N/m^2$)

soundproof ①隔声,消声②隔声的,消声的

sound radar 声(雷)达(声波定位器,声波测距器,声波探测仪,声呐,＝sound locatersound ranger)

sound radiation 声音辐射

sound scope (汽车发动机等用)听诊器

sound-sensitive vehicle detector 声感式侦车器,声感式车辆检测器(由车辆通过所产生的声波来引动)

sound spectrometer 声频频谱计

sound speed 声速

sound system 音响系统

sound track 声迹,声道

sound transmission 声的传播,噪声传播

sound transmission coefficient 声透射系数,声透射率(通常用τ表示,$\tau = T/I$,式中:I—射入材料的声能;T—透过材料的声能)

sound truck 广播车(装有扩音设备的汽车,＝public-address truck)

sound vibration 声的振动

sound wave 声波(＝sonic wave,振动频率在 20~20000Hz 的机械波,产生的引起耳教膜振动会人听到的声音,故名声波。频率高于 20000Hz 的叶超声波 supersonic wave,低于20Hz的叫汐声波 infrasonic wave)

souped-up 经改造或调整使功率提高了的

souping 对发动机多供燃油

soup up 改装汽车、发动机,以提高其性能、增加功率(＝[美] hop up)

sour ①含硫的（汽油）②变酸的，酸性的③酸味，酸性物质④变酸，变坏⑤用稀酸溶液处理

source ①源（如：电源，能源，动力源，信号源，光源，振源）②根源（如：故障原因）

source contact （场效应晶体管）管源（极）接点

source terminal （场效应晶体管）源（极）端子，源极接线柱

sour gasoline 酸性汽油，含硫汽油（经硫酸精制而未进行碱处理的汽油）

sour oil 酸性油，未中和油

south pole 南极（代号 S，见 north pole）

Southwest Research Institute ［美］西南研究院（简称 SwRI）

SP ①自行的（self-propelled）②程序编制器（sequence programmer）③串联并联，混联（series parallel）④肩点（shoulder point）⑤单相（single phase）⑥单极，单柱（single pole）⑦配件，备件（spare parts）⑧火花（spark）⑨专门论文（special paper）⑩特殊功用（special purpose）⑪防溅的（splash-proof）⑫标准压力（standard pressure）⑬标准程序（standard procedure）⑭起点（starting point）⑮静压力（static pressure）⑯钢板（steel plate）⑰研究计划（study program）

space ①空间②间距，空隙

space between twin wheels （货车等双胎并装车轮的）双胎间距（双胎中心平面间的距离）

space cavity 空腔

space charge 空间电荷

space charge limited condition 空间电荷限制条件

space configuration 空间构形

space-constrained 空间狭窄的，受空间限制的

space curve 空间曲线，挠曲线

spaced 间距的，间隔的

spaced out 留有间隙的，留有宽间隙的

space frame （汽车的桁架式）立体车架（汽车的三维结构形式的整体骨架，全部车身板件均由该骨架支承，取代承载式车身或常规的车架，多用于赛车）

space heater ①（车厢）热风取暖装置②空间对流加热器

space interval （公共汽车）站距；路段

space length 空间距离，间距

space mean speed 区段平均车速，空间平均车速（指某瞬间 t，道路上某区间 L 内 n 辆车地面车速分布的平均值，$\bar{v}_s = \dfrac{L}{\frac{1}{n}\sum_{i} t_i} = \dfrac{1}{\frac{1}{n}\sum_{i=1}^{n}\frac{1}{v_i}}$）

space of tooth 齿间距

spacer 隔件（将二者隔开的任何部件的通称，如：隔板，隔离物，隔套，垫片，垫圈，衬套，衬垫，定位架，调整垫，调距板，间隔确定装置；撑挡）

spacer bar 间隔棒（参见 distance bar）

spacer-expander （活塞）油环的胀圈（见 spacer ring②）

spacer ring ①隔圈，隔环②（油环的）胀圈（= expander spacer，或 spacer-expander）

spacer shim 间隙片

spacer sleeve 隔套（= spacer tube）

space-saving 空间节约，节约空间，紧凑的

space thin walled construction 空间薄壁结构（用金属蒙皮制成的中空薄壁结构，在客车车身上一般都采用有骨架的结构形式，蒙皮就固定在骨架上）

space time 时空

space tube frame 管梁式空间车架（见 space frame）

space velocity（**of exhaust gases**）（废气催化转化器的）空间速度（在标准温度和压力的状态下测得的废气流量除以催化剂体积，即为空间速度）

space vision warning 空间视觉警告灯（呈空间虚像感的警告灯）

space washer 定位垫圈，间隔垫圈

space wastage （货物堆放不合理时的）空位损失，面积损失，（仓库）容积损失

space width 齿槽宽（槽宽，在锥齿轮上，一个齿槽的两侧齿面之间的分度圆弧长）

space width half angle 槽宽半角（指在直齿锥齿轮和圆柱齿轮的分度圆所在平面上，齿槽宽所对圆心角的一半）

spacing 间隔，间距，节距

spacing block 分隔块；分隔零件

spacing collar 间隔环，分隔环，隔环，分离垫圈，隔圈；分隔套，隔套

spacing hole 限位孔

spacing inaccuracy 位置误差；节距误差（如：齿轮的周节误差）

spacing piece 定距片

spacing ring 隔环，定距环

spacing shim 调节间距的垫片

spacing sleeve 隔套

spacing tube 定距管（= distance tube）

spacing washer 间隔垫圈（= distance washer）

spacious （空间）宽敞的

spacious comfort （车身内部）宽敞舒适性

spaciousness of the body 车身（内部）宽敞度

spade terminal 多芯电缆接头

spaghetti 绝缘套管

spalling ①剥落，裂蚀 ②削，割，研，打击 ③裂，散裂，碎

spalling resistance ①耐热冲击性（耐热震性，耐激冷激热性，抗热急变性，= thermal shock resistance, resistance to thermal shocks）②抗热急强度（= spalling strength）

spall point （路面）碎裂地段，碎裂点

span ①跨度，跨距，径间，间距 ②（相邻）刻度单位的间隔 ③一拃宽（约 23cm）④（气流的）宽度 ⑤（一段）时间，期间 ⑥量距（仪表零点到最高标定点的距离）⑦跨越，跨过，横跨 ⑧span 量程（范围上限值与下限值的代数差）

span control （仪表）满刻度校正

span drift 量距漂移（如：废气检测中，HC 检测仪在规定的时间周期内所发生的量距气刻度的漂移）

span error 量程误差（在参比工作条件下，实际输出量程与规定输出量程之差，以规定输出量程的百分数表示）

span gas 量距气［用于校正 HC、CO 和 NO_x 检测仪的］已知浓度的标准混合气。"量距"指检测的零点和高刻度设定点之间的间距，亦称标准气体，校正气 "calibrating gas"］

span-in bearing 离心浇铸轴承

span-in casting 离心铸造（法）（= centrifugal casting）

spanner 扳手

spanning ability （车辆）越沟能力

span shift 量程迁移，量程偏移（指由于某些影响量引起的输出量程的变化）

spar 翼梁，悬臂杆

spare ①备件 ②备用的，储备的，附加的，多余的

spare battery 备用蓄电池

spare cover holder 备胎架（= spare wheel holder）
spare detail 附件；备用零件（= spare parts）
spare engine 备用发动机
spare-less car 不需要带备用轮胎的轿车（见 four-tire car）
spare space 空位
spare time 业余时间，空余时间
spare tire 备胎，备用胎（指装有轮胎的备用车轮，= spare wheel）
spare tyre holder 备胎架（= spare tyre carrier, spare wheel bracket, spare wheel carrier）
spare wheel 备用车轮（亦称 emergency wheel，带轮胎的备用车轮，= spare tyre）
spare wheel carrier locking post bracket 备胎架锁紧柱支架
spare wheel dust cover 备胎防尘罩
spare wheel folding bracket 备胎折叠式托架
spare wheel safety lock 备胎安全锁，备胎防盗锁
spark ①火花，电火花 ②发火花，电火花点火
spark advance 点火提前（亦称 ignition advance 或 advanced ignition，指火花塞提前到活塞到达上止点前跳火，其提前量用活塞到达上止点前的曲轴转角度数表示，称点火提前角 spark advance angle）
spark advancer 点火提前装置（亦称 ignition advancer, advance mechanism）
spark arrester （排气）火花消除器（防止火花外射的装置）
spark arrester muffler 防火花消声器（无火花消声器）
spark assisted methanol diesel engine 电火花助燃甲醇柴油机（柴油机改用甲醇燃料加装助燃点火系统）
spark at breaking 电路断开产生的火花
sparkbite （胎面胶）因臭氧作用损坏
spark calorimeter （火花塞）火花热值测定器
spark chamber 火花摄影室（由一组平行金属板组成，板间电场升到击穿电压，通过拍摄电离后的火花，研究电离微粒的轨迹）
spark channel （转子发动机）火花塞室通路
spark clearance 火花间隙（指火花塞电极间隙）
spark coil 点火线圈
spark condenser 点火系电容器（灭火花用电容器）
spark control 点火正时控制（亦称 ignition timing control）
spark control valve 点火正时控制阀（由发动机冷却水温控制真空点火正时的真空通路的阀门，简称 SCV）
spark current 火花电流（在规定瞬时所测得流经火花电极间的电流）
spark delay valve （真空控制）点火延时阀（简称 SDV）
spark discharge 火花放电
spark discharger 电火花放电器（简称 SD）
spark duration 火花持续时间（指火花塞电极间电弧放电始点到终点的时间）
spark energy 火花能量（在火花间隙电极间所释放的能量）
sparker 电火花器
spark erosion 电火花腐蚀，电火花加工
spark extinguisher 火花消除器
spark failure （发动机）点火故障（缺火、漏火、断火）
spark flame 电火花，电火花闪光
spark formative time 火花形成时间
spark frequency 火花频率（跳火频

率）
spark gap 火花间隙（一个含有两个或多个电极用以在特定情况下产生火花的器件的电极间的放电间隙）
spark generator 火花发生器
spark hand-lever tube 点火调节手柄
spark-ignited diesel 火花点燃式柴油机（见 Texaco Controlled Combustion System engine）
spark ignition engine 火花点火式发动机（指 Otto 循环式发动机及任何形式的用电火花点燃燃料—空气混合气的往复式内燃机）
spark ignition fuel-injection engine 火花点火燃油喷射式发动机
spark-ignition heavy-fuel injection RC engine 重油喷射火花点火式转子发动机
spark ignition passenger car 汽油（机）轿车（电火花点火式发动机轿车）
sparking 跳火（指产生火花）
sparking at the brushes 电刷跳火花
sparking coil [英] 点火线圈（= ignition coil）
sparking distance 火花间隙，跳火间隙，火花长度
sparking plug boss 火花塞凸台（火花塞止挡部分）
sparking plug cable cover strip 火花塞高压线连接套（将火花塞接头、火花塞高压线、分电器盖和点火线圈高压接头合成一体的连接系统）
sparking plug cable loom 火花塞高压线架（一般为带高压线导孔和塑料线塞的 T 形钢制线夹，可将高压线可靠定位并防止漏电）
sparking plug spanner 火花塞扳手
sparking voltage test （火花塞）放电电压试验
spark intensifier 火花增强器（如：采用双重火花间隙的火花增强装置）

spark intensity 火花强度
spark jump 跳火花，放电
spark knock 点火爆燃（指点火提前角过大而不是其他原因引起的爆燃，亦称 ignition knock）
spark lag 点火延迟（从分电器接通电流开始到汽缸内火花塞跳出火花并点燃可燃混合气为止的一段时间。以曲轴转角表示，亦是汽油机的滞燃期）
spark length 火花长度
sparkless 无火花的
spark lever 点火提前调整杆
spark line （发动机示波器基本波形火花部分的）火花线（表示火花放电的电压及放电时间的长短）
spark of rust 锈点，锈斑
spark output （福特公司的 EEC IV 系统的电子控制总成 ECA 向其点火控制模块发出的）点火指令（该指令为脉冲信号，其脉冲的前沿为点火线圈初级电路断开指令，后沿为初级电路接通指令，简称 spout）
spark plug 火花塞（火花塞是内燃机电点火系统的点火元件，借助于脉冲高电压击穿火花间隙而形成电火花，点燃燃烧室内的燃料空气混合气，亦写作 sparking plug）
spark-plug body 火花塞壳体
spark plug body hexagonal part 火花塞的六角形部分
spark-plug cable 火花塞高压线
spark-plug cables protecting tube 火花塞高压线套管
spark-plug cleaner 火花塞清洁器，火花塞清洁工具
spark-plug cleaner and tester 火花塞清洁和试验器
spark-plug double end wrench 火花塞双头扳手
spark-plug electrode 火花塞电极
spark-plug extension 火花塞伸长部
spark-plug file 火花塞电极锉

spark-plug fouling　火花塞积污，火花塞积炭

spark plug gap　火花塞（电极间的）间隙（简称 spark gap）

spark-plug gap gauge　火花塞电极间隙测量规

spark-plug gapper　火花塞电极间隙校正钳（只要将该钳夹紧火花塞电极部分，便能得到正确的间隙）

spark-plug gasket　火花塞垫圈

spark-plug gland　火花塞绝缘子压紧螺套

spark plug heat chamber　火花塞热腔（火花塞电极端绝缘体与外壳间的高温空腔）

spark-plug heat range　火花塞的热分类（热特性）（根据火花塞中央电极绝缘瓷尖到发动机冷却介质的传热路程，路程短、传热快的称为冷式"cold type"，路程长的称为热式"hot type"，路程长度在两者之间的，称为均式"average plug"）

spark-plug heat value　火花塞热值

spark-plug hole　火花塞孔

spark-plug insert　火花塞（孔）镶套

spark-plug insulator　火花塞绝缘瓷体

spark-plug lead　火花塞高压线

spark-plug location　火花塞位置（火花塞位置的布置）

spark-plug nipple　火花塞螺纹接套

spark-plug points　火花塞电极

spark-plug porcelain　火花塞瓷芯

spark-plug reamer tap　火花塞孔螺纹修整用丝锥

spark-plug rubber cap　火花塞橡皮帽

spark-plug shell　火花塞（金属）壳体

spark-plug shell body nut　火花塞壳体螺母

spark-plug side electrode　火花塞侧电极

spark-plug socket　火花塞套筒扳手

spark-plug's reach　火花塞的伸入长度（指火花塞伸入燃烧室的长度，即自火花塞与缸盖接触的垫圈面至螺纹部分末端的距离）

spark-plug taps　火花塞孔（专用）丝锥

spark-plug terminal　火花塞接线头

spark-plug tester　火花塞检查仪（检查火花强度等）

spark-plug thread　火花塞螺纹

spark-plug tip　火花塞电极

spark-plug type pressure sensor　火花塞式压力传感器（压力传感器与火花塞制成一体，测量缸内压力不需另开传感器孔）

spark-plug washer　火花塞垫圈

spark-plug well　（汽缸盖上）火花塞凹窝

spark-plug wire　火花塞高压线

spark-plug wrench　火花塞扳手（亦称 sparking plug spanner）

spark port　点火角真空控制信号孔

spark potential　跳火电压，击穿电压

spark protractor　点火定时分度仪

spark rate　点火频率，火花频率，火花放电频率

spark retardation　点火延迟，点火迟后（亦称 spark retard, ignition retard）

spark retard system　点火延迟系统（遇爆燃时延迟点火的控制系统）

spark spacer　（点火系）分电器（= current distributor）

sparks per minute　（火花塞）每分钟发火次数

spark test　火花试验

spark timing　点火正时（= ignition timing）

spark timing maintained at minimum for best torque　最佳转矩最小点火提前角（简称 mbt spark timing）

spark-torch ignition　火花-火炬点火

（预燃室火焰点火，火炬点火，汽油机的一种点火方式，常用于稀燃均质充气汽油机，或分层充气汽油机，在燃烧室内分隔出一个副燃烧室，其中为喷入主燃烧室，点燃其中的稀混合气，亦称 torch ignition, flame ignition）

spark trap 火花捕集器，灭火花器

spark voltage 火花电压（在规定瞬间，火花间隙两端所测得的电压）

spark wear 电火花烧蚀（触点）

spark welding 电弧焊

spat 流线型轮罩

spate 大量出现，纷纷涌现（如：某种新型装置或结构在短时间内大量推广应用）

spatial 立体的，（占据）空间的，（存在于）空间的

spatial accommodation 容纳空间

spatial brightness 空间亮度

spatial cognition 空间认知能力

spatial distribution （城市运输的）空间分布，空间布置

spatial variation of heat transfer 热传导的空间变化（零件的热传导率随零件部位的变化）

spatiotemporal 时间空间的，时空的，存在于时空的（亦写作：spatial & temporal，如：可再现实际发生的环境和时间的车辆混杂状况和事故现场的交通信息模式等）

spats （装在车身底板下面）减轻风阻的悬架和车轮的盖板

spatter 溅，洒

7-sp auto-cl man 带自动离合器的7挡手动变速器（7-speed auto-clutch manual 的简称）

spd ①速率（speed）②（变速器）挡速（speed）③备件车间（见 spare parts department）

15 spd road ranger gearbox 15前进挡齿轮变速器（其中 spd 亦写作 speed）

SPE [美]石油工程师学会（Society of Petroleum Engineers）

speaker 扬声器，话筒

speaking tube 话筒，传声筒（= voice tube, listening tube）

speak injection pressure 最高喷射压力（燃油系统高压油管中的峰值压力）

spec ①标准，规格（= specification）②说明书，加工单 ③特种的；专门的（special）④样品，试样（= specimen）⑤光谱，频谱（spectrum）

special 特别的，特种的；专用的，专门的；特制的

special alloy steel 特种合金钢

special ambient test 特种环境试验（在特种环境试验室内，模拟高原低气压、低温或高寒、高温、高湿度等条件所做的试验。这种试验可以是单项或多项条件的模拟试验）

special construction vehicle 特种结构汽车（具有各种特殊结构的专用汽车和专用挂车）

special energy （蓄电池的）比能（能量密度，能量通量，亦称 energy density, 指蓄电池单位重量的容量，Wh/kg）

special fixture 专用夹具

special gasoline 特种汽油

special heavy duty truck 专用重型载货汽车（简称 SHD）

Specialised Carriers & Rigging Association [美]特种运输与装备协会（从事特种货物运输，为特种货物运输提供专门的装载固定装备和服务的行业协会，简称 SC&RA）

specialism ①专门学科，专门化 ②（学科等）专长

Speciality Equipment Manufacturer's Association [美]专用设备制造商协会（简称 SEMA）

Speciality Vehicle Institute of America

美国专用汽车协会（缩写 SVIA）
specialization 专业化，专门化
specialize 专门研究，使专业化，使专门化，特殊化，把……用于专门目的；限制……的范围；特别指明，列举，逐条详述
specialized knowledge 专业知识，专门知识
specialized motor transportation enterprise 专用汽车运输企业（使用专用车辆或特种车辆，专门经营集装箱、特种货物或某些种类货物的运输企业）
specialloid piston 特种高硅铝合金活塞
specially-built 专门订制（的）（按特种设计要求制造的）
special paper 专门论文，专论（简称 SP）
special passenger car 特种轿车（特种用途的轿车，如：检阅车，指挥车）
special phosphor-bronze 特种磷青铜
special pipe 异形管
special power 比功率（功能密度，亦称 power density，如：蓄电池每单位重量所能提供的最大功率，Wh/kg）
special publications 特种出版物
special purpose vehicle 专用汽车，特种用途汽车
special quality 高质量的，特殊质量的
specials ①异形管②专用部件③专用车辆
special school bus 中、小学专用大客车［各国均规定有特殊的安全要求，供接送中、小学生用的大客车，简称 school bus（校车）］
special service tools for automotive parts 汽车零件拆装维修专用工具
special steel 特（殊）种钢
special tipper 专用自卸汽车（装有由本车发动机驱动的液压举升机构，能将车箱卸下或使车箱倾斜一定角度，使货物能依靠自重而自行卸下的专用汽车）
special transformation of sound fields 声场空间变换法（简称 STSF，测量汽车噪声辐射的一种方法，利用汽车近距离声场的测量数据，推算远距离声场的声压、声强分布）
special transportation vehicle 专用运输车辆（专门用于运输某种运输对象或具有特殊用途的客、货运输车辆）
special truck 特种货运汽车（为运输货物而具有特殊装备的货车，如：液罐车"tank lorry"等）
special tuning 特别调整，专门调校（指包括提高发动机功率的改造、加工等作业的调校）
special tyre 特种轮胎，专用轮胎
special version 特别说明
special warehouse 专用仓库（储存和保管特种或特定货物，并配有相应设施的货物仓库）
species 种类，物种
specific ①比的（如：比重，比热等）②特定条件的，专用的，特有的，一定的，指定的
specific air consumption 空气消耗率（内燃机每千瓦小时所消耗的空气量）
specification ①说明书②规格，规范③（复）技术条件，技术要求④（复）参数
specification chart 规范一览表
specification control 规范控制，控制技术要求（简称 SC）
specification decal 技术规范铭牌，技术规格铭牌
specification fuel 符合一定技术要求的燃油，特定规格的燃料
specification sheets 说明书，样本
specific capacity 比容（比容量，单

位重量的体积）
specific character 特点，特性
specific conductance 电导率，传导系数
specific consumption of fuel 燃料消耗率（比油耗，比燃料消耗，见 specific fuel consumption）
specific damping capacity 阻尼比容（单位阻尼能与单位应变能之比）
specific density 比重，比密度，相对密度
specific diffusion constant 比扩散常数（其大小决定于扩散微粒的平均速度）
specific duty 单位生产量，单位功率工作量
specific elongation 比延伸，延伸率
specific energy 比能（如：蓄电池的比能指其单位重量的电能容量，用 Wh/kg 表示）
specific energy consumption 能量比耗（能量消耗率，指单位时间内产生单位功率所消耗的能量）
specific fuel consumption 燃料消耗率比油耗（单位时间内单位功率的燃料消耗量，一般以 g/(Ps·h)，g/(kW·h)，cm³/(Ps·h)，cm³/(kW·h)，m³/(Ps·h)，m³/(kW·h) 等单位表示，简称 SFC）
specific gas leakage （汽缸的）比漏气率（＝实际漏气量/汽缸排量×100%）
specific gravity 比重（简称 SG，＝specific weight）
specific gravity bottle 比重瓶
specific ground pressure 地面单位压力，接地压强
specific heat 比热（简称 sp. ht.）
specific heat at constant pressure 定压比热容（c_p）
specific heat at constant volume 定容比热容（c_V）
specific heat consumption 热量消耗率，比热耗，比耗热量
specific inductance capacity 介电常数，电容率（亦称 specific inductive capacity，简称 SIC）
specific items 特殊条款，特别项目
specific load 比荷载
specific lub-oil consumption 机油消耗率（内燃机每千瓦小时所消耗的机油量，以质量计）
specific oil consumption 机油消耗率
specific power 比功率，功率系数
specific power output 比输出功率，比功率输出（内燃机一般指每升排量 L 所产生的千瓦 kW）
specific pressure 压强（单位压力）
specific resistance ①比电阻（电阻率）②单位阻力，比阻力（简称 SR）
specific sliding ①（齿面间）相对滑动率 ②（轮胎对路面的）滑移率
specific speed ①比速（如：水泵每分钟泵送总水头 1ft 的水，其叶轮每分钟的转数，该转数随水泵叶轮尺寸及泵水量 gal 和水头而变）②有效速率 ③特有速率
specific-speeds network chart 比速网络图
specific strength 比强度（单位强度）
specific surface area of catalyst 催化剂比表面积（指单位质量的总表面积，包括载体微孔的表面积，单位为 m²/g）
specific thrust 比切线牵引力，比驱动力，比推进力
specific viscosity 比黏度
specific volume 比容（简称 SV）
specific wear 比磨损
specific wearability 磨损率，磨耗率
specific weight 比重（＝specific gravity）
specified （技术条件）规定的，详细规定的

specified characteristic curve 规定特性曲线（如：在规定条件下，表明仪器仪表应有的输出量稳态值与一个输入量之间函数关系的曲线）

specified criteria 明细规范，给定（技术）条件，专用标准

specified fuel consumption 说明书规定的燃油消耗量，额定燃油消耗率

specified horsepower 说明书规定的功率，铭牌功率，额定功率

specified load 规定荷载，特定荷载

specified operating conditions 特定的使用条件

specified speed 规定速度

specified time 给定时间，规定时间

specified waiting time for loading 额定待装时间（车辆按约定时间到达指定装货地点至装车前允许等待的时间）

specified waiting time for unloading 额定待卸时间（车辆到达指定卸货地点至卸车前允许等待的时间）

specify 指定，规定，确定；详细说明；列举

specimen 样品，试件（简称 spec）

specimen damping energy 试样阻尼能（均质试样在简谐荷载作用下，一个周期内由于材料内阻尼而耗散的能量）

specimen strain energy 试样应变能（均质试样在简谐荷载作用下，一个周期内所储存的应变能）

specimen temperature 试件温度（试件试验截面上的平均温度）

specimen test 样品试验，样机试验

speck 点，斑点，污点

specs 规格，规范；技术要求（specification 的简称）

spectacle-bearing plate 双联式轴承板（眼镜式轴承板）

spectacles 眼镜

spectra 频谱，光谱（spectrum 的复数）

spectral analysis 光谱分析，频谱分析

spectral band 光谱带

spectral density 频谱密度

spectral distribution curve 频谱分布曲线（如：表示光源的放射波长与放射能量的曲线关系）

spectral function 频谱函数

spectrally-sensitive pyrometer 光谱灵敏高温计

spectral radiant emittance 光谱辐射量（每单位波长期间的辐射量）

spectral radiant power 光谱辐射功率（每单位波长期间的辐射功率）

spectral response curve 振动响应频谱曲线

spectro-chemical testing 光谱化学试验，光谱化学分析

spectrogram （光）谱图

spectrograph 摄谱仪，分光摄像仪，光谱仪，光谱分析仪

spectrometer ①分光仪，光谱仪②频谱仪③能谱仪，摄谱仪

spectrometric 光谱量测的，频谱分析的

spectrometry 光谱测定法，频谱测定法

spectrophotometer 分光光度计（测定光谱透射率、光谱反射率、相对光谱放射率的装置）

spectrophotometry 光谱光度测定法

spectropyrometer 分光高温计

spectroscope 分光镜，分光仪

spectroscopic test 光谱分析

spectroscopy 能谱学，光谱学，频谱学，分光学

spectrum ①谱，光谱，波谱，质谱，频谱②领域，范围，系列，各种各样（简称 spec）

spectrum analyser 频谱分析器，光谱分析仪

spectrum colour 光谱色

spectrum distribution 光谱分布，频

谱分布
spectrum level 频谱级
spectrum loading 谱荷载（疲劳荷载中，所有峰值荷载不等，或所有谷值荷载不等，或两者均不等的荷载，也称为变幅荷载或不规则荷载）
spectrum of loads 负荷频谱
spectrum of road surface roughness 路面（平面度）谱（亦称道路谱）
spectrum of sensation through man's body 人体感觉频谱
spectrum test 频谱试验
specular ①反射的，有金属光泽的，助视力的②镜的，镜状的，镜面的，反射镜的
specularity 反射性，镜面性（像镜子那样的特性）
specular reflection 镜面反射
specular reflector 镜面反射板
speech amplifier 声频放大器（= voice amplifier）
speech interface （车载信息服务系统的）语言接口
speech interference level （噪声的）谈话干扰级
speech recognition system 语音识别系统
speech synthesis 声音合成（指由大规模集成电路电子系统合成人类的声音的技术）
speed ①速度，转速②（变速器）挡位③加速，加快
speed adaptive coefficient 转速适应性系数（发动机额定转速与最大扭矩转速之比值）
speed alarm 车速警报器
speed along 飞跑，飞驰，急驶，急行，汽车开出违章速度（= speed away）
speed and delay study 车速及延迟调查（研究一条道路上的运行车速、延迟的原因及时间）

speed at maximum torque 最大转矩转速（内燃机发出最大转矩时的转速）
5 speed auto 5挡自动变速器
speed belt 变速传动带
speed bump （装在路面上的防超速行驶的）横挡（见 sleeping policeman）
speed-change 变速，换挡
speed-change area ①（公路的）变速区；变速路段（合流驶入主线前需加速，分流驶出主线后需减速，为此在连接主线处设置的变速路段，亦称，speed-change lane 变速车道）②（公路加宽的）超车区
speed-change belt drive 变速式传动带驱动；变速式传动带驱动装置
speed(-change) box 变速器（= change-speed box）
speed-change gearbox 齿轮式变速器，变速箱（= speed-change box）
speed characteristic 速度特性曲线
speed chart 速度表
speed controlled exhaust recirculation 发动机转速控制的废气再循环
speed controller 速度调节器，速控制器，调速器（= speed regulator）
speed control signal 控速信号（警示驾驶人员将车速控制在规定范围内的信号）
speed control vacuum control solenoid 车速控制（系统真空执行器的）真空控制电磁阀（简称 SCVAC，根据电子控制模块的指令控制节气门开度真空执行器的真空通路电磁阀，见 vehicle speed control system）
speed control vacuum vent solenoid 车速控制（系统真空执行器的）大气控制电磁阀（根据电子控制模块的指令控制节气门开度真空执行器的大气通路电磁阀，见 vehicle speed control system）

speed cop [美俚]管理汽车违反规定速度的警察

speed counter 车速表，转速表

speed demon ①（爱开）快车的驾驶员，快车鬼（俗）②乘高速交通工具的旅行者

speed density engine control system 速度密度式发动机汽油喷射系统（见 speed density formula）

speed density formula （空气容积流量式汽油喷射系统电子控制模块确定进气空气质量用的）转速密度公式［汽缸内的进气空气密度 = $(EP \times EGR \times VE \times MAP)/AT$。式中：$EP$—发动机参数、节气门开度、发动机转速等；$EGR$—废气再循环流量；$VE$—容积效率；$MAP$—进气歧管绝对温度；$AT$—空气温度。利用这一公式计算空气质量的方法称转速密度法（speed density approach），采用速度密度法实现的喷油量控制，称速度密度控制（speed density control）]

speed-dependent 取决于速度的（随速度的变化而变化的，取决于速度大小的）

speed diagram 车速特性曲线图（表示在各种挡位下，发动机转速与车速的关系）

speed difference 速度差，车速差（亦称 speed disrepane，两辆汽车的速度差，发动机的转速差，转速表显示值与实际值之间的误差）

speed-down ①减速②沿…急驰

speed drop 速度降；速度下降

speeder ①增速器，调速器，调速装置②加快工作的工具，快速回转的工具③乱开快车的驾驶员（= speed fiend, speed hog, speed merchant）

speed factor 速度系数，速度因素，速率因数

speed flash 频闪放电管（见 speed light）

speed fluctuation rate 转速波动率（衡量发动机运转是否均衡的一项指标）

speed fluctuation test 转速波动率试验（测定内燃机在规定的工况下稳定运转时的转速波动率的试验）

speed for flying mile （汽车动力性试验时）起步加速行驶 1mile 后的车速

speed gauge 速度表（= velocity gauge）

speed gear box 齿轮变速器

speed governing 调速（由速度调节机构将内燃机转速调节到所需之转速）

speed governing characteristics 调速特性（将调速手柄置于某一工况位置，使发动机无马荷空转，然后逐渐增加负荷，恢复原来工况，其间由调速器自动控制相应的供油量的大小。在此过程中内燃机功率、转矩等参数随转速改变而变化的关系称为调速特性）

speed governing feedback control （发动机）转速反馈控制

speed governor 转速调节器，调速器

speed increasing gear pair 增速齿轮副（从动轮角速度大于主动轮角速度的齿轮副）

speed increasing gear train 增速齿轮系（末端从动轮的角速度大于始端主动轮角速度的齿轮系）

speed increasing ratio 增速比（增齿轮副或增速齿轮系的传动比）

speed indicator ①车速指示装置（如：车速表等）②（大型车辆风窗玻璃上方安装的三个黄绿色）车速指示灯（车速超过 40km/h 以下时，左灯亮；40~60km/h 时，左、右灯亮；60km/h 以上时，左、中、右三灯齐亮）

speed induction mechanism 转速感应机构（将旋转件的转速转换成某

元件的直线运动等形式的机构，如：用以感应喷油泵凸轮轴或柴油机转速变化的飞重等部件）

speeding 违章超速行驶

speeding-up （汽车）加速

speed-insensitive 对速度不灵敏的，非速敏的（如：速度变化时，性能、参数等保持稳定的）

speed law 限速法规

speed light 闪光管，频闪放电管（= speed flash）

speed-limit device 限速装置（亦称 speed limiter, speed limiting device, 欧洲、日本均以法律形式规定大型货车必须安装车速限制器）

speed-limit road sign 限速路标

speed loss 速度损失

speed meter tester 车速表试验台

speed of advance 前进速度

speed of combustion 燃烧速度

speed of loading 加载速度，装载速度

speed of propagation （火焰前锋）传播速率

speed of response 响应速度

speed of revolutions 转速

speed of vision 视觉速度（看到观察对象所需时间的倒数）

speedometer ①车速表，车速里程表 ②转速表

speedometer cable 车速表传动软轴，里程表传动软轴（亦称 speedometer drive cable, speedometer flexible shaft）

speedometer drive worm 车速表驱动蜗杆

speedometer error 速度表误差

speedometer tester 车速表检测台（检测汽车车速表是否准确地指示真实车速）

speedometer trip reset 车速里程表读数回零

speedostat 自动限速仪

speed pickup 速度传感器（将转速信号转换成电信号的装置，亦称 speed sensor）

speed pulley （传动带式连续无级变速器的变径）传动带轮（亦称 variable speed pulleys, variable speed cones）

speed rate 速率

speed ratio 传动比，转速比，速比（指驱动件与被驱动件之间的速度比）

speed reaction type power door lock 车速反应式电动门锁（当车速达到某规定值，如：10km/h 时，便将车门自动锁死，防止忘锁车门造成的事故）

speed reaction type power steering (system) ①车速响应式动力转向（系统，即转向盘的轻重随汽车的行驶速度而变，车速越高，助力越小，转向盘越重。亦称 vehicle-speed reaction type power steering）②发动机转速响应式动力转向系统（系统，即转向盘轻重随发动机转速而变。由该系统使用的液压泵的特性所决定，发动机转速越高，液压泵所产生的助力越小，转向盘越重，转速越低，助力越大，转向盘越轻。亦称 engine-speed reaction type power steering system。由于其液压泵产生的助力随发动机转速升高而下降，故又称下降型动力转向系 dropping type power steering system

speed recorder 速度记录仪

speed recovery time 转速稳定时间（带有调速器的内燃机运转时，负荷突变后转速从开始变化到恢复稳定所需的时间）

speed reducer 减速器

speed reducing gear pair 减速齿轮副（从动轮角速度小于主动轮角速度的齿轮副）

speed reducing gear train 减速齿轮

系（末端从动轮的角速度小于始端主动角速度的齿轮系）

speed reducing ratio 减速比（减速齿轮副或减速齿轮系的传动比）

speed reduction gear ①（变速器）减速挡②减速挡齿轮③齿轮减速机构

speed regulator 调速器，速度调节器（= speed controller, speed regulating device）

speed-related steering control （转动转向盘所需的力的大小）随车速而变的转向控制系统

speed sense （驾驶人员的）速度感

speed-sensing bearing 转速传感轴承（在轴承内圈装有简单的电子传感元件，可测定轴的转速、加速度和角位移，供自动控制或量测用）

speed sensing height-adjusting air suspension 速敏调高（型）空气悬架（具有按车速调整车身高度的能力，如：当车速大于89km/h时，其电子控制模块将车身较正常高度降低20mm，以减小空气阻力，改善高速行驶时的燃油经济性和操纵性，而当车速低于72km/h时，电子控制模块即将车身高度恢复正常）

speed-sensitive, electronic variable-orifice power steering system 车速感知式可变节流孔径式动力转向系（液压节流孔可随车速而变的动力转向系）

speed-sensitive shut-off valve regulator 转速感知断油阀式调节器

speed-sensitive switch 速度传感开关

speed sensitivity characteristics 速度敏感特性，速度灵敏特性

speed sensor 速度传感器

speed set button 速度选择按钮（= set-speed button）

speed-slackening signal 减速信号，制动减速信号

speedster 双座高速敞篷跑车

speed switch 转速开关，转速控制开关

speed symbol （轮胎的）速度符号（按规定充气后，在相应的负荷下，轮胎最高行驶速度的特定符号）

speed timing 按速调时（如：①相应于车速来调整、改变绿灯的延长时间②根据转速改变点火、喷油时刻）

speed-torque characteristic 转矩-转速特性曲线（发动机转矩随转速而变化的曲线，= torque-speed characteristic）

7-speed torque converter auto 7挡变矩器型自动变速器

speed track 快速路（= speedway）

speed transforming gear 变速齿轮，变速机构

speed transforming transmission 变速传动装置，变速器

speed transition zone 速度变换区

speed transmission 变速器，变速箱

speed trap （汽车）速度监视站，车速监视哨

speed trial 速度试验

speed under load 有负载速度，负载速率，工作速率（= load speed, 相对于无负荷怠速而言）

speed-voltage generator 测速发电机

speed wagon ①高速厢式运货车②高速旅行车

speedway ①汽车及摩托车的竞赛跑道（= motor race track）②（一般指收费的）高速公路③快速公路

Speedway Control Board [英]高速公路管理局（简称SCB）

speed without load 空转速度，无负载速率

speed zone ahead sign 车速限制区预告标志

SPEG 集体设计鉴定小组，集体规划评定小组（staff planning evaluation group）

spelter ①（一般指含锌98%~99%的）粗锌锭 ②锌铜焊料
spelter solder 硬钎焊料（锌铜焊料，铜50%~53%，铅<0.5%，其余锌）
spend 花费，消费，消耗，浪费，耗尽，用完
spent 废的，失去效用的，余下的，耗尽的
spent anolyte 废阳极电解液，阳极废液（见 anolyte）
sp. gr. 比重（specific gravity）
spherangular roller bearing 球面滚子止推轴承（= spherical roller bearing）
spherax （一种）导电橡胶（商品名，见 conductive elastomer）
sphere ①球，球体 ②范围，区域
spherical 球面的，球形的，球状的，圆的
spherical accumulator 球形蓄压器，球形储能器
spherical angle 球面角
spherical cam 球形凸轮，球面凸轮
spherical combustion chamber 球形燃烧室
spherical condenser 球形电容器
spherical connection 球头节，球窝节，球节；球形连接，球面连接（= ball joint）
spherical coordinates 球面坐标
spherical dome 球面穹面
spherical end 球形端
spherical four-bar linkage 球头四连杆机构（一种汽车转向机构）
spherical guide 滚珠导轨
spherical head 球形头
spherical head piston 圆顶活塞
spherical helix 球面螺旋线
spherical housing 球形外壳
spherical involute 球面渐开线［球面上的一个大圆（发生圆）沿着位于同一球面上的一个固定的小圆（基圆）作纯滚动时，位于该大圆上的一个任意点在球面上的运动轨迹］
spherical involute helicoid 球面渐开螺旋面（平面沿着一个固定的圆锥面作纯滚动时，此平面上的一条以恒定的角度与基圆锥的轴线倾斜交错的直线在固定空间内的轨迹曲面，称为球面渐开螺旋面）
spherical joint 球铰接，球形接合；球关节
spherical-roller thrust bearing 球面滚子推力轴承（简称 spherical roller bearing, = spherangular roller bearing）
spherical seating ring bearing 带球面垫圈的推力滚动轴承
spherical seat nut 球座螺母
spherical segment combustion chamber 半球形燃烧室
spherical shell 球形壳
spherical space 球面空间
spherical surface 球面，球率曲面
spherical valve 球面阀，球形阀，球阀
spherical vortex 球面旋涡
spherical washer 球面垫圈，球底垫圈
spherical wave 球面波
spherical wheel vehicle 球形车轮车辆（车轮为球形，可做横向运动）
spherodization 球化处理，球化现象，球化作用
spheroidal 球状的，球体的
spheroidal cementite （钢铁的）球状结晶（= nodular cementite）
spheroidal-graphite cast iron 球墨铸铁，球状石墨铸铁（简称 spheroidal graphite iron, = nodular iron）
spheroidizing ①球化（处理）②延期热处理
spheroidizing annealing 球化退火（使钢中的碳化物球状化而进行的

退火，亦称 spheroidal annealing）
sphero-joint 球接头
sphero-meter 球面计，球径计，球径仪，球曲面率计，测球仪
sp. ht. 比热（specific heat）
SPI ①单点式（汽油）喷射（系统）（见 single point injection system）②［美］塑料工业学会（Society of the Plastic Industry Inc 的简称）③声压级（见 sound pressure level）
spider （原意为蜘蛛，在汽车上指类似蜘蛛，具有由中心向外伸出的轴颈或分支的各种零件）①（十字轴式万向节的）十字轴（亦称 cross，为在同一平面内具有四个径向均布轴颈的中间传动元件）②（三球销万向节的）三销架（在同一平面内具有三个径向均布的轴颈和内花键的元件）③（三销式万向节的）三销轴（一对由三个轴颈组成的"T"形元件，其垂直方向的一个轴颈与水平方向的两个轴颈不在同一平面上）④轮辐［特指铸造成形铝合金车轮（cast aluminum wheel）和某些冲压成形的钢车轮（steel pressed 或 forged, stamped wheel）中连接轮辋和轮毂的部分，呈整板型，带圆孔或异形孔板形或宽幅条形］⑤十字形轮毂螺母扳手（可安装四种不同尺寸的套筒）⑥（各种）星形轮⑦星形多头接头⑧（汽车静液压变速器可变容积轨道泵的）星形泵芯（见 orbiter）⑨［德，意］高性能跑车（亦写作 spyder）
spider beam ①十字梁②（特指半挂牵引车转盘式牵引架机械式控制装置的转盘）底横梁（中间穿纵轴，两端带支架支撑销）
spider center ①辐条式轮毂②（万向节）十字轴中心
spider gear 行星齿轮

spider of tripod universal joint （三球销式万向节的）三销架（在同一平面内具有三个径向均布轴颈和内花键的元件，亦称 tripod，见 tripod universal joint）
spider pin （差速器行星齿轮）十字轴
spider single check valve 十字形止回阀（用以分开各条管路而不致相互影响的双止回阀）
spider steering wheel 辐条式转向盘
spider wheel 辐条式车轮（指轮辋由若干辐条联结到轮毂上的车轮，亦称 spoke wheel）
spiel truck 商业广告车，宣传车
SPI engine 单点喷射汽油机（single-point injection engine 的简称，见 single point injection system）
spigot and socket joint ①榫—槽接合②套筒接合
spigot bearing ①导向轴承，定位轴承②（特指变速器）第一轴轴承
spigot joint ①窝接②插头联结器③套筒接合
spigot sleeve （中空的）衬套式插销
spike ①长钉，销钉②（脉冲）尖峰③峰值，最大值
spike brake application 猛踩踏制动（按 SAE J294 的规定，对液压制动车辆，指以 2500lb/s 的速率施加 200lbf 的踩踏力，该踩踏力保持到汽车停住；对气压制动车辆，指在 0.25s 的时间内，将踏板踩到底，使全部制动气室的压力达到 60lbf/in^2）
spike stop 猛制动停车（见 spike brake application）
spike tire 防滑钉轮胎（轮面具有特殊的超硬质合金制的防滑钉，在冰冻路面上使用）
spike type electrode （一种火花塞的）尖端形侧电极
spike tyre （胎冠上镶有）防滑钉

（的）轮胎（20世纪90年代以后，已不再使用）

spill ①溢出，流出，倒出；骤降，跌落②溢出物，溢出量，流出量③小栓，小塞子，销子

spillage ①漏溢，漏失，漏耗②溢出量，泄漏量

spillage test （油箱等容器的）渗漏试验

spill guard 防溢栏板

spill port （柴油机喷油泵柱塞套上的）回油孔（亦称 cutoff hole，当柱塞上升至其斜槽与该孔相通时喷油结束）

spill pressure 回油压力，溢出压力

spill valve 溢流阀，旁通阀；回流阀

spill valve type fuel injection pump 溢流阀式喷油泵

spin ①（一切绕自身轴线的高速）旋转②（当车轮驱动力大于轮胎与路面的摩擦力时，车轮原地）空转，滑转③（当汽车单侧车轮的驱动力或制动力大于路面与轮胎的摩擦力，或质心前后受到侧面碰撞时，出现整车绕其瞬时中心的）回转④用起动机起动发动机⑤乘车短途旅行

spinal cord 脊髓

spinal injury （车辆乘员的）脊椎伤损

spinal kinematics and kinetics of human 人体脊椎骨运动学和动力学

spinal support 座位靠背

spinal- support type comfort seat 脊椎支撑型舒适座椅（亦称 comfort seat with spinal- supporting function，其特点是靠背的形状及其上、下软垫的分割比例可缓解腰-背肌肉受力状况，促进血液流通，据称可减轻30%的长时间坐车疲劳）

spin axis （车轮等旋转体的）旋转轴线（简称 SA）

spin-burst strength （轮胎等旋转件的）抗高速旋转爆裂强度

spindle ①轴，芯轴，轴销，轴颈②转向主销③转向节轴（安装前轮轴承和前轮的短轴）④（柴油机喷油器）挺杆（在调压弹簧与针阀之间起传动等作用的杆件）

spindle arm 转向节臂（= steering knuckle arm，指装在转向节上，与非独立悬架式转向桥的直拉杆或独立悬架式转向桥及齿轮齿条式转向机构的横拉杆连接，传递其转向力，使转向节带动车轮绕主销或转向轴线转动，以实现转向的杆件，有的文献中，亦将转向节臂与转向梯形臂，通称为 steering arm）

spindle arm gauge 杆式前轴前束测量器

spindle axis 主轴线

spindle connecting rod ①（非独立悬架式转向桥的）转向直拉杆②（独立悬架式转向桥的）转向横拉杆（或分段式横拉杆的外端杆）

spindle drive motor 主轴电动机（= spindle motor）

spindle keyway 转轴或芯轴上的键槽

spindle tilt 转向节轴倾角（指由于车轮外倾而引起的转向节轴相对于水平面的倾斜）

spine frame 中央独梁式车架（其特点是中央一根大圆形或矩形断面的脊梁做主承载件，亦称 spine back，spine chassis 或 backbone frame，backbone chassis）

spin into the ground 车轮原地旋转以致压入土中

spin loss （汽车旋转件的）旋转损失（一般指轴承及齿轮等的摩擦损失，故亦称轴承损失，= bearing loss）

spin moment 自转力矩，自旋力矩

spinner ①（各种）旋转件，旋转装置，旋转器（的通称）②（离合

器）从动盘（俗称）③敲击式车轮中心螺母（见 knock off/on wheel nut）

spin-on 压转安装的，旋装的（如：插头等压入插座后转动一定角度即可装妥）

spin-on oil filter 离心式机油滤清器

spin out 拉长，拖长，延长；持续；消磨（时间）

spin resistant differential 防（车轮）滑转差速器（简称 SRD）

spin resonance 自旋共振，自转共振

spin turn ①回旋转向（履带式车辆或轮式非道路车辆单侧驱动，另一侧完全制动，使车辆绕其垂直轴线旋转而实现转向的方法）②滑转转向（赛车驾驶技术之一，汽车瞬间大幅度侧滑，借以实现汽车转向）

spin velocity 自转（角）速度，旋转（角）速度

spiral ①螺旋，螺旋线②螺旋的，螺旋线的

spiral angle at a point 任意点螺旋角（在曲线齿锥齿轮上，基线齿线任意点处的切线与通过该点的分锥母线之间所夹的锐角）

spiral bevel axle 装有曲线齿锥齿轮副主减速器的驱动桥

spiral bevel gear 曲线齿锥齿轮［产形冠轮上的齿线呈某种平面曲线的锥齿轮，如：汽车主减速器使用的弧齿锥齿轮（Gleason spiral bevel gear）和摆线锥齿轮（Oerlikon spiral bevel gear）］

spiral-bevel gearing 曲线齿锥齿轮传动

spiral burr 螺纹

spiral chute 螺旋槽

spiral coil 螺旋形线圈（亦称 spiral winding，= helical coil, helical winding）

spiral conveyor 螺旋输送器

spiral driving worm box 螺旋传动蜗杆箱

spiral gear drive 曲线齿齿轮传动

spiral groove 螺旋槽

spiral inlet duct 螺旋进气道（使新鲜充量进入汽缸时带绕汽缸中心旋转的涡流）

spiral instability （汽车的）螺线形不稳定性，螺旋式不稳定状态（指汽车行驶方向不能稳定控制，以不断减小的回转半径急速转向，致使行驶轨迹呈螺旋状）

spiral jaw clutch 螺旋牙嵌式离合器

spiral line 螺旋线

spiral marking 螺旋形条纹；螺旋形条纹标记（如：导线的彩色螺旋形条纹标记）

spiral movement 螺旋运动

spiral nozzle （柴油机的）螺旋式喷嘴（孔式喷嘴的一种，但其针阀端部不呈尖形，而是一螺旋面，喷油时针阀升起，燃油便从螺旋面所形成的孔隙中喷出，其喷射压力较高，可达 15~30MPa）

spiral of Archimedes 阿基米德螺旋线

spiral oil groove 螺旋油槽

spiral pump 螺旋泵，离心泵

spiral ratchet screwdriver 螺旋棘轮螺钉旋具

spiral roller bearing 螺旋滚子轴承（= flexible roller bearing, wound roller bearing）

spiral-rotor compressor type super charge 螺旋转子（空气）压缩机型（进气）增压器

spiral scroll 螺旋槽（= spiral slot）

spiral spring suspension 螺旋弹簧悬架

spiral test （测金属流动性的）螺旋试验

spiral tooth （曲线齿锥齿轮的）曲线齿

spiral vane flowmeter 螺旋叶片式流

量计
spiral vortex 旋涡
spiral wound roller bearing 螺旋滚子轴承
spirit 酒精（乙醇，= alcohol）
spirit-lamp 酒精灯
spirit-level 酒精水准仪，气泡水平仪
Spirit of Bied 拜得魂（1990年澳大利亚世界太阳能汽车赛夺得第一名的太阳能汽车的车名）
spirit of Detroit [美俚]福特汽车
spirit varnish 酒精清漆
spiroid 锥蜗杆（分度曲面为圆锥面的蜗杆，有一条或若干条等导程的锥螺纹）
spiroid gear 锥涡轮（与锥蜗杆配对的、其外形类似锥齿轮的涡轮）
spiroid gear pair 锥蜗杆和锥涡轮副（锥蜗杆和锥涡轮组成的交错轴齿轮副）
spit back 回火，反喷
spit-pump station 多种燃料加油站
spivot 尖轴
SPL 声压级（见 sound pressure level）
splash 飞溅
splasher （连杆上的）溅油匙
splash guard [美]挡泥板（一般指挂在车较后的防溅片，亦称 splash apron, splash block, splash plafe, splash shield, splash wind, mud wing）
splash pit （试车场）试车浅水槽（亦称 splash pond）
splash-proof 防溅的（简称 SP, 亦称 splash-protection）
splash-proof enclosure 防溅机壳, 防溅外壳
splash test （车辆通过浅水池的）车身密封性试验
splash trough （飞溅润滑的）溅油槽，油池，油盘（亦称 splash basin, 如: 发动机油底壳）
splay-elastic constant 展曲的弹性常数（见 splay of liquid crystal）
splaying-out effect （前轮的）前张效应（汽车行驶时，在推力和滚动阻力等作用下，前轮前端向外张开的现象）
splay of liquid crystal 液晶展曲（使平行排列的液晶分子由原指向矢方向向两侧呈扇面状展开的连续弹性曲率形变）
SPLC 座椅底板负荷传感器（见 seat pan load cell）
splendid 有光彩的, 灿烂的, 壮丽的, 辉煌的, 杰出的
splice ①铰接, 镶接, 拼接 ②铰接物; 铰接处, （铰）接头
splice angle 铰接角
splice cracking of inner tube 内胎接头裂纹（内胎接头处裂开的细小纹路）
splice joint 铰接, 拼合接头, 鱼尾板接合
splice plate 镶接板, 拼接板
splicer 铰接器, 镶接器, 接合器
splice ridge （内胎）接头起棱（接头不平、接头过厚, 内胎和垫带处的凸起现象）
splicing sleeve 牙嵌式接合套, 连接套管
spline ①用花键接合 ②曲线板, 云线规, 云形板（= french curve）③花键 ④齿条 ⑤齿槽
splined 带花键的
splined coupling 花键连接（输出件与输入件以花键连接的形式, 亦称 splined joint）
splined hob 花键座, 花键套
splined hole 花键孔
splined portion of shaft 轴的花键部分
splined shaft 花键轴
splined sleeve 花键套筒（亦称

splined tube)

spline function 样条函数（是逼近曲线的一种方法。工程上，制图员用柔软材质的"样条"在图上特定点之间配绘光滑曲线。数学上的样条就是将上述"样条"代之以一条弹性线，然后再用逐段三次曲线逼近后者。这条逐段三次曲线在两个三次曲线连接处的结点上，允许有一定的导数不连续性）

spline grunt （花键连接承受荷载、低速滑动时产生的）低沉噪声

spline plug gauge 花键塞规

splinter-proof glass 防碎玻璃（＝shatterproof glass）

splintery fracture 碎片状断裂

split ①缝，裂缝 ②分开，分裂，裂开

split axle 组合式驱动桥，组合式轴

split axle casing （由两半壳用螺栓紧固在一起的）组合式桥壳

split beam 组合梁

split bearing 对分式轴承（由上、下两轴瓦组成的滑动轴承，如：曲轴主轴瓦）

split beltpulley 对开传动带轮

split-bench seat （轿车车厢内中间带可向前放平的小靠背，且左、右各有独立靠背的）分开式长座椅

split brake system 双管路制动系统（亦称 split braking system, split service brake, 见 dual-circuit braking system）

split braking 前、后轮独立制动（＝divided braking）

split bush(ing) ①剖分式轴瓦，可卸的瓦片 ②开槽的轴套，开口轴套

split cable 分股电缆

split clamping bearing 开槽的压紧套（可利用轴套压紧程度来调整轴承间隙）

split coefficient braking （左、右车轮所在路面）附着系数不同时的制动

split coefficient stopping testing （左、右车轮路面）不同附着系数道路制动停车试验

split-coefficient surface 双附着系数路面（如：半边结冰的水泥路面等）

split collar 对开环，对开圈，对开垫圈，对开式轴环；对开式轴套，对开套

split conical bushing 切口式锥形衬套，拼合式锥形衬套

split cotter 开口销，开尾销

split crankcase （由两个或多个部分组合而成的）组合式曲轴箱（一般是在曲轴主轴颈轴线平面上装合，以便于曲轴的安装）

split crankshaft （由多段接装成的）组装式曲轴

split cycle engine 分缸循环式发动机（指循环的各个行程分别在两个汽缸内完成的发动机）

split drive transmission 功率分流式传动

splited cords in first ply （轮胎）第一层帘线裂缝（胎里第一层帘线局部裂开的现象）

split-feed control 分路馈给控制

split flow pump 分流油泵

split folding rear seat （轿车或大客车的）每个座位的，靠背都可单独放倒或调节的长条后座椅

split frame 分段式构架，分段式车架

split fuel injection 燃油分股喷射，燃油分段喷射

split gear 拼合齿轮

split housing ①分开式壳体 ②分段式桥壳，分开式桥壳（＝separable housing）

split inner race bearing 双半内圈（内圈径向剖分式）滚动轴承

split lever end 叉状杠杆端部

split manifold 分隔式排气歧管（其中央有隔板，将排气歧管分成两半，每一半都有一独立的排气管将废气引出）

split nut 拼合螺母，开缝螺母，对开螺母

split outer race bearing 外圈径向剖分式滚动轴承

split-phase motor 分相（感应）电动机

split pin 开尾销，开口销（= cotter pin）

split-pin synchronizer 开尾销式同步器

split-pump hydraulic system 分流式油泵液压系统

split rim 对开式轮辋（由两半组合成的组合式轮辋）

split rotor gear （转子发动机的）可分式转子内齿圈，拼装式转子相位齿圈

split rotor shaft （多缸转子发动机）拼装式主轴，拼装式偏心轴，多缸拼装式主轴

split screen （小客车后排座的）分开式（DVD）显示屏（每座一个）

split-second 快速的，极快速的，瞬时的

split-second hand 双秒针

split series servomotor 双绕组串励伺服电动机

split shackle 组合式吊耳

split shaft 半轴

split shell 分开式轴瓦

split side ring 可拆式轮辋边圈

split single 双缸单室式内燃机（指其两个活塞由一个曲柄驱动，且其两个汽缸共用一个燃烧室的两冲程内燃机，亦称 U-cylinder, U-engine）

split skirt piston ［美］裙部开槽的活塞（裙部开槽，以补偿热变形）

split socket 对开式球窝

μ-split surface 左、右车轮所在区域附系数值不同的路面

split-system hydraulic brakes 双管路式液压制动系（= divided-system hydraulic brakes, dual-circuit hydraulic braking system, split hydraulic brake system）

split taper cotter ①开口锥形销，锥形开口锁销 ②（气门弹簧）对开锁瓣

splitter ①机械式变速器的副变速器（亦称 gear group、auxiliary box，一般具有 1~3 个挡位，附装于主变速器前端或后端，用来增加变速器挡位，以扩大变速器传动比范围的齿轮传动装置）②动力分流装置，分动装置

splitter gear （动力）分流齿轮机构

splitter transmission ①（带副变速器的）组合式机械变速器（亦称 splitter box、combinary transmission、compound transmission、two-box transmission，由主变速器与副变速器组合而成的多挡位变速器，其副变速器通常通过自动挡位预选机构挂挡）②（有时仅指组合式变速器中的）副变速器（= splitter）

split tie rod type ackermann geometry 分段式梯形机构（转向横拉杆是分段的梯形机构）

splitting 裂缝，裂开，分隔，分解，分裂，劈开，蜕变

splitting-off 裂口，脱裂，分裂，分离

split torque drive transmission （转矩）分流式液力变速器（从输入端到输出端具有两条或两条以上功率流的液力变速器）

split-train drive 拼合齿轮系传动

split type crankcase 组合式曲轴箱（= split crankcase）

split wheel 对开式车轮（亦称 devided wheel，车轮的轮辋由两个对开零件组成，用螺栓紧固在一起而形成具有两个固定轮缘的车轮）

SPMF （液压泵和液压马达的）旋转斜盘的力矩波动（swash plate moment fluctuations 的简称）

SPMM （汽车）悬架特性参数测试机（suspension parameter measurement machine 的简称，用于测定悬架系统的动态与随变特性）

spoil 腐烂，变坏

spoiler 扰流板（汽车车身上任一种横向布置或纵向布置、用于减小空气阻力的各种空气动力学导流板件的通称，但一般多指用于减小高速时空气浮升力的翼形板件，将空气动力转变为汽车对地面的压力，从而提高轮胎与路面的附着力，可制成各种外形和装于车身的各个部分，如：front spoiler、rear spoiler、roof spoiler、whale tail 等）

spoke 辐条

spoked disk wheel 辐板式车轮（具有带孔的冲压辐板 = disc wheel with holes）

spoked flywheel 辐条式飞轮（= fan flywheel）

spoked wheel 辐条式车轮（亦称 spider wheel 或 spoke wheel）

spoke of the steering wheel 转向盘辐条

spokesperson （机关、部门、企业、公司等）发言人

5-spoke wheel 五轮辐车轮

spoke wire 钢丝辐条

sponge ①海绵②泡沫材料，多孔塑料，海绵状物，疏松多孔金属③海绵状

sponge filter 海绵芯滤清器

sponge plastic 泡沫塑料（= aerated plastic）

sponge rubber upholstery 泡沫橡胶垫（= all-sponge rubber upholstery）

sponginess ①海绵性，海绵状②（液压系统内存在空气时，制动器加踏板的）海绵感

spongy 海绵状的，多孔的

spongy lead （青灰色）海绵状铅（Pb，新的或充电后的蓄电池负极板上的活性物质）

spongy pedal 踏板的海绵现象，踏板海绵感（液压制动系管路内漏入空气，产生气阻等故障时，踩下踏板时的感觉）

sponsor ①发起人，创议人，保证人②发起，主办，提倡，保证，赞助

spontaneous 自发的

spontaneous combustion 自燃（= spontaneous ignition）

spontaneous combustion temperature 自燃温度（= spontaneous ignition temperature）

spontaneously inflammable 易燃的，有自燃倾向的（= liable to spontaneous ignition）

spontaneous polarization 自发极化，自然极化

spool ①卷轴，绕钢丝绳的轴，线轴，线圈；卷盘，线管，双端突缘管，短管②滑阀

spool balance valve （自动变速器液压系统的）滑阀式平衡阀（由一弹簧控制输入压力、保持其平衡，以输出控制元件所需的稳定液压）

spool land 滑阀密封段

spool position 滑阀位置

spool stroke 滑阀行程

spool type control valve 滑柱式控制阀

spool-type rubber bushing 套管式橡胶衬套

spool valve ①滑阀，滑柱阀（液压控制系中的液流方向控制阀）②轴向滑动阀，（线轴形）滑阀③柱塞式滑阀（多用作液压系统液流方向控制阀）

spool valve type steering control valve 滑阀式转向控制阀（滑阀相对于阀体作直线移动的转向控制阀）

spoon 匙，勺，匙状物

spoon of blade 叶片曲面

sportbutton （多功能汽车）运动模式（的）启动按钮，跑车模式启动按钮

sport car ①跑车，运动型轿车（将驾驶汽车作为一种娱乐和户外运动，使用高性能发动机，加速性能好的高速双座敞篷低车身轿车，亦写作 sports car, sportycar, 或称 sportster）②（国际竞赛法规附则A规定的）竞赛轿车（要求在12个月内至少生产50辆，装有在公路上行驶所要求的各个装置的高性能轿车）

sport chassis 运动底盘，跑车底盘

sport (ing) cabriolet 双座敞篷跑车

sport (ing) coupé 单排座轿式跑车

sportive derivative 跑车变形车

sport mode （电子控制悬架的）运动模式［亦称硬模式（hard mode）（firm male）］

sport roadster 双门敞篷跑车

sport(s) body 跑车车身

2+2 sports car 2+2型运动车，2+2型跑车（前、后轮驱动系相互独立，二者间无机械联系的跑车）

sports car platform 基础运动车平台（指加装不同的设置可制造成各种不同系列和型号的运动车的基础车）

sports-hatchback 跑车型舱门式后背小轿车（指具有跑车功能的掀背式轿车，见 hatch back）

sports multi-function leather steering wheel 运动型多功能真皮（包裹）转向盘

sports pattern （行驶模式可变汽车的）运动模式（指不计较能耗，仅要求对加速踏板响应灵敏，能快捷加速、动力强劲的行驶模式）

sport-touring car 旅游运动车，运动旅游两用车

Sport trim （非运动型车辆，如 pick-up 等的）运动型（内、外）装饰和配置（等）

sport-tuned steering system （按运动型多功能车性能要求设计制造的）运动适应型转向系

sport utility vehicle 运动型多功能车（简称SUV, 亦称 sports utility vehicle, 有时亦写作"Sport", 指大功率、高性能、通常为三排座的高通过性箱式轿车，如 Audi Q7、BMW X6、Buick Enclave、Cadillac SRX、Chevrolet Suburban、Dodge Durango、Ford Expedition/EL、Honda CR-v、Infiniti QX、Hyundai Santa Fe、Jeep Grand Cherokee、land Land Rove Ramge Rover Sport、Lexus Rx、Mercedes-Benz G-dass、GL-class 等）

sport wagon 运动型旅行车（= sport station wagon、sport estate）

sporty （论及汽车时指）又快又靓的（汽车，sportiest "最快最靓的"）

sporty layout 跑车变形布置

sporty seat （越野的）运动型座椅

sporty sedan 两排座轿式跑车

spot ①地点，场所，位置②点，斑点，污点，光点③局部

spot check 现场调查，现场核对；抽样检查，抽查；单项检查，部位检查

spot cure 局部硫化，局部固化

spot facing 接触面修平作业，表面修平作业；凸台平面加工，孔口凸台平面加工

spot friction welding 摩擦点焊

spot hardening 局部淬火（= local hardening）

spot heating 局部加热

spot lamp （远距离照射的）聚光灯（亦称 spot light、long range lamp，

1511

装在车前方的窄光束强光射灯，照射方向可由驾驶人员确定，通常只限于停车后使用）

spotlight bulb 聚光灯泡
spot light function 见 smart headlamp
spot of light 光点，光斑
spot repair 现场修理
spot speed ①瞬间速度，即时速度②点速度（车辆通过某观测点时的速度）
spot speed study 定点车速调查（道路上某一定点的交通车速调查）
spot test ①当场试验，现场试验②硝酸浸蚀试验法
spotting ①（故障）位置探查②斑痕
spotting tool 定中心工具
spot turn 原地掉头（= pivot turn）
spotty 多斑点的，有斑点的，有污点的，有缺点的，缺陷多的，不调和的，不规则的，质量不均匀的
spot type disc brake 钳盘式制动器（见 disc brake）
spotty tread wear 胎面斑状磨损（不均匀磨损）
spot weldability （车身金属板材的）点焊性能
spot welder 点焊机
spot welding 点焊（= point welding）
spout ①排出口，排出管，流出槽②水流，气流③（特指发动机排气）尾管（= tail pipe）
spout 见 spark output
spout cleaner 气动压差吸尘器
spout signal （由动力控制模块"PCM"发送给点火控制模块 ICM 的）点火指令信号（spark out signal 的简称，该信号告诉 ICM 以下内容：下一个应点火的是哪一个或哪一组汽缸②其点火提前角是多少，即在该汽缸上止点前多少度点火。然后 ICM 便在所指定的精确时间内切断点火线圈初级电路，使该

火花塞跳火）

sprag ①（自由轮单向离合器的）楔块②三角木，撑木
sprag clutch 楔块式单向离合器，楔块式自由轮（= sprag type overrunning clutch、overrunning sprag clutch、free wheeling sprag clutch，在其内、外座圈间装有只允许外座圈单方向相对内座圈旋转的弹簧加载式楔块）
spray ①喷束，喷雾束②喷射，喷雾，飞溅
sprayability 喷雾性能
spray angle 喷束锥角，喷雾锥角，喷射角
spray application （用喷枪）喷涂
spray atomizer 喷雾器
spray (atomizing) carburettor 喷射式化油器（= spraying carburettor）
spray chamber 喷漆室，喷涂室
spray characteristic 喷雾特性（与喷注破碎、弥散、雾化等有关的特性，如：雾珠细microscopy分布、雾珠的蒸发与扩散、喷雾的偏转、喷雾的干扰等）
spray combustion 喷雾燃烧
spray cone angle 喷雾锥角（喷注离喷孔口后，由于射流扩散效应和背压的阻力作用，形成锥形喷雾，其锥角称喷雾锥角，简称 spray angle）
spray-droplet 喷射油滴，喷雾油滴
spray, drying, coating production line （汽车车身的）喷漆-烘干-涂装生产线
spray(ed) coating 喷涂；喷镀层
sprayer 喷雾器，喷洒器，喷漆枪
spray exposure 在盐水喷雾下的暴露试验
spray gun 喷枪
spraying hardening 喷雾淬火（压缩空气通过喷嘴使水雾化，而后喷到工件上进行冷却）

spraying nozzle 喷口，喷嘴（亦称 spraying jet，spraying nipple）

spray metal coating ①金属喷镀②金属喷镀层

spray meter 喷雾计，喷射计

spray orifice 喷孔（如：针阀体头部或孔板中部喷射出雾状燃油的小孔，亦称 spray hole）

spray-painted 喷漆的

spray penetration （燃油）喷雾穿透深度，喷射深度，（燃油）喷雾射程，喷注贯穿距离（从喷孔口起到喷注前锋所能达到的最大直线距离，简称贯穿距离）

spray penetration curve 喷注贯穿曲线（表示喷注贯穿直线距离随时间或曲轴转角的变化规律的曲线）

spray penetration ratio 喷注贯穿率（滞燃期内喷注的贯穿距离与从喷孔口沿喷孔轴线方向到燃烧室壁的直线距离的比值，简称贯穿率）

spray pipe passage 喷雾管路

spray ring （燃气涡轮）喷嘴环，环状喷嘴

spray shape 射束形状（亦称 spray pattern）

spray test ①喷射腐蚀试验（用喷射腐蚀性溶液的方法来检查材料、制件的抗腐蚀能力）②（喷嘴的）喷射试验

spray tip 喷油嘴喷头（= nozzle tip）

spray truck 喷洒车，喷水车

spray valve ①喷射阀（如：喷油器内的针阀，= needle valve）②喷油器

spray washer 喷射式清洗机

spray wire 喷镀用的金属丝

spread ①范围，间距②散布，分散，扩散③（金属）延压④拆开，铺开⑤（轴承）盈量⑥总传动比（= overall gear ratio）

spreader ①撒布机，扩张器②（间隔）撑柱，撑杆，撑板

spreader-trailer 牵引式撒布机

spreading 扩展，扩散，散布；撒布，摊铺，延压

spreading beam （大灯）散光束

spreading of load （双功率流传动装置的）荷载分布

spread tandem axle 分开式双轴并装车桥（双轴并装车桥总成中两车轴之间的距离超过轮胎外径的1.5倍以上者，用于回避法规对常规并装双桥的轴重限制）

spring ①春（季）②泉；源泉，根源③跳跃；弹回，返跳④弹力，弹性⑤弹簧（在汽车上按 SAE J274 规定，包括钢板弹簧、螺旋弹簧、扭力杆、橡皮弹簧、空气弹簧等）

spring accumulator 弹簧式蓄压器，弹簧式储能器

spring-actuated 弹簧作动的

spring adaptor 弹簧座（用于定位弹簧的零件，= spring abutment）

spring aid （悬架）弹簧（橡胶或其他弹性元件制成的压缩行程）缓冲限位块（亦称 bump stop）

spring (anchorage) bracket 钢板弹簧支架

spring-and-guide assembly 带导向件的弹性元件总成（如：螺旋弹簧及导杆总成）

spring and piston ring elasticity tester 弹簧和活塞环弹性检查器

spring arch 钢板弹簧拱度

spring arrangement 弹簧布置（如：悬架弹簧布置）

spring(-) back 回跳，回弹（弹性变形回复）

spring-backed 弹簧支撑的

spring-backed piston ring 带胀圈的活塞环

spring ball joint 带弹簧缓冲的球关节

spring base （汽车悬架）弹簧间距（左右弹簧的车身或车架支撑点间

的距离)
spring beam 弹性梁
spring bearer plate (在车架上固定车厢的)弹性压板
spring blade 钢板弹簧片(= spring leaf)
spring block 弹簧座(亦称 spring bearing, spring bolster)
spring bolt ①钢板弹簧中心螺栓 ②钢板弹簧吊耳销
spring bolt thread bushing 钢板弹簧销螺纹衬套
spring booster (增加重载时,悬架弹簧承载能力的)弹簧加力装置(如:重型货车钢板弹簧式非独立悬架在承重超过某规定值、主钢板弹簧被压平到一定程度时起作用的副板弹簧)
spring boot 钢板弹簧防尘罩
spring-borne 弹簧悬架的
spring brake 见 energy storage spring brake
spring breakage 弹簧断裂
spring buckle 钢板弹簧吊耳(= spring shackle)
spring buffer ①弹簧缓冲器 ②(钢板)弹簧缓冲块(= spring bumper, spring buffer stopper)
spring bumper ①弹簧缓冲器 ②(钢板)弹簧限位块(= spring limiting stopper)
spring bushing 钢板弹簧吊耳孔内的衬套
spring caliper(s) (带)弹簧(的)卡钳,测径规
spring camber (钢板)弹簧挠度(= camber of spring)
spring cap (气门)弹簧座(= valve spring retainer)
spring capacity 弹簧容量(弹簧承载能力)
spring capacity at ground (钢板)弹簧弯曲或变形至其最大正常承载位置时地面所承载的汽车总重(此时的簧上质量与簧下质量之和)
spring capacity at pad (钢板)弹簧弯曲或变形至其正常满负荷位置时,(钢板)弹簧所承载的汽车簧上质量的总重
spring carrier 弹簧支架
spring carrier arm 弹簧支臂
spring catapult (撞车试验用的)弹簧弹射器
spring centre clip 钢板弹簧中央夹箍(指钢板弹簧中央的两端带螺纹的U形螺栓,= U bolt,亦称 spring centre bend, spring centre bolt, spring centre clamp)
spring-centred 弹簧定心的
spring centre hump 钢板弹簧垫中部凸起处
spring centrifugal clutch 弹簧延动式离心离合器(弹簧使离心操纵机构延缓作用,达到一定高速后,离合器才能接合)
spring chair ①弹簧椅 ②弹簧坐垫(= spring perch) ③弹簧座(= spring seat)
spring chamber parking brake 弹簧室式驻车制动器(弹簧室内的气压,即:制动系的气压低于某规定值时,弹簧即伸张而推动蹄片将制动器抱死)
spring clamp 弹簧夹(亦称 spring clip)
spring clamping plate 弹簧夹板
spring clip bar 弹簧夹条
spring clip of headlamp (汽车)前照灯弹簧夹箍
spring clutch 弹簧离合器
spring coil 螺旋弹簧
spring collar 弹簧挡圈,弹簧座圈
spring compressor ①弹簧帽,弹簧罩(= spring cap) ②(拆卸弹簧件时使用的)弹簧压缩器(如:拆卸悬架螺旋弹簧时,将其压缩,便于

拆卸紧固件，保证安全）
spring constant 弹簧常数（弹簧的刚度参数，每单位变形所需的负荷，N/cm）
spring contact 弹簧触点
spring controlled valve 弹簧控制阀，弹簧调节阀
spring cotter 开口销，开尾销，弹簧锁销
spring damper 弹簧减振器，弹簧缓冲器
spring damper coil 减振螺旋弹簧（如：装在离合器从动片上的减振弹簧）
spring deflection 弹簧变形；钢板弹簧挠度，钢板弹簧变形；
spring-driven 弹簧驱动的，发条驱动的
spring equalizing device 弹簧平衡装置
spring eye 钢板弹簧卷耳
spring eye bushing 钢板弹簧卷耳孔衬套
spring eye pin 钢板弹簧卷耳销
spring fastener 弹簧扣
spring fixed end 钢板弹簧固定端
spring flange （两件式轮辋的可折式）弹性挡圈（detachable spring flange 的简称，起卡住轮胎胎圈的作用）
spring force 弹簧弹力（弹簧刚度×变形量）
spring free end sliding plate 钢板弹簧自由端滑板
spring front end bracket 钢板弹簧前吊架
spring hammer 弹簧锤
spring hanger 弹簧吊架（汽车底盘上的钢板弹簧卷耳端悬架装置，亦称 spring bracket）
spring hanger bushing replacer 钢板弹簧吊架衬套拆装工具
spring holding pressure （弹簧制动器的）弹簧保持压力
spring insert 钢板弹簧的片间垫块
spring key 弹簧键
spring knockout （拆装用）弹簧式顶出工具，（车身维修用）弹簧式顶出器
spring lateral rate 弹簧侧向角刚度（弹簧质量所受侧向力矩与其产生侧向角的比值，即产生单位侧向角的侧向力矩）
spring leaf 钢板弹簧片
spring(-leaf) opener 拆开钢板弹簧的工具
spring leaf retainer 钢板弹簧片夹
springless 无弹性的，无弹簧元件的
springless flow control valve 无弹簧的流量控制阀
springless oil seal 无弹簧式油封
spring liner 钢板弹簧的片间（软材料）衬垫
spring loaded apex seal 弹簧加载径向密封片（转子发动机中的径向密封片后面装有片簧，使密封片与缸壁保持接触）
spring loaded clutch 弹簧加载式离合器（指弹簧加载常啮合式离合器）
spring loaded length 钢板弹簧在承载状态下的长度
spring loaded oil piston ring 弹簧加载式活塞油环（指带胀圈的活塞油环）
spring loaded plunger （喷油泵等）带复位弹簧的柱塞
spring lock washer 弹簧锁紧垫圈
spring main leaf camber 弹簧钢板主片拱度
spring mandrel 螺旋弹簧（的）芯轴
spring-mass system 弹簧质量系统
spring motor 发条驱动装置，发条传动装置
spring mounted 弹簧悬架的

spring mounting ①弹簧座（= spring fastening）②钢板弹簧吊架

springness 弹性

spring offset 单边弹簧式，弹簧偏置式（换向阀等）

spring oiler 钢板弹簧润滑油嘴，钢板弹簧加油器

spring pad （前后桥壳的）钢板弹簧坐垫

spring pocket （车身底板或车架或其他板件上安装）螺旋弹簧（的）凹座（= spring seat）

spring rate 弹簧刚度（指弹簧或弹性系统在单位荷载下的变形量或其单位变形量所需的荷载）

spring rate control （电子控制悬架系统）弹簧刚度控制

spring rebound clip （钢板）弹簧回跳卡箍

spring resonance 弹簧共振

spring rotating mechanical seal 弹簧旋转式机械密封（弹性元件随轴旋转的机械密封）

spring scale ①弹簧刚度测定器 ②（复）弹簧秤

spring seat 弹簧座

spring seat angle （钢板弹簧）座角（= seat angle）

spring shackle （钢板弹簧）吊耳（见 shackle①）

spring shackle bolt （钢板）弹簧吊耳销（= spring eye bolt）

spring shackle bushing, spring shackle pin 钢板弹簧吊耳衬套

spring single coil 单圈螺旋弹簧

spring spacer 钢板弹簧隔片（亦称 spring separator）

spring-spoked steering wheel 弹性辐条转向盘（= spring-spoke steering wheel）

spring-spoked wheel 弹性辐条车轮

spring spreader 弹簧扩张器，弹簧拉长器

spring squeak 弹簧吱吱声

spring standing mechanical seal 弹簧静止式机械密封（弹性元件不随轴旋转的机械密封）

spring starter （发动机）弹簧起动器

spring static deflection 弹簧静挠度（= L_s/R_s，式中：L_s—弹簧的静载荷；R_s—弹簧的静载荷刚度）

spring steel 弹簧钢

spring steering wheel 弹性转向盘（自动复位转向盘）

spring stiffness 弹簧刚度

spring-strut assembly （悬架的）螺旋弹簧滑柱总成

spring surge frequency 弹簧颤动频率

spring tab 弹簧（弹力的）调整片

spring tension 弹簧张力

spring-tensioned oil seal 弹簧自紧油封（亦称 spring loaded oil seal）

spring tension tester 弹簧弹力试验器

spring thrust （汽车）悬架弹簧传递的切线推力（驱动力）

spring tower （悬架螺旋）弹簧（的）凸盘形支座

spring U-bolt 钢板弹簧 U 形螺栓（钢板弹簧骑马螺栓，亦称 spring U-clips）

spring valve plate (of shock absorber's damping valve) （减振器阻尼阀的）弹簧阀片

spring wagon 一种装有弹簧悬架的轻型货车（以往多用于农业）

spring washer with external teeth 外齿形弹簧垫圈

spring washer with internal teeth 内齿形弹簧垫圈

spring weight ①弹簧支撑的重量 ②弹簧自重

spring wheel 弹簧悬架车轮（亦称 spring hud wheel）

spring wind-up 钢板弹簧卷曲（指汽车驱动轿的钢板弹簧，在制动或加速时产生的扭转荷载的作用力矩下变成 S 形的现象，= wind-up of spring）

spring wire 弹簧钢丝

spring with compression shackles 带承压吊耳的钢板弹簧

spring with tension shackles 带承拉吊耳的钢板弹簧

springy ①具有弹力的，似弹簧的②湿润的，湿的③轻快的

sprinkler ①洒水车（= sprinkler truck，亦称 sprinkler tank wagon，sprinkler wagon, sprinkling car, sprinkling tank wagon, sprinkling truck, sprinkling wagon）②洒水设备，喷水设备，喷水装置③人工降雨装置

sprocket chain 传动链

sprocket drive 链传动（= chain drive）

sprocket dynamometer （履带式机械）驱动链轮测力计（用来测定传递给驱动链轮的转矩）

sprocket wheel 链轮（简称 sprocket, = chain wheel）

SPRs 自钻铆接（见 self piercing rivets）

sprung empty weight 空车簧上重量（空车悬架质量的旧称）

sprung mass 簧上质量（悬架弹性元件以上负荷的质量，再计入传动轴、悬架系、制动系、转向系中起簧上质量作用的那部分质量）

sprung parts 簧上部件（指支在弹簧上的部件）

sprung seat 弹簧座椅

sprung-to-unsprung weight ratio （汽车）弹簧上重量与弹簧下重量比（弹簧上质量与弹簧下质量之比的旧称）

SPT ①支柱②（器材-技术）保证（support 的简称）③在标准状态下（在标准气压和温度下，即 101 kPa，0℃下，under standard pressure and temperature 的简称）

spun bearing 离心浇铸轴承

spun casting 离心铸造，离心浇铸法

spun-in 离心浇铸

spun-in metal 离心浇铸（轴承）合金

spun yarn packing 麻纱软垫

spur ①直齿②抓地齿

spur action 抓地齿作用，防滑钉作用

spur bevel gear 直齿锥齿轮（= straight bevel gear，指齿线是分度圆锥面的直母线的直齿轮）

spur differential 直齿圆柱齿轮差速器〔spur gear differential 的简称，使用直齿圆柱齿轮的差速器，但目前，差速器广泛采用的是直齿锥齿轮（straight bevel gear）〕

spur friction wheel 筒形摩擦轮

spur gear 直齿圆柱齿轮（直齿轮，齿线是分度圆柱面直母线的圆柱齿轮）

spur geared wheel reductor 外啮合圆柱齿轮式轮边减速器（由一对外啮合的圆柱齿轮所构成的轮边减速器）

spur-gear-hub drive 圆柱齿轮轮边传动，圆柱齿轮侧传动

spur gear pair 直齿圆柱齿轮副（由两个配对的直齿圆柱齿轮组成的平行轴齿轮副）

spur gear pump 外啮合直齿齿轮泵

spur gear road wheel reduction axle 带直齿圆柱齿轮轮边减速器的驱动桥

spurious signal 虚假信号，错误信号

spur rack 直齿条（其齿线是垂直于齿的运动方向的直线的齿条）

spur road 岔路

spurt 喷流，喷出

spurt hole 喷（出）口（见 squirt

1517

hole)

spur type planetary reducer 直齿式行星齿轮减速装置

sputter ①（发动机）噼啪作响②喷镀金属③溅射，喷射

sputtering ①溅射（一种金属薄膜形成法）②阴极真空喷镀，喷涂，飞溅③溅蚀（离子对结构表面冲击引起的材料损耗）④爆裂，发出噼啪响声

sputtering of injector 喷油嘴吐沫

SPWM 正弦波脉宽调制（sinusoidal pulse width modulation 的简称）

sq. 平方；正方形（= square）

sq. cm 平方厘米（= square centimeter）

sq. ft 平方英尺（= square foot）

sq. in 平方英寸（= square inch）

sq. m 平方米（= square meter）

sq. mm 平方毫米（= square milimeter）

squab bracket 座椅靠背支架

squab inclination 座椅靠背倾斜度

squad car （高速公路）巡视车（= patrol car）

square ①正方形，平方；直角尺②正方形的，平方的，直角的，垂直的③使相互成直角

square back （轿车或客车的）方形车身后壁

square bearer 方框托架，方框支撑座

square bend 90°曲管，直角弯头

square crossing 十字形交叉；十字形交叉路口

square-dressed pavement 方块石（铺砌的）路面

square drive ①（电动或气动冲击式扳手的）方形驱动头（用于接装套筒扳头）②（手动套筒扳手接套筒扳头的）方形扭杆

square elbow 直角弯管，直角弯头

square engine ①方形发动机，等径程发动机（活塞行程等于汽缸内径的发动机，缸径行程比等于1，亦称 square stroke engine）②方形四缸发动机（= square-four engine）

square foot 平方英尺（ft², 1ft² = 0.092 903 04m²）

square-law 按变量平方变化的；平方律

square neck carriage bolt 方颈车身螺栓

squareness ①方形②垂直度，直角度

square parking line 广场驻车标线

square pole 方杆（英美面积单位，简称 sq. pole, 1 sq. pole = 30.25 sq. yard, = square rod）

square root 平方根

square wave 矩形（脉冲）波（方波）

squaring amplifier 矩形波形成-放大器

squaring circuit 矩形波形成-整形电路

squash 压碎，压扁，压挤，高度压缩

squash type 挤压式（燃烧室）[如：楔形燃烧室（wedge type）]

squawk （制动器）低频咯咯响声（频率在900Hz以下）

squeab （座椅的）靠背

squeab panel （轿车车身支撑后座靠背并分隔客厢与后行李舱的横向布置的垂直）后壁板（亦称 rear squeab panel）

squeak （车身、弹簧等的）吱吱声，制动刺耳尖声

squeal ①（轮胎在路面上的）滑移噪音②（制动器总成的）高频振动噪音

squeegee ①轮胎帘布层间的隔离胶②橡皮滚子，橡皮刮板，路刮

squeegee action （制动和驱动时使轮胎胎体变形的）挤压作用

squeeze ①压，夹，压榨，压出，挤压；使…缩减，压实，塞入，压出 ②压印，压出物

squeeze (moulding) machine 压实造型机

squeezing 紧压，压缩，压实，挤压，夹紧

squelch ①轮胎噪声（高温干燥的条件下，在平坦的道路上直线行驶时产生的轮胎噪声）②压扁，压碎；制止，使…终止；发出沙沙噪声

squelch-circuit 噪声抑制电路，静噪电路

squib ①（安全气囊等的）引爆装置 ②（商品）标签 ③引爆 ④扩孔底

squill vice 弓形虎钳，C形夹，C形夹钳（= C-clamp）

squirm ①摇摆；扭曲；蠕动 ②（轮胎因受挤压，扭曲而引起的胎面与路面间的相对）滑磨

"squirrel cage" AC induction motor 鼠笼式交流感应电动机

squirrel cage blower 鼠笼式鼓风机（由电动机直接驱动，装在形似松鼠笼的外壳内的风扇，用于汽车空调—暖风系统）

squirt ①喷出，喷流 ②喷注器

squirt hole （连杆小头中）机油喷射孔，喷油孔（亦称 spur hole）

squish ①挤气（指内燃机压缩行程终了活塞到达上止点，将其与汽缸盖底平面之间的间隙内的可燃混合气挤至靠近火花塞附近的空间和挤入活塞顶内燃烧室中形成涡流的过程）②挤气面积（见 squish area）③压扁，压碎；压入（= squash）

squish area 挤气面积〔指活塞到达上止点后，活塞顶与汽缸盖底面间隙最小时的燃烧室面积，亦称挤气带（squish band）〕

squish lip （英国 Perkins 发动机公司提出的一种新型无增压，直喷式柴油机活塞顶燃烧室的环形）挤压边

squish motor 挤气型发动机（指其燃烧室可产生强烈挤压气流的发动机）

squish swirl 挤压涡流（当活塞接近压缩行程终点时，活塞顶部非燃烧室表面和缸盖底面之间的狭小空间内的混合气，以向心方向被挤入活塞顶的凹窝燃烧室内而产生的径向气体涡流）

squish type chamber 挤流型燃烧室（具有挤压面的燃烧室）

sr ①（电机）集流环，（离合器）分离推力环（= slip-ring）②比阻力（= specific resistance）③球面度（立体角单位，1 球面弧度等于某球体半径平方大小的球面所对应的该球体中心的立体角，见 steradian）

SR ①扫气比（见 scavenge ratio）②防滑性（skid resistance 的简称）

SRAM （汽车电子控制系统中的）静态随机存储器（static access memory 的简称）

SRC 溶剂精制煤（solvent refined coal）

SRD ①开关磁阻电动机驱动系统（switch reluctance drive 的简称，见 SRM）②防滑转差速器（spin resistant differential）

SRFF （两级式气门升程可变系统的）换位滚子头气门挺杆（switching roller finger follower 的简称）

SRL ［美］斯柯特实验研究所（Scott Research Laboratories）

SRM ①开关磁阻电动机（switch reluctance motor 的简称，20 世纪 70 年代以后开发的一种磁阻同步电动机和电子开关电路相结合的机电一体化产品，其转子无绕组也无永磁体，定子极上绕有集中绕组，径向相对的两个绕组串联成一个两极磁极，称为一相，可以设计成多相结构）②标准参考材料（standard ref-

SROM 单纯转动活塞机（single rotating piston machines, similar to SIM）

SRP 坐姿基准点（seating reference point 的简称）

SRS ①乘员约束型辅助保护装置（supplemental restraint system 的简称，一般指安全带以外的碰撞时防止乘员受伤的正面和侧面安全气囊等，该术语多不单独使用，而与安全气囊的商品名等合用）②（底特律公司柴油机电子控制系统的）同步基准（信号）传感器（synchronous reference sensor 的简称，向电子控制模块发送发动机转速信号）

SRS light 安全气囊及安全带警报灯

SRT （车辆的）标准修理时间（standard repair times 的简称）

SRU 自记录装置（self-recording unit）

S²RV （福特公司的）智能、安全研究车（Smart, Safe Research Vehicle 的简称，该车用于显示本田公司在今后将用于大批量生产车上的各种智能和安全技术的开发与研制成果）

SRV 安全研究车（Safety Research Vehicle）

SS ①闪烁谱仪（scintillation spectrometer）②固定螺钉；调节螺钉（set screw）③剪切强度（shear strength）④换挡电磁阀（shift solenoid）⑤信号装置（signalling set）⑥单信号（single signal）⑦跑车型轿车（sport sedan）⑧稳定系统（stabilization system）⑨不锈钢（stainless steel）⑩过热蒸汽（superheated steam）⑪开关选择器（switching selector）⑫转向传感器（steering sensor 的简称，将转向盘的转动角速度及扭矩变为电信号输出至电子控制模块）

SSA [美]汽车安全标准咨询委员会（Automotive Safety Standards Advisory Committees）

S11 Salisbury axle 一种杆式独立悬架车桥（商品名，其悬架由减振器、螺旋弹簧和支撑杆组成，用于越野车辆）

SSC 起动—停机自动控制（系统）（见 start-stop control）

SSCC [美]雪地汽车安全与鉴定委员会（Snowmobile Safety and Certification Committee）

S-S condition 稳定工况，稳态（steady-state condition）

S-shaped curve S形曲线

SSHEV （日本富士重工的）顺序串联式混合动力电动车（商品名，sequential series hybrid electric vehicle 的简称）

SSI 小规模集成电路（见 small scale integrated circuit）

SSL [美]壳牌石油公司精选燃油（Shell selected fuel）

SSM 悬架转向（电子控制）模块（suspension steering module 的简称，控制悬架与转向系统的车用电子计算机）

S-spanner S形扳钳，S形双头呆扳手

S spring S形弹簧（如：呈连续S形的汽车座椅软垫钢丝弹簧）

SSR 固态继电器（solid-state relay 的简称）

SSST 见 Sequential Spot Shift Transmission

SSU ①赛氏通用黏度秒（Saybolt Seconds Universal）②信号选择装置（= signal selector unit）

SSVS [日] 超级智能汽车系统（super-smart vehicle systems 的简称，包括：障碍物探测，道路几何形状探测，碰撞预警，自动制动/转向，行人探测，驾驶支援，自动线路跟踪，事故防止等项功能和系统）

SSW 特大旅行轿车（参见 super space wagon）；准旅行轿车（Semi-station wagon）

ST ①维修工具（= service tools）②单曲柄曲轴（= single-throw）③专用工具（= special tools）④标准温度（= standard temperature）⑤起动（= start）⑥静推力（= static thrust）⑦蒸汽（steam）

St 沱（见 stoke）

stabilised voltage supply 稳压电源

stabilitic annealing 稳定化正火（在加热、保温和缓冷过程中消除内应力工艺）

stabilitic heat treatment 热定型处理（如：用冷拔钢丝绕制的冷卷弹簧，必须在 200~300°C 加热以消除冷卷造成的内应力并使弹簧定型）

Stabilitrak ①（卡迪拉克/德尔福的汽车）稳定性控制系统（商品名，参见 vehicle stability assist system）②（Seville STS 的）稳迹（动态稳定性控制系统的商品名，该系统与前、后轮牵引力分配系统及悬架阻尼自动调节系统 CVRSS 配合工作，当汽车的实际转向角与驾驶者意图比较，不足时，对弯道内侧前轮施加制动，过度时，对弯道外侧的前轮施加制动，同时控制发动机扭矩和悬架硬度，以校正行驶方向，保持稳定转向，见 turn-rate control system）

stability 稳定性（①汽车的稳定性，指汽车受到外界干扰后，维持或迅速恢复原运动状态的能力②汽车各系统的稳定性指受到外界干扰时，仍能保持其原有工作能力和性能的能力③材料物理化学性质的稳定性一般指抗化变化的性能）

stability characteristic test 稳态特性试验（指稳态工况下的特性试验）

stability condition 稳定条件，稳定状况

stability criterion 稳定性标准

stability factor 稳定性因素（①指汽车的侧翻的稳定性因素：稳定力矩与翻倾力矩的比值%，其倒数称稳定性裕度，见 stability margin）②指角跃输入下稳态转向特性的稳定性因素 k。若 $k=0$，汽车呈中性转向特性，$k>0$，汽车呈不足转向特性，$k<0$，汽车呈过度转向特性）

stability in use 使用稳定性

stability limit 稳定极限

stability margin 稳定性裕度（用裕度百分率来表示汽车稳定性的好坏，与稳定系数的关系式为：稳定裕度% = 稳定性因数$^{-1}$ × 100%，= margin of stability）

stability pressure chamber 稳压室

stability test 稳定性试验（= stability trial）

stabilization of austenite 奥氏体稳定化（使奥氏体稳定，不易转变为马氏体）

stabilization period 稳定期（如：装有调速器的发动机，从负荷变动时开始，到达转速稳定时为止所经过的时间）

stabilization system 稳定系统（简称 SS）

stabilizator rod 稳定杆（防止车身侧倾的悬架杆件，亦称 stabilizer bar）

stabilize （使）稳定，稳定化，安定，减摇；使⋯坚固，使⋯牢固，耐⋯，抗⋯；消除内应力

stabilized combustion system 稳定燃烧系统（简称 SCS，日本马自达汽车的废气净化系统）

stabilized conditions 稳定状态

stabilized earth road 稳定（处理的）土路

stabilized gasoline 经过稳定性处理的汽油（降低其蒸汽压）

stabilized speed 稳定速度；稳定

转速

stabilizer ①稳定器②汽车独立悬架系统的稳定杆［亦称 stabilizer bar, anti-roll bar, sway bar, stabilizer rod, stabilizator bar, stabilizator rod, 为一根连接左、右两车轮独立悬架下控制臂的横向弹性杆件。它的作用是使左、右车轮中任一方车轮的垂直运动都会受到另一方车轮的制约，从而减小汽车的侧倾趋势，故英文称抗侧倾杆（anti-roll bar 或 roll bar）］

stabilizer crank （履带拖拉机的）导向机构曲柄

stabilizer ply （带束斜交胎和子午线轮胎紧贴轮胎胎面橡胶层下面、宽度在两侧胎肩之间、紧箍胎体的帘线层，总称：）带束层（亦称 stabilizer belt，简称 belt）

stabilizing 起稳定作用的

stabilizing beam ①平衡梁，平衡杆②（铰接式客车机械连接装置的）梭梁（位于中间框架底部，并受等分机构约束而使其始终处于转角平分线上的横梁）

stabilizing fin 稳定翼板，稳定鳍板

stabilizing jack 支撑千斤顶（汽车吊或挂车用的支撑脚）

stabilizing moment 稳定力矩

stabilizing spoiler 稳定导流板

stabilizing tester （汽车的）稳定性试验台（倾翻角试验台）

stabilizing treatment （金相组织的）稳定性处理

stabilizing valve （液压式防侧倾稳定杆的）稳定阀

stabilometer ①稳定仪（量测稳定性）②稳定性记录仪

stable 确定的，安定的，牢固的

stable equilibrium 稳定平衡

stable output configuration of a sequential circuit 时序电路的稳定输出组态［亦称 output pattern（输出图形），一种在产生它的激励或维持它的其他激励被非激励的输入组态（输入图形）代替后，或者在没有激励情况下，仍保持不变的电路输出组态、输出图形］

stack ①堆积，层叠，捆束，组，套②一堆（木材计量单位 = $108 in^3$），木材堆

stacked cell 组合气室（用于 NDIR 的组合样气室，由几个样气室叠置而成。用于对特定成分进行多量程测定）

stacker ①堆货机，码垛机②叠式存储器

stack gas 烟气

stack height （多片式钢板弹簧总成）中部厚度

stacking fault 晶格内原子排列的缺陷

stacking test 堆码试验（在包装件或包装容器上放置重物，评定包装件或包装容器承受堆积静载的能力和包装对内装物保护能力的试验）

stacking up 堆垛（按照货物运输和保管要求，将货物堆齐码好的作业）

stack pointer 栈指针（存储当前栈项地址，即：最近存入的数据项的存储单元的地址的寄存器）

stack transfer 倒垛（将货垛翻动和重新堆码的作业）

stack type filter 叠片式滤清器

staff aerial （金属）棒天线，杆状天线（= rod aerial, staff antenna, rod antenna）

staff car 指挥车

staff costs per seat （客车、公共汽车等）分摊到每位旅客上的乘务员开支费用，每客座乘务员费用，每客座乘务费

staffs （全体）工作人员

stage ①级（液力变矩器的级指位于其他叶轮元件之间刚性连接的涡轮

元件数）②阶段，步骤，时期
③台，台架
stage coach 台阶式厢式大客车
（1830 年英国人 Gold Worthy Gurney
设计的装用蒸汽机的厢式客车）
stage efficiency （压气机、涡轮机
的）级效率
stage filter 分级式滤清器
stage heat drop （压气机、涡轮机
的）级间热降，级间焓降
stage improvement ①（交通路口）
行车通过信号的相段改进（主要指
红、绿灯的显示时间及方法的改
进）②（产品等的）分阶段改进
stage pressure ratio 级压力比（多级
压缩机中任一级的压力比，其排气
取中间冷却器前的值）
stage pump 多级泵
2-stage rotary engine 双级（压燃
式）转子发动机
stage-time curve 级时曲线
stage turbine 分级式涡轮机
stagger ①斜罩，罩②交错排列；参
差，交错装置，摇摆，跳动；摆
（动）（误）差；回路失调
stagger angle （轴流式涡轮的）叶
片安装角，排列角，交错角
staggered 交错排列的，交错的
staggered arrangement 交错排列
staggered bumps （试验跑道上）左
右交错布置的人造凸起障碍物（使
左右车轮交替跳动）
staggered cylinders 交错直列式汽缸
（排成一列，但不在一轴线上）
staggered doors 车身左右侧不对称
布置的车门
staggered fan 叶片不对称排列的
风扇
staggered seam 间断焊缝
staggered seats 交错排列的座位
staggered section view 阶梯剖视图
staggered spokes 交错辐条
staggered tooth double-helical gear
交错齿人字齿轮
staggered tube radiator 叠管式散热
器；交错排列管式散热器
staggered valves 交叉布置的阀门
staggered V-engine （Lancia 公司研
制的汽缸）交错式 V 形发动机（两
排汽缸体成小锐角 V 形排列，每一
排中的汽缸交错排开，正好与另一
排中交错排开的汽缸对合，使发动
机尺寸更为紧凑）
stagnant air 不流动的空气（静区，
= dead air ①）
stagnation conditions 滞止状态，停
滞状态
stagnation point 静点，驻点，滞点
stagnation temperature 滞流温度，
滞点温度，静滞温度，临界温度
（见 total temperature）
stain ①着色剂②污点；锈③生锈
stained glass 有色玻璃，彩色玻璃，
彩画玻璃
stainless ①不锈的②无斑的，无污
点的，无瑕疵的，纯洁的
stainless property 抗锈蚀性能（=
rustless property）
stainless steel 不锈钢（指含有铬、
镍等合金元素的耐腐蚀、抗氧化合
金钢，简称 SS）
stainless steel clad 不锈钢包覆的
stainless steel mesh type brake hose
不锈钢网式制动软管
stain remover 去污剂，除渍剂，除
锈剂
stain spots 斑点，污点，锈蚀点
stair case 楼梯，楼梯间
stake ①桩，标杆，柱杆②底架；小
铁钻③用桩围住④（螺母垫圈的）
卷边锁紧
staked-side trailer 两侧插有桩杆的
挂车
stake truck 四周带桩柱的平板车身
（stake body）载货汽车
staking （螺母垫圈的）卷边锁紧

stale air 不流通的空气（见 dead air）

stale gasoline 陈（旧）汽油（放置很久，含有胶质及水分等沉淀杂质，起动性变差）

stalk control 杆式操纵（件）

stalk-mounted 装有转向盘管柱上的

stall ①（机器等的）停车，停住 ②（发动机）超载熄火（由于突然加载、制动、供油不足而熄火的现象）③（液力变矩器）零速（涡轮负载过大而停止转动，但泵轮仍保持旋转，因而只有输入而无输出，即发动机转动、汽车却不动的现象）④汽车间，汽车停存处⑤前排座位⑥焙烧室⑦阻止，拖延，妨害，使（汽车发动机等承受大负荷而）停车

stall characteristic 零速特性（液力传动装置在零速工况下的特性）

stall condition 零速状态（液力变矩器指输入轴转速 n 与输出转速 n_1 之比 $n_1/n = 0$；机械式离合器指离合器从动片不动，飞轮打滑时的状态等）

stalled car 库存（待销）轿车

stalled engine 熄火的发动机（= dead engine）

stall flow （涡轮）零速流量（见 stall speed）

stalling ①（发动机）熄火 ②（液力变矩器的）零速（见 stall speed）

stalling torque 零速转矩（液力变矩器输出轴完全被迫停转时的最大转矩）

stall limit （涡轮性能曲线）零速线

stall margin （发动机等的）喘振边界；零速边际

stall output speed 零速转速（见 stall speed）

stall point 零速点（= stall spot，在一定输入转矩下，液力变矩器的输入轴转速与输出轴转速之比 = 0 时

的输入转速，亦称零速转速 stall speed、stall output speed）

stall speed （液力变矩器等的）零速转速（亦称零速点，指在规定的输入扭矩下，由于负荷过大而涡轮停止转动时的输入转速，γ/min，= stall output speed，亦称零速点，= stall point）

stall spot ①（气流）分离区，分离点②零速点（见 stall point）

stall start （装有液力变矩器的汽车的）零速起步（指首先踏下离合器和制动踏板，将汽车制动，油门全开，在发动机达到最大零速转速后立即接合离合器和松开制动器，使汽车起步）

stall torque 零速转矩（迫使运转中的发动机、电动机等的转速下降到零的负荷扭矩）

stall torque ratio （变矩器）零速变矩比（液力变矩器涡轮转速为零时的输入—输出扭矩比）

stamina 持久力（持续工作能力），耐力

stamp ①印模，图章②特征，性质③标记，记号④印痕，痕迹⑤模压器；冲压装置⑥冲压，模压，压花

stamped-steel engine （用）钢板模压（成型的）发动机

stamping (aluminum, copper, fibre, steel, flat) washer 冲压（成型的铝、铜、纤维、钢、平）垫圈

stamping of foreign matter 杂质印痕（外胎、内胎、垫带的表面和胎里上的杂质压印痕迹）

stampings 冲压制品，冲压废料，捣碎物

stamping steel sheet frame 钢板冲压车架

stamp tester （制动及加速路试时使用的）路面印痕机（在踩踏制动踏板的同时，在试验路面上打出记

号,用以测定制动距离,有的印痕机除制动始点印痕外,还可以每隔1/2、1/4s等任意时间间隔打出印痕)

stance (汽车的)姿势

stanchion ①支柱,柱子,标桩,撑杆②用柱子支撑

stanchion sign (道路上可移动的)柱座标志

stand ①台,架;试验台②机座,底座,支座③站住,站立④经受住

stand-alone 独立的[用于说明独立于其他系统、程序、装置、终端等,如:stand-alone network system (独立网络系统)、stand-alone modem(独立调制调解器)、stand-alone terminal(独立终端、stand-alone module 独立控制模块等)]

standard ①标准,规格;标准样品②机架,架子,支架,立柱③标准的,典型的

standard atmosphere 标准大气压(简称 atm 或 SA, 1atm = 101.325kN/m² = 14.6959 lbf/in²)

standard atmosphere condition 标准大气压条件

standard atmospheric pressure 标准大气压力(= 101kPa)

standard automotive ignition system 标准汽车点火系

standard bar 标准轴,检验轴

standard basic rack tooth profile of bevel gears 锥齿轮的基本齿廓(锥齿轮的当量圆柱齿轮的基本齿廓,见 basic rack tooth profile)

standard bicarbonate 标准碳酸氢盐(简称 SB)

standard block gauge 标准块规

standard coal 标准煤(能源计算单位,1吨标准煤的热能 = 29.31MJ。我国一般计算1吨原煤 = 0.714吨标准煤,1吨石油 = 1.429吨标准煤)

standard condition 标准状态,标准条件(简称 SC)

standard conductivity 标准电导率(简称 SC)

standard container 标准(集装)箱

standard copper 标准铜(含铜 > 96%的工业铜)

standard deviation 标准偏差[简称 SD,指(平)均(平)方(偏)差,亦称 standard dispersion, standard error, 简称 SE]

standard deviation of a single measurement in a series of measurements 测量列中单项测量的标准(偏)差(表征同一被测量值 n 次测量所得结果分散性的参数)

standard deviation of the arithmetic mean of a series of measurements 测量列算术平均值的标准(偏)差(表征同一被测量值的独立测量列中算术平均值分散性的参数)

standard deviation of weighted arithmetic mean 加权算术平均值的标准(偏)差(在多组测量中,表征测量结果中加"权"算术平均值分散性的参数)

standard discharge condition 标准排气状态

standard discharge point 标准排气点(压缩机上认为有代表性的排气位置。此位置随压缩机的结构及安装方式而变化)

standard electrode potential 标准电极电位(= standard potential)

standard (engine) rotation (发动机)标准旋转方向(指从输出端看反时针旋转,即发动机正转)

standard flame ionization analyzer 标准火焰电离分析仪

standard floor model 标准落地式

standard fractional dimension 标准分级尺寸

standard gas 标准气(由待测成分

或其模拟气体与空气或其他适当的平衡气混合而成,且浓度经标定已知的气体)

standard gauge 标准量规

standard head-loss meter 标准压力头损失计

standard hole system 基孔制

standard horsepower 标准功率(铭牌功率)

standard inlet condition 标准吸气状态(亦称 standard suction condition)

standard inlet point 标准吸气点(压缩机上认为有代表性的吸气位置。此位置随压缩机的结构和安装方式而变化,亦称 standard suction point)

standardization 标准化,规格化;标定,校准

standardized 标准的(如:标准化的,标准尺寸的,标准大小的)

standardized installed power output 标准装机功率(装车发动机在标准状态下的输出功率)

standardized performance 标准性能(如:发动机在标准大气状态下的性能)

standardized power (发动机的)标准功率(在标准大气条件下的输出功率,= corrected power)

standardized signal 标准化信号(具有标准化的上、下范围值的信号)

standardizing reagent 标定试剂(指具有标定的被测试物质含量的试剂,用于仪器校准,及确定试样测试物质含量等的比较标准等)

Standard Methods of Testing Rubber Hose (美国材料试验协会的)橡皮软管标准试验法(ASTM D 380)

standard of comparison 对比标准样品

standard of USSR (前)苏联标准

standard potential 标准电位(以标准氢电极作为零电位电极而测出任一材料的相对电极电位)

standard power 标准功率(在标准大气状态下测得的功率)

standard pressure 标准压力(简称 SP)

standard procedure 标准程序(简称 SP)

standard production vehicle 标准生产样车(新汽车在大量生产前,专门生产的一定数量的标准样车,供大量生产审批测试用,见 prototype vehicle)

standard reference condition 标准环境状况(如:确定内燃机功率、油耗率而规定的标准环境条件,包括环境温度、环境压力和相对湿度、增压器进气温度等)

standard reference material 标准参照材料(试验时用,如:标准气,简称 SRM)

standard rotor (转子发动机的)标准(凹坑形)转子(指转子工作面凹坑,不偏前,不偏后,形状对称)

standard shaft system 基轴制

standard system 标准体系(一定范围内的标准按其内在联系形成的科学有机整体)

standard volume rate of flow 压缩机标准容积流量[亦称 standard capacity(标准排气量),经压缩并排出的气体,在标准排气位置的实际容积流量。该流量应换算到标准工况]

standard wire gauge 标准线规(简称 SWG)

stand-by ①备用设备,备用器 ②备用的,预备的;等待用的,应急的,可代用的 ③准备,等待

stand-by lighting 备用照明(事故工作照明,在正常照明系统失效时,使工作能继续进行的照明)

stand-by system 应急系统,备用系统

standby time 待命时间（汽车处于完好状态，但不进行工作的时间）

stand-down 停工，暂时停止工作

standee （公共汽车等的）站立乘客，无座乘客

standing 停止的，停滞的，站立的，不变的，不在运转的；固定的

standing area 停车场地

standing balance 静平衡（= static balance）

standing capacity 站客定员（指允许的最多站立乘客人数）

standing charges （运行的）固定费用

standing costs 固定开支，固定成本

standing height 固定高度，稳定高度，标准高度

standing operating procedure 标准操作规程

standing passenger （公共汽车等的）站立乘客

standing period （发动机等的）停止运转时间

standing room （公共汽车内的）站客空间，站立空间

standing start acceleration （汽车的）静止起步加速度

standing start with dead engine 冷机起步（指从发动机不运转状态下开始汽车起步操作，= dead engine start）

standing start with running engine 热机起步（在发动机运转状态下，开始汽车起步操作）

standing time 停歇时间（汽车停驶时间，公共汽车到站的停车时间）

standing vehicle 暂停车辆（装卸货物或上下乘客等原因短时间停在路上的车辆）

standing water （道路上的）积水

standing wave 驻波（弹性体旋转件高转旋转时产生的看上去形状不变的波状变形）

standing wave of tire （轮胎的）驻波（轮胎高速转动时沿圆周形成的驻波状变形，= ripple wave of tire, traction wave of tire）

standing weight 恒重（将被测量物反复烘干，其重力保持稳定时的重量）

standpipe 竖管（亦写作 stand pipe，如：牵引车后端的竖立的压缩空气管，该管顶端接装挂车连接牵引车制动系的压缩空气软管）

standpoint 观点，立场

standstill 停滞不前，停止，停顿，停歇；搁浅；静止状态

stand test 台架试验

staple ①主要成分，主要原料，原材料；主要产品，常用品②商业中心，重要市场③主题，要领④纤维（平均）长度⑤化学纤维，棉毛纤维，棉丝⑥来源地⑦肘钉，U 形钉；钩环，锁环⑧底板，底子，基底⑨主要的，大量供应的，恒定的，经常需要的，常用的；纺织纤维的⑩用 U 形螺栓固定，用锁环固定；按纤维长度分级

staple commodity 大宗货物，主要物资，重要商品

Star alloy 星牌轴承合金（商品名，锑 17% ~ 19%，锡 9% ~ 10.5%，铜 1%，其余为铅）

starch 淀粉（starch paste 糨糊）

star-delta connection 星形三角接线法（Y-Δ 接线）

star-delta starter 星形三角起动机（Y-Δ 起动机）

star-delta switch 星形-三角形转换开关

star diagnosis 诊断之星（奔驰汽车专用诊断仪的商品名）

5 star front and side impact rating by Euro NCAP 欧洲新车安全评价计划组织的五星制正面和侧面碰撞安全等级（见 Euro NCAP）

star gear 星形齿轮
star handwheel 星形手轮
star junction 星形交叉点（辐射式交叉点）
star knob 星形捏手
star-like curve 星状曲线
star member （万向节的）十字轴（=cross spider, cross）
2-star petrol 两星级汽油（亦称regular petrol，最低一级汽油）
3-star petrol 三星级汽油（中等级别的汽油）
4-star petrol 四星级汽油（一般指辛烷值为98的含铅优质汽油）
5-star (petrol) 五星级汽油（辛烷值100的含铅汽油）
star pinion 小星形轮（小链轮）
StaRR car 自动变换公路-轨道两用车（self-transit rail and road car 的简称）
starred value 标有星号(★)的数值
star section 十字截面
star-shaped disposition 星形排列，星形布置
star-star connection （线路的）Y-Y连接，Y-Y线制
start ①（发动机）起动②（汽车）起步
startability 起动性能，（发动机的）起动性
startability of (motor) fuel （发动机）燃油起动性能
startability of oil 机油（低温）起动性能
start bit 起始位（表示起始信号的二进制位）
start clutch （装在CVT输出轴上的汽车）起步离合器
starter carburettor （发动机的一种冷机）起动化油器（参见Zenith fully automatic starter）
starter control ①起动机控制②起动机操纵件（发动机起动装置的手或脚操纵件）
starter drive 起动机驱动机构
starter engine 起动用发动机
starter field coil 起动机励磁线圈
starter field coil equalizer 起动(电)机磁场线圈中间接头
starter front cover 起动机前盖
starter gear 起动机驱动齿轮
starter gear housing 起动机齿轮传动壳体
starter generator 起动—发电两用机（发动机起动时当作起动机使用，发动机起动后当作充电发电机使用的一台直流电机，亦称，starter/charger，[美] cranking motor，= starter-generator motor）
starter pinion to ring ratio （起动机）小齿轮与（飞轮）齿圈的传动比
starter relay （大型起动机的）起动继电器（起动开关仅流过控制继电器吸引线圈的小电流，而驱动起动机的大电流则由吸引线圈吸合的继电器触点电路供给）
starter rheostat 起动机变阻器
starter ring (gear) （与起动机啮合的）飞轮齿圈
starter shifting lever 起动机接合杆
starter solenoid 起动机电磁开关（由电磁力控制起动机电流接通和断开，从而驱动拨叉，推动驱动小齿轮与飞轮齿圈啮合及脱开的电磁开关）
starter solenoid relay cover 起动机电磁线圈继电器盖
starter solenoid switch 起动机电磁开关（由电磁力控制起动电流接通及断开，并驱动拨叉，推动驱动齿轮与飞轮齿环啮合及脱开的开关，亦简称 starter solenoid 或 solenoid）
starter with internal reduction gear 内带减速器的起动机
Star Tester （福特公司早期自诊断系统使用的）故障诊断仪（商品

名，利用插接线与自诊断插座和蓄电池连接，通过闪光次数显示故障代码）

startindicator light 起动指示信号灯（向驾驶者发出发动机已处于可起动状态的信号灯）

starting ability ①（发动机的）起动性能 ②（汽车的）起步性能

starting acceleration 起步加速（度）(= acceleration from dead stop)

starting aids 起动辅助设备，起动辅助措施

starting air （柴油机等）起动用压缩空气

starting air consumption （柴油机等）起动用压缩空气消耗量

starting and acceleration performance （车辆）起步与加速性能

starting anode （整流器的）起动阳极

starting button 起动按钮开关 (= starter push-button, starter button)

starting cable 起动电缆（连接蓄电池到起动机的带接头的电线）

starting cold 冷（机）起动

starting compensator （电动机）起动自耦变压器

starting compressor 起动用空气压缩机，起动压气机

starting course 起步路段 (= starting distance)

starting crank handle 起动摇把

starting current 起动电流

starting cycle 起动操作循环

starting decompressor 起动减压装置（起动时减少发动机汽缸内的压缩阻力）

starting difficulty 起动困难

starting distance 起动距离（从起步时起，到加速至所规定车速时的距离）

starting engine 起动用发动机 (= barring engine)

starting enriching device （混合气）起动加浓装置（亦称 starting excess fuel device，起动时能增加供油量，起动后自动停止加浓的装置）

starting fare 起步票价（为出租汽车的最低票价）

starting fluid 起动液（柴油机等的起动燃油，= primer fluid）

starting fluid capsule （发动机）起动液囊

starting fluid ignition 起动燃料（引燃）点火 (= auxiliary-fluid ignition)

starting fluid injector 起动液喷射装置

starting force 起动力（起步加速力）

starting friction 起动摩擦

starting fuel （柴油机）冷车起动用燃料

starting fuel fraction 燃油的初始馏分

starting gear ①起步挡（见 first gear）②起动机构，起动装置

starting impulse 起动冲击

starting lag 起动滞后

starting lever 起动机操纵杆，起动操纵杆

starting-lighting-ignition cell 起动-点火-照明用电池（简称 SLI cell）

starting load 起动负载，起步负载

starting material 原材料

starting mode （喷油系统等的）起动工况

starting pedal 起动机踏板（起动机脚踏开关，= starter pedal）

starting performance 起动性能（反映内燃机起动温度、起动时间、起动转速、起动可靠性和起动适应性等的性能）

starting plate （电镀）底层

starting point 起点，基点，始点（简称 SP）

starting preheater boiler bracket

（发动机）起动预热锅炉支架

starting preheater burner （发动机）起动预热燃烧器（如：动预热喷灯）

starting receiver （发动机）起动用高压储气筒

starting resistance 起动阻力

starting rheostat 起动变阻器

starting sequence 起动程序

starting shock 起动冲击，起动振动

starting signal 起动信号

starting speed 起动转速（能够使内燃机起动的最低转速）

starting spring 起动弹簧（柴油机起动时，可使喷油泵油量调节机构处于供油量超供位置，以利于起动的弹簧）

starting switch 起动开关

starting system ①起动（加浓）系②（柴油机等的）起动用汽油机化油器（= starter carburetor, starting carburetor）③（由起动机等组成的发动机）起动系统

starting test 起动试验（包括起动转速、起动时间、环境温度、起动压力、耗气量、耗电量等）的试验

starting time ①（发动机）起动时间②（汽车）起步加速时间

starting time interval （发动机）起动间隔时间

starting torque 起动力矩（指起动时，所需施加的力矩）

starting turbine 起动涡轮机

starting unloader 起动用卸荷装置（减轻起动负荷用装置）

starting-up 起动

starting-up to speed 起步加速

starting valve 起动阀

starting velocity 起始速度（初始速度，初速）

starting work 起动（时消耗的）功

"start" light 起动灯（见"wait" light）

start-off traction （汽车的）起步牵引力（汽车起步时的地面推动力）

start-quantity stop with thermal expansion element （柴油机喷油泵的）热膨胀件（控制型）起动（加浓）喷油量停止机构

start signal 起动信号

start/start system （柴油机的）预热/起动系统（指共用一个开关的预热和起动装置，起动前先将开关转动，通过热敏开关和时间继电器接通预热塞，当燃烧室内达到一定的温度持续一定的时间后，仪表板上的指示灯指示驾驶员进一步转动开关，接通起动机，驱动发动机，启动后即自动断开，亦称两次起动装置）

start-stop control 起动-停机自动控制（系统）（简称SSC，由独立的电子模块控制的节油和减少排放的系统。发动机怠速运转时自动停机，而再次踩踏加速踏板时自动起动）

start-stop lever 开关控制杆，起停操纵杆

start-stop (operation) system 自动起动-停机运转系统（只要踩下离合器或制动踏板发动机即自动停机，松开离合器或制动踏板发动机即自动起动恢复运转）

start-stop synchronism 起止同步

start-stop system 起止装置，启闭装置

start-up groan （变速器轴产生的）起步挂挡（低频）噪声

start-up period 起动期

start-up time ①（发动机的）起动时间②（汽车的）起步时间

start-up wear 起动磨损

starvation 供给不足，缺乏

star washer 星齿垫圈（防松垫圈）

star wheel 星形轮（如：制动器蹄片与制动鼓间隙调整用星轮）

state ①状态,情况 ②指出,表示,叙述

State Development Planning Commission (中国)国家发展计划委员会(原称 State Planning Commission)

state diagram 工况图

state function (热力学)状态函数(见 thermodynamic function)

state highway (美国的)州道,州级公路(属于各州的公路,与 federal highway 等有别),省级公路,省道

state-level appraisal 国家级鉴定

state locus (系统的)状态轨迹(以阻尼系统为例:若以位移 y 为横坐标,速度 dy/dt 为纵坐标,则描述每一时刻 y 与 dy/dt 的点的连线便是该系统的状态轨迹)

statement 叙述,申明,阐述,陈述,报告书

state of charge (蓄电池等的)充电状态(简称 SOC,指所测得的蓄电池容量 Ah)

state of equilibrium 平衡状态

state of motion 运动状态

state of stress 应力状态

state of system 系统的状态(任一系统的状态定义为由 x_1, x_2, x_3, …, x_n, 表述的一组最小数目的变量。若已知这组变量在 $t=t_0$ 时刻的值及 $t>t_0$ 时刻的输入值,则该组变量决定任何未来 $t>t_0$ 时刻系统的状态)

state-of-the-art data 最新技术资料

state-of-the-art facility 现代化设备

state-owned bus company 国有公共汽车公司

state-owned corporation 国有公司

state space method (现代控制理论的)状态空间法(将系统的状态、状态变量、状态轨迹等概念推广至高阶系统,形成一状态空间。状态空间中的一个点对应系统中的某一状态)

state-specified standards 国家标准(国家规定的标准)

State Testing Institution [瑞典]国家试验所

state vector 状态向量[亦称状态矢量,以阻尼系统为例:若其状态变量 $x_1 = y$ "位移", $x_2 = dy/dt$ "速度" 看作是 $X(t)$ 的各个分量,则该二维或多维向量列 $X = [x_1, x_2]'$ 便是该阻尼系统的状态向量]

static 静力的,静态的,静止的

statical equilibrium 静态平衡(= static balance)

statically balanced crankshaft (经过)静平衡(的)曲轴

statically determinate 静定的

statically indeterminate 静不定的(超静定的)

statically restoring moment 静回复力矩(静回正力矩,静回原力矩)

static(al) stability 静力稳定性

statical stress 静应力

statical unstability 静不稳定性

static axle weight 车桥静荷载(汽车静止时,分配在车桥上的荷载)

static balance 静平衡(亦称=statical equilibrium,指旋转体,如:车轮的重量绕其旋转轴线均匀分布)

static balance test 静平衡试验(如:按标准规定,在平衡试验机上测定轮胎在静态中不平衡度的试验)

static beaming test 静(态)弯曲试验(见 beaming test)

static breakaway (离合器等的)静打滑始点

static calibration 静力校准,静态校准

static characteristic(s) 静特性,静态特性

static common emitter characteristics 共发射极静态特性曲线

static cornering light (相对于动态弯道照明而言的)静态转弯照明灯,

1531

固定式弯道照明（= fixed bending light，多与雾灯组装在一起，见 adaptive front-lighting system②）

static crash(ing) test 静载碰撞试验（用加一相当于冲击荷载的静荷载来进行汽车的碰撞试验）

static deflection 静载挠度，静载变形

static deflection of suspension 悬架的静挠度（对于刚度不变的悬架，指汽车满载时静态荷载下悬架的变形值。对于变刚度悬架，指汽车满载时悬架的静载与其相应的瞬时刚度的比值）

static discharger 静电放射器

static drive （液晶显示的）静态驱动（空间分割驱动方式。显示像素相应的两电极之间加有持续驱动的信号）

static electricity 静电（指两物体间摩擦产生的电荷，将一直保持于其中的某一物体，直到释放）

static eliminator （无线电）防干扰电容器（= radio interference suppressor）

static energy 静能，位能，势能

static equilibrium 见 static balance

static eraser 静电消除装置（如：装运汽油的罐车车体上挂装的与地接触的链条等）

static-free 无电波干扰的，不受电波干扰的

static friction coefficient 静摩擦系数（指两物体间最大静摩擦力与该两物体表面间压力的比值）

static friction in the suspension 悬架系统中的静摩擦力

static head 静水头，静压，落差

static ignition timing （发动机）静态点火正时（指发动机非工作状态下的起始点火正时，如：一般发动机是以飞轮外壳上的刻度线与飞轮上的正时符号或正时齿轮盖上的箭头与曲轴端皮带轮上的正时符号对准，来确定所规定的静态，即起始点火提前角，同时利用仪表等将断电器触点调到正好处于刚刚分开的位置）

static interference 静电干扰

static joint 静接合（两静止面间的结合）

static load 静载，恒载

static loaded deflection test 静负荷变形试验（轮胎安装在静负荷试验机上，在规定的内压及相应的静负荷下，测定轮胎变形值的试验）

static loaded radius 静负荷半径（轮胎在静止状态下受法向负荷作用后，从轮轴中心到支撑平面的垂直距离，简称 static radius）

static loading 静荷载，静荷加载

static (loading) stress 静应力，静载应力

static margin 静态裕度（汽车质心到中性转向线的水平距离与轴距的比值。汽车质心在中心转向线的前方时，该值为正，简称 SM）

static measurement 静态测量（对测量期间其值可认为是恒定的量的测量）

static parameters 静态参数（用来表示集成电路和元器件直流特性的电参数。如：直流电压，直流电压比等）

static-plate brake tester 静板式制动试验台

static pressure 静压力，静压（简称 SP）

static RAM 静态随机存取存储器（静态 RAM）

static read/write memory 静态读写存储器（在没有控制信号时，仍能保持数据内容的一种存储器）

static register 静态寄存器

static resistance 静态阻力

static response 静态响应特性，静态响应

static road-adhesion coefficient 道路

静附着系数
statics 静力学；天电干扰；大气干扰；电波干扰
static screen 无线电防干扰屏蔽装置（= radio interference suppressor）
static seal 静态密封件（指在两个固定的表面间起密封作用，防止渗漏和保持压力的部件）
static sent out 静电放射，静电发射
static spring deflection （钢板）弹簧静载变形，（钢板）弹簧静载挠度
static spring rate 弹簧静载刚度
static steering effort test 静态操舵力试验（评价汽车在静止状态下转动转向盘时操舵力大小的试验）
static steering friction coefficient 静态转向（地面）摩擦系数
static suppression 静电干扰抑制（减弱或消除引起无线电静电干扰，如：发啸声，嚓啪声的有害电磁波）
static temperature 静温度（不受流体速度影响所测得的流体温度）
static test 静态试验，静载试验（= static trial）
static timing 静点火正时（最低怠速下，即真空点火提前装置不起作用时的点火正时）
static tire deflection 轮胎静载变形
static tire rate 轮胎静载刚度
static toe （汽车车轮的）静载前束（静载正、负前束的总称。指站在汽车的前方观测，在静荷载下，同一轴两端的车轮轮辋的最前端点间的距离 A 与最后端点间的距离 B 的差值。若 $A<B$，则称静载正前束（static positive toe in），简称"static toe in"。若 $A>B$，则称静载负前束（static negative toe in），或（static toe out）。静态正前束，一般简称前束，静态负前束，亦称前张）
static toe-in 静态前束
static toe-out 静态负前束，静态前张
static torque 静回转转矩
static torsional and beaming test 静载扭转及弯曲试验，静态弯扭试验
static track sinkage 静止履带沉陷量
static trial 静力试验，静态试验（= static test）
static type RAM 静态（型）随机存取存储器（见 RAM）
static unbalance 静力不平衡，静不平衡度（轮胎在静态中的不平衡量。通常以重点与轻点之间的重力矩差表示）
static vehicle weight 静态车重
static weight 静态重力（静荷载）
static wheel balancer 车轮静平衡试验机
station ①站，基地，岗位，台，车站 ②安置，放置
stationarity 固定性
stationary ①固定的，不变的 ②紧配合的
stationary axle 固定轴（指支承轴，= solid axle）
stationary blade 固定叶片，定子叶片
stationary body cylinder 固定缸体式油缸
stationary cabriolet 两门轿车（= coupe）
stationary caliper （盘式制动器的）固定式制动钳（相对浮动式制动钳而言，见 floating caliper）
stationary contact 固定触点
stationary drive attachment 固定作业动力输出附加装置
stationary electromagnets 定子电磁铁组
stationary engine ①固定式发动机（= fixed engine）②固定式内燃机（在固定地点使用的内燃机）
stationary flame front 固定火焰前锋（参见 fixed flame front）

stationary gasoline measuring　固定式汽油计量装置

stationary housing　①固定壳体　②（转子发动机的）固定缸体

stationary housing（KKM）engine　固定缸体转子发动机（固定缸体行星式旋转发动机，= circuitous piston engine）

stationary pole-piece　定子极靴

stationary reaction gear　固定反馈齿轮（如：转子发动机的相位齿轮系中固定于端盖上的齿轮）

stationary ring　静止环（静环）（不随轴做旋转运动的密封环）

stationary rod cylinder　固定活塞杆式油缸（相对于固定缸体式活塞而言）

stationary shaft（DKM）Wankel engine　固定轴式转子发动机（一种内外两转子的发动机，内转子为活塞，外转子为缸体，两转子都围绕同一固定轴旋转，无偏心距，其外转子即旋转缸体，带动输出轴）

stationary shaft transmission　固定轴式机械变速器

stationary state　静止状态，固定状态

stationary test　平稳性检验（鉴别数据的平稳性。即时间历程的统计特征是否随时间的推移而变化。只有随时间的推移，统计特征不变，即平稳的数据，才可以用任意一段时间的样本，来估计母体的统计特征）

stationary torus　环形定子

stationary value　逗留值，固定值

stationary vane　静叶片

stationary vehicle　固定作业用的车辆

stationary wheel balancer　固定式车轮动平衡设备（离车式车轮平衡仪，将车轮拆下进行动平衡测试）

station equipment　车站设施

station utility vehicle　旅行型多用途车（简称SUV，亦称 recreational vehicle。较轿车可提供更大的空间、更多的用途，这类车族起始于Jeep，大致包括：①轻型越野车　②multipurpose vehicle，简称MPV，多用途车，美国称 minivan　③三厢旅行车　④pick up，客货两用车，轿车型客货两用车，俗称皮卡）

station wagon　接站车，旅行车（美，四门厢式小客车的变形，车身延长，后座的后面尚有可放置行李、货物等的空间，车身后端设有车门，车身常为木制，= 英 estate car、estate wagon、universal car，简称 wagon）

statistical accelerometer　统计加速度仪

statistic(al) analysis　统计分析

statistical analysis monitor　（质量管理系统中使用的）统计分析监视器（自动采集生产过程中产品"合格-不合格"的情报，供质量控制统计分析用，简称SAM）

statistical assurance　统计可靠性

statistical cost model　统计估算成本模型（以统计期运输生产过程中实际发生的运输费用与运输量的统计值为依据建立的运输费用估算数学模型——通常为线性回归数学模型）

statistical data　统计资料，统计数据

statistical error　统计误差

statistical estimation　统计评价（= statistical evaluation，statistical validation）

statistical experiment　统计性试验

statistical figures　统计数字

statistical hypothesis　统计假设

statistical independence　统计的独立（性）

statistical inference　统计推断

statistical life　统计寿命（一批机械失效率达某一百分比时的工作寿

statistically significant sample （足以作产品性能统计评价的）有统计意义的样品

statistically significant verification 统计性的有效证明（有意义的统计性核证）

statistical mechanics 统计力学

statistical method 统计法

statistical models evaluation 统计模型评价

statistical property 统计特性

statistical quality control 质量统计管理，质量统计控制

statistical sampling 统计采样

statistical table 统计表

statistical theory 统计理论

statistical uncertainty 统计误差

statistics 统计学

stator 定子［指旋转件系中与旋转件转子（rotor）相对应的不动部分或部分，如：①电机的定子：直流发电机和起动机指由磁场绕组、磁极和机壳组成的磁场部分的整体；交流发动机，则指由三相绕组组成的电枢部分的整体②电容器指其定片③液力减速器的定子，指液力减速器中带有叶片的固定件④液力变矩器，指迫使液流改变方向，给涡轮一个反作用力矩，从而增大涡轮输出转矩的导轮（guide wheel）中未装单向离合器的固定式导轮，此时称定轮，亦称 stator wheel ⑤涡轮机的固定壳体⑥转子发动机的固定缸体］

stator assembly 定子总成（①直流发电机、起动机中由磁场绕组、磁极和机壳组成的磁场部分整体②交流发电机中由三相绕组组成的发电机电枢部分整体，亦称 field frame assembly ③液力减速器中带有叶片的固定件）

stator blade ①定子叶片②（变矩器的）定轮（固定式导轮）叶片

stator bore （转子发动机的）固定缸体（固定缸筒）

stator case 定子壳体

stator coil terminal 定子线圈接线柱（= relay terminal）

stator core 定子铁芯（定子总成的铁芯部分）

stator-rotor play 定子-转子间隙（转子与定子之间的间隙）

stature 站立乘员的身高（从地板到头顶）

status 状况，状态，地位

status display 状态显示器（用于显示某一系统或装置技术状态的变化与完好程度的部件）

statute ①法令，法规②（学校，公司等的）章程，条例，规章制度

statute mile 法定英里（= 5280 ft 或 1609.3m，见 mile）

statutory 规定的，法定的，法规性的，法令的

statutory inspection 法定检验

stay ①支撑物，支柱②支撑

stay alloy 含铜、钛压铸铝合金

staying ①拉、撑，加劲，固定，紧固②刚性结合

staying power 持久力，耐久性

staying quality 持久性

stay-in-grade 不变质的，质量稳定的

stay retainer 固定件（辅助支撑，固定位置、稳定结构用的杆、架、板等，亦称 holder，firming part）

stay tube （支）撑管，支撑管（= stay pipe）

STC 起动牵引力控制系统（start traction control system 的简称，通过施加制动的方法，阻止起步时车轮滑转）

STC system （Cummins 公司柴油机的）分级正时控制燃油喷射系统（step timing control system 的简称）

std 标准，规格（standard）

steadiness test （内燃机运转）稳定性试验（内燃机连续运转较长时间时，测定其主要性能参数稳定性的试验）

steadite 斯氏体，磷化物共晶体

steady 平稳（运动）的，稳定的，固定的

steady acceleration 等加速度

steady creep 等速蠕变率

steady energy input 稳定能量输入

steady flow 稳流（恒态流，定型流）

steady-flow swirl test 稳流涡流试验

steady gradient 均坡

steadying effect 旋转质量惯性效应（=flywheel effect）

steady load test 稳定负荷试验

steady planar detonation 稳定平面爆震

steady pressure 稳定压力

steady pull 稳定的牵引力

steady rolling conditions 稳定滚动条件

steady rotation 稳定旋转（匀速转动）

steady sine excitation test 稳态正弦激振试验（利用激振设备对结构施加正弦激振力，待结构作稳态振动后采集结构对输入响应的数据，经过数据处理得到传递函数或机械阻抗，并采用参数识别方法获得结构的模态参数）

steady speed 稳定速度（均匀速度，定速）

steady state 稳态（加在汽车上的外力，包括道路响应及空气动力不随时间发生变化或汽车操纵输入为常数时的汽车运动状态）

steady-state characteristics 稳态特性（=steady-state performance）

steady-state condition 稳态工况（相对于加速、减速等过渡工况而言，如：发动机在稳定的转速、负荷以及稳定的温度和压力下的工作状态，简称 S-S condition，亦称 steady working condition）

steady state cornering test （汽车）稳态回转试验（改变横向加速度，以一定车速在固定半径的圆弧上行驶，对汽车的不足转向及过多转向特性、侧倾特性、最大横向加速度、保舵力等进行评价的试验）

steady-state engine speed difference 发动机稳态转速差

steady-state error 稳态误差（定常误差，稳定状态误差）

steady state gain in yaw velocity （汽车）横摆角速度稳态增益（=$\frac{1}{1+KV^2} \cdot \frac{V}{l}$，式中：$K$—稳定性因素；$V$—车速；$l$—轴距）

steady-state lateral acceleration （汽车转向的）稳态横向加速度（稳态转向离心加速度，指汽车以等速、等转弯半径转向时的离心加速度）

steady-state ramp delay time （乘法 DAC 的）稳态斜坡延迟时间［基准电压为斜坡电压时，在输出稳态斜坡建立时间结束之后，模拟输出的实际曲线与理论曲线（无延迟）之间的时间间隔］

steady state response 稳态响应（汽车稳态状况下的对外力的响应）

steady-state response test of wheel suspension system 车轮悬架系统稳态响应试验

steady-state solution 稳态解

steady state speed governing rate （柴油机调整器的）稳态调速率

steady-state speed regulation 稳定调速率（由于突变负荷引起转速变化的调速率，其表达式为：$\left|\frac{n_3-n_1}{n}\right| \times 100\%$。式中：$n$—标定转速；$n_1$—突变负荷前的转速；$n_3$—突变负荷后

的稳定转速）

steady-state temperature 稳定工况温度

steady-state turn （汽车的）稳态转弯（等速、等半径转弯）

steady state vibration 稳态振动（振动物体以一定的频率和振幅不断地振动。其若振动频率与外力所施加于振动物体的频率 f_F 一样，则其振幅 x_0 不仅与外来频率 f_F 及外力形成的强迫振动振幅 y_0 有关，而且与本身的固有频率 f_N 有关，即，$x_0 = y_0 / \left[1 - \left(\frac{f_F}{f_N} \right)^2 \right]$，当 $f_F = f_N$ 时，振动物体的振幅 x_0，在理论上变为无穷大，称为共振）

steady state yaw velocity gain 稳态横摆角速度增益（汽车等速圆周行驶时，其横摆角速度 r 与前轮转角 δ 之比，常用来表征汽车的稳态响应）

steady stress 静应力

steady turn 平稳转弯（= sweeping turn）

steady yellow 黄灯信号（绿灯通行信号终止后，红灯禁止通行信号未出现前之的过渡信号）

stealthy 隐形的

Steam Automobile Club of America 美国蒸汽机汽车俱乐部（简称 SACA）

steam blast 蒸汽喷洗

steam bus 蒸汽（机）客车

steam cleaner 蒸汽冲洗机

steam cock 蒸汽阀（蒸汽排出阀，排气阀，放汽阀）

steam engine 蒸汽机

steamer ①蒸汽发生器②蒸汽汽车③蒸汽机

steam-gas 过热蒸汽（= superheated steam）

steam hammer 汽锤

steam heating 蒸汽加热（法）

steaming 汽蒸（蒸烘，用蒸汽处理）

steam jet chiller 蒸汽喷射式冷冻机

steam-operated 用蒸汽机运转的

steam pocket （冷却水套中的）蒸汽泡

steam-powered 蒸汽动力的

steam-powered rotary engine 蒸汽转子发动机

steam pressure 蒸汽压力

steam propulsion system 蒸汽驱动系统，蒸汽动力系统

steam reforming process 水蒸气重整（制氢）法（将水蒸气和碳氢化合物燃料混合，通过在高温中的镍触媒，产生出氢气和一氧化碳，作为汽车用燃料，亦简称 steam reforming，或 steam reformation）

steam-tight 汽密的，不漏气的

steam treatment 蒸汽处理（将工件放在 500～560℃的饱和热蒸汽中加热氧化，使其表面生成一层均匀、坚实、多孔且带有磁性的蓝色四氧化三铁 Fe_3O_4 薄膜，其厚度约 3～5μm，能牢固地附着在工件表面）

steam turbine 蒸汽涡轮机

steam unit 蒸汽（动力）系统，蒸汽装置

steam vulcanizer 蒸汽硫化器

steatite 皂石（= soapstone）

steel ①钢（指含碳量在 0.04%～2.06% 范围内的铁炭合金）②钢制工具；钢制品

steel-angle bearing 大锥角圆锥滚子轴承

steel-armored 装甲的

steel-backed （轴瓦，轴套等）钢背的（亦写作 steel backing）

steel-backed bimetal bearing 钢背双金属轴瓦

steel-backed bronze-faced washer 钢背青铜面双金属推力垫片

steel belt ①钢带②（子午胎胎体帘线层与胎面橡胶层之间，由钢丝帘

线橡胶带制成的)钢丝束带(用以加强胎面部位,保证轮胎周向外形尺寸不变,并将胎体全周紧紧箍住,防止胎面的周向和横向的伸张和压缩,提高胎面的刚性,故亦称钢丝增强层)

steel-belted piston 箍有钢环的活塞
steel belted radial tire 钢丝带束子午线轮胎
steel cable bumper decelerator (汽车)保险杠钢索减速装置
steel casting(s) 钢铸件(简称SC)
steel cord tire 钢丝帘布层轮胎
steel framed structure 钢架结构
steel hoop 钢箍,环形钢筋
steel I-beam 工字钢梁
steel link belt (连续无级变速器CVT使用的一种)钢链节片型传动带(见 metallic belt)
steel magnet 磁钢
steel pack muffler 金属屑片填充式消声器(由金属屑片包围的一多孔管组成的无隔板直通式排气消声器)
steel sandwich 夹层薄钢板(由夹在两层薄钢皮间的聚丙热塑性复合材料芯板组成,可在不降低强度的条件下减轻重量50%,用于制造仪表板、备胎架等)
steel sections 型钢(= steel shapes)
steel-sheet 薄钢板的
steel-sheet disc wheel (冲压)钢板辐板式车轮
steel shell bearing (滑动轴承的)钢背轴瓦
steel-spoke wheel 钢轮辐车轮
steel-studded tire 胎面带金属防滑钉的轮胎(雪地防滑轮胎)
steel tank rectifier 钢壳汞弧整流器(其阳极为钢壳)
steel tip trailer 钢制车身自卸挂车
steel top cab 钢顶驾驶室
steel tube seat 钢管构架座椅

steel vest gasket 夹软钢片爪的石棉橡胶密封垫片
steel welded integral body construction 钢件焊接整体式车身结构
steel wire brush 钢丝刷
steel wire rope 钢丝绳,钢丝索
steel wool filter 钢丝棉芯滤清器
steep grade 陡坡(亦称 steep gradient、heavy gradient、steep incline、sharp incline、steep slope)
steeple head rivet 尖头铆钉
steepness 陡度
steep road 陡峭险路
steep taper 陡锥体(大锥度、大角度的锥体)
steep variation 急剧变化
steer ①驾驶②转向
steer ability 转向性能,转向操纵性
steerability ①可转向性②转向性能
steerable trailer 可转向式挂车(可操纵式挂车)
steerage ①驾驶,操纵,控制②驾驶装置,控制设备
steerage gear 转向机构
steer axle 转向桥(= steering axle)
steer-by-wire controller 线控转向控制器
steered wheel 转向车轮,转向轮(亦称 steerable wheel,指可绕主销轴线回转,实现汽车转向的前轮等,注意与 steering wheel 区分,后者指驾驶人员操纵的转向盘)
steering ①转向②转向机构
steering actuation cylinder 转向助力缸
steering actuator (电子控制液压转向系的)转向执行器(将转向液压变换为推动车轮转向的机械运动的器件)
steering added lighting lamp 转向辅助照明灯(见 DynaView™)
steering angle 转向角(车辆纵向对称平面和转向车轮中心平面与路面

交线间的夹角,亦称 steer angle, cramp angle)

steering angle indicator ①(前轮)转向角指示器②(转向盘)转角指示器

steering angle ratio (四轮转向系前、后轮的)转向角比

steering angle sensor 转向角传感器

steering apparatus 转向装置

steering arm 转向臂[转向杆系中车轮转向节的臂件的通称,亦称 knuckle arm, steering knuckle arm, ①一般指非独立悬架式车辆梯形转向杆系中转向横拉杆与左、右转向节的连杆臂,称转向梯形臂或转向横拉杆臂(tie rod arm)②指非独立悬架梯形转向杆系中与转向直拉杆或独立悬架式转向桥及齿轮齿条式转向机构的转向横拉杆连接带动转向节转动实现转向的臂件,多称 spindle arm,或 steering knuckle arm]

steering arm adjusting screw wrench 转向臂调节螺钉扳手

steering arm pin 转向节臂销

steering arm shaft 转向节臂轴

steering arm shaft felt washer cup 转向节臂轴毡垫盖

steering-assisted vehicle stability control system 见 S-VSC

steering assist rate (动力转向)转向助力率(= fa/Fs%, fa-转向助力, Fs-转向总力,随车速变化,高速时助力率高,而低速时助力率低)

steering assist ratio 转向助力比

steering axis (亦称 steering swivel axis)①(非独立悬架转向桥的)转向主销轴线(= kingpin axis)②(独立悬架转向桥相当于转向主销轴线的、车轮转向时绕之回转的)转向轴线(即:双横臂式独立悬架上、下横臂与转向节连接的球节中心的连线)

steering axis inclination (独立悬架的)转向轴线内倾(简称 SAI,= ball joint axis inclination,见 kingpin inclination)

steering axle 转向桥(装有转向轮的车桥)

steering ball joint (转向轮独立悬架的)转向球节(上、下横臂与转向节连接的球节)

steering band (履带车辆)转向离合器制动带

steering behavior 转向性能(操纵特性,转向特性)

steering bogie 并装转向双桥(如:半挂车的并装双桥有时做成转向桥)

steering box ①转向器(亦称 steering gearbox, steering gear,将驾驶人员操纵的转向盘轴的转动转化为推动转向直拉杆的摇臂的摆动或推动转向横拉杆的齿条横向运动,并按一定比例放大其作用力的机构)②转向器壳体③转向器带壳总成

steering box cover 转向器盖(= steering gear case cover、steering gear housing cover、cover of steering gear)

steering box side cover 转向器侧盖

steering by wire 线控转向(指电子控制模块根据转向盘传递的驾驶者的转向意图,指挥电动机通过齿条-齿轮等转向执行机构实现的车轮转向控制,同时传感元件将路面对轮胎的反作用力,即:原机械式转向机构产生的驾驶者的手感反馈至电子控制模块,以修正转向执行机构的转向力度,确保准确地再现驾驶者的转向意图。此外,电子控制模块还可根据车载摄像系统的信息,自动修正车辆的行驶方向,确保车辆稳定地直线行驶)

steering characteristics 转向特性

steering clutch (履带式车辆的)转向离合器

steering clutch brake （履带式车辆的）转向离合器制动器（＝steering brake）

steering clutch control （履带式车辆的）转向离合器操纵机构（如：转向离合器踏板）

steering clutch driven disk （履带式车辆）转向离合器从动片

steering clutch driving drum 转向离合器主动鼓

steering clutch release （履带拖拉机）转向离合器分离叉

steering clutch release crank axle （履带式车辆）转向离合器分离操纵曲轴

steering clutch release rocking lever （履带式车辆）转向离合器分离摇臂

steering clutch release yoke （履带式拖拉机）转向离合器拨叉

steering clutch shaft （履带式车辆）转向离合器轴

steering clutch spring 转向离合器弹簧

steering-column gear control 转向盘管柱变速杆（位于转向盘柱上的变速换挡机构，＝steering-column gear change，美称 steering column gear shift）

steering-column selector 装在转向柱上的选速杆（装在转向盘柱上的变速杆）

steering-column support 转向柱支架

steering column switch centre 转向盘柱开关中心（指装在转向盘柱上的起动、停机、转向及换挡等按钮和拨杆开关组合件）

steering control 转向操纵件（控制车辆行驶方向的操纵件，如：转向盘）

steering control modes 转向控制方式（驾驶员通过转向系统控制汽车行驶的方式分为 position control 与 force control 两类）

steering control rearward displacement （车辆发生碰撞时）转向控制件（转向盘等）的后移量

steering control valve （动力转向系统由转向盘转角操纵的）转向控制阀

steering control valve pressure losses characteristic 转向控制阀压力特性（阀的压力降与油泵流量之间的关系）

steering control valve response characteristic 转向控制阀灵敏度特性（转向控制阀响应特性，阀的输出口压力与其位移之间的关系）

steering coupling 转向联轴节

steering crank 转向机构曲柄（由转向臂通至横拉杆的中间连接件）

steering cross rod jaw 转向横拉杆接头

steering cross tie-rod 转向横拉杆

steering cross tube 管状转向横拉杆

steering curve 转向曲线（汽车沿给定曲线行驶时，其前桥中心的轨迹）

steering cylinder 转向助力缸

steering damper (unit) 转向（机构中的）减振器（用以减轻在不平道路上行驶时，前轮摆动等引起的转向盘振摆，亦称 steering wheel damper, steering shock eliminator）

steering drag link 转向直拉杆（在转向摇臂和转向节臂之间传递力和运动的杆件）

steering drive axle 转向驱动桥（除有驱动桥的作用外，还有转向桥的作用）

steering drop arm 转向垂臂（亦称 steering gear arm、drop arm）

steering effort 操舵力（操纵转向盘的力）

steering effort generator 见 steering reactive torque generator

steering effort test 操舵力试验(评价汽车在静止状态、极低速、中速、高速和大转弯时操舵力适宜性的试验)

steering evaluator 转向检测器(测定转向机构自由行程等)

steering feel 转向路感(驾驶人员从转向盘上感觉到的车辆、路面对转向操作输入的响应状况,见 road feel)

steering feeling (驾驶者操纵转向盘的) 操舵感

steering force ①(作用于转向盘上的)转向操作力,操舵力②(汽车的)转弯力(路面对轮胎的侧向反作用力,见 cornering force)

steering force characteristic 转向力特性(①在机械转向系中,摇臂轴输出力矩与转向轴输入力矩之间的关系②在动力转向系中,在额定工况下,系统压力与转向轴的输入力矩之间的关系)

steering force for keeping a given control 保舵力(为了保持汽车给定运动状态而加在转向盘上的切向力)

steering front wheel 前转向轮(亦称 steered front wheel)

steering gain 转向增益(见 steering sensitivity)

steering gear angle ratio 转向器角传动比(转向盘转角的增量与转向摇臂轴转角的相应增量之比)

steering gear angle ratio characteristic 转向器角传动比特性(转向器角传动比与转向盘轴转角之间的关系)

steering gear angle ratio characters 转向器转角传动比特性

steering gear arm 转向摇臂(见 pitman arm)

steering gear backlash 转向传动件间的背隙(= backlash in the steering)

steering gear case cover 转向器盖(= steering box cover, steering gear housing cover)

steering gear checker 转向机构检测器

steering gear checking scales 测转向力的弹簧秤

steering gear clearance 转向器传动间隙(转向器各传动副之间的传动间隙之和)

steering gear clearance characteristics 转向器传动间隙特性(转向器传动间隙与转向盘轴转角之间的关系)

steering gear connecting rod end 转向直拉杆端头(见 drag linked)

steering gear connection 转向机构控制杆系(= steering linkage)

steering gear efficiency 转向器传动效率(转向器输出功率与输入功率之比)

steering gear efficiency characteristic 转向器传动效率特性(转向器传动效率与转向盘轴转角之间的关系)

steering gear efficiency test 转向器传动效率试验

steering gear forward efficiency 转向器正效率[指转向盘的输入由转向摇臂输出时的效率, = ($P_1 - P_2$)/P_1. 式中: P_1—作用在转向盘上的功率; P_2—转向器中的摩擦功率]

steering gear lock 转向角限止器(= steering lock、steering motion stop、steering stop)

steering gear max. output 转向器最大输出力矩(设计中规定的转向器允许最大输出力矩)

steering gear reduction ratio 转向齿轮机构减速比

steering gear reverse efficiency 转向器逆效率(指由转向摇臂输入、转向盘输出时的效率, = ($P_3 - P_2$)/P_3, 式中: P_3—作用于转向摇臂轴上的功率; P_2—转向器中的摩擦功率)

steering gear slider （蜗杆指销式转向机"worm and peg steering gear"中的）指销（转向盘轴转动时，该指销沿转向盘轴上的转向蜗杆螺旋槽滑动，通过其销臂和销臂轴将转向盘轴的运动传给转向摇臂，亦称 peg 或 stud）

steering gear strength test 转向器强度试验（包括静扭、落锤冲击及疲劳强度试验）

steering gear with variable ratio 变传动比转向器（其传动比随车速的改变而改变）

steering geometry ①转向几何图形 [指用点、线、面来表示转向杆系的布置形式和运动关系及在各种布置形式下，杆件的长度和相对间角度关系的几何图形，如：阿克曼转向机构（Ackermann steering mechanism）的几何图形为梯形] ②转向几何学（关于用几何学方法表示转向杆系布置形式、运动关系及在各种布置形式下，各杆件的长度和角度及角度变化的数值的学科）

steering head （摩托车和自行车主车架前端插装并支撑前轮叉与方向把的）方向柱管，方向柱（亦称 steering support stem）

steering head angle （摩托车）方向柱后倾角（方向柱轴线与其延长线接地点的垂直线间的夹角，相当于汽车转向主销后倾角）

steering head axle （摩托车）方向柱轴线

steering inner articulated shaft 转向传动轴（转向管柱内通过万向节与转向盘轴连接的转向力矩传动轴）

steering inner tube 转向柱内管（= steering column tube）

steering jack 转向伺服液压油缸（转向助力油缸）

steering kingpin 转向主销（亦称 steering kingbolt、steering knuckle bolt、steering knuckle pin、steering knuckle pivot pin、steering swivel pin、steering yoke pin）

steering knuckle 转向节 [亦称 steering swivel，装在非独立悬架前桥梁两端或独立悬架控制臂端，安装前轮并使前轮在转向拉杆的操纵下绕其转向盘轴线回转实现转向的组合件或整体件，由带前轮轴承的转向节轴（stub axle）和安装转向主销或控制臂球销的销孔的转向节体和转向节臂（steering arm）组成，有的还包括梯形臂（tie rod arm）]

steering knuckle angle 转向节夹角 [转向节（的轮毂）轴与轴向轴线（转向主销）间的夹角，亦称 included angle]

steering knuckle arm 转向节臂（亦称 steering knuckle gear rod arm、steering arm、track arm）

steering knuckle bracket （独立悬架）转向节支架

steering knuckle bush 转向节（主销）衬套

steering knuckle bushing 转向节主销衬套（= pivot pin bush）

steering knuckle kingpin dust washer 转向节主销防尘垫

steering knuckle lever ①转向节臂 ②转向横拉杆臂

steering knuckle spindle 转向节（的轮毂）轴（亦称 steering stub、steering stub axle）

steering knuckle stop screw 转向节限位螺钉

steering knuckle support （独立悬架）转向节支架

steering knuckle thrust bearing 转向节推力轴承

steering knuckle thrust washer 转向节推力垫片

steering knuckle tie rod 转向横拉杆

steering knuckle tie rod ball seat 转

向横拉杆球节座
steering knuckle tie rod end 转向横拉杆端头（= tie rod end）
steering knuckle tie rod spring 转向（节）横拉杆弹簧
steering knuckle tie rod yoke 转向横拉杆叉
steering knuckle type 转向节形式
steering link 转向拉杆
steering linkage ①转向传动杆系（指将转向器的运动传递至转向节臂的全部传动杆件）②（履带车辆）转向离合器操纵杆系
steering linkage angle ratio 转向传动机构（杆系）角传动比（转向摇臂转角的增量与同侧转向节转角的相应增量之比）
steering linkage layout 转向杆系的布置
steering linkage reduction ratio 转向杆系减速比
steering lock ①转向角限止器（= steering gear lock）②转向盘锁（如：当点火开关断开时，将转向盘锁死的防盗装置）
steering lock angle 最大转向角（= angle of lock、steering locking angle）
steering manipulator 转向操作装置（如：转向盘等）
steering moment 操舵力矩（转动转向盘的力矩。操舵力与转向盘有效半径的乘积）
steering moment for keeping a given control 保舵力矩（保舵力与转向盘有效半径的乘积）
steering pad （汽车）转向试验场
steering pillar 转向柱管（转向盘柱管）
steering pillar shell 转向盘柱壳，转向柱壳
steering pinion 转向齿轮
steering pitman arm 转向摇臂（= steering gear arm）

steering planetary （履带式车辆）行星转向机构
steering post 转向盘柱（见 steering column）
steering post gearshift 转向盘柱变速（变速操纵杆在方向盘下方转向柱上，= column gearshift）
steering pump 转向助力油泵
steering rack （齿条式转向器的）转向器齿条
steering range 转向轮转向角度范围
steering reaction force （车轮经转向机构传至转向盘的）转向反作用力
steering reactive torque generator （供驾驶模拟装置使用的）转向反作用力矩发生器（亦称 steering effort generator）
steering (reduction) ratio ①转向减速比（转向变速比，亦称 steering box ratio、steering gear ratio）②转向系角传动比（指转向盘转角与转向轮转角之比，见 steering system angle ratio）
steering reference position 转向基准位置（一般车辆为后桥中心点）
steering resisting torque 转向阻力矩（转向轮转向时，地面作用于转向轮上的阻力矩）
steering response 转向响应［施加在（汽车转向）操纵部件上的输入所引起的汽车运动，包括驾驶员加在制动踏板、加速踏板上的输入，以及各种外力干扰所引起的转向响应］
steering response rate （电子控制转向系统的）转向响应速率
steering reversal 转向回正
steering robot （控制）转向盘（的）机器人（用于汽车无人驾驶路试输入转向信息）
steering sensitivity 转向敏感性［操纵输入增加规定量时，稳态响应增益的增加量，主要指横向加速度、

横摆角速度等,亦称 steering gain (转向增益)]

steering sensor (丰田公司 TEMS 等上使用的)转向传感器[测定转向盘轴(steering shaft)转动方向和转动量(转角)的传感器]

steering shaft thrust bearing 转向盘轴推力轴承

steering shaft with worm 带蜗杆的转向盘轴

steering shock eliminator 转向机构减振器(亦称 steering shock absorber)

steering side tube (连接转向摇臂与转向节臂的)转向直拉杆(位于转向机侧,故名,= drag link)

steering spindle 转向节轴(安装转向车轮轮毂轴承和车轮的短轴,亦称 steering stub axle、steering axle、steering stub)

steering stability (汽车的)转向稳定性(指在转向过程中,受到外界干扰时,维持或迅速恢复原运动状态的能力)

steering stabilizer 转向稳定器

steering stem (摩托车的)方向柱(见 steering head)

steering stiffness test 转向器刚性试验(将转向器安装在刚性试验台上,固定其摇臂末端不动,在转向盘轴上施加力矩,然后测绘转向盘轴上所受力矩值及其相应的扭转角度值的关系曲线,算出其刚度值)

steering stops 转向角限位器,转向限止装置(确定转向角的极限,常见限止机构由转向节臂上的凸耳与前横梁上的可调止动螺栓组成)

steering stub 转向节轴(见 steering spindle)

steering swivel 转向节(见 steering knuckle)

steering swivel bush 转向节主销衬套(= pivot pin bush)

steering system angle ratio 转向系角传动比(转向盘转角的增量与同侧转向节转角的相应增量之比)

steering system ratio 转向系传动比(包括两部分:即转向系角传动比和力传动比。角传动比是指转向盘的转角和驾驶员同侧的转向车轮转角之比。转向系力传动比是指从轮胎接地面中心作用在两转向轮上的合力与作用在转向盘上的操舵力之比)

steering system stiffness 转向系刚度(转向节固定,转向盘输入的力矩增量与其产生的角位移增量之比)

steering tie-rod 转向横拉杆[非独立悬架式转向梯形机构中连接左、右转向节梯形臂(steering arm),将某一车轮转向节的运动传给另一车轮的横向拉杆。独立悬架式转向传动杆系中,中央拉杆等两端与转向节臂连接的横杆件]

steering tie rod 转向横拉杆(连接左、右梯形臂,并传递力和运动的杆件)

steering torque indicator 转向力矩指示仪

steering track rod 转向(横)拉杆

steering trapezium 转向梯形(结构)

steering tube 转向柱管(转向盘柱管,= steering-column tube, steering wheel tube)

steering tube bush 转向盘柱管衬套

steering universal joint 转向万向节

steering wheel (驾驶人员操纵的)转向盘[注意勿与 steered wheel(转向车轮)混淆]

steering-wheel actuator 转向盘使动器(汽车诊断、性能测试等时,由电子计算机控制、代替人工操纵转向盘的装置)

steering wheel adjustment control 转向盘调节装置操纵件(调节转向盘相对于驾驶员位置的装置的操纵

件)

steering-wheel air bag 装于转向盘上的(驾驶员安全)气囊

steering wheel angle ①转向盘转角(以汽车直行时左、右转向轮平均转向角为零时转向盘的位置为基准测定的转向盘角位移) ②转向盘(倾斜)角(转向盘上平面与水平面间的夹角)

steering-wheel-angle responsive 4 wheel steering system 转向盘转角响应式四轮转向系[亦称 steering-wheel-angle sensitive (或 dependent) 4 wheel steering system, 转向盘转角小时, 前、后轮向同一方向转向, 当转向盘转角大时, 前、后轮向不同方向转向。这样既可保证高速转向稳定性, 又可减小低速时的转向半径]

steering wheel angle sensor 转向盘转角传感器

steering wheel angular velocity sensor 转向盘(转动)角速度传感器

steering-wheel arm 转向盘辐条

(steering-wheel attached) brake lever (装在转向盘上的)制动操纵杆

steering wheel centre 转向盘中心(转向盘上平面中心)

steering-wheel cover (汽车)转向盘罩

steering wheel diameter 转向盘的直径(转向盘的外径)

steering wheel extreme lower point 转向盘下缘最低点(转向盘下边缘与 Z 平面相切的点)

steering-wheel flutter 转向盘摆振

steering wheel force-steering angle tester 转向盘转动力-转角测试仪

steering wheel free play gauge 转向盘间隙测量仪(由转向盘指示器和轮胎转动检测器组成, 用于检测汽车转向机构的自由间隙)

steering-wheel gear change 转向盘柱变速装置

steering-wheel geometry 转向盘安装几何位置(转向盘几何定位)

steering-wheel hub 转向盘毂

steering wheel impulse input test 转向盘转角脉冲输入响应试验(以脉冲形式进行转向盘转角输入, 汽车横摆角速度、侧倾角等为输出来评价汽车的响应特性试验)

steering-wheel lock 转向盘锁, 转向器锁(= steering lock)

steering-wheel-mounted 安装在转向盘上的

steering wheel out-side edge 转向盘外缘(转向盘外径的边缘)

steering-wheel play 转向盘自由间隙

steering-wheel puller 转向盘拉具(拆卸转向盘的专用拉器)

steering-wheel rim 转向盘轮缘

steering-wheel (rim) effort 转向盘操纵力, 操舵力

steering wheels adjustment control 转向盘调节装置操纵件(调节转向盘相对于驾驶员位置的装置的操纵件)

steering wheel speed responsive method (电子控制动力转向系转向助力的)转向盘角速度响应法(转向助力的大小随车速和转向盘转动的角速度而变, 车速越高, 转向助力越小; 转向盘角速度越快, 转向助力越高。当车速一定时, 转向助力则随转向盘角速度的加速而升高, 而在转向盘的某一角速度下, 车速变高, 则转向助力变小, 采用这一方法的系统称 steering wheel speed responsive type hybrid power steering, 复合动力是指液压泵的输出流量取决于由车速控制的液压泵驱动电动机和控制转向盘转速的驾驶人员两个动力源转向盘转速响应型复合动力转向系)

steering-wheel tilting angle 转向盘倾

斜角（见 steering wheel angle②）
steering-wheel torque 转向盘转矩
steering wheel tube 转向柱管（= steering tube）
steering wheel with steel-wire arm ①钢丝辐条转向盘②（有时亦指）钢丝辐条转向轮
steering worm （蜗杆滚轮式转向器等的）转向蜗杆
steering worm gear 转向机构蜗杆涡轮传动
steering worm sector shaft 转向蜗杆扇形齿轮轴
steering yoke 转向节叉
steering yoke bolt 转向节主销，转向主销（= steering kingpin）
steersman （汽车等机动车辆）驾驶人，驾驶员
steers'manship ①驾驶术②驾驶人员
stellite 司太立特合金（商品名，耐高温、耐磨、硬度高，含钴70%~90%、铬10%~25%或少量钨硅的钨铬钴合金）
stellite cast valve seat insert 钨铬钴合金铸造气门座镶口
stellite faced valve 钴铬钨合金镶面的气门
stem 杆，柄
stem gear 连轴齿轮（与齿轮制成一整体的轴）
stem-to-guide clearance 气门杆与导管间的间隙
step ①级②台阶，阶梯③步调，步骤④手段，方法，措施⑤节距⑥（上、下车的）脚踏板
step and repeat process 分步重复工序
step attenuator 分级衰减器，步进衰减器
step bearing 立式推力轴承
step bolt 半圆头方颈螺栓（车身踏脚板固定螺栓）
step-bore cylinder 异径缸（阶梯径缸，塔形缸）
step-by-step 逐级的，步进的，逐步的
step-by-step approach （检查故障原因的）逐步（排查）法
step-by-step construction 阶梯式结构
step-by-step method 步进法，逐步法
step-by-step variable (speed) transmission 多级变速传动装置
step change 有级变速
step climbing capability （乘客上车时）登上踏脚板的能力
step-ditch-obstacle performance （车辆）过台阶-壕沟的越障性能
step-down ①降低电压的；变低的，降低的，逐步降下的 ②下车，下台；逐步缩小，逐步降低
step-down frame 台阶式车架（亦称 cranked frame，低架平板挂车和半挂车的车架，其前方转向部分离地较高，后方下降至离地很低，而呈阶梯状，以便降低装货高度和便于装卸重物，简称 step frame）
step-down gear 减速挡，减速齿轮，减速传动
step-down transformer 降压变压器
step drive system 步进式驱动系统
step feeler gauge 阶形厚薄规
step frame semitrailer 台阶式车架半挂车
step-free entrance 无踏板的（车厢）入口
step-gear transmission 分级换挡变速器（即常用的齿轮换挡式变速器）
step-head piston 阶梯顶活塞
step height ①踏步高（两踏步板上平面之间的距离）②台阶高度（在模拟—数字和数学—模拟转换曲线中，两相邻台阶之间台阶值之差的绝对值，亦称 step size）
step lamp 踏板照明灯（亦称 step

light, running-board lamp)

stepless acceleration 无级加速（连续加速）

steplessly variable automatic transmission 无级自动变速器（= continuously variable transmission, infinitely variable transmission，速比可连续无级变化的变速器的通称）

stepless type power window 无级式电动车窗（压住按钮时，不断升降，松开按钮立即停止升降）

step load(ing) program （零部件试验）递增加载规程

stepney （汽车）备用轮胎,备胎

step of an analogue-to-digital or digital-to-analogue conversion 模拟—数字或数字—模拟转换的台阶（在转换代码中，指各组独立对应关系中的任一组；在转换曲线中，与独立对应关系相等的曲线中的任一部分；在 ADC 中，代表模拟输入值的一小区段和相应的数字输出码；在 DAC 中，代表数字输入码与相应的不连续模拟输出值）

step on the gas 踩踏加速踏板（= step on the accelerator）

stepped automatic transmission 分级式自动变速器［指常规的液力或电子控制液力自动变速器,相对于无级式连续变速自动变速器（stepless continuously variable automatic transmission）而言］

stepped bore 阶梯式孔

stepped control 有级控制（步进式控制,步进式操纵）

stepped reflector （汽车前照灯等的）双焦反光镜（具有两个不同焦距的抛物面形反光镜）

stepped rim 阶梯式(断面)轮辋

stepper motor type idle air control device 步进电动机式怠速空气控制装置（亦写作 stepper motor type IAC，见 IAC）

stepping accuracy （步进电动机的）步进精度（用步进角%表示）

stepping angle （步进电机的）步进角

stepping motor 步进电动机（由电脉冲信号控制旋转的电动机。一般，一个脉冲信号电动机转动一定的角度，亦称 pulse motor、step motor、stepped motor, stepped motor，用于电子控制式燃油喷射系统的怠速控制、减振器的阻尼控制、旁通进气道和油路通过面积的调节等）

stepping of spring leaves 钢板弹簧的梯状层叠

stepping relay 步进式继电器

step (ping) switch 步进开关（分挡开关,分级转换开关）

step plate 踏步板（乘员上、下车踏脚的构件）

step response 阶跃响应（汽车对以阶跃形式进行的转向输入的响应）

step response test 阶跃响应试验（以阶跃形式进行转向输入,按横摆角速度、侧倾角等评价汽车响应特性的试验）

step response time 阶跃响应时间（当输入产生阶跃变化时,输出由初始值第一次达到最终稳态值与初始稳态值之差的规定百分数时的时间）

step seal 阶式密封

step signal 阶跃信号

step-stress test 递增应力疲劳试验

step-test procedure 逐步试验法

step transformer 分级变压器

steptronic 多挡电控（宝马公司电子控制五前进挡自动变速器商品名）

step-up 升高（电压）,升压；加速,促进,逐步增加,使…断断续续；上车

step-up coil 升压线圈

step-up gear 加速挡

step-up instrument 无零点仪表（=

suppressed zero instrument）

step-up jet （化油器的）省油器量孔（= power jet ②）

step-up planetary-gear set （可使所传递的转速增大的）加速式行星齿轮系

step-up transformer 升压变压器（输出电压高于输入电压，亦称 step up converter）

step value（of a DAC） （DAC）台阶值（表示数字输入码的模拟输出值）

step valve 阶梯式滑阀，级阀

step width（of an ADC） （ADC的）台阶宽度（对应于一个台阶范围化的两端模拟值之差的绝对值）

stepwise technique 逐步回归法

steradian 球面度（亦称 sterad，国际单位制的立体角单位，代号为 sr，1 球面度为 1 立体角，其顶点为球心，它在球面上所对应的面积等于以球半径为边长的正方形的面积，整个球面所包的立体角为 4π sr）

stereo ①立体②立体

stereo acuity 立体视力（双眼对立体性及物体相对距离的分辨能力）

stereo autographic drawing instrument 立体影像（自动）绘图机

stereo effect （车用无线电话及收音机等的）立体声响效应

stereo lithographic model 立体影像模型（计算机辅助设计中的计算机屏幕显示的立体设计物模型）

stereoscopic 立体的，体视的

stereoscopic "bird view" navigation system 立体鸟瞰图导航系统

stereoscopic vision 立体影像，立体视觉，立体视力（= stereopsis）

stereo tape player 立体声磁带唱机

sterilizer 消毒器

sterilizing vehicle 消毒车

stethoscope ①听诊器，听筒 ②用听诊器检查

Stevens loudness level 斯特闻斯响度级（为噪声响度级中最常用的一种）

Steyr 斯太尔（奥地利 Steyr 公司生产的重型汽车牌名，中国重型汽车工业公司 1984 年引进该车型系列产品的制造技术）

StG SW 装在转向盘上的各种（控制）开关（= switches installed on the steering wheel）

stick ①棒，杆，柄 ②黏着，卡住

stick control 手柄控制

sticking 卡住，黏附，发涩，烧结（如：活塞环黏结，触点烧结，电刷卡死，制动拖滞，气门黏结等）

stickness 黏着性，发涩性，黏性

stick shift （手动变速器的）换挡杆换挡

stick-slip （滑动件处于边界润滑和大静摩擦力状态下的不正常）滞着滑动，黏滑现象

stick transmission 变速杆换挡型变速器

sticky 黏性的，胶黏的，发涩的，黏住的

stiffen 加强，加劲，使坚固

stiffener ①加强肋，加强杆，加强条，加强梁（等加强件）②增强剂，硬化剂

stiffener angle 加强角钢

stiffening ①固化②强化，加强③变稠，稠化

stiffening liner （车身板件等的）加强衬里

stiffening member ①加强件（= stiffener①）②加强梁（= stiffening beam）

stiffening rib 加强肋

stiffness 刚度（弹性体所受外力的增量与其所产生的位移或转角的增量之比）

stiffness constant 刚度常数

stiff shaft 刚性轴

stiff spring 刚度大的弹簧

still ①蒸馏器,蒸锅②静止的,平静的,不流动的,没有活力的,不含气泡的③使静止;蒸馏

stillson wrench 管子扳手(= pipe wrench)

still tube 蒸馏管

stilt tractor 高架式拖拉机,高跨式拖拉机

stimulate 促进,刺激

stipulate ①规定,限定,约定②保证③坚持要求以…为协议条件

stir ①搅拌,搅动②激起,鼓动

Stirling cycle 斯特林循环(亦称 stirling gas cycle,1816 年英国人 Robert stirling 发明并制造出了第一台使用空气作为工质的斯特林发动机,整个循环由等温压缩、等容加热、等温膨胀、等容冷却组成,其循环热效率理论上可达 60%～65%,但除去机械摩擦、附件驱动、工质流动压力损失等,实际效率最高为 30%～40%)

Stirling-electric(series) hybrid 斯特林发动机/电力装置复合动力汽车(采用斯特林发动机与蓄电池储能-电动系统相串联,作为复合动力的汽车)

Stirling engine 斯特林发动机[按实际斯特林循环工作的连续燃烧、往复式活塞外燃机,由热膨胀区、加热装置、热交换器、冷却装置、冷压缩区、汽缸、活塞及将往复运动变为旋转运动的机构组成。定量的气体工质封闭在发动机中,交替加热与冷却,加热时工质膨胀,推动活塞下行做功,冷却时,压力下降,活塞上行。最早用空气作工质,1960 年后采用氢气作工质,可用煤、柴油等任一种燃料作能源。它工作平顺,燃烧易于控制,低污染。早期的斯特林发动机为一缸两个相位相差 90°活塞的菱形驱动形式,称驱气活塞 displaser 型,其结构复杂,不适宜于汽车使用。目前各国研制的多为一缸一个活塞的四缸连通斜盘驱动型(swash plate type)或称双作用型(double acting type)]

stirring torque 搅拌力矩(机械密封正常运转时由旋转组件对流体的搅拌作用而引起的力矩)

stitch bonding 连续点焊,缝焊(= stitch welding,亦称 continuous spot welding)

stitched flow rotor housing cooling system 转子发动机缸体穿梭流动式冷却系(冷却液沿缸体上的轴向通道往复流动)

STLR 半挂车(semitrailer 的简称)

1st/2nd speeds striking rod (机械式变速器的)1/2 挡(换挡)拨叉轴

stochastic(al) 随机的(= random)

stochastic convergence 随机收敛(依概率收敛)

stochastic industrial processes 随机工业过程,随机工业法(将马尔科夫过程、排队论等原理应用于换代对策,机器、车辆维修及供求分析等)

stochastic process 随机过程(= random process)

stochastic queuing systems (公路交通等的)随机排队系统(随机排队方法,随机排队模式)

stochastic sampling 随机采样

stock ①余量,储备②毛坯,原料③现货④(工具的)柄,把,架

stockage maintenance 存放维护,存库维护

stock allowance 机械加工留量,机械加工裕量

stock car ①成批大量生产的汽车②存库待售汽车③标准系列汽车(指一般大量生产,在市场上销售

的汽车)④以大量生产的车型为基础的赛车(在美国特指由全国市场销售车辆赛车协会规定作为赛车用的轴距120in,排量7000mL以下的普通大量生产车)

stock car race (成批生产的)普通汽车比赛(区别于竞赛专用赛车比赛)

stock engine ①市场出售的大量生产的发动机②库存发动机(供总成互换修理时换用)③装在 stock car 上的发动机(参见 stock car④)

stock holding network (供应部门向制造厂提供原材料的)料库网

stock ignition system 储能型点火系(能量存储型点火系)

stock production 大量生产,成批生产(= mass production)

stock rack-body truck (运输大牲畜用的)栅栏式载货汽车

stock size ①标准尺寸②常备货量,库存量

stock solution 储(备溶)液,备用溶液

stocky driver 粗柄螺丝起子(= stubby driver)

Stoichi D-4 system 理论空燃比(混合料燃油)直接喷射(燃烧)系统(的简称,亦称λ = 1 direct injection combustion system,相对于直接喷射稀混合气分层燃烧系统而言,"-4"表示4型)

stoichiometric air-fuel ratio 化学计量空燃比,理论空燃比(简称 stoichiometric ratio,化学计算理论上完全燃烧所要求的空气/燃油比。汽油的理论混合比为14.7:1,甲苯为13.1:1,异辛烷为15.05:1)

stoichiometric(al) 化学计算的,化学计量的,化学当量的

stoichiometrical fuel-air ratio 燃空当量比(燃空比与理论燃空比的比值,简称当量比)

stoichiometric composition 化学计量成分,理想配比成分

stoichiometric deficiency 理想配比不足(化学计量欠缺)

stoichiometric excess 理想配比过剩(化学计量过剩)

stoichiometric impurity 化学计算杂质,理想配比杂质

stoichiometric mixture 理论混合气(= theoretically correct mixture)

stoichiometric mixture direct injection combustion system 见 Stoichi D-4 system

stoichiometric mixture ratio 理论混合比(= theoretically correct mixing ratio、chemically correct air-fuel ratio、stoichometric ratio 的旧称)

stoichiometric mixture strength 化学计算混合气浓度,理论混合气浓度,理论计算混合气强度(= stoichiometric MS、theoretically correct MS,见 mixture strength)

stoichiometry 化学计量学

stoke ①沱(运动黏度单位,简称 St,1 沱 = 1cm²/s,参见 kinematic viscosity) ②添加燃料,供给燃料③连续烧结

stolen car 被偷盗的轿车

stone ①石料,石头②宝石③英石(英制常衡重量单位,代号 st,1st = 14lb,但实际应用中肉类为 8lb,羊毛是 24lb,麻是 32lb,玻璃是 5lb 等,见 avoirdupois weights)

stone blocks 石块

stone bolt 地脚螺栓

stone bruise 由于碰撞石块而造成的轮胎损伤

stone deflector (汽车车身的)防飞石护板(亦称 rock guard、stone guard、stone shield,一般装于前保险杠下或后翼板前边,防止碎石击伤车身)

stone guard 砂石防护罩(板)(=

rock guard)
stone pavement 石料路面，石路面
stooge 副驾驶员，驾驶助手
stool ①平板②垫板③托架
stool plate 垫板
stop ①停止，停车，阻碍，阻止，妨碍，停留②车站③限位器，定位器，止动器；挡块
stop ahead sign "前面(临时)停止通行"标志（置于临时停止通行标志之前的预告标志）
stop-and-go bucking motion 汽车窜动（汽车在减速后猛然加速时所产生的现象，主要是由于发动机的转速突然升高而引起的，参见 bucking）
stop-and-go driving （城市行车等）停停走走驾驶，停-走式行车（指经常停车、起动的行车）
stop-and-go operation 停停走走的运行（= stop-and-start operation）
stop and go signal 停止和通行信号（交替指示停止和通行的信号，红、绿灯交替指示信号）
stop-and-go test （汽车）停车-起步试验（= stop-start test）
stop and license plate light 制动和牌照灯的组合灯（= stop-license plate light）
stop-and-start operation 停停走走运行（汽车在经常停车、起步的市区条件下的使用，= stop-and-go operation）
stop and start system 停机与起动系统（亦称"stop & go" system，停车急速运转时发动机自动停机，踩踏加速踏板时发动机自动起动，此项技术称为 auto stop /start tech）
stop and tail light 制动和尾灯的组合灯（= stop-tail light）
stop bit 停止位（表示停止信号的二进制位）
stop button 停止按钮（如：制动按钮，断流按钮）
stop chain 止动链（参见 snubber chain）
stop check valve 止回阀
stop-controlled intersection 停车控制式交叉路口（车流停止控制式交叉路口，红绿灯管理式交叉路口）
stop control lever 停机杆（柴油机喷油泵的停止供油杆）
stop counter 停车次数计数器
stop frequency （车辆在运行中的）停车频率
stop hitch 带脱钩装置的挂钩（= clutch release hitch）
stoping place 停车场
stop interval 停车间隔时间
stop lamp combined with number plate and tail lamp 将牌照灯和制动灯组合在一起的停车尾灯
stop lamp switch 制动灯开关
stoplight drag （红灯时不熄火，发动机高速运转至离合器打滑，不惜付出离合器磨损和变速器振动代价，以便等到红灯过后的瞬间）高速起步（亦称 jack-rabbit start）
stop(-light) switch 制动信号灯开关
stop line （汽车）停车线，停止线，止动线（= stop mark）
stop mechanism 制动机构，停车机构
stopmeter 制动距离记录仪
stop nut 防松螺母（锁紧螺母）
stop-off material （在电镀件非电镀表面上涂覆的）隔镀材料（及类似作用的隔离材料）
stoppage ①阻止，阻塞，阻碍②中止，停止，停歇，停工③（机器运转中的）故障
stopped time 停止时间，停车时间（旅程中由于交通上的理由而停车的时间）
stopper ①止动器，挡块②塞子，堵头，螺塞

stopper ring 止动环（定位环，挡环）

stop piece 挡块，行程限制块

stop pin 止动销

stopping ability 制动能力（= stop ability）

stopping and starting test 停车-起步试验（= stop-start test）

stopping brake 坡道驻车制动器，斜坡停车制动器［= hill holder，注意与一般驻车制动器（parking brake）不同］

stopping capacity （汽车制动系的）制动停车能力

stopping distance ①（一般指）停车距离（指驾驶员反应时间的行车距离 + 制动距离）②（偶见指）制动距离（= braking distance，指自踩制动踏板起至车停的距离）

stopping distance from 20 miles per hour 在20mile/h初速下的制动距离

stopping distance test ①制动距离试验②停车距离试验

stopping sight distance 停车视距（指能看见障碍物时，车辆与障碍物间的距离是否足以使汽车制动停车，见 minimum non-passing sight distance）

stopping time （制动）停车时间（从驾驶员感官受到"必须停车"的刺激的瞬间起，到汽车停止时止的时间，= stop time，比 braking time 多一段驾驶员反应时间）

stop plate 止动板，断流片

stop rod 止动杆，定位杆

stop screw 限位螺钉，止动螺钉

stop sign 停车标志（设在无信号控制的交叉路口，要求汽车完全停止在路口停车线前，在确保安全的前提下，按规则通过交叉口，= stop signal）

stop spring 止动弹簧

stop-start economy （发动机）在经常性的反复停车和起步工况下的燃料经济性（如：在市区行驶的条件下）

stop-start test ①（汽车）停车-起步试验②（发动机）停机-起动试验（亦称 stop-start trial）

stop street （车辆进入干道，主要街道前）停车等待通行的街道

stop, tail and reversing light 制动灯、尾灯和倒车灯的组合灯

stop (tail) lamp ［美］制动信号灯（亦称 stop light，踩踏制动踏板时该灯发亮，一般装在车身后部，英称 brake lamp）

stop valve 截止阀（如：断流阀，停气阀，停止阀）

stop washer 止动垫圈

stop watch 停表（秒表，跑表）

stop watch figures 秒表读数

stopway 停车道

storage ①仓库，堆栈，储藏室②（电子计算机）存储器③积累，积储，保存，储存，储藏

storage ability 可存放性，长期存放稳定性

storage battery ①（由多个单格电池组成的）蓄电池②可充电电池（= secondary cell）

storage bin （客车等的）储物舱

storage capacitor 蓄电型电容器

storage capacity ①储藏量，库容量②蓄存容量；存储器容量③（蓄池）容量

storage cell （组成蓄电池的）单格电池

storage energy in primary capacitor （电容放电点火系）储存在初级电容器中的能量（单位：J，= 1/2CV^2，式中：C—初级电容器电容量，F；V—放电时电容器两端的电压，V）

storage failure rate 长期储存损耗率

storage fuel tank （燃料油）储油罐

storage garage 长期停车库（汽车存车库）

storage gate 存储栅（一种加上电压可使电荷存储的电极，它与半导体之间用绝缘层或结隔开）

storage life 保存期限，储存寿命（＝shelf life）

storage life before unpack 封存期（内燃机出厂时油封并采用规定的方法保存而不锈蚀机件的期限）

storage lifetime 存放寿命（器件能正常工作的最长存放时间）

storage mode （液晶显示的）存储型（撤销驱动信号后，仍可保持可视信息的显示类型）

storage modulus of elasticity 储能弹性模量（复弹性模量的实部）

storage pad （汽车）存放场

storage register 存储寄存器（亦称memory register，从主存储器中取出的信息、数据临处理前的存储区）

storage shear modulus of elasticity 储能切变模量（复切变模量的实部）

storage space 储藏室容量，储藏空间

storage/stake truck 仓栅式汽车（具有仓笼式、栅栏式结构的车厢，用于运输散装颗粒食物、畜禽等货物）

storage stiffness 储能刚度（复刚度的实部）

storage system ①储备系统②存储系统

storage tank corrosion protection 存储罐防锈（装置）

storage temperature range 储存温度范围（可保存，不会使材料和器件变质的温度范围）

storage test 储存寿命试验

storage tire rack 轮胎储放架

storage trailer 仓库挂车（作为一种临时性的移动仓库）

storage zone of data 数据存储区（存储器内包含一个或几个存储单元的小区，它是存储器可供选择的最小部分）

stored energy constant （储能式飞轮等的）储能常数（见 factor of inertia）

stored energy function 储能函数

stored energy in ignition coil （电感点火系统）储存于点火线圈中的能量（单位：J，$= 1/2LI^2$。式中：L—初级电感，H；I—断电电流，A）

stored energy transmission 储能式传动装置（如：储能飞轮等，简称SET）

stored heat 储存热，蓄热

stored inert gas pressure sensor （安全气囊复合式充气器储气罐内的）惰性气体存储压力传感器

stored program 存储程序

storeroom 仓库，储藏室

store tank 存储罐（＝storage tank）

storing stability 储存安全性，储存稳定性

storm 暴风雨（雪）（见 whole gale）

storm curtain （篷顶车的）防雨篷帘

stovebolt （通用公司的）雪佛兰直列六缸顶置气门式汽油机（绰号）

stoving 烘干，焙干

stoving finish （车身用的）烤漆（工艺），烘干清漆

stow ①装载，装填，堆置②收藏，隐藏，包装

stowage ①仓库，存放处，存储物②存放费，保险费③储藏，存放

stow-away arm rest 折叠扶手，可翻藏的扶手

STR ①（发动机）短时额定功率（short time rating）②直线，直的（straight）③滤网；拉紧装置（strainer）④窄条，跑道（＝strip）

strada mode （跑车、赛车等的行驶模式之一的）道路行驶模式
straddle 跨，跨立
straddle attachment ①跨装附件②跨装法
straddle carrier ①龙门式吊装运输车（采用门架式结构，驾驶室及发动机一般在门架上方，吊装设备在门架下方，行走机构在门架底部）②高架长货运输车，木材运输专用车
straddle-mounted bearings 跨式安装的轴承（轴承布置在加载点的两侧）
straddle-mounted pinion （轴承）跨式安装（于两端的）主动小锥齿轮
straddle truck 龙门式吊运车
straddle type 跨装式（如：主降速器驱动小齿轮的前后两端都用轴承支撑的方式）
straight ①（跑道，道路）直线部分；直线区段，直线布置②直的，直线的，直线前进的
straight-ahead 正向前方的
straight-ahead position of steering wheels 转向轮在直前行驶时的位置
straight-air shift system 气动换挡系统
straight alcohol 纯乙醇（纯酒精）
straight angle 平角（= flat angle）
straight axle 直轴
straight bar seal （转子发动机转子）端面直线密封条
straight base rim 平底轮辋
straight beam 平行光束
straight bevel gear 直齿锥齿轮（指齿线是分度圆锥面的直母线的锥齿轮）
straight-braced frame 带直加强横梁的车架
straight chain paraffins 直链烷烃

straight check valve 直通式止回阀
straight cock 直旋塞（= straight way cock）
straight connecting rod 直连杆
straight-cut gear 直齿齿轮（= straight-tooth gear, 见 spur gear）
straight cylinder 直列式多缸发动机（= cylinder in line engine）
straight diesel 直列式柴油机
straight drive 直接挡驱动
straight-eight 直列八缸（发动机）（= eight cylinder engine）
straight engine 直列式发动机（= in-line engine）
straightening 校直，矫直，矫正
straight face piston ring 平活塞环
straight flute 直槽，直沟
straight forward ①顺向的②流水作业的③简单明了的，易懂的
straight frame semitrailer 直纵梁车架半挂车
straight gasoline 直馏汽油
straight gear（wheel） 直齿轮
straight-line 直线
straight-line approximation method 直线近似法
straight-line body 直线型车身
straight-lined 直线的
straight-line depreciation 直线折旧（法）（与使用年限或里程成正比的折旧价格计算方法）
straight-line distance 直线距离（= air-line distance, crow-light distance）
straight-line engine 直列式发动机（= in-line engine, straight-type engine, 简称 straight engine）
straight-line motion 直线运动
straight-line pattern 直线花型
straight-line running characteristics 直线行驶特性
straight line stability （汽车）直线行驶稳定性
straight-line stopping test 直线停车

制动试验
straight-line stopping testing 直线制动停车试验
straight mineral oil 直馏矿物油
straight motion stability 直线行驶稳定性（汽车直线行驶状态受到外部干扰后，保持或恢复原来行驶状态的特性）
straightness 正直度（平直度，直线性）
straight oil 无添加剂的纯矿物油
straight-on 直通的
straight pin 直销
straight pipe thread 圆柱管螺纹
straight pipe union 直管接头
straight roller bearing 直滚柱轴承
straight-run ①直馏的②直馏馏分，直馏产品③直的
straight-run gasoline 直馏汽油（=distilled gasoline）
straight-running 立即可工作的（完好的，技术状况良好的）
straight-run of pipe 一段直管
straight sided axial worm-worm 轴向直廓蜗杆（亦称 ZA-worm，齿面为阿基米德螺旋面的圆柱蜗杆。其端面齿廓是阿基米德螺旋线，轴向齿廓是直线，故亦称阿基米德蜗杆，=Archimedes worm）
straight-side deep centre rim 直边深槽轮辋
straight-sided flank （凸轮型面）直线腹部（直线工作侧面）
straight sided normal worm 法向直廓蜗杆（亦称 ZN 蜗杆，在垂直于齿线的法平面内，或垂直于齿槽中点螺旋线的法平面内，或垂直于齿厚中点螺旋线的法平面内的齿廓为直线的圆柱蜗杆，均称为法向直廓蜗杆）
straight-side flat rim 直边平底轮辋
straight-side profile 直线齿廓（齿廓为直线）

straight-side tyre 直边轮胎
straight skidding （车辆）纵向滑移
straight thread 圆柱螺纹
straight-through 直通的，直流的
straight-through arrangement 直线排列，直线布置
straight-through combustion chamber （燃气轮机）直流式燃烧室
straight-through drive 通轴式传动（=through drive）
straight-through transmission 通轴式变速器（输入、输出轴在同一轴线上）
straight-tooth bevel gear 直齿锥齿轮
straight (toothed) spur gear 直齿圆柱齿轮
straight truck 不带挂车的载货汽车，单（个货）车（=rigid lorry）
straight valve （内胎）直气门嘴
straight-vaned fluid flywheel 直叶片（叶轮式）液力耦合器
straightway ①直线跑道，直线段，直线道路②没有弯曲的，笔直的；直线行进的；作用于一个方向的③易懂的，立刻
straight worm 圆柱形蜗杆（=cylindrical worm）
strain ①张紧，拉紧；拉力，张力②应变[由外力所引起的物体原始尺寸或形状的相对变化，通常以百分数（%）表示]；变形③过滤
strain ageing impact absorbing energy 应变时效冲击吸收功（经规定应变人工时效后试件的冲击吸收功）
strain ageing impact toughness 应变时效冲击韧度（试件缺口底部单位横截面积上的应变时效冲击吸收功）
strain amplitude 应变幅（应变范围的一半）
strain analysis 应变解析（分析）
strain cracking 应变裂纹
strain energy （材料的）应变能

(弹性势能)

strainer ①滤清器（多指全流式粗滤器）②滤网③筛子，网筛④拉紧装置，拉条

strainer cartridge 滤油器芯

strain figure 应变图

strain-gage accelerometer 应变仪式加速度计

strain-gage active length 应变片有效长度

strain-gage torque meter 应变仪型扭矩测量仪

strain ga(u)ge 应变仪（将应变量转变为电信号的传感元器件）

strain-ga(u)ge indicator 应变仪指示器

strain hardenability （金属材料的）应变硬化性

strain hardening exponent 应变硬化指数（亦称 n-value "n值"，指经验的真实应力与真实应变关系式 $\sigma = K\varepsilon^n$ 中的指数 n）

strain-optical coefficient 应变光学系数

strain rate 变形率，应变率

strain ratio 应变比（一次应变循环中两个规定应变值的代数比值，通常有：①最小应变与最大应变之比②应变幅与平均应变之比）

strain-recording equipment 应变记录仪器（= strain-recording instrument）

strain sensor 应变传感器

strain tensor 应变张量

strait 狭窄的

strake 抓地齿，（车轮）铁箍

strand ①（合股的，导线或绳索的）股②要素，成分

stranded ignition wire 多股点火高压线

stranded wire 合股线（= twisted wire）

strangler （化油器）阻风门（choke 的旧称）

strangler overrun valve 阻风门旁通阀

strangling of gas 气阻

strap ①带，皮带，金属带②嵌条，狭条③窄板④搭接片（线），蓄电池各单格电池同极性接线柱的连接片⑤搭接；用带子捆扎；用带子测桶的周长，围测

strap brake 带式制动器（= band brake）

strap drive 传力片驱动（指离合器盖通过沿圆周切向布置的弹性传力钢片结构来带动压盘随飞轮一起旋转，这种传动结构形式可在轴向和旋转方向提供一定程度的挠性，克服了凸台—窗孔式驱动结构的缺点，目前用得较多）

strap tension 制动带的张紧度（制动带的拉力）

strap wire 带状电线(如：蓄电池的接地线)

strategic petroleum reserve 战略石油储备（指一个国家根据战略性目标储备的石油量）

strategy ①策略，谋略②控制模式，运转模式，工作模式（= mode）

stratification 层次，层；分层；层理；层叠形成；成层作用；层化

stratification effect 分层（充气和燃烧）效应

stratification process 分层混合气形成过程（见 stratified charge）

stratified charge 分层充气（为扩大稀混合气稳定工作的极限，在火花塞附近形成浓混合气，在其他部位形成稀混合气的分层充气方式）

stratified charge engine 层状充气发动机，分层充气发动机（简称 stratified engine，采用分层充气方式的汽油发动机，见 stratified charge）

stratified charge fuel injection 分层充气燃油喷射

stratified combustion 分层燃烧(指汽油机先在火花周围燃烧较浓的混合气,而当有了高温燃烧火焰以后,再喷向主要燃烧室,用喷焰点火法使那里的稀混合气着火燃烧的分层、分阶段的稀薄燃烧)

stratified mixtures 分层混合气(指层状燃烧发动机中,在电火花附近形成的浓混合气层和在主燃烧室内形成的稀混合气层)

stratified sampling 分层采样

stratosphere ①同温层②平流层

stratospheric ozone 同温层臭氧

stratum 地层,岩层,层[(复)strata]

stray ①(复)杂散电容,寄生电容②无线电干扰

stray current ①涡流②涡电流(= eddy current, foucault current)

stray light (使对面来车驾驶员有炫目危险的汽车前照灯)杂散光,散射光

stray parameter 寄生参数,杂散参数

strain(o)meter 应变仪,应变计

streak ①条纹,斑纹,条痕,画线;拖影,条状擦纹,条状擦伤②擦伤;加条纹,形成条纹;疾驰

streak line ①(气流或液流的)流线;流脉②条纹线

streak line method (汽车空气动力学气流可见化技术中的)流脉法(如:在风洞试验中使用可见烟实现气流流脉可见的方法)

stream ①流(如:车流,气流,液流)②流线③流动,流出,倾,注

streamer (车身在风洞里做试验时采用的)飘带

stream filament 流束,流线

stream friction 流动摩擦

stream function 流量函数

stream hardening 喷水淬火

streamline ①流线(型)(的)②气流③流水线④把…设计成流线型,使流线型化;使产生层流

streamline body ①流线型物体(在空气中运动时,其外形廓线处处与当地相对气流方向平行,亦即不发生气流分离的物体,所受阻力较小)②流线型车身

streamline contour 流线型外廓

streamlined 流线型的

streamlined reefer housing (装在厢式货车车厢前部,驾驶室上方的)流线型导风罩,导流罩

streamlined section 流线型断面

streamlined tail 流线型车尾

streamlined truck 流线型载货汽车,流线型货车

streamline fairing 流线型罩(见AOA device)

streamline fender 流线型翼子板

streamline flow 层流(流线型流,= laminar flow)

streamline form 流线型(= stream line shape, aerodynamic form)

streamline mudguard 流线型挡泥板

streamliner 流线型物(如:流线型车辆)

streamline wing 流线型翼子板

stream velocity 流速

street 街道,道路

street car [美]市内有轨电车(亦称tram-car,或简称tram)

street car detector 有轨电车探测器

street cleaning vehicle 街道清扫车(= street vehicle, street cleaner, street-sweeping vehicle, street sweeper)

street crossing 十字街口

street curb 街道路缘石

street elbow 异径弯(头)管,带内外螺纹的弯管接头,长臂肘管

street flusher 街道清洗车(= roadway flusher,参见 motor water car)

street lighting 街道照明

street loading zone ①（街道上的）装卸区②（公共汽车和电车乘客上下的）站台

street name sign 路名标志，街名标志

street network （城市）街道网

street plate （用于街上行驶的）履带板

street rod （稍加改造使之适合在市区街道行驶的）加速赛用车

street sprinkler 街道洒水车（= street sprinking truck）

street traffic 街道交通，市内交通，市区交通

street (type) version 适用于城市行驶的变形车

street washer 街道冲洗车（= motor water）

strength ①强度（金属抵抗永久变形和断裂的能力。常用的强度判据有屈服点、抗拉强度等）②（溶液）浓度③力度

strength analysis 强度分析

strength asymptote 强度渐近线

strength at pulsating load 脉冲荷载强度

strength at repeated alternation 交变荷载强度（疲劳强度）

strength-deformation characteristic 强度-变形特性

strengthen 加强，增强，强化；加固，巩固；硬化；使放大

strengthening rib 加强肋

strength factor 强度系数，强度因数

strength margin 强度安全系数（强度裕度，后备强度系数，最大容许负荷对实际额定负荷之比）

strength of charging current 充电电流强度

strength of material ①材料强度②材料力学

strength of pressure 压强

strength per unit area 单位面积强度

strength under shock （耐）冲击强度

strenuous condition 紧张状态；受力状态，受力状态

stress 应力（物体受外力作用后所导致物体内部之间的相互作用力称为内力，单位面积上的内力即为应力）

stress alternation 应力交替变化（变负载）

stress amplitude 应力幅（应力循环中最大应力和最小应力代数差的一半）

stress amplitude ratio 应力比（见 stress ratio）

stress area 应力面积

stress coat 应力涂层（检验应力用的涂料层，= brittle lacquer coating）

stress concentration 应力集中

stress corrosion 应力腐蚀（因金属材料应力过大而引起的腐蚀）

stress crack (ing) 应力裂纹（①应力过大引起的零部件腐蚀裂纹，亦称 stress corrosion cracking②应力检测中使用的涂层产生的裂纹，亦称 stress cracks）

stress distribution 应力分布（= distribution of stress）

stressed 受应力的（受荷载的）

stressed skin car （由车身壳体板件承受荷载的整体无车架）应力壳式车身轿车（= unitized car, frameless body car）

stressed skin construction body （大客车的）应力外壳结构型车身（车身外壳板与构架焊接成一整体，其构架承受轴向力，而外壳板承受剪切力，参见 skeleton construction body）

stress-elongation curve 应力-延伸曲线

stress fluctuation 应力脉动，应力波动

stress function 应力函数
stress gradient effect 应力斜率效应（应力梯度效应）
stress history 应力变化历程（应力随有关参数的变化曲线）
stress intensity 应力强度
stress-intensity calibration 应力强度标定（亦称 K calibration，K 标定，一种基于经验和解析结果的数学表达式，它表明特定条件下应力强度因子与载荷及裂纹长度的关系）
stress-intensity factor 应力强度因子（均匀线弹性体中特定形式的理想裂纹尖端应力场的量值）
stressless corrosion 非应力腐蚀（与应力无关的金属腐蚀）
stress-number of cycles to failure curve 应力-疲劳曲线（导致试件损坏的应力循环次数曲线，简称 stress cycle diagram, S-N curve）
stressometer 应力计
stress-optical coefficient 应力光学系数
stress-optic law 应力光学定律
stress peening （表面）喷丸强化（曲轴圆角等处的一种喷丸强化处理工艺）
stress producing force 引起应力的外力
stress ratio 应力比（不对称应力循环中最大应力与平均应力之比，= stress amplitude ratio）
stress recorder 应力记录仪
stress relaxation 应力松弛（在规定温度及初始变形位或位移恒定的条件下，金属材料的应力随时间而减小的现象）
stress relaxation curve 应力松弛曲线（用剩余应力作为时间的函数所绘制的曲线）
stress relaxation rate 应力松弛速率（单位时间的应力下降值，即给定瞬间的应力松弛曲线的斜率）

stress relaxation test 应力松弛试验（在规定温度下，保持试件初始变形或位移恒定，测定试件上应力随时间变化关系的试验）
stress-relief 消除应力的
stress relief annealed 消除应力退火的（低温退火的）
stress-relief tempering 消除残余应力的回火
stress-relieving 消除应力处理（稳定化处理，如：低温退火）
stress reversal 应力反向
stress-rupture limit 持久强度极限（在规定温度下，试件达到规定时间而不断裂的最大应力）
stress-rupture notch sensitivity factor 持久缺口敏感系数（缺口持久试件与光滑试件断裂时间相同时的应力比率或应力相同时断裂时间的比率）
stress-rupture plasticity 持久塑性（材料在一定温度及恒定试验力长期作用下的塑性变形）
stress-rupture test 持久强度试验（在规定温度及恒定试验力作用下，测定试件至断裂的持续时间及持久强度极限的试验）
stress-strain curve 应力-应变曲线（应力与应变的关系曲线，亦称 stress-strain diagram）
stress-strain gauge 应力-应变计
stress tensor 应力张量
stress time superposition 应力时间叠加作用
stress to rupture 断裂应力
stress wave 应力波
stretch ①伸长，伸展，延伸 ②拉长，拉直，拉紧 ③加宽，扩大，扩张 ④铺设 ⑤一段路程，（一次通过的）距离，路段 ⑥可拉伸的
stretch bend test 拉伸弯曲试验（简称 SBT）
stretch elongation 拉伸延伸率（=

tensile elongation)
stretcher （绳，索，带等的）拉紧装置
stretcher level(1)er 拉伸矫直机
stretcher strain 拉伸应变（亦称 luder lines）
stretch factor 拉伸系数，伸展系数
stretching device 拉伸装置，张紧机构（= tightening device, stretcher）
stretching force 拉力，张力
stretching resistance 抗拉强度（= stretch resistance）
stretching screw 拉紧螺杆
stretching skin 张拉蒙皮（先将外或内蒙皮张紧，然后固定在客车车身骨架上，此时蒙皮受应力，可增加蒙皮刚性，减轻由于蒙皮振动而引起的噪声）
stretch of road 路段
stretch resistance 抗拉强度（= stretching resistance）
stribeck curve 斯萃伯克曲线（指滑动轴承摩擦面间的摩擦力 F 随 ZN/P 而变化的关系曲线。其中，Z—润滑油黏度；N—摩擦面间相对速度；P—摩擦面间压力，可表征摩擦面间的润滑状态，如：边界摩擦、混合摩擦或全液体摩擦，及其润滑状态的转变等）
strickle ①刮平，刮光②刮扳③磨石，油石
strict ①严格的，严密的，严谨的②精确的
strident 轧轧响的，吱吱叫的
striker ①差速锁②（车门）闩眼，（发动机罩或行李舱）闩眼③（变速器）换挡拨叉，变速叉；（离合器）拨叉
striker clutch 拨叉式离合器
striker (clutch) fork （离合器）分离拨叉（= clutch fork, clutch throwout yoke, release clutch yoke, clutch release fork）

striker mechanism （车门的）锁销碰锁机构
striker plate （车门锁扣等带闩眼的）碰板
striking ①打击；冲击；放电；触发；起弧②显著的，惊人的
striking current 起弧电流（击穿电流）
striking energy 冲击能量
striking film 起镀膜（开始的一层电镀膜）
striking fork （机械式变速器各挡位换挡拨叉轴上的）凹形碰栓（变速杆选挡头通过该碰栓推动换挡拨叉轴）
striking potential 起弧电位（引燃电位，放电电位）
striking rod （机械式变速器的换挡）拨叉轴（美称换挡拨叉滑轨"shift rail"，见 selector rod①）
striking velocity 撞击速度
striking voltage 起弧电压；放电电压
striking wrench 冲击扳手（= impact wrench）
string ①弦（线）；线，带，细绳②一串，一列
string drive 弦线传动
string electrometer 弦线式静电计
stringency （规则的）严格性
stringency of test 试验规则的严格性（试验结果精度）
stringent 迫切需要的，紧急的；严格的，精确的，必须遵守的；有说服力的
stringer ①纵桁，桁条，系梁，纵梁②纵向加强肋，纵枕木③吊绳，架设装置
strip ①拆卸，拆散，拆开②除去，取去，摘取③（轮齿）折断④剥去，剥落；（齿面的）剥伤，（螺纹）磨伤⑤简易跑道⑥簧片，带钢⑦狭片，长条，窄条，棒，束

strip chart （自动记录仪）纸带记录图

stripe ①条纹，镶条，包条②（公路上的）车道③种，类，派④加上条纹，在…上画线，使成条纹状

strip heater 电热丝式加热器

strip inspection （机器）解体检查（拆成零件进行检查）

stripped 拆开的

stripped-down vehicle ①减少装备的车辆（减少某些附件和设备）②拆散的车辆，解体的车辆

stripped engine 无附件发动机（基本发动机，= bare engine, basic engine）

stripped plasma 完全（电离的）等离子体

stripped thread 已滑牙的螺纹

stripped weight （不带驾驶室及车身，但加满燃料的）空车重量

stripper ①拆卸器②剥皮机；去膜机；涂层消除剂③汽提塔（用蒸馏法从气体状态的原料油中提出轻质油分的塔）

stripping ①拆开，拆卸②剥离，去掉覆盖层

stripping and re-assembly 拆装（拆散重装）

strip solder 钎焊焊条

strip steel 带钢，扁钢

strip(-type) fuse 熔断片（片状熔断件）

strip type seals 片式密封装置（条状密封装置）

strip wiring 带状的线束

strobe 频闪测试仪（见 stroboscope）

strobe flash 频闪光（指频闪观测器的闪光，闪光放电管的闪光，亦写作 stroboflash）

strobe propagation time 选通传输时间（在选通或类似的控制输入端与规定输出端之间的传输时间）

strobe timing light 频闪正时灯

strobophonometer 爆震测声计（爆震强度计，测汽油发动机爆震时的声响强度）

stroboscope 频闪测试仪（包括点火正时用的频闪测试灯在内的各种利用频闪原理进行测试的装置的通称，俗称 strobe，或 strobe lamp，strobe light）

stroboscopic effect 频闪效应（荧光灯及其他气体放电灯点燃后，由于交流电频率的影响，使发射出的光线产生相应频率变化的效应）

stroboscopic instrument 频闪测速仪（亦称 strobotac）

stroke ①行程（a. 指往复运动件两端止点间的距离，= stroke distance，如：活塞行程指活塞上、下止点间距的长度；b. 指在从一止点到另一止点运动期间所发生的过程，= working process，如：活塞的进气行程，指活塞从上止点向下止点运动中发生的新鲜充量进入汽缸内的过程）②（指改装不同的曲轴以加长或缩短活塞行程来）增减发动机排量

stroke adjustment 行程调整(机构)

stroke bore ratio 行程缸径比（活塞行程与汽缸直径的比值，亦称 stroke-diameter ratio）

stroke coefficient 行程系数

stroke counter 冲程计数器

stroked crankshaft 加长行程曲轴（可使活塞行程加长的曲轴）

stroke limiter 行程限制器

stroker （使用）加长行程曲轴的发动机

stroke simulator ①（线控制动系统中可使驾驶者产生踏踩常规制动踏板的感觉的制动踏板）行程模拟器②制动踏板行程发生器（丰田电子控制制动系统中，装在制动主缸总成内的液压件。当电子控制系统执行控制功能时，产生与驾驶员制动

踏板力相对应的踏板行程）

strokes per minute 每分钟行程（数）

stroke volume （发动机的）汽缸工作容积（行程容积，汽缸排量，亦称 piston displacement, piston swept volume, stroke capacity, stroke volume, swept volume, = 活塞顶面积×行程）

stroking 通过增加行程来增加汽缸工作容积

stroking test 使零件在往复运动中经受考核的试验（如：使制动液压部件的皮碗、活塞不断地进行往复运动以试验其寿命）

strong 强的，有力的

strong gale 烈风（九级风，风速 20.8～24.4m/s）

strong parallel HEV 超强并联式混合动力车系统（亦写作 strong parallel HV。Bosch 公司推出的并联式混合动力车系统商品名，该系统用于两款 VW 的混合动力车。其动力为一台 3.6L, 245 kW, 440N·m, V 型汽油机和一台 38kW, 300N·m, 连续最高转速 6700r/min, 最高转速 8500r/min 的一体式直流电动机-发电机）

strontium 锶（Sr）

struck car （在碰撞事故中）被撞击的轿车

2-S1-2 truck-trailer combination 2-S1-2 拖挂列车（即一辆双轴牵引车，拖一辆单轴半挂车，再拖一辆双轴全挂车，其符号 S 代表半挂车，数字代表轴数，= tractor semi-trailer with a full trailer）

2-S1 truck-trailer combination 2-S1 拖挂列车（即二轴牵引车拖一辆单轴半挂车，其中 S 代表半挂车，1 代表单轴）

structual height （车辆的）结构高度

structual length （车辆的）结构长度

structual width （车辆的）结构宽度

structural adhesive 结构用黏合剂（用于黏结车身等的各种构件）

structural analogue 结构模拟

structural analysis 结构分析

structural battery 车身结构板件蓄电池（见 battery skin）

structural dynamics modification 结构动态修正，结构动态修改（简称 SDM, 利用模态分析得到的频率、阻尼数据及振型，对汽车车架的结构刚度、阻尼、质量等进行修正，参见 simulation mode analysis）

structural failure 结构故障（制件等的结构破坏，损坏）

structural features 结构特征，结构特点

structural integrity test 结构完善性试验（根据规定的试验要求和程序，如：制动系是通过多次频繁制动等来试验结构是否完善）

structural machinability 结构工艺性（指在一定的生产规模和生产条件下，零件结构在机械加工和装配时的难易程度。它是评价零件结构优劣性的技术经济指标之一）

structural parts 结构元件，结构件

structural shapes 结构用型钢

structural stability 结构稳定性

structural steel 结构钢

structural testing setup 结构试验装置

structural weaknesses 结构的薄弱环节

structural weight 结构重量（结构质量的旧称）

structure ①结构，构造②建筑物，构造物③装置；组织；机构

structure analysis 结构分析

structure-borne 构造物产生的，固体结构产生的（如：噪声、振动等）

structure classification symbol 结构分类标志（结构承载等级标志）

structure design 结构设计

structure diagram 结构图

structured problem 结构化问题（指人类面临的问题，可分两类：充分结构化问题和弱结构化问题，可用数学模型来描述和求解，而弱结构化问题，则必须用人工智能、智能控制、知识工程等方法进行处理，智能运输系统 ITS 的理论依据之一）

structure drawing 结构图

structure material 构造用材料；建筑用材料

structure model 结构模型

structure transformation 相变（指金属材料在热处理过程中，由于加热温度、保温时间和冷却速度的不同，在金属内部产生不同的组织转变）

strut rod ①支撑杆（各种起支撑作用的杆件，= strut bar）②（双横臂式前桥独立悬架中使用单铰接式下横臂的）斜撑杆（其一端连接车架，一端连接下横臂，用来保持下横臂的设定位置，以及前轮定位的正确位置③有时在悬架系统中指半径杆，= radius rod，radius arm 或 radius link，见 radius rod）

strut/shock absorber （麦弗逊滑柱式悬架的）滑柱/减振器（内含减振器结构的滑柱）

strut suspension ①滑柱式悬架（独式、麦弗逊式等使用滑柱的滑柱摆臂，或称滑柱控制臂式，滑柱连杆式悬架的通称）②（一般多指）麦弗逊滑柱式悬架（见 Macpherson strut type suspension）

strut suspension combined with variable rate air spring assembly 带变刚度空气弹簧的滑柱式悬架总成（变刚度空气弹簧与滑柱式悬架制成一体，空气弹簧的变刚度执行器也组装在滑柱内）

strut suspension with electric actuator 带电动执行器的滑柱式悬架（执行器根据电子控制模块的指令通过其电磁型流量控制阀改变悬架滑柱伸缩行程中其油、气腔阻尼孔径，实现悬架阻尼特性，即其软-硬程度的变换）

strutting ①支撑②支柱，支撑物

strut tower bar （车身上的）（麦弗逊悬架）滑柱上端支座的加强板件

strut with coil spring type suspension 带螺旋弹簧的滑柱式悬架

STSF （噪声源定位和分级的）声场空间传输技术（spatial transformation of sound fields 的简称）

stub 桩（粗短立柱）

stub arm 短粗臂

stub axle ①短轴，丁字轴，枢轴②（特指）转向节轴（亦称 knuckle spindle，stud axle spindle，简称 spindle，转向节上安装车轮的短轴）

stubby driver 大柄木螺丝旋具（短粗柄螺丝刀，= stocky driver）

stub-frame car 短车架式轿车（半车架式轿车）

stuck piston 卡滞住的活塞（= seized piston）

stuck-tight 紧紧卡住的，不能动的

stud ①双头螺栓，螺柱②饰钮③键，销子；短轴④接线柱⑤钉靴（安装在雪地车的履带上以增大驱动力）⑥（轮胎的）防滑钉⑦（循环球-曲柄销式转向器和蜗杆指销式转向器的）指销（亦称 peg）

stud bolt hole 螺柱孔

studded tire 防滑钉轮胎（装有防滑钉的轮胎）

stud driver 螺柱拆装工具（亦称 stud setter and remover）

Student Engineered Economy Design rally （美国举办的世界性）大学生汽车改造经济性设计竞赛（简称 SEED rally）

studio buck （在车身外形设计过程中使用的）造型模型（用黏土、木材或其他材料制成，用于表现造型风格而不考虑细节的缩尺模型）

stud link 日字环链节

stud nut 螺柱螺母

stud puller 螺柱拉器（亦称 stud extractor, stud remover）

study 研究，考查，探讨，分析，学习

study program 研究计划，学习计划（简称 SP）

study scope 研究范围

stuff ①材料，原料②涂料③填料④本质，素质，品质⑤（毛）织品，呢绒

stuffing ①填料，填密料，填塞物，填充剂②填充，装塞

stuffing box 填料函，填料箱，填密槽（= parking box, packed gland）

stuffing box gland 密封压盖，填料盖，密封套

stuffy driver 短粗旋具

stumble ①失误，失败；过失②（发动机）不稳定，忽快忽慢③不稳定地运行

stunt-driving exhibition （汽车等的）特技驾驶表演

sturdy 强度高的，不易破损的，坚固的，结实的；加强的，强力的

S-turn ①S 状转弯②S 形弯道

STW 锯齿波（saw tooth wave 的简称）

S-twist S 形扭曲

style 形式，式样，造型，风格

style A arbor A 型柄轴

styled disc wheel with ribs 带棱条的（特殊）造型辐板式车轮

styling designer （车身）造型设计师（= stylist）

stylized ①具有独特风格的（车身造型等）②虚幻的，非写实的

stylus ①触针，测头②记录笔尖，记录针（亦称 stylus point）

styrene ①苯乙烯，苯代乙撑（= phenylethylene $C_6H_5CH:CH_2$）②苯次乙基（$Ph_1CHCH_2—$）

styrene acrylonitrile 苯乙烯丙烯腈（塑料的一种，简称 SAN）

styrene-butadiene copolymer 苯乙烯-丁二烯共聚物

styrene-butadiene rubber 苯乙烯-丁二烯橡胶（简称 SBR）

styrene insulation 苯乙烯绝缘材料

styrenemalefic anhydride 苯乙烯顺丁烯二酸酐（简称 SMA，车用塑料，制作对尺寸稳定性、抗蠕变性、高温稳定性及强度要求高的大型形状复杂的模铸构件）

sub 副，辅助，次，在下，低于

sub accumulator 副蓄液筒

SUBARU 斯巴鲁（日本富士重工轿车产品名，日文音译，意为"六连星"，即"昴星"。1984 年世界首创的电子控制无级连续变速器"ECVT"研制成功，1987 年首部装有 ECVT 的 SUBARU Justy 轿车问世）

Subaru Exhaust Emission Control 富士重工汽车排气净化系统（简称 SEEC）

Subaru Exhaust Emission Control Technique engine （日本）富士重工（汽车）排气净化技术发动机（简称 SEEC-Tengine）

Subaru legacy car 富士重工雷格斯轿车（日本富士重工公司生产的中档轿车，1990 年、1991 年获加拿大、日本的最佳轿车称号，装用 16 气门水平对置四缸发动机，电子燃油喷射，最大功率 80kW，最大转矩 149N·m，最高车速 170km/h）

Subaru viki car 富士重工维佳轿车（日本富士重工公司生产的微型轿车，装用直列四缸发动机，排量 800mL，最大转矩 6N·m，最大功

率 31hp，最高车速 120km/h，整备质量 655kg）

subassembler 附件总成装配工

subassembly 分总成（附件总成）

sub-audible 亚音频的

sub(-) battery （通常指混合动力车为增加电容量而加装的）副蓄电池

subcalibre 小于规定口径的

subcarrier 副载波

subcompact car 次小型轿车（发动机排量大于1L且小于或等于1.6L的小型轿车）

sub cooled boiling 亚冷沸腾（液体温度低于饱和温度，而加热温度很高时产生的沸腾）

sub cooling 局部冷却（分支冷却）

subcritical 低于临界的

subcritical annealing 亚临界退火（在临界温度以下退火）

sub critical exhaust 亚临界排气（在自由排气时，当汽缸内压力与排气管内压力的比值小于临界压比时的排气过程）

subcutaneous tissue 皮下组织

subframe （汽车车身或车架的）副架（辅助构架，一般指可从底盘上拆下的供安装发动机、悬架、转向机构等的附加机架，亦写作 subframe）

subfreezing temperature 冰点以下的温度（零下温度）

sub grade-traffic factor 路基承载交通密度系数（交通密度与路基强度的相对关系）

sub-harness 辅助配线（指可从汽车电系主配线系统上断开的附加配线）

subject 论题，题目，学科，科目

subjective brightness ①主观亮度（见 brightness）②视亮度（人眼对物体的明亮程度的主观感觉。视亮度受视觉敏锐度、适应亮度水平的影响）

subjective evaluation 主观感觉评价（依靠评价人员乘坐的主观感觉进行评价）

sub layer 下层，次层，底层

sub link （多连杆式悬架系统中控制杆间的）副杆

submarine 海底的，潜水的

submarining （汽车乘员安全带）松滑（故障）（指发生碰撞时，挂上安全带的乘员们向前滑窜的现象）

submember 副件（辅助机件，附属机件）

submerged 浸入水中的（被淹没的）

submerged arc-welding 潜弧焊（埋弧焊，= shielded arc-welding）

submerged motor pump 潜水泵

submerged oil pump 浸没式机油泵

submerged rib 暗肋条（轮胎胎面花纹间的低肋条，亦称副胎面花纹条，= sub-tread）

submersed filter 浸入式滤清器

submersible motor ①潜水发动机（= submersible engine）②潜水电动机

submersion-proof ignition （供涉水汽车用的）防水点火系统

submicro ①亚微型（比微型还小的，超微型）②亚微米（比微米还小的，超微米）

subminiature 微型（的）

sub miniature camera 微型摄像机

sub motor-generator 见 ECO Motor③

sub optimal control 准最佳控制（次最佳控制）

sub ordinate 辅助的，从属的，下级的

sub-program 子程序（亦称 subroutine）

sub-program selection push button 子程序选择按钮开关

sub-quality products 次品（副品，不合格产品）

sub

sub regular gasoline 低级汽油（研究法辛烷值低于常规汽油，见premium gasoline）

sub sample 复抽样（从抽样中再抽样）

subscale prototype test 原型（样机）的缩尺模型试验

subscript ①脚码，下标，脚注②标在字母右下方的

subsequent 接着发生的，以后的，其次的

subsequent treatment 顺序处理（加工）

subshaft 副轴

subsidence ①沉淀，沉陷，沉降 ②凹陷，凹下去 ③减退，衰耗（= subsidency）

subsidence transient 衰减瞬变过程（= damping transient）

subsidiary ①辅助的，附属的，次要的，补足的 ②附属品，附属者，子公司

subsidiary air supply （燃烧器、排气净化反应器）二次空气供给

subsidiary battery 辅助蓄电池

subsidiary combustion chamber 副燃室（分开式燃烧室中涡流室、预燃室、储能室等的统称，简称副室）

subsidiary experiment 辅助试验

subsidiary road 辅助道路（= minor highway）

subsonic axial compressor 亚音速轴流压气机

subsonic diffuser 亚音速扩压管

subsonic flow 亚音速流

substance ①物质 ②物体，实体 ③添加物 ④内容，大意，要点

substandard 非标准的（不合技术条件的）

substantial convergence 实质收敛

substantiate 证实，使……具体化

substantive 实质性的，实在的

substitute 代用品，代用物

substitute fuel 代用燃料

substitute function （电子控制系统的）置换功能

substitution ①代换，置换；代入；代替 ②替代物

substitution method of measurement 替代测量法（将选定的且已知其值的量替代被测量，使在指示装置上得到相同效应以确定被测量值的测量方法）

substrate ①（催化转化器的）载体（催化床的一个组成部分，所用材料是一种热稳定物质，通常在催化方面是惰性的，起骨架作用。催化剂活性材料添入、嵌入、附着其表面或用其他方法与它结合在一起）②（电子电路或集成电路的）衬底（在其表面和内部制造器件或电路元件的材料），基片（对膜电路元器件和/或外贴元件形成支撑基体的片状材料）③（化学）基质（被酶作用物）④基底，底板

substrate PNP transistor PNP基片型晶体管

substructure ①基础 ②基础结构（下部结构，底层结构，如：路基，= substruction）

sub supplier 供应零部件的协作厂

subsurface corrosion 表层下的腐蚀（表皮下腐蚀）

subsurface discontinuities （零件）表层下组织的不密实

subsurface failure （路面）下层的损坏

subsurface hardness 表层下硬度

subsystem 子系统

sub-throttle position sensor 副节气门位置传感器

subtle ①不明显的，不易察觉的 ②淡淡的（色彩、气味、照明等）

subtraction ①减法 ②减去，减少，扣除，去掉

sub-tread 副胎面花纹条（胎面花纹

沟底的低花纹肋条, = depressed rib)

suburb 郊区 (常用复数 suburbs)

suburban(-type) motor bus 近郊公共汽车 (装有横排座,使客座尽量增多,并有车顶行李架,亦称 shuttle bus)

subvitrieous 半玻璃质的 (光泽不如玻璃的)

subway ①地下车道 (如:地铁) ②地下管道

subway crossing (交叉口处的) 地下横道 (地下人行过道)

subwoofer (仅产生低于200Hz的低音的) 亚重低音喇叭

subzero ①零度下的 [英、美习惯上仍指 0°F (−17.8℃) 以下的] ②适于零度以下低温使用的 ③低凝固点的 ④负的,零下的

subzero oil 低温润滑油 [指凝固点低于 0°F (−17.8℃) 的润滑油]

subzero winterization (车辆) 在低温条件下的运行装备,寒带运行装备

SU carburetor SU 化油器 (英国 Skinnor Union 公司生产的一种可变喉管化油器商品名)

successive approximation 逐步近似 (计算) 法 (= progressive approximation),逐步求近法

successive vehicles 车队列

successor (某种车型的同类) 后继车

succinic acids 丁二酸,琥珀酸

succinimide 琥珀酰亚胺 [(CH$_2$CO)$_2$NH, 发动机用机油分散净化剂的一种]

suck ①吸,吸入 ②吸力

sucker ①吸管,进气管 ②(泵的) 活塞

suction ①吸,吸入 ②真空度 (= vacuum)

suction air 吸入的空气 (= induction air)

suction chamber (泵的) 吸入腔

suction cup 吸盘 (吸碗,吸杯,如: 研磨气阀时用以吸持气阀的橡皮吸杯)

suction cup tread tyre 吸盘胎面花纹形轮胎

suction draught 抽吸力

suction fan 抽风扇 (= drawing fan)

suction filter 吸入式滤清器

suction gage ①吸力计 ②真空计 (= vacuum gauge)

suction gas engine 吸入式煤气机 (煤气发生炉和进气系统构成一个整体,参见 suction gas producer)

suction gas producer 吸入式煤气发生炉 (用于吸入式煤气机,与发动机进气系直接连接,利用进气管吸力为煤气炉发生的煤气吸入汽缸)

suction governor 真空调速器 (见 vacuum governor)

suction head 吸入压头 (吸入真空度,吸入压差,亦称 suction lift)

suction line ①(示动图) 进气曲线 ②进气管道 ③低压管路

suction manifold 进气歧管 (亦称 intake manifold)

suction of intake pressure 进气吸力

suction period 进气期 (= charging period)

suction pipe 吸入管,流入管 (如: 进水管,进液管,进气管,吸气管, = suction tube)

suction pipe injection system 进气管喷油系 (进气道喷油系,燃油喷射到进气歧管、进气口等处, = manifold injection system, suction port injection system)

suction pressure 吸入压力 (一般指进气管内的进气压力, = intake pressure)

suction pressure gage 进气压力计 (测试进气压力的装置。当无增压

时则为负压计或真空计)

suction pulsation 进气脉冲

suction pump 抽吸泵（如：抽水泵，抽汽泵，吸气泵）

suction pyrometer 吸入式高温计（用于测定高温气体等的温度，将高温气体吸入温度计的内管直接由热传导测温）

suction resistance 吸入阻力（进气阻力）

suction screen 吸气滤网（进气滤网）

suction strainer 吸入（口）滤网（如：油底壳内的机油集滤器）

suction stroke 进气行程（四冲程内燃机汽缸内，充量进入汽缸时相应的活塞行程，亦称 induction stroke, intake stroke）

suction surface （翼型的）真空面

suction sweeper 吸尘式清扫车

suction system 进气系统

suction throttling valve （装在空调系统蒸发器和压缩机之间控制蒸发器压力，使之既可提供最大冷却效果，又不致使蒸发器芯子结冰的）吸入节流阀

suction tube 进气管，吸入管（= suction pipe）

suction type carburetor 吸气型化油器（装在增压器前，见 pressure type carburetor）

suction-type sewer scavenger 吸污车（装备有储运罐、真空泵等设施，用于吸除水坑、阴沟洞和下水道里污浊物的罐式汽车）

suction-type tumbrel tanker 真空吸粪车（装备有真空泵，靠罐内真空度将总含水量85%以上的粪便吸入罐体内，利用气压或自流排放出罐体的罐式汽车）

suction valve cone 进气门座（= suction valve seat）

suction valve spring 进气门弹簧

suction ventilator 吸气式通风机

suction vortex 进气涡流

suction wiper 真空式刮水器

sudden change in tire-road friction （遇路面脏污、泥水或结冰区产生的）路面与轮胎附着力的突变

sudden closure 突然闭合，紧急停闭（= sudden stoppage）

sudden contraction （断面）突然缩小

sudden engagement 突然接合，急剧地接合

sudden failure 突然失效（不能预先防止的故障）

sudden lane change test 突然变换车道试验（简称 SLCT）

sudden load change test （内燃机）突变负荷试验（在标定工况下，突卸全部或部分负荷，或从空载突加全部或部分负荷，观察内燃机工作适应性的试验）

sudden movements （周边行人或车辆的）突发性举动，突然行动

sudden-obstacle avoidance 突现障碍物避让

sudden stop 紧急制动，急刹车

sudden stoppage ①紧急停闭，急速闭合，突然锁合（= sudden closure）②切断，急速停止

sufficiency 足够，足量

sufficient 充分的，足够的

suffix ①接尾字，接尾词②词尾，尾标；下标，添标

suggestion 建议

suggestion system 建议制度（充分调动从业人员的积极性，鼓励对工厂、企业广泛提出合理化建议等的制度）

suit ①适合，配合，适应②一套，一组

suitability 适应性，适用性；相配，相宜

suitable 适合的，适当的，相适应的

suitable for EURO 6 and EURO 7 technology 达到欧6和欧7排放标准要求的技术

SULEV （按美国加利福尼亚排放标准的）超级低排放车（Super-Ultra-Low-Emissions Vehicle 的简称）

sulfanilic acid 磺胺酸（对氨基苯磺酸，$NH_2C_6H_4SO_3H$）

sulfate bath （电镀等时使用的）硫酸盐镀槽，硫酸盐镀液

sulfated ash （油料等）硫酸盐灰分

sulfation 硫化现象（硫酸盐化，= sulphation）

sulfonate ［美］①磺化（使变成磺酸盐或用磺酸处理）②磺酸盐（$HOSO_2R$，用作分散清净剂或去垢剂）（亦写作 sulphonate）

sulfone 砜（RSO_2R，亦写作 sulphone）

sulfonic acid 磺酸（RSO_3H）

sulfur 硫，硫黄（亦写作 sulphur）

sulfur content 硫分，含硫量

sulfur-free diesel fuel 无硫柴油

sulfur-free fuel 无硫燃料

sulfur fuel 含硫燃料

sulfuric acid refining 硫酸精制

sulfur removal 脱硫，除硫

sulphate ①硫酸盐 M_2SO_4 ②硫酸酯 R_2SO_4 ③用硫酸（盐）处理，使成硫酸盐，硫酸（盐）化（亦写作 sulfate）

sulphation of plate 铅板硫化

sulpha(tiza)tion 硫酸盐化

sulphide ①硫化物，硫醚②用硫化物处理，使变成硫化物

sulphocyaniding 硫氰酸盐化，硫氰酸酯化

sulphur ①硫（S，第16号元素，原子量32.06，原子序数16）②硫化的，加硫的③硫化（用硫处理，用亚硫酸盐处理，= sulphurate）

sulphuration 渗硫（将钢件放入含硫介质中加热，使钢的表面形成一层硫化铁 FeS 和 FeS_2 薄膜的热处理工艺，提高零件的耐磨性和抗咬合能力，降低摩擦系数）

sulphur content 硫分，含硫量

sulphur elimination 脱硫，除硫

sulphur-free 无硫的，不含硫的，去硫的

sulphuric acid 硫酸

sulphurization 硫化处理，硫化作用

sulphurized lub oil 硫化润滑油

sulphurizing 硫化，加硫，硫化处理（= sulphurization）

sulphur limit 含硫量极限

sulphur oxides 氧化硫（硫的多种氧化物的通称，美写作 sulfur oxides）

sulphur removal 脱硫

sum ①和，总和，总数②概要③合计，加起来④总结，概括

Sumitomo Rubber Industries ［日］住友橡胶公司（1990年世界轮胎市场占有率6.0%）

summary 摘要，概括

summary counter 累积计数器

summation 求和（法）；累加；合计，总计

summation meter 累计表，累计器

summation point （控制信号等的）相加点

summer capacity （冷却系的）夏季冷却能力（夏季冷却容量）

summer (compound) oil 夏季田（合成）润滑油

summer grade 夏季用（润滑油）品级

summer oil level 夏季润滑油液面高度

summit ①极高点，顶点②凸部，凸处；道路纵断凸起部分③最高的，最高级的

sum of vertical amplitudes of vehicle vibration per unit distance 单位距离内车辆垂直振幅和

sump ①（发动机）油底壳（美称 oil pan）②润滑油壶③沉淀器，沉

淀池④贮槽
sump slope 油底壳底面倾斜度
sump strainer （油底壳内）机油集滤器
sump test （工件表面）印模试验法
sum total 总数
sun and planet gear 行星齿轮传动，行星齿轮机构（亦称 epicyclic gear）
sun arc 太阳灯（见 sun-lamp）
sunday driver 周日（私人汽车）驾驶者
sundeck （旅游车等）可透日光的车顶
sundries ①杂货，杂物②杂费（= sundry charges）
Sunflower fuel （车用）向日葵油（基于 Joule 公司的微生物分泌专利技术，由 Audi 和 Joule 公司联合研制的新型清洁燃料的商品名，亦称 Joule fuel，其原料为清洁的水和工厂或动力机械放排的 CO_2，而不使用任何食用或非食用农作物，柴油机用者称 Sunflower -D fuel，汽油机用者称 Sunflower -E fuel）
sun gear 太阳轮（指行星齿轮传动中的外齿中心轮，亦称 center gear, sun wheel）
sunk 埋头的，沉下的
sunk head rivet 埋头铆钉
sunk key 埋头键（= sink key）
sunk spot 沉陷点
sun-lamp 太阳灯（一种模拟太阳光的弧光灯，放射出从紫外线到红外线的各种光波，常用于烘烤、强光照明等，亦称 sun arc）
sunlight 阳光（直射光，指昼光天然光中的直射光部分）
sunlight aging 日光老化作用
sunlight exposure 阳光曝晒试验
sunload sensor （汽车空调电子控制系统中装在仪表板上的）阳光强度传感器（为一光敏二极管，用于测定阳光是否照入车内及其光照强度）
sunny 阳光（日本 Nisson 公司的一种轿车牌名，排量 1.6L）
sun-proof 耐晒的（抗日晒老化的）
sunray to electricity conversion rate 日光电转换(效)率
sun-roof ①凉栅，遮阳篷顶②遮阳的③防晒的④（车顶上的）天窗
sunshine body 顶盖可打开的车厢，敞篷式车厢
sun visor 遮阳板（悬挂式遮挡件，防止阳光直射驾驶或乘坐人员眼睛，= anti-dazzle visor, sun screen, sunshade visor, sun shield）
sun wheel 太阳（齿）轮（亦称 sun gear, center gear, 行星齿轮中央的直齿圆柱齿轮）
SUP ①固体尿烷塑料（solid urethane plastics）②电源，馈电（supply）
super 超级的，优等的，特等的
super aerodynamic regime ①稀薄气动力状态②超音速空气动力状态
superalloy 超耐热合金（如：①超耐热不锈钢，碳<0.1%，铬16%，铜1.0%，硅1.0%，锰0.4%，其余铁②超耐热高应力耐蚀高镍钴合金，含铝、铬、钼、钛、锆、氮化物、碳化钨，耐 600~1000℃高温）
superb 极好的（无比的，最上等的）
super balloon tire 超低压轮胎（亦称 super pneumatic tire）
super car 超级车，超级汽车（特指使用大功率发动机，加速性能优异的高速轿车）
super car project 超级汽车项目（20世纪90年代美国政府提出将国家实验室的技术转让给汽车业，以提高美国汽车在国际市场上的竞争力的一项计划、项目，由副总统监督，1999财政年底拨款 2.77 亿美元资助这一项目，该项目又称"新一代

汽车伙伴计划" Partnership for a New Generation of Vehicles)
supercharge (发动机)增压进气(亦称 forced charge, forced induction, 指不单单依靠活塞下行在汽缸内形成的真空, 在大气压力下进气, 而是利用发动机曲轴驱动的鼓风装置, 如: blower 或利用排气能量驱动的废气涡轮增压器"turbocharger"将空气压入汽缸, 有时亦写为 S'change)
supercharged engine 增压内燃机(进入汽缸的空气或可燃混合气已经压气机压缩, 借以增大充量密度的内燃机, 亦称 engine with supercharger, forced induction engine)
supercharged natural gas engine ignited with gas oil 柴油(喷射)点火、(进气)增压式天然气(-空气混合气)发动机
supercharged Wankel engine 增压式汪克尔转子发动机(增压式汪克尔旋转活塞发动机, 增压转子发动机)
supercharger (发动机)进气增压器(一般指由曲轴驱动的机械增压器, 如: 罗兹式增压器"Roots blower"等, 以区别于以排气能量为动力的废气涡轮增压器"turbocharger")
supercharge ratio 增压比
supercharger blast gate 增压器的出风阀
supercharger control bypass valve 控制增压器风量的旁通阀
supercharger-cut test 增压器停机试验(测定增压内燃机在部分或全部增压器停止工作时继续工作的最大能力的试验)
supercharger impeller 增压器叶轮
supercharger outlet temperature 增压器出口温度(指增压器压气机的出口温度)
supercharger speed 增压器转速

supercharging 增压(提高内燃机进气的压力, 即增加其进气充量密度而提高其功率的技术, 亦称 super charging boosting)
supercharging level 增压度(内燃机增压后的标定功率与增压前的标定功率的差值与增压前标定功率的比值。增压度表明增压后功率增加的程度)
supercharging performance 增压特性
supercompressibility 超压缩性
supercompression 超压缩
super computer 超级计算机(指运算速度可达到每秒 1 亿次浮点计算"MFLOPS"的巨型计算机)
super concentrated 超浓缩的
superconducting 超导的
superconducting bolometer 超导式辐射热测量计(超导体电阻测温计)
super conductivity ①超导性(超导现象, 某些导体在温度、电流密度和磁场强度均低于临界值时, 其电阻几乎为零的特性和现象) ②超导(电)率
superconductor 超导(电)体
supercool 过冷
supercritical exhaust 超临界排气(在自由排气中, 当汽缸压力与排气管内压力的比值大于临界压比时, 汽缸内的废气以当地音速流出排气门或排气口的排气过程)
supercritical flow 超临界流
supercritical rotor 超临界转子(工作转速高于临界转速的转子)
supercushion 高级软垫(用于乘员保护系统, 特指一种装在驾驶员前方仪表板上的头胸保护装置)
Super CVT-i 超智能型无级连续变速器(丰田公司开发的新型无级连续变速器, Super CVT-intelligent 的简称)
super directional microphone (车厢

内使用的）超高方向性话筒（通过非线性信号处理，可消减背景音而确保主方向声音清晰传送）
super-dry air 超级干燥空气
super duralumin 超硬铝
superelevated-and-widened curve 外侧超高和加宽的弯道（弯道处的加宽路面具有横向倾斜度，外侧高起，用以克服汽车转弯的离心力）
superelevation angle （路面的）超高角（横向倾斜角，亦称 cant angle）
superficial 表面的
superficial cementation 表面渗碳（＝surface cementation）
superficial damage 表面损坏
superficial layer 表面层
superfine ①超细的，微的（小于 10μm）②特级的，最上等的
superfine adjustment 微调
superfine file 最细锉，极细锉
superfines 超细粉末（小于 10μm）
superfinish surface 超精加工面
superfluous 过剩的，多余的，过多的
super flywheel （驱动车辆等用）高能飞轮（高容量储能飞轮）
super frequency 超高频
super-fuel 超级燃料（在热值及燃烧特性等方面，均优于其他燃料）
super gasoline 超级汽油（高抗爆性汽油）
super-grade ①巨型的，大型的②超级的
superhardened 超硬的
super heat 过热（＝over heat）
superheated compression 过热压缩
superheated steam 过热蒸汽（有时称为 steam gas）
super heat switch （空调系统的压缩机）防过热保护开关（亦称 compressor protection switch，为一温度和/或压力传感开关，防止压缩机因润滑油不足和过热而损坏）
superheat temperature 过热温度
superheavy 超重的
superhigh 超高的
superhigh pressure-charging 超高增压（通常指增压压力 p_b > 0.35MPa 的增压）
superhigh speed 超高速的
super huge 特大型的
super ignition plug 超级火花塞（一种中心电极和接地电极的尺寸均很细小的高点火能力和长寿命新型火花塞）
superimpose 加上，重叠，叠加
superimposed layer 叠加层
superimposed load 超载，过载
superinvar 超级殷钢（超级镍钴钢，镍 31.5%～32%，钴 5%，其余为铁，热膨胀系数近于零）
superior 优越的，优秀的；在上的，较高的，较大的，较多的
superiority 优越性，优势
superior limit 上限
super laminated windshield 超叠层风窗玻璃（10～20 层安全风窗玻璃）
super-lean mixture 超稀混合气（一般指空燃比 18:1 以上的稀混合气）
super light tracer ①高亮度示迹器 ②高亮度示踪物
super live sound system 超级高保真音响系统（丰田公司由 7～10 个音箱组成的轿车高级音响系统的商品名）
super low section tyre 超低断面轮胎（轮胎断面高宽比低于 0.70 的充气轮胎）
super lube （汽车用）大型滑脂加注器
super-luxury model car 超豪华型轿车
supermarket 超级市场（＝large self-service department store）

super Monocock Body （马自达公司）高刚度整体式车身（的商品名）

super oilite 多孔储油铁铜合金（铁75%，铜25%）

superplastic Al/Cu alloy 高塑性铝铜合金

superplasticity 超塑性（一些金属在特定组织状态下，主要是超晶细粒，特定温度范围内和一定变形速度下表现极高的塑性，其伸长率可达百分之几百甚至百分之几千）

superpneumatic tire 超低压轮胎（= super balloon tire）

superpose 重合，叠加

superposed force 叠加力

superposed leaf spring 叠片式钢板弹簧

super premium gasoline 超高级汽油（见 premium gasoline，指研究法辛烷值高于高级汽油）

superpressure ①超压（超过周围大气压的气压）②超压（状态）的

supersaturated mixture 过饱和混合气（过浓混合气，= overrich mixture）

supersaturation 过饱和

superscalar 超量标（说明微处理器在给定的时钟周期内能执行多条指令的能力）

superscenic windshield 全景风窗玻璃（= panoramic windshield）

supersede ①替代，更换②废除，废弃；撤销

super single （供货车道路行驶使用的）大尺寸重型单胎（用于取替并装双胎，以减轻车重）

super smart vehicle system 超智能汽车系统（简称 SSVS，见 intelligent vehicle）

supersonic detector 超声波检验仪

supersonic effuser 超音速喷管

supersonic expansion 超音速膨胀（气流）

supersonic machining 超声波加工

supersonic molecular beam 超音速分子流束

supersonic nozzle 超音速喷管（嘴）

supersonic road (condition) sensor 超声波路况传感器（一般装在车身最前端，如：保险杠上，由超声波发射与接收器件组成，根据路面的超声波反射时间，向电子控制模块提供路况信息，借以在瞬间将可变阻尼悬架系统的阻尼力调到与实际路况相适应的最佳值）

supersonic road sensor 超声波路况传感器

supersonic sounding 超声探测（法）

supers pace wagon ①特大旅行轿车（具有特大车身内部空间的旅行轿车，简称 SSW）②特大厢式车身

superspeed 超高速（的）

superspeed radial tire 超高速子午线轮胎

superstrength adhesion 超高强度胶

superstructure 上部结构，上层结构

supertanker 超大型液罐车

super-thin 超薄的

super tire 超级（加强）轮胎

super-toe-control-rear-suspension （日产公司开发的）超级前束控制式后悬架（用于前轮驱动式轿车，当后轮悬架受压缩时，可自动使两后轮向内侧偏转，形成前束）

super transport truck 超级货运汽车

Super Ultra Low Emission Vehicle 见 SULEV

super video compact disk 超小影碟（简称 SVCD，见 video compact disk）

supervision 监督，管理；监控，检查，检验；观测；操纵，控制

supervision of freight transportation 货运监督

supervisor 检验员

supervisory circuit 监控电路

supervisory engineering staff 工程监理人员

supervisory management zone （企业的）监督管理部门

super wide angle detection 超广角探测

supplement ①补充，追加，附加，添加②添加物，附加物

supplemental equipment 附加装置

supplemental fuel 添加燃料（如：添加入主燃料内的酒精、氢等）

supplemental instruction 补充说明（附加说明，附注）

supplemental restraint system 辅助约束性安全系统（简称SRS，指车辆在发生碰撞事故时，约束乘员不动，避免二次碰伤，如：安全带、安全气囊等。无特别说明时，SRS常指安全带之外又追加的安全气囊系统）

supplemental side air bag 侧面副安全气囊

supplement angle 补角

supplementary 补充的，辅助的，副的（= supplemental）

supplementary air reservoir 备份储气筒（附加储气筒，副储气筒）

supplementary-air valve 辅助空气阀（副空气阀）

supplementary driving lamp 辅助远光灯

supplementary engine 辅助发动机（= donkey engine）

supplementary gearbox 副变速器

supplementary handling 辅助装卸作业（装卸过程中对货物进行的捆绑、加固、稳定等作业）

supplementary instrument 辅助仪表

supplementary means 辅助手段

supplementary parts 补充零件

supplementary passing lamp 辅助近光灯

supplementary pressure 补充压力

supplementary reservoir 副油箱（辅助油箱，辅助储存器）

supplementary spring 副钢板弹簧（见 auxiliary spring）

supplementary test 补充试验（追加试验）

supplemented hydrogen-gasoline engine 添氢-汽油发动机（一种层状燃烧发动机，主燃烧室内为汽油空气稀混合气，过量空气系数一般为2，将氢气喷入辅助小燃烧室中，用电火花点燃后，从该通道中喷出，点燃主燃烧室内的汽油稀混合气）

supplier company （协作件）供应公司

Supplier Cost Reduction Effort （美国克莱斯勒等公司开展的配套件）供应商降低成本运动（简称SCORE）

supply ①供给，供应②供应品，物资

supply chamber 供给室（如：液力制动主缸上部的储液室，= reservoir）

supply current 电源电流（在规定条件不，由电源供给电路的电流）

supply depot 补给仓库

supply dump valve （牵引车-挂车汽车列车双回路气制动系统中的）气压监控平衡阀（用于监测与平衡主挂车制动系统的气压，以保证主、挂车间制动力的平衡）

supply lead 电源线（= power lead）

supply line 供给管（线）路（如：将挂车制动能介质或信号从牵引车传输给挂车储气罐之间的专用管线路）

supply of heat 供热

supply plant （为汽车制造厂提供总成、组合件或装置的）配件供应厂（协作供应厂）

supply port of hydraulic pressure control valve 液压控制阀的进液孔

(油泵供油孔，油泵泵送的油液经该孔进入控制阀)

supply-pressure-reaction type open/close valve 供油压力响应式开/闭阀(当压力超过规定值时开启，压力低于规定值时关闭的压力控制阀)

supply voltage 供电电压，馈电电压(电源电压)

supply-voltage rejection ratio (线性放大器)电源电压抑制比(其他电源电压保持不变，一个电源电压变化与由此引起的输入失调电压变化之比的绝对值)

supply-voltage sensitivity (线性放大器)电源电压灵敏度(其他电源电压保持不变，输入失调电压变化与一个电源电压相应变化之比的绝对值)

support ①支撑，支援，援助②支座，支柱，托架

supportability 支撑能力，承载能力

support abutment 支座

support arm shaft 支臂轴

support beam 支撑梁

support bracket 支架(支撑其他总成、零件的构件，亦称 supporter)

support frame 承载构架(= support framework)

supporting area 支撑面积

supporting axle 支重桥(多轴汽车驱动桥后的)非驱动桥(= trailing axle)

supporting capacity 承载能力(承载量，承重量，= supporting power, supporting value)

supporting facility 支持设施(支援设施，辅助设施，辅助装备)

supporting force 支撑力

supporting frame 承载构架(= load-bearing frame)

support(ing) structure 承载结构

supporting surface 支撑面，承载面

supporting technology 基础技术，支持(…的)技术

supporting-tractive parameters of mobility 汽车机动性的承载-牵引能力参数(表征汽车以足够高的平均速度通过各种坏路和无路地带的能力，主要指标有：滚动阻力系数，附着系数，车轮对地面的单位压力、附着质量和最大动力因数等)

supporting wheels (半挂车的)支地轮(= ground wheel)

support post (货车栏板式车身的)栏板立柱(栏板中的加强骨架)

support saddle 鞍形支架

supposition 想象，推测，假定

suppress 镇定，抑制，消灭，扑灭

suppressant 抑制剂

suppressed type spark plug 抑制型火花塞(装有干扰抑制器的火花塞)

suppressed zero instrument 无零点仪表(刻度的零点不在该仪表的量程范围内，即：刻度不是从零点开始的，= inferred-zero instrument, set-up instrument, set-up-scale instrument, set-up-zero instrument, step-up instrument)

suppressing device 无线电干扰排除器(= radio interference suppressor)

suppression 抑制，镇定，熄灭

suppression of torsional vibration 扭振减振

suppressor ①(消除点火和汽车其他电器产生的电磁波对无线电干扰的)抑制装置(如：suppressor chock "扼流圈", suppressor condenser "抑制电容器", suppressor grid "抑制栅")②各种消、减、阻尼装置(如：foam suppressor "消泡剂", noise suppressor "消声器", knock suppressor "抗爆剂", shock suppressor "减振器"等)

suppressor condenser 防干扰电容器

（抑制干扰的电容器,亦称 suppression condenser）

suppressor kit 抑制无线电干扰的成套装置

suppressor resistor ①阻尼电阻（具有抑制火花对无线电干扰能力的电阻）②防干扰电阻器

supreme ①最高的②最主要的③极度（大）的④终极的,最后的

sure brake 安全制动器（一种四轮防滑系统的商品名）

sure-grip differential （可向前、后桥提供驱动力的）高牵引力差速器

surface 面,表面

surface abrasion 表面磨损

surface active agent 表面活化剂（合成洗涤剂,工业用分散剂,浸透剂,乳化剂的总称）

surface active property 表面活性

surface analyzer 表面质量分析仪（如:表面粗糙度检查仪）

surface blowhole 表面气孔

surface blow off cock 从水面排出浮渣、浮垢的旋塞（= scum cock）

surface boiling 表面沸腾（当液体的平均温度低于饱和温度且低于加热面温度时,而在加热面上引起的沸腾, = local boiling）

surface carburization 表面渗碳（处理）

surface channel 表面沟道（在半导体—绝缘体界面上的电荷转移沟道）

surface checking ①表面检验②表面龟裂（表面出现网状细裂纹）

surface cleaning 表面清洗

surface coating technique 表面镀覆技术

surface cock （容器等检查或控制液面高度的）液面阀

surface condition 表面状况,表面质量,表面条件

surface-cooled 表面冷却的

surface crack 表面裂纹

surface damage 表面损伤（如:外胎、内胎、垫带和轮胎气门嘴表面的机械损伤)

surface decarbonization 表面脱碳（= skin decarbonization）

surface deficiency 表面缺陷

surface density 表面密度

surface deterioration 表面损坏

surface discharge plug 表面放电火花塞（绝缘面放电火花塞,亦称 surface gap sparking plug"沿面间隙放电型火花塞",与常规火花塞的区别,在于两电极之间的放电处,用半导体绝缘材料隔开,与高能装置配合,用于某些火花点火发动机,亦常用于燃气轮机的起动点火,与之相对的是常规的 air gap sparking plug）

surface discontinuity ①（工件的）表面破伤（如裂纹,裂口等）②表面的不连续性

surface durability 表面耐久性（表面层的疲劳强度,接触应力疲劳强度）

surfaced width of road 路面宽度

surface effect vehicle ①地面效应器（指气垫车）②水面效应器（指气垫船）（简称 SEV）

surface engineering 表面工程（机械零件运动副摩擦面的处理、变化等技术）

surface exposed to air 暴露在空气中的表面

surface field-effect transistor 面场效应晶体（三极）管

surface filter element 多孔表面滤芯

surface finish ①表面粗糙度②表面抛光（表面精整）③表面最后精加工

surface finish indicator 表面精加工检查仪（表面粗糙度指示器）

surface gap spark plug 沿面间隙

（放电）火花塞（电火花沿中心电极及壳体之间的绝缘体裙部端面放电的火花塞，见 surface discharge plug）

surface hardening 表面淬火，表面硬化（= face hardening, shell hardening）

surface haze 表面蒙上薄雾

surface heat 表面发热，表面加热

surface ignition 热面点火（汽油机混合气由炽热燃烧室表面或炽热点等所点燃，形成不正常燃烧的现象）

surface imperfection 表面缺陷

surface in contact 接触面

surface indicator ①表面检查仪（检查表面凹凸，径向振摆等）②平面规

surface irregularities 表面平面度（表面粗糙度）

surface layer 表层（面层）

surface line method （汽车空气动力学气流可视化技术中的）表面流脉可见法（如：在风洞试验中将油液涂复于车身表面实现气流沿车身表面的流脉可见的方法）

surface morphing computer technology 计算机表面成型技术（如：制造厂采用该技术确定冲模工作面形状等）

surface-mount 表面安装的，装在表面上的，装在表面层内的

surface of action （齿轮啮合的）啮合曲面（啮合面，指一对相啮合的齿面，在其整个啮合过程中，其瞬时接触线在固定空间内的轨迹曲面，称为啮合曲面。对于平行轴齿轮副，啮合曲面也就是该齿轮副在各个端截面上的端面啮合线互相连接而成的曲面）

surface of contact 接触面

surface of evaporation 蒸发表面

surface of fracture 断裂面，折断面

surface of perfect black body 完全黑体表面

surface passivation 表面钝化（在P区、N区和PN结形成以后，在半导体表面生长或涂敷一层保护膜的过程）

surface plate ①平板（检验平整度用）②画线台

surface polishing 表面抛光

surface pressure 表面压力

surface pyrometer 表面高温计

surface quality 表面质量

surface residual stress 表面残余应力（表层残余应力）

surface roughness 表面不平（①指表面凹凸不平、麻面、斑痕②指外胎、内胎、垫带表面局部粗糙和不应有的凹凸痕迹）

surface roughness meter 表面粗糙度检测仪（表面粗糙度测试仪）

surface roughness specimen 表面粗糙度标准片（凭感觉或视觉比较测定表面粗糙度用的标准片，以及表面粗糙度测试仪用的标准片）

surface roughness tester 表面粗糙度测试仪（有触针式、光切断式、光干涉式多种）

surface scale 表面氧化皮（表面锈皮，表面垢皮）

surface scarfing 表面嵌接

surface street 地面街道（以别于高层街道或地下车道）

surface stress 表面应力，表层应力

surface tackiness 表面黏着性

surface temperature 表面温度

surface tension （液体）表面张力

surface tester 表面检查仪

surface texture 表面结构（表面组织）

surface thermocouple 表面温差电偶

surface traction 地面牵引力（路面牵引力）

surface transportation 陆上运输，地

1577

面运输（参见 land transportation）

surface treatment 表面处理，表面处置

surface vehicle 陆运车辆，陆地运输车（= land vehicle）

surface viscosity 表面黏度

surface-volume ratio of combustion chamber 燃烧室面容比［燃烧室的表面积（含主、副燃烧室）与其容积的比值］

surfacing spoon （钣金工用）匙形工具

surfacing welding electrode 堆焊焊条

surfactant ①表面活化剂（surface active agent 的简称，用以改变液体与固体之间的面际张力，如：a.肥皂、洗涤剂等；b.添加在燃油、机油中的将所生成的胶质和酸性不溶物溶解或分散，以防止它们沉积于零件表面的清净分散剂）②表面定向剂（为得到所需液晶分子排列，在基板上涂覆的材料）

surge ①（汽车）速度波动现象（如：猛然前串等）②（发动机）喘振（指转速的非控制性瞬间冲高现象）③（电）电涌④冲击，波动，急变⑤（液压系统内过渡性）压力波动⑥（绳索）滑脱⑦（车轮）空转打滑，向后滑⑧冲击波

surge chamber 稳压室，缓冲腔

surge damper ①电涌吸收器②波动阻尼器

surge flow ①湍流②浪涌电流

surge line 喘振线（压气机特性曲线上表示喘振状态的临界线）

surge pressure （仪器、仪表的）冲击压力（当泵启动、阀关闭等时在极短时间内仪器仪表所可能承受的工作压力加上超过工作压力的增量）

surge tank 稳压箱，缓冲箱

surging 冲击，波动，电涌

surpass 优于，胜过，超过

surplus ①过剩，剩余，多余，盈余，超过额②剩余的，多余的，过剩的

surrealistic vehicle 超现实车（梦想车，预想车，指目前尚不存在，但从技术上看是可行的未来的各种车辆）

surrogate ①代替，代理②代用品，代用件③代理人，代表

surround 包围，围绕

surround camera system 环绕摄像系统，全景摄像系统

surrounding air 大气（周围空气，环境空气）

surround view camera （四周）全景式摄像机

surveillance 监视，监督

surveillance test 监视性试验（监视性抽样检查）

survey 测量，测绘，调查，勘查，预测，展望

survey simulator ①评价用模拟装置②评价用数学模型

Survey Simulator to Evaluate Safety System （汽车）预防性安全系统效果模拟器（见 ASSESS）

survival ①幸存，生存，保全，救生，残存，遗物，残存物，（肇事后）未死的人②保留了生命的，残存的，活命的，保命的

survival probability 幸存概率

survival rate 成活率（活命率，指汽车等肇事后，保存生命的比率）

survivor's curve 残存概率曲线

SUS 赛氏通用黏度秒（见 Saybolt Universal Second）

susceptance 电纳

susceptibility ①敏感性（敏感度）②磁化系数（磁化率）

susceptible 敏感的（易受影响的，易感染的）

susceptiveness 敏感性（感受性）

suspend ①吊，悬，挂②悬浮
suspendability （机油等的机械微粒）悬浮性能（使微粒、胶质或酸性不溶物等悬浮于油中的能力，避免这些物质沉积于零件表面，以便最后由滤清器滤除，亦称清净分散性）
suspended item 保留项目，（试验）中止项目
suspended mass （弹）簧上质量（悬架质量，见 sprung mass）
suspended particles 悬浮颗粒
suspended type loading equipment 悬挂式装货器（安装在运输车辆上的一种轻型装卸机械）
suspended type pedal 吊装式踏板（= pendant pedal，见 pendant type pe-dal）
suspending dust 浮游尘埃，悬浮尘埃
suspension ①悬架（位于车架或车身与车轴或车轮之间，缓和并衰减由地面引起的冲击和振动，同时传递作用在车轮和车架或车身之间的各种力和力矩的装置）②（任何悬浮于液体或气体中的固体微粒）悬浮物
suspension actuator 悬架执行器（根据电子控制模块的指令改变空气弹簧、液压弹簧、减振器等悬架器件阻尼特性，即：软-硬程度的执行器件。按其控制的对象又可分为减振器执行器"shock absorber actuator"和油/汽弹簧执行器"air/oil spring actuator"）
suspension air control system （空气）悬架的气压控制系统（通过对各车桥或车轮的悬架空气弹簧气压的控制与调节，保证在汽车行驶中，车身的正确高度与姿势的系统的泛称）
suspension arm 悬架控制臂（悬架臂，悬挂的支撑臂）
suspension (attachment) points 悬架固定点
suspension bracket 悬架托架
suspension bridge 吊桥（悬索桥）
suspension by cross springs 横向钢板弹簧悬架
suspension damper （汽车悬架系统的）悬架减振器（用以吸收悬挂弹簧起落时车辆的振动能量）
suspension dynamics 悬架动力学
suspension firing 悬浮燃烧（浮游燃烧，将煤粉吸入燃烧室内，使之在悬浮状态中燃烧）
suspension fork （汽车独立）悬架叉形臂
suspension gear 悬架装置
suspension geometry ①悬架几何学（关于悬架系统部件及杆系的几何布置和在各种布置的几何图形下其部件和杆件的长度和角度的数值的学科）②悬形（部件与杆系布置的）几何图形（指用点、线、面来表示悬架部件和杆系的布置形式及其长度和角度数值的图形）
suspension lever （独立悬架的）杆件（摆杆，拉杆，推杆，支撑杆等）
suspension lever pivot pin 悬架臂杆枢轴
suspension link （独立悬架）连杆
suspension longitudinal stiffness 悬架纵向刚度（车轮中心与车体纵向相对变化单位距离时，所对应的车轮中心纵向力的增量）
suspension mounting reinforcement 悬架支撑加强件
suspension natural frequency 悬架的固有频率
suspension ride rate 悬架有效刚度（在一定荷载时，簧上质量与地面间垂直距离的单位增量所对应的轮胎垂直荷载的减量，简称 suspension rate）
suspension roll 悬架侧倾（①以左、

右车轮中心连线为基准,车身绕纵向轴即坐标系 x 轴的旋转运动②有时指汽车簧上质量的侧倾,含轮胎变形)

suspension roll angle 悬架侧倾角(由悬架侧倾产生的角位移)

suspension roll center 悬架侧倾中心(簧上质量不产生侧倾的横向力作用点,该点在通过同一轴两车轮中心的横向铅垂面内)

suspension roll geometry effect (汽车的)悬架系统侧倾效应(由于悬架系统的侧向几何变形,引起汽车本身及车轮等的侧倾对汽车性能产生的影响,见 roll camber, roll camber steer)

suspension roll stiffness 悬架侧倾刚度(悬架侧倾角单位增量所对应的悬架系传到簧上质量的恢复力矩的增量,恢复力矩中不包含衰减力矩)

suspension seat (汽车驾驶员的)悬架式座椅(弹性元件支撑式座椅)

suspension shackle 悬架吊耳

suspension stability control 悬架稳定性控制

suspension stiffness 悬架刚度(悬架有效刚度、垂直刚度、横向刚度及侧倾刚度的统称,分别见 suspension ride rate, suspension roll, transverse stiffness, vertical stiffness)

suspension strut (麦弗逊式和烛式独立悬架的)滑柱

suspension system 悬挂系统,悬架系统(指将车身等簧上质量支撑在车桥或车轮上的各种弹簧件、减振器、控制臂和连接及承力杆件等组成的系统)

suspension transmissibility 悬架传递振动的性能

suspension transverse stiffness 悬架横向刚度(车轮中心与车体横向相对变化单位距离时,所对应的车轮中心横向力的增量)

suspension vertical stiffness (汽车的)悬架系统垂直刚度(悬架系统在垂直方向产生 1mm 的变形量所需的负荷,单位为:kg/mm,或在一定荷载状态下,簧上质心与车轮中心间垂直距离的单位增量所对应的轮胎垂直负荷的减量)

suspension wheelbase 悬架轴距(指多轴车辆中,双轴并装车桥两轴之间的距离,见 tandem)

sustain 支持,维持,持续,经受,证实,确认

sustainability (能源和自然资源的)合理利用,(利用过程中)不破坏生态平衡

sustained grade 持续坡度(连续坡度)

sustained load 持续荷载(长期荷载)

sustained operating torque 连续工作扭矩(= continuous torque)

sustained oscillation 持续等幅振荡

sustained overload 持续超载(长时间过载)

sustained speed 持续速度

sustained use 持续使用(长期使用)

sustainer 支点,支座,支撑

SUT 运动型多功能货车(sport utility truck 的简称,雪佛兰 Chevrolet 一款具有多功能运动车 SUV 的性能和 pickup 功能的客货两用车,亦称 sport utility pickup 或半 SUV/半货车混合动力车 half-SUV/half-truck hybrid)

sutruck 无挂车的载货汽车(单辆货车)

SUV ①多用途旅行车(见 station utility vehicle)②运动型多功能车(见 sport utility vehicle)

SUZUKI [日本]铃木汽车

Suzuki Cappuccino Sport car 铃木卡

布西诺跑车（日本铃木公司1991年产品，装用直列四缸DOHC发动机，排量657mL，压缩比8.3，最大功率47kW，最大扭矩87N·m，最高车速176km/h）

Suzuki Motor Corporation （日本）铃木汽车公司

S/V （燃烧室）面/容比（surface/volume ratio）

SV ①电（磁螺线开关）控（制）真空阀（solenoid vacuum valve）②比容（specific volume）

SVC （福特公司在欧洲等地的）小型和中型汽车中心（Small and Medium Vehicle Center）

SVCD 超小影碟（super video compact disk）

SVIA 美国专用汽车协会（Speciality Vehicle Institute of America 的简称）

S-VSC 转向辅助式车辆稳定系统（steering-assisting vehicle stability system 的简称，通过电子控制转向响应来修正过度转向和不足转向，以保持车辆方向稳定性）

SVT （福特工程师、经销商及热心高性能车改装发烧友组成的）特种汽车队（Special Vehicle Team 的简称）

S-VT 序序式气门正时（机构）（Sequential Valve Timing 的简称，日本马自达公司进气凸轮相位可变式气门正时机构的商品名）

S/W 真空开关（vacuum switch）

SW ①短波（short-wave）②开关（switch）

swag ①挠度，垂度②下沉，下垂③摇晃，侧倾

swage block 型砧，花砧

swaged forging 型锻

swale 沼地，洼地，滩地，湿地

swamp （汽车越野赛线路中的）沼泽地，沼泽

swamp buggy 沼泽地带用轮式越野汽车（= marsh buggy）

swamp(ed) ground 湿地（沼泽地，= swampy ground，swamp land）

swampy caterpillar tractor 沼泽地用履带牵引车，湿地履带牵引车

swan-neck 鹅颈状的

swap body 互换式（货车）箱式车身（为一独立的货箱，或集装箱，可装放在专用的货车底盘上载运，本身大都带有可收放的支撑腿，以便于在专用货车底盘上的装卸、互换，亦称 swop body 或 demountable body）

Swarm theory 斯瓦姆理论（液晶常出现白色混浊现象，这是由于分子凝集聚结的作用形成斯瓦姆畴，在畴内的各分子方向趋于一致，在畴间相互作用减弱，而各个畴取向随机，于是有强烈光散射现象）

swashplate ①旋转斜盘（斜置的旋转圆盘，用于将往复运动转变为旋转运动，亦写作 swash plate，有时称 wobble plate）②挡板，隔板

swashplate angle 旋转斜盘角（旋转斜盘斜角）

swashplate axial piston pump 旋转斜盘式轴向活塞泵

swashplate cam 旋转斜盘凸轮

swash plate engine 旋转斜盘式发动机（用旋转斜盘机构取代曲柄，将活塞的往复运动变为旋转运动的发动机）

swashplate motor 旋转斜盘液压马达（旋转斜盘液动机）

swashplate pump 旋转斜盘式液压泵（斜盘式液压马达用的液压泵）

sway ①倾斜，偏向，歪斜②摇摆，摇动

sway bar link 横向稳定杆（两端与左、右车轮悬架下控制臂连接的杆件，亦称 sway bar，sway rod，见 stabilizer bar）

sway eliminator （汽车）侧倾（横

向角振动）消减器

SWCNT 单壁碳纳米管（single-walled carbon nanotubes 的简称，含（按重量）50%的纳米级铁粒子，在 $10 \sim 150 \mathrm{W/cm^2}$ 的光强度照射下可激活着火）

S4WD 可选择式四轮驱动（selectable four wheel drive 的简称，可在四轮与二轮驱动模式间选择的非全时四轮驱动，= part-time 4WD）

sweat 压接加热钎焊（将钎焊料置于两金属焊接件间，然后将二者夹紧加热到焊料熔化）

sweat cooling 发汗冷却（渗透冷却，蒸发冷却）

sweating 出汗（渗出湿气）

sweating rate （评价驾驶人员心理压力的）出汗率

sweep ①扫，扫过，扫动（来回摆动）②扫除，清扫③扫视④扫描（在计算机图形处理中，指沿以某一定点为中心的弧的移动；在电视成像技术中，指阴极射线在荧光屏上的反复运动）

sweepback vane 后弯式叶片（= backward bent vane）

sweep-delay circuit 扫描延迟电路

sweeper ①清扫机，清扫车（sweeper-collector 清扫-垃圾收集车，sweeper-flusher 清扫冲洗车）②扫描仪③（车身门、窗等的）密封唇边

sweep frequency ①扫描频率②（风窗玻璃刮水器）刮扫频率

sweep of vision （观察者目光扫过的）视野范围

sweep oscillator 扫描振荡器

sweep rate ①扫描速率（扫描是指可控变量连续经过或往返某一区间的过程。扫描过程中，可控变量的移动距离对时间的变化率称为扫描速率）②（绕某一中心的）摆动速率

sweep-sight windshield 全景风窗玻璃（= panoramic windshield）

sweep speedometer 圆形刻度盘指针式车速里程表

swell ①（铸件的）鼓胀②（漆面，橡胶制品）肿胀，泡胀，膨胀；隆起③表面外凸，增厚，增大，增长

swell factor 膨胀系数

swelling 膨胀，胀大

swell-shrink characteristics 胀缩性，鼓胀-收缩特性

swell test （橡胶浸油）膨胀试验

swept area （盘式制动器制动钳摩擦块与制动盘的）摩擦面积

swept-back 后掠式

swept-body tipper 摆臂式自装卸汽车（装备有可回转的起重摆臂，车斗或集装货物悬吊在起重摆臂上，随起重摆臂回转、平移起落，实现货物的自装自卸，又能实现散装货物的自行装卸的自卸式汽车）

swept capacity （发动机）排量（= swept volume capacity）

swept circle （汽车的）转弯通道圆外圈（转向盘转到极限位置时，包含车辆所有点在其支撑平面上的投影的最小外圆，亦称 outside circle of turning clearance circles）

swept circle diameter （汽车的）转弯通道圆外圈直径（见 swept circle）

swept frame arch （车桥上方）车架拱形弯曲（以降低车身高度，亦称 swept wheel arch）

swept-out ［英］流线型的

swept volume ①扫气容积（= displacement volume, cubic capacity, a. 指汽缸工作容积，见 piston swept volume b. 指发动机排量，见 engine swept volume）②（滤纸式烟度计的）抽气量（抽气泵一次抽入的排气动态容积）

swept volume for a displacement com-

pressor 压缩机扫气容积（压缩机第一级压缩元件在一转内所扫过的容积）

swept volume of a single chamber 单室工作容积（参见 chamber displacement）

swerve ①转弯，转向；偏向②（突然）改变方向③弯曲④滑出，逸出

SWG 标准线规（standard wire gauge）

SWIFT 短（振动）波中间频率轮胎模型（荷兰 Delft 工业大学和 TNO 联合开发的模拟轮胎在短（振动）波不平路面动特性的刚性环主流模型，Short Wave Intermediate Frequency Tire model 的简称）

swiftly moving traffic 高速交通（= fast traffic）

swift sedan 快速轿车

SWIFT-TIRE 荷兰 Pacejka 教授开发的硬环轮胎模型（rigid ring tyre model）名

swimmability （车辆）浮渡性能

swimmer kit 供汽车浮渡用的成套装备

swimming truck 水陆两用载货汽车（= amphibian truck）

swing ①摇摆，摆动，旋摆②摆幅

swing angle ①倾斜角（见 angle of inclination）②偏摆角③摆角

swing angularity of apex seal （转子发动机）径向密封片摆动角度（= angle of inclination）

swing arm ①摆臂（亦称 rocker arm, 泛指各种可绕其支点摆动的臂件）②（在顶置凸轮轴式发动机中，指由凸轮直接推压的）摇臂（其一端为铰接支点，另一端顶压气门，在凸轮轴凸轮的推顶下，绕支点摆动）③（摆臂式车桥中的）摆动臂（亦称 sway bar，连接车架车身与车轮轴并可使车轮上、下摆动的各种形式的杆件或控制臂件，亦称 oscillating arm, 见 swing axle）

swing arm type equalizing suspension （带后从动轴的双轴并装式后桥的）摆臂式平衡悬架（仅在并装双轴的前驱动轴下方装有一架钢板弹簧，该钢板弹簧的前端通过吊架与支架铰接，后端则与后轴摆臂的前端铰接，摆臂的中部与车架铰接，而摆臂的后端支撑后从动轴）

swing axle 摆动桥（亦称 articulated axle, divided axle, oscillating axle, pivoted axle, 一般为独立悬架断开式驱动桥，两半桥分别铰接于中央差速器壳左、右两侧，可在一定范围内摆动。车轮外倾角随半桥的摆动而变化，且其变化角度恒等于半桥的摆角。亦见有用于非驱动桥者，此时，左、右半桥由一个中央铰接头连接，称单铰接接式摆动桥"single joint swing axle"。上述驱动桥的摆动桥左、右半桥各有一个铰接接头者，称双铰接接式摆动桥"double joint swing axle"）

swing-beam diesel 摆臂式柴油机（一种活塞对置式二冲程可变压缩比柴油机，由连接活塞与连杆的摆杆控制活塞行程，而改变压缩比）

swing bearing 摆动支座（见 rocker bearing）

swing bevel gear 摆动锥齿轮（作摆动或同时作回转运动的锥齿轮）

swing bolt 铰节螺栓（指铰接支点枢轴）

swing boom 起重机旋转臂

swing cam 摇摆凸轮

swing center 摆动中心

swing check valve 回转式止回阀

swing clearance 推车的摆径（转向中牵引车转向盘转到极限位置时，挂车前角所画出的最大外圆的直径）

swing diameter of work 工件回转直径

swing drawbar 摆动式牵引装置

swing drive axle 见 swing axle

swinging caliper （液压盘式制动器的）摆钳（制动钳总成可绕其下端的枢轴转动，以适应磨损或变形）

swing(ing) crane 旋臂式起重机

swinging gear 回转机构，摆动机构

swinging half-axle （摆动桥的）摆动半轴（见 swing axle）

swing(ing) link 摆杆

swinging radius （起重机臂）摆动半径，伸出距

swinging shackle （钢板弹簧的）吊耳（连接钢板弹簧卷耳与弹簧支架的构件，可绕支架销摆动，允许弹簧钢板长度方向移动，简称 shackle）

swinging type windshield 铰链式风窗玻璃，翻转式风窗玻璃

swing joint 铰链连接

swing-type check mechanism 回转止回机构（回转式单向机构）

swing-up rear door 向上翻开的后门

swirl （横向）旋流，（横向）旋涡，横涡（见 tumble）

swirl atomiser 涡流喷雾器（涡流喷射阀，涡流喷嘴，涡流雾化器）

swirl chamber 涡流室（一般指涡流室式柴油机汽缸盖内的球形、平底形或扁钟形小室，与主燃烧室之间有通道相连。压缩行程中柴油喷入该室内产生的强烈涡流中，形成浓混合气并遇高温而着火，经切向通道冲入主燃烧室内，在主燃烧室内形成二次涡流并与主燃烧室内的压缩空气进一步混合形成较稀混合气并完成层状燃烧过程。近年来某些层状充气和燃烧式汽油机也采用涡流室式结构，如日本本田的CCTV）

swirl chamber diesel engine 涡流室柴油机（见 diesel engine with turbulence）

swirl control valve 见 SCV

swirl duct 涡流型进气通路

swirler 离心式喷雾器（涡流式喷雾器）

swirl flame stabilization （燃气轮机）涡流火焰稳定化

swirl number 涡流数，涡流值

swirl port 涡流式进气孔

swirl rate 涡流比（汽缸或燃烧室内气流旋转运动的转速与发动机转速的比值）

swirl ratio 横向旋涡比

swirl reducing baffle 防旋流挡板

swirl sprayer 涡旋式喷嘴

swirl stratified combustion 涡流分层燃烧

swirl tube air cleaner 旋流管式空气滤清器（空气在旋流管中强烈旋转，靠离心力将大部分灰尘从空气中分离出去，并沿管壁落到底壳内）

switch ①电开关，开关 ②转换，转接

switched sensor 开关型传感器（当所传感的物理量达到某规定值以上时，输出为"1"，表示接通状态"on"，而低于该规定值时，输出为"0"，表示断开状态"off"的传感器，其设定值仅上述的"开"、"关"两个状态，而且表示"开"与"关"状态的"1"和"0"，可直接输入微机进行处理）

switching amplification circuit 开关放大电路（同时起开关与放大作用的电路）

switching arrangement ①开关装置 ②配电系统

switching current amplifier 开关电流放大器（开关电流放大电路）

switching regulator 开关式调节器

switching roller finger follower （两级式气门升程可变系统的）换位滚子头气门挺杆（简称SRFF）

switching selector 开关选择器（简

称 SS)
switching transistor 开关三极管
switching valve 开关阀
switch key 钥匙开关
switch knob 按钮开关
switch-over filter 带转换阀的并联滤清器
switch over valve 转换开关阀（如：在 ABS/ASR 系统中由正常制动转换为 ASR 功能的开关阀）
switch panel ①开关板②插线板③插接板
switch plug 插接头（插头式开关）
switch seat 插头式开关座
switch starting 起动开关（接通起动开关）
switch-style transfer case control system 开关型分动箱控制系统［通常旧式分动箱控制系统为杠杆手柄式 (lever type)］
switch terminal 开关接线端子，开关接线端
switch type actuator 开关式执行机构
switch type braking sensor 开关式制动传感器（为一装在制动控制阀总成内的常开式开关器件。当踩踏制动踏板，制动液压达到规定值时，该开关闭合，向电子控制模块发送制动信号，亦称 braking pressure switch，braking switch，braking sensor)
switch-type (mode-) changeable 4 WD system 开关式（模式）可选择型四轮驱动系统（可通过模式选择开关选择不同的四轮驱动模式，见 4 WD ECO, 4 WD AUTO, 4 WD LOOK)
swivel ①绕轴回转，回旋②带转轴的链环
swiveling offset 转向轴线偏距（指转向轴线或转向主销的延长线与车轮支持平面的交点至车轮中心平面与车轮支持平面的交线间的距离，亦称 king ping offset、steering offset、wheel offset、scrub radius)
swiveling spotlight 回转式聚光灯（美写作 swivelling spotlight)
swivelling radius （转向车轮绕主销的）回转半径（转向节主销中心线延长线的接地点与车轮中心平面在地面上的距离）
swivel motion （绕支轴的）回转运动
swivel-mounted (second) seat 可回转式（第二排）座椅
swivel nozzle 旋转喷嘴
swivel nut 螺套（如：套装在转臂式气门嘴嘴体上，连接嘴体和嘴座的紧固件）
swivel pin ①枢轴销，铰接销②转向主销（= kingpin, anchor pin)
swivel pin angle 主销内倾（见 kingpin inclination)
swivel plate 转盘
swivel seat （可）旋转式座椅（一般用作旅居车或商务汽车等的前排座椅，可回转180°，与后排座椅对向而座）
swivel style hydraulic tube fittings 可转动式液压管接头
swivel window 旋转式车窗（= hinged window)
S-wrench S 形扳手
SwRI ［美］西南研究院（Souhwest Research Institute 的简称）
SWS ①智能线路系统（见 smart wiring system)②简化配线系统（参见 simplified wiring system)
symbol 符号，记号，象征
symbolic assembly language 符号汇编语言（= assembly language)
symbolic diagram 示意图
symbol of a unit (of measurement) （测量）单位的符号（标志测量单位的约定记号）

symbol of numeral 数字符号
symbol of operation 运算符号
symcenter 对称中心（symmetriccal center 的简称）
symmetrical attenuator 对称衰减器（输入和输出镜像阻抗相等的衰减器）
symmetrical beam ①（左、右）对称的前照灯配光②对称光（以屏幕 V 线为中心，左右对称的光）
symmetrical blade 对称式叶片
symmetrical depression （转子发动机转子工作面的）对称（燃烧）凹坑（凹坑在转子工作面上前后左右对称）
symmetrical wave 对称波
symmetric rim 对称式轮辋
symmetric tire tread pattern 对称型胎面花纹（亦称 symmetric tire tread design，简称 symmetric tire tread，symmetric tread）
symmetry ①对称（对称性，对称现象）②匀称，和谐
symmetry of an equivalence relation 等价关系的对称性
symmetry of three phases （三相电流）三相位的对称性
sympathetic 共鸣的，共振的，谐和的
sympathetic body panel oscillation 车身板件共振，车身板件谐振
sympathetic vibration 共振，谐振
symposium ①论文集②讨论会
symptom 迹象，症候
symptom of vehicle failure 汽车故障症状（汽车故障的具体表现）
syn(c) ①同步的（synchronizing 的简称）②同步（synchronization 的简称）
SYNC 车载多媒体通信娱乐系统（商品名）
sync （通用公司和克莱斯勒公司对）凸轮轴位置传感器（的称谓，

= 福特公司的 CID，见 CMP）
synchro ①自动同步（selsyn）②同步的（采用同步方式的）③同步啮合机构（同步器，同步啮合装置，同步啮合系，= synchronizer，synchromesh device，synchromesh gear，synchromesh system）④（使）同步（= synchronize）
synchro angle 同步角
synchro-circlip seat 同步器弹簧卡环座
synchromesh ①同步啮合②同步啮合机构（= synchro ③）
synchromesh change gear ①同步变速齿轮②同步变速机构
synchromesh clutch gear 同步啮合齿套（= synchronizing clutch gear）
synchromesh gear ①同步啮合齿轮②同步啮合装置
synchromesh gearbox 同步器式变速器（亦称 synchromesh type transmission，synchronized gear transmission。①指部分前进挡位装有同步器的变速器，以别于全同步器式变速器，见 all synchromesh transmission②各种带同步器的变速器的泛称）
synchromesh sliding sleeve （机械式齿轮变速器的）同步（器）接合（滑）套（为装在变速器第二轴花键毂上带拨叉环槽的内花键滑套。换挡时，在拨叉推动下带动摩擦件，使齿轮转速同步并将第二轴花键毂与所换挡位齿轮的外花键齿圈套合在一起，而实现换挡，亦称 synchronizer sleeve）
synchromesh transmission ［美］同步器式变速器（部分前进挡位装有同步器，使啮合元件间的转速迅速同步的变速器，= 英 synchromesh gear-box）
synchromotor 同步电动机（synchronous motor 的简称）
synchronism ①同步（同步性，=

synchronization,简称 syn（c））②同期（同时，并发）

synchronized countershaft transmission 同步器式中间轴齿轮变速器（见 counter shaft transmission）

synchronized shift 同步换挡

synchronizer （机械式齿轮变速器的）同步器（亦写作 synchronizator, synchromesh gear, synchromesh unit, synchromesh device，使换挡时将要啮合的一对齿轮的圆周转速接近一致或相等，以保证二者平顺无冲击地啮合的装置，常用的有常压式"constant pressure type"和惯性式"inertia type"等两大类）

synchronizer cone 同步器（花键毂，同步环等部件的）锥形摩擦面（亦称 synchronizing cone）

synchronizer hub 同步器花键毂（亦称 synchro-mesh hub）

synchronizer ring 同步器的同步环（亦称 synchro-mesh ring）

synchronizer sleeve （机械式变速器的）同步器接合套（亦称 synchromesh clutch gear, synchromesh sliding sleeve, synchronising sleeve）

synchronizer test 同步器试验（评价其同步能力、同步平稳性等）

synchronizer trigger 同步触发器

synchronizing adhesion coefficient 同步附着系数（实际制动器制动力分配曲线与理想制动器制动力分配曲线交点处的轮胎-道路附着系数）

synchronizing angle 同步角

synchronizing controls 同步控制机构（同步调节装置）

synchronizing drum 同步转鼓

synchronizing indicator 同步（状态）指示器

synchronizing voltage 同步电压

synchronous alternator 同步交流发电机

synchronous belt 同步传动带（可使曲轴和凸轮轴同步旋转的弹性齿形传动带）

synchronous braking 同步制动

synchronous cancellation system for engine vibration 发动机振动的同步减振系统（积极式减振系统的一种，由发动机振动传感器、同步反波形振动波发生器及发动机的反振动波支座等组成，可完全抵消发动机的各种振动，见 active noise control）

synchronous circuit 同步电路

synchronous feedback （积极式噪声控制中的）同步反馈法（从噪声源取出控制信号，产生与有害噪声同步的反噪声，见 antinoise）

synchronous generator 同步发电机

synchronous motor controller 同步电动机控制器（电动机与电源频率同步）

synchronous muscular activities （驾驶者左右部位）肌肉同步动作

synchronous supervision mechanism 同步监控装置

synchronous transmission 同步传输

synchro pickup （发动机示波器的）同步传感器

synchroscope 同步示波器

synchro-spiral gearbox 斜齿轮同步换挡变速器

sync notch 同步缺口（通用公司的电子控制无分电器式点火系统"IDI"，"DIS"的变磁阻曲轴位置与转速传感器的变磁阻齿盘上共有 7 个使其永磁线圈磁路磁阻发生变化、而在线圈中感生电压脉冲信号的缺口，其中 6 个各相间隔 60°，在第 1 个缺口与第 6 个缺口间，有一个与第 6 个缺口仅隔 10°的第 7 个缺口，电子控制模块利用该缺口产生的脉冲信号，使线圈的点火顺序与发动机的曲轴"位置"同步，该缺口便是"同步缺口"，亦称 cylinder event notch）

sync pickup （克莱斯勒公司多点式汽油喷射系统中的）同步传感器（除基准传感器"reference pickup"以外的另一个装在分电器上的霍尔效应传感器，分电器轴每半转即180°产生一个矩形脉冲信号，该矩形脉冲的前、后沿分别供电子控制模块的功率电路决定在收到逻辑电路的喷油指令后接通哪一组喷油器，供逻辑电路与其他传感器的信息一起决定喷油脉冲宽度，亦称 sync sensor）

syncro piston 同步活塞（见 variable valve stop mechanism）

syncrude 合成原油（synthetic crude 的简称）

sync sensor 同步传感器（通用公司等对其霍尔效应凸轮轴传感器的称谓，= camshaft sensor，该传感器的信号亦称同步信号，用来告知电子控制模块接下来点火或喷油的应轮到哪一缸或哪一组汽缸点火、喷油，即确保各汽缸的点火和喷油与规定的点火—喷油顺序同步。有的同步传感器与曲轴位置传感器组成一体并不装在凸轮轴上，见 sync notch）

sync signal 同步信号（由凸轮轴位置传感器或曲轴位置传感器上的同步信号槽等产生的脉冲信号，电子控制模块根据该信号确定点火和喷油顺序，即接下来应该是哪一缸或哪一组汽缸点火和喷油，见 sync sensor, sync notch）

syndet 合成洗涤剂（synthetic detergent 的简称）

synergistic 协和的，复合的，叠加的，合作的，协同的

synergy 最佳协同作用

synfuel 合成燃料（synthetic fuel 的简称）

synlube 合成润滑油（synthetic lubricant 的简称）

syntactic foam 复合（酚醛树脂）泡沫塑料（由铸塑树脂，如：环氧树脂，和轻质填充物，如：泡沫酚醛树脂制成的混合物）

synthesis 综合，合成法；综合性

synthesis of field load spectrum 场负荷频谱综合

synthesized hydrocarbon-based engine oil 烃基合成机油

synthesizer 综合器，合成器，合成装置

synthetic ①人造的，合成的②合成剂；（化学）合成物，合成纤维织物③综合的④合成，综合

synthetic brake shoe 合成材料制动蹄

synthetic crude 合成原油（如：煤的加氢液化合成的石油）

synthetic fabrics 合成纤维织物（亦写作 synthetic fibres）

synthetic fuel 合成燃料（简称 synfuel）

synthetic skin 人造皮肤（供汽车试验时模拟人皮用）

synthetic study 综合研究

synthetic utilization 综合利用

synthol 合成醇（用作合成燃料）

syntholube 合成润滑油

syntony 谐振，共振

syphon ①虹吸②虹吸管

syphon circulation 虹吸循环

syphon feed 虹吸供油（利用虹吸原理供给燃油）

syren 警报器（亦写作 siren）

syringe ①喷射器（注油器，注水器）②注射，冲洗

system ①系统，体系②方式，方法③制度④系统图，线路图

system acceptance tests ①（由一系列试验组成的）系统验收试验（简称 SAT）②（对某一）系统（进行的）验收试验

system (analysis) engineering 系统（分析）工程，系统工程学

systematic ①系统的②有次序的,有规则的,整齐的;有计划的,非偶然的③分类上的

systematic approach 系统工程方法

systematic error 系统误差(在同一被测量的多次测量过程中保持常数或其变化是可预计的一个系统的累加总和误差,亦称 system error)

systematic mathematical analysis 系统(的)数学分析法

systematization 系统化

system controller (控制整个系统的)系统控制器

system design 系统设计

system diagram 系统图(亦称 system drawing)

system function [相对于单一功能(one function)而言的]一系列功能,多功能

system model technique (车辆设计的)系统(数字)模型技术

system of axes 坐标系

system of conics 二次曲线系

system of connections ①管路图②线路图

system of fits 配合制

system of linear equations 一次方程组(系)(线性方程组)

system of units (of measurement) (测量)单位制(为给定量制建立的一组单位)

system of vehicle maintenance and repair 汽车维修制度

system-on-a-programmable chip 可编程单芯片式系统(指整个系统组装在一块可编程的芯片上)

system on a ship 单片系统(简称 SOS,指中央处理器、存储器、接口电路等均装在一块芯片上的控制系统)

system on/off switch 系统接通/断开开关

system parameter identification method 系统参数识别法(利用现有的理论分析模型,只对装置或系统进行试验,而不必对内部每个组件分别进行试验测量,就可获得理论分析所必需的参数值,从而确定数学模型的方法)

system protection valve (气制动系的)系统保护阀(当某一储气筒损伤时,可接通另一储气筒提供所设定的制动气压)

system read indicator 系统状态指示装置

system research 系统研究

system resilience 系统容错能力(见 fault tolerance)

systems analysis 系统分析

systems approach 系统(研究)法(利用系统工程理论研究解决问题的方法)

systems engineering 系统工程

systems modelling 系统模型化,系统模拟试验

system synthesis technique 系统综合技术

system transfer function 系统的传递函数

system-wide 全系统的,整个系统范围内的

system with one degree of freedom 一自由度系统

Système International d'Unitès 国际单位制(代号 SI)

T ①绝对温度（absolute temperature）②表面张力（surface tension）③合成热塑性塑料（synthetic thermoplastics）④液罐车（tanker）⑤目标（target）⑥三通接头（tee）⑦无线电遥测（telemetering）⑧电话（telephone）⑨温度（temperature）⑩拉力（tension）⑪张量，伸张器（tensor）⑫万亿（tera）⑬术语；项（term）⑭特斯拉（磁通量单位 tesla）⑮温度计（thermometer）⑯厚度（thickness）⑰手柄（tiler）⑱时间，次数（time）⑲齿厚（tooth thickness）⑳塔；支柱（tower）㉑处理；交易（transaction）㉒运输；公共交通（transit）㉓转换平移（translation）㉔运输［transport（ation）］㉕横向的；横梁（transverse）

TA 技术评估，技术鉴定（technology assessment）

Ta 钽（tantalum）

TAA 美国运输协会（Transportation As-sociation of America）

TAB ①货车-飞机-轮船（指陆空海运输工具，truck，airplane，boat）②横向比例分配制动系统（transverse apportioning brake system）

tab ①接头（片），小片；薄片，链形物，供拉手或悬挂用的吊环、凸耳等小的凸出部；（锁紧垫圈、检索卡片等的）凸舌；标记，标签，标志牌；阻力板 ②给⋯加上小突出部，用接头片固定；选出，指定，把⋯列表

TAB and TAD solenoid 热反应器的二次空气旁通阀和分配阀的真空通路控制电磁阀（见 TAB and TAD valve）

TAB and TAD valves 热反应器二次空气旁通阀和分配阀（thermactor air bypass and thermactor air divert valves 的简称，这两个阀组装在一个阀体内，其中旁通阀将空气泵输入的空气引向分配阀或排出至大气，而分配阀则将旁通阀送来的空气送至排气歧管或催化转化器）

table ①桌子，台，工作台 ②表，表格，图表 ③平板，平台，平面

table control lever 工作台控制手柄

table dispatching method 表上调度法（按货物流量、流向，利用制表法，调整求出最优调运方案的调度方法）

table-like ①表格式的 ②平台状的

table looking up control 查表法控制（见 feedforward control）

table of contents 目录，目次

table of threads 螺纹表

tabular ①表格式的 ②平面状的；平板状的；平台状的

tabulation ①表格化（以表格的形式

表示）②列表（制表）
tabulation method in optimization　最优化（求解中的）表上作业法（求解线性规划中运输问题简便而有效的计算方法）
TAB valve　见 thermactor air bypass valve
tab washer　带耳的止动垫圈
TAC　①恒温控制式空气滤清器（thermostatic controlled air cleaner）②加拿大运输协会（Transportation Association of Canada）
tach　见 tachometer
tachoalternator　测速发电机
tachograph　行车自动记录仪（通常指将汽车的运用数据，如：车速、行程、停车次数、停车时间等随时间而变化的曲线形式记录在圆盘形记录纸上的装置，简称 tacho）
tachometer　①测速表，转速计（简称 tach 或 tacho = revolution counter 或 rev counter）②流速计
tachometer signal　测速信号
tachomotor　测速电动机
tachoscope　闪频转速计
tachymeter　快速（测定距离、方位等用的）视距仪
tackiness　黏性
tack positioned weld　定位点焊（简称 tack-weld）
tacky　黏性的，黏的
tact　①（自动生产线的）生产节拍②节拍，拍子
tactical problem dynamics　战术问题动力学（从战术要求考虑动力问题）
tactical truck fleet　战术货车车队（简称 TTF）
tactical vehicle　战术车辆
tactile　有触觉的，能触知的
tactile sense　触觉
tact timing　生产节拍时间的计算（确定等）

TACV　①气垫运输车（transport air-cushion vehicle）②有轨气垫车（tracked air cushion vehicle）
tag　①吊耳，提手，凸耳②（金属）箍，终端接头③标签，标记④加装凸耳、箍等附属物；加装标签
TAG　技术援助组（technical assistance group）
tag axle　后支重桥（中桥驱动的6×2汽车中间驱动桥后面的从动桥）
Tag open cup apparatus　泰氏开式闪点仪（泰格敞口杯式闪点测定装置）
Tag Open Cup Method　泰格敞口（闪点）测定法
tag tanden　（仅前面的车轴为驱动轴，而后面的车轴为支重轴的）后支重轴式并装双桥
tail　①尾，尾部，末端②（电子管）引线③石油产品的残余馏分
tail-and-stop lamp　后灯和制动灯的组合灯（亦称 tail-and-stop light, tail-stop light）
tail board　①尾板，后面板②（栏板式车身货车的）后栏板
tail-end　①末端，尾端；后部，部；结束时期②最后的，终结的
tail-engined car　后置发动机式汽车
tail fuel fraction　燃油的尾馏分
tail-gas law　（汽车）尾气排放法规
tailgate chain, hinge and hook　（栏板式货车车箱）后栏板挂链，铰链和链钩
tailgate step　（车箱）后栏板登车阶梯
tailgate window　车厢的后门窗
tailing　（HC检测中的）拖尾（由于排气中高沸点碳氢成分吸附在管道系统中或滞留在检测器中造成开始时读数较低，接着读数又较高的现象。拖尾过分，将产生读数误差，亦称 hang up）
tail lamp　后灯，尾灯

tail lift ①后栏板举升器（安装在后栏板上的举升机构或后栏板本身就是举升板）②（制动时，重量转移造成汽车前部下沉）后部抬升现象（亦称制动点头，见 brake dive）

tail-lift truck 后栏板起重式货车（以本车动力驱动后栏板起重装置，使后栏板能自行升降，用于起重货物的汽车）

tail light （汽车）后灯，尾灯（指后部照明和信号灯）

tailored 改装的，改编的；定制的，配制的，按要求特制的；作装潢（修饰）用的

tailor-made 订制的，特制的

tailpiece 尾部机件，尾部构件

tailpipe ①（排气系的）尾管（亦称 kick-up pipe，将废气排入大气的最后一节管子）②（当使用两级消声器时，偶见指主消声器与副消声器间的）连接管

tailpipe emission 尾管排放（在发动机排气尾管处检测到的排放污染物）

tailpipe NOx sensor 排气尾管 NOx 传感器（检测尾管排出的废气中的 NOx 含量）

tailrace 放水管路，排水管道（一般指从水泵排水口至储水处之间的连接管道）

tail shaft 尾轴（指从发动机、变速器或其他旋转机械壳体伸出的驱动轴或输出轴）

tail shaft governor （燃料喷射系的）尾轴调速器（机械式调速器的一种，装在发动机驱动的变矩器上，监测其尾轴，即：输出轴转速，通过机械方式与发动机燃料喷射泵的调速器连接，控制发动机的转速，使尾轴在扭矩负荷变化时转速保持不变）

tail water 废水

tail wind 顺风（= following wind）

take ①拿，取②量出，读出③记下，拍摄④接受，承担，收受⑤订购⑥推断，认为，以为⑦（齿轮）啮合⑧乘，坐（汽车等）

take a wrong bus 错乘，误乘（客车）（旅客乘坐与所持客票规定的路线、车次不符的班车）

take charge （机械、车辆等的）滥用，乱用，任性开动（如：开车超过规定车速疾驶）

take down the shutters 打开（散热器的）百叶窗

take fire 着火，点燃，开始燃烧（= catch fire）

take-off ①脱开，断开②取出，输出，引出（功率等）③起步④输出轴，输出器⑤（变速器）取力器（见 power take off）

take-off maximum revolving speed （汽车取力器、动力输出器等的）最大动力输出转速

take-off output （汽车取力器、动力输出器等的）输出功率

take-out ①取出②断开③卸荷

take stock of 估量，估计，鉴定

take to pieces 拆散（将机器拆成零件）

take-up ①张紧机构，张紧轮②张紧，拧紧

take up the back lash ①消除背隙②走完空程

taking-over 验收，接收

talc ①滑石，滑石粉②撒滑石粉

tallow （动物）脂

tally 货签，标签

tally clerk 理货员（从事货物分拣、签证等理货业务的人员）

tallying of cargoes 理货（在货物储存、装卸过程中，对货物的分票、计数、清理残损、签证和交接等作业）

TAME 三甲基戊醚（见 tertiary amyl methyl ether）

tamper ①夯实，捣固②夯实，捣固用工具
tamper hardening 回火硬化
tampering action 碰击作用，碰撞作用；碰击，撞击（如：车门碰击门框）
tamper-proof 防止乱动的，防止乱调的
Tan 总酸值（total acid number 的简称）
tandem ①串列，并列布置②串联的，串列的，前后并列的
tandem anti-lock system 双轴并装车桥制动抱死系统
tandem axles 双轴并列式车桥（货车、客车、挂车的前后串接且中心轴线间距在 1～2.4m 之间的双轴或多轴组成的双轴或多轴并装式车桥，多为后驱动桥）
tandem brake master cylinder （双管路制动系的）串列双腔式制动主缸（见 series dual-chamber brake master cylinder）
tandem dual diaphragm type vacuum booster 串联双膜片式真空助力器
tandem engine ①串联式发动机（多级串联式发动机）②同轴式多级膨胀型蒸汽机（指各汽缸布置在同一根轴上的多级膨胀蒸汽机）
tandem mechanical seal 串联机械密封（由两套或两套以上同向布置的单端面机械密封所组成的机械密封）
tandem piston 串联活塞
tandem pump 串联泵
tandem seat 前后二人座（如：摩托车座）
tandem wiper 双联刮水器
tang ①尾，尾部，柄②锁紧垫片的凸舌③（叉子的）齿④（与被动件上的凹槽相配合的驱动件上的）凸榫
tangency point 切点（亦写作 tangent point）
tangent ①切线，正切②道路的直线区段③切向的，切线的，正切的
tangent division method （车身外形线的）正切分割绘制法
tangential acceleration 切向加速度
tangential acting hydrodynamic mechanical seal 切向作用流体动压式机械密封（能在切向形成流体动压分布的流体动压式机械密封）
tangential brush 切向（配置）电刷（= tangent brush, diagonal brush）
tangential cam 切线凸轮（= tangent cam）
tangential component 切向分力
tangential deflection 切向变形量（构件任一点在切向方向产生的变形量）
tangential inlet duct 切向进气道（可产生进气涡流，以加速混合气形成和燃烧）
tangential path ①连接弯道的直线路段②（曲线间的）共切线段
tangential shaving 切向剃齿法
tangential speed 切线速度
tangent(ial) spoke wheel 切线轮辐式车轮
tangential tractive force 切向牵引力
tangent modulus 切线模量（在弹性范围内轴向应力与轴向应变关系曲线上任一规定应力或应变处的斜率）
tangent screw 切向螺旋（微动螺旋）
tangent surface 切线曲面，切曲面
tangent to helix 螺旋切线
tangent vector 切矢量
tangle ①（导线、软管等）缠结②弄乱，混乱
tank 箱，罐，桶（等容器，如：油箱，水箱，气罐）
tankage ①储存在容器内，储存在罐车内②储油罐容量③在容器内

（如：油罐内）的沉积物④油罐储存的费用

tank air-mover 油箱（中的）空气排除装置

tank and hose fittings 油箱和软管接头

tank -body 油罐车身

tank breathing diaphragm 油罐的通气隔膜

tank capacity 油箱容积，油罐容量

tank charge level 液箱加液的液面（高度）

tank collapsing 油箱（因碰撞等原因被）压扁

tank container 液罐集装箱（液罐装在框架内，框架的外廓尺寸及形状同一般集装箱）

tank engine 坦克用发动机（用作坦克或装甲车动力的发动机）

tanker 罐式汽车（如：油罐车，水罐车，装有罐状容器，通常带有工作泵，用于运输液体、气体或粉状物资，以及完成特定作业任务的专用车辆）

tanker-trailer （油、水、奶等）液罐挂车

tank fleet 液罐车车队

tank for coolant 冷却液箱

tank for edible liquids 饮料用罐车

tank gauge unit （油箱油量表的）油箱液面高度传感器（一般为可变电阻器）

tank monitor 油罐监视器（监视漏气、漏油情况）

tank motor truck （运输水、油等用的）液罐车（一般装有输液泵，=英tank motorlorry, tank lorry, 简称 tanker）

tankoscope （油罐）内窥灯（自加油口伸入罐内窥察）

tank pressure sensor 油箱压力传感器

tank regulator 气（液）罐调压器

tank sludge 油罐淤渣，油箱残渣

tank vapor pressure sensor 油箱燃油蒸汽压力传感器

tantalum rectifier 钽整流器

tap ①丝攻，丝锥②开关，龙头③放液孔，放液管④塞子，栓⑤用丝锥攻丝⑥放出（液体），分流，分接⑦轻敲，轻拍

TAP ①温控加速泵（thermostatic accelerating pump）②交通分析程序（transportation analysis program）

tap -and-die set 成套丝锥与板牙

tap down （用锤）轻轻敲入

tape ①皮尺，卷尺，软尺，带尺②带，布带，胶带，绝缘胶带，记录纸带，磁带，录音带③用带卷绕，用卷尺测量，用磁带记录

tape-controlled ride simulator 磁带控制（汽车）行驶模拟装置，磁带控制（汽车）乘坐平顺性模拟装置

tape-controlled test 用磁带或穿孔带控制的程序试验，磁带控制的模拟试验

tape data 磁带（纸带）上记录的数据

taped disc wheel 锥形断面（变厚度）辐板式车轮

tape deck （录音机磁带）走带装置

tape gauge 帷度规

tape player 磁带播放机

taper ①锥度，斜度，坡度②带喇叭口的管子③带锥度的，拔销的，逐渐变细的；渐减的，递减的④使具有锥度，使倾斜，使成坡度，使逐渐减小

taper bearing 锥形轴承

taper clamping sleeve （滚动轴承的）紧定套

tapered 锥形的，锥体的，楔形的，斜削的，削尖的，渐减的

tapered adapter sleeve 锥形接头套筒

tapered bead seat rim 楔边式轮辋（如：自行车轮胎的轮辋）

tapered blade 锥形叶片
tapered bushing 锥形衬套
taper(ed) hole 锥孔
tapered inlet 喇叭(形)进口
taper(ed) journal 锥形轴颈
tapered pin 锥形销
tapered plane 斜平面
tapered roller(thrust) bearing 圆锥滚子推力轴承(= conical roller bearing)
tapered (screw) plug 锥形螺塞
tapered shaft 锥形轴(做轴向移动,通过紧贴其锥面的随动件将其轴向移动转换为随动件垂直其移动方向的横向或竖向移动)
tapered snorkel (空气滤清器)锥形进气管
tapered splined joint 锥形花键接合(= conic splined joint)
tapered spring 变截面弹簧(变断面板材制成的弹簧)
tapered steering-wheel hub 锥形转向盘毂
tapered thickness gauge 楔形厚度规
tapered workpiece 锥形工件
taper-face piston ring 锥面活塞环
taper fitting 锥度配合(拔销配合)
taper flat file 尖扁锉(断面成长方形,宽度和厚度向着端部逐渐变小)
tapering ①圆锥度②形成锥度的
taper joint 锥柄连接(带锥度的连接)
taper key 锥形键(斜键)
taper-leaf spring 叶片两头渐窄的钢板弹簧
taper pin hole 锥形销孔
taper plug gauge 锥度塞规
taper profile 锥形剖面
taper ratio 锥度比
taper ring 锥形环
taper ring gauge 锥度环规
taper roller bearing 圆锥滚子轴承(推力轴承的一种, = conical roller bearing)
taper-seat valve 锥形座面阀门(如:锥形座面气门, bevel seated valve)
taper section 锥形断面
taper thrust bearing 锥形滚子推力轴承(= conical roller thrust bearing)
taper washer 锥形垫圈
tap fit 轻打配合,轻迫配合(轻轻打击便可装入的配合)
tap hole 塞孔,螺塞孔,放液孔
tap off 放出,泄出
tapped ①攻有内螺纹的②分支的,分流的,分叉的③抽头的(电绕组)
tapped blind hole 螺纹盲孔
tapped circuit 具有分接头的电路
tapped coil 多接头线圈
tapped hole 螺纹孔
tappet 挺柱(压靠在凸轮上并在导套上滑动,传递往复运动的组件),(气门)挺杆(凸轮随动件, = valve lifter)
tappet adjusting device 挺杆调节装置(如:tappet adjusting screw)
tappet assembly 挺柱体部件(由挺柱、滚轮和滚轮销等组成的部件,将凸轮轴的旋转运动转换成柱塞的往复运动)
tappet clearance 气门间隙(气门挺杆间隙)
tappet guide 挺柱导套(挺柱的导向零件),(气门)挺杆导管
tappet head 挺杆头部
tappet lever 气门挺杆
tappet noise 气门挺杆等的间隙产生的噪音
tappet oil gallery (气门)挺杆润滑油道
tappet pad 挺柱垫块(调整柱塞预行程用的垫块,设置在柱塞尾端与挺柱之间)
tappet plunger (液压)挺杆柱塞

(= valve tappet plunger)

tappet rod guide 挺杆导管（ = lifter guide）

tappet roller （凸轮轴）挺柱滚轮（将凸轮升程传递给挺柱的滚轮）

tappet screw 挺杆间隙调节螺钉

tappet spanner （调节用）气门挺杆扳手

tappet stem 推杆，挺柱

tappet valve （凸轮）挺杆驱动式气门

tappet wear surface 挺杆磨损面

tappet wrench 气门间隙调整扳手，挺杆扳手

tapping ①轻微敲击声，敲击声②攻丝③管道分叉④绕组抽头⑤放出，泄出

tap（ping）bolt 自攻螺钉（被紧固件只有无螺纹的光孔或无孔，而由螺钉本身外螺纹攻出螺纹或螺纹孔，利用拧紧螺钉头的扭矩紧固， = tapping screw，cap screw）

tap（ping）drill 螺孔钻，螺纹底孔钻

tap transformer 抽头变压器

tap water （城市等的）自来水

tar ①柏油，煤焦油，焦油②涂柏油，浇柏油

tar content 焦油含量，含焦油量，胶状物含量

tar cuts 焦油馏分

tare ①皮重（货物包装重，容器重）②不良成分，起阻碍作用的东西③确定皮重；除去皮重

tare and tret 扣除皮重计算法

tare weight 自重，皮重

target ①任务，计划；对象，目标，目的，靶子；终点，到达地点②（交通指挥上的）信号盘③以…作为目标，瞄准

target address 目标地址（信息预定传输的网点的地址，一般指该网点的物理地址）

target date 预定日期（如：预定开始的日期，预定结束的日期，目标日期）

target gauge 标线窗孔式检测仪（带有标线窗孔的检测仪器，如：柴油机喷油嘴喷射角的标线窗孔式检测仪等）

target gear （自动变速器由换挡点特性曲线决定的）目标挡位

target output 目标输出功率（如：研制发动机时所要达到的设计功率，亦称 target power）

target timing for market introduction （新车等）投放市场的目标时间

target tracking 目标跟踪

target weight （设计给定的）目标重量

tariff ①税，关税，税率；收费，用费，（运）费率②确定税率，定税；确定收费标准，定费率

tariff for luggage 行包价目表

tarnish ①（因锈蚀，生锈造成的）表面褪色②使失去光泽，使褪色

tarnish film 氧化膜，锈皮

tarnishing test 表面光泽退化试验（锈蚀试验的一种）

tar oil 煤焦油（焦油，柏油）

TARP ［美］减少交通事故计划（Traffic Accident Reduction Program）

tarp 篷布（见 tarpaulin）

tarpaulin ①篷布，漆布，油布，防雨布，涂油的帆布，帆布篷②（油布）防水衣（简称 tarp）

tarpaulin rod （铰接式客车伸缩篷的）篷杆（位于中间框架两侧主要承受伸缩篷重力的"∏"形构件）

tarpaulin rope hook （车厢）篷布索固定钩

tarpaulin top 帆布篷顶

tarp hook 雨篷挂钩（tarpaulin rope hook 的简称）

tar-spraying car 沥青摊铺车

TAS ①节流阀调整螺钉（throttle adjust screw 的简称）②防盗警报系统（theft alarm system 的简称）

taseometer 应力计

Tauras 金牛座（轿车牌名，美国福特汽车公司 20 世纪 80 年代的成功产品，V6 发动机，24 气门，6L 排量）

taut 拉紧的，张紧的

tautness 拉紧程度，张紧度

TAV system （美国福特汽车公司）温控真空系（temperature activated vacuum system。由温度控制点火提前或废气再循环的真空信号）

tax 税；收税，征税

taxable horsepower 捐功率（国家用来确定汽车捐锐的发动机功率，亦称 duty horsepower）

taxation ①征税②税收，税款

tax-exempt vehicle 免税车辆（亦称 exempt vehicle）

tax-free 免税的（简称 tax-exempt）

taxi depot 出租汽车站，出租汽车场

taximeter （出租汽车的）自动计费、计程表

taxi operation 出租汽车型运行（指汽车在运行过程中时停时走）

taxi productivity 出租汽车运输生产率（指平均每单位时间出租车辆所完成的收费里程和收费停歇时间，用以评价出租汽车营运效率）

taxi stand 出租汽车停车处（= taxi rank）

taxi style （公共交通）出租轿车型（无固定线路，按乘客要求直接送达目的地）

taxonomy （科技文献等的）分类法，分类学

Taylor's principle 泰勒原理（1905 年英国人 W. Taylor 提出确定通过规通过端和不通过端的形状的原则）

T-bar T 形断面棒材

T-bar roof 滑顶式两门轿车（其车身顶部有一可沿 T 形顶梁的纵梁滑动开启的顶盖，开启后可获得敞篷车的行驶感）

TBB （中央单点喷油系统电子控制模块中的）节气门体（喷油）备份控制电路（throttle body backup 的简称，亦称 fuel backup circuit，当电子控制模块发生无法执行其喷油控制程序的故障时，该电路即接替其工作，向喷油器电磁阀发送喷油脉冲指令，该备份电路及其控制数据和控制程序一般装在一种直接插装在电子控制模块专门的插座内的称为 calpak 的插装式计量程序包内，见 calpak）

TBEA [美] 载货汽车车身与设备协会（Truck Body and Equipment Association, Inc 的简称）

T-beam T 形断面梁

T-bend T 形弯头（三通弯头）

TBI 节气门体（汽油）喷射系统（Throttle Body Injection 的简称，通用公司 20 世纪 80 年代的单点式汽油喷射系统的商品名，见 single point injection system）

TBN 总碱值（= total base number）

T-bolt T 字（形）螺栓

TBO（tbo） 大修间隔期，大修周期（time between overhauls）

TBP sensor 废气涡轮增压压力传感器（turbocharger boost pressure sensor 的简称）

T&BT [澳] 载货汽车与客车运输（杂志）（Truck & Bus Transportation 的简称）

TC ①技术通报（technical circular）②技术委员会（technical committee）③温度系数（temperature coefficient）④试验指导人（test conductor）⑤热电耦（thermo-couple）⑥上止点（top center）⑦跟踪摄影机（tracking camera）⑧运输部队（transportation corps）⑨形式合格证

(type certificate)

TC22 (ISO/TC22) 国际标准组织第 22（汽车）委员会（Technical Committee 22 of the ISO 的简称）

TCC ①交通管理中心（traffic control centre）②交通管理电子计算机（traffic control computer）③自动变速器液力变矩器离合器（torque converter clutch 或 transmission converter clutch 的简称）

Tccc solenoid 液力变矩器锁止离合器控制电磁阀（torque converter clutch control selenoid 的简称，由电子控制模块以占空比控制的电磁阀，用于控制 Tcc shift valve 的液压通路）

TCC PWM solenoid 变矩器离合器脉冲宽度调制电磁阀（其中 TCC PWM 为 torque converter clutch pulse width modulation solenoid 的简称，用于控制变矩器锁止离合器接合与分离的速率，使其锁止和分离平顺柔和，减小振动及噪声）

TCCS ①特克瑟科控制燃烧系统发动机（Taxaco controlled combustion system engine 的简称）②丰田电子计算机控制系统（Toyota computer controlled system 的简称，丰田公司使用微型电子计算机对汽油喷射、点火提前、爆燃、急速、自动变速器、牵引力、制动、空调和自诊断等进行统一控制的系统的商品名）

TCC shift valve 液力变矩器锁止合器（由电磁阀控制的）液压控制阀，见 CCC valve

TCC test lead 变速器液力变矩器离合器测试线（可使用电压表或测示灯检测液力变矩器离合器电路的工作情况）

TCE 总综合误差（total composite error）

TCI ①离地间隙计，离地高度计，绝对高度计（terrain clearance indicator）②受控涡流进气（turbulence controlled induction）

TCIL 变速器控制指示灯（transmission control indicator light 的简称）

TCI unit 受控涡流进气导栅（见 TCI③和 jetted grid）

TCL （三菱公司研制的）牵引力控制系统（商品名，Traction control 的简称，该系统的功能是①防止牵引力大于路面与轮胎间附着力时，车轮滑转②防止弯道行驶时，车速过高，冲出弯道，以保证汽车按驾驶员意图转向和弯道行驶）

TCLU 液力变矩器锁止装置（见 torque converter lock-up unit）

TCM ①（自动）变速器控制模块（transmission control module 的简称，一般柴油车由单独的 TCM 控制挡位，而汽油车挡位变换与控制功能合拼在动力控制模块内）②变速驱动桥电子控制模块（transaxle control module 的简称）

T cock 三通旋塞（three-way cock 的简称）

TCP 移镀法（参见 transplant coating process）

TCP engine 特克瑟科分层燃烧发动机（Texaco Combustion Process engine 的简称）

TCR ①电阻温度系数（temperature coefficient of resistance）②工具交付记录（tool consignment record）③示踪物，故障检测仪（tracer）

TCS ①交通管理系统（traffic control system）②变速器控制真空点火提前系统（见 TCS system）③牵引力控制系统（traction control system 当某驱动轮出现因牵引力大于路面附着力而滑转时，通过减小牵引力的方法来消除滑转的系统，一般与防抱死制动系统合为一体。具有牵引力控制功能的防抱死系统使用的电子控制模块称制动和牵引力电子控制模块，见 EBTCM。控制牵引力的方法见 ABC with traction control）④进气增压控制系统（turbo-charge control system）

TCS button （某些自动）变速器（超速挡）控制开关按钮（transmission O/D control switch button 的简称，该开关按钮装在变速器换挡手柄上。用于防止汽车在山区公路上行驶时挂超速挡，按下该按钮后，自动变速器控制指示灯"TCIL"发亮，此时可阻止变速器挂超速挡，而只可在其他挡位上正常运行）

TCS motor （电动式）牵引力控制系统电动机（traction control system motor 的简称，当车轮滑转时，该电动机通过球面螺杆-螺母机构推动液压活塞对滑转的车轮施加制动）

TCS system 变速器控制真空点火提前系（transmission controlled vacuum spark advanced system，挂低速挡时，切断分电器真空源并使之和化油器节流阀上的空气孔相通；挂高速挡时，接通真空源，使点火提前）

TCTL 直接偶合型晶体管逻辑电路（direct coupling transistor logic 的简称）

TCV （电子控制式柴油机喷油泵的）喷油时刻控制阀（timing control valve 的简称）

TD 废气涡轮增压型柴油机（turbo-charged diesel 的简称）

TDC 上止点（top dead center 的简称，活塞顶离曲轴中心线最近时的止点）

TDCL 总故障诊断插座（total diagnostic communication link，车装式自诊断系统中读取故障代码的总插座，一般位于汽车驾驶室仪表板下方，或发动机附近，OBD-II 规定为 16 针插座）

TDC sensor 上止点传感器（top dead center sensor 的简称）

TDI ①涡轮增压直接喷射（式柴油机）（turbo direct injection 的简称）②（日本）丰田（公司的）直接点火系统（商品名，Toyota Direct Ignition system 的简称，每一个火花塞上均装有一点火线圈，直接向火花塞输送高压点火脉冲）

TDM ①（汽车）防盗系统电子控制模块（thief deterrent module 的简称）②技术演示模型（technology demonstration model）

TDMA 时间分割多路复用存取（time division multiple access 的简称，在汽车电子系统中，指每一个电子控制装置都分配有一段排他性的独自占用总线的时间片，用于存取、传输信息，完成访问等）

TDS 感温开关（temperature detect switch）

Te 碲（= tellurium）

teak brown 柚木棕（车身颜色）

team ①组，队，班②编成一组，组成机组

team spirit （比赛车队等的）团队精神

tear ①裂口，裂缝②扯开，撕裂，刺破；擦伤，钩破，划破

teardrop body 流线型车身（streamlined body）

tearing test （抗）撕裂试验（亦称 tear resistance test）

tear-proof 抗撕裂的

tear seam （控制安全气囊充气速度和压力的）破裂缝（当爆发过猛、充气速度和压力超出规定的安全阈值时，该缝即破裂减压，以免炸伤乘员，亦称 inflation control "safety" seam）

tear strength 抗撕裂强度（亦称 tear resistance）

teat 凸出部，凸台，凸座

4TEC （英 Land Rover Discovery SerialsII 车上的）全轮牵引力电子控制

系统（4-wheel traction electronic control 的简称）

Tec -High Park 高科驻（一种全自动驻车系统的商品名，见 automatic parking system）

technic ①技巧，手法②技术性的，工艺的

technical 技术的

technical and economic index 技术经济指标（在一定时期内，用平均数和相对数反映所有工作车辆在运行中的技术经济效果）

technical appraisal 技术鉴定书（由主管部门鉴认的技术文件）

technical assistance 技术援助

technical atmosphere 工程大气压（简称 at，1at = 98.0665kPa = 14.2233lbf/in²）

technical checking 技术检验（按规定的技术要求，确定汽车、总成、零部件技术状况所实施的检查）

technical classification of motor vehicle 汽车技术等级 temperature field 温度场

technical committee 技术委员会

Technical Committee 22（Automobile）of the ISO 国际标准化组织第22（汽车）委员会（简称 TC22，亦称国际标准化组织汽车专业委员会，或道路车辆技术委员会，秘书处设在法国标准化协会）

technical condition of vehicle 车辆的技术状况（车辆状况和技术性能参数的综合表征）

technical data 技术数据

technical exchange 技术交流

technical failure 技术故障（技术失效）

technical feasibility 技术可行性

technical feature 技术特征，技术特点

technical information file 技术信息文件（简称 TIF）

technical inspection 技术检验（技术检测）

technical life of vehicle 车辆的技术寿命

technical maintenance 技术维护

technical materials 技术资料

technical norms 技术标准，技术规范

technical parameter 技术参数

technical performance 技术性能

technical personnel 技术人员

technical regulation ①技术手册（= technical manual）②技术规范（= technical specification）

technical regulations 技术规程，技术规范，技术条件，技术说明书，技术细则，技术定额

technical requirement（s） 技术要求

technical risk 技术风险

technical speed 技术速度（车辆在运行时间内平均每小时的行程）

technical standard of vehicle repair 汽车修理技术标准（对汽车修理全过程的技术要求、检验规则所做的统一规定）

technical supervision 技术管理，技术检验

technical terms 技术名词，技术词汇，专门术语，术语

technical vehicle inspection 车辆技术检验

techni characteristics 技术规格，技术特性

technique ①技术，工艺，技能，手法②技术装备，工艺装备

technologic（al） 工艺的，工艺性的，技术的；因工业技术发展而引起的

technological advance 技术进步

technological analysis 工艺分析，技术分析

technological characteristics 工艺特

性,技术特性

technological chart 工艺卡,工艺图表(= technological card)

technological document 工艺文件,技术文件

technological equipment of vehicle maintenance and repair 汽车维修工艺设备

technological forecasting 技术预测,技术预报

technological improvement 技术改革,技改

technological innovation 技术革新,工艺新技术

technological process 工艺过程,工艺规程,制造过程,生产过程

technological process of vehicle maintenanceand repair 汽车维修工艺过程

technological standpoint 技术观点

technology 工艺,工艺学;技术

technology assessment 技术鉴定,技术评价,技术认证

technology demonstration model 技术示范模型(简称TDM)

technology development project 技术开发项目

technology innovation 技术创新

technology liaison activity 技术交流活动(技术联络活动,技术协作活动)

technology of metals 金属工艺学

Technology of the Year "Best 10" (日本《自动车工学》期刊每年一次评选的)本年度"10项最佳技术"奖

technology of vehicle maintenance 汽车维护工艺

technology of vehicle repair 汽车修理工艺

Tech Z (通用公司某些车型使用的故障)诊断软件名

tee ①T字形,丁字形②T字形零件(如: tee coupling, tee fitting, tee joint, tee tube, tee union 等各种三通件)

TEE 试验设备工程学(test equipment engineering)

TEEAR 试验设备误差分析报告(test equipment error analysis report)

tee-head cylinder T形头汽缸(T形燃烧室汽缸)

tee-scopic damper 伸缩筒式减振器

tee-section T形断面

tee-slot T形槽

teeter (如跷跷板似的)上下往复运动

teeth 齿,牙,轮齿

teethed type coupling 齿型联轴节

teethed wheel type pulse generator 齿轮式脉冲发生器

teeth spacing 齿距

teeth washer 带齿垫圈

tee valve 三通阀(= T valve)

teflon 特氟隆(一种聚四氟乙烯塑料的商品名,热可塑性合成树脂之一,见polytetrafluoroeth,其机械强度、耐磨性、耐油性均好,可用于节气门等的轴承)

teflon-coated 涂有特氟隆的(有特氟隆涂层的)

teflon fluorocarbon plastic 特氟隆碳氟化合物塑料(聚四氟乙烯碳氟塑料)

teflon-lined 聚四氟乙烯内衬的

TEL ①四乙基铅(tetraethyl lead)②试验仪器清单(test equipment list)③电话(telephone)④望远镜(telescope)

tele ①远,远距离②电信;电传

tele adjusting ①远距离调节②可远距离调节的

teleaid system (奔驰的)电传呼救系统(汽车因故障而途中抛锚时,该系统会自动通知紧急服务中心)

telecar 收发报汽车

telecommunication 电信学（复），电信

telecommunication date-transmitting technology 远距离数据传输技术

telecommunication field service truck 电信工程车（用于通信系统的线路维修和建设作业及运输线杆、线盘等）

telecommunication terminal system 无线电信终端系统

telecontrol 遥控（远距离控制，远距离操纵）

telegauge 遥测仪表

telehoist 套筒伸缩臂起重机

telematics ①无线电话信息通信服务（指20世纪90年代末出现的车载式IT machines 与外部 service center 通过移动电话联络，向驾驶者提供各种服务的系统，见 IT machine, service center）②电讯信息（学）（telecommunication and informatics 的简称）

telemechanic system 远距离操纵机械系统

telemeter ①遥测仪（用于远距离测量、记录、发送测量数据的测试仪器的通称）②遥测（指用遥测仪进行测试和通过远程通信设施传送测量数据）

telemetering instrument 遥测仪器仪表（对被测装置或系统进行远距离测量的仪器仪表）

telemetering system 遥测系统

telemetric evaluation 遥测评价（使用遥测技术对车辆上的某项装置或系统的性能或参数进行评定）

telemetry 遥测，遥测术，遥测装置（=telemetering）

Telemp 天帘布（商品名，棉毛混纺织物，用于座位蒙布等）

telephone cable 电话线，通信电缆

telephoto lens 遥摄镜头

telescope ①望远镜；望远装置②嵌进，插进拔出③（汽车等）相撞而嵌进

telescope (d) joint 套筒接头（伸缩管接头，套管连接装置，插接）

telescope jack 伸缩式举升器（伸缩式举升油缸）

telescope tube 伸缩套筒

telescopic 望远镜（式）的（可伸缩的，套筒式的）

telescopic aerial 套筒式天线

telescopic shaft coupling 伸缩式联轴节（轴内可自由伸缩的联轴节）

telescopic shock absorber 伸缩筒式减振器（亦称 telescopic type absorber, telescopic type damper, cylinder type absorber）

telescopic steering column 伸缩式转向盘柱（转向盘高度、位置可调，亦简称 telescopic steering）

telescopic strut 伸缩撑杆

telescopic tarpaulin （铰接式客车的）伸缩篷（主、副车间可相对运动的软篷）

telescoping gauge 伸缩式测量仪（伸缩规）

telescoping hydraulic cylinder 伸缩式液力缸

telescoping jack 伸缩式举升器

tele service 远程（维修等）服务

teleswitch 遥控开关

teletachometer 遥测转数计（遥测转速表）

telethermometer 遥测温度计

television ①电视（学）②电视机（简称TV）

television car 电视车

television reporting van 电视（传送）车

tell-tale hole 警报孔（如：压力超过某极限值的，气或液即由该孔喷出，以示警报）

tell-tales 信号装置（用光信号或音响信号显示车辆及其部件的功能状

况的信号装置）
tell-tale signal 警报信号
tellurium 碲（Te）
telpher ①电动吊车（天车）②电动（架空单轨）缆车③高架索道，架空索道
Telstar ［美］福特卫星（福特汽车公司轿车牌名，V6发动机排量1995mL，功率118kW）
TEMD 驾驶员眼点与后视镜中心的横向距离（transverse distance between the driver eye point and the mirror center）
temp 温度（temperature的简称）
temper ①回火，回火度②硬度，韧度③调质④缓和，减轻，变柔软⑤调和物
temperament （原指人的气质、性情、秉性，现亦用于形容汽车造型等的）风格
temperate 适度的，温和的，有节制的
temperate zone 温带
temperature 温度（简称temp）
temperature adjustable fluid （密封件的）调温流体（不与密封端面接触的能使密封件得到冷却或加热的外部循环流体）
temperature alarm 温度警报器（过热报警装置）
temperature balance 温度平衡
temperature booster 加热器
temperature bulb 测温泡（测温度的热敏元件）
temperature buzzer 温度警报蜂鸣器
temperature coefficient of regulated output current（of a current regulator）（电流调整器的）调整输出电流的温度系数（当其他条件保持不变时，输出电流的相对变化与规定温度的变化之比）
temperature coefficient of regulated output voltage（of a voltage regulator）（电压调整器的）调整输出电压的温度系数（当其他条件保持不变时，输出电压的相对变化与规定温度的变化之比）
temperature compensating circuit 温度补偿电路（抵消温度变化造成的影响的电路）
temperature compensator 温度补偿器（对因温度或温度变化而造成的各种不利影响进行补偿的装置的总称，如：temperature-compensated flasher"温度补偿闪光断续器"，temperature-compensated regulator"温度补偿调节器"）
temperature conditions 温度条件，温度状况
temperature conductivity 热导率（=thermal conductivity）
temperature controlled（modulated）air cleaner 温控式空气滤清器（使空气滤清器吸入的空气保持适当温度的装置。此装置通常包括预热器、导管和控制阀）
temperature control valve 温度控制阀
temperature correction 温度校正
temperature dependence of velocity 速度与温度关系（曲线）
temperature-dependent 随温度而变的
temperature detector 温度传感器
temperature detect switch 温控开关（感温开关，简称TDS）
temperature difference 温差
temperature distribution 温度分布
temperature drift 温度偏离
temperature drive 温差促动，温度驱动
temperature drop 温度降
temperature effect 温度效应
temperature efficiency 温度（交换）效率（在热交换器中，高温流体A将热量传给低温流体B时的比值

1603

$(t_{B_2} - t_{B_1}) / (t_{A_1} - t_{A_2})$，即 B 的温升与 A 的温降的比值

temperature error 温度误差

temperature factor 温度系数，温度因素

temperature fall 温度落差；温度降

temperature-gradient 温度梯度，温度陡度

temperature increment 温度增量，温度升高值

temperature-independent 与温度无关的（不随温度变化而变化的）

temperature indicator ①温度指示器 ②温度指示剂（当温度超过某阈值时，变色的材料，溶于涂料或制成各种形状，用来测定装置或部件的工作温度是否超过规定值）

temperature limit 温度极限

temperature limited condition 温度限制条件

temperature loss 热量损失，温度损失

temperature-modulated air cleaner 调温式空气滤清器（装有可调温式预热器）

temperature-modulated choke system 调温式阻风门系统

temperature of solidification 凝固温度

temperature of superheat 过热温度

temperature-pressure curve 温度-压力曲线

temperature range 温度范围；温度极限

temperature recorder 温度记录仪

temperature regulator 温度调节器（节温器）

temperature-resistant 耐热的，抗热的，热稳定的

temperature scale 温（度）标

temperature-sensing 感温的（对温度变化敏感的，热敏的）

temperature-sensing element 温度传感元件

temperature-sensing valve 感温阀

temperature-sensitive bimetallic element 感温式双金属片元件

temperature-sensitive capsule 感温盒（见 silicon fluid）

temperature-sensitive shim 感温垫片（感温填隙片，尺寸可随温度变化的垫片）

temperature setting switch （汽车空调系统的）温度设定开关

temperature shock 温度冲击（温度骤变，温度剧增，温度急降）

temperature susceptibility 温度敏感度，温度敏感性

temperature swing ［发动机汽缸燃烧室壁面形成的低热传导率、低热容量的隔热层（heat insulation）的］温度（紧随汽缸内进气和燃气温度的变化而）快速变化（既可防止壁面加热进入汽缸的新鲜混合气，又可减低混合气燃烧后随缸壁传导的热损失）

temperature switch 温度开关（如：根据冷却水温度或进气温度发出信号、操纵控制电路的接通或断开的传感器）

temperature time curve 温度-时间曲线

temperature transducer 温度传感器（= temperature sensor）

temperature traverse （沿着某条直线的）温度分布（温度变化）

temperature variation 温度变化

temperature warning tell-tale 温度警报灯（表示发动机的冷却液和机油温度低于或高于规定的信号灯）

temperature warping （由于）热（应力引起的）翘曲（变形）

temperaure equalisation system 温度均衡系统（如：转子发动机缸体上的预热及冷却装置，以使冷区和热区的温度趋于平衡）

temperaure gauge 温度计，温度表（= heat indicator）

temper bend test 加热弯曲试验（将加热至指定的温度状态下的试件弯折，检查是否出现裂纹的试验）

temper brittleness 回火脆性（= blue brittleness）

temper color （钢的）回火色

tempered 经过回火处理的

tempered air 预热空气

tempered glass 钢化玻璃（淬火玻璃、强化玻璃，利用加热到软化点附近然后骤冷的方法，提高强度和热稳定性，一旦破坏，碎片无尖利棱角的安全玻璃）

tempered-hardness 回火硬度

tempered heat-absorbing glass 吸热钢化玻璃（玻璃本身含有着色氧化物，因而具有吸热效果的钢化玻璃）

tempered masonite backing 梅索奈特软纤维衬板（柔韧贴面纤维衬板，常用于大客车车身，衬板外盖，装饰性的铝板面）

temper hardening 回火硬化

tempering ①回火，人工时效 ②混合，调和，调合

temper rolling ①硬化冷轧 ②表面光轧，表面平整

temper test 回火韧度试验，调质试验

template ①制取图样，取样，画样，打样，放样 ②模板，样板，模型，样规，仿形板；靠模

template eyepiece 样板目镜（标准图板接目镜，工具显微镜，万能显微镜等画有螺纹形状、圆弧、圆等大量标准图形的玻璃板，可在焦点面上回转的接目镜）

template process 仿形加工法（如：仿形切削法，仿形铣齿法）

templet 样板，模板，模型，样规，仿形板，靠模

templug 测温塞

TEMPMATIC (Benz 带花粉、微粒过滤系统和在风窗玻璃上装有可测定阳光强度和方向的日光传感器的) 电子控制自动恒温空调系统（商品名）

temporary bridge 便桥，临时桥

temporary hardness 暂时硬度（见 temporary hardwater）

temporary hardwater 暂时硬水（含有 Ca(HCO$_3$)$_2$, Mg(HCO$_3$)$_2$ 等重碳酸盐的硬水，经煮沸后，碳酸盐即可沉淀除去，这种硬水称为暂时硬水，这些盐类造成的硬度称为暂时硬度）

temporary magnet 暂时磁铁（如：电磁铁）

temporary marker 临时路标（因事故或道路施工等临时性的原因需更改路线时设置的路标）

temporary repair 临时修理，小修（= running repair）

temporary route 临时线路（供临时交通使用的道路）

temporary storage register 暂时性存储寄存器（简称暂存存储器"temporary storage"，汽车电子控制系统电子控制模块保存中间结果的存储单元）

TEMS system 丰田电子调制悬架系统（Toyota Electronic modulated suspension system 的简称，其减振器的阻尼特性可作多级调制，并可由驾驶者根据路状和个人喜好调至舒适或运动模式）

tenacious ①坚韧的；黏滞的 ②黏着力强的 ③紧握的，抓紧的

tenacity of the lubricating film 润滑油膜韧度

tendency to detonate 爆震倾向

tendency to soot 形成积炭的倾向

tender ①柔软的，脆弱的；稳定性差的；敏感的 ②提出，申请

tending 维护，保养，照料

tenon ①榫舌，榫头 ②用榫联结；在…上开榫

ten ply tyre 十层帘布线轮胎

ten point road test 十项道路试验，十项路试（美国规定的一种路试法）

tensible force ①拉力 ②牵引力（= tractive effort）

tensile ①抗拉（张）的 ②拉（张）力的 ③拉伸的，受拉的；可伸长的；能伸展的，有延性的

tensile adhesion 抗拉黏着强度（抗拉黏着力）

tensile and compression test 拉伸和压缩试验

tensile component （承受）拉伸（的）零件

tensile cord （传动带等的）拉力帘线

tensile elongation 拉伸延伸率（= stretch elongation）

tensile failure 拉断（拉伸破坏）

tensile fatigue test 拉伸疲劳试验

tensile force 拉力，张力

tensile impact test 拉伸冲击试验（= tensile shock test）

tensile load 张力负载，拉伸负载

tensile retention 拉伸保持（力）

tensile strain 拉伸应变

tensile strength limit 抗拉强度极限

tensile-stress skin 拉伸应力表面

tensile tester 拉伸试验机（= tensile test machine）

tensile testing 拉伸试验（用静拉伸力对试样轴向拉伸，测量力和相应的伸长，一般拉至断裂，测定其力学性能的试验）

tensile yield point 拉伸屈服点（张力屈服点，简称 tensile YP）

tensiometer 张力计，拉力计；伸长计

tension ①张力，拉力（= stretching force）②压强，（流体）压力 ③电压（= voltage）④张紧状态 ⑤使拉紧，使张紧

tension adjusting gear 张紧力调整机构

tension coil spring 张力卷簧，拉伸卷簧

tension-compression fatigue limit 拉伸-压缩疲劳极限（指交替受拉、受压时材料的疲劳极限）

tension dynamometer 牵引力计，拉力计

tensioner 张紧装置（如：传动带的张紧轮）

tensioner eccentric （链条等的）张紧装置的偏心轮

tensioner sprocket 张紧链轮

tension gauge 张力规，张力计（= tensimeter）

tension gauge factor 张力计的灵敏度系数

tension indicating wrench 扭力扳手，测力扳手

tension indicator 扭力计，拉力计

tensioning device （汽车发动机凸轮轴驱动带等的）张紧装置

tensioning pulley 张紧带轮（压靠在传动带上，调节传动带张紧度的滚轮）

tensioning wheel of chain 链条张紧轮（压靠在链条上，调节链条张紧度的轮子）

tension leaf 副钢板弹簧片（= auxiliary leaf）

tension limiter safety belt 拉紧力限制式安全带

tension link ①张力调节杆 ②拉杆（亦称 tensioning lever）

tension load 拉伸负载

tension (loaded) ball joint （承受）拉伸载荷式球节

tension member 受拉件，抗拉件

tension pulley 传动带张紧轮

tension reducer （安全带的）张紧减

压器（用于减轻乘员承受的安全带的压迫力，当汽车受到冲击时，该装置可利用紧急收紧锁死装置将安全带收紧锁死）

tension rod 拉杆（承受拉力的杆）

tension roller 张力滚柱

tension shackle （钢板弹簧）抗拉吊耳

tension side 拉力边（皮带紧边，皮带主动边）

tension spring 拉簧

tension tester 拉力试验机

tension washer 张紧垫圈

tension wrench 扭力扳手（= torque wrench）

tensometer 张力计，拉力计；应变计

tensor ①张量②磁张线③伸张器（简称 T）

TENT ①试验性的；暂行的②假设的（tentative 的简称）

tent 帐篷，篷布

tentative ①试验性的，尝试性的，试探性的；暂行的，试行的（试用的标准、规范等，简称 TENT）②假设的

tentative data 假设数据，试用数据

tentative design 草案（性质的）设计

tentatives ①试验（性）的，暂时的②试验③假说

tentative specification 暂行技术规范（试用规范）

tentative standard 暂行标准（试用标准）

tenth highest annual hourly volume 一年内的第十位最高小时交通量

tent-shaped combustion chamber 篷顶式燃烧室

tenuity ①（气体的）稀薄度②纤细，单薄③贫乏④微弱

tenuity factor 真空度系数（空气稀薄系数）

TEOM （微粒物测定的）锥形件振荡微平衡法（tapered element oscillating microbalance 的简称）

tera- 万亿，兆（词头，代号为 T = 10^{12}。旧称 megamega，代号为 MM）

term ①术语，专用语，专门名词②期限，期间；学期，任期，限期③条，条款，项④终端，终点（terminal 的简称）⑤结束，终止，终端（装置），终端（负载）（= termination）

terminal ①（运输）总站，终点站，转运基地，装卸站②（货物）集散点；中转库③接线柱，引线，接头，线端④终端设备，终端符号⑤终端，末端，终点⑥末端的，终点的，终站的

terminal-based conformity （仪表的）端基一致性（通过调整将校准曲线接近规定的特性曲线，使两曲线的范围上限值和下限值分别重合时的一致程度）

terminal-based linearity （测量仪表的）端基线性度（指通过调整将校准曲线接近规定曲线，使两者范围的上限值和下限值分别重合时的一致程度）

terminal block 接线盒，接线板（亦称 terminal board）

terminal bolt 接线柱螺栓

terminal charges 装卸费

terminal check 最后检验，最终校核；终点（站）检验

terminal circle of involute profile on internal circular spline 刚轮齿渐开线终止圆（在内齿刚轮齿廓上接近齿根处终止渐开线齿廓的圆）

terminal connector 接线柱

terminal delay 终点站停车延误（时间）

terminal face 端面

terminal facilities 车站设施

terminal garage 起点或终点站车库
terminal holder 接线夹，线夹，接线柱
terminal insulated plate 接（电）线柱绝缘底板
terminal kit 电气线路的成套接头和接线柱
terminal life 总使用寿命（最终寿命，报废前的使用期限）
terminal of semiconductor device 半导体器件的引出端（规定的外部可用连接点）
terminal of spark plug 火花塞接线头
terminal point 终点（到达站，到达地点）
terminal pole loosening 电桩头松动
terminal post 接线柱（带螺纹或不带螺纹的接线端）
terminal pressure 终点压力（如：膨胀终了时的压力，管道终点压力）
terminal speed 末速（临界速率，极限速率，终点车速）
terminal state 终态（极限状态，临界状态，极限状态）
terminal station 终点站（简称terminal）
terminal-to-terminal time 从起点到终点的路程运行时间
terminal velocity 终端速度（最大速度，末速度；稳定状态速度，极限速度）
terminal voltage 端电压（如：蓄电池各单格电池的总电压）
terminating traffic 到达交通（以某一地区为目的地到达这个地区的交通）
termination 终止（作用），结束，结尾，归结，终端（装置），终端（负荷）；端接（法）；终点站；界限
termini terminus 的复数

terminology 专门名词（专门词汇，术语）
terminus ①（汽车线路的）终点站 ②极限，目标，界限，界标，终点
term of service 使用期限，使用期
term of validity 有效期限
terms 条件，关系，条款，约定，约章；要求额；价钱，费用
terms of delivery 移交条件，交货条件
terms of reference ①职责范围②参考条款
ternary ①三合一②三元，三重；三进制③三个一套的，三元的，三重的；三进制的
ternary alloy（s） 三元合金
terne ①镀锡铅合金的薄铁皮，薄钢板（=terneplate）②铅锡合金（=terne metal）
terned 镀锡铅合金的（亦称terne-coated）
terne metal 铅锡合金（铅80%~80.5%，锑1.5%~2%，锡18%或铅85%~90%，锡10%~15%，=terne alloy）
terrain ①地面，地表面②地形，地势③地域，地带
terrain break angle 相邻坡面夹角
terrain clearance 离地高度，离地间隙（简称TC）
terrain-hugging vehicle 气垫车（=air-cushion vehicle）
terrain-measuring instrumentation 地形测量仪（亦称terrain profilometer）
terrain Response system （新型Land Rover上配装的）路况地形反应系统（商品名，随行驶条件及地形、路况的变化，实时改变车辆的有关工况）
terrain-tech package （汽车的）越野包（整套越野技术装备，亦称off-road package）
terrain trafficability （车辆的）地面

通过能力
terrain vehicle system statistical evaluation 地面车辆系统的统计评价
terrapin 水陆两用汽车
terra-tyre 超低压轮胎（高通过性轮胎）
terra-tyred transporter 超低压轮胎运输车辆（= terra-tyred vehicle）
terrestrial ①地球的 ②地上的，陆上的
terrestrial gravitation 地球引力（重力）
terrestrial transport 陆上运输
terrestrial vehicle 地面车辆（陆用车辆，区别于水陆两用车辆）
tertiary air 三次空气（指燃气轮机的燃烧器中，与燃烧完了的废气混合，降低其温度的空气，而燃料燃烧所需的空气，按供给顺序称为一次空气和二次空气）
tertiary amyl methyl ether 三甲基戊醚（用作为汽油混合成分的氧化剂）
tertiary creep 第三阶段蠕变（蠕变破坏段）
tertiary highways 三级公路（在公路网中较地方公路范围更小的公路）
Terzaghi's bearing capacity coefficient 泰查基氏土壤承载系数
tesla 特斯拉（国际单位制的磁通密度及磁感应强度单位，代号T，每平方米有1韦伯的磁通量，$1T = 1Wb/m^2 = 10^4 Gs$）
test 试验
testability 可测试性
test air tunnel 试验风洞
test club 试验用功率吸收风扇（= test fan）
test code 试验规范
test coil 试验用线圈（试验时使用的标准线圈等）
test conditions 试验条件

test coupon 试件，试样
test criteria 试验标准
test cycle 试验循环（由模拟发动机或汽车各种运行工况组成的燃油经济性或排放等的测试循环，如：欧洲ECE 15工况试验循环由包括模拟冷起动、怠速、加速、稳速、减速等15种严格按规定的顺序、时间及转速和运行条件的工况组成的排放物测试循环）
test data 试验数据（在试验中得到的观测数据）
test distance 试验距离（试验行程长度，路试里程）
test drive ①试验驾驶，试车 ②试驱动
test driver 试车驾驶员
test driving time （车辆）路试时间
test drum （转鼓试验台的）转鼓
test duration 试验持续期（试验持续时间）
test dust 试验用粉尘
testee 测试对象（被测试物）
test engine ①被试验的发动机 ②进行试验研究用的发动机
test equipment error analysis report 试验设备误差分析报告（简称TEEAR）
test equipment tester 测试设备检验装置（简称TET）
tester ①试验员，试验人员 ②试验装置，试验台 ③测试仪表
tester for licence plate illumination 汽车牌照灯测试器（由遮光板、亮度计等组成，可在白昼及室外测试牌照灯等的亮度、光分布的均匀度等，遮光板用于遮断外部光源，亮度计一般由光电池、晶体管放大电路等组成）
tester lift （汽车的）单端举升器（只将汽车的一端顶起，= end lift）
tester probe （气体、液体分析试验装置等的）试样采集头（取样头，

采样头)

test evaluation time 评价试验(所需)时间

test facilities 试验设备,试验装置,(=test equipment)

test failure 试验时发生的故障

test failure load 试验性破坏载荷

test fan (发动机试验用的)功率吸收风扇

test for convergence 收敛检验法

test for durability 耐久性试验(寿命试验)

test for ground (检查仪表,电器接地情况的)接地试验

test for non-transmission of an internal explosion 隔爆性能试验(检验隔爆型仪器仪表内部规定的爆炸性气体混合物爆炸时能否点燃其周围同一爆炸性气体混合物的试验)

test for parallelism 平行度检查

test for short-circuit 短路检查

test for suitability (对所提要求的)适应性试验

test for thermal stability 热稳定性试验

test function 试验功能

test gauge 样板,校核用标准量规,校核用仪具

testing car 测试(用)车(一般指车内装有各种测试设备,用来进行各种试验、测定、检查作业)

test(ing) certificate 试验证明书,试验合格证

testing ground 试验场,试车场(=proof ground, proving ground)

testing method for calorific value 热值测试法

testing method for distillation 分馏试验法

testing method for oxidation characteristics 氧化稳定性试验法

testing method of color (滑油的)色度测试法

testing of destruction 破坏性试验

testing of hypothesis 假设的验证

testing of materials 材料试验

Testing Operation Fuel Economy Program [美]燃油经济性试验操作规程(简称 TOFEP)

testing procedure 试验程序

test(ing) program(me) 试验大纲,测试方案

testing record sheet 试验记录表

testing regulations 试验规程

testing track 试车跑道(试验车道)

testing without destruction 非破坏性试验

test interval 两次试验的间隔时间

test in the field (相对于实验室试验的)现场试验(=field test)

test lamp (电路等的)故障检查灯(亦称 test light)

test length 试验持续时间

test loop ①试验回路,测试回路 ②环形试验线路

test number ①试验次数 ②试验编号(简称 TN)

test of braking on curve 弯道制动试验(评价汽车在转弯行驶时,进行制动时的稳定性试验)

test of braking stability 制动稳定性试验(汽车直线行驶中进行制动时的稳定性试验,可用横向位移、横摆角速度等进行评价)

test of burst response of tire 轮胎爆破响应试验(评价汽车在行驶中轮胎爆破后,驾驶员控制汽车难易程度的试验)

test of control at breakaway 收油门后控制试验(汽车沿圆周行驶,当侧向加速度达到预先指定值时,迅速松开加速踏板,急收油门,评价此时驾驶员控制汽车难易程度的试验)

test of cross-wind stability 横风稳定性试验(当送风装置产生的横向

风,或自然风作用于行驶的汽车上时,用横向位移、横摆角速度、转向盘转角的修正额度及转向角等评价汽车行驶方向稳定性的试验)

test of effect of sudden power change 功率突然变化影响试验(汽车在转弯行驶中,控制加速踏板,评价汽车突然加速及突然减速时的稳定性试验)

test of "J" turn "J"形转弯试验(评价汽车由直线行驶急剧进入"J"形曲线行驶时的抗翻倾性、轮辋错动等的试验)

test of overturning immunity 抗翻倾试验(评价汽车耐翻倾程度的试验。可用"J"形转弯试验、蛇行试验、转弯制动试验代替,参见 test of "J" turn)

test of pavement irregularity sensitivity 路面不平敏感性试验(评价汽车对路面不平响应敏感性的试验)

test of rated performance 额定性能试验(指发动机处于额定状态下运转时的油耗、功率及其他性能的测试)

test of returnability 回正性试验(评价汽车在转弯行驶中松开转向盘时,克服汽车横摆加速度等变量恢复直线行驶状态的试验)

test of significance 显著性检定(见 significance test)

test of stability of steer-off motion on a straight-ahead driving 撒手稳定性试验(汽车以一定车速直线行驶,突然转动转向盘并立即撒手,评价汽车运动收敛性的试验)

test of steering wheel returnability 转向盘回正性试验(评价转向盘过某一角度松开后,转向盘恢复直行位置的试验)

test of time 经时试验(经受时间考验,指代产品或材料等经受一定时间的考验来试验其性能的可靠性和稳定性,如:让产品预先经受一定时间的运转考验,再投入使用、材料保护层的风蚀暴露试验等, = time test)

test oil 试验用油

test OK (试验结果表明)正常,无故障

test on sand 砂地试验(测定车辆在砂地的运行能力等)

test on the road (道)路试(验)(= road test)

test oscillator 测试用振荡器

test parameters 试验参数

test paraphernalia 试验用附属装置

test pattern 试验模式

test piece 试验样品,试件

test piece model 试件模型

test plan table 表格形式的试验大纲

test plug 试验插头

test point scattering 试验点分布(区)

test procedure 试验程序,测试工艺过程

test prod 探针

test profile 试验结果的曲线图

test requirement specification 试验技术规范,试验规范,试验要求规程

test rig 试验台架,试验设备(亦称 test bed, testjig, testing stand, test rack)

test-rig failure ①台架故障(台架损坏)②台架试验时的损坏(台试时的故障)

test rig panel board 试验台控制板

test road 试车道路

test routine 试验程序

test run ①试验运行②(汽车)试运行,试车

test sample 试(验)样(品)

test session 试验阶段(试验期,试车期)

test set 试验装置

test socket 试验(接线)插座

test specifications 试验规程

test stand performance 试验台性能；台架性能

test station truck 流动试验车（装有试验用仪器设备的试验车）

test summary sheet 试验报告摘要表

test support equipment 试验支持设备（简称TSE）

test to destruction 损坏性试验（= test to failure）

test track 试验车道（汽车路试车道）

test tractor 试验用牵引车

test under load 负荷试验

test validation 根据试验结果做出的评定

test weight ①在试验时的重量②试验重量（试验质量的旧称）

test zone ①试验区，试验区域②试验范围

TET ①测试设备组（test equipment team）②测试设备检验装置（test equipment tester）③测试设备工具（test equipment tool）④四氯化物（tetrachloride）

tether 栓，栓件，紧固件，卡装件

tethered testing 系杆试验（法）（用于汽车操纵性试验）

tetraethyl 四乙基

tetraethyl lead 四乙基铅 [$Pb(C_2H_5)_4$，汽油用抗爆剂，简称TEL]

tetrafluoroethylene fiber 四氟乙烯纤维

tetrafluoroethylene resin 四氟乙烯树脂

tetragonal structure ①四方晶体结构 ②四角形结构；四边形结构

tetralin 萘满，1、2、3、4—四氢化萘 $C_6H_4CH_2(CH_2)_2CH_2$（容易形成萘满过氧化物，是一种爆震诱导剂，也是一种危险的着火加速剂）

tetramethyl lead 四甲基铅（$Pb(CH_3)_4$）（一种抗爆剂，简称TML）

tetrode 四极管

Teves Mark II type ABS 特佛斯·马克II型防抱死制动系统（一种氮气压缩式储压器液压助力整体式防抱死制动系统的商品名）

Teves Mark IV ABS 特佛斯·马克IV型防抱死制动系统（用于美国通用、福特、克莱斯勒等公司生产的多种型号的轿车的四通道ABS，其电子控制模块操纵四个常开型加压电磁阀和四个常闭型减压电磁阀，控制车轮分泵的制动液压，实现防抱死制动。某些Teves Mark IV型系统复合有牵引力控制功能，这时装有两个防止实施牵引力控制时制动液从电动泵流向制动总泵的隔离阀）

Teves Mark IV（system） 特佛斯·马克IV（系统）（带防滑转牵引力控制功能，利用制动控制牵引力的ABS系统的商品名）

Texaco Controlled-Combustion System engine （美国）特克斯科控制燃烧系统发动机（美特克斯科公司多年研制的直喷式层状充气发动机，在汽缸内形成强烈的旋流，在压缩冲程末期，按所要求的点火时刻，通过喷嘴将燃油直接喷至火花塞附近、进气旋转方向的上方，使之在火花塞附近形成混合气，为火花所点燃，并且边喷边燃，由于这种发动机燃油是直接喷入汽缸的，类似柴油机，但又是由火花塞点燃的，故又称为半柴油机"semidiesel"或火花点火式柴油机"spark-ignited diesel"）

texrope drive V带传动（三角带传动）

textile rope 纤维绳（泛指麻、尼龙等化学纤维合股编成的绳索）

text massaging （车用）文本信息传送显示

textolite 夹布胶木

texture ①组织，结构，构造，构成；织品（织品）质地；（木材）纹理；特性，性格，本质②使具有某种结构，使具有……组织

texture profile recorder 构造物外廓记录仪（如：道路路面外形自动记录仪）

TFC/IW 惯性重量比油耗率（total fuel consumption divided by inertia weight 的简称，总油耗除以惯性重量）

TFE resin （聚）四氟乙烯树脂（美称 PTFE, polytetrafluorethylene 的简称）

TFFT 薄膜场效应晶体管（thin film field effect transistor）

TFI 薄膜集成电路（thin film integrated circuit 的简称）

T-fixture T字（形）夹具

T-flip flop 反转触发器

TFSI ①涡轮增压燃油顺序喷射式（发动机）（turbocharged fuel sequential injection 的简称）②涡轮增压燃油分层喷射式（发动机）（turbocharged fuel straitified injection 的简称）③涡轮增压燃油火花点火式（发动机）（turbocharged fuel spark ignition 的简称）

TFTL 薄膜晶体管液晶显示（thin film transistor liquid crystal display 的简称，亦简称 TFT LCD）

TFV 牵引力变动（tractive force variation 的简称）

TG 扭矩梯度（torque gradient 的简称）

T-girder T形架

TGP 紊流生成罐（见 turbulence generating pot）

TGP combustion system 紊流罐燃烧系统（turbulence generating pot combustion system 的简称）

"T"-grade separation T型立体交叉口（立体化的 T 形三路交叉口，有喇叭式 T 形立体交叉或直接连接式 T 形立体交叉，亦称 trumpet-grade separation）

Th ①钍（thorium）②节气门，节流阀（throttle）

T-handle T形手柄

thawing test 解冻试验（熔化试验）

thaw out 使……熔化，使……溶解

THC 总碳氢（total hydrocarbons 的简称，排气排放物中各种碳氢化合物的总称）

THC analyzer 总碳氢化合物分析仪（见 Total Hydrocarbon Analyzer）

THCT 涡轮液力传动循环试验（turbo hydromatic cycling test 的简称）

T-head T型汽缸盖（指进、排气门分别位于汽缸盖的两侧）

T-head bolt T形头螺栓

T-head cylinder 侧置气门汽缸，T形头缸盖汽缸（= T-type cylinder，进、排气门分别置于汽缸两侧）

Theater package （豪华车内配置的）剧院（型）声响影乐娱乐设备

theater type seat （豪华车的）剧院式座椅

the disabled 残疾人

The European Communities 欧洲共同体（简称 EC）

the first stage of creep 蠕变第一阶段（蠕变速率随时间逐渐降低的期间）

the first stage of stress relaxation 应力松弛第一阶段（应力松弛速度随时间逐渐减慢的期间）

theftalarm system （汽车）防盗警报系统（简称 TAS）

theft deterrent system （汽车）防盗系统（简称 TDS）

theft-proof 防盗的

The Institution of Automobile Engineers ［英］汽车工程师学会（简称 IAE）

The Institution of Mechanical Engi-

neers [英]机械工程师学会(创立于1847年,该会设有汽车和铁道工程两个部门)

The International Standardize Organization Technical Committee 104 国际标准化组织104技术委员会(简称ISO/TC104)

The Journal of Automotive Engineering 汽车工程杂志(英国机械工程师学会编,简称JAE)

theodolite 经纬仪

theorem 定理,原理,法则,定律,理论

theorem of minimum energy 最小能量定理

theoretical 理论的

theoretical air-fuel ratio 理论空(气)燃(料)比(计算空燃比,按化学反应式 $C_7H_{16} + 11O_2 \longrightarrow 7CO_2 + 8H_2O$ 计算,每千克汽油需要15.5kg空气,就可完全燃烧,所以一般汽油混合气的理论空燃比为15.5:1)

theoretical amount of air 理论空气量(理论计算空气量,一般指完全燃烧时所必需的最小空气量,可由燃料成分及燃烧方程式计算求得,亦称theoretical air quantity)

theoretical amount of combustion gas 理论燃烧气体量(按燃料成分计算,完全燃烧时所产生的最小气体量)

theoretical combustion temperature 理论燃烧温度(根据燃烧前后的能量平衡而从理论上推算出来的燃烧生成气体的温度)

theoretical correct MS 理论计算混合气强度(= stoichiometric mixture strength, 见 MS)

theoretical cutoff frequency 理论截止频率

theoretical cycle 理论循环

theoretical displacement of oil pump 油泵理论排量(设计油泵时所规定的每转输油量)

theoretical efficiency 理论效率(理论功率与指示功率之比。按所选定的可逆基准过程,理论效率可以有多变效率、等熵效率及等温效率)

theoretical error 理论误差

theoretical fuel-air ratio 理论燃油-空气混合比(理论燃-空比,按 $C_7H_{16} + 11O_2 \longrightarrow 7CO_2 + 8H_2O$ 化学反应式计算的燃-空比,即1摩尔的 C_7H_{16},重为100g,和11摩尔的 O_2,重为352g,相混合,两者恰好完全燃烧。其中 C_7H_{16} 代表燃油的平均摩尔100g,而 $11O_2$ 代表空气1550g,因此理论燃-空比为1:15.5,亦称 stoich iometric mixture ratio, theoretical mixture ratio)

theoretically correct mixture 理论混合气(理论计算混合气,化学计算混合气,按理论混合比混合,即 air-fuel ratio = 15, fuel-air ratio = 0.066, MS = 1 的混合气, = stoichiometric mixture)

theoretical mass of charge (发动机的)理论充气量

theoretical mean effective pressure 理论平均有效压力

theoretical mechanics 理论力学

theoretical required power 理论功率(理论上所需要消耗的功率)

theoretical rim 理论轮辋(轮辋名义宽度与轮胎名义断面宽度具有规定比值的轮辋)

theoretical running radius of tire 轮胎的理论滚动半径(汽车在最大载重下,无加速、制动、横偏等现象,定速行驶时,轮胎转一周,汽车移动距离,除以 2π)

theoretical size 理论尺寸(计算尺寸)

theoretical specific energy requirement 理论所需比能(理论比功率,按所

选定的基准过程压缩单位质量气体或单位容积气体所需要的功,分别称为理论质量比能、质量比功率或理论容积比能、容积比功率)

theoretical stress concentration factor 理论应力集中系数(按弹性理论计算所得缺口或其他应力集中源的最大应力与相应的标称应力的比值)

theoretical thermal efficiency 理论热效率

theoretical value 理论值

theoretical water power 理论水功率

theory of approximation 近似理论

theory of cumulative damage in fatigue 累积疲劳损伤理论

theory of errors 误差论

theory of field 场论

theory of finite deformation 有限变形理论

theory of functions 函数论

theory of plane stress 平面应力理论

theory of probability 概率论(几率论,亦称 theory of chances)

theory of similarity 相似理论

theory of structure 结构力学

theory of types 类型论

thermac 恒温进气空气滤清器(通用公司用语,thermostatic air cleaner 的简称)

thermactor 福特公司二次空气的空气泵的商品名

thermactor air bypass valve 福特公司二次空气喷射"热反应系统"的二次空气旁通阀(简称 TABvalve,见 thermactor system)

thermactor (air control) system 热反应系统[福特公司二次空气喷射系统的商品名,由电子控制模块控制的二次空气泵、两个真空通路电磁阀(见 TAB 和 TAD solenoid)及其控制的真空膜片式旁通阀(称 thermactor air bypass valve, 简称 TAB valve) 和真空膜片式换向阀(称 thermactor air divert valve, 简称 TAD valve)组成。当发动机起动、冷却水温低于 10℃时,换向阀关闭,旁通阀开启,将二次空气排入大气。当水温达到或超过 10℃时,旁通阀关闭,换向阀开放,将二次空气引入排气歧管,而当冷却水温达到 88℃时,换向阀将二次空气引入催化转化器。当发动机急速运转、加速或节气门全开,以及 O_2 传感器产生故障时,电子控制模块亦将旁通阀开启,二次空气排入大气,以免催化转化器过热]

thermactor air divert valve (福特公司二次空气喷射"热反应系统"的)二次空气换向阀(简称 TADvalve,见 thermactor system)

thermal 热的

thermal abrasion 热蚀

thermal accumulator 储热器(一切形式的储热装置和系统的总称,=heat accumulator,亦可 heat regenerator)

thermal actuator 热力执行器(如:双金属片执行装置等)

thermal aging 加热时效处理(加热老化;热老化)

thermal ammeter 热线式安培计(温差电流表)

thermal and vibration combine fatigue 热和振动复合疲劳

thermal baffle 绝热板(=heat baffle)

thermal balance 热平衡(热力平衡,温度平衡)

thermal barrier 热障

thermal battery 温差电池(热电池,热偶电池,一组不同金属的接点在受热后产生电压)

thermal boundary layer 热边界层(温度边界层)

thermal breakdown 热破坏

thermal capacity 热容量
thermal car 热力轿车（用热机驱动的轿车）
thermal characteristics 热特性
thermal coefficient of expansion 热膨胀系数
thermal conduction 热传导（指物质不移动，而在物体内热移动的现象，= heat conduction）
thermal conduction per unit area 单位面积的传热量（单位面积的导热量）
thermal conductivity ①导热系数（热导率）②导热性（= heat conductivity）
thermal content 热焓（含热量，= heat content）
thermal convection 热对流（= heat convection）
thermal crack 热裂纹
thermal cracking ①（石油的）热裂化，热裂炼②热分解；加热分解③（金属的）热裂纹（= heat cracking）
thermal current 热流（热空气流，热气流）
thermal cycling 热循环（温度的循环变化）
thermal decomposition 热分解
thermal deformation 热变形
thermal design 热计算，热力计算
thermal diffusion 热扩散（= heat diffusion）
thermal diffusivity 热扩散性
thermal dispersion 热散逸
thermal dissociation 热分解（热离解，由于加热，物质分解成较小的分子、原子、离子等的现象）
thermal distortion 热变形
thermal drop 温度降（= temperature drop）
thermal effect 热效应［= heat (ing) effect］

thermal efficiency （发动机）热效率（= heat efficiency，指燃料中所含的热能在内燃机中转变为功的份额用百分数表示。分为指示热效率和有效热效率，见 indicated thermal efficiency）
thermal electric current 温差电流
thermal element ①热敏元件（热电偶，温差电偶）②熔断器，熔断丝
thermal endurance 耐热性（耐热持续时间，= heat endurance）
thermal energy 热能（= heat energy）
thermal engine 热机（热力发动机，= heat engine）
thermal engineering 热工学
thermal equilibrium 热平衡
thermal equivalent 热当量（热功当量，一般指每千卡热量所相当的功，即：1kcal = 4186.8J，= thermal equivalent of work）
thermal expansion 热膨胀（= heat expansion）
thermal expansion coefficient 热膨胀系数
thermal expansion valve 热膨胀阀
thermal expansivity 热膨胀性
thermal fatigue 热疲劳（受热疲劳，物体由于反复受热和冷却，内部产生热应力，而使材料疲劳破损的现象）
thermal flasher 热效闪光灯（热敏闪光信号器，热敏断续电路开关）
thermal flow 热流（热通量，= thermal flux, heat flow, thermal current）
thermal gradient 温度梯度（热梯度）
thermal history 温度历程（温度随时间变化曲线，温度与时间关系，温度变化历程）
thermal hysteresis 热滞（温度滞后）
thermal impact 热冲击
thermal insulating material 绝热材

料（=thermal insulator）

thermal insulation 隔热（在标准耐火试验中，元件或材料防止过量传热的能力），热绝缘（=heat insulation）

thermal insulation ceramic combustion chamber engine 绝热陶瓷（材料）燃烧室发动机（无须冷却系，重量轻，尺寸小，热效率可高达35.1%）

thermal insulation test 隔热性能试验

thermal insulator ①绝热材料（=thermal insulating material）②绝热件

thermal lag 热滞迟

thermal limit 热极限

thermal load 热负荷（如：内燃机汽缸、燃烧室及其周围的零件承受温度、热应力、热流量等的强烈程度）

thermal loss 热量损失

thermalloy （铁镍）耐热合金

thermally sensitive resistor 热敏电阻器，热变电阻（器）（亦称thermally dependent resistor）

thermal mechanical fatigue 热机械疲劳（温度循环与应变循环叠加所导致的疲劳）

thermal output 热量输出（放热量，放热率）

thermal plastic urethane 热塑性尿烷（简称TPU）

thermal pressure welding 热压焊接

thermal-radiating 热辐射的

thermal radiation 热辐射（指物体以辐射形式放出或吸收热能，热辐射与物体表面温度、表面性质有关，单位面积、单位时间辐射的热量，与该表面的绝对温度的四次方成比例）

thermal rating （齿轮等的）热限额定负载，热限额定功率（变速器的温度升高，不超过规定限度时，齿轮箱所能允许传递的最大功率）

thermal reactor 热反应器（利用废气高温使有害排放物，如：HC、CO氧化的装置的总称。一般位于排气歧管内或附近，使废气从发动机燃烧室排出后仍保持在高温状态并停留一定时间，同时喷入或引入新鲜空气，使废气中的HC、CO继续燃烧，简称thermactor）

thermal refining 调质（热）处理

thermal regeneration 热回收

thermalregeneration unit （排放净化系统的）热再生装置

thermal relay 热敏继电器（温度控制继电器，温差继电器）

thermal resistance ①耐热性②热阻

thermal resistivity 热阻率

thermal resistor 热敏电阻

thermal shock 热冲击（物体突然加热和冷却等产生冲击性的温度变化和非稳定的、非常态的温度分布，而引起大的热应力及热变形）

thermal shock crack 热冲击裂纹（由于高低温度反复变化，造成表面龟裂）

thermal shock resistance 抗热冲击性能（抵抗高温冲击的能力，=spalling resistance）

thermal shock test 热冲击试验（耐温度急剧变化试验）

thermal sponge 海绵状储热材料

thermal spray 热喷镀

thermal stability 热稳定性（耐热性）

thermal state 热（状）态

thermal strain 热应变

thermal strength 热强度（指材料抵抗热疲劳破坏的能力）

thermal stress 热应力（由于温度变化而产生的应力）

thermal switch 热敏开关

thermal time constant 热时间常数

thermal transmission 传热，热传递

(= heat transmission)

thermal transmitter 热传感器，感温感传器（如：一般发动机水温表的感温塞）

thermal treatment 热处理（ = heat treatment)

thermal unit 热量单位

thermal vacuum valve 温控真空阀（简称TVV，TV valve，如：当发动机水温达到某规定值时该阀开放或关闭控制用真空通路，亦称thermal vacuum switch，如：装在空气滤清器上由进气温度控制的温控真空开关阀）

thermal value 热值（发热量）

thermal vibration 热致振动

thermauto stat ①自动恒温箱②恒温器

thermel （装有热电偶的）热电温度计

thermic ①热的②由于热而造成的

thermic equivalent 热功当量（ = thermal equivalent)

thermic piston 防热变形活塞（ = autothermic piston)

thermic wear （零件等因高温引起的）热磨损

thermionic conduction 热离子传导

thermionic tube 热离子管，热阴极电子管，热发射电子管（亦称thermionic valve)

thermionic work function 热离子功函数，热离子逸出功（加热物射出一个电子所需的能量）

thermistor 热敏电阻（电阻值随介质温度而变化的器件，在汽车上用作水温和进气温度传感器。有随温度上升，其电阻值增加的正温度特性型和其阻值下降的负温度特性型两种，汽车上一般使用后者）

thermistor bolometer 热敏电阻式辐射热测量仪（热敏电阻测热计，亦称 **thermistor-bolometer detector**, thermistor heat detector cell)

thermistor nomogram 热敏电阻列线图（计算热变电阻的诺谟图）

thermistor temperature sensor 热敏电阻式温度传感器（利用热敏电阻电阻值随温度的变化而变化的特性将温度变化变为电信号输出的传感器）

thermit ①热熔剂（铝粉与氧化铁粉的混合物，用于焊接剂或制造燃烧弹）②铝熔剂焊接法

Thermit metal 瑟米特合金（铅基重型轴承合金的商品名，锑14% ~ 16%，锡5% ~ 7%，铜0.8% ~ 1.2%，镍0.7% ~ 1.5%，砷0.3% ~ 0.8%，镉0.7% ~ 1.5%，其余为铅）

thermit welding process 铝热剂焊接法（ = thermit welding method)

THERMO 恒温器（thermostat的简称）

thermoammeter （测量微电流用）热电偶安培计（温差电偶安培计，热电流表）

thermobarometer ①（根据水的沸点测定海拔高度的）温度气压计，温压表②（可用作温度计的）虹吸气压表

thermochemical calorie 热化学卡（热化学采用的热量单位，= 4.184丁）

thermochemical engine 热化学发动机

thermochemistry 热化学

thermocompression bonding 热压接（热压接装，热压焊，压焊接）

thermo-couple probe 热电偶探头

thermo-couple pyrometer 热电偶高温计

thermocurrent 热电流（温差电流）

thermodetector ①热检波器（温差电检波器）②温差测探器（测温计）

1618

thermo-diffusive 热扩散的

thermoduric 耐热的

thermodynamic cycle 热力循环（着重研究工质热力状态和热力过程的工作循环）

thermodynamic efficiency 热力学效率（热机工质的全部热降 H_a 与扣除诸如机械损失等之后的有效功 H_e 之比，即 $\eta_e = H_e/H_a$）

thermodynamic equilibrium 热力平衡

thermodynamic function 热力学函数（温度、压力、体积、熵、焓等表示物体固体、液体、气体的热力学状态的量的总称，亦称状态函数，状态量，= quantity of state, state function）

thermodynamic instability 热力学不稳定性

thermodynamic phase 热力学相位

thermodynamics 热力学

thermodynamic temperature 热力学温度（绝对温度）

thermoeiectric sealing 电热密封法

thermoelastic deformation 热弹性变形（高温引起的弹性变形）

thermoelasticity 热弹性

thermoelecrtic cooling 热电冷却

thermoelecrtic couple 热电偶（温差电偶，= thermal couple）

thermoelectric（al） 热电的（由温差产生电流的）

thermoelectrical effect 热电效应（温差电效应）

thermoelectric cell 温差电池，温差电偶，热电元件，亦称（thermoelectric generator）

thermoelectric cycle 热电循环（直流电经过不同金属构成的冷、热两接点）

thermoelectric element 热电元件（热电偶）

thermoelectricity 热电学，热电现象

thermoelectric power 热电（动）势率（温差电（动）势率）

thermoelectric power station 热电厂

thermoelectric thermometer 热电温度计（温差电偶温度计，利用两种不同金属丝两端连接而形成闭合回路时，若两连接点温度变化，便会产生电动势的原理制成的温度计。只要知道一个连接点的温度，测出电动势，即可测定另一连接点的温度，这种温度计的测温范围 -200 ~ +1600℃，精度可达 0.1℃，因而亦称热电高温计 thermoelectric pyrometer，在工业上应用很广）

thermoelectromagnetic 热电磁的

thermo-electrometer 热电计

thermoelectromotive force 温差电动势

thermoelectron 热电子

thermoelement ①热电偶（温差电偶）②热电元件（温差电元件）

thermo-emf 热电势（温差电动势）

thermo fan drive system 温控风扇驱动系统（达到一定温度后，自动开动风扇）

thermo form（ing） 热成型（热压加工）

thermogram 自记温度曲线（温谱图）

thermograph 自记式温度计（温度变化曲线记录仪）

thermo-hamper effect 热束缚效应（当喷油贯穿距离过小，燃油聚集在燃烧室中央区，或燃烧开始后喷入汽缸内的燃油过多，造成燃油过多地处于高温燃烧产物集聚的中央区，这些燃油不能及时地得到足够的空气，而处于被束缚状态，易于在高温下裂解成炭烟，而燃烧室周边区的空气却未充分利用，导致燃烧不完善的现象）

thermo jar （美国规格型号的丰田复合动力车 Prius 的内燃机冷却液的）

暖罐〔装在左前叶子板内、容积为2.5L的暖罐，发动机熄火后使冷却液温度全天保持在某规定值，可使该车满足"先进技术-零排放车"（见AT-ZEV）冷起动排放要求〕

thermojunction 热电偶工作端

thermolabile 不耐热的，热不稳定的（指受热，如：55℃以上，即分解或受热后改变性能的）

thermolize （表面）热处理

thermo (-) mechanical 热机械的

thermomechanical treatment 热机械加工（如：锻、铸，相对于冷机械加工，如：车削、铣、磨而言）

thermometal 双金属片（= bi-metallic plate）

thermometal cut-out 双金属片式温控断电器（当温度超过规定值时，双金属片臂变形，使触点分离而断电）

thermometer 温度计，温度表

thermometer bulb 温度表感温泡

thermometric correction 测热修正（温度量测修正）

thermometric instruments 温度测量仪器

thermometric scale 温度标

thermometrograph 温度记录器（自记式温度计）

thermometry 测温学，测温法，测温技术

thermo-mixture effect 热分层效应（热混合效应，指在有适当涡流强度的活塞顶内燃烧室中，燃油喷到燃烧室周边地区，由于涡流造成的离心力场，使燃烧后或正在燃烧的高温燃烧产物或燃气，因其密度小而被吸到燃烧室中央；而尚未参加燃烧新鲜空气、燃油蒸气及其混合气，因其密度大而被离心力甩至周边区，形成分层混合燃烧，从而充分利用了周边区的空气，使燃烧完善的现象）

thermomotive 热动力的

thermomotive flasher 温控偶断续器；温控闪光器

thermonegative 吸热的

thermonuclear reaction 核反应（亦称 thermonuclear fusion）

thermo-optic effect （液晶的）热光效应（液晶的光学性质随外界温度变化而变化的现象）

thermo-physical engine 热物理发动机

thermopile 热电堆（温差电堆），热电池（温差电池），热电元件（热电偶）

thermoplastic ①热塑性②热塑性塑料③热塑的，热范的，加热软化的

thermoplastic base resin 热塑性树脂

thermoplastic elastomer 见 TPE

thermoplastic heat exchanger 耐热塑料热交换器（如：替代金属散热器，以减轻重量，防锈、抗冲击等的尼龙散热器）

thermoplastic hub cap 热塑性塑料轮毂帽

thermoplastic insulation 热塑绝缘

thermoplasticity 热塑性

thermoplastic rubber 热塑橡胶

thermoplastics 热塑性塑料（= thermoplastic plastics，加热熔融，冷却硬化，呈线状构造的热可塑性树脂的总称）

thermoplastics bodied vehicle 热塑料车身汽车

thermoplastic synthetic rubber material 热塑性合成橡胶材料

thermoplastic vulcanizate 热塑性硫化橡胶

thermopneumatic actuator 温控气动执行器

thermo-polymerization 热聚合作用

thermopositive 放热的

thermo regulator 温度调节器

thermo-relay 热继电器（温差电偶

继电器)

thermoresponsive (snap) switch 热敏(速动)开关

thermo sensor 温度传感器

thermoset ①热冲击性(加热变硬,热凝) ②热固的,热成型的(加热成型即硬化的)

thermoset material 热固性材料(亦称thermosets,由硬化反应形成网状化的高分子结构,受热不再熔融的热固性树脂、热固性塑料)

thermosetting 热固的(热凝的,加热成型后即硬化的)

thermosetting varnish 热固性油漆

thermo-shock test 热冲击试验(使内燃机反复突加和突卸负荷,并相应突变冷却水温度后,使零件受突热、突冷的试验。它是一种低周波热疲劳的试验)

thermosiphon 热虹吸管

thermosiphon circulation system 热虹吸循环系统(温差对流循环系统)

thermosiphon water cooling 温差对流循环水冷却

thermos-like tank 保温瓶式绝热储存箱(如:氢燃料汽车的保温瓶式绝热液态氢储存箱)

thermostable 热稳定的

thermostart (柴油机)加热起动装置

thermostat ①恒温装置,温度自动调节装置 ②(在发动机中一般特指装在发动机缸盖与散热器之间冷却管道内,随水温控制冷却水流向和流量,而确保发动机保持相对恒定的冷却水温的)节温器,恒温器

thermostat control 恒温器控制(装置)

thermostatic accelerating pump 温控加速泵(低温时喷油量大,高温时喷油量少,简称TAP)

thermostatic air cleaner 恒温空气滤清器 (= thermostatically controlled air cleaner,简称TAC)

thermostatic air shutters 恒温自动调节式百叶窗

thermostatically controlled 恒温控制的(亦称thermostatic operated, thermostatic regulated,指由恒温装置控制、操纵、调节的)

thermostatically controlled air cleaner 恒温控制式空气滤清器 (= thermostatic air cleaner,简称TAC)

thermostatic coil-vacuum diaphragm type chock opener 双金属温控卷簧—真空膜片型阻风门开启器(该开启器由两部分组成,装在进气歧管处的双金属卷簧在冷机状态下收缩,使节气门关闭,而发动机起动升温后双金属卷簧伸展,节气门逐步开启,直至全开。与此同时,有一由进气管真空控制的膜片,只要发动机一起动,其进气歧管真空便吸动膜片使阻风门微开,发动机热起后,双金属卷簧已使阻风门全开,真空膜片不再起作用,见chock opener)

thermostatic fan (可随水温升降自动控制转速,以维持冷却水温相对恒定的)恒温式风扇

thermostatic interrupter (防止照明电路因短路、漏电等故障而过热的)恒温断电器

thermostatic switch 恒温开关,温控开关(当温度达到某预定值时自动接通或断开电路的热敏开关)

thermostatic vacuum switching valve (恒)温控(制)式真空通路开关阀(简称TVSV或thermovacuum switch,亦称thermostatic vacuum transmitting valve,简称TVTV)

thermostat metal 双金属片

thermostat valve 恒温控制阀(如:冷却系的节温器阀,恒温阀)

thermostat varnish 耐热漆(热稳定

thermoswitch 热敏开关（温控开关，热电偶继电器）

thermo-syphon cooling system 温差虹吸式冷却系（无冷却水泵，借助热虹吸作用，实现冷却水循环的冷却系）

thermo syphon radiator （利用冷-热水比重差异而实现冷却液循环的）温差虹吸式（冷却）散热器

thermo-time switch 热控时间开关（指用双金属片式电路触点开关）

THERMOTRONIC （Benz 的）分区控制智能型空调系统（驾驶者、前排和后排乘员均可各自按需单独设定适宜的温度和气候风格）

thermotropic liquid crystal 热致液晶（因温度变化而形成液晶态的物质）

thermovoltmeter 热电偶伏特计

The Royal Automobile Club [英]皇家汽车俱乐部（简称 RAC）

the second best in quality 质量上属于第二级的（用符号 B 表示）

the second stage of creep 蠕变第二阶段（蠕变速率恒定的期间）

the second stage of stress relaxation 应力松弛第二阶段（应力松弛速度保持恒定的期间）

the third stage of creep 蠕变第三阶段（蠕变速率随时间逐渐增加的期间）

the Tire and Rim Association, Inc. [美] 轮胎和轮辋协会（简称 TRA）

thick 厚的，粗的，浓的，稠密的，密集的

thicken （使）变厚，变浓，变稠；稠化；变浑浊；使更浓，使更稠，使更浑浊；使复杂化，变复杂

thickened gasoline 稠化汽油（增稠汽油）

thickener ①增稠剂（稠化剂）②浓缩器（稠化器）③沉降槽

thick film 厚膜（相对薄膜而言，通常用丝网印刷等工艺在陶瓷基片上淀积的导体或绝缘材料膜，构成电阻、电容及导线等无源元件）

thick film hybrid circuit 厚膜混合电路

thick film ignition module 厚膜电路点火控制模块

thick-film integrated circuit 厚膜集成电路（采用印刷、丝网印刷技术或其他有关技术形成膜的膜集成电路）

thick-film metallic electrode 厚膜金属电极

thick film temperature-sensing resistor 厚膜感温电阻（厚膜热敏电阻）

thick film temperature sensor 厚膜温度传感器

thick glue 稠胶

thick grease 稠脂

thick line 粗线

thickness at root of tooth 齿根厚度

thick oil 稠油（高黏度润滑油）

thick-wall compression ring 厚壁压缩环（环的径向壁最大厚度达直径的 1/20 者）

thicness measuring instrument 厚度量具（如：thickness gauge 厚度量规，厚度规，厚薄规，thickness indicator 测厚仪，厚度指示仪，thickness piece 厚薄规，测隙规，厚薄片，thickness tester 厚度计）

thief-proofer （汽车）防盗装置

thigh central line （人体）大腿的中心线

thigh support (height) adjuster switch （座椅的）大腿支撑垫（高度）调节开关

thimble connector 套管接头，卡箍接头

thin ①薄的，细的，瘦的 ②稀薄的，稀少的，微弱的 ③没有内容的，不充实的 ④稀薄，稀薄处，细

小部分⑤使变稀,压薄,使变细⑥削去,磨去,磨修
thin circular cylinder 薄壁圆筒(如:薄壁汽缸, = thin cylinder)
thin coating 薄层涂覆
thin-down 变细,变薄,变弱,变稀薄
thin fan shaped spray (缝口式喷嘴喷出的)薄扇面形喷雾
thin film 薄膜(用真空蒸发、溅射及化学气相淀积等生长工艺在基片上淀积形成的几个分子厚的膜)
thin-film integrated circuit 薄膜集成电路(采用真空淀积技术,也可辅以其他淀积技术形成的几个分子厚的膜的膜集成电路)
thin-film lubrication 薄膜润滑(= boundary lubrication)
thin-film magnetoresistive sensor 薄膜磁阻传感器
thin film oxidation test (滑油的)薄膜氧化试验(在含氧的大气中,使滑油通过一只加热的旋转金属盘,测定滑油薄膜的高温稳定性)
thin-film plastic resistor 薄膜塑性电阻器
thin-film pressure sensor 薄膜式压力传感器
thin glue 稀胶
THINK+ (一种)车载多功能信息系统(的商品名,具有电话通信、语言导航、影音娱乐、安全警告、驻车引导等多项功能)
thinner 稀释剂
thinness of walls 壁的薄度
thinning 压薄,磨薄;稀化,稀薄化
thinning limits 稀释限度
thin oil 稀油(低黏度润滑油)
thin out 稀释,稀化
thin section ①薄壁断面②薄壁型材
thin sheet structure 薄板结构(如:车身)

thin-wall bearing shell 薄壁轴瓦(指瓦背厚度与合金层厚度之和与轴瓦内径之比为 0.02~0.05,厚度为 1.5~7mm,合金层厚度为 0.2~0.7mm 的轴瓦)
thio 硫,含硫的,硫代
thio-alcohol 硫醇(汽油中的一种硫化物杂质)
thiokol 聚硫橡胶(乙硫橡胶)
third ①第三,三分之一②(变速器)第三挡(= third gear)
third and fourth gear switches 变速器三-四挡开关(挂三挡或四挡时,三挡或四挡开关接通,向电子控制模块发送变速器挂三挡或四挡的信号)
third axle 第三轴,第三桥(一般指三轴汽车最后端的驱动桥或支重桥,见 tag axle)
third brush (发电机上控制电流输出的)第三(电)刷
third-brush generator 三刷发电机
third differential 第三差速器(多轴汽车双驱动桥的桥间差速器)
third-generation 第三代的
third lane 第三车道(多车道道路中,靠左行驶时为前进方向从左起的第三车道,靠右行驶时为前进方向从右起的第三车道)
third law of motion 第三运动定律
third main type engine 第三大类发动机(一般指多种燃料发动机)
third-octave analyzer 1/3 倍(频)带分析器
third party insurance 第三者保险(事故中第三者人身及购物损失保险,不包括投保人本身及其所驾驶车辆)
third piston land 第三槽岸(指第二和第三活塞环槽间的凸岸)
third power 三次幂(立方)
third-row screen (三排座轿车的)后排显示屏

third valve 第三气门（层状充气发动机预燃室的辅助进气门，专门吸入浓混合气，而主进气门只吸入稀混合气）

thirtieth highest annual hourly volume 一年间第30个最高小时交通量（美国公路设计中，取指定年度中按小时交通量的第30个最高数值作为设计依据）

thixotropic 触变的，摇溶的（指振动液化的）

thixotropic compound 摇溶剂

thixotropy 摇溶现象（指固态体经搅动或摇动便会液化而呈液态的现象或特性）

thorax injury （碰撞事故中乘员）胸部撞伤

thorax trauma （汽车碰撞事故中乘员的）胸外伤

thorium 钍(Th)

thoroughbred ①最好的汽车，最高级的赛车②高尚的，优美的

thorough burning 完全燃烧

thoroughfare ①干线公路，干道；大街②通行（= passage，transit）

thoroughly repaired 大修过的

thou ①千分之一英寸（英国用的长度单位之一，亦称 mil）②［美］一千元③［英］一千磅

THP ①驱动轮推进马力（thrust horsepower）②牵引马力（tractive horsepower）

thrash ①激烈摇动，剧烈摆动（如：传动皮带激烈横向振动等）②颠簸③拍击

thread ①螺纹，螺线，螺旋线②丝状物，线状物，细丝，纤维③加工螺纹，切割螺纹

threadbare ①（螺纹）磨薄的（磨损了的）②磨损的，陈旧的

thread caliper 螺纹卡尺（螺纹规）

thread comparator 螺纹比较仪（螺纹有效直径测定仪，由千分表指示两球形或螺纹形测头间距，与标准螺纹规比较，即可迅速测定螺纹有效半径）

threaded bushing 带螺旋油槽的衬套

threaded cap （带）螺纹（的）盖（塞）

threaded fastener 螺纹紧固件（螺栓、螺杆、螺钉、螺母等的总称）

threaded hole 螺纹孔

threaded joint 螺纹连接

thread(ed) plug gauge 螺纹塞规

threaded valve stem 末端带螺纹的气门杆

thread fit 螺纹配合

thread form 牙形（牙型）

thread-forming screw 自攻螺钉

thread hand 螺纹方向（指左旋，右旋）

thread locking adhesive 螺纹密封胶（拧装螺钉前，涂于螺纹处，可保证螺纹密封）

thread micrometer 螺纹千分尺

thread pitch 螺距

thread pitch gauge 螺距规

thread runout 螺纹偏心度（指螺钉的杆身、头部和螺纹之间的总偏差）

thread runout sleeve gauge 螺纹偏心度套筒量规

threads per inch 每英寸螺纹数

thread standard 螺纹标准

thread tolerance 螺纹公差

threat ①（对车辆构成）危险；（对安全构成）威胁②危险物，威胁物③恶兆（可能发生事故等的预兆）

threatening object （对汽车行驶）有危险的物体（如：可能与汽车撞碰的对向行驶的车辆等）

three-abreast seats 三人并肩座椅

three-apexed rotor （转子发动机的）三角转子（三角旋转活塞，亦称 three-cornered rotor）

three-axis simulator 三度空间模拟

装置
three axle rigid 三桥汽车（未带挂车的三轴货车）
three ball and trunnion universal joint 三球枢轴式（等角速）万向节，三球销式万向节（见 tripot universal joint）
three-bank cylinders W 形缸体
three-bar bumper 三杆保险杠
three bearing crankshaft 三主轴承曲轴（具有两端主轴颈和一个中间主轴颈的典型轻型四缸发动机曲轴）
three box 三厢式（轿车）（指前有发动机舱，中有客厢，后有行李舱的 4 门软、硬顶轿车，亦写作 3-box）
three brush dynamo 三刷式直流发电机（旧式的由第三电刷控制输出电流直流发电机）
three button remote key 三按钮式遥控钥匙（在钥匙柄上装有开、闭车门、发动机罩及行李舱盖的遥控信号发射按钮。根据不同车型按钮数量亦不尽相同。有的遥控钥匙还带有机械钥匙插头，称"with mechanical key"）
three-car interaction 三车相互作用（交通流量理论）
three-chamber air reservoir 三腔贮气筒
three-component ①三元的 ②三分量的 ③三部分组成的
three-component velocity vector field 三分量速度矢量场
three coordinates measuring equipment 三向坐标测量装置（三维坐标仪，一种用来快速测量和绘制汽车车身表面曲线的装置）
three-cylinder two-stroke engine 三缸二冲程发动机（= three-port two-stroke engine）
three-D 见 three-dimensional
three diaphragm brake chamber 三膜片制动气室
three-dimensional 三度空间的，三维的（简称 three-D）
three-dimensional CAD technology 三维计算机辅助设计技术（在计算机辅助设计时，电视屏幕可现出设计的三维图像）
three dimensional flow 三维流（流线要用空间曲线来表示的三次元流）
three-dimensional front （火焰的）三维前锋
three dimensional fundamental form 三维（度）基本形
three-dimensional milli (meter)-wave scan radar 见 milli (meter) -wave scan radar
three-dimensional viscous fluid analysis technique 三维黏性流体分析技术
three-dimension cam （直喷式柴油机连续可变排气正时机构中使用的）三维凸轮
three-dimension image processing technology 三维图像处理技术
three-dimension piston slap simulation technique 三维活塞敲击缸壁模拟技术（用于在研制新型发动机时，评定活塞裙与缸壁的接触状态）
three disk wave generator （谐波齿轮）三圆盘波发生器（由三个等直径圆盘对称偏心设置于输入轴的非积极控制式双波发生器）
three "E"s 能源、经济、环境（energy, economy, environment）
three fold 3 倍（于）（增加 2 倍的）
three horn set 三音喇叭（= triple horn set）
three-in-one brake valve 三合一制动阀
three-joint drive shaft 三万向节传动轴（传动轴分为两根，使用三个万向节，中部加装中间支撑的传动装置）

three-lane road 三车道公路（对向交通各占用一条车道，中间的车道则供超车使用的双向无分隔带公路）

three-layer 三层（的）

three leaved rose curve 三瓣玫瑰线

three-link rear-axle suspension （福特 2005 年型 Mustang 轿车的）三连杆式后桥悬架（由一根固定于差速器前上端的中央扭矩控制臂 "center torque-control arm" 和两根分别位于该桥各端附近的纵臂 "trailing arm" 组成）

three lobe epitrochoidal bore （转子发动机）三弧外旋轮线缸体

three-lobe rotor （转子发动机的）三弧旋转活塞（三弧转子，三角转子）

three-minute charge test 三分钟充电试验（用快速充电器，大电流对蓄电池充电 3min，测试极板硫化程度）

three o'clock wind 右侧风（口语）

three-phase alternating current motor 三相交流电动机

three-phase full-wave rectifier 三相全波整流器

three-phase induction motor 三相感应电动机

three-phase sinusoidal AC voltage 三相正弦交流电压

three-phase stator winding （交流发电机的）三相定子绕组

three-piece apex seal （转子发动机的）三片式径向密封片

three-piece construction rim 三件式轮辋（亦称 three-piece type rim，指由轮辋体 "rim base"、挡圈 "detachable endless flange" 和锁圈 "lock ring" 组成的可拆式轮辋）

three-piece flat base rim 三件式平底轮辋

three-piece hydraulic tube fittings 三元件式液压管接头（螺母-套管扩口式管接头，卡套式管接头）

three-piece radiator 三件式散热器（指由上水箱、散热器芯子、下水箱组成的散热器）

three-plate clutch 三片式离合器

three-ply fabric 三层织物（= triple fabric）

three-ply wood 三层板（三合板）

three-point attachment 三点悬架装置，三点连接装置

three-point belt 三点式安全带（= lap and shoulder belt）

three-point contact ball bearing 三点接触式球轴承（每一滚球与内外圈三点接触）

three-point drive 三点式传动（指三个传动带盘组成的传动带传动系）

three-point hitch 三点式挂接装置（= three-link hitch）

three-point suspension 三点式悬架装置

three-polar 三极（的）（亦称 three-pole）

three-port two-stroke engine 三缸二冲程发动机（= three-cylinder two-stroke engine）

three-position control 三位控制

three-quarter elliptic spring 3/4 椭圆形钢板弹簧

three-quarter race camshaft （赛车用）3/4 型凸轮轴（按用户要求的赛车用凸轮轴凸轮磨制的形式，亦表示其用途，此外还有：1/4 型 "one-quarter race"，全赛车型 "full-race"，和街区型 "street-grind" 等）

three-quarter tracked vehicle 3/4 履带式车辆

three-range transmission 三级变速器（参见 multiple-range transmission）

three-seater car 三座轿车

three sensor, three channel ABS 三传感器、三通道式 ABS（两个前轮

分别装有一个转速传感器并分别各由一条独立的通道控制,而由一个装在差速器上的传感器向电子控制模块传送两后轮的转速信息,并由一条液压通道控制两后轮)

three-shaft turbine 三轴式汽轮机

three-shoe brake 三蹄式制动器

three-side tipper truck 三向倾卸式自倾货车

three-speed gear (变速器的)三挡齿轮

three-speed tandem through drive axles 三挡贯通式并装双驱动桥

three-speed transmission 三挡变速器

three-stage gas sealing system 三级气密封系统

three-stage gas turbine 三级式燃气轮机

three stage jack 三级举升器

three-stage potassium vapor turbine 三级钾蒸汽轮机

three-stage torque converter 三级变矩器

three-start screw 三头螺纹

three-state output (数字集成电路的)三态输出(在高电平和低电平时呈相对的低阻抗的源点或汇点,且在适当的输入条件下,提供近似于开路的高阻态的二进制电路的输出)

three-step(ped) 三级的

three-throw crankshaft 三曲柄曲轴

three-throw pump 三联泵,三缸泵(指装在同一壳体内的三个柱塞泵或活塞泵,共用一根曲轴,相位相差120°,曲轴每转一周,产生三个输出行程)

three-toned 三音调的

three-ton truck 三吨载货汽车,三吨货车(=3-ton truck)

three trunnion universal joint 三销式万向节(由两个三销轴连接的两个偏心轴叉组成的准等速万向节,亦称 Joint homocinétique à 3 pivots[法])

three-valve engine 三气门发动机(每一汽缸有三个气门:①两个常规气门,一个空气或极稀混合气气门②一个排气门,两个进气门,以增大进气效率)

three-venturi 三喉管的

three-way 三通式,三路式(指可向三个方向流通或可向三个方向,如:前后、左右倾斜或调整用的)

three-way analyzer 三用分析仪,三项分析仪

three-way catalyst 三效催化剂(一种氧化碳氢化合物和一氧化碳并同时还原氮氧化物的催化剂。为了获得最佳转化率,发动机必须在很狭窄,接近理论配比状态的空燃比范围)

three-way catalytic converter 三效催化转化器[简称 TWC,亦称 three unique catalytic converter 三元催化转化器,指可使 NO_x、CO、HC 三种有害排放物均得到净化处理的催化转化器。分单床式"single-bed",和双床式"dual-bed"两类。单床式指在催化箱内只有一个装有可同时氧化 HC、CO 和还原 NO_x 的三效催化剂"three-way catalyst"的容器,而双床式指在催化箱内串联着两个催化剂容器,形成两级净化。一般第一个容器(第一床)内装的是涂覆有贵金属催化剂铂"platinum Pt"、铑"rhodium Rh"的蜂窝状整体式载体"monolith substrate"的三效整体式催化剂"monolith catalytic 或 unit catalyst",用来将 NO_x 还原为 N_2 和 O_2。第二个容器内(第二床)装的是涂覆有贵金属钯"plladium, Pd"和铂的整体式催化剂,用来使 CO、HC 及第一床内热反应生成的 NH_3 氧化。此外,有的第一容器内装的只是还原性催化

剂，也有两个容器内都装三效催化剂的。除了使用整体式载体和整体式催化剂外，还有将贵金属催化剂涂覆于微小的颗粒状载体"pelleted substrate"上的颗粒状催化剂"pellets catalyst"。为了提高氧化床的净化效果，一般将新鲜空气泵入第一、二床之间的空间，即中间床"mid-bed"内，随由第一床还原处理后的废气进入第二床]

three-way cock 三通开关，三通阀

three way control valve 三通路控制阀（具有三个通路和两个工作位置的控制阀）

three-way dump body 三向倾卸车车身（= three-way tipping body，左、右、后）三向倾卸

three-way intersection 三路交叉口（= three-leg intersection）

three-way pipe 三通管

three-way switch 三路开关（三通开关）

three-way van （左、右、后）三门厢式货车

three-wheel(ed) car 三轮轿车（车身为轿车车身，底盘为三轮摩托车底盘，= three wheeler，美称 tricar）

three-wheeled delivery van 三轮送货车（= three wheeler delivery van）

three-wire compensator 三相自耦变压器

three-wire generator 三线发电机（三相发电机）

threshold ①门槛，门口，门限②界限，限度，范围，边界③临界点，分界点④阈，阈值

threshold contrast 阈限对比（如：在阈限可见度时的亮度对比值）

threshold in fatigue crack propagation 疲劳裂纹扩展门槛值（已存在的疲劳裂纹不发生扩展的应力强度因子值，在平面应变条件下，以 10^{-6} ~ 10^{-7} mm/次所对应的应力强度因子范围 ΔK 值表示）

threshold of audibility 可听阈（听觉界限，可听限度）

threshold of sensitivity 灵敏度界限

threshold value ①阈值（一种确定阈函数结果的值）②界限值，临界值（= critical value）

threshold velocity 界限速度，临界速度

threshold visibility 阈限可见度（似见非见细节或目标时的可见度）

threshold voltage （液晶显示的）阈值电压（低于此电压值时，器件的电光特性只有微小变化）

thrill ①振颤，振动；激动②使振颤，使振动

throat ①喉管（狭窄的通道，咽喉状部分）②（焊缝的）最小截面处③切口，车槽，环槽

throat area 喉口面积（喉管通过断面）

throat body injection system （电子控制式）节气门体（汽油）喷射系统（节气门体装在进气歧管上方，原来安装化油器的位置，其作用与化油器的节气门相同，但其节气门仅用来控制进入发动机的空气量。一般四缸发动机有一个节气门体，一个节气门，V6 和 V8 发动机多装有双节气门体和两个节气门。汽油由一个或两个喷油器喷入节气体节气门前方的进气空气流中，随空气进入进气歧管内分配到各个汽缸，简称 TBI，亦称单点式汽油喷射系统"single point injection system SPI"）

throat depth 焊缝厚度（= throat thickness）

throat diameter （喉管的）喉部直径（临界截面直径）

throat geometry 喉管的几何形状（喉管的几何尺寸）

throat velocity （混合气在喉管内）

喉部流速（临界截面流速）

throttle ①节气门，节流阀（= throttle valve）②节流③加速踏板（控制节气门的踏板，= accelerator pedal）

throttle actuator 加速踏板操纵器（如：汽车自动诊断时，由电子计算机控制，代替人工操纵加速踏板的装置）

throttle adjust screw 节气门调节螺钉（简称 TAS）

throttle angle position transducer 节气门开度传感器（简称 TAP sensor, 亦称 throttle position sensor 或 throttle angle position sensor）

throttle body ①节气门段（包括节气门及其轴的区段）②（单点式汽油喷射系统的）节气门体

throttle body temperature sensor 节气门体温度传感器（用于测定节气门体式单点汽油喷射系统节气门体内的汽油温度，供电子控制模块计算热机再起动空燃比）

throttle bush 节气门衬套

throttle butterfly 节气门蝶阀（蝶形节流阀）

throttle button 节气门操纵按钮

throttle chamber 节气门室

throttle characteristics 节流特性（节流阀流量特性）

throttle compensating valve 加速补偿阀，节气门补偿阀（参见 compensator valve）

throttle dash pot 节气门缓闭器（为减少减速时的排气污染物，使节气门延迟关闭的空气阻尼器）

throttled directional valve 节流方向阀

throttled engine 节气门关闭状态下的发动机（一般指节气门全闭怠速状况的发动机）

throttled exhaust pipe 节流排气管（排气管口处有节流装置的排气管系统，用以增加排气流速）

throttled nut 槽形螺母

throttle down 减速（节流）

throttled-wide （一般指节气门全开的）节气门开大的

throttle-free part load control 无节气门（的发动机）部分负荷控制

throttle full open 节气门全开（= throttle wide open）

throttle governing 节流调节（指利用调节节气门开度来调节发动机输出功率、转速等）

throttle governor 节流调节器（如：节流阀，节气门）

throttle kicker 节气门顶开器（简称 TK，发动机怠速运转期间，若发动机温度低于或高于规定值或发动机在高海拔地区工作，以及使用空调等系统时，由电子控制模块通过电磁阀直接控制或通过电磁真空阀控制，使该顶开器的顶头伸出，适当加大节气门开度，提高怠速转速，亦称 throttle cracker, vacuum-operated throttle modulator）

throttle kicker vacuum actuator 节气门顶开器真空执行器（见 throttle kicker）

throttle motor （电子控制系统中控制节气门开度的）节气门电动机

throttle nozzle （柴油机的）节流式喷嘴（倒锥针式喷嘴、闭式喷嘴的一种，其针阀下端的密封锥面底部还向下延伸出一倒锥形锥头，使喷孔成圆环状狭缝，喷油时油雾成锥形，与柱针式比较，喷油初期只喷出少量燃油，针阀开到一定升程时，才进行主喷射，参见 pintle nozzle）

throttle opener 节气门强制开启装置（当强制怠速时，进气管真空超过规定值时，该装置即在真空作用下拉开节气门，简称 TO）

throttle opening 节气门开度

throttle pedal 加速踏板，油门踏板 (= accelerator pedal)

throttle pedal position sensor 加速踏板位置传感器（节气门控制踏板的位置传感器）

throttle plate 节气门（见 throttle valve①）；节气门片

throttle positioner 节气门怠速开度控制阀（松开加速踏板后，该阀可使节气门暂时保持大于怠速开度的开启，以防止节气门猛关，燃烧不完全，过一定时间后，再让节气门徐徐关闭到怠速开度，简称 TP)

throttle position sensor 节气门位置传感器（测定节气门开度的传感器，有仅测定节气门怠速、中速、满负荷位置的触点式"point-type"和连续测定节气门开度的线性式"linear type"两种，前者亦称 throttle position switch）

throttle position switch 节气门位置开关（根据节气门开度发出电信号，操纵控制电路的接通或断开的开关型传感器，见 throttle position sensor）

throttle potentiometer 节气门电位器（节气门位置传感器的一种）

throttle pressure （自动变速器行星齿轮机构液压控制系的）加速踏板控制液压（即加速踏板控制的液压阀的输出液压，随加速踏板或节气门位置而变化，用来作为发动机扭矩信号，见 throttle valve）

throttle regulator motor （电动式牵引力控制系统的）节气门（开度）调节器电动机（当驱动轮出现滑转时，该直流电动机通过拉索机构使节气门向减小节气门开度的方向运动，以降低发动机的输出扭矩，简称 throttle regulator）

throttle resistance 节流阻力

throttle response （发动机）对节气门开度的响应灵敏度

throttle response lag （对）节气门（开度）反应滞后，（对）油门反应迟后

throttle return check 见 throttle return damper

throttle return damper 节气门回位缓冲器（当松开加速踏板减速时，该缓冲器可延缓节气门的关闭速度，以减小排气中 HC 的浓度和防止熄灭，亦称 throttle return dashpot）

throttle return dashpot 见 throttle return damper

throttle sensor 节气门（位置）传感器 (= 发动机负荷传感器"engine load sensor")

throttle-sensor switch 节气门开关式传感器（仅发送两种节气门位置信号，即：开启、关闭信号的节气门位置传感器）

throttle stop 节气门限位器（一般用来调节发动机怠速运转时节气门的开度，借以调节怠速转速）

throttle stop switch 节气门关闭开关（某些 O_2 反馈控制系统不使用节气门开度传感器，而改用节气门杆作用的触点式传感器，向电子控制模块提供节气门关闭信息）

throttle valve ①（发动机燃油系的）节气门 (= throttle plate, 由驾驶者通过加速踏板控制其开度，借以控制进入发动机汽缸的空气或混合气流量的阀门)②（自动变速器中控制液压系统主压力的）节气门（开度控制）阀（该阀随发动机节气门开度控制输入换挡阀的液压，节气门开度越大，输入换挡阀的压力越高）

throttle valve control 节气门开度控制（在 ASR 系统中指节气门开度调节执行器）

throttle valve controlled EGR system 节气门控制式 EGR 系统（与节气门机构联动的 EGR 阀来控制再循环

排气量)

throttle-valve fuzzy controller 节气门模糊控制器

throttle valve's response time 节气门响应时间

throttling calorimeter 节流型量热器（测定湿蒸气干度用的仪器）

throttling governing 节流控制（变量控制,见 quantitative governing）

throttling governor 节流调节器,节流调速器

throttling loss 节流损失,节气损失（如:节气门所造成的吸气损失）

throttling pintle nozzle 节流轴针式喷油嘴（亦写作 throttling pintel nozzle,节流升程较大的一种轴针式喷油嘴）

throttling section 节流断面

through 穿透的,通过的,贯穿的,直通的,直达的,过境的

through band 有效绿波波宽（连续通行时距,按连续绿波系统的设计车速行驶时,在全系统任一路口的绿灯信号都不致停止的条件下,所能通行的第一辆车与最后一辆车的时间,s）

through beam 连续梁

through bridge 下承式公路桥（= bottom-road bridge）

through-coupling ①直接联轴节②直接耦合

through crack 贯穿裂缝（透缝;穿透裂纹）

through drive 贯通轴传动（= straight-through drive）

through drive axle 贯通轴驱动桥

through highway 直达公路（见 major road）

through hole 通孔（透孔）（= open-end hole）

through loading 直达装运

throughput ①通过量（如:流量、气量、流通量）②生产量,生产能力,生产率③容许量,容许能力④（计算机的）解题能力

throughput capacity ①生产能力②流通能力③通过能力

through repair 大修（= general overh-aul）

through-scavenging （二冲程发动机的）直流扫气（见 uniflow scavenging）

through-station 通过站（中间站,中途站）

through street ①公路干线（城市）干道（= arterial）②大街,主要街道（= major street）

through transportation 直达运输（从始发站或起运地不经中转将旅客、货物送达终点站或卸货地的运输）

through welding 焊透

throw ①急冲,碰撞,投掷②偏心距③曲柄半径④曲柄,曲拐⑤偏心行程,冲程⑥摆幅,摆动距离⑦推动,转动（手柄等）

throwaway engine 报废的发动机

throw-back seat 靠背可向后倒的座椅

throw bearing 曲轴连杆（大端）轴承

throw down ①倾覆,翻倒②拆毁,扔下③（使）沉淀

thrower ①喷洒装置,飞溅装置;撒布装置,撒布机,喷雾器②抛油环,甩油环,溅油圈

thrower ring 甩油圈（离心集油环）

throw in 接入（接通,如:接合离合器,使齿轮啮合）

throwing action （钢板弹簧等的）回跳作用

throw in second gear 挂（上）二挡

throw into action ①起动,开动,投入运转②接入,接合,啮合（齿轮）

thrown solder 脱焊

throw of crankshaft 曲柄半径（亦称 throw of crank）
throw of eccentric ①偏心轮升程 ②偏心距
throw of lever ①杠杆行程，②杠杆臂
throw of piston 活塞行程
throw of pointer 指针（偏摆）行程
throw of pump 泵的扬程
throw out ①切断，断开②分离（离合器）③脱开（齿轮啮合），脱（钩）④放（热，光），放射出⑤使产生误差，使产生偏差
throw-out bearing [美]（离合器）分离轴承（= clutch release bearing）
throw-out（bearing）sleeve 分离轴承套（安装离合器分离轴承的滑套）
throw-out collar 离合器分离推力环
throw-out equalizer （离合器）分离叉均衡器
throw-out fork [美]分离叉（推动离合器分离轴承使离合器分离的叉形件，亦称 thrust bearing actuating lever, throwout lever, clutch release-fork, operation fork, withdrawal fork）
throw-out the clutch 脱开离合器（踩下离合器踏板，= clutch out）
throw-over switch 双向开关
thru-bolt 贯穿螺栓（螺柱，= through bolt）
thru-drive 贯通式主减速器（除向轮边输出功率以外，还能向汽车前方或后方输出功率的主减速器）
thru fastener 贯穿系固件（双面紧固件，如：贯穿螺栓，常规铆钉等）
thru hole 透孔（贯穿孔，通孔）
thru shaft 贯通轴
thrust ①推力，轴向推力，轴向荷载②水头，压头③推动，推进，冲，插，冲入，插入
thrust axle 推力轴
thrust bar 推力杆，推杆
thrust bearing 推力轴承（承受推力，即轴向负荷的轴承，如：离合器的分离轴承）
thrust bearing actuating lever [美]（离合器分离轴承）分离叉（= 英 clutch release bearing lever，见 clutch throwout fork）
thrust block 推力座
thrust button 按钮（= push button）
thrust capacity 承推能力（承受轴向负荷的能力）
thrust cup 承推块（嵌入凸轮从动件或摇臂的推杆接触凹坑中承受推杆压力的零件）
thrust due to temperature 温度致生推力（由于温度变化，热膨胀或冷收缩而产生的推力）
thrust fan （气垫车的）推进风扇
thrust fitting 推力接头
thrust force 推力
thrust-forward front fender 前伸的前翼子板
thrust horsepower （按马力计算的驱动轮）推动功率（切线牵引功率）
thrust load 推力荷载（亦称轴向荷载"axial load"）
thrust of pump 泵的压头
thrust on spring （汽车钢板）弹簧推力（钢板弹簧所传递的切线牵引力，即驱动力）
thrust plate ①推力片（轴向游隙调整片）②（离合器）从动盘（= clutch driven plate）
thrust plug 防过载螺塞（= overload plug）
thrust roller bearing 推力滚柱轴承（= roller thrust bearing）
thrust shoe 斜盘滑履
thrust surface 推力面（亦称 thrust face）
thrust taper roller bearing 推力锥形

滚子轴承（= conical roller thrust bearing）

thrust wall 推力板（承受推力的板，如：浮钳式盘式制动器摩擦衬块的背板）

thrust washer 推力垫圈

thruway ［美］直达公路（= through way, express way, superhighway）

thruway skid cart 路面抗滑（能力）测定车（路面摩擦系数测定车）

THS 丰田复合动力系统（Toyota Hybrid System 的简称，日本丰田公司推出的汽油机——三相交流电动机复合动力系统的商品名。该系统发动机只在效率高的大扭矩转速范围内运转，通过以下三种运转模式实现车辆的低油耗、低排放行驶：①发动机单独驱动汽车行驶②发动机、电动机同时运转，但发动机的动力仅用于发电，而由电动机驱动汽车行驶③发动机停止，由电动机单独驱动汽车行驶。制动减速工况时，车轮带动电动机反转发电，回收车辆的动能转变为电能由蓄电池存储。其中带无级变速器CVT者，称THS–C；第二代者称THS–Ⅱ，中级者称THS–M，M为Mild的简称）

50th simulating dummy 第50%模拟假人（指比美国50%的男人的体重和坐姿高大的假人）

thumb ①拇指②要求搭便车（者）的手势③用拇指压入

thumb-button push rod 按钮推杆

thumb fit 拇指压入配合

thumbnail sketch 草图，略图，简图

thumb nut 元宝螺母（= wing nut, 用手可拧紧的带翼蝶形螺母）

thumbwheel switch 手指转轮式开关（拇指旋拧开关）

thump ①（汽车）振动，低沉噪声②（特指）轮胎击地噪声（车辆在以40~80km/h的速度行驶时，由于轮胎不平衡而每转产生一次40~150Hz的噪声）③重击（声），捶击，砰然声④重击，捶击

THW （丰田公司开发的）冷却水温传感器（商品名，Toyota therm-water 的简称）

T/H wind 顺/逆风（tail/head wind 的简称）

thyristor-impulse control 闸流晶体管-脉冲控制

Ti 钛（titanium）

TIC ［美］运输保险公司（Transport Insurance Co.）

ticket vending machine 自动售票机

tickler ①汽油泵②（发动机）起动注油器（在起动前给汽缸注入少量燃料）③反馈线圈（无线电）

tick over （发动机）怠速运转，在极慢的转速下运转

tidal traffic 潮状交通（对向交通中，交通量多的一方的方向随着时间或周期性变化）

tie ①系杆，拉杆，连接杆②带，条，绳③构架横梁；枕木；桁架的杆件（腹杆，系杆）④系，拉，结，捆，缚；约束，限制；用拉杆拉紧

tie bar ①连接杆（任一连接两个部件或机件的杆件）②（特指梯形转向传动机构中，连接左、右转向节梯形臂的转向）横拉杆（亦称 tie rod）

tie-bar of pattern 花纹加强筋（胎面花纹沟底部突起的增强胶）

tie bolt 拉紧螺栓（连接螺栓）

tie distance 系杆间的距离

tiedown ①系紧，束缚，捆扎，拴紧②系紧装置，捆绑装置，固定装置

tie-down cable ①限位索（底盘测功机检测前轮驱动车辆时，用以防止前轮左右移位）②捆绑用绳索

tier ①层；行；列；盘；定向无线

元件；捆扎装置；等级②堆积成层，层层排列，（货物）堆垛③（阶梯的）一排（一层，一列）④一排座位

tiering truck 带堆垛设备的载货汽车

tie rod 拉杆（在构件或杆系中，任一种承受拉力的杆件，如：①非独立悬架整体式梯形机构中，连接左、右转向梯形臂的整根横拉杆，亦称 cross rod, track rod②在独立悬架分段式梯形机构中，或齿轮—齿条式转向器式转向杆系中连接左、右转向节臂并传递转向摇臂或齿条运动的左、右两节式横拉杆，亦称 side rod 或 part of track rod, 有时也称 track rod）③贯穿螺栓（使几个固定件在预紧力下紧固的螺栓或拉杆）

tie-rod adjusting sleeve 转向横拉杆（长度）调节套管

tie-rod end 转向横拉杆接头 (= steering knuckle tie rod end。横拉杆球形接头称 tie-rod ball, U形接头称 tie-rod yoke 或 tie-rod clevis, 窝形接头称 tie-rod socket)

tie rod linkage 转向拉杆机构（使左、右转向轮按一定关系进行偏转的机构，亦称阿克曼梯形机构，Ackerman geometry）

Tier 1 suppliers 一级供应商，一级销售商

tie-strut （保持车身与车桥的相互位置的）支撑拉杆

tie-up （道路）阻塞，（交通）堵塞

TIF 技术信息资料（technical information file）

tight ①坚固的，牢固的，结实的，密实的，不透气的，密封的，紧的，张紧的，拉紧的，紧配合的，楔紧的，贴紧的②拉紧，紧固，拧紧③上紧（有时用 taut, 其含义是一直拉紧，以致继续再加力拉紧，就会出现断裂）

tight black oxide 密实的黑色（抗剥落）氧化膜

tight connection 紧配合接头 (= tight joint)

tight corner braking phenomena （非全时四轮驱动车辆挂四轮驱动挡后产生的）急转弯制动现象（由于急转弯时前、后车轮转速相同，但行驶距离却不同，因而就会像踩了制动踏板一样，在车轮上产生制动力的现象，严重时会导致发动机熄火）

tighten 上紧，拧紧，紧固；拉紧，拴紧，张紧；密封，密闭

tightened sampling inspection 严格抽样检查

tightening ①上紧，拧紧，紧固；拉紧，张紧，拴紧②密封，密闭

tightening device 张紧装置（亦称 = stretching device, tightener, 如：传动带传动中的张紧轮"tightening pulley"）

tightening flap 捆索，绷带 (= rope tourniquet)

tightening of bearing 轴承的预紧

tightening order 紧固顺序（如：缸盖螺母的上紧顺序等，亦称 tightening sequence）

tightening torque （螺纹连接的）扭紧力矩

tight fit 紧配合

tightly looped distributed processing 紧密耦合分布处理（指多路复用网络内的多个控制器件分布在不同部位，在事件发生的实际时间内各自进行实时控制的处理模式）

tightly packed 用填料密封紧的、压实了的

tightness ①紧密性，密封性，不透性②配合紧度

tight pivot 紧铰接点

tight-sealing 密封（的）

tight-tolerance 精密公差 (= close-

tolerance)
tight turn (车辆)急转弯；(道路的)急弯(= sharp turn)
tight weld 防漏焊接(以防止焊缝处漏气、液等为目的的密实性焊接)
tig weld 惰性气体保护钨极电弧焊(= inert gas shielded tungsten arc welding)
TIG welding 钨极惰性气体保护焊(tungsten inert gas welding 的简称)
tiller steering gear 手柄操纵的杠杆式转向机构(如：履带拖拉机的手柄转向操纵机构)
tilt ①倾斜，斜度，斜面，斜坡②车用篷布，帐篷③倾卸
tiltable 可倾斜的，可倾翻的，可翻倒的
tilt-and-telescope steering wheel 斜度可调整的伸缩式转向盘
tilt angle ①倾斜角②倾卸角③(液晶的)预倾角(液晶分子长轴方向与基板之间的夹角)
tilt(-bed) trailer 自卸挂车(= tipping trailer)
tilt body (平头车的)前翻倾式驾驶室(= tilt cab)
tilt camber 转向节主销内倾(inclination of steering knuckle pivot)
tilt control 倾卸货物操纵件(使货箱倾斜卸货的手操纵件)
tilt cylinder (自卸车的)倾卸用油缸
tilt deck 自动倾卸式车(其货箱底板可全部或部分相对于底盘倾斜，以便于倾卸货物的货车、半挂车和全挂车的总称)
tilted-body motor 斜置式液力马达(= bent-axis motor)
tilt fore and aft (angle) 前后倾斜角
tilting axle 斜置轴，斜轴，斜度可调节的轴
tilting bearing 调心轴承，自位轴承(= tip bearing)
tilting equipment for truck unloading 货车倾卸机构(可使车身倾斜，以倾卸汽车车箱内散粒状货物的机构)
tilting force 倾翻力，倾覆力，翻转力
tilting lamp bracket 能改变倾角的前照灯支架
tilting of the piston (在活塞与汽缸间隙范围内的)活塞的晃动；活塞的歪斜
tilting seat 靠背斜度可调节的座椅
tilting stand 翻转式装配架
tilting steering wheel 倾斜度可调的转向盘
tilting test (自卸车)倾卸试验
tilt motor 见 power tilt mechanism
tilt switch 倾斜开关(当车身向任一方向倾斜度超过某规定值时，该开关闭合，向控制模块发生险性信号。由一顶部装有永久磁铁的摇筒和感知该摇筒摇摆度霍尔元件组成)
tilt-telescoping steering column 倾斜度可调的伸缩式转向柱
TIM 胎压监测器(tire inflation monitor 的简称)
timber ①木材，木料②原木，梁木
timber body 木材运输车身
timber carriage 木材运输车
timber carrying one axle trailer 单轴圆木运输挂车
timber constructed body 木结构车身
timber drag 拖曳木材的阻力，集材阻力
timbered crossing 铺有枕木的横道(如：横穿铁路的横道等)
timber preservation 木材防腐
timber truck 木材运输车(= log truck)
time ①时，时间；时期，阶段，时代②次数，回数，倍数

time adjusting device 时间调整装置（定时装置）

time-area diagram 时间—断面积图，（发动机气门开启时气门口气流的通过断面积和对应开启时间的乘积，用来评价气门的通过能力）

time-area value 时面值（进、排气门或口开启的流通面积随时间或曲轴转角而变化的曲线所包含的面积值）

time-averaged measurement of steady-state flows 稳态流的时间平均测定

time-base 时基，时标，时轴，时间坐标

time base accuracy 时基精度（时标精度，时轴精度）

time(-base) diagram 以时间为横坐标的曲线图

time-base diagram 随时间而变的曲线图（= time curve）

time between failures 两次损坏间的时间

time between overhauls 大修间隔时间

time bill [英]时刻表，时间表

time book 工时记录器，时间记录本

time clock 定时器，时钟，（自动润滑系统的）调时装置

time compression 时间压缩（如：模拟处理磁带上的信号时，采用比原记录快若干倍的速度重放磁带，以压缩信号的时间）

time-compression curve 时间-压缩（压力）曲线（压缩压力随时间而变的曲线）

time constant 时间常数（在由阶跃或脉冲输入引起的一阶线性系统中，输出完成总上升或总下降的63.2%所需的时间）

time-consuming 费时的（需要花费大量时间的，大劳动量的）

time contour map 等时线图（交通分析用，表示等时到达地点）

time controller 时间控制装置（自动定时仪；定时器，正时器）

time course 时间历程（测试获得的某物理量的瞬时幅值随时间而变化的记录）

time-critical function 时间限制功能（电子控制系统软件优先级的一种分配功能）

time-critical message 时间限制性信息（指在实时控制所要求的时间范围内必须处理完的信息）

time cut-out 定时断路器

timed 定时的，计时的，时控的

timed acceleration 定时加速

time-deformation curve 时间-形变图（时间-形变曲线）

time delay 时间滞后（时间迟后）

time-delay switch 延时开关

time delay valve 延时阀

timed engine-starting system 发动机定时起动装置

time-dependent 随时间而变化的（与时间有关的，依赖于时间的）

time-dependent system 时间相关系统

timed fuel injection 燃油定时喷射（指燃油在规定时刻喷射，如：进气门开启时喷射等）

timed induction with supercharge 定时进气增压（提高转子发动机转矩的一种方法，通过一个专门的进气门，只在进气行程中由空气泵将一部分附加空气泵入燃烧室，简称TISC）

timed injection 定时喷射（如：喷射式汽油机中，在规定的时刻将适量的汽油喷到进气管等处的喷射方式）

time-displacement curve 时间-位移曲线

time distance （变化过程中）两点间的时间间隔

time-distance graph （表示车辆加

速性能的）时间-行程曲线图
time division 时间分割，时分（如：在汽车电子系统中，将总信道进行时间分割，各个装置按一定顺序和预先规定的长短轮流占用其中的一段时间与主控计算机之间传递信息）
time division multiplex 时间分割多路传输，时分多路复用传输
time division mutiple access 时间分割多路复用存取（见TDMA）
time domain 时间范畴
timed unit 时控装置，计时装置，定时装置
time element （继电器）延时元件
time expand 延时
time exposure 长时间曝光（拍摄的照片，超过1/2s的曝光）
time factor 时间因数
time for acceleration 加速时间
time function 时间函数
time function iteration trip distribution method （预测交通量的）时间函数迭代旅行分配法
time gap 时间间隔
time growth constant 逐时增长常数
time headway 车头时距（以车辆某一对应点为基准测定的车辆连续通过特定点的时间间隔，亦称 time interval）
time history （某一参数）随时间而变化的历程（与时间的关系曲线）
time-independent 不随时间而变化的，与时间无关的
time in service 使用时间（使用寿命）
time integration stage 时间积分级
time interval ①车头时距（见 time headway）②时间间隔，时程，时节
time interval recorder 时间间隔记录仪
time(-)invariant 不随时间而变化的
timekeeping circuit 计时电路，测时电路
time lag 时滞（时间延迟、滞后）
time-lagged 延时的，滞时的，迟后的
time lag of inflammation 着火延迟期
time lag relay 延时继电器
time length 时间长度（持续时间）
time lever （照相装置的）长时间曝光用快门拨杆（手控速度B门拨杆）
time-like 类时的
time limit 期限，限期
time marker pickup 时间标记脉冲发生器
time mean speed 时间平均车速（= average speed, average spot speed）
time of acceleration 加速时间
time of climb （汽车）爬坡持续时间
time of driver's reaction 驾驶员反应时间
time of heat 加热时间
time of idling stop waiting for green light 等待绿灯信号的怠速停车时间
time of ignition 点火时刻（= firing point）
time of oscillation 振动周期
time of run 运行时间，运转时间
time-on-target threshold 到达目标物的时间界限
time on test 试验（延续）时间
time-out 暂停，中断
timepiece 时计（如：钟表，秒表）
time piston （喷油时刻控制电磁阀的）正时柱塞
time-pressure area 时间-压力曲线下的面积
time-prohibitive 受时间限制（的）
time-proof 长寿命的，耐久的，耐用的
timer ①计时器，秒表，时速表，定时器，定时装置②计时员，测时员③自动按时操作装置，延时调节

器，延时继电器，时间继电器，时间传感器，定时标记，时标④时间信号发生器⑤程序装置，程序调节器⑥正时器⑦（计算机的）时间暂存器（一种寄存器"registe"，其内容按固定的时刻间隔改变，用这种方法来测量时间，亦称 time register, clock register）

timer core （装在分电盘式电子点火系分电器轴端，带齿的）正时齿轮状转子（位于电磁感应传感线圈的中央，其齿数与汽缸数相同，分电器轴旋转时，其齿转动，使感应线圈内感生出电压脉冲，向电子控制模块发送发动机转速和曲轴位置信号，作为电子控制模块控制点火的基准信号）

timer distributor 分电器，配电器（见 distributor）

time recorder 时间记录器，时间记录仪

time reference 时间基准（时间参考点，时间控制标记，时间参照点）

time reference line 时间基线（时间基准线）

time register （计算机）时间寄存器（时间暂存器，见 timer⑦）

time relay 时间继电器（定时继电器）

time reliability （交通运输的）准时性

time resolution 时间分辨率

time response 时间响应（一个输入量的规定变化引起输出量随时间的变化）

timer-operated 定时器控制的

timer rotor 定时转子（在无触点点火系统中，分电器轴上带有凸起或齿形的转子）

timer shaft 分电器轴

time-saving 节约时间的，省时的

time scale 时间标度（时标、时间刻度）

time schedule 时间表（如：工作进程表，施工进度表，行车时刻表）

time schedule control 时序控制（= time variable control）

time-schedule controller 时序控制器

time-sensing element 时间传感元件

time sequencing 时间顺序

time series 时间序列

time series reliability model （碰撞回避制动系统等按）时间顺序（分析的作用）可靠性（的数学）模型

time-shared multiplexing system 时间分割多路传输系统（分时多路传输系统）

time sheet ①计时卡②时间表（= time card）

time slicing principle 时间分隔法（分时法，见 time slot principle）

time slot 时隙（时间分割多路复用传输系统中时间分割片的时间间隔）

time slot principle 时隙法，时间分隔法，分时法（将时间分片，以实现信息的并行传输式处理方法，简称 TSP，亦称 time slicing principle）

time-space diagram 时间-空间运行图（时间距离图、时距图、车辆的运行坐标图，横坐标表示经过时间，纵坐标表示行驶距离）

time span 时间间隔

time study 工时标定，工时分析，工时调查

time switch 时控开关（自动按一定时间启闭的电动开关）

time table 时刻表，时间表

time-taking 计时，测时

time taxi 计时出租汽车，计时出租车

time-temperature switch 时间-温度开关

time-tested 经过长期运行试验的，经受过时间考验的

time tick 报时信号（时间分段信号）

time-to-digital converter 时间-数字变换器

time-to-market (新产品的)投放市场时间,上市所需时间(产品从设计开始到提供给市场所需的时间)

time to peak ①过冲时间(阶跃响应中,过度偏差达到过冲量的时间)②到达峰值的时间

time-to-peak pressure (安全气囊等)到达最大压力所需的时间

time totalizer 总计时

time-travel curve 时间-行程曲线

time triggered protocol 时间触发协议(见TTP/C)

time unit 时间单位

time variable control 时序控制(= time schedule control)

time-varying image processing (technologies) (随)时间连续变化的影像处理(技术)

time vector 时间矢(量)(时间直线)

time-work 计时工作

time worn 用旧了的,陈旧的;过时的,古老的

time zero 计时起点,时间零点

timing ①配时,调时,正时,定时 ②计时,测时,校时 ③(发动机指)气门正时,点火正时,喷油正时(见 valve timing, spark timing 及 ignition timing)④(自动变速器)换挡正时(见 gear change timing)

timing advance tester 点火提前角测试仪

timing-and-recording equipment 测时记录装置

timing belt (发动机的)正时带(由曲轴带动凸轮轴旋转的内圈带齿的传动带)

timing chain (发动机)正时链(曲轴带动凸轮轴的驱动链)

timing circuit 定时电路

timing control 定时控制,时间控制,延时控制

timing cycle 定期循环

timing cylinder 正时汽缸(定时汽缸,确定点火时间的汽缸,如:多缸发动机的第一缸)

timing data map (存储在电子控制模块内的点火或喷油等)正时数据曲面图(见 map)

timing device ①计时器(时间信号发生器)②(点火、喷油时刻的正时器)

timing device plunger (电子控制柴油机燃油系统的)正时机构柱塞(根据控制模块指令转动分配式喷油泵分配环或推动柱塞式喷油泵调节齿条,使喷油时刻提前的执行件)

timing diagram 正时图(表示气门开、闭,点火,喷油等的时刻和延续时间的图示)

timing equipment 测时装置

timing gear ①正时齿轮(曲轴带动凸轮轴的驱动齿轮)②正时机构

timing generator 定时信号发生器(时标振荡器)

timing hole 点火正时标记检视孔

timing hut 汽车路试时的测时亭

timing lamp 正时灯(调整点火正时用的频闪观测灯,亦称 timing test lamp, timing light, 手机形正时灯称 timing gun)

timing length (汽车路试)计时长度

timing lever (点火或喷油)正时调整杆

timing light-tachometer 正时灯-转速仪

timing mark ①正时标记(发动机飞轮、曲轮、凸轮轴或其他零件上供确定气门、点火、喷油时刻的基准标记)②时(间)标(记)

timing of engine 发动机气门正时(见 valve timing);发动机点火或喷

油正时（见 ignition timing 和 injection timing）

timing of piston 活塞在汽缸内位置的测定（为了校准气门和点火正时）

timing of port events （二冲程发动机，转子发动机进排）气口开闭正时

timing pulse generator 时标脉冲发生器

timing reference 时间基准

timing relay 时间继电器（定时继电器，时限继电器）

timing ring （分配式喷油泵的）正时环（用作几何供油始点记号的圆环形零部件）

timing scatter 点火时刻离散（高速时，由于机械式或真空式点火提前机构的特性造成的实际点火时刻与调定的最佳点火时刻的前、后偏差）

timing shaft [美]分电器轴（= distributor shaft）

timing sprocket （曲轴、凸轮轴的）正时链轮

timing tach tester 点火正时灯-转速表检验仪

timing variator （电子控制）正时机构

Timken 铬镍钼耐热钢

timken test （润滑油、脂的）抗磨和抗挤压特性试验

Timken X 镍镍钼钴铁耐热合金（钴 30.7%，镍 28.6%，铬 16.8%，钼 10.5%，铁 11%，锰 1.4%，硅 0.75%）

TIMS （汽车）运输信息管理系统（Transportation Information Management Systems）

tin ①锡（Sn）②锡焊③镀锡

TIN 车辆变速器出厂编号（见 vehicle transmission identification number）

tin bar 锡棒料

tin-base babbit(t) 锡基巴氏合金

tin-base bearing metal 锡基滑动轴承合金

tin can ①镀锡白铁罐②小型廉价汽车；轻快轿车

tin-coated 镀锡的

tin-containing 含锡的

tine （锯、耙的）齿，尖头，端头，叉

tin foil 锡箔（= leaf tin）

tin glazed steel plate 镀锡钢板

tin-indium film 锡-铟薄膜（透明，导电，涂于汽车风窗玻璃，作为电热融霜薄膜）

tinlizzie 廉价轿车（原为美福特产 T 型轿车的诨名，现泛指廉价的小型轿车）

tinned ①镀锡的②包锡的③包马口铁的④罐装的

tinning solder 焊锡（软钎焊焊料，Sn91%，Zn9%）

tinplate 马口铁（镀锡铁皮，白铁皮，= tin sheet）马口铁

tin-plating 镀锡（的）

tin solder 锡钎焊焊料

tin(-)soldering 锡焊钎

tint ①色调，颜色的浓淡；涂色 ②浅色，涂漆

tinted glass 着色防眩玻璃（= antiglare glass，tinted window，简称 tints）

tinted transparent top 有色透明车顶

"T"-intersection T 形交叉口，丁字形交叉口（美，一路与其他两路成直角的三路交叉口，= "T"-junction）

tin-type （美俗）福特汽车

tiny lamp 小灯泡，微型灯泡

TiO_2 type oxygen sensor 二氧化钛型氧传感器（亦称 titanate type oxygen sensor，titanium dioxide oxygen sensor，与 ZrO_2 型氧传感器不同之处在于它是作为传感器电路中的一个可变电阻元件，以改变电压的方式工作。

当空燃比浓时，TiO_2 的阻值降低，输出高电压（1.2V）信号，而空燃比稀时，TiO_2 阻值高，输出 0.2V 低电压信号）

tip ①端（如：火花塞绝缘体端），尖，梢②接头，触点，插头尖端③（天平等仪器的）刀口④倾斜，倾卸，翻转⑤装（包）尖头，装（镶）刀片

tip-and-slide seat 靠背可放平的滑动式座椅

tip angle 顶圆锥角（亦称顶锥角，锥齿轮轴线与顶锥母线之间的夹角，轮齿位于顶锥角之内）

tip-back 后倾（后倾翻，后倾卸）

tip bearing 自位轴承（= tilting bearing）

tip car 自卸车（= tilter）

tip chute 倾卸滑槽，倾卸斜道

tip circle 齿顶圆（锥齿轮指共顶锥与背锥的交线。圆柱齿轮和摆线轮及涡轮指齿顶圆柱面与端平面的交线）

tip clearance 径向间隙（指：螺纹顶的间隙、齿顶间隙等）

tip cone 齿顶圆锥面（简称顶锥、锥齿轮的齿顶曲面）

tip cylinder 齿顶圆柱面（齿顶面上呈圆柱面形状的那一部分齿顶表面，如：圆柱齿轮的齿顶曲面、摆线轮的齿顶曲面）

tip diameter 齿顶圆直径（锥齿轮齿顶圆的直径、圆柱齿轮齿顶圆柱面和齿顶圆的直径）

tip distance （锥齿轮）轮冠距（齿顶圆所在平面至定位面的距离）

tip edge engagement 顶缘啮合（轮齿廓相接触的啮合）

tip leakage （压气机或涡轮机）叶片顶部处的泄漏

tip-off ①脱焊，开焊，熔下②（故障，损坏等的）预兆，预告，警报③翻倒

tip-over seat 可翻平的座椅

tippable vehicle cab 前翻式驾驶室

tipper ①自动倾卸车，翻斗车（= dump car）②倾卸装置，倾翻机构（= tippler）

tipping stability （汽车的）抗翻倾稳定性，抗侧翻稳定性

tipping trailer 自卸挂车（= self-emptying trailer, tilt(-bed) trailer, tilt-deck trailer）

tip relief 修缘（齿廓修形的一种，指在齿顶附近对齿廓形状进行有意识的修削）

tip rod 转向横拉杆（= tie rod）

Tipshift （奔驰轿车的）五前进挡自动变速器商品名

tip surface 齿顶曲面（①对齿轮指包含齿轮各个齿的齿顶面的假想曲面②对涡轮指位于涡轮或蜗杆的轮齿顶部的曲面，它用于确定蜗轮或蜗杆的齿凸出于分度曲面之外的高度。对于圆柱蜗杆，其齿顶曲面为圆柱面。对于涡轮和环面蜗杆，其齿顶曲面为圆锥面，或者由圆环面和圆柱面组合而成。对于锥蜗杆和锥涡轮，其齿顶曲面为圆锥面）

Tiptronic 手动/自动-体式变速器（亦写作 tiptronical，其换挡拨片多装在多功能方向盘上）

tip up 竖起，向上翻起

tire [美]①轮胎（= 英 tyre，凡遇到 tire 为首的词组可查阅 tyre）②装配轮胎

tire accessories ①轮胎附件（防滑链等）②安装修理轮胎用的附件（撬棒等）

tire adhesion coefficient 轮胎（与地面的）附着系数

tire air pump （汽车上的）轮胎充气泵（= tire air inflater）

tire aligning torque 轮胎回正力矩（指路面作用在轮胎上的力旋矢量使轮胎绕轮胎坐标系 z' 轴旋转的分

1641

tir

量)

tire alignment 车轮定位(= wheel alignment)

tire aquaplaning 轮胎浮滑(车轮水滑)

tire aspect-ratio deflection sensor 轮胎高宽比变化传感器

tire attachment 轮胎防滑件(如:防滑带,防滑链等)

tire axis system 轮胎坐标系(以轮胎接地中心为原点的右手直角坐标系。x'轴为车轮中心平面和道路平面的交线,车轮中心平面行进方向为正;z'轴为铅垂线,向上为正;y'轴在道路平面内,方向按右手法则确定)

tire balancing equipment 轮胎平衡机

tire band 轮胎捆带(= rope tourniquet②)

tire bead breaker (轮胎)胎圈拆卸器

tire bead unseating 轮胎胎圈脱座

tire break 轮胎破裂

tire brushing washer 车轮刷洗机

tire-camber wear 外倾角不当引起的轮胎磨损

tire capacity 轮胎承载量(轮胎承载能力)

tire carcass (轮胎的)胎体(见carcass)

tire carcass resistance 轮胎胎体变形阻力

tire carrier bracket 备胎架(亦称tire carrier frame)

tire casing ①(轮胎的)胎面和胎肩②胎体(= tire carcass,见carcass)

tire casing analyzer 胎体检验仪(亦称tire casing inspector)

tire cavity noise devices (装在车轮上的)轮胎胎腔气柱共鸣噪声消减装置

tire chain repair tool 轮胎防滑链维修工具

tire changer 轮胎拆装机

tire characteristics 轮胎特性

tire compliance 轮胎柔度

tire-contact area 轮胎触地面积(轮胎接地面积)

tire-contact center 轮胎(与路面)的接触印痕中心(亦称 tire center on road)

tire contact force fluctuation 轮胎接地力波动(作为评价轮胎路线保持性能的指标性参数之一)

tire cord 轮胎帘线

tire cornering force 轮胎转弯力(见 cornering force)

tire cornering test vehicle 轮胎转弯试验用车(测试车辆转弯时,轮胎的各项指标)

tire cornering wear (转向轮面)转向磨损

tire cover 胎面

tire cushion 轮胎缓冲层

tire cut 轮胎割痕

tire deformation work 轮胎变形功(由于轮胎变形消耗的功,亦称 tire-flexure wor)

tire demountor 轮胎拆卸器

tire design 轮胎设计;轮胎结构

tire drag 轮胎滚动阻力

tire flange 轮胎胎圈(= tyre bead)

tire flap 轮胎衬带

tire flexibility 轮胎挠性

tire footprint 轮胎印痕(指轮胎接地印痕)

tire force ①轮胎力(指路面对轮胎的各种反作用力)②轮胎转弯力(= tire cornering force)

tire girdle 轮胎防滑套箍

tire groove 轮胎花纹凹槽

tire gross contact 轮胎总接地面积

tire-ground braking force 轮胎—地面制动力(制动时地面作用于轮

胎的切线力，是使汽车制动而减速的外力）

tire ground contact length 轮胎接地长度

tire-ground elasticity 轮胎-路面弹性（指轮胎和路面的相对弹性及迟滞性）

Tire HILS 轮胎硬件连线模拟器（亦简称 HILS，为 tire hardware-in-loop simulator 的简称，由硬件"轮胎及转鼓式轮胎试验机"与之连线的软件"汽车数字模型系统"两部分组成，二者通过接口和电子计算机连接。由于使用真实轮胎作为实机试验，测试结果准确可靠）

tire holder 备胎架

tire hysteresis 轮胎弹性滞后（及其引起的滚动阻力）

tire indicator ①轮胎气压表（tire pressure indicator）②轮胎磨损指示片（见 tire wear indicator）

tire inflation pressure 轮胎充气压力（= tire pressure）

tire inflation pressure sensor 轮胎充气压力传感器（简称 TIPS）

tire kerfs 轮胎花纹上的横向狭槽

tire lateral flexibility 轮胎在侧向荷载作用下的挠性

tire lateral force 轮胎横向力（见 lateral force of tire）

tire lateral pressure sensor 轮胎横向压力传感器（简称 TLPS）

tire load capacity factor 轮胎负载系数（指汽车总质量与全部轮胎允许荷载之比值）

tire load transfer （汽车的）轮胎负载转移（一般指汽车转弯时，外胎负载增大，内胎负载减小；制动时前轮负荷增大，后轮负荷减小；加速时前轮负荷减少，后轮负荷增大的现象）

tire mark on pavement （制动时）路面上（留下的）轮胎拖痕

tire monitoring and inflation system 胎压监测和（自动）充气系统

tire noise 轮胎噪音（轮胎在行驶中产生的各种噪音的总称）

tire overhang 轮胎外悬量（轮胎中心至轮毂轴承中心的距离）

tire overinflation wear 轮胎充气过度引起的磨损

tire overload 轮胎超载

tire patch kit 修补汽车轮胎用的工具包

tire percent deflection （受静载时）轮胎变形与断面高度之百分比

tire performance criteria 轮胎性能规范（简称 TPC）

tire placard （固定在汽车上的）轮胎说明牌（说明轮胎荷载、充气压力等信息的永久性铭牌）

tire power loss 轮胎的功率损失（指被轮胎转换为热量的机械输入功率）

tire press 轮胎压床（外胎硫化或拆装用压力机）

tire pressure 轮胎气压，胎压（= tire inflation，tire inflation pressure）

tire pressure control system 胎压控制系统

tire(-pressure) gauge 轮胎气压表

tire pressure indicator ①胎压指示器，胎压警报器（简称 tire indicator）②胎压表

tire pressure monitor 胎压监测器

tire pressure monitor system （轮）胎（充）气（压）力）监测系统（简称 TPMS）

tire print 轮胎印迹

tire protection chain 轮胎保护链

tire pull force （由于轮胎本身制造上的缺陷，如：帘线层不对称、胎体失圆等原因造成的在平整地面上行驶时使轮胎向左侧或右侧偏行趋势的）轮胎侧拉力（该力与转向系和悬架系的几何布置无关）

tire radial flexibility 轮胎在径向荷载作用下的挠性

tire radial run out 轮胎径向跳动（指安装在车轴上轮胎转动时，其胎面在中心平面内半径的变动）

tire radius under load 轮胎静载半径

tire radius under no load 轮胎无负荷半径（轮胎充气至规定的最大压力时，在无负荷状态下的半径）

tire rate 轮胎弹性常数（一定内压下，车轮载荷变化与车轴和地面间的距离变化之比，= tire spring rate）

tire recapping 轮胎翻修（工艺），胎面翻新（工艺）

tire removing-and-replacing tool 轮胎拆装工具

tire repair compounds 轮胎修补配料

tire repair kit 轮胎维修包（包括气动表面擦洗机、扩孔器，以及其他手工具，还包括补胎材料"patch materials"）

tire research facility 轮胎研究设备，轮胎研究装置（简称TIRF）

tire ride quality 轮胎的行驶平顺性

tire rim 轮辋（见 rim）

tire-rim locking ring 轮辋锁环

tire-road adhesion utilization curve 轮胎-路面附着系数利用曲线（车轮不致抱死所要求的轮胎-路面附着系数与制动减速度的关系曲线）

tire-road adhesion utilization factor 轮胎—道路附着力利用率

tire road grip 轮胎的路面抓着力（轮胎与道路的附着力）

tire road holding performance 轮胎的路线保持性能（保持行驶方向的能力）

tire road noise 轮胎（在）道路（上滚动时产生的）噪声

tire-road traction properties 轮胎-路面的牵引力特性

tire roller 轮式压路机

tire rupture test 轮胎断裂试验

tire scrub （在侧向力作用下产生一定侧偏角时直行轮胎单位行走距离的横向偏移量，可以在侧滑试验台上测出，称）横向滑移量（用m/km，mm/m为单位，亦称 tire lateral slip 或 tire slip，为侧偏角对汽车行驶方向产生的实际结果）

tire scuff detector 轮胎磨损检测器

tire seat （轮辋的）轮胎胎圈座面

tire section 轮胎断面

tire section height 轮胎断面高度

tire section height sensor 轮胎断面高度传感器

tire self-aligning torque 轮胎自回正力矩

tire service equipment 轮胎维修机具

tire side wear 轮胎胎侧磨损

tire size 轮胎尺寸

tire sizing 轮胎尺寸选配

tire slots 胎面花纹槽

tire spreader 轮胎撑开器

tire spring rate 轮胎弹性常数（见 tire rate）

tire squeak 轮胎噪声（= tire squeal）

tire stiffness 轮胎刚度（轮胎的径向刚度、侧向刚度和切向刚度的统称）

tire stud 轮胎防滑钉

tire sundries 轮胎小配件

tire surface temperature sensor 胎面温度传感器（简称TST sensor）

tire temperature sensor 轮胎温度传感器

tire testing machine 轮胎试验机（简称TTM，= tire tester）

tire thump （在高速行驶时）轮胎（发出的）敲击声

tire toe-in wear 前束引起的轮胎磨损

tire toe-out wear 前轮负前束引起的轮胎磨损（前轮共张引起的轮胎磨损）

tire-to-road slip 轮胎与路面间的滑

移率（见 slip⑥）
tire traction properties　轮胎牵引（力）特性
tire tread design　轮胎胎面设计；轮胎胎面花纹结构
tire tread face　轮胎胎面行驶面
tire tread height　轮胎胎面花纹高度
tire truing machine　轮胎整形机（将胎面微小的凸点削除，保证轮胎正圆，以免高速行驶时引起振动）
tire tube　轮胎内胎（＝inner tube）
tire (tube) valve　轮胎气门嘴（见 inflation valve）
tire under inflation wear　轮胎充气不足引起的磨损
tire uniformity machine　轮胎均匀性检查机
tire wear indicator　轮胎磨损指示件（该指示件位于胎面层的一定深处，当胎面磨损到该处时，即显露出来，表示达到翻修极限，简称 tire indicator）
tire well　车身备胎室，备胎腔（放置备胎的腔室）
tire wheel nut wrench　轮胎螺母扳手
TIRF　轮胎研究装置（tire research facility）
Tirrill (type) regulator　梯瑞尔电压调节器（触点式调节器，利用触点的开闭，控制发电机的输出电压）
TISC　定时进气增压（见 timed induction with supercharge）
TISS　变速器输入转速传感器（transmission input speed sensor 的简称）
titanate　钛酸盐；钛酸酯
titania sensor　二氧化钛（TiO_2）废气氧含量传感器（用于三元废气催化净化系统）
titanium　钛（Ti）
titanium-base alloy　钛基合金
titanium coated　镀钛的
titanium dioxide　二氧化钛（TiO_2）
Titanium Fluid Strength Technology（机油等）流体加钛强化技术
titanium-iron alloy　钛铁合金（用于吸收、储存氢气，供氢气汽车使用）
title　题目，标题，名称，图标
Ti-VCT　双独立凸轮轴可变正时系统（Twin independed-Variable Camshaft Timing 的简称）
TI-worm　渐开面包络环面蜗杆（亦称 TI 蜗杆，指以直齿的或斜齿的渐开线圆柱，齿轮为产形轮所发展成的环面蜗杆）
T-joint　①T 字形管接头，三通管接头（＝Tee union）②（金属板的）T 形焊接
T-junction　T 形交叉，丁字形交叉口（＝"T"-intersection）
t-km　吨-公里（ton-kilometer）
TK solenoid　节气门顶开器电磁阀（见 throttle kicker）
TK-worm　锥面包络环面蜗杆（亦称 TK 蜗杆，由齿面呈圆锥面形状的产形轮所展成的环面蜗杆）
TLEV　过渡时期低排放车辆（如：美联邦环境保护法规规定从 1994 年至 1997 年期间的过渡性低排放车辆 Transition Low Emission Vehicle 的简称，见 LEV）
TLM　①遥测装置（＝telemeter）②遥测技术（＝telemetry）
TLOCE　交通信号灯操作控制设备（traffic light operating control equipment）
t/m^3　吨/米³（国际单位制密度单位，$1t/m^3 = 1kg/L = 1g/cm^3 = 0.7525$ $ton/yd^3 = 62.43$ $lb/ft^3 = 0.03613$ $lb/in^3 = 10.02$ $lb/imp.\ gal$）
TM　①技术手册（technical manual）②技术备忘录（technical memorandum）③温度计（temperature me-

ter) ④时间调制（time modulation）⑤吨英里（ton-miles）⑥商标（trade mark）⑦扭转力矩（twisting moment）

TMC ①交通管理中心（Traffic Management Center 的简称）②［日］丰田汽车公司（见 Toyota Motor Co.）③交通信息频道（traffic message channel 的简称）

TMEC 丰田汽车研究中心（中国）有限公司［Toyota Motor Engineering &Manufacturing（China）Co., Ltol. 的中文名，位于江苏无锡］

TML 四甲基铅（抗爆剂）（tetraethyl lead 的简称）

TMS ①轮胎管理系统（tire management system 的简称，测定实际胎压）②运输监控系统（transport monitor system）

TMT ①四甲基秋兰姆化二硫；联二甲氨硫酸基（tetramethyl thiuram disulphide）②热机械加工（thermo mechanical-treatment）

TN ①技术备忘录（technical note）②试验次数；试验编号（test number）③吨（ton）④商品名（trade name）

TO 节气门强制开启装置（见 throttle opener）

to-and-fro movement 往返运动，往复运动

to and fro route 往复式路线，来回路线（指车辆在完成运输任务中，多次重复于两个货运点之间的运行路线）

toe ①端，前端，尖端（如：齿顶，齿顶高，斜钉，轴踵；柄尖，焊缝边缘，胎趾）②前束（toe-in 的简称）

toe board （驾驶室的驾驶员）搁脚板（驾驶室前壁下的斜地板，＝pedal panel, toe board panel）

toe brake 行车制动器（＝foot brake）

toe button 脚踏（开关）钮

toe contact 齿顶接触，齿尖接触（齿轮啮合时由于齿宽不足的一种不正常接触现象）

toe control arm （悬架的）前束控制臂

toe control hub （后轮）前束控制轮毂（如：在 Savanna RX-7 型轿车后桥悬架上采用有这一机构。当后轮上施加驱动力或制动力，或汽车低速转弯时，该机构可使左、右后轮向内转动某一角度，形成前束。）

toe controlled rear suspension 前束控制式后悬架（当发生侧倾等后悬架受压缩时，能自动使其后轮向内偏转一定的角度，即形成前束。因而，当汽车弯道行驶时，车轮能自动偏向弯道内侧，保持车辆姿势稳定）

toe controlling strut type front suspension 前束控制滑柱式前悬架

toe control link （悬架的）前束控制连杆（见 toe-correct bushing）

toe-correct bushing （某些纵臂式悬架的）前束校正衬套（纵臂通过该衬套与车身连接，当受到横向力作用时，该衬套产生反作用力使前束保持稳定。有的纵臂式悬架使用 toe control link "前束控制连杆"，其作用与此相同）

toe end of shoe （制动器的）蹄片窄端

toe end of tooth （锥齿轮）齿的小端

toe-in 前束（亦简称 toe，指同一轴两端车轮中心平面在水平地面上的投影线前端间距 B 与其后端间距 A 的差距，即 toe-in = A-B（mm）。当 A-B＞0 时为正前束，简称前束，A-B＜0 时为负前束或称前张 "toe-out"。为前束时，上述两投影线延长线的交点在车辆的前方，二者的

夹角称前束角"toe-in angle")
toe-in checking rule (车轮)前束检验尺
toe-in controladjusting cam (悬架的)前束调节凸轮
toe-in gauge 前束量规(测量、调整前束的装置)
toe of bead 胎趾(见 bead toe)
toe-out (车轮的)负前束,前张(见 toe-in)
toe-out angle 车轮前张角,车轮负前束角(见 toe-in)
toe-out on turns 转弯时(由内侧前轮转角大于外侧前轮等原因造成的)转向轮的负前束(转弯时车轮的前张)
toe-setting alignment 前束定位(作业)
TOFEP 燃油经济性试验操作规程(Testing Operation of Fuel Economy Program)
toggle ①曲柄,曲拐;弯杆,肘节(=bent lever) ②触发器,双态元(器)件(指可接通两种方式、两种状态且在接通后保持稳定状态的开关,任何具有两个稳态的器件,=flip-flop)
toggle flip-flop 反转触发器
toggle switch 拨杆开关,扳柄开关
Tokyo Motor Show 东京汽车展览会
tolerable 可容许的,允许的,相当的,相当好的,过得去的
tolerance ①公差,容差,容限 ②容许,容忍 ③耐受度,耐力
tolerance and fit 公差及配合
tolerance deviation 容许偏差
tolerance limit 容许界限,容许极限;公差限度
tolerance of dimension 尺寸公差
tolerance of fit 配合公差(=tolerance on fit, fit tolerance)
tolerance range 公差范围
tolerance unit 公差单位

tolerance zone 公差带,公差范围
tolerate 容许,准许
tolerate stress 容许应力
toll ①税费(如:通行税,过境税;过桥费;养路费,通行费) ②运费 ③收税,收费;纳税,缴费
toll expressway 收费快速公路(=turnpike ②)
toll-free expressway 免费快速公路(=freeway ②)
tollgate (收费公路上的)收费站
toluene 甲苯($CH_3C_6H_5$, =methylbenzene)
toluene number 甲苯值(早期使用的燃油抗爆指数,现已为辛烷值"octane number"所取代)
tommy wrench T字柄扳手(如:火花塞扳手,亦称 tommy bar)
Tom Tom 一种汽车导航系统的商品名
ton 吨 ①重量单位。英吨亦称 long ton,为2240lb;美吨亦称 short ton,为2000lb。米吨或吨为 1000kg = 2204.6lb ②货物的容积单位:木材等为 40in³;石料为 16in³;小麦是 20bushels,煤是 49bushels;船只的排水吨(=displacement ton=海水 35in³)
tonality ①音调(由频率决定的声音的高低) ②(由泛音的数目、频率和振幅决定的)音品,音色 ③(由基频及其倍音频组成的)谐音(如:轮胎在平整路面上等行驶时发出的唰唰声)
tonal noise 周期性正弦波噪声(亦称 periodic noise,其频率为基础频率的整倍数)
tone ①音调,音色;色调 ②调和,协调;调色,上色
tone control 音调调节,色调控制
tone wheel (车轮转速传感器的截磁路)齿轮(亦写作 tonewheel, = toothed wheel, 亦称 teethed wheel type pulse generator)

tonf/in² 吨力/英寸²（英制单位的压力倍数单位，每平方英寸受1t的力）

ton-force 吨力（= 9810N，代号 tonf）

tongs ①钳，夹具，铗②（机械手的）抓手

tongue ①舌，舌状物（如：舌片，舌簧，舌板；榫舌，火焰的火舌）②牵引杆③磅秤指针④榫，榫头（构件两部分利用凸凹接合的凸出部分）

tongue and groove coupling （凸块式万向节"Tracta universal joint"的）榫槽凸块

tongue(d)-and-groove(d) joint 榫头—榫槽结合，榫头—榫眼结合［亦称 tongue(d)-and-mortise(d) joint］

tongued flange 阳突缘（带凸台的法兰，= male flange）

tongued washer 带舌垫圈

ton-kilometerage volume 吨公里运量，（货物周转量，在一定时期内运送的货物吨数与运送里程的乘积，单位：t·km）

ton miles per gallon 吨英里/加仑（货运汽车燃料经济性的一种评价指标，即一加仑燃油所能完成的货物周转量，吨英里，简称 ton-mpg）

tonnage 吨数；吨位；装载质量；总吨数（= gross ton）

tonnage capability 载重能力

tonnage of cargo handled 货物操作量（一个完整操作过程所进行的装卸、搬运货物的数量，以操作吨表示）

tonnage rating 额定吨位，额定吨数

tonne 吨（= metric ton）

tonneau ①（特指与驾驶区隔开的旧式厢式轿车的）客厢②敞篷轿车的客厢

tonneau cover （敞篷轿车停放时，罩上去防风雨露晒的）客厢保护套罩

tonneau light 室内灯（见 room light）

tonneau panel （四门轿车等的车身）后翼板（遮盖后车轮的车身外板，亦称 rear fender, rear wing）

tonne-km 吨公里

32-tonner 32 吨级车辆

ton of refrigeration 冷冻吨位

1 $\frac{1}{2}$ ton truck 一吨半货车（= one and a half ton truck）

ton/yd³ 英吨/码³（英制密度单位，1 ton/yd³ = 1.329t/m³ = 82.96 lb/ft³ = 0.04801 lb/in³ = 13.32 lb/imp.gal）

tooch contact area 轮齿接触面积

tool ①工具，刀具，刃具②机床通称

toolbox 工具箱

tool carbon steel 碳素工具钢

tool for mounting and removing valve spring 气门弹簧拆装工具

tool(s) for frame straightening 车架校正设备

tool truck 修理工程车（= machine shop truck, tool vehicle, repair vehicle）

tooth ①齿；牙；齿形物②［动］切齿，加工齿；使啮合，使用齿啮合

tooth addendum 齿顶高（见 addendum）

tooth bending fatigue 轮齿弯曲疲劳极限（亦称额定强度值 "strength rating"）

tooth breakdown test （齿轮）轮齿的断裂试验（齿轮轮齿的弯曲疲劳试验）

tooth caliper 测齿规；齿厚卡钳

tooth clearance 齿隙（一般指两相啮合齿轮的顶隙，即：两轮齿啮合时，一轮齿顶与另一轮齿根间的间隙，见 bottom clearance）

tooth control ring 调节齿圈（齿杆式供油量调节机构中的一个零件）

tooth crown 齿冠（冠齿轮，见 crown gear）

tooth crushing pressure 轮齿破坏压力

tooth dedendum 齿根高（见 dedendum）

tooth depth 齿高（圆柱齿轮，指顶圆与齿根圆之间的径向距离。锥齿轮，指齿顶圆至齿根圆之间沿背锥母线量度的距离。对于圆柱蜗杆，指齿顶圆柱面与齿根圆柱面之间的径向距离。对于涡轮和环面蜗杆，指的是喉圆与齿根圆之间的径向距离）

toothed 齿的，带齿的，齿形的，锯齿状的

toothed belt 齿形传动带（亦称 cogged belt，其内表面带平行的横直齿条，与驱动轮和被驱动轮的齿槽啮合的强化橡胶带，可实现无打滑的可靠传动。在汽车上一般用于气门正时机构，称 timing belt，以代替原先使用的三角传动带或传动链）

toothed flywheel 带齿圈飞轮（= flywheel with toothing）

toothed gear 齿传动件（简称 gear，任意一个有齿的机械零件，只要它能利用它的齿与另一个有齿元件连续啮合，从而将动力传递给后者，或从后者接受动力时，就称为 toothed gear，其圆形者称齿轮）

toothed quadrant 扇形齿板，齿扇（亦称 toothed segment, tooth sector, gear segment）

toothed rack 齿条（亦称 toothed bar, toothed rail, toothed bar, rack bar，见 rack）

toothed ring 齿圈，（内齿圈，= ring gear）

toothed timing belt （发动机的）带齿正时皮带

toothed wheel stator （汽车防滑系车轮转速传感器等的）齿轮形定子

tooth flank 齿面（位于齿顶曲面和齿根曲面之间的轮齿侧表面）

tooth form 齿形

tooth heel 齿根（亦称 gear root）

tooth load 轮齿荷载

tooth lock washer 带齿形锁紧片的垫圈（亦称 toothed washer）

tooth mesh leakage （齿轮泵）齿轮啮合处泄漏

tooth outline 齿轮外形，齿廓

tooth power loss 齿轮传动中的功率损失

tooth pressure 轮齿接触压力

tooth profile 齿廓（齿面被一个与齿线相交的既定曲面所截的截线）

tooth space 齿槽（齿轮上两邻轮齿之间的空间）

tooth surface fatigue 轮齿表面疲劳极限

tooth surfaces 轮齿表面（注意：齿轮表面指齿轮上的各个表面，不单指齿面，见 tooth flank）

tooth thickness 齿厚（轮齿的两侧齿面之间的分度圆弧长）

tooth thickness half angle 齿厚半角（端面齿厚所对圆心角的一半）

tooth tip 齿棱（齿面与齿顶曲面的交线，简称 tip）

tooth trace 齿线（齿面与分度曲面的交线）

tooth (type) coupling 齿式联轴节

tooth width （齿轮）齿宽（见 facewidth）

tooth working depth （齿轮）轮齿的工作高度（= working depth of tooth）

top ①顶，盖；车篷②最高的，顶部的，主要的③到…的顶部，上升到…顶点④装顶，加盖⑤最高档（top gear 的简称）

top antenna 车顶天线（= top aerial,

overcar aerial）

TOPAZ catalyst （日本大发公司开发的耐高温）全顶级催化剂（商品名，由 top "顶级"和从头到尾 A～Z 组成，该项研究成果获日本《自动车工学》期刊 2002 年度 "10 项最佳技术"大奖）

Topaz Metallic （车身外壳的）金属光泽黄宝石色，黄玉金属漆色

top capping 外胎胎面翻新，外胎花纹层的翻修

top center 上止点（top dead center 的简称）

top circle ①顶圆，外圆②（齿轮）齿顶圆（见 tip circle）

top clearance 余隙高度（亦称顶隙，活塞在上止点时，活塞最高顶面与汽缸盖底平面之间的垂直距离）

top clearance of tooth 齿顶间隙（见 bottom clearance）

top cloth 折叠式车顶用的篷布

top coat ①外涂层，面涂层②外套，外罩

top compression ring 第一道压缩环（第一道气环）

top dead-center indicator 上止点标记

top deck （双层公共汽车的）上层，顶层（= upper deck）

top down motoring （活顶小轿车）敞篷驾驶

top dust hood 上部的防尘罩（顶部防尘罩）

top engine 高质量的发动机

top fabric （汽车）篷冇

top fastener 汽车顶篷的扣紧装置

top feed injector 顶部进油式喷油器

top feed type 顶部供油式

topflight 第一流的，高级的，最高的

top-gear speed on gradient 最高挡上坡时的车速

top groove 活塞第一道环槽

top half 上半部

top holder （车厢）活动篷顶支架

topic 题目，论题，主题

top inch 汽缸内表面距顶端 1in 的部位（离顶端约 25mm，第一道活塞环的上止点位于该处，该处不仅温度高而且润滑困难，承受活塞顶部振动，因而常产生最大磨损）

top iron （车辆）篷顶拱形支架

top land ①齿顶面（位于齿顶部、被齿顶曲面所包含的那一部分轮齿表面。对于外齿轮，它是轮齿上与齿轮轴线相距最远的一个表面；对于内齿轮，它是与轴线相距最近的一个表面，亦称 crest）②第一道环槽岸（活塞头部外圆柱表面第一道环槽至活塞顶之间的区域）

top-land clearance 顶环岸间隙（活塞第一道气环到活塞顶之间的活塞外圆面与缸壁形成的间隙）

top leaf of spring 钢板弹簧主片（= main leaf of spring, top spring leaf）

topless 敞篷车

top lighting 顶部照明

top luggage rail 车顶行李架（= luggage rail on top）

top mounted double reduction final drive 上置式双级主减速器（装在桥壳上方的双级主减速器）

top off 加满

topological optimization 拓扑最佳化（如：决定网络单元如何互连既最经济又能实现全部性能目标和要求条件）

topology 拓扑（拓扑学，研究网络中各个网点的物理和逻辑布局）

top petrol tank 上置式汽油箱，顶置油箱

top piston land 第一（活塞环槽）槽岸（指活塞头部外圆柱表面，第一活塞环槽上边至活塞顶的区域）

top piston ring 第一道活塞环

topple 翻转，倾倒

top(-) quality ①高质量②高质量的，最优质的

top-roof inner decoration 车顶内饰

top sleeper （位于货车驾驶室顶部的）车顶卧铺间

top speed 最大速度，最高车速，全速（= full speed，对汽车一般指在无风条件下平路上所测定的最高稳定车速）

top speed capability 最高速度能力（①指车辆能产生的最高速度②指汽车雷达控制的安全装置等能保证安全的最高车速）

top speed limiting 最高车速限制

top surface of piston ring 活塞环上平面

top up ①充气，加油，充液，注水，加燃料，添加滑油，加足汽油，装满…②完成，竣工，终止，结束

top view 上视图，顶视图

top wishbone （双横臂式独立悬架的）上 Y 形横臂

torch ignition 火焰点火，火炬点火（预燃室火焰喷射点火，= flame ignition）

Torchinsky's coefficient of vibration 托氏（车辆垂直）振动系数（单位长度路程平面度总和与垂直振幅总和之比值）

torch lamp 喷灯（= blow lamp）

torch welding 气焊（= gas welding）

tor-con 变矩器（torque converter 的简称）

tore 环面，管环（见 torus ③）

torn 撕破的，划破的，裂开的；不平的（表面），有划痕的

torn-up 磨损的，剥伤的（摩擦表面）

toroid 圆环面［一个圆（母圆）围绕着位于圆周之外，但与此圆在同一平面内的一条直线（轴线）做旋转运动；于是，此圆在固定空间内的轨迹曲面就称为圆环面］

toroidal cavity 环形空腔

toroidal combustion chamber ω 形燃烧室（是半开式燃烧室的一种，其剖面近似 ω 形，故亦称 ω-combustion chamber，在压缩过程中，ω 形燃烧室内部的气流兼有进气涡流和挤压涡流，可促进混合气形成和完全燃烧）

toroidal coordinates 圆环坐标

toroidal CVT （日本日产公司于 20 世纪 90 年代末期在批量生产的轿车上使用的）摩擦盘式无级连续变速器（商品名，toroidal continuously variable transmission 的简称，见 CVT）

toroidal swirl type 环形旋涡式（燃烧室，直接喷射式柴油机燃烧室的一种，活塞顶上有环形凹面）

toroid transmission 见 EXTROID CVT

torpedo body 鱼雷型车身（长度较大，头部线型圆滑流畅，形似鱼雷的车身，= gunboat body）

torqmatic transmission "自动变矩"变速器（美国一种自动变速器的商品名，由液力变矩器和内啮双排行星齿轮系组成）

torque 扭矩，转矩

torque adaptive coefficient 转矩适应系数（发动机最大转矩与额定转速转矩的比值）

torque amplifier 增矩器，转矩放大器

torque arm 转矩杆，扭矩臂（①任一种承受或传递转矩的杆件②特指悬架杆系中装在驱动桥壳和车架之间，加速或制动时防止桥壳扭转而承受扭力的杆件，亦称半径杆，= torque bar，torque reaction rod，reaction rod，torque rod，traction rod）

torque arm and track bar type rigid axle suspension 扭转臂-横向推力杆式刚性车桥非独立悬架（由支撑车身或车架的纵向布置的扭转臂和

横向推力杆及螺旋弹簧组成的非独立悬架）

torque arm center in braking 制动时转矩杆的瞬时中心

torque at peak hp （发动机）最大功率转矩

torque back up （发动机）后备转矩

torque balance 扭力计，扭力秤（＝torsion balance）

torque-balance system ①转矩平衡法（遥测技术中使用的平衡法的一种，将所测量的量变换为转矩，同时利用电磁的方法产生另一转矩，不断地与该转矩自动保持平衡，而将这时所要求的电流的变化量作为遥测信号传送到远方）②转矩平衡系统

torque ball （某些转矩套管式传动结构中）转矩套管（前端容纳传动轴万向节的）球形壳（见 torque tube transmission）

torque bar 见 torque arm

torque beam （测功器测量转矩用的）转矩反作用臂

torque-biasing full-time four-wheel drive 转矩差动型全时四轮驱动

torque box 抗扭的箱形断面元件

torque bridge 电桥式转矩指示器（利用电桥将转矩变为电量，通过仪表直接显示出转矩量）

torque capacity 额定转矩（额定转矩容量）

torque chain 转矩传递链

torque coefficient 转矩系数（令工作流体传给叶轮的转矩为 Q，流体的密度为 ρ，叶轮的转速为 n，直径为 D，则下式表示的无因次系数 K_Q 称为转矩系数；$K_Q = Q/\rho n^2 D^5$，亦称转矩常数 "torque constant"）

torque command-feedback engine control 转矩指令反馈发动机控制系统（以发动机输出转矩反馈信号进行的转矩闭路控制系统，亦称 torque governing feedback control）

torque constant 转矩常数（见 torque coefficient）

torque control （紧固件拧紧时的）转矩控制（指将紧固件拧紧到规定的转矩值）

torque controller 校正器（调速器中对速度特性上的供油量起校正作用的机构）

torque conversion 转矩变换，转矩转换

torque conversion range （液力变矩器的）变矩区（指输出转矩 M_t 与输入转矩 M_p 之比 $M_t/M_p > 1$ 时的变矩范围）

torque converter 液力变矩器（动液传动装置的一种，在传递动力的过程中能改变转矩，转矩比为速比的函数）

torque converter blade system parameters 液力变矩器叶栅系统参数（指泵轮、导轮进出口角，泵轮叶片进、出口半径，泵轮进、出口导流截面积等）

torque converter characteristics （液力变矩器的）变矩特性曲线

torque converter clutch 液力变矩器（锁止）离合器（简称 TCC，亦称 torque converter lock up clucth, lock out clutch 或 transmission converter cluctch，汽车以基本稳定的速度行驶时，该离合器接合，发动机与传动系之间由液力传动转变为机械传动，以消除液力传动损失和变矩器发热，提高燃油经济性）

torque converter clutch valve 液力变矩锁止离合器阀（控制液力变矩器锁止离合器的液压阀）

torque converter-coupling 液力变矩-耦合器，液力耦合-变矩器（相当于将液力耦合器和变矩器合到一台装置上，既具有耦合工作区，又具有变矩工作区）

torque converter fluid 液力变矩器用工作油液（简称 torque fluid）

torque converter level tell-tale 液力变矩器工作液面高度指示灯

torque converter lever 液力变矩器操纵杆

torque converter lock-up unit 液力变矩器锁止装置（简称 TCLU，见 torque converter clutch）

torque converter oil temperature tell-tale 液力变矩器油温警告灯

torque converter pump 液力变矩器泵轮（亦称 torque converter impeller，由发动机带动旋转，使变矩器环形内腔的工作油液以高速进入涡轮，推动涡轮旋转而输出动力，同时，接受导轮改变液流方向产生的反作用力矩，而增大涡轮的输出转矩）

torque converter reactor 液力变矩器导轮（液力变矩器的反作用轮，通过单向离合器或直接地固定于壳体，液流经导轮改变方向又流入泵轮，给涡轮一个反作用力矩，从而增大涡轮的输出转矩）

torque converter regulator valve 液力变矩器液压控制阀（根据汽车的行驶状态对供给液力变矩器的液压作最佳控制）

torque converter size 液力变矩器尺寸（一般指液力变矩循环流道的最大直径，英美多用英寸为单位，亦称变矩器有效直径）

torque converter transmission 带液力变矩器的变速器

torque converter with planetary gear box 带行星齿轮变速器的液力变矩器

torque converter with reversal reactor 导轮可反转的变矩器

torque detector 转矩测定器

torque diagram 转矩特性曲线图，转矩曲线图

torque distribution coefficient of differential 差速器的转矩分配系数（$\zeta = M_2/M_o$，式中：M_2—半轴的转矩；M_o—差速器壳传递的转矩）

torque divider 分动箱（= power divider）

torque drop 转矩降

torque factor 转矩系数（评价液力元件传递功率能力大小的参数，见 torque coefficient）

torque fluctuation diagram 转矩波动图

torque fluid 液力变矩器（中使用的低黏度、高稳定性）工作油液

torque force 扭力

torque gear shift 转矩传送不中断换挡（不切断功率换挡）

torque gradient 转矩梯度（简称 TG）

torque-indicating wrench 转矩扳手（= torque-control wrench, torque indicator hand wrench, torque-measuring wrench）

torque indicator 转矩指示仪

torque insulator （消除发动机曲轴扭振的）转振减振器

torque-limiting screw-driver 限矩螺钉旋具

torque/litre （发动机）转矩/排量比，比转矩（N·m/L）

torque load 扭转荷载

torque machine 低速大转矩动力机械的总称

torque maintain(ing) gearbox 换挡时转矩传递不中断的变速器

torque/mass ratio 转矩/质量比（比转矩，发动机最大转矩与汽车总质量之比，= specific torque）

torquemeter 扭力计，转矩仪（torsiometer）

torque moment 转矩

torque motor 转矩马达（气动或液压系统内用于开闭阀门、喷嘴等的

执行器件。有电动式和气动式两种。前者利用永久磁铁和线圈的相互作用，后者是利用气压作用使一活动件绕支点摆动，而产生开启或关闭阀门、喷嘴等的转矩）

torque multiplication （液力变矩器的）转矩增大比

torque multiplier 转矩放大器

torque multipling transmission （增大扭矩的）增矩传动装置

torque-on-demand control system 转矩按需控制系统（按照驾驶者的意图和车辆在各种运行状态下的要求控制发动机输出转矩）

torque-output characteristics （动力装置的）转矩输出特性

torque per liter （发动机的）升转矩（指每升排量所发出的最大有效转矩）

torque plate ①转矩扳（泛指各种承受扭转力矩的板件）②（特指盘式制动器制动钳的）安装底板（见 caliper anchor bracket）

torque range 转矩范围

torque rating 额定转矩；转矩标定

torque ratio （转矩变换机构，如：变速器，液力变矩器的）变矩比（输入、输出转矩比）

torque reaction 反作用转矩

torque reaction rod 转矩杆（见 torque arm②）

torque reaction stand 反力式转矩测试台

torque receiver 转矩接收器

torque retention （螺纹连接拧紧）转矩保持量

torque ring （增加车身结构强度的）（抗）转矩箍

torque rod ①转矩杆（见 torque arm②）②转力杆（= torsion bar）

torque rod joint 扭杆连接

torque rod suspension 扭力杆式悬架

torque scatter （紧固件等的拧紧）转矩的偏差范围（如：±10%等）

torque screw driver 测力旋具，扭力旋具

torque sensing coupling 转矩传感联轴节

torque-sensing differential 见 torsen differential

torque sensing LSD 转矩感知式防滑差速器（LSD为 limited slip differential 的简称）

torque sensor 转矩传感器

torque shuffling sport differential at the rear 后桥左、右轮转矩分配式差速器

torque-slip curve 转矩-滑移率曲线

torque slitting center differential 中央转矩分配式差速器（指前、后桥间转矩分配式差速器）

torque spanner 扭力扳手，转矩扳手（= torque wrench）

torque-speed characteristic （发动机）转矩-转速特性曲线（= torque speed curve，参见 speed-torque characteristic）

torque split 4DW 转矩分配式4轮驱动系统（日产公司电子控制式四轮驱动系统的商品名，用于 Skyline 牌轿车，平时为后两轮驱动，当路面状况不良时，电子控制模块根据各种传感器输送的信息实现四个车轮间转矩的最佳分配，而成为全轮驱动）

torque-split system 转矩分配系统（简称 TSS，指在同一车桥左、右两车轮或四轮驱动车辆前、后驱动桥间分配转矩的系统，见 power distribution）

torque stay 转矩撑杆，扭力杆

torque steer （汽车的）转矩转向（汽车由于各种原因形成的车轮间转矩不平衡，所引起行驶方向的偏转现象）

torque synchro 转矩传递同步器

torque-torsional angle curve 转矩-扭转角曲线（转矩对扭转角的关系曲线）

torque-to-yield bolt （在制造厂已拧紧到材料预定屈服点的）屈服点扭紧力矩螺栓

torque trailer 牵引杆长度可调节的长货挂车（参见 pole trailer）

torque transducer 转矩传感器

torque transfer 分动器（如：四轮驱动车辆前、后桥间转矩传送与分配装置，= transfer gear, transfer, power transfer, torque transmitter）

torque tube (drive) type suspension 转矩管（传动）式悬架（指转矩管传动式车辆使用的后悬架，一般多为半椭圆形钢板弹簧，通过支座装在后桥壳上，该悬架不再承受驱动力与制动力及其反作用力矩，仅起支撑作用，仅通过前、后两个吊耳架与车架连接，见 torque tube transmission）

torque tube propeller shaft 装在转矩管内的单万向节传动轴（见 torque tube transmission）

torque tube transmission 转矩套管式传动（亦称 torque tube drive，其传动轴整个封闭在一个与后桥壳和差速器壳形成一整体的刚性套管"转矩管 torque tube"中，该套管的前端经球铰装在变速器后端或车架上，起着传递后桥驱动力和制动力及抵抗其反作用转矩的作用，装在后桥壳上的悬架不再承受驱动力和制动力及其反作用力矩，传动轴只需要用一个万向节与变速器连接而无须通过万向节与主传动连接。此外，后桥还可绕转矩管前端与变速器或车架的铰接点，以该点到后桥中心线为半径摆动。）

torque-twist diagram （零件的）转矩-扭转角曲线图

torque type power meter 转矩式功率计

torque variable clutch 转矩可变型离合器

torque vectoring 转矩定向的

torque vibration damper 扭转振动阻尼器 [= torsional (oscillation) damper]

torque-weight ratio （汽车的）车重-转矩比 [车重与最大转矩的比值，即每单位转矩所承担的车重，单位为 kg/(N·m)，其值越小，汽车的加速性越好]

torque wrench 扭力扳手，转矩扳手（= tension wrench）

torquey engine 大转矩发动机

torque yield 扭转时的屈服极限

torquing on the line 在装配线上以规定的扭力拧紧（紧固件）

torr 托（真空单位，相当于 1mmHg 的压力，1torr = 1mmHg = 133.322Pa）

torrid zone 热带

torsal line (of a surface) （曲面上的）挠点线

torsal plane 挠切面

torsal point 挠切点

torsen differential 转矩感知式差速器（torque-sensing differential 的简称，亦称 helical/skew differential，装有蜗杆—滚轮机构的防滑差速器。利用蜗杆可驱动滚轮但滚轮不能反过来驱动蜗杆的原理，当左、右两车轮因地面附着力差而产生转速差时，该机构可"感知"二者转矩差而自动锁止，亦称 torsen limited-slip differential, torsen locking differential，或简称 torsen LSD）

torsen four-wheel drive 带转矩感知式差速器的常四轮驱动（见 torsen differential）

torsiogram 扭挠图，转矩示波图

torsiograph 扭力计，转矩仪

torsiometer 扭力计，转矩仪（=

torquemeter)
torsion 扭转（变形）（由于受转矩作用而产生的应变）
torsion(al) load 扭转载荷
torsional 扭转的，扭力的
torsional angle 扭转角（在转矩作用下构件两端横截面相对旋转的角度）
torsional capacity 抗扭能力
torsional couple 扭转力偶
torsional damper 扭振减振器（亦称 vibration damper, torsional vibration balancer, torsional vibration damper, ①指发动机曲轴或变速器输出轴的机械或流体阻尼式、弹性摆动式、弹性—阻尼式等扭振动的消减装置②指悬架的摇臂式减振器, = lever type shock absorber, lever type suspension damper③指扭杆弹簧减振器)
torsional damping arrangement 扭转减振器（可吸收与消耗扭振动能量的部件的画称，见 clutch damper）
torsional distribution graph 车身（的）扭曲变形分布图，扭转变形分布图（用两条曲线分别表示车身底板和外壳沿纵轴各点的扭曲变形值，以评定车身结构的扭曲连续性、底板和外壳、车顶和支柱之间连接的可靠性）
torsional elasticity 扭转弹性
torsional endurance limit 扭转疲劳极限
torsional exciter system 扭振激发装置（转矩发生系统，可产生静、动扭力，供扭振试验使用）
torsional fatigue 扭转疲劳
torsional force 扭力（= twisting force)
torsional frequency 扭转振动频率
torsional mode 扭转（振动）模式
torsional moment 转矩
torsional oscillation method 扭转振动法（用来测定物体绕垂直轴线的惯性矩）
torsion(al) oscillations 扭转振动
torsion(al) pendulum 扭（转）摆
torsional (piston) ring 扭曲式活塞环（带内沉肩，工作时受力，略呈扭曲状，以提高其气密性）
torsional resilience 扭转弹性
torsional rigidity 扭转刚度（在扭转力矩的作用下，构件抗扭转变形的能力）
torsional shake 扭转振摆
torsion(al) spring 扭转弹簧
torsional stability 扭转稳定性，扭曲稳定性
torsional stabilizer 抗扭转稳定杆
torsional stiffness 扭转刚度，抗扭刚度（车身结构每扭转一度所承受的转矩, = torsional rigidity)
torsional stiffness graph （车身的）扭转刚度图（表示不同转矩下的扭曲变形值）
torsional stiffness of steering gear 转向器扭转刚度（摇臂轴固定，转向器输入的力矩增量与其产生的角位移增量之比）
torsional strain 扭转应变
torsional strength 抗扭强度（工件在扭断前所承受的最大转矩，按弹性扭转公式计算的工件表面最大切应力）
torsional stress 扭应力（由扭转作用而引起的横截面内的切应力）
torsional suspension 扭力杆式悬架（见 torsion bar suspension）
torsional vibration 扭（转）振（动）（因扭力变动，曲轴等旋转轴上发生的角振动）
torsion analogy 扭振模拟
torsion angle 扭转角，扭曲角
torsion balance ①扭力秤，扭力天平 ②扭力平衡（= torque balance)
torsion balancer 扭力平衡器，均

扭器
torsion bar 扭（力）杆，(= torque rod，一切承受扭力作用的杆状弹性件的通称，亦称扭杆弹簧，扭力杆簧"torsion bar spring, torsion rod spring"）

torsion bar anchor 扭力杆支座（扭杆支架）

torsion bar belt-force-limiter 扭杆式（汽车乘员安全带）负荷限制器

torsion bar stabilizer 扭力杆式稳定器（稳定扭杆）

torsion bar suspension 扭力杆式悬架（指使用杆状或管状弹簧元件替代钢板弹簧或螺旋弹簧等的悬架，该扭力杆一般装在双纵臂式悬架的上控制臂与车架或车身之间，当车架或车身上、下运动时，该扭力杆承受扭力，见 double trailling arm tyne suspension)

torsion beam 扭力梁（承受扭力的梁形杆件）

torsion beam axle 扭力梁式车桥（由扭力梁制成的非驱动桥）

torsion beam axle (type) suspension 扭转梁式车桥悬架（指装在不使用整根刚性轴而使用整根扭力梁制成的非驱动车桥上支撑车架或车身的悬架形式，故亦称半独立式悬架，有多种类型，但大多由纵向控制臂，或螺旋弹簧-减振器总成，或纵向控制臂+螺旋弹簧-减振器总成等组成）

torsion coefficient 扭转系数

torsion coil spring 扭力螺旋弹簧（承受绕其轴心的扭力的卷簧）

torsion damper 扭振阻尼器（见 torsional damper）

torsion dynamics ①（传动轴等的）扭转动态特性②扭动力学

torsion dynamometer 扭力测力计，扭力计

torsion frequency 扭振频率

torsion gum 扭振橡胶弹簧（承受扭力的橡胶件，见 torsion rubber spring)

torsion Hooke's law 扭曲虎克定理（理想弹性轴的扭曲角与转矩成正比）

torsion impact test 扭转冲击试验

torsion indicator 扭转角测量指示仪

torsion levelling suspension 扭杆调平式悬架

torsion meter 扭力计，转矩计

torsion proof 防扭的，抗扭转的

torsion rig 扭转试验台

torsion rod 扭力杆（承受扭力的杆件，亦称"torsion bar"，某些悬架中，用来取代钢板弹簧等作为悬架的弹性元件，称扭杆弹簧"torsion bar spring"）

torsion rubber spring 橡胶扭转弹簧（利用其扭转变形起缓冲作用和减振作用的橡胶件）

torsion-shaft ①传动轴（传递转矩的轴）②扭转轴（承受扭力的轴）

torsion strain sensor 扭转应变传感器（亦称 twist sensor）

torsion test 扭转试验（对试件两端施加静转矩，测量转矩和相应的转角，一般转至断裂，测定其力学性能的试验）

torso 躯干（指人体不包括头和四肢的部分）

torso line （乘员的）躯干线（指人体平面图形上，双肩基准点与臀点之间的连线）

tortuosity 弯折，曲折

tortuous 曲折的（迂回的、盘旋的）

torture test track 具有特殊不平路面的试验跑道

torus ①（液力耦合器等的）叶轮（参见 front torus 及 rear torus）②（液力变矩器等的）循环圆（见 torus section）③圆环，环面，环形（圈），（圆形断面的）圆环体，环

形圆纹曲面(=tore)④环形柔性联轴节

torus pattern (液力变矩器叶轮元件等的)环路(见torus section)

torus ring (液力变矩器)环腔

torus section 循环圆(液力变矩器或液力耦合器各叶轮元件的环路,指在变矩器或耦合器径向平面内液流循环的范围,即:工作油液在叶轮间所形成的环形油路,亦称torus pattern,简称torus)

tosecan 平面规,划线盘(=surface gage)

to size 达到应有的尺寸,达到规定的大小

T(O)SS 变速器(输出)转速传感器[transmission (output) speed sensor的简称,向电子控制模块提供变速器输出转速信息]

tossing test 振动试验(颠簸试验)

total ①总数,总计,合计②总计的,全部的,完全的

total acid number 总酸值(简称TAN,亦称total acid value,见acid number)

total air 活塞发动机每一循环经进气道进入的空气总量

total air-fuel ratio 总空燃比[每循环流过进气门(口)的空气与喷入汽缸内燃料的质量比值]

total amplitude 总振幅,全振幅(=振幅×2)

total angle of transmission (齿轮的)总作用角(其总作用弧所对圆心角,对于锥齿轮,其值应在冠轮上量度)

total arc of transmission 总作用弧(齿轮在其啮合过程中,它的一个齿面从啮合到啮合终止所转过的分度圆弧长)

total area of nozzle holes 喷孔总面积(一个喷油器全部喷孔的总面积)

total bag sampling 全量袋式取样法(汽车按规定的行驶工况运行时,所排出的废气全部收入取样袋中)

total base number 总碱值(简称TBN)

total braking distance 总制动距离(汽车或汽车列车在总制动时间内行驶的距离)

total braking force 总制动力(由制动系的作用而产生在全部车轮与地面接触之间并与车辆运动或运动趋势方向相反的制动力总和)

total braking time 总制动时间(从控制力作用于控制装置的部件使其开始动作,至制动力消失为止所经过的时间。若车辆在制动力消失前停止,则至车辆停止时所经过的时间作为总制动时间)

total carbon 碳总含量

total case annealing 完全退火,相变退火

total charge (电子电路电荷转移器件的)总电荷(存储在势阱或旱链器件分立区域中所有的电荷)

total contact 全(面)接触

total contact ratio (齿轮的)总重合度(指总作用角与齿距角的比值。对于锥齿轮,其值应在冠轮上量度)

total content 总含量

total cooling power 总冷却功率(冷却所吸收的总功率)

total curvature 全曲率

total displacement ①(发动机)总排量②总位移

total driving resistance (汽车)总行驶阻力(汽车行驶时的滚动阻力、空气阻力和上坡力、加速阻力之和)

total efficiency 总效率

total enclosure 全密封机壳

total excess air ratio 总过量空气系数(一个工作循环内流过进气门或进气口的空气总量与汽缸内燃料完

全燃烧所需的理论空气量的质量比值。总过量空气系数等于过量空气系数与扫气系数的乘积）

total external characteristics 全外特性

total failure 完全失效（=complete failure）

total flow 总流量

total fuel consumption divided by inertia weight 单位惯性质量燃油消耗量（惯性质量除以总油耗，简称TFC/IW）

total gear ratio （汽车的）总减速比（变速器的减速比乘以主传动的减速比）

total generic failure 一般性故障（通常发生的故障）

total hardening 全部淬火（区别于局部淬火）

total head 总压头

total heat 总热量（热焓，焓，=heat content）

total heat consumption （发动机的）总耗热量（指供给发动机的全部热量，由所消耗的全部燃油量按低热值计算）

total heating value （燃料）高热值（见 high heating value）

total height 总高度

total hydrocarbon analyzer 总碳氢化合物分析仪（测定样气中碳氢化合物总量，简称THC的分析仪，通常使用FID，简称THC analyzer）

total hydrogen operation （发动机的）全氢运转（完全用氢气作为燃料）

totality 总数，总额，总体，全体，完全，全部

totalizator 总额（=tote）

totalizer 加法器，累计器（=totaliser）

totalizing instrument 总计仪器仪表（通过对被测量的各部分值的求和来确定被测量值的测量仪器仪表。这些部分值可以同时或依次从一个或多个来源中获得）

total length 总长度

total load 总负载（总负荷）

total loss 总赔（发生车祸不得不放弃原车时，投保人可选择现金或相同的车作赔偿的方式）

total loss lubrication system （滑油）全耗润滑系统（滑油完成润滑作用时，全部耗尽。如：某些二冲程发动机滑油和汽油混合，随进气进入汽缸的润滑法）

totally continuous 完全连续的

totally disconnected 完全不连通的（全不相连的）

totally-opened play of steering control valve 转向控制阀全开隙（转向时，转向阀肩相对于阀体台肩之间的轴向间隙或角度）

total mass （汽车）总质量（汽车整车整备质量与装载质量之和，见 vehicle kerb mass, vehicle laden mass）

total mileage 总行驶里程（英里数）

Total Mobility tire 全机动胎（美国邓禄普公司生产的一种宽胎面、高强度、厚胎壁，胎内装有六个盛润滑液的小筒的无内胎式轮胎的商品名。装在窄轮辋上，当轮胎完全泄气时，小筒内的润滑液被压出，充填于胎壁和胎面之间，将轮胎撑起，同时迅速封补穿刺孔，这些润滑液受热后产生蒸气，在胎内形成的气压可保证汽车以近200km/h的速度平稳地行驶近100km以上）

total motion resistance 总运动阻力（车辆内外行驶阻力之和）

total number of coils 螺旋弹簧的总圈数（见 number of spring coils）

total number of steering gear 转向器总圈数（转向器的转向轴从一个极端位置转到另一极端位置所转过的

圈数)

total number of steering wheel turns 转向盘总圈数(汽车转向盘从一个极端位置转到另一极端位置时所转过的圈数)

total odometer 累计行程表(行驶里程累计表)

total output 总生产量,总生产能力;总工作容量,总输出功率

total payload kilometrage 总有效载运里程[亦称 total vehicle ton (seat) kilometer]

total pitch error 节距总误差

total pressure 全压力(静压力和动压力之和。它表示流体的动能被无损耗地转变为压力能后的压力。流体在静止状态下,静压力和全压力的数值相等)

total pressure ratio 全压力比(排气压力与吸气压力之比)

total preventive maintenance time 总维护时间(维护准备与维护实施时间之和)

total production system 总体生产系统(20世纪90年代末期,GM为了适应经常变化的市场及剧烈的销售竞争,提出总体生产系统的新思路,要求生产系统更加精简"leaner",快速"faster",灵活"flexible")

total quality control 全面质量管理(简称TQC)

total radiation pyrometer 全辐射高温计

total reduction ratio 总减速比

total reflection prism 全反射棱镜(等边直角棱镜)

total requirement 总需求量(简称TRQ)

total response time (线性放大器的)全响应时间(延迟时间、斜坡时间和脉动时间的总和)

total revolution counter 累计转数表

total square deviation 总方差(相对平方差之总和,如:汽车横摆角速度响应与转向盘、转角或力的相对平方差之总和)

total stroke volume (发动机)总排量(总工作容积)

total suspended particles (大气中)总悬浮微粒量,悬浮微粒总量(简称TSP,参见API)

total temperature 总温,全温度(将温度计定为流体,测量温度时,温度计所显示的温度为流体的实际温度T。加上流量所受温度计阻力而产生的热能所反映的温度,故称为全温度。若上述热量仅是在绝热状况下产生的,则该温度称为滞点温度, = stagnation temperature)

total transmission error 传动总误差(简称TTE)

total trim 全面修整

total turns of steering gear 转向器总圈数(转向器的转向轴从一个极端位置转到另一极端位置时所转过的圈数)

total understeer 不足转向总量(= overall understeer)

total valve event 气门总开启度

total vehicle 整车

total vehicle curb weight 整车整备质量(装满燃润料、水、各种工作液和随车装备等的车辆总自重, = complete vehicle kerb mass)

total vehicle days 总车日(在一定时期内,每天在用营运车辆数量的累计)

total vehicle evaluator 整车性能测定装置

total vehicle ton (seat)-days 总车吨(客)位日[在一定时期内,每天在用营运车辆吨(客)位数量的累计]

total vehicle ton (seat) kilometer 总车吨(客位)公里(见 total payload kilometrage）

total weight in working order （汽车等处于可工作状态时的）总重

total weight per hp 每单位马力车重（=汽车总重/发动机马力）

total wheel base 全轴距（指多轴汽车最前、后两轴中心间的水平距离）

total width 总宽

tote ［美俗］①运输，搬运，举起②总额

tote bin 搬运箱，运输箱，装运箱

tote pan （放置洗净的零件，使免被污染的）零件搬运盘

toter 运载装置，运输工具，装载起重机

TOT sensor ①（自动）变速器油温传感器（transmission oil temperature sensor 的简称，亦称 transmission fluid temperature sensor，简称TFT。变速器电子控制模块，根据该传感器的信号确定是否开启冷起动换挡程序，即：当该传感器测得变速器油温低于某规定值时，电子控制模块便阻止变矩器锁止，并操纵电子调压电磁阀"EPC"修正液压，以适应冷态运行）②变速驱动桥油温传感器（transaxle oil temperature sensor 的简称）

TOU 故障探测装置（trace operate unit）

touch ①接触②微量，痕迹③涉及，论及④（直线）切（圆）等⑤接近，达到⑥修改，（汽车等的结构，设置）改动，改变

touch area 接触面积（如：轮胎与路面的接触面积）

touch block 接线板（见 terminal block）

touch feel （对内饰件，材料）摸触的感觉

touch-screen 触摸式显示屏

touch screen navigation system 触摸屏式导航系统

touch-sensitive control architecture 触摸控制式结构

touch switch 触摸开关

touch temperature 触觉温度（触摸温度，触摸转向盘及各种操纵手柄等时的温度感）

touchtronic auto 触摸式电子控制自动变速器

touch-type-intelligent sunroof 轻触式智能天窗

tough ①坚固的，坚韧的，牢固的②黏稠的，黏着的

tough alloy steel 韧性合金钢

tough-brittle transition （塑料）由塑性状态变到脆性状态的过渡（转变）

toughened glass 韧化玻璃，（=tempered glass，受冲击后不会破碎，而至多形成网状裂纹）

toughened polystyrene 韧化聚苯乙烯

tough hardness 韧硬度

tough metal 韧性金属

toughness 韧性（金属在断裂前吸收变形能量的能力。金属的韧性通常随加载速度提高、温度降低、应力集中程度等的加剧而减小）

tourer 旅行车，旅游车（一种早期的敞篷小客车，一般为四门，两排横座，并有折叠式篷顶，=phaeton, touring car）②可供旅游者住宿的挂车③旅游者，旅行者，游客

tourniquet ①捆索，绷带（=rope tourniquet）②压脉带，止血带

tow ①拖曳，牵引②纤维束，（短）麻屑

towability 牵引能力；可牵引性，可拖曳性

towable length 拖挂设备的容许长度

towage ①拖挂，拖拉，牵引②拖挂费用，牵引费

tow-away theft （将上锁的车辆偷着拖走的）拖车偷盗

tow bar （拖带挂车等时使用的）牵引杆（美称 hitch bar）
tow cable 牵引钢索（= towing cable）
tow car ①牵引车，拖车 ②拖走故障车的救援车（= tow truck）
tow chain 拖车链，牵引链
towed （被）牵引的，拖挂的
towed load 牵引负荷
towed mass 拖挂质量（牵引车能够牵引的全挂车或半挂车的最大总质量）
tower ①塔 ②支架，支撑，支柱
tower crane 塔式起重机（= tower hoist）
tower vehicle （供修理电车线路、路灯等用的）带升降塔架的车辆
tower visibility （高置驾驶座的）俯视视野
tower wagon （供修理电车线路、路灯等用的）带升降塔架的挂车（= trailer tower wagon）
tow-hook 拖钩，挂钩（= drawbar hook）
towing ①牵引，拖曳 ②牵引的；拖挂的
towing ambulance ①（将发生事故或故障的车辆拖至修理厂等的）急救拖挂车（由拉杆、车轮和拖架组成，故障车某端的车轮置于该支架上，而另一端车轮仍着地拖行）②拖挂救护车（可拖带挂车的救护车）
towing ball 牵引球节（美称 hitch ball）
towing bracket 牵引架（用以装置球铰机构，并分别与主车和副车车架相连接的部件）
towing fork （牵引车上的挂车）拖挂装置，挂钩（亦称 towing jaw，towing hook，美称 trailer hitch）
towing performance 牵引性能
towing vehicle 牵引车（专门或主要用于牵引挂车的汽车）
town house car 城市房车（1991年3月第61届日内瓦国际汽车展，日本本田公司展出的一种未来型轿车，竖立起来似城市内的一幢房子，放下来就是一辆可行驶的轿车）
township highway 镇区公路（交通量小，与 secondary county highways 等，都称为 land access roads）
town traffic 城市交通
tow rod 拉杆，牵引杆
tow-rope horsepower 有效牵引功率（= drawbar horsepower）
tow starting 牵引起动
toxic ①有毒的，毒性的 ②毒剂，毒物
toxic atmosphere 有毒大气
toxic emission 有毒性排放（物）
toxic fume 有毒臭气
Toyo Kogyo Co. Ltd 日本东洋股份有限公司
Toyota （日本）丰田（汽车公司）
Toyota Axv Ivcar 丰田埃斯维微型轿车（日本丰田公司产品，装用二冲程、双缸10气门发动机，排量809mL，最大功率47kW，整备质量450 kg，最高车速170km/h）
Toyota computer controlled system 丰田电子计算机控制系统（见 TCCS②）
Toyota Corolla 1500SE car 丰田花冠轿车（日本丰田公司的普通型轿车，1988年、1990年两度评为美国十佳轿车，装用4缸DOHC发动机，排量1492mL，最大功率77kW，4挡自动变速）
Toyota Crown Majesta car 丰田皇冠马驾斯塔轿车（日本丰田公司1991年推出的高级轿车，装用V8四凸轮轴，32气门发动机，排量3968mL，压缩比10，最大功率191kW，4挡自动变速）
Toyota Electro-Multivision 丰田多用

彩显（丰田公司 1987 年至 20 世纪 90 年代初推出的日本第一代汽车 GPS—电子图像屏显导航系统的商品名，除导航地图显示车辆所在位置及路线外，还包括 AM—FM 收音、CD 播放，彩电收视等多项功能）

Toyota electronic automatic transmission 丰田电子控制式自动变速器（简称 TOYOTAEAT，日本丰田公司 20 世纪 80 年代初使用的电子控制 A32 型自动变速器的商品名。为在原 A30 型机械式自动变速器上加装模拟计算机控制的变形，模拟计算机根据运行条件确定速比，通过电磁阀控制液压实现变速）

Toyota Highlander Hybrid 丰田海兰德复合动力车

Toyota Hybrid System （丰田 Plus-Ⅱ 上使用的）混合动力系统（简称 THS-Ⅱ，一种行星齿轮机构，其齿轮架与发动机输出轴连接，太阳轮与起动机/发电机连接，内齿圈与驱动用电动机连接，因此可以实现发动机单独驱动、驱动用电动机单独驱动及发动机-电动机共同驱动的混合动力工况）

Toyota Lexus LS400 car 丰田凌志 400 轿车（系日本丰田公司 1990 年推出的豪华轿车，当年被评为美国十佳轿车之一，装用发动机排量 3969mL，最大功率 191kW，最高车速 235km/h）

Toyota Motor Corporation ［日］丰田汽车公司（由 1933 年丰田自动编织机制作所的汽车部发展起来的，1937 年成立丰田汽车工业公司，1982 年与丰田汽车销售公司合并，改用现名，1994 年年产汽车 350 万辆，位居美国通用、福特之后，占世界总产量的 9.8%，简称 TMC）

Toyota Total Clean System ［日］丰田综合排气净化系统（简称 TTC-S）

TP 节气门位置传感器（美国政府规定从 1995 年 1 月 1 日起一律将 throttle position sensor 简称为 TP，而取代原通用、福特、克莱斯勒公司使用的 TPS）

TPC 轮胎性能标准（tire performance criteria）

TPCS 轮胎气压控制系统（tyre pressure control system 的简称）

TPCV 燃油箱压力控制阀（tank pressure control valve 的简称，该阀装在燃油箱与活性炭罐之间的燃油蒸汽管道中，有一进气歧管真空管通入该阀，当发动机运转时，进气歧管内的真空使该阀开启，燃油箱内的燃油蒸汽便经该阀进入活性炭罐。发动机不工作时，只要燃油箱内的蒸汽压力超过规定值也可将该阀顶开，而让燃油蒸汽经该阀进入活性炭罐存储）

TPE 热塑性弹性材料（thermoplastic elastomer 的简称）

TPI 见 port fuel injection

T-piece T 形件

T-pipe to rear brake 通后制动器的 T 形管

TPIS 变速器挡位指示器开关（transmission position indicator switch）

T-plug （转子发动机位于缸体短轴线以下的）下位火花塞

TPM（S） （轮）胎（充气）压（力）监测（系统）[tire pressure monitor system 的简称，亦称 tire pressure warning system（轮）胎（充气）压（力）警告系统，简称 TPWS]

TPS ①韧化聚苯乙烯（toughened polystyrene）②油箱压力传感（tank pressure sensing）③防热系统（thermal protection system）④节气门开

度传感器（throttle position sensor）

TPU 热塑性尿烷（= thermal plastic urethane）

TPV ①热塑性硫化材料（thermoplastic vulcanizate 的简称）②牵引车安全保护阀（tractor protection valve 的简称）

TPX 四甲基-戊烯1聚合物的商品名（poly 4-methyl-pentene-1）

TQC 全面质量管理（total quality control）

TR （发动机废气）热反应（净化）器（thermal reactor）

TRA [美]轮胎和轮辋协会（The Tire and Rim Association, Inc.）

trace ①痕迹，踪迹②微量，少许③标出（与out连用），描绘④追踪，探索，寻找

traceability （测量结果的）溯源性

trace amount 微量，痕量

trace command 跟踪指令

trace control 轨迹控制（三菱公司开发的牵引力控制系统"TCL"中的一个子系统。若汽车进入弯道的速度过大，便有可能冲出弯道外侧，此时，牵引控制系统中轨迹控制功能开始起作用，自动降低发动机功率并加大转向角，使汽车保持预定的弯道行车轨迹）

trace down (the short) 检查线路（短路）故障

trace element ①微量元素②示踪元素（亦写作 tracer element）

trace impurity 微量杂质

trace-knock level （发动机的）轻微爆震级（可听见的最低爆震级）

tracer test 示踪（原子）试验，（同位素）示踪试验 亦称 tracer experiment

tracing ability （密封件的）追随性（当机械密封存在跳动、振动和转轴的窜动时，补偿环对于非补偿环保持贴合的性能。如果这种性能不良，密封端面将会分离从而导致较大的泄漏）

tracing (for) troubles 找寻故障（故障检验，故障诊断）

track ①（车辆等经过后留下的）踪迹，痕迹，车辙②（两条钢轨组成的）轨道（注意，不同于单根的钢轨"rail"，如：single track，指由两条钢轨组成的单轨，= one pair of rails。double track，指由四条钢轨组成的，双向行车的双轨，= two pairs of rails）③（赛车的）跑道（= motor racing track）④（履带车辆的）履带（= caterpillar）⑤路径、路线⑥（轮式车辆的）轮距（指同一车轴左、右车轮某规定点之，如：轮胎接地中心间的距离），（履带式车辆的）轨距⑦（磁记录媒体的）道（磁道，记录道）⑧追踪，尾随

track adhesion 履带附着力

track adjusting bracket 履带张紧机构支架

track adjusting lever 履带张紧度调整杆

track adjusting wheel 履带张紧轮，导向轮

track-alignment gauge 履带定位仪，履带轨距定位仪

track area (at zero penetration) （不下陷时）履带接地面积

track arm ①（独立悬架系统中的）横臂（亦称 track control arm, transverse arm, 指横向布置的铰接式控制臂，用于限制车轮的横向移动，如：与铰接式滑柱组成麦弗逊式"Macpherson type"独立悬架的铰接式下横臂）②（有时指转向杆系中的）横拉杆（= track rod）

track bar ①（车身）横向减振杆（见 track rod）②（某些汽车差速器与车架间的斜置）横后斜拉杆③转向横拉杆（= tie rod）

track block 履带板（= caterpillar block, tread block）
track bolt 轨条螺栓
track bushing 履带链节轴销套（= track link bushing）
track carrying wheel （履带行走装置）托链轮（= carrying wheel, upper track wheel）
track center distance 履带轨距
track chain 履带
track control arm 横臂（悬架系统中横向布置的控制臂，见 track arm）
track crossing 横穿铁路的交叉口，轨道交叉点，路轨交叉点，交叉路口
track curvature （赛车）跑道曲度，跑道曲率
track (driving) sprocket 履带驱动轮（亦称 track driving wheel）
tracked air cushion vehicle 轨道气垫车（简称 TACV）
tracked cross-country vehicle 履带式越野车辆
tracked vehicle 履带式车辆（= endless-track vehicle, tracklaying vehicle）
tracker ①跟踪系统，追踪装置，跟踪仪 ②示踪物
track eradicator （拖拉机）辙迹消除器
track frame pivot shaft 履带台车架摆动轴
track gauge （履带车辆）轨距仪
track ground contact length 履带接地长度
track ground contact pressure 履带接地压力
track grouser 履带履刺
track grouser height 履刺高度
track grouser spacing 履刺间距
track guard 履带护罩
track guiding wheel （履带行走装置）导向轮，张紧轮（亦称 track idler）
track idler bracket 履带导向轮支架
track idler guard 履带导向轮护罩
track idler recoil spring 履带导向轮缓冲弹簧
track idler yoke 履带张紧轮叉
track idler yoke arm 履带张紧轮叉形架臂（= track release yokearm）
tracking ①形成轮辙 ②追迹行驶（顺前车旧辙行车）③随动，跟踪，追迹 ④（因潮湿等原因引起的高压电沿导线或分电器盖等的）绝缘体表面漏电 ⑤积炭形成的漏电通路（= carbon tracking）⑥火花塞电极端因积炭而短路 ⑦（汽车转向和悬架系构件的）定位（及为保持其所要求的几何位置所进行的）调整
tracking behavio(u)r （汽车列车或多节铰接车辆的）同辙性（前后车轮轮辙的重合性）
tracking error （对转向和轮胎磨损产生不良影响的车轮）定位误差，定位失调
tracking system 追踪系统
tracklayer 履带式机械（车辆）
tracklayer tractor chassis 履带牵引车底盘（= crawler tractorchassis）
tracklaying crane 履带式起重机
tracklaying drive 履带驱动
trackless 无轨的
track link bushing 履带链节轴销套；履带销轴套（= track bushing）
track (link) pin 履带链节轴销
track master link bushing 履带闭合链节轴套 [= master (track) bushing]
track of tyres 轮距（左右轮胎触地中心距离）
track-oriented （悬架等）着重于保持行车路线的（相对于以保持平顺性为重点的而言）
track pin hole 履带链节轴销孔

track pitch 履带节距
track plate 履带板
track propulsion 履带推进,履带驱动
track protection 履带防护装置
track racing 汽车跑道竞赛,车道赛车
track ring (径向柱塞泵的)内凸轮环
track rod (转向传动杆系中的)横拉杆(指连接或间接传递转向摇臂的力和运动的整体式或分段式横向布置的杆件,见 tie rod)
track rod end (转向)横拉杆铰接式球节端,横拉杆球头
track rod joint 转向横拉杆接头
track rod lever 横拉杆臂(转向杆系中任一被横拉杆推动或推动横拉杆的杆件,如:整体式梯形机构的左、右梯形臂,分段式梯形机构的左、右转向节臂及某些转向机构中的转向摇臂等,亦称 track rod arm)
track roller frame 履带支重轮架
track roller frame guard 履带支重轮护罩
track shoe 履带板,履板
track shoe face 履板接地面
track slide motor and switch (座椅)沿滑轨移动调节前、后位置的电动机和开关
track slip 履带打滑
track sprocket shaft 履带驱动轮轴
track tension device 履带张紧机构
track test 跑道试验(在专门试车跑道上的试验)
track trailer 履带式挂车
track-while-scan radar 跟踪搜索雷达(扫描跟踪雷达)
trac off (牵引力控制系统的)"无牵引力控制"警报灯(①当电子控制模块测得制动摩擦片由于持续控制牵引力时间过长,而温度高于某规定值时,便点亮该警报灯 ②当驾驶者按压仪表板上的牵引力控制开关时,该警报灯亮,指示牵引力控制系统停止工作,直至下一次按压该牵引力控制开关恢复其工作)
Trac off light 牵引力控制系统控制功能中止指示灯
tracta universal joint 凸块式万向节(亦称 Bendix-tracta joint,简称 tracta joint,由两个凸轮叉,一个凹槽凸块和一个榫槽凸块组成的准等速万向节,见 fork yoke, tongue and groove coupling, groove coupling。这种万向节需要外部支撑定心和密封装置)
tracted load 牵引负荷,挂钩荷载
traction ①牵引力(= pulling force)②(地面与轮胎的)附着力(= adhesive friction between the tire and road surface)③(轮胎的)抓着力(= gripping power)
traction aids 增加附着力的辅助装置
traction assist (system) (福特公司的)牵引力控制系统(商品名,= traction control system)
traction avant 前轮驱动(英语中使用的法文,= front-wheel drive)
traction bar ①转矩杆(悬架系统中装在驱动桥壳上承受扭转负荷和防止或减轻车桥扭转和跳振的杆件和支撑件)②推力杆(位于驱动桥与车架之间,传递推力和推力矩的杆件)
traction battery 动力用蓄电池
traction bite (车轮等)与土壤的附着
traction booster 驱动轮配重
traction booster drawbar 具有驱动轮加载作用的牵引杆
traction booster system 牵引力增强系统(牵引增重系统,驱动轮加载系统)
traction chain 防滑链
traction coefficient 牵引力系数,附

着力系数
traction control actuator 牵引力控制执行器（如：防滑转系统中的节气门开度控制阀"throttle-valve opening control valve"）
traction control switch 牵引力控制开关（仪表板上由驾驶者操纵的利用制动对牵引力进行控制的防滑转功能开关。按压该开关，牵引力控制功能停止，直至下一次按压开关，使该功能恢复）
traction control system 牵引力控制系统（见 TRC system）
traction device 行走机构的牵引装置（指车辆行走机构中与地面相互作用而产生牵引力的装置，如：车轮、履带机构等）
traction differential 防滑差速器（通过锁止作用，可防止驱动轮打滑的差速器，"limited-slip differential"的别称）
traction dynamometer 牵引力测力计（= towing dynamometer）
traction element （车辆行走装置的）牵引元件（如：轮胎、履带等）
traction engine ①牵引发动机②（早期使用的蒸汽动力）牵引车，拖拉机
traction force 牵引力（= tractive force, propelling force）
traction grade （汽车轮胎的）附着性能等级（表征其使车辆在湿路上制动停车的能力的文字代码系统）
traction horsepower （以马力为单位的）牵引功率（亦称 tractive horsepower, 简称 THP）
traction indicator 牵引力计
tractionless 无附着力的, 无牵引力的
traction motor （电动汽车的）牵引电动机（作为电动车主动力源的电动机，亦称 drive motor）

traction resistance 牵引阻力（= tractive resistance）
traction rod 转矩杆（见 torque arm ②）
traction spring 牵引缓冲弹簧
traction test 牵引试验（拖拉机、机车等用的内燃机，为考核其牵引性能的整车试验）
traction truck （带挂车的）牵引（货车）（= towing truck）
traction-type cell 牵引型电池（动力用电池，= motive-power battery）
traction-type tyre 大牵引力型驱动轮轮胎
traction wave of tire 轮胎的驻波（见 standing wave of tire）
tractive 牵引的, 拖曳的
tractive ability 牵引能力
tractive characteristics 牵引特性
tractive effort 牵引力（汽车牵引能力的量化指标）
tractive force 牵引力（由路面作用在轮胎接地中心的力矢量沿前进方向的分量，它等于横向力乘以侧偏角的正弦加上纵向力乘以侧偏角的余弦，= traction force）
tractive force balance 牵引力平衡（亦称 traction balance）
tractive force chart （汽车的）牵引力图（表征牵引力、道路附着系数和荷载分配之间的相互关系）
tractive force diagram （汽车的）牵引力平衡图（图上绘出在不同车速下的滚动阻力曲线、空气阻力曲线、各种坡度的爬坡阻力曲线，以及各种排挡下驱动轮上的牵引力曲线，根据这些曲线计算汽车的有关性能）
tractive force limit （汽车的）牵引力极限（最大牵引力，即：根据驱动桥动载荷 W_d 和道路附着系数 μ，所确定的最大牵引力 P_{max}，其关系式为：$P_{max} = W_d \mu$）

tractive force method （汽车的）牵引力图解法（参见 tractive force diagram）

tractive force sensor 牵引力传感器

tractive force variation 牵引力变动（承受负荷的轮胎在旋转时某一半径上产生的）前后方向力的变动（亦称 tangential force variation，简称 TFV）

tractive grip 牵引元件（轮胎或履带对地面的）抓着力

tractive output 牵引功率

tractive performance 牵引性能，动力性能

tractive power 牵引功率（亦称 propelling power）

tractive unit ①牵引装置（如：牵引车）②牵引电机③牵引用发动机

tractive wheel 驱动轮（= traction wheel）

tractometer 测功计，工况仪，牵引力计

tractor ①拖拉机②牵引车（如：半挂车的牵引车）

tractor-drawn 牵引车拖挂的，牵引车牵引的（= tractor-dragged, tractor-hauled, tractor-hitched）

tractor driver 牵引车驾驶员

tractor engine 拖拉机用内燃机

tractor on pneumatics 轮式牵引车（= air-tired tractor）

tractor proportioning valve 牵引车（制动）比例分配阀（参见 proportioning valve）

tractor protection valve 制动系统的牵引车保护阀（挂车脱离牵引车时，封断牵引车通向挂车的制动气管，以保护牵引车制动系的阀门）

tractor-semitrailer combination 牵引车-半挂车列车

tractor-semitrailer with a full trailer 牵引车-半挂车-全挂车列车（= 2-SI-2 truck trailer combination）

tractor stability automatic control system 牵引车稳定性自动控制系统

tractor suspension cab 牵引车悬架式驾驶室

tractor track car 履带牵引车

tractor-trailer combination 牵引车带全挂车汽车列车（= tractor-trailer train）

tractor-trailer transportation 拖挂运输（牵引车拖带挂车装载旅客或货物的运输，tractor-trailer trucking 拖挂货运）

tractor vibration spectrum 牵引车振动频谱

tractor wagon 箱式牵引车

tractor winch 牵引车绞盘

trade ①贸易，交易，商业；行业，手工业②从事贸易，经营商业，做交易；交换，对换；购物

trade association 商会，贸易协会

trade-in ①以实物作价购买货物（如：以旧车折价购买新车）②折价的

trade mark 厂牌，商标

trade name 商品名

trade nego(tiation) 贸易谈判，贸易洽谈

traditional logic 传统逻辑

traffic ①交通，交通量；运输；运输量②车流（指沿道路行驶的车辆）③运务④交易，来往；通信⑤电讯，（传输）信息量

trafficability ①（车辆）通过性，通过能力（车辆通过各种复杂地形的能力）②（道路）可行驶性，通行能力③（物品，机器等）可运输性（如：机器装在平板车上不至超高、超宽等）

trafficability curve of soil 土壤可通行性曲线

trafficability test ①（道路的）可行驶性（可通行性）试验②（车辆的）通过性试验，通过能力试验

trafficable 可通行的，可通过的

traffic accident reconstruction 交通事故再现（分析事故原因的一种方法）

Traffic Accident Reduction Program [美]减少交通事故规划（简称 TARP）

traffic-actuated 车辆触动的（由车辆或车流通过时触发启动记录装置、摄像装置、各种开关或控制装置等）

traffic-actuated controller 车辆触动式交通控制器（一种由车流信号触动的管理交通信号的自动控制器）

traffic-actuated signal 车辆触动式交通信号

traffic actuation detector 车辆及行人传感器和检测器（的统称）

trafficator ①指示道路方向的路标 ②（旧时汽车的）转向信号指示臂（= trafficator arm）③（现在亦指）转向信号灯 ④指各种表示停车、转向等的信号装置（traffic indicator 的简称）

trafficator control light （驾驶室仪表板上的）转向信号指示灯（使驾驶员知道方向指示灯是否正常，= direction-indicator control light）

trafficator switch 转向信号灯开关

traffic beam （汽车前照灯）远光

traffic behavior 交通现象，行车动态（指道路上行驶的车辆在一定时间和一定空间范围内的动态）

traffic blackspot 交通事故多发地点（= traffic accident blackspot，美称 traffic high-accident location 或 hazardous location）

traffic block 交通阻塞

traffic bollard （双柱）交通标志牌

traffic bottleneck 交通瓶颈（交通拥挤地段，交通狭道，道路狭窄地段）

traffic-bound road 压实的道路，车辆压实的道路（= traffic-compacted road）

traffic button 交通路钮（路面标线用路钮，路钉）

traffic cameras （道路）车流摄像机

traffic capacity investigation （道路）交通容量调查，交通容量测试

traffic capacity of public service 公用运输业的运输能力

traffic chaos 交通混乱（= traffic snarls）

traffic circle 交通环形交叉口（= rotary intersection，traffic circuit，美称 roundabout）

traffic computer management system 计算机交通管理系统

traffic concentration 交通密度（见 traffic density）

traffic conflict technique 交通交错技术

traffic-congestion 交通堵塞

traffic constable [英]交通警察

traffic control system 交通控制系统（简称 TCS，亦称交通监理系统）

traffic control vehicle 交通监理车（装备有警报器、监测仪器和宣传设施，用于监理公路交通、处理事故的厢式汽车）

traffic cop （美俗）交通警察

traffic crawled 交通阻滞车辆缓行

traffic death 交通死亡事故

traffic demand 交通需求（指对车辆的需求；trip demand 指人的出行需求；travel demand 指旅游对交通的需求；transportation demand 则是包含空运、陆运、水运等的综合交通需求；但这几个词常常混用，统称交通运输需求）

traffic density 交通密度（指某瞬间在单位长度车道上的车辆总数，通常其单位为：车辆数/公里路段，= traffic concentration）

traffic diagram 交通图

traffic distribution 交通分布（指交通量分布，交通车辆流量分布，= trip distribution，但含义有时是有区别的，traffic 主要讲车辆，而 trip 主要讲人）

traffic disturbance 交通紊乱

traffic diversion 交通分流；交通改道，交通绕行（= diversion of traffic）

traffic engineering 交通工程（指道路交通工程，由工程 engineering，教育 education，法规 enforcement，能源 energy，环境 environment 五方面的内容组成，故亦称 5-E engineering）

traffic fatality 交通肇事伤亡

traffic flow ①交通流（量）（见 traffic volume）②车流（= traffic current）

traffic flow analysis 交通流分析（研究分析交通车流相互之间的关系，车流间隔的组成，交叉路口的交通特性及流量、流向等）

traffic flow diagram 交通流量图（在公路网或城市道路网中，一定时间内道路各区段间通过的交通量以连线的粗细来表明，这种图式称为交通流量图）

traffic flow theory 交通流（量）理论（包括交通流的数学理论，车辆跟随模式，运动波理论，交通信号灯光的概率模式，信号化交通交叉路口的最佳化管理，运输网路上的交通流量等）

traffic forecasting technique 交通预测技术

traffic-free 无车辆通行的，无交通往来的（= traffic-less）

traffic halt 交通停车（交通拥挤、交叉路口停车信号等造成的停车）

traffic indicator ①交通指示器②交通（指挥）信号装置③车辆信号灯（装在车上向其他车辆或行人表示汽车转向、制动的信号灯，如：direction-indicating device, direction indicator lamp, directional turn signal, turn signal lamp, turn indicator, stop lamp 等）

traffic information 交通信息，交通情报，交通资料

traffic interaction 交通干扰，交通流的相互（干扰）作用

traffic interchange 立体交叉口（= flyover junction）

traffic in transit 过境交通（= through traffic）

traffic island 交通岛（分车岛，导向岛，安全岛）

traffic jam 交通拥挤，交通阻塞

traffic jam queues 交通拥挤排队（现象），车辆阻塞排队（现象）

traffic lane divider 行车道分道线

traffic less 无车通行的（参见 traffic-free）

traffic light 交通信号灯

traffic-light creep 汽车驶近交通指挥灯、信号灯时的缓慢行驶

traffic light operating control equipment 交通信号灯操作控制设备（简称 TLOCE）

traffic lights （包括红、绿灯在内的所有）交通管制信号灯

traffic loop （交叉口）环行道，绕行道

traffic management 交通管理

traffic master system 交通主信息机系统（一种装在汽车仪表板上，表明行驶于高速公路上的车流长度、车速、位置等，供驾驶人安全运行参考的信息系统的商品名）

traffic offence 交通违章，违章行车

Traffic Safety and Nuisance Research Institute 交通安全与公害研究所（属日本国运输省，简称 TSNRI）

Traffic Safety and Nuisance Research Institutes Type Approval Test

Standard ［日］（运输省）交通安全与公害研究所（制定的）汽车试验标准（法）（简称 TRIAS）

Traffic Safety Institute ［美］交通安全协会（简称 TSI）

Traffic Safety Research (Corporation) ［美］交通安全研究公司（简称 TSR）

traffic sign 交通标志

traffic signal 交通信号，交通信号灯

traffic signal speed sign 交通信号系统规定的速度标志

traffic stream 车流（同方向一条或几条车道上行驶的车辆交通，= traffic flow）

traffic strip （车道间）分隔带

traffic throughput 交通流量

traffic ticket 汽车驾驶员违反交通规章的传票（简称 T ticket）

traffic-type truck 平头货车，亦称 cab-over (engine) truck

traffic violation 交通违章事项（违反交通规章、条例的事项）

traffic violation aggravated by alcohol 酒后驾驶交通违章（简称 TVAA）

traffic volume 交通流量（一定时间内通过道路上某定点的车辆、行人等，除专门说明者外，均指两个方向的合计值，亦称 traffic flow）

traffic volume characteristic 交通流量（随时间等的）变化特性

traffic way 车行道

traffic/weather/routing information 交通-气候-线路信息

trail ①痕迹，轨迹，轮迹②尾部，后缘，车尾③小路，小径④牵引杆，拖杆⑤主销后倾拖距（指主销中心线接地点与车轮中心地面投影点之间的距离）⑥拉，拖，曳；拖行；跟踪，追迹，尾随，跟在后面走；伸展开

trail-and-error procedure 尝试法，试探法，试算法

trail arm type rigid beam axle suspension 纵臂式刚性梁车桥悬架（由纵向控制臂、横向推力杆及螺旋弹簧-减振器等组成的非独立式悬架。注意：若车桥不是刚性梁而是扭转梁，这类悬架则为半独立式悬架，见 torsion beam axle suspension）

trailblazer 路径导向标（近旁的高速公路、桥梁等的标示牌）

trail car 挂车（= trailer）

trailed tank 拖挂式罐车

trailer ①挂车（一般指全挂车 full trailer，半挂车为 semitrailer）②被拖曳者，尾部③用挂车运输

trailer axle alignment 挂车轴定位（确保挂车拖挂销中心点与挂车轴中点之连线与挂车轴中心线垂直）

trailer axle alignment gage 挂车轴定位仪（挂车轴定位测量设备）

trailer bed （平板挂车的）平板货台

trailer brake controller （装在主车上的）挂车制动控制器

trailer braking protection valve 挂车制动保护阀（控制挂车的制动作用，且在牵引车和挂车之间的跨接软管损坏或漏气时，能保护牵引车制动气压的部件）

trailer braking relax valve 挂车制动放松阀（挂车在脱挂自行制动后，用以放松挂车制动的部件）

trailer braking relay emergency valve 挂车制动应急继动阀（由牵引车气制动阀和继动阀的输出气压来控制，使挂车制动或放松，或者当挂车供给管路和控制管路断裂或漏气以及脱挂时，使挂车自行应急制动的部件）

trailer braking valve 挂车制动阀（按照牵引车气制动阀的输出气压作用控制挂车制动的部件）

trailer bus 挂车式客车（= trailer coach）

trailer cable plug　挂车插头

trailer camp　①活动旅居挂车群②活动旅居挂车停车场（= trailer court, trailer park, trailer house park）③旅游起居车宿营地（一般在场地上有自来水、煤气、电源接头，供车辆连接使用）

trailer (converter) dolly　半挂车拖挂桥（一种货车拖挂半挂车时仅用的单轴或双轴独立车桥，本身具有牵引杆及承载半挂车的转盘，常规货车用它来拖带半挂车）

trailer coupling　拖挂装置，牵引机构

trailer drawgear　挂车牵引机构

trailer dropped and picked up transportation　甩挂运输（牵引车拖带挂车到货物到达站后，将整个挂车甩在到达站，然后再重新牵引其他装货挂车起运至相应到达站的运输）

trailer dump　挂车倾卸机构

trailerette　单轴挂车

trailer gear　（轿车、货车和大客车等的）挂车拖挂装置

trailer hitch　[美]（牵引车拖带）挂车的拖挂装置（= towing fork, towing jaws）

trailer hitch guidance　挂车钩挂引导（系统一体）

trailer house　旅居挂车（由汽车牵引的全挂式旅居房，= trailer coach, trailer home）

trailerite　居住在汽车拖曳活动房屋中的人

trailerized tank　拖挂式罐车

trailer kingpin　挂车主销（挂车与牵引车连接主销）

trailer lamp socket　挂车车灯电线插座

trailer landing gear　（半）挂车支地轮起落装置

trailer-mounted　装在挂车上的

trailer nose　挂车前鼻（挂车头部，挂车前端）

trailer on flat car　（可由铁路驮运的）驮运用挂车（简称 TOFC, = piggyback trailer）

trailer overrunning brake　挂车超速制动器（防止挂车速度超过主车速度，一般是当挂车因速度超过主车速度而撞推拖挂装置时，该制动器即起作用）

trailer pull　挂车反拖力（挂车对牵引车的反拉力）

trailer pump　汽车牵引的移动式消防泵

trailer reflector　挂车反光镜

trailer reverse park guidance　挂车倒车入库、驻车引导（系统）

trailer shaft altitude　（全）挂车牵引杆离地高度

trailer shaft reach　（全）挂车牵引杆牵引端至前轴中心线距离

trailer support　挂车支撑（挂车支架，如：半挂车在未拖挂时，依靠装在车架下的支架，负载前端重量）

trailer sway damping　挂车横摆抑制（装置）

trailer swing　挂车甩摆（美称 trailer sway, 指挂车绕与牵引车的连接点横向摆动的现象）

trailer swing mitigation system　防挂车摆振系统（简称 TSM, 美称 trailer sway mitigation）

trailer tipped side-ways　侧倾式自卸挂车

trailer towability　（汽车）牵引挂车的能力

trailer tow bar eye　挂车拖拽环

trailer tower wagon　带升降台架的挂车（= tower wagon）

trailer-towing vehicle　全挂车牵引车（如：牵引全挂车的常规货车）

trailer train　挂车列车

trailer with adjustable drawbar height 牵引杆高度可调式挂车
trailer with canvas cover 帆布顶篷挂车
trailer with detachable rear axle 后轴可拆卸式挂车（= trailer with withdrawable rear axle）
trailer with loading skids 带装卸货物用滑板的挂车
trailer with oscillating axles 带摆动桥的挂车
trailer with shaft length （全）挂车带牵引杆全长
trailing ①拖曳，牵引②（制动器）拖滞③拖挂的，牵引的④后面的，尾随的
trailing angle ①（转子发动机转子顶尖与缸面法线的）后面夹角（后夹角，尾随夹角）②（汽车的）后悬角
trailing arm （悬架的）纵臂（纵向布置的控制臂，亦称 trailing link，见 control arm，单纵臂式悬架称 single trailing arm type suspension；双纵臂式悬架称 double trailing arm type suspension；双纵臂式悬架的上纵臂称 upper trailing arm，下纵臂称 under trailing arm，一般纵臂都为后拖式，即：车轮支承在纵臂后端，见 leading arm）
trailing axle （特指中桥驱动三轴汽车的）后从动尾桥（尾随桥）
trailing (brake) shoe （内张型鼓式制动器制动蹄中的）从蹄（张开时的转动方向与制动鼓的转动方向相反的制动蹄）
trailing cable 拖动式电缆（移动式发电机组等的可跟着机组移动的拖动式电缆）
trailing cable socket 挂车插座
trailing chamber （转子发动机的）后方工作室（后一个工作室，按转子旋转方向，相对于前一个工作室而言）
trailing characteristics 牵引特性（机动车用的内燃机按牵引功率运行的性能）
trailing combustion chamber ①转子发动机的后置燃烧室（后置转子燃烧凹坑，指转子工作面凹坑偏置后方）②（转子发动机的）后燃烧室（转子工作面后凹坑，指凹坑的后部）
trailing edge ①（凸轮）下降面②（叶片）后缘③（转子发动机径向密封片）后棱（见 following edge）④（板件等的）后边缘⑤脉冲的后缘
trailing effect （被拖带车轮的）拖带（回正）效应（= self-right effect）
trailing plug （转子发动机的）后置火花塞（装置在燃烧室尾部区域）
trailing portion 后段，后部分，尾随部分，被拖动的部分，从动部分，下垂部分
trailing vortex 尾流旋涡（如：汽车行驶中的空气尾流旋涡）
trail pipe （发动机的）排气尾管
trail road 试用道路
trail run 试运行，试运转
train ①列车②系，系列（如：齿轮系）
training 训练，教练，培训
training car （培训新驾驶员的）教练车
training field （如：汽车驾驶）教练场
train of gears 齿轮系
train of mechanism 机构链，机构系（如：由原动机构和必需的从动机构组成的可完成某一独立作业的机构组合）
train of vehicles 车队，汽车队
train resistance （汽车）列车行驶阻力（行驶时遇到的各种阻力，

如：滚动阻力、加速阻力、空气阻力、上坡阻力等的总称）

train-type vehicle 多节铰接式车辆（如：汽车列车）

trait ①特色，特点，特征，特性 ②外形

TRAJ 轨迹（trajectory 的简称）

trajectory 轨迹，弹道（简称 TRAJ）

traking filter 跟迹滤波器

tram ①有轨电车，轨道车 ②轨道 ③椭圆规 ④调整机器部件用规 ⑤正确位置，正确调整

trambus 平头式（车厢）公共汽车，有轨电车

tramcar ①市内有轨电车 ②轨道运输车辆，矿车，高架索道缆车

tramp ①步行，徒步行走 ②（汽车同一车桥左、右两个车轮）反相跳振（亦称 tramping）

tramp iron rejector 金属夹杂物分离器

transaxle ①变速驱动桥（transmission axle 的简称，在这种驱动桥系统中，变速器与主减速器和差速器组装在一起，成为一个总成，多用于前轮驱动式轿车。此时，该总成装在横置式发动机的后端，发动机的动力由离合器经变速器主减速器带差速器总成两端的半轴直接驱动左、右前轮）②（仅指上述系统中的）变速器带主减速器差速器总成（亦称 final driving transmission。其变速器分手动与自动两种，自动型由电子模块控制的，称 electronic automatic transaxle，简称 EATX，其控制模块称 EATX module，简称 EATXM）

transaxle-mounted motor （电动汽车的）安装在驱动桥内的电动机（电动机-减速齿轮-差速器均布置在驱动桥壳内成一整体总成）

transbus 公共轿车（1970 年美国研制的一种乘坐性能类似轿车的公共汽车，以替代市区轿车行驶，并采用宽车门、低地板、备有跳板，以便轮椅上下）

transceiver ①发送-接收器（兼有发送和接收功能的器件，transmitter 和 receiver 的组合词，亦写作 receiver-transmitter）②（微处理机系统的）选择性接口（有选择地使微处理机与输入和输出相连接）

transcend 超出，超越，胜过

transconductance 互导（转移电导，跨导）

transcontinental coach （横贯大陆的）长途大客车

transcriber （数据，信息的）转录装置，转录器（将数据从一个媒体转储到另一个媒体）

transcription ①复制，转录；录制 ②（记录数据、信息的）再生，再现，重播

transduce ①转换（换能，传感）②变换（变送，变频）

transducer ①变换器（可将能量或物理量从一种形式变换成另一形式的装置）②（当在汽车电子控制系统中，将温度、压力、流量、速度、位移等物理量，变换为电信号输送给电子控制模块的变换器称为）传感器（= sensor）

transducer amplifier 传感器放大器（传感信号放大器）

transducer valve 传感阀

transesterification reaction 交酯化反应

trans-European 横贯欧洲的，全欧洲的

transfer ①移动，移位，搬运 ②转换，变换 ③传递，传输，传送，传导 ④换车，转运 ⑤进位 ⑥数据的记录与读出

transferable torque 可传递的转矩

transfer box 分动器（亦称 transfer gear, transfer gearbox, 美称 transfer case,全轮驱动车辆中将动力分配给各驱动桥的齿轮箱。非全时全轮驱动式车辆使用的分动器,尚起接通与断开前桥或中间桥动力的作用。有的分动器还可以改变传动比兼起副变速器、辅助变速器的作用)

transfer case 分动器(见 transfer box)

transfer case control 分动器操纵机构(指使分动器离合或进行换挡的控制机构)

transfer case cover 分动器盖

transfer case gearshift cover 分动器换挡盖

transfer case oil capacity 分动器滑油容量(分动器齿轮箱容量)

transfer channel 转移沟道(电荷转移器件中的区域,电荷流动被限制在这区域中)

transfer characteristic ①传输特性②(放大设备等的)瞬态特性

transfer constant 传输常数

transfer crane 门式起重机

transfer drive ①(全轮驱动车辆的)分动器驱动②锐角传动箱(指输入轴与输出轴成锐角布置的锥齿轮变速器,主要用于发动机横向后置式大客车,以便将动力由该变速器传至传动轴)

transfer efficiency ①转换系数②传输系数③(合金)过渡系数

transfer function 传递函数〔在规定的条件范围内,表达输入量与相应输出量间关系的函数,线性系统中,当初始条件为零时,系统输出(响应)与输入(激励)的拉普拉斯(Laplace)变换之比,常记为 $W(s)$ 或 $H(s)$(s 为复参数),是描述线性系统固有传递关系的重要特性〕

transfer function analyzer 传递函数分析器

transfer gantry 龙门吊车,龙门吊

transfer gate 转移栅(一种加上电压可使电荷转移的电极,它与半导体之间用绝缘层或结来隔开)

transfer gear ①分动器(见 transfer)②(美指)低输出轴变速器(见 drop box)

transfer gearbox 分动器(见 transfer box)

transfer hole ①传递孔,传送孔②(转子发动机的)喷焰孔(指连接火花塞小室和旋轮线缸体型面燃烧室之间的小孔,= shoot hole, transfer port)

transfer indicator lamp 分动器挡位指示灯

transfer of energy ①能量传递②能量转换

transfer of heat 热传递,传热(= heat transfer)

transfer of technology 技术移植(技术引进)

transfer plate (液力自动变速器控制阀的)油路连接板

transfer port ①旁通孔,溢流孔(亦称 transfer hole)②(特指曲轴箱压缩式二冲程发动机中,被压缩的新鲜可燃混合气由曲轴箱进入汽缸的)进气道

transfer port injection system (二冲程发动机)进气口(燃油)直接喷射系统

transfer switch 转换开关

transfer valve ①输送阀②旁通阀③溢流阀

transform ①变换,变化,转变,转化②换算,折算③变换式

transformation ①变换,变化,转变,转换②换算

transformation induced plastic steel 见 TRIP steel

transformed value (of a measured) (被测量的)变换值(表示与被测

量有函数关系的量值)

transformer ①变压器 ②变换器(如:将图像等放大、缩小、转动、平移等的装置)

transformer amplifier 变压器耦合放大器

transformer coil 变压器线圈(感应线圈)

transformer effect 变压器效应

transformer impedance 变压器阻抗

transformer imput current 变压器输入电流

transformer oil 变压器油

transformer ratio 变压比

transformer tap 变压器抽头

transient ①过渡历程,过渡过程;瞬态过程,不稳定过程 ②瞬时状态;过渡状态,不稳定状态;不稳定工况,过渡工况 ③过渡的,不固定的,不稳定的;暂态的,瞬态的;非定常的

transient adaptation factor (眼睛的)瞬时适应因数(表示眼睛从一种背景亮度改变到另一种背景亮度时重新适应所降低的等效对比的一个因数,简称TAF)

transient behavio(u)r 瞬态特性(非稳定状态下的性能,瞬态状况下的性能)

transient circumferential profile of contact pressure (轮胎)接触压力的瞬态圆周分布图

transient compensating (发动机)过渡(性工况喷油量)补偿(如:加速加浓等)

transient creep 瞬时蠕变

transient drag 瞬时阻力

transient flow 瞬态流(非稳定流)

transient-free 稳定的(指无过渡、瞬态历程的)

transient load 瞬(时荷)载

transient overshoot 瞬时过冲(在阶跃响应中,输出量超出其最终稳态值的最大瞬态偏差)

transient performance of control system 控制系统瞬时特性(控制系过渡特性)

transient phenomenon 瞬变现象

transient protection (电器仪表的)瞬态(电压)保护

transient response test (汽车)瞬态响应试验(操纵输入或加、减速输入随时间而变化,用横摆角速度、侧倾角等评价汽车过渡过程响应特性的试验)

transient speed regulation 瞬时调速率(由于突变负荷引起转速变化瞬时幅度的状况,其表达式为:$|(n_2-n_1)/n| \times 100\%$,式中:$n_1$—突变负荷前的转速;$n_2$—突变负荷时转速的最大或最小值;$n$—标定转速)

transient state 瞬态(过渡状态,非稳定状况,加在汽车上的外力或操纵及汽车的运动响应随时间而改变时的汽车状态,简称TS)

transient (state) response 瞬态响应(瞬变响应,过渡响应,汽车瞬态状况下的运动响应)

transient state yaw velocity response to a stepped input of steering wheel angle 转向盘转角阶跃输入瞬态横摆角速度响应(指汽车等速直线行驶时,突然将转向盘转一角度,汽车不会立即进入等横摆角速度的稳态,而要经过的一个横摆角速度随时间而变化的过渡过程)

transient-suppressing capacitor 瞬时抑制电容器

transient thermal analysis 瞬时温度分析,瞬时热态分析

transient through resonance 共振过渡过程

transient time 瞬态时间(瞬时,建立时间,过渡时间)

transient vibration 瞬态振动(对稳

态振动而言，见 steady state vibration)

transient voltage 瞬态电压（过渡电压）

transient voltage suppression 瞬态电压抑制

transient working condition 过渡工况（运转状态变化过程中的工况）

transinformation 传递信息（互传信息）

transistor 晶体（三极）管（用于开关电路或放大信号）

transistor amplifier 晶体管放大器

transistor base 晶体管基极

transistor checker 晶体管测试仪

transistor collector 晶体管集电极

transistor-controlled ignition 晶体管（开关电路）点火，（= transistorized ignition）

transistor diode 半导体二极管，晶体二极管，二极管

transistor emitter 晶体管发射极

transistor flasher 晶体管闪光器（利用晶体管的开关特性控制的闪光器）

transistor horn 晶体管电喇叭（利用晶体管电路激励膜片振动产生音响的警告装置）

transistorized ignition 晶体管点火（系）（在电子点火发展初期，是指在常规机械触点式断电器点火系初级电路中加装晶体管电路，初级电流经该电路接入点火线圈初级绕组，而不再通过断电器触点，通过断电器触点的只是微弱的晶体管基极电流的点火系。随着电子点火技术的发展，晶体管点火一词曾泛指各种无触点式电子点火系，但目前已不再使用。美国政府规定，从1995年／月起，按 SAE J1930 推荐的术语，无分电器电子点火系一律称 electronic ignition，简称 EI，有分电器式电子点火系一律称 distributor ignition，简称 DI)

transistor sound scope （根据杂音和振动，判断发动机及各种机械技术状况用的）晶体管听诊器

transistor trigger 晶体管触发电路

transit ①通行，通过；越过，过渡②运输；转运；过境运输③运输线；公共交通系统④转变，变换

transit company 运输公司

Transit Connect Electric 全顺全电动车［福特公司2010年在美国2011年在欧洲推出的全电池动力车（full battery electric vehicle）的车名］

transit curve ①过渡曲线②（弯道）过渡段（= transition curve）

transit information 运输信息，交通资料，交通信息

transition 经过，通过；过渡，渐增；渐变段，过渡段

transitional 过渡的，瞬变的，不稳定的，转变的

Transitional Low Emission Vehicle （美国加利福尼亚）过渡性低排放车（指符合美国加州制定的过渡性低排放车排放标准的车辆，简称 TLEV）

transitional-road-surface braking test 变附着系数变化的路面制动试验（指在各路段附着系数不同的路面上进行的制动试验）

transitional road surface braking testing 瞬变性路面制动试验（包括棋盘路和附着系数不断由低变高或由高变低的各种路面）

transitional yaw center （车身的）瞬时横摆中心

transition capacitance 过渡电容（瞬变电容）

transition condition 过渡状态（瞬时状态，瞬态）

transition curve 过渡曲线（= transit curve）

transition fit 过渡配合，静配合

transition frequency 过渡频率（交界频率，交叉频率）

transition length （公路）缓和段长度（缓和曲线路段的长度）

transition line 过渡线（界线，转变线）

transition loss 过渡损失

transition-operated input （数字集成电路的）转换工作输入（一种只有在两个转换方向之一时才有效的，引起激励的输入；或只有从一个电平到另一个电平的转换速率足够大时才引起激励的输入）

transition region 过滤区域（转变区域，迁移区域，如：层流层到紊流层的过渡区域）

transition stage 过渡阶段（瞬时阶段）

transition temperature ①相变温度（转变温度，转变点，指物质由一种状态转变为另一种状态，即：一相转变为他相的过程中，有一个两相共存的平衡状态，这时的温度称为转变温度，或相变温度）②跃迁温度（跃迁点，一般指金属材料的性质急剧变化时的温度）③（结晶构造和磁性等的）变态温度（变态点）

transition time 过渡历程时间（从一状态到另一状态的过渡时间）

transition type 过渡型（中间型）

transition zone 过渡区（缓和区；溶化区）

transit mode 交通模式

transit-oriented structure 以公共交通为方向的（城市建设）结构

transit routes 运输路线（运输线路，交通线路）

transit system theory 快速客运系统理论

transit traffic 过境交通（＝through traffic）

transit type bus 长途客车（长途公共汽车，国际交通用的公共汽车）

transit vehicle 过境车辆

translating ①变换，调换，转化②转移，移动，平移③翻译，解释，说明

translating gear 变换齿轮；中间齿轮

translation ①翻译（一般指笔译），译文②转化，转变，转换，换算③移动，平移，位移；平移运动，直线运动④调动，调换⑤（电讯）中继，转接

translational motion 平移运动，平动

translational velocity 平移速度（直线运动速度）

translation cam 直动凸轮（直线运动凸轮，指将旋转运动变为从动件的直线运动的凸轮）

translation circuit 变换电路，转接电路，译码电路

translation loss 平移损失

translation surface 平移曲面

translation wave 平移波

translator ①变换器，转换器②转发器，中继器，发射机③译码器，翻译机④译员，译者（一般指笔译）

translatory 平移的

translatory acceleration 平移运动加速度（直线运动加速度）

translatory mass 平移质量（直线运动的质量，见 translatory motion）

translatory motion 平移运动（平动，运动物体的全部质点，都沿着同一方向，以同样的速度运动）

translatory resistance 平移阻力（平移运动阻力）

translot 横缝，横沟，横槽（transverse slot）

translucent ①透亮的，透明的（＝transparent）②明显的，坦率的，清楚的，显而易见的

transmissibility ①传输率，传递能

力,传导能力②通过能力,可透性,可传递性③传递率(当线性系统的响应与激励取为同一物理量,如:力或运动时,响应与激励的傅里叶变换之比)

transmissibility of vibration ①振动传递率②振动的可传性

transmissibility spectrum (振动)传递频谱

transmission ①传动系,传动装置(英,指离合器、变速器、传动轴、主减速器和差速器、半轴等将动力从发动机传至车轮的整个系统中各个总成与部件的通称,亦称 drive line,power train)②(美指)变速器,变速箱(=英 gear box)③传递,传送,传输,传动,传导④透射,透过⑤发射,发送

transmission accuracy 传动精度(在工作状态下,输入轴单向旋转时,输出轴的实际转角相对于理论转角的接近程度。传动精度的高低用传动误差大小来衡量,误差小、精度高,误差大、精度低)

transmission adapter 异型变速器接装器(将型号或生产年份不同的变速器接装在发动机上的装置)

transmission-axle 见 transaxle

transmission band (液力变速器中使用的)带式离合器(液力驱动,离合带将离合器鼓箍紧时,鼓不再旋转,亦称 band type clutch,或带式制动器"band type brake")

transmission brake 传动系制动器(指不直接装在车轮上,而装在汽车传动系某一部件,如:传动轴等处的制动装置)

transmission characteristics of electromagnetic waves 电磁波传播特性(表征在发射天线与接收天线之间的电磁波传播场内,电磁波的反射、吸收、散射、折射等现象对电磁波传播的影响的特性)

transmission controlled 变速器控制的(挡位控制的,如:挂低速挡时,真空点火提前装置便不起作用等)

transmission countershaft (=轴式)变速器中间轴(亦称变速器副轴)

transmission countershaft reverse gear (=轴式)变速器中间轴倒挡齿轮

transmission device ①(制动系的)传能装置(制动系中用以将制动能量输送到制动促动器的部件。②(泛指各种)传动装置(包括变速器)

transmission diagram 挡位图

transmission diameter (前照灯)透光直径(光线透过配光镜有效面积的直径)

transmission distance 传送距离;传动距离

transmission driven power take-off 变速器功率输出轴

transmission dynamometer 传动式测功器(不吸收能量的测功器)

transmission error 传动误差(在工作状态下,当输入轴单向旋转时,输出轴的实际转角与理论转角之差)

transmission (fluid) cooler 自动变速器液力传动油冷却器(一般与发动机散热器组装成一体,利用冷却水冷却液力传动油,有的文献亦称 transmission oil cooler)

transmission gear ratio [美]变速器速比(指变速器输入轴与输出轴的转速比,亦称变速器挡位速比,简称 transmission ratio,=英 change gear ratio)

transmission identification number (车辆的)变速器出厂编号(变速器识别号码,简称 TIN)

transmission input shaft 变速器第一轴(输入轴)

transmission loss 传动（功率）损失（传动系或变速器中的功率损失）

transmission main shaft 变速器第二轴（主轴，输出轴，亦写作 transmission mainshaft）main shaft

transmission main shaft pilot bearing 变速器第二轴导向（前）轴承

transmission media 传输媒介

transmission noise test 变速器噪声试验（测定在不同工况下，各类变速器不同部分产生的噪声强度及其来源的试验）

transmission of rear axle pushing 后桥推力的传递

transmission of vibration 振动的传递，传振

transmission oil 传动系用的润滑油（如：变速器油，齿轮油）

transmission output speed 变速器第二轴转速，变速器输出转速

transmission output torque 传动系（或变速器）输出轴转矩

transmission position indicator switch 变速器挡位指示器开关（简称TPIS）

transmission position sensor 变速器挡位传感器

transmission ratio 传动比（在齿轮副或齿轮系中，基始端主动轮与末端从动轮的角速度比值，或其输入角速度与输出角速度的比值）

transmission resistance 传动系阻力（指离合器、变速器、万向节、差速器以及轴承等的功率耗损）

transmission retarder （大客车用的）变速器缓速器（利用变速器反拖阻力使车辆减速）

transmission reverse gear shaft 变速器倒挡轴（变速器倒挡齿轮轴）

transmission reverse idler gear 变速器倒挡中间齿轮

transmission shaft 传动轴（＝英propeller shaft，指将动力从变速器传至驱动桥，或从发动机传至变速驱动桥的万向节管）

transmission sliding clutch 变速器滑动式啮合器

transmission sliding gear hub 变速器滑动齿轮轮毂

transmission slip （液力）传动打滑（输入输出转速差）

transmission switch 变速器挡位开关（向电子控制模块输送变速器挡位信息）

transmission system ①传动系（汽车从发动机至驱动桥的各传动机构的总称）②（在美国有时仅指）变速装置

transmission temperature switch 自动变速器温度开关（见TTS）

transmission tester ①变速器测试台 ②传动系试验台

transmission tube 传动轴管

transmission tunnel （轿车车身底板中央凸起的）变速器-传动轴通道

transmission wind-up 传动系统自身轴线角振动

transmission without overrunning clutches 无单向离合器式自动变速器（由电子控制模块通过液压调节电磁阀对换挡件精确控制的最完善的自动变速器，已无须使用单向超越离合器，其装配尺寸可显著减小）

transmissive 能传递的，能传送的；可透过的

transmissive type display 透射型显示（在显示屏背后配置照明光源，用显示屏改变透过光的光强进行显示的方式）

transmissivity ①透明度，可透性 ②透光系数（见transmittance）

transmisson cooler （自动）变速器冷却器（用于冷却工作油液）

transmisson oil pressure sensor 变速器油压传感器

transmit 传递，传送，传动，传达；

传热，导热；发射，发送；透射，透光，使透过

transmittance 透光率（透光度，由光源传来的光，透过一条被排烟变暗的通道，到达仪器接收装置的部分所占的百分率，$T = 1 - \dfrac{N}{100}$。其中 N 为不透光率，见 opacity）

transmitter ①传感器，变送器 ②（信号）发送器，发送装置 ③（无线电）发射机，传送机

transmitting frequency 发射频率

transmitting medium 传导介质（包括电、光、热、声、力、能等的传导）

transmitting radar antenna 雷达发射天线

transmitting ratio 传动比

transom ①横梁，横挡 ②固定座椅 ③门顶窗，气窗

transparency 透明；透明度；透明体

transparency of torque converter 液力变矩器的透穿性（指液力变矩器泵轮转速不变时，荷载变化引起输入轴力矩变化的性能，其评价指标为穿透数"transparent number"）

transparent 透明的，透穿的，可透的

transparent conductive coating 透明导电膜（可导电的透明薄膜）

transpire ①蒸发，汽化 ②（气体）渗漏 ③排出，流溢

transplant 移植，移植厂（= transplant factory，如：日本丰田汽车公司移植到美国 Kentucky、California 等地的 Toyota plant）

transplant coating process 移植镀覆法（移镀工艺，在不易镀覆的金属表面上，先敷盖一层易镀覆的金属，然后再进行镀覆。如：转子发动机的铝缸体上不易镀铬，就先在铝缸壁上喷镀一层薄钢，然后再镀铬，简称 TCP）

transplant die-casting 移植压铸法

transponder （信号）转发器（①在通信技术中一种可以接收信号并将它再发送出去的装置 ②在卫星通信中将接收的信号放大，再以另一种频率重新发射出去的装置）

transport ①运输，运送，搬运 ②运输工具（= means of transport）

transport air-cushion vehicle 气垫运输车（简称 TACV）

Transport and Road Research Laboratory （英国环境保护厅所属的）运输和道路研究所（简称 TRRL）

transportation 运输，搬运，运送

transportation administration ①运输管理（运输行政管理）②运输管理机构（如：交通局、运输处等运政部门）

Transportation Association of America 美国运输协会（简称 TAA）

Transportation Association of Canada 加拿大运输协会（简称 TAC，原名道路及运输协会"Roads and Transportation Association of Canada"，简称 RTAC，于 1990 年改用现名）

Transportation Research Board 运输研究会（属于美国交通科学研究院，简称 TRB）

Transportation Research Center 运输研究中心（属美国联邦政府国家公路交通安全管理局，简称 TRC）

Transportation Research Information System 运输研究信息系统（属于美国交通科学研究院，简称 TRIS）

Transporter ①运输带，传送带，皮带运输机 ②传送装置 ③运输工具 ④（有时指运输其他车辆或超大型货物用的）汽车列车

transport ergonomics 运输人机工程学

Transport Insurance Co. ［美］运输保险公司（简称 TIC）

transport mixer 混凝土搅拌车（= concrete mixer truck）

transport monitor system 运输监控系统（简称 TMS）

transport vehicle 运输车辆（简称 TV）

transport width 车辆运货时的外廓宽度

transpose ①（位置的）置换，改换 ②（公式、方程等的）移项 ③（声音的）变调、移调

trans-provincial highway 跨省公路

transrapid system 高速运输系统

transversal ①横向的，横断的，横贯的 ②切割线，相贯线

transversal leaf spring type suspension 横置板簧式悬架（钢板弹簧与车轴平行布置的悬架形式）

transversal surface 横截面，横断面

transversce distance between the driver eye point and the mirror center 驾驶员眼点与后视镜中心的横向距离（简称 TEMC）

transverse ①横向的，横放的 ②横断的 ③横向物（如：横梁，横轴）

transverse angle of transmission （齿轮）端面作用角（端面作用弧所对圆心角。对于锥齿轮，其值应在冠轮上量度）

transverse apportioning brake system 横向（制动力）比例（分配）制动系（简称 TAB，由英国 Automotive Products 研制成功，防止车辆在转弯制动时由于重量侧向转移而出现过度转向或内侧车轮抱死的装置，结构简单，只是在每一车轮的液压管道中装有一个阀门，由各车轮的载荷通过一套控制杆系控制，如：当转向内侧的车较趋于抱死时，使内侧车轮的制动液压降低）

transverse arc 端面作用弧（齿轮在其啮合过程中，它的一个端面齿廓从啮合开始到啮合终止所转过的分度圆弧长。对于锥齿轮，指的是背锥齿廓在相应的啮合期间所转过的分度圆弧长）

transverse arm （悬架）横臂（横向布置的控制臂，可分上横臂、下横臂）

transverse base pitch 端面基圆齿距（亦称端面基节，基节。指在渐开线圆柱齿轮的一个端平面上，相邻的两个同侧齿廓的渐开线起始点之间的基圆弧长。它与这两个端面齿廓之间恒定的法向距离在数值上相等）

transverse base thickness 端面基圆齿厚（基圆齿厚，在渐开线圆柱齿轮的一个端平面上，一个齿的两侧端面齿廓的渐开线起始点之间的基圆弧长）

transverse bearing 向心轴承（径向轴承，= radial bearing）

transverse bending resilience 横向弯曲弹性（= transverse elasticity）

transverse bending strength 横向抗弯强度

transverse (bending) test 横向（弯曲）试验

transverse chordal tooth thickness 端面弦齿厚（简称弦齿厚，在齿轮的一个端平面上，一个齿的两侧端面齿廓之间的分度圆弧所对应的弦长）

transverse contact ratio （齿轮）端面重合度（端面作用角与齿距角的比值）

transverse crack 横裂纹

transverse deflection 横向挠度，横向弯度

transverse diametral pitch 端面径节（圆周率 π 除以以毫米计的端面齿距所得到的商，其值等于端面模数的倒数）

transverse displacement 横向位移

transverse distribution 横向分布

(如：在行车道横断方向上车辆行驶位置的分布)

transverse elasticity 弯曲弹性

transverse engine 横置式发动机（发动机曲轴中心线与行车方向成90°角的横向安装的发动机，亦称crosswise engine, transversally mounted engine）

transverse force 横向力（= cross force）

transverse front-wheel-drive power units 横置式前轮驱动动力装置（指横置式前轮驱动发动机-传动系机组）

transverse grade [美] 横向坡度（英 = transverse gradient）

transverse leaf-spring and rocker arm type suspension 横置板簧与单横摆臂式悬架（由一架横向布置，两端分别支承左、右车轮的钢板弹簧和左、右车轮各一根与车架连接的单横向控制臂组成的悬架系统）

transverse leaf suspension 横置式钢板弹簧悬架（与汽车纵轴线呈90°布置）

transverse link 横杆，横臂（任一机械杆系，特别是悬架系中横向布置的杆件，如：横向推力杆"lateral rod"，横向控制臂"transverse arm"，横向稳定杆"track rod"等）

transverse load 横向载荷

transverse module 端面模数（端面齿距除以圆周率π所得到的商，以毫米计）

transverse path of contact 端面啮合线（简称 path of contact，啮合线，平行轴圆柱齿轮副中的任意一对相啮合的端面齿廓，在其整个啮合过程中，其瞬时接触点在端平面上的运动轨迹，称为端面啮合线。在渐开线齿轮副中，其端面啮合线与两相啮齿廓在其接触点处的、介于从动轮的齿顶圆与主动轮的齿顶圆两者之间的那一段公法线相重合）

transverse pattern （胎面）横向花纹（按轮胎周向排列的胎面花纹）

transverse pitch 端面齿距（简称齿距，指两个相邻而同侧的端面齿廓之间的分度圆弧长，不应称为周节）

transverse plane 端平面（在圆柱齿轮或圆柱蜗杆上，垂直于齿轮轴线的平面）

transverse pressure angle at a point 任意点的端面压力角（简称任意点压力角，在端平面内，过端面齿廓上任意点处的径向直线与齿廓在该点外的切线所夹的锐角）

transverse profile 端面齿廓（圆柱齿轮和圆柱涡轮齿面被端平面所截的截线）

transverse rib 横肋，横向加强筋，横向肋

transverse section 横断面（横剖面）

transverse shear 横向剪切力

transverse slide 横向滑动

transverse space width 端面齿槽宽（槽宽，在端平面上，一个齿槽的两侧齿廓之间的分度圆弧长）

transverse spring （汽车悬架系的）横置（钢板）弹簧

transverse stiffness 横向刚度

transverse strain 横向应变（垂直于试样纵向轴的平面上的线性应变）

transverse strength 横向强度（如：抗弯强度，挠曲强度）

transverse stress 横向应力

transverse swirl 横涡涡流，横向涡流

transverse tooth thickness 端面齿厚（对于圆柱齿轮，指其端平面上，一个齿的两侧端面齿廓之间的分度圆弧长。对于鼓形齿，是在鼓形齿面的最高处度量）

transverse vibration applied to the human body 作用于人体的横向振动

transverse wall 横隔板（= cross wall）

transverse warping 横向翘曲

transverse windshield wiper 横刮式风窗玻璃刮水器

transveyer 运送机，输送机

TRANSYT 交通网络研究工具（英国交通与道路研究所20世纪60年代开发的电子计算机交通网络研究系统名，Traffic Network Study Tool 的简称）

trap ①（油、水、汽、尘、液、污物、射线、火焰、电子、电波、噪音、杂质等的）捕集、阻隔、滤除装置 ②捕集、阻挡、截集、吸收、分离

trap bottom wagon 活底箱式货车

trap circuit ①吸收滤波器电路 ②陷波电路

trap crust 冻雪的松脆表层

trap door 活门，活板门

trapezium ①不规则四边形（指无平行边的四边形）②梯形（指仅两边平行而另两边不平行的四边形）

trapezoidal waveform 梯形波

trapezoid belt 梯形传动带

trapezoid divisor （车身外形线的）梯形分割绘制法

trapezoid thread 梯形螺纹

trap oxidizer （微粒）捕集器氧化装置（捕集器补燃器，为了防止捕集装置堵塞而在一定条件下燃烧捕集装置捕集到的微粒物的装置）

trapped air-fuel ratio （缸内）实际存留空-燃比（即汽缸内实际保留下来的空气质量和实际保留下来的燃油质量之比）

trapped dirt 收集的污物

trapped-line pressure valve 管路压力保持阀（停止使用制动器时使液压制动管路中保持某规定值液压的单向阀）

trapped particles （滤清器）捕集的微粒

trapping efficiency ①有效充气率（$\eta_{tr} = W_c / W_{hc}$. 式中：W_c—换气终了后实际保留在汽缸内的新鲜充量的质量；W_{hc}—换气期间流入汽缸的全部新鲜充量的质量）②扫气利用系数（见 scavenging utilization efficiency）

trash packer 带液压压实装置的垃圾汽车

trash truck 垃圾车，= garbage (-removal) truck

trasmission efficiency ①变速器效率 ②传动（系）效率

trauma severity （撞车后的）人体外伤严重程度

travel ①移动，移位 ②行驶，行走，行进 ③旅行 ④行程（指机械零件执行某项作业时的移动距离，如：活塞行程，= piston stroke）

travelable 可移动的，活动的，便于通行的

travel direction 行驶方向，运动的方向（= direction of travel）

travel efficiency 行程效率，行走效率（牵引能力的一项指标，指有载荷时驱动轮每转一转的车辆前进距离和无载荷时驱动轮每转一转的车辆前进距离之百分比）

traveler information system 旅行者信息系统（ITS 的一项分支，亦称驾驶人信息系统，= driver information system）

travelled distance 已驶过的距离

travelling (bridge) crane 移动式（桥式）起重机

travelling comfort （汽车）乘坐舒适性

travelling contact 活动触点，动接触

travelling gauntry 移动式龙门起重机

travelling portal jib crane 移动式悬臂吊车

travelling speed 行驶速度

travelling time 行驶时间（运行时间，路程时间，运程时间）

travelling wave 行进波

travelling-wave tube 行波管（微波信号放大的真空管）

Travelpilot 行车向导（由 Etak 和 Bosch 公司联合研制的第二代 Navigator 产品的商品名，见 Etak Navigator）

travel sensor 行程传感器

travel speed 行程车速（车辆行驶里程与时间之比。行驶时间包括有效行驶时间及途中停车和延误的时间，但不包括起、终点掉头等路外停车及延误的时间）

travel time 出行时间，旅程时间（= journey time）

travel to stop 制动停车距离

travel trailer 旅行挂车，旅宿挂车（一般指拖在轿车后，供旅宿生活用的厢式挂车，= tourist trailer）

travel way 行车路线，运行路线；行车道

traverser ①停车场内横向移动车辆的装置②活动平台③转车台④横梁，横臂，横挡；横过物

Trav Tek Driver Information system 〔美〕Trav Tek 驾驶员信息系统（集卫星导航、线路选择和引导、实时交流信息、旅行者信息、蜂窝电话服务于一体的车载屏显信息系统）

tray ①盘，槽，盘状容器②（盘状）底壳，底板，底架，托架，托盘

tray type frame 盘式车架（半承载式车架，车架与部分车身底板制成一体，= semi frameless construction, platform type frame）

TRB （美国交通科学研究院下属）运输研究会（Transportation Research Board）

TRC ①牵引力控制系统（traction control 的简称）②运输研究中心（Transportation Research Center 的简称）

TRC actuator solenoid 牵引力控制系统执行器电磁阀

TRC brake main relay 牵引力控制系统制动主继电器

TRC sub-throttle relay 牵引力控制系统副节气门继电器

TRC sub-throttle step motor circuit 牵引力控制系统副节气门步进电动机电路

TRC system 牵引力控制系统（traction control system 的简称。通过对车轮实施制动或降低发动机输出功率等方式控制车轮上的牵引力，防止起步或加速时，车轮因牵引力大于路面附着力而滑转）

TRC·VSC system （丰田公司复合动力车的）牵引力控制·车辆稳定性控制系统（通过对前、后轮驱动力和制动力作最佳控制，以保证车辆在加速和转向时的方向稳定性，见 TRC, VSC）

TREAD 〔美〕运输车辆召回强化、义务与提供真实文件法（Transportation Recall Enhancement, Accountability and Documentation Act 的简称，美国保护消费者权益的一项大法，规定强化缺陷车召回、厂家的责任和义务，以及厂家必须向用户提供与真实情况相符的说明文件等）

tread ①（轮胎）胎面（轮胎胎冠部位缓冲层，或带束层，或帘布层以上的、与地路接触的外层胶层）②（轮胎的）胎面花纹表面③车辙，轮辙④〔美〕轮距，轨距（= 英 track）⑤履带

treadable tire 胎面可再生的轮胎

tread air groove resonance 胎面空气沟槽共振（轮胎道路噪音源之一）

tread arc width 胎面弧宽（沿胎面

轮廓测量的轮胎两角之间的弧长)
tread axis 轮距中线
tread bar contact area (轮胎)胎面凸起花纹接地面积
tread bar contact pressure (轮胎)凸起花纹接地压力
tread bar profile (轮胎)凸起花纹截面轮廓
tread bars 胎面磨损指示条(当胎面严重磨损到必须更换时,该条显露)
tread base 胎面基部(胎面花纹沟底部以下至缓冲层或带束层或帘布层之间的胶层,分为基部胶和过渡胶)
tread base deflection 胎面基部偏移
tread base rotation 胎面基部转动
tread block 胎面花纹块(胎面花纹相互之间有一定距离,而又各自独立或部分连接的凸起部分)
tread bracing 增强胎面(在胎面内部掺入其他增强材料所构成的胎面)
tread cap 胎面行驶面(通常指胎面花纹沟底部以上地面正常的接触的胶层)
tread caterpillar 履带
tread change (悬架产生挠度时的)轮距变化
tread chord width 胎面弦宽
tread contact length 轮胎接地面长度(通常在车轮中心平面上测定)
tread contact width 轮胎接地面宽度(在规定的荷载和充气压力下,侧偏角为零时,沿与车轮轴线平行的方向,测得的轮胎接地面两侧边间的最大距离)
tread contour 胎面轮廓(轮胎按规定压力充气后未加载时其胎面横截面的形状,胎面花纹凹处略而不计)
tread cushioning layer 胎面缓冲层
tread depth 胎面花纹深度(指花纹凹底面至其两相邻花纹表面公切线间的距离)
tread detachment 胎面剥离
tread footprint 胎面印痕
tread gauge 胎面厚度规(胎面磨损量规)
tread groove 胎面花纹沟(胎面花纹块或花纹条之间凹下的部分)
tread groove width 胎面花纹沟宽度(两相邻的胎面花纹块或花纹条之间的花纹沟,在胎面行驶外表面上的距离)
tread hysteresis 轮胎胎面滞后阻力
treadle drive 踏板驱动(= pedal drive)
treadle effort 踏板力(= pedal effort)
treadle valve 踏板操纵的阀门
tread life (轮胎)胎面使用寿命
tread lug 胎面突起花纹,胎面突纹
tread noise 胎面噪声(车辆行驶时轮胎胎面花纹与路面相互作用而产生的各种除啸叫和拍打声外的噪声)
tread pattern 胎面花纹(模压或刻制在外胎胎面上的凹凸部分)
tread pattern depth 胎面花纹深度(胎面花纹沟底部到胎面行驶面外表面的垂直距离)
tread pattern groove 胎面花纹的凹槽
tread pattern pitch 胎面花纹节距(沿胎面中心线,一个完整胎面花纹的循环单元长度)
tread pattern pitch variation (tyre)胎面花纹变间距轮胎(胎面花纹不均匀,间距变化的轮胎,以降低行驶噪音)
tread pattern plan 胎面花纹展开图(胎面花纹展开的平面图)
tread profile 胎面横断面形状(从横截面观察,看到的轮胎胎面的形状)

tread radius 胎面（横向弧度）半径
tread range 轮距变化范围
tread regrooving 胎面再刻花（标有"可再刻花"标志的轮胎，当胎面磨损到规定深度时，在胎面胶上再刻花纹或修正花纹形状的工艺）
tread reinforcement fillet 胎面花纹加强筋条
tread rib 胎面花纹条（胎面花纹连续的条状凸起部分，亦称 tread bar）
tread rig 胎面横向肋式花纹
tread-rubber （轮胎的）胎面胶
tread running surface 轮胎滚动面
tread separation 胎面脱壳，胎面剥层，胎面剥落
tread shoulder 胎肩（见 shoulder）
tread sipe 胎面花纹细缝（胎面花纹凸起部分上的细缝，其宽度通常不大于 1.5mm）
tread surface （轮胎）胎面花纹表面（= tread face）
tread thickness 胎面高度
tread void 胎面花纹沟槽（= tread groove）
tread wear grade （表示轮胎耐磨性的数字）标号
tread wear indicator 胎面磨耗标记（指示胎面已经磨损到必须进行翻新的标记）
tread-wear life 胎面磨损寿命
tread wear per mile 每英里行驶里程的胎面磨耗量
tread-wear-X （某些轮胎胎壁上标示的）胎面耐磨性指数（X 为加在 tread-wear-后面带的数字，该数字越大越耐磨）
tread width 胎面宽度
treated water 经处理的水
treatment 处理
treble ①3倍的，三重的②尖锐刺耳的（噪声）③（最）高音的
treeing 树枝状结晶（树枝状组织，不规则金属淀积，海绵状金属沉积物）
tree-like 树枝状的（组织）
trees building method 树枝法（为求得最优解常用的一种网络分析方法）
trellis work 栅格结构（桁架结构）
tremble 振颤，摇摆
trembler ①振动子②断续器③蜂鸣器
trembler coil ①振动器线圈②（将低压变换成高压输出的）感应升压线圈
trembling 振颤的
trench 沟，槽
trench crossing capacity 越沟能力（通过沟壕的能力，亦称 trench-spanning capacity）
trend 倾向，趋势；走向，动向，发展方向
trend of staircase （客车）车梯倾斜度
trends anticipation 发展趋势预测
trend term 趋势项（测量中若存在系统性因素的干扰，测量记录数据会呈现某种缓慢变化的趋势。通常把连续信号中变化周期大于记录时间的频率分量称为趋势项）
trespass （原意为侵占、侵犯、侵害，特别是未经允许侵入私人住宅、土地。写在公共汽车登车口上的"No Trespass"则是指：不得）强行拥挤、插队或不遵守规则、未经允许窜上公共汽车
trestle ①支架，台架，门架，高架②高架桥，栈桥（= trestle bridge）
TRI ①技术报告说明书（technical report instruction）②三极管（triode 的简称）
trial ①试验，实验；尝试，探索②试验性的，尝试性的，探索性的
trial(-) and(-) error method 试错法（尝试法，试算法，逐步逼近法）

trial and error test 渐近校正试验（试探试验，边试边改试验，试改试验，逐次逼近试验）

trial drive 试车，试驱动，试驾驶

trial ground 试验场

trial installation 试验设备（= test installation）

trial operation 试运转，试验性的使用

trial speed 试车速度

trial trip 试车行程，试车路线

triangle 三角形，三角板，三角铁

triangle belt 三角（形断面）传动带

triangle collision 三角碰撞（三车碰撞）

triangle crossing （道路）三岔路口

triangle of velocities 速度三角形（= velocity triangle）

triangular asperities technique 三角形凸点密封技术（在刚体密封件的表面上，按一定的排列方法，加工出很多密布的三角形凸点，用以密封滑油）

triangular belt 三角（形断面）传动带（= V-belt）

triangular cam 三角凸轮

triangular cast-iron end piece （转子发动机三片式径向密封件的）三角形铸铁端片（三角形铸铁副片，铸铁密封楔，铸铁密封片）

triangular corner seal （转子发动机三片式径向密封件的）三角形角密封片（三角副片，密封楔，三角角片）

triangular divisor （车身外形线的）三角形分割绘制法

triangular rotor 三角转子（三角形旋转活塞）

triangular thread 三角（形断面）螺纹，V形螺纹

triangular waveform 三角波形

TRIAS （日本运输省）交通安全与公害研究所形式认证试验标准（Traffic Safety and Nuisance Research Institute's Type Approved Test Standard）

triaxial 三轴的（三度的，三维的，三元的，空间的）

triaxial load cell 三轴向负载传感器（可将相互垂直的三个轴向 x、y、z 的负载转变为电信号输出的传感元件）

triaxial road simulator 三轴向道路模拟机（从三个方向同时对汽车激振，模拟汽车在道路上行驶时所受振动的试验装置）

triaxial stress 三维应力（三度空间应力）

tri-axle drive 三驱动桥驱动

tri-axle semitrailer 并装三桥半挂车

tribochemistry 摩擦化学（研究机械运动副摩擦过程中的化学现象）

triboelectrification 摩擦起电

tribology 摩擦学，摩擦润滑学（研究相对运动的接触表面的摩擦、润滑、磨损等理论和技术的总称）

tribometer 摩擦计（摩擦力测量仪）

tribophysic 摩擦物理学

tricar ①（特指）乘客座位在车前部的机动三轮车 ②三轮汽车，机动三轮车（= three wheeler tricar, motor tricycle, three wheeled motor-car, three wheeler）

trichlene 三氯乙烯（的商品名）

trichloroethylene 三氯乙烯（$ClCH:CCl_2$，无色液体，相对密度1.459，溶点 $-70℃$，沸点 $87℃$，橡胶、油脂、树脂、涂料等的良好溶剂，为汽车零件等的有效清洗剂，但有毒性，亦称 trichlorethylene）

trichotomy law 三分律

trickle charge （蓄电池等的）连续补充充电，点滴式充电，弱电流充电，涓流充电（一般指用于补充电瓶在存放期间自放电所消耗的电量的充电）

triclene 三氯乙烯（= trichloroethylene）

tri-cresylphosphate （壳牌石油公司发明的一种）防早燃添加剂（见 ignition control additive）

trid equip 拖挂装置（= trailed equipment 的简称）

T-Ride suspension T 型悬架（Volvo 公司生产的货车上使用的一种悬架系统，由两片中间向上凸起、两端逐渐减薄的抛物线形钢板及支撑于两端的橡皮伸缩筒形弹簧组成）

tridrive 三（驱动）桥驱动

trier ①试验仪器②取（试）样工具

trig ①（制动）三角木②刹住，制住，用三角木制动

trigger ①触发器，启动器②触发电路③触发脉冲，触发信号④触发，启动

trigger amplifier 触发信号放大器（触发脉冲放大器）

trigger circuit 触发电路（指一种至少具有一个稳态或若干稳态或不稳态的电路，该电路设计成输入一个规定的脉冲便可实现所要求的状态转换）

trigger command 触发指令

trigger diode 触发二极管

triggering level 触发电平

triggering pulse 触发脉冲（亦称 trigger pulse，trigging pulse）

triggering time 触发时间

trigger point 触发点

trigger rod （松开驻车制动器等的）手操纵杆

trigger shaper 触发脉冲形成器

trigger sharpener 触发脉冲锐化电路

trigonal 三角的，三角形的

trihedral 有三面的，有三边的，三面角的，三棱的，三面体的；三面形

trihedral angle 三面角

trilinear coordinates 三线坐标（亦称 trilinear line coordinates，trilinear point coordinates）

trim ①纵向坡角②车辆翘头③平衡性，荷重、货物的平衡分配④（汽车外部和内部的）装潢，装饰物⑤修整，修饰⑥微调，调谐⑦（零件的）去毛刺，修边，倒角⑧整洁的，整齐的⑨准备，预备⑩（汽车的技术）状态

trim alloy 装饰用合金

trim angle of vehicle 车辆的后坐角

trim board 装饰板（车门内蒙板）

trim buck 车身内部的全尺寸模型（= interior buck）

trimer 三聚物

tri-metal （滑动轴承的）三层金属的轴瓦，三层式轴瓦（一般指用软钢皮作轴瓦底片，油膜合金为中间层，白色合金为表面减磨层，见 kelmet，white metal）

2,2,4-trimethylpentane 2,2,4—三甲基戊烷（C_8H_{18}），异辛烷（= isooctane）

trimmer 微调电容器

trimmer pressure modulator （自动变速器控制系统）缓冲控制阀（利用节气门开度控制压力调制缓冲压力的阀）

trimmer valve （液力变速器控制系统）缓冲阀（调整换挡元件或锁止离合器接合压力增长特性，从而降低换挡冲击的阀）

trimming ①修整，修饰②微调③（车身内部）装饰，装饰件（起装饰、美化作用的零件，亦称 finisher，molding，garnish）

trimming cloth 修饰用布料，装饰布料

trimming moment 平衡力矩

trimming screw 调整螺钉

trim molding （车身的）装饰花边，装饰线脚，装饰边带，装饰用冲压件

trim（of vehicle state） （汽车稳定状况）的工作点（由稳态汽车响应及控制或扰动输入决定。在非线性汽车的操纵分析中，工作点是用来分析汽车稳定性的参考点）

trim packing 汽车内部装潢用衬垫

trim panel 内装饰（衬）板

trim retainer （车厢）内部装潢饰条固定卡

trim strip 压条（起固定和装饰作用的条形零件，亦称 binding）

trim surface of sealing element 唇型油封修剪面，密封件的修整面

triniding 一种气体渗氮法（将零件置于成批型连续热处理炉内，在566℃下将氮扩散至零件表面层中）

trio 由三个组成的一组（如：由三种车型组成的一个车型系列）

triode 三极管（单栅管）

trip ①行程，旅程，运程，里程；短途交通，短途行驶②棘爪，卡锁③自动断开（断路，跳闸，分离）装置，解脱机构④释放，松开，断开，断路，触脱

Trip Computer 行车电脑（美国Cadillac公司生产的驾驶员信息系统的商品名，可向驾驶员提供平均车速、油耗、每单位行驶里程燃油费用、估计到达预定目的地的时间及距离、累计行驶里程等行车信息，见 driver-information system）

trip counter 短程里程器（具有调零功能的汽车短距离行驶里程计算装置，亦称 trip indicator）

triphibian （水、陆、空）三栖的

trip information （汽车）运行参数信息（如：行车时间、里程、油耗、车速等）

trip inspection （车辆）回场检查（出车后检查）

triple ①3倍的，三行的，三次的，三重的，由三个组成的②3倍数，三个一组③3倍于，使增至3倍

triple action skid control brake system 三级降压防滑制动系统（三级降压防抱死制动系统）

triple belt 三层传动带（= triple-ply belt）

triple-bend valve 三弯式气门嘴（嘴体杆部有三处弯曲的气门嘴）

triple-chamber air brake valve 三腔气制动阀（由三个膜片或活塞分别构成三个工作腔，用单一动作控制三条独立回路的气制动阀）

triple chrome piston ring 三面（顶面、底面、外圆面）镀铬型活塞环

triple circuit system 三管路系统（一般指前桥、后桥及挂车，分别由独立的三条管路控制的制动系统）

triple cone synchronizer （变速器的）三锥形同步器

triple-decker 三层立体交叉，三层道路

triple differential locks 三级差速器锁

triple diffuser （化油器的）三重喉管

triple-expansion engine 三级膨胀式发动机（蒸汽等工质顺序在三个尺寸逐步加大的高、中、低压缸内膨胀，驱动同一曲轴，见 multiple-expansion engine）

triple fabric 三层织物（= three-ply fabric）

triple geared drive 三联齿轮传动

triple horn set 三音喇叭（组）（= three horn set）

triple jet 三孔喷嘴（三束喷嘴）

triple mode catalytic converter 三元催化转换器

triple mode emission control system 三作用式排放控制系统（一种在起动、正常运转及使用稀混合气时分别采用不同方式实现废气催化反应及再燃烧的排气净化系统）

trip length 旅程长度（路程距离）

triple plate clutch 三片式离合器（= three-plate clutch）

triple-ply belt 三层式传动带（triple belt）

triple point ①三相点（物质的三相能够同时存在的温度和压力）②三重点，三重切点

triple point of water 水的三相点温度（在密封的真空烧瓶中，同时存在纯冰、液态水和水蒸气时的平衡状态温度，0.01°C 或 293.16K）

triple-post lift 三柱式车库用举升器

triple-reduction axle （重型汽车的）三级减速驱动桥

triple reduction gear 三级减速器

triple-roller wave generator （谐波齿轮）三滚轮波发生器（在滚轮架上装有三个均布滚轮的波发生器）

triple-safe air brake system 三合一安全气制动系（常用、紧急、驻车制动共用同一个制动器，但分别由三个系统控制）

triple screw 三纹螺旋（三头螺纹）

triple sealing system 三层密封系统（如：豪华轿车车门的密封系统）

triple seat 三人座椅

triple servo brake 带有加力器的三蹄块式制动器

triple start worm 三线蜗杆

Triple steel 高速钢（$W_4Cr_4V_2Mo_2$，碳 0.9%，锰 0.4%，铬 3.5%~4%，钼 2.5%，钒 2.5%，钨 3.5%~4%）

triplet ①三座汽车②三人座③三件一套④三合一⑤T形接头，三通接头，三通管⑥三联的

triple-thread screw 三头螺纹螺钉，三线螺纹，三纹螺旋

triple-tone horn 三（重）音（调）喇叭

triple-trailer combination 三挂车汽车列车

triple valve 三通阀，三通开关

triplex ①三倍的，三重的，三部的，三联的；有三种作用的，发生三种效果的②（汽车风窗用）三层式安全玻璃（原为一种夹层结构的高强度安全玻璃的商品名"Triplex"，现泛指三层式夹层安全玻璃，亦称 triplex glass, triplex safety glass）

trip map 行程图（路程图）

trip meter （通常组合在车速表内的）行程表（亦称 trip mileage counter, trip odometer, trip recorder，可以随时调零，记录某一段行程的里程）

trip mileage indicator 旅程记录仪（旅行里程自动显示装置）

Tripminder 行车电脑（福特公司商品名，= trip computer）

tripod ①三脚架，三脚台，三脚支撑物（= tripod rest）②三面角③（三球销万向节的）三销架（见 spider②）

tripod jack 三脚举升器

trip odometer 里程计数器，旅程记录表（可手动归零，因而可记录并显示车辆区段行驶里程的装置，亦称 trip recorder）

tripod universal joint 三球销万向节（亦称 three ball and trunnion universal joint，在同一个平面内通过三个径向均匀分布的装有球环的三销架将壳体与轴连接起来以允许轴向相对滑动的径向自承式等速万向节，亦写作 tri-pot universal joint，简称 tri-pot joint）

tripolar lead-cobalt battery 三极式铅-钴（蓄）电池

tri-pot joint 三球销万向节（见 tripod universal joint）

tripper ①自动断开（断路，分离，解脱，转换）装置②自卸车③卸到机构④卸料（撒抛）装置

tripping ①断开，解脱，脱钩；倾翻②断开的，脱钩的；倾翻的

tripping car 自动倾卸车

tripping device ①跳闸机构②脱扣装置

trip ring ①挡圈,弹簧挡圈②扣环,定位环③开口环

TRIP steel 相变诱导塑性钢(先进高强度钢的一种,transformation induced plastic steel 的简称,主要组织是铁素体、贝氏体和5%~15%的残余奥氏体,具有高延伸率,见 AHSS)

trip trigger 制动掣子(制动棘轮爪)

trirectangular quadrilateral 三直角的四边形

tri-rotor pump 三转子泵

TRIS 交通运输研究信息系统(Transportation Research Information System)

trisection of an angle 角的三等分,三等分角

trislot 带有三条切槽的(如:具有三道环槽的活塞)

tristimulus values (of a light) (光线的)三刺激值(三色值,形成三色制中任一标准颜色所需的三种原色的各原色值)

tritanopia (一种)蓝黄色盲(将蓝色和黄色看成灰色,对蓝色的光感较正常视力弱)

tritium ①氚(T)②超重氢(H_3)

tritone horn 三音喇叭(用三只具有不同音调的喇叭组成的喇叭组)

trivial name 俗名

TRLA [美](载)货(汽)车租赁协会(Truck Renting and Leasing Association)

trld equip 拖挂装置(trailed equipment 的简称)

trochoid 摆线(亦称旋轮线,为外摆线"epicycloid",长幅外摆线"prolate epicycloid",短幅外摆线"curtate epicycloid"和摆线"cycloid",长幅摆线"prolate cycloid",短幅摆线"curtate cycloid",内摆线"hypocycloid",长幅内摆线"prolate hypocycloid",短幅内摆线"curtate hypocyloid"的总称。当说明汪克式三角活塞转子发动机内腔的型线和转子三个角运动时的轨迹时,是指其中的一个滚动圆沿一固定圆的外侧作外切线滚动,且该固定圆半径正好是滚动圆半径的两倍,此滚动圆半径上的一点 P 的轨迹,即上述特定条件下的短幅外摆线"curtate epicycloid"或因其形状,称双弧长短轴圆外旋轮线,P 点称创成点"generating point",P 至滚动圆中心的距离称偏心距"eccentric distance",滚动圆中心与固定圆中心的距离称创成半径"generating radius")

trochoidal rotor (汪克三角活塞式旋转发动机的)短幅外摆线型(或称双弧长短幅圆外旋轮线型)三角转子(指其外形是由其缸体短幅外摆线内腔型面导出的三角形旋转活塞,以保证该活塞运动时,三个角始终与缸体内腔表面接触,见 trochoid)

trochoid chatter wear (转子发动机的)旋轮线缸壁震纹磨损,旋轮线型面震颤磨损

trochoid coating (转子发动机的)旋轮线缸壁镀盖层

trochoid deposits (转子发动机的)缸壁沉积物

trochoid housing (转子发动机的)旋轮线缸体

trochoid pump 旋轮线泵(见 internal external rotary pump, gerotor pump)

trochoid surface (转子发动机的)旋轮线缸壁面

trochoid varnish (转子发动机上)旋轮线缸壁漆状亮膜

trochoid waist （外）旋轮线型细腰部

trochoid wear treatment （转子发动机的）旋轮线缸壁抗磨处理

Troland 特罗蓝德（网膜的受光度单位，为通过 1mm² 的瞳孔看亮度为 1 新烛光/米² 的表面时网膜接受的光亮度，简称 Trol）

trolley ①手推车，（装有脚轮的）小车②（美由架空线供电的城市载客）电车（= 英 train）③（城市电车与架空电源线间的）触轮

trolley track ①触轮滑轨②门轮滑轨

troop carrier 士兵运输车

troop-carrying 军事运输；军事运输的

troop-carrying coach 军用客车

troop-carrying company 为军事运输服务的汽车运输连，部队汽车运输连

troop transporter 装甲运兵车

troostite 屈氏体（金相组织）

troosto-sorbite 屈氏-索贝体（金相组织）

tropic 热带；热带的

tropicalization test 热带气候适应性试验（在人工模拟热带气候条件下的试验，亦称 tropical trial，= hot-weather trial）

Tropical Test Center ［美］（汽车）热带试验中心（简称 TTC）

tropical test chamber 人工热带气候试验室

tropical year 回归年（atrop, 太阳连续两次通过平均春分点所经历的时间）

trottoir 人行道（法语）

trouble 故障，事故，毛病，损坏，麻烦

trouble car 故障检修车

trouble crew 故障车救援队

trouble finder 故障探测仪

trouble-free life 无故障使用期

trouble-free performance 无故障性能（保持无故障运行的能力）

trouble hunting 故障检测，故障诊断（找出故障所在或故障原因）

trouble lamp 故障信号灯（故障指示灯）

trouble-locating 故障探测（确定发生故障的部位）

trouble location 故障部位

trouble-proof 防故障的

trouble-proof tyre 防爆轮胎（见 puncture-proof tyre）

trouble recorder 故障记录仪

trouble removal 故障排除

trouble-saving 预防故障的；故障清除的

trouble-shooter 故障诊断装置

trouble-shooting oscilloscope 探测故障用示波器（故障诊断用示波器）

trouble-shooting time 寻找故障所需时间

trouble spots ①故障部位②（结构的）薄弱部位

trouble tracing 故障排查

trouble truck （排除故障的）检修服务车

trough ①沟槽，凹槽；水槽，油槽②盘，盆，浅长的容器③波谷④槽形的

trough method （故障分析的）平均故障率法（亦称 range/mean method，指在规定的考察行程内，故障发生次数与累计行程之比）

trough-shaped pavement 凹形路面

trough truck 带槽式车厢的货车

troy ounce 金衡盎司（代号 troy oz, 1 troy oz = 1/12 troy lb = 480 grains）

troy weights 金衡（衡量金、银、宝石等，金衡制的基本单位为金衡磅"troy pound"，金衡制在英国已为非法定衡制，在美国仍为法定衡制，1 troy pound = 0.3732kg = 0.82286 常衡磅 = 13.1577 常衡盎司；金衡制

内：1 金衡磅 = 12 金磅盎司"ounce"，1 金衡盎司 = 20 本尼威特"pennyweight"，1 本尼威特 = 24 格令"grains"）

TR pressure switch assembly 自动变速器挡位压力开关总成（其中 TR 为 transmission range "挡位"的简称，指自动变速器的驻车挡、倒挡、各前进挡等，亦称挡区的压力开关，用来向电子控制模块发送换挡手柄的位置信息）

TRQ 总需要量（total requirements）

TRRL ［英］运输和道路研究试验所（Transport and Road Research Laboratory）

TRS ①（底特律公司柴油机电子控制系统的）喷油正时基准（信号）传感器（timing reference sensor 的简称，电子控制模块根据其电压信号确定喷油器电磁线圈的喷油接通时刻，相当于汽油机电子控制系统中的 crankshaft position sensor）②试验规范（test requirement specification）

T（R）SP 挂车稳定性（控制）程序（trailer roll-over stability programmer 的简称）

TRS +1 system （美福特汽车公司的）变速器控制真空点火提前及废气再循环系统（由变速器的挡位控制真空点火系及废气再循环系统，见 TRS system）

TRS system （美福特汽车公司的）变速器真空点火提前控制系统（transmission regulated spark control system，由真空控制阀、温控开关及变速器开关组成，其作用为仅在高速挡时真空提前系统才能起作用）

truck ①载货汽车、货车（1896 年德国 Daimler 工厂研制成一种专门载货的汽车，命名 truck，因而得名，美国一直沿用，= 英 lorry）②装上货车，用货车运输；驾驶货车③货车的

Truck Body and Equipment Association Inc ［美］载货汽车车身与设备协会（简称 TBEA）

Truck & Bus Transportation ［澳］载货汽车与客车运输（杂志）（简称 T&BT）

truck cab levelling 货车驾驶室自动调平

truck capacity 货车的装载能力（载货汽车装载量）

truck chassis 货车底盘（一般指由车架、车桥、悬架、发动机、传动系统及其他有关机件组成的不包括驾驶室、叶子板和车身，虽不完整，但已可行驶的货车基体）

truck electrical center 货车电控中心

truck elevator 货车（自带的）升降设备（货车举升器）

truck equivalency 货车当量（相当于一辆货车的轿车等车辆的数量，用于计算交通容量）

trucker 货车驾驶员；货车运输从业人员

truck evaporator 载货汽车（驾驶室空调系统用的）蒸发器

truck heater 货车驾驶室暖风装置（货车暖风机）

truck hoist 汽车式起重机，汽车吊

trucking company 汽车货运公司

trucking industry 货（运汽）车工业，货车制造业

truck leasing firm 载货汽车租赁公司

truck-leasing industry 货车租赁业

truck-like all-drive tractor 货车型全轮驱动牵引车

truck loader 货车式装载机

truck mixer 混凝土搅拌车

truck motor lorry 载货汽车

truck-mounted launcher 汽车式火箭发射装置（安装在载货汽车底盘上的发射装置）

truck (mounted) shovel 汽车挖土机（装在汽车上的挖土铲）

truck plant 载货汽车制造厂，货车制造厂

truck population 货车保有量

truck productivity 货运汽车运输生产率（货车每单位时间内所完成的货运量或货物周转量）

truck racing 货车赛（货车锦标赛，1984年欧洲始创的一种赛车爱好者的业余赛事，由普通货车驾驶员驾驶不装货箱，只有发动机和底盘的货车参赛，参赛车按排量分为三级）

Truck Renting and Leasing Association ［美］载货汽车租赁协会（简称TRLA）

truck-road transportation 公路干线运输（= trunk transportation）

Truck Safety Equipment Institute （美国）载货汽车安全设备学会（简称TSEI）

truck scale 货车磅，货车地秤

truck scraper 货车型铲运机

TruckSim 载货汽车（性能测试用数学）模拟模型

truck spreader （装在货车上的）撒布装置（撒布车）

truck stop 载货汽车停车场地

truck tanker 油罐车，油槽车

truck-tire remover 载货汽车轮胎拆卸工具

truck ton production （汽车）车吨（位）产量（货运汽车在统计期内，平均每个吨位所完成的货物周转量：车吨产量 = 货物总周转量/货运车吨位总数）

truck-tractor 货车牵引车（一般指半挂车的牵引车，本身承载半挂车的一部分载荷和质量）

truck tractor fifth wheel coupling displacement 半挂牵引车转盘式牵引架的（前后方向）可移动长度

truck-tractor semitrailer 载货牵引车半挂车

truck trailer 载货汽车挂车（= lorry trailer，包括全挂车"full trailer"与半挂车"semi-trailer"。当无说明时，一般指全挂车）

truck-trailer combination 货车-挂车列车，货车带挂列车

truck tyre 载重汽车轮胎（主要用于载货汽车、客车及其挂车上的充气轮胎。分为重型、中型和轻型等三类）

truck washing system 货车清洗装置

truck with end dump body 后倾卸式自卸车（= rear-dump truck）

truck with loading crane 带起重设备的货车（装有臂架式随车起重机，能实现货物自行装卸的汽车）

true annealing 全退火

true course 正北方向行驶的路线

true epitrochoid 理论外旋轮线（相对实际缸壁旋轮线而言，即滚动圆在基圆上滚动时，创成点所行的轨迹，见 epitrochoid）

true horsepower 实际功率

true joint angle 万向节夹角（万向节输入轴和输出轴的旋转轴线相交所构成的锐角。该角应在两轴线所在的平面内测量）

trueness 精确度，准确度；真实性

true proof stress of non-proportional shear strain 真实规定非比例扭转应力（扭转试验中，圆形试样标距部分外表面上的非比例切应变达到规定数值时，按刘德维克-卡曼公式计算的切应力）

true representation 真实的表现（表示），准确的表现（表示）

true representation of surface 曲面的准确表示

true-running 纯转动（无径向跳动的转动）

true specific heat 实际比热

true strain 真应变（在轴向加力试验中，试样瞬间标距与原始标距之比的自然对数）

true stress 实际应力（实际应力，当连续体内某一微小面积 ΔA，由于荷载作用而产生变形 $\Delta A'$ 时，形成内力 ΔF，该面积上的实际应力 $=\Delta F/\Delta A'$，亦称 actual stress。而 $\Delta F/\Delta A$，则称 nominal stress "标称应力"）

true time 真实时间

true torsional strength 真实抗扭强度（扭转试验中，圆形试样扭断时，按刘德维克—卡曼公式计算的最大切应力）

true-to-shape 形状正确的（有正确断面的）

true-to-size 尺寸准确的

true-up 校正，校准，调整

true value（of a quantity）（量的）真值（表征在研究某量时所处条件下严密定义的量的值）

truing 调整，校正，整形

truing face 修正面

truing tool 修正工具（= dressing tool）

truing unit 整形装置，精密修整设备

trumpet ①漏斗状筒，喇叭管，喇叭口②喇叭声，像喇叭的声音

trumpet grade separation 喇叭形立体交叉（通常为三路 T 型的立体交叉只有一边有套形连接匝道）

trumpet interchange 喇叭形互通式立体交叉口（通常三路相交只有一边有套形连接匝道的互通式立体交叉口）

trumpet projector 扬声筒（把膜片振动产生的声音加以扩大并传播到远处的筒形件）

trumpet-type axle housing 整体式桥壳（与主减速器铸成一体，并在两个或多个铸件的接合处用螺栓连接起来构成一整体的桥壳，亦称 Banjo axle housing）

trumpet type horn 筒形电喇叭（具有细长扬声筒的电喇叭）

truncate ①截断；修剪，缩短②削去头的；截面的；缩短了的

truncated cone 斜截头圆锥体（斜截锥）

truncated corner ①修圆的角②抄近路转角

truncated cylinder 斜截柱

truncation 截去，剪断，缩短，切断，尖端钝化

trundle ①脚轮②带脚轮的手推车

trunk ①干线，干路，主干道②总管道③（电信）连接总线，中继线④[美]（轿车）后行李舱（= rear baggage compartment, 亦称 boot, luggage compartment, luggage hold）⑤（气垫车）裙部⑥干线的⑦箱形的

trunk depth （气垫车）支撑表面至喷嘴之间的距离

trunk drag （气垫车）空气垫与不平路面的摩擦阻力

trunk engine 单动式发动机（= single-acting engine）

trunk highway 干线公路（= main highway）

trunking ①（导线）槽②管道

trunk line 干线，（公路）主干线，躯干线（人体躯干的中心线）

trunk-piston engine 筒形活塞式发动机（用活塞销连接活塞与连杆的发动机）

trunk rack 行李架

trunk roominess （轿车的）行李舱容积

trunk vehicle 干线长途运输用车辆

trunnion ①枢轴，耳轴，摆动轴，转动轴②（万向节）十字轴③摆动支座④轴颈

trunnion axle 枢轴式车桥（指中央悬架梁式车桥，在侧倾中，如：在

1696

trunnion base 平衡轴支座（固定在车架上，用以支撑钢板弹簧及平衡轴等的构件），心轴支座（见 trunning shaft）

trunnion bearing （万向节十字轴）轴颈（滚针）轴承

trunnion block 万向节十字架总成

trunnion bracket 枢轴支架

trunnion cross 万向节十字轴

trunnion joint 球销式万向接（= muff coupling joint）

trunnion shaft （货车双轴并装式后桥平衡悬架中支撑平衡臂或起平衡臂作用的钢板弹簧的）心轴（亦称平衡轴"equalizing shaft"）

trunnion spring （转子发动机径向密封的）密封销弹簧

Trurck Trailer MFRS, Inc [美] 载货汽车挂车制造商协会（简称 TTMI）

truss ①桁架，构架②一捆，一束

trussed beam 格构梁（桁架）

trussed pole 桁构式直柱

truss frame ①桁架②桁架式构架③（汽车）桁架式车架

truss panel 桁架边板，构架加强板

trust ①信任②联合公司（托拉斯）

truth ①（配合的）精确度②（安装的）准确性③真实，真理，真相

truth table （用于数字变量间的关系的）真值表（给出一个或多个数字自变量与一个或多个数字因变量之间的逻辑关系的表格）

truth value 真值（指真值表中列出的输入或输出的值）

try 试验，试用，尝试；企图，力图

try and error method 试凑法（逐步逼近法，= cut and try method）

try cock 试验开关（= test cock）

T/S 试验台架（test stand）

TS ①锥形柄（taper shank）②温度开关（temperature switch）③抗拉强度（tensile strength）④工具钢（tool steel）⑤绝密（top secret）⑥追踪系统（tracking system）⑦瞬态，非稳定状态（transient state）

TSCV （进气系统中的）涡流控制阀（tumble-swirl control valve 的简称，见 vortex）

TSE 试验辅助设备（test support equipment）

T-section ①T（字）形断面②T形（钢）材

TSEI [美] 载货汽车安全设备学会（Truck Safety Equipment Institute）

T-shape（d） T形的，T形截面的

T-shaped apex seal （转子发动机）T型径向密封件

TSI ①（有两种怠速转速的）双速怠速（系统）（two speed idle 的简称）②[美] 交通安全学会（Traffic Safety Institute 的简称）

tsi 吨/英寸² （tons per square inch）

TSI engine 涡轮增压式火花点火（汽油缸内直接喷射式）发动机（turbocharged spark ignition engine 的简称）

"T" simbol sign T形交叉标志

T-slot T形槽

T-slot piston 裙部带T形槽切的活塞

TSM 见 trailer sway mitigation

TSNRI 交通安全与公害研究所（Traffic Safety and Nuisance Research Institute）

T-socket T形套管，T形套筒

TSOP 丰田超级链烯烃聚合物

TSOSC 试验装置操作信号变换器（test set operational signal converter）

TSP ①时间分隔法（分时法，见 time slot principle）②（大气中）悬浮粉尘总量（total suspended partides 的简称，见 API）

T-spoked wheel T形（三辐条）转向盘

T-square 丁字尺

TSR ［美］交通安全研究公司（Traffic Safety Research Corporation）

TSS 转矩分配系统（见 torque-split system）

TST 测验，试验（test 的简称）

T-steel 丁字钢

TTA （丰田公司开发的）进气空气温度传感器（商品名，TOYOTA thermo-air 的简称）

TTC ①丰田总合排气净化系统（Toyota Total Clean System 的简称）②［美］（汽车）热带试验中心（Tropical Test Center）

TT CAN 时间触发通信 CAN（time-trigger CAN 的简称，为 CAN 的升级版，因为 CAN 协议并未改变，故在同一物理层上既可实现传输时间触发报文，也可实现传输事件触发报文，见 CAN）

TTCAN （汽车的）时间触发控制器局域网（Time trigger CAN 的简称）

TTCE 齿隙综合误差（包括齿厚的变化，齿廓的偏差，相邻齿节的误差，齿的调整误差等，tooth to tooth composite error 的简称）

TTE ①临时试验设备（temporary test equipment）②挂车试验设备（trailer test equipment）③设备暂定目录（tentative tables of equipments）④传动系总误差（total transmission error）

TTF 战术载货汽车车队（tactical truck fleet）

T ticket 交通违章传票（= traffic ticket）

TTL 晶体管-晶体管逻辑（电路）（亦写作 T²L，transistor-transistor logic 的简称）

TTM 轮胎试验机（tire testing machine）

TTMI ［美］载货汽车挂车制造商协会（Truck Trailer MFRS, Inc.）

TTP 时间触发协议（time triggered protocol 的简称）

TTP/C 时间触发协议（time triggered protocol 的简称，指在汽车电子系统中采用的一种通信协议，允许计算机网点按分时法使用通信媒体。C 表示美国汽车工程学会有关标准规定的通信系统分类中的 C 级，见 SAE categories of communication systems）

T-traffic 货车交通（= truck traffic）

TTS 自动变速器温度开关（transmission temperature switch 的简称，当自动变速器因节气门大开或下长坡，其工作油液温度超过某规定值，如：135℃ 时，该开关断开，向电子控制模块发送警报信号。当电子控制模块收到温度过高警报信号时，立即使自动变速器液力变矩器离合器接合，借以减少液力变矩器中产生的热量）

T tube T字形管，T形三通管（亦称 three way tube）

T-type cylinder 双侧置气门汽缸（= T-head cylinder）

T-type highway 货运公路（主要供载货汽车使用的公路，T-type 为 truck-type 的简称）

TU ①热量单位（thermal unit）②电子管，真空管（tube）③训练单位（training unit）

tub 桶，盆，槽

tube ①管子②电子管③内胎④使成管状；装上管子；敷设管道

tube and corrugated fin core 皱纹片-管式（散热器）芯子

tube and plate fin core 片管式散热器芯子（= finned tubular radiator core）

tube arrangement 管道布置

tube axial fan 轴流式风扇

tube block radiator 分段管式散热器
tube caulker 管子卷边工具
tube clamp 管夹（=tube clip）
tube coil 管状线圈（=tubular coil）
tube connector 管接头
tubed tyre 有内胎轮胎（外胎内腔中需要配有内胎的充气轮胎）
tube flaring and cutting tool 管子扩口及切割工具
tubeless tyre 无内胎轮胎（由胎里气密层及胎圈与轮辋的密合作用保持内压，不需要配用内胎的充气轮胎）
tube nozzle 管式喷嘴
tube plate （散热器上、下水室）集管板
tube-structure type chassis 管结构底盘
tub-shaped seat 斗式座椅
tubular ①管状的，筒形的 ②用管子造成的；有管子的
tubular-backbone type frame 中央管材独梁车架（亦称 tubular backbone chassis, tubular spine chassis, 简称 tubular frame, tubular spine chassis, 见 backbone type frame）
tubular battery 管栅状阳极板蓄电池（阳极板制成管栅状，以增加极板面-容比的一种高能电池，亦称 tubular plate battery）
tubular cross bearer 管状横梁（亦称 tubular cross member）
tubular drive shaft 管材传动轴（亦称 tubular propeller shaft）
tubular heat exchanger 管式热交换器
tubular inside micrometer 管形内径千分尺
tubular journal 空心轴颈
tubular linear motor 管状直线感应电机
tubular pipe type chassis base contruction 钢管式底盘基架

tubular positive plate （管栅状阳极板蓄电池的）管栅状阳极板（见 tubular battery）
tubular radiator core 管式散热器芯子
tubular side-rail 管材大梁
tubular spoke 管形轮辐
tuck in 卷入（在回转运动中，急松加速踏板或急踩离合器，汽车向内转的现象）
Tudor phaeton [英] 都铎王室式活顶四门轿车
tufftride method 扩散渗氮法（德国研制成的一种表面低温热处理法，采用一种特殊的氰化钾盐溶剂，使金属表面形成一种含氮、碳的耐磨、耐疲劳、耐腐蚀的合金属）
tug （用力或猛地）拉，扯，拖，拽
tugger 卷扬机，绞盘
Tukon microhardness instrument 杜孔显微硬度计
tulip (shaped) valve 郁金香花形阀（亦称 tulip type valve, 钟形阀门，喇叭形气门，如：在高速发动机中，为了减轻气门的质量和便于冷却，气门头制成中空的喇叭形气门）
tumble ①跌落，滚落 ②翻滚 ③乱流，搅流，紊流 ④使杂乱，搅乱 ⑤纵向旋流，纵向旋涡，纵涡（见 swirl）
tumble and swirl multiplex intake port 直涡和横涡多重紊流进气孔
tumble forming valve 见 tumble plate
tumble motion 紊流，乱流，纵向紊流，纵向涡流
tumble plate （装在汽缸进气口前方进气道内的）纵（向）涡（流）板（将进气道分隔成上、下两层的薄片状结构，使进气流生成最佳强度的纵向涡流，亦称 tumble forming valve）

tumbler ①倾翻机构，翻斗机，倾倒机②换向齿轮，齿轮换向器，换向机构③铸件清砂用滚筒
tumble ratio 纵涡比
tumbler switch 拨动式开关（倒扳开关，翻转开关）
tumbling barrel 研磨滚筒，滚光筒（工作、材料在筒内相互摩擦，而使表面抛光，= tumbling box）
tunable ①可调谐的，可调音的②音调优美的
tune ①音调，曲调，语调②和谐，协调③调整，调试④调谐
tuned intake pressure charging 谐振增压充气（调整进气管长度，使进气系统的进气脉冲声速谐振与发动机转速匹配，起谐振管的作用，以增加可燃混合气进气量，亦称 tuned intake tube charging，见 harmonic induction）
tuned intake supercharging system 谐波进气增压系统（在进气系统中装有谐振器，如：谐振箱和谐振管等的增压系统）
tuned port injection 见 port fuel injection
tuned ports （汽油喷射式发动机经精心设计，各缸进气阻力均一且最小的）精调进气孔
tune in 调谐，调准（波长）
tune out 失调，失谐，匹配不当，解谐
tuner 调谐器
tune-up ①调整，调节②（为了提高发动机功率而进行的）改革，改进，改造③（汽车）调试（一项重要的维护工艺，对整车进行全面检查、测试、调整，使各部分性能恢复到出厂标准或最佳状态，= tunning up）
tune-up center ①（发动机等的）调试中心，调试站②（各种诊断、调整仪表装成一整体的）联合调试-诊断器，集中调试-诊断器
tune-up data 调试数据（调整、调试用数据，亦称 tune-up specifications）
tune-up decal 调试图表板（有的汽车将需要调试的项目、数据印在板上，置于发动机罩下，以便调试工应用）
tune-up master 发动机多功能调整测试仪（由转速表、分电器凸轮闭合角测定仪、正时灯及真空表等部分组成的整体式测试仪器，= twin tuner）
tune-up specialty shop （汽车）专业调试店
tune-up tester 调整试验器，调试台（如：engine analyzer, chassis dynamometer 等）
tungar bulb 钨氩管（钨氩整流管，用于蓄电池充电等的大电流整流，简称 tungar）
tung oil 桐油（见 china wood oil）
tungsten 钨（W）
tungsten carbide 碳化钨（硬质合金，WC，W_2C，W_3C）
tungsten chromium (tool) steel 钨铬（工具）钢
tungsten-halogen bulb 钨丝卤素灯泡（充有卤素的钨丝灯泡，见 halogen head lamp 和 halogen regenerative cycle）
tungsten inert gas welding 钨极惰性气体保护焊，惰性气体保护钨电极电弧焊（简称 tig welding, TIG，亦称 inert-gas tungsten-arc welding）
tungsten point 钨接点，钨触点
tungsten-wire cathode 钨丝阴极
tuning ①调整，调节，校准②调谐
tunnel ①隧道，涵洞②管道，孔道，烟道③风洞
tunnel-lighting ①地道照明②风洞照明
tunnel section （车身）筒腔部分

（指轿车车身前后车门之间的部分）

tunnel velocity 风洞空气流速

tunnel wall interference 洞壁干扰（如：风洞壁干涉）

turbidity ①混浊②混浊度（= turbidness）

turbidity point 混浊点，浊点

turbine ①涡轮（亦称 turbine wheel，如：废气涡轮增压器中废气驱动的叶轮，液力变矩器和液力耦合器中输出动力的叶轮）②燃气轮机（= gas turbine engine）

turbine casing 涡轮机外壳（亦称 turbine housing）

turbine crown 涡轮的轮缘，涡轮叶轮的轮缘

turbine efficiency ratio 涡轮机效率比

turbine engine 燃气（涡）轮（发动）机（= gas-turbine engine）

turbine-engined vehicle 燃气轮机车辆（指以燃气轮机为动力的轿车、货车等，亦称 turbine-powered vehicle，turbine-engine vehicle）

turbine-exit temperature 涡轮机出口温度

turbine inlet casing 涡轮进气壳（具有一个或几个进气通道的涡轮壳体部分，通常带有涡轮喷嘴环）

turbine nozzle ring 涡轮喷嘴环（涡轮工作轮入口处将废气的压力能部分地转变为动能的一种固定的或可调节的通道装置）

turbine outlet casing 涡轮排气壳（涡轮壳体的排气部分）

turbine pump 涡轮（式）泵，叶轮泵

turbine-reciprocating engine combination （燃气）涡轮机-往复活塞机组

turbine runner （液力变矩器的）涡轮

turbine speed sensor （自动变速器变矩器）涡轮转速传感器（向电子控制模块传送变矩器涡轮的输出转速信号）

turbine thermodynamic efficiency 燃气轮机热（力学）效率

turbine-type rotary interchange 涡轮式环形交叉口（车辆进入和离开交叉口时均沿切线方向行驶）

turbo(-) ①涡轮机（turbine 的简称）②涡轮增压器（turbo-supercharger 的简称）③直接与驱动涡轮连接、耦合的（如：turbofan, turbo-alternator 等）④由涡轮机组成或本身就是涡轮机的（如：turbo motor 等）

turbo-alternator 涡轮交流发电机

turbo-blower 涡轮鼓风机（涡轮增压器）

turbo boost control 废气涡轮增压压力控制（系统）（turbocharger boost control 的简称，当出现爆燃趋势时，降低进气增压压力，见 waste gate）

turbo boost pressure sensor 废气涡轮进气增压压力传感器（简称 TBP sensor）

turbo-chamber ignition 涡流燃烧室点火

turbocharged edition 废气涡轮增压版（指废气涡轮增压型的，废气涡轮增压式的）

turbocharged knock-limited engine 防爆燃控制式废气涡轮增压型发动机（将增压控制在不致产生爆燃的极限下工作）

turbocharged spark ignition engine 涡轮增压式火花点火发动机（简称 TSI engine）

turbo-charger 涡轮增压器（亦称 turbo supercharger，用废气涡轮驱动压气机实现进气增压的装置）

turbocharger aftercooling （进气）增压后冷却

turbocharger boost control solenoid 废气涡轮进气增压压力控制电磁阀

(用于开、闭废气排出阀,以控制废气增压压力)

turbocharger compressor (废气)涡轮增压器压气机(简称 turbocompressor)

turbocharger compressor performance 废气涡轮增压器压气机性能曲线

turbocharger matching test 增压器配机试验(调整或测定增压内燃机增压器与内燃机的匹配使用性能的试验)

turbocharger wastegate regulation valve (见 turbocharging pressure vacuum solenoid valve)

turbo-charging pressure vacuum solenoid valve (控制)废气涡轮驱动压力(的)真空通路(的)电磁开关阀(= turbo-charging pressure vacuum switching valve,简称 turbo-charging pressure VSV,当驱动废气涡轮的废气压力超过规定值时,阀开启,进气管的真空经该阀进入废气旁通阀的真空执行器而将该旁通阀开启,废气压力随之降低。当废气压力低于规定值时,该阀关闭,故该阀亦称 turbocharging wastegate regulation valve)

turbocompounded engine 废气涡轮复合式发动机(利用废气涡轮将废气能量的一部分通过传动机构送回曲轴,从而形成复合动力的发动机系统,以提高热效率)

turbodiesel 涡轮增压式柴油机

turbo-diesel passenger car 废气涡轮增压式柴油机轿车

turbo-electric hybrid system 燃气轮机-发电机-电动机复合驱动系统

turbo fan ①涡轮鼓风机(与驱动涡轮直接耦合的风扇, = turbo blower)②涡轮空气压缩机(与驱动涡轮直接耦合的压气机, = turbo compressor)

turbo-four and 6A combo 涡轮增压4缸发动机和6挡自动变速器机组

turbogenerator 涡轮发电机

turbo hydromatic cycling test 涡轮液力传动循环试验(简称 THCT)

turbojet engine 涡轮喷气发动机(简称 turbojet)

1.6 turbo1.6 L 涡轮增压发动机

turbo lag (发动机增压系的)增压滞后(发动机加速至一定转速后增压系才起作用的现象)

turbo lator valve 涡流气门(指具有导流片等的气门,可在气门区形成一定的涡流)

turbopetrol 涡轮增压式汽油机

twin (separate) scroll turbocharger 双(分)式涡形进气道涡轮增压器(每一对排气行程的汽缸分别从一个进气道排送废气)

turbopump 涡轮泵

turboramjet 涡轮冲压式喷气发动机

turbo-supercharged engine 废气涡轮增压发动机(一般称 turbocharged engine,装有由废气驱动的涡轮机和由该涡轮机带动的压气机组成的进气增压系统的发动机)

turbulence amplifier 紊流增强装置

turbulence-chamber engine 紊流燃烧室式发动机

turbulence combustion chamber 紊流式燃烧室

turbulence controlled induction 受控紊流进气(在进气过程中使新鲜混合气按所要求的方向、流速等产生紊流,以改善燃油的分布特性等,简称 TCI)

turbulence generating pot 紊流生成罐(电火花先将罐内浓混合气点燃,利用由罐内喷出的火焰形成强烈紊流,点燃主燃烧室内全部稀混合气体,日本大发公司及丰田公司等采用的稀混合气稳定燃烧净化、节油型罐状预燃室,简称 TGP)

turbulence intensity 紊流强度

turbulence nozzle 紊流喷嘴（喷出的油柱形成紊流）

turbulence resistance 紊流阻力

turbulence statistics 紊流统计学

turbulent boundary layer 紊流边界层

turbulent diffusion combustion 紊流扩散燃烧

turbulent flame 紊流火焰

turbulent flow 紊流，乱流；湍流（= turbulent current）

turbulent motion 紊流运动（= eddy motion）

turbulent noise 乱噪音（杂乱无序的混合噪音）

turbulent velocity 紊流速度

turfary 沼泽，泥沼地

turn ①回转，旋转②转弯，转向，掉头③一圈，一转，一回④圈数，转数，（线圈的）匝数⑤转角，弯角，转折点⑥变化，转变⑦顺序，次序

turnability （车辆）转向性能，回转性能

turnabout ①180°转弯（掉头，亦称 turnround，turn-around）②掉头路段，回车道③往返周期，工作（检修）周期④周转时间

turnaround time ①作业周期（某项作业，如建模、原型制作等，从接受任务到完成该任务的整个时间）②（货车运输终点的）货物装、卸时间③转机、好转④（观点等的）彻底转变

turned-up 向上翻起

turning 盘车（为进行检查和调整，以外力使内燃机曲轴缓慢转动）

turning ability （汽车的）转弯能力（= cornering ability）

turning angle （汽车）转向角，回转角

turning back of car 汽车掉头

turning caster aligner （汽车的）前轮转角及主销纵倾角测试台（由前轮回转角测定器和主销纵倾角测试器组成，可精确测定主销后倾、负后倾等纵倾角）

turning center （汽车的瞬时）转弯中心（指汽车作平面回转运动时的速度瞬心，即：前外轮转过任一角度时，其滚动方向的垂线与后轴延长线的交点）

turning circle （汽车的）转弯圆（汽车作回转运动时，以其瞬时转向中心为圆心，以其瞬时转弯半径为半径所做的回转圆，见 turning center，tuning radius）

turning (circle) radius （汽车）转弯半径（指汽车转弯时的回转圆半径。对汽车作转向运动动力学分析时，若取后轴中点 B 为固定于汽车的动坐标系原点，则转弯半径 $R = OB = L/\tan\alpha$。式中：O—转弯中心；L—轴距；α—动坐标系 x 轴转角。说明汽车结构尺寸时，见 turning circles diameters）

turning circles diameters 转弯圆直径（转向盘转到极限位置时，车辆内外转向轮上 A 点在 X 平面上的轨迹圆直径。车辆外转向轮上 A 点在 X 平面上的轨迹圆直径为车辆最小转弯直径）

turning clearance circles 转弯通道圆（转向盘转到极限位置时，下述两圆形成的通道称车辆转弯通道圆：①车辆所有点在地面上的投影均位于圆外的最大内圆②包含车辆所有点在地面上的投影的最小外圆，分为左转和右转通道圆，亦称 vehicle clearance circles）

turning clearance width 转弯通道宽度（当车辆转弯时，转弯通道圆的内外圆半径之差）

turning clockwise 顺时针方向旋转（向右转动，右转弯）

turning crane 旋臂起重机，回转臂

turning effort ①圆周力②转动力③转弯时转向盘操纵力（操舵力）

turning fit 自由转动配合

turning force 旋转力，转向力，转弯力

turning gear 回转机构

turning joint 活动关节，铰链

turning movement ①转动，回转运动，旋转运动②（车辆左转或右转的）转向运行，转弯动作

turning pair 转动力偶

turning path （车辆的）转弯轨迹，转向轨迹（转向时车上某定点的轨迹）

turning point ①转折点，转机②转弯点（转向中心）

turning-point in time series 时间序列中的转折点

turning radius ①回转半径②转弯半径（汽车转向中心至最外轮胎触地中心的距离）

turning radius gauge （汽车转向轮）转弯半径测定器（测出各转向轮绕主销回转的角度 θ 后，按下式可求出汽车的最小转弯半径：$r = L/\sin\theta$。式中：L—轴距。因此，该测定器亦称回转角测定仪"turning angle tester"）

turning roadway （交叉口处的）转弯（分）车道

turning roadway terminal （高速公路）转弯车道出入口（转弯车道连接主线的岔口，驶离主线的交通所经岔口称为驶出口，驶入主线的交通所经岔口称为驶入口）

turning test 转弯试验（转向性能试验，测定最小转弯半径等）

turning time 转弯时间

turning track ①转向轨迹（转向时轮胎的轨迹）②转向轨距（车辆转向时，最外轮胎触地中心转向半径和最内轮胎触地中心转向半径之差，车轮为双胎时，以两胎之中间线计）

turning track width 转向轨迹宽度（转向车辆的前外轮胎外侧轨迹与后轮内胎外侧轨迹之间的距离，沿半径方向测得的宽度）

turning traffic 转弯行车，弯道行车

turning valve 转阀（旋转式滑阀）

turn light indicator 转向指示灯（安装在驾驶室内指示汽车转向信号灯是否开放的灯具，亦称 turn signal indicator，turn indicator）

turn marking （在交叉口的车辆）转向路面标示

turnoff ①断开，断路，关闭②让车道，岔道，支路③避开，让开

turnoff the fuel 切断燃油供给

turnon 接通，接入，开动

turnon left 左转弯

turn on (off) time 延迟时间（输入信号开始或终止和到达对比度的相应最大波幅10%和90%之间的时间）

turnon right 右转弯

turnon time 接通时间（如：晶体三极管由截止转换为通导所需的时间）

turnout ①断开，断路，关闭②岔道，让车道（指道路允许两车相错或超越的较宽阔段）③让车，避车

turnover ①（货物）周转量，周转额，营业额②翻车，翻倒，翻转，倒置，倒转，倾覆

turnover job 大修理

turnover mechanism （离合器的踏板）弹簧式助力器（将离合器踏板踩下一定角度时，其弹簧力开始起作用，可减轻离合器踏板的踩踏力）

turnover of freight 货物周转量（货物装载量与运输里程的乘积，单位为：$t \cdot km$，为货物运输产量的单位，= freight turnover）

turnpike ①(收费公路的)收费处栅门,栅杆(= toll bar, toll gate, toll pike,简称 pike) ②收费公路(= turnpike road, toll road, toll expressway) ③免费公路(= free road) ④免费快速公路(= freee xpressway,特指原先收费现已免费的高速公路) ⑤干道,干线公路(= main road)

turn-plate ①(车辆)转弯、掉头的场地 ②转车台,转盘(= turntable)

turn prohibition sign 禁止转向标志(禁止左转弯或禁止右转弯等运行的标志)

turn rate 转向率(指汽车实际转向角与转向盘转角所对应的转向轮理论转向角之间的%比)

turn-rate control system 转向率控制系统(通过对发动机输出转矩的控制和对相应车轮施加制动的方式,保证车辆在转弯或在弯道上行驶时,按照驾驶者的意图稳定转向,防止汽车实际转向角不足,而冲出弯道外侧,或实际转向过度,而甩出弯道内侧。目前各厂家大都将这一系统称为"dynamic stability control"动态稳定性控制系统,但各厂家的商品名各不相同,见 AHS, ESP, DSC, PSM, PSTC, Stabilitrak, VDC, VSC)

turn-signal control lamp 转向信号指示灯(= turn light indicator)

turn signal flasher 转向信号闪光灯(转向闪光信号灯)

turn signal lamp 转向信号灯(装在车外,向其他车辆和行人发出转向信号的灯具)

turn signal switch 转向信号灯开关

turns lock to lock 转向盘总转数(从向右转到底到向左转到底的总圈数)

turntable 转盘,转台

turntable supporting 回转式支座(可转动的支架,可转动的支撑装置)

turn through 180° 转过 180°

turn under (车身侧面腰线以下)向内倾斜

turpentine oil 松节油,松脂油(亦称 turpentine, terebene)

turpentine varnish 松节油清漆

turret 转台,转动架,转塔

turret steps 螺旋梯

turtle top 龟背式车顶(一般四座轿车用整块钢板压制成的车顶,如:大众甲壳虫轿车车顶, = turret deck)

tuyere [法]风管,风口,风嘴

TV ①电视(television) ②末速,最大(的极限)速度(terminal velocity) ③测试电压(test voltage) ④运输车辆(transport vehicle)

TVAA 酒后驾驶交通违章(traffic violation aggravated by alcohol)

T-valve T 形阀(三通阀,三通开关, = tee valve)

TVC (弯道)驱动转矩分配系统

T-VIS 丰田可变进气系统(Toyota-Variable Induction System 的简称,丰田公司推出的电子控制进气通道断面可变系统的商品名。该系统将进气歧管各汽缸的进气管中间隔开,形成两个通道,在其中的一个通道上装有由发动机电子控制模块通过进气管真空控制阀操纵的进气通道控制阀。在发动机低—中速区域,该阀关闭,进气通道断面减小,高速运转时,该阀门开启,进气通道断面加大)

T/V pressure 节气门压力(自动变速器中随节气门位置而变化的调制压力,为发动机的转矩信号,throttle/valve pressure 的简称)

TVPS 节气门开度传感器(throttle valve position sensor 的简称)

TVR 电视录像(television recording)

TV relaying vehicle 电视转播车

TV rod (机械液压式自动变速器的)节气门阀杆(transmission valve rod 的简称,指从加速踏板杆系伸至自动变速器节气门阀的控制杆)

TVS diode 瞬变电压抑制二极管(transient voltage suppressing diode 的简称)

TVSV 温控真空开关(thermostatic vacuum switch 的简称)

TVTV 温控真空通路阀(= thermostatic vacuum transmitting valve 的简称)

TVV 温控真空阀(thermal vacuum valve 的简称,为一热敏蜡元件柱塞阀,用于根据所规定的温度关闭或开通真空通道,以阻止或引入控制用的真空。如:装在机械式蒸发排放物控制系统进气歧管与活性炭罐之间的清除软管中的 TVV,当冷却水温低于某规定值,如:35℃时,该阀关闭进气歧管与活性炭罐之间的清除软管;水温高于此温度时,该阀开通清除软管,存储在活性炭罐内的燃油蒸汽便被进气歧管真空吸入进气歧管)

TW ①软化水(tempered water)②总重(total weight) ③扭曲的,弯曲的(twisted) ④打印机(typewriter) ⑤轮胎宽度(tyre width)

TWC (**twc**) ①总工作费用,总工作成本(total work cost 的简称)②三效催化剂(three way catalyst)③三效催化转化(three way conversion)

tweak 对机器、系统、数据等稍作调整

'tween drive spindle 中间传动轴

T-welded joint T 字形焊缝,T 形焊道

twelve-cylinder car 12 缸发动机轿车

twelve-cylinder engine 12 缸发动机(有时简称 twelve、twelve-cylinder)

twelve o'clock wind 顶风,逆风(口语)

twelve point socket wrench 十二方套筒扳手(= bihexagon wrench)

twentieth highest annual hourly volume 一年间第 20 个最高小时交通量

twice 两次,两倍

twice the life 使寿命增加一倍

twin ①成双的,成对的,两倍的 ②成对的物件

twin-action brake 双作动式制动器

twin-bar bumper 双杆保险杠

twin barrel carburetor 双腔化油器(亦称双阻风门化油器"twin choke carburetor")

twin-bead tire 双胎圈轮胎(= double-bead tire)

twin beam oscilloscope 双像示波器

twin bench-type seat 双人(型)座椅

twin cable 双芯电缆

twin camshaft 双凸轮轴[简称 twin cam,指每列汽缸体具有平行布置的两根凸轮轴,分别用于进、排气门,亦称 dual camshaft,不一定是顶置式。参见 twin(或 dual)overhead camshaft]

twin camshaft chain drive 双凸轮轴的链传动装置

twin carburetor 双联的双化油器(简称 twin carb,指一台发动机使用两个相同型号的化油器,多用于 V 型发动机或汽缸水平对置式发动机等)

twin-cast cylinders 成对铸造的汽缸

Twin Ceramic Turbo (日本丰田公司 IJZ·GT6 缸汽油机上使用的)双陶瓷涡轮机式增压器(的商品名,该增压器由两个废气涡轮机带动一个压气机实现进气增压,每三

个汽缸的废气驱动一个涡轮机)

twin channel system 双信道制，双通路制

twin-choke carburetor 双阻风门化油器（指具有两个喉管的化油器，亦称 dual venturi carburetor)

twin-clutch layshaft gearbox 双离合器中间轴型齿轮变速器（亦称 double shift gearbox, 简称DSG）

twin-coach 通道式公共汽车（铰接式大客车）

twin-countershaft transmission 双中间轴变速器（带两中间轴的变速器）

twin crankshaft engine 双曲轴发动机

twin-cylinder 双缸的

Twin Damper system （马自达公司开发的机械式）双减振器系统（由主、副减振器组成，可根据道路状况自动以最佳配合方式参与减振用）

twin-deck bus 双层客车

twin-disc clutch 双片式离合器（= double disc clutch）

twin-disc resilient drive 双盘弹性传动器（可吸收扭转振动的柔性万向传动装置）

twin drive 双电动机驱动

twin duplex carburetor 双联分动式化油器（四腔化油器）

twin engine vehicle 双发动机汽车（前、后端都装有发动机）

twin exhaust pipes 双排气管

twin filter 并联滤清器

twin-flow turbine （废气涡轮增压器的）双流式涡轮机（发动机低速运转时，废气由一个进气口进入涡轮机，以保证所要求的废气压力，高速时，废气分别从两个进气口进入涡轮机。丰田公司的商品名为 Twin Enrty Turbo, 马自达公司的商品名为 Twin Scroll Turbo）

twin frame lift 双柱式车身底架支撑型举升器（见 frame lift）

twin helical gear 人字齿轮

twin-horn set 双音喇叭

Twin·hybrid system 孪生儿（牌）混合动力车（日五十铃由一台小型3缸发动机和一台装在发动机与液力变矩器之间、直接与自动变速器连接的交流同步助力电动机组成的并联型混合动力车系统的商品名）

twin intake twin exhaust system 双进、排气系统（V型8缸发动机两侧分别各采用一套独立的进、排气系统）

twin-jet nozzle 双喷嘴

twin-layshaft configuration （变速器）双中间轴式结构

twin-lever roller-mounted stud steering gear 曲柄销安装在滚子轴承上的曲柄双销式转向机构

twin-lobe cam 双凸角凸轮（由两个轮廓完全相同的凸角，驱动同一只气门）

twin master cylinder and shuttle valve brake system 双主缸及梭行阀制动系统

twin muffler type exhaust system 双消声器型排气系统

twinned 成双的，成对的

twin overhead camshaft 双顶置式凸轮轴（每列汽缸顶部平行布置有两根顶置式凸轮轴，分别用于进、排气，亦称 dual overhead camshaft）

twin plug engine 每一缸有两个火花塞的发动机

twin post auto lift 双柱式汽车举升器

TwinPower Turbo technology （BMW推出的）双动力-增压技术（如采用该技术的 BMW 1.5 liter TwinPower Turbo petrol engine 由一台废气涡轮增压式3缸汽油机和单独驱动时可使汽车行驶30 km的电动机两种

动力共用一套传动-变速系统组成。这一技术包括：燃油缸内直喷、废气涡轮增压、气门正时-升程可变及自动停机-起动等多项 BMW Efficient Dynamics 技术，既用于汽油机又用于柴油机）

twin pump 双联泵

twin rear wheel 双胎并装后轮，双轮并装后轮

twin rear window 双后窗（分成两半的后窗，见 divided rear window）

twin roller cam 蜗杆-双排滚子（式转向器）

twin rotor engine 双缸转子发动机

twin-rotor housing （转子发动机的）双缸体（指双缸转子发动机的两个缸都在同一根轴上，但缸体是独立的，都有自己的前后端盖）

twin-rotor side-intake-port engine 双缸端面进气转子发动机

twin-shaft transmission 两轴式变速器（无中间轴的固定轴式变速器）

twin-six engine V 型 12 缸发动机

twin-spark ignition 双火花点火（简称 twin ignition，= double-spark ignition）

twin-speed power take-off 双挡位功率输出轴

twin-steer 双转向装置，双转向机构

Twin sunroof 双天窗

twin throttle body fuel injection system 双节气门体燃油喷射系统

twin tire 并装双胎（= dual tire）

twin-toned horn 双音喇叭（= double-tone horn）

twin-trailer (road) train 双挂车汽车列车

twin-turbine torque converter 双涡轮液力变矩器

twin-turbo (charged) engine 双涡轮增压发动机

twin turbo (charger) 双联式废气涡轮增压器（由两个相对较小的废气涡轮组成，各由一排汽缸排出的废气驱动，可保证发动机低、高速时均能获得较佳的增压效果，同时又减少汽缸间排气干扰）

twin-type lever steering （取代常规圆形转向盘的）双操纵杆式转向杆

twin-volute waterpump 双蜗壳水泵

twist ①一股，一绞 ②扭转，扭曲 ③缠绕，弯卷 ④螺旋运动 ⑤螺旋状 ⑥搓，捻，绞，拧，卷成螺旋状

twist angle 扭转角，扭曲角

twist-beam suspension 扭力梁式悬架（半独立悬架的一种）

twist centre 扭转中心，扭曲中心

twist counter gauge length 扭转计标距（用扭转计测量试件扭转角所使用试件部分的长度）

twist course （车架，车身）扭曲试验跑道

twisted nematic mode （液晶显示）扭曲向列型（液晶分子在两基板间呈扭曲排列，在液晶盒两面分别配置偏振片，利用外加电场改变液晶旋光性进行显示的方式）

twisted-pair-line CAN bus network 双绞线 CAN 总线网络（指用双绞线作为传输介质的 CAN 总线，见 CAN）

twisted spur gear 斜直齿圆柱齿轮

twisted wire 双股扭绞线，合股线（绞合电缆，由多股扭绞成的绞合线，= stranded wire）

twist elastic constant 扭曲（的）弹性常数

twist grip （摩托车油门控制器油门钢索等的可转动式）操纵把

twisting coefficient 扭曲系数，扭曲率

twisting couple 扭力力偶

twisting effect 扭转效应

twisting force 扭转力（= torsional force）

twisting of frame 车架扭弯，车架

扭歪

twisting resistance 扭转阻力，扭绞阻力

twisting strain 扭转应变

twisting strength 抗扭强度

twisting stress 扭应力

twisting tester 扭力试验器，扭转试验器（= torsion tester）

twist joint （导线、钢索等）扭绞连接

twistlock 手动拧紧式锁紧装置

twist moment 扭转力矩

twist off 拧开，拧松；拧断，使（螺纹）滑扣

twist of liguid crystal 液晶扭曲（使平行排列的液晶分子各层指向矢逐渐扭转，产生螺旋状的连续弹性曲率形变）

twist type piston ring 扭曲式活塞环（断面不对称，在与缸壁摩擦时扭曲的活塞环）

two and half box 见 two box

two-arm yoke 双臂叉形件（如：双臂轭，双臂支架）

two-axle engine 双轴式发动机（一般指双轴式燃气轮机）

two-axle full trailer 双轴全挂车

two-axle motor unit 双轴汽车，双轴牵引车（相对挂车而言）

two axle rigid （常规的单桥或双桥驱动的）双桥式载货汽车

two-axle semitrailer 双轴半挂车

two-bank 双排的，双列的，双行的

two-bank engine 双排汽缸型发动机（如：V形发动机）

two-barrel dual carburetor 双腔并动化油器（相当于一台多缸汽油机装用两只相同的单腔化油器，每只化油器分别供给几只汽缸以同样的混合气，避免各缸在进气时相互抢气）

two-barrel duplex carburetor 双腔分动化油器（有主、副两腔，按发动机工况要求，分别单独工作或同时工作，主副腔各有一组喉管和喷嘴系统）

two-bearing crankshaft 双轴承曲轴

two-bladed fan 双叶风扇

two box 两厢式轿车（只有发动机舱和客厢的轿车。亦写作 2 box，有的两厢式轿车后面也有一个小行李舱，有人称之为 two and half box 或 2.5 box

two-box transmission 具有两变速器（主变速器和副变速器）的传动系

two car test 双车试验（一种规定的路试）

two-chamber air reservoir 双室储气筒

two chamber brake cylinder 双腔制动缸

2 (two) channel automatic transmission with overdrive gear （丰田公司研制的）带超速挡的双路自动变速器（商品名，所谓双路是指有两条动力传递线路。挂低挡时，动力通过液力变矩器工况输出，挂超速挡时动力通过机锁止式离合器工况输出）

two circuit hydraulic braking system 双管路液压制动系

two-clutch （转换两个传动系统的）双向离合器

two convolution oblong section bellow type pneumatic spring 双椭圆鼓形波纹箱式空气弹簧

two cycle ①二冲程循环（= two stroke cycle）②（有时指）二冲程发动机

two-cycle opposed piston diesel engine 二冲程对置活塞柴油机

two-dimensional device 二维装置（平面装置）

two-dimensional drafting template 二维人体样板（是一种根据大量人体统计数据，用赛璐珞或有机玻

璃、密实的纸板或胶合板裁制的人体侧面外形样板)
two-dimensional field 二维(度)场
two-dimensional flow 二维流(二次元流,以 x, y 直角坐标或 r, θ 极坐标讨论的流动,即平面流)
two-dimensional fundamental form 二维(度)基本形
two-dimensional positioning system 二维定位系统(平面定位装置)
two-dimensional space 二维(度)空间
two-dimensional stress 二维应力(二次元应力,考虑某一点的应力状态时,若三个主应力 σ_1、σ_2、σ_3 中有一个为零,即:只有两个主应力作用,则称为二次元应力)
two-direction thrust bearing 双向推力轴承
two disk wave generator (谐波齿轮)双圆盘波发生器(两个等直径圆盘对称偏心设置于输入轴上的非积极控制式波发生器)
two-door car 两门轿车(左右两侧各一个车门,如:双门敞篷跑车)
two-engined 双发动机的(亦称 twin-engined)
two-filament bulb 双丝灯泡(= bifilar bulb)
two flank gear rolling tester (齿轮)双面啮合检查仪
two-fold ①2 倍的,双重的 ②双折的
two-frequency addressing scheme (液晶显示)双频驱动方式(利用电光特性与频率的相关性,在选择点和非选择点上分别施加不同频率电压的驱动方式)
two-group approach (汽油喷射系统的)两组喷油法(如:8 缸发动机,以每 4 个汽缸为一组,发动机曲轴每转一周,对其中的一组 4 个汽缸同时喷油一次)

two-hand(ed) control 双手控制,双手操纵
two hole injector 双喷孔式喷嘴(四气门式发动机采用的分别向两个方向喷射燃油、具有两个喷油孔的喷嘴)
two independent ignition 双源独立点火
two intake ports technology 双进气孔技术(20 世纪 90 年代后期汽油直接喷射式发动机多采用此技术。两个进气孔一个为直孔,一个为涡旋孔。直孔由电子控制的涡流控制阀开、闭,当该阀关闭时空气流由涡旋孔充入,产生强烈进气涡流。当该阀开放时,空气流由两个孔同时充入,涡流减弱,但充气量增加)
two-into(one) pipe 二合一"Y"管(亦称 Y pipe, bifurcated pipe)
two jet 双喷嘴的
two-joint inboard slip drive shaft 双万向节内侧滑动的传动轴(轴向滑动由双万向节之间的内侧元件保证的双万向节传动轴)
two-joint outboard slip drive shaft 双万向节外侧滑动传动轴(轴向滑动由两万向节外侧元件保证的双万向节传动轴)
two-lane road 双车道道路(具有两条车道的双向无分隔带道路)
two-layer formed in one-piece facing 双(层)合一式衬面(如:由两层不同材料制成的摩擦衬片,底层注重强度,表层注重摩擦性能)
two-layer ironnitride surface (表面渗氮处理后形成的)双氮化铁层表面
two-layer type center console box 双层型中(央)控(制)箱
two lay shaft gearbox 双中间轴变速器(双副轴变速器,= twin counter shafts transmission)

two leading shoe brake 双领蹄式制动器（简称 2L type brake，指当制动鼓正向旋转时，两制动蹄均为领蹄的内张型鼓式制动器）

two-leafed door 双扇门

two leaf-spring thrust-rod type equalizing suspension （货车双轴并装式后桥的）双架钢板弹簧推力杆式平衡悬架（两后轴上各装有一架钢板弹簧，两钢板弹簧的外侧通过吊架或滑座与车架连接，而两钢板弹簧的内侧则与一称为平衡臂的构件铰接，平衡臂通过心轴，亦称平衡轴装在车架的平衡臂支座上，两钢板弹簧只承受垂直力和侧向力，驱动力和制动力及其相应的反作用力矩由两根两端分别与两后轴和平衡臂支架铰接的推力杆"thrust rod"支撑）

two-level fork junction 双层 Y 型交叉口

two-level rotor 双层分火头（如：转子发动机使用的双分火头式分电器，有两层，其中一层控制前置火花塞的发火，另一层控制后置火花塞的发火）

two-level signal 双（级）亮度信号灯

two lever steering 双杆式转向操舵（机构）

two-light headlamp 双光前照灯（带远、近两灯泡或两灯丝）

two-line brake system 双管路制动系（产生制动力所需的能量，由两条回路传送，若其中一条回路的某处失效，则另一条回路仍可传递制动力所需的能量，以保证安全行车）

two-lip seal 双唇密封件

two-liter car 2 升排量发动机汽车

two-lobed epitrochoidal housing （转子发动机的）双弧外旋轮线缸体

two-lobed epitrochoidal working chamber （转子发动机的）双弧外旋轮线工作室

two-lobed epitrochoid rotary mechanism 双弧外旋轮线旋转机械

two-lobe epitrochoidal bore （转子发动机的）双弧长短幅外旋轮线汽缸，双弧外旋轮线缸筒

two-lobe epitrochoidal shape 双弧长短辐外旋轮线形状（指转子发动机缸体）

two-men (operation) bus 配备两名工作人员（一名驾驶员，一名售票员）的公共汽车

two-mile advance sign 两英里前置标志（在高速公路的交叉口前两英里处设置的预告标志）

two-motor drive ①双发动机驱动 ②双电动机驱动

two-motor system 双发动机系统（= two-engine system）

two-motor type 4WD 双电动机型四轮驱动式（电动）汽车（两前轮和两后轮各由一台电动机驱动）

two-part bearing 对开式滑动轴承

two-part crankshaft 两段式曲轴（由两部分组成的曲轴）

two-part flywheel （两部分）拼合式飞轮（= two piece flywheel）

two parts ①三分之二 ②两部分

two passenger commuter 双座通勤车

two-passenger seating （装有）单排双乘员座椅的

two-pass radiator 双通道散热器

two-pedal control 双踏板控制（双踏板操纵装置）

two-phase coupling 两相耦合器（见 phase）

two-phase current 两相电流

two-phase premixed charge compression ignition combustion engine 双相预混合充气式压燃机（指使用天然气-空气混合气作为主燃料而喷入少量柴油作为引火源的压燃式发动

机）

two-phase single stage torque converter with variable blade reactor 双相单级可变叶片导轮式液力变矩器（见 phase 和 stage）

two-phase supercharger 两级增压器

two-piece 由两件组成的

two-piece apex seal （转子发动机的）双片式径向密封片（主密封片只有一端装有三角形端密封片）

two-piece bearing （由上、下轴瓦组成的）对开式滑动轴承

two-piece construction rim 两件式轮辋（亦称 two-piece type rim，指由轮辋体"rim base"和可拆式弹性挡圈"detachable spring flange"组成的可拆式轮辋）

two-piece flywheel 两件装合式飞轮（= two-part flywheel）

two-piece housing 两件装合式的壳体

two-piece piston 两件组合式活塞

two-piece rim 两件式轮辋

two-piece screen 两级滤网（= two-part screen）

two-piece wheel 两件对合式轮辋车轮（轮辋由各带一个辋圈的半边轮辋组成）

two-pin plug 双脚插头（= double-contact plug，two-wire plug）

two piston brake master cylinder （双独立回路式制动系的）双活塞式制动主缸 [series dual chamber brake master cylinder（串列双腔制动主缸）的别称]

two-piston caliper （盘式制动器的）双活塞式制动钳

two-places coupe 单排双座厢式轿车（= two seater，two-seater saloon motor car）

two plane type （齿轮啮合位置的）双面式

two plate clutch 双片式离合器

two-ply 双层的，双股的，双重的

two-point belt 两点式安全带

two-point breaker 双触点断电器（= double contact breaker）

two-point drive 两点式传动（指两个带盘组成的传动带传动系）

two pointer type 双针式（指示仪表）

two point suspension 两点式悬架装置

two-polar 二极的（亦称 two-pole）

two-post (car) lift 双柱汽车举升器

two-power bus 双动力客车（如：电动机和内燃机）

two-range transmission 两级变速器（高低挡副变速器）

two-reflector headlamp 双反光镜前照灯（近光和远光各有独自的反光镜）

two ring piston 双环式活塞

two-rod piston 双活塞杆式活塞

two-rotors rotary combustion engine 双缸转子发动机（简称 RC-2 engine）

two-row ball bearing 双列球轴承

two row (cylinder) 双排（汽缸）

two self-energizing shoes （制动器）双自加力蹄（双领蹄，双紧蹄）

two separate intake pork （汽油发动机各汽缸的）双独立进气管口

two-shaft free power turbine engine 双轴自由燃气轮机（压气机和驱动它的涡轮装在一条轴上，输出功率的涡轮装在另一条轴上）

two shoe brake 双蹄式制动器

two-sided manifold ①双侧簇（流形）②两侧式（进、排气）歧管

two-spark ignition 双火花点火（①指一个火花塞两次跳火，= double-fire ignition ②指每一汽缸由两个火花塞点火，= double-plug ignition）

two-speed axle 两挡主减速器式驱动桥（two-speed final drive type axle 的

简称,指其主减速器具有两种减速比可获得两倍于变速器的挡位,一般可分锥齿轮—行星齿轮式和锥齿轮—圆柱齿轮式两种,常采用电磁式、气压式或电磁气压式操纵机构控制其行星齿轮或圆柱齿轮变换啮合方式,而获得不同速比,亦称 double-reduction axle 或 two speed final drive。注意不要与由两级减速齿轮组成、但只有一种减速比的双级主减速器式驱动桥"two-stage reduction axle"混淆)

two-speed-axle electric shift system (货车的)两挡式驱动桥的电动变速系统

two speed double reduction final drive 双级双速主减速器(由一对锥齿轮和两对圆柱齿轮组成的双速主减速器)

two-speed gear 双速齿轮变速装置(两挡齿轮变速器,泛指可将输入轴的转速变为两种不同转速输出的齿轮变速机构)

two speed governor 双速调速器(仅在柴油机怠速和最高转速时起作用,怠速时防止熄火,高速时防止飞车)

two-speed power take-off gear 两挡功率输出装置

two-spool compressor 双转子压气机

two-spool engine 双路式燃气轮机(亦称 two-spool gas turbine,见 supercharged gas turbine engine)

two-spring non-reactive suspension (由纵向推力杆和两架钢板弹簧组成的双轴并装驱动桥的)非反力式双钢板弹簧式悬架(并装双轴驱动桥的每一轴上装有一架钢板弹簧和一根推力杆。两钢板弹簧的两相邻端通过同一个平衡轴支座与车架相连,而两外端则通过各自的吊架与车架相连。这种悬架只传递垂直和侧向力,驱动和制动力及其反作用力由推杆承受,亦称 dual-spring balanced suspension,见 single spring non-reactive suspension)

two-stage ①双级(液力变矩器)(见 stage) ②分两阶段的,分二期的 (= two-step)

two-stage air compressor 两级式空气压缩机(有往复式和离心式多种,其共同特点为:压缩分两级进行,第一级压缩缸输出的中压空气,经中间冷却,再由第二级压缩缸压缩成高压空气)

two-stage carburetor 两级化油器(两个性能不同的化油器联动或者构成一体,按工况要求,分段起作用,见 primary carburetor, secondary carburetor)

two-stage combination filter 复合式(干、油浴)双级(空气)滤清器

two stage combustion engine 两级燃烧发动机(分层充气燃烧发动机,见 stratified charge engine)

two-stage compression ignition RC engine 两级压燃转子发动机(两级压缩柴油转子发动机)

two -stage control type air bag 两级控制式安全气囊(可根据碰撞剧烈程度分级充气)

two-stage converter 两级液力变矩器

two-stage epicyclic reduction 两级行星齿轮减速器

two-stage explosion belt 双级燃爆式安全带

two-stage for barrel carburetor 双腔分动式化油器

two-stage fuel injection 两级燃油喷射,两级喷油

two-stage gas turbine 两级式燃气轮机

two-stage harmonic gear drive 双级谐波齿轮传动(由两个单级谐波齿轮传动串联组合而成的传动)

two-stage induction system (转子发

动机的）两级进气系统（具有主、副进气口，一般讲，主进气口用于怠速和小负荷，副进气口较大，用于高速、大负荷）

two-stage pump 两级泵

two-stage reduction（final drive type）axle 双级主减速器式驱动桥（当单级主减速比不能满足要求时，重型汽车或某些中型汽车驱动桥采用由两套减速齿轮组成的双级主减速器，其总主减速比 i_o 固定，不能变换，一般 $7 < i_o \leqslant 12$，见 double-reduction final drive）

two-stage rotary engine 双级转子发动机（指第一级为压缩级，第二级为动力级的转子发动机，既可作为汽油机，又可作为柴油机）

two stage supercharging 二级增压（增压空气分两次压缩，第一次压缩并使空气冷却后，再进行第二次压缩，以提高压缩总效率。二级增压能满足二冲程柴油机低负荷运行或大功率柴油机高压比的需要）

two-stage throttle position sensor 两级节气门位置传感器（亦称 two-stage throttle position switch，简称 two-stage TPS，仅向电子控制模块发送"全闭"、"全开"两级信息）

two stage type automatic roof （敞篷车的）两级式自动车篷（如：按一下按钮，车篷后缩 40 cm，呈天窗效果；按两下按钮，车篷完全收置于后座后方）

two-stage type through drive axles （双桥并装后驱动式车辆的）双级型贯通式驱动桥

two-stage type turbocharging 两级型涡轮增压（①见 two-stage supercharging②指具有大、小两个涡轮增压器的废气涡轮增压系统，发动机低转速时小涡轮增压器工作，高转速时大涡轮增压器工作，中间转速时由电子控制模块从小、大涡轮增压器中选用最符合当时的运转条件者工作）

two-stage unit lift 两级式总成举升器

two-stage voltage regulator 两级电压调节器

two-start screw 双头螺纹

two-step 双级的，两级的，两阶的

two-step supercharger 两级增压器

two-stop-per-mile driving cycle 每英里两次停车驾驶循环（美国的一种驾驶测试模式，1mile 内以 37mile/h 等速行驶，中间以 2ft/s^2 减速度，停止两次，每次停 10s，两次加速，加速度为 2ft/s^2）

two-stroke cycle 二冲程循环（指在发动机曲轴一转活塞的两个行程内完成进气、压缩、做功、排气等四个工作过程的火花点火或压燃式发动机的热力循环）

two-stroke cycle engine 二冲程发动机（= two-stroke engine，two-cycle engine，亦称 two stroker）

two-sump-mounted engine （装有）双油底壳（的）发动机

two-thread worm 双头蜗杆（= double-thread worm）

two-throw crankshaft 双拐曲轴，双曲柄曲轴

two-throw pump 二联泵，双缸泵（两个活塞泵或柱塞泵共装于一个壳体内，相位相差 180°，共用一根曲轴，曲轴每转一转，泵液两次）

two-tone color 双色（车身上下部分别为两种颜色）

two-tone finish （车身的）双色涂装

two-tone horn 双音喇叭（double-tone horn）

two-to-one gear 2 比 1 齿轮传动（指输入轴每转两转，输出轴转一转的齿轮传动装置）

two trailing arms and torsion bars type suspension 双纵臂、扭杆式

悬架（由两根纵向布置，前端与车架连接，后端与车轮连接的控制臂及一根扭杆弹簧组成的悬架）

two trailing shoe brake 双从蹄式制动器（当制动鼓正向旋转时，两制动蹄均为从蹄，即张开时的旋转方向与制动鼓旋转方向相反的内张型鼓式制动器，简称2T brake）

two transversely mounted leaf-springs type suspension 双横置板簧式悬架（两架横向布置、两端分别支承左、右车轮的钢板弹簧悬架系统）

two transverse rocker arms type suspension 双横摇臂式悬架（由上、下两根横向布置的控制臂连接车轮与车架或车身的悬架，亦称 double transverse swing arm type suspension，若该两根控制臂接近于平行布置，则亦称 parallel link type suspension）

two-value capacitor motor 双值电容式电动机（起动与运转采用两个不同的电容值）

two-valve combustion system 双气门燃烧系统（指常规内燃机每缸有一个进气门、一个排气门的燃烧系统）

two-way ①双向的，双路的 ②双频道的 ③两用的

two-way cock 双通开关，双通阀

two-way converter 双效催化转化器（指使用镀铂和钯的颗粒状或整体蜂窝状载体的氧化型转化器，只能将 CO 与 HC 两种有害物氧化成 H_2O）

two-way cylinder 双向作用缸

two-way dump truck 二面倾卸货车

two-way radio 双向无线电通信装置

two-way road 双向交通道路（同时对向通行的道路，有分隔带的，也有无分隔带的）

two-way shock absorber 双向减振器（= double-acting shock absorber）

two-way traffic 双向交通

two-wheeled trailer with power take-off (to) drive 带动力输出轴驱动装置的单轴双轮挂车（挂车有驱动桥）

two-wire system 双线电路（不搭铁电路）

T-wrench T形扳手

TWT 三轮式涡轮增压器（three wheel turbocharger，用以改善涡轮增压柴油机汽车的起步加速性能等）

type 类型，形式，式样，形式（同一种产品按其形状、结构、特征的不同所划分的类别）

type A fire （汽车的）A 型火灾（亦称 class A fire，指由木料、纸张、织物、衣物、引起的火灾。由汽油、润滑油、脂及其他易燃液体引起的火灾，称 B 型火灾"type B fire"，由电器设备、电动机、开关等引起的火灾，称 C 型火灾"type C fire"）

type and class of elastomeric materials （汽车用）橡胶材料的类型与级别（美国 SAE 及 ASTM 根据耐热老化温度分型"type"，根据耐油浸泡胀率分级"class"）

type approval test 形式认证试验（对新车型是否符合国家或国际标准要求的官方认证）

type by type classification 逐型分类，按型号逐一分类

Type C-B-Diesel fuel oil ［美］城市客车用柴油机油（其中 C，B 为 city bus 的简称）

type certificate 形式合格证（简称 TC，形式认证书）

type designations 型号标记（名称）

type 2K-H planetary gear drive mechanism 2K-H 型行星齿轮传动机构（由两个中心轮和一个行星架组成的行星齿轮传动机构。中心轮用 K 表示，行星架用 H 表示）

type number 型号

type of file teeth 锉刀牙型（美国分为三级，粗：bastard，细：2nd cut，精：smooth）

type of protection of an instrument for explosive atmosphere （仪表的）防爆形式（为防止点燃周围爆炸性混合物对仪器仪表采取各种特定措施的形式）

types of transportation 运输形式（按运输作用、组织方法或营运范围的不同，对公路运输的划分）

2/2 type solenoid valve 两位双通电磁阀（具有两个工位、两个出入口和一条出入通路的电磁控制液压阀，2/3 type，指具有两个工位、三个出入口和两条不同出入通路的两位三通电磁控制液压阀。3/3 type，指具有三个工位、三个出入口和两条不同出入通路的三位三通电磁控制液压阀）

type test 典型试验，标准试验；定型试验，形式认证试验，形式试验，形式检验（为证明设计符合一定规范和要求，对按设计制造的一台或多台仪器仪表设备、装置、机械等所进行的全性能检验）

type test procedure ①典型试验方法 ②形式（认证）试验程序

Type T-T-Fuel [美]货车、拖拉机用柴油（其中 T-T 为 truck，tractor 的简称）

typical 典型的

tyre 轮胎（= tire）

tyre axis system 轮胎坐标系（原点为轮胎接地中心，x' 轴为车轮平面中心线和地平面的交线）

tyre balance 轮胎平衡

tyre bead breaker 撬胎器（拆换轮胎用的撬胎边工具）

tyre bead flange area 轮胎胎圈（与轮辋）轮缘的接触面积（= tyre chafer area, tyre flange area）

tyre blow-out 轮胎爆破

tyre buttress area 轮胎上部侧壁面积（= tyre upper sidewall area）

tyre canvas 轮胎帘布（层）

tyre capacity 轮胎的承载能力（= tire capacity）

tyre carcass 胎体（帘布层、缓冲层、外层胶等部分的总称，简称 carcass）

tyre cavity 胎里（外胎的内表面）

tyre chafer 轮胎胎圈包布

tyre chafer area 轮胎胎圈包布（与轮辋轮缘的）接触面积（= tyre bead flange area）

tyre chafing strip 轮胎胎圈包布条（胎圈最外层的胶布层）

tyre chain 轮胎防滑链

tyre changer 换胎（时所用的）工具

tyre cold patching cement 冷补胎胶

tyre collapse 轮胎（气压不足，承受重负荷时被）压瘪

tyre contact patch 轮胎接地面

tyre cord 轮胎帘线（轮胎橡胶帘布层中的帘线）

tyre core 外胎的胎圈芯（见 bead core）

tyre-cornering-characteristics diagram 轮胎转弯力特性图（= Gough's tyre-characteristic diagram，见 cornering force）

tyre cover 备胎罩（备胎套）

tyre crane 轮式起重机

tyre curing 轮胎硫化

tyre cushioning capacity 轮胎减振能力（轮胎缓冲能力）

tyre cut 轮胎割痕

tyre defect indicator 轮胎损伤指示器

tyre engraving （轮胎）胎面花纹

tyre fitting ①轮胎安装（= tyre mounting）②轮胎固定件

tyre flange area 轮胎胎圈与轮辋轮缘的接触面积（= tyre bead flange

area)

tyre flap 轮胎胎圈包布条（= tyre chafing strip, rim band strip, flap）

tyre flat 轮胎漏气，轮胎气压过低

tyre force effect 轮胎（横向）力效应（指轮胎在横向力的作用下，由于弹性变形而侧偏对行驶方向、车轮侧倾及车身姿势等造成的影响。见 lateral force compliance steer; lateral force compliance camber）

tyre gaiter 轮胎套，轮胎罩

tyre-ground braking force 地面制动力（指制动时地面作用用轮胎的切线反作用力，是使汽车减速、停车的外力，其最大值取决于轮胎与地面的附着力）

tyre-ground braking force 轮胎-地面制动力

tyre hot patch 轮胎热补胶片

tyre inflation pressure warning telltale 轮胎充气压力警报灯（表示轮胎的充气压力已低于或高于规定压力的信号灯）

tyre iron ［美］拆轮胎棒，撬胎棒（= tyre lever）

tyre irregular wear 轮胎非正常磨损

tyre lever 撬胎棒（= tyre iron）

tyre load 轮胎负载

tyre locking ring 轮胎锁圈

tyre marking 轮胎标志（轮胎上的商标、厂名、规格、生产编号和材料等的模痕或印记）

tyre moment effect 轮胎（回正）力矩效应（弹性轮胎自回正力矩对汽车行驶方向性的影响，见 tire aligning torque）

tyre mounting and demounting device 轮胎拆装装置

tyre paint 轮胎涂料（轮胎上色涂料）

tyre patch center （汽车的）轮胎接地面中心（一般指轮胎瞬时接地面中心）

tyre pitch sequence 轮胎花纹排列

tyre pressure sensor 轮胎充气压力传感器

tyre recapping shop 轮胎翻新车间（= recapping shop）

tyre reconditioning 轮胎修补，轮胎翻修

tyre refinish 轮胎修整（不需要用材料就可消除轮胎外观缺陷的操作，需要用材料消除外观缺陷的操作称 tyre repair）

tyre removing and replacing machine 轮胎拆装机

tyre repair cement 补胎胶

tyre resistance coefficient （胎体弹性变形引起的）轮胎（滚动）阻力系数

tyre retreading 轮胎翻新（轮胎翻新方法的总称。可以仅指更换胎面胶，也可指更换胎面胶和胎侧胶等）

tyre-road adhesion coefficient 轮胎-路面附着系数（最大地面制动力与车轮垂直载荷之比）

tyre rolling circumference 轮胎滚动周长

tyre rotation 轮胎换位（按车辆保养规定，对装配在同一车辆上的轮胎作调换安装位置的操作）

tyre rough 轮胎毛坯（指硫化前已成形的轮胎）

tyre safe load 轮胎安全负载（轮胎容许负载，= tyre working load）

tyre sculpture 轮胎花纹

tyre series 轮胎系列（用相同的轮胎名义高宽比，对同一结构类型轮胎的特定分类）

tyre service 轮胎维护，轮胎维修

tyre side wall 轮胎侧壁

tyre size 轮胎规格（由名义的轮胎外直径、轮胎断面宽度、轮辋外直径组合所表示的轮胎尺寸）

tyre slip ①轮胎侧偏（指轮胎侧向弹性变形，= tyre side slip）②轮胎滑移（指轮胎相对路面相对滑移，= tyre skidding）

tyre slip angle 轮胎侧偏角（弹性车轮在侧向力的作用下，由于车轮的侧向弹性变形，其实际运动的方向不再是车轮平面所指的方向，而与其差一角度，这一现象称为轮胎侧偏，所偏的角度称为车轮轮胎侧偏角，即：车轮中心平面方向与轮胎接地中心行进方向间的夹角，= wheel slip angle，简称 slip angle）

tyre slip factor 轮胎侧偏系数（= slip factor）

tyre soling 轮胎修理，轮胎翻新（口语）

tyre spreader 张胎机，扩胎机（= tyre opener）

tyre squealing 轮胎啸响，轮胎发出噪音

tyre strap 轮胎衬带

tyre talc 轮胎粉（轮胎用滑石粉，用于内外胎之间）

tyre tape 轮胎衬带

tyre tread imprint 轮胎胎面印迹

tyre upper sidewall area 轮胎上部侧壁面积（= tyre buttress area）

tyre valve 轮胎气门嘴（用于轮胎充放气体或液体，并能保持和检测内压的止回阀门）

tyre valve core 轮胎气门芯

tyre valve hole misalignment 轮胎气门嘴孔位置不正（内胎、垫带上的轮胎气门嘴孔位置偏离设计尺寸的现象）

tyre valve rubber pad 轮胎气门嘴胶垫（将轮胎气门嘴与内胎胎身黏着为一体的胶垫）

tyre vulcanization 轮胎硫化

tyre vulcanizer 轮胎硫化器，轮胎热补机

tyre vulcanizing cement 热补胎胶

tyre weight coefficient 轮胎重量系数（重量与负荷、尺寸关系式中的系数）

tyre-well （汽车的）备胎舱，备胎腔

tyre width 轮胎宽度（简称 TW）

tyre with adjustable inflation pressure 调压轮胎（可根据使用条件大幅度调节轮胎内压的充气轮胎）

tyre working load 轮胎容许负荷（= tyre safe load）

UAES 联合汽车电子有限公司（中联汽车电子有限公司与罗伯特·博世有限公司在上海的合资企业 United Automotive Electronic Systems Co. Ltd 的简称）

UART （汽车电子控制系统中采用的）通用异步接收传输系统（信号的接收和发送是由控制字符控制的，而不是同步或按一定时间顺序的，universal asynchronous receiver transmitter system 的简称）

UART data link （通用公司 OBD Ⅱ 系统的）万能异步收发数据链线（universal asynchronized receive-transmit data link 的简称）

U-bar (-beam) 槽钢

U-bend U形弯管，U形弯头，U形弯道（=return bend）

ubiquitous 十分普遍的，处处可见的，尽人皆知的

u-bolt block U型螺栓垫块（固定U形螺栓的垫块）

u-bolt plate U型螺栓垫片（固定U形螺栓的板件）

U bolt wrench U形螺栓专用扳手（骑马螺栓专用扳手）

U-bottom （水陆两用汽车壳体的）U形底

UCC system ①底盘集中控制系统（undercarriage centralized control system 的简称，该系统由一个电子控制模块将制动、转向、悬架、传动等系统集中统一控制，共用传感器，资源共享，使整车的动力、操纵、稳定性等处于最佳状态）②整体式中央控制系统（unitized central control system 的简称，指由一个电子控制模块，对制动、转向悬架等做统一综合控制的电子系统）

U. C. engine 均质（混合气）充气发动机（uniform charge engine 的简称）

UCO 见 Waste cooking oil derived biodiesel

U Connect （Daimler Chrysler 公司推出的）蓝牙免提车载工具包（商品名）

U-core U型磁铁心

U-cylinder engine U 形发动机（=V-type engine，见 U-engine）

UD （变速器的）超低挡（underdrive gear 的简称，亦称爬行挡 "crawling gear"，用于爬坡或重载）

UDC 上止点（upper dead centre 的简称）

UDDS ［美］城市运行（模式）底盘测功器（排放和燃油经济性）测试程序（Urban Dynamometer Driving Schedule 的简称，该试验程序的时间为 22min 52s）

U drive-it-car 自驾驶式租赁轿车（指租来自己驾驶的汽车，大的出

租公司一般是，开到目的地后即可交给该公司在当地的营业处，= rental car, Rent-A-Car）

UEC ①欧洲客车制造商联盟（Union of European Coach Builders）②欧洲消费者联盟（Union of European Consumers）③万能电子控制器（universal electronic control）

U-engine U 型内燃机（由一个曲柄驱动两个平行布置的活塞且共用一个燃烧室的二冲程发动机，在工作循环的大部分时间内，这两个活塞的运动方向是相同的，有时亦称双缸单室式内燃机"split-single"）

UF ①脲醛树脂，脲醛塑料（urea formal-dehyde）②特细的（ultra-fine）

UFA 见 unsaturated fatty acids

U-frame U 形（车）架

U-gauge U 形压力计

U-girder U 形梁

UHF (uhf) 超高频（ultra-high-frequency 的简称，指 $3 \times 10^8 \sim 3 \times 10^9$ 的频率）

Uiper （克莱斯勒道奇）维帕牌轿车（Chrysler Dodge 厂生产的双座跑车，V10 发动机，排量 1990mL，功率 325kW，最高车速 288km/h，整备质量 1500kg）

U-iron U 形铁，槽钢

UIS （美国通用公司的）整体式点火系（见 DLI①）

UJ 万向节（U-joint, universal joint 的简称）

UK 联合王国（大不列颠及北爱尔兰联合王国，是英国的正式称号，United Kingdom 的简称）

UK bsh 英国蒲式耳（imperial bushel，=36.368 立方分米）

UK gallon 英国加仑（imperial gallon）

UK qt 英国夸（脱）（imperial quart，1/4 加仑）

ULCCC （英国政府的）超低碳（排放）轿车挑战（计划）（Ultra Low Carbon Car Challenge 的简称）

Ulcony metal 尤尔康尼轴承合金（重载荷铜铅轴承合金，铜 65%，铅 35%）

ULEV （美国 20 世纪 80 年代加利福尼亚州提出的）超低排放车（ultra-low emission vehicle 的简称，指新车在行驶 8 万 km 后，其排放限值仍能满足以下要求的车辆：非甲烷有机气体 0.04g/mile，NO_x 0.2g/mile，CO 1.7g/mile，且同一公司，一个车型年中出售的汽车排放平均值的总碳氢"THC"限值必须降低到 2001 年车型实际执行的 0.07g/mile）

ulf 超低频（ultra-low-frequency）

ULG 无铅汽油（unleaded gasoline 的简称，见 ULP）

U-link U 形联杆，U 形拉杆

ullage ①液罐中液面上部的空隙②（容器的）缺量，不足量③漏损量，漏耗量④用测定液罐内液面上部空间高度的办法来测定罐内液体容积的方法⑤测定液罐中液面某点到罐面的空间高度

ullage rule 量测液罐中液体容积用的、只测液面上部空间高度而不浸入液体中的量液尺（参见 ullage）

ULP 无铅汽油（unleaded petrol 的简称，按美国 ASTM 的标准，每 1L 汽油含铅量不超 0.018g 的汽油，亦称 ULG）

ULSAB 超轻钢制汽车车身（ultra-light steel automotive body 的简称，20 世纪 90 年代全球 34 家钢厂组成新联合共同体出资开展的一系列减轻汽车质量的研究项目之一，此外还有超轻钢制汽车覆盖件"ULSAC"，C 为 cover 的简称和超轻钢制汽车悬架"ULSAS"，S 为 suspention 的简称等研究课题）

ULSD 超低含硫量柴油（亦称 ULS diesel fuel，ultra low sulphur diesel fuel 的简称）

ultimate ①最终的，最后的，极端的；极限的，临界的；②基本的，主要的，首要的；③极限，终极，顶点

ultimate motor fuel 发动机用的最佳燃料

ultimate slope angle 极限坡道角

ultimate tensile stress 极限抗拉应力（最大抗拉应力，在拉伸试验中，金属试件被拉断时的最大负荷除以试件的原始断面面积，即金属每单位断面面积上所能承受的最大拉力，亦称 tenacity）

ultra-acoustics 超声学

ultra-capacitor 超级储电器（商品名，日本本田公司生产的汽油机-电动双动力轿车制动减速时由发电机以电能形式回收的能量的存储装置）

ultraca pa citorsystem 超级电容器系统（起蓄电池作用的大电容量充—放电型电容器组，用于复合动力车或燃料电池车）

ultra-compact 超紧凑的，超小型的

ultra-fine particles 超细微粒物（指直径 50nm 以下的微粒物）

ultra-high-frequency sound wave generator 超高频声波发生器

ultra-high-tensile steel 超高抗拉强度钢

ultra-high vacuum 超高真空

ultra lean combustion 超稀燃烧（使用超稀混合气燃烧，亦称 ultra lean burn）

ultralight hybrid car 微型混合动力车（超轻型双动力车，见 hybrid electric car）

ultra-light machine element 超轻量机械零件

ultra light steel automotive body 超轻钢车身（简称 ULSAB，20 世纪 90 年代欧亚等国家的 32 家钢铁公司联合开发的一种高强度超轻钢材制造的车身，较一般钢材车身轻 35%，强度增加一倍，保时捷公司使用这种钢材设计的 5 座轿车车身仅重 205kg）

ultra-linear amplifier 超高线性放大器

ultra-low carbon dioxide emission 超低二氧化碳（CO_2）排放

ultra-low emission vehicle 超低排放车（见 ULEV）

ultra-low inertia AC motor 超低惯性式交流电动机

ultra-low PM reduction system 超低微粒物排放减少系统

ultra-low sulfur diesel fuel 超低硫柴（油机燃）油

ultra-luxury mode 超豪华型

ultramicro 超微的（小于百万分之一的）

ultramicroscope 超高倍显微镜

ultramicrotechnique 超微技术

ultramodern 超现代的（尖端的，最新式的，极其现代化的）

ultraportable 超轻便式，超轻型的（简称 up）

ultra-precise control 超精密控制

ultrared gas analyzer 红外线气体分析仪

ultrared laser four-wheel alignment system 红外线激光四轮定位仪

ultrared ray 红外线（= infrared ray）

ultrared ray dryer 红外线烘干机，红外线烘干装置

ultrared spectrophotometer 红外线分光光度计

ultra rich mixture 过浓混合气

UltraShift 超级换挡（美 Eaton 公司供 8 级货车用的自动换挡 10 挡变速器的商品名）

ULTRA shine （轿车车身的）超光

亮水晶打蜡（商品名）
ultrashort journey 极短的运程
ultrashort-waves 超短波
ultrasonator 超音速振荡器（超声波发生装置）
ultrasonic ①超声波②超声波的
ultrasonic bonding ①超声波焊接②超声波黏结
ultrasonic cleaning 超声波清洗
ultrasonic current meter 超声波流速计（利用超声波在流体中的传播速度随流体流速的变化而变化的特性制成的流速计）
ultrasonic degreasing 超声波去油
ultrasonic detector of defects 超声波探伤器（= ultrasonic inspector, ultrasonic flaw detector）
ultrasonic digital thickness gauge 超声波数字型厚度计
ultrasonic dip tank 超声波（零件）浸洗槽
ultrasonic flow meter 超声波流量计
ultrasonic generator 超声波发生器
ultrasonic guidance system 超声波导向系统
ultrasonic inspection 超声波探伤（= ultrasonic detection of defects）
ultrasonic measurement karman vortices air flow meter 超声波计量（型）卡尔曼涡流式空气流量计（见 karman vortices air flow meter）
ultrasonic motor ①超声波马达（一种精密的控制系统用压电型执行器，亦称 ultrasonic traveling-wave motor 或 traveling-wave motor，具有高转矩，可达 1.3 N·m，低转速，30～130 r/min，精确定位，运转无声等特点）②超声波电动机（利用压电原理感生超声行进电压波、推动转子旋转的新型电动机）
ultrasonic noise generator 超声波噪声发生装置

ultrasonic nozzle 超声波喷嘴（利用超声波振动，将燃油击成极细小的微粒）
ultrasonic propagation 超声波传播
ultrasonic rain-cleaning mirror 超声波除雨后视镜（简称 ultrasonic mirror，利用超声波产生的振动及电加热器将后视镜上的雨水除净）
ultrasonic receiver 超声波接收器
ultrasonics 超声学
ultrasonic soldering 超声波（软）钎焊
ultrasonic tester 超声波检验仪
ultrasonic transducer 超声波传感器
ultrasonic transmitter 超声波发射器
ultrasonic vehicle detector 超声波侦车器（在道路上方或一侧设置的超声波车辆感知器，利用汽车通过时超声波反射的变化来侦车）
ultrasonic welding 超声波焊接
ultrasonoscope 超声波（探测）仪
ultrasound anti-collision technology 超声波防撞技术
ultra-sound wave 超声波（= ultrasonic wave，指频率 20 kHz 以上的声波）
ultra-thin type piston ring 超薄型活塞环（如：丰田第二代复合动力系统发动机活塞头道压缩环仅 0.8 mm，以减小摩擦损失）
ultraviolet ①紫外线的，产生紫外线的②紫外线（简称 UV）
ultraviolet impulse 紫外线光脉冲
ultraviolet radiation 紫外线辐射
ultraviolet rays flaw detector 紫外线探伤器（用紫外线照射涂有渗透性发光剂及显像液的零件表面，具有裂纹等损伤的部分，即产生人眼极易辨别的荧光）
ultraviolet stability 抗紫外线（光）稳定性
ultro low sulfur engine oil 超低含硫量机油

ULV (发动机的)超轻气门,简称 ultra light (engine) valve

umbilical cord 脐状电缆(集中于一处的多根导线端)

umbilic piont 脐点(亦称 umbilical point)

UMTA [美]都市公共交通署(Urban Mass Transportation Administration 的简称)

unaided ignition 非助燃点火(自发点火)

unalloyed 非合金的(纯金属的)

unassembled bus 客车散件(指未组装成整车的全套客车散件)

unauthorized vehicle 未经审验许可使用的车辆

unavailable ①无用的,无效的,不可利用的②得不到的

unbalance 不平衡;失去平衡

unbalanced attenuator (无源集成电路的)非补偿衰减器(一个输入端对一个输出端有效地短路的衰减器)

unbalanced camber (车轮的)不平衡外倾(指车轮的前束和外倾在 side slip tester 上测试的侧偏值为零,即两者相互平衡后,外倾角的单独改变量)

unbalanced gasoline 稳定性不良的汽油

unbalanced load 不平衡载荷(不均匀载荷)

unbalanced mechanical seal 非平衡式机械密封(载荷系数 $K \geqslant 1$ 的机械密封,见 load factor)

unbalanced moment 不平衡力矩

unbalanced toe-in (车轮的)不平衡前束(参见 unbalanced camber,即前束与外倾平衡后,前束单独的改变量)

unbalanced weight 不平衡重

unbanked slope 无横向倾斜的坡道,无超高坡道

unban (test) cycle (汽车经济性及排放等测试模拟市区行车的)市区测试循环(一般包括加速、减速、等速、怠速等工况)

unbelted 未系安全带的(指驾驶员、乘员)

unbend 矫正,调整,压平,校直

unbender 矫直机

unblock 开启,开放,接通;放行,通行

unblown edition 非增压型,非增压版(柴油机等)

unbolt 松开螺栓

unbreakable glass 不碎玻璃

unbuffered 无缓冲装置的

unburned HC emission 废气中未燃烧的 HC 排放(见 unburned hydrocarbons 及 exhaust hydrocarbon emission)

unburned hydrocarbons 未燃烧的碳氢化合物(特指由于燃料在发动机内未燃烧或燃烧不完全而产生的随废气排至大气的 HC 排放)

unburnedness 未燃尽(程)度

uncertainty of measurement 测量不确定度(表征被测量的真值在某个量值范围内的一种估计)

unclear marking 标志不清

uncombined carbon 游离碳

uncompensated brake linkage 无补偿的制动机构杆系

uncompensated ring 非补偿环(不具有轴向补偿能力的密封环)

uncompensated ring adaptor 非补偿环座(用于装嵌非补偿环的零件)

uncompressed cushion 未承压软垫(自由状态的软垫)

unconditional 无条件的

unconditional stability 无条件稳定

uncongealable 不冻的

uncontinuous change ①非连续变速,非无级变速②非连续变化

uncontrollable 不可控制的,不能调

uncontrolled combustion phase 非受控制燃烧期（自由燃烧期，指柴油机诱导期后的爆炸燃烧期）

uncontrolled variables 非受控变量（非调节变量）

uncorrected result 未修正结果（有系统误差存在而未加修正的测量结果）

uncounter-weighted crankshaft 无平衡重曲轴

uncouple 脱开，分开，松脱，拆开，解除连接（耦合）

uncoupling 拆开；脱开联轴节，非耦合

uncover 揭开盖子，移去覆盖物；使露出，暴露，揭露

uncovered 无盖的，无外壳的；裸露的，暴露的

uncrossed 不相交的

UNC thread [英] 全国统一粗螺纹（Unified National Coarse thread 的简称）

unctuosity 润滑性；油（腻）性

unctuous 油性的，油滑的，含油脂的，腻滑的

unctuousness 润滑性；油（腻）性

uncultivated 未开发的，未耕种的（土地）

undamped control 无阻尼控制，不带阻尼器的调节装置

undamped natural frequency 无衰减固有频率（指无阻尼自由振动的频率，见 undamped vibration）

undamped oscillations 无阻尼振荡（指无衰减等幅振荡）

undamped vibration 无阻尼振动（振幅不随时间而衰减的振动）

undecane 十一烷（烃）

underbalance 平衡不足（未完全平衡，未达平衡标准）

underbead crack 焊道下（面的内部）裂纹

underbody ①物体下部，底部 ②（轿车承载式车身结构中的）底板（= floor pan, floor board, 包括车身地板、轮口板和加强件）③车底④（在与空气动力有关的上、下文中，指）车底的有效轮廓

underbody aeroacoustic sources 车身底板下方的气动噪声源

underbody assembly （轿车承载式车身的）底板总成（= floor pan assembly）

underbody belly pan 车身下腹板（车身底部导流板，可使气流平顺，减少风阻）

underbody coating 车底保护涂层（亦称 underbody protection）

underbody flow 车底气流（指流过车底的气流，以及由此而产生的空气动力学特性）

underbody hardware ①车身底部的结构件 ②车身底部的各种装置

underbody press 车身底板压力机（车身底部构件冲压设备）

underbody sealing compound 车身底面的防锈、消声、密封、保护涂层（简称 underseal, 美称 undercoat）

underbody wind noise （汽车行驶时车身底板下方高速空气流产生的）底板风噪音

under bonnet area （轿车、长头货等的）发动机舱（= engine compartment）

under-bonnet light（ing） 发动机罩下照明（亦称 under-hood light）

underbridge （立体多层交叉的上跨线桥下的下穿式）跨线桥

underbridge clearance 桥下净空（桥洞距路面的高度）

under bumper apron （汽车）保险杠下方的挡风板（起减小空气浮升力的作用，见 apron）

under car aerial 底盘天线（= chassis aerial）

undercarriage ①底架，脚架；起落架，下支架②（车辆的）行走部分（行走机构，包括车轮、车桥和悬架系统，主要指货车）

under charge 燃油供应不足；充电不足

undercoat ①底漆②[美]（车身）底部表面保护涂层（隔热，防水，隔音，防震，防尘 = underseal）③上底漆，涂敷（车身）底部表面保护涂层

under construction （公路）在施工中（公路上的标志）

under cooling ①过度冷却，过冷（= supercooling）②冷却不足

undercord ①（传动带等）拉力帘线层下面的②（传动皮带拉力帘线层下面的）橡胶层

undercover 底罩（装在车身下的罩，用来减小噪声和空气阻力等）

under crossing （道路的）下穿式立体交叉

under crown 活塞顶（本身的）底面（指活塞筒腔内的顶面）

undercut 挖根（对齿轮轮齿的齿根过渡曲面进行有意识的修削）

under cutting （电机整流子云母片等的）修割作业（割低作业）

under dash unit 泛指安装在汽车仪表板下面的装置或设备

underfilm corrosion 漆层下金属面锈蚀（亦称 creepage）

underfloor airflow management 车底气流控制

under-floor battery （全电动汽车等装在）车身底扳下的（动力）电池（组）

underfloor catalytic converter （安装在）车厢地板下的催化转换器

underfloor-engine（d）bus 发动机置于车厢地板下的客车

underfloor inspection （车辆）地板下部检查

underfloor mid-engine 车身地板下中置式发动机（发动机位于车身底板下，前、后桥中间位置）

underfloor-mounted 在车厢底板下安装的

underfloor shield （车身）底板下面的防护板

underframe 车身底板构架

underground garage 地下车库，地下停车场

underground gasoline tank 地下汽油罐

underground passage way 地下通道

under hood ①发动机舱（= engine compartment）②（指）发动机及发动机舱内的各种附件

under-hood light 发动机罩下照明灯（= under-bonnet light）

under-hood temperature （汽车的）发动机罩下温度

underhung spring （位于车轴下的）悬吊式钢板弹簧

under inflation wear of tire 轮胎充气不足（造成的）磨损

under interlayer （汽车用夹层玻璃）胶合层缩卷（胶合层端面自玻璃的边缘向内部收缩的现象）

underloaded 装载不足的（未满载的，未能达到额定荷载量，部分荷载的）

underload wear 轻荷载时的磨损

underlying 隐含的、潜在的

under personalized repair method （要求被修复的零件或总成装回原车的）原装修理法

underpin ①支撑，支持②作为…的基础③在…下面加基础

underpinning ①加支柱②支柱，支持物，支撑结构

under powered （发动机）功率不足的

underpriming （发动机起动时）注入燃油不足的

underrated 低于额定的,低于标定的,低于定额的;低于规定的

under repair(s) 在修理中(正在修理的)

underride 钻撞(特指汽车相撞时,一车被压于另一车下的现象)

underrun protection ①(货车后部的)防止钻撞(防止小客车等碰撞货车的后部时钻入货车车厢下面而使乘员受伤害)②防钻撞装置(如:underride guard 车尾防钻撞护栅,underrun bumper 防钻撞保险杠,= underrun protection bar, underrider, underrun crash barrier 大型货车后端的防钻撞板,防钻撞栅杆)

undersaturated 未饱和的,欠饱和的

underscreen 见 undershield

under seal 见 under coating

undersealing 密封不严

under seat engine vehicle 发动机位于驾驶员座位下的汽车

under seat heater 安装在座椅下的取暖器

under seat panel (车身底板的)座椅板(见 seat pan)

under-sensitive 灵敏度不足的

under service conditions 在使用条件下

undershield (发动机舱或整个车身的)底面护板,底面挡泥板(亦称 underscreen)

undersize ①减小尺寸(指小于标准的尺寸)②尺寸过小的,尺寸不够的

undersize bearing (供修理用的)较标准尺寸小的轴承

undersize spare parts 减小尺寸的(修理用)备件(如:轴瓦)

underslung bearing 悬盖轴承,吊装轴承(如:曲轴主轴承)

underslung frame 凹式车架(= drop frame,指前、后桥间的部分,呈凹形、低于车桥的车架,亦称 underslung platform chassis 低货台底盘)

underslung spring (位于车轴下的)悬吊式钢板弹簧

underslung type suspension 下置板簧式悬架(钢板弹簧安装在车轴下面的悬架形式)

underslung worm 下置式蜗杆(蜗杆置于涡轮之下)

underslung worm drive 见 underslung worm transmission

underslung worm transmission 下置式蜗杆传动装置(指蜗杆位于涡轮下方的涡轮-蜗杆传动装置,可降低蜗杆轴的高度,亦称 underslung worm drive)

underspeed ①速度不足②低速③降低速度

under square engine (行程/缸径比大于1的)长行程发动机(,亦称 undersquare engine 亚方型发动机 long stroke engine)

understandability test (路标的)可分辨性试验

understeer (汽车的)不足转向(特性)(简称 US,指:①在车速一定而改变横向加速度时,若名义转向角"normal steering angle"的斜率大于阿克曼转向角"Ackerman steering angle"的斜率,该汽车的转向特性为不足转向,该特性相当于静态裕度"static margin"的负值②汽车对转向输入的响应不足,直线稳速行驶时转向盘转过 θ 角短暂时间后,前轮侧偏比后轮侧偏严重,即前桥侧偏角大于后桥侧偏角,汽车的转弯半径越来越大。具有这一转向特性的汽车在直线行驶时,遇横向力作用,具有恢复直线行驶的良好稳定性③车辆对转向输入的响应的特征为横摆率"yaw rate"递增,因而驾驶员必须加大转向角才能保持想要的转弯半径)

under-the-hood parts (指所有装

在）发动机罩下的部件

under thick of inner tube 内胎厚度不够（内胎胎身厚度局部低于标准规定的尺寸）

undertighten 稍微拧紧，不拧足

under-tread ①胎面基部（= tread base，指胎面花纹沟底以下至缓冲层或带束层和帘布层之间的胶层）②（泛指）胎面下的加强帘布层

under-tyred vehicle 轮胎小于规定尺寸的车辆

under-water kit 供车辆潜渡用的成套装备

under-water test 水下试验

under way refueling （汽车）路上加油

under weight 质量不足（质量低于额定值、不符合要求）

undesired gear shifting 意外换挡（故障）

undesired sound 噪声（不希望有的及令人不愉快的、起干扰作用的声音的总称，= noise）

undetected failure time 失效未发现时间（从失效发生到被发现的时间）

unditching gear 汽车自救拖曳绞盘装置

undivided road 无分隔带道路（俗称一块板路，对向交通之间没有分隔带）

undo ①拆卸，拆散，解体，拧松②取消，废除③破坏，毁坏

undue wear 过度磨损，不正常磨损

undulated sheet iron 波纹铁皮，瓦楞铁皮

undulating terrain 起伏不平的（丘陵）地带

undulations of ground 地面的起伏平面度

UN Earth Summit 地球宪章（联合国环境与发展大会，1992年6月3~14日在巴西首都举行，全世界178个国家1.5万名代表参会，110个国家首脑出席会议，通过了里约环境与发展宣言）

unequal addendum（gear）system 不等齿顶高齿轮系

unequal length arm suspension 不等长控制臂式悬架［指上、下控制臂长度不同的双纵臂或双横臂式悬架，亦称长-短臂式悬架（short-long arm），简称SLA suspension］

unequal length driver shaft 变长度传动轴（可伸缩式传动轴）

unequal-length wishbone suspension 不等长双A形横臂式（独立）悬架（亦称unequal wishbones，其上A形臂比下A形臂短，可减轻轮胎磨损）

unequally loaded 不均匀负载的

unequally spaced coil spring 不等节距螺旋弹簧

unequally spaced teeth 不等距的齿

unequal stress 不均匀应力

UNESCO 联合国教科文组织（United-Nations Educational Scientific and Cultural Organization的简称）

uneven ①不平整的，不平坦的，不平的②不均匀的，参差不齐的③不稳的，易变化的

uneven bead width 胎圈宽窄不一（两侧胎圈宽度不一致的现象）

uneven heating 不均匀加热

unevenness 不均匀性，不均匀度，不均衡度；不平整度，粗糙度

uneven running 不平稳运转

uneven tread wear 轮胎胎面的不均匀磨损

unexpected failure 意外的损坏，意外失效

unexpected injury of passenger 旅客意外伤害

unexpended 未耗尽的

unexplosive 非爆炸性的材料

unfading ①（摩擦材料）不衰退的

（抗衰退性能高的）②不褪色的
unfair hole 不通孔（见 closed hole）
UNF thread ［英］全国统一细螺纹（Unified National Fine thread 的简称）
ungear 脱离啮合（状态），脱开传动装置
unhydrous 不含水的（无水的，干的）
uniaxial 同轴的，同心的；单轴的（结晶）
uniaxiality 同轴性，（结晶的）单轴性
unibody （无车架的承载式）整体（单壳）车身（见 unitary construction）
unicontrol 单操纵杆控制（指不用踏板和转向盘而只用一根操纵杆，前推控制加速，后拉控制减速，左右推动控制转向的汽车操纵系统）
unidirectional ①单向的（不可逆向的）②单自由度的③单方面的
unidirectional clutch 单向离合器
unidirectional (flow) scavenging 见 uniflow scavenging
unified coarse thread 统一标准粗牙螺纹（简称 UNC）
unified fine thread 统一标准细牙螺纹（简称 UNF）
uniflow ①单向流动，直流，顺流 ②单向流动的，直流的，顺流的
uniflow cooling 单向流动冷却
uniflow scavenging （二冲程发动机）直流扫气［充量从汽缸的一端进入，驱使废气沿汽缸中心线方向从汽缸另一端排出的扫气方式，亦称 unidirectional (flow) scavenging］
uniflow suction valve 单向吸气阀（亦称 single suction valve）
uniform acceleration cam 等加速凸轮
uniform angular velocity 匀角速度
uniform charge engine 均质充气发动机（均质燃烧发动机，亦称 uniform-charge Otto-engine，指燃烧室内混合气为均质的 Otto 发动机，以区别于分层充气发动机。简称 UC engine，参见 stratified charge engine）
uniform circular motion 等速圆周运动
uniform combustion 均匀燃烧
uniform continuity 均匀连续（性），一致连续（性）
uniform convergence （均）匀（收）敛，一致收敛
uniform corrosion （相对于局部腐蚀"localized corrosion"而言的暴露表面的）整体腐蚀
uniform distribution 均匀分布（= rectangular distribution）
uniform divergence 均匀发散，一致发散
uniform-geometry technique 规则形状技术（指用形状一定的标准化元器件装配微型结构的技术）
uniform grade 均匀坡度
uniforming of flow （液流、气流等的）整流（指使涡流、紊流通过整流格栅等转变为单向流动的层流）
uniformity 均匀性，匀质性；一致性，同一性，统一性
uniformity of illuminance 照度均匀度（表示给定平面上照度变化的度量。可用最小与平均照度之比或最小与最大照度之比表示）
uniformity of mixture composition 可燃混合气成分的均匀性
uniformity of pulverization 雾化的均匀性，喷雾的均匀性
uniformity of tire ①轮胎运转的均匀性（指承受负荷的轮胎旋转时，一定半径上产生的各种力及这些力变化的均匀性）②轮胎质地结构的均一性
uniformity test （轮胎的）均匀性试验（在直线等速恒定负荷下测定轮

胎旋转轴中心位置变化的试验，或在直线等速恒定动负荷半径下测定轮胎受力变化的试验）

uniformly distributed load 均匀分布的载荷

uniformly varying load 等变负载（匀变负载）

uniformly varying stress 等变应力

uniform material 均质材料（宏观均匀或宏观连续的材料）

uniform motion cam 等速凸轮（如：使气门在整个升程中速度不变的凸轮）

uniform service road （高速道路等的）流量调节路（如：保证山区等起伏较长的高速公路车流均匀的侧道）

uniform specimen 均质试样（由单一均质材料构成的试样）

uniform structure 均匀的（金相）组织

uniform thickness 等厚度

Uniform Tire Quality Grading Standards [美] 轮胎质量分级统一标准（简称 UTQGS）

Uniform Vehicle Code [美] 车辆统一规范（简称 UVC）

uniform velocity motion 等速运动

uniform wear 均匀磨损

uniframe 与车身制成一体的车架

unignited 未点燃的

unijet 稳喷（意大利 Alfa Romeo 公司生产的世界第一台批量生产的柴油机共用高压储油歧管直喷系统的商品名，见 common rail direct injection system）

unijunction transistor 单结型晶体管（单晶管）

unilateral ①单向的，单向作用的 ②单方面的

unilateral conductivity 单向导电率

unilateral surface 单侧曲面

unilateral tolerance 单向公差

unilateral waiting （道路）单边停放车辆（一边禁止停车制）

Unimate （原为一种机械手的商品名，现已成为）通用机械手（的通称）

uninflammable 不易燃烧的，不易着火的

uninspected 未经检查的，未经检验的

uninsured 未保险的

unintended fueling sensor （电子控制燃油系统中向控制模块发送执行器件漏油信息的）执行器件漏油传感器

uninterrupted 非断续性的（连续的）

uninterrupted power supply 不间断供电装置（连续供电装置，指外来电源断电时，能短时间内保持继续供电的装置，简称 UPS）

union ①联合，联合体，联邦，联盟 ②连接，接合 ③连接器，接头，连管节

union adaptor 联轴接头，联管接头

unionarc welding 磁性焊剂二氧化碳保护焊

union body 承载式车身

union coupling 联管节，管接头（亦称 union fitting, union joint, 简称 union）

union-hose connector 软管管节头

unionmelt welding 埋弧自动焊（焊剂层下自动焊）

Union of European Coach Builders 欧洲客车制造商联盟（简称 UEC）

Union of European Consumers 欧洲消费者联盟（简称 UEC）

union of tire 轮胎缓冲层边缘的橡胶衬带

union pipe 连接管

Uniontown procedure （车用汽油的道路辛烷值的）联点测定法（在试验条件下，节气门全开，使汽车的车

速由 10mile/h 加速到 50~60mile/h。车速每升高 5mile/h 就记录一次发动机的爆震强度，做出车速与发动机爆震强度的关系曲线。汽油试样的上述曲线和用异辛烷正庚烷标准混合油做出的曲线相比较，汽油试样的道路辛烷值即等于与其最大爆震强度相同的标准燃油所含的异辛烷体积百分率值，见 roadknock rating method)

unipolar armature 单极电枢
unipolar pulse 单极脉冲
unipolar transistor 单极晶体管
unipump 组合泵，内燃（机）泵
unique solution 唯一解
uni-servo brake 单向伺服式制动器（简称 US brake，仅在制动鼓的某一旋转方向上，才能借助摩擦力的作用使施加力的效能增高的内张型鼓式制动器，亦称单向自增力式制动器，单向自助力式制动器)
UNISIST 通用科学技术信息系统（Universal System for Information in Science and Technology 的简称)
unisometric drawing 不等角制图法（采用不等角投影的绘图方法，一般用于绘制易于理解的立体简图)
unisometric projection 不等角投影法（不等角制图法中使用的投影方法，即立体投影时，互相相交的三个侧边，分别用不同的角度表示的投影)
unisurface system 统一平面法（车身硬模的一种数字控制加工法)
unit ①单位，单元，组合件②装置，设备，机器，仪器③全套装备，成套设备，机组
unit area 单位面积
unitary body 承载式车身（整体式车身，见 monocoque body)
unitary braking system （汽车列车的）统一式制动系统（主车及挂车的制动系在正常情况下，都由主车上的制动踏板控制，主车与挂车一旦脱钩，挂车即自动地制动)
unitary construction 整体式结构（美称 unitized construction，①对汽车的驱动系统，指发动机离合器和变速器组成一个总成，但仍可分件拆开的结构②对车身，指无车架的承载式整体车身结构)
unitary construction body 承载式车身（指全部荷载都由车身承受无独立车架的整体式结构车身，亦称 chassisless body, full-monocoque body, integral body, monocoque body, unibody, unitary body, unit body, unit construction body)
unitary underframe 单体式底板，整体式底板（车身底板与底架合并成一个整体构件)
unit assembled window 车窗总成（包括窗框，升降、开启关闭机构及车窗玻璃，有时亦包括刮水器、喷洗器等附件)
unit assembly drawing 总成装配图，组件装配图
unit bore system 基孔制
unit-cast 整体浇铸的
unit compressive stress 单位压缩应力
unit construction system 整体结构系统
unit cost 单价
unit damping energy 单位阻尼能（单位体积均质材料在简谐应力作用下，一个周期内由于材料内阻尼而耗散的能量)
unit design （机器）整体结构设计，整体设计
United Automotive Electronic System Co. Ltd （中德合资）联合汽车电子有限公司（简称 UAES，中联汽车电子有限公司与德国 Bosh 有限公司的合资企业，1996 年 5 月 11 日正式开业，年产 120 万套规模，

总部设在上海，下设技术中心，及上海、无锡、西安三个分厂）

United States Bureau of Standards 美国标准局（简称 USBS）

United States Council for Automotive Research 美国汽车研究会（建立于1992年，为了协调与促进克莱斯勒、福特与通用汽车公司之间的研究工作，简称 USCAR）

United States gauge 美国标准量规（简称 USG）

United States of America Standards 美国标准（简称 USAS）

United States Snowmobile Association 美国雪地汽车协会（USSA）

United States standard screw thread 美国标准螺纹

United States Testing Company Inc 美国试验公司（试验安全带，玻璃和头盔等，简称 USTC）

unit elements of projective coordinate system 投影坐标系的单位元素

unit elongation 单位伸长度（伸长率）

unit engine （发动机和变速器组装在一个壳体内的）整体发动机

unite parcel service （美国的汽车运输办理的）联运包裹服务（相当于我国的零担运输，简称 UPS）

unit exchange repairing method 总成互换修理法（用储备的完好总成替换汽车上的不可用总成的修理方法）

unit extension （绿灯的）单位延长（感知有车辆存在时，绿灯再延续一段的最少时间）

unit flow 单位流量

unit force 单位力

unit fuel injection pump 分列式喷油泵（不自带驱动凸轮轴的柱塞式喷油泵）

unit in combination （汽车列车的）各组成单元（牵引车、半挂车或挂车）

unit injector 整体式泵-喷油器（高压油泵与喷油器组成一体、同时泵油和喷油的装置）

unitize ①（零、部件的）规格化，标准化设计，规格化，统一化②将货物包装成标准尺寸的运输单元，货物包装集装箱化③单元化，积木化，组合化

unitized 组合的，成套的，成组的，合成的，组成的，统一的，划一的；整体的；通用化的，规格化的

unitized body 整体式承载车身（= monocoque body, body integral with frame）

unitized car 承载式整体车身轿车，(= frameless car, stressed-skin car, unitary car, single unit car, monocoque car)

unitized carrier-type axle housing 整体式桥壳（将减速器壳与桥壳的中间部分铸成一体，两端压入无缝钢管后，用塞焊将其与中间部分焊接在一起）

unitized design 通用化设计，规格化设计，标准化设计

unitized drive shaft ①组合式传动轴（由金属与复合材料组合而成的传动轴。在薄壁的金属管内，用复合材料制成的分层轴衬从内部加强）②整体式传动轴

unitized housing 整体式壳体（= onepiece housing）

Unitized Ignition System （美国通用公司的）整体式点火系（商品名，简称 UIS，见 DLI①）

unitized shipment 集装箱运货

unitized track 可拆卸式钢板路面（一种试验跑道）

unit of understeer （汽车的）不足转向度单位（常用基准侧偏角的单位 deg/g 表示，见 reference steer angle）

unit repair plant for vehicle 汽车总

unit strain energy 单位应变能（单位体积均质材料在简谐作用下，一个周期内所储存的应变能）

unit type crankshaft 整体式曲轴

unit type fuel injection system 整体式燃油喷射系统（由凸轮轴通过推杆和摇臂等直接驱动各缸单独的喷油泵-喷嘴组成一体，同时进行泵油和喷油的系统）

unit vehicle repair method 总成修理法（用储备的完好总成更换汽车上需要修理的总成）

unit velocity 单位速度（如：指气流或液流单位流量通过的时间等）

unit volume （转子发动机的）单室容积（=cell volume）

unit wear 单位磨耗（简称单耗，如：胎面花纹深度每磨耗1mm所行驶的km数）

unit wheel bearing 整体式轮毂轴承（亦称 one piece wheel bearing 单件式轮毂轴承）

unity feed back control system 直接反馈控制系统［传输函数 ω（s）=1 的反馈控制系］

unity slope 单位斜率

unity thread 统一标准螺纹

UNIVAC 通用型自动计算机（universal automatic computer 的简称，亦写作 univac）

universal ①万能的，通用的②万向的

universal asynchronous receiver/transmitter 见 bidirectional data link

universal ball joint 万向球节（=universal spheric joint）

universal bevel protractor 万能量角器，活动量角器

universal brand 通用品种

universal car 多用途轿车

universal container 通用集装箱

universal coupling 万向节（=universal joint）

universal drawbar 通用牵引装置，通用牵引杆

universal drive belt 多用传动带（如：可同时驱动凸轮轴、风扇、发电机、油泵、水泵、液压泵、空气压缩机等全部装置的一根皮带）

universal electric tester 万能电气试验台

universal electronic control 万能电子控制器，通用电子控制器（简称 UEC）

universal engineering tractor 通用型工程机械牵引车

universal gear 齿轮式万向节（由带齿的轮盘组成，两轴夹角可大至为90°）

universal gear tester 万能测齿仪

universal gravitation 万有引力

universal joint 万向节（在两轴夹角不变或改变时，均能够将转矩和旋转运动从一根轴传到另一根轴的关节式的机械装置，简称UJ，亦称 universal coupling）

universal joint（center）cross 万向节十字轴（=universal center cross, universal joint cross-head, universal joint pin, universal joint spider, universal joint trunnion）

universal joint flange 万向节突缘

universal joint flange yoke 万向节突缘叉

universal joint fork 万向节叉（亦称 universal joint jaw）

universal joint needle bearing 万向节滚针轴承

universal joint roller 万向节滚针，万向节滚子

universal joint shaft 万向节传动轴（=propeller shaft）

universal joint shaft tube 万向节传动轴管（=cardan tube）

universal joint sleeve yoke 万向节套筒叉
universal joint sliding yoke 万向节滑动叉（亦称 universal joint slip yoke）
universal joint type output mechanism 万向节型输出机构（采用万向节作为输出机构）
universally jointed axle 万向节连接的半轴
universal machine 万能工作机械
universal meter 万用（电）表
universal motor 通用电动机（交直流两用电动机）
universal protractor 万能量角器
universal puller 通用拉器
universal receiver 通用接收机（= allmains receiver）
universal slip joint 滑动花键式万向节（= sliding universal joint）
universal small car engine 通用小型车用发动机
universal spheric joint 万向球节（= universal ball joint）
universal strength tester 万能强度试验机
Universal Traffic Management System 全面交通管理系统（见 UTMS）
universal turbulence constant 通用紊流常数
unjointed beam （无焊缝、铆接、螺栓的）整体梁
unjustified 未确定的
unknown 未知的，待求的（如：unknown number"未知数"，unknown quantity"未知量"，unknown term"未知项"）
unladen 卸载的，空载的
unladen static deflection 自重引起的静载挠度
unladen vehicle mass 车辆空载质量（对载货汽车或客车一般理解为加上驾驶员和助手及所有服务设施，但未装货物或乘客的整车整备质量）
unladen weight ①空载重量②（汽车的）整备重量（整备质量的旧称，= kerb mass，见 curb mass）
unladen weight group 按空载质量分级的（运输车辆）组
unleaded gasoline ［美］无铅汽油（美国 ASTM 规定，不加含铅的添加剂，含铅量不多于 0.018g/L，= unleaded petrol）
unleaded premium gasoline 高级无铅汽油（无铅添加剂的高辛烷值汽油）
unlicensed cabbies 无证出租汽车（无营业证的出租汽车）
unload 卸载，卸下，卸除，卸荷
unloaded ball joint 非承载球节（如：steering ball joint）
unloaded kilometrage 空车行程公里数（= empty vehicle kilometer）
unloaded spring 自由状态弹簧
unloaded weight 空车重
unloader ①卸载机，卸货机②卸荷器，减压器
unloader lever 卸荷杆
unloader valve （= delivery valve）①卸荷阀，放泄阀，卸载阀②（气制动系统中的）限压阀（当气压超过规定值时，该阀开启，将压缩空气放出至大气）
unloading circuit ①（液压系统的）释压回路（卸荷回路，卸载回路）②卸载电路
unloading cone spin-resistant differential 卸荷锥式防滑转差速器
unloading valve 卸荷阀（卸载阀）
unlock 开启，开锁，断开，脱开，分离，解除连锁
unlubricated sliding 无润滑滑动
unmachinable 不能机械加工的
unmanned vehicle （无线电操纵的）无人驾驶车辆
unmatched ①不相配的，不相称的

②无比的，不可比拟的
unmetalled ①（表面）没有金属保护层的②没有硬质路面的（道路）
unmilitary 非军事的（非军用的）
unmodified polystyrene 通用聚苯乙烯（未经改性处理的聚苯乙烯）
unnotched bearing 不带装球缺口的球轴承
unobstructed floor space （车厢）地板的无障碍面积
unobstructed front view 无阻挡的前方视野
unoil 除油（清除机油）；脱脂
unoperating rate 停驶率（全部营运车辆的总车日中，停驶车日所占的比率）
unorthodox 非传统的，非常规的，非正统的
U-notch U形缺口，U形刻槽
unpackaged 未包装的，散装的
unpassable 不能通过的，通不过的
unpatented 未得到专利权的
(UN) peace keeping vehicle （联合国）维和（战）车
unplated 未镀的，无涂层的
unpowered 无动力装置的，非机动的
unpredictable 不可预测的，不能预报的
unprogrammed state （EPROM的）未编程状态
unqualified truck （经检验）不合（规）格的载货汽车
unreactable （化学）不起反应的
unrefined 非精制的，非精炼的
unregulated variable 非调节变量
unreliability of service 使用的不可靠性
unrenewable 不能再生（更新）的
unrestrained 无约束的（如：未系安全带的）
unroad worthy 不适于在路上行驶的
uns 不对称的（unsymmetrical 的简称）

unsafe action probability （驾驶者）非安全操作概率
unsalvageable component 不可修复利用的废件
unsatfy 理由不充分的，不能解决问题的，不能令人满意的（unsatisfactory 的简称）
unsaturated fatty acids 不饱和脂肪酸（简称 UFA，作为润滑性添加剂加入压燃机等发动机的燃料中）
unsaturated hydrocarbon 不饱和烃
unsaturated logic circuit 非饱和逻辑电路
unscheduled ①非计划性的②不定期的，没有预定时间的
unscheduled maintenance and repair 非计划性维修（不是按计划而是根据车辆的具体技术状况进行维修）
unscreened ①未筛过的（未经粒度分级的）②未过滤的③未屏蔽的
unscrew ①解体检修（= overhaul）②拆卸螺钉，拧松螺钉③拆开，拆散
unseating ①脱座，座合不良②接触面贴合不良，配合面接触不良
unselected element （液晶显示）非选择点（在多路驱动中，扫描电极和信号电极都不施加驱动信号的像素）
unshielded 未屏蔽的，无防护的
unsignalized intersection 无（红绿灯等交通管制）信号（设施）的交叉路口
unspecified （技术条件中）未规定的
unsplinterable glass 不碎玻璃（防碎安全玻璃）
unsplit crankcase 不可分开的整体式曲轴箱
unsprung ①没有安装弹簧的，不加弹簧垫的②不在弹簧上的，非悬架的，弹簧下的
unsprung mass （汽车的）簧下质量

（指不由悬架承载的质量，包括固定在前、后轴上的车轮及各种零部件的质量，再计入传动轴、悬架系、制动系、转向系中起簧上质量作用的那部分质量。簧下质量就是汽车质量与簧上质量之差。有的定义，将弹簧与减振器质量的一半也算作簧下质量，亦写作 unspringing mass）

unsprung mass vibration 簧下质量的振动（= secondary vibration，亦称 unsprung oscillations）

unsprung weight 汽车的簧下重量（亦写作 unspringing weight，①指用重力单位表示的簧下质量②若不严格定义，可视为簧下质量的同义词或旧称）

unstability 不稳定性

unstable 不稳定的

unstable balance 不稳定平衡（亦称 unstable equilibrium）

unstainable 不锈的

unsteady flow 不稳定流（流场任意点的流体的速度、压力或温度，都随时间而变化的流）

unstrained 无应变的，未变形的；不紧张的，自然的

unstratified engine 非分层充气的（常规）发动机

unsupercharged engine 非增压充气的（自然吸气式）发动机

unsupported length 无支撑长度（悬臂长度）

unsymmetrical 不对称的（简称 UN-SYM 或 unsym）

unsymmetrical passing beam 不对称（近光）光束

unsymmetrical placement 不对称的布置

unsymmetrical spring 非对称弹簧

unsymmetric pattern tyre 非对称花纹式轮胎（指内侧花纹与外侧花纹不同的轮胎）

untempered 未经调质的，未回火的

unthreaded portion （螺栓或螺钉的）无螺纹部分

untimely ignition ①不适时点火（点火时刻不当）②过早或过迟点火

untrafficable area 不通行区（不通车地区）

untrained driver 未经训练的驾驶员

untreated 未经处理的

untrue ①不真实的，不正确的，不精确的②（旋转体）有径向振摆的

untuned ①未调谐的②未调节的，未调整的

U-nut U 形螺母

up ①超轻型的（ultraportable）②不合格的（under-proof）③上面的（= upper）④向上地，朝上地⑤上面的，朝上的，向上面的⑥上升，上坡⑦提高，增加

U-packing U 形断面密封件

up-and-down motion 上下运动

up current 上升（气）流

UPD 均匀概率设计（uniform probability design 的简称）

update ①修正，校正②更新，革新，不断改进，使现代化，使适合新的要求③现代化，最新资料

updating formula 校正公式

UP/DN button 升、降调节按钮

up/down open type rear gate （厢式车身的）上、下对开型（两扇式）后门

up-draft carburetor ［美］上吸式化油器（= updraught carburetor，指空气由下方吸入，向上流过喉管内的主量孔喷嘴的化油器）

up-flow ①上升气流②向上的流动

up flow type converter 上流式转化器（排气向上方流动与催化剂接触的催化转化器）

up-front costs ①前期费用，前期成本②预付费用，预交费用

up-grade ①提高（提高质量等级，升级）②加强，加固，加浓 ③上坡，升坡

upgrading version （车辆等的）升级版

uphill ①上坡，上山 ②上坡的，向上行的

uphill axle （行驶于坡道上汽车的）坡上车桥（位于坡度上位的车桥，如：上坡行驶时的前桥，下坡行驶时的后桥）

uphill-downhill operation （汽车在山区或丘陵地区经常）上、下坡运行

uphill gradient 上坡坡度

uphill-pointing vehicle （坡道上）上坡的车辆

uphill pull 爬坡牵引力

uphill-race （汽车）爬坡竞赛

uphill road 上坡路

uphill slope 上山路坡度

uphill starting （汽车）（上）坡道起步

uphill startup assist and control （车辆）坡道起步辅助和控制（系统）（当车辆在上坡道上起步时，该系统可提供足够的转矩，防止车辆向坡下滑动，保证平稳起步。此外，在山地行驶时，该系统可根据山路的坡度和车辆载荷，将驱动转矩保持在控制程序所设定的最佳值的范围内）

upholstered cab 内部装潢过的驾驶室

upholstered seat 软座

upholstery ①（室内，车厢内的）装潢，装饰品 ②（车身，座椅等的）蒙皮装饰，蒙皮材料（= upholstering）

upholstery border （车身及车厢内部的）装饰条，装饰边

upholstery of leather substitute 人造革蒙皮

U-piston engine U型活塞发动机（两个并列的汽缸，共同一个燃烧室，两缸内各有一个活塞，同时向同方向运动）

upland ①高地，山地，高原（= upland plain）②高地的，山地的，高原的

uplift ①举起，升起 ②（地面）隆起 ③向上运动，浮升，上升

upper and lower A-arm type suspension 上下（布置的双）A形臂式悬架（由上、下两根A型横臂组成的独立悬架）

(upper-and-lower-parts) divided type side mirror （上、下部分）分割型车侧后视镜（可扩大照视范围和清晰度）

upper arm ①（双臂式悬架的）上臂 ②位于悬架上方的控制臂（只就其布置位置而言，不涉及其形状等）

upper back panel （轿车）后围上盖板（后窗下部与行李舱盖或后置发动机罩前缘连接的外层盖板，亦称 rear waist panel, back window lower panel, rear deck panel）

upper beam （汽车前照灯）远光，= long distance beam (light), full beam

upper beam indicator lamp 汽车前照灯远光指示灯

upper bearing （轴瓦式滑动轴承的）上轴瓦

upper block 见 open deck type block

upper bound 上界，上限（亦称 upper boundary）

upper change point 上变点（上临界点，如：碳化铁全部溶入γ铁中，形成奥氏体的温度）

upper control arm （独立悬架）上控制臂

upper control limit 控制上限

upper crankcase 上曲轴箱

upper curve 上曲线

upper cut 细切削，二次切削

upper cut-off frequency 上限截止频率

upper cylinder bore wear 缸壁上部磨损（上止点附近的汽缸壁磨损）

upper dead center （内燃机）上止点，上死点（简称 UDC，= top dead center）

upper deck （双层公共汽车的）上层车厢（= top deck）

upper deviation 上偏差（公差带的上限）

upper extreme point 上端（点）

upper front wing （轿车车身）前上翼子板

upper header 散热器上水室

upper hitch pin （悬架装置）上拉杆连接销

upper insulator gasket （火花塞）绝缘上密封垫

upper limit ①上限尺寸（最大尺寸）②上限

upper limiting frequency for full output voltage swing 满输出电压幅度上限频率（放大器满输出幅度对应的最高工作频率）

upper limit to obstacle performance （车辆）越障性能上限

upper link 上连接杆，上臂（= top link）

uppermost layer 外表层，面层

upper plastic limit 塑性上限

upper pressure spring injector 调压弹簧上置式喷油器（具有长挺杆结构，调压弹簧靠近喷油嘴的喷油器）

upper sidewall 胎侧上部（胎肩，= shoulder of tyre）

upper suspension arm 悬架上控制臂（= upper control arm）

upper tonneau panel （轿车车身）后上侧板（参见 rear quarter panel）

upper torso restraint （乘客）身躯上部的约束性安全装置（如：安全肩带等）

upper valve-gear housing 顶置式气门室罩壳

upper variation of tolerance 上偏差

upper V-arm （某些悬架杆系中的）V 形上控制臂

upper yield (ing) point 上屈服点（试件发生屈服而作用力首次下降前的最大应力，见 yield point）

upper yield stress 上屈服应力

up (-) rate ①提高功率②提高性能指标

uprated engine 强化的发动机（= hopped up engine）

uprated test 超（额定）负荷试验，超额定工况试验

uprating 强化（提高额定值）

upright ①立柱（直立支撑件）②直立的，垂直的，立式的③立起，竖立，竖起

upright cylinder 直立式汽缸

upright dial gauge 立式指示表

upright engine 直立式发动机

upright post 立柱

upright projection 垂直投影

upright shaft 立轴

upright valve 直置式气门（垂直安装，相对于斜置气门而言）

UPS 不间断供电装置（uninterrupted power supply）

upset ①缩锻，镦锻，镦（粗）②推翻，颠覆，翻倒③扰乱，干扰④使失常，使乱⑤固定的，一定的

upset welding 电热压对接焊（热压对接焊，电阻焊的一种，对接焊件间通过强大的电流，被焊接部分电阻发热，达到适当高温后，施加轴向压力而将工作焊牢，= upset butt welding）

upshift 升挡（挂高速挡，换高速挡，指一切在原挡位基础上降低转矩比，提高速比的换挡操作）

upstream O₂ sensor 上游传感器（指装在催化转化器前方的 O_2 传感器，用于测定废气进入催化转化器之前的 O_2 含量，亦称主 O_2 传感器）

upstream pressure （液压元件）上游压力（阀前压力）

upstroke （活塞）向上冲程（如：压缩冲程，排气冲程，= upward stroke）

upsweep ①向上弯曲②向上弯曲部分

upswept frame 凹形车架（为了降低车身高度，车架两端，即在车桥上方的部分向上拱起，而两桥之间的部分降低，整个车架呈凹形，以降低重心，便于货物装卸，= kickup frame）

uptake ①了解，领会②吸收

up-to-date 最新（式）的，现代化的

upturned spring eye 钢板弹簧的向上卷耳

upward 向上的，朝上的

upwards angle of visibility 上视角（通过眼点的 Z 平面与眼至风窗上缘的直线之间的夹角）

upwards or downwards adjustable range of seat 座椅上下调节范围（座椅调至最上与最下位置时的垂直位移量）

upward ventilation 上吸式通风（= updraft）

uranium 铀 U（92 号金属元属，地球上出产的铀称为天然铀，其成分比为 $U^{234} : U^{235} : U^{238} = 0.01 : 0.71 : 99.28$。其中 U^{235} 为分裂性物质，可用作为原子反应堆燃料，U^{238} 吸收中子即变成 pu^{239}，pu^{239} 也是原子反应堆燃料）

urban area 市区（都市及其邻近地区，= city district）

urban bus 市区公共汽车（= city bus）

urban-city transportation 市内运输（= city transportation）

urban clearway （在特定的高峰时间内）禁止停车的市区街道

urban cycle （汽车台架测试的）市区（多工况）运行循环（模拟市区典型行车工况组成的测试运转循环）

urban drive 市区行车（美称 metro driving）

urban dynamometer driving schedule 见 UDDS

urban freeway 城市高速道路

urban fuel economy 市区运行燃料经济性

Urban Mass Transportation Administration ［美］都市公共交通署（简称 UMTA，1991 年改组为联邦公共交通署 FTA）

urban traffic control system 城市交通控制系统（城市交通管理系统，简称 UTCS）

urea-fed catalytic converter 尿素喷射型催化转化器（欧洲规定从 2007 年起全部柴油机货车均须安装这种转化器，以减少 NO_x 排量）

urea formaldehyde resin 脲醛树脂（尿素甲醛树脂）为热固性树脂的一种，机械强度、硬度、电性能、耐溶剂性等良好，耐水性较差

urea injection type SCR system 尿素喷射式选择性催化还原系统（在废气进入选择性还原催化转化器前先在废气流中喷入尿素还原剂后的 NO_x 净化系统）

ureareductant （NO_x 的）尿素还原剂

urethane 氨基甲酸乙酯，尿烷

urethane adhesive 氨基甲酸乙酯胶粘剂

urethane elastomer 氨基甲酸乙酯树脂（尿烷树脂，尿烷人造橡胶）

urethane foam 尿烷泡沫塑料（氨基

甲酸乙酯泡沫弹性材料，用于喷覆汽车车身外底板、管件等，可防止锈蚀）

urge 推动，推进；促使，催促；加力，增加推动力，加荷，（发动机）强化

urgency ①紧急②紧急情况（紧急状态）

urgency level 紧急程度（紧急级别）

urgent 紧急的，紧迫的

urgent signal 紧急信号

USA ①美国陆军（United States Army）②美国，美利坚合众国（United States of America）

USABC 美国先进蓄电池联合开发组织（United States Advanced Battery Consortium 的简称，由美国福特、克莱斯勒和通用三大汽车公司共同组建的联合体。1992 年 USABC 与美国政府投资 2.6 亿美元启动电动汽车高效储能系统的研制计划，研究除铅酸蓄电池以外的多种新型蓄电池）

usability 使用性能，可用性

usable cargo space 有效载货容积

usable dimensions of rear body 汽车货箱的有效尺寸（可用尺寸）

usable flank 可用齿面（齿轮齿面上的一个区域。其面积大小，只取决于刀具切削刃的几何形状以及刀具切齿时与工件的相对位置，而不受该齿轮本身的及其配对齿轮的工作位置的影响）

usable height 有效高度，有用高度

usable horsepower （用马力为单位的）有用功率（可用的功率），有效功率

USAC 美国汽车俱乐部（United States Auto Club）

USAEC 美国原子能委员会（United States Atomic Energy Commission）

usage ①使用②用法

usage factor 利用率（利用系数）

USAS 美国标准（United States of America Standards）

USATECOM 美国陆军试验与评价部（United States Army Test and Evaluation Command）

USATRECOM 美国陆军运输研究部（United States Army Transportation Research Command）

U. S. Auto Club 美国汽车俱乐部（= USAC）

USB 通用串行总线（universal serial bus 的简称）

USB interface and adapter cable USB 接口和接插线

USBS 美国标准局（United States Bureau of Standards）

US-built 美国制的

USC 超声波清洗（ultrasonic cleaning）

US characteristic 不足转向特性（understeering characteristics）

USC measurements 美制惯用计量单位（U. S. customary measurements 的简称，长度单位为英寸、英尺、英里；质量单位为磅、盎司等）

U. S. Council for Automotive Research Department of Commerce 美国汽车研究委员会（其执行委员会由通用、福特、克莱斯勒三大公司的副总裁组成，简称 USCAR）

USD body 极限刚度结构车身（Ultimate Stiffness Design body 的简称）

U. S. Department of Commerce 美国商业部

U. S. Department of Defense 美国国防部（简称 U. S. DOD）

U. S. Department of Transportation 美国运输部

use 使用，利用，运用

U section （汽车车身底板及其承架结构中的）U 形断面板材构件（比箱形断面少一面，呈 U 形）

U-sectioned twist beam U形断面扭力梁

used car market 旧(汽)车市场, 在用(汽)车市场(= used vehicle market)

used car test 旧车测试

used cooking oil biodiesel 见 Waste cooking oil derived biodiesel

used oil reclaimer 废油回收装置

used oil regenerator 废油再生装置

used-ticket box (公共汽车上的)废票箱

used-up 使用至极限的,完全磨损了的,用完了的;疲劳不堪的

use factor 利用系数(= utilization factor)

useful 有用的,有效的

useful life 使用寿命(对可修复的设备、装置,在规定使用条件下,具有可接受的失效率的时间区间)

useful work 有用功(= effective work)

useless 无用的,无效的

US EPA heavy duty diesel engine transient test cycle 美国环保局重型柴油机瞬态法(美国对13人以上客车和6000lb以上货车用柴油机排放物测定的台架试验工况法)

US EPA heavy duty gasoline engine transient test cycle 美国环保局重型车汽油机瞬态试验法(对13座以上客车和总质量6000lb以上货车用汽油机的排放测定所采用的台架试验工况法)

US EPA LA-4C test procedure 美国环保局LA-4C测试法(1972~1974年间,对总质量6000lb以下货车,12座以下客车,实行的排放测试法,LA-4C系模拟汽车在 Los Angelos 市郊区到市区的行驶工况,C表示冷起动循环)

US EPA 9-Mode test cycle 美国环保局9工况法(自1974年起对13座以上客车和总质量6000lb以上货车用汽油机排放的台架试验工况法。1984年后亦可采用瞬态试验工况法)

US EPA 13-mode test cycle 美国环保局13工况法(美国从1974年起对13人以上大客车及总重6000lb以上载货汽车所用柴油机实行的测定排气排放物的台架试验工况法。从1984年起也可采用瞬态法)

US EPA smoke emission test cycle 美国环保局排烟工况测试法(1970年起对总质量6000lb以上货车、13座以上客车用柴油机实行的多工况排烟测试法)

use-proved 经使用检验过的

user 使用者,用户

user adjustment 用户调整(允许用户进行的调整)

use reliability 使用可靠性

user-friendly (对)用户友好的(指用户使用起来高效、方便、容易、顺手的)

user interface facilities (汽车内的)用户(电器)接口设施

user selectable function 用户(可)选用(的)功能

user test 用户(进行的)试验(= user trial)

use test 使用试验

US Federal LEV (Ⅱ) emission requirement 美国联邦(二)级排放标准要求(相当于 Euro 4)

USG 美国标准(线,量)规(United States gauge)

US gallon 美国加仑[有干、液之分,干加仑用于量干货,液加仑用于量液体,为美国常用的容积单位,干加仑较液加仑大,1US gal(干)= 268.8 in^3, 1US gal(液)= 231 in^3 = 3.7854美液加仑,亦称 wine gallon, liquid gallon]

US gal/min 美加仑/分(美制容积

流量单位,1US gal/min = 3.785L/min = 0.0038m³/min)

U-shaped　U形的(马蹄形的)

U-shaped clamp　U形夹

U-shaped door side protection　U形车门侧护栏

usher　①引导(引入,引进)②预示(预告,预报,宣示)③引导者(引导物)④(一种系列新车型中的)第一种型号的车种(引出它以后的众多同系列车型)

U-slot piston　裙部带U形槽的活塞

USNCAP　美国新车碰撞测试机构(见NCAP)

U. S. New Car Assessment Program　美国新(轿)车评审程序(按星级标准对新车进行评价)

USSA　美国雪地汽车协会(United States Snowmobile Association 的简称)

USS screw thread　美国标准螺纹(亦称塞勒螺纹 "seller's screw thread")

USS(t)　美国标准(United States Standard 的简称)

USTC　美国(安全)试验公司(United States Testing Company Inc. 的简称)

U-steel　U字钢(槽钢)

U-strap　(钢板弹簧)U形(回跳限位)箍

UTCS　城市交通控制系统(urban traffic control system 的简称)

ute　(澳俚)轻型货车,多功能车,客货两用轻型货车(utility truck 的简称, = pick-up truck)

utility　有多种用途的,通用的,多功能的

utility analysis　用途(的)分析,使用分析

utility body　多功能车身

utility factor　设备利用系数

utility seat　(客货两用车)可折叠式座椅

utility trailer　多功能挂车(特指客车牵引的装行李、用具等的小挂车,通用性能高)

utility truck　多功能轻型载货汽车(美国军车分类指载重1/4~1t多种功能通用货车, = light truck)

utility-type　万能的,通用的,一般用途的

utility-type tractor　多功能牵引车(= universal tractor)

utility vehicle　(轻型高通过性)多功能车(jeep, land-rover, pickup, land-cruiser 等的总称)

utilization factor　利用系数(利用率, = use factor)

utilization factor of payload of loaded vehicl (rate of tonnage of seats)　重车载质(客)量利用率(亦称 rate of tonnage or seats "吨、客位利用率",指全部工作车辆完成的主要自载换算周转量占重车行程装载质量的比率,反映重车吨或客位的行程公里的利用程度)

utilization of debris　废物利用

utilization rate　使用率

util service　公用服务事业(utility service 的简称,亦称 public utility)

UTMS　全面交通管理系统(Universal Traffic Management System 的简称,日本 ITS 的开发项目之一)

UTQGS　[美]统一轮胎质量分级标准(Uniform Tire Quality Grading Standards 的缩写)

UTS　极限抗拉强度(ultimate tensile strength 的简称)

U-tube manometer　U形管压力计

U-turn　①U形转弯②(汽车)掉头

UUE　用完为止(use until exhausted 的简称)

UV　①紫外线②紫外线的(ultraviolet 的简称)

UV absorber　紫外线吸收剂(亦称

UV stabilizer,涂于塑料或橡胶制件表面,可将紫外线辐射能释解为无害能,以减少制件受紫外光照的影响)

UVC [美国] 车辆统一统码(Uniform Vehicle Code)
UV free glass 防紫外线玻璃
UW 超声波(ultrasonic wave 的简称)
U-washer U形垫圈(开口垫圈)

V- 4 (V-6, V-8, V-10, V-12) V形四缸（六缸，八缸，十缸，十二缸）发动机

V ①气门（valve）②真空管（valve）③矢量（vector）④速度（velocity）⑤伏（volt，电位单位）⑥电压（voltage）⑦电压表（voltmeter）⑧容积，体积（volume）⑨运动黏度（kinematic viscosity）⑩比容（specific volume）⑪V形的⑫轮胎侧壁表示最高设计车速为210km/h的字母⑬先进技术—零排放车（advanced technology-zero emission vehicle 的简称，指采用多种先进技术实现零排放的车辆）

VA ①价值分析（value analysis）②可变区域（variable-area）③乙烯基醋酸酯（vinyl acetate）④伏安（volt-ampere）

VAB （化油器）可变空气量孔（variable air bleed）

Vac 真空（vacuum 的简称）

vacancy 空地；空位，空额，空白

vacillate 摇摆，振荡，波动

vac-metal 镍铬电热丝合金

vacpup 真空泵（vacuum pump 的简称）

VAC sensor 真空度传感器（vacuum sensor 的简称，亦称压差传感器"pressure differential sensor"）

vac switch 真空开关（vacuum switch 的简称）

vacua 真空（vacuum 的复数）

vacuity 真空度（稀薄度）

vacumatic transmission 真空自动控制变速器

vacuometer 真空计（= vacuum meter，亦写作 vacuumometer）

vacural （一种）高压真空铸造法

vacuum ①造成真空②用真空吸尘器吸尘③真空

vacuum actuator 真空（驱动的）执行器（如：真空马达"vacuum motor"）

vacuum advance angle 真空提前角（由进气歧管真空控制，根据发动机负荷提前点火的角度）

vacuum advance control valve 真空点火提前控制阀（该阀可随发动机负荷，即：进气管内的真空度改变点火提前角，以减少 CO、HC 排出量）

vacuum advance mechanism 真空提前机构（根据发动机负荷自动地改变点火时刻的机构，亦称 vacuum ignition advancer）

vacuum amplifier 真空放大器（如：利用喉管负压作为信号，控制进气管真空通道，可将真空信号放大10倍，简称 V-AMP）

vacuum and spring operated EGR valve 真空-弹簧控制型废气再循环

阀

vacuum aneroid capsule type actuator 真空膜盒式执行器

vacuum apparatus 真空设备

vacuum-assisted 真空助力的（真空加力的）

vacuum-assisted hydraulic brake system 真空助力式液压制动（系）（利用进气管或真空室真空与大气压力差作为动力源的伺服机构来增补驾驶员施加于踏板上的力的液压制动系统，亦称 vacuum booster brake system，vacuum servo brake system，vacuum-over-hydraulic brake system）

vacuum booster pump 真空助力泵

vacuum (brake) booster 真空（制动）助力器（利用进气管或其他真空源负压来增补驾驶员施加于踏板上的力的部件，亦称 master vac，vacuum servo）

vacuum brake hose 制动器真空软管

vacuum brake system 真空液压制动系（亦称 vacuum operated brake system，为真空助力式和增压式液压制动系的总称，二者的区别在于前者 vacuum assisted type 助力机构设在踏板与制动主缸之间，用于增补踏板力，而后者 vacuum intensified type 增压机构在制动主缸之后，用于提高制动管路压力）

vacuum car 垃圾抽吸车，污水抽吸车（俗称 honey car）

vacuum carburizing 真空渗碳（法）（工件装入渗碳炉后，在 50μmHg 真空下加热到渗碳温度，将渗碳气 CH_4，或 C_3H_8、C_4H_{10} 输入炉内渗碳，至炉内压力达 $300\sim350$mmHg；停止输入渗碳气，排出气体，使炉内气压低于 50μmHg，进行规定时间的扩散处理；调质，淬火）

vacuum casting 真空模铸（一种模铸技术，将熔融金属吸入模腔内）

vacuum chamber 真空室（亦称 vacuum capsule，一般指膜片式，利用膜片两侧压力差产生短程调节运动的真空气动式执行器）

vacuum check valve （真空传输管道系统中防止真空泄漏的）真空止回阀

vacuum cleaner 真空吸尘器

vacuum cleaning robot 真空清洁机器人

vacuum connection 真空系统的管道连接；真空管道接头

vacuum controlled 真空控制的

vacuum (controlled) advance 真空（控制）点火提前（装置）（vacuum ignition advance）

vacuum-controlled automatic clutch 真空控制式自动离合器

vacuum controlled gearshift 真空控制换挡

vacuum control modulator valve 真空控制调节阀（简称 VCM）

vacuum control valve 真空控制阀（由进气管或其他真空源真空控制的各种阀门、开关的统称，简称 VCV）

vacuum corrector 真空校正器

vacuum cup 真空吸杯

vacuum cup tread （对地面有吸附力的）凸形真空吸杯效应胎面花纹

vacuum cylinder 真空缸（指真空动力缸或真空助力缸）

vacuum cylinder and plunger assembly 真空缸筒及柱塞总成

vacuum-deposited 真空沉积的

vacuum desiccator 真空干燥器（将要干燥的物体置于一密闭容器内，由抽气机减压，而在低压下进行干燥的装置）

vacuum diaphragm chamber ①真空膜片室（室内膜片的一侧通大气并装有压力弹簧，另一侧通真空，膜片的位置随真空度的变化而改变，

借以通过与膜片联动的扭件推动或拉动受控部件）②（真空膜片室的）真空腔

vacuum diaphragm cylinder 膜片式真空缸（vacuum diaphragm chamber 的别称）

vacuum distillation 真空蒸馏

vacuum ejector 真空喷射器（喷射式真空泵）

vacuum evaporation 真空蒸发（在减压、加温的条件下，使某种金属、合金或化合物直接气化并随即冷凝且沉积在被镀覆的表面上，形成很薄的固态膜）

vacuum evaporator 真空蒸发器

vacuum fan 抽气扇（= drawing fan）

vacuum feed 真空供给

vacuum filter 真空信号去噪滤波器（从真空传感器发送至电子控制模块的真空信号中消除电噪声的滤波器）

vacuum fluorescent 真空荧光的

vacuum fluorescent display （汽车仪表等的）真空荧光显示（简称 VFD）

vacuum-formed 真空成形的（低压成形的）

vacuum-fuel tester （汽油发动机）真空及燃油泵输出压力测试仪

vacuum gauge 真空计（真空压力计，= suction gauge）

vacuum gear shift 真空助力换挡

vacuum governor （燃油喷射系的）真空调速器（气力式调速器的一种，利用发动机进气管内负压变化控制的调速器，= suction governor）

vacuum horn 真空喇叭（利用负压产生鸣响的喇叭）

vacuum hose 真空软管（真空驱动的执行机构与真空源之间的连接软管）

vacuum ignition advancer 真空点火提前装置（见 vacuum advance mechanism）

vacuum ignition timing control 真空点火正时控制（= vacuum controlled retard adjustment, vacuum controlled spark adjustment, vacuum controlled spark timing, vacuum ignition advance, vacuum controlled advance, vacuum ignition adjustment，利用发动机进气管真空控制点火提前角）

vacuum incandescent lamp 真空白炽灯

vacuum intensifier 真空增压器（利用负压来增高制动管路压力、加速制动动作的部件）

vacuum limiter （强制怠速工况的进气管）真空抑制阀（简称 VL）

vacuum line 真空管路

vacuum loader 真空吸盘式装载机（利用真空吸力将散装货等装入汽车）

vacuum-meter 真空表（= vacuumometer, vacuum-gauge, vacuum indicator）

vacuum modulated EGR 真空调节式 EGR（利用发动机进气真空调节再循环废气量的 EGR 系统，亦称真空控制 EGR 系统 "vacuum control EGR"）

vacuum modulator 真空式调节器（利用发动机进气系统真空进行某项控制的装置的总称。如：在自动变速器中，指利用发动机真空控制其节气门阀的装置）

vacuum modulator pressure （自动变速器液力控制系的）真空调制液压（随发动机进气管的真空度而变化的调制压力，用来作为发动机的转矩信号）

vacuum motor 真空马达（真空驱动装置，以真空作为动力的驱动装置）

vacuum-operated clutch 真空驱动式离合器

vacuum-operated emission control 真空控制式排气净化

vacuum-operated hydraulic brake 真空驱动式液压制动器（指利用真空源负压推动的液压制动器）

vacuum-operated spark control 真空控制点火时刻控制装置（= vacuum-operated timing gear）

vacuum-operated throttle modulator 真空控制式节气门怠速开度调节器（简称 VOTM, 见 throttle kicker）

vacuum-operated timing gear 真空控制（点火）正时装置（亦称 vacuum-operated spark controller）

vacuum pan 真空盘（在真空下使溶液浓缩、结晶的装置）

vacuum powered booster （制动踏板）真空加力器

vacuum-power gear change 真空动力换挡（亦称 vacuum-power gear shift）

vacuum pressure indicator lamp 真空压力指示灯

vacuum pump 真空泵（用于将容器内的空气抽出，即：vacuum pumping 抽真空，作业以形成真空）

vacuum reducer valve （限制真空点火提前机构真空量的）真空减量阀（如：在某些发动机中，当冷却水温高于104℃时，该阀限制输入真空点火提前装置的真空量，以减少点火提前量，防止爆燃，简称 VRV）

vacuum reservoir 真空罐（呈真空状态的罐状容器，用作存储真空及真空源）

vacuum sensing line 真空传感管（真空信号输送管、真空信号源和真空传感器之间的管道）

vacuum sensor 真空传感器（如：向电子控制模块发送进气歧管负压值及其变化的传感器，有膜片式、压电晶体式等多种，见 pressure sensor）

vacuum servo ABS 真空助力式防抱死制动系统

vacuum servo hydraulic brake system 真空伺服液压制动系统（利用真空源负压助力的制动系统）

vacuum servo system 真空伺服系统（在汽车上，指利用大气压与真空或负压源的压力差来增补人的作用力，以推动机械或液压系统运转的系统，如：真空助力制动系）

vacuum solenoid 真空电磁阀（控制真空通道，从而控制真空流量的电磁阀）

vacuum space 真空容积；真空区

vacuum-stable 在真空条件下保持性能稳定的

vacuum suction cup （吸平板玻璃等的）真空吸盘

vacuum suspended type 真空浮动式（制动助力器活塞或膜片的两侧，在不制动时都保持真空，制动时一侧引入空气）

vacuum sweeper 真空吸尘清扫车

vacuum switch 真空控制开关（由负压控制触点闭合与断开，简称 vsw, vacswitch）

vacuum switching valve 真空通道控制开关阀（简称 VSV）

vacuum tank 真空箱（呈真空状态或负压状态的密封箱体，用作为真空源）

vacuum thermometer 真空式温度计

vacuum-tight 真空气密的（指不漏真空的）

vacuum transducer （进气管或节气门孔道的）真空度传感器

vacuum-treated 真空处理的

vacuum tube 真空管（电子管）

vacuum-type pneumatic micrometer 真空式气动测微计（气动式测微器的一种，其读数在广范围内成直线，受到大气压力变动的影响时易

于修正）

vacuum unit （发动机点火提前装置等的）真空控制装置（亦称 vacuum control unit）

vacuum vapor deposition method 真空蒸发淀积法（形成薄膜镀覆层的一种方法）

vacuum ventilation system 真空式通风系统

vacuum vessel 真空室

vacuum warning switch 真空报警开关（当真空度低于规定值时，该开关闭合，警报灯或有关电路接通）

vacuum windshield wiper 风窗玻璃真空刮水器（亦称 vacuum windshield cleaner）

VAFC system 车辆加速度反馈控制系统（vehicle acceleration feedback control system 的简称，以测得或根据发动机转矩、变速器速比等算出的实际加速度作为输入，对根据车速和踩踏加速踏板的速度和行程算出的驾驶者的目标加速度值进行对比和实时修正，以保证车辆的实际加速度不因路况、坡度等因素的变化而偏离目标值波动）

VAF sensor 叶片式空气流量传感器（vane air flow sensor 的简称）

vagueness 不清楚（含混，模糊）

valance ①帷幔，布帘，挡板②化合价，原子价（=valency）

valance panel （轿车车身）发动机室侧壁板，前轮罩板，前翼子板侧板（=front wheelhouse panel, fender side shield, front wheel arch, valance of front wing）

valence bond （化合）价键，价键耦合

valence electron 化合价电子，原子价电子

valent weight （化合价）当量

valeting 清扫作业（特指汽车内部的清扫）

valeting station 汽车（车身内部）清扫站

valid 有效的，有法律效力的，经过正当手续的，强有力的

validate ①验证，确证，证明正确 ②使合法，使生效

validation ①认证，论证，确认 ②审批（使合法，生效）

valid period of claim 索赔时限（理赔方规定提出索赔要求的有效时间）

valid time （集成数字电路）有效时间（在输出信号是有效的，或者输入信号必须是有效期间的时间间隔）

valley current 谷值电流（最小电流）

valley line （曲线的）谷线

valley load 谷值荷载（疲劳荷载中，荷载为时间函数的一阶导数从负号变至正号处的荷载，恒幅荷载中的最小荷载）

valuable ①有价值的，重要的 ②可评价的，可估价的

value ①价值，价格 ②值，数值，大小

value-added tax 增值税（简称 VAT）

value analysis （设计）价格分析，价值分析（学）（简称 VA）

value chain 价格链

value engineering 价值工程（学）（简称 VE）

value of a quantity 量值（用一个数和一个适当的测量单位表示的量）

value of scale division 标度分格值（格值，指标度中对应两相邻标度标记的被测量值之差）

value of service 使用价值，服务价值

value of thrust 推力值

valve ①阀；气门 ②电子管，真空管 ③装上阀门，用阀调节

θ valve θ形板阀（指转轴在阀板中央的转动式阀门）

valve actuating mechanism ①（发动机）气门驱动机构②（各种）阀门驱动机构［亦称 valve (-actuating) gear］

valve adjuster 气门调整器（如：气门间隙的调节螺钉）

valve area 气门开启最大面积（菌状气门开启的最大面积 $A = \pi \times$ 气门头最大直径×最大开启高度）

valve arm 气门摇臂（= valve lever, rocking lever, valve rocker arm, rocking arm, rocker arm, rocker lever, rocker actuator）

valve arrangement （发动机）气门布置（气门位置）

valve at side 侧置气门（= side-by-side valve；valve in block, side valves）

valve barrel 滑阀套筒

valve base ①阀座②（轮胎）气门嘴基座（= valve seat, valve holder, valve socket）

valve beat-in 气门（因气门座磨损而）下陷 亦称 valve recession, valve sink, valve sinkage）

valve block 阀体（亦称 valve body）

valve blow-by 气门漏气

valve bonnet 气门嘴帽

valve bounce 气门（关闭时因弹簧谐振或速度过高而在气门座上）回跳

valve bridge 气门（摇臂传动中的）横臂（由一个摇臂传动两个以上气门的过桥零件，亦称 bridge piece）

valve cage 气门壳（在其内部装有气门，本身具有密封锥面，能从汽缸盖或机体中分离出来的零件，被冷却的气门壳附有"Cooled"的标志）

valve cap ①（轮胎）气门嘴帽②（顶置式气门机构的）汽缸盖罩③（缸盖与缸体铸成一个整体件的侧置式气门发动机上的）气门螺塞（为一可卸式螺塞，为气门提供调整、拆装孔口）④防护帽（对气门嘴芯腔和气门芯起防护作用的顶帽，分为密封帽、非密封帽和扳手帽三类）

valve case 气门（机构）室（= valve-gear housing）

valve chain 气门驱动链条（正时链）

valve chamber （发动机）气门室，气阀室

valve characteristics control method 阀特性控制法（指利用控制阀件的工作特性制某种参数的方法，如：在液压动力转向系中，利用装在动力缸输入液压管路中的具有开度随控制电流量而变化的特性的电磁阀来控制动力缸的输出液压的方法。其控制电流量为车速的函数，因而可实现转向动力随车速而变化的要求）

valve chatter 气门颤动作响

valve chest 气门箱（= airbox），气门室，气阀室（= valve-gear housing）

valve clack 气门撞击声

valve clearance 气门间隙（气门关闭且挺杆完全回位后气门杆端与挺杆端的间隙，亦称 valve lash）

valve clearance depression （顶置式气门发动机活塞顶上的）气门凹窝（防止气门开启时碰及活塞）

valve clear diameter 气门座孔内径

valve clogging 气门积炭（= valve fouling）

valve-closing retard 气门关闭延迟

valve-closing time 气门关闭时间（一般用曲轴上止点后的转角度数表示）

valve collar ①气门套管②气门头肩部

valve cone ①气门座锥面②气门锥面 (= valve poppet)

valve control scavenging 阀门控制式扫气

valve cover 气门罩（气门室盖，美称摇臂罩"rocker cover"）

valve crash speed 气门落座速度

valve crossover point （进、排气门叠开期间的）气门等高度点（排气门升程降到与进气门升程增加到相同高度的一点，用曲轴或凸轮轴上止点前、后的转角表示）

valve crown 气门头（亦称 valve head）

valve cup 气门防油罩

valve cut-out （某些每缸四气门式发动机低速时只用两个气门工作，另两个气门关闭，高速时四个气门才同时工作的）气门关闭机构

valve diagram 气门配气相位图（气门正时图，气门升程曲线图）

valve duration 气门开启期（用曲轴转角度数量与表示气门的开启时间）

valve edge ①气门边，阀缘②滑阀工作棱

valve EGR 排气门控制式废气再循环（在进气行程中，排气门部分开启，直接由进气门吸入数量严格控制的废气再循环系统）

valve extractor 气门拆卸器，气门拉器

valve-face width 气门工作面宽度

valve fillet 气门（杆和气门头底面间的）过渡曲面（用以增加气门的强度）

valve flap 阀瓣（蝶形活门）

valve float ①（高速时的）气门浮升现象②（由于气门弹簧弹力不足，造成气门关闭滞后，出现的）气门浮动

valve flutter 阀门的颤振

valve follower [美]气门滚轮（式）挺柱（亦称 cam follower, valve roller lifter 或 roller tappet, 指具有滚轮与凸轮直接接触的挺柱）

valve fouling 气门结污（气门积炭，= valve clogging）

valve gapper 气门间隙调整器

valve gear drive 气门机构驱动装置

valve gear housing 气门（机构）室 (= valve box, valve case, valve chest, valve housing, valve enclosure)

valve gear member 气门机构构件

valve guide splitted bushing 对开式气门导管衬套

valve gutter 气门头端面的研磨工具槽

valve guttering 气门工作表面（由于磨损）形成沟槽

valve hammering 气门发响（气门发出敲击声）

valve head ①气门头（亦称 valve crown）②气门盘（指气门顶面）

valve head margin ①（菌状气门头顶面与锥形工作面之间的）环边②（该）环边厚度

valve head slot 气门顶部（研磨工具）槽

valve-in-block engine 侧置气门发动机（气门装在汽缸体侧的发动机，= side valve engine）

valve-in-head engine 顶置气门发动机（气门装在汽缸盖上的发动机，= overhead valve engine, valve-in-the-head engine）

valve-in-head type ①顶置气门单向换气式，顶置气门单向扫气式（二冲程柴油机增压扫气的一种，新鲜空气流由汽缸下部的进气孔流入而由装在缸盖上的排气门扫除废气）②顶置气门式

valve lag 气门（开、闭）迟后

valve lap （进、排）气门的重叠度（气门叠开度，= valve overlap ping）

valve lash 气门间隙（见 valve clearance）

valve lead 气门提前量（气门提前关闭或开启期的曲轴转角度数）

valve leakage 气门漏气

valveless 无阀门的，无气门的，无活门的；无电子管的

valveless engine 无气门发动机（亦称 valveless motor）

valvelet 小气门（=valvula, valvule）

valve lever 气门摇臂（=valve rocker lever）

valve lift 气门升程（气门升起的高度随时间变化的瞬时值。但亦常把气门最大升程简称为气门升程）

valve lift curve 气门升程曲线图（=valve-lift diagram）

valve lifter ①气门挺柱（在气门驱动系统中直接由凸轮轴凸轮顶推的杆件，亦称 valve tappet, valve-lifting plunger 或凸轮随动件"cam follower"）②起阀器（气门拆卸工具）

valve-lifting speed 气门挺升速度（亦称 valve-lifting velocity）

valve-lift period 气门上升期

valve liner 阀套（滑阀套）

valve link 滑阀阀杆

valve linkage 气门（驱动机构）杆系

valve lock 气门弹簧座锁片（亦称 valve keeper）

valve margin 气门头柱面宽度（指气门顶面至气门锥面间的柱面宽度，该宽度过窄会因过热而导致早燃式气门烧损）

valve metering characteristics 阀的计量特性曲线

valve needle 阀针（见 nozzle needle）

valve oil seal 气门油封（见 valve seal）

valve oil shield 阀防油罩

valve-on-the-side 侧置气门（=valve at side）

valve opening diagram 气门开度图，气门正时图

valve opening duration 气门开启延续时间（=duration of valve opening）

valve-opening period 气门开启期

valve-opening pressure 气门开启压力

valve-opening time 气门开启时间

valve outer spring 阀外簧，气门外弹簧

valve overlap 气门叠开（=valve lap, 指进、排气门同时开启）

valve overlap area （进、排气门升程随曲轴转角而变化的气门正时曲线图中进、排）气门叠开期面积

valve overlap duration 气门叠开期（简称 valve overlap, 用曲轴转角表示）

valve plate axial piston pump 配流盘式轴向活塞泵

valve plunger guide 气门挺杆导管（=valve tappet guide）

valve poppet （菌式）气门的锥形头部（=valve cone）

valve principle （早期 ABS 系统使用电磁阀控制制动液压的）阀门式（见 plunger principle）

valve push rod cover 气门推杆盖（板）

valve reamer 气门座绞刀

valve recession 见 valve beat-in

valve reconditioning machine 气门修磨机［如 valve refacer 磨气门机, valve regrinding machine （修）磨气门机, valve reseater 气门座修整机］

valve response 气门（开、闭）响应特性

valve-retainer cotter pin 气门弹簧座卡销

valve retainer lock 气门弹簧座锁片

valve return ①滑阀的回位②气门回

程

valve rim 气门头部的环边（见 valve head margin）

valve rocker 气门摇臂（气门驱动系中，传感推杆运动并改变方向和升程的零件，亦称 valve-rocker lever, valve lever, valve-rocking lever）

valve-rotator （发动机）转阀器（气门转动机构，使气门在作往复运动的同时，缓慢转动的组件，亦称 rotor cap）

valve rotator cover 转阀器罩盖（通过气门弹簧座碟形弹簧和滚珠，传递气门弹簧力于气门并使气门缓慢转动的支承零件）

valve scavenging 气门扫气

valve seal ①（限制润滑油进入气门导管的）气门杆密封圈②阀门油封

valve seat angle 气门座锥角，气门座工作面锥角

valve-seat area 气门座接触面（积），气门锥面（= valve face, valve-seat face）

valve seat (er) 气门座（= valve base）

valve seat grinder 气门座研磨机，磨气门座机（= valve seat grinding machine）

valve-seating machine 镶气门座圈机，铣气门座工具（= valve reseating machine）

valve-seating velocity 气门回位速度

valve-seat insert 镶嵌式气门座圈（镶嵌于发动机进、排气孔，与气门盘形成密封副的可更换零件，= insert of seat, inserted valve seat, detachable valve seat, valve seat ring）

valve-seat jacket 气门座（冷却）水套

valve sim 气门（间隙调节）垫片

valve sink 见 valve beat-in

valve sleeve 阀套（见 valve beat-in）

valve slot ①气门顶部研磨工具槽②（轮辋上的）气门嘴槽

valve spanner 气门扳手

valve split collet (ter) s 气门锁夹（气门弹簧座的一对半圆锁瓣，亦称 valve keepers, valve keys）

valve spool （滑阀的）柱塞

valve-spring damper 气门弹簧（颤振）阻尼器（= valve surge damper）

valve spring keepers 气门弹簧锁夹

valve-spring remover 气门弹簧拆卸器（亦称 valve-spring lifter）

valve-spring retainer 气门弹簧座（= valve retainer, valve-spring retaining collar）

valve-spring retainer lock 气门弹簧锁夹（简称 valve lock，亦称 valve collets）

valve-spring retaining collar 气门弹簧座圈（= valve-spring retainer）

valve-spring surge 气门弹簧颤振

valve steel 气门用钢材，气门用钢

valve stem ①气门杆②嘴体（气门嘴中具有芯腔或安装芯套的部位的零件，它直接或通过嘴座与内胎或轮辋连接）

valve stem clearance 气门杆导管间隙

valve stem guide 气门导管（= valve guide）

valve sticking （因积炭、结胶而导致）气门黏滞，气门黏住

valve stroke 气门升程，阀门行程

valve surge damper 气门弹簧阻尼器（= valve spring damper）

valve surging point 气门颤振点，气门振动点（气门开始产生颤振现象时的发动机转速）

valve-tappet clearance 气门推杆间隙

valve tappet clearance adjuster 气门挺杆间隙调节器

valve-tappet guide 气门挺杆导管（= valve lifter guide, valve plunger guide）

valve-tappet plunger 气门液压挺杆柱塞

valve timing angle 气门正时角,气门开闭角(由上止点前、后曲轴转角表示的气门开、闭时刻)

valve timing diagram 配气相位图,配气定时图

valve timing gear 气门正时齿轮,气门正时齿轮机构(= timing gear)

valve timing sign 气门正时标记

valve train ①气门传动机构(将凸轮轴的运动传至气门的各种杆件、臂件及其支承件)②气门系(指包括凸轮轴直至气门在内的整个气门系统)

valve train clearance 气门系(膨胀)间隙(气门挺杆、摇臂和气门之间的热膨胀间隙)

valve travel 气门行程,气门升程,气门升起高度

valvetronic (宝马公司的)电子气门(电子控制可变气门升程系统的商品名,该系统取代传统的节气门功能,气门的升程可根据发动机负荷和转速的要求而改变,改变的范围从急速的 0.2mm 到满负荷的 9.85mm,向发动机各种工况提供最佳进气量)

valve umbrella (顶置式气门的)伞形油封(防止过多的机油进入气门杆与气门导管之间)

valve voltmeter 电子管伏特计(电子管电压表)

VAMP 光-声-磁压强(visual-acoustic-magnetic pressure)

V-AMP 真空放大器(= vacuum amplifier)

VAN ①汽车局域网(vehicle area network 的简称,指汽车范围内的局域网,见 area network)②可变截面喷嘴(variable area nozzle)

van 厢式汽车(具有独立的封闭结构的车厢或驾驶室联成一体的整体式封闭结构车厢,装有专用设施,用于载运人员、货物或承担专门作业的专用汽车)

VAN 汽车局域网(Vehicle Area Network 的简称,ISO 推出的中等速率的串行通信总线系统)

vanadium 钒(V,铁灰色硬金属元素,熔点 1717℃,相对密度 5.98,为炼制弹簧钢、高速钢等的元素)

vanadium attack 氧化钒浸蚀(五氧化二钒浸蚀)

vanadium bronze 钒青铜

vanadium steel 钒钢

van body 厢式车身(有顶的封闭车箱)

van container 集装箱

van cooler 冷藏车,冷冻车

vandalic 破坏性的

vandal-proof 防破坏的,防损坏的;防破损的

Van der Waals' equation of state 冯·魏尔氏状态方程式[实际气体的压力 p、比容积 V 与绝对温度 T 的关系远较 $pV=RT$ 复杂。冯·魏尔氏提出了其近似式:$(p+a/V^2)(V-b)=RT$,式中:R—气体常数;a,b—气体分子间力所确定的常数]

vane ①叶片,轮叶②(特指涡轮机内的)定子叶片

vane airflow sensor 叶片式空气流量传感器(简称 VAF sensor)

vane air temperature sensor (叶片式传感器中的)进气空气温度传感器(见 vane meter)

vane anemometer 翼式风速器

vaned diffuser 带导流片的扩压器

vane fuel supply pump 滑片式输油泵(泵油元件为带有滑片的内转子和外偏心环的输油泵)

vane-in-rotor pump 滑动叶片转子泵(= sliding-van pump)

vaneless diffuser 无导流片的扩压器

vane meter 叶片式传感器（装在空气滤清器和节气门体之间，由叶片式空气容积流量传感器"vane airflow sensor"及其空气入口处的空气温度传感器"vane air temperature sensor"组成，用于测定电子控制模块计算实际进入汽缸的空气质量所需的发动机的进气空气容积流量及温度）

vane motor 叶轮液压马达（叶片式液力马达，叶轮液动机）

vane switch 叶片转子式开关（Hall vane switch 的简称，指叶片转子式霍尔效开关，利用转子叶片遮蔽气隙，将霍尔元件与磁力线隔开，而产生矩形输出信号的开关元件）

vane tip 叶片顶端（= blade tip）

vane-type blower 叶片式鼓风机

vane type flasher 翼片式闪光器（以热丝的伸缩转变为翼片突变动作的闪光器）

vane (type) pump 叶轮泵（叶片式离心泵）

vane-type shock absorber 摆臂式减振器（亦称 lever-type shock absorber）

vane-type shutter 百叶窗

vane-type supercharger 叶片式增压器

vane wheel 叶轮

vane wheel impeller 带径向直叶片的泵轮

vane-within-a-vane-type pump 套装叶片式泵

vanity lamp 化妆灯

vanity plate （汽车的）个性化牌照（亦称 personal 或 personalized number plate，如：牌照上，标出车主姓名或车主要求的特殊文字、数字等）

vantage 优势，优越性

vapipe 汽化管（一种安装在进气管前端利用废气的热量使燃油进一步汽化的装置）

vapor ［美］蒸气（= vapour）

vaporability 蒸发性，挥发性，汽化性

vaporable 可挥发的，可蒸发的，可汽化的

vapor-air release valve 蒸气-空气阀（装在散热器上水箱盖内，当发动机温度正常时，蒸气阀和空气阀均关闭，将冷却系与大气隔开而使冷却系内的压力稍高于大气压力，从而提高冷却水的沸点，增强冷却系的散热能力。当水温过高，散热器内蒸气压力超过规定值时，蒸气阀开启，而当水温过低，散热器内压力低于规定值时，空气阀开启）

vaporator temperature sensor （空调系统）蒸发器温度传感器

vaporblast operation 蒸气喷砂处理

vapor compression refrigeration cycle 蒸气压缩制冷循环

vapor-cooling ①蒸发冷却的②蒸发冷却

vapor degreasing 蒸气除油（蒸气去脂）

vapor density 蒸气密度

vapor diffusion 蒸气扩散

vapor heating equipment 蒸气供暖装置，蒸气加热装置

vaporific 产生蒸气的，多蒸气的，汽化的，蒸气状的，雾状的

vaporization 蒸发，汽化

vaporization cooling 蒸发冷却（法）

vaporized fuel 已挥发的燃料，已汽化的燃油

vaporized gasoline metering system 汽化汽油计量系统

vaporizer 蒸发器，喷雾器

vaporizing chamber 汽化室，蒸发室，混合室

vaporizing combustion chamber 汽化式燃烧室，汽化式燃烧器（燃气轮机的燃烧室的一种，室内具有燃料蒸发装置，使燃油蒸发而充分燃

烧）

vapor/liquid ratio 气-液比（指在不同温度下，在标准容器内测得的汽油气体体积与液体体积的百分比值。为汽油规格中表征汽油气阻趋势的指标之一，一般写成 V/L）

vapor-liquid separator 气-液分离器

vapor lock 气阻（因管道内有油蒸气或空气而造成的油、液路堵塞，亦写作 vapor locking）

vapor lock index （汽油的）气阻指数（指用蒸气压"vapor pressure"和气液比"vapor/liquid ratio"两项指标，来衡量汽油发生气阻的趋势。蒸气压力指在38℃下，在密闭容器内测定的雷德蒸气压，气液比指在不同温度下测得的标准容器内的汽油蒸气体积与液体体积的百分比值。二者的值越高，发生气阻的趋势越强，在汽油规格中规定有具体的最高值）

vapor-lock test （供油系统中）气阻试验

vaporous 蒸气的，汽化的，雾状的

vapor phase 蒸气相（气相，蒸气状态）

vapor phase inhibitor 气相氧化抑制剂（气相防蚀剂，气相防锈剂，一种制成粉状、粒状或块状的挥发性固体，置于装箱的或库存的金属制件、总成、装置等的封装物内，其挥发而形成的蒸气，可保护金属免于氧化锈蚀）

vapor phase reaction 气相反应

vapor plating 气相渗镀（气相扩散渗镀，将易与涂覆表面起反应的蒸气或气体，通过涂覆表面进行反应，而在表面上形成固态化合物的薄膜）

vapor pressure ①蒸气压力②（大气中）蒸气分压力

vapor pressure curve 蒸气压力曲线

vapor proof ①汽密的②不受蒸气侵蚀的

vapor recovery system 蒸气回收系统（如：汽油蒸气回收装置）

vapor rectifier 汞弧整流器（水银蒸气整流器）

vapor tight 不漏气的，汽密的

vapor trail 雾化尾迹，凝气尾迹

vapo（u）r 蒸气，汽化物

vapo（u）r canister 收集-存储燃油蒸发排放物的活性炭罐（亦称 evaporative emission canister, 简称 EVAP canister）

vapour canister 活性炭罐（见 activated carbon canister）

vapour separator 蒸汽分离器（将液—汽分离的各种装置的通称）

VAP PRF 汽密的（vapor proof 的简称）

var 乏（无功功率的单位，电抗功率单位，var 是 volts-ampere reactive 的简称，见 reactive power）

varactor （可）变（电）抗器（变容二极管，可变电抗二极管，= varactor diode）

var-hour 乏-小时（无功伏安小时）

variability of volume 体积的可变性（如：体积的可压缩性）

variable ①可变的，变化的，不定的 ②变数，变量

variable-acceleration 变加速度（= non-uniform acceleration）

variable-air bleed 可变空气量孔（通过断面积可变的空气量孔，简称 VAB）

variable-amplitude test 变幅应力疲劳试验

variable-angle nozzle 可变角度的喷嘴

variable-area 可变区域，可变区

variable-area carburetor 活动喉管化油器（可变喉管断面化油器，= variable-venturi carburetor）

variable-area nozzle 可变截面喷嘴，

可变截面喷管（简称 VAN）

variable-area turbocharger 可变截面涡轮增压器（简称 VAT）

variable asist steering 可变助力转向（系）

variable belt transmission 连续可变传动带式无级变速器（使用 V 形传动带，通过改变其主、从动盘的工作直径，实现传动速比的连续无级变换，由冯·多尔勒 ven Doorne 为 DAF 牌轿车研制，后用于 Volvo 340 型轿车，其商品名为 Varimatic transmission）

variable blade 可变叶片（可改变其角度位置，从而改变液流方向的叶片）

variable-braking vehicle 参数可变的制动试验车（分析研究制动参数用的一种试验车，简称 vbv）

variable brightness control （灯具的）可变亮度控制

variable-capacitance parametron 可变电容参变元件

variable capacity converter 转矩容量可变式液力变矩器（亦称 adjustable torque convertor）

variable-coefficient damper 可变系数阻尼器

variable combustion (sequential) engine 可变燃烧顺序式发动机

variable-compression-ratio engine 可变压缩比发动机（简称 VCR engine）

variable-compression-ratio piston 可变压缩比活塞（由销座部分和可相对销座部分移动的冠部组成，借助于冠部与销座部分的相对移动，改变活塞顶面与活塞销中心的间距，而使汽缸的压缩比改变，简称 VCR piston）

variable condenser 可变电容器

variable-contour cam 可变外形凸轮（可变升程凸轮，亦称 variable lift cam）

variable crank-throw engine 可变曲柄半径式发动机

variable cycle 可变周期

variable cylinder management technology 可变工作缸数管理技术（如：当需要的功率较小时，V6 发动机自动转为仅 3 个汽缸工作，以节油，简称 VCM，亦称 variable displacement technology）

variable damper system （阻尼特性）可变减振器系统

variable-damping-force (type) shock absober 可变阻尼力（型）减振器

variable-delivery check valve pump 止回阀式变量泵

variable delivery pump 变量输送泵

variable density 可变密度

vari able-deploy-force type air bag 可变展开力式安全气囊（其展开力可随碰撞力度而变）

variable depression carburetor 可变压降式化油器（指固定喉管式化油器，在工作过程中，其喉管处的压力降随节气门开度而变，见 fixed chock carburetor）

variable-dilution sampling 变稀释度取样（定容取样）

variable displacement engine 可变排量发动机（如：电子控制模块根据汽车的行驶状况通过液压执行机构，使进气门关闭或停止供油的方式改变工作缸数，实现排量变化，达到节油和减少排放的目的）

variable-displacement orbital pump （汽车用静液压变速器的）可变排量轨道泵

variable-drive power take-off 可变速式功率输出轴

variable driving pattern system （汽车的）可变行驶模式系统［亦称 variable driving mode system，如：3

driving pattern system、5 driving mode system 等，可由驾驶者通过拨杆或按钮等选择装置选择节油的经济模式（economic mode），动力澎湃、加速迅猛的运动模式（sports mode）或正常行驶的标准模式（normal mode）等]

variable dwell 可变闭合角，= dwell angle control，指①断电器触点闭合角控制②点火线圈初级绕组通电时间（按曲轴转角计）控制

variable dynamic testing vehicle 可变动态性能测试车（简称 VDTV。美国20世纪90年代为智能运输系统中在自动公路系统内进行各种动态性能检测用的试验车，参见 ITS，AHS. Ⅳ)

variable element ①变参数，可变元素②可变元件

variable epicycloid circular arc spur gear 变幅外摆线圆弧直齿轮（齿廓曲线为变幅外摆线的等距线的圆弧直齿轮）

variable flow control valve 可变流量控制阀

variable flow muffler 可变流量消声器（亦称 variable displacement muffler）

variable flywheel cluster 可变惯量飞轮组

variable-frequency generator 可变频率发生器

variable front bumper 可变式前保险杠

variable fuel vehicle 可变燃料汽车（指可用两种或两种以上不同燃料的汽车，= flexible-fuel vehicle）

variable gear ratio steering 变速比转向机构（可根据汽车行驶状况，自动改变齿轮速比，以满足高速行驶时转向盘操纵力较重，而低速大转向角入库时，转向盘操纵力较轻的要求）

variable-geometry chassis 几何形状可变底盘

variable-geometry cooling fan 可变几何形状冷却风扇（发动机转速增加时，风扇叶片变平，风量随之减少）

variable geometry turbocharger 几何尺寸可变型废气涡轮增压器[简称 VGT，= variable volume turbocharger（可变容量型废气涡轮增压器）]

variable half vane 半活动叶片（叶片后缘可调节）

variable induction system 可变进气系统（可根据发动机工况改变进气通路的长度或通过断面，即进气量，以满足不同工况对进气的要求，如：其中进气通路长度可变者称 variable length induction system，用于进气惯性增压）

variable inlet guide vanes 可变进气导流片（简称 VIGV）

variable intake-exhaust cams phasing 可变进、排气门凸轮相位

variable intake manifold flap type air control valve 可变进气歧管阻风板式控制阀（简称 intake air control valve）

variable involute circular arc spur gear 变幅渐开线圆弧直齿轮（齿廓曲线是圆心运动轨迹为变幅渐开线的等距曲线的圆弧直齿轮）

variable length intake runner （滑动式）可变长度进气管

variable length word （长度可变的）可变长字（信息数据中的一个字符占一个地址，而不是固定字长）

variable-lift cam 可变升程凸轮（= variable-contour cam）

variable limited-slip axle differential 可变转矩比防滑式驱动桥差速器（用电子控制多片离合器式作为防滑装置的左、右轮转矩分配比可变式差速器）

variable limited-slip centre differential 可变转矩比防滑式中央差速器（电子控制的可变转矩分配比的全轮驱动的前、后桥间差速器）

variable linear system 可变线性系统

variable-locking differential 可变锁止差速器（如：ASR 系统中的可反馈式控制的电子控制液压离合器型可锁止差速器，向其离合器片加压即可实现锁止功能，压力来自 ASR 系统储压器供给的高压油液，压力值大小由电子控制模块根据防滑转的要求控制，其锁止范围可从基本锁止到完全锁止）

variable message sign （公路）可变信息标志（简称 VMS）

variable modulus of elasticity 可变弹性模量（见 modulus of elasticity）

variable motor 变速电动机

variable-nozzle turbocharger 可变（截面）喷嘴涡轮增压器

variable of state （系统的）状况变量（指可说明系统状态、确定系统性质和行为的最少数目的一组变量。如：阻尼系统的动态过程涉及位移、速度和加速度三项变量。若两项已知，则第三项就可"唯一地"确定。这两项已知的变量是可确定系统行为的最少数目的一组变量，即：状态变量）

variable μ pentode 变 μ 五极管

variable-pitch blade 可变节距叶片

variable-pitch control （液力变矩器的）变角度操纵，变角度操纵机构（导轮叶片的角度可由驾驶员操纵改变。汽车常速行驶时用较小的角度，要瞬间加速或增加转矩时，由驾驶员加大导轮叶片角度）

variable-pitch fan 变倾角风扇（风扇叶片的倾角可调，以改变风量与风压）

variable-pitch pulley 可变径节传动带轮（有效传动直径可变式传动带盘，由两半个锥形传动带盘拼合组成，两盘或一盘可沿轴向移动，而改变其有效传动带轮直径，用于无级变速装置）

variable-pitch spring 变距弹簧

variable-pitch stator （液力变矩器）叶片角可变的导轮（其叶片角度可随负荷而变）

variable-pressure circuit 压力可变回路，可变压力回路（一般指压力在工作期间可随要求由人控或自动变化的液压回路等）

variable-pressure solenoid 变压电磁阀（由行程可变式电磁阀的衔铁直接控制的滑动柱塞的压力调节阀，亦称 pressure regulator solenoid）

variable-pressure wind tunnel 变风压风洞

variable-preswirl assembly 可调预旋导向叶片总成

variable-pulley transmission 可变速比传动带盘式（无级）变速器

variable pump 变量泵

variable quantity 变量（其值可变且通常可测出的量或状态，亦简称 variable）

variable-rate power steering 可变速比动力转向

variable-rate spring 变刚度弹簧

variable-rate suspension 变刚度悬架

variable-ratio braking system 前后车轮制动力比可变式制动系（如：装有比例分配阀制动系）

variable-ratio steering 可变传动比转向装置

variable-reluctance magnetic device 变磁阻式电磁装置（多用作传感器）

variable reluctance rotor 变磁阻转子

variable reluctance speed sensor 变磁阻转速传感器（简称 VR speed sensor）

variable-reluctance step motor 变磁阻式步进电动机（亦称 neutral magnetic circuit step motor "中性磁路步进电动机"）

variable resistance fuel level sensor 可变电阻式燃油油量传感器（利用燃油液面高度的变化改变电阻值大小而工作的传感器）

variable resistance oil pressure sensor 可变电阻式油压表传感器（利用压力的变化使电阻变化而工作的传感器）

Variable Resonance Induction System 可变谐振式进气系统（见 VRIS）

variable rheostat 可变电阻器

variable section 可变截面

variable sensitivity control （液压传动）可变灵敏度控制

variable-speed belt cone 传动带式无级变速装置的锥形传动带盘

variable-speed drive 变速传动装置

variable-speed fan clutch 可变速风扇离合器

variable-speed friction wheel 变速摩擦轮

variable-speed governor （燃油喷射系的）全程式调速器（在发动机整个转速范围内的任何转速下都可自动控制喷油量的调速器，= all speed governor, adjustable speed governor）

variable-speed hydraulic transmission 无级变速液力（动液或静液）传动

variable-speed pulley 可变速式传动带盘

variable-stability car （专供试验用的）稳定性可变的轿车

variable-stress level test 变应力（疲劳）试验

variable stroke engine 可变冲程发动机

variable-stroke (fuel) injection pump 可变行程式（燃油）喷射泵

variable-stroke plunger type metering pump 变行程柱塞式计量泵

variable swirl 可变（进气）涡流

variable-threshold logic 变阈逻辑电路

variable-timing camshaft （发动机的）可变气门正时凸轮轴（可根据发动机工况改变气门正时）

variable torque distribution system （四轮驱动汽车的前、后桥）可变转矩分配系统（可根据前、后桥的载荷，改变桥间的转矩分配比例，亦称 variable torque dividing system, variable torque split system）

variable-track wheels 轮距可调车轮

variable transformer 可调变压器

variable-tune control valve 可变进气通道控制阀（由电子控制模块通过可逆转式电动机根据发动机转速和节气门位置控制的进气歧管通过断面的调节阀）

variable twin turbocharger system 见 VTT system

variable two cycling circuit cooling system （发动机）可变双环路冷却系统（缸盖与缸体分为两个冷却环路，水温低于95℃时缸体冷环道关闭，冷却水仅在缸盖环道内循环，使缸体迅速升温）

variable valve actuation 可变气门驱动机构（简称VVA，指发动机进排气门的气门升程、气门开启时刻及开启延续时间都可随发动机运转工况的变化而变化的气门驱动机构，见 VVT)

Variable Valve Lift and Timing system 可变气门升程与正时系统（简称 VVL system）

variable valve stop mechanism （可变工作缸数发动机的）可变气门闭合机构［当根据车辆行驶状况的要求，六缸发动机只需使用三个汽缸工作时，可通过一个称为 syncro piston（同步活塞）的机构，使六缸中的三个汽缸的进、排气门全部关闭，同时停止对其喷油，以达到节油和减排的目的]

variable valve timing 可变气门正时（发动机气门启闭时间可随着转速的变化而变化，简称VVT）

variable valve timing and valve lift electronic control 电子控制可变气门正时和升程机构（日本本田公司20世纪80年代在摩托车上试用，20世纪90年代用于轿车，见VTEC）

variable-venturi carburetor 可变喉管化油器（活动喉管化油器，喉管截面随发动机工况变化的化油器，= variable area choke carburetor, 简称 VV carburetor, 亦称 constant depression carburetor）

variable voltage welding machine 可变电压焊接机，自动变压电焊机（电流增加时，电压自动下降，而使电流保持不变）

variable volume 可变容积

variable volume turbocharger 可变容量型废气涡轮增压器（简称VVT）

variable working condition 变工况（运转状态，如：速度、负荷、功率等频繁变化的工况）

variance ①变化，变异，变动②差异，不同③不符合，不一致，分歧④偏离，偏；离散（值）⑤（均）方差（标准偏差的平方）⑥分散⑦色散⑧散度，变化度

variance analysis 差值分析

variance ratio 方差比

variant ①变型车（只改变车身结构，保持原车底盘不变）②变形，变体

variation ①变化，变更，变动②变量，偏差，偏转，差异

variation in flow ①流量变化②车流变化，交通量变化

variation of sign 符号的变更，正负号（符号）替换

variation of tolerance 公差带

variator ①（无级）变速器（= speed variator）②变换器，变化器③伸缩（接）缝，伸胀缝

variety ①变化，多样化，多样性，多种类型②变型，变种，变体③簇④品种（产品按其性能、成分等方面的特征所划分的类别）

varimatic transmission 见 variable belt transmission

Vario Cam Plus （保时捷911Targa跑车上使用的）可变气门系统（的商品名）

variode 变容二极管（参量二极管，= varactor diode）

variodenser 可变电容器

VarioFlex （Skoda的）可调节式后座（adjustable rear seat的商品名）

variohm 可变电阻器（变阻器）

variomatic transmission 自动变速器（荷兰Van Doorn公司产品，通过改变传动带的主动与从动盘的直径比实现速比无级连续变化的小轿车用变速器的商品名）

variometer ①可变电感器，变感器②磁力比较器，磁偏计③气压测量器，变压表

vario-roof （轿车的）摺合式硬顶（Benz公司的商品名）

varistor ①压敏电阻②可变电阻③压敏变阻器（由具有"+"、"-"两个电极的半导体器件组成，其电阻值随两电极间电压而呈非线性变化。当加在其电极间的电压增加时，其电阻值急剧下降）

varistor compensated circuit 可变电阻补偿电路

varistor rectifier 变阻整流器

varnish ①清漆②漆膜状沉积物

varnish deposit 漆膜状沉积物（=

lacquer deposit，简称 varnish）

varnished 上清漆的，涂（清）漆的

varnished cable 漆包线（= varnished wire）

varnished cloth 漆布

varsal 万能的，通用的

vary 改变，变更，变化

varying ①变动的，变化的，改变的 ②不定的，不同的，不等的

VAS 车辆警报系统（vehicle alarm system 的简称，该系统由中央处理单元即 CPU，周边探测器和传感器，声、光警报信号系统及停车装置等组成。当测得车门、行李舱盖等非正常开启，驾驶室倾斜，挂车脱钩，断电或对车辆有干扰或入侵等紧急情况时，即通过警报系统发出相应警报，必要时自动停机或停车）

vaseline 凡士林（见 petroleum jelly）

VAT ①可变截面涡轮增压器（variable area turbocharger）②增值税（value added tax）③电压-电流测试表，伏—安表（voltage amperage tester）

vat 大桶，大槽，大盆，大缸

VATE 万能自动测试设备（versatile automatic test equipment）

VAT sensor 叶片型空气流量传感器空气进口处的空气温度传感器（vane air temperature sensor 的简称）

vaucher alloy 锌基轴承合金（锌75%，锡18%，铅4.5%，锑2.5%）

vaulted 拱状的（拱顶的，双曲拱的）

V-belt 三角（传动）带（= triangular belt，wedge belt）

V-block ①V 形缸体②V 形块，V 形铁

V-body （自卸汽车等的）V 形车身，V 形车槽

v bolt U 型螺栓（如：将钢板弹簧固定在车轴上或连接货箱与车架的 U 型螺栓）

VBRA ［英］车辆制造商和修理商协会（Vehicle Builders and Repairers Association 的简称）

VBS 车身结构（vehicle body structure）

vbv 参数可变的制动试验车（variable braking vehicle）

VC ①黏性耦合器（见 viscous coupling）②竖曲线（vertical curve）

VCC ①见 viscous converter clutch ②（Volvo 的）多功能概念车（Versatility Concept Car 的简称，该车的概念是：舒适性追求车 "a car pursuing the comfort"）

VCCO （电）压控（制）晶体振荡器（voltage controlled crystal oscillator 的简称，见 VCO）

VCC piston 可变（压缩比）燃烧室活塞（variable combustion chamber piston 的简称）

VCC temperature sensor 液力变矩器的黏性离合器温度传感器（viscous converter clutch temperature sensor 的简称）

VCD ①可视小光盘（video compact disk）②影碟机（video compact disk player）

VCG ①车辆重心（vehicle center of gravity）②重心的垂直方向的位置（vertical location of the center of gravity）

VCI 见 C1

VCL 垂直中心线（vertical center line）

VCM ①（通用公司的）整车控制模块（该模块执行动力控制，ABS 控制和爆燃传感器模块功能，vehicle control module 的简称）②见 variable cylinder management technology

VCM technology 可变工作缸数控制技术（variable cylinder management

technology 的简称,如:在平坦的公路上行驶时,6缸发动机仅3个汽缸工作,以节约燃油)

VCM valve 真空控制调节阀(vacuum control modulator valve)

VCO (电)压控(制)振荡器(voltage controlled oscillator 的简称,其振荡频率随电压而变,可用作模/数变换器)

V-configuration V型的

VCO type nozzle 阀盖孔式喷嘴(VCO 为 valve covered orifice 的简称)

VCR crankshaft 可变压缩比曲轴(variable-compression ratio crankshaft 的简称,通过偏心轴承机构,控制曲轴上、下位置,改变压缩比)

VCSI 车辆碰撞严重程度指数(vehicle crash severity index)

VCU 电压-电流控制装置(voltage and current control unit 的简称)

VCV ①真空控制阀(vacuum control valve 的简称,利用真空与大气压的压力差起控制作用的执行器件) ②真空开关阀(vacuum switch valve 的简称,控制真空通路的开关阀)

V-cylinder arrangement 汽缸V型排列(= V-type cylinder arrangement)

vd 蒸气密度(vapour density)

VDA 德国汽车工业联合会(Verband der Automobile industrie)

VDC (**s**) 车辆动态控制系统[Vehicle Dynamic Control (System) 的简称,日产公司车辆稳定性控制系统的商品名。该系统是在原牵引力控制系统(TCS)和防抱死制动系统(ABS)的基础上,增加一个车身横向加速度传感器(lateral accelerometer)、转向盘转角传感器(steering angle sensor)和横摆率传感器(yaw ratesensor),除了可以防止制动时因车轮制动力大于路面附着力,以致车轮抱死而造成的侧滑和车辆起步、加速及路面过滑时,牵引力大于路面附着力,以致车轮原地滑转所造成的侧滑或甩尾外,还可以防止车辆急剧在改变车道、转向和回避前方障碍物时,产生的过度转向和不足转向趋势,以保持车辆的回转运动稳定性。由于VDC 与 ABS 和 TCS 共用一个控制模块、各种传感器和执行机构,因而合三为一,又称为 VDC/TCS/ABS]

VDCW 直流工作电压(volts, direct current working 或 direct current working volts 的简称)

VDI ①德国工程师学会(Verein Deutscher Ingenieure) ②车辆(碰撞)变形指数(vehicle deformation index)

VDI -Guide lines 德国工程师学会提出的行驶舒适性曲线

VDM (丰田公司复合动力车 Highlander hybrid 和 Lexus RX 400h 等车型上使用的)车辆动态管理(系统)(vehicle dynamic management 的简称,为丰田公司常规的车辆稳定性控制系统"vehicle stability control"的升级版,该系统综合运用车辆稳定性控制系统和电子控制制动系统的功能,通过对节气门和制动器的控制,可预先确保车辆动态稳定性)

VDR 压敏电阻(voltage dependent resistor 的简称)

VDS (铭牌中)车型说明部分(见 vehicle descriptor section)

VDT belt (无级连续变速器的)VDT 传动带(VDT 传动带是德国博世公司在荷兰的子公司 Van Doorne Transmission 生产的专利产品。在传动过程中该传动带传递推力,称为挤压型或推力型传动带,使用这种传动带的 CVT 称推力型 CVT

"push"或"pusher type CVT")
VE ①价值工程(value engineering) ②充气效率(volumetric efficiency)
VECI 车辆排放控制信息(Vehicle Emission Control Information 的简称,按规定贴在车上直接表明该车排放控制信息的标签)
vector 矢量,矢,向量
vector computer ①阵列计算机(亦称 array computer,指具有多项控制或/和多个数据流的计算机)②阵列处理器
vectored injection 定向喷射
vector encoding 矢量编码法
vector of unit length 单位矢量
vector potential 矢量势(矢量位,矢势,矢位)
vector quantity 矢量
vector sum 矢量和,向量和,矢和
vector triangle 矢量三角形
vecto vector encoded digital road map 矢量编码数字化路线(地)图
vee (英文字母)V
vee-belt 三角形传动带
vee engine V 型发动机(= V-type engine,具有两个或两列汽缸,其中心线夹角呈 V 形,且共用一根曲轴输出功率的内燃机)
vee formation (发动机汽缸的)V 型布置
vee-(grooved) pulley V 形槽传动带轮,三角形传动带盘
vee-section V 形截面的
vee-shaped radiator front V 型散热器前脸
vee-thread 三角螺纹(的)
vegetable oil 植物油
vegetarian car 植物燃料车
vehicle ①任一种陆上交通运输工具的通称(一般指轮式车辆,如:手推车、马车、摩托车、货运与客运汽车等,有时亦指雪橇等非轮式运载工具)②(传达思想、感情的)媒体,媒介,手段
vehicle acceleration feedback control system 汽车的加速度反馈控制系统(见 VAFC system)
vehicle acceleration feedback control system 见 VAFC system
vehicle accelerator crash simulator 汽车加速碰撞模拟装置
vehicle-actuated road signal 车控交通信号(由车辆控制的道路交通信号,一种装在路面上,由行驶汽车触发的传感装置所控制的交通信号,亦称 vehicle-actuated traffic signal)
vehicle anchor (试验台)车辆固定装置
vehicle-application dependent 取决于车辆运用的,与车辆运用有关的
Vehicle Area Network 见 VAN
vehicle attitude 汽车姿势(汽车纵向、横向、垂直等轴线与所在路面的相对位置,常用姿势角来表示,即汽车上述各轴线与路面之间的夹角)
vehicle attitude angle 汽车姿势角(见 vehicle attitude)
vehicle attitude change 汽车姿势变化(指绕纵向轴线的左右摇动,或绕横向轴线的前后波动,或绕垂直轴线的左右摆动,变化的大小,常用姿势变化角来表示,即汽车姿势未变化前的轴线与变化后的轴线之间的夹角)
vehicle attitude control 车身姿势控制(如:自动升高或降低车身前端、后端或某一角,以保持车身水平姿势)
vehicle automatic longitudinal control 车辆自动纵向姿势控制
vehicle axis system 汽车坐标系(x、y、z,以簧上质心为原点的右手直角坐标系。该坐标系随同簧上质量一起运动和旋转。在静止状态下,x

轴在水平平面内，指向前方，y 轴在水平平面内，指向左方，z 轴指向上方）

vehicle behaviour 车辆（的运动）特性

vehicle body engineering 车身工程

(vehicle) body rotational motion 车身的（回）转（运）动（指车身绕其坐标系 x、y、z 轴的回转运动，如：侧倾、横摆、纵倾等）

(vehicle-body) shaker test （汽车车身的）振动机（振动）试验

vehicle body structure 车身结构（简称 VBS）

vehicle break-down time 车辆故障时间（指营运车辆由于机件损坏、失效而发生故障影响其正常运行的平均时间）

vehicle capacity （运输）车辆装载量

vehicle-center 2 way communication-system 车辆-（控制）中心间的双向通信系统

vehicle characteristic tester 车辆特性试验台

vehicle classification sign 车辆分级标志

vehicle clearance ①汽车的最小离地间隙（见 ground clearance）②汽车的侧隙（见 side clearance）③汽车的净空高度（见 headroom②）

vehicle clearance circle 汽车的转弯通道圆（见 turning clearance circles）

vehicle collision avoidance system 车辆防撞系统

vehicle collision avoidance system using civil radar 民用雷达车辆防撞系统

vehicle compatibility 车辆适应性

vehicle cone index （确定车辆行驶时土壤阻力和推力特性的）车辆圆锥贯入指数（简称 vci）

vehicle configurations 汽车造型

vehicle consumption factor 车辆（每昼夜燃料）能耗指数

vehicle contour 车身外形，车形轮廓

vehicle conversion 车辆换代，车辆换型

vehicle crash protection system 车辆碰撞保护系统

vehicle crash severity index 车辆碰撞严重程度指数（简称 VCSI）

vehicle damage index 车辆损坏指数，车损指数（简称 VDI）

vehicle data communication network 汽车数据通信网络（指汽车电子控制系统的通信网络，美国 SAE 将汽车网络分为 A、B、C 三级。class A network 指多项信号均通过在各网点间的同一条信号总线发送和接收的多路复用系统，以减少车内导线。class B network 指在各网点间传送多种数据的多路复用系统，以省去重复的传感器和系统元件。class C network 指通过信号总线传输各实时控制系统，如：发动机控制系统、防抱死制动系统等的高数据传输率信号的多路复用系统，便于实现分布式控制和进一步减少汽车内的导线。B 级包括 A 级的功能，C 级包括 B、A 级功能）

vehicle deformation index 车辆变形指数（表示机动车碰撞的变形程度，简称 VDI）

vehicle density 汽车饱和度（每辆汽车所分摊的居民人数）

vehicle descriptor section （车辆牌号中的）车型说明部分（如：挂车牌号中包括有牌名、挂车型、轴数、长度、挂车结构、主要材料等项的代号，简称 VDS）

vehicle detecting equipment （道路）侦车设备（车辆感知设备）

vehicle detecting test station 汽车检测站

vehicle detector 车辆传感器（检测

车辆通过和存在的装置)

vehicle detector pad 车辆传感板(装设在路面上,当车辆从该板通过时即可发出相应信号的传感装置)

vehicle diagnosis 汽车诊断(在不解体或仅卸下个别小件的条件下,确定汽车技术状况、查明故障部位及原因的检测与判断作业)

vehicle diagnostic station 汽车诊断站

vehicle dive 汽车点头(在汽车制动时由于质量前移而使前悬架系统较正常情况负荷加大,引起汽车前端下倾的现象)

vehicle-driving environment 车辆驾驶环境

vehicle-driving environment detecting system (车装式)车辆驾驶环境探测系统(使用车载摄像与屏显装置观测路面状况、周围车辆及探测其接近速度和接近距离等)

vehicle driving stability 车辆驱动稳定性

vehicle dry mass (汽车)整车干质量(见 complete vehicle dry mass,旧称 vehicle dry weight)

vehicle dry weight 汽车干重(指装备有车身、全部电气设备,但未加燃料、润滑油、冷却水、备胎、随车工具、附属设备,也未载客、货时的汽车质量)

vehicle dynamic area [美]汽车动态试验场(亦称 skid pad,用以测试汽车的操纵稳定性等性能,有人亦称汽车转向试验场)

vehicle dynamic control 车辆动态控制系统(见 VDC)

vehicle dynamic management 见 VDM

vehicle dynamic response 车辆的动态响应特性

vehicle dynamics 汽车(动)力学,车辆动力学

vehicle dynamics control during non-braking maneuvers 非制动驾驶操作时的车辆动态控制

vehicle economy 车辆(燃料)经济性(简称 DE)

vehicle electric test system 车辆电气试验系统(简称 VETS)

vehicle electronic navigation system 车辆电子导航系统(汽车电子导行装备,简称 VELNAS)

vehicle electronics ①汽车电子(学) ②汽车电子系统,汽车电子设备(= auto electronics)

vehicle emissions 汽车排放(一般指车辆排放到大气中的各种污染物,如:排出的废气、燃料蒸汽等)

vehicle emission sensor 汽车排放传感器

vehicle encroachment 车辆转弯时的占用空间

vehicle engine identification number 车辆发动机识别号(不一定与车辆出厂号码相同,但一台发动机有一个号码,一般规定一定年限,如:十年内不准重复)

Vehicle Equipment Safety Commission [美]车辆装备安全委员会(简称 VESC)

vehicle exhaust fan 车辆排风扇

vehicle experimental research facility 车辆试验研究设备(简称 VERF)

vehicle exterior safety 车辆的对外安全性(指对道路行人等的安全性等)

vehicle fog (在寒冷天气)车辆发动机工作时形成的雾气

vehicle following control for autonomous driving 无人自动驾驶的车辆跟随控制

vehicle for construction 建筑用车辆(各种砂、土料自倾车,吊车,挖掘机,铲运机,平地机等土建工程

用车辆、机械的总称）

vehicle form-size-power aggregate 车辆形状-尺寸-功率汇编集

vehicle fuel efficiency 车辆燃料（使用）效率

vehicle glare shield 汽车用炫目防护装置（如：在风窗玻璃框遮阳板上的防眩板）

vehicle glass 车用玻璃

vehicle green tax 汽车环境保护税

vehicle gross weight per power 比功率（单位功率车重，指汽车总重与发动机功率之比值）

vehicle handling quality 车辆操纵性能

vehicle heading 车辆行驶方向

vehicle heading direction 汽车车头（所对的）方向（指汽车纵轴的方向）

vehicle height control system 车辆高度控制系统

vehicle hight locking device （越野车辆的）车身高度锁定器

vehicle hoist 汽车举升器，车辆举升器

vehicle hour 车时（每辆车的运行小时）

vehicle identification number 车辆识别号（亦称车辆的出厂号，由制造厂编制并打在规定位置上，供车辆注册与识别用的由字母和数字代码组成的编号，一般包括以下内容：制造国名、公司名、生产厂名、车型、年型、车身类型、发动机型号及汽车出厂序号等，简称 VIN）

vehicle identification number derivative 汽车出厂号的附加号（指除汽车出厂号外，厂家还打印在汽车发动机、变速器、主减速器、车桥、轮胎、排放控制装置及车身等处，向用户提供更多具体识别该车各总成的信息的代码号）

vehicle identification plate 汽车出厂号牌（指打有出厂号的金属小牌，美国车该号牌一般固定在仪表板上，驾驶员的侧方，从车外通过风窗玻璃能看见的位置上）

vehicle immobilizing system ①汽车停机装置（如：停止供油或切断点火等装置）②汽车防盗系统

vehicle impact testing 汽车碰撞试验

vehicle indicator section （车辆牌号中的）编号部分（包括车型、编号等，简称 VIS）

Vehicle Information and Communication System 车辆信息和通信系统（见 VICS）

vehicle information communication system 车辆信息交流系统（车辆接收公路通行状况的信息，选择最佳行驶路线，避免交通阻塞，提高交通速度，简称 VICS，与 IVHS 的功能类似，见 ITS）

Vehicle Inspection Association [日]车辆检测协会（简称 VIA）

vehicle inspection station 车辆检测站

vehicle interference 车辆（造成的无线电）干扰

vehicle interior safety 车辆的内部安全性（指乘员的安全性）

vehicle interior safety constraint systems 车辆内部的乘员拘束性安全保护系统（见 vehicle interior safety）

vehicle in use 在用车辆（简称 VIU）

vehicle kerb mass （汽车）整车整备质量（见 complete vehicle kerb mass）

vehicle kilometers traveled 车辆已行驶的公里数

vehicle laden mass 汽车装载质量（汽车所载运的人和物的总质量）

vehicle license plate reading system 汽车牌照自动识别读入系统

vehicle life span 车辆使用寿命期

vehicle lift 车辆举升机

vehicle limit drivability 车辆的极限

操纵性能（指在极限条件下的操纵性）

vehicle load limits （道路的）车辆装载限制

vehicle load monitor （货车的）车辆荷载监测器

vehicle location system 车辆定位系统（汽车所在位置自动测报系统，见 GPS）

vehicle longitudinal symmetric plane 车辆纵向对称平面（简称基准 Y 平面"zero Y plane"，指过车辆的线段 AB 的垂直平分平面。A 和 B 两点为通过同一轴上两端车轮轴线的车辆支撑平面，简称基准 Z 平面"zero Z plane"的垂线同车轮中心平面的交线与基准 Z 平面的交点）

vehicle maintenance 车辆维护（为维持汽车完好技术状况和工作能力而进行的作业，旧称车辆保养）

vehicle management 车辆管理

vehicle maneuverability 汽车方向操纵机动性（如：在弯弯曲曲的道路上行驶的操纵性能）

vehicle manufacturer 车辆制造厂

vehicle manufacturing industry 汽车制造业

vehicle mechanics 车辆力学（汽车力学）

vehicle-miles traveled 行驶车英里（英美常用年行驶车英里数"annual vehicle-miles traveled"来表示每年的工作量，或总的车队工作量）

vehicle mission simulation 车辆运输任务模拟

vehicle model （数学模拟中的）汽车模型（如：以驾驶者的操作量等为输入考虑行车条件而计算出汽车位置坐标的数学模型等）

vehicle model with Chinese specification （国外厂家按其拟定的）中国规格（标准生产的）车型

vehicle morphological analysis 车辆形态学分析（车辆表面几何形状分析研究）

vehicle mounted instrument 车装仪表

vehicle mounted on wheels 轮式车辆（= wheeled vehicle）

vehicle operating cost 车辆营运成本（简称 VOC）

vehicle operation 车辆的使用，车辆的运用

vehicle park 停车场（简称 VP）

vehicle path （车道的）车辆占用宽度（一辆汽车实际占用的路面带状部分）

vehicle performance 车辆性能

vehicle performance-limit 车辆性能极限（包括牵引极限、车速极限、加速度极限、爬坡度极限等）

vehicle performance monitoring system 车辆性能监测系统（由传感系、信号处理系及数据记录系等部分组成，用于车辆路试及台试时，记录整理测试数据，如：车速、发动机转速、燃烧及喷油压力、废气温度、冷却水温、润滑油压、燃油流量和温度、车身加速度等）

vehicle pitch angle (θ) 车辆纵倾角（θ）（车辆以簧上质心为原点的汽车坐标系的 x 轴与 $x-y$ 平面间所夹的锐角）

vehicle polar inertia 汽车极惯量（绕垂直轴线转动惯量）

vehicle population 车辆保有量

vehicle power diagram 汽车功率平衡图（图上绘出在不同车速下，克服各种坡度阻力、滚动阻力、空气阻力所消耗的功率曲线，以及在各个挡速下，发动机传到驱动轴的功率曲线，根据这些曲线，解析计算汽车的相关性能）

vehicle queue length 车辆堵车排队长度

vehicle range 汽车可行驶里程（亦

称 diving range, operating range, 一般用公里或英里数表示)

vehicle refitting 车辆改装

vehicle refueling emission 车辆加油排放(车辆加注燃油时产生的有害排出物,如:车辆加注燃油时,排出的 HC 等)

vehicle registration document 车辆注册文件

vehicle repair depot (亦称 vehicle repair plant)汽车修理厂点

vehicle reserve depot 备用车辆车库

vehicle response time 汽车响应时间(接受输入到产生输出的时间)

vehicle road test simulation 车辆道路试验模拟(装置)(如:底盘测动机等装置用来模拟道路试验,简称 VRTS)

Vehicle Road Traffic Intelligence society [日]道路交通车辆智能促进会(简称 VER-TIS,是日本研究智能化交通系统的组织,见 JTS)

vehicle roll angle (φ) 汽车侧倾角(φ)(以簧上质心为原点的汽车坐标系的 y 轴与地面固定坐标系 X-Y 平面间所夹的锐角)

vehicle roll effect 汽车侧倾效应(由于各种原因引起汽车簧上质量的侧倾,使悬架系统的几何形状,以及车轮的转向角、外倾角等发生变化的现象)

vehicle roll susceptibility 汽车侧倾敏感度(汽车在横向力的作用下侧倾的敏感程度,常用单位 deg/g,即:汽车受到产生一个重力加速度 g 的横向力时,所产生的侧倾角)

vehicle rotational motion behaviour measurement system 车辆回转运动特性测试系统(见 body rotational motion)

vehicle safe spacing indicator 车辆安全距离指示器(亦称车辆安全制动距离指示器"vehicle safe braking distance indicator",装在汽车上自动指示该车与前方行驶汽车之间安全距离和该车与前后两车之间的相对速度)

vehicle safety support system 车辆安全支持系统(车上与路上及路外向驾驶人员提供安全信息,或协助驾驶人员控制与操纵车辆确保安全的各种系统的统称)

vehicle's angle of break 车辆纵向最小通过角

vehicle's center of gravity 车辆重心(简称 VCG)

vehicle's condition 车况

vehicle's crush zone 车辆(碰撞时的)挤压区

vehicle seat angle adjuster 汽车座位角度调节器

vehicle seat production 车客座产量(运输企业在统计期内平均每个客位所完成的旅客周转量)

vehicle security system 车辆安全保护系统

vehicle sensitive emergency-locking retractor 汽车安全带紧急状态感知-锁紧式收紧装置

vehicle's holiday 汽车假日(指有些城市为了净化大气,缓解交通拥挤,减小汽车流量,某天不允许某一尾号的汽车上街行驶,令这些汽车在这一天"放假休息")

vehicle side slip angle 汽车侧偏角(亦称 side slip angle of vehicle, angle of slip,指以汽车质心为坐标原点的汽车运动坐标系 x_0 轴在地面上的投影与质心处的车速在路面上的投影间的夹角)

vehicle side slip angle control system 整车侧偏角控制系统(通过对前、后轮转向比的控制,使汽车在各种车速下转向时的整车偏侧角均为零,见 side slip angle of vehicle)

vehicle sinkage ①车辆下陷②车辆涉

渡入水量

vehicle skid torque 车轮滑转转矩（引起滑转的驱动轮力矩）

vehicle-slope-elevation curves 车辆-坡度-升高曲线

vehicle slope operation test 车辆坡度运行试验

(vehicle's) night vision system （车辆的）夜视系统

Vehicle Sound Level Committee [美]（汽车工程师学会的）车辆声级委员会（简称 VSLC）

vehicle speed 车速（质心速度的水平分量）

vehicle speed control system 车速控制系统（福特等公司早期的定速巡行控制系统，简称 VSC system，由电子控制模块对实际车速和驾驶者选定的车速进行比较，当实际车速低于选定车速时，控制模块向其真空控制电磁阀"speed control vacuum control solenoid"发出指令使其车速控制执行器"speed control servo"与真空源相通，加大节气门开度，提高车速，而当实际车速高于选定车速时，则向大气控制电磁阀"speed control vacuum vent solenoid"发出指令，使车速控制执行器与大气相通，减小节气门开度，降低车速）

vehicle speed/front (-) wheel steering angle/steering wheel velocity responsive type electronic-hydraulic control 4WS system 车速/前轮转向角/转向盘角速度响应型电子-液压控制四轮转向系（电子控制模块根据前轮转向角和转向盘转动角速度，及车速直接通过电磁阀控制后轮转动方向及转向角。如：当转向盘在中等车速下急速转动之初，后轮反向转向，以改善车辆机动性）

vehicle speed/front-wheel steering angle/yaw velocity responsive type electronic-hydraulic-mechanical control 4WS system 车速/前轮转向角/横摆速率响应式电子-液压-机械控制四轮转向系

vehicle speed/lateral acceleration responsive type electronic-hydraulic control 4WS system 车速/横向加速度响应型电子-液压控制四轮转向系（其后轮与前轮同向转向，因此主要保证转向时车辆稳定性，而不着眼于减小转向半径，其后轮转角则不仅决定前轮转角，而且随车速及横向加速度而变）

vehicle speed limiter 车辆速度限制器，限速器（简称 VSL）

vehicle speed-responsive pump discharge flow volume control type electronically controlled full hydraulic power steering system 车速响应泵输出流量控制型电子控制全液压式动力转向系统（由电子控制模块根据车速传感器等的信息，通过电磁阀控制液压泵输出流量，借以实现从停车状态到高速行驶全速度范围内转向助力率的连续平滑变化：低速时，转向助力大；高速时，助力小）

vehicle speed (sensing) power steering 车速感知型动力转向（动力转向特性随车速而变）

vehicle speed sensor calibrating module 车速传感器标定模块（简称 VSSCM）

vehicles per mile （道路上的）每英里车辆数（= vehicles to the mile）

vehicle's slip angle control 4WS 车辆侧偏角控制式四轮转向系统

vehicle's static stability factor （美国国家公路交通安全管理局用来确定车辆翻车倾向的两项指标之一的）车辆静态稳定性系数（$= D/2 \times H$，式中：D—轮距；H—重心高度）

vehicle stability 车辆（行驶）稳定

性

vehicle stability Assist System 见 VSA system

vehicle Stability Control system 车辆稳定性控制系统（见 VSC system）

vehicle stability enhancement system 见 VSES

vehicle stability management 车辆稳定性管理系统（简称 VSM）

vehicle stopping distance 制动停车距离（从驾驶员开始踩踏制动踏板的瞬间起，到车辆停止时止所驶过的距离）

vehicle structural mechanics 汽车结构力学

vehicle structure 车辆结构，汽车结构

vehicle structure torsional stiffness 汽车整体结构扭曲刚度

vehicle supporting plane 车辆支撑平面（简称 Z plane，指支撑车轮的平坦、坚实的水平面）

vehicle suspension spring rate ①汽车悬架弹簧变化率（指悬架弹簧高度随着轮胎接地面垂直压力变化的变化率）②汽车悬架弹簧常数（指悬架弹簧的负载对变形的比值，单位为 kg/cm 或 kg/mm）

vehicle swimmability 车辆浮渡性能

vehicle symptom 汽车故障症状

vehicle system analysis program 车辆系统分析程序（简称 VSAP）

vehicle tax ①汽车运输税（= road tax，通常根据货物质量及运距来抽税）②（泛指各种因）车辆（发生的）税（收）

vehicle-terrain interaction 车辆-地面间的相互作用

vehicle testing capability （整车测试站的）车辆测试能力（根据测试技术装备条件，计算所得的年测试车辆数，或称年可测试车数）

vehicle (test) voltmeter 汽车测试用电压表

vehicle test weight 车辆（在）试验（时的）重量

vehicle tilt 车辆倾斜度，车辆倾斜角

vehicle -tilt sensor （防盗系统防止盗贼拖车）车辆倾斜传感器

vehicle ton production 车吨位产量（指运输车辆在统计期内平均每个吨位所完成的货物周转量）

vehicle to vehicle communication 车间通信（车际通信，汽车与汽车之间的无线电通信）

vehicle tracking system 车辆跟踪系统（指实时掌握车辆的行车路线和所在方位的电子系统）

vehicle traction coefficient 车辆牵引力系数（汽车动力因素，单位车重的牵引力，牵引力与车重的比值）

vehicle traction performance 汽车的动力性能（指表征汽车的最高车速、所能克服的最大坡度和加速性能）

vehicle trajectory measurement system 车辆轨迹测定系统

vehicle transmission identification number 车辆变速器出厂号码（变速器识别号，简称 VIN）

vehicle travel activity logger 车辆行驶状况记录仪

vehicle unladed height 空车高（未装载货物式乘员的车辆最高点至 X 平面的距离）

vehicle upkeep operation 车辆技术维护作业

vehicle use pattern (s) 车辆使用模式

vehicle washing equipment 汽车清洗设备

vehicle waterproofing 车辆的防水（密封）性

vehicle wear out 汽车耗损（各种损坏和磨损的总称）

vehicle width 车宽［分别过车辆两

侧固定突出部位(不包括后视镜、侧面标志灯、示位灯、转向指示灯、挠性挡泥板、折叠式踏板、防滑链以及轮胎与地面接触变成部分)最外侧点且平行于 Y 平面的两平面之间的距离。Y 平面,见 y plane]

vehicle with frame construction 车架式汽车(具有由大梁构成的车架,供安装悬架弹簧、车轴、发动机及车厢等)

vehicle yaw 2WS system 车辆横摆型 2 轮转向系(vehicle yaw two-wheel steering system 的简称)

vehicular ①用车辆运载的②供车辆使用的③车辆的

vehicular battery-charging system 车辆(本身的)蓄电池充电系统

vehicular casualty 行车伤亡事故,行车事故

vehicular diesel engine 车用柴油机(指陆地非轨道车辆驱动用 1000 马力以下的压燃式内燃机)

vehicular distance (车队中)汽车之间的间距(= inter vehicular distance)

vehicular electro-magnetic interference 汽车电磁波干扰(简称 VEMI)

vehicular emission 机动车排放,汽车排放

vehicular gap 车间间隔(先行车后端与后随车前端之间的时间间隔或距离间隔)

vehicular gas turbine engine 汽车用燃气涡轮发动机

vehicular intrusion alarm 汽车防盗(贼入侵)警报装置

vehicularized 机动(车辆)化的,摩托化的

vehicular lane 车辆行驶道,车行道

vehicular (movement) phase (交通信号系统的)车行信号相(分配给车辆交通的信号相)

vehicular planimetric dead-reckoning computer 车辆平面测量推算定位用计算机(根据左右车轮转速及其转速差,确定车辆行驶距离和曲线行驶角度,从而确定车辆所在位置的计算装置)

vehicular radio 车用无线电装置

vehicular thermal energy storage power system 车用热能存储式动力系统

V-eight engine V 形八缸发动机

veiling reflection 光幕反射(在视觉作业上镜面反射与漫反射重叠出现的现象。光幕反射降低了作业与背景之间的亮度对比,致使部分地或全部地看不清它的细节)

Velcro (钩环式)尼龙拉链(的商品名,每平方英寸可承受 10~15lbf 的剪切力)

VELNAS 汽车电子导行系统(vehicle electronic navigation system 的简称)

velocimeter ①速度计②(风速,流速等的)测速仪

velocity 速度(与 speed 的区别在于,velocity 是一种矢量,除了和 speed 一样表示单位时间内的移动距离或转动角度外,还表示移动的方向,即 velocity 不仅表示 speed of motian,还表示 direction of motion)

velocity coefficient of chemical reaction 化学反应速度系数

velocity component 速度分量

velocity (-) dependent 取决于速度的(由速度决定的,随速度而变的)

velocity-distance curve 速度-距离曲线

velocity distribution 速度分布

velocity error constant 速度误差常数

velocity gauge 速度表(= speed gauge)

velocity governor 调速器
velocity gradient 速度梯度
velocity head （流体的）速度头（速头，速位差，指单位质量的流体由于速度所具有的能量，亦称 kinetic head。假设流体中某一点的流速为 v (m/s)，则该点的速度头为 $v^2/2g$，式中：g—重力加速度，m/s²）
velocity lag 速度滞后
velocity limit 速度极限
velocity limited （受）速度（所）限制的
velocity limiter 限速器
velocity modulation 速度调制，调速
velocity of discharge ①放电速度 ②排出速度（= discharge velocity）
velocity of flapping 拍击速度，打击速度
velocity of flow 流速
velocity of impact 冲击速度，撞击速度（= impact velocity）
velocity of propagation 传播速度
velocity of sound 声速（= acoustic velocity）
velocity of whirl 涡流速度
velocity potential 速度势（当流体在直角坐标系 x、y 平面内无涡流地流动时，必有一函数 $\varphi(x, y, t)$ 存在，某时刻 t，该流体在某一点 x、y 方向的分速度 u、v 分别为：$u = d\varphi/dx$，$v = d\varphi/dy$，该函数称为速度势）
velocity pressure 速度压力（流体动压，因速度头而产生的压力，见 velocity head）
velocity profile 速度分布图
velocity range 速度范围
velocity ratio 速比（传动比）
velocity ratio for optimum efficiency （传动装置的）最佳效率速比
velocity resonance 速度谐振
velocity restriction ①限速 ②限速装置
velocity rod 浮棒流速计（流速测定浮棒，亦称 rod float）
velocity sensor 速度传感器（亦称 velocity transducer）
velocity type governor （根据速度进行调节的）速度型调节器
velocity vector at center of mass 质心速度矢量（汽车质心或簧上质心的三维速度矢量）
velocity vibrograph 振动速度计（振动计的一种）
velodrome 机器脚踏车竞赛场，（自行车等的）室内赛车场
velograph 速度计录仪
velometer 速度表
VEMI 汽车电磁波干扰（vehicular electro-magnetic interference 的简称）
veneer 表面饰板，镶面板，表面镶饰件，饰面，护面
V-8 engine V 型八缸发动机
vent ①孔，口；出口，通道 ②通风（口），排气（口），通气（口），烟囱 ③漏洞，孔隙，裂口 ④（美指轿车的小）三角通风窗
vent cap 通气盖，通风盖
vent cock 放气开关，放气阀（如：汽油泵的空气排放阀等）
vent cover 通气孔盖，通风孔盖
vented (brake) disc （盘式制动器的）通风式制动盘
vent fan 通风扇（= draft fan）
ventilated box car 通风式厢式货车（蔬菜、水果等要求通风的货物的专用货车，车厢各处都设有通风装置）
ventilated disc （盘式制动器的）通风式制动盘（由中间隔以冷却筋，以便冷却空气流通过的两层金属盘组成的制动盘，亦称 ventilated rotor）
ventilated disk brake 通风（冷却）式盘式制动器

ventilated dynamo 强制通风冷却型电机（如：带冷却风扇的电机）

ventilating device 通风装置，通风设备

ventilation ①通风，换气②通风量

ventilation and heating blower switch 通风和暖气鼓风机开关

ventilation by extraction 抽气通风（= drawing ventilation）

ventilation by pressure 压力通风

ventilation loss ①风扇损失（消耗在冷却风扇上的功率损耗）②通风损失

ventilation orifice 通风口，换气孔

ventilation rate 换气率，通风率（单位时间内的换气量与需要换气的空间的总容积之比）

ventilation resistance 通风阻力

ventilation window 通风窗（= air vent window）

ventilator ①通风装置（通风机，风扇等的总称，亦称 ventilating equipment）②通风口，通风孔③通风窗

ventilator valve ①曲轴箱通风量控制阀（= PCV valve）②（泛指）通风量控制阀

venting quality 透气性

venting screw 排气螺钉

ventipane 车顶通风窗

vent panel 通风孔盖板

vent-plug 通气孔螺塞

vent tube 通气管（= ventilator tube, 简称 ventube）

venture mixing unit （液化石油气或液化天然气汽车发动机的）喉管型混合器（亦称 venturi mixer，液化石油气或液化天然气在此气化并与空气混合形成可燃混合气）

venturi-meter 文氏管流量计（喉管流量计，由文氏管和气压计组成，根据管径收缩前和最小断面处的压力差求出流量值）

venturimeter coefficient 文氏管流量计系数

venturi nozzle 文丘里管型喷嘴（消声器内的喉管形喷嘴，用于减小低频噪声）

venturi principle 文丘里原理（管道内稳定流体的流速与管道通过断面面积成反比，而其压力则与通过断面面积成正比，即：在断面积最大处流速最低，压力最大，而在断面积最小处流速最高，压力最小，1791年由物理学家文丘里 venturi 提出，故名）

venturi tube ①文丘里管（应用文丘里原理制成的缩径管，可使流过它的流体加速和减压，用于流量计等）②（在汽车化油器中指应用文丘里原理的）喉管（简称 venturi, 亦称 chock tube，利用进气空气流流过喉管时形成的负压，将燃油吸出）

venturi vacuum controlled EGR system 喉管真空控制式废气再循环系统（以化油器喉管处的真空度作为控制信号来控制再循环废气量）

vent window （汽车车身的）通风窗（可转动的小边窗，= flipper window）

VEP 视觉性（脑皮）激发电位（visual evoked potential）

-ve plate （蓄电池）负极板（= negative plate）

+ve plate （蓄电池）正极板（= positive plate）

VERF 车辆试验研究设备（vehicle experimental research facility）

verge ①边缘，边界，界限②接近，毗连③路边，路肩

verification 检验，验证；核算，核实，证实，证明

verification and adjusting equipment 校验和调节设备

verification regulation 验证规程，检定规程，鉴定规程

verification test 验证试验（指已定型产品转厂生产后对试生产的产品进行试验，以考核转产厂所用工艺是否能保证原设计要求）

verify 检验，验证；核实，核对，查对

verifying bench 检验平台，检校工作台

vernier 副尺，游标，游标尺（以发明人法国数学家命名）

vernier calliper 游标卡尺（泛指带游标的卡钳式量具）

vernier control 微动控制

vernier coupling 微调式联轴节（能保证任意相对位置内的两轴的连接）

vernier micrometer 游标千分尺，游标测微器

vernier protractor 游标量角器

vernier scale 游标尺

vernier stator construction 微调定子结构（步进电动机）

versatile 通用的，多用途的

versatile additive 多用（途）添加剂

versatile automatic test equipment 万能自动测试设备（简称VATE）

versatile cab system 通用驾驶室系统（为了降低车身的造价，实现车身组件的通用化，以简化工艺装备）

versatile dinette （旅游车上的）多用餐室

versatile distributor type diesel injection pump 多用型分配式柴油喷射泵

versatile oil 多用途润滑油

versatile pulse shaper 多用途脉冲形成电路

versatile spindle 万向轴

versatility 通用性，多功能性

version ①形式，模型②变型，改型③见解

vertex ①（曲线）顶点②（曲线族的）共同点

vertex angle 顶角

vertex distance at large end 圆锥齿轮分度锥锥顶至大端齿顶的轴向距离

vertex distance at small end 圆锥齿轮分度锥锥顶至小端齿顶轴向距离

vertex sealing bar （转子发动机的）径向密封件（径向密封片，= apex seal）

vertical ①垂（直）线②垂直的

vertical acceleration 垂直加速度（质心加速度矢量沿z轴方向的分量）

vertical adjustment 垂直调整

vertical aerodynamic force coefficient 垂直空气动力系数 [z_0轴方向空气动力分量的无量纲系数，定义为：$G_Z = F_{AZ}/(q \cdot A)$，见 side aerodynamic force coefficient]

vertical air tunnel 立式风洞（= vertical wind tunnel）

vertical boot side panel （轿车车身的）行李舱侧壁直板

vertical camshaft drive 顶置式凸轮轴的垂直轴式驱动系统（由一垂直布置的传动轴及其两端分别与曲轴和凸轮轴端啮合的锥齿轮副组成的驱动系统）

vertical clearance ①垂直净空②垂直间隙

vertical clearance of wheel 车轮的铅垂行程（车轮从车辆厂定最大总质量时的位置起，可能相对于车架或车身上移的极限铅垂距离）

vertical component 垂直分力

vertical curb 直立式路沿石（沿石面在20°以下或垂直的沿石，汽车车轮不易或不能越过）

vertical deformation 竖向变形

vertical displacement 垂直位移

vertical drive 垂直传动，垂直驱动

vertical engine 立式内燃机（汽缸布置于曲轴上方且汽缸中心线垂直于

水平面的内燃机)
vertical face 立面
vertical force 垂直力(作用在汽车上的力矢量沿 z_0 轴方向的分量)
vertical force of tire 轮胎垂直力(路面作用在轮胎上的力沿轮胎坐标系 z' 轴方向的分量,见 tire axis system)
vertical glass type rear window (敞篷车的)垂直玻璃型后窗
vertical gravitation switch (翻车传感器系统中的)重力开关(亦称 vertical acceleration switch,当车轮脱离地面时,该开关向电子控制模块发出翻车信号)
vertical G sensor 垂直方向加速度传感器(亦称上、下加速度传感器 up and down G force sensor)
vertical harmonic gear drive 立式谐波齿轮传动(输出轴呈垂直配置的谐波齿轮传动)
vertical illuminance 垂直照度(垂直面上一点的照度)
vertical line 垂直线,铅垂线
vertically pivoted 绕垂直轴摆动的
vertically split brake system 垂直分立式制动系统(指两个前轮和两个后轮各共用一条回路的双回路制动系统)
vertical motion 垂直运动
vertical obstacle 直立障碍物
vertical outline (车辆)纵向中心平面轮廓图
vertical plane 垂面(垂直于基准 Z 平面的任一平面)
vertical play 上下方向的间隙(上下方向自由行)
vertical polarization 垂直偏振
vertical polarized component 垂直偏振分量
vertical post 立柱,立杆
vertical pressure 垂直压力
vertical projection 垂直投影

verticals 铅垂线
vertical seat adjustability 座位高度可调性
vertical shaft turbine 立轴式涡轮机
vertical shake 垂直振动(一般指车身低频垂直振动)
vertical stiffness 垂直刚度
vertical swirl 纵向涡流,垂直涡流
vertical up and down movement 垂直上下运动
vertical velocity 垂直速度(质心速度沿垂直轴的分量)
vertical vibration 垂直振动(沿汽车垂直轴方向的直线振动)
vertical view 俯视图
VER-TIS [日]道路交通车辆智能促进会(Vehicle Road Traffic Intelligence Society)
very large scale integrated circuit 超大规模集成电路(简称 VLSI,亦称 super-large-scale integrated circuit,指集装在一块基片上的元件超过 10 万个的集成电路)
VESC [美]车辆装备安全委员会(Vehicle Equipment Safety Commission)
vesicular 多孔的(蜂窝状的)
vesicular tissue 多孔状组织(蜂窝状组织)
vessel 容器(器皿,罐)
vestibule diaphragm (通道式客车前、后车厢)连接通道的围幛,连接通道的软篷
vestibule train (两车厢相通的)通道式(客车)列车
veteran car 古老名车(结构仍保持原样的早年生产的名车,年代并无定论,一般多指英皇爱德华二世以前,即 1900 年以前生产的古典名车)
veteran rally 老爷车拉力赛(早年制造的老式汽车的长途连续行驶的比赛)

VETS 车辆电气试验系统（vehicle electric test system）

VFC ①电压—频率变换器（voltage-frequency converter）②电子调压电磁阀（variable force control solenoid 的简称）

VFD ①真空荧光显示管（vacuum fluorescent display tube 的简称，炽热型三极真空管，其炽热丝即负极放射出来的高温电子束撞击玻璃面板上的荧光体薄膜，而以荧光的形式显示数字或图案）②真空荧光显示（系统）（vacuum fluorescent display 的简称，由真空射线管发射的电子束激发的荧光活动显示系统）

V-feel 速度感觉

VF glass tube 真空荧光玻璃管（vacuum fluorescent glass tube 的简称）

V-four engine V形四缸发动机

V-fronted radiator V形前脸散热器

V-front (ed) windscreen V形风窗玻璃

VFV 可变燃料车（variable fuel vehicle 的简称，如：既可使用汽油，又可燃用 M100 全甲醇等的汽车，亦称 flexible fuel vehicle）

vfy 鉴定，证明，检验（verify 的简称）

V-groove V形断面槽

V-groove pulley V形传动带轮，三角传动带轮

VGT 见 variable geometry turbocharger

V-guide way V型导轨

VH ①排气孔，通风孔（vent hole）②维氏硬度（Vickers hardness）

VHDL 极高速集成电路硬件描述语言（VHSIC hardware description language 的简称，其中 VHSIC 为 very-high-speed integrated circuit 的简称，为美国国防部开发的行为级电路设计硬件描述语言）

VHIPS （Volvo的）头部保护系统（Volvo Head Impact Protecting System 的简称）

VHSIC 极高速集成电路（very-high-speed integrated circuit 的简称，见 VHDC）

V/H test of spiral bevel gear 螺旋锥齿轮的垂直/水平检验

VI ①黏度指数（viscosity index）②视觉指示器（visual indicator）③音量指示器（volume indicator）

VIA ［日］车辆检测协会（Vehicle Inspection Association）

viability 耐久性（寿命，使用期限）

viaduct ①高架桥②高架道路

vialog （= viameter） ①路面平面度测量仪②（车辆颠簸）测振仪③路程计

VIAMOTO （美 Motorola 公司的）地图与导航信息软件系统（商品名，用于提供具体方位与导航信息，可将可以进行数据传输的手机及其他车内无线电设备转换成导航系统、本地信息指南和移动个人助手。当驾驶者转向错误时，VIAMOTO 能帮助驾驶者重新规划线路，并沿途告知路名并逐一发出转向指令）

vibrant 振动的

vibrate 振动

vibrating breaker 振动式断续器

vibrating diaphragm 振动膜片

vibrating membrane 振动膜

vibrating reed 振动片（振簧，舌簧）

vibrating screen 振动筛（振动筛分机，= vibrating grizzly，vibrating sieve）

vibrating sensor 振动传感器

vibrating system 振动系统

vibrating table 振动（试验）台

vibrating wire strain gauge 线振应变仪（钢弦式应变计）

vibration 振动

vibrational load 振动荷载
vibration applied to particular parts of the human body 人体局部振动（通过操纵机构的手柄、踏板、转向盘、乘员的扶手和头枕等机件作用于人体各部位的振动）
vibration dampening characteristic 振动衰减特性
vibration damper ①减振器（亦称 vibration dampener, vibration absorber, 泛指各种利用机械式、流体摩擦阻尼，及弹性材料弹性阻尼来吸收振动能量，消减振动的装置，如：汽车悬架系统消减冲击振动的减振器"shock absorber"，"oscillation damper"等）②（发动机曲轴或变速器输出轴的）扭转振动减振器（= torsional vibration damper, 详见 torsional damper①及 harmonic balancer）
vibration damping 振动阻尼，振动衰减
vibration damping steel sheet 减振钢板（中间夹有沥青、橡胶或塑性材料的夹层钢板，可通过将振动能量转化为热能消散。轿车上用于制作车身底板等）
vibration detector 测振仪，振动传感器
vibration exciter 激振器
vibration exposure time 振动暴露时间（处于振动状态下的时间）
vibration frequency 振动频率
vibration gauge 示振仪，振动仪，测振计（= vibration meter, vibration measurer, vibrometer, vibroscope）
vibration isolating component 隔振元件
vibration isolation 隔振，避震
vibration isolator 隔振器，避震器
vibration laboratory 振动试验室
vibrationless 无振动；不振动的
vibration machine （汽车实验室模拟振动试验的）振动机（振动装置，加振装置）
vibration measurement axis （车辆乘员的）振动测定轴线（沿该轴线的方向测定振幅和振动频率及加速度）
vibration nodal point 振动节点
vibration of normal mode 固有振动（物体在本身弹性复原力作用下产生的自由振动）
vibration period 振动周期
vibration-proof 耐振的，防振的，抗振的
vibration rig 振动试验设备
vibration sensor 振动传感器（亦称 vibration pickup）
vibration severity 振动强度（指振动强烈度）
vibration strength 抗振强度（指耐振强度）
vibration stress 振动应力
vibration table 振动（试验）台
vibration test 振动试验（= vibratory test）
vibration TMT 振动形变热处理（vibrationthermo-mechanical-treatment 的简称）
vibration transducer 振动传感器
vibration transmissibility 传递振动的能力，传振性能
vibration transmission rate 振动传递率
vibrator ①振动器，振子②振荡筛③振动式铆钉枪④断续器
vibrator coil 振动（火花断续）线圈，带断续器的线圈
vibrator horn 振动式喇叭
vibrator type induction coil 振动式感应线圈
vibratory 振动的，振荡的
vibratory impulse 振动脉冲
vibratory linear shear apparatus 振动式直线剪切装置，振动式直线剪

切机
vibratory milling 振动球磨
vibratory shock load 振动冲击荷载
vibro-bench 振动台
vibrograph 测振计，振动仪（用光学或电气方法测定振幅、振速、振动加速度等的装置，亦称 vibrometer）
VIC （本田公司电子）气门正时控制系统（商品名，valve timing control 的简称）
vicinity 附近（区域），邻近（地区）
Vickers hardness test 维氏硬度试验[将相对面夹角为136°的正四棱锥体金刚石压头以选定的试验力(49.03~980.7N)压入试样表面，经规定保持时间后卸除试验力，用测量的压痕对角线长度计算压印面积，然后按单位面积所承受的压力表征其硬度值的一种压痕硬度试验]
Vickers micro hardness test 显微维氏硬度试验（试验力在1.961N以下的维氏硬度试验）
VICS ①[日]车辆信息与控制系统（Vehicle Information and Control System）②车辆信息和通信系统（Vehicle Information and Communication System 的简称，日本 ITS 的开发项目之一）
video amplifier 视频放大器
video anti-collision technology 视频防撞技术
videocamera sensor 摄像机传感器
video carrier 视频载波
video cast 电视广播
video compact disk player 影碟机（简称 VCD player）
video compositing 影像合成
video conference 电视会议
video data 视频数据（数据显示在荧光屏上）

video event data recorder 事件数据影像记录仪
videognosis 电视 X 射线诊断术
video information 视频信息
videophone 电视电话（通话双方可见影像）
videoplayer 放像机
video projector 视频投影仪，影像投放机
video recorder 录像机
video recording vehicle 电视录像车
view ①视野，视界，视力 ②观看，观察
view aid system （驾驶人员）视野辅助系统
viewing angle 视角（垂直于发光或反光面的直线和观察者的视线间的夹角，= visual angle）
viewing distance 目测距离
viewing test 观察试验
vigorous 强烈的，猛烈的；强有力的
VIGV 可变进气导流片（variable inlet guide vanes 的简称）
VI improver 黏度指数改善剂（viscosity index improver 的简称）
village-run auto assembling factory 乡镇经营的汽车装配厂
VIM 可变进气歧管（variable intake manifold 的简称）
VIN ①可变截面废气涡轮增压器喷嘴（variable turbine nozzle 的简称）②汽车的出厂号（vehicle identification number 的简称）
vintage ①古老的，过时的，属于某的时期的 ②酒，美酒，酒的 ③（同年代的一批产品，制造的时期）
vintage car （在结构上仍保持原状的）古旧名车（早年生产的名车，年代并无定论，一般指英皇爱德华二世以后，即20世纪20~30年代生产的古典名车）
vintage truck 运酒车

vinyl acetate 乙烯基醋酸盐（或酯）($CH_2 : CHCH_2COOM$)

vinyl acetylene 乙烯（基）乙炔（氯丁二烯橡胶原料）

vinyl chloride 氯乙烯

vinyl covered cord 乙烯基包皮电线

vinyl ester resin 乙烯基酯树脂

vinyl top molding clip 车顶用维尼龙装饰卡条

violet 紫色

virgin 未使用过的（未开发的，新的）

Virial coefficient （流体力学的）维里系数（理想气体的状态方程，$pV = A + B/V + C/V^2 \cdots$，式中：$A$，$B$，$C$ 等为温度的函数，称为维里系数）

VIRTTEX （福特公司的）虚拟路试系统（Virtual Test Track Experiment 的简称，为电子控制球形驾驶室模拟装置，内部装有多个摄录机和红外线传感器等，以监测受测试的驾驶者在操作车内各种系统时的行为和眼部活动，借以获取发展更安全的设计所需的资料）

virtual ①实际的（但未公开或未被承认的）事实上的②有效的③虚的，虚拟的

virtual center 瞬时中心（回转运动瞬时中心，亦称 instantaneous center of rotation）

virtual cylindrical gear of bevel gear 锥齿轮的当量圆柱齿轮［一个假想的圆柱齿轮，其分度圆半径等于所研究的锥齿轮的背锥距，并且其端面模数等于此锥齿轮的大端端面模数（在锥齿轮的大端端面即背锥面的情况下）时，这个假想的圆锥齿轮就称为该锥齿轮的当量圆柱齿轮］

virtual cylindrical gear pair 当量圆柱齿轮副（在锥齿轮副中，它的两个锥齿轮的相啮合的当量齿轮副，称为当量圆柱齿轮副）

virtual environment 虚拟环境

virtual number of teeth 当量齿数（当量齿轮的齿数，亦称 equivalent number of teeth）

virtual prototype （计算机）虚拟原型（简称VP）

virtual prototyping technique ［指相对于实体车辆原型（real physical vehicle prototype）开发技术而言的、使用计算机平台进行的］虚拟（车辆）原型（virtual vehicle prototype）开发技术［通常包括：①创建原型车的 CAE 模型（build CAD model）②对该模型进行数模分析（execute numerical analysis）③对虚拟车辆原型进行计算机平台各项虚拟试验（virtual tests）④检验该虚拟原型车性能（judge vehicle performances）］⑤继续运用该计算机平台研究、拟定、进行下一步修正、改进、测试、评价等任务（study next step）］

virtual reality （计算机）虚拟实体技术（简称VR）

virtual spur gear 斜齿轮的当量齿轮（简称 virtual gear "当量齿轮"，对于斜齿轮，其齿线上某一点处的法平面与分度圆柱面的交线是一个椭圆；以此椭圆的最大曲率半径作为某一个假想直齿轮的分度圆半径，并以此斜齿轮的法向模数和法向压力角作为上述的假想直齿的端面模数和端面压力角；于是此假想直齿轮就称为所述的斜齿轮的当量齿轮）

virtual technology （计算机的）虚拟技术（包括虚拟实体，虚拟原型机开发，虚拟制造，见 VR，VP）

virtual vehicle validation （新车设计的设计概念阶段的）拟议车辆论证

VIS ①可变进气系统（variable intake system 的简称，一般指进气通路长度或进气量可随工况要求而变的进气系统，通常多指前者）

② (车辆牌号中) 编号部分 (vehicle indicator section)

viscid ①黏的,黏性的②稠的,半流体的

visco-control unit 黏性耦合器 (见 viscous coupling)

visco-differential 黏性耦合式差速器 (见 viscous coupling differential)

viscoelastic fluid 黏弹性流体 [非牛顿流体的一种,其剪切速度 D 与剪切应力 τ 间的函数式为 $D=f(\tau,s)$,式中: s—剪切应变,见 non-Newtonian fluid]

viscoelastic materials 黏弹性材料 [指在规定温度和恒定力的作用下,产生随时间而增加的塑性变形 (蠕变),而在规定温度和初始变形恒定的条件下,其应力随时间而减小 (应力松弛),当除去作用力后,经过一段时间可缓慢恢复原形的材料]

viscometer calibrating liquid 黏度计校正液 (黏度校正、标定用标准液,一般用蒸馏水)

viscosimeter 黏度计 (黏度测定仪, = viscometer)

viscosity ①黏度 [对牛顿黏性流体,使流体流动所需的力 (即其剪切应力) F 与剪切变形 (即其剪切速度) S 成正比,两者间固有的比例常数称为黏性系数或简称黏度 η, $F=\eta S$。绝对黏度的单位为 $g/(cm \cdot s)$,代号 P,见 poise。绝对黏度除以该温度下流体的密度,称运动黏度,单位为 cm^2/s,见 stoke] ②黏性 (指流体抵抗剪切变形的能力,黏性的强弱用黏度表示)

viscosity classification 黏度分类 (指包括润滑油在内的工业、工程、汽车用油液按 cts 黏度的分类)

viscosity down 黏度降低 (亦称 viscosity loss)

viscosity factor 黏度系数 (见 viscosity①)

viscosity gauge 黏度式真空计,分子真空计 (气体的黏度在其压力低于 13.32Pa 时,随压力的降低而减少,因而测定在压力极低的气体中的振动体的衰减,即可知道该气体的压力,这种真空计的测定范围为 $1.332^{-5} \sim 1.332\text{Pa}$)

viscosity index 黏度指数 (简称 VI,指油品黏度随温度而变化的程度,即:表明其黏度-温度关系特性好坏的系定量值,从 0~100,该指数越高,说明黏度随温度的变化小,其黏温特性好,亦称 viscosity-temperature coefficient, viscosity coefficient 或 viscosity factor)

viscosity index improver (机油的)黏度指数改善剂 (黏度指数提高剂,简称 VI improver,为 viscosity modifier 的旧称)

viscosity modifier (机油的) 黏度指数提高剂 (温黏特性改善剂,可减缓油温升高时机油变稀,即黏度降低的趋势,旧称 viscosity improver 或 viscosity index improver,见 viscosity index)

viscosity-pressure coefficient 黏度-压力系数 (一般液体的黏度随压力增加而增加,两者关系的经验式为: $\eta = Ae^{BP}$,式中: η—黏度; e—压力; A, B—常数,其中 B 为黏度-压力系数)

viscosity ratio 黏度比 (指使用中的机油与新机油的黏度比值,用以表征其劣化的程度)

viscosity resistance 黏性阻力,黏滞阻力

viscosity retention (滑油的) 黏度保持性

viscosity slope (润滑油的黏度随温度变化的) 温黏曲线的斜率

viscosity stability (滑油的) 黏度稳定性

viscosity-temperature characteristics 黏温特性（黏度-温度关系特性）

viscous 黏的，黏性的

viscous clutch-type transfer case （四轮驱动车辆的）黏液离合器型分动器

viscous converter clutch 液力变矩器黏性锁止离合器（简称 VCC，其作用与 torque converter clutch 相同，但它通过硅油实现"锁止"，因此在发动机与变速器间还保留一定比例的滑移率，可避免机械锁止时出现的"粗暴"）

viscous coupling 黏性耦合器（简称 VC，亦称 visco-control unit，通常过黏性油液，如：硅油，传递转矩的装置。一般为一充满硅油等黏性传动液的圆桶形密封壳体，类似多片式离合器，不过其输入端耦合器盘与输出端的耦合器盘间保持一定间隔。当输入端转速高于输出端时，便通过硅油的摩擦力将转矩传给输出端，直至二者转速相等，这种耦合器在汽车上多用于四轮驱动系统）

viscous coupling differential 黏性耦合式差速器（使用黏性耦合器作为防滑装置的防滑式差速器）

viscous-damping 黏性阻尼（①指振动中由于本身材料内阻尼力引起的振动能量消耗作用，见 linear viscous damping, non-linear viscous damping ②指处于黏性液体中的振动件，由于液体黏性的摩擦阻尼而消耗能量，使振动衰减的作用）

viscous fan drive （发动机冷却）风扇黏性驱动（装置）（指硅油离合器，黏性联轴器等风扇驱动装置）

viscous flow 黏性（液体的）流动；黏滞流动

viscous fluid 黏性流体（相对于理想流体而言，指具有黏性的流体）

viscous fluid clutch 黏液离合器（利用黏稠液体的剪切力特性的离合器）

viscous friction 黏性摩擦（流体黏性所造成的摩擦，如：轴承油膜剪切力所造成的摩擦阻力）

viscous loss 黏滞损失

viscous mode （黏性耦合器的）黏液耦合工况（输入端与输出端的耦合器盘通过黏性介质，如：硅油传递转矩的工作模式）

viscous oil 高黏度润滑油（稠油）

viscous resistance 黏滞阻力

viscous silicone fluid 高黏度硅油

viscous sublayer 黏性底层（紊流中靠近壁面，因而受分子黏性影响显著的底层）

viscous transmission 黏性耦合式差速器的四轮驱动传动系统（简称 VT）

viscous type damper 黏液型减振器 [利用液体的黏滞剪切力产生的阻尼减振，如：一般汽车悬架系的液力减振器，亦称 viscous (vibration) damper]

vise 虎钳，台虎钳（=美，vice）

visibility ①可见度，能见度 ②视界，视野，视距

visibility distance 能见距离（= sight distance, vision distance）

visibility level 可见度水平（简称 VL，一个作业的视觉显示的等效对比超过一个观察者在相同的作业背景亮度水平时，对同样显示的可见度阈限的程度。可见度水平是用观察者的阈限对比为单位来度量的，见 threshold contrast）

visibility meter 能见度测定仪

visibility scale 能见度等级

visibility test after fracture （车玻璃）破碎后的能见度试验（确定安全玻璃一旦破坏时，能否保留一定的能见度的试验。用尖锤子等工具将试样击碎后，按所衬的照相纸上记录

的主视区中碎片的数目及其尺寸来评定)

visible 可见的,能见的;明显的,显著的

visible concept(car) 透视型概念车(指由玻璃材料制成的外壳,可直接观看其内部的透明概念展览车)

visible crack 可见裂纹

visible error 视(觉)差(错)

visible line 外形线(轮廓线,亦称 visible outline)

visible oil flow gauge 目测滑油流量计

visible signal 可见信号,视觉信号

visible spectrum 可见光谱

vision ①视力②视觉③视线

vision area (汽车的)视区(风窗玻璃中适用于驾驶车辆的区域)

vision coordinate system (计算机视觉的)视坐标系

vision device 视野测定装置

vision electronics recording apparatus 电子录像机

vision information 视觉信息(自眼睛获取的信息)

visionoccupant sensor (由摄像系统组成的)乘员观察传感器

vision screen headlight tester 映幕式前照灯试验台

vision sensor 图像传感器(显像型传感器)

vision system (Navlab系统中装在车上的)图像系统(由装在车身前、后两侧的雷达和激光扫描系统、电视摄像系统,以及图像信息处理系统组成,该系统的输出用于控制汽车转向,制动,加、减速,避开障碍物,保持或改变车道以及定速巡行等,见Navlab)

visor ①护目镜,遮光板,遮阳板②头盔,面具③观察孔

Vista roof 全自动全景天窗(商品名)

visual ①视觉的,视力的②看得见的,可见的

visual-acoustic-magnetic pressure 可见光-声-磁压强(简称VAMP)

visual acuity ①(驾驶者的)视觉敏锐度②(后视镜的)照视范围和清晰度

visual adaptation 视觉适应(视觉器官的感觉随着接收的亮度和颜色的刺激而变化的过程和它的最终状态)

visual alarm 可见报警(灯光报警信号)

visual angle 视觉角(指被观察的物体在眼球节点所对的角,该角的大小决定视网膜上的映象尺寸,= viewing angle)

visual check 目测检查

visual environmental space 视觉环境空间(当转动头部和眼睛时,从一个工作地点所能看到的整个空间)

visual ergonomics 视觉工效学(研究人所处的光环境对人是否合适,以获得最佳的工作效能、安全和舒适的科学)

visual evoked potential 视觉性(脑波)激发电位(简称VEP)

visual field 视界,视野(指在给定时刻内作用于不动的眼睛上的全部视觉刺激)

Visu-aligner 维肖定位仪(光学式车轮定位调整仪的商品名)

visual information system 可见信息系统(如:电视屏显信息系统等)

visual intensity 可见(光)强度

visualization ①可视化(如:使汽缸内燃烧的气流可见化试验 visualization experiment等)②形象化,具体化③目测(方法),目视观察④显影

visual perception 视知觉(人脑将进入眼睛的光刺激转化为整体经验的

过程，包括：察觉物体存在，确定其空间位置，与其他事物的关系，辨认其运动、颜色、明亮度和形状等）

visual performance 视觉功效（人的视觉器官完成给定视觉作业的定量评价）

visual task 视觉作业（在工作和活动中，必须观察的呈现在背景前的细节或目标）

vital circuit 关键性电路

viton 氟（化）橡胶

viton O-ring O形断面氟化橡胶密封环

vitreous enamel 透明釉（釉瓷，搪瓷，珐琅，美称 porous enamel）

vitrified wheel 陶瓷砂轮

VIU 在用车辆（vehicle in use）

vizor ①护目镜②遮阳板③面盔（= visor）

V·J·Jandasek theory V·J·简达瑟科（液力变矩器设计）理论（Jandasek，美，于1961年发表 Design of single-stage, Three-Element Torque Converter 一文）

V-junction V形交叉（路口）

V. K. D 见 complex-split torque paths type hydromechanic drive

V-kool 车晾（一种汽车风窗玻璃用防碎隔热贴膜的商品名，这种贴膜透光率可达73.2%~83%，但却可反射阳光紫外线的98%~99%和红外线的57%~94%，保持车内阳光直射下凉爽，同时可防止玻璃破碎）

VKT 车辆已行驶公里数（vehicle-kilometers traveled）

V/L 汽液比（vapor/liquid）

VL （强制怠速工况下）进气管真空度限制阀（vacuum limiter）

VLES 限大涡流模拟（very large eddy simulation 的简称，用于研究内燃机燃烧过程的数学模型）

VLI 气阻指数（vapor lock index）

V8-like performance （指缸数较少的发动机，如：V6发动机的复合动力可产生）如V8发动机般的性能

VLSI 超大规模集成电路（见 very large scale integrated circuit）

VLTC system （日产公司）气门升程和正时控制系统

V Master [美]（Horton公司）风扇驱动装置的商品名

V-motor V形发动机

VMT 车辆已行驶里程英里数（vehicle miles of travel）

VMV （燃油）蒸气控制阀（vapour management valve 的简称，由动力控制模块操纵，用于控制由活性炭罐流入进气歧管的燃油蒸气量）

Vne 不允许超过的速度（velocity never to exceed）

VOC 车辆营运成本（vehicle operating costs）

VOC emission 挥发性有机物排放（volatile organic compound emission 的简称）

VOD 视频点播（video on demand 的简称）

voice activated control 声控

voice alert (system) 语言警报（系统）

voice amplifier 声频放大器（speech amplifier）

voice control 声控

voice interactive control 复合声控系（联动声控系统）

voice recognition 语言识别（识别语音指令的能力）

voice-recognition system （蓝牙）声音识别系统

voice synthesis 声音合成技术

voice tube 话筒（= speaking tube）

void ①间隙，空隙，空穴，空白点（如：轮胎胎面凸起的花纹条、块之间的空隙、气孔砂眼等）②空

的，真空的③没有的；无效的，无益的④排空，放出⑤使无效，使成废品⑥取消，放弃

void ratio of film 滤膜孔隙率（滤膜单位体积吸收水分的百分率）

void volume 空隙容积

voiture ［法］双座敞篷轿车（亦称 voiturette）

volatile fuel fraction 燃油的易挥发馏分

volatile matter 挥发性物质

volatile memory 易失性存储器（当不再加电时，其数据内容即行消失的一种存储器）

volatile organic compound 挥发性有机化合物（简称 VOC）

volatile RAM 易失性只读存储器（亦称 keep-alive memory，其存储内容断电后即消失，因而在汽车电子控制系统直接通过熔丝与蓄电池连接）

volatility characteristic（s）（燃油等的）挥发性

volatility test （燃油）挥发性试验

volatilization loss 挥发损失

Volkswagen of America Inc. 美国大众汽车公司（德国大众汽车公司的子公司，简称 VWA 或 VWoA）

Volkswagen Werke AG 大众汽车公司（德国的最大汽车集团，创立于 1937 年，生产 Audi, Golf, Jetta 等轿车）

volometer 伏安表（伏特安培计）

volt ①伏（特）（国际单位制的电位，电位差，电动势，电压单位，代号 V。导体两点之间的电位差为 1V 时，通过 1A 的电流消耗的功率为 1W，即 1V = 1W/A）② voltage 的简称

voltage 电压（电动势"emf"或电位差"pd"的值，单位为 V，参见 volt）

voltage alarm 电压警报

voltage amplifier 电压放大器

voltage averaging circuit 电压平均电路（为一积分器电路，将直流脉冲电压值积分并转换为平均值后输出）

voltage boost ①升压（指提高电压）②升压增功（指使用提高电源电压的方法，增加电动机的输出功率）

voltage break down 电压击穿

voltage coil 电压线圈（一般指发电机电压调节器中，当发电机输出电压超过规定值时，接通磁场线圈电阻；而当电压低于规定值时，断开该电阻，从而保证电压稳定的铁心线圈）

voltage comparator 电压比较器［能对差动输入电压做出响应，并能输出数字信号（通常是电压）的集成电路，也可以包括一个选通端］

voltage control 电压控制

voltage control system 电压控制系统

voltage control unit 电压调节装置（稳压器，调压器 = voltage regulator）

voltage converter （安全气囊诊断和储能模块存储器的升压）变压器（亦称 step-up converter，用于使储能器的电压保持始终高于蓄电池的正常电压）

voltage-current characteristic 电压-电流特性（伏安特性）

voltage（current）compliance（of a DAC） （DAC 的）顺从电压（电流）［当 DAC 的电流（或电压）作为输出量，其规范值有效时，相应输出电压（或电流）的允许范围］

voltage-depended 电压控制的（指随电压变化而变化的、对电压敏感的，压敏的）

voltage-divider 分压器

voltage divider circuit 分压电路（分压器）

voltage-drive 电压激励
voltage drop 电压降（=drop in voltage）
voltage excursion 电压偏移
voltage follower circuit 电压跟随电路（电压输出电路）
voltage gain 电压增益（电压放大系数）
voltage generator ①电压发生器（脉冲电压发生器，亦称voltage impulse generator）②测速发电机（转速传感器，将转速变为电压信号的装置）
voltage level (1) er 电压电平器
voltage multiplier 电压倍增器（倍压器）
voltage pulse 电压脉冲
voltage rating 额定电压（标定电压）
voltage reducing device 降（电）压装置
voltage regulator 电压调节器（①将发电机输出电压控制在规定范围的调节装置②负载电压相对独立于负载电流或输入电压波动的集成电路）
voltage regulator contact point arm 电压调节器触点臂
voltage reserve （见 high voltage reserve）
voltage sensing circuit 电压传感电路
voltage spike 电压脉冲尖峰
voltage stabilizer 电压稳定器（稳压器）
voltage-to-digital converter 电压-数字变换器
voltage transformer 变压器（电压变换器）
voltammeter 伏-安表（电压-电流表）
volt-amp alternator tester 交流发电机（测验用）伏安表
voltampere 伏安（电测量单位之一，伏特与安培的乘积，国际单位制视在功率的单位，代号VA或V·A，在直流电路中1V·A=1W。在交流电路中，只用于视在功率，见 apparent power）
voltmeter 伏特表（电位计，电压表）
volt-ohmmeter 伏特欧姆计（电压-电阻表，=voltohmist, voltohmyst）
voltol oil 高压电聚合油（矿物油或矿物油与脂肪油混合后，经高压电流无声放电而聚合成的油液，其黏度高，油性好）
volume ①容积，体积 ②音量，响度 ③卷，册，合订本 ④大量，许多 ⑤大量的
volume air flow sensor 空气体积流量传感器（简称VAF sensor）
volume car 大量生产的轿车
volume change 容积变化
volume contraction 容积缩小，容积收缩
volume control ①流量调控 ②容量调整 ③音量调控
volume efficiency ①（液压泵、马达的）容积效率 ②（发动机）升功率 ③（发动机）充气系数（充气效率，=volumetric efficiency）
volume elasticity 容积弹性
volume flow 体积流量（按体积计的流量，单位为 m^3/s）
volume gain 容积增益（容积增大）
volume level （声响）响度级
volume mil 毫升（=国际单位制的毫升，代号为mL）
volume modulus of elasticity 弹性容积模数
volume of cylinder 汽缸容积（=cylinder volume）
volume of sound 声音响度，音量
volume of traffic 交通量，交通密度
volume (-produced) vehicle 大量生产的货车，成批生产的车辆

volume production　大量生产，批量生产

Volumer　容积型底盘（Benz 公司对运输相对密度小、重量轻的货物的货车底盘的称呼，而将运输相对密度大、重的货物的货车底盘称为 Loader）

volume ratio of combustion chamber　燃烧室容积比（①在分开式燃烧室中，是指副燃烧室容积与燃烧室总容积，即汽缸余隙容积的比值②在半开式燃烧室中，是指活塞顶内或汽缸盖内燃烧室的容积与燃烧室总容积的比值）

volume resistance　①体积变形阻力②体积电阻

volume resistivity　体积电阻率

volume stability　体积稳定性

volumeter　容积计（体积计，容量表，= volumometer）

Volumetrically-distributed ignition　（汽缸内液体燃料喷雾的）体积内分散着火

volumetric calorific value　容积热值

volumetric capacity　排量，容量

volumetric displacement　（发动机等的）排量

volumetric efficiency　充量系数（亦称充气效率、容积效率，指每一工作循环进入汽缸的实际充量与进气状态下能充满汽缸工作容积的理论充量的质量比值）

volumetric efficiency of compressor　压缩机容积效率（压缩机的实际容积流量与压缩机的理想容积流量之比。可考虑冷凝的影响）

volumetric expansion coefficient　体膨胀系数，体积膨胀系数（= cubic expansion coefficient）

volumetric expansion ratio　体积膨胀比

volumetric flow detector　容积式流量计（可连续测量，常用于汽车道路试验中测量燃油消耗量，= volumetric flow meter）

volumetric flow rate　体积流速（容量流速）

volumetric fuel meter　容积式（燃）油耗计

volumetric mixture ratio　体积混合比（在标准状态下气体燃料与空气以体积计量的混合比）

volumetric protection　（对汽车的）容积保护（指用来检测对驾驶室、乘客舱入侵及其内部非正常情况的装置，参见 perimeter protection）

volumetric strain　体积应变（物体在外力作用下变形时，包含在其内部的任意一点 P 的微小体积单元 ΔV 产生体积变化 Δq，则在 P 点的体积应变 ε_w 具有下式所规定的定义：
$$\varepsilon_w = \lim_{\Delta V \to 0} \frac{\Delta q}{\Delta V}$$

volume unit　①体积单位，容积单位②声量单位，响度单位

volume weight　容重，容积重力，单位体积质量

voluminous　①体积大的（庞大的）②大量的

voluntary expense　自愿承担费用（指车主在发生车祸时，自愿分担的责任）

voluntary injury level　志愿者允许碰撞强度（由志愿者担任汽车碰撞试验时的人体允许碰撞值，一般较致伤碰撞强度低，见 human tolerance level 及 injury threshold）

voluntary vehicle inspection　按（车主）要求进行的车辆检查

voluptuous　（车身外形等）令人愉悦的，让人感到舒适的

volute　①（离心式水泵、鼓风机的）蜗壳②螺旋形，涡旋形

volute casing　蜗壳

volute chamber　（蜗壳式鼓风机或离心式水泵的）蜗形室

volute pump 蜗壳离心泵,蜗壳泵(离心泵的一种,泵壳呈蜗形,蜗形室壁直接对着叶轮外周,如:发动机冷却水泵等,= volute-type centrifugal pump)

volute spring 蜗形螺旋簧(锥形螺旋弹簧)

Volvo 沃尔沃汽车集团(Aktien-bolay Volvo 之简称,创立于 1926 年,瑞典最大的汽车制造厂)

Volvo dual power plant 沃尔沃双动力装置(装有一台多燃料对置活塞式柴油机和一台燃气涡轮机,用一套自动变矩器联结在一起)

Volvo Truck Corp [瑞典]沃尔沃载货汽车公司(简称VTC)

Von Neumann John 约翰·冯·诺伊曼(1903~1957年,现代计算机之父)

vortex ①旋涡,涡流(横向涡流"swirl"、与纵向涡流"turbulence"的总称)②涡旋的,涡流的

vortex cavity ①涡流式燃烧室②涡流腔

vortex chamber 涡流室(如:柴油机的涡流室等,= swirl chamber, turbulence chamber)

vortex characteristic 旋涡特性

vortex cone 涡流锥,涡核(心)

vortex current dynamometer 电涡流型测功机(亦称 eddy current type dynamometer, eddy current absorption dynamometer, vortices current power meter,发动机带动一置于电磁场内的铜板旋转,在铜板内产生涡电流,而形成阻止发动机旋转的负荷,测定此时的铜板转矩和转速,即可测出发动机的输出功率。该负荷通过加减磁场励磁电流来调整,亦可用于底盘测功)

vortex drag 涡阻

vortex filament 涡旋线,涡形丝

vortex flow ①涡流,旋流②(传动液在液力变矩器和液力耦合器内的)循环流(指工作液由泵轮至涡轮、导轮等又流回泵轮的循环流,即:绕内壁在轴向平面内的循环流动的液流)

vortex-free 无旋涡的

vortex horn 蜗形喇叭

vortex incline degree (进气孔口的)涡流倾斜角度数

vortex induced drag (汽车行驶时空气阻力中的)涡流诱导阻力(指由于车身后面形成涡流区造成车身的迎面与背面空气压力不等而诱生的阻力,见 induced drag)

vortex line 涡(旋)线

vortex motion 涡流运动(= eddy motion)

vortex pair 涡偶(汽车行驶时车后两列交替换位的平行涡流尾流,亦称 vortex street)

vortex path 涡旋迹,涡道

vortex-ring 环形涡流,旋涡环

vortex stabilizer ①(汽车车身的)涡流稳定件(指任一种应用空气动力学原理,使车身尾涡有序形成,以减少空气阻力的板件)②(特指箱式半挂车车厢的)涡流稳定板(阻挡在横风下,横向气流从驾驶室后方的空间流过,用以稳定驾驶室与半挂车车箱间的涡流)

vortex stabilizer 稳涡装置(安装在货车或箱式挂车货箱前围上部的空气动力学附加装置。目的是稳定相对气流在驾驶室与货箱之间产生的非定常涡,以减小风阻)

vortex stratified combustion system 涡流式分层充气燃烧系统

vortex streets 涡旋迹(见 vortex path)

vortex theory 涡流理论

vortex trail 涡旋尾迹

vorticity ①涡旋(状态),旋涡②涡旋强度,涡(流强)度,涡量

VOT 电话传输视频点播（video dial tone 的简称）

VOX 声控传输（语音控制传输，voice-operated transmission 的简称）

VP ①停车场（vehicle park）②车辆保有量（vehicle population）③见 virtual prototyping

V8-powered car V型八缸轿车（装用八缸V型发动机的轿车）

V-pulley ①（三角形传动带的）三角形槽传动盘②（特指传动带式无级变速器的直径可变的）V形槽主、从动盘

VPW 可变脉冲宽度（variable pulse width 的简称）

VPWM 可变脉冲宽度调制（亦写作 VPW modulation, variable pulse-width modulation 的简称）

VR （计算机）虚拟实体技术（virtual reality 的简称，见 virtual prototyping）

VRD ①汽车修理场（vehicle repair depot）②备用汽车车库（vehicle reserve depot）

VREF 基准电压（reference voltage 的简称）

VR engine 小夹角V形发动机（V-reduced engine 的简称，介于直列式和V形发动机之间，其V形缸体夹角仅15°左右，与常规V形发动机不同的另一点是，它只用一个汽缸盖盖住两排汽缸）

VRI ［美］车辆研究所（Vehicle Rese-arch Institute）

VRIS 可变谐振式进气系统［Variable Resonance Induction System 的简称，日本马自达公司推出的充分利用进气脉冲惯性增压和谐振增压效应的进气管长度可变式进气系统的商品名。该系统由加装在进气管路中的谐振箱（surge tank）和关闭阀（shut-off valve）及其控制系统组成。当发动机高速或低速运转时，该阀关闭，进气管道变短，而当发动机中速运转时，该阀开启，进气管道变长，以充分利用进气过程的惯性增压和谐振增压效果，改善充气效率］

V-rope drive V形钢索传动

VRS 变磁阻传感器（variable reluctance sensor 的简称）

VR sensor 可变磁阻式（速度，加速度）传感器（variable reluctance sensor 的简称）

VRTS 车辆道路试验模拟（装置）（vehicle road test simulation）

VRV ①真空减量阀（见 vacuum reducer valve）②真空调节阀（vacuum regulator valve 的简称）

VS （吸入的）进气空气量（volume of suction air 的简称）

VSA （本田公司的）汽车行驶稳定性辅助控制系统（vehicle stability assists 的简称，见 vehicle stability assist system）

VSA control system 车辆稳定性辅助控制系统（vehicle stability auxiliary control system 的简称）

VSAP 车辆系统分析程序（vehicle system analysis program）

VSA system 车辆稳定性支持系统［本田公司 Vehicle Stability Assist System 的简称，保证车辆转向时的稳定性、防止车辆过度转向或不足转向的系统。该系统与原TCS、ABS共用一个电子控制模块，由车轮速度传感器、VSA调制器（VSA modulator）、横向加速传感器（lateral acceleration sensor）、横摆传感器（yaw sensor）、转向盘转角传感器等构成。当VSA控制模块根据上述传感器输入的信号判断车辆出现过度转向趋势时，对外侧车轮施以相应的制动，使车辆产生向外的转矩，而抵消过度转向倾向；当判断车辆出现不足转向趋势时，便对内

侧车轮施以相应的制动力,使车辆产生向内的转矩,而减轻其不足转向趋势]

VSC ①(Lexus车的)车辆侧滑控制系统(汽车弯道动态稳定系统的商品名,vehicle skid control 的简称,当电子控制模块测得汽车弯道行驶的方向偏离驾驶者意图、转向不足时,减小发动机输出转矩,同时对弯道外侧后轮施加比弯道内侧后轮大的制动力;转向过度时,在降低发动机输出转矩的同时,对弯道外侧的前轮施加制动,以校正车辆的弯道行驶方向,见 turn-rate control system)②车速控制(vehicle speed control 的简称)

VSC buzzer 车辆稳定性控制系统故障警报蜂鸣器(当VSC发生故障时,该蜂鸣器发出断续警报声)

VSC system (丰田公司的)车辆稳定性控制系统(vehicle stability control system 的简称,保证车辆转向时方向稳定性的电子控制系统。电子控制模块根据转向盘转角、车速、车辆横摆角速度、车辆横向加速度等传感器的信息,确定转向时车辆的姿势。若认定此时前轮侧偏倾向大于后轮,导致车辆的实际转向角小于驾驶者的目标值时,则相应控制驱动力,同时对转向外侧的前轮和内侧的前、后轮施加制动。若认定此时后轮侧偏倾向大于前轮,以导致车辆的实际转向角大于目标值时,对转向外侧的前、后轮施加制动。通过上述控制,保持车辆转向或弯道行驶时的方向稳定性。类似的系统,Benz公司称ESP,保时捷称PSM,宝马公司称DSC)

VSC warning lamp 车辆稳定性控制系统故障警报灯(车辆稳定性控制系统发生故障时,该灯闪光,并通过闪光模式表示故障诊断代码,见VSC)

VSE 可变冲程发动机(variable stroke engine)

VSES 车辆稳定性加强系统(通用公司 vehicle stability enhancement system 的简称,该系统的商品名为 StabiliTrak,该系统将ABS、动态制动力比例分配系统、牵引力控制系统和横摆稳定性控制系统集成控制、传感器共用,通过对节气门开度和制动的自动控制,使车辆即使在雨天或冰雪路上均可保持稳定行驶)

VSG motor 变速式电动机(variable speed gear motor 的简称)

V-shaped apex seal (转子发动机)V形径向密封件(V形径向密封片)

V-shaped brake V形制动器

V-shaped cylinder arrangement 汽缸V形排列(= V-type cylinder arrangement)

V-shaped cylinders (多缸发动机的)V形汽缸体

V-shaped radiator front V形的散热器前部格栅(散热器V形前脸)

V-shaped rest (挂车的)V形支脚(V形支架)

V-shaped windscreen V形风窗玻璃

V sheave 三角形传动带轮

V-six engine V型6缸发动机(简称V-6)

VSL 车辆速度限制器(vehicle speed limiter 的简称)

VSLC [美](汽车工程师学会SAE的)车辆声级委员会(Vehicle Sound Level Committee 的简称)

V-slot V型槽(三角形槽)

VSM 车辆稳定性管理系统(vehicle stability management 的简称)

V-spoke V形轮辐

VSR (安全带的)车辆紧急状态传感锁紧式收紧装置(vehicle-sensitive emergence locking retractor 的简称）

VSS 车速传感器（vehicle speed sensor 的简称，一般装在两轮驱动车的变速器或主传动壳、四轮驱动车辆的分动箱壳内，检测并向电子控制模块发送驱动轮转速信息的传感器件）

VSS buffer 车速传感器缓冲器（VSS 产生的幅度和频率随车速而变化的模拟信号通过该缓冲器转换为一定频率的脉冲信号输入电子控制模块）

V-strapped V 型带的

VSV （废气再循环阀的）真空通路开关阀（真空换向阀，vacuum switch valve 的简称）

VSW 真空控制开关（vacuum switch 的简称）

VT 见 viscous transmission

VTC （本田公司研制的）可变气门相位控制系统（variable timing control system 的简称，电子控制模块通过液压执行系统，使凸轮轴转动一定的角度，改变其正时相位，以获得低速区最佳转矩，最佳油耗控制和中、高速区的最佳转矩控制）

VTC actuator VTC 执行机构（见 VTC）

VTC cam sensor VTC 凸轮传感器（见 VTC）

V-TCS 黏性耦合器式防滑差速器和牵引力控制系统（Viscous Lsd and Traction Control System 的简称，防滑差速器与牵引力综合电子控制系统）

VTD system （四轮驱动车辆前、后轮的）可变转矩分配系统（variable torque distribution system 的简称）

VTEC （日本本田公司研制的）可变气门正时与升程电子控制（系统）（商品名，variable valve timing and valve lift electronic control system 的简称，该系统每缸有两个进气门、两个排气门，其进气门凸轮轴上每缸有三个轮廓和升程均不相同的进气门凸轮，其中两个为低速凸轮，一个为大升程高速凸轮。发动机低速运转时，两个低速凸轮各控制一个进气门，有一个升程很小发动机中、高速运转时，由一个高速凸轮同时控制两个进气门，发动机在低、中、高速运转区都能获得最佳气门正时、气门升程和叠开时间，实现低油耗、高输出功率二者兼得，亦简称气门正时电子控制系统（valve timing electronic control）

V-ten engine V 形 10 缸发动机（简称 V-10）

V-thread V 形螺纹（三角螺纹，管螺纹，= triangular thread, sharp thread, pipe thread）

VTL 变阈逻辑电路（variable threshold logic）

VTM-4 （四轮驱动车辆的前、后轮）可变转矩（分配）机构（variable torque mechanism 的简称，其中，4 表示 4WD "四轮驱动"）

V-tooth gear 人字（形齿）齿轮（= herringbone gear）

VTP （美国能源部 "U. S. Department of Energy" 的）汽车技术（发展）规划（Vehicle Technologies Program 的简称）

VTR 磁带录像机（video tape recorder）

VTSS module 车辆防盗系统模块（vehicle theft security system module 的简称，该模块一般与 BCM 合成一体）

VTT 可变双废气涡轮增压系统（variable twin turbocharger system 的简称，由大、小两个废气涡轮增压器和电子控制模块控制的废气阀和空气阀组成。发动机低速、小负荷运转时，废气阀关闭，全部废气流向小涡轮增压器的废气涡轮，对进气空气实施增压。发动机高速、大负荷运转时,废气阀开启,大部分废气流向大涡轮增压器的废气涡轮,对进气空气实施增压。无须改变增压器的几何形状,便可适应发动机不同工况的要求)

VTV 真空传输阀(vacuum transmitting valve)

V-type cylinder arrangement 汽缸V形排列(= V-cylinder arrangement, V-shaped cylinder arrangement)

V-type engine V型发动机(= V-engine, Vee engine)

V-type fan belt V型风扇传动带

V type fuel injection pump V形喷油泵(两列柱塞偶件轴线呈V形排列,带单根凸轮轴的合成式喷油泵。见drive shaft fuel injection pump)

V-type radiator V形散热器

V type spark plug V形槽火花塞(指中心电极或侧电极上切有V形或U形凹槽的火花塞,可减轻电极对焰核的冷却作用而改善怠速和低速时的点火性能)

V-type step pulley V形塔轮

V-type thread V形螺纹(60°螺纹)

V-type windshield V形风窗玻璃

vulcanization ①(橡胶)硫化,硫化作用②热补(轮胎)

vulcanization accelerator 硫化促进剂,硫化加速剂

vulcanize ①硫化(指使天然橡胶或某些热塑性材料与硫或其他添加剂加热反应,以改变其物理性质,特别是提高其弹性和强度,亦写作vulcanise)②热补(轮胎)

vulcanized elastomeric material 硫化弹性材料(硫化天然橡胶、硫化再生橡胶、硫化合成橡胶等的总称)

vulcanized fabric 硫化橡胶织物

vulcanized rubber 硫化橡胶

vulcanizer ①(橡胶)硫化器,硫化机,硫化设备②(橡胶)硬化剂,(橡胶)硫化剂③轮胎热补机,轮胎热补装置

vulnerable ①易损伤的,易损坏的②有弱点的,有缺点的,薄弱的

vulnerable part 薄弱部分

VU meter 响度单位计(volume units meter)

V2V communication network 车-车间通信网络

VV 可变喉管(variable-venturi的简称)

VVA 可变气门执行机构(variable valve actuation)

ΔV-value 速度变化值(如:汽车发生碰撞期间的减速度随时间的变化值)

VVL 可变气门正时和升程(variable valve timing and lift的简称)

VVLT system 可变气门升程与正时系统(Variable Valve Lift and Timing System的简称,日本日产公司发动机低、高速运转时,气门开闭时刻及升程切换系统的商品名。该系统使用两组形状不同的低速与高速凸轮,分别在发动机低、高速运转时起作用,因而可实现进排气门开、闭时刻及气门升程的最佳控制)

VVT ①可变气门正时,可变配气相位(variable valve timing)②喉管真空度传感器(venturi vacuum transducer)

VVT camshaft 可变气门正时凸轮轴(= variable valve timing camshaft)

VVT-i controller (丰田公司可变气门正时和升程系统的)智能型可变气门正时控制器(variable valve timing intelligent controller的简称)

VW 大众汽车公司(德国Volkswagen Werks AG的简称)

VWA 美国大众汽车公司(= VWoA, Volkswagen of America Inc.的简称)

VWJ 日本大众(汽车)公司(Volkswagen Japan的简称)

W ①腰（中间细的部分，waist 的简称）②壁（wall）③暖，变暖（warm）④废物；损耗（waste）⑤水（water）⑥瓦（特）（watt）⑦天气（weather）⑧周，星期（week）⑨质量（weight）⑩西（west）⑪湿的；水分（wet）⑫白色的（white）⑬（大门上的）小门、窗口（wicket）⑭宽度（width）⑮风；绕组（wind）⑯导线（wire）⑰木质的（wooden）⑱功（work）⑲错误的（wrong）

W.A 水量表［water gag（u）ge 的简称］

wabbler mechanism 摆摆机构

wabbling ①晃动②偏摆③运转不均匀（见 wobbling）

Wabco ［美］威斯汀豪斯气压制动器公司（Westinghouse air brake company 的简称）

4 W ABS （马自达公司的）四轮防抱死制动系统（的商品名）

WAC 节气门全开空调自动切断器（wide-open throttle air conditioner cut-off 的简称，亦写作 wide-open A/C cut-off）

wadding 填塞（物），填料，衬料

wadding filter 棉絮滤芯滤清器

waddle （汽车行驶中）摇摆（亦称 lateral runout，左右摇摆，多由悬架损坏或转胎失圆引起）

wade 涉水，涉渡

wafer ①晶片（一种半导体材料或将这种半导体材料沉积到衬底上形成的圆形薄片或扁圆片，在它上面可同时制作出一个或若干个器件，然后将它们分割成芯片）②（各种）薄片、薄板、薄膜

waffle clutch 烤蛋饼形离合器（其摩擦片上开有十字格冷却槽，酷似一种鸡蛋烤饼：waffle，故名）

wag （上、下、左、右、来回）摆动，摇摆

waggon ①旅行车（见 station wagon）②厢式货车（= wagon）③泛指车，车辆

wagon balance 车辆地秤

wagon body 旅行车车厢，厢式车厢

wagon drill 汽车式钻机，移动式钻机，汽车钻

wagonette 小型厢式运货车（源于乘坐 6~8 人的四轮马车）

wagon ferry ①车辆轮渡（指由渡船运送车辆渡河等）②车辆渡轮③车辆渡口

wagon for transporting long timber 长木材运输车

wagon of calibrating 磅秤校验车（= weight-testing car）

wagon truck 厢式货车（= panel-body truck）

wagon-type bus 厢式客车（平头式

wagon type cab （货车的双排座）平头型驾驶室

wainscoting ①（车身侧壁等的）内蒙板，内面板，内壁板（用于保温、装饰等目的，不包括车身顶部的壁板，亦称 wainscot，= inside panel）②内壁板装修工作，安装（车身）内壁板③（车身等）内面板材料

waist 腰部（中间细部，收敛部分）

waist line 腰线（车身腰部水平线，美称 belt line）

waistline of the working chamber （转子发动机的）工作室细腰（外旋轮线缸筒的短轴处）

waist member （车身等的）腰带（亦称 waist rail）

waist molding 汽车车身腰线的金属或塑料模制装饰边条

waist pillar （客车车身）腰立柱（侧围骨架中直接支承腰梁的立柱）

waist rail （客车车身）腰梁（侧围骨架中位于窗台部位的纵梁）

waited worm roller steering gear 细腰型蜗杆滚轮式转向器（由细腰型蜗杆滚轮副组成的转向器）

waiting bay （短时）停车道，（短时）停车弯道（道路上专为离开行驶车流短时停车用的地段，美称 turn-out lane）

waiting-line theory 排队论

waiting room （车站）候车室

wait（ing）time 等待时间

waiting time on loading and unloading 装卸停歇时间

"wait" light （柴油车的起动）等待灯（装在仪表板上，当将起动电钮旋到第一挡时，等待灯闪光，过 15～60s，等待灯停止闪光，继续旋动电钮到第二挡，"start" light 闪光，表示电热塞预热，已达到可以起动的程度）

wait to repair 待修

wake ①激发，引起（反响等）；注意到（to）②（道路上的）车迹，车辙③（气流中的）尾流，涡区④（in the wake of）跟在…的后边，紧随…

wake flame 尾焰

4 WAL braking system 四轮防抱死制动系统 [four wheel antilock braking system 的简称，对桥四轮车辆亦称 full wheel antilock braking system 简称 FWA braking system（全轮防抱死系统）]

walk ①行走，步行②人行道

walk in（device） 上、下车机构（两门双排座轿车后排座乘员上、下车时，只要踩一下助手座椅后的该机构踏板，其后背便会自动向前倾倒且整个座椅向前滑动）

walking beam （重型货车或越野货车并装双轴式后桥的平衡式悬架的）摆臂（其两端各支撑一副双轴并装式后桥的钢板弹簧的摆动式吊架，亦称 working beam，相当于平衡臂 balance beam 或 equalizer）

walking-out of mesh ①（齿轮，凸轮）脱离啮合②（变速器齿轮自动）脱接，跳挡

walking robot 步行式机器人（类人机器人，见 humanoid robot）

walking root sinkage 行走机械的脚的沉陷量

walking time 步行时间（在客运公共交通企业服务区域内，乘客由出发地或出行目的地到最近公共交通停车站的平均步行时间）

walking vehicle 步行式车辆（以步行系统代替常规车轮系统的高通过性车辆）

walk on left sign （指示行人）靠左走标志

walk path 人行道（= walkway）

walk point [美] 偏移点（不足转

向车辆转向轮转向时，明显失去路面附着力的始点的俚称)

walk-roll principle （步行车辆）步行-滚动原理

walk-through layout （离地高度很小的）跨入式，步入式（驾驶室等）

walkway ①车身两边的走道（如：水陆两用车、洒水车、油罐车身上两旁的走道）②人行道，走道，通道

wall 墙壁，隔板，隔墙

wall action 壁面作用

wall bracket 墙装托架，壁装支架

wall climbing effect 爬墙效应（在峡谷式街道内，汽车排放污染物向上空扩散过程中，沿着街边建筑物的背风墙面向上扩散的现象，以致建筑物高层的污染物浓度大于低层）

wall covering （车身）壁面涂覆，壁面衬覆

wall crane 墙装起重机，壁装起吊设备

wall effect 壁面效应

wall-film （附着于管道、零件等的）壁面附着膜（如：壁面油膜，壁面漆膜，壁面污膜）

wall friction 壁面摩擦

Wall guide direct injection 缸壁导向型（燃油）直接喷射

wall-mounted 壁装式的，壁装的（镶装或挂装在墙壁上的）

wall of hole 孔壁

wall of piston ring 活塞环壁（活塞环径向厚度）

wall panel 壁板

wall quenching effect 壁面冷激效应（汽油机燃烧室壁面温度过低时，火焰从核心传播到接近壁面时，自行熄灭的现象）

wall temperature 壁温（如：汽缸壁、曲轴厢壁等的温度）

wall thickness 壁厚

wall thickness of cylinder 柔轮筒体壁厚（柔轮光滑体段之壁厚）

wall thickness of flexspline 柔轮齿圈壁厚（指柔轮齿根至柔轮内壁或外壁的壁厚）

wall-to-wall turning diameter （车身）外侧最小转弯半径（区别于轮胎外侧最小转弯半径）

wall wetting 壁湿（指冷机时，进入发动机的燃油蒸气遇进气管和燃烧室的低温表面而冷凝并附着于这些表面的现象）

wall-wetting dynamics 湿壁动力学（见 wall-wetting effect）

wall-wetting effect 湿壁效应（指未汽化的油滴微粒附着于进气系统壁面而造成的影响）

walnut timber 胡桃木（车室内装饰用）

WAN 广域网（wide area network 的简称，指连接分散在广阔地域内的大量终端和计算机的一种综合多态网络）

wander ①徘徊②漂游，漂动③偏离（预定的行驶）方向④摆动（车辆行驶方向来回摆动）⑤（汽车列车，多节挂车的）甩摆

wandering effect 汽车行驶时的摆动效应

Wankel ①汪克尔（德国人 Felix Heinrich Wankel，生于1902年，汪克尔转子发动机的发明人）②转子发动机（三角旋转活塞发动机）

Wankel automotive engine 汽车用汪克尔转子发动机（汽车用汪克尔旋转活塞发动机）

Wankel engine's displacement 汪克尔转子发动机排量（通常指它的整机当量排量，有时则指转子每一转的实际总排量，此时等于 3 × 单室排量 × 缸数，见 chamber displacement）

Wankel PLM engine 汪克尔行星旋

转式三角活塞发动机（汪克尔行星旋转式转子发动机，见 PLM）

Wankel RC engine 汪克尔旋转燃烧发动机（汪克尔转子发动机，Wankel rotary combustion engine 的简称）

Wankel rotary compressor 汪克尔旋转（活塞）压缩机（亦称 Wankel-type compressor）

Wankel sealing grid （转子发动机等采用的）汪克尔密封栅（汪克尔密封系统）

Wankel SIM engine 汪克尔单纯旋转式发动机（见 SIM）

Wankel's rotating piston 汪克尔转子发动机的旋转活塞（一般为三角转子）

warding file 薄片锉，极薄锉（形状与平锉相同，但厚度很小，用于锉修缝隙等）

Wardis Auto World ［美］华德汽车世界（杂志）（简称 WAW）

Ward-Leonard drive 发动机-电动机（组合）传动（因发明人渥特-勒奥那多而得名）

warehouse 仓库，堆栈，储存室

warhead trailer 运弹头的挂车

warm ①加温，加热；预热，暖机 ②温的，热的

warm engine ①经预热的发动机 ②热发动机，热机

warm(ing) up period （发动机）暖机期（= heating-up period，指从发动机起动到达到其稳定运转温度的升温期，热起期）

warm-up control unit （K-Jetronic 汽油喷射系统的发动机起动后）暖机期（混合气浓度）控制装置（冷机起动后，暖机运转时，发动机温度逐步升高，该装置通过对汽油分配器"fuel distributor"控制油压的调节，使混合气的加浓随发动机温度的上升而减少，直至停止，该装置又称控制油压调节器"control pressure regulator"）

warm-up enrichment （发动机起动后的）暖机（期）（混合气）加浓（起动后暖机初始期，发动机温度尚低，要求一定量的冷机加浓，但随着发动机暖机运转，其温度逐步上升，混合气的加浓度亦应随温度上升而减少，直到暖机终了，发动机达到正常工作温度时，暖机加浓停止，因此，"暖机加浓"是指逐步减少加浓度直至终止加浓的过程）

warm-up regulator （低温起动后的）升温期喷油量调节器

warm wheel sector 蜗杆齿扇式转向器中的）齿扇

warn 警告，预告

warnet 警报器

warning ①警告，预报；警报信号，警告标志 ②警告的，预报的

warning blinker 闪光警报灯（亦称 warning flasher，warning winker）

warning lamp 警告灯，警报灯（有时用 warning light）

warning (road) sign （道路）安全性警告标志（向驾驶人表明现有或潜在的危险的标志）

warning triangle 三角形警告标志

warp ①扭曲（= twist）②弯曲（= bend）③（织物中的）经线

warpage （车用玻璃的）弯曲度（玻璃板的平面度，以弯起的高度与边长之比来表示）

warpage test 扭曲试验

warped surface 扭曲面，弯曲面

warranted period 保用期（如：内燃机在正常使用条件下，保证不发生因产品质量而引起的重大故障的期限。在此期限内若出现较大故障或损坏，应由制造厂免费负责修理、更换或赔偿）

warrant(y) ①保证 ②保证书，保

单，证书③理由④批准，授权

warranty-covered 属于保证范围内的

warranty life 保用寿命（保证使用期限）

warranty test 保用（鉴定）试验（保证产品在保用期内符合规定技术条件的试验）

4 WAS 见 4 wheel Antiskid Brake System

wash 洗涤，清洗

washboard 搓板（如：搓板状路面，滚动轴承内、外圈的搓板状磨损等）

washboard pavement 搓板（状）路面

washcoat （排气催化转化器中）载体涂料（用来增加载体上沉积催化剂的表面积的物质）

washer ①垫圈②垫片③清洗机，洗涤设备，洗涤器

washer-drier 清洗-干燥机（带有干燥设备的清洗机）

washer face （螺栓头部等的）垫圈面（指接触垫圈的一面）

washer motor 洗涤电动机（带有洗涤泵的电动机）

washer-shaped piezoelectric sensor 垫圈型压电传感器

washer solvent 洗涤剂（洗涤用溶剂，洗涤液，亦称 washing solution）

washing gun （清洗汽车等使用的）冲洗（水）枪

washing heads ①（洒水车的）洒水头②（清洗机的）喷水头

washing lane 汽车清洗作业线

washing mark 冲洗痕迹

wash-leather （揩拭用的）麂皮，软皮

wash off resistance test 耐冲洗试验（亦称 washout resistance test）

washout ①冲洗，冲刷②路面上被雨水冲刷出的凹坑、凹槽

wash rack 清洗台

wash/wipe switch （车身后窗等的）清洗/刮水（装置控制）开关

wasp-waisted tractor 蜂腰式拖拉机

wastage ①损失，损耗（量），损漏（量），磨损量②残渣，废料，垃圾

waste ①损失，损耗②废物，废料，残渣③废弃的；无用的

waste cooking oil derived biodiesel 废食用油提炼的生物柴油，地沟油柴油，泔水油柴油（亦称 used cooking oil biodiesel，简称 UCO biodiesel）

wasted car 废弃车辆，废汽车

wasted power 损耗功率

waste-gas heater 废气加热器（利用废气余热加热、取暖的装置）

wastegate control system （废气涡轮增压系统的）废气泄放阀控制系统

wastegate valve 废气泄放阀（由手动或进气歧管压力、伺服电动机等控制，当废气涡轮增压压力超过某规定值时，该阀开启，使部分废气不再经过废气涡轮，而直接通过消声器排出，以降低废气涡轮转速和增压压力，保护废气增压器和发动机，简称 wastegate）

waste-heat boiler 废热锅炉（用于利用废气余热的暖气设备或回收废气余热，提高热效率的动力回收系统）

waste-heat loss 废（气）热（量）损失

waste-heat recover 废热回收

waste-heat utilization 废热利用

waste of compression 压缩（过程的）能量）损失

waste of energy 能量损耗（= energy waste）

waste oil collection equipment 废机油收集设备

waste oil drain （供汽车发动机、变速器等更换滑油时使用的）废油接

装桶

waster section 代蚀件（代损件，为了减少相互接触的两金属构件间的自发电池腐蚀，在该两构件间加装一个小的活性金属件，以"代替"大的阳极基础构件"承受"腐蚀）

waste-skip ①废料搬运车，垃圾车 ②石料输送车

waste spark 无用火花（在某些无分电器电子控制点火系统中，每两个汽缸的火花塞共用一个点火线圈，即由一个点火线圈同时向两个火花塞提供跳火高压，每一循环内都有一个汽缸的火花塞在压缩冲程终了时跳火，另一个汽缸的火花塞在排气冲程中跳火，后者称无用火花）

waste spark method 无用火花法（采用"无用火花"的点火控制方法）

watch ①钟，表②观察，注视，监视

watch-dog 看守狗（监视器，监控设备的俗称）

watchdog micro controller 监视微控制器（电子控制系统中，用来判断某些特定状态在预定的时间间隔内是否出现的装置，简称 watchdog micro）

watch-dog timer 监视计时器

watch glass test （测定汽油中的胶质等的）表玻璃试验

watch window 观察窗，检视窗

water absorption test 吸水性试验

water addition in fuel 燃油掺水

water analog 水模拟法（一种测涡流场的方法，可用来测发动机缸内进气涡流的结构等）

water-ballasted tire 充水轮胎

water ballasting of wheels 轮胎充水配重

water based paint 水基涂料

water boggy tire 沼泽地用轮胎（= marsh tire）

water bottom （油）箱底沉积水，（油）罐底残水

water brake 水力测功制动器

water bug 轻型的水陆两用汽车（口语）

water bus 水上客机（指起飞降落都在水面上的客机）

water bypass system （汽车发动机的）冷却水旁通系（统）

water capacity of cooling system 冷却系的水容量

water cart ①洒水车②运水车

water chamber ①水箱（储）水室 ②水套

water channel 排水槽，水沟，水管道

water check valve 单向放水阀，单向水阀

water-circulating pump 循环水泵（亦称 water-circulation pump）

water-circulation gauge 循环水压力表

water cistern 水（罐）槽车

water column pressure 水柱压力

water consumption 水消耗量

water content 含水量（水分）

water coolant 冷却水

water-cooled brake 水冷式制动器

water-cooled condenser 水冷凝器

water cooled EGR 水冷却废气再循环（冷却式废气再循环的一种，废气先通过水冷却器降温后再经 EGR 阀进入进气管）

water-cooled EGR 水冷却式废气再循环（系统）（再循环的废气经过水冷却器冷却后再经 EGR 阀进入进气歧管）

water-cooled generator 水冷式发电机

water crack 水淬裂纹

water-crossing （汽车）越过水域（如：过河等）

water deposit 水垢（指由水中析出

的固体沉淀物）

water detector 水分传感器（柴油机燃油系中，检测水分含量的传感元件）

water distributing gallery （发动机冷却系缸体）冷却水分配道，配水道

water drive （水陆两用车辆的）螺旋桨驱动

water ejection （轮胎的）排水性能

water emulsified fuel 水乳化燃油（一般指用水乳化柴油，以降低排放）

water engine ①水动机（水马达，水力马达，液压马达，液动机，指将水力或液力转变为旋转运动输出的机械，= hydraulic motor, water motor）②救火车③抽水机

water expulsion 脱水（除去水分，干燥）

water filling car 加水车

water from combustion （发动机）燃烧生成的水分

water-gas generator 水煤气发生器

water-ga(u)ge ①水量表（如：锅炉上装的玻璃管显示锅内的水面高度）②水柱压力表（用以测量气体的气压，或测量压力差，其单位用水柱的米数表示者，称为 meter）

water-gauge cock 水面量测旋塞

water-glass 水玻璃（硅酸钠）

water-hammer 水锤（现象）（水击作用）

water-hammer shock absorber 水锤冲击吸收器（液力冲击吸收器，液力冲击缓冲器）

water-hardening 水冷硬化（淬火）

water-head 水头（水位差，表示流体位能的大小）

water-heated light alloy induction manifold 水暖式轻合金进气歧管

water hole 水孔（注水孔；流水孔）

water horsepower 水马力（水功率 $L = \gamma Q h / 75$ 马力。式中：γ—水的容重，$9.8 N/m^3$；Q—水泵流量，m^3/s；h—水泵有效水头，m）

water hose 水（箱）软管

watering car 洒水汽车

water-injection（cooled）engine 喷水（冷却）式发动机（将水喷入进气歧管与可燃混合气混合进入汽缸或直接喷入汽缸内，利用水的蒸发作用，使缸套、活塞等零件保持在一定的温度界限下，以代替一般的水套冷却或空气冷却，或降低燃烧温度减少 NO_x 形成，防止爆燃，或利用喷水节油等）

water injector 水喷嘴，喷水嘴

water inlet ①进水孔，进水道②进水

water in oil test 油中含水量测试

water jacket （汽缸体或缸盖内的）冷却水套

water-jet ①喷水器，喷水量孔②水束，水射流

water level sensor 水位传感器

water loving 亲水（的）

water-methanol mixture 水-甲醇混合液

water motor 水马达（水力马达，水动机，见 water engine）

water paint 水溶性涂料（用水作为稀释剂的涂料）

water passage 水道（如：冷却水道等）

water performance of amphibian 水陆两用车辆水中行驶性能

water pollution 水污染

water power 水动力（水电力，水力，水能）

water pressure 水压（力）

waterproof 防水的，不透水的

waterproof packaging 防水包装

waterproof seal 防水密封件（水密封件）

waterproof test 防水性试验（水密性试验）

water propeller transfer case （水陆两用汽车）螺旋桨分动器壳

water pump body 水泵壳体（亦称 water pump housing）

water pump gland ring 水泵密封环

water pump impeller 水泵叶轮（= water pump vane）

water pump shaft 水泵轴（亦称 water pump spindle）

water pump shaft gear 水泵轴传动齿轮

water pump suction pipe 水泵吸水管

water purification vehicle 带净水设备的车辆（= purification vehicle）

water purifier 净水器

water quality 水质

water-quench（ing） 水淬火

water-raising engine 抽水机（扬水机，升水机）

water rate 耗水量（一般指蒸汽机或蒸汽轮机每马力消耗的水量）

water ratio 含水率（含水量百分率，以%计算）

water-recovery test （制动器）浸水后效能恢复试验

water-reducible finish 防水（用）罩面漆

water regulating valve 水量调节阀（冷却水流量调节阀）

water removal 脱水，除水

water-resistance test 耐水性能试验

water-resisting properties 耐水性，抗水性

water-retaining 保水的

water rheostat 水介质可变电阻器（将电极置于水中，而利用电极间的水作为电阻器，其阻值随电极间距、面积而变化）

water-seal 水封

water-sealed bearing （带水封的）防水轴承

water-separator 水分离器（亦称 water-segregator）

water-softener ①水软化剂②水质软化器

water-solubility 水溶性

water-soluble oil 水溶性油

water speed （水陆两用汽车或气垫车的）水面行驶速度

water splash 试车浅水池（试车场检查车身密封性专设的水池）

water sprayer 洒水车（亦称 water sprinkler）

water spray test 喷淋试验

water supply 供水，给水

water-tank lorry 水罐车（= water-tank truck, water truck）

water temperature indicator ①水温表②冷却水水温表（= radiator thermometer, water thermometer, water temperature gauge）

water temperature sensor （发动机）水温传感器

water temperature switch 水温开关（当冷却水温达到某规定值时，其触点断开或闭合的开关装置）

water tempering 水浴回火

watertight 水密的，不漏水的，防渗水的（亦写作 water tight，简称 WT）

watertight instrument 水密式仪器仪表（能在完全沉入水中后防止水侵入的仪器仪表）

watertight packing 防水包装，不透水的封装

water tight test 水密封试验（如试验汽缸体等水套的裂纹，简称 water test）

water tolerance 耐水性

water trap ①水分离器，脱水器②（机油滤清器内的）水分沉积室

water treatment 水质处理

water-tube boiler 水管式锅炉

water-tube cleaner 水管清洁器（清除水管道内的水垢、污泥等）

water turbine 水轮机（借助叶轮将

水的能量——速度、压力转变为机械能的装置)

water under the keel (水陆两用汽车)龙骨下的水深

water vapour permeability 水蒸气渗透性

water vapour proof packaging 防潮包装

water wall ①水壁,水墙②冷却水套壁

water washing chamber 水洗箱(一种串联在排气管路中的水箱,能对柴油机排出的气体起一定的清洁作用)

water washout grease test 润滑脂抗水洗能力的试验

watery solution 水溶液

watt 瓦(特)(国际单位制的功率单位,代号W,1W指每秒钟做1J的功,1W=1J/s)

wattage 瓦特功率(电路的总功率,$=V\cdot A$)

watt（age）loss 电功率损耗

watt-hour capacity 瓦特小时容量(瓦时容量)

watt-hour meter 瓦(特小)时计(电表,电度表,简称 watt-hr meter)

wattless component of current 无功电流 (= reactive current)

wattmeter 瓦特计(电功率表,亦称 indicating wattmeter)

watt's horsepower 英制马力

watt's linkage 瓦特式三杆件悬架(一种刚性车轴的非独立悬架,由两根内端分别与装在车轴中央的垂直摆杆上、下端连接,而外端则分别通过铰接件支撑车身左、右两端的横向布置的半径杆组成)

wave 波

wave band 波段,频带

wave changer 波段(选择)开关

wave crest 波峰(峰值)

wave filter 滤波器

waveform 波形(荷载、应变、位移、电压等作为时间的函数的曲线从峰值变到谷值,再由谷值变到峰值的形状)

waveform generator 波形发生器(可产生一组脉冲波形的电路)

waveform washer 波浪式垫圈

wave frequency 波的频率

wave front 波阵面,波前锋

wave generator (谐波齿轮传动中的)波发生器(使柔性齿轮按一定变形规律产生弹性变形波的构件)

wave generator of positive control (谐波齿轮)积极控制式波发生器(柔性齿轮整周变形后受到波发生器的确实控制的波发生器)

wave guides 波导,波导管

wave height 波高(从波谷底到波峰顶的高度)

wavelength 波长(在连续周期波形中,某一相位点到下一周期中同相位点的距离)

wave-mechanics 波动力学

wavemeter 波频计,波长计

wave phenomena (轮胎高速时的)波动现象(或振动现象)

wave propagation 波的传播

wave radiation 波的辐射

wave-shaped 波形修整(如:将梯形波边角修圆等)的

wave spring 波状弹簧(如:活塞环衬环)

wave trough 波谷

wave velocity 波速(波的传播速度)(= phase velocity,波长与频率的乘积)

wave winding ①波形绕线,波状绕组②波形绕法,波卷

waviness (表面)波动度,波纹度

waviness height 波峰高度

waviness width (加工表面波状不平)相邻波峰间的节距,波纹宽度

wavy fracture 波状断裂面

WAW [美]华德汽车世界(杂志)(Wardis Auto World)

wax ①蜡,石蜡(=paraffin) ②蜜蜂蜡,鲸鱼蜡等固态脂 ③车身抛光蜡(=body wax,主要成分为paraffin) ④打蜡

wax capsule (节温装置的)蜡囊,蜡丸,蜡球(亦称 wax pelleg)

waxed paper (包装用)蜡纸(=paraffin paper)

wax element thermostat 蜡质节温器(=wax-type thermostat,利用蜡随温度变化而溶化或凝固时体积的变化来控制冷却水的冷却通道的阀门,使冷却水温稳定在一定范围内的装置。当蜡芯为丸状物时,称蜡丸恒温器"wax pellet thermostat")

waxing ①(燃油,特别是柴油,在低温下)蜡结晶析出与长大趋势 ②打蜡(上蜡抛光)

wax plugging 蜡阻(低温下,柴油析出的蜡结晶堵塞柴油机燃油管道的现象)

wax spraying arch (洗车设备中的)喷(上光)蜡拱门

way ①路(通路,路线,路程,路途) ②状态,方式,方法

13-way connector 13通路接头(牵引车与挂车间的13个插接点的电路接头)

way Exhaust Control System (日本丰田皇冠V8发动机的)双通道排气控制系统(商品名,随发动机转速不同由电子控制开放或关闭其消声器内的两个排气通道,以减小排气阻力,保证发动机性能)

wayfarer 旅行人(尤指徒步旅行者)

way point (主要站点之间的)小站(一般直通车或快车不停的中间站,=美 way station)

8-way-power seat (上下、前后、左右及靠背前后倾斜角度均可调节的汽车)8位电动座椅

wayside ①路边,路旁 ②路边的

Wb 韦伯(磁通量单位,见 Weber)

WBR (汽车碰撞试验中的假人)全躯体反应(whole-body response 的简称)

4WB system 四轮(独立)制动系统(four wheel brake system 的简称,电子控制模块根据各种传感器的信息综合判断各个车轮的滑移和滑转率,对四个车轮的制动力分别作最佳控制,防止抱死、侧滑、滑转和过度及不足转向等)

WC 小心轻放(货运包装标记)(with care)

WCAC 水冷式空调(water-cooling air conditioning 的简称)

WCLD 水冷式(的)(water-cooled 的简称)

W-curve W形曲线

W/D 质量排量比(weight-displacement ratio)

WD 线路图,布线图(wiring diagram)

WD-40 (一种专利)防水喷剂(的商品名)

4 WD AUTO mode 四轮驱动自动模式(当使用模式可选择型四轮驱动系统的模式选择开关选择该模式时,会随着路面状况和行驶条件的变化瞬时在两轮驱动和四轮驱动间自动切换)

WDCR 宽基深轮辋(wide base drop center rim 的简称)

4 WD ECO mode 四轮驱动节能模式(当使用模式可选择型四轮驱动系统的模式选择开关选择该模式时,平时为节油仅两前轮驱动,只有当路面打滑时,才瞬时自动切换为四轮驱动,过后仍恢复前轮驱动)

4WD「e4Mitic」 四轮电动机驱动(系统)(商品名,四个车轮均使用

轮内电动机驱动,可分别控制转矩的全轮驱动系统)

4 WD hybrid vehicle 四轮驱动混合动力车(通常由汽油机-电动机混合动力系统驱动前桥或后桥,而由制动能量回收的再生发电-电动机系统驱动另一车桥)

4 WD LOCK mode 四轮驱动锁定模式(当使用模式可选择型四轮驱动系统的模式选择开关选择该模式时,无论在何种路面和行驶条件下均为强劲有力的四轮驱动行驶)

4WD mode selecting switch (模式可选择型)四轮驱动系统的模式选择开关[见 switch-type(mode-)changeable 4WD system]

4WD NORMAL mode (超级)四轮驱动常规模式(见 S-AWC)

4 WD SNOW mode 四轮驱动雪地模式(提高在雪地、冰冻等打滑地面上行驶时的稳定性)

2 WD / 4 WD selector (分时四轮驱动系统的)二/四轮驱动选择开关

We 净重,空车重(weight empty)

weak ①弱的,薄弱的,脆弱的②稀薄的,淡薄的

weak current 弱电流

weaken 减弱,削弱,减薄,变稀;衰减

weakening of spring 弹簧变软(弹簧弹力减小)

weakly adhering oil film 黏附力很弱的润滑油膜

weak machine 功率小的机器

weak mixture 稀混合气(指空燃比大于理论混合气空燃比的混合气,=lean mixture, poor mixture)

weaknesses ①缺点,弱点②结构中的薄弱环节

weak solution 稀溶液

weapon carrier 武器运输车(军械运输车辆)

wear 磨损,磨耗

wearability 耐磨性,抗磨性

wear adjuster (制动器的制动衬片与制动鼓或制动盘间的)间隙调节装置(以补制动衬片的磨损,=lash adjusting device)

wear allowance 磨损留量(容许磨耗)

wear bars 轮胎胎面磨损指示标(亦称 tread wear indicator)

wear-causing 引起磨损的

wear characteristics 磨损特性

wear compensation device 磨损补偿器(如:摩擦式制动器摩擦衬片磨损后间隙自动补偿装置)

wear curve 磨损曲线(磨损量与时间或摩擦行程之间的关系曲线。曲线一般具有三个阶段:磨合阶段、稳定磨损阶段和剧烈磨损阶段)

wear-in 磨合,走合(亦称 wearing-in)

wear indicator 磨损指示器(如:制动蹄摩擦片磨损警报标志)

wearing capacity 磨损容量

wearing coat ①耐磨涂层,耐磨镀覆表层②磨耗表层,磨耗面,磨损面(亦称 wearing face, wearing layer, wearing surface)

wearing depth 磨损深度

wearing of side slipping (轮胎)侧滑(造成的)磨损

wearing-resistance property 耐磨性(用体积磨损或质量磨损表征的抵抗磨损的性能指标)

wearing ring 耐磨环(由耐磨材料制成,镶装于易受磨损的部位的圆环)

wearing test 耐磨性试验,磨耗试验

wear inhibitor 抗磨损添加剂

wearlessness 耐磨性,抗磨性

wear-life 磨损期限,抗磨寿命

wear limit 磨损极限

wear loose 磨松(磨损造成的松动)

wear of mass 质量磨损(磨损试验

后试件失去的质量,有时亦写作 wear of weight)

wear of volume 体积磨损(磨损试验后试件失去的体积)

wear-out failure ①磨损性破坏,磨损性故障②耗损失效(由于老化、磨损、损耗、疲劳等原因引起的失效)

wear-out reliability 耐磨损可靠性

wear particle 致磨颗粒,磨料微粒

wear pattern 磨损模式(显示磨损面等的式样的图形)

wear plate 防磨耗板

wearproof 防磨损的(耐磨的,抗磨的)

wear rate ①磨损速率②磨耗率(磨损程度,指磨损量与产生磨损的行程和时间之比)

wear reference point 磨损参考点(磨损测量的基本尺寸)

wear resistant coating ①抗磨镀层,耐磨镀层②耐磨覆层,耐磨覆盖层

wear-resistant steel 耐磨钢

wear ring (装在旋转或滑动接合处,防止贵重的主件磨损的)磨损环

wear sensor (各种摩擦件,如制动蹄片等的)磨损(程度)传感器

wear sleeve (易更换的)承磨衬套

wear smooth 磨光,磨滑

wear strip 耐磨衬条,磨损补偿楔形条,防磨损条,防磨损板条

wear tester 磨损试验机

wear trace 磨损痕迹(亦称 wear track,如:磨损表面的沟槽)

wear value 磨耗值

wear washer 抗磨垫圈(耐磨垫圈)

weasel 水陆两用车辆(如:雪地和沼泽地工作的超越野履带式运输机械)

wea T 不透风雨的(防风雨的,weather tight 的简称)

weather ①天气,气候,气象(简称 W)②气候影响(大气影响、风化等作用)③露天时效(露天老化,风吹雨打、日晒引起的老化)

weatherability 抗天气影响的稳定性(如:抗侵蚀性,抗风化性,抗老化性等,参见 exposure test)

weather-bound ①受气候限制的②因气候不良而引起停运的

weather cracking 风蚀裂纹(轮胎或其他橡胶件表面因大气中臭氧等引起的裂纹)

weather effects 气候的影响,气候效应

weather exposure 暴露于大气中(风化,日晒雨淋)

weather exposure test 气候暴露试验,(亦称 weathering test,见 exposure test)

weather forecast 天气预报

weather guard auto shelter (尼龙、帆布等制成,可将整个汽车罩住的)汽车防晒风雨罩

weathering ①天气的自然作用(如:大气的侵蚀、风蚀、气候的自然老化、自然时效、大气的风化作用等)②天气自然作用试验,抗天气影响稳定性试验,风蚀暴露试验(见 exposure test)

weathering quality (车身外壳等的)耐风蚀性,耐气候老化性,抗风雨性

weather interference 气候干扰

weather joint 泄水缝

weather minimum 最低气象条件

weatherometer 气象仪,气象(风雨,气压等的)测定仪器;耐风蚀测试仪,老化测试器

weather-pack connector (电气设备中导线的)防风雨接头(可防止风、雨及尘埃浸蚀的密封插套式导线接头)

weather-proof 不受气候影响的(经得起各种天气变化的,如,weather-proof color 抗气候风化的颜色,

weather-proof paint 防风化漆，耐日晒风雨浸蚀的涂料，weather-proof wire 防潮绝缘电线，weather protected machine，抗大气影响的机器，可防风雨及有防风雨设备的机器)

weather-related error 气候所造成的误差

weather report 气象报告

weather resistance 抗风蚀性；抗气候性，耐风雨性，耐老化，抗风化能力，耐候性（指材料在各种气候条件下，如：日晒、雨淋、盐蚀、高温、冷冻等的耐久性)

weather-resistance test 抗天气影响稳定性试验（见 exposure test)

weather sealing 密封件（起密封作用的零部件)

weather-strip（ping） （车身门、窗的风、雨、尘埃）密封条

weathertight 不透风雨的，防风雨的

weather tunnel （试验汽车用）人造气候风洞

weather vane 风向指示计（风向标，亦称 wind indicator)

weave 摇动，摇晃，摆动

weaver brake tester 跑板式制动试验台

weaver-type side slip tester （汽车车轮的）平移型侧偏试验台（试验台板作横向平行移动的板式侧向偏移试验台，根据其移动量，求出前轮等的侧偏值，即：我国汽车检测界所谓的"侧滑量"，m/km)

weaving （车辆）交织（指两股以上的车流以小角度汇合同一方向前进，然后交叉穿过而分流离开)

weaving space （道路行车的）交织路段，交织区（美国亦称 weaving section，见 weaving)

web ①腹板，连接板（如：工字梁的梁腹，T形钢的立段，角钢的一股等）②辐板，轮辐（如：齿轮的轮辐，车轮的辐板）③筋，蹼④（板件之间的）内加强件⑤金属薄片（如：刀片，锯片，散热片等）⑥曲柄臂（= crank web）⑦丝（织）网，网膜，网状物

Web 万维网（见 world wide web)

web-based information provision system 基于网页的信息提供系统

webbed 有腹板的，有加强筋的，有横隔板的，有筋片的

webbing 纺织带（如：作为汽车安全带的纺织尼龙带)

webbing grabber （汽车突然制动或发生碰撞时）安全带收紧装置

webbing sensitive emergency locking retractor （汽车乘员安全带的）安全带加速度感知式紧急锁紧型收紧装置

Weber 韦伯（国际单位制的磁通量单位，代号 Wb，即在一只线圈中，磁通量以每秒钟 1Wb 的均匀速率变化，则感应出 1V 的电动势。1Wb = 1Vs = 10^8 maxwell)

web of crank （曲轴的）曲柄臂（亦称 crankshaft web)

web of wheel 车轮的辐板

web-plate 腹板，筋片，肋板，肋片

web-type flywheel 辐板式飞轮，盘式飞轮

web wheel 盘式车轮（= disk wheel)

wedge ①楔，尖劈②V形件，楔状物③（车用玻璃的）平行度（呈楔形）④楔入，楔住，楔紧

wedge-actuated brake 外张楔式制动器（= expanding wedge brake)

wedge adjuster 调整楔（= adjusting wedge)

wedge angle 楔角

wedge belt 三角传动带（= V-belt)

wedge brake 楔形制动器（大型车用制动器的一种，由气动缸或液压缸顶压楔形凸轮件"wedge expander"，使制动蹄张开，与旧式 S 凸轮型制动器比较，效率较高，= expanding wedge brake, wedge-operated brake)

wedge clamp 楔形压板

wedged 楔形的，楔状的

wedged tenon 楔榫

wedge expander （鼓式制动器使制动蹄张开的）楔形凸轮（见 wedge brake）

wedge gap 楔形缝，楔状间隙

wedge lock （防止半挂车牵引主销滑出牵引座钩销板的）楔形锁止板

wedge-operated brake 见 wedge brake

wedge seal （转子发动机径向密封片）楔状密封片（角密封片，一般指三片式径向密封片，两端的三角形密封楔）

wedge shape car 楔形车（车身前低后高的轿车，以减小空气阻力）

wedge-shaped combustion chamber 楔形燃烧室（横剖面呈楔形，顶置气门式汽油机的一种燃烧室。气门纵向排列，呈倾斜安置，倾斜角一般为 0°～16°，亦称 wedge-section combustion chamber，简称 wedge combustion chamber）

wedge tensile strength test （螺钉等的）楔垫抗拉强度试验（用带有斜度的楔形垫片代替平垫圈，在钉头的承压面受力不均的条件下，旋紧螺钉，测定抗拉强度）

wedge valve 楔形阀

wedging action 楔紧作用

weep ①滴漏②滴漏处

weeping pipe 滴流管

W/EGR 带有废气再循环的（= with EGR）

Weibull distribution 威布尔分布（如：材料的疲劳寿命之概率分布，服从威布尔分布）

Weibull scale 威氏概率数值表

weigh 称重，过秤，衡量

weighing ①称重②加权③权重

weighing apparatus 秤（物体质量或重力测定装置的总称，= weighing instrument, balance, scale）

weighing bottle 比重瓶

weigh (ing) bridge 地秤（= platform scale）

weigh-in-motion 动态称量（汽车在公路上行驶过程中测量其动态载荷，简称 W-I-M）

weigh-shaft 秤轴

weight ①重量[指物体所受重力大小的物理量，单位为牛（N）。质量（mass）表示物体所含物质多少的物理量，单位为千克（kg）。物体的质量是不变的，而重量则随地点而改变。至今英美汽车文献中所谓的"Weight"，实际上是指物体不随地点而变的质量，因此，为避免质量与重量混淆，宜用"重力"一词表示重量，但按习惯，英、美仍沿用重量"weight"一词]②重物；重块，重锤，载重，荷载，荷重③砝码，秤砣；平衡重，配重④加权值，权重⑤加载，加荷重，装载，加砝码，加配重，加权

weight and load regulations 车辆重量和载重法规（公路、桥梁限制汽车重量及载重的规定）

weight ballasting of wheels 车轮的配重块

weight box 配重箱

weight by volume 容积重量（= volume weight）

weight carried per wheel （每个）车轮承重，车轮负重

weight-carrying capacity 载重量（载重量的旧称）

weight class （汽车的）载重量等级（按载重量分的等级。质量级、装载质量等级的旧称）

weight coefficient 重量系数（重量功率比，发动机重量对其额定功率之比，kg/kW，亦称 weight-power ratio。质量系数、质量功率比的旧称）

weight component 重力分力（分重

weight counterbalance 平衡重（平衡块，= balance weight）
weight density 重（量密）度
weight-dependent limit 与车重有关的（汽车性能）极限（如：车速极限，拖杆拉力极限）
weight-displacement ratio （发动机的）重量—排量比（发动机的一项评价指标，重量排量比愈小，发动机的结构设计质量愈好，简称 W/D）
weight-distance tax 一种根据重量及运输距离收取的汽车运输税
weight distribution effect （汽车的）重量分配效应（由于汽车前后桥的载荷分配比的变化，而影响汽车制动、转向等作用的现象）
weight-distribution factor （汽车的）重量分配系数，载荷分配率（驱动桥动载荷 W_d 与汽车总重 W 之比，即 W_d/W）
weight distribution oversteer （汽车的）重量分配过度转向（由于载荷分配而引起的负不足转向，见 oversteer 及 weight distribution understeer）
weight distribution ratio 重量分配比（如：轴间重力分配的百分比）
weight distribution understeer （汽车的）重量分配不足转向（由于载荷分配引起的不足转向，见 understeer）
weighted ①负载的，载重的 ②加权的，计权的
weighted acceleration 加权加速度
weighted approximation 加权近似值
weighted arithmetic mean 加权算术平均值（在对某一量值的多组测量中，考虑到每组测量结果的"权"后，计算出这一列测量结果的算术平均值）
weighted average 加权平均值（= weighted mean）

weighted average traffic 加权平均车辆通过数（车公里除以路线长度）
weighted check 加权校验
weighted creep ratio 加权蠕变比
weighted error 加权误差
weight/hp ratio 车重马力比
weighting factor 加权系数（亦称 weighting coefficient）
weighting method （测定车用液体清洁度的）重量法（将带有杂质的混浊液通过过滤器并测得杂质质量的方法）
weight in running order 车辆在运行状态下的重量（车辆满载并加满燃料、冷却水、润滑油、工作油液时的车重）
weight limit sign 车重限制标志
weight-loaded accumulator 重物加载式蓄压器
weight moment of inertia 重力转动惯量（美国常用，= 重量转动惯量×重力加速度 g）
weight of car 车重（简称 WOC）
weight of chassis 底盘重
weight on front axle 前桥荷重
weight-payload ratio 自重-载重比
weight penalty 重量损失（评价构件材料的指标，指材料质量造成的功率损失等，如：某材料的质量损失越大，说明该材料制成的零件越重）
weight per axle 车桥载重（= axle weight）
weight per brake horsepower 发动机重量制动马力比（公斤/马力）
weight-performance ratio （汽车的）重量性能比（重力功率比，= weight-power ratio，一般用 kW/t 或 PS/t 为单位）
weight per gallon （液罐车）每加仑运载液体的车重
weight per inch of tire width 轮胎每英寸宽度上的载重

weight per output 单位输出功率的发动机重

weight per unit area 单位面积的重量（表征油漆层等的厚度）

weight per unit volume 单位体积重量（见 volume weight）

weight-power ratio 重量功率比（= weight coefficient）

weight printer 车重打印机（可自动打出货车等的总重、装载量等）

weight-reduction technology （汽车等的）自重减小技术，自重减轻技术

weight-rigidity ratio （车身底盘等的）重量-刚度比

weight-saving 轻量的，轻量化的，可减小重力的

weight sensor 重力传感器

weight-testing car （货运站等处使用的）地秤校验车（用于校验大型地秤，一般装有标准砝码和砝码起吊设备，亦称 wagon for calibrating）

weight ton 长吨（见 long ton）

weight transfer （制动或加速时引起的）重力转移（亦称 weight shift）

weight tray 运货托盘

weight utilization factor （车辆）重量利用系数

weight when empty 空车重量（= empty weight）

Weissach axle 韦萨奇悬架式车桥（由四根非等长控制臂组成的一种四连杆式悬架车桥，每一车轮由两根杆臂控制，可减弱由于制动和转向中松开加速踏板时的转向轮突然前张现象造成的转向输入，及将过度转向问题减到最小，由 Porshe 为其 928S 型轿车研制）

Weiss constant velocity universal joint 韦斯式球叉等角速万向节，球叉式等角速万向节（= Bendix-weiss constant velocity joint, 简称 Bendix-weiss joint, Weiss universal joint, Weiss coupling, 见 Weiss universal joint）

Weiss' domains 韦斯磁畴（指磁铁体中尺寸从 0.01~1mm 随机分布的磁性微粒，即使无外来磁场作用，这些微粒本身也是一个个小的天然单元磁铁，但由于它们的分布杂乱无章，磁场相互抵消，以致铁磁体对外界不显磁性。当受外界磁场作用时，它们的磁场方向基本相同，对外显出磁性）

weiss universal joint 球叉式万向节（由一组钢球和连接钢球的两个球叉组成的等速万向节。这一组钢球中有一个带销孔和销的定心钢球，见 ball yoke, centering ball）

weld ①焊，焊接，熔焊，熔接；锻焊②焊缝，焊接点，焊接接头③焊接的

weld-ability test 可焊性试验（= welding test）

weldable 可以焊接的，可焊的

weld bead ①焊珠②焊缝，焊道

weld-bond joint 黏接点焊（为了提高铝等构件的黏接强度，先用金属黏接剂将两构件的连接边重接，然后再加点焊）

weld drive shaft tube assembly 传动轴管焊接合件（由花键轴管和轴管叉焊接成的合件）

welding electrode(s) 焊条（亦称 welding rod）

welding flux 焊剂（焊药）

welding generator 电焊机（作为焊接电源的发电机，= welding dynamo）

welding grade gas 焊接用保护气（如：氩 argon）

welding ground 电焊地线（指施焊时接在被焊基体金属或焊接台上的地线）

welding motor generator 电动机-发

电机电焊机组

welding stress 焊接应力（焊接时，溶焊金属冷却收缩而不能自由变形所产生的残余应力）

welding truck 装备有焊接设备的修理工程车

welding wear （高温摩擦引起的摩擦件表面间的）熔合（黏合）磨损

welding wire 焊丝（= filler wire, filling wire）

weldless pipe 无焊缝管（亦称 weldless tube）

weld nut 焊装螺孔塞（用于需要螺纹紧固而不能攻螺孔的薄板构件，将带螺孔的塞形件焊于板件事先钻好的孔中，以形成螺孔，多用于车身等不易从两面紧固的构件）

weld yoke （万向节）焊接叉

welfare vehicle （备有轮椅等设备，车内设计考虑老弱病残人士需要并可保证高速、安全、舒适运送上述人士的）福利车

well ①井（油井，水井，矿井）②穴，凹室，凹腔③井状结构

well-appointed 配备齐全的，设备完善的

well-base rim 槽底式轮辋（指轮辋底部有足够深度和宽度的凹槽，以便于轮胎跨过轮辋的轮缘或胎圈座进行拆装，包括深槽轮辋"drop center rim"，深槽宽轮辋"wide drop center rim"和半深槽轮辋"semi-drop center rim"等）

well-base tire 用于槽底式轮辋的轮胎

well car 凹形车身大型载货汽车（亦称 depressed centre car）

well-conditioned 条件较好的，情况良好的

well-distributed 均匀分布的，分布良好的

well-equipped 装备良好的

well-floor ①凹形底板的（车身等）②（车身的）凹地板

well maintenance vehicle 修井车（装备有动力输出装置、减速装置、远距离操纵控制系统和伸缩式井架，用于不同油、水、气井维修的专用汽车）

well-oversquare engine 超方形发动机（指缸径大于活塞行程的扁形发动机）

well-rounded 良好过渡圆角的（曲线）

well-worn 严重磨损的

welt ①贴边，镶边 ②（车身蒙皮）盖缝的镶条，衬板

welted edge ①搭接缝，搭接边 ②贴边，翻边，折边

W-engine W 形内燃机（具有三列汽缸，其中心线呈 W 形）

west ①西，西方，西部（简称 W）②西方的，在西方；西的

Westing (house) -arc welding [美] 西屋电弧焊（惰性气体保护金属极电弧焊）

Weston cell 韦斯顿电池（一种恒定端电压的汞、镉原电池）

Weston photronic cell 韦斯顿光电管

West type motor 韦斯特式液压马达

wet ①潮湿，湿气 ②湿的，潮湿的

wetability ①可湿性，湿润性 ②表面保护润滑油的能力

wet and dry-bulb thermometer 干湿球温度计

wet basis emission concentration 湿基排放浓度（发动机排出的 CO、HC 和 NO_x 气体的体积占排气总体积的百万分数）

wet-bulb temperature 湿球温度（指在感温部分用湿布卷包的湿球温度计测出的温度）

wet-chemical etching 湿化学刻蚀，湿化学腐蚀

wet cleaner 湿式滤清器（指油浴湿式空气滤清器）

wet clutch 湿式离合器（亦称油浴式离合器"oil immersed clutch"）

wet combustion chamber 湿式燃烧室，喷水燃烧室，液态排渣式燃烧室（= wet chamber）

wet corrosion 潮湿腐蚀，水浸腐蚀

wet disc brake 湿式盘式制动器（油浸型盘式制动器）

wet fouling （火花塞）油污

wet friction 液体摩擦

wet grip （轮胎的）湿路面抓着力（指轮胎与湿路面间的附着力）

wet hub rotor （转子发动机）湿毂式转子（湿毂式旋转活塞，其毂部直接抵住端盖，起轴向推力轴承作用，限制转子轴向窜动，而且有封油作用，以减轻转子油封负荷，转子毂部在转子油封圈内，充满滑油）

wet liner 湿式汽缸套（美称 wet sleeve，严格说，它并不是缸套，而是仅上、下端由缸体支撑的薄壁硬金属汽缸筒，其中部直接与冷却水接触，故名）

wet loss 湿损失（气动件受到压缩气中的水滴作用而造成的损失）

wet mixture 湿混合气（带有液态燃油的混合气）

wet natural gas 湿天然气（饱含液态燃料蒸气的天然气）

wet -proof 防湿的，防潮的

wets 潮地用赛车轮胎（俚称）

wet sleeve 湿式缸套（见 wet liner）

wet solenoid （液压系统的）湿式电磁阀（其衔铁和极板位于液压通路内同时起阀杆和阀门的作用，直接开启和关闭通路的出、入口，而电磁线圈和电路则位于液压通路之外）

wet steam 湿蒸气

wet storage battery 湿蓄电池（带电解液的）

wet-sump engine 湿油底壳式发动机（相对于干底壳发动机而言，油底壳润滑式发动机）

wet sump lubrication 湿油底壳润滑（润滑油储存在油底壳内的发动机润滑形式）

wet tank 油-水箱（气制动系中存储从压缩空气中排除的水和油的容器）

wetted area ①受577面积，液浸面积 ②（液冷系统中）液流经过的面积，冷却液所及的面积 ③（水陆两用车）入水面积

wetted surface （水陆两用车）入水表面

wetting power 湿润能力，浸润力

wetting property （油膜等的）防湿性能（防潮性）

wet-tire traction 轮胎在潮湿路面上的牵引力

wet traction test 潮湿路面的牵引试验（轮胎和潮湿路面的附着力试验）

wet-type cleaner 湿式空气滤清器（油浴式空气滤清器，= oil-bath air cleaner）

wet vapor 湿（蒸）气

wet weather 潮湿气候

wet weight （车辆）湿重（加满燃油、冷却水、润滑油、工作液的车辆自重）

WEVA 世界电动车联合会（the World Electric Vehicle Association 的简称）

W-fold ①W 形折叠的 ②W 形折

WFSW 世界科学工作者协会（World Federation of Scientific Workers 的简称）

W G ①（研究或从事某一项目的）工作组（work group 的简称）②见 water gag（u）ge

Wh 瓦（特小）时（watt-hour）

whack 猛击，重击

whale tail 大包尾（俚，指装在汽车

尾部的大型导流板）

Wheatstone bridge 惠斯登电桥（由四个电阻 R_1、R_2、R_3、R_X 连成的四边形电桥，其中 R_X 为待测电阻，R_{1-3} 为已知可调电阻，利用电桥平衡条件，可准确地测量 R_X 的电阻值）

wheel 轮（齿轮，飞轮，车轮，叶轮，滚轮，砂轮转向盘等轮形物）

60 wheel 60 轮胎（指其扁平率为 60 的轮胎，见 aspect ratio）

4 wheel ABS 见 4 wheel Antilock Brake System

wheel aligner ①车轮校正器②车轮定位器

wheel aligner templet 前轮定位角样板

wheel alignment ①车轮校正，（一般指）前轮校正②车轮定位（以往一般指前轮定位，目前，已发展为全轮定位）

wheel alignment gauge 车轮定位仪（wheel alignment indicator 车轮定位测试仪，一般指转向轮定位指示仪，wheel alignment tester 车轮定位试验台）

wheel and axle press 车轮压装机（将车轮压装到车轴上用的液压机等）

4 wheel Antilock Brake System （丰田公司的）四轮防抱死制动系统（的商品名，简称 4 wheel ABS）

wheel arch ①轮口（车身裙部供车轮安装与转动的区域，即车身侧面供车轮装卸与转向回旋的开口，= wheel opening, wheel house, wheel well, wheel cutout）②车轮拱板，车轮拱罩（指车身底板为容纳车轮而拱起的挡泥部分）

wheel-arch area （客车车身地板下，避免妨碍车轮旋转的）车轮拱形结构区（车身地板越低，地板向上拱起的区域就越大）

wheel arch panel （轿车车身的）车轮罩板，车轮拱板

wheel arch screen （轿车车身）后轮口挡板

wheel axis 车轮轴线

wheel axis system 车轮坐标系（亦称车轮固定位标系，见 wheel-fixed axis system）

wheel balancer 车轮平衡机（= wheel demonstrator，车轮动、静平衡试验机的通称）

wheel balance weight 车轮平衡配重

wheel base ①（车辆的）轴距（亦写作 wheelbase，= wheel space，指同一侧相邻两车轮中心间的距离。三轴以上的车辆的总轴距为各轴距之和）②（车辆的）车轮接地面积（车轮轮胎触地点围起的面积）

wheel base angle （梯形转向机构车辆转向瞬心处）轴距弦张角

wheel bearing washer and packer 轮毂轴承清洗和润滑机

wheel bore 轮毂孔

wheel boss 轮毂，轮心

wheel bouncing 车轮（在不平道路上的）跳动

wheel-braking cylinder 制动器轮缸，制动轮泵（= wheel cylinder）

wheel camber ①车轮外倾②车轮外倾角（见 camber）

wheel-camber-and-castor tester 前轮外倾和转向主销后倾角测定仪

wheel cap ①车轮罩（= wheel cover）②轮毂盖（= wheel hub cap）

wheel caster （转向轮的）主销纵倾（一般指①主销后倾②主销后倾角，见 caster）

wheel center 车轮中心（车轮中心平面与车轮旋转中心线的交点）

wheel center cap 车轮中心罩

wheel center distance ①轮距（左右车轮中心距）②轴距（同侧两车轮中心距）

wheel center plane 车轮中心平面（单式车轮：指与车轮轮辋两侧内边缘等距的平面；双式车轮：与外车轮轮辋内缘和内车轮轮外缘等距的平面）

wheel chair lift van 带（残疾人）轮椅举起装置的箱式车身

wheel changing 更换车轮（指用好车轮更换损坏的车轮，勿与 wheel rotation 混淆）

wheel chock 车轮垫木（阻止车辆溜坡用的三角楔木）

wheel clamp （锁住违章停放车辆的）车轮锁夹（美亦称 Denver boot，简称 boot）

wheel clearance 轮胎间隙（一般指双轮并装时轮胎与轮胎的间隙，有时指车胎与车架、轮胎与车身之间的间隙）

wheel contact stress 车轮触地应力

wheel cover ①（叶子板外侧半圆形）车轮护盖②车轮装饰盖（装在轮毂上，= wheel cap）

wheel cowl 车轮罩

wheel crane 轮式起重机（= auto crane，truck crane）

wheel cutout （车身的）轮口（见 wheel arch）

wheel cylinder 轮缸（车轮制动缸，将制动主缸产生的液压，转换成推动制动蹄的作用力的部件）

wheel cylinder bleeder screw （制动）轮缸放气螺塞

wheel cylinder brake 轮缸式制动器（利用轮缸活塞推动制动蹄张开和紧压到旋转件上而产生制动作用的摩擦式制动器）

wheel cylinder clamp （维修时使用的）轮缸夹具，（修理制动分泵时用于分泵定位的）分泵夹

wheel cylinder pressure sensor 制动轮缸（输入）液压传感器

wheel demonstrator 车轮平衡试验机（= wheel balancer）

wheel disc rim embellisher 车轮装饰罩（装饰轮辋的罩壳）

wheel disk 车轮辐板（车轮轮毂与轮辋之间的板状轮辐）

wheel drawer 车轮拆卸器（= wheel puller）

wheeled military vehicle 轮式军用车辆（= military wheeled vehicle）

wheeled mobile robot 轮式移动机器人

wheeled-skidder 轮式雪橇（一种轮式木材搬动车）

wheeled tractor 轮式拖拉机，轮式牵引车（= wheel-type tractor）

wheel felloe 轮辋（亦称 wheel felly，= wheel rim）

wheel fender 翼子板（遮盖车轮的板件，亦 wing）

wheel (field) dynamic balancer （就车式）车轮动平衡仪[= wheel (field) balancing equipment]

wheel fight （作用在转向车轮上的力引起的）转向盘摆振

wheel-fixed axis system 车轮固定坐标系（x_w, y_w, z_w）（以车轮中心为原点的右手直角坐标系。x_w 轴和 z_w 轴在车轮中心平面内，x_w 轴水平向前，y_w 轴为车轮旋转轴。转向角为 x_0 和 x_w 间的夹角，车轮外倾角为 z_0 和 z_w 间的夹角）

wheel flange 轮辋突缘

wheel flutter 转向轮（绕转向主销）的摆振（亦称 wheel wobble，通常，其频率大于车轮的旋转频率）

wheel-frame system 车轮-车架系

wheel free lift （可使车轮自由转动的）悬轮型举升装置

wheel front support arm 双臂式独立悬架的下控制臂（= lower control arm）

wheel gauge （左右）车轮轮胎内侧间距（决定车辆可安全通过的最小

桥面宽度等，=back gauge, gauge of tyres, distance between tyres）

wheel-ground orientation 车轮地面定位（一般指指向轮定位，指转向轮和转向节主销相对于地面的方位）

wheel guard height 轮罩高（与轮罩相切的 Z 平面至最近地板的垂直距离）

wheel hop 车轮垂直跳振（亦称 wheel patter）

wheel house ①（车身翼子板所包围的）轮口区②（有时指）内翼子板③轮口（见 wheel arch）

wheelhouse frame 车轮上方弯成弧拱的车架

wheel house panel （车身）轮口区护板（形状与轮口相近的钢板件，防止翼子板内表面受泥水沙石飞溅），车轮挡泥罩（起挡泥作用的车轮罩板）

wheel housing 轮罩（①货车驾驶室内车轮的挡泥罩②轿车起挡泥作用的车轮罩板）

wheel hub 轮毂（见 hub①）

wheel-hub drive 轮毂驱动（见 hub drive）

wheel hub drive by spur gears 直齿圆柱齿轮轮边驱动

wheel hub puller 轮毂拉器（=wheel puller）

wheel hub starting torque 车轮的起动转矩

wheelie bars （赛车的）防前轮抬升杆（装在车身后端带接地轮的支撑杆，防止猛加速时赛车前端过度抬离地面）

wheel imbalance 车轮不平衡

4 wheel independed hydraulic brake system 四轮独立液压制动系统（每一个车轮都有一条独立的制动管路，其中任一管路发生泄漏都只会影响一个车轮的制动）

4-wheel independent driving & steering system 四轮独立驱动和转向系统（四个车轮均装有一台独立的轮内电动机和转向执行器，因此每个车轮均可在电子控制系统操纵下独立回转和驱动，整车可原地回转 360°，并可左、右横向行驶）

wheel information transmitter （汽车的）车轮信息发送器（将车轮气压等信息发射到驾驶室内的接收器。如：当胎压超过危险极限，即由接收装置发出危险信号）

wheel judder 前轮左右快速摆振（=shimmy）

wheeless vehicle 无轮汽车（气垫车等）

wheel lift 车轮抬升（在离心力作用下，汽车转向时一侧前轮或后轮抬离路面的现象）

wheel load ①车轮载荷（指车轮所承载的车重）②（地面承受的）车轮载重

wheel load distribution 车轮的负荷分配

wheel loader 轮式装载机（参见 loader）

wheel lock ①车轮抱死（=wheel lock-up，指制动力大于车轮与路面附着力时产生的车轮被刹死，不再转动的现象。在制动过程中，车轮抱死的结果常常是车轮打滑）②车轮（防盗）锁

wheel lock coefficient 车轮抱死系数，车轮抱死率（简称 WLC）

wheel lug 车轮的轮毂螺栓（亦称 lug bolt）

wheelmark eradicator 轮迹消除器

wheel marking 车轮（轮辐上表示制造厂商标、编号、轮辋尺寸、生产日期等的）标志

wheel motor ①（大型车辆电动车轮内安装的）车轮电动机（亦称 wheel-in motor）②车轮马达（装在

车轮毂内直接驱动车轮的液力马达、气力马达等的通称)

wheel-mounted front-end loader 轮式前端装载机

wheel-mounted paddle 装在转向盘上的(换挡等的)拨杆

wheel-mounted paddles (装在)转向盘(上的)换挡拨杆

wheel movement-laden to bump (悬架)受压时的车轮运动

wheel movement-laden to rebump (悬架)回跳时的车轮运动

wheel nave 车轮轮毂

wheel nut 车轮螺母(美称 lug nut)

wheel nut spanner 车轮螺母扳手(= wheel nut wrench)

wheel nut spider 车轮螺母的十字形四头套筒扳手

wheel offset 车轮偏置距(轮辋中心面与轮毂装配面间的距离)

wheel opening flare (车身裙部的)轮口外接板(亦称 wheel arch extension,其密封垫条称 wheel opening flare pad 或 wheel arch extension seal)

wheel orientation 车轮定位(一般指前轮定位,= wheel alignment)

wheel panel (翼子板内围绕轮口的)轮口薄板

wheel path 车轮轨迹,轮辙

wheel patter 车轮垂直跳动(亦称 wheel hop)

wheel plane 车轮(垂直于其旋转轴的)中心平面

wheel puller 车轮拆卸器

wheel pump propulsion system (水陆两用车等的)车轮泵推进系统

wheel rate 轮胎刚度(= 载质量/压缩量,kg/mm)

wheel reduction cylindrical pinion 轮边减速器(主动)小圆柱齿轮

wheel reduction gear ①轮边减速器(将原中央主减速器的第二级圆柱齿轮分置于左、右车轮两侧的减速装置,可得到更大的减速比,= wheel reductor,亦称 hub reductor)②(轮边减速器的)减速齿轮(指由小齿轮驱动的从动大齿轮)

wheel rib 轮辐

wheel rim 轮辋(车轮上支撑和安装轮胎的部件,简称 rim)

wheel rotation 见 tyre rotation

wheel runout (车轮或轮胎失圆造成的)车轮径向跳动

wheel scotch 车轮的三角垫木(= wheel chock)

wheel scraper 轮式铲运机(轮式刮土机)

wheel sensor 车轮转数传感器(用于导航系统根据转数确定冲程,根据各车轮的转数差确定行驶方向)

wheel shaft 半轴(参见 differential axle)

wheel shield 车轮挡板,车轮护板

wheel shimmy (由于不平衡等原因引起的)车轮低振幅机械振动(简称 shimmy),前轮摆振(简称 shimmy,亦称 wheel shudder, wheel judder)

wheel side rim with lock ring 轮辋边圈带锁环

wheel sinkage 车轮下陷

wheel slip ①车轮滑移(指车轮制动力大于胎面与路面间的附着力时产生的胎面与路面间的相对滑移。此时,车速 v > 车轮圆周线速度 rw,亦称 wheel skid, wheel slide)②车轮滑转(见 wheel spin)③车轮滑移率(见 slip⑥)

wheel slip angle 车轮侧偏角(见 side-slip angle, wheel slip)

wheel slip brake control system 车轮防滑制动系(= anti-lock braking system 车轮防抱死控制系)

wheel slip tester ①轮胎滑移(率)测定装置②轮胎侧向偏移测定装置

wheels-locked testing 车轮抱死试验

wheel space （汽车）轴距（见 wheel base）

wheel spacer 轮距调节垫圈，轮距调节套

wheel spacing ①并装双胎间距②（汽车）轮距（=wheel span）

wheel speed sensor 车轮转速传感器

wheel spider 车轮轮辐

wheel spin 车轮滑转（指车轮驱动力大于胎面与路面间的附着力时产生的胎面相对于路面的滑转，有的文献亦称 wheel slip。此时，车速 $v<$ 车轮圆周线速度 rw）

wheel spindle （转向节上安装前轮的）轮轴（见 knuckle spindle）

wheel spinner （动平衡用的）车轮旋转装置

wheel splash guard 车轮挡泥板

wheel spoke 轮辐

wheels spin sinkage 车轮滑转沉陷

wheel steering 车轮转向

wheel stroke 车轮上、下活动距离（指独立悬架车轮的最大上、下活动量）

wheel support 备轮支架（备胎支架）

wheel suspension travel （悬架装置允许的）车轮的上、下振幅

wheel swarf 轮胎磨屑

wheel-tire tractor 轮（胎）式牵引车，轮式拖拉机

wheel torque meter 车轮转矩仪（装在汽车驱动轮上，测量行驶中传递给车轮的转矩）

wheel trace 车轮运动轨迹

wheel track ①轮距②轮迹，轮辙

wheel tramp 车轮径向跳动（亦称 wheel radial run-out）

wheel tramping 车轮的角振动

wheel transducer （汽车试验设备中的）车轮传感器（一般指将车轮的转速，转向角，倾向角，横偏角，横向位移，加、减速度转变为电信号输出的传感装置）

wheel-tread ①轮（辙）距②轮胎面花纹

wheel tree 车轮（专用树状）支架（长期存放车辆用）

wheel trim ①（汽车车轮上的）车轮装饰件②（轮毂上粘贴的塑料制）商标（亦称 wheel trim emblem）

wheel tub （车身地板轮口上方的）车轮凸区

wheel turn adjusting screw 车轮最大转向角调整螺钉

wheel turning angle 车轮转向角

wheel type 车轮形式（一般指轮辐形式）

wheel (type) tractor 轮式牵引车（=wheeled tractor）

wheel weight ①车轮载重②车轮自重③车轮总重

wheel weight tool 车轮平衡作业用工具

wheel well ①轮口（见 wheel arch①）②轮辋凹区（轮辋两侧轮缘间的区域，包括轮辋的胎圈座、胎圈座圆角和轮圈槽底等）

wheel with drop center rim 装有深（凹）式轮辋的车轮

wheel wobble ①（由于不平衡或定位不当引起的）车轮（绕主销与旋转频率相同的）摆振②转向轮（绕主销的）自激摆振（产生时无明显地跳动）

wheel wrench 胎轮螺母扳手

whim 绞车，绞盘，卷扬机

whip ①搅动，搅起泡沫②上下（或左右）的急速抖动③（张紧的绳索，高速旋转的轴等的）横向颤振

whip aerial 鞭状天线

whip lash ①头-颈碰伤（特指汽车碰撞事故中，由于颈部受到强烈弯曲、拉扯，头部前后碰撞所造成的颈脊骨伤害和脑震荡）②（引起上述碰伤的）头部突然的前、后运动

whiplash injury lessening seat （碰撞中）乘员颈部伤害减轻座椅（简称 WIL seat）

whipping ①抖动，甩动，拍打②（传动带，绳索，传动轴等的）弦振（见 whirling）

whipping of the cardan shaft 十字轴万向节传动轴的拍振

WHIPS （Volvo 的）颈部碰伤防护系统（whiplash protection system 的简称，当车辆受到来自后方的激烈碰撞时，座位的靠背和头枕可紧随座位上的乘员身体一起移动，而避免乘员颈部受伤）

whirl chamber 涡流室（= vortex chamber, whirl pool chamber）

whirling ①涡流，涡流运动，涡旋②涡流的③（传动轴，曲轴等长轴高速旋转时，共振引起的）弦振（如：乐器中的琴弦振动模式，来回振颤，美称 whipping）

whirling current 涡流

whirling flywheel 端面偏摆的飞轮

whirling motion 涡（流运）动（= eddy motion）

whirling needle 剧烈摆动的指针

whirling speed ①涡流速度，旋动速度②弦振转速（长轴产生弦振时的转速，见 whirling③）

whirlpool chamber 涡流燃烧室（= whirl chamber）

whirl vane 旋流叶片（见 prewhirl vane）

whirl velocity 涡流速度

whisk broom （汽车坐垫）清扫刷

whistle 汽笛；哨声

whistle signal 哨音信号

white ①白色②白色的

white alloy 白色合金，假银

white assembly 白色总成（原色总成，未上漆及修饰加工的总成）

white cast iron 白口铸铁

white design （车身等的）造型及结构设计

white gold 白金（铂）色（车身颜色）

white-heart malleable iron 白心可锻铸铁

white LED technology 白色发光二极管技术（其中 LED 为 light-emitting diode 的简称）

white line 车身装配线（指车身上漆以前的装配线）

white lithium grease 白色锂基润滑脂

white metal ①铅基或锡基减摩合金的通称（= antifriction metal, bearing metal，如：Babbitt metal）②白色合金的通称（如：锡铅合金等）③白（冰）铜，铜锍（含 Cu 80%，S 20%，完全不含 Fe，= copper matte）

white noise 白色噪音（白噪音，指在足够宽的任意频带内，具有大体相等谱值的噪音）

white noise generator 白噪音发生器

white pig iron 白口（生）铁，白铸铁

white room （高标准实验室等的）绝尘室

white rust 白色蚀痕（锌板件上的松孔状氧化痕）

white-side tire 白色胎壁轮胎（= white-wall tire, white sidewall tire）

white smoke 白烟（指发动机排气流中，由凝结的水蒸气、未燃烧的液态燃油和润滑油的微滴所组成的烟雾，参见 black smoke）

white tin 白锡

white wall ring （车轮的）卡装式胎侧装饰性白环（卡装在轮胎与轮辋之间的白色橡胶宽环或窄环，以造成白色胎侧效果，亦称 white wall topper）

whitewall tyre 白色胎侧式轮胎

Whitworth gauge 惠氏螺纹规

Whitworth quick return motion 惠

氏急回转运动
Whitworth（standard）screw thread 惠氏标准螺纹（英制，55°牙形角螺纹，代号 W，= Whit thread）
WHO （联合国）国际卫生组织（World Health Organization）
whole-body human surrogate （汽车试验用）全躯体假人（整身体模拟人）
whole body response （汽车碰撞试验时人体的）全身体反应（全躯反应，简称 WBR）
whole body vibration （人体）全身振动（通过地板、座椅传给整个人体的振动）
whole gale 狂风（十级风，风速 $24.5 \sim 28.4$ m/s，= storm）
whole number 整数
whole of life 全部寿命（寿命期，简称 WOL）
whole performance map （发动机的）万有特性图（见 performance map）
whole rim 整体式轮辋
whole solution through filtering 全液过滤（过滤全部混浊液的方法）
whole wheel driven truck 全轮驱动式载货汽车
WI [英] 焊接学会（the Welding Institute）
wick（-feed）lubrication 油绳供油润滑（法），油绳润滑
wicking ①（油绳润滑中的）油绳吸油 ②灯芯现象（如：线路某处触腐蚀物质后，该物质被吸至整个线路）
Wickman gauge 威氏螺纹规（凹口螺纹量规）
wide ①宽的，宽阔的，广泛的，广大的 ②充分张开的，开得很大的
wide-angle joint 大偏角万向节
wide area network 广域网（见 WAN）

wide base drop center rim 深式宽底轮辋（简称 WDCR，= wide base drop well rim）
wide-base removable rim 宽底可拆式轮辋
wide base tyre 宽基轮胎（轮辋宽度与轮胎断面宽度比约为 0.80 以上的工程机械轮胎）
wide-beam（head）lamp 宽光前照灯（= broad-beam headlamp, widespread light）
wide-boiling cut 宽馏分（宽沸点馏分，指沸点在某一较宽范围的馏分）
wide-center axles 宽轴距车桥
wide cross-section tire 宽断面轮胎（宽体轮胎，宽胎，断面比普通轮胎宽 $0.5 \sim 1$ 倍的轮胎，亦称 wide section tire）
wide-cut gasoline 宽馏分汽油
wide fender （50 或 60cm 以上的）宽挡泥板
wide flange beam 宽缘工字梁
wide frequency band 宽频带（宽的频率范围）
wide front bumper 大包围前保险杠
wide gate 宽门电路（宽选择脉冲）
wide inner ring bearing 宽内圈滚动轴承
wide line （车身）宽度线
wide meter 宽刻度表（宽量程仪表）
wide-open throttle [美] 节气门全开（简称 WOT，= full throttle）
wide-open throttle acceleration 节气门全开加速度
wide-open throttle A/C cut-off relay 节气门全开（时）空调停开继电器（节气门全开时，该继电器断开，空调停止运转）
wide-open throttle kick-down valve （自动变速器液力控制系的）节气门全开强制换挡阀（参见 shift overcontrol valve）

wide-range 大量程，宽量程，宽波段；大范围

wide-range A/F sensor 宽程型空燃比传感器（可同时供 λ = 1 的理论空燃比混合气和 λ > 1 的稀混合气闭路控制系统用的氧传感器，分为 single cell type "单氧浓度电池型"和 dual-cell type "双氧浓度电池型"两种，亦写作 wide-range air-fuel ratio sensor）

wide-range ohmmeter 大量程欧姆表，宽量程电阻表

wide-range plug 通用火花塞（泛用火花塞，指高、低负荷发动机都适用的火花塞）

wide rim wheel 宽轮辋车轮

wide scope 宽频带示波器

wide-tread ①宽轮距的②宽胎面的

wide treads 宽胎（亦称 wide oval, wide tire，指高/宽 ≥ 70% 的宽轮胎）

wide-type 4×4 radial mud tire 四轮驱动宽型泥泞地用子午胎

wide variety of operating condition 各种各样的使用条件；使用条件的多样性

wide-zone toughened windshield 宽视野钢化风窗玻璃

widia ［德］钨系硬质合金（碳化钨硬质合金）

width 宽度

width angle 齿宽角（涡轮齿宽所对应的蜗杆圆心角）

width between centers 中心距

width indicator ①（车身）宽度指示灯②宽度标志

width lamp 示宽灯

width of gather 前束宽度（= width of toe-in）

width regulations 载货汽车宽度法规（限制车身和所运货物最大宽度的规定）

Wi-Fi （基于 IEEE802.11b 标准的）无线局域网（Local Wireless Fidelity 的简称）

WIFsensor 油中含水量传感器（water in fuel sensor 的简称，= water in fuel detector）

wiggle 摆动，摇晃

wigwag motion 左右摆动（如：风窗刮水器的运动）

wigwag signal 摇摆式信号（如：灯光或旗语信号）

wildhaber-worm 平面包络环面蜗杆（以直齿或斜齿的平面涡轮为铲形轮展成的环面蜗杆，亦称 TP-worm "TP 蜗杆"）

wildhaber-worm wheel 平面涡轮（亦称 TP-worm wheel，一个齿形状为平面的齿轮，它与环面蜗杆啮合而组成交错轴齿轮副时，就称为平面涡轮。平面涡轮的齿面可以与轮轴线平行或不平行。齿面与轴线平行的平面涡轮称直齿平面涡轮齿面与轴线不平行的平面涡轮称斜齿平面涡轮），

wild ping 激烈的爆震声

Willian's line method 威廉测试法（以发明人名命名的一种柴油机无负荷运转时的机械损失的测试方法）

Willot's transportation plan 威里奥特变位图（用图解法求平面桁架的变形，即各节点的变位）

Will's lock-nut 卫氏锁紧螺母（一种带有切口的防松螺母）

wills ring 金属 O 形密封环（= metal O-ring seal）

WIL seat 见 whiplash injury lessening seat

Wilson gearbox 威尔逊变速器（以发明人，英 W. G. Wilson 命名的预选挡位式行星齿轮变速器，用于客车）

WIM 动态称量（见 weight-in-motion）

Wim scale 动态称（动态称重器）

winch ①绞盘，绞车，卷扬机②用绞盘提升，用卷扬机拉动

Winchester bushel 温且斯特蒲式耳（英制容积单位，用以衡量干物，等于内径 $18\frac{1}{2}$in、深 8in 的缸的容积，等于 $2150.42in^3$，同美国 bushel，见 bushel）

winch truck ①带自救用绞盘的越野汽车②绞盘工程车

wind 风

windage ①风阻（空气阻力）②风偏（汽车方向因风而产生的偏移）③（汽车高速行驶引起的）气流，车风④风力影响，风力修正量

windage losses （汽车行驶的）空气阻力损失，风阻损失

wind ahead 逆风（迎面风，顶头风）

wind area 迎风面积（受风面积，挡风面积，风阻面积）

wind calculator 风速计算器（风速仪）

wind catcher 集风口

wind channel 风洞

wind circulation 空气循环

wind component 风的分力

wind cord 车身接缝密封嵌线

wind cowl 通风罩，通风帽

wind deflector （装在驾驶室顶前方、减小空气阻力的）导风板

wind deflector 导流罩（安装在货车或拖车驾驶室顶盖的整流装置。主要是为了改善撞在拖车前围上的气流特性，以减小阻力）

wind demister 风窗去雾装置

wind direction 风向

wind-down 见 axle wind down

winder front 散热器罩（= radiator cover）

wind flutter （汽车行驶时）风致颤振噪声（= wind throb）

wind force 风力

wind-gauge 风速表（风力计，风压计）

windheaded bolt 蝶形头螺钉（元宝螺钉，= flyheaded screw）

wind indicator 风向标（风标，风向指示器，亦称 weather vane）

winding ①绕组，线圈②卷缠，缠绕，绕法③（用绞车）卷起，提升④缠绕的，曲折的，弯弯曲曲的

winding machine 卷（绕）线机

winding pitch 绕组节距

winding road 曲折盘旋弯道

winding road sign 连续弯道标志（连续五个以上弯道的警告标志）

wind-lace （车身接缝）密封嵌线（密封嵌条）

wind load 风载荷（空气阻力）

wind noise （汽车行驶时产生的）风笛噪音（闭窗时，由窗框边的小缝隙漏入车内空气而在车内听到的噪声，以及开窗时，由于车外突出物产生空气涡流而在车内听到的噪音，其声如吹笛）

window ①窗（窗口，窗孔）②（催化剂的）高效带（在理论空燃比附近，三效催化剂能高效发挥功能的一段狭窄的空燃比范围）

window amplifier "窗"放大器（上下限幅放大器）

window aperture （车身）窗洞

window arch 窗的拱弧

window channel(ing) ①车窗玻璃密封条②车窗玻璃密封槽，车窗玻璃（滑动）槽（美称 glass channel）

window cleaner 车窗玻璃清扫器（如：风窗玻璃刮水器）

window control 车窗控制（指窗玻璃升降，车窗开闭）

window defroster 风窗玻璃防霜冻装置（窗玻璃去霜器，窗玻璃热风防霜装置）

window frame 窗框（亦称 window

border)
window gasket 车窗密封条
window-glass channel 车窗玻璃槽
window lift 车窗玻璃升降机构（= window regulator）
window lift motor 门窗电动机（驱动门窗升降机构的电动机）
window line （车身的）腰线（= waistline）
window pillar 窗立柱
window rail seal 车窗玻璃升降槽密封条
window recess 车窗凹距（指凹入车身外表面的车窗与车身外表面间的距离，亦称 window reveal）
window regulator 玻璃升降器（操纵窗玻璃升降的机构，亦称 window lifter）
window sill 窗台梁（窗框底梁，窗槛）
window type air conditioner 窗式空调器
window van 有窗厢式车身
window ventilator 车窗通风装置
window visor 遮阳板（= sun visor）
wind pressure 风压（与风速平方成正比）
wind pressure meter 风压计（测定气流对车身压力及其与车辆行驶方向的夹角）
wind protection 防风（工作），防风措施
wind resistance 风阻力，风阻
wind rush noise （汽车的）风窗噪音（风通过风窗栅柱区时产生的噪音）
wind-screen 风窗玻璃（美称 windshield，指汽车正前方前围上的挡风窗玻璃，亦写作 windscreen）
windscreen aperture 风窗玻璃窗洞
windscreen corner panel 风窗玻璃角板
windscreen electric heater tell-tale 风窗电加热器信号灯（表示前风窗电加热器已接通的信号灯）
windscreen header (panel) 风窗玻璃框上方的车顶骨架的加强板（呈箱形，或双层板）
wind-screen pillar ①（货车驾驶室、轿车车身的）前柱（指支撑顶盖，安装风窗玻璃与前门的立柱，见 A pillar）②（客车的）前围立柱（指前围骨架两侧起支撑顶盖及安装风窗玻璃的立柱，亦称 front wall pillar）
wind-screen rail （敞篷车身的）风窗篷条（= canopy rail）
windscreen washer control 风窗玻璃洗涤器操纵件（控制前风窗玻璃洗涤器工作的操纵件）
windscreen wash/wipe system 风窗玻璃冲洗/刮水系统
windscreen wiper 风窗玻璃刮水器（= windshield wiper，简称 wind wiper）
windscreen wiper motor 风窗玻璃刮水器电动机
windshield adjusting arm bracket 风窗开度调节臂支架
windshield angle 风窗玻璃（相对于水平或垂直面的）斜角（亦称 windshield inclination angle，相对于垂直面的斜角称 windshield rake）
windshield antidazzle glass 防炫光风窗玻璃（在夹层玻璃的一面镀有特殊胶膜，既能防止炫光又能保留驾驶员清晰视野的风窗玻璃）
windshield central bar 风窗中立柱（= windshield central post；亦称 windshield central post，风窗框架中部的支柱）
windshield cross sill 风窗框下横梁（风窗框架下部的横梁）
windshield defroster （汽车）风窗玻璃除霜器（= windshield heater）
windshield films （汽车）风窗玻璃

（上的）遮阳膜

windshield for rear seat 后风窗玻璃

windshield frame 风窗框架（供安装风窗玻璃用的框架）

windshield header crossbar 风窗框上横梁（风窗框架上部的横梁）

windshield heater 风窗玻璃加热装置（指风窗玻璃防霜装置，= windshield defroster）

windshield left adjusting arm 风窗玻璃刮水器左调节臂

windshield lower edge 风窗下缘（风窗玻璃下透光边缘）

windshield rake 风窗玻璃（相对于垂直面的）斜角

windshield regulator 风窗玻璃开度调整装置

windshield sill 风窗框底梁

windshield testing 汽车风窗玻璃试验（如：测定其强度、安全性、破碎时对乘员的划伤程度等）

windshield upper edge 风窗上缘（风窗玻璃上透光边缘）

windshield visor 风窗玻璃遮阳板

wind speed relative to ground or to vehicle 相对于地面或车辆的风速

wind spring 卷簧，发条

wind surface 迎风面

wind throb （汽车行驶时产生的）风颤振噪音（= wind flutter）

wind tone horn ①气动膜片式喇叭②螺旋形电喇叭（具有螺旋状扬声筒的电喇叭，亦称 shell type horn）

wind-tunnel reshaping test 风洞改形试验

wind tunnel test 风洞试验（利用风洞进行试验，用以评价汽车的空气动力特性）

wind-up degrees 扭转角的度数

wind-up of spring 钢板弹簧卷曲（见 spring wind-up）

wind-up torque 钢板弹簧扭曲力偶（由切线牵引力或制动力引起的作用在弹簧纵向平面的使钢板弹簧扭曲的力偶）

wind-up window （车窗玻璃可摇上摇下的）手摇升降车窗

wind vector 风（速）矢量

wind velocity 风速

wine gallon 液加仑（古时用以量酒，等于高 6in、直径为 7in 的圆柱体。美国用以量液体的加仑 US gallon，量酒液时，1 液加仑 = 6 reputed quarts）

wing ①翼，翼状物②（车身）翼子板，挡泥板（美称 fender）

wing body 翼形车身（①货车车身两侧栏板可翻起，如：翼状，装卸方便②轿车两侧门板向上翻起供乘员进出）

wing-headed bolt 蝶形头螺栓（= flyheaded screw）

wing lamp 翼子板灯（= mudguard lamp）

wingless oil pan 无侧边型机油盘

winglets （高速车辆，如：赛车等的）水平布置的小型导风板

wing mirror 装在翼子板上的后视镜（美称 side mirror）

wing nut 蝶形螺母（= butterfly nut, thumb nut）

wing pump 叶轮泵

wing stay 翼子板托架

winking lights ①（泛指各种）闪光信号灯②汽车转向信号灯（亦称 winker，= turn signal lamp, direction signal）

winking trafficator （汽车）闪光信号灯（一般指转向信号灯）

winter driving 冬季行车（冬季驾驶）

winter front 冬季用的散热器前方保温罩

winter grade gasoline 冬季汽油，冬季用汽油

winterization 准备过冬（提供防寒

设施,加装防寒装置,做冬季行车准备)

winterization kit (供汽车在)冬季(严寒条件下使用的成套)装备

winterized equipment 冬季防寒、防冻设备

winter maintenance 冬季维护(简称WM)

winter oil 冬季润滑油(低凝点润滑油)

winter package (汽车的)整套冬季装备

winter-proofing 防寒,防冻

winter red 冬季红(车身颜色)

winter salt (道路)防冰冻用盐

wip 工作在进行中(work in progress 的简称)

wipe 擦,拭,抹,揩

wipe contact type distributor 滑动接触点式分电器

wiped joint 拭接,热接,焊接,焊接点(=solder joint, brazed joint)

wipe-dry 擦干

wiper 擦拭物件、器具的装置的总称(如:汽车车窗玻璃或前照灯玻璃的刮水器)

wiper blade 刮水器片(windshield wiper blade 的简称)

wiper cam 刮水器凸轮(使刮水件产生摆动运动)

wiper compression ring 刮油式气环(带刮油槽的第二、三道压缩环)

wiper groove (活塞环外圆的)刮油槽

wiper of rubber 橡胶防尘圈(用于防止外界灰尘等污染物进入密封装置的橡胶密封圈)

wiper scraper seal 刮片式密封件

wiper-washer system 车窗及车灯玻璃等的)刮水冲洗系统

wire ①金属丝②导线,电线③金属丝制品,金属丝网④布线,架线,敷设导线

wire bead core (胎圈)钢丝芯

wire bonding 引线键合(为了使细金属丝与芯片上规定的金属化区域或底座上规定的区域形成欧姆接触,而对它们施加应力的过程)

wire bridge (公路上的)钢索桥(悬索桥,铁索桥,吊桥,=suspension bridge)

wire cable 钢索(钢丝绳)

wire conduit 电线导管,电缆管道(=wire duct)

wire connection (电)线接头

wire-cutter 剪丝钳(=wire cutting pliers)

wire filter cloth 金属丝滤布

wire fuse 熔断丝

wire gauge 线规

wire gauge number (车用)电线标号(指美国 SAE 规定电线尺寸、电阻值等的标号)

wire gauge size (车用)电线标准尺寸(SAE 用英寸表示,公制用 mm 表示)

wire gauze filter (金属)丝网滤清器(金属丝滤网)

wire glass 嵌丝玻璃(一种安全防碎玻璃,亦称 wired glass)

wire glow plug (裸露)电热丝型预热塞

wire guard 钢丝护网

wire guide (操纵)索导向装置(如:拉索导管)

wire inserted asbestos yarn 加金属丝的石棉线

wire-laying vehicle 电缆敷设车辆(=cable-laying vehicle)

wireless ①无线的②无线电,无线电报

wireless area network 无线局域网

wireless car 带无线电装置的汽车

wireless charging system (电动汽车的)无线充电系统[亦称非接触充电系统(non-contact charging system），如：将电动汽车停在地面下设有无线电源的场地上，无须接线即可充电的系统］

wireless door lock 遥控门锁

wireless energy source （为电动汽车无线充电系统提供电源的）无线电源

wireless fixing 无线电定位（= radio fixing）

wireless guidance system （汽车的）无线导向系统（指靠外部无线电信息的导行系统，包括 GPS 和固定电台导行系统"fixed radio station guidance system"）

wireless local area network system （实现车内通信与信息传递的）无线局域网系统

wireless proximity sensor 无线式临近传感器（该传感器可将两车已临近的信息"我已在你跟前"通过无线电彼此传送给对方车辆防碰撞系统的电子控制模块）

wireless ream-time data collection 无线实时数据收集

wireless telematics system （IBM 公司最新研制的）无线电通信与信息系统（这一系统已用于生产厂家与货运车辆及车队之间的车辆运行状况、车辆实时位置、车辆维修资料及维修指导、卫星导航、车辆临修警告、车辆性能监测、车辆各系统及附件远程监测以及车辆故障远程诊断等的声响和图像通信）

wireless telephonic communication 无线电话通信

wireless transmitter 无线信号发射器

wireline networks 有线网络

wire mesh ①金属丝网②（特指在使用整体式蜂窝状催化剂载体催化转化器中，用来作为蜂窝状载体的吸振支承件的）不锈钢丝编织网

wire nipple 导线接头

wire-resistance (strain) gauge 电阻丝应变仪

wire rope tester 钢丝绳检测仪（检查钢丝绳是否有断线、腐蚀、磨损等，亦称 wire cable tester）

wire solder 焊丝

wire spoke wheel 钢丝辐条车轮（= wire wheel①）

wire spring 钢丝弹簧

wire straightener 线材拉直机

wire strand （钢索、电缆等的）股

wire stripper 导线剥皮器（可剥去各种规格导线绝缘皮而不损伤导线本身）

wire tape 钢丝带

wire terminal 接线柱

wire truck 电缆敷设车（= reel truck）

wire type tire 金属丝帘布层轮胎（= metal-cord tire）

wire wheel ①钢丝辐条式车轮（= wire spoke wheel）②钢丝轮刷（轮子周围装有钢丝，用以清洁钢铁制品等）

wire-wound piston 周围嵌缠钢丝的活塞（防止热膨胀）

wiring arrangement （电）线路布置

wiring diagram （电气）线路图（布线图，电路图，= diagram of wiring）

wiring harness ①铠装线束（装在一个保护套管内的多条成束的导线，以便于作为一个整件安装，亦称 wiring loom）②导线束（指由一组导线及其接头件和其他有关附件，如：熔断丝、过载自动断路器等电路保护件，以及护罩、线夹等外包装保护件组成一体的所要求长度导线束件）③电线束（带接头、插头或插座的多种电线组合在一起的接线部件）

wiring loom 导线的绝缘套管（见 wiring harness）

wiring pigtail （元器件的）导线抽头（由元器件电路中抽出的带接头的短引线）

wiring tube 电线（套）管

wishbone （独立悬架中横向布置的）A 形控制臂（亦称 wishbone arm，形状如鸟胸叉骨，故名，美称 A-arm，其单头端通过球节"ball joint"与转向节连接，其分叉的双头端通过衬套套装在承载式车身、车架或前桥梁上的支撑轴的两端，形成可绕该轴转动的两个枢轴"pivot"式接头，故 A 形控制臂亦称 double pivot control arm，双枢轴式横臂。注意，某些车辆只是上横臂"upper transverse control arm"使用 A 形控制臂，而下横臂"lower control arm"使用无分叉端的单枢轴式横臂"single pivot lower control arm"，而某些车辆则上、下横臂均使用 A 形控制臂，此时悬架称双 A 形控制臂式"double wishbone arm type"）

wishbone arm shaft A 形控制臂（分叉端的）枢轴

wishbone bushing A 形控制臂（分叉头的）衬套

wishbone shim A 形控制臂（分叉端的）垫片（用于调节叉形控制臂轴的位置，借以调节前轮定位）

wishbone-type independent suspension A 形控制臂式独立悬架（指上、下横臂或仅上横臂使用 A 形控制臂的双枢轴式横臂独立悬架，简称 wishbone suspension，亦称 double pivot control-arm type independent suspension）

WIT 最坏喷油正时（worst injection timing 的简称）

withdraw ①收起，收回，缩回②取出，抽出③撤销，取消

withdrawable 可抽出的；可收起的

withdrawal bearing （离合器中的）分离轴承（= clutch release bearing，美称 throwout bearing）

withdrawal fork （离合器的）分离叉（= throw-out fork, clutch fork，驱动分离轴承的叉形件）

withdrawal lever 分离操纵杆

withdrawal load 压配合中拔出、压入零件所需的力

withdrawal plate （某些离合器结构中使用的）分离盘（使压盘与从动盘分离的圆盘形件）

withdrawal tool 拉器（拆卸工具，亦称 withdrawer, = puller）

withdraw collar 离合器分离轴承推力环（= throw-out collar）

within reach 在可达到的范围内

without EGR 无废气再循环（见 EGR，简称 WO/EGR）

withstanding 耐……的

witness mark 零件的安装位置标记

witness test 有订货者在场的试验

WLC 车轮抱死系数（wheel lock coefficient）

W/m² 瓦/米²（国际单位制散热率单位，每平方米面积每秒散出 1J 的热量，见 watt）

W/（m·℃） 瓦/（米·度）（国际单位制的热传导系数单位，每米长度，每降低 1℃，每秒钟导出 1J 的热量，见 watt 及 thermal conductivity）

W/（m²·℃） 瓦/（米²·度）（国际单位制的散热系数单位，即每平方米的面积上，每降低 1℃，每秒钟散出 1J 的热量，见 watt）

WM 冬季技术维护（winter maintenance）

Wobbe index 鄂伯指数，鄂伯值（亦称 Wobbe number，表示可燃气体的发热量与其比重的关系，鄂伯值 K = 热值/$\sqrt{比重}$）

wobble ①摇摆，摇晃，摆动，晃动；颤振，颤动（= wabble，如：

轮缘一类的盘形件在旋转时横向摆动）②摆振（= shimmy）③不均匀的运动，不稳定运动④（陀螺仪）摆动⑤（声音）变量，变度

wobble plate pump 斜盘泵（泵芯是一个斜装在回转轴上的圆盘，多用于抽送重油等高黏度液体）

wobbler ①摇动器，摆动试验台②偏心轮，偏心装置摆动轮③（液压马达的）旋转斜盘（= wabbler，亦称 wobble plate，见 swash plate）

wobbler shaft 斜盘轴

wobble wheel 摆动轮

wobbling of wheels 车轮摆动

WOC 车重（weight of car 的简称）

WO/EGR 无废气再循环的（= without EGR）

WOF （某些国家汽车经安全检查后颁发的）合格证（Warrant of Fitness 的简称，亦简写成 WoF。它不同于这些国家的 pre-purchase inspection，只检查轮胎、制动、结构件、灯光、风窗玻璃、安全带、门窗、车速表、转向、悬架、排气系统及燃油系统是否符合安全标准）

WOG 水—油—气（water-oil-gas）

WOL 寿命期（whole of life）

wolfram ①钨（W, = tungsten）②钨锰铁矿

wolfram-carbide alloy 碳化钨合金

wood ①木材；木制品②木制的，木质的

 wood alcohol 木精（亦称 = wood spirit, 指甲醇"methanol"）

wooden 木质的，木制的

wooden base ①木底型，木底架②（车身黏土模型的）木模架，木模底，木模基

wooden car 木车身汽车

wooden fender 木质的（车身）翼子板（= wood wing）

wood filler （装在车厢与车架之间的）枕木

wood filler block 纵梁垫木（货箱纵梁与底盘车架间的垫木，亦称 main sill liner）

wood-grained 漆成木纹的，木纹的

wood handle ①木质旋柄②木质手柄

woodie （美俚）旅行车（见 shooting brake）

wood oil 桐油

wood paneling 木镶板，镶木

wood partition 木隔板（亦称 wood separator）

Wood's metal 伍德合金（Bi50%，Pb24%，Sn14%，Cd12%，熔点 66~71℃）

wool 羊毛，羊毛织品

woolly-type engine 低速（大马力）发动机

wool tuft 羊毛簇（羊毛纤维簇，风洞试验时，贴于车身，以观察车身上的气流状态）

word ①语言②文字③字④（在汽车电子控制系统中指被看作一个整体或一个单位串的字符串或二进制位的）计算机字（字的位数多少称字长，随计算机，即电子控制模块类型与型号不同而不同，32 位微处理器字长为每字由 32 个二进制位数组成）

word marking （交通标志中）文字标志

word-oriented organization 按字编排（存储器的一种编排方式，其中每个存储区由组成字的一定数量的存储单元构成）

work ①工作，劳动；操作，作业；加工；研究②工件，工作物，机件，结构③功④制品，成品；著作，成果⑤工程，工事⑥运转，运行；操纵，开动；加工，处理，制造

workable automobile （指轿车研制达到可使用阶段的）实用轿车

work due to friction 摩擦功

work-hardened steels 表面加工硬化

钢（表面冷作，表面摩擦，使表面硬化）

working ability of vehicle 汽车工作能力（汽车按技术文件规定的使用性能指标执行其设定功能的能力）

working accuracy 加工精度

working addendum 节圆齿顶高（在涡轮上，喉圆与节圆之间的径向距离）

working backlash 啮合侧隙（当一对相啮合的摆线轮与针轮处于理论啮合位置时，在某一针齿中心与节点的连线上，摆线轮齿廓与针齿廓之间量度的最短距离。摆线轮轮齿和针轮轮齿在不同位置啮合时，其啮合侧隙不相等）

working cycle 工作循环

working cylinder 工作缸（如：双筒减振器的内油缸）

working dedendum 节圆齿根高（在涡轮上，节圆与根圆之间的径向距离）

working depth 工作高度（对圆柱齿轮，指两个配对齿轮的齿顶圆柱面各与连心线相交，所得到的两交点之间的最短距离。一对锥齿轮互相啮合时，指两者的顶圆与两背锥的公共母线各有一个交点，这两个交点之间沿上述公共母线量度的最短距离。对蜗杆副，指涡轮和蜗杆两者的齿顶曲面之间在连心线上量度的最短距离）

work (ing) efficiency 工作效率，加工效率

working flanks 工作齿面（轮齿上的一个齿面，它与配对齿轮的齿面相啮合并传递运动）

working fluid 工作液体（工作油液，工质）

working medium 工质

working medium volume 汽缸容积（活塞顶面所封闭的汽缸瞬时容积，亦称 cylinder capacity, cylinder volume）

working mixture 工作混合气（指在发动机汽缸内工作的混合气，为新鲜充量与废气的混合物）

working $p_c v$ valve 许用 $p_c v$ 值（极限 $p_c v$ 值除以安全系数，见 pv value, limiting pv value）

working pitch 节圆齿距（齿距，在涡轮上，介于两个相邻的同侧齿廓之间的节圆弧长，称为节圆齿距。它等于配对蜗杆的轴向齿距。在此定义中，所谓的节圆指的是涡轮中间平面上的一个和分度圆同心的圆）

working pressure angle 啮合角（在一般情况下，两相啮轮齿的端面齿廓在接触点处的公法线与两节圆的内公切线所夹的锐角，称为啮合角。对于渐开线齿轮，指的是两相啮轮齿在节点上的端面压力角）

working pv value 许用 pv 值（极限 pv 值除以安全系数，见 pv value, limiting pv value）

work (ing) speed 工作速度

work-piece 工件

work plane 工作面（通常指在其上面进行工作的平面。如：当没有其他规定时，一般把室内照明的工作面假设为离地面0.75m高的水平面）

work sampling 工况随机抽样分析（根据概率理论，对处理对象进行随机抽样测定，经统计处理推算出所要测定的数和量）

work-saving device 省工装置

workshop truck 修理工程车（亦称 machine shop truck，=workshop lorry）

work-site 工作现场

works-reconditioned 在工厂修理好的

works trailer 厂内运输用挂车（指只在厂内或工作地附近特许的公路上使用的工业用挂车）

work study 劳动研究（对劳动者的工作方法、工作量进行研究测定的

通称。全面考察劳动者的工作，系统地调查、研究并改进影响劳动效率和生产成本的有关因素）

work study engineer 劳动工程师，劳动研究工程技术人员（见 work study）

world car 世界车（在 1973 年石油危机以后，各国都缩小汽车尺寸，生产紧凑型省油轿车，这种轿车当时称为世界车）

world-class vehicle 世界级汽车（指世界领先的车辆，如：世界最畅销车，世界上最先进设计的车等）

World Intellectual Property Organization 世界知识产权组织

world SID （国际标准化组织"ISO"宣布的）世界（协调统一）侧碰撞假人（world side-impact dummy 的简称）

World's leading 世界领先的

World Solar Car Challenge 世界太阳能汽车赛（第一次于 1987 年，第二次于 1991 年澳大利亚，参加国有加拿大、德国、英国、丹麦、新西兰）

world speed record 速度的世界纪录

World Trade Organization 世界贸易组织（简称 WTO，见 General Agreement on Tariffs and Trade）

world wide web 万维网（简称 WWW 或 Web，见 Internet）

worm 蜗杆（一个齿轮，当它只具有一个或几个螺旋齿，并且与涡轮啮合而组成交错轴齿轮副时，就称为蜗杆。其分度曲面可以是圆柱面、圆锥面或圆环面）

worm-and-double-nut steering gear 蜗杆双螺母式转向器（= screw-and-double-nut steering gear）

worm-and-double-roller steering gear （球面）蜗杆双滚轮式转向器（亦称 warm-and-twin roller steering gear）

worm and lever steering (gear) 蜗杆式转向器（由蜗杆及其随动件副组成的转向器的总称，包括 Marles steering gear, worm and roller steering, worm and nut steering, worm and peg steering, worm and sector steering 等，这类转向器将转向盘轴的旋转运动通过蜗杆传给其随动件，再由随动件传至转向摇臂"pitman arm"转换为摆动输出，故亦称摇臂式转向机"pitman arm steering gear"，相对于无转向摇臂的齿轮—齿条式转向器而言）

worm and nut steering gear ①蜗杆—螺母式转向器（蜗杆的随动件为由 a. 套在蜗杆上的转向螺母"steering nut" b. 转向螺母与蜗杆间减少摩擦的循环球"recirculating ball" c. 转向螺母带动的转向摇臂轴驱动件，如：齿扇"sector"、曲柄销"lever and peg 或 spigot on crank arm"等组成的传动副，亦称循环球式转向器"recirculating ball steering gear"）②（有时专指）循环球曲柄销式转向器（recirculating ball-lever and peg steering gear）

worm and peg steering gear 蜗杆指销式转向器（指蜗杆的随动件为带一个或两个指销的曲柄，即具有蜗杆、曲柄指销传动副的转向器）

worm and roller steering gear 蜗杆滚轮式转向器（由蜗杆滚轮副组成的转向器）

worm and sector steering gear 蜗杆—齿扇式转向器（指蜗杆随动件为齿扇的转向器，亦称循环球—齿条齿扇式转向器"recirculating ball—rack and sector steering gear"，即具有齿条、齿扇传动副的循环球式转向器，见 worm and nut steering gear）

worm-and-single-peg steering gear 蜗杆单指销式转向器

worm-and-single-roller steering gear （球面）蜗杆单滚轮式转向器

worm-and-spiral-teeth sector steering gear 蜗杆与螺旋齿扇转向器

worm-and-taper pin steering gear 蜗杆-锥销式转向器

worm-and-three-teeth sector steering gear 蜗杆与三齿式齿扇转向器

worm-and-twin-peg steering gear 蜗杆双指销式转向器

worm-and-wheel axle 蜗杆涡轮式驱动桥

worm-and-wheel gear 涡轮蜗杆机构

worm bearing 蜗杆轴承

worm bending strength 蜗杆抗弯强度

worm box 涡轮传动箱

worm brake 涡轮制动器

worm case 蜗杆罩,蜗杆壳体

worm clip 蜗杆式夹紧机构,蜗杆拉紧式夹箍

worm couple (涡轮)蜗杆副

worm drive of rear axle 后桥涡轮传动(= worm-rear-axle drive)

worm face width 蜗杆齿宽(圆柱蜗杆的有齿或螺纹部分、在分度圆柱面上沿轴线方向量度的宽度)

worm gear ①涡轮②涡轮蜗杆机构③涡轮传动

worm-gear cam drive 涡轮凸轮传动

worm-gear conjugation tester 涡轮副配对检查仪

worm-gear differential 涡轮式差速器

worm (-gear) drive 涡轮-蜗杆传动,涡轮传动

worm-gear drive ratio 涡轮传动比

worm gear final drive 蜗杆涡轮式主传动(涡轮蜗杆式主减速器)

worm gear pair 蜗杆副(由蜗杆及其配对涡轮组成的交错轴齿轮副)

worm housing 涡轮(减速)箱壳体

worm lock 蜗杆止动锁

worm mesh 蜗杆啮合

worm pipe 蛇形管

worm screw 蜗杆螺钉

worm sector 扇形涡轮(亦称 worm segment)

worm shaft roller conical bearing 蜗杆锥形滚子轴承

worm wheel 涡轮(一个齿轮,它作为交错轴齿轮副中的大轮而与配对蜗杆相啮合时,就称为涡轮。其分度曲面可以是圆柱面、圆锥面或圆环面。通常,它和配对的蜗杆呈线接触状态,亦称 worm gear)

worn 磨损的,磨耗的,用旧的

worn-in 磨合,走合

worn-off 磨损,磨破

worn on a taper 磨损成锥度的

worn-out 磨损了的;用坏了的;陈旧的,破烂的;耗尽的,没有用的;衰弱的

worn-part reclamation 旧件修复(磨损零件修复)

worn tyre 花纹磨平轮胎(胎面花纹凸起部分已经磨损到胎面磨损标记的轮胎)

worst-case design 最坏条件设计(在汽车电子系统中,指即使所有元件均处于在允许的最坏条件下,线路仍能保证正常工作的电路设计方法,参见 worst case)

worst possible conditions 可能发生的最坏条件

WOT 节气门全开(见 wide-open throttle)

would-be car buyer 潜在的轿车买主(愿意购轿车而尚未购轿车的客户)

wound roller bearing without inner-ring 无内圈螺旋滚子轴承

wound roller bearing with solid outer race 整体外圈式螺旋滚子轴承

wound roller bearing with split outer race 双半外圈(外圈径向剖分式)螺旋滚子轴承

woven belt 编织带

woven facing (离合器等用的)石

棉织物摩擦衬片
woven lining 织物衬片
WP29 世界车辆法规协调论坛（下设制动及底盘工作组"GRBF"，一般安全工作组"GRSG"，被动安全工作组"GRSP"，污染与能源工作组"GRPE"等多个工作组）
WP ①防水的（waterproof）②全天候（weather-proof）③工作点，着力点（working point）④工作压力（working pressure）
(WP29/GRSG) RE5 （世界车辆法规协调论坛一般安全工作组完成的）在全球技术法规中使用的统一定义和规程的联合决议（该决议规定了所有轮式车辆、装备和部件的全球技术法规"Global Technology Regulation"中使用的标准术语，为制定其他各项全球统一性汽车技术法规的基础性文件，见 WP29）
WPI class 世界专利索引分类（world patents index class 的简称）
WPMI 世界零部件厂家识别标志（world parts manufacturer identifier）
WPP 防水填料（= water proof packing）
wrap ①卷，包，缠绕②覆盖，掩饰，遮蔽，掩蔽③叠起③外罩，封套，包封物，包皮，外壳④（线）匝
wrap-around grille 全包式散热器护栅（两侧包覆车身的曲面散热器护栅，作为汽车前部的一种装饰格栅）
wrap-around rear glass 曲面后窗玻璃（全景后窗玻璃）
wrap-around tread 圆肩胎面
wrap-around windshield （包覆左、右两侧，形成左、右曲面的）全景风窗玻璃（亦称 panoramic window）
wrap (ping) angle 包覆角（包角）
wrapround （由车身前面或后面向两侧）包覆（而形成圆角曲面）的
wrapround bumper （前、后保险杠均延伸至车身两侧的轮口的）大包角式保险杠
wrapround dash design 曲面仪表板
wrap test （细弹簧钢丝等的）缠绕试验（缠绕在一定尺寸的芯轴上，观察钢丝表皮是否有裂纹等）
wreck ①肇事，事故②肇事车辆
wreckage ①失事，事故②（车、船）失事后的残骸或残存物
wreck crane 救险用起重机
wreck derrick 救险用的转臂起重机
wrecked vehicle 事故毁损车辆（因事故等原因损坏的车辆，发生故障的车辆）
wrecker ①救险车，救援车（备有随车起吊装置，可将事故车、故障车及违章停放车辆等的前端或后端吊起拖至修理厂或检查站）②救险车驾驶员，救援者，救济者
wrecker rail 救援车拖引导轨
wrench 扳手
wrench socket 扳手套筒
wring ①收缩量，过盈量（简称 W）②拧出，拧入，绞出，扭紧，扭变形；挤出③黏合，研合④歪曲，曲解
wring fit 轻打配合，轻迫配合，紧推配合，紧（动）配合，转入配合（= wringing fit）
wrinkle ①起皱，生皱纹②皱纹③方法，技巧④错误，缺点⑤新设计，新花样，好主意，好方法
wrinkled, buckled or torn chafer 胎圈包布打褶、翘起或破损（胎圈包布局部呈褶皱、脱开或破裂的现象）
wrinkled cords in tyre cavity 胎里帘线起褶（胎里帘线局部起褶棱的现象）
wrinkled inner tube 内胎褶子（内胎折叠起皱纹的现象，包括死褶子和活褶子，出褶，打褶）
wrinkle laminar flame 皱纹层流火焰
wrinkle resistance 抗皱折性能
wrist 肘节，肘杆，耳轴，销轴，腕

（关节）

wrist pin ［美］活塞销（= piston pin, gudgeon pin）

wrist-pin bush 活塞销衬套（偶见称 wrist-pin bearing）

wrist-pin end 连杆小头（= connecting rod small end）

wrist-pin hole 连杆小头的活塞销孔

write cycle time 写周期（存储器一个写循环起止的时间间隔）

write enable 允许写入（指令存储器允许写入数据的控制信号）

write-enable input 写允许输入（一种当其有效时允许数据进入存储器的输入）

write-off ①报废（装备）②注销，取消

write/read cycle time 写读周期（存储器数据写入，然后存储器读出这一循环起止的时间间隔）

write recovery time 写恢复时间（存储器一个写脉冲的终止与新循环起始的时间间隔，是供存储器从写操作恢复到正确动作的时间）

writing circuit 记录电路

wrong (-) way caution system 错车道行驶警报系统［亦称 wrong (-) way driving prevention device 或 system。有两种：①置于无中央隔离带双向行驶的公路路侧的摄像-警报系统②装在车上的雷达探测系统。二者作用相同，都是测到车辆偏离规定的车道越线行驶时，即向驾驶者发出相应的警报，以避免与对向行驶的车辆正面碰撞，并可保留录像在万一发生事故时作为事故分析的依据］

wrought ①可锻的②锻造的，锻制的

4WS 四轮转向系统（4 wheel steering system 的简称）

WS and D 风速与风向（wind speed and direction 的简称）

W-speed-rated all-season performance tire W 额定速度级全季节高性能轮胎（指额定速度值为 270km/h 的高性能轮胎，见 rated speed of car-tire）

WS system 四轮转向系统（four-wheel steering system 的简称）

W-surface W 形曲面

WT ①警告标志（= warning tag）②不透水的（watertight）③（车前）横木（= whiffle-tree，结构试验用）④防冻试验，冬季行车试验（= winterization test）⑤无线电报（= wireless telegraphy）

wt ①瓦（特）（watt）②质量（weight）

wthp 单位质量马力（weight horsepower）

WTO 世界贸易组织（World Trade Organization）

W-type engine W 型发动机（双 V 型发动机，汽缸作 W 状排列）

WU-OC 速热型氧化催化转化器（warm-up oxidation catalytic converter 的简称，其安装位置靠近排气歧管，可快速升到工作温度）

WV ①工作电压（working voltage）②［德］大众汽车公司（Volkswagen 的简称）

WW 风窗刮水器（windshield wiper 的简称）

WW system 风窗玻璃刮水器系统（windshield wiper system 的简称）

WWW 万维网（world wide web 的简称，由世界各地无数网站组织起来的世界范围互联网，这无数的网站是万维网的基本要素，而组织和连接这些网站使之形成网状体系结构的是用于唯一标志不同网站的 IP 地址以及替代 IP 地址使用的网址）

wye-wound stator winding （交流发电机的）星型接法定子绕组（亦写作 Y-wound stator winding）

X-alloy 铜铝合金（铜3.5%，铁1.25%，镁0.6%，镍0.6%，硅0.6%，其余铝）

X-axis X坐标轴

X-axle ①X型轴，X形车桥②横轴

X-band (frequency) X频带，X波段（5200~10900MC，用于雷达）

X-by-wire （通用公司）线传电子控制系统

X drive （宝马轿车）智能全轮驱动系统（商品名）

xDrive X驱动（宝马全轮驱动轿车作为标准件使用的前-后驱动力分配系统的商品名。传统的全轮驱动系统前、后驱动力按前40%、后60%的固定比例分配转矩。如：如果后轮因路面附着力不足而完全滑转时，由于行星齿轮式分动器的特性，即使前轮具有良好的抓着力，也不可能将转矩传送至地面，这时必须制动干涉制止后轮滑转，才能将固定比例40%的转矩传至前轮，60%的转矩白白损失于制动，而且这一过程约需要0.5s的时间。xDrive系统此时则无须制动干涉，且可在0.1s的时间内将100%的发动机转矩传给前轮。该系统由微处理器根据发动机的输出转矩、车辆的横摆和横向加速度、制动、节气门开度、各车轮的转速、转向盘转角等信息控制的电动机驱动多片式离合器，实现前、后驱动力的连续最佳分配。此外，该系统还具有控制动态稳定性功能）

XDS 电子控制型差速锁（商品名，Xtronic differential system 的简称）

xenon 氙（Xe）（无色、无味气体）

xenon-filled 充氙气的

xenon (-filled) flash tube 氙闪光管

xenon headlamp system 氙气前照灯系统（由照明控制模块"light control module"和充有氙气并具有放电电极的气体放电灯泡组成。照明控制模块一般装在灯泡下方，它的作用是将蓄电池输入的电压迅速提升到20000V，同时保持电流、电压稳定和保证安全，在高压下，灯泡内的氙气在电极间产生气体放电而发出强光）

xenon lamp 氙气灯

xerogel 干凝胶

xeroprinting 静电印刷（的）

X-factor 乘数，倍率（= multiplying factor）

X-flow cylinder head 横流式汽缸盖（见 cross-flow cylinder head）

XFMR 变压器（transformer 的简称）

X-form cross member X形横梁（= X-shaped cross member, X-type cross member, cruciform member）

x-gear 变位齿轮（= gear with addendum modification）

x-gear pair 变位齿轮副（至少包含一个变位齿轮的齿轮副）

X impact acceleration （汽车及乘员的）负纵向碰撞加速度，碰撞时的负纵向加速度（指向着行车方向后方的加速度）

X LWB 超长轴距（extra long wheelbase 的简称）

XMSN 传送，传动装置，变速器（trans-mission 的简称）

"X"-nonskid tyre chain X 形轮胎防滑链

XOne （美国 Michlin 公司供大客车使用的）钢丝子午胎（商品名，扁平率达 45%，其基本理念是用一条 XOne 代替两条普通轮胎）

x plane X 平面（平行于基准 X 平面的任一平面）

XPS 多孔聚苯乙烯（= expanded polystyrene）

X-ray analysis X 光分析，X 射线分析

X-ray defectoscopy X 射线探伤法

X-ray density X 射线密度（伦琴射线密度）

X-ray detector X 射线探伤器

X-ray generator X 射线发生装置（伦琴射线发生装置）

X-ray inspection X 射线检查

X-ray photograph X 光照片

X-rays X 射线（伦琴射线 "Röntgen rays"，1895 年，德国物理学家 W·K·Röntgen 发现当高速电子撞击某些物质时，产生的一种穿透能力很强的射线，称 X 射线或伦琴射线，它可使乳胶片感光，空气及不少物质产生电离）

X-ray spectrum X 射线谱

X-ray tube X 射线管

X-shaped cross member X 形横梁（= X-form cross member, X type cross member）

X-th decimal place 小数点后 x 位

X-TRAIC （日产公司生产的）氢燃料电池车（商品名）

X tronic 电子控制的（亦写作 xtronic，商品名用语，如：日产公司的带 7 挡手动拨片换挡、1400 种变速模式的电子控制式无级连续变速器的商名品为 "Xtronic CVT"，见 CVT）

X-type engine X 形发动机（以一根曲轴为中心，汽缸按 X 形布置的多缸发动机，简称 x-engine）

X-type frame X 形车架（= cruciform frame，指两侧大梁中部带 X 形加强梁，两头带横梁的车架，亦称 frame with cruciform bearing, cross-braced frame, diagonally braced frame ladder and X-brace frame, X-member frame）

X type safety belt X 形安全带（在三点式安全带的基础上又添加一条由肩至臀的斜肩带，由此组成一组交叉于乘员胸前的 X 形安全带）

X unit X 单位（波长单位 = 10^{-11} cm）

xylol 混合二甲苯（用于擦拭浸没物镜上的杉木油）

xylonite 赛璐珞

X-Y plotter X-Y 坐标图描绘器（用以描绘出以 X，Y 正交轴作为坐标轴的图像）

X-Y recorder X，Y 坐标曲线自动记录器

x-zero gear pair 非变位齿轮副

Y-alloy Y 合金，铜-镍-锰-铝合金（制造活塞用的轻合金的一种，其标准成分为：Cu 3.5% ~ 4.5%，Ni1.7% ~ 2.3%，Mg1.2% ~ 1.8%，微量 Fe、Si、Ti、Zn，余为 Al。抗拉强度：294MPa；硬度：HB90；热传导率：1.5kJ；热膨胀系数：(22.5 ~ 23.9) ×10^{-6}/℃；熔点 640~650℃)

Yanmar Diesel Engine Co. Ltd. （日本）洋马柴油机股份有限公司

yard ①码（英制的长度基本单位，代号 yd，1963 年规定的英国标准码为 1yd = 3ft = 0.9144m；1 码长的东西）②工（作）场；制造场；停车场③堆置场，围场

yardage ①以立方码计的容积②以平方码计的面积③以码计的长度

yard-crane （车）场内（移动式）起重机

yarding-in-transit （转口运输、过境运输、途中的）货物管理（卸货、保管、储存、分类等）

yardstick 码尺（1 码长的量尺）

yardwork 车场工作，车场作业，货场作业，维修场作业，维护场作业

yaw 横摆（汽车质量产生横摆角或横摆角的变化）

yaw angle ①横摆角（汽车质量绕汽车坐标系 z 轴旋转的角度）②汽车的侧偏角（= sideslip angle of vehicle，指汽车的对称平面，即汽车坐标系 x_0 轴与汽车实际行驶方向的夹角，见 beading angel②)

yaw control system （汽车）横摆控制系统

yaw inertia 横摆惯量

yawing moment 横摆力矩（亦称 yaw moment，作用在汽车上的力矩矢量使汽车绕运动坐标系 z_0 轴旋转的分量，见 moving axis system）

yawing moment coefficient （空气动力矩的）横摆力矩系数（绕 z_0 轴的空气动力矩分量的无量纲系数，根据作用在车辆上空气动力的分布求出的横摆力矩 M_{AZ} 导出)

yawing moment of inertia of sprung mass 簧上质量横摆惯性矩（簧上质量绕 z 轴旋转的惯性矩）

yawing moment of inertia of vehicle 汽车横摆惯性矩（整车质量绕通过质心的铅垂轴的惯性矩）

yawing rate ①（汽车的）横摆角速度（= yaw rate）②（汽车的）横摆振动频率

yawing velocity 横摆角速度（汽车质量绕以簧上质心为原点的汽车坐标系 z 轴旋转的角速度，见 vehicle axis system，单位为：deg/s）

yaw meter （汽车）横摆测定仪（使用可绕垂直轴自由回转的陀螺仪来测定汽车的横摆角等）

yaw moment （作用于汽车的侧向

力的合力中心与汽车质心不重合时产生的绕质心的）横摆力矩

yaw-moment controller 横摆力矩控制器（指通过控制左、右、前、后车轮制动力和牵引力来产生所希望的大小和方向的横摆力矩，以提高车辆稳定性和操纵性的电子控制模块）

yaw-motion of the rear axle 汽车后桥横摆（指后桥非悬架质量绕其重心之铅垂线的角振动，= rear-axle yaw）

yawn ①开口，裂缝，间隙，缝隙 ②裂开

yaw rate ①（汽车的）横摆角速度 [= yaw (angular) velocity] ②横摆率（亦称 yaw velocity "横摆角速度"，单位：deg/s）

yaw rate gain 横摆角速度增益 [简称 yaw gain, 指横摆角速度 r 与车轮转角 θ 的比值：r/θ。当车轮转角为常数时，称 r/θ 为稳态横摆角速度增益（yaw rate stabilized gain）。为保证车辆低速时转向轻快，高速时转向稳定，应使 r/θ 值随车速的提高而降低]

Yaw rate-G sensor （车身横摆角速度传感器和车身前后左右加速度传感器制成一体的）Y-G 传感器

yaw rate sensor （车辆）横摆角速度传感器（通过检测传感器压电陶瓷元件的应变量和应变方向来测定车辆绕其横摆轴线自转的方向和角速度，亦称横摆率传感器，单位 deg/s）

yaw rate wave 横摆率波形

yaw response 汽车的横摆响应（在操纵输入或外部扰动输入时，汽车的横摆运动响应）

yaw sensor （汽车的）横摆传感器（根据汽车行驶时在外力，如：横风的影响下，姿态与方向发生的变化，检测其横摆角及横摆角速度信息的传感器，如 yaw rate sensor）

yaw stability 横摆稳定性

yaw velocity 横摆角速度（汽车质量绕汽车坐标系 z 轴旋转的角速度，亦称横摆率"yaw rate"，见 vehicle axis system）

yaw velocity model following control system 横摆速度（数学）模型追随控制系统

yaw vibration 横摆振动（汽车绕过重心垂直轴的角振动）

y-axis y 轴，y 轴线

Y belt （汽车婴儿座椅约束婴儿用的）Y 形安全带

Y-bend Y 形弯头

Y-configuration （交流发电机三个定子绕组的）Y 形接线法（亦称 Y-shaped connection, Y connection, 亦写作 wye connection, = star connection "星形接线法"）

yd 码（= yard）

yearbook 年鉴

5 year guarantee on repair （车辆等的）五年保修

yearly traffic pattern 年小时交通量变化图（横坐标轴为一年内各小时的交通量按大小的排列次序，纵坐标为各小时的实际交通量对年平均日交通量的比值）

year round type 全年通用式

yellow ①黄色 ②黄色的

yellow brass 黄铜（铜65%，锌35%）

yellow cabbies 有证出租汽车（合法有证出租汽车的车身漆成黄色，以区别于无证出租汽车）

yellow flame 黄焰（混合气燃烧中，碳氢化合物裂化成碳时的火焰色，亦称 luminous flame）

yellow flasher lamp （交通控制机用）黄色闪光灯

yellow glass bulb 黄色玻璃灯泡

yellow signal light 黄色信号灯

yellow soil 黄土

Y-engine Y 型发动机（三缸星形发动机）

Y-grade separation 三路交叉口（见

Y-intersection)

yield ①产量，产出率②收益，获益率③出产④屈服（指可延性材料在外力作用下由弹性状态进入塑性状态）

yield factor 屈服（极限储备）系数

yielding condition 屈服条件（弹性破损的应力条件）

yield（ing）strength 屈服强度（软化强度，抗屈强度，简称 ys）

yield limit-strength limit ratio 屈强比（指材料的屈服极限与强度极限的比值）

yield load 屈服载荷（引起残余变形的载荷）

yield point 屈服点[试样在试验过程中力不增加（保持恒定）仍能继续伸长（变形）时的应力]

yield point elongation 屈服点延伸率（简称 YPE）

yield point in torsion 扭转屈服点（扭转试验中，扭角增加而转矩不增加保持恒定时，按弹性扭转公式计算的切应力）

yield sign 让路标志（从支路或环道进入交叉口或干道时，让干道车辆先行）

yield strain 屈服（点）应变

yield stress 屈服应力

yield stress controlled bonding （在高于屈服点应力作用下的）受控屈服应力黏结

Y-intersection Y 形交叉口（三路交叉口中，交角在 75°~105°者称为 T 形，交角小于 75°或大于 105°者称为 Y 形，亦称 Y-junction，Y-grade separation）

Y-joint 叉形接头，Y 形接头，Y 形接合（亦称 Y-junction）

Y-motor Y 形发动机（见 Y-type engine）

yoke ①轭，轭状物②叉，叉形物，叉形件（如：拨叉，叉状定位架）

yoke bolt 离合器分离叉调节螺栓

yoke bracket 拨叉支架

yoked connecting rod 叉头形连杆，叉形连杆（多用于 V 形发动机，= forked connecting rod）

yoke of cardan type universal joint （十字轴式万向节的）万向节叉（用来传递转矩和旋转运动，并具有某种对连接结构的输入和输出叉形元件，包括 slip yoke，flange yoke 和 slip shaft yoke 等）

yoke shifter 拨叉

Young's modulus in compression 压缩杨氏模量（轴向压缩应力与轴向压缩应变呈线性比例关系范围内的轴向压缩应力与轴向压缩应变之比）

Young's modulus in tension 拉伸杨氏模量（轴向拉伸应力与轴向拉伸应变呈线性比例关系范围内的轴向拉伸应力与轴向拉伸应变之比）

YPE 屈服点延伸率(yield point elongation)

Y pipe Y 形管(亦称 breeches pipe)

Y-pipe joint Y 形管接头（= Y-piece）

Y plane Y 平面(平行于基准 Y 平面的任一平面，见 vehicle longitudinal symmetric plane)

5-yr./750000mi. warranty （新车）5 年/750000 英里保用期

YS ①屈服强度(yield strength)②屈服应力(yield stress)

ytterbium oxide 氧化镱（Yb_2O_3，与二氧化锆 Z_rO_2 混合，作为氧传感器的固体陶瓷电解质材料，加入 Yb_2O_3 可提高离子传导率，热稳定性和机械强度）

Y type ABS 三通道式防抱死制动系统(左、右前轮都装有速度传感器,其制动液压分别由两条液压通道控制,而后两轮分别装两个或共用一个速度传感器,后轮制动液压由一条液压通道控制的防抱死制动系统)

Y-type engine Y 形发动机（汽缸绕曲轴成 Y 形布置的发动机，亦称 Y-motor）

zapon lacquer 硝化纤维清漆（硝基清漆，亦称 zapon varnish，简称 zapon）

Z-axis Z 坐标轴

Z-axle （宝马轿车的）Z 形后桥（其每侧车轮的悬挂由一纵臂、一根上方的横连杆、一根下方的斜连杆和一架螺旋弹簧组成，此外，还装有一根防侧倾的稳定杆）

Z-bar ①Z 形断面型材（= Zee-bar）②补偿弹簧③（二冲程发动机曲轴箱的）齐默曼阀型圆盘式进气阀（= Zimmermann valve type of rank-case induction valve）

ZDDP 二烷基二硫代磷酸锌（zinc dialkyl dithiophosphate 的简称，发动机润滑油添加剂）

zebra crossing 斑马纹人行横道（无控制人行横道的一种，由斑马条纹的路面标志表明，行人要优先于车辆通过）

zebrano 斑马木（一种带条纹的硬木，为胡桃木内饰的廉价代用品，亦称 zebrawood）

Zeiss optimeter ［德］蔡司光学比较仪

zener diode 齐纳二极管（加上一较小的，如：数 V 反向电压，便会被击穿而通导的二极管，齐纳二极管被击穿时的电压称齐纳电压。将齐纳管用于稳压电路，可保证电压稳定在齐纳电压的范围内）

zener rectifier 齐纳二极管整流器

Zener voltage 齐纳电压（齐纳二极管击穿电压）

Z-engine （日本日产公司生产的）急速燃烧发动机（每一汽缸内具有两个火花塞，火焰传播距离短，缩短燃烧时间，见 NAPS-Z）

Zenith fully automatic starter 栽尼斯全自动冷起动器（可确保在 -30℃时发动机起动，简称 Autostarter）

Zeolite 沸石（Na-Y）

zeolite trap 沸石捕集器（用于吸附排气中的 HC）

zerk fitting 润滑脂加注嘴（简称 zerk，= grease nipple）

zero adjuster 零位调节器（零点调整机构）

zero air void density 无空隙密实度

zero allowance 零公差

zero-ash 无灰分的（滑油等）

zero axial ①通过零点的②通过坐标原点的

zero-backlash automatic adjuster 背隙自动消除器（自动消除间隙的调节装置）

zero balance 零位平衡，零点调整

zero-based conformity （仪表的）零基一致性（通过调整校准曲线接近规定特定曲线，使两者曲线的范围

下限值重合且最大的正偏差和负偏差相等时的一致程度)

zero-based linearity (仪表的)零基线性度(通过调整将校准曲线接近规定直线,使两者的范围下限值重合且最大的正偏差和负偏差相等时的一致程度)

zero bevel gear 零度锥齿轮(中点螺旋角为零度的曲线齿锥齿轮)

zero camber (前轮)零外倾(外倾角等于零),零外倾角

zero caster (转向节)零主销零纵倾,零后倾(后倾角为零)

zero centre (type) meter 中心指式仪表

zero control (仪表)零位控制(零位调整)

zero crossings 零值交叉[疲劳载荷中,载荷-时间历程在其给定长度内与具有正斜率(或负斜率,或两者,按规定)的零值载荷水平交叉的次数]

zero damage 无损伤,无损害

zero-decrement 零衰减量,无衰减,无阻尼;无衰减的,无阻尼的

zero-defects 无缺陷的,无损伤的

zero drift 零位偏移,零位漂移,零点位移,零点漂移(亦称 zero creep,零漂,指范围下限值上的点漂。当下限值不为零值时亦称为始点漂移)

zero elimination 消零(法)

zero-emission car 零排放轿车(无污染轿车)

zero emission vehicle 零排放汽车(无污染汽车,简称ZEV,指燃料电池汽车、太阳能汽车等无HC、CO、NO等有害排放的汽车)

zero energy 零级能量(= energy of absolute zero)

zero-error 无误差,零点误差(在参比工作条件下,当输入处于范围下限值时实际输出值与规定输出范围下限值之差。当下限值不为零值时,亦称为始点误差)

zero-error reference 零误差基准线

zero gas 零位气体(仪器调零用气体,指不含测定物质的气体,用于测定仪表调零,见 zero grade gas)

zero grade gas 零点气(含以甲烷为当量基础计的碳氢化合物 1×10^{-6} 以下、一氧化碳 1×10^{-6} 以下、二氧化碳 400×10^{-6} 以下和氮氧化物 0.1×10^{-6} 以下的气体。这种气体通常是用作调整碳氢化合物、一氧化碳、二氧化碳和氮氧化物分析仪的零点,但不能用作调整测量环境中二氧化碳浓度或接近浓度的分析仪的零点,= zero gas)

zero graduation 零刻度

zeroing 零位调整,定(对准)零点,调零

zero-kilometer car 零公里轿车(指尚未行驶的新车,促销用语,亦称 zero-mileage car)

zero-lapped 零重叠度的,无重叠的

zero-lash 无游隙的,无间隙的

zero-lash valve tappet 无间隙的气门挺杆

zerol bevel gear 零度螺旋锥齿轮(螺旋角为零度的螺旋锥齿轮,简称 zerol gear)

zero lift angle 零升力角(无浮升力角,指车身各板件在汽车行驶时不产生空气浮升的角度)

zero line 零位线

zero-load flow 无负荷流量

zero method 零位法(利用独立于被测对象的、可调整的已知量与被测的未知量平衡,而根据已知量确定未知量的方法,亦称 null method)

zero motor 低速马达(转速从 0 ~ 300r/min,带减速器的电动机)

zero of a measuring instrument 测量仪器仪表的零位(当测量仪器仪表工作所需要的任何辅助能源都接通

和被测量值为零时,仪器仪表的直接示值)

zero offset ①零点偏移②零主销偏距

zero offset steering 零主销偏距转向(见 centre point steering 及 kingpin offset)

Zero-phosphorus oil 无磷机油,零磷油

zero point correction (量测仪具的)零点校准(调零,校零)

zero position 零位(= null position)

zero potential 零电位,零电势(简称ZP)

zero pressure 零压力(一般指大气压)

zero pressure tyre 零压轮胎(大气压轮胎)

zero-rating capacity (蓄电池的)零度放电额定容量(蓄电池低温起动能力的质量指标,如:6V蓄电池充好电后,当电液温度为0°F,即 -17.8℃时以300A放电,其端电压下降至3V时所需的时间,以分计)

zero reading 零位读数,零起点读数

zero-rush tappet (气门的)零冲击式挺杆(无隙挺杆,指无气门间隙的挺杆结构,工作可靠、无声、不需调整,如:液压挺杆等)

zero scale error(of a linear ADC or DAC)(线性ADC或DAC的)零度误差(在规定的零度时,实际台阶中心值与标称台阶中心值或实际台阶值与标称台阶值之间的差)

zero scale mark 零(标度)标记(零标度线,指标度盘或标度板上标有"零"数字的标度标记或标度线)

zero scale(of an ADC or a DAC with true zero)(有真实零点的ADC或DAC的)零度(表示标称台阶中心值或标称台阶值等于零的台阶特性)

zero scrub radius 零磨胎半径(转向轴线或转向主销轴线的延长线正好落在车轮接地面积的纵向中心线上)

zero seepage 完全无渗漏

zero setting (仪表)零位调整(置零,调到零点,调零)

zero shift 零点迁移(亦称零点偏移,指当输入值处于范围下限值时,由于某些影响引起的输出值的变化。当下限值不为零值时,亦称为始点迁移或始点偏移)

zero slip 无滑移

Zero slip angle 4WS control algorithm 零侧偏角4轮转向控制算法(为4轮转向基本控制算法,该算法控制后轮转向,使车身的侧偏角 β 始终为零,亦简称 $β_0$ control algorithm)

zero teeth difference type output mechanism 零齿差输出机构(由具有较大的法向侧隙,且齿数相等的内齿轮副或锥齿轮副构成的输出机构)

zero temperature 零温度(参考点温度,基准点温度)

zero-time reference 零时参考点(计时起点)

zero-to-sixty acceleration times (汽车)0~60mile/h 加速时间(指汽车从静止起步至车速提高到60mile/h所需的时间)

zero treatment 零化处理(中心化处理,试验数据处理时,为简化计算,避免低频成分的畸变,常把原始信号转换为具有零均值的信号进行处理)

zero vector 零矢量

zero visibility 零能见度(极为不良的能见度)

zero X plane 基准 X 平面(通过前轮中心,并垂直于基准 Y 平面和基准 Z 平面的平面)

zero Y plane 基准 Y 平面(车辆纵

向对称平面）

zero Z plane 基准 Z 平面（通过客车底架上平面，并垂直于基准 Y 平面的平面）

zeta function ξ 函数

ZEV 零排放车辆（zero emission vehicle 的简称，美国联邦环境保护法规规定 2003 年以后，已有 10% 的汽车零排放，且其无甲烷有机气体"NMOG"的排放只许 0.06 克/英里）

zig fastener 拉链（= slide fastener）

zigzag ①之字形，Z 字形，锯齿形②之字形的，Z 字形的；交错的；锯齿形的

zigzagging 之字形运动

zigzag spring （汽车座椅等使用的）Z 字形钢丝弹簧

zigzag tooth (teeth) 交错齿

zinc ①锌（Zn）②在…上镀锌，包锌，用锌处理

zinc-air battery 锌-空气电池（亦称 zinc-air cell，电动汽车用新型电池，用空气中的氧为正极，锌为负极）

zinc anode 锌阳极

zinc-base bearing metal 锌基轴承合金

zinc-base die cast alloy 锌基压铸合金

zinc bath 镀锌槽

zinc casting 锌铸件

zinc chromate primer 锌铬酸盐底漆（车身喷漆前的一种带色底漆）

zinc-coated 镀锌的

zinc coating ①镀锌层（锌镀层）②镀锌

zinc dialkyl dithiophosphate 锌二烃基二硫代膦酸酯（润滑油极压添加剂的一种，加入黏度低的发动机机油中，作为装配后的磨合机油，简称 ZDDP）

zinc-galvanized （电）镀锌的

zinciflcation ①镀锌②加锌③包锌④锌腐蚀

zincing steel sheet 镀锌钢板

zincode （电池的）锌极

zinc oxide separator （燃料电池）氧化锌分离器

zinc phosphate coating 磷酸锌镀层

zinc plate 锌板

zinc-plating 镀锌

zinc-rich 高锌的（锌占 95% 左右的）

zinc-rich paint 富锌涂料

zinc sheet 锌片

zinc splash condenser 锌雾冷凝器（在封闭的熔锌槽内，冷凝锌蒸气）

zinc spraying 锌喷镀（将锌丝或锌粉熔化，用喷枪喷到需要镀的表面上，一般用来修补防锈镀层）

zinc vapour deposition 锌蒸气（真空）沉积镀（简称 ZVD）

zinc white 锌白（80% 氧化锌，20% 硫酸钡的混合物）

zip fastener 拉链（简称 zip）

zipper ①拉链，拉锁②用拉链扣上

zipping （安装）风窗玻璃的装配工序（口语）

zircon 锆石

zirconia （二）氧化锆（ZrO_2，在汽车上利用其离子传导性，制作 O_2 传感器）

zirconia oxygen sensor 氧化锆氧传感器

zirconium ceramic 氧化锆镀膜陶瓷

zirconium-dioxide 二氧化锆（ZrO_2）

zirconium dioxide 氧化锆（ZrO_2，白色晶体，315℃ 时，成为氧离子的导体）

zirconium tube （氧传感器的）锆管

ZMBI 巯基苯并咪唑锌（zinc mercaptobenzimidazole）

zone ①带，区，地段②范围，区域，区段

zone body （发生碰撞时吸收碰撞能

量保护乘员免受损伤的）分区结构车身（通常将汽车分为前变形缓冲区、中高强度座舱区、后变形缓冲区等三个结构分区。当发生正前方碰撞时通过前变形缓冲区的前纵梁、上边梁、副车架等结构件的变形来分散、吸收冲击能量，当发生正后方追尾碰撞时，左、右后纵梁变形来分散、吸收冲击能量，以减轻对座舱的冲击）

zone body concept 分区车身方案，指车身不同区域采用不同结构（如：前、后两端采用能吸收碰撞能量的结构，称为 crushable zone，车身中部采用高强度结构，同时采用避免侧碰撞的结构和厚车门等，称 safety zone。日本 Nissan 公司 Cedric 等车型采用。这样的车身称：zone body construction 分区轴结构）

zone control air conditioning system 分区控制式空调系统（可根据车厢内不同区域的气温状况分别吹送不同温度的冷、热风）

zoned tempered glass 区域钢化玻璃（分区域控制钢化程序的钢化安全玻璃，一旦破坏，总体上符合安全玻璃对断裂碎片的要求，同时又提供了一个不妨碍驾驶的视区）

zone of action 啮合区域（在平行轴渐开线齿轮副中，啮合平面上的一个矩形区域，称为啮合区域，此区域以有效齿宽和端面啮合线为边界）

zone of adhesion （车轮或履带牵引元件与地面的）附着区域

zone of dispersion （图表上数据的）离散区域

zone of flame 火焰区

zone of negative pressure 负压区

zone toughened windshield 分区钢化的风窗玻璃

zoning 分区，区划；分区制

zoom 图像缩放（无说明时指图像放大）

zoom lens 变焦镜

ZP 零电位（zero potential）

Z plane Z 平面（平行于基准 Z 平面的任一平面）

ZP RWAL （通用公司的）零压后轮防抱死系统（商品名，Zero Pressure Rear Wheel Anti-lock 的简称，其双电磁液压阀总成中的蓄能器容积较大，防抱死制动减压工况时，后轮制动轮缸的制动液通过快泄阀大量的进入蓄能器，后轮制动压可迅速大幅度降低，至所谓的"零压"）

ZrO_2 NO_x-A/F sensor 二氧化锆型氮氧化物与空燃比传感器

Z-section Z 形截面